Longman Anthology of World Literature by Women

1875–1975

Marian Arkin
City University of New York, La Guardia

and

Barbara Shollar
City University of New York, Queens College

Longman
New York & London

Longman Anthology of World Literature by Women

Longman Inc., 95 Church Street, White Plains, N.Y. 10601

Associated companies:
Longman Group Ltd., London
Longman Cheshire Pty., Melbourne
Longman Paul Pty., Auckland
Copp Clark Pitman, Toronto
Pitman Publishing Inc., New York

Because of their length, Permissions Credits appear at the back of the book.
Frontis illustration: Alfred Stieglitz, *Paula*, 1889,
black and white photograph,
courtesy International Museum of Photography
at George Eastman House, Rochester, N.Y.

Executive editor: Gordon T. R. Anderson
Developmental and production editor: Elsa van Bergen
Text design: Lynn Luchetti
Photo research: Kristie Jayne
Production supervisor: Judith Millman

Library of Congress Cataloging in Publication Data

Longman anthology of world literature by women/Marian Arkin and Barbara Shollar.
   p.   cm.
  Bibliography: p.
  Includes index.
  ISBN 0-582-28559-3
  1. Literature—Women authors—Collections.   I. Arkin, Marian, 1943–
II. Shollar, Barbara.
PN6069.W65L66 1989
808.8'99287—dc 19

88–8274
CIP

ISBN 0-582-285593

88 89 90 91 92 9 8 7 6 5 4 3 2 1

To Anna, who grew up with this book,
and to Brian, who waited

To Ellen
"Oh, there's something about the women"

Contents

An alternative List of Writers and Selections by Region appears before the index.

WOMEN'S LITERARY TRADITIONS: REGIONAL ESSAYS

Board of Advisors

Marian Arkin received her M.A. in English and her Ph.D. in Comparative Literature from New York University. Professor of English at City University of New York (LaGuardia), she is Founding Director of the Writing Center at LaGuardia; she designed and taught the first women's literature courses in the early 1970s and has been active in curriculum design of women's literature courses ever since.

Prof. Arkin is managing editor of the American Association of Australian Literary Studies' journal, *Antipodes,* for which she will guest edit a special issue on Australian women writers in Spring 1989.

Prof. Arkin's publications include several books on pedagogy and articles on women writers, Commonwealth literature, and the teaching of writing for such journals as *Modern Fiction Studies, Comparative Literature Studies*, and *The Connecticut English Journal.* She is a nationally recognized consultant on writing and tutoring and has done extensive work on the teaching of writing using computers.

Katherine Carlitz is Adjunct Assistant Professor of Chinese literature at the University of Pittsburgh. She received her B.S. in Chemistry from UCLA and her Ph.D. in Chinese literature from the University of Chicago. Her publications include articles on traditional Chinese vernacular fiction and drama, and translations of classical and modern Chinese short stories. Her study of the major sixteenth-century Chinese vernacular novel *Jin ping mei* (*The Rhetoric of Chin p'ing mei*) was published by Indiana University Press in 1986.

Ingrid Claréus was born and educated in Sweden, where she completed her M.A. (Fil. mag.) degree in Scandinavian Languages and Literature at the University of Stockholm. After studies of English literature at the University of Bristol, England, she lived for six years in Brazil, where she taught English at the British Council School. She taught at the University of Wisconsin, Madison, in the Department of Scandinavian Studies from the early 1960s to June, 1987, when she was awarded the rank of Assistant Professor Emeritus there. Professor Claréus has written and published extensively on Scandinavian women writers; her current project, *An Anthology of Scandinavian Women's Prose, from the 1880s to the 1980s* will be published by Greenwood. She has done numerous translations from

Swedish and reviews Scandinavian contemporary writers for *World Literature Today* and *Scandinavian Review.* Professor Claréus resides in Stockholm.

Alice R. Clemente is Professor of Spanish and Portuguese and of Comparative Literature at Smith College. She received her Ph.D. from Brown University in Spanish and in her teaching she concentrates heavily on Spanish literature from the Middle Ages through the seventeenth century. For the last ten years, however, her writing has dealt with Portuguese women's literature, primarily in the contemporary period. She is now working on two books: a study of Portuguese women's fiction in the ten years following the revolution of 1974 and an anthology of that same material.

Natalia Costa-Zalessow received her Ph.D. in Romance Languages and Literatures, with emphasis in Italian, in 1967 from the University of California, Berkeley. At present she is Professor of Italian in the Department of Foreign Languages and Literatures at San Francisco State University. She has written a book on Italian women writers (*Scrittrici italiane dal XIII al XX secolo, Testi e critica* (Women Writers from the 18th to the 20th Century), Ravenna, Longo Editore, 1982), contributed articles to *Italica, Ausonia, Forum Italicum*, and *Italian Quarterly*, as well as entry articles to the foreign language series of Magill's *Critical Survey of Drama, Critical Survey of Long Fiction*, and *Critical Survey of Short Fiction.*

Gillian Davies was born and educated in Great Britain and taught in the Caribbean for three years before moving to Canada in 1966. Fluent in French and English, she has taught Québécois and Acadian literature for the last fourteen years. She publishes articles, essays, and reviews on Acadian and Québécois fiction on a regular basis and was Associate Editor of *Studies in Canadian Literature* from its inception to 1985. Present research efforts include a Harvard doctoral dissertation on the Québécois novel and a comparative study of the Acadian/Cajun oral and literary traditions. Her publications include *Of Princes and Scarecrows: A Look at Contemporary Québec Fiction; A Far Cry from Longfellow: A Look at Contemporary Acadian Literature*; and the introduction to Jacques Godbout's *Le couteau sur la table* (The Knife on the Table).

master's degree and doctorate in Japanese literature from the University of Chicago. She has been in Japan a number of times for research study and has written *The Saga of Dazai Osamu: A Critical Study with Translations*; she won the 1983 Japan-U.S. Friendship Fund Translation Prize for this volume. Her articles and reviews have appeared in such journals as the *Harvard Journal of Asiatic Studies* and *The Journal of Asian Studies*. For her study of the dominance of the autobiographical mode as both a tone and a distinct genre in modern Japanese fiction, she received a full year grant in 1987–1988 from the National Endowment of the Humanities.

Mona N. Mikhail is currently Associate Professor of Arabic Literature and Islamic Studies in the Department of Near Eastern Languages and Literatures, New York University. She occasionally teaches courses also for the Department of Comparative Literature there.

Born in Egypt, she obtained degrees from Cairo University and The University of Michigan and served on the faculties of Cairo University, the University of Michigan, Ann Arbor, and Princeton University. Her publications include *Images of Arab Women: Fact and Fiction* (1979), *Seeds of Corruption* (1980), and numerous translations of fiction and poetry.

Chieko Mulhern was born in Japan and came to the U.S. as a student in 1959. She earned her B.A. in English Literature at Brooklyn College, her M.A. and Ph.D. in Japanese Literature from Columbia University. Having taught Japanese at Columbia and Princeton Universities, she is currently Associate Professor of Japanese and Comparative Literature at the University of Illinois, Urbana-Champaign. Her recent publications related to women's literature include articles for *Southern Folklore Quarterly*, *Journal of Asian Studies*, and *Review of National Literatures*, the book *Japanese TV Drama For, By, and About Women*, and the forthcoming books *Heroic With Grace: Legendary Women of Japan* and *Japanese Women Writers: A Bio-critical Source Book*.

Maria Luisa Nunes was born in Providence, RI, and holds degrees from Radcliffe-Harvard, Columbia University, and City University of New York. Professor Nunes is currently a fellow at the Center for Advanced Study in the Behavioral Sciences at Stanford, California. She is on leave from the State University of New York at Stony Brook, where she is Associate Professor of Portuguese. She has published monographs on Eça de Queiroz, Machado de Assis, has edited books on Lima Barreto and the Cape Verdean experience in America, and is published extensively in journals devoted to Luso-Brazilian and Hispanic literatures.

Margarite Fernández Olmos is an Associate Professor of Spanish at Brooklyn College of the City University of New York, where she also teaches Women's Studies. A recipient of a Ford Foundation Fellowship and a Postdoctoral Fellow of the National Research Council, she has lived and studied in Europe and Latin America. Professor Fernández Olmos has lectured and written on contemporary Latin American literature for journals such as *Studies in Afro-Hispanic Literature*, *Revista / Review Interamericana*, *Hispania*, *The Lion and the Unicorn*, *La revista canadiense de estudios hispánicos*, *Heresies*, and *Third Woman*, as well as several critical anthologies of Puerto Rican literature. She is author of a book on the Dominican writer Juan Bosch, and co-editor with Doris Meyer of *Contemporary Women Authors of Latin America: New Translations* and *Introductory Essays* (1983).

Christopher Robinson studied classics, then French and Modern Greek at Oxford, 1960–1966. He was a lecturer in French at the University of Lancaster, 1966–1971. Since then Professor Robinson has held a Combined University Lectureship and Fellowship at Christ Church, Oxford and is a member of the sub-faculties of both French and Modern Greek there. He has published books on Erasmus, on nineteenth and twentieth century French literature, and on the classical satirist Lucian and his influence in Europe, as well as articles on various aspects of Modern Greek poetry. He is currently writing a book on Cavafy.

Barbara Shollar currently teaches writing at Queens College, City University of New York. Beginning her academic career as a director of developmental education and academic support, she developed pedagogical programs and curriculum in writing, tutoring, and the computer for students and faculty and co-authored *The Tutor Book* and *Tutoring Writing*; she also wrote a book on reading instruction. She has served as consultant for evaluation and staff development to colleges and to the New York City Board of Education. Her most recent work includes presentations on the women's literary cannon/curriculum and on immigrant women's autobiography. She is completing her dissertation on the immigrant women's autobiographical tradition in American literature.

Susie Tharu is Reader in English Literature, Central Institute of English and Foreign Languages. Her recent book, *The Sense of Performance* (1983), is a study of embodiment as form and its implications for a critical, spectator-centered theatre. Other publications, on Indian literature in English, critical theory, and women's studies focus on structure and change as evidenced in literary and other cultural discourses. She is a member of the National Association of Women's Studies and of Stree Shakti Sangatana, Hyderabad, India.

Elizabeth Webby is Associate Professor in the Englsh Department, University of Sydney, Australia. She teaches courses in Australian literature, South Pacific literature, the short story, and nineteenth

century theater. Her publications include *Early Australian Poetry* (1982) and, as joint editor, *Happy Endings: Stories by Women from Australia and New Zealand* (1987) and the *Penguin New Literary History of Australia* (1988). In 1988 she became editor of Australia's senior literary quarterly, *Southerly*.

Phyllis Zatlin is Professor of Spanish at Rutgers, The State University of New Jersey. She holds a B.A. from Rollins College and M.A. and Ph.D. degrees from the University of Florida. A specialist in contemporary Spanish women writers and contemporary Spanish theater, she has published extensively in these areas. She has authored books in the Twayne World Authors Series on Elena Quiroga, Victor Ruiz Iriarte, and Jaime Salom, and has prepared editions in Spain of works by several playwrights. With Martha Halsey, she is co-editor of *The Contemporary Spanish Theater: A Collection of Critical Essays*. At present she directs the advanced undergraduate and masters level translation options in the Department of Spanish and Portuguese.

Acknowledgments

With a book such as this, the number of people who contribute to it feels almost limitless and we apologize for any persons who go unmentioned. The editors would like to thank the following especially.

For help on the Australia/New Zealand section Marian Arkin would like to thank her good friends, Julianne Schultz of the New South Wales Institute of Technology and Ian Reinecke of the University of Woollangong, who helped with everything from selections to advisors. Thanks also to Drusilla Modjeska, also of the New South Wales Institute of Technology, and to the Association for the Study of Australian Literature for bringing me to their 1986 conference to experience their glorious literature firsthand. Thanks to Amelia Simpson, and to Carmelo Virgillo of Arizona State University, who translated and also wrote headnotes for the Brazilian section, and to my colleague at LaGuardia, Elizabeth Woodruff, who first introduced me to the diary of Carolina Maria deJesus. For the Greek section, where barely any primary or secondary material on women writers exists in English, I am indebted to translator Peter Bien of Dartmouth for sharing with me his invaluable resources on Greek women writers and to my colleague Joan Richardson at LaGuardia for her continuing interest in the project. Yael Feldman, of Columbia University, was an immense help for the section on Israel. Not only did she provide aid in making the selections, but she edited manuscript and translated where necessary. Kathrine Jason, Claire Siegel, and Joan Borrelli did excellent translations for the Italian section as did Patti Firth, Maureen Ahern of Arizona State College, Doris Meyer of Connecticut College, and Tona Wilson in the Latin American section. Thanks to Loretta Slover, Boston University, and Jean Longland for initial work on the Portuguese section and especial gratitude to Alexis Levitin of the State University of New York at Plattsburgh, whose painstaking translations are much appreciated. For the Spanish section, many thanks to Micaela Misiego, formerly of Rutgers University, for her loving translations from the Catalan, and to Carol Maier, University of Illinois, Champaign-Urbana, for her Spanish translation.

The Scandinavian section was especially difficult, as it was so large and inclusive of so many traditions. I would especially like to thank Marna Feldt of the Swedish Consulate General Information Service, Rose-Marie Oster of the University of Maryland, and George Blecher of Lehman College for help in the beginning stages and to Sara Death, Linda Schenck, Rochelle Wright of the University of Illinois, Barbara Wilson, and Verne Moberg for translations and headnotes. Thanks particularly to Stina Katchadourian for her prompt, eleventh-hour translations of Solveig von Schoultz's poetry.

For the United Kingdom and Ireland section, thanks so much to those of my colleagues at LaGuardia who read and critiqued my essay: Brian Gallagher, Gail Green, Roberta Matthews (thanks also to Roberta for research in Portugal), Cecilia Macheski, Ellen Keck Stauder at Reed College and Nan Albinski at Penn State University. Also, gratitude to John Isom for his diligent and enthusiastic headnotes and to Jane Marcus, whose seminar on twentieth-century English women writers at the Graduate School, City University of New York, during Fall 1987, inspired all who attended. I am particularly grateful to Meic Stephens of the Welsh Arts Council for his advice on the Welsh selections. So little is known about Welsh literature in this country and his *Oxford Companion to Literature in Welsh*, as well as his epistolary advice was immensely useful. Thanks again to Brian Gallagher, and to Eilean ní Chuilleanain of Trinity College, Dublin and to Mary Elizabeth Carter of the Keshkarrigan Bookstore for helping me with the Irish section.

Thanks to Joan Hartman of the College of Staten Island, for information and support during a difficult period in the book's final phase.

Finally, although not last in importance by any means, is the institutional help I received: my thanks to Dean Richard Barsam of the City University Office of Academic Affairs and Dean Martin Moed of LaGuardia for a curriculum development grant that allowed me to develop a course on the international woman writer, to the two chairpeople of the English Department during the long period of this project, Daniel Lynch and Sandra Hanson, who understood and cheered me on, and to the fine secretaries in the department, particularly Florence Pasternak, Genevieve Schiefer, Rosemary Prinz, and Arlene Semoff. Also, much gratitude to the Bobst Library at New York University for help from its research staff and especially to the Baker Library at Dartmouth College for extensive interlibrary loan assistance, for reference librarians with a dedication and compassion unlike any I have known, for its exceptional primary collection, and for its warm, friendly atmosphere, which made me feel welcome and at home during four years of long summer days.

Barbara Shollar would like to express her appreciation to Richard Stites, Georgetown University; Sara Lennox, University of Massachusetts at Amherst; Diane Marting, formerly of Rutgers University; Frank Peters, New York University; Gayatri Chakravorty Spivak, University of Pittsburgh; and George Blecher, Lehman College, whose prompt response and early generosity made the road ahead seem easy. And to Margaret Fete, Ohio Wesleyan University, whose important unpublished bibliography of francophone African women writers made the task of identification of women in that tradition less problematic than it would have been, and whose annotations can be traced in the introductions to those women; Sue Houchins, formerly of Scripps College, and Lloyd Brown, University of California, San Diego, for assistance with African selections. Thanks go to Talat Sait Halman, New York University, and especially, Ellen Ervin, who undertook to provide translations and introductions for Turkish prose writers; Astrid Hustvedt and Brian Baer, both of New York University, and Carole Ciano, Graduate School of the City University of New York, for excellent French translations for the French and Middle Eastern sections; Ruth Nybbaken, Ohio University, and Donald Holoch and Shu-ying Tsau, both of York University (Ontario), who contributed headnotes and translations to the Chinese section; Hiroaki Sato, who provided helpful annotative material as well as elegant translations, Barbara Ruch, Columbia University, who sent me in the right direction at a crucial stage, and Laurel Rodd, Arizona State University, who also provided new translations—all for the Japanese section. Appreciated is the assistance provided by Fred Cogswell and John Patterson, both of the University of New Brunswick, for their translations of Francophone Canadian poetry and prose; Salma al-Khadra al-Jayyusi, Director of the Project of Translating Arabic Literature into English (PROTA), for her advice and discussion of Middle Eastern literature, and Zeina Matar and Pamela Vittoria for their translations of that literature; Kathryn Szczepanska for her translation from the Russian; Judith Preckshot, University of Minnesota for her introduction to Joyce Mansour: Enakshi Chatterjee, Mahua Bhattacharya, and the authors Amrita Pritam, Mahasveta Devi, and C. S. Lakshmi, all of whom obliged me with biographical material, translations, and other helpful information regarding their work, included in the Indian section. Thanks also to Bette Weidman, Queens College, whose interest in native American literature led me to the works of Victoria Howard, and their redactions by Dell Hymes; Dell Hymes, University of Virginia, who graciously permitted the use of his new translations of Victoria Howard and to whose feminist re-readings and pioneering scholarship in ethnopoetics the notes and introduction to Howard are much indebted; Charles Molesworth, Harriet Zinnes, Marie Ponsot, and Jay Miskowiec, all of Queens College, who provided translations of and introductions to various French and American authors, some of which we were ultimately unable to include; Clara Lomas, Colorado College, Inés Hernandez, San Francisco State University, and Sonia Saldívar-Woodhull, University of Texas at Austin, whose commitment to the Chicana, Amer-Indian, and Hispanic traditions made possible the inclusion of these traditions within the United States section and whose goodness and spirit buoyed me during a difficult period; Shirley Lim, Rockland County Community College, and especially, Amy Ling, Rutgers University, whose helpful discussions on the Asian-American tradition insured that it too would be incorporated into the selections and the United States essay. And to Claire Quintal, Director of the Institut Français at Assumption College, Worcester, Massachusetts, who provided helpful information on the francophone contribution to the literature of the United States, and to Dominque Polfliet for her translation of some of this material; Lois Kuznets, San Diego State University who gave me an afternoon by the pool and much information on the women writing children's literature that I could not include; Toyo Suyemoto, who shared with me something of her life and some of her work, which appears in this book; Tom Trusky, Boise State University, whose sympathetic knowledge of and good humor about the anthologizing task made the last labors less burdensome; Marie Ponsot, Queens College, without whom the poets of the American section might never have been selected; Con Davis,

Ronald Schleifer, both of the University of Oklahoma, Patricia Yeager, Yale University, and especially, Françoise Burgess and Susan Harris, both of Queens College, and Mary Dearborn, Heyman Center for the Humanities, Columbia University, and Thomas Rocco, Empire State College whose review of earlier versions of the essay on women's writing in the United States contributed to its merits; Ellen Doherty, whose help with selections for the American section and reading of various parts of the manuscript was invaluable; Jane Marcus, whose savvy and feistiness did much to make another trying period less anxious. Thanks must also go to those who provided research assistance and drafted introductions: Pamela Vittorio (Middle East), New York University, Catherine Liu (France and francophone Africa), Leslie Camhi, Bill Mullen, and especially, my friend Eric Mendelsohn (United States), all of The Graduate School, City University of New York. My appreciation to Terri Faup for typing certain sections of the manuscript. At least half of this work would not have been completed in a timely fashion—or at all—without the efficient and comprehensive help of the Inter-library loan staff of the Paul Klapper Library, Queens College, under the able direction of Isabel Thaler. I want also to express appreciation to the staffs of the libraries at SUNY New Paltz and San Diego State University for their assistance during summers of research and reading away from home.

Finally, my thanks to the English Department of Queens College, CUNY. I would most especially like to acknowledge my colleague Marie Ponsot for her faith in me and in this project and Helen Cairns, Dean of Graduate Studies at the college, who provided both timely encouragement and financial support. Above all, they *understood*, and their understanding was golden.

There are others who do not provide professional expertise and institutional support but put dinners on the table, clean the house, and hand you aspirins and coffee for the long haul; they bear with your fits of anxiety, despair, and tension, knowing the elation will eventually come. They listen. They give you courage. To those who sustained me— Gerald Hudson, Penny von Eschen, and Ellen Doherty—as well as Lois Kuznets, my thanks.

Both editors want to acknowledge the support we received from each other. Little did we know the Amazonian task that lay before us on that fateful day when we divided the world between us—for Marian, anglophone Canada, Australia and New Zealand, Scandinavia and Finland, Spanish America and Brazil, Great Britain, Greece, Italy, Peninsular Spain, Portugal, and Israel; for Barbara, Africa, China, France, francophone Canada, Germany, India, Japan, the Middle East and Turkey, the U.S., and the U.S.S.R. It is our primary collaboration that made the project feasible, that made all the other collaborations which contributed to the book possible. Ours has survived our differences to nurture us.

We also are especially grateful to our editors at Longman. Gordon Anderson and Elsa van Bergen, as well as to Laura McCormick and Emma Roderick, for their enthusiasm for this work and the support—financial and otherwise—that such an undertaking required.

And last, but not least, we are grateful to our advisors, who heard our complaints, listened to our concerns, responded to our requests, assisted with proofreading, and provided us with that specialized knowledge, network, and shared sense of commitment, which made the production of this text possible.

M.A.
B.S.

Robert Montenegro, Indian Singers, *ca. 1950, oil on canvas. © 1986 Sotheby's, Inc.*

Introduction

I told you in the course of this paper that Shakespeare had a sister; but do not look for her in Sir Sidney Lee's life of the poet. She died young—alas, she never wrote a word. She lies buried where the omnibuses stop, opposite the Elephant and Castle. Now my belief is that this poet who never wrote a word and was buried at the crossroads still lives. She lives in you and in me and in many other women who are not here tonight, for they are washing up the dishes, and putting the children to bed. But she lives; for great poets do not die; they are continuing presences; they need only the opportunity to walk among us in the flesh.

—Virginia Woolf, *A Room of One's Own*

In the course of history (history is an archive of deeds undertaken by men and all that remains outside it belongs to the realm of conjecture, fables, legend, or lie) more than a natural phenomenon, a component of society or a human creature, women have been myth.

—Rosario Castellanos, "Woman and Her Image"

When Virginia Woolf wrote *A Room of One's Own*, she had every reason to believe that Shakespeare's sister—her idea of the archetypal woman writer—was "buried at the crossroads" waiting to be recovered, discovered, "given an opportunity to walk among us in the flesh." Woolf herself had written about a number of then-obscure English women writers (e.g., Aphra Behn, Margaret Cavendish), but her resources were limited and she worked in virtual isolation. The fruits of persistent work by artists, scholars, and critics half a century later would have surprised even her. Rosario Castellanos, too, would have been surprised at the achievements of literary women, in the years since her death, to demythologize women, to give them substantiality, and to privilege their creativity.

Thanks to painstaking work by an international body of scholars who have been researching the feminist literary tradition in their own countries—and who, like Woolf and Castellanos, have been unsupported and, until recently, in isolation—the study of women's literature has gained official status and academic prestige. Yet this anthology is the first to reflect the scholarship in the field done worldwide over the past two decades, and to attempt a survey of women writers in the modern historical period that both is international and indicates the variety of genres in which women wrote. Many of the works in this anthology were translated specifically for this project and are available for the first time in English in this text. Also, because there is little or no secondary information, at least in English, about many of these writers we have provided readers with two major sources of contextual material: (1) information about the life and work of each writer to introduce the selection; (2) bibliographical essays, written by members of a distinguished editorial board, that trace women's literary tradition in most of the countries represented in the anthology, providing a social and historical context for the writings we have included. (Many of these essays are the first scholarly and critical efforts to survey the spectrum of women's literature in particular countries.)

In this introduction, we discuss some of the general issues that are relevant to a consideration of women's literature, and those that are pertinent to the study of a worldwide literary tradition.

ESTHETIC CRITERIA / PATRIARCHAL ESTHETICS

An anthology is an organ for developing a *canon*, a list of works that are accepted as representative of a particular tradition or literature. It is—consciously or unconsciously—a political, or ideological, project, preserving certain texts over others, and, almost equally, a conservative one, tending to preserve those texts *previously* considered worthy of preservation.

The representative quality of an anthology, however, may be variously defined: one may argue, for example, that the selections reflect those themes or concerns that are considered to be peculiarly relevant to a certain category of literature. In that light, previous anthologies of women's literature have emphasized particular aspects of female experience such as motherhood, marriage, sisterhood, and sexuality, or those images of women that have pervaded particular societies or literatures, whether they be angel or whore, *mujer sufrida* or *La Malinche*. Editors of national literatures may in turn select works that express nationalist characteristics or identities.

An editor may also define "representative" according to a more "universal" criteria, the "best" that has been thought or said, regardless of time or place. Such "universal" criteria is usually formalist in nature, based on considerations of esthetic value. This last approach tends to favor an ahistorical understanding, in which a special preserve for art is isolated, one that will transcend local concerns. It also sharply demarcates the creations of a high culture from the works of popular culture.

Within these critical contexts, many different kinds of writing are disregarded. Formalist criteria tend to exclude literary speeches, philosophical treatises and sermons, diaries, letters, and journals, as well as popular novels, tales, and other anecdotal narratives, expository forms, and moral genres. Much of women's art, which has made use of more fragmentary and less "artful" forms, tended also to be pragmatic, not to say moralistic, in its concerns. Moreover, women often used more ephemeral outlets for mass production and distribution or as frequently (and conversely) used more intimate and communal forms of communication, both oral and written. Women's writing, to a greater degree than men's, has been categorized as "regional" or "provincial," or to use another rubric, labelled as "merely women's" literature and thus less than "universal."

Within the last twenty years, as prevailing literary philosophies have been examined critically, feminism has led critics and scholars to reassess both who became part of the canon and what esthetic criteria or literary values were used to define that canon. They found that works were "canonized" because of values that, arguably, were more gender-defined than they were "national" or "universal"; that is, a phallocentric (patriarchal or "masculinist") esthetic rather than an abstract or pure esthetic or literary value was at work to determine both the process of selection and its "representative" nature. (For whom? Of what? literary feminists asked.)

The question of canon is further complicated by the international issue. Any international anthology published in the West will reflect a bias that may be considered Eurocentric. Those works that are European, and those traditions that are seen as deriving from Europe, are likely to be emphasized in the table of contents; traditions more remote are perceived as less accessible. Like those who have discussed these questions in regard to minorities and colonial peoples, feminists recognize that this is the literary equivalent of imperialism in the geopolitical sphere. Both points of view are critical of patriarchy as the determining principle.

The difficulties of evaluation can be found in our own anthology in regard to the Eastern European and Slavic section. One of the editors and an advisor spent weeks compiling lists of Estonian, Ukranian, Hungarian, Polish, and Russian writers and reading material by these authors. Gradually they made the anguished decisions to eliminate each of the countries in turn until they were left with only those of Poland and Russia. As they labored over these two groups, they considered the current interest in Poland that had been fueled by the Solidarity movement, the fact that few if any of the Polish writers, including the "greatest" of them, had been translated into English, and, conversely, that the Russian authors were generally far more accessible. Moreover, they were forced to recognize that they could not adequately represent both Russian and Polish traditions: one would have to be sacrificed to the other. Their feeling was that the Polish tradition needed to be given expression much more than the Russian; their intellectual training and backgrounds also forced them to admit that they could not include Polish literature *without* including Russian literature. The Polish women writers went by the wayside, even though they may be as "great" as or "greater" than their female Russian counterparts. To our minds, the process illuminated yet again the way in which sociopolitical considerations (the U.S.S.R. has a higher status in the world political hierarchy than Poland) may influence cultural dominance (Russian literature has been awarded "greater" literary eminence within academic institutions by Western standards).

The criteria for "representative" selections are also questionable. How, for example, might we apply a "universal" or formalist criterion? Can we assume that the standards for literary "greatness" are unvarying from culture to culture, or from period to period (not to speak of from gender to gender)? Or that, to put it another way, the formalist criterion is not itself derivative from certain literatures of certain times and places? Might we, like Aristotle, be in danger of arriving at a definition of the great tragedy, or of tragedy in general, merely by analyzing one play (in his case, that of Sophocles' *Oedipus Rex*)? Not surprisingly, many literary histories, particularly those dealing with literatures of the Third World or of the East, define certain pivotal points in these literatures in relation to the adoption of Western forms, particularly the short story and the (psychological) novel, and indicate that these forms give birth to the modern literature of these countries. *Realism, naturalism, modernism*, their various offshoots—movements that define the literary tradition in the West—and the signal documents that express them achieve high status in the literary hierarchy.

In fact, our research has taught us that *each* literature is, in part, tied to a distinctive body of traditions, movements, and critical and literary apparatuses. French women's writing has a place within a specifically French culture, history, and tradition as much as Chinese women's writing must be understood within the context of specifically Chinese historical, social, and literary forces. Even within these traditions, there exist diverse class and cultural universes: Chinese texts, for example, engage a variety of languages and esthetic frames. Rather than argue for a universal criteria, we have based our selections on historical, national, and ethnic considerations. To conclude, we have created a women's anthology of international/national/indigenous literatures. As an act of compensation, restoration, and recuperation, this canon challenges already existing canons.

WOMEN AND THE INTERNATIONAL LITERARY CANON

In choosing to create a specifically *women's* anthology, we also were forced to ask questions regarding a gender-specific esthetic, what Elaine Showalter has called "gynocriticism," and an international women's tradition. International women's literature is not firmly a field (there are, as yet, few courses, and few critical books about the subject), and there is little theory to inform it. What follows is a consideration of issues that may contribute to the development of cross-cultural perspectives and a feminist comparatist theory. These considerations shaped our selections.

The Politics of Selection

The re-examination of the women's literary tradition has taken two major directions: first, recovering and discovering many female writers; and second, reassessing the many different forms of women's writing. In regard to the first project, feminist critics argued that women had been omitted from the canon of their literatures precisely because they were women. Those who were *not* excluded tended to be included either because they wrote like men (e.g., Willa Cather, Yosano Akiko, Cecília Meireles, Marguerite Yourcenar) or because they accepted the traditional female role that was conferred upon them (e.g., Juana de Ibarbourou, Sigrid Undset, Germaine Guèvremont, Fadwa Tuqan). Both groups have been included in our anthology. We have done so because they reflect, in part, the historical, social, and literary roles women have played within the so-called mainstream.

Among female writers, critics have sought to recover and discover are those previously rated as minor or relegated to advanced study known only to specialists. These might include the German Marie von Ebner-Eschenbach, the Peruvian Clorinda Matto de Turner, the Indian Svarnakumari Devi, the Chinese Ding Ling, the Russian Zinaída Nikoláevna Gíppius, the Japanese

Higuchi Ichiyō, the South African Olive Schreiner, the French writer Renée Vivien, the English Christina Rossetti, the American Zora Neale Hurston— all of whom are to be found in this collection.

It can be argued that many of those writers outside the literary mainstream were marginalized on the basis of race (or ethnicity) and class, in addition to gender. This was particularly the case when these factors interacted with their texts and produced literature that was defined by "alien" themes, motifs, subject matter, and structure. Difficult as it was, it was not as difficult for the aristocratic Clorinda Matto de Turner to have access to the literary critics and writers of Lima in the late nineteenth century as it was for the working-class Alfonsina Storni in Buenos Aires in the early twentieth century. Nonetheless, Matto de Turner, sympathetic to the indigenous populations of her country and increasingly critical of the social establishment, was eventually forced to flee her country, precisely because her texts challenged the social hierarchy and status quo of Peru. Zora Neale Hurston, it is said, has not gained an appropriate place in American literature, first because she was black and she wrote a literature about blacks and then because she chose to reject certain conventions regarding the way blacks were depicted in traditional literature; she drew instead on an indigenous folk culture that her reading public was unprepared to understand or honor. Others like the Clackamas Victoria Howard, who created her work within the frame of an oral, Amerindian tradition or Mahasveta Devi, who inscribes a political text within Bengali, have yet to be incorporated into their respective canons of American or Indian (Southeast Asian) literatures.

Similarly, those who chose to raise issues of sexuality or to assert a female identity inconsistent with male-defined standards of a particular period or place did not appear in the literary mainstream. Only recently has Kate Chopin been incorporated into the American literary canon, Tove Ditlevson into the Danish, Qiu Jin into the Chinese, Jean Rhys into the British, and Marya Fiamengo into the Canadian literary canon.

The second project—reassessing the many different forms of women's writing—involves reconsidering genre. As we have suggested, formalist esthetic values were frequently used to exclude writing by women. Interdisciplinary studies of the last fifteen years have created in us new awareness of a variety of prose forms. Definitions of what constitutes literature have been broadened. Thus, not only novels, short stories, poetry, and drama are included in this anthology but journalism, autobiography, and letters and diaries as well. For example: the journalistic essays of Canadians Sara Jeannette Duncan and Nellie McClung and of the English Rebecca West; the journal entries of Catherine Pozzi, Marie Lenéru, Beatrice Webb, Carolina Maria de Jesus, and of Victoria Benedictsson; autobiographical works by Elizabeth Stuart Phelps Ward, Tove Jansson, and Glora Fuertes; the letters of Flannery O'Connor. Essays were selected from such critical feminist texts as Qui Jin's "A Warning To My Sisters," Simone de Beauvoir's *The Second Sex*, Virginia Woolf's "Women and Fiction," and Rosario Castellanos's "Woman and Her Image."

Women as Writers / The Question of "Women's" Literature

The question of a canon of woman writers leads us back to the vexing albeit crucial question of whether or not there is a specifically female literature and how and by what characteristics such a literature is to be defined. Masculinist critics' categorization, "women's literature," has in the past carried with it a badge of inferiority; it signified a lack or absence, a failure to transcend the limits of *genre* that *gender* imposed. Historically, women artists responded in diverse ways: some sought to escape the category by assuming male "author"-ity, using a variety of "transvestite" strategies, including male pseudonyms and male personas, studiously avoiding traditional female subject matter and themes. Other writers accepted traditional definitions of their gender/genre roles. The positive limit of the continuum is defined perhaps by women artists who proclaimed the necessity and importance of writing as a woman for and to women. And a few recognized that until women were no longer defined solely in terms of gender, they were required to contend with the woman question.

In the most recent period, the resurgence of feminism and a new feminist consciousness has led women to *célebrate* the female; second-wave women artists have self-consciously created a "woman's literature" or, as it is known in feminist criticism, *un literatur féminin*. What then distinguishes women's assumption of this sign/definition from the masculinists' attribution? Put this way, the question answers itself. Women have *chosen* this "label" as a sign of their *self*-definition. More important, the definition of gender is no longer a single, unified field. It is not a monolithic category into which women must fit themselves or their art. Instead, gender is seen as a polysystem, a multiplicity of ideas and ways of being that constitute the female. Such a notion celebrates difference, and literature narrates the diversity of female experience— whether constituted by class, ethnicity, geography, political and nationalist affiliation, or sexuality. Affirming diversity, women's writing has nonetheless been marked by characteristic language, mythology, subject matter, and themes.

Women have always been associated metonymically with language in gender-defined terms: silence was equated with chastity and women's talk was the linguistic equivalent of her shrewish nature and sexual promiscuity. To affirm one's creative identity through sexuality is to overturn these traditional definitions. Beyond the mere fact of authorship, however, many women have written (preserved, created) a distinctly female language— understood as encompassing a variety of female languages. Ethnologists have recorded formal and grammatical differences between men and women's speech in such different languages as Koasati, Inuit, Carib, Amerindian, Thai, and Japanese; linguists have pointed to the differences between men and women in speech habits (the relative frequency with which they make use of certain words, constructions, and grammatical moods and the different patterns of verbal intercourse).[1] In recent history, French feminists have been extremely influential in awakening women to the potential of female languages and especially the radical possibilities inherent in such languages in subverting gendered systems of thought and social organization, and writers otherwise as different as Verena Stefan in Germany (not included in our text), Monique Wittig in France, Shiraishi Kazuko in Japan, and Fawziyya Abu-Khalid in Saudi Arabia have used their linguistic practice to undermine traditional definitions of gender. Women have asserted their right to "dirty" words, as Susan Suleiman has suggested.[2] The use of such words by women is but one means writers have used to accomplish their ends.

Female language is tied not only to how things are said but to what is discussed, the subject matter of women's words. If language is gender-defined, it is also intimately related to sexuality. Traditionally, women have been seen as sexual objects in the narratives of both male and female writers. But women writers have especially sought to constitute the female as *subject*, asserting varieties of female sexuality and exploring female eroticism. By a process of linguistic transfer, the body has eroticized the narrative itself, charging the text with a new sexual energy.

More traditional but no less meaningful is women's concern with the body social—especially the relations between men and women and those manifold relations contained within the social definitions of woman. Women writers have dealt with the many stages of female growth and development. Relations with women, symbolized by "sisterhood," has been the subject of intense interest at different periods and within different national and ethnic cultures, whether it be between female siblings, mother and daughter, female lovers, or the community of women. These subjects are often translated into a thematics: biological maternity, for instance, may be translated into the theme of mothering, while the domestic sphere frequently takes on sociopolitical and metaphysical significance.

A female thematics also lies behind the efforts of women to create a distinctly female mythology. Frequently, woman artists have made use of traditional mythological figures—the Medusa, Demeter, the Spider Woman of certain Amerindian tribes, Lakshmi; but they also have created new texts for these legendary figures. This use of a distinct female mythology creates a matrilineal geneology and becomes the basis of a matrilineal inheritance, a gynological order that is perhaps most evidenced in the text of Wittig's *Les Guérillères*, concerned with the successful revolutionary uprising of the Amazons and their overturning of the patriarchy. It is also in evidence in *Sultana's Dream* (1905; not included here but reprinted by Feminist Press, 1987), apparently the earliest feminist utopia, written by the Bengali Muslim activist Rokeya Sakhawat Hossein [1880–1932].

A counterpart to this use of the legendary and mythological is women's rewriting of history in the formulation of *herstory*: history as understood and perceived from women's perspectives and with women as subject. The phenomenon is perhaps best exemplified in our text by women's insistent concern with the topic of war and various historical acts of aggression. Thus Nellie McClung's "What Do Women Think of War? (Not That It Matters)" asks the reader to consider a woman's perspective, and, in doing so, puts into question the ways in which such a perspective has been excluded from the social realities of decision making. On the eve of World War II, Colette's

story gives us an epiphanic revelation of the meaning war has for women.
Yosano Akiko, contending with the jingoistic climate within Japan during the
Russo-Japanese War of 1905, insists "Brother, You Must Not Die," and
argues against the exaltation of the military state and the imperialist mytho-
logies used to install it. Enid Bagnold, too, writing during World War I,
wishing to unsettle propagandistic notions of military heroism, takes us
beyond the glory of the battlefield into a hospital ward, there to reveal a
different courage but also to expose the underside of the heroic ideal and its
ultimate corruption. Narrating the roles of women in war, these artists
inevitably dismantle previous histories written by the phallocentric pen to
create herstories that cross over and undercut male-defined views of reality.

Women's Literature and the International Scene

The continuity and coherence of women's literature depends in part on
women writers' acknowledgment of and affiliation with a female literary
tradition. Most frequently such acknowledgment is *intra*national but it is
occasionally international as well. Thus the German writer Christa Wolf has
frequently written about her eighteenth-century predecessors as well as honoring Anna Seghers as her literary mentor and the mother of German (FRG)
literature. Doris Lessing from Rhodesia (now Zimbabwe) and Nadine Gordimer from South Africa have paid homage to the South African Olive
Schreiner, and Canadian Gabrielle Roy has pointed to the influence of her
earlier United States contemporary Willa Cather, while her fellow Canadian
Modernist Isabella Valancy Crawford collaborated with the American Amy
Lowell. The Japanese Tomioka Taeko has honored the American Gertrude
Stein by translating her *Three Lives* into Japanese. Hélène Cixous has rein-
scribed the myths and content of the Portuguese writings of Brazilian Clarice
Lispector into the French context. Perhaps the most significant symbolic
statement of literary sisterhood in recent times was the collaboration of three
Portuguese women writers whose *Novas Cartas Portuguesas* (New Portuguese Letters, 1973) attempted to recreate women's history up to modern
times. When the book was seized and its writers arrested on morals charges,
it became an international feminist cause célèbre. It was as if women everywhere acknowledged their literary collaboration in creating the female text.

It was Ellen Moers who first suggested that there existed a women's
literary tradition that extended from England to the European continent and
across the Atlantic to the United States. Tracking the crisscrossing web of
global influences may be beyond the ken of current feminist scholarship. Yet
an international canon of women writers may establish certain literary check-
points that can be used to further such inquiry.

What we can say with some confidence, and what this book helps us
more clearly to see, is that women writers have with great frequency achieved
international status and worldwide renown. Political feminist writers such as
the American Charlotte Perkins Gilman, the South African Olive Schreiner,
the Swedish Ellen Key (not included in our text), the French Simone de
Beauvoir, the British Virginia Woolf, the Egyptian Nawal al-Saadawi as well
as younger American and French feminists have exerted pervasive worldwide

influence upon women. If other writers included in this text appear in English for the first time, equally as many—if not more—have not only been translated into or appeared in English; they have been translated into anywhere from half a dozen to thirty other languages: writers such as the Swedish Selma Lagerlöf, the French Colette, the Chilean Gabriela Mistral, the New Zealand Katherine Mansfield, the German Anna Seghers, the French-Canadian Gabrielle Roy, the Danish Isak Dinesen, the Brazilian Clarice Lispector, the Russian Anna Akhmátova, the Indian Amrita Pritam. They thus contribute to an imaginary library of *weltliteratur*, or world literature, an ideal canon that locates itself in the country of memory.

For many women artists "making it" on the international scene gave them the opportunity to transcend national boundaries. For some it provided the imaginative means for reappropriating a homeland that otherwise no longer had any existence except perhaps in the writer's mind: Palestinian writers must locate their works on this landscape, as do many emigrant writers. The case of Doris Lessing is exemplary. Born in Persia (now Iran), bred in Rhodesia (now Zimbabwe), Lessing did not begin to publish until she immigrated to England: her first trilogy was a combined *bildungsroman* and saga of her Rhodesian homeland. Decolonized, part of a past even she would not wish to have survived into the present, the world of her growing up exists no longer save in her work.

For other writers, the issue of publication is such that often an international scene is the only landscape on which the writer can be located. Nadine Gordimer and Nawal al-Sadaawi are two major examples of this phenomenon: their work is frequently banned in their own countries; al-Saadawi is prevented from publishing in Egypt, the country where she was born.

Women as Readers

From Charlotte Brontë's Jane Eyre to the provincial heroines of Guèvremont and Schreiner, women as readers have been inscribed within women's texts, writing the significance of women reading. Women as readers also implies a reciprocal relationship, as women inscribe texts within their own lives, and use the plots and scenarios to develop strategies for living.

In our own time, feminist critics and artists have developed theories and practices for reading literature. Two major trends can be discerned: reading women's writing and reading men's. Judith Fetterly has suggested the latter requires "resisting" masculinist interpretations of women as objects, frequently maimed, killed, or otherwise eliminated or rendered invisible.[3] The woman reader's task here lies in deconstructing or "exposing" the "cover-up" practiced by literary texts and their perpetrators.

One aspect of reassessing women's writings is re-evaluating those categories traditionally devalued. Thus readers such as Domna Stanton and Barbara Harlow, respectively, have alerted us to the ways in which women have structured the world within diaries and letters and prison writings just as Modleski, Flynn, and Schweikert have alerted us to the narrative strategies in such popular genres as the soap opera, romance, and gothic novel.[4] Women readers have also refused the confines of traditional genres and preferred to read as well as fashion new forms of the autobiography and what we now call speculative fiction, in part because women would not be constrained by the premises, plots, and characters of what was once called science fiction.

Within this context, we might also discover a further justification for including what we have called the canonical writers. Their works frequently have been given a new life or a different literary life by feminist (re)readings. Through them, we have discovered texts different from those canonized by phallocentric esthetic, or "new" texts, different *by virtue of their having been read in new ways*. They have been read differently, to use the critical terminology of a new literary discourse.

Thus within the American canon, we have learned to admire and value the later, epic works of H. D., those incarnating a female mythology, rather than her earlier imagist poems, which won the early and influential imprimatur of poet Ezra Pound and the consequent approval of the male establishment. Anglo-Canadian Isabella Valancy Crawford has always been recognized within the standard poetry anthologies and literary histories; only recently, however, has the recognition of her remarkable mythopoetic powers resulted in the development of a "new" text. Such "rereadings" have had a particularly acute impact on our understanding of what might be defined as encoded lesbian texts: thus we are learning to read differently the modernist works of Gertrude Stein, who is now known to have written or rewritten narratives of lesbian relationships. Consider *Melanctha*, originally read as a startling early use of stream-of-consciousness technique to bring us into the mind of a black woman servant betrayed by her husband; likewise Marguerite Yourcenar's male-identified stories of homosexual love and desire may be reread in terms of a lesbian code/coded lesbianism.

Language

There are some 5,000 languages spoken in the world. As early as 1813, Madame de Staël argued that there was a dynamic relationship between a language and the character and history of a people. Yet the use of a particular language may be a conscious decision on the part of the writer, defined by questions of education, audience, and means of publication; it should not surprise us that the decision is complicated by social, historical, and geographical circumstances, shaped by what might be called the politics of language.

Under colonialism—the condition that prevails thoughout the period encompassed by our anthology—the cultural dominance of a language reflected economic and social domination. Within the West, and for large portions of Southeast Asia and Africa, English and French became universal languages; more recently, Russia, China, and Japan have emerged as linguistic as well as political powers. Thus the decision *not* to write in English, French, Russian, or Japanese as the period wears on is one strategy of decolonization. The impulse of nationalism, of ethnic striving, is parallel to the feminist impulse to throw off the chains of a male-defined language and create a female language.

For writers who live in countries with an official language, or countries defined as monolingual or linguistically homogeneous, using a dialect or regional language is part of an effort to preserve a particular character, history, and culture. Thus Marion Angus was intrumental in laying the groundwork of the Scots literary revival; Clementina Arderiu extended the possibilities of the Catalan language; Ismat Chugtai introduced a new comic wit and stylistic verve as well as subjects and words previously taboo into Urdu. Each of these writers helped to sustain her culture by creating linguistic attachments to it.

On the other hand, writers who chose to continue to write in English or French have likewise insisted that these languages are in fact more suitable for survival in the postcolonial world. How else might India, for example, with its 700 languages (and many dialects), communicate with its people? Only through those semi-universal languages could writers reach the audiences (within their countries) who most need to hear their messages, and to reach those (beyond their national boundaries) who might be in a position to respond to their demands. The choices that individual writers have made are part of an ongoing debate that has its special permutations and most expressive resonances in India, Africa, Canada, as well as parts of the United States, and those countries or regions dominated earlier by China and later by Japan.

Some writers have marked this debate by writing on the *linguistic border*, using a macaronic language that combines the different languages of their world like so many strands of spaghetti. We have included their texts, which serve to highlight the tensions and strains of living in different linguistic universes, to point to differences in what can be or is said in different languages, to signal the consequences of imperial/colonial dualities.

For women writers, the debate was further complicated by the question of gender. The early tradition of Japanese women writers is exemplary in this regard. Women recorded their texts in native *kana* rather than in Chinese, the language of literature, simply because they were prevented from learning the literary language used by men. Even within China, women writers were limited by education from inscribing their texts within the learned Mandarin that was thus *literally* the preserve of men. In more recent history, British and later American empires frequently brought with them feminist notions that had great impact on women's lives. For those in the upper classes and aristocracies of their countries, English and French was the vehicle of education and liberation, power and knowledge. Of perhaps prime importance, women writers lacked a female audience in their own languages, since the majority of women remained uneducated and illiterate. Thus, improvements in women's education and literacy have been as critical as nationalistic impulses in determining the decisions of women to write in indigenous languages. Writers such as Nawal al-Saadawi and Kannuta Banuna write now in Arabic, while their precursors characteristically wrote in French—or not at all; in India, Mahasveta Devi and Indira Sant write in Bengali and Marathi, respectively, drawing on indigenous oral sources while being confident that there are audiences for their *writing* within their own linguistic communities. Within nationalist (con)texts, women have inserted their narratives, inscribed women's characters, (re)written their countries' stories to take account of their role in both public and private domains. And they have frequently given previously unwritten questions of class and race a text.

In the face of such linguistic complexity one cannot help but be reminded of the biblical story in which architects and craftsmen came together to build a tower that would lead them to god, only to have the divinity prevent them from achieving their aspiration by causing them to speak different languages; no longer able to communicate with one another, the builders could not complete the tower of Babel, and the proper noun, which designated a city of God, now became a synonym for linguistic chaos and confusion. The story is in effect another version of the Fall, the expulsion from Eden. However, it can be seen in a positive light, as well, an example of the "Fortunate Fall." If, as some linguists and linguistic philosophers have suggested, language is a construct of reality, then linguistic diversity gives us access to different ways of seeing the world. To understand a Chinese text, for example, is to learn something of the Chinese landscape as well as its social organization; if we "read" its narrative correctly, we discover something of its beliefs and understand its customs. Languages are the verbal maps of culture. In this context, the multiplicity of tongues is a gift rather than a punishment, for insofar as language reflects different habits of consciousness and thus expresses different realities, it offers the reader different ways of seeing the world, ways not otherwise accessible to her. Ideally, of course, we would all learn as many languages as possible in order to gain access to the different realities contained within them. In a less than ideal world, we turn to translations.

SCOPE AND CONTENTS OF THIS ANTHOLOGY

Before you read any single selection in this book, may we ask you to look at the Table of Contents. It will reveal that this is a book about remarkable fruition—fruition, in many cases, against nearly impossible odds and in the face of enormous struggle. Women were writing in Africa in the nineteenth century, in Spanish America, in Japan, Australia, India, indeed, in most countries of the world; not only were they writing, some were writing profusely, and, in the main, getting published. People in their own countries knew about them, read them, admired them. They were writing in different modes, on many subjects, in many languages, and for different purposes. We have compiled this anthology to pay homage to these writers by giving them the readers they deserve. Our ultimate goal is to reveal an international women's literary tradition, one that is multilingual, multiracial, multigeneric, and of long standing.

This book contains literature written or published by women between the years 1875 and 1975, the period we see as the first vigorous flowering of women's writing on an international scale. The beginning date coincides with the beginnings of the modern women's struggle, a struggle which experienced a renaissance one hundred years later in the late 1960s and early-to-mid-1970s. The terminal date of the anthology brings us to the era that stimulated an immense flowering of women's writing, one which we feel sure will be examined by future historians and critics as a separate phenomenon. This recent period has not yet had its end, and we provided but a few of the most significant texts and included only a few representatives of those whose major work is perhaps yet to come. We hope this anthology will create enough interest in, and awareness of, the field so that a work, or series of works, is compiled to give a more complete picture of contemporary women's writing.

Organization of the Text

In the text, writers appear chronologically. Our aim in organizing the text by date of the author's birth rather than by country or themes is to emphasize that women's literature developed within a historical context; at the same time, such an order recognizes the primacy of the individual writer. The writer's life serves as the matrix within which the work comes into being. The organization was also the one most frequently requested by teachers and students of the field.

An alternative "table of contents" grouping writers by country and region appears after the regional essays, to enable students and teachers to study the development of indigenous traditions and selected nationalities. Some courses might then focus exclusively on the Third World, or Europe, or the Eastern or Western traditions.

Selections

The selections themselves represent a variety of genres. We have included not only short stories, poetry, and drama (as well as excerpts from novels), but oral works, journalistic essays, literary criticism, letters, diaries, and excerpts from autobiographies in the recognition that the definition of what constitutes literature has been broadened. In a variety of ways, the selections reflect the major social, political, and historical movements and events shaping the writer's world during the period in question. They frequently touch both directly and indirectly on women's roles, aspects of female development, and feminist issues as well as feminist interpretations of cultural and world events.

We might note that each nation or region elicited or favored a consideration of a particular kind of literature that exists in some measure in other literatures. Thus, the Russian political picture compelled us to address the question and include examples of expatriate/émigré writers who addressed themselves to a large Russian community living outside the national boundaries of their country and who wrote about the changes wrought by desettlement, while presuming their connection to and participation in a Russian literary canon. Similarly, the vagaries of Russian political history demanded a consideration of prison memoirs. A parallel case is the inclusion of examples of the oral traditions in India and Africa, where we know women have been equal contributors both to the more traditional forms and to its more modern permutations, but we might just as well have included examples from China, Latin America, or the United States. Another category is that of indigenous languages: here the United States and, to a greater extent, India are used to illustrate linguistic diversity. We hope that readers will recognize that the examples are intended as synecdochal representatives of such genres and languages everywhere and that the absence of a particular genre, tradition, or theme in one area is compensated for by its presence in another area. We regret the absence of those writers we strongly wished to include but for whose work proper permission clearance was not forthcoming.

Headnotes

Biobibliographical introductions precede the selection(s) for each author. Each note includes facts about her life, notes the writer's major works, and characterizes the writer's major themes, literary style, and subject matter. The introductions also provide a literary, historical, and social context for the author's production. They place the writer within the national landscape and on the international scene. Discussion of her literary standing is also included, and where criticism is available, this may also be mentioned.

Historical and Literary Essays

The regional essays that appear at the end of the book provide historical background for the writers surveyed in this anthology. Written by critics, scholars, and translators who are recognized specialists in their respective language and literatures, the essays are designed to introduce both faculty and students to the women's literary tradition of a particular language, nation, or region prior to 1875 and to briefly suggest developments after 1975; the main focus, however, is the period covered by the text. They cover most of the areas from which our selections have been drawn.

The essays stress not only historical events affecting a particular country or region but those social factors specifically affecting women. Many authors take note that women's writing was often stimulated by new opportunities available to women, and that women's literary productivity was often but one expression or form that women seized upon and fashioned, part of a larger ferment. In addition, these discussions emphasize those writers at work during this period whom we have been unable to include for reasons of space. The intention here on the part of most essay authors was to suggest the wealth of writers in this period, historical knowledge that would give the lie to statements like: "There really aren't many women writers in_____ —(name your favorite country)" or "We know that there were perhaps a few fine women writers, but in general women have not made extensive contributions to the_____(name your own favorite genre/field)."

Individual differences among the essays do exist. Some of these derive from the different perspectives our advisors took on the material, and the contexts that a given writer felt most beginning students should have in reading the literature of a particular literary tradition. Other differences emerge as a result of the relative distance of certain cultures from our own, and the degree of basic research done by critics in the field. Thus, for example, Colette Gaudin, in writing about the French literary tradition, presumes there is less need to make students aware of French history and the social backgrounds of her writers than Gillian Davies writing on the francophone Canadian tradition; the former chooses instead to emphasize the significant developments in French literary history that have led to the suppression of French women writers. In a related vein, Barbara Harlow, writing under the influence of deconstruction and concerned with a tradition frequently perceived in the West as "alien," is at pains to dismantle the colonialist "text" and its relation to female "narrative" in the Middle East; her essay is concerned to provide us with feminism as the perspective for analyzing more strictly literary production, and indirectly makes us aware of how necessary basic literary research is. Marguerite Olmos, writing about Spanish American women writers, and influenced by a Marxist perspective, chooses to stress the political and social factors that shape the female literary tradition.

Furthermore, a comparative review of the essays will enable students to note trends and differences in particular countries. There is no doubt that increasing educational and professional work opportunities for women, for example, laid the groundwork worldwide for both new readers as well as new writers; however, such opportunities and their consequences occur at different periods of particular national histories. Within the literary sphere, the phenomenon of "westernization" is also a pattern that occurs differentially, as does the phenomenon that emphasizes indigenous traditions, even as these patterns reflect decolonization and liberation movements, also occurring at different periods in countries' histories.

Introductory bibliographies follow each essay and include sociohistorical texts, general literary histories, and texts on the women's literary tradition or on specific groups or individual women writers. Contributors have also noted series titles, which include discussions of women writers. These bibliographies generally include only works written in English. This will permit students interested in a particular literature or period to do further research in the areas that interest them.

EDITORIAL MATTERS

This work employs certain conventions and styles, as explained below, to facilitate communication of pertinent information.

Languages, Names, and Alphabets

Transliterations in Arabic are based on the system used in the Wehr Dictionary. Two major letters that do not have adequate English equivalents are the *hamza*, which is represented by an apostrophe (') and the *ain*, which is represented by a reverse apostrophe ('). However, where names or words are commonly known to the English reader, their established American spellings are used. Dates and ages derive from the Western rather than the Muslim calendar.

All Chinese names and terms in these selections have been transliterated according to Pinyin, the standard romanization system used in the People's Republic of China. A guide to Pinyin pronunciation can be found in any textbook or Chinese-English dictionary published in the People's Republic of China. Most consonants and vowels are pronounced roughly the same as in English, and the brief list that follows will explain the exceptions that appear in the selections. The sounds *si, ri, zhi,* and *shi* are pronounced "sz," "ir," (as in *girl*), "jr," and "shr," respectively. *X* is pronounced like the "sh" in *sheep, zh* is pronounced like the "G" in *George, ui* is pronounced like "way" (so that *shui* rhymes with *sway*), *q* is pronounced like the "ch" in *cheap, z* is pronounced "dz," *c* is pronounced "ts," and *you* rhymes with *snow.* Until recently the standard romanization from Chinese into English was the Wade-Giles system (a guide to which can be found in *Mathews' Chinese-English Dictionary*), and Wade-Giles romanization is given in parentheses beside each author's name. In the introductory essay, the names of expatriate writers are given in Wade-Giles romanization, since this is the spelling by which their names are known in the West. Chinese surnames are almost always mono-syllabic, and they precede given names, which are either monosyllabic or bisyllabic.

Indian names and concepts have been spelled phonetically according to common usage in American texts. Indian names vary according to the usage of the individual, although the name order generally follows western tradi-tion; in some parts of the south where a matrilineal society pertains, names are given in reverse order, with the mother's family name, and sometimes the father's family name, followed by the given name. In either case, women are rarely addressed by their surname or family name: Women have traditionally followed their first name with the honorific titles *Bai* or *Devi*; the latter literally means "goddess," but both are loosely used to mean "named woman." Somewhat like our use of Ms. or, more aptly, the British use of "Lady," as in Lady Diane, these terms are markers of respect or status indicating the given name that precedes them is the name of a woman. Some writers use Western-style names, such as Amrita Pritam, whose given name is Amrita and whose surname, or family or father's name, is Pritam. Others such as Lalithambika Antherjanam use as their "last name," their caste name: Antherjanam means "woman inside," or woman of the Namboodiri caste. Lakshmi is a common woman's name, referring to the "goddess of fortune," and given to female children in the prayerful hope that she will bring the family prosperity.

Japanese ideograms have been transliterated using the Roman alphabet; an American reader can assume that words sound much as they are spelled. *Ch* has the sound of *church* and the *g* is pronounced as in *go*; vowels are pronounced as in Italian. A macron is used to indicate a long vowel in all words, proper names, and place-names, except for major cities. Japanese names appear in Japanese order, surname first; writers may be referred to by their first names, using the common critical practice for both male and female authors. The Japanese traditionally reckon age by assigning one year at birth and adding a year each New Year; ages are converted to Western count.

The transliteration system used here for the Russian Cyrillic alphabet is the one generally accepted for a nonspecialized audience. This system allows the nonspecialist to pronounce Russian names with some degree of accuracy.

This same consideration prompted the placement of stress marks on all Russian words and names. All Russian names consist of a given name, a patronymic, and a surname. The patronymic is the father's name with the feminine suffix -*ovna* or -*evna* (meaning *son of*). Masculine *surnames* that end in the suffix -*in*, -*ov*, -*sky*, or -*tsky* have the feminine variants -*ina*, -*ova* (not to be confused with the patronymic -*ovna*), -*skaya* and -*tskaya*. All other surnames have no gender distinction. The Western calendar has been used in regard to all dates and ages.

In 1928 the Turkish Parliament changed the alphabet from the Arabic to the Latin. Arabic, with its lack of written vowels, was not suited to Turkish, which has eight vowels, and it posed various other spelling difficulties. The new alphabet was developed in less than a year. It has one sound per letter and, because it was introduced so recently, is still phonetic. The principal differences from the letters found in Western European languages are that *c* in Turkish is pronounced like the letter "j" in *judge*, and a *ç* is the "ch" in *church*, *ş* is the "sh" in *ship*, and the *ğ* is not pronounced like our "g" but lengthens the preceding vowel. The *i* is reserved for the "ee" in *beet*, and there is a new letter, *ı*, which sounds like the "a" in *cereal*. Although last names were introduced in the early 1930s, people have continued to use only first names in social address about as often as do Americans today. The usual equivalent of Mr. is *Bey*, and *Hanim* (also written as Hanum in English) is the equivalent of Mrs., Miss, and Ms. *after* the first name; there is no distinction made in Turkish between Miss and Mrs. and no grammatical gender.

British spellings have been retained if the original work employed them.

Country of Origin

In assigning countries to our writers, we have generally considered the relevance to the writer's publication, and secondarily, to the writer's life. Many of our writers were more cosmopolitan or peripatetic than usual, traveling frequently and living abroad for somewhat extended periods of time. There is no hard and fast line that can be drawn as a consequence. A few examples may be offered to suggest our strategies. Renée Vivien was an Anglo-American, but because her identity is defined as French by her use of the pseudonymous *Vivien* and by the fact that she lived out her life there, and because her literary production appeared originally in French and is part of France's literary history, she is assigned only to France. Halide Adib-Adivar did write in English, and she herself lived in both England and the United States, but we have chosen to identify her solely with Turkey since she returned there in later life and is defined/identifies herself as a Turk even when, or perhaps especially when, writing in English. Though born in Greece, Mathilde Serao wrote in Italian as an Italian, and though born in what was then Persia, Doris Lessing wrote of the country in which she grew up as the country of her adoption; the former is assigned to Italy, but not to Greece, the latter to Rhodesia *and* England, but not to Persia. On the other hand, though Gertrude Stein wrote in English and intended an English audience, she lived out her entire maturity in France and is associated in literary history with the expatriate community, and her "French connection" is privileged, while Isak Dinesen's link with Kenya, for better or worse, is also given "official" identification through her categorization under Africa. Finally, one need not have even moved to have found oneself living in another country: witness, for example, those writers who grew up in Russia and died in the Union of the Soviet Socialist Republic, or those who were born in Germany and now find themselves either part of the German Federal Republic or the German Democratic Republic.

Titles, Dates, and Notes

In the headnote, or introduction to a writer's work, any work that has appeared in translation has the title of that translation in italics (or, for shorter works, in quotation marks) following the original title; otherwise the translation of the title appears in Roman print. The year given is that of publication of the original work.

Every effort has been made to ascertain correct birth/death dates in headnotes, essays, and of course for the book's basic chronology. Where information is unavailable or not precise, we have used "fl." for *flourishing*, if we know a writer published during a certain period, or *contemporary* (contemp.).

Notes to selections are from the author herself *only* when so marked; they are otherwise provided by translators, editors, and advisors of this volume, or by those associated with previous publication of the material.

NOTES

1. George Steiner, *After Babel: Aspects of Language and Translation* (New York: Oxford University Press, 1975), pp. 38–56. Steiner's book also influences the discussion on translation that later follows.
2. "(Re)writing the Body: The Politics and Poetics of Female Eroticism," *The Female Body in Western Culture: Contemporary Perspectives*, ed. Susan Rubin Suleiman (Cambridge: Harvard University Press, 1986), pp. 7–29. Suleiman's article is also reflected in the discussion on the characteristics of women's writing later in the text.
3. In *The Resisting Reader: A Feminist Approach to American Fiction*. (Bloomington/London: Indiana University Press, 1978).
4. See Domna Stanton, ed., *The Female Autograph: Theory and Practice of Autobiography from the Tenth to the Twentieth Century* (Chicago/London: University of Chicago Press, 1987); Barbara Harlow, "From the Woman's Prison: Third World Women's Narratives of Prison, "*Feminist Studies* 12, 3 (1986): 501–524. Tania Modleski, *Loving with a Vengeance: Mass-Produced Fantasies for Women* (New York: Methuen, 1984); Elizabeth A. Flynn and Patrocinio P. Schweickart, *Gender and Reading: Essays on Readers, Texts, and Contexts* (Baltimore: Johns Hopkins University Press, 1986).

BIBLIOGRAPHY

Bernard, Jessie. *The Female World from a Global Perspective*. Bloomington: Indiana University Press,

Benstock, Shari, ed. *Feminist Issues in Literary Scholarship*. Bloomington: Indiana University Press, 1987.
Boxer, Marilyn J. and Jean H. Quataert. *Connecting Spheres: Women in the Western World, 1500 to the Present*. New York: Oxford University Press, 1987.

Chafetz, Janet Salzman and Anthony Gary Dworkin. *Female Revolt: Women's Movements in World and Historical Perspective*. Totowa, N.J.: Rowman and Allanheld, 1986.

de Lauretis, Teresa, ed. *Feminist Studies/Critical Studies*. Bloomington: Indiana University Press, 1987.

Duley, Margot I. and Mary I. Edwards, eds. *The Cross-Cultural Study of Women: A Comprehensive Guide*. New York: Feminist Press, 1986.

Encyclopedia of Continental Women Writers. New York: Garland Publishing, 1987.

Evans, Richard J. *The Feminists: Women's Emancipation Movements in Europe, America and Australia, 1840–1920*. New York: Barnes and Noble, 1977.

Jayawardena, Kumari. *Feminism and Nationalism in the Third World*. London: Zed Books, 1987.

Lerner, Gerda. *The Creation of Patriarchy*. New York: Oxford University Press, 1986.

Matthiasson, Carolyn J. *Many Sisters: Women in Cross-Cultural Perspective*. New York: Free Press, 1979.
Newton, Judith and Deborah Rosenfelt, eds. *Feminist Criticism and Social Change: Sex, Class and Race in Literature and Culture*. New York: Methuen, 1986.

Robinson, Lillian S. *Sex, Class, and Culture*. New York: Methuen, 1986.

Russ, Johanna. *How To Suppress Women's Writing*. Austin: University of Texas Press, 1983.

Ruthven, K.K. *Feminist Literary Studies: An Introduction*. New York: Cambridge University Press, 1984.
Said, Edward. *Orientalism*. New York: Vintage Books, 1979.

Schipper, Mineke, ed. *Unheard Words: Women and Literature in Africa, the Arab World, the Caribbean and Latin America*. Trans. Barbara Potter Fasting. New York: Allison & Busby, 1985.

Snitow, Ann, Christine Stansell, and Sharon Thompson, eds. *Powers of Desire: The Politics of Sexuality*. New York: Monthly Review Press, 1983.

Spivak, Gayatri Chakravorty. *In Other Worlds: Essays in Cultural Politics*. New York: Rutledge, 1988.

Women's Studies in Western Europe: A Resource Guide. Eds. Stephen Lehmann and Eva Sartori. Chicago: Association of College and Research Libraries/American Library Association, 1987.

Worsley, Peter. *The Three Worlds: Culture and World Development*. Chicago: University of Chicago Press, 1984.

Material on Translations: Following are standard references for seeking out works in translation; despite their pretensions to completeness, however, the nonfeminist sources frequently omit works by women. They should be supplemented by bibliographies of specific literatures, bibliographies devoted to women's studies of specific cultures or areas, and women's literary bibliographies.

Chicorel Index to Plays. 5 vols. 1970–1974.

Chicorel Index to Poetry in Anthologies and Collections in Print. 4 vols. 1974.,

Chicorel Index to Poetry in Anthologies and Collections: Retrospective. 4 vols. 1975.

Chicorel Index to Short Stories in Anthologies and Collections. 4 vols. 1974.

Index translationum: Cumulative Index to English Translations, 1948–1968. Lists only books.

"List of Translations," 1960–. *Yearbook of Comparative and General Literature*, nos. 10–, 1961–. (Annual)

Literature of the World in English Translation: A Bibliography. Eds. George B. Parks and Ruth Z. Temple. 1967–. Volume 2 covers Slavic literatures; vol. 3, pt. 1 includes Catalan, Italian, Portuguese, Brazilian, Rumanian, Spanish, Spanish-American literatures; pt. 2 is devoted to French literature. Volume 4 will? cover Celtic, Germanic, and other European literatures and Volume 5 will deal with literatures of Asia and Africa.

Resnick, Margery and Isabelle de Courtivron. *Women Writers in Translation: An Annotated Bibliography, 1945–1982*. New York/London: Garland Publishing, 1984. Covers books devoted to a single author almost exclusively for Brazil and Portugal, France, Francophone countries, German-speaking countries, Italy, Japan, Russian, Spain, and Spanish America.

The Selections

Thórarinn B. Thorláksson,
Woman at a Window,
1899, oil on canvas. Private
Collection, Reykjavik,
Iceland

Anonymous

Ethiopia, 19th century

Anonymous was a woman. This selection stands as a dedication to all the women who are part of the oral tradition, which exists as the unexplored subtext of this book. The song is representative of but one of a multitude of strains in that tradition—a secular, witty lament for a male lover. It was originally spoken in Amharic, in Ethiopia.

TROUSERS OF WIND

> Trousers of wind and buttons of hail,
> A lump of Shoa earth, at Gondar nothing left;
> A hyena bearing meat, led by a leather thong;
> Some water in a glass left standing by the fire;
> A measure of water thrown on the hearth;
> A horse of mist and a swollen ford;
> Useless for anything, useful to no one;
> Why am I in love with such a man as he?

Translated by Sylvia Pankhurst, assisted by Ato Menghestu Lemme

Emily Dickinson   *US, 1830–1886*

The events of Dickinson's life were few. She was born and died in her father's house in the small college town of Amherst, Massachusetts. She never married and rarely left home. The greatest lyric poet of nineteenth-century America was part of no literary movement, championed no public causes, and had few readers beyond an intimate circle of family and friends. In isolation, she was prolific. Of the 1,755 poems and fragments that have been found since her death, a mere six were printed in newspapers and magazines during her lifetime. Rarely has a poet's voice been more insistently powerful or more private.

Dickinson was the daughter of a prominent family steeped in the traditions of Puritan New England, committed to education, industry, and public service. Her father was a Massachusetts judge and a U.S. Congressman. Her mother was a near invalid and remote from the poet, her brother and sister. Dickinson attended Amherst Academy and Mount Holyoke Female Seminary, before "delicate health" (or possibly, emotional sensitivity and intellectual frustration) put an end to her formal education. Increasingly, she withdrew from the world. By her thirtieth year, she barely left her garden, received few visitors, and wore only white. For most would-be guests, a message had to suffice.

"The Soul selects her own Society—/Then—shuts the Door" (poem 303), and we can only guess at her reasons. Critics have fruitlessly speculated that she was unhappy in love. More probably, as Suzanne Juhasz has suggested, the fostering of literary genius in a woman of the nineteenth century required some form of social or personal violence, and isolation was her choice.[1]

Dickinson had written hundreds of verses by 1862, when she began her correspondence with Thomas Wentworth Higginson, an editor for *Atlantic Monthly* magazine to whom she submitted four poems. In her letters, she addressed him as "Preceptor," and humbly posed as his student. A man of mediocre and conventional taste, he discouraged her from publishing, yet continued to offer advice on her work for twenty years.

From a life narrow by conventional standards, and from the household tasks that women have performed silently for generations, Dickinson drew the material for metaphysical speculation. Baking, sweeping, caring for the ill, mourning the dead, and observing the quiet nature of a garden, were the occasions for sudden mysteries. "A Route of Evanescence" (poem 1463) is a verbal picture of a hummingbird. She used the quotidian and small to illuminate great uncertainties.

Ambivalent religious attitudes, together with the themes of death, immortality, and eternity, permeate her work. The Puritan sense of spiritual mystery inhabiting the circumstances of everyday life informs her minute observations of nature. Her meter is adapted from eighteenth-century hymns. But hers was "that religion/That doubts as fervently as it believes" (poem 1144), holding more in common with such Transcendentalist thinkers as Emerson and Thoreau.

Four years after her death, Dickinson's family and friends published the first selection of her poems. They added titles, conventionalized her elliptical grammar, and altered her words. Many critics at first received her poetry with hostility or condescension, but readers educated in a modernist tradition have begun to catch up with her unorthodox rhythms and difficult thoughts. Her work was revived by the Imagists in the 1920s and during the 1950s by the New Critics. Since the publication of an authoritative text of her poems in 1955, and with feminist considerations of her work abounding,[2] appreciation of her work has grown. Only recently have we begun to gain an understanding of her incalculable influence on American (and other) women from Genevieve Taggard, Toyo Suyemoto, and Dorothy Parker to Adrienne Rich.

Leslie Camhi

NOTES

1. *Naked and Fiery Forms; Modern American Poetry by Women, a New Tradition* (New York: Harper & Row, 1976).
2. See, for example, *Feminist Critics Read Emily Dickinson*, ed. Suzanne Juhasz (Bloomington: Indiana University Press, 1983).

SELECTED POEMS

219

She sweeps with many-colored Brooms—
And leaves the Shreds behind—
Oh Housewife in the Evening West—
Come back, and dust the Pond!

You dropped an Amber thread—
And now you've littered all the East
With Duds of Emerald!

And still, she plies her spotted Brooms,
And still the Aprons fly,
Till Brooms fade softly into stars—
And then I come away—

245

I held a Jewel in my fingers—
And went to sleep—
The day was warm, and winds were prosy—
I said "Twill keep"—
I woke—and chid my honest fingers,
The Gem was gone—
And now, an Amethyst remembrance
Is all I own—

258

There's a certain Slant of light,
Winter Afternoons—
That oppressess, like the Heft
Of Cathedral Tunes—

Heavenly Hurt, it gives us—
We can find no scar,
But internal difference,
Where the Meanings, are—

None may teach it—Any—
'Tis the Seal Despair—
An imperial affliction
Sent us of the Air—

When it comes, the Landscape listens—
Shadows—hold their breath—
When it goes, 'tis like the Distance
On the look of Death—

320

We play at Paste—
Till Qualified, for Pearl—
Then, drop the Paste—
And deem ourself a fool—

The Shapes—though—were similar—
And our new Hands
Learned *Gem*-Tactics—
Practicing *Sands*—

613

They shut me up in Prose—
As when a little Girl
They put me in the Closet—
Because they liked me "still"—

Still! Could themself have peeped—
And seen my Brain—go round—
They might as wise have lodged a Bird
For Treason—in the Pound—

Himself has but to will
And easy as a Star
Abolish his Captivity—
And laugh—No more have I—

1078

The Bustle in a House
The Morning after Death
Is solemnest of industries
Enacted upon Earth—

The Sweeping up the Heart
And putting Love away
We shall not want to use again
Until Eternity.

1207

He preached upon "Breadth" till it argued
                                        him narrow—
The Broad are too broad to define
And of "Truth" until it proclaimed him a
                                                    Liar—
The Truth never flaunted a Sign—

Simplicity fled from his counterfeit presence
As Gold the Pyrites* would shun—
What confusion would cover the innocent
                                                        Jesus
To meet so enabled a Man!

NOTE

* A lustrous yellow mineral, also called Fool's Gold.

1540

As imperceptibly as Grief
The Summer lapsed away—
Too imperceptible at last
To seem like Perfidy—
A Quietness distilled
As Twilight long begun,
Or Nature spending with herself
Sequestered Afternoon—
The Dusk drew earlier in—
The Morning foreign shone—
A courteous, yet harrowing Grace,
As Guest, that would be gone—
And thus, without a Wing
Or service of a Keel
Our Summer made her light escape
Into the Beautiful.

1545

The Bible is an antique Volume—
Written by faded Men
At the suggestion of Holy Spectres—
Subjects—Bethlehem—
Eden—the ancient Homestead—
Satan—the Brigadier—
Judas—the Great Defaulter—
David—the Troubadour—
Sin—a distinguished Precipice
Others must resist—
Boys that "believe" are very lonesome—
Other Boys are "lost"—
Had but the Tale a warbling Teller—
All the Boys would come—
Orpheus' Sermon captivated—
It did not condemn—

Marie von Ebner-Eschenbach   *Austria, 1830–1916*

Marie von Ebner-Eschenbach, born Countess Dubsky into an aristocratic Czech-German family, grew up summering on the family estate in Mähren and wintering in Vienna. Although frequent visits to the Viennese Burgtheater inspired her to write plays, her eventual literary success derived from fiction and aphorisms. She was married at age 18 to von Ebner-Eschenbach, her cousin, and she continued to live the life of a noble lady, moving between country estate and city palace. The social contours of this life are outlined in the title of the short story collection that brought her the greatest recognition, *Dorf- und Schlossgeschichten* (Tales of the Village and the Palace), which she published in 1883 during the waning years of the Austro-Hungarian Empire, in the fin-de-siècle atmosphere that was to breed such writers and thinkers as Nietzsche, Freud, and Kafka. The collection, together with some six other volumes of short stories, depicts the ethnic and class divisions between the Slavo-German peasants and their aristocratic Austrian rulers. "The District Doctor" and "Jacob Szela," for example, are set during the bloody peasant uprisings of 1846 in Galicia. Altogether, Ebner-Eschenbach's works provide an acute observation of her time as well as a critique of the landed gentry from a conservative Catholic point of view.

Her best-known work was the novel *Das Gemeindekind* (Child of the Parish, 1887). Ebner-Eschenbach also published a few poems. Her highly regarded volume of aphorisms appeared in 1880. In 1900 she became the first woman to be given a honorary doctorate by the University of Vienna.

Marilyn Sibley Fries

SELECTED APHORISMS

An aphorism is the last link in a long chain of thoughts.

He who no longer remembers clearly his own childhood is a poor teacher.

Let us not look for truthfulness in women so long as they are reared in the belief that their chief end in life is—to please.

The genius of a language reveals itself most clearly in its untranslatable idioms.

Manuscripts turn moldy in the desk, or come to maturity there.

Not to join in the intellectual advances of one's time is to be retarded morally.

What is still to be done, ponder over that; what you have already done, forget.

All earthly power has its base in violence.

We are in mortal fear that love of our neighbor should become too widespread, and we erect barricades against it—nationalities.

The little troubles of life often help us over the great misery of it.

When a woman learned to read, the woman question arose in the world.

Translated by G.H. Needler

Christina Rossetti   *UK (England), 1830–1894*

Born in London, English poet Christina Rossetti was the daughter of a museum curator, Dante scholar, and poet who had fled Italy in 1824 because of his involvement with the Carabinieri, Neopolitan separatists. Her mother, Anglo-Italian, was thoroughly English in custom and tradition.

The artistic Rossetti family were very loving and nurturing of one another's writing, painting, and reading. Christina, the youngest of the four children (Maria, a Dante scholar herself; Dante Gabriel, an artist; and William, a man of letters) took to writing poetry as early as the age of 5. By 12 she was writing verse regularly, although she hid her composing from her family, and in 1847, her grandfather, Gaetano Polidori, collected her first poems and printed them privately.

Throughout her youth, Christina was greatly affected and encouraged by her brother Dante Gabriel to whom she was similar in temperament. However, her passionate temperament was cloaked both by Victorian attitudes toward women and by her own devotion to her Anglo-Catholic religion, a religion that was at once fired by the romanticism of the day and restrained by its austere views, self-negation, piety, and rationality. Christina's devotion to and search for God apparently led her to reject two suitors whose religious devotion and affiliation were at issue. If Christina's piety was outwardly constraining, it was a fount of emotion and poetic creativity, empowering and informing all she wrote.

During the 1840s and early 1850s, the fortunes of the Rossetti family declined. The father became ill in 1843 and soon after was forced to leave his teaching position at King's College, London. Christina became ill too; absorbed in the care of her father, who died in 1854, and of herself, she rarely left home. Her many years of seclusion and ill health led her to be, in her brother William's words, "compelled, even if not naturally disposed, to regard this world as a valley of the shadow of death."

In 1848, Dante Gabriel and six other artist cohorts formed the Pre-Raphaelite Brotherhood, and Christina became involved with the group as a model for Dante's paintings. In 1850, she published seven poems in the Pre-Raphaelite's periodical *Germ*. These, along with "Heart's Chill Between," published in 1848 in *Athenaeum*, were her first poems to appear in print. In 1862, she published the collection *Goblin's Market*, about two sisters, one tempted by goblins (thought to be a metaphor for "evil" sexuality), the other risking her own life to save her. This work met with immediate and universal acclaim. In 1866, *The Prince's Progress* appeared, and although its success put Christina on public display in a way she felt to be unsuitable to her religious values, it also established her reputation as a writer. Both works contained illustrations and woodprints by Dante. In 1872, Christina published a delightful collection of children's verse entitled *Sing-Song, A Nursery Rhyme Book*, followed in 1874 by a collection of children's stories, *Speaking of Likenesses*. Much of her poetry was infused with religious devotion, and it was in the 1870s that she also began to write religious tracts, several of them published by the Society for Propagating Christian Knowledge.

The 1870s, which brought Christina continued acclaim, also brought an end to the health and unity of the Rossetti family. Christina became ill with Grave's disease, which left her partially invalided and physically disfigured. Maria became an Anglican nun in 1872 and died in 1876. William married in 1874, and in 1876 he and his wife moved out of the Rossetti home. For several years, Dante suffered from insomnia, and began to rely heavily on whiskey and drugs; on Easter day in 1882, he died.

Christina published two more volumes of poetry: *A Pageant and other Poems* (1881), which contains the sonnets of troubled love reprinted here, "Monna Innominata"; and *Verses* (1893). In 1883, her one-time suitor and lifelong friend Charles Bagot Cayley died, and her mother in 1886, leaving Christina ill and alone. She died of cancer in 1894.

John Isom

MONNA INNOMINATA[1]

A Sonnet Of Sonnets

1.

"Lo dì che han detto a' dolci amici addio."—DANTE.
"Amor, con quanto sforzo oggi mi vinci!"
——PETRARCA.[2]

Come back to me, who wait and watch for
you:—
  Or come not yet, for it is over then.
  And long it is before you come again,
So far between my pleasures are and few.
While, when you come not, what I do I do
  Thinking "Now when he comes," my
sweetest "when:"
  For one man is my world of all the men
This wide world holds; O love, my world is
you.
Howbeit, to meet you grows almost a pang
  Because the pang of parting comes so soon;
  My hope hangs waning, waxing, like a moon
  Between the heavenly days on which we
meet:
Ah me, but where are now the songs I sang
  When life was sweet because you called
them sweet?

2.

"Era già l'ora che volge il desio."—DANTE.
"Ricorro al tempo ch'io vi vidi prima."—PETRARCA.

I wish I could remember, that first day,
  First hour, first moment of your meeting me,
  If bright or dim the season, it might be
Summer or Winter for aught I can say;
So unrecorded did it slip away,
  So blind was I to see and to foresee,
  So dull to mark the budding of my tree
That would not blossom yet for many a May.
If only I could recollect it, such
  A day of days! I let it come and go
  As traceless as a thaw of bygone snow;
It seemed to mean so little, meant so much;
If only now I could recall that touch,
  First touch of hand in hand—Did one but
know!

3.

> "O ombre vane, fuor che ne l'aspetto!"—DANTE.
> "Immaginata guida la conduce."—PETRARCA.

I dream of you to wake: would that I might
   Dream of you and not wake but slumber on;
   Nor find with dreams the dear companion
                        gone,
As Summer ended Summer birds take flight.
In happy dreams I hold you full in sight,
   I blush again who waking look so wan;
   Brighter than sunniest day that ever shone,
In happy dreams your smile makes day of
                        night.
Thus only in a dream we are as one.
   Thus only in a dream we give and take
     The faith that maketh rich who take or give;
If thus to sleep is sweeter than to wake,
   To die were surely sweeter than to live,
Tho' there be nothing new beneath the sun.

4.

> "Poca favilla gran fiamma seconda."—DANTE.
> "Ogni altra cosa, ogni pensier va fore,
> E sol ivi con voi rimansi amore."—PETRARCA.

I loved you first: but afterwards your love
   Outsoaring mine, sang such a loftier song
As drowned the friendly cooings of my dove.
   Which owes the other most? my love was
                        long,
   And yours one moment seemed to wax
                  more strong;
I loved and guessed at you, you construed me
And loved me for what might or might not be—
   Nay, weights and measures do us both a
                      wrong.
For verily love knows not "mine" or "thine;"
   With separate "I" and "thou" free love has
                      done,
   For one is both and both are one in love:
Rich love knows nought of "thine that is not
                   mine;"
   Both have the strength and both the
                length thereof,
Both of us, of the love which makes us one.

5.

> "Amor che a nulla amato amar perdona."—DANTE.
> "Amor m'addusse in sì gioiosa spene."—PETRARCA.

O my heart's heart, and you who are to me
   More than myself myself, God be with you.
   Keep you in strong obedience leal and true
To Him whose noble service setteth free,
Give you all good we see or can foresee,
   Make your joys many and your sorrows few,
   Bless you in what you bear and what you do.
Yea, perfect you as He would have you be.
So much for you; but what for me, dear friend?
   To love you without stint and all I can
Today, tomorrow, world without an end;
   To love you much and yet to love you
                      more,
   As Jordan at his flood sweeps either
                    shore;
Since woman is the helpmeet made for man.

6.

> "Or puoi la quantitate
> Comprender de l'amor che a te mi scalda."—
>   DANTE.
> "Non vo' che da tal nodo amor mi scioglia."—
>   PETRARCA.

Trust me, I have not earned your dear rebuke,
   I love, as you would have me, God the most;
   Would lose not Him, but you, must one be
                      lost,
Nor with Lot's wife cast back a faithless look
Unready to forego what I forsook;
   This say I, having counted up the cost,
   This, tho' I be the feeblest of God's host,
The sorriest sheep Christ shepherds with His
                    crook.
Yet while I love my God the most, I deem
   That I can never love you overmuch;
    I love Him more, so let me love you too;
    Yea, as I apprehend it, love is such
I cannot love you if I love not Him,
   I cannot love Him if I love not you.

7.

"Qui primavera sempre ed ogni frutto."—DANTE.
"Ragionando con meco ed io con lui."—PETRARCA.

"Love me, for I love you"—and answer me,
   "Love me, for I love you"—so shall we stand
   As happy equals in the flowering land
Of love, that knows not a dividing sea.
Love builds the house on rock and not on sand,
   Love laughs what while the winds rave
                   desperately;
   And who hath found love's citadel unmanned?
   And who hath held in bonds love's liberty?
My heart's a coward tho' my words are brave—
   We meet so seldom, yet we surely part
   So often; there's a problem for your art!
   Still I find comfort in his Book, who saith,
Tho' jealously be cruel as the grave,
   And death be strong, yet love is strong as
                   death.

8.

"Come dicesse a Dio: D'altro non calme."—
   DANTE.
"Spero trovar pietà non che perdono."—PETRARCA.

"I, if I perish, perish"—Esther spake:
   And bride of life or death she made her fair
   In all the lustre of her perfumed hair
And smiles that kindle longing but to slake.
She put on pomp of loveliness, to take
   Her husband thro' his eyes at unaware;
   She spread abroad her beauty for a snare,
Harmless as doves and subtle as a snake.
She trapped him with one mesh of silken hair,
   She vanquished him by wisdom of her wit,
   And built her people's house that it should
                 stand:
   If I might take my life so in my hand,
And for my love to Love put up my prayer,
   And for love's sake by Love be granted it!

9.

"O dignitosa coscienza e netta!"—DANTE.
"Spirto più acceso di virtuti ardenti."—PETRARCA.

Thinking of you, and all that was, and all
   That might have been and now can never be,
   I feel your honoured excellence, and see
Myself unworthy of the happier call:
For woe is me who walk so apt to fall,
   So apt to shrink afraid, so apt to flee,
   Apt to lie down and die (ah, woe is me!)
Faithless and hopeless turning to the wall.
And yet not hopeless quite nor faithless quite.
Because not loveless; love may toil all night,
   But take at morning; wrestle till the break
   Of day, but then wield power with God
                 and man:—
   So take I heart of grace as best I can,
   Ready to spend and be spent for your
                   sake.

10.

"Con miglior corso e con migliore stella."—DANTE.
"La vita fugge e non s'arresta un' ora."—PETRARCA.

Time flies, hope flags, life plies a wearied wing;
   Death following hard on life gains ground
                   apace;
   Faith runs with each and rears an eager face,
Outruns the rest, makes light of everything,
Spurns earth, and still finds breath to pray and
                   sing;
   While love ahead of all uplifts his praise,
   Still asks for grace and still gives thanks for
                   grace,
Content with all day brings and night will bring.
Life wanes; and when love folds his wings above
   Tired hope, and less we feel his conscious
                   pulse,
   Let us go fall asleep, dear friend, in peace:
   A little while, and age and sorrow cease;
   A little while, and life reborn annuls
Loss and decay and death, and all is love.

11.

"Vien dietro a me e lascia dir le genti."—DANTE.
"Contando i casi della vita nostra."—PETRARCA.

Many in aftertimes will say of you
    "He loved her"—while of me what will
                        they say?
    Not that I loved you more than just in play,
For fashion's sake as idle women do.
Even let them prate; who know not what we
                        knew
    Of love and parting in exceeding pain.
    Of parting hopeless here to meet again,
Hopeless on earth, and heaven is out of view.
But by my heart of love laid bare to you,
    My love that you can make not void nor
                        vain,
Love that foregoes you but to claim anew
    Beyond this passage of the gate of death,
    I charge you at the Judgment make it plain
    My love of you was life and not a breath.

12.

"Amor, che ne la mente mi ragiona."—DANTE.
"Amor vien nel bel viso di costei."—PETRARCA.

If there be any one can take my place
    And make you happy whom I grieve to grieve,
    Think not that I can grudge it, but believe
I do commend you to that nobler grace,
That readier wit than mine, that sweeter face;
    Yea, since your riches make me rich, conceive
    I too am crowned, while bridal crowns I
                        weave,
And thread the bridal dance with jocund pace.
For if I did not love you, it might be
    That I should grudge you some one dear
                        delight;
    But since the heart is yours that was mine
                        own,
    Your pleasure is my pleasure, right my right,
Your honourable freedom makes me free,
    And you companioned I am not alone.

13.

"E drizzeremo gli occhi al Primo Amore."—DANTE.
"Ma trovo peso non da le mie braccia."—PETRARCA.

If I could trust mine own self with your fate,
    Shall I not rather trust it in God's hand?
    Without Whose Will one lily doth not stand,
Nor sparrow fall at his appointed date;
    Who numbereth the innumerable sand.
Who weighs the wind and water with a weight,
To Whom the world is neither small nor great,
    Whose knowledge foreknew every plan we
                        planned.
Searching my heart for all that touches you,
    I find there only love and love's goodwill
Helpless to help and impotent to do,
    Of understanding dull, of sight most dim;
    And therefore I commend you back to Him
Whose love your love's capacity call fill.

14.

"E la Sua Volontade è nostra pace."—DANTE.
"Sol con questi pensier, con altre chiome."—
    PETRARCA.

Youth gone, and beauty gone if ever there
    Dwelt beauty in so poor a face as this;
    Youth gone and beauty, what remains of
                        bliss?
I will not bind fresh roses in my hair,
To shame a cheek at best but little fair,—
    Leave youth his roses, who can bear a
                        thorn,—
I will not seek for blossoms anywhere,
    Except such common flowers as blow with
                        corn.
Youth gone and beauty gone, what doth remain?
    The longing of a heart pent up forlorn,
    A silent heart whose silence loves and
                        longs;
    The silence of a heart which sang its songs
While youth and beauty made a summer
                        morn,
Silence of love that cannot sing again.

NOTES

1. The Latin title refers literally to the nameless women poets and muses of the Middle Ages and particularly to Beatrice and Laura, the muses of Italian poets Dante Alighieri (1265–1321) and Francesco Petrarca (1304–1374). Lines from their works, which deal with the poetic quest for spiritual salvation through transcendent love, inform Rossetti's major theme in her sonnet sequence, are translated by her brother William (1829–1919):

2. Translations of the epigraphs:
    1. The day that they have said adieu to their sweet friends.
       Love, with how great a stress dost thou vanquish me today!
    2. It was already the hour which turns back the desire.
       I recur to the time when I first saw thee.
    3. Oh shades, empty save in semblance!
       An imaginary guide conducts her.
    4. A small spark fosters a great flame.
       Every other thing, every thought, goes off, and love alone remains there with you.
    5. Love, who exempts no loved one from loving.
       Love led me into such joyous hope.
6. Now canst thou comprehend the quantity of the love which glows in me towards thee.
    I do not choose that Love should release me from such a tie.
7. Here always Spring and every fruit.
    Conversing with me, and I with him.
8. As if he were to say to God, "I care for nought else."
    I hope to find pity, and not only pardon.
9. O dignified and pure conscience!
    Spirit more lit with burning virtues.
10. With better course and with better star.
    Life flees, and stays not an hour.
11. Come after me, and leave folk to talk.
    Relating the casualties of our life.
12. Love, who speaks within my mind.
    Love comes in the beautiful face of this lady.
13. And we will direct our eyes to the Primal Love.
    But I find a burden to which my arms suffice not.
14. And His will is our peace.
    Only with these thoughts, with different locks.

Rosalía de Castro   *Spain, 1837–1885*

The illegitimate child of the daughter of a wealthy family from Galicia, Rosalía de Castro was raised in the country with peasants, as was the custom of upperclass families of the time. She was only brought to live with her mother when a young woman, at which point she received the traditional "woman's education," which included instruction in art, music, languages, and sewing.

De Castro began writing as early as 11 and published her first book of poetry *La flor* (The Flower) in 1857, at the age of 20. This work was soon followed by her three novels *La hija de mar* (Daughter of the Sea, 1859), *Flavio* (1861) and *El caballero de las botas azules* (The Gentleman with the Blue Boots, 1867). These works, written in Spanish, were quite favorably reviewed. However, the time de Castro spent as a child with the Galician peasantry, learning traditional songs and stories, greatly influenced her, and the beautifully lyrical poems she wrote in the ancient language of the region are among her best works. Her two books of poetry in Galician were *Cantares gallegos* (Galician Songs, 1863) and *Follas novas* (New Leaves, 1880), both considered exquisite examples of the poetry of a language which was once the preferred poetic language of Spain and Portugal. The following poems were taken from her final work, *En las orillas de Sar* (On the Banks of the Sar, 1884), written in Spanish and published shortly before her death from cancer.

Rosalía de Castro's life was not a happy one. Her marriage to the eminent Galician folklorist Manuel Murguía was marked by poverty and ill treatment on his part. Of her six children, three died while still young. And critical recognition came slowly; her reputation as one of the finest nineteenth century Spanish and Galician poets was not achieved until nearly fifty years after her death.

THE BELLS
Las campanas

I love them, I listen to them
As I listen to the wind's whisper,
Or to the fountain's murmur
Or the bleating of the lamb.

The bells are like the birds,
Their cries and echoes welcome
The earliest ray of daybreak
That opens up the skies.

And their notes, pealing out
Across the plains and the peaks,
Keep in them something candid,
Something serene and sweet.

Were their tongues forever dumb,
What gloom in the air and in the sky!
What silence in all the churches!
What strangeness among the dead!

Translated by Edwin Morgan

THE SPRING DOES NOT FLOW NOW...
Ya no mana la fuente...

The spring does not flow now, the stream is
                                    quite dry;
No traveler goes to quench his thirst there.
The grass does not grow now, no daffodil
                                    blooms.
No fragrance of lilies floats on the air.
Only the sandy bed of the dried-up river
Fills the parched traveler with the horror of
                                    death.
No matter; in the distance another stream
                                    murmurs
Where timid violets perfume the air.
And willow boughs, seeing themselves in the
                                    ripples.
Spread about the water the coolest of shade.
The thirsty traveler, crossing the highway,
Moistens his lips with the limpid water
Of the stream shaded by the tree's branches,
And gladly forgets the spring now dry.

Translated by Muriel Kittel

Minna Canth   *Finland, 1844–1897*

Born in Tampere, Finland, and educated at the Finnish Teacher's College in Jyvasyla, Minna Canth married, in 1865, the professor of sciences at the college. After his death in 1879, she was left with seven children to support. Taking over her father's drapery shop, she succeeded in making a living for herself and her children while pursuing a career as a writer.

A radical feminist writer since the 1880s, Canth became as important to the emancipation of women in Finland as Mathilde Fibinger, Camilla Collett, and Fredrika Bremer had been during the 1850s in their respective countries of Denmark, Norway, and Sweden. Canth wrote both plays and short stories dealing with the exploitation of the working class, the poor, and women. Her writing was considered radical at the time, and her focus on women's rights can be viewed as modern. She was, moreover, extremely critical of society's hypocrisy, especially regarding sexual morality.

A very successful playwright, Canth is still considered one of Finland's best. At the time of their original production, her plays were controversial for their radical social views and on occasion condemned for being too shocking. In one of them she explores divorce, which at the time was legal in Finland but extremely difficult for a woman to obtain. In the play *Sylvi*, written in Swedish and first performed at the Swedish Theater of Helsinki in 1893, certain similarities with Ibsen's *A Doll's House* and Flaubert's *Madame Bovary* are quite apparent.

In "Lapsenpiika" ("The Nursemaid," 1892), the short story included here, Canth explores the exploitation of a poor nursemaid by her middle-class employers.

Ingrid Claréus

THE NURSEMAID
Lapsenpiika

"Emmi, wake up! Can't you hear Madam ringing? Emmi! How that girl sleeps, Emmi, Emmi!"

Finally, Silja got a response from her. Emmi sat up, grumbled, and rubbed her eyes. She was still terribly sleepy.

"What time is it?"

"It's way after four."

Way after four? She had been in bed three hours; not until one-thirty had she finished wiping the dishes, for last night they had had guests, as they so frequently did. And before that, she had had to stay up for two whole nights because of Lilli; Madam had gone to a wedding and the child would not settle for the sugartit. Was it any wonder, then, that she was sleepy?

She was going on fourteen. Her legs always ached in the mornings, so that it was quite difficult to step on them at first. Silja, who slept with her in the same bed, said it was because she was growing. Her legs should be bled, Silja thought, but Emmi was afraid it would hurt. And they were thin even now. What would they be if blood was let from them? When she slept, her legs never ached, but as soon as she woke up, the aching would begin. Then, if she managed to fall asleep again, they stopped aching at once.

Even now, as she sat in the bed, her legs ached from the knees down to the heels. Her head dropped back into the bed, sank so heavily, that it was impossible to get up. Would she ever in this world be lucky enough to be allowed to sleep as long as she wanted to even for one single morning?

Sitting up again, Emmi rubbed her legs. Her head dropped so low that her chin touched her breast and her eyes closed. Her hands stopped moving, she breathed deeply and slowly. In no time, she sank back into the bed.

The bell jingled again. Silja poked Emmi in the side with her elbow.

"Isn't it strange that we can't get this little brat to obey. Get up!"

She poked Emmi once more with her sharp elbow, and it hit so sharply on Emmi's breast that she cried out in pain.

"What's the matter with you that you have to be called ten times before you'll get up?"

Emmi staggered to her feet, she felt dizzy and almost fell over.

"Rinse your eyes with cold water, it'll help you wake up," Silja advised.

But Emmi didn't have time to do that, for the bell sounded once again. She managed to put on her dress, smoothed down her hair with both hands, rubbed her eyes from time to time, and hurried in to Madam.

"I have rung three times," said Madam.

Emmi didn't speak, she just took Lilli, who lay beside Madam in the bed, into her arms.

"Put something dry on her and take her to

the cradle, she won't fall asleep beside me any more anyhow."

Madam turned over on her other side and closed her eyes. The cradle was in the next room, where Emmi now took the child. After changing Lilli, she began to sing and rock the cradle. From time to time, an idea would pop into her mind, not a great or complicated one, but strong enough to break into the singing.

"Hs hss s. Aa aa aa a. —Sleep, my Child, sleep. —Hs hss s. Aa aa aa a. —Oh, god how sleepy I am. —I came along the Turku road, I rested on the Pori road. —Silja, lucky girl, is still sleeping—I came along the Turku road, I rested on the Pori road. —Hs hss hss s. Aa aa aa aa a—."

Lilli fell asleep. Emmi then stretched out on the floor beside the cradle. She put her arm beneath her head and before long she was sound asleep. Emmi was unaware that Lilli awakened almost at the same time as she fell asleep; Lilli rubbed her nose and looked around in wonder, for no one was with her. She tried to stand up, but couldn't; however, she managed to move to one side of the cradle and got her head over the edge. Now Lilli noticed Emmi, was delighted, and prattling, reached to touch her. The cradle tipped. She tumbled out and hit her forehead on the rocker of the cradle. The shriek of pain suddenly awakened everyone.

"God help me!"

Emmi turned deathly pale when she saw the child on the floor beside her. She grabbed the child into her arms, tried to quiet her, and still very pale, kept swinging her in her arms. Madam must have heard it, Emmi, terrified, kept thinking the whole time. In her panic she forgot to check whether the child was hurt, or whether she was just crying from fright. Madam opened the door.

Emmi thought she would faint, the whole world turned black before her eyes.

"What happened to her?"

"Nothing."

Emmi didn't know what she answered. Instinctively, she blurted out words which she hoped would, if possible, save her.

"Why is she crying like that then? Certainly there has to be a reason."

In vain Emmi tried everything to calm the child.

"Give her to me," said Madam. "Oh, Child, my Dear, what is wrong? My god, she's got a black and blue mark on her forehead!"

She looked at Emmi, who stood helpless.

"How did it get there? Are you struck dumb?"

"I don't know..."

"You must have dropped her. From the cradle I suppose."

Emmi was silent and looked down.

"So, you can no longer deny it. What an incompetent and careless thing you are. First you drop the child and then, furthermore, you lie. Poor me, that I ever took you in. But now I want you to know that we will not keep you here next year. Get another place for yourself, wherever you can find one. I certainly don't want you, even if I never get a nursemaid again...Sssh, my Darling, sssh, mamma's own Child. Mamma will find you a better nursemaid next year. Don't cry, don't cry."

Lilli stopped crying when she found the breast, and after a little while, she smiled with contentment, even though teardrops still glistened in her eyes.

"Oh, my Darling, are you smiling at Mamma already? My own Child, what a good girl you are. And now you have that ugly black and blue mark on your forehead."

Lilli didn't cry any more that day; she was as happy as before, perhaps even a little happier. She laughed for Emmi, stuck her finger into Emmi's mouth, and tugged at Emmi's hair. Emmi brushed her own cheeks with Lilli's delicate hand, for teardrops the size of beads rolled down her cheeks all day. And when she remembered that in six weeks she would no longer hold this soft, sweet child in her arms, nor even see her except for perhaps just a glimpse at the window, when she, a miserable outcast, would walk past on the street; it was then, when she thought of this, or felt rather than thought it, that the teardrops followed each other so quickly that they joined together and formed a small pool on the table.

"Look at that, look at that," she said to Lilli, who began at once to splash in it with the palms of her hands.

Before noon, Madam received guests, Doctor Vinter's wife and Headmaster Siven's wife, elegant and refined, both of them, although they were not nearly as elegant as our Madam, Silja said, and Emmi thought so too.

When Silja brought in the coffee, Madam asked her to tell Emmi to bring Lilli in for the guests to see. Emmi put on Lilli's prettiest bonnet and also a brand new bib. These made the child look so lovely that Emmi had to call Silja to come and look before she brought Lilli to the guests.

How charmed the women were as soon as the two appeared in the doorway.

"Oh, how sweet!"

And then, vying with each other, they took Lilli into their arms, kissed her, and squeezed her, and laughed.

"How sweet, how sweet!"

Emmi stood in the back and smiled. She didn't really understand what "how sweet, how sweet" meant, since the women spoke in Swedish, but she concluded from it all that it must mean something really good.

But suddenly the women became very grave. Madam was telling them—whatever it was she was telling them. Emmi didn't understand it, since she spoke in Swedish. However, she suspected what it was when she saw the shocked expressions on the women's faces.

"My god, my god, no just think of it, poor Child."

Three pairs of eyes turned at the same time to look, first, with extreme compassion, at the black and blue mark on Lilli's forehead, and then, repulsed, at Emmi.

"What a wretched creature!"

Emmi looked down at the carpet on the floor and waited for something to drop on her from the ceiling, something that in one swoop would dash her to pieces, or smite her deep into the ground. For certainly there was no one in the whole world as worthless as she, miserable wretch. She did not dare to look up, but she knew, and felt in the very tips of her fingers and toes, that they were still looking at her. These elegant, refined women, who themselves never made mistakes. How would that even be possible, since they were so very wise and so much better than ordinary people.

"You may take Lilli away," she heard Madam say.

Emmi's hands had suddenly become so limp that she was afraid of dropping the child if she took her into her arms now.

"Do you hear?"

"There you see now, what she is like."

Emmi staggered forward and somehow managed to take those few steps to Madam's chair. Her desire to get away from their sight back to the nursery provided the strength she needed. Or was it just her old routine that made her arms once again obey and carry out their tasks as always before. She lowered Lilli into the cradle, and sat on the footstool beside it and showed her playthings. But Lilli had lifted both feet straight up into the air and was grasping at them with her hands. She thought this was such fun that she laughed out loud. Emmi would have laughed too if her guilt and the choking sensation in her throat would have allowed it. As she sat there, she wondered why she hadn't remembered at all this morning the trick which she had often used to fight off sleep; namely, to prick and scratch her arms with a needle. This forgetfulness had caused the whole, horrible accident, which could not be undone, and which was now ruining her whole life.

Late that night, when everyone had gone to bed, Emmi went outside into the yard. It was gray and dark there and quiet, but above, the sky was filled with stars. She sat down on the lowest step to think about her present and her future. But just thinking about it didn't solve anything, for her situation was just as gray and dark as the night around her. So she left her cares behind and looked into the dark blue up high, where heaven's candles burned brightly. Who were the lucky ones near them? And who of those living now would get to go there? Probably no servant girls? But, of course, all the gentry. This was certain, since they were already so very much better down here. Furthermore, she wondered who lit those candles every night, the angels or the humans? Or did humans become angels there? What about small children who die very young? Who rocked them and cared for them? Or didn't they perhaps need care in heaven?

Silja opened the door and urged her to come inside.

"Why on earth are you sitting out there in the cold?"

"Listen, Silja," said Emmi later as she was undressing, "why is it that we servant girls are so bad?"

"Don't you know?"

"No."

"Because we have to stay awake so much. We have all the more time to sin. You see, since the gentry sleep late in the mornings, until nine or ten, they avoid many a bad deed."

That was probably it. If she, too, had been allowed to sleep longer in the morning, Lilli would not have fallen from the cradle because of her.

The following Sunday was the third Sunday for hiring servants. Emmi was given her reference paper, and told to go to the churchyard.

There was a big crowd there, those who were hiring and those who hoped to be hired. They were standing in their large sleighs; they all seemed to know one another and to be in league together. Emmi felt deserted and alone. Who would care to hire her, tiny and frail as she was? She stood next to the wall of the church with her reference paper, and waited. Masters and mistresses crisscrossed in front of her, but didn't even glance at her. Some young men were sitting nearby on the church steps.

"Ho, there, girl, come over here," said one of them. The others laughed and whispered among themselves.

"Come, come, how about it? Come and sit beside me here."

Emmi blushed and moved farther away. At the same time, she happened to come face to face with a gentleman and his wife. Or were they real members of the gentry, since the woman was wearing a scarf over her head and the man's clothes were quite worn.

"What about that one?" said the gentleman, pointing at Emmi with his cane. "She certainly can't be asking very high wages. What do you ask?"

"Whatever the master and mistress wish to give me. I will be happy with that," answered Emmi softly. A faint hope rose in her breast.

"What use is she to us? Has she even got the strength to carry water tubs?"

"I do have the strength for that."

"And do you know how to wash clothes?"

"I've done that too."

"Let's take her; she seems decent and quiet," said the master. But the mistress still was doubtful.

"She might be sickly, being so thin."

Emmi remembered her legs, but she didn't dare to say anything about them, for then they would have rejected her immediately.

"Are you sickly?" asked the master, looking at Emmi's reference paper, which he had snatched from her hand.

"No," whispered Emmi.

In her mind she decided never to complain again, no matter how much her legs ached.

The master tucked the reference paper

into his pocket, gave her a couple of marks as wages paid in advance, and so the matter was settled.

"You are to come in the evening of All Saints' Day to the Karvonen estate and ask for the Hartonen family," said the mistress. "But be sure to be there by the evening of All Saints' Day!"

Emmi went home.

"You'll be going to a bad household," said Silja, who knew the Hartonen family. "Living there is miserable and poor, and the mistress is such a good-for-nothing that ser-vants never stay for the full year. They say that she doesn't even give food except in portions, and very small ones at that."

Emmi blushed. But she recovered quickly and answered, "Not everyone can get the best places. Some have to settle for poorer places and be grateful that they don't have to go out into the world as beggars."

She took Lilli into her arms and pressed her face against the child's warm breast. Lilli grabbed Emmi's hair with both hands and babbled, "Ta, ta, ta."

Translated by Inkeri Väänänen-Jensen

Elizabeth Stuart Phelps Ward   *US, 1844–1911*

Elizabeth Stuart Phelps Ward was born Mary Gray in Boston to parents whose differences came to define a tension in her writing. Her father, Austin Phelps, like her maternal grandfather, taught sacred rhetoric at Andover Theological Seminary. His Calvinist views on women were apparently a source of some frustration to Ward's mother, Elizabeth Stuart Phelps, an established author whose portraits of women's day-to-day lives inspired her daughter's writing. So closely did Ward identify with her mother that sometime after the latter's death in 1852, Ward assumed her name.

Ward was educated at the Abbot Academy and Mrs. Edwards' School for Young Ladies, where she was greatly influenced by Elizabeth Barrett Browning's *Aurora Leigh* (1857). She wrote several unremarkable religious works until a story published in *The Atlantic Monthly*, "The Tenth of January" (1868) about the Pemberton Mill Fire in Lawrence, Massachusetts, brought her literary recognition and the support of friend and neighbor Harriet Beecher Stowe (1811–1896) and other prominent women writers. An active supporter of women's rights, Ward authored feminist articles for *The Independent* and other periodicals. In 1876, she delivered the "George Eliot" lectures at Boston University. When she was 44 she married Herbert Dickenson Ward, a 27-year-old journalist, with whom she col-laborated on two novels. The couple spent their summers together in Ward's house (formerly, her "Old Maid's Paradise") in Gloucester, Massachusetts, and their winters apart. It was in Gloucester that Ward was converted to the temperance movement.

Beginning with the immensely popular and widely translated *The Gates Ajar* (1868), which sold 100,000 copies, inspired a small industry of popular songs and trademark mementos, and moved Mark Twain to parody, Ward spun off *Beyond the Gates* (1883) and *The Gates Between* (1887). In the Gates trilogy, which anticipates the Utopian literature of the 1890s, the humanity of society is measured by the condition of women, and inversely, women are a source of utopian values. In a series of novels, including *Hedged In* (1870), which deals with the situation of a single mother and the disruption of a friendship between two women by marriage, and *The Silent Partner* (1871), in which two women from contrasting backgrounds choose reformist social projects over marriage, Ward probed the institution of marriage. The particularly noteworthy *Story of Avis* (1877), alluding to Ward's and her mother's life, appraises the conflict between domesticity and creativity. Like her friend Sarah Orne Jewett (1849–1909), Ward also wrote about a woman's becoming a doctor in *Doctor Zay* (1882); unlike Jewett's protagonist, Ward's heroine chooses to marry, making her right to pursue her career a condition of her commitment.

Ward's autobiography *Chapters from a Life* (1896) recounts her meetings with Ralph Waldo Emerson and provides portraits of prominent members of the New England literary establishment, including Henry Wadsworth Longfellow and John Whittier, and of female literary figures like poet and essayist Celia Thaxter (1835–1894), working-class autobiographer Lucy Larcom (1824–1893), and romance writer and reformer Lydia Child (1802–1880). In the work, Ward is also concerned to describe the genesis of her texts (not without humor) and the critical as well as reader response to them; she is fully prepared to justify her professionalism. Among the more poignant aspects of these memoirs is Ward's description of the onset of her invalidism; it is a revelation of what it cost an early feminist to pursue her ambition and creative independence. It is but one reflection of the conflict Ward never fully resolved between her father's misogynist views and her mother's creative model. Nonetheless, in the best of her some forty-odd books, Ward fashioned from regional materials a morally-informed feminist realism.

Eric Mendelsohn

from CHAPTERS FROM A LIFE

For my first effort to sail the sea of letters, it occurs to me that I ought to say that my father's literary reputation cannot be held responsible.

I had reached (to take a step backwards in the story) the mature age of thirteen. I was a little girl in low-necked gingham dresses, I know, because I remember I had on one (of a purple shade, and incredibly unbecoming to a half-grown, brunette girl) one evening when my first gentleman caller came to see me.

I felt that the fact that he was my Sunday-school teacher detracted from the importance of the occasion, but did not extinguish it.

It was perhaps half-past eight, and, obediently to law and gospel, I had gone upstairs.

The actual troubles of life have never dulled my sense of mortification at overhearing from my little room at the head of the stairs, where I was struggling to get into that gingham gown and present a tardy appearance, a voice distinctly excusing me on the ground that it was past her usual bedtime, and she had gone to bed.

Whether the anguish of that occasion so far aged me that it had anything to do with my first literary undertaking, I cannot say; but I am sure that it was during this particular year that I determined to become an individual and contribute to the "Youth's Companion."

I did so. My contribution was accepted and paid for by the appearance in my father's post-office box of the paper for a year; and my impression is that I wore high-necked dresses pretty soon thereafter, and was allowed to sit up till nine o'clock. At any rate, these memorable events are distinctly intertwined in my mind.

This was in the days when even the "Companion," the oldest and most delightful of children's journals, printed things like these:—

Why Julia B. Loved The Country.

"Julia B. loved the country because whenever she walked out she could see God in the face of Nature."

I really think that the semi-column which I sent to that distinguished paper was a tone or two above this. But I can remember nothing about it, except that there was a sister who neglected her little brothers, and hence defeated the first object to existence in a woman-child. It was very proper, and very pious, and very much like what well-brought-up little girls were taught to do, to be, to suffer, or to write in those days. I have often intended to ask Mr. Ford if the staff discovered any signs of literary promise in that funny little performance.

At all events, my literary ambitions, with this solitary exercise, came to a sudden suspension. I have no recollection of having written or of having wanted to write anything more for a long time.

It is impossible to remember how or when the idea of the book [*The Gates Ajar*] first visited me. Its publication bears the date of 1869, but I am told that the exact time was in 1868; since publishers sometimes give to an Autumn book the date of the coming year. My impressions are that it may have been towards the close of 1864 that the work began; for there was work in it, more than its imperfect and

youthful character might lead one ignorant of the art of book-making to suppose.

It was not until 1863 that I left school, being then just about at my nineteenth birthday. It is probable that the magazine stories and Sunday-school books and hack work occupied from one to two years without interruption; but I have no more temperament for dates in my own affairs than I have for those of history. At the most, I could not have been far from twenty when the book was written; possibly approaching twenty-one.

At that time, it will be remembered, our country was dark with sorrowing women. The regiments came home, but the mourners went about the streets.

The Grand Review passed through Washington; four hundred thousand ghosts of murdered men kept invisible march to the drum-beats, and lifted to the stained and tattered flags the proud and unreturned gaze of the dead who have died in their glory.

Our gayest scenes were black with crape. The drawn faces of bereaved wife, mother, sister, and widowed girl showed piteously everywhere. Gray-haired parents knelt at the grave of the boy whose enviable fortune it was to be brought home in time to die in his mother's room. Towards the nameless mounds of Arlington, of Gettysburg, and the rest, the yearning of desolated homes went out in those waves of anguish which seem to choke the very air that the happier and more fortunate must breathe.

Is there not an actual, occult force in the existence of a general grief? It swells to a tide whose invisible flow covers all the little resistance of common, human joyousness. It is not a material miasma. The gayest man breathes it, if he breathe at all; and the most superficial cannot escape it.

Into that great world of woe my little book stole forth, trembling. So far as I can remember having had any "object" at all in its creation, I wished to say something that would comfort some few—I did not think at all about comforting many, not daring to suppose that incredible privilege possible—of the women whose misery crowded the land. The smoke of their torment ascended, and the sky was blackened by it. I do not think I thought so much about the suffering of men—the fathers, the brothers, the sons—bereft; but the women, —the helpless, outnumbering, unconsulted women; they whom war trampled down, without a choice or protest; the patient, limited, domestic women, who thought little, but loved much, and, loving, had lost all,—to them I would have spoken.

For it came to seem to me, as I pondered these things in my own heart, that even the best and kindest forms of our prevailing beliefs had nothing to say to an afflicted woman that could help her much. Creeds and commentaries and sermons were made by men. What tenderest of men knows how to comfort his own daughter when her heart is broken? What can the doctrines do for the desolated by death? They were chains of rusty iron, eating into raw hearts. The prayer of the preacher was not much better; it sounded like the language of an unknown race to a despairing girl. Listen to the hymn. It falls like icicles on snow. Or, if it happen to be one of the old genuine outcries of the church, sprung from real human anguish or hope, it maddens the listener, and she flees from it, too sore a thing to bear the touch of holy music.

At this time, be it said, I had no interest at all in any especial movement for the peculiar needs of women as a class. I was reared in circles which did not concern themselves with those whom we should probably have called agitators. I was taught the old ideas of womanhood, in the old way, and had not to any important extent begun to resent them.

Perhaps I am wrong here. Individually, I may have begun to recoil from them, but only in a purely selfish, personal way, beyond which I had evolved neither theory nor conscience, much less the smallest tendency towards sympathy with any public movement of the question.

In the course of two or three years spent in exceptional solitude, I had read a good deal in the direction of my ruling thoughts and feeling, and came to the writing of my little book, not ignorant of what had been written for and by the mourning. The results of this reading, of course, went into the book, and seemed to me at the time by far the most useful part of it.

How the book grew, who can say? More of nature than of purpose, surely. It moved like a tear or a sigh or a prayer. In a sense I scarcely knew that I wrote it. Yet it signified labor and time, crude and young as it looks to me now; and often as I have wondered, from my soul, why it has known the history that it has, I have at least a certain respect for it, myself, in that it did not represent shiftlessness or sloth, but steady and conscientious toil. There was not a page in it which had not been subjected to such study as the writer then knew how to offer to her manuscripts.

Every sentence had received the best attention which it was in the power of my inexperience and youth to give. I wrote and rewrote. The book was revised so many times that I could have said it by heart. The process of forming and writing *The Gates Ajar* lasted, I think, nearly two years.

I had no study or place to myself in those days; only the little room whose one window looked upon the garden cross, and which it was not expected would be warmed in winter.

The room contained no chimney, and, until I was sixteen, no fire for any purpose. At that time, it being supposed that some delicacy of the lungs had threatened serious results, my father, who always moved the sods beneath him and the skies above him to care for a sick child, had managed to insert a little stove into the room, to soften its chill when needed. But I did not have consumption, only life; and one was not expected to burn wood all day for private convenience in our furnace-heated house. Was there not the great dining-room where the children studied?

It was not so long since I, too, had learned my lessons off the dining-room table, or in the corner by the register, that it should occur to any member of the family that these opportunities for privacy could not answer my needs.

Equally, it did not occur to me to ask for any abnormal luxuries. I therefore made the best of my conditions, though I do remember sorely longing for quiet.

This, at that time, in that house, it was impossible for me to compass. There was a growing family of noisy boys,—four of them,—of whom I was the only sister, as I was the oldest child. When the baby did not cry (I have always maintained that the baby cried pretty steadily both day and night, but this is a point upon which their mother and I have affectionately agreed to differ), the boys were shouting about the grounds, chasing each other through the large house, up and down the cellar stairs, and through the wide halls, a whirlwind of vigor and fun. They were merry, healthy boys, and everything was done to keep them so. I sometimes doubt if there are any happier children growing anywhere than the boys and girls of Andover used to be. I was very fond of the boys, and cherished no objection to their privileges in the house. But when one went down, on a cold day, to the register, to write one's chapter on the nature of amusements in the life to come, and found the dining-room neatly laid out in the form of a church congregation, to which a certain proportion of brothers were enthusiastically performing the duties of an active pastor and parish, the environment was a definite check to inspiration.

Anna Radius Zuccari   *Italy, 1846–1918*

Anna Zuccari, whose mother died when Zuccari was 10, grew up cared for by two old aunts. She envied her brothers who, being male, could find diversion in their studies and friends. In 1871 she married Adolfo Radius, a lawyer, and although they had children, her husband encouraged her to write; she published her first short story in 1875, using the pseudonym Neera, under which she later became famous as a novelist and essayist; she is now known under her proper name.

Zuccari depicted the world of women, regardless of their social class, with fine psychological penetration. In 1880 the writer and critic Luigi Capuana, in an important review of her early prose, defined her art as *rêverie*. Having started to write in a period when all over Europe women were fighting for emancipation, Zuccari frequently depicted her heroines as victims of a society controlled by men. Yet she did not feel that men and women were rivals, and she did not fight for equal political and professional rights for women. She simply asked that women have the right to a personal life, something frequently denied to them by their families, where men's interests came first. She elaborated on these ideas in *Battaglie per un'idea* (Struggles for an Idea, 1898) and *Le idee di una donna* (The Ideas of a Woman, 1903), in which she states that women are not inferior, superior, nor equal to men; rather, men and women complement each other. A woman's position is tied to progress and turns on her social standing. Although Zuccari did not deny women the right to an education and freedom to choose a profession, she did believe that many were content as homemakers and thus did not need these rights. Ironically, in Zuccari's novels we find very few happy wives or mothers.

Teresa (1886), her best novel, excerpted here, depicts the sad story of a first-born girl who helps her mother raise the younger children and in the process is deprived of a personal life. The family's money having gone to send the only boy to college—with poor results—Teresa is not permitted to marry the man she loves, for her father needs her as a housekeeper after her mother's death. Only at the very end, prematurely old and bitter, does Teresa find the courage to leave her paternal house, to serve as nurse for her former love. In the powerful novel *L'indomani* (The Day After, 1890), Zuccari describes a young wife's attempt to reach out to her husband, a good and kind person but incapable of understanding her needs and affections.

Zuccari keeps sentimentality at a minimum. Her feminism is reflected above all in her heroines' thoughts and in descriptions of their daily routines, which tend to suffocate them. Her style is brisk and unadorned, characteristics that did not seem very praiseworthy to the great Italian critic Benedetto Croce, who prepared an edition of her novels in 1943, having directed his attention to her as early as 1905. A very popular and prolific writer, Zuccari published about forty books. Some of her novels were reprinted more than ten times, and the best ones were translated into German and French; only *Anima sola* (*The Soul of an Artist*, 1894) has appeared in English.

Natalia Costa-Zalessow

from TERESA

Sitting on the divan with a stool under her feet, pale as always, undone by her recent maternity, Signora Soave nursed the little one. Teresina came and went with the baby's clothes and pap, carrying orders and counter-orders to the servant in the kitchen. When she was able to rest for a moment, she sat in a small chair at the top of the steps and worked on.

Her mother looked at her tenderly, distressed by this daughter who was so good. Who knew if she would be lucky! At least luckier than she....

When assailed by such thoughts, she would lower her eyes to her slight breast, from which hung yet another baby, and she would become even sadder.

Signor Caccia seldom entered the women's room, but if by chance he did appear, the sweet intimacy between mother and daughter seemed to suspend itself. They would both look at him expectantly, fearing to find him in bad humor, ready to obey him at the slightest sign.

After he had gone, the mother would once again take up her melancholic, contemplative calm; and Teresina, in the simple serenity of her fifteen years, would smile, finding the nightmare over....

Later, contemplating her situation, she thought of how the talk at home recently, ever since they had sent Carlino to Parma to go to school, was always about money. They had to pay his room and board each month; they no longer had the servant woman, and she herself had been waiting for a new pair of boots for three months....

Sewing, under the window in the half-darkened sitting room, she imagined groups of boys, laughing and creating an uproar; and across the way, in the Palazzo Varisi, now completely dark and shut-up, she thought she saw, passing in a luminous halo, the beautiful daughter of the Marquis, dressed all in white, with a black velvet flower on her bosom.

In the middle of this reverie, a cry from little Ida or a lament from her mother would wake her abruptly, and she would shift, without transition, into one of the long jeremiads on economy that Signora Soave recited in her resigned voice. There were no more sheets in the wardrobe, the twins needed new dresses, and they could no longer put off having the copper pots tinned. And Carlino cost so much! . . . But what could be done? The only boy, it was indeed necessary to give him a good education, and with the education came all the rest.

Teresina carried these discourses in the marrow of her bones; they were a part of her diet, in the air that she breathed.

Then, on the occasions when Signor Caccia would thunder on about the luxury of a woman's life, preaching to them modesty, humility, silent activity within the domestic walls, obedience to the stronger sex, and spontaneous recognition of their duties in the face of the rights of the male, it was at these moments that she felt so abased that there would remain with her for the rest of the day a feeling of discouragement; her mother's tired voice penetrated more deeply, and she understood more clearly the look in those large, melancholy, opaque eyes. . . .

Without realizing it, that boy of eighteen, their only son, their hope for the future, absorbed the entire family.

When he shut himself in his room to study, there was complete silence; even Ida had to refrain, because the two exams that he would be repeating in October were the most important of all the matters that troubled the household.

He, the father, was a nobody, and a presumptuous one, who hid his nothingness under a great air of arrogant surliness; true to aristocratic tradition, he was a coarse, petty tyrant. He had established, with his precedence, the absolute rule of the stronger sex.

Carlino found the ground prepared, with no resistance, no struggle; he lay in it as in a bed. . . .

What could she do? Rebel against her father, break her mother's heart, ignore family tradition, be remiss in her duties as an obedient and submissive daughter?

Slavery bound her on all sides. Affection, custom, religion, society, each imposed on her its own tie. She saw happiness and could not touch it. Was she free perhaps? A girl is never free, she isn't even given the liberty to show her suffering. She was obliged to pretend with her mother out of love, with her father out of fear, and with her sisters out of shame.

And it was worse when she went out. People observed her like some rare beast on two legs. All those who had envied her the conquest of Orlandi took their revenge, laughing in her face, mocking her. The more prudent ones murmured under their breaths. Men looked her directly in the eyes, unabashed.

None of these inquisitive onlookers considered love seriously. They were disposed to find only a diversion, considering love a trifle, a reason to laugh, an indecent joke. Love, indeed, is a drama for whoever recites it and a farce for whoever looks on. . . .

She had reflected many times—not without hesitation, fearing to be a bad sister— that if it hadn't been for Carlino and his studies, perhaps she might have been assigned a small dowry. How things would have been simplified in that case!

She understood her father's reasons. She had lived in those surroundings, and only those, for too long not to be persuaded that her condition as a woman imposed on her, first of all, resignation towards her destiny—a destiny that she was not free to direct—that she was obliged to accept, however it came to her, stifled by the demands of her family, subordinated to the needs and desires of others. Yes, of all this she was convinced. But even a blind man is convinced that he cannot hope to see yet asks of the sighted world why he alone must be the victim.

Translated by Claire Siegel

Victoria Benedictsson   *Sweden, 1850–1888*

Victoria Benedictsson was a major Swedish naturalist of the 1880s and the most important writer of the first generation of women authors in Sweden. Her road to writing, however, was roundabout.

Growing up in southern Sweden, Victoria Bruzelius wanted to be a painter, but her father refused to send her to the art academy in Stockholm. Accordingly, she worked as a governess for a time to earn her own expenses for art school, but once she had done so and again approached her father, he rejected her a second time. In despair, she accepted the marriage proposal of a man twenty-eight years her senior: Christian Benedictsson, a well-meaning, dull-minded postmaster in a sleepy village in Sweden's South. The next years she spent diligently trying to be a dutiful wife and a good mother to his family of five, now six children. But then she fell ill and was confined to bed for several years; it was during this period that she began to write—sketches, short stories, and diary entries at first, but eventually also a semiautobiographical novel.

This novel, *Pengar* (Money, 1885), about an unfulfilled woman artist, established Benedictsson in Scandinavian literary circles (thanks in part to some lobbying by feminist critics). At first in Stockholm and then in Copenhagen, she met the top writers of the day, including an intellectual deemed Europe's most exciting literary critic, Georg Brandes. Obsessed with trying to please Brandes, Benedictsson set to work on her next novel, about a woman who *made* herself adjust to marriage. The result, *Fru Marianne* (Mrs. Marianne, 1887), Brandes privately dismissed as a "ladies' novel," even though Brandes never reviewed women's literature; Benedictsson was shaken. Several times before she had attempted suicide, and this time she succeeded. On the night of July 21, 1888, she watched in a mirror as she slit her carotid artery with a razor.

In her own period Benedictsson was appreciated primarily for her novels and short stories, but at least equally interesting today is her journal, *Stora boken* (The Big Book), including her intimate observations on family life as well as sketches for her fictional works. However, so controversial was her journal that an unexpurgated edition of it became available in Sweden only recently. The following excerpt, for example, was censored from the early posthumous editions of her work and first became available in Swedish in 1982.

Verne Moberg

from THE BIG BOOK
Stora boken

Hörby, the 23rd of August, 1886

Yesterday we were in Sextorp. We walked up the slope behind the house. It was just as the sun had sunk down behind a light, hazy wall of cloud. The lake was still, in gray-blue gauze. All the contours were drawn together as if with a wide, soft brush. Ellen Key and I were sitting alone on the bench, and on another, farther away, Hilda, Hilma, Matti, and Karl.[1]

Ellen sat talking about the intensity that the sense of external details can have during exceptionally strong psychic movements....

While we talked about this, the others sat making small talk off on the bench. "Aren't you Schultz in *Erik Grane*?"[2] said Hilda, impudently unabashed, as usual. "Not completely, but there probably are certain traits." And with this he cast such a strange glance at Mathilda. This abrupt utterance must clearly have broken the mood, and Matti felt a need to dismiss it.

"Look, there's a single round window up there; what a lovely view they must have from there," she said.

"Come on, let's see if there's one like it on the other side," he replied, and they walked alone to the top of the hill, where they stopped and looked out on the lake. And then it came:

"Buddy, do you think you can care for me?"[3]

On our way home, we all sat very quietly. I sat thinking how lovely Matti had grown —more beautiful for each day since he'd come....

In the evening we had colored lanterns in the garden. Christian came home from Sven Thor's wake, had been drinking, was talking nonsense over Ellen Key and being unbearable. To get rid of him, we started walking around in the garden together.... It was completely dark. Matti and Karl disappeared. I wondered if they had it settled or if he was proposing then.

After the lanterns were extinguished, we went into the parlor....

When everybody had gone, I called to Matti.

"You know, he was in here swearing to Ellen that you two never got any peace, with Hilda around." Matti looked oddly indifferent. Something strange had come over her. "You know, Mama, when we were up there in Sextorp," she began drily, unexpressively, in a narrative tone, "he asked if I could care for him. And then he said that he'd been in love with Anna Whitlock[4] for three years and that he'd been sick, and that he had lived the way young men usually did, and that I would probably never be able to care for him now. And, Mama, you know, when he told me this—and he was in such a state—so terribly upset—I felt so sorry for him. He was so pale, and he cried, and he was just devastated."

"Oh? What about *you*?"

"I was so cold, I felt completely dead inside. It was all over." She dropped her voice to a whisper. "You know, Mama, I felt such disgust."

"Yes, but you knew that he'd been living that way, didn't you? And it hasn't been since he got to know you, has it?"

"Yes." Oh, there was such a heavy sense of shame.

"What are you saying?"

"Yes, I asked him. It had been since. It had been last winter."

The rigid look of horror on her face gripped me so, I trembled deep in my soul. I had never before seen how repulsive and hideous this was. I saw it now in this young face with its composed seriousness, its heavy sorrow, its tearless gaze. She looked as if life's happiness had passed her by and was now going far, far away, never to return. Only when I saw this warm, young full-blooded woman shrink back in the presence of this thing did I realize to my horror what it was: to drag one's best, most human feelings through the mud and then offer them up to the one person who has kept her own living clean. He had turned away from this wholesome young woman, for whom his feeling had begun to waken, and had gone to the sad gray sirens of the streets; he had touched them with his hands, and now he reached out these same hands to my child, for her to put her whole life into them, her whole world of feeling. And people don't call this arrogance! For me it was upsetting, frighteningly hideous. I asked if she would still think of him with the same feeling.

Yes. She couldn't feel anything but cold disgust.

Was it over Anna Whitlock or the other?

It was the other. She could not understand how—after he'd already begun showing her attention—it had been possible for him to go to the others. It was so disgusting.

I was afraid. A whole spider's nest of self-reproach was overturned upon me. Of course, I had known or at least surmised about his life, and not thought it was anything special: he'd lived like the others, and I hadn't felt repulsed by that, I could have kept them from getting together but had not done so.

I said that if she felt indifferent to him now, then she shouldn't keep from putting an end to it because of what people would say.

No, she cared for him. She didn't think she could put an end to it. (She said this with such suppressed anguish, it went right to the roots of my heart like a pang of conscience.) But she didn't know how she could get over the feeling of cold and repugnance that had closed in upon her like an iron door.

It will be up to him to get rid of it. Don't worry about it because he can, if only you care for each other. . . .

Also, I told her that she mustn't go now and keep it all quiet and keep a check on herself; on the contrary, it would be her duty to talk, and only in complete openness would there be liberation for them both. Without compassion and without paying the slightest regard for his pain, she should disclose all her feelings to him, gather them up from all the nooks and crannies inside her and bring them out for him. Not one bit of doubt was she allowed to tuck away, not one unpleasant sensation, not one fear or suspicion. She should bring it all out now, so he might be able to clear it up, behead all the dragons. "And if he can't, then you can also be sure

there isn't any love between you, but the whole thing is a mistake, and it's best that you separate. I don't have to be afraid of giving you this advice, for nothing I could say to discourage or dissuade you is going to have the slightest effect, if you love him. And all the doubts I can bring up are less than nothing to him, if you care for him. Because if you do, then a single word is enough. The whole world can stand up and testify, and it won't have any effect: you believe him, you can't help believing, you believe despite yourself, despite everything that can be said, despite the whole world. That's the test, child, and if you cannot believe him, then you don't love him either. . . .

"So you have to talk now, before it's settled, because you should learn now to understand each other and to be open; otherwise you'll never learn it. And you mustn't give in to your shyness, not grope for words, because now you have to have them, wherever they come from. Talk, and talk honestly, that's the first and last piece of advice I have to give you. And always remember, that love is a glorious thing, worth striving for and worth having, but that it's nothing if respect doesn't go along with it."

"Naturally you can't sleep. Lie there thinking over everything you have to say and don't forget anything."

It was late, it was past midnight, and we got up to go to our rest.

I asked if she hadn't intended to turn to me, if I hadn't called her.

No. She probably would have wanted to, but not been able to. She felt shy and didn't know how to begin. She'd felt ashamed of what she had heard—it was as if she were paralyzed. She was glad that I'd spoken to her. She thanked me. She had been walking around in a dull anguish, not knowing where to turn. Now she felt more secure, now anything could happen, and she would obey the advice I had given her; she would talk.

It was as if the constraint in her being had opened up. There were tears in her eyes, she embraced me warmly, and the coloring had come back into her voice.

Translated by Verne Moberg

NOTES

After Victoria Benedictsson committed suicide in 1888, her stepdaughter Matti and Karl af Geijerstam married. Matti gave birth to three sons, the youngest after the death of his father, eleven years later. She raised the boys alone and lived to her eighties.

1. Ellen Key was an important and controversial figure in the Swedish women's movement and Victoria Benedictsson's best friend. Hilda Benedictsson was the author's biological child, and Hilma and Mathilda (Matti) Benedictsson were her stepdaughters. Matti, her stepmother's favorite, was being visited by Karl of Geijerstam, from Stockholm.

2. A reference to the 1885 novel by Gustaf of Geijerstam, brother to Karl. Schultz, an old friend of the title character, goes to Germany in attempt to cure his syphilis. One of the implicit messages of the novel is that the wife of Erik Grane made the correct moral choice in goodnaturedly opting to "adjust" to his syphilis. See the article "Truth Against Syphilis: Victoria Benedictsson's Remedy for a Dreaded Disease," by Verne Moberg, *Edda* (1982–1983).

3. "Buddy" (in Swedish, *pysen* = "junior" or "squirt," etc.) was Victoria Benedictsson's nickname for Matti.

4. Anna Whitlock (1852–1930) was the founder of an experimental private girls' school in Stockholm where both she and Ellen Key taught. After the turn of the century Whitlock became an important figure in the fight for woman's suffrage in Sweden. She never married.

Isabella Valancy Crawford   *Canada, 1850–1887*

Isabella Valancy Crawford, her brief life beset with domestic tragedy and poverty, emerges against all odds as Canada's first major English-language poet. Lacking all material advantages, Crawford produced long narrative poems, dramatic monologues in blank verse, dialect poems, and intensely evocative lyrics, as well as humorous sketches, short romantic stories, and two novels, publishing them in Toronto and New York newspapers and magazines. Northrop Frye has called hers "the most remarkable mythopoeic imagination in Canadian poetry," yet Crawford's life remains strangely obscure. Much of her fiction is still in manuscript form, and neither a definitive edition of her poetry nor a full-length study of her writing exists.

Born in Dublin, the sixth of thirteen children of an immigrant Irish family that settled in the village of Paisley, Canada West (Ontario), in the decade before Confederation, her heavy-drinking father was doctor and town treasurer (eventually surrounding the family in scandal). Crawford was educated at home, reading the classics and developing a sensitive knowledge of English, French, and American literature. After the family's move to Lakefield, where the immigrant British writers Susanna Moodie and Catharine Parr Traill lived, Crawford perhaps found encouragement for her writing, and, from the Stony Indians on a nearby reserve, a knowledge of Indian legend that influences some of her most distinctive poems.

Moving to Peterborough, then to Toronto, Crawford eked out her living by writing, supporting herself and her widowed mother in rented rooms above a Toronto grocery store. Only one book, *Old Spookses' Pass, Malcolm's Katie and Other Poems* (1884) was published during her lifetime. Brought out at her own expense, it sold only fifty copies, despite favorable notices in London journals such as the *Spectator* and the *Saturday Review*. "Malcolm's Katie," a long pioneer idyll, remains her most enduring achievement. Two serialized novels, which have not survived, were published in the 1880s; ten other novels were left unfinished at her death from heart failure at the age of 36.

Interest in Canada's first woman poet in recent years has led to the reprinting of Crawford's posthumously published *Collected Poems* (1905, reprinted 1972) and of a sampling of her fiction in *Selected Stories* (1975), *Fairy Tales of Isabella Valancy Crawford* (1977), and *The Halton Boys: A Story for Boys* (1979). A long unfinished poem, which contemporary poet Dorothy Livesay discovered in the Queen's University Archives, has been published as *Hugh and Ion* (1977). Crawford's use of Amer-Indian lore and sexual imagery and her registering of a female perspective (in poems such as "The Hidden Room," "The Rolling Pin," "Esther," and "Vashti, the Queen") are highly innovative. "Said the Canoe," regarded as her most powerful lyric, and "The Lily Bed," later incorporated into *Hugh and Ion*, illustrate some of her central concerns and techniques.

Wendy Robbins Keitner

SAID THE CANOE[1]

My masters twain made me a bed
Of pine-boughs resinous, and cedar;
Of moss, a soft and gentle breeder
Of dreams of rest; and me they spread
With furry skins and, laughing, said:
'Now she shall lay her polished sides
As queens do rest, or dainty brides,
Our slender lady of the tides!'

My masters twain their camp-soul[2] lit;
Streamed incense from the hissing cones;
Large crimson flashes grew and whirled;
Thin golden nerves of sly light curled
Round the dun camp; and rose faint zones,
Half way about each grim bole knit,
Like a shy child that would bedeck
With its soft clasp a Brave's red neck,
Yet sees the rough shield on his breast,
The awful plumes shake on his crest,
And, fearful, drops his timid face,
Nor dares complete the sweet embrace.

Into the hollow hearts of brakes—
Yet warm from sides of does and stags
Passed to the crisp, dark river-flags—
Sinuous, red as copper-snakes,
Sharp-headed serpents, made of light,
Glided and hid themselves in night.

My masters twain the slaughtered deer

Hung on forked boughs with thongs of leather:
Bound were his stiff, slim feet together,
His eyes like dead stars cold and drear.
The wandering firelight drew near
And laid its wide palm, red and anxious,
On the sharp splendour of his branches,
On the white foam grown hard and sere
    On flank and shoulder.
Death—hard as breast of granite boulder—
    Under his lashes
Peered thro' his eyes at his life's grey ashes.

My masters twain sang songs that wove—
As they burnished hunting-blade and rifle—
A golden thread with a cobweb trifle,
Loud of the chase and low of love:

'O Love! art thou a silver fish,
Shy of the line and shy of gaffing,
Which we do follow, fierce, yet laughing,
Casting at thee the light-winged wish?
And at the last shall we bring thee up
From the crystal darkness, under the cup
    Of lily folden
    On broad leaves golden?

'O Love! art thou a silver deer
With feet as swift as wing of swallow,
While we with rushing arrows follow?
And at the last shall we draw near

And o'er thy velvet neck cast thongs
Woven of roses, stars and songs—
   New chains all moulden
   Of rare gems olden?'

They hung the slaughtered fish like swords
   On saplings slender; like scimitars,
   Bright, and ruddied from new-dead wars,
Blazed in the light the scaly hordes.

They piled up boughs beneath the trees,
   Of cedar web and green fir tassel.
   Low did the pointed pine tops rustle,
The camp-fire blushed to the tender breeze.

The bounds laid dewlaps on the ground
   With needles of pine, sweet, soft and rusty,
   Dreamed of the dead stag stout and lusty;
A bat by the red flames wove its round.

The darkenss built its wigwam walls
   Close round the camp, and at its curtain
   Pressed shapes, thin, woven and uncertain
As white locks of tall waterfalls.

NOTES

1. Originally titled "The Canoe."
2. The campfire.

THE LILY BED

His cedar paddle, scented, red,
He thrust down through the lily bed;

Cloaked in a golden pause he lay,
Locked in the arms of the placid bay.

Trembled alone his bark canoe
As shocks of bursting lilies flew

Thro' the still crystal of the tide,
And smote the frail boat's birchen side;

Or, when beside the sedges thin
Rose the sharp silver of a fin;

Or when, a wizard swift and cold,
A dragon-fly beat out in gold

And jewels all the widening rings
Of waters singing to his wings;

Or, like a winged and burning soul,
Dropped from the gloom an oriole

On the cool wave, as to the balm
Of the Great Spirit's open palm

The freed soul flies. And silence clung
To the still hours, as tendrils hung,

In darkness carven, from the trees,
Sedge-buried to their burly knees.

Stillness sat in his lodge of leaves;
Clung golden shadows to its eaves,

And on its cone-spiced floor, like maize,
Red-ripe, fell sheaves of knotted rays.

The wood, a proud and crested brave;
Bead-bright, a maiden, stood the wave.

And he had spoke his soul of love
With voice of eagle and of dove.

Of loud, strong pines his tongue was made;
His lips, soft blossoms in the shade,

That kissed her silver lips—her's cool
As lilies on his inmost pool—

Till now he stood, in triumph's rest,
His image painted in her breast.

One isle 'tween blue and blue did melt,—
A bead of wampum from the belt

Of Manitou—a purple rise
On the far shore heaved to the skies.

His cedar paddle, scented, red,
He drew up from the lily bed;

All lily-locked, all lily-locked,
His light bark in the blossoms rocked.

Their cool lips round the sharp prow sang,
Their soft clasp to the frail sides sprang,

With breast and lip they wove a bar.
Stole from her lodge the Evening Star;

With golden hand she grasped the mane
Of a red cloud on her azure plain.

It by the peaked, red sunset flew;
Cool winds from its bright nostrils blew.

They swayed the high, dark trees, and low
Swept the locked lilies to and fro.

With cedar paddle, scented, red,
He pushed out from the lily bed.

Nathalie Gontcharova, Gardening, 1908, oil on canvas. The Tate Gallery, London
© A.D.A.G.P., Paris/V.A.G.A., New York, 1987

Kate Chopin

US, 1851–1904

Kate Chopin was born Katherine O'Flaherty in St. Louis to an immigrant Irish father and a mother descended from the St. Louis Creole elite. After the death of her father, she was raised by three generations of widows. The education Chopin received from her aristocratic maternal grandmother, and her reading of the "indelicate" French novelist Gustave Flaubert, seem to have influenced her rejection of Victorian literary values. Married to Oscar Chopin at the age of 19, Chopin moved with her husband first to New Orleans, where she gave birth to five sons in twice as many years, and then to a Red River plantation. Her husband died young from swamp fever and she returned to her mother's house in St. Louis, then an active cultural community. Upon her mother's death, resisting remarriage, Chopin commenced work as a writer.

She took as her model the detached and morally relativistic stories of French writer Guy de Maupassant, a representative—like Flaubert—of European naturalism, a literary creed considered by many prominent critics, including W.D.

Howells, to be an affront to American "innocence." Even in her awkward first novel *At Fault* (1890), in which her protagonist's Christian doctrine, inflexibly applied, destroys the very person whose interests she has taken to heart, Chopin breaks with the tradition of domestic sentimentality. Chopin came to associate the earthy, sophisticated French Creole and Acadian cultures of Louisiana, celebrated in her two collections of short stories *Bayou Folk* (1894) and *A Night in Acadie* (1897), with the awakening of feminine sexuality. Chopin's clearsighted depiction of women's desire, and the general sexual ambiance of her work, made for a complicated publishing history. When she could not find a publisher for the second novel, she destroyed it. She never even attempted to publish "The Storm," a story—one of her best—that refuses to condemn adultery.

Yet up to a point, Chopin opted for publication, and her extensive use of ambiguous and ironic plots as well as her lack of commentary—whether conscious or unconscious—as in "A Respectable Woman" reprinted here can be seen as narrative strategies for evading censorship.

The novel *The Awakening* (1899) owes something to Flaubert's *Madame Bovary*, to modern science, especially Darwin, and to the American Transcendentalists Ralph Waldo Emerson and Walt Whitman. It takes up the themes of the emergence of suppressed sexuality and of female autonomy. Edna, a young woman from Kentucky, marries into a Creole family, the Pontelliers. The Creoles of Grand Isle, on the Gulf of Mexico, manage to reconcile openness and chastity, tolerance, and morality. Edna, however, feels torn between her feelings for her children (she has already lost them for her husband) and her feelings for herself; rather than effect a compromise, she experiments inconclusively with adultery, and finally destroys herself in the sea. In this work, as in the much anthologized "Desirée's Baby," feminine autonomy seems tragically constrained by biology, an outcome consistent with naturalism, and perhaps more significantly, with prevailing moral standards.

Chopin's attitude—neither rejecting nor automatically accepting the family—led her to a properly modern treatment of sexuality, and earned *The Awakening* blatantly unfair critical reviews. Suffering from this rejection, she produced little in the remaining years of her life; nevertheless, she remains an example of unblinking and undespairing literary and personal autonomy.

Eric Mendelsohn

A RESPECTABLE WOMAN

Mrs. Baroda was a little provoked to learn that her husband expected his friend, Gouvernail, up to spend a week or two on the plantation.

They had entertained a good deal during the winter; much of the time had also been passed in New Orleans in various forms of mild dissipation. She was looking forward to a period of unbroken rest, now, and undisturbed tête-à-tête with her husband, when he informed her that Gouvernail was coming up to stay a week or two.

This was a man she had heard much of but never seen. He had been her husband's college friend; was now a journalist, and in no sense a society man or "a man about town," which were, perhaps, some of the reasons she had never met him. But she had unconsciously formed an image of him in her mind. She pictured him tall, slim, cynical; with eyeglasses, and his hands in his pockets; and she did not like him. Gouvernail was slim enough, but he wasn't very tall nor very cynical; neither did he wear eye-glasses nor carry his hands in his pockets. And she rather liked him when he first presented himself.

But why she liked him she could not explain satisfactorily to herself when she partly attempted to do so. She could discover in him none of those brilliant and promising traits which Gaston, her husband, had often assured her that he possessed. On the contrary, he sat rather mute and receptive before her chatty eagerness to make him feel at home and in face of Gaston's frank and wordy hospitality. His manner was as courteous toward her as the most exacting woman could require; but he made no direct appeal to her approval or even esteem.

Once settled at the plantation he seemed to like to sit upon the wide portico in the shade of one of the big Corinthian pillars, smoking his cigar lazily and listening attentively to Gaston's experience as a sugar planter.

"This is what I call living," he would utter with deep satisfaction, as the air that swept across the sugar field caressed him with its warm and scented velvety touch. It pleased him also to get on familiar terms with the big dogs that came about him, rubbing themselves sociably against his legs. He did not care to fish, and displayed no eagerness to go out and kill grosbecs when Gaston proposed doing so.

Gouvernail's personality puzzled Mrs. Baroda, but she liked him. Indeed, he was a lovable, inoffensive fellow. After a few days, when she could understand him no better than at first, she gave over being puzzled and remained piqued. In this mood she left her husband and her guest, for the most part, alone together. Then finding that Gouvernail took no

manner of exception to her action, she imposed her society upon him, accompanying him in his idle strolls to the mill and walks along the batture. She persistently sought to penetrate the reserve in which he had unconsciously enveloped himself.

"When is he going—your friend?" she one day asked her husband. "For my part, he tires me frightfully."

"Not for a week yet, dear. I can't understand; he gives you no trouble."

"No. I should like him better if he did; if he were more like others, and I had to plan somewhat for his comfort and enjoyment."

Gaston took his wife's pretty face between his hands and looked tenderly and laughingly into her troubled eyes. They were making a bit of toilet sociably together in Mrs. Baroda's dressing-room.

"You are full of surprises, ma belle," he said to her. "Even I can never count upon how you are going to act under given conditions." He kissed her and turned to fasten his cravat before the mirror.

"Here you are," he went on, "taking poor Gouvernail seriously and making a commotion over him, the last thing he would desire or expect."

"Commotion!" she hotly resented. "Nonsense! How can you say such a thing? Commotion, indeed! But, you know, you said he was clever."

"So he is. But the poor fellow is run down by overwork now. That's why I asked him here to take a rest."

"You used to say he was a man of ideas," she retorted, unconciliated. "I expected him to be interesting, at least. I'm going to the city in the morning to have my spring gowns fitted. Let met know when Mr. Gouvernail is gone; I shall be at my Aunt Octavie's."

That night she went and sat alone upon a bench that stood beneath a live oak tree at the edge of the gravel walk.

She had never known her thoughts or her intentions to be confused. She could gather nothing from them but the feeling of a distinct necessity to quit her home in the morning.

Mrs. Baroda heard footsteps crunching the gravel; but could discern in the darkness only the approaching red point of a lighted cigar. She knew it was Gouvernail, for her husband did not smoke. She hoped to remain unnoticed, but her white gown revealed her to him. He threw away his cigar and seated himself upon the bench beside her; without a suspicion that she might object to his presence.

"Your husband told me to bring this to you, Mrs. Baroda," he said, handing her a filmy, white scarf with which she sometimes enveloped her head and shoulders. She accepted the scarf from him with a murmur of thanks, and let it lie in her lap.

He made some commonplace observation upon the baneful effect of the night air at that season. Then as his gaze reached out into the darkness, he murmured, half to himself:

"'Night of south winds—night of the large few stars!
Still nodding night—'"

She made no reply to this apostrophe to the night, which indeed, was not addressed to her.

Gouvernail was in no sense a diffident man, for he was not a self-conscious one. His periods of reserve were not constitutional, but the result of moods. Sitting there beside Mrs. Baroda, his silence melted for the time.

He talked freely and intimately in a low, hesitating drawl that was not unpleasant to hear. He talked of the old college days when he and Gaston had been a good deal to each other; of the days of keen and blind ambitions and large intentions. Now there was left with him, at least, a philosophic acquiescence to the existing order—only a desire to be permitted to exist, with now and then a little whiff of genuine life, such as he was breathing now.

Her mind only vaguely grasped what he was saying. Her physical being was for the moment predominant. She was not thinking of his words, only drinking in the tones of his voice. She wanted to reach out her hand in the darkness and touch him with the sensitive tips of her fingers upon the face or the lips. She wanted to draw close to him and whisper against his cheek—she did not care what—as she might have done if she had not been a respectable woman.

The stronger the impulse grew to bring herself near him, the further, in fact, did she draw away from him. As soon as she could do so without an appearance of too great rudeness, she rose and left him there alone.

Before she reached the house, Gouvernail had lighted a fresh cigar and ended his apostrophe to the night.

Mrs. Baroda was greatly tempted that night to tell her husband—who was also her friend—of this folly that had seized her. But she did not yield to the temptation. Beside being a respectable woman she was a very sensible one; and she knew there are some battles in life which a human being must fight alone.

When Gaston arose in the morning, his wife had already departed. She had taken an early morning train to the city. She did not return till Gouvernail was gone from under her roof.

There was some talk of having him back during the summer that followed. That is, Gaston greatly desired it; but this desire yielded to his wife's strenuous opposition.

However, before the year ended, she proposed, wholly from herself, to have Gouvernail visit them again. Her husband was surprised and delighted with the suggestion coming from her.

"I am glad, chère amie, to know that you have finally overcome your dislike for him; truly he did not deserve it."

"Oh," she told him, laughingly, after pressing a long, tender kiss upon his lips, "I have overcome everything! you will see. This time I shall be very nice to him."

Véra Nikoláevna Fígner   *Russia/USSR, 1852–1942*

Véra Fígner represents "the grim distinction" Russian women achieved in the late nineteenth century in advance of those in all Western nations, except the United States. Armed with higher education and an unusual political consciousness, and repressed by increasingly harsh governmental decrees, Fígner and others like her moved from feminism to revolutionary politics, achieving full equality in the practice of terrorism. Her literary importance lies in the significant contribution she made to the related genres of autobiography and "prison literature": in "Studéncheskie gódy" (Student Days, 1872–1873) and the monumental *Zapechatlénnyi trúd* (*A Graven Work*, 1921–1922), she traces the growth and development of her political beliefs and details the harrowing experience of her twenty-year incarceration in the notorious Schlüsselburg Fortress. Her experience of her first day there is reprinted here.

Raised in Kazan the eldest of six children, Fígner agreed to marry the man her father had chosen for her on the condition that he would travel to Zurich, where, along with some one hundred other Russian women, she was able to study medicine in the early 1870s. She and her husband underwent a painful separation as she grew more political, studying first in what was called the Fritsche Circle, and then allying herself with the populist movement *Zemlya i Volya* (Land and Will). With the capture and death of activists stemming from the trials of 1877 and 1878, Fígner felt compelled to return to Russia before she completed her degree, and with her sister, she settled and worked among the peasants of Samara and Saratov as a medic and teacher from 1877 to 1879. At the age of 25, Fígner emerged as one of the leaders of *Naródnaya Volya* (The People's Will) a new "political" phase of populism: the "propaganda of the word" and "flying propaganda" gave way to the "propaganda of the deed"—terrorist activities against government officials that culminated in the assassination of Alexander II in March, 1881.

Finally captured in 1883, Fígner was sentenced to death in the Trial of Fourteen, her sentence later commuted to indefinite imprisonment. Fígner was pardoned in 1905, only to be left homeless when her family estate was burned in the turmoil that followed. From 1907 to 1917, she lived in Western Europe. On her return to Russia, she enlisted in the feminist cause rather than allying herself with either the Bolsheviks or other revolutionary parties and focused primarily on achieving suffrage and full equality for women. Though she refused to become a Communist, the Soviet government treated her with the respect and honor accorded an older revolutionary generation. Fígner herself recognized that she lived a posthumous existence, when she refused official offers of aid before the German siege in 1941 with the response to "concern yourself with the living."

from A GRAVEN WORK
Zapechatlénnyi trúd

The two stories of the prison were separated by nothing save a netting, and a narrow walk which ran like a balcony along the row of cells on the upper story. Owing to this arrangement, one could see at once the whole interior of the prison, all the forty iron doors of the cells.

The rope net was divided in the middle by a narrow bridge, which led to Cell 26. "The bridge of sighs," I thought, as I was being led across it, I recalled the palace of the Venetian doges, where the bridge of that name was the only road over which the rebels of Venice walked from their cells to the block. The Schlüsselburg bridge of sighs I crossed every day for many, many years. I was locked up in Number 26. The door slammed, and I dropped, exhausted, on my cot.

A new life began. A life amidst deathly stillness, that stillness to which you always listen and which you hear; the stillness which little by little overpowers you, envelops you, penetrates into all the pores of your body, into your reason, your very soul. How dreadful it is in its dumbness, how terrible it is in its soundlessness and in its chance interruptions. Gradually there steals from it to you the sense that some mystery is close at hand; everything becomes unusual, puzzling, as on a moonlit night, in solitude, in the shadow of a still forest. Everything is mysterious, incomprehensible. In this stillness the real becomes vague and unreal, and the imaginary seems real. Everything is tangled up, confused. The long gray day, wearying in its idleness, resembles a sleep without dreams; and at night you have such bright and glowing dreams that you have continually to assure yourself that they are only the fruit of your imagination. You live in such a way that dream seems life, and life, a dream.

And the sounds! Accursed sounds which suddenly and unexpectedly break in upon you, frighten you, and vanish. Somewhere begins a loud hissing, as though an enormous snake were creeping from under the floor, to enwrap you in its cold, slippery coils. But it is only water hissing somewhere below, in the pipes. You imagine people immured within stony sacks. You hear a very soft, suppressed groan, and it seems as though someone were suffocating beneath a heap of stones. But no! It is only the faint, very faint, dry cough of a tubercular prisoner. If a dish clatters somewhere, or the metal leg of a cot drops on the floor, your imagination pictures men rattling their chains and fetters.

What, then, is real here? What is actually here, and what is nonexisting? It is still and quiet as in a grave, when suddenly you hear a light rustling at the door—the gendarme has looked into the peephole and has covered it with the slide. It seems as if the wire of an electric battery were stretched from there. The current has touched your body for a minute, and the shock runs through your frame and strikes your hands and feet; fine needles plunge into the ends of your fingers, and your whole body, your foolish, silly body, after one violent shock, keeps trembling long and painfully. It fears something, and your heart quivers, and refuses to lie still.

And the dreams by night! Those mad dreams! You see flights, pursuits, gendarmes, fusillades, arrests. Somebody is being led to execution. The crowd is agitated and angry; red faces are distorted with malice. But most often you see torture. They torture with hot steam which escapes through hundreds of thin pipes in the wall, the ceiling, the floor; it burns, it beats, it is terrible, and there is no escape from it. The cell is locked, it is empty, quite empty, it is filled only with hot stream-lets. Or they torture you with electricity. You sit on a wooden chair, like those they have at the guardhouse, and you cannot rise; some invisible jailer is sending a current through you. Once, twice—you wake up—your nerves all along the arms twitching, or a convulsion has bound the muscles of your leg into a lump as hard as iron.

There is only one sound place in your soul, and it repeats to you:

"Have courage, Véra, and be firm! Re-member the Russian people, and how it lives! Recall all the world's unfortunates, recall their crushing toil, life without the light of joy; re-call humiliation, hunger, sickness, and poverty.

"Be resolute. Do not weep if your mother has been taken away from you, though they do not inflict such punishment even on an in-famous seducer or a greedy murderer. Do not weep over the failures of the struggle, over the comrades who have perished. Do not weep over the ruins that have covered the field of your life!

"Do not fear. Do not fear. In this myste-rious stillness, behind these deaf stones your friends are invisibly present. It is not you alone who are oppressed here; they too are suffering. Think of them. They are invisible, but they are here. You do not hear them, but they are here. They watch over you and guard you, like dis-embodied spirits. Nothing will happen, no-thing will happen. You are not alone, you are not alone!"

Translator Unknown

Mary Wilkins Freeman   *US, 1852–1930*

Mary Freeman was born into a religious family in Randolph, Massachsetts; of four siblings, she alone survived into adulthood. The decline of Randolph's shoe factor-ies, which had been her family's livelihood, drove the Wilkins family to Brattleboro, Vermont, where her mother found work as a maid. At the age of 18, Freeman—like Emily Dickinson before her—attended, found too strenuous, and left Mount Holyoke Female Seminary, completing her formal education at Mrs. Hosford's Glenwood Seminary. After the deaths of her parents, Freeman returned to Ran-dolph. At the age of 49, she married Charles Freeman, a man seven years her junior. The couple moved to New Jersey. A doctor turned successful lumber dealer, Mr. Freeman played the ponies, chased women, and was frequently hospitalized for alcoholism. They separated in 1923; the following year he died, having disin-herited his wife.

In 1926, Freeman, the author of more than twenty-five books, was awarded the Howells Medal For Fiction from the American Academy of Arts and Letters, and was elected to membership in the National Institute of Arts and Letters—like Edith Wharton, one of the first women to be so honored.

Freeman was already an established author of children's literature when she turned to adult fiction, depicting the New England villager's endurance of grinding material and spiritual poverty, and acute awareness of the role of gender. In some of the stories collected in *A Humble Romance* (1887) and *A New England Nun* (1887) Freeman's heroines adhere at great personal expense to Christian morality. In others, the sympathetic characters are rebels who feel the narrowness of folk culture (unlike the heros and heroines of Sarah Orne Jewett [1849–1909], Freeman's contemporary and fellow local-colorist, who mostly identify with folk culture). Spinsterhood is portrayed as a metaphor for lives thwarted by history.

Freeman's unromantic treatment of New England village life, as in *Jane Field* (1893), reveals a tendency toward naturalism. Her multi-sided, and probably her best, novel, *Pembroke* (1894), the story of an engagement ruined by the stubbornness of two men, indicts a sexually repressive New England culture. Influenced by Rebecca Harding Davis (1831–1910), *Jerome, a Poor Man* (1897) and *The Portion of Labor* (1901) focus specifically on the working class.

Recently, feminist criticism has rescued Freeman from the local-color ghetto of "women's writing." In her introduction to a new edition of Freeman's stories, Marjorie Pryse places the works of Freeman, Jewett, Elizabeth Stuart Phelps Ward, Harriet Beecher Stowe, and others in a "world transformed into a quasimatriarchal one both by the casualties of the Civil War and by the departure of a substantial proportion of the region's remaining young healthy male population." Disputing the notion that "the strong and adventurous left New England (to travel west) while the weak and conservative remained," Pryse argues that "the vision of nineteenth-century American life that Freeman offers suggests that in collaborative, cooperative, and communal endeavors we have found symbols most conducive to supporting human life. Instead of man alone against the wilderness, Freeman depicts two women or women in small groups...facing life together."

In a recent article, Julia Bader has suggested that the historical reality may be understood in literary terms: Freeman and other women writers of the period experienced the collapse of the illusion that the "male order" is essentially an extension of nature. Rather, the "male order" is a displacement of nature; the female author strives to recenter the world through emotional symbolism. The selection included here from *Six Trees* (1903) highlights Freeman's symbolist mode. Despite the revival of Freeman's work by feminist critics, the book has never been reprinted: it deserves to be read as a whole. Each story in the volume intends the revelation of personality through the natural symbol of the tree. Thus Freeman displays a genuinely feminine relationship with nature, a gentleness nurtured in the shadows of the drive to dominate nature.

Eric Mendelsohn

THE GREAT PINE

It was in the summertime that the great pine sang his loudest song of winter, for always the voice of the tree seemed to arouse in the listener a realization of that which was past and to come, rather than of the present. In the winter the tree seemed to sing of the slumberous peace under his gently fanning boughs, and the deep swell of his aromatic breath in burning noons, and when the summer traveler up the mountain-side threw himself, spent and heated, beneath his shade, then the winter song was at its best. When the wind swelled high came the song of the ice-fields, of the frozen mountain-torrents, of the trees wearing hoary beards and bent double like old men, of the little wild things trembling in their covers when the sharp reports of the frost sounded through the rigid hush of the arctic night and death was abroad.

The man who lay beneath the tree had much uncultivated imagination, and, though hampered by exceeding ignorance, he yet saw and heard that which was beyond mere observation. When exhausted by the summer heat, he reflected upon the winter with that keen pleasure that comes from the mental grasp of contrast to discomfort. He did not know that he heard the voice of the tree and not his own thought, so did the personality of the great pine mingle with his own. He was a sailor, and had climbed different heights from mountains, even masts made from the kindred of the tree.

Presently he threw his head back, and stared up and up, and reflected what a fine mast the tree would make, if only it were not soft pine. There was a stir in a branch, and a bird which lived in the tree in summer cast a small, wary glance at him from an eye like a point of bright intelligence, but the man did not see it. He drew a long breath, and looked irresolutely at the upward slope beyond the tree. It was time for him to be up and on if he would cross the mountain before nightfall. He was a wayfarer without resources. He was as poor as the tree, or any of the wild creatures which were in hiding around him on the mountain. He was even poorer, for he had not their feudal tenure of an abiding-place for root and foot on the mountain by the inalienable right of past generations of his race. Even the little, wary-eyed, feathered thing had its small freehold in the branches of the great pine, but the man had nothing. He had returned to primitive conditions; he was portionless save for that with which he came into the world, except for two garments that were nearly past their use as such. His skin showed through the rents; the pockets were empty. Adam expelled from Eden was not in much worse case, and this man also had at his back the flaming sword of punishment for wrong-doing. The man arose. He stood for a moment, letting the cool wind fan his forehead a little longer; then he bent his shoulders doggedly and resumed his climb up the dry bed of a brook which was in winter a fierce conduit for the melting ice and snow. Presently he came to such a choke of fallen trees across the bed that he had to leave it; then there was a sheer rock ascent which he had to skirt and go lower down the mountain to avoid.

The tree was left alone. He stood quiescent with the wind in his green plumes. He belonged to that simplest form of life which cannot project itself beyond its own existence to judge of it. He did not know when presently the man returned and threw himself down with a violent thud against his trunk, though there was a slight shock to his majesty. But the man looked up at the tree and cursed it. He had lost his way through avoiding the rocky precipice, and had circled back to the tree. He remained there a few minutes to gain breath; then he rose, for the western sunlight was filtering in gold drops through the foliage below the pine, and plodded heavily on again.

It might have been twenty minutes before he returned. When he saw the pine he cursed more loudly than before. The sun was quite low. The mountain seemed to be growing in size, the valleys were fast becoming gulfs of black mystery. The man looked at the tree malignantly. He felt in his pocket for a knife which he used to own, then for a match, the accompaniment of the tobacco and pipe which formerly comforted him, but there was none there. The thought of the lost pipe and tobacco filled him with a childish savagery. He felt that he must vent his spite upon something outside himself. He picked up two dry sticks, and began rubbing them together. He had some skill in woodcraft. Presently a spark gleamed; then another. He scraped up a handful of dry leaves. Presently smoke arose pungently in his face, then a flame leaped to life. The man kept on his way, leaving a fire behind him, and swore with an oath that he would not be trapped by the tree again.

He struggled up the old waterway, turning aside for the prostrate skeletons of giant trees, clambering over heaps of stones which might have been the cairns of others, and clawing up precipices like a panther. After one fierce scramble he paused for breath, and, standing on a sheer rock ledge, gazed downward. Below him was a swaying, folding gloom full of vague whispers and rustlings. It seemed to wave and eddy before him like the sea from the deck of a ship, and, indeed, it was another deep, only of air instead of water. Suddenly he realized that there was no light, that the fire which he had kindled must have gone out. He stared into the waving darkness below, and sniffed hard. He could smell smoke faintly, although he could see no fire. Then all at once came a gleam of red, then a leap of orange flame. Then—no human being could have told how it happened, he himself least of all, what swift motive born of deeds and experiences in his own life, born perhaps of deeds and experiences of long-dead ancestors, actuated him. He leaped back down the mountain, stumbling headlong, falling at times, and scrambled to his feet again, sending loose stones down in avalanches, running risks of life and limb, but never faltering until he was beside the pine, standing, singing in the growing glare of the fire. Then he began beating the fire fiercely with sticks, trampling it until he blistered his feet. At last the fire was out. People on a hotel piazza down in the valley, who had been watching it, turned away. "The fire is out," they said, with the regret of those who miss a spectacular delight, although admitting the pity and shame of it, yet coddling with fierce and defiant joy the secret lust of destruction of the whole race. "The fire is out," they said; but more than the fire had burned low, and was out, on the mountain. The man who had evoked destruction to satisfy his own wrath and bitterness of spirit, and then repented, sat for a few minutes outside the blackened circle around the great pine, breathing hard. He drew his rough coat-sleeve across his wet forehead, and stared up at the tree, which loomed above him like a prophet with solemnly waving arms of benediction, prophesying in a great

unknown language of his own. He gaped as he stared; his face looked vacant. He felt in his pocket for his departed pipe, then withdrew his hand forcibly, dashing it against the ground. Then he sighed, swore mildly under his breath an oath of weariness and misery rather than of wrath. Then he pulled himself up by successive stages of his stiff muscles, like an old camel, and resumed his journey.

After a while he again paused and looked back. The moon had arisen, and he could see quite plainly the great pine standing crowned with white light, tossing his boughs like spears and lances of silver. "Thunderin' big tree," he muttered, with a certain pride and self-approbation. He felt that that majestic thing owed its being to him, to his forbearance with his own hard fate. Had it not been for that it would have been a mere blackened trunk. At that moment, for the first time in his history, he rose superior to his own life. In some unknown fashion this seemingly trivial happening had, as it were, tuned him to a higher place in the scale of things than he had ever held. He, through saving the tree from himself, gained a greater spiritual growth than the tree had gained in height since it first quickened with life. Who shall determine the limit at which the intimate connection and reciprocal influence of all forms of visible creation upon one another may stop? A man may cut down a tree and plant one. Who knows what effect the tree may have upon the man, to his raising or undoing?

Presently the man frowned and shook his head in a curious fashion, as if he questioned his own identity; then he resumed his climb. After the summit was gained he went down the other side of the mountain, then northward through a narrow gorge of valley to which the moonbeams did not yet penetrate. This valley, between mighty walls of silver-crested darkness, was terrifying. The man felt his own smallness and the largeness of nature which seemed about to fall upon him. Spirit was intimidated by matter. The man, rude and unlettered, brutalized and dulled by his life, yet realized it. He rolled his eyes aloft from side to side, and ran as if pursued.

When he had reached the brow of a little decline in the valley road he paused and searched eagerly with straining eyes the side of the mountain on the right. Then he drew a long breath of relief. He had seen what he wished to see—a feeble glimmer of lamplight from a window of a house, the only one on that lonely road for five miles in either direction. It was the dwelling-house on a small farm which had been owned by the father of the woman whom the man had married fifteen years before. Ten years ago, when he had run away, there had been his wife, his little girl, and his wife's mother living on the farm. The old farmer father had died two years before that, and the man, who had wild blood in his veins, had rebelled at the hard grind necessary to wrest a livelihood by himself from the mountain soil. So one morning he was gone, leaving a note saying that he had gone to sea, and would write and send money, that he could earn more than on a farm. But he never wrote, and he never sent the money. He had met with sin and diasster, and at last he started homeward, shorn, and, if not repentant, weary of wrong-doing and its hard wages. He had retreated from the broad way with an ignoble impulse, desiring the safety of the narrow, and the loaves and fishes, which, after all, can be found in it with greater certainty; but now, as he hastened along, he became conscious of something better than that. One good impulse begat others by some law of spiritual reproduction. He began to think how he would perhaps do more work than he had formerly, and please his wife and her mother.

He looked at the light in the window ahead with something akin to thankfulness. He remembered how very gentle his wife had been, and how fond of him. His wife's mother also had been a mild woman, with reproving eyes only, never with a tongue of reproach. He remembered his little girl with a thrill of

tenderness and curiosity. She would be a big girl now; she would be like her mother. He began picturing to himself what they would do and say, what they would give him for supper. He thought he would like a slice of ham cut from one of those cured on the farm, that and some new-laid eggs. He would have some of those biscuits that his wife's mother used to make, and some fresh butter, and honey from the home bees. He would have tea and cream. He seemed to smell the tea and the ham. A hunger which was sorer than any hunger of the flesh came over him. All at once the wanderer starved for home. He had been shipwrecked and at the point of death from hunger, but never was hunger like this. He had planned speeches of contrition; now he planned nothing. He feared no blame from those whom he had wronged; he feared nothing except his own need of them. Faster and faster he went. He seemed to be running a race. At last he was quite close to the house. The light was in a window facing the road, and the curtain was up. He could see a figure steadily passing and repassing it. He went closer, and saw that it was a little girl with a baby in her arms, and she was walking up and down hushing it. A feeble cry smote his ears, though the doors and windows were closed. It was chilly even in midsummer in the mountains. He went around the house to the side door. He noticed that the field on the left was waving with tall, dry grass, which should have been cut long ago; he noticed that there were no beanpoles in the garden. He noticed that the house looked gray and shabby even in the moonlight, that some blinds were gone and a window broken. He leaned a second against the door. Then he opened it and entered. He came into a little, square entry; on one side was the kitchen door, on the other the room where the light was. He opened the door leading to this room. He stood staring, for nothing which he had anticipated met his eyes, except the little girl. She stood gazing at him, half in alarm, half in surprise, clutching close the baby, which was puny, but evidently about a year old. Two little boys stood near the table on which the lamp was burning, and they stared at him with wide-open mouths and round eyes. But the sight which filled the intruder with the most amazement and dismay was that of a man in the bed in the corner. He recognized him at once as a farmer who had lived, at the time of his departure, five miles away in the village. He remembered that his wife was recently dead when he left. The man, whose blue, ghastly face was sunken in the pillows, looked up at him. He thrust out a cadaverous hand as if to threaten. The little girl with the baby and the two little boys edged nearer the bed, as if for protection.

Who be you?" inquired the sick man, with feeble menace. "What d' ye want comin' in here this way?" It was like the growl of a sick dog.

The other man went close to the bed. "Where is my wife?" he asked, in a strange voice. It was expressive of horror and anger and a rage of disappointment.

"You ain't—Dick?" gasped the man in bed.

"Yes, I be; and I know you, Johnny Willet. Where is my wife? What are you here for?"

"Your wife is dead," answered the man, in a choking voice. He began to cough; he half raised himself on one elbow. His eyes bulged. He crowed like a child with the croup. The little girl promptly laid the baby on the bed and ran to a chimney cupboard for a bottle of medicine, which she administered with a spoon. The sick man lay back, gasping for breath. He looked as if already dead; his jaw dropped; there were awful blue hollows in his face.

"Dead!" repeated the visitor, thinking of his wife, and not of the other image of death before him.

"Yes, she's dead."

"Where's my little girl?"

The sick man raised one shaking hand and pointed to the little girl who had taken up the whimpering baby.

"That?"

The sick man nodded.

The other eyed the little girl, rather tall for her age, but very slim, her narrow shoulders already bent with toil. She regarded him, with serious blue eyes in a little face, with an expression of gentleness so pronounced that it gave the impression of a smile. The man's eyes wandered from the girl to the baby in her arms and the two little boys.

"What be you all a-doin' here?" he demanded, gruffly, and made a movement towards the bed. The little girl turned pale, and clutched the baby more closely. The sick man made a feeble sound of protest and deprecation. "What be you all a-doin' here?" demanded the other again.

"I married your wife after we heard your ship was lost. We knew you was aboard her from Abel Dennison. He come home, and said you was dead for sure, some eight year ago, and then she said she'd marry me. I'd been after her some time. My wife died, and my house burned down, and I was left alone without any home, and I'd always liked her. She wasn't any too willin', but finally she give in."

The man whom he had called Dick glared at him speechlessly.

"We both thought you was dead, sure," said the sick man, in a voice of mild deprecation, which was ludicrously out of proportion to the subject.

Dick looked at the children.

"We had 'em," said the sick man. "She died when the baby was two months old, and your girl Lottie has been taking care of it. It has been pretty hard for her, but I was took sick, and 'ain't been able to do anything. I can jest crawl round a little, and that's all. Lottie can milk—we've got one cow left—and she feeds the hens, and my first wife's brother has given us some flour and meal, and cuts up some wood to burn, and we've worried along, but we can't stand it when winter comes, anyhow. Somethin' has got to be done." Suddenly

an expression of blank surprise before an acquisition of knowledge came over his face.
"Good Lord! Dick," he gasped out, "it's all
yours. It's all yours, anyway, now."

"Where's the old woman?" asked Dick,
abruptly, ignoring what the other said.

"Your wife's mother? She died of pneumonia about two year ago. Your wife she took
it to heart pretty bad. She was a heap of help
about the children."

Dick nodded. "The old woman always
was smart to work," he assented.

"Yes, and your wife she wa'n't over-
strong."

"Never was."

"No."

"S'pose there was enough to put her away
decent?"

"I sold the wood-lot on the back road.
There's a gravestone. Luckily I had it done
before I was took sick."

"S'pose you're pretty hard pinched now?"

"Awful hard. We can't get along so much
longer. There's enough wood to cut, if I could
do it, that would bring in somethin'; and
there's the hay, that's spoilin'. I can't do
nothin'. There's nothin' but this house over
our heads." Suddenly that look of surprised
knowledge came over his face again. "Lord!
it's all yours, and the girl's, anyhow," he muttered.

"She's been doin' the work?" asked Dick,
pointing to the girl.

"Yes; she does the best she can, but she
ain't very big, and the children 'ain't got
enough to be decent, and we can't get much
cooked."

Dick made a resolute step towards the
door.

"Where be you a-goin', Dick?" asked the
sick man, with a curious wistfulness. "You
ain't goin' tonight?"

"What is there in the house to eat?"

"What's in the house, Lottie?"

"There's some meal and milk and eggs,"
answered the child, in a high, sweet voice.

"Come here and give us a kiss, Lottie,"
said Dick, suddenly.

The little girl approached him timidly,
staggering under the weight of the baby. She
lifted her face, and the man kissed her with a
sort of solemnity. "I'm your father, Lottie,"
said he.

The two looked at each other, the child
shrinking, yet smiling.

"Glad I got home?" asked the man.

"Yes, sir."

Dick went out into the kitchen, and the
children followed and stood in the doorway,
watching. He gravely set to work with such
utensils and materials as he found, which were
scanty enough. He kindled a fire and made a
corn-cake. He made porridge for the sick man
and carried him a bowl of it smoking hot.
"'Ain't had nothin' like this sence she died,"
said the sick man.

After supper Dick cleaned the kitchen. He
also tidied up the other room and made the
bed, and milked, and split some wood wherewith to cook breakfast.

"You ain't goin' tonight, Dick?" the sick
man said, anxiously, when he came in after the
work was done.

"No, I ain't."

"Lord! I forgot; it's your house," said the
sick man.

"I wa'n't goin' anyhow," said Dick.

"Well, there's a bed upstairs. You 'ain't
got any more clothes than what you've got on,
have you?"

"No, I 'ain't," replied Dick, shortly.

"Well, there's mine in the closet out of
this room, and you might jest as well wear 'em
till I get up. There's some shirts and some
pants."

"All right," said Dick.

The next morning Dick got the breakfast,
cooking eggs with wonderful skill and frying
corn-cakes. Then, dressed in the sick man's
shirt and trousers, he set forth, axe in hand.
He toiled all day in the woods; he toiled every
day until he had sufficient wood cut, then

he hired a horse, to be paid for when the wood was sold. He carted loads to the hotels and farmhouses where summer boarders were taken. He arose before dawn and worked in the field and garden. He cut the hay. He was up half the night setting the house to rights. He washed and ironed like a woman. The whole establishment was transformed. He got a doctor for the sick man, but he gave small encouragement. He had consumption, although he might linger long. "Who's going to take care of the poor fellow, I don't know," said the doctor.

"I be," said Dick.

"Then there are the children," said the doctor.

"One of 'em is mine, and I'll take care of his," said Dick.

The doctor stared, as one stares who sees a good deed in a naughty world, with a mixture of awe, of contempt, and of incredulity.

"Well," he said, "it's lucky you came along."

After that Dick simply continued in his new path of life. He worked and nursed. It was inconceivable how much the man accomplished. He developed an enormous capacity for work. In the autumn he painted the house; the cellar was full of winter vegetables, the woodpile was compact. The children were warmly clad, and Lottie went to school. Her father had bought an old horse for a song, and he carried her to school every day. Once in January he had occasion to drive around the other side of the mountain which he had climbed the night of his return. He started early in the afternoon, that he might be in season to go for Lottie.

It was a clear, cold day. Snow was on the ground, a deep, glittering level, with a hard crust of ice. The sleigh slid over the frozen surface with long hisses. The trees were all bare and had suffered frightfully in the last storm. The rain had frozen as it fell, and there had been a high gale. The ice-mauled branches had snapped, and sometimes whole trees. Dick, slipping along on the white line of road below, gazed up at the side of the mountain. He looked and looked again. Then he desisted. He reached over and cut the horse's back with the reins. "Get up!" he cried, harshly.

The great pine had fallen from his high estate. He was no more to be seen dominating the other trees, standing out in solitary majesty among his kind. The storm had killed him. He lay prostrate on the mountain.

And the man on the road below passed like the wind, and left the mountain and the dead tree behind.

Lady Augusta Gregory

Ireland, 1852–1932

Lady Isabella Augusta Persse was born in County Galway, Ireland, the youngest of seven daughters. Her family was from the landed gentry, Protestants in a Catholic Ireland. Her heritage seemed to destine her for a life of detached leisure in a country of poverty and political strife. Yet this playwright, essayist, and pamphleteer, cofounder of Ireland's Abbey Theatre and preeminent collector of Irish folktales and folklore, chose her own destiny. By the time of her death in 1932, she had worked tirelessly as an artist, a custodian of the arts, and a preserver of Irish culture and history. George Bernard Shaw called her "the greatest living Irish woman."

Gregory was affected early in life by the lore and literature of Ireland. Her Catholic nurse, Mary Sheridan, recounted to her stories and fables in Irish, and

Gregory later responded by collecting tales about the traditional Irish hero Cuchulain and Irish legends (*Gods and Fighting Men*, 1904). Her sympathy for Ireland in an era of England's domination of the country and its culture continued following her marriage in 1880 to Sir William Gregory, Irish politician and former governor of Ceylon, who was thirty-five years older than she. He encouraged her to write, and the results were seasoned political essays and pamphlets on such issues as the support of Irish cottage industries, taxes, and home rule. It was during these years that she began a lifelong preoccupation with the collecting, compiling, and editing of Irish folktales and folklore. A part of Ireland's oppressed culture and history, these tales were often incorporated into Gregory's plays, like *Spreading the News*, first published in 1909 and included here.

It was not until she was almost 50 that she began to devote her artistic abilities to playwriting. With W. B. Yeats, Douglas Hyde, George Moore, Edward Martyn, and other young artists, Gregory sought to establish an Irish literary theater. The Abbey Theatre was born, and Gregory became its benefactor, with financial and artistic support for its early writers.

In her own writing, she became devoted to restoring the language and literature of Ireland. She sought to resurrect the dialects of Ireland with one-act comedies like the one below and with folk history plays, carrying them to the villages and rural regions of Ireland. As one of the Abbey's leading writers, she took care in her characterization and in the delicate balance of dialogue and dialect. She had a keen awareness of what was possible on the stage, and she relied on the interplay of characters' intentions and beliefs to bring about comic mischief and consequences. Always her audience was the Irish people and their language and culture.

One of Gregory's greatest plays, *Kincora* (1909), led Yeats to say "it gives me the greatest joy—colour, speech, all has music." Indeed, it was Yeats who gave depth and memorial to Gregory's literary genius in his two poems "Coole Park" and "Coole Park and Ballylee." And for Yeats she was "mother, friend, sister, and brother. I cannot realize the world without her—she brought to my wavering thoughts steadfast nobility."

John Isom

SPREADING THE NEWS

────────────────────────── PERSONS ──────────────────────────

BARTLEY FALLON

MRS. FALLON

JACK SMITH

SHAWN EARLY

TIM CASEY

JAMES RYAN

MRS. TARPEY

MRS. TULLY

A POLICEMAN (JO MULDOON).

A REMOVABLE MAGISTRATE

SCENE. *The outskirts of a Fair. An Apple Stall.* MRS. TARPEY *sitting at it.* MAGISTRATE *and* POLICEMAN *enter.*

MAGISTRATE: So that is the Fair Green. Cattle and sheep and mud. No system. What a repulsive sight!

POLICEMAN: That is so, indeed.

MAGISTRATE: I suppose there is a good deal of disorder in this place?

POLICEMAN: There is.

MAGISTRATE: Common assault?

POLICEMAN: It's common enough.

MAGISTRATE: Agrarian crime, no doubt?

POLICEMAN: That is so.

MAGISTRATE: Boycotting? Maiming of cattle? Firing into houses?

POLICEMAN: There was one time, and there might be again.

MAGISTRATE: That is bad. Does it go any farther than that?

POLICEMAN: Far enough, indeed.

MAGISTRATE: Homicide, then! This district has been shamefully neglected! I will change all that. When I was in the Andaman Islands, my system never failed. Yes, yes, I will change all that. What has that woman on her stall?

POLICEMAN: Apples mostly—and sweets.

MAGISTRATE: Just see if there are any unlicensed goods underneath—spirits or the like. We had evasions of the salt tax in the Andaman Islands.

POLICEMAN: (*sniffing cautiously and upsetting a heap of apples*) I see no spirits here—or salt.

MAGISTRATE: (*to* MRS. TARPEY) Do you know this town well, my good woman?

MRS. TARPEY: (*holding out some apples*). A penny the half-dozen, your honour.

POLICEMAN: (*shouting*) The gentleman is asking do you know the town! He's the new magistrate!

MRS. TARPEY: (*rising and ducking*). Do I know the town? I do, to be sure.

MAGISTRATE: (*shouting*) What is its chief business?

MRS. TARPEY: Business, is it? What business would the people here have but to be minding one another's business?

MAGISTRATE: I mean what trade have they?

MRS. TARPEY: Not a trade. No trade at all but to be talking.

MAGISTRATE: I shall learn nothing here.

(JAMES RYAN *comes in, pipe in mouth. Seeing* MAGISTRATE *he retreats quickly, taking pipe from mouth.*)

MAGISTRATE: The smoke from that man's pipe had a greenish look; he may be growing unlicensed tobacco at home. I wish I had brought my telescope to this district. Come to the post-office, I will telegraph for it. I found it very useful in the Andaman Islands.

(MAGISTRATE *and* POLICEMAN *go out left.*)

MRS. TARPEY: Bad luck to Jo Muldoon, knocking my apples this way and that way. (*Begins arranging them.*) Showing off he was to the new magistrate.

(*Enter* BARTLEY FALLON *and* MRS. FALLON.)

BARTLEY: Indeed it's a poor country and a scarce country to be living in. But I'm thinking if I went to America it's long ago the day I'd be dead!

MRS. FALLON: So you might, indeed.

(*She puts her basket on a barrel and begins putting parcels in it, taking them from under her cloak.*)

BARTLEY: And it's a great expense for a poor man to be buried in America.

MRS. FALLON: Never fear, Bartley Fallon, but I'll give you a good burying the day you'll die.

BARTLEY: Maybe it's yourself will be buried in the graveyard of Cloonmara before me, Mary Fallon, and I myself that will be dying unbeknownst some night, and no one a-near me. And the cat itself may be gone straying through the country, and the mice squealing over the quilt.

MRS. FALLON: Leave off talking of dying. It might be twenty years you'll be living yet.

BARTLEY: (*with a deep sigh*) I'm thinking if I'll be living at the end of twenty years, it's a very old man I'll be then!

MRS. TARPEY: (*turns and sees them*) Good morrow, Bartley Fallon; good morrow, Mrs. Fallon. Well, Bartley, you'll find no cause for complaining to-day; they are all saying it was a good fair.

BARTLEY: (*raising his voice*) It was not a good fair, Mrs. Tarpey. It was a scattered sort of a fair. If we didn't expect more, we got less. That's the way with me always; whatever I have to sell goes down and whatever I have to buy goes up. If there's ever any misfortune coming to this world, it's on myself it pitches, like a flock of crows on seed potatoes.

MRS. FALLON: Leave off talking of misfortunes, and listen to Jack Smith that is coming the way, and he singing.

(*Voice of* JACK SMITH *heard singing:*)

I thought, my first love,
  There'd be but one house between you and me,
And I thought I would find
  Yourself coaxing my child on your knee.
Over the tide
  I would leap with the leap of a swan,
Till I came to the side
  Of the wife of the Red-haired man!

(JACK SMITH *comes in; he is a red-haired man, and is carrying a hayfork.*)

MRS. TARPEY: That should be a good song if I had my hearing.

MRS. FALLON: (*shouting*) It's "The Red-haired Man's Wife."

MRS. TARPEY: I know it well. That's the song that has a skin on it!

(*She turns her back to them and goes on arranging her apples.*)

MRS. FALLON: Where's herself, Jack Smith?

JACK SMITH: She was delayed with her washing; bleaching the clothes on the hedge she is, and she daren't leave them, with all the tinkers that do be passing to the fair. It isn't to the fair I came myself, but up to the Five Acre Meadow I'm going, where I have a contract for the hay. We'll get a share of it into tramps today.

(*He lays down hayfork and lights his pipe.*)

BARTLEY: You will not get it into tramps to-day. The rain will be down on it by evening, and on myself too. It's seldom I ever started on a journey but the rain would come down on me before I'd find any place of shelter.

JACK SMITH: If it didn't itself, Bartley, it is my belief you would carry a leaky pail on your head in place of a hat, the way you'd not be without some cause of complaining.

(*A voice heard, "Go on, now, go on out o' that. Go on I say."*)

JACK SMITH: Look at that young mare of Pat Ryan's that is backing into Shaughnessy's bullocks with the dint of the crowd! Don't be daunted, Pat, I'll give you a hand with her.

(*He goes out, leaving his hayfork.*)

MRS. FALLON: It's time for ourselves to be going home. I have all I bought put in the basket. Look at there, Jack Smith's hayfork he left after him! He'll be wanting it. (*Calls.*) Jack Smith! Jack Smith!—He's gone through the crowd—hurry after him, Bartley, he'll be wanting it.

BARTLEY: I'll do that. This is no safe place to be leaving it. (*He takes up fork awkwardly and upsets the basket.*) Look at that now! If there is any basket in the fair upset, it must be our own basket!

(*He goes out to right.*)

MRS. FALLON: Get out of that! It is your own fault, it is. Talk of misfortunes and misfortunes will come. Glory be! Look at my new egg-cups rolling in every part—and my two pound of sugar with the paper broke—

MRS. TARPEY: (*turning from stall*) God help us, Mrs. Fallon, what happened to your basket?

MRS. FALLON: It's himself that knocked it down, bad manners to him. (*Putting things up.*) My grand sugar that's destroyed, and he'll not drink his tea without it. I had best go back to the shop for more, much good may it do him!

(*Enter* TIM CASEY.)

TIM CASEY: Where is Bartley Fallon, Mrs. Fallon? I want a word with him before he'll leave the fair. I was afraid he might have gone home by this, for he's a temperate man.

MRS. FALLON: I wish he did go home! It'd be best for me if he went home straight from the fair green, or if he never came with me at all? Where is he, is it? He's gone up the road (*jerks elbow*) following Jack Smith with a hayfork.

(*She goes out to left.*)

TIM CASEY: Following Jack Smith with a hayfork! Did ever any one hear the like of that. (*Shouts.*) Did you hear that news, Mrs. Tarpey?

MRS. TARPEY: I heard no news at all.

TIM CASEY: Some dispute I suppose it was that rose betwen Jack Smith and Bartley Fallon, and it seems Jack made off, and Bartley is following him with a hayfork!

MRS. TARPEY: Is he now? Well, that was quick work! It's not ten minutes since the two of them were here, Bartley going home and Jack going to the Five Acre Meadow; and I had my apples to settle up, that Jo Muldoon of the police had scattered, and when I looked round again Jack Smith was gone, and Bartley Fallon was gone, and Mrs. Fallon's basket upset, and all in it strewed upon the ground—the tea here—the two pound of sugar there—the egg-cups there—Look, now, what a great hardship the deafness puts upon me, that I didn't hear the com-mencement of the fight! Wait till I tell James Ryan that I see below; he is a neighbour of Bartley's, it would be a pity if he wouldn't hear the news!

(*She goes out. Enter* SHAWN EARLY *and* MRS. TULLY.)

TIM CASEY.: Listen, Shawn Early! Listen, Mrs. Tully, to the news! Jack Smith and Bartley Fallon had a falling out, and Jack knocked Mrs. Fallon's basket into the road, and Bartley made an attack on him with a hayfork, and away with Jack, and Bartley after him. Look at the sugar here yet on the road!

SHAWN EARLY: Do you tell me so? Well, that's a queer thing, and Bartley Fallon so quiet a man!

MRS. TULLY: I wouldn't wonder at all. I would never think well of a man that would have that sort of a mouldering look. It's likely he has overtaken Jack by this.

(*Enter* JAMES RYAN *and* MRS. TARPEY.)

JAMES RYAN: That is great news Mrs. Tarpey was telling me! I suppose that's what brought the police and the magistrate up this way. I was wondering to see them in it a while ago.

SHAWN EARLY: The police after them? Bartley Fallon must have injured Jack so. They wouldn't meddle in a fight that was only for show!

MRS. TULLY: Why wouldn't he injure him? There was many a man killed with no more of a weapon than a hayfork.

JAMES RYAN: Wait till I run north as far as Kelly's bar to spread the news!

(*He goes out.*)

TIM CASEY: I'll go tell Jack Smith's first cousin that is standing there south of the church after selling his lambs.

(*Goes out.*)

MRS. TULLY: I'll go telling a few of the neighbours I see beyond to the west.

(*Goes out.*)

SHAWN EARLY: I'll give word of it beyond at the east of the green.

(*Is going out when* MRS. TARPEY *seizes hold of him.*)

MRS. TARPEY: Stop a minute, Shawn Early, and tell me did you see red Jack Smith's wife, Kitty Keary, in any place?

SHAWN EARLY: I did. At her own house she was, drying clothes on the hedge as I passed.

MRS. TARPEY: What did you say she was doing?

SHAWN EARLY: (*breaking away*) Laying out a sheet on the hedge.

(*He goes.*)

MRS. TARPEY: Laying out a sheet for the dead! The Lord have mercy on us! Jack Smith dead, and his wife laying out a sheet for his burying! (*Calls out.*) Why didn't you tell me that before, Shawn Early? Isn't the deafness the great hardship? Half the world might be dead without me knowing of it or getting word of it all! (*She sits down and rocks herself.*) O my poor Jack Smith! To be going to his work so nice and so hearty, and to be left stretched on the ground in the full light of the day!

(*Enter* TIM CASEY.)

TIM CASEY: What is it, Mrs. Tarpey? What happened since?

MRS. TARPEY: O my poor Jack Smith!

TIM CASEY: Did Bartley overtake him?

MRS. TARPEY: O the poor man!

TIM CASEY: Is it killed he is?

MRS. TARPEY: Stretched in the Five Acre Meadow!

TIM CASEY: The Lord have mercy on us! Is that a fact?

MRS. TARPEY: Without the rites of the Church or a ha'porth!

TIM CASEY: Who was telling you?

MRS. TARPEY: And the wife laying out a sheet for his corpse. (*Sits up and wipes her eyes.*) I suppose they'll wake him the same as another?

(*Enter* MRS. TULLY, SHAWN EARLY, *and* JAMES RYAN.)

MRS. TULLY: There is great talk about this work in every quarter of the fair.

MRS. TARPEY: Ochone! cold and dead. And myself maybe the last he was speaking to!

JAMES RYAN: The Lord save us! Is it dead he is?

TIM CASEY: Dead surely, and the wife getting provision for the wake.

SHAWN EARLY: Well, now, hadn't Bartley Fallon great venom in him?

MRS. TULLY: You may be sure he had some cause. Why would he have made an end of him if he had not? (*To* MRS. TARPEY, *raising her voice*) What was it rose the dispute at all, Mrs. Tarpey?

MRS. TARPEY: Not a one of me knows. The last I saw of them, Jack Smith was standing there, and Bartley Fallon was standing there, quiet and easy, and he listening to "The Red-haired Man's Wife."

MRS. TULLY: Do you hear that, Tim Casey? Do you hear that, Shawn Early and James Ryan? Bartley Fallon was here this morning listening to red Jack Smith's wife, Kitty Keary that was! Listening to her and whispering with her! It was she started the fight so!

SHAWN EARLY: She must have followed him from her own house. It is likely some person roused him.

TIM CASEY: I never knew, before, Bartley Fallon was great with Jack Smith's wife.

MRS. TULLY: How would you know it? Sure it's not in the streets they would be calling it. If Mrs. Fallon didn't know of it, and if I that have the next house to them didn't know of it, and if Jack Smith himself didn't know of it, it is not likely you would know of it, Tim Casey.

SHAWN EARLY: Let Bartley Fallon take charge of her from this out so, and let him provide for her. It is little pity she will get from any person in this parish.

TIM CASEY: How can he take charge of her? Sure he has a wife of his own. Sure you don't think he'd turn souper and marry her in a Protestant church?

JAMES RYAN: It would be easy for him to marry her if he brought her to America.

SHAWN EARLY: With or without Kitty Keary, believe me it is for America he's making at this minute. I saw the new magistrate and Jo Muldoon of the police going into the post-office as I came up—there was hurry on them—you may be sure it was to telegraph they went, the way he'll be stopped in the docks at Queenstown!

MRS TULLY: It's likely Kitty Keary is gone with him, and not minding a sheet or a wake at all. The poor man, to be deserted by his own wife, and the breath hardly gone out yet from his body that is lying bloody in the field!

(*Enter* MRS. FALLON.)

MRS. FALLON: What is it the whole of the town is talking about? And what is it you yourselves are talking about? Is it about my man Bartley Fallon you are talking? Is it lies about him you are telling, saying that he went killing Jack Smith? My grief that ever he came into this place at all!

JAMES RYAN: Be easy now, Mrs. Fallon. Sure there is no one at all in the whole fair but is sorry for you!

MRS. FALLON: Sorry for me, is it? Why would any one be sorry for me? Let you be sorry for yourselves, and that there may be shame on you for ever and at the day of judgment, for the words you are saying and the lies you are telling to take away the character of my poor man, and to take the good name off of him, and to drive him to destruction! That is what you are doing!

SHAWN EARLY: Take comfort now, Mrs. Fallon. The police are not so smart as they think. Sure he might give them the slip yet, the same as Lynchehaun.

MRS. TULLY: If they do get him, and if they do put a rope around his neck, there is no one can say he does not deserve it!

MRS FALLON: Is that what you are saying, Bridget Tully, and is that what you think? I tell you it's too much talk you have, making yourself out to be such a great one, and to be running down every respectable person! A rope, is it? It isn't much of a rope was needed to tie up your own furniture the day you came into Martin Tully's house, and you never bringing as much as a blanket, or a penny, or a suit of clothes with you and I myself bringing seventy pounds and two feather beds. And now you are stiffer than a woman would have a hundred pounds! It is too much talk the whole of you have. A rope is it? I tell you the whole of this town is full of liars and schemers that would hang you up for half a glass of whiskey. (*Turning to go.*) People they are you wouldn't believe as much as daylight from without you'd get up to have a look at it yourself. Killing Jack Smith indeed! Where are you at all, Bartley, till I bring you out of this? My nice quiet little man! My decent comrade! He that is as kind and as harmless as an innocent beast of the field! He'll be doing no harm at all if he'll shed the blood of some of you after this day's work! That much would be no harm at all. (*Calls out*) Bartley! Bartley Fallon! Where are you? (*Going out*) Did any one see Bartley Fallon?

(*All turn to look after her*.)

JAMES RYAN: It is hard for her to believe any such a thing, God help her!

(*Enter* BARTLEY FALLON *from right, carrying hayfork*.)

BARTLEY: It is what I often said to myself, if there is ever any misfortune coming to this world it is on myself it is sure to come!

(*All turn round and face him*.)

BARTLEY: To be going about with this fork and to find no one to take it, and no place to leave it down, and I wanting to be gone out of this—Is that you, Shawn Early? (*Holds out fork*.) It's well I met you. You have no call to be leaving the fair for a while the way I have, and how can I go till I'm rid of this fork? Will you take it and keep it until such time as Jack Smith—

SHAWN EARLY: (*backing*) I will not take it, Bartley Fallon, I'm very thankful to you!

BARTLEY: (*turning to apple stall*). Look at it now, Mrs. Tarpey, it was here I got it; let me thrust it in under the stall. It will lie there safe enough, and no one will take notice of it until such time as Jack Smith—

MRS. TARPEY: Take your fork out of that! Is it to put trouble on me and to destroy me you want? Putting it there for the police to be rooting it out maybe.

(*Thrusts him back*.)

BARTLEY: That is a very unneighbourly thing for you to do, Mrs. Tarpey. Hadn't I enough care on me with that fork before this, running up and down with it like the swinging of a clock, and afeard to lay it down in any place! I wish I never touched it or meddled with it at all!

JAMES RYAN: It is a pity, indeed, you ever did.

BARTLEY: Will you yourself take it, James Ryan? You were always a neighbourly man.

JAMES RYAN: (*backing*) There is many a thing I would do for you, Bartley Fallon, but I won't do that!

SHAWN EARLY: I tell you there is no man will give you any help or any encouragement for this day's work. If it was something agrarian now—

BARTLEY: If no one at all will take it, maybe it's best to give it up to the police.

TIM CASEY: There'd be a welcome for it with them surely!

(*Laughter*.)

MRS. TULLY: And it is to the police Kitty Keary herself will be brought.

MRS. TARPEY: (*rocking to and fro*) I wonder now who will take the expense of the wake for poor Jack Smith?

BARTLEY: The wake for Jack Smith!

TIM CASEY: Why wouldn't he get a wake as well as another? Would you begrudge him that much?

BARTLEY: Red Jack Smith dead! Who was telling you?

SHAWN EARLY: The whole town knows of it by this.

BARTLEY: Do they say what way did he die?

JAMES RYAN: You don't know that yourself, I suppose, Bartley Fallon? You don't know he was followed and that he was laid dead with the stab of a hayfork?

BARTLEY: The stab of a hayfork!

SHAWN EARLY: You don't know, I suppose, that the body was found in the Five Acre Meadow?

BARTLEY: The Five Acre Meadow!

TIM CASEY: It is likely you don't know that the police are after the man that did it?

BARTLEY: The man that did it!

MRS. TULLY: You don't know, maybe, that he was made away with for the sake of Kitty Keary, his wife?

BARTLEY: Kitty Keary, his wife!

(*Sits down bewildered*.)

MRS. TULLY: And what have you to say now, Bartley Fallon?

BARTLEY: (*crossing himself*) I to bring that fork here, and to find that news before me! It is much if I can ever stir from this place at all, or reach as far as the road!

TIM CASEY: Look, boys, at the new magistrate, and Jo Muldoon along with him! It's best for us to quit this.

SHAWN EARLY: That is so. It is best not to be mixed in this business at all.

JAMES RYAN: Bad as he is, I wouldn't like to be an informer against any man.

(*All hurry away except Mrs. Tarpey, who remains behind her stall. Enter magistrate and policeman*.)

MAGISTRATE: I knew the district was in a bad state, but I did not expect to be confronted with a murder at the first fair I came to.

POLICEMAN: I am sure you did not, indeed.

MAGISTRATE: It was well I had not gone home. I caught a few words here and there that roused my suspicions.

POLICEMAN: So they would, too.

MAGISTRATE: You heard the same story from everyone you asked?

POLICEMAN: The same story—or if it was not altogether the same, anyway it was no less than the first story.

MAGISTRATE: What is that man doing? He is sitting alone with a hayfork. He has a guilty look. The murder was done with a hayfork!

POLICEMAN: (in a whisper) That's the very man they say did the act; Bartley Fallon himself!

MAGISTRATE: He must have found escape difficult—he is trying to brazen it out. A convict in the Andaman Islands tried the same game, but he could not escape my system! Stand aside—Don't go far—have the handcuffs ready. (He walks up to Bartley, folds his arms, and stands before him.) Here, my man, do you know anything of John Smith?

BARTLEY: Of John Smith! Who is he, now?

POLICEMAN: Jack Smith, sir—Red Jack Smith!

MAGISTRATE: (coming a step nearer and tapping him on the shoulder) Where is Jack Smith?

BARTLEY: (with a deep sigh, and shaking his head slowly) Where is he, indeed?

MAGISTRATE: What have you to tell?

BARTLEY: It is where he was this morning, standing in this spot, singing his share of songs—no, but lighting his pipe—scraping a match on the sole of his shoes—

MAGISTRATE: I ask you, for the third time, where is he?

BARTLEY: I wouldn't like to say that. It is a great mystery, and it is hard to say of any man, did he earn hatred or love.

MAGISTRATE: Tell me all you know.

BARTLEY: All that I know—Well, there are the three estates; there is Limbo, and there is Purgatory, and there is—

MAGISTRATE: Nonsense! This is trifling! Get to the point.

BARTLEY: Maybe you don't hold with the clergy so? That is the teaching of the clergy. Maybe you hold with the old people. It is what they do be saying, that the shadow goes wandering, and the soul is tired, and the body is taking a rest—The shadow! (Starts up.) I was nearly sure I saw Jack Smith not ten minutes ago at the corner of the forge, and I lost him again—Was it his ghost I saw, do you think?

MAGISTRATE: (to policeman) Conscience-struck! He will confess all now!

BARTLEY: His ghost to come before me! It is likely it was on account of the fork! I to have it and he to have no way to defend himself the time he met with his death!

MAGISTRATE: (to policeman) I must note down his words. (Takes out notebook.) (To Bartley.) I warn you that your words are being noted.

BARTLEY: If I had ha' run faster in the beginning, this terror would not be on me at the latter end! Maybe he will cast it up against me at the day of judgment—I wouldn't wonder at all at that.

MAGISTRATE: (writing) At the day of judgment—

BARTLEY: It was soon for his ghost to appear to me—is it coming after me always by day it will be, and stripping the clothes off in the night time?—I wouldn't wonder at all at that, being as I am an unfortunate man!

MAGISTRATE: (sternly) Tell me this truly. What was the motive of this crime?

BARTLEY: The motive, is it?

MAGISTRATE: Yes; the motive; the cause.

BARTLEY: I'd sooner not say that.

MAGISTRATE: You had better tell me truly. Was it money?

BARTLEY: Not at all! What did poor Jack Smith ever have in his pockets unless it might be his hands that would be in them?

MAGISTRATE: Any dispute about land?

BARTLEY: (indignantly) Not at all! He never was a grabber or grabbed from anyone!

MAGISTRATE: You will find it better for you if you tell me at once.

BARTLEY: I tell you I wouldn't for the whole world wish to say what it was—it is a thing I would not like to be talking about.

MAGISTRATE: There is no use in hiding it. It will be discovered in the end.

BARTLEY: Well, I suppose it will, seeing that mostly everybody knows it before. Whisper here now. I will tell no lie; where would be the use? (*Puts his hand to his mouth, and Magistrate stoops.*) Don't be putting the blame on the parish, for such a thing was never done in the parish before—it was done for the sake of Kitty Keary, Jack Smith's wife.

MAGISTRATE: (*to policeman*) Put on the handcuffs. We have been saved some trouble. I knew he would confess if taken in the right way.

(*Policeman puts on handcuffs.*)

BARTLEY: Handcuffs now! Glory be! I always said, if there was ever any misfortune coming to this place it was on myself it would fall. I to be in handcuffs! There's no wonder at all in that.

(*Enter Mrs. Fallon, followed by the rest. She is looking back at them as she speaks.*)

MRS. FALLON: Telling lies the whole of people of this town are; telling lies, telling lies as fast as a dog will trot! Speaking against my poor respectable man! Saying he made an end of Jack Smith! My decent comrade! There is no better man and no kinder man in the whole of the five parishes! It's little annoyance he ever gave to any one! (*Turns and sees him.*) What in the earthly world do I see before me? Bartley Fallon in charge of the police! Handcuffs on him! O Bartley, what did you do at all at all?

BARTLEY: O Mary, there has a great misfortune come upon me! It is what I always said, that if there is ever any misfortune—

MRS. FALLON: What did he do at all, or is it bewitched I am?

MAGISTRATE: This man has been arrested on a charge of murder.

MRS. FALLON: Whose charge is that? Don't believe them! They are all liars in this place! Give me back my man!

MAGISTRATE: It is natural you should take his part, but you have no cause of complaint against your neighbours. He has been arrested for the murder of John Smith, on his own confession.

MRS. FALLON: The saints of heaven protect us! And what did he want killing Jack Smith?

MAGISTRATE: It is best you should know all. He did it on account of a love affair with the murdered man's wife.

MRS. FALLON: (*Sitting down*) With Jack Smith's wife! With Kitty Keary!—Ochone, the traitor!

THE CROWD: A great shame, indeed. He is a traitor indeed.

MRS. TULLY: To America he was bringing her, Mrs. Fallon.

BARTLEY: What are you saying, Mary? I tell you—

MRS. FALLON Don't say a word! I won't listen to any word you'll say! (*Stops her ears.*) O, isn't he the treacherous villain? Ochone go deo!

BARTLEY: Be quiet till I speak! Listen to what I say!

MRS. FALLON: Sitting beside me on the ass-car coming to the town, so quiet and so respectable, and treachery like that in his heart!

BARTLEY: Is it your wits you have lost or is it I myself that have lost my wits?

MRS. FALLON: And it's hard I earned you, slaving—and you grumbling, and sighing, and coughing, and discontented, and the priest wore out anointing you, with all the times you threatened to die!

BARTLEY: Let you be quiet till I tell you!

MRS. FALLON: You to bring such a disgrace into the parish. A thing that was never heard of before!

BARTLEY: Will you shut you mouth and hear me speaking?

MRS. FALLON: And if it was for any sort of a fine handsome woman, but for a little fistful of a woman like Kitty Keary, that's not four feet high hardly, and not three teeth in her head unless she got new ones! May God reward you, Bartley Fallon, for the black treachery in your heart and the wickedness in your mind, and the red blood of poor Jack Smith that is wet upon your hand!

(*Voice of Jack Smith heard singing.*)

> The sea shall be dry,
>   The earth under mourning and ban!
> Then loud shall he cry
>   For the wife of the red-haired man!

BARTLEY: It's Jack Smith's voice—I never knew a ghost to sing before—. It is after myself and the fork he is coming! (*Goes back. Enter Jack Smith.*) Let one of you give him the fork and I will be clear of him now and for eternity!

MRS. TARPEY: The Lord have mercy on us! Red Jack Smith! The man that was going to be waked!

JAMES RYAN: Is it back from the grave you are come?

SHAWN EARLY: Is it alive you are, or is it dead you are?

TIM CASEY: Is it yourself at all that's in it?

MRS. TULLY: Is it letting on you were to be dead?

MRS. FALLON: Dead or alive, let you stop Kitty Keary, your wife, from bringing my man away with her to America!

JACK SMITH: It is what I think, the wits are gone astray on the whole of you. What would my wife want bringing Bartley Fallon to America?

MRS. FALLON: To leave yourself, and to get quit of you she wants, Jack Smith, and to bring him away from myself. That's what the two of them had settled together.

JACK SMITH: I'll break the head of any man that says that! Who is it says it? (*To Tim Casey*) Was it you said it? (*To Shawn Early*) Was it you?

ALL TOGETHER: (*backing and shaking their heads*). It wasn't I said it!

JACK SMITH: Tell me the name of any man that said it!

ALL TOGETHER: (*pointing to Bartley*). It was him that said it!

JACK SMITH: Let me at him till I break his head!

(*Bartley backs in terror. Neighbours hold Jack Smith back.*)

JACK SMITH: (*trying to free himself*). Let me at him! Isn't he the pleasant sort of a scarecrow for any woman to be crossing the ocean with! It's back from the docks of New York he'd be turned (*trying to rush at him again*), with a lie in his mouth and treachery in his heart, and another man's wife by his side, and he passing her off as his own! Let me at him, can't you.

(*Makes another rush, but is held back.*)

MAGISTRATE: (*pointing to Jack Smith*). Policeman, put the handcuffs on this man. I see it all now. A case of false impersonation, a conspiracy to defeat the ends of justice. There was a case in the Andaman Islands, a murderer of the Mopsa tribe, a religious enthusiast—

POLICEMAN: So he might be, too.

MAGISTRATE: We must take both these men to the scene of the murder. We must confront them with the body of the real Jack Smith.

JACK SMITH: I'll break the head of any man that will find my dead body!

MAGISTRATE: I'll call more help from the barracks. (*Blows Policeman's whistle.*)

BARTLEY: It is what I am thinking, if myself and Jack Smith are put together in the one cell for the night, the handcuffs will be taken off him, and his hands will be free, and murder will be done that time surely!

MAGISTRATE: Come on! (*They turn to the right.*)

Curtain.

Clorinda Matto de Turner   *Peru, 1854–1909*

Married at 19 to an English doctor, Clorinda Matto de Turner went to live on her husband's ranch in Peru and began publishing her stories and essays under a variety of pseudonyms in local periodicals. In 1876 she founded a cultural review that published important contemporary writers from all over Latin America. The journal was so successful that Matto de Turner was accepted into the tight literary community in Lima, frequently visiting the salon of Indianist writer Juana Manuela Gorritti, and eventually founding her own salon.

The years between 1880 and 1890 were busy ones for Matto de Turner. After her husband's death in 1881 she became editor of a newspaper in Arequipa, in rural Peru, and published several important books on the subject for which she would become famous—the rights of the indigenous people of Peru, including *Tradiciones cuzqueñas: Leyendas, biografías y hojas sueltas* (Traditions of Cuzco. Legends, Biographies and Other Subjects, 1884–1886, and *Hima-Sumac*, 1892, a play in prose. At around the same time, she published her manual on women's education. *Elementos de literatura: para el bello sexo* (Elements of Literature for the Fair Sex, 1881), which outlines her goals for a healthy society based on love and a sound education for the young and elevates the role of women in the home to its critical place in the society at large.

In 1889 Matto de Turner became editor of *El Perú Illustrado* (Peru Illustrated) an important journal in Lima, and she published *Aves sin nido* (Birds Without a Nest), the work for which she is best known. *Birds* focuses on the oppression by landowners, government officials, and the Catholic church, of the Indian people in Peru. Her work inspired a whole genre of novels on that theme but made her very unpopular with the people she criticized. She was excommunicated and attacks on her, both verbal and physical, were so great she was forced into exile in neighboring Argentina, where she died in 1909.

from BIRDS WITHOUT A NEST
Aves sin nido

Prologue

If history is the mirror in which generations to come may contemplate the image of generations that were, then the novel must be the photograph which stereotypes the vices and virtues of a people, in order to correct the former and praise the latter.

Therefore the importance of the "novel of customs" is such that in its pages it often contains the secret of the reform of certain types, if not their extinction.

In countries like ours, where LITERATURE is still in its infancy, the novel must exert the greatest influence on the transformation of the people's customs. Therefore, when a work comes to light which exhibits tendencies raised to regions above those in which purely romantic or entertaining novels are born and live, it may well implore the attention of its public so that, reaching out their hands, they can deliver its message to the common people.

Who knows whether, upon turning the last page of this book, the reader may be struck by a sudden realization of the importance of carefully monitoring the civil and ecclesiastical personnel empowered to rule the destinies of those who live in the farflung villages of Peru's interior?

Who knows whether he may recognize as a social necessity the marriage of the clergy?

In the expression of this hope I am inspired by the exactitude with which I have taken my tableaux, from reality, presenting the copy to the reader that he may judge and pass sentence.

I feel a great love and tenderness toward the native race of Peru, not the least because I have had the opportunity to closely observe their simple and therefore charming customs, and the objection into which they are forced by overbearing village bosses who, whatever their designations, never fail to qualify as tyrants. For generally, priests, town governors, *caciques** and mayors are no better than tyrants.

For fifteen years, moved by my affection for them, I have observed many incidents which, if they took place in Switzerland, Provence or Savoy, would inspire a poet, novelist or historian to immortalize them with lyre or pen; but in the farflung reaches of my country, they can barely attract a sister's faded pencil.

I repeat that, in giving this work over to the reader's verdict, it is with the hope that he will decide on the necessity of bettering conditions in the small towns of Peru. Even if it only calls forth compassion, the author of these pages will have achieved her objectives, recording that in our country there are brothers who suffer, exploited in the night of ignorance, tortured in that blackness that begs for light; pointing out ideas of no small importance in regard to our national progress; and *creating*, at the same time, Peruvian literature. . . .

_____

On that same morning, when the sun had just risen from the darkness of his bed, causing both bird and flower to leap up to greet him in the subjection of their love and gratitude, a peasant crossed the plaza driving his team of oxen, carrying the equipment for ploughing and his ration of food for the day. A yoke, a prod and a leather yoke-strap for the day's work, the traditional colored woven *chuspa* containing its coca leaves and *llipta* biscuits for breakfast.

On his way past the church door, he reverently removed his fringed cloth cap, murmuring something similar to an invocation; and continued on his way, at intervals turning his head to look sadly at the hut he was leaving behind.

Was it fear or doubt, love or hope, which stirred in his soul at those moments?

It was clear he was deeply moved by some emotion.

Along the stone wall which borders the south side of the plaza, a head peeked out, and then as quickly as a fox was hidden again behind the stones, but not before revealing the well-formed head of a woman. Her black tresses, long and limp, were parted in two sections, serving as a frame for her pretty face; her red-tinted cheeks, even brighter where the many capillaries woven beneath the surface stood out in her copper-colored skin.

No sooner had the peasant disappeared over the distant hill of Cañas than the head hidden behind the wall took on a body, jumping to the other side. She was a healthy, strapping young woman, striking in her Peruvian beauty. She was about thirty years old, but with her fresh good looks, no one would guess her to be more than twenty-eight at most. She wore a flowing dark blue overskirt of baize cloth; and her torso was graced by a bodice of coffee-colored velveteen with decorations at the neckline, cuffs of fake silver, and bone buttons.

As best she could, she shook off the muddy dirt that had fallen on her clothes as she jumped the wall; and she immediately headed toward a small white house with a tiled roof. A woman stood in the doorway; she was elegantly dressed in a lead-colored grenadine dressing gown, with silk lace, fastened by pearl-shell buttons. She was none other than Señora Lucía, wife of Don Fernando Marín; the couple had taken up residence temporarily in the country.

The new arrival spoke up without preface to Lucía, saying, "In the name of the Holy Virgin, *señoracha*, please help a whole family in disgrace this day. The one that went out to the fields today, carrying all his work hodgepodge with him, and that passed right by you, that was Juan Yupanqui, my husband, father of two little girls. Ay, señoracha! He went out with his heart half-dead, because he knows today will be the day of the distribution visit, and since the cacique works sowing barley, he can't hide either, because besides getting locked up he'll have to pay a fine of eight reales for not showing up, and we don't have any money. I stayed there crying near Rosacha, who sleeps next to the hearth, and all of a sudden my heart told me that you're a good person; and without Juan knowing I came to beg for your help, for the holy Virgin's sake, señoracha, ay! ay!"

The petition was ended by tears, leaving Lucía mystified. Having lived there only a few months, she knew nothing of the local customs and could not comprehend the urgency of the poor woman's situation, which of course aroused her curiosity.

It was necessary to see these poor disinherited creatures up close, and to hear them tell their own story in their own expressive manner of speaking, to understand the pity that springs forth unexpectedly in noble hearts, and how they begin to share the same pain, even when their original motive has been a mere scholarly interest in the observation of customs little-known by the majority of Peruvians and lamented by very few.

Lucía's goodness was a natural quality, and the interest awakened by the other woman's words continued to increase. She asked, "And who are you?"

"I am Marcela, señoracha, wife of Juan Yupanqui, poor and helpless," the woman answered, drying her eyes on the sleeve of her bodice.

Lucía put her hand affectionately on the woman's shoulder, and invited her to come in and rest on the stone bench in the white house's garden.

"Sit down, Marcela, wipe those tears that darken the skies of your countenance, and let's talk calmly," said Lucía, greatly interested in getting to know the Indian customs.

Marcela's pain was calmed, and, perhaps in the hope of her salvation, she responded in minute detail to Lucía's questions; and as she talked she began to trust Lucía so much that she would have been willing to confess even her darkest deeds, even those bad thoughts, which are the breath of vicious germs in humans. Therefore in a confiding manner she said to Lucía, "Since you're not from around here, childling, you don't know what tortures the collector, the cacique, and the papa priest put us through. Ay! Ay! Why didn't the plague just kill us all, so we could be sleeping now in the ground?"

"My poor Marcela, why do you get so upset?" interrupted Lucía. "It can't be that bad; you're a mother and in one life, a mother's heart has as many lives as she has children."

"Yes, childling," responded Marcela, "You have the face of the Virgin to whom we pray the Hail Mary, and that's why I came to ask you. I want to save my husband. As he left he said to me, 'One of these days I'm going to throw myself in the river because I can't stand my life anymore, and I would want to kill you first before giving up my body to the water,' and you can see, señoracha, how crazy it is to talk like that."

"That's a terrible thought, it's insanity, poor Juan!" said Lucía sorrowfully, and looking closely at her companion, she continued, "And what is your urgent problem today?

Speak, Marcela, as if you were speaking to your own soul."

"Last year," the Indian woman responded frankly, "they left us ten pesos in our hut for two hundred-weights of wool. We spent that money in the fair buying the things I'm wearing now, because Juan said we would get plenty of fleeces during the year, but it was impossible because he has no one to help him in his tasks; and because my mother-in-law died at Christmas, the papa priest took our potato crop as payment for the burial and the prayers. Now I will have to go work as a forced servant in the parish house, and leave my hut and my little girls, and while I'm gone, who knows if Juan will go crazy and die? Who knows what will happen to me there, because the women who go in there to work as forced servants come out...looking at the ground!"

"Enough! Don't tell me any more," broke in Lucía, frightened by the direction Marcela's story was taking. Her last words had alarmed the open, good-hearted woman, who was beginning to see that those she had thought civilized might actually be monsters of greed and even lust.

"Today I will speak with the governor and the priest, and maybe by tomorrow your problems will be solved," promised Don Fernando's wife, and added as a farewell, "Go on now to take care of your daughters, and when Juan comes back, calm him down, tell him that you've talked to me, and tell him to come and see me."

The Indian woman, for her part, sighed contentedly for the first time in her life.

It is such a solemn moment when a person in the depths of despair encounters a generous hand reaching out to help him, the heart doesn't know whether to bathe the kindly hand with tears or cover it with kisses, or just burst out with cries of blessing. This is what is happening in those moments in Marcela's heart.

Those who do good to the unfortunate can never measure the magnitude of a single kind word, a sweet smile that for the fallen one, the unhappy one, is like a ray of sunlight that restores life to limbs numbed by the ice of misfortune....

In the provinces where the alpaca is bred, and the wool industry is the principal source of wealth, there exists, with few exceptions, the custom of advance distribution by the powerful merchants, generally among the richest people in the area.

For the forced cash advances the *wool dealers* make, they fix such a low price for each hundred-weight of wool that the cost of the yield exceeds by five-hundred percent the capital provided, a usury which, along with the extortions which accompany it, almost makes life a living hell for those savages.

The Indians who own alpacas move out of their huts at distribution time, in order not to receive the advance money, which for them comes to be as accursed as the thirteen coins of Judas. But do the abandonment of their homes, their wanderings in the solitude of the mountain peaks, save them? No....

The collector, the same man that does the distribution, breaks into the hut with ease owing to the flimsy lock on the cowhide door: he leaves the money on the wool-press and departs at once, only to return a year later with the executory LIST, which is the only judge and witness for the wretched forced debtor.

When the year is up, the collector shows up with his retinue of ten or twelve *mestizos*, sometimes disguised as soldiers, and he takes, using a special scale with stone counter-weights, fifty pounds of wool for twenty-five. And if the Indian hides his only property, if he protests and curses, he is subjected to tortures the likes of which the pen cannot bear to write, despite asking pardon for those cases in which the ink changes color.

The PASTORAL LETTER of one of the most renowned bishops of the Peruvian church mentions those excesses, but did not dare to speak of the cold-water enemas used in some places to make the Indians confess where their resources are hidden. The Indian fears that even more than the lash of the whip, and those inhuman monsters who abide by the letter and not the sense of the law, allege that whipping is forbidden in Peru, but that the barbarities which they inflict upon their unfortunate brothers are not.

Oh! May God in his goodness someday decree the extinction of the native race, which after having worn imperial greatness, now drinks the mud of opprobrium. May God will its extinction, since it is not possible for it to regain its dignity nor exercise its rights!

Marcela's bitter weeping and desperation upon contemplating the forthcoming arrival of the collector were, therefore, the justified explosion of anguish of one who saw in her presence a whole world of poverty and shameful pain. . . .

Shortness of stature, flat head, dark complexion, thick nose with prominent nostrils, thick lips, small gray eyes; a short neck encircled by black and white beads, a sparse and ill-shaven beard; dressed in an imitation cassock of black cloth, shiny, poorly tailored, and cared for even worse, a hat of Guayaquil straw in the right hand; such was the appearance of the first personage, who stepped forward and whom Lucía greeted first, with marked manifestations of respect, saying, "God grant you good afternoon, Reverend Pascual."

The priest Pascual Vargas, successor to Don Pedro Miranda y Claro in the curacy of Killac, inspired grave doubts from the first moment one met him that he had ever studied or learned Theology or Latin; the latter being a language that sat poorly in a mouth shielded by two walls of very large and white teeth. He was about fifty years of age, and his manners very seriously accentuated Marcela's fears when she spoke of entering as a servant into the parish house, from which, according to the native phrase, women came out "looking at the ground."

To a physiological observer, the general appearance of the Reverend Pascual could be compared to a nest of lecherous snakes, quick to awaken at the slightest sound of a woman's voice.

The question also rapidly crossed Lucía's mind as to how such an ill-favored personage could have reached the highest of ministries; for a basic tenet of her religious convictions was the sublimity of the priesthood which on this earth is charged with the education of man, greeting him in the cradle with the baptismal waters, laying him to rest in the tomb with the rain of sanctified water, and during his journey through the valley of pain, sweetening his bitternesses with sound words of advice and the soft voice of hope.

Lucía had forgotten that the explanation for its propensities to error lay in the fact that its mission was dependent on human will, and she was not aware of the general nature of the pastors of remote parishes.

The other personage who followed the Reverend Pascual was wrapped in a wide Spanish cape, the very mention of which was worth fourteen testimonials, and which might represent his ancient titles, if not his genealogical tree; this was Don Sebastián Pancorbo, a name received by his lordship in a baptismal ceremony which included a tall cross, a new cape, a silver saltcellar and the voice of the organ, when he was three days old.

Don Sebastián, a very unique sort, judging by his apparel, is tall and bony; his face is never troubled by the masculine annoyances of moustache and beard; his black eyes, bright and greedy, bear witness, in a glance that tends toward the left, that he is not indifferent to the sound of metal, nor to the metal of a female voice. He twisted the little finger of his right hand when he was a boy, upon administering a blow to a friend of his, and since then he has used a half-glove of vicuña fur, though he manages that hand with a peculiar grace. The man has not one atom of nitroglycerin in his blood: he seems made for peace, but his natural weakness frequently causes him to become the center of ridiculous scenes which are greatly enjoyed by his dinner companions. He strums the guitar with such lack of skill and of musical sense that he has achieved prominence for the same, though he drinks like an army musician.

Don Sebastián received such primary education as time permitted in the three years he spent in a city school; and after returning to the village, he was made keeper of the keys on Holy Thursday; he married Doña Petronila Hinojosa, daughter of a *prominent man*; and immediately became governor; that is to say, he arrived at the highest post known of and aspired to in any village.

The two personages settled themselves comfortably into armchairs indicated by Lucía.

Marín's wife summoned up all of her affability and reason so that she might sway her interlocutors in Marcela's favor, and speaking especially to the parish priest, she said, "In the name of the Christian religion, which is pure love, tenderness and hope; in the name of our Teacher, who bid us give all to the poor, I ask of you, Reverend Father, that you consider as cancelled the debt which weighs heavily on the family of Juan Yupanqui. Oh! You will receive in exchange a doubled reward in heaven..."

"My dear young lady," replied the Reverend Pascual, sprawling in his seat and resting both hands on the arms of the chair, "all these are pretty bits of nonsense, but when all is said and done, God help us, who can live without income? Nowadays, with the increase in ecclesiastical contributions and the fancy new civilization that will come with the railroads, the emoluments will end and...and ...once and for all, Doña Lucía, forget about priests; we'll all starve to death!"

"So that's what's going on with the Indian Yupanqui?" added the governor, in support of the priest. And in a tone of triumph he ended, stressing the sentence for Lucía, "Frankly, you'd better learn, Señorita, that our customs are our law, and no one's going to take our customs away from us, hmmm?"...

"Gentlemen, charity is also a law of the heart," argued Lucía, interrupting.

"So this is Juan's doing, eh? Frankly, we'll see if that Indian scoundrel tries to pull any more fast ones on us," continued Don Sebastián, ignoring Lucía's words, and with a certain threatening scorn, which did not go unnoticed by Don Fernando's wife, whose heart trembled with fear. The brief sentences exchanged among them had clearly revealed the moral values of those men, from whom there was nothing to hope for, and everything to fear.

Her plan was thoroughly upset; but her heart was still firmly concerned with Marcela's family, and she was determined to protect them from any harm. Her dove's heart felt its self-esteem wounded, and pallor clouded her countenance.

At that moment, it was necessary to make a decisive sortie, and Lucía found it in the energy with which she responded: "A sad reality, gentlemen! Very well! I am becoming convinced that vile interest has dried up the most beautiful flowers of human emotion in these parts, where I expected to find patriarchal families living together in brotherhood. Nothing has been said here today; and the Indian Juan's family will never ask for your favors or your protection." Upon heatedly speaking these last words, Lucía fixed her lovely eyes, with the look of one giving a command, on the door-screen.

The two potentates of Kíllac were baffled by such an unexpected attitude, and seeing no way to reopen a discussion which, moreover, it was in their best interests to flee, took their hats.

"Señora Lucía, don't be offended by this, and believe I am always your chaplain," said the priest, turning his straw hat over between his hands; and Don Sebastián hurried to say brusquely, "Good afternoon, Señora Lucía."

Lucía cut short the usual formulas of farewell, satisfying herself with a mere nod of the head; and watching them go, those men who had made the deepest impression on her angel's soul, she said to herself, trembling and with vehemence, "No, no, that man is an insult to the Catholic priesthood; I have seen better men than him in the city, gray-haired men, walking silently, in mystery, to seek out the poor and orphaned to help and console them; I have seen the self-sacrificing Catholic priest by the bedside of a dying man; pure before the sacrificial altar; weeping and humble in the home of the widow and orphan; I have seen him take his last piece of bread and offer it to the poor man, depriving himself of food and thanking God for his mercy. And that is the Reverend Pascual?...Oh! priests of these hamlets! ...And the other one, his soul cast in a thin miser's mold, the governor, he also doesn't deserve the dignity which surrounds an honorable man in this world. Good riddance to them, for all I need to do is plead with my Fernando, and carry the flowers of satisfaction to our home!"

The sound of the family clock striking five made Lucía realize how much time had passed, and announced to her that dinner was served.

Senor Marín's wife, her cheeks flushed with the heat of her impressions, passed through various corridors and arrived at the dining room, where she took her usual seat.

The walls and ceiling of the white house's dining room were oak-colored; at intervals luxurious oil paintings were hung, depicting here a half-plucked partridge, there a Castilian rabbit ready to be thrown into the stewing casserole. A cedar sideboard with quicksilvered moons, identical to the table implements placed symmetrically, stood on the left-hand wall. On the right-hand wall stood two small tables, one holding a chess board, the other a roulette game; for this was the space chosen by the mine employees to spend their free time. The dining table, in the center of the room, covered with freshly pressed white cloths, boasted a country table service of blue china with colored borders.

The soup gave off a thick vapor that, along with its fragrance, identified it as the substantial meat-porridge made of ground loin with spices, walnuts, and biscuits, all dissolved in the watery gravy and broth; it was followed by three fine dishes, including the delicious patchwork stew.

They were serving Carabaya coffee which, clear, hot, and strong, sent out an inspirational aroma from within the small porcelain cups, when a messenger arrived bearing a letter for Lucía, who took it with interest and, recognizing Fernando's handwriting, tore open the envelope and began to read it. By the changes on Lucía's face, an observer could have guessed the contents of the letter, in which Senor Marín said that he would arrive home the next morning, because the landslides caused by recurrent snowfalls in the Andes had paralyzed the miners' work for the time being. He asked that she send ahead a fresh horse to relieve the one he was riding, which was without horseshoes.

Translated by Patti Firth

NOTE

* Indian leader.

Vittoria Aganoor Pompilj   *Italy, 1855–1910*

Vittoria Aganoor was fortunate enough to study under the guidance of two distinguished poets, Giacomo Zanella and Enrico Nencioni. A member of a well-to-do family, she led a life that seemed serene but was apparently disturbed by a number of emotional disappointments; indeed, in 1903 the critic and poet Domenico Gnoli (1838–1915) published under the name of Giulio Orsini a volume of love poems inspired in part by Pompilj. In 1901 she married Guido Pompilj, a member of Parliament, with whom she enjoyed domestic serenity. Her death, following an operation, was rendered more dramatic by the fact that her husband committed suicide a few hours later beside her body.

Reluctant at first to publish her poems, except for a few that appeared in journals, Pompilj put together a collection entitled *Leggenda eterna* (Eternal Legend, 1900), in which the poems below were published. It was well received and was reprinted in 1903. She dealt mainly with unrequited love and the resulting disenchantment and bitter solitude, partly reflecting her own experiences. Frequently posing questions to which there are no answers, Pompilj expresses in her poetry a sad restlessness and pessimism that anticipates the later works of the existentialists. She was familiar with the Romantic and Decadent poets and, like Pirandello, went beyond conventional realism to capture some of the disturbing aspects of modern life, such as people's inability to understand others, for each person interprets words in a different way. Some of her poems have been translated into English and anthologized. *Nuove liriche* (New Lyrics, 1908) was reprinted, together with her first collection, under the title *Le poesie complete* (Complete Poems, 1912), edited by Alfredo Grilli.

Natalia Costa-Zalessow

DIALOGUE
Dialogo

We talk, but do I know
what you really mean to say?
And did you understand
anything of what I meant?
Words flow and a subtle
veil of laughter
often masks the intent.

We talk . . . You hear only
the sound of another's voice;
I likewise heed the strange
echo of another's speech.
Conversing are
two sepulchres
each to each.

We laugh, also, we laugh
loudly, and the joy
flashes in our eyes
at a fine joke's quick leaping.
In what abyss of the heart
who, then, meanwhile
bursts in a rain of weeping?

Translated by Joan Borrelli

EQUIVOCATION
Equivoco

—Are you smiling? I read in your heart, plainly:
you see a future
of joy.—

    —You are wrong; I was pondering
a love loved vainly
long past,—

    —Are you sighing? I read
in your heart: the memory
poisons your every pure
dream.—

    —You are wrong! In me
a peace has at last descended.
I was pondering...that the soul
reposes only now
when every dream is ended.—

—Yet you were sighing!—

        —Oh ruthless

inquisitress! The vain
love, the battles, the tears
were life, alas!
but this silence of the heart
which at love's every breath
has barred its every door,
this silence...is, perhaps,
(I was thinking a while before) my death?

Translated by Joan Borrelli

Olive Schreiner   *South Africa/UK(England), 1855–1920*

Olive Schreiner has been immortalized as the writer of the first novel of white South Africa; because she never wrote anything commensurate with *Story of an African Farm* (1883), her feminist critics, taking her at her own word, have tended to overemphasize her *literary* career as thwarted by self-conflict, while neglecting her social and political achievement. Instead, it may be argued that Schreiner used her youthful celebrity to mobilize her society against capitalism, imperialism, and male chauvinism.

Her allegorical novel *Trooper Peter Halket of Mashonaland* (1897) was an angry denunciation of the jingoistic adventurism of Cecil Rhodes and his British South Africa Company. Her articles and essays (collected in *Thoughts on South*

Africa, 1923), advocated the cause of South Africa and peaceful coexistence between the Boers and the British, while recognizing the exploitation of blacks (though her view of the "black race" shows that she did not escape the prejudices of her time). Her *Women and Labor* (1911), contemporaneous with Charlotte Perkins Gilman's *Women and Economics*, became a "bible for feminists"—a complex effort to analyze the ambiguous status of bourgeois women as oppressors and oppressed, which transcends the contemporary social conditions it describes, as Doris Lessing notes. The unfinished novel *From Man to Man* (1927) also exposed the economic inequality that distorted male and female relations. Finally, she poured considerable energy into public life: she was apparently an inspired speaker in prophesying and then opposing the Anglo-Boer War (1899–1902); in supporting a democratic constitution for South Africa; and, as founder and then Vice-President of the Women's Enfranchisement League, in advocating women's rights.

A freethinker who became a socialist, Schreiner overcame the constraints of a parochial environment and a harsh Calvinist upbringing largely through self-education by reading such writers as George Eliot, the Brontë sisters, John Stuart Mill, John Ruskin, Ralph Waldo Emerson, and Herbert Spencer. Their legacy of mid-Victorian morality undoubtedly caused Schreiner to place social and political reform above literary accomplishment.

Schreiner described her early years in *Undine*, her first novel, begun when she was 20 and published only after her death. Born the ninth of twelve children to missionary parents, Schreiner at an early age was forced to go into service with the Boers she had been taught to despise, after her father declared bankruptcy and the family was dispersed. It was then that she developed the asthma that would plague her for the rest of her life, sapping her energies and finally killing her.

Supported by a brother in Cambridge, Schreiner came to England in 1881 to study nursing, bringing with her the manuscript of *Story of an African Farm*. Published in 1883 under the pseudonym of Ralph Iron and reprinted three times in the same year, it was immediately acclaimed—as much for its intense realization of the African landscape and its people as for its daring portrayal of a young woman who bears an illegitimate child. For contemporary readers, this work was as momentous as *A Doll's House* by Ibsen. Notable too was a new style of allegorical realism.

Having made a reputation for herself, Schreiner was befriended by the psychologist Havelock Ellis and later by the feminist-socialist Eleanor Marx. She became involved in the Men and Women's Club, a discussion group that was committed to intellectual cooperation between men and women in exploring issues of marriage, prostitution, and human sexuality. Her own correspondence reveals a women uncomfortable with her own sexuality and doubtful that a woman could write and have a full emotional life with a man at the same time.

In 1889, she decided to leave England to return to South Africa for her health and in order to have leisure to write. In the meantime, Ellis had *Dreams* published in England in 1890; like the posthumous *Stories, Dreams, and Allegories* (1923), it uses psychological dream imagery and fable structures in an effort to break the stranglehold of a tyrannical realism that, arguably, helps to sustain the status quo.

At the age of 38, in 1894, Schreiner married Samuel Cronwright and in the following year gave birth to a baby girl, who died sixteen hours later. Her husband, who was eight years younger than she, took her name along with his own, supported her writing, and worked on the political goals they shared. In 1913, however, Schreiner returned alone to England on the verge of the First World War. Committed to a pacifism largely abandoned by her old suffragette and socialist allies, she experienced a social isolation that was intensified by her illness. Against the advice of her doctors, she returned to her homeland, to die in 1920.

"The Dawn of Civilisation," published posthumously in 1921 in *The London Nation and Athenaeum* is reprinted here.

THE DAWN OF CIVILISATION

(Her Last Words, in 1920)

Stray Thoughts on Peace and War.
The Homely Personal Confession of a Believer in Human Unity

I—INTRODUCTION

I have thrown these scattered thoughts, written at intervals during illness, into a somewhat personal form. I have done so intentionally, because I have felt that many persons, even those of high intellectual attainments, were not able to understand what the question of peace and war in its widest aspects meant to certain among us; that, for us, it stands for something far more intimate, personal, and of a far more organic nature than any mere intellectual conclusion—that, for some among us, as a man is compelled to feel the beating of his own heart and cannot shake himself from the consciousness of it, whether he will or no, so we are under a certain psychic compulsion to hold that view which we do hold with regard to war, and are organically unable to hold any other.

There are many ways in which a man at the present day may conscientiously object to war. His forebears may have been objectors and have handed down to him a tradition, which, from his earliest years, has impressed on him the view that war is an evil, not to be trafficked with. His ancestors may have been imprisoned and punished by the men of their own day, for holding what were then entirely new and objectionable views; but, where once

a man can prove that he holds any opinions as a matter of inheritance and that they are shared by a certain number of his fellows under a recognised collective name, the bulk of human beings in his society may not agree with him, may even severely condemn him and desire to punish him; but, since the majority of human creatures accept their politics, their religion, their manners and their ideals purely as a matter of inheritance, the mass of men who differ from him are, at least, able to understand *how* he comes by his views. They do not regard him as a monstrosity and an impossibility, and are able to extend to him in some cases a certain limited tolerance; he comes by his views exactly as they come by theirs; and in so far they are able to understand him.

But a man may conscientiously object to war in quite another fashion. He may object to a definite and given war, for some definite, limited reason. He may believe that war to have been led up to by a false and mad diplomacy, to be based on a mistaken judgment of the national interests; to be even suicidal; and therefore he may feel compelled to oppose that particular war while the bulk of men and women in his society desire and approve of it. The unthinking herd, unable to understand or tolerate any opposition to the herd-will of the moment, may regard him as incomprehensibly wicked; but, at least, an appreciable number of intelligent persons, not sharing his view, will understand that a man may be sincerely compelled to oppose certain lines of public action which the majority of his fellows approve. They may hate him for opposing their will, they may attempt to ostracise and crush him; but, in their calmest and most reasonable moments, they do understand that they might themselves under certain circumstances be compelled to act in the same manner, and are willing, therefore, to allow him the virtue of possible sincerity, if nothing else.

But a man may object to war in another and far wider way. His objection to it may not be based on any hereditary tradition, or on the teaching of any organised society, or of any of the great historic figures of the past; and, while he may indeed object to any definite war for certain limited and material reasons, these are subordinate to the real ground on which his objection rests. He may fully recognise the difference in type between one war and another; between a war for dominance, trade expansion, glory, or the maintenance of Empire, and a war in which a class or race struggles against a power seeking permanently to crush and subject it, or in which a man fights in the land of his birth for the soil on which he first saw light, against the strangers seeking to dispossess him; but, while recognising the immeasurable difference between these types (exactly as the man who objects to private murder must recognise the wide difference between the man who stabs one who has a knife at his throat and the man who slowpoisons another to obtain a great inheritance), he is yet an objector to all war. And he is bound to object, not only to the final expression of war in the slaying of men's bodies; he is bound to object, if possible, more strongly to those ideals and aims and those institutions and methods of action which make the existence of war possible and inevitable among men.

Also, while he may most fully allow that certain immediate and definite ends may be gained by the slaughter of man by man—not merely as where Jezebel gained possession of Naboth's vineyard, for a time, by destroying him, or David acquired Uriah's wife by putting him in the forefront of battle,* but aims even otherwise excusable or even laudable—he is yet compelled to hold that no immediate gain conferred by war, however great, can compensate for the evils it ultimately entails on the human race. He is therefore unable to assist not merely in the actual carnage of war, but, as far as possible, in all that leads to its success.

This is the man, often not belonging to any organised religion, not basing his conviction on the teachings of authority external to himself, whom it appears so difficult, if not impossible, for many persons, sometimes even of keen and critical intellectual gifts, to understand.

We have, in South Africa, a version of a certain well-known story. According to this, an old Boer from the backveld goes for the first time to the Zoological Gardens at Pretoria and sees there some of the, to him, new and quite unknown beasts. He stands long and solemnly before one, and looks at it intently; and then, slowly shaking his head, he turns away, "Daar is nie zoo'n dier nie!" ("There is not such a beast") he remarks calmly, as he walks away.

This story returns often to the mind at the present day, when watching the action of certain bodies of men called upon to pass judgment on the psychic conditions of their fellows, on the matter of slaughter and war. The good shopkeeper, the worthy farmer, the town councillor, the country gentleman, and dashing young military man may understand perfectly their own businesses of weighing and measuring goods, rearing cattle, levying rates, or polo playing, or the best way to cut and thrust in the slaughter of war; but, when suddenly called upon to adjudge on psychological phenomena of which they have no personal experience, they are almost compelled to come to the conclusion of the good old backveld Boer—"Daar *is* nie zoo'n dier nie!" "There *is* no such thing as a Conscientious Objector! He may stand before us; he may tell us what he feels; but we have no experience of such feelings. We know, therefore, that such a being *cannot* exist—and, therefore, it *does* not!"

In the few pages that follow I have

allowed, as I said, a personal element to enter, and I have done so intentionally. As a rule, the more the personal element is eliminated in dealing with the large impersonal problems of human life, the wiser the treatment will be; and it is perhaps always painful in dealing with that to be viewed by those not in sympathy, to touch on those phases of life sacred to the individual as they never can be to any other. But I have felt that, perhaps only by a very simple statement of what one insignificant human creature has felt and does feel, it might perhaps be possible for me to make clear to some of my fellows that such a being as the universal conscientious objector to war does exist.

We are a reality! We do exist. We are as real as a bayonet with human blood and brains along its edge; we are as much a part of the Universe as coal or lead or iron; you have to count us in! You may think us fools, you may hate us, you may wish we were all dead; but it is at least something if you recognise that we are. "To understand all is to forgive all," it has been said; and it is sometimes even something more; it is to sympathise, and even to love, where we cannot yet fully agree. And therefore, perhaps, even the feeblest little attempt to make human beings understand how and why their fellows feel as they feel and are as they are, is not quite nothing.

II—SOMEWHERE, SOMETIME, SOMEPLACE!

When a child, not yet nine years old, I walked out one morning along the mountain tops on which my home stood. The sun had not yet risen, and the mountain grass was heavy with dew; as I looked back I could see the marks my feet had made on the long, grassy slope behind me. I walked till I came to a place where a little stream ran, which farther on passed over the precipices into the deep valley below. Here it passed between soft, earthy banks; at one place a large slice of earth had fallen away from the bank on the other side, and it had made a little island a few feet wide

with water flowing all round it. It was covered with wild mint and a weed with yellow flowers and long waving grasses. I sat down on the bank at the foot of a dwarfed olive tree, the only tree near. All the plants on the island were dark with the heavy night's dew, and the sun had not yet risen.

I had got up so early because I had been awake much in the night and could not sleep longer. My heart was heavy; my physical heart seemed to have a pain in it, as if small, sharp crystals were cutting into it. All the world seemed wrong to me. It was not only that sense of the small misunderstandings and tiny injustices of daily life, which perhaps all sensitive children feel at some time pressing down on them; but the whole Universe seemed to be weighing on me.

I had grown up in a land where wars were common. From my earliest years I had heard of bloodshed and battles and hairbreadth escapes; I had heard them told of by those who had seen and taken part in them. In my native country dark men were killed and their lands taken from them by white men armed with superior weapons; even near to me such things had happened. I knew also how white men fought white men; the stronger even hanging the weaker on gallows when they did not submit; and I had see how white men used the dark as beasts of labour, often without any thought for their good or happiness. Three times I had seen an ox striving to pull a heavily loaded wagon up a hill, the blood and foam streaming from its mouth and nostrils as it struggled, and I had seen it fall dead, under the lash. In the bush in the kloof below I had seen bush-bucks and little long-tailed monkeys that I loved so shot dead, not from any necessity but for the pleasure of killing, and the cock-o-veets and the honey-suckers and the wood-doves that made the bush so beautiful to me. And sometimes I had seen bands of convicts going past to work on the roads, and had heard the chains clanking which went round their waists and passed between their legs to the irons on their feet; I had seen the terrible look in their eyes of a wild creature, when every man's hand is against it, and no one loves it, and it only hates and fears. I had got up early in the morning to drop small bits of tobacco at the roadside, hoping they would find them and pick them up. I had wanted to say to them, "Someone loves you"; but the man with the gun was always there. Once I had seen a pack of dogs set on by men to attack a strange dog, which had come among them and had done no harm to anyone. I had watched it torn to pieces, though I had done all I could to save it. Why did everyone press on everyone and try to make them do what they wanted? Why did the strong always crush the weak? Why did we hate and kill and torture? Why was it all as it was? Why had the world ever been made? Why, oh why, had I ever been born?

The little sharp crystals seemed to cut deeper into my heart.

And then, as I sat looking at that little, damp, dark island, the sun began to rise. It shot its light across the long, grassy slopes of the mountains and struck the little mound of earth in the water. All the leaves and flowers and grasses on it turned bright gold, and the dewdrops hanging from them were like diamonds; and the water in the stream glinted as it ran. And, as I looked at that almost intolerable beauty, a curious feeling came over me. It was not what I *thought* put into exact words, but I seemed to *see* a world in which creatures no more hated and crushed, in which the strong helped the weak, and men understood each other, and forgave each other, and did not try to crush others, but to help. I did not think of it, as something to be in a distant picture; it was there, about me, and I was in it, and a part of it. And there came to me, as I sat there, a joy such as never besides have I experienced, except perhaps once, a joy without limit.

And then, as I sat on there, the sun rose higher and higher, and shone hot on my back, and the morning light was everywhere. And slowly and slowly the vision vanished, and I began to think and question myself.

How could that glory ever really be? In a world where creature preys on creature, and man, the strongest of all, preys more than all, how could this be? And my mind went back to the dark thoughts I had in the night. In a world where the little ant-lion digs his hole in the sand and lies hidden at the bottom for the small ant to fall in and be eaten, and the leopard's eyes gleam yellow through bushes as it watches the little bush-buck coming down to the fountain to drink, and millions and millions of human beings use all they know, and their wonderful hands, to kill and press down others, what hope could there ever be? The world was as it was! And what was I? A tiny, miserable worm, a speck within a speck, an imperceptible atom, a less than a nothing! What did it matter what I did, how I lifted my hands, and how I cried out? The great world would roll on, and on, just as it had! What if nowhere, at no time, in no place, was there anything else?

The band about my heart seemed to grow tighter and tighter. A helpless, tiny, miserable worm! Could I prevent one man from torturing an animal that was in his power; stop one armed man from going out to kill? In my own heart, was there not bitterness, the anger against those who injured me or others, till my heart was like a burning coal? If the world had been made so, so it was! But, why, oh why, had I ever been born? Why did the Universe exist?

And then, as I sat on there, another thought came to me; and in some form or other it has remained with me ever since, all my life. It was like this: You cannot by willing it alter the vast world outside of you; you cannot, perhaps, cut the lash from one whip; you cannot stop the march of even one armed man going out to kill; you cannot, perhaps, strike the handcuff from one chained hand; you cannot even remake your own soul so that there shall be no tendency to evil in it; the great world rolls on, and *you* cannot reshape it; but this one thing only you can do—in that one, small, minute, almost infinitesimal spot in the Universe, where your will rules, there, where alone you are as God, *strive* to make that you hunger for real! No man can prevent you there. In your own heart strive to kill out all hate, all desire to see evil come even to those who have injured you or another; what is weaker than yourself try to help; whatever is in pain or unjustly treated and cries out, say, "I am here! I, little, weak, feeble, but I will do what I can for you." This is all you can do; but do it; it is not nothing! And then this feeling came to me, a feeling it is not easy to put into words, but it was like this: You also are part of the great Universe; what you strive for something strives for; *and nothing in the Universe is quite alone*; you are moving on towards something.

And as I walked back that morning over the grass slopes, I was not sorry I was going back to the old life. I did not wish I was dead and that the Universe had never existed. I, also, had something to live for—and even if I failed to reach it utterly—somewhere, some time, some place, it was! I was not alone.

More than a generation has passed since that day, but it remains to me the most important and unforgettable of my life. In the darkest hour its light has never quite died out.

In the long years which have passed, the adult has seen much of which the young child knew nothing.

In my native land I have seen the horror of a great war. Smoke has risen from burning homesteads; women and children by thousands have been thrown into great camps to perish there; men whom I have known have been tied in chairs and executed for fighting against strangers in the land of their own birth. In the world's great cities I have seen how everywhere the upper stone grinds hard on the nether, and men and women feed upon the toil of their fellow men without any increase of spiritual beauty or joy for themselves, only a heavy congestion; while those who are fed upon grow bitter and narrow from the loss of the life that is sucked from them. Within my own soul I have perceived elements militating against all I hungered for, of which the young child knew nothing; I have watched closely the great, terrible world of public life, of politics, diplomacy, and international relations, where, as under a terrible magnifying glass, the greed, the ambition, the cruelty and falsehood of the individual soul are seen, in so hideously enlarged and wholly unrestrained a form that it might be forgiven to one who cried out to the powers that lie behind life: "Is it not possible to put out a sponge and wipe up humanity from the earth? It is stain!" I have realised that the struggle against the primitive, self-seeking instincts in human nature, whether in the individual or in the larger social organism, is a life-and-death struggle, to be renewed by the individual till death, by the race through the ages. I have tried to wear no blinkers. I have not held a veil before my eyes, that I might profess that cruelty, injustice, and mental and physical anguish were not. I have tried to look nakedly in the face those facts which make most against all hope—and yet, in the darkest hour, the consciousness which I carried back with me that morning has never wholly deserted me; even as a man who clings with one hand to a rock, though the waves pass over his head, yet knows what his hand touches.

But, in the course of the long years which have passed, something else has happened. That which was for the young child only a vision, a flash of almost blinding light, which it could hardly even to itself translate, has, in the course of a long life's experience, become a hope, which I think the cool reason can find grounds to justify, and which a growing knowledge of human nature and human life does endorse.

Somewhere, sometime, someplace—even on earth!

NOTE

* See 1 Kings: 41–46; 21:1–16 and 2 Samuel 11. Uriah's wife is Bathshebaa.

Svarnakumari Devi   *India, 1855–1932*

During the time when Calcutta was the capital of British India, Svarnakumari Devi was born there, the tenth child and fourth daughter of the illustrious and cultured Tagore family. She was already writing at the age of 13, when she married Janakinath Ghosal and soon bore the first of her three children. When her husband went to England to study law, she traveled with him, studying English and gaining access to the most exclusive Bombay circles there, including the leaders of the Indian National Congress. Although she did not become extensively involved in the Nationalist movement, her writings reveal the influence of nationalist ideas.

Prominent as a writer, Svarnakumari Devi turned to civic reform, involving herself in women's issues. From 1882 to 1886, she began and was head of a theosophical society for women; later she established a charitable organization, *Sakhi Samiti*, to help widows and orphaned girls become self-sustaining; it collected funds for the education of women, organized trade fairs for women, and eventually established a center for handicrafts by women. In 1889 and 1890, Svarnakumari Devi was the female delegate to the Indian National Congress. She also fostered Bengali letters, editing the literary journal, *Bharati*, for almost thirty years until her husband's death in 1913, and befriending other contemporary women writers, including Girindra Mohini, Sarat Kumari Chaudhurani, and Anurupa Devi. Svarnakumari Devi was elected chair of the literary section of the Bangiya Sahitya Sammelan, and in recognition of her achievements became the first woman to receive the Jagattarini Gold Medal of Calcutta in 1927.

A prolific writer, Svarnakumari Devi was completely bilingual and published in both English and Bengali, although her major output was in Bengali. In that language, she made important contributions to the early development of the modern novel, writing historical romances that were the dominant form in a period that exhalted patriotic, even nationalist, ideas. Although her writing owed much to conventions of older classical forms as well as to potboilers written in English, they did appeal to a newly risen middle class and helped to create and shape a reading public.

Out of her large and varied oeuvre, certain works have historical, political, and feminist significance. Her second and third books, *Chinamukul* (A Picked Flower) and *Malati* (the name of the protagonist), both written in 1879, are warm explorations of friendship and love between sisters. On the other hand, *Vidaba Katha*, sketches published in 1898, offer glimpses, frequently satirical in nature, into the secluded world of women. *Mewar Raj* (the name of the ruling dynasty) and its sequel, *Vidroha* (Revolt), both depict conflicts of indigenous groups (known as tribals) with the ruling Rajputs; although these works are filled with ancient superstition and astrological schemes, they also describe realistic tribal customs, rituals, and ways of life, and *Vidroha* especially is important for its use of tribal dialect. In contrast to the grander plots and the exotic settings often invoked by her male contemporaries, Svarnakumari Devi depicted the world in which she moved: in the two-volume *Snehalata* (1890, 1892) and in *Kahaki* (The Unfinished Song, 1898), Svarnakumari Devi takes as her theme middle-class life in Calcutta and deals with its "minor" ripples with humor and realism.

In addition to her novels, nonfiction prose, and letters, Svarnakumari Devi also wrote poetry considered remarkable for its lyrical beauty; *Gatha* (1880) is a long philosophical poem modeled along classical lines, and *Sangit Satak* (One Hundred Songs) was extremely popular in her own time and the songs are still sung today. In drama too she made her mark in the sphere of farcical and musical plays: *Basanta Utsab* (Spring Festival, 1879) and *Koney Badal* (Evening Clouds, 1906) are predecessors of her brother's work; *Pakachakra* (The Wheel of Fortune, 1911) contains some scathing commentary on the dowry system.

Although short stories were not her forte, in such works as "Samadre," "Darjeeling," and "Mutiny," the title story of an English collection published in 1919 and included here, Svarnakumari Devi's style and wit are evident. A modern reading would take note of the interesting use of the frame to bracket—structurally and thematically—questions of national loyalty, sexuality, and even race— "writing" what remains "unsaid." Various elements in the story also indicate the ways in which power underwrites social and political legitimacy, serving as a critique of both imperialism and war. The mutiny that is "behind" the text is the First War of Indian Independence, also known in the West as the Sepoy Rebellion (1875–1858), named after the Bengali soldiers who initiated the fighting against British soldiers that quickly spread through northern India before the insurrection was finally quelled. The most important result was the transfer of the rule of India from the East India Company to the British Crown. The story itself takes place at the time of World War I.

NOTE

The editors gratefully acknowledge the unpublished translation of an essay by Bani Ray, "Introduction to the Life and Work of Svarnakumari Devi," by Enakshi Chatterjee, as the primary source of the material and point of view presented here.

MUTINY

(A true story)

We—my son and I—were staying by the sea at Alibag, in the Bombay Presidency, and dining at the house of Mrs. A, when this true story was related by our hostess. The gentlemen lingered, in English fashion over their wine, while we ladies chatted on the verandah of the bungalow.

It was a beautiful night. Silvery moonbeams danced on the dark sea that stretched in front of us. The mighty water, swelling and heaving with the rising tide, seemed to be unable to contain its deep emotions and to strive, passionately, to flood the whole world. After washing the Fort of Kolaba nearby, and over flowing the far-reaching expanse of white sand, the sea ran up to a mass of black rock near the bungalow, just in front of which stood two pillars, dedicated to two Satis.[1] Here, at the foot of the pillars, the foaming, heaving water for a moment seemed to come to a sudden standstill. It was as though at the sacred touch of the pillars, its boldness vanished, and it sank back in wonder and awe, after paying its repeated homage to the Satis, and singing them a hundred hymns of praise.

Far away, in the west, the dark forms of the two island forts of Andhari and Kandari were dimly discernable in the moonlight. Not so very long ago, only in the eighteenth century, the famous pirate chieftain Kanhoji Angray is said to have kept his captives imprisoned on one of these islands. The reader will remember that this notorious Mahratta was in his time the terror by land and sea of English, Portuguese, and Moguls alike.[2] Europeans called him "pirate," and such in truth he was; but in the days when might was right, what chief, or ruler, or founder of a dynasty was not a robber or a pirate? With success, piracy only receives another name. Angray had many noble qualities, and his soldiers worshipped him like a Napoleon. His power extended far and wide, and Balaji, the Mahratta ruler of that time, was obliged to make him the Raja of the provinces that he had brought under his control.[3] Angray's descendants, though bereft of most of their ancestral possessions, still hold the title of Raja. The two forts stand out proudly towards the sea, and tell their own story of the glory of the past. The incessant washing of the waves has not broken away one stone. None could subdue the indomitable spirit of Angray but Death. And the island forts—his monuments—still stand erect and strong defying the waves of the ocean. Andari is now a complete desert, and Kandhari has been converted into a lighthouse. And a lighthouse keeper, with one servant for a companion, tends the revolving light on the Kandari Fort, which flashed before our eyes as we sat on the verandah and talked, then gradually grew dim and for a moment disappeared altogether, like the intermittent glow of a firefly.

With such a scene in front of us, we talked about the great war that is now convulsing the world.

Conversation turned on the topic of national courage, and our hostess proudly declared that one Frenchman is equal to five Germans, and one Englishman the equal of three Frenchmen.

Proud words these, and true, perhaps! I, too, felt a glow of pride, as at the praise of a dear friend; for are not the English the most intimately related to us? And have we not cast in our lot with them as the sharer of their destiny? Do we not pray for the victory of the English as fervently as they do themselves and feel proud to sacrifice our men and money to save the honour of England?

In this connection, I, too, could have remarked with pride that our sepoys are in no degree inferior to the soldiers of other nations—that, led by good officers, they show exceptional courage and bravery on the battlefield; and that they are the first to march forward fearlessly into the jaws of death. But if I pressed my views would they be appreciated? Most probably not. Now is a time of misunderstanding and is not mere suspicion positive proof against lifelong loyalty? Then who knows what next—indictment, or internment? So one has to think twice even before giving utterance to the simplest truth.

Moreover, however proud we may feel at the bravery of our sepoys, can we call it a national pride? Alas! have we not lost the privilege of calling ourselves a nation? What nation do we belong to? Our Rulers are of the West and we are not a bit less loyal for it— possibly more. For it is the English who have made modern India, for which we are supremely grateful. But still the shoe pinches somewhere. Our king is not one but many. The merest boy even if he be a half-caste, thinks himself a king in India, demands our allegiance and arrogates to himself privileges which are denied to us. Of these thousands of kings we must be the lawful and loyal subjects. But even the simple rights which loyal citizens expect do not belong to us. We are not treated as equals, nor do we receive the affection that according to our own national ideas, rulers should show to their subjects. If one among so many millions of us shows a disloyal spirit, then we are all considered to be deserving of the gallows. And lest one or two should go wrong we are deprived of the privilege of carrying firearms with which to defend ourselves even from wild beasts!

Of what nation are we then? Certainly we are not one with our rulers. We have not the rights of children of the soil that belong to us. Surely our forefathers, asleep in heaven, would be disturbed by the very idea, and curse us for our degeneracy! Was it not in this ancient land that science, literature, and the arts flourished at the dawn of time? Our very posterity, also, will rise up in anger against so preposterous a notion, since at this very moment are we not renowned among the nations, in the things of the mind. We are, then, in the position of our mythological hero Harischandra's father Trisangu, who could find no place either in heaven or on earth, and remained suspended in vacant space.[4] So it is natural that Occidentals should look upon our courage as reflected glory, and our loyalty and self-sacrifice as cringing, doglike virtues!

And I kept silence.

Never before had I been made to feel my racial inequality in my intercourse with English people. I had always been treated as one of themselves. But this deference and friendliness had been paid to me individually, as being due to my social position. Today, these expressions of a woman belonging to a free nation, made me feel myself an utter stranger among English people. Humbled and mortified, I called to mind our past Aryan glory, and with a suppressed sigh, I asked rather abruptly:—"Are not those Sati pillars yonder in memory of Raja Angray's wives?"

Mrs. B—, another guest, replied: "So they say. What a terrible custom!"

"What terrible courage!" said I.

Mrs. B— was silent, but her curling lip seemed to say: "Courage indeed! To allow oneself to be burnt alive and not to have the power to utter a word! That is your courage! To be trodden under the heel of subjugation and feel it to be the happiness of virtue. This is indeed natural for a brave people like you."

If she had really spoken these words, what could I have said in reply? Could ever faith, love, and devotion stand the test of argument? They are part and parcel of the divinity and a thing apart from human logic. Fortunately I was not put to such a test. Said Mrs. A—: "Are not those two islands Raja Angray's prisons? How daring he must have been!"

"And how horrid!" exclaimed Mrs. B—. "For he was only a pirate."

(True enough! What is bravery in a victorious nation is contemptible courage and babarism in the conquered.)

Miss C—, who was staying with Mrs. A— and who had just come out from England, thought we were talking about the Mutiny and exclaimed:—"Oh! How dreadful! Were you here during the Mutiny?"

"No, I was not," laughed Mrs. A—, "and for the good reason that I was not born at the time. But my father was in India then."

Scotch people are said by their English neighbours to be wanting in humour, so we all looked at Miss C— while she asked, quite simply: "Had your father any experiences of the Mutiny?"

"No," replied Mrs. A—, "he was not a soldier, but I went through a Mutiny once."

"How awful!" exclaimed Miss C—

"Really?" said Mrs. B—." But was there ever a Mutiny in this part of India?"

We were all eager to hear the story, and begged Mrs. A— to tell it to us. And when it was finished, I did not know whether to laugh or to cry.

MRS. A—'S STORY

I had just come out to India after my marriage. Years before, when I was quite a child, I had once been in Bengal—but I was too young at that time to remember anything, and this was, in fact, my first experience of this country and the people in it. My husband was an Assistant Collector in Sukkar, and we settled down in our new home quite comfortably. When my husband went "on tour" I always accompanied him, and after knocking about for a few days in Camp, we were always glad to return to our cosy little bungalow and thoroughly enjoyed the rest and quiet of homelife. Only once I stayed at home alone. My husband had to go to a small village for two or three days, and I decided not to go with him. The house was full of servants and sepoys, so I felt that I should be quite safe during my husband's absence. But my friends in the Station thought differently. They were filled with anxiety on my account, and the Superintendent of Police offered to let me have a guard of his own sepoys. I thanked him for his kindness, but refused, saying it would show want of confidence in our own men. Before coming to India, I had had the impression that the servants of this country are cruel and treacherous. Horrible accounts of the Mutiny had given me this idea, but my actual experience after coming to India had proved quite different, and I had found the servants and the sepoys docile, and very faithful and intelligent. I trusted our own sepoys and felt that I should be quite safe in their care, and I thought the Police Sahib's proposal quite unnecessary and even ventured to tell him so. My husband laughed at my enthusiasm; but the Police Sahib seemed annoyed and tried to make me change my mind. But I declined to do so, and I thought the matter had ended there.

My husband had gone away, and I had retired for the night, feeling quite safe and happy. Little did I think that I was to pay so heavily and so soon for my independence! My ayah was the sole attendant in my room, and when I fell asleep, she was lying on the floor beside my bed. At about midnight, I awoke, hearing a noise outside the house. I was startled and only half conscious, and I heard cries, and the sound of firearms. A horrible feeling of fear overcame me. The thought of the Mutiny of 1857 came to my mind, and I remembered that rumour of a disturbance in the interior had reached us. That this was another mutiny I felt certain.

"Oh! God, save me," I cried.

Like a drowning man who clutches at a straw, I called out, "Ayah, Ayah!"

But she was not in the room. Had she, too, joined the mutineers? Ah! why had I been so sanguine, why had I not listened to those who knew the people of the land?

Stricken with utter terror, I lay in bed, motionless, in a half-conscious state, and inwardly praying. Just then the ayah returned.

"Madam Sahib!" she said, and her voice was respectful and natural as usual.

Thus reassured and finding a friend near me, I recovered from my state of stupor, and confidence in our own men returned. But still I thought that the sepoys of the Sukkar Fort had rebelled, and an attack had been made on the bungalow and that our few men had been fighting to save me.

All this flashed through my mind, and I asked in a trembling voice: "What is this noise, Ayah? What has happened? Where are our men?"

The ayah in reply said many things, but I had not learnt the language well enough to understand more than that "Police," "Sepoy," "Fighting." So I was right. I had heard that there were a great many soldiers kept in secret in the Fort of Sukkar. A mutiny must have broken out among them. (I did not know then the difference between a court sepoy and a soldier sepoy.) I cried out wildly, "Fighting! Mutiny! Are they going to kill me? Oh! help, help, help!"

The ayah, although she did not understand English, could see that I was very much frightened, and she said "No, no, Madam Sahib, no, no." But I thought there was no help for me. The noise of arms and the cries seemed to come nearer and to grow louder. Frantic with terror, I tried to rise, but unable to do so, fell back unconscious. Oh! what a dreadful night!

Mrs. A— paused, and Miss C— gave vent to her feelings.

"Dreadful is not the word for it," she said, "But go on. What happened then?"

"I was not killed, that's certain," said Mrs. A— laughing, "for I have lived to tell you the tale."

"But what was the end? Was it really a mutiny?"

"No, I am afraid it was not. It was only a tempest in a teapot. On returning to consciousness, I found that it was morning and the ayah was standing beside me. All was quiet outside. It could not have been a dream, a nightmare. So I asked my ayah: "I think I heard a noise outside during the night. Has anything happened?"

"No, Madam Sahib," she said, "Go, sleep."

But I could not sleep then, for the sun was up, and I asked again: "Ayah, I thought I heard a noise outside last night. What was it?"

She began to talk volubly, but I could not understand what she said. So I sent her for a sepoy who could speak a little English and he told me the whole truth. The Police Sahib had been at the bottom of it all. In spite of my declining to have his sepoys, he had sent a guard to the bungalow at night. My men had been angry and had told them to go away; and at last, it had come to blows. The Police Sahib, however, as I learnt later on, had not been solely to blame. The God of Love had had something to do with it. Since my ayah was sought in marriage by one of our sepoys, and a young sepoy of the Police force was also in love with her, the two rivals had found it a good opportunity to fight out their quarrel, and the noise of their fighting, in the silence of the night, had been exaggerated a hundredfold by my wild imagination and fears. I felt very angry at the Police Sahib's well-meant interference, which had terrified me out of my senses and nearly killed me with alarm. But when my husband returned, I said very little about it, for

I think I was a little ashamed of myself."

At this juncture the gentlemen came into the verandah, and one of them said to us: "A cable had just arrived saying that Indian troops have been safely landed in Europe, and the French people have covered them with flowers."

"And England feels proud to have them!" exclaimed our host. "Brave warriors of an ancient civilization, to fight side by side with English soldiers against the common enemy."

Since then, "les Hindues," as the Indian troops are called by the French, have gone to the front, have thrown themselves into the thick of the fight and have saved the "Izzat"[5] of their motherland and earned the highest praises of their king and commanders by their wholehearted camaraderie and brilliant achievements. The bravery of the Indian troops is on every tongue in England; and the English soldiers desire that they should share with them the Victoria Cross and other coveted military honours. And the government? It, too, has been touched by this enthusiastic self-sacrifice, and it is believed that after the war is over, India will receive her just demands.

All honour to our brave countrymen, and to the foreigners who appreciate their gallant efforts.

NOTES

1. *Sati* (lit. a virtuous wife): practice of the immolation of a widow on the husband's funeral pyre. The practice is not mentioned in the early Vedic texts but can be traced back to the sixth century when sati stones were erected. It was initially restricted to the Kshatriya (royalty/fighting castes) families in Bengal and among the Rajputs, but in later centuries appears among the Brahmins. Steps to prohibit it were initially taken by the Mughal emperor Humayun and his son, Akbar, and the practice was finally banned in 1829 after a controversial social movement against it. However, sporadic instances continue.

2. Muslim domination of India, or the Mogul Empire reached its peak in the mid-seventeenth century: thereafter the Mahratta peoples in Western India gained the

ascendency; the latter were the chief opponents of British control until they were subdued by England in 1818.

3. Balaji: son of Baji Rao I, founder of the Mahratta Empire. Succeeded to the throne in 1740 and continued to rule until a major defeat in battle in 1761.

4. In Hindu mythology, related in the *Mahabarata* and other narratives, Harischandra is subject to Job-like sufferings and gains immortality by his humility and good works. His father, for having committed the three "sins" of adultery, cow-killing, and beef-eating, is barred from heaven but his expulsion is halted in the empyrean where he forms the constellation of the Southern Cross.

5. *Izzat*: Urdu word for honor, now commonly used all over India.

Matilde Serao   *Italy, 1856–1927*

Matilde Serao was born in Greece of a Greek mother and Italian father, who was in exile there. Returning to Naples in 1860, he was poor provider and soon separated from his wife, who survived by giving private lessons as a language teacher. The miserable environment in which mother and daughter lived was later described by Serao in the short story "Terno secco" ("A Stroke of Fortune"). Serao received a teacher's diploma and recalled her school years in the story "Scuola normale femminile" (Girls' School), which concludes with a poignant epilogue about the sad destinies of her friends who became teachers. She herself did not teach; instead, she took a job with the State Telegraph Office, documented in a story bearing the agency's name, "Telegrafi dello stato," from which we learn that women received much less pay than men for the same work and were fired when they got married or grew old.

In 1881, Serao went to Rome and succeeded as a journalist. She married Edoardo Scarfoglio, with whom she founded and coedited a newspaper. But her marriage was not happy; and the newspaper promulgated her husband's political ideals, which she did not share. In 1904, having cut all ties with him, she founded her own newspaper, *Il Giorno*. During the First World War she remained neutral, her only concern being for the bereaved mothers of soldiers: she herself had four sons to worry about. Later her paper assumed an antifascist position, while her husband's (*Il Mattino*) was profascist. In 1926, when she was a candidate for the Nobel Prize, the regime of Benito Mussolini did not support her because of her novel *Mors tua* (*The Harvest*, 1926), which was critical of the war of 1914–1918. Nonetheless, in 1927 Mussolini paid an unexpected visit to her in Rome, trying in vain to win her to the fascist cause. She died in August 1927, and her funeral on August 27 in Naples was spectacular, for she had become a legendary figure there.

Serao is at her best when describing the environment of the Neapolitan poor of the *petit bourgeois*, or of the impoverished nobility. She has a journalistic style and a sharp eye, and she handles her characters with understanding. Her realism is frequently reportorial and anecdotal, especially in the autobiographical stories mentioned above. However, her books (about sixty) vary in style and form: some are realistic, others are mundane or overly sentimental; many point out a social injustice. In *Il paese di cuccagna* (*The Land of Cockayne*, 1891), Serao scores the Neapolitan passion for playing the state lottery, which served to further impoverish the poor. Similarly in *Suor Giovanna della Croce* (Sister Joan of the Holy Cross,

1901), she laments the new Italian monarchy's closing of convents, which forced many old nuns to reenter a secular life for which they were unprepared and where they were exploited. As she records the protogonist's growing decadence, Serao's interest is not in the religious but in the social problems.

Other novels by Serao translated into English are *Fantasia* (*Fantasy*, 1883); *La conquista di Roma* (*The Conquest of Rome*, 1885); *Addio, Amore* (*Farewell Love*, 1890), a best-seller in its day; *La ballerina* (*The Ballet Dancer*, 1899); *Dopo il perdono* (*After the Pardon*, 1906); *Evviva la vita* (*The Desire of Life*, 1909); *La mano tagliata* (*The Severed Hand*, 1912); and *Ella non rispose* (*Souls Divided*, 1914).

Natalia Costa-Zalessow

from A STROKE OF FORTUNE
Terno secco

...That Saturday morning, like any other, Tommasina stirred the ashes of the hearth to find some live coal that she always left there on purpose in the evening and muttered, "In the name of God."

It was the morning invocation, the one that all the working women of Naples make before setting to work. Now she blew on the coals to rekindle them, throwing herself backward every so often because the stink of carbon dioxide was nauseating her. When she had put on the kettle to reboil a bit of leftover coffee from the previous day, she rummaged in her basket and fished out an egg well-wrapped in paper. Trying to make as little noise as possible, she beat this egg in a glass, just the yolk, with some white sugar, and stifled the sound so as not to awaken those asleep in the tiny flat. But from one of the two rooms which comprised the apartment came a bout of coughing, followed by another, and another, not too loud, not too piercing, but insistent. Then there was a pause, followed by a deep sigh, after which the cough began again for another three or four minutes and finally let up all at once. Continuing to beat the egg in the glass, Tommasina crossed a small room which served as both parlor and dining room and, pushing open the leaves of the folding door, entered the bedroom where someone was sleeping.

"Good morning, ladies," said the servant girl, turning toward the wide bed.

"Good morning, Tommasina," answered a voice that had been resonant but that a filminess now clouded. "What time is it?"

"About seven-thirty."

"It's late. It's late," murmured the muffled female voice. The woman raised herself on the pillows to get up, and two long braids of blonde hair, already mixed with white, cascaded onto her nightgown. She was a woman of forty, with a flawless profile, with a pair of very sweet grey eyes, almond-shaped, and with hands so fine and so unblemished that they seemed those of a little girl.

"Caterina, Caterina," said the signora, turning toward the person lying next to her.

But the latter did not even budge. With her head flung back on the pillow, with two long brown pigtails straggling across the whiteness of the pillowcase, with her red mouth open, she was sleeping so blessedly, so profoundly, that the signora, her mother, called her yet again, but very gently, as if she didn't have the heart to awaken her.

"Poor girl," she then said softly, as one talking to herself, and she folded her delicate white hands on the blanket. Tommasina, leaning on the back of the bed in a casual way, was gazing at Caterina, the fourteen-year-old girl with the bushy black eyebrows and a snub nose.

"Why do you say 'poor girl'? She's very well off, God bless her . . ."

"I wish she could sleep till late and didn't have to go to school," said the mother, while quietly, modestly, she began to get dressed.

"She goes to school and she learns *culture*," said Tommasina sententiously. "If I knew how to read, I wouldn't be a servant."

The *signora*, who was before the mirror, shook her head sadly. Petite, slender, with a very graceful figure, she did not even look into that greenish sphere, where faces seemed so pallid. She slowly passed the comb through her long blonde hair, abundantly rich and just barely mixed with white. And she began to cough again.

"That phosphorous from yesterday evening has made me sick, Tommasina," she said in a low voice, after the deep sigh that she always gave following the coughing.

"And it didn't do any good," answered the young servant, ceasing to beat the egg already turned into a whitish cream.

In the evenings, this apartment of the old house in one of the old quarters of Naples, although it appeared clean enough, was overrun by cockroaches that gushed out of certain holes, that came up from the drainpipe of the kitchen sink in troops, that invaded the kitchen and the so-called parlor, so that mother and daughter, in disgust, did not dare receive anyone in the evenings but, overcome by nausea, went out, although they did not feel like it, although the signora was very tired from too much talking during the day. Recently, Tommasina had devised a method of spreading phosphorous as an ointment on fresh romaine lettuce leaves in order to kill those ugly beasts: but the little home had filled with a bad smell and with a phosphoric light, without obtaining any result.

"And yet I do everything to keep it clean," mumbled Tommasina, squeezing into the narrow space between the wall and the huge double bed in order to rouse the big girl who was always sleeping.

The signora, as she finished dressing, cast a glance around. The house was so poorly furnished that little was needed to keep it clean. The small bedroom was taken up by the great iron bed, truly Neapolitan and scarcely forged; there was a chest of drawers with a top of plain wood instead of the usual marble, a tiny vanity, very paltry, in walnut but painted over, a coatstand and a couple of chairs. The parlor furniture consisted of a sofa of the so-called Genoese style that could be converted into a bed, made of iron and horsehair and shabbily covered with a drapery of cretonne discolored by too many washings; four hard chairs, austere, of a very antiquated shape; two bookshelves; and a round table topped with marble, solid, lustrous, the luxury of the house. There they ate, there they wrote, there they worked, and it was clean, white, cold— the pride of the signora and her daughter. There was nothing more. Not the ghost of an easy chair, of a rug, of a curtain; the floor bricks bare; the windows bare; an icy nudity.

But Caterina resisted Tommasina, who wanted to get her up: she turned away smiling, mumbling, complaining that she was sleepy, that she had slept too little, and she cried out every now and again as if for refuge:

"Oh Mama, Mama . . ."

"Up, little one, up," answered the mother caressingly, as if talking to a child of four.

Caterina asserted that it was a holiday, it was Sunday; no, Miss, it was Saturday, contradicted the servant, and the poor girl from Cilento, who was lean, olive-brown, as devoted to the two women as a faithful dog, pulling a little, laughing a little, almost forced Caterina to get dressed, promising her that tomorrow, Sunday, she could sleep till ten; promising to put a beaten egg in *her* coffee, too, because it was Sunday. The signora, who had to talk all day long giving lessons in English and French, permitted herself this luxury that cost three cents and that did her chest good: but, as a scruple, she did not have breakfast and went until five without anything but that egg. Seated now, pensive, she observed Tommasina, who was tying her girl's skirt. Caterina had a robust build, not at all graceful. She was growing exuberantly and bursting everything, dresses, shoes, stockings. This little grey wool dress, for example, had been worn away at the elbows, had become short, and let a bit of the legs be seen. Caterina looked at her shoes and her elbows with a downcast face, while her mother, who in May was still wearing a heavy winter suit of brown wool, maintained a grand, aristocratic air.

"You rip everything, my little daughter," the mother said sweetly.

"It rips, Mama. What can I do about it? And didn't you promise me a new dress for the exams?"

"Certainly, certainly," murmured the signora with a vague smile.

"We'll give this one to Tommasina, then, for her baby," exclaimed the girl.

Growing pale, the servant looked away. Whenever they talked to her about this child, whose birth was imminent and for whom she had, as yet, not a thing ready, not even a diaper, she worried, shuddered, already a mother, already trembling with love and with pity for her child. Then she looked into the eyes of her signora and the two mothers understood one another implicitly, so great was the agitation of the younger woman, so great the affectionate compassion of the older. But Caterina, redoing her pigtails, running through the house, searching for her books and notebooks, was humming, already wearing eyeglasses on her sharp, upturned nose, and lifting her head with finesse. She had drunk her black coffee, with a one-cent bun, happily, while the signora took her coffee with the egg, offering some to her girl every so often, almost remorseful for that luxury which she permitted herself and in which her daughter did not take part. Tommasina had returned to the kitchen, sipping a sediment of coffee from a glass, since the cups in the house numbered only two. The *signora*, with hat on, came to the kitchen door and spoke very softly for a while with the servant. She told her to gauge herself a little in the shopping that day because she could give her only three lire in all, and she handed them to her and looked the poor servant girl in the face, kindly, almost wanting to invoke some benevolence for her. And the other looked at the three silver lire in the palm of her hand without speaking, making mental calculations.

"Will it be enough?" asked the signora.

"We'll soon see," answered the other, still thinking. . . .

Mother and daughter went out of the house, the daughter with a burden of books and notebooks and a small box of compasses for design under one arm, the other arm tucked under the arm of her mother.

"Oh, Mama, you're pulling me," she said, descending the stairs.

"But it's *you* who is pushing *me*, little one," responded the mother.

Before going out to shop, Tommasina, left alone, began to clean the house. According to Neapolitan custom, she unmade the bed, removing the cushions and sheets, and she piled the mattresses at the head, where they would remain until the afternoon to air. She was doing all this very painfully because of her troublesome pregnancy when, shaking out the sheets, she saw fall to the floor a small piece of paper. She first thought it might be the wrapper from the codeine lozenges, which, at times, when tormented by the coughing during the night, the signora would put in her mouth to calm herself, to sleep. But there was some writing on the little paper, which Tommasina picked up in order to save. She gave it a glance, although she did not know how to read. She did not know how to read, the poor peasant girl from Cilento, who, because the soil must be tilled, had not been able to go to the school at Giffoni. But she knew her numbers perfectly—and on the paper were written three numbers in a clear, round pen.

"Three, forty-two, eighty-four: it's a triple*," thought Tommasina, after having read.

She mechanically stuck the paper into the pocket of her cotton apron. It was worth a try, when she went down to do the shopping, to play this triple, since it was Saturday and since it was, perhaps, a gift that God was sending. But how did that paper come to be in the signora's bed? It really was a triple; it was neither an envelope for a letter, nor a recipe nor a calling-card: it was a paper with three numbers on it, without doubt for betting. And puzzling, puzzling, Tommasina tried reconstructing all the facts. Maybe someone, a priest or a friar or some good, devout soul, had given those three numbers to the signora yesterday, Friday: or maybe she, who was truly sainted, had thought of them just like that, by chance. And as it is the habit of one who bets in Naples an uncertain triple, and to whom it means so much, the signora had run a test. In other words, before going to bed Friday night, she had written the three numbers on a scrap of paper, putting them unfolded under the pillow and thinking about them, thinking about them intensely during the night between Friday and Saturday. If these numbers are dreamt in that night, it means they are good and that they will surely come out. If they are not dreamt, it means they are bad and that it's not worth the trouble risking even two cents on them. The signora must have done this, and being so extremely good, she could not but dream and recognize the winning numbers.

"Who knows!" thought Tommasina. "Who knows! The signora probably gave me only three *lire* for the shopping so she could bet a little more. May the Madonna bless her and help me, too..."

Translated by Joan Borrelli

NOTE

* The term "triple" refers to a system of betting (as in horse racing) in which the bettor must pick the first, second, and third-place finishers in that sequence in order to win, a difficult combination but one that yields a greater prize. This type of fixed combination of three corresponds to the Italian *terno* used in the lottery at Naples.

Barbara Baynton   *Australia, 1857–1929*

Despite her very small output—a handful of stories and one novel—Barbara Baynton has never dropped from sight, thanks to her striking portraits of life in turn-of-the-century outback Australia. Her presentation of bush life from a woman's point of view has been seen as a useful corrective to the often romantic pictures of mateship and heroism painted by the great pioneer Australian writers "Banjo" Paterson and, at times, Henry Lawson.

Baynton's life was far more romantic than any of her stories, though recent research has revealed that she was not, as she claimed, born in 1862, the illegitimate daughter of an Indian Army officer, but born five years earlier the daughter of a small-town carpenter. The decidedly upward social mobility of her two marriages may perhaps account for her desire for a less ordinary parentage. Her first marriage ended in divorce when her husband ran off with a servant. She soon remarried a wealthy, elderly doctor, Thomas Baynton, and so gained entry to Sydney's literary and academic circles. Most of her fiction was written during her second marriage, though informed by the events of her first and her earlier life in the bush.

A highly edited version of "The Chosen Vessel," entitled "The Tramp," first appeared in the Sydney *Bulletin* in 1896. Most of the second half of the story, the episode involving Peter Hennessey, was cut out, presumably because of the blasphemous implications of equating a rape victim with the Holy Mother. Baynton later had the complete story privately printed in Sydney and this version, included here, appeared in her collection *Bush Studies* (1902). Her only novel, *Human Toll* (1907) also contains some remarkably frank questioning of religious and sexual issues for its time.

After Dr. Baynton's death in 1904, Baynton was left a wealthy woman and divided her time between England and Australia, collecting antiques and opals. In 1921, she completed her social apotheosis when a brief marriage to a member of the English aristocracy made her Lady Headley.

Elizabeth Webby

THE CHOSEN VESSEL

She laid the stick and her baby on the grass while she untied the rope that tethered the calf. The length of the rope separated them. The cow was near the calf, and both were lying down. Feed along the creek was plentiful, and every day she found a fresh place to tether it, since tether it she must, for if she did not, it would stray with the cow out on the plain. She had plenty of time to go after it, but then there was baby; and if the cow turned on her out on the plain, and she with baby—she had been a town girl and was afraid of the cow, but she did not want the cow to know it. She used to run at first when it bellowed its protest against the penning up of its calf. This satisfied the cow, also the calf, but the woman's husband was angry, and called her—the noun was cur. It was he who forced her to run and meet the advancing cow, brandishing a stick, and uttering threatening words till the enemy turned and ran. "That's the way!" the man said, laughing at her white face. In many things he was worse than the cow, and she wondered if the same rule would apply to the man, but she was not one to provoke skirmishes even with the cow.

It was early for the calf to go "to bed"— nearly an hour earlier than usual; but she had felt so restless all day. Partly because it was Monday, and the end of the week that would bring her and baby the companionship of its father, was so far off. He was a shearer, and had gone to his shed before daylight that morning. Fifteen miles as the crow flies separated them.

There was a track in front of the house, for it had once been a wine shanty, and a few travelers passed along at intervals. She was not afraid of horsemen; but swagmen,[1] going to, or worse, coming from the dismal, drunken little township, a day's journey beyond, terrified her. One had called at the house today, and asked for tucker.[2]

Ah! that was why she had penned up the calf so early! She feared more from the look of his eyes, and the gleam of his teeth, as he watched her newly awakened baby beat its impatient fists upon her covered breasts, than from the knife that was sheathed in the belt at his waist.

She had given him bread and meat. Her husband, she told him, was sick. She always said that when she was alone, and a swagman came, and she had gone in from the kitchen to the bedroom, and asked questions and replied to them in the best man's voice she could assume. Then he had asked to go into the kitchen to boil his billy,[3] but she gave him tea, and he drank it on the wood-heap. He had walked round and round the house, and there were cracks in some places, and after the last time he had asked for tobacco. She had none to give him, and he had grinned, because there was a broken clay pipe near the wood-heap where he stood, and if there were a man inside, there ought to have been tobacco. Then he asked for money, but women in the bush never have money.

At last he had gone, and she, watching through the cracks, saw him when about a quarter of a mile away, turn and look back at the house. He had stood so for some moments with a pretence of fixing his swag, and then, apparently satisfied, moved to the left towards the creek. The creek made a bow round the house, and when he came to it she lost sight of him. Hours after, watching intently for signs of smoke, she saw the man's dog chasing some sheep that had gone to the creek for water, and saw it slink back suddenly, as if the man had called it.

More than once she thought of taking her baby and going to her husband. But in the past, when she had dared to speak of the dangers to which her loneliness exposed her, he had taunted and sneered at her. She need not flatter herself, he had coarsely told her, that anybody would want to run away with her.

Long before nightfall she placed food on the kitchen table, and beside it laid the big brooch that had been her mother's. It was the only thing of value that she had. And she left the kitchen door wide open.

The doors inside she securely fastened. Beside the bolt in the back one she drove in the steel and scissors; against it she piled the table and the stools. Underneath the lock of the front door she forced the handle of the spade, and the blade between the cracks in the flooring boards. Then the prop-stick, cut into lengths, held the top, as the spade held the middle. The windows were little more than portholes; she had nothing to fear through them.

She ate a few mouthfuls of food and drank a cup of milk. But she lighted no fire, and when night came, no candle, but crept with her baby to bed.

What woke her? The wonder was that she had slept—she had not meant to. But she was young, very young. Perhaps the shrinking of the galvanized roof—yet hardly, since that was so usual. Something had set her heart beating wildly; but she lay quite still, only she put her arm over her baby. Then she had both round it, and she prayed, "Little baby, little baby, don't wake!"

The moon's rays shone on the front of the house, and she saw one of the open cracks, quite close to where she lay, darken with a shadow. Then a protesting growl reached her; and she could fancy she heard the man turn hastily. She plainly heard the thud of something striking the dog's ribs, and the long flying strides of the animal as it howled and ran. Still watching, she saw the shadow darken every crack along the wall. She knew by the sounds that the man was trying every standpoint that might help him to see in; but how much he saw she could not tell. She thought of many things she might do to deceive him into the idea that she was not alone. But the sound of her voice would wake baby, and she dreaded that as though it were the only danger that threatened her. So she prayed, "Little baby, don't wake, don't cry!"

Stealthily the man crept about. She knew he had his boots off, because of the vibration that his feet caused as he walked along the veranda to gauge the width of the little window in her room, and the resistance of the front door.

Then he went to the other end, and the uncertainty of what he was doing became unendurable. She had felt safer, far safer, while he was close, and she could watch and listen. She felt she must watch, but the great fear of wakening baby again assailed her. She suddenly recalled that one of the slabs on that side of the house had shrunk in length as well as in width, and had once fallen out. It was held in position only by a wedge of wood underneath. What if he should discover that! The uncertainty increased her terror. She prayed as she gently raised herself with her little one in her arms, held tightly to her breast.

She thought of the knife, and shielded her child's body with her hands and arms. Even its little feet she covered with its white gown, and baby never murmured—it liked to be held so. Noiselessly she crossed to the other side, and stood where she could see and hear, but not be seen. He was trying every slab, and was very near to that with the wedge under it. Then she saw him find it; and heard the sound of the knife as bit by bit he began to cut away the wooden support.

She waited motionless, with her baby pressed tightly to her, though she knew that in another few minutes this man with the cruel eyes, lascivious mouth, and gleaming knife, would enter. One side of the slab tilted; he had only to cut away the remaining little end, when the slab, unless he held it, would fall outside.

She heard his jerked breathing as it kept time with the cuts of the knife, and the brush of his clothes as he rubbed the wall in his movements, for she was so still and quiet, that she did not even tremble. She knew when he ceased, and wondered why. She stood well concealed; she knew he could not see her, and that he would not fear if he did, yet she heard him move cautiously away. Perhaps he expected the slab to fall. Still his motive puzzled her, and she moved even closer, and bent her body the better to listen. Ah! what sound was that? "Listen! Listen!" she bade her heart—her heart that had kept so still, but now bounded with tumultuous throbs that dulled her ears. Nearer and nearer came the sounds, till the welcome thud of a horse's hoof rang out clearly.

"Oh, God! Oh, God! Oh, God!" she cried, for they were very close before she could make sure. She turned to the door, and with her baby in her arms tore frantically at its bolts and bars.

Out she darted at last, and running madly along, saw the horseman beyond her in the distance. She called to him in Christ's name, in her babe's name, still flying like the wind with the speed that deadly peril gives. But the distance grew greater and greater between them, and when she reached the creek her prayers turned to wild shrieks, for there crouched the man she feared, with outstretched arms that caught her as she fell. She knew he was offering terms if she ceased to struggle and cry for help, though louder and louder did she cry for it, but it was only when the man's hand gripped her throat, that the cry of "Murder" came from her lips. And when she ceased, the startled curlews took up the awful sound, and flew shrieking over the horseman's head.

By God!" said the boundary rider,[4] "it's been a dingo right enough! Eight killed up here, and there's more down in the creek—a ewe and a lamb, I'll bet; and the lamb's alive!" And he shut out the sky with his hand, and watched the crows that were circling round and round, nearing the earth one moment, and the next shooting skywards. By that he knew the lamb must be alive; even a dingo will spare a lamb sometimes.

Yes, the lamb was alive, and after the manner of lambs of its kind did not know its mother when the light came. It had sucked the still warm breasts, and laid its little head on her bosom, and slept till the morn. Then, when it looked at the swollen disfigured face, it wept and would have crept away, but for the hand that still clutched its little gown. Sleep was nodding its golden head and swaying its small body, and the crows were close, so close, to the mother's wide-open eyes, when the boundary rider galloped down.

"Jesus Christ!" he said, covering his eyes. He told afterwards how the little child held out its arms to him, and how he was forced to cut its gown that the dead hand held.

It was election time, and as usual the priest had selected a candidate. His choice was so obviously in the interests of the squatter,[5] that Peter Hennessey's reason, for once in his life, had over-ridden superstition, and he had dared promise his vote to another. Yet he was uneasy, and every time he woke in the night (and it was often) he heard the murmur of his mother's voice. It came through the partition, or under the door. If through the partition, he knew she was praying in her bed; but when the sounds came under the door, she was on her knees before the little altar in the corner that enshrined the statue of the Blessed Virgin and Child.

"Mary, Mother of Christ! save my son! Save him!" prayed she in the dairy as she strained and set the evening's milking. "Sweet Mary! for the love of Christ, save him!" The grief in her old face made the morning meal so bitter, that to avoid her he came late to his dinner. It made him so cowardly, that he could not say goodbye to her, and when night fell on the eve of the election day, he rode off secretly.

He had thirty miles to ride to the township to record his vote. He cantered briskly along the great stretch of plain that had nothing but stunted cottonbush to play shadow to the full moon, which glorified a sky of earliest spring. The bruised incense of the flowering clover rose up to him, and the glory of the night appealed vaguely to his imagination, but he was preoccupied with his present act of revolt.

Vividly he saw his mother's agony when she would find him gone. At that moment, he felt sure, she was praying.

"Mary! Mother of Christ!" He repeated the invocation, half unconsciously. And suddenly, out of the stillness, came Christ's name to him—called loudly in despairing accents.

"For Christ's sake! Christ's sake! Christ's sake!" called the voice. Good Catholic that he had been, he crossed himself before he dared to look back. Gliding across a ghostly patch of pipe-clay, he saw a white-robed figure with a babe clasped to her bosom.

All the superstitious awe of his race and religion swayed his brain. The moonlight on the gleaming clay was a "heavenly light" to him, and he knew the white figure not for flesh and blood, but for the Virgin and Child of his mother's prayers. Then, good Catholic that once more he was, he put spurs to his horse's sides and galloped madly away.

His mother's prayers were answered.

Hennessey was the first to record his vote—for the priest's candidate. Then he sought the priest at home, but found that he was out rallying the voters. Still, under the influence of his blessed vision, Hennessey would not go near the public-houses, but wandered about the outskirts of the town for hours, keeping apart from the townspeople, and fasting as penance. He was subdued and mildly ecstatic, feeling as a repentant chastened child, who awaits only the kiss of peace.

And at last, as he stood in the graveyard crossing himself with reverent awe, he heard in the gathering twilight the roar of many voices crying the name of the victor at the election. It was well with the priest.

Again Hennessey sought him. He was at home, the housekeeper said, and led him into the dimly-lighted study. His seat was immediately opposite a large picture, and as the housekeeper turned up the lamp, once more the face of the Madonna and Child looked down on him, but this time silently, peacefully. The half-parted lips of the Virgin were smiling with compassionate tenderness; her eyes seemed to beam with the forgiveness of an earthly mother for her erring but beloved child!

He fell on his knees in adoration. Transfixed, the wondering priest stood, for, mingled with the adoration, "My Lord and my God!" was the exaltation, "And hast Thou chosen me?"

"What is it, Peter?" said the priest.

"Father," he answered reverently, and with loosened tongue he poured forth the story of his vision.

"Great God!" shouted the priest, "and you did not stop to save her! Have you not heard?"

Many miles further down the creek a man kept throwing an old cap into a waterhole. The dog would bring it out and lay it on the opposite side to where the man stood, but would not allow the man to catch him, though it was only to wash the blood of the sheep from his mouth and throat, for the sight of blood made the man tremble.

NOTES

1. Tramp.
2. Food.
3. Cooking pot.
4. One who patrols sheep on cattle stations.
5. Owner of big sheep farm.

Emilia Pardo Bazán   *Spain, 1857–1921*

Emilia Pardo Bazán was a major force in late nineteenth-century Spanish literature, as a writer in the naturalistic and symbolist modes, as a critic, and as a feminist. She wrote more than twenty novels, the most important being the naturalistic *Los Pazos de Ulloa* (*The Son of the Bondswoman*, 1886), many short stories, and criticism. She frequently wrote on the woman's question, and her essays, particularly "La España moderna" ("The Women of Spain," 1889) and "La educación del hombre y de la mujer: sus diferencias" ("The Education of Men and Women: The Differences" 1892) were strong indictments of the oppression of women in Spanish society. As a critic she is best known for the controversial *La cuestion palpitante* (The Burning Question, 1883), an explanation of naturalism and a discussion of the differences between Spanish naturalism, which she saw as closer to realism (in the tradition of Cervantes) and European naturalism defined by its adherence to determinism. Married, with three children, Pardo Bazán separated from her husband over her championing this "scandalous" movement.

She was one of the most influential literary figures of her time and was much honored; as the only child of the Count and Countess of Pardo Bazán, she inherited the papal title of Countess. This hereditary title was converted into a Castilian title in 1908 by Alfonso XII in honor of her literary accomplishment. Nonetheless, Pardo Bazán was denied admission into the Spanish Royal Academy because of her gender. It was more than a half century after her death before the first woman was chosen for that honor.

The following work was originally published in 1895 in the newspaper *El Imparcial* (The Impartial) and was later included in her collection *El fondo del alma. Interiores* (The Bottom of the Soul. Interiors) in *Obras completas* (Complete Works, 1907).

THE REVOLVER
El revólver

In a burst of confidence, one of those provoked by the familiarity and companionship of bathing resorts, the woman suffering from heart trouble told me about her illness, with all the details of chokings, violent palpitations, dizziness, fainting spells, and collapses, in which one sees the final hour approach.... As she spoke, I looked her over carefully. She was a woman of about thirty-five or thirty-six, maimed by suffering; at least I thought so, but, on closer scrutiny, I began to suspect that there was something more than the physical in her ruin. As a matter of fact, she spoke and expressed herself like someone who had suffered a good deal, and I know that the ills of the body, when not of imminent gravity, are usually not enough to produce such a wasting away, such extreme dejection. And, noting how the broad leaves of the plane tree, touched with carmine by the artistic hand of autumn, fell to the ground majestically and lay stretched out like severed hands, I remarked, in order to gain her confidence, on the passing of all life, the melancholy of the transitoriness of everything...

"Nothing is anything," she answered, understanding at once that not curiosity but compassion was beckoning at the gates of her spirit. "Nothing is anything...unless we ourselves convert that nothing into something. Would to God we could see everything, always, with the slight but sad emotion produced in us by the fall of this foliage on the sand."

The sickly flush of her cheeks deepened, and then I realized that she had probably been very beautiful, although her beauty was effaced and gone, like the colors of a fine picture over which is passed cotton saturated with alcohol. Her blond, silky hair showed traces of ash, premature gray hair. Her features had withered away; her complexion especially revealed those disturbances of the blood which are slow poisonings, decompositions of the organism. Her soft blue eyes, veined with black, must have once been attractive, but now they were disfigured by something worse than age; a kind of aberration, which at certain moments lent them the glitter of blindness.

We grew silent: but my way of contemplating her expressed my pity so plainly that she, sighing for a chance to unburden her heavy heart, made up her mind, and stopping from time to time to breathe and regain her strength, she told me the strange story.

"When I married, I was very much in love.... My husband was, compared to me, advanced in years; he was bordering on forty, and I was only nineteen. My temperament was gay and lively; I retained a childlike disposition, and when he was not home I would devote my time to singing, playing the piano, chatting and laughing with girl-friends who came to see me and envied me my happiness, my brilliant marriage, my devoted husband, and my brilliant social position.

"This lasted a year—the wonderful year of the honeymoon. The following spring, on our wedding anniversary, I began to notice that Reinaldo's disposition was changing. He was often in a gloomy mood, and, without my knowing the cause, he spoke to me harshly, and had outbursts of anger. But it was not long before I understood the origins of his transformation: Reinaldo had conceived a violent, irrational jealousy, a jealousy without object or cause, which, for that very reason, was doubly cruel and difficult to cure.

"If we went out together, he was watchful lest people stare at me or tell me, in passing, one of those silly things people say to young women; if he went out alone, he was suspicious of what I was doing in the house, and of the people who came to see me; if I went out alone, his suspicions and suppositions were even more defamatory....

"If I proposed, pleadingly, that we stay home together, he was watchful of my saddened expression, of my supposed boredom, of my work, of an instant when, passing in front of the window, I happened to look outside ... He was watchful, above all, when he noticed that my birdlike disposition, my good, childlike humor, had disappeared, and that on many afternoons, when I turned on the lights, he found my skin shining with the damp, ardent trace of tears. Deprived of my innocent amusements, now separated from my friends and relatives, and from my own family, because Reinaldo interpreted as treacherous artifices the desire to communicate and look at faces other than his, I often wept, and did not respond to Reinaldo's transports of passion with the sweet abandonment of earlier times.

"One day, after one of the usual bitter scenes, my husband said:

"'Flora, I may be a madman, but I am not a fool. I have alienated your love, and although perhaps you would not have thought of deceiving me, in the future, without being able to remedy it, you would. Now I shall never again be your beloved. The swallows that have left do not return. But because, unfortunately, I love you more each day, and love you without peace, with eagerness and fever, I wish to point out that I have thought of a way which will prevent questions, quarrels, or tears between us—and once and for all you will know what our future will be.'"

"Speaking thus, he took me by the arm and led me toward the bedroom.

"I went trembling; cruel presentiments froze me. Reinaldo opened the drawer of the small inlaid cabinet where he kept tobacco, a watch, and handkerchiefs and showed me a large revolver, a sinister weapon.

"'Here,' he said, 'is your guarantee that in the future your life will be peaceful and pleasant. I shall never again demand an accounting of how you spend your time, or of your friends, or of your amusements. You are free, free as the air. But the day I see something that wounds me to the quick...that day, I swear by my mother! Without complaints or scenes, or the slightest sign that I am displeased, oh no, not that! I will get up quietly at night, take the weapon, put it to your temple and you will wake up in eternity. Now you have been warned....

"As for me, I was in a daze, unconscious. It was necessary to send for the doctor, inasmuch as the fainting spell lasted. When I recovered consciousness and remembered, the convulsion took place. I must point out that I have a mortal fear of firearms; a younger brother of mine died of an accidental shot. My eyes, staring wildly, would not leave the drawer of the cabinet that held the revolver.

"I could not doubt, from Reinaldo's tone and the look on his face, that he was prepared to carry out his threat, and knowing also how easily his imagination grew confused, I began to consider myself as dead. As a matter of fact, Reinaldo kept his promise, and left me complete mistress of myself, without directing the slightest censure my way, or showing, even by a look, that he was opposed to any of my wishes or disapproved of my actions; but this itself frightened me, because it indicated the strength and tyranny of a resolute will...and, victim of a terror which every day grew more profound, I remained motionless, not daring to take a step. I would always see the steely reflection of the gun barrel.

"At night, insomnia kept my eyes open, and I imagined I felt the metallic cold of a steel circle on my temple; or if I got to sleep, I woke up startled with palpitations that made my heart seem to leap from my breast, because I dreamed that an awful report was ripping apart the bones of my skull and blowing my brains out, dashing them against the wall...And this lasted four years, four years without a single peaceful moment, when I never took a step without fearing that that step might give rise to tragedy."

"And how did that horrible situation end?" I asked, in order to bring her story to a close, because I saw her gasping for breath.

"It ended...with Reinaldo, who was thrown by a horse, and had some internal injury, being killed on the spot.

"Then, and only then, I knew that I still loved him, and I mourned him quite sincerely, although he was my executioner, and a systematic one at that!"

"And did you pick up the revolver to throw it out the window?"

"You'll see," she murmured. "Something rather extraordinary happened. I sent Reinaldo's manservant to remove the revolver from my room, because in my dreams I continued to see the shot and feel the chill on my temple.... And after he carried out the order, the manservant came to tell me: 'Señora, there was no cause for alarm.... This revolver wasn't loaded.'

"'It wasn't loaded'"

"'No, Señora, and it looks to me as though it never was... As a matter of fact, the poor master never got around to buying the cartridges. Why, I would even ask him at times if he wanted me to go to the gunsmith's and get them, but he didn't answer, and then he never spoke of the matter again.'"

"And so," added the sufferer from heart disease, "an unloaded revolver shot me, not in the head, but in the center of my heart, and believe me when I tell you that, in spite of digitalis and baths and all the remedies, the bullet is unsparing...."

Translated by Angel Flores

Selma Lagerlöf $\qquad$ *Sweden, 1858–1940*

Selma Lagerlöf is a central figure in Swedish literature, as an artist whose writing won her the Nobel Prize in 1909 and as a humanist who worked throughout her life for world peace, feminism, and temperance and against poverty.

Lagerlöf was born on her family estate, Mårbacka, in Värmland, Sweden, a beautiful rural district that figures very importantly in her work. Värmland is an area with a long cultural tradition—many writers and artists came from there and the area is rich in folk tales and legends. She spent many hours listening to these tales, some of which found their way into her own stories and novels. Her childhood at Mårbacka is captured in her three memoirs: *Mårbacka* (*Mårbacka*, 1922); *Mårbacka 2: Ettbarns memoarer* (*Memories of My Childhood*, 1930), and *Mårbacka 3: Dogbok* (*The Diary of Selma Lagerlöf*, 1932).

Although it was beautiful at Mårbacka, it was also remote and lonely for the children. While Lagerlöf's two brothers were sent to university, the three girls remained home, as was the custom. In that remote location, Lagerlöf read voraciously and began writing as a young child, creating plays and puppet theater for her family. When she was a young woman, encouragement from a prominent Swedish feminist, Eva Fryxhall, inspired Lagerlöf to leave home to study in Stockholm, at a teacher's college. In Stockholm, involved in the cultural life of the times, she began to write. She was teaching in 1890 when she won first prize from the women's magazine *Idun* for the first five chapters of *Gösta Berlings Saga* (*The Story of Gösta Berling*, 1891). The novel, really a collection of loosely connected episodes, received little favorable response until the great Danish critic Georg Brandes praised it. From then on, and with all her succeeding works, Selma

Lagerlöf was immensely popular. Lagerlöf's works have been translated into more than forty languages and have been made into films and television dramas.

Gösta Berling, the story of a defrocked priest and his band of dissolute cavaliers who write a contract with the devil, is her most important work artistically. It represented a dramatic turn from naturalism, the dominant literary style of the day in Scandinavia, blending the fantastic and the real to capture eloquently the spirit of her childhood province of Värmland. *Jerusalem 1 & 2* (*Jerusalem*, 1901–1902) is also about Värmland, but this novel's portrayal of country life is realistic, based on an historic event, the emigration of a Swedish religious community to the Holy Land. Lagerlöf's best known work is *Nils Holgersson 1 & 2* (*The Wonderful Adventures of Nils*, 1906–1907), a fantasy about a young boy shrunk to Tom Thumb size, who flies over Sweden on the back of a goose. Commissioned by the Swedish National Teacher's Society, this book was written to instruct young children in both the geography of Sweden and Christian morality. An underlying theme in most of Lagerlöf's works is the triumph of good over evil.

Of her later work, the most important are *Kejsarn av Portugallien* (*The Emperor of Portugallia*, 1914) about a poor farming community, and *Löwensköldska ringen; Charlotte Löwensköld;* and *Anna Svärd* (*The Ring of the Löwenskölds*, 1925–1927), a ghost story as well as a family saga, containing themes of revenge, love, and loss of love. An important novel of her middle period is *Herr Arnes Penningar* (*The Treasure*, 1904).

Lagerlöf's politics are not directly reflected in her works. However, she did work for political causes and is remembered for her speech "Home and State," delivered at the World Congress of Women in 1911, in which she spoke of women as creators of home and family and men as creators of the State—which is in need of women's help to give it humanity and compassion. In addition to winning the Nobel Prize, Lagerlöf received much honor in her country. She was awarded an honorary doctorate from the University of Uppsala in 1907 and in 1914 was the first woman admitted to the Swedish Academy.

The following story was first published in the collection *Höst* (Cough), 1933.

SISTER KARIN AND SISTER SISLA
Syster Karin och Syster Sisla

Long ago, when Luther's Reformation had just begun, there was a poor nun at Riseberga Abbey in Närke, who was so slow and dull and useless that all the other sisters made a laughingstock of her.

Now, this kind of behavior in such holy places might strike you as surprising, but after all, people are only human no matter where they are; these pent-up ladies of the veil, who had nothing to do but work and pray, might have needed some distraction now and then, and they found it by ridiculing poor, hopeless Sister Karin.

If truth be told, Sister Karin was the best-looking nun in the whole abbey. She was a head taller than all the others, and only plump enough to lend stature to her height. She had small hands and feet, a little head of fair hair, a clear complexion, and blue eyes, and she was far from unattractive. Moreover, there was a strange aura of dignity about her. At first glance, you might have taken this impressive nun for a princess, at the very least.

Anyone watching her a little more closely, however, couldn't help but notice her unchanging expression. Whatever was going on around her, she had the same kind and serene look in her eyes. Another odd thing was that she never moved; she just sat silent and motionless on her bench. But she was always conscious of looking dignified. She would never have leaned back or crossed her legs. And no matter how much the other sisters provoked her, she was never upset and she never answered back.

She wasn't sickly, nor was she simpleminded. She had just grown lazy and listless, and there really is nothing more annoying than the sight of a person in full possession of her health and senses forever sitting with her hands clasped, doing nothing at all. Neither the sister librarian, nor the sister gatekeeper, nor the sister housekeeper, nor the sister storekeeper, nor the sister seamstress, nor the sister gardener, nor the sister bursar, nor the sister who cared for the sick, nor the sister who distributed alms from the abbey could find any excuse for a sister who wanted no occupation and no share in the labors and duties of the others.

There was also a nun there called Cecilia, but known to everyone as Sister Sisla. She was witty and cheerful and eager and active, and the one who badgered Sister Karin most. She once overheard another nun saying Sister Karin was so lazy even her thoughts stood still. "Yes, Sister Karin is really lazy," said Sister Sisla. "But at least there are three things she never tires of doing. The first is sleeping, the second is eating, and the third is doing nothing."

This conversation took place in the presence of the abbess, who hastened to add a fourth thing Sister Karin never tired of doing, which was singing the praises of Our Lord.

And this was true, for never once had Sister Karin missed a service or meditation.

Moreover, they had noticed long ago that the abbess was more positive about Sister Karin than anyone else. Sister Karin had a big appetite and it was the abbess who made sure she had enough to eat. The abbess sometimes gave her little tasks she could do without too much effort. She had her darn and mend the other sisters' clothes and arrange and light the altar candles, so it wouldn't always be said that Sister Karin never did anything.

The abbess must have thought Sister Karin could not help or change her behavior. "The good Lord has placed her among us to test our charity and forbearance," she said. "He will deliver her from her indolence when he finds us deserving thereof."

Sister Sisla always found it hard to understand why the abbess was so partial to Sister Karin. It was easy to see why Sister Sisla herself was much favored. She was learned, she was the abbey librarian, she could understand Latin and could copy books. She brought the abbey both profit and honor. But Sister Karin! Why, she couldn't even print her own name!

Well, this was the state of affairs at Riseberga Abbey when Martin Luther set about his great religious improvement.

How shall I describe it? It must have felt as if the earth beneath your feet began to quake and jolt, as if everything around you was about to collapse, and no ground in the whole world was firm enough to stand on.

Or it might have been as if you possessed a vast fortune in gold and silver all safely stored in an iron-bound chest, and then the lid was opened one day and all the gold and silver were gone, the chest filled with nothing but stones and ashes.

Well, imagine how you would feel today, safe and secure, certain nothing unfortunate or unpleasant could possibly happen in this life or the hereafter, if you were suddenly deprived not only of all your worldly prosperity but of all your heavenly prospects, too.

What did being a nun mean, a nun at Riseberga Abbey, for instance, in those days?

Well, for one thing, it meant that two hundred and twenty-four farmers had to pay an annual tithe of oxen and sheep, swine and geese, hops and malt, grain and game, fish and turnips for her upkeep. For another, it meant she could expect to have her hand humbly kissed by any stranger who appeared at the abbey to ask for hospitality or help of any kind. It meant enjoying the admiration and respect of all men because she was doing penance not only for her own sins but the sins of the whole world, by living the holy life. It meant amassing a fortune through fasting and prayer in a land where no thieves stalk by night. Now suddenly all this was taken from her. Now it was said nuns and monks were no use. Now they were no better than anyone else. This might have been all right, but now they were regarded as far worse, and became the object of more slander than even the Turks and pagans.

They must have felt as if they were aboard a ship on a storm-tossed sea. Perhaps they couldn't even help wondering why He who held sway over weather and wind did not extend His arm and bid the storm die down.

Try to imagine this. One day at Riseberga all the sisters have gathered in the chapter. The abbess is sitting under a carved canopy at the far end of the room, and all the other nuns are seated around the sides. They are dressed in habit and wimple, but otherwise there is nothing strange about them; they all have decent Swedish faces and names. Deep down in their souls they are worried and frightened but they look outwardly placid and unconcerned, old and young alike. It makes the abbess feel better to have them there. They love their abbey and they love her. They sit there like dear, virtuous daughters around a virtuous and dear mother.

In an unsteady voice the abbess says she has summoned them to read out the concessions the Assembly of Estates made to the king, at the meeting in Västerås.

She reads and they sit listening, dignified and calm—well, except that an occasional mocking laugh is heard. So the king is to have the right to appropriate the surplus property of churches and abbeys, is he? What does that matter to them? These poor nuns don't have superfluous possessions. They have no farms or mills or fishing waters or merchants' residences to surrender. And what they do own is already pledged to the Lord. Would even the king be so bold as to seize what was pledged to the Lord?

The nuns and monks were henceforth free to come and go at will. So, that's what he said, this Gustav Eriksson! Well, no one had ever told them they were in *his* service, or that *he* was to issue their marching orders. They had always considered themselves in the service of the Lord.

Sister Sisla, the most learned person among them, stands up and holds forth about Saint Bernard, the monks and nuns of his holy order, and the great works they have performed, and about the sisters of Riseberga, and all the service they have given their country. "Pity the Swedish people," she says, "when there are no more monks or nuns to teach them farming, how to tend their herb gardens, care for their bees, cook their food, dip their candles, and bake their bread. Where will the daughters of the nobility learn manners, and who will care for the poor and shelter the wayfarer when the convents are gone? Not to mention," Sister Sisla goes on, "the blessings endowed upon a country through the intercessions of pious, God-fearing women. I'll not even mention them because this Gustav Eriksson says they are not in demand. I speak only of the worldly services we render, which he should have the sense to appreciate."

All the sisters, old and young, are heartened and encouraged by listening to Sister Sisla. One by one, they rise and swear to stay at the abbey, come what may.

They give each other strength and conviction. Their country cannot possibly do without its monks and nuns. They know no evil can befall them. Help is sure to be forthcoming. They will show the king that neither force nor arms can be of any avail against them.

Not a single nun fails to speak up with a pledge and a promise except, of course, Sister Karin. She sits bolt upright on her bench, face calm and beautiful, hands clasped; she says not a word.

Now even the abbess feels her indolence has gone too far, and the time has come for a reprimand. "Sister Karin, do you have nothing to say about these evil tidings?" she asks.

Sister Karin turns to face the abbess, but with no sign of haste, of course, so Sister Sisla has time to pass comment: "Sister Karin may be thinking of going out into the world to make a good marriage."

For the first time in her life, Sister Karin leaps from her bench in fury, shouting loudly and startling the other nuns: "Mark my words—I shall not break my vow of chastity until the day Sister Cecilia breaks hers."

There is total silence in the chapter, for Sister Sisla is the most devout of them all, and the very idea that she might renounce her vows is worse than saying such a thing about the abbess herself. Sister Sisla looks ready to fly at Sister Karin and slap her face.

The abbess clearly fears something of the sort, for she stands up quickly to indicate the conclusion of the meeting. All the nuns rise and bow to her, and she raises her arms in blessing, asking God to make their hearts strong.

That night the abbess went to bed feeling reassured. It had all gone as well as she could have hoped, and if Sister Karin had given Sister Sisla a taste of her own medicine, the abbess didn't really mind. For people are only human, no matter where they are.

If only things had settled down after that, and the earth had not begun to quake anew.

To begin with, the novices and young nuns started leaving. The first one ran away by night, scaling the abbey wall, and at least having the decency to be ashamed. But after a while young nuns began leaving in broad daylight and in full view of the abbess and Sister Sisla. There was no point running after them or

flogging them or bundling them into the abbey cellar. This would only have led to the lodging of complaints with King Gustav, and there was no question whose side he would take.

If only that had been the end of it.

If it hadn't been for the fortune to be paid to the Crown in taxes, if only the rightful heirs to farms left to the abbey long ago hadn't come demanding the restoration of their estates, if only there had been an end to the lawsuits and hearings and examination of old deeds, if only the king hadn't kept sending his soldiers to confiscate church silver and bells and vestments, if only the farmers hadn't decided they no longer needed to pay tithes, if only so many malicious tracts hadn't been distributed telling people what self-seeking parasites the fat lazy monks were, living off their poverty-stricken country, if only so many strange, vicious rumors about the impious habits of popes, cardinals, and bishops hadn't been spread, if only there hadn't been so many other misfortunes and adversities, the abbess might have been able to bear up.

But it was no good. In the end she had to submit to the godless king and his godless chancellor, beseeching him to take over all the possessions of the abbey and the abbey itself. She had to relinquish all power, on condition that she and her fellow sisters be allowed to stay there at the abbey for the rest of their lives. It was like being deposed and impoverished, forced to accept gratefully whatever alms it pleased the king to distribute.

What a bitter pill this was for the woman who had once been lord-and-lady of all Riseberga; church and abbey, larders and barns, kitchens and stables, two hundred and twenty-four farmers, mills and smithies, fishing waters and interests in silver and copper mines.

That evening, when all was settled, when the document had been copied and signed and the great seal of the abbey used for the last time, the abbess retired to her chamber and shut the door, refusing to see anyone.

But two people met in the passage outside the abbess' door, and they were Sister Karin and Sister Sisla.

Sister Sisla was the abbess' trusted and devoted helper, and no one at the abbey was so eloquent. It was only natural for her to wait outside the abbess' door to be let in. She wished to comfort and console the abbess, that was obvious.

But Sister Karin, what was Sister Karin doing there? Nothing she could say or do would console the dethroned regent kneeling on the other side of the door, praying to God to grant her patience.

Admittedly, Sister Karin had changed. That evening in the chapter must have roused her from her apathy, and she now worked and earned her keep. Of course she was still quite clumsy and awkward—she could not become as quick and clever as the other sisters overnight. She did just enough to make it clear she was trying. Still, no one would have expected to find her wanting to comfort the abbess.

So when the two met outside the door, Sister Sisla could not help giving Sister Karin an indignant look, as if to say she had no right to be there. Not that she hadn't improved, but this task was beyond her means.

Sister Karin went up to Sister Sisla and took her hand. "I know full well I cannot be of the slightest help to our mother. I only wanted to hear the wise and gentle words you would speak," she said.

Sister Sisla was touched. One of the many things she had always disliked about Sister Karin was that her own wisdom and good counsel never seemed to impress her in the least. She hastened to embrace Sister Karin. "Come along. We'll go in and see her together," she said.

The abbess was kneeling at her prie-dieu when she heard their voices. She imagined Sister Sisla wanted to complain about Sister Karin. "Why does she have to bother me in my hour of need?" she wondered.

She opened the door to tell them to go away and leave her alone, but then she saw Sister Sisla with her arm around Sister Karin.

Before they could say a word the pain began to leave the abbess' face. She made the sign of the cross over them. "Nothing but seeing the two of you as friends could have made me so happy on a day like this. It makes me believe that the Lord has not abandoned us."

After this things seemed to improve somewhat for the nuns at Riseberga. True, the church was stripped bare and even the gold cross the abbess wore around her neck had to be relinquished to the Crown. True, the bailiff tried to cut the allowances to the abbeys, but at least they were left in peace. They still had their fine convent and the other buildings, Sister Sisla could still sit in the library copying books, the garden still bore herbs and fruit, the bees still made honey and wax, and the occasional monk still came on foot from Varnhem or Alvastra and could hear their confessions and read mass.

Peace of mind returned to the abbess; song rang out anew in the church, and Sister Karin grew slow and lazy once more, usually finding it unnecessary to say anything.

No new nuns found their way to the abbey, but neither did tracts nor awful rumors, and the seven remaining nuns began to hope they would be able to go on living there peacefully for the rest of their lives.

But one windy night a fire broke out. It didn't seem too serious at first, but then the wind carried the flames to a row of old wooden buildings. Thus the fire was fueled, and the abbey was soon engulfed in a sea of flames.

By morning, the devastation was complete. The abbess and the seven faithful sisters were saved, but they now had no chapter, no library, no refectory, no dormitory, no larder, no kitchen. In fact, they did not have so much as a church in which to prostrate themselves before God and lament this scourge. The church, too, had burned down, and nothing but four naked walls remained.

The abbess must have considered this a sign from God that Riseberga Abbey would be no more, and she informed the sisters their Lord had now discharged them from his service. She reminded them how they all came from good families and had wealthy relations, to whom they should now turn for favor and protection, as they could no longer stay there.

No one objected, so the abbess contacted the bailiff who was responsible for the Riseberga properties, asking him to arrange for horses and a decent escort, to ensure that she and the seven sisters arrived safely at the homes of their friends and families.

A few days later eight horses with sidesaddles, and a number of armed men to escort the travelers, stood assembled around the pitiful heaps of scorched debris and fallen walls, which were all that remained of Riseberga Abbey. The poor homeless women soon joined them, and before long each one was seated in a saddle, except of course Sister Karin, who always had to be last.

They spent a long time looking for her, and when she finally appeared she was every bit the old Sister Karin, dull and apathetic, incapable of either action or speech.

The abbess ordered her sternly to mount her horse at once, but Sister Karin just stood there, appearing not to understand.

There was a great flurry. The abbess repeated the order. Sister Sisla tried to persuade and cajole her, but Sister Karin just stood proud and beautiful, and wouldn't move.

"What do you want to stay for?" Sister Sisla cried. "You can't hold a service, you can't give alms, you can't offer wayfarers a roof over their heads."

Sister Karin did not reply. She just stood there, indifferent and slow, as if she had no idea what was going on.

So the abbess motioned to the bailiff that she was ready to depart, thinking if Sister Karin saw her ride off with the others, her resistance would break and she would hurry to mount her horse and follow.

But Sister Sisla had a different idea. When the others had begun to move off, she leapt from the saddle and ran to Sister Karin, saying firmly, "Sister Karin, if you are staying at Riseberga, then so am I." For Sister Sisla thought if a good-hearted woman like Sister Karin saw someone prepared to be self-sacrificing for her sake, she would be so touched she would hurry to her horse, to save the other from living in such misery.

Sister Karin really did seem moved when she saw Sister Sisla was willing to stay. She no longer stood there dull and still, but leaned forward and gave her an eager, penetrating look. Quickly, she knelt before Sister Sisla and kissed her feet. "Oh, Sister Sisla, will you really stay on for my sake? Thank you. Thank you."

Sister Sisla could tell Sister Karin was deeply moved. She was trembling from head to toe, speaking loudly, with tears streaming down her cheeks.

"Will you really not ride away and leave a poor, wretched woman like me?" asked Sister Karin.

Sister Sisla thought Sister Karin's resistance might be breaking, as the Abbess had anticipated. At the same time she saw Sister Karin must care very deeply for her, since her staying meant so much. At this her own heart was touched, and she cried: "Of course I shall stay, Sister Karin. I shall never leave you. . . ."

In 1556, ten years after the fire at Riseberga Abbey, two young scholars who had the right to ride freely through the parishes of Närke, begging for food and lodging, rode past the abbey. It was a lovely summer's day and they were in no hurry, so they decided to have a look at the ruins.

Nothing had been cleared away after the fire. Charred beams lay just as they had fallen, and chimneys and the remains of walls rose from the debris that covered the ground. The only new thing seemed to be the raspberry canes growing everywhere, and the youths were pleased to see they were full of ripe berries.

They began eating heartily, but were soon halted by the anxious cries of two old nuns who were sitting beside the abbey wall spinning flax. One was tall, beautiful and gray-haired, the other small and wizened, but with lively eyes and hair that was still dark. Their old, gray homespun habits were very worn but decently darned and mended. The nuns were quick and nimble with their spindles, and looked mild and gentle, but slightly mournful. They had shouted to warn the young men that the stone mound where the raspberries were growing was infested with vipers and to say that if they were hungry the nuns would be happy to share the little they had. So they brought out beer, bread, and honey, and the youths sat on the ground at their feet, eating and drinking.

Imagine these young scholars. Brought up in fear of all things popish, they might never have met a monk or nun before. It worried them that they might be jeopardizing their salvation if they had anything to do with these Catholic sisters, but as they were very hungry they thought they would take the risk.

The two old ladies of the veil were very talkative. They asked the wayfarers who they were and where they came from, and when they identified themselves as scholars from Strängnäs, the dark-haired woman exchanged a few Latin phrases with them to show she was learned as well.

The nuns asked about all kinds of things, about the king and the state of the country and about their travels. They wanted to know if Swedish farmers were really so well off that it was worthwhile begging from farm to farm.

The young men were all praise. They said trade was flourishing now that Sweden was rid of the Lubeckians. Under the king's personal supervision, the farmers were tilling their fields with such energy and good sense that their crops had tripled. Things were peaceful and orderly everywhere and times really had improved. Gustav Eriksson was the greatest king ever to sit on the throne. The nuns looked at one another and sighed, but before long they were smiling again. "We are pleased to know that all is going well for the country," they said mildly.

At last the young men worked up the courage to ask the sisters some questions. Why did they stay on here in such misery? They looked like high-born women, and must have friends and patrons who would take them in.

At this the old women laughed, and the dark one replied that this was their abbey, and although it was ruined they did not want to leave it. They lacked for nothing. There was an allowance from the bailiff, and the cellar to live in, but when the weather was fine, as it was today, they enjoyed working in the sunshine.

They were so good and gentle that the young men felt drawn to them and hated to think of leaving them in the ruins. They asked if they knew that nowadays monks and nuns could live wherever they pleased.

The nuns looked into each other's eyes, and then the dark-haired one, who was the more talkative, said the Lord they served had not yet discharged them. They hoped to remain in his service for a long while, in fact it was all they desired.

With each remark the young men grew more impatient. They asked how they could be content to live in a cellar, after their former splendor. The women got up and showed the young men around the debris, describing the many large buildings, and how each room had been decorated and furnished.

Good Protestants though they were, the young men couldn't help feeling sad at the thought of all this magnificence having come to nothing. They said they could see why the nuns didn't have much liking for the Lutheran religious improvement.

This started the small, dark nun railing against the heretical doctrine being preached in Sweden, but the gray-haired one must have noticed the young men's discomfort. She gestured to her companion to be silent, and in her mild voice she said: "Dear sister, you know these young men mean well. Tell them something that will please them. Tell them how once upon a time there was a nun at this abbey called Sister Karin. She was so slow and dull and useless that all the other sisters made a laughingstock of her but the good Lord, who can change all things for the better, sent the Lutheran doctrine to this country, which roused her from her apathy."

When she had said this, Sister Sisla ceased to rail. "It would be even better to tell them about Sister Sisla," she said. "She was witty and learned, eager and industrious, but she had grown harsh and haughty and would have died in sin if our all-merciful Lord had not taught her humility when this abbey fell into poverty and disrepair through the evil progress of the Lutherans."

They extended their hands and bid the young men farewell, assuring them they need not grieve on their account. For what harm can come to those who know that pain and suffering, sickness and distress, bitterness and humiliation all come from God, who can turn all trials into blessings?

Translated by Linda Schenck

Beatrice Webb

UK(England), 1858–1943

Beatrice Potter Webb was born at Standish House near Gloucester, England. Her father, a well-known merchant, and his brothers, were the politically radical Potters, who were very active in the reform movement in the mid-nineteenth century. Her father helped found the Manchester Grammar School and *The Manchester Guardian* newspaper. The youngest of eight daughters, Webb had a lonely childhood, exacerbated by frequent illness. Although she had virtually no formal education, her home provided her with a fine library and her father's distinguished visitors with their stimulating conversation and guidance. A particular mentor of her early years was philosopher Herbert Spencer.

Webb's mother died when Webb was in her early twenties, and as her seven sisters were all married, it became her responsibility to serve as her father's housekeeper, companion, and secretary. In these roles she was able to meet the important left-wing political thinkers of her time, including the capitalist imperialist Joseph Chamberlain, whom she almost married.

Webb became concerned about the conditions of laborers in the 1890s when she took part in a study of London laborers organized by her cousin Charles Booth. Using a false identity, she researched the conditions of garment workers by actually working in a factory for several weeks, and she gave evidence on her experience there at a governmental hearing. She also researched cooperative societies, writing her book *The Cooperative Movement* in 1891.

Webb's research on labor unions led her to seek the help of Sidney Webb (1859–1947), an early member of the Fabian Society, an organization formed in 1883 by predominantly middle-class English intellectuals to promote socialism through the gradual assimilation of their ideas into the mainstream political party structure. Although her first reaction to Webb was less than positive—she found him very ugly—she grew to love him and the two married in 1892. The couple had the motto *pro bono publico* (for the public good) inscribed in the rings they exchanged at their wedding, and indeed they lived a life committed to public service. They researched and wrote many works together, although at first she was seen as the fact-gatherer and he the diplomat and committeeman. They wrote the classic *The History of Trade Unionism* in 1894, *Industrial Democracy* in 1897, and the ten-volume *English Local Governments* from 1906 to 1929. Also very involved in English education, the Webbs cofounded the London School of Economics. Another involvement of theirs was the movement to repeal the Poor Laws and to institute a form of social insurance. As part of the Royal Commission on the Poor Laws, Beatrice Webb wrote the "Minority Report," which showed remarkable prescience; much of the legislation it called for was effected, although not until two years after her death in 1945. The Webbs founded the influential journal *The New Statesman* in 1913, in which many of their social and political theories were analyzed and promulgated. After the First World War, the Webbs became involved in many committees to stabilize and reconstruct postwar Britain. To that end, Beatrice Webb wrote, in 1919, *The Wages of Men and Women: Should They Be Equal?* for the Government Committee on Equal Pay, a minority report that unfortunately was never enacted, although considered a classic.

The Webbs believed in the inevitability of socialism through gradual changes in policy and law. However, little of what they wanted was realized in their lifetimes, and during the latter part of their lives they turned to Soviet Russia as an ideal, concomitantly seeing the justification for revolutionary action and publishing the two-volume *Soviet Communism: A New Civilization?* in 1935.

Although Beatrice Webb is hardly valued for her prose style which in many of her written studies was dull and plodding, at times that style was accomplished and even brilliant. Her memoirs *My Apprenticeship* (1926) and *Our Partnership* (1948), are beautifully written descriptions of her life up to and after her marriage. In them she interweaves extracts from her diaries. The complete diaries, published in 1985, from which the following selections are taken, are vivid first-hand accounts of a remarkable life.

from THE DIARIES OF BEATRICE WEBB, 1888

4 March. [London]

Trying to grasp my subject—the trade and labour question of East End tailoring. Wish I had more strength and pluck.

28 March. Good Friday.
[Devonshire House Hotel]

So the first six weeks of my inquiry ends. Think I have broken the crust and am now grabbing at the roots of the subject. But much definite work I have not done. Most of my time spent in training as a "plain hand," and it remains to be seen whether my training will be of real use. Anyway, it has given me an insight into the organization, or, in this case, into the want of organization, of a workshop, and into the actual handicraft of tailoring. Otherwise my life has been extremely interesting, and I am more than ever assured that, *if I have capacity,* I have found the life that suits me, in which I am happiest, in which I can be of most use to my fellow-mortals. My work now absolutely absorbs me. When I am too tired to work I pray; when I am too exhausted to pray I simply rest in the faith that my work is useful if I give it my best energy and my whole heart. And now there are no conflicting desires and few conflicting duties. Society, even now that it is unusually gracious and flattering, has no charm for me, and the other night after I had come back from a distinguished party to which I had been enticed, I felt that I should not regret the loss of attraction (as I shall inevitably lose it), for I did not care for the result. Only in work should I fear the loss of a woman's charm, for undoubtedly it smooths out obstacles, but then I am so planning my life that the work I need it for will be done before I lose it!

Of my family I see less and less but that is unavoidable in my present hurried life—every bit of spare time must be devoted to work.

11 April. [London lodgings]

Settled at 56 Great Prescott St. to begin life as a working woman. With a very queer feeling I left the house in my old clothes and walked straight off to Princes Street and Wood Street, a nest of tailors. No bills up, except for "good tailoress," and at these places I daren't apply, feeling myself rather an imposter. I wandered on, until my heart sank within me, my legs and back began to ache, and I felt all the feelings of "out o' work." At last I summoned up courage and knocked at the door of a tailor wanting a "good tailoress." A fat and comfortable Jewess opened the door.

"Do you want a plain 'and?" said I, trying to effect a working-class accent.

"No," was the reply.

"I can do everything except buttonholes," I insisted.

"Where have you worked?"

"With my father, a master tailor. I've come from Manchester."

"Rebecca," shouted the fat Jewess to her daughter down the street, "do you want a hand?"

"Suited," shouted back Rebecca, to my mingled disappointment and relief. "You will find plenty of bills in the next street," she added in a kindly voice.

So I trudged on, asked at one or two other places, but all were "suited." Thought I, "Is it because it's middle of the week, or because they suspect I'm not genuine?" and looked sensitively into the next shop window at my reflection; certainly I looked shabby enough. I pass by a shop where a long list of "hands wanted" is nailed; but I have neither pencil nor paper and cannot in my dazed nervousness remember addresses and names—and how can I walk any longer? I feel quite strained. So in a fit of listless despair I take the top of the tram down Mile End Rd. It is warm and balmy, and with a little rest from that weary trudge I pick up my pluck again. A large placard strikes my eye. "Trouser and vest hands wanted immediately." I descend quickly and am soon inside the shop. A large crowded room with a stout, clever-looking Jewess presiding at the top of the table, at which some thirty girls are working.

"Do you want trouser hands?"

"Yes, we do," answered the Jewess.

"I'm a trouser finisher."

The Jewess looks at me from top to toe; and somewhat superciliously glances at my draggled old dress.

"Call tomorrow half-past eight."

"What price do you pay?" say I with firmness.

"Why, according to the work; all prices," answers she laconically.

"Then tomorrow, half-past eight," and I leave the shop feeling triumphant to have secured a place, but a little doubtful of my power of finishing trousers. So I hurry back to my little room, throw off my disguise, gulp down a cup of tea and rush off to a friendly Cooperative workroom to "finish a pair of trousers" which I accomplish without difficulty in two hours. If they only expect "finishing" I'm safe. Basting I have not really mastered.

12 April. [London]

Thursday morning I reappear at 198 Mile End Road. It is a long irregular-shaped room running backward from the retail shop to the kitchen. Two small tables by the gas jets (used for heating irons) serve for the two pressers. Then a long table with forms on either side and chairs at top and bottom, for the trouser finishers. Two other tables for machinists and vest hands and a high table for the trouser-basters complete the furniture of the room. It is barely 8.30 but the 30 girls are crowding in and taking their seats in front of their work and boxes on the tables. The "missus" has not yet come down; the two pressers, English lads of about 22, saunter lazily into the room a little after the half-hour. The head woman calls for a pair of trousers and hands them to me. I look at them puzzled to know what to do; I have no materials wherewith to begin. The woman next to me explains: "You will have to bring trimmings, but I'll lend you some to begin with." "What ought I to buy?" say I, feeling very helpless. At this moment the "missus" bustles into the room. She is a big woman, enormously developed in the hips and legs, with strongly Jewish features and only one eye. Her hair is crisp and has been jet black; now in places it is quite grey. Her dress is stamped cotton velvet of a large flowery pattern; she has a heavy watch-chain, plentiful rings; and a spotlessly clean apron.

"Good morning to you," she says good-temperedly to the whole assemblage. "Esther, have you given that young person some work?"

"Yes," replied Esther. "3½ trousers."

"I have not got any trimmings. I did not know that I had to supply them. Where I worked before they were given," I ejaculate humbly.

"That's easily managed; the shop is just around the corner, or Esther," she calls out across the table, "you're going out; get this young person her trimmings. The lady next you will tell you what you want," she says in a lower tone bending over between us. The lady next me is a good-tempered married woman of a certain age. She, like all the other trouser-hands, works piecework; but in spite of that she is ready to give me up a good deal of time in explaining how I am to set about my work.

"You'll feel a bit strange the first day. Have you been long out 'o work?"

"Yes," I answer abruptly.

"Ah, that accounts for your feeling awkward like. One's fingers feel like so many thumbs at first."

And certainly mine do. The work is quite different from the Cooperative shop [in which I learnt the work?]; much coarser and not so well arranged. And then I feel nervous, very much "on trial," and the heat of the room, the crowded table and the general strangeness of the position, all these circumstances unite to incapacitate me for even decent work.

However, happily for me, no one pays much attention. There is plenty of row, what with the machines, the singing of the girls at the other end of the room, the chattering that goes on at the upper end of one table, at which sits the mistress. Chaff and bad language is freely thrown from the two lads at the pressing-tables to the girls at our table. Offers of kisses, sending to the Devil and his abode, and a constant repetition of the inevitable adjective [bloody] form the staple of the conversation between the lads and workgirls; the elder women whisper bits of gossip or news in each other's ears. There is a free giving and taking of each other's trimmings, and a general supervision of each other's work, altogether a hearty geniality of a rough sort. The missus joins in the chatter, encourages or scolds as the case may be.

"The missus has 16 children," says Mrs. Read (the woman next me), "8 of her own and 8 of her husband's. All those girls at the last table are her daughters."

I look down the room: the girls there are smartly dressed, but are working quite as hard as the others and appear on terms of equality.

"They are a nice-looking set," say I in a complimentary tone.

"Yes, it's a pity some of the girls are not like them," mutters the woman. "They're an awful bad lot, some o' them. Why bless you, that young woman just behind us has had three babies by her father, and another here has had one by her brother."

"Yes," remarks the person next to her (a regular woman of the slums), "it's ill thinking of what you may have to touch in these sort of places."

"Well," replies Mrs. Read, "I've worked here these eight years and never yet had any words with anyone. There's regular work and no one need grumble who wishes to work. There's no need to mix yourself up with others whose look you don't like. There's some of all sorts here."

"I'm one of those sort," continues the slum woman, "that answers a person back when they call me bl—y names. I'll give the last word to no one."

"I don't choose to hold conversation with such as they," replies Mrs. Read with conscious superiority. "It isn't as if I 'ad to work for my living. My 'usband is in regular work; it's only for the extras that I work; and just for those times, per'aps three or four weeks, when the building trade is slack."

This effectually silences the woman of the slums. Her husband comes home drunk every night, and spends his time lounging about the publics (so [I] was afterwards informed by Mrs. Read). She has an ill-looking daughter next her, with whom she exchanges work and bad language and shares victuals.

So we go on; my attention divided between my work and picking up bits of conversation. Evidently much of the work is for export, chiefly for Parnells [a wholesale house]. Other work is for sale in the front shop; the trousers we are finishing for 3½ up to 5d are sold from 4s 6d up to 8s 6d. Coats and vests for 17s up to 22s. Coats must be made out. The coarser trousers are also made out in large quantities and are probably paid 2½ for finishing.

"One o'clock," shouts a shrill boy's voice. "Stop work," orders the missus.

"I wish I could finish this bit," say I to the woman next me.

"You mustn't. It's dinner-time."

So I put on my bonnet and jacket and go out into the Mile End Road heartily glad to get a breath of fresh air and a change from the cramped position. I take the tram up and down to Aldgate and end by turning into a clean shop for a cup of tea and a bun. Back again at two.

"You must work a little quicker for your own sake," says the missus, who has been inspecting my work. "We've had worse buttonholers than this," she says in a kindly voice, "but it don't look as if you have been 'customed to much work."

But now begins the drama of the day. The two pressers come in ten minutes after hour. This brings down upon them the ire of the Jewess. They, however, seem masters of the situation, for they answer her back in even choicer language than she has advanced to them. They taunt her with putting the 5s she rings out of them on horses; they declare their right to come when they choose, and if they want a day off, to take it. And then begins a perfect volley of abuse, in which the girls at one of the tables join in, taking the "missus" side against the pressers. At this critical point enter the master.

Mr. Marks is a somewhat sleepy-looking well-dressed Jew, with an evident desire to keep the peace. I think also he has himself suffered from the missus' tongue and feels the masculine side of the question with the bevy of women shouting on all sides. Anyway, he is inclined to take an impartial view of the row. "Now just you be quiet," he shouts to the two pressers. "Go on with your work and don't speak to my wife." And then to his wife in a lower tone, "Why can't you leave them alone and not answer them?" and the rest of his speech I cannot hear but it is evidently taking the form of expostulation.

"Why, if you were only a bit of a man," says the missus, raising her voice so that all may hear, "you would throw these two bl—y rascals out. Why, I'd throw them out at any price. The idea of saying how I spend my money. What's that to him? And that Joe says he'll call the Factory Man in. He may call the Devil in, if he likes, and the only person as he'll notice will be himself. The idea of his saying that I spend my money on horses; as if I couldn't spend my money on anything I like. As if you wouldn't give me money, as I earn, when I ask you, Mr. Marks; and never ask where it goes to," she adds, looking threateningly at Mr Marks. The betting on horses is evidently a sore point.

"It's not their business what you do with your money," says the master soothingly. "But just let them alone, and tell the girls to be quiet." But the pressers have caught the word "devil" and reply in due form. The quick firing of words between missus and men goes on: the tall young man, Joe by name, shouts the loudest and the longest, but as Mrs. Read remarks to me, "It's Harry as makes the bullets; just listen to him; but it's Joe that fires them."

At last it subsides. Women (outdoor workers) come in and turn the mistress' attention off the pressers on to their work. They, like most of the indoor hands, are Christians but, unlike the former, they are nearly all married women.

"Come in on Monday, Mrs. South. But mind it's Monday morning and not Tuesday morning. You understand English, don't you? Monday morning."

A boy comes into the shop with a bundle of trousers unfinished.

"What do you think of this, Esther? Mrs. Hall says she was washing on Monday, cleaning on Tuesday, and I suppose the Devil on Wednesday; for here on Thursday the work is sent in undone," and the missus, as she throws the bundle on to the table, says, "Now,

girls, be quick with your work; there's all this to be done extra before Friday for Parnells. Strike her name off the book, Esther."

At last tea-time breaks the working day. All, or nearly all, the women have their own teapots on the gas stove and have with them bread as a relish. The missus takes her tea at the top of the table. The obnoxious pressers have left for the half-hour. The missus' feelings break out. "Pay them 5s a day to abuse you; as if I couldn't spend my money on what I like; and as if Mr. Marks would ever ask—I'd like to see him ask me how the money had gone."

All the women sympathize with her, and exchange abuse of the absent pressers. "It's awful, their language," says the slum woman. "If I were the missus, I would give the bl—y scoundrels tit for tat."

"As for the Factory Man," continues the mistress, turning to another sore point, "just fancy threatening me with him. Why, they aren't fit to work in a respectable shop— they're d—d spies. I'd throw them out, if I were Mr. Marks, if it cost me £100. If he were half a man he would."

"You have nothing to fear," venture I, "from the Factory man. You keep the regulations exactly."

However, the pressers are not "thrown out." The truth being that in the busy season it would be difficult to supply their place.

The women on either side of me offer me tea, which I resolutely refuse. An hour afterwards I have finished my second pair of trousers.

"This won't do," says the missus, pulling the work to piece. "Here, take and undo that one. I'll set this one to rights. Better have respectable persons who know little to work here than blackguards who know a lot and a deal too much too," she mutters, still smarting over the taunt of money laid on horses.

"Eight o'clock by the Brewery clock," cries out the shrill voice.

"Ten minutes to," shouts the missus, looking at her watch. "However, it ain't worth while breaking the law for a few minutes. Stop work."

This is most welcome to me. The heat, since the gas has been lit, is terrific and my fingers are horribly sore and my back aches as if it would break. The women bundle up their work and one or two take it home. Everyone leaves their trimmings on the table with scissors and thimble.

The freshness of the evening air is delicious, and as I walk up Mile End Road the physical sensation of free movement and rest to the weary eyes and fingers is keen enjoyment. Back in my little lodging and eat my supper and tumble into bed.

13 April. [London]

Friday morning I have trimmings to buy before I sit down to work. But this morning I feel hopelessly tired, my fingers clammy and a general shakiness all over. The needle will not pierce the hard shoddy stuff; my stitches will go all awry and the dampness of my fingers stretches the linings out of place. Altogether I feel on the brink of deep disgrace as a needlewoman....

"This will never do," says the missus as she looks over the work. "This work won't suit me. You want to go and learn somewhere first. This will never do. This won't suit me," she repeats slowly. All the women at the table look at me pityingly and I retire to my place feeling very small. There is a dead silence, during which I arrange any trimmings so as to be ready to take my leave if the missus persists. Presently she beckons to me. "I'll see what I can do with you. You sit between those two young ladies and they'll show you. You must help one another," she says to the two girls....

Tea-time the missus addresses me: "Now I am very much interested in you; there is something in your face that is uncommon. The women here will tell you that I have made an exception for you. I should have bundled you out long ago if it had not been for your face and your voice. Directly you open your mouth, anyone can see that you are different from others. What have you been?"

"I used not to have to work for my living," I reply, evading the question. "I am looking out for different work now, but I had to take to something."

"A nice-looking person like you ought to get married to a respectable man; you're more fit for that than to earn your living," says the shrewd Jewess. "But since you have come here, I'll see what I can do with you."

I have my cup of tea. The pale weary girl is munching her bread and butter.

"Won't you have some?" she says, pushing the paper towards me.

"No, thank you," I answer.

"Sure?" she says. And then, without more to-do, she lays a piece on my lap and turns away to avoid my thanks. A little bit of human kindness that goes to my heart and brings tears into my eyes. Work begins again. My friend has finished her trousers and is waiting for another pair. She covers her head with her hand and in her grey eyes there is an intense look of weariness, weariness of body and of mind. Another pair is handed to her and she begins again. She is a quick worker but, work as hard as she may, she cannot make much over a 1s a day, discounting trimmings. A shilling a day is about the price of unskilled woman's labour.

Another two hours and I say "goodnight" to the mistress and leave this workshop and its inhabitants to work on its way day after day and to become to me only a memory....

Charlotte Perkins Gilman   *US, 1860–1935*

Despite the poverty and sadness of her childhood, and the psychic difficulties and social controversies that marked periods of her adult life, Charlotte Gilman was an indefatigable author and lecturer—a prototypic feminist intellectual. Inspired early by the examples of her great aunts Harriet Beecher Stowe and Catherine Beecher, and later by Olive Schreiner, she became the leading American theorist of the women's movement during the first two decades of the twentieth century, the first to articulate an "androcentric" theory of female inequality and to envision the "new woman" within the context of a reconstructed social order.[1] Gary Scharnhorst, in his critical biography, has illuminated the relationship between Gilman's work and her life.

One of two surviving children born in Hartford, Connecticut, Gilman grew up in dire poverty after her parents separated soon after her birth; the family moved nineteen times in eighteen years for work, and for charity. Gilman completed a course of study at the Rhode Island School of Design and began her career as a commercial artist and art teacher. Reluctant to repeat the mistakes of her parents, she married Charles Stetson only after prolonged vacillation, in 1884. The birth of a daughter brought on a severe mental depression, recounted in *The Living of Charlotte Perkins Gilman: An Autobiography* (1935): "Here was a charming home, a loving and devoted husband; an exquisite baby, healthy, intelligent and good; a highly competent mother to run things; a wholly satisfactory servant—and I lay all day on the lounge and cried." Her husband urged willpower; for the sake of her sanity, Gilman divorced him in 1894. The prolonged divorce, Stetson's remarriage to Gilman's closest friend, and the pragmatic arrangements concerning their daughter, who went to live with her father and "co-mother," as Gilman called her, scandalized Hearst readers in California and Boston and traumatized Gilman: When she subsequently married her cousin George, she negotiated a marriage of equality and economic independence.

During the period of trial separation that ended in her divorce, Gilman resettled in California and supported her daughter and destitute mother by writing, lecturing on women, labor, and social organization to women's clubs, labor unions, and suffrage groups. She was associated, like other progressive intellectuals, with the nativist Nationalist movement—a reform movement inspired by Edward Ballamy's utopia, *Looking Backward* (1888); later, she edited the journal of the Pacific Coast Women's Press Association, afterwards becoming its President, and organized a variety of women's congresses. Her commitment to socialism led her to become a delegate to the 1896 International Socialist and Labor Congress, where she met George Bernard Shaw and Beatrice Webb, among others, and was enlisted in the Fabian cause. This was to be the first of several major European tours. After *Economic Relation of the Sexes* and other social works brought her great fame but increasingly fewer outlets for publication, Gilman wrote, edited and published a monthly, the *Forerunner* (1909–1916), the equivalent, she estimated, of four books a year. Her husband died in 1934. The following year, Gilman decided that she "preferred chloroform to cancer," and managed to stir controversy even with her own death, contributing to debate on euthanasia, part of the eugenics rage of the period.

Gilman's earliest literary efforts were poems on economic and social themes: *In This Our World* (1893) was hailed by critic William Dean Howells and achieved a modest public success, going through three different editions. Though marred by her stilted versification and the moral didacticism that pervades all her work, it is refreshing in its use of a direct and forceful colloquial diction and for its satirical wit and irony in framing discussion of serious social and political issues. Her current literary reputation rests primarily on "The Yellow Wallpaper" (1899; reissued by Feminist Press in 1973), which has elicited most interesting and consciousness-raising feminist interpretations; and to a lesser extent, on one of several utopias, *Herland* (1915).

In her own day, Gilman's fame rested principally on the major works of social theory and reform—her second book *Economic Relation of the Sexes As a Factor in Social Development* (1898, reissued in 1966 as *Women and Economics*), *The Home: Its Work and Influence* (1903), and *The Man-Made World* (1911). *Women in Economics* went through seven editions by 1911, and was soon translated into seven languages, including Russian and Japanese, making Gilman world-famous. Influenced by Fabianism and by the writings of Lester Frank Ward, Gilman argued cogently for female economic independence, shocking the reader by juxtaposing, for instance, traditional marriage and prostitution.[2] She also used her novels to put forth proposals for sweeping domestic reforms, including cooperative living arrangements and professional childcare.

Today it is easy to see that Gilman's feminism is limited by its assumption of maternal and other female instincts and its appeal to middle-class interests, her socialism in reality a benevolent capitalism vitiated by racist thinking; in her own day, however, she argued for a more radical view than that of the liberal suffragists, and did as much as any writer to link women's fate to a wider human destiny.

NOTES

1. Catherine Beecher (1800–1878): Important educator and founder of the Hartford Female Seminary (1823) and three female colleges in the midwest, as well as prolific author; her most important work is *A Treatise on Domestic Economy* (1841).
2. Lester Frank Ward (1841–1913): Founder of American sociology, he stressed the biological supremacy of the female sex and social equality of women while propounding a revisionist interpretation of the prevailing Social Darwinist thought of the period; he emphasized human intervention and collective action to shape evolutionary advance as against the individual survival of the fittest and accumulation of material wealth.

HOMES

We are the smiling comfortable homes
With happy families enthroned therein,
Where baby souls are brought to meet the
                                                    world,
Where women end their duties and desires,
For which men labor as the goal of life,
That people worship now instead of God.

Do we not teach the child to worship God?—
Whose soul's young range is bounded by the
                                                    homes
Of those he loves, and where he learns that
                                                    life
Is all constrained to serve the wants therein,
Domestic needs and personal desires,—
These are the early limits of his world.

And are we not the woman's perfect world
Prescribed by nature and ordained by God,
Beyond which she can have no right desires,
No need for service other than in homes?
For doth she not bring up her young therein?
And is not rearing young the end of life?

And man? What other need hath he in life
Than to go forth and labor on the world,
And struggle sore with other men therein?
Not to serve other men, nor yet his God,
But to maintain these comfortable homes,—
The end of all a normal man's desires.

Shall not the soul's most measureless desires
Learn that the very flower and fruit of life
Lies all attained in comfortable homes,
With which life's purpose is to dot the world
And consummate the utmost will of God,
By sitting down to eat and drink therein.
Yea, in the processes that work therein—
Fulfilment of our natural desires—
Surely man finds the proof that mighty God
For to maintain and reproduce his life
Created him and set him in the world,
And this high end is best attained in homes.

Are we not homes? and is not all therein?
Wring dry the world to meet our wide desires!
We crown all life! We are the aim of God!

EXILES

Exiled from home. The far sea rolls
Between them and the country of their birth;
The childhood-turning impulse of their souls
            Pulls half across the earth.

Exiled from home. No mother to take care
That they work not too hard, grieve not too
                                                    sore;
No older brother nor small sister fair;
            No father any more.

Exiled from home; from all familiar things;
The low-browed roof, the grass surrounded
                                                    door;
Accustomed labors that gave daylight wings;
            Loved steps on the worn floor.

Exiled from home. Young girls sent forth alone
When most their hearts need close
                                                    companioning;
No love and hardly friendship may they own,
            No voice of welcoming.

Blinded with homesick tears the exile stands;
To toil for alien household gods she comes;
A servant and a stranger in our lands,
            Homeless within our homes.

(opposite) Thomas Eakins, The Pathetic Song, *1881, oil on canvas. Collection of The Corcoran Gallery of Art, Washington, D.C., Museum Purchase, Gallery Fund*

Victoria Howard

US, 1860–1930

Victoria Howard was one of the last and indubitably one of the greatest oral storytellers of the Clackamas Chinook people. Born on the Grand Ronde Reservation in northwestern Oregon, she and her mother returned to her mother's family household upon her father's death. When her mother remarried, Victoria remained with her grandmother until at the age of 15 she married Eustace Howard; a year later, she gave birth to a daughter. Part Molale, part Clackamas, Howard was proficient in English and both Amer-Indian languages. The myths she recorded in the last two years of her life were those that had been handed down to her by her mother-in-law and her grandmother. In these, as well as in the Clackamas, Molale, and Kalapuya songs she dictated, Melville Jacobs discerns a "fine humor, sharp intelligence, and excellent diction," as well as a rare "mastery of literary repertoire and technique." Recent redactions by Dell Hymes have also revealed her as a fine poet.

The first two selections here are not traditional myths but anecdotes. In a two-step exchange, a second "turn" reframes the first, through saying something that invites the audience to entertain as true something contrary to expectation. The second turn "tops" the first; but commonly the respondent who attempts to rival his or her opponent also become the subject of humor, thus providing a dual perspective.

The themes reflected in the three selections here may be seen as part of a larger pattern in which Howard's gender (as well as those from whom she inherited these tales) serves to reshape the oral tradition, providing a more detailed handling of female actors and focusing on myths in which female actors are dominant and take a more active role than in those versions recited by men.

LAUGHING AT MISSIONARIES[1]

It must have been the *very* first time a preacher got to this country he told them:
"You must *always* pray,
"the Chief Above will see you.
"In case you do not accept it for yourselves,
"now, you will get yourselves tails,[2]
"Like things chased about,
"creatures in the forest.
Now my mother-in-law would say:
"Oh *dear* oh *dear*!
"(It) may be strange (as) we keep playing
shinny.[3]
"Our tails will keep whipping us!"

Translated by Dell Hymes

NOTES

1. "Laughing at Missionaries" refers to the arrival of Father Adrian Croquet in the year of Howard's birth and four years after the first Amer-Indians were moved to the Grande Ronde Reservation. The anecdote tops the priest on his own terms and more generally makes fun of attempts at conversion and their associated threats of of punishment.
2. The motif of the "tailed Englishman" appears in Scottish songs as early as 1332 and is to be found in the life of St. Augustine in *The Golden Legend*; it has been well known since the Middle Ages.
3. A favorite game of women.

'MAYBE IT'S MILT' *

Our house (was) near the road
Someone will pass by us.
She will look at them.
Now she will laugh and laugh,
she will say:
"Dear oh dear...
"A light one!
"Maybe it's milt!"
Now she will sing,
this is what she will say:
"The Honorable Milt!
"I supposed him for myself."

Translated by Dell Hymes

NOTE

* This selection derives from a myth in which a widow wishes that the milt (sperm-filled reproductive glands) saved from a fine male salmon were a person and wakes to find a man beside her, only to have him be stolen and herself mocked by another woman. Thereupon, the widow extends her spirit-power and turns the man once again to milt. The myth itself contains derogatory implications concerning "half-breeds" and barrenness. The short narrative also suggests that the white person may not be really human. The first mention of milt in this anecdote demeans the white; the second raises the possibility that he is but a figment of Indian imagination, existing on Indian sufferance. The power of transformation belonging to the Indian would, on another level, bring salmon again "exclusively under Indian control."

SEAL AND HER YOUNGER BROTHER LIVED THERE[1]
Wálxayu iCámxix gahxílayt

[I. THE "WIFE" COMES]

They lived there, Seal, her daughter, her younger brother.
After some time, now a woman got to Seal's younger brother.
They lived there.
        They would 'go out' outside in the evening.[2]
The girl would say,
        she would tell her mother:
        "Mother! Something is different about my uncle's wife.
        "It sounds just like a man when she 'goes out.'"
"Shush! Your uncle's wife!"
A long long time they lived there like that.
        In the evening they would each 'go out.'"
Now she would tell her:
        "Mother! Something is different about my uncle's wife.
        "When she 'goes out' it sounds just like a man."
"Shush!"

[II. THE UNCLE DIES]

Her uncle, his wife, would 'lie down' up above on the bed.[3]
Pretty soon the other two would lie down close to the fire,
        they would lie down beside each other.
Some time during the night, something comes on to her face.
She shook her mother,
        she told her:
        "Mother! Something comes on to my face."
"mmmmm. Shush, Your uncle, they are 'going.'"
Pretty soon now again, she heard something escaping.
She told her:
        "Mother! Something is going t'úq t'úq.
        "I hear something."
"Shush. Your uncle, they are 'going.'"
The girl got up,
        she fixed the fire,
                she lit pitch,
                        she looked where the two were:
                                Ah! Ah! Blood!
She raised her light to it, thus,
        her uncle is on his bed,
                his neck cut,
                        he is dead.
                                She screamed.

[III. THE WOMEN LAMENT]

She told her mother:
   "I told you,
     'Something is dripping.'
   "You told me,
     'Shush, they are "going."'
   "I had told you,
     'Something is different about my uncle's wife.
     'She would "go out"
       with a sound just like a man she would urinate.'
   "You would tell me,
     'Shush!'"
She wept.
Seal said:
     "Younger brother! My younger brother!
     "They are valuable standing there.
     "My younger brother!"
She kept saying that
As for that girl, she wept.
She said:
   "In vain I tried to tell you,
     'Not like a woman,
     'With a sound just like a man she would urinate,
       my uncle's wife.'
   "You told me,
     "Shush!"
   "Oh oh my uncle!
   "Oh my uncle!"
She wept, that girl.

                         * * *

"Now I remember only that far."

Translated by Dell Hymes

NOTES

1. This selection is a myth, traditionally interpreted by anthropologists as a narrative concerned with homophobic tensions and rivalry between in-laws within the Clackamas community; more recent interpretation suggests that it focuses on tensions between mother and daughter and concerns the daughter's movement from innocence to experience and from ignorance to knowledge of sexuality and death, an interpretation in which the daughter is "implicitly the heroine." In characteristically Howardian fashion, the daughter voices the concern for personal loyalty as against social propriety; awards the reality of sensory experience over the ideal of verbal convention; and prizes personal feeling above the formal expression of grief.
2. The verb and onomatopoeic particle combine to make this a euphemism for urination, suggesting specifically the sound made by a male; also later, a euphemistic pun on sexual climax.
3. The Clackamas euphemistent equivalent for the English "going to bed; having sexual intercourse."

Sara Jeannette Duncan   *Canada/India, 1861–1922*

Sara Jeannette Duncan, born in Brantford, Ontario, and a graduate of the Toronto
Normal School, began her writing career in the 1880s—a period of social ferment
in which the "woman question" was hotly debated. Duncan, the first full-time
woman journalist hired by the Toronto *Globe*, ranks as the first woman to work in
the editorial department of any leading Canadian newspaper. (She managed the
Globe's "Woman's World" department.) She also wrote editorials, book reviews,
parliamentary reports, and regular columns for several other papers, including the
Washington *Post*, the New York *World*, the Montreal *Star*, Goldwin Smith's
journal of ideas, *The Week*, and, later, the paper her husband edited, the *Indian
Daily News*.

Typifying the "new woman," Duncan set off with a sister journalist in 1888
on an ambitious round-the-world tour, traveling across Canada to Vancouver on
the newly completed Canadian Pacific Railway, then continuing by boat to the
Orient. Her travels, undertaken as correspondent, are recorded in her first book,
the very popular *A Social Departure* (1890). Her reputation as a novelist was
secured with the appearance of *An American Girl in London* (1891), the story of a
self-reliant young Chicago heiress traveling alone. In India, Duncan met, and in
1891 married, Everard Cotes of the Indian Museum in Calcutta. Living in Calcutta
and Simla for most of the next three decades, Duncan was able to write from a
crosscultural perspective.

The author of twenty-two books, Duncan's major works are *The Simple
Adventures of a Memsahib* (1893), centered on a pair of contrasting women; *His
Honour, and a Lady (1896)*, her first serious study of Indian politics; and the two
novels she set in Canada. These are *The Imperialist* (1904, repr. 1971, 1985), a
study of love and politics in her small Ontario hometown, and in which the
passionately intellectual heroine is an autobiographical character; and *Cousin
Cinderella* (1908), an exploration of imperial and colonial attitudes, which traces
the experiences of an idealistic young Canadian woman who attempts to gain
social recognition in London.

Duncan, who died in 1922, shortly after she and her husband had retired to
England, recognized the importance of her role as witness to "the making of a
nation," and her reputation as one of the most perceptive observers of Canadian
society in her time is secure. Her novels and her journalism (much of the latter
published under the pseudonym Garth Grafton) comment with intelligence, wit,
and incisiveness on a wide variety of social, cultural, and political issues; but
nowhere, perhaps, does she write with more energy and acumen than in those
articles—such as "Advantages of Being a Modern Woman" (following)—
addressed to her "sisters" on the subject of "the possibility of other than domestic
channels for your womanly activity."

Wendy Robbins Keitner

ADVANTAGES OF BEING A MODERN WOMAN

The Globe, November 17, 1886

As you are probably well aware, my sisters, tomorrow is Thanksgiving Day. It is not so very long since we imported the laudable custom of our American cousins, but quite long enough for one of its chief features to have taken such strong hold upon our affections as to make the approach of the occasion very evident to every housekeeper. Thanksgiving turkey, with all that doth accompany or flow therefrom, may be said to have become an incorporated fact in Canadian domesticity. We have not gone the length of compounding mince meat out of its due season, as the New Englanders do, nor have we taken the typical Thanksgiving pumpkin pie into our affections to any great extent as yet, but we have shown remarkable unanimity in adopting the dinner extraordinary as an indispensable feature of all true gratitude. It is both stimulative and illustrative and we have not been slow to appreciate these advantages.

So by your plenished larder, and your hot cheeks, and your floury apron, and the arrival of half a score of friends and relations, you know very well that tomorrow you will be called upon to give thanks with the rest of the people of this Dominion of Canada for all your manifold and multiplied mercies, national, social, family, civil, and religious. I have no doubt you will lump them. People always do, although the particularity with which they enumerate their tribulations is most painstaking. This department has frequently been given over to such enumeration, but will seize the present propitious occasion to make a few specifications of the other sort.

To begin at the very beginning your start in the world was made under auspices for which you would have been grateful doubtless, at the time, if you had been able to form any idea of the woes you escaped. You were not constantly jig-trotted on your nurse's knee to induce repose of mind and body. You were not swathed in uncounted yards of baby linen, which would have utterly repressed your reasonable and infantile desire to kick, and left your natural spirits no outlet but your lungs. You were not made acquainted with distilled liquor and the necessity of prohibition as a preventive of cruelty to infants, at the early age of three days. You were not fed until your small organs of deglutition and digestion utterly rebelled and your whole wretched little internal structure arose in a colicky protest. You were not put to sleep by the assistance of laudanum and Mrs. Winslow, and occasionally, when you wept for it, you were given a mouthful of water! All of which was reversed in the experience of the babies of the last generation.

Froebel hadn't influenced modern educational ideas as he did later when you were a very small girl, and there were no kindergartens. But your father and mother knew that romping and fresh air were important factors in your development, and while you may have learned your alphabet under the old system, you were not compelled to sit in the house and sew samplers and keep your petticoats clean, your slippers in shape, and your hair in curl, because you were a little girl. You climbed apple trees and fences and tore your clothes and raced and rioted and had as generally good and uproarious a time as your brothers had. Perhaps you even played hockey with them—I did, with crooked sticks and wrinkled horse-chestnuts, in intervals of taffy-making, over a big kitchen floor. And all this helped to lay the foundation for your excellent constitution which meets the wear and tear of the world's demand upon it so well today.

But the small creatures in pinafores of your mother's day were served not so.

When you went to school you were permitted to learn Latin if you wanted to, and to revel in the higher mathematics if you were so inclined. You had the fun of beating your cousin Tom at trigonometry, and topping the class in an examination in Greek prose. Science invited you, and you ruined three aprons, nearly deprived yourself of your right thumb, and burst twenty-seven glass tubes in learning how to make a certain acid with a most inexpressible smell. True, you couldn't make it now, even if you wanted to, and you don't remember much of your chemical research, and you couldn't analyze your own baking powder, nevertheless one Julia Jones who researched at the same time you did now occupies an excellent position in a ladies' college by virtue of the opportunity. Then you could have matriculated if you had so decided, and if it had not been for Jack no doubt you would have been today a graduate of a university of which he is now the president, and faculty, and Senate combined.

Which educational advantages were not known to the maidens of the last generation.

Jack was not the first who attempted to interfere with your university career by several people. But the possibility of other than domestic channels for your womanly activity made you critical and careful. So you said "No" till you couldn't help "Yes," which is a course so admirable that it is here held up for emulation by every young woman whose eyes

rest upon your causes for thanksgiving. You could afford to wait till Jack came or to dispense with a matrimonial prospect altogether, although Jack was an incident you rather hoped for and have never regretted.

But in the olden time the girl who refused a man who was willing and able to support her in comfort assumed a responsibility for her future that is rather alarming to think of.

And now that you and Jack are housekeeping, haven't you got a patent cradle, and an improved kitchen range, and hot and cold water, and stationary wash tubs, and a magic sewing machine silent and dexterous, and a carpet-sweeper, and a book which tells you how to furnish a house artistically with red flannel and empty flour barrels for three hundred and fifty dollars, and photogravures and Public Library books, and ten cent editions of the philosophers, and the prospect of casting an early and unbiased vote, and the sweetest baby girl in the world who will have a great many more advantages than her mother ever had!

Yes, if you follow Old Aunt Chloe's advice and "Tink ob y'er mercies," it is very evident that your meditations will be long and not unprofitable tomorrow; and it is tolerably certain, too, that however Jack may rail at the deplorable feminine tendencies of the age, upon hearing your enumeration of them, his thankfulness will not be less than yours.

E. Pauline Johnson (Tekahionwake)   *Canada, 1861–1913*

Born in the colonial era on the Six Nations Indian Reserve near Brantford, Canada West (Ontario), her mother English and her father a Mohawk chief, Emily Pauline Johnson was, under patriarchal law, Indian. Although she received little formal education, she read at home the poetry of Byron, Scott, Longfellow, Tennyson, and Keats, and she listened to Indian tales and legends told by her paternal grandfather. In 1886 she adopted the ancestral name Tekahionwake (Double Wampum) and, as many of her poems make clear, she identified with and bitterly resented the bigoted treatment Indians (and whites who mixed with them) had endured historically and often still endured in a race-conscious Canadian society. Poems such as "The Pilot of the Plains" and the autobiographical four-part short story, "My Mother," or the early "A Red's Girl's Reasoning," depict the tension between Indians and whites, and highlight Johnson's dual loyalties.

Johnson's first poems appeared in the New York magazine *Gems of Poetry* in 1884, and thereafter in several British and North American magazines, including *The Week*. Two of her nature poems were anthologized by W.D. Lighthall in *Songs of the Great Dominion* (1889), and her work was singled out for special praise in *Athenaeum* by its reviewer Theodore Watts-Dunton, whom she afterwards regarded as a mentor. Johnson's reputation was firmly established by her popular public readings, during which she wore elegant evening clothes and, for her Indian poems, ornate Indian attire; she made highly successful tours through Canada and the United States, and made two trips to London, in 1894 and 1906. (Johnson's wide popularity may be judged by the fact that her poem "The Song My Paddle Sings" is known by heart by the young heroine of Margaret Laurence's autobiographical short story "Loons.") Johnson's books of poetry are *The White Wampum* (1895), *Canadian Born* (1903), and *Flint and Feather* (1912, repr. 1972). Near the end of her life, having retired to the West Coast, she published *Legends of Vancouver* (1911), from which the following story is taken; it is a collection of tales and legends she heard from her friend Joe Capilano, a Squamish chief. Two posthumously published collections of short sentimental and didactic fiction, including some previously published boys' adventure stories, appeared in 1913 as *The Moccasin Maker* and *The Shagganappi*.

Johnson's two central themes are love of nature and pride of race. The stripped-down lines and imagistic depictions of nature in poems such as "Marsh-lands" or "The Camper" and the recurrent image of the Indian woman as a sturdy paddler of her own canoe ("My arm as strong as steel") provide an antidote to the stereotypical image of the delicate, fussy, reclusive Victorian poetess. Johnson's use of native legends and history—in such poems as the famous "As Red Men Die," "Silhouette," and the mellifluous "Lullaby of the Iroquois"— and especially her portraits of fiercely loyal Indian women—in "Ojistoh," "The Cattle Thief," "Dawendine," and "The Corn Husker"—make current a perspective on history that is all too little known. A feminist as well as an Indian interest accrues also to several of the West Coast legends she transcribed. "The Lost Salmon-Run" centers on the vital importance of girls and women to a tribe; "The Two Sisters" brings to the surface a buried vision—but one which seems strikingly contemporary—of female solidarity in the cause of peace.

Wendy Robbins Keitner

THE TWO SISTERS

THE LIONS

You can see them as you look towards the north and the west, where the dream-hills swim into the sky amid their ever-drifting clouds of pearl and grey. They catch the earliest hint of sunrise, they hold the last colour of sunset. Twin mountains they are, lifting their twin peaks above the fairest city in all Canada, and known throughout the British Empire as "The Lions of Vancouver."

Sometimes the smoke of forest fires blurs them until they gleam like opals in a purple atmosphere, too beautiful for words to paint. Sometimes the slanting rains festoon scarves of mist about their crests, and the peaks fade into shadowy outlines, melting, melting, forever melting into the distances. But for most days in the year the sun circles the twin glories with a sweep of gold. The moon washes them with a torrent of silver. Oftentimes, when the city is shrouded in rain, the sun yellows their snows to a deep orange; but through sun and shadow they stand immovable, smiling westward above the waters of the restless Pacific, eastward above the superb beauty of the Capilano Canyon. But the Indian tribes do not know these peaks as "The Lions." Even the chief whose feet have so recently wandered to the Happy Hunting Grounds never heard the name given them until I mentioned it to him one dreamy August day, as together we followed the trail leading to the canyon. He seemed so surprised at the name that I mentioned the reason it had been applied to them, asking him if he recalled the Landseer Lions in Trafalgar Square. Yes, he remembered those splendid sculptures, and his quick eye saw the resemblance instantly. It appeared to please him, and his fine face expressed the haunting memories of the far-away roar of Old London. But the "call of the blood" was stronger, and presently he referred to the Indian legend of those peaks—a legend that I have reason to believe is absolutely unknown to thousands of Pale-faces who look upon "The Lions" daily, without the love for them that is in the Indian heart, without knowledge of the secret of "The Two Sisters." The legend was intensely fascinating as it left his lips in the quaint broken English that is never so dulcet as when it slips from an Indian tongue. His inimitable gestures, strong, graceful, comprehensive, were like a perfectly chosen frame embracing a delicate

painting, and his brooding eyes were as the light in which the picture hung. "Many thousands of years ago," he began, "there were no twin peaks like sentinels guarding the outposts of this sunset coast. They were placed there long after the first creation, when the Sagalie Tyee moulded the mountains, and patterned the mighty rivers where the salmon run, because of His love for His Indian children, and His wisdom for their necessities. In those times there were many and mighty Indian tribes along the Pacific—in the mountain ranges, at the shores and sources of the great Fraser River. Indian law ruled the land. Indian customs prevailed. Indian beliefs were regarded. Those were the legend-making ages when great things occurred to make the traditions we repeat to our children today. Perhaps the greatest of these traditions is the story of 'The Two Sisters,' for they are known to us as 'The Chief's Daughters,' and to them we owe the Great Peace in which we live, and have lived for many countless moons. There is an ancient custom amongst the coast tribes that, when our daughters step from childhood into the great world of womanhood, the occasion must be made one of extreme rejoicing. The being who possesses the possibility of some day mothering a man-child, a warrior, a brave, receives much consideration in most nations; but to us, the Sunset tribes, she is honored above all people. The parents usually give a great potlatch, and a feast that lasts many days. The entire tribe and the surrounding tribes are bidden to this festival. More than that, sometimes when a great Tyee celebrates for his daughter, the tribes from far up the coast, from the distant north, from inland, from the island, from the Cariboo country, are gathered as guests to the feast. During these days of rejoicing the girl is placed in a high seat, an exalted position, for is she not marriageable? And does not marriage mean motherhood? And does not motherhood mean a vaster nation of brave sons and of gentle daughters, who, in their turn, will give us sons and daughters of their own?

"But it was many thousands of years ago that a great Tyee had two daughters that grew to womanhood at the same springtime, when the first great run of salmon thronged the rivers, and the ollallie bushes were heavy with blossoms. These two daughters were young, lovable, and oh! very beautiful. Their father, the great Tyee, prepared to make a feast such as the Coast had never seen. There were to be days and days of rejoicing, the people were to come for many leagues, were to bring gifts to the girls and to receive gifts of great value from the chief, and hospitality was to reign as long as pleasuring feet could dance, and enjoying lips could laugh, and mouths partake of the excellence of the chief's fish, game, and ollallies.

"The only shadow on the joy of it all was war, for the tribe of the great Tyee was at war with the Upper Coast Indians, those who lived north, near what is named by the Pale-face as the port of Prince Rupert. Giant war-canoes slipped along the entire coast, war-parties paddled up and down, war-songs broke the silences of the nights, hatred, vengeance, strife, horror festered everywhere like sores on the surface of the earth. But the great Tyee, after warring for weeks, turned and laughed at the battle and the bloodshed, for he had been victor in every encounter, and he could well afford to leave the strife for a brief week and feast in his daughters' honor, nor permit any mere enemy to come between him and the traditions of his race and household. So he turned insultingly deaf ears to their war-cries; he ignored with arrogant indifference their paddle-dips that encroached within his own coast waters, and he prepared, as a great Tyee should, to royally entertain his tribesmen in honor of his daughters.

"But seven suns before the great feast, these two maidens came before him, hand clasped in hand.

"'Oh! our father,' they said, 'may we speak?'

"'Speak, my daughters, my girls with the eyes of April, the hearts of June'" (early spring and early summer would be the more accurate Indian phrasing).

"'Some day, oh! our father, we may mother a man-child, who may grow to be just such a powerful Tyee as you are, and for this honor that may some day be ours we have come to crave a favour of you—you, Oh! our father.'

"'It is your privilege at this celebration to receive any favour your hearts may wish,' he replied graciously, placing his fingers beneath their girlish chins. 'The favour is yours before you ask it, my daughters.'

"'Will you, for our sakes, invite the great northern hostile tribe—the tribe you war upon—to this, our feast?' they asked fearlessly.

"'To a peaceful feast, a feast in the honor of women?' he exclaimed incredulously.

"'So we would desire it,' they answered.

"'And so shall it be,' he declared. 'I can deny you nothing this day, and some time you may bear sons to bless this peace you have asked, and to bless their mother's sire for granting it.' Then he turned to all the young men of the tribe and commanded: 'Build fires at sunset on all the coast headlands—fires of welcome. Man your canoes and face the north, greet the enemy, and tell them that I, the Tyee of the Capilanos, ask—no, command—that they join me for a great feast in honor of my two daughters.' And when the northern tribe got this invitation they flocked down the coast to this feast of a Great Peace. They brought their women and their children; they brought game and fish, gold and white stone beads, baskets and carven ladles, and wonderful woven blankets to lay at the feet of their now acknowledged ruler, the great Tyee. And he, in turn, gave such a potlatch that nothing but tradition can vie with it. There were long, glad days of joyousness, long, pleasurable nights of dancing and camp-fires, and vast quantities of food. The war-canoes were emptied of their deadly weapons and filled with the daily catch of salmon. The hostile war-songs ceased, and in their place were heard the soft shuffle of dancing feet, the singing voices of women, the play-games of the children of two powerful tribes which had been until now ancient enemies, for a great and lasting brotherhood was sealed between them—their warsongs were ended for ever.

"Then the Sagalie Tyee smiled on His Indian children: 'I will make these young-eyed maidens immortal,' He said. In the cup of His hands He lifted the chief's two daughters and set them forever in a high place, for they had borne two offspring—Peace and Brother-hood—each of which is now a great Tyee ruling this land.

"And on the mountain crest the chief's daughters can be seen wrapped in the suns, the snows, the stars of all seasons, for they have stood in this high place for thousands of years, and will stand for thousands of years to come, guarding the peace of the Pacific Coast and the quiet of the Capilano Canyon." . . .

This is the Indian legend of "The Lions of Vancouver" as I had it from one who will tell me no more the traditions of his people.

Mary Gilmore   *Australia, 1864–1962*

During her long life, Mary Gilmore passed through many changes of role, from country schoolteacher to South American emigrant, from writer for left-wing newspapers to Dame of the British Empire. Though she published eight volumes of poetry and three of prose, besides much journalism, she owed her honors and repute as much to her campaigns for the underprivileged and her encouragement and help of other writers.

Gilmore was born Mary Jean Cameron in southern New South Wales and at an early age became a pupil-teacher in bush schools there. Two years spent teaching in the mining district of Broken Hill awakened her lifelong interest in the Labour movement. In 1890 she moved to Sydney, where she met writers and radical intellectuals, becoming for a time romantically involved with the great Australian writer Henry Lawson. In 1896 she took part in William Lane's attempt to found an ideal socialist community at Cosme in Paraguay. Here she married William Gilmore, a sheep shearer, and they returned to Australia in 1902.

In 1908 Gilmore became editor of the women's page of the Sydney newspaper *The Worker*, a position she maintained until 1931. Many of her poems, and prose works such as *Old Days, Old Ways* (1934), record pioneer times, but not in a mood of unalloyed celebration. Like Judith Wright, a poet she appears to have influenced, Gilmore mourns the destruction of Aboriginal tribes and of the countryside.

"Eve-Song," from Gilmore's second collection, *The Passionate Heart* (1918), is a celebration of the sorrows and joys of being a woman. "The Brucedale Scandal," from her third collection, *The Tilted Cart* (1925), shows Gilmore in a more humorous and colloquial vein, making fun of small-town gossips and their notions of decorum. Although it has been praised for its strong lyricism and outspokenness, Gilmore's poetry is no longer in print.

Elizabeth Webby

EVE-SONG

I span and Eve span
A thread to bind the heart of man;
But the heart of man was a wandering thing
That came and went with little to bring;
Nothing he minded what we made,
As here he loitered, and there he stayed.

I span and Eve span
A thread to bind the heart of man;
But the more we span the more we found
It wasn't his heart but ours we bound.
For children gathered about our knees:
The thread was a chain that stole our ease.
And one of us learned in our children's eyes
That more than man was love and prize.
But deep in the heart of one of us lay
A root of loss and hidden dismay.

He said he was strong. He had no strength
But that which comes of breadth and length.
He said he was fond. But his fondness proved
The flame of an hour when he was moved.
He said he was true. His truth was but
A door that winds could open and shut.

And yet, and yet, as he came back,
Wandering in from the outward track,
We held our arms, and gave him our breast,
As a pillowing place for his head to rest.
I span and Eve span,
A thread to bind the heart of man!

THE BRUCEDALE SCANDAL

Himself and me put in the trap
    And daundered into town,
And there we found a whirlygig,
    A circus and a clown;
We took a ticket for the two,
    Without a thought of shame,
And never knew till we got home
    The loss of our good name.

'Twas Mrs Dinny met us first,
    Says she, "What's this I hear?
Ye're gaddin' round like young gossoons
    Instid of sixty year!"
Says she, "I heard a shockin' thing
    About a horse ye rid!..."
Says I, "The divel take your ears—
    I don't care if ye did!"

Says she, "I've had respect for you;
    I've held ye up to all;
And now my heart is broke in two
    To think ye've had a fall;
For sure I never thought to find
    The frivolous in you..."
Says I, for I was feelin' warm,
    "I don't care if ye do!"

We turned and left her where she stood,
    A poor astonished thing,
Whose wildest dissipation was
    A sober Highland Fling;
But when we came to Kelly's gate
    We got another knock,
For there was John O'Brien's Joe,
    Who looked his naked shock!

Says he (to Dan he whispers it)
    "They say—" says he, "they say..."
"Be damned to what they say," says Dan;
    Says I, "Do asses bray?"
The poor misfortune stared at me
    As if he thought me daft,
But, me, I looked him eye for eye,
    Until he felt a draught.

(continued)

The next was Mrs Tracy's Mick;
  Who said, "I'm hearin' things!"
Says I, "We'd never need to ride
  If gossipin' was wings!"
Says he, "There's decency you know;
  Ye mustn't go too far.
I'm that much shocked . . ." "Tut, tut," says I,
  "I don't care if ye are!"

But dear old Gran O'Shaughnessy
  She met us at the door,
And said, "Since first I heard the news
  My foot's wore out the floor!
I never laughed so much," says she,
  "Not once in all me days,
As when I heard that you and Dan
  Was took to shameless ways.

"I'm keepin' up the fire," she said,
  "Through all this blessed day.
My wan eye on the kittle, and
  Me other up the way;
And when I heard ye on the road,
  And thought of what ye'd done,
I felt me longest years slip off
  For thinkin' of your fun!"

"Sure then," say I, "it's not myself
  That would begrudge the tale,
And jokes, like butter on the shelf,
  If left too long grow stale."
I told her how I rid the horse
  In that there jig-ma-gee,
And when I said how I fell off,
  "A-w-w, did ye now!" says she.

I told her of the circus clown,
  And all the things he did.
She said, "He wasn't half the fun
  Of that there horse ye rid;
And though my bones is eighty-six,
  I wisht I was wi' ye!"
Says I, "Myself, I wisht it, too!"
  "I bet ye did!" says she.

"Aw, gir," she said, "ye've had your day,
  If Brucedale has the talk;
Ye've ate the apple to the core,
  So let them chew the stalk!"
They chewed the stalk from Rapley's gate
  To Cartwright's on the hill—
"Bedad," says Dan, "though years is gone,
  There's some that's chewin' still!"

Marie Dauguet   *France, 1865–1942*

In contrast with the large number of women poets of that generation who expressed their delicate feelings and dreams, Marie Dauguet created a sensation at the turn
of the century with her vigorous, almost realistic, poetry of nature. After the
publication of *À travers le voile* (Through the Veil) in 1902, the critic Emile Faguet
saluted her as a real poet, "neither classic, nor romantic, nor decadent," and
compared her to André Chénier.[1]

Marie Dauguet spent most of her life in her native province in the Southern
Vosges, making only brief visits to Paris. "My curiosity is universal. . . .I believe I
love science—natural sciences—as much as the arts. I wasted a lot of time in
various dilettante studies, from physiology to botany; fascinated by plants, animals, by everything that lives; sharing my time between fields, gardens, barns,
painting, music, and books" (letter to Alphonse Séché, 1908). She tells how she
came to writing by chance, when, one day, feeling sad and weary, she began to
scribble verse in the margin of one of her drawings.

It seems that writing poetry finally gave her a way to realize fully her pantheistic perception of nature. She reacted against the somewhat formalist rules of the
Parnassian masters, even against the imperative of musicality set by Verlaine,[2] in
order to reassert the rights of personal emotion. "A poem does not give me
satisfaction if it is not highly personal, full of color and harmony—not just any
correct harmony, but one closely related to what it expresses." With her 1908
volume, *Les Pastorales*, she demonstrated fully her ability to infuse new life into
the pallid genre of pastoral poetry. Her "duty" as an artist was to enjoy life in
flesh, heart and soul, and to celebrate it with the same passionate attention. She
nevertheless advocated a strict artistic control, accepting, for example, the discipline of verse forms for the crispness and brilliance they can give to the expression
of feelings. Only later in her career, in *Ce n'est rien, C'est la vie* (It's Nothing, It's
Life, 1924), did she use free verse.

Dauguet's poetry stands the test of time better than that of many of her
famous contemporaries. While Anna de Noailles' inventions sometimes border on
the precious, the artificial, or the narcissistic, Dauguet always retains a convincing
sincerity and directness. Rather than celebrating the self in nature, she tends to
dissolve herself in it. Looking, as she says, for "the synesthetic vibrance of Life,"
she creates original correspondances between sensations given by the most ordinary aspects of nature. Hers is a sensuous poetry exuding both mysticism and
paganism. Some of her poems achieve a transcendent eroticism no less direct,
however, than her descriptions of nature. There are echoes of *The Song of Songs* in
the selection from *L'Amant* (1924), a daring poem glorifying the lover's body.

Colette Gaudin

NOTES

1. André Chenier (1762–1794) was considered the greatest French poet of the eighteenth century.
2. See Note 2. to Renée Vivien.

from THE LOVER
L'Amant

You are the vigor of the sun
And your sap smells sweet,
It is a brook in May beneath the hawthorne,
Sweeter than the flower of the elder tree.
You hold yourself erect and you are the force
                    of the forest,
Its movement in the sun.
Your chest is rough beneath my cheek,
Your loins hurt my clenched hands.
You are hard like an oak.
I kissed you like a robin in my hand.
I gorge myself on your savage smell,
You smell of woods and marsh,
You are handsome like the wolf;
You shoot out like a beech tree
Whose energy swells its bark;
Your drunken gaze is beautiful
When it resembles that of a brute beast
Filled with some divine spirit.
Your head, swollen with instinct, is heavy
And your fists are weighty;
Desire tinges your eyelashes crimson,
The knot of your shoulders is hard beneath my
                    hands.
The axis of the world is in your flesh;
You are its rose of delights.
You are the hoarse wind and the cry of the oak.
Your spasm is beautiful like the wind
That changes the face of water.
You are a rough burden,
You are a delicious burden.
Your heart is the hammer that forges
In this beautiful red forge;
You are the divine blacksmith
Who forges life with full breath,
In the red forge.
You are the secret fountain
On which the lips come to rest;
The sweet savage source
On which the mouth comes to rest
And the warm bird in my hand.
Pride is in your eyes
That command; divine death
Is in your pure eyes that close,

When you fall back on the hollow of one
                    shoulder.
I caressed you like the grass and the beast
And the wind; I put my hand on your forehead
And I laughed, for you know nothing
Of what you are,
No more than the bull or the cornflower.
Are you The One Theresa loved? *
Will you have the nobility of the wolf
Or that of a field of wheat?
Or will you be nothing
But the one who disrupts the order of the
                    world
And its beauty?—All possibilities are in you,
All promises and all lies,
"Wonderful monster."
But I will praise your savage cry,
But I will praise your sweet-smelling body.
It is a savage wood of hearty flowers.
I will praise your brutality
And the hoarse sob of your flesh,
And I will praise your immeasurable sap
Where the universe is potential,
I will praise your fists and how they open
All of a sudden, when you fall back
On the hollow of one shoulder,
More gentle than a small child
And more innocent than an angel.

Translated by Brian Baer

NOTE

* This is probably a reference to St. Thérèse de Lisieux (1873–1879), Carmelite nun canonized 1925 and celebrated for her autobiography, *Little Way*, which emphasizes the sanctity of common life.

Marion Angus   *UK(Scotland), 1866–1946*

The daughter of a Presbyterian minister, Marion Angus was born in Arbroath and moved to Aberdeen, where she spent most of her life. She began writing when she was over 50, the best of her poems being in Scots, although the most frequently anthologized, "Alas! Poor Queen" (included here) is in Standard English.

Seen as a transitional figure between nineteenth-century literature and the new Scots writing of the Scottish Renaissance, Angus' poetry is serious and lyrical, and shows the influence of traditonal Scottish ballads. Christopher Murray-Grieve, the great leader of the Scottish Renaissance movement, considered her, along with Lewis Spence, "at the head of the New Movement in Vernacular poetry" (poetry written in the new Scots).

Angus published six collections of poems in her lifetime, most of them in the 1920s. "Alas/Poor Queen" is from *The Turn of the Day* (1931) and Mary's Song" from *Sun and Candlelight* (1927). Her *Selected Poems* were edited by Maurice Lindsay in 1950, to which Helen Cruickshank, fellow Scots poet and close friend, added a personal memoir.

ALAS! POOR QUEEN*

She was skilled in music and the dance
And the old arts of love
At the court of the poisoned rose
And the perfumed glove,
And gave her beautiful hand
To the pale Dauphin
A triple crown to win—
And she loved little dogs
      And parrots
    And red-legged partridges
And the golden fishes of the Duc de Guise
And a pigeon with a blue ruff
She had from Monsieur d'Elbœuf.

Master John Knox was no friend to her;
She spoke him soft and kind,
Her honeyed words were Satan's lure
The unwary soul to bind.
"Good sir, doth a lissome shape
And a comely face
Offend your God His Grace
Whose Wisdom maketh these
Golden fishes of the Duc de Guise?"

NOTE

* Mary Stuart (1542–1547), the only child of James V of Scotland, who died shortly after her birth; known as

Mary Queen of Scots. Raised in France, she married the Dauphin and ruled with him for a year until he died, leaving her in the center of political struggles between her uncle, the Duc de Guise's faction, and that of the New Queen of France. Returning as queen and Catholic to Scotland, recently reformed, she was bheaded by order of Queen Elizabeth of England after years of turmoil.

MARY'S SONG

I wad ha'e gi'en him my lips tae kiss,
Had I been his, had I been his;
Barley breid[1] and elder wine,
Had I been his as he is mine.

The wanderin' bee it seeks the rose;
Tae the lochan's[2] bosom the burnie goes;
The grey bird cries at evenin's fa',[3]
"My luve, my fair one, come awa'."

My beloved sall ha'e this he'rt tae break,
Reid, reid wine and the barley cake,
A he'rt tae break, and a mou'[4] tae kiss,
Tho, he be nae mine, as I am his.

NOTES

1. Bread.
2. Little loch.
3. Fall.
4. Mouth.

Zinaída Nikoláevna Gíppius   *Russia/France, 1869–1945*

Grouped with the Russian Symbolists who rejected materialism and realist critical tenets in favor of a poetry that would "materialize the spiritual," Gíppius was a member of the first wave of what is called the Russian Silver Age. The poetry, published in five volumes, the last of which is *Siyániya* (Radiances, 1938), constitutes only part of her oeuvre; in seven volumes of short stories (1894–1921), plays, critical and political essays, literary reminiscences, and memoirs, as well as diaries and journals, Gíppius concretizes a wide-reaching and constantly evolving dynamic philosophy and documents the aspirations and dislocations of her epoch.

Born to a well-to-do family, Gíppius at the age of 19 met and shortly afterward married the Symbolist poet and philosopher Dmítry Merezhkóvsky and lived with him in a perhaps platonic but extremely close intellectual and artistic relationship for over fifty years. Their St. Petersburg home became the center of a literary, philosophical, and religious circle that was to have an enormous impact on Russian culture. The Merezhkóvskys also participated in the publication of *Novyi put* (The New Way, 1903–1904) as a vehicle for their ideal synthesis of spirituality and art. At this time also began a long-term relationship—artistic, intellectual, and sexual—with Dmítry Filósofov (1872–1940). The years of the "Cause" lasted from 1905 to 1917 and were commemorated by Gíppius in a volume by that name; during this period she also supported the revolutions of 1905 and 1917 as possible heralds of a new society.

With the Bolshevik takeover, however, Gíppius's opposition to the state became total, and on Christmas Eve of 1919 she made her way illegally to Poland, before relocating in Paris in 1921. Gíppius remained politically active: her extreme positions antagonized editors of the emigré press, and she was forced to rely on friends, and her two sisters who had remained in Russia, for support. Though impoverished, the Merezhkóvskys once again became the center of significant influence, especially in the late 1920s, with the establishment of regular Sunday *soirées* that were held until the beginning of World II, the founding of Zelyónaya lámpa (The Green Lamp), a literary and philosophical society, and in 1938, Gíppius's editorship of the *Literary Review*. After Merezhkóvsky's death in late 1941, Gíppius spent the remainder of her life in penury. She sustained herself by writing her memoirs and the biography of Merezhkóvsky, which was published posthumously in 1951.

Gíppius's work is significant both formally and thematically. As Simon Karlinsky notes, her poetry "expanded the boundaries of traditional Russian metrics, popularized the use of accentual verse,...and initiated the use of assonance rhymes.:" Influenced by the mystical writings of Vladímir Solovyóv, as well as the philosophy of Dostóyevsky, Gíppius's work manifests a belief in a tragic Christian ideal: only through individual suffering can one come to an enduring spiritual reality. Moreover, she insists on the reality of the "devil," that is to say, on the presence of evil and death in the world as obstacles to freedom and love. Gíppius's stories are notable both for their philosophical seriousness and their sexual frankness. Her dramatic production has undergone reassessment. In addition to *Mákov tsvét* (Poppy Blossoms, 1908) and *Svyatáya Króv* (Sacred Blood, 1901), there is

Zelyónoe Koltsó (The Green Ring, 1916), which Karlinsky considers "one of the finest genuinely revolutionary poetic plays in the Russian language." Also memorable are the two-volume *Zhivyé lítsa* (Living Portraits, 1925) and important critical essays about Pasternák, Blók, Sologúb, and Tsvetáeva (whom Gíppius rejected as a misguided experimenter). Because of Gíppius's extreme anti-Soviet stance, her work was entirely suppressed in Soviet Russia from 1920 to the mid-1960s, when liberalization made at least her early work available.

INDIFFERENCE
Ravnodúshie

He came to me—I don't know who
he is.
He hid his face behind a cape...
                                                      1906

Again he came, he looks at me with
scorn
I don't know who he is,
just Someone in a cape...
                                                      1918*

Now he's different when he comes.
He assumes a slave-like guise.
  And bows down so very humbly,
Sits down quietly in the corner,
At a distance from me, on the floor,
  Snickering insincerely.

He whispers: "I dropped by, my love,
Just like that, just to have a look.
  I won't bother you—I wouldn't dare.
I'll sit for a while in my corner.
If you're tired, I shall amuse you,
  I can do a whole lot of tricks.

Want to look into your fellow men?
You'll just die, it's so screamingly funny!
  Name me anyone you like,
Point out anyone to me,
And I'll change you into him
  Just like that, on my word of honor,

For an instant, but not forever,
So you'll stand in his shoes for a while.
  If you're in them for only a moment,
You will know what is truth, what is lies.
You will see through him—through and
                                                      through.

Once you do, you won't soon forget.
What's the matter with you? Chat with me.
It's no fun? Now wait just a minute,
  I know some other tricks too."
Thus he whispered and babbled in his corner,
Wretched, puny, he sat on the floor,
  Wringing his thin little hands.

And a secret fear consumed him:
Of my answer. He waited and withered,
  Promising me he'd be good.
But this time, too, I did not raise my eyes
From my work to look at him.
  I stayed silent and—indifferent.

Go away or stay here with me;
Go ahead and writhe, but my calm
  Won't be ruined by the likes of you.
And he melted before my eyes,
Before my eyes he dissolved into dust,
  Because I was—indifferent.

Translated by Vladimir Zlobin

NOTE

* The epigraphs are taken from two other poems in which Gíppius wrote about her encounter with the devil: "Into a Line," dated 1906 and "The Hour of Victory," dated 1918, after the Revolution had occurred; "Indifference" was written after her emigration.

RELENTLESS
Neotstúpnoe

I'll not go from the door,
Let the night last, let the wind rage.
I'll knock until I fall,
I'll knock until Thou givest answer.
I won't give up, nor step aside,
I'll knock, I'll call Thee without fear:
Give me back the one I love!
Raise her from the ashes!
Return her to her Father's roof,
Even if she is guilty—grant forgiveness!
Spread Thy purifying cover
Over sinful Russia!

And grant to me, your stubborn slave,
To see her yet among the living.
Open up!
                    While she is in the grave,
I will not leave our Father's door.
The fire in my soul is inextinguishable,
I knock, the door hinges shake.
I call to Thee—oh, hurry!
I shout to Thee—oh, don't delay!

Translated by Vladimir Zlobin

Charlotte Mew   *UK(England), 1869–1928*

A frail-looking woman, English poet Charlotte Mew lived a life of seclusion with her sister Anne and her ailing mother. Her devotion to them and her own fear of becoming insane like her two youngest siblings made her later life tortured. The death of her mother in 1923 and of Anne by cancer in 1927 drove Mew to suicide in 1928.

Mew's early life, on the other hand, was relatively peaceful. The first child of Anne Kendall Mew and Frederick Mew, she had a typical Victorian middle-class childhood with her family in the Bloomsbury section of London. Early in life, she and her sister Anne became devoted to each other and when their younger sister, Freda, and brother, Henry, became mentally ill, the two older sisters vowed never to marry in order not to pass on this hereditary illness. When their father died, both women began working, Anne as a restorer of antique furniture and Charlotte as a writer. Mew had already become a regular contributor of stories to *The Temple Bar*, and it was in 1894 that her first work, a story entitled "Passed," appeared in the literary journal *The Yellow Book*. Soon after, her poetry, essays, and stories began to appear in *The Nation, The New Statesman, The English Woman*, and *The Egoist*.

By 1912, the diminuitive Mew, often dressed in a tweed coat, porkpie hat and boots, was a familiar sight among the London literati. This was also the year in which "Farmer's Bride," her most significant poem, was published in *The Nation*. Alida Klemantaski, wife of the Georgian poet Harold Monro, having read the poem and fallen in love with it, memorized it and four years later published seventeen of Mew's poems under the title *The Farmer's Bride*, from which the following selections are taken. The poems were greeted warmly. Thomas Hardy, who later became one of Mew's good friends, called her "the least pretentious but undoubtedly the best woman poet of [the] day."

Many of Mew's poems are spoken by or to women, and often in a sensual and sexually intimate manner that contrasts sharply with Mew's own apparent austerity. By 1916, Mew had virtually stopped writing. She would produce no prose and only a handful of poems in the last twelve years of her life, and only one other collection of poems would be published in her lifetime, *The Rambling Sailor* (1928).

John Isom

THE FARMER'S BRIDE

Three Summers since I chose a maid,
Too young maybe—but more's to do
At harvest-time than bide and woo.
    When us was wed she turned afraid
Of love and me and all things human;
Like the shut of a winter's day.
Her smile went out, and 'twasn't a
                    woman—
    More like a little frightened fay.
      One night, in the Fall, she
              runned away.

"Out 'mong the sheep, her be," they said,
'Should properly have been abed;
But sure enough she wasn't there
Lying awake with her wide brown stare.
So over seven-acre field and up-along across
                  the down
We chased her, flying like a hare
Before our lanterns. To Church-Town
    All in a shiver and a scare
We caught her, fetched her home at last
    And turned the key upon her, fast.

She does the work about the house
As well as most, but like a mouse:
    Happy enough to chat and play
    With birds and rabbits and such as
           they,
    So long as men-folk keep away.

"Not near, not near!" her eyes beseech
When one of us comes within reach.
    The women say that beasts in stall
    Look round like children at her call.
    I've hardly heard her speak at all.
Shy as a leveret, swift as he,
Straight and slight as a young larch tree,
Sweet as the first wild violets, she,
To her wild self. But what to me?

The short days shorten and the oaks are
                brown,
    The blue smoke rises to the low grey
                sky,
One leaf in the still air falls slowly down,
    A magpie's spotted feathers lie
On the black earth spread white with rime,
The berries redden up to Christmas-time.
    What's Christmas-time without there
               be
    Some other in the house than we!

She sleeps up in the attic there
    Alone, poor maid, 'Tis but a stair
Betwixt us. Oh! my God! the down,
    The soft young down of her, the brown,
The brown of her—her eyes, her hair, her hair!

THE NARROW DOOR

The narrow door, the narrow door
On the three steps of which the café
children play
Mostly at shop with pebbles from the shore,
It is always shut this narrow door
But open for a little while to-day.

And round it, each with pebbles in his hand,
A silenced crowd the café children stand
To see the long box jerking down the bend
Of twisted stair; then set on end,
Quite filling up the narrow door
Till it comes out and does not go in any more.

Along the quay you see it wind,
The slow back line. Someone pulls up the blind
Of the small window just above the narrow
door—
"Tiens! que veux-tu achéter?"[1] Renée cries,
"Mais, pour quat'sous, des oignons,"[2]
Jean
replies
And one pays down with pebbles from the
shore.

NOTES

1. "Wait! What do you want to buy?"
2. "But, for four sous, some onions."

Blanche Baughan   *New Zealand, 1870–1958*

Blanche Baughan is considered to be the first notable New Zealand writer, or at least the first to respond wholeheartedly to the possibilities of this new environment and its new way of life. Born and educated in England, she attended London University, despite the wishes of her father, a London stockbroker, graduating in 1892 with honors in Greek. At that time she became a suffragette and also worked to help the London poor.

Baughan arrived in New Zealand early in the new century and traveled widely throughout the country. She supported hereself writing journalism and tourist brochures about New Zealand beauty spots, later collected as *Studies of New Zealand Scenery* (1916) and *Glimpses of New Zealand Scenery* (1922). She also wrote a lively collection of stories and sketches, *Brown Bread from a Colonial Oven* (1912), and four volumes of poetry.

"A Bush Section," reproduced in part here, comes from her third collection, *Shingle-Short and Other Verses* (1908). Here Baughan, clearly influenced by the American Walt Whitman, dramatizes the colonial experience through "little Thor Rayden," symbol of both the European past and the New Zealand future, as he gazes at the destruction white settlement has brought to the countryside.

After a serious illness in 1910, Baughan felt that her talent for writing had deserted her. She devoted the rest of her life to community and social work, being particularly active in the cause of prison reform. She never married.

Elizabeth Webby

from A BUSH SECTION

Logs, at the door, by the fence; logs, broadcast over the paddock;
Sprawling in motionless thousands away down the green of the gully,
Logs, grey-black. And the opposite rampart of ridges
Bristles against the sky, all the tawny, tumultuous landscape
Is stuck, and prickled, and spiked with the standing back and grey splinters,
Strewn, all over its hollows and hills, with the long, prone, grey-black logs.

> For along the paddock, and down the gully,
> Over the multitudinous ridges,
> Through valley and spur,
> Fire has been!

Ay, the Fire went through and the Bush has departed,
The green Bush departed, green Clearing is not yet come.

> 'Tis a silent, skeleton world;
> Dead, and not yet re-born,
> Made, unmade, and scarcely as yet in the making;
> Ruin'd, forlorn, and blank.

At the little raw farm on the edge of the desolate hillside,
Perch'd on the brink, overlooking the desolate valley,
To-night, now the milking is finish'd, and all the calves fed,
The kindling all split, and the dishes all wash'd after supper:
Thorold von Reden, the last of a long line of nobles,
Little 'Thor Rayden', the twice-orphan'd son of a drunkard,
Dependent on strangers, the taciturn, grave ten-year-old,
Stands and looks from the garden of cabbage and larkspur, looks over
The one little stump-spotted rye-patched, so gratefully green,
Out, on this desert of logs, on this dead disconsolate ocean
Of billows arrested, of currents stay'd, that never awake and flow.
Day after day,
The hills stand out on the sky,
The splinters stand on the hills,
In the paddock the logs lie prone.
The prone logs never arise,
The erect ones never grow green,
Leaves never rustle, the birds went away with the Bush,—
There is no change, nothing stirs!
And to-night there is no change;
All is mute, monotonous, stark;
In the whole wide sweep round the low little hut of the settler
No life to be seen; nothing stirs.

> Yet, see! past the cow-bails,
> Down, deep in the gully,
> What glimmers? What silver
> Streaks the grey dusk?

(continued)

'Tis the River, the River! Ah, gladly Thor thinks of the River,
His playmate, his comrade,
Down there all day,
All the long day, betwixt lumber and cumber,
Sparkling and singing;
Lively glancing, adventurously speeding,
Busy and bright as a needle in knitting
Running in, running out, running over and under
The logs that bridge it, the logs that block it,
The logs that helplessly trail in its waters,
The jamm'd-up jetsam, the rooted snags.
Twigs of konini, bronze leaf-boats of wineberry
Launch'd in the River, they also will run with it,
They cannot stop themselves, twisting and twirling
They too will keep running, away and away.
Yes; for on runs the River, it presses, it passes
On—by the fence, by the bails, by the landslip, away down the gully,
On, ever onward and on!
The hills remain, the logs and the gully remain,
Changeless as ever, and still;
But the River changes, the River passes.
Nothing else stirring about it,
It stirs, it is quick, 'tis alive!
        'What is the River, the running River?
        Where does it come from?
        Where does it go?'
            Listen! Listen! . . .
Far away, down the voiceless valley,
Thro' league-long spaces of empty air,
A sound! as of thunder.
            Look! ah, look!
Yonder, deep in the clear dark distance,
At the foot of the shaggy, snow-hooded ranges,—
Out on the houseless and homeless country
Suddenly issuing, eddying, volleying—
Smoke, bright smoke! Not the soft blue vapour
By day, in the paddock there, wreathing and wavering,
O'er the red spark well at work in the stumps:
Not the poor little misty pale pillar
Here straggling up, close at hand, from the crazy tin chimney:—
No! but an airy river of riches,
Irrepressibly billowing, volume on volume
Rolling, unrolling, tempestuously tossing,
Ah! like the glorious hair of some else-invisible Angel
Rushing splendidly forth in the darkness—
Gold! gold on the gloom!

...Floating, fleeing, flying...
Thor catches his breath...All, flown!
Gone! Yes, the torrent of glory,
The Voice and the Vision are gone—
For over the viaduct, out of the valley,
It is gone, the wonderful Train!
Gone, yet still going on: on: on! to the far-away township
(Ten miles off, down the track, and the mud of the metal-less roadway:
Seen, once at Christmas, and once on a fine summer Sunday:
Always a dream, with its dozens of passing people,
Its three beneficent stores)...
And past the township, and on!
—The hills and the gully remain;
One day is just like another;
In the paddock the logs lie still;
But the Train is not still; every evening it sparkles out, streams by and goes.
     'What is the Train, that it travels?
     Where does it come from?
     Where does it go?'

Luisa Giaconi   *Italy, 1870–1908*

Not much is known about the life of Luisa Giaconi. She spent a lonely childhood, first in boarding schools and then with her father, a math teacher, who was constantly on the move. After his death she studied painting in Florence and lived from the sale of copies she made of famous masterworks.

Her poems, including the following selection, were scattered in the periodical *Marzocco*, collected by G.S. Gargano after her death and published under the title *Tebaide* (Thebais, 1909); they went unnoticed at first. Only later did critics do justice to her. She is now considered to be one of the best Italian women poets based on the richness and intensity of her poetic inspiration. Influenced by the late Romantics and European Decadent writers, her refined poems acquired an original intonation through a particularly musical rhythm, under which her restless sensibility seems to vibrate. Giaconi was abandoned by her lover for another woman, and her poems, in the form of interior monologues, are a spiritual diary of her unhappy love.

Natalia Costa-Zalessow

DIANORA

Draw back into distance. Your day of love
is done, your hour of sun spent, Dianora;
to your wandering step, that inlet,
doorway, goal once so secret
is shut, your reign of love
over. At hush of vespers who, now,
silently tends the lamp of the Poet,
smiles through his wakeful night,
kisses his laden sight,
who, now, Dianora?
Who, at your dream eternal, smiled with another dawn's splendor
of love, and extinguished you, quick not-quite-vanished star
oh Dianora?

With eternal charm she now wins the man who is dreaming,
his eternal fever she soothes as you did, Dianora.
Warm at his hearth she lies
and they listen to quiet sighs
of wind bringing from the hills a harmony
of bagpipes, and they wonder if, at shore,
a glittering sickle moon may still tremble on the tide.
And through the darkness her heart glows
and she sinks not into doubt's shadows
as you do, Dianora.
She knows not that Love is a wind's breath, and no more,
over the sonorous lyre, and neither hinders nor bars the path to glory,
oh Dianora.

Draw back, draw back into distance; on your long way
seek not your dreams but your death, Dianora;
oh lamp that bore luster,
oh earth that bore flower,
heart that bore its fate,
eyes that cried, oh Dianora.
Go, then, down some desert track yet unknown to you,
through land barren and brutal
where the last peace may lull
those who wept and loved, Dianora.
Rest at some cypress, await the hour
when all shall seem as null, vast and futile,
oh Dianora.

Translated by Joan Borrelli

Henry Handel Richardson (Ethel Florence Lindesay Richardson)

Australia/UK(England), 1870–1946

Henry Handel Richardson was the pseudonym of Ethel Florence Lindesay Richardson, who was born in Melbourne in 1870. After a few years of prosperity, Richardson's father, an Irish physician who had come to Victoria during the 1850s gold rushes, suffered heavy financial losses, and he found it increasingly difficult to support his family. His desperation and increasing mental instability, leading to his death in 1879, overshadowed Richardson's childhood. Her historical trilogy, *The Fortunes of Richard Mahony* (1930), can be seen as an attempt to fit her father's life into some sort of explicable pattern. The first two volumes, *Australia Felix* (1917) and *The Way Home* (1925), attracted little attention but *Ultima Thule* (1929) was a bestseller that, for a time, gave Richardson an international reputation.

Mary Richardson, Ethel Richardson's mother, supported her family by working as a postmistress in various country towns and in 1883 was able to send Richardson to board at the Presbyterian Ladies' College, then Melbourne's leading girls' school. The five years spent there are reflected in Richardson's satirical novel, *The Getting of Wisdom* (1910), with the usual novelist's license. She does not, for example, record her musical achievements, which in 1888 led her mother to take the family to Europe so that Richardson could pursue her piano studies at the Leipzig Conservatorium.

Though Richardson successfully completed her studies in Germany, she felt she was temperamentally unsuited to a career as a concert pianist and did not wish to become a music teacher. Moreover, she had met, and in 1895 married, a Scottish student of German literature, J.G. Robertson, who encouraged her to read widely in European literature and to try writing. In 1897 she began her first novel. *Maurice Guest* (1908), based on her student years in Leipzig. For its period, it is remarkably forthright in its treatment of both homosexuality and women's sexual needs.

After Robertson became Professor of German at London University in 1903, Richardson lived a fairly reclusive life in London, devoting herself to her writing. "'And Women Must Weep'" comes from her only collection of stories, *The End of a Childhood* (1934), where it forms part of a sequence, "Growing Pains," focused on the problems girls encounter as they pass from babyhood to maturity. It has been seen as a response to Katherine Mansfield's story "Her First Ball."

Richardson's final novel, *The Young Cosima* (1939), a semidocumentary account of the early life of Cosima Wagner, does not meet the high standard of her earlier works. She obviously suffered from the loss of the help and encouragement given by her husband, who had died in 1933. Richardson herself died in 1946, leaving her autobiography, *Myself When Young* (1948), to be finished and published by her long-time companion, Olga Roncoroni.

Elizabeth Webby

"AND WOMEN MUST WEEP"

"For men must work"*

She was ready at last, the last bow tied, the last strengthening pin in place, and they said to her—Auntie Cha and Miss Biddons—to sit down and rest while Auntie Cha "climbed into her own togs": "Or you'll be tired before the evening begins." But she could not bring herself to sit, for fear of crushing her dress—it was so light, so airy. How glad she felt now that she had chosen muslin, and not silk as Auntie Cha had tried to persuade her. The gossamerlike stuff seemed to float around her as she moved, and the cut of the dress made her look so tall and so different from everyday that she hardly recognised herself in the glass; the girl reflected there—in palest blue, with a wreath of cornflowers in her hair—might have been a stranger. Never had she thought she was so pretty...nor had Auntie and Miss Biddons either; though all they said was: "Well, Dolly, you'll *do*," and: "Yes, I think she will be a credit to you." Something hot and stinging came up her throat at this: a kind of gratitude for her pinky-white skin, her big blue eyes and fair curly hair, and pity for those girls who hadn't got them. Or an Auntie Cha either, to dress them and see that everything was "just so."

Instead of sitting, she stood very stiff and straight at the window, pretending to watch for the cab, her long white gloves hanging loose over one arm so as not to soil them. But her heart was beating pit-a-pat. For this was her first real grown-up ball. It was to be held in a public hall, and Auntie Cha, where she was staying, had bought tickets and was taking her.

True, Miss Biddons rather spoilt things at the end by saying: "Now mind you don't forget your steps in the waltz. One, two, together; four, five, six." And in the wagonette, with her dress filling one seat, Auntie Cha's the other, Auntie said: "Now, Dolly, remember not to look too *serious*. Or you'll frighten the gentleman off."

But she was only doing it now because of her dress: cabs were so cramped, the seats so narrow.

Alas! in getting out a little accident happened. She caught the bottom of one of her flounces—the skirt was made of nothing else—on the iron step, and ripped off the selvedge. Auntie Cha said: "My *dear*, how clumsy!" She could have cried with vexation.

The woman who took their cloaks hunted everywhere, but could only find black cotton; so the torn selvedge—there was nearly half a yard of it—had just to be cut off. This left a raw edge, and when they went into the hall and walked across the enormous floor, with people sitting all around, staring, it seemed to Dolly as if every one had their eyes fixed on it. Auntie Cha sat down in the front row of chairs beside a lady friend; but she slid into a chair behind.

The first dance was already over, and they were hardly seated before partners began to be taken for the second. Shyly she mustered the assembly. In the cloakroom, she had expected the woman to exclaim: "What a sweet pretty frock!" when she handled it. (When all she did say was: "This sort of stuff's bound to fray.") And now Dolly saw that the hall was full of *lovely* dresses, some much, much prettier than hers, which suddenly began to seem rather too plain, even a little dowdy; perhaps after all it would have been better to have chosen silk.

She wondered if Auntie Cha thought so, too. For Auntie suddenly turned and looked at her, quite hard, and then said snappily: "Come, come, child, you mustn't tuck yourself away like that, or the gentlemen will think you don't want to dance." So she had to come out and sit in the front; and show that she had a programme, by holding it open on her lap.

When other ladies were being requested for the third time, and still nobody had asked to be introduced, Auntie began making signs and beckoning with her head to the Master of Ceremonies—a funny little fat man with a bright red beard. He waddled across the floor, and Auntie whispered to him...behind her fan. (But she heard. And heard him answer: "Wants a partner? Why, certainly.") And then he went away and they could see him offering her to several gentlemen. Some pointed to the ladies they were sitting with or standing in front of; some showed their programmes that these were full. One or two turned their heads and looked at her. But it was no good. So he came back and said: "Will the little lady do *me* the favour?" and she had to look glad and say: "With pleasure," and get up and dance with him. Perhaps she was a little slow about it ...at any rate Auntie Cha made great round eyes at her. But she felt sure every one would know why he was asking her. It was the lancers, too, and he swung her off her feet at the corners, and was comic when he set to partners—putting one hand on his hip and the other over his head, as if he were dancing the hornpipe—and the rest of the set laughed. She was glad when it was over and she could go back to her place.

Auntie Cha's lady friend had a son, and he was beckoned to next and there was more whispering. But he was engaged to be married, and of course perferred to dance with his financée. When he came and bowed—to oblige his mother—he looked quite grumpy, and didn't trouble to say all of "May I have the pleasure?" but just "The pleasure?" While she had to say "Certainly," and pretend to be very pleased, though she didn't feel it, and really didn't want much to dance with him, knowing he didn't, and that it was only out of charity. Besides, all the time they went round he was explaining things to the other girl with his eyes...making faces over her head. She saw him, quite plainly.

After he had brought her back—and Auntie had talked to him again—he went to a gentleman who hadn't danced at all yet, but just stood looking on. And this one needed a lot of persuasion. He was ugly, and lanky, and as soon as they stood up, said quite rudely: "I'm no earthly good at this kind of thing, you know." And he wasn't. He trod on her foot and put her out of step, and they got into the most dreadful muddle, right out in the middle of the floor. It was a waltz, and remembering what Miss Biddons had said, she got more and more nervous, and then went wrong herself and had to say: "I beg your pardon," to which he said: "Granted." She saw them in a mirror as they passed, and her face was red as red.

It didn't get cool again either, for she had to go on sitting out, and she felt sure he was spreading it that *she* couldn't dance. She didn't know whether Auntie Cha had seen her mistakes, but now Auntie sort of went for her. "It's no use, Dolly, if you don't do *your* share. For goodness sake, try and look more agreeable!"

So after this, in the intervals between the dances, she sat with a stiff little smile gummed to her lips. And, did any likely-looking partner approach the corner where they were, this widened till she felt what it was really saying was: "Here I am! Oh, *please*, take *me*!"

She had several false hopes. Men, looking so splendid in their white shirt fronts, would walk across the floor and *seem* to be coming...and then it was always not her. Their eyes wouldn't stay on her. There she sat, with her false little smile, and *her* eyes fixed on them; but theirs always got away...flitted past...moved on. Once she felt quite sure. Ever such a handsome young man looked as if he were making straight for her. She stretched her lips, showing all her teeth (they were very good) and for an instant his eyes seemed to linger...really to take her in, in her pretty blue dress and the cornflowers. And then at the last minute they ran away—and it wasn't her at all, but a girl sitting three seats further on; one who wasn't even pretty, or her dress either.— But her own dress was beginning to get quite tashy, from the way she squeezed her hot hands down in her lap.

Quite the worst part of all was having to go on sitting in the front row, pretending you were enjoying yourself. It was so hard to know what to do with your eyes. There was nothing but the floor for them to look at—if you watched the other couples dancing they would think you were envying them. At first she made a show of studying her programme; but you couldn't go on staring at a programme forever; and presently her shame at its emptiness grew till she could bear it no longer, and, seizing a moment when people were dancing, she slipped it down the front of her dress. Now she could say she'd lost it, if anyone asked to see it. But they didn't; they went on dancing with other girls. Oh, these men, who walked round and chose just who they fancied and left who they didn't...how she hated them! It wasn't fair...it wasn't fair. And when there was a "leap-year dance" where the ladies invited the gentlemen, and Auntie Cha tried to push her up and make her go and said: "Now then, Dolly, here's your chance!" she shook her head hard and dug herself deeper into her seat. She wasn't going to ask them when they never asked her. So she said her head ached and she'd rather not. And to this she clung, sitting the while wishing with her whole heart that her dress was black and her hair grey, like Auntie Cha's. Nobody expected Auntie to dance, or thought it shameful if she didn't: she could do and be just as she liked. Yes, tonight she wished she was old...an old, old woman. Or that she was safe at home in bed...this dreadful evening, to which she had once counted the days, behind her. Even, as the night wore on, that she was dead.

At supper she sat with Auntie and the other lady, and the son and the girl came, too. There were lovely cakes and things, but she could not eat them. Her throat was so dry that a sandwich stuck in it and nearly choked her. Perhaps the son felt a little sorry for her (or else his mother had whispered again), for afterwards he said something to the girl, and then asked *her* to dance. They stood up together;

but it wasn't a success. Her legs seemed to have forgotten how to jump, heavy as lead they were...as heavy as she felt inside...and she couldn't think of a thing to say. So now he would put her down as stupid, as well.

Her only other partner was a boy younger than she was—almost a schoolboy—who she heard them say was "making a positive nuisance of himself." This was to a *very* pretty girl called the "belle of the ball." And he didn't seem to mind how badly he danced (with her), for he couldn't take his eyes off this other girl; but went on staring at her all the time, and very fiercely, because she was talking and laughing with somebody else. Besides, he hopped like a grasshopper, and didn't wear gloves, and his hands were hot and sticky. She hadn't come there to dance with little boys.

They left before anybody else; there was nothing to stay for. And the drive home in the wagonette, which had to be fetched, they were so early, was dreadful: Auntie Cha just sat and pressed her lips and didn't say a word. She herself kept her face turned the other way, because her mouth was jumping in and out as if it might have to cry.

At the sound of wheels Miss Biddons came running to the front door with questions and exclamations, dreadfully curious to know why they were back so soon. Dolly fled to her own little room and turned the key in the lock. She wanted only to be alone, quite alone, where nobody could see her...where nobody would ever see her again. But the walls were thin, and as she tore off the wreath and ripped open her dress, now crushed to nothing from so much sitting, and threw them from her anywhere, anyhow, she could hear the two voices going on, Auntie Cha's telling and telling, and winding up at last, quite out loud, with: "Well, I don't know what it was, but the plain truth is, she didn't *take*!"

Oh, the shame of it!...the sting and the shame. Her first ball, and not to have "taken," to have failed to "attract the gentlemen"—this was a slur that would rest on her all her life. And yet…and yet…in spite of everything, a small voice that wouldn't be silenced kept on saying: "It wasn't my fault…it wasn't my *fault*!" (Or at least not except for the one silly mistake in the steps of the waltz.) She had tried her hardest, done everything she was told to: had dressed up to please and look pretty, sat in the front row offering her programme, smiled when she didn't feel a bit like smiling…and almost more than anything she thought she hated the memory of that smile (it was like trying to make people buy something they didn't think worthwhile). For really, truly, right deep down in her, she hadn't wanted "the gentlemen" any more than they'd wanted her: she had only had to pretend to. And they showed only too plainly they didn't, by choosing other girls, who were not even pretty, and dancing with them, and laughing and talking and enjoying them.—And now, the many slights and humiliations of the evening crowding upon her, the long-repressed tears broke through; and with the blanket pulled up over her head, her face driven deep into the pillow, she cried till she could cry no more.

NOTE

* "And Women Must Weep" is a quote from *The Three Fishers* (1851) by English poet Charles Kingsley. The entire line reads: "For men must work and women must weep, And there's little to earn and many to keep, Though the harbor bar be moaning."

Grazia Deledda   *Italy, 1871–1936*

The Nobel laureate Grazia Deledda was a self-made woman. She attended only the first four grades of elementary school and received some private lessons later on. She received a more practical education, however, from her brother Andrea, who took her with him on his visits to shepherds in the mountains and to various local festivities. In the autobiographical novel *Cosima* (1937), excerpted here, she described her difficult life against the background of her native Sardinia, and Sardinia, indeed, is featured in her best novels.

Deledda's writing career started when she secretly sent a short story to a women's journal. It was published; she subsequently wrote novels, which, admired by readers, caught the attention of the writer and critic Luigi Capuana, but caused scandal at home: Deledda was even accused of immorality by her illiterate aunts. After marrying Palmiro Madesani, she moved to Rome, where she led a quiet life with him and their two sons, dedicating the greater part of her day to writing. She published thirty-three novels and nineteen collections of short stories. Her best novels are *Dopo il divorzio* (*After the Divorce*, 1902); *Elias Portolu* (1903); *Cenere* (*Ashes*, 1904); *L'edera* (Ivy, 1908); *Colombi e sparvieri* (Doves and Hawks, 1912); *Canne al vento* (Reeds in the Wind, 1913); *Le colpe altrui* (Misdeeds of Others, 1914); *Marianna Sirca* (1915); and *La madre* (*Mother*, or *The Woman and the Priest*, 1920). All these books deal with the basic human problems of simple people who live in rustic Sardinia, where nature, as seen through the author's eyes, becomes symbolic of the protagonists' various passions. Deledda's heroes and heroines are shepherds, peasants, landowners, servants, bandits, beggars, priests, and sorceresses, who follow natural instincts that never seem corrupt; they usually repent misdeeds and seek redemption from society and religion at the end, which gives them a magical and universal quality. For example, *Canne al vento* is the story of the Pintor sisters and Efix, their servant, who helps the youngest of them escape from home to go to Naples and then spends the rest of his life working free of charge for his impoverished ladies because he considers himself responsible for their father's death. In her later novels Deledda abandoned the Sardinian milieu, but the result was less rewarding.

Natalia Costa-Zalessow

from COSIMA

Cosima learned more in her time spent with her brother Andrea than she did in any of her lessons. He introduced her to old shepherds who told stories more wonderful than anything contained in books, and he took her on excursions to the most typical villages of the region, or to rural feasts and to the sheepfolds scattered over the lonely pastures or hidden like nests in the forested valleys.

One of these excursions was also memorable because of the good company in which it was made.... The two were accompanied by friends of Andrea, most of them failed students who preferred the tormenting joys of the accordion to those of the dictionary. They would create their own Odyssey, doing battle over some local Helen, only to be reconciled at a feast where the bones of fire-roasted lamb would pile high at their feet as they had at the tables of the heroes of Homer.

Just such a feast was prepared that day in the sheepfold of Andrea and Cosima's paternal *tancas*. The swineherds had finished their season and had been replaced by shepherds and goatherds. Sheep grazed on dried asphodel, crunching the long golden stems between their teeth like breadsticks; and black goats with their diabolical heads could be seen outlined against the mother-of-pearl of the rocky peaks.

Certainly Cosima learned more that day then she would have in ten lessons with her literature teacher. She learned to distinguish the notched leaves of the oak from the spear-shaped ones of the holm-oak; and the aromatic flowers of the verbascum from those of the bearbine. And, from a castle of boulders over which falcons flew as if drawn to the sun the way moths are drawn to a light at nighttime,

she saw a great shining sword at the foot of the cliff, as if to indicate that the island had been cut from the continent and must remain so forever. It was the sea that Cosima was seeing for the first time.

Certainly it was an unforgettable day, like the one on which a child who firmly believes in God is confirmed and, cleansed of all sin, feels closer to Him. Everything seemed extraordinary to Cosima, even the predatory cries of the jays and the spiny thistles growing among the sun-baked rocks; but instead of exalting, she felt small and humble, standing alongside rocks that shimmered as if covered with scales and, beside them, the centuries-old holm-oaks. If some small cloud crossed the sky, it seemed that it attached itself to the highest peaks over certain small openings in the forest, like a child peering into a well. But the feast was served on the ground, of course, in a clearing surrounded by a colonnade of tree trunks, like a royal drawing room. For Cosima, Andrea prepared a comfortable seat out of a saddle and saddle-bag; the best bits of food were given to her, the lamb's kidney, sweet and tender as a berry, the top of the spit-roasted cheese, and the bunch of early grapes brought especially on her account by her solicitous brother.

The guests noticed this kindness bordering on gallantry, and began to nudge one another; and, as if a command passed among them with this gesture, they all turned at once and pointed their odd stick-forks at her, each strung with meat, bread, cheese, whatever food could be found on the table.

She reddened but said nothing. She hadn't opened her mouth once during the entire meal and seemed like a stranger on her saddle covered with an ancient blanket, her big silent eyes the green of the dark forest shadow. She was like one of those fairies, perhaps good, perhaps bad, one isn't sure which, who live in the mountain caves and who for millennia weave, on their looms of gold, nets to imprison falcons, winds, clouds, and the dreams of men.

She was cross that her brother had exposed her to the attention of his companions, however respectful it might be. She stopped eating, and as soon as no one was watching, turned and leaped from the saddle as if from a racehorse. She moved away quickly through the ferns of the clearing, brushing them with her open arms like a swallow flying low at the approach of a storm. She returned to the top of the cliff from which the sea could be seen. The sea: the great mystery, the barren land of blue shrubs, the bank of white flowering hawthorne, the desert that the swallow dreamed of crossing to the marvelous regions of the continent. If she could have, she would have liked to remain on that hard stone cliff like a solitary lady of a manor, looking at the horizon, hoping to see appear there a sail, an emblem of hope; or perhaps Prince Charming disembarking, dressed in the color of the sea.

The yells of the boys in the clearing called her back to earth; whistles of the shepherds rounding up their flocks could be heard as well; each voice, each sound, vibrated in the immense silence, a clear echo in a house of crystal. The sun was descending opposite her in the sky above the mountains beyond the valley, and the goats, still climbing along the peaks, had red falconlike eyes. It was time to go home. The sea in front of her, and above, the sunset-reddened precipices, she remembered her childish days, enlivened only by the stories she told herself; and she felt like a little goat on the craggy mountain rim, who would imitate the flight of the falcon but who, at the whistle of the shepherd, must return to the stable.

Instead, a sharper whistle, different from the others, reached her like an arrow, followed by the taunting imitations of the others. It was Andrea calling, warning her not to take advantage of his lenience. The derision of her brother's companions reminded her even more that such an incursion would be withstood only once by the laws of the community in which she was destined to live. So she stood up, stretched her arms once more toward the sea, seeming to brush the waves as she had not long before brushed the ferns in the clearing, like a swallow who migrates after the warm but sterile winter of the Libyan plains, toward the land of the sun, the red summer twilights, the love that alone concedes the gift of eternity.

Translated by Claire Siegel

Higuchi Ichiyō   *Japan, 1872–1896*

Higuchi Ichiyō is probably the most famous Japanese woman writer of the pre-World War II period. Natsu (her real first name) was the daughter of an ambitious minor official of the city of Tokyo who, only shortly before the samurai class was abolished, had managed to buy his way up from the peasantry. The father's ambition transferred to the daughter: although her mother refused to allow Higuchi formal education past the fourth grade (as improper for a woman), she did permit her to enter an all-women's upper-class, conservative poetry academy in 1886, the Haginoya (run by the well-known female poet Nakajimo Utako). There Higuchi's love for poetry vied with her sense of defiant defensiveness as leader of the "commoners' squad" (*heimin-gumi*). The death of her eldest brother, and of her father after failure at business, reduced Higuchi and her mother and younger sister to doing laundry and sewing to stay alive. Her engagement to her childhood sweetheart was broken off by his family. These and other hardships and bitter disappointments became the plights and challenges of the abused women in her stories. She wrote largely not about people who were successes in the rapidly modernizing world of the 1890s but about those left behind by choice or circumstance.

It was the success of a Haginoya classmate at selling her stories that spurred Higuchi to begin writing fiction in 1890. She fell secretly in love with her writing mentor, Nakarai Tōsui, a less-than-first-rate newpaper novelist; her diary, published as *Wakabakage* (In the Shade of Spring Leaves), recounts her private joys and despair as she eventually felt compelled to break away from Nakarai because of fear of public scandal. As Robert Danly suggests, the epigraph she wrote for that work captures the tone of unfulfilled longing that characterizes her life and art:

> If only I could live
> In the shade of spring leaves
> Instead of in a world
> Of disillusion
> And despair

Higuchi's best writing (including the selection [1896]) comes from the last two years of her life, and it has left the literary world lamenting the loss of what might have been had she lived longer than her 24 years. A ten-month unsuccessful attempt to make a living running a sundries shop just outside the gates of the licensed-prostitution quarter of Tokyo, the Yoshiwara, gave Higuchi new insight into forms of oppression of women, who were victimized by the paternalistic Meiji civil codes and the still-feudal mores. Prostitution, unhappy marriage, servants' misery are the subjects of such stories as "Ōtsugomori" ("The Last Day of the Year," 1894), "Nigorie" ("Muddy Bay," 1895), "Jūsan'ya" ("The Thirteenth Night," 1895), and Higuchi's masterpiece, "Takekurabe" ("Comparing Heights," 1895–1896). In fusing the poetic traditions and conventions of court poetry with a realistic subject matter that focused on individuals caught in the contradictions of modern life, Higuchi succeeded in revitalizing fiction.

This achievement brought Higuchi the acclaim of leading writers of the day and support from the influential journal *Bungakukai* (Literary World), but she was already ill with tuberculosis, of which she died late in 1896. The romantic tragedy of her life, her fierce determination to succeed as a writer, and the excellence of her stories produced a kind of posthumous celebrity unmatched by any other Japanese woman writer. Danly's critical work, which includes a study of Higuchi and translations of her work, is the first full-length work in English devoted to one modern Japanese woman writer.

Phyllis I. Lyons

SEPARATE WAYS
Wakare Michi

There was someone outside, tapping at her window.

"Okyō? Are you home?"

"Who is it? I'm already in bed," she lied. "Come back in the morning."

"I don't care if you are in bed. Open up! It's me—Kichizō, from the umbrella shop."

"What a bothersome boy you are. Why do you come so late at night? I suppose you want some rice cakes again," she chuckled. "Just a minute. I'm coming."

Okyō, a stylish woman in her early twenties, put her sewing down and hurried into the front hall. Her abundant hair was tied back simply—she was too busy to fuss with it—and over her kimono she wore a long apron and a jacket. She opened the lattice, then the storm door.

"Sorry," Kichizō said as he barged in.

Dwarf, they called him. He was a pugnacious little one. He was sixteen, and he worked as an apprentice at the umbrella shop, but to look at him one would think he was eleven or twelve. He had spindly shoulders and a small face. He was a bright-looking boy, but so short that people teased him and dubbed him "Dwarf."

"Pardon me." He went right for the brazier.

"You won't find enough fire in there to toast any of your rice cakes. Go get some charcoal from the cinder box in the kitchen. You can heat the cakes yourself. I've got to get this done tonight." She took up her sewing again. "The owner of the pawnshop on the corner ordered it to wear on New Year's."

"Hmm. What a waste, on that old baldie. Why don't I wear it first?"

"Don't be ridiculous. Don't you know what they say? 'He who wears another's clothes will never get anywhere in life.' You're a hopeless one, you are. You shouldn't say such things."

"I never did expect to be successful. I'll wear anybody's clothes—it's all the same to me. Remember what you promised once? When your luck changes, you said you'd make me a good kimono. Will you really?" He wasn't joking now.

"If only I could sew you a nice kimono, it would be a happy day. I'd gladly do it. But look at me. I don't have enough money to dress myself properly. I'm sewing to support myself. These aren't gifts I'm making." She smiled at him. "It's a dream, that promise."

"That's all right. I'm not asking for it now. Wait until some good luck comes. At least say you will. Don't you want to make me happy? That would be a sight, though, wouldn't it?" The boy had a wistful smile on his face. "Me dressed up in a fancy kimono!"

"And if you succeed first, Kichizō, promise me you'll do the same. That's a pledge I'd like to see come true."

"Don't count on it. I'm not going to succeed."

"How do you know?"

"I know, that's all. Even if someone came along and insisted on helping me, I'd still rather stay where I am. Oiling umbrellas suits me fine. I was born to wear a plain kimono with workman's sleeves[1] and a short band around my waist. To me, all 'good luck' means is squeezing a little money from the change when I'm sent to buy persimmon juice.[2] If I hit the target someday, shooting arrows through a bamboo pole,[3] that's about all the good luck I can hope for. But someone like you, from a good family—why, fortune will come to greet you in a carriage. I don't mean a man's going to come and take you for his mistress, or something. Don't get the wrong idea." He toyed with the fire in the brazier and sighed over his fate.

"It won't be a fine carriage that comes for me. I'll be going to hell in a handcart."[4] Okyō leaned against her yardstick and turned to Kichizō. "I've had so many troubles on my mind, sometimes it feels as if my heart's on fire."

Kichizō went to fetch the charcoal from the kitchen, as he always did.

"Aren't you going to have any rice cakes?" Okyō shook her head. "No thank you."

"Then I'll go ahead. That old tightwad at the umbrella shop is always complaining. He doesn't know how to treat people properly. I was sorry when the old woman died. *She* was never like that. These new people! I don't talk to any of them. Okyō, what do you think of Hanji at the shop? He's a mean one, isn't he? He's so stuck-up. He's the owner's son, but, you know, I still can't think of him as a future boss. Whenever I have the chance, I like to pick a fight and cut him down to size." Kichizō set the rice cakes on the wire net above the brazier. "Oh, it's hot!" he shouted, blowing on his fingers. "I wonder why it is—you seem almost like a sister to me, Okyō. Are you sure you never had a younger brother?"

"I was an only child. I never had any brothers or sisters."

"So there really is no connection between us. Boy, I'd sure be glad if someone like you would come and tell me she was my sister. I'd hug her so tight…After that, I wouldn't care if I died. What was I, born from a piece of wood? I've never run into anyone who was a relative of mine. You don't know how many times I've thought about it: if I'm never, ever going to meet anyone from my own family, I'd be better off dying right now. Wouldn't I? But it's odd. I still want to go on living. I have this funny dream. The few people who've been the least bit kind to me all of a sudden turn out to be my mother and father and my brother and sister. And then I think, I want to live a little longer. Maybe if I wait another year, someone will tell me the truth. So I go on oiling umbrellas, even if it doesn't interest me a bit. Do you suppose there's anyone in the world as strange as I am? I don't have a mother or a father, Okyō. How could a child be born without either parent? It makes me pretty odd." He tapped at the rice cakes and decided they were done.

"Don't you have some kind of proof of

your identity? A charm with your name on it, for instance?[5] There must be something you have, some clue to your family's whereabouts."

"Nothing. My friends used to tease me. They said I was left underneath a bridge when I was born, so I'd be taken for a beggar's baby. It may be true. Who knows? I may be the child of a tramp. One of those men who pass by in rags every day could be a kinsman. That old crippled lady with one eye who comes begging every morning—for all I know, she could be my mother. I used to wear a lion's mask and do acrobatics in the street," he said dejectedly, "before I worked at the umbrella shop. Okyō, if I were a beggar's boy, you wouldn't have been so nice to me, would you? You wouldn't have given me a second look."

"You shouldn't joke like that, Kichizō. I don't know what kind of people your parents were, but it makes no difference to me. These silly things you're saying—you're not yourself tonight. If I were you, I wouldn't let it bother me. Even if I were the child of an outcast. I'd make something of myself, whether I had any parents or not, no matter who my brothers were. Why are you whining around so?"

"I don't know," he said, staring at the floor. "There's something wrong with me. I don't seem to have any get-up-and-go."

She was dead now, but in the last generation the old woman Omatsu, fat as a *sumō* wrestler, had made a tidy fortune at the umbrella shop. It was a winter's night six years before that she had picked up Kichizō, performing his tumbler's act along the road, as she was returning from a pilgrimage.

"It's all right," she had assured him. "If the master gives us any trouble, we'll worry about it when the time comes. I'll tell him what a poor boy you are, how your companions abandoned you when your feet were too sore to go on walking. Don't worry about it. No one will raise an eyebrow. There's always room for a child or two. Who's going to care if we spread out a few boards for you to sleep on in the kitchen, and give you a little bit to eat? There's no risk in that. Why, even with a formal apprenticeship boys have been known to disappear. It doesn't prevent them from running off with things that don't belong to them. There are all kinds of people in this world. You know what they say: 'You don't know a horse till you ride it.' How can we tell whether we can use you in the shop if we don't give you a try? But listen, if you don't want to go back to that slum of yours, you're going to have to work hard. And learn how things are done. You'll have to make up your mind: this is where your home is. You're going to have to work, you know."

And work he did. Today, by himself, Kichizō could treat as many umbrellas as three adults, humming a tune as he went about his business. Seeing this, people would praise the dead lady's foresight: "Granny knew what she was doing."

The old woman, to whom he owed so much, had been dead two years now, and the present owners of the shop and their son Hanji were hard for Kichizō to take. But what was he to do? Even if he didn't like them, he had nowhere else to go. Had not his anger and resentment at them caused his very bones and muscles to contract? "Dwarf! Dwarf!" everybody taunted him. "Eating fish on the anniversary of your parents' death! It serves you right that you're so short. Round and round we go—look at him! The tiny monk who'll never grow!"[6]

In his work, he could take revenge on the sniveling bullies, and he was perfectly ready to answer them with a clenched fist. But his valor sometimes left him. He didn't even know the date of his parents' death, he had no way to observe the yearly abstinences. It made him miserable, and he would throw himself down underneath the umbrellas drying in the yard and push his face against the ground to stifle his tears.

The boy was a little fireball. He had a violence about him that frightened the entire neighborhood. The sleeves of his plain kimono

would swing as he flailed his arms, and the smell of oil from the umbrellas followed him through every season. There was no one to calm his temper, and he suffered all the more. If anyone were to show Kichizō a moment's kindness, he knew that he would cling to him and find it hard ever to let go.

In the spring Okyō the seamstress had moved into the neighborhood. With her quick wit, she was soon friendly with everyone. Her landlord was the owner of the umbrella shop, and so she was especially cordial to the members of the shop. "Bring over your mending any time, boys. I don't care what condition it's in. There are so many people at your house, the mistress won't have time to tend to it. I'm always sewing anyway, one more stitch is nothing. Come and visit when you have time. I get lonely living by myself. I like people who speak their minds, and that rambunctious Kichizō—he's one of my favorites. Listen, the next time you lose your temper," she would tell him, "instead of hitting the little dog at the rice shop, come over to my place. I'll give you my mallet, and you can take out your anger on the fulling block.[7] That way, people won't be so upset with you. And you'll be helping me—it'll do us both good."

In no time Kichizō began to make himself at home. It was "Okyō, this" and "Okyō, that" until he had given the other workmen at the shop something new to tease him about. "Why, he's the mirror image of the great Chōemon!" they would laugh.[8] "At the River Katsura, Ohan will have to carry *him*! Can't you see the little runt perched on top of her sash for the ride across the river? What a farce!"

Kichizō was not without retort. "If you're so manly, why don't you ever visit Okyō? Which one of you can tell me each day what sweets she's put in the cookie jar? Take the pawnbroker with the bald spot. He's head over heels in love with her, always ordering sewing from her and coming round on one pretext or another, sending her aprons and neckpieces and sashes—trying to win her over. But she's

never given him the time of day. Let alone
treat him the way she does me! Kichizō from
the umbrella shop—*I'm* the one who can go
there any hour of the night, and when she
hears it's me, she'll open the door in her nightgown. 'You haven't come to see me all day.
Did something happen? I've been worried
about you.' That's how she greets me. Who
else gets treated that way? 'Hulking men are
like big trees: not always good supports.'[9] Size
has nothing to do with it. Look at how the tiny
peppercorn is prized."[10]

"Listen to him!" they would yell, pelting
Kichizō across the back.

But all he did was smile nonchalantly.
"Thank you very much." If only he had a little
height, no one would dare to tease him. As it
was, the disdain he showed them was dismissed
as nothing more than the impertinence of a
little fool. He was the butt of all their jokes
and the gossip they exchanged over tobacco.

On the night of the thirtieth of December,
Kichizō was returning home. He had been up
the hill to call on a customer with apologies
for the late filling of an order. On his way back
now he kept his arms folded across his chest
and walked briskly, kicking a stone with the
tip of his sandal. It rolled to the left and then
to the right, and finally Kichizō kicked it into a
ditch, chuckling aloud to himself. Three was
no one around to hear him. The moon above
shone brightly on the white winter roads, but
the boy was oblivious to the cold. He felt
invigorated. He thought he would stop by
Okyō's on the way home. As he crossed over
to the back street, he was suddenly startled:
someone appeared from behind him and covered his eyes. Whoever it was, the person
could not keep from laughing.

"Who is it? Come on, who is it?" When he
touched the hands held over his eyes, he knew
who it was. "Ah, Okyō! I can tell by your
snaky fingers.[11] You shouldn't scare people."

Kichizō freed himself and Okyō laughed.
"Oh, too bad! I've been discovered."

Over her usual jacket she was wearing a

hood that came down almost to her eyes. She
looked smart tonight, Kichizō thought as he
surveyed her appearance. "Where've you been?
I thought you told me you were too busy even
to eat the next few days." The boy did not
hide his suspicion. "Were you taking something to a customer?"

"I went to make some of my New Year's
calls early," she said innocently.

"You're lying. No one receives greetings on the
thirtieth. Where did you go? To your relatives?"

"As a matter of fact, I *am* goin to a
relative's—to live with a relative I hardly
know. Tomorrow I'll be moving. It's so sudden, it probably surprises you. It *is* unexpected, even I feel a little startled. Anyway,
you should be happy for me. It's not a bad
thing that's happened."

"Really? You're not teasing, are you? You
shouldn't scare me like this. If you went away,
what would I do for fun? Don't ever joke
about such things. You and your nonsense!"
He shook his head at her.

"I'm not joking. It's just as you said
once—good luck has come riding in a fancy
carriage. So I can't very well stay on in a back
tenement, can I? Now I'll be able to sew you
that kimono, Kichizō."

"I don't want it. When you say 'Good
luck has come,' you mean you're going off
some place worthless. That's what Hanji said
the other day. 'You know Okyō the seamstress?' he said. 'Her uncle—the one who gives
rubdowns over by the vegetable market—he's
helped her find a new position. She's going
into service with some rich family. Or so they
say. But it sounds fishy to me—she's too old to
learn sewing from some housewife. Somebody's going to set her up. I'm sure of it. She'll
be wearing tasseled coats the next time we see
her, la-de-da, and her hair all done up in ring-
lets, like a kept woman. You wait. With a face
like hers, you don't think she's about to spend
her whole life sewing, do you?' That's what he
said. I told him he was full of it, and we had a
big fight. But you *are* going to do it, aren't you?
You're going off to be someone's mistress!"

"It's not that I want to. I don't have much choice. I suppose I won't be able to see you any more, Kichizō, will I?"

With these few words, Kichizō withered. "I don't know, maybe it's a step up for you, but don't do it. It's not as if you can't make a living with your sewing. The only one you have to feed is yourself. When you're good at your work, why give it up for something so stupid? It's disgusting of you. Don't go through with it. It's not too late to change your mind." The boy was unyielding in his notion of integrity.

"Oh, dear," Okyō sighed. She stopped walking. "Kichizō, I'm sick of all this washing and sewing. Anything would be better. I'm tired of these drab clothes. I'd like to wear a crepe kimono, too, for a change—even if it is tainted."

They were bold words, and yet it didn't sound as if she herself fully comprehended them. "Anyway," she laughed, "come home with me. Hurry up now."

"What! I'm too disgusted. You go ahead," he said, but his long, sad shadow followed after her.

Soon they came to their street. Okyō stopped beneath the window where Kichizō always tapped for her. "Every night you come and knock at this window. After tomorrow night," she sighed, "I won't be able to hear your voice calling any more. How terrible the world is."

"It's not the world. It's you."

Okyō went in first and lit a lamp. "Kichizō, come get warm," she called when she had the fire in the brazier going.

He stood by the pillar. "No, thanks."

"Aren't you chilly? It won't do to catch a cold."

"I don't care." He looked down at the floor as he spoke. "Leave me alone."

"What's the matter with you? You're acting funny. Is it something I said? If it is, please tell me. When you stand around with a long face like that and won't talk to me, it makes me worry."

"You don't have to worry about anything. This is Kichizō from the umbrella shop you're talking to. I don't need any woman to take care of me." He rubbed his back against the pillar. "How pointless everything turns out. What a life! People are friendly, and then they disappear. It's always the ones I like. Granny at the umbrella shop, and Kinu, the one with short hair, at the dyer's shop. First Granny dies of palsy. Then Kinu goes and throws herself into the well behind the dyer's—she didn't want to marry. Now you're going off. I'm always disappointed in the end. Why should I be surprised, I suppose? What am I but a boy who oils umbrellas? So what if I do the work of a hundred men? I'm not going to win any prizes for it. Morning and night, the only title I ever hear is 'Dwarf'...'Dwarf'! I wonder if I'll ever get any taller. 'All things come to him who waits,'[12] they say, but I wait and wait, and all I get is more unhappiness. Just the day before yesterday I had a fight with Hanji over you. Ha! I was so sure he was wrong. I told him you were the last person rotten enough to go off and do that kind of thing. Not five days have passed, and I have to eat crow. How could I have thought of you as a sister? You, with all your lies and tricks, and your selfishness. This is the last you'll ever see of me. Ever. Thanks for your kindness. Go on and do what you want. From now on, I won't have anything to do with anyone. It's not worth it. Good-by, Okyō."

He went to the front door and began to put his sandals on.

"Kichizō! You're wrong. I'm leaving here, but I'm not abandoning you. You're like my little brother. How can you turn on me?" From behind, she hugged him with all her might. "You're too impatient. You jump to conclusions."

"You mean you're not going to be someone's mistress?" Kichizō turned around.

"It's not the sort of thing anybody wants to do. But it's been decided. You can't change things."

He stared at her with tears in his eyes.

"Take your hands off me, Okyō."

Translated by Robert Danly

NOTES

1. Narrow sleeves (*tsutsu-sode*), the better to work in.
2. Persimmon tannin was used to treat umbrellas.
3. A kind of carnival game, in which arrows were blown through a bamboo tube, with a prize for hitting the target.
4. ...The fiery cart has two meanings: (1) the carriage that drives sinners through hell, and (2) straitened circumstances....
5. Paper charms with a child's name written on them were placed inside a brocade bag and carried by the child for good luck and protection. The little charm-bags thus became a means of identification.
6. A song from a game that children played, forming a ring around one of their number and chanting....
7. A block on which cloth was cleaned, shrunk, and thickened with moisture, heat, and pressure.

8. An allusion to the puppet play *Katsuragawa Renri no Shigarami* (The River Katsura and the Floodgate of Eternal Love, 1858) by Suga Sensuke. In the play, Choemon, the head of a draper's shop, is a middle-aged man charged with watching after a 14-year-old girl, Ohan, when her father dies; in one scene he carries her across the Katsura River. Here, in an analogy to Kichizō's dependence on Okyō, the roles are reversed: Choemon rides to safety on Ohan's back.
9. The saying was that great, gawky trees would never make good pillars....
10. This too is based on a proverb:...A grain of pepper may be small, but it is very hot....
11. ...So-called because the first joint of the finger would bend, but not the second.
12. Literally, "Honey comes to him who waits."

Téffi   (Nadézhda Aleksandrovna Buchínskaya)

Russia/France, 1872–1952

Born Nadézhda Aleksandrovna Lokhvítskaya (later Buchínskaya), Téffi was the daughter of a well-known lawyer and criminologist and the younger sister of the famous Decadent poet Mírra (1869–1905, sometimes called the Russian Sappho). Although Téffi began her career as a poet obviously influenced by her sister and the Symbolist circle of which she was a part, only "Passiflóra" (1923) is considered of critical significance. Téffi's real importance rests instead on the largely comic plays, short stories, and journalistic sketches that she began publishing in 1910, in such journals as *Nóvaya zhizn* (The New Life, the first legal Bolshevik journal) and *Satirikon*, and in book form in some fifteen volumes, beginning in 1911. The most significant work of her Russian period is considered *Nezhivoy zvér* (The Lifeless Beast, 1916). Often compared to such satirical humorists as Chekov, Averchenko, and Zóshchenko, Téffi achieved such fame that, as with Colette, consumer products like candy and perfume were marketed and sold under her name.

Téffi's popularity with both liberal and conservative Russians at home (she herself supported the 1905 and 1917 revolutions) assured her a prominant place in the publications of the emgré community when she arrived in Paris in 1920—the journals *Gryadúshchaya Rossíya* (Russia of the Future) and *Poslednie novosti* (The Latest News). Moreover, her satirical wit and lucid dialogue made her words proverbial for the chaos and illusion that characterized emigré life. In addition to short stories, she wrote an adventure novel, *Avantyurnyi roman* (1932), a volume of reminiscences, *Vospominániya* (1932), and a collection of plays (1934), two of which were later successfully produced. Her most ambitious works of this period appear in *Vechérnii den* (The Nocturnal Day, 1924).

Between 1939 and the end of World War II, having been forced to live under the Nazi regime she despised, Téffi first sunk into anonymity and then reemerged, old, sick, and impoverished. Nonetheless, she continued to write—*Vsyó o lyubví* (*All about Love*, 1930), from which the selection here is taken, and *Zemnáya raduga* (The Earthly Rainbow), published posthumously in 1952. Her painful last years are documented in letters to Andréy Sedýkh (1963). Like many other emigré writers, Téffi experienced a decline in her reputation in the Soviet Union in the late 1920s, and her works disappeared until the post-Khrushchev era, when volumes of her poetry, sketches, and finally short stories were published there.

THE NIGHTMARE
Koshmár

The nightmare lasted four years.

Four years poor Véra Sergéevna knew no peace or night. Day and night she was conscious of the fact that her happiness was dangling on a thread, that today or tomorrow that insolent hussy Elíza Gértz might steal Nikoláy Andréevich away from her once and for all. He was already enamoured of her.

Poor Véra Sergéevna fought for her heart and hearth with every resource that modern civilization had placed in the hands of a sensible and energetic woman: she wrote herself anonymous letters and then showed them to her wayward husband; she assured him constantly of their son's brilliant intellect and emphasized how important firm family foundations were for the nurturance of such a chosen creature; she created a comfortable and cozy domestic life and planned interesting parties, to which she invited prominent people; she took care of her appearance, exercised, was massaged, painstakingly performed her toilette, did everything she could to be young, intelligent, and beautiful in the eyes of her husband. Never, even in the first years of their married life, had she been so in love with him as in these four years of the nightmare.

And indeed, if Nikoláy Andréevich could have been attractive to anyone, it would have been during these four years. He had become elegant, vigorous, and mysterious, now stormily cheerful, now melancholy. He recited verse and gave his wife presents, even compliments —mainly, we suppose, as he was hurrying out of the house, afraid of being detained.

"Darling, how attractive you are today," he would mutter distractedly, kissing her forehead. "You should always wear that dress."

Or: "Are you having guests today!? I'm terribly sorry I can't be here. But I'll send you a basket of flowers. Let everyone see that I'm still in love with my kitten."

He always smelled of stirring scents, although he himself didn't use any. He was always humming something, exuding an air of infatuation—at which everyone would smile uneasily, casting sly glances at each other and tittering themes of love.

Once a year Elíza Gértz gave a concert. Véra Sergéevna would order a magnificent toilette for that evening. She'd gather her friends together at dinner and then invite them to her loge. Nikoláy Andréevich would sit separately in the parterre, and she would follow the expression of his face with her opera glasses.

Nikoláy Andréevich really was enchanted with Elíza Gértz. His quiet, careful, businesslike nature was as unlike Elíza's personality as the land from the sea, yet he swam in her, dove, and snorted with pleasure. All her elegant rabble amazed and moved him: the polished dandies with stomachs rumbling with hunger; the languishing ladies with glued-on eyelashes, whose belongings were always being held by some hotel for non-payment of their rooms; the breakfasts at five in the evening, dinners at one in the morning, unexpected dances—all the intricacies of the relationships between these strange and fascinating people. And the strangest and most fascinating of all— incomprehensible, unknown to the end, tormenting both herself and others, brilliant, talented, goddess, devil, snake—was Elíza Gértz.

In all four years Nikoláy Andréevich was not for a single day calm or sure of what the next day would bring. He never understood a thing about her.

One day she returned she expensive bracelet he had sent her, scrawling in pencil on a scrap of paper: "I didn't expect such boorishness. I'm embarrassed for you." Confused and humiliated, he did not dare appear before her for two whole days and wracked his brains to understand why she could have taken such offense when just three days earlier he had given her twenty thousand which she nonchalantly dropped into her purse, actually yawning in the process.

Another time, after receiving a basket of oranges from him, she got down on her knees before him and said there was so much innocent beauty in this action of his that she had cried tears of ecstasy all morning, then ordered a compote made from the oranges.

He never knew what was awaiting him. He often returned home offended and humiliated and sought consolation in Véra Sergéevna's devotion.

"Verúsya, you're an angel, and I'm a pig," he would say. "But you know even a pig has a right to demand his share of respect and affection. Hug me, tell me, is our Volódya really a remarkable boy? I want to live for you and for him only. Really, just for the two of you!"

Sometimes, like a meteor, like a meteor sparkling with joy, he would run home for just a moment, humming an operetta tune: "Goodbye, Verúsya. You are my life. Don't hold me back—some boring business is calling. Tra-la-la! Boring, tra-la-la! Business, la-de-da!"

And off he'd go again.

The nightmare ended unexpectedly.

For a long time Elíza had been talking about a singing engagement in Argentina. Nikoláy Andréevich had grown used to these discussions and didn't pay any particular attention to them. From time to time he had to sign checks made out to some middleman, but then he often had to give out money for the most incomprehensible needs—for some sort of advertising (what sort he didn't know), for liquidating a debt from a concert that was absolutely assured to bring in a profit, and so on. Consequently, he didn't give special significance to these middlemen. Then suddenly it turned out that the Argentinian tour was not a mirage at all, but an imminent reality, and Elíza had only to secure a passport to leave right away.

The proposed half-year's separation didn't particularly bother Nikoláy Andréevich, though, at least not at first. "I'll relax, have a long sleep, and conduct my business affairs," he cheered himself.

Elíza's whole set went to see her off in Marseilles. It was an intoxicating, merry occasion.

For a long time Nikoláy Andréevich could not tear himself away from Elíza's life. He made the rounds of restaurants with her friend Milúsha in order to talk about Elíza, try to learn more about her and verify certain facts he already had.

Then he got tired of Milúsha. She was dumb and unattractive and wore Elíza's old dresses. And everything she said about her friend somehow simplified Elíza, made her comprehensible, deprived her of anxieties and mysteries.

He soon got rid of Milúsha.

Then a letter came from Elíza with tales of raging success and a request for money.

With great delight he immediately sent the sum demanded.

Five months later a second demand arrived.

He fulfilled that, too, but no longer with delight.

Her letters smelled of a new perfume, like incense. Very disagreeable.

Nikoláy Andréevich became bored.

Weariness from the sleepless nights, the drinking binges, and the anxieties of the past year soon told on him. He took to lazily dealing out solitaire, grumbling at his wife, and falling into bed at ten o'clock.

At first Véra Sergéevna regarded the happy change in her life with pleasure. Then she began to worry because her flighty husband, who had always given her complete freedom, suddenly sat immobile at home. Twice he expressed great indignation when she returned home late from her bridge game. She felt some annoyance and even boredom from such behavior on his part.

"Well, this shouldn't last long," she consoled herself. "That woman will return soon enough and everything will be as it was before."

But everything wasn't as it was before.

Nikoláy Andréevich received a new demand from Argentina, which he venomously answered by telegram: "You will receive it only if we meet in person." The answer came over the wire, a single word in roman letters: "Bastard."

Véra Sergéevna, who by rights of an innocent sufferer often rummaged through her unfaithful husband's desk (she had even equipped herself very cleverly with a small button hook for this purpose), read this telegram with mixed emotions of despair and delight.

Delight sang: the nightmare is over.

Despair moaned: what will happen now?

And despair was right.

The once fascinating and tender Nikoláy Andréevich, now like a dishevelled boar, leapt out of his study with bills in his hands and gave his poor suffering wife such a chewing out for the dress from Chanel and the hat from Desca that she bitterly longed for the difficult years of the nightmare.

And then a new misfortune appeared: their "brilliant" boy turned out to be dumb. He had failed to get his diploma for the third time, and when his father—with reason—called him an idiot, the young scion, sticking

his upper lip out like a trunk, said very clearly: "Idiot? It must be hereditary."

Suddenly the parents noticed with horror that he was lop-eared, with a low forehead and a dirty neck. In general, he was nothing to be proud of. But it was already too late to thrash him. Véra Sergéevna reproached her husband for neglecting the child, and her husband reproached her for fussing over him too much. Everything was unpleasant and dull.

In such an atmosphere it was no use even thinking about maintaining their former way of life. What need was there for parties with refined guests? And on top of everything else, Nikoláy Andréevich was becoming carping and stingy. He hung around the house, eternally sticking his nose into everything. It got to the point that when Véra Sergéevna bought a piece of smoked sturgeon for dinner, he called her, in front of the servant, a witch, always choosing a word inappropriate to the given occasion, but one which was nonetheless very insulting and coarse.

So that's how things were.

Nikoláy Andréevich tried to rouse himself. He took a young ballerina out to dinner. But he was so bored with her that later, when she began to call him every day on the telephone, he asked his wife, Véra Sergéevna, to put the ballerina in her place for him.

Véra Sergéevna stopped dressing up and taking care of herself. She unravelled at the seams and aged quickly.

She often fell to thinking bitterly: "Yes! Not too long ago I was a woman who lived a full life. I loved, envied, and sought oblivion in the whirl of society."

"How boring Paris has become," she would sigh. "Not at all the same atmosphere. Everything is somehow extinguished and gloomy."

"It's all on account of the recession," friends explained to her.

She would shake her head mistrustfully, and one time, turning pale and flushing, she asked the old profligate, Colonel Eróshin, her husband's friend: "Tell me, do you know why that singer, Elíza Gértz, doesn't return from South America?"

"God knows," the Colonel answered indifferently. "Maybe she doesn't have the money to come back."

"Don't you think it would be worth it to send her money for the trip?" Véra Sergéevna asked, even more agitated. "Maybe you could talk it over with my husband? Hm?"

Translated by Darra Goldstein

Willa Cather   *US, 1873–1947*

Born in Virginia, Willa Cather was the eldest of seven children. When she was 10, her family moved to Nebraska, then a frontier state, and the setting for Cather's most famous novels. She graduated from the University of Nebraska in 1895 and lived in Pittsburgh, Pennsylania, for ten years with her lover, Isabelle McClung, honing her journalistic skills at several periodicals, and teaching high school. Cather moved to New York City and became managing editor of *McClure's* magazine, whose namesake was Cather's mentor and the subject of "Ardessa" (1918), an early story. In New York Cather became involved with Edith Lewis, who wrote an unexceptional memoir of Cather. Before leaving *McClure's* to concentrate on her art, she published a book of poetry, a book of stories, *The Troll Garden* (1905), and wrote her first novel, *Alexander's Bridge* (1912), under the influence of Henry James.

Sharon O'Brien, in *Willa Cather: The Emerging Voice* (1987), has identified a conflict in Cather's early work and life between the traditional role of a woman, defined in relation to others, and the more compelling role of the solitary artist. Symptomatically, Cather's first novel, and some of the later ones, have male narrators. Moreover, some of her early stories, aesthetically unfinished and psychologically naked, reveal a troubled sense of the relations between mothers and daughters. Her second novel, *O Pioneers*! (1913), about the stamina of heroic frontier women, transforms these conflicts into a sophisticated work of art. Cather here breaks with the influence of Henry James, to fashion out of "native" materials an indigenous realism. She dedicated the novel to the prominent local-colorist, and Cather's latest mentor, Sarah Orne Jewett (1849–1909).

The Song of the Lark (1915) and *Lucy Gayheart* (1935) examine the music world, a favored subject in Cather's oeuvre. Her criticism, which includes essays on Christina Rossetti, George Eliot, and Katherine Mansfield, is collected in two volumes, *The Kingdom of Art: Willa Cather's First Principles and Critical Statements, 1893 to 1896* (Ed. B. Slote, 1966), and *The World and the Parish: Willa Cather's Articles and Reviews, 1893–1902* (Ed. W.M. Curtin, 1970). In the significantly titled *Not Under Forty* (1936), a late collection assembled by Cather herself, from which the selection is taken, Cather suggests that her writer's credo has no attraction for a new generation—as if, after the Great War, the "world broke in two."

Her most popular novel, *My Antonía* (1918), tells the story of an eastern lawyer's admiration for an immigrant pioneer woman who partakes of "eternal" values. Because she seems less a real woman, and more a personification of male desire, critics dispute the interpretation of Antonía, a situation complicated by Cather's homosexuality. In *The Professor's House* (1925), also narrated by a man, Cather explores the psychology of regression, the unfulfillable desire to retreat, as if from post–World War I American technology and materialism, to a simpler state of connectedness. After the death of her father, Cather entered a religious phase, writing *Death Comes for the Archbishop* (1927). In the final phase of her career her writing evokes her family's past and her complex feelings for her mother.

Cather's significant literary reputation has primarily been based on a few of her works, perceived as nostalgia pieces: the much anthologized story "Paul's Case," *My Antonía*, and *Death Comes for the Archbishop*. Supported by the University of Nebraska, Bernice Slote and other recent feminist critics have won critical recognition for Cather's so-called minor works: *A Lost Lady* (1923) and *My Mortal Enemy* (1926), among others, which do not have Nebraska or the South as their exclusive settings. These works reveal a writer less provincial in locale and narrative technique than some of her more favored works would indicate.

Eric Mendelsohn

THE NOVEL *DÉMEUBLÉ*[1]

The novel, for a long while, has been over-furnished. The property-man has been so busy on its pages, the importance of material objects and their vivid presentation have been so stressed, that we take it for granted whoever can observe, and can write the English language, can write a novel. Often the latter qualification is considered unnecessary.

In any discussion of the novel, one must make it clear whether one is talking about the novel as a form of amusement, or as a form of art; since they serve very different purposes and in very different ways. One does not wish the egg one eats for breakfast, or the morning paper, to be made of the stuff of immortality. The novel manufactured to entertain great multitudes of people must be considered exactly like a cheap soap or a cheap perfume, or cheap furniture. Fine quality is a distinct disadvantage in articles made for great numbers of people who do not want quality but quantity, who do not want a thing that "wears," but who want change—a succession of new things

that are quickly threadbare and can be lightly thrown away. Does anyone pretend that if the Woolworth store windows were piled high with Tanagra figurines[2] at ten cents, they could for a moment compete with Kewpie[3] brides in the popular esteem? Amusement is one thing; enjoyment of art is another.

Every writer who is an artist knows that his "power of observation," and his "power of description," form but a low part of his equipment. He must have both, to be sure; but he knows that the most trivial of writers often have a very good observation. Mérimée said in his remarkable essay on Gogol: "L'art de choisir parmi les innombrable traits que nous offre la nature est, après tout, bien plus difficile que celui de les observer avec attention et de les rendre avec exactitude."[4]

There is a popular superstition that "realism" asserts itself in the cataloguing of a great number of material objects, in explaining mechanical processes, the methods of operating manufactories and trades, and in minutely and unsparingly describing physical sensations. But is not realism, more than it is anything else, an attitude of mind on the part of the writer toward his material, a vague indication of the sympathy and candor with which he accepts, rather than chooses, his theme? Is the story of a banker who is unfaithful to his wife and who ruins himself by speculation in trying to gratify the caprices of his mistresses, at all reinforced by a masterly exposition of banking, our whole system of credits, the methods of the Stock Exchange? Of course, if the story is thin, these things do reinforce it in a sense—any amount of red meat thrown into the scale to make the beam dip. But are the banking system and the Stock Exchange worth being written about at all? Have such things any proper place in imaginative art?

The automatic reply to this question is the name of Balzac.[5] Yes, certainly, Balzac tried out the value of literalness in the novel, tried it out to the uttermost, as Wagner did the value of scenic literalness in the music drama. He tried it, too, with the passion of discovery, with the inflamed zest of an unexampled curiosity. If the heat of that furnace could not give hardness and sharpness to material accessories, no other brain will ever do it. To reproduce on paper the actual city of Paris; the houses, the upholstery, the food, the wines, the game of pleasure, the game of business, the game of finance: a stupendous ambition—but, after all, unworthy of an artist. In exactly so far as he succeeded in pouring out on his pages that mass of brick and mortar and furniture and proceedings in bankruptcy, in exactly so far he defeated his end. The things by which he still lives, the types of greed and avarice and ambition and vanity and lost innocence of heart which he created—are as vital today as they were then. But their material surroundings, upon which he expended such labor and pains...the eye glides over them. We have had too much of the interior decorator and the "romance of business" since his day. The city

he built on paper is already crumbling. Stevenson[6] said he wanted to blue-pencil a great deal of Balzac's "presentation"—and he loved him beyond all modern novelists. But where is the man who could cut one sentence from the stories of Mérimée? And who wants any more detail as to how Carmencita and her fellow factory-girls made cigars? Another sort of novel? Truly. Isn't it a better sort?

In this discussion another great name naturally occurs. Tolstoi[7] was almost as great a lover of material things as Balzac, almost as much interested in the way dishes were cooked, and people were dressed, and houses were furnished. But there is this determining difference: the clothes, the dishes, the haunting interiors of those old Moscow houses, are always so much a part of the emotions of the people that they are perfectly synthesized; they seem to exist, not so much in the author's mind, as in the emotional penumbra of the characters themselves. When it is fused like this, literalness ceases to be literalness—it is merely part of the experience.

If the novel is a form of imaginative art, it cannot be at the same time a vivid and brilliant form of journalism. Out of the teeming, gleaming stream of the present it must select the eternal material of art. There are hopeful signs that some of the younger writers are trying to break away from mere verisimilitude, and, following the development of modern painting, to interpret imaginatively the material and social investiture of their characters; to present their scene by suggestion rather than by enumeration. The higher processes of art are all processes of simplification. The novelist must learn to write, and then he must unlearn it; just as the modern painter learns to draw, and then learns when utterly to disregard his accomplishment, when to subordinate it to a higher and truer effect. In this direction only, it seems to me, can the novel develop into anything more varied and perfect than all the many novels that have gone before.

One of the very earliest American romances might well serve as a suggestion to later writers. In *The Scarlet Letter* how truly in the spirit of art is the mise-en-scène presented. That drudge, the theme-writing high-school student, could scarcely be sent there for information regarding the manners and dress and interiors of Puritan society. The material investiture of the story is presented as if unconsciously; by the reserved, fastidious hand of an artist, not by the gaudy fingers of a showman or the mechanical industry of a department store window-dresser. As I remember it, in the twilight melancholy of that book, in its consistent mood, one can scarcely ever see the actual surroundings of the people; one feels them, rather, in the dusk.

Whatever is felt upon the page without being specifically named there—that, one might say, is created. It is the inexplicable presence of the thing not named, of the overtone divined by the ear but not heard by it, the verbal mood, the emotional aura of the fact or the thing or the deed, that gives high quality to the novel or the drama, as well as to poetry itself.

Literalness, when applied to the presenting of mental reactions and of physical sensations, seems to be no more effective than when it is applied to material things. A novel crowded with physical sensations is no less a catalogue than one crowded with furniture. A book like *The Rainbow* by D.H. Lawrence[8] sharply reminds one how vast a distance lies between emotion and mere sensory reactions. Characters can be almost dehumanized by a laboratory study of the behavior of their bodily organs under sensory stimuli—can be reduced, indeed, to mere animal pulp. Can one imagine anything more terrible than the story of *Romeo and Juliet* rewritten in prose by D.H. Lawrence?

How wonderful it would be if we could throw all the furniture out of the window; and along with it, all the meaningless reiterations concerning physical sensations, all the tiresome old patterns, and leave the room as bare as the stage of a Greek theatre, or as that house into which the glory of Pentecost descended; leave the scene bare for the play of emotions, great and little—for the nursery tale, no less than the tragedy, is killed by tasteless amplitude. The elder Dumas enunciated a great principle when he said that to make a drama, a man needed one passion, and four walls.[9]

NOTES

1. Literally, unfurnished; uncluttered, unadorned.
2. Third-century terra cotta figurines, usually of elegantly draped women, mass produced at Tanagra in Mycenaean Greece.
3. Mass-produced dolls of the twentieth century, modelled after the illustrated adventure story of the Kewpies, by Rose O'Neil (1874–1944) that appeared in *Ladies Home Journal*, beginning in 1909.
4. Prosper Mérimée (1803–1870): French experimental short story writer, transitional figure between romanticism and realism; among the first to appreciate Russian writers of literature. Nikolai Gogol (1809–1852): his short fiction for inspiration on native materials; combining the realistic and the grotesque, he is considered a highly moral, spiritual writer.
   "The art of choosing among innumerable traits that nature offer us is after all more difficult than that of observing them with attention and rendering them with exactitude."
5. Honoré de Balzac (1799–1850). Politically reactionary, in *La Comedie humaine* (*The Human Comedy*), he sought to document life under the Bourbon restoration (1814–1830) and the July Monarchy.
6. Robert Louis Stevenson (1850–1894): popular Scottish novelist, essayist, and poet, occasional resident of and writer about America. He sought to restore the romance and is best known for *Dr. Jekyll and Mr. Hyde*.
7. Leo Tolstoy (1828–1910): Russian novelist and moralist; author of *War and Peace* and *Anna Karenina*.
8. D.H. Lawrence (1885–1930): British modernist novelist who glorified sexuality in such works as *Sons and Lovers* (1913), *the Rainbow* (1915) and *Women in Love* (1926).
9. The elder Dumas (1802–1870): French writer of the popular Romantic novels *The Three Musketeers* (1884) and *The Count of Monte Cristo* (1845).

Colette   (Sidonie-Gabrielle Colette)   *France, 1873–1954*

In a period spanning eight of the ten decades covered by this anthology, Colette was mime, actress, journalist, critic, lecturer, novelist, and short story writer, businesswoman and promoter, daughter and mother, three times a wife, and many times a lover. It is difficult to reduce her life and its varied achievements, as well as commentary on her works, to a small compass.

Born Sidonie-Gabrielle Colette, the youngest child of the woman she called "the most important person of all my life" and whom she immortalized as Sido (*Sido*, 1930), Colette seems to have owed her resources to her happy childhood in the Burgundian countryside. She evoked that period of her life in the book that marked a turning point in her fiction, *La Retraite sentimentale* (*The Retreat from Love*, 1907), as well as in *Dialogues de bêtes* (*Barks and Purrs*, 1904) and *La Maison de Claudine* (*My Mother's House*, 1922), all of them bringing a new sensuality and pastorality to French literature. In 1893 she moved to Paris with her first husband, the notorious Willy (Henri Gauthier-Villars), who in the now legendary story initiated her writing career by claiming poverty and forcing her to write the *Claudine* and *Minne* series (1900–1905) that he then published under his own name. Leaving him in 1906, Colette became a music-hall performer, a famous if scandalous figure of *la belle époque* known for her lesbian affairs; this part of her life came to an end with her second marriage to Henry de Jouvenel and the birth of a daughter when Colette was 40. Ten years later, when she was already an acknowledged star of the modern novel, along with Proust and Gide, Colette once again embarked on a tempestuous affair and journalistic career with Maurice Goudeket, whom she married in 1935. Her life with him was interrupted only when he was arrested and held briefly by the Gestapo in 1941. During her last years, she was confined by painful arthritis, but her public still grew when *Gigi* (1944) was adapted for the stage (1951) and then issued as a hugely popular film.

Colette's life and works are inseparable: she herself proved "her greatest fictional character," as Elaine Marks has commented. Colette was hailed for her uncanny ability to evoke a particular milieu: the evocation of nature, animals, and childhood, on the one hand; the world of Paris between the wars and the demimonde, of which she was a part, on the other. But Colette's greatness transcends her stylistic achievements. It lies first in her psychology of the feminine: with *The Vagabond* (1911), Colette first posed the great twentieth-century conflict between marriage and career; and from that work to *L'etoile Vesper* (The Evening Star, 1946), Colette's "free and fettered" heroines never renounce love while learning painfully not to lose themselves in its mirage. It lies second in her awareness of the conditions of modernity: with the publication of *Chéri* (1920) and *The Last of Chéri* (1926), Colette conveyed what Mauriac called "the wretchedness of man without God" and what other critics have seen as the power—and illusion—of sexuality.

For this greatness, Colette was widely recognized, by, among others, Proust and the Comtesse Anna de Noailles, whom she was chosen to replace in the Académie Royale de Langue et de Littérature Françaises de Belgiques in 1936. In

1945, she was the second woman to be elected to the Académie Goncourt. At her death, she was accorded a state funeral. A new biography by Michèle Sarde, making extensive use of Colette's letters and diaries, pays homage to her life and work.

Colettes collected works' were published beginning in 1948. The selection, taken from *Paysages et Portraits* (Country Scenes and Portraits, 1958), written some time in the 1920s, is shadowed by World War I. The story evokes both the fashion of the Romantic era of the 1830s as well as the rage for short hair that swept the fashionable world when "the "flapper" and her French equivalent "la garçonne" became the new woman of the twentieth century. The selection may also allude to the rage of Maeterlinck's opera *Pelléas et Mélisande* (1892) in which Mélisande's long hair is an important symbol of something less than emancipation.

from MY FRIEND, VALENTINE
Mon amie Valentine

My friend Valentine sat down, powdered the wings of her nose, the hollow of her chin and, after a friendly exchange of compliments, was silent. I viewed this with some surprise, for on days when we have nothing to say to each other, my friend Valentine embroiders with ease on that theme "Ah, subjects of conversation are becoming so rare!"—a good three-quarters of an hour of scintillating palaver...

She was quiet and I saw that she had changed something about the carriage of her head. With a slightly timid air, she had lowered her head and was looking at me from under her jutting brow.

"I've cut my hair," she confessed suddenly, and took off her hat.

The beautiful blond hair on the nape of her neck showed its fresh cut, still rebelling against the metal, and from a part on the left a big Chateaubriand-style wave swept down across her forehead.

"It doesn't look too bad on me, does it?" my friend asked with false daring.

"Surely not."

"I was just at the Hickses', they gave me hundreds of compliments, Monsieur Hicks told me I look like...guess."

"Like someone convalescing from typhoid fever?"

"Very funny, really...but that's not it."

"Like Dujardin-Beaumetz, only more shorn? Like Drummont, without his glasses?"

"Wrong again. Like an English peeress, my dear!"

"The Hickses know some English peeresses, do they?"

"You're sidestepping the question, as usual. Does it look good or bad on me?"

"Good. Very good, in fact, But I'm thinking about that long hair which is nothing but dead, golden grass now. Tell me, why did you have your hair cut too, like everybody else?"

My friend Valentine shrugged her shoulders. "How do I know?... Just an idea, that's all. I couldn't stand myself in long hair anymore...And then, it's the fashion. In England, it seems that..."

"Yes, yes, but why else?"

"Well, Charlotte Lysès cut hers," she says evasively. "And even Sorel. I haven't seen her, but I heard that she's wearing her hair 'like a Roman gladiator.' And Annie de Pène, and hundreds of other women of taste whose names I could mention, and..."

"And Polaire."

My friend paused in astonishment. "Polaire? She hasn't had her hair cut."

"I thought she had."

"She has very long short hair. That doesn't have anything to do with the current fashion. Polaire wears her hair like Polaire. I didn't think of Polaire for a minute when I was having my hair cut."

"What did you think of? I would like to try and understand, through you, why women are contagiously clipping their hair, level with the ear, so much hair which until now was pampered, waved, perfumed..."

She stood up impatiently, and walked around, tossing her romantic forelock.

"You're funny...I don't know. I couldn't stand my long hair anymore, I'm telling you. And besides it's hot. And at night that long braid would pull at the back of my neck, and it would get rolled up around my arm..."

"Thirty years wasn't long enough for you to get used to that thick, beautiful cable?"

"It seems that way. You question me, and I answer you, only because I'm so nice. Oh, yes, the other morning, my braid got caught in a dresser drawer I'd pushed shut. I hate that. And when we were having those air-raid alerts, it became a scourge; no one enjoys looking grotesque even in a cellar, now do they, with a chignon that's collapsing on one side and

unraveling on the other. I could have died a thousand deaths because of that hair...And then, in the end, it can't be reasoned about. I cut my hair because I cut my hair."

In front of the mirror, she subdued her curls, and aired her 1830s wave, with newly acquired gestures. How many newly shorn women have already invoked, in order to excuse the same vandalism, reasons of coquetry, herd instinct, anglophilia—and even economy — before arriving at: "How do I know?"

One came up with "My neuralgia..."

"You understand, I had had it with bleaching, I just had to do something new with my hair..." explained another.

"It's cleaner," imagined a third. "You can wash your hair at the same time as the rest, in the bath..."

My friend Valentine did not add a novel lie of her own to this lot of modest verities. But her attitude, like theirs, is that of a prisoner who has just broken her chains. So I can assume myself—in the free coquetry of a head no longer weighed down by a pinned-up coil of hair, in the pride of a forehead on which the wind scatters a slightly masculine curliness—I can amuse myself by reading or imagining in it the joy of having shaken off an old fear that the war, the approach of the enemy had roused from a long oblivion, and the barely conscious memory of the frantic flight of women before the barbarians when they ran naked and the flag of their hair, behind them, was suddenly knotted in the fist of their ravisher...

Nellie McClung   *Canada, 1873–1951*

Writer, reformer, suffragist, and mother of five, Nellie Letitia Mooney McClung is the personification of early twentieth-century Canadian feminism. A "maternal suffragist," McClung believed that only women had the spiritual and moral resources to reform society, and she worked tirelessly for female suffrage, prohibition, property and pension rights for women, and factory safety legislation, her motto being "Never retract, never explain, never apologize—get the thing done and let them howl."

Born near Chatsworth, Grey County, Ontario, the youngest of six children and raised on a Manitoba homestead, McClung did not attend school until she was 10. At 16, she graduated from the Manitoba Normal School in Winnipeg, and she taught in a rural school until she married Robert McClung, a pharmacist (and later insurance dealer), in 1896. She gained prominence through the Woman's Christian Temperance Union, of which her beloved mother-in-law was provincial president, an association working for prohibition and women's rights. McClung was catapulated to national fame with the publication in 1908 of her best-selling first novel, *Sowing Seeds in Danny*, loosely based on her own life and focussed on young Pearl Watson and her courageous rural family. This was followed by fifteen other books, including *In Times Like These* (1915, reprinted 1972), excerpted below, a classic statement of Canadian feminism.

In Winnipeg after the First World War, McClung played a leading role in the Liberal victory over Sir Rodmond Roblin's Conservative government, which in 1916 won the vote for the women of Manitoba—the first in Canada. Eschewing the violence of their British counterparts, the Manitoba suffragists appealed directly to Roblin to extend the franchise. When their pleas failed, they staged a satire in the form of a mock parliament, with McClung playing the part of the premier as the women in power reject the request for votes for men, stating that "men's place is on the farm."

Moving to Edmonton, Alberta, McClung served as the only woman on the Dominion War Council in 1918, as Canada's only woman representative both at the League of Nations in 1918 and also at the Ecumenical Council of the Methodist Church in 1921, the year she was elected a Liberal Member of the Legislative Assembly for Edmonton (placing her amongst the first women in the British Empire to serve in a provincial legislature). Her greatest triumph came in 1929 before the Privy Council in London, England. She was one of the "famous five" appellants, who successfully challenged the British North America Act, which had denied that women were "persons" (a stand upheld by the Supreme Court of Canada), thereby finally gaining women the right to sit as senators.

In the 1930s, McClung settled on Vancouver Island, writing two autobiographical volumes—*Clearing in the West* (1935) and *The Stream Runs Fast* (1945)—and serving as the first woman on the Board of Governors of the Canadian Broadcasting Corporation. Following her death in 1951, the Women's Institute of Grey County, Ontario, erected a monument on the property on which McClung was born, honoring the achievements of this famous crusader whose extraordinary life demonstrated her conviction that "nothing is too good to be true."

Wendy Robbins Keitner

WHAT DO WOMEN THINK OF WAR?
(NOT THAT IT MATTERS)

Bands in the street, and resounding cheers,
And honor to him whom the army led!
But his mother moans thro' her
                              blinding tears—
'My boy is dead—is dead!'

"Madam," said Charles XI of Sweden to his wife when she appealed to him for mercy to some prisoner, "I married you to give me children, not to give me advice." That was said a long time ago, and the haughty old Emperor put it rather crudely, but he put it straight. This is still the attitude of the world towards women. That men are human beings, but women are women, with one reason for their existence, has long been the dictum of the world.

More recent philosophers have been more adroit—they have sought to soften the blow, and so they palaver the women by telling them what a tremendous power they are for good. They quote the men who have said: "All that I am my mother made me." They also quote that old iniquitous lie, about the hand that rocks the cradle ruling the world.

For a long time men have been able to hush women up by these means; and many women have gladly allowed themselves to be deceived. Sometimes when a little child goes driving with his father he is allowed to hold the ends of the reins, and encouraged to believe that he is driving, and it works quite well with a very small child. Women have been deceived in the same way into believing that they are the controlling factor in the world. Here and there, there have been doubters among women who have said: "If it be true that the hand that rocks the cradle rules the world, how comes the liquor traffic and the white slave traffic to prevail among us unchecked? Do women wish for these things? Do the gentle mothers whose hands rule the world declare in favor of these things?" Every day the number of doubters has increased, and now women everywhere realize that a bad old lie has been put over on them for years. The hand that rocks the cradle does not rule the world. If it did, human life would be held dearer and the world would be a sweeter, cleaner, safer place than it is now!

Women are naturally the guardians of the race, and every normal woman desires children. Children are not a handicap in the race of life either, they are an inspiration. We hear too much about the burden of motherhood and too little of its benefits. The average child does well for his parents, and teaches them many things. Bless his little soft hands—he broadens our outlook, quickens our sympathies, and leads us, if we will but let him, into all truth. A child pays well for his board and keep.

Deeply rooted in every woman's heart is the love and care of children. A little girl's first toy is a doll, and so, too, her first great sorrow is when her doll has its eyes poked out by her little brother. Dolls have suffered many things at the hands of their maternal uncles.

There, little girl, don't cry,
They have broken your doll, I know,

contains in it the universal note of woman's woe!

But just as the woman's greatest sorrow has come through her children, so has her greatest development. Women learned to cook, so that their children might be fed; they learned to sew that their children might be clothed, and women are learning to think so that their children may be guided.

Since the war broke out women have done a great deal of knitting. Looking at this great army of women struggling with rib and back seam, some have seen nothing in it but a "fad" which has supplanted for the time tatting and bridge. But it is more than that. It is the desire to help, to care for, to minister; it is the same spirit which inspires our nurses to go out and bind up the wounded and care for the dying. The woman's outlook on life is to save, to care for, to help. Men make wounds and women bind them up, and so the women, with their hearts filled with love and sorrow, sit in their quiet homes and knit.

Comforter—they call it—yes—
So it is for my distress,
For it gives my restless hands
Blessed work. God understands
How we women yearn to be
Doing something ceaselessly.

Women have not only been knitting— they have been thinking. Among other things they have thought about the German women, those faithful, patient, homeloving, obedient women, who never interfere in public affairs, nor question man's ruling. The Kaiser says women have only two concerns in life, cooking and children, and the German women have accepted his dictum. They are good cooks and faithful nurses to their children.

According to the theories of the world, the sons of such women should be the gentlest men on earth. Their home has been so sacred, and well-kept; their mother has been so gentle, patient and unworldly—she has never lowered the standard of her womanhood by asking to vote, or to mingle in the "hurly burly" of politics. She has been humble, and loving, and always hoped for the best.

According to the theories of the world, the gentle sons of gentle mothers will respect and reverence all womankind everywhere. Yet, we know that in the invasion of Belgium, the German soldiers made a shield of Belgian women and children in front of their army; no child was too young, no woman too old, to escape their cruelty; no mother's prayers, no child's appeal could stay their fury! These chivalrous sons of gentle, loving mothers marched through the land of Belgium, their nearest neighbor, leaving behind them smoking trails of ruin, black as their own hard hearts!

What, then, is the matter with the theory? Nothing, except that there is nothing in it— it will not work. Women who set a low value on themselves make life hard for all women. The German woman's ways have been ways of pleasantness, but her paths have not been paths of peace; and now, women everywhere are thinking of her, rather bitterly. Her peaceful, humble, patient ways have suddenly ceased to appear virtuous in our eyes and we see now, it is not so much a woman's duty to bring children into the world, as to see what sort of a world she is bringing them into, and what their contribution will be to it. Bertha Krupp has made good guns and the German women have raised good soldiers—if guns and soldiers can be called "good"—and between them they have manned the most terrible and destructive war machine that the world has ever known. We are not grateful to either of them.

The nimble fingers of the knitting women are transforming balls of wool into socks and comforters, but even a greater change is being wrought in their own hearts. Into their gentle souls have come bitter thoughts of rebellion. They realize now how little human life is valued, as opposed to the greed and ambition of nations. They think bitterly of Napoleon's utterance on the subject of women—that the greatest woman in the world is the one who brings into the world the greatest number of sons; they also remember that he said that a boy could stop a bullet as well as a man, and that God is on the side of the heaviest artillery. From these three statements they get the military idea of women, children, and God, and the heart of the knitting woman recoils in horror from the cold brutality of it all. They realize now something of what is back of all the opposition to the woman's advancement into all lines of activity and a share in government.

Women are intended for two things, to bring children into the world and to make men comfortable, and then they must keep quiet and if their hearts break with grief, let them break quietly—that's all. No woman is so unpopular as the noisy woman who protests against these things.

The knitting women know now why the militant suffragettes broke windows and destroyed property, and went to jail for it joyously, and without a murmur—it was the protest of brave women against the world's estimate of woman's position. It was the world-old struggle for liberty. The knitting women remember now with shame and sorrow that they have said hard things about the suffragettes, and thought they were unwomanly and hysterical. Now they know that womanliness, and peaceful gentle ways, prayers, petitions and tears have long been tried but are found wanting; and now they know that these brave women in England, maligned, ridiculed, persecuted, as they were, have been fighting every woman's battle, fighting for the recognition of human life, and the mother's point of view. Many of the knitting women have seen a light shine around their pathway, as they have passed down the road from the heel to the toe, and they know now that the explanation cannot be accepted any longer that the English women are "crazy." That has been offered so often and been accepted.

Crazy! That's such an easy way to explain actions which we do not understand. Crazy! and it gives such a delightful thrill of sanity to the one who says it—such a pleasurable flash of superiority!

Oh, no, they have not been crazy, unless acts of heroism and suffering for the sake of others can be described as crazy! The knitting women wish now that there had been "crazy!" women in Germany to direct the thought of the nation to the brutality of the military system, to have aroused the women to struggle for a human civilization, instead of a masculine civilization such as they have now. They would have fared badly of course, even worse than the women in England, but they are far-

ing badly now, and to what purpose? The women of Belgium* have fared badly. After all, the greatest thing in life is not to live comfortably—it is to live honorably, and when that becomes impossible, to die honorably!

The woman who knits is thinking sadly of the glad days of peace, now unhappily gone by, when she was so sure it was her duty to bring children into the world. She thinks of the glad rapture with which she looked into the sweet face of her first-born twenty years ago—the brave lad who went with the first contingent, and is now at the front. She was so sure then that she had done a noble thing in giving this young life to the world. He was to have been a great doctor, a great healer, one who bound up wounds, and made weak men strong—and now—in the trenches, he stands, this lad of hers, with the weapons of death in his hands, with bitter hatred in his heart, not binding wounds, but making them, sending poor human beings out in the dark to meet their Maker, unprepared, surrounded by sights and sounds that must harden his heart or break it. Oh! her sunny-hearted lad! So full of love and tenderness and pity, so full of ambition and high resolves and noble impulses, he is dead—dead already—and in his place there stands "private 355," a man of hate, a man of blood! Many a time the knitting has to be laid aside, for the bitter tears blur the stitches.

The woman who knits thinks of all this and now she feels that she who brought this boy into the world, who is responsible for his existence, has some way been to blame. Is life really such a boon that any should crave it? Do we really confer a favor on the innocent little souls we bring into the world, or do we owe them an apology?

She thinks now of Abraham's sacrifice, when he was willing at God's command to offer his dearly beloved son on the altar; and now she knows it was not so hard for Abraham, for he knew it was God who asked it, and he had God's voice to guide him! Abraham was sure, but about this—who knows?

Then she thinks of the little one who dropped out of the race before it was well begun, and of the inexplicable smile of peace which lay on his small white face, that day, so many years ago now, when they laid him away with such sorrow, and such agony of loss. She understands now why the little one smiled, while all around him wept.

And she thinks enviously of her neighbor across the way, who had no son to give, the childless woman for whom in the old days she felt so sorry, but whom now she envies. She is the happiest woman of all—so thinks the knitting woman, as she sits alone in her quiet house; for thoughts can grow very bitter when the house is still and the boyish voice is heard no more shouting, "Mother" in the hall.

There, little girl, don't cry!
They have broken your heart, I know.

NOTE

* The German army invaded Belgium in 1914 and kept it under brutal occupation.

Dorothy Richardson   *UK(England), 1873–1957*

Dorothy Richardson is probably best known as being one of the first writers to use stream-of-consciousness techniques, popularized by Modernists such as James Joyce and Virginia Woolf. The term, in fact, was coined by writer May Sinclair in a commentary on Richardson's massive opus *Pilgrimage* (1915–1957), the autobiographical account of the minutiae of one woman's consciousness. Written over a forty-year span, *Pilgrimage* was actually a series of thirteen novels chronicling the details of the life of Miriam Henderson, details that mirror those of Richardson's.

Richardson was born in 1873 in Abingdon, Berkshire, the third of four daughters of a gentleman of unsound finances. While her father was doing well, she was able to get a good education and was sent to one of the few schools of the time where women were taught academic subjects. When her father started having financial difficulties, she had to leave school, and she continued her education in a very different role, as a student teacher in Hanover, Germany, and then in North London. Richardson returned from Germany to be with her mother, who was mentally ill. While she was accompanying her mother on a rest cure, her mother killed herself, an action that was that source of great guilt for the young girl.

After her mother's death, Richardson moved to London. There she became friendly with several members of the London avant-garde of the early twentieth century, including H. G. Wells, who became both mentor and lover. During this time, Richardson wrote reviews and essays about literature, politics, and economic theory for such magazines as *The Saturday Review* and, while working as a secretary at a dentist's office, *The Dental Record*.

Pointed Roofs came out in 1915, several years after Richardson had left the dental office to live by writing. The mixed reviews that met its publication were characteristic of the response to all of *Pilgrimage*. Many readers did not understand or appreciate what she was trying to achieve. Some found the work too long and tedious. However, many praised her writing for the depth and immediacy with which it explores the female consciousness, and Virginia Woolf even claimed Richardson invented the female sentence. Moreover, Richardson was nominated for the French Femina-Vie-Heureuse in 1928; John Cowper Powys wrote an extremely favorable critical analysis of her work in 1931 (*Dorothy Richardson*), and American poet Conrad Aiken in the *New York Evening Post* praised *Pilgrimage* in a long essay about it.

In 1938, a compact edition of all her works to that date was published by Dent & Cresset, who erroneously labled the work the complete *Pilgrimage*, although one more volume was to appear ten years after Richardson's death.

After her busy early years in London, Richardson decided to remove herself from active participation in society to concentrate on her massive work and other writings. In 1917, at the age of 44, she married an artist, Alan Odle, as devoted an aesthete as she, and the two of them spent the next thirty years moving between their London and Cornwall homes, finally retiring to Cornwall in 1939. Richardson continued writing essays, doing translations, writing short stories, and continuing to work on *Pilgrimage*. The story "Visit" was written in 1944 and was published in *Life and Letters Magazine*.

John Isom

VISIT

The carriage door is shut. The guard shows all his teeth again, touches his cap to Mary, blows his whistle and goes away to get into the train. The train gives a jolt and the platform, with Mary on it waving her hand, moves away until the station has gone and there are fields. This is the Journey. There is Pug, opposite. But not like she is at home. Like a stranger. Berry feels alone.

The wheels keep saying: Going-to, going-to, Bilberry Hill, Bilberry Hill, Bilberry Hill. If they went more slowly, they would be saying something else. But they hurry because they know they must get to Bilberry Hill. All the time it is coming nearer. Not like it was in the garden, when Mother said about going, and Berry and Pug had danced round the lawn singing Off to Philadelphy. Berry looks across at Pug and sees that she knows it is not the same.

When another station has come, the guard looks in at the window with his teeth and goes away, waving his flag. The wheels begin again, slowly. Aunt*bertha*, they say, Uncle*henry*, Uncle*albert*, Greataunt*stone*.

Another station and the guard comes and says: 'Next station, young ladies!' and Berry

thanks him politely and looks at Pug as soon as he is gone, to try and feel happy. But Pug's face says there is no help. Home is gone, for three whole days. Berry stares at Pug, trying to think of something to make her say something instead of just sitting there with her pug-face, nose all screwed up, like looking out of the window when it rains on a holiday.

"Watery-boughtery-*ceive*,' says Pug, and looks away, trying to show she does not care. But she does care. She is thinking of the strange place and strangers.

'Great-aunt Stone won't say grace for *tea*,' says Berry, and feels better. Busy, with things to explain to Pug. Pug is wondering about blind Great-aunt Stone. She has never seen a private blind person. 'Pug, if you think Great-aunt Stone will be wearing a cardboard label, she won't.'

It is a little station, with wet bushes. Nobody there. The guard comes and lifts them out into a smell of sweetbriar.

'There's yer uncle that's Mr. Albert, getting out of the chaise.'

Berry stands looking. Her feet won't move. A countryman is coming in at the little gate, looking above jerking his head, with his eyes nearly shut because the sun is in them. He comes across the platform, to take them to Uncle Albert.

'Ber-rie an' Nan-cie?'

It can't be Uncle Albert. But it is Uncle Albert. His mouth is pulled sideways to pretend he is not frightened. But he is frightened.

'I'll drive y'long.' He turns round and waits a second as if he is not sure Berry and Pug will follow, and then goes on, in a jerky walk, showing off, all to himself.

The chaise is very low, almost on the ground, so that the dusty, fat pony looks too large. When they are inside with the little portmanteau standing on end, they all seem too large and close together. Close together, and all alone. Uncle Albert has to sit sideways to drive. All the time, every day, he is frightened, ashamed, like a little boy in disgrace. But now he is being very grand because there is nobody there.

'Chee-er up!'

He has seen we think him dreadful and are not liking the bumpy drive in the little basket.

'I'm sure,' Berry says, and hears her voice come out frightfully loud; 'we shall be very happy.'

'Chee-er *up*, Carrie!' says Uncle Albert, flicking the pony with his whip. He is not thinking about us at all. Berry sits quite still, with the blush burning her face, and looks at the shining back of the pony where the big bones move under the fat. They are going downhill and the chaise shakes and bumps, and a polite cough Pug gives comes out in two pieces.

'How's all at home?'

'Quite-well-thank-you.' Pug has not said anything yet. But she is sitting up nicely and her face is looking polite. A village has come. Uncle Albert stops at a butcher-shop.

'Got that for me, Mr. Pi-ther?' he shouts in a high, squeaky voice.

Pug is pinching Berry's arm and looking up the street. 'Look!' she says in a loud whisper: 'Bald-faced Stag!' Berry pretends not to hear. 'Berry! Bald—' 'Sh' says Berry and feels like Miss Webb. Pug is quiet at once. She knows it is rude to make remarks. And she is silly to expect a village public-house to be called The Northumberland Arms. There is honeysuckle somewhere. But Pug doesn't smell it because she is still looking out for something funny.

Mr. Pither comes out of his shop in a large white apron, with a parcel, and looks. He has no whites to his eyes; like a horse.

'Nice after the sha-oo-er. So ye found the little misses.' He smiles into the chaise with his eyelids down as he puts in the parcel. Berry watches the eyelids to say good afternoon when they come up. Uncle Albert says thankee Mr. Pi-ther and gives a click and the pony moves and Mr. Pither looks down the street. He is thinking about the village, the only place he knows.

A cottage, hidden in dark creepers, joined on to another cottage, plain white. As Berry goes up the little path, the strange cottage seems to be one she has been into before. She knows she has never been into it, and yet feels her face suddenly get unhappy because she must go again into a place she doesn't like.

'Come in, children!'

Aunt Bertha's voice, in a room. It is low and small and musty, sending away the summer. Aunt Bertha is there, twisted round in her chair, to welcome. While Berry kisses her she sees home and the mornings with Aunt Bertha, making the Text, and Aunt Bertha smiles and sees them, too, but after Pug has quickly kissed her she only says now go and give your Great-auntie a kiss, and the little room is full of Great-aunt Stone sitting in a low armchair with no arms. The back of it, going up beyond her head, looks like half a pipe.

Aunt Stone does not move or speak as Berry goes towards her. Her eyes are open, staring at nothing, with a film over them like the fish on the slab at Pratt's.

'Mother! Berry!'

So Great-aunt Stone is deaf as well as blind. What is the good of her, sitting there? That is what happens if you are eighty-five. You sit somewhere being no good.

'How do you do, Aunt Stone?' Berry asks, speaking very loud, to be heard. And now Aunt Stone knows she is there, because the dreadful mauve lips are going to speak and one of the twisted hands, with the big mauve veins standing up on it, comes a little way off her knee.

'Give me a kiss, my-little-dear.'

When her own face is near enough to the dreadful old face she must kiss, Berry shuts her eyes. But just before her eyelids go down she sees a piece of sunlight on the wall behind the chair and stays in it while she gives her kiss and thinks of how she will be able to look at it again presently; but remembers politeness:

'This is my sister Nancy,' she shouts, and bumps into Pug standing too near behind.

It is rude to be seeing Aunt Bertha frowning and being cross. Every day, for every meal, someone has to get her to the table like this. Perhaps Uncle Albert always makes the same mistakes, making her angry. At home she clung on to the servants' arms and made little jokes as she came, and made funny faces at Pug and me to make us laugh. Aunt Bertha on a visit happy and polite. This is Aunt Bertha at home. Quite different. Angry like a little girl, and making Uncle Albert frightened. She knows I have seen, and is smiling at me now that she is sitting down; and I can't smile back.

Those things she can see on the other side of the room as she sits at the tea-table beside Pug have always been there, making a home like other things make other homes; a grandfather clock with a private face, high up above everybody; plush frames on the walls with bunches of flowers inside, painted by hand; a sheffa-near with a mirror and photographs in plush frames and a bowl, like the bowl of dried rose-leaves at home: po-pooery. I am on

a visit to all of them, and not to the uncles and aunts. They are always there, whatever happens. And the little patch of sunlight is often there, like someone saying something special.

There is no bread-and-butter. The *loaf* is on the table and a dish with a large round of butter with a picture of a cow on the top, and a little china beehive. No cake. A dish with a Yorkshire pudding in it. But jam, and a bowl of cream. Uncle Albert is cutting bread-and-butter, screwing up his face and being almost as grand as he was in the chaise. Aunt Bertha is looking at him, frowning. Suddenly she tells Berry to begin. As if she has been seeing her without looking, and knows she has not begun. And now she and Pug are eating lovely new crusty bread-and-butter. Bilberry Hill. It goes down being Bilberry Hill, not tasting of the musty smell in the room. Berry looks at the lovely little beehive, munching and thinking how unkind it is to be happy without caring about the aunts and Uncle Albert although it is their bread-and-butter and their beehive. Perhaps they are happy, too? She looks at Aunt Bertha, and Aunt Bertha is smiling at her like she used to do at home. And now she is leaning over and helping Berry to honey out of the beehive.

'Would Berry like a piece of lardy-cake?'

Berry quickly says yes please and looks all round the table again, for cake. But there is not any cake. Uncle Albert is cutting out a corner of the Yorkshire pudding, and now he has slid it on to her plate. When she has taken a small bite, she wants to talk about it. It is like the outside of very brown doughnuts, only much nicer and crisp. Uncle Albert is looking at her with his head on one side and is going to speak. She wishes he wouldn't, wishes nobody would look or speak to her. The cake won't go on tasting so good if she must think of people too.

'Ye won't get that,' Uncle Albert's voice is angry, as if I had done something wrong—'not outside Burksheer.'

'Did ye get that bitta brisket, Albert?'

Now they are all attending to Aunt Stone and something they all know about. I am alone with the lardy-cake and Pug. She is eating her piece neatly, in nice little bites, but listening too.

Suddenly Pug's voice comes out: 'We have all our meat done in a roasting-jack in front of the fire.'

'That'll be Jo-erge,' says Uncle Albert.

'And Father cuts the usparrygus; not gardener.'

Berry kicks hard, sideways, and hits Pug's ankle and Pug stops and Berry quickly sighs and says I'm awfully happy, to make up for Pug showing off, and as soon as she has said this without meaning it, she means it, and wants to be staying at Bilberry Hill for a long time, long enough to see everything there is, instead of just three days.

Eliza picks up the candle and says good night little misses and opens the door. She doesn't want to stay and she doesn't want to go. Her footsteps creak, like her voice. They are the only footsteps and voice she has. She will have them when she is back in the kitchen.

Black darkness. Taking away the walls. You can only tell it is the same room by the musty smell. All the things are in it like they were when the candle was there. The Chair. No, no, NO! I *won't* see the Chair.

'Pug,' very quietly, just to show she is there, even if she is asleep. She is asleep. Berry pokes her eyelids, to make colours. Where do they come from, these pretty colours? When the colours are gone, the Chair is there, inside her eyes, with Great-uncle Stone sitting in it. Dead. Like Eliza said they found him. But with certainly a gold watch-chain. Look at the watch-chain. All gold and shining, like it was when he was going about the house and going out. Going to Wesleen chapel. But one day he couldn't go out. He came upstairs and sat in that Chair. For ten years.

'Pug!'

Pug is asleep, far away. Berry turns quick-

ly round, to be nearer to her. The quilt crackles as she turns, telling her to remember the pink roses on it. They are still there, in the dark. And it isn't quite, quite dark. Over there, in the corner, is a little square of faint light showing through the window curtain, telling about getting up in the morning, with Pug.

Rose leaves and roses, coming in at the window, almost touching the little washstand. Berry washes very slowly, to be staying as long as possible, with her back to the room, in this corner where the morning comes in with the roses. Not talking to Pug. Just being altogether Berry.

Downstairs, it is dark. In the Morning. Uncle Henry is still not there. Uncle Albert has a shiny face and a Cambridge blue tie; for Sunday. But he cuts large slices of the cold bacon, and it is lovely; very mild and with pink fading away into the fat part.

After breakfast Uncle Henry suddenly comes in. He has a black beard, but all the same is short like Uncle Albert. He says some of the things relations say, only in the funny way they all speak at Bilberry Hill. Then he goes away behind his beard and is sad. And frightened too. But not of people, like Uncle Albert.

It is nice running down the lane with Uncle Henry, joining hands and running and laughing, out in the sunlight. When he laughs, his white teeth come out of his black beard. But the land ends in a muddy yard, with pigs running about and grunting. Pug says aren't they funny. But they are not funny. They are dirty and frightened.

'Race you back,' says Uncle Henry, and runs up the lane very fast and into the house. And now there is only the sitting-room again, and Uncle Henry gone away somewhere. There's nothing to do but look through the glass of the door that goes into the garden; until Aunt Bertha comes down to read Line upon Line. Perhaps she can find the piece about a bell and a pomegranate, a bell and a pomegranate, round about the hem of Aaron's robe.

Aunt Bertha said not to play in the garden until tomorrow. But we can just open the door and look. There is a little pavement outside, running along the back of the cottage.

'Come along, Pug. This isn't the garden.'

The little path is very nice. Secret. Pug is just behind me, liking it too. Only somewhere in front, further along there is a dreadful harmonium sound; wheezy and out of tune. The path reaches the plain white part of the cottage, and the slow, dismal sound is quite near. Just inside this door. Another sitting-room. Perhaps that is where Uncle Henry went. Berry opens the door: Uncle Albert. All alone, sitting at a crooked harmonium, playing How Sweet the Name in a bare room with no carpet, and bulging sacks lying about on the floor. Poor Uncle Albert playing, all out of tune and out of time, the only Sunday music he knows. Holding on to it; all alone.

Quickly Berry closes the door, pushes past Pug, runs back along the little path. Half-way along, she is back again at the creeper-covered cottage. Where to go? Where is Sunday? Why don't chapel people stop being chapel? Why aren't they taken to church, and *shown*? But Sunday must be here; somewhere. Perhaps at the far end of the path, near that tree.

'Is 'Enery back?' Great-aunt Stone's voice, shaky, calling from her room upstairs. 'Tellim I wantim to cut my toe-nails.'

'Come on Pug, come in!' Somewhere inside is Uncle Henry and his beard, being looked for. He is Aunt Stone's favourite and must do this dreadful thing for her. Perhaps this afternoon he'll take us out somewhere. Away. Tomorrow we can go in the garden. The next day we shall be at home. But all the things here will be the same when we're not seeing them.

Not a real garden. No lawn. Nowhere to play. Nowhere to forget yesterday in. Only this one little path going along between the vegetables and gooseberry-bushes to the end: trees, and thick shrubs and a wall. And Pug coming along the path not very happy, waiting for something nice and already seeing there's nothing.

It is a wooden door, right in the middle of the wall; nearly covered with creepers.

'Pug!' Pug comes running; is near. Good little Pug, not saying anything, waiting to be told what to do. I can smell the lineny smell of her pinafore. The gate won't move. It *won't*.

'Hold on to me, and pull!'

Wudge. It's open.

A green hill, going up into the sky. A little path at the bottom for people to walk and go somewhere.

'Pug. *Pug*!'

Berry runs up the bright green grass. Into nowhere. Sees the wind moving the grass. Feels it in her hair. No one knows about this hill. No one knows it is there. Near the top she stands still, to remember how it looked from the door; long, long ago. It will always look like that. Always. Always. She lies down, to smell the grass, puts her cheek against it, feels grass-blades in her ear.

'*Pug*! This is the country. Bilberry Hill. We've found it.'

Pug looks down at her, standing still, waiting. Berry hides her face in the grass, to be alone.

'Berry! Aren't you glad we are going home tomorrow?'

'I don't know.'

Lakshmibai Tilak

India, 1873–1936

Lakshmibai was born in Nasik the third of five children into the Brahmin Gokhale family; she was raised by an aunt who was childless. In the first chapter of her autobiography, Lakshmibai Tilak recounts, from the point of view of the women in the household, the death of her maternal grandfather, killed by British officials in the 1857 Mutiny as it is known in the West, and the First War of Independence as it is known in India. Her father was an extremely orthodox Hindu, and something of a tyrant as well. As was the custom, Tilak was married as a child to a young man of 17 who was soon to become a Christian.* This placed Lakshmibai on the horns of a dilemma: on one hand, she found herself angered by her family's treatment of him, and on the other, she was unable to cast aside her Brahmin upbringing and live with a husband who was, according to its traditions, "defiled." Supported and sustained by her family, she separated from him for a period, but finally returned with their son, Dattu, eventually adopting her husband's religion and carrying on his work after him.

Smritichitre (Memory Sketches), an autobiographical record of her life, brought Tilak great fame when it was published in Marathi in four volumes between 1934 and 1936. The work is not only important for its insight into Tilak but for the distinctive voice which expressed, with humor and in a vivid narrative style, life in a changing world. Its colloquial charm and wit enlivened the Marathi language and helped to shape it as a medium for modern literature. Translated in 1950 after Tilak's death and retitled *I Follow After*(!), the English version is a considerably abridged, more tendentious book intended for use by missionaries. The following excerpts include two separate incidents that are indicative of Tilak's point of view. Her reference in the second section is to a novel that is now lost, a casualty of the neglect of women's literature.

NOTE

* Narayan Waman Tilak (1862–1912). A poet and a clergyman, he also composed many very popular Marathi hymns. At a time when missionary control was still strong, Tilak fought a lone—and losing—battle to Indianize the culture of Christianity.

from I FOLLOW AFTER
Smritichitre

I WAIT EIGHT YEARS

....Dattu was about eighteen years old. I began to enjoy happy visions. I imagined my son the most learned man in all the world. He was such a good boy, and had now gone to college! I was his mother. I never saw any fault in him. I used to wonder why, since he was so good, no offer of marriage came for him. Unlike high-caste Hindus, among Christians the girl's parents do not look for a husband. The boy's people ask for the girl. Having no personal experience of this custom I forgot all about it.

In Nagar there was a matron called Rakhmabai Kukas, and between the two of us there was much coming and going. I used to unburden my mind to her, and she used to comfort me.

"Lakshmibai, you have to ask for the girl here. The bridegroom's people have to look for the bride. Besides, your son is not so very old yet."

I, however, did not agree to this.

"What does it matter if the boy is not old enough?" said I. "He will continue his studies in college, and the girl [can] stay with us."

We had decided to go to Nasik that year in the hot weather. Rakhmabai's brother Krishnarao Sarode, from Bombay, was there also for a change of air. We stayed nearby and shared a woman who cooked for both of us, which meant that for two months we did not need to bother ourselves with either cooking or shopping. We met the Sarodes twice a day at meal times because the woman did the serving in our house. Sarode's party took a great pride in the Marathi tongue, so they got on well with Tilak. They were very good people and sociable, and in no time we were fast friends.

I was extremely anxious that Dattu should be married, or at least that his marriage should be arranged. Had we been Hindus I should already have had a little daughter-in-law at my right hand, but among Christians this seemed impossible. If no offer could come from some girl's parents, then that could not be helped; but there was no reason why one should not put out a feeler oneself, and see what would happen.

Without telling Tilak I dropped a hint or two, only to get the answer:

"But, Bai, the boy is still only studying. Why are you so bent on marrying him off now?"

I, however, could not agree.

Sarode's daughter Ruth and Dattu had become good friends in Nasik, and I began to think I would like her for a daughter-in-law. She was good, virtuous and clever, so all was well, and it was easy to see they liked each other.

Ruth at this time was in the fifth standard English, and she was only fourteen years old. Among Christians this is by no means the age for marrying: there is no thought even of mar-

riage, and now among Hindus too this age is considered too young. Nothing daunted, I took Ruth aside, and when we were alone asked her if she would be my daughter-in-law.

"What can I say?" she replied. "If you like, ask my father."

I set about goading Tilak on. It was not possible to have a wedding, but what was there to prevent an engagement? In the end he gave in, and asked Krishnarao Sarode. He said he would ask his sister before replying. Naturally my mind was in a ferment again. Now they will go to Bombay! Then ask the sister! Then write to us! How could I have so much patience?

It was the end of the hot weather by now. We returned to Nagar, Dattu went to college, but no letter came from Sarode. After waiting one or two months Tilak wrote to him; needless to say, because I told him to. He was in no hurry, though I was. I was consumed with the desire to see my son married. At long last, Sarode's letter came saying they would agree to give their daughter, but only after a certain time. There was to be no mention of marriage until she had passed her Matriculation examination. Tilak replied that he would be in no hurry till his son had passed his B.A. And so, though there was no wedding and no little daughter-in-law to keep me company, at least I knew who would be my daughter-in-law four years hence, and I was completely satisfied.

They say thoughts of marriage upset a boy's studies. What did I know? So people say, but it was not the case with these two. Ruth passed her Matriculation and in the whole University examination stood first in English, and took a prize.

On the other hand, when Dattu got his B.A., the agreement that they should be married immediately was shelved, and not until the education of both of them was complete, that is, till she had her B.A. too, were they married. I, who was not willing to put off my son's wedding for eight months, had to wait through an eight years' engagement.

MY NOVEL

Needs no explantation

I took in hand the writing of a social novel. As I was writing I would be held up every now and again by a compound letter, then having turned all our books inside out and outside in and found the word, my cart would rumble along the road again.

One day, my novel was thus galloping along merrily when my horse stopped. I could not write the Marathi word for "man," I turned topsyturvy all the books on which I could lay my hands, but I could find "man" nowhere. I was sitting lost in thought, before me the books all tumbled down, the unfinished work of the house crying out to be done.

At that moment Thombre came in. Seeing the picture I presented, he said:

"Why are you sitting like this, Lakshmibai? Do you want anything?"

"What shall I do? I want 'a man'. I have turned everything upside down and can find 'a man' nowhere!"

Thombre stepped before me, and laid his hand upon his chest.

"Why all this turn-up? See, here stands a man! If you want any more just come outside, I shall show you as many men as you want. There is no lack of them. The whole world is full of men. No lack of men!"

"Tush, I do not want a human man. I want 'a man' as written in a book." We both laughed then, and Thombre wrote out the word for me.

Another day I asked Thombre to read my novel. He read it and wrote the review given below:

Review:
The hole of this novl i hav red. Such
an other novl in the sweat Marathi tung
will not be scene.

> Tri-bunk Bomb-poji
> Htombre
> Aha Mud Nagre

Adver tis ne ment
Uncompirabl Buk-Uncompirabl Buk-Uncompirabl Buk

> Tak noat...Tak noat...Tak noat
> No Sekund Chans.

I still have the above page with this review. No name was given to the novel, but Thombre wrote at the top in big letters,

LUX-UMM-BOY'S NOVL

This page has been engulfed in the maw of time. It is twenty years since it all happened. I can now write much better, but in those days my spelling was the butt of all the boys.

Translated by Josephine Inkster

Mary Ursula Bethell   *New Zealand, 1874–1945*

Ursula Bethell's finely controlled, understated lyrics have long been recognized as among the best poetry written in New Zealand between the wars. Often focused on details of her garden, the poems reach out to embrace much larger themes, as in the two printed here.

Bethell was born in England while her father, a New Zealand farmer, and mother were taking an extended honeymoon. She grew up near Christchurch in New Zealand's South Island, returning to England to complete her schooling and later studying painting and music in Germany. For a time she worked as a social worker in South London before returning to New Zealand in 1924. With a close friend, Effie Pollen, she lived in a cottage near Christchurch, tended her garden, and began, at the age of 50, to write poetry. Three collections appeared in her lifetime and *Collected Poems* in 1950.

"Response" shows the close ties between England and New Zealand, which were so much a part of Bethell's own life. Indeed, for New Zealanders of her generation, England was home even if they had never been there. In "Pause," Bethell, unlike earlier colonial poets, who loved to celebrate pioneering achievements, speculates on the triviality of human endeavors set alongside the forces of nature. A critical study of her work (*Mary Ursula Bethell*, 1975), has been written by M.H. Holcroft and is one of the few critical studies yet made of a New Zealand woman poet.

Elizabeth Webby

RESPONSE

When you wrote your letter it was April,
And you were glad that it was spring weather,
And that the sun shone out in turn with
                                        showers of rain.

I write in waning May and it is autumn,
And I am glad that my chrysanthemums
Are tied up fast to strong posts,
So that the south winds cannot beat them
                                        down.

I am glad that they are tawny coloured,
And fiery in the low west evening light.
And I am glad that one bush warbler
Still sings in the honey-scented wattle...

But oh, we have remembering hearts,
And we say 'How green it was in such and
                                        such an April,'
And 'Such and such an autumn was very
                                        golden,'
And 'Everything is for a very short time.'

PAUSE

When I am very earnestly digging
I lift my head sometimes, and look at the
                                        mountains,
And muse upon them, muscles relaxing.

I think how freely the wild grasses flower there,
How grandly the storm-shaped trees are
                                        massed in their gorges
And the rain-worn rocks strewn in magnificent
                                        heaps.

Pioneer plants on those uplands find their own
                                        footing;
No vigorous growth, there, is an evil weed:
All weathers are salutary.

It is only a little while since this hillside
Lay untrammelled likewise,
Unceasingly swept by transmarine winds.

In a very little while, it may be,
When our impulsive limbs and our superior
                                        skulls
Have to the soil restored several ounces of
                                        fertiliser,

The Mother of all will take charge again,
And soon wipe away with her elements
Our small fond human enclosures.

Alice Barber Stevens, Female Life Class, *1879, grisalle modello on board.*
Courtesy The Pennsylvania Academy of the Fine Arts, Philadelphia, Pennsylvania

Gertrude Stein   *US/France, 1874–1946*

Stein was the youngest of seven children in an affluent Jewish family with whom she traveled through Europe before settling in Oakland, California. When she was 14 Stein's mother died; three years later, her father died. She attended Radcliffe College where she studied psychology with the eminent William James. Later she became one of few women to attend Johns Hopkins Medical School, but soon lost her interest in medicine.

In 1903 Stein joined her brother Leo in Paris, where they were the patrons and friends of modern artists. The Saturday evening salon in their apartment at 27 rue de Fleurus was a center for artists and writers, such as Matisse, Braque, Juan Gris, and Guillaume Apollinaire. Stein became Picasso's close friend when his work was mostly unknown, and he painted her portrait. In 1907 she met Alice B. Toklas, who became her lover, inseparable companion, unofficial secretary, receptionist, housekeeper, and sometime publisher, for the rest of their lives. Stein finished her epic, *The Making of Americans*, and separated from Leo, who disparaged her work. During World War I, the two women did relief work in France, and afterwards their home became a meeting place for expatriate Americans. Stein knew and influenced Hemingway, Sherwood Anderson, and F. Scott Fitzgerald, but her own work remained for the most part unpublished. With the success of *The Autobiography of Alice B. Toklas* (1933), however, her reputation quickly grew. As a celebrity, she toured America, but more attention was paid to her person than to her work.

The range of Stein's work is enormous, and almost all of it explores the limits of its particular genre. Her novels in poetic prose vary in length from one to 1,000 pages. (One example from 1926 is presented here.) She wrote other people's autobiographies; five-act plays in four pages; experimental poetry; and explanations of her method that are as dense as her most difficult work. She invented the 'portrait' as well as other genres for which critics have not found names.

Though an expatriate for most of her life, Stein expanded the possibilities of American English. *The Making of Americans*, completed in 1911, was to be the story of every American "who ever can or is or was or will be living," using the history of Stein's own family. As an exploration of language, its style is also "democratic": each character and each clause has equal importance and weight within the whole. Investigating her theory that "everyone said the same thing over and over again," Stein used repetition to express character and organize her work.

Three Lives (1909) concerns the experience of three working-class immigrant and minority women, and uses a different syntax to describe each of the different characters and her thoughts. Brief portraits of Picasso, Matisse, and others, written between 1908 and 1913, continue this stylistic exploration. Like Cubist portraits of the period, Stein built a complex style out of a limited vocabulary, using repetition, ambiguity, and shifting syntax to represent different facets of a personality. The result is an abstract portrait from conflicting viewpoints rather than a realistic description.

Stein continued experimentation with her notoriously hermetic *Tender Buttons* (1914). Like the poem "Lifting Belly" (1915–1917), a lesbian classic, *Tender Buttons* explores the mysteries of the female body. Testing a new form of prose,

Stein refused all reference to a predominantly male literary tradition. In the abstract "Patriarchal Poetry" (1927), a brief excerpt of which follows, and in the long sequence *Stanzas in Meditation* (1932), she refers only to herself, the experience of composition, and the material properties of language.

Stein's plays, included in *Geography and Plays* (1922), and *Operas and Plays* (1932), are often idiosyncratic. Her opera, "Four Saints in Three Acts" (1927), was set to music by the American composer Virgil Thompson, who compared the sound of her words to atonal music.

Recently revived (1986), it is, along with *The Autobiography of Alice B. Toklas*, Stein's most accessible work.

Other works include *Q.E.D.* (1950), her first novel; *Lucy Church Amiably* (1931), meditations on a landscape; *The Geographical History of America* (1936), a treatise on consciousness; *The World is Round* (1939), a children's book; *Everybody's Autobiography* (1937), *Paris France* (1940), and *Wars I Have Seen* (1945), chronicles of her later life; and *Mrs. Reynolds* (1952) and *Brewsie and Willie* (1946), her last novels. Eight volumes of previously unprinted manuscripts were published after her death.

Although the American critic Edmund Wilson did much to insure Stein's critical standing by including her in *Axel's Castle* (1931), it was not until Yale University began printing a standard edition of her unpublished writings (1951–1958) and James R. Mellow (1974) and Richard Birdgman (1870) published their works of literary biography and criticism that Stein began to receive the attention due her. Recent criticism has tended to place her within a characteristically American, and frequently female, tradition, though little has been done to explore her influence on experimental theater. But Wendy Steiner's *Exact Resemblance to Exact Resemblance: The Literary Portraiture of Gertrude Stein* (1978), Catherine Stimpson's "The Mind, the Body, and Gertrude Stein," (*Critical Inquiry*, Spring 1977), Anna Gibb's article in *Meanjin* (September, 1979) connecting her with *l'écriture féminine* (feminine writing) of Hélène Cixous, and Mary Dearborn's *Pochahantas' Daughters* (1986) have done much to develop a reading public for this prolific and inventive modernist.

Leslie Camhi

A LITTLE NOVEL

Fourteen people have been known to come again. One came. They asked her name. One after one another. Fourteen is not very many and fourteen came. One after another. Six were known to be at once. Welcomed. How do you do. Who is pleasant. How often do they think kindly. May they be earnest.

What is the wish.

They have fourteen. One is in a way troubled may he succeed. They asked his name. It is very often a habit in mentioning a name to mention his name. He mentioned his name.

Earnest is partly their habit.

She is without doubt welcome.

Once or twice four or five there are many which is admirable.

May I ask politely that they are well and wishes.

Cleanly and orderly.

Benjamin Charles may amount to it he is wounded by their doubt.

Or for or fortunately.

No blame is a blemish.

Once upon a time a dog intended to be

mended. He would be vainly thought to be pleasant. Or just or join or clearly. Or with or mind or flowery. Or should or be a value.

Benjamin James was troubled. He had been certain. He had perused. He had learned. To labor and to wait.

Or why should he be rich. He was. He was lamentable and discovered. He had tried to sin. Or with perplexity.

She may be judicious.

Many will be led in hope.

He was conveniently placed for observation. They will. They may well

Be happy.

Any and every one is an authority.

Does it make any difference who comes first.

She neglected to ask it of him. Will he like gardening. She neglected to ask her to be very often. Made pleasantly happy. They were never strange. It is unnecessary never to know them.

And they

When this you see remarkably.

Patriarchal poetry needs rectification and there about it.

Come to a distance and it still bears their name.

Prosperity and theirs prosperity left to it.

To be told to be harsh to be told to be harsh to be to them.

One.

To be told to be harsh to be told to be harsh to them.

None.

To be told to be harsh to be told to be harsh to them.

When.

To be told to be harsh to be told to be harsh to them.

Then.

What is the result.

The result is that they know the difference between instead and instead and made and made and said and said.

The result is that they might be as very well two and as soon three and to be sure, four and which is why they might not be.

Elegant replaced by delicate and tender, delicate and tender replaced by one from there instead of five from there, there is not there this is what has happened evidently.

Why while while why while why why identity identity why while while why. Why while while while while identity.

Patriarchal Poetry is the same as Patriotic poetry is the same as patriarchal poetry is the same as Patriotic poetry is the same as patriarchal poetry is the same.

Patriarchal poetry is the same.

If in in crossing there is a if in crossing if in in crossing nearly there is a distance if in crossing there is a distance between measurement and exact if in in crossing if in in crossing there is a measurement between and in in exact she says I must be careful and I will.

If in in crossing there is an opportunity not only but also and in in looking in looking in regarding if in in looking if in in regarding if in in regarding there is an opportunity if in in looking there is an opportunity if in in regarding there is an opportunity to verify verify sometimes as more sometimes as more sometimes as more.

Fish eggs commonly fish eggs. Architects commonly fortunately indicatively architects indicatively architects. Elaborated at a time with it with it at a time with it at a time attentively today.

Does she know how to ask her brother is there any difference between turning it again again and again and again or turning it again and again. In resembling two brothers.

That makes patriarchal poetry apart.

Intermediate or patriarchal poetry.

If at once sixty-five have come one by one if at once sixty five have come one by one if at once sixty-five have come one by one. This took two and two have been added to by Jenny. Never to name Jenny. Have been added to by two. Never have named Helen Jenny never have named Agnes Helen never have named Helen Jenny. There is no difference between having been born in Brittany and having been born in Algeria.

from PATRIARCHAL POETRY

These words containing as they do neither reproaches nor satisfaction may be finally very nearly rearranged and why, because they mean to be partly left alone. Patriarchal poetry and kindly, it would be very kind in him in him of him of him to be as much obliged as that. Patriotic poetry. It would be as plainly an advantage if not only but altogether repeatedly it should be left not only to them but for them but for them. Explain to them by for them. Explain shall it be explain will it be explain can it be explain as it is to be explain letting it be had as if he had had more than wishes. More than wishes.

    Patriarchal poetry more than wishes.
    Assigned to Patriarchal Poetry.

Assigned to patriarchal poetry too sue sue sue sue shall sue sell and magnificent can as coming let the same shall shall shall shall let it share is share is share shall shall shall shall shell shell shall share is share shell can shell be shell be shell moving in in in inner moving move inner in in inner in meant meant might might may collect collected recollected to refuse what it is is it.

    Having started at once at once.
    Put it with it with it and it and it come to ten.
    Put it with it with it and it and it for it for it made to be extra.
    With it put it put it prepare it prepare it add it add it or it or it would it would it and make it all at once.

Marie Lenéru
France, 1875–1918

Marie Lenéru died prematurely during the flu epidemics of 1918, leaving a slim but original body of work strongly marked by the circumstances of her life. During the years preceding the war, she achieved notoriety for her accomplishments in the theater, a genre in which no woman had yet really succeeded. Her plays are firmly constructed around ethical or ideological conflicts in the manner of her model François de Curel.[1] They show her belief in the right and duty of the individual to rise against the constraints of conventional morality. After *Les Affranchis* (The Free Ones, 1910), she was criticized for not showing enough feminine sensitivity in this highly intellectual work. She was also accused of making a disguised apology for Dreyfus in *Le Redoutable* (The Invincible One, 1912), a play dealing with treason aboard a military ship. In *La Triomphatrice* (The Triumphant Woman, 1928)—staged by the *Comédie Française*—her heroine is a Nobel Prize laureate who loses the man she loves because of her success.

Modern readers are more likely to be interested in her diary—published posthumously in 1922—which she started at the age of 11 and continued until her death. She stopped writing it only between 1889 and 1893, when she had to adjust to the infirmities that were to plague her all her life. She was born in the Brittany port town of Brest to a family of marine officers. She never knew her father who died while on duty abroad, but she very early absorbed his sense of honor through the reading of his diary. After an illness, she began losing her hearing at the age of 13 ("Things suddenly became quiet," she wrote); then her eyesight diminished to the point where she could read only with the help of a strong magnifying glass.

These were hard blows to the spirited adolescent who lived with music and books, and had manifested early her intense love for life. She reacted to her bad fortune with remarkable strength, and was greatly encouraged by her mother. Although she never stopped deploring the loss of sensations she could only remember and no longer enjoy, and the lack of experiences that would have enlarged her horizon, she expressed this loss without self-pity, bitterness toward others, or stoic posturing.

She imposed on herself a rigorous program of studies in philosophy, literature, and ancient and modern languages. Nietzsche and Schopenhauer, along with Maurice Barrès and the Latin Stoics, strongly influenced her thinking.[2] In her search for lucidity and self-integrity she moved further and further away from the religious faith of her childhood. Suzanne Lavaud, her biographer, characteristically noted in 1932: "Her mind acquired an unusual virility."

Although she lived, mostly in Brittany, a life she herself compared to that of a Carmelite, Marie Lenéru spent a few years in Paris, where she came in contact with the literary world of the turn of the century. Léon Blum (1872–1950), then famous as a literary critic before being a prominent political figure, became one of her good friends. After an attempt at fiction writing, she began a study of the French revolutionary Saint-Just, (1767–1794), "A professor of energy," which she intended to publish under a male pseudonym. She abandoned it to turn her attention to Helen Keller, the subject of a prose poem, *La Vivante* (An Alive Woman, 1908). She ultimately devoted her writing to the theater, in order "to involve the public in the play of ideas."

Her diary provides a fascinating reflection of the cultural atmosphere of her time besides being a remarkable personal document. It shows a young woman capable of tempering her passionate admirations with lucid criticism. On the hotly debated subject of feminism, she castigates the baseness of antifeminist attitudes while being also critical of women. Lenéru's style in her diary is very seldom lyrical. It is marked by a talent for lapidary phrases such as the one she wrote at the end of the war, summarizing her pacifist beliefs with the words: "Une victoire ne se chante pas, elle se pleure" ("A victory should not be celebrated; it should be mourned").

Colette Gaudin

NOTES

1. François de Curel (1854–1928): part of a general movement articulating the play of ideas, considered a distinguished playwright who brought a keen psychological insight and perhaps proto-symbolic technique to his dramas.
2. Friedrich Wilhelm Nietzsche (1844–1900): German philosopher influenced by Schopenhauer. His teachings emphasized a heroic life-affirming morality, incarnated by a race of supermen, distinguished by their "will to power."

   Arthur Schopenhauer (1788–1860): German philosopher. His notion of a blind, impelling force manifested within the individual is compensated for by as Hindu-influenced concept of renunciation as the means for achieving pleasure.

   Maurice Barrès (1862–1923): French philosopher, politician, and statesman; theorist of nationalism who believed the individual as well as the nation was formed by ancestry and the land.

   Latin Stoics: school founded by Zeno about 300 B.C., which emphasized resignation in the face of human mortality: wisdom lay in being superior to passion, joy, and grief.

from THE JOURNAL OF MARIE LENÉRU
Le Journal de Marie Lenéru

Le Trez-Hir, 1899

I instinctively mistrust manual work. How it keeps women in a state of lethargy!

If they didn't have that miserable occupation ready and waiting for them—which doesn't occupy them any more than beating time with their feet, and which is just as useless—they would then be forced to take the initiative to do something else.

If women must have reassuringly humble occupations, cooking at least has its charm, as does the skillful running of the household, which not one in a hundred attain. But these two things still require too much use of intelligence. After that, if they can neither converse, nor read, nor play music, let them go to the poor, by God! and to the Church. But a bit too much charity and piety are also more beyond their reach than you'd think.

"Our current literature" is certainly spoken of rather badly! Yet where do we find talents more intelligent, more accomplished, more original? I love my contemporaries down to their warts.

Horrid day. I so declare my bad mood and say in jest all manner of things too outrageous to be taken seriously, and which allow me to complain incognito. They find that very amusing: "You should be in a bad mood every day." Oh Molière,[1] how amusing you must have been when you passed away for good amidst the pointed hats and all the pomp and ceremony!

How I react to my reading astonishes them: authors who see things in a vulgar or comical manner or simply turn up their noses in disgust, my God! moral authors have shocked me more, have seemed to me less "decent" than the others who adore everything in life and don't seem to suspect that a fly might fall in their glass.

I have no tolerance for romantic misdeeds, but to speak of them with distaste, seems to me as vulgar as the abject laugh caused by deceived husbands.

Since everything is a matter of opinion, as the stoics would say, it's in seeing dirt that things become dirty.

April 2, 1900

I read an article by Mirbeau[2]: "Gallant Remarks about Women." They are rather vulgar, quite masculine jokes against feminism.

How can they not imagine that, *from the material point of view itself*, a woman must have in her life, her own activities, interests, and abilities "beyond" her children? Well brought up children will not readily have an enthusiastic adoration for the good mother, who uses them as a pretext for her existence, and whose life depends on their flannel vests, and their concoctions, and their problems, and their gossip, and their good grades, and their promotions, and their exams and their matrimonial projects.

Read, instead, the letters of Auguste de Staël[3] after the death of his mother, saying how much their family life had declined along with their conversation and interests.

And how can men not feel that love must grow with the woman? It might be said that they are taking out their vengeance on intelligent women for the fools they have been forced to love.

But the comment I want to make is this: most of the literary hacks who argue about feminism are not men of that world where men and women consider themselves on an equal footing.

The first woman writers were highborn ladies and that didn't bother in the least their salon companions who encouraged them.

When Catherine II[4] wanted to command her fleet, she made inquiries as to whether she would be considered ridiculous. Those gentlemen replied that that would depend on just how well she handled it.

In masculine opposition to feminism, I sense something commonplace, the habit of seeing women in the role of servant or housewife. A gentleman who has always seen his mother cut a brilliant figure in the company of distinguished men, the son of a peeress in her own right, a minister like Lord Melbourne who "would prefer to have to deal with ten kings than with one queen" so extremely conscientious did Victoria's royal scruples seem to him,[5] those people find less amusement in feminism.

May 8, 1901

Sometimes, I listen. It's an extraordinary respite. Memories from long ago return and help me recognize the stranger I've become.

It seems to me that things, the least little things that exist outside myself are more myself than I, and that in gathering my thoughts, I lose myself. Scatterbrain that you are, don't try "to get back into yourself." There's nothing within. I know that for having been made to stand in the corner at a time when there were as yet no memories.

And it's always tunes that bring me back the best. Has anyone ever noticed that tunes are the only human things in the world that don't change...? An old tune comes down to us from further back than the words which accompany it: and yet the language has already outlived the race. We can be sure that, somewhere in the world, can still be heard the warblings of the first voice that sang.

To learn, to grasp: *apprendre*, to seize in passing, to hang on to, to cling to.

One must live to take revenge on death.

"From which it follows, in reasoning as we are doing, that wisdom is not moderation, wisdom being inseparable from Beauty; because there's no way to deny that the moderate actions in the course of life never—or with very few exceptions—appear more beautiful to us than those accomplished with energy and speed...

"And even though, my dear, there might well be as many actions enhanced in beauty by moderation as by speed and vigor, you wouldn't have the right, based on that, to say that wisdom consists rather in action with moderation than with speed and vigor... Nor that a moderate life is sounder than a life without moderation." (Charmide)[6]

Villa Saïd, November 11, 1907

Mesdames de Noailles, de Régnier, Delarue-Mardus, yes these women are talents and rivals. Mesdames Tynaire and Colette Yver are intelligent; and yet, they're not. Why? They're not writers. *They don't rethink what they see.*

They're storytellers and talkers, when they write they aren't engaged in feeling, they don't create a new style that relates to life. They don't have strong sensibilities, we have nothing to inherit from them.

In literature there is: written, heartfelt literature, and spoken literature, devoid of energy. The first three lines of a book immediately classify it as one or the other, they reveal the laziness or the attention given to the process.

A man who writes a hackneyed sentence such as: "the violin that sings and cries like a human voice"—I just read it in Rod[7]—is a man who doesn't distinguish himself, and who doesn't distinguish style from the notions of his own orignality. Maupassant had neither a brilliant mind nor an extraordinary sensibility, but he'd had the method hammered into his head, and his work emerges alive, not only from the milieu he examines but from his very being as a writer.

Spoken literature is quickly written, but it doesn't bring to the mind the driving force of style, the joyful expansion of effort. It doesn't take its man very far. It gives him perhaps the power over his work, but not this creation of oneself by oneself, which makes of a few writers the best representatives of humanity, the most accomplished, complete beings who exist, along with monks and saints.

To write, not in order to speak, not even for the sake of writing: but rather *to be*, to become deeper in one's mind and in one's heart.

Translated by Carole Ciano

NOTES

1. Molière (1622–1673): French playwright (and actor) best known for his satirial comedies *Tartuffe* (1664), *Le Misanthrope* (1666), and *Le Bourgeois Gentilhomme* (1670). He died on stage, at the end of *Le Malade imaginaire*.
2. Octave Mirbeau (1848–1917): French journalist and novelist. His best known work, *The Diary of a Chambermaid* (1900) exemplifies the misogyny, sensuality, and social satire that characterizes his writings.
3. Auguste de Staël (1790–1826): the son of the famous writer Madame de Staël. After she died, he devoted his energies to the publication of her works.
4. Catherine II (1729–1796): she ruled Russia from 1762–1796. A patron of arts and literature, she herself wrote memoirs, comedies, and stories.
5. Lord Melbourne (1779–1848): British statesman and prime minister. A favorite of Queen Victoria, he was her mentor in statecraft. He was married to British novelist Lady Caroline Lamb (1785–1828).
6. Charmide: (*Charmides*): one of the earlier Plato's Dialogues, in which Socrates engages the young Charmides on the relation between self-knowledge and the conduct of life.
7. Edouard Rod (1857–1910), Swiss novelist.

Qiu Jin (Ch'iu Chin)

China, 1875–1907

Qiu Jin's brief life ended just before the Republican Revolution of 1911 that brought Imperial China to an end, and it is in many ways an important emblem for the transition between pre-Modern China and the China of the republican era. Qiu Jin wrote mainly in traditional literary forms to express a revolutionary spirit and modern feminism. She advocated new freedoms for women but expressed her own individuality by dressing and acting like a martial male hero. She created a legend out of traditional heroic and religious stereotypes (the male or female warrior, the compassionate—usually female—*bodhisattva*, or Buddha on earth, who saves others from suffering) that served the next generation in its struggle to cast off tradition.

Qiu Jin was born in the prosperous region of Shaoxing, in Zhejiang province, the only daughter in a family that had produced scholar-officials for government service over several generations. Despite a decline in the family's fortunes, Qiu Jin received the excellent traditional literary education reserved for girls whose families could afford the kind of family-operated school she attended. She also engaged in the same pursuits as her brothers: she not only wrote poetry, she also practiced horseback riding and swordsmanship. Married in 1896 at the relatively late age of 21, to the son of an official and colleague of her father's, she experienced restriction on the freedoms she had heretofore enjoyed. She found a measure of freedom once again when her husband took advantage of the corruption of late-Qing officialdom to purchase a position in Peking in 1901. Here she made friends with women who participated actively in the cosmopolitan milieu that was open to Western influence and to change in general. She became increasingly politically aware, and her patriotic fervor was strengthened as China's humiliation grew at Japanese and Western hands. Finally, in 1903, after eight years of marriage and the birth of a son and a daughter, she ended her marriage and left China to study in Japan. Her own family took her children in and aided her financially.

In Japan she devoted most of her time to radical politics, and was named the Zhejiang recruiter for the Revolutionary Alliance, a group dedicated to the overthrow of the old regime. (In Japan she also developed her iconoclastic personal style, dressing as a man and carrying a sword.) In 1906 she returned to China to work for the revolution, and during some months spent in Shanghai, developed a variety of important feminist contacts. Feminist journals had already been started in Shanghai and Peking, but she found them inadequate to the task of moving the masses of Chinese women, so in 1907 she and friends founded the *Zhongguo nübao* (Chinese Women's Journal), a selection from whose first issue (only two were ever published) is included here. Feminism for Qiu Jin was inseparable from the revolutionary mentality generally: she saw the new era to come as one in which barriers to her sex would be swept away along with the humiliation her country was suffering under its corrupt and rigid rulers.

During the last months of her life, she held a position at the Datung (Great Unity) revolutionary training school. With male associates she planned an uprising in Anhui province, but plans went awry, and she was captured, tortured and executed on July 15, 1907. Her poems and the heroic persona she had created immediately became legendary.

Qiu Jin's total literary output is contained in one slim volume, consisting of essays (mostly in classical Chinese, except for the vernacular essays published in the Chinese Women's Journal), poems, letters, and song-poetry in classical Chinese, and a fragment of a vernacular narrative called *Jingwei shih* (Stones of the Jingwei Bird), in a traditional prose-verse form called a *tanci*. (The traditional form expresses modern content: the narrative is about five heroic "modern girls," as Chinese of the time referred to women like Qiu Jin, and their triumphs and troubles.) In her own lifetime, only selections from her diaries and material she wrote for the Chinese Women's Journal were published, but publication of her poetry, essays, and letters began almost immediately after her death. She is revered in the People's Republic of China today, where modern critical editions of her collected works have been published.

Katharine Carlitz

NOTE

For biographical information on Qiu Jin, I am indebted to Mary Rankin, "The Emergence of Women at the End of the Ch'ing: The Case of Ch'iu Chin," in *Women in Chinese Society*, ed. Margery Wolf and Roxane Witke (Stanford, CA: Stanford University Press, 1975), pp. 39–46.

A WARNING TO MY SISTERS
Jinggao Jiemeimen

My beloved sisters: though I am not a person of great scholarly attainments, I am someone who loves her country and her compatriots with all her heart. And isn't it true that we now number some four hundred million? But the two hundred million who are men have gradually begun to take part in the enlightenment of the modern age: their knowledge has increased, their outlook has broadened, their level of scholarship has risen, and their reputation is advancing day by day. This is all due to the fact that they have access to books and periodicals. Isn't theirs an enviable position? That is why people say that reading books and periodicals is the easiest way to broaden the intellect. But alas, while these two hundred million men and boys have entered the enlightened new age, my two hundred million countrywomen are still mired in the darkness of the eighteen levels of their earthly prison, with no thought of advancing even a single stage.* Their feet are bound small, their hair is dressed to a shine; they wear ornaments of buds and blossoms, carved and inlaid; on their bodies are silk and satin, rippling and shimmering, and to their faces they apply the whitest powder and the reddest rouge. Their whole lives long they learn nothing but how to comply with men, and for what they wear and eat they rely upon men entirely. They flatter and coax with their yielding and compliant bodies; they despondently endure cruel treatment, they are frequently driven to tears, and their lives are spent trying to please others—lifelong captives, half-living beasts of burden. Let me ask you, sisters, have you ever in your lives experienced the delights of independence? Consider the lot of the woman who enjoys wealth and honor in a prosperous household, with a hundred servants to answer every call, surrounded by crowds of attendants—when she steps outside, the crowds part before her and throng after her. She is magnificent beyond words. Within her household she can make her orders known by her expression alone—there are no limits to the awe she inspires. Such a woman thinks to herself that it must be her fortunate destiny, prepared by the accumulation of merit in a former life, to be able to rely on a good husband and to pass her days in a life of comfort and respect. And her words are echoed by outsiders who burst into exclamations of envy and admiration—what a happy destiny that lady has! How fortunate she is! How magnificent! How greatly to be respected!—such are their cries of praise, but how little they know of the

anger and bitterness she endures within her walls! The buds and blossoms are like locks of jade and fetters of gold, and the silk and satin are like ropes of brocade or embroidered tethers, binding her ever more tightly. Her servants guard her like jailers and wardens, not to mention her husband, [who is like] the magistrate and the governor of the prison! All orders proceed from the pleasure or anger of this one man. Let me ask you, then: do these wives and mothers, even in their comfortable circumstances, possess in fact the slightest shred of authority? In short, man is the master and woman the slave. Because she chooses to rely on someone else, she hasn't the least bit of independence. And this captive in her secluded women's quarters doesn't even experience her lot as bitterness.

Alas, sisters, there is no one the world over who would willingly be called a slave—so why is it that you, by contrast, consider it no disgrace? It must be that you say to yourselves that we women can't earn our own living, we have no skills, our glory or disgrace depend entirely on our husbands and sons, and so we have no alternative but to submit to every kind of vexation. But if you are content to abandon ambition and dismiss *this* as fate—oh! the only thing anyone has to fear is not having a will of one's own. With will and ambition, one can demand the basis for independence, the skills for self-support. At present, women's schools have increased in number, women's crafts have begun to flourish, and if we study scientific techniques and industrial arts, pursue education and open factories, why can we not support ourselves? No longer will we have to eat our bread in idleness, dependent on father and brother, husband and son. On the one hand we can increase our families' fortunes, and on the other, we can win the respect of men, cleansing ourselves of our reputation for uselessness, and receiving the blessings of self-reliance. Returning home we will gain the welcome and acceptance of our relatives, and out in the world, the lessons and examples of our friends. Husband and wife can take hands and wander about together, sisters can sit and chat side by side [literally, "sleeves touching"]; all pretexts for domestic quarreling will be gone. And with even higher ambition and keener intellect, some of us will achieve high honors, some of us will accomplish glorious deeds—we will be exalted within and without our country, and receive the respect and admiration of all nations. How does the prospect of such an exquisite, enlightened world strike you? Can it be that we are really content with the life of slaves and beasts of burden, with no thought of saving ourselves? If so, it is simply because we are deep in the seclusion of the women's quarters, unable to learn about the affairs of the world, and without the books and periodicals that could broaden our knowledge and intellect. The *Women's Scholarly Journal* existed, but it ceased publication after only three or four numbers, and at present the level of language in the journal *Women's World* is excessively elevated. Eighty or ninety percent of my sisters are still unable to understand classical Chinese, but if there were a periodical written in simple language, they could use their knowledge of the vernacular to read it. If a periodical is too abstruse, however, they simply won't be able to understand it. In publishing the *Chinese Women's Journal*, this is what I have tried to respond to. The language and style [of my paper] are all simple and in common usage, in order to enable my sisters to understand it at first glance, even though great pains were in fact taken for their benefit.

But publishing a journal is only easy to do if sufficient money is available for expenses; if there is not enough money, then all kinds of difficulties unavoidably arise. So my first thought has been to accumulate a capital of 10,000 yuan (in shares of twenty yuan each), rent a building, set up a press to print the newspaper and produce books, and hire reporters, editors, and managers, so that I could bring glory to my two hundred million sisters by producing a high-quality Chinese women's journal and insuring its continued publication. If we can show that we are not backward, that we can establish the basis for our own independence, then things will become a great deal easier for us to accomplish. To this end I've published the prospectus for the *Chinese Women's Journal* in domestic and foreign newspapers, and sent individual copies of the prospectus to all the women's schools. I expect that you sisters have all already seen it. But some time has now elapsed, and aside from four or five people who have bought shares, not a soul has so much as asked about it! This just gives you some idea of the state of our women's world—it's enough to make one's heart ache.

As I reach this point, my tears fall, my heart is sore, and my pen cannot write another word. But wouldn't this attitude simply keep the *Chinese Women's Journal* from ever being published? Moreover, I cannot bear to keep my beloved sisters bound in their earthly prison—I have to exert myself to accumulate a bit of the money I need for expenses, and join my blood and tears to publish what I can for my sisters' reading pleasure. Today, though we've produced our first number, and will exert every effort to follow it with others, money still remains quite a problem. But all things under heaven are difficult to do alone and easy to do when many join together. If there are ardent sisters willing to unite their efforts with mine, then fortune will smile on the *Chinese Women's Journal* and on the whole world of Chinese women.

Translated by Katherine Carlitz

NOTE

* The eighteen levels refer to the Buddhist classification of the afterlife; even for those who were not religious, the term denoted the worst possible fate imaginable.

Leonor Villegas de Magnon   *Mexico/US, 1876–1955*

Leonor Villegas de Magnon was born near Nuevo Laredo, Mexico along the Texas-United States border on June 12, 1876, a few days after Porfirio Díaz, who was to be Mexico's dictator for the next thirty-four years, had triumphantly taken Mexico City. On that day, her father affectionately called her the *Rebelde* (rebel), after military men searching the area for insurgents suspected that the newborn child's cry was that of a hiding rebel. Later, she would grow into the name when she opposed the Díaz dictatorship, rebelling against the ideals of her aristocratic class and against the traditional role of women in her society.

Educated in San Antonio and New York's Bedford Park Convent, where she received her teaching degree, Leonor Villegas married a United States citizen, Adolpho Magnon, and bore three children. With her husband, she moved to Mexico City in 1901, where she wrote various articles against the dictatorship, voicing her revolutionary sentiments and signing them with her family name. Shortly before the revolutionary movement broke out in 1910, she left for the border with her children to see her seriously ill father. On his deathbed, he expressed admiration for her courage, but warned her that the revolution would severely jeopardize their family interests. Her previous writing, however, was only the beginning of her collaboration with the revolutionary efforts; ironically, she would later exhaust her inheritance from her father in support of the revolutionary cause.

Separated from her husband during the first years of the revolution, Villegas de Magnon became actively involved in the political arena in the Laredo, Texas area, specifically as a member of the *Junta Revolucionaria* (Revolutionary Council). She used her fiery pen to inform the general public of the latest developments in the revolutionary movement as a guest writer to Texas-Mexican newspapers *La Crónica* (The Chronicle) and *El Progreso* (The Progressive) and organized some of the first women's civic organizations in the area such as Unión, Progreso y Caridad (Unity, Progress and Charity). As part of a concerted effort to provide an alternative school system to instruct children of Mexican ancestry in their native language, she opened a kindergarten in her Laredo home.

On March 17, 1913, when Nuevo Laredo was under attack by Jesus Carranza's revolutionary troops, Villegas de Magnon recruited women from her organizations and formed a medical relief group to care for wounded soldiers. This group later became La Cruz Blanca (The White Cross), the medical auxiliary that would accompany the *Carrancistas*, the revolutionary forces, from the border region to Mexico City.

Many women, from both sides of the border, were to risk their lives and leave their families in support of the revolutionary cause. Years later, however, when their participation had still not been acknowledged and their contribution to the revolutionary cause was running the risk of being forgotten, Villegas de Magnon decided to write her personal account of these historic events. She originally composed two versions—one in English, the other in Spanish. The English manuscript has been lost, apparently stolen by an unscrupulous publisher. The Spanish manuscript entitled *La Rebelde* (The Rebellious Woman), covers the period from

1876 through the 1920s, and documents episodes and incidents that focus on the heroic actions by women including long lists of the participants' names. Written in third person and with romantic fervor—reminiscent of Latin America's literary tradition in which romanticism and the struggle for freedom are inseparable—the narrative voice interweaves the *Rebelde's* life story with La Cruz Blanca's saga. The following excerpt captures the first moments of its creation, and women's involvement in the revolution.

Villegas de Magnon's life story exemplifies the realities of a people whose daily existence transcends the limitations imposed by political and national boundaries. Until now her written contributions have remained virtually unrecognized—peripheral to both countries, fragmented by a border. Not only does her work attest to the vitality, strength and involvement of women in socio-political concerns, but it stands as one of the very few written documents which consciously challenges stereotyped misconceptions of the Texas Mexicans held by both Mexican-and Anglo-Americans during that historical period. Retrieval of works such as hers is filling a gap in the tradition of precursors to contemporary Chicana writers and feminism, whose peripheral "nonexistence" has denied them influence in Chicano literature.

Clara Lomas

from THE REBELLIOUS WOMAN
La Rebelde

The huge and powerful state of Texas, whose lands were fertilized by Mexican blood years ago, also responded to the call of a noble cause, cursed Cain, and took pity at the just call for sacrifice.

This was the *Rebelde's* announcement to the *Junta Revolucionaria* in Laredo, Texas, after a twenty-six hour automobile journey along the border from Brownsville to El Paso, while in the Mexican towns on the other side of the border, the loyalists were grouping themselves, ready for battle.

Arriving enthusiastically with her observations, the *Rebelde* seized Mr. Melquiades García's beautiful Mexican flag, gave it to a faithful servant of Juárez's[1] country mounting a fiery horse, and told him: "Parade this throughout the entire city of Laredo." As he did, a multitude of more than five thousand people followed the colors, outraged by the Usurpation and raised to renewed dignity by the strong man of Coahuila.

On March 17 of the tragic year, Don Jesús Carranza attacked the well-fortified plaza of Nuevo Laredo guarded by Guardiola. Moved by an irresistible impulse when she heard the first shots fired, the *Rebelde* quickly dressed and wrote the following message on a piece of paper: "Children: when you get up, go to your uncle's house. Wait for me there. I'll be back soon."

Although it was only six in the morning, the deserted streets did not discourage her from proceding. She resolved to cross the bridge [border] and volunteer as a nurse.

Her fate was decided in a few moments. Many years earlier, her mother had suggested that she hoist the white flag of compassion that cares for and heals the wounded in war. The *Rebelde* now did not hesitate.

Just as she was about to get into her automobile, another vehicle arrived from the neighboring city. In it were a group of young women who, following the example of many other people, had preferred to escape from the battle zone. The *Rebelde* convinced them that it was necessary to return. They got out of their car to get into hers.

Among these women was Jovita Idar,[2] who had spent the night in Nuevo Laredo and who, as a reporter, was well informed about the events. Since Jovita was near her house (the weekly newspaper office, *La Crónica*), she went in to say hello to her father and ask his permission to cross the river again, in order to collaborate with the *Rebelde*. While the latter was waiting for her friend, she entered the editorial room. Unexpectedly, she noticed a white towel hanging on the back of a chair. Suddenly inspired, she reached for it, but clumsily dropped it on top of a can of red paint used in the presses. Coincidences can sometimes occur but are only rarely realized. Seeing a brush inside the can, the *Rebelde* took it, drew a cross on the piece of cloth, for its symbolic significance, and hung it from the automobile's windshield. The ambulance service that would so effectively assist the revolutionary movement was thus begun.

That improvised flag accompanied the *Rebelde* in her initiation as a nurse in the battlefield. The first unit of the auxiliary service was formed by Elvira and Jovita Idar, María Alegría, Araceli García, Rosa Chávez, Mrs. Antonia S. de Garza, Refugio Garza Góngora, with the *Rebelde* as its leader.[3]

During the battle between the *Carrancistas* and the *Federales* (government troops) in the Nuevo Laredo plaza, these volunteer women arrived well prepared with medical and other appropriate supplies. They were welcomed with evident satisfaction and promptly moved forward to aid those wounded in the armed battlefield. The local authorities arranged to have them take charge at the Civil Hospital, and the wounded and dead soldiers were brought there.

The relief provided by these nurses was invaluable from the very first moments. Risking their own lives, they entered the battlefield

to care for the fallen soldiers. One by one, they were carefully collected and tended to, then taken to the hospital in large automobiles, accompanied by nurses. Once there, they were put under the best care of volunteer American doctors, Hamilton, Wilcox, and McGregor, and Mexican doctors, Salinas Puga, Juan F. de la Garza, Garza Gutiérrez, Francisco Canesco, García Cantú, Serrano.

The *Rebelde* was the last to leave the almost deserted battlefield. Carranza's defeated troops had been forced to retreat. Only one soldier was still standing: the flag carrier. Realizing he was alone and too close to the *Federales*, he pulled the flag from the pole, wrapped it around himself and slowly retreated to join his platoon. A serene, heroic action meriting mention.

The *Rebelde* stood stunned, watching the brave warrior, when nearby, government officer Salvador Gonzales raised his rifle and aimed. With lightening speed, the *Rebelde* ran out, snatched his arm and pushed the gun aside to prevent him from shooting. Infuriated she cried, "No! Who is more noble of the two? That brother of yours who is serving as a flagpole or you who spares his life, honoring your own flag!"

"You're right," replied the government soldier.

Silently, he accompanied the *Rebelde* to pick up the flagpole left in the field. "This flagpole is yours. Put *La Cruz Blanca*'s flag here." The last *Carrancista* was out of sight.

They returned to the hospital together and met with the nurses and the doctors. They signed a deed that read: "We have witnessed the actions of the nurses headed by the *Rebelde* and attest to their bravery and spirit of sacrifice."

They cared for the wounded Constitutionalist soldiers[4] for several weeks in their enemies' territory, without the latter ever noticing the true political colors of the nurses.

It was necessary to remain there to protect the lives of those who, when they had recuperated, would be executed. Once they were doing much better, the nurses began advising every one of the prisoners to escape that very night by taking the road closest to the river, where deep ravines were located.

The river—which ceases to be the Río Bravo and becomes the Río Grande (grandiose for its tranquility and hospitality)—protected the fugitives and led them to safety. The pitch-dark night collaborated in the feat, as well as the festival taking place in the plaza, where the Federal Army leaders and officials were happily enjoying themselves.

Pancho's loyal companion, Julia, had died.[5] Pancho was still living in the same house near the riverbank but was no longer a candy vendor. Some time earlier, Don Joaquín had bought him a skiff, oars, and a pole, with which he made his living by transporting passengers. He had captured everyone's heart on both banks and was able to continue his modest business even after the construction of the pedestrian bridge.

The *Rebelde* went to look for him. They agreed to have him wait for the wounded. He gave her the necessary details and counter-signs, then undertook the dangerous adventure alone. Meanwhile, at the hospital, the rebels were scaling the adobe wall one by one, covered by nurses keeping the soldiers occupied while others remade the beds with large pillows to look like the convalescents. Late into the night, when the festival was at its peak and the thirty wounded soldiers had escaped, the nurses began to leave telling the guards they were going to the festivities. They were allowed to pass. Moments later, in a car specially prepared for them, they crossed the bridge never to return. The hospital was left in the hands of the *Federales*.

The *Rebelde* returned to wait for Pancho at his house, accompanied by Araceli, the young nurse who had stayed in the hospital until she saw the last prisoner leave. Since several hours would go by before Pancho would return, both women covered themselves with some dark blankets and cautiously went down to the riverbank where, with a view of Nuevo Laredo, they continued the wait.

In the city before them, window lights gradually faded. The illumination of the streets fused slowly with the arrival of dawn.

Translated by Clara Lomas

NOTES

1. Benito Juárez (1806–1872): an Indian Lawyer, military and political leader, and statesman. He helped to overthrow the Mexican dictatorship in 1855, led the liberals to victory in the War of the Reform (1858–1861) and was Pressident of Mexico from 1857 to 1865 and then again from 1867 until his death. Responsible for limiting the power of the church and the army, and the transfer of power from Spanish descendants to the indigenous population, he also defeated France's attempt to colonize the country.

2. Along with her father, and her brothers, Jovita Idar published *La Crónica* and organized the *Primer Congreso Mexicanista* (The First Mexicanist Congress) in 1911. Jovita Idar also formed the *Liga Femenil Mexicana*. These two organizations provided a political forum to deal with racial discrimination. See José Limón, "El Primer Congreso Mexicanista de 1911: Precursor to Contemporary Chicanismo," *Aztlán*, Spring and Fall 1974, pp. 85–117.

3. This is a brief example of the long lists of women participants that Villegas de Magnon provides throughout the entire text.

4. Read revolutionary soldiers.

5. Julia and Pancho were house servants of the Villegas family until Don Jaoquín, the *Rebelde's* father, remarried and was forced to let them go. He felt compelled to provide for their well being and helped them in any way he could, as the *Rebelde* recounts.

Renée Vivien   (Pauline Tarn)   *France, 1877–1909*

Renée Vivien was born Pauline Tarn in England of an English father and American mother; she chose to live the last ten years of her brief life—she died at 32, as a result of a combination of alcoholism, drug abuse, and what today would be called anorexia nervosa—in France, and to use the French language to incarnate a homoerotic ideal. Although little is known either about her upbringing or education,[1] the decision to seek exile in Paris was probably based on her desire to be near the author Violet Stilleto, whom she had met in 1890 and who was to die in 1901.

In Paris, Vivien became part of a significant lesbian community devoted to the arts and comprised in part of a number of well-to-do American expatriates, including the Philadelphia socialite Natalie Clifford Barney, who became her lover and with whom she traveled to the Greek island of Mytilene in 1904 in a failed effort to established a Sapphic community of poets. During this period, when Colette herself was involved in homosexual affairs, the two writers were friendly, and Colette later wrote of Vivien and her circle, not without ambivalence, in several pieces, including *The Pure and the Impure* (1932).

Making her literary début in 1901 with *Études et préludes*, Vivien published twelve more volumes within ten years: Although she wrote short stories, novellas, prose poems (some of which have been published in translation under the title of *The Women of the Wolf and Other Stories*, 1983), and a novel that displays an appealing humor and satiric bent not found in her poetry, it was her poetry that created a sensation and won her critical acclaim, marking her as one of the "Amazones" during her own day. She created what Sandia Belgrade, one of her translators, has called "a legitimizing mythology" for lesbians, based on the historical figure of the poet Sappho of Lesbos—an aspect that served to reawaken interest in Vivien's works and caused them to be translated in the most recent wave of feminism.

In her own day, Vivien was acclaimed for her ability to capture a sensuous Greek ideal of beauty in a highly wrought, Parnassian, verse; others detected the more modern influences of Verlaine and Baudelaire, particularly the decadent poet of *Fleurs du mal*.[2] The selections here are taken from *A L'heure des mains jointes*, (*The Sweet Hour of Hand in Hand*, derived from an English line by the pre-Raphaelite poet Dante Rossetti, 1906) and *Sillages* (Traces, 1908).

NOTES

1. The critical biography by Karla Jay, *The Amazon and the Page: Natalie Clifford Barney and Renée Vivien* (Bloomington: Indiana University Press, 1988) should add to our knowledge of Vivien's life.
2. Parnassian. The norm of French poetry between the Romantic era and the Symbolists, characterized by formalist precision and the use of exotic and classical subject matter: related to a school of nineteenth-century French poets named after their journal *Parnasse contemporain* (Contemporary Parnassus, 1866–1876) who were influenced by the doctrine of art for art's sake. Paul Verlaine (1844–1896): his early work is identified with the Parnassian school, and his later work established him as an important Symbolist. Charles Baudelaire (1821–1867): great precursor of the Symbolist movement in poetry. *Les Fleurs du mal* (1857) caused him to be tried and found guilty of offenses against religion and public decency.

ONE-EYED LOVE
L'Amour Borgne

I love you with my single eye, I leer at you
Like a Chinese at opium:
I love you with my one-eyed love,
Young girl as white as arum.
I want your dark brown eyelids,
And your voice slower than a timbrel;
I love you with my sinister eye
Where shines the anger of rum.

I follow you with my stare, like a wanton ape,
Drunk like a balloon without ballast.
Your fickle soul of a Sphinx
Floats between middling nonsense
And I pant toward the bait
Of vibrant breasts, of supple torso
Where grace marries force,
And of eyes green like the west.

Your face is blurred across the curtains;
And you meditate, a dry fruit
Between your Florentine lips
Where a Greek smile is appeased.
I die at your brief words...
I want you with your teeth
To pierce my eye where dreams boil over
Like a macaw, with one sharp peck.

Translated by Sandia Belgrade

DRESSED
Vêtue

I

Your dress is part of your enchanted being.
Oh my beloved!...It is a trace of your beauty.

Inhaling it, your scent is what I steal.
Your intimate heart lives in the folds of your
                                                    dress.

The odor of our past kisses, lies in these
                                                    folds...
It recalls our divine oblivion.

In my deepest being I am almost jealous
Of the clinging fabric which your body weds.

I dare confess, some night unsure
When it's at last expressed...We both love
                                                    you.

To have been so near your supreme softness,
Your dress is my rival, and yet I love her...

II

You no longer love this ancient dress.
Long and silky like an unreal iris.

But I love and want and guard it.
The past remains, time gone by slows for me.

I adore the folds of this transparent veil
Which no longer covers your indifferent body.

Keep for me, like a mummy thus perfumed,
Your dress of a beautiful past, oh my friend!

Translated by Jay Miskowiec

Yosano Akiko   *Japan, 1878–1942*

Yosano Akiko (her maiden name was Hō), one of the pioneers of new poetry and an early feminist writer, published her first poetry in the journal of the Kansai Youth Literary Society in 1899. The daughter of a confectioner in Sakai, she soon became active with the *Shinshisha* (New Poetry) group of poets led by Yosano Tekkan, the charismatic poetry reformer, whose journal, *Myōjō* (Venus) began publication in 1900. Later that year, Tekkan made a tour of the Kansai area and Akiko met him at that time. Several months later she left her family home and moved with Tekkan in Tokyo; they married the following year. In the course of their long marriage (Tekkan died in 1935), Akiko raised eleven children, published nearly two dozen volumes of poetry, supported new writers and poets, wrote children's stories, and wrote on such women's issues as suffrage and education.

Akiko's first volume of poetry *Midaregami* (*Tangled Hair*), appeared in 1901. The sensuality of the nearly four hundred poems, inspired by her love affair with Tekkan, brought her passing notoriety and lasting fame. The new style and openly passionate content of her poetry were both a model for and example of the efforts of the *Myōjō* group: although the New Poetry movement was short-lived (*Myōjō* ceased publication in 1908), both Akiko and Tekkan were instrumental in breaking new ground for poetic diction and expression. In particular, Akiko revitalized the classical *tanka* form, lending it a new immediacy (of the kind that characterizes the western lyric, with which it may be compared). And like lyrics, Akiko's *tanka* are often written in the guise of various persona—the priest, the lonely traveler, the geisha or *maiko* (dancing girl), as well as a variety of lovers.

During the Russo-Japanese War (1904–1905) and later, Akiko was an outspoken critic of the military. Of note is the poem printed here, which she wrote in response to rumors that a suicide mission might attempt to take Port Arthur and in fear that her brother might be tempted to participate. Antinationalist, if not antiwar, the poem managed to evade Meiji censorship but incurred scurrilous attacks of the sort that became the battlecry of witch hunters for the next forty years.*

In addition to her writing and lecturing on social issues, Akiko is remembered for her commentaries on, and translations into modern Japanese of a number of classical literary masterpieces, including *Genji monogatari* (*The Tale of Genji*). Her last major work was a collaboration with a number of other poets in producing The New *Manyōshū* (hearkening back to the earliest collection of Japanese poetry, the eighth-century "Collection of Ten Thousand Leaves"). Although she was ill and often bedridden in her last years, her major literary contributions and the romantic aura that gathered around her early life made her one of the few prewar woman writers who has always been recognized in the largely male Japanese literary world.

Phyllis I. Lyons

NOTE

* Jay Rubin, *Injurious to Public Morals: Writers and the Meiji State* (Seattle: University of Washington Press, 1984) pp. 57–58: See also Masao Maruyama, *Thought and Behaviour in Modern Japanese Politics* (Oxford: Oxford University Press, 1963) pp. 154–156.

from TANGLED HAIR*
Midaregami

do not ask
if I have any songs
in me now   slender
koto strings without bridges   all
twenty-five echo soundlessly

in the spring breeze
cherry petals flutter to   earth
near the many-tiered
pagoda   on the wings of doves
I will write my new poems

all I've seen are
those green dreams of youth
thin weightless dreams
ah   forgive me   traveler
I lack the stuff of stories

the dancing girl
drifts off to sleep   how lovely
her slumbering face
this morning   aboard the riverboat
of spring   leaving the capital

spring is short
what is there in life that
does not decay
I let him caress
these breasts   their vital force

to punish men
those men of heavy sins
was I created
with skin clean and pure
with black hair hanging long
                    Translated by Laurel Rasplica Rodd

In my bath—
Submerged like some graceful lily
At the bottom of a spring,
How beautiful
This body of twenty summers.

With this ax
I strike my koto!
Listen!
The sound of life's end!
Of God's will!

Having rowed out to see the lotus
And now back at dusk—
Was it red flowers or white,
Priest,
That so detained you?

Morning wisteria,
Soft murmurs of love,
His hand on the back of my neck,
O powerless to detain him,
My lover of one night!

Still yearning
After the good,
The true, the beautiful?
O, my love, this flower in my hand
Is dazzling red!

A thousand lines
Of black black hair
All tangled, tangled—
And tangled too
My thoughts of love!

Sleeve raised
As if to strike her love,
She tries to turn the gesture
Into
A dance!

When the gods of doubt
And unbelief
Stole upon me,
Suddenly colorless
The spring flowers!

Weren't
The many poems of love
We exchanged
By candlelight last night
Too wordy?
                    Translated by Sandford Goldstein
                    and Shinoda Seishi

NOTE

* The *tanka*, also known as the *waka*, 31-syllable verses in
a 5−7−5−7−7 pattern, was a form already in use in the
early classical period (784−1100); they also came to be
arranged into coherent sequences to form, in effect, long
poems in the mid-classical period (1100−1241). Traditionally used to express tenderness, yearning, and melancholy, tanka were often part of the courtship ritual; this
also made them amenable to the Romantic influence of
Byron, Goethe, and Shakespeare, who had, by the time
Akiko began writing, been translated into Japanese. The
form was regulated by the Imperial Poetry Bureau beginning in 1871.

Color imagery and nature symbols are very much
part of the Japanese tradition; the former is especially
characteristic of the school with which Akiko was
associated. Some knowledge of these may be helpful in
reading her: The lotus is associated with the Buddha;
who is often depicted sitting on lotus leaves; cherry
blossoms are associated with spring and wisteria with
late spring and the approach of summer and are often
used to symbolize mutability. Cherry blossom festivals
were held in the old capitol Kyoto (and elsewhere), the
center of famed Buddhist temples. Red, as in the West, is
associated with passion, white with purity; white flowers
are also associated with mourning and death.

MY BROTHER,
YOU MUST NOT DIE
Kimi Shinitamō Koto nakare

My young brother, I weep for you.
My brother, you must not die.
You, the last born,
Apple of our parents' eyes.
Did they teach you to hold a sword,
Teach you to kill?
Did they nurture you for twenty-four years
And send you to kill and die?

You are to carry on the name
Of a proud old house,
Merchants of Sakai.
My brother, you must not die.
Whether the fortress at Port Arthur falls
Or not—what does it matter?
Should it concern you? War is not
The tradition of a merchant house.

My brother, you must not die.
Let the Emperor himself go
Off to war.
"Die like beasts,
Leaving pools of human blood.
In death is your glory."
If that majestic heart is truly wise,
He cannot have such thoughts.

Ah, my young brother,
You must not die in battle.
Since this past autumn, your aged mother,
Widowed,
Has been pathetic in her grief.
Now she's sent her son away and keeps the
house alone.
Even in this "secure and joyful" reign
Her white hairs increase.

Weeping in the shadow of the shop curtain,
Your young bride
Of but ten months—
Have you forgotten her? Do you not yearn for
her?
Imagine her misery
If you to whom she would turn in sorrow
Were gone.
Oh no, my brother, you must not die.

Translated by Laurel Rasplica Rodd

FIRST LABOR PAINS

Today I am in pain,
Physical pain.
Silently, eyes open,
I lie on the birthing bed.

Why, I wonder,
As death flickers before my eyes,
Does the young doctor comfort me
With talk of the joys of childbirth?
Those I know—far better than he—
But can that help me now?

Knowledge is not reality.
Experience, too, belongs to the past.
All of you—please hush!

Keep to your roles as spectators.
I am alone,
Unique in heaven and on earth.
My teeth bite into my lip
As I await the inevitable.

For now giving birth is
The only reality.
The explosion comes from within me.
There is no choice; nothing else exists.
With the first labor pains
The sun goes pale,
The indifferent world quiets,
And I—I am alone.

Translated by Laurel Rasplica Rodd

Sarojini Naidu   *India, 1879–1949*

Sarojini Chattopadhyay was born the eldest of six children into an ancient Bengali Brahmin family. Her mother was Varada Sundari, her father Aghorenath Chatto-Padhyay, the first Indian to gain a doctorate in science and the founder of Nizam College. Their home in Hyderabad was a center of culture that encompassed Hindu and Muslim and East and West, and was a source of enlightened opinion on caste and the position of women. Sarojini received an advanced education, matriculating at Madras University at the age of 13 and studying in England from 1895 to 1898 before returning to India to marry the non-Brahmin Dr. Govindurajulu Naidu, a widower ten years her senior, to whom she bore four children, two sons and two daughters.

Naidu's mature life clearly falls into two major parts. That of her poetic achievement is concentrated mainly in the period from 1898 to 1914. The political involvement, initiated as early as 1904 and crystallized when she met Mahatma Gandhi in 1914 and became his lifelong disciple and friend, continued to her death in 1949.

Naidu refused to speak English until the age of 9, but by the age of 11 she had written her first poem in that language. Initially influenced by her reading of the English Romantic and Victorian poets (as in her first volume, *Songs*, published 1895), she later indicated her indebtedness to the Decadent movement by dedicating *The Golden Threshold* (1905) to Edmund Gosse; the book also carried a prefatory essay by Arthur Symons. (She had met them and other members of the Rhymers Club while studying at Cambridge.) It was followed by *The Bird of Fame* (1912; its title derives from the opening lines of the *Rubáiyát*) and *The Broken Wing* (1917). Her collected works were published in *The Sceptred Flute* in 1928.

The Feather of the Dawn was published posthumously in 1961. Her work is characterized by the use of traditional poetic diction and verse forms and an intense lyricism that often borders on the erotic and melancholy. Part of an Indo-Anglian tradition initiated in the 1830s, Naidu's oeuvre contributes a jeweled and sophisticated style as well as a distinctively Indian subject matter and tonality to poetry written in English.

Naidu's political achievement is intertwined with India's successful efforts to free itself from colonial rule. It begins with her active involvement in the fight for women's rights: the liberation of women becomes inseparable from the liberation of India. Some of the highlights of the career include the founding of the Women's Indian Association and the introduction of resolutions for the franchise of women; her first speech in 1916 before the Indian National Congress—the organization leading the fight against British imperial domination—and her subsequent election as its president in 1925; her activities as a sort of roving ambassador—in Africa in 1924 and 1929, in America and Canada in 1928 and 1929; and her participation in and leadership of Gandhi's *Satyagraha* and the Quit India movements, for which she was arrested and imprisoned three times, in 1930, 1932, and then again in 1942. In 1947 she was asked to preside over the Asian Relations Conference, and after independence, she became the first woman governor, appointed to head the state of Uttar Pradesh. One of the great women in Indian history, Sarojini Naidu was accorded full state honors at her death.

SUTTEE*

Lamp of my life, the lips of Death
Hath blown thee out with their sudden breath;
Naught shall revive thy vanished spark . . .
Love, must I dwell in the living dark?

Tree of my life, Death's cruel foot
Hath crushed thee down to thy hidden root;
Naught shall restore thy glory fled . . .
Shall the blossom live when the tree is dead?

Life of my life, Death's bitter sword
Hath severed us like a broken word,
Rent us in twain who are but one . . .
Shall the flesh survive when the soul is gone?

NOTE

* Also *sati*: ritual burning of a Rajput widow on her husband's funeral pyre, it spread after 300 A.D. to the Brahmins and later to all castes; the practice, said to be voluntary, was virtually eradicated during the nineteenth century, though it is difficult to estimate how pervasive or systemic it actually was. The religious justification was that by sacrificing herself, the wife won eternal merit and broke the karmic cycle.

TO INDIA

O young through all thy immemorial years!
Rise, Mother, rise, regenerate from thy gloom
And, like a bride high-mated with the spheres,
Beget new glories from thine ageless womb!
The nations that in fettered darkness weep
Crave thee to lead them where great mornings
                                        break . . . .

Mother, O Mother, wherefore dost thou sleep?
Arise and answer for thy children's sake!

They Future calls thee with a manifold sound
To crescent honours, splendours, victories
                                                vast;
Waken, O slumbering Mother, and be
                                        crowned,
Who once wert empress of the sovereign Past.

EDUCATION OF INDIAN WOMEN

The following is a lecture delivered at the Indian Social Conference, Calcutta, 1906.

It seems to me a paradox, at once touched with humour and tragedy, that on the very threshold of the twentieth century, it should still be necessary for us to stand upon public platforms and pass resolutions in favor of what is called female education in India—in all places in India, which, at the beginning of the first century was already ripe with civilization and had contributed to the world's progress radiant examples of women of the highest genius and widest culture. But as by some irony of evolution the paradox stands to our shame, it is time for us to consider how best we can remove such a reproach, how we can best achieve something more fruitful than the passing of empty resolutions in favor of female education from year to year. At this great moment of stress and striving, when the Indian races are seeking for the ultimate unity of a common national ideal, it is well for us to remember that the success of the whole movement lies centerd in what is known as the woman question. It is not you but we who are the true nation-builders. But it seems to me that there is not even an unanimous acceptance of the fact that the education of women is a essential factor in the process of nation-building. Many of you will remember that, some years ago, when Mrs. Sathianadhan first started "The Indian Ladies' Magazine," a lively correspondence went on as to whether we should or should not educate our women. The women themselves with one voice pleaded their own cause most eloquently, but when it came to the man there was division in the camp. Many men doubtless proved themselves true patriots by proving themselves the true friends of education for the mothers of the people. But others there were who took fright at the very word. "What," they cried, "educate our women? What then will become of the comfortable domestic ideals as exemplified by the luscious 'halwa' and the savoury 'ome-

lette'?" Others again were neither "for Jove nor for Jehovah," but were for compromise, bringing forward a whole syllabus of compromises. "Teach this," they said, "and not that." But, my friends, in the matter of education you cannot say *thus far and no further*. Neither can you say to the winds of Heaven "Blow not where ye list," nor forbid the waves to cross their boundaries, nor yet the human soul to soar beyond the bounds of arbitrary limitations. The word education is the worst misunderstood word in any language. The Italians, who are an imaginative people, with their subtle instinct for the inner meaning of words, have made a positive difference between *instruction* and *education* and we should do well to accept and acknowledge that difference. *Instruction* being merely the accumulation of knowledge might, indeed, lend itself to conventional definition but *education* is an immeasurable, beautiful, indispensable atmosphere in which we live and move and have our being. Does one man dare to deprive another of his birthright to God's pure air which nourishes his body? How then shall a man dare to deprive a human soul of its immemorial inheritance of liberty and life? And yet, my friends, man has so dared in the case of Indian women. That is why you men of India are today what you are: because your fathers, in depriving your mothers of that immemorial birthright, have robbed you, their sons, of your just inheritance. Therefore, I charge you, restore to your women their ancient rights, for, as I have said it is we, and not you, who are the real nation-builders, and without our active co-operation at all points of progress all your Congresses and Conferences are in vain. Educate your women and the nation will take care of itself, for it is true today as it was yesterday and will be to the end of human life that the hand that rocks the cradle is the power that rules the world.

Bahinabai Chowdhary   *India, ca. 1880–1951*

An illiterate Marathi peasant poet from Jalgaon, Bahinabai represents a significant oral tradition that is largely absent from this volume, because so little of it has been recorded. She was named after a seventeenth-century Bhakti* poet, Bahinabai (1625–1700), another peasant woman who wrote, besides a large number of poems, an autobiography in verse that traced her spiritual journey not only in this life, but in her twelve previous lives. Bahinabai Chowdhary's son, Sopandev, is also a poet. He dedicated his first collection to his mother with this line: "I lay at your feet your own achievement." Twenty years later, at her death, he published a volume of her songs under the title *Bahinaichi gani* (Bahinabai's Songs) recorded by him and by her brother. These poems caused something of a stir in the literary world, for quite apart from their significance as individual works they gave evidence of the continuing creativity and the tremendous range of the oral tradition.

The poems themselves are composed in the Khandeshi-Varhadi dialect in the traditional meter and rhyme scheme used by women to create children's lullabies, field chants, and songs sung to accompany the grinding of grain with the *chakki* or handmill: four-line stanzas using the *ovi* meter with second and fourth lines rhyming. Like the autobiography of Lakshmibai Tilak, these songs have vitalized the Marathi literary language, expanding the literary horizon by their philosophic depth and imaginative reinterpretation of tradition. Though not always noted in histories of Marathi literature, the songs have become standard reading in textbooks and popular music to a generation that heard them sung in a film on Bahinabai that appeared in the 1960s.

NOTE

* *Bhakti movement:* (ca. 12th to 16th centuries) a popular social and religious movement critical of the empty formalism of ritual and the ower of the priestly Brahmins. It emphasized individual ecstatic or mystic experience. The philosophers and poet-saints of the movement were weavers, blacksmiths, cobblers, and others drawn from the traditionally lower castes. Among them were many major women poets.

THE MIND*
Mun

The mind, a roving cow
Loose among the crop.
Drive it off again, again,
It still keeps coming back.

The mind unbridled, loose,
It goes so many ways,
Like ripples on the water
Running with the wind.

The mind so fickle, fickle,
Who can catch it in his hand?
Breaking out and running
Like the blowing of the wind.

The mind has poison, poison,
Far worse than any other.
Snake or scorpion bite at least
Can be cured by charms.

(*continued*)

The mind a bird, a bird,
What words can catch its flash?
Here on earth a moment
Then gone into the sky.

The mind is darting, darting,
It never can stay still.
A lightning bolt again, again,
It falls and strikes the earth.

The mind how tiny, tiny,
As small as poppyseed.
The mind how vast, how vast,
The whole sky cannot fill it.

God, how could you give the mind?
There's nothing in the world like it.
How did you do it, Yogi?
A marvel you created.

God, how could the mind be like this,
How could it come to be?
Here when you were wide awake
How could you dream this dream?

**Translated by Philip Engblom, Maxine Berntsen,
and Jayant Karve**

NOTE

* The Marathi *mun* encompasses the imaginative and
emotional aspects as well as the cognitive.

ONCE THE LINE OF FATE LAY HIDDEN
Lāpé Kārāmāci Rékhá

Once the line of Fate lay hidden
Underneath a spot of red
When my kumkum was erased
It revealed the line of Fate
Oh dear Lord in your house too
Has the fount of wealth run dry
I see here upon my palm,
My Fate carves a cruel path
Oh Lord tell me no tales now
Be they true or be they false.
For good fortune does not show
In the lines upon my palm.
Say what is this thing called Fate
Which my feet to faintness drives
I go round and round again
Living through these nine long lives
Oh Lord bless my darling jewels
This is all the grace I ask.
For good fortune there does lie
It is not found in almanacs.
No do not dear astrologer
Do not try to read my palm
For I know my Fate already
I don't need you at my door.

Translated by Shanta Gokhale

WHAT IT SHOULD NOT BE CALLED
Kshalé Kaya Mhenū Nahi

If it does not open out,
    It should not be called a cotton boll.

        If it does not speak the name of Hari.
            It should not be called a mouth.

                If it does not move with the blowing wind,
                    It should not be called a leaf.

If it does not hear the name of Hari,
    It should not be called an ear.

        If there are no wells or channels,
            It should not be called an orchard.

                If it has not seen God's image.
                    It should not be called an eye.

What makes you sleep on an empty belly
Should not be called night.

If it withdraws itself from giving,
It should not be called a hand.

What has no water in it
Should not be called a stream.

What draws back from cries for help
Should not be called feet.

What comes up empty from the well
Should not be called a water bucket.

What feeds none but itself alone
Should just be called a belly.

She that does not recognize her calf
Should not be called a cow.

She whose breasts do not fill with milk
Should not be called a mother.

No, the rope lying in the path
Should never be called a snake.

He who sells his very own daughter
Should not be called a father.

The milk that's gone bad and sour
Should not be called cream.

She whose love can disappear
Should not be called a mother.

He who forgets his own honor
Should not be called faithful.

He who is ungrateful to his parents
Should not be called a son.

That in which there is no feeling
Should not be called devotion.

That in which there is no real goal
Should not be called strength.

Translated by Philip Engblom and Jayant Karve

Cora Sandel   *Norway/Sweden, 1880–1974*

Cora Sandel is one of the few Scandinavian women writers to have remained in print in English over the past twenty-five years. Considered a classic author in Norway and Sweden, Sandel's spare, ironic yet compassionate style, and feminist grasp of the essentials of women's lives make her accessible to a wide variety of readers.

Born Sara Fabricius in Oslo, she grew up in Tromsø, well within the Arctic Circle. Her earliest ambition was to be an artist, and she moved to Paris in her twenties to study painting. She stayed fifteen years and married the Swedish sculptor Anders Jönsson. Returning with him and their young son to Sweden in 1921, she made the decision to give up painting for writing. She and Jönsson divorced, and Sandel spent most of the rest of her life in Sweden, dying there in 1974.

Sandel is best known for her Alberte trilogy *Alberte og Jakob*; *Alberte og friheten*; and *Bare Alberte* (Alberta and Jacob; Alberta and Freedom; and Alberta Alone, 1926–1939), the semi-autobiographical novels of a young woman's struggle to become a writer. In addition to two other novels *Kranes konditori* (Krane's Cafe, 1945) and *Kjøp ikke Dondi* (The Leech, 1958), Sandel also published five volumes of short stories. Their subjects range from growing up female to bitter relationships between men and women, from touching but nonsentimental stories about animals to humorous sketches from her atelier days in Paris.

The selection "Kunsten å Myrde" (The Art of Murder) is one of her best-known stories. It was originally published in 1935, in the collection *Mange Takk, Doctor* (Thank you, Doctor).

Barbara Wilson

THE ART OF MURDER
Kunsten å Myrde

Grand Sables, 1920

Francine arrives.

I say, "Francine, you've come after all! You're not too tired then?"

"Oh no," answers Francine. "Not so I can't manage the washing up and children's clothes, Madame."

With that she bends her small, serious, early-faded, war-widow face over her tasks and gets to work. Francine has children to provide for. She works as house help for the summer visitors and is paid by the hour. Besides, she is a sensible and dependable person who understands that when you're needed, you're needed.

Today we didn't expect her. She's trekked eighteen kilometers, nine there and nine back, and been to a funeral. It wouldn't have surprised anyone if she hadn't returned to work. But now she stands here after all, rattling our plates.

The whole thing was unexpected. Someone came running, out of breath, over the meadows from the direction of the village shop where the telephone is. A relative of Fran-

cine's, a cousin, had died suddenly and was going to be buried this morning. Would Francine be able to come? "I suppose I'd better," said Francine, stopping her work a moment and considering, while scouring what she held in her hands even harder. When we asked her if she wouldn't rather quit for the day, go home and gather her thoughts a little, perhaps phone the house of mourning, she answered, "No thank you, that's not necessary." And we breathed a sigh of relief. We really do need Francine.

The messenger sat down by the kitchen door and caught his breath.

After a little while Francine turned to him and said, "It was Germaine, wasn't it? It wasn't the sister?"

"They said Germaine on the telephone."

"Good." Francine isn't someone who shows her feelings, either by words or by the expression of her face. Now she was plainly reassured. She almost looked pleased. It seemed a little strange, but Germaine was unmarried and the sister had several small children. Francine probably saw it from that perspective.

All the same it was a pity. I asked, "How did it happen, Francine? A young person like that?"

"Don't know, Madame. She died suddenly, according to what they say."

Francine pressed her lips together and I didn't want to ask more.

I've seen Germaine. I saw her last year. She came driving a cart full of apples for us from the people she worked for—rennet apples, big as children's heads, choice fruit without a spot, a hundred of them. Francine had arranged the purchase.

Germaine was a pretty girl with something gentle but also quite dispirited in her manner. She couldn't be persuaded to sit down, chat a little, drink a glass of cider. She helped us take the apples inside and then wanted to be on her way.

I said, 'But she has to rest a minute. And what about the horse?"

"She'll rest the horse down by the bend," said Francine, who answered for the both of them. "She has acquaintances there." Germaine drove off and Francine explained, "She's shy and a little unsocial, Madame."

"But why? Such a pretty girl!"

"She's like that," said Francine and shrugged her shoulders.

Now she's buried. It's over with.

I should be content with that. Even Francine gives no sign of being otherwise. Taciturn as usual, absorbed in her work.

Yet I've *seen* Germaine, I remember her, however vaguely, and feel I should show my sympathy.

"It must have been hard for the parents, Francine."

Francine doesn't answer right away. Then she says, "Well, it was a daughter..."

"Yes..." I persist, slightly bewildered. And I come out with my thought about the children, using one of those cheap observations we have ready for these occasions, "But if something tragic had to happen—I mean, for the little ones' sakes..."

Francine turns her head a bit and looks at me with a small half smile, as if she finds me more than a little naive. "She did leave a boy, Madame; she had one too. He's five years old."

That puts me in my place. It's not as simple and straightforward as it seems. She did leave a boy; she had one too. It may be worse in every way that this mother and not the other is gone. I've gotten myself into a muddle and had better keep quiet.

Whether or not she means to give me a clearer picture of the case, Francine says, "He's with her parents, naturally. Where else would he be? The father...? A foreign sailor, so we believe. Germaine took a trip to Lorient and then..."

And Francine shrugs her shoulders again.

"So she was out earning a living?"

"She had to, Madame. With a child to support. This last month she was home, though."

"Was she ill then?"

Francine smiles her half smile. It comes and goes so quickly that you can't be sure she really smiled. "Ill? If you want to put it that way, Madame."

An ambiguous answer. It must indicate that Francine is reluctant to talk about it. Well, there are certainly all sorts of illnesses. In order to say something I remark, "It's good, at least, that the boy has a home."

"Yes, of course," allows Francine. "It is." She opens her mouth to say more. Closes it firmly again as if, on thinking it over, she finds it better to be silent about certain things. The situation definitely has a number of angles. It's easy to stand outside, to say, "It's good, at least, that..." These people aren't rich, even though they have a house and a little land, a couple of cows and a pig. Francine, usually so uncommunicative, told me that once. But they're not poor either. And Germaine contributed to the boy's keep.

An intimate question slips from my tongue. Francine's revelations are so strangely unsatisfactory that it would be better if she said nothing. "They do like him, Francine? The boy, I mean? There at the farm?"

"They're not bad to him," answers Francine with reserve.

"Well, I should hope not."

"They're Christian people..."

"Of course."

"It's not his fault."

"No, that's certain."

"But he's a bastard, isn't he? That's always a misfortune."

Francine is absolutely right. And words don't need to mean more than exactly what they say. That it's a misfortune to be a bastard, even for those who have a home, can't be denied. But if you interpret them so that ...interpret them so that...

I wish I'd never gotten into this conversation with oracular Francine. She has a tendency to express herself in double meanings that can be taken many ways, just like those of Delphi. It's all about a parentless little boy, a poor thing five years old, for whom you can't do anything. I get up to go.

Then Francine says—and she says it in an almost cheerful tone, and without any intention of involving us in any drama, "It was over quickly anyway. She did it herself."

"What? Did what?"

"She did it herself, Madame. She took her own life, as they say."

"But good God, Francine—was she *so* unhappy?"

Francine has her own interpretation of the word *unhappy*. She answers, "Oh no, Madame, she wasn't unhappy. But her parents had told her that if it happened again, she'd just have to manage by herself with the first one and the other. And then..."

"And then, Francine? Had it happened. Was she...?"

"Yes, Madame. It appeared that way."

I sit down again. Now I see Germaine plainly before me, remember things about her I didn't know I'd noticed. Pale, diffident, eyes frightened, an uncertain smile...

"But then she was unhappy, Francine."

"She wasn't unhappy, Madame."

"If neither her parents or the child's father..."

"She only had to conduct herself properly. The rest of us do. She could have as well."

I have on the tip of my tongue that that's easy to say. I don't say it. Instead I ask about the child's father. Wasn't it possible to make him responsible this time either? It was his duty...

"Oh..." Francine rubs a plate, holds it up to the light and rubs anew, neat and conscientious. "It was an old man, Madame."

An old man. I'm dumb a second, then say, "Then he could have paid up in any case, if he was an old man."

"Somebody who'd been put away on the farm where she worked, Madame. An old man. They said he was always after her."

I don't know what more to say. I sigh, then I say, "Poor girl." And mean many things by that.

But Francine still has her own opinion and she is determined to make her point. "She had nothing to complain of, Madame. She could have behaved herself decently. We were all sorry for her because she couldn't behave herself decently. So when she got that way again and there already was a boy to raise... then..."

"So they were nasty to her."

"Not nasty. They said what they thought."

"She paid for her son, Francine."

"Not much. There was scarcely enough for one. If there had been two..."

"Now they have to support the boy alone," I say, pleased in a spiteful way.

"There could have been more, Madame. The way she was. And when she barely earned enough for one..."

Francine obviously feels on the side of the majority. She continues to stand there. On the dead woman's side no one stood. The icy breath of loneliness is all around her. She was one of the fragile vessels, perhaps one of those beyond saving. She'd probably have gotten pregnant anyway. It's hopeless to take on her case.

Once again, to emphasize the lighter sides, Francine says, "It wasn't such a great loss, Madame. She had already started to act a little queer."

"What are you saying, Francine?"

"I'm saying she was a little strange lately. She didn't answer anymore if they spoke to her. It was like she didn't see people at all, like she was walking around in a daze. Her reason was almost gone, as they say. And when that's happened, it's almost better..."

Francine doesn't finish. What purpose would it serve? I should be able to understand the general family relief. Why pretend anything else? How much shame, how many expenses, how much stir is avoided now. It's only too reasonable that no one is crying.

But since details of this sort always have interest, Francine informs me, "She hung herself. She tied a cord around her neck and hung herself. It was to be expected, Madame. It was good she didn't throw herself in the well. They were afraid she might think of that. And a

well... It supposedly happened very quickly."

"It wasn't right in front of people?" I no longer know what I should believe and ask absurd questions.

"Oh no, oh no, Madame. Her mother had just turned her back on her. And then she went into the clothes closet. The door was half-way closed so no one heard it. But a few minutes later someone had to go in there and then they found her. She was already dead, so you see it was over quickly. They had hung up clothes-lines there, and she used them..."

I see. That I can't avoid. See above all a mother's back. Wide or narrow, it goes away and doesn't turn. If it had...

I catch myself thinking that it's probably best as it is. She did what was most useful, what they expected of her. And she didn't throw herself into the well. She saw the cord in the storeroom, understood how it could be used...

"It wasn't such a great loss, Madame," says Francine once more. "When a person no longer has her reason..."

She calmly stacks the plates together and puts them back where they belong.

Translated by Barbara Wilson

Sara Estela Ramirez   *Mexico/US, 1881–1910*

Teacher, journalist, labor organizer, political activist, and feminist, the poet Sara Estela Ramirez participated in the ground-laying for the Mexican Revolution of 1910 as a member of the PLM, the Partido Liberal Mexicano (Mexican Liberal Party), and as a member of the anti-clerical Club Redención (Redemption Club), as well as the feminist organization Regeneración y Concordia (Regeneration and Concord). Her association with these groups, and with the alternative press movement that encompassed and united them all, becomes highlighted when seen in relation to the close friendships she formed with the leadership of these organizations; she was an intimate and respected colleague of persons such as Dolores Jimenez y Muro (1848–1925), Elisa Acuña y Rosetti (?–1946), Juana Gutierrez Belén de Mendoza (1875–1942), and Ricardo Flores Magón (1874–1922); her letters to Magón (which are located in the Flores Magón Archives in Tlaltelolco Convent, Mexico, D.F.), in fact, provide a great part of the biographical information available to date about Ramirez. The other primary sources of biographical information are the four eulogies written on the occasion of her death in the

Texas-Mexican newspapers, *El Demócrata Fronterizo* (The Border Democrat) and *La Crónica* (The Chronicle), now located in the Barker Texas History Collection at the University of Texas at Austin.

The eulogies provide details of her early childhood and family life and suggest the high esteem with which she was regarded as a poet and an intellectual. The letters to Magón reveal her own perceptions of the revolutionary struggle and the internal politics within the PLM, her wishes for harmony, clarity, and understanding to govern within the group, and in the midst of it all, her own personal needs as a poet to see her work in published form. Her personal, poetic voice needs to be understood in the context of the collective, public voice that she was a part of; that is, as a worker of the word, Ramirez mediated the struggles that she felt personally and perceived socially and politically amongst her colleagues and loved ones. Not the least of these struggles was the apparent constant physical pain that her illness subjected her to.

Ramirez was born in 1881 at Villa de Progreso, Coahuila. She grew up during the Porfiriato, the period in Mexican history that marked the thirty-four year dictatorship (1877–1911) of the despot Porfirio Diaz (1830–1913), a period of severe national unrest and intense repression of political dissidents. Orphaned of her mother at an early age, Ramirez assumed the responsibility of caring for her aged father and her younger sister. She received her teacher's certificate from the school Ateneo Fuentes, in Saltillo, Coahuila, when she was about 15, and shortly after traveled to Laredo, Texas. There she was integrated into the Texas-Mexican community as a teacher in the alternative schools (where she taught the Spanish language and Mexican culture), and as a member of a growing group of radical journalists (including the well-known Idar family) whose political consciousness spanned north as well as south of the Rio Grande, and who defended vehemently the right of Mexicans to a better and just life. In 1901, at the age of 20, Ramirez began her association with Richardo Flores Magón and the Mexican Liberal Party and also founded the newspaper *La Corregidora* (The Corregidor's Wife), in honor of Josefa Ortíz de Dominguez, a famous heroine of the 1810 Mexican War for Independence; Ramirez placed *La Corregidora* at the service of the Liberal cause. Even though she traveled to Mexico City at times, Ramirez was part of the network of organizers in the northern sector of activity; her responsibility, then, was to serve as a link between Mexicans on either side of the border. As a woman organizer, she was one of the leadership who insisted that women's rights be integrated into the revolutionary struggle.

There are no known copies of *La Corregidora*, nor are there any of *Aurora*, a literary magazine that Ramirez founded in late 1909 or early 1910, which was well received and saluted as a "new paladin of modern ideas" (*La Crónica*, 19 March 1910). The extant body of her poetry appears in the Texas-Mexican newspapers *La Crónica* and *El Demócrata Fronterizo*; these poems can be grouped into four main categories: poems of sisterhood, poems of male-female relationships, philosophical poems, political poems. The poems of sisterhood are generally the most hopeful.

Ramirez died at the age of 29, just before the official beginning of the Mexican Revolution that she helped to shape.

Inés Hernandez

HOW I LOVE YOU!
Cuánto te quiero

For María—on her day—

Last shadow of my family,
Of my loves the supreme ideal,
Faith that strong winds do not sweep away,
Light that lasts with an eternal ray
Over the ruins of my hope
and the despoiling of my dreams,
How I bless your sweet name
and your existence....How I love you!

In my darkness you are a star,
For my sorrows you are consolation,
You have lullabies for my tears,
Your caresses are as a mother's,
For this, sister, I bless your love
And in you I condense
All the world of my immaculate
and lasting love.

How I love you with all my soul,
How your arms form my refuge!
How your life is for my life
The chaste kiss!
I would so wish to give you for your nights
The most beautiful of stars,
I would so wish to give you for your days
The most divine of all dreams,
And in your sanctuary place as page
a good angel
Who would care for you as I do,
Who would love you as I love you.

As long as your sweet life lasts
I bless the heavens,
As long as my life lasts
It will be your incense.

Last shadow of my family,
Of my loves the supreme ideal,
Faith that strong winds do not sweep away,
Light that lasts with an eternal ray
Over the ruins of my hope
and the darkness of my universe,
How I bless your sweet name
and your existence....How I love you!
(1907)

Translated by Inés Hernandez

21 OF MARCH
21 de Marzo

To Juárez*

It is true that the deeds of my homeland,
        which I adore,
As well as her heroes
Number in the thousands.
How many pages of gold
In that history of epic songs!
How many sublime strophes on those pages
Where liberty traced her name
With clear, indelible, red letters!

Sweet truth that I evoke with pride:
How many times has the lofty eagle
Of that holy flag been raised to celebrate
        one of her sons!
Whether for a hero honorably fallen
Or for a triumph honorably celebrated
See how she flies there greatly and beautiful,
Recalling for the nation its epic
A happy day, a memorable day
When that liberator, who, without fortune,
In the rocks of Ixtlan had a cradle
Which the descendants of a king would envy.

How many titans, how many gladiators
With arms of steel destroying
The thrones of rude oppressors!
How many fervent lives sacrificed
on the fields of struggle,
Sustaining their honor with their swords!

Of all these the past speaks to us
And all these are—who would believe it!—
A prologue sublime and irresolute
To the hidden and sought after paradise
Known as Redemption,[2] that yet awaits us.

All those feats,
Cheers that the mountains repeat
Like an echo of the Creator, drive us mad:
And it is for this that on going from mouth
                                        to mouth,

From heart to heart, it is forgotten
That the glory of the present is little,
And the work for the good is unfinished.

(continued)

Is it the fault of chance? It does not
                                        prophesy!
Is it the fault of destiny? I do not believe it!
It is only the fault of human effort
Which will forgive me if I find it to be the
                                        culprit!

How well I know that the conquest of
                                        the good
          that man yearns for
Is not the undertaking of an instant.
That difficult and tremendous task
That begins within the walls of the school
Is yet most distant from us.

Oh pages of yesterday, blessed, holy,
You are the pedestal of glory
To which our feet direct us.

          Let us go forward with persistence,
Now that we have our tutelary gods,
Such as the unconquered Juarez,
Who guides our steps.
Juarez, oh! when the name of the athlete
Rises to my lips with divine accent,
I am happy, because I feel my heart
Shout like a prophet:
You, the indomitable Mexican people,
Look at the past and think of tomorrow,
You are yet most distant from your goal.
(1908)

                              Translated by Inés Hernandez

NOTES

1. Benito Juárez (1806–1872). See notes to de Magnon
   selection.
2. Ramirez's use of the word "Redemptión" must be
   considered in light of the anti-clerical Club Redención
   to which she belonged, along with the Magonista
   position that placed the "redemptive" power of the
   revolution before what was felt to be the false and
   misleading teachings of the Church, which sought to
   convince the people that the true redemption was in the
   afterlife.

REEF
Escollo

If the reef does not cause anger, if it does
          not discourage
To be wounded twice on the same rock;
If not two times, then not a hundred; the
          arena of combat
Provokes triumph and not surrender.

And it is necessary to triumph. Upon the reef
That one day scratched with its cutting
                                        blade,
Is placed the foot that tripped, tranquil,
Making of it an indestructible support.

This obstacle would not terrify a giant.
And in struggle, those souls are giants
Who expose themselves to disaster with the
                                        fiber of stone,
The firmness of diamonds.

Sometimes one vacillates...in the fall,
Phoenix the heart, wanting breath,
Seems to succumb, except in her wound
She drinks faith to climb higher.

Higher still, without fear of thorns,
Nor of audacious blades of smooth stone;
Let them wound! Wounds are divine
When they are sustained by a brave heart.

Blessed be the reef that relieves pain!
Blessed be Lucifer for the rude assault!
Blessed the obstacle that teaches us
To struggle and always to climb higher!
(1908)

                              Translated by Inés Hernandez

Catherine Pozzi

France, 1882–1934

Catherine Pozzi was born in Paris in 1882. Her father was an eminent surgeon and a professor at the Faculté de Médecine. As the senator of Dordogne, he was also a man engaged in politics. Attention was given to literary matters as well: Leconte de Lisle, Montesquiou, Bourget, and Barrès numbered among the family friends; Pozzi's mother was the cousin of poet Jean Lahor who was a great friend of Mallarmé and Verlaine. Pozzi had a classical education from childhood, and she spoke English and German fluently. She did not take her baccalaureate then, however; few girls at the time were encouraged to study for degrees. At the age of 20, she went to England to study at Oxford, where she was a brilliant student. In 1909, she married Edouard Bourdet by whom she had a son. She divorced him shortly after the end of the First World War.

Pozzi had been very athletic as a young woman, but her health gradually declined after childbirth, and she was obliged to give up many activities. Asthma made long conversations a strain for her. More and more, she devoted herself to scientific inquiry in isolation. Purely on the basis of this independent study, she was able to pass the baccalaureate. She returned to Paris from the south of France, where she had been living since the end of the war, to pursue research at the Faculté des Sciences.

Writing became a significant outlet, as she struggled against poor health. Occasionally, her illness left its mark even on the subject of her poetry, as in "Scopolamine" (a sleep potion). Her letters, charming, witty, and literate, soon became the only way she could communicate with many of her acquaintances. Among her correspondents she counted Valéry (who greatly admired her poetry), Rilke, and later, Paulhan, Julien Benda, and Pierre Jean Jouve. Her small poetic œuvre was published at the time of her death, and her diaries in 1987, but her letters remain unpublished. An example of her poetry is included here.

Her philosophy is invoked in *Peau d'âme*, a collection of fragments published posthumously in 1935 (and translated here for the first time), which present her intense meditations on the nature of knowledge and sensory perception, at a time when psychology was trying to reduce these to quantitative terms. In her contemplation of the "present" or the "instant," she reacts against this reductionism. The title is perhaps also an allusion to "Peau d'âne," the fairy tale by Perrault about the princess who hides under a donkey skin. Her thinking was heavily influenced by the Gnostics and Indian religions as well as by genetics theory. Late in life Pozzi came to embrace her own, idiosyncratic form of Catholicism. In the selection that follows, Pozzi names the universe and sensation "yesterday," because, as she says, there is no *first* sensation. The idea may be compared to the concept of the Deconstructionist philosopher, Jacques Derrida (b. 1930) of the "already always" written language, with its capacity to create rather than merely transmit meaning.

Save for scientific articles, the only work that Pozzi published during her lifetime was a novel, *Agnes*, in 1927. Her work is not well-known and the standard literary reference *Dictionnaire des littératures de langue français* (1984) does not mention her. With the recent feminist revival, she is beginning to be discovered.

Colette Gaudin

from THE SKIN OF THE SOUL
Peau d'âme

Are you there, Universe?

—Yes; my name is "Yesterday"...

According to Weber's law,[1] a sensation is more intense if it has been *preceded* by sensations of the same order, and less intense if equivalent impressions are *simultaneous*. This would still be a banality if Fechner[2] had not made use of it in seeking a mathematical equation of feeling, which he established after 24,576 observations and which is false.

However, on that day, you thought tenderly of Weber and Fechner, because you were so close to discovering their secret of the world.

To feel, to feel more. One feels more if one has felt. One feels what one has felt. How could one feel if one had never felt?

WOULD ONE FEEL?

One single day would be clear water, but on that day, the lost universe had come together: the water is sweet or bitter...Today! I call you "Yesterday," and I speak to you in verse.

Yes; and these gentlemen have done a great deal of research to determine what Today would be without Yesterday. The crème de la crème of all professors and even more: Herbert Spencer, Taine, Williams James[3]... Let us not offend the living.

Today without yesterday, they call that a pure sensation.

Even if it were a sensation—well, you understand. Without yesterday, it was pure, at any rate. Unfortunately, it was extremely difficult to erase yesterday. To put it simply, it could not be done. They had to resort to taking a new-born baby; that creature who had never felt anything started from sensation number one.

But, what was even more unfortunate, sensation number one was impossible.

And if it were impossible for a sensation to be the first, it's because it was impossible for a subject to feel a sign of the world that would be the first one.

There is no first sign of the universe for us.

Now, as Perrault said, "That was the magic key."

Translated by Carole Ciano

NOTES

1. Ernst Weber (1795–1878): German physiologist who studied sensory experience and established that ratios, not absolute differences, determine sensory discrimination of least perceptible differences.
2. Gustav Fechner (1801–1877): the creator of psychophysics, gave mathematical form to the relation empirically discovered by Weber between stimulus and sensation, and called it Weber's law.
3. Herbert Spencer (1820–1903): English philosopher chiefly responsible for the popularization of Darwin's theory of evolution and its social application; he coined the phrase "the survival of the fittest." Hippolyte Taine (1828–1893): French thinker, literary and art critic, and historian, champion of the cult of the scientific method in all disciplines. William James (1842–1910): American philosopher and psychologist.

NYX

To Louise also from Lyon and Italy

Oh you my nights, my darkness awaited
Oh proud country, oh secrets unyielded
Oh looks lingering, oh thunderous clouds
Oh flight allowed beyond heaven's bounds

Oh great desire, oh surprise expanding
Oh splendrous journey of the spirit enchanted
Oh evil of evil, oh diminished grace
Oh open door where none had passed

I know not why I'm drowning, dying
Before reaching the eternal dwelling.
I do not know whose prey I am.
I do not know whose love I am.
(1934)

Translated by Carole Ciano

Sigrid Undset   *Norway, 1882–1949*

Sigrid Undset, Norway's 1928 Nobel laureate, was born in a small town in Denmark and moved to Christiania (now Oslo) at age 2.

It was her father, a noted archeologist, and his many colleagues who first interested her in Norway's past, providing her with the setting of her most important works, the *Kristin Lavransdatter* trilogy (*Kristin Lavransdatter*, 1920–1922) and *The Master of Hestviken* quartet (*Olav Audunssön*, 1925–1930), both of which take place during Norway's Middle Ages. Undset studied at a commercial college in Oslo and proceeded to work in an office for ten years. During that time she began writing, publishing within three years a novella, a tale, a collection of short stories, a one-act play, and some poems. The short stories *Den Lykkelige Alder* (The Happy Age, 1908) are particularly interesting in dealing with the lives of young working girls in Oslo. *Fru Marta Oulie* (Mrs. Marta Oulie, 1907) about an adulterous relationship, introduces a popular subject in her works, that of sexual fidelity and moral responsibility; that theme was more artistically developed in *Jenny* (*Jenny*, 1911), which is about a "liberated" woman's moral struggle when confronting the meaninglessness of her life. *Jenny* was extremely controversial; hailed for its frank discussion of female sexuality, including pregnancy and child-birth, its unhappy ending—Jenny's suicide—and overall theme was seen, correctly, by feminists as an attack on women's liberation.

In 1909 Undset received a year's scholarship to study in Italy and there met her future husband, artist Anders C. Svarstad, whom she married in 1912. They had three children (one was mentally retarded and one died in World War II). The next ten years were difficult for Undset, who had to care for her husband's three children from his former marriage as well as her own. However, she continued writing, at night, after the children were asleep. She felt it right that she sacrifice her career to her children and explained her beliefs about woman's role in a collection of essays entitled *Et kvindesynspunkt* (A Woman's Point of View, 1919). Although she doesn't object to woman's emancipation, she believed woman's primary obligation and source of fulfillment must come from motherhood; if a woman couldn't harmonize motherhood and career, career must go.

These beliefs show very clearly in her writing. *Kristin Lavransdatter* is about a young woman who goes against family and community for an illicit love. Although Kristin's marriage is doomed, she is saved by her love for her children and by her devotion to God. (Undset was, while writing this work, becoming increasingly devout, and in 1924 she converted to Catholicism, simultaneously annulling her marriage.) Despite the strong Catholic ideology of the novel, the moral messages are not intrusive in this work as they are in many of Undset's later novels. Instead, one is transported by the work's deep psychological analysis and realistic historical detail.

Many of Undset's later works focus on people's relationship to God, particularly *Gymnadenia* (*The Wild Orchid*, 1929) and its sequal *Den braendende busk* (The Burning Bush, 1930), while *Ida Elisabeth* (*Ida Elisabeth*, 1933) and the less critically successful *Den trofaste hustru* (*The Faithful Wife*, 1933) explore modern marriage within a religious context. In all her works Undset is concerned with ethical development. Her characters all must make moral and ethical decisions, and, because of her ideological commitment to Catholicism, those decisions often seem contrived; characters suffer and are punished to the degree that they believe and act according to their/her moral beliefs. On the other hand, much of her writing is very realistic and her characters profoundly well realized.

Undset's moral fervor made her an enemy of the Nazis, and she fled Norway for the United States in 1940. In the five years she lived there, she published many essays against the Nazis and also wrote several children's books. She traveled much in this country and received honorary degrees from Rollins College in 1942 and Smith College in 1943. In 1947, after her return to Norway, she received the Grand Cross of the Order of St. Olav for her patriotic contribution to her country's freedom, an award only once before given to a woman. Her last major work was a biography of St. Catherine of Siena, a heroic portrait realistically drawn and published posthumously in 1951.

The following selection is excerpted from *Fru Hjelde* (*Images in a Mirror*, 1917), four closely related stories about the domestic difficulties of a young couple told from the wife's point of view.

from IMAGES IN A MIRROR
Fru Hjelde

"Fine, healthy child," said Sister Bergljot, glancing at the new-born infant in Uni's arm. "I expect you're glad it's another boy, aren't you? Two girls and two boys, that's just as it should be.—Perhaps I'd better put these sheets in the bathtub, then I can give them a soak tomorrow. Towels—aren't there any more in here?" she asked the midwife. "I'll go and get them—I know my way about here," she explained once more; "I've looked after Fru Hjelde every time she's had a baby, except the first one."

Kristian knocked at the door and announced that the taxi was at the door, and the midwife, a slim, blonde young woman who let you know very clearly that she was a lady and businesslike, said good-bye and left.

"She gives herself some airs, doesn't she? But she's clever, oh yes, she's clever. I was out nursing in Asker last winter at a place where they had her—well, a nice state of things it was and we phoned and phoned for all the doctors we could think of—but Fru Klausen was pleasanter to get on with; didn't you like Fru Klausen better? Fancy, they say her husband's going to marry her sister's adopted daughter. Well, now we'll put the boy into the baby carriage, so you can get a little sleep— come along, baby, good little boy, Mamma's tired now, you see. Wonder if they weren't up to something while Fru Klausen was alive. Ah, poor thing, she didn't have much of a time, no, and so kind she was to him, *he* never earned the price of his drinks, I'm sure; ah, talk about midwives' husbands! You haven't had the baby carriage done up this time? Lasse hasn't been very careful with it either, I can see.—Do you know what? I think he looks like the little one you lost, I do."

"Yes—I think so too, he has a look of Lars Kristian," said Uni softly.

"Oh, that was a pretty child! Lasse wasn't at all pretty, but he's improved a lot in his looks, I could see that when we carried out his cot. But Karen Inga's the pick of them—bless me, how fond I've always been of that child! But now you really must lie down and go to sleep, Fru Hjelde—are you in pain?"

"Oh yes." Uni closed her eyes.

"Well, isn't it funny?—the after-pains get worse every time. There's one consolation, you get the business over all the easier."

"Perhaps. Oh, but, Sister Bergljot, I think it's just as cruel every time."

"No, look here! You really ought to be ashamed to say such a thing, Fru Hjelde, seeing how you've always got over it so easy. Ah, you don't know what some poor women have to go through. Like that one I was nursing in April before I went to the Johannesens'—"

Sister Bergljot had finished clearing up the room and taken off her nurse's uniform. She put on her flannel dressing-gown and crept up into Kristian's bed. Uni closed her eyes to shut out the gray light of eary summer morning that came through the white blinds and fell asleep while the nurse was describing all the frightful confinements she had witnessed.

At about half past seven Kristian came in with Lasse on his arm. He was to take the child up to Torbjörg Bakke, who lived at Grefsen, before going to the office. The little girls were going there from school, and all three were to stay there while their mother was in bed.

Kristian lifted up the boy so that he could see the new arrival in the baby carriage. "Well, Lasse, do you think he's sweet? Aren't you glad you've got a brother?"

"Is he ours?" asked Lasse. "Will he still be here when I come back from Aunt's?"

"Yes, he will always be here, Lasse," said his mother. "With God's help," she whispered.

"Now, you mustn't have any sad thoughts, Uni," said Kristian in a low voice. "The little girls would like to come in and say good-morning to Mummy and the new little brother."

The little girls were quiet and rather bewildered. They had been roused at midnight, when their sofa bed was moved into the sitting-room; they found their father and Lasse there too, when they woke in the morning.

Memories of former occasions returned; they wondered, rather bashfully.

"What dear little hands he's got, Mummy!" said Nora; and Karen Inga went over to her mother's bed:

"Have you got a headache, Mummy?"

"Oh yes, a little, my dear." Their mother kissed the three little faces that bent down to her. "And, for God's sake, be very careful, girls. Look out when you're getting on or off the streetcar—and mind you look both ways, do you hear? Remember that your poor mother is going to be terribly anxious till she has you safely home again. And *never* let Lasse go beyond the garden—and keep him out of mischief—and be very nice and obedient to Aunt Torbjörg. And above all be careful about the street cars."

"But my dearest Uni, they're big enough to be sensible—and Torbjörg's at home all day, she's not acting in this piece, you know. You really mustn't worry yourself like this."

The children went out. Sister Bergljot came and made her patient's bed. She preached steadily, but there was something very soothing in her chatter and in the sight of her agreeable person in the well-ironed blue and white uniform. She had the kind of freckled complexion which reminded one of a pale custard sprinkled with cinnamon; even her arms were a creamy white with little brown specks and reddish-golden down. Uni measured her thigh as the nurse turned back the blanket; yes, her fingers could almost span the thickest part of it.

"Oh, nonsense," said the nurse; "you know you'll soon put on flesh again when you start taking beer posset.—No, nobody can come in," she called out as there was a hard knock at the door.

"It's only me," cried Fröken Bomann; "I only want to leave this—I couldn't help coming to congratulate, I heard them moving out the bed and so I asked Ingrid this morning— well, all my best wishes—I'm *so* looking forward to seeing the new little prince—good morning—I'm sure the little girls are delighted—and your husband—well, now I must fly." She stood shouting in through the door till the nurse had finished making Uni's bed; then she was allowed to peep in and admire the baby; and there she stood talking till she herself declared she would be late at the office. Then at last she departed after a few concluding remarks.

Sister Bergljot went to see what she had left outside the door. Some lovely tulips, a parcel containing a knitted baby jacket, and a bag of hot rolls.

"Dear goodness, how kind she is!" said Uni.

"Lovely white rolls," said the nurse. "And Ingrid's made such delicious coffee—that's a fine girl, I tell you!"

"Well, now you've done your duty as a citizen for this time," said Torbjörg Bakke when she came to call on the fourth day. "You've made your demonstration against the small-family system and the materialism of this pleasure-loving age and all that. And now I think you can give it up, Uni.—Certainly, children *are* sweet—"

"Do have some cake," said Uni. "It'll only get sour. It's a shame the children can't have a taste of it, poor dears; I don't know when they last had cream cake."

"Oh, they get such a lot of good things at our house, Uni. Papa, the old sinner, is so wild about these children of yours—he positively forgets the distress of being sober, simply because he has to play with. You can guess he and Lasse are great chums—he works away with hammer and nails, knocking together the oddest contraptions. God knows, perhaps if I'd made him a grandfather he might have been reformed at the eleventh hour. We're so glad to have them, Uni—just don't think about them, my dear, don't worry yourself." She stroked her friend's forehead. "Bless my soul, sister, how she's perspiring—am I talking too much, Uni?"

"It's only the nipple that's rather raw," said Uni, compressing her lips. "He's so rough," and she tenderly stroked the little red head of the sucking child.

"Aren't you coming in to have some of your own cake and wine, Fru Helseth?" Torbjörg called to Aunt Bendikte, whose sewing machine was buzzing in the next room.

"Just a moment." Aunt Bendikte appeared in the doorway and laid the sleeves of a child's coat on the bed. "Do you see, Uni?—I've made up this sleeve from seven patches, but it won't show like that—I shall get two *nice* coats out of your old street-dress, Fröken Bakke."

"You're so handy at needlework, Aunt; I feel quite ashamed of myself," said Uni, and Torbjörg examined the sleeve.

"Why, this is nothing short of applied geometry!"

"Oh, I dare say"—Aunt Bendikte settled herself comfortably in a chair and took a piece of the cake she had sent—"we didn't learn any geometry or that kind of thing in my time, but we learned what would be useful. Now I'm just an ordinary woman, and I've never pretended to be anything else either, and I've never said I knew anything about art and such things, though I've every respect for it—I do enjoy going to the theatre now and then—thanks for the tickets, Fröken Bakke—but, my word, what a disgusting play! I was quite ashamed sitting looking at it, but *you* were great—no, I'm blest if I know how you can do it, just like looking at a stewardess on one of those boats, it was—there was one on the west-coast boat three years ago when I was going to Hilda's funeral, I couldn't help thinking of her the whole time, and didn't I laugh! Though to be sure it made me sad too, thinking about poor Hilda—oh, I meant to tell you, Uni, I expect Birgit will look in this afternoon—"

"That's good, then she can take a piece of the cake for her boy."

"Well, it was meant for you, my girl. You know, you can't have any milk for the baby if you won't eat anything. Look here, drink another glass of wine, it won't do you any harm.—But I was just going to say, I was uncommonly glad nobody of mine was acting in that piece. But I do think a lot of art when it's a nice play. No, all I wanted to say was that all those years Uni was studying and had set her heart on being an actress and then those years on the stage—I call all that so much waste of time—what has it done for you now? Just think if you'd learned housekeeping and dressmaking and so on while you were young, how much easier it would have come to you now!"

"No, look here, Fru Helseth, you can't say Uni's not clever."

"I know, I know—I've often said myself she's ever so much smarter than anyone would have expected—"

"Aunt's quite right!" said Uni excitedly. "I should have got on much better, and what's more, it wouldn't have taken so much out of me, if I hadn't spent all those years imagining I was going to be a great artist. The only time I have anything to show for was when I went to Aunt Hilda as nursemaid without pay."

Torbjörg took hold of her friend's thin, hot hand. "Who gave you that lovely rose-tree?" she asked, to change the subject.

"Fru Waage—she lives here just across the hallway."

"A divorced woman," explained Aunt Bendikte.

"I don't know her at all—so it was awfully kind of her."

"Oh, Harriet Waage—the one who married the ironfounder—now she's taken up with Damm, the lawyer, the man who perpetrates poetry."

"She lost her only little boy in such a terrible way—he was drowned." Uni's voice trembled.

"Ah, that makes it easier to understand—I don't mean her choosing Henning Damm, but that she should wish to take up a new part. But have you heard that Tilla's gone and done

it now—run away from her Einar and all her three youngsters?"

"God knows she didn't have much of a time with him," said Uni.

"No, but the children. God bless my soul, to give up three live youngsters for one single lover! If she'd given up *one* child for three lovers I might have understood it."

"Now, really, Fröken Bakke—"

"I mean it, Fru Helseth. Up to a certain point I can understand her getting sick at last of making soup and mending breeches, begging for every penny for herself and the children, and preferring to go out and amuse herself. But if one insists on love as one's form of amusement, then the more one plays with, the merrier. For you can't tell me there's any man alive who has more than a limited amount of fun in his composition. But this silly creature blithers about Paulsen being her first and greatest love and says she's going to begin life anew—just as if she can begin anew with three boys running loose that she herself has brought into the world."

"Grögaard wasn't a bit kind to Tilla, Torbjörg—fearfully inconsiderate."

"Inconsiderate! You have to put up with that, if you're a natural human being and disposed to choose a partner of the opposite sex. It's possible one can live on terms of consideration and good understanding with a person of one's own sex, but that would be called perverse. Well, I'll go so far as to say that there's a touch of perversity in this talk about consideration and understanding. We're inconsiderate and stupid enough with our menfolk, in all conscience, and they with us, and I dare say God meant to teach us to put up with as much as that. 'O women of a bygone age'—they had some sense—they didn't think you could make a silk purse out of a sow's ear!"

Aunt Bendikte laughed with delight. "I'm one with you there, Fröken Bakke! No, in my time—I knew very well that poor Helseth was no god; I knew he was a frail and sinful creature, but I knew I wasn't any more than that either; but he before whom we stood to pro-mise each other fidelity and help in weal and woe was the faithful and almighty God.

"Well, now I'll have to be going home, Uni dear. No, thank you, I'm sure Fröken Bak-ke's meat loaf's delicious, but I *must* get home—phew, it's going to be warm, but—Then I'll come in this afternoon and finish the coats, and tomorrow I'll do the darning. I can well remember how one frets about all the work that piles up when one's confined—I'll do all your mending for you till you're up again."

"It's funny that you and Aunt Bendikte should get on so well," said Uni when her aunt had gone. Torbjörg's hats and dresses were always in the very latest fashion and she used the powder-puff more liberally than was altogether becoming.

Torbjörg gave a little laugh. "She reminds me of Sven Dufva—an old soldier who de-serves to die, knitting needles in hand. I might have been like that myself if I'd ever had a home of my own. What she said about the two poor sinful creatures before the altar of almighty God—I liked that. Poor you, I'm sure we must have talked you nearly to death. Goodness, how you're sweating! Is that child still devouring you?"

"No, he's asleep. It's so warm in bed," said Uni.

The mild wind, which fluttered the curtain a little, brought a scent of hot rolls and of cutlets grilling at Fru Waage's. There was a clatter of the lids on some kitchen range and somebody was pounding meat—all the kitchen windows were wide open in the heat.

"Your garden must be looking lovely now," said Uni. "Kristian told me yesterday that the lilacs were coming out already."

It was the 4th of June.

Translated by Arthur Chater

Li Shuang, Dancers, ca. 1980, oil on canvas, Courtesy the artist and Sabrina Fung, New York

Elin Wägner   *Sweden, 1882–1949*

Born in Lund in the south of Sweden, Elin Wägner lost her mother at an early age
and had a rather melancholy childhood and an undistinguished school career. She
is remembered today for her life's work as journalist, prolific novelist, short-story
writer, feminist, pacifist, and friend of the earth. She was a prominent figure in the
campaign for women's suffrage in Sweden, and subsequently helped to found the
radical women's weekly *Tidevarvet* (The Epoch) and the Women Citizens' College
at Fogelstad, both initiatives designed to raise women's political consciousness.

Many of her novels reflect her strong ideological commitments. Among her
finest novels are *Pennskaftet* (Penwoman, 1910), *Åsa-Hanna* (Hanna from Ridge
Farm, 1918), *Silverforsen* (The Silver Stream, 1924), *Vändkorset* (The Turnstile,
1935) and *Vinden vände bladen* (The Wind Turned the Leaves Over, 1947). In
these, as in all her fiction, she is noted for the fine psychological portraits of her
characters. Her nonfiction includes biographies of sister writers, social and political
commentaries on inter-war Europe, and cultural and women's history. She was
awarded the major prize of the Swedish literary society Samfundet De Nio in 1923,
and in 1944 became only the second woman to be elected to the prestigious
Swedish Academy. Her novels have yet to be published in English translation,
despite their indisputable interest for today's readership.

The piece that follows is from her collection of interlinked short stories,
Gammalrödja: skildring av en bygd som ömsar skinn (Gammalrödja: A Country
District Sheds its Old Skin), published in 1931, and its title literally means "Making
Cheese with Bought Rennet." Its setting and its central themes are in many respects
typical of Elin Wägner's fiction as a whole; the question of women's power and
powerlessness was one to which she returned again and again.

Sarah Death

THE CHEESEMAKING
Yste med Köpelöpe

A large, impressive-looking lady drove her
shiny Chevrolet with casual skill along the
main road that ran through Gammalrödja village. Sitting inside the car, she might have been
indoors, hatless as she was, and dressed only in
a thin, pale-gray summer frock. The breeze
ruffled her gray curls, and she looked every
inch the sophisticated foreigner, but her eyes
were gleaming Gammalrödja blue with child-
like anticipation as she negotiated Guardsman
Skott's new road, which led to Bridge End
Farm. For this was indeed none other than
Hilma Skott's sister, who had gone off to
America many years before, leaving behind

only the lasting memory of her dazzling good
looks. It must be clear from this introduction
that things had turned out very nicely for her.
She had married well, had three children, doubled her weight, and got herself a car, some
gold fillings, and various other things to be
revealed in due course.

The idea of arriving to visit her sister un-
announced had appealed to her. Gammalrödja
people are always in, so there was no risk in
making it a surprise visit. In her mind she
could still picture the gloomy, out of the way
old cottage, and she almost believed she might
be able to jump across the footbridges as lightly

as she used to. She kept herself fit, so she ought to be able to manage it. But finding that Hilma now had a proper road, and land that had been cleared of rocks and stones, she had to admit that things were changing even in old Gammalrödja. And yet, when she stepped into the familiar old kitchen and found four women, with ages ranging from six to sixty, busily scrubbing out copper pans and wicker-work cheese molds, and discussing the pros and cons of home-produced rennet, and the newfangled sort they made you buy nowadays, then she knew she was home.

"Well I'm blessed, Hilma," she said loudly, lapsing into her native dialect, "Fancy you having a cheesemaking here today!"

Hilma turned round and stared.

Agda and the little girls stared too. There was a long pause.

"How old and ugly she's grown," thought Emerentia, regarding the handsome Hilma.

"Heavens, how fine and grand she is," thought Hilma enviously at the sight of her flabby sister.

"Yes, it's today they're all bringing their milk to make the cheese," she said at last, and went to the cupboard for an extra cup and saucer for Emerentia.

Before the sisters had a chance to start exchanging all their news, Agda's eldest girl piped up, "I can hear them coming."

Soon, the grown-ups too could hear the cheerful buzz of conversation from down by the gate. The guests were in high spirits, for the women of Gammalrödja were still just as fond as in the old days of putting on their best clothes on a fine summer's afternoon and going along to a cheesemaking.

They didn't care if their menfolk jeered at them in a good-natured way because they still went to each other's houses with milk for making cheese, when there was a new dairy that bought the milk and sold them cheese at a good price.

"It must be the coffee you go for," the menfolk would say.

But it wasn't the coffee at all; they could indulge their taste for that just as well at home. No, the secret fascination of going to a cheese-making was that it was an old custom dating back to the days when everyone helped everyone else with the really big jobs on the farm. When they came together to make cheese, they were transported back for a while to that time of mutual friendship and support, and it made them feel comfortable. The menfolk just didn't feel the same about it, for although many years had gone by since the common land had been parcelled out, the idea of being their own bosses and looking after their own affairs hadn't lost its fascination for them, and if anyone came up with a new idea for some collective venture, their mutual distrust soon put an end to the scheme. They continued to thrive, like plants, on their own reserves of food, trying not to think about what the future might have in store for them.

Emerentia posted herself eagerly at the window. What a bit of luck that the cheese-making happened to be today, almost as if it had been laid on specially for her. Now she would be able to see all her old acquaintances, and show off to them a little.

Here came the churchwarden's wife from Foxes Farm. You could tell it was her from her cotton dress: the stripes were just the same blue and black as they had been in the old days. Otherwise though, she'd certainly changed, grown old and wizened.

"Trust her to have brought such a small jug," said Hilma, who was still nursing a grudge. She hadn't forgotten that Foxes Farm had tried to send her to the workhouse because she couldn't pay the rent, before she had come into money and been able to live decently.

"Oh look, here comes my old friend Märta from our confirmation class. She used to pass the time of day with the lad from Ravens Farm, even before I left, and now she looks very hoity-toity."

"Well, she married into the family at

Ravens Farm, and her husband's a magistrate now," Hilma said.

And here comes a young woman who's the very image of Sara of Scriveners Farm, except that her hair is shingled and waved, and she's wearing...

"Bless my soul, then that'll be Berta, her daughter," said Hilma in surprise, leaving the coffeepot on the stove to come and look. "Where did you say you saw her? Well, fancy her turning up! And don't you recognize Sara herself, now?"

"What, the old woman with her? But who's that man coming along carrying two jugs, and who are those women he's got with him?"

Hilma had to come and look again. Oh yes, that was Verner of West Southacres Farm with his mother Fia, and the other one, in the black checked dress that didn't look home-woven, was Viktoria from the East Farm, whose clothes were still in mourning for her husband, though they do say she did away with him herself.

Verner said his goodbyes out by the front porch, but even from indoors they could hear him saying that he'd call back when he'd finished at the peat bog and ask whether any-one wanted a lift home. The ladies were in such high spirits that they even went so far as to joke about how it just happened that Verner had to go to the peat bog the same day Fia and Viktoria were going cheesemaking at Hilma's. But Viktoria pursed her lips and blushed. Someone else, from outside the parish, was courting her now, and anyway she had thought it was a secret.

Mrs. Emerentia Nelson was so convinced that she hadn't really changed very much in twenty-five years, that she attributed the sud-den silence when they saw her to her rings and crepe de chine. But although the guests had spotted the car, and Emerentia's name had sprung to mind, they remembered her as the prettiest girl in seven parishes, and it took them a moment to find her blue eyes and de-licate features in among all the layers of fat. Once they were certain, they greeted her with-out any fuss; it took more than silk and rings and even the most well-endowed pair of hips to surprise the ladies of Gammalrödja. And they had no fears about their own appearances, be-cause their cotton frocks were all made along the same lines as Berta's, cut in one piece with a sash round the hips. Berta had given the dressmaker strict instructions not to copy her pattern, because it wouldn't suit the village wives half as well as their usual skirts and bodices, you know. But they didn't care about that, and nor did the dressmaker, because why should Berta be the only one wearing the latest fashion? So it was only Sara, Berta's poor old mother, who was in a full skirt and traditional jacket.

While the guests were emptying their jugs into the big copper vat, Emerentia condes-cended to help carry out the things they would need for the coffee to the pretty group of gar-den seats with its leafy canopy. That's where they were all sitting now, all except Agda, who was in the kitchen waiting for the magic mo-ment when the milk curdled.

The sisters from Bridge End Farm hadn't been in touch with one another for years.

"You didn't write and let us know your boy had been killed," Emerentia said, "but anyway here's a stone I took from his grave when I was there!" She took a little white stone from out of her bag, and said, with her mouth full of cake, "I found it just by the cross on Ernst's grave."

No one was interested in the stone, which was just an ordinary stone, but the news was a different matter. How come Emerentia had been in France? What was the name of the place where Ernst was buried? Notre Dame de la Lorette! How strange it sounded! How on earth had she found her way there?

Berta, though, bent forward and picked up the little stone in her hand, because it had lain near his cross. Her heart jumped, as it did at every reminder of her obstinate, wayward,

good-looking boy. Elegant Miss Berta Skri-
vare, who worked in the food hall of Stockholm's smartest store and sat on the committee
of the new shop assistants' union, and was so
busy, always took the long way round to avoid
passing a plaque which bore Ernst's name, until even the detour pained her.

Now she carefully drew back out of the
circle with the stone in her hand; she had
decided that she wasn't going to give it back.
You want to forget, but if a memento comes to
hand, you steal it.... She didn't stop dreaming until Emerentia dropped her bombshell.

"You want to know how I came to be in
France, Märta? Well then, I'll tell you. I sacrificed my eldest boy too, just like Hilma. I've
got a grave as well, not far from hers. I went
with a group of two hundred mourning
mothers from Minnesota to visit our graves in
France."

So saying, she produced from her bag
something far more remarkable than the stone.
It was a star-shaped medal, rather like the one
Reverend Springer, the dean, wore for weddings, only bigger and showier. Its owner fastened it on in the same place, so to speak, as
the Reverend wore his.

"We were all wearing these when we went
to France," she said, and, lapsing into American speech, "You bet we made a sensation."

Hilma felt a sort of pang inside.

"Your husband must be well off," she
said.

"You don't think he gave me the star, do
you? You fool, it's a decoration awarded by
the American authorities to all the mothers
who've sacrificed a son. We all belong to an
association called the Mothers of the Star. This
is the Star, see, and I'm the Mother."

"What did you have to do to get it then?"

"What did I have to do? Well first I had
the boy. You must know how you do that.
And then I let him go off to war."

"You let him?"

"Yes, me. I sacrificed the dearest thing
I had, because we were fighting for 'a high

ideal', as we say over there. Then he was killed
in action, poor boy."

"But I think those who were killed should
have had the stars themselves," said Berta.

Emerentia looked the young girl slowly up
and down.

"You needn't worry yourself. The authorities took care of all that. But over there, they
think that a mother who's given the best thing
she had for her country ought to get some
recognition too. But of course, you can't
understand that over here in old Sweden.
You're so used to doing yourselves down."

"Well we haven't had a war, thank God,
and surely there won't be one now?" said Viktoria in alarm.

"Yes, may God protect our sons..."

"Why do you want Him to, when you
could get a star on your breast like her, and a
soldier's mother's pension," Berta said, in a
voice which somehow spoiled the pleasant cof-
feetime atmosphere. She was a bundle of
nerves these days, and this self-satisfied, star-
decorated mother had infuriated her. Ernst
was hers, wasn't he, and she'd sacrificed him,
but what was she left with? A stone. A sting.

Her mother, alarmed, stopped her from
going on by saying, "Why don't you go in,
dear, and take over from Agda with the cheese,
so she can come out for her coffee?"

Emerentia started fishing about in her bag
again.

"If Berta's going in, she can take these
with her to show Agda. They're her cousins."

But when the others heard this, they
wouldn't let Berta go until they had seen
Emerentia's children too. There they were: the
eldest son who was dead and the daughter
who was still alive, both in uniform. They
were just as good-looking as their mother had
been, but the son, hero though he was, paled
into insignificance beside Mary H. Nelson—H
for Hilma. It wasn't particularly remarkable
that she should be slim and elegant, with curls
and a smile; what caught their eye was the fact
that she was wearing a jacket and trousers and

a braid-trimmed cap. Hanging from her shoulders she had a broad, becoming military greatcoat, but even that wasn't as incredible as— the sword. Yes, a sword! She was like something in a painting, standing there to present arms to a very distinguished and very smug-looking gentleman with lots of stripes on his sleeve.

"Oh," said Berta, "she's in films."

"Films indeed!" snorted Emerentia. "It's plain you can't understand English, Berta, or you'd have seen it says here at the bottom, 'Colonel Mary H. Nelson.' 'Colonel' is an American military rank, and a colonel is what she is, not a film star."

"Heavens, aren't there any men left over there?" Hilma asked, thinking, "Then how will they be able to carry on paying my pension?"

"Are you mad, you fool," Emerentia retorted, "Mary's the colonel of a proper regiment with proper men. This is the whole corps of trainee reserve officers here, see. They were standing behind her when it was taken. And the one she's facing, that's General Field, who'd come to inspect the regiment. You just can't imagine what a sight they made. Even my Nelson cried, and as for little John, our youngest, I could hardly control him. And me, I clean forgot about my Charles in his grave."

"Mercy me, whatever next!"

"Did you ever see the like of it? What's that newspaper you've got there?"

"Well, wouldn't you like to hear what they wrote about her in the Minnesota Star?" Emerentia opened the newspaper and translated rapidly, as though she knew most of it by heart. "It's grand being a soldier, when the officers are as sweet as Mary H. Nelson, Newfield, Minn. Dressed in full uniform, and making even a sword look graceful, the little colonel leads parades, troop reviews and exercises. But when it's time for the regimental ball, she exchanges her uniform for something more feminine, and takes her place as the belle of the ball. If war breaks out, she says, she

intends to go to the front and lead her boys into battle herself."

The women exchanged glances. They had learned to accept milking machines and airplanes, and some of the younger ones had even been to the cinema, but this they just *could not believe*. Any minute they expected Emerentia to start laughing at them.

"Good Lord, the things they think of!" they said cautiously. That could be taken to mean Emerentia herself, or the American government.

But Berta could understand a bit of English, and she could see that Emerentia had given a faithful translation. It was ridiculous and absurd, but none the less true for that.

"You know what, Hilma," she said to her hostess, "I think the authorities up in Stockholm have been downright unfair to you. You didn't get a star in exchange for Ernst, and Agda didn't get a sword, either."

Viktoria tittered. "I can just see Agda with a sword," she said.

Hilma had just been wondering whether perhaps she was far more special and deserving of much more recognition than she'd imagined.

"I've been too modest," thought the woman who believed that God had started the World War in response to her prayers. So she said, a trifle sourly, "What me, a poor old woman from a little province like Småland?"

Emerentia was disappointed in her old friends; they were too stupid to be properly knocked flat by what she had shown them. The vague stirrings of envy in Hilma were something, at least, and now she would play her trump card.

"Do you want to see me, when I was with the Royal Family in England?" she asked.

"You never were?"

The tone was one of mistrust, but even the doubters had to admit defeat, because there before their eyes, on the front page of an illustrated magazine, stood none other than Mrs. Emerentia Nelson with a crowd of other blissfully smiling Mothers of the Star, and who was that fine young gentleman in their midst but the heir to the British throne? Berta couldn't deny that she recognized him.

"Did he shake hands with you?"

"Yes, to greet us and when he said goodbye."

"I expect you could feel it right through you?"

"You just have to have been there; you can't describe it."

"Who's that he's talking to?"

"That's a lady who lost two sons. She was the leader of our group."

Poor Hilma, nothing like that would ever happen to her, even though Ernst had undoubtedly shot just as many idle Frenchmen and was just as dead as Charles.

"Come on, Hilma dear, you try on the Star and we'll take your photograph," said Emerentia generously.

They all watched while Hilma was decorated.

"Those two from Bridge End Farm, they always have to go one better," thought the magistrate's wife from Ravens Farm. "Even when we were girls, they were better-looking than the rest of us, and now they've got medals and pensions and shake hands with royalty."

"Of course, you think we're just cat's dirt here in Gamalrödja," she said. Emerentia protested lamely. "But all the same, Father and I are going into town on Saturday to visit our boy, who's in military service. We parents have got printed cards inviting us to see round the barracks, and stay to dinner afterwards. The card's got *Regimental Commander* at the bottom."

The others had already heard this remarkable bit of news, and they knew too what a stir it had caused in every household to think that the *wives* were being invited along to see the barracks and even being offered a meal there. Only Mia from Foxes Farm, who couldn't always follow what was happening, was taken by surprise. It was almost too much for her,

after she'd had six sons do military service, and not got so much as a cup of coffee for it. She wasn't interested in the food, and fortunately for her she could manage without a pension or a star, but it was a blow that it should be Märta, wife of her enemy at Ravens Farm, sitting there boasting.

"Well, I must be getting back," she said, and got up.

They could all see that the fun was over for old Mia the church warden's wife. When she was killed, a week later, by her son Anton, they felt pangs of conscience, but just now they really didn't care.

"There, there, mother Mia," said Emerentia, pushing her back down into her seat. "Stay and have another cup of coffee, and then I'll give you a lift home in my car. Aren't you glad to hear that they're starting to appreciate the mothers in this country too? I certainly am. I would never have thought.... One of these days it'll be your turn too. You've got six boys, haven't you? It's people like you the authorities need to stay well in with."

"How strange," said Berta, "It's topsy-turvy world."

Her mother looked at her in alarm. She knew what it meant when Berta's eyes narrowed and she bit her top lip.

But Emerentia didn't recognize the danger signs, and she asked provocatively, "In what way?"

"Well, I've heard from Father that they used to bribe the authorities when they came to inspect the roads and collect the taxes, and things weren't quite up to scratch. But it's something new when *those at the top* bribe the women. The Swedish authorities just couldn't...no, I don't understand all this."

"There's no need to start on about bribery, Berta," said Vendla from North Farm. "No one had to bribe me to send my lads to learn to defend their country. I come from the Five Lakes, where the Danes overran us like hordes of Turks, so I know very well that ours need to learn. Don't you laugh, Berta; it says in the history books that my family home was burnt down in 1643, and it's been called the Derelict Farm ever since."

"I'm not laughing at you, but I was just thinking that your lads haven't much to fear from the Danes these days."

"You never can tell," declared the magistrate's wife firmly. "Just when you think there's peace, along comes a war."

If the chairman of the district council, the magistrate, and the churchwarden could have seen their wives now, they would undoubtedly have been more astonished by them than by Emerentia and Mary H. Nelson with her sword. The womenfolk might talk as much as they liked about household chores, the weather, the neighbors, childbirth, and deathbeds, but it was customary and proper that they should stay silent or keep away when the men got onto politics and tried to work out who had started the war.

No one thought of asking them whether they had any views on the matter, and old Mia hadn't had a chance to put forward her idea that the whole cause of the war had been silk stockings.

What would the men have said, if they had heard Emerentia explaining that in other countries, the men didn't dare get into a war without buttering up the womenfolk first. They might just about have explained it away by saying that they have some funny ways in these foreign parts. But if they had seen Ebba, Sara, and Mia taking the regimental commander's invitation as a sign that things were the same in Sweden, they would have thought matters were getting quite absurdly out of hand. Was old Sweden so far gone that the king and his subjects couldn't manage to cope with defending the country without enlisting the women's support?

"I've never thought about it before, but I'm sure Emerentia's right," said Märta the magistrate's wife suddenly, reaching the end of her train of thought. "After all, how far would the authorities get without our lads?"

"What do you think would happen if we all said we weren't going to let our lads go?" said old Mia in the most scornful tone she could muster.

"I'll tell you what would happen," said Emerentia, "There wouldn't be a war."

"Is that so?" said Berta, furious with rage, and glaring at the fat lady who had got a star for her son. "Well then, I think you ought to get on and do it."

"I think you're all getting carried away," said mild-mannered old Sara, patting her daughter soothingly on the shoulder, which merely made her wilder. "We women don't run things, after all."

"Nor do the men," old Mia put in.

"You never know what God might be trying to do with a war," said Hilma, thinking of her own experience.

"Don't blame God!" cried Berta, beside herself, "It's not God!"

"Oh, so God's not in charge of the world any longer?"

"You watch out, talking about God like that! Jesus told us to love our enemies, didn't he? The men are the ones who've decided to kill each other. And if you mothers can stop it, but don't, and go prancing about wearing stars instead, like those poor Negro women who give away their poor little children in exchange for glass beads, then just you watch out, their blood will be on your hands."

She burst into tears and left the garden.

They all sat very quiet, feeling embarrassed. Were they powerless? Were they powerful? They didn't know. No, it couldn't be their fault. None of them wanted blood on their hands. They pulled themselves together. Poor Berta, Stockholm had been too much for her. The blood had always been on the hands of the Danes or the Russians or some other good-for-nothing lot of foreigners before.

Poor Viktoria was feeling, as she often did, that life was getting harder to live every day. It was hard enough for a widow to run a farm, when prices kept on falling, and now they said you were to blame for the war as well.

It was as though Berta's mother had guessed what everyone was thinking. "It's not easy when you've got a broken heart," she said softly. "Once it's broken, nothing can help."

"Time heals," said Märta from Ravens Farm.

"No, not even time," said old Sara.

A sigh came from old Mia, another from Vendla. This human suffering for something so hopeless brought home to them an echo of what war was really like. A young man was dead. The girl who had cared for him had grieved until she had made herself ill. For one short moment, they all understood what that meant, even Hilma with her pension and the star-bedecked Emerentia who had shaken hands with the Prince of Wales.

At that moment, Agda came bursting out of the house, crying out in a voice that shook with fear and desperation.

"It won't curdle!"

"Jesus, girl, have you heated it up properly?"

"Three times! But there must be some bad milk in it, sure as I've ever made cheese before."

"Well! So it's our fault is it? The Foxes Farm milk, I suppose?"

"Or North Farm's?"

"Give me back my jug!"

"I can tell you this is the last time I'll be coming here to make cheese!"

"It's that bought rennet, of course. Anyone can see that."

They forgot all about the war.

Translated by Sarah Death

Virginia Woolf

UK(England), 1882–1941

Considered by many the first modern feminist critic, Virginia Woolf was as much a groundbreaker in fiction as she was in literary criticism. Her ten novels were crucial works in modernist writing. *A Room of One's Own* (1929) contains a brilliant and perspicacious critique of society's oppression of women writers; her essays about English women writers, many of whom were unrecognized and forgotten, began the process of recovery of women's literature which has waited for the modern women's movement to reach fruition. She also wrote reviews, diaries, short stories, and many essays. She has been immensely influential to women writers and students of women's literature the world over, a beacon of radical dissent against traditional standards and mores.

Looking at her background, class, and time, Woolf was hardly a likely candidate for taking radical positions. She was born in Victorian England, in an upper-middle-class home, the daughter of Sir Leslie Stephen, writer and editor of the *Dictionary of Literary Biography*, and Julia Duckworth Stephen. It was a house filled with children: her sister, Vanessa, and two brothers, Adrian and Thoby, from her parents' first marriages. However, the comfortable Victorian façade of domesticity was all too soon beset by loss. Her mother died when Woolf was just 13. One of her half-sister's was mentally retarded; her other half-sister, Stella, died young from complications of childbirth, and her brother Thoby from typhoid. Her stepbrothers made sexual advances to her. And plaguing Woolf from her early teens was the mental illness that was eventually to provoke her suicide by drowning in 1941.

Despite periods of severe psychosis, however, Woolf was extraordinarily productive. Although she received no formal education, as was common with women of her class, Woolf was able to educate herself, using her father's substantial library for reference. She had the opportunity to articulate what she had learned whenever her brother Thoby's Cambridge friends gathered together with the Stephen sisters during the first part of the century. That group of young intellectuals, now thought of as cultural avatars of Edwardian society, was unofficially named "the Bloomsbury Group" because the Stephens lived in the section of London of the same name. Aside from the Stephens, members of this group included such brilliant thinkers as biographer Lytton Strachey, economist J.M. Keynes, writer E.M. Forster, and writer/critic Leonard Woolf whom Virginia Stephen married in 1912. Bloomsbury, known for its devotion to aesthetics and for its radical views on personal and sexual freedom, became, for many, an emblem of the coming of modernism.

Virginia and Leonard Woolf were able to act on their aesthetic and intellectual convictions after 1917 when they founded the Hogarth Press and published some of the best and most avant-garde international voices of their day: Katherine Mansfield, Chekov, T.S. Eliot, E.M. Forster, Sigmund Freud, Robert Graves, and, of course, Virgina Woolf, among others. From the inception of the Hogarth Press, Woolf was to have free access to publication. Nearly all her books were published by the press, books that might not have been published by more conventional firms, particularly *Mrs. Dalloway*, (1925) *To the Lighthouse* (1927), and *The Waves* (1931). These works have helped to change the course of the modern novel through their innovations with language—making full use of the interior monologue—and structure. The story "The Introduction," written in 1925 but not published until 1973 (in *Mrs. Dalloway's Party: A Short Story Sequence*), was selected for inclusion here because it contains characters and motifs to be found more fully developed in *Mrs. Dalloway* and *To the Lighthouse*.

It was in the 1920s that Woolf produced her most original and influential works and most important essays. In 1925 Woolf wrote her brilliant attack on realism, "Mrs. Bennett and Mrs. Brown," and in 1929 *A Room of One's Own*, called by Sandra Gilbert and Susan Gubar "the first major achievement of feminist criticism in the English language." The essay represented here, "Women and Fiction," first appeared in *The Forum* in 1929 and was reprinted in her collection of essays *Granite and Rainbow* (1958).

Although Woolf was recognized in her lifetime as an important modern writer, she did not receive substantial critical attention until the 1970s. In the past two decades, however, much has been written about her, including the two-volume biography by her nephew Quentin Bell in 1972; most of her writing has been put back in print and reissued in paperback. No course in women's studies is considered complete without using one of her essays, and no course in twentieth-century literature can omit assigning one of her novels. Woolf was a major voice in this century, and her work continues to be studied for its substance and for its example.

WOMEN AND FICTION

The title of this article can be read in two ways: it may allude to women and the fiction that they write, or to women and the fiction that is written about them. The ambiguity is intentional, for in dealing with women as writers, as much elasticity as possible is desirable; it is necessary to leave onself room to deal with other things besides their work, so much has that work been influenced by conditions that have nothing whatever to do with art.

The most superficial inquiry into women's writing instantly raises a host of questions. Why, we ask at once, was there no continuous writing done by women before the eighteenth century? Why did they then write almost as habitually as men, and in the course of that writing produce, one after another, some of the classics of English fiction? And why did their art then, and why to some extent does their art still, take the form of fiction?

A little thought will show us that we are asking questions to which we shall get, as answer, only further fiction. The answer lies at present locked in old diaries, stuffed away in old drawers, half-obliterated in the memories of the aged. It is to be found in the lives of the obscure—in those almost unlit corridors of history where the figures of generations of women are so dimly, so fitfully perceived. For very little is known about women. The history of England is the history of the male line, not of the female. Of our fathers we know always some fact, some distinction. They were soldiers or they were sailors; they filled that office or they made that law. But of our mothers, our grandmothers, our great-grandmothers, what remains? Nothing but a tradition. One was beautiful; one was red-haired; one was kissed by a Queen. We know nothing of them except their names and the dates of their marriages and the number of children they bore.

Thus, if we wish to know why at any particular time women did this or that, why they wrote nothing, why on the other hand they wrote masterpieces, it is extremely difficult to tell. Anyone who should seek among those old papers, who should turn history wrong side out and so construct a faithful picture of the daily life of the ordinary women in Shakespeare's time, in Milton's time, in Johnson's time, would not only write a book of astonishing interest, but would furnish the critic with a weapon which he now lacks. The extraordinary woman depends on the ordinary woman. It is only when we know what were the conditions of the average woman's life—the number of her children, whether she had money of her own, if she had a room to herself, whether she had help in bringing up her family, if she had servants, whether part of the housework was her task—it is only when we can measure the way of life and the experience of life made possible to the ordinary woman that we can account for the success or failure of the extraordinary woman as a writer.

Strange spaces of silence seem to separate one period of activity from another. There was Sappho and a little group of women all writing poetry on a Greek island six hundred years before the birth of Christ. They fall silent. Then about the year 1000 we find a certain court lady, the Lady Murasaki, writing a very long and beautiful novel in Japan. But in England in the sixteenth century, when the dramatists and poets were most active, the women were dumb. Elizabethan literature is exclusively masculine. Then, at the end of the eighteenth century and in the beginning of the nineteenth, we find women again writing—this time in England—with extraordinary frequency and success.

Law and custom were of course largely responsible for these strange intermissions of silence and speech. When a woman was liable, as she was in the fifteenth century, to be beaten and flung about the room if she did not marry the man of her parents' choice, the spiritual atmosphere was not favourable to the production of works of art. When she was married without her own consent to a man who thereupon became her lord and master, "so far at least as law and custom could make him", as she was in the time of the Stuarts, it is likely she had little time for writing, and less encouragement. The immense effect of environment and suggestion upon the mind, we in our psychoanalytical age are beginning to realize. Again, with memoirs and letters to help us, we are beginning to understand how abnormal is the effort needed to produce a work of art, and what shelter and what support the mind of the artist requires. Of those facts the lives and letters of men like Keats and Carlyle and Flaubert assure us.

Thus it is clear that the extraordinary outburst of fiction in the beginning of the nineteenth century in England was heralded by innumerable slight changes in law and customs and manners. And women of the nineteenth century had some leisure; they had some education. It was no longer the exception for women of the middle and upper classes to choose their own husbands. And it is significant that of the four great women novelists— Jane Austen, Emily Brontë, Charlotte Brontë, and George Eliot—not one had a child, and two were unmarried.

Yet, though it is clear that the ban upon writing had been removed, there was still, it would seem, considerable pressure upon women to write novels. No four women can have been more unlike in genius and character than these four. Jane Austen can have had nothing in common with George Eliot; George Eliot was the direct opposite of Emily Brontë. Yet all were trained for the same profession; all, when they wrote, wrote novels.

Fiction was, as fiction still is, the easiest thing for a woman to write. Nor is it difficult to find the reason. A novel is the least concentrated form of art. A novel can be taken up or put down more easily than a play or a poem. George Eliot left her work to nurse her father. Charlotte Brontë put down her pen to pick the

eyes out of the potatoes. And living as she did in the common sitting-room, surrounded by people, a woman was trained to use her mind in observation and upon the analysis of character. She was trained to be a novelist and not to be a poet.

Even in the nineteenth century, a woman lived almost solely in her home and her emotions. And those nineteenth-century novels, remarkable as they were, were profoundly influenced by the fact that the women who wrote them were excluded by their sex from certain kinds of experience. That experience has a great influence upon fiction is indisputable. The best part of Conrad's novels, for instance, would be destroyed if it had been impossible for him to be a sailor. Take away all that Tolstoi knew of war as a soldier, of life and society as a rich young man whose education admitted him to all sorts of experience, and *War and Peace* would be incredibly impoverished.

Yet *Pride and Prejudice, Wuthering Heights, Villette,* and *Middlemarch* were written by women from whom was forcibly withheld all experience save that which could be met with in a middle-class drawing-room. No first-hand experience of war or seafaring or politics or business was possible for them. Even their emotional life was strictly regulated by law and custom. When George Eliot ventured to live with Mr. Lewes without being his wife, public opinion was scandalized. Under its pressure she withdrew into a suburban seclusion which, inevitably, had the worst possible effects upon her work. She wrote that unless people asked of their own accord to come and see her, she never invited them. At the same time, on the other side of Europe, Tolstoi was living a free life as a soldier, with men and women of all classes, for which nobody censured him and from which his novels drew much of their astonishing breadth and vigour.

But the novels of women were not affected only by the necessarily narrow range of the writer's experience. They showed, at least in the nineteenth century, another characteristic which may be traced to the writer's sex. In *Middlemarch* and in *Jane Eyre* we are conscious not merely of the writer's character, as we are conscious of the character of Charles Dickens, but we are conscious of a woman's presence—of someone resenting the treatment of her sex and pleading for its rights. This brings into women's writing an element which is entirely absent from a man's, unless, indeed, he happens to be a working-man, a Negro, or one who for some other reason is conscious of disability. It introduces a distortion and is frequently the cause of weakness. The desire to plead some personal cause or to make a character the mouthpiece of some personal discontent or grievance always has a distressing effect, as if the spot at which the reader's attention is directed were suddenly twofold instead of single.

The genius of Jane Austen and Emily Brontë is never more convincing than in their power to ignore such claims and solicitations and to hold on their way unperturbed by scorn or censure. But it needed a very serene or a very powerful mind to resist the temptation to anger. The ridicule, the censure, the assurance of inferiority in one form or another which were lavished upon women who practised an art, provoked such reactions naturally enough. One sees the effect in Charlotte Brontë's indignation, in George Eliot's resignation. Again and again one finds it in the work of the lesser women writers—in their choice of a subject, in their unnatural self-assertiveness, in their unnatural docility. Moreover, insincerity leaks in almost unconsciously. They adopt a view in deference to authority. The vision becomes too masculine or it becomes too feminine; it loses its perfect integrity and, with that, its most essential quality as a work of art.

The great change that has crept into women's writing is, it would seem, a change of attitude. The woman writer is no longer bitter. She is no longer angry. She is no longer pleading and protesting as she writes. We are approaching, if we have not yet reached, the time when her writing will have little or no foreign influence to disturb it. She will be able to concentrate upon her vision without distraction from outside. The aloofness that was once within the reach of genius and originality is only now coming within reach of ordinary women. Therefore the average novel by a woman is far more genuine and far more interesting today than it was a hundred or even fifty years ago.

But it is still true that before a woman can write exactly as she wishes to write, she has many difficulties to face. To begin with, there is the technical difficulty—so simple, apparently; in reality, so baffling—that the very form of the sentence does not fit her. It is a sentence made by men; it is too loose, too heavy, too pompous for a woman's use. Yet in a novel, which covers so wide a stretch of ground, an ordinary and usual type of sentence has to be found to carry the reader on easily and naturally from one end of the book to the other. And this a woman must make for herself, altering and adapting the current sentence until she writes one that takes the natural shape of her thought without crushing or distorting it.

But that, after all, is only a means to an end, and the end is still to be reached only when a woman has the courage to surmount opposition and the determination to be true to herself. For a novel, after all, is a statement about a thousand different objects—human, natural, divine; it is an attempt to relate them to each other. In every novel of merit these different elements are held in place by the force of the writer's vision. But they have another order also, which is the order imposed upon them by convention. And as men are the arbiters of that convention, as they have established an order of values in life, so too, since fiction is largely based on life, these values prevail there also to a very great extent.

It is probable, however, that both in life and in art the values of a woman are not the values of a man. Thus, when a woman comes to write a novel, she will find that she is perpetually wishing to alter the established values—to make serious what appears insignificant to a man, and trivial what is to him important. And for that, of course, she will be criticized; for the critic of the opposite sex will be genuinely puzzled and surprised by an attempt to alter the current scale of values, and will see in it not merely a difference of view, but a view that is weak, or trivial, or sentimental, because it differs from his own.

But here, too, women are coming to be more independent of opinion. They are beginning to respect their own sense of values. And for this reason the subject matter of their novels begins to show certain changes. They are less interested, it would seem, in themselves; on the other hand, they are more interrested in other women. In the early nineteenth century, women's novels were largely autobiographical. One of the motives that led them to write was the desire to expose their own suffering, to plead their own cause. Now that this desire is no longer so urgent, women are beginning to explore their own sex, to write of women as women have never been written of before; for of course, until very lately, women in literature were the creation of men.

Here again there are difficulties to overcome, for, if one may generalize, not only do women submit less readily to observation than men, but their lives are far less tested and examined by the ordinary processes of life. Often nothing tangible remains of a woman's day. The food that has been cooked is eaten; the children that have been nursed have gone out into the world. Where does the accent fall? What is the salient point for the novelist to seize upon? It is difficult to say. Her life has an anonymous character which is baffling and puzzling in the extreme. For the first time, this dark country is beginning to be explored in fiction; and at the same moment a woman has also to record the changes in women's minds and habits which the opening of the professions has introduced. She has to observe how their lives are ceasing to run underground; she has to discover what new colours and shadows are showing in them now that they are exposed to the outer world.

If, then, one should try to sum up the character of women's fiction at the present moment, one would say that it is courageous; it is sincere; it keeps closely to what women feel. It is not bitter. It does not insist upon its femininity. But at the same time, a woman's book is not written as a man would write it. These qualities are much commoner than they were, and they give even to second- and third-rate work the value of truth and the interest of sincerity.

But in addition to these good qualities, there are two that call for a word more of discussion. The change which has turned the English woman from a nondescript influence, fluctuating and vague, to a voter, a wage-earner, a responsible citizen, has given her both in her life and in her art a turn towards the impersonal. Her relations now are not only emotional; they are intellectual, they are political. The old system which condemned her to squint askance at things through the eyes or through the interests of husband or brother, has given place to the direct and practical interests of one who must act for herself, and not merely influence the acts of others. Hence her attention is being directed away from the personal centre which engaged it exclusively in the past to the impersonal, and her novels naturally become more critical of society, and less analytical of individual lives.

We may expect that the office of gadfly to the state, which has been so far a male prerogative, will now be discharged by women also. Their novels will deal with social evils and remedies. Their men and women will not be observed wholly in relation to each other emotionally, but as they cohere and clash in groups and classes and races. That is one change of some importance. But there is another more interesting to those who prefer the butterfly to the gadfly—that is to say, the artist to the reformer. The greater impersonality of women's lives will encourage the poetic spirit, and it is in poetry that women's fiction is still weakest. It will lead them to be less absorbed in facts and no longer content to record with astonishing acuteness the minute details which fall under their own observation. They will look beyond the personal and political relationships to the wider questions which the poet tries to solve—of our destiny and the meaning of life.

The basis of the poetic attitude is of course largely founded upon material things. It depends upon leisure, and a little money, and the chance which money and leisure give to observe impersonally and dispassionately. With money and leisure at their service, women will naturally occupy themselves more than has hitherto been possible with the craft of letters. They will make a fuller and a more subtle use of the instrument of writing. Their technique will become bolder and richer.

In the past, the virtue of women's writing often lay in its divine spontaneity, like that of the blackbird's song or the thrush's. It was untaught; it was from the heart. But it was also, and much more often, chattering and garrulous—mere talk spilt over paper and left to dry in pools and blots. In future, granted time and books and a little space in the house for herself, literature will become for women, as for men, an art to be studied. Women's gift will be trained and strengthened. The novel will cease to be the dumping-ground for the personal emotions. It will become, more than at present, a work of art like any other, and its resources and its limitations will be explored.

From this it is a short step to the practice of the sophisticated arts, hitherto so little practised by women—to the writing of essays and criticism, of history and biography. And that, too, if we are considering the novel, will be of advantage; for besides improving the quality of the novel itself, it will draw off the aliens who have been attracted to fiction by its accessibility while their hearts lay elsewhere. Thus will the novel be rid of those excrescences of his-

tory and fact which, in our time, have made it so shapeless.

So, if we may prophesy, women in time to come will write fewer novels, but better novels; and not novels only, but poetry and criticism and history. But in this, to be sure, one is looking ahead to that golden, that perhaps fabulous, age when women will have what has so long been denied them—leisure, and money, and a room to themselves.

THE INTRODUCTION

Lily Everit saw Mrs. Dalloway bearing down on her from the other side of the room, and could have prayed her not to come and disturb her; and yet, as Mrs. Dalloway approached with her right hand raised and a smile which Lily knew (though this was her first party) meant: "But you've got to come out of your corner and talk," a smile at once benevolent and drastic, commanding, she felt the strangest mixture of excitement and fear, of desire to be left alone and of longing to be taken out and thrown down, down into the boiling depths. But Mrs. Dalloway was intercepted; caught by an old gentleman with white moustaches, and thus Lily Everit had two minutes' respite in which to hug to herself, like a spar in the sea, to sip, like a glass of wine, the thought of her essay upon the character of Dean Swift which Professor Miller had marked that morning with three red stars; First rate. First rate; she repeated that to herself, but the cordial was ever so much weaker now than it had been when she stood before the long glass being finished off (a pat here, a dab there) by her sister and Mildred, the housemaid. For as their hands moved about her, she felt that they were fidgeting agreeably on the surface but beneath lay untouched like a lump of glowing metal her essay on the character of Dean Swift, and all their praises when she came downstairs and stood in the hall waiting for a cab—Rupert had come out of his room and said what a swell she looked—ruffled the surface, went like a breeze among ribbons, but no more. One divided life (she felt sure of it) into fact, this essay, and into fiction, this going out, into rock and into wave, she thought, driving along and seeing things with such intensity that for ever she would see the truth and herself, a white reflection in the driver's dark back inextricably mixed: the moment of vision. Then as she came into the house, at the very first sight of people moving up stairs, down stairs, this hard lump (her essay on the character of Swift) wobbled, began melting, she could not keep hold of it, and all her being (no longer sharp as a diamond cleaving the heart of life asunder) turned to a mist of alarm, apprehension, and defence as she stood at bay in her corner. This was the famous place: the world.

Looking out, Lily Everit instinctively hid that essay of hers, so ashamed was she now, so bewildered too, and on tiptoe nevertheless to adjust her focus and get into right proportions (the old having been shamefully wrong) these diminishing and expanding things (what could one call them? people—impressions of people's lives?) which seemed to menace her and mount over her, to turn everything to water, leaving her only—for that she would not resign—the power to stand at bay.

Now Mrs. Dalloway, who had never quite dropped her arm, had shown by the way she moved it while she stood talking that she remembered, was only interrupted by the old soldier with the white moustaches, raised it again definitely and came straight down on her, and said to the shy charming girl, with her pale skin, her bright eyes, the dark hair which clustered poetically round her head and the thin body in a dress which seemed slipping off,

"Come and let me introduce you," and there Mrs. Dalloway hesitated, and then remembering that Lily was the clever one, who read poetry, looked about for some young man, some young man just down from Oxford, who would have read everything and could talk about Shelley. And holding Lily Everit's hand [she] led her towards a group where there were young people talking, and Bob Brinsley.

Lily Everit hung back a little, might have been the wayward sailing boat curtseying in the wake of a steamer, and felt as Mrs. Dalloway led her on, that it was now going to happen; that nothing could prevent it now; or save her (and she only wanted it to be over now) from being flung into a whirlpool where either she would perish or be saved. But what was the whirlpool?

Oh it was made of a million things and each was distinct to her; Westminster Abbey; the sense of enormously high solemn buildings surrounding them; being a woman. Perhaps that was the thing that came out, that remained, it was partly the dress, but all the little chivalries and respects of the drawing-room— all made her feel that she had come out of her chrysalis and was being proclaimed what in the comfortable darkness of childhood she had never been—this frail and beautiful creature, before whom men bowed, this limited and circumscribed creature who could not do what she liked, this butterfly with a thousand facets to its eyes and delicate fine plumage, and difficulties and sensibilities and sadnesses innumerable; a woman.

As she walked with Mrs. Dalloway across the room she accepted the part which was now laid on her and, naturally, overdid it a little as a soldier, proud of the traditions of an old and famous uniform might overdo it, feeling conscious as she walked, of her finery; of her tight shoes; of her coiled and twisted hair; and how if she dropped a handkerchief (this had happened) a man would stoop precipitately and give it her; thus accentuating the delicacy, the artificiality of her bearing unnaturally, for they were not hers after all.

Hers it was, rather, to run and hurry and ponder on long solitary walks, climbing gates, stepping through the mud, and through the blur, the dream, the ecstasy of loneliness, to see the plover's wheel and surprise the rabbits, and come in the hearts of woods or wide lonely moors upon little ceremonies which had no audience, private rites, pure beauty offered by beetles and lilies of the valley and dead leaves and still pools, without any care whatever what human beings thought of them, which filled her mind with rapture and wonder and held her there till she must touch the gate post to recollect herself—all this was, until tonight her ordinary being, by which she knew and liked herself and crept into the heart of mother and father and brothers and sisters; and this other was a flower which had opened in ten minutes. As the flower opened so too [came], incontrovertibly, the flower's world, so different, so strange; the towers of Westminster; the high and formal buildings; talk; this civilisation, she felt, hanging back, as Mrs. Dalloway led her on, this regulated way of life, which fell like a yoke about her neck, softly, indomitably, from the skies, a statement which there was no gainsaying. Glancing at her essay, the three red stars dulled to obscurity, but peacefully, pensively, as if yielding to the pressure of unquestionable might, that is the conviction that it was not hers to dominate, or to assert; rather to air and embellish this orderly life where all was done already; high towers, solemn bells, flats built every brick of them by men's toil, churches built by men's toil, parliaments too; and even the criss-cross of telegraph wires she thought looking at the window as she walked. What had she to oppose to this massive masculine achievement? An essay on the character of Dean Swift! And as she came up to the group, which Bob Brinsley dominated (with his heel on the fender, and his head back), with his great honest forehead, and his self-assurance, and his delicacy, and honour and robust physical well being, and sunburn, and airiness and direct descent from Shakespeare, what could she do but lay her essay, oh and the whole of her being, on the floor as a cloak for him to trample on, as a rose for him to rifle. Which she did, emphatically, when Mrs. Dalloway said, still holding her hand as if she would run away from this supreme trial, this introduction, "Mr. Brinsley —Miss Everit. Both of you love Shelley." But hers was not love compared with his.

Saying this, Mrs. Dalloway felt, as she always felt remembering her youth, absurdly moved; youth meeting youth at her hands, and there flashing, as at the concussion of steel upon flint (both stiffened to her feeling perceptibly) the loveliest and most ancient of all fires as she saw in Bob Brinsley's change of expression from carelessness to conformity, to formality, as he shook hands, which foreboded Clarissa thought, the tenderness, the goodness, the carefulness of women latent in all men, to her a sight to bring tears to the eyes, as it moved her even more intimately, to see in Lily herself the shy look, the startled look, surely the loveliest of all looks on a girl's face; and man feeling this for woman, and woman that for man, and there flowing from that contact all those homes, trials, sorrows, profound joy and ultimate staunchness in the face of catastrophe, humanity was sweet at its heart, thought Clarissa, and her own life (to introduce a couple made her think of meeting Richard for the first time!) infinitely blessed. And on she went.

But, thought Lily Everit. But—but—but what?

Oh nothing, she thought hastily smothering down softly her sharp instinct. Yes, she said. She did like reading.

"And I suppose you write?" he said, "poems presumably?"

"Essays," she said. And she would not let this horror get possession of her. Churches and parliaments, flats, even the telegraph wires— all, she told herself, made by men's toil, and this young man, she told herself, is in direct descent from Shakespeare, so she would not let this terror, this suspicion of something different, get hold of her and shrivel up her wings and drive her out into loneliness. But as she said this, she saw him—how else could she describe it—kill a fly. He tore the wings off a fly, standing with his foot on the fender, his head thrown back, talking insolently about himself, arrogantly, but she didn't mind how insolent and arrogant he was to her, if only he had not been brutal to flies.

But she said, fidgeting as she smothered down that idea, why not, since he is the greatest of all worldly objects? And to worship, to adorn, to embellish was her task, and to be worshipped, her wings were for that. But he talked; but he looked; but he laughed; he tore the wings off a fly. He pulled the wings off its back with his clever strong hands, and she saw him do it; and she could not hide the knowledge from herself. But it is necessary that it should be so, she argued, thinking of the churches, of the parliaments and the blocks of flats, and so tried to crouch and cower and fold the wings down flat on her back. But— but, what was it why was it? In spite of all she could do her essay upon the character of Swift became more and more obtrusive and the three stars burnt quite bright again, only no longer clear and brilliant, but troubled and blood-stained as if this man, this great Mr. Brinsley, had just by pulling the wings off a fly as he talked (about his essay, about himself and once laughing, about a girl there) charged her light being with cloud, and confused her for ever and ever and shrivelled her wings on her back, and, as he turned away from her, he made her think of the towers and civilisation with horror, and the yoke that had fallen from the skies onto her neck crushed her, and she felt like a naked wretch who having sought shelter in some shady garden is turned out and told—no, that there are no sanctuaries, or butterflies, in this world, and this civilisation, churches, parliaments and flats—this civilisation, said Lily Everit to herself, as she accepted the kind compliments of old Mrs. Bromley on her appearance[, depends upon me,] and Mrs. Bromley said later that like all the Everits Lily looked "as if she had the weight of the world upon her shoulders".

Myrtiótissa   (Theoni Drakopoúlou)   *Greece, 1883–1973*

Myrtiótissa is the pseudonym of Theoni Drakopoúlou, who was born in Constantinople in 1883, and educated at a boarding school in Athens, to which city her family moved in 1901. Early she developed a passion for contemporary Greek poetry and for the theater. She gained experience in amateur acting (e.g., as Desdemona in *Othello*) but was prevented by her family from becoming a professional actress. At the period such a profession was unthinkable for a girl of good family. Obliged to marry, she rejected the first suitor proposed by her family, but capitulated and agreed to the second match proposed—a cousin who lived in Paris. The marriage was a disaster: Myrtiótissa could find no common ground with her husband and was desperately unhappy in Paris. She soon separated from him and returned to Greece with her baby son (later the actor George Pappás). In Athens, Myrtiótissa fell in love with the much older poet Loréntzos Mavílis, the last great poet of the so-called "School of the Ionian Islands." She was, therefore, devastated when Mavílis was killed in 1912, fighting as a volunteer in the Greco-Bulgarian War. However, she found some consolation in the poetic circles to which her friendship with Mavílis had given her access, notably in her acquaintanceship with Kostís Palamás, the "grand old man" of Greek poetry, who encouraged her to write. Her main works are *Tragoúdia* (Songs, 1919), *Kítrines Floyés* (Yellow Flames, 1925, with a preface by Palamás), *Ta dóra tis agápis* (The Gifts of Love, 1932), which won the Poetry Prize of the Academy of Athens, and *Kravyés* (Cries, 1939), which won the State Poetry Prize, and in which "Women of Suli" appears.

In 1928 she published her translations of a selection of the poems of the Comtesse de Noailles, who was an important influence on her own work, and also translated Sophocles' *Medea*. In 1952 she published a touching memoir on the childhood of her son George, who preceded her to the grave. She herself died in the very house where Palamás had lived at the end of his life.

The sense of a woman haunted by others and yet unsure whether she wishes to escape that haunting marks Myrtiótissa's poetry, which contains many of the conventional themes of pre–First World War Greek poetry, particularly love and nature. It is essentially lyrical in character. But through these conventional themes she reveals a divided and uncertain self. She yearns to be relieved of the responsibility for herself, yet she struggles against the oppressive effects of outside forces. In her best poems emotional intensity comes through very strongly.

Christopher Robinson

WOMEN OF SULI*
Souliótisses

Ah! You who wakened in my child's soul
the first quiver of phantasy and wonder,
who first opened the deeps of my heart
for the sublime breath of poetry to enter!

Ah! You who wakened in me a vast pride,
what if my life is a starless night,
what if a wasteland, bitter and black, surround
                                                            me,
if only a drop of your blood beats in my heart!

As a child, I leaned on my grandmother's knee
to hear of princesses most fair and mighty
                                                            kings,
but always at the end, I remembered to ask
                                                about you,
"Tell me your story, Grandma, the true story."

And as she began, I saw you passing before me,
one by one, like high-breasted, beautiful
                                                    princesses,
and singing still, you plunged into the dragon's
                                                            cave
imbedded at the base of the cliff.

Then terrified I closed my eyes and always
the moan of your wild song would reach my
                                                            ears,
weaving a living circle in my mind,
yawning mouths of an unseen monster.

But though my early years were full of you,
                                    your meaning
escaped me, for it was greater than my mind
                                                could grasp,
I loved you with a seven year old heart
I thought of you with timid, quivering love.

As my emotion deepened and thought matured,
once as I stood beneath the spreading red-gold
                                                            light
diffused over Zalongo before the sun went
                                                            down,
I saw a miraculous vision of your tragic dance!

And I saw you like young does ascending
with your children, a sheer and rugged peak,
the sun crowning the serpents of your hair,
rags covering your bodies teeming with life.

And you tossed down your children, and ah
                                    me, the infants
seemed to be playing a happy mad game;
at the foot of the cliff were piled roses
                                                and lilies
that shone like an April garden, softly.

And then of a sudden you started a frenzied
celebration,
One by one, dropping into space, you left the
dance,
and you wheeled in ever narrowing circles
and the wind flailed many colored rags and
hair!

Abruptly my heart shook, a worshipping bell,
for you were left the last, alone on the peak,
and I quaked like a terrified mother
but you were rigid and still, last woman of
Suli!

Ah! When your scream had trailed away, your
feet were in space,
when the tight-clenched fingers flew apart like
birds,
and you saw about you only thorns and stones
in the frightful and infinite gloom enclosing you,
did horror not glide snake-like through your
heart,
did doubt not face you for a moment
as you measured the yawning abyss before you,
did death not seem a foe worse than the Turk?

The others rested sweetly in the feathery arms
of glory,
leaned down from the whirl of their sacred
dance,
but you were awakened bitterly by silence
fixing its cold glance upon you.

Then, did your beloved country scenes not
haunt you?

The rough path leading to the village?
Did you not feel your mother's trembling touch
under the pine shading your house, like a
mighty guardian?
Did you not hear your dogs bay mournfully?
Did you not see the old folks left alone?
Did you not hear nature keening over you
through the crying of birds and the North
Wind?

Your breasts that swelled with abundant milk,
your vigorous wholesome mountain body,
as you leaned far over the rocky hollow
did it not say *no* to you, did it not oppose you?

The sun set and with it the vision of you,
but I stood fixed as stone before the sacred
mountain,
and for long I felt deeply throbbing within me
the warmth of your blood, the freshness of
your hair,
Women of Suli! Where your bodies are one
with the rocks,
the stony earth is adorned with wild flowers,
but on the peak there blooms a single lily to
honor
the last Suli woman, foam of your fragrance.
                                    Translated by Rae Dalvin

NOTE

* Before the Greek War of Independence of 1821, all the
  women of Suli leaped to their death with their children
  in their arms from the cliffs of Zalongo in Epirus, rather
  than surrender to the Turks.

Katharine Susannah Prichard   *Australia, 1883–1969*

Katharine Susannah Prichard has been one of Australia's most controversial women writers and debate still continues over her standing in Australian literature. Though the title of her autobiography, *Child of the Hurricane* (1963), was a reference to the circumstances of her birth, it also appears appropriate given much that happened to her later in life.

Prichard was born in Fiji, where her Australian journalist father was editing a local newspaper. She grew up in Tasmania and later in Melbourne where she began writing, publishing her first story at the age of 16 in a Melbourne newspaper. Unable to attend university because of family poverty, she worked as a governess on large country estates, and later as a teacher and journalist in Melbourne.

Though an ardent Australian nationalist, Prichard, like most Australian writers of her generation and later, felt the need to go overseas to further her career. While she was working in London as a journalist, her first novel, *The Pioneers* (1915), about the settlement of Australia, won an English publisher's competition and was filmed in Australia in 1916. Prichard returned to Australia and in 1919 married the World War I hero Hugo Throssell and moved to his home near Perth.

Many of Prichard's later novels are set in Western Australia, including the two usually regarded as her finest, *Working Bullocks* (1926) and *Coonardoo* (1929). The latter won a fiction award in 1928 but upset many because of its frank portrayal of sexual relations between Aboriginal women and white men; *Brumby Innes*, a play dealing with the same material, won a 1927 award for best Australian play, but had to wait until 1940 for publication and 1972 for stage production.

Like these two prize-winning works, "The Cooboo," included here, was based on Prichard's experiences during a visit to an isolated cattle station in north-west Western Australia, where she came to admire Aboriginals and their culture. It was published in her first, and best, collection of stories, *Kiss on the Lips* (1932).

Prichard's sympathetic portrayal of Aboriginals and open treatment of sexuality were by no means the only controversial areas of her life and writings. She had always been involved in socialist and radical causes and in 1920 became a founding member of the Communist Party of Australia. In 1933 she visited the Soviet Union, a trip recorded in her non-fiction book, *The Real Russia* (1934). While she was away, her husband committed suicide as a result of business and financial worries. Prichard, however, feared that he had read the draft of her novel *Intimate Strangers* (1937), which originally ended with the husband committing suicide. She changed the ending because of his suicide to one of reconciliation between husband and wife. Many critics have felt that Prichard's work after this period never again reached the standards of her earlier books.

Altogether, Prichard published twelve novels, five collections of stories, two volumes of poetry and two plays, besides her book on Russia, her autobiography and many articles and political pamphlets. Some of her articles have been collected by her son, Ric Throssell, in *Straight Left* (1982). Prichard's many unpublished plays suggest that she had the potential to have been at least as fine a dramatist as a novelist had the possibility of stage productions been available to her.

Elizabeth Webby

THE COOBOO[1]

They had been mustering all day on the wide plains of Murndoo station. Over the red earth, black with ironstone pebbles, through mulga and curari bush, across the ridges which make a blue wall along the horizon. And the rosy, garish light of sunset was on plains, hills, moving cattle, men and horses.

Through red dust the bullocks mooched, restless and scary still, a wild mob from the hills. John Gray, in the rear with Arra, the boy who was his shadow; Wongana, on the right with his gin,[2] Rose; Frank, the half-caste, on the left with Minni.

A steer breaking from the mob before Rose, she wheeled and went after him. Faint and wailing, a cry followed her, as though her horse had stepped on and crushed some small creature. But the steer was getting away. Arra went after him, stretched along his horse's neck, rounded the beast and rode him back to the mob, sulky and blethering. The mob swayed; it had broken three times that day, but was settling to the road.

John Gray called: "Yienda (you) damn fool, Rosey. Finish!"

The gin, on her slight, rough-haired horse, pulled up scowling.

"Tell Meetchie, Thirty Mile, tomorrow," John Gray said. "Miah, new moon."

Rose slewed her horse away from the mob of men and cattle. That wailing, thin and hard as hair-string, moved with her.

"Minni!"

John Gray jerked his head towards Rose. Minni's bare heels struck her horse's belly; with a turn of the wrist she swung her horse off from the mob, turned, leaned forward, rising in her stirrups, and came up with Rose.

Thin, dark figures on their wiry station-bred horses, the gins rode into the haze of sunset towards the hills. The dull, dirty blue of the trousers wrapped round their legs was torn; their short, fairish hair tousled by the wind. But the glitter and tumult of Rose's eyes, Minni looked away from them.

At a little distance, when men and cattle were a moving cloud of red dust, Rose's anger gushed after them.

"Koo!"[3]

Fierce as the cry of a hawk flew her last note of derision and defiance.

A far-away rattle of laughter drifted back across country. The men had heard and were laughing at her. The women walked their horses. Alone they would have been afraid, as darkness coming up behind was hovering near them, secreting itself among the low, writhen trees and bushes; afraid of the evil spirits who wander over the plains and stony ridges when the light of day is withdrawn. But together they were not so afraid. Twenty miles away, over there, below that dent in the hills where Nyedee Creek made a sandy bed for itself among white-bodied gums, was Murndoo homestead and the uloo[4] of their people.

There was no track; and in the first darkness, which would be thick as wool after the glow of sunset faded, only their instinct would keep them moving in the direction of the homestead and their own low, round huts of bagging, rusty tin and dead boughs.

Both were Wongana's women: Rose, tall, gaunt and masterful; Minni, younger, fat and jolly. Rose had been a good stockman in her day: one of the best. Minni did not ride or track nearly as well as Rose.

And yet, as they rode along, Minni pattered complacently of how well she had worked that day; of how she was flashed, this way and that, heading-off breakaways, dashing after them, turning them back to the mob so smartly that John had said, "Good man, Minni!" There was the white bullock—he had rushed near the yards. Had Rose seen the chestnut mare stumble in a crab-hole and send Arra flying? But Minni had chased the white bullock, chased him for a couple of miles, and brought him back to the yards. No doubt there would be nammery[5] for her and a new gina-gina[6] when the men came in from the muster.

She pulled a pipe from her belt, shook the ashes out, and with reins looped over one arm stuffed the bowl with tobacco from a tin tied to her belt. Stooping down, she struck a match on her stirrup-iron, guarded the flame to the pipe between her short, white teeth, and smoked contentedly.

The scowl on Rose's face deepened, darkened. That thin, fretted wailing came from her breast.

She unslung from her neck the rag rope by which the baby had been held against her body, and gave him a sagging breast to suck. Holding him with one arm, she rode slowly, her horse picking his way over the rough, stony earth.

It had been a hard day. The gins were mustering with the men at sunrise. Camped at Nyedee well the night before, in order to get a good start, they had been riding through the timbered ridges all the morning, rounding up wild cows, calves and young bullocks, and driving them down to the yards at Nyedee, where John Gray cut out the fats, left old Jimmy and a couple of boys to brand calves, turn the cows and calves back to the ridge again while he took on the mob for trucking at Meekatharra. The bullocks were as wild as birds: needed watching all day. And all the time that small, whimpering bundle against her breast had hampered Rose's movements.

There was nothing the gins liked better than a muster, riding after cattle. And they could ride, were quicker in their movements, more alert than the men; sharper at picking up tracks. They did not go mustering very often nowadays when there was work to do at the homestead. Since John Gray had married, and there was a woman on Murndoo, she found plenty of washing, scrubbing and sweeping for the gins to do; would not spare them often to go after cattle. But John was short-handed. He had said he must have Rose and Minni to muster Nyedee. And all day her baby's crying had irritated Rose. The cooboo had wailed and wailed as she rode with him tied to her body.

The cooboo was responsible for the wrong things she had done that day. Stupid things. Rose was furious. The men had yelled at her. Wongana, her man, blackguarding her before everybody, had called her "a hen who did not know where she laid her eggs." And John Gray, with his "Yienda, damn fool, Rosey, Finish!" had sent her home like a naughty child.

Now, here was Minni jabbering of the tobacco she would get and the new gina-gina. How pleased Wongana would be with her! And the cooboo, wailing, wailing. He wailed as he chewed Rose's empty breast, squirming, against her; wailed and gnawed.

She cried out with hurt and impatience. Rage, irritated to madness, rushed through her; rushed like waters coming down the dry creek-beds after heavy rain. Rose wrenched the cooboo from her breast and flung him from her to the ground. There was a crack as of twigs breaking.

Minni glanced aside. "Wiah!" she gasped with widening eyes. But Rose rode on, gazing ahead over the rosy, garish plains and wall of the hills, darkening from blue to purple and indigo.

When the women came into the station kitchen, earth, hills and trees were dark; the sky heavy with stars. Minni gave John's wife his message: that he would be home with the new moon, in about a fortnight.

Meetchie, as the blacks called Mrs. John Gray, could not make out why the gins were so stiff and quiet: why Rose stalked, scowling and sulky-fellow, sombre eyes just glancing, and away again. Meetchie wanted to ask about the muster, what sort of conditions the bullocks had on; how many were on the road; if many calves had been branded at Nyedee. But she knew them too well to ask questions when they looked like that.

Only when she had given them bread and a tin of jam, cut off hunks of corned beef for them, filled their billies with strong black tea, put sugar in their empty tins, and they were going off to the uloo, she was surprised to see Rose without her baby.

"Why, Rose," she exclaimed, "where's the cooboo?"

Rose stalked off into the night. Minni glanced back with scared eyes, and followed Rose.

In the dawn, when a cry, remote and anguished, flew through the clear air, Meetchie wondered who was dead in the camp by the creek. She remembered Rose: how she had looked the night before. And the cooboo—where was he?

for her cooboo in the dawn; Rose cutting herself with stones until her body bled; Rose screaming in a fury of unavailing grief.

NOTES

1. Aboriginal for 'baby.'
2. Woman.
3. An Aborigine cry.
4. Camp.
5. Reward.
6. Dress.

Halide Edib-Adıvar   *Turkey, 1884–1964*

Halide Edib, or Halide Edib-Adıvar as she became known after last names were adopted in the 1930s and she took the last name of her husband, Dr. Adnan Adıvar, is perhaps the best-known modern Turkish woman to date. She was an active member of the National Liberation movement and a riveting public speaker in the crucial years immediately after the First World War, when her native Istanbul was occupied by the Allies, Turkey having fought on the side of the Germans. She escaped to Anatolia and fought alongside Mustafa Kemal Atatürk during the War of Independence (1919–1922), ending the war with the rank of staff sergeant. This ability to put up with primitive conditions might not have been predicted of a woman raised in aristocratic surroundings, the daughter of a palace official of the Ottoman Empire. However, before the First World War, Halide Edib had already graduated from the American College for Girls at Üsküdar in Istanbul where the language of instruction was English; studied philosophy, sociology, and mathematics privately; married and given birth to two sons; written articles for the Istanbul newspapers which necessitated that she flee the country for a while to escape the wrath of the autocratic sultan; become a teacher and school inspector; and become interested in the education of women and in women's suffrage.

After the foundation of the Turkish Republic, in the years between 1923 and 1938, Halide Edib lived mostly in England and the United States. She wrote first in English and published in England and the United States two volumes of memoirs, *The Memoirs of Halide Edib* (1926) and *The Turkish Ordeal* (1928); and a novel, *The Clown and His Daughter* (1935; *Sinekli Bakkal,* 1936), followed in 1930 in the United States by *Turkey Faces West*, a historical essay. Many of her more than thirty novels written in Turkish are still in print, and several have been made into newspaper "photo novel" serials, while others have been adapted for cinema, television, or radio. In the section of her autobiographical writings included here, Halide Edib describes her stay with the black slave and wet nurse Nevres, and Nevre's husband, by extension her "milk father," and their participation in the Moslem fast period. In the story, Halide Edib refers to Nevres as 'sister.'

Halide Edib became a Professor of English Literature at Istanbul University in 1939, teaching there continuously until her death except for a four-year period (1950–1954) when she was a member of Parliament from Izmir.

Ellen Ervin

from MEMOIRS

...The young moon which started the Rama-zan rejoicings had been seen by someone late in the night. Just as I was feeling immured by the rocky hardness of the lightless room, soft lights from outside lit up the white curtains as boys and men passed along the street with lanterns in their hands, singing and beating a tremendous drum. This made milk-mother get up, make a light, and begin to bustle round, getting ready for the first *sahur* (the night meal which is eaten after midnight in Ramazan in preparation for the next day's fasting), which every one would begin the next day.

The next morning when I woke, milk-father was snoring in his bed. Only milk-mother was up, probably to prepare my morning milk; and I had to have a lonely meal listening to the extraordinary silence which seemed to fill the house as well as the streets. It was only at three in the afternoon that the world began to wake up and we got ready for the visit to the mosques.

This part of Istamboul is a vast burnt waste, islanded with patches of charming dark wooden houses with shadowy eaves. Between these we passed, she holding my hand fast, that I might not get lost. The streets were full. Groups of women, in *charshafs*[1] of many col-ors, moved along, the young with thick veils but the old with their faces uncovered, all with rosaries in hand and tight lips occasionally whispering a prayer. Every one carried a ros-ary, beautifully and fancifully colored, each mosque having had a fair where one could buy rosaries, pipes, women's trinkets, dried fruit, and all imaginable delicacies, especially spices. Men from all over the empire stood there, picturesquely dressed, crying their goods in musical tones and in their own languages. Arabs predominated in numbers, their stalls full of henna and kohl in pretty red leather tubes, which they pretended to have brought from Mecca, and which made their goods con-sidered almost like holy relics and therefore to be much sought after. Besides holy tradition said that it was pleasing to Mohammed for women to dye their eyes with kohl and their fingers with henna.

Finally Suleymanié mosque was reached, where we were to hear preaching or *mukabelé*.[2] The sight of that gray and impos-ing group of buildings made me almost drunk with pleasure. It seemed to be composed of myriads of open cells through which pene-trated this gray mass rising in the blue air. The feeling inside me was of a fluid motion, flood-ing and moving in a divine harmony through my little body. I have often thought since that a child's perception of beauty is superior to that of a grown-up. It is not a beauty of words. It is color; it is sound; it is harmony and line all combined yet producing a single sensation.

A moment's pause at the door to give one's shoes to the old man,[3] the lifting of the corner of the huge worn curtain, beside which one looked like a tiny rabbit, and then the entrance!

A gray endless upward sweep of dome, holding a hazy gray atmosphere in which hung the constellation of the tiny oil lamplets.[4] The light through the colored windows must have added a rosy hue, but the warmth of its pink-ish shade was rather felt than seen. It was diffused in that gray air and added a faint tone which prevented the gray from being sad and somber, as it usually is on sea and sky. The magic of genius has given the mosque of Suleymanié the proportions which make one fancy it the largest building one has ever seen, so imposing is the sense of space and grandeur reduced to its simplest expression. Near the *mihrab*,[5] under different groups of lamps, sat various men in white turbans and loose black gowns, swinging their bodies in rhythm with the lilt of their minor chants. Everything seemed part of the simple majestic gray space with its invisible rosy hue and its invisible pulsations. In the pulpits sat men in the same dresses as the chanters. They were preaching and waving their arms in more passionate rhythm than the chanting ones, but everything became toned down and swallowed up in the conquering silence, in the invisible pulsation of the air. Nevres sat down where she could listen to some man who was chanting for the souls of the dead. Some of these chanters were old and some young, but all had the transparent amber pallor and the hectic eyes of those who are fasting. In no time I felt caught up into the general sway and began moving my body unconsciously to and fro in the same harmonious manner as the rest. I became a part of the whole and could not have moved otherwise than under the dominating pulsations of the place. No false note, no discordant gesture was possible.

There were more groups of women than men around the preachers, and as Badji always went to listen to the chanters, I quietly sneaked away and knelt before a preacher's pulpit. A pale man with eyes of liquid flame was speaking, condemning every human being to eternal fire, since his standard for a good Moslem was such that it was quite impracticable to get to heaven. As the natural dwelling-place of Moslem mortals therefore, he described all the quarters of hell—the place where people are burned, the place where they are tortured in all sorts of ways. It seemed to be a case of either endless suffering in this world or the next; that at any rate is the effect which has stayed in my memory as being what he wanted to impress upon us. His arms in their long loose black sleeves had prophetic gestures; his voice had a troubling tone, something so burning, so colored lending itself to the wonderful rhythm and beauty of the verses of the Koran which he read and interpreted. It was really sublime nonsense, rendered in most artistic gestures and tones. I sneaked back to Badji and hid my face in her ample *charshaf*. I was frightened and troubled for the first time with a vague sense of religion.

In the evening the great guns were fired, signaling the time to break the fast, and we gathered about the round low tray on which jams, olives, cheese, spiced meats, eggs, and all sorts of highly flavored pastries were arranged. Milk-father got back his good humor as he ate. In Ramazan the Moslem spoils his stomach as one spoils a beloved child, even the poorest allowing himself variety and plenty.

Our evening prayers received only scant observance that night, for we had to hurry out for the Ramazan prayer, milk-father leading with a lantern in his hand; but turning back he soon lifted me on his shoulders, and swinging the lantern in his other hand, he walked by Badji's side, talking and joking. The streets were lighted by hundreds of these moving lanterns. Men, women, and children flickered forward like a swarm of fireflies, drums were sounding in the distance, and from every minaret the muezzin was calling, "*Allah Ekber, Allah Ekber....*"[6] The grand harmony came nearer or grew more distant as we moved on. Then suddenly above the dimly lighted houses, above the mass of moving lights, a circle of light came into view high over our heads in the dark blue air. The tiny balcony of some dim minaret was now traced out as though by magic in a slender illusive ring of light. These light circles multiplied into hundreds, standing out in the bluish heaven, softly lighting up the picturesque masses of the wooden buildings below them, or the melting lines of the domes. And now in the same air, hanging in fact between minaret and minaret, other beautiful lines of light as if by a miracle interlaced and wove themselves into wonderful writing: "Welcome, O Ramazan!" Belshazzar's surprise when he saw the invisible fingers writing on the wall differed from mine only in quality.[7] I was on the shoulders of the tallest man in the crowd. Below me the lights of the lanterns swung in the dark depths of the long winding mysterious streets. Above me light circles and gigantic letterings, also in light, hung in the blue void, while the illusive tracery of the minarets, the soft droop of the domes, appeared dimly or disappeared in the thickness of blue distance as we walked on. And so once more we reached Suleymanié and plunged into the great crowd gathered inside.

The gray space was now a golden haze. Around the hundreds of tremulous oil lights a vast golden atmosphere thickened, and under it thousands of men sat on their knees in orderly rows; not one single space was empty, and this compact mass, this human carpet presented a design made up of all costumes, ages, and ranks. The women prayed in the gallery above.

Nevres Badji left me to watch it all while she found herself a proper place in a regular row. Suddenly came the unique grand call—"*Sal-li-a-la Mohammed!*"[8] and then the rise of the entire human mass. The imam stood in front of the *mihrab*, his back to the people, and opened the prayer. It is wonderful to pray led by an imam. He chants aloud the verses you usually repeat in lonely prayer. You bow, you kneel, your forehead touches the floor. Each movement is a vast and complicated rhythm, the rising and falling controlled by the invisible voices of the several muezzins. There is a beautiful minor chant. The refrain is taken up again and again by the muezzins. There is a continual rhythmic thud and rustle as the thousands fall and rise. The rest belongs to the eternal silence.

It seems as if we should go on rising and falling, rising and falling for the rest of our lives, till all of a sudden people remain longer on their knees than before, and a chorus of, "*Amin, amin.*" sets the pulsing air into an almost frantic rhythm.

Then we leave the mosque.

I have often prayed in most of the mosques of Istamboul, but I have never entered Suleymanié again, although I have walked many times around it and visited the museum which used to be its soup-kitchen in earlier times. I did not want to alter the memory of the divine and esthetic emotion which I had had in the days of my early childhood, and I knew it was not possible to repeat it without destroying the intensity of that first impression.

Whatever my feelings are toward some parts of the Ottoman past, I am grateful to its conception of beauty as expressed by Sinan[9] in that wonderful dome. The gorgeous coloring of the Byzantines, the magic tracery, and the delicate, lace-like ornament of the Arab influenced him in many ways, but he surely brought that flawless beauty of line and that sober majesty in his Turkish heart from its original home in the wild steppes. There is a manliness and lack of self-consciousness here which I have never seen in any other temple, yet the work is far from being primitive or elemental. It combines genius and science, as well as the personal sense of holy beauty which is characteristic of the Ottoman, and it can hold its own with the architectural triumphs of any age.

NOTES (by author: 2–5, 7, 8)

1. An outer garment traditionally worn by women covering the body from head to foot.
2. Every family had a *hafiz*, a man who knows the Koran by heart and the musical rules of the chanting. He has to chant the Koran for the soul of the dead. One heard them in every mosque, some being famous and more sought after for beauty of voice or rendering.
3. No one may pollute a mosque by walking in it with shoes dirty with the impurities of the street. Huge padded curtains hang over the mosque doorways.
4. Until recently all mosques were lit by tiny lamps, each lamp consisting of a small, cup-like glass filled with oil on which floated a wick. From the ceiling of the dome an iron framework was hung by heavy chains, and in this framework the lamps were placed; but so slight and delicate was it that, when the lamps were lit, the framework was unseen and the impression was of stars hanging in the sky of the dome.
5. The part of a mosque which shows the direction of Mecca.
6. God is great—the beginning of the usual call to prayer.
7. Daniel 4:9; 5: 25–28, 30–31.
8. Pray in the name of Mohammed.
9. Sinan is the celebrated Turkish architect who lived in the sixteenth and seventeenth centuries and built endless mosques, bridges, *türbahs*, fountains, and kitchens for the poor.

Anna Wickham   (Edith Alice Mary Harper)

UK(England), 1884 – 1947

Anna Wickham was born Edith Alice Mary Harper in Wimbledon, Surrey. At the age of 6, she and her family went to Australia, and lived in Queensland, New South Wales. She returned to London when she was 21, and from there went to Paris to study opera; however, her studies came to an abrupt end in 1906 when she married Patrick Hepburn, a solicitor and amateur balloonist and astronomer. The marriage was not always a happy one for the spirited Wickham, who rebelled against a standard Victorian marriage. The couple had four children.

Wickham started writing while quite young and by 1911 had already privately published a small collection of verse plays. During the teens, Wickham became a part of Harold and Alice Monro's Poetry Bookshop literary circle, and it was the Monros who were responsible for bringing her emotional candor and unschooled style to maturity. In June 1914 some of her poems were printed in *Poetry and Drama*, and then in 1915 *The Contemplative Quarry* appeared.

Many of Wickham's poems are quite musical in impulse and feeling. They are emotionally very powerful in a tempestuous and jarring way. Some of the best poems are but epithets and epigrams, poems that are barely a couplet or stanza in length. Regardless of the length, her themes about women's need for liberty and equality, quite modern for their time, come through very strongly. Three volumes of poems that followed *The Contemplative Quarry: The Man with a Hammer were Verses* in 1916, *The Little Old House* in 1921, and *Thirty-Six Poems* in 1936. Her poems received modest acclaim in America and France but she has been little known in her native England except among the artists and literati of her time, including D.H. Lawrence, Dylan Thomas and Kate O'Brien. A collection of her work, *The Writings of Anna Wickham*, was published in 1984. The following poems are from *The Little Old House*.

John Isom

THE AFFINITY

I have to thank God I'm a woman
For in these ordered days a woman only
Is free to be very hungry, very lonely.

It is said for Feminism, but still clear
That man, more often than women, is a
                                    pioneer.

If I would confide a new thought,
First to a man must it be brought.

Now, for our sins, it is my bitter fate
That such a man wills soon to be my mate,
And so of friendship is quick end:
When I have gained a love I lose a friend.

It is well within the order of things
That man should listen when his mate sings;
But the true male never yet walked
Who liked to listen when his mate talked.

I would be married to a full man,
As would all women since the world began;
But from a wealth of living I have proved
I must be silent, if I would be loved.

(continued)

Now of my silence I have much wealth,
I have to do my thinking all by stealth.
My thought may never see the day;
My mind is like a catacomb where early
                                        Christians pray.

And of my silence I have much pain,
But of these pangs I have great gain;
For I must take to drugs or drink,
Or I must write the things I think.

If my sex would let me speak,
I would be very lazy and most weak;
I should speak only, and the things I spoke
Would fill the air a while, and clear like
                                        smoke.

The things I think now I write down,
And some day I will show them to the Town.
When I am sad I make thought clear;
I can re-read it all next year.

I have to thank God I'm a woman,
For in these ordered days a woman only
Is free to be very hungry, very lonely.

MEDITATION AT KEW*

Alas! for all the pretty women who marry dull
                                        men,
Go into the suburbs and never come out again,
Who lose their pretty faces, and dim their
                                        pretty eyes,
Because no one has skill or courage to
                                        organize.

What do these pretty women suffer when they
                                        marry?
They bear a boy who is like Uncle Harry,
A girl, who is like Aunt Eliza, and not new,
These old, dull races must breed true.

I would enclose a common in the sun,
And let the young wives out to laugh and run;
I would steal their dull clothes and go away,
And leave the pretty naked things to play.

Then I would make a contract with hard Fate
That they see all the men in the world and
                                        choose a mate,
And I would summon all the pipers in the
                                        town
That they dance with Love at a feast, and
                                        dance him down.

From the gay unions of choice
We'd have a race of splendid beauty, and of
                                        thrilling voice.
The World whips frank, gay love with rods,
But frankly gaily shall we get the gods.

NOTE

* A south London suburb.

Isak Dinesen   (Karen Blixen)   *Denmark/Kenya, 1885–1962*

Isak Dinesen (pseudonym of Karen Blixen) has had a decidedly erratic relationship with the public. At times, she has been extremely popular, most recently in 1986 when the film of her autobiographical book *pen afrikanske farm* (*Out of Africa*, 1937) was released. The first rush of popularity came in 1935 when she first published *syv fantastiske fortællinger* (*Seven Gothic Tales*) her first literary production, which, despite its exotic subject matter and difficult, allusive, ironic style was immensely well received in the U.S. where it was first published, as was her autobiography two years later. (She wrote these works first in English.) Reception in Denmark was not as favorable; the book was viewed there, intially, as aristocratic and decadent. She then fell out of the popular limelight until the late 1950s when she again aroused public interest because she was a wonderful reader of her own stories, and because of her unusual appearance—in the last phases of illness she was extremely gaunt, with an eerie, skeletal appearance. People now think she looked like Meryl Streep, who played Dinesen in the movie and Isak is once more the object of curiosity, although it is her seemingly glamorous life in Africa, in the main, rather than her writing, which is the subject of the public's interest.

Isak Dinesen was born to an old Danish family. Her father, a military man and an adventurer, was also a writer, publishing several noted books in the late nineteenth century about his exploits. His suicide, when Dinesen was 10, was a profoundly traumatic event in the young girl's life. Dinesen was tutored at home and, at 15, studied art in several European cities. Her illfated marriage to her second cousin, Baron Bror Blixen, took her to Kenya to run a coffee plantation; she continued running it alone after her divorce a few years later. When the coffee crop eventually failed, seventeen years after her arrival in Africa, she left, and, to support herself, became a writer. (She had long been an accomplished storyteller and had begun writing in Kenya.) *Seven Gothic Tales*, her tragi-comic romances about hope, love, and the imagination, brought her immediate fame. *Out of Africa* and its successor *Shadows in the Grass* (*Skygger paa Graesset*, 1960), were about her time in Africa. Extremely realistic, they make her exotic life there a real and yet artistic creation, bound as it is by the towering figure of Karen, creator and narrator. Her love for the adventurer Denys Finch-Hatton is moving and dramatic, and his death tragic. Karen's character is very believable. Further information is available in *Letters From Africa 1914–1931*, published first in two volumes in Danish (1978; translation, 1981).

Dinesen did not write a great deal, partly because she started so late (at age 50) and partly because she suffered from the increasingly disabling disease of syphilis, which she contracted during her brief marriage and which, with the removal of most of her stomach, resulted in her extreme emaciation. Her small opus, some of it written first in English, and most of it translated into English (often by the author) has been very well received by critics, however, especially *Winter's Tales* (*Vinter-Eventyr* 1942), and *Last Tales* (*Sidste Fortællinger*, 1957), centering on the theme of the interrelation between art and life. The story presented here is from *Last Tales* and was translated by Dinesen. She also wrote, pseudonymously, *The Angelic Avengers* (*Gengaeldelsens Veie*, 1944), a political allegory about the Nazi occupation of Denmark.

Dinesen's persona was always strangely anachronistic, more suited to the distant past than to the present. Many of her works are set in the eighteenth and nineteenth centuries and feature aristocratic characters and settings. She lived in the five-hundred-year-old house, Rungsted, purchased by her father in the late nineteenth century and once occupied by the poet Johannes Ewald, who lodged there in the eighteenth century when the house was an inn. For poetic inspiration, Dinesen used Ewald's room as her study. She despaired of the loss of the elegance and nobility of pre-World War I Europe and, indeed, was seen as a great influence on the Heretica movement, based on the journal of the same name (1948–1953), whose constituents bemoaned the materialism of the modern world, calling for a return to the cultural unity of earlier periods (e.g., the Middle Ages).

Dinesen, with her sense of noblesse oblige, left her house to the people of Denmark as a foundation for the study of culture and science and its grounds as a park and bird sanctuary. Royalties from her book sales (and film rights) are used to maintain the property.

TALES OF TWO OLD GENTLEMEN

Two old gentlemen, both of them widowers, played piquet[1] in a small salon next to a ballroom. When they had finished their game, they had their chairs turned round, so that through the open doors they could watch the dancers. They sat on contentedly, sipping their wine, their delicate noses turned up a little and taking in, with the melancholic superiority of age, the fragrance of youth before them. They first talked of ancient scandals in high society—for they had known each other as boys and young men—and of the sad fate of common friends, then of political and dynastic matters, and at last of the complexity of the universe in general. When they got there, there was a pause.

"My grandfather," the one old gentleman said at the end of it, "who was a very happy man and particularly happy in his married life, had built up a philosophy of his own, which in the course of my life from time to time has been brought back to me."

"I remember your grandfather quite well, my good Matteo," said the other, "a highly corpulent, but still graceful figure, with a smooth, rosy face. He did not speak much."

"He did not speak much, my good Taddeo," Matteo agreed, "for he did, in accordance with his philosophy, admit the futility of argumentation. It is from my brilliant grandmother, his wife, that I have inherited my taste for a discussion. Yet one evening, while I was still quite a young boy, he benignly condescended to develop his theory to me. It happened, I remember, at a ball like this, and I myself was all the time longing to get away from the lecture. But my grandfather, his mind once opened upon the matter, did not dismiss his youthful listener till he had set forth to him his entire train of ideas. He said:

"'We suffer much. We go through many dark hours of doubt, dread and despair, because we cannot reconcile our idea of divinity with the state of things in the universe round us. I myself as a young man brooded a good deal over the problem. Later on I arrived at the conviction that we should, more easily and more thoroughly than we now do or ever have done, understand the nature and the laws of the Cosmos if we would from the beginning recognize its originator and upholder as being of the female sex.

"'We speak about Providence and announce: The Lord is my shepherd, He will provide. But in our hearts we know that we should demand from our own shepherds—'

"—for my grandfather," the narrator here interrupted himself, "drew most of his wealth from his vast sheep farms in the province of Marche.

"'—a providential care of our sheep very different from the one to which we are ourselves submitted, and which appears mainly to provide us with blood and tears.

"'But say instead, of Providence: "She is my shepherdess"—and you will at once realize in what way you may expect to be provided for.

"'For to a shepherdess tears are convenient and precious, like rain—as in the old song *il pleut, il pleut, bergère*[2]—like pearls, or like falling stars running over the firmament—all phenomena in themselves divine, and symbolic of the highest and the deepest spheres of human knowledge. And as to the shedding of blood, this to our shepherdess—as to any lady—is a high privilege and is inseparably united with the sublimest moments of existence, with promotion and beatification. What little girl will not joyously shed her blood in order to become a virgin,[3] what bride not hers in order to become a wife, what young wife not hers to become a mother?

"'Man, troubled and perplexed about the relation between divinity and humanity, is ever striving to find a foothold in the matter by drawing on his own normal experience. He will view it in the light of relations between tutor and pupil, or of commander and soldier, and he will lose breath—and heart—in search and investigation. The ladies, whose nature is nearer to the nature of the deity, take no such trouble; they see the relation between the Cosmos and the Creator quite plainly as a love affair. And in a love affair search and investigation is an absurdity, and unseemly. There are, thus, no genuine female atheists. If a lady tells you that she is an atheist, she is either, still, an adorable person, and it is coquetry, or she is a depraved creature, and it is a lie. Woman even wonders at man's perseverance in questioning, for they are aware that he will never get any other kind of answer than the kind which King Alexander the Great got from the Sibylla of Babylon. You may have forgotten the tale, I shall recount it to you.

"'King Alexander, on his triumphant return from the Indies, in Babylon heard of a young Sibylla who was able to foretell the future, and had her brought before him. When the black-eyed woman demanded a price to part with her knowledge, he let a soldier bring up a box filled with precious stones which had been collected over half the world. The Sibylla rummaged in the box and picked out two emeralds and a pearl; then she gave in to the King's wish and promised to tell him what till now she had told nobody.

"'Very slowly and conscientiously, all the time holding up one finger and begging him—since she must never speak any word of hers over again—to give his utmost attention to her words, she explained to him with what rare woods to build up the sacred pile, with what incantations to kindle it, and what parts of a cat and a crocodile to place upon it. After that she was silent for a long time. "Now, King Alexander," she at last said, "I am coming to the core of my secret. But I shall not speak one more word unless you give me the big ruby which, before your soldier brought up the box, you told him to lay aside." Alexander was loath to part with the ruby, for he had meant to give it to his mistress Thaïs at home, but by this time he felt that he could not live without having been told the final part of the spell, so had it brought and handed over to her.

"'"Listen then, Alexander," the woman said, laying her finger on the King's lips. "At the moment when you gaze into the smoke, you must not think of the left eye of a camel. To think of its right eye is dangerous enough. But to think of the left is perdition."'"

"So much for my grandfather's philosophy," said Matteo.

Taddeo smiled a little at the account of his friend.

"It was," Matteo went on after a while, "this time brought back to me by the sight of the young ladies before us, moving with such perfect freedom in such severely regulated figures. Almost all of them, you will know, have been brought up in convents, and have been taken out from there to be married a few years, a year—or perhaps a week—ago.

"How, now, is the Cosmos made to look to a girl in a convent school? From my cousin, who is Mother Superior of the most ancient of such schools, I have some knowledge of the matter. You will not, my friend, find a mirror in the whole building, and a girl may spend ten years in it and come out not knowing whether she be plain or pretty. The little cells are whitewashed, the nuns are dressed in black and white, and the young pupils are put in gray smocks, as if there were in the whole world but the two colors, and the cheerless mixture of them. The old gardener in charge of the convent garden has a small bell tied round his leg, so that by the tinkling of it the maidens may be warned of the approach of a man and may absent themselves like fawns before the huntsman. Any little sisterly kisses or caresses between school friends—light and innocent butterflies of Eros—by the alarmed nuns are chased off the grounds with fly-flaps, as if they were wasps.

"From this stronghold of unworldliness our blossoming virginal ascetic is fetched out into the world and is married. What is now, from the very first day, the object of her existence? To make herself desirable to all men and the incarnation of desire to one. The mirror is given her as her chief instructress and confidante; the knowledge of fashion, of silks, laces and fans, becomes her chief study; the care of her fair body, from the brushing and curling of the hair to the polishing of the toenails, the occupation of her day; and the embrace and caresses of an ardent young husband is the prize for her teachability.

"My friend—a boy brought up for his task in life in an equally incongruous manner would protest and argue, and storm against his tutor—as, alas, all men do protest, argue and storm against the Almighty! But a young girl agrees with her mother, with her mother's mother and with the common, divine Mother of the Universe, that the only method of turning out a dazzling and adorable woman of the world is a convent education.

"I might," he said after a pause, "tell you a story which goes to prove in what good understanding a young girl is with the Paradox."

"A nobleman married a girl fresh from the convent, with whom he was deeply in love, and on the evening of their wedding drove with her to his villa. In the coach he said to her: 'My beloved, I am this evening going to make some alterations in my household, and to hand over to you a proportion of my property. But I must tell you beforehand that there is in my house one object which I am keeping to myself, and to the ownership of which you must never make any claim. I beg you: ask me no questions, and make no investigation in the matter.'

"In the frescoed room within which he sat down to sup with his wife he called before him the master of his stables and said to him: 'Listen to my order and mark it well. From this hour my stables, and everything in them, are the property of the Princess my wife. None of my horses or coaches, none of my saddlery or harness, down to the coachman's whips, in the future belongs to me myself.'"

"He next called up his steward and said to him: 'Mark my words well. From this hour all objects of value in my house, all gold and silver, all pictures and statues are the property of the Princess my wife, and I myself shall have nothing to say over them.'

"In the same way he had the housekeeper of the villa called and told her: 'From today all linen and silk bedding, all lace and satin curtains within my house belong to the Princess my wife, and I myself renounce all rights of property in them. Be not forgetful of my bidding, but behave according to it.'

"In the end he called in the old woman who had been maid to his mother and grandmother, and informed her: 'My faithful Gelsomina, hear me. All jewelry, which has before belonged to my mother, my grandmother, or to any former mistress of the house, from tonight belongs solely to the Princess my wife—who will wear it with the same grace as my mama and grandmama—to do with what she likes.'

"He here kissed his wife's hand and offered her his arm. 'You will now, dear heart,' he said, 'come with me, in order that I may show you the one precious object which, alone of all my belongings, I am keeping to myself.'

"With these words he led her upstairs to her bedroom and set her, all puzzled, in the middle of the floor. He lifted the bridal veil from her head and removed her pearls and diamonds. He undid her heavy bridal gown with its long train and made her step out of it, and one by one he took off her petticoats, stays and shift, until she stood before him, blushing and confused, as lovely as Eve in Paradise in her first hour with Adam. Very gently he turned her round to the tall mirror on the wall.

"'There,' he said, 'is the one thing of my estate solely reserved for me myself.'

"My friend," Matteo said, "a soldier receiving from his commander-in-chief corresponding instructions would shake his head at them and protest that surely this was no strategy to adopt, and that if he could, he would desert. But a young woman, faced with the instructions, nods her head."

"But," Taddeo asked, "did the nobleman of your tale, good Matteo, succeed in making his wife happy?"

"It is always, good Taddeo," Matteo answered, "difficult for a husband to know whether he is making his wife happy or not. But as to the husband and wife of my tale, the lady, on the twentieth anniversary of their wedding, took her husband's hand, gazed archly into his eyes and asked him whether he still remembered this first evening of their married life. 'My God,' she said, 'how terrified was I not then for half an hour, how did I not tremble. Why!' she exclaimed, throwing herself into his arms, 'if you had not included in your directions that last clause of yours, I should have felt disdained and betrayed! My God, I should have been lost!'"

The contradance before the two old gentlemen changed into a waltz, and the whole ballroom waved and swayed like a garden under a summer breeze. The seductive Viennese tune then again died away.

"I should like to tell you," Taddeo said, "another tale. It may go to support your grandfather's theology, or it may not."

"A nobleman of an ambitious nature, and with a brilliant career behind him, when he was no longer quite young decided to marry and looked round for a wife. On a visit to the town of Bergamo he made the acquaintance of a family of an ancient, great name but of modest means. There were at the time seven daughters in the tall gloomy palazzo, and at the end of the pretty row an only son, who was still a child. The seven young sisters were fully aware that their individual existence might with reason be disputed or denied, since they had come into the world as failures in the attempt at acquiring an heir to the name, and were—so to say—blanks drawn by their ancient house in its lottery on life and death. But their family arrogance was fierce enough to make them bear their sad lot high-handedly, as a privilege out of reach to the common people.

"It so happened that the youngest sister, the one whose arrival, he felt, to the poor Prince and Princess would have been the hardest blow of all, caught our nobleman's eye, so that he returned to the house, and again returned.

"The girl, who was then but seventeen years old, was far from being the prettiest of the group. But the visitor was a connoisseur of feminine loveliness, and spied in her youthful face and form the promise of coming, unusual beauty. Yet much more than by this, he was attracted by a particular trait in her. He guessed behind her demure and disciplined bearing the fruit of an excellent education, an ambition kindred to his own, but more powerful because less blasé, a longing—and an energy to satisfy the longing—a long way out of the ordinary. It would be, he reflected, a pleasant, an entertaining experience to encourage this youthful ambition, still but faintly conscious of itself, to fledge the cygnet and watch it soaring. At the same time, he thought, a young wife of high birth and brought up in Spartan simplicity, with a nostalgia for glory, would be an asset in his future career. He applied for the girl's hand, and her father and mother, surprised and delighted at having their daughter make such a splendid match, handed her over to him.

"Our nobleman had every reason to congratulate himself on his decision. The flight feathers of his young bird grew with surprising quickness; soon in his brilliant circle one would not find a lady of greater beauty and finer grace, of more exquisite and dignified comportment, or of more punctilious tact. She wore the heavy ornaments that he gave her with as much ease as a rosebush its roses, and had he, he thought, been able to set a crown on her head, the world would have felt her to be born with it. And she was still soaring, inspired by, as well as enraptured with, her success. He himself, within the first two years of their married life, acquired two supreme decorations at his native and at a foreign court.

"But when he and his wife had been married for three years he observed a change in her. She became pensive, as if stirred by some new mighty emotion, obscure to him. At times she did not hear what he spoke to her. It also seemed to him that she would now prefer to show herself in the world on such occasions where he was not with her, and to excuse herself from others where she would have to appear by his side. 'I have spoilt her,' he reflected. 'Is it indeed possible that, against the very order of things, her ambition and her vanity now make her aspire to outshine her lord, to whom she owes all?' His feelings were naturally badly hurt at the idea of so much ingratitude, and at last, on an evening when they were alone together, he resolved to take her to account.

"'Surely, my dear,' he said to her, 'you will realize that I am not going to play the part of that husband in the fairy tale who, owing to his connection with higher powers, raised his wife to the rank of queen and empress, only to hear her, in the end, demanding to have the sun rise at her word. Recall to yourself the place from which I took you, and remember that the response of higher powers to the too indulgent husband forwarding his wife's claim was this: "Return, and find her back in her hovel."'

"His wife for a long time did not answer him; in the end she rose from her chair as if about to leave the room. She was tall and willowy; her ample skirts at each of her movements made a little chirping sound.

"'My husband,' she said in her low, sonorous voice. 'Surely you will realize that to an ambitious woman it comes hard, in entering a ballroom, to know that she is entering it on the arm of a cuckold.'

"As, very quietly and without another word, she had gone out of the door, the nobleman sat on, wondering, as till now he had never done, at the complexity of the Universe."

NOTES

1. Card game for two players.
2. "It rains, it rains shepherd."
3. Probably referring to menstruation.

Delmira Agustini   *Uruguay, 1886–1914*

When Delmira Agustini published her third book of poetry, *Los cálices vacíos* (The Empty Chalices) in 1913, Montevidean society was scandalized by its erotic content. She became, wrongly, identified as an erotic, or merely "feminine" writer (the word feminine associated with superficial love poetry) because critics of her work concentrated only on the sensuality in the poems. Recent analyses of her work, however, place her firmly in the modernist tradition—in which eroticism is used to reach a deep poetic reality—and see her romantic themes inspired by the aesthetic philosophy of Friedrich Nietzsche.

Agustini's life was as untraditional as her poetry. Born into the extremely conservative middle-class of Montevideo, Agustini had a very sheltered life, and was extremely introspective and solitary. Privately educated in the arts and music, she began writing poetry quite young (some say at 7), and published her first poem, "Poesía," in the journal *Rojo y Blanco* (Red and White) at age 16; a year later Agustini was featured as a "*poetisa precoz*" (precocious poetess) in a Montevidean weekly called *La Alborada* (Dawn), for which she wrote a weekly column the following year, signing herself "*Joujou*." She published two books of poetry, *El libro blanco* (The White Book, 1907) and *Cantos de la mañana* (Songs of the Morning, 1910) by the time she was 24. In 1913, Agustini married a young, wealthy Uruguayan, Enrique Job Reyes, but left him shortly after the marriage; she continued to see him secretly, however, and during one of their rendezvous he murdered her, apparently because of jealousy, and then killed himself.

The following selections are from *Los cálices vacíos* and the posthumous *Obras completas* (Complete Works, 1924).

VISION
Visión

Maybe all I saw was the mirror
of my desires, an illusory
frame around it all...
Or it's simply a miracle: did I really
see you the other night, watching me sleep?
Loneliness and terror had made my bedroom
huge; you appeared at my side
like a giant fungus, both dead and alive,
in the corners of the night,
damp with silence,
greased with solitude and darkness.

You leaned toward me, utterly
toward me—as toward the lake, the crystal
                                        cup
on the desert's tablecloth.

You leaned toward me as an invalid
leans toward the drugs that won't fail him,
toward the stone bandages of death.

You leaned toward me as a believer
toward the blessed communion wafer—
the snowflake that tastes
of stars, nourishing the lilies of man's flesh;
God's spark, a star for man.

You leaned toward me as sadness, the large
                                        willow,
leans toward silence, its deep pools.
You leaned toward me like pride's tower,
its marble quarried by the monster sadness,
leaning toward its own shadow, its great sister.
You leaned toward me as if my body

in this dark page of a bed
was where your destiny began.
You leaned toward me as toward a window
                                     looking out
upon whatever follows death.
And you leaned even more!
My vision was a snake
aimed through eyelashes of brambles
toward your body, oh reverent swan.
And my lust was a snake
gliding through dark canyons
toward your body, oh statue of lilies.
You leaned farther and farther, and so far,
you leaned so far,
that my sexual flowers grew to twice their size
and my star has been larger since then.
Your whole life was imprinted on mine.

Anxious, uncertain, I waited
for the rustling wings that signal a magnificent
                                               embrace,
a miraculous and passionate embrace,
an embrace of four arms; flight!
The enchanted arms can be
four roots of a new race.

Anxious, uncertain, I waited
for the rustling wings that signal a magnificent
                                       embrace...
                                          And when
I opened my eyes—like a soul—to you:
I saw you'd fallen back, you were wrapped
in some huge fold of darkness!

Translated by Marti Moody

NOCTURNE
Nocturno

Outside, the sad night clothed in tragedy's
                              garments is sobbing,
Just like a huge widow who holds her face
                              close to my window.
My room...
Through a beautiful miracle wrought by the
                              fire and the light,
My room is a grotto of gold and of very rare gems;
It has a deep moss that is fashioned from
                              tapestries' softness,
And it is so vivid, so warm and so sweet, I
                              imagine
Myself in a heart.
My bed, all arrayed in pure white, is as white
                              and as cloudlike
As the flower of innocence,
As the froth upon vice.
This night makes me sleepless;
Black nights come at times, oh so black, yet
                              that wear on their brow
A bright rose like the sun.
Nobody can sleep on the nights that are black
                              and yet bright.

I love you, O Winter!
I imagine you old,
I imagine you wise,
With body divinely created of quivering marble,
That trails like the mantles of royalty Time's
                              heavy weight.
O Winter, I love you, and I am the Springtime.
I am rosy; you, snow;
You, because you know all,
I, because I dream all.

Let us then love each other!
On my bed dressed in white,
As white and as cloudlike as innocence's fragile
                              white flower,
As the froth upon vice,
Winter, Winter, O Winter,
Come now; let us fall in a cluster of roses and
                              lilies!

Translated by Mildred E. Johnson

Helen Cruickshank   *UK(Scotland), 1886–1975*

Helen Burness Cruickshank was born in Hillside, Angus, Scotland, and educated at the village school and at Montrose Academy. At 17, she went to London and got a job with the post office there; she returned to Scotland ten years later to work for the new National Health Service in Edinburgh. In Edinburgh, she became very friendly with Christopher Murray-Grieve and other members of the new Scottish Renaissance movement, and became secretary of the newly formed Scottish P.E.N. Club, a position she kept for many years. That post brought her in touch with a wide circle of writers, and she is as important for her work in support of the arts, especially for her enthusiastic encouragement of young writers, as for her poetry.

Cruickshank's first poems were published in the *Scottish Chapbook* and *Northern Nembus*, both edited by Murray-Grieve. Her first book of poems, *Up the Noran Water*, was published in 1934. She went on to publish six volumes of poetry in all, the last posthumously in 1978. She was a close friend of Scots' poet Marion Angus, and her memoir about Angus introduces her *Selected Poems* in 1950.

Cruickshank writes in both Scots and English, although she is better regarded for her poetry in Scots. The following poems are from *Sea Buckthorn* (1954).

COMFORT IN PUIRTITH

The man that mates wi' Poverty,
  An' clasps her tae his banes,
Will faither lean an' lively thochts,
  A host o eident weans[1]
But wow! they'll warstle tae the fore
  Wi' hunger-sharpit brains!

But he that lies wi' creeshy[2] W'alth
  Will breed a pudden thrang,[3]
Owre cosh[4] tae ken their foziness,[5]
  Owre bien[6] tae mak' a sang—
A routh o'donnert[7] feckless fules
  Wha dinna coont a dang!

NOTES

1. Diligent brats.
2. Fat.
3. Throng.
4. Sung.
5. Stupidity.
6. Well-off.
7. Stupefied.

SHY GEORDIE

Up the Noran Water
In by Inglismaddy,
Annie's got a bairnie
That hasna got a daddy.
Some say it's Tamma's,
An' some say it's Chay's;
An' naebody expec'it it,
Wi' Annie's quiet ways.

Up the Noran Water
The bonny little mannie
Is dandled an' cuddled close
By Inglismaddy's Annie.
Wha the bairnie's daddy is
The lassie never says;
But some think it's Tammas's,
An' some think it's Clay's.

Up the Noran Water
The country folk are kind;
An' wha the bairnie's daddy is
They dinna muckle mind.
But oh! the bairn at Annie's breist,
They love in Annie's e'e—
They mak' me wish wi' a' my micht
They lucky lad was me!

H.D.   (Hilda Doolittle)   *US/UK(England), 1886–1961*

Born in Bethlehem, Pennsylvania, Hilda Doolittle received her early formal education in private school and spiritual tutelage in a local Moravian seminary. She was
the only daughter of five children born to her father, Charles, an astronomy
professor, and her artistic mother Helen, a fact that may account for a lifelong
sense of feminine distinction and isolation. In 1904 she enrolled at Bryn Mawr
College but withdrew in 1906 after a minor breakdown. She returned home to
study until 1911 when she traveled to London to be reunited with Ezra Pound, a
former University of Pennsylvania student to whom, six years earlier, she had been
briefly engaged.

In London Pound introduced her to numerous artists including F.S. Flint, T.E.
Hulme and Richard Aldington, who together formed the short-lived Imagist movement. In 1913 she married Aldington and with Pound's direct urging published her
first poems. Her first major poetry publication, *Sea Garden* (1916), was a deftly
personal collection that helped earn her the persistent label "perfect imagist." In
1917 she assumed editorship of *The Egoist*, but with literary success came personal
disaster. A miscarriage, the deaths of her father and older brother, and separation
from Aldington (they were to be divorced in 1938) pushed her in 1919 to the brink
of what she called "psychic death."

Spiritual and literary regeneration came from Winifred Ellerman, a novelist
with the pseudonym Bryher who had come to see Doolittle in 1918 after admiring
her early poems. They became lovers, and along with Doolittle's newborn daughter, Perdita, traveled to Greece, back to America, and to Egypt. The exposure to
homophilic love and first-hand contact with a new iconography altered Dolittle's
poetic landscape and persona. Always interested in ancient Greece (she had published a translation of Euripides' *Ion* in 1919), H.D. now turned more fervently
towards self-definition via the mythic patterns of the classical world. She published
Heliodora and Other Poems (1924), an interior monologue in which gods and
goddesses became projections of subject/object, feminine/masculine dualisms. In
1925, her reputation was established with *Collected Poems of H.D.*, based in part
on the private disasters of her preceding years. *Hippolytus Temporizes* (1927), a
verse play, broadened her formal artistic scope and advanced her claim as a
modernist immersed in what Amy Lowell called "the frank, unartificial paganism
of a new world." "Wine Bowl is an example of this aspect of H.D.'s work.

From 1933 to 1934, Doolittle underwent analysis with Freud, an experience
that served as material for the poem "The Master" and for her later psychobiogra-
phy, *Tribute to Freud* (1956). More importantly, the self-analytic process intensified Doolittle's inward quest and her fascination with sexual/political aspects of
the feminine self. Hence modern critics have tended to view Doolittle's career as a
gradual assertion of what one critic has called a "feminist theology" with female
iconography. Her early imagist poems, once stigmatized as discrete and formalistic,
are now seen as powerful private encodings of sexual and emotional longings. The
first selection, "Dream," shows still another side of H.D. that she frequently
suppressed—that of mother in dialogue with her child.

Critical emphasis on Doolittle has shifted away from the early imagist poems to two later works: the war-inspired *Trilogy: The Walls Do Not Fall, Tribute to the Angels,* and *The Flowering of the Rod*, composed in sections between 1944 and 1946 and published together in 1973, and her late feminist epic *Helen in Egypt* (1961). In *Walls*, the poet unfolds a dream of spiritual and symbolic unification interwoven with allusions to Christianity, and Egyptian and Greek mythology. The lines "the bone-frame was made for/no such shock knit within terror, yet the skeleton stood up to it" suggest an intensely resilient response to layers of personal and historical horror. *Helen in Egypt* recasts Homer's version of the Trojan War from a feminine perspective; Helen is the poem's controlling consciousness, and her flight with Paris is an act of affirmation and rebellion rather than betrayal. Here especially critics have identified Doolittle's emerging feminist consciousness. "I am awake/. . . . I *see* things clearly at last, the old pictures are really there" says the poem's protagonist. In these lines of close personal identification, Doolittle overleaps wars and patriarchies of both the ancient and modern order.

Doolittle's recent critical revival has also refocused attention on the prose and autobiographical works she wrote continually throughout her career, many just re-issued or published for the first time. They include *HERmione* (1981), a roman à clef based on the years 1905–1911, *Notes on Thought and Vision and The Wise Sappho* (1982), an experiment in self-reflexivity, and most recently *Nights* (1986) published under the pen name John Helforth, one of half a dozen pseudonyms under which her writing sometimes appeared. Final evaluations of these previously neglected works will help determine the range and depth of Doolittle's contribution to literature.

Bill Mullen

DREAM

"I tell you it couldn't have been;
you couldn't have a dream
until you're ten."

"But I had
a five year old one—
it's always the same."

"What?"

"The dream."

"People don't dream
until they're ten."

"But *I* had one."

"You don't even know
what a dream is;
how did it come?"

"It didn't come,
it *was* there."

"Where?"

"In my eyes,
here."

"You made it up,
you were awake."

"No, asleep,
it was a picture—"

"you made up
any one could tell *that*—"

"no, no it was real—
a kitten and his cat."

WINE BOWL

I will rise
from my troth
with the dead,
I will sweeten my cup
and my bread
with a gift;
I will chisel a bowl for the wine,
for the white wine
and red;
I will summon a Satyr to dance,
a Centaur,
a Nymph
and a Faun;
I will picture
a warrior King,
a Giant,
a Naiad,
a Monster;
I will cut round the rim of the crater,
some simple
familiar thing,
vine leaves
or the sea-swallow's wing;
I will work at each separate part
till my mind is worn out
and my heart:
in my skull,
where the vision had birth,
will come wine,
would pour song
of the hot earth,
of the flower and the sweet
of the hill,
thyme,
meadow-plant,
grass-blade and sorrel;
in my skull,
from which vision took flight,
will come wine
will pour song
of the cool night,
of the silver and blade of the moon,
of the star,
of the sun's kiss at mid-noon;
I will challenge the reed-pipe
and stringed lyre,

to sing sweeter,
pipe wilder,
praise louder
the fragrance and sweet
of the wine-jar,
till each lover
must summon another,
to proffer a rose
where all flowers are,
in the depths of the exquisite crater;
flower will fall upon flower
till the red shower
inflame all
with intimate fervour;
till:
men who travel afar
will look up,
sensing grape
and hill-slope
in the cup;
men who sleep by the wood
will arise,
hearing ripple and fall
of the tide,
being drawn by the spell of the sea;
the bowl will ensnare and enchant
men who crouch by the hearth
till they want
but the riot of stars in the night;
those who dwell far inland
will seek ships;
the deep-sea fisher,
plying his nets,
will forsake them
for wheat-sheaves and loam;
men who wander
will yearn for their home,
men at home
will depart.

I will rise
from my troth with the dead,
I will sweeten my cup
and my bread
with a gift;
I will chisel a bowl for the wine,
for the white wine
and red.

Mayy Ziyadah   *Palestine/Egypt, 1886–1941*

A renowned writer, reviewer, and critic, Mayy Ziyadah was born on February 11, 1886 in Nazareth, Palestine. Christened Mary by her Palestinian mother, Nuzha Khalil Mu'mar, and Lebanese father, Elias Zakhur Ziyadah, she changed her name to Mayy and later to May because she felt it was more poetic.

Ziyadah's education began in a small school in Nazareth, and she spent five years at the 'Aintourah Institute for Girls in Lebanon. In 1908 the Ziyadah family moved to the literary capital of the Arab world—Cairo, Egypt. There, Elias Ziyadah embarked on a journalistic career, eventually becoming the editorial manager of *al-Mahrūsah* (The Guarded One), a popular daily paper. He was a primary nurturer of his daughter's interest in literature and her writing talents: Ziyadah later occupied her father's position at the newspaper.

Ziyadah's first major literary work was published in 1911 under the pseudonym Isis Copia (probably after the ancient Egyptian goddess). The work, "Fleurs de Rêve" (Flowers of Fantasy), represents the influence of the Francophone education she had received. She went on to publish in several periodicals and newspapers in addition to *al-Mahrūsah*, including *al-Fajr* (Dawn), from which the essay here is taken. An impressionistic sketch of an important Turkish-born poet and intellectual who lived from 1873 to 1921, the essay suggests the relatively free intellectual climate of Egypt during this period, free from the Ottoman censorship that prevailed in greater Syria (Syria, Lebanon, and what was then Palestine).

In 1912, Ziyadah began an intellectual, literary correspondence with Gibran Kahlil Gibran (1883–1931), an acclaimed Lebanese writer and poet whose works have been compared to those of William Blake. Gibran's letters progressed from opinions and discussions about Ziyadah's reviews and critiques to a form of poetic eloquence that evolved into an epistolary love affair, although the two never met. Gibran symbolized their relationship in a sketch of his hand embracing a blue flame as one of harmony and deep understanding, but Ziyadah, apparently torn between desire and diffidence, frequently found the relationship a strain. Only six edited letters, one of which is translated here, have been released by her family. In it, Ziyadah comments on Gibran's novella *Broken Wings* (1912) and in her exquisite style and impassioned tone, debates the subject of marriage.

Though Ziyadah attracted the attention of many other men who deemed her the "muse" and "inspirer," she chose to live independently. She became very interested in the woman's emancipation movement in Egypt, and during her years at the Egyptian National University, she came into close contact with suffragette leader Huda Shaarawi (1879–1947). Ziyadah's subjects were thus influenced by her feminist involvement, as reflected by her essay and book on Bahithat al-Badiyya (pseudonym of Malak Hifni Nasif [1836–1918]), another noted feminist of the day.

During the last fifteen years of her life, Ziyadah suffered tragic personal losses. After the deaths within five years of her parents, a very close friend, and Gibran, she went into a deep depression. Travel to Italy, France, and England between the years 1932 and 1934 did little to overcome her anguish, and after a suicide attempt, she was committed to a mental asylum in Lebanon for an extended period. Finally rehabilitated, she made some public appearances, including one at the American University of Beirut, where she spoke on the role of the writer in Arab society, before returning to Cairo in 1939. She died there in 1941.

Some of Ziyadah's important works are *Sawānih Fatāh* (The Thoughts of a Young Girl, 1922) and *Zulumāt wa Ashi'ah* (Darkness and Sunlight, 1923). There are also two biographical studies, one of al-Badiyya and the other on the Francophone woman writer 'Ai'shah Taymouriyya, as well as translations, reviews, and a handful of poems.

With her fresh and spontaneous approach, Ziyadah explored various topics with unusual honesty of feeling and insight. She holds a significant place in Arabic literature as the most influential woman writer of the early twentieth century. Gibran wrote of her: "You, Mayy, are a voice crying in the wilderness; you are a divine voice, and divine voices remain reverberating in the ethereal expanse until the end of time..."[1]

Pamela Vittorio

NOTE

* The quotation and biographical material derives largely from Suheil Bushrui and Salma Kuzbari, eds. and introd., *The Blue Flame: The Letters of Kahlil Gibran to Mayy Ziadah* (White Plains, NY: Longman, 1983).

from A LETTER TO KAHLIL GIBRAN

12 May 1912

To Gibran,

...Gibran, you and I do not agree about marriage. I respect your thoughts and esteem your principles because I know that you are honest in advocating them and sincere in defending them; indeed, they all represent noble aspirations.

I also believe—as you do—in the basic premise of freedom for women: just like men, women must be completely free to choose their husbands by following their own inclinations and intuition, rather than conforming to the mold prescribed for them by neighbors and acquaintances. When she chooses her companion, a woman becomes wholly bound by the duties of this partnership.

You call them heavy chains woven by past generations, and I say that they are heavy chains too, but they were tightened by Nature itself, which made women what they are. Even if the mind manages to break the bondages which have been set by custom and conven-

tion, it will never succeed in breaking those of Nature, because the laws of Nature transcend all other laws. This is the answer to the question "Why can a woman not meet with her beloved without her husband's knowledge?": a secret meeting, however innocent, means that the woman is betraying not only her husband and the name which she took of her own volition, but also the human society in which she is an active member.

When she marries, a woman vows fidelity; mental and physical faithfulness are equally important and equally meaningful. When she marries, a woman pledges to make her husband happy; therefore, when she secretly meets with another man, she is guilty before Society, the Family, and Duty. You may disagree and say that Duty is a vague term which is often difficult to define and that it is sufficient to know what makes a family in order to learn about the duties which are imposed upon its members. The woman's role in the family is the hardest, humblest, and bitterest of roles.

I strongly feel those chains which bind women, chains made of silk, as delicate as a spider's web and as firm as golden threads. Let us allow Salma—that is Salma Karma, the heroine of the story, and every woman whose feelings, pride, and intelligence are not unlike Salma's—to meet with an honorable friend, dear to her heart; does this mean that every woman who does not find in marriage the happiness which filled her dreams as a young girl can therefore rightfully choose a (male) companion other than her husband and meet with him without the latter's knowledge, even if the purpose of their meeting is only a prayer made to the one crucified of old?

Mayy

Translated by Zeina Matar

SOMETHING ABOUT WALI AL-DIN YAKIN
Shay'an Wali al-Din Yakin

In the replies given to the questions of a referendum,[1] my attention was drawn by the words of a young girl saying that her wish was to die by drowning. I had heard this wish expressed before, not by a young girl, but by Wali al-Din Yakin, a poet whose imaginings were so gentle that they could indeed have been conceived in the mind of a young girl.

The life of Wali al-Din Yakin was filled with tragic events. This man, who belonged to a Muslim family great in both the East and the West, and certainly to the greatest Egyptian family, brought upon himself the wrath of his relatives when he married a Greek Christian woman. His love of freedom provoked the anger of Abd al-Hamid[2] and he lost his high position in the Turkish government. Moreover, this proud and noble individual lived through poverty, detention, exile, and separation from kin and country. He finally returned to Egypt, but his troubles increased over the last few years: his younger son electrocuted himself and

died suddenly at sixteen; then his mother died; and his pain was made even greater by the loss of his sister, whom he loved dearly and who had married a member of the Yakin family. And here he is today, in Hilwan, seeking a cure from a disease that has struck him, having isolated himself from all acquaintances and friends. We in Egypt, like people in Syria and other lands, can hear the moans [which come across] in his writings.

In spite of his misfortunes, Wali al-Din Yakin remained a charming and cultured man whose sense of humor showed in every sentence he uttered. He used to make strange comparisons, as for instance, when he saw the handwriting of the late Doctor Shumayyil,[3] who was famous for his bad script. Wali al-Din bey placed his finger on a letter and said: "I like this *a* because it looks like a club." His dislike of the word *also* had no limits: whenever he referred to it, it was in such a manner that the people who were present would laugh until they cried and avoid the use of the word as much as possible. I, for example, sometimes wrote two or three words, or even a complete sentence, so as to avoid *also*. When I was forced to write, read, or hear it, I would remember the satirical way in which Wali al-Din described the term and regret using the word, however reluctantly.

I once asked Wali al-Din Yakin about his response to a writer who was debating him in the columns of a newspaper. He said in all seriousness: "How can I discuss anything with a man who inserts 'also' twenty times in one article and does not die from it? Were I to respond to him, I would have to say: 'What have I to do with you, O "also"?'"

Wali al-Din Yakin was once present at a party well attended by ministers and other distinguished personalities. After about an hour had gone by, he rose unexpectedly and quickly left the hall. When the party was over, he came back and apologized to those who had been standing near him and had witnessed his sud-

den move in dismay. He apologized for not
having known so-and-so was present and he
said that he would not be seen in the same
room as that man. Someone said: "You hate
so-and-so; but suppose that he likes you and
seeks your friendship, what would you do
then?" He replied immediately: "Kill myself!"

The strangest thing was that there was no
connection between himself and the object of
his hatred; some say that they had never even
spoken with each other!

Wali al-Din Yakin had no affectation
whatsoever; he was, right or wrong, honest in
both his likes and dislikes.

Tunes and colors had a profound effect on
Wali al-Din Yakin. Upon hearing a young girl
sing softly, he said that her voice reminded him
of the breeze which came from the Bosphorus.
Whenever he saw the piano open, he would
instantly ask someone to play a composition
known as "Carmen Silva," a tune to which
people also danced. During one of his visits to
us, I saw him stare far into the distance and
when I asked him the reason for it he said:
"That," pointing at a lilac flower on my dress.
"The color saddens me." As I tried to remove
the flower he said: "Please do not! I am sad to
see it but I would be even sadder to see it taken
away." That evening, we recited some verses
of his melancholy poetry.

If his loathing and revulsion toward some people were intense, so too was his love and
admiration of others. He used to enjoy drawing, the principle of which he had learned in
exile—and it was not uncommon to find in his
poetry words which he expressed by a drawing. For instance, in "the bird sang," he would
write "sang" and then draw a bird. He was
also very fond of Khalil Mutran[4] and his poetry; I recall once noticing his trouble and the
change in his expression as he heard verses
from "The Crying Lion":

I am the crying lion, I am the hill of sorrow,
I am the grave which walks bleeding over other
                                                    graves.

O my love's farthest horizon and that of desire,
My soul's joy transcends the misery of my senses.
I have called you for consolation, so fulfill my wish,
Even if you do not know that you are the cause of
                                                    my suffering.

Wali al-Din exclaimed: "Enough!" After a
short silence, he went on: "O Khalil, Khalil! If
I were asked to tell how I wish my funeral to
be, I would say that I wish to be eulogized in
the poetry of Khalil Mutran, recited by Aziz
Nasr while my bier is carried. I want to be
escorted to my last abode in this way, in a
cortege organized by Salim Sarkis."

I have written all of this about Wali al-Din bey
because I know that he is a writer well loved in
Syria and news of him is important to those
readers who do not have access to such information from the daily press. The pleasant
manner which characterizes this man's de-
meanor is that of one who has been given an
excellent education; but it could not exist
without some inherent quality. He is a man of
many longings, worn out, rebellious yet steady,
whose sensitivity and gentleness sometimes
brought him to the verge of illness. When the
moment came for him to act, he was reckless
in his courage, heedless and bold. It is no wonder that the sea attracted him and awakened in
him unusual yearnings, and it is no wonder
that we should hear this from him: "I would
rather drown than die in my bed, confined
between oppressive walls and after days of
pain and hours of death throes. I want to die
by drowning in the sea, unprepared, because
such a poetic death carries greatness and a
sense of the extraordinary."

Translated by Zeina Matar

NOTES

1. Possibly a newspaper poll on an issue affecting women.
2. Abd al-Hamid II: Ottoman Sultan, reigned 1876.
3. A family friend, a physician and a member of Ziyadah's
   literary circle, he was a writer of mediocre verse.
4. Khalil Mutran (1872–1949). Lebanese poet and journalist, he lived in Egypt from 1892 until his death. Aziz
   Nasr and Salim Sarkis, mentioned later, have not been
   identified. They were probably intellectuals.

Marianne Moore

Marianne Moore was born in 1887, in a suburb of St. Louis, Missouri. Her maternal grandfather was a minister who had some slight acquaintance with the minister-grandfather of T.S. Eliot in the same city. Following H.D., Moore attended Bryn Mawr College, graduating in 1909, when the President of the college was M. Carey Thomas, an important figure in women's higher education and feminist causes. Moore herself marched in suffragette demonstrations. She moved to New York City with her mother in 1918, and there spent the rest of her life, living in Greenwich Village and later in Brooklyn. She died in 1972, generally acknowledged as the peer of Eliot, Ezra Pound, and William Carlos Williams.

Her writing career actually began in college, but in 1921 her first book of poetry, *Poems*, appeared in England, published by her friends Bryher and H.D. Her chap-book containing a single poem, *Marriage*, was published in 1923 by a small house. A second full-length volume of poetry, entitled *Observations*, appeared in 1924, and she was given the *Dial* Award for that year. The next year she became the editor of the *Dial*, then arguably the most important literary journal in the English-speaking world. She remained its editor until the journal ceased publication in 1929. Throughout the 1920s Moore was an active and well-known figure in the artistic circles of Greenwich Village.

The 1930s saw a lessening of public activity, though some of her best poems, included here, were written and published in this decade. In the decade that included World War II Moore published *What Are Years* (1941), represented by "The Paper Nautilus," and *Nevertheless* (1944). Her *Collected Poems* (1951) secured a reputation that already had several major awards supporting it. In 1955 she was elected to the American Academy of Arts and Letters. Her translation of La Fontaine's *Fables* (1954) added to her stature and made it clearer than ever that her work was based on conjunction of stylistic grace and serious moral intelligence.

Tell Me, Tell Me (1966), from which "To A Giraffe" is taken, preceded the appearance of her *Complete Poems* (1967, corrected edition, 1981) and her *Complete Prose* (1987), which delighted her readers and made her work more generally known. In addition, her celebrity as the woman who wrote about the Brooklyn Dodgers, and who wore distinctive tricorne hats and was photographed by Cecil Beaton and dined with Mohammed Ali, was a distinctive blending of American publicity and American "eccentricity." It is partly this "character" who is captured in Elizabeth Bishop's encomium to her precursor: "Invitation to Miss Marianne Moore." Moore as a poet was experimental yet serious, fanciful yet highly educated, stylized yet often pointed and direct. Her best critics early on were T.S. Eliot, who wrote a preface to her *Selected Poems* (1935), and Kenneth Burke, her associate at the *Dial*. More recently her work has been explored in a feminist context by Bonnie Costello (*Imaginary Possessions*, 1981) and Taffy Martin (*Marianne Moore: Subversive Modernist*, 1987). Because she doesn't take as her subject such issues as sexual identity, her work was not particularly championed by the first wave of feminist criticism in the early 1970s, but increasingly reflective accounts of the relation between style and gender have focused on her distinctive achievement. Younger poets, too, among them Tess Gallagher, have begun to acknowledge her influence.

Noted for her intricate forms and patterns (along with an eye for the poem's look on the page), her beast iconography, aphoristic wit and unlikely metaphoric combinations, Moore brought a new self-consciousness to poetry, quintessentially realized in "Poetry," which is as much about itself as it is an expression of and clue to her special art. Moore's linguistic invention was matched by her unusual prosody, which, as Robert Beloof has explained, relies early on free verse but later on syllable count: the pattern is established by the number of syllables (as in the haiku) rather than by meter; by varying the length of her line and using a somewhat unpredictable or blurred rhyme scheme, she emphasized the stanza rather than the line as the basic unit. It is this combination of diction and form that allows Moore to capture, as Robert Lowell said, "the splendor and variety of prose in very compressed spaces."[1]

Charles Molesworth

POETRY*

I, too, dislike it: there are things that are important beyond all this fiddle.
     Reading it, however, with a perfect contempt for it one discovers in
     it after all, a place for the genuine.
          Hands that can grasp, eyes
          that can dilate, hair that can rise
               if it must, these things are important not because a

high-sounding interpretation can be put upon them but because they are
     useful. When they become so derivative as to become unintelligible,
the same thing may be said for all of us, that we
     do not admire what
     we cannot understand: the bat
          holding on upside down or in quest of something to

eat, elephants pushing, a wild horse taking a roll, a tireless wolf under
     a tree, the immovable critic twitching his skin like a horse that feels a flea, the

                                                                                                   base-
     ball fan, the statistician—
     nor is it valid
          to discriminate against "business documents and

school-books"; all these phenomena are important. One must make a distinction
     however: when dragged into prominence by half poets, the result is not poetry,
     nor till the poets among us can be
          "literalists of
          the imagination"—above
               insolence and triviality and can present

for inspection, "imaginary gardens with real toads in them," shall we have
     it. In the meantime, if you demand on the one hand,
     the raw material of poetry in
          all its rawness and
          that which is on the other hand
               genuine, you are interested in poetry.

NOTES (all line commentaries are by Moore)

* The original version of this poem published in *Observations* was only thirteen lines; this is the expanded version first published in *Selected Poems* (1935), which Moore placed in the appendix of her *Complete Poems*; she always supplied the sources for the quotations she used in her poems.

line 23: "Where the boundary between prose and poetry lies, I shall never be able to understand. The question is raised in manuals of style, yet the answer to it lies beyond me. Poetry is verse: prose is not verse. Or else poetry is everything with the exception of business documents and school books." from *The Diary of Tolstoy*, p. 84.

line 29: "The limitation of his idea was from the very intensity of his vision; he was a too literal realist of imagination, as others are of nature; and because he believed that the figures seen by the mind's eye, when exalted by inspiration, were 'eternal existences,' symbols of divine essences, he hated every grace of style that might obscure their lineaments," in regard to William Butler Yeats, in *Ideas of Good and Evil* by A.H. Bullen (1903), p. 182.

AN EGYPTIAN PULLED GLASS BOTTLE IN THE SHAPE OF A FISH

Here we have thirst
and patience, from the first,
   and art, as in a wave held up for us to see
   in its essential perpendicularity;

not brittle but
intense—the spectrum, that
   spectacular and nimble animal the fish,
   whose scales turn aside the sun's sword by
              their polish.

TO A SNAIL

If "compression is the first grace of style,"*
you have it. Contractility is a virtue
as modesty is a virtue.
It is not the acquisition of any one thing
that is able to adorn,
or the incidental quality that occurs
as a concomitant of something well said,
that we value in style,
but the principle that is hid:
in the absence of feet, "a method of
                 conclusions";
"a knowledge of principles,"
in the curious phenomenon of your occipital
                 horn.

NOTE (by Moore)

* line 1: "The very first grace of style is that which comes from compression." In *Demetrius on Style*, translated by W. Hamilton Fyfe (London: Heinemann, 1932).

SOJOURN IN THE WHALE

Trying to open locked doors with a sword,
                 threading
   the points of needles, planting shade trees
   upside down; swallowed by the opaqueness
           of one whom the seas
love better than they love you, Ireland—
you have lived and lived on every kind of
                shortage.
   You have been compelled by hags to spin
   gold thread from straw and have heard men
          say:
"There is a feminine temperament in direct
           contrast to ours
which makes her do these things.
            Circumscribed by a
   heritage of blindness and native
   incompetence, she will become wise and will
           be forced to give in.
Compelled by experience, she will turn back;
water seeks its own level":
   and you have smiled. "Water in motion is
           far*
   from level." You have seen it, when
          obstacles happened to bar
   the path, rise automatically.

NOTE (by Moore)

* lines 14–15: "Water in motion is far from level." *Literary Digest*.

THE PAPER NAUTILUS

For authorities whose hopes
are shaped by mercenaries?
    Writers entrapped by
    teatime fame and by
commuters' comforts? Not for these
    the paper nautilus
    constructs her thin glass shell.

    Giving her perishable
souvenir of hope, a dull
    white outside and smooth-
    edged inner surface
glossy as the sea, the watchful
    maker of it guards it
    day and night; she scarcely

    eats until the eggs are hatched.
Buried eightfold in her eight
    arms, for she is in
    a sense a devil-
fish, her glass ram's-horn-cradled freight
    is hid but is not crushed;
    as Hercules, bitten

    by a crab loyal to the hydra,
was hindered to succeed,
    the intensively
    watched eggs coming from
the shell free it when they are freed—
    leaving its wasp-nest flaws
    of white on white, and close-

    laid Ionic chiton-folds
like the lines in the mane of
    a Parthenon horse,
    round which the arms had
wound themselves as if they knew love
    is the only fortress
    strong enough to trust to.

TO A GIRAFFE

If it is unpermissible, in fact fatal
to be personal and undesirable

to be literal—detrimental as well
if the eye is not innocent—does it mean that

one can live only on top leaves that are small
reachable only by a beast that is tall?—

of which the giraffe is the best example—
the unconversational animal.

When plagued by the psychological,
a creature can be unbearable

that could have been irresistible;
or to be exact, exceptional

since less conversational
than some emotionally-tied-in-knots animal.

    After all
consolations of the metaphysical
    can be profound. In Homer, existence

is flawed; transcendence, conditional;
"the journey from sin to redemption,
                                    perpetual."*

NOTE (by Moore)

* Ennis Rees summarizes the *Odyssey*, I feel, when he
finds expressed in it the conditional nature of existence,
the consolations of the metaphysical: the journey from
sin to redemption.

Carmen Lyra (or Lira) (María Isabel Carvajal)

Costa Rica, 1888–1949

A teacher, labor organizer, and journalist, Carmen Lyra is best known as a writer of children's stories and theater, although her "adult" novel, *En un sillón de ruedas* (In a Wheelchair, 1943), is highly regarded by critics. The following selection is the prologue to *Los cuentos de mi tía Panchita* (The Tales of My Aunt Panchita, 1920), which is a collection of folktales about Brer Rabbit and his friends. These witty, spirited tales originated in India and were adapted to the Costa Rican setting and socio-cultural environment by Lyra, as were those written by Joel Chandler Harris to life in Georgia.

Prologue to THE TALES OF MY AUNT PANCHITA
from Los cuentos de mi tía Panchita

My Aunt Panchita was a short, slight little woman, who wore her gray hair in two braids, had a broad forehead and little, twinkling eyes. She was always dressed in mourning, and around the house she protected her black skirt with a snow-white apron. From her ears swung two of my baby teeth set in gold. Perhaps for this reason I once dreamed that I was tiny, tiny—the size of a bean—and that I was swinging in a golden swing fastened to one of Aunt Panchita's ears. I swung back and forth, tickling her withered face with my feet, which sent her into peals of laughter. She used to say that she had those teeth imprisoned there in punishment for the bites they gave her when they were fast in the mouth of their owner, who was a terrible little wild Indian.

Diligent and hardworking as an ant was the old lady, and ready to turn an honest penny at anything that came along. But this it must be said: she was not in the least like the smug ant of the fable, and on more than one occasion I have caught her sharing her provisions with some flibbertigibbet grasshopper.

She lived with my Aunt Jesusa, whose hands were crippled with rheumatism, in a neat little house near El Morazán. People always spoke of them as "the girls," and even their brothers Pablo and Joaquín, when they sent me to see them, would say:

"Go over to the girls—"

They made a thousand different kinds of sweetmeats, which sold like hotcakes and were famous all over the city. A big cupboard with glass doors which stood in the little entrance hall displayed the wares created by their hands for the delectation of the inhabitants of San José: boxes of the most delicious candied coconut and orange I have ever eaten in my life; *cidrachayote* preserves that often proved too strong a temptation for me to resist; little dolls and strange beasts of a snowy-white sugar paste such as I have never since encountered; cakes and tamales that attracted customers from distant sections of the city. There were glass jars holding fragrant cakes of Matina chocolate that made a drink whose taste was like nectar, and which crowned the cups with foam an inch high.

It was she who told me most of the stories that transported me to a land of wonder.

The other members of my family—sober, sensible people—scolded the old lady for filling the young fry's heads full of those tales of fairies, witches, ghosts which, in their opinion, were bad for the mind. These sound reflections seemed nonsense to me. All I can say is that none of my other relatives won my confidence; nor did their sensible conversation or their uplifting little stories, which almost always trailed some clumsy moral behind them, interest me in the least. My Uncle Pablo, who taught logic and ethics in one of the schools of the city, used to refer disdainfully to Aunt Panchita's tales as poppycock and rubbish. It may be that people who think like Uncle Pablo will have the same opinion of them, and they will be right according to their lights. But as for me, who have never been able to find a satisfactory explanation for the things that happen around me every minute, who look on in gaping-mouthed wonder every time I see a flower open, Aunt Panchita's "lies" are just as credible as the scientific explanations I have received from very solemn and learned professors.

What a world of colorful, ineffable suggestions was awakened in our childish imaginations by the words of her stories, many of which had been invented in a way the grammar would never have sanctioned, and which were meaningless to the minds of those weighed down with years and learning!

The tales of Aunt Panchita were humble iron keys that opened up treasure chests of dreams.

In the back yard of her house there was a well under a chayote vine that hung a canopy of coolness over the curb.

Often, especially during the heat of March, my mouth recalls the water of that well, the coolest, clearest it has ever tasted, and which is no more, for the heat has dried it up; and without intending to, at the same time my heart recalls the memory of the happiness I knew then, crystalline and cool, which is no more, for sorrow has dried it up.

Seated beside the well, the old lady told me lies that entranced me: at the bottom there was a crystal palace whose lamps were stars. In it there lived a king and queen, who had two beautiful daughters: one dark, with black hair that reached to her knees, and a mole shaped like a flower on her cheek; and the other fair, with golden hair that touched the ground, and a blue mole shaped like a star on her cheek. The fair one was my favorite, and the blue star-shaped mole on her cheek was a fountain of dreams to me.

My greatest pleasure was when Aunt Panchita took her bucket and started for the well. I skipped along in front of her, as though we were going to a festival.

What strange, fascinating sounds arose from that dark, deep hole in whose depths lights seemed to be winking on and off! (Now I know they were the flecks of sunshine that glinted through the foliage overhead, but then I believed they were the lamps the old lady had told me about.) The curb and the sides of the well were covered with a greenish-golden moss. The drops that fell from them made such charming music. Tin! Tan! Aunt Panchita said they were the silver bells the princesses' little dogs wore hanging from a gold chain about their necks.

If Aunt Panchita had on occasion been able to read my thoughts, she would have been horrified at the effects of her beguiling lies, and would have trembled for my life, for I wanted nothing so much as to go and play with the princesses and their dogs in the crystal palace. And the smile of deprecating triumph that would have curved the lips of Uncle Pablo, professor of logic and ethics, if he could have turned his glasses upon the fields of my fancy cultivated by his sister, who, according to him, had a couple of screws loose. Probably those of common sense and logic. Now I close my eyes, and the memory of the beloved old lady, a thousand times dearer to me than Uncle Pablo, in spite of the fact that she did not know there were such things as logic and ethics, seats itself in her little, low chair, while her busy fingers roll cigarettes. I am at her feet on the little leather stool Uncle Joaquín made for me. I can smell the tobacco cured with fig leaves, brandy, and honey. It is in a big room with whitewashed walls and a brick floor. Somewhere there hangs a picture of a shepherdess putting a garland of flowers upon her lamb. On a chest of drawers a bell glass protects a scene of the Passion from the inclemencies of the weather, and beside it sit two china hens, each in her own nest.

Among the stories were the ever-beloved *Cinderella, Puss in Boots, Snow White, Little Red Riding Hood, The Bluebird,* which later on I found in books. And other stories that perhaps are not to be found in books. Some of these I have since met, not in books, but on other lips.

Where did Aunt Panchita get them? What long-vanished imagination of America wove them out of scraps picked up here and there and bits of straw filched from tales created in the dim past of the Old World? She put into them the charm of her words and expression which disappeared with her.

Dear Aunt Panchita, who knew nothing of logic or ethics, but who had the gift of making children laugh and dream.

Translated by Harriet de Onís

Katherine Mansfield (Kathleen Mansfield Beauchamp)
New Zealand/UK(England), 1888–1923

Katherine Mansfield was the first woman writer from either Australia or New Zealand to achieve an international reputation. Though she spent most of her adult life away from New Zealand, and is often regarded as an English writer, one of her continuing aims was to bring the "undiscovered country" of her birth to life for the rest of the world.

Mansfield was born Kathleen Mansfield Beauchamp in Wellington, New Zealand's capital, into an increasingly prosperous family. In the colonial fashion of her time and class, Mansfield and her sisters were sent "home" to London in 1903, to be educated at Queen's College. There she read Ibsen and Wilde, determined to become a writer, and formed a life-long, if at times mutually exasperating, friendship with "L.M.," (Ida Baker), a school friend of Mansfield's and author of *Katherine Mansfield. The Memories of L.M.* (1971).

Mansfield returned to New Zealand in 1906 but soon persuaded her father to let her go back to London with a small allowance. During these first independent years in London she experimented with life as well as literature, enduring a miscarriage, a very brief marriage, and a venereal infection. In 1912 she began living with the literary critic John Middleton Murry whom she eventually married in 1918. Theirs was a stormy relationship, marked by infidelities on both sides; their marriage became increasingly difficult after Mansfield's tuberculosis was diagnosed in 1917 and she was forced to spend winters away from Murry in a warmer climate than London's.

Only three collections of stories appeared during Mansfield's life, "A Dill Pickle" coming from the second, *Bliss* (1920). Its themes of male egotism and female isolation and frustration are typical of her work. Its subtle use of symbol and image, such as the "untouched cream" of the ending, indicates one of the major ways in which Mansfield contributed to the development of the modern short story. Mansfield gained the admiration of many critics during her brief lifetime for her highly innovative and accomplished writing. Indeed Virginia Woolf saw Mansfield as her major competitor.

After her death, Middleton Murry assiduously cultivated his wife's literary remains, publishing another two volumes of stories, besides collections of her poetry and book reviews and editions of her letters and journals. As recent scholarship has increasingly revealed, the latter were carefully edited by Murry to build up an image of Mansfield as a "bright spirit," someone too good to stay long in this world. The real Mansfield was a much tougher and more complex person who deserves recognition for her innovations in form and style rather than for her "sensitivity."

Ellizabeth Webby

A DILL PICKLE

And then, after six years, she saw him again. He was seated at one of those little bamboo tables decorated with a Japanese vase of paper daffodils. There was a tall plate of fruit in front of him, and very carefully, in a way she recognized immediately as his "special" way, he was peeling an orange.

He must have felt that shock of recognition in her, for he looked up and met her eyes. Incredible! He didn't know her! She smiled; he frowned. She came towards him. He closed his eyes an instant, but opening them his face lit up as though he had struck a match in a dark room. He laid down the orange and pushed back his chair, and she took her little warm hand out of her muff and gave it to him.

"Vera!" he exclaimed. "How strange. Really, for a moment I didn't know you. Won't you sit down? You've had lunch? Won't you have some coffee?"

She hesitated, but of course she meant to.

"Yes, I'd like some coffee." And she sat down opposite him.

"You've changed. You've changed very much," he said, staring at her with that eager, lighted look. "You look so well. I've never seen you look so well before."

"Really?" She raised her veil and unbuttoned her high fur collar. "I don't feel very well. I can't bear this weather, you know."

"Ah, no. You hate the cold...."

"Loathe it." She shuddered. "And the worst of it is that the older one grows..."

He interrupted her. "Excuse me," and tapped on the table for the waitress. "Please bring some coffee and cream." To her: "You are sure you won't eat anything? Some fruit, perhaps. The fruit here is very good."

"No, thanks. Nothing."

"Then that's settled." And smiling just a hint too broadly he took up the orange again. "You were saying—the older one grows—"

"The colder," she laughed. But she was thinking how well she remembered that trick of his—the trick of interrupting her—and of how it used to exasperate her six years ago. She used to feel then as though he, quite suddenly, in the middle of what she was saying, put his hand over her lips, turned from her, attended to something different, and then took his hand away, and with just the same slightly too broad smile, gave her his attention again.... Now we are ready. That is settled.

"The colder!" He echoed her words,

laughing too. "Ah, ah. You still say the same things. And there is another thing about you that is not changed at all—your beautiful voice—your beautiful way of speaking." Now he was very grave; he leaned towards her, and she smelled the warm, stinging scent of the orange peel. "You have only to say one word and I would know your voice among all other voices. I don't know what it is—I've often wondered—that makes your voice such a— haunting memory.... Do you remember that first afternoon we spent together at Kew Gardens? You were so surprised because I did not know the names of any flowers. I am still just as ignorant for all your telling me. But whenever it is very fine and warm, and I see some bright colours—it's awfully strange—I hear your voice saying: 'Geranium, marigold and verbena.' And I feel those three words are all I recall of some forgotten heavenly language.... You remember that afternoon?"

"Oh, yes, very well." She drew a long, soft breath, as though the paper daffodils between them were almost too sweet to bear. Yet, what had remained in her mind of that particular afternoon was an absurd scene over the tea table. A great many people taking tea in a Chinese pagoda, and he behaving like a maniac about the wasps—waving them away, flapping at them with his straw hat, serious and infuriated out of all proportion to the occasion. How delighted the sniggering tea drinkers had been. And how she had suffered.

But now, as he spoke, the memory faded. His was the truer. Yes, it had been a wonderful afternoon, full of geranium and marigold and verbena, and—warm sunshine. Her thoughts lingered over the last two words as though she sang them.

In the warmth, as it were, another memory unfolded. She saw herself sitting on a lawn. He lay beside her, and suddenly, after a long silence, he rolled over and put his head in her lap.

"I wish," he said, in a low, troubled voice,

"I wish that I had taken poison and were about to die—here now!"

At that moment a little girl in a white dress, holding a long, dripping water lily, dodged from behind a bush, stared at them, and dodged back again. But he did not see. She leaned over him.

"Ah, why do you say that? I could not say that."

But he gave a kind of soft moan, and taking her hand he held it to his cheek.

"Because I know I am going to love you too much—far too much. And I shall suffer so terribly, Vera, because you never, never will love me."

He was certainly far better looking now than he had been then. He had lost all that dreamy vagueness and indecision. Now he had the air of a man who has found his place in life, and fills it with a confidence and an assurance which was, to say the least, impressive. He must have made money, too. His clothes were admirable, and at that moment he pulled a Russian cigarette case out of his pocket.

"Won't you smoke?"

"Yes, I will." She hovered over them. "They look very good."

"I think they are. I get them made for me by a little man in St. James's Street. I don't smoke very much. I'm not like you—but when I do, they must be delicious, very fresh cigarettes. Smoking isn't a habit with me; it's a luxury—like perfume. Are you still so fond of perfumes? Ah, when I was in Russia..."

She broke in: "You've really been to Russia?"

"Oh, yes. I was there for over a year. Have you forgotten how we used to talk of going there?"

"No, I've not forgotten."

He gave a strange half laugh and leaned back in his chair. "Isn't it curious. I have really carried out all those journeys that we planned. Yes, I have been to all those places that we talked of, and stayed in them long enough to—as you used to say, 'air oneself' in them. In fact, I have spent the last three years of my life travelling all the time. Spain, Corsica, Siberia, Russia, Egypt. The only country left is China, and I mean to go there, too, when the war is over."

As he spoke, so lightly, tapping the end of his cigarette against the ash tray, she felt the strange beast that had slumbered so long within her bosom stir, stretch itself, yawn, prick up its ears, and suddenly bound to its feet, and fix its longing, hungry stare upon those far away places. But all she said was, smiling gently: "How I envy you."

He accepted that. "It has been," he said, "very wonderful—especially Russia. Russia was all that we had imagined, and far, far more. I even spent some days on a river boat on the Volga. Do you remember that boatman's song that you used to play?"

"Yes." It began to play in her mind as she spoke.

"Do you ever play it now?"

"No, I've no piano."

He was amazed at that. "But what has become of your beautiful piano?"

She made a little grimace. "Sold. Ages ago."

"But you were so fond of music," he wondered.

"I've no time for it now," said she.

He let it go at that. "That river life," he went on, "is something quite special. After a day or two you cannot realize that you have ever known another. And it is not necessary to know the language—the life of the boat creates a bond between you and the people that's more than sufficient. You eat with them, pass the day with them, and in the evening there is that endless singing."

She shivered, hearing the boatman's song break out again loud and tragic, and seeing the boat floating on the darkening river with melancholy trees on either side... "Yes, I should like that," said she, stroking her muff.

"You'd like almost everything about Russian life," he said warmly. "It's so informal, so

impulsive, so free without question. And then the peasants are so splendid. They are such human beings—yes, that is it. Even the man who drives your carriage has—has some real part in what is happening. I remember the evening a party of us, two friends of mine and the wife of one of them, went for a picnic by the Black Sea. We took supper and champagne and ate and drank on the grass. And while we were eating the coachman came up. 'Have a dill pickle,' he said. He wanted to share with us. That seemed to me so right, so—you know what I mean?"

And she seemed at the moment to be sitting on the grass beside the mysteriously Black Sea, black as velvet, and rippling against the banks in silent, velvet waves. She saw the carriage drawn up to one side of the road, and the little group on the grass, their faces and hands white in the moonlight. She saw the pale dress of the woman outspread and her folded parasol, lying on the grass like a huge pearl crochet hook. Apart from them, with his supper in a cloth on his knees, sat the coachman. "Have a dill pickle," said he, and although she was not certain what a dill pickle was, she saw the greenish glass jar with a red chili like a parrot's beak glimmering through. She sucked in her cheeks; the dill pickle was terribly sour....

"Yes, I know perfectly what you mean," she said.

In the pause that followed they looked at each other. In the past when they had looked at each other like that they had felt such a boundless understanding between them that their souls had, as it were, put their arms round each other and dropped into the same sea, content to be drowned, like mournful lovers. But now, the surprising thing was that it was he who held back. He who said:

"What a marvellous listener you are. When you look at me with those wild eyes I feel that I could tell you things that I would never breathe to another human being."

Was there just a hint of mockery in his voice or was it her fancy? She could not be sure.

"Before I met you," he said, "I had never spoken of myself to anybody. How well I remember one night, the night that I brought you the little Christmas tree, telling you all about my childhood. And of how I was so miserable that I ran away and lived under a cart in our yard for two days without being discovered. And you listened, and your eyes shone, and I felt that you had even made the little Christmas tree listen too, as in a fairy story."

But of that evening she had remembered a little pot of caviare. It had cost seven and sixpence. He could not get over it. Think of it—a tiny jar like that costing seven and sixpence. While she ate it he watched her, delighted and shocked.

"No, really, that is eating money. You could not get seven shillings into a little pot that size. Only think of the profit they must make...." And he had begun some immensely complicated calculations.... But now goodbye to the caviare. The Christmas tree was on the table, and the little boy lay under the cart with his head pillowed on the yard dog.

"The dog was called Bosun," she cried delightedly.

But he did not follow. "Which dog? Had you a dog? I don't remember a dog at all."

"No, no. I mean the yard dog when you were a little boy." He laughed and snapped the cigarette case to.

"Was he? Do you know I had forgotten that. It seems such ages ago. I cannot believe that it is only six years. After I had recognized you today—I had to take such a leap—I had to take a leap over my whole life to get back to that time. I was such a kid then." He drummed on the table. "I've often thought how I must have bored you. And now I understand so perfectly why you wrote to me as you did— although at the time that letter nearly finished my life. I found it again the other day, and I couldn't help laughing as I read it. It was so clever—such a true picture of me." He glanced up. "You're not going?"

She had buttoned her collar again and drawn down her veil.

"Yes, I am afraid I must," she said, and managed a smile. Now she knew that he had been mocking.

"Ah, no, please," he pleaded. "Don't go just for a moment," and he caught up one of her gloves from the table and clutched at it as if that would hold her. "I see so few people to talk to nowadays, that I have turned into a sort of barbarian," he said. "Have I said something to hurt you?"

"Not a bit," she lied. But as she watched him draw her glove through his fingers, gently, gently, her anger really did die down, and besides, at the moment he looked more like himself of six years ago....

"What I really wanted then," he said softly, "was to be a sort of carpet—to make myself into a sort of carpet for you to walk on so that you need not be hurt by the sharp stones and the mud that you hated so. It was nothing more positive than that—nothing more selfish. Only I did desire, eventually, to turn into a magic carpet and carry you away to all those lands you longed to see."

As he spoke she lifted her head as though she drank something; the strange beast in her bosom began to purr....

"I felt that you were more lonely than anybody else in the world," he went on, "and yet, perhaps, that you were the only person in the world who was really, truly alive. Born out of your time," he murmured, stroking the glove, "fated."

Ah, God! What had she done! How had she dared to throw away her happiness like this. This was the only man who had ever understood her. Was it too late? Could it be too late? *She* was that glove that he held in his fingers....

"And then the fact that you had no friends and never had made friends with people. How I understood that, for neither had I. Is it just the same now?"

"Yes," she breathed. "Just the same. I am as alone as ever."

"So am I," he laughed gently, "just the same."

Suddenly with a quick gesture he handed her back the glove and scraped his chair on the floor. "But what seemed to me so mysterious then is perfectly plain to me now. And to you, too, of course. . . .It simply was that we were such egoists, so self-engrossed, so wrapped up in ourselves that we hadn't a corner in our hearts for anybody else. Do you know," he cried, naïve and hearty, and dreadfully like another side of that old self again, "I began studying a Mind System when I was in Russia, and I found that we were not peculiar at all. It's quite a well known form of. . ."

She had gone. He sat there, thunderstruck, astounded beyond words. . . . And then he asked the waitress for his bill.

"But the cream has not been touched," he said. "Please do not charge me for it."

Ánna Akhmátova   (Ánna Andréevna Gorénko)

Russia/USSR, 1889–1966

Ánna Andréevna Gorénko was born on June 11, 1889 near Odessa and was raised in Tsárskoe Seló (now Pushkin), the summer residence of the czars. While attending the girls' Gymnasium there she met the future founder of the Acmeist movement Nikoláy Sergéevich Gumilyóv (1886–1921), in whose Paris journal *Sirius* her first poems appeared in 1907, and whom she married in 1910. She then transferred to Petersburg to study literature, where in 1912 she bore her son Lev and published her first collection of poetry *Vécher* (Evening) under the pseudonym Ánna Akhmátova (the Tatar surname of her great grandmother). After the publication of *Chyótki* (The Rosary, 1914) and *Bélaya stáya* (The White Flock, 1917), "Akhmátova School" among the young generation of Russian poets was already evident.

With the October Revolution in 1917 and her divorce from Gumilyóv in 1918, Akhmátova withdrew from literary society. Her collection *Podorózhnik* (Plantain, 1921) reflects the violent days of the Revolution and the ensuing Civil War, in which the crumbling of Akhmátova's whole world was compounded by personal loss. In August her friend and the greatest Russian Symbolist poet Aleksándr Aleksándrovich Blók (b. 1880) died, and two weeks later, Gumilyóv was executed as a counterrevolutionary. The publication of *Anno Domini MCMXXI* in 1922 was Akhmátova's last for almost two decades. She continued to write, however (although her second husband burned her manuscripts), and her poems were a favorite critical subject, particularly of the Formalists. Negative criticism from Party critics, who labelled her a "bourgeois relic," prevailed by the end of the decade. Although she was not harrassed, her son Lev was subject to several arrests before (and after) the Second World War, and Akhmátova's third husband, the art critic Nikoláy Púnin, with whom she lived from 1926 to 1940, was also arrested and died in 1953 after imprisonment and deportation.

In the relaxation of literary restraints at the outset of the war, Akhmátova was allowed to publish again and a collection *Iz shestí kníg* (From Six Books), including her earlier works and a new cycle, appeared in 1940 only to be recalled six months later. In 1943, *Ízbrannoe* (Selected Works), including very moving war poetry that had been copied and recited in the bomb shelters during the Leningrad seige, was published in Tashként.

After the war the Party once again clamped down on literature. In 1946 Akhmátova (along with the famous writer and satirist Zóshchenko) was subjected to vicious attack, expelled from the Union of Soviet Writers, and denied the right to publish. Until her partial rehabilitation in 1956, Akhmátova supported herself by translating other writers' works from various languages, including a volume of Korean classical poetry. In 1958 her last collection, *Bég vrémeni* (The Course of Time), was published, and included *Sedmáya kníga* (The Seventh Book, from which the following cycle is taken), *Trostník* (The Reed, containing poems written between 1922 and 1940 during her enforced silence), fragments from "Rékviem" ("Requiem") and "Poéma bez geróya" ("Poem Without a Hero"), as well as selected poems from her early period. Subsequent editions included later additions and revisions she made to her book.

Akhmátova was not fully rehabilitated until 1964 when her entire published work was officially accepted. She was also finally recognized in the West: Robert Frost visited her in the Soviet Union; she traveled to Italy to receive the Taormina Prize for Poetry in 1964; and she received an honorary degree from Oxford in 1965. Her death was mourned not only as the passing of a great poet and woman of dignity and integrity, but also as the loss of the last link with pre-Revolutionary Russian culture.

The one dominating theme of Akhmátova's poetry is the grief and betrayal of love, presented in infinite variety. In accordance with the dictates of Acmeism, her verse is characterized by precision and concrete detail. Akhmátova was deeply tied to the traditions of Russian culture, which had made it impossible for her to emigrate in the early 1920s as so many of her colleagues had done (homelessness was for her the greatest tragedy), and these traditions made their way into her poetry through imagery and diction. Yet a single word or phrase evokes many layers of meaning and belies her supposed simplicity. In her later work, Akhmátova also addressed the process of artistic creation, the force of history, and culture. Her "Poem Without a Hero," particularly, is an extremely complex, sometimes indecipherable multilayered work, with literary and biographical allusions, that may be said to "memorialize a bygone era."

Dobrochna Dyrcz-Freeman

THE SWEETBRIAR FLOWERS
Shipóvnik tsvetyót

From a burnt notebook

> And thou art distant in humanity
> (KEATS)[1]

Instead of the festive congratulations
this wind, hard and dry,
will bring you only the smell of decay,
the foretaste of smoke and poems
written in my hand.
(1961)

1. BURNT NOTEBOOK

Your happy sister
is already showing off on the book shelf,
and over you the fragments of starry flocks,
and under you the coals of the bonfire.
How you prayed, how you wanted to live,
how you feared the acrid fire!
But suddenly your body trembled
and a voice flying off cursed me.
And immediately all the pines started rustling
and were reflected in the depth of moon
                                                    waters,
and round the fire the most sacred springtimes
already led the round dance by the grave.
(1961)

2. AWAKE

Away with time, away with space,
I saw everything through the white night,
the narcissus in the crystal vase on your table,
and the blue smoke of a cigar,
and that mirror where you could now
be reflected as in clear water.
Away with time, away with space...
but even you cannot help me.
(1946)

3. IN A DREAM

I bear equally with you
the black, permanent separation.
Why are you crying? Rather give me your
                                                    hand,
promise to come again in a dream.
You and I are a mountain of grief...
You and I will never meet on this earth.
If only you could send me at midnight
a greeting through the stars.
(1946)

4. FIRST SONG

The triumphs of the secret
non-meeting are empty.
Unspoken speech,
unpronounced words.
Uncrossed glances
do not know where to lie,
and only tears are happy
because they can flow a long time.
The sweetbriar of the Moscow countryside,
alas, it's nothing...
and all this they call
immortal love.
(1956)

5. ANOTHER SONG

I will no longer repeat
unspoken speeches.
But in memory of that non-meeting
I will plant a sweetbriar.
The miracle of our meeting
Shone and sang there,
I did not want to return
anywhere from there.
Happiness instead of duty
was my bitter sweetness,
I talked with someone I shouldn't have
I talked for a long time.
Let passion choke lovers,
demanding an answer,
but we, my darling, are only souls
on the edge of the earth.
(1956)

6. DREAM

Is it sweet to see unearthly dreams?[2]
(A. BLOK)

This dream was prophetic or not prophetic...
Mars shone among the stars in the sky,
it became crimson, giving off sparks,
                                        malevolent,
and that night I dreamed of your coming.

It was in everything...in Bach's chaconne,[3]
in the roses that blossomed in vain,
and in the ringing of the village bell
above the blackness of the ploughed earth.

And in the autumn that approached in earnest
and suddenly after some thought hid itself
                                        again.
O my August, how could you return
such news on this terrible anniversary!

How shall I repay the royal present?
Where shall I go and with whom shall I
                                        celebrate?
And now I write my poems in the burnt
                                        notebook
as before without smudges.
(14th August 1956, Near Kolomna)

7.

Along that road where Dmitry Donskoy[4]
once led his great host,
where the wind remembers the enemy,
where the moon is yellow and horned,
I walked as though in the sea's depth...
The sweetbriar was so scented
that it even turned into a word
and I was ready to meet
the ninth wave of my fate.

8.

You thought me up. There is no such person,
there couldn't be such a person on earth.
Neither will the doctor cure him, nor will the
                                poet slake his thirst,
the shadow of a ghost alarms you by day and
                                        night.

You and I met in an improbable year,
when already the powers of the world had
                                        dried up,
everything was in mourning, everything wilted
                                from adversity,
and only the graves were fresh.
Without lamps the Neva was black as pitch.
The night surrounded me like a wall...
So it was then my voice challenged you.
What I did I still did not understand.
And you came to me as though led by a star,
treading through the tragic autumn,
into the house emptied for ever,
from where the flock of burnt poems was
                                        carried away.

(18 August 1956)

9. THE SHATTERED MIRROR

I listened to words that could not be taken
                                        back
on that starry evening,
and my head began to swim
as though it were over a flaming abyss.
And destruction howled by the gates.
And the black garden hooted like an eagle owl,
and the city, deathly weak,
was more ancient than Troy in this hour.
That hour was unbearably clear
and it seems was ringing till tears fell.
You did not give me the present
which you had brought from afar.
It seemed to be an empty amusement
in that evening that was fiery for you.
And it became the slow poison
in my enigmatic fate.
And it was the precursor of all my troubles—
let us not remember it!
The meeting that never took place
still weeps behind the corner.
(1956)

(continued)

10.

> You are with me again, my friend Autumn!
> (INNOKÉNTY ANNENSKY)[5]

Let someone still rest in the South
and bask in the heavenly garden.
Here it is very northerly and this year
I took autumn as my friend.

I live as if in a strange house that I dreamed of,
where perhaps I died,
where the mirrors save for themselves
something strange in the evening languor.

I walk through the black squat firs,
there the heather is like the wind,
and the dull fragment of the moon shines
like an old serrated knife.
I brought here the blessed memory
of my last non-meeting with you—
the cold, clear, light flame
of my victory over fate.
(1957)

11.

> Against my will, o queen, I left your shore
> (AENEID 6)[6]

Don't be afraid—I can still picture
more like us.
Are you a ghost, or a passing man,
for some reason I preserve your shade.

Not for long were you my Aeneas.
I was then separated by the fire of sacrifice.
We know how to be silent about each other.
And you forgot my damned house.

You forgot those hands stretched
through the fire in terror and torture
and the news of cursed hope.

You don't know what they forgave you...
Rome is founded, the flocks of flotillas sail
and flattery glorifies the victory.
(Komarovo 1962)

12.

You want my poems directly...
You'll live somehow even without them.
Not a gramme was left in the blood
that has not sucked their bitterness.
We burn up the gold and fine days
of this unrealizable life,
and the night fires do not whisper
to us of a meeting in the celestial fatherland.

And a little cold wave streams
from our great acts,
as though at a mysterious crypt
we trembled and read out some names.

We cannot think up a more fathomless parting,
better immediately, outright.
And without doubt there has never been

                                   anyone
more parted than us.
(Moscow 1963)

13.[7]

And the cunning moon
hiding by the gates
saw how that evening
I changed my posthumous fame.
Now they will forget me,
books will rot in the cupboard.
They will call
no street or avenue Akhmátova.
(1946)

14.

And this will become for the people
like the times of Vespasian[8]
and this was only a wound
and a little cloud of torture over it.
(18th December 1964, Rome Night)

Translated by Richard McKane

NOTES

1. From "Isabella; or The Pot of Basil," stanza xxxix, 1.312, by the English Romantic poet (1795–1821).
2. From "*Shagí Komandóra*" (Steps of the Commander).
3. Musical form using triple meter and a recurring harmonic pattern of four or eight bars, popular during the Baroque period. One of the most popular and well-known examples is the Chaconne from the D Minor Violin Suite by J.S. Bach (1685–1750).
4. Dmítry Donskóy, or Donskoi (1350–1389): popular Russian hero who challenged the Mongolian Tatar invaders and successfully resisted Lithuanian attempts to invade Moscow; the subject of the most famous epic of his period.
5. The first line of that untitled poem by Innokénty Fyódorovich Annensky (1856–1909). Poet, playwright, and literary critic, he belonged to no literary movement but was considered "a poet's poet." Acmeists, particularly Gumilyóv and Akhmátova considered Annensky a mentor, especially in his opposition to the mysticism of Russian symbolism.
6. Said by Aeneas to his lover Dido, ruler of Carthage, whom he abandons to continue his journey, in the first-century B.C. Roman epic by Virgil.
7. The Soviet edition omits this poem; although she has been rehabilitated, there can be no mention of the time when Akhmátova was in disfavor.
8. Vespasian (9–79 A.D.): reigned 69 to 79 A.D., fostered classical historical literature.

William Orpen, The Wash House, *1905, oil on canvas. Courtesy The National Gallery of Ireland, Dublin*

Enid Bagnold   *UK(England), 1889–1981*

Though she is best known for her drama, English author and playwright Enid
Bagnold's artistic life was marked by versatility. She wrote for the stage and for
children; she wrote novels, poems, and a classic non-fiction work about life in a
World War I hospital. Bagnold drew largely from her own life, a life of adventure,
bohemian culture, and high society. Her fiction is far-ranging in its audience
appeal. Still, though she said that her career, from age 9, was "simply writing," she
never published with the regularity or in the volume of many other writers.

Enid Bagnold was born in Rochester, Kent, England, the daughter of Ethel
Alger and Col. Arthur Henry Bagnold. In 1899, the family went to Jamaica, West
Indies, and returned in 1902. Bagnold attended Priors Field, an exclusive girls'
school and later went to finishing schools in Switzerland ("a school from which I
ran away" she said), Germany, and France before studying drawing and painting
in London in 1909. There, with her teacher, Walter Sickert, the British impression-
ist, she led a bohemian's life, earning a living as an artist's model and artist, and
then later working on the staff of *Hearth and Home* and *Modern Society*.

Bagnold's career as a writer began in 1917 with the publication of her only
volume of poetry, *The Sailing Ship and Other Poems*. While the World War was
raging, she worked as a volunteer in the Royal Herbert Hospital, writing about her
experience as a nurse's aide in her classic, *A Diary Without Dates* (1918), excerpted here. The book was found to be too close to the truth and she was expelled
from the hospital for breaching "military discipline." *The Happy Foreigner* (1920)
was Bagnold's first novel and was based on her experience with the French as an
ambulance driver toward the end of the war. Its heroine is the first of many of
Bagnold's characters who are incapable of sustaining intimate relationships.

Bagnold's marriage to Sir Roderick Jones brought her into a world of international society, a life that she relished and which often served as the source of her
fiction. *Serena Blandish* (1924), her second novel, was published, like the first,
under the pseudonym "A Lady of Quality," an anonymity taken out of deference
to her family. Six years passed before Bagnold published *Alice and Thomas and
Jane* (1930), a children's book which, along with the internationally known
National Velvet (1935), was illustrated by her adolescent daughter, Laurian.

Bagnold's first play, *Lottie Dundass* (1942), is the story of an egocentric
young actress who murders the woman for whose role she is understudy. For
Bagnold, the play was a chance to carry out an impossible wish. She had once been
asked to recite the prologue of a new play because the original actor had fallen ill.
She excitedly accepted, only to be dropped when the original reader recovered.
Though encouraged by the play's modest success (it ran for ninety-three performances), Bagnold continued to write only sporadically. *Poor Judas* (1946) won the
Arts Theatre Prize in 1951 for a new play of "contemporary significance" but the
play received mixed critical reviews. *Gertie* (1952) was, by Bagnold's account, "a
flop."

It took nearly two years to bring about the production of *The Chalk Garden*
(1955), Bagnold's most powerful and moving play. It is the story of an aging
society woman and her attempts to shape first her daughter and then her grand-

daughter. Critics hailed the play, which won an Award of Merit Medal of the American Academy of Arts and Letters. *The Chinese Prime Minister* (1964) is Bagnold's only other successful play. In it, a seventy-year-old retired actress seeks to make aging a time of fulfillment, as do the Chinese. The play's power lies in its theme of the significance of old age, and in its strong, realistic dialogue.

Bagnold was named Commander of the British Empire in 1976.

John Isom

from A DIARY WITHOUT DATES

A warded M.O. is pathetic. He knows he can't get well quicker than time will let him. He has no faith.

Tomorrow I have to take down all the decorations that I put up for Christmas. When I put them up I never thought I should be the one to take them down. When I was born no one thought I should be old.

While I was untying a piece of holly from the electric-light cords on the ceiling and a patient was holding the ladder for me, a young *padre* came and pretended to help us, but while he stood with us he whispered to the patient, "Are you a communicant?" I felt a wave of heat and anger; I could have dropped the holly on him.

They hung up their stockings on Christmas night on walking-sticks hitched over the ends of the beds and under the mattresses. Such big stockings! Many of them must have played Father Christmas in their own homes, to their own children, on other Christmases.

On Christmas Eve I didn't leave the hospital till long after the Day-Sisters had gone and the Night-Sisters came on. The wards were all quiet as I walked down the corridor, and to left and right through the glass doors hung the rows of expectant stockings.

Final and despairing postscript on Mr. Pettitt.

When a woman says she cannot come to lunch it is because she doesn't want to.

Let this serve as an axiom to every lover: A woman who refuses lunch refuses everything.

The hospital is alive; I feel it like a living being.

The hospital is like a dream. I am afraid of walking up and finding it commonplace.

The white Sisters, the ceaselessly changing patients, the long passages, the sudden plunges into the brilliant wards...their scenery hypnotizes me.

Sometimes in the late evening one walks busily up and down the ward doing this and that, forgetting that there is anything beyond the drawn blinds, engrossed in the patients, one's tasks—bed-making, washing, one errand and another—and then suddenly a blind will blow out and almost up to the ceiling, and through it you will catch a glimpse that makes you gasp, of a black night crossed with bladed searchlights, of a moon behind a crooked tree.

The lifting of the blind is a miracle; I do not believe in the wind.

A new Sister on tonight...very severe. We had to make the beds like white cardboard. I wonder what she thinks of me.

Mr. Pettitt (who really is going tomorrow) wandered up into the ward and limped near me. "Sister..." he began. He *will* call me "Sister." I frowned at him. The new Sister glanced at him and blinked.

He was very persistent. "Sister," he said again, "do you think I can have a word with you?"

"Not now," I whispered as I hurried past him.

"Oh, is that so?" he said, as though I had

made an interesting statement, and limped away, looking backwards at me. I suppose he wants to say good-bye.

He sat beside Mr. Wicks's bed (Mr. Wicks who is paralysed) and looked at me from time to time with that stare of his which contains so little offence.

It is curious to think that I once saw Mr. Wicks on a tennis-lawn, walking across the grass...Mr. Wicks, who will never put his foot on grass again, but, lying in his bed, continues to say, as all Tommies say, "I feel well in meself."

So he does; he feels well in himself. But he isn't going to live, all the same.

Still his routine goes on: he plays his game of cards, he has his joke: "Lemonade, please, nurse; but it's not from choice!"

When I go to clear his ashtray at night I always say, "Well, now I've got something worth clearing at last!"

And he chuckles and answers: "Thought you'd be pleased. It's the others gets round my bed and leaves their bits."

He was once a sergeant: he got his commission a year ago.

My ruined charms cry aloud for help.

The cap wears away my front hair; my feet are widening from the everlasting boards; my hands won't take my rings.

I was advised last night on the telephone to marry immediately before it was too late.

A desperate remedy. I will try cold cream and hair tonics first.

There is a tuberculosis ward across the landing. They call it the T.B. ward.

It is a den of coughs and harrowing noises.

One night I saw a negro standing in the doorway with his long hair done up in hair-pins. He is the pet of the T.B. ward; they call him Henry.

Henry came in to help us with our Christmas decorations on Christmas Eve, and as he

cleverly made wreaths my Sister whispered to me, "He's ever spitting...in the ward!"

But he wasn't, it was part of his language—little clicks and ticks. He comes from somewhere in Central Africa, and one of the T.B.'s told me, "He's only got one wife, nurse."

He is very proud of his austerity, for he has somehow discovered that he has hit on a country where it is the nutty thing only to have one wife.

No one can speak a word of his language, no one knows exactly where he comes from; but he can say in English, "Good morning, Sister!" and "Christmas Box!" and "One!"

Directly one takes any notice of him he laughs and clicks, holding up one finger, crying, "One!"

Then a proud T.B. (they regard him as the Creator might regard a hummingbird) explains: "He means he's only got one wife, nurse."

Then he did his second trick. He came to me with outstretched black hand and took my apron, fingering it. Its whiteness slipped between his fingers. He dropped it and, holding up the hand with its fellow, ducked his head to watch me with his glinting eyes.

"He means," explained the versatile T.B., "that he has ten piccaninnies in his village and they're all dressed in white."

It took my breath away; I looked at Henry for corroboration. He nodded earnestly, coughed and whispered, "Ten!"

"How do you know he means that?" I asked. "How can you possibly have found out?"

"We got pictures, nurse. We showed 'im kids, and 'e said 'e got ten—six girls and four boys. We showed 'im pictures of kids."

I had never seen Henry before, never knew he existed. But in the ward opposite the poor T.B.'s had been holding conversations with him in window-seats, showing him pictures, painfully establishing a communion with him...Henry, with his hair done up in hair-pins!

Although they showed him off with conscious pride, I don't think he really appeared strange to them, beyond his colour. I believe they imagine his wife as appearing much as their own wives, his children as the little children who run about their own doorsteps. They do not stretch their imaginations to conceive any strangeness about his home surroundings to correspond with his own strangeness.

To them Henry has the dignity of a man and a householder, possibly a ratepayer.

He seems quite happy and amused. I see him carrying a bucket sometimes, sharing its handle with a flushed T.B. They carry on animated conversations as they go downstairs, the T.B. talking the most. It reminds me of a child and a dog.

What strange machinery is there for getting him back? Part of the cargo of a ship... one day..."a nigger for Central Africa..."

"Where's his unit?"

"Who knows! One nigger and his bundle...for Central Africa!"

The ward has put Mr. Wicks to Coventry* because he has been abusive and violent-tempered for three days.

He lies flat in his bed and frowns; no more jokes over the lemonade, no wilfulness over the thermometer.

It is in these days that Mr. Wicks faces the truth.

I lingered by his bed last night, after I had put his teatray on his table, and looked down at him; he pretended to be inanimate, his open eyes fixed upon the white rail of the bed. His bedclothes were stretched about him as though he had not moved since his bed was made, hours before.

His worldly pleasures were beside him—his reading lamp, his Christmas box of cigars, his *Star*—but his eyes, disregarding them, were upon that sober vision that hung around the bedrail.

He began a bitter conversation:

"Nurse, I'm only a ranker, but I had a bit saved. I went to a private doctor and paid for myself. And I went to a specialist, and he told me I should never get this. I paid for it myself out of what I had saved."

We might have been alone in the world, he and I. Far down at the other end of the room the men sat crouched about the fire, their trays before them on chairs. The sheet of window behind Mr. Wicks's head was flecked with the morsels of snow which, hunted by the gale, obtained a second's refuge before oblivion.

"I'd sooner be dead than lying here; I would, reely." You hear that often in the world. "I'd sooner be dead than—" But Mr. Wicks meant it; he would sooner be dead than lying there. And death is a horror, an end. Yet he says lying there is worse.

"You see, I paid for a specialist myself, and he told me I should never be like this."

There was nothing to be said...One must have one's tea. I went down the ward to the bunk, and we cut the pink iced cake left over from Christmas....

NOTE

* To isolate someone.

Gabriela Mistral   (Lucila Godoy de Alcayaga)   *Chile, 1889–1957*

Perhaps the best known woman writer from Latin America, Gabriela Mistral was the first Latin American to win the Nobel Prize (1945). Using folk and religious imagery, Mistral wrote simple, sincere poems on the theme of love, death, and motherhood.

Unlike most Latin American women writers of her time, Mistral came from a poor family. She went to school only until age 11 and began teaching at 15. At age 18 she fell in love with a young man who later killed himself over financial difficulties. It is thought that his suicide and a later unhappy love affair inspired much of her poetry, especially that focusing on love and loss.

Mistral published her first poem in 1904 and continued to write poems and essays for journals, eventually establishing a reputation in the Chilean world of letters. In 1914 she won the prestigious Santiago Poetry Prize for "Los sonetos de la muerte" ("Sonnets of Death"), a series of three poems. From that point on, Mistral was a personality in Latin American literature, corresponding with the most important writers of her time.

During these early years Mistral continued working in education and became recognized in that area as well as in writing. In 1922 she was invited to Mexico to help reform the school system there. It was also in 1922 that her first book of poetry, *Desolación* (*Desolation*), from which the following poems were taken, was published by Columbia University Press in New York City on the insistence of Frederico de Onís who had become familiar with her work. A year later the book was published in Chile, and her anthology of Latin American literature directed towards women, *Lecturas para mujeres destinadas a la enseñanza del lenguaje* (Reading for Women Emphasizing Education in Language), was published in Mexico. In 1924 she published *Ternura* (Tenderness), her first book on the theme of children and *for* children.

After leaving Mexico, Mistral worked for many years in international diplomacy, traveling through Europe and the United States working for peace and education. In the U.S. she taught at Barnard, Vassar, Middlebury colleges, and at the University of Puerto Rico. During that time, she published no poems until *Tala* (Felling) was published by Sur Press containing poems written between 1922 and 1938; proceeds from the book were dedicated to the relief of children made homeless by the Spanish Civil War.

Many of the poems in Mistral's final book of poetry *Lagar* (Wine Press, 1954) were her saddest and most dreamlike. They express the desolation of her last years brought on by the death of her nephew (who was her ward) as well as of close friends, the World War, and her own sickness.

PRAYER
El Ruego

Lord, you know with what frenzy fine
Your help for strangers I have often sought.
Now I come to plead for one who was mine,
honeycomb of my mouth, spring of my
                                        drought.

Lime of my bones, sweet reason to be,
birdsong at my ear, a belt my waist to trim.
I have sought help for others who meant
                              nothing to me.
Do not turn Your head now when I plead for
                                          him.

I tell You he was good, and I say
his heart like a flower in his breast did sing,
gentle of nature, frank as the light of day,
bursting with miracles as is the Spring.

Unworthy of my pleas is he, You sternly say,
since no sign of prayer crossed his fevered face
and one day, with no nod from You, he went
                                        away,
shattering his temples like a fragile vase.

But I tell you, Lord, I once caressed
his gentle and tormented heart—
as a lily might his brow have pressed—
and found it silky as a bud when petals part.

You say he was cruel? You forget I loved him
                                          ever.
He knew my wounded flesh was his to shatter.
Now the waters of my gladness he disturbs
                                      forever?
I loved him! You know, I loved him—so that
                              does not matter.

To love (as You well understand) is a bitter
                                        task—
eyelids wet with tears may be,
kisses in prickly tresses may bask,
beneath them guarding eyes of ecstasy.

Translated by Langston Hughes

HOLY LAW
La Sagrada Ley

They say that life has flown from my body,
                                      that my
veins have spouted like wine presses: but I feel
                                        only
the relief a breast knows after a long sigh.
"Who am I," I say to myself, "to have a son
                                on my knee?"
And I myself answer, "A woman who loved,
                              and whose love,
when he kissed me, asked for eternity."
Let the Earth observe me with my son in my
                                    arms, and
bless me, because now I am fruitful like the
                                    palm trees
and furrows in the earth.

Translated by Langston Hughes

TELL ME, MOTHER
Cuéntame, Madre

Mother, tell me all you have learned from your
                                          own
pain. Tell me how he is born and how from
                                    within me
all entangled comes a little body.
Tell me if he will seek my breast alone, or if I
should offer it to him, coaxing.
Now teach me the science of love, mother.
                                      Show me
new caresses, gentle ones, gentler than those
                                        of a
husband.
How, in days to come, shall I wash his little
                                        head?
And how shall I swaddle him so as not to hurt
                                          him?
Teach me that lullaby, mother, you sang to
                                    rock me
to sleep. It will make him sleep better than any
                              other songs.

Translated by Langston Hughes

Rahel Bluwstein   *Russia/Palestine, 1890–1931*

Rahel Bluwstein was born and educated in Russia, attending a Hebrew public school, a Russian gymnasium, and the art school in Kiev. Her earliest poetry is in Russian. She immigrated to Israel (then called Palestine) in 1909 where she did agricultural work on a kibbutz. Later, she went to France and pursued her interests in agriculture until she had to return to Russia when World War I began. When she went back to Palestine at the end of the war she was ill with tuberculosis and was to be in and out of hospitals during the last ten years of her life. Rahel (her literary name) died in 1931, having produced two volumes of Hebrew poetry during her lifetime, *Safiah* (Aftergrowth, 1927) and *Mineged* (From the Other Side, 1930), and two posthumous works *Nevo* (Mt. Nebo, 1932) and *Shirat Rahel* (The Poetry of Rahel, 1949). "Only of Myself I Knew How to Tell" and "Here on Earth" are from *Shirat Rahel*.

If Rahel's poetry manifests an intense sensitivity combined with a tone of resignation and melancholy, it is probably because she composed most of her works while she was terminally ill. She was extremely nationalistic, and her poetry also gives voice to her pride and joy in the pioneer spirit of her adopted country's settlers. Seen as an embodiment of this spirit, Rahel is one of the most popular Hebrew poets; she has been widely anthologized in Israel and many of her poems have even been set to music.

ONLY OF MYSELF I KNEW HOW TO TELL
Rak al atzmi lesaper yadati

Only of myself I knew how to tell,
My world like the ant's compressed.
Also my burdens I carried like her,
Too many, too heavy for my thin shoulder.

Also my path—like hers to the treetop—
Was a path of pain, a path of toil.
A giant hand, sure and malicious,
A teasing hand lay over all.

All my ways trembled and wept
At this giant hand, in constant fright.
Why did you call me, shores of wonder?
Why disappoint me, distant lights?

Translated by Ruth Mintz

HERE ON EARTH
Kan al pnei ha'adama

Here on the earth—not in high clouds—
On this mother earth that is close:
To sorrow in her sadness, exult in her meager
                                                              joy
That knows, so well, how to console.
Not nebulous tomorrow but today: solid,
                                                   warm, mighty,
Today materialized in the hand:
Of this single, short day to drink deep
Here in our own land.

Before night falls—come, oh come all!
A unified stubborn effort, awake
With a thousand arms. Is it impossible to roll
The stone from the mouth of the well?

Translated by Ruth Mintz

Lesbia Harford   *Australia, 1891–1927*

It has taken readers a long time to catch up with the remarkable modernity, in both style and subject matter, of Lesbia Harford's poetry. Years after her early death from a heart condition that had plagued her all her life, Harford's friend, the critic Nettie Palmer, managed to bring out a small collection of her poems (1941). Published in wartime, they attracted little attention and not a great deal more has been accorded the recent *Poems of Lesbia Harford* (1985), edited by Drusilla Modjeska and Marjorie Pizer. Harford's supposedly lost novel, *The Invaluable Mystery,* was published in 1987.

Lesbia Keogh Harford was born in Melbourne and appears to have had a happy and comfortable childhood until her father deserted the family around 1900. Her mother, left to support four children, was determined that they should have a good education. Harford graduated from Melbourne University in Law in 1916 but, an ardent social reformer and feminist, she did not practice her profession. Despite poor health, she worked in clothing factories, and many of her poems deal with the poor conditions of women workers. Along with her poems protesting class and gender roles, Harford wrote many love poems, some to her first lover, a woman, as well as to men.

Only a handful of Harford's poems were published during her lifetime since she did not actively seek publication. "I take my poetry seriously, and am in no hurry to be read," she told one anthologist. She did, however, attempt unsuccessfully to find a publisher for her novel.

Harford was involved in antiwar and anticonscription protests during World War I and later joined the International Workers of the World. In 1918 she moved to Sydney and two years later married Pat Harford, an artist and fellow I.W.W. worker. Within a few years they had separated; she returned to Melbourne and resumed her legal training, but died soon afterward.

Elizabeth Webby

PERIODICITY

My friend declares
Being woman and virgin she
Takes small account of periodicity

And she is right.
Her days are calmly spent
For her sex-function is irrelevant.

But I whose life
Is monthly broke in twain
Must seek some sort of meaning in my pain.

Women, I say,
Are beautiful in change,
Remote, immortal, like the moon they range.

Or call my pain
A skirmish in the whole
Tremendous conflict between body and soul.

Meaning must lie,
Some beauty surely dwell
In the fierce depths and uttermost pits of hell.

Yet still I seek,
Month after month in vain,
Meaning and beauty in recurrent pain.
(June, 1917)

MACHINISTS TALKING

I sit at my machine
Hourlong beside me, Vera, aged nineteen,
Babbles her sweet and innocent tale of sex.

Her boy, she hopes, will prove
Unlike his father in the act of love.
Twelve children are too many for her taste.

She looks sidelong, blue-eyed,
And tells a girlish story of a bride
With the sweet licence of Arabian queens.

Her child, she says, saw light
Minute for minute, nine months from the night
The mother first lay in her lover's arms.

She says a friend of hers
Is a man's mistress who gives jewels and furs
But will not have her soft limbs cased in stays.

I open my small store
And tell of a young delicate girl, a whore,
Stole from her mother many months ago.

Fate made the woman seem
To have a tiger's loveliness, to gleam
Strong and fantastic as a beast of prey.

I sit at my machine.
Hourlong beside me, Vera, aged nineteen,
Babbles her sweet and innocent tale of sex.
(February 20, 1917)

Zora Neale Hurston   US, 1891–1960

Zora Neale Hurston was born in Eatonville, an all-black town in Florida. Her mother died when Hurston was 9 and she was raised by relatives. Unschooled, she supported herself with domestic work, managing to attend, and in 1918 to graduate from, Morgan College in Baltimore. In 1920, Hurston received an associate degree from Howard University, a center of black scholarship and intellectual ferment. At a time when blacks were still subject to blatant discrimination, Hurston won a scholarship to Barnard College in New York City, where she worked with the important anthropologist Franz Boas and became secretary to a well-known writer, Fannie Hurst. Upon her graduation in 1928, Dr. Boas arranged for Hurston to return to the South to collect black folk tales. Hurston had already published short fiction, including a series of thumbnail sketches of characters from her hometown, *The Eatonsville Anthology* (1926); a selection from this appears here. Her trip south resulted in a classic collection of folklore, *Mules and Men* (1935). Unfortunately, this anthropological work has tended to complicate Hurston's identity as a writer, evoking questions about the significance for authorship of racial heritage.

A deathbed scene in her first novel, *Jonah's Gourd Vine* (1934), loosely based on her parent's lives, intimates that Hurston's relationship to folk culture is ambivalent. The protagonist's mother begs her daughter to forgo the traditional death rituals, but when her father and the other adults disregard her protests, the girl cannot fulfill her mother's wishes. Despite this symbolism, Hurston was firmly attached to the vernacular traditions she researched. In fact, amidst an awakening of black art in the Harlem Renaissance of the 1920s, some prominent black critics bitterly attacked, as either inartistic or demeaning, her use of folk culture.

The financial support received by Harlem Renaissance artists from white patrons such as Carl Van Vechten, himself a controversial chronicler of Harlem life, complicated the controversy over Hurston's use of folklore. Hurston, like the poet Langston Hughes, for years accepted help from Mrs. Rufus Osgood Mason, a Park Avenue matron and "connoisseur" of black folk culture. Critics accused Hurston of catering to Mason, "trading" folklore for support. Hurston and other black artists evidently needed financial help; Hurston, as recounted in her auto-biography, *Dust Tracks on A Road* (1942), also needed to break with Mason to write her first novel.

In the masterpiece *Their Eyes Were Watching God* (1937), the story of Janie Woods' search for autonomy within the folk community, Hurston very successfully fused folklore and imaginative writing. Sadly, novelist Richard Wright, who depicted urban black life naturalistically in *Native Son* (1940), accused Hurston of pandering to whites with unthreatening, apolitical images of blacks. Wright's attack was influenced by the political esthetics of the Communist, but other critics followed his lead, and controversy haunted Hurston, exacerbated by her paradoxically conservative political assertions. Despite the claims of conservatism, the second selection here, "Crazy for Democracy" (1945) connects racism in the United States and colonialism in the Third World, notwithstanding shallow proclamations, here and abroad, of democracy.

In the last decades of her life, Hurston's health and finances declined. She and her second husband divorced. In 1948 she was charged in New York with molesting a 10-year-old boy. The district attorney dismissed the case but the charges devastated Hurston. Eventually she returned to Florida, to less writing and low-paying jobs, dying in a county welfare home on January 28, 1960, interred in an unmarked grave.

Amidst the current revival of interest in women's writing, Alice Walker, seeking her own artistic roots, has successfully championed Hurston, reversing the prevailing negative assessment of her work. With *Zora Neale Hurston: A Literary Biography* (1977) by Southern critic Robert Hemenway, a not uncritical advocate, Hurston, "the most significant unread author in America," became the subject of the first full-length literary biography of a black American woman writer. *Spunk* (1985), a recent anthology of works by Hurston, is another result of the new critical attention Hurston has garnered.

Eric Mendelsohn

THE HEAD OF THE NAIL

Daisy Taylor was the town vamp. Not that she was pretty. But sirens were all but non-existent in the town. Perhaps she was forced to it by circumstances. She was quite dark, with little bushy patches of hair squatting over her head. These were held down by shingle-nails often. No one knows whether she did this for artistic effect or for lack of hairpins, but there they were shining in the little patches of hair when she got all dressed for the afternoon and came up to Clarke's store to see if there was any mail for her.

It was seldom that anyone wrote to Daisy, but she knew that the men of the town would be assembled there by five o'clock, and some one could usually be induced to buy her some soda water or peanuts.

Daisy flirted with married men. There

were only two single men in town. Lum Boger, who was engaged to the assistant school-teacher and Hiram Lester, who had been off to school at Tuskegee and wouldn't look at a person like Daisy. In addition to other draw-backs, she was pigeon-toed and her petticoat was always showing so perhaps he was jus-tified. There was nothing else to do except flirt with married men.

This went on for a long time. First one wife and then another complained of her, or drove her from the preserves by threat.

But the affair with Crooms was the most prolonged and serious. He was even known to have bought her a pair of shoes.

Mrs. Laura Crooms was a meek little woman who took all of her troubles crying, and talked a great deal of leaving things in the hands of God.

The affair came to a head one night in orange picking time. Crooms was over at Oneido picking oranges. Many fruit pickers move from one town to the other during the season.

The *town* was collected at the store-postoffice as is customary on Saturday nights. The *town* has had its bath and with its week's pay in pocket fares forth to be merry. The men tell stories and treat the ladies to soda water, peanuts and peppermint candy.

Daisy was trying to get treats, but the porch was cold to her that night.

"Ah don't keer if you don't treat me. What's a dirty lil nickel?" She flung this at Walter Thomas. "The everloving Mister Crooms will gimme anything atall Ah wants."

"You better shet up yo' mouf talking 'bout Albert Crooms. Heah his wife comes right now."

Daisy went akimbo. "Who? Me! Ah don't keer whut Laura Crooms think. If she ain't a heavy hip-ted Mama enough to keep him, she don't need to come crying to me."

She stood making goo-goo eyes as Mrs. Crooms walked upon the porch. Daisy laughed loud, made several references to Albert Crooms, and when she saw the mail-bag come in from Maitland she said, "Ah better go in an' see if Ah ain't got a letter from Oneido."

The more Daisy played the game of get-ting Mrs. Crooms' goat, the better she liked it. She ran in and out of the store laughing until she could scarcely stand. Some of the people present began to talk to Mrs. Crooms—to egg her on to halt Daisy's boasting, but she was for leaving it all in the hands of God. Walter Thom-as kept on after Mrs. Crooms until she stif-fened and resolved to fight. Daisy was inside when she came to this resolve and never dreamed anything of the kind could happen. She had gotten hold of an envelope and came laughing and shouting, "Oh, Ah can't stand to see Oneido lose!"

There was a box of ax-handles on display on the porch, propped up against the door jamb. As Daisy stepped upon the porch, Mrs. Crooms leaned the heavy end of one of those handles heavily upon her head. She staggered from the porch to the ground and the timid Laura, fearful of a counter-attack, struck again and Daisy toppled into the town ditch. There was not enough water in there to do more than muss her up. Every time she tried to rise, down would come that ax-handle again. Laura was fighting a scared fight. With Daisy thoroughly licked, she retired to the store porch and left her fallen enemy in the ditch. But Elijah Moseley, who was some distance down the street when the trouble began, arrived as the victor was withdrawing. He rushed up and picked Daisy out of the mud and began feeling her head.

"Is she hurt much?" Joe Clarke asked from the doorway.

"I don't know," Elijah answered, "I was just looking to see if Laura had been lucky enough to hit one of those nails on the head and drive it in."

Before a week was up, Daisy moved to Orlando. There in a wider sphere, perhaps, her talents as a vamp were appreciated.

CRAZY FOR THIS DEMOCRACY

They tell me this democracy form of government is a wonderful thing. It has freedom, equality, justice, in short, everything! Since 1937 nobody has talked about anything else.

The late Franklin D. Roosevelt sort of redecorated it, and called these United States the boastful name of "The Arsenal of Democracy."

The radio, the newspapers, and the columnists inside the newspapers, have said how lovely it was.

And this talk and praise-giving has got me in the notion to try some of the stuff. All I want to do is to get hold of a sample of the thing, and I declare, I sure will try it. I don't know for myself, but I have been told that it is really wonderful.

Like the late Will Rogers, all I know is what I see by the papers. It seems like now, I do not know geography as well as I ought to, or I would not get the wrong idea about so many things. I heard so much about "global" "world-freedom" and things like that, that I must have gotten mixed up about oceans.

I thought that when they said Atlantic Charter,[1] that meant me and everybody in Africa and Asia and everywhere. But it seems like the Atlantic is an ocean that does not touch anywhere but North America and Europe.

Just the other day, seeing how things were going in Asia, I went out and bought myself an atlas and found out how narrow this Atlantic ocean was. No wonder that those Four Freedoms couldn't get no further than they did! Why, that poor little ocean can't even wash up some things right here in America, let alone places like India, Burma, Indo-China, and the Netherlands East Indies. We need two more whole oceans for that.

Maybe, I need to go out and buy me a dictionary, too. Or perhaps a spelling-book would help me out a lot. Or it could be that I just mistook the words. Maybe I mistook a British pronunciation for a plain American word. Did F.D.R., aristocrat from Groton and Harvard, using the British language say "arse-and-all" of Democracy when I thought he said plain arsenal? Maybe he did, and I have been mistaken all this time. From what is going on, I think that is what he must have said.

That must be what he said, for from what is happening over on the other, unmentioned ocean, we look like the Ass-and-All of Democracy. Our weapons, money, and the blood of millions of our men have been used to carry the English, French and Dutch and lead them back on the millions of unwilling Asiatics. The Ass-and-all-he-has has been very useful.

The Indo-Chinese are fighting the French now in Indo-China to keep the freedom that they have enjoyed for five or six years now. The Indonesians are trying to stay free from the Dutch, and the Burmese and Malayans from the British.

But American soldiers and sailors are fighting along with the French, Dutch and English to rivet these chains back on their former slaves. How can we so admire the fire and determination of Toussaint Louverture to resist the orders of Napoleon to "Rip the gold braids off those Haitian slaves and put them back to work" after four years of freedom,[2] and be indifferent to these Asiatics for the same feelings under the same circumstances?

Have we not noted that not one word has been uttered about the freedom of the Africans? On the contrary, there have been mutterings in undertones about being fair and giving different nations sources of raw materials there? The Ass-and-All of Democracy has shouldered the load of subjugating the dark world completely.

The only Asiatic power able to offer any effective resistance has been double-teamed by the combined powers of the Occident and rendered incapable of offering or encouraging resistance, and likewise removed as an example to the dark people of the world.

The inference is that God has restated the superiority of the West. God always does like that when a thousand white people surround one dark one. Dark people are always "bad" when they do not admit the Divine Plan like that. A certain Javanese man who sticks up for Indonesian Independence is very lowdown by the papers, and suspected of being a Japanese puppet. Wanting the Dutch to go back to Holland and go to work for themselves! The very idea! A very, very bad man, that Javanese.

As for me, I am just as sceptical as this contrary Javanese. I accept this idea of Democracy. I am all for trying it out. It must be a good thing if everybody praises it like that. If our government has been willing to go to war and to sacrifice billions of dollars and millions of men for the idea, I think that I ought to give the thing a trial.

The only thing that keeps me from pitching headlong into the thing is the presence of numerous Jim Crow laws on the statute books of the nation. I am crazy about the idea of this Democracy. I want to see how it feels. Therefore, I am all for the repeal of every Jim Crow law in the nation here and now. Not in another generation or so. The Hurstons have already been waiting eighty years for that. I want it here and now.

And why not? A lot of people in these United States have been saying all this time that things ought to be equal. Numerous instances of inequality have been pointed out, and fought over in the courts and in the newspapers. That seems like a waste of time to me.

The patient has the smallpox. Segregation and things like that are the bumps and blisters on the skin, and not the disease, but evidence and symptoms of the sickness. The doctors around the bedside of the patient are desperately picking bumps. Some assume that the opening of one blister will cure the case. Some strangely assert that a change of climate is all that is needed to kill the virus in the blood!

But why this sentimental over-simplification in diagnosis? Do the doctors not know anything about the widespread occurrence of this disease? It is *not* peculiar to the South.

Canada, once the refuge of escaping slaves, has now its denomination of second-class citizens, and they are the Japanese and other non-Caucasians. The war cannot explain it, because enemy Germans are not put in that second class.

Jim Crow is the rule in South Africa, and is even more extensive than in America. More rigid and grinding. No East Indian may ride first-class in the trains of British-held India. Jim Crow is common in all colonial Africa, Asia and the Netherlands East Indies. There, too, a Javanese male is punished for flirting back at a white female. So why this stupid assumption that "moving North" will do away with social smallpox? Events in northern cities do not bear out this juvenile contention.

So why the waste of good time and energy, and further delay the recovery of the patient by picking him over bump by bump and blister to blister? Why not the shot of serum that will kill the thing in the blood? The bumps are symptoms. The symptoms cannot disappear until the cause is cured.

These Jim Crow laws have been put on the books for a purpose, and that purpose is psychological. It has two edges to the thing. By physical evidence, back seats in trains, back doors of houses, exclusion from certain places and activities, to promote in the mind of the smallest white child the conviction of First by Birth, eternal and irrevocable like the place assigned to the Levites by Moses over the other tribes of the Hebrews [Num 3:23ff.]. Talent, capabilities, nothing has anything to do with the case. Just *first by birth*.

No one of darker skin can ever be considered an equal. Seeing the daily humiliations of the darker people confirms the child in its superiority, so that it comes to feel it [is] the arrangement of God. By the same means, the smallest dark child is to be convinced of its inferiority, so that it is to be convinced that competition is out of the question, and against all nature and God.

All physical and emotional things flow

from this premise. It perpetuates itself. The unnatural exaltation of one ego, and the equally unnatural grinding down of the other. The business of some whites to help pick a bump or so is even part of the pattern. Not a human right, but a concession from the throne has been made. Otherwise why do they not take the attitude of Robert Ingersoll[3] that all of it is wrong? Why the necessity for the little concession? Why not go for the underskin injection? Is it a bargaining with a detail to save the whole intact? It is something to think about.

As for me, I am committed to the hypodermic and the serum. I see no point in the picking of a bump. Others can erupt too easily. That same one can burst out again. Witness the easy scrapping of FEPC [Fair Employment Practices Commission].[4] No, I give my hand, my heart and my head to the total struggle. I am for complete repeal of all Jim Crow Laws in the United States once and for all, and right now. For the benefit of this nation and as a precedent to the world.

I have been made to believe in this democracy thing, and I am all for tasting this democracy out. The flavor must be good. If the Occident is so intent in keeping the taste out of darker mouths that it spends all those billions and expends all those millions of lives, colored ones too, to keep it among themselves, then it must be something good. I crave to sample this gorgeous thing. So I cannot say anything different from repeal of all Jim Crow laws! Not in some future generation, but repeal *now* and forever!!

NOTES

1. An agreement reached August 14, 1941 between President Franklin Delano Roosevelt and the British Prime Minister Winston Churchill to supply U.S. allies with all necessary supplies. This was made possible by Lend-Lease legislation previously approved by Congress; the message to Congress making this request included a statement of the Four Freedoms referred to below. They are freedom of speech and expression, freedom of worship, freedom from want, and freedom from fear.
2. Toussaint L'Ouverture (ca. 1774–1803): Symbol of successful and heroic revolt, this self-educated freed slave joined the black rebellion to liberate the slaves in Haiti in 1791, forced the British to withdraw in 1798, quelled a mulatto uprising in 1799, and resisted a French invasion in 1802, having successfully established an autonomous government. L'Ouverture was treacherously betrayed by the French, and died in a dungeon in France.
3. Hurston may be referring to the famed nineteenth-century agnostic lawyer who preached equality, Robert Green Ingersoll (1833–1899).
4. Created in 1941 by Executive Order, after A. Philip Randolph organized a movement called the March on Washington, which threatened to bring 100,000 blacks to the seat of the national government unless Roosevelt responded to a series of demands including more equal job opportunities for blacks, it had a mixed record of achievement and was allowed to lapse after World War II.

Teresa de la Parra   *Venezuela, 1891–1936*

Teresa de la Parra (originally Ana Teresa Parra-Sanojo, but legally changed) was born to an aristocratic family; Parra was Venezuelan, although she was actually born in Paris and did not see her native country until she was 2 years old. She spent the years between the ages 2 and 10 on a sugar plantation outside of Caracas, the setting of her masterpiece, *Las memorias de Mamá Blanca* (*Mama Blanca's Souvenirs*, 1929) from which the following selection was taken. For the next twelve years of her life, Parra was at a convent school near Valencia in Spain, which was to provide some of the inspiration for her other great novel, *Ifigenia, Diario de una señorita que se fastidiaba* (Iphigenia, Diary of a Young Lady's

Boredom, 1924). Once out of school, she divided her time between Caracas and Europe, particularly Paris where she was friendly with many important writers and diplomats and where she met Francis de Miomandre, who was to translate *Ifigenia* into French. In the last years of her life, Parra lived and traveled with Cuban writer Lydia Cabrera. She died in Spain of tuberculosis at the age of 45.

Both of Teresa de la Parra's books were extremely popular, although their strong themes of social protest were perhaps underemphasized by critics. Actually, *Ifigenia* is one of the first Spanish-American books to explore the oppressive role assigned to upperclass women by society. *Mamá Blanca* describes the patriarchal tradition in turn-of-the-century Venezuela, although Parra's main interest is in the subtleties of the female experience.

NO MORE MILL,
from MAMA BLANCA'S SOUVENIRS
Se Acabó Trapiche,
from Las memorias de Mamá Blanca

We were playing in the orchard one day. Violeta, whose love of adventure impelled her to the most daring feats, one of which was disobedience with its risk of scoldings and punishment, Violeta, as I say, had gone to the dining room and got herself a knife. With it she cut off branches, whittled them to a point, and stuck them in the ground saying:

"These are my cane fields; these are my coffee groves; these are my gardens, all this is my plantation, and nobody is to come near it."

One of the maids who was watching came over and asked her to be good enough to set up her plantation without the use of a knife, for both Mama and Evelyn had absolutely forbidden us to play with fire, inkwells, or knives. Violeta told her to go away and not bother her with repeated nonsense. To wash her hands of all responsibility, the maid went off and told Evelyn. Evelyn arrived at the very moment that Violeta was sharpening a branch. The knife gleamed and flashed in the air. Seeing what was going on with her own eyes, Evelyn said firmly:

"Violeta, give me that knife."

"No," answered Violeta.

Evelyn's authority translated itself from word to deed. Grabbing Violeta by the wrist, she took the knife from her with the other hand. Violeta, surprised and disarmed, gave her an insolent look, and in self-defense and a clear voice:

"———."

Wham! Out came an epithet, unexpected, unqualified, and unthinkable, gender and number in perfect agreement, one single word.

Where had she picked it up? A complete mystery. That was one of Violeta's specialties, knowing things nobody else knew, without knowing herself where she had learned it. In spite of the fact that the word was new, all the rest of us instantly grasped the fact that the word suited Evelyn like an ugly hat, that is to say, it fitted her without becoming her. When the two maids who were present heard the term whose meaning admitted of no doubt, they began to shriek with laughter. With their mirth the appellation took on heightened proportions and enveloped Evelyn's person more closely. Outraged more by the laughter than by the unexpected word, Evelyn was speechless for a moment. Then she inquired:

"Where did you learn that word, Violeta, which has made your mouth dirty, black as coal? Where did you learn it?"

Violeta rubbed her hand over her mouth to see if it was really dirty, but she did not deign to answer. As Evelyn had to hit upon some condign punishment, without waiting for the culprit's reply she suddenly arrived at this ominous conclusion:

"You learned it at the mill! All right, there'll be no more mill, now or ever."

"No more mill," and all because of Violeta and the two maids! It was one of those infamous, arbitrary decisions that fall upon the innocent because of the violence of those in power or the crimes of a group. And without further explanation, the law went into effect as of that moment.

"No more mill!" What unprecedented punishment! What a tragedy!

To our rustic souls the mill was club, theater, city. There was no pleasure comparable to the hour we spent at the stream and in the mill. It seemed heaven to us, and we were right, it was. Everything about it pleased sight, smell, taste, ear. Just as the syrup boiled in the great kettles, so life in the vicinity of the mill bubbled frank and hearty. All the elements and all the colors met and came together there: water, fire, sun, all walked untrammeled and in harmony to the rhythm set by the great meek, majestic wheel of the mill. None of that ugly, inexplicable, gloomy boredom of factories moved by steam or electricity. No. There was nothing mysterious or hidden in the mill. Everything was in plain view. Everyone knew why things happened and the door stood open to anyone who wanted to come in, the elements, people, animals.

First in importance, the commander-in-chief, the ruling spirit of the mill, was the water. From on high it came piped in from the dam, and flung itself upon the great wheel singing as it went with its chorus of streams and drops. The slow-turning wheel accompa-nied it with the rosary of its buckets, with intervals of empty space against a background of ferns and moss. To the turning of the wheel three masses moved: the cane oozing juice as it was crushed; the hands of the feeders moving among the canes; and the hands of the bagasse loaders who carried away the poor dead remains of the cane on stretchers of leather to spread it in the sun. There under the sun the crushed corpses underwent a resurrection and, piled into heaps, became the brides of fire.

In the vast, generous mill there were almost no walls or doors. Nothing was shut in. Everybody was welcome. The sun came in, the air, the rain, legions of golden, buzzing wasps in search of sweets. The slow ox-teams came in with the broad carts piled high with tightly packed cane which the hands unloaded quickly and left piled on the ground behind the carts. And in search of sweets, like the wasps, came the children of the workers with a pan in their hands, asking: "Mama wants to know if you will be good enough to give me some scrapings or a piece of broken sugar loaf for *guarapo* tonight." Like the wasps, they were given their scrapings or piece of broken sugar loaf, for nobody was turned away.

In a swarm, with Evelyn and the maids behind, buzzing and flying, like the wasps, like the workers' children, between the ox-teams, the piles of cane, and the bagasse litters, came the girls in search of sweets, interfering with the work and getting in everyone's way.

The first thing we did was to rush to stick a foot into the hardened, grayish foam the sugar cane formed as it went through a trough toward the boiling room. After imprinting on the foam the greatest possible number of feet, the next thing was to call out to Vicente Cochocho, if he happened to be present, and if not, to the group of loaders:

"When are you going to stop grinding? Hurry up, it's time now. Time for lunch. Time for lunch!"

To "stop the grinding" or "lunch" was to

halt the wheel and the cylinders and release the water through a cement conduit which emptied into a pool where, among vines, bamboo tufts, and a spreading *huisache*, we had our daily bath in the sunshine, to the roaring of the stream, amidst the whirlpools it set up, and the perfume the water released from the earth and the mossy stones as it touched them.

The big mill wheel and the noise of the water drowned out our voices. But by our gestures and moving lips the loaders knew what we wanted, and they limited themselves to answering by signs that it was not time to turn off the mill yet, and to round out their explanation they pointed out to us the pile of cane still to be ground.

While waiting for the water, we each ran our separate ways to one of the hands asking him to peel us a piece of cane. The peon had to stop what he was doing, select a cane, peel it with his machete, slice it into pieces, and each little girl went off with her sugar cane, sucking it and dribbling juice on herself. Up and down the mill they went, from one end to the other, and the more questions, the better.

I don't know about my sisters, but, for myself, I can assure you that there in the mill, awaiting the moment for the water to be released, sucking stalks of cane with hands sticky and rivulets of juice running down my neck and arms, I spent the pleasantest hours of my life.

People did not gather at the mill to amuse themselves; that was what made it so pleasant and agreeable. To watch what was going on one did not have to take a seat as in the theater and sit motionless without talking for hours, with a pair of opera glasses in hand, one's leg gone to sleep, watching gestures and listening to banalities against a background of painted cloth and boards. At the mill it was not like a dance, where one whirls solemnly on teetering heels in time to the music, nor was it necessary to mouth, with a sandwich in one hand and a glass of champagne in the other, all those commonplaces which most of our interlocutors, far

more eloquent than we, affirm with such vehemence and assurance brilliantly, emphatically.

What went on at the mill, so varied, so full of life and color, did not chain one's attention, nor tyrannize over one's movements. While watching the skimming cauldron, the testing of the syrup, the molasses flowing through the pipes, the stirring of the thickening sugar, the filling of the molds, one could move freely from side to side like a dancer, and at the same time suck cane, eat molasses candy, and think about anything one liked.

At the mill it was possible to fire a dozen questions at the sugar-tester, and walk off before he had a chance to answer, and ask the same questions of the skimmer of the first cauldron, without bothering to ask either of them first, "May I ask you something, sir?" At the mill solid body or winged spirit could go whither it listed, like the wasps, lighting here, there, when and where it pleased. Freedom of movement and freedom of thought—are not these two of the indispensable elements of happiness? Not to mention that delicious smell that kettles and pans gave off. Nor the beautiful golden hue of high grade brown sugar of fine quality cane. Or the drab color of the cheap variety from skimmings or poor cane. And the melodious cry of the tester calling out through a grating, like the Angelus in the afternoon:

"Fiiire!"

And the way everyone took his ease. Nobody in the boiling room, or the grinding room, or in the bagasse shed rushed about with brusque movements denoting activity, graceless and overbearing, as though shouting: "I am the big noise here; I am the one who makes the mare go, hurry up, look at me, look what I can do." None of that. Everything moved at a gentle pace in the friendly mill. Nobody was pretending to set the world on fire. The long process of sugar boiling, like the work of nature rather than industry, seemed to accomplish itself, taking all the time it needed; little by little, little by little. The thirty or forty mill hands took part in the sugar making as though it were a birth: a little help, lots of patience, talk, and nothing more.

In a word, the mill was simple, good well-being. And Violeta had wiped it all out with a single word. Violeta was strong because she was enterprising and aggressive. Her words, as you have seen, like those of certain congressmen and senators, changed the calm course of life. Peaceful multitudes then had to suffer the consequences.

Now, with the severe sanction in force, before we could go to bathe we had to stay up the hill near the dam, where the mill wheel was located. To catch a glimpse of our beloved mill we had to peep over the wall. With a great effort, standing tiptoe on a stone, we could manage to get eyes and nose over it, but rarely our mouths. There, as best we could, we proferred our daily prayer:

"When are you going to stop grinding? It's time for lunch. Go on, go on. It's time now."

A prayer that was swallowed up in the dark night of unnoticed things. Nobody paid any attention to us, inasmuch as lost up there, between the wall and the noise of the water, we could neither be seen nor heard.

In justice I must mention one thing. Although the prohibition was strictly enforced, as I have said, occasionally Evelyn gathered us together after our bath, and announced:

"Today, as you've all been good girls, you can come with me to the mill."

Our shrieks of delight were deafening, and our headlong flight wild. When all is said and done I believe that if Violeta had never said that word with its disastrous results the memory of the mill would undoubtedly have vanished amidst the myriad places, persons, scenes which lie buried under the dust of my memory as in a graveyard. Violeta provoked Evelyn's stern reprisal, and Evelyn's sternness saved the mill from oblivion. The mill gleams, the mill scintillates among my recollections.

Excellent Evelyn. Your good influence filled our childhood with joys and saved it from the black, the cruel boredom which afflicts the soul of those children who have everything, pitiful victims of satiety, frail buds blasted by disillusion. By forbidding us things and places, Evelyn imbued them with life. Breathing like God upon the dust, she gave it a soul, the soul which animates anything worth loving.

If my childhood was happy, if my childhood comes back to me, smiles upon me throughout the years, it is because it transpired in the arms of nature, and because, though channeled, it flowed as freely as a river between its banks. My sisters and I were never shut up within four walls, sated with candy, dolls, wagons, rocking horses, all those gloomy toys which, like the cares of adult life, bow down the shoulders of childhood. When one of us was given a doll, we fondled it as long as the novelty lasted. In two hours the sight of those staring eyes, those rigid legs and arms no longer interested us, and away with the dead thing! We never touched it again, and we were right.

We made our favorite toys ourselves out under the trees of leaves, stones, water, green fruit, mud, old bottles, and empty tin cans. Like artists, we were possessed by the divine fire of creation, and like poets, we discovered secret affinities and mysterious relations between the most diverse objects. For example, we would take an old can, and with a nail or stone make a hole in it into which we fitted a stick as a tongue, attaching a pair of corncobs to serve as oxen, with two curved thorns stuck into each cob for horns, and with a reed for a goad. Our creation finished, we imitated the voice of the ox-drivers, shouting at the stubborn corncobs:

"Gee, ox! Back, Swallow! Get over, Blaze!"

With the old can, the two cobs, and the four thorns we had made an ox-cart with its team, and also a poem.

The rest of my life was to transpire under the same kindly and stern regime as my early childhood. Life imitated Evelyn; it gave me to taste of all its pleasant things, but sparingly, frugally, so that surfeit never dulled the edge of desire. The passing of the indifferent years did not carry off treasures of beauty, of love, or honors. I do not misprize my own bygone years, nor those which have not yet passed for others. Time, as it laid its lips upon my hair, has tenderly crowned me with the white snow of my own name, and has never left the teeth-marks of bitterness in my soul. For all my seventy-five years, my heart still leaps up at the prospect of an automobile ride into the country for a picnic under the mountain sunshine, and my hands still tremble with excitement and impatience as they undo the knots of ribbon that adorn the surprise of a present.

Translated by Harriet de Onís

Kate Roberts

UK(Wales), 1891–1985

Kate Roberts, considered the most important twentieth-century Welsh prose stylist, was born in the exclusively Welsh-speaking slate quarrying town of Rhosgadfan, near Caernarfon. She studied literary Welsh at the University College of North Wales in Bangor with two important scholars of Welsh, John Morris Jones and Ifor Williams.

Roberts taught school for thirteen years until she and her new husband, Morris Williams, bought the publishing house *Gwasg Gee* that put out the powerful radical weekly newspaper *Baner Ac Amserau Cymru* (The Banner and Times of Wales), popularly called *Y Faner*, which did much to influence political and cultural life in Wales. Roberts wrote for *Y Faner* on many different subjects, including politics and literature. Extremely committed to Welsh nationalism, she was a member of the Nationalist Party from its beginning, and incorporated her politics into both her journalism and her fiction.

Roberts began writing after the First World War as therapy, she said, for her family's losses (one brother was killed, another injured). Her early works, such as *Traed Mewn Cyffion* (*Feet in Chains*, 1936), depicts the suffering of the Welsh working class. Her later books, after her husband's death in 1946, *Stryd y Glep* (Gossip, 1949) deal with women and the elderly trying to cope with the pain and suffering of modern existence. Many of her works focus on the female experience as the center of domestic life.

Very few of Roberts' many works have been translated into English. The following story is from an English-language collection of some of her stories, *A Summer's Day and Other Stories* (1946); it was introduced by the English writer Storm Jameson.

FOLDED HANDS

"Hello there!" The cry resounded through the house. Dafydd Gruffydd waking up to go to work in the quarry, six o'clock in the morning, on his seventieth birthday.

As soon as he answered her call, his wife Beti went to the kitchen and began cutting bread and butter for his food tin. Eight slices, the length of the loaf, and as she pressed them into the tin, her ring sank into the bread. By the time she had put tea and sugar into the old mustard tin, he was washing in the back kitchen, the water spluttering away from his mouth.

Breakfast over, he turned his chair to the fire, threw one leg over its arm and reached out for his pipe. Then he got up and looked out at the weather.

"Going to rain today?" he asked.

"No, I don't think so," she replied. "But you'd better take your coat."

He took it from behind the back kitchen door, picked up his two tins and pushed them into the inside pockets of his linen jacket. Beti heard the click of the gate and the voice of his partner, Twm, asking, "How's the health with you today, Dafydd?" Then the sound of the two men passing the side of the house, and others following them, quarrymen's voices pitched low in the morning, so much lower than in the evening.

And that was how Dafydd Gruffydd went to work each day. For thirty-two years he and his partner had met at the gate at half past six, without a break. But this was the first time Beti had realized it: today, she saw and heard everything as if it were new. It struck her that now, having reached the age of seventy, he would have to leave the quarry and live on his pension, and that all he had done on this and on every other morning for so many years would come to an end. How wise the Government must be, how well versed in the Scriptures, to pension a man at seventy when it was time for him to die.

She pondered thus awhile and then went to fetch the cows that were grazing upon the common. She waited until she reached the top of the fields before calling to them, waited every morning, as if she feared to wake the people in the houses, blinds down in most of them, down for the dead it might be. Quietly she called the cattle, "Trw bach, trw bach," quietly enough to wake no one, and the two cows lifted their heads together as on the word of command and moved slowly towards the byre,[1] their udders swaying, teats splayed out, a bridle of slaver bright against the sheen of their dark coats.

"Near up, lass!" The chain clicked round the neck as each cow licked the Indian corn from her bucket and rattled the handle. The milk came blue and thin at first, a thin sound in the pail. Then free and rich and heavy. The cow lifted her head and breathed heavily, dozed and twitched in her sleep, but Beti kept on milking. And kept on thinking—something she had not done for many years, for life was too full for much thought. Mostly a matter of sleeping tonight to wake up tomorrow, and work to fill the time between waking and sleeping. Always the same kind of work, like lessons in a school timetable, the one and the many each day of the week. She had lived long enough to see the odd days of holiday relapse into an item in her timetable. If the quarry were working on Ascension Day, the day Dafydd Gruffydd's club walked, the even pattern of her life would have been broken. Into the same uniformity fell the day on which she took the children to the seaside each year. If you had asked her which Saturday they went, she could not have told you with any certainty. But she knew that it was always the same Saturday in July, that something of the quality of that day could be apprehended beforehand, so that when it came, neither she nor the children had any doubt that this was the day for the seaside.

Of course there were times when marriage

and death broke into this uniformity—the day her daughter Meri died, a little girl of four. God in heaven! The bitter pain and hard. She thought then that she could never live without her, but even in her own life she had proved the truth of the old saying that the grave is the home of the forgotten. Today it called for an effort of memory even to remember the birth of her child. She had kept a lock of her hair in a drawer upstairs, and a white petticoat embroidered at the edge, but now the hair was faded and lackluster, like a doll's hair, and the petticoat was yellow with age.

Then the children got married, emptying for a while the house and the family purse, but she quickly grew accustomed to that, and now she and Dafydd had lived alone for so many years that she thought nothing could ever change their way of life. She had always been a stay-at-home. There was little room in life for anything but housework, milking, and butter-making. Her house was her world, and if her interest in anything outside it was ever stirred, it was by something in a book or the newspaper. She read one or two books—*The Maid of Eithinfynydd* was one—with intense delight, and her favorite newspaper was the *Weekly Echo*. And if there was no romance in her own life, the columns of the *Echo* showed that there was plenty in the lives of others. But she would not go out of her way to find romance. Now and then she went to chapel, and occasionally to town. On her own testimony, she had never been to a Quarterly preaching meeting, an eis-teddfod[2] or a circus: she always named them in that order, and they all meant much the same to her. She had never been to the quarry, and had not the faintest idea of the conditions in which her husband worked. His food tin, his working clothes, and his money thick with slate dust—they were the closest links between her and the quarry. Today, many such thoughts filled her mind.

She took the milk pails out and sent the cows into the field, and after sieving the milk she began to churn. She did not usually churn on a Saturday, but the cows were yielding their best and there would be too much milk to keep until Monday. She shut her eyes as she churned, and with each turn of the handle her head followed the drop of her arm. How hot the day was: the butter was sure to lie like scum on top of the milk, not in clots, as in winter. And so it was, all set and sticking to the dish. In winter she could catch the butter on the back of the "thin" saucer, hard enough to throw at you: today it lay on the dish like a pancake. But she was not to be defeated by soft butter on a warm day—she kept squeezing it together and patting it and running ridges into it with the thin saucer while the water dropped out and over the table into the pail below.

By the time Dayfdd Gruffydd came home midday, there were five pounds of butter on the round slate slab, the churn was drying in the sun, and the house all clean. After his dinner of new potatoes and buttermilk, he set out to cut the thorns in the fields—his Satur-day afternoon task. His evenings he gave to working about the farm: he was never idle. In one sense, his world was as small as his wife's, widened only by his contacts in the quarry.

Today, for the first time, she suggested that he should go to bed after dinner, and he looked at her as if he thought she was taking leave of her senses.

"Indeed you'd better go," she insisted. "Here you are, seventy years old today, and I can't ever remember seeing you with folded hands."

"I must go and cut those thorns while it's dry," he replied.

"Wet or fine, if you were dead you'd have to let them be."

She knew it was no use saying any more, but she had succeeded in expressing a thought that had troubled her mind all morning.

After washing up, she went to fetch water from the spring in the top field. The day was fine, and on her way back she sat in the field where he was working. The aftermath was fresh and green, the rasp of the cows as they grazed pleasant to the ear. Not so the sound of her husband's billhook, the twigs flying off like a jack-in-the-box, falling spread-armed to die in the ditch.

Her eyes dwelt upon him: she had not thought so much about him since the days before they were married. Then, he was one man in a thousand, but living with him had reduced him to something very much like the rest of the thousand. She had too much sense to deceive herself into believing that romantic love lasted long after the wedding. There he stood in his working clothes, an old hat on his head, its color lost in slate dust, a sweat stain on the ribbon in front. A strip of the sleeve of his jacket hung like a streamer, swaying as his arm moved, reminding her that she must mend his clean clothes before going to bed. A wave of pity engulfed her. There was a time when he was handsome. Long ago, the hat he wore for the May Day Fair was black, much blacker than this one, and the crease in his pepper-and-salt trousers straighter than the ribs in his corduroys today. And although he worked most

Saturday afternoons helping his father, it was a straighter frame that carried his clothes in those days. Today he looked so much older, older even than yesterday, she thought. She had grown so used to him that this had not occurred to her before.

Looking back over the years, she could see in his life nothing but work, work, and but little rest. If all that work were piled together into one heap, it would surely reach to the sky, a monument of monotony. And he the author of it all, Dafydd Gruffydd, standing there today, cutting thorns. She watched him swinging the billhook up and down, a faint sigh echoing each stroke, and murmured to herself, "Soon, it's in that graveyard he'll lie, his hands folded for all time."

Translated by Wyn Griffith

NOTES

1. A cowshed.
2. A festival of Welsh culture.

Nelly (Leonie) Sachs   *Germany/Sweden, 1891–1970*

Nelly Sachs, recognized as one of the most powerful writers of what has come to be known as "holocaust literature," was born in Berlin on December 10, 1891, an only child in a wealthy Jewish family. Poor health caused her to be educated mainly at home by private tutors. In 1907 she began a correspondence with the Swedish author Selma Lagerlöf that not only led to Sachs' early attempts at poetry but was also instrumental years later when Lagerlöf assisted Sachs in fleeing from Nazi Germany to Sweden with her mother on May 16, 1940—the virtual evening of their threatened deportation to a concentration camp. Sachs lived the rest of her life in Stockholm, interrupting her stay there in 1960 for a trip to Zürich and Paris. On her return to Sweden, she suffered a severe mental breakdown and required frequent treatment. She died in Stockholm on May 12, 1970, and was buried in the Jewish cemetery there.

Recognition of Sachs' contribution to the memory of her people has come in several forms. The city of Berlin named her an honorary citizen in 1967; the Kungliga Library in Stockholm established a Nelly Sachs Room in 1971; she was awarded numerous literary prizes, including the Nobel Prize for Literature (together with Schmu'el Josef Agnon) in 1966. Her poems have been widely translated and may be seen in their entirety as a eulogy to the Jews. They exemplify her lifelong attempt to "say the unsayable," and testify to the power of language to stave off madness and to erect verbal monuments as a means of fighting against the "ideology of forgetting."

Sach's writing career is generally divided into three phases. Her first two volumes of poetry, *In den Wohnungen des Todes* (*In the Habitations of Death*, 1947), and *Sternverdunkelung* (*Eclipse of the Stars*, 1949), deal directly with the horrors of Auschwitz and thematize her forced exile. Her use of themes, motifs, and imagery betray the strong influence of the Old Testament in this early phase. The first two selections here are taken from those two volumes, respectively. Sachs' style changes noticeably around 1955 after intensive study of the Cabala. *Und niemand weiß weiter* (*And No One Knows How To Go On*, 1957) is the first volume of her second phase, followed in 1959 by *Flucht und Verwandlung* (*Flight and Metamorphosis*), in which she concentrates ever more heavily on a metaphysical idea of transformation, often symbolized by the butterfly as seen in the third of the selections. Her late poetry, finally, is thought to begin with the publication of *Noch feiert Tod das Leben* (*Death Still Celebrates Life*, 1961). She no longer relies so heavily on traditional sources, but reveals instead a tendency to mysticism: symbols no longer name the concrete or refer to things commonly recognized, but stand for the unspeakable that exists only in a private realm.

Marilyn Sibley Fries

BUTTERFLY
Schmetterling

What lovely aftermath
is painted in your dust.
You were led through the flaming
core of earth,
through its stony shell,
webs of farewell in the transient measure.

Butterfly
blessed night of all beings!
The weights of life and death
sink down with your wings
on the rose
which withers with the light ripening
                                    homewards.

What lovely aftermath
is painted in your dust.
What royal sign
in the secret of the air.

Translated by Ruth and Matthew Mead

FLEEING
In der Flucht

Fleeing,
what a great reception
on the way—
Wrapped
in the wind's shawl
feet in the prayer of sand
which can never say amen
compelled
from fin to wing
and further—

The sick butterfly
will soon learn again of the sea—
This stone
with the fly's inscription
gave itself into my hand—

I hold instead of a homeland
the metamorphoses of the world—

Translated by Ruth and Matthew Mead

O THE CHIMNEYS
O die Schornsteine

> And though after my skin worms destroy this
> body, yet in my flesh shall I see God.—Job, 19:26

O the chimneys
On the ingeniously devised habitations of
                        death
When Israel's body drifted as smoke
Through the air—
Was welcomed by a star, a chimney sweep,
A star that turned black
Or was it a ray of sun?

O the chimneys!
Freedomway for Jeremiah and Job's dust—
Who devised you and laid stone upon stone
The road for refugees of smoke?

O the habitations of death,
Invitingly appointed
For the host who used to be a guest—
O you fingers
Laying the threshold
Like a knife between life and death—

O you chimneys,
O you fingers
And Israel's body as smoke through the air!

Translated by Michael Roloff

Irene Lisboa   *Portugal, 1892–1958*

Irene Lisboa was a poet and prose writer of considerable talent. Yet it is only in recent years that her work has begun to receive recognition. She was the illegitimate daughter of an elderly man and a young peasant woman whom he seduced and who in turn abandoned him and their young daughter in favor of another lover. The young Irene found herself in outcast la her home, unwanted by the series of women who took her mother's place. After a primary education in a convent, she was sent off to Lisbon at the age of 15. She completed a course in primary education and continued her studies of pedagogy on a scholarship in Switzerland, Belgium and France before returning to Lisbon to teach and to pursue a solitary life in the city.

Irene Lisboa's work falls into two major categories: studies on pedagogical subjects published under the pseudonym of Manuel Soares until 1942 and after that under her own name; books of poetry and prose, again published under a male pseudonym (João Falco) until 1942 and, subsequently, under her own name. The books on pedagogy reveal her as an innovative thinker on that subject in a vein similar to that of Montessori,* whom she admired. So innovative was she that she was removed from her teaching post for her radical positions. Her purely literary works were no more successful than her pedagogical writings in her day, but she was not deterred by apparent failure. She produced seventeen books of prose and poetry between 1926 and the end of her life, in addition to the half dozen works on pedagogy. All of the former speak of the plight of an educated woman entrapped in a traditional environment, emotionally deprived and alone. They range from sensitive meditations on her own life and trials to vivid and perceptive observations of the world around her: the shopkeepers, construction workers, and serving-women who peopled the streets of Lisbon and provided some relief from her solitude. There are books of poetry and collections of vignettes and short stories that incorporate into her own clear, precise idiom the popular language of the street. From among the many titles, one could single out *Solidão* (Solitude, 1939), *Começa Uma Vida* (A Life Begins, 1940), and *Solidão II* (Solitude II) published posthumously in 1966. The following story is from *O Pouco e o Muito. Crônica Urbana* (A Little and A lot/Urban Tales, 1956).

The present reputation of Irene Lisboa began to emerge several years after her death and has grown to the point where her work is being reedited. She has received public recognition of another kind as well: a street has been named after her in Lisbon and, in Oporto, a school.

Alice Clemente

NOTE

* Maria Montessori (1870–1952). Italian educator and doctor, known for her innovative system of education for preschool children.

LAURINDA

Where Laurinda came from, now that I really couldn't say, she just turned up....As for her sojourn with me, that too was of "no" great consequence. Her ways, her manners, the stories she told, however, might indeed prove interesting. But no sooner do I begin to write, then, you know what, I feel like stopping....How come? Because of the diverse faces subsumed within that single Laurinda. What a woman! Of her one could well say that she is, or at least encompasses, all of the known and all of the unknown within her narrow bounds. Always gnawed at by a thousand and one worries, crude, random, scattered, she defines herself by and simultaneously confounds herself with the rest of her sort. She is fickle, simple, and coarse to perfection.

For a while, when she first comes to a house, Laurinda is ready to serve, almost cheerful, nicely composed and punctual, yes, indeed; but this doesn't last long, it has to change, and Laurinda goes back to odd jobs: she runs errands, first for one, then for another, empties out boxes, sells rags and old bottles, does various chores, and, at last, she vanishes away, her whereabouts unknown.

She is not a woman who talks much, quite the contrary. Once she gains confidence in her new house, she even has fits of ill humor, usually provoked by her own life outside. She gets grouchy and mutters curses, looking askance, with those tiny little eyes of hers half shut and her nose, sharpened to a point, drooping down.

I wish I could paint a true portrait of Laurinda! To project her onto this screen of the written word without serious disfigurements, just as I remember her and still see her. But it will be difficult for me. Laurinda, just like each of us, is one and many....I began to know her better after she abandoned my house. Inside, she seemed to me quite ordinary. She cleaned and washed like anyone else, spoke little, as I've already said, bought many things that suited her taste from street vendors coming to the door of the glassed-in balcony, bras, aprons...she would tell me one story or another about Lourinhã, where she comes from, or about a sister who lives here and takes care of her daughter (who she claims to have had by a waiter), but then she made it vaguely clear that she was going to go home, and finally she disappeared, leaving behind a banana-debt to a local grocer.

It was thanks to Laurinda that I came to see that those poor vendors, going from street to street, from door to door: *cheap! real cheap!* loaded down with showy, badly made things, always do good business. Lovely, sparkling blouses, held together by a couple of stitches and displayed on little hangers, can be as tempting as fox furs and costly *manteaux*.[1] If Laurinda were to pass through the Chiado, she wouldn't even notice what was displayed in the shopwindows, she wasn't used to all that, it didn't interest her; but with the street vendors she would lose herself utterly.

And yet, no matter how much Laurinda bought or got hold of, no matter how much they gave her, no matter how much she varied her style, she never managed to look like the other women. Nothing kept its blossom on that body, spots and stains were always in hot pursuit. Even so, she had her vanities: she would dress in something new or even something second hand (she also bought a lot of such stuff) and liked to be stared at.

Before I came to know her, Laurinda was with a sidewalk cobbler, also for a short time. According to her, the little guy was a tight-fisted and cocksure booby, coming on to anything in a skirt. So she upped and left him, hit the road, why not?

Along the staircase where he had his little shop, other rumors ran—that the two would fight and she was a sloven. However, it was clear that the little guy exploited women. He would share with them his cubicle and his bed, true enough, but when it came to food...let them earn it themselves, if they wanted any. For lunch, he'd put a few potatoes and a slice of codfish on the counter, and as for them, if they wanted to join him, they'd have to put up their equal share. When the potatoes finished cooking, he would count them.

After they separated, and even after he had taken another woman—they were always there, so many of them, at his door: Senhor José, my shoes, aren't my shoes ready yet, Senhor José, and my heels?—Laurinda still stayed on there to wash the landing. In fact,

the whole building was hers. Sometimes she would whitewash the kitchen on the third floor, sometimes run errands for the fourth floor, or else mop up two or three flights of stairs. Laurinda would wash down the entrance way, the benches, and the small counter at the shoemaker's, but the latter's new girl friend seemed not to like it. And she kept her eye on her. Then one day she saw her rival enter the man's cubicle and very quickly, throughout the neighborhood, she spread the word, whether true or not, that the two of them once again had an understanding. One even heard that she gave, or promised to give, Laurinda a real licking. What's for sure is that the latter kept out of sight for a while. A short while that passed quickly, with Laurinda re-appearing, as usual, for her customers in the building. It was through them, in fact, that I went on following her life.

Laurinda was not a woman to harbor grudges, much less dwell on doubts. When there were no houses to do, she would sell fish, and in the fig season she would naturally sell figs. As she had neither a wicker basket nor a license, she couldn't cry out her wares (she didn't even have the voice, she admitted), and so she carried the fish around in a small basket over her arm. She would sell them door-to-door to women she knew, keeping muddled accounts with all of them: don't pay now, forget it, take some, here, take, take, here's something for the cat...nothing worth arguing about, why get mad about such a little thing....One could see that Laurinda was quite liberal, when she felt like it. In the end, if sales gave her barely enough to pay them off at the Riverfront, there would at least be some fish left over for her to eat, some little mackerel, some little hake or other....

Gone were the days when she also did the rounds of the market fairs.

Ah, the markets! What a pity Laurinda expressed herself so badly! She was not very explicit, and in fact, at times she was even distrustful. What was it she sold? Well, then, what should she be selling? Fruit, sweet bread, lupine beans, periwinkles...and pumpkin seeds, or whatever. All the people who came out to these fairs would pass and buy things. She also would fry fish in the midway stalls. Hey folks, right this way! She had the knack. Wherever she'd set up, everything would go. Fried fish and a green salad...the country bumpkins loved it and the Lisbon locals loved it even more. She would also work selling sodas and snacks on Sundays at the beach, she would!

She seemed a slave to work, this woman, but she was nothing more than an adventuress, poor thing, and second rate, at that. She would chase whatever destiny, run after anything or anyone. She would tell lies just like that, beg with indifference, accept everything that others scorned. And so she went on, always enmeshed deep in the bowels of some business or other. She had even worked in the theater, dressing chorus girls: there she was, always ready with needle in hand, on her knees in front of them ...no, there was no time to lose...hurry-scurry! Helter-skelter!

But despite being tossed from here to there, erratic, backsliding, appearing and disappearing, Laurinda never was a bore. Those who shook her off today rehired her tomorrow. Did one have to do a house-cleaning or to send for something at the station? Who could one call? Laurinda! Anyone would know her whereabouts.

One such necessity brought her again to my house, useful as no one else, she with her barrage of "oh, dearies!" At that time she had a new preoccupation, one which she didn't hide.

For three years now Laurinda had had a real man, and taking care of him, as well as keeping an eye on him, were her great labors. He, too, was a jack-of-all-trades; he sold lottery tickets, had been a waiter in cafés, a street crier with various wares...had fought bulls in the Algés Ring and out in the provinces, had been a "spear-carrier" in the theater...in one of the last reviews at the Parque Mayer, it was

none other than he who had crossed the stage with an empty box on his back! He was colored, but those who knew them both thought that Laurinda didn't deserve him. To such an extent that she became quite submissive: she took care of his food and his clothes and kept a sharp eye on him....

Marques, that was his family name, went back to her hometown with her one time, and there he was held in high regard. But now and then he was offered contracts elsewhere, and Laurinda would remain behind on tenterhooks. Might he not leave her? So she would mount strategies to attract him anew: she would invent illnesses, declare herself pregnant.

Once, when Marques had gone north and had stayed there beyond his limit, Laurinda truly thought herself abandoned. And as she knew that he would have liked to have a son, she sent messages to him by whomever, announcing her pregnancy. She told me all this afterwards.

"How did you work it out, in the end?" I asked her.

"Well, just like a customer of mine, I pretended to have a miscarriage; it's the easiest thing in the world. Go out and buy a piece of cow liver, you know, then tear it to shreds; they don't notice a thing, they fall for it...."

Her Marques was now filled with the idea of taking sail, it was an obsession, no one could get it out of his head! He had already gone to hand in his name and had even sent away for his birth certificate.

However, Laurinda had something of her own in mind. She wanted to get married before his departure. Just some added security, right?

"But will he go for it?" someone asked her.

She bridled and, almost hissing, shot back: "Why shouldn't he? Does he lose by it? We live and we die!"

Laurinda threw herself into calculations: "nowadays they have these marriages arranged by benefactresses, that's just the kind that suits me; but what about catechism,[2] catechism,

catechism? The worst of all is catechism, where am I going to find the brains and the time to learn catechism. For that my Marques has got the better head."

Whoever heard her, with that unrestrained vulgarity of speech flowing to right and to left, interrupted from time to time by bursts of laughter, might well have supposed her seriously interested. But no, Laurinda imagined herself getting married and her man sailing off just for a lark, just like that. Her calculations meant about as much to her as a handful of rags. She no longer even remembered that she might lose her Marques. That's where it all had driven her.

"This is all crazy!" she would confess at times, modestly, "but there are those who say it's worth it...."

One day, with smiles and an air of delicacy, she told me how their courtship had begun. How they had met on the street, right there on the Travessa de Santo Domingos, how he had fallen in beside her, the gruff answers she gave him, the handkerchief he lent her, the conversations they later had in the public garden, seated together (she the whole time eluding and ensnaring him: she was going to leave, she was going to leave, and she did), the letter that he wrote her to her hometown, which, by the way, astonished everyone....

Credulous, I listened on.

The life of Marques, which also had its particularities, seemed to her equally worth the telling. And thus it was that Laurinda, knife in hand, beside the sink, scaling and washing a piece of fish for dinner, began to unfold it before me, there between truths and lies.

Marques was from the Cape Verde Islands. He had been brought here by a family from the islands when he was still little and had never seen his mother again. Here he had come and here he had stayed. One day his boss said to him, he was already full grown at the time: "Wait here!" They were in front of a movie house. It was something he never forgot, Marques! Wait here, the boss told him, but

some men were passing by, men with signboards on their backs, advertisements for the theaters, and, with a snap decision, he fell in behind them. He never saw his boss again, nor did his boss see him again. Just one of those things! He lived for a few days from hand to mouth...a crust here, a few pennies there...until a guy in Aterro, a guy with an eating-house, took him up. And he became a good waiter, but they never paid him his salary. And now he'd gone to see if the boss's son, now that the boss had died, would pay him some back wages. That would suit her fine, with him sailing off...but...oh, well!

"You may become a widow yet," I told her, half seriously, at the end of that endless harangue.

She laughed, but not really knowing at what, just to laugh.

Summer passed and I no longer saw Laurinda. She had gone to her hometown with Marques to say her good-byes. After that, I heard news of her through some tenants from the shoemaker's stairwell, where she continued to work. I learned then that she had returned from Lourinhã feeling pleased and honored thanks to the fine figure the two of them had made. As always happens to her after an encounter with the fluctuations of life, it seems that Laurinda maintained, for a brief period, a certain serene and proper manner. And who would not forgive her this irregularity? One knows that if one day she appears late, another she comes early, if one day she mops the stairs badly and splashes the trousers of whoever is going up and down, another she washes the clothes to perfection. No one asks more of Laurinda. She may never be steadily conscious, poor devil, but she has her fits and starts of reflection. To such effect that once, before she met Marques, when she was looking around for a room, miserable and irritated, I said to her: "sleep here, for the time being, you know I don't have a maid," and she answered with some spirit: "oh no, I wouldn't want to tarnish your house."

Marques, in the end, didn't sail off and Laurinda no longer thought about the whole affair.

Finally, in fact, they did marry, but what she had to go through to satisfy that dream! She wanted a best man and a maid of honor, but didn't want to pay the priest, and she had lost faith in the efficacy of those benefactresses. She wanted to get married on a Sunday and have a real celebration, but on a Sunday she'd have to fork over twenty-five escudos there and then....And what about the best man and maid of honor? She had just the ones, just right she knew...but they, well, they refused to go along with it....

And there was still the permanent; yes, she was no less than the rest of them—but would it cost a lot? The dress she would pay for by the month. It came from an acquaintance who had passed it on to her. A dress, second hand, but still good!

When someone mentioned underwear to her she laughed. The permanent, the permanent was what she considered indispensable.

So they arranged things as best they could. Marques wore a borrowed coat that was only a little too large. And they had a best man and a maid of honor. They left the church arm in arm, profoundly composed and grave. There were even some who came to watch. There was no doubt that Laurinda was impressed and took her wedding seriously; she behaved with politeness and reserve. But afterwards, either because the luxury of the ceremony had already given what it could give or because her husband had irritated her, she returned to her former restiveness. She would puff into the iron with obstinance, mutter under her breath, mope and scowl, go out without saying where she was going..."I'll be right back, I'll be right back!" was the assurance she gave her employers. If her mood were right, she would come out with it upon returning.

On one of these expeditions, she shadowed Marques. As usual, he was hanging out near the Condes Cinema selling lottery tickets.

She saw him go into the movie house, but soon after he left...she wasn't going to give up that easily. He was following a blonde! She watched the two of them: at first they didn't speak, but around the first corner...that bastard! Yes, indeed, for she had already caught him with photos in his wallet, having had her suspicions for some time....That dirty bastard!

Head down, Laurinda gave vent to it all, chewing over what she had to say, as if she were already getting revenge. But the most beautiful of her stories came to me first hand, straight from the horse's mouth, a short time later. It was the one about winning the lottery!

I was entering the Largo do Rato, when I bumped into Laurinda, one foot in, one out, of a small dairy bar. She hadn't expected to see me, nor I her.

"You, here?" I said to her.

"Well, Marques was left with a whole series of lottery tickets and the winning numbers are out...."

"Poor guy!"

"No, he won, he won second prize" and her gaze wandered all around.

And I: "Congratulations, but are you sure?"

"That's what they told me down at the Rosario, just like that: it was the colored guy who had the second-prize ticket."

"Well, then, Laurinda, what now?"

She laughed, but without looking me in the eye, vague, mouth agape. That's when I noticed that she had retained only a few of her little mouse teeth. She showed me a mouth with nothing but gums. But Laurinda isn't old yet, she is rather of an indefinable age; one can't call her old, but she's already begun to turn repulsive.

Her wedding dress, which she must never have taken off, was graced with a huge brooch, only it seemed covered with spittle.

"He went in there to settle his account at the tobacco shop," she explained, seeing me standing in her way. "That's where he's always gotten his tickets. He's been running a tab for a long time, but now...."

"Well, then, good-bye, good luck!" I said.

She laughed and stayed at her post, her head restive. She was keeping a sharp lookout, she had been following him. In Rossio she had heard them spreading the news...she had dropped everything.

The rest of the story I heard from the family for which she was working that day: Marques left the tobacco shop and Laurinda wouldn't let him get away, dodging here, dodging there. She even put on some sunglasses that she had bought in the summer for six escudos, even then for just such a purpose. But Marques discovered her game: suddenly he turns, she's on top of him, they burst out laughing. Lady Luck? What Lady? There had been a mistake, one number had been wrong. It was always like that! Just another ninety escudos on his tab for the lottery tickets, that's all that had come of it. The computations that Laurinda had made in the blink of an eye were the following: first she would send five hundred escudos to her mother, only later would she send the rest—people had been known to die from such things: she would pay her landlady everything she owed her and a little over ...there was that story of the rabbits...she would rent her own separate house....But Lady Luck never looked her way!

After this unfortunate grand event, her landlady gave her notice. She was a real pig and had killed those rabbits with rat poison, the creature threw it in her face. "*She* was the pig!" Laurinda shot back. Whose fault was it that those rabbits were running around loose in the house? And she wouldn't leave if she didn't feel like it, she had the law on her side, so said Marques, and he knew very well what he was saying. But in fact she would leave, she'd had enough of that woman's mug. And so she placed an ad: "Room for a couple, just four walls."

A couple! Wasn't that nice? Laurinda and Marques...a couple, at last.

With her weasel face and heavy legs, often swollen, with her vile and garbled speech, her bad temper and her cheerful tomfoolery, such as tossing water down the back staircase on the coalmen and the baker's boys, Laurinda had and still has style, character, why she's a local personality, a real Lisbon *alfacinha*,[3] a personification of a certain life, a life with no rules and a misery of toil.

Conclusion

We have no one, we know nothing....

And how it rains!

Penned in by the rain and by the flu, watching clouds go by, how they fly! and catching, surprised, the rattle of hail on the windowpanes, or else listening to the heavy fall of a cloudburst beating down on the pavement and on invisible, neighboring rooftops, despondent, I repeat to myself: no one, nothing....

The world covered by water! Tragedies without a name. Two, three words have left their mark on me, inadvertent words, written by chance, escaped from a reporter's pen: silence...fields, flooded and dead and silent.

And all of a sudden, I am disturbed by literary impropriety, that kind of mental masturbation of certain types who because of these masses of murderous water, give forth sweet meows, a lyric rhetoric, diffusive, tearful, flowery. Which we must read and yet deny.

But my "no one and nothing" covers the rain, preceding and then following it.

And uselessness, our indescribable uselessness? An exciting, menacing sensation. Our, my incapacity for...for everything. And I, what do I do? What is this "writing"? Self-inquiry, no, I don't even question myself, I get discouraged. I cannot write, I have nothing to say, nothing is worth my saying. Language, what is language? And is language enough? There may still be some who think it is....But I feel empty. Useless, empty.

Spent? Worse than all that. Alone.

And how it rains!

Each of us is an island—floating islands in deep and vast, vast seas of solitude. Abandonment.

Ever-changing solitude: now agitated and tempestuous, anxious and dissatisfied, now dead. But companion everlasting; dust, mist that never fades, never disappears from before certain eyes.

Penned in by the flu and the rain. . . .

Whole days, who knows whether short or long, whole, shadowy, empty, solitary, without hearing a voice, nauseated by false literary lyricism and thirsting for I don't know what, as yet. Still alive; doesn't it seem impossible? Defeated, almost amputated of feelings and senses, but like a lizard's tail, unconsciously quivering, agitated.

May a period be put to what is written.

Why write? Not to be accepted even in the cheap cabbage leaves, called literary, of one's time! But that's not what troubles me most. What troubles me are the lost worlds.

I got up last night to write these half dozen words:

I suffered for a long time because my world was shrinking, in any case not expanding. Straitened, I suffered. And today, more than ever, I suffer from irremediable solitude.

I'm not interested in moralizing, nor was I ever; what interests me, what I'd really like to do, is to close a book, as vain as all that are written, with this confession: lost worlds, lost worlds, all that we've never known and all that we've missed. . . .

But a world dead and known, submerged, drowned along with us, a troublesome and grievous entity—this one, this world of irremediable solitude.

Translated by Alexis Levitin

NOTES

1. Cloak.
2. Religious instruction.
3. Slang for a native of Lisbon.

Edith Södergran   *Russia/Finland, 1892–1923*

Edith Södergran introduced modernist poetry to Scandinavia. When she died in a remote village in eastern Finland at the age of 31, her greatness as a poet was appreciated only by a handful of admirers. Today, she is widely regarded as one of the supreme lyrical poets of all time, a unique and passionate voice of universal proportions. Södergran's production was very small. She published four thin volumes of poetry and a collection of aphorisms. A fifth volume of poetry was published posthumously.

Edith Södergran was born in St. Petersburg, in tsarist Russia. Both of her parents belonged to the Swedish-speaking minority of Finland, which at that time was a Grand Duchy under the tsar. Södergran attended a German-language school and wrote her first poetry in German while still in her teens. At 16, she contracted tuberculosis, which had claimed the life of her father two years earlier. She was forced to abandon her schooling and spent some time in Finnish and Swiss sanatoriums. In 1914, she returned with her mother to the Finnish village where she spent the rest of her life under increasingly difficult conditions—partly as a result of the Russian Revolution of 1917 and the subsequent civil war in Finland, and partly because of her own poverty and declining health.

Undaunted by her harsh circumstances, she continued to write poetry—now in her native Swedish—and made her debut with *Dikter* (Poems) in 1916. The volume, which represents one of the first attempts to do away with rhyme and meter in Scandinavian poetry, was met with ridicule and indifference by the public and by most critics. In 1918 she followed with *Septemberlyran* (The September Lyre), in 1919 came *Rosenaltaret* (The Rose Altar), and in 1920 *Framtidens skugga* (The Shadow of the Future)—all three volumes inspired by Nietzsche and containing cosmic visions of the future of mankind. The critics continued to heap their scorn, and some seriously questioned her mental state. Södergran's last collection, *Landet som icke är* (The Land That Does Not Exist) was published posthumously in 1925 and includes some of her early, lyrical poetry as well as a few late poems imbued with a religious feeling and a closeness to nature.

The last decade has seen a number of translations of her poetry into English. Book-length translations include Martin Allwood's *The Collected Poems of Edith Södergran* (1980), David McDuff's *Complete Poems of Edith Södergran* (1984), and Stina Katchadourian's bilingual selection *Edith Södergran: Love and Solitude: Selected Poems: 1916–1923* (1985). The following poems are taken from *Love and Solitude*.

Stina Katchadourian

THE DAY COOLS...
Dagen Svalnar...

I

The day cools toward evening...
Drink the warmth from my hand,
it throbs with spring's own blood,
Take my hand, take my white arm,
take the longing of my slender shoulders...
How strange if I could feel,
one single night, a night like this,
your heavy head against my breast.

II

You cast your love's red rose
into my white womb—
and with my burning hands I hold
your love's red rose that soon will wilt...
Oh master with your frozen eyes,
I will accept the crown you give me,
which bends my head toward my heart.

III

Today, for the first time, I saw my master.
Shivering, I recognized him at once.
Already I feel his heavy hand on my light
                                                    arm...
Where is my ringing maidenly laughter,
my womanly freedom with head carried high?
Now I feel his tight grip on my shaking body,
Now I hear the hard ring of reality
against my sheer, sheer dreams.

IV

You looked for a flower
and found a fruit.
You looked for a well
and found an ocean.
You looked for a woman
and found a soul—
you are disappointed.

Translated by Stina Katchadourian

WE WOMEN
Vi Kvinnor

We women, we are so close to the brown earth.
We ask the cuckoo what he expects of spring,
we embrace the rugged fir tree,
we look in the sunset for signs and counsel.
Once I loved a man, he believed in nothing...
He came on a cold day with empty eyes,
he left on a heavy day with lost memories on
                                                                                  his brow.
If my child does not live, it is his...

Translated by Stina Katchadourian

Alfonsina Storni   *Argentina, 1892–1938*

Alfonsina Storni is best known for her early works, which are overtly feminist, denouncing woman's traditionally dependent role in Latin American society. Storni also writes of the absurdity and oppression of middle-class morality typified by the double standard she had to face when she was trying to support herself and her illegitimate son while writing her poetry in post–World War I Buenos Aires. One of her early poems, "Yo tengo un hijo, fruto del amor sin ley...." ("I Have a Son, the Fruit of an Unsanctified Love," 1917), publicly displayed her rebelliousness towards that society. Such courage and talent served her well. She was one of the first women to be accepted into Buenos Aires literary circles.

Although considered a true Buenos Aires poet, Alfonsina Storni was born in Switzerland, and came to the province of San Juan, Argentina when she was 3. Her childhood was relatively unsupervised and the young Storni was allowed to roam around at will. When the family's finances became desperate, Storni went to work, holding a number of jobs, including acting with a traveling theater; eventually she attended teacher's college, and, upon receiving her teaching license, went to Buenos Aires with her infant son. In the capital she worked as a teacher, actor, and clerk to support herself and her child.

Storni's first book of poetry, *La inquietud del Rosal* (The Restlessness of the Rose Garden), published in 1916, was immediately successful. During the next four years she wrote three more books of poetry: *El duce daño* (Sweet Danger, 1918), *Irremediablemente* (Incurably, 1919) and *Languidez* (Langor, 1920). *Languidez* won the First Municipal Prize and the Second National Prize. These early poems are her most popular because they are quite accessible. Beginning in 1925, with the collection *Ocre* (Ocher) her work became more intellectual and experimental. It is this later work, including her two subsequent collections *Poemas de amor* (Love Poems, 1926) and *Mundo de siete pozos* (World of Seven Wells, 1934), she preferred and for which she wished to be remembered.

Suffering from terminal cancer, Storni committed suicide in 1938 by walking into the Mar del Plata in Buenos Aires. The following poems were published in *El dulce dano* and *Obra poètica* (Poetic Works, 1946).

YOU WANT ME WHITE
Tú me quieres blanca

You'd like me to be white as dawn,
You'd like me to be made of foam,
You wish I were mother of pearl,
A lily
Chaste above all others.
Of delicate perfume.
A closed bud.

Not one ray of the moon
Should have filtered me,
Not one daisy
Should have called me sister
You want me to be snowy,
You want me to be white,
You want me to be like dawn.

You who have held all the wineglasses
In your hand,
Your lips stained purple
With fruit and honey.
You who in the banquet
Crowned with young vines
Made toasts with your flesh to Bacchus.
You who in the gardens
Black with Deceit
Dressed in red
Ran to your Ruin.

You who keep your skeleton
Well preserved, intact,
I don't know yet
Through what miracles
You want to make me white
(God forgive you),
You want to make me chaste
(God forgive you),
You want to make me like dawn!

Run away to the woods;
Go to the mountain;
Wash your mouth;
Get to know the wet earth
With your hands;
Feed your body
With bitter roots;
Drink from the rocks;
Sleep on the white frost;

Renew your tissue
With the salt of rocks and water;
Talk to the birds
And get up at dawn.
And when your flesh
Has returned to you,
And when you have put
Your soul back into it,
Your soul which was left entangled
In all the bedrooms,
Then, my good man,
Ask me to be white,
Ask me to be snowy,
Ask me to be chaste.
Translated by Marion Freeman and Mary Crow

SQUARES AND ANGLES
Cuadros y ángulos

Houses in a row, houses in a row,
Houses in a row.
Block after block, block after block,
Houses in a row.
People even have rectangular-shaped souls,
Ideas in a line,
And angles on their backs.
Even I myself shed yesterday a tear,
That was. . . my goodness!. . . square.
Translated by Mildred E. Johnson

ANCESTRAL WEIGHT
Peso ancestral

You said to me, "My father did not weep."
You said to me, "Grandfather did not cry.
The menfolk of my race have never wept.
They were of steel."

And as you spoke a tear gushed from your eye,
And then fell down upon my mouth; more
                                        poison
I never drank in any other glass
That was so small.
Weak, pitiable woman who can understand,
I knew the pain of centuries of drinking,
Alas, my soul can not endure the burden
Of all its weight.
Translated by Mildred E. Johnson

Marína Ivánovna Tsvetáeva   *Russia/France/USSR, 1892–1941*

Born one of three children to an upper-class family whose father was an art historian, Tsvetáeva grew up among the leading intellectuals of Moscow. An indifferent and rebellious student, she was nonetheless an accomplished linguist in Russian, French, and German. By the time she married Sergéy Efrón in 1912 and gave birth to the first of their three children, this love of words made Tsvetáeva a published and acclaimed poet. From 1917 to 1922 Efrón fought with the White Army against the Bolsheviks in the south; the civil war provided Tsvetáeva the substance of a new political poetry in *Lebedínyi stán* (*The Demesne of the Swans*, 1917–1921, published 1957). Yet Tsvetáeva was unable to support her family, and her second daughter died of malnutrition in a state orphanage.

Tsvetáeva's exile dates from 1922 to 1939, begun when she joined her husband in Berlin, moved to Prague and then to Paris in 1925. During this period of relative tranquility, Tsvetáeva began her major work: *Remesló* (*Craft*, 1923), *Posle Rossíi* (*After Russia*, 1928), including the "Poem of the Hill," and "Poem of the End"; the chief dramatic works, "Tezéi-Ariádna" (Theseus-Ariadne, 1927), followed by "Fédra" (1928), intended as part of a trilogy on the destructive power of love and the theme of renunciation; and the major social and political satire in six cantos based on the legend of the Pied Piper, "Krysolóv" (1925–1926), in which the Rat-catcher artist is at odds with the scornful bourgeoisie and the revolutionary rodents against which it is pitted.

In Paris, Tsvetáeva devoted herself increasingly to prose—autobiographical memoirs and literary reminiscences and criticism: together they constitute a mythic recreation of the poet's life and a major statement on poetry. Examples are: "Poét i vrémya" (The Poet and Time) and "Iskússtvo pri svéte sóvesti" ("Art in the Light of Conscience") published in 1932, "Mát i múzyka" ("Mother and Music," 1935), and "Móy Púshkin" ("My Pushkin," 1937).

However, Tsvetáeva grew more and more isolated—the result of many factors: increasing impoverishment; her praise of Soviet poets Mayakóvsky and Pasternák while denouncing their emigré critics *and* the Soviet regime, effectively cutting her off from either audience; her own poetic practice, constantly experimental and frequently allusive; and the intensified pro-Soviet politics of her family which culminated in her daughter's return to Russia in 1937 and in her husband's exposure as a Soviet spy and subsequent flight at about the same time.

At the height of mass arrests and purges, Tsvetáeva returned to the USSR. Soon after the family's reunion, her sister and daughter were both imprisoned and her husband executed as an enemy of the people. With Germany's invasion in 1941, her son entered the army (and was lost at the front), while she was evacuated from Moscow to the Tatar Autonomous Republic. Alone and unknown, Tsvetáeva hanged herself in Elabuga.

Tsvetáeva's early work was influenced by the Romantics of the second half of the nineteenth century and the early Symbolists of the 1890–1910 period; the new voice that emerged in the 1920s exploits real speech and draws on the oral folk tradition that lies beneath Western-influenced literary versions. At the same time, a new classicism based on the reading of Homer and other Western classics (drama especially) lends a philosophical depth to an intensely lyrical poetry; Tsvetáeva turns both to *poèma*, long verse narratives—either epic or autobiographical—and to drama. Her mature work is characterized by a variety of Russian "languages," highly inventive rhythmic and stanzaic forms, and the extreme exploitation of phonetic-semantic relationships. Both the poetry and prose are remarkable for their use of imagery and a highly elliptical syntax.

After Russia was the last complete volume published in Tsvetáeva's lifetime. An important new collection of her work appeared in the Soviet Union in 1965, when the circumstances of her death were first made public; a complete five-volume edition of her verse was begun in 1980 by Russica Publishers in New York.

from POEMS FOR AKHMÁTOVA
Stikhí k Akmátovoy

Muse of lament, you are the most beautiful of
  all muses, a crazy emanation of white night:
and you have sent a black snow storm over all
                                        Russia.
  We are pierced with the arrows of your cries
so that we shy like horses at the muffled
  many times uttered pledge—Ah!—Anna
Akhmátova—the name is a vast sigh
  and it falls into depths without name
and we wear crowns only through stamping
  the same earth as you, with the same sky
                                      over us.
Whoever shares the pain of your deathly
                                    power will
  lie down immortal upon his death bed.
In my melodious town the domes are burning
  and the blind wanderer praises our shining
                                        Lord.
I give you my town of many bells,
  Akhmátova, and with the gift: my heart.
(1916)

                Translated by Elaine Feinstein

I UNSEALED MY VEINS: UNSTOPPABLE
Vskrýla zhíly: neostanovímo

I unsealed my veins: unstoppable,
irreparable, life gushes out—
place basins and plates underneath!
Every plate is too shallow,
every basin flat.

            Over the ground and *beyond*
into the black earth and nourishing the reed,
irrevocable, unstoppable,
irreparable—poems rush out.
(**January 6, 1934**)

                Translated by Mary Maddock

HOMESICKNESS!
Toská po ródine! Davnó

Homesickness! that long
exposed weariness!
It's all the same to me now
where I am   altogether lonely

or what stones I wander over
home with a shopping bag to
a house that is no more mine
than a hospital or a barracks

It's all the same to me, captive
lion   what faces I move through
bristling, or what human crowd will
cast me out   as it must

into myself, into my separate internal
world, a Kamchatka bear without ice.
Where I fail to fit in (and I'm not trying) or
where I'm humiliated   it's all the same

And I won't be seduced by the thought of
my native language, its milky call.
How can it matter   in what tongue I
am misunderstood by whoever I meet

(or by what readers, swallowing
newsprint, squeezing for gossip?)
They all belong to the twentieth
century, and   I am before time,

stunned, like a log left
behind from an avenue of trees.
People are all the same to me, everything
is the same, and it may be the most

indifferent of all   are these
signs and tokens which once were
native   but the dates have been
rubbed out: the soul was born somewhere.

For my country has taken so little care
of me that even the sharpest spy could
go over my whole spirit and would
detect no native stain there.

Houses are alien, churches are empty
everything   is the same:
But if by the side of the path one
particular bush rises

                    the rowanberry...
(1934)   *Translated by Elaine Feinstein*

from MOTHER AND MUSIC
Mát i múzyka

A hot day. A blue day. Fly-like music and torment. The piano is right next to the window, as if trying hopelessly, with all its elephantine inertness to use it—to leave, and right in the window, coming halfway through it like a live person—is the jasmine. Sweat pours, red fingers—I am playing with my whole body, with my whole not-inconsiderable strength, with my whole weight, my whole thrust, and—the main thing—with my whole repulsion for playing. I look at my wrist, which in mother's childhood you had to keep on the same line (of tensed effort) with the elbow and the first finger joints, and so unmovingly that the hand wouldn't spill—(think of the perfidy!)—a Sèvres cup of boiling coffee placed on top, so unmovingly a silver ruble wouldn't roll off, and which now in my childhood you had to maintain in continuous free motion, alternating downward dips with upward thrusts to make the playing hand, together with the elbow, the wrist and the fingertips act like a drinking swan, the wrist on the back of which I have a blue vein that makes a clear letter N when I press down—the N of the Nikolái whom I will marry, so the German woman claims, in twelve years—but the French woman says it stands for Henri.[1] Everyone is at liberty: Andryúsha and Pápa have gone swimming, Máma and Ásya have gone "to the stumps." Valéria has gone to the post office in Tarusa. There's only the cook left pounding her knife on the cutlets, and I—pounding on the keys. Or it's autumn: Andryúsha is sharpening a stick, Ásya, her tongue stuck out, is drawing houses, Máma is reading Eckermann,[2] Valéria is writing a letter to Véra Murómtseva, I am the only one—"playing." (Why??)

"No, you don't love music" mother would say getting angry (and her anger was literally heartfelt) in answer to my unashamedly open, blissful jump off the piano stool after two hours of sitting. "No, you do *not* love music."

Oh no—I did love it. I loved music. Only I didn't love—my music. For a child there is no future, there is only right now (which means—now and for always). And right now there were scales and canons and miserable little "pieces" that insulted me by their childishness. And my future virtuosity meant no more than marrying that Nikolai or Henri. It was fine for her, she who could do everything on the piano, she who descended onto the keyboard like a swan onto the water, she who, within my memory, learned to play the guitar in three lessons and played concert pieces on it, she who read from a page of music the way I read from the page of a book, it was fine for her to "love music." In her were mingled two streams of musical blood, her father's and her mother's, mingled into one, and it was those two that gave her everything! And she didn't take into account that she herself through her marriage had set her own, melodious, lyric, mono-elemental blood running counter to another blood: philological and clearly continental, a blood that could not mingle and did not mingle with hers.

Mother deluged us with music. (We never again floated free from that music turned into Lyricism—out into the light of day!) Mother flooded us like an inundation. Her children, like those poor people's shacks on the banks of all great rivers, were doomed from their inception. Mother deluged us with all the bitterness of her own unrealized vocation, her own unrealized life, she deluged us with music as if with blood, the blood of a second birth. I can say that I was born not *ins Leben*, but *in die Musik hinein*.[3] From the beginning I heard the best of everything that could be heard (including the *future*). How could I, after the unbearable magic of those streams every evening (those very Undinian, forest-kingly,[4] "pearly streams") even hear my own honest, dreary "playing" that crawled out from under my skin to my own counting and the metronome's clicking? And how could I not feel repulsion for it? A born musician would have subdued it. But I was not a born musician. (I remember,

however, that one of her best-beloved Russian books was *The Blind Musician*, which she constantly used in order to reproach me, the same way she used the three-year-old Mozart, and her four-year-old self, and later, Músya Potápov who was jumping ahead of me, and whom *didn't* she use, just whom didn't she use!...)

The click of a metronome. In my life there are several firmly fixed joys: *not* to go to the *Gymnasium, not* to wake up in Moscow of 1919,[5] and *not* to hear a metronome. How is it that musical ears endure it? (Or are musical ears something different from musical souls?) Until the age of four, I even liked the metronome, almost the same as the clock with the cuckoo and for the same reason: because there too someone lived inside, although who lived there—was unknown, because I was the one who made him come back to life in his house. It was a house in which I myself wanted to live. (Children always want to live in something inconceivable; thus my son at the age of six yearned to live in a street lamp: bright, warm, high up, a good view on everything. "And what if they throw a stone at your house?"—"Then I'll attack them with fire!") But as soon as I was *subjected* to its methodical click, I started hating it and fearing it until my heart beat faster, until I felt faint, until I turned cold, just as now nights I am afraid of an alarm clock, of every regular sound in the night. That sound seems to go right through my soul! Someone is standing over your soul and hurrying you, and holding you back and not letting you take a breath or swallow, and will go on hurrying you that way and holding you back when you go away—clicking all alone in the empty music room over the empty piano stool, over the closed piano lid, because they forgot to stop it—and on and on, until the mechanism gives out. The lifeless over the living, that which has no existence over that which does. And what if the mechanism—never gives out, and what if I—never get up from the piano stool, never get out from under the tick tock, tick tock....It was truly Death itself standing over a soul, a living soul which could die—deathless (already dead) Death. The metronome was—a coffin, and in it there lived—death. In my horror of the sound I would even forget the horror of its look; a steel stick, crawling out like a finger and oscillating with maniacal obtuseness behind a living backbone. That was my first encounter with technology, decisive for all subsequent encounters, technology in all its freshness, its steel bouquet, its first, for me, steel flowerbud. Oh, I never lagged behind the metronome! It held me fast—not only to the beat, it physically riveted me to the piano stool. The open metronome was the best guarantee that I wouldn't look around at the clock. But mother, fortunately, would sometimes forget and no protestant honesty of mine—of hers!—could force me to doom myself to that torture by a reminder. If ever I wanted to kill someone—it was the metronome. And my eyes have never ceased sending out that look of voluptuous revenge that I presented to it when I had played my way to freedom and I went by the music shelf and looked at it with a carefree face over my haughty shoulder: I—am going, and you—are stuck!...

Translated by J. Marin King

NOTES

1. The letter "N" in the Cyrillic alphabet looks like the Roman letter "H," hence the two interpretations.
2. Johann Peter Eckermann (1792–1854): Goethe's secretary and author of *Goethe's Conversations with Eckermann (1836–1848)*.
3. "...into life....into music"
4. This alludes to two different poems, "Erlkönig," (1782) written by Goethe, and "Lesnóy Tsár," (1818) written by Zhukóvsky, of which Tsvetáeva did a study, *Dvá lesnykh tsaryá* (The Two Forest Kings, 1933). Johann Wolfgang von Goethe (1749–1832) was a German poet, playwright, statesman, and scientist; he is considered the founder of modern German literature and the chief exponent of German Romanticism. Vasíly Andréevich Zhukóvsky (1783–1852) is the leading representative of early Russian Romanticism; he contributed to the creation of a poetic language, and inspired Púshkin and other poets of the Golden Age of Russian poetry.
5. A time of extreme hardship when even basic necessities were unavailable to city dwellers.

Rebecca West (Cicily Isabel Fairchild) *Ireland/UK(England), 1892–1983*

At the age of 19, Cicily Isabel Fairchild took the name Rebecca West, the feminist heroine of Henrik Ibsen's *Rosmersholm*. More than a stage name for the young actress, it signaled a conscious choice of identity. She was to speak of and for women in an age of Victorian repression.

West was born in County Kerry, Ireland, on Christmas day, to Captain Charles Fairchild, an impoverished socialist writer, and Isabella MacKenzie, a Scottish pianist. Upon her father's death when West was 10, the family left Ireland for Edinburgh. There West attended George Watson's Ladies' College, but left at 16 for London where she eventually enrolled at the Royal Academy of Dramatic Art.

A journalist, feminist, novelist, and essayist, Rebecca West's early writings focused on societal problems, particularly those experienced by women. Writing in the socialist periodicals *The Clarion, The Freewoman*, and *The New Freewoman*, West's essays dealt with such concerns as conservative divorce laws, rape, the suffragist movement, and unwed mothers. In 1916, West published her first book, a critical study of writer Henry James (*Henry James*), the first such critique written after his death. In her second book, *The Return of the Soldier* (1918), West examines the paradox that a denial of life can bring about a deeper appreciation of life. Although West wrote several other novels in the next twenty years, she was not successful until 1936 with *The Thinking Reed*. Her best novel is probably *The Fountain Overflows* (1956), about a turn-of-the-century family. Her nonfiction work of social history, *1900* (1982) is often seen as its sequel.

The work that established West as a master journalist is undoubtedly *Black Lamb and Gray Falcon* (1941), in which she turns a travelogue of her journey through the Balkan States into a judicious meditation on the patterns of Western history, art, religion, morals, and politics. West sets about to present truthfully the facts, both historical and contemporary. Such facts, she said, "are the face of the age...[and] if people do not have the face of the age set before them, they begin to imagine it." In such imaginings, the face of the age was fast becoming Nazism. These concerns led West to cover the treason trials of Englishmen who had broadcast for the Nazis in Germany during World War II in *The Meaning of Treason* (1947), and the Nüremberg trial of Nazi war criminals in *A Train of Powder* (1955), excerpted here. In these, West accomplished what William Shirer has called the "elevation of journalism to art."

West's personal life was as rebellious and strongly stated as her professional life. For many years a lover of H.G. Wells (1866–1946), the couple had a son, Anthony (b. 1914), who took his mother's pseudonym of West. A successful writer, he was to repudiate his mother in a 1984 book called *H.G. Wells: Aspects of a Life*. In 1930 Rebecca West married banker Henry Maxwell Andrews, who was a source of great sustenance to West throughout her life. By the 1950s, West's radical ideas changed direction. A devoted socialist, she became discouraged by Stalin's excesses and was a vocal anti-Communist.

West received many awards throughout her life, including the Order of the British Empire in 1949 and Dame Commander in 1959. She received honorary degrees from New York University, Yale, and Edinburgh University. She continued to write until her death in 1983 at the age of 91.

John Isom

from GREENHOUSE WITH CYCLAMENS I

There rushed up towards the plane the astonishing face of the world's enemy: pine woods on little hills, grey-green glossy lakes, too small ever to be anything but smooth, gardens tall with red-tongued beans, fields striped with copper wheat, russet-roofed villages with headlong gables and pumpkin-steeple churches that no architect over seven could have designed. Another minute and the plane dropped to the heart of the world's enemy: Nüremberg. It took not many more minutes to get to the courtroom where the world's enemy was being tried for his sins;[1] but immediately those sins were forgotten in wonder at a conflict which was going on in that court, though it had nothing to do with the indictments considered by it. The trial was then in its eleventh month, and the courtroom was a citadel of boredom. Every person within its walk was in the grip of extreme tedium. This is not to say that the work in hand was being performed languidly. An iron discipline met that tedium head on and did not yield an inch to it. But all the same the most spectacular process in the court was by then a certain tug-of-war concerning time. Some of those present were fiercely desiring that that tedium should come to an end at the first possible moment, and the others were as fiercely desiring that it should last for ever and ever.

The people in court who wanted the tedium to endure eternally were the twenty-one defendants in the dock, who disconcerted the spectator by presenting the blatant appearance that historical characters, particularly in distress, assume in bad pictures. They looked what they were as crudely as Mary Queen of Scots at Fotheringay or Napoleon on St. Helena in a mid-Victorian Academy success.[2] But it was, of course, an unusually ghastly picture. They were wreathed in suggestions of death. Not only were they in peril of the death sentence, there was constant talk about millions of dead and arguments whether these had died because of these men or not; knowing so well what death is, and experiencing it by anticipation, these men preferred the monotony of the trial to its cessation. So they clung to the procedure through their lawyers and stretched it to the limits of its texture; and thus they aroused in the rest of the court, the people who had a prospect of leaving Nüremberg and going back to life, a savage impatience. This the iron discipline of the court prevented from finding an expression for itself. But it made the air more tense.

It seemed ridiculous for the defendants to make any effort to stave off the end, for they admitted by their appearance that nothing was to go well with them again on this earth. These Nazi leaders, self-dedicated to the breaking of all rules, broke last of all the rule that the verdict of a court must not be foretold. Their appearance announced what they believed. The Russians had asked for the death penalty for all of them, and it was plain that the defendants thought that wish would be granted. Believing that they were to lose everything, they forgot what possession had been. Not the slightest trace of their power and their glory remained; none of them looked as if he could ever have exercised any valid authority. Göring still used imperial gestures, but they were so vulgar that they did not suggest that he had really filled any great position; it merely seemed probable that in certain bars the frequenters had called him by some such nickname as "The Emperor." These people were also surrendering physical characteristics which might have been thought inalienable during life, such as the colour and texture of their skins and the moulding of their features. Most of them, except Schacht, who was white-haired, and Speer, who was black like a monkey, were neither dark nor fair any more; and there was amongst them no leanness that did not sag and no plumpness that seemed more than inflation by some thin gas. So diminished were their personalities that it was hard to keep in mind which was which, even after one had sat and looked at them for days; and those who stood out defined themselves by oddity rather than character.

Hess was noticeable because he was so plainly mad: so plainly mad that it seemed shameful that he should be tried. His skin was ashen, and he had that odd faculty, peculiar to lunatics, of falling into strained positions which no normal person could maintain for more than a few minutes, and staying fixed in contortion for hours. He had the classless air characteristic of asylum inmates; evidently his distracted personality had torn up all clues to his past. He looked as if his mind had no surface, as if every part of it had been blasted away except the depth where the nightmares live. Schacht was as noticeable because he was so far from mad, so completely his ordinary self in these extraordinary circumstances. He sat twisted in his seat so that his tall body, stiff as a plank, was propped against the end of the dock, which ought to have been at his side. Thus he sat at right angles to his fellow defendants and looked past them and over their heads: it was always his argument that he was far superior to Hitler's gang. Thus, too, he sat at right angles to the judges on the bench confronting him: it was his argument that he was a leading international banker, a most respectable man, and no court on earth could have the right to try him. He was petrified by rage because this court was pretending to have this right. He might have been a corpse frozen by rigor mortis, a disagreeable corpse who had contrived to aggravate the process so that he should be specially difficult to fit into his coffin.

A few others were still individuals. Streicher was pitiable, because it was plainly the community and not he who was guilty of his sins. He was a dirty old man of the sort that gives trouble in parks, and a sane Germany would have sent him to an asylum long before. Baldur von Schirach, the Youth Leader, startled because he was like a woman in a way not common among men who looked like women. It was as if a neat and mousy governess sat there, not pretty, but with never a hair out of place, and always to be trusted never to intrude when there were visitors: as it might be Jane Eyre.[3] And though one had read surprising news of Göring for years, he still surprised. He was so very soft. Sometimes he wore a German Air Force uniform, and sometimes a light beach suit in the worst of playful taste, and both hung loosely on him, giving him an air of pregnancy. He had thick brown young hair, the coarse bright skin of an actor who has used grease paint for decades, and the preternaturally deep wrinkles of the drug addict. It added up to something like the head of a ventriloquist's dummy. He looked infinitely corrupt, and acted naïvely. When the other defendants' lawyers came to the door to receive instruc-

tions, he often intervened and insisted on instructing them himself, in spite of the evident fury of the defendants, which, indeed, must have been poignant, since most of them might well have felt that, had it not been for him, they never would have had to employ these lawyers at all. One of these lawyers was a tiny little man of very Jewish appearance, and when he stood in front of the dock, his head hardly reaching to the top of it, and flapped his gown in annoyance because Göring's smiling wooden mask was bearing down between him and his client, it was as if a ventriloquist had staged a quarrel between two dummies.

Göring's appearance made a strong but obscure allusion to sex. It is a matter of history that his love affairs with women played a decisive part in the development of the Nazi party at various stages, but he looked as one who would never lift a hand against a woman save in something much more peculiar than kindness. He did not look like any recognized type of homosexual, yet he was feminine. Sometimes, particularly when his humour was good, he recalled the madam of a brothel. His like are to be seen in the late morning in doorways along the steep streets of Marseilles, the professional mask of geniality still hard on their faces though they stand relaxed in leisure, their fat cats rubbing against their spread skirts. Certainly there had been a concentration on appetite, and on elaborate schemes for gratifying it; and yet there was a sense of desert thirst. No matter what aqueducts he had built to bring water to his encampment, some perversity in the architecture had let it run out and spill on the sands long before it reached him. Sometimes even now his wide lips smacked together as if he were a well-fed man who had heard no news as yet that his meals were to stop. He was the only one of all these defendants who, if he had the chance, would have walked out of the Palace of Justice and taken over Germany again, and turned it into the stage for the enactment of the private fantasy which had brought him to the dock.

As these men gave up the effort to be themselves, they joined to make a common pattern which simply reiterated the plea of not guilty. All the time they made quite unidiosyncratic gestures expressive of innocence and outraged common sense, and in the intervals they stood up and chatted among themselves, forming little protesting groups, each one of which, painted as a mural, would be instantly recognized as a holy band that had tried to save the world but had been frustrated by mistaken men. But this performance they rendered more weakly every day. They were visibly receding from the field of existence and were, perhaps, no longer conscious of the recession. It is possible that they never thought directly of death or even of imprisonment, and there was nothing positive in them at all except their desire to hold time still. They were all praying with their sharp-set nerves: "Let this trial never finish, let it go on for ever and ever, without end."

The nerves of all others present in the Palace of Justice were sending out a counter-prayer: the eight judges on the bench, who were plainly dragging the proceedings over the threshold of their consciousness by sheer force of will; the lawyers and the secretaries who sat sagged in their seats at the tables in the well of the court; the interpreters twittering unhappily in their glass box like cage-birds kept awake by a bright light, feeding the microphones with French and Russian and English versions of the proceedings for the spectators' earphones; the guards who stood with their arms gripping their white truncheons behind their backs, all still and hard as metal save their childish faces, which were puffy with boredom. All these people wanted to leave Nüremberg as urgently as a dental patient enduring the drill wants to up and leave the chair; and they would have had as much difficulty as the dental patient in explaining the cause of that urgency. Modern drills do not inflict real pain, only discomfort. But all the same the patients on whom they are used feel that they will go mad if that grinding does not stop. The people at Nüremberg were all well fed, well clothed, well housed, and well cared for by their organizations, on a standard well above their recent experience. This was obviously true of the soldiers who had campaigned in the war, and of the British and French civilians at work in the court; and it was, to an extent that would have surprised most Europeans, true of the American civilians. It never crossed the Atlantic, the news of just how uncomfortable life became in the United States during the war: what the gasoline shortage did to make life untenable in the pretty townships planned on the supposition that every householder had an automobile; how the titanic munitions programme had often to plant factories in little towns that could not offer a room apiece to the incoming workers; what it was like to live in an all-electric house when electric equipment was impossible to replace or repair. By contrast, what Nüremberg gave was the life of Riley, but it was also the water-torture, boredom falling drop by drop on the same spot on the soul.

What irked was the isolation in a small area, cut off from normal life by the barbed wire of army regulations; the perpetual confrontation with the dreary details of an ugly chapter in history which the surrounding rubble seemed to prove to have been torn out of the book and to require no further discussion; the continued enslavement by the war machine. To live in Nüremberg was, even for the victors, in itself physical captivity. The old town had been destroyed. There was left the uninteresting new town, in which certain grubby hotels improvised accommodation for Allied personnel, and were the sole places in which they might sleep and eat and amuse themselves. On five days a week, from ten to five, and often on Saturday mornings, their duties compelled them to the Palace of Justice of Nüremberg, an extreme example of the German tendency to overbuild, which has done much to get them into the recurring financial troubles that make them look to war for release. Every German who wanted to prove himself a man of substance built himself a house with more rooms than he needed and put more bricks into it than it needed; and every German city put up municipal buildings that were as much demonstrations of solidity as for use. Even though the Nüremberg Palace of Justice housed various agencies we would not find in a British or American or French law court, such as a Labour Exchange, its mass could not be excused, for much of it was a mere waste of masonry and an expense of shame, in obese walls and distended corridors. It recalled Civil War architecture but lacked the homeliness; and it made the young American heart sicken with nostalgia for the clean-run concrete and glass and plastic of modern office buildings. From its clumsy tripes the personnel could escape at the end of the working day to the tennis courts and the swimming pools, provided that they were doing only routine work. Those who were more deeply involved had to go home and work on their papers, with little time for any recreation but dinner parties, which themselves, owing to the unique character of the Nüremberg event, were quite unrefreshing. For the guests at these parties had either to be co-workers grown deadly familiar with the passing months or V.I.P.s come to see the show, who, as most were allowed to stay only two days, had nothing to bring to the occasion except the first superficial impressions, so apt to be the same in every case. The symbol of Nüremberg was a yawn.

The Allies reacted according to their histories. The French, many of whom had been in concentration camps, rested and read; no nation has endured more wars, or been more persistent in its creation of a culture, and it has been done this way. The British reconstituted an Indian hill station; anybody who wants to know what they were like in Nüremberg need only read the early works of Rudyard Kipling. In villas set among the Bavarian pines, amid German modernist furniture, each piece of which seemed to have an enormous behind, a

triple feat of reconstitution was performed: people who were in Germany pretended they were people in the jungle who were pretending they were in England. The Americans gave those huge parties of which the type was fixed in pioneering days, when the folks in the scattered homesteads could meet so rarely that it would have been tiring out the horses for nothing not to let geniality go all up the scale; and for the rest they contended with disappointment. Do what you will with America, it remains vast, and it follows that most towns are small in a land where the people are enthralled by the conception of the big town. Here were children of that people, who had crossed a great ocean in the belief that they were going to see the prodigious, and were back in a small town smaller than any of the small towns they had fled.

For a small town is a place where there is nothing to buy with money; and in Nüremberg, as in all German towns at that time, purchase was a forgotten faculty. The Nürembergers went to work in shabby streetcars hooked three together; so presumably they paid their fares. They bought the few foodstuffs available to them in shops so bare that it was hard to associate them with the satisfaction of an appetite. They bought fuel, not much, as it was summer, but enough to cook by and give what they felt to be, much more urgently than might have been supposed, the necessity of light. In the old town a twisted tower leaned backward against the city wall, and of this the top floor had miraculously remained roofed and weather-tight. To get to it one had to walk a long way over the rubble, which exhaled the double stench of disinfectant and of that which was irredeemably infected, for it concealed thirty thousand dead; and then one had to walk up the sagging concave exterior of the tower, and go in through a window. It would seem that people who had to live in such a home would not care to stay awake when darkness fell; but at night a weak light burned in the canted window. Such minuscule extravagance was as far as expenditure could go, except for grubby peddling in the black market. One could not buy a new hat, a new kettle, a yard of ribbon, a baby's diaper. There was no money, there were only cigarettes. A judge's wife, come out for a visit, said to a woman staying in the same villa, who had said she was going into the town, "Will you buy me some silver paint? I want to touch up my evening shoes," and everyone in earshot, even the G.I. guards at the door, burst into laughter.

It was hysterical laughter. Merely to go into a shop and buy something is to exercise choice and to enjoy the freedom of the will; and when this is checked it hurts. True, the Allied personnel in Nüremberg could go into their own stores and buy what they wanted; but that was not the full healthy process, for they knew with a deadly particularity every item in their own stores, and the traveller does not feel he has made terms with the country he visits till the people have sold him their goods. Without that interchange he is like a ghost among the living. The Allied personnel were like ghosts, and it might have been that the story would have a supernatural ending. If Allah of the Arabian Nights had governed this dispensation an angel would have appeared and struck dead all the defendants, and would have cried out that the rest of the court might do what it willed, and they would have run

towards the East, towards France, towards the Atlantic, and by its surf would have taken off from the ground and risen into the air on the force of their desire, and travelled in a black compact cloud across the ocean, back to America, back to peace, back to life.

NOTES

1. After World War II, many Nazi leaders were tried for war crimes in the German city of Nüremberg. These trials, conducted by the Allied armies of the U.S., England, Russia, and France, is the subject of the entire piece, excerpted here. Hermann Göring (1893–1946), the creator of Hitler's air force, and Julius Streicher (1885–1946), a sadistic leader of anti-Semitic propaganda, were both convicted and sentenced to the hanged, although Göring committed suicide before the sentence could be carried out. Rudolf Hess (1894–1987), Hitler's deputy commander, was given life imprisonment, while Albert Speer, Hitler's architect, was imprisoned for twenty years, as was Nazi youth leader Baldur von Schirach (1907–1974). Banker Hjalmar Schacht (1877–1970) was acquitted.

2. West compares the aspect of the defendants to how Mary Stuart, Queen of Scots (1542–1587), who was beheaded by order of Queen Elizabeth I at Fotheringay in central England, and French general Napoleon Bonaparte (1769–1821), who conquered much of Europe, was himself finally conquered, and ended his days as a prisoner of war on the British island of Saint Helena, might appear if painted during the mid-ninteenth century by a very traditional British artist.

3. Jane Eyre, the main character in Charlotte Brontë's novel of the same name (1847) was, indeed, portrayed as a mousy, albeit passionate governess.

Clementina Arderiu   *Spain, 1893–1976*

Clementina Arderiu was born in Barcelona in 1893. She received a degree in piano and music theory and also studied languages. Her first poem was published in 1911 and her first book, *Poems i elegies* (Poems and Elegies) appeared in 1916, the year she married Carlos Riba (a well-known Catalan poet) and began to participate actively in the Catalan literary life. For the next two decades, she traveled through Europe and published *L'alta Llibertat* (The Heights of Freedom, 1920) and *Cant i paraules* (Words and Music, 1936). In 1938, during the Spanish Civil War, she was awarded the Joaquim Folguera Prize for *Sempre i ara* (Now and Always, 1946) and, as she sympathized with the defeated Republican cause, the next year she went into exile in France. Arderiu returned to Barcelona in 1943 and participated in the silent (and clandestine) literary activity of those years. In the late 1950s she received two important literary prizes—the Ossa Menor Prize and the Lletra d'or for her book *Es a dir* (That Is to Say). In 1969 she published her last book of poems *L'esperança encara* (There's Still Hope). All her work appeared in one volume, *Obra poètica* (Poetic Works), in 1973, three years before her death. The poems selected for this anthology appeared in *Cant i paraules* and in *L'esperança encara.*

Micaela Misiego

UNEASINESS
Desassossec

They give me turbid water
—I see the golden wine.

I do not hear the bell
—it rings within my heart.

What anguish in the air!
—the trees are full of fruit.

How pitiful the yieldings!
—I am richer than ever.

If I must be shipwrecked
I'll jump into the sea.

Translated by Micaela Misiego

FEAR
Basarda

Fear,
you spoil my afternoon;
you take away the roads
of my dreams. Miserable,
ugly birds
are fluttering in the air.
Good-bye, sweet light,
Good-bye, scent
of spring!
Today you have come
uncouth and ill-formed.
And I will not have
peace in the afternoon,
because fear
with its subtle threads
brings perverse murmurs
to my ears.

Translated by Micaela Misiego

THE CLIFF
El Salt

The first step was swift,
as the loosening of a ribbon;
and the mouth was smiling,
and the cheek was blushing.
That was the first step of one hundred
that followed
at the beginning of the climb.
    Good-bye, beloved; this is a path
    where you cannot follow me.

How hard the rocks, how hot the breeze,
and how annoying the droning of that

                                 wasp . . .

But up here there is much light,
and a soft wind to breathe.
I shiver, when I look around me!
The road behind me is there no more.
    You will never be able to reach me
    without the road.

What will I find, what will I do
if I reach the summit?
They say there is a cliff, and this scares me;
a painful feeling tries to stop me,
but to go back now is impossible.
I have to climb, and I will be
heavier still, and will go slowly.
    But wait for me at the end
    of my road.

A dreadful fear of emptiness has shocked me;
there is no step, no flight, no strength of arms;
death seems to be my only neighbor,
and death is sifting me through a thousand
                                 sieves.
Far below, the eyes of my beloved,
and his two arms as magnets.
    How strong you had to be
    to hear my moaning!

Then came the piercing cry, and the valley
full of sunlight was once again around me;
I was at peace, under a linen
sheet soft as a silken rose,
and lying by my side I had
the sum of all my love.
    What does the rough road matter,
                        beloved,
    when our child is here?

Translated by Micaela Misiego

THE OBSTINATE ONE
L'obstinada

The pride of victory contracts her moistened
                                lips,
her torso is still erect and her breast feels the
                             tension;
from her cruel and calculated last outburst
the enraged whip is shivering in her raised
                         right hand.
She has lashed the face of that courageous
                         child
who, full of joy and following the rhythm of a
                         song
promising glory, will appear sometimes
and, collecting your formerly scattered wishes,
will put them softly together to give you
                         happiness.
But she, the obstinate one, with the tortuous
                         heart,
suspects a fraud, and when the child donning a
                       new disguise
seeks her, he finds her stubbornly believing
the fortress of her heart to be invulnerable.
Alas, poor heart, languishing in the coldness of
                         death
of the flesh that surrounds it!

Translated by Micaela Misiego

WAITING
Espera encara

Death has left me drained
forever.
There are no birds, there are no swaying
flowers;
in this wasteland only the rocks
surface.
And I can still hear that voice
guiding me!
I have the words written to me
and keep them!

But I cannot find that steady
hand,
that strong and gentle hand, so selflessly
offered.
Enraged, I cannot go on. I look
behind me...
I can see Angels of God that
look at me,
they fold their wings and with their eyes
they tell me:
"You need still more virtue.
Wait."

Translated by Micaela Misiego

Nella Larsen

US, 1893–1963

The rediscovery in the 1970s of the women writers of the Harlem Renaissance brought renewed attention to the novels of Nella Larsen. A mulatto, born in Chicago to a Danish mother and a West Indian father, Larsen was raised as black; after her father died while Larsen was still a young girl, her mother remarried a white man who disliked his new daughter: both aspects lie behind Larsen's novels, *Quicksand* (1928) and *Passing* (1929), which probed female sexuality and worried the boundaries between white and black. Larsen studied science at Fisk University in Tennessee and married Elmer S. Imes, a physics professor. She visited relatives in Denmark and audited classes at the University of Copenhagen. In 1915 she graduated from the Lincoln Hospital Training School for Nurses in New York. She worked as a superintendent of nurses in Alabama and then as a nurse and a children's librarian in New York City, where she began to write.

Quicksand won Larsen second prize in literature from the Harmon Foundation, and praise from the leading black intellectual of the period, W.E.B. Du Bois. *Passing* received excellent reviews, and in 1930 Larsen became the first black woman to win a Guggenheim award for study abroad. That same year, however, following the publication of her story "Sanctuary," reprinted here for the first time since its original publication, Larsen was charged, apparently unfairly, with plagiarism. The charge marks the end of her career. She never finished her third novel, or anything else, working as a nurse in Brooklyn and dying in obscurity in 1963.

The backdrop of Larsen's writing and career is the tortured political esthetics of the Harlem Renaissance. Black writers struggled with contradictory impulses: fostering racial pride and protest and capturing without uplifting clichés the undeniable vitality of Harlem street life. The conflict between a "politically correct" but essentially sentimental style and a properly modernist concern with forbidden experience was especially acute for black women writers, who were often tempted to replace racist images of black women as "erotic primitives" with their opposite, images of pure, virginal black women. This difficulty shows up in Larsen's novels in her abruptly conventional or melodramatic endings.

In *Quicksand*, Helga Crane, a mulatto like Larsen, torn between wanting respectability and wanting sexual fulfillment, undergoes an ambiguous, sexually charged religious conversion and then enters an equally ambiguous marriage. Desire is subordinated to motherhood, the self to the other: "And hardly had she left her bed and become able to walk again without pain, hardly had the children returned from the home of the neighbors, when she began to have her fifth child." In *Passing*, the story of Irene Redfield and Clare Kendry, near-white "society Negros," Larsen renews her exploration of sexuality in a race-conscious society before lapsing into thirty years of silence.

Eric Mendelsohn

SANCTUARY

I

On the Southern coast, between Merton and Shawboro, there is a strip of desolation some half a mile wide and nearly ten miles long between the sea and old fields of ruined plantations. Skirting the edge of this narrow jungle is a partly grown-over road which still shows traces of furrows made by the wheels of wagons that have long since rotted away or been cut into firewood. This road is little used, now that the state has built its new highway a bit to the west and wagons are less numerous than automobiles.

In the forsaken road a man was walking swiftly. But in spite of his hurry, at every step he set down his feet with infinite care, for the night was windless and the heavy silence intensified each sound; even the breaking of a twig could be plainly heard. And the man had need of caution as well as haste.

Before a lonely cottage that shrank timidly back from the road the man hesitated a moment, then struck out across the patch of green in front of it. Stepping behind a clump of bushes close to the house, he looked in through the lighted window at Annie Poole, standing at her kitchen table mixing the supper biscuits.

He was a big, black man with pale brown eyes in which there was an odd mixture of fear and amazement. The light showed streaks of gray soil on his heavy, sweating face and great hands, and on his torn clothes. In his woolly hair clung bits of dried leaves and dead grass.

He made a gesture as if to tap on the window, but turned away to the door instead. Without knocking he opened it and went in.

II

The woman's brown gaze was immediately on him, though she did not move. She said, "You ain't in no hurry, is you, Jim Hammer?" It wasn't, however, entirely a question.

"Ah's in trubble, Mis' Poole," the man explained, his voice shaking, his fingers twitching.

"W'at you done done now?"

"Shot a man, Mis' Poole."

"Trufe?" The woman seemed calm. But the word was spat out.

"Yas'm. Shot 'im." In the man's tone was something of wonder, as if he himself could not quite believe that he had really done this thing which he affirmed.

"Daid?"

"Dunno, Mis' Poole. Dunno."

"White man o' niggah?"

"Cain't say, Mis' Poole. White man, Ah reckons."

Annie Poole looked at him with cold contempt. She was a tiny, withered woman—fifty perhaps—with a wrinkled face the color of old copper, framed by a crinkly mass of white hair. But about her small figure was some quality of hardness that belied her appearance of frailty. At last she spoke, boring her sharp little eyes into those of the anxious creature before her.

"An' w'at am you lookin' foh me to do 'bout et?"

"Jes' lemme stop till dey's gone by. Hide me till dey passes. Reckon dey ain't fur off now." His begging voice changed to a frightened whimper. "Foh de Lawd's sake, Mis' Poole, lemme stop."

And why, the woman inquired caustically, should she run the dangerous risk of hiding him?

"Obadiah, he'd lemme stop ef he was to home," the man whined.

Annie Poole sighed. "Yas," she admitted, slowly, reluctantly, "Ah spec' he would. Obadiah, he's too good to youall no 'count trash." Her slight shoulders lifted in a hopeless shrug. "Yas, Ah reckon he'd do et. Emspecial' seein how he allus set such a heap o' store by you. Cain't see w'at foh, mahse'f. Ah shuah don' see nuffin' in you but a heap o' dirt."

But a look of irony, of cunning, of complicity passed over her face. She went on, "Still, 'siderin' all an' all, how Obadiah's right fon' o'you, an' how white folks is white folks, Ah'm a-gwine hide you dis one time."

Crossing the kitchen, she opened a door leading into a small bedroom, saying, "Git yo'se'f in dat dere feather baid an' Ah'm a-gwine put de clo's on de top. Don' reckon dey'll fin' you ef dey does look foh you in mah house. An Ah don' spec' dey'll go foh to do dat. Not lessen you been keerless an' let 'em smell you out gittin' hyah." She turned on him a withering look. "But you allus been triflin'. Cain't do nuffin propah. An' Ah'm a-tellin' you ef dey warn't white folks an' you a po' niggah, Ah shuah wouldn't be lettin' you mess up mah feather baid dis ebenin', 'cose Ah jes' plain don' want you hyah. Ah done kep' mahse'f outen trubble all mah life. So's Obadiah."

"Ah's powahful 'bliged to you, Mis' Poole. You shuah am one good 'oman. De Lawd'll mos' suttinly—"

Annie Poole cut him off. "Dis ain't no time foh all dat kin' o' fiddle-de-roll. Ah does mah duty as Ah sees et 'thout no thanks from you. Ef de Lawd had gib you a white face 'stead o' dat dere black one, Ah shuah would turn you out. Now hush yo' mouf an' git yo'se'f in. An' don' git movin' and scrunchin' undah dose covahs and git yo'se'f kotched in mah house."

Without further comment the man did as he was told. After he had laid his soiled body and grimy garments between her snowy sheets, Annie Poole carefully rearranged the covering and placed piles of freshly laundered linen on top. Then she gave a pat here and there, eyed the result, and finding it satisfactory, went back to her cooking.

III

Jim Hammer settled down to the racking business of waiting until the approaching danger should have passed him by. Soon savory odors seeped in to him and he realized that he was hungry. He wished that Annie Poole would bring him something to eat. Just one biscuit. But she wouldn't, he knew. Not she. She was a hard one, Obadiah's mother.

By and by he fell into a sleep from which he was dragged back by the rumbling sound of wheels in the road outside. For a second, fear clutched so tightly at him that he almost leaped from the suffocating shelter of the bed in order to make some active attempt to escape the horror that his capture meant. There was a spasm at his heart, a pain so sharp, so slashing that he had to suppress an impulse to cry out. He felt himself falling. Down, down down.... Everything grew dim and very distant in his memory....Vanished....Came rushing back.

Outside there was silence. He strained his ears. Nothing. No footsteps. No voices. They had gone on then. Gone without even stopping to ask Annie Poole if she had seen him pass that way. A sigh of relief slipped from him. His thick lips curled in an ugly, cunning smile. It had been smart of him to think of coming to Obadiah's mother's to hide. She was an old demon, but he was safe in her house.

He lay a short while longer listening intently, and, hearing nothing, started to get up. But immediately he stopped, his yellow eyes glowing like pale flames. He had heard the unmistakable sound of men coming toward the house. Swiftly he slid back into the heavy, hot stuffiness of the bed and lay listening fearfully.

The terrifying sounds drew nearer. Slowly. Heavily. Just for a moment he thought they were not coming in—they took so long. But there was a light knock and the noise of a door being opened. His whole body went taut. His feet felt frozen, his hands clammy, his tongue like a weighted, dying thing. His pounding heart made it hard for his straining ears to hear what they were saying out there.

"Ebenin', Mistah Lowndes." Annie Poole's voice sounded as it always did, sharp and dry.

There was no answer. Or had he missed it? With slow care he shifted his position, bringing his head nearer the edge of the bed. Still he heard nothing. What were they waiting for? Why didn't they ask about him?

Annie Poole, it seemed, was of the same mind. "Ah don' reckon youall done traipsed 'way out hyah jes' foh yo' healf," she hinted.

"There's bad news for you, Annie, I'm 'fraid." The sheriff's voice was low and queer.

Jim Hammer visualized him standing out

there—a tall, stooped man, his white tobacco-stained mustache drooping limply at the ends, his nose hooked and sharp, his eyes blue and cold. Bill Lowndes was a hard one too. And white.

"W'atall bad news, Mistah Lowndes?" The woman put the question quietly, directly.

"Obadiah—" the sheriff began—hesitated —began again. "Obadiah—ah—er he's outside, Annie. I'm 'fraid—"

"Shucks! You done missed. Obadiah, he ain't done nuffin', Mistah Lowndes. Obadiah!" she called stridently, "Obadiah! git hyah an' splain yo'se'f."

But Obadiah didn't answer, didn't come in. Other men came in. Came in with steps that dragged and halted. No one spoke. Not even Annie Poole. Something was laid carefully upon the floor.

"Obadiah, chile," his mother said softly, "Obadiah, chile." Then, with sudden alarm, "He ain't daid, is he? Mistah Lowndes! Obadiah, he ain't daid?"

Jim Hammer didn't catch the answer to that pleading question. A new fear was stealing over him.

"There was a to-do, Annie," Bill Lowndes explained gently, "at the garage back o' the factory. Fellow tryin' to steal tires. Obadiah heerd a noise an' run out with two or three others. Scared the rascal all right. Fired off his gun an' run. We allow et to be Jim Hammer. Picked up his cap back there. Never was no 'count. Thievin' an' sly. But we'll git 'im; Annie. We'll git 'im."

The man huddled in the feather bed prayed silently. "Oh, Lawd! Ah didn't go to do et. Not Obadiah, Lawd. You knows dat. You knows et." And into his frenzied brain came the thought that it would be better for him to get up and go out to them before Annie Poole gave him away. For he was lost now. With all his great strength he tried to get himself out of the bed. But he couldn't.

"Oh Lawd" he moaned, "Oh Lawd!" His thoughts were bitter and they ran through his mind like panic. He knew that it had come to pass as it said somewhere in the Bible about the wicked. The Lord had stretched out his hand and smitten him. He was paralyzed. He couldn't move hand or foot. He moaned again. It was all there was left for him to do. For in the terror of this new calamity that had come upon him he had forgotten the waiting danger which was so near out there in the kitchen.

His hunters, however, didn't hear him. Bill Lowndes was saying, "We been a-lookin' for Jim out along the old road. Figured he'd make tracks for Shawboro. You ain't noticed anybody pass this evenin', Annie?"

The reply came promptly, unwaveringly. "No, Ah ain't sees nobody pass. Not yet."

IV

Jim Hammer caught his breath.

"Well," the sheriff concluded, "we'll be gittin' along. Obadiah was a mighty fine boy. Ef they was all like him—. I'm sorry, Annie. Anything I c'n do let me know."

"Thank you, Mistah Lowndes."

With the sound of the door closing on the departing men, power to move came back to the man in the bedroom. He pushed his dirt-caked feet out from the covers and rose up, but crouched down again. He wasn't cold now, but hot all over and burning. Almost he wished that Bill Lowndes and his men had taken him with them.

Annie Poole had come into the room.

It seemed a long time before Obadiah's mother spoke. When she did there were no tears, no reproaches; but there was a raging fury in her voice as she lashed out, "Git outen mah feather baid, Jim Hammer, an' outen mah house, an' don' nevah stop thankin' yo' Jesus he done gib you dat black face."

Sylvia Townsend Warner   *UK(England), 1893–1978*

Sylvia Townsend Warner was an extremely gifted and prolific writer—she published seven novels, ten volumes of short stories, and regularly had her stories published in *The New Yorker* (144 in all). Her first novel, *Lolly Willowes or The Loving Huntsman* (1926) was a Book-of-the-Month Club first selection and her second novel, *Mr. Fortune's Maggot* (1927) a Literary Guild selection. Nevertheless, despite some fine reviews, she has received little critical attention, a fate one reviewer, Eleanor Perenyi, ascribes to "the difficulty of placing her" in a category. For she is not really a historical novelist, although her novels tend to have chronologically remote settings, nor a socio-political novelist, although many of her works explore or explain political and economic realities.

Warner was born in Middlesex, England. Her father was a French master at the famous boy's school, Harrow; she, however, was educated at home and, although she had her father's large library to peruse, she deeply resented the system that sent its young boys to the best schools to be educated and expected the girls to make do at home. "A Spirit Rises," one of her most widely anthologized stories, describes her semi-autobiographical protagonist's feelings of deprivation as she calls herself "her father's Cinderella [who] went barefoot like a cobbler's child in the adage." Warner did get to study music at Harrow—informally—with one of the music masters, and went on to work as a musicologist, editing, with a committee, the ten-volume *Tudor Church Music* (1923–29).

Warner began her literary career by writing poetry; however, she is most important for her prose fiction. *Lolly Willowes* is about a "spinster" turned witch, and explores social conventions. *Mr. Fortune's Maggot* tells the story of a failed missionary on a South Sea island who, instead of saving, is "saved" by the islanders. *The Corner That Held Them* (1948) is about the day-to-day social and economic realities of life in a fourteenth-century English nunnery. The story presented here, "The Old Nun," is from Warner's short story collection *A Spirit Rises*.

Warner's ideology is not directly apparent in most of her writing (although *The Corner that Held Them* has been called Marxist); nonetheless she was a member of the Communist party for a number of years and quite active in left-wing politics. She shared her home near Dorchester in southwest England with her lover, the poet Valentine Ackland, from 1930 until Ackland's death in 1969. Warner was a fellow of the Royal Society of Literature and an honorary member of the American Academy of Arts and Letters.

THE OLD NUN

After the unpredictable current of living had swirled her past the point of death and back into life again (and in such an old woman, and one so tired, the Mother Superior's recovery seemed like a miracle to them all) and Dr. Kennedy, saying, "Well, Madam, you're not dead this time," had declared her out of danger, her married sister was allowed to visit her for a quarter of an hour. Into the extreme cleanliness and dispassionateness of the room Everina brought a smell of hot pavements, smoke, and car exhaust, as if some part of the industrial Thames-side town had shoved in with her. A large bouquet of white China asters shook with the pulse of her hand; her grey hair stuck out in tufts beneath a hat that was too small and too alert for her broad emotional face, and as she sat down a bus ticket dropped on to the floor.

"Oh, Chrissie, my love, what a scare you've given us! Not that I believed it. I never did. I wasn't going to give in. I just wouldn't believe it."

"No, dear. You never had much faith, had you?"

"Oh! Oh, you wretch! Well, I can see you're yourself again, biting my head off as usual, the same old catnip—and that's a comfort." Tweaked back from that imminent fit of weeping, she settled herself more squarely on the bentwood chair, drew a deep breath as if she were about to say a great deal and instead remained silent, obedient, and smiling.

"Well, Everina. Go on, I can see you're bursting."

"Chrissie, I am. I've got a piece of news for you, and thank God you're alive to hear it, for it's good news this time. Poor Ellen's Mary is out of the hospital and walking as well as ever. And that's not all. She's going to be married, and I couldn't like him better if I'd chosen him myself—the house surgeon at the hospital, and he was in love with her from the moment he saw her carried in all over blood on a stretcher. He's called Vincent Jones, he's got five brothers and three sisters, his father's a farmer in Herefordshire, I've seen all their photographs, and they've written the nicest letters. Such a good steady young man! Even Ellen's pleased, and she's coming out of black for the wedding. In October, and then he's going to a practice in Cumberland, the Lake district, think how romantic! Will you ever forget that evening we went in a boat on Ullswater? And, Chrissie, best of all, there's a house with it, so she can have all the children she wants without disobliging anyone. Five bridesmaids, no less. Three of ours and two of his. I've tacked up our three's already—taffeta, the colour of Petit-Beurre biscuits, with brown velvet muffs. Chrissie, I'm just beginning to feel I can enjoy it! It hasn't really seemed true till now—now, when I've seen with my own eyes that you're not dying. That's the worst of being my age—your heart's all over the place so!"

To the woman listening, it seemed true enough for her to ask, "And what's happening about Ellen?"

"Ellen? Well, she's coming to me. After all, she's my own daughter-in-law, and she can't be left alone with poor Billy. I'm really looking forward to Billy; it's nice to think there's one grandchild who'll never be anything but a baby."

"If you've no great talent for faith, you'll make up for it with charity. Now tell me about yourself."

"Me? There's nothing to tell about me. Or do you mean what shall I wear for the wedding? Do you think it would be positively indecent if I wore pink? I do so adore pink, and I shall never get another chance."

When Everina was gone—taken out after exactly fifteen minutes, as if she were some precise feat in cookery—though the room resumed its stillness, the stillness was not of the same quality. Listening had brought sounds into it—the creaking of the chair that had been so excitedly sat on, the hooting of the tugs on the river. There had been a night when she thought the tugs were trying to get her away, but try as they might, poor dutiful creatures, they could not budge her, for the weight of her limbs pinned her to the bed. And so Mary, God bless the child, was going to be married in pink. No, not in pink—what nonsense!—but she would go in a boat on Lake Ullswater with a good steady young man whose name was Vincent Jones. It was the sky that would be pink, the evening sky; and as the sunset faded, and the westward hills darkened and put on cloaks of contourless velvet, and every stroke of the oars cut a deeper swathe of darkness, and the ripples smacked with louder, lonelier exclamations, against indistincter banks, the

brows of the eastward fells would be clear and detailed in a hoary light, like moonlight, or like a powdering of frost. But it *was* moonlight, and the music had come with it, dance music sounding in the hollow shell of the tall hillsides; and now, as the boat rounded the bend, she could see, behind the silhouette of the oarsman, the lighted windows of the house on the shore, streaming with light, and flung open so that the music could be heard far and wide, calling impatiently for the dancers to come to it. So now she must stand up in the boat and dress herself in her ball dress. But which? The boat was full of them, a cargo of ball dresses, for she had not been able to decide among them before she set out, so she had brought them all with her. It was really rather silly to be standing up in a silk petticoat, bare-necked and bare-armed on such a chilly evening, dressing oneself on a boat in the middle of Lake Ullswater, and all because one had not been able to make up one's mind what to wear. Here was a dress that would do very nicely. It was made of white lace, and the scarf that matched it was sewn with milk-white sequins in a pattern of little Japanese fish. But in a ballroom one white dress is very much like another, and this dress hooked up at the back, a difficult dress to get into standing in a small rowing boat, so the yellow dress that was narrowly pleated like Greek statuary would be better, if she could find the scarlet sandals that went with it. When she had found the sandals under the bilge board, they were sopping wet; but here was a charming pair of grey slippers, quite dry, and warm, too, being lined with grey swansdown. Yes, that was it, and the dress had grey swansdown round the bosom and was the changing colour of blue-grey hydrangeas. She was half-way into it, and the trombones in the band were heavily breathing out the strong beat of a waltz measure, saying, 'Coom, Coom,' in their Cumberland accents, when she remembered that the dress she wanted to wear was the dress of pink tinsel. But when she picked it up from the floor of the boat where it lay glimmering and pale as the drowned Ophelia it turned itself into a dress of green velvet that had never belonged to her, wouldn't fit her, and had a most inconvenient fan fastened to it, that clattered like a Venetian blind. How tiresome it was to have so many dresses, and to be obliged to decide among them! And the lighted house was now so near (for the boatman, whose beard flowed down his waistcoat like a waterfall, was rowing faster and faster) that she could see the polished empty floor and the trombone's gigantic shadow shooting back and forth across it. If only there were not so many dresses, if only each had not some small thing wrong with it, if only she could make up her mind! Well, at any rate, here was a pair of long white kid gloves.

She was trembling so violently with cold and fluster that she could scarcely pull them on. She gave a tug; immediately a rent appeared in the floor of the boat, and the boatman, growing thin as a waterweed, disappeared through it; but not before he had handed her a packet of starch.... She opened her eyes and saw her old woman's hands, that not even a month's idleness had been able to blanch or supple. Practised in wakings, she observed that there was no change in the light of the room, and that Sister Mary Innocent

must have been standing there for quite a minute, long enough for her beads to have left off swinging while she stood looking down in quiet approval on an old woman taking a little nap.

"Yes, I have been asleep. And I'm glad to wake up, too, for I dreamed I was back in the world and obliged to choose what dress I would put on. It was most disagreeable, most unsatisfactory. We take God's mercies too much for granted, my child, but I assure you, we ought to be especially thankful for our habit.'

Safe ashore from her dream, she felt inclined to go into considerably more detail, and proffer the funny side of it as well as the spiritual bouquet. A woman of her age, and who had so recently been nose to nose with the King of Terrors, to be wobbling in a skiff in that skimpy petticoat...Lord, what is man, that he boasteth himself? But few things are more unedifying than the girlishness of Superiors, and few would feel this more correctly than Sister Mary Innocent. So she asked if Mrs. Kelly's flowers had been put in the chapel, and if their stalks had been snipped first; both answers being as satisfactory as she had known they would be she then said that her nap had given her quite an appetite, and that she thought she would venture on a poached egg.

Florbela Espanca   *Portugal, 1894–1930*

It is no exaggeration to call Florbela Espanca one of the greatest Portuguese poets of the twentieth century. She was unique in many respects. As the illegitimate daughter of a businessman and a domestic servant, Florbela (as she is commonly called) knew a series of mother figures, products of her father's libertine ways. Indeed, the only stable person in her early life was a brother who was to leave her desolate when he perished in one of the country's earliest aviation disasters. While it did not provide her with stability, her family did give her an education that culminated in three years of study in the Faculty of Law at the University of Lisbon. Florbela never became a lawyer. While still a student, she embarked on the first of three marital adventures and the two divorces that she obtained before divorce was outlawed by the dictator Salazar.

Florbela Espanca was a sickly, troubled, hypersensitive individual. Whether this was a consequence or a cause of her psychological and social imbalance is difficult to determine. What is obvious is that there was a certain amount of theatricality in her makeup that manifested itself not only in her mannered appearance but in the cultivation of a persona that flowed from life into poetry. Her untimely death in 1930 has yet to be satisfactorily explained.

The poetry of this attractive but troubled woman is characterized by a profound lyricism. It is filled with longing intricately linked with a dualistic eroticism that is at once seductive and chaste, and with a profound metaphysical quality that is again dualistic in that it impels her equally toward the experience of life and the desire for death. Her poetry also reveals a profound love for the soil of her native Alentejo. Formally, Florbela was drawn, above all, to the sonnet in all its expressive intensity.

As a writer, Florbela Espanca was critically marginal. She remained independent of the lively literary milieu of her day. That her work was nevertheless well received is attested to at once by the ease with which it found publication and by her voluminous correspondence with a variety of notable figures. Her first book of poems *Livro de Mágoas* (Book of Sorrows, 1919) was followed by *Livro de Soror Saudade* (Book of Sister Longing, 1923), and finally by *Charneca em Flor* (Heath in Bloom, 1930). A fourth book of poems, *Reliquiae* (Of Relics), and two collections of short stories, *As Máscaras do Destino* (The Masks of Destiny) and *O Dominó Preto* (The Black Domino), were published posthumously in 1931. A monumental edition of her complete works published in 1985 nearly doubled her known *oeuvre* with the addition of previously unedited stories and poems. It is a fitting testimony to the esteem in which she is held today. The following poems are from *Sonetos Completos* (Complete Sonnets, 1952).

Alice Clemente

PRINCE CHARMING
Prince Charmant...

In the languid fading of love-filled
afternoons that voluptuously expire,
I searched the crowd for Him whom I desire;
I searched for Him as well when all was stilled.

Oh, thick-gloomed nights of my soul!
Mouths, bleeding kisses, a flower's scent.
Eyes, fixed on a dream, humble, intent,
Hands, filled with violets, with roses, like a
        bowl...

And I never found my Prince of gleaming light.
Perhaps He still will come, fearless, with grace,
Out of morning mists, like a storybook
        knight.

Throughout our life glides the chimera, fate,
weaving with fragile fingers fragile lace...
We never meet the One for whom we wait.

Translated by Alexis Levitin

NIHIL NOVUM[1]

In the shadow of the magic portico
of Bruges[2] I've lived, in quite another age;
with Pierre Loti[3] I've seen Egyptian temples on
                                         a desert stage;
in India, I've cast flowers on the sacred river's
                                                  flow.

Along a horizon where opal mists curl,
facing the Bosphorus,[4] I've wandered, thinking
                                              of you.
And I have known the stillness of a cloister
                                          through
brocaded sunsets, Mother-of-pearl.

In Isfahan,[5] white roses were my bane.
Always, when I bit, the taste of ash.
Always a wild, empty moor,

sad, blooming, eager somewhat—in vain.
And life—always an illness, strange, obscure,
And the heart—always that same raw gash.

Translated by Alexis Levitin

MAN OF THE ALENTEJO
Alentejano

Hot sun, as the noon bell tolls,
kisses sad heather on the rolling hills.
At it since dawn, harvesters reap, still
happy in the gulleys between knolls.

Singing softly, young girls hold
witchery in black eyes, a strange shine,
and there are hidden features, dark and fine,
among those blades of high and burning gold.

The earth clasps in its sensuous fingers
blond tresses, wheat waving as it unfurls
beneath the gentle blessing of the sky.

And there's the long and drawn-out wail of
                                         singers...

And I am one of those young girls,
and calling out "God bless you all," you pass
                                             by.

Translated by Alexis Levitin

NOTES

1. Latin for "nothing new."
2. A city in Belgium with much of its medieval architecture intact.
3. A French author (1850–1923) whose romantic novels were often set in exotic lands.
4. A narrow strait of water between Europe and Asia.
5. The second largest city in Iran.

Jean Rhys   (Ellen Gwendoline Rhys Williams)

Dominica/UK(England), 1894–1979

Jean Rhys grew up on the island of Dominica in the West Indies. Its Negro and Creole cultures, the isolation of the colonial whites, the passivity and subordination of the white woman, and the quiet light and colors of the island are reflected in her writing, most dramatically in *Wide Sargasso Sea*. Rhys' stories of lonely, passive women, of desperate emotions and isolation, come out of her own life story: "If you want to write the truth...you must write from yourself," she wrote. "It must go out from yourself....I am the only truth I know."

Jean Rhys was born Ellen Gwendoline Rhys Williams, the fourth of five children. Her father, Rhys Williams, was a Welsh doctor who had come to

Dominica to practice; her mother, Minna Lockhart, was a third-generation Dominican Creole. Never close to her siblings, Rhys was a quiet, private child. Convent educated, an important part of her childhood revolved around the Catholic Church despite the fact that her parents were not strong believers. Another strong attraction in childhood was the Negro culture of the island. She wanted to be black, she said, because the women attended Mass in the most beautiful of dresses. So she learned Negro hymns and spent time with her Negro servants and, in her adolescence, wrote poetry expressing her alienation from white Dominican culture.

In her late teens she went to Europe with her aunt, attending first the Perse School and then the Royal Academy of Dramatic Arts. Her father's death a year later cut off financial support, and Rhys began doing odd jobs such as film extra and chorus girl. In 1919 she married a French man, Jean Langlet de Neve, and moved to Paris. It was there she met the American novelist Ford Maddox Ford (1873–1939), her eventual lover and patron.

Encouraged by Ford, Rhys began writing, partly as a means of supporting herself. In 1927, she published *The Left Bank: Sketches and Studies of Present-Day Bohemian Paris*. The book, a collection of twenty-two sketches, was introduced by Ford. *The Left Bank* stories portray, in Ford's words, a "spirit of undisciplined and unconventional youth, of hardship, of disillusion, of loose and nervous and artificial existence." Her characters live in the dregs, unable to get out of predicaments, incapable of feeling another's emotional distress, and isolated from others. Although early works, the stories show strong artistic control.

The Left Bank was followed in 1928 by *Postures* (reprinted in 1969 as *Quartet*), a novel based partly on her affair with Ford. In 1930 she published *After Leaving Mr. Mackenzie*. Her works by this time had begun to reflect her own life. Her heroines are unconscious and alienated, powerless underdogs who live in a cruel paternalistic society, victimized by men who do not consciously seek out power or domination but are compelled to power by the same unseen forces that drive Rhys' women to seek out the cruel comforts of these men.

Several more works followed, but although her books were well received, they were never popular. In 1939, *Good Morning, Midnight* was published. It was adapted for the stage by the actress Selma Vaz Dias. The monologue was broadcast by the BBC in 1957 and Rhys finally started to get the public attention she craved.

Despite a heart attack Rhys managed to finish her 1966 masterpiece, *Wide* Sargasso Sea (the story of Mr. Rochester's first wife, the second being Jane Eyre). This publication was timely in that it coincided with the resurgence of feminism. The woman's movement brought Rhys much praise for her delicate portraits of unexceptional women and earlier works were reprinted after being unavailable for a long while. When she died, a semi-recluse living in Devon, she was a writer of considerable fame.

The following story is from her 1968 collection, *Tigers are Better Looking*.

John Isom

NOTE

* Mr. Rochester and Jane Eyre are characters in Charlotte Brontë's novel *Jane Eyre* (1847).

THE LOTUS

"Garland says she's a tart."

"A tart! My dear Christine, have you seen her? After all, there are limits."

"What, round about the Portobello Road? I very much doubt it."

"Nonsense," Ronnie said, "She's writing a novel. Yes, dearie—" he opened his eyes very wide and turned the corners of his mouth down—"all about a girl who gets seduced—"

"Well, well."

"On a haystack." Ronnie roared with laughter.

"Perhaps we'll have a bit of luck; she may get tight earlier than usual tonight and not turn up."

"Not turn up? You bet she will."

Christine said, "I can't imagine why you asked her here at all."

"Well, she borrowed a book the other day, and she said she was coming up to return it. What was I to do?"

While they were still arguing there was a knock on the door and he called, "Come in....Christine, this is Mrs. Heath, Lotus Heath."

"Good evening," Lotus said in a hoarse voice. "How are you? Quite well, I hope ....Good evening, Mr. Miles. I've brought your book. *Most* enjoyable."

She was a middle-aged woman, short and stout. Her plump arms were bare, the finger nails varnished bright red. She had rouged her mouth unskilfully to match her nails, but her face was very pale. The front of her black dress was grey with powder.

"The way these windows rattle!" Christine said. "Hysterical, I call it." She wedged a piece of newspaper into the sash, then sat down on the divan. Lotus immediately moved over to her side and leaned forward.

"You do like me, dear, don't you? Say you like me."

"Of course I do."

"I think it's so nice of you to ask me up here." Lotus said. Her sad eyes, set very wide apart, rolled vaguely round the room, which was distempered yellow and decorated with steamship posters—"Morocco, Land of Sunshine," "Come to Beautiful Bali." "I get fed up, I can tell you, sitting by myself in the basement night after night. And day after day too if it comes to that."

Christine remarked primly, "This is a horribly depressing part of London, I always think."

Her nostrils dilated. Then she pressed her arms close against her sides, edged away and lit a cigarette, breathing the smoke in deeply.

"But you've got it very nice up here, haven't you? Is that a photograph of your father on the mantelpiece? You are like him."

Ronnie glanced at his wife and coughed. "Well, how's the poetry going?" he asked, smiling slyly as he said thw word "poetry" as if at an improper joke. "And the novel, how's that getting on?"

"Not too fast," Lotus said, looking at the whisky decanter. Ronnie got up hospitably.

She took the glass he handed to her, screwed up her eyes, emptied it at a gulp and watched him refill it with an absentminded expression.

"But it's wonderful the way it comes to me," she said. "It's going to be a long book. I'm going to get everything in—the whole damn thing. I'm going to write a book like nobody's ever written before."

"You're quite right, Mrs. Heath, make it a long book," Ronnie advised.

His politely interested expression annoyed Christine. "Is he trying to be funny?" she thought, and felt prickles of irritation all over her body. She got up, murmuring, "I'll see if there's any more whisky. It's sure to be needed."

"The awful thing," Lotus said as she was going out, "is not knowing the words. That's the torture—knowing the thing and not knowing the words."

In the bedroom next door Christine could

still hear her monotonous, sing-song voice, the voice of a woman who often talked to herself. "Springing this ghastly old creature on me!" she thought. "Ronnie must be mad."

"This place is getting me down," she thought. The front door was painted a bland blue. There were four small brass plates and bell-pushes on the right-hand side—Mr. and Mrs. Garland, Mr. and Mrs. Miles, Mrs. Spencer, Miss Reid, and a dirty visiting-card tacked underneath—Mrs. Lotus Heath. A painted finger pointed downwards.

Christine powdered her face and made up her mouth carefully. What could the fool be talking about?

"Is it as hopeless as all that?" she said, when she opened the sitting-room door. Lotus was in tears.

"Very good." Ronnie looked bashful and shuffled his feet. "Very good indeed, but a bit sad. Really, a bit on the sad side, don't you think?"

Christine laughed softly.

"That's what my friend told me," Lotus said, ignoring her hostess. "'Whatever you do, don't be gloomy,' he said, 'because that gets on people's nerves. And don't write about anything you know, for then you get excited and say too much, and that gets under their skins too. Make it up; use your imagination.' And what about my book? That isn't sad, is it? I'm using my imagination. All the same, I wish I could write down some of things that have happened to me, just write them down straight, sad or not sad. I've had my bit of fun too; I'll say I have."

Ronnie looked at Christine, but instead of responding she looked away and pushed the decanter across the table.

"Have another drink before you tell us any more. Do, please. That's what the whisky's here for. Make the most of it, because I'm sorry to say there isn't any more in the kitchen and the pub is shut now."

"She thinks I'm drinking too much of your Scotch," Lotus said to Ronnie.

"No, I'm sure she doesn't think that."

"Well, don't think that, dear—what's your name?—Christine. I've got a bottle of port downstairs and I'll go and get it in a minute."

"Do," Christine said, "Let's be really matey."

"That's right, dear. Well, as I was saying to Mr. Miles, the best thing I ever wrote was poetry. I don't give a damn about the novel, just between you and me. Only to make some money, the novel is. Poetry's what I really like. All the same, the memory I've got, you wouldn't believe. Do you know, I can remember things people have said to me ever so long ago? If I try, I can hear the words and I can remember the voice saying them. It's wonderful, the memory I've got. Of course, I can't do it as well now as I used to, but there you are, nobody stays young for ever."

"No, isn't it distressing?" Christine remarked to no one in particular. "Most people go on living long after they ought to be dead, don't they? Especially women."

"Sarcastic, isn't she? A dainty little thing, but sarcastic." Lotus got up, swayed and held on to the mantelpiece. "Are you a mother, dear?"

"Do you mean me?"

"No, I can see you're not—and never will be if you can help it. You're too fly, aren't you? Well, anyway, I've just finished a poem. I wrote it with the tears running down my face and it's the best thing I ever wrote. It was as if somebody was saying into my ears all the time, 'Write it, write it.' Just like that. It's about a woman and she's in court and she hears the judge condemning her son to death. 'You must die,' he says. 'No, no, no,' the woman says, 'he's too young.' But the old judge keeps on. 'Till you die,' he says. And, you see—" her voice rose—"he's not real. He's a dummy, like one of those things ventriloquists have, he's not *real*. And nobody knows it. But she knows it. And so she says—wait, I'll recite it to you."

She walked into the middle of the room and stood very straight, with her head thrown back and her feet together. Then she clasped her hands loosely behind her back and announced in a high, artificial voice, "The Convict's Mother."

Christine began to laugh. "This is too funny. You mustn't think me rude, I can't help it. Recitations always make me behave badly." She went to the gramophone and turned over the records. "Dance for us instead. I'm sure you dance beautifully. Here's the very thing— *Just One More Chance.* That'll do, won't it?"

"Don't take any notice of her," Ronnie said. "You go on with the poem."

"Not much I won't. What's the good, if your wife doesn't like poetry?"

"Oh, she's only a silly kid."

"Tell me what you laugh at, and I'll tell you what you are," Lotus said. "Most people laugh when you're unhappy, that's when they laugh. I've lived long enough to know that— and maybe I'll live long enough to see them laugh the other side of their faces, too."

"Don't you take any notice of her," Ronnie repeated. "She's like that." He nodded at Christine's back, speaking in a proud and tender voice. "She was telling me only this morning that she doesn't believe in being sentimental about other people. Weren't you, Christine?"

"I didn't tell you anything of the sort." Christine turned round, her face scarlet. "I said I was tired of slop—that's what I said. And I said I was sick of being asked to pity people who are only getting what they deserve. When people have a rotten time you can bet it's their own fault."

"Go on," said Lotus. "You're talking like a bloody fool, dear. You've never felt anything in your life, or you wouldn't be able to say that. Rudimentary heart, that's your trouble. Your father may be a clergyman, but you've got a rudimentary heart all the same." She was still standing in the middle of the room, with her hands behind her back. "You tell her, Mr. What's-your-name? Tell the truth and shame the devil. Go on, tell your little friend she's talking like a bloody fool."

"Now, now, now, what's all this about?" Ronnie shifted uncomfortably. He reached out for the decanter and tilted it upside down into his glass. "It's always when you want a drink really badly that there isn't any more. Have you ever noticed it? What about that port?"

The two women were glaring at each other. Neither answered him.

"What about that port, Mrs. Heath? Let's have a look at that port you promised us."

"Oh yes, the port," Lotus said, "the port. All right, I'll get it."

As soon as she had gone Christine began to walk up and down the room furiously. "What's the idea? Why are you encouraging that horrible woman? 'Your little friend,' did you hear that? Does she think I'm your concubine or something? Do you like her to insult me?"

"Oh, don't be silly, she didn't mean to insult you," Ronnie argued. "She's tight— that's what's the matter with her. I think she's damned comic. She's the funniest old relic of the past I've struck for a long time."

Christine went on as if she had not heard him. "This hellish, filthy slum and my hellish life in it! And now you must produce this creature, who stinks of whisky and all the rest better left unsaid, to *talk* to me. To talk to me! There are limits, as you said yourself, there are limits....Seduced on a haystack, my God!...She oughtn't to be touched with a barge-pole."

"I say, look out," Ronnie said. "She's coming back. She'll hear you."

"Let her hear me," said Christine.

She went on to the landing and stood there. When she saw the top of Lotus' head she said in a clear, high voice, "I really can't stay any longer in the same room as that woman. The mixture of whisky and mustiness is too awful."

She went into the bedroom, sat down on the bed and began to laugh. Soon she was laughing so heartily that she had to put the back of her hand over her mouth to stop the noise.

"Hullo," Ronnie said, "so here you are."

"I couldn't find the port."

"That's all right. Don't you worry about that."

"I did have some."

"That's quite all right....My wife's not very well. She's had to go to bed."

"I know when I've had the bird, Mr. Miles," Lotus said. "Only give us another drink. I bet you've got some put away somewhere."

There was some sherry in the cupboard.

"Thanks muchly."

"Won't you sit down?"

"No, I'm going. But see me downstairs. It's so dark, and I don't know where the lights are."

"Certainly, certainly."

He went ahead, turning on the lights at each landing, and she followed him, holding on to the banisters.

Outside, the rain had stopped but the wind was still blowing strong and very cold.

"Help me down these damned steps, will you? I don't feel too good."

He put his hand under her arm and they went down the area steps. She got her key out of her bag and opened the door of the basement flat.

"Come on in for a minute. I've got a lovely fire going."

The room was small and crowded with furniture. Four straight-backed chairs with rococo legs, armchairs with the stuffing coming out, piles of old magazines, photographs of Lotus herself, always in elaborate evening dress, smiling and lifeless.

Ronnie stood rocking himself from heel to toe. He liked the photographs. "Must have been a good-looking girl twenty years ago," he thought, and as if in answer Lotus said in a tearful voice, "I had everything; my God, I had. Eyes, hair, teeth, figure, the whole damned thing. And what was the good of it?"

The window was shut and a brown curtain was drawn across it. The room was full of the sour smell of the three dustbins that stood in the area outside.

"What d'you pay for this place?" Ronnie said, stroking his chin.

"Thirty bob a week, unfurnished."

"Do you know that woman owns four houses along this street? And every floor let, basements and all. But there you are—money makes money, and if you haven't any you can whistle for it. Yes, money makes money."

"Let it," said Lotus. "I don't care a damn."

"Now then, don't talk so wildly."

"I don't care a damn. Tell the world I said it. Not a damn. That was never what I wanted. I don't care about the things you care about."

"Cracked, poor old soul," he thought, and said: "Well, I'll be getting along if you're all right."

"You know—that port. I really had some. I wouldn't have told you I had some if I hadn't. I'm not that sort of person at all. You believe me, don't you?"

"Of course I do." He patted her shoulder. "Don't you worry about a little thing like that."

"When I came down it had gone. And I don't need anybody to tell me where it went, either."

"Ah?"

"Some people are blighters; some people are proper blighters. He takes everything he can lay his hands on. Never comes to see me except it's to grab something." She put her elbows on her knees and her head in her hands and began to cry. "I've had enough. I've had enough, I can tell you. The things people say! My Christ, the things they say...."

"Oh, don't let them get you down," Ronnie said. "That'll never do. Better luck next time."

She did not answer or look at him. He fidgeted. "Well, I must be running along, I'm afraid. Cheerio. Remember—better luck next time."

As soon as he got upstairs Christine called out from the bedroom, and when he went in she told him that they must get away, that it wasn't any good saying he couldn't afford a better flat, he must afford a better flat.

Ronnie thought that on the whole she was right, but she talked and talked and after a while it got on his nerves. So he went back into the sitting room and read a list of second-hand gramophone records for sale at a shop near by, underlining the titles that attracted him. *I'm a Dreamer, Aren't We All? I've Got You Under My Skin*—that one certainly; he underlined it twice. Then he collected the glasses and took them into the kitchen for the charwoman to wash up the next morning.

He opened the window and looked out at the wet street. "I've got you under my skin," he hummed softly.

The street was dark as a country lane, bordered with lopped trees. It glistened—rather wickedly, he thought.

"Deep in the heart of me," he hummed. Then he shivered—a very cold wind for the time of year—turned away from the window and wrote a note to the charwoman: "Mrs. Bryan. Please call me as soon as you get here." He underlined "soon" and propped the envelope up against one of the dirty dishes. As he did so he heard an odd, squeaking noise. He looked out of the window again. A white figure was rushing up the street, looking very small and strange in the darkness.

"But she's got nothing on," he said aloud, and craned out eagerly.

A police whistle sounded. The squeaking continued, and the Garlands' window above him went up.

Two policemen half supported, half dragged Lotus along. One of them had wrapped her in his cape, which hung down to her knees. Her legs were moving unsteadily below it. The trio went down the area steps.

Christine had come into the kitchen and was looking over his shoulder. "Good Lord," she said. "Well, that's one way of attracting attention if all else fails."

The bell rang.

"It's one of the policemen," said Ronnie.

"What's he want to ring our bell for? We don't know anything about her. Why doesn't he ring somebody else's bell?"

The bell rang again.

"I'd better go down," Ronnie said.

"Do you know anything about Mrs. Heath, Mrs. Lotus Heath, who lives in the basement flat?" the policeman asked.

"I know her by sight," Ronnie answered cautiously.

"She's a bit of a mess," said the policeman.

"Oh, dear!"

"She's passed out stone cold," the policeman went on confidentially. "And she looks as if there's something more than drink the matter, if you ask me."

Ronnie said in a shocked voice—he did not know why—"Is she dying?"

"Dying? No!" said the policeman, and when he said "No!" death became unthinkable, the invention of hysteria, something that simply didn't happen. Not to ordinary people. "She'll be all right. There'll be an ambulance here in a minute. Do you know anything about the person?"

"Nothing," Ronnie said, "nothing."

"Ah?" The policeman wrote in his notebook. "Is there anybody else in the house, do you think, who'd give us some information?" He shone a light on the brass plates on the door post. "Mr. Garland?"

"Not Mr. Garland," Ronnie answered hurriedly. "I'm sure not. She's not at all friendly with the Garlands, I know that for a fact. She didn't have much to do with anybody."

"Thank you very much," the policeman said. Was his voice ironical?

He pressed Miss Reid's bell and when no answer came looked upwards darkly. But he didn't get any change out of Number Six, Albion Crescent. Everybody had put their lights out and shut their windows.

"You see—" Ronnie began.

"Yes, I see," the policeman said.

When Ronnie got upstairs again Christine was in bed.

"Well, what was it all about?"

"She seems to have conked out. They're getting an ambulance."

"Really? Poor devil." ("Poor devil" she said, but it did not mean anything.) "I thought she looked awful, didn't you? That dead-white face, and her lips such a funny colour after her lipstick got rubbed off. Did you notice?"

A car stopped outside and Ronnie saw the procession coming up the area steps, everybody looking very solemn and important. And it was pretty slick, too—the way they put the stretcher into the ambulance. He knew that the Garlands were watching from the top floor and Mrs. Spencer from the floor below. Miss Reid's floor was in darkness because she was away for a few days.

"Funny how this street gives me goose-flesh tonight," he thought. "Somebody walking over my grave, as they say."

He could not help admiring the way Christine ignored the whole sordid affair, lying there with her eyes shut and the eiderdown pulled up under her chin, smiling a little. She looked very pretty, warm and happy like a child when you have given it a sweet to suck. And peaceful.

A lovely child. So lovely that he had to tell her how lovely she was, and start kissing her.

Gertrude Kasebier, The Sketch, *ca. 1902, black and white photograph.*
Courtesy International Museum of Photography at George Eastman House, Rochester, N.Y.

Genevieve Taggard   *US, 1894–1948*

Genevieve Taggard was born in a small town in Washington State to parents who were members of a fundamentalist sect, the Disciples of Christ. As a young child she moved to Hawaii, the relative freedom and luxuriance of which contrasted sharply with the temper of her missionary parents and the small town of her origin: her experience there was to be an important subject of her poetry (*Hawaiian Hilltop*, 1923; later expanded and reprinted as *Origin: Hawaii*, 1947). She attended the University of California at Berkeley, where she met and befriended the writer Josephine Herbst, the poets Josephine Miles and Hildegarde Flanner, and others, who were to be associated with the founding of the artists' colony in Carmel, California. By the time she graduated in 1920, she knew what she wanted to do with her life. She had begun writing poetry at an early age, and she had become interested in politics and social causes. She matured at a time when such a combination of interests, if possible and even desirable, was far from easy. She was to continue throughout her life to struggle with the often conflicting demands of social reform and artistic concentration.

She moved to New York City, married Robert L. Wolf (by whom she had one daughter), and took a job in publishing; after Wolf's mental breakdown and institutionalization, she was left to raise her daughter on her own. In 1934, she married Kenneth Durant. She began writing for *The Liberator*, edited by Max Eastman. She also wrote for the *Freeman*, an important left-wing journal of the 1920s and 1930s, and she published many of her poems in *New Masses*, the successor to the radical journal *Masses*. But her poetry also appeared in the *New Yorker*, hardly a left-wing magazine. In 1925, Taggard edited a significant anthology of verse from *Masses-Liberator* (the successor of those two publications), entitled *May Days*, notable for including many now-forgotten women whose work she believed reflected the era; in her introduction, she argued for the "cross-pollenizing" of "social passion and creative beauty."

In *Collected Poems (1918–1938)*, we can read in one of her longer poems, "Ice Age," an extended meditation on the end of the world (this long before the so-called nuclear age) that combines a lyric love of nature's powers of replenishment with a primitive fascination with the absence of culture that is one of modernism's favorite themes. "They'll touch Cautiously their children and their lovers—clutch/Anything alive." Another long poem, "Evening of Self-Love," dwells on the theme of one's autonomy and the threats against such autonomy presented by other people and the social demands of living. The main figure is a New England farm woman who watches a sunset and tries to come to terms with her solitude; the poem owes something to Robert Frost's monologues, but it is equally indebted to modern psychology and its concern with the forces of gender and economic and social limits. In such works as "Remote Design," "Problem of Evil into Cocoon," and "Exchange of Awe," we can trace the influence of Emily Dickinson, about whom Taggard had published a book in 1930. Nonetheless, Taggard's poems frequently map the geography of her varied travels as much as they graph the individuality of her vision, a fact emphasized by the most recent selection of her works *To the Natural World* (1980).

Edmund Wilson discussed her work in his book *The Shores of Light* (1952), as did Daniel Aaron in *Writers on the Left* (1961). Nonetheless, Taggard's work was not at all fashionable in the academic world of the 1950s, and so her reputation has suffered considerably since her death. With the renewed interest in the traditions of women's writing as well as that of socially conscious literature, Taggard's work may well find a place in the canon.

Charles Molesworth

TO MR. MAUNDER MAUNDER, PROFESSIONAL POET

I'll be your Gigadibs,—despise
  You, root and branch and lock and barrel;
The filmy way you use your eyes;
  The words you take for your apparel;
The way you edit with discretion;
The poetry you pick for nice
Work of a safe and sane profession.

You should be shown the edge of the sword,
  And taught to die for a stubborn phrase
Or burn on pyres for a word!
  And have swift passions, in a horde
Run up and peer into your face
And jeer your petty, petty grace—
Have mercy on Thy Poets, Lord!

Here, learn the temper of the tool
  You wield so avid for success.
I will not touch your "beautiful"—
  Carve beauty more and rant her less...
The English Language is no whore—
What are you making rhyme-schemes for?
(New York City 1927)

DETAIL

On a New York evening of thin tedium
A woman with blue eyes and some feeling read
A poem; while the city like a drum
Heavied her voice. Casually, she was dead

A little later. I recall and cannot find
The poem. It was a poem then,
About a clock that ticked and would unwind
In an old house, and strike out nine or ten

While sparrows chaffered and feathered on
                    outside.

By Thomas Hardy. Three quatrains.
We were not friends. We were polite. She died
In a meagre way, I think, of minor pains....

And in the deckle edges of his thick
Books I have looked, but I cannot find
The poem. Still the clock does tick
Somewhere, and the springs unwind.
(And the insignificant woman, and the dull,
                        polite
Evening...the subway crammed and
                      stale....)
Goodnight, goodnight, goodnight, goodnight,
                  goodnight,
Woman and poem in limbo.
               Detail, detail,
Of the infallible city of our failure, drawn to
                    scale.

(Winterton, New York 1927)

TURN TO THE EAST

Not Tu Fu,[1] nor the copyist's brush-stroke soft,
Nor rice wine in jade cups.
Not three tones of ink in vista-far crags:
Distance and the ages composed in inches;
Nor the autumn rains on yards of old silk in
                                    museums,
Nor Kuan Yin, mercy goddess in gold,
Nor fat buddhas in gold rows, gold upon
                                    cedar,
Nor gongs sombre and brassy....
These are the husks of China. China in a book.

Not trips sold in job lots to tourists;
Not the hymn sung off-key in the mission,
No junk dragons, junk temple bells, slick
                                    brocades,
No hotel flappers, Hollywood stuff, no hop for
                                    addicts...

China has moved. Now no longer even
The paper dragon twisting pantomime
Down the village street under fire-cracker noise
Down the mud street under dry bamboo...
Nor the little object, art of real glaze
Best in the world, art of pure porcelain,
The superlative shade of good yellow;
Now none of these.
China has crawled away and left its skin for
                                    your museum,
For your elegant little home.
For China the face of Chu Teh[2] rising out of
                                    deep Asia,
Chu Teh on a banner, Sun Yat Sen on a banner,
Blowing in a big wind, higher than the
                                    Emperor's falcon flew,
Over a marching horde
Longer than the Wall.

A newsreel, not a painting on silk, a far-away
                                    film, come close,
Beautiful and harsh, a flicker on a screen in
                                    Manhattan.
Close-up of the face of a slim girl in denim.
She looks direct at you under her short hair.
Her shoes are of straw. *Greetings to comrades
                                    in Spain.*

Then empty land and on the beige plain
Four little mongolian ponies trotting,
                                    galloping,
With short legs, very fat in the belly, and four
                                    men riding, out-posts,
All going hard over the plain into a big wind.
Disregarded the whining and flirting of fans on
                                    the stage
To the tiddle of sticks.
No more for American globe trotters, the loot
                                    of bazaars.
For those who stay at home and collect fine
                                    feelings, no more
Silence and melancholy after we read aloud
The River Merchant's Wife, purified by
                                    restraint of centuries
Re-written by Ezra.[3]
          No, now they create, they re-create
China in the tall image, the ancestor on a
                                    banner.
No more mandarin papas. The hand with the
                                    fine brush
Trembles in the silk sleeve; the telephone rings.
The jade collectors had better go home quick.
The puny children of the consul say good-bye
                                    to their good old Amah,
The corrupt legations can put up their shutters
                                    now and fade.
A big wind is beginning to blow
In the teeth of the barbarian. All over Asia
People migrate and arm. They laugh direct into
                                    the camera.
Tax collectors run by in a litter of leaves.
The spies stay and are shot; one, two, three,
                                    they fall
Like fat pigeons. People migrate and arm.
I wouldn't try to get up the Yangtse, lady.
Wind and poppy fields yellow with a big angry
                                    river.

China is a long caravan, longer and stronger
                         than the Wall.
A moving Wall no Emperor made,
A Wall against the barbarian.
The film shows: a little rice, pamphlets, and a
                              clean gun.

(Lake Champlain 1938)

NOTES

1. Tu Fu (712–770): great poet of the T'ang dynasty, known for his portrayal of the social and political disorders of his time, when China was being ruined by military rebellions and wars with border tribes; remarkable for his powers of description, he excelled in a difficult verse form known as lü-shih, or regulated verse.

2. Chu Teh (1886–1976): Chinese Communist soldier who led his section of the Red Army on the Long March to northwest China (1934–1935). He later became Deputy Chairman of the People's Republic of China, beginning 1954, and of the National People's Congress, beginning 1959.

3. The poem referred to appears in Ezra Pound's *Cathay* (1915); although Pound used the version by the 8th-century Japanese poet Rihaku, the original was by the Chinese Li Po (?–762 A.D.), known as the Great White Light, or the Heavenly Poet.

Anna Banti   (Lucia Lopresti Longhi)   *Italy, 1895–1985*

The novelist, critic, biographer and translator Anna Banti (born Lucia Lopresti) graduated from the University of Florence with a degree in the history of art. She married the distinguished art critic Roberto Longhi and became literary editor of the periodical *Paragone*, which they founded together. Her book on Lorenzo Lotto stands out among her contributions to art criticism, and Thackeray's *Vanity Fair* and Virginia Woolf's *Jacob's Room* are the best among her translations. She also produced, in 1965, the finest Italian biography of Matilde Serao. Turning to literature, she first published *Itinerario di Paolina* (Paolina's Itinerary, 1937), defined as autobiographical prose, then followed it with a collection of short stories, *Il coraggio delle donne* (The Courage of Women, 1940), a genre she cultivated with excellent results. *Le donne muoiono* (Women Die, 1951), was awarded the Viareggio Prize and *La monaca di Sciangai* (The Nun from Shanghai, 1957) won the Veillon Prize. *Da un paese vicino* (From a Country Near By, 1975) was her last collection.

Her second novel, *Artemisia* (1947), excerpted here, is a fictitious recreation of the life of the Baroque painter Artemisia Gentileschi, whom the author considers as one of the first women to have obtained, through hard work and talent, the right to a career and parity of sex. *Allarme sul lago* (Alarm on the Lake, 1954), is the life story of three women, narrated to a fourth.

Anna Banti has a unique, masterful, and complex narrative style. She frequently intertwines past and present with her own life and that of her heroines. Her basic theme is always that of the painful solitude of intelligent women and their struggle to have their creative work recognized in a society that does not give them professional and spiritual equality. She is, indeed, one of the strongest and most original feminist voices in Italian literature.

Banti also experimented with various structural forms. In the novel *Le mosche d'oro* (Golden Flies, 1962), she structures her story on two parallels: the odd-numbered chapters are dedicated to the male protagonist, the even-numbered chapters to the female protagonist. The basic theme is feminist. *Noi credevamo* (We Believed, 1967), on the other hand, is actually the biography of Domenico Lopresti (1809–1883), Banti's ancestor, written in the form of memoirs, starting with old age and regressing to his childhood. It is a work full of pessimism and void of all nostalgic heroism.

In *La camicia bruciata* (The Burned Nightgown, 1973), Banti recreates, in her own original way, the life of Marguerite-Louise of Orléans, wife of Cosimo III of Tuscany, and their children, the last of the Medici.* She concluded her literary work with the autobiographical novel *Un grido lacerante* (A Rending Cry, 1981) and *Quando anche le donne si misero a dipingere* (When Women Too Started Painting, 1982), which consists of short narrative biographies of twelve women painters.

Natalia Costa-Zalessow

NOTE

* The Medici were an Italian family that controlled Florence and much of Tuscany from the fifteenth to the mid-eighteenth century.

from ARTEMISIA

To the Reader

A new drawing near and converging of life past and life present; a new historical-literary concoction; an attempt to let our old and very potable fonts of everyday speech into the misbegotten swamp of literary Italian in circulation: such were the ambitions of the story entitled *Artemisia* which had reached its final pages in the spring of 1944. That summer, through events of war having, unfortunately, nothing of the exceptional about them, the manuscript was destroyed.

In the following years, my memory did not weary of keeping faith with a protagonist perhaps too beloved, and these new pages should, at least, justify my heartsore obstinacy. But because this time the need for telling was sustained by only a commemorative form of the fragment, and the story linked itself instinctively to personal emotion too pressing to be obliterated or betrayed, I believe the reader deserves some data on the circumstances of Artemisia Gentileschi, an extremely talented woman painter among the few that history records. Born in 1598, in Rome, to a Pisan

family. Daughter of Orazio, himself an excellent painter. Violated, in honor and in love, while yet a young girl. Humiliated victim of a public trial for rape. Who maintained a school of painting in Naples. Who hazarded to journey into heretical England in 1638. One of the first women to uphold, in word and in deed, the right to congenial work and parity of spirit between the two sexes.

The biographies do not indicate the year of her death.

(**A.B.**)

"Don't cry." In the silence that divides my sobs, one from the other, this voice conjures up a little girl who has climbed the hill and who wants to dispatch an urgent report. I do not raise my head. "Don't cry": the syllables repeat rapidly like a hailstone, a message, in summer's heat, from the high, cold skies. I do not raise my head; no one is near me.

Few things exist for me in this fatiguing and white August dawn in which I sit, in my nightgown, on the gravel of a little path in the

Boboli Gardens,[1] as in dream. From my stomach to my head I am wrung with tears, I cannot consciously help it, and I press my face against my knees. Beneath me, among the pebbles, my bare, gray feet; above me, as waves over a drowned man, the dull coming and going of people who ascend and descend the incline where I am, and who cannot care about a woman crouched in sobbing. People who, at four in the morning, are pushing forward like frightened sheep to gaze at the devastation of their country, to confront the terrors of a night during which the German mines, one after the other, overturned the crust of the earth. Without realizing it, I am crying for what each of them will see from Belvedere,[2] and my sobs go on boiling; irrational, flashing, wild snatches, the bridge of Santa Trinita, gilded towers, a floral-patterned cup that I used to drink from as a child. And again, while I stop an instant and I gather, in my emptiness, that I must yet get up, that sound, "don't cry," touches me hurriedly like a wave withdrawing. I finally raise my head which is already a memory and in this pose I listen for those words. I grow quiet, stunned by the discovery of my most grievous loss.

Under the debris of my house, I have lost Artemisia, my companion of three centuries ago, who was gently breathing, cradled by me on one hundred pages of script. I have recognized her voice while, from arcane wounds in my spirit, there gush forth tumultuous images that are, at the same time: Artemisia, stung, desperate, convulsed before dying, like a crushed dog; images all clean, clear, glittering under a May sun: the child Artemisia who hops among the artichokes of the monks on Monte Pincio, a few paces from home; the girl Artemisia, shut in a room with a handkerchief to her mouth so that no one will hear her crying; and furious, with hand raised in imprecation, her eyebrows crossed; and the young beauty, head bent and with slight smile, in a somewhat plain party dress, who passes through these streets, through these very streets. . . .

I see her grow distant with that bearing of Diana that she had about her at the age of eighteen or twenty when, married for expediency, she wanted no husband and lived in solitude.

I find her again in the meadow up near Belvedere where she is reclining on the warm grass in risk of the machine guns. "I defied people's talk, the whole neighborhood of Santo Spirito, of Sant'Onofrio.[3] I walked straight ahead, eyes open, without looking at anyone. I would go out alone, for disdain. . ." Mutely she wails like a Medusa among serpents and once again is stretched out on the ground, dispelled in a sleep white with dust, and turns her head aside, like a dead girl seeking a last breath. The twilight hovers above; last night all the stones of Florence were strong, all the things they sheltered were intact. There below, the last beams give way: they say that mysterious fires burn among the rubble. The cursed night begins again, but among the pacts of my lethargic sleep, on the terrified floor of a palace, a new presence wants to be recognized at any cost. . . .In the darkness, in the brutality of war's thunder, beneath my eyelids forced shut, the face of Artemisia, like that of a belligerent woman, catches fire: I could touch it, and I see in the middle of her forehead that vertical line, there since childhood, which only grew deeper. Like a raging sleepwalker, she begins to shout into my ear. She has a hoarse voice and the clipped accent of the Borgo commoners, worn-out yet inexhaustible means by which a desperate people seek to express themselves, to justify themselves. And what else did Artemisia do but justify herself from the age of fourteen on?. . .

"We were alone in the parlor. Madonna Tuzia was pounding at the cutting board in the kitchen. I said, I have a fever, leave me alone. He said, I have more fever than you; and he took me by the hand, he wanted us to walk up and down. The door to my bedroom was open. He forced me onto the bed and kept me there with his fists and his teeth, but I had seen Francesco's knife on the trunk. I stretched, I grasped it, and I drew it from below, cutting my palm." This testimony of bewildered anatomical precision from the girl Artemisia cannot take place between us. The words the midwives taught her after having examined her, have passed through my memory like sparks, leaving somber ash. And not even the tender Artemisia remembers them now. She leans her head, a sparrow's weight, on my shoulder and with convalescent voice: "Afterwards I bled every time and Agostino said I was of poor complexion." The look of disdain no longer serves; the large eyes become fixed without rancor, eyes of an innocent whom the secret of life will never convince. . . .

. . . Custom has not changed and Artemisia, despite the heat, closes the blind in full day so that no one will see her. Her brothers are working, Marco at leather, Giulio at a shop, Francesco at the plasterer's. They are as free as adults and, in the evening, they dine at the tavern *al fresco*. At this hour, a greenish hue tinges the face of the recluse Artemisia. Her hair hangs upon her cheeks like skeins of opaque silk. She sits and draws until dark and then, without opening the window, lights the lantern. Her models, dressed-up dolls and statuettes, are supplied by the studio of her father who works, eats and sleeps at Monte Cavallo. With the ribbons and silk that belong to her sparse trousseau, she touches up the subjects; in addition, there are flowers, fruits, a skull. Sometimes those well arranged and silent scenes terrify her, if her attention slackens. Then she rises, takes a few steps through the room which is the kitchen; this house has no parlor. She stops at the window without opening it. She is intent upon listening to the great noise of the courtyard whose every sound she recognizes. . . . Another few steps and an unimportant gesture, moving a basin from the kneading-board to the drain, filling a glass of water, and the girl is again seated with pencil-holder between her fingers. The lantern's light,

growing increasingly less hindered by the twilight, multiplies the shadowplay on the drapes and revives an interest in the subject; a new white page is begun.

Well into evening, her brothers return and Artemisia has not yet taken the liberty of opening the window for a breath of air, though no one would see her. She is still drawing with a sensible diligence that almost erases the signs of fatigue, the pinched eyes with their blue-black circles. Giulio and Marco go right to bed, but Francesco stays to lounge about the kitchen, pats the cat, snuffs out a light and always finds a way to stop for a second to look over his sister's shoulder: a split second and no more, because he well knows how Artemisia dislikes being watched while she works. Finally, he cannot resist the temptation to take a stool and sit with paper before him, charcoal in hand. He is content with a slice of the table and the portion of the model that is visible from where he sits. His hand, stiff from manual labor, loosens little by little and the nocturnal silence seems also to loosen in that exercise which, for the Gentileschi, is like a conversation. In monosyllables, in brief phrases, the real conversation gets started and now Francesco's drawing proceeds slowly and distractedly, his eyes wander from his paper and from the model in order to rest upon Artemisia's hands, upon her work. Now he no longer fears annoying her if he should follow the movement of her pencil and if, leaning towards her, he should linger to look at her drawing. The determination, secret yet evident, in the small, thin hand, slightly freckled at the back, is enough for two artists, and the boy ends by urging her on, applauding her freely. . . . And often Francesco saves his surprise, the spark of joy, till the very last moment: "In the shop of Angelo the sculptor, a painter from Modena said: I'd like to know how to paint like that young girl who lives at San Spirito, the daughter of Gentileschi." It is not easy, even for Francesco, to decipher the emotion in Artemisia's face. She withdraws, bending to gather

her papers, to pick up the pencil that has fallen to the floor. But the harmony of the gestures with which brother and sister straighten the table and put out the lamp is worth a handshake of thanks. Before disappearing to his straw cot behind the green drape, the boy opens the window, and the cold night air is like a gift that he leaves for Artemisia. She stops to breathe it in, on her way to bed, and grows a little dizzy, almost dismayed at the grand sky, high and distant, against which seems to beat the great bell of St. Peter's. Up there, the stars form their designs as if sifted to a luminous dust that awaits a giant brush. With hot palms touching the cold marble, knees on the stool, Artemisia abandons her head to the windowsill, feeling as if she were sailing towards her fate.

Translated by Joan Borrelli

NOTES

1. The beautiful gardens of the Boboli Palace in Florence are now a public park.
2. A spot in Florence from which you can see much of the city.
3. Florentine neighborhoods.

Juana de Ibarbourou   *Uruguay, 1895–1979*

Because she is known for writing "feminine" poetry, that is, lyrical poems on themes of love and death, Juana de Ibarbourou is often linked with Delmira Agustini, Alfonsina Storni, and Gabriela Mistral. Her first published collection of poems, *Las lenguas de diamante* (Diamond Tongues, 1919) was extraordinarily successful, the poems, acclaimed for their joyous spontaneity and sensuality, and her succeeding collections, *El cántaro fresco* (The Cool Pitcher, 1920) and *Raíz salvaje* (Savage Root, 1922) were equally popular. She quickly became known throughout Latin America as well as internationally, and was given the name of Juana de América by the Uruguayan legislature because her writings did so much to familiarize people with Latin American culture. Her presence was also felt within the Uruguayan artistic community, where she was known for her generous support of young writers.

While it was the early poems, with their primitive eroticism, that made Ibarbourou famous and to which her public continued to respond, it is her later work, like that in *La rosa de los vientos* (The Rose of the Winds, 1930) that she herself preferred. The later poems deal with the destructive power of time, especially as it affects women's physical beauty (a theme chosen, perhaps, because of the poet's own extraordinary beauty), and the constancy of their lovers. These poems are, naturally, more dour and cynical in tone than her earlier work. Her later work also included books on pedagogy, stories and poems for children, and devotional literature.

Married to an army officer, Juana de Ibarbourou had one son. The following poems are from *Las lenguas de diamante* and *Raíz salvaje*.

DEJECTION
Despecho

Oh how weary I am! I have laughed for so long.
For so long that the tears now appear in my
eyes;
For so long that the twitch now contracting
my mouth
Is the trace my mad laughter has left in this
guise.
For so long, this intense look of pallor I wear,
(That the portraits of all my old ancestors
show,)
Merely comes from fatigue caused by laughing
so madly,
And the lethargy that all my nerves sadly know.
Oh how weary I am! Let me now fall to sleep,
For it anguish brings illness, it comes from joy
too.

How peculiar it is that you think I am sad!
When, if ever, have I appeared gayer to you?
What a lie! I feel naught of unrest or of longing;
Nor do feelings of pain, doubt or jealousy
throng.
If there shines in my eyes the faint moisture of
weeping,
It is due to the effort of laughing so long.

Translated by Mildred E. Johnson

CLINGING TO LIFE
Vida-Garfio

If I should die, beloved, take me to no cemetery,
But let my sepulcher be opened just below the
ground,
Close to some aviary with its heavenly laughing
noise,
Or else close to a fountain with its charming
chatting sound.
Beloved, just below the ground. And almost on
the earth,
So that the sun may give my bones its warmth,
and where my eyes,
Prolonged within the stems of plants may rise
to see anew
The sunsets light their savage lamp in crimson
western skies.

Beloved, just below the ground. Let the
transition thus
Be briefer. I foretell
My body will be struggling always to return
above,
So it may feel the freshness of the wind in
every cell.
I am quite certain that my hands when
underground can never
Stay quietly at rest;
But as if moles, they will be always scratching
at the earth,
Within the darkness where they are so crowded
and compressed.
Throw seeds upon me. I desire that they might
there take root
Within the yellow clay remaining from my
wretched bones.
Along the dark gray ladder that the living roots
have made
I shall ascend to look at you from lilies' purple
tones.

Translated by Mildred E. Johnson

WOMAN
Mujer

Oh, if I were a man, how I should get my fill
Of silence and of shade, and of the moon's fair
light!
How I should wander then while facing
toward the sea,
And through the quiet fields, alone night after
night!
Oh, if I were a man, then what a strange,
erratic,
Persistent vagabond I should become no
doubt!
A friend of all the roads whose lengthiness
invites
Each one to travel far and never turn about!
When thus desires to roam beset me urgently,
How deeply I regret my femininity!

Translated by Mildred E. Johnson

Germaine Guèvremont   *Canada, 1896–1968*

Born in Saint-Jérôme and educated in Québec, Lachine, and Toronto, Germaine Grignon came from a family of writers, including the well-known Claude-Henri Grignon. She married Hyacinthe Guèvremont before joining him as a reporter on the staff of *Le Courrier de Sorel*. For her first book, *En pleine terre* (The Wide World) published in 1942, after she had already settled in Montréal, Guèvremont drew on her early observations of the Québec countryside where she had first worked, and where her husband's family lived.

A prolific journalist, Guèvremont wrote for the Montréal *Gazette*, the revue *Paysana*, *L'Oeil*, and *Le Nouveau Journal*. Her writings included short stories, interviews with women who had "succeeded" in life, childhood memories, and a serialized novel entitled "Tu seras journaliste" (You Will Become a Journalist), as well as a variety of short pieces inspired by local, national, and international events, literary figures and other celebrities. At the end of her life, she turned to another medium and wrote three radio plays: In 1960 she wrote "Une grosse nouvelle" (A Tremendous Piece of News) and "Les Demoiselles Mondor" (The Mondor Girls); her final work, "L'Adieu aux îles" (Goodbye to the Islands), was produced the year of her death.

But the works that brought Guèvremont lasting fame were *Le Survenant* (1945) and *Marie-Didace* (1947), both printed in 1950 under the title of *The Outlander*. For this achievement, she won several prizes in France and Québec as well as the coveted Canadian Governor General's Award. The diptych concerns a prairie community whose hero is the aging farmer and widower Didace (actually Hyacinthe's grandfather). It is he who takes in the stranger, and thus secures his acceptance in the community, and eventually marries another outsider, the Acadian Blanche Varieur: both disrupt the rhythms and rituals sanctioned and sanctified by the family, the church, and the land.

For some critics, Guèvremont served as the modern guardian of an already archaic literary tradition: *le terroir* or *la roman de la terre*, the novel of the earth. In its initial form, it represented an indigenous literature celebrating the rural life of French-Canada; as it evolved, the genre served increasingly to represent a pastoral ideal that no longer had any basis in reality; instead, it ratified a hierarchy in which the individual was part of the great chain of being and subordinate to the patriarchy of the family, church, and state. To such critics, the outsider is only a variant of "the absent, or treasonous, son," often the dominant theme of books in this tradition, as Maroussia Hajdukowski-Ahmed suggests. For other critics, Guèvremont's outsider permanently darkens the rural landscape with his shadow; for these, the work contains within itself the death knell for the very tradition in which it is written. In this context *The Outlander* is often compared with Ringuet's *Trente arpents* (*Thirty Acres*, 1938), which offered a harshly realistic picture of peasant life.

For the reader new to the francophone tradition, however, different aspects emerge: the monumentality of the characters, the sense of the community as a collectivity, the ceremonious structure achieved by counterpointing the liturgical and seasonal calendars, and the elegiac mood that shapes the novel.

from THE OUTLANDER
Le Survenant

As they came out from Mass a few flakes of snow fluttered down and dropped delicately, as though with infinite caution, onto the ground.

"It's white weather. Is the snow coming, do you think?"

"It's beginning to snow."

"It's snowing," said Phonsine joyously.

The men smiled. "Snowing" meant to them a heavy fall, a deep coating on the houses, a solid bridge on the winter roads between the river buoys, a thickened stream that clung to the river banks. But not these silly feathers. . . .

Phonsine held out a hand to catch a flake or two. The small, isolated drops quivered against the warmth of her skin.

A few days later, in the milky light that flooded into the room, the Stranger realized on awakening that the expected transformation had come at last. He jumped out of bed. Beneath the lowering sky the snow was obliterating everything; it unified the whole countryside in a white immobility. The snow was falling heavily, not in silly feathers as on the previous Sunday. The snow was falling, fine and dense and abundant, to feast the earth.

Toward noon the sun came out, pale among pale clouds; and yet it kindled myriads of stars in the fields.

"The snow will lie," said Didace.

And the snow did lie.

With the definite arrival of the snow an atmosphere of calm descended upon the house. All attended to their duties with increased energy. The Stranger had transformed the bakehouse into a workshop which only Didace was allowed to enter. From their talk it could be gathered that the boat was making progress, but no one had had a glimpse of it.

The first time the roads were usable the two men made their way to Sorel. They did not reappear until the evening, hilarious and rather drunk, and apparently fellow conspir-

ators in a project which they took a childish pleasure in concealing.

In the middle of the following week Marie-Amanda arrived from the Ile de Grâce. She had not been expected so soon. With a child in each hand; and heavy with the third, which she was expecting in the spring—tall and strong and honest-eyed, refreshing in her health and serenity—she walked up to the paternal house.

"I was so afraid that the ice bridge wouldn't form in time for the holidays."

Alphonsine understood that Marie-Amanda wanted to lighten her father's regret for the first New Year's Day without Mathilde Beauchemin.

"Will you take me in, Father?" asked Marie-Amanda, with an affectionate smile on her lips.

Didace, touched and delighted, turned to his daughter-in-law and said with affected surliness, "What do you think, little woman? Shall we take her in?"

Phonsine entered into the game.

"I daresay we can manage with her for a day or two."

It was from that moment that the house really recovered its quality. The very day after her arrival Marie-Amanda undertook the great house cleaning which Alphonsine had always been putting off. For one whole day the pulleys creaked under the weight of the rope from which hung the various items of household linen. Toward evening the women carried armfuls of it into the kitchen, aching all over from their labors. A smell of cleanliness and comfort pervaded the whole house, and the men took unwonted care not to soil anything.

"You'll wear yourself out," Didace kept on saying to Marie-Amanda.

But she would not relax until everything was in order. The window curtains had to be meticulously starched, as in the days of Mathilde Beauchemin, the feather beds thoroughly shaken up, and at the head of them, the stiff, square pillows decorously enthroned. One was embroidered in red thread with the design of a sleeping child; the other, an awakened child, with the legend underneath "Good morning—Good night." In the darkness of the chest of drawers, hand-woven carpets and round plaited table covers awaited their turn to lend a festive air to the house.

In the kitchen (apart from table, stove, and chairs) a single piece of furniture, propped level across a corner of the room by a wooden wedge under one end, served both as a sideboard and a chest of drawers. On a mat of unbleached linen embroidered with a pattern in red thread, a crystal decanter stood as centerpiece. Made of unconvincing pink glass engraved with gilded doves carrying a white message coiling from their beaks and surrounded by six small glasses, its fanciful appearance clashed with the other workaday objects. When he caught sight of it Didace had peevishly remarked, "It looks like a redneck with its brood." In the early days, when he noticed someone eyeing it with atonishment, rather taken aback by the presence of such frivolity in the house, he felt impelled to explain how it had come there, "It's my daughter-in-law's . . . ." Alphonsine had won it at a fair at Sorel, at the same time as the teacup and saucer which she alone used.

Then the pigs were killed. Angelina offered to make the gut-cased sausage and the black pudding.

"I won't say no," Phonsine hurriedly replied. She was feeling utterly exhausted.

But Marie-Amanda, far from overdoing with all the work, never complained of being tired. At the most she sometimes laid her hands on her hips and stretched her waist in rather exaggerated fashion, to ease her back for a moment of the weight of her fecundity.

Work seemed to her natural and easy. The eye was soothed by seeing her bring to the accomplishment of all these things such precise and serene movements. With a faithful and a confident hand she dressed the dishes or kneaded the bread, just as she wrung out the linen and did the housework. If anything was needed in the house she had but to say so, and someone would promptly harness Gaillarde and dash off to Sainte-Anne, or even to Sorel, to buy whatever it was, without question from anybody. The Stranger even taught her how to make bread without yeast. Phonsine, who had so much trouble in getting Amable to help her, envied Marie-Amanda's knack of getting such ready assistance from everyone. And Angelina, seeing the Stranger so assiduous in his attentions to Marie-Amanda, secretly set herself to copy her friend's methods.

Christmas was at hand. The Stranger could never keep the wood bin full. He even picked out the best sort of wood, and was particularly on the lookout for birch, that was renowned for making a good, hot fire.

After having prepared, as usual at this time, the festal meal with the best of what could be found upon the earth, on the morning of the twenty-fourth of December Marie-Amanda began to come and go as usual between the storeroom and the house. The hour had come to bring in the jar of doughnuts powdered with sugar, the stew with the meat balls floating in rich gravy, pies that melted in the mouth, and lavishly spiced mince. In the depths of the iron cauldron a shoulder of young pork simmered gently with a bit of chine set aside for Phonsine, who did not like garlic. As usual, too, the turkey was thawing out in the small stove. And on the top shelf of the cupboard in Didace's room, safely out of sight of the children, sweets and oranges and apples reposed behind a pile of sheets.

Just like old days, thought Marie-Amanda. But the carefree joy of those old days had gone. Her heart was in the grip of bitter recollections: Ephrem had been drowned one day in July; he was not yet sixteen. Mathilde Beauchemin was no longer in the world to try to soothe Didace when Amable became peevish or the two men were at odds. And grandmother no longer pottered about the kitchen lamenting that pralines weren't made as they used to be.

And yet Marie-Amanda would not utter the words that might have relieved her anguish; she did not want to depress the others. She merely walked to the window and stood looking out, as though to beg the unchanging countryside for a reflection of its stability. Dusk was falling, casting a blue shadow on the snow mantling the fields, and the line of mountains, usually humped against the hollow of the sky, was now blended with the plain. Through the mist of her tears Marie-Amanda could scarcely see the landscape. She, at thirty, was already the oldest of women in the family. It was for her, the eldest daughter, to give a good example. Was life like the river, intent only upon its course, heedless of the banks that it fertilizes or lays waste? Were human beings rushes, impotent to restrain it from obeying its own law—blue rushes, full of vigor in the morning, and by the evening shrunk into dismal husks, sapless and straw-colored? Young rushes would grow up in their place. Inexorable, the river continued on its course; neither she nor anyone could prevent it.

Little Mathilde, astonished to see her mother motionless for so long, clung to Marie-Amanda's skirts.

"Mum-my!"

Little Ephrem, tottering on his small legs, copied her.

"Mum-my...Mum-my!"

Marie-Amanda turned. She still felt sick at heart, but she seemed comforted, and said quietly to Alphonsine, "If only we made pralines as in my time...."

Little Mathilde clapped her hands.

"Some pralines, Mummy—I want some pralines."

Marie-Amanda swung the child up into her arms and smothered her with kisses. The Stranger took her very gently, but said rather sharply to the mother, "You really oughtn't to carry her. She's much too heavy for you at present."

Soon afterward the shopman from Sainte-Anne arrived. He marched into the kitchen accompanied by a blast of frozen air. He always arrived like a gust of wind, and he looked the sort of man that wouldn't stay a moment longer than was needed; and yet at every house he spent enough time to smoke his pipe and inquire after every member of the family.

"So old Didace is still a widower, eh? Well, the old boy has held out properly, hasn't he? I expect the creatures* frightened him, that's how it was."

Phonsine, for the pleasure of getting him to talk, remarked, "They aren't very dangerous, after all."

"Ah, my girl, you never know. I've known some that were very alarming—very alarming indeed."

"What sort were they?"

"Creatures with hair like straw mattresses."

Every other moment he kept jumping to his feet, as though he were dashing off once more; but he merely lifted a lid of the stove to spit in the fire, and came back and settled down in his chair, with his two feet outstretched toward the heat.

"And what about you, Phonsine—when's the child expected? And how's Amable? And the Stranger? And Ludger? And the little dog, does he bark as much as ever?"

He went through the whole list. When he came to the turn of Marie-Amanda, he did no more than peer slantwise from where he sat poised on the edge of his chair.

"And the folks from the Ile de Grâce? They look as if they were doing pretty well, as far as I can see."

His budget of news expanded at every house he visited, and he lingered longer at each stage of his round. One might almost have thought that that was his main object, rather than the disposal of his wares.

Marie-Amanda took a special joy in attending Midnight Mass. At Didace's request, the Stranger undertook to mind the house. Indeed he needed no persuasion. Marie-Amanda assured him that the children never woke up at night. Her husband, Ludger Aubuchon, joined her at the Sainte-Anne church, and after Mass, the dwellers on the Inlet returned in procession. A whole file of sleighs stood like a dotted line along the road, in the blue night that silvered the hamlet. David Desmarais and Angelina accepted the invitation to eat their midnight supper at the Beauchemins'. Angelina had never known a happier Christmas. "What a lovely Christmas!" she kept on repeating in her heart, in which a pious joy was blended with the image of the Stranger.

On their arrival home the Stranger was asleep in his chair. He started up at the same time as the dog, and in a bound he was on his feet. No sooner had the wick of the lamp been turned up than an exclamation burst from Alphonsine.

"Where on earth did you pick up that armchair?"

The armchair from which the Stranger had just risen—a genuine Voltaire armchair, with molded feet and a high, concave back as though to fit the body of the sitter, and the defects that betokened the hand of a local maker—stood imposingly beside the stove.

Still half asleep, the Stranger said with a yawn, "Well, Didace and Amable have their own special chairs in this house. It's about time I had mine too."

They spoke of the Midnight Mass, the beautiful singing, and the crèche, but the conversation kept insensibly reverting to the armchair. Everyone wanted to try it and sat themselves down in it with an air of high importance. It seemed to mold exactly to the body. "I've seldom seen such a handsome chair. My word, it's a grand bit of work!"

"You may well boast that you're a good carpenter," remarked Ludger Aubuchon.

Alphonsine, who was busy making the forcemeat stew, suddenly dropped the ladle and planted herself in front of the Stranger.

"So that was the great Christmas surprise you were so anxious to conceal from me."

Angelina wanted to know all about the making of it, and with what it had been stuffed. The Stranger couldn't answer everybody at the same time.

"I stuffed it," he explained, "with the old salt bags. It has a smell of the water's edge, don't you think?"

"I know some English women at Sorel," put in Angelina, "who would pay you well to repair their furniture."

"Hi, Father-in-law," cried Alphonsine rapturously. "Do you hear what Angelina says?"

But Marie-Amanda gave the signal to sit down to table. After the long drive in the fresh air everyone would celebrate Christmas with good heart and appetite. At the moment of sitting down, there was a minute of deep emotion at the sight of Mathilde's empty chair; since her death it had been left unoccupied. Marie-Amanda fetched her little girl and sat her down in it; a leaf falls from the trees, another leaf replaces it.

Translated by Eric Sutton

NOTE

* An old Québécois term for women.

Gianna Manzini

Italy, 1896–1974

After receiving a doctorate in literature from the University of Florence, Gianna Manzini began to contribute to *Solaria* and other leading periodicals. Her first novel, *Tempo innamorato* (Time of Love, 1928), already includes the major focus of her work, a constant search for psychological symmetries and secret ties between protagonists and the things surrounding them. Greatly influenced by Virginia Woolf, as she herself states, Manzini frequently creates irrational transfigurations that approach the surrealistic. Underlying much of Manzini's work are autobiographical recollections. Few writers have been able to become one with their style as she did, for her syntax is a perennial invention, where lexical finesse and images fuse perfectly. The result is a complex style, difficult to follow, which explains why Manzini never became "popular" with many readers in Italy. Moreover, the problems involved in translating her intricate images, which are based on a complicated sequence of perceptions and an original use of language, explain why she has also been neglected abroad, although she is one of the foremost novelists of her time.

Noteworthy among her short stories are the two collections *Venti racconti* (Twenty Stories, 1941), from which comes "Gentilina" (below), and *Forte come un leone* (As Strong as a Lion, 1944). Perhaps her best novel is *La sparviera* (The Sparrow Hawk, 1956), where the bird of prey that is made a character in the novel is the bronchial illness that constantly pursues the male protagonist from his early childhood—an original transposition of the author's own torments. It was awarded the Viareggio Prize.

Ritratto in piedi (Full-length Portrait, 1971) is a delicate reconstruction of her father's life; he died in a Fascist prison, a victim of his anarchic ideas that left him open to exploitation by all. This novel received the Campiello Prize. Her last work, *Sulla soglia* (On the Threshold, 1973), consists of four short stories, all dealing with the relationship between life and death; together they read almost like a novel. It is Manzini's most daring work, a true virtuoso performance, where life and death are seen as a continuum.

Natalia Costa-Zalessow

GENTILINA

The petunias on the window sill, looking out and protected behind the glass, in the distance a young larch, all movement dainty and quick, feminine; and along the same line of vision, in the "V" between two mountains, a piece of blue faded by the sun: the pale one thinks to find behind the sky.

Small, too ornamented, the window spills over with excessive comfort, behind which trembles a mournful presence. And descending from there like an overturned rainbow, in order to touch, approvingly, the afflicted tree and again rising up, sustained by a flow of breeze to the horizon, a stroke of melancholy, almost a tear in the blue. It has sprung from my window sill to carry me far away, to a time vanished and new to memory. With a sense of languid parting I venture without courage. And suddenly this band of stale sadness sways like a cradle, like a swing. Soon it will become an apparition, perhaps a face. There: a doll dying of consumption. So many years ago, in summer. Her name was Gentilina.

She came to me unwrapped, with an independence that frightened me. She was dressed in white lace trimmed with little pink flowers. She wore leather shoes and crocheted half gloves.

What an uneasy awe I felt upon viewing her clothing and the excessive grace of her hand, with its little finger raised and arched, as if playing the harp. A respectful friendship was born, one that could never concede to familiarity; the most regal of gifts, to value without hope of profit, the smile and the amiable blue of her eyes.

Taking her in my arms seemed like abducting her. At once all the garden offered itself to her, and in homage lessened the clash of its vehement colors, pitiless for a summer bleached so pale.

The twilight now touches the dense green of the meadow, dilutes it, unravels it, while a cloud bursting with presumptuous white becomes lighter and combs a benevolent church-like light, into which the velvety luster of these flowers surrenders itself, almost resigning itself to sweetness. It's then that, just as a bird would begin to sing, a little cluster of carnations suddenly puts forth its scent. Fragrance rediscovered, nay revived, even the ghost of a fragrance, in fact slightly funereal. It seems that I can listen to it. Lightly it comes upon me, interrogates me, disquiets me, it finds me in my bygone years, unveils this yet untouched memory.

Thus I realize that I no longer think of Gentilina this evening, for I accompany her apparition, perhaps her ghost.

Through her adventures I entered, promoted without merit, into an everyday fairy tale. The world set itself in verse and in rhyme, became *cantabile*.[1] Next to her delicate dress, I saw the condensed red of an amaranth courteously veil itself (in this manner the colors bow and lower their eyes) and I saw a bum-

blebee hide, almost spiraling into a bud, only to yield its place, with touching politeness, to a scarab.

Called to table, I left her in the cradle of a flowerbed trimmed with verbena.

The garden gathered around her, closing ever tighter, together with so many bees that circled near her deafeningly. A buzzing cloud detached itself from her upon my return; and that swarm seemed a frenetic and delicate festivity, like doll-cherubims.

But Gentilina had grown pale, and with no color left in her face, her eyes took on a reckless, feverish prominence. I approached. She was sweating. Struck dumb with amazement, suspended with me, all the garden fell silent.

As she lay face to face with the blue, she no longer belonged to me. Her irises fixed firmly like mirrors, had cast a spell on the terrified white of the sky that, discoloring her, had then descended upon her together with all those expert bees in an improvised uproar of offensive curiosity on a face of wax, reawakening a remote life, fluid and disturbing (*this perfume in waves moves the image of her, makes her breathe*) and had departed again in ever widening circles, leaving her alone and ruined, almost shamed.

I lightly passed a handkerchief over her face, barely brushing her, but it was sufficient: her nose elongated and bent, making her suddenly elderly and severe.

Still less than a shiver, in the mountains, and instantly the landscape frowns, and even the trees become estranged from one another, while the birds that flit back and forth between treetops no longer find messages to carry.

It's seems she's had smallpox," said my mother, and quickly added "you'll see how pretty she'll be with a veil."

On a little hat of pink horsehair was pinned a white veil, that, circling under her chin, was fastened on the curls. Only her eyes shone through, lively, ever newer, and her elusive rosy smile, truly secret.

She seemed taller and foreign; and her hand rendered precious by the whimsical movements of the fingers in the half glove acquired meaning; and it was clear that I now had to call her *signorina*.

But just that independent little finger fell sick: softened, almost decomposed, it had to be amputated. And Gentilina got full gloves with a finger stuffed, and she let a ragged hand weigh upon her still-starched skirt, like a beggar. Anxiety and a sense of illness, while I carried her about with a parasol, pushing the little carriage along the hedged paths cut into the vineyard. Always some meddling bee (*even the scent that pours forth from these flowers, lined with a padding, alluring, from deep, twisting gorges smells of wax: losing control, almost as if wings were no longer the celestial symbol that they are, these buzzing creatures frenziedly plunge into them*) followed us, persuading us too, that summer, imperious and resonant, with that unremitting whirling over our heads, was indicating to the fruit a maximum circle of maturity, a sickening turgidity.

And the earth was shrivelling and drying up, cracking in order to help the grapes fill out and the bursting plums powder themselves like young girls and the peaches swell and sweeten. Those ostentations, of an intimate pink, like gums (what a pacifying, elegant decorum instead in the arid pinks of Gentilina), plump, cloven and moreover having completely escaped the shelter of the foliage, offended me. I looked disdainfully upon the really yellow ones, those in which summer concentrates itself, almost resides with a joyless contentedness, like a wealthy man overly sated. And I grew ever more tender towards Gentilina, who continued to melt and waste away, truly alone, estranged and contrary to so much rivalry to accumulate weight and sweetness.

At the bottom of the slope, next to the wall, opulence was becoming a malady. The enormous pumpkins of an ocher fired to orange or corrupted into violet, decrepit newborns, with a few curls of dried green vines on top,

were supported by trestles and planks, out of kindness for the meager stems. The grapevines were defending in paper sacks clusters of grapes so swollen that if a bee touched them, juice would flow; the pears, on overburdened branches looked like adult faces distorted by mumps. Under her veil Gentilina was hiding a chaste and nocturnal pallor and flat cheeks, truly spiritual.

Squeezed from the white cloud that retreats into the softened blue at day's end, a melancholy splendor has come down in which the façade, no, the face of the church stands out, at first far away, perhaps distracted, now fully descried in the minimal peak, almost an accent on the vertex; an acute face; and the landscape feels such a new presence because it arises without haughtiness, as in a sigh.

I do not remember. I let myself be led. Gentilina, revived by this moment that suspends a band of melancholy between my window and the horizon, takes me back, with insistence, to that countryside dulled by sultriness. *I find once again the meaning of full summer: equal to the longing drowsing of an infant.* But Gentilina remained clear-eyed, wide awake, not at all compromised by that sweet-wine drunkenness that is August in a valley bursting with fruit.

She was beautiful. (*This larch, now I realize it, with its spent nobility, bestows upon her a sorrowful prestige: it actually resembles her, paled as it is by consumption of its foliage.*)

Yet it seemed necessary to give her a bit of color: minium-red on her lips and a soft lilac-pink on her cheeks. I presented her like this at breakfast.

Comfortable, the dining room, and cheerful as mint. Closed, filtered light from the blinds and the curtains, it seems like a galleria: one enters somewhat hesitant, with a slight air of ceremony. The women wear light dresses in pastels and necklaces that quickly harmonize with the glittering gaiety of the table (precious, the ice in the glasses) so that a bosom no longer seems an inconvenience against the tablecloth, which, submitting affably to arm-level, lifts, almost fortifies that expanse of white.

We had just sat down when my cousin, planting a spiteful elbow next to her plate, said (and her voice seemed mirrored on the blade of the knife):

"I can't stand her anymore, that consumptive doll facing me. She's absolutely indecent!"

Everyone turned towards Gentilina, and even I leaned over to look at her. That tone and those words had disfigured her: I saw her nose reduced to nothing, the mouth enlarged by lipstick, perhaps a bit crooked, the smeared cheeks, and her eyes seemed larger than ever. Who knows if at any given moment, she might have started to roll them in order to scare us. She was moribund yet very much alive.

Thus I began to fear her.

Hidden between the drapes and the parapet we would look at each other for hours: I would tremble, and since I was holding her with both hands, she too trembled with me. With an ear pressed against her back I would urge her: "Say '*trentatré*,'[2] say '*trentatré*' . . ." fearful that she might indeed say it. And again, examining her closely: "She's really sick. She's consumptive. She's going to cough pretty soon." Awaiting, terrified, that bout of cough, I ended up insisting that she cough immediately in order to dispense with that thrill and enter into the circle of a more defined fear. I would slap her on the back and cough to provoke her.

The day bitterly plunges between the mountains. A heartbeat and the light is cut off like hair and falls into the river which hastily steals it. At once the birds fall silent without having finished singing, while the mountain peaks become redder from the reflection of the water. There is an air of misfortune in the succeeding silence, veiled, not unlike that which arises when a little girl and a doll gaze at each other in that way.

"Tonight Uncle will take Gentilina into town to the doctor. As soon as she gets better, she'll come back."

I passively played along: "As soon as she gets better she'll come back," but what an impression to see her actually leave, at night, with those wide-opened eyes, alone in the middle of the car seat, accompanied by my uncle who was driving and would never even turn to look at her.

Because a cat (an eccentric tabby, enemy to chickens and breaker of glasses) carried away at night in the same way, tied up in a sack, had returned after many months from a place far away (of course not returned: an apparition: haggard, he presented himself in the kitchen, knocking down whatever was on the sink; he looked everyone in the face; he confidently ran through corridors, bedrooms, and parlors in search of his masters, in order to fix reproving eyes on each one; he went out through the back door, off to the nearby woods to die), I proceeded to wait year in year out for Gentilina to reappear. And yet, the moment they took her from my arms, I had guessed the gesture of my uncle who, before entering the city, without so much as stopping, would reach back to take her and toss her into a ditch, where the doll would remain with her skirt entangled in the hawthorne, face up, already exposed for the next day to the needling curiosity of the bees that meddle destructively in the secrets of a waxen face.

Today she has come back. And it took the window sill decorated with swinging vines and delicate flowers (bells of silk so soft and susceptible that you look at them with caution and you grieve) to make Gentilina truly present with her meticulously designed hand, too lovely.

I have seen her. This delicate, compromised moment that trembles of its own secrets, summoned her ghost. And Gentilina has appeared with her possessed eyes (*it doesn't take much in the mountains, the lifting of a cloud, the waning of the light on the peak that towers above us, a sudden hush of the wind, for certain spaces to widen in a steadiness that engages the heart, and for us to become fright-*

ened: "say 'trentatré,' say 'trentatré'..." ") with her emaciated look (*more than ever the treetops let themselves droop and waste away this evening from the amorous solicitude of the air, here disturbed in a minimal, acute manner*) with her face paling and thinning, and her veil.

She appeared so that this certainty of unusual presence having increased, even the ghost of a toy, my fantasy would be richer, more allusive; and also so that I would be able to say to myself: "If I hadn't seen a doll fall sick with real consumption when I was eleven...," I could imagine my whole life differently from then to now.

In the possibility of so doubling and re-newing my time, I recognize a gift, the last from Gentilina, who disappears in this moment without even a wave of farewell (*the twilight by now wet with dew and ebbing*) from her hand completely gloved, with its padded little finger.

Translated as a class project by J. Borrelli, D. Beyeler, L. O'Connell, C. Platamorne, C. Siegel, C. Wallace, and V. Wolcott, students of Italian at San Francisco State University, Fall 1985

NOTE

1. Songlike.
2. Means thirty-three in Italian, and was said by children during medical examinations so the doctor could listen to their chests.

Elizabeth Bowen   *Ireland/UK(England), 1899–1973*

Elizabeth Bowen was born near Dublin, Ireland. Her father, the heir to the three-century-old estate of Bowen's Court, near Kildorrey, County Cork, apparently suffered a mental breakdown in 1905 because of his inability to sire a male heir. The debilitation and eventual death of her mother when Bowen was just 10 left the child in the care of numerous geographically distant relatives. Bowen's ten novels, over seventy short stories, and many essays reflect such a life—of loneliness and emotional deprivation and disability, of the search for sense of place and a settled life.

Writing at the time of the birth of modern psychology, Bowen demonstrated early a gift for careful, yet bold examination of human emotions. Her first collection of short stories, *Encounters* (1923), begins a lifelong exploration of characters who are lonely, yet without recourse to self-examination. A second and equally powerful theme found in Bowen's works is the relationship between the world of children and that of adults. Her masterpiece, *The Death of the Heart* (1938), deals with Portia, an orphan living with her brother and his wife. Here, the natural and spontaneous child is subjected to the routine of conformity and the domination and control of adults. Portia's response to this oppression is to live through her imagination and the illusions that it creates. Such illusions, says Bowen, "are art."

Bowen often refuses to allow for the resolution of conflicts or the fulfillment of dreams. Such endings, she feels, do not bring about an understanding of human emotion or a sense of security, and to dream of these is dangerous. This sense of insecurity is beautifully resonant in Bowen's novels, for instance, *The Heat of the Day* (1949) set in London during World War II, and stories, including "The Cat Jumps," from a collection of stories of the same title (1934).

Bowen was named Commander of the British Empire for her relief work in World War II. She received honorary degrees from Trinity College, Dublin, in 1949, and from Oxford in 1956.

John Isom

THE CAT JUMPS

After the Bentley murder, Rose Hill stood empty two years. Lawns mounted to meadows; white paint peeled from the balconies; the sun, looking more constantly, less fearfully in that sightseer's eyes through the naked windows, bleached the floral wallpapers. The week after the execution Harold Bentley's legatees had placed the house on the books of the principal agents, London and local. But though sunny, up to date, and convenient, though so delightfully situated over the Thames valley (above flooded level), within easy reach of a golfcourse, Rose Hill, while frequently viewed, remained unpurchased. Dreadful associations apart, the privacy of the place had been violated; with its terraced garden, lily-pond and pergola cheerfully rose-encrusted, the public had been made too familiar. On the domestic scene too many eyes had burnt the impress of their horror. Moreover, that pearly bathroom, that bedroom with wide outlook over a loop of the Thames... "*The Rose Hill Horror*": headlines flashed up at the very sound of the name. "Oh, *no*, dear!" many wives had exclaimed, drawing their husbands hurriedly from the gate. "Come away!" they had urged crumpling the agent's order to view as though the house were advancing upon them. And husbands came away—with a backward glance at the garage. Funny to think a chap who was hanged had kept his car there.

The Harold Wrights, however, were not deterred. They had light, bright, shadowless, thoroughly disinfected minds. They believed that they disbelieved in most things but were unprejudiced; they enjoyed frank discussions. They dreaded nothing but inhibitions: they had no inhibitions. They were pious agnostics, earnest for social reform; they explained everything to their children, and were annoyed to find their children could not sleep at night because they thought there was a complex under the bed. They knew all crime to be pathological, and read their murders only in

scientific books. They had vita glass put into all their windows. No family, in fact, could have been more unlike the mistaken Harold Bentleys.

Rose Hill, from the first glance, suited the Wrights admirably. They were in search of a cheerful weekend house with a nice atmosphere, where their friends could join them for frank discussions, and their own and their friends' children "run wild" during the summer months. Harold Wright, who had a good head, got the agent to knock six hundred off the quoted price of the house. "That unfortunate affair," he murmured. Jocelyn commended his inspiration. Otherwise, they did not give the Bentleys another thought.

The Wrights had the floral wallpapers all stripped off and the walls cream-washed; they removed some disagreeably thick pink shades from the electricity and had the paint renewed inside and out. (The front of the house was bracketed over with balconies, like an overmantel.) Their bedroom mantelpiece, stained by the late Mrs. Bentley's cosmetics, had to be scrubbed with chemicals. Also, they had removed from the rock garden Mrs. Bentley's little dog's memorial tablet, with a quotation on it from *Indian Love Lyrics*. Jocelyn Wright, looking into the unfortunate bath—*the* bath, so square and opulent, with its surround of nacreous tiles—said, laughing lightly, she supposed anyone *else* would have had that bath changed. "Not that that would be possible," she added; "the bath's built in...I've always wanted a built-in bath."

Harold and Jocelyn turned from the bath to look down at the cheerful river shimmering under a spring haze. All the way down the slope cherry trees were in blossom. Life should be simplified for the Wrights; they were fortunate in their mentality.

After an experimental weekend, without guests or children, only one thing troubled them: a resolute stuffiness, upstairs and down

—due presumably, to the house's having been so long shut up—a smell of unsavoury habitation, of rich cigarette smoke stale in the folds of unaired curtains, of scent spilled on unbrushed carpets, an alcoholic smell—persistent in their perhaps too sensitive nostrils after days of airing, doors and windows open, in rooms drenched thoroughly with sun and wind. They told each other it came from the parquet; they didn't like it, somehow. They had the parquet taken up—at great expense—and put down plain oak floors.

In their practical way, the Wrights now set out to expel, live out, live down, almost (had the word had place in their vocabulary) to 'lay' the Bentleys. Deferred by trouble over the parquet, their occupation of Rose Hill, which should have dated from mid-April, did not begin till the end of May. Throughout a week, Jocelyn had motored from town daily, so that the final installation of themselves and the children was able to coincide with their first weekend party—they asked down five of their friends to warm the house.

That first Friday, everything was auspicious; afternoon sky blue as the garden irises; later, a full moon pendent over the river; a night so warm that, after midnight, their enlightened friends, in pyjamas, could run on the blanched lawns in a state of high though rational excitement. Jane, Jacob and Janet, their admirably spaced-out children, kept awake by the moonlight, hailed their elders out of the nursery skylight. Jocelyn waved to them: they never had been repressed.

The girl Muriel Barker was found looking up the terraces at the house a shade doubtfully. "You know," she said, "I do rather wonder they don't feel . . . *sometimes* . . . you know what I mean?"

"No," replied her companion, a young scientist.

Muriel sighed. "No one would mind if it had been just a short sharp shooting. But it was so . . . prolonged. It went on all over the house. Do you remember?" she said timidly.

"No," replied Mr. Cartaret. "It didn't interest me."

"Oh, nor me either!" agreed Muriel quickly, but added: "How he must have hated her . . . ."

The scientist, sleepy, yawned frankly and referred her to Krafft-Ebing.[1] But Muriel went to bed with *Alice in Wonderland*; she went to sleep with the lights on. She was not, as Jocelyn realized later, the sort of girl to have asked at all.

Next morning was overcast; in the afternoon it rained, suddenly and heavily—interrupting, for some, tennis, for others, a pleasant discussion, in a punt, on marriage under the Soviet. Defeated, they all rushed in. Jocelyn went round from room to room, shutting tightly the rain-lashed casements along the front of the house. These continued to rattle; the balconies creaked. An early dusk set in; an oppressive, almost visible moisture, up from the darkening river, pressed on the panes like a presence and slid through the house. The party gathered in the library, round an expansive but thinly burning fire. Harold circulated photographs of modern architecture; they discussed these tendencies. Then Mrs. Monkhouse, sniffing, exclaimed: "Who uses 'Trèfle Incarnat'?"

"Now, *who* ever would—" her hostess began scornfully. Then from the hall came a howl, scuffle, a thin shriek. They sat too still; in the dusky library Mr. Cartaret laughed out loud. Harold Wright, indignantly throwing open the door, revealed Jane and Jacob rolling at the foot of the stairs, biting each other, their faces dark with uninhibited passion. Bumping alternate heads against the foot of the banisters, they shrieked in concert.

"Extraordinary," said Harold; "they've never done that before. They have always understood each other so well."

"I wouldn't do that," advised Jocelyn, raising her voice slightly; "you'll hurt your teeth. Other teeth won't grow at once, you know."

"You should let them find that out for themselves," disapproved Edward Cartaret, taking up the *New Statesman*. Harold, in perplexity, shut the door on his children, who soon stunned each other to silence.

Meanwhile, Sara and Talbot Monkhouse, Muriel Barker and Theodora Smith, had drawn together over the fire in a tight little knot. Their voices twanged with excitement. By that shock, just now, something seemed to have been released. Even Cartaret gave them half his attention. They were discussing *crime passionnel*.

"Of course, if that's what they really *want* to discuss..." thought Jocelyn. But it did seem unfortunate. Partly from an innocent desire to annoy her visitors, partly because the room felt awful—you would have thought fifty people had been there for a week—she went across and opened one of the windows, admitting a pounce of damp wind. They all turned, startled, to hear rain crash on the lead of an upstairs balcony. Muriel's voice was left in forlorn solo: "Dragged herself...whining 'Harold'..."

Harold Wright looked remarkably conscious. Jocelyn said brightly, "Whatever *are* you talking about?" But, unfortunately, Harold, on almost the same breath, suggested: "Let's leave that family alone, shall we?" Their friends all felt they might not be asked again. Though they did feel, plaintively, that they had been being natural. However, they disowned Muriel, who, getting up abruptly, said she thought she'd like to go for a walk in the rain before dinner. Nobody accompanied her.

Later, overtaking Mrs. Monkhouse on the stairs, Muriel confided: absolutely, she could not stand Edward Cartaret. She could hardly bear to be in the room with him. He seemed so...cruel. Cold-blooded? No, she meant cruel. Sara Monkhouse, going into Jocelyn's room for a chat (at her entrance Jocelyn started violently), told Jocelyn that Muriel could not stand Edward, could hardly bear to be in a room with him. "Pity," said Jocelyn. "I

had thought they might do for each other." Jocelyn and Sara agreed that Muriel was unrealized: what she ought to have was a baby. But when Sara, dressing, told Talbot Monkhouse that Muriel could not stand Edward, and Talbot said Muriel was unrealized, Sara was furious. The Monkhouses, who never did quarrel, quarrelled bitterly, and were late for dinner. They would have been later if the meal itself had not been delayed by an outburst of sex-antagonism between the nice Jacksons, a couple imported from London to run the house. Mrs. Jackson, putting everything in the oven, had locked herself into her room.

"Curious," said Harold; "the Jacksons' relations to each other always seemed so modern. They have the most intelligent discussions."

Theodora said she had been re-reading Shakespeare—this brought them point-blank up against *Othello*. Harold, with titanic force, wrenched round the conversation to relativity: about this no one seemed to have anything to say but Edward Cartaret. And Muriel, who by some mischance had again been placed beside him, sat deathly, turning down her dark-rimmed eyes. In fact, on the intelligent sharp-featured faces all round the table something—perhaps simply a clearness—seemed to be lacking, as though these were wax faces for one fatal instant exposed to a furnace. Voices came out from some dark interiority; in each conversational interchange a mutual vote of no confidence was implicit. You would have said that each personality had been attacked by some kind of decomposition.

"No moon tonight," complained Sara Monkhouse. Never mind, they would have a cosy evening; they would play paper games, Jocelyn promised.

"If you can see," said Harold. "Something seems to be going wrong with the light."

Did Harold think so? They had all noticed the light seemed to be losing quality, as though a film, smoke-like, were creeping over the bulbs. The light, thinning, darkening, seemed to contract round each lamp into a blurred aura. They had noticed, but, each with a proper dread of his own subjectivity, had not spoken.

"Funny stuff, electricity." Harold said.

Mr. Cartaret could not agree with him.

Though it was late, though they yawned and would not play paper games, they were reluctant to go to bed. You would have supposed a delightful evening. Jocelyn was not gratified.

The library stools, rugs and divans were strewn with Krafft-Ebing, Freud, Forel, Weiniger and the heterosexual volume of Havelock Ellis.[1] (Harold had thought it right to install his reference library; his friends hated to discuss without basis.) The volumes were pressed open with paper-knives and small pieces of modern statuary; stooping from one to another, purposeful as a bee, Edward Cartaret read extracts aloud to Harold, to Talbot Monkhouse, and to Theodora Smith, who stitched *gros point* with resolution. At the far end of the library under a sallow drip from a group of electric candles, Mrs. Monkhouse and Miss Barker shared an ottoman, spines pressed rigid against the wall. Tensely one spoke, one listened.

"And these," thought Jocelyn, leaning back with her eyes shut between the two groups, "are the friends I liked to have in my life. Pellucid, sane...."

It was remarkable how much Muriel knew. Sara, very much shocked, edged up till their thighs touched. You would have thought the Harold Bentleys had been Muriel's relatives. Surely, Sara attempted, in one's large, bright world one did not think of these things? Practically, they did not exist! Surely Muriel should not....But Muriel looked at her strangely.

"Did you know," she said, "that one of Mrs. Bentley's hands was found in the library?"

Sara, smiling a little awkwardly, licked her lip. "Oh," she said.

"But the fingers were in the dining room. He began there."

"Why isn't he in Broadmoor?"[2]

"That defence failed. He didn't really subscribe to it. He said having done what he wanted was worth anything."

"Oh!"

"Yes, he was nearly lynched....She dragged herself upstairs. She couldn't lock any doors—naturally. One maid—her maid—got shut into the house with them: he'd sent all the others away. For a long time everything seemed so quiet: the maid crept out and saw Harold Bentley sitting halfway upstairs, finishing a cigarette. All the lights were full on. He nodded to her and dropped the cigarette through the banisters. Then she saw the...the state of the hall. He went upstairs after Mrs. Bentley, saying: "Lucinda!" He looked into room after room, whistling; then he said "*Here we are*," and shut a door after him.

"The maid fainted. When she came to, it was still going on, upstairs...Harold Bentley had locked all the garden doors; there were locks even on the French windows. The maid couldn't get out. Everything she touched was ...sticky. At last she broke a pane and got through. As she ran down the garden—the lights were on all over the house—she saw Harold Bentley moving about in the bathroom. She fell right over the edge of a terrace and one of the tradesmen picked her up next day.

'Doesn't it seem odd, Sara, to think of Jocelyn in that bath?'

Finishing her recital, Muriel turned on Sara an ecstatic and brooding look that made her almost beautiful. Sara fumbled with a cigarette; match after match failed her. "Muriel, *you* ought to see a specialist."

Muriel held out her hand for a cigarette. "He put her heart in her hatbox. He said it belonged in there."

"You had no right to come here. It was most unfair to Jocelyn. Most...indelicate."

Muriel, to whom the word was, properly, unfamiliar, eyed incredulously Sara's lips.

"How dared you come?"

"I thought I might like it. I thought I ought to fulfil myself. I'd never had any experience of these things."

"*Muriel*..."

"Besides, I wanted to meet Edward Cartaret. Several people said we were made for each other. Now, of course, I shall never marry. Look what comes of it...I must say, Sara, I wouldn't be you or Jocelyn. Shut up all night with a man all alone—I don't know how you dare sleep. I've arranged to sleep with Theodora, and we shall barricade the door. I noticed something about Edward Cartaret the moment I arrived: a kind of insane glitter. He is utterly pathological. He's got instruments in his room, in that black bag. Yes, I looked. Did you notice the way he went on and on about cutting up that cat, and the way Talbot and Harold listened?"

Sara, looking furtively round the room, saw Mr. Cartaret making passes over the head of Theodora Smith with a paper knife. Both appeared to laugh heartily, but in silence.

"Here we are," said Harold, showing his teeth, smiling.

He stood over Muriel with a siphon in one hand, glass in the other.

At this point Jocelyn, rising, said she, for one, intended to go to bed.

Jocelyn's bedroom curtains swelled a little over the noisy window. The room was stuffy and—insupportable, so that she did not know where to turn. The house, fingered outwardly by the wind that dragged unceasingly past the walls, was, within, a solid silence: silence heavy as flesh. Jocelyn dropped her wrap to the floor, then watched how its feathered edges crept a little. A draught came in, under her bathroom door.

Jocelyn turned away in despair and hostility from the strained, pale woman looking at her from her oblong glass. She said aloud, "There *is* no fear"; then, within herself, heard this taken up: "But the death fear, that one is not there to relate! If the spirit, dismembered

in agony, dies before the body! If the spirit, in the whole knowledge of its dissolution, drags from chamber to chamber, drops from plane to plane of awareness (as from knife to knife down an oubliette), shedding, receiving agony! Till, long afterwards, death, with its little pain, is established in the indifferent body." There was no comfort: death (now at every turn and instant claiming her) was, in its every possible manifestation, violent death: ultimately, she was to be given up to terror.

Undressing, shocked by the iteration of her reflected movements, she flung a towel over the glass. With what desperate eyes of appeal, at Sara's door, she and Sara had looked at each other, clung with their looks—and parted. She could have sworn she heard Sara's bolt slide softly to. But what then, subsequently, of Talbot? And what—she eyed her own bolt, so bright (and, for the late Mrs. Bentley, so ineffective)—what of Harold?

"It's atavistic!" she said aloud, in the dark-lit room, and, kicking her slippers away, got into bed. She took *Erewhon*[3] from the rack, but lay rigid, listening. As though snatched by a movement, the towel slipped from the mirror beyond her bed-end. She faced the two eyes of an animal in extremity, eyes black, mindless. The clock struck two: she had been waiting an hour.

On the floor, her feathered wrap shivered again all over. She heard the other door of the bathroom very stealthily open, then shut. Harold moved in softly, heavily, knocked against the side of the bath, and stood still. He was quietly whistling.

"Why didn't I understand? He must always have hated me. It's tonight he's been waiting for...*He wanted this house.* His look, as we went upstairs...."

She shrieked: "Harold!"

Harold, so softly whistling, remained behind the imperturbable door, remained quite still..."He's *listening* for me..." One pinpoint of hope at the tunnel-end: to get to Sara, to Theodora, to Muriel. Unmasked, incautious, with a long tearing sound of displaced air, Jocelyn leapt from the bed to the door.

But her door had been locked from the outside.

With a strange rueful smile, like an actress, Jocelyn, skirting the foot of the two beds, approached the door of the bathroom. "At least I have still...my feet." For some time the heavy body of Mrs. Bentley, tenacious of life, had been dragging itself from room to room. "*Harold*!" she said to the silence, face close to the door.

The door opened on Harold, looking more dreadfully at her than she had imagined. With a quick, vague movement he roused himself from his meditation. Therein he had assumed the entire burden of Harold Bentley. Forces he did not know of assembling darkly, he had faced for untold ages the imperturbable door to his wife's room. She would be there, densely, smotheringly there. She lay like a great cat, always, over the mouth of his life.

The Harolds, superimposed on each other, stood searching the bedroom srangely. Taking a step forward, shutting the door behind him: "Here we are," said Harold.

Jocelyn went down heavily. Harold watched.

Harold Wright was appalled. Jocelyn had fainted: Jocelyn never had fainted before. He shook, he fanned, he applied restoratives. His perplexed thoughts fled to Sara—oh, Sara certainly. "Hi!" he cried, "Sara!" and successively fled from each to each of the locked doors. There was no way out.

Across the passage a door throbbed to the maniac drumming of Sara Monkhouse. She had been locked in. For Talbot, agonized with solicitude, it was equally impossible to emerge from his dressingroom. Further down the passage, Edward Cartaret, interested by this nocturnal manifestation, wrenched and rattled his door-handle in vain.

Muriel, on her silent way through the house to Theodora's bedroom, had turned all the keys on the outside, impartially. She did not know which door might be Edward Cartaret's. Muriel was a woman who took no chances.

NOTES

1. Richard Von Krafft-Ebing (1840–1907), Sigmund Freud (1856–1939), Auguste-Henri Forel (1848–1931), Otto Weiniger (1880–1903), and Havelock Ellis (1859–1939) all wrote on sexual psychopathology.
2. An institution for the criminally insane in southeastern England.
3. *Erewhon* (1872) is a satirical novel by Samuel Butler; the title is an anagram for "nowhere."

Claudia Lars (Carmen Brannon de Samoya) *El Salvador, 1899–1974*

Born in a rural village in El Salvador, Claudia Lars went to the United States after completing her studies; she married there and did not return to her native country until 1949 following the breakup of her marriage. She began writing poetry while in the United States and published her first book of poems, *Estrellas en el pozo* (*Stars in the Hole*, 1934) in the style of García Lorca, her major influence at that time. Her own unique style, one of subtle intensity, is evident in her later work.

Following her return to El Salvador, Lars held several diplomatic posts, her most important in the Ministry of Culture, where she oversaw the production of many exciting creative projects from all over Latin America. Lars' reputation today is quite strong; considered by many to be one of Latin America's most important poets, she is often compared with Gabriela Mistral, for the intensity, honesty, and compassion of her poems. She wrote thirteen volumes of poetry between 1934 and 1974, several of them for children. An additional fifteen love poems, written in 1972 in response to three sonnets she had received forty years earlier from an unnamed lover, were published posthumously in 1975 as *Apuntes. Obra inédita. Cartas escritas cuando crece la noche* (*Notes. Unpublished Work. Letters Written at Nightfall*). The following year a series of poems dedicated to Lars were published by the same anonymous poet.

The following is from *Canción redonda* (Round Song, 1937).

SKETCH OF THE FRONTIER WOMAN
Dibujo de la mujer que llega

Standing erect in the mire.
Unlike the flower's stalk
and the butterfly's eagerness...
Without roots or fluttering:
more upright, more sure,
and more free.

Familiar with the shadow and the thorn.
With the miracle uplifted
in her triumphant arms.
With the barrier and the abyss
beneath her leap.

Absolute mistress of her flesh
to make it the core of her spirit:
vessel of the heavenly,
domus aurea,
a lump of earth from which rise, budding,
the corn and the tuberose.

Forgotten the Gioconda* smile.
Broken the spell of centuries.
Vanquisher of fears.
Clear and naked in the limpid day.

Lover without equal
in a love so lofty
that today no one divines it.
Sweet,
with a filtered sweetness
that neither harms nor intoxicates him who
                            tastes it.

Maternal always,
without the caress that hinders flight,
or the tenderness that confines,
or the petty yieldings that must be redeemed.

Pioneer of the clouds.
Guide to the labyrinth.
Weaver of tissues and songs.
Her only adornment, simplicity.

She rises from the dust...
Unlike the flower's stalk
which is less than beauty.

Translated by Donald Walsh

NOTE

* La Gioconda is the "Mona Lisa," the famous painting by Leonardo da Vinci.

EVOCATION OF GABRIELA MISTRAL
Evocación de Gabriela Mistral

(at her house in Santa Barbara, California)

Your hideaway barely picked up
rumors of the mechanized city:
island for insane travelers,
full of books and plums

> I don't forget our readings
> under the lamp,
> nor the Norwegian writer's visits
> who spoke of the fourth dimension
> as if he spoke of Oslo.
> I'm easily returned to the blue poplars
> and certain morning chores
> among the beets and cabbage

Butterflies with no direction
wanted to rest on your head
and the dog, destroyer of beetles,
on hearing your voice, turned
into a docile lamb.

> A marble Buddha had a seat
> near the most Christian book of all
> and the medieval Christ on his Friday
> cross
> agonized on top of the console.

Your profound gaze
went from the tranquil compassionate one to
　　　　　　　　　　　　　　the loving martyr
affirming that both could light the whole earth
from the same source.

> Such a clean quiet house
> made me walk on tiptoes
> and I received your words of
> gold, gently, without asking.

I enjoyed an undeserved summer
and I burst through the soul's nights
wanting to discover chasms.
That's why you finally said with resignation:
"Most curious friend:
You have arrived at my very bones to observe
　　　　　　　　　　　　　　　　　　me
and you see now: my own dead have killed
　　　　　　　　　　　　　　　　　　me."

> Then I understood the lines
> of an austere face
> and now I suffer the fire
> of all your poems.

Translated by Naomi Wieser

Nadézhda Yákovlevna Mandelshtám   *Russia/USSR, 1899–1980*

Nadézhda Yákovlevna Kházina grew up in the artistic and intellectual circles of pre-Revolutionary Kiev. She was well-read, traveled widely, knew several languages, including English, and studied art in the studio of Aleksándra Ékster. But, in her own words, "My life began when I met Mandelshtám." Osip Emílievich Mandelshtám (1891–1938) was already a published poet and essayist, and one of the core members of the Acmeist movement,[1] when he met Nadézhda Yákovlevna on May 1, 1919 in a basement cabaret in Kiev. They were married three years later.

　　Beginning in 1923 Mandelshtám's husband found it difficult to publish. His critical attitude toward the regime and his disassociation from Soviet literature eventually led to the suppression of his work and then to his arrest, in May 1934, and subsequent exile, first in Cherdyn, and later Voronezh.

It is the last four years of their life together that Mandelshtám describes in the first of her two volumes of memoirs *Vospominaniya* (*Hope Against Hope*, 1970), from which the selection is taken. The Mandelshtáms were allowed to live together, but, denied the possibility of working, they survived largely on money given them by friends. When O. M. (as Mandelshtám refers to her husband in her writings) was arrested again on May 1, 1938, Mandelshtám quickly traveled to Kalinin via Moscow, barely escaping arrest herself, to collect her husband's manuscripts stored there. She worked the night shift at a factory in a small town outside Moscow so that she could spend her days in line at the jail passing in food parcels for O. M. and vainly seeking news of her husband. She learned of his death only when one of her packages was returned with a note saying "addressee dead" in early 1939. Ordered by the secret police to leave Moscow, she lived first in Kalinin until the German invasion, then for the next twenty-three years moved from city to city (Dzhambul, Tashkent, Ulyanovsk, Chita, Cheboksary, Pskov, among others), supporting herself largely by teaching. In 1956 O. M. was posthumously rehabilitated and an edition of his works contemplated, and in 1964 Mandelshtám herself was finally granted permission to live in Moscow, where she spent her remaining years.

Mandelshtám had published two short stories in 1961 in *Pages from Tarusa* under a pseudonym, and in 1964 the first volume of her memoirs was first circulated in *Samizdat*,[2] then published abroad in Russian and several other languages. The second volume, *Vtoraya kniga* (*Hope Abandoned*, 1972), published in Russian in Paris, concentrates on her own life and on ruthlessly attacking the moral blindness which allowed the Stalinist terror to take place. Both books offer a brilliant commentary on her husband's poetry (the preservation of which was the central concern of the last forty-two years of her life), the various literary figures and party officials around her, and the fear and terror of life under Stalin. In the first volume particularly, she strives for strict objectivity and tries to make the reader understand the essence of survival under impossible conditions. Her prose is lucid, her memory astounding (although some have questioned it), her erudition impressive, and her faith in and devotion to her husband unwavering. In her memoirs Nadézhda Mandelshtám has created "an aesthetic structure," as Edward Brown suggests, that far surpasses mere document.

Dobrochna Dyrcz-Freeman

NOTES

1. A school of Russian poets that included Akhmátova, and Gumilyóv; founded 1912, it emphasized concrete and precise imagery and clarity of expression. Similar to American imagism, which appeared about the same time.
2. Handwritten or typed rather than printed texts that are "privately" circulated so as to evade the censorship of Soviet authorities, they consititute an "underground" literature in the Soviet Union.

COW OR POETRY READING?
from HOPE AGAINST HOPE
Vospomináni ya

Like everybody else, we tried to devise ways of saving ourselves. It is only in the East that people voluntarily throw themselves into the flames, but we still thought of ourselves as Europeans. Both O. M. and I had different plans—all they had in common was their absolute unfeasibility.

My plan was summed up by the word "cow." In our country, where all means of earning a livelihood are in the hands of the State, there are only two ways of maintaining a private existence: begging, or keeping a cow. We had tried begging, but found it unbearable. Everybody shies away from beggars and nobody wants to give alms, particularly as all they have comes to them by courtesy of the State. There had been a time when the ordinary people in Russia always took pity on prisoners and convicts, and the intelligentsia regarded it as a duty to support anyone persecuted for political reasons. All this disappeared together with "abstract humanism." Apart from this, people were frightened of us—we were not only beggars, we were also lepers. Everybody was afraid of everybody else: not even the "safest" person was immune—they could even come at night for someone who had just published an article in *Pravda* denouncing the "enemies of the people." Every arrest was followed by a chain reaction of others—the relatives and friends of the arrested man, as well as those whose telephone numbers were scribbled in his notebook, or in whose company he had celebrated the New Year. . . . People were frightened of every meeting and of every conversation, but they gave a particularly wide berth to people like us who had already been touched by the plague. And we ourselves felt that we were spreading the infection and wanted nothing more than to hide away and not see anybody.

This was why I dreamed of a cow. Thanks to the vagaries of our economic system, a family could support itself for many years by keeping a cow. Millions lived in wretched huts, feeding themselves from the products of their tiny plots of land (on which they grew potatoes, cabbage, cucumbers, beets, turnips and onions) and their cow. Some of the milk had to be sold to buy hay, but there was always enough left over to add a little richness to the cabbage soup. A cow gives people some independence and, without over-exerting themselves, they can earn a little extra to buy bread. The State is still in a quandary about this relic of the old world: if people are allowed to buy hay to feed their cow, then they do only the very minimum of work on the kolkhoz;[1] if, on the other hand, you take their cows away, they will die of hunger. The result is that the cow is alternately forbidden and then permitted again. But the number of cows is gradually decreasing, because the peasant women no longer have the strength to fight for them.

A cow would have saved us, and I was sure I would be able to learn how to milk it. We would have merged with the background somewhere, living very obscurely and never leaving our house. But to buy a house and cow you needed money—even now I wouldn't be able to afford them. Peasant women came to us in Savelovo, offering us their frame houses for a song, and nothing could have been more tempting. But to settle in the countryside you need to have been born there and inherit a hut with a leaking roof and a broken fence from some old peasant woman. Perhaps in capitalist countries there might be people eccentric enough to give an exiled poet the money to buy himself a peasant hut and a cow, but there could be no question of it here. To do so would have been regarded as a crime, and the benefactors themselves would speedily have ended up in a labor camp.

O. M. was not keen on my plan. Apart from the fact that we had no money to bring it about, the idea itself did not appeal to him. "Nothing ever comes of such schemes," he said. His plan was the reverse of mine— instead of merging with the background, he wanted to attract attention to himself. He believed that if only he could induce the Union of Writers to arrange a public reading of his poetry, then it would be impossible to refuse him work. He still harbored the illusion that you could win people over with poetry. This was something he had felt in his youth, when he once said to me that nobody could deny him anything if he wrote verse. It was probably quite true—things had been good for him in those days, his friends valued and protected him. But it was of course meaningless to apply those standards to the Moscow of 1937. Moscow no longer had faith in anything, and the order of the day was: every man for himself. Moscow now had no time for any civilized values, let alone for poetry. We knew this well enough, but O. M. was restless by nature and could not just sit waiting on events. Morever, an outcast could live only if he kept on the move—O. M. was not to be given a moment's respite until his death.

Lakhuti[2] seized on the idea of a poetry reading, which he too thought might save O. M. I know nothing at all of Lakhuti, except that he was friendly and kind to us. In the brutal atmosphere of those days, his friendliness seemed like a miracle. Neither he nor Stávsky[3] could decide the question of a reading without consulting higher authority. While this matter of State was being considered "up above," we waited in Savelovo, occasionally coming in to Moscow and going to the Union to see whether there was any progress. On one of these visits O. M. had a conversation with Surkóv[4] in the corridor, and when he came out, he found 300 roubles in his pocket. Sur-

kóv must have put them there without O. M. noticing. Not everybody would have risked such a thing—the consequences could have been very unpleasant. In any final estimate of Surkov, one should not forget this gift of money to O. M. It was rather like the onion which, in Russian tradition, the sinner must hang on to if he wants the Virgin to pull him into heaven at the last moment.

For a long time there was no word about the poetry reading, but then suddenly O. M.'s brother Evgény had a phone call from the Union and was asked to inform O. M. urgently that it had been fixed for the next evening. Cables were very unreliable and, rather than take chances, Evgény rushed to the station and caught the last train out to Savelovo. At that moment he too no doubt thought that O. M. might be saved by a poetry reading.

The next day we traveled to Moscow and went to the Union of Writers at the stated time. The secretaries were still there, but nobody knew anything about a poetry reading— they had only heard some vague rumor, but couldn't remember exactly what. All the rooms it could have been held in were locked, and there were no posters announcing it.

It only remained to find out whether anybody had received a circular about it. Shklóvsky[5] told us that nothing had been sent to him, but he advised us to ring one of the poets—invitations were generally sent around only to members of the relevant section. We happened to have Aséev's[6] telephone number and O. M. phoned him to ask whether he had received a notice. After a moment or two O. M. turned pale and hung up: Aséev said that he had heard something vaguely, but that he couldn't talk just now because he was about to leave for the Bolshoi Theater to see *The Snow Maiden*[7] . . . . O. M. didn't have the heart to try anybody else.

We were never able to unravel the mystery of the poetry reading. Somebody had certainly rung Evgény from the Union of Writers, but we never discovered who. It might have been the personnel department (always closely connected with the secret police) which had not bothered to inform the secretaries and given them no instructions—it was they who usually attended to the practical arrangements for such things. But why would the personnel department have been involved? The thought crossed our minds that it had all been a trap designed to lure O. M. from Savelovo for the purpose of arresting him in Moscow, but that nothing had come of it because somebody had forgotten to get top-level clearance—perhaps from Stalin himself. Since Stalin had been personally interested in O. M.'s case, this may well have been so. Otherwise O. M. might have been picked up in a way which had now become common practice for the overworked secret police—instead of going to arrest people in their homes, they lured them on some pretext to a convenient place from which they could be sent straight to the Lubyánka. There were many stories about such cases. But there was no point in speculating about it, so we returned to Savelovo and pretended to be vacationers again.

Both our plans for salvation thus collapsed—O. M.'s suddenly, and mine more gradually. Such dreams offered no way out.

It was quite natural that Aséev should have mentioned *The Snow Maiden*, rather than some other opera, as his excuse for not being able to talk: the poetic faction to which he belonged had once shown a weakness for pre-Christian Russia. But we omitted to inquire what was being performed that evening at the Bolshoi Theater and whether, indeed, it had not already been closed for the summer. I am told that in his old age Aséev was lonely and isolated. He explained his isolation by saying that he had lost his standing because of his fight against the "cult of personality." Friends of Kochetov[8] write articles to say that even he (Kochetov) fought against the "cult of personality." It now seems there were no Stalinists at all, only brave fighters against the "cult of personality." I can testify that nobody I knew fought—all they did was to lie low. This was the most that people with a conscience could do—and even that required real courage.

Translated by Max Howard

NOTES

1. Collective farm.
2. Abolhasem Akhmedzade Lakhuti (1887–1957): Persian poet and revolutionary.
3. V.P. Stávsky (d. 1943): writer believed to have collaborated with the government and to have contributed to the case against O. M.
4. Alekséy Aleksándrovich Surkóv (b. 1899): poet, essayist, editor, and functionary within the Writer's Union and the Communist Party.
5. Víktor Borísovich Shklóvsky (b. 1893): literary scholar, essayist, and novelist, one of the founders of the Formalist movement in Russian literary scholarship in the 1920s.
6. Nikoláy Nikoláevich Aséev (1889–1963): poet; proponent of various forms of Futurism and a follower of the poet Mayakóvsky.
7. An opera by Rímsky-Kórsakov (1844–1908) based on a Russian fairy tale.
8. Vsévolod Anísimovich Kóchetov (1912–1973): novelist and editor, he was extremely pro-Stalin and a powerful functionary in official writers' organizations.

Miyamoto Yuriko

Japan, 1899–1951

A writer whose whole life was a witness to a woman's personal struggle for self-definition and dedication to social activism, Miyamoto Yuriko was born a member of the social and intellectual elite. Her father was a Cambridge-educated architect, her mother the daugher of a founder of one of the leading modern intellectual journals, *Meiroku zasshi* (Meiji Period Journal). Miyamoto (her maiden name was Chūjō) began writing when she was 12, and she read such Western writers as Tolstoy and Dostoevsky while she was a student at Ochanomizu Women's High School (now Ochanomizu University). Her first novel, *Mazushiki hitobito no mure* (A Crowd of Poor People), was published in the important journal *Chūō kōron* (Central Review) when she was 17; it revealed the humanitarian commitment to social betterment that was to be her lifelong work.

Miyamoto traveled to New York with her father in 1918, where she met and married, despite family objections, a scholar fifteen years her senior. The disastrous marriage, which ended in divorce in 1924, is the subject of her first autobiographical novel, *Nobuko* (1924–1926, 1928; a portion is included here); the "I-novel," chronicles her own resistance to traditional notions about marriage and her efforts toward self-fulfillment. A nearly three-year stay in Russia and travel in Europe between 1927 and 1930 are the subject of *Dōhyō*, (Road Signs, 1947–1950); her relations after her divorce with the woman poet Yuasa Yoshiko and the decision to go to Russia are covered in *Futatsu no niwa* (Two Gardens, 1947).

On her return to Japan in 1930, Miyamoto joined the All-Japan Proletarian Artists' Association and edited its journal, *Hataraku fujin* (Working Women). In 1931 she joined the Japanese Communist Party and met Miyamoto Kenji, a communist literary critic nine years her junior (and later long-reigning Chairman of the Party). They were married in 1932. Government suppression of leftist activities in the early 1930s led to Kenji's arrest in 1933; he remained imprisoned until the end of World War II in 1945. Yuriko was arrested ten times between 1932 and 1943, experiences which broke her health but did not impair her political commitment.

During the war, Miyamoto wrote mainly literary criticism and essays on women writers, published together in 1948 as *Fujin to bungaku* (Women and Writing). After the war, she began writing novels again; *Banshū heiya* (*Bansū Plain*, 1946–1947) speaks of the hardships of the war years and the confusion of defeat, and *Fuchisō* (*The Weathervane Plant*, 1946) tells of her reunion with her husband after his release from prison. While not innovative in technique, Miyamoto's I-novels introduced subject matter that was radically new—the independent woman, the woman as artist. Later her political thought also led her to clarify the social and historical forces at work in shaping individual behavior. Ultimately, the I-novel was significant for its power to reveal the inner thought of the protagonist, thus exposing the disparities between burdensome social codes and the individual's response to them. Miyamoto's fiction shows the struggle of a woman to liberate herself from her bourgeois background; her essays deal with the relationship between literature and politics, and to the end of her life, Miyamoto remained devoted to public and private issues of human welfare.

Phyllis I. Lyons

from NOBUKO

The vortex of emotions into which they had been caught was fierce and complicated and Nobuko found her existence growing more painful by the day. With her simple and passionate nature, she responded with every fiber of her being to each provocation from her mother [Takeyo] or [her husband] Tsukuda. No sooner had she rebounded from one collision than there would be another—Nobuko began to long for the mental composure which would enable her to write. Her mind was a turbulent chaos of all that she had felt and experienced since Tsukuda's return, upon which she could impose no semblance of order.

"Lately I've rather been wanting to settle down and write," Nobuko told Tsukuda one day.

"That sounds like a good idea."

"I think that means I'm going to have to do some moving, though." Tsukuda glanced at Nobuko with an air of anxiety and suspicion.

"Oh, I don't mean moving out. All we have to do is move my desk somewhere. It's difficult for both of us to concentrate with two people coming in and out of here all the time, so I thought I would use my old room."

Tsukuda was silent for a moment. He took Nobuko's hand. "Is it really because you want to study?"

"Of course." At the moment she said this Nobuko felt a doubt, like a microscopic larva, flutter somewhere deep in her heart. Was that really all there was to it? "Absolutely." Nobuko reaffirmed her statement even more brightly than before. "So, will you help me?"

"Certainly."

Already, both of them were wearing spring clothes of light serge. Each of them took one side of the oaken desk Nobuko had inherited from her grandfather and they carried it through the verandah bordering the garden to a corner of one of the guest rooms.

"Isn't it dark in here?" Tsukuda asked.

"But I like this room, don't you?"

Only these guest rooms and the front entrance of the Sasa house still stood as its former owner, a master of the tea ceremony, had had them built. This room, in a part of the house which faced out on a small, old-fashioned garden, was now covered with the dust of many years. Some of its frameposts were even beginning to crumble. Nobuko and Tsukuda sat down, she facing the desk which they had set down after sweeping off one part of the tatami, Tsukuda on the verandah at the entrance of the room.

"Ah, spring is here. Do you see the *fuki* sprouts there under the pine tree?"

"Look!"

"What is it?"

"A salamander!"

The early summer sun fell across the garden moss as they chatted, lighting up the brushmarks on the wainscot of the white wall. Childhood memories welled up one after another in Nobuko's heart when she sat in this room. She remembered playing alone in the garden one summer day, that she had absently turned over a square tile set in the ground as a steppingstone. Caked, dry earth swelled up luxuriantly in the place where the tile had been, and Nobuko was surprised to see what seemed to be tiny grains of rice scattered all over it. A swarm of ants rushed to the place, grabbed the rice grains in their jaws, and fled. Nobuko could almost hear the rustle of their moving legs.

The scene which had unexpectedly opened up before her startled Nobuko. But as she watched, a sense of curiosity intensified within her. Picking up a bamboo pole, she poked over another tile. The place was empty. She tried another. There they were! Intoxicated by the physical sensation of that moment when she caught sight of the rice grains, Nobuko turned over one tile after another in the hot sun. Today, Nobuko remembered the ants' eggs with a pang of nostalgia. There was a transparent intensity to that girlish excitement, she thought, which she would never experience again. She sat with her paper spread out on her desk. But with her mind in its present state, she could find no way to bring order out of her complex emotions. Just as life itself right now seemed beyond her ability to cope with, its latent artistic content seemed beyond the limits of her skill.

Several days passed with Nobuko, Tsukuda, and her mother living in different parts of the house. Nobuko in her small study, Tsukuda in his room in front of the store house, and Takeyo in the diningroom, all avoided the precipitous vortex which so often whirled up out of even the most petty arguments.

"Anyone home?" One afternoon, Takeyo, her hair done up in Western style, ducked her head under the doorframe and entered Nobuko's room.

"I hadn't thought you would get such a good breeze in here."

"It's the lattice-work window."

Takeyo made a sweep of the room with her eye, as if she had entered someone else's house. "Will Tsukuda be home tonight?"

"I suppose so. He didn't mention anything to the contrary."

"In that case, it can just as well wait, but..." A change came into Takeyo's voice. "I've been thinking things over lately."

Nobuko said nothing.

"Come, come now. Don't sit there as if it had nothing to do with you!"

"Then what do you want?" Nobuko was unable to repress the harshness in her tone.

"If that's the way you feel about it, I can just as well let it pass, you know."

"Oh, mother, come out with it!"

"I've been thinking about you, you see, the two of you...That Tsukuda—you told me he wasn't his family's oldest son, didn't you?"

Nobuko felt suspicious. "Yes, I said that. Why?" She stared into her mother's face.

"Well, that means he can be adopted into another family, doesn't it?"

"It does."

"I think so. As long as there's one heir to a household, the other sons are free, aren't they? To tell you the truth, your father and I have been talking about this lately, and we feel if you must continue living with Tsukuda, it would be better to take him into the family as an adopted son. Don't you think so?"

Nobuko's eyes were wide with astonishment. "What do you mean? That's absurd! Why, you already have Waichiro to take over the house."

"That's true. But you don't think it's the house we're worried about, do you? How do you think we could have conceived of such a plan if we weren't thinking of you two?"

Nobuko could not quite fathom what her mother was trying to say. At the same time, she felt a strong, instinctive sense of caution. "For us? But we're doing fine by ourselves!"

"You see! That's just what I've been saying." Takeyo reprimanded Nobuko irritably. "You two don't know a thing about life! For one thing, take this school that Tsukuda is working in. You don't mean to tell me it wasn't precisely because of your father's introduction that Mr. Tsumura was so ready to offer him the position, do you? Without that, I can't imagine anyone being so receptive to a man with no name, no background, like Tsukuda."

Nobuko sensed something heartless in Takeyo's nature which prevented her from offering a kindness until she had made the recipient painfully aware of the nature and extent of her generosity. So zealous was Takeyo in advertising her charity that one inevitably began to suspect her motivations. Now, as so often in the past, Nobuko found herself listening to her mother's words in pained silence.

"I can't tell you what a difference it would make if he became Sasa instead of Tsukuda... a name nobody knows from Adam."

Nobuko boiled over. Her words tumbled out roughly. "If that's what you're trying to do for Tsukuda, he can do without it! Tsukuda is fine as Tsukuda. Do you think a human being's worth can be determined as simply as that?"

"Right now, you have smoke in your eyes, Nobuko." Takeyo pronounced her words slowly, letting each one hit its mark. "We all understand that Tsukuda must seem like a magnificent being to you. I think if you'd come down out of the clouds a bit, you'd notice we've been put in a slightly awkward position by his honorable presence."

The insult leveled at herself and her husband made Nobuko's face redden. "Why should we mind a little awkwardness? I still can't see why we have to adopt him into the family because of it." She steadied herself and tried to explain to Takeyo. "Mother, you don't understand my feelings at all. Haven't I already told you? The goals of my life are fundamentally different from yours. And there's more to it than that. This name Sasa that you set so much store by—if you think in broader terms, ours is a name nobody knows from Adam either. It's just that the only world you've ever experienced is one where everybody knows who the Sasa family is."

"No doubt my world is rather limited. But in this case, the facts will prove me right."

"Then that's all the more reason for me to refuse."

Takeyo laughed sarcastically. "Well, talk it over with your husband and see what he thinks. You may not like the idea, but I have a feeling Tsukuda will be different."

In fact, Nobuko never mentioned the matter to Tsukuda. One evening several days after the conversation, however, when Takeyo happened to find both Tsukuda and Nobuko together on the verandah, she suddenly brought the proposition up again. "Well, what do you think? You've mentioned the matter we discussed the other day to Mr. Tsukuda, I presume."

"I haven't," Nobuko said awkwardly.

"What matter?" Tsukuda asked from the side. Seeing that Nobuko made no attempt to answer the question, Takeyo began. "It con-

cerns the future, you see. Father and I aren't going to be around forever, of course, so lately we've been discussing a certain matter.... Nobuko, you mean to say you haven't told him for me?"

Nobuko could not help but feel a touch of fondness at this slight hesitation of the usually aggressive Takeyo. "You don't have to. It's alright," she said.

But Takeyo rejoined, "You think you can dismiss the matter so easily?"

Moonlight illuminated the garden, making the broad surfaces of the *pawlonia* and *yatsude* leaves glisten as if they were wet. In the depths of the shadowy branches across from them, Nobuko sensed an uncanny darkness, as if the garden itself were bearing down on her with some extraordinary oppressive force. She sat, hugging her knees, staring out into the garden, listening intently to the exchange between her mother and Tsukuda. Surely Tsukuda would refuse, she thought, surely....

"Well, that's what we've been thinking about." Takeyo concluded her explanation and waited for Tsukuda's response. "Nobuko is completely in a huff over this, as if we'd offered her an insult of some kind. But, of course, you know her personality as well as I do."

Nobuko, concentrating so hard her ears almost turned inside out, waited for Tsukuda's response.

"So what do you think?" Takeyo prodded. "I don't see what harm could come from it..."

"I'll certainly think it over and let you know."

Nobuko whirled around. "Why on earth should you have to think over a thing like this?" She was almost shouting at Tsukuda. "You don't mean you're really going to think it over, do you?"

"Nobuko, you stay out of this. Mr. Tsukuda has his own opinions," said Takeyo, who had succeeded in manipulating the unknowing Tsukuda this way and that at her will, and was now trying through him to bring Nobuko, too, more tightly into her grasp. Should she ever achieve this, Nobuko felt, it would be the end. Rather than love for the mother who was trying desperately to hold on to her, Nobuko felt a dread as if the very roots of her existence were being threatened. The fact that Tsukuda had not then and there dismissed the matter with a laugh, with an outright refusal, as she had anticipated, filled her with deep anxiety.

When Tsukuda rose and walked off the verandah, Nobuko followed at his heels. "Dear, is that really something you have to think about?" Tsukuda stood taller than Nobuko, and she looked up into his face. "As far as I'm concerned, I'll have nothing to do with it, you know." Tsukuda still said nothing. "If she has her way, our life together will simply disappear!"

"Of course, that's why I told her I would have to think it over."

"Oh, I see. You were being polite?"

Again, silence from Tsukuda.

"But tell me. It's only me you have to tell, but hurry! What do you really think? You wouldn't even consider it, of course?"

"Hmmmm. I suppose not....But if it would make you happy, darling. After all, my life is in your hands."

Tsukuda's answer, which by its very failure to clarify his real desires seemed to compel Nobuko to feel grateful to him, darkened Nobuko's heart. The ambiguity of his words recalled to her mind her mother's stinging criticism of Tsukuda, and Nobuko was wracked with doubt. "My life is in your hands." Nobuko was not so naïve as to take these words at face value without feeling a sense of repulsion. At the same time, frightening as it was, she suspected there was something more than mere unctuousness to Tsukuda's turn of phrase. Her reason informed her that Tsukuda's answer was complex in nature: it was not inconceivable that what his vague words implied was that it would not bother him tremendously to

become an adopted son. Far from it, he might even be pleased to become one were it not that he feared what Nobuko would think. More than anything else, however, Nobuko regretted that Tsukuda had answered just as her mother had expected. In her heart of hearts, Takeyo was certainly gloating over this victory. For victory to her would be simply the confirmation of her suspicions that Tsukuda, just as she had predicted, was shrewdly plotting how to make his way in the world and that he had inveigled Nobuko into marriage itself in order to use her. Nobuko, for the sake of their love, could not bear to think that this prophecy might come true. For herself and Tsukuda, for her mother, for all that was untainted in that authentic love that the human heart can hold, she resolved to prevent this matter from developing any further. She knew that Takeyo, who was suspicious of people on principle and who even took a kind of pride in seeing her doubts about a person materialize, would through this recent development grow even more confirmed in her cynical view of human nature. Yet if one possibility out of a hundred thousand (truly one out of a hundred thousand, Nobuko hoped with all her heart) proved true, and there was some unclean calculation in Tsukuda's marriage to her, Tsukuda would have to learn that this world was not a place where one could trample others underfoot so easily. For how could Nobuko believe that the love which she was striving to make pure and genuine at the price even of confrontation with her parents and defiance of the society around her, was simply the fruit of Tsukuda's manipulation of her own stupidity by feigning to love her? That night, Nobuko felt sick with sorrow. "If only Tsukuda would stand firm!" she thought, crying to herself. The sense of her aloneness in life made her weep.

"Well, what have you decided?" Takeyo asked several times in the days that followed.

"It won't work." Nobuko would tell her. "Let's forget we ever discussed the matter." After these exchanges Nobuko would plead with Tsukuda. "Can't you put an end to all this by giving her a definite answer now? You must see how much better it would be to simply refuse!"

Takeyo, too, in Nobuko's presence and even in her absence, found her opportunities to corner Tsukuda and pressure him for an answer. "After all you said about being ready to do anything for Nobuko's sake, you're not going to go back on your word, are you? We have the letters you wrote from America, you know, with those very words."

Tsukuda, his skin turning to gooseflesh, would answer nervously, "One of these days, I'm sure, you'll come to understand how committed I am." But whether he would become an adopted son of the Sasa family or not, whether he liked or detested the idea, he never said clearly. For some reason, when it came to this point, Tsukuda displayed extraordinary caution and stubbornness in his refusal to divulge his intentions. Takeyo, gradually losing patience, began to bring the matter up if she so much as caught sight of Nobuko.

Nobuko finally reached the limits of her endurance. "Mother, it doesn't matter what you say, I refuse," she declared one day. "Even if Tsukuda goes along with you, I'm against it. Imagine what will happen if Tsukuda agrees, whatever his motivations may be. Do you really think you'll be happy afterwards? I find the very idea of this scheme hateful. It degrades the entire family."

Takeyo, although surely she would have reacted just as Nobuko predicted if things developed as she wanted them to now, flared up as if she had been dealt a blow. She spoke with tears in her eyes, "Ah, how true it is, 'The child has not heart for its parents.' Why do you make us suffer so? You realize that when a woman marries she becomes part of another house, don't you? Once I die, your tie to the Sasa family is gone. Don't disinherit yourself, Nobuko. You've brought us enough shame as it is."

Nobuko, too, broke down in tears.

"Mother, think of it this way. Even cedar saplings have to be separated from each other as they grow. People are no different. Someday I think you'll be happy I insisted on this so strongly. It's not without reason I've been so stubborn." During this exchange, Nobuko's brother and sister, who had been standing next to them, left the room one by one.

Takeyo nevertheless went ahead and made preparations to have Tsukuda adopted into the family. Nobuko, completely unaware of this, was sitting at her desk one day when the maid called her: "Your mother would like to see you."

"Why, Mother, what's wrong?" Takeyo was clearly so upset about something she was unable to work.

"This Tsukuda fellow frightens me, you know."

"What do you mean?"

"You should ask! You've known all along he couldn't become an adopted son, haven't you?"

Nobuko, baffled, was silent.

"Your father met Ida-san at a meeting the other day and they discussed the possibility of adopting Tsukuda into the family. Ida later made some inquiries into the matter. Just yesterday he reported back to us that it was legally impossible. The head of one family can't be adopted into another." As it turned out, Tsukuda, although he had been born as the second son in the Okamoto family, was the legal heir of the name of a distant relative, Tsukuda.

"Of course I had completely forgotten about that."

"Really? Well no doubt the news comes as quite a relief to you. But the gall of him doing that to us! And I'm sure behind our backs he was getting a good laugh out of it all the while."

"That's ridiculous. He was as oblivious of the problem as you were."

"I wonder. It certainly is strange. It seems to me a man who managed to keep himself afloat in American society for fifteen years should have at least that much savoir-faire. He knew perfectly well that one simple, outright 'no' from him would have ended his game of acting like a son of ours."

"Ah!" Nobuko let out a loud sign of despair. "My poor husband! You'd think he was born into this world just for the purpose of having people speak ill of him. 'If thou art born human,'" she ended with a laugh, "'become not Nobuko's husband!'"

The discovery that Tsukuda could not be adopted into the family changed Takeyo's feelings toward him completely. She now began to insist that, if Tsukuda had no shameful intentions regarding them, he should leave the Sasa household immediately as proof. "I know you don't want this separation any more than I do," she told Nobuko, "but I've endured as much as I can. The sooner you leave the better."

Her despair at seeing her daughter slowly but surely being wrested away from her seemed to find its only outlet in tears and vilifications. For Takeyo's proud personality could not bear having her sadness interpreted as weakness, or becoming an object of sympathy. She would lash out as if she were about to burn up with the intensity of her feelings.

"I know the longer I'm around, the more of a nuisance I am to you two. But think of [your sister] Tsuyako, she's still so young . . . for her sake, let me live a little while longer. At least it should be interesting to you to watch how all this drives me to the grave."

"Ah, ah!" Nobuko, at a loss for how to express the love she felt for her mother, wept. From the time of her childhood, she and Takeyo had been linked by a passion quite different from the usual feeling between mother and daughter. Over the years, they had borne each other both deep love and deep hate. As a woman, Takeyo had been for Nobuko at times wholly mother, at times friend, at times a rival. At all times, at any rate, she had lived her life facing Nobuko, thrusting force-

fully at her daughter every angle of existence, however raw. In Nobuko's life, too, Takeyo had been a focal point which demanded every ounce of her energy—for it was no half-hearted effort that Nobuko had expended in becoming aware of the difference between herself and her mother, in criticizing her mother's way of life, in short, in striving to form herself into a woman who was not a carbon copy of Takeyo. It was in the strange flash of light produced by this combustion of their lives that Takeyo and Nobuko were united, a bond utterly different from the usual sense of rest and fondness which link mother and daughter.

Now, when the time had come to pass through that gate which separates one stage of life from the next, how could Nobuko communicate to her mother the painful, dazzling rush of memories that filled her soul? Yes, she thought between her sobs, what an unusual love it was that she and Takeyo bore each other! It was a love so deep that it was only in this way, by wounding and striking out at each other with all their might, that they could separate.

For Sasa, who was less passionate, more peaceful in nature than his wife and daughter, it was difficult to deal with the battle of hearts that raged between them. On the one hand, he tried to comfort and mollify Takeyo; on the other, he appealed to Nobuko with heartfelt pleas.

"Why is it always you who causes trouble in this family? Can't you be a little bit more tender-hearted? We love you. Why don't you accept our love and let us all live in peace? Get rid of these theories of yours that bring nothing but suffering to you and everyone else!"

"Father," Nobuko's sadness was so great she could barely speak the words. "This has nothing to do with theories."

"Then get out!" Sasa shouted. But he, too, his heart filled with sorrow, could manage only a simple, mechanical rage. "If you can turn your back on your parents, I can do without a child. Get out of this house forever!"

Translated by Brett DeBary

Karin Boye   *Sweden, 1900—1941*

Karin Boye was born in Göteborg (Gothenburg), where her father was a civil
engineer; later the family moved to Stockholm. After receiving a diploma from
Teacher's College in 1921, Boye continued her studies at the Universities of
Uppsala and Stockholm, receiving an M.A. in 1928. She was a teacher at a folk
high school from 1936 to 1938, but primarily functioned as a writer and critic.
Married for a short time in a kind of friendship union, she later preferred lesbian
relationships. After several nervous breakdowns and chronic depression, she finally
committed suicide.

As a student in Uppsala, Boye joined the left-wing organization *Clarté* (Clarity), founded in France by Henri Barbusse, and wrote for their magazine, which
featured articles about Marx, Freud and psychoanalysis. During the 1930s, she was
a co-founder of the Stockholm literary journal *Spectrum*, introducing T.S. Eliot
and the Surrealists to the Swedish reader. Together with the critic Erik Mesterton,
she translated T.S. Eliot's *The Waste Land* (*Det Öde Landet, 1931*).

Boye is probably most read as a poet. Influenced by Buddhism in her early
poems, later by Schopenhauer, and finally by Nietzsche, the poetic style of her
works changed from a strict classical form in the 1920s—like *Clouds* (1922) from
which "You Are My Purest Consolation" is taken, and *Gömda Land* (Hidden
Lands, 1924) in which "A Wish" first appeared—to a modernistic, expressionistic
form in her later collections. Of these later works, *För trädets skull* (*For the Sake
of the Tree*, 1935) in which "Farewell" appears, is considered her best. Her poetry
deals mainly with dualism in life, the outer and inner self, the split personality, the
person who is both strong and weak—an Amazon, ready to fight, "armed and
erect," and, at the same time, a vegetative, introverted person who cannot cope
with the outside world.

Her best known novel, *Kallocain* (1940), was published in an English translation in 1966 under the same title. A utopian novel, it is a kind of psychoanalytic
description of people who, through a truth serum, come to understand and express
their innermost selves.

Boye's poetry has had a considerable impact on contemporary Scandinavian
poets. As a prose writer, her influence has been felt both in Scandinavia and in the
English-speaking world, through *Kallocain*, which in some respects can be seen as
a link between George Orwell's *Brave New World* and *1984*. Translations of her
work can be found in *A Selection from Modern Swedish Poetry* (1929), *Twentieth-
Century Scandinavian Poetry* (1950) and *Twentieth-Century Women's Poetry in
Translation. The Other Voice* (1976).

Ingrid Claréus

YOU ARE MY PUREST CONSOLATION
Du är min renaste tröst

You are my purest consolation,
You are my strongest protection,
You are the best I've got,
for nothing hurts like you.

Yes, nothing hurts like you.
You burn like ice and fire,
You cut like steel my soul—
You are the best I've got.

Translated by Ingrid Claréus

A WISH
Önskan

Oh, let me really live
and really die once,
so that I may touch reality
in good as in bad.
And let me be quiet
and honor what I see,
so that this will be this
and nothing more.

If out of my long life
only one day was left,
then I would seek the most beautiful
there is on earth.
The most beautiful on earth
is honesty,
and that alone makes life to life
and reality.

The whole wide world is
a buttercup leaf
and in its cup rests
a drop of clear water.
This single drop
is the essence of life.
Oh make me worthy to look at it!
Oh make me pure!

Translated by Ingrid Claréus

FAREWELL
Avsked

I wanted to wake you to a nakedness like a
                        naked spring evening,
when the stars overflow
and the earth burns under melting snow.
I wanted to see you just once
sink into the darkness of creative chaos,
wanted to see your eyes like a wide-opened
                                        space,
ready to be filled,
wanted to see your hands like opened flowers,
empty, new, awaiting,
You are leaving, and nothing of this have I given
                                        you.
I never reached where your soul lies bare.
You are leaving, you take nothing of me with
                                        you—
leaving me to my defeat.

I remember another farewell:
we were cast from the melting pot as one being.
and when we parted, we no longer knew
what was I or you . . .
But you—like a bowl of glass you have left my
                                        hand,
so complete as only a dead thing and so
                                        unchanged,
with no memories other than light fingermarks
to be washed away in water.
I wanted to wake you to a formlessness like a
                        formless flickering flame,
which finds at last its living shape, its own, . . .
Defeat, oh defeat!

Translated by Ingrid Claréus

Lydia Cabrera   *Cuba/US, b. 1900*

Born into Cuba's white aristocracy, Lydia Cabrera was one of the first "archivists" of traditional black Afro-Caribbean literature. She began her creative life as a painter and went to Paris, where many artists from Latin America congregated in the 1920s and 1930s, including Venezuelan Teresa de la Parra, with whom she lived for several years. It was there she became interested in Afro-Cuban folklore, some of which she had heard as a child from her black nursemaid. Her many years of research resulted in stories, essays, and poems by and about a virtually unknown and rapidly disappearing culture.

Dedicated to Teresa de la Parra, *Cuentos negros de Cuba* (Stories from the Negroes of Cuba, 1940), from which the following story is taken, was first published in French, in Paris, in 1936, its translator the eminent writer Francis Miomandre. Four years later it appeared in Cuba, with an introduction by the great pioneer in Afro-Cuban studies, Fernando Ortiz. Among her other Africanist works, Cabrera has published a collection of Negro proverbs *Refranes de Negros Viejos* (Proverbs by Old Negroes, 1955), a scholarly book on the magic, superstition, and folklore of African Cubans, *El monte* (The Mountain, 1968), and a dictionary of Lucumi, which is the Yoruba (an African language) they speak in Cuba.

An exile from Cuba, Cabrera lives in southern Florida.

WALO-WILA

There were once two sisters, Walo-Wila and Ayere Kénde—or Kénde Ayere. Walo-Wila never went outdoors. No one had ever seen her.

Ayere Kénde leaned over the balcony. With her elbows on the railing, Ayere Kénde was enjoying the evening coolness which came up from the sea.

A wooden horse with music went by. He said, "A little water, please."

Ayere Kénde had a golden goblet. She filled it with water and gave it [to] him to drink.

Said the horse, "What a handsome goblet, Ayere Kénde. I've never seen anything to equal it in all my life!"

"Oh, fairer, far fairer, is my sister...!"

"Then I want to see her, Ayere Kénde. Let me in."

"If you marry her you'll see her, brother," said Ayere Kénde.

Walo-Wila lived and died behind the closed shutters. Died and lived.

Kénde Ayere sang:

"Walo-Wila, Walo Kénde,
   Ayere Kénde,
Here is a visitor, Kénde Ayere!"

Walo-Wila asked:

"Walo-Wila, Walo Kénde,
   Ayere Kénde,
Who is the visitor, Kénde Ayere?"

"Walo-Wila, Walo Kénde,
   Ayere Kénde,
Brother Horse, Kénde Ayere."

"Walo-Wila, Walo Kénde,
   Ayere Kénde,
What does Brother Horse want, Kénde
                              Ayere?"

"Walo-Wila, Walo Kénde,
   Ayere Kénde,
What but marriage, Kénde Ayere."

"Walo-Wila, Walo Kénde,
   Ayere Kénde,
Tell Brother Horse that I am ugly, Kénde
                              Ayere.

Walo-Wila, Walo Kénde,
  Ayere Kénde,
That I am one-eyed, Kénde Ayere.

Walo-Wila, Walo Kénde,
  Ayere Kénde,
That I have boils, Kénde Ayere.

Walo-Wila, Walo Kénde,
  Ayere Kénde,
That I am putrid, Kénde Ayere!"

"Farewell, farewell!" said the horse.

Ayere Kénde was on her balcony. The Goat-Man passed, the Bull-Man, and the Water-Tortoise-Man.

The Tiger-Man passed, the Elephant-Man and the Lion-Man. Each of them was thirsty. When Ayere Kénde offered them her goblet of fine gold, they all praised the goblet, and she would say, "Fairer, far fairer, is my invisible sister."

And they all wanted to see her, but Walo-Wila sang, like a shadow singing behind the shutters:

"Alas, for I am ugly,
For I am one-eyed,
For I am bandy-legged,
For I have scurvy!"

And they went away in disgust.

Stag, the son of the Honeysuckle, had not yet drunk from the golden goblet.

Ayere Kénde was enjoying the coolness of evening on her balcony; she was rocking in the rocker while the breeze rocked the balcony. (With far-off dreams in her eyes.)

Stag approached. He said, "Ayere Kénde, give me a drink in your golden goblet."

Ayere Kénde offered him the full goblet.

Said Stag, "I have never seen anything fairer."

"Oh, fairer, far fairer, is my sister whom no one has seen!"

"Show her to me, Ayere Kénde. I shall know the right way to look at her."

"Your eyes are gentle. If you marry her you'll see her, brother: you may not touch her. Wait, wait."

"Walo-Wila, Walo Kénde,
  Ayere Kénde,
Here is a visitor, Kénde Ayere."

And Walo-Wila replied, sad as nightfall at the window:

"Tell him that I am ugly,
That I am a cripple,
That I am one-eyed,
That I have boils..."

"I'll marry her," promised Stag.

Then said Walo-Wila, "My sister's mother lives at the bottom of the sea. My sister's mother is called Kariempembe."

At midnight Walo-Wila gave Ayere Kénde a pumpkin filled with pearls.

At midnight Kénde Ayere spilled out the pearls. She called Stag and handed him the pumpkin, now empty.

"Go down to the bottom of the sea."

Stag ran to the shore. The whole shore was saying, "Walo-Wila, Walo-Wila, Walo-Wila, Walo-Wila."

And he went in, between the moon-sharpened waves.

Ayere Kénde kept vigil all night on her balcony. At dawn Stag returned. He brought the pumpkin brimming with blue water from the sapphire depths of Olokun...

Said Ayere Kénde, "Go into my sister's chamber."

And Walo-Wila was fairer, far fairer than the goblet of Ayere Kénde.

When the moon kisses the sea...

Translator Unknown

Nathalie Sarraute   (Nathalie Tcherniak Ivanovo-Vozenssenk)

France, b. 1900

Nathalie Sarraute was born Nathalie Tcherniak Ivanovo-Voznessenk in Russia. After her parents' divorce when she was 2, she lived in France but shuttled for years between her native country and her adopted one. Educated primarily in

France where she obtained a degree in English, she also studied at Oxford (1920–1921) and Berlin (1921–1922).

After having completed a law degree, she passed the bar in Paris, although she never practiced law with great enthusiasm. Sarraute began writing in 1932 and published a collection of her works as *Tropismes* (*Tropisms*, 1938; expanded version, 1957), which went basically unnoticed. In 1949, *Portrait d'un Inconnu* (*Portrait of a Man Unknown*) appeared with a preface by Jean-Paul Sartre, who described it as an "anti-novel."[1] This was one of the earliest critical efforts to place Sarraute and to define what eventually came to be called the *nouveau roman* (the "New Novel");[2] Sarraute was one of its pioneers as well as one of its most interesting theoreticians, as suggested by the following excerpt from her critical writings, collected under the title of *L'Ere du Soupçon* (*The Age of Suspicion*, 1956). After the success of *Le Planétarium* (*Planetarium*, 1959), she received official acclaim when she was awarded the International Literature Prize.

Sarraute's work makes transparent the complexity masked by the most banal and commonplace gestures and situations without betraying the absolutely elusive character of human existence. According to Sarraute, her first book, *Tropisms* (from which a selection follows), contained the seeds of what she would develop in her later works: the moment that is always moving beyond the limits of consciousness, and that, significantly, constitutes the hidden origin of what we say and do. Sarraute's novels are highly experimental, yet they also reflect a relentless attempt to rediscover a common ground between human beings. At the same time that they mine the psychological oddities of human character, they provide a scathingly satirical critique of bourgeois conventionality. Though Sarraute has now begun to explore a new genre with her first autobiographical volume *Enfance* (*Childhood*, 1983), she is still committed to revealing the "shadowy secrets" that are for her the only subject of literature.

In 1982 Sarraute was awarded the Prix national des lettres. Her latest book, published in 1986, is *Paul Valéry et l'enfant d'éléphant* (Paul Valéry and the Elephant Child), a work of literary criticism; it refers to a tale in Rudyard Kipling's *Just So Stories*. Composed of previously published essays on Valéry (1947; 1984 revised) and Flaubert (1965), the book is particularly daring in its unflattering assessment of the poet, who is admired to the point of idolatry by French critics. She has won acclaim both in France and abroad for this intellectual independence as well as her literary quality, and her works are much translated into English.

NOTES

1. Jean-Paul Sartre (1905–1980). Existentialist philosopher, novelist, critic, and editor of the influential review *Les Temps Modernes* (Modern Times), he was the leading intellectual authority of the post–World War II period along with his companion Simone de Beauvoir.
2. The name given by critics and journalists to a group of novelists who, in spite of their marked differences and their refusal to be considered a "school," were all pursuing a renewal of novelistic form during the years following World War II. Alain Robbe-Grillet (b. 1922) and Claude Simon (b. 1913) were prominent representatives of this group.

from TROPISMS
Tropismes

They were ugly, they were dull, commonplace, without personality, they were really too out-of-date, clichés, she thought, which she had already seen described everywhere, so many times, in the works of Balzac, of Maupassant, in *Madame Bovary*,[1] clichés, copies, copies of copies, she decided.

She would have so liked to repulse them, seize them and hurl them away. But they stood quietly about her, they smiled at her, pleasantly, but dignifiedly, very decorously, they had been working all week, all their lives they had counted on nobody but themselves, they asked for nothing, except to see her from time to time; to rearrange a little the tie between them and her, feel that it was there, still in place, the tie that bound them to her. They wanted nothing more than to ask her—as was natural, as everybody did, when they went to call on friends, or on relatives—to ask her what she had been doing that was nice, if she had been reading a lot lately, if she had gone out often, if she had seen that, didn't she think those films were good...They, themselves, had so enjoyed Michel Simon, Jouvet,[2] they had laughed so hard, had had such a delightful evening...

And as for all that, clichés, copies, Balzac, Flaubert, *Madame Bovary*, oh! they knew very well, they were acquainted with it all, but they were not afraid—they looked at her kindly, they smiled, they seemed to feel that they were safe with her, they seemed to know that they had been observed, depicted, described so often, been so sucked on, that they had become as smooth as pebbles, all shiny, without a nick, without a single hold. She could not get at them. They were safe.

They surrounded her, held out their hands to her: "Michel Simon...Jouvet...Ah! she had been obliged to book seats well ahead of time, had she not...Later, there would have been no tickets to be had, except at exorbitant prices, nothing but boxes, or in the orchestra..." They tightened the tie a little more, very gently, unobtrusively, without hurting her, they rearranged the slender tie, pulled...

And little by little a certain weakness, a certain slackness, a need to approach them, to have them approach her, made her join in the game with them. She sensed how docilely (Oh! yes...Michel Simon...Jouvet...) very docilely, like a good, amenable little girl, she gave them her hand and walked in a ring with them.

Ah! here we are at last all together, good as gold, doing what our parents would have approved of, here we all are then, well behaved, singing together like good little children that an invisible adult is looking after, while they walk gently around in a circle giving one another their sad, moist little hands.

Translated by Maria Jolas

NOTES

1. *Madame Bovary*: the realistic novel by Gustave Flaubert concerning the illusions and adulterous affairs of the provincial Emma, who may be taken as an exemplary heroine of the sort the narrator refers to. When the novel was published in 1856, Flaubert was prosecuted for and acquitted of immorality.
2. Michel Simon (1895–1975): French actor; Louis Jouvet (1887–1951): French actor, producer and director, at the time of the Athenée theater in Paris.

from CONVERSATION AND SUBCONVERSATION, *in* THE AGE OF SUSPICION
Ere du soupçon

...Lacking actions, we can use words. And words possess the qualities needed to seize upon, protect and bring out into the open these subterranean movements that are at once impatient and afraid.

They have in their favor their suppleness, their freedom, the iridescent richness of their shading, their transparency or their opaqueness.

Their rapid, abundant flow, with its restless shimmer, allows the more imprudent of them to slip by, to let themselves be borne along and disappear at the slightest sign of danger. But they risk little danger. Their reputation for gratuitousness, lightness, inconsistency—they are, after all, pre-eminently the instruments of frivolous pastimes and games—protects them from suspicion and from minute examination: we are generally content to make purely formal verification of them; they are subject to rather lax regulations; they rarely result in serious sanctions.

Consequently, provided they present a more or less harmless, commonplace appearance, they can be and, in fact, without anyone's taking exception, without the victim's even daring to admit it frankly to himself, they often are the daily, insidious and very effective weapon responsible for countless minor crimes.

For there is nothing to equal the rapidity with which they attain to the other person at the moment when he is least on his guard, often giving him merely a sensation of disagreeable tickling or slight burning; or the precision with which they enter straight into him at his most secret and most vulnerable points, and lodge in his innermost recesses, without his having the desire, the means or the time to retort. But once they are deposited inside him, they begin to swell, to explode, they give rise around them to waves and eddies which, in turn, come up to the surface and spread out in words. By virtue of this game of actions and reactions that they make possible, they constitute for the novelist a most valuable tool.

And this, no doubt, is why, as Henry Green* has noted, characters in fiction have become so talkative.

But this dialogue, which tends more and more, in the modern novel, to take the place left by action, does not adapt itself easily to the forms imposed by the traditional novel. For it is above all the outward continuation of subterranean movements which the author—and with him the reader—must make at the same time as the character...

It is therefore permissible to dream—without blinding ourselves to all that separates the dream from its reality—of a technique that might succeed in plunging the reader into the stream of these subterranean dramas of which Proust only had time to obtain a rapid aerial view, and concerning which he observed and reproduced nothing but the broad motionless lines. This technique would give the reader the illusion of repeating these actions himself, in a more clearly aware, more orderly, distinct and forceful manner than he can do in life, without their losing that element of indetermination, of opacity and mystery that one's own actions always have for the one who lives them.

The dialogue, which would be merely the outcome or, at times, one of the phases of these dramas, would then, quite naturally, free itself of the conventions and restraints that were made indispensable by the methods of the traditional novel. And thus, imperceptibly, through a change of rhythm or form, which would espouse and at the same time accentuate his own sensation, the reader would become aware that the action has moved from inside to outside.

The dialogue, having become vibrant and swollen with these movements that propel and subtend it, would be as revealing as theatrical dialogue, however commonplace it might seem in appearance.

Translated by Maria Jolas

NOTE

* Henry Green (b. 1905): English comic novelist and critic known for his allusive and poetic style.

Anna Seghers   (Netty Reiling)   *Germany/GDR, 1900–1983*

Born in the Rhineland in 1900, Netty Reiling used the pseudonym Anna Seghers for the publication of her first story, "Der Aufstand der Fischer von St. Barbara" (The Revolt of the Fishermen of St. Barbara, 1928). The daughter of an influential art dealer, she studied art history and earned a doctorate in 1924 with a dissertation on Rembrandt. She joined the German Communist Party in 1928 and became one of the most vociferous and eloquent spokespeople in the discussions that raged during the 1930s concerning Marxist-Leninist aesthetics and the relative virtues and drawbacks of expressionism and realism. As a critical theoretician, she is especially well known for her correspondence with the Hungarian critic-philosopher Georg Lukács (1885–1971), which took place during those years while she was in exile in Paris, he in Moscow.

Her membership in the Communist Party and her strongly-held ideological beliefs led both to her exile, which took her first to France and ultimately to Mexico, and to her return after the Second World War to the G.D.R. Active during the years of the Weimar Republic in various Communist organizations, she was forced to leave Germany in 1933 after her books were banned and then burned. She wrote some of her best works during that period of exile, including the novel for which she is perhaps best known, and which was made into a Hollywood film, *Das siebte Kreuz* (*The Seventh Cross*, 1942), a tale of Communist resistance to Nazi persecution. Another work that has been widely translated and hailed as a classic for its intricate weaving of past and present and its depth of feeling is her novella "Der Ausflug der toten Mädchen" ("The Outing of the Dead Girls," 1946).

Seghers was one of the most ardent proponents and able practitioners of "socialist realism," generally avoiding autobiographical reference and choosing in her novels and stories always to portray simple but paradigmatic characters successfully confronting the problems of the everyday world. On this basis, Annemarie Auer argues that she has created an "unbroken and consistently progressive epic of contemporary German society." Her central purpose in writing was to bring about a change of consciousness on the part of her readers.

In the G.D.R., Seghers was honored as one of the few writers who could provide continuity between the earlier German Communist movement and the new Communist state. She became the *grande dame* of East German letters, held some high offices in the party's cultural bureaucracy, and was very influential both in determining cultural polices and in serving as a model to be emulated by younger writers. Christa Wolf in particular paid multifold tribute to Seghers in her essays and elsewhere. Recognized in both Germanies as a major writer of this century, Seghers received, among other awards, the Büchner Prize in 1947, the National Prize for Literature of the G.D.R. (1951 and 1959), and the Stalin Peace Price (1951).

Her works from the period between 1947 and her death in 1983 include two long novels, essays, and speeches, and several collections of short stories, among them *Die Kraft der Schwachen* (The Strength of the Weak Ones, 1965), from which "The Prophet" is taken.

Marilyn Sibley Fries

THE PROPHET
Der Prophet

Stefan published his first article when he was fifteen, during the First World War. The paper in which it was printed was run off the press secretly in a suburb of Budapest—a few hundred copies—and distributed at once.

He was a printer's apprentice. He had also helped to print and distribute the paper. His heart was filled with happy pride because for the first time he had written an article which had been accepted by those he respected. Now it was to be printed and read by many people.

When he was handing out the folded sheet—for the paper was no more than that—under the eyes of the police, at various factory gates when the shifts changed Stefan seldom thought of the danger, because he felt so happy that all these people would soon be reading his thoughts, properly expressed, and would take them to heart if not the same day, then the day after. And even if it's not always the people we actually give the paper to, thought Stefan, then others will hear about our ideas and perhaps understand them better than the first readers.

Stefan, who had not yet finished his apprenticeship, was soon asked by his friends to write another article; this pleased them and him, too, even more than the first. Their thoughts and efforts were aimed at putting an end to the war and therefore at stirring up strikes in the big munitions factories. But the cellar in which they had run off the paper was discovered—or someone betrayed them—and surrounded. The editors were arrested. So as to avoid any delay, it was decided to print the paper in a house which a friend offered. Stefan wrote various articles under various names, which gave the impression that the arrests had left no gap and only unimportant people had been caught.

Those in power could not and would not believe that their end was coming; they dared one last big move in their atrocious game and a new wave of arrests began. Stefan was caught, brought up for questioning and beaten. One of the men who had distributed the paper had already been arrested. He had given way under the beating and had betrayed Stefan. When they tried to force Stefan to betray other names he took the entire blame on himself and insisted that he had written the entire paper, from beginning to end. Nobody believed him; they did not even believe he was the author of the articles, for he looked like a boy of less than fifteen. He had grown up in dark city flats and workshops and was small and weak. The cross-questioning ended with broken teeth and blood-spitting in a mass cell.

The revolution in his country which followed the October Revolution freed him from prison, and he joined the editorial staff of the youth paper. When Horthy put down the revolution with the help of Rumanian troops Stefan managed to escape to Austria.[1] Many of his comrades were murdered. His friend, a printer's apprentice, was drowned in the Danube, his feet tied together and weighted down with a stone.

After that Stefan kept body and soul together in various European countries, mostly by the work of his hands. Sometimes he wrote an article for the Party paper of the country in which he had found asylum. People remembered his name subconsciously, because he wrote simply and truthfully and his explanations provided a guiding line for many people to hold on to in hard, uneasy times when they could not help themselves. But this effect only made itself felt slowly, in the course of the years. Every time he saw his ideas in print again, translated into the language of the country that sheltered him, he felt the same secret, happy pride as he had had in his first article, written when he was fifteen. But of course he only earned a few pence, if anything at all—not enough to keep body and soul together—for an article on which he had worked long and carefully, until it said exactly what he wanted to say, without unnecessary frills or confusing abbreviations. But he could not rest until he had put down each of his thoughts in the most exact form possible. He understood and learned foreign languages quickly; he argued over every sentence with every translator who helped him.

This was the work he was doing at the end of the twenties and the early thirties. He was glad to be able to get enough casual work to keep his family more or less fed and clothed. For he had married in the meantime and had a wife and two children to look after. His wife was delicate and not attractive, but the happiness she felt when she sensed her husband's pride in a new article lent her a kind of beauty. She loved the expression on his face at such times. Experience made him appear old but at the same time youthful, and his eyes were good and wide-awake. And he was a little ashamed when she noticed his pride and her own face reflected it.

Stefan and his wife Therese were completely surprised, and pleasantly shocked when he was suddenly appointed to the editorial staff of a big workers' journal that appeared in many countries in a number of languages. But readers expressed their approval of his appointment. His analyses, which he had been writing for some time and on varied occasions and which were becoming well known, gave them a goal to look forward to in the hard times that lay ahead.

Stefan was living in Berlin at that time, shortly before Hitler seized power. He was now relieved of the need to do casual work and had time to study and write, but this did not make life easier for him. He traveled a great deal in order to follow events himself, to see the effects on people with his own eyes, in various cities in Europe, not only in Berlin and other German citices.

His wife fell ill. She tried to keep her illness a secret from him. Since he had always seen only her smile and her eyes, it was a long time before he noticed how thin and pale she

had become. When he was at home—seldom enough in that year—she hid her suffering. He had thrown himself whole-heartedly into his work; armed with his experience, which steadily increased, he wrote day and night. It may be that he only understood in the last few days that his personal happiness was coming to an end. After his wife's death his daughter, still a schoolgirl, kept house for him.

At that time his articles were eagerly read in at least two dozen countries, because they gave people a glimmer of the truth in the terribly confused times between the Reichstag Fire and the outbreak of the Second World War.

Stefan went to Spain several times during the Civil War,[2] although he hated traveling, by air, rail or car. He grew prematurely heavy and found traveling more and more difficult. And when he returned from a journey he could never get used to the fact that Therese was not there waiting for him. His clever eyes always looked sadly out from behind his spectacles.

He was in France when the Munich Agreement was signed, and he wrote an article about what he thought of Chamberlain's "Peace in our time."[3] He shook people into awareness with this article, warning them against senseless optimism and drawing attention to the signs of coming war.

The following year, he wrote from his little attic hotel room in Paris that the French government was making use of the war to introduce emergency laws against their own workers and that they did not dare to make an alliance with the Soviet Union against Hitler. This article was published in many languages and it again helped many people to think over and understand what had been happening.

The Wehrmacht marched into France.[4] Paris was occupied. Although he had known what was coming, Stefan made his arrangements to leave too late, as he was delayed by empty promises and finally left in the lurch. He saw very clearly what was going on in the world at large, but hardly ever saw into the minds of individuals with whom he came into contact.

Long before the occupation the Gestapo had discovered the whereabouts of a number of people and had had them watched. And Stefan, sitting and thinking in his hotel room on the Left Bank, and writing the articles which many people read so eagerly, was a nuisance to the Nazis. Since the car promised him did not appear, he had decided to go on foot to a station outside Paris and take a train from there. But he was arrested in his room before he could even make the attempt and was sent to a concentration camp in Germany.

What they did to him there—all the humiliations and torture—he watched with grief and close attention, as if it were happening to someone else. Many others around him were treated in the same way and he took notice of everything, as if he would have to give an exact account of it for his newspaper.

He was completely helpless after they beat him on the head and his spectacles were knocked off and broken. Many prisoners tried to show how greatly they respected him, giving him a helping hand, a crust of bread or a friendly word. But soon Stefan, weak and helpless as he was, radiated a feeling of strength in the midst of their almost unbearable life. The prisoners tried to catch every word he said, his explanations were passed on from one to another, especially after Hitler invaded the Soviet Union and penetrated deep into the country in the blitz attack.

One night Stefan was awakened. He was led before the camp commandant, who sat at supper with his young adjutant and a number of SS officers. They had probably only just had the idea of having him called in. Conversation dried up, they stared at him. They had reached the stage between nervous watchfulness and complete drunkenness. The commandant, who was still fairly sober, said they knew that Stefan was a prophet for the Jews and Communists and had always foretold the future for them. He had even prophesied that Hitler would seize power and gain control of Europe. He could now exercise his office as prophet again, but for the real rulers this time. He could sit down in a room alone and undisturbed and write down what Europe would be like in three years' time.

Stefan replied that he was prepared to do this, but he could not write without spectacles.

The commandant laughed and said this would be no obstacle. He ordered a camp doctor to get hold of suitable glasses at once.

Stefan was sent back to the barracks again until the order had been carried out. In this way he was able to tell one of his fellow prisoners what they had told him to do. He took leave of him and, through him, of all friends.

Early the next morning he was taken to the room set aside for him. Here he found a pair of new glasses, paper and pen on the table, and also a good breakfast, just as if he were suddenly no longer a prisoner. He asked for a map, because he needed to write down everything exactly.

He had often told his fellow sufferers why Hitler could never achieve any final result through his blitz war against the Soviet Union —because he had the entire nation against him; he was bound to fail there, just as Napoleon had failed, and there were plenty of signs of the decline of his power. Stefan had counted these again and again, to comfort them and keep up their courage.

Stefan was now determined to make the most of the quiet and the opportunity to think undisturbed that had been given him once more. He weighed each word he wrote. In his analysis the end of Hitler's power was as clear and as indisputable as the answer to a sum. He sought patiently for the right word to express each of his thoughts, as if the article was to be printed and distributed at once and must bring strength and confidence to countless people. He had no doubt at all as to what he would get for it. He wrote carefully in his neat handwriting, which had no flourishes and was easy to read.

Then he folded the sheets and said to the guard at the door, "I'm finished." And the guard quickly brought the sheets to the camp commandant, as he had been ordered.

The commandant burst into a sharp, cackling laugh as he read. He slid the pages across to the young adjutant, his favorite. Then he suddenly turned scarlet with rage, snatched the pages from the box and shouted, "Into the fire with them!" While the adjutant crumpled the paper and thrust it into the stove, the commandant considered whether it would be better to send the prophet to be burnt like his prophecies or whether, instead of waiting for the next transport to the death camp, he should make an end of him here at once.

He shouted to the guard who dealt with such matters, "Bunker A!" and they both knew when he gave the order that no one ever left Bunker A alive.

When Stefan was fetched from the stone quarry after only just beginning to work, he saw what was coming from their faces and from the direction their blows and kicks sent him, and finally from the bare, reddish, windowless walls, behind which many of his comrades had vanished forever.

The icy cold killed him, not fire. He knew this with the last flicker of his brain, the last of his being to be extinguished in his stone coffin.

When the guard unlocked the door he did not need to shoot, and there was no point in his kick either. The prisoner was frozen stiff.

His name was never again mentioned in the camp. It was to be as if he had never been there, as if he had never prophesied anything. He had vanished without a sound while the world war shrieked towards its end through hundreds of thousands of guns.

But the prisoner in whom he had confided when he was brought back once more to the barracks before writing down his thoughts saw to it that an account of how his life ended was passed on from one prisoner to the next.

Translated by Joan Becker

NOTES

1. The October Revolution was one of several in 1917 that established a soviet-style government in Russia. Hungary, an independent republic formed after World War I, established a socialist government under Béla Kun (1886–1939?) in 1919.

    Nikolaus Horthy (1868–1957), an Austro-Hungarian Marine admiral formed and led the counterrevolutionary army that squelched the republic in 1920. He ruled until 1944, when the Axis ally was invaded by the USSR.
2. Spanish Civil War (1936–1939) in which the conservative and fascist forces overthrew the Loyalists to the democratic second Spanish republic. Voluntary international brigades formed to support the Loyalist cause.
3. British prime minister (1869–1940), chiefly responsible for the agreement (1938) surrendering most of Czechoslovakia to Germany, widely regarded as a symbol of appeasement, which failed: World War II began about a year later.
4. Hitler's army, which invaded France in 1940.

Zoë Karélli   (Chrysoúla Pendzíki Argyriádou)   *Greece, b. 1901*

Born in Thessaloniki in 1901, Zoë Karélli's real name is Chrysoúla Pendzíki; she is the sister of the poet and novelist N.G. Pendzíkis. Like many of her class she studied languages privately—English, French, German and Italian—also music and dance. She married at 17 (her married name is Argyriádou), and then took courses in literature at the University of Thessaloniki. Widowed in 1953, she has two sons.

Zoë Karélli's writing initially attracted public attention in 1934 but her first collection of poems did not appear until 1940. She has since published nine more books of poetry, including *Epoché tou thanátou* (Season of Death, 1948), *Tis monaxiás ke tis éparsis* (Of Solitude and Arrogance, 1951), *Kassándra ke álla piímata* (Cassandra and Other Poems, 1955), and *O kathréftis tou mesonyktíov* (The Mirror of Midnight, 1958). She was awarded the Palmes Academiques by the French Ministry of Educaton in 1959; she shared the Second State Prize for poetry in 1955 and won the First State Prize for poetry in 1974 (the year in which the second volume of her collected works appeared); and she was given the Ouranis Award by the Academy of Athens in 1978.

She has also written three poetic dramas with strong affinities to both ancient Greek and modern symbolist drama. It is therefore not surprising to find that she has translated two of T.S. Eliot's plays (*The Cocktail Party* and *The Family Reunion*).* Her translations also include works by the American modernist poets William Carlos Williams and Djuna Barnes. Her critical articles and books have ranged over such subjects as the plays of Beckett, Claudel, Gogol, and Pirandello, the novels of Camus, Dostoyevski, Joyce, and Kafka, and the philosophy of Kierkegaard.

Called by Katarina Anghelaki-Rooke in her article on Greek Women Poets "probably the best living Greek woman poet," Zoë Karélli is a very difficult writer, very conscious of contemporary philosophical dilemmas, believing that new ideas need new forms and a new poetic language in which to express them. The most European of twentieth-century Greek women poets, she has been accused of elitism and criticized for excessive intellectuality and hermeticism. Karélli's position is made more complex by her identification of the relationship between her self and her body with the wider metaphysical crisis of identity and physical context. From the outset, then, her poems express both man's alienation in a meaningless universe, and her own difficulty in maintaining personal intellectual and moral integrity in the modern world. Karélli has tried to make doubt and division into positive forces. *Antithéseis* (Antitheses, 1957), in which "Man, Feminine Gender" appeared, marked a significant new development in her writing; it led to a final acceptance of "reality" and of the need for the self to have a context in humanity as a whole, however "meaningless" philosophically that context might appear to be.

Karélli has consciously rejected the older style of lyricism, though she is capable of lyrical images. While interested in the problems of the nature of language—hence much word play which cannot survive in translation—she is also struggling to find new poetic forms capable of making her abstract ideas "tangible." Indeed, she has said of her own move into writing for the theater: "I turned to the theater, to poetic drama, as an escape from becoming too inward-looking. I believed that by trying to create characters in action, my own character would cease to concern me."

The first selection appeared in *Fantasia tou chronou* (Fantasies of Time, 1949).

Christopher Robinson

NOTE

* The writings of Anglo-American writer T.S. Eliot (1886–1965) owe much to Greek drama and to the work of French symbolist writers of the late nineteenth century.

WORKER IN THE WORKSHOPS OF TIME
Ergátis sta ergastíria tou chrónou

As he wrought the shape,
a worker, a blower of glass,
felt his love profoundly
for the material
into which he blew his breath.
At times crystal or like pearl,
mother-of-pearl, precious ivory
or opal with misty colors
drifting toward azure.
All these were materials that became shapes,
erotic shapes for whatever exists
within time.

The shape, receptacle of time,
enclosed it erotically,
an offering to time,
expectation and acceptance both,
that form which is an embrace of time,
the singular shape he wrought
out of his own essence,
his own imagination.

But as his material hand
caressed the final shape afterward,
he understood the materiality of time
as his own hand
together with the shape
and the precious, erotic material
were transformed into the diaphanous meaning
                                                    of time.

All together,
but particularly he.

                                    Translated by Kimon Friar

MAN, FEMININE GENDER
I ánthropos

I, woman, "man" in the feminine gender,
have always sought Thy face;
it was, until this moment, man's,
and I could not otherwise know it.
Who is more alone now,
and in what way,
intensely, despairingly alone,
he or I?
I believe I exist, shall exist,
but when did I exist without him,
and now, how do I stand, in what light,
what is my sorrow still?
O how I suffer doubly,
continuously lost,
when Thou are not my guide.
How shall I look upon my face
how shall I accept my spirit
when I struggle so
yet cannot find accord.
Because it is through Thee
*that man and woman find their concord.**
The tragedy of the impersonal
is not yet revealed, nor can I even
imagine it still, still.
What can I do since I know so well
so many things, and know better than to think
that Thou plucked me from out his side.
And I say that I am "man," completed
and alone. I could not have been formed
                                                    without him
but now I *am* and am capable,
and we are a separated pair, he
and I, and I have my own light.
I was never the moon,
but I said I would not depend on the sun,
and I have such pride
that I am trying to reach his
and to surpass myself, I
and again I,
who now in learning about myself, learn
completely that I want to resist him,
that I want to accept
nothing from him, that I do not want to wait.

I neither weep nor chant a song,
but my own violent separation, which I am

                                        preparing,
is becoming more painful
that I may know the world through myself,
that I may speak my own word,
I, who until this moment existed
to marvel and esteem and to love.
I no longer belong to him,
and I must be alone,
I, "man" in the feminine gender.

Translated by Kimon Friar

NOTE

* From the marriage ceremony of the Greek Orthodox
  Church.

Marie Luise Kaschnitz   *Germany/FRG, 1901–1974*

Marie Luise Kaschnitz is one of the most highly regarded German women poets of
the twentieth century. Her creative life spanned Germany's most difficult decades
and witnessed the progression, interrupted by two wars, from the Wilhelmenian
Empire to the Weimar Republic, from Hitler's Third Reich to the Federal Republic
of Germany. Kaschnitz was born into the aristocratic family of Holzing-Berstett
in Karlsruhe on January 1, 1901. She spent her childhood and youth mainly in
Potsdam and Berlin, apprenticed as a book dealer in Weimar, and then worked in
that business in Munich and Rome. She was married in 1925 to the Austrian
archeologist Guido Kaschnitz von Weinberg, with whom she traveled widely,
primarily to the Mediterranean. After his death in 1958, she lived in Frankfurt and
continued to make extended visits to Rome, her favorite city, where she died at the
home of her daughter on October 10, 1974.

Kaschnitz was honored with some of the most prestigious literary prizes her
country has to offer, including the Georg Büchner Prize (1955), the Goethe Plaque
of the City of Frankfurt (1966), an Honorary Doctorate from the University of
Frankfurt (1968), and the Johann Peter Hebel Prize (1970). She was also the guest
professor for poetics at the University of Frankfurt in 1960 (a position also held by
Ingeborg Bachmann and Christa Wolf).

Always an observer of herself and her social surroundings, Kaschnitz uses her
writing to comment on society's faults; while highly critical, however, she never
regarded herself as an activist, but preferred to think of herself as a "watchman."

Like many writers who chose to remain in Nazi Germany, she had practiced
an "inner emigration" that led to extreme self-censorship and distorted literary
positions. For this reason, at the end of World War II, she quickly abandoned her

earlier attitude of art for art's sake and repudiated most of her writings of the 1930s and 1940s.

Her publications from the 1940s until her husband's death comprise her second creative period. In this period she moves from the celebratory hope of a new beginning immediately after the war to a disillusioned resignation prompted by the recognition that little had changed (*Neue Gedichte* [New Poems, 1957], from which "A Map of Sicily" and "The Frog Prince Bridegroom" come). The death of the man to whom she was so close seems to have been quite devastating; after a considerable period of silence, she grappled with that loss in *Dein Schweigen—meine Stimme* (Your Silence—My Voice, 1962), source of "By Writing." This work initiates her last and perhaps greatest phase, one that turned increasingly subjective as the author anticipated her own death in *Ein Wort weiter* (One Word Further, 1965) and *Kein Zauberspruch* (No Magic Formula, 1972), her last and most important volume of poetry, which included "Broadcast for Women." Much of this work has been made available in translation, from which the selections have been taken. Kaschnitz also began writing short stories shortly after the war (most notably *Lange Schatten* [*Long Shadows*], 1960) and produced several radio plays during that genre's most popular period in the 1950s. In all her works, she assumes a dialogical stance, always directly or indirectly involving the reader. Her continued significance and recognition in Germany is underscored by the current publication of her complete works in eight volumes, of which the first five have appeared to date. These include her nine collections of poetry, more than a dozen volumes of fiction, essays, radio plays, and her diary, *Tage, Tage, Jahre* (Days, Days, Years), the reflections of an aging woman, which are considered by some critics to define the high point of her literary achievement.

Marilyn Sibley Fries

THE FROG PRINCE BRIDEGROOM
Bräutigam Froschkönig

How ugly he is
Your bridegroom
Mistress Life

With a gas mask for a face
A cartridge belt for hips
A flame thrower for a hand

Your bridegroom the frog prince flies with you
(Wheels spinning in all directions)
Over the houses of the dead

Between Doomsday
And Doomsday
He eases himself
Into your body

In the darkness
All you touch is
His damp hair

Only when it dawns
Only when
It dawns
Only when

Do you discover his
Sad
Beautiful
Eyes.

Translated by Lisel Müller

A MAP OF SICILY
Karte von Sizilien

I'll draw the outline for you. It's a wing
From the shoulder of a victory goddess.
The side view is a chunk of rugged mountain
Arrested in the brightness of the sun,
The sea around it covering the plain
With sand and seaweed and with schools of
                              fish.
Striated lines are for steep elevations.
The seven river valleys are left blank.
The toothed crown means the mountain where
                         the wedding
Of fire and ice takes place. Move in a little
Around the table. Look, I tip the oil jug.
Wherever you see drops fall on the table
Is where the black and silver olives grow.
Wherever I drop breadcrumbs, think of crops
On the red hills, the wide range of the
                         plowshares.
The salt I pour, this whiteness in the east,
Stands for food from the ocean, salt and fish;
The lemon wedge, a piece of the yellow moon,
For shade of arbors, sweetly scented flowers,
I'll draw red arrows clear across the ocean,
One from the mainland, one from Africa,
One from Peloponnesus, one from Spain,
To show you the routes of foreign conquerors.
Now run out to the garden path and bring
Some small white pebbles. Don't they look to
                         you
Like cupolas and temples in the moonlight—
But watch, I'll stamp my feet
And they shake and dance;
Nothing can keep from falling in an earthquake.
I'll pull the lamp forward and push it back,
Pull it forward again. Now light. Now darkness.
Splendor and death, eternal argument.

Where is the little peasant that I kneaded
Out of a piece of bread? Still there, as always
Hands on his hoe. Bent down a little more
Than at the start. And now, what is all this?
Bread, blood and stone. A piece of the Western
                         world.
Translated by Lisel Müller

BY WRITING
Schreibend

By writing I wanted
To save my soul.
I tried to make poems
It did not work.
I tried to tell stories
It did not work.
You cannot write
To save your soul.
Given up, it drifts and does the singing.
Translated by Lisel Müller

BROADCAST FOR WOMEN
Frauenfunk

I give a talk on the radio
Toward morning when no one is listening
I offer my recipes

Pour milk into the telephone
Let your cats sleep
In the dishwashers
Smash the clocks in your washing machines
Leave your shoes behind

Season your peaches with paprika
And your soup meat with honey

Teach your children the alphabet of foxes
Turn the leaves in your gardens silver side up
Take the advice of the owl

When summer arrives put on your furs
Go meet the ones with the bagpipes
Who come from inside the mountains
Leave your shoes behind

Don't be too sure
Evening will come
Don't be too sure
That God loves you.
Translated by Lisel Müller

Cecília Meireles   *Brazil, 1901–1964*

Cecília Meireles was one of Latin America's foremost poets. Known as a "Spiritualist," she wrote poetry akin to that of European Symbolists but transformed by the Brazilian *modernismo** movement. She and her husband, who was also a writer, were part of a group of late-modernist Catholic writers in the 1920s and 1930s known as the *espiritualistas* (Spiritualists) for whose journal, *Festa*, Meireles contributed many works. Unlike some other Brazilian Modernists, however, her work does not have a national flavor, but is abstract and universal; some of her most frequent themes are of nature and the elements. Her language is simple and direct.

Cecília Meireles' parents and her three older brothers died when the poet was quite young, and she was raised by her Azorean grandmother. She became a teacher and was able to publish her first volume of poetry, *Espectros* (Ghosts), when she was just 18, in 1919. Although very popular in Portugal, Meireles waited a long time for success in her native country. This first volume of poetry, and its successors, *Nunca mais...e poema dos poemas* (Nothing more...and poem of poems, 1923) and *Baladas para el-rei* (Ballads for the King, 1925) were not very well regarded by critics because they were out of step with the prevailing Modernist movement. It was not until 1939, when her collection *Viagem* (Voyages) was awarded the Olavo Bilac prize by the Brazilian Academy of Letters (in a controversial election in which two important men of letters publicly feuded for and against her), that she received support and praise from the critical establishment in her own country. *Mar absoluto e outros poemas* (Absolute Sea and Other Poems, 1945) is considered the best expression of her major themes of death, alienation, and loneliness, themes that express her tragically lonely childhood and the suicide of her first husband. At her death, Meireles' collected works contained more than seven hundred poems, numerous translations, *crônicas*, essays, plays, as well as children's literature.

Meireles lectured in Brazilian literature at the Federal University of Rio and, for a year, at the University of Texas. As director of Rio's Department of Children she founded Brazil's first children's library. She traveled widely.

The following poems are from *Viagem, Retrato Natural* (Natural Portrait, 1949), and *Metal Rosicler* (Pyrargyrite Metal, 1960).

NOTE

* Symbolism was a literary movement, begun in France in the late nineteenth century, which stressed evocation and suggestion over literal depictions of reality. It was a strong influence in Spanish American *modernismo*, a literary movement epitomized by Nicaraguan poet Rubén Darío (1867–1916) that involved experimentation with form and meter. *Modernismo* in Brazil began later than in the rest of Latin America and was more influenced by prevailing movements in Europe: expressionism, futurism, and cubism. Brazilian *modernismo* called for a return to Brazilian folk culture, its literature and language. It remained the predominant influence in Brazilian literature until the 1940s.

PORTRAIT
Retrato

I did not have this face of today
So calm
So sad
So thin.

Nor these eyes so empty
Nor this bitter mouth.

I did not have these strengthless hands
So still
And cold
And dead.

I did not have this heart
That does not even show itself.

I did not realize this change
So simple
So certain
So easy.

In what mirror did I lose my face?

Translated by John Nist

MOTIVE
Motivo

I sing because the moment exists
And my life is complete.
I am not gay, I am not sad:
I am a poet.

Brother of fugitive things,
I feel no delight or torment.
I cross nights and days
In the wind.

Whether I destroy or build,
Whether I persist or disperse,
—I don't know, I don't know.
I don't know if I stay or go.

I know that I sing.
The song is everything.
The rhythmic wing has eternal blood,
And I know that one day I shall be dumb:
—Nothing more.

Translated by John Nist

THE DEAD HORSE
O Cavalo Morto

I saw the early morning mist
make silver passes, shift
densities of opal
within sleep's portico.

On the frontier, a dead horse.

Crystal grains were rolling down
his lustrous flanks, and the breeze
twisted his mane in a littlest,
lightest arabesque, sorry adornment
—and his tail stirred, the dead horse.

Still the stars were shining,
and that day's flowers, sad to say,
had not yet come to light
—but his body was a plot,
garden of lilies, the dead horse.

Many a traveler took note
of fluid music, the dewfall
of big emerald flies
arriving in a noisy gush.

He was listing sorely, the dead horse.

And some live horses could be seen
slender and tall as ships,
galloping through the keen air
in profile, joyously dreaming.

White and green the dead horse
in the enormous field without recourse
—and slowly the world between
his eyelashes revolved, all blurred
as in red mirror moons.

Sun shone on the teeth of the dead horse.

But everybody was in a frantic rush
and could not feel how earth
kept searching league upon league
for the nimble, the immense, the ethereal breath
which had escaped that skeleton.

O heavy breast of the dead horse!

Translated by James Merrill

THE GATES OF MIDNIGHT
Metal Rosicler 37

The angels come to open the gates of midnight,
at that very moment when sleep is deepest and
                                        silence most pervasive.
The gates wheel open and unexpectedly we
                                        sigh.
The angels come with their golden music,
their tunics billowing with celestial breezes,
and they sing in their fluid incomprehensible
                                        tongue.

Then the trees burst forth with blossoms and
                                        fruit,
the moon and the sun intertwine their beams,
the rainbow unwinds its ribbons
and all the animals appear,
mingled with the stars.

The angels come to open the gates of midnight.

And we understand that there is no more time,
that this is the last vision,
that our hands are already lifted for goodbyes,
that our feet at last are freed from the earth,
freed for that flight, announced and dreamed
since the beginning of births.

The angels extend us their divine invitations.
And we dream that we are no longer dreaming.

Translated by John Nist

Christina Stead   *Australia, 1902–1983*

Christina Stead, whose work was neglected for many years, is now increasingly being recognized not only as one of Australia's leading novelists but as one of the foremost English-language writers of this century. The international character of her fiction and her life—she lived in England, France, Spain, Switzerland, and the U.S. as well as Australia—that was, in part, responsible for her neglect, is also part of her excellence. She does not fit easily into any literary tradition; even less into any national one.

Stead was born in Sydney, where her father was a leading biologist and fisheries expert. As her mother died when she was barely 2, Stead was largely raised by her father, to whom she attributed much of her love of storytelling and what she saw as her naturalist's outlook on life. After his remarriage in 1907, she helped to raise a large family of half-brothers and sisters. These experiences are reflected in one of the most highly regarded of her novels, *The Man Who Loved Children* (1940), though, in order to protect her family's privacy, its locale was shifted from Sydney to Washington, D.C.

After graduating from Sydney Teacher's College in 1921, Stead found that her voice was too weak to cope with the demands of a teaching career. For several years she worked in an office, saving money towards the European trip that then, and for many years after, was the goal of all educated young Australians. Again, these experiences are reflected in her fiction, in the novel *For Love Alone* (1944), which also questions conventional notions of love and female sexuality.

Though women's experiences are central to most of Stead's fiction, she resisted feminist readings of her work, in part because she associated feminism with antimale attitudes. Her own long and successful partnership with the banker and writer William Blake, whom she married in London in 1929, was clearly the basis for her belief that men and women were meant to be friends rather than enemies.

After spending 1929–1937 in France and Spain, Stead and Blake moved to the United States where she worked for a time as a Hollywood writer. After the Second World War they returned to Europe and lived in England from 1953 until Blake's death in 1968. In 1982 she was made an honorary member of the American Academy and Institute of Arts and Letters. Stead spent the final years of her life back in Australia; she died in Sydney in 1983.

Most of the eleven novels published in her lifetime appeared between 1934 and 1952. She also published a collection of novellas and a remarkable early collection of stories, *The Salzburg Tales* (1934), from which "Day of Wrath" is taken. As the echo of Chaucer's *Canterbury Tales* in the title suggests, this is a series of stories told by a group of people, of widely different ages, occupations, and nationalities, gathered in Salzburg for the annual music festival. "Day of Wrath," based on an actual Sydney Harbor ferry disaster, is told by the Schoolboy. Its scornful attitude to suburban morality is in keeping with his character, and is also a reflection of Stead's.

Two posthumous works have so far appeared: another collection of stories, *Ocean of Story* (1986); and a novel, *I'm Dying Laughing* (1987), a major addition to Stead's works, which focuses on the life of a left-wing American writer and her husband from the 1930s to the 1950s.

Elizabeth Webby

DAY OF WRATH

THE SCHOOLBOY'S TALE

Do the mountains wear black for the death of a bee in the old world? Not so in the new. Perhaps Ardennes[1] wept over the "unreturning brave," but I saw death ride naked on a tropic shore and his breath never darkened the water nor brushed the sky: nature's children drowned, curdled the water with their blood, while she painted her cheeks, wreathed in smiles, and the hills sparkled with jollity by the pacific sea.

I lived in Avallon, a waterside village in a seaport. A woman in the district was divorced for adultery. Her husband was a cabinet minister, a rich man, coarse, luxurious and tyrannical. Public opinion was bitter against his wife because she had left his house and gone to live with her lover, and it was proved that because they were poor, she had slept with her two children nightly in her lover's bed. The children had to appear in court and give this evidence. The father renounced these children, who he declared were not of his blood, and he left all three in great poverty: this was not condemned, for a woman who forsakes wealth for poverty is obviously poor-spirited, and beneath commiseration: even the poor despise her.

The son was ten years old, the daughter fourteen. I knew her, her name was Viola. She was pretty, but thin, with long black hair, and rather smart with her tongue. Certainly she suffered in such an honest city, where the "Decameron"[2] is forbidden, and England's colonial history is expurgated for the school books.

I saw her mother once, a pretty, dark, sweet woman, who ventured timidly into the ladies' cabin on the ferry, and looked quickly but without expectation of greeting at the female faces decorating the walls. When I raised my hat to her she smiled with pleasure, but with indulgence also: she knew I pitied her, but she regarded us all very calmly from another world. The ladies were indignant that she continued to live in our district. "She should have at least the delicacy to go where she is not known," said my maiden aunt. Society, great beast of tender skin, blind, with elephant ears, felt indignant, lashed its little tail and got hot round the rump. It required a sacrifice, and when Jumbo wants something the gods themselves obey.

One Wednesday afternoon, the four o'clock ferry, which carried the schoolchildren home from town, was stuck amidships by an ocean liner and sank immediately, carrying down more than fifty souls. Thirty children were drowned, and all those who died were from our village of Avallon. I went down to catch the four-thirty ferry and saw the stretchers with bodies brought in already by the rescuers. All the way home, with my books on the seat, I watched the lustrous tide flow in, bearing planks, seats, lifebuoys and splintered wood up into the bays and rivers. Eddies of soot and oil floated past. In a few minutes we reached the spot where the ferry lay with her passengers, and I felt paralysed with a strange and almost voluptuous cramp, and my spirit being wound out of me like a *djinn*[13] out of a pot. We went dead slow, with our flag at half-mast, and there was a silence on the boat. I thought of those people sitting below, almost living, with a glow on their cheeks still through the green gloom of the deep-water channel; they seemed a company that had gone apart for some conclave. I believed my two young sisters were there, waiting for me with open eyes, and wanted to dive in, but I could not move. When we neared home I saw my little brother running and jumping on our lawn, so I was reassured.

After a few days, when the last rumours and hopes had died out, and the whole village was in mourning, in the lovely weather, only one piece of fantasy remained: Viola alone had not been found. She must have been carried away, or been lost in the deeper mud of the bottom; the ferry itself had moved several hundred feet. It seemed to my mother and aunt that this was the "judgment of God"; though for what mortal sins the other bereaved women had been punished, no one thought to conjecture.

At the end of a week Viola was found on one end of the wreck, standing upright, uninjured, her right foot simply entangled in a rope. The founts of pity at this word broke the seals and jetted in each breast, and everyone that night had before his eye the image of Viola standing in the green gloom for a week, upright, looking for the rescuers, astonished that they did not come for her, perhaps with a lively word on her lips at their slowness, and then, prisoned by her poor weak foot, decaying, but with her arms still floating up; a watermaiden tangled in a lily-root, and not able to reach the surface. I cried and thought how she died in that attitude to ask pity.

In fact, it turned out that way; or at least, if the church and justice were not moved, for they should be above the frailties of flesh and blood, the women began to lament on her mother's account, to say she was well punished and one could even pity her. The beast was appeased, as in ancient days, by the sacrifice of a virgin.

NOTES

1. The Ardennes is a heavily wooded area of mountains and plateaus in southwest Belgium used often as a battleground during World War I.
2. *The Decameron* was a collection of a hundred tales, many about love, by Italian writer Giovanni Boccaccio (1313–1375).
3. *Djinn*, or genie, is Arabic for a supernatural being.

Marguerite Yourcenar (Marguerite de Crayencour)

France/US, 1903–1987

It was only in 1980, when Yourcenar became the first woman elected to the Académie Française, that her accomplishments gained full critical recognition. Until then, her somewhat nomadic existence and her independence of mind had kept her out of the literary debates and the limelight, although she enjoyed a solid reputation among limited circles and had received several literary prizes.

Marguerite de Crayencour was born in Brussels to a Belgian mother and a French father, both from wealthy, well-established families. She never knew her mother, who died shortly after giving birth. She was raised and educated by her father, an avid reader and traveler. Although she never attended any regular school, she passed the French baccalaureate in Greek and Latin at the age of 16. After the death of her father in 1929, Marguerite Yourcenar—who had published a book of poems under this anagram of her family name in 1921—continued to write and to study history and literature on her own, while traveling throughout Europe. The years 1934–1938 in particular were largely devoted to her exploration of Greece and the Greek sites of the Middle East. Grace Frick, a Yale student she had met in Paris, invited her to New Haven in 1937. Yourcenar's second visit to Yale coincided with the outbreak of World War II, which led her to settle in the United States. To support herself, she went to work for the first time in her life, lecturing throughout the country and teaching part time at Sarah Lawrence College (1942–1949). In 1950, she and Grace Frick bought a small house on Mount Desert Island in Maine, where they lived and worked together until Frick's death in 1979; Yourcenar continued residence in Maine, traveling widely and working on several projects up until her death at 84.

She made a controversial debut as a novelist with *Alexis* (1929), a first-person epistolary novel that dealt with male homosexual desire. Written by a woman then only 24, it was a literary performance to be repeated on a grander, more elaborate scale in *Memoirs of Hadrian.* Her other fiction of the prewar period include a novel inspired by a trip to Italy during the first years of fascism, *Denier du rêve, A Coin in Nine Hands,* 1934), her *Nouvelles orientales* (*Oriental Tales,* 1938; revised 1963, 1978), which draw on legends and ballads from Eastern Europe and China, and the short novel *Coup de Grâce* (1939). In *Feux* (*Fires,* 1936), a very unusual book composed of prose poems interspersed with fragments of her diary, she transposed classical mythological figures into incarnations of "abstract passions."

Yourcenar characterized the period of the war as being for her a "night of the soul." Her literary activities were then limited to the translation of Negro spirituals and the writing of plays based on Greek mythology. She started writing fiction again when she found her notes for a novel on a Roman emperor. The result was *Memoirs of Hadrian* (1951), which won her widespread acclaim. This fictitious autobiography, from which the following excerpt is taken, and which most critics consider her masterpiece, is a probing portrayal of a powerful Emperor, hungry for knowledge and driven by an ascetic self-discipline. Yourcenar's other tour de force in historical fiction is *L'Oeuvre au noir* (*The Abyss,* 1968), a chronicle of Renaissance Europe centered on the story of an imaginary philosopher and scientist she called Zeno. She also directed her fascination with the past to reconstructing, with the same blend of "erudition and magic" she used in her historical novels, the story of both her maternal and her paternal families in *Souvenirs pieux* (Pious Memories, 1974) and *Archives du Nord* (Archives of the North, 1977). These two volumes were tentatively part of a larger project entitled *The Labyrinth of the World*. The labyrinth was in fact one of Yourcenar's favorite images, designating both the complexity of the world and our situation within it.

Yourcenar's work as a translator and essayist, with a special interest in Greek poetry, ran parallel to her writing of fiction. She translated Virginia Woolf's *The Waves*, Henry James' *What Maisie Knew*, and in 1979 published an anthology of twelve centuries of Greek verse, *La Couronne et la Lyre*, (The Crown and the Lyre). Her last critical work was her study of the Japanese novelist Yukio Mishima (1980), now available in English.

Yourcenar drew most usually on eras, cultures, and landscapes remote from our own, with a remarkable talent for historical recreation. It is striking also that the most important of her novels are centered around a male character (often speaking in the first person within an epistolary or memoir frame). Through heroes such as Hadrian and Zeno—who are dominantly homosexual—she explored the relation between knowledge, power, and sexuality. While some critics are satisfied with admiring her meticulous attention to historical sources and her "classical" style, others have noted that her erudite documentation only enhances the modernity and ambiguity of her characters. Feminist critics have been disturbed by the work of a woman who writes mainly with a male voice. Some have suggested that her distant settings serve to seal off the taboo topic of homosexuality or that her treatment of male homosexuality is a disguise that displaces (and perhaps distorts) the issue of lesbianism.

Yourcenar spoke of herself as a "poet-historian-novelist." The work of many years, sometimes decades, her texts underwent successive transformations that give the narratives, secreted like the shell of a mollusc, a characteristic ceremoniousness. Critical commentary and author's notes provided for the translations and new editions add still other layers of meaning to her work, thus creating a paradoxical combination of lucidity and density.

Criticism on Yourcenar is just beginning to appear: a summary work published as part of the Twayne World Authors Series (1985) and some few articles on *Hadrian* by J. Whatley (*University of Toronto Quarterly* no. 50, 1981), on *Fires* by C.F. Farrell and E.R. Farrell (*Kentucky Romance Quarterly* no. 29, 1982), and on her prefaces by C. Gaudin (*Studies in Twentieth Century Literature* 10, no. 1, 1985).

from MEMOIRS OF HADRIAN[1]
Mémoires d' Hadrien

I fought against my grief, battling as if it were gangrene: I recalled his occasional stubbornness and lies; I told myself that he would have changed, growing older and heavy. Such efforts proved futile; instead, like some painstaking workman who toils to copy a masterpiece, I exhausted myself in tasking my memory for fanatic exactitude, evoking that smooth chest, high and rounded as a shield. Sometimes the image leaped to mind of itself, and a flood of tenderness swept over me: once again I caught sight of an orchard in Tibur, and the youth gathering up autumn fruits in his tunic, for lack of a basket. I had lost everything at once, the companion of the night's delights and the young friend squatting low to his heels to help Euphorion with the folds of my toga. If one were to believe the priests, the shade was also in torment, regretting the warm shelter of its body and haunting its familiar habitations with many a moan, so far and yet so near, but for the time too weak to signify his presence to me. If that were true my deafness was worse than death itself. But after all had I so well understood, on that morning, the living boy who sobbed at my side?

One evening Chabrias called me to show me a star, till then hardly visible, in the constellation of the Eagle; it flashed like a gem and pulsated like a heart. I chose it for his star and his sign. Each night I would follow its course until utterly wearied; in that part of the sky I have seen strange radiance. Folk thought me mad, but that was of little consequence.

Death is hideous, but life is too. Everything seemed awry. The founding of Antinoöpolis was a ludicrous endeavor, after all, just one more city to shelter fraudulent trading, official extortion, prostitution, disorder, and those cowards who weep for a while over their dead before forgetting them. Apotheosis was but empty ceremony: such public honors would serve only to make of the boy a pretext for adulation or irony, a posthumous object of cheap desire, or of scandal, one of those legends already tainted which clutter history's recesses. Perhaps my grief itself was only a form of license, a vulgar debauch: I was still the one who profited from the experience and tasted it to the full, for the beloved one was giving me even his death for my indulgence. A man frustrated was weeping over himself.

Ideas jarred upon each other; words ground on without meaning; voices rasped and buzzed like locusts in the desert or flies on a dung pile; our ships with sails swelling out like doves' breasts were carriers for intrigue and lies; on the human countenance stupidity reigned. Death, in its aspect of weakness or decay, came to the surface everywhere: the weakness or decay, came to the surface everywhere: the bad spot on a fruit, some imperceptible rent at the edge of a hanging, a carrion body on the shore, the pustules of a face, the mark of scourges on a bargeman's back. My hands seemed always somewhat soiled. At the hour of the bath, as I extended my legs for the slaves to shave, I looked with disgust upon this solid body, this almost indestructible machine which absorbed food, walked, and managed to sleep, and would, I knew, reaccustom itself one day or another to the routines of love. I could no longer bear the presence of any but those few servants who remembered the departed one; in their way they had loved him. My sorrow found an echo in the rather foolish mourning of a masseur, or of the old negro who tended the lamps. But their grief did not keep them from laughing softly amongst themselves as they took the evening air along the river bank. One morning as I leaned on the taffrail I noticed a slave at work in the quarters reserved for the kitchens; he was cleaning one of those chickens which Egypt hatches by the thousands in its dirty incubators; he gathered the slimy entrails into his hands and threw them into the water. I had barely time to turn away to vomit. At our stop in Philae, during a reception offered us by the governor, a child of three met with an accident: son of a Nubian porter and dark as bronze, he had crept into the balconies to watch the dancing, and fell from that height. They did the best they could to hide the whole thing; the porter held back his sobs for fear of disturbing his master's guests, and was led out with the body through the kitchen doors; in spite of such precautions I caught a glimpse of his shoulders rising and falling convulsively, as under the blows of a whip. I had the feeling of taking that father's grief to myself much as I had taken on the sorrow of Hercules, of Alexander, of Plato, each of whom wept for a dead friend. I sent a few gold pieces to this poor fellow; one could do nothing more. Two or three days later I saw him again; he was contentedly picking at lice as he lay in the sun at the doorway.

Messages flooded in; Pancrates sent me his poem, finished at last; it was only a mediocre assemblage of Homeric hexameters,[2] but the name which figured in almost every line made it more moving for me than many a masterpiece. Numenius sent me a *Consolation* written according to the usual formulas for such works; I passed a night reading it, although it contained every possible platitude. These feeble defenses raised by man against death were developed along two lines: the first consisted in presenting death to us as an inevitable evil, and in reminding us that neither beauty, youth, nor love escapes decay; life and its train of ills are thus proved even more horrible than death itself, and it is better, accordingly, to die than to grow old. Such truths are cited to incline us toward resignation, but they justify chiefly despair. The second line of argument contradicts the first, but our philosophers care little for such niceties: the theme was no longer resignation to death but negation of it. Only the soul was important, they said, arrogantly positing as a fact the immortality of that vague entity which we have never seen function in the absence of the body, and the existence of which they had not yet taken the trouble to prove. I was not so certain: since the smile, the expression of the eyes, the voice, these imponderable realities, had ceased to be, then why not the soul, too? Was it necessarily more immaterial than the body's heat? They attached no importance to those remains wherein the soul no longer dwelt; that body, however, was the only thing left to me, my sole proof that the living boy had existed. The immortality of the race was supposed to make up in some way for each individual death, but it was hardly consoling to me that whole generations of Bithynians would succeed each other to the end of time along the banks of the Sangarius. We speak of glory, that fine word which swells the heart, but there is willful confusion between it and immortality, as if the mere trace of a person were the same thing as his presence. They would have had me see the resplendent god in place of the corpse, but I had created that god; I believed in him, in my way, but a brilliant posthumous destiny in the midst of the stellar spheres failed to compensate for so brief a life; the god did not take the place of the living being I had lost.

Translated by Grace Frick

NOTES

1. Hadrian (A.D. 76–138). Roman emperor. A ward of Trajan, he was named to succeed him after proving himself as an administrator and commander. He reversed the expansionist policies of Rome and sought to replace extensive military support by direct supervision: consequently he traveled widely throughout the Empire. Known for his patronage of the arts, and especially for his love of architecture and the beautifying of cities, he built Hadrian's Wall, the Parthenon, and the Castel Sant'Angelo, as well as his palace on the Tibur (modern Tivoli). His well-known regard for young Antinous (ca. 110–130) was recorded by sculptors and architects as well as poets of the period. Various legends arose after the death of Antinous by drowning in the Nile, including one that said that Antinous died trying to save Hadrian's life; Yourcenar has Hadrian assume that Antinous committed suicide. Hadrian mourned him greatly, founding the city of Antinoöpolis in Egypt and renaming Antinous's birthplace Bythia in his honor.

2. The 6-foot dactylic measure is to classical Greek what the iambic pentameter is to English and the Alexandrine to French; traditionally used in epic poetry and, subsequently, in elegiac works.

Ding Ling   (Ting Ling) (Jiang Bingzhi; Chiang Ping-chih)
China, 1904–1986

Born Jiang Bingzhi into a well-known but impoverished landed gentry family of Hunan province, Ding Ling benefited from her mother's emancipation. In effect a member of the first generation of feminists, who focused their demands on access to education, Ding Ling's mother enrolled in a normal school recently established by the Nationalist regime and became a teacher to support her family. Ding Ling herself participated in the May 4th demonstrations and received a progressive education, studying modern vernacular literature as well as foreign authors, first in Changsha, then in Shanghai, and later at Beijing University. There she met the poet Hu Yepin, with whom she lived the bohemian life of an artist, while actively engaging in Communist demonstrations and espousing feminist causes of the "second generation," that is, the demand for equality and the right to inherit property. While there is no simple relationship between Ding Ling's life and work, the three major phases of her literary production can be demarcated by the social and political events that swept over Chinese society. This relationship has been traced in Mei Feuerwerker's pioneering book, *Ding Ling's Fiction* (1982).

The first phase consists of approximately thirteen stories that she wrote between 1927 and 1930 after coming to Shanghai. Influenced especially by Flaubert's *Madame Bovary* and Alexandre Dumas' *La Dame aux Camilles*, they are characterized by their experimental style and technique, a highly subjective point of view, and their bold exploration of women's feelings. "Shafei nüshi de riji" ("The Diary of Miss Sophie," 1928), the major and oft-translated work of this phase is exemplary: typical of the female artist-intellectuals of the period, Miss Sophie is depicted as a victim of men, institutions, cultural mores, as well as her own feelings (*Miss Sophie's Diary and Other Stories*, 1986).

In 1931, shortly after Ding Ling gave birth to their child, Hu Yepin, along with four other writers, was executed by the Nationalists. Ding Ling became increasingly politically committed; she was also editor of *Beidou* (Big Dipper), the journal of the League of Left-Wing Writers. Her writing now entered a second phase, broadening its subject matter and expanding the range of its characters. "Shui" (Flood) is considered a landmark story of proletarian fiction. Also from this period is the story "From Night to Morning," included here: it combines the earlier concern with the self and the meaning of writing with a new sense of their relation to social and political realities.

From 1933 to 1936 Ding Ling was under arrest and presumed executed until she escaped and made her way to the Communist stronghold in the North where she was greeted by Mao Zedong who later wrote several poems in her honor. There Ding Ling organized the Red Army Guard unit responsible for mobilizing villagers as part of the War of Resistance against Japan beginning in 1937. *Yinian* (One Year) is the powerful documentary record of that experience, one which gave Ding Ling new insight into the possibilities for *dazhonghua*, a popular literature. Her essay, "Sanba jie you gan" (Thoughts on March 8), written and published in 1942, is the last major work of this phase. An impassioned report on the exploitation of women even in the areas liberated by the Communists, it expresses Ding

Ling's special concern for women and her commitment to a "critical realism" that would permit literature to reflect "the dark side" of socialist life, as she had expressed it in some twenty-five short stories and novellas.

With the rectification campaign that culminated in the famed Yan'an Talks of 1942, all cultural activity was subordinated to revolutionary goals: literature was to present models for emulation. This new accommodation between fiction and reality is reflected in Ding Ling's last major period and exemplified by her monumental novel on the early phase of land reform, *Taiyang zhao zai Sangganhe shang* (*The Sun Shines on the Sanggan River*, 1948). Though the book was awarded the Stalin Prize in 1951 and Ding Ling held many influential positions, she was later accused of "maligning the masses in her fiction," expelled from the party, and forced into exile after 1957. Eventually permitted to engage in agricultural and cultural activity, Ding Ling was working in the northern provinces, when in 1966, under the aegis of the Cultural Revolution, she was continually attacked and abused by the Red Guard; from 1970 to 1975 she was imprisoned in solitary confinement—one cell away from her husband (she had married some thirty years earlier).

In 1978 she was allowed to return to Beijing, and with her rehabilitation, she was given a prominent position in the Writers' Union. Though permitted to publish again for the first time in thirty years, Ding Ling did not add to her fictional corpus. She remained committed to the Revolution until her death.

FROM NIGHT TO MORNING
Cong yewan dao tianliang

"Quiet lane, crescent moon hanging high in the sky, sparkling stars, trolley wheels creaking along the rails, and that child, how adorable he is from the back! The two people he's walking between must be his parents...Oh! Damn it! This is all so senseless..."

She was a woman thinking of many things, blotting out others, not really knowing what she should think about as she walked down the street, very much alone, in the direction of her so-called "home."

She sighed. "Today's the day my little brother died, so many years ago....From the train I saw so many graves draped with paper money, and I don't even know where he's buried. Won't Mother be grieving today too? No, Little Ping can make her forget the past, but still...." She sighed again. "Why do I think about these things!"

After crossing the avenue, she turned onto an even quieter street lined with trees. The street lamp cast shadows by her feet of the sparse leaves that had just appeared on the branches, and she heard the clicking sound of her heels on the cement pavement.

"And Mother's letter! Humph! How can she talk about good fortune and happiness? If I told you the truth, mother, I'm afraid you might...but what does that matter? Little Ping does have a mother—is he really so unfortunate?"

Several figures suddenly loomed in front of her. She quickly jumped to the side.

"Why do you look at me like that?" she thought angrily. "I'm not afraid of you!"

From a house along the street came the faint notes of a violin. What a sorrowful melody—it said so much about the bitterness of life! She stopped for a while to listen, then hurried on.

"I won't listen; I can't bear it!"

She ran as far as the lane where she lived.

Kitchens along the way gave off odors of cooking oil, in living rooms red gauze lanterns were lit, and one could hear the light tinkle of pianos. She reached a house reeking of opium smoke, rapped sharply at the back door, and yelled:

"It's me from upstairs! Please open the door!"

It always took a long time before the sallow, skinny little servant-girl came softly to open the door. Once inside she had to hold her nose and dash to the staircase.

"Hey! You had a visitor." The little servant with her long, long hair stood beside the staircase.

"Oh? Was there any message?"

"No." A pitiable look appeared on the girl's dirty face.

"Well, what does it matter!" She bolted on up the stairs.

Her room looked barren and the glare from the light hurt her eyes. She collapsed on a chair; her head throbbed as if something were pounding at it. She cast a weak glance about the room, but saw only a face with tear-filled eyes. It was Ah-dian, her childhood self. She let out a wide, unrestrained laugh. In that innocent childish heart she could still discern a mood of passionate longing. Oh! That poor girl, that miserable childhood, that lonely— unforgettably lonely—childhood!

Totally exhausted, her head still aching, she closed her eyes hoping to rest for a while, but the vast ocean spread out again before her and, in the boundless sky, she saw a carefree seagull, that proud wanderer! She had knocked herself out, she had gone downtown with Yang, but what did she get out of it?

"....Together we will die in pursuit of the starlight." This was a line from one of his poems. But what was there to say now?

"Is there anything I can say? No, nothing. I must understand.

"Ocean, grasslands, what do they mean to me? I wander about the whole day indifferent to everything.

"But why? I shouldn't think this way. There's nothing unique about me. I'm just like anyone else...."

And she wasn't indifferent. She recalled coming back from Wusong and getting on the trolley at North Sichuan Road. Through the window she saw the back of a man in a heavy beige overcoat—it was that familiar shape! She was so happy she nearly called out, "Hey! Ping!" when she suddenly remembered. Heartbroken, she leaned her head against the window and held back her tears. Still, she couldn't resist looking again, wanting to find him in that group of young people, vaguely hoping that familiar face might detach itself from the crowd and come to her. But it was impossible—she knew that. That trolley took her as far as the main avenue downtown. There she ran into Mrs. F. And that encounter was the beginning of what was to cause her untold grief.

Swept along in the crowds, she and Yang entered the Yongan Department Store. There were powdered faces everywhere, and from the phonograph came the singing voice of a movie star. They ran up to the second floor with no particular purpose, then came down again. By chance they found themselves in the department selling children's Western-style clothing. Without realizing it, she lingered here. She found exactly what she wanted: a two-piece outfit, blue and cream-colored. It was just the right size, slightly smaller than others of the same type. She kept looking at it while she counted the money in her purse—one dollar and eighty cents. It wasn't enough—far from enough. Disheartened, she thought about the last letter from home. It said the child was so adorable people couldn't get over it. But those taking care of him felt very sorry for him and hoped the parents could manage somehow to send a little money so they could provide better food and clothing for him. Besides, they were almost out of powdered milk....The children's clothes looked so bright and attractive, she couldn't tear herself away. Some pink silk dresses caught her eye, and she was about to go over and look at them when Yang nudged her. Surprised, she looked up and saw Yang signal her with her eyes, and just then she saw an attractive young married woman standing beside her. The woman, too, was absorbed in fingering a colorful little garment. Looking at the woman's black cat-fur coat, long hair, and pretty face with only a touch of makeup, she was taken aback and felt a little dazed, but getting a grip on herself she walked over and touched Mrs. F's arm lightly. It was clear from her expression that Mrs. F. was also surprised. "Oh, my goodness," she exclaimed in her usual soft way of speaking. "It's been so long!" Her tone of voice conveyed affection and sympathy.

What could she say to Mrs. F? She felt at a loss for words.

"How are you? Are you still living in the same place?" The questions seemed rather pointless, but she wanted to say something.

"Yes, we're still there. I heard you sent your child back home." Mrs. F. continued to speak softly.

"Yes...yes...that's right. Are you buying clothes?"

"No, powdered milk." Mrs. F. held up a large container of powdered milk that she had bought.

Powdered milk...the letter said they were almost out.... Again she felt a little dizzy. Then moved by a sudden impulse, she said in a quivering voice, "Come to visit me and bring your child!"

"All right, I will. Are you living alone? Where do you live?"

For a moment she hesitated, then slowly gave Mrs. F. the address. She hoped she had remembered it correctly.

"Well then, see you later!" she moved away from the counter but after a moment glanced back and saw that Mrs. F. was gone too. She hadn't bought that small dress.

"What a pity!" Yang said with emotion. "She's from a good family—how could she marry such a...?"

"They love each other. They live on love." She still felt a little weak and unsteady on her feet.

"I think there are a lot of contradictions there." Yang herself was a person of contradictions.

She followed Yang's advice and took a rickshaw; they said goodbye and she went on her way alone. Now she couldn't hold back the tears. But how could she cry? Who would understand? Mrs. F. would never imagine that she could make this strong-willed woman cry. And then the memory of a night in the past came to her—a terrible night when the wind howled and blew cold drizzle into her face. Driven by a frantic sense of uneasiness, she had searched everywhere. Desperate, she had been to three likely places but with no success. Finally she went to Mr. F.'s place and when she saw the reddish light at the third-floor window, she dared to hope for a moment. She pounded at the door but there was no response. She went around the the back door; still nobody answered. Her anguish was unimaginable. She stood in the street and shouted, "Mr. F.! Mr. F.!" Her voice was probably drowned out by the street noises because the windows on the third floor remained shut. A helpful passer-by knocked at the door and she yelled from the other side of the street. Then, suddenly, the light went out. Her hopes dashed, the words screamed in her head, "They have gone to bed." She could picture the three of them sleeping together in an embrace. She looked at the window again. Behind it lay tranquility and happiness. She didn't want to call out again. Gazing at the window, she burst into tears. She thought of her newborn infant and the man who had disappeared into a mysterious darkness. She cried for a long time. She felt her hair thoroughly drenched, from the rain but also from her tears. At last she made her way home, running through the wind and rain. That night her fate was sealed. She would never again see the one she loved. Everything was over—that boundless peace and happiness! Two persons' hopes and plans for the future! Was *everything* over? Those unforgettable dreams!

On the rickshaw she cried without a sound. She was constrained by another kind of force.

Now tonight the still-youthful face of Mrs. F. again appeared to her. She tried not to feel the dull pain in the back of her mind.

"They're still happy," she thought. "I saw them; I saw their happiness. Their life is just what ours used to be, just what we thought of as the ideal. And by now their child must have grown. She's probably at that age when children are so much fun to dress up. I don't think she bought that dress, though. They surely don't have money to spare...."

She thought of something else that had happened fairly recently. One day when she was changing Little Ping's diaper, she noticed that his cotton quilt was slightly small. Smiling and patting his little bottom, she said, "You little rascal! You should try to be more considerate of your parents. Don't make trouble for them. Don't you know you're growing too fast?" At that time the baby's father was stretched out on a chair reading. He added, also with a smile, "This is why I picked a good name for him a long time ago. 'Little Troublemaker'—it fits him perfectly! Oh—the F.'s child hasn't got enough to wear either. They told me her cotton quilt was already too small and thin." At this time, she had picked the child up and was holding him high.

"Okay," she said, "if we make a cotton quilt, we'll make an extra one. Are the F.'s short of money too?"

"Of course they are! How could they not be? Mr. F. told me they've been living exclusively on the sale of two bookcases of foreign books, but in another month they don't know what they'll do...."

"Another month." That month had passed long ago. What had they been living on? Without realizing it, she felt concerned about them. Of course in her eyes, they were happy—even to think about it was painful. Just the same, she wondered what they were living on

these days. The thought took hold of her and she started to feel anxious.

"She must be really unhappy about not buying that little dress. Naturally this isn't the kind of thing that's important to them, but still, as a mother, she probably can't help feeling unhappy. Maybe at this very moment she is telling him about the dress and imagining what it would look like on her lovable little girl...."

It was true, they were happy. F. was exactly like the man she loved and Mrs. F. was still young and beautiful. She wished they could be like that forever. Perhaps they'll be lucky. Perhaps they won't encounter any trouble, but....Her head started spinning again and she was enveloped by a whirling darkness.

"Mrs. F...." She again pictured that lightly powdered face. "Oh! She's happy now, even though she probably doesn't realize it. How can I not love and envy her? She is the exact image of what I was in the past! Could *I* do anything to give her a little pleasure, make her even happier? I know! I'll buy that small dress for her."

This thought made her excited. She jumped to her feet, grabbed her purse and rushed out. It wasn't until she was on the avenue that she seemed to remember something. She glanced at her watch; it was 9:15. Yes, that's the solution! And she went into a pawn shop, got five dollars and hurried in the direction of Shafei Road.

Some shops were already closed, but in others the lights were still on. She couldn't say precisely how many times she had been there in the past, but she knew exactly where to find what she was looking for. Previously she had paid close attention to all those things that small children need. She went into a shop. Countless times before she had lingered in front of those glass counters. Hadn't she figured out many times with Little Ping's father when they would need this or that small item? Wasn't it a spring like this one that they had discussed taking the child out in a stroller when he was big enough? But she hadn't come back here until now; she was alone and had come to buy a small dress. She saw a lot of familiar things she had once dreamed she would have. She suppressed her sorrow and thought, "I want to give her something! I want her to be happy!"

A kindly old foreign woman brought her a big pile of dresses and looked at her with a warm smile, the kind one gives to a happy young mother. She found a pink silk dress embroidered with a flower. What luck! The price had been reduced and it was only six dollars and twenty cents.

Outside she heard the noise from the trolley and the incessant honking of automobile horns. A clean-shaven young foreigner, his beautiful tie flapping in the wind, had his arm around his sweetheart. They were strolling casually; they stopped now and then in front of the store windows and pointed out the jewelry that was displayed with particular care. A flower vendor was there too. From the musical instruments shop drifted the strains of an intoxicating song. Oh! Everything was just the same as before. In the past she too had strolled there casually.

After she returned to her room, she again examined that small dress. It really was perfect! She folded it up again and thought contentedly, "Maybe this will make her happy. I hope so." She wrote an accompanying letter— a very polite and reserved one because she didn't want anyone else to know how she was feeling.

She finished everything easily and felt she was gratifying a cherished desire. She lay down on the bed, but her thoughts turned to herself. She thoughts of the present, the past, the child whose powdered milk was running out. And for the first time since she had been living by herself she didn't hold back, but abandoned herself to her tears.

"Why do I want to cry? I should forget everything! When I was in the arms of my lover—that's when I should have cried. But now I need to brace up and be strong...."

"But why shouldn't I cry? I've endured so much. If only I could be the way I was. I want to do what I feel like—to destroy everything, sabotage everything. All I want is to be happy for a while...."

Her head felt heavy and her heart ached as if it had been wounded. She had a little of the feeling: "This might be the end of my life."

What time was it? It was so quiet— frighteningly so. The light was too bright and her face pale and haggard.

She didn't know when she dozed off into a death-like, dreamless sleep.

The day gradually dawned. The yellow light still burned. As usual, she woke with a start and sat up immediately. Once awake she never allowed herself to lie in bed. She was afraid her precious mornings would be taken up by those worthless dreams. Every day she took advantage of the best hours when her spirit was fresh to write a few pages. Seeing she had forgotten to switch off the light, she cursed herself softly.

She jumped out of bed, stood on the floor and breathed in the fresh air coming through the window.

A small package caught her eye. She picked it up gently and opened it. It was only that small pink dress. Like someone waking from a drunken sleep she remembered everything that had happened during the night. As she picked up the letter, she let the small dress fall to the floor. And soon the letter, in two shreds, fluttered away from her hand.

"What a ridiculous idea!" she said to herself. "I'm still living in some kind of illusory world! Shouldn't I live the way other people imagine I do—steadfast, in control, moving ahead in spite of the obstacles? I mustn't behave like this anymore! What a total waste!"

Grabbing a big towel, she ran down the stairs to the water tap.

The manuscript paper was spread out on the table. She had written only twelve pages— up to the point where the farmer's youngest daughter, an innocent, young girl, was sitting with Third Miss in front of the earthen house. They were talking about their childhood. She continued to write. She described Elder Brother who was repairing the raised paths in a field not far away. He stood barefooted, his sleeves rolled up high. He was a strapping, healthy youth. The girls were calling him but he didn't answer. And since he couldn't get an answer out, he was overwhelmed by a dull kind of pain which was indescribable....

She had written this far when she turned around and saw the small dress lying on the floor pathetically. She sighed and turned back to her story.

"Reason—you're a fraud! You will only destroy natural human feeling....

"But never mind. Besides, maybe I'm wrong...."

She continued writing. She had already reached page fifteen.

Translated by Ruth Nybakken

Molly Keane

Ireland, b. 1904

Known as M.J. Farrell for most of her professional life, Molly Keane, the author of twelve novels, was apparently not destined to be a writer. She was born in County Kildare into an upper-class Anglo-Irish family, and into a society that was cut off from the political and economic realities of life within its impoverished, predominantly Catholic country. At that time, women of her class were barely educated and certainly not expected to work. They married, had children, partied, and hunted. Keane was saved from that vapid life by a neighboring family who, taking an interest in her, exposed her to modern culture. Her own parents were not interested in their children. Her father was reclusive and cared only for his horses; her mother, under the pseudonym of Moira O'Neill, was a minor writer of "folkloric" poetry and was known as "The Poet of the Seven Glens."

Keane married young and began writing for "pin money." She took the pseudonym M.J. Farrell from an Irish pub near her home and used it in order to avoid offending her friends. Her early works, such as *Young Entry* (1928) and *Devoted Ladies* (1934), were lighthearted novels about the people and life she knew. The former was about how the upper-class Anglo-Irish behave towards Irish workers, and the latter dealt with a love triangle, including two women in a lesbian relationship and the man who "saves" one of the women. These early works were extremely successful as were her plays, all directed by John Gielgud, such as *Spring Meeting* (1938) and *Ducks and Drakes* (1942), which were compared to the plays of Noël Coward.

When her husband died, quite young, and her fourth play failed, partially because it was out of date, she stopped writing for many years, beginning again when she was in her seventies with *Good Behavior* (1981) and *Time after Time* (1983). These she published under her own name and they were critically very well received. In fact, *Good Behavior* almost won the coveted Booker Prize and was adapted for TV. These later books deal with subjects similar to the earlier ones, but their vision of life is far darker. Keane presently lives in County Waterford, Northern Ireland, and has two daughters.

The segment we have selected for this anthology is from *Rising Tide*, first published in 1937, and reprinted as part of the Virago series, which has also reprinted *Devoted Ladies* and plans also to republish *Mad Puppetstown* (1931), *Full House* (1935), and *Two Days in Aragon* (1944). It describes the life of an Anglo-Irish family in 1900 and was chosen because it gives such a rich facsimile of Edwardian life among the moneyed Anglo-Irish. Life among the Anglo-Irish is Keane's preoccupation and her novels evoke that lost world, which was her world, with a remarkable precision and clarity.

from RISING TIDE

What don't we know about the Early Nineteen Hundreds. 1901 and 2 and 3 and up to '14 we can feel about only very dimly. Leisure and Richness and Space and Motor-veils and the bravery of those who flew in the earliest aeroplanes impress us. But we can't feel about those years really. Not in the way we feel about the War. There we are conscious.

It requires an effort to realise the necessities, pleasures, colossal bad taste, Romance, trust, suspicion, pride of those years. The War is forced on us, horror is so actual. But those years, the years of our cousins' youth, avoid us and will not be known. We almost forget how deeply that youth was influenced by the generation that got it. Influenced and prescribed for in a way we can't know about. So much and such nearly complete power was in those elder hands. Over the trivialities or fatalities of Life our cousins and aunts accepted so much and really managed it with admirable smoothness and dignity.

Pain they endured and accepted.

Endless Chaperonage.

Supervision of their correspondence.

The fact that Mother Knew Best.

That Father Says So.

That there is no more to be said on the subject, they accepted.

They accepted their leisure without boredom.

They accepted having occupations found for this leisure.

They accepted trivialities and treated them with that carefulness and detail which rounds such perfect smallness and makes it an acceptable part of life.

With all this acceptance they could pre-serve a death-like romantical obstinacy where their hearts were concerned—they had a true romantical outlook, infinitely less destructible than the quick love encounters we so often know. On absence their Romances throve. They were not afraid of sentimentality—they were not afraid of being thought girlish. They never needed to explain their emotions to themselves or to their friends. The indecency of knowing what it was all about would have been appalling to them; they didn't want to know—the mystery and the thrill enough and most secretly their own. Hence much rapture and much failure, and a certain dignity too. This outward smoothness of Life which at all costs they struggled to achieve was a politeness of living which we may envy them.

"Eleven o'clock—more than bedtime!" Lady Charlotte French-McGrath had four daughters, and at these words Muriel immediately folded up her work. Enid ceased tracing a picture of a stag's head into her album called Sunlight and Shadow. Violet gathered up the cards with which she and her father had been playing picquet, and only Diana, Little Diana, showed no speed in closing her book. Really, Mother might not have spoken——

"Bed-time, I think, Diana."

Diana shut her book guiltily and was the first of the four to kiss her father good-night.

"Ha," he said. "Ha-Ha. Bed-time. Bed-time, I suppose. Good-night, my dear. Candles, now, let me see, candles." He crossed the room to that small, dark table where immemorially the candlesticks were set out and lit the five candles. Giving each daughter a kiss and a candlestick and the same to his wife, he followed them with a very satisfied eye as they went out of the door, crossed the hall one behind another and mounted the stairs in the same pretty succession.

Muriel first with her fluffy brown hair, thin neck and little birdy body. Poor little Muriel—time she was finding a husband. Twenty-four and nothing satisfactory turning up yet. Enid then, with her purple eyes, deep voice and dark hair. She would have been a beauty if Violet had not come after her, and Violet was an Edwardian classic. Skin like shells and peaches, bosom like the prow of a ship, smooth thighs, features of bland and simple beauty and a head crowned by obedient golden hair and unhampered by brains. A satisfactory daughter. And then Diana—little Diana—there was not much of the Edwardian classic about Diana. Her mother could not find her very satisfactory, since she had neither the charm nor the biddable disposition of her elder sisters. And none of their beauty. Small and dark and angular and inclined even at the age of seventeen to a dark and downy growth of hair (ignored by her family, for what could be done about it?) Diana was hardly due for success in 1900.

Lady Charlotte French-McGrath mounting the stairs in her daughters' wake was a shocking despot, really swollen with family conceit and a terrifying pride of race. She had a strange sense of her own power, made real indeed by a life spent chiefly at Garonlea with her obedient husband, frightened children and many tenants and dependants. Here she had lived and suffered and here she was supreme.

Married at the age of eighteen to a man of good family and one who owned moreover the best woodcock shoot in the west of Ireland, Lady Charlotte had borne six children in the first eight years of her married life—four daughters and two sons; one son unhappily died of convulsions when an infant. She was mean, although not so mean as her husband whom she had taught to be mean. She ran Garonlea like a court—her daughters like the ladies in waiting.

"Muriel, write my notes for me——"

"Enid, how about your little job of washing the china in my boudoir this afternoon——"

Such awful little employments—the walks and messages to the needy tenantry, bestowals of charities and reprimands, piano practising and "Lying Down," that cure for all ills.

God should have chastened Lady Charlotte with one malformed or unsatisfactory child. But they were all miracles of aristocratic good looks—inclined to anæmia perhaps, except for the divine Violet.

One by one the Lady Charlotte French-McGrath presented her daughters to their sovereign. But as far as entering the social contest and finding them husbands went, God or Garonlea and its famous woodcock shoot might do the rest. So far, whatever God might send them in that lonely countryside, the woodcock shoot produced for the most part only their father's friends and contemporaries. Determined as she was that the girls should marry men of Property and Title, Lady Charlotte did nothing at all about collecting these mythical and appropriate husbands. She showed such marked disapproval of any young friend that her son Desmond ever brought to stay, should the friend fulfil neither of these requirements, and such embarrassingly obvious tactics should he fulfil either or both that Desmond desisted in disgust, for he was a charming creature and entirely free from his mother's influence. His sisters adored him and it was his firm intention to do all in his power for the girls when he should marry. Until then he looked on them as rather boring princesses set for a time in a castle beyond a wood.

Meantime it would be unfair to her not to allow that Lady Charlotte loved her daughters with a passion none the less genuine if it demanded first their unquestioning obedience, and fed itself on a profound jealousy of any interest in their lives other than those she might herself prompt or provide. She felt that her children owed to her as a mother, not as a person, love, confidence and obedience. She felt this tremendously. It was a true thing with her. Among all the travails and secret adventures of her own life both mental and physical she had endured, raising no manner of complaining, shyness as much as stoicism helping her here. She absolutely required that her children should prove a justification, as she should see it, of herself.

So they were—they were practically all that she required. Her son Desmond and Violet were the two at the top of her estimation but she trusted herself to keep this sacred maternal secret safely from the other three daughters. "I love all my children equally," she was very fond of saying. Although vaguely impressed by the proper feeling she thus displayed, the three less-favoured daughters were never slow to employ either Desmond or Violet as their intermediary if for any reason matters should be strained between themselves and their mother.

Tonight at the stairhead they parted from her.

"Good-night, Mother dear."

A gold head bobbed for a kiss in the candlelight.

"Good-night, my child. Don't let me hear you and Muriel talking at one o'clock as I did last night on my way to—the bathroom. Please, Violet."

"Good-night, Mother dear."

"Good-night, Muriel. Now remember."

"Good-night, Mother dear."

"Good-night, Enid. Have you been taking your senna regularly? I see you have another spot on your chin."

"Oh, but I have been taking it."

"Always remember, darling, a bad skin is most unattractive to gentlemen."

Enid flushed up to her beautiful brow. Oh, the shame of those spots, the shame and the recurring horror.

"Couldn't we perhaps ask Doctor Maxwell if he knows of a cure," she had once

asked her mother; but the answer, "Some things are best left to *Nature*, Enid," had quelled the ardour of her vanity.

"Good-night, Mother."

Diana as usual trying to be a little different from the rest.

"Good-night, Diana—*dear*."

The quick brush and escape of lips. Strange the lack of confidence in that child. Sad for her. A pity.

Lady Charlotte trailed the length of her oyster satin skirt down the passage to her bedroom and with the help of her maid undressed so far as those black satin corsets which had been in her trousseau. Then she slipped the fine white flannel nightgown over her head and fumbled under it for a long time before she thrust her arms into its sleeves.

In the blue-and-white bedroom at the other end of the house the three sisters were gathered solicitously round Violet, who lay on her bed in a state of pretty severe pain. Now that the long formality of the evening was over she could collapse and leave go that curious control which worked somewhere outside herself because it must.

"Let me help you with your stays, Violet dearest. You'll feel so much more comfy in your nightie."

"Oh, don't touch me, please, I'm in such pain." Violet sank her face into her pillow for a moment, then sat up bending herself together taut and convulsive with pain. The hair on her forehead and on the back of her neck was wet and sticking to her flesh. She was entirely in pain and moaned helplessly.

"I must go and tell Mother," Enid said in a frightened voice. "She'd give you a glass of ginger."

Violet signed to her desperately not to go.

Muriel was crying quietly for she adored Violet.

Diana said, "Mother ought to see how bad Violet is."

They all felt quite desperate and quite helpless as they stood round that neat brass bedstead where Violet lay suffering so horridly at the hands of Mother Nature. Each of them knew that the glass of hot water and ginger, their mother's sovereign remedy in such times of stress, was calculated rather to make the sufferer vomit than to relieve her pain. The only thing it did relieve was their mother's sense of responsibility towards sickness. That and "Lying down," were her two invariable specifics for all female ills.

Violet whispered, "I'm so dreadfully cold."

Muriel sobbed, "I'll sleep with you darling, and warm you."

This not very hygenic plan these sisters often followed, for fires and hot-water bottles alike were considered vaguely sybaritic influences and seldom appeared in either the Blue and White or the Pink and White bedroom. Tonight the Blue and White room was full of October air, cold and hollow as an October mist. Between the window panes that flattened the outside night and the white curtains it was present and in the room too, circling bluely the candle flames when the girls had put down their candlesticks here and there at unequal levels and distances. They shivered a little in their low dresses and put a flannel dressing-gown tenderly over their poor sister at whom they continued to gaze in helpless concern.

"But where has Diana gone?" Enid whispered to Muriel. "To Mother's room?"

"Or do you think the bath-room?"

"Oh, dear, shall I go and see?"

"She's not in our room and she's not in the bathroom," Enid reported, important with omen. "Can she have gone to Mother?"

"Well, if she has and Mother catches you in here there'll be trouble. Oh, dear, do go to your own room."

With many a backward and pitying look at Violet, Enid retired as advised. She had plaited her hair in its two soft dark plaits and put on her frilled nightdress and blue padded silk dressing-gown before Diana came in.

Diana was so sharp and aggressive, tearing off her dress and her corsets and doing her

Swedish exercises in her black silk stockings and her chemise. Really she didn't seem to mind at all...Enid couldn't always look. Embarrassing.

"Where did you go to?" she asked when she had poured her senna out of the window and hopped into bed. "Poor Violet, wasn't it awful!"

"If you did drink that senna you wouldn't have so many spots," Diana told her, still exercising with energy.

"Oh, but I simply can't. I would if I could. I hate deceiving dear Mother. But where did you go, Diana?"

"I went down to the kitchen and got some hot milk and brandy for Violet and a hot-water bottle."

"Brandy—Diana, but what would Mother say? And a hot-water bottle. You'll catch it if she finds out."

"Why should she find out? Anyhow Violet's better now. The hot milk acted like a charm."

"The hot milk? Oh, Diana, I'm afraid it may have been the brandy." Enid said this sadly without a ray of amusement. She saw nothing either funny or comforting in her sister relaxing into a drunken stupor. The thought of such pain as she had seen assuaged hardly touched her.

"I don't care whether it was the milk or the brandy or the hot-water bottle, she's better now than if we'd left it all to Nature," Diana said this in the hard unappealing way which Enid admired while secretly feeling repelled by it. Now she said as she tested the almost damp cold of her bed with her thin blue feet:

"Oh, Diana, it is cold. Shall we sleep together?"

Diana said quickly, "Oh, no it's not cold enough for that." She had a dreadful inner feeling about sleeping with Enid and never did so if it could be avoided. Enid slept with her only for warmth as sheep sleep and huddle together, but Diana was afraid about this. Afraid only of herself. Obscurely obstinate in her avoidance of such contacts.

Ling Shuhua   (Ling Ruitang; Ling Jui-t'ang)

China/UK(England), b. 1904

Born Ling Ruitang in Beijing to the fourth of her father's six marriage partners, Ling grew up in a highly privileged household; as her father's favorite, she was permitted educational and social advantages unusual even then for a woman of her class. Her education led to a B.A. in foreign literature (English, French, Japanese) at Beijing's Yanjing University (1923–1926), followed by a year in Tokyo studying modern Japanese literature. In 1924 Ling Shuhua began to write in the vernacular despite the opposition of her father, who considered classical Chinese the only respectable literary medium. At the same time, her father began training her to carry on the family name in traditional painting and calligraphy, thus setting the stage for Ling's dual career as writer and as artist.

In 1925 Ling joined the 'right-wing' literary group, Xinyue (the Crescent Moon), which first published "Songche" ("The Sendoff," 1929), later included in *Nüren* (Women). Another early story, "Jiuhou" (After Wine, 1925), was turned into a one-act play by the prominent dramatist Ding Xilin. Ling Shuhua's fame rests primarily on these and some forty other short stories that she published between 1924 and 1936, later collected in *Hua Zhi Si* (Temple of Flowers, 1928), *Nüren* (1930), and *Xiao Ger Lia* (Two Little Brothers, 1935). They demonstrate her skill in characterization through dialogue and her alertness to the significance of seemingly routine detail, particularly in the lives of women. In her dispassionate narration everyday trivia emerges as a veneer over terrible institutionalized anguish. Such a devastating description and indictment of patriarchal society won her the respect of writers all across the political spectrum, from Hu Shi to Lu Xun, including Ding Ling, Zheng Zhenduo, Ba Jin and Xiao Qian, all of whom published her work.

In 1926 Ling married professor Chen Yuan (1896–1970); in 1938 they joined the exodus of Wuhan University to Sichuan to avoid the advancing Japanese armies. A government appointment brought Chen Yuan to London in 1945 as China's representative to UNESCO. There Ling Shuhua joined him with their only child, a daughter, in 1947, and there she has made her home for most of the last forty years.

After a period of child care and adjustment to her new surroundings, Ling Shuhua resumed her writing and artistic career in the 1950s with the publication of a volume of reminiscences in English, *Ancient Melodies* (1953); a collection of some two dozen essays, many on art and travel, *Dreams from a Mountain-Lover's Studio* (1960); and an album of her paintings with a foreword by André Maurois, based on the well-reviewed 1962–1963 exhibition of her work at the Chernuschi Museum in Paris. In 1983 Oxford's Ashmolean Museum mounted another exhibition, entitled "The Paintings of Ling Shuhua and Her Friends."

Donald Holoch

THE SENDOFF
Songche

"You think our cook is honest?" Mrs. Bai spat out the hull of a roasted melonseed, a shrewd smile appearing on her face as she took another seed, and then went on: "You have yet to run a house, Miss Wang; how could you know the bad side of servants? Ah there's simply not a one that's honest! The other day I sent him to buy a chicken, obviously one pound eight and a tiny fraction when I weighed it, yet he claimed one pound nine. Bean sprouts are fourteen cents a pound. When I asked a few days ago, he said no one would sell for less than fifteen—too bad the man of the house is fond of sprouts—so I had to let him buy them, and that's not bad, to make a penny a pound on vegetables, two cents on two pounds, not to mention his rip-off on every pound of fish and every pound of meat. I can't be far wrong, it's no wonder he's even wearing new winter pants and day before yesterday he went out in a pair of black serge shoes—shoes alone must cost you two dollars; in fact I can't tell how much more he pockets without my knowledge." Mrs. Bai's frown deepened as she went on, apparently having discovered something dangerous.

"Well, things are dear nowadays, a dollar or two for shoes alone, so if people make only three or four dollars a month, how can they get by?" replied Miss Wang.

"Things are far more dear than they've been in years. This year what isn't dear! It used to be, before I was married, a bushel of the best white rice cost two twenty, and a maid's wages were only three strings of cash, not a dollar like now.* In those days you just couldn't count all the servants in our family: in our rooms, two for the light work, three for the heavy work, one to look after baby sister; in the rooms of the older sister-in-law, one for the light work, two wetnurses, one for the heavy work; the second sister-in-law was fussy, she had two for the light work—"

"Here come Mrs. Zhou and her daughter." Sitting apart and reading his paper, the husband had seen them through the window and interrupted his wife's interminable talk.

Mrs. Bai suddenly remembered: "Oh yes, yesterday we arranged to see Mrs. Xu off at the station." Yet she took her time going to the door, inviting them in with a smile.

"Mrs. Zhou, please do come in. But your eldest isn't with you; studying again for her tests, I imagine....The girls want to be tops in school just like the boys. Actually she's already as lovely to look at as anyone could wish, and still she studies, recites poems, writes couplets for occasions; who knows how many hearts she'll break!" She concluded with a complacent chuckle.

"Without fail, Mrs. Bai, you always ask after our Crystal; if you had a grown son I would engage her to him right now. I know you'd never be a domineering mother-in-law."

"If I ever found a daughter-in-law like her, how could I do enough for her? Domineering is out of the question." Mrs. Bai followed her guests in, grinning at the second daughter as she spoke:

"The young lady must be ten by now, really as fresh and tender as springtime. With a daughter like this I wouldn't let her go to any school. To have her home and dress her up is all I'd need to be happy."

"If you like her so much, let me engage her to your boy."

The words were hardly uttered before the embarrassed girl was trying somehow to hide behind her mother.

"Seriously? A promise is a promise, eh, Mrs. Zhou. And we do have a son about the same age, but I don't know if he's worthy of her. Pompom. Come here, come meet your mother-in-law.

"...Pompom! Eh, Pompom?"

The house was now filled with the wife's

high-strung voice and her complacent laughter. The husband opened his eyes to see a flurry of figures passing in front of him but didn't catch the conversation.

"Pompom? Go look for him, Papa, bring him here," said the wife through her loud laughter, "or else you won't be a father-in-law."

"Pompom is still at school," he said, glancing at the clock. "Aren't you seeing someone off on the 4:20 train? It's already 3:50. Better get going."

"Don't worry, this clock may be fast," replied the wife.

"Not likely if it was set by the noon gun."

"Sometimes Pompom winds it; he often makes it fast. Give me a minute, Mrs. Zhou, I still have to change." She was hurrying from the parlor, giving orders to the maid: "Li Ma, bring the sponge cake out on a plate, same with the thousand-layer cake in the cupboard, a plateful of sliced pears, tell the young lady not to be shy. I'll be right there."

The sound of clumping up the stairs, the staccato crossing of the floor to open a closet, the concomitant rattle of the windows, the staccato recrossing of the floor, the tea-table clinking of porcelain bowls and cups as in a moving train.

"Li Ma, where are my keys? Has the skirt been ironed?"

Li Ma hastened up to her, her bound feet on the stairs making the same sound her mistress had.

"How come you didn't grab them, let the little one play with them? Genius, come here, where did you go with Mommy's keys?...

"...Li Ma says you took them, get them for me. I'm going out to buy you cookies.... Li Ma, check what he has on. Yesterday they turned up in one of his pockets.... Ah, on the floor. Never mind, Li Ma, hurry with the skirt....

"Now where's my compact? Genius, did you take it?" The last phrase sounded more rushed than anything she'd said so far. At a

train station, she thought, with all those people, a compact was a must.

"Ma! Am I going too?" little Genius was whining.

"You wouldn't like it, what would you do? At home you can get Li Ma to play with you."

"No! I'm going!" and the boy started to scream.

"What a nuisance! Li Ma, come and change the young man's clothes, put that Western suit on him, hurry up. Change his socks too, just look at these holes, not even mended for him, what can you be doing all day long?"

"Where would I get the time? All day it's 'Do this, Do that'..." Li Ma muttered under her breath.

"Ma, I want an umbrella," the boy shouted.

"Skip the umbrella, let's get going."

"But its cloudy, it'll rain; what if my new suit gets all wet later on?"

"Cut it out. Papa, would you get him the umbrella on top of the closet?" She shouted as they came, mother and son, clumping down the stairs.

"The train's about to leave, forget the send-off. If you ask people here shouldn't you be ready on time...." The husband was mumbling but the wife, preoccupied, had grabbed the umbrella and hurried into the parlor calling out:

"It's a bit windy, will you all be warm enough? Have another piece of sponge cake, young lady, I made it myself, and there's no snacks at the station, have another piece, don't worry, this you can't get sick on...." Such hearty pressure to eat was like a prelude to exile, not a trip to the station.

"Mrs. Bai, it's four already," said Miss Wang as she rose to go.

"Will we make it to the station? It's already 4:10 by my watch, faster than yours." Smiling, Mrs. Zhou stood up.

"Yours must not be right either. Go next

door, Wang Sheng, to Public Security, and ask Mr. Zhu."

Wang Sheng, who was just then pouring tea, promptly left the room.

"If you're going, go. Why keep asking? Each delay makes you that much later." The husband strode from the room as he spoke, visibly disgruntled and frustrated.

Mrs. Zhou said, "If we dash right now perhaps we'll still make it."

"Wang Sheng will be right back. There! He's running back. If it is too late we'll be wasting cab fare and getting a mouthful of wind to boot."

Wang Sheng came in to say that the clock over there was in fact five minutes slower than here. That still left a mere quarter hour till departure and, as they all agreed after some chatter, only a taxi could get them there in time.

So they phoned a company to order a cab; it would be dispatched right away.

The ladies sat down again to wait, as before Mrs. Bai's speech flowed incessantly, the two children sat at the tea-table nibbling, and the relaxed atmosphere was promptly restored.

The desk clock ticked off the seconds, and when the thousand-layer cake had vanished into various stomachs, ten minutes had elapsed, the cab hadn't come yet, the train would be leaving, and they couldn't make it.

"Now what? The cab isn't here and the train must be leaving." Finally Mrs. Bai was anxious. "Such unreliable companies, promise plain as day to come right away, still not here when it's too late. Wang Sheng! Wang Sheng! What's the name of the company you phoned?"

"Great Eastern, I phoned twice to hurry them up, both times they said it had left long ago and would be right here."

"Right here, ah, what good would it be now, the train is leaving."

"There's no way to catch the train. We don't need a cab any more." It had apparently occurred to Mrs. Zhou that it was a two-dollar minimum if a taxi were sent, so she hastily made her position clear.

"They've already dispatched the cab," said Wang Sheng awkwardly.

"Tell him to just go back. Is it my fault it takes him so long to get here?"

"It takes gas to get here. No one would give in just like that," said Wang Sheng under his breath as he walked out.

Mrs. Bai now switched to her favorite topic, the trouble with hired help:

"Did you hear him butt in on the side of the company? I wonder how much commission they promised him."

"You can't let servants handle anything. They all have sticky fingers." The theme was also a favorite with Mrs. Zhou, and her tone was resonant.

"Buying rice, buying coal, buying groceries, they always make a commission on it, that goes without saying. If you happen to have anything delivered to the door, they're on the ball asking you for money; honestly, 'One more servant, one more thief,' at least ten cents out of every dollar you spend must go to them."

"Just consider it an added tax," put in Miss Wang with a smile.

"Send them shopping and you've added three or four taxes." Mrs. Zhou forcefully flung a handful of melonseed hulls at the cuspidor, as if to vent old frustrations.

"Isn't that the truth. Yesterday I called the cook in and told him myself that everybody buys chicken at forty-five a pound, like the day Mrs. Zhang bought hers it was forty-five, so how come it has to be forty-six when we buy? Imagine how irritating to hear him say, 'The Zhangs bought a tough chicken, good for soup but not to eat; if that's what you want I can get it for you at forty-four.' I said, 'How about your carp at twenty-eight a pound, other people only pay twenty-six?' He was quite irritating; he said, 'Ma'am, the best would be to shop yourself, then the price would always be right.' If I went shopping myself, what would I need the cook for?"

"You can be thankful that your cook merely talks back, ours will even sneak oil and rice home with him." Mrs. Zhou's voice now dropped to a whisper, as if it were all top secret, and it was considerate, to keep this cook from getting wind of it; gratitude and sympathy showed on Mrs. Bai's face. "To measure the rice for cooking he'd always have to come to me for the keys; that way, the cook couldn't take rice home, could he? But when he was measuring rice he'd measure out an extra bowl or two, so once I thought of a method, to watch him till he soaked the rice in water, then he'd have no way to take it home. Ach, several days later under the kitchen table I found a little fiber sack of moldy rice, too sticky and gooey to wash and use. I was so angry I would have fired him on the spot, but my husband really likes his cooking and wouldn't agree to let him go. It made me so angry I spent two or three whole days in bed. Ah, aren't you lucky, Mrs. Bai, yours leaves everything up to you."

"In running the house, he does leave it all up to me." A smug expression surfaced as she spoke.

"But everybody says your husband has a bit of a temper." This was Mrs. Zhou's riposte to the other woman's smug expression.

"A temper he does have. In raising the children he refuses to yield a fraction of an inch, they look at him like poor little imps at an ogre." With a pang of regret at having compared her own children to little imps, she checked her tongue.

"But 'spare the rod and spoil the child.'" Mrs. Zhou hastened to add the proverb that came to mind.

"As far as husbands go," Mrs. Bai reverted to the earlier idea, "I'd say Mrs. Xu's is tops. It's wild what's up to her. He goes to the movies with her one day, to the opera the next, they go wherever the action is; a pair of adorable children all dolled up follow her everywhere, it makes you happy just to see them. Mrs. Xu can't be too old yet; in the three years

I've known her, her skin is forever soft. She hasn't changed."

"And doesn't have to worry over fuel and rice. Whatever he makes the husband hands it all to her, it's up to her to enjoy la dolce vita, so she ages gracefully." There seemed to be desire and jealously in Mrs. Zhou's voice.

"Not everyone's as stupid as we are, leading this life for a man's sake, saving every penny we can, making old bitches out of ourselves—nothing but take care of the house, take care of the children...." Mrs. Bai's cool assessment turned into self-pity.

"You said it," sighed Mrs. Zhou. It was getting to her as well. "Not only has it made us into this—the husbands aren't bound to praise us for it either—but they meet that sort of free-spending woman and desire her." This of course was aimed at Mrs. Xu, and Mrs. Bai knew it.

"It's the old saying about wives," exclaimed Mrs. Bai: "First Wife: decorum; Second Wife: love; Third Wife: for worship, like Buddha above. They say she's the third to fill his wife's shoes, may the others rest in peace."

"Rest in peace? Those two are still living, stuck in the country. Hers was a free-love marriage...." Mrs. Zhou displayed a disdainful smile, too embarrassed to go on.

"As a matter of fact what is free love, that's what I asked mine the other day, and he said, what do you want to know for?"

"You are naïve, Mrs. Bai, not knowing even that. They say that when parents arrange it, with matchmaker and proper ceremony as ours did, it doesn't amount to a free-love marriage. Who knows what you're supposed to call our kind—as if the word 'marriage' were gross—Crystal told it to me once, how did I forget it?" Mrs. Zhou thought back for a while but couldn't come up with it.

Mrs. Zhou's explanation suddenly reminded Mrs. Bai of the impatient looks she often got from her own man especially at any reference to marriage. The free marriage she usually had in mind was the tightly embracing or kissing couples she had seen in the movies. She had often cursed it as shameless yet at the same time wondered what if her husband were just that sort of man....

"Anyway, I don't think much of that sort of marriage. Our sort may not have let us choose but it was right and proper, and if anyone doubts our affection, look at all those children." Mrs. Bai suddenly displayed a triumphant smile.

"Perfectly right!" Mrs. Zhou also smiled with satisfaction. "We too have raised quite a few children. Thinking of Mrs. Xu, I still haven't told you yet—now that she's gone we might as well talk about it—what she told me was," at this point she moved closer and lowered her voice, "one day at her house your husband complained there was no pleasure in home life and said he was a victim of the old-fashioned marriage."

"And yet his family sent the bridal sedan to ask for me." Mrs. Bai felt a rising surge of resentment, a frustrated urge to seek relief in smashing something. "No pleasure my eye, doesn't he have two helpings every meal?"

"Yes, and so I was outraged, in fact I was peeved at him for saying old-fashioned marriage. I contradicted her then and there —What's this 'no pleasure'—when they already have four children?" Mrs. Zhou was indignant.

"Hunh, it's simply that our sort aren't up on mascara and making eyes, dressing in red today and green tomorrow all to tickle our husband, so the men think it's boring." Mrs. Bai was fuming as she spoke, though she was staring blankly at the table; soon she knew she had something to let the other woman know:

"This is a thing I've never told you before, but when my husband came home from their house that day, he said they said you're eight years older than your husband, you look like his mother. That sounds like Mrs. Xu to me, maybe she's the one who said it."

"What she says is her business, at least we're not the third or fourth to fill a wife's shoes for anyone. Sounds nice but it's gross. Some wife! she's more like a kept woman if you ask me. High and mighty, is she?" Mrs. Zhou's temper was up and she added, "Our not seeing her off this time probably gives her something to gab about. It seems she used to be friends with you but later on you weren't too close?"

"I saw all of you had something to do with her, so I just joined the crowd to be sociable."

"Her husband is a hot official and lots of people even flock to her. That's a lady not to be offended." The words whispered by Mrs. Zhou instantly silenced Mrs. Bai.

"I hear that her husband now has even more influence. Miss Wang, do you know what post Mr. Xu was just promoted to?" asked Mrs. Zhou.

"Something like the Attorney General's Staff?" Miss Wang replied.

"That's it, and this Attorney General's Staff has great power." Mrs. Zhou got worried as she spoke: because she had missed the send-off, that woman might slander her husband and ruin his career. If she told him when she got home, she might have to put up with his anger. Suddenly the worry became agitation, but there was no outlet for it.

Between grievance and rage, Mrs. Bai too was speechless for a moment, just when Wang Sheng came walking in to say the cab was here, they'd had a long argument and the man refused to leave, because he couldn't waste gas for nothing and couldn't justify it back at the company.

"Is it my fault he got here late and made us miss the sendoff? I'm not paying that money, just tell him that." Mrs. Bai exploded with rage.

"But at the time we phoned him there were only ten minutes or so before the train left, he says, and it takes seven minutes to get here at the quickest."

"Why do you always take his side? Is he

some sort of relative, getting all this support from you? Oh no, I haven't set foot in his cab, so I don't pay!"

"You just tell him, if we haven't taken his cab we don't pay," put in Mrs. Zhou, since she too was involved.

"Look at it this way, Mrs. Zhou. When they make a trip it uses up their gas, so they better not come for nothing. You can see the point without...."

Mrs. Zhou raised her voice and stopped Wang Sheng in mid-sentence:

"What do you mean, 'see the point'? I do see there's no need to pay for not riding. I don't need cabbie's backtalk from you, and you can tell him I said so."

Crestfallen Wang Sheng was reluctant to go. Mrs. Bai shouted:

"Go on and talk to him. Don't hold things up around here." When he wouldn't go, she raised her voice again: "Go on!"

"I did, I talked to him, but did he listen? Just now if it hadn't been for the neighbor, Mr. Zhang, I might have been beaten up. As if I hadn't talked to him...." Wang Sheng himself was hopping mad.

"If you won't go, tell the cook to go." Mrs. Bai turned to call through a back window to the cook. Standing in the courtyard plucking a chicken, the cook replied with a smile.

"I'm even worse at talking, Ma'am. If Wang there couldn't talk him round, I sure couldn't, I'd be wasting time."

"You mean you two are sticking together. What kind of favors do you get from the cab company that you take his side like this?" Yelling this way did give Mrs. Bai some relief from her recent frustration but further relief was needed.

She stepped into the rear courtyard and called, "Husband, come take a look at these two gentlemen, they simply won't take orders. Suppose you come and handle it. I simply can't run the house any more with these lofty gentlemen around. You hired both of them, suppose you give them orders!"

The husband's curt response was to send Wang Sheng out with some change, thus averting the end of the world.

After she heard the cab drive away, Mrs. Zhou graciously took her leave, joined by Miss Wang. Mrs. Bai quickly saw them out, returned to the house where her husband, reclining on the chaise longue, was reading in total silence and frowning slightly as if he were preoccupied. This expression fed her anxiety but, embarrassed to come right out with it, she seized on the latest incident.

"Honestly," she said, "I might as well let you know, if I've told you once I've told you a thousand times, till I'm blue in the face, and you still won't believe me, that each day this cook and this servant work here is a year off my life. If I put up with any more of it I'll have a heart attack!"

Brow still furrowed, her husband kept reading, pretending to ignore her, so she launched into her speech. "Of course, with me as your old lady what if anger is the death of me? Fine, you remarry someone who suits your fancy; the pity of it is the four children...." Her voice choking, she sat down overwhelmed by her grievances and began to weep softly.

"The servants you don't like you can just dismiss, why all this beating around the bush?" Putting down his book, her husband sighed.

"All you do is read, your mind's on someone's...." 'Woman' was the word she dared not utter but she pretended she was choked by tears.

Her husband still staying nothing but picking up his book again, she went on, "All you do is go by the face; you hire this slow-witted cook and say he's honest; well, if he's honest he wouldn't buy a one pound eight ounce chicken and claim it's one pound nine; if he wasn't pocketing money, how could he afford black serge shoes? Wang Sheng is also something, a fifty-six cent pack of cigarettes he claims is fifty-eight. Don't just see the two-cent difference, two cents amounts to eight cash, enough to buy four rolls, four rolls are enough for a meal. Day before yesterday he obviously pocketed a solid dime on the tangerines...."

The wife just opening up the floodgates, the husband tossed his book aside and stopped her: "How about changing the subject? Don't you get sick of harping on them?"

These words too evoked the latest gossip, depressing the wife. She finally said, "What can I talk about if not this, after all I'm no good at that sort of *dolce vita* talk, besides, I don't think much of those..."

Only she herself heard the rest of it.

Translated by Donald Holoch

NOTE

* The Chinese denominations *fen, mao,* and *kuai* are translated as cent, dime, and dollar, respectively. During this period money consisted of a debased copper coinage, round with a square hole in the center for stringing. A string of cash was normally 100 coins.

Henriqueta Lisboa   *Brazil, 1904–1985*

Henriqueta Lisboa, a native of Lambari, in the state of Minas Gerais, was acclaimed as one of Brazil's leading writers and intellectuals. She was unquestionably the country's most celebrated poet, a fact attested to by several prizes accorded to her over a fifty-year career. In 1984, she won the coveted Machado de Assis Award, conferred by the Brazilian Academy, which had honored Lisboa once before. In recognition of her better than thirty volumes of poetry, essays, monographic studies, translations, and anthologies of children's literature, the Minas Gerais State Academy of Letters welcomed her as its first woman member. Lisboa's popularity abroad is evidenced by translations of her works into a number of languages. She is widely anthologized and studied.

Although Lisboa's verse (1929–1982) reflects all the spiritual anguish and a great many of the techniques that characterize Brazil's poetry, from symbolism to the 1920s avantgarde *modernismo*, in many respects it makes a contribution of its own. It reveals an individual possessing an extraordinary awareness of the dichotomy, complexity, and elusiveness of life. The aesthetic implications of her worldview are most readily perceived in her many varied themes. Herein womanhood and Minas Gerais tradition, solitude and universal solidarity, are perfectly consonant, as are happy childhood recollections and terrified reflections on death. However, one motif stands out above all others, as it runs throughout her poetry: mysticism, allowing the poet to look underneath the surface of things—the credo espoused in the title poem of one of her collections, *Além da imagem* (Beyond Image, 1963) from which "Fruitescence" was taken—and to probe into the essence of those things. Thus her compositions are marked by an apparent concern with the external configuration of the world: nature, history, philosophy, humanitarianism, God, and the self. Eventually, the reader becomes aware that such themes, whose presence is justifiable on purely aesthetic grounds, also transcend conventional reality and are transmuted into immanent elements of a quest for eternal truth. It may be said that Lisboa's deceptively simple, crystal clear language, used ostensibly to touch upon the obvious and the human, harbors a complex symbolic imagery whose intent is to delve into the invisible, the indescribable, and the unspeakable. "Experience" is from the collection *Prisioneira da noite* (Prisoner of Night, 1939).

Carmelo Virgillo

EXPERIENCE
Experiência

Night and darkness, darkness and night
(but life is present, life is present).
Night blinds your eyes,
feet slip—how wretched!

Your soul is gone, the night is dark,
your flesh is weak, your body's falling.

In darkness, though, your hand gropes
seeking the lamp, lifting it high,
and there is light, pure,
over your fallen body.

Perhaps, perhaps tomorrow,
some other pilgrim your straying
steps will follow.

And the glow atop the marsh
will set you back on course
toward that once lost future.

Translated by Carmelo Virgillo

FRUITESCENCE
Frutescência

In solitude fruit
ripens snatched from her branch
before the sun could rise.
Before the winds could lull her
in the rustling of the grove.
Before the moon could visit her
from her high and quiet domains.
Before the rains could touch
her tenuous skin at will.
Before the bird could taste
the juice of her palpitating
sap in their first embrace.

In solitude fruit is tested
her sourness squeezed out.

But all along her essence
now without root, trunk or stem
her password miraculously endures.

Then in darkness she divines
the sun who transfigures her into sun
with soft, slow dabs.
And hears the secret of those woods
where the winds fell still.
And dreams of invisible dewdrops
next to her sun-scorched skin.
And conceives the image of the moon
within her own whiteness.
And accepts the bird that has no resting place
who teaches her, with his sweetness, to be
even sweeter.

Translated by Carmelo Virgillo

Melpo Axióti   *Greece, 1905–1973*

Melpo Axióti was born in Athens in 1905, of a wealthy family from Mykonos. Her parents' marriage was a failure, and this doubtless contributed to the chilly atmosphere of what seems to have been a loveless household. She was brought up by her father after her mother deserted them, and the figure of a lonely and frightened small girl, growing up in an unfeeling, upper-class environment, is a frequent motif in her fiction. Between the ages of 13 and 17 she was educated at the Ursaline convent on Tinos, which accounts for her fluent command of French and her interest in French literature—she was later to translate both from Greek into French (folksongs, and poems by Yiannópoulos and Astéris) and from French into Greek (e.g., works by Radiguet and Ionesco). On leaving school she went back to her family island of Mykonos, but after an unsuccessful, though apparently perfectly amiable, four-year marriage to one of her former teachers, she settled in Athens in 1930, dabbled in various unsuccessful jobs (including studying technical drawing), and began writing.

Her attraction to cultural activities was perhaps influenced by her family background. Her father, Giorgos, had studied music in Italy, founded the Piraeus Conservatory, and composed songs and orchestral works. He also founded the artistic and literary review *Kritiki* in 1903, and himself wrote articles on cultural topics. Melpo Axióti was also influenced by her close friendship with her cousin, the music critic Loukia Photopoulou, who was able to introduce her into Modernist literary circles, where she met writers such as Engonopoulos, Kavvadias, Seferis, and Theotokas, and critics such as Malanos and Kleon Paraschos.

Axióti's career began with two short stories in the short-lived periodical *Mykoniatiká Chroniká* (Chronicles of Mykonos), in 1933–1934, but what made her name was her first novel, *Dýskoles Nýchtes* (Difficult Nights), written in 1937, published in 1938, and awarded first prize by the Gynaikeios Syllogos Grammaton kai Technon (Women's Association of Letters and Arts) in 1939. *Dýskoles Nýchtes* became the subject of controversy, being greeted with both critical acclaim and ridicule. To what can be seen as her first period of writing also belong the long poems *Sýmptose* (Coincidence, 1939), and the short novel *Thélete na chorépsome María?* (Shall We Dance Maria?, 1940).

As she was just becoming acquainted with the Modernists, Melpo Axióti began to be involved in left-wing politics, and in 1936 joined the KKE (the Greek Communist Party). During the Occupation and its aftermath she worked for EAM (the left-wing Resistance movement), in particular contributing to the underground press. Her most important contributions at this period, which marks the beginning of the second or "committed" phase of her writing, were the four *Chroniká* (Chronicles) that appeared in 1945: *Apándisi se 5 erotímata,* (Reply to 5 questions), *Protomayiés 1886–1945* (Maydays 1886–1945), *I Ellenídes phrouroí tes Elládas* (Greek Women, Guardians of Greece), and *Athena 1941–45* (Athens 1941–45). This non-fiction work was followed by a series of ten short stories based on similar material, and the novel *Eíkostos eónas* (Twentieth Century, 1949), excerpted in this collection, a poem to the Greek women who valiantly resisted fascism.

Early in 1947 Axióti found herself obliged to go into exile in France, where she continued her political activity through articles in *Humanité and Les lettres françaises*, and other public pronouncements. She became acquainted with the leading members of the French intellectual Left, including Louis Aragon, Elsa Triolet, and Paul Eluard (Eluard adapted her translations of Yannópoulos and Astéris; Aragon wrote the preface to the French translation of *Eíkostos eiónas*). But in 1950, as the result of pressure brought to bear on the French government by the new Greek government, she was expelled, along with other self-exiled intellectuals, to East Germany. Her creative work of this period is slight—a volume of stories *Sýntrophoi kaliméra* (Good Morning Comrades, 1953), a critical essay *Mia katagraphé stin periochí tis logotechnías* (Signing Up for Literature, 1955) a one-act play for children and a translation of Hans Christian Andersen's fairy tales—but we still find some of the same concern as in *Eíkostos eónas* for blending political commitment with poetic sensibility.

The start of the third phase of Axióti's creative life coincided with her second period of residence in East Berlin, from 1958 to 1964, when she was given a job teaching Modern Greek language and literature in the Classical Institute of the Humboldt University. She acquired a greater freedom to travel, including four much-valued trips to Italy, which brought her into contact with other writers. Through the publication of her second long poem, *Kontrabándo* (Contraband) in 1959 she renewed her acquaintance with Yiannis Ritsos, who devoted himself to overseeing the publication of her works from 1959 to 1964. Among other things, Axióti collaborated with Dimitris Chatzis on a German anthology of Modern Greek short stories; published a cycle of four poems, *Thalassiná* (Things of the Sea); wrote a critical article "I poíisi kai oi peripéteies tis" (Poetry and Its Adventures) in *Epitheórisi Téchnis* (Art Review, the progressive arts magazine in Greece); and began the translation of stories and plays by Chekov. One of the major works of this period, which she classified as a "diegesi" (in French, *recit*), *To spíti mou*, (My House), written in 1959, was not in fact published until 1965.

In 1964 she was finally allowed to return to Greece. Her return marked the beginning of a final creative burst, notably in the form of articles for *Epitheórisi Téchnis* and more translations. Her return also signalled that it was safe to republish her early works in Greece: *Dýskoles Nýchtes* was reissued in 1964, *Eíkostos eónas* in 1966, and *Thélete na Chorépsome María?* in 1967. Her last, work of fiction, the short novel *I Kadmó* (Cadmo), came out in 1972. She died in 1973. Her complete works have now been republished in nine volumes by the publishing house Kedros.

Christopher Robinson

from TWENTIETH CENTURY
Eikostos eónas

Thirty women were walking around, putting a few bits of clothing on the ground.

"I'm leaving my sweater. If anyone survives, will they take it to my mother for me?" The echo could be heard in the neighborhood beyond.

"I call on our friends to carry on our work unflinchingly in our places," said a slip of a girl in a thin, high voice.

"That's the right spirit, comrade," said Polyxena beside her.

"Don't call me comrade. I'm not. You know I don't like political parties. I've never wanted anything to do with them."

"Today's the day you're going to die," said Polyxena. "Aren't you ready?"

"Yes," said the girl, "I'm ready."

"Well, stupid, that's what I meant by calling you comrade. Comrades in death..."

The girl stared at her, at a loss for words. Some of the others were in tears.

"Don't cry for us, those of you who are left behind," said Polyxena. "It isn't just us. Think of China, Southeast Asia, Czechoslovakia. Weep for all those everywhere who are going to their death every day."

Who would stay...who would go....

There was no time for anything else. The guards pushed them out into courtyard.

It was a bright day in May.

They walked like soldiers. Other women joined them from the cells. Their numbers swelled.

As Polyxena walked, her mind was ticking over like a well-wound watch. She was seeing the wall for the last time. Every stone meant death; every inch meant blood.

There, that's where the poor idiot fell. He used to go around calling out "Mercy! Mercy!" One morning Fischer had emptied his pistol into his temple. Polyxena looked at the stain on the stone. She kept walking.

They were forming ranks. The women were taking their places.

There, that's where they executed the syphilitics. "Anyone sick..." they said at roll-call. Twelve men came forward, thinking they would be saved, and there was a cook as well, thinking he would be saved, too. They took them forward a few steps and then cut them down from behind. From the women's room she was looking straight down on it. She saw convoys. Some coming, some going. Some men into the earth, others to the crematoria, they were heading for Europe, the Haidari prison emptied and filled again straight away, like a gypsy's bellows.

The day before yesterday had been the First of May. The bloody First.

There, that's where the disabled soldiers were standing before they left. I used to wheel them around, I washed their feet, they were my children, thought Polyxena. "Put the radio on for us," they used to call, "quick, fetch me my crutches from the carpenter's." They rounded them up in November, two thousand of them.

They didn't have time to bring their crutches with them: for months they had to drag themselves along the ground on their backsides to go and relieve themselves....

"What's put the wind up you?" they asked the soldiers. "Are you scared of our crutches? Is that why you've brought us in?"

"And when they come back short of a leg, they'll come begging for a drachma and *I* shan't give them one!" Yes, she could remember the unknown man who had said that to her. Later they took them out a few at a time and shot them. The last lot went the day before yesterday. The First of May.

A phalanx of naked men going to their deaths. The roll had stopped at number 200. "Let me get a bit of warmth from the sun, it's the first time I've seen it in eight years. I'm from Akronauplion," someone had been heard to say. From up in the women's room they could see them capering and singing. And Death and the Resistance had made no exceptions that day, not even for a man who hadn't seen daylight for eight years.

Now the roll-call was beginning. Everyone held their breath. First, those about to die. Haidari was empty. The men were still asleep. The sun had not yet risen. It was damp. The prison van with its great black cage was there. In the road. In front of the bars. The women heard their names. They called them out. A man with a foreign accent called them out. You could hardly recognize your own name.

The third was Maria. Polyxena was the fourth. She had never been first in anything in her whole life, she knew that from her childhood. They took a few steps forward. Steps which separated them from the others. Steps which took them away from life, took them elsewhere.

Phroso and her daughter went into the cage together. The girl with the thin, high voice went in with her sister. In the van Fifi met her husband. Soula found Lefteri, who had lost both his feet: the two of them had been arrested at her house.

They all set off together.

On the road they were traveling spring was dancing merrily. It was now completely light. One of the men wrote something on a little card, and as they went along, threw it out of the back of the van. The wind tossed it right up, then blew it back to the ground. They saw an old woman, far, far behind them, stoop down and pick it up. "Pavlos Karatzas" it said, "exiled since 1936, on his way to execution."

Since 1936. Now it was 1944.

They all took courage from his action. One of the girls threw her engagement ring. It was all she had. Another tore a strip off her dress and threw it. The tokens of their identity danced on the Maytime earth.

The van drove on, through suburbs with people going to and fro. "Maria," said Polyxena, "Maria, do you remember? 'Little old men and shoe-shine boys, little kids with little toys...' That's what we are dying for. That was Greece. Now you know...."

They arrived at the cypresses. There was less light there. They reached the field, and there they had to get out. They were led forward to the sacrificial altar. Then they saw the wall in front of them.

When I was a kid I wanted to be a man. I was jealous of Fifino, thought Polyxena. Now I'm dying a man's death.

The putrid smell from the trench filled her lungs. It was alien. Brains and blood had been squeezed out there. And now her smell would mingle with the rest. The May sun would drink her in, too, and they would all be indistinguishable from each other.

"Maria, do you remember," Polyxena said again," "'That's the stink of rich men's shit!' You taught me that first; I've never forgotten it. But here we're all the same, rich and poor...I used to dream of it."

Foreign men killed Polyxena, men brought from the cold north, who never in their lives had children, or a wife to touch their hair when they were sad. But when she was dead it was her own kind, local moles, who raised her up.

When the group moved forward, she moved with them, and they went to the wall, and stood like books on a shelf in front of the firing squad. Half-naked as she was she could see the mole she had always had on her breast. Emilios was the first to touch her. Death was the last. The crossfire from two huge machine-guns on steel legs pierced her through and through. She flew into the air and was tossed to heaven like a dead dove. On the hills of Kaisariani the trumpet cried "Revenge!" In the valley, somewhere far away, a bell rang and called the people together. Between a church and a chemist's shop a girl called Polyxena once came into the world. And now, she made her exit.

Translated by Christopher Robinson

Tess Slesinger   *US, 1905–1945*

Born on July 16, 1905, in New York City, dead a mere thirty-nine years later in Los Angeles, Tess Slesinger was the daughter of a mediocre businessman and an exceptional mother. An immigrant, Anthony Slesinger was pressured into the garment business by his father-in-law, while, given the roles assigned to women during the first half of this century, Augusta Singer Slesinger was free to develop her considerable talents and become a social-welfare worker, an administrator, a founder of the famous New School for Social Research, and a lay analyst. Despite the couple's growing incompatibility, their marriage ended only after their fiftieth wedding anniversary.

Meanwhile, their daughter grew up in an unusually progressive, highly assimilated middle-class environment; encouraged to become educated and to develop a career, Slesinger attended the Ethical Culture School, then Swarthmore College, before graduating in 1927 from Columbia University's School of Journalism. Her marriage the following year to Herbert Solow gained her entry to a left-wing, largely Jewish coterie of intellectuals who ultimately came to be known as the New York literary left, of which she was at once both participant and observer. In the early 1930s she developed her theme, the conflict between the public and the private, the political and the sexual.

In 1934 Slesinger divorced her husband; two years later she published *The Unpossessed*, a satiric look at the sexual and other games of politicized intellectuals. Subsequently reprinted in 1966 (with an afterword by a member of her circle, Lionel Trilling) and again in 1984; when it first appeared the book was reviewed disparagingly by the left-wing press, highly praised by the establishment press, and well-received by the public. A year later, Slesinger released a collection of short stories, *Time, the Present*, recently reprinted as *On Being Told That Her Second Husband Has Taken His First Lover* (1971), including the now-famous 1935 prize-winning story "A Life in the Day of A Writer," which turns on the male narrator's analogy of writing and sexual conquest. The story reprinted here is taken from this collection. The only other piece of note is an autobiographical essay Slesinger published in *Vanity Fair*, "Memoirs of An Ex-Flapper" (1934). Soon after, Slesinger moved to Hollywood: like many leftist writers of her generation, she saw film as a means of reaching and transforming an audience beyond the scope of the written word.

In Hollywood Slesinger wrote screenplays, some in collaboration with her second husband, the producer Frank Davis, including those for Pearl Buck's *The Good Earth* (1937), the proto-feminist film *Dance, Girls, Dance* (1940), and Betty Smith's *A Tree Grows in Brooklyn* (1945). She had a child. She participated in many political causes, including the struggle to establish the Screen Writers Guild. In 1945, Slesinger died of cancer, leaving behind the unfinished manuscript for a projected novel about Hollywood.

One can only mourn the loss of such a talent: were it not for her limited and relatively youthful production, she would undoubtedly rank as a major American artist. As Janet Sharistanian has suggested, Slesinger managed to combine and maintain in rare balance political awareness that was both social and individual with a fidelity to her craft. Both her artistry and her feminist perspective seemed to provide her with the necessary objectivity to create critical fiction. Her accomplishment can be understood in terms of the remarkable synthesis she performed, wedding the experimental techniques of literary modernism—stream of consciousness, and shifting points of view especially—to the political subject matter of realism and naturalism.

THE TIMES SO UNSETTLED ARE[1]

The little Austrian girl Mariedel, sitting numbly in her deck-chair (they were passing Ellis Island now and soon would dock), had not cried for twenty years, since she was ten. Then they had brought home the body of her brother, killed on the Italian front, and Mariedel and her mother had wept unceasingly for three days. Her mother had virtually never stopped; meals and sleep and occasional bursts of gayety were merely interludes for Mariedel's mother, for her real life had been given over for almost twenty years to weeping. But Mariedel had never had a tear again—not for her father, horribly wounded toward the end of the War, nor for her second brother dead of some mysterious disease in the trenches; not even for her sweetheart Heinrich who had died two months ago, shot down on the parapets of the Karl Marx Workers' Home which he had always predicted would some day serve as barricades. Heinrich is dead, they said to her very gently—her weeping mother, her crippled father, her friends—Heinrich has been killed, Mariedel, don't you understand, don't you hear us? Yes, said Mariedel over and over again; I understand; Heinrich is dead—and I am going to America; the Amerikaners, Richard and die schöne[2] Mahli, they always asked us to come, but now Heinrich is dead and so I am going alone; excuse me, but I cannot weep. For she had cried herself out in 1914 and no tears were left for Heinrich, whom she loved the most.

What had died really for Mariedel was Vienna her beloved city. It was not the Vienna her parents had known, of course—all her life she heard them tell sadly of the music now withdrawn from the cafés, of the balls and excursions and military splendor that were gone forever. But that was not Mariedel's Vienna. Mariedel's Wien was a tortured little city with the bravest and saddest and oldest young people in the world. Night after night they sat in the cafés, Mariedel and Heinrich

and their contemporaries, and talked of Vienna's future, so bound up with their own—and most of them looked to Socialism as their parents had to God. Five of their number had killed themselves—one apparently for love, the others for vaguer reasons; yet no one was particularly shocked, reasons were not sought for long; they all understood, the rest of them, meeting again to drink coffee in the Herrenhof, that Karl or Mitzi or Hans had been pushed just so much farther than he or she could endure, and that at any moment it might happen to one of the surviving coffee-drinkers. The times are so unsettled, they said, explaining to themselves, and to the childish emotional Richard and Mahli from Amerika; and nodded much as their elders did, and went on drinking their coffee.

They had gone in, too, their little band, for resolutions to leave Vienna, to strike out for Berlin which they hated, or America which they feared. There things always seemed to go better; one could have a job that might lead somewhere; one might marry and raise children; one might take part in a government less deadlocked than their own—there might perhaps be a future more vital than drinking coffee in the same Café-Haus every night. But none of them ever left. And when the Amerikaners, die schöne Molly (who signed her letters 'Mahli' when she wrote to Mariedel, because that was Mariedel's way of saying it) and Richard, came and were taken into their midst for the brief and lovely month of their honeymoon, and begged them all to come to America and start life over again, they had all of them laughed and shrugged their shoulders and said "vielleicht"[3] and known very well that they would never leave Vienna. Richard and Mahli had laughed too, and said that when they came to celebrate their golden wedding, they would undoubtedly find their old friends in the same Café-Haus, at the same round table in the corner, the men with long white beards—all laughing and promising to come to America and ordering another cup of coffee: with Schlagobers[4] when they could afford it.

Richard and Mahli had been particular friends of Heinrich and Mariedel, even though Heinrich was never gay and always distrustful of strangers, especially tourists, especially Americans, of anyone who was not a Socialist, in short. But they were so warming, Richard and Mahli, so happy together, and so much in love that everybody fell in love with the pair of them—just as they fell in love with everyone they met and the whole little city of Vienna, which they never tired of comparing with their own New York. They talked German so badly, especially Mahli, and so eagerly—it was so funny to hear them addressing each other as "sie" because they could not learn the ramifications of the personal pronoun. And they looked so hopelessly, so ridiculously American—Mahli like a tall American chorus girl in the pink and blue peasant Dierndel which she wore about their rooms, with her boyish hair-cut and her tiny American breasts which scarcely bulged above the apron; and Richard, attempting on Sundays to resemble his Viennese comrades on their Ausflüge,[5] continued to look like a cartoon of an American in his baggy knickers and shoes with saddles, and his horn-rimmed glasses through which his eyes looked so straight and pleasantly clear. The most disillusioned of their little band had fallen in love with these Americans, even Heinrich, bitten with distrust and worse (for Heinrich had stopped believing in God more suddenly than was good for him), but even Heinrich had let the Americans laugh at him and tease him, and sometimes he was almost able to joke back, just like Mariedel.

The Americans had chosen Heinrich and Mariedel for their particular friends because they saw that they too were in love. But Mariedel knew that theirs was a different sort of love; they had been brought up, Mariedel and Heinrich, in too much poverty and change, and their love was more of a refuge than a source of gayety to them, it was a necessity as bitter as the need for bread. They loved each other in the way that sole survivors on a ship must love—and they did not doubt each other, but they doubted themselves and everything about them. For in a shipwreck such as theirs, where brothers turned on brothers and fathers against their sons, how could they be sure even of their love enduring? And Heinrich was so bitter that he even doubted love—in his mind, that is; in his bitter mind; for his heart (which Heinrich believed as poor a word as God) had really never failed her. No, Heinrich, snatched from the University and forced to earn a living for his widowed mother and his sisters, who hated him for supporting them and hated him for being a Socialist, starving and living in wretched, disease-ridden quarters, could not allow himself to be happy in the "unsettled times." He could enjoy nothing that was not whole and lasting, could trust nothing that was not severe.

He had been an ardent Socialist; but when the Socialists took over Vienna, had Heinrich permitted himself to be really happy? to rejoice? Not for long. There were his Socialists, doing all the things he had wanted them to do; they taxed the rich; they housed the poor—but Heinrich was never satisfied: they must tax the rich ever harder, they must house the poor better and faster, they must carry on the fight in the country outside Vienna, or Heinrich predicted their downfall. Mariedel and Heinrich would wander arm in arm through the fine courts of the Workers' Houses, where the poor were quickly learning the cleanliness and healthful habits of the rich, they would look into the community stores lining the streets below, they would visit the charming practical apartments where sunlight and plenty of heat entered every room—and Mariedel had felt happy, happy as she had been in her childhood before the War, when everything was good and gay and plentiful. Look, Heinrich, look at the little children wading in the community fountain—two months ago they would not have known what it is to have a bath. Look, Heinrich, the mothers, so proud of their new homes, their clean children; how well they care for the gardens, they who a short time before saw only a potted flower now and then. Look, Heinrich, at the new building going up over the hill, how fast it rises, the workmen love what they are building, the bricks fly into place as though they loved it too. Everyone, everything, working together, Heinrich, for the poor, at last, for the majority, the real people, look, Heinrich, is it not beautiful and gay? But the lean look never went from Heinrich's eyes, not altogether; yes, there would be pride in them as he saw how swiftly building after building mounted the old streets, how each house was better than the last—but he would run his hand along the parapets above the courtyards where the children played: "Some day these all will be barricades, Mariedel, it cannot be done through peace, we must have more bloodshed, Mariedel, before the rich will permit such houses to stand for the poor." His eyes would sweep the dingy sections of old Vienna, spread below them. "All that must be wiped out and built over, Mariedel, work must be done faster, we must be stronger, more inexorable, like the Communists—too many of our Socialists are dreamers, and these houses, they are so few, Mariedel, they are built on dreams instead of power." He would not take transient happiness; in the same way he would not really take her love. Perhaps he was waiting till the world too should be wiped out and built over, a fit thing to house their love.

"But you poor silly children," the happy Mahli had cried, out of her own joy and love; "you are in love, you live together when you can, why don't you get married and do it properly?" Mariedel and Heinrich laughed and shrugged their shoulders; naturally Mariedel would have married Heinrich any time he said, but in her heart she knew it was wrong as long as either of them had a reservation. She too longed for a whole country that could live and eat in peace and security, a world which could

wipe out the memory of a brother brought home dead from the Italian front and causing a little sister to shed the last of her tears. "Oh, Mahli," she had said often in her faulty English, "the times here so unsettled are." And Richard and Mahli had laughed at her English and hugged each other and hugged Mariedel and Heinrich, and sung over and over again, "Oh Mahli, the times so unsettled are."

"But you ought to come back with us!" Richard and Mahli had cried together. "We'll finds jobs for you somehow, Richard, your father, darrling—you could live right next door to us, we'd find them a place, wouldn't we, darrling—you bet we would, beloved—and then you could be married and live the way we do, the way you ought to. Vienna is lovely for a honeymoon (thank you, Richard darrling) but for young people starting out it's dead from the neck down isn't it, beloved? Of course it is, darrling. So do come back with us," they cried together, "Mariedel and Heinrich, won't you, couldn't you really now?"

Mariedel had smiled softly across the table to Heinrich. To tell him that if he went to America of course she would come too; to tell him that if he stayed behind in Vienna and spent the rest of his life fighting and being underfed, she would stay with him anyway; to tell him that she loved him. Heinrich had always the same answer to make in his precise, cold, studied English—but smiling, for he loved these Americans and their contentment was infectious: "If Vienna is dead, then Mariedel and I are dead too, Vienna is our city. We will live with it or die with it. If we do not marry, it is because we do not believe in marriage; marriage does not stop a husband from being killed in war or revolution, it does not stop a wife from having too little to feed her children, it does not even ensure love. Yes, we would like to be married, if it would mean that we could live as we believe people should. But, for us in Vienna, we must fight and keep on fighting..." And Mariedel, loving him and aching for him, painfully wishing to be loyal and to be thought loyal in the eyes of the

Americans, would look across at Mahli and try to make her understand by making her laugh: "With us, it is so different, Mahli—the times so unsettled are."

In the end, of course, everything that Heinrich said was proven right. The Socialists had not lasted, their dreams had been put down by bloodshed, bloodshed in which Heinrich himself, who loved peace and wanted peace more than anything in life, more even perhaps than he wanted Mariedel, in whom he sought it, had voluntarily taken part. And he was right too, it was as well to be still young and to lose one's life-long lover as it would have been to lose a husband; however it was, Mariedel, on hearing her father and her mother and all her friends murmur gently, Mariedel, Heinrich has been killed, can't you understand?—Mariedel could not weep. It was as if she had wept for the death of Heinrich almost twenty years before, when she wept for the death of her brother. The old folks went on weeping when once they got started—Mariedel's mother had never left off again; but Mariedel was still of that younger stock, that had shed their last tears with their first, and Mariedel could not weep, she must go on living somehow. Almost at once the memory of Mahli and Richard had come back to her like a little island of safety in the middle of all the chaos. She would go to America. They would revive that little month in which she and Heinrich had been so nearly happy with their American friends; and in any case, Mariedel would find something to shock her from this numbness. And so she had written to Mahli, saying that Heinrich was dead; saying to forgive her for not writing in nearly three years but that the times so *very* unsettled had been that there had seemed somehow little use; and that now Mariedel would like to come along to America—since the Socialists were finished, and many of her friends now dead or scattered, and Wien, as Heinrich had prophesied, as the lieber[6] Richard had said too, was dead as well. Mahli's cablegram had been prompt, the first thing after Heinrich's death that meant

anything to Mariedel: "Come soon as you can arrange to sorry about Heinrich visit me as long as you like love Mahli." She had even remembered to sign her name "Mahli!"

So it was all over with Heinrich and Vienna and the Socialists, thought Mariedel, sitting numbly in her steamer-chair when they told her they would be landing in thirty minutes now. She thought she would never go back, unless it were to die. And she remembered that last sight of the crumbling Workers' Home—which would now, her old father said, be turned over to the rich to do anything with they liked, while the poor would be thrown out on the streets again—where Heinrich had met his death. Broken glass and legs of furniture lay scattered on the ramparts; there were bloodstains on the parapets which Heinrich had rightfully seen as barricades. She had stood there, as numb as she was now in her steamer-chair, with twenty-years-old tears frozen in her throat. They had all hoped that the sight of the ruined Home where Heinrich had died would make Mariedel weep again; they wanted her to weep, to weep as she had when she was a child, because they thought that was nature's way of healing. Mariedel had wanted to weep too. But she could only stand there, wondering if Heinrich had been right— that the Socialists should have trained an army and fought with the weapons of their enemies, even though their end was peace; and wondering too if Heinrich had been right about that other thing that he always so passionately declared, that there was no God, that the sooner people knew it the better it would be for them.

For Heinrich, of course, with all the unhappy youths of his age, had been a violent atheist. Mariedel herself never went to church, not since they had been to the funeral of her second brother; and she knew that her mother went only to find another place in which to weep and remember, and weep more hotly. No, Mariedel did not believe in any sort of church-God; and yet she never brought herself to curse the thought, as Heinrich had. It was as if Heinrich, expecting things from some King of Kings, turned his disappointment to denial that that King had ever existed. Mariedel expected very little, except perhaps Heinrich's love—and perhaps that was it, for her, perhaps that was why in the inner parts of her brain, or her heart (which Heinrich never let her talk about, because it sounded synonymous with God) she nevertheless held some sort of belief in something. If it had been Mariedel who had been killed, she felt now, instead of Heinrich, then Heinrich would have seen in her death still further proof that there was no God; but Mariedel, not even able to weep for Heinrich, knew that there had been *something* between them, which no chemical could account for and no revolution wipe out—something in their hearts which not even Heinrich's death could end. She had it still, she had his love for her and her love for him, and sitting there in her deck-chair, not speaking to a soul on board, remembering numbly how her city and her lover and all that they had stood for were dead, she still could not say there was no God, she still felt that something went on which outwitted death and outlasted life ...And perhaps it was this that she was really going to America for, to find it again in the lives of Richard and Mahli and keep it somehow vicariously lighted in herself through them.

Now the great city of New York was in her sight for the first time, and again she thought that there must be something, *something*, beyond greed and restlessness, which led people to building up great towns and preparing for so much life. The city looked to her like a city of closely packed cathedrals, and she imagined that the streets must run like dark little aisles at their feet. And this was where Mahli and Richard belonged, probably they lived back in the heart of the magnificence somewhere, out of sight of the sea and the dividing rivers, protected forever by these looming towers. Heinrich's words about the barricades came into her mind for a moment, as she stood with her hand on the rail, and she thought perhaps some day all those many windows might be crenelles, the buildings

fortresses. Perhaps she was slightly dizzy, as the boat ceased motion. For the buildings swayed a bit before her eyes, and for a moment looked less like cathedrals than like spears, like bayonets, marching in line over the heads of dead and living soldiers...

"Mariedel, Mariedel!" Richard and Mahli, her dear Americans, were kissing her one moment and lightly weeping the next—they were unchanged in these seven years, Richard with his mild steady glare through his horn-rimmed spectacles, and Molly, tall and American as ever, with a gentle fringed bang to her eyebrows now, and her bright mouth painted redder than before, and her wonderful chic clothing that made her look like a mannequin. Mariedel stood dazed, allowing herself to be kissed and wept over—how easily happy people wept, either for joy or for sorrow!—and then stood with her hand through Mahli's while Richard did wonderful American things to find and get rid of her luggage. "This is a real reunion," said Richard, coming back, and speaking unconsciously a little louder to Mariedel as he always had, as Americans were always doing, as though foreigners must be slightly deaf, "a real reunion, and we ought to celebrate—in a real American Café-Haus, Mariedel?"

"In the Childs, in the Childs," said Mariedel eagerly remembering, "where you said you would some day show Heinrich and me, the very table where you sat and figured on paper napkins how you could marry and you forgot to leave out for the laundry, do you not remember, Richard and Mahli?"

"But—" began Mahli. They hesitated a bit, those dear Americans of hers, and Mariedel felt she guessed the reason. "No, no, you think I am sad, that it will make me sad, because of Heinrich, but it will make me gay—it is what I have come to America for," she begged them; "I want to see where Richard told Mahli, and Mahli told Richard, and about the laundry, and the lady making jack-flaps in the window—"

"Flapjacks, you darling," said Mahli, hugging Mariedel again. And Richard said, "A real reunion, Molly, we might as well do it up brown," and Mariedel felt again their delicacy, their shyness with each other in her presence, because they didn't want to hurt her. She must explain it to them, how she had come all the way across an ocean to see them with each other. Richard said again. "What do you say, Molly?" and Molly, taking Mariedel's arm, cried, "Off for the reunion in Vienna!" So then everything was beginning to be all right again, and they found a taxi and Richard said solemnly to the driver, "Childs, on Fifth Avenue, where the best paper napkins are," and Mariedel sat between them holding both their hands and chattering briskly to put them at their ease about her and looking out at the strange streets and feeling thankful to God that she was here with them.

They came into the big clean restaurant, Mariedel dancing on her sea-legs, and because it was late afternoon it was fairly empty, and Richard and Mahli were able to find the same table in a corner that they had sat at years ago. "It is a reunion, a reunion," Richard kept saying, with his steady clear American eyes on his Molly—and Molly was beginning to look at him, and Mariedel felt happy that her Americans were remembering things and perfectly happy to be left out for the moment. "Only I am going to have a cocktail this time," said Mahli gayly, "just think, Mariedel, in those days one could not drink cocktails except in practically cellars, and now, right here in Childs . . ." "I wish you would take just butter-cakes and coffee," said Mahli's Richard softly, "then it would be a real reunion . . ." "Reunion, reunion, who's got the reunion," said Mahli merrily; and Mariedel knew it was an American joke of some kind and laughed in order to be one of them, and then saw that neither of them was laughing as Mahli turned to the waitress and repeated firmly, "Yes, a Manhattan, please."

"Tell us, Mariedel," said Richard gently, "about your poor Heinrich, how terrible it must have been for you."

"No, no," cried Mariedel, "I do not want to talk about Heinrich, I want to talk about Richard and Mahli, I want to hear again how you say Darrling to each other, and then there was something Richard used to say—"

"Oh, don't talk about *us*," cried Mahli, tipping her little velvet beret deeper over the fringe, "we want to hear all about Vienna, so terribly sad, awful about those beautiful houses and everything—"

"But I do not want to talk about all that," Mariedel explained to her Americans, "I want, I have come such a long way, just to see two people happy once more. Do you see, I have remembered so much, it gives me only joy to see you two happy, just as in Wien seven years ago . . . Always Darrling this and Darrling that—and that other word, Richard used to say—"

"I think I will have a cocktail too," said Richard suddenly. "How are the Manhattans, M—Beloved?"

"That is it, that is it—Beloved!" cried Mariedel, clapping her hands joyfully. "Ah, now it is like the old days! Heinrich and Mariedel, Richard and Mahli . . ."

"The Manhattans are swell, Darrling," said Mahli quietly. "Here's to you, Beloved," said Richard, lifting his little glass and staring at her through his spectacles. "To you, Mariedel darrling," said Mahli, but her eyes were returning Richard's gaze, and Mariedel could see that the two of them, Richard with his level eyes and Mahli with her red mouth made up for laughing were growing soft and misty again. Because this was where they had come Mariedel thought happily (refusing herself to drink anything but coffee), this was where they had come and figured on paper napkins how they could make do, with Richard's little salary. It was not much like the Herrenhof, where Heinrich and Mariedel had come every night and figured on the marble table tops how they could *not* make do—but it was lovely and clean and gay, and Richard was looking at his Mahli, not *quite* as Heinrich had ever been able to do, but surely as he had wanted to, as he had been meant to, if only so much misfortune, so much unsettledness...

But her Americans had put down their glasses and remembered her again. "And what do you think of our skyline, gnädiges Fräulein,"[7] Richard was trying to say.

"Ah, do you not remember her, Richard," cried Mariedel, waving his nonsense away, "do you not remember her as she must have looked that night? In a blue sweater, you said—?"

"Yes," said Richard, nodding gravely. "Yes, she was wearing a bright blue sweater and a bright blue hat, and it was summer and both of us had come out without our hats. She looked rather remarkably beautiful that night, if my memory doesn't play me tricks—"

"Though he couldn't have possibly seen me, Mariedel," said Mahli, "because he was so nervous he kept taking off his glasses and wiping them and doing tricks like making the cream stay on top of the coffee—"

"Whereas she, Mariedel," said Richard, "she was so calm and poised that she spilled most of hers all over that bright blue skirt."

"I did not, you fancy liar, it was you, you admitted it."

"Always a gentleman, Beloved."

"How silly we are, how boring to Mariedel," murmured Mahli.

"No, it is lovely," said Mariedel, "please, you have not come to the part about the laundry yet." She saw how the drinks were making them grow less shy before her, how each time they started speaking to her and ended by addressing one another as though they had no audience. "It was a terribly hot evening," she helped them out, "there was Donner und Blitzen," she prompted Richard...

"and she pretended to be frightened"

"and we went on drinking coffee even though it was so hot because we didn't want to ever go home and end that evening"

"we sat through three shifts of waitresses, Beloved"

"I must have journeyed to the Ladies' Room four times"

"and when we'd checked through telephone bills—and were going to save by using candles instead of electricity—"

"then suddenly we discovered about the laundry, Darrling"

"and Beloved do you remember I said something about how I wanted a dependable wife"

"and I was simply scared to death Darrling, I almost burst out crying, I thought you were going to tell me I wouldn't do or something."

There was a mild diminuendo in their sweet gay American *Tristan*, and Mariedel saw that they both had tears, these Americans, as volatile as children—even Mahli with her bright red lips not made up for crying at all.

"And there was that frightened little moment after we had both said yes to each other when we thought that we would never again have anything to talk about"

"Oh, it was terrible, Mariedel," said Mahli, wiping her eyes, "we sat there and were afraid to look at one another—"

"and then—" said Richard.

"and then luckily we both started laughing at the same moment and that saved the day, Darrling"

"we confessed to each other, Beloved, how scared to death we were"

"and then we weren't any more, because we knew that—"

"because we thought—"

They were silent for a moment and Mariedel sat poised and expectant.

"We thought we could always laugh together in the bad moments," said Mahli softly.

"We nearly always did, Beloved."

"Only of course there are some things, Darrling."

"Yes, there are some things, Molly."

There was a curious hiatus in their song now, coming, thought Mariedel, in the wrong place, just as they had been mounting to the allegro—and she sat perfectly still, feeling that perhaps they were going on with it silently, between themselves, in some other, private realms she mustn't enter. They looked at each other for a long time, and then looked away at the same moment. "It wasn't our fault," said Richard, setting down his glass. "No, it wasn't anybody's fault," said Molly, the tears rolling down past her bright red lips and falling into her empty cocktail. "Shall we have another drink, Molly?" said Richard, leaning across the table as though he were asking her something else. "No, I think not," said Molly, lifting her head and beginning to blink away her tears, "I think then nobody would be able to laugh at anything any more." And as Mariedel sat bewildered, out came Molly's purse and from it a little red stick, with which Molly painted on another laughing mouth. "Heavens above," cried Molly gaily, "what awful fools Mariedel must think Americans are—and here we sit and sit with all of the sights ahead of us still, we must think what we would like to do this evening, Mariedel darrling—"

"Shall I—" began Richard, taking out his watch but looking at Molly instead.

"Yes, please, Richard, I think it would be better," said Molly smiling brightly through her new red lips.

"I guess you're right," said Richard, and to Mariedel's surprise he cheerfully whipped his watch back into his pocket again and rose and tossed his paper napkin on the table. "It's been a beautiful reunion, Mariedel, hasn't it?"

"You—you are going?" said Mariedel, feeling suddenly frightened and lonely.

"Why yes, I have to be going," said Richard easily; "but I'll see you again, Mariedel, for sure."

"You have to *go*?" said Mariedel, feeling stupid and shy.

"Yes, he has to go, Mariedel," said Mahli gravely. "Goodbye, Darrling, it was a beautiful reunion."

"Goodbye, Beloved. Goodbye, Mariedel."

"But what is it," cried Mariedel, feeling as she had twenty years ago when her mother had opened the telegram from the War Office, black apprehensive despair and her limbs gone hollow, her heart beating like somebody else's heart—"what is it," she cried again, feeling

she was a stupid Austrian girl, that perhaps her life, the death of Heinrich, everything, had unhinged her more than she knew.

"It wasn't anybody's fault, Mariedel," said Molly, putting her too-red lips to the empty cocktail glass. "It wasn't her fault and it wasn't mine," said Richard, standing now and putting his hands on both their shoulders—almost impersonal he was, Mariedel thought, as though he wished to comfort them, to apologize, for something none of them could help. "It was just as you used to say, Mariedel," said Molly, smiling and grave—and Mariedel could hear Heinrich telling her bleakly, through his bitten lips, that there was no God, that marriage did not ensure food, or peace, or even love—"here in America too—the times unsettled are."

Suddenly Mariedel was crying, crying as she had when the first thing went out of her life, for now the last thing was going too—and Molly with her red mouth not made up for crying, was crying too, and comforting her, as Richard walked away.

NOTE

1. Briefly, the historical context of this story is as follows: Austria established a democratic republic and coalition government following World War I; given a loose federation, Vienna, the capital city, and an established center of culture, was elevated to the rank of a state, and from 1925 on, controlled by Socialists embarked on an ambitious program of working-class housing, including the famed Karl-Marx hof, health care, and adult education that gave "Red Vienna" its name and unique reputation in Europe. Beginning in 1927, the country was subject to internal civil strife, exacerbated by the Great Depression in 1929 and increasing support for the Nazis after 1932. *Anschluss*, or union, was accomplished when Nazi Germany annexed Austria in 1938, although the Allies chose to perpetuate a myth of Austrian independence.
2. The beautiful.
3. Perhaps.
4. Whipped cream.
5. Outings.
6. Beloved, dear.
7. Gracious miss.

Robin Hyde (Iris Guiver Wilkinson) *New Zealand, 1906–1939*

Robin Hyde could be regarded as a child of the British Empire. She was born in Capetown, South Africa, as Iris Guiver Wilkinson, of an English father and an Australian mother, and came to live in New Zealand as a baby. She began writing poetry as a child and achieved some recognition for it while still at school but, after the age of 17, Hyde was forced to put most of her energy into supporting herself as a journalist. Soon afterward she began to suffer from the ill health and related depression which were to dog her for the rest of her life. At the age of 20 she went across to Australia to bear an illegitimate child, who died soon after birth. A son was born in 1930.

After 1933, Hyde's poor health caused her to retire from full-time journalism, though she supported herself by writing fiction and nonfiction. Of her five novels, published between 1936 and 1938, the best known is the largely autobiographical *The Godwits Fly* (1938). Hyde's longing to travel overseas, recorded in this novel, was finally satisfied in 1938.

Headed for England, instead of taking the most direct route she went via China, where she attempted to earn money by reporting on the Sino-Japanese War, which was then raging. After spending two extremely trying months in a village captured by the Japanese, Hyde managed to escape. Her experiences in China produced several poems, including "The Deserted Village," as well as a book, *Dragon Rampant* (1939).

Hyde finally reached England toward the end of 1938 but was too ill with a tropical disease she caught in China to work as a journalist as she had planned. Worn out and depressed by illness and financial worries, she committed suicide in London, at the age of 33.

Though Hyde has been best known in New Zealand for her fiction, her poetry was what really mattered to her. Three collections appeared during her life, but her better poems, written in her last years, were not collected until the posthumous *Houses by the Sea* (1952), source of the two poems reprinted here. The recent appearance of a *Selected Poems* (1984) will, one hopes, bring further attention to Hyde's poetry.

Elizabeth Webby

THE LAST ONES

But the last black horse of all
Stood munching the green-bud wind,
And the last of the raupo[1] huts
Let down its light behind.
Sullen and shadow-clipped
He tugged at the evening star,
New-mown silvers swished like straw
Across the manuka.[2]

As for the hut, it said
No word but its meagre light,
Its people slept as the dead,
Bedded in Maori night.
"And there is the world's last door,
And the last world's horse," sang the wind,
"With little enough before,
And what you have seen behind."

NOTES

1. Maori for 'bulrush."
2. Maori for "the tea-tree, a small tree or shrub.

THE DESERTED VILLAGE

In the deserted village, sunken down
With a shrug of last weak old age, pulled back
                                      to earth,
All people are fled or killed. The cotton crop
                                      rots,
Not one mild house leans sideways, a man on
                                      crutches,
Not a sparrow earns from the naked floors,
Walls look, but cannot live without the folk
                                      they loved—
It would be a bad thing to awaken them.
Having broken the rice-bowl, seek not to fill it
                                      again.

The village temple, well built, with five smashed
                                      gods, ten whole ones,
Does not want prayers. Its last vain prayer
                                      bled up
When the women ran outside to be slain.
A temple must house its sparrows or fall asleep,
Therefore a long time, under his crown of snails,
The gilded Buddha demands to meditate.

No little flowering fires on the incense-strings
Startle Kwan-Yin, whom they dressed in satin—
Old women sewing beads like pearls in her
                                      hair.
This was a temple for the very poor ones:
Their gods were mud and lath: but artfully
Some village painter coloured them all.
Wooden dragons were carefully carved.
Finding in mangled wood one smiling childish
                                      tree,
Roses and bells not one foot high,
I set it back, at the feet of Kwan-Yin.
A woman's prayer-bag,
Having within her papers prayers, paid for in
                                      copper,
Seeing it torn, I gathered it up.
I shall often think, "The woman I did not see
Voiced here her dying wish.
But the gods dreamed on. So low her voice, so
                                      loud
The guns, all that death-night, who would stoop
                                      to hear?"

I. Grékova   (Yeléna Sergéevna Vénttsel)   *Russia/USSR, b. 1907*

Yeléna Sergéevna Vénttsel was born in 1907 in Reval (now Tallinn, Estonia). She holds a doctoral degree in mathematics and was Professor of Cybernetics at the Moscow Air Force Academy from 1955 to 1967. Her pseudonym, I. Grékova, comes from the Russian "igrek," which is an "x" in mathematical terminology meaning "the unknown." She started writing as an avocation at the age of 50, and her first novella, *Za prokhodnóy* (*Beyond the Entryway*, 1962) met with immediate success: she was acclaimed as one of the "new voices in Russian literature." This first story exhibits many of the elements that are characteristic of her work. The setting is a science laboratory, the narrator a woman who is a member of the research team. The narrator describes her coworkers, often with humor, adeptly reproducing their characteristic idiom, and within this context, discusses the relative merits of science and lyric poetry.

I. Grékova's second novella, *Dámskiy máster* (*The Ladies' Hairdresser*, 1963), from which the following selection is taken, is artistically one of her best. The heroine, Maríya Vladímirovna Kovalyóva, is a single parent of two teen-aged sons and head of a Moscow computer institute. Her desire to improve her physical appearance brings her to a beauty parlor and the young hairdresser, Vitály. Vitály is very creative and devoted to his profession, as well as to his touching if misguided efforts to "improve himself." Both of them are stifled in their professional ambitions by the forces of conformity within their respective work collectives.

The story "Na ispytániyakh," (During the Tests, 1967) is set in a Siberian settlement in 1952, where a group of ballistics experts conduct military experiments. Grékova's description of the shallowness, pettiness, suspicion and fear of these scientists caused her dismissal from the Air Force Academy.

Grékova's other works include the stories "Létom v górode" (Summer in the City, 1965), "Málenkiy Gárusov" (Little Garusov, 1970), "Khozyáyka gostínitsy" ("The Hotel Manager," 1976), the novel *Pod fonaryom* (Under the Streetlamp, 1966) and the collection of novellas published under the title of *Kafédra* (The Faculty, 1981). A novella from this work, (*Vdóviy parokhód* [*The Ship of Widows*], 1981), with its obvious pun on Ship of Fools, has recently been translated. A group of five widows living communally form a microcosm of Soviet society; as Priscilla Meyer suggests, their treatment of one another is reflective of the indignities of everyday life in the Soviet Union.

These women are Grékova's typical protagonists. Grékova is particularly good at reproducing the special idiom of each character, usually in well-structured dialogues, or internal monologues, although her male figures tend to be flat. Her style is introspective, though not lacking in humor. She invariably raises moral questions, but does not supply answers to them.

Dobrochna Dyrcz-Freeman

from THE LADIES' HAIRDRESSER
Dámskiy máster

"Who wants to be next?" called a young lad in a sharp voice. I started. Next to the line stood an eighteen-year-old kid with a tuft of hair sticking up on top of his head. He wasn't just thin, he was all angles: slim arms bare to the elbow, and a pale, wild face with fiery dark eyes. Like a young deer or a wolf cub.

"Who wants to be next?" he repeated. He looked at the ladies on line with contempt, as though they should be serving him and not he them.

"I do."

"So do I."

"Me, too."

"I got here first!"

"No, I did!"

"Incidentally," said the kid, "I am obliged to inform you that I am not a full-fledged hairdresser—I'm only a trainee and am quite capable of disfiguring you."

The women fell silent.

"No, thanks. We'd better stay in our nice little line," sighed the middle-aged one.

I made up my mind, "Let's go to it, disfigure me."

The kid started to laugh. There was something wild not only in his eyes but also in his smile. He had sharp, bright white teeth.

"I like the way you put that—'disfigure me.' I shall do my best not to do so. Come in."

He took me into a rear cubbyhole instead of the salon. Two hairdressers in black instead of the familiar white coats were muttering incantations over two female heads bent back over tarnished iron basins. One was applying coloring with a shaving brush while the other scrutinized a green liquid in a measuring glass. Do they really dye hair green?

It smelled different back there, pungent and stuffy. At the rear door, two suspicious-looking punks in tight pants and with slanting sideburns were carrying on a cryptic conversation in low tones that reeked of the black market.

"Thirty bottles of the blonde stuff and fifty setting lotions along with them," said one.

"Don't worry," said my trainee, "I'll do your hair behind this screen."

The flimsy blue screen wobbled unsteadily. On the wall in a cheap gold frame hung a certificate, "A Leader among Enterprises." I sat down in the chair.

"Take out the pins," the kid ordered. I took them out. He picked up a lock of hair, felt it, ran it through his fingers, and tested another one.

"Your hair is splitting," he said, "the result of curling it yourself. What would you like?"

"A cut...and a six-month perm, if that's possible."

"Everything is possible, including a six-month perm. But I warn you that in today's world that method is old fashioned. If it were up to me I would suggest a chemical wave."

"A chemical wave?"

"Precisely. It's the most modern kind of coiffure. Kindly remember that they've practically stopped doing six-month perms abroad; they've all gone over to chemical waves."

"How's that different from the six-month one?"

"Day and night. The six-month perm makes one look like a ram. Perhaps some people are fond of rams, but personally I'm opposed to them. Chemical waves give a more interesting line to the coiffure, as though it were fluttering in the wind."

I suddenly wanted my hairdo to flutter in the wind.

"Well, go ahead with it," I said. "Will it take long?"

"At least four hours. You can do hack work in two hours, but I'm not in the habit of doing hack work."

"That means till eleven?"

"Or eleven-thirty."

I thought of [my teenaged kids] Kólya and Kóstya sitting at home with no dinner, and wondered if those dummies were bright enough to buy themselves something. Well, they had to get used to it sometime.

"O.K.," I said, "let's get going."

"Don't worry," the kid said suddenly, "my qualifications are equal to those of a full-fledged hairdresser; perhaps even better. Right now it's more profitable for me to be a trainee than a full-fledged hairdresser. I don't have to fulfill a plan,* I've got less responsibility, and I can experiment freely with anyone who gives me her head to practice on."

"I'm not worried," I replied. "The stakes aren't high this time around. Just think what great beauty you could destroy."

He again laughed his peculiar laugh, flashing his teeth for a second.

"You put that nicely. 'Just think, what great beauty.' That's true."

Well, so much for that. I was asking for it.

Translated by Michael Petrov

NOTE (by translator)

* Plan refers to the production quotas, assigned in advance, that all Soviet enterprises must fulfill.

Solveig von Schoultz   *Finland, b. 1907*

Born on August 5, 1907, Solveig von Schoultz grew up in the small town of Borgå, Finland. Her father was a high school teacher and her mother, Hanna Frosterus-Segerstråle, a painter whom she has described in *Porträtt av Hanna* (Portrait of Hanna, 1978).

Youngest of eight siblings, she wished to become a sculptor but after her father's death had to choose a more secure profession and became a grade school teacher. She married young and had two daughters, both of whom are now psychologists. As a trained educator of children, she studied and annotated the behavior of her two daughters during their first year and published the result in a book *De sju dagarna. Två barn skapar sin värld.* (The Seven Days. Two children create their world, 1942). This work is considered one of the most informative accounts about parents and children in Swedish literature. She has also written books for children, some of which have been used in Finnish grade schools.

Primarily a poet and a short story writer, von Schoultz has also written numerous radio plays. Her literary style, both in poetry and prose, is condensed and sparse. Her poetry is rich in symbols and metaphors borrowed from earth, sun, water, and trees—all expressing creativity and life. Her short stories generally depict women's changing thoughts and feelings. Her main theme is the relationship between people: intimacy and misunderstanding, problems of married life, and the generation gap. She often addresses the external and internal emancipation of women. Von Schoultz stresses how important it is that women not give up fighting for their independence and always remain open to new life situations. Her own strict Lutheran upbringing is reflected in two semi-autobiographical books: *Ansa och samvetet* (Ansa and her conscience, 1954), a collection of short stories about the girl Ansa from the age of six to puberty, who struggles with feelings of rejection, and *Där Står du* (There you are, 1973) which carries Ansa to her fifteenth birthday, at which point she is a woman whose self-esteem has been crushed and who has been taught to regard modesty as the highest of virtues.

Only a few of von Schoultz's poems and short stories have been translated into English. Of the following poems "Vila" (Rest) is from *Sänk Ditt Ljus* (Lower Your Light, 1967, "Till Jorden" (Back to the Earth) is from *Klippbok* (Scrapbook, 1968) and "Ögat" (The Eye) is from *De Fyra Flöjtspelarna* (The Four Flute Players, 1975)

Ingrid Claréus

REST
Vila

Inside disaster everything is quiet, everyone has
                                        passed by,
all doors are shut, you can't hear any sounds.
It's sparsely furnished, the air is stale and it's
                                        dark
but rest,
face and body against hard floor
but rest
and strange dream about God.

Translated by Stina Katchadourian

BACK TO THE EARTH
Till Jorden

Why such a hurry back to the earth?
Why not in stages:
  first be a cow
  thoughtful, in the shade
  ruminating the past
  reflecting in the eye all that passes
      (as I have done)

then, a cat
with claws pulled into the paws
    (as I have walked)
softly, with contracted pupils
carrying kittens in the mouth

then, a mole
already smelling the earth, fast
already smaller

then an earthworm
full of soil and moving slowly.

Translated by Stina Katchadourian

THE EYE
Ögat

Remaining:
just the eye.
Hands and feet already quiet
and stretched out under the blanket
weight and silence.

Hands and feet:
whose?
And whose that old shattered heart?
All this preparing to resume its place
in the nameless
in the vast laboratory that alters everything.
For a few decades it had belonged
to whom?
Someone had determined actions and steps
decided, hoped, been deceived, still believed
slept to get strength, continued
but who
who had painstakingly gathered what she had
                                        seen
what she had felt what she finally knew
and for whom?

The mouth silent.
She must pass on
the uttermost the last—

overflowing
it filled the eye
pleading its way
to whom?

Translated by Stina Katchadourian

Simone de Beauvoir   *France, 1908–1986*

The political and theoretical impact of Simone de Beauvoir's work upon the history of ideas in the twentieth century is immeasurable. Her seminal study on the oppression of women within the patriarchal structures of power, *The Second Sex*, lay the groundwork for the feminist critique of male-dominated structures of sexual difference that would be launched through literature, theory, the visual arts, politics, and the economy in the years following its publication in France in 1949 and, in a severely abridged version, in the United States in 1952.

The anger and the passion that she felt about the subject is evident in the book, but they emerged from and are coupled with immense learning: the book traces the concept of the female as it is defined by the biology of sex, the history of women in the West, and the psychology and sociology of women in modern life. Led to the following conclusion, which was absolutely disturbing and shocking when it first appeared, de Beauvoir wrote: "One is not born, but rather, becomes a woman. No biological, psychological, or economic fate determines the figure that the human female presents in society; it is civilization as a whole that produces this creature, intermediate between male and eunuch, which is described as feminine." This assertion in *The Second Sex* was to become one of the fundamental tenets of the feminist movement in the United States as well as France. The selection that follows is taken from the historical section of the book.

Born in Paris in 1908, de Beauvoir received a rather classical, if not conventional, education. After secondary school, she went on to the Sorbonne where she earned her *agrégation* in philosophy in 1929. It was there that she met Jean-Paul Sartre, three years her senior. She wrote later in life about this critical encounter: "It was the first time in my life that I felt intellectually inferior to anyone else." She and Sartre were to become lifelong companions as well as intellectual and political partners, and leaders of the most significant philosophical movement to emerge in the postwar period—Existentialism. Although de Beauvoir refused Sartre's proposals of marriage, she saw him almost daily until his death in 1980.*

After receiving her degree, de Beauvoir taught philosophy in Marseilles and Rouen before returning to Paris in 1938. By 1943, she had given up teaching in order to devote herself more fully to her writing, and in 1945, she joined Sartre in editing *Les Temps Modernes* (Modern Times), a leading journal of intellectual ferment.

With Sartre, de Beauvoir brought her intellectual leadership to bear on a variety of causes during their lifetime. She was a committed leftist despite her disillusionment with Soviet communism. Moreover, she remained a harsh and outspoken critic of the United States as an imperialist power: her opinion can be found in *L'Amérique au jour le jour* (*America Day by Day*), which she wrote after she had toured this country in 1953. In 1960, she and Sartre were banned from French radio and television for having signed a manifesto supporting the rights of young men who refused to do military service in Algeria. In 1970, the two of them were arrested for distributing a banned Maoist newsletter. In 1971, de Beauvoir signed a petition in which she revealed for the first time having had an illegal abortion (abortion was not legalized in France until 1974).

In addition to her philosophical and political work, de Beauvoir was also a literary artist. Her first novel, *L'Invitée* (*She Came To Stay*, 1943) was about a triangular relationship involving a man and a woman who are both attached to a second, younger woman. *Le Sang des autres* (*The Blood of Others*, 1945) depicted the fusion of the personal and the political during the French Resistance. It was followed by *Tous les hommes sont mortels* (*All Men Are Mortal*) and her essay "Pour une morale de l'ambiguité" ("Towards an Ambiguous Morality") in 1947. In 1954, when her novel, *Les Mandarins* (*The Mandarins*), won the Prix Goncourt, a scandal arose because of its thinly disguised portraits of Sartre, Camus, and other leading intellectuals. De Beauvoir has said that her fiction was influenced by Hemingway's style and her admiration for the work of Joyce, Proust, and Kafka. However, her tendency to write "romans à clef" and "romans à thèse" or novels of ideas in which characters seem propelled by particular philosophical or political positions has subjected her to critical attack. Notwithstanding, the feminist literary revival that she did so much to inspire has precipitated the reprinting of her works in translation, which include a collection of fine early short stories under the title of *Quand Prime le Spirituel* (*When Things of the Spirit Come First*, 1982). Many contemporary critics have re-examined her work in light of new feminist positions.

Given her staunch feminism and her position in the intellectual life of postwar France, it is not surprising that readers looked forward to the publication of de Beauvoir's four volumes of autobiography: *Memoirs of a Dutiful Daughter*, *Mémoires d'une fille rangée* (1958), *Force of Circumstance*, *La Force des choses* (1963), *La Force de l'age* (*The Coming of Age*, 1960), and *Tout compte faite* (*All Said and Done*, 1972). In the vanguard regarding the great social ideas of the age, de Beauvoir also made early, powerful contributions to the movement which seeks to criticize "ageism" in modern Western society.

Simone de Beauvoir died in 1986 at the Cochin Hospital in Paris at the age of 78.

NOTE

* This famous and supposedly paradigmatic modern heterosexual relationship was troubled by traditional inequalities that de Beauvoir was unwilling to acknowledge directly though they are hinted at in some of her fictions. Sartre was a notorious womanizer; he legally adopted his last mistress and she thus inherited all his writings, library, and personal effects. See John Weightman. "Summing Up Sartre," *New York Review of Books* XXIV (August 13, 1987) 13: 42–46, for this and recent critical and biographical works on both Sartre and de Beauvoir.

    For other recent scholarship, see Hélène Vivienne Wenzel, Ed., "Simone de Beauvoir: Witness to a Century," *Yale French Studies* No. 72 (1986).

from THE SECOND SEX
Le Deuxième Sexe

. . . The masses of women are on the margin of history, and circumstances are an obstacle for each individual, not a springboard. In order to change the face of the world, it is first neces-sary to be firmly anchored in it; but the women who are firmly rooted in society are those who are in subjection to it; unless de-signated for action by divine authority—and then they have shown themselves to be as capable as men—the ambitious woman and the heroine are strange monsters. It is only since women have begun to feel themselves at home on the earth that we have seen a Rosa Luxemburg, a Mme Curie appear.[1] They brilliantly demonstrate that it is not the inferiority of women that has caused their historical insignificance: it is rather their historical insignificance that has doomed them to inferiority.[2]

This fact is glaringly clear in the domain in which women have best succeeded in asserting themselves—that is, the domain of culture. Their lot has been deeply bound up with that of arts and letters; among the ancient Germans the functions of prophetess and priestess were already appropriate to women. Because of woman's marginal position in the world, men will turn to her when they strive through culture to go beyond the boundaries of their universe and gain access to something other than what they have known. Courtly mysticism, humanist curiosity, the taste for beauty which flourished in the Italian Renaissance, the preciosity of the seventeenth century, the progressive idealism of the eighteenth—all brought about under different forms an exaltation of femininity. Woman was thus the guiding star of poetry, the subject matter of the work of art; her leisure allowed her to consecrate herself to the pleasures of the spirit: inspiration, critic, and public of the writer, she became his rival; she it was who often made prevail a mode of sensibility, an ethic that fed masculine hearts, and thus she intervened in her own destiny—the education of women was in large part a feminine conquest. And yet, however important this collective role of the intellectual woman may have been, the individual contributions have been in general of less value. It is because she has not been engaged in action that woman has had a privileged place in the domains of thought and of art; but art and thought have their living springs in action. To be situated at the margin of the world is not a position favorable for one who aims at crea-

ting anew; here again, to emerge beyond the given, it is necessary first to be deeply rooted in it. Personal accomplishment is almost impossible in the human categories that are maintained collectively in an inferior situation. "Where would you have one go, with skirts on?" Marie Bashkirtsev wanted to know.[3] And Stendhal said: "All the geniuses who are born *women* are lost to the public good." To tell the truth, one is not born a genius: one becomes a genius; and the feminine situation has up to the present rendered this becoming practically impossible.

The antifeminists obtain from the study of history two contradictory arguments: (1) women have never created anything great; and (2) the situation of woman has never prevented the flowering of great feminine personalities. There is bad faith in these two statements; the successes of a privileged few do not counterbalance or excuse the systematic lowering of the collective level; and that these successes are rare and limited proves precisely that circumstances are unfavorable for them. As has been maintained by Christine de Pisan, Poulain de la Barre, Condorcet, John Stuart Mill, and Stendhal, in no domain has woman ever really had her chance.[4] That is why a great many women today demand a new status; and once again their demand is not that they be exalted in their femininity: they wish that in themselves, as in humanity in general, transcendence may prevail over immanence; they wish to be accorded at last the abstract rights and concrete possibilities without the concurrence of which liberty is only a mockery.[5]

This wish is on the way to fulfillment. But the period in which we live is a period of transition; this world, which has always belonged to the men, is still in their hands; the institutions and the values of the patriarchal civilization still survive in large part. Abstract rights are far from being completely granted everywhere to women: in Switzerland they do not yet vote; in France the law of 1942 maintains in attenuated form the privileges of the husband.[6] And abstract rights, as I have just been saying have never sufficed to assure to woman a definite hold on the world: true equality between the two sexes does not exist even today.

In the first place, the burdens of marriage weigh much more heavily upon woman than upon man. We have noted that servitude to maternity has been reduced by the use—admitted or clandestine—of birth control; but the practice has not spread everywhere nor is it invariably used. Abortion being officially forbidden, many women either risk their health in unsupervised efforts to abort or find themselves overwhelmed by their numerous pregnancies. The care of children like the upkeep of the home is still undertaken almost exclusively by woman. Especially in France the antifeminist tradition is so tenacious that a man would feel that he was lowering himself by helping with tasks hitherto assigned to women. The result is that it is more difficult for woman than for man to reconcile her family life with her role as worker. Whenever society demands this effort, her life is much harder than her husband's....

Every benefit always has as its bad side some burden; but if the burden is too heavy, the benefit seems no longer to be anything more than a servitude. For the majority of laborers, labor is today a thankless drudgery, but in the case of woman this is not compensated for by a definite conquest of her social dignity, her freedom of behavior, or her economic independence; it is natural enough for many woman workers and employees to see in the right to work only an obligation from which marriage will deliver them. Because of the fact that she has taken on awareness of self, however, and because she can also free herself from marriage through a job, woman no longer accepts domestic subjection with docility. What she would hope is that the reconciliation of family life with a job should not require of her an exhausting, difficult performance. Even

then, as long as the temptations of convenience exist—in the economic inequality that favors certain individuals and the recognized right of woman to sell herself to one of these privileged men—she will need to make a greater moral effort than would a man in choosing the road of independence. It has not been sufficiently realized that the temptation is also an obstacle, and even one of the most dangerous. Here it is accompanied by a hoax, since in fact there will be only one winner out of thousands in the lottery of marriage. The present epoch invites, even compels women to work; but it flashes before their eyes paradises of idleness and delight: it exalts the winners far above those who remain tied down to earth.

The privileged place held by men in economic life, their social usefulness, the prestige of marriage, the value of masculine backing, all this makes women wish ardently to please men. Women are still, for the most part, in a state of subjection. It follows that woman sees herself and makes her choices not in accordance with her true nature in itself, but as man defines her.

Translated by H. M. Parshley

NOTES

1. Rosa Luxemburg (1870–1919): Polish-born revolutionary and theorist, she was a leader of the international Socialist movement and of the Socialist Democrat Party (SPD) and founder of the German Communist Party (KPD). She was brutally murdered by soldiers quelling the revolt of German workers known as the Spartacist Uprising following World War I. Marie Curie (1867–1934) Polish-born French physicist who pioneered in radioactive research, discovering radium and polonium, and was among the first "anti-nuclear" peace activists.

2. It is remarkable that out of a thousand statues in Paris (excepting the queens that for a purely architectural reason form the corbel of the Luxembourg) there should be only ten raised to women. Three are consecrated to Joan of Arc. The others are statues of Mme de Ségur, George Sand, Sarah Bernhardt, Mme Boucicaut and the Baroness de Hirsch, Maria Deraismes, and Rosa Bonheur. (Author's note)

3. Marie Bashkirtsev (1860–1884): Russian-born French memoirist whose posthumously published *Journal*

(1885) created a worldwide sensation; in it she expressed a desire to live to the utmost and an ambition for greatness that found no outlet in her short life.

4. All these writers, including the early French feminist *Catherine de Pisan* (1363?–1431), championed egalitarian theories and defended the dignity of women.

5. Here again the antifeminists take an equivocal line. Now, regarding abstract liberty as nothing, they expatiate on the great concrete role that the enslaved woman can play in the world—what then, is she asking for? Again, they disregard the fact that negative license opens no concrete possibilities, and they reproach women who are abstractly emancipated for not having produced evidence of their abilities. (Author's note)

6. Switzerland finally granted the vote to women in 1971. The French law of 1942 *theoretically* abolished the authority of a husband over his wife. A married woman was no longer considered a minor; the law had to be revised again in 1965.

Kathleen Raine   *UK(England), b. 1908*

"Since the age of ten, when I...returned to the suburb[s] [of London], I have lived in exile." Indeed, English poet Kathleen Raine's artistic exile from the wild Northumberland farmlands of her childhood has been relieved only by those moments when her poetry has been able to recapture for her the natural beauty of the Northumberland, Cumberland, and Scottish countryside.

Poet, scholar, translator, Kathleen Jessie Raine was born to a Northumberland farmer and itinerant lecturer for non-conformist churches, and a Scottish school mistress. She spent much of her childhood with her maternal grandmother in Northumberland, and it was there, in "the noble country and dignified way of life...of farmers and shepherds of Northumberland," as she put it, that she found "the epitome of all that I have ever loved."

Given scholarships to Girton College, Cambridge, she studied zoology, botany, and geology and completed her M.A. in 1929. It was at Cambridge that she made friends with other poets, including William Empson and her second husband, Charles Madge, and began to write poetry, a poetry she has said, of "spontaneous inspirations." Her poetry found inspiration in her studies of the natural sciences; what has emerged is a visionary poetry that expresses the abstract nature of the natural science. Since her first collection in 1943, *Stone and Flower: Poems of 1935–43*, with illustrations by Barbara Hepworth, Raine has published numerous poems. She has also edited and written critical studies of Yeats, Shelley, Coleridge, and Blake, among others, and has translated writers Denis de Rougement and Honoré de Balzac from the French. She has received many awards, including a research fellowship to Cambridge from 1955 to 1961, an Andrew Mellon Lectureship at the National Gallery of Art in Washington, D.C. in 1962, the Harriet Monroe Memorial Prize in 1952, the Oscar Blumenthal Award in 1961, and the Smith Literary Award in 1972. She was given a D. Litt from Leicester University in 1974.

Kathleen Raine has sought to establish and explore a view of the world in which, she says, she would like to reaffirm "the sacred dimension of life," and "man as a spiritual and immortal being." Hers is a mystical poetry, poetry as archetype rather than poetry as a delineation of the emotions or ideas. It is a poetry much informed by the visual arts. The following poems are from *Stone and Flower* (1943).

John Isom

MATERNAL GRIEF

I am not human,
I am not human,
Nor am I divine.

To whom,
to whom can I cry,
'I am thine'?

I have picked my grandsire's corpse to the
bone,
I have found no ghost in brisket or chine.

I have shed the blood of my female kin,
but they never return to speak again.

I am not human,
I am not human,
How shall I feed my hungry children?

I make the porridge of meal and wine
and pour it out in the troughs for swine.

The ghosts are hungry, the ghosts are divine,
but the pigs eat the meal, and the priests drink
the wine.

LONDON REVISITED

Haunting these shattered walls, hung with our
past
That no electron and no sun can pierce,
We visit rooms in dreams
Where we ourselves are ghosts.

There is no foothold for our solid world,
No hanging Babylon for the certain mind
In rooms tattered by wind, wept on by rain.

Wild as the tomb, wild as the mountainside
A storm of hours has shaken the finespun
world
Tearing away our palaces, our faces, and our
days.

Lalithambika Antherjanam   *India, 1909–1987*

Though Lalithambika was born into a traditional Namboodiri *illam* (household), her parents were progressive thinkers, and as a writer she broke away from tradition and orthodoxy to recount stories of the community. The Namboodiris were powerful feudal aristocrats, but also a priestly community, famed for their rigid adherence to tradition. Women in this society were not only kept in strict seclusion, they had to face the hardships that arose from the Namboodiri custom that only the eldest son married a woman from his own community. Younger sons usually made alliances in the matrilineal Nair community. Though this tradition ensured that the land was not fragmented, it also meant that it became difficult for Namboodiri women, who were not allowed to marry into a lower caste, to find husbands. Large dowries had to be paid and it was not uncommon for an eldest son to marry several times. A young girl might become the third or fourth wife of a much older man and run the risk of becoming widowed while she was still very young.

Early twentieth-century movements for reform emphasized the need for education, for more freedom for the women, and for a change in marriage customs. Orthodoxy was outraged at this questioning, and reformers like Lalithambika came in for constant attack. Though she started as a social reformer, Lalithambika joined the Gandhian movement for Independence and continued to champion the cause of oppressed womanhood. Only as we set her writings within this context does the significance of her work, spread over five decades, really emerge.

Lalithambika is considered one of the important writers of the "second generation"—those writing in the thirties and forties who followed the reformist pioneers but embued fiction with a new social and political consciousness and a passionate commitment to change in the era prior to Independence. Lalithambika was commended for the subtle psychology of her characters, especially for the sensitivity with which she depicts the plight of Namboodiri women trying to escape the boundaries of their traditional *illam*. K.M. Pannikar, one of Kerala's most distinguished historians who was also a novelist, wrote the preface to an early collection of short stories *Ambikanjali* (Ambika's Offerings, 1938) supporting her efforts. Though she was primarily a short story writer, her novel, *Agni Sakshi* (Witness by Fire, 1976) was widely acclaimed. Set in early twentieth-century Kerala it tells the story of two women who rebel in different ways against the deadening restrictions of custom and practice. "My husband does not seem to know how to love anyone," Thetikutty says. "He's afraid of everyone and everything—of Aphan, of Mother, of custom—why, he's even afraid of God. Brother was right. If I live too long in this house, I might also lose my senses out of fear."

Lalithambika earned her reputation with the romantic poetry of *Lalitanjali* (Simple Offerings/Lalitha's offerings, 1937). Later she published *Nissabdhasangitam* (Wordless Songs, 1955) and in 1969, as part of her sixtieth birthday-celebration, a collected edition *Ayirathiri* (A Thousand Tapers) was published. She is principally known as the author of more than two dozen prose works in Malayalam. Among her better known collections of short stories are *Adyathe Kathakal* (First Stories, 1937), *Koddunkatil Ninnu* (From a Whirlwind, 1951), *Takarna Talamura* (Ruined Generation, 1953), *Muddupadatil* (Behind the Veil, 1955), and *Agni Pushpangal* (Flowers of Fire, 1960). The Writers Co-operative published a major critical edition of her stories, *Therenjedutha Kathakal* (Selected Stories) in 1966. She has won many awards including Sahitya Academy ones for her children's book *Gosayi Paranja Katha* (The Story Gosayi Told, 1965); her study of women characters in the *Ramayana* of Valmiki and the Vyasa* *Mahabharata Seetha Muthal Sathyavathivare* (From Seeta to Satyavathi, 1974); and her novel *Agni Sakshi* in 1976. The selection was first published in 1940.

Jancy George and Susie Tharu

NOTE

* *Ramayana*: an epic work in 24,000 couplets centered around. Rama, a righteous king and incarnation of the sacred Hindu divinity, Vishnu, credited to Valmiki (ca. fourth century B.C.), considered to be the first poet. The earliest surviving manuscript dates from the eleventh century. Vyasa, or "arranger," is the title given to several unknown authors who compiled and recorded versions of the *Mahabharata*, another epic dating back to the first century A.D.

THE CONFESSION
Kuttasammatham

The *thing*, put under taboo because of suspected adultery spoke thus before the community court. "I am guilty. You can throw me out. The entire fault is mine. No one else is a party to my action."

There was some agitation in that assembly

of Brahmin priests. How defiant the woman was! She, a pregnant widow, dared to say that no one shared her guilt. How then had she become guilty?

The *Smarta*[1] roared: "You adulteress! You have fallen into evil. Can't you speak the truth at least now?"

From within the "taboo-room" a faint voice sobbed out.

As God is my witness, I tell you, I do not know who is guilty in this matter. Was it the solitude of that night? Or my youthfulness? Or the compelling drive of some emotions I had never experienced? You know that I am a child widow. My *tali*[2] was cut and removed when I was fourteen. Twenty years are gone by since then. Has there ever been any stain on my name? Have I ever neglected a single religious fast or vigil? Or holy baths or sacred rituals? Have I ever been slack in worshipping at Guruvayoor[3] or Thrippangot? Why, then, did God turn my head just for that one night? I have never talked to any man but my father. I was frightened at the very thought of "man." There is only one man a woman should know. I did not have him.

My world was confined to the kitchen and the women's apartments. Never have I opened the door of the inner rooms, not even to take a peep at the world outside. You might ask me how such a thing could have happened to me. I shall tell you that story. Believe me or not, this is the truth....

What an unexpected counter-argument! The court was stupefied. How could this fallen woman justify her obvious guilt? The priest who was the prosecutor was annoyed. He gave a curt order, "Say what you have to, and do it quickly."

The door of the "taboo-room" opened a little. Words flowed out like a stream through a breach in a dam.

To hear my story—even to listen to my words—I know you would consider a sacrilege. I also once thought as you do, didn't I, that an ostracized Namboodiri woman is more despicable than an evil spirit? Did I not shrink from the polluting touch of even the wind that blew in from where such sinners were? I did not care to visit sister Tatri even when she lay on her deathbed. May be, I am paying for that sin now.

I will not enter into that story now. Were not all of you present there at the feast conducted by Aditiri?[4] Why did you fix such a marriage? You decided that the thirty-year-old daughter of the eldest son of that family was to be married to my father, and I just eleven years and three months old, to that old man. An exchange of fathers in wedlock! My grandmother used to say, "I am glad that at least this girl can be given away before she attained puberty. But God knows, how she is going to get along with those wretched folks.

But I did not have to stay with them for long. My father's new wife—my husband's daughter—was a sick woman. She died soon. I was just a burden to my husband. In such circumstances, women naturally return to their father's place. I was happy there because my mother was my father's favorite wife.

I have looked at my husband only once. At the sight of his gray beard and pot belly, I felt bewildered rather than frightened. Even though my grandmother insisted, I never entered his room. He who had four wives in his caste and forty elsewhere, never bothered to come there again. Scarcely had two years passed and....Do you think it could be a punishment for my omission?

It was during the Onam days.[5] One afternoon I was in the courtyard playing with my friends. I heard some servant had come there. My father whispered something to my mother. "Alas! my girl! Oh God! What have you done to us!" My mother cried out and beat her breast. She fell down in a swoon. People began gathering there. They were all whispering something. Someone dragged me away from my playmates into the house. There was loud wailing in the women's rooms. But I did not cry. I did not even know why I should cry. I had to take a dip, and all wet, I was taken to a dark room. My bronze bangles were removed. The *tilak*[6] on my forehead was wiped off. I was quite submissive to whatever was being done.

But when the senior daughter-in-law of the house tried to cut my *tali* I could not help protesting: "No, no, I won't give this. This *tali* alone you needn't ask of me. It is touching this thread that I chant everyday the thousand and eight holy names. Ask my mother whether it is so or not.

My obstinate protests and weeping reached my father's ears.

He came to the door, his tired old face looking very sad. "Give it, my daughter," he said, "Let it go, that useless old string! I will buy you, my child, a better chain. Just wait for ten days."

Once my father said he would do something, I knew he would keep his word. After the funeral rites, I got a rosary of gold to replace my *tali*. How it sparkled! how pretty it was! My girlish desire to deck myself was quite satisfied. How I wish I could always have remained ignorant as during my girlhood days— of the difference between a rosary and a *tali*!

In the course of time, I got used to the changes I had to bring about in my way of life. I could not touch the auspicious lamp or the *ashtamangalya*.[7] I could not apply *kajalf*[8] to my eyes, or *kumkum* or sandalwood paste on my forehead. I could eat rice only once a day. My grandmother instructed me in all the new ways I had to observe in dress and manners. I used to lie on her lap listening to her old tales. It was in those days that I heard for the first time the stories of Krishna and the *gopis* and Vrindavan.[9] In a rather melancholy voice, she would tell me, "You must always chant 'Bhagavan,[10] Lord of Guruvayoor, Krishna!' Your life should be devoted to that." "Where is He, grandma?" I asked her. "He is everywhere," was her reply. "If you look for Him, you can see Him." "Really? Have you seen Him yourself?" I asked her eagerly. "I? Am I so lucky, my child? But *Bhattathiri*[11] and

others have seen Him. They have said that when they were reading the *Bhagavatham*,[12] He appeared before them. They have seen Him clad in yellow silk and with a peacock feather and flute. Oh! Krishna! Harikrishna! Krishna!"

Her fingers trembling on the beads of her rosary, my grandmother would close her eyes in an ecstasy of adoration. One would feel that God was there, standing right in front of her. I did not know anything about Bhattathiri or his readings, but I felt greatly drawn to Sri Krishna. Which girl could help loving that cowherd-boy who sang and danced?

It became my responsibility to get everything ready for the daily *puja*.[13] I had to get up in the early dawn and bathe, prepare garlands, light the oil lamp and pour holy water on the idols. Of the numerous idols, I liked that of Vishnu with Lakshmi best.[14] He seemed the personification of love. Smiling he held Lakshmi to his heart, with His hands that bore the sacred symbols of the conch and the disc. There was something in His face that excited me. That idol I would polish and decorate with garlands. I would put a sandalwood paste mark on His forehead. My love of decking out myself, a love I could never indulge in again, was transferred to that idol and became part of the pujarites. On some dreamlike dawns or evening twilight-hours, fragrant with the scent of puja flowers, warm with incense smoke and the flames of the oil lamp, while kneeling before the enchanting idol of my favorite deity, I felt disturbed by a faint desire—could I not wear some of those flowers? Could I not have a sandalwood paste *tilak*? No. I could have nothing but the ashes of my burnt-up hopes.

Even while breathing her last, my grandmother was anxious about me. Her last words were, "My son! look after her well. She is so very young." No one knew then that her words were a warning from fate. But I felt a strange foreboding. What was there to be so anxious about me who was so utterly self-effacing and harmless?

Years went by, but I did not realize that I

had become a young woman. Bathing, doing *puja*, and chanting holy names, I found my days roll by. In fact, I was not conscious of myself till my elder brother married and brought his bride home. Why was my sister-in-law so pretty? Why did she laugh so gaily? Every evening she would bathe and wear jasmines in her hair. With what pretty folds she used to wear her gold-bordered *dhoti*[15]! A way of life I had not seen till then, was unfolded before my eyes. Every night, when the doors of their room closed with a bang against my ears! ...I pray you, do not be angry with me. It is sorrow which makes me say all this, not envy. I do not envy my sister-in-law or anyone else at all. But still, my heart breaks into fragments when I think how different my life is from hers. And she only six months older than I.

A widow is more afraid of laughter than of tears. Gaiety hurts her, irrespective of who is gay. To watch another person—even if he or she is a near one—enjoy the pleasures and joys lost to her for ever—great Brahmins! Can you understand how it hurts and burns? In your inner apartments there is this slow consuming fire burning constantly.

We quarrelled—my sister-in-law and I. There were many provocations. I could not get a single flower from my pet jasmine creeper for my *puja*. The *chempak* sapling which I had nurtured with such love and care put forth its first bud, but soon it had vanished. In sorrow and spiteful anger I growled, "What seductress is stealing my puja flowers to decorate herself? It is not for that I grow flowers." "What are flowers for, if not to be worn by women blessed with a long married life? Just because you cannot wear them, you should not grudge them to others." Such was the piercing reply. The seeds were sown for a family strife. We fought, wept, abused, and cursed each other over all sorts of trifles. I was always the winner in those quarrels. How could it be otherwise when my parents were there? My sister-in-law, defeated, would gnash her teeth and mutter, "A time will come when I can have my revenge. Just wait till then."

I learnt how relentless such calculated vengeance could be. Perhaps I learnt more. You know what position women have in their father's house. Because of troubles in the husband's house, we stay most of the time with our parents. As long as they are alive, we have no difficulty. We even succeed in humiliating the women married into the family. Things begin to change when the reins pass into the hands of the father's younger brother. Those who flatter his wife and children find things easy for them. Next when the eldest son of the family becomes the head, we the orphaned women, quarrelsome and helpless, run hither and thither for shelter. Even a maid servant, if she is gossipy enough to win the favor of the mistress of the house, can scold us defiantly. All this I saw, experienced, endured. During the mourning for my mother's death, it was with tears in my eyes that I left my house for my husband's.

His three senior wives had six or seven daughters, all of them grown up and unmarried. There were some ten children in that house and also four of his daughters older than I. I got into that crowd. From the corners of the rain-drenched, dilapidated house, all that could be heard were the wailings of hunger and suppressed desires. There was no master, or rather everybody was master. But I had a right there. It was my own house. Nobody could ask me to leave, and even if somebody did, I didn't have to pay any heed.

My heart had become too hardened to be wounded by the stinging remarks of the elder wives. I too gave stinging replies. I had no children and no other responsibilities. A childless widow is not likely to know what kindness is. We live, we have to live, simply because we do not die.

I used to observe every fast, and bow wherever a lamp was lit. I have fasted for fifteen days at a stretch. Did not people speak of me in those days as a *sanyasini*?[16] How soon is all that reputation lost! Perhaps you will condemn me as a fake ascetic. Say whatever you like and mock me as much as you please. But let me ask you one thing. You consider yourselves the guardians of chastity and morality. Have you ever done the slightest thing for the protection of these pitiable women who have never known what life is? You decreed that this world was not for us. We go from gate to gate seeking that peace and comfort which you say are in the next world. Irrepressible hopes—uncontrollable emotions—these are stone steps slimy with instinctive sensuality. One little slip and pitiless priestdom is there with its cruel punishment of pushing you down into the bottomless pit of hell....Oh God! Can nothing save me from here, neither the Lord of Guruvayoor nor Vadakkunathan,[17] nor all the fasts and vigils I have observed!

Through the gap between the doors, a warm whiff of air blew. Was it not a suppressed burning sigh? The Brahmins listened to it in silence. Didn't they have at least a trace of human kindness? Nobody felt like saying anything. After a brief silence, the confession was resumed in a steadier tone:

I do not blame anyone. It was my fate that this should happen. How many Brahmin women go to listen to the *Bhagavatham* reading? But has such a thing as this happened to any of them? In this temple itself, the reading is an annual custom, and lots of Brahmin women crowd to hear it. We go not merely out of pious desire to hear the stories of the Lord. We also like to have an outing even though hidden under our "umbrella and shawl." There is also the eagerness to hear a man's voice at least sneakingly. Moreover, there is spiritual merit to be acquired through listening to the reading. *Bhajans,*[18] spiritual readings and so on, are such opportunities for us to go anywhere without displeasing anyone. We have only to be a little careful. Thus the frustrated widows, ill-treated co-wives, and forgotten spinsters all get together behind the temple granary. What a confluence there is of aches, tears and sighs!

My house, as you know, is conveniently close to the temple. I used to get up very early and after my bath and puja. wait for the hour of reading in the temple. What ardent enthusiasm I had for it! My grandmother used to say, "If Meppathoor of Swamiyar calls the Bhagavan, He is there before them. Just think of it, my child, how blessed one has to be to reach that stage. One has to be even more blessed to listen to their reading."

Our "reader" was no *sanyasin*, nor was he an old man who had reached the stage of self-denial and turned to religious devotion. But such was the brightness of his face that people got up from their seats when he came in with bookstand in hand. In his well-laundered dhoti fresh from his bath, he would sit crosslegged before the bright oil-lamp. He was about thirty-five, fair and well built. His chest was broad. He wore a length of yellow silk; there were puja flowers on his hair. Whenever he raised his head to explain the lines he had read, his diamond studs sparkled even as his eyes sparkled with expression. Every woman there adored him as the incarnation of Lord Krishna.

What music, what humor, what eloquence there was in his reading! A mother who had lost her little son recently, wept on hearing of the pranks of the darling little Krishna. An old lady listening to the miracles of Sri Krishna shed tears of joy and cried out, "Oh! Lord of Guruvayoor! Saviour of devotees!" Old people who knew what was what nodded their heads in appreciation and commented, "This man excels even Vazhakkunnam."[19]

I was not much interested in the frolics of Balagopal. What is so delightful about the pranks of a little boy? I do not have a child and I will never have one. Then why should I bother about such stories? I was more interested in looking at the man who read, than in listening to his reading. The reading proceeded to Krishna's amorous play with the *gopis*. That, of course, is the best part of the Bhagavatha. As the audience in the inner room swelled, the reader's enthusiasm too increased. His eyes opened wider, his tongue became more eloquent, he himself seemed to have become Krishna. He said there was some hidden meaning in Krishna's stealing the garments of the gopis. Krishna was a human being only apparently. He said that in the woods on the banks of the Yamuna, Krishna sported with a thousand gopis, at midnight when everyone slept. He would explain every line in detail. Hearing those exciting descriptions, the unmarried girls would shyly bend their heads, the wives would smile, and the widows, their memories stirred, would sigh and chant the name of the Lord. But I was different. I had neither hope, nor experience, nor memories. Coldly, indifferently, I listened, and I stored up, for my next birth, whenever that might be, the essence of those feelings and that blessedness of the spirit.

He read a beautiful verse from the song of the gopis and said, "Ah how blessed was Radhika! Did she not give up husband and children and all duties and run all by herself seeking that golden lute? Believing that Love is the only refuge, did she not sport with Him? Bhagavan! Lord of Guruvayoor! Who can understand your cosmic play? Sin and holiness, justice and duty, are all mere illusions. Before the infinite rapture of love, what other duty has the human heart? We can forget the Ten Incarnations, we can forget everything else in the story of Krishna, but not his love of the gopis. Those fascinating scenes from Vrindavan reach us even today through the stretch of centuries and immerse us in the nectar of bliss. Love is devotion, love is salvation, the ecstatic thrill of love is oneness with God." I sat there, my eyes fixed on his face. I longed for an explanation beyond the power of words. Love is salvation, love is bliss. What did it mean—this fulfilment of love?

In the halo of the sacred lamp, with the open book in front of him, he sat, his eyes half-closed, his palms folded in worship. He seemed to me the personification of love. For a moment, his eyes flashed into the inner room. It was then that I realized that I was in the forefront, closest to the door. Startled, I drew my head back. What a strange emotion filled my heart. Was it shame, or shyness, or embarrassment? I was frightened. Did he see me? With my pale cheeks and unkempt hair, how ugly I might have seemed to him!

One of my nephews had a small mirror. That evening I secretly looked at my face in it. It was long since I had seen myself. As in the beautiful but wan face of Radha,[20] griefstricken by separation from Krishna, was there not something of a faint charm in my pale and melancholy face?

Next morning after my bath, I did not forget to comb my hair. Instead of sacred ashes, I applied a little sandalwood paste to my forehead. I also put a string of the ten sacred flowers on my hair. With my shawl and umbrella, I went to the temple as usual. On the platform at the entrance someone was chanting the holy names. How sweet that voice was! Slanting my umbrella a little, I stole a glance at him. He too was looking at me. I was overcome by some strange agitation of mind. My legs became unsteady, my eyes could not see clearly. I came away without completing my circumambulation of the shrine. Thereafter, when I went for the reading, I would sit only at the back. I felt too shy to look at anyone's face. All the same, I could not help going to the reading. It may have been because of the power of the Lord's name that it had become an indispensable consolation to my heart to be somewhere so close to the reader. Eating or sleeping, I had no other thought but this: the banks of the Yamuna beautiful with *Kadamba* trees in bloom; Radha in an ecstasy of love, Krishna amorously sporting. Ah, whose form is it? That yellow garment and the diamond studs and flashing smile: does Krishna look like this? He can, of course, assume any form.

In the chilly dawns of *Magha*[21] I used to bathe in the temple tank and worship daily at the hour of *nirmalya puja.*[22] I had begun this habit a long time back when someone had told me that it would fulfil my heart's desires. I had no desire; yet I continued the practice without break. Recently when I went to bathe, I could hear from the next bathing that someone was singing hymns, singing in such a way that even the misty dawn became thrilling. There were ripples in the water—someone must have been bathing—some lonely creature like me.

Even though my mind had become utterly exhausted by the incessant fight against delusive desires, I can swear to you that I never, never for a moment, expected what happened that day.

Seeing the pallor of the shadows in the *Magha*-moonlight, I thought the day had dawned. I ran to the tank, forgetting even to call the maidservant who was my escort. It would be a pity, I thought, if I missed the *puja* at dawn. In my hurry to reach the temple in time, I took a hasty dip, and had dried my hair when I heard the nightingale twittering from the asoka tree. A cold breeze blew, bearing the fragrance of the midnight flower. As the moon was declining towards the west, the shadow of the bathhouse grew darker and longer behind me. In front of me, between the moonlight and the shadows, the large tank lay like a woman's heart full of silent emotion.

It may be because I had been listening to the readings that a poetic thought came into my mind too. Could it be that the lovely nights on the banks of the Yamuna were like this same night? On one side lay the Govardhana mountain covered with green silk and glistening in the moonlight. A playful little wind, full of the excitement of the new spring, was dancing about. On the other side plunged in darkness lay the sleeping *gopa*-houses[23] with many a deadened heart and repressive rule.

Amidst these different scenes, the slow Kalindi river flowed like a dream, the starry sky reflected in her clear bosom, and the lotuses and water-lily buds gently swaying in her waves. Centuries ago, the sweet lute-song of pure love had risen from the banks of this river. The echoes of that song reach down through the ages to this day and sprinkle the nectar of revitalizing hope even on withered creatures like me. As I stood there lost in my

thoughts, almost unconsciously I sang a song from the *Ashtapadi*[24] which I had learnt long ago.

It is an incurable weakness of human nature that on some occasions, in certain circumstances, try however hard, it cannot submit to self-control. It is so with even great men like you. Then how can you blame a poor woman like me? Even in that dreamy swooning mood, when two warm arms clasped me from behind, I was really startled. Who was this? Could it be Bhagavan Himself? I have heard that He has often appeared before His devotees. But my commonsense waking up, protested, "No, it is impossible. In *Kaliyuga*[25] there is no direct knowledge of the Lord." Alas! then who could it be? The cry that rose from the depths of my soul was smothered by a soft kiss on my lips. My vain writhing could not but yield to a strong embrace. All my resistance ebbed away in the surging tide of emotions. Was it the waking up of a new knowledge of a hundred experiences I had never known before, or was I sinking into a swoon? It was not sleep. It was no dream. In that fight against nature, I too was defeated like everybody else. If it was a sin, I am prepared to give my entire life in exchange for it.

Do not ask me whether that meeting was repeated. And do not seek to know who that "god" was. I am guilty. You can punish me. I tell you again, no one else is a party to my guilt.

Translated by Smt B. Hrdaya Kumari

NOTES

1. *Smarta*: a scholar of *Smriti*, or the code of ethics derived from the ancient Hindu scriptures known as the Vedas; he acted as the prosecutor of the community court established to determine the guilt or innocence of the Namboori woman accused of adultery. During the "trial," the woman was kept in isolation.
2. A gold pendant strung on a yellow thread and tied around the bride's neck during the Hindu marriage ritual; it is considered a sacred symbol.
3. *Guruvayoor* is literally, the 'guru's gate," a center of

worship, specifically in north Kerala, and resting place for weary travelers.

4. A sect of Malayalam Brahmins.

5. *Onam*: harvest festival; most important of the festivals celebrated in Kerala. The legend is that Mahabali, whose reign symbolizes prosperity and justice visits his kingdom each year during the ten days of Onam.

6. An alternate term for *bindi*, the red mark worn especially by Hindu women on their foreheads; it is usually restricted to those who are married and of a certain caste and affirms their feminine power and the fecund divine energy. It is also associated with the Third Eye, a mystical center through which the soul leaves the body in certain stages of meditation and in death.

7. An essential feature of the decorations for auspicious occasions, it consists of a tray on which are arranged rice, kumkum, a mirror, cloth, and other symbolic objects necessary to holiday rituals.

8. The charcoal eye makeup *kumkum* is the red paste traditionally made from sandalwood used to form the tilak.

9. *Krishna*: one of the most important avatars, or incarnations of the sacred Hindu deity, Vishnu, manifested in and guiding the world. In one of his forms, the sensuous and erotic Krishna is a low-caste cowherd who mingles with *gopis* or girls who tend cattle, and his sexual union with them symbolizes God's love in its most intense form. *Vrindavan* (or *Brindavan*) was a nature goddess (a transcendent form of the gopi) who was to marry Krishna; literally, "grove of the group goddess," the word is also the name of an important center of Krishna worship.

10. *Bhagavan*: the most general, all-encompassing term for God; Godhead; any manifestation of the divine;

11. Meppathur *Bhattathiri*: (1559–1665) reknowned Sanskrit scholar, grammarian, and poet; a devotee of Krishnia, he composed his *Narayananiyam* in praise of the deity.

12. *Bhagavatha(m)*: the leading *purana* or narrative work dealing with ancient kings, sages, and the gods, composed in South India in the ninth and tenth centuries, it is comprised of 12 sections or skandhas of a lofty and difficult form of Sanskrit. The tenth skandha tells the story of the Lord Krishna.

13. A common form of ceremonial worship performed by an individual to honor gods and images of various forms and types, done according to strict rules and formulas and demanding proper preparation and dress; it is intended to direct the devotee's attention and concentration inward.

14. *Vishnu*: Along with Brahma and Shiva, the three great gods of Hinduism traceable to the early *Upanishads* (prior to 600 B.C.) *Lakshmi* one of the rare female divinities of the *Vedas* or Indian scriptures (1700–1200 B.C.), she is the goddess of fortune and the consort of Vishnu, sometimes also a wife of Krishna. As the goddess of beauty, she is known as Sri Lakshmi.

15. A garment formed by wrapping cloth around the waist.

16. *sanyasini* female form of *sanyasin*: one who has renounced the ordinary obligation of this world to seek salvation; he or she may act individually or as part of an order and is not considered an outcast but an exemplar to be admired and envied; the community provides food and shelter for such people.

17. *Vadakkunnathan*: Lord of the North, another name for Shiva; a temple with three shrines facing west located in the heart of Trichur is dedicated to him.

18. The hymns chanted or sung in the local language honoring either local or universal deities.

19. *Vazhakkunnam*: (ca. 1910–1985): a reknowned Malayalan Brahmin, master of hypnotism and magical arts.

20. *Radhika*: Also known as *Radha* (literally, "success"); historically a late figure (twelfth century), now the most famous of all the gopis, the embodiment of their selfless love, celebrated in medieval and later mystical-erotic cults and the poetry and song that grew out of them.

21. *Magha*: January–February

22. The earliest puja in a temple, performed just before dawn.

23. Houses in which the gopi, or shepherdesses live.

24. *Ashtapadi*: the name of the erotic poem describing the love story of Radha and Krishna.

25. *Kaliyuga*: Yuga is an age or measurement of time on a cosmic scale; Kaliyuga is the present age and the last of four yugas, an era characterized by vice, weakness, and the lessening of all forms of goodness and beauty.

Nellie Campobello   *Mexico, b. 1909*

Born in Villa Ocampo, in the Mexican State of Durango, Nellie Campobello came
to Mexico City when she was very young and published her first book *Yo* (I,
Verses for Francisca, 1928) when she was only 19. For most of her life, however,
Campobello was a professional dancer; she held the post of director of the
National School of Dance, which is part of the National Institute of Fine Arts and
wrote a book on indigenous Mexican folk dances.

Campobello is included here because of her two important novels about the
Mexican Revolution. In her clear, direct style, *Las manos de mamá* (Mama's
Hands, 1937) tells of her mother and all the mothers who suffered during that
period. *Cartucho* (Cartridge, 1931) (excerpted below) is a child's macabre view of
the revolution; the fragments and sketches about revolutionaries (generally *Villistas**) are bound by the young girl's reaction to the events around her.

NOTE

* Followers of Mexican revolutionary Pancho Villa (1878–1923). Villa was one of the leading generals
  during the revolution, a bloody period in Mexican history; beginning in the early 1900s and lasting,
  in its violent phase, nearly two decades, this populist movement succeeded in overthrowing oppressive
  dictator Porfirió Diaz in 1911 albeit with the sacrifice of a million Mexican lives.

from CARTRIDGE: TALES OF THE STRUGGLE IN NORTHERN MEXICO
from Cartucho[1]

GENERAL RUEDA

A tall man with a blond mustache. He spoke
forcefully. He had come into the house with
ten men, and was insulting Mama, saying:

"Do you claim you're not a Villa partisan? Do you deny that? There are firearms
here. If you don't give them to us, along with
the money and the ammunition, I'll burn down
your house!" He spoke walking back and forth
in front of her. Lauro Ruiz (from the town of
Balleza) was the name of another man with
him. They all shoved and bullied us. The man
with the blond mustache was about to hit
Mama, then he said:

"Tear the place apart. Look everywhere."
They poked their bayonets into everything,
pushing my little brothers and sisters toward
Mama, but he wouldn't allow us to get close
to her. I rebelled and went over to her, but he
gave me a shove and I fell down. Mama didn't

cry. She told them to do what they pleased but
not to touch her children. Even with a machine
gun, she couldn't have fought them all. The
soldiers stepped on my brothers and sisters
and broke everything. Since they didn't find
firearms, they carried off what they wanted,
and the blond man said:

"If you complain, I'll come and burn your
house down." Mama's eyes, grown large with
revolt, did not cry. They had hardened, re-
loaded in the rifle barrel of her memory.

I have never forgotten the picture of my
mother, back up against the wall, eyes fixed
on the black table, listening to the insults.
That blond man, too, has been engraved in my
memory ever since.

Two years later, we went to live in Chihuahua. I saw him going up the steps of the
Government Palace. He had a smaller mus-

tache then. That day everything was ruined for me: I couldn't study, I spent it thinking about being a man, having my own pistol and firing a hundred shots into him.

Another time, he was with some people in one of the windows of the Palace, laughing with his mouth open and his mustache shaking. I don't want to say what I saw him do, nor what he said, because it would seem an exaggeration. Again I dreamed of having a pistol.

One day, here in Mexico City, I saw a photograph in a newspaper with this caption: "General Alfredo Ruedo Quijano, before a summary court martial." It was the same blond man (his mustache was even smaller). Mama was no longer with us. Without being sick, she closed her eyes one day and remained asleep, back in Chihuahua. (I know Mama was tired of hearing the 30–30s.) Today they were going to shoot him, here in the capital. The people felt sorry for him, admired him, and made a great scene over his death, so he could shout out loud, just as he shouted at Mama the night of the attack.

The soldiers who fired at him had taken hold of my pistol with a hundred shots.

All night long, I kept saying to myself: "They killed him because he abused Mama, because he was bad to her." Mama's hardened eyes were mine now, and I repeated, "He was bad to Mama. That's why they shot him."

When I saw his picture on the front page of the Mexico City newspapers, I sent a child's smile to those soldiers who held in their hands my pistol with its hundred bullets, turned into a carbine resting against their shoulders.

GENERAL SOBARZO'S GUTS

At about three in the afternoon, we were by the big rock on San Francisco Street. As we went down La Pila de Cirilo Reyes alleyway, we saw some soldiers coming our way, carrying a tray above their heads, talking and laughing. "Hey, what's that pretty thing you're carrying?" From up the street we had been able to see that there was something pretty and

red in the basin. The soldiers smiled at each other, lowered the tray, and showed it to us. "They're guts," said the youngest one, fixing his eyes on the two of us to see if we were frightened. When we heard "they're guts," we moved up close to see them. They were all rolled together, as if they had no end. "Guts! How nice! Whose are they?" we said, our curiosity showing in our eyes. "They belong to General Sobarzo," said the same soldier. "We're taking them to be buried in the cemetery." And off they went, all in step, without another word. We told Mama that we'd seen Sobarzo's guts. She had seen them too going along the iron bridge.

I don't remember if they were on the attack for five days, but that time the Villistas weren't able to take the plaza. I believe the commanding officer's name was Luis Manuel Sobarzo and that he was killed near La Cruz hill or near the station. He was from Sonora. They embalmed him and put him on a train. His guts stayed in Parral.

THE HANGED MAN

The man whose hand was sticking out the train window—bruised and with nails so black it looked strangled—was talking so fervently that the *macuchi*[2] cigarette behind his ear kept moving and looked like it would fall to the floor. I was hoping to see it fall. "Machines, land, plows, nothing but machinery and more machinery!" he said with his arms open, his ideas swaying with the movement of the coach. "The government doesn't understand. It doesn't see." No one answered him. When the water vendor came by, everyone asked for a bottle. They offered him one. "No, I never drink water. My whole life, coffee, only coffee. Water tastes bad to me," he said, clearing his throat. "When we get to Camargo, I'll have my coffee."

He spoke in ten different tones of voice, always asking some phantom for the same thing: machinery.

In Santa Rosalia de Camargo everyone was eating watermelon. My freckled nose was buried in a slice Mama gave me when, suddenly, we saw a bunch of men on horseback next to a telegraph post, trying to throw a rope over it. When they succeeded, they handed the end to one man, who jammed his spurs into his horse. The horse leapt into motion. On the other end was the man they were hanging. The one on horseback stopped at a certain distance, when the rope was taut, and looked toward the post as if trying to read an advertisement from far away. Then he moved back little by little until the hanged man was at the right height. The others cut the rope, and they all rode off, carrying along a cloud of dust in their horses's hooves. Mama said nothing, but she stopped eating the watermelon. The seat opposite us was vacant. The man who dangled his hand out the window was hanging in front of the train, not ten meters from where we were. The *macuchi* cigarette had fallen from his ear, and the hanged man looked as though he was searching for it with his tongue. Slowly the train pulled out of the station, leaving behind, swinging from a post, the man who drank coffee all his life.

FROM A WINDOW

A window two meters above a street corner. Two girls looking down on a group of ten men with their weapons drawn, aiming at a young man on his knees, unshaven and grimey, who was begging desperately. Terribly sick, he writhed in terror, stretching out his hands toward the soldiers. He was dying of fear. The officer next to them was giving signals with his sword. When he raised it, as if to stab the sky,

ten bursts of fire left the 30–30s and embedded themselves in the young man's body, swollen with alcohol and cowardice. Lifted into the air by the shots, he then fell, blood pouring out of him through many holes. His hands stayed clapped over his mouth. There he lay for three days. One afternoon, somebody or other carried him away.

Since he lay there for three nights, I became accustomed to seeing the scrawl of his body, fallen toward the left with his hands on his face, sleeping there, next to me. That dead man seemed mine. There were moments when, fearful he would be taken away, I would get up and run to the window. He was my obsession at night. I liked to look at him because I thought he was very afraid.

One day, after dinner, I went running to see him from the window, but he wasn't there any more. Someone had stolen the timid dead man. The ground remained marked and desolate. That night I went to sleep dreaming they would shoot someone else and hoping it would be next to my house.

Translated by Doris Meyer

NOTES

1. *Cartucho* = cartridge; a tube of metal or paper containing the charge for a firearm, usually consisting of powder and shot, sometimes only powder. Campobello also uses this word metaphorically to convey the idea that a person living in the midst of the Mexican Revolution could be ready to explode at any moment with highly charged emotions.
2. A cigarette made with tobacco of common or inferior quality from Northern Mexico.

(opposite) *Kathe Kollwitz,* Self-Portrait with a Pencil, *1933, charcoal on paper. National Gallery of Art, Washington, D.C.; Rosenwald Collection*

Dorothy Livesay

Canada, b. 1909

Dorothy Livesay's career as Canada's first major feminist poet spans seven decades, from the 1920s through the 1980s. The length and strength of her career, and her deep concern for social justice (her writing manifests strong commitments to socialism, feminism, and the peace movement) have earned Livesay a prominent position as the *doyenne* of Canadian poetry. As *Collected Poems* (1972) demonstrates, her thematic and technical range includes subtle Imagist evocations, strident left-wing polemics, *engagé* documentary drama, and intensely personal lyrics—but her style is consistently spare, being, at its best, eloquent in utter simplicity.

Born in Winnipeg, Manitoba, to a literary family—both her parents wrote for the Winnipeg *Telegram*, and her mother, Florence Randal Livesay, was also a poet—Livesay moved to Toronto in 1920 when her father became manager of the Canadian Press. Attending Glen Mawr, a private school for girls, she studied Shaw and Ibsen, read Emily Dickinson and H.D. (Hilda Doolittle), and was introduced to atheism, socialism, and women's rights, attending Emma Goldman's lecture series in Toronto in 1926. Later this same year, Livesay entered Trinity College, University of Toronto, to study French and Italian; in 1928, while still in her teens, she published her first book of poems. After graduation in 1931, she studied at the Sorbonne in Paris, where she was moved by the workers' plight in the Depression so deeply that she returned, in 1932, to the University of Toronto to train as a social worker; she also joined the Communist Party.

457

One of Canada's most important social poets and a highly original love poet, Livesay's central themes are freedom and connection, identity and intimacy, and the tension that exists between them. The political poems on working-class life in *Day and Night* (1944) broke new ground in Canadian poetry; both this book and *Poems for People* (1947) earned Governor General's Awards. But Livesay was experiencing conflict and near despair at a time when the feminine mystique dominated North American society; she was split between her vocation as poet, and her daily life as the wife of accountant Duncan Macnair (whom she had married in 1938) and the mother of two children. This can be felt in the emotional power of poems such as "The Three Emily's" and "Ballad of Me." These touching, first-person explorations serve as important landmarks in the development of women's poetry in Canada.

Widowed in the late 1950s, Livesay struck out alone, teaching English for UNESCO in Zambia from 1960 to 1963; rejuvenated, she returned to Canada to work on a master's degree in education at the University of British Columbia. To coincide with the changes in her life, she altered her poetry to more boldly express herself—a sexually passionate and aging woman. Some of her best work dates from this period: *The Unquiet Bed* (1967), *Plainsongs* (1969), *Ice Age* (1975), and *The Woman I Am* (1977). The following poems are in *Ice Age* and *Collected Poems*.

Livesay has served Canadian literature unstintingly, as writer-in-residence at the University of New Brunswick and elsewhere, as editor of the pioneering anthology Forty Women Poets of Canada (1972), and as founder of the journal CV/II. A grandmother of seven, Livesay now lives in a community of artists on Galiano Island, near Vancouver, traveling frequently to distant parts of the world to give poetry readings.

Wendy Robbins Keitner

GRANDMOTHER

O lovely raw red wild
autumn turning
it's time to think of the blood
the red searing

Pale pale the poets and poetasters
moving along the midnight mists
those riverbanks where girls
white flanked, never refuse
yield all their mysteries

Give me instead
a small child noting
holly and rowan berry ripen
a small hand clasped

Who's there? What's that?
O, to survive
what must we do
to believe?
In the trees, my grandson.
In these roots. In these leaves.

THE THREE EMILY'S*

These women crying in my head
Walk alone, uncomforted:
The Emily's, these three
Cry to be set free—
And others whom I will not name
Each different, each the same.

Yet they had liberty!
Their kingdom was the sky:
They batted clouds with easy hand,
Found a mountain for their stand;
From wandering lonely they could catch
The inner magic of a heath—
A lake their palette, any tree
Their brush could be.

And still they cry to me
As in reproach—
I, born to hear their inner storm
Of separate man in woman's form,
I yet possess another kingdom, barred
To them, these three, this Emily.

I move as mother in a frame,
My arteries
Flow the immemorial way
Towards the child, the man;
And only for brief span
Am I an Emily on mountain snows
And one of these.

And so the whole that I possess
Is still much less—
They move triumphant through my head:
I am the one
Uncomforted.

NOTE

* Emily Brontë (1818–1848), Emily Dickinson (1830–1886), and Emily Carr (1871–1945), respectively an English novelist, an American poet, and a Canadian painter and writer.

Mercè Rodoreda   *Spain, 1909–1983*

Mercè Rodoreda, called by her American translator, David Rosenthal, "the greatest contemporary Catalan novelist and possibly the best Mediterranean woman author since Sappho" spent most of her productive years outside of her native Spain in exile from the Fascist government that banned the use of the Catalan language in which she wrote. Before 1939, when the use of Catalan was still permitted, she had published five novels and had won a major prize, the Premi Crexells for *Aloma* in 1937; however, in 1939, when the Civil War ended she, a Catalonian and Republican sympathizer, had to leave Spain. She lived in Paris and then Geneva, not writing again until 1959, when she published *Vint-i-dos contes* (Twenty-two Stories). *La Plaça del Diamant* (*The Time of the Dove*, 1962) established Rodoreda as one of the major Catalan writers; it has been widely translated and was recently made into a film. She returned to Spain in 1979, after Franco's death, and the use of Catalan was legalized. The selection here is taken from *La mera Christina i altres contes* (*My Christina and Other Stories*, 1967).

Rodoreda is known for her subtle evocation of setting and skillful characterization, aided by a vivid use of dialogue. Her women are, in the main, strong characters intent on making productive lives for themselves. Her major themes are the themes of postwar Europe: loneliness, alienation, and despair. Even so, there is great humor in her writing, and enormous human sympathy.

THE NURSEMAID
La mainadera

...Come here, little snaily snippet of lizard tail! Laugh! Go on! Laugh! Silly little creature, show me your toothies...Let's see. One, two, three...and a half! Coming down from the gummywum. Lift your arms, lift...You know what the ladies are doing? They're sitting in the parlor eating cakes and they're all saying "My husband, my husband..." while you and I have fun, shittypants, worse than shittypants. Let's see your tummy...plump as a little pigeon, a wee rabbit, a newborn baby partridge, a chickee-wickee, a tiny turtle, an itsy bitsy blackbird, a disgusting little pissypants...Lift up your armees. Say "housefly, housefly, housefly..." Buuum! Look at the garden. Put your arm around my neck...Like this, see? A nice silk scarfy. See the drizzle coming down? Look at that shiny tree, and the drops on the bellies of those leaves, dripping down so the lovely wormies and butterflies can get fat. Hear how they never stop talking? Those-are-the-ladies...Adelina, teach the girl to say papa and mama. If you sit in front of her and say pa-pa, ma-ma very slowly, so she can see how you move your lips...That's how you teach them, little by little, small children are excellent imitators...The child must learn to say papa before my husband's Saint's Day...Say nitwit! Nit-wit, nit-wit...See the little swallow, see the greenyfinch, see the blackbirdie running with three worms in his beak...look, look...here comes another lady, you see? Neus is going with a red umbrella to open the gate and they're saying something to each other and now she'll eat cream puffs with a little golden fork and her pinky raised, and soon I'll warm up your milk, just as white as a lily. Aren't we happy by ourselves? Shall we open the balcony door? Be brave like a lady, put your footsies in the little puddle. You like it? It's cool, it comes from heaven, the man with the beard makes it fall, who lives up there above everything, with his pants and his cap made of clouds, and he says amen. Play patty-cake...don't you know how? Aren't you just the smallest most delightful little girl ever made? You are? And you're my little girl and we love each other? Now into your crib. I'll dry your footsies with the yellow towel...nice and dry. So we won't catch cold and get a runny nosy. What's in your hand? A hair? Don't do that, it's naughty. Mustn't pull your hair out. It's dirty, you hear? And your hands must always be like coral...Little witch! If the boogie man comes he'll eat you up. First one toey-woey, then another, then your footsies and kneesies...and your little sparrow tummy. Yes indeed, don't wrinkle your nose at me. He'll have you for tea and throw away your bones, to make the glowworms laugh. Indeed he would. So you be good. Say...pa-pa, ma-ma...Now one of the ladies is leaving, with her hair curled and a girdle, and you look prettier with your hair all messed up like a toilet brush. Say nitwit! Nitwit, nit-wit...You must know how to say nitwit by your father's Saint's Day. Shall we go back out on the balcony? Come...you feel a little sick to your stomach? Don't you know up from down?...I'll make you a little clown suit and we'll go to the fair and we'll laugh and dance...You'll go dressed as a clown...

Translated by David H. Rosenthal

Gabrielle Roy   *Canada, 1909–1983*

Gabrielle Roy is one of Canada's most important and revered novelists, short-story writers, and essayists. Twice winner of Canada's prestigious Governor General's Award, recipient of its highest literary honor, the Prix David, and the first woman admitted to the Royal Society, she is hailed for putting Canada on the international literary map. Her importance to the Canadian tradition lies in her representation of a new urban subject matter and the creation of an ethnic landscape that includes groups marginal to Canadian society and previously unrepresented in its literature. Yet her naturalism is often tempered by a lyrical style and spiritual vision.

A teacher, an actress of significant local fame, and a journalist, Roy had traveled and studied in England and France before she published her first novel at the age of 36, thereafter marrying Marcel Carbotte and settling in Montreal. *Bonheur d'occasion* (1945) was also published in France, where it won her immediate celebrity and the critically prestigious Prix Femina. Soon translated for an American and British audience as *The Tin Flute*, it remained unpublished in anglophone Canada until 1958, when political ferment created interest in francophone literature. Using her reportorial skill, Roy depicted the squalor of a working-class neighborhood in Montreal during the Great Depression; the novel thus heralded a shift from the rural landscape and pastoral tradition of the Canadian novel. In the chief character, Rose-Anna, Roy also created a *mater dolorosa*, as Hugh McPherson has called her, the first of many strong mother figures in Roy's fiction.

The Tin Flute and other works that focus on the city, alternate with the prairie of Roy's native Manitoba as a setting for her fiction. A clue to this contrast lies in the leading role that Roy played in shaping the themes of Expo '67, the World's Fair held in Canada. In her essay *"Terre des hommes"* (1967) which takes as its title the fair's theme as well as Frenchman Antoine de Saint-Exupéry's work *Terre des hommes*, or Man and this World, known in the U.S., as *Wind, Sand and Stars*, Roy defines progress as that which emerges from the human capacity to respect cultural difference. The fair and its motif was to become a crucial symbol for younger artists of the Quiet Revolution. For Roy, it would seem to be the context for work that increasingly drew on the Canadian mosaic: the Inuit heroine of the novella *La rivière sans repos* (Windflower, 1970) and the immigrants from the Ukraine and from China, as well as those from Quebec, depicted in *Un jardin au bout du monde* (*Garden in the Wind*, 1975) and *Ces Enfants de ma vie* (*Children of My Heart*, 1977)—all in various ways caught between two worlds.

Akin to the work of the American Willa Cather, whom Roy greatly admired, the fiction also parallels the work of anglophone Canadian prairie writers such as Margaret Laurence. It also draws on the realities of Roy's own background: a mother whose family of Acadian descent had migrated from Quebec and a father who had served as an immigration officer during the open-door policy of the Liberal administration. Roy was neither a part of the francophone mainstream centered in Quebec nor the anglophone mainstream of Manitoba. Yet her work has contributed greatly to heal the "two solitudes" of Canada.

In earlier works by Roy, the autobiographical strain takes a different form. *Rue Deschambault* (*Street of Riches*, 1955) is a series of loosely connected stories centered around an apprentice writer growing up in Manitoba; Christine is also the semiautobiographical heroine of the episodically structured *La Route d'Altamont* (1966). As Barbara Godard suggests, these are novels in the *kunstlerroman* tradition, portraying the growth and development of the female artist, with the structural motif of the journey serving as a metaphor for the voyage of (self-) discovery. As important in the latter book are the matriarchal relations it delineates among grandmother, mother, and daughter.

In an early part of the book, Christine's grandmother makes a doll "out of nothing"; the incident offers the grandmother a respite from advancing age and senility and her granddaughter relief from boredom, leaving the narrator "haunted by the idea that it could not possibly be a man who made the world. But perhaps an old woman with extremely capable hands." In the selection here, Christine has reached young adulthood, is teaching and living with her mother. Soon she will leave to travel abroad. But today mother and daughter are returning from an annual visit to the family homestead on the prairie, and for the second time they "lose" their way and find themselves, amongst the Pembina Mountains.

from THE ROAD PAST ALTAMONT
La route d' Altamont

Maman was half asleep. Her head nodded slightly. From time to time she partly opened her eyes, undoubtedly struggling against her tiredness with that fear I had known in her all her life, the fear that if she rested for a minute or even dozed off, in that precise instant she would miss the best and most interesting thing that could happen. The heat and the monotony overcame her curiosity in spite of her. Her head fell forward again, her eyelids beat heavily, and, as they slipped over her eyes, I noticed in their expression a physical weariness so great that soon perhaps all Maman's eagerness and love of life would no longer be able to prevail against it. And I remember I said to myself something like: I mustn't wait too long to give Maman happiness. She may not be able to wait for it much longer. At that time I imagined that it was on the whole rather easy to make someone happy, that a tender word, a caress, or a smile could be enough. I imagined that it was in our power to fulfill the deepest needs of the heart, not yet knowing that tragic desires for perfection haunt some people till the end or, on the other hand, desires of such purity and simplicity that even the best will in the world would not know how to satisfy them.

I was perhaps slightly annoyed with my mother for wishing something other than what I considered it right to wish for her. If the truth be told, I was astonished that, old and sometimes weary as she was, Maman still entertained desires that seemed to me to be those of youth. I said to myself: Either one is young and it is time to strike out to know the world or one is old and it is time to rest and give up.

So a hundred times a day I said to Maman, "Rest. Haven't you done enough? It's time for you to rest."

And, as if I had insulted her, she would reply, "Rest! Believe me, it will soon enough be time for that."

Then, becoming thoughtful, she would say, "You know, I spoke that way to my own mother when she seemed to me to be growing old. 'When are you ever going to give up and rest?' I used to say to her, and only now can I see how provoking it must have been."

Our quiet, haphazardly chosen road had seemed for some time to be climbing, without perceptible strain, by slight and very gentle slopes, no doubt. However, the motor was puffing a little, and, if this hadn't been enough to tell me. I would have realized from the drier, more invigorating air that we were gaining altitude, sensitive as I have always been to the slightest atmospheric variation. With closed eyes, I think, I would recognize from the first breath the air of the ocean, the air of the plain, and certainly that of the high plateaus, because of the delightful feeling of lightness it communicates to me, as if I shed weight as I climbed—or mistakes.

Then, as we continued to rise, I seemed to see, spread against the sky, a distant, half-transparent range of small blue hills.

I was accustomed to the mirages of the prairies and this was the time of day when they arose, extraordinary or completely reasonable—sometimes great stretches of shimmering water, heavy, lifeless lakes. Often the Dead Sea itself appeared among us, level with the horizon; at other times phantom villages around their grain elevators. And once in my childhood an entire city rose from the ground at the end of the prairie especially for me, a strange city with cupolas.

Those are only clouds, I told myself, nothing more—and yet I pressed on as if to reach those gentle little hills before they were effaced.

But they did not melt away, like an illusion, sooner or later. Time and again, when I had rested my glance elsewhere, I found them still there when I looked back. They seemed to sharpen, to increase in size, and even perhaps become more beautiful. Then—did I dream all this? In so many things in our life an element of the imprecise and inexplicable persists, which makes us doubt their reality—the prairie, which since the beginning of the ages had been level and submissive, appeared to revolt. First it exploded in swellings, in crevices, in eroded cracks; boulders broke the sur-

face. Then it split more deeply; ridges sprang up, took on height and came rushing from every side as if, delivered from its heavy immobility, the land was beginning to move and was coming toward me in waves quite as much as I was going toward it. Finally, there was no more doubt possible. Little hills formed on either side of us; they accompanied us at a fixed distance, then suddenly drew near and now we were completely enclosed.

Now, moreover, the dirt road was perceptibly climbing, without pretense, with a sort of elation, in joyous little bounds, in leaps like a young dog straining at the leash, and I had to change gears in mid-hill. From time to time as we passed, a liquid voice, some flow of water over the rocks, struck my ear.

Ah, Maman is right, I thought. Hills are exciting, playing a game of waiting and withholding with us, keeping us always in suspense.

And soon, just as my mother had wished, they showed themselves to be covered with dry bushes, with small trees insecurely rooted on inclining slopes but warmed by the sun, shot with ardent light, the luminous tones of their foliage trembling in the sunlit air. All this—the patches of scorched rock, the red berries on their slender branches, the scarlet leaves of the underbrush—was delightfully tangled together, almost dead, and yet meanwhile what a shout of life it gave!

Then, abruptly, my mother woke up.

Had she been informed during her sleep that the hills had been found again? At any rate, when the landscape was at its most beautiful, she opened her eyes, just as I was about to pull her by the sleeve and say, "Look, just look what's happened to you, Mamatchka!"

At first she appeared to be sunk in a profound bewilderment. Did she believe she had been carried back to the land of her childhood, returned to her starting point with her whole long life to be lived over again? Or did it seem to her that the landscape was mocking at her desires, offering her only an illusion?

But I still didn't know her. Always prompter to faith and to reality than I was, Maman soon realized the simple, delightful truth.

"Can you believe it, Christine!" she cried. "We're in the Pembina Mountains. You know —the only range of mountains in southern Manitoba. I've always wanted to see them. Your uncle assured me there was no way in. But there is, there is, and you, dear child, have discovered it!"

How would I dare to touch her joy that day, much less try to take it apart to grasp its inmost spring? All joy is so mysterious that I am always most conscious in its presence of the clumsiness of words and of the impiety of wishing to be always analyzing, trying to take the human heart by surprise.

And then everything that took place between Maman and the little hills was so silent. I went slowly to let her look at them at her ease, watching the way her eyes flew from one side of the road to the other. We were still climbing, and the hills continued to hurry to the right, then to the left, as if to see us pass, since they in their isolation could not have seen human beings any oftener than we saw hills. Then I stopped; I turned off the engine. In her anxiety to get out, Maman no longer knew which handle to turn to open the door. I helped her. Then, without a word, she set out alone into the hills.

She began to climb, between the dry bushes that caught for an instant at her skirt, surprisingly agile, with the movements of a young goat, raising her head from time to time toward the height...then I lost sight of her. When she reappeared a short time later, she was right on top of one of the steepest hills, a silhouette diminished by the distance, completely alone on the farthermost point of the rock. Beside her leaned a small twisted fir tree, which had found its niche up there among the winds. And the curious thought came to me as I saw them there side by side, Maman and the tree, that it is perhaps necessary to be quite alone at times in order to find oneself.

What did they say to each other that day, Maman and the little hills? Did the hills really give Maman back her joyous childhood heart? And why is it that a human being knows no greater happiness in old age than to find in himself once more the face he wore as a child? Wouldn't this be rather an infinitely cruel thing? Whence comes the happiness of such an encounter? Perhaps, full of pity for the vanished youthful soul, the aged soul calls to it tenderly across the years, like an echo. "See," it says, "I can still feel what you felt... love what you loved...." And the echo undoubtedly answers something...but what? I knew nothing of this dialogue at that time. I merely wondered what could hold my mother for so long, in the open wind, on the rock. And if it was her past life she was finding there, how could there be happiness in this? How could it be good at seventy to give one's hand to one's childhood on a little hill? And if this is what life is, to find one's childhood again, at that moment then, when in their own good time childhood and old age come together again, the round must be almost finished, the festival over. I was suddenly terribly eager to see Maman back with me once more.

At last she came down from the hill. To conceal her emotion, she plucked a branch of red glowing leaves from a half-dead bush and, as she came toward me, caressed her bowed cheek with this. For she kept her eyes hidden from me as she approached and did not reveal them to me till quite a long time later, when there was no longer anything but ordinary things between us.

She sat down beside me without saying a word. We drove on in silence. From time to time I looked at her stealthily; I saw joy sparkling in her eyes like far-off water and even, for an instant, break to the surface in real moisture. So what she had seen was so disturbing? I was anxious all at once. The hills seemed different now, humped and rather cheerless; I longed to find the frank clear plain again.

Then Maman seized my arm in agitation.

"Christine," she asked, "did you just find this marvelous road by mistake?"

"So the thoughtlessness of youth is good for something!" I said jokingly.

But I saw that she was really troubled.

"In fact," she said, "you may not be able to find it again when we're coming back from your uncle's next year. You may never be able to find it again. There are roads, Christine, that one loses forever."

"What would you have me do?" I teased her gently. "Scatter bread crumbs like Tom Thumb?"

At that moment the hills opened out a little and, lodged completely in a crevice between fir trees, a tiny settlement appeared, rather like a mountain village with its four or five houses clinging at different levels to the uneven ground. On one of them shone a red Post Office sign. We had scarcely glimpsed the poor hamlet before it was hidden from our sight, though the singing of a stream, somewhere on the rocks, followed us for a moment longer. Maman had had time to catch the name of the place from the Post Office sign, a name that had, I think, fixed itself like an arrow in her spirit.

"It's Altamont," she said, glowing.

"Well, there's your landmark," I said, "since you're determined to have something definite about the journey."

"Yes," she said, "and let's never forget it, Christine. Let's engrave it in our memories. It's our only key to these hills, all we know for certain, the Altamont road."

And as she was speaking, our hills abruptly subsided, dwindled into scarcely raised mounds of earth, and almost at once the prairie received us stretching away on every side in its obliterating changelessness, denying everything that was not itself. With one accord Maman and I turned to look behind us. Of the hills that were already beginning to withdraw into the night almost nothing remained, only a faint contour against the sky, a barely perceptible line such as children make when they amuse themselves drawing the earth and the sky.

Translated by Joyce Marshall

Simone Weil   *France, 1909–1943*

Simone Weil is a controversial and compelling figure in the history of French letters. An important philosopher and thinker of the twentieth century, Weil as mystic and activist influenced generations of young people who saw in her a model of political and spiritual engagement. Given her refusal to isolate learning from politics and spirituality, intellectuals find her difficult to classify and to assimilate: She has been characterized by some as the greatest mystic of the century and by others as a revolutionary anarchist.

Weil was born into a comfortably upper-middle-class Jewish family in Paris. She received a rigorous classical education, as did other European intellectuals of her time. In 1928 she entered the Ecole Normale Supérieure, a prestigious institution of higher learning that sends its graduates to the best posts in the French university system; received her *agrégation* in philosophy; and was appointed to a teaching position in Le Puy, a small town in the center of France. She veered sharply from the predictable path of the academic when in 1934 she took a sabbatical to work in a Renault factory, believing that the only way to understand the plight of the working class was to live it, an experience she then described in *La Condition ouvrière* (The Condition of the Workers, 1951). In 1936, at the outbreak of the Spanish Civil War, she went to Barcelona, where she worked behind the lines for the Republicans.

Not only did Weil reject her bourgeois past; she also rejected the religious tradition of her family, because of the harshness of the Old Testament on which it was based, to embrace mystical Catholicism. Weil described her conversion experiences in *Attente de Dieu* (*Waiting for God*) and *Intuitions Préchrétiennes* (*Intimations of Christianity*, 1951); however, she was an outspoken critic of the Church, and refused to be baptised. Traditional Catholics accused her of being a heretic.

After the Germans invaded France, Weil was barred from the French university system because of her Jewish background and had to seek refuge in the provinces, where she was an agricultural worker for a time before escaping in 1942, to England, where she worked with other expatriates for French liberation. Finally, her health gave way after many self-inflicted and externally imposed privations, and she died of malnutrition and tuberculosis at the age of 33.

During her short life Weil refused to have any of her works published, with the exception of some articles that appeared in a number of journals, including *Révolution prolétarienne* and *Critique sociale*. Most of her writings were preserved through the efforts of her friends (including Albert Camus). The first volume to appear was *La Pesanteur et la grâce* (*Gravity and Grace*, 1947), which was edited from her voluminous notebooks. Like many of her other works, it is somewhat autobiographical in nature, combining philosopical reflections, political theorizing, and personal testimony. *L'Enracinement* (*The Need for Roots*, 1949), from which the selection here is taken, is an unusual document. It is a report, commissioned by Free France (a coalition of various groups in exile in England, including the provisional government established by de Gaulle) that sets forth a rationale and method for restructuring the French economy and educational system in the postwar period; it is a text remarkable for its attempt to realize an ideal while demanding nothing less than the regeneration of Western civilizaton and the reconstitution of an entirely new society. Along with "Reflections Concerning the Causes of Liberty and Social Oppression," (translated in *L'Oppression et la liberté* [*Oppression and Liberty, 1955*]), it is considered her finest political work.

Some of her most lyrical work appears in *La Source Grecque* (The Greek Source), which contains her meditations on the love of God; an unfinished tragedy *Venise sauvée* (Venice Saved, 1965); and a collection of poems (1968).

T.S. Eliot wrote the first major critical English-language introduction to Weil's writings; his commentary, published as a preface to *The Need for Roots*, is indicative of the ambivalence that Weil has generated. A new era in criticism began in the 1970s with the publication of Weil's three-volume *Cahiers* (Notebooks, 1970–1974) and the appearance of Simone Pétrement's biography. With critics like Elizabeth Hardwick and Conor Cruise O'Brien commenting on her work, discussion moved to a high level. Historians, political scientists, and philosophers like George Abbot White, John Hellman, Richard Reeves, John M. Dunaway, and Dorothy McFarland have written book-length works on her, while others such as Peter Winch, G.W. Weil, and Jean Bethke Elshtain have made important essayistic contributions. While segments of Weil's work have regularly appeared in translation, a team of scholars now preparing a new edition of Weil's writings in French should lead to a better sense of her oeuvre and its scope and the interrelationship of the various aspects of her thought.

from THE NEED FOR ROOTS
L'enracinement

UPROOTEDNESS

To be rooted is perhaps the most important and least recognized need of the human soul. It is one of the hardest to define. A human being has roots by virtue of his real, active, and natural participation in the life of a community, which preserves in living shape certain particular treasures of the past and certain particular expectations for the future. This participation is a natural one, in the sense that it is automatically brought about by place, conditions of birth, profession, and social surroundings. Every human being needs to have multiple roots. It is necessary for him to draw well-nigh the whole of his moral, intellectual, and spiritual life by way of the environment of which he forms a natural part.

Reciprocal exchanges by which different sorts of environment exert influence on one another are no less vital than to be rooted in natural surroundings. But a given environment should not receive an outside influence as something additional to itself, but as a stimulant intensifying its own particular way of life. It should draw nourishment from outside contributions only after having digested them, and the human beings who compose it should receive such contributions only from its hands. When a really talented painter walks into a picture gallery, his own originality is thereby confirmed. The same thing should apply to the various communities throughout the world and the different social environments.

Uprootedness occurs whenever there is a military conquest, and in this sense conquest is nearly always an evil. There is the minimum of uprootedness when the conquerors are migrants who settle down in the conquered country, intermarry with the inhabitants, and take root themselves. Such was the case with the Hellenes in Greece, the Celts in Gaul, and the Moors in Spain. But when the conqueror remains a stranger in the land of which he has taken possession, uprootedness becomes an almost mortal disease among the subdued population. It reaches its most acute stage when there are deportations on a massive scale, as in Europe under the German occupation, or along the upper loop of the Niger, or where there is any brutal suppression of all local traditions, as in the French possessions in the Pacific (if Gauguin and Alain Gerbault are to be believed).[1]

Even without a military conquest, money, power and economic domination can so impose a foreign influence as actually to provoke this disease of uprootedness.

Finally, the social relations existing in any one country can be very dangerous factors in connection with uprootedness. In all parts of our country at the present time—and setting aside the question of the conquest—there are two poisons at work spreading this disease. One of them is money. Money destroys human roots wherever it is able to penetrate, by turning desire for gain into the sole motive. It easily manages to outweigh all other motives, because the effort it demands of the mind is so very much less. Nothing is so clear and so simple as a row of figures.

UPROOTEDNESS IN THE TOWNS

There are social conditions in which an absolute and continuous dependence on money prevails—those of the wage-earning class, especially now that work by the piece obliges each workman to have his attention continually taken up with the subject of his pay. It is in these social conditions that the disease of uprootedness is most acute. Bernanos has said that our workmen are not, after all, immigrants like those of Mr. Ford.[2] The major social difficulty of our age proceeds from the fact that in a certain sense they *are* like them. Although they have remained geographically stationary, they have been morally uprooted, banished, and then reinstated, as it were on sufferance, in the form of industrial brawn. Unemployment is, of course, an uprootedness raised to the second power. They are unable to feel themselves at home whether it be in the factories, their own dwellings, the parties and trade-unions ostensibly created on their behalf, places of amusement, or in intellectual activities if they attempt to acquire some culture.

For the second factor making for uprootedness is education as it is understood nowadays. The Renaissance everywhere brought about a break between people of culture and the mass of the population; but while abstracting culture from national tradition, it did at least cause it to be steeped in Greek tradition. Since then, links with the national traditions have not been renewed, but Greece has been forgotten. The result has been a culture which has developed in a very restricted medium, removed from the world, in a stovepipe atmosphere—a culture very strongly directed toward and influenced by technical science, very strongly tinged with pragmatism, extremely broken up by specialization, entirely deprived both of contact with this world and, at the same time, of any window opening onto the world beyond....

To take but one example of the deformation of our culture: The concern—a perfectly legitimate one—to preserve for geometrical reasoning its character of necessity, causes geometry to be presented to *lycée* [high school] boys as something without any relation at all to the outside world. The only interest they can take

in it is as in some game, or else in order to get good marks. How could they be expected to see any truth in it?

The majority of them will always remain ignorant of the fact that nearly all our actions, the simple ones as well as the judiciously combined ones, are applications of geometrical principles; that the universe we inhabit is a network of geometrical relations, and that it is to geometrical necessity that we are in fact bound, as creatures enclosed in space and time. This geometrical necessity is presented to them in such a way that it appears arbitrary. Could anything be more absurd than an arbitrary necessity? By definition, necessity is something which is imposed.

On the other hand, when it is sought to popularize geometry and relate it to experience, the demonstrations are omitted. All that remains then is a few formulas totally devoid of interest. Geometry has then lost its savor, its very essence. For its essence lies in being a branch of study devoted to the subject of necessity—that same necessity which is sovereign in this material world.

Both these deformations could be easily avoided. There is no need to choose between demonstration and experience. It is as easy to demonstrate with some wood or iron as it is with a piece of chalk.

It is urgent, therefore, to consider a plan for re-establishing the working class by the roots. Tentative proposals for such are summarized below.

Large factories would be abolished. A big concern would be composed of an assembly shop connected with a number of little workshops, each containing one or more workmen, dispersed throughout the country. It would be these same workmen, and not specialists, who would take it in turns to go and work for a time in the central assembly shop, and there ought to be a holiday atmosphere about such occasions. Only half a day's work would be required, the rest of the time being taken up with hobnobbing with others similarly engaged, the development of feelings of loyalty to the concern, technical demonstrations showing each worker the exact function of the parts he makes and the various difficulties overcome by the work of others, geography lectures pointing out where the products they help to manufacture go to, the sort of human beings who use them, and the type of social surroundings, daily existence, or human atmosphere in which these products have a part to play, and how big this part is. To this could be added general cultural information. A workman's university would be in the vicinity of each central assembly shop. It would act in close liaison with the management of the concern, but would not form part of the later's property.

The machines would not belong to the concern. They would belong to the minute workshops scattered about everywhere, and these would, in their turn, be the property of the workmen, either individually or collectively. Every workman would, besides, own a house and a bit of land.

This triple proprietorship comprising machine, house, and land would be bestowed on him by the State as a gift on his marriage, and provided he had successfully passed a difficult technical examination, accompanied by a test to check the level of his intelligence and general culture.

The choice of a machine would be made to depend in the first place on the individual workman's tastes and natural abilities, and secondly on very general requirements from the point of view of production. It should be, of course, as far as possible, an adjustable automatic machine with a variety of uses.

The triple proprietorship could be neither transmitted by inheritance, nor sold, nor alienated in any way whatever. (The machine alone could, under certain circumstances, be exchanged.) The individual having the use of it would only be able to relinquish it purely and simply. In that event, it should be made difficult, but not impossible, for him later on to obtain an equivalent one elsewhere.

On a workman's death, this property would return to the State, which would, of course, if need be, be bound to maintain the well-being of the wife and children at the same level as before. If the woman was capable of doing the work, she could keep the property.

All such gifts would be financed out of taxes, either levied directly on business profits or indirectly on the sale of business products. They would be administered by a board composed of government officials, owners of business undertakings, trade-unionists, and representatives of the Chamber of Deputies.[3]

This right to property could be withdrawn on account of professional incapacity after sentence by a court of law. This, of course, presupposes the adoption of analogous penal measures for punishing, if necessary, professional incapacity on the part of the owner of a business undertaking.

A workman who wanted to become the owner of a small workshop would first have to obtain permission from a professional organization authorized to grant the same with discretion, and would then be given facilities for the purchase of two or three extra machines; but no more than that.

A workman unable to pass the technical examination would remain in the position of a wage earner. But he would be able throughout the whole of his life, at whatever age, to make fresh attempts to satisfy the conditions. He would also at any age, and on several occasions, be able to ask to be sent on a free course of some months at a training school.

These wages earners through incapacity would work either in little workshops not run on a co-operative basis, as assistants to a man working on his own, or as hands in the assembly shops. But only a small number of them should be allowed to stay in industry. The majority should be sent to fill jobs as manual laborers and pen pushers, which are indispensable to the carrying on of the public services and trade.

Up to the time he gets married and settles down somewhere for the remainder of his life—that is to say, depending on the individual character, up to the age of twenty-two, twenty-five, or thirty—a young man would be regarded as being still in a state of apprenticeship.

During childhood, enough time should be left out of school to enable children to spend many, many hours pottering about in their father's company while at work. Semiattendance at school—a few hours' study followed by a few hours' work—should then go on for some considerable time. Later, a very varied existence is what is needed: journeys of the *Tour de France* type, working courses spent, now with artisans working on their own, now in little co-operative workshops, now in assembly shops belonging to different concerns, now in youth associations of the *chantiers* or *compagnons* type;[4] working courses which, according to individual tastes and capacities, could be several times repeated and further prolonged by attendance at workmen's colleges for periods varying between a few weeks and two years. The ability to go on such working courses should, moreover, under certain conditions, be made possible at any age. They should be entirely free of charge, and not carry with them any sort of social advantages.

When the young workman, gorged and glutted with variety, began to think of settling down, he would be ripe for planting his roots. A wife, children, a garden supplying him with a great part of his food, work associating him with an enterprise he could love, be proud of,

and which was to him as a window opened wide on to the outside world—all this is surely enough for the earthly happiness of any human being.

Naturally, such a conception of the young workingman's development implies a complete recasting of the present prisonlike system.

Translated by Arthur Wills

NOTES

1. Paul Gauguin (1848–1903), the modern artist, described his experiences in Tahiti (1891–1893 and 1896–1901) in his journals and letters; Alain Gerbault (1893–1941) was a widely published and widely translated author who wrote of his solitary voyages across the Atlantic, in the Pacific, and to various South Pacific islands providing descriptions of the natives' degradation.
2. Georges Bernanos (1888–1948): French Catholic novelist, known for his passionate refusal to compromise with complacent bourgeois values.
3. The French chamber of parliament whose members are directly elected.
4. One of the last vestiges of the guild or corporation system of the Middle Ages. Young workmen serving their apprenticeship were known as *compagnons*, and in order to perfect themselves in their trade, used to undertake a journey on foot across France, following a fixed itinerary which took them to the principal centers of production. The arrival of the railway gradually caused this very ancient custom to die out.

     chantier de jeunesse: a type of instructional center created by the Vichy government with the object of giving young people on leaving school a supplementary education and practical experience in a trade.

Eudora Welty   *US, b. 1909*

Eudora Welty is a first-generation Southerner, the eldest child and only daughter of mixed American Protestant stock: her father, who became part of the new American managerial middle class, was from an Ohio farming family, and her mother was from West Virginia of people who were mostly teachers, lawyers, and preachers. "Chessie" Andrews Welty used the money she earned as a teacher in a one-room school to put herself through college, and although she chose not to follow in her mother's path, Welty frequently creates teacher heroines, most notably Miss Eckart in "June Recital" and Julia Mortimer in *Losing Battles*.

Born in Jackson, Mississippi, where she has lived most of her "sheltered life," as she calls it in her autobiography (*A Writer's Beginnings*, 1984), Welty completed her B.A. at the University of Wisconsin (1927–1929); studied advertising at Columbia Graduate School of Business (1930–1931) in New York City, to reassure her father that she would have some economic security; and then traveled throughout Mississippi in her first job as a publicity agent for the Works Progress Administration (WPA) during the early years of the Great Depression. Later, a Guggenheim Fellowship permitted her to travel to Europe (1949–1950); subsequent awards, honors, and attendance at writers' conferences and symposiums, as well as appointments as artist-in-residence in places such as Oxford and Cambridge, have marked her increasing literary stature.

Welty is representative of a new kind of experimental writer whose fiction left behind the politicized literary debates and modes of expression of the 1930s and established a link between traditional and modernist literature. This characteristic and implicitly feminist vision that has only recently begun to be acknowledged are perhaps reflected in the diverse precursors that Welty acknowledges: Jane Austen, Virginia Woolf, Mark Twain, and the Southern humorists.

Welty began her career as a writer by publishing in important literary magazines such as *Manuscript* and *Southern Review*, supported by such fellow Southerners as Cleanth Brooks and Robert Penn Warren (whose 1944 essay "The Love and Separateness of Miss Welty" was highly influential in setting the tone and direction of much of the early Welty criticism), followed by Ford Madox Ford and Katherine Anne Porter, who respectively sought to find a publisher for her first collection *A Curtain of Green* (1941) and wrote the introduction for it. This collection includes Welty's first-published story "Death of a Traveling Salesman" and the much anthologized "Why I Live at the P.O.," "Petrified Man," "Powerhouse" (loosely based on jazz pianist Fats Waller), and "A Worn Path." Still considered her finest achievement by some, these stories also anticipate the characteristic features of her later work: the country and small-town whose characters' provincialism often makes them the subject of comedy; the use of dramatic monologue and dialogue; colloquial diction derived from the Southern art of storytelling; and precise detail and rich imagery.

Welty's second and third collections, *The Wide Net* (1943) and *The Bride of Innisfallen* (1955), influenced by the writers Henry Green and Elizabeth Bowen (also a close friend, to whom the latter book is dedicated), puzzled reviewers and critics by their its impressionistic lyrical style and obvious but enigmatic symbolism. In *The Golden Apples* (1949), a collection of related stories, Welty was able to balance her lyrical exploration into the mystery of the human heart with mythical structures, motifs, and tropes that lend clarity to the work, making it one of the most highly regarded books in her canon. The title, taken from William Butler Yeats's poem "Song of the Wandering Aengus," evokes the myth of Atalanta's golden apples and the fruit of the Hesperides; the story reprinted here rewrites Yeats's famous poem "Leda and the Swan." Also unifying the stories is their sense of place and the thematic continuity of family life and community, centered on the eight, main families of Morgana and Maclain in the Mississippi delta region and stretching over a forty-year period.

Welty published her first novel, *Delta Wedding*, in 1946. Publication of *The Ponder Heart* (1954) brought Welty increased critical attention; and *Losing Battles* (1970), her first book after sixteen years, was the first to make the bestseller lists, evidence of a new reading public coming into being. Set in the hill country of the northeast Mississippi of the Great Depression years during a family reunion for Granny Vaughan's ninetieth birthday, the latter is the occasion for superb dialogue and tale-telling (in both senses) that span a century of living. This major novel, along with *The Optimist's Daughter* (1972), won a popular success richly deserved by one who has shown an unusual appreciation of and respect for the common reader.

Criticism on Welty is plentiful and generally illuminating. Elizabeth Evans's work is a good introduction. Ruth M. Vande Kieft's revised book (1987) stands as the most comprehensive study of her fiction; Michael Kreyling's *Eudora Welty's Achievement of Order* (1980) has been much praised for its insights. Important collections include special issues published by *Shenandoah* (1961) and *Mississippi Quarterly* (Fall 1973 and Fall 1986) and those edited by John F. Diamond, by Louis Dollarheide and Ann J. Abadie, and by Peggy Premshaw. Premshaw has also been foremost in assessing Welty's work from a feminist perspective. Other important feminist considerations of Welty's work are those of Danièle Pitavy-Souques and Louise Westling (*Sacred Groves and Ravaged Gardens*, 1985).

SIR RABBIT

He looked around first one side of the tree and then the other. And not a word!

"Oh-oh. I know you, Mr. King Mac-Lain!" Mattie Will cried, but the impudence—which still seemed marvelous to her since she'd never laid eyes on him close or thought of opening her mouth to him—all the impudence was carried off on the batting spring wind. "I know the way you do." When it came down to it, scared or not, she wanted to show him she'd heard all about King MacLain and his way. And scared or not, the air made her light-headed.

If it was Mr. King, he was, suddenly, looking around both sides of the tree at once—two eyes here and two eyes there, two little Adam's apples, and all those little brown hands. She shut her eyes, then her mouth. She planted her hoe in front of her toes and stood her ground by the bait can, too old—fifteen—to call out now that something was happening, but she took back what she'd said.

Then as she peeped, it was two MacLains that came out from behind the hickory nut tree.

Mr. MacLain's twins, his sons of course. Who would have believed they'd grown up?—or almost; for they were scared. They must be as old as herself, thought Mattie Will. People aren't prepared for twins having to grow up like ordinary people but see them always miniature and young somewhere. And here they were coming—the very spit of Mr. King their father.

Mattie Will waited on them. She yawned—strangely, for she felt at that moment as though somewhere a little boat was going out on a lake, never to come back—to see two little meanies coming now that she'd never dreamed of, instead of the one that would have terrified her for the rest of her days.

Those twins were town boys. They had their own pop stand by the post office stile on Saturdays in summer. Out here in the country they had undone their knee buckles and came jingling. Their fair bangs lifted and fell in the soft downy light under the dark tree, with its flowers so few you could still count them, it was so early in spring. They trotted down and up through the little gully like a pony pair that could keep time to music in the Ringling Brothers', touching shoulders until the last.

They made a tinkling circle around her. They didn't give her a chance to begin her own commotion, only lifted away her hoe that she stretched out and leaned it on the big vines. They didn't have one smile between them; instead, little matching frowns were furrowing their foreheads, so that she wanted to press them out with the flat of her finger.

One of the twins took hold of her by the apron sash and the other one ran under and she was down. One of them pinned her arms and the other one jumped her bare, naked feet. Biting their lips, they sat on her. One small hand, smelling of a recent lightning-bug (so early in the year?), blindfolded her eyes. The strong fresh smell of the place—which she had found first—came up and they rolled over on the turned-up mold, where the old foolish worms were coming out in their blindness.

At moments the sun would take hold of their arms with a bold dart of light, or rest on their wetted, shaken hair, or splash over their pretty clothes like the torn petals of a sunflower. She felt the soft and babylike heads, and the nuzzle of little cool noses. Whose nose was whose? She might have felt more anger than confusion, except that to keep twins straight had fallen her lot. And it seemed to her that from now on, having a visit go the visitor's way would come before giving trouble. She who had kicked Old Man Flewellyn out of the dewberry patch, an old smiling man! She had set her teeth in a small pointed ear that had the fuzz of a peach, and did not bite. Then she rolled her head and dared the other twin, with her teeth at his ear, since they were all in this together, all in here equally now, where it had been quiet as moonrise to her, and now while one black crow after another beat his wings across a turned-over field no distance at all beyond.

When they sat up in a circle with their skinned knees propped up in the playing light that came down like a fountain, she and the MacLain twins ate candy—as many sticks of candy as they felt like eating out of one paper sack for three people. The MacLain twins had brought the sack away out here with them and had put it in a safe place ahead of time, as far from the scene as the pin oak—needlessly far. Their forethought cast a pall on all three as they sucked and held their candy in their mouths like old men's pipes. One crow hollered over their heads and they all got to their feet as though a clock struck.

"Now."

What did it matter which twin said that word, like a little bark? It was the parting word. There was her hoe held up in a grandfather vine, gone a little further in its fall, and there was her bucket. After they'd walked away from her—backwards for a piece—then she, jumping at them to chase them off, screamed into the veil of leaves, "I just did it because your mama's a poor albino!"

She would think afterwards, married, when she had the time to sit down—churning, for instance—"Who had the least sense and the least care, for fifteen? They did. I did. But it wasn't fair to tease me. To try to make me dizzy, and run a ring around me, or make me think that first minute I was going to be carried off by their pa. Teasing because I had to open my mouth about Mr. King MacLain before I knew what was coming."

Tumbling on the wet spring ground with the goody-goody MacLain twins was something Junior Holifield would have given her a licking for, just for making such a story up, supposing, after she married Junior, she had put anything in words. Or he would have said he'd lick her for it if she told it *again*.

Poor Junior!

II

"Oh, good afternoon, sir. Don't shoot me, it's King MacLain. I'm in the habit of hunting these parts."

Junior had just knocked off a dead, double-headed pine cone and Blackstone was aiming at the telephone wire when the light voice with the fast words running together came out of the tree above the gully.

"Thought I'd see if the birds around here still tasted as sweet as they used to." And there he was—that is, he showed for a minute and then was gone behind a reddening sweetgum tree.

But fall coming or not, poor little quails weren't any of his business, with him darting around tree trunks in a starched white suit, even if he did carry a gun for looks, Mattie Will thought. She studied the empty arch between two trees with a far-sighted look. If that was Mr. King MacLain, nobody was ever going to shoot him. Shoot *him*? Let him go on ahead in his Sunday best from one tree to another without giving warning or being so fussy about wild shots from the low scrub. He was Mr. King, all right. Up there back of the leaves his voice laughed and made fun this minute.

Junior looked up and said, "Well, we come out to use up some old ammunition." He lifted his upper lip. He had another pine cone on his mind. He pinged it.

"You hear me?" said the voice.

"It sure did look like Mr. MacLain to me, Junior," Mattie Will whispered, pretending to be as slow as Junior was. She squinted against the small sun points that came at her cheeks through the braid of her hat. Then she pushed her way around her husband.

"Well. And we come out to shoot up some old ammunition on Saturday," Junior told her. "This *is* Saturday." He pulled her back.

"You boys been sighting any birds this way?" the white glimmer asked courteously, and then it passed behind another tree. "Seen my dog, then?" And the invisible mouth whistled, from east right around to west, they could hear the clean round of it. Mr. King even *whistled* with manners. And with familiarity.

And what two men in the world whistle the same? Mattie Will believed she must have heard him and seen him closer-to than she thought. Nobody could have *told* her how sweet the old rascal whistled, but it didn't surprise her.

Wilbur, the Holifield dog, flailed his tail and took a single bound toward the bank. Of course he had been barking the whole time, answered tolerantly by some dogs in town who—as certainly as if you could see them—were lying in front of the barbershop.

"Sighted e'er bird? Just one cuckoo," Junior said now, with his baby-mouth drawn down as if he would cry, which meant he was being funny, and so Blackstone, his distance behind in the plum thicket, hopped on one foot for Junior, but Junior said, "Be still, Blackstone, no call for you to start cutting up yet."

"No, sir. Never pass by these parts without bringing down a few plump, juicy birds for my supper," said the voice. It was far-away for the moment; Mr. MacLain must have turned and looked at the view from the hilltop. You could see all Morgana from there, and he could have picked out his own house.

"My name is Holifield. We was just out using up some old ammunition on Saturday, me and a nigger. And as long as you don't get no closer to us, we ain't liable to hit you," said Junior.

That echoed a little. They both happened to get behind gum trees just then, Mr. MacLain and Junior. *Junior* was behind a tree! And she was between them. Mattie Will put her hand over her laughing mouth. Blackstone in the thicket broke a stick and chunked the pieces in the air. "And we won't pay no attention what you do in your part of the woods," Junior said, a dignified gaze on the falling chips.

"Suits me, sir!"

"Truth is—" Junior always kept right on! Just as he would do eating, at the table, and to his sorrow. "I ain't prepared to believe you come after birds, hardly, Mr. MacLain, if it is you. *We* are the ones come after what birds they is, if they is any birds. You're trespassing."

"Trespassing," said the voice presently. "Well—don't shoot me for that."

"Oho ho, Mr. Junior! Know what? *He* gawn shoot *us*! Shoot us!" In the ecstasy of knowing the end of it ahead of time, Blackstone flew out in the open and sang it like a bird, and beat his pants.

"You hush up, or if he don't shoot you, I will," Junior said. "Look, what happened to your gun, you lost it agin?"

Mr. MacLain was moving waywardly along, and sometimes got as completely hidden by even a skinny little wild cherry as if he'd melted into it.

Ping!

"One more redbird!" sighed Mattie Will.

"Ain't we two hunting men letting each other by and about their own business?" asked Mr. MacLain, suddenly loud upon them. They saw part of him, looking out there at the head of the gully, one hand on a knee. "Look—this is the stretch of woods I always did like the best. Why don't you try a different stretch?"

"*See there*?"

Mr. MacLain laughed agreeably at accusation.

"There's something else ain't what you think," Junior said in his most Holifield way. "Ain't e'er young lady folling after me, that you can catch a holt of—white or black."

Wilbur spraddled right up the bank to Mr. MacLain suddenly, before they knew it, and fawned on him before they got him back. He was named Wilbur after Mr. Morrison, who had printed Mattie Will's and Junior's marriage in the newspaper.

Mr. MacLain withdrew, and Junior was patting Wilbur, hammerlike.

"Junior," Mattie Will called softly through the cup of her hand. "Looks like you really scared that man away. Wonder who he was?"

"Bless God. Come out in the open, young lady. I can hear you but not see you," Mr. MacLain called, appearing immediately from the waist up.

So poor Junior had got one thing right. Mr. MacLain had been counting on it all the time—that young girl-wives not tied down yet could generally be found following after their husbands, if the husbands went out with a .22 on a nice enough day in October.

"Won't you come out and explain something mysterious to me, young lady?"

But it sounded as if he'd just thought of it, and called it mysterious.

Mattie Will, who was crouched to her knees, bent her head. She took a June bug off a leaf, a late June bug. She was thinking to herself, Mr. MacLain must be up in years, and they said he never did feel constrained to live in Morgana like other people and just visited Mrs. MacLain a little now and then. He roamed the country end on end, living up north and where-all, on funds; and might at any time appear and then, over night, disappear. Who could have guessed today he was this close?

"Show yourself, young lady. Are you a Holifield too? I don't think you are. Come out here and let me ask you something." But he went bobbing on to another tree while he was cajoling, bright as a lantern that swayed in a wind.

"Show yourself and I'll brain you directly, Mattie Will," Junior said. "You heard who he said he was and you done heard what he was, all your life, or you ain't a girl." Junior squeezed up to his .22 and trained it, immediately changing his voice to a little high singsong. "He's the one gits ever'thing he wants shootin' from around trees, like the MacLains been doing since Time. Killed folks trespassin' when he was growin' up, or his pa did, if it so pleased him. MacLains begun killin' when they begun settlin.' And don't nobody know how many chirren he has. Don't let him git no closer to me than he is now, you all."

Mattie Will ran the June bug up and

down her arm and remembered once when she was little and her mother and father had both been taken with the prevalent sickness, and it was Mrs. MacLain from Morgana—who before that was known only by sight to her—who had come out to the farm and nursed and cooked for them, since there was nobody. She served them light-bread toast, and not biscuit, and didn't believe in molasses. She was not afraid of all the mud. She was in the congregation, always, a sweet-looking Presbyterian albino lady. Nothing was her fault. Mrs. MacLain came by herself to church, without boy or man, her lace collar fastened down by a cluster-pearl pin just like a little ice cream spoon, loaded. Going down the aisle she held up her head for the benefit of them all, while they considered Mr. MacLain a thousand miles away. And when they sang in church with her, they might as well have sung,

> "A thousand miles away.
>   A thousand miles away."

It made church holier.

"I'll just start up that little bank till I see what he's after, Junior," Mattie Will said, rising.

Junior just looked at her stubbornly.

She pinched him. "Didn't you hear him ask me a question? Don't be so country: I'm going to answer it. And who's trespassing, if it's not us all three and a nigger? These whole woods belongs to you know who, Old Lady Stark. She'd like to see us all in Coventry this minute." She pointed overhead, without looking, where the signs said,

> Posted.
> No Pigs With or Without Rings.
> No Hunting.
> This Means You.

STARK

While he looked at those, and even Mr. MacLain looked at them, Mattie Will made her way up the bank.

"You see?" Junior cried again. "Yonder comes Mattie Will. It's just a good thing I got my gun too, Mr. MacLain. You're so smart. I didn't even know you was near enough to flush out, Mr. MacLain. You back to stay? Come on, Blackstone, let's me and you shoot him right now if he budges to catch a holt of Mattie Will, don't care what happens to us or who we hit, whether we both go to the 'lectric chair or not."

Mr. MacLain then looked out from a pin oak and fired a load of buckshot down, the way he'd throw a bone. Mattie Will's tongue ran out too, to show Junior how he'd acted in public.

Blackstone was howling out from his plum thicket, "Now it be's our turn and I found my old gun and we done used up every bit of ammunition we had on turtles an' trash! You see, you see."

Mattie Will looked up at Mr. MacLain and he beamed at her. He sent another load out, this one down over her where she held to some roots on the bank, and right over Junior's head.

It peppered his hat. Baby holes shamed it all over, blush-like. Junior threw away his gun.

Big red hand spread out on his shirt (he would always think he was shot through the heart if anybody's gun but his went off), Junior rose in the air and got a holler out. And then—he seemed determined about the way to come down, like Mister Holifield down from a ladder; no man more set in his ways than he, even Mister Holifield—he kicked and came down backwards. There was a fallen tree, a big fresh-cut magnolia some good-for-nothing had amused himself chopping down. Across that Junior decided to light, instead of on green moss—head and body on one side of the tree, feet and legs on the other. Then he went limp from the middle out, before their eyes. He was dead to the world; as immune as if asleep in his pew, but bent the opposite way.

Mr. MacLain appeared on top of the gully, wearing a yellow Panama hat and a white linen suit with the sleeves as ridgy as two washboards. He looked like the preternatural month of June. He came light of foot and let his gunstock trail carefree through the periwinkle, which would bind it a little and then let go.

He went to Junior first, taking the bank in three or four knee-deep steps down.

He bent over and laid his ear to Junior. He thumped him, like a melon he tested, and let him lie—too green. As if lighting a match from his side, he drew a finger down Junior's brown pants leg, and stepped away. Mr. MacLain's linen shoulders, white as a goose's back in the sun, shrugged and twinkled in the glade.

To his back, he was not so very big, not so flashy and splendid as, for example, some brand-new evangelist come into the midst. He turned around and threw off his hat, and showed a thatch of straight, biscuit-colored hair. He smiled. His puckered face was like a little boy's, with square brown teeth.

Mattie Will slid down the bank. Mr. MacLain stood with head cocked while the wind swelled and blew across the top of the ridge, turning over the green and gold leaves high up around them all, stirring along suspicions of burning leaves and gunpowder smoke and the juice of the magnolia, and then he dropped his gun flat in the vines. Mattie Will saw he was coming now.

"Turn *your* self around and start picking plums!" she called, joining her hands, and Blackstone turned around, just in time.

When she laid eyes on Mr. MacLain close, she staggered, he had such grandeur, and then she was caught by the hair and brought down as suddenly to earth as if whacked by an unseen shillelagh. Presently she lifted her eyes in a lazy dread and saw those eyes above hers, as keenly bright and unwavering and apart from her life as the flowers on a tree.

But he put on her, with the affront of his body, the affront of his sense too. No pleasure in that! She had to put on what he knew with what he did—maybe because he was so grand

it was a thorn to him. Like submitting to another way to talk, she could answer to his burden now, his whole blithe, smiling, superior, frantic existence. And no matter what happened to her, she had to remember, disappointments are not to be borne by Mr. MacLain, or he'll go away again.

Now he clasped her to his shoulder, and her tongue tasted sweet starch for the last time. Her arms dropped back to the mossiness, and she was Mr. MacLain's Doom, or Mr. MacLain's Weakness, like the rest, and neither Mrs. Junior Holifield nor Mattie Will Sojourner; now she was something she had always heard of. She did not stir.

Then when he let her fall and walked off, when he was out of hearing in the woods, and the birds and woods-sounds and the wood-chopping throbbed clearly, she lay there on one elbow, wide awake. A dove feather came turning down through the light that was like golden smoke. She caught it with a dart of the hand, and brushed her chin; she was never displeased to catch anything. Nothing more fell.

But she moved. She was the mover in the family. She jumped up. Besides, she heard plums falling into the bucket—sounds of pure complaint by this time. She threw Blackstone a glance. He picked plums and had a lizard to play with, and his cap unretrieved from his first sailing delight still hung in a tree. The Holifield dog licked Blackstone on the seat patch and then trotted over and licked Junior on the stone-like hand, and looked back over his shoulder with the expression of a lady soloist to whose song nobody has really listened. For ages he might have been making a little path back and forth between Junior and Blackstone, but she could not think of his name, or would not, just as Junior would not wake up.

She wasn't going to call a one of them, man or dog, to his senses. There was Junior suspended dead to the world over a tree that was big enough around for two of him half as willful. He was hooped in the middle like the bridge over Little Chunky. Fools could set foot on him, walk over him. Even a young mule could run across him, the one he wanted to buy. His old brown pants hung halfway up his legs, and there in his poky middle pitifully gleamed the belt buckle anybody would know him by, even in a hundred years. J for Junior. A pang reached her and she took a step. It could be he was scared more than half to death—but no, not with that sleeping face, still with its look of "How come?," or its speckled lashes, quiet as the tails of sitting birds, in the shade of his brow.

"Let the church bells wake him!" said Mattie Will to Wilbur. "Ain't tomorrow Sunday? Blackstone, you have your cap to climb up after."

In the woods she heard sounds, the dry creek beginning to run or a strange man calling, one or the other, she thought, but she walked right up on Mr. MacLain again, asleep—snoring. He slept sitting up with his back against a tree, his head pillowed in the luminous Panama, his snorting mouth drawn round in a perfect heart open to the green turning world around him.

She stamped her foot, nothing happened, then she approached softly, and down on hands and knees contemplated him. Her hair fell over her eyes and she steadily blew a part in it; his head went back and forth appearing to say "No." Of course she was not denying a thing in this world, but now had time to look at anything she pleased and study it.

With her almost motherly sway of the head and arms to help her, she gazed at the sounding-off, sleeping head, and the neck like a little porch column in town, at the one hand, the other hand, the bent leg and the straight, all those parts looking no more driven than her man's now, or of any more use than a heap of cane thrown up by the mill and left in the pit to dry. But they were, and would be. He snored as if all the frogs of spring were inside

him—but to him an old song. Or to him little bells, little bells for the light air, that rose up and sank between his two hands, never to be let fall.

His coat hung loosely out from him, and a letter suddenly dropped a little way out from a pocket—whiter than white.

Mattie Will subsided forward onto her arms. Her rear stayed up in the sky, which seemed to brush it with little feathers. She lay there and listened to the world go round.

But presently Mr. MacLain leaped to his feet, bolt awake, with a flourish of legs. He looked horrified—that he had been seen asleep? and by Mattie Will? And he did not know that there was nothing she could or would take away from him—Mr. King MacLain?

> In the night time,
> At the right time,
>   So I've understood,
>   'Tis the habit of Sir Rabbit
>   To dance in the wood—

That was all that went through Mattie Will's head.

"What you doing here, girl?" Mr. MacLain beat his snowy arms up and down. "Go on! Go on off! Go to Guinea!"

She got up and skedaddled.

She pressed through a haw thicket and through the cherry trees. With a tree-high seesawing of boughs a squirrel chase ran ahead of her through the woods—Morgan's Woods, as it used to be called. Fat birds were rocking on their perches. A little quail ran on the woods floor. Down an arch, some old cedar lane up here, Mattie Will could look away into the big West. She could see the drift of it all, the stretched land below the little hills, and the Big Black, clear to MacLain's Courthouse, almost, the Stark place plain and the fields, and their farm, everybody's house above trees, the

MacLains'—the white floating peak—and even Blackstone's granny's cabin, where there had been a murder one time. And Morgana all in rays, like a giant sunflower in the dust of Saturday.

But as she ran down through the woods and vines, this side and that, on the way to get Junior home, it stole back into her mind about those two gawky boys, the MacLain twins. They were soft and jumpy! That day, with their brown, bright eyes popping and blinking, and their little aching Adam's apples—they were like young deer, or even remoter creatures...kangaroos...For the first time Mattie Will thought they were mysterious and sweet —gamboling now she knew not where.

Ólga Fyódorovna Berggólts   *Russia/USSR, 1910–1975*

Born in St. Petersburg, now Leningrad, the daughter of a physician, Berggólts graduated from Leningrad University in 1930 with a degree in philology and began work as a journalist and, later, as a radio correspondent, becoming noted for her daily broadcasts during the period of the 900-day Leningrad seige. Though it is omitted in or contradicted by Soviet sources, emigré writers indicate that two daughters died during the 1930s; her first husband, the poet Borís Kornílov, was executed during the Stalinist purges of 1938; and her second husband died of hunger during the Leningrad blockade in 1942. Despite her loyalty to the regime, Berggólts has wrested admiration from Western critics for her courage in opposing it and her ability to maintain a measure of intellectual and artistic integrity. In 1954, she opened the afternoon session of the second Soviet Writers' Congress with a speech entitled "Second-Class Writers"; the now-famous lines, completed only in *Literatúrnaya gazéta*, read, "You don't need literature. You need just one writer and even then...a dead one."

Her first collection, *Stikhotvoréniya* (Poems), appeared in 1934, followed by *Kníga pésen* (Book of Songs, 1935) and *Listopád* (Fall, 1938). Her best works emerge from and document the wartime experience—*Leningrádskaya tetrád* (Leningrad Notebook, 1942) as well as *Leningrád* (1944) and *Tvóy pút* (Your Road, 1945); they fuse the personal and the epic and build a monument to the city and its people. Though she won a State Prize in 1951 for her verse epic "Pervorossísk" (1950), in later works written during a period of greater liberalization—*Uzel* (The Knot, 1965), *Dnevnikí dalókikh lét* (Diaries of Bygone Years, 1967), *Ispytánie* (The Trial, 1967), and her last volume *Pamyat* (Memory, 1972)—Berggólts not only draws on historical events but also depicts the savage repression that preceded and followed the Soviet's finest hour, endurance during both the Leningrad blockade and more generally during World War II. The first two poems are from the wartime collections; the last is from her most recent work.

THE ARMY
'Armiya'

I hear "The Army..."
                                        I recall the day
in winter, January, forty-two.
My friend was walking with her children, home.
They carried bottles—water—from the river.
Their path was frightening,
                                        although not far.
A person in a coat came up to them:
He looked—and then took out his rationed bread,
three hundred grams, encrusted all in ice.
He broke it up and gave it to those children
and stood a while until they finished eating.
The mother, with a hand as gray as smoke,
reached out to barely touch his greatcoat's sleeve.
She touched, her face not brightening at all...
The world has never witnessed greater thanks!
We know our armies' lives entirely
that stood with us, engirded, in the city.
...They left, the mother turning to the right,
the soldier forward, through the snow and ice.
He went to Narvsk, an outpost on the front,
from hunger reeling, always on the move.
He went to Narvsk, in torment burning
with shame of father, of a man and soldier.
The giant city died away behind him
in graying rays of January's sunset.
He went to Narvsk, and conquering his delirium,
remembered how—no, not remembered—knew
there was a woman watching as he left
who thanked him and did not reproach.
He gulped down snow and felt with some annoyance
the rifle on his shoulder hung too heavy.
He reached the front and crawled away in ambush
to slay the enemy, exterminate...
So now you understand the reason why
there is no army anywhere more loved,
none more devoted to its native people,
none more self-giving, nor invincible.
(January, 1942)

Translated by Kathryn Szczepanska

from FEBRUARY DIARY
Fevrálsky Dnevník

The city was adorned in sleepy rime.
The district snowdrifts, silence...
Beneath the snow the tram rails can't be found
and only sounds of sleighbells now are heard.

They squeak, they squeak, those runners, down the Nevsky.
On narrow, funny, children's sleds
they carry pots of deep blue water,
and firewood and baggage, and the dying and the sick...

Thus from December city people wander
for many miles, in thick and foggy murk,
in backwoods of the blind, iced-over buildings,
in search of slightly warmer nooks.

And look—a woman takes her husband somewhere,
a grayish half-mask on her face,
her hands are holding cans, the soup for dinner.
The shells are whistling and the frost grows fierce...
—Friends! We are in a fiery circle.

A girl with frosted-over cheeks
who clenches stubbornly her darkened mouth
is taking to the Okhtinsk cemetery
a body shrouded in a blanket.

She, rocking, takes him—might be there by evening...
Her eyes impassively look to the darkness.
Take off your hat, O citizen! here passes
a man who perished at his post.

The city sleighs, they squeak and creak...
We cannot count the many we have lost!
But we cry not; they speak the truth who say
that Leningrader's tears are frozen solid.

No, we cry not. Our tears are precious little.
Our hatred will not let us cry.
Our hatred has become our pledge to life:
it centers us, it burns, it drives us on.

So that I not forgive and not forget,
So that I take my vengeance as I can,
My brother's grave before me now appears
in Okhtinsk cemetery, on the right.

Translated by Kathryn Szczepanska

I KEEP REMEMBERING....
Nó yá vsyó vrémya pómnyu pro odnú

But I keep remembering one of them,
that first spring of the blockade...

How many rusty beds and bunks
littered the streets those days!
They hunched down among the ruins
senselessly trying to screen them.
Their somber, bony dance twirled
everywhere the ground was being dug for vegetables...
And for no particular reason they gathered
here and there on the embankment—
                                                          dark and bare,

as though Dystrophia, the enemy,
wanted a place to rest up nights.

You walk, you count—but they are countless...
Their former owners cannot sleep on them—they cannot!
The sovereign earth tends these beds
and covers them with an iron down...

How many times I tugged at your hearts
with my implacable inventory of losses.
I spoke out loud of the most terrible things,
which even in a whisper are not spoken of.
But Leningrad,
                      my father,
                                          home,
                                                          life's path,
sending me ever into new terrains,
you say to me:
                        'Do not forget—that's all!'
And as you see now:
                                I have not forgotten.

1964   *Translated by J.R. Rowland*

María Luisa Bombal   *Chile, 1910–1980*

"When they name the best [Latin American writers she] is never missing from the
list." So said the celebrated Jorge Luis Borges[1] about the distinguished writer,
María Luisa Bombal. Born in Viña de Mar, Chile, María Luisa Bombal received
her formal education in France; when at the Sorbonne she majored in philosophy
and literature. There she was greatly influenced by the Surrealists. After she

graduated, she went to Buenos Aires, where she lived for a short time with Pablo Neruda[2] and his wife, writing the novella *La última niebla* (House of Mist, 1934) on the kitchen counter of their apartment. It was published by Victoria Ocampo's Sur Press. Immediately successful, *La última niebla* went through many editions and was widely translated. The novella uses surrealistic elements to create a mythic and dreamlike atmosphere.

In addition to *La última niebla* she wrote only one novel, *La amortajada* (The Shrouded Woman, 1938) and a novella, *La historia de María Griselda* (The Story of Maria Griselda, 1976) in which the following story, "Trenzas" (Braids) originally appeared; the English-language *New Islands and Other Stories* (1982) from which the translation of the selection was taken is a collection of short stories which, except for "Braids," first appeared in *La última niebla*. Bombal also wrote screenplays for Argentinian film for several years. Despite her small output, Bombal is considered to be an extremely important figure in Latin American literature, especially as having influenced magical realism and other experimental approaches to writing.

As Chile's representative to the P.E.N. conference in the United States in 1940, Bombal met and married the Count Raphael de Saint-Phalle, and lived with him in the United States until his death in 1970, when she returned to her native Chile for the remaining years of her life. She received the prestigious Chilean Academy of Arts and Letters annual prize for *La historia de María Griselda* in 1977, shortly before her death.

NOTES

1. Jorge Luis Borges (1899–1986): Argentinan writer of poetry, short stories, and criticism, he was for many years one of Latin America's leading literati.
2. Pablo Neruda (1904–1973): poet and political leader, he was extremely active in the Communist party and died during the military coup in 1973.

BRAIDS
Trenzas

Day by day, proud human beings that we are, we have a tendency to renounce our elemental roots, which accounts for the fact that women no longer appreciate their braids.

Being rationalists nowadays, women in cutting off their braids ignore that in effect they are severing their ties with those magic currents which issue from the very heart of the earth.

Because a woman's hair springs from the most profound and mysterious source, whence is born the first trembling seed of life—evolving therefrom to struggle and grow among many entangling forces, thrusting through the vegetal surface into the air and on upwards to the privileged forehead of its choice.

Did not the dark and lustrous braids of Isolde,[1] princess of Ireland, absorb this mysterious power even as her lips took the first drop of the enchanted potion?

Was it not owing perhaps to the length of her braids that the potion led her so swiftly to her fate? For there is no doubt that her swirling hair murmured like underground fountains, sighed like the breeze whispering through leaves. Murmur and sighing—which held Tristram spellbound on those nights of moonlight and love, when he undid her tresses and listened in ecstasy to the far-off singing, persistent and secret...the song of nature emanating from her hair.

And I know that even when Isolde was asleep her tousled hair maintained its power—on the elegant pillows of Tintagel Castle as well as in the wheat fields of exile...and her braids blossomed from those exotic flowers that she uprooted in fear with every dawn.

And Queen Mélisande's[2] blond braids, longer even than her delicate body.

Braids that, as she leaned over her tower in the autumn twilight, came to rest imprudently on the strong shoulders of the king's brother.

"Mélisande," Pelléas cries in awe. Then, quaking, daring at last to let his heart speak: "Mélisande," he murmurs, "your braids, I can finally touch your braids, kiss them, enfold myself in them."

In answer—only a sigh from the top of the tower. The braids had already unwittingly confessed that shy and timid truth their owner was hiding within her heart.

And why not at this point recall the braids of our sweet María from the novel by Jorge Isaacs?[3] Disembodied braids wrapped in that blue apron she wore when watering her small garden.

Braids covered with dried butterflies and memories which slept under Efraín's pillow during his long night of grief.

Dead braids, and yet somehow a living testament that obliged him to go on living, if only to remember her.

Bluebeard's eighth wife—have you forgotten her?[4] Forgotten how her severe and extravagant husband, before leaving on an unexpected journey, entrusted his mischievous young bride with the keys to every chamber in that vast and sumptuous mansion, prohibiting only the use of that rusty little key which opened the last room in a forbidding and uncarpeted corridor?

Needless to say, during this welcome marital separation, in the midst of much amusement, laughing friends, and genteel courtiers, the game that intrigued and tempted her the most was the only game forbidden: inserting that mysterious little key into the lock of that innermost, abandoned room.

Now, it is well known that, in women as well as cats, curiosity dominates all other passions. And so, when her lord and master returned without warning, the disobedient, quivering wife surrendered the keys, among them one of the fearful knight, in spite of her attempts to disguise it, found not only rusty but flecked with blood.

"You, my lady, have betrayed me!" he roared. "For which your fate shall be to join your wretched predecessors at the end of the corridor."

Having said this, he unsheathed his sword...

And what is the relevance of this old story that we learn in our childhood, you must be wondering. It has nothing to do with braids...

Ah, but it does! I reply vehemently. You fail to understand that what saved her was not the brief reprieve granted by her enraged husband to say her last prayers; nor was it her pleading, or the terrified cries the frightened Anne sent forth from the tower, beseeching help for her sister.

Nor was it the coincidental appearance of her two warrior brothers, who at that very moment were riding toward the castle for a visit.

No, none of these circumstances saved her.

It was her braids, and only her braids, intricately wound in a hundred silky, capricious coils that, when her implacable husband threw her brutally at his feet to consummate his crime, seized and obstructed his murderous fingers so that he found himself snarled up to the sword hilt in those desperate curls protecting her delicate head until the providential arrival of the aforementioned warriors, her well-beloved brothers, who had been invited earlier by our curious heroine.

You must admit it was not in vain that during her innocent and happy youth the girl who later became the foolish Castilian and last wife of Bluebeard sang as she brushed her hair, endowing it with vigor and beauty.

"She was very pale, like those women who have long hair," Balzac describes one of his enigmatic heroines.[5]

And that was no verbal caprice.

Because undoubtedly Balzac must have been blessed with an intuition of the ultimate relationship that can exist between human beings and the profound mystery of the earth.

And I am here to verify and illustrate his affirmation with a tale of a strange event witnessed by so many of us only a few years ago.

Of what use are names and places? Those who are familiar know; the rest can guess.

Two sisters.

The declining days of an old, brilliant, powerful family—albeit one amply beset by hidden passions, unexpected deaths, and suicides.

The older sister, who since her youth had endured a loveless existence, cut her hair short one day, dressed herself in a simple poncho made of vicuña wool, and, in spite of her parents' grief-stricken protests, retired to the family's large southern hacienda—which she was determined to administer with an iron hand. The gentle country people soon named her the Amazon.[6] She was stubborn but fair. Ugly but with an aristocratic carriage and a generous smile. A spinster...no one knew why.

By contrast, the younger sister had become a widow voluntarily—having shot her adulterous husband out of wounded pride. She was very beautiful, but suffered from extremely fragile health.

She also lived alone, in the family's old mansion in the city. She had a soft voice, quiet brown eyes, but the single red braid that she wore in a circlet around her small head cast a resplendent light over her pale complexion.

Yes, she was a sweet and terrible woman. She would fall in love and love madly.

It all began on the hacienda that autumn night when the gamekeeper ran down to the dale shouting: "Fire!"

For some time, however, her forehead pressed against the windowpane, the Amazon had been gazing with fascination at that precocious and purple dawn beginning to blaze up there on her hills...Then, in her usual calm manner, she gave the necessary instructions to the servants of the manor, ordered her horse brought, and set off toward the fire, accompanied by her foremen.

Meanwhile, in the city, the younger sister, just returned from a ball, lay on the rug of the salon, victim of a sudden faint.

Her suitors were gone, her servants asleep, she was hidden in the shadow of the candelabra she had been in the act of extinguishing. Like a devious accomplice, a gust of cold wind stirred the balcony drapes, billowing them, to settle on the defenseless woman's forehead, shoulders, and exposed breasts.

In the southern hacienda, the Amazon and her retinue were climbing the hills, penetrating the woods, the fires. Another blast of wind, hot and acrid, swept over them, carrying a cloud of scorched leaves, blinded birds, burning nests.

She knew beforehand that she was beaten. No one could have stopped the fury of those flames.

Later, sitting on the trunk of a dead tree that had fallen many years ago, the Amazon stoically resigned herself to the distant spectacle of the catastrophe, with the sullen dignity of a despised millionaire witnessing the ransacking and destruction of his riches.

The forest was burning almost silently before her eyes, trees falling one by one, row after row, like the columns of a familiar cathedral, while, as in a dream, she contemplated her loss...thinking, remembering, allowing herself, after so many years, to suffer...

That enormous hazelnut tree being consumed...Hadn't her brother and sisters gathered with their governess under its avalanche of hard fruit to enjoy their special picnics?

And behind that gigantic trunk, I forget its name, she would run to hide after a prank ...and those little mushrooms they used to pick under the cedar...and that eucalyptus she had embraced—very young, crying stupidly after experiencing her first disillusionment: that grief she never confessed, that pain which drove her to cut her hair, to become the Amazon, resolving never to love again...never...

There, in the city, dawn was breaking over the carpet on which lay the still form of her sister—the one who dared to love—sinking gradually, with gentle spasms, into what is called death, unseen, beyond help...though her red braid was still vivid, seemingly alive.

And suddenly, down there on the hacienda, the final act: the exodus of brave horses returning with singed hair standing on end, having saved their almost asphyxiated riders.

From the immense ruined forest rose enormous tongues of smoke, climbing high and straight as the trees which had once stood there.

And for a brief moment the ghost of a forest wavered before the eyes of the owner and her weeping servants. She did not cry, however.

Then: debris, ashes, silence.

When they came to close the balcony doors and carry the fragile woman to her bed, trying in vain to revive her, to warm her, it was too late.

The doctor concluded that she had taken all night to die.

You see, the forest had to die along with her and her hair, because they shared the same roots.

Because the green climbing plants that twine on the trees, the sweet algae clinging to the rocks, are but strands of hair: are the word, the coming and soaring of nature—its happiness and melancholy, the means of expression by which she gently instills her magic and wisdom into all living things.

And it is for this reason that women nowadays, having renounced their braids, have lost their prophetic powers, no longer have premonitions, or feel absurd joy, or have their old magetism.

And as a result their dreams are but a sad sea tide bringing and rebringing faded images, or some other domestic nightmare.

Translated by Richard and Lucia Cunningham

NOTES

1. Isolde; in Arthurian legend, the Irish Isolde was betrothed to King Mark of Cornwall. However a magic potion compels her to forever love Sir Tristram, Mark's nephew, and he Isolde.
2. *Pélleas et Mélisande* is a play by Maurice Maeterlinck about forbidden love. First performed in 1893, it was the basis for the famous 1902 opera by Charles Debussy.
3. Jorge Isaacs (1837–1895), Colombian novelist, wrote the immensely successful romantic novel *Marla* in 1867.
4. Bluebeard was the nickname of the nobleman Raoul, a character in a fairytale by Charles Perrault, whose wife Fatima discovers in a locked room the bodies of her husband's former wives, whom he had murdered.
5. Honoré de Balzac (1799–1850): the great French novelist whose many novels and short stories depict the details of everyday French life.
6. In Greek mythology, a member of a tribe of women warriors.

Josephine W. Johnson   *US, b. 1910*

Josephine Winslow Johnson was born a few years before World War I in Kirk-wood, Missouri, to parents of Irish, Scotch, and English ancestry, people fiercely attached to their land. When she was 12, the family moved to a one-hundred-acre farm in south-central Missouri where she conceived a lifelong passion for nature. She studied English and painting at Washington University in St. Louis and left without graduating, as she tells us in her autobiography *Seven Houses: A Memoir of Time and Places*, (1973), to paint and to write on "sharecroppers and local strike and relief conditions" for the St. Louis *Post-Dispatch* and *Star-Times*, hoping that she would thus contribute to "abolishing the 'profit system'" and establishing "a true democracy—economically as well as politically." In 1938, Johnson served as president of the Consumer Co-operative organization. She married twice, in 1939 to a lawyer, then three years later to Grant Cannon, with whom she raised three children. Johnson's initial output spans the Depression and World War II.

Journalist, teacher, short story writer, and novelist, Johnson is both a product and expression of the 1930s and the Depression. In her work, this is reflected by an abiding passion for the land and a sense of the intractability of both man and nature, especially in the face of human need. In her recently reprinted Pulitzer Prize-winning *Now in November* (1934), nature thwarted returns as catastrophe. In an era of acute agricultural crisis, the 24-year-old author depicted the struggles of a family of poor indebted farmers in Missouri, continuing a tradition established in the 1920s by such writers as Edith Summers Kelly and Dorothy Scarborough.

In *Jordanstown* (1937), led by her sympathy for the socially dispossessed, Johnson attempted proletarian realism. Her novel of a grocer's clerk who at night edits the radical *Jordanstown Voice* and writes editorials denouncing the smug and well-to-do, earned Johnson kindly advice from well-meaning critics disappointed by her failure to reach the lyric heights of *Now in November*. That same year, the "neurotic" and "original" poems of *Year's End* received better reviews.

Johnson published a much-praised collection of short stories *Winter Orchard* (1935); here, too, a lyric symbolism and stream of consciousness techniques underwrote an identification with the poor, the marginal, and notably, with blacks, the focus of several stories. The excellent "Gedacht," is a subjective portrait of a World War I veteran blinded by poison who briefly regains his sight; "The Preacher's Pilgrimage" is a moralistic but nonetheless moving tale of a preacher who seeks to regain his stature in the face of onslaughts by social leaders who have proposed political solutions as an alternative to spiritual resignation; he sacrifices his own and the hard-earned savings of his congregation for a trip to the Holy Land. When he arrives in New York to begin his transatlantic journey it is only to discover that the trip is for whites only. In another story, a black boy who discovers a dead body fears lynching rather than gratitude will be the recompense for his announcement.

Johnson continued to produce significant short fiction: "Night Flight," originally published in *Harper's* and subsequently anthologized in a collection of writing on World War II, was much remembered by her generation. The story, if atypical in mood and tone, does indicate her interest in experimental modes, and enlists fantasy as an aid to subversiveness.

After a twenty-year hiatus, Johnson was drawn once again to literary and political activism by the Vietnam War and other events of the 1960s: the developing ecological movement attracted someone who had always been interested in "pigs, hedgehogs, hawks, bats, sheep, and all the others too." She returned to print with the well-received novel *The Dark Traveller* (1963), about a sensitive boy's struggles to endure life under the brutal pounding of his coarse father. In other books that crossed nature writing and political protest—particularly *Inland Island* (1969)—Johnson also suggests a new fusion of her old themes of nature and social reform.

Eric Mendelsohn

NIGHT FLIGHT

Beating slowly, a little wearily back across the long Kansas pastures, Joe thought it all over and decided it was good. Almost the real thing. He thought of her face when she had finally seen him sitting there on the bed, and forgot the creeping ache in his arms as he shot on forward. Only five hundred miles to go, but the air had the warning cold of dawn.

He smiled a little to himself. God, the things that a woman thought of to do before she let herself go to bed! And the nightgowns she wore when he wasn't there!—long-sleeved cotton, with buttons down the front. She'd looked like a cute little shoebox in it. And the ironing, ironing, ironing, while he'd paced up and down half-wild, and she'd stood there mashing down a tablecloth, pleating up a skirt, looking straight at him and not knowing he was there. Then she'd just sighed and folded up in a chair and taken off her shoes. He'd noticed how little her feet looked in the damp stockings with three runs up the side.

Then she'd got up and gone to the icebox and made herself a little sandwich of bread and butter and a slice of cold sweet potato, and drunk some milk straight out of the bottle, and wiped her mouth on her sleeve. It had made him hungry and he'd almost reached over her shoulder and grabbed a cold slice of ham, but remembered Polocheck's warning just in time: "Don't eat, Joe. Don't

drink. You might ground yourself coming back. It has happened." He had shaken his head in an ominous and warning way, and in his silence Joe read some unspeakable fate.

Then Charlotte had puttered and puttered and puttered. Washing her stockings and hanging them first in one place and then in another, and brushing her lovely, thick black hair and looking at herself in the mirror to see how much bigger she'd got round the waist, and then just standing there like a kid making faces at herself and whispering.

He loved her so much he thought his heart would crack, and then he thought he would let loose and crack her too if she didn't quit dawdling.

Then, finally, she'd turned out the lights and sat down on the bed facing west, and looked out at the moon and spoken his name once or twice, and that was all the praying she seemed to do; and then she'd gone to sleep and found him there.

"Jesus!" Joe said quietly to the Kansas prairies, "she was sure surprised!"

It hadn't taken as much explaining though as he'd expected. Apparently she had thought of it too and wanted him to teach her how. But he'd said no, he wasn't going to have her flying around at night, and besides, his bunk wasn't very big, and for God's sake suppose they had a night alarm and inspection. "This isn't like the Mexican army, baby," he'd said. "It's for adults only, and all of those adults male."

She had thought him wonderful to have learned so quickly, and since she pointed it out he realized it *was* pretty wonderful, come to think of it. This was only Monday, and Sunday morning Polocheck had told him of his dream. "...And in the dream I ran from these dogs—but I see no reason why I ran. I could have flown." He looked at Joe and slowly lifted his glass of beer. "I often fly."

"Home?"

"Home to Czechoslovakia." He looked calmly into Joe's grinning eyes. "Tonight when it is dark I will teach you how." He raised a round, warning hand above his glass: "Hush." His blue eyes glittered behind his glasses: "We want no *more* fliers. The nights are wide and peaceful now."

Joe had leaned forward and whispered behind his hand: "When?"

"Eight o'clock."

"Do many know?"

"Some."

"Who?"

Josef's eyes had twinkled. "You would be surprised."

"Okay," Joe said.

It had been a bad morning. He wanted to forget it. Even acting like nuts out in the middle of the desert in a madman's prank was preferable to remembering. "It wasn't so much that it happened to me," he growled into her warm and patient ear, "but that it could happen at all! The fool—the damn young fool!" He re-enacted the scene. The Major's office, young pudgy Major Lewis whose wife once offered Joe a bag of peanuts and who summered in New England and early-autumned in New York. It had all been trivial and nasty. The matter of a desk. The desk drawer stuck, and the Major wanted another desk and he knew where another was. He wanted it moved in, and his own desk moved out, and he needed a truck and about five men, and he started writing out communications all over

the place. Joe had been standing there and listening and finally he said: "Why don't you just have the desk drawer fixed?" Somewhere along the line he had put in a "sir."

And the Major had turned with his vapid young face suddenly interesting with hate, and shouted: "Who spoke to you? Wait till you're spoken to, soldier!"

Well, that was that. But it was there like a ten-word brand,

"...And then I just went out with Josef, and he showed me how..."

"You learned so quickly, darling!" She had looked at him with love and adoration. Sometimes Charlotte got God and Joe confused.

He laughed and hugged her and muttered that it was something that any fool could do. He told her how it had felt, his spirit slipping quietly between the beds, shuffling out into the moonlight desert....He had paused and taken in the incomparable beauty of this early autumn night. South the wide snowstreaked peaks, beautiful and barren in the white moonlight. The clean icy air poured down his lungs. All round him the silent tarboard barracks and the sand, sleeping in the great white flooded light. The army trucks huddled row on row like shrouded beasts.

Quietly Joe had lifted one long arm and then the other. He whirled them round like a ship's propeller, and felt the blood race through his veins. "Contact," he whispered, grinning.

Then, warmed up, he had started taxiing across the sand, his long mountain legs casting wild shadows from the moon. He aimed for the eastern fence and planned to take off and soar above the spiked wire in a gesture of derision. But halfway down the road he slowed down suddenly and crouched. By shadowy sound his spirit's sensitive ears detected another traveler, and he whirled and flattened against a barracks building. From a door of the officers' quarters a short and heavy form came striding, and paused in the open moonlight. Major Lewis hesitated, reconnoitered, and seeing only the dry, unspeaking sand, the bright expressionless autumn moon, seemed satisfied. Over his face came a silly, expectant look, and his mouth opened and shut like a toad devouring flies. After a few minutes Joe realized that the Major was singing as he flailed his arms and warmed up for the flight: "*From the desert I come to thee,*" he was singing, "*On a stallion shod with fire...*"

"Oh, my God," Joe muttered. "Oh, my God."

Then the Major was running, beating his arms in perfect form, and heading for the gate with terrific speed. Breathless, Joe watched him and saw him suddenly leap, click his heels together and soar upward with a roar like a little four-engine bomber. The perfect take-off of long practice.

Joe sighed with envy and slid out from the shadow. "Bastard," he murmured. "Bastard!"

Then his eyes filled with a deep and cynical scorn. The Major had shot like a bullet westward and not toward the high towers of Manhattan, which seemed an odd thing for a man whose wife never went farther westward than Hot Springs, Virginia.

"*From the desert I come to thee,*" Joe whinnied derisively, "*On a stallion shod with fire...*" He stamped his big feet in the sand. "Did I speak to you?" he muttered fiercely. "Wait till you're spoken to, soldier!"

A flame of intolerable hate flared up in him and then he remembered it was growing late, and started to run, forgetting the Major and concentrating with all his might on Polocheck's lesson and his warnings: "*Flail those arms. Pick up the feet. Then jump—so—leap. Beat. Beat. Right, left, together: beat.*" He felt himself soaring upward in a wild rush, clearing the barrack fence and heading like a comet for the sky.

"Watch you level off!" Polocheck had warned him. "Once I forgot. My God, the stars!"

He had leveled off then and flown eastward in the moonlight. Brownsville, Indiana,

here I come! Below him the dry autumn fields of Colorado, the bony creek beds twisting whitely, the forms of sleeping cattle soaked in moonlight. The cold pure air whistled by his ears. It was an extraordinary and exhilarating experience. He felt as though he had been doing it all his life, and wanted to try a nose dive just for the hell of it.

Josef was too cautious. "Keep level," he'd said. "Don't fuss round. You got to go fast." But Indiana wasn't Europe, and Joe turned down his right hand, raised his left, and bore down with a mighty rush. The cattle lifted up stricken faces and poured over the pastures, their wet hooves glittering. Joe grinned and swept on eastward.

Above the Solomon River he had hit an air pocket and dropped downward with a sickening rush, but recovered himself and pulled up again, beating his way above the cold, scaly water, the river smell chilling his throat.

Sometimes he thought he saw other forms far off, dim wingshapes of soldiers passing, but was not sure. Not till he pulled past Topeka, lights burning like a handful of embers on a plain, did he meet another nocturnal flier close enough to speak. Here he was overtaken by a young Negro sergeant bound for Carolina and traveling fast. Joe acknowledged his coming with a right-arm sweep and motioned as though to shake his hand. "Cold, Sergeant?"

"Cold!"

"Been at this flying long?"

"Learned last week. Been home every night since." He laughed as at something secret and very pleasant.

"First flight for me," Joe said. "I don't know how it'll be. Not sure of all the rules."

The sergeant laughed. "Me neither." He winged in closer. "You learn something new every time. Las' night I landed late and I walked up the backyard after my wife was asleep—she can't see you till she sleeps—and the lights were all out, only a bright moon so you could see everything white, and the moon-flowers hanging on the fence. Well, I walk up and past that old broken swing the kids still use, and suddenly I stop. I'm not kidding you: I stopped like a man shot dead. And there, sitting down on the swing, scuffing his boots and looking all out of joints, was the mortal soul of my First Lieutenant!"

He laughed very loudly, and after a moment of uncertainty Joe laughed too.

"He couldn't get in!" the sergeant gloated. "That's one of the things you learn. She never thought about *him*. She didn't never know he was there!"

Joe took an exulting leap. "What'd you do?"

The sergeant shrugged. "Jus' let him swing. A man's got a right to dream, I guess. He was gone when I come out again. Only a scuff place under the swing." He laughed again.

They flew on for a minute in silence, and then they saw the lights of St. Louis and the sluggish silvery mud of the Mississippi. "Here's where I leave you, brother," the sergeant said. "Take it slow and easy. Don't eat. Don't drink. And a long night to you!" He was gone, winging darkly southward, and soon lost in the shadows.

Not long now for Joe. Fly east, young man. Familiar hills and farmlands going under, but he could not see them well in the night. "I was sure afraid," he told Charlotte. "I thought I'd pass over and land in Brooklyn! 'You'll know,' Josef kept telling me, but I got the jitters. No map, no compass—how'd I know Brownsville from Ashtabula?"

"How did you know?" Charlotte whispered.

He held her and laughed. There had been no question about his finding her. He had flown lower and lower, peering at highways

and little billboards and the silent, impassive roofs of towns.

Suddenly he realized that he was gliding slowly downward as in the grip of a thick, receding tide. "I just knew," he said.

Now, crossing the Kansas border and beating on, he knew he would find the camp all right, not by any love-gravity of the heart, but because it was so damn big that he could not miss it.

He felt calm and happy. Tomorrow was tomorrow, and to hell with yesterday. He saw the white, shining, snow-cold peaks and the canyoned towns. And then the camp stretched out far below him. There wasn't much time, but he circled slowly above it, hunting hawk-like for signs of some living thing on the outskirts of plain. Then he saw what he was seeking.

A mile westward from the camp, a small fat form, like a two-legged dusty beetle, scurried across the sand.

Leisurely, heartlessly, like a falcon over a wounded hare, Joe circled nearer and lower. He knew the Major's odd hummocky run. "He ate too much, and he drank too much, and a lot of other things too much, and he foundered all right," he thought. "*On the wings of the desert, I come to thee*!" Joe sang in a loud, sweet voice. He swooped low, and the wind of his swooping swept the Major's hat from his round, blond head. It gleamed like a moonflower opening wide in the pale gray desert air. "Get a horse, Bud!" Joe shouted coarsely. "Get a horse!"

Then happily Joe soared upward with firm, triumphant strokes and plummeted swiftly toward the barracks, taking care to avoid the soul of Josef, returning in haste from Europe, the dawn like a white Gestapo at his heels.

Melissánthi   (Hébe Skandhaláki)   *Greece, b. 1910*

Melissánthi is the pseudonym of Hébe Skandhaláki (née Kóuyia), who was born in
Athens in 1910 and educated there at the French Institute and the German School.
After studying music drama, and dance, Melissánthi taught French in private
schools and night colleges. (She is proficient in German and English as well.)
Deeply interested in theological and philosophical problems, Melissánthi's own
religious crisis was probably precipitated or heightened by an attack of tuberculosis, from which she recuperated for eighteen months in a Swiss sanatorium. She
married the politician and writer Yiánnis Skandalákis in 1939.

Melissánthi published her first poems *Phonés endómou* (Insect Voices) in
1930; in it "Repentance" first appeared. It was her second collection, *Prophiteíes*
(Prophecies, 1931) that brought her attention. She was encouraged in her writing
by Malakases, the last major poet of the "School of Palamas." The inspiration for
her prewar poetry was religious. (Note the Biblical titles: *Phlegómeni vátos* (Burning Bush, 1935, from which "Atonement" is taken); *Yirismós tou asótou* (Return
of the Prodigal, 1936), of which the second edition in 1938 received an honorable
mention from the Academy of Athens; *Hosánna ke oramatismós* (Hosannah and
Visionary Power, 1939.) All these early works reflect a search for truth and
meaning (for God, if you like) in herself and the world around her. She moved
gradually, however, to what could loosely be called an existentialist standpoint. Sin
and guilt become the existentialist burden of awareness: humans are condemned to
the awareness of their own pointlessness and their own total responsibility for the
self. Her first postwar collection, *Lyrikí omoloyía* (Lyrical Confession, 1945)
received honorable mention from the judges of the Palamas Prize. She continued
publishing collections of poetry with *I epohí tou ýpnou ke tis agrypnías* (The
Season of Sleep and Wakefulness, 1950). In 1960 she wrote a play, *O mikrós
adelfós* (The Little Brother), which won the Skiaridhion Prize for Children's Theatre
awarded by the Women's Literary Association. Further poetic collections followed:
To Anthropinó schéma (Human Shape, 1961); *To frágma tis siopís* (The Barrier of
Silence, 1961), which won the State Prize for Literature; and two volumes of
selected works (1965 and 1970). In 1965 she was awarded the Golden Cross of the
Royal Order of Benefaction for her services to literature and she received the State
Second Prize for Poetry as well; in 1979 she was awarded the State First Prize for
Poetry.

Melissánthi is still writing. Her poems of the period from 1974 to 1982 were
published in 1982 under the title *Ta néa piímata* (The New Poems); her most
recent collection appeared in 1985. She is also very active as a literary critic, not
only of Greek poets (including Zoë Karélli) but of English and American poets
(notably Robert Frost, Emily Dickinson, and Henry Wadsworth Longfellow). She
contributed critical commentary on contemporary literature to Greek radio for
fifteen years. A volume of tributes to her by many leading Greek writers and critics
(including Katerina Anghelaki-Rooke, Elli Alexíou, Zoë Karélli, and Tatiána Stávrou) was published in 1985 under the title *Ton órthron ton erhómenon* (The
Coming Dawn). Outside Greece, her work has received particular attention in
Germany.

Melissánthi's imagery owes much to Ancient Greek myth and literature as well as to biblical influences. She is very much a poet of tensions—notably of the mind versus external reality, of intellect versus emotion, of freedom versus constraint, of human isolation and despair versus hope. Not completely negative, she ultimately has faith in the power of human love to create meaning, however transitory.

Christopher Robinson

REPENTANCE
Metamélya

Tonight, I said to myself you won me at last,
now that my desires have all become rosy-hued
flowers.
But before the cock crowed three times
dear Lord, I had again denied you.

Passions, hatred still slowly burn me—
haven't I yet reached the end of my sins?
If only the fountain of your grace would open
then perhaps even my pitcher would be filled.

What I have suffered since that night
when I left our bridal bed empty
and I refused to look into your eyes!

If you do not believe, look at my wounds—
give me your hand; look here and here.
Well then; do you know me now? Tell me?

Translated by Rae Dalvin

ATONEMENT
Exiléosi

Every time I sinned a door half opened, and
the Angels
who in my virtue had never found me beautiful,
tipped over the full amphora of their flower
souls;
every time I sinned, it was as though a door
had opened,
and tears of sweet compassion dripped among
the grasses.
But if the sword of my remorse chased me
from heaven,
every time I sinned a door half opened, and
though men
thought me most ugly, the angels thought me
beautiful.

Translated by Kimon Friar

Rachel de Queiroz
Brazil, b. 1910

Rachel (or Raquel) de Queiroz, the first women to be elected to Brazil's Academy of Letters (1977) in its eighty-year history, is best known for her semiautobiographical *As tres Marias* (*The Three Marias*), excerpted below, an outstanding example of the socially aware "novel of the Northeast." Published in 1939, the novel is important for its simple, clear characterization and its critical social vision: in it de Queiroz explores societal norms and probes into women's place in the arch-conservative Northeast. She was born and raised there on the family ranch in the drought-wracked backlands of Ceará State. This area, described especially in her popular novel *O quinze* (*The year '15*, 1930) about the effects of the severe drought of 1915, remains an important source of imagery in her work.

Long a national figure in Brazil, de Queiroz has been known not only for her novels but for her journalism, which, like the novels is frequently topical and politically involved. She also wrote plays and *crônicas*, (the short essaylike works that are an outstanding feature of Brazilian journalism), did many translations from European, English, and American writers; and wrote literature for children and for the theater. Her style is clear and direct and realistically evokes her settings, which include the streets of Rio as well as her native state. Her themes frequently involve the poor and oppressed, often women and workers, struggling for a better life. She won many prizes, the most prestigious being the Graça Aranha Foundation Prize in 1931 for her first novel, *O quinze*, and the Machado de Assis Prize in 1957 for her lifelong contribution to Brazilian literature.

from THE THREE MARIAS
As tres Marias

It was our teacher, Sister Germana, who suggested our nickname, for the first time calling us "the three Marias."

It happened during an afternoon study period, and while everyone was reading or writing exercises in their notebooks, Maria José, Glória, and I sat in the back of the room conversing secretively.

Sister Germana suddenly came in, sounded the clack sharply: "Maria José, Maria Augusta, Maria Glória, why don't you keep still? You three are inseparable! Have you ever noticed, girls? Those three spend all their time together chatting, idling, avoiding everyone else. They are the three Marias. A fine thing, the Lord knows, if they only lived together like the three in the Gospel! But I'll wager they're frittering away their time in dissipation."

Glória looked at me, I looked at Maria José. We smiled. "The Three Marias!" The three Biblical Marias? The three heavenly stars?

The class found this amusing and the nickname stuck. We ourselves took pride in it, we felt ourselves to be set apart in an aristocratic and celestial trinity, in the midst of all the other plebeians. Heavenly personages have a prestige that has always dazzled humans; and comparing us to the stars was like an intoxication newly experienced, a pretext for fantasies and whimsy. We loftily adopted the device. In our books, in our notebooks, a drawing of three stars together was our symbol: the three Marias of the heavens.

At night we would stay out on the patio gazing at our stars, identifying ourselves with them. Glória was the first star, dazzling and close. Maria José chose the one on the other extremity, tiny and twinkling. To my lot fell the middle one, perhaps the nicest of all; a serene star of bluish light, that undoubtedly was some tranquil sun warming distant worlds, happy worlds, that I could only imagine to be nocturnal and moonlike.

Maria José was the one who thought up the idea of tattooing ourselves. It had to be on the thigh, so that the Sisters wouldn't see. For our tastes it should have been on the arms, the neck, the shoulders; but it was necessary to avoid having the nuns find out, or having some counselor run tattle to Sister Germana.

Hidden out behind the lavatories—our regular headquarters—sitting on the ground, with our stockings pulled down, we used the point of a scissors to make the row of three stars on our thighs.

It was painful. It was done with light scraping, until the blood came. I made my cut decisively, with my teeth clenched. Glória, fainthearted and patient, made her scratches very, very slowly. And Maria José lost her courage on the last star, and it was necessary for Glória to come help her with her soft hand. From time to time she would make a face and groan, and Glória would raise her hand: "Do you want me to stop?"

She shook her head. She had to keep going until the end. And I recalled, when my own insignia was finished, that you could fill the stars with ink and they would never fade away. I had read some place (I don't know where) that the Japanese put ink inside a tattoo right away.

Glória, who was afraid of germs and who always kept a bottle of iodine in her desk, was opposed and said apprehensively, "Who knows what ink is made of? It might be something filthy, and cause infection, tetanus, gangrene."

"You're crazy, Glória. Ink is made out of the sap of plants."

"It's also made with Prussian blue. Who can say that it's not the same as prussic acid, the worst poison in the world?"

I quit the discussion, engrossed in contemplating my own tattoo, without looking at the others'. Red with blood, the three stars shone on my white skin as if they had flowered from the flesh.

We had our stars and several other problems. The problem of Jandira, for example. A case of a bad beginning and an obscure outcome. Jandira was an illegitimate child; what's worse, the child of an adultery. Her father was a married man and her mother a humble, mixblood prostitute. Jandira didn't have any definite home, she lived with her aunts, her father's sisters—three old maids, only one of whom esteemed her—and she did not know what kind of future lay ahead of her.

People think that children are unaware of life's dramas. And they forget that these dramas do not obey discretion or choose a proper moment; naked and fearsome, they reveal themselves indifferently to the eyes of adults and to the eyes of children. For example, Jandira's history, unsuitable for minors, raised terrible questions for us and attracted and disturbed us unceasingly.

Jandira hated her other two aunts. She felt they treated her like a miserable, importuning animal, like a bedraggled cat which has been let in during a thunderstorm at night, and which has a right only to the crumbs of charity—to its saucer of milk on the floor and to a humble spot on the hearth, without ever being permitted to curl up on the living-room pillows.

And Jandira was ambitious, precocious, imaginative.

She wanted a place at life's feast, and not the least, nor the most obscure. And she used to fight for it. She slept late, polished her nails, turned up her nose at certain dishes on the table. She stood at the window, watching the young military cadet who was strutting with the air of an aristocrat and showing off his golden epaulets. She would smile at him and later boast of receiving his military salute and of the number of times she made him turn back down the street.

Dondom, her youngest aunt, who was myopic and ill-humored, used to observe: "Know your place, my child." And it was as if she had struck her in the face.

Jandira would come to the Colégio, throw herself into our arms, purple with desperation: "I'd rather she had given me a beating! I'd rather she had killed me!"

And nothing moved them, these diabolical old women, not the achievements which the girl threw in their faces, nor her honorable mention at school, her success in public speaking, her pride, her invincible ambition.

"Know your place, my child—" (That is: "Think about who you are, about the mother who had you, a woman without a husband and beyond the law, who abandoned you to be brought up by charity. Ahead of you life looks beautiful, attractive, glittering. But for you it's only a showcase: don't stick out your hand; you'll hit the glass; and don't break the glass; you'll come out bleeding—Be satisfied to look, and, if you like, you may even desire. But stop at that. Go to the Colégio: study with the others, wear what they wear, laugh with them, play with them. In matters of the heart, be like them, and, if you like, learn what love is, read books about it and dream! But when your time comes, stand back, don't have anything to do with the sentimental lad who will come to serenade you, don't dare think about a boy of good family, but look for someone of your own kind. Never forget, because no one will ever let you forget, your original stigma, the blemished womb that formed you, and the day that ever saw you born had best be put out of mind."

Injustice was a familiar thing to us, and in general we did not go into the reason for things. To us, orphans were orphans; sick people were sick people; poor people were poor people. But injustice, in Jandira's case, was all too close and evident. It hurt us all.

In Maria José's opinion, Jandira should have gone and become a nun: "Since the world doesn't want her, let her seek out the arms of Our Lord."

And I would comment, with bitter irritation: "A nun? What order would take her in? Do you think that there is room for her in any convent? Only as a lay sister, in certain orders, or as a penitent, in the Order of the Good Shepherd—"

As if Jandira would ever agree to being a lay sister or a penitent! Mother Superior, abbess, prioress, nothing less.

Jandira was an extern. She saw much more of the world than we—the avenues, the movie houses, the young men—and she felt its attraction at closer range. And at times she went through strange phases. She forgot all about the question of "her place," calmly occupied the place she wished, and fraternized with her tyrants. She chose friends from the aristocratic circles of the Colégio, fell in love with the brothers of these girls, deluded herself, laid plans, courted the enemy, and perhaps even made over him a bit.

We felt we had been betrayed and anxiously awaited the inevitable comedown. And the comedown came, as suddenly and brutally as a slap on the face. Someone had said to her, in one way or another, somewhere on the most unexpected occasion, the same old line: "Who do you think you are? Know your place."

And we took her in, sympathized with her, planned vengeance. We dreamed up impossible marriages, as in books. It is true that in books one always finds out that the little schoolmistress with no one in the world is of noble origin, the daughter of a count and countess. And with Jandira inescapable reality was always there, present, scoffing: her mother still living, taking lovers, degrading herself, bearing more children, as invincible and unconscious as a force of nature.

And I would murmur, looking up at the dark sky, my hands joined behind my neck, thinking of something that, in last analysis, might perhaps be a solution: "I am afraid that she is going to finally kill herself."

I was about to reach my fourteenth birthday when, for the first time, I had a desire to kill myself.

Naturally I had no reason. I believe that what we customarily call "motive" is in such cases of secondary importance: that is, some concrete, immediate cause which is responsible for the suicidal impulse. Those who need such a motive kill themselves by accident. But the person who wants to kill himself does not need a great and irremediably tragic pretext; he kills himself indeed by reason of that obscure aspiration of his to die; he kills himself because something within him calls, because he feels a violent and invincible attraction.

It is like love. Why does a woman passionately desire a particular man, why does her flesh quiver at his touch, at the barest brush of his hands, at the simple suggestion of a caress? Perhaps love for death is like love for a man, and she is satisfied, is consoled, and is cured only after being possessed and exhausted.

I know that since that time I have always considered myself to have suicidal tendencies. I was afraid, afraid of the act, afraid of the pain (now I am back to my analogy), and my fear was mingled with desire.

And I consoled myself a little, for my dissatisfaction, by talking and thinking about it, by planning gentle and obscure deaths—sleeping pills in the silent hours of the night, or a dash into the sea from the solitude of a deserted beach.

And when I spoke in confidence about this, no one believed me. Maria José and Glória called me crazy, Jandira mentioned the holy Scripture: "that a suicide is the same as a murderer."

They would laugh, make up verses about me, ridicule me; and if they talked about me, it is because that age loves discussions and takes pleasure in controversy.

And they doubted me to such an extent, they so summarily ruled out my fantasies, after proving their logical impossibility, that I myself was at times convinced that my morbid desires were a farce, that I was engaged in play-acting.

Meanwhile, my secret aspiration remained, and has always remained. Today I have it more than ever.

Sleepless nights, long interminable nights; my eyes dried up, my body tossing in bed without finding a soft place to rest, my hands digging soft holes in the pillow, weariness, such a weariness! The sluggishness of the dawning day, of eternal, immutable things which are going to be implacably repeated. And dreams, dreams of an impossible blissfulness, of a sweet and rapid death without pain and without misery, a death as joyful and cunning as a dream, precisely like the dream that I never have.

Before the holidays of the final year, Jandira surprised us with sensational news: she was engaged to be married. For some months she had acted aloof: we thought that her studies were occupying her, whereas she was concentrating on her plans, preparing all alone her escape, fearful perhaps that we might put objections and difficulties in her way and take away her courage.

Her fiancé was a seaman, slow of speech and deep-voiced, lumbering in his gait, a sim-

ple soul; he gave no heed to the tragic origin of his bride-to-be; he wanted only a wife and he wanted Jandira.

His romantic calling compensated for their inequality, and eliminated certain distances. A seaman is unconsciously a kind of poet and the sea is the ideal backdrop for all lyrical tales. He had a gasoline launch and transported cargo from the ships to shore. Jandira didn't tell us if she loved him and perhaps didn't even think of that. It was enough that he loved her. (Strange and marvelous thing for her—she who was always supposed to know her place"—to feel that she was first in the mind and heart of another.)

And she showed us the gifts from the man she was to marry, the cuttings of silk, the bottles of perfume, the heavy wedding ring, her wrist watch. However, she never showed us his letters, those he wrote on a trip he made to Camocim. She told us merely that they were terribly passionate and lovesick, and so bold that if Dondom had seen them she perhaps would have called off the wedding, scandalized and enraged.

One day I saw his handwriting in a book he had given her. Irregular, awkward, child-like. And from his handwriting I imagined his letters. That is why Jandira never showed them to us.

Jandira married on the day she became eighteen.

The altar was decorated with roses and lilies, and the bride wore on her breast the blue ribbon of the Daughters of Maria, along with her white silks and veil.

I never understood why—whether out of spite for her aunts, vengeance, mockery, or simple human kindness—Jandira had her mother attend the ceremony, her ignored and unacknowledged mother, the cause of all her humiliations. She discovered her, I don't know where, dressed her up, showed her off, and fell into her arms after the wedding. And her mother did not disappoint her: simple, modest, wearing a plain, dark coat, she gave her blessing discreetly to her daughter, smiled tenderly, and disappeared.

Her aunts wept, especially the eldest, who thought well of Jandira, who used to hold her in her lap when she was little, and tell her stories; we knew that when the girl got engaged her aunt gave her for her trousseau her own "hope chest" of lace—lovely, tenuous lace yellowed by the years in the shadows of the drawer, collected for her own wedding, which had never come, faded and ancient like dried flowers.

Jandira embraced the old woman, hung on her neck, and wept as one forsaken, wept as I had wept the day I entered the school. Our eyes were also filled with tears, and the bridegroom, touched and bewildered, timidly smiled and seemed to be asking forgiveness for being the cause of it all.

Finally a car drew up to the sidewalk, and Jandira got in it with her new husband and her mother-in-law.

At night, lying in our dormitory beds, we would think about her, who was our age, and who was already wearing a gold wedding band on her finger, already walking on the arm of a companion along new and free roads.

The atmosphere there oppressed us, and it seemed to us that they were imposing excessive years of childhood upon us. We felt a humiliating sensation of failure, delay, lost youth.

No longer a child, but still not a mature woman, I was taken from the warm and cozy retreat of the Colégio—and I finally came to know the world.

After the holidays that followed upon our diplomas, I found myself at last in the city—settled—on my own.

I was supposed to have stayed at Crato; the holidays weren't supposed to be holidays, merely the beginning of my new life at home with my family. I, however, did not go along with that, and I spent those months at home as in a hotel, as in a way station. It embarrassed me to say so, but I did not consider that to be my proper home, or what's worse, I felt no need of a home, and everything seemed to me boring, monotonous, and inappropriate.

At school, in all our compositions and in all the songs at year's end, one sang about the beauties and the delights of home. For that reason, perhaps, my deception was so great.

The youngsters bothered me, I had no love for them. I felt toward them merely that conventional tenderness that I had been taught in books, "the loving kindness one should show to his younger brothers and sisters." I found them hostile, spiteful, obstinate. They broke in on my moments of meditation with their arguments and crying spells, they constantly fought, yelled, soiled themselves, and were malicious, thoughtless, and cruel.

It was only with the passing of time that my love for children became developed. On that occasion, I was seeing my brothers and sisters too close up, children I was not acquainted with, who merely wearied and frightened me.

Later on, I always had that same fear and that same uncomfortable vague fatigue whenever I found myself in the disturbing and incalculable proximity of a crowd.

When I first got back from school, I would with great enthusiasm run to them with open arms. I expected that they would ask me to tell them stories, that they would sit on my lap, sweet smelling and angelic. But the youngsters were continually dirty, wanted nothing to do with me, and, in the midst of fights and confusion, never got interested in stories except very vaguely. And if I attempted to be helpful they would poke their hands in my face.

At home the monotony was so oppressive, so constant, that it came to be as painful as a bruise. I started turning black and blue with boredom.

On the very next day after my arrival a solemn session was held, in which, after a brief prologue, Godmother explained my new duties as a daughter and older sister, and spoke of the help that the family expected from me. And, oh, how horrified I was, Our Lady of mine, at the beds to be made, the stockings to be darned, the tables to be set and cleared, those never-to-be-forgotten weeks that I was supposed to alternate in the kitchen with my stepmother! The much-lauded aim of all that was to prepare me to be the future mother of a family, the wifely producer of a brood. I, meanwhile, merely felt that they wished to take advantage of my presence in the house, to get work out of me, and this of the most uninteresting and inglorious sort.

And no one understood me, and they wondered why, after so many years of cloistered discipline, I should only wish, only aspire to, freedom and prohibited pleasures. As if the prisoner ever got used to prison, and as if he, after being freed, should desire nothing more than to return to his prison uniform and his evening rounds in the patio!

My dream was to sleep late, without screaming children, without the sound of the broom throughout the house, without that laborious and exasperating movement of a beehive at dawn. Without the voice of Godmother, who would open the door to my room, clap her hands, and say sonorously:

"Maria Augusta, look what time it is! You know your father doesn't like for you to sleep so late! We're already having our coffee."

I, who would still be taking my ease, thinking vaguely about things pleasant and indefinite, would leap from my bed in fury and embarrassment, slip on my dress in all haste, go and wash my teeth at the window of the dining room; there I would forget myself once more and daydream, my mouth full of foam, looking out at the beds of zinnias.

Implacably, with the shrillness of something mechanical, Godmother's voice would be raised anew:

"Did you make your bed, Daughter?"

All my blood would rush to my face, I would rinse my teeth in haste, run to my bedroom, and pull the blanket over the wrinkled sheet. I still heard Godmother's comment of veiled censure, to Papa:

"After so many years of school! How is it possible that she never got the habit?"

But, Lord in Heaven, she couldn't see, Papa couldn't see, no one could see, that the sole desire in my heart was to uproot my habits, forget about the slavery of the school bell, prayers, made-up beds. Why get out of school, why be a woman after all, if life was going to be the same and if growing up had not delivered me from childhood?

It is hard for me to express in a few lines everything that that decisive period meant to me, which would perhaps require a book, and nothing less, to speak of my rebellions, my nighttime tears, my desperate wish to run away, which got to be almost an obsession.

The best thing to do is to move along.

So then when I saw in the newspaper the public announcement of a competitive examination for a typist's job in Fortaleza, I clung to that hope with such tenacity and energy that Godmother gave in, Papa gave in, and he brought me to take the examination, saw some friends of his, and got me the job.

I began work. And it seemed to me that my happiness was about to begin. To live by myself, to live for myself, to live on my own, to be free of my family, to be free of my roots, to be alone, to be free!

And in the city, life was equally monotonous, full of other little tedious duties. Everything ran along in a routine which I steadfastly wished to believe temporary, but which became implacably fixed.

I was eighteen when I started to work, and six months later I had already started to fear getting old without ever knowing what the world was all about.

The world—my thirst for it was great.

Not for pleasures, or rather, not solely for pleasures. My soul was like that of the soldier in the folktale of Pedro Malasarte who abandons everything, sets out with his knapsack on his shoulder, experiences hunger and persecutions, walks covered with dust and weariness through strange cities governed by cruel and crafty kings, all plotting his downfall. He, however, a slave to his desire to "see," to "know," confronts all things, continues eternally in search of the impossible surprise, of things never seen, journeying always ahead, beneath the sun and through peril.

I felt I was like him, that the two of us were brother and sister, the soldier and I, and I was his sister who stayed behind, who could not accompany him, and who held out her arms to him and wept.

Translated by Fred P. Ellison

Leah Goldberg   *Lithuania/Palestine/Israel, 1911–1971*

Born in Kovno, Lithuania, Leah Goldberg graduated from the Hebrew Gymnasium there and did graduate work in philosophy and Semitic languages at the universities of Berlin and Bonn, receiving a doctorate for her work on Semitic languages. An early and fervent Zionist, she emigrated to Israel in 1935 and, as a commitment to her adopted home, chose Hebrew as her written language, although her first language was Russian. Goldberg worked as a journalist for many years on the then-Palestine newspapers *Davar* (Object) and *Ha-Mishmar* (On Guard) as drama and literature critic. She also taught theater history at a drama school and did some writing for the theater. In 1954 she became a lecturer of comparative literature at Hebrew University in Jerusalem and was later appointed to the chair of comparative literature there.

On arriving in Jerusalem, Goldberg quickly became a member of the Yachdav literary group, whose leaders Avraham Shlonsky (1900–1973) and Natan Alterman (1910–1970) were at the forefront of the avant-garde literary scene. Although considered modern in theme, her works are not "modernist" in that they do not emphasize experimentation with language and structure. They are quite lyrical and filled with deep expression.

Goldberg published five books of poems, including *Al ha-Pericha* (Of the Blossom, 1948), from which the selection here, "Remembrance of the Beginnings of Things," was taken. "From My Mother's Home" was taken from *Shirim Nivharim* (*Selected Poems*), edited and translated by Robert Friend posthumously in 1976. Goldberg also wrote criticism (e.g. *Amanut ha-sippur* [The Art of Narrative]) did translations from Shakespeare, Rilke, Ibsen, Petrarch, among others, and wrote children's stories and poems. She died in 1971 of cancer.

FROM MY MOTHER'S HOME
Mibéyt Imí

My mother's mother died
in the spring of her days.   And her daughter
did not remember her face.   Her portrait
                                        engraved
in my grandfather's heart
was struck from the world of images
after his death.

Only her mirror remains, sunk deeper with age
into its silver frame.
And I, her pale granddaughter, who does not
                                  resemble her,
peer into it today as if it were a pool
hiding its treasures under the water.

Deep deep beyond my face
I see a young woman
pink-cheeked and smiling,
a wig on her head.
She is putting
a long earring into the lobe of her ear.
                                  Threading it
through a tiny hole in the delicate flesh.

Deep deep beyond my face
shines her eyes' bright gold.
The mirror carries on
the family tradition:
that she was beautiful.

Translated by Robert Friend

REMEMBRANCE OF THE BEGINNINGS OF THINGS
Zichron reshit dvarim

We shall remember the wheat stalk in the
                      greenness of her youth,
The time she stood erect with head to heaven,
Thin was her blade but straight and proud.
And now bent is her head to the ground,
For heavy is the gold of her ripeness,
The crown of her full pregnancy.
Beautiful are her seasons.

We shall remember the tree in the middle of
                              his spring:
His blossoms were white and pink,
Trembling sunbeams glimmered in him on the
                              branch
And the sweet resin dropped to earth
Like the bride's tears on the day of her heart's
                              joy.
Now he stands in the abundance of his apples
Carrying his beautiful burden motionless
Knowing the spring of things to come.

We shall surely remember these things
In the change of the year's circuit and in the
                              passage of day and night,
How the moon was fragile
And very full, then round and died,
Yet its youth would be renewed.

We shall surely remember the beginning of our
                              love
When she was tremulous as a fawn,
A beautiful doe lowering her eyes,
And there she has become full grown
With her open face
And her deep voice.
Beautiful are her seasons.

Translated by Ruth Mintz

Xiao Hong (Hsiao Hung; Chang Nai-Ying)   *China, 1911–1942*

Xiao Hong's biography reads like a story by her older contemporary and friend Ding Ling. A woman who sought liberation, Xiao lived a marginal and vagabond life, a victim of the social instability of the period, of the men in her life, and of herself. Born Chang Nai-Ying in Hulan county, her grandfather the only source of love, compassion, and justice, as documented in her semiautobiographical *Hulanho chuan* (*Tales of Hulan River*), she fled to Harbin with an unknown lover to escape the marriage her family had arranged for her. Pregnant and soon abandoned, Xiao herself abandoned the child she had given birth to. After a period of vagrancy and isolation, she met and, from 1934 to 1938, lived with another writer, Xiao Jun, also from the Northeast; their impoverished Harbin life is the subject of her autobiographical *Shang-shi chieh* (*Market Street*, 1936). Fleeing the Japanese occupation of Manchuria, they settled in the commercial and cultural center of Shanghai, where they began their writing careers and soon rose to prominence as the protegés of the great modern writer Lu Xun (1881–1936), about whom Xiao wrote an important literary portrait and reminiscence (1940). With the fall of Shanghai in 1937, though the relationship with Xiao Jun was already disintegrating Xiao moved with him from place to place in the Nationalist-controlled interior until she met Duonmu Hongliang, another Northeastern writer. She lived intermittently with Duonmu from 1938 on, eventually migrating with him to Hong Kong, where he abandoned her in her illness. Invalided by tuberculosis, mistakenly operated on, and then lacking medical care as a result of the invasion by the Japanese, Xiao Hong died at the age of 31.

Xiao Hong's works redeem her life. With the publication of *Sheng si chang* (*The Field of Life and Death*) in 1935, Xiao became an orginator of anti-Japanese fiction and revealed her talent for describing rural settings, and conveying the harsh realities of peasant life and character; though this is the book most lauded by Communist critics, Western writers find Xiao Hong's promise fulfilled by the posthumously published work *Hulan River* (1941). Unified by place, time, and the point of view of the child narrator, these sketches alternate somber portrayals with humorous satire to capture life in an early twentieth-century Chinese rural village, the society of Xiao's childhood. This work and such short stories from her three collections as *Shou* (Hands), *Niu-che shang* (On the Oxcart) and *Xiao cheng san yue* (Spring in a Small Town) also reveal Xiao's special concern with the plight of women in a partriarchal society. In *Ma Bolou* (1940), Xiao departed radically from the "line" of the period, as well as the mainstream of her own work, creating a successful wartime satire, in an urban setting, which directed much of its humor at the Chinese themselves. A selection of her works appeared in Peking in 1958. A critical biography entitled *Hsiao Hung* (1976) by Howard Goldblatt has given her English-speaking audience a better understanding of the relationship between her life and her works.

from TALES OF HULAN RIVER
Hulanho chuan

In addition to The Crossroads, there are two other streets, one called Road Two East and the other called Road Two West. Both streets run from north to south, probably for five or six *li*.[1] There is nothing much on these two streets worth noting—a few temples, several stands where flatcakes are sold, and a number of grain storehouses....

As for Road Two West, not only is it without a fire mill, it has but one school, a Moslem school situated in the Temple of the City God. With this exception, it is precisely like Road Two East, dusty and barren. When carts and horses pass over these roads they raise up clouds of dust, and whenever it rains the roads are covered with a layer of mud. There is an added feature on Road Two East: a five- or six-foot-deep quagmire. During dry periods the consistency of the mud inside is about that of gruel, but once it starts to rain the quagmire turns into a river. The people who live nearby suffer because of it: when they are splashed with its water, they come away covered with mud; and when the waters subside as the sun reappears in the clearing sky, hordes of mosquitos emerge and fly around their homes. The longer the sun shines, the more homogenized the quagmire becomes, as though someone were trying to refine something inside it. If more than a month goes by without any rain, that big quagmire becomes even more homogenized in makeup. All the water having evaporated, the mud has turned black and has become stickier than the gummy residue on a gruel pot, stickier even than paste. It takes on the appearance of a big melting vat, gummy black with an oily glisten to it, and even flies and mosquitos that swarm around stick to it as they land....

One very rainy day a young child fell into the quagmire and was rescued by a bean-curd peddler. Once they got him out they discovered he was the son of the principal of the Agricultural School. A lively discussion ensued. Someone said that it happened because the Agricultural School was located in the Dragon King Temple, which angered the venerable Dragon King. He claimed it was the Dragon King who caused the heavy downpour in order to drown the child.

Someone disagreed with him completely, saying that the cause of the incident rested with the father, for during his highly animated lectures in the classroom he had once said that the venerable Dragon King was not responsible for any rainfall, and for that matter, did not even exist. "Knowing how furious that would make the venerable Dragon King, you can imagine how he would find some way to vent his anger! So he grabbed hold of the son as a means of gaining retribution."

Someone else said that the students at the school were so incorrigible that one had even climbed up onto the old Dragon King's head and capped him with a straw hat. "What are the times coming to when a child who isn't even dry behind the ears would dare to invite such tremendous calamities down upon himself? How could the old Dragon King not seek retribution? Mark my word, it's not finished yet; don't you get the idea that the venerable Dragon King is some kind of moron! Do you think he'd just let you off once you've provoked his anger? It's not like dealing with a ricksha boy or a vegetable peddler whom you can kick at will, then let him be on his way. This is the venerable Dragon King we're talking about! Do you think that the venerable Dragon King is someone who can easily be pushed around?"

Then there was someone who said that the students at that school were truly undisciplined, and that with his own eyes he had once seen some of them in the main hall putting silkworms into the old Dragon King's hands. "Now just how do you think the old Dragon King could stand for something like that?"

Another person said that the schools were no good at all, and that anyone with children should on no account allow them to go to school, since they immediately lose respect for everyone and everything.

Someone remarked that he was going to the school to get his son and take him home—there would be no more school for him.

Someone else commented that the more the children study, the worse they become. "Take, for example, when their souls are frightened out of their bodies; the minute their mothers call for the souls to return, what do you think they say? They announce that this is nothing but superstition! Now what in the world do you think they'll be saying if they continue going to school?"

And so they talked, drifting further and further away from the original topic.

Before many days had passed, the big quagmire receded once again and pedestrians were soon passing along either side unimpeded. More days passed without any new rainfall, and the quagmire began to dry up, at which time carts and horses recommenced their crossings; then more overturned carts, more horses falling into it and thrashing around; again the ropes and levers appeared, again they were used to lift and drag the horses out. As the righted carts drove off, more followed: into the quagmire, and the lifting began anew.

How many carts and horses are extricated from this quagmire every year may never be known. But, you ask, does no one ever think of solving the problem by filling it in with dirt? No, not a single one.

An elderly member of the gentry once fell into the quagmire at high water. As soon as he crawled out he said: "This street is too narrow. When you have to pass by this water hazard there isn't even room to walk. Why don't the two families whose gardens are on either side take down their walls and open up some paths?"

As he was saying this, an old woman sit-ting in her garden on the other side of the wall chimed in with the comment that the walls could not be taken down, and that the best course of action would be to plant some trees; if a row of trees were planted alongside the wall, then when it rained the people could cross over by holding on to the trees.

Some advise taking down walls and some advise planting trees, but as for filling up the quagmire with dirt, there isn't a single person who advocates that.

Many pigs meet their end by drowning in this quagmire; dogs are suffocated in the mud, cats too; chickens and ducks often lose their lives there as well. This is because the quagmire is covered with a layer of husks; the animals are unaware that there is a trap lying below, and once they realize that fact it is already too late. Whether they come on foot or by air, the instant they alight on the husk-covered mire they cannot free themselves. If it happens in the daytime there is still a chance that someone passing by might save them, but once night falls they are doomed. They struggle all alone until they exhaust their strength, then begin to sink gradually into the mire. If, on the contrary, they continue to struggle, they might sink even faster. Some even die there without sinking below the surface, but that's the sort of thing that happens when the mud is gummier than usual.

What might happen then is that some cheap pork will suddenly appear in the marketplace, and everyone's thoughts turn to the quagmire. "Has another pig drowned in that quagmire?" they ask.

Once the word is out, those who are fast on their feet lose no time in running to their neighbors with the news: "Hurry over and get some cheap pork. Hurry, hurry, before it's all gone."

After it is bought and brought home, a closer look reveals that there seems to be something wrong with it. Why is the meat all dark and discolored? Maybe this pork is in-fected. But on second thought, how could it really be infected? No, it must have been a pig that drowned in the quagmire. So then family after family sautés, fries, steams, boils, and then eats this cheap pork. But though they eat it, they feel always that it doesn't have a fragrant enough aroma, and they fear that it might have been infected after all. But then they think: "Infected pork would be unpalatable, so this must be from a pig that drowned in the quagmire!"

Actually, only one or two pigs drown each year in the quagmire, perhaps three, and some years not a single one. How the residents manage to eat the meat of a drowned pig so often is hard to imagine, and I'm afraid only the Dragon King knows the answer.

Though the people who eat the meat say it is from a pig drowned in the quagmire, there are still those who get sick from it, and those unfortunates are ready with their opinions: "Even if the pork was from a drowned pig, it still shouldn't have been sold in the marketplace; meat from animals that have died isn't fresh, and the revenue office isn't doing its job if it allows meat like this to be sold on the street in broad daylight!"

Those who do not become ill are of a different opinion: "That's what you say, but you're letting your suspicions get the best of you. If you'd just eat it and not give it another thought, everything would be all right. Look at the rest of us; we ate it too, so how come we're not sick?"

Now and then a child lacking in common sense will tell people that his mother wouldn't allow him to eat the pork since it was infected. No one likes this kind of child. Everyone gives him hard looks and accuses him of speaking nonsense.

For example, a child says that the pork is definitely infected—this he tells a neighbor right in front of his mother. There is little reaction from the neighbor who hears him say this, but the mother's face immediately turns beet-red. She reaches out and smacks him.

But he is a stubborn child, and he keeps saying: "The pork is infected!"

His mother, feeling terribly embarrassed, picks up a poker that is lying by the door and strikes him on the shoulder, sending him crying into the house. As he enters the room he sees his maternal grandmother sitting on the edge of the *kang*,[2] so he runs into her arms. "Grannie," he sobs, "wasn't that pork you ate infected? Mama just hit me."

Now this maternal grandmother wants to comfort the poor abused child, but just then she looks up to see the wet nurse of the Li family who shares the compound standing in the doorway looking at her. So she lifts up the back of the child's shirttail and begins spanking him loudly on the behind. "Whoever saw a child as small as you speaking such utter nonsense!" she exclaims. She continues spanking him until the wet nurse walks away with the Li's child in her arms. The spanked child is by then screaming and crying uncontrollably, so hard that no one can make heads or tails of his shouts of "infected pork this" and "infected pork that."

In all, this quagmire brings two benefits to the residents of the area: the first is that the overturned carts and horses and the drowned chickens and ducks always produce a lot of excitement, which keeps the inhabitants buzzing for some time and gives them something to while away the hours.

The second is in relation to the matter of pork. Were there no quagmire, how could they have their infected pork? Naturally, they might still eat it, but how are they to explain it away? If they simply admit they are eating infected pork, it would be too unsanitary for words, but with the presence of the quagmire their problem is solved: infected pork becomes the meat of drowned pigs, which means that when they buy the meat, not only is it economical, but there are no sanitation problems either.

Translated by Howard Goldblatt

NOTES

1. A measure equal to 654 yards or 598.02 meters.
2. Brick platform running along the side of a room and warmed by fire providing sitting and sleeping space.

Brenda Chamberlain   *UK(Wales), 1912–1971*

The Anglo-Welsh writer Brenda Chamberlain is thought of primarily as a fine artist. She studied painting at the Royal Academy of Art and worked as an artist throughout her life. Moreover, she did not start writing seriously until relatively late in life, publishing her first book in 1958 when she was 46. However, she took her writing quite seriously, considering her poetry as significant as her artwork; critics think her prose work *Tide Race* (1962) the most important of her writings.

Chamberlain was born in Bangor, Wales, in 1912. She was educated at home until she was 19, when she went to study art in London. In 1936 she married fellow artist John Betts. The couple moved to Llanllechid, Caerns, and together published the *Caseg Broadsheets*, a series of six broadsheets including poems by poets of her generation like Alun Lewis and Dylan Thomas that served to popularize Welsh poetry outside Wales. Illustrated by Chamberlain and her husband, they also included some of Chamberlain's first poems.

Chamberlain was divorced from Betts in 1946 and went to live by herself on Bardsey, an island off the coast of western Wales. While there she wrote *Tide Race* (1962), a work of prose-poetry about the daily life of this small, Welsh-speaking community. Illustrated by Chamberlain with drawings and paintings, the work spanned several genres, including fairy tales, poems and narrative. She also published the first of her two books of poetry there. *The Green Heart* (1958), the first, reflects the world around her on Bardsey, that of fishermen and mountain dwellers. It won an Arts Council award; two poems from it appear here. The Second, *A Rope of Sands* (1965), is often seen as a sequel to *Tide Race* because, as its subtitle, "Journal from a Greek Island," tells us, it is a chronicle of daily life on a small Greek island, Ydra, where Chamberlain lived for several years. Chamberlain's visit to postwar Germany is reflected in *Water Castle* (1964), her only novel. Chamberlain published *Poems with Drawings* in 1969. She also wrote a play, *The Protagonists*, which was performed in Bangor but never published.

ISLANDMAN

Full of years and seasoned like a salt timber
The island fisherman has come to terms with
                                        death.
His crabbed fingers are coldly afire with
                                  phosphorus
From the night-sea he fishes for bright-
                          armoured herring.

Lifting his lobster pots at sunrise,
He is not surprised when drowned sailors
Wearing ropes of pearl round green throats,
Nod their heads at him from underwater forests.

His black-browed wife who sits at home
Before the red hearth, does not guess
That only a fishscale breastplate protects him
When he sets out across ranges of winter sea.

DEAD PONIES

There is death enough in Europe without these
Dead ponies on the mountain.
They are the underlining, the emphasis of death.
It is not wonderful that when they live
Their eyes are shadowed under mats of hair.
Despair and famine do not gripe so hard
When the bound earth and sky are kept remote
Behind clogged hairs.
The snows engulfed them, pressed their
               withered haunches flat,
Filled up their nostrils, burdened the cage of
               their ribs.

The snow retreated. Their bodies sink to heaven,
Potently crying out to raven hawk and dog;
Come! Pick us clean; cleanse our fine bones of
               blood.

They were never lovely save as foals,
Before their necks grew long, uncrested;
But the wildness of the mountain was in their
               stepping,
The pride of Spring burnt in their haunches,
They were tawny as the rushes of the marsh.
The prey-birds have had their fill, and preen
               their feathers:
Soft entrails have gone to make the hawk
               arrogant.

Hilde Domin   *Germany/FRG, b. 1912*

Born into the upper middle class (her father was a lawyer) in Cologne, Hilde Domin studied law, economics, sociology, and philosophy, completing her studies in 1935, her dissertation entitled "Pontanus as a Predecessor of Machiavelli." In 1936 she married Erwin Palm, an archeologist, and spent the years between 1939 and 1954 away from Germany, primarily in the Dominican Republic. Living among Latin Americans was to have a strong influence on her way of seeing and of writing, and it endowed her poetry with a particular use of metaphor rooted in the Spanish tradition that would separate her works from the models of postwar German literature. Domin initially earned her living as a language teacher and translator, translating into and from Italian, English, French, and Spanish.

Domin began writing poetry in 1951 and designates that period as the start of a new phase of her life. Her first volume of poetry, *Nur eine Rose als Stütze* (Only a Rose as Support), appeared in1959; she has subsequently published seven volumes of poetry, together with numerous critical essays, editions of poetry and prose, and two volumes of autobiographical writings. She has received several literary awards and has been a member of PEN since 1964 and of the German Academy for Language and Poetry since 1978. She has resided in Heidelberg since 1960.

Few other authors give in their works as pronounced an evidence of the experience of exile as an impulse for poetry. Domin describes her exile as a "language odyssey," in which she loses her language and then finds it again. Like so many others, she was banished not only from her homeland but also from her native language; the mother tongue became the language of the persecutors, the language of the enemy and of death. Language becomes the central theme of her poetry, but unlike those who are overcome by skepticism, Domin insists on the potential of words to carry meaning, preferring to regard them metaphorically as "birds with roots." The metaphor in the title of her first volume of poetry, in which the rose is equated with the newly discovered German language, captures the paradoxical nature of her entire oeuvre. In her third volume of poetry, *Hier* (*Here*, 1964), she provides this telling definition of poetry: "the non-word/ stretched out between/word and word." Domin's belief in the positive power of the word is underscored in the poems included here, all of which date from the 1960s.

Marilyn Sibley Fries

NOT TO BE STOPPED
Unaufhaltsam

Your own word
who will retrieve it,
the living
a moment ago unspoken
word?

Where the word flies by
grasses wither,
leaves yellow,
snow falls.
A bird may come back to you.
Not your word,
a moment ago unspoken
word into your mouth.
You send out other words
to catch it,
words with colored, soft feathers.
The word is quicker,
the black word.
It always arrives,
it never stops
arriving.

Better a knife than a word.
A knife can be blunt.
A knife often
misses the heart.
Not the word.

At the end is the word
always
at the end
the word.

Translated by Agnes Stein

MESSENGERS
Die Botschafter

The messengers
come from afar
from the other side of the wall

barefoot
they come
the long way

in order to deliver this word.
One stands before you
in clothes from afar

he brings the word I
he spreads his arms wide
he says the word I

with this parting word
just now you looked at each other
he gives himself over

continues in you.

Translated by Agnes Stein

ABEL ARISE*
Abel steh auf

Abel arise
it must be played again
daily it must be played again
daily the answer must lie ahead
the answer yes must be made possible
if you don't arise Abel
how shall the answer
the only significant answer
how shall it ever change
we can close all churches
abolish all law books
in all the languages of the globe
if only you rise
and make it unspoken
the first false answer
to the only question
that counts
arise
so that Cain says
so that he may say
I am your keeper
Brother
how could I not be your keeper
daily arise
that it may lie ahead
this yes I am here
I
your brother
so that the children of Abel
may no longer be afraid
because Cain will not be Cain
I am writing this
I a child of Abel
daily afraid
of the answer
the air in my lungs diminishes
as I wait for the answer

Abel arise
that there may be new beginnings
among all of us
The fires that burn
the fire that burns on the earth
shall be the fire of Abel
and at the missiles' tail
shall be the fire of Abel

Translated by Agnes Stein

NOTE

* Genesis 4:2

ECCE HOMO*

Less than the hopes set in him
that is man
one-armed
always
Only the crucified
both arms
wide open
the Here-I-Am

Translated by Hilde Domin and Tudor Morris

NOTE

* Literally, "behold the man," from the Vulgate version of
the words spoken by Pilate in presenting Christ wearing
the crown of the thorns to the Jews (John 19:5), now
also understood to symbolize the man of sorrows or a
representation of Christ crowned with thorns.

Mary Lavin

Mary Lavin had a love- and security-filled childhood. She loved learning and the nuns who taught her. She spent memorable days with her mother's family in the Irish village of Athenry and on a large farm north of Dublin. All are celebrated in her often autobiographical short stories. Later, after years of struggling through personal tragedy, financial problems, and long creative droughts, she could write in the short story "Happiness": "You see, annoyance and fatigue...and even illness and pain, could coexist with happiness."

Born in East Walpole, Massachusetts, Mary Lavin was an only child. When Lavin was 9, the family decided to return to Ireland and she and her mother, who was unhappy in the United States, went first, staying in Athenry, County Galway. The town and its people affected her to the degree that, "For years, whenever I wrote a story, no matter what gave me the idea, I had to recast it in terms of the people of that town." Her father joined them the next year, and the family settled in Dublin. Here, Lavin went to the Loreto Convent, where she developed a deep and lasting love for reading and learning. Encouraged by the nuns, Lavin received honors in French and English. She then went to University College, Dublin, in 1930, continuing her studies in literature, and by 1936 she had submitted her masters' thesis on Jane Austen and the novel. She then taught French and English at the Loreto Convent while doing her doctoral work and preparing to write on Virginia Woolf.

Lavin began writing fiction around this time, and her first story, "Miss Holland" was published by *Dublin Magazine* in 1938. The following year "The Green Grave and the Black Grave" was published in the *Atlantic Monthly* in the United States. In 1943, she was awarded the James Tait Black Memorial Book Prize for *Tales from Bective Bridge* (1942), her first collection of short stories. The year 1943 also saw the birth of the first of Lavin's three children (Lavin had married William Walsh, a lawyer, in 1942). Understandably, her three children made great demands on her time, which is why she chose the short story as her primary mode of expression. Lavin was able to produce four collections of stories between 1944 and 1951, as well as two novels, *The House on Cleve Street* (1945) and *Mary O'Grady* (1950).

In 1946, with an inheritance from her father's death the previous year, Lavin purchased the Abbey Farm at Bective, an estate that her father had managed for nearly twenty years. Though the farm served as a sustaining source of inspiration to Lavin, her life changed abruptly in 1954 when her husband died. She was left with little financial or emotional support, and despair all but halted her writing. She did rebound, however, with the help of an Australian Jesuit priest she had known at University College and whom she married when he left the order in 1969.

Lavin has produced nearly fifteen volumes of short stories, to date, many of which were originally published in *The New Yorker*, with which she has had a relationship for the past three decades. Her stories, written in the realistic mode, concern sensitive, often lonely, tortured characters involved in moral struggles in which they invariably are sacrificed to a "greater good." Many of her stories have an autobiographical basis, including a number on widowhood and several based on her beloved father. The selection here is from *Collected Stories* (1971). Lavin has received many awards for her work, including the Katharine Mansfield Prize in 1961, an honorary doctorate from University College, in 1968, several Guggenheim Fellowships, the Ella Lyman Cabot Award in 1972, the Eire Society Medal, and the prestigious Gregory Medal in 1975.

John Isom

A VISIT TO THE CEMETERY

"What a pity she had to be buried here!" said Alice, for the hundredth time since their mother died, as she took the key from her younger sister Liddy and struggled with the iron gate of the Old Cemetery.

The New Plot was about a mile outside the town, on a nice dry hill that commanded a fine view of the countryside. And it was just a nice walk out to it, not too far, but above all not too near.

"I can't think why on earth they ever put a cemetery here in the middle of the town," cried Alice, as the key turned at last in the corroded lock, but the heavy old gate refused to budge.

"Oh, Alice!" Liddy had to laugh at her older sister's ignorance, because of course the cemetery was far older than the town. It was the site of an ancient friary of which only one stump now remained, sticking up like an old tooth rotted down to its obstinate root, but which must once, upon the open fields, have floated free as an island.

Alice, however, was not concerned with antiquity.

"Come on," she cried. She had got the gate to open. The next minute they were inside, finding their way through the neglected grass and high rank nettles, following the faint track of the funeral still visible after four months. There was no real path anywhere now, and funerals had to make their way on foot, in and out, wormlike, between tottering tombstones. No hearse had entered the place in living memory; coffins had to be shouldered to their last resting place.

"Mind your clothes!" cried Alice sharply. She still had memories of the humiliation she suffered at the funeral, when the mourners came out into the street with burrs stuck all over their good black clothes.

"I'm all right," said Liddy. She was holding up her skirt. All the same they both had to stop more than once where their dresses caught in the briers.

But at last they came to their mother's grave and knelt down quickly, crossing themselves before their knees touched the clay. And, as they brought their hands together again in front of them, they closed their eyes tightly.

For the next second or so their lips moved with the quick pecking movements of a bird, as they got through what might almost have been a prearranged ration of prayer, so neatly did they come to an end together. Yet they did not immediately make the sign of the cross, neither wanting to be the first to move. But someone had to be the first, and so at last Liddy glanced across at Alice and raised her eyebrows questioningly.

At once, just as if she had been audibly addressed, Alice answered.

"I am. Are you?" she said, and she blessed herself and got to her feet. Liddy also scrambled to her feet.

"That grass was damp," she said crossly, and she began to rub her knees.

"It's always damp in this old place," Alice said very crossly. "I always say I'll bring something with me to kneel on—even an old newspaper—but I forget every time." She, too, rubbed her knees, but it was her black dress that concerned her most, and lifting up the hem, she submitted her skirt to a close scrutiny. "I'll never forget those burrs."

"Nor I," said Liddy, but she didn't bother to look at her dress, because after all they had to make their way back to the gate again. Wasn't it a wonder no one took any care of the place? Even to scythe the weeds would help. But then of course hardly anyone ever came here, except themselves. What a lonely place it was. And although where she stood she could hear the people talking in the street outside, and only a little farther away the thudding of a ball in the ball-alley, it seemed that she was cut off from them so that they would not hear her, not even if she were to scream at the top of her voice. But that was absurd. Why should she scream? It was broad daylight and there was Alice a few feet away calling out to her impatiently.

"Are you coming?" Alice cried.

But Liddy still loitered, and as if she had never before been in it, she looked around the old cemetery. As far as they could be made out in the rank growth in which they were submerged, there wasn't a tombstone or a headstone that wasn't slanted or tottering. It was almost as if the earth had quaked and the quiet dead—momentarily dislodged—had settled down again in postures, unquiet and disorderly. And ah—just behind their mother's headstone there was an unsightly grave where a rabbit—no, it must have been a badger—had burrowed, and from it—yes—though Liddy quickly averted her eyes—yes, from it a large bleached bone stuck upward. Almost falling forward into the high grass she ran after Alice, and caught her by the sleeve.

"Poor Mother!" she cried. "I can't help thinking how much nicer and cleaner it would have been for her in the new cemetery!"

"Isn't that what I'm always saying!" Alice looked at her. Liddy was slow sometimes. "Are you coming or are you not?" Pulling her sleeve free, she went on a few steps.

"Alice?"

Alice didn't want to turn around, but there was something in Liddy's voice that compelled her to turn. Liddy was standing just where she had left her, looking back at their mother's grave.

"What?"

Alice knew her voice was grumpy, but she really wanted to get out of the gate. How she hated it! And Liddy looked as if she were prepared to stay there forever.

"Do you ever think about it at all, Alice?"

What Liddy meant Alice both knew and did not know, so she hedged. "I don't know what you're talking about," she said.

Liddy turned around slowly and in her eyes there was an expression that could not be misread.

"It's so awful, isn't it?" She shuddered.

Almost as quickly as Liddy herself had averted her eyes from the grave, Alice averted hers from her sister.

"Oh, Liddy! If I'd thought you were going to take on like this I'd never have come with you." She paused, casting around in her mind for something to say that might get them over the silence that fell. "After all we must all die—we know that," she said lamely.

But Liddy was incorrigible. "That's what I mean," she said quietly.

Alice was at a loss. "Well, after all we can console ourselves that it's only the body that is buried, the soul..."

Not exactly rudely, however, and not exactly impatiently, Liddy shrugged her shoulders.

"I sometimes think that's the worst of it," she said, in a voice so low Alice had to bend to hear. "I can never believe that I won't go on feeling: feeling the cold and the damp—you know, even after—"

"Liddy! Liddy!" Alice stumbled toward her across the tufted grass. If Liddy had said a single other word she would have clapped her hands over her sister's mouth.

But Liddy didn't finish it. She had begun to sob softly.

"And to think," she said after a minute, "that in a few years, perhaps sooner, poor Father—" she sobbed, "just think of it—poor Father will be put down here too."

This was dreadful. Alice felt helpless. She always knew Liddy took things differently from her, but she never knew her to carry on like this. She couldn't think what to do, and when at that moment near her foot she saw a bone she gave it a kick. Hateful place: it was all bones. That one might have been brought in by some mongrel, but it could just as easily be a human bone. The place was disgusting. It was enough to give anyone the creeps. Oh, if only Mother had been buried in the new cemetery where everything was so neat and orderly, Liddy would not have got into this state! The gravedigger up there always boasted that he'd give five pounds to anyone who found a bone after him!

"Well, thanks be to goodness we won't be buried here, anyway!" she said impulsively.

"We won't?" Liddy looked up in such surprise a tear that was slowly rolling down her cheeks was jerked into the air.

"Of course not," Alice cried. "Not unless we are old maids!" But that seemed so untoward a thing that she made a playful face. Then, seeing that Liddy had smiled, if wanly, she put on an arch expression. "We'll be buried with our husbands."

"Oh, Alice!" Liddy knew that Alice used to talk about boys with her friends, but she had never said anything like this to her before and she felt herself blushing. She was furious with herself about it until she saw that Alice was blushing a little too.

"It's true!" said Alice defensively. "The first death in the family means that you have to buy a plot. Surely you know that! That's why Mother was buried here, because of that baby she had before any of us, the one that died. Father bought a plot here then, and even though it was years ago, and there is a new cemetery now, poor Mother had to be buried here. And so will Father himself. But there aren't any more plots to be got here now, thanks be to God, so our husbands will have to provide them—in the new cemetery—thanks be to God again!"

Their husbands: it was an intoxicating thought. Liddy looked up at the sky. It was turning out to be a beautiful evening, although you wouldn't notice it so much in the old graveyard, where the ivy made everything so dark, and the shadow of stones overlapping made a sort of double gloom.

Although there was hardly room for two to walk together, she recklessly linked her arm in her sister's and began to draw her toward the gate. A great feeling of sisterly affection had come over her, and it seemed to her that it wasn't just a matter of chance that they had picked this evening to come out together. It was as if something for a long time suppressed had at last begun to force upward toward the light.

"Just think, Alice—about that baby, I mean. Mother was younger than us—than you, anyway—when that baby was born, and we—" she hesitated.

"I know," said Alice glumly. "I was thinking that myself a few minutes ago. But times were different then; girls were encouraged to have boys then. Not like now."

"You mean Father would—"

"He'd be just wild. You know that as well as me. And he will probably be ten times stricter now because he used to rely on Mother to look after us."

"Poor Mother! She wasn't strict at all."

"I expect that was because she was so ill for the past few years. You remember everyone said it was a happy release for her."

"I suppose it was too," Liddy said.

But they had reached the gate at last, and she sighed. Their adventure for the day was over. It was a pity they had started out so early in a way; if they had started half an hour later they would be coming in the gate now instead of going out. And she was right about the evening; there was a remarkable change in the air. It was like an evening in spring. Just as they stepped out into the street a breeze that came up out of nowhere, oh, so fresh and sweet, blew their skirts around their legs like an umbrella around its stem. It would be such a nice evening to go for a walk outside the town; to hold up their faces, to look, to smell and above all to talk; to talk.

"Oh, isn't it too bad, Alice," she cried, as if it was the first time anyone had expressed the idea—

"—that she wasn't buried in the new cemetery?"

Liddy nodded. "It must be lovely up there on an evening like this: we could walk around and read the names on the stones—they're all names we know, not like in this old place. I don't suppose—" she hesitated—"I wonder if we might—"

"You mean—walk out that way?" said Alice, taking up her meaning immediately, but she looked frightened. "We didn't tell them at home that we were going for a walk."

"We said we were going to the cemetery, didn't we?" cried Liddy. "We didn't say which one!" She gave Alice's arm a pull. "Oh, come on, I've something to tell you, anyway. I've kept it a secret, but I think I could tell you now."

For an instant Alice was almost livid with jealously. Could it be that Liddy had a boy? Liddy who was two years younger than her. And she hadn't had a single flutter. Unless you could count what happened after the choir the other evening. She wondered what Liddy would think about that? She might tell her as they went along.

"Come on so," she cried. "We'll chance it."

They almost forgot to lock the gate.

"What about this?" Liddy held up the key which she managed to get out of the lock.

They were supposed to hand it back where they got it, at the parochial house.

"Oh, we'll leave it back on the way home," said Alice. She was impatient to start.

But before they set out, one after the other, the sisters gave the gate a push to see that it was locked, and to make doubly sure Liddy put her shoulder to it.

"It's locked all right," she said. "Come on."

Elsa Morante

Italy, 1912–1985

Elsa Morante was born in 1912 (not 1918 as she liked to claim). She married the writer Alberto Moravia in 1941 but later separated from him. Her first book of short stories, *Il gioco segreto* (The Secret Game, 1941), was noticed for its magic realism and her first novel *Menzogna e sortilegio* (*House of Liars*, 1948), received the Viareggio Prize, launching her as an original writer of the postwar generation. In the novel, the heroine narrates the saga of three generations of her family ruined because its members tried to live out their rebellious fantasies. Highly unrealistic, the novel emphasizes memory and the intensity of feelings through its lyric prose. In *L'isola di Arturo* (*Arturo's Island*, 1957), which won the Strega Prize, the dreamlike world of an adolescent crumbles at the discoveries of his father's homosexuality and his love for his young stepmother.

Scialle andaluso (Andalusian Shawl, 1963) is a book of short stories, some of them published previously. Of the two books of poetry, *Alibi* (Alibi, 1958) and *Il mondo salvato dai ragazzini* (The World Saved by Children, 1968), the latter is more powerful. In spite of Morante's pessimistic vision of the world, there is hope at the end: the very young are capable of love and honesty, leading to salvation.

Morante's desire to reach out to the poor and humble resulted in the novel *La Storia* (*History: A Novel*, 1974), which depicts the life of Iduzza, a part-Jewish school teacher living in Rome, and her two sons against the historic events of 1941–1947. In spite of its rather simple vision, the novel became a bestseller, probably because of its touching, humanistic portrayal of characters. An excerpt from *History* follows.

Her last novel, *Aracoeli* (*Aracoeli: A Novel*, 1982), is an attempt to comprehend the contemporary world—in this case peopled by drug addicts and homosexuals—by following a man on a trip to Spain in search of his mother's roots; recovering his childhood in flashbacks, the man realizes, at the end that he has never had his father's love although he always longed for it.

Natalia Costa-Zalessow

from HISTORY: A NOVEL
La Storia

Giuseppe Ramundo, at the time of his death, was fifty-eight; and Nora, sixty-six when she was widowed, was already retired. She never went to visit her husband's grave, prevented by a kind of sacred terror of burial-places; but still it is certain that her deepest bond, which made her stay in the city of Cosenza, was his nearness, since he dwelt there still, in that cemetery.

She would never leave the old house, which had become her lair. She went out only rarely, in the early morning to buy food, or on the days when she had to draw her pension or send the usual money-order to Giuseppe's ancient parents. To them, as also to Ida, she wrote long letters, which the illiterate old couple had to have read to them. But in her letters, she took care never to refer, even in the most indirect and reticent way, to her own pressing terrors for the future: by now she suspected censorship and informers everywhere. And in those frequent and endless communications of hers, she did nothing but repeat the same notion in every possible variation:

"How strange and unnatural destiny is. I married a man eight years younger than myself, and according to the law of nature I should have been the first to die, with Him at my side. Instead, it was my destiny to witness His death."

In speaking of Giuseppe, she always wrote Him, with a capital letter. Her style was prolix, repetitive, but with a certain academic nobility; and her handwriting was elongated, fine, even elegant. (However, in her final decline, her letters grew shorter and shorter. Her style became amputated and disjointed; and her written words, all shaky and twisted, groped across the page, uncertain of their direction.)

Besides this correspondence, which occupied her like a mania, her usual pastimes were reading illustrated magazines or love stories or listening to the radio. For some time now, the tales of racial persecution in Germany had alarmed her, like a precise signal confirming her old forebodings. But when, towards spring of 1938, Italy also intoned the official choros of anti-Semitic propaganda, she saw the thunderous magnitude of destiny advancing towards her door, growing more enormous day by day. The news broadcasts, with their pompous and menacing voices, already seemed to be physically invading her little rooms, sowing panic; but to be prepared, she felt more and more obliged to listen to the news. And she spent her days and evenings on guard, alert to the news-broadcast schedules, like a little, wounded fox that has gone to earth and strains to hear the barking of the pack.

Some minor Fascist officials arrived from Catanzaro one day and spread the unofficial word of an imminent census of all Italian Jews, each of whom would be required to report himself. And after that moment, Nora no longer turned on the radio, in her terror of hearing the official announcement of the government's order, with a time-limit for reporting.

It was the beginning of summer. Already the previous winter, Nora, now sixty-eight, had begun to suffer a worsening of her ailments, due to the arteriosclerosis that had been undermining her for some time. With other people, too, her behavior (which had been shy before, but always tempered by an inner sweetness) had become angry and harsh. She no longer spoke if someone greeted her, not even when it was a former student, now grown up, perhaps one who had until then remained dear to her. On certain nights, she had raving fits, when she tore her gown with her fingernails. One night, she fell out of bed in her sleep, and she found herself lying on the floor, her head aching and buzzing. She often would wheel around, frowning and furious on the slightest pretext, sensing mysterious insults even in innocent gestures or words.

Of all the possible measures threatened against the Jews, the one that most immediately frightened her was the predicted obligation to report oneself for the census! All imaginable forms of near and future persecutions, even the most wicked and disastrous, were confused in her mind like wavering phantoms, among which the terrible spotlight of that single decree froze her in its beam! At the thought of having to declare publicly her fatal secret, which she had always hidden as something infamous, she promptly said to herself: it's impossible. Since she never saw the newspapers or listened to the radio anymore, she suspected the famous decree was by now promulgated and already in effect (whereas, in reality, no racial decree had so far been issued); and indeed, she became convinced, in her isolation, that the time-limit for reporting oneself was already up. She was careful, all the same, not to make inquiries or, worse, present herself at City Hall. As each new day dawned, she repeated: it's impossible, spending the hours then in this constant fear, until the city offices' closing-time, only to find herself, the next day, with the same obsessive problem. In her rooted conviction that she was already late, and hence subject to all sorts of unknown sanctions, she began to fear the calendar, dates, the sun's daily rising. And though the days went by without any suspect sign, she lived every moment from then on in the expectation of some forthcoming, terrible event. She expected to be summoned to the city offices to explain her transgression, then publicly given the lie, charged with perjury. Or else someone from City Hall or Police Headquarters would come looking for her; she might even be arrested.

She no longer left the house, not even for her daily needs, which she asked the concierge's wife to buy for her. One morning, however, when the woman showed up at the door for her list, Nora drove her off with bestial cries, hurling a cup she had in her hand. But people suspected nothing and had always esteemed her, so they forgave her these shrewish moods, attributing them to grief for her husband.

She began to suffer hallucinations. Her blood, rising with effort to her brain, would pound and roar in her hardened arteries, and she would think she heard violent blows in the street, hammering at the front door, footsteps or heavy breathing on the stairs. At evening, if she suddenly turned on the electric light, her failing eyesight transformed the furniture and its shadows into the motionless shapes of informers or armed police who had come to take her by surprise and arrest her. And one night when, for the second time, she happened to fall out of bed in her sleep, she imagined one of these men, having entered by stealth, had thrown her to the ground, and was still roaming about the house.

She thought of leaving Cosenza, of moving somewhere else. But where? And to whom? Padua, with her few Jewish relatives, was impossible. At her daughter's in Rome, or at her in-laws', down in the country below Reggio, her alien presence would be more noticeable than ever, would be recorded, and would compromise the others too. And besides, how could she impose the intrusion of a neurasthenic, haunted old woman on those who already had so many worries and torments of their own? She had never asked anything of anyone; she had been independent, since her girlhood. She always remembered two verses heard in the Ghetto, from an aged rabbi:

Unhappy the man who needs other men!
Happy the man who needs only God.

Why not leave then for some other city or anonymous town, where no one knew her? But, in any place, she would have to report her presence, produce her papers. She pondered escaping to a foreign country, where there were no racial laws. But she had never been abroad, had no passport; and acquiring a passport meant, again, questions at the registry office, the police, the frontiers: all places and rooms denied her, menacing, as if to an outlaw.

She was not poor, as perhaps everyone believed. Through those years (precisely to guarantee her own future independence, in the case of illness or other unforeseen eventualities) she had habitually put aside, little by little, some savings which now amounted to three thousand lire. This sum, in three one-thousand bills, was sewn into a handkerchief which at night she kept under her pillow and the rest of the time always on her person, pinned inside a stocking.

In her inexperienced mind, which was already clouding over, she assumed that, with such a sum, she could pay for any foreign journey, even an exotic one! At certain moments, like a young girl, she would daydream about metropolises that, as a spinster, in her Bovaresque dreams,[1] she had longed for as sublime destinations: London, Paris! But suddenly she would remember that she was alone now; and how could a lone old woman find her way amid those cosmopolitan and tumultuous throngs?! If only Giuseppe were with her, then traveling would indeed still be beautiful! But Giuseppe no longer existed, he was not to be found here or anywhere. Perhaps even his body, so big and heavy, had now dissolved into the earth. There was no longer anyone on earth to reassure her in her terrors, as he used to do, saying to her: "How silly you are! You crazy little thing!"

Though she continued proposing various plans to herself, examining all the continents and countries, for her, in the entire globe, there was no place. And yet, as the days went by, the necessity, the urgency of escape were impressed on her feverish brain.

In the course of the last months, she had heard, perhaps over the radio, talk of Jewish emigrations from all Europe to Palestine. She knew absolutely nothing about Zionism, if she even knew the word. And of Palestine she knew only that it was the Biblical homeland of the Hebrews and that its capital was Jerusalem. But still, she came to the conclusion that the only place where she could be received, as a fugitive Jew among a people of Jews, was Palestine.

And as the summer heat was already advancing, one evening she suddenly decided to flee, then and there, even without a passport. She could cross the border illegally, or else she would stow away in the hold of a ship, as she had heard about in tales of illegal emigrants.

She took no baggage with her, not even a change of linen. She had on her, as always, her three thousand lire hidden inside the stocking.

And at the last minute, noticing one of those old Calabrian cloaks Giuseppe used to wear in winter still hanging from a hook in the hall, she took it along, folded over her arm, with the thought of protecting herself if perhaps she went to a cold climate.

It is certain she was already delirious. But still she must have reasoned that to go from Cosenza to Jerusalem overland was not a good idea, because she headed for the sea, choosing the alternative of a ship as the only solution. Some people vaguely recall having seen her, in her little summer dress of black artificial silk with a blue pattern, on the last evening train heading for the beach at Paola. And in fact it is there, in that area, that she was found. Perhaps she wandered for a while along that beach without ports, searching for some freighter flying an Asiatic flag, more lost and confused than a five-year-old boy who runs away to sign on as a cabin boy and see the world.

In any event, though such endurance seems incredible in her condition, we have to believe that, from the station where she arrived, she covered a long distance on foot. In fact, the specific spot where they found her on the sand is several miles away from the Paola beach, towards Fuscaldo. Along that stretch of the coastline, beyond the railroad track, there are hilly fields of corn whose swaying expanse in the darkness, to her crazed eyes, may have created the effect of the sea opening out ahead.

It was a beautiful moonless night, calm and starry. Perhaps she was reminded of that one little song from her parts that she could sing:

What a fine night this is for stealing girls.

But even in that serene and tepid air, at a certain point in her walk, she felt cold. And she covered herself with that man's cloak she had brought along, taking care to fasten the buckle at the throat. It was an old mantle of dark brown country wool, which had been the right length for Giuseppe, but was too long for her, falling to her feet. A local man seeing her go by in the distance, cloaked in that way, could have taken her for the *monacheddu*, the little domestic brigand disguised as a monk, who roams about at night, they say, entering houses by dropping down the chimney. Apparently, however, nobody encountered her, naturally enough, on that isolated shore, seldom visited, especially at night.

The first to find her were some boatmen coming in at dawn from their fishing; and immediately they thought she was a suicide, brought ashore by the sea's currents. But the position of the drowned woman and the condition of her body did not agree with that hasty conclusion.

She was lying below the waterline, on sand still wet from the recent tide, in a relaxed and natural attitude, like someone surprised by death in a state of unconsciousness or in sleep. Her head was on the sand, which the light flux had made even and clean, without seaweed or flotsam; and the rest of her body was on the great man's cloak, held at the collar by the buckle and spread out at her sides, open, all soaked with water. The little artificial silk dress, damp and smoothed by the water, clung decorously to her thin body, which seemed unharmed, not swollen or abused as bodies washed in by the tide usually look. And the tiny blue carnations printed on the silk appeared new, brightened by the water, against the dark background of the cloak.

The sea's only violence had been to tear off her little shoes and undo her hair which, despite her age, had remained long and abundant, and only partly graying, so that now, wet, it seemed black again, and had fallen all down one side, almost gracefully. The current had not even slipped from her emaciated hand the little gold wedding ring, whose slight, precious gleam was distinct in the day's advancing light.

This was all the gold she possessed. In spite of her patriotic comformity (unlike her timid daughter Ida), she had not wanted to part with it even when the government had invited the people to "give gold to the Fatherland" to aid the Abyssinian conquest.[2]

On her wrist, not yet spotted with rust, there remained her cheap little metal watch, stopped at four o'clock.

The examination of the body confirmed beyond a doubt her death by drowning; but she had left no sign or farewell message that indicated any suicidal intention. They found on her, hidden in the usual place beneath her stocking, her secret treasure in banknotes, still recognizable, though reduced by the water to a valueless pulp. Knowing Nora's character, we can be sure that if she had meant to do away with herself, she would first have taken care, wherever she was, to save from destruction that capital, so huge for her, accumulated with such perseverance.

Moreover, if she had really abandoned herself to the great mass of the sea, deliberately seeking death, we can suppose that the cloak's weight, increased by the water, would have dragged her to the bottom.

The case was closed, with the verdict: *accidental death by drowning*. And this, in my opinion, is the most logical explanation. I believe that death caught her unawares, perhaps when she had fallen into one of those spells she had been prone to for some time.

At that part of the coast, and in that season, the tides are light, especially at the new moon. In her futile, haunted, and almost blind journey in the darkness of the night, she must have lost all sense of direction and even all sensory signals. And inadvertently she must have advanced too far on the strip washed by the tide, perhaps confused between the ocean of corn and the windless sea, or perhaps in some deranged move towards the ghost outline of a ship. There she fell, and the tide, already turning, covered her, just enough to drown her, but without assaulting her or striking her, and with no other sound save its own sucking imperceptible in the calm air. Meanwhile, the water-logged mantle, its edges buried under layers of sand, held her body on the damp slope, restraining it, lifeless, on the beach until the first hours of daylight.

I know Nora only from a photograph taken in the days of her engagement. She is standing against the background of a paper landscape, unfolding a fan, which covers the front of her blouse, and her pensive but formal pose betrays her grave yet sentimental nature. She is tiny and slim, with a woolen skirt, almost straight, pleated, tight-fitting at the waist, and a white muslin blouse with starched cuffs, buttoned up to the throat. With her free arm she is leaning, with almost histrionic abandon, on a little console, typical of middle-class photographers at the end of the century. Her hair is combed tight over her forehead and loose on top of her head in a gentle circle, like a geisha's. Her eyes are deeply fervent, behind a veil of melancholy. And the rest of the face is delicately made but ordinary.

On the photograph's lower margin, a yellowed white, printed on thick cardboard as they were then, in addition to the ornate printed legend customary at the time (*Format*, etc.) the dedication is still legible, in her gentle, diligent, and fine hand:

For You, beloved Giuseppe!
   from your
     Eleonora

In the lower left-hand corner there is the date: *20 May 1902*; and a bit farther down, on the right, in the same little hand, there follows the sentiment:

With You forever
as long as I live and beyond.

Translated by William Weaver

NOTES

1. Madame Bovary (1856), written by Gustave Flaubert (1821–1880), is a novel about a woman, bored in marriage, who enters into a romantic, yet adulterous, relationship only to be rejected and to kill herself.
2. Abyssinia, now called Ethiopia, was invaded in 1935 by Italy, which ruled it until 1941.

Marguerite Taos Amrouche   *Tunisia/France, 1913–1976*

Marguerite Taos Amrouche was born in Tunis to a family of Christian converts. Her mother, Fadhma Aïth Mansour Amrouche, and her brother Jean were both writers as well: the Amrouches were an extraordinary literary family whose sense of religious exile in their own country was the obverse of their deep passion for and attachment to Tunisia and the Berber tradition. Marguerite Amrouche once wrote, "Facing the incomprehension of strangers is bearable, but there is nothing more cruel than the incomprehension of one's brothers."[1]

The family eventually immigrated to France, where Amrouche was supposed to study for the entrance examination to the École normale of Sèvres, a prestigious school of higher learning. She abandoned this goal however, and in 1936 became interested in the preservation and reconstitution of Berber songs and chants, which her mother had sung to her and her brother when they were children. From 1937 to 1938, in Paris and Munich, Amrouche performed for the public the repertory of Berber songs that she had been working on. In 1939, having received a scholarship to study at the Casa Valasquez in Spain, she gathered legends, tales, and proverbs of the nomadic North tribe, which she published under the title *Le grain magique*, (The Magic Grain, reprinted 1966), dedicated to her mother—"the last link in a chain of aedes" (Greek poets of a primitive era).

Her novel *Jacinthe noire* (Black Hyacinth, 1947), excerpted and translated here for the first time, is one of the first Maghrebine (or northwest African) novels written in French. It is set in a Parisian rooming house for young women. A young Tunisian woman, named simply Reine (literally, Queen), arrives and disrupts the monotonous lives of the sheltered young French women; they are both seduced and repulsed by her passion, her loneliness, and her exotic past. The narrator, a lonely young woman from the French provinces who works as a tutor for a wealthy family by day and is supposed to be studying for an entrance examination for university at night, falls madly in love with Reine but must disguise her obsession with the young Tunisian from the curiosity of other young women. The narrator feels that only under Reine's ardent gaze will she herself be made whole. Not only is the novel a wonderful portrait of adolescent female desire, it is also evocative of the bitterness of exile and the politics of difference and otherness. It is clearly ahead of its time, anticipating much of the recent theoretical work on Orientalism done in the United States and France. Experimental, too, in style, its shifting tenses are used to convey the inner moods of the character.

In *La rue des tambourins* (The Street of Drums, 1960), Amrouche draws on the events of her childhood in Tunis. The mother figure in the novel maintains the integrity of the Berber tradition for her children but does not allow them to indulge in nostalgia for an irretrievable past. Her last novel, *L'amant imaginaire* (The Imaginary Lover, 1975), describes the marginality of North Africans in France.

The trajectory of Amrouche's life and writing is parallel to those of certain other artists of her generation. Like Zora Neale Hurston in the United States, Amrouche inserted her people into the ethnographic narrative. Like the francophone Canadian Gabrielle Roy, she voiced her marginality in two cultures, transforming her solitude into communication.

from BLACK HYACINTH
Jacinthe noire

When the weather is mild, Mic and I are in the garden. I'm in charge of watching him while he does his homework. In principle I'm not supposed to help him. In the morning we work together but in the afternoon he's on his own. Once a week I accompany him to his class. Mic is sitting on a tall chair, his feet curled behind the cross-bar. His small white neck is delicate, fragile. A chestnut tree shields us. I was stretched out comfortably on a reclining chair. We were surrounded by beautiful dahlias on bending stems. Some reminded me of heads weighing heavily on shoulders, while others, arrogant and open, held themselves up proudly. I leaned over to pick a purple one in full bloom. I put it in my lap and almost callously began to slowly pull off its petals. The dahlia is a magnificent flower but it doesn't have a soul. I made two more stitches in my knitting and then set it aside. I read several pages of the novel Elisabeth had lent me. Never before had reading seemed so strange.

There in the garden, with Mic's gentle presence and the stronger one of the trees and flowers, I wanted to remain perfectly still to feel the wind on my forehead. I cared little for the impression I made, since I knew that I bore within me, like a dense, almost painful fruit, the conviction of my inner life. I began to think about Reine, and soon the worries about my sister and my friend from Spain found their way into my thoughts. To quiet my anxiety I decided to write to them. While I can now recall even the tiniest details from that time, including the precise contents of Madame d'Angillaire's meals, I have only a vague memory of those two letters. I wasn't close enough to my sister to make her understand the miracle that had overwhelmed me. As for my friend from Spain, the distance between us paralyzed me. But then, perhaps I hadn't really resolved to share everything with her. . . .I can imagine smiling at her—that same smile that used to make Reine angry. I remember those two letters as two empty shells. I only mailed the one to Marie-Hélène. The other was forgotten in a cabinet in my room in Versailles. After a month went by, and I still hadn't received a response, I accused my friend of negligence.

From that day on, because I had to give time to Reine, I tried to stay busy and occupied my free time with knitting, reading, and writing. In front of the d'Angillaires I avoided idleness and daydreaming: I was always on my best behavior. In the presence of Miss Anatole I wore a mask. But it was not time yet to abandon this image of me. In Paris, no one except for Reine saw me as I really was. And besides, I had been determined for so long to hide that the only time I showed my real face was on my night off. It took all of Reine's power—her insistent questioning—to touch me and slowly expose that face. It surfaced like a moon with blurred contours, reluctantly lifted from the bottom of a well. But before I could see it clearly, it sank back into the depths of myself. For there was a time when that smile did not exist, that smile that took the place of words and became automatic. But it appeared one day, and ever since then I haven't been able to keep it from my face, from blocking the passage of any heartfelt expression. It isolated me from my surroundings and even from my friends. It inspired so little confidence that I got none in return; any trust in me was killed before it could be born. Only Reine was able to break through it. After all, it was nothing more than a smile of habit, a defense.

When I finished writing my letters it was around four o'clock. Mic had done his homework, the temperature was dropping, and we walked back to the house, where we had our afternoon snack. Michel walked quietly to his little wicker chair. When he had eaten his sandwiches, he looked longingly at me. I could see that he was burning to hear the end of the story. We moved next to the large bay window, Mic dragging his chair behind him like a snail. Shadows were advancing into the room; only the bay window remained in the light. My cheek was pressed against the pane. As the last ray of light disappeared, I read the last line: "And they lived happily ever after." Mic sat motionless, his little hands clasped tightly together, his eyes lit like green stars. I touched his shoulder; he got up and followed me. It was time for us to leave each other. On the verge of returning to Paris, I was overcome by sadness of my room on X Street. I cut an armful of red dahlias and hurried toward the train station.

Translated by Astrid Hustvedt

Carolina Maria de Jesus   *Brazil, 1913–1977*

Born in a small town in rural Brazil of an unmarried farm worker, Carolina de Jesus ran off to São Paulo when she was 16, became pregnant, and moved into a *favela*, one of many slum areas encircling the large metropolitan centers of Brazil. She had several more children, supporting herself by collecting scrap paper and selling it for pennies. A reporter visiting the *favela* during a local election heard about a diary de Jesus was keeping and, after convincing her to let him read it, helped her to publish it. He also helped her to edit it by suggesting ways she could make it less repetitious and wordy; it is generally believed that he did not help her to write or rewrite it, despite accusations by some critics, who found it hard to believe a woman with a second-grade education could write so eloquently. The book, *Quarto de despejo*, (*Child of the Dark: The Diary of Carolina Maria de Jesus*, 1960), from which the following extract was taken, was extremely successful; it was translated into thirteen languages and sold well enough for her to move out of the *favela* and to buy a farm near her native city and to support her family. For a while she was a public personality. However, her further attempts at writing were unsuccessful.

from CHILD OF THE DARK
Quarto de despejo

May 2, 1958. I'm not lazy. There are times when I try to keep up my diary. But then I think it's not worth it and figure I'm wasting my time.

I've made a promise to myself. I want to treat people that I know with more consideration. I want to have a pleasant smile for children and the employed.

I received a summons to appear at 8 P.M. at police station number 12. I spent the day looking for paper. At night my feet pained me so I couldn't walk. It started to rain. I went to the station and took José Carlos with me. The summons was for him. José Carlos is nine years old.

May 3. I went to the market at Carlos de Campos Street looking for any old thing. I got a lot of greens. But it didn't help much, for I've got no cooking fat. The children are upset because there's nothing to eat. . . .

May 9. I looked for paper but I didn't like it. Then I thought: I'll pretend that I'm dreaming.

May 10. I went to the police station and talked to the lieutenant. What a pleasant man! If I had known he was going to be so pleasant, I'd have gone on the first summons. The lieutenant was interested in my boys' education. He said the favelas have an unhealthy atmosphere where the people have more chance to go wrong than to become useful to state and country. I thought: if he knows this why doesn't he make a report and send it to the politicians? To Jánio Quadros, Kubitschek,[1] and Dr. Adhemar de Barros? Now he tells me this, I a poor garbage collector. I can't even solve my own problems.

Brazil needs to be led by a person who has known hunger. Hunger is also a teacher.

Who has gone hungry learns to think of the future and of the children.

May 11. Today is Mother's Day. The sky is blue and white. It seems that even nature wants to pay homage to the mothers who feel unhappy because they can't realize the desires of their children.

The sun keeps climbing. Today it's not going to rain. Today is our day.

Dona Teresinha came to vist me. She gave me fifteen cruzeiros and said it was for Vera to go to the circus. But I'm going to use the money to buy bread tomorrow because I only have four cruzeiros.

Yesterday I got half a pig's head at the slaughterhouse. We ate the meat and saved the bones. Today I put the bones on to boil and into the broth I put some potatoes. My children are always hungry. When they are starving they aren't so fussy about what they eat.

Night came. The stars are hidden. The shack is filled with mosquitoes. I lit a page from a newspaper and ran it over the walls. This is the way the favela dwellers kill mosquitoes.

May 13. At dawn it was raining. Today is a nice day for me, it's the anniversary of the Abolition. The day we celebrate the freeing of the slaves. In the jails the Negroes were the scapegoats. But now the whites are more educated and don't treat us any more with contempt. May God enlighten the whites so that the Negroes may have a happier life.[2]

It continued to rain and I only have beans and salt. The rain is strong but even so I sent the boys to school. I'm writing until the rain goes away so I can go to Senhor Manuel and sell scrap. With that money I'm going to buy rice and sausage. The rain has stopped for a while. I'm going out.

I feel so sorry for my children. When they see the things to eat that I come home with they shout:

"*Viva Mama!*"

Their outbursts please me. But I've lost the habit of smiling. Ten minutes later they want more food. I sent João to ask Dona Ida for a little pork fat. She didn't have any. I sent her a note:

"Dona Ida, I beg you to help me get a little pork fat, so I can make soup for the children. Today it's raining and I can't go looking for paper. Thank you, Carolina."

It rained and got colder. Winter had arrived and in winter people eat more. Vera asked for food, and I didn't have any. It was the same old show. I had two cruzeiros and wanted to buy a little flour to make a *virado*.[3] I went to ask Dona Alice for a little pork. She gave me pork and rice. It was 9 at night when we ate.

And that is the way on May 13, 1958 I fought against the real slavery—hunger!...

May 19. I left the bed at 5 A.M. The sparrows have just begun their morning symphony. The birds must be happier than we are. Perhaps happiness and equality reign among them. The world of the birds must be better than that of the *favelados*, who lie down but don't sleep because they go to bed hungry.

What our President Senhor Juscelino has in his favor is his voice. He sings like a bird and his voice is pleasant to the ears. And now the bird is living in a golden cage called Catete Palace. Be careful, little bird, that you don't lose this cage, because cats when they are hungry think of birds in cages. The favelados are the cats, and they are hungry.

I broke my train of thought when I heard the voice of the baker:

"Here you go! Fresh bread, and right on time for breakfast!"

How little he knows that in the favela there are only a few who have breakfast. The favelados eat only when they have something to eat. All the families who live in the favela have children. A Spanish woman lives here named Dona Maria Puerta. She bought some land and started to economize so she could build a house. When she finished construction her children were weak with pneumonia. And there are eight children.

There have been people who visited us and said:

"Only pigs could live in a place like this. This is the pigsty of São Paulo."

I'm starting to lose my interest in life. It's beginning to revolt me and my revulsion is just.

I washed the floor because I'm expecting a visit from a future deputy and he wants me to make some speeches for him. He says he wants to know the favelas and if he is elected he's going to abolish them.

The sky was the color of indigo, and I understood that I adore my Brazil. My glance went over the trees that are planted at the beginning of Pedro Vicente Street. The leaves moved by themselves. I thought: they are applauding my gesture of love to my country. I went on looking for paper. Vera was smiling and I thought of Casemiro de Abreu, the Brazilian poet who said: "Laugh, child. Life is beautiful." Life was good in that era. Because now in this era it's necessary to say: "Cry, child. Life is bitter."

I went on so preoccupied that I didn't even notice the gardens of the city. It's the season for white flowers, the predominating color. And in the month of May the altars must be adorned with white flowers. We must thank God or Nature, who gave us the stars that adorn the sky, for the flowers that adorn the parks and the fields and the forests.

When I was going up Southern Cross Avenue I saw a woman with blue shoes and a blue handbag. Vera told me:

"Look, Mama, what a beautiful woman. She is going in my car."

My daughter Vera Eunice says she is going to buy a car and will only drive beautiful people in it. The woman smiled and Vera went on:

"You smell so good!"

I saw that my daughter knew how to flatter. The woman opened her bag and gave me twenty cruzeiros.

Here in the favela almost everyone has a difficult fight to live. But I am the only one who writes of what suffering is. I do this for the good of the others. Many look in the garbage for shoes to wear. But the shoes are weak and only last six days. In the old days, that is from 1950–1958, the favelados sang. They had parties. 1957, 1958 life was getting tougher and tougher. Now there isn't even money for them to buy *pinga*.[4] The parties were shortened until they snuffed themselves out. The other day I met a policeman. He asked me:

"You still live in the favela?"

"Why?"

"Because your family has left the Radio Patrol in peace."

"There's no money left over to buy booze!" I snapped.

I put João and Vera to bed and went looking for José Carlos. I telephoned the Central Police Station. The phone doesn't always resolve things. I took a streetcar and went there. I didn't feel cold. I felt as if my blood was 40 degrees. I spoke with the Female Police who told me that José Carlos was at Asdrubal Nascimento Street (juvenile court). What a relief! Only a mother could appreciate it.

I went toward Asdrubal Nascimento. I don't know how to walk at night. The glare of the lights turns me around. I have to keep asking. I like the night only to contemplate the shining stars, to read and to write. During the night it is quieter.

I arrived at Asdrubal Nascimento and the guard told me to wait. I looked at the children. Some were crying but others were furious with the interference of a law that didn't permit them to do as they pleased. José Carlos was crying. When he heard my voice he became happy. I could feel his contentment. He looked at me and it was the tenderest look I have ever received in my life.

At 8:30 that night I was in the favela breathing the smell of excrement mixed with the rotten earth. When I am in the city I have the impression that I am in a living room with crystal chandeliers, rugs of velvet, and satin cushions. And when I'm in the favela I have the impression that I'm a useless object, destined to be forever in a garbage dump.

May 20.   Day was breaking when I got out of bed. Vera woke up and sang and asked me to sing with her. We sang. Then José Carlos and João joined in.

The morning was damp and foggy. The sun was rising but its heat didn't chase away the cold. I stayed thinking: there are seasons when the sun dominates. There's a season for the rain. There's a season for the wind. Now is the time for the cold. Among them there are no rivalries. Each one has a time.

I opened the window and watched the women passing by with their coats discolored and worn by time. It won't be long until these coats which they got from others, and which should be in a museum, will be replaced by others. The politicians must give us things. That includes me too, because I'm also a favelado. I'm one of the discarded. I'm in the garbage dump and those in the garbage dump either burn themselves or throw themselves into ruin.

The women that I see passing are going to church begging for bread for their children. Brother Luiz gives it to them while their husbands remain home under the blankets. Some because they can't find jobs. Others because they are sick. Others because they are drunk.

I don't bother myself about their men. If they give a ball and I don't show up, it's because I don't like to dance. I only get involved in fights when I think I can prevent a crime. I don't know what started this unfriendliness of mine. I have a hard cold look for both men and women. My smile and my soft smooth words I save for children.

There is a teen-ager named Julião who beats his father at times. When he hits his father it is with such sadism and pleasure. He thinks he is unconquerable. He beats the old man as if he were beating a drum. The father wants him to study law. When Julião was arrested the father went with him with his eyes filled with tears. As if he was accompanying a saint in a procession. Julião is a rebel, but without a cause. They don't need to live in a favela; they have a home on Villa Maria hill.

Sometimes families move into the favela with children. In the beginning they are educated, friendly. Days later they use foul language, are mean and quarrelsome. They are diamonds turned to lead. They are transformed from objects that were in the living room to objects banished to the garbage dump.

For me the world instead of evolving is turning primitive. Those who don't know hunger will say: "Whoever wrote this is crazy." But who has gone hungry can say:

"Well, Dona Carolina. The basic necessities must be within reach of everyone."

How horrible it is to see a child eat and ask: "Is there more?" This word "more" keeps ringing in the mother's head as she looks in the pot and doesn't have any more.

When a politician tells us in his speeches that he is on the side of the people, that he is only in politics in order to improve our living conditions, asking for our votes, promising to freeze prices, he is well aware that by touching on these grave problems he will win at the polls. Afterward he divorces himself from the people. He looks at them with half-closed eyes, and with a pride that hurts us.

When I arrived from the Palace that is the city, my children ran to tell me that they had found some macaroni in the garbage. As the food supply was low I cooked some of the macaroni with beans. And my son João said to me:

"Uh, huh. You told me we weren't going to eat any more things from the garbage."

It was the first time I had failed to keep my word. I said:

"I had faith in President Kubitschek."

"You had faith, and now you don't have it any more?"

"No, my son, democracy is losing its followers. In our country everything is weakening. The money is weak. Democracy is weak and the politicians are very weak. Everything that is weak dies one day."

The politicians know that I am a poetess. And that a poet will even face death when he sees his people oppressed.

May 21. I spent a horrible night. I dreamt I lived in a decent house that had a bathroom, kitchen, pantry, and even a maid's room. I was going to celebrate the birthday of my daughter Vera Eunice. I went and bought some small pots that I had wanted for a long time. Because I was able to buy. I sat at the table to eat. The tablecloth was white as a lily. I ate a steak, bread and butter, fried potatoes, and a salad. When I reached for another steak I woke up. What bitter reality! I don't live in the city. I live in the favela. In the mud on the banks of the Tieté River. And with only nine cruzeiros. I don't even have sugar, because yesterday after I went out the children ate what little I had.

Who must be a leader is he who has the ability. He who has pity and friendship for the people. Those who govern our country are those who have money, who don't know what

hunger is, or pain or poverty. If the majority revolt, what can the minority do? I am on the side of the poor, who are an arm. An undernourished arm. We must free the country of the profiteering politicians.

Yesterday I ate that macaroni from the garbage with fear of death, because in 1953 I sold scrap over there in Zinho. There was a pretty little black boy. He also went to sell scrap in Zinho. He was young and said that those who should look for paper were the old. One day I was collecting scrap when I stopped at Bom Jardim Avenue. Someone had thrown meat into the garbage, and he was picking out the pieces. He told me:

"Take some, Carolina. It's still fit to eat."

He gave me some, and so as not to hurt his feelings, I accepted. I tried to convince him not to eat that meat, or the hard bread gnawed by the rats. He told me no, because it was two days since he had eaten. He made a fire and roasted the meat. His hunger was so great that he couldn't wait for the meat to cook. He heated it and ate. So as not to remember that scene, I left thinking: I'm going to pretend I wasn't there. This can't be real in a rich country like mine. I was disgusted with that Social Service that had been created to readjust the maladjusted, but took no notice of us marginal people. I sold the scrap at Zinho and returned to São Paulo's back yard, the favela.

The next day I found that little black boy dead. His toes were spread apart. The space must have been eight inches between them. He had blown up as if made out of rubber. His toes looked like a fan. He had no documents. He was buried like any other "Joe." Nobody tried to find out his name. The marginal people don't have names.

Once every four years the politicians change without solving the problem of hunger that has its headquarters in the favela and its branch offices in the workers' homes.

When I went to get water I saw a poor woman collapse near the pump because last night she slept without dinner. She was undernourished. The doctors that we have in politics know this.

Now I'm going to Dona Julita's house to work for her. I went looking for paper. Senhor Samuel weighed it. I got 12 cruzeiros. I went up Tiradentes Avenue looking for paper. I came to Brother Antonio Santana de Galvão Street, number 17, to work for Dona Julita. She told me not to fool with men because I might have another baby and that afterward men won't give anything to take care of the child. I smiled and thought: In relations with men, I've had some bitter experiences. Now I'm mature, reached a stage of life where my judgment has grown roots.

I found a sweet potato and a carrot in the garbage. When I got back to the favela my boys were gnawing on a piece of hard bread. I thought: for them to eat this bread, they need electric teeth.

I don't have any lard. I put meat on the fire with some tomatoes that I found at the Peixe canning factory. I put in the carrot and the sweet potato and water. As soon as it was boiling I put in the macaroni that the boys found in the garbage. The favelados are the few who are convinced that in order to live, they must imitate the vultures. I don't see any help from the Social Service regarding the favelados. Tomorrow I'm not going to have bread. I'm going to cook a sweet potato.

Translated by David St. Clair

NOTES

1. Juscelino Kubitschek: President of Brazil from 1956 to 1961.
2. Slavery was abolished in Brazil in 1888.
3. A dish of black beans, manioc flour, pork, and eggs.
4. *Pinga* has two meanings in Brazilian Portuguese: the very strong homebrewed liquor drunk mainly by poor people, or as a coarse word for the male genitalia.

Muriel Rukeyser   *US, 1913–1980*

Muriel Rukeyser is one in a line of American writers whose literary career and critical reputation are inextricably bound up with politics. Once hailed by Kenneth Rexroth as the "best poet of her exact generation," Rukeyser and her formidable literary achievement—she published more than twenty books—have been obscured by persisting debate about the merits of her lifelong commitment to reformist politics. Thus her literary standing is uncertain and a balanced appreciation of her work is still to be written.

Rukeyser was born in New York City in 1913. After a youthful period of political neutrality and education at Vassar College and Columbia University, Rukeyser, like so many writers of the 1930s, was stunned by the economic devastation of the Great Depression and subsequently embraced a leftist agenda that shaped her literary career. Yet Rukeyser transcended the dogmas of right and left that dominated period esthetics. Preferring Whitman to Marx, personal theology to formal doctrine, myth-making to the purely dialectic, Rukeyser remained attuned in the 1930s and 1940s to "the desperate music poetry makes." Written when she was 21, her first major collection, *Theory of Flight* (1935), like Hart Crane's *The Bridge* (1931), welded American technology and the oracular poetic tradition into a prophetic, celebratory myth. Though Rukeyser was later to qualify her optimistic belief in boundless scientific advance, she here fused personal experience and the romance of flight (she had studied piloting briefly at the Roosevelt

Aviation School) to create in *Theory* symbols of hope and beneficent social change. Poetry as "human energy," as she identified it in her important treatise *The Life of Poetry* (1949), is "very close to...science" and a "meeting place between all kinds of imagination." Readers of poetry are thus not passive spectators but "witnesses" who partake of its energy. The result is a kind of emotional fission in which poetry, to reverse Auden, *makes* something happen: "the imagination leads us to surpass ourselves."

Rukeyser's belief that the sources of poetry should be "everyday, infinite and commonplace as a look" also moved her briefly, along with contemporary novelists John Dos Passos and John Steinbeck, into the vanguard of formal realist experimentation. In *U.S. 1* (1938) she combined factual investigation, reportage, scientific formula and a "camera-eye" perspective to commemorate the on-the-job deaths of West Virginia miners—selections from which follow. Later volumes of her middle age, including *Breaking Open* (1973) and *The Gates* (1976), take a retrospective look at earlier radicalisms and feature personal poems of visionary scope. In "To Be a Jew in the Twentieth Century" Rukeyser celebrates the paradox of "suffering to be free / Daring to live for the impossible." In "Facing Sentencing," impending arrest for antiwar protest becomes the occasion for a paean to the history of left-wing American resistance. Finally, in poem 8 of *The Gates*, the poet culminates a lifelong celebration of the durable feminine conscience—"Women seen as a slender instrument, / Woman at vigil in the prison yard."

Rukeyser will likely never escape criticisms—many legitimate, of rhetorical excess, political naiveté, and romantic idolatry. Yet she is undoubtedly the most bardic female poet America has produced and the only one to fully adopt the prophet's voice.

Bill Mullen

from THE BOOK OF THE DEAD, in U.S.1

WEST VIRGINIA

They saw rivers flow west and hoped again.
Virginia speeding to another sea!
1671—Thomes Batts, Robert Fallam,
Thomas Wood, the Indian Perecute,
and an unnamed indentured English servant
followed the forest past blazed trees, pillars of God,
were the first whites emergent from the east.
They left a record to our heritage,
breaking of records. Hoped now for the sea,
for all mountains have their descents about them,
waters, descending naturally, doe alwaies resort
unto the seas invironing those lands...
yea, at home amongst the mountaines in England.

Coming where this road comes,
flat stones spilled water which the still pools fed.
Kanawha Falls, the rapids of the mind,
fast waters spilling west.

Found Indian fields, standing how cornstalks left,
learned three Mohetons planted them; found-land
farmland, the planted home, discovered!

War-born:
The battle at Point Pleasant, Cornstalk's tribes,
last stand, Fort Henry, a revolution won;
the granite SITE OF THE precursor EXECUTION
sabres, apostles OF JOHN BROWN LEADER OF THE
War's brilliant cloudy RAID AT HARPERS FERRY.*
Floods, heavy wind this spring, the beaten land
blown high by wind, fought wars, forming a state,
a surf, frontier defines two fighting halves,
two hundred battles in the four years: troops
here in Gauley Bridge, Union headquarters, lines
bring in the military telegraph.
Wires over the gash of gorge and height of pine.

But it was always the water
the power flying deep
green rivers cut the rock
rapids boiled down,
a scene of power.

Done by the dead.
Discovery learned it.
And the living?

Live country filling west,
knotted the glassy rivers;
like valleys, opening mines,
coming to life.

NOTE

* John Brown (1800–1859): American abolitionist; with a group of twenty-one followers, he
captured the U.S. arsenal at Harper's Ferry in what is now West Virginia as part of a plan to liberate
Southern slaves. Captured by Robert E. Lee and hanged, Brown is considered a martyr to the cause.

(continued)

STATEMENT: PHILIPPA ALLEN

—You like the State of West Virginia very much, do you not?

—I do very much, in the summertime.

—How much time have you spent in West Virginia?

—During the summer of 1934, when I was doing social work down there, I first
    heard of what we were pleased to call the Gauley tunnel tragedy, which
    involved about 2,000 men.

—What was their salary?

—It started at 40¢ and dropped to 25¢ an hour.

—You have met these people personally?

—I have talked to people; yes.

  According to estimates of contractors

  2,000 men were

      employed there

      period, about 2 years

      drilling, 3.75 miles of tunnel.

      To divert water (from New River)

      to a hydroelectric plant (at Gauley Junction).

  The rock through which they were boring was of a high silica content.

  In tunnel No. 1 it ran 97–99% pure silica.

  The contractors

      knowing pure silica

      30 years' experience

      must have known danger for every man

neglected to provide the workmen with any safety device. . . .

—As a matter of fact, they originally intended to dig that tunnel a certain size?

—Yes.

—And then enlarged the size of the tunnel, due to the fact that they discovered
    silica and wanted to get it out?

—That is true for tunnel No. 1.

  The tunnel is part of a huge water-power project

      begun, latter part of 1929

      direction: New Kanawha Power Co.

             subsidiary of Union Carbide & Carbon Co.

      That company—licensed:

      to develop power for public sale.

      Ostensibly it was to do that; but

      (in reality) it was formed to sell all the power to

          the Electro-Metallurgical Co.

          subsidiary of Union Carbide & Carbon Co.

             which by an act of the State legislature

             was allowed to buy up

          New Kanawha Power Co. in 1933.

—They were developing the power. What I am trying to get at, Miss Allen, is, did
    they use this silica from the tunnel; did they afterward sell it and use it in
    commerce?

—They used it in the electro-processing of steel.
SiO_2 SiO_2
The richest deposit.
Shipped on the C & O down to Alloy.
It was so pure that
                    SiO_2
they used it without refining.
—Where did you stay?
—I stayed at Cedar Grove. Some days I would have to hitch into Charleston,
    other days to Gauley Bridge.
—You found the people of West Virginia very happy to pick you up on the
    highway, did you not?
—Yes; they are delightfully obliging.
    (All were bewildered. Again at Vanetta they are asking, "What can be done
        about this?")
    I feel that this investigation may help in some manner.
    I do hope it may.
    I am now making a very general statement as a beginning. There are many
        points that I should like to develop later, but I shall try to give you a general
        history of this condition first. . . .

ABSALOM*

I first discovered what was killing these men.
I had three sons who worked with their father in the tunnel:
Cecil, aged 23, Owen, aged 21, Shirley, aged 17.
They used to work in a coal mine, not steady work
for the mines were not going much of the time.
A power Co. foreman learned that we made home brew,
he formed a habit of dropping in evenings to drink,
persuading the boys and my husband—
give up their jobs and take this other work.
It would pay them better.
Shirley was my youngest son; the boy.
He went into the tunnel.

   My heart   my mother   my heart   my mother
   My heart   my coming into being.

My husband is not able to work.
He has it, according to the doctor.
We have been having a very hard time making a living since this trouble came to us.
I saw the dust in the bottom of the tub.
The boy worked there about eighteen months,
came home one evening with a shortness of breath.
He said, "Mother, I cannot get my breath."
Shirley was sick about three months.

(*continued*)

I would carry him from his bed to the table,
from his bed to the porch, in my arms.

My heart is mine in the place of hearts,
They gave me back my heart, it lies in me.

When they took sick, right at the start, I saw a doctor.
I tried to get Dr. Harless to X-ray the boys.
He was the only man I had any confidence in,
the company doctor in the Kopper's mine,
but he would not see Shirley.
He did not know where his money was coming from.
I promised him half if he'd work to get compensation,
but even then he would not do anything.
I went on the road and begged the X-ray money,
the Charleston hospital made the lung pictures,
he took the case after the pictures were made.
And two or three doctors said the same thing.
The youngest boy did not get to go down there with me,
he lay and said, "Mother, when I die,
"I want you to have them open me up and
"see if that dust killed me.
"Try to get compensation,
"you will not have any way of making your living
"when we are gone,
"and the rest are going too."

I have gained mastery over my heart
I have gained mastery over my two hands
I have gained mastery over the waters
I have gained mastery over the river.

The case of my son was the first of the line of lawsuits.
They sent the lawyers down and the doctors down;
they closed the electric sockets in the camps.
There was Shirley, and Cecil, Jeffrey and Oren,
Raymond Johnson, Clev and Oscar Anders,
Frank Lynch, Henry Palf, Mr. Pitch, a foreman;
a slim fellow who carried steel with my boys,
his name was Darnell, I believe. There were many others,
the towns of Glen Ferris, Alloy, where the white rock lies,
six miles away; Vanetta, Gauley Bridge,
Gamoca, Lockwood, the gullies,
the whole valley is witness.
I hitchhike eighteen miles, they make checks out.
They asked me how I keep the cow on $2.
I said one week, feed for the cow, one week, the children's flour.
The oldest son was twenty-three.
The next son was twenty-one.
The youngest son was eighteen.

They called it pneumonia at first.
They would pronounce it fever.
Shirley asked that we try to find out.
That's how they learned what the trouble was.

> *I open out a way, they have covered my sky with crystal*
> *I come forth by day; I am born a second time,*
> *I force a way through, and I know the gate*
> *I shall journey over the earth among the living.*

He shall not be diminished, never;
I shall give a mouth to my son.

NOTE

* Beloved son of David who murdered his brother Amnon. Forgiven by his father, he returned to stir up rebellion, dying in the fray. (2 Sam. 13–19)

THE BILL

The subcommittee submits:
Your committee held hearings, heard many witnesses; finds:
THAT the Hawk's Nest tunnel was constructed
        Dennis and Rinehart, Charlottesville, Va., for
        New Kanawha Power Co., subsidiary of
        Union Carbide & Carbon Co.
THAT a tunnel was drilled
        app. dist. 3.75 mis.
        to divert water (from New River)
        to hydroelectric plant (Gauley Junction).
THAT in most of the tunnel, drilled rock contained
        90—even 99 percent pure silica.
This is a fact that was known.
THAT silica is dangerous to lungs of human beings.
        When submitted to contact. Silicosis.
THAT the effects are well known.
        Disease incurable.
        Physical incapacity, cases fatal.
THAT the Bureau of Mines has warned for twenty years.
THAT prevention is: wet drilling, ventilation,
                                respirators, vacuum drills.
        Disregard: utter. Dust: collected. Visibility: low.
        Workmen left work, white with dust.
        Air system: inadequate.
        It was quite cloudy in there.
        When the drills were going, in all the smoke and dust,
        it seemed like a gang of airplanes going through that tunnel.   *(continued)*

Respirators, not furnished.
I have seen men with masks, but simply on their breasts.
I have seen two wear them.
Drills: dry drilling, for speed, for saving.
A fellow could drill three holes dry for one hole wet.
They went so fast they didn't square at the top.
Locomotives: gasoline. Suffering from monoxide gas.
There have been men that fell in the tunnel. They had to be carried out.
The driving of the tunnel.
   It was begun, continued, completed, with gravest disregard.
   And the employees? Their health, lives, future?
Results and infection.
   Many died. Many are not yet dead.
   Of negligence. Wilful or inexcusable.
Further findings:
   Prevalence: many States, mine, tunnel operations.
   A greatest menace.
We suggest hearings be read.
   This is the dark. Lights strung up all the way.
   Depression; and, driven deeper in,
   by hunger, pistols, and despair,
   they took the tunnel.
Of the contracting firm
     P.H. Faulconer, Pres.
     E.J. Perkins, Vice-Pres.
   have declined to appear.
   They have no knowledge of deaths from silicosis.
   However, their firm paid claims.
   I want to point out that under the statute $500 or $1000, but no more, may
    be recovered.

We recommend.
   Bring them. Their books and records.
   Investigate. Require.
Can do no more.
   These citizens from many States
   paying the price for electric power,
   To Be Vindicated.

"If by their suffering and death they will have made a future life safer for work beneath the earth, if they will have been able to establish a new and greater regard for human life in industry, their suffering may not have been in vain."
        Respectfully,
        Glenn Griswold
       Chairman, Subcommittee

        Vito Marcantonio
        W.P. Lambertson
        Matthew A. Dunn

The subcommitte subcommits.

Words on a monument.
Capitoline thunder. It cannot be enough.
The origin of storms is not in clouds,
our lightning strikes when the earth rises,
spillways free authentic power:
dead John Brown's body walking from a tunnel
to break the armored and concluded mind.

W. Eugene Smith, The Spinner,
1951, black and white photograph.
Courtesy International Museum
of Photography at George
Eastman House, Rochester,
New York

Bint al-Shati ('Aisha Abd al-Rahman)   *Egypt, b. 1913*

Born 'Aisha Abd al-Rahman, Bint al-Shati received her education at Cairo University, and after completing her doctorate began working there as a lecturer in Arabic literature and language. Her academic career then led her to Ain Shams University (1950–1962), until she became a full professor at the University College for Women. After 1942, she also worked for the Ministry of Education for a time.

Her literary production falls into three overlapping categories: nonfiction prose, fiction, and literary biography and criticism. Significant as a social critic, at a time when people of her class painted an exotic picture of the Middle East, of which the harem was the symbolic center, al-Shati turned to the world around her, writing a path-breaking series of articles in the late 1930s describing the dismal conditions of the Egyptian countryside and the harsh life of those living there.

In the fiction category, for which she has received numerous literary awards between the years 1936 and 1960, of special note are *Imra'a Khāṭi'a* (Story of a Fallen Woman, 1944) and *Ṣuwar min hayātihinna* (Pictures from Their Lives, 1959), a collection of twenty-four short stories. Both of these works focus on the problems facing emancipated Arab women. In her work as a writer of belles-lettres, al-Shati has also been forward-looking: both *Qiyam Jadīdah lil-Adab al-'Arabi* (New Values in Arabic Literature, 1961) and *Al-Qur'an wa-al-Tafsīr al-Asrī* (The Koran: A Literary Interpretation, 1962) are obvious testimony to her humanism as well as to the more liberal and secular intellectual climate of that period. And in such work as *Contemporary Arab Women Poets* (1963), *The Arab Woman Writer: Yesterday and Today* (1967), as well as six books on illustrious women of Islam, including *Nīsa' al-Nabī* (The Wives of the Prophet, 1973), al-Shati attests to her feminist commitment.

The selection here is taken from *Al-Khansa'* (2nd ed. 1963), another one of al-Shati's literary biographies, and describes the status, among her contemporaries, of Al-Khansa' (literally, female gazelle), a famed poet who lived at the beginning of the Islamic era (ca. A.D. 645). Born into the influential tribal family of al-Sharid in the north of the Arabian peninsula, al-Khansa' married twice and bore six children, all of them also poets. She is said to have produced over one thousand verses, the subject of which is her hero "Sakhr," modeled after her brother, to whom she was intensely devoted. The prophet Muhammad is said to have held her poetry in highest regard and admired her greatly. Undoubtedly, the influence of al-Khansa', including her oeuvre, did much to solidify and ensure the spread of Islam. Her contemporary Hassan ibn Thabit, also an esteemed poet of the time, was very fond of her, and the two of them would recite their poems in the market of Ukaz, in what is now Saudi Arabia.

Pamela Vittorio

from AL-KHANSA'

Al-Khansa'[1] won the praises of the critics and the scholars when she was—and still is today—the topic of interest. Indeed, in Arab literary history she was depicted with an unusually high degree of esteem, especially for a woman. And if we pursued the fate of al-

Khansa' among the Arab poets, and familiarized ourselves with her, she would give us more than we could have expected from someone within the cultural environment which brought together pre-Islamic poetry and the heart of Islam—while her contemporaries' status would diminish.

She was destined to witness her own fame and to charm the ears of the dignitaries of poetry as well as the masters of rhetoric, in the market of Ukaz.[2] It is believed that whenever she visited the market and the distinguished poet-genius al-Nabighah al-Dhubyani[3] was sitting as a judge between the poets, she recited some of her elegies to Sakhr, but only after she had been preceeded by other poets, among whom was the blind poet al-A'sha and Hassan ibn Thabit.[4]

Al-Dhubyani would tell her: "By God, had Abu Basir not preceded you and recited to me already, I would have said that you are far more poetic than he among the festival's contestants."

In another account, he was reported to have said: "Had not al-A'sha come before you, I would have said you are more poetic than man or demon!"

It is said that Hasan was enraged and told al-Dhubyani: "By God, I am far more poetic than you or she!"

The accounts of the end of the story after Hassan spoke these words are controversial.

In "Poetry and Poets," al-Dhubyani grabbed Hassan's hand, saying: "My dear nephew, you are not enhanced by speaking such words. You are like the night, it is your rationality—and perhaps your prominence has made you bitter."

He then said to al-Khansa': "Recite for him." And thus, she did so. And He said: "By God, I have yet to see a poet greater than you!"

And al-Khansa' replied: "And by God, this one is not Male!"

In the "Critique of Poetry," al-Dhubyani asks Hassan for a more poetic verse; and Hassan recited: "The barren grapevines glitter in the morning light—and our swords drip with the blood of courage."

Al-Dhubyani the judge said to him that his word "grapevines" was merely a plural of scarcity and it could have been preferable to say "white" instead of "barren" because "barrenness" is rarely of another color. As to "glitter in the morning light" he ought to have said "in the gloom of the darkness," which would have been better....On the other hand, had he used "flowing" it would have been more desirable than "dripping"—"flowing" being more expressive than "dripping."

Abu al-Farj[5] narrated this story in a similar manner in regard to the critique of Hassan's verse by al-Dhubyani, as did another historian, al-Marzubani, who related it in a summary.

On the other hand, Ibn Qutayba[6] confirmed the critique of al-Khansa', and so did the medieval historian Sharisha. This is the report that has been quoted by most publishers of our time, even those who denounced her and criticized her writings.

Translated by Ouafae Benhallam

NOTES

1. Pre-Islamic poetess, who lived up to the time of Islam, to which she became a convert—her two brothers, of whom Sakhr was one, were killed and much of her poetry is in the form of elegies.
2. A marketplace outside of Mecca where poetry contests were held.
3. Nickname of Ziyad ibn Mu'awiya, a court poet who lived just before Islam. His poems both extol princes and reveal information on the internal affairs and conflicts of the tribe of Dubyan.
4. al-A'sha ("the dimsighted"): versatile poet, wrote songs of drinking, hunting and nature, satire and panegyric. Later joined the Prophet in Mecca. Hassan ibn Thabit (d. 673–4): author of drinking and love songs; when he later joined the Prophet Muhammad, he turned to writing poems in praise of the Prophet.
5. Poet of Isfahan (10th century).
6. Ibn Qutayba died towards the end of the ninth century; critic who maintained that ancients and moderns should be judged according to merit, not age.

Julia de Burgos   *US(Puerto Rico), 1914–1953*

Julia de Burgos was born and raised in rural Puerto Rico and died, unknown, on the streets of New York City, where she had lived for the last sixteen years of her life. She has since been recognized as a major Puerto Rican poet, one of lyric intensity and immediacy. De Burgos had a tragic personal life. Her first marriage ended in divorce and her second was unhappy. She had a passionate but masochistic attachment to a man she called "X." And she waged a losing struggle with alcoholism that led to her death. Yet her lifelong commitment to social justice, to the rights of the poor, blacks, women, and laborers is as much a part of her writing as is her desperate passion.

Two collections of her poetry were published in de Burgos' lifetime: *Poema en veinte surcos* (Poem in Twenty Furrows, 1938) and *Cancion de la verdad sencilla* (Song of the Simple Truth, 1939). A third collection, *El mar y tu* (The Sea and You) was published the year following her death. The following poems were taken from *Obra Poetica* (Poetic Works, 1961).

POEM WITH THE FINAL TUNE
Poema con la tonada última

Are you asking where I'm going with these sad
                        faces
and the bubbling of wounded veins on my
                        forehead?

I'm going to cast roses into the sea,
to vanish under waves higher than the birds,
to pull out roads that by now had burrowed
                through me like roots...
I'm going to give up stars,
and dews,
and the brief rivulets where I loved the passion
              that ravaged my mountains,
and a special cooing
of doves,
and words...

I am going to remain alone, without songs or
                      skin,
like the inside of a tunnel,
where its own silence goes crazy
        and kills itself.

Translated by Julio Marzán

TO JULIA DE BURGOS
A Julia de Burgos

Already people murmur that I am your enemy
because, they say, I give you to the world in
                      verse.

They lie, Julia de Burgos. They lie, Julia de Burgos.
The voice which rises in my verses is not your
                      voice;
it is my voice;
for you are only the covering and I am the
                    essence;
and there is a deep abyss between the two.

You are the cold doll of social lies,
and I, the virile spark of human truth.

You, honey of courtly hypocrisies; not I;
in all my poems I bare my heart.

You are egotistical like your world; not I;
I risk everything to be what I am.

You are the serious, respectable lady;
not I; I am the life, the strength, the woman.

You belong to your husband, to your master;
                    not I;
I belong to no one or to everyone,
because I give myself to all, to all, through my
clear thoughts and feelings.

You curl your hair and paint your face; not I;
the wind curls me and I am painted by the sun.
You are the lady of the house, resigned,
                                        submissive.
tied to the prejudices of men;
not I; I am Rocinante* running wild
sniffing the horizons of God's justice.
You do not rule yourself; everyone else rules
                                        you:
your husband, your parents, your relatives,
the priest, the dressmaker, the theatre, the
                                        casino,
the car, the jewelry, the banquet, the
                                        champagne,
heaven and earth, and "what will people say?"
But I am ruled only by my heart, my thoughts;
I am the one who rules in me.
You, flower of the aristocracy;
and I the flower of the common people.
You have everything and owe everything,
while I, my nothing I owe to no one.

You, nailed to the static ancestral dividend,
and I, a mere one in the figure of the social
                                        divisor;
we are the duel to death which fatally
                                        approaches.
When the multitudes run in revolt, leaving
                                        behind
the ashes of burned injustices,
and when they run with the torch of the seven
                                        virtues
after the seven sins,
against you, and against everything unjust and
                                        inhuman,
I will run in their midst with the torch high in
                                        my hand.

Translated by Julia Price

NOTE

* Don Quixote's horse, in the seventeenth-century Spanish
  epic by Miguel de Cervantes Sauvedra.

Marguerite Duras   *France, b. 1914*

In *Un barrage contre le Pacifique* (*Sea Wall*, 1950) and *L'Amant* (*The Lover*, 1984), Marguerite Duras describes her childhood in what was then known as French Indochina, evoking the humiliation of poverty, the tension and fear of living with a deranged and sometimes cruel mother, the violence of an adolescent passion and the desperate ambivalence of being white, French, and poor in a colony. The only girl and middle child, Duras was born in GiaDinh; her father, a professor of mathematics, died when she was 4, and her mother supplemented her meager income from teaching by playing the piano at a local moviehouse—the Eden Cinema. She finally invested the savings of twenty years in a piece of unarable land in Cambodia, and the entire family nearly died many times in an attempt to live off the land. At the age of 18, Duras fled to Paris, where she studied law, mathematics, and political science. She married Robert Antelme and left him in 1942 for Dionys Mascolo, by whom she had a son, Jean. Along with many French intellectuals, she joined the French Communist Party around this time but left it after becoming disillusioned with Stalinism.

Although Duras published her first novel *Les Impudents* (The Impudent Ones) in 1943, it was not until 1960 that she gained recognition, when a film for which she wrote the screenplay, *Hiroshima mon amour* (directed by Alain Resnais) achieved spectacular success at the International Film Festival at Cannes. Set against the backdrop of occupied France and postwar Japan, the film tells the story of a French woman who goes to Hiroshima to make a film about peace and falls in love, for the second time in her life, with a Japanese man. About memory and oblivion, unbearable passion and irrevocable loss, the film captures the personal devastation of those who must live in a world of unimaginable destruction brought on by the nuclear bomb.

In 1964, with the publication of *Le Ravissement de Lol V. Stein* (*The Ravishing of Lol V. Stein*), Duras entered a new stage of literary creation. Jacques Lacan, the famous French revisionist of Freud, said of the novel: "Duras manifests a knowledge without me of what I teach." Her works, always haunted by the unspeakable, by harrowing absences, by inexplicable trauma, became ever more cinematic and theatrical as the author began to develop a style that her critics speak of as "Durassian." *Détruire dit-elle* (*Destroy She Said*, 1969) was the culmination of this trend in her oeuvre. The title itself evokes the violence of the time in which it was written—the height of student revolt throughout the country and the energetic insurgency of the left in France.

In the decade that followed, Duras turned increasingly to film as her preferred medium, although her scenarios were commonly drawn from her own texts. Her trilogy of films on India is considered among her strongest.

A frequent motif in Duras' work is the crime of passion that fuses love and destruction; for a period, her characters escape temporarily from the emptiness of their lives. The mise en scène is usually at some boundary or limit (a park, a square, at the sea), the topographical equivalent of her marginal characters; and these places are often oppressively hot, evoking the tropical climes in which Duras grew up, and serving as correlative of the characters' enervation and passivity. Durassian language is also musical and hypnotic; through rhythm and repetition, indirect and often flat dialogue, the reader is made to experience the work subjectively, that is, at another level of consciousness, out of which the characters seem to act out their destiny. Thus Susan Laffredo sums up Duras' oeuvre. In *Dix heures et demie du soir en été* (*Ten-Thirty on a Summer Night*, 1960), from which a selection follows, Maria and Pierre are on a holiday in Spain with their daughter Judith and friend Claire when they find themselves caught in a village the police have barricaded to hunt down a worker who has just murdered his adulterous wife and her lover.

Sometimes identified with the "New Novelists," those postwar writers who sought to break with traditional forms and styles, Duras goes beyond them in scope and breadth. With the publication of her autobiographical works and a return to a more linear narrative style in such writing as *La Douleur* (*War*, 1985), Duras has achieved a degree of commercial success and popularity as well. Her most recent novel is *Les Yeux bleus, cheveux noirs* (Blue Eyes, Black Hair, 1986). Translated into many different languages, including Chinese and Japanese, Duras' work is internationally acclaimed. In 1986, New York honored the 73-year old artist with a month-long festival that included the American premiere of her play *l'Eden-Cinéma* (*The Eden Cinema*, 1977).

from TEN-THIRTY ON A SUMMER NIGHT
Dix heures et demie du soir en été

Again the police started their search. They returned as the storm subsided. They marched through the mud again. Maria leaned over the railing of the balcony and saw them. One of them laughed. At regular intervals, the whole town rang with the sound of whistling. Just more pauses in the waiting period, which was going to last until morning.

In addition to the balcony where Maria was standing, there were others on the north side of the hotel. They were empty, except one, just one, on Maria's right, one flight above. They must have been there for a very short time. Maria hadn't seen them arrive. She moved back slightly into the corridor where people were now asleep.

This must have been the first time they had kissed. Maria put out her cigarette. She could see them fully outlined against the moving sky. While Pierre kissed her, his hands touched Claire's breasts. They were probably talking. But very softly. They must have been speaking the first words of love. Irrepressible, bursting words which came to their lips between two kisses.

The lightning made the town look livid. It was unforeseeable, striking irregularly. But every time it made their kisses livid too, as well as their single, nearly blinding shape. Was it on her eyes, behind the screen formed by the dark sky, that he had first kissed her? How could one know. Your eyes were the color of your fear in the afternoon, the color of rain at that very moment, Claire, your eyes, I could hardly see them, how could I have noticed it before, your eyes must be gray.

Opposite these kisses, a few yards away, Rodrigo Paestra wrapped in his brown blanket was waiting for the infernal night to end. At dawn, it would be all over.

A new phase of the storm was coming up that was going to separate them and prevent Maria from seeing them.

As he did it, so did she, bringing her hands to her lonely breasts, then her hands fell and, useless, grasped the balcony. While she had moved too far out onto the balcony while they were merging into a single, nearly blinding shape, she now moved back a little from the balcony, toward the corridor where the new wind was already sweeping into the lamp chimneys. No, she couldn't help seeing them. She could still see them. And their shadows were on that roof. Now their bodies broke apart. The wind raised her skirt, and, in a flash, they laughed. The same wind that had raised her skirt, again crossed the whole town, bumping up against the edges of the rooftops.

Two more minutes, and the storm would come, sweeping over the whole town, emptying the streets, the balconies. He must have stepped back in order to hold her better, to be reunited with her for the first time, their happiness intensified by the suffering he created by holding her far from him. They didn't know, they were still unaware that the storm would separate them for the night.

More waiting. And the impatience of the waiting grew so intense it reached its climax, and at last calm set in. One of Pierre's hands was moving all over another woman's body. His other hand held her close against him. It was done now, forever.

It was ten-thirty. And summer.

And then it was a little later. Night had come at last, completely. There was no room that night, in that town, for love. Maria lowered her eyes before this reality: their thirst for love would remain unfulfilled, the town was bulging, in this summer night made for their love. The flashes of lightning kept lighting up the shape of their desire. They were still there, folded in each other's arms, and motionless, his hand now resting on her hip, hers forever, while she, she, her hands unable to move as they clung to his shoulders, her mouth against his mouth, she was devouring him.

The same flashes, at the same time, lit up the roof opposite them and on its top, around a chimney, the shrouded shape of Rodrigo Paestra, the murderer.

The wind increased, swept into the hallway and moved over the sleeping children. A lamp had gone out. But nothing would wake them. The town was dark and asleep. In the rooms there was silence. Judith was good.

They had disappeared from the balcony as suddenly as they had come. He must have led her away without letting go of her—how could he—into the shadow of the sleeping corridor. The balcony was deserted. Maria looked at her watch once again. It was almost eleven. Because of the wind that was still growing stronger, one of the children—it wasn't that one—uttered a cry, isolated, turned over and fell back to sleep.

The rain. And again its ineffable smell, its lifeless smell of muddy streets. Just as it did on the fields, the rain was falling on the dead shape of Rodrigo Paestra, dead of sorrow, dead of love.

Where could they have found a place to be together that night, in that hotel? Where would he take off her light skirt, that very night? How beautiful she is. How beautiful you are, God how beautiful. With the rain, their shapes had vanished from the balcony.

Summer was everywhere, in the rain, in the streets, in the courtyards, in the bathrooms, in the kitchens, summer, everywhere, summer was everywhere for their love. Maria stretched, went back in, lay down in the hallway, stretched again. Was it done now? Perhaps there was no one in another dark, stifling corridor—could anyone know all of them?—the corridor extending from their balcony, for example, right above this one, in this miraculously forgotten corridor, along the wall, on the floor, was it done?

Tomorrow would be there in a few hours. You had to wait. The shower was longer than the previous one. It kept coming down with force. And also on the skylight, echoing horribly throughout the hotel.

"We wait for you, Maria," Pierre said.

They appeared with the end of the shower. She saw their two shadows move toward her while she was lying next to Judith, two huge shadows. Claire's skirt had risen above her knees, bulging around her hips. The wind in the corridor. Too fast. They hadn't had much time between leaving the balcony and arriving there, next to Maria. They were smiling. So that hope had been foolish. Love hadn't been fulfilled that night in the hotel. More waiting. The rest of the night.

"You said you would be back, Maria," Pierre said again.

"Well, I was tired."

She had seen him looking for her on the floor of the corridor carefully, almost walk past her, and stop in front of her; she was the last one, just where the corridor ended, engulfed in the darkness of the dining room. Claire was following him.

"Well," Maria repeated—she was pointing at Judith—"she would have been afraid."

Pierre smiled. He stopped looking at Maria and discovered an open window leading onto a balcony at the end of the corridor.

"What weather," he said.

He brushed away his discovery of the window at the very moment he made it. Was it fear?

"And it will last all night," he said. "It will end by daybreak."

She could have told just from his voice, trembling, shaky, affected by desire for that woman.

Then Claire also smiled at Judith. At the small, lopsided shape, wrapped in a brown blanket. Her hair was still wet from the rain on the balcony. Her eyes in the yellow light of the oil lamp. Your eyes, blue stones. I'll eat your eyes, he was telling her, your eyes. The youthfulness of her breasts showed clearly under her white sweater. Her blue gaze was haggard, paralyzed by frustration, by the very fulfillment of frustration. Her gaze left Judith and moved back to Pierre.

"Did you go back to a café, Maria?"

"No. I stayed here."

"A good thing we didn't leave for Madrid," Pierre said. "You see."

He turned again toward the open window.

"A good thing, yes."

In the street alongside the hotel, a whistle rang out. Was it over? There was no second whistle. The three of them waited. No. Once more, just a pause in the waiting period. Steps made heavy by the mud in the streets moved toward the northern part of town. They didn't talk about it.

"She isn't warm tonight," Claire said.

Maria stroked Judith's forehead.

"Not really. Less than usual. It's comfortable."

Maria could have told just from Claire's breasts that they were in love. They were going to lie down there, next to her, separated while torn and tortured by desire. And both were smiling, equally guilty, terrified and happy.

"We waited for you," Pierre repeated.

Even Claire raised her eyes. Then she lowered them and only a vague, indelible smile remained on her face. Maria would have known just from seeing her eyes lowered on that smile. What glory. On what glory were those eyes closing? They must have looked, looked all over the hotel for a spot. It had been impossible. They had had to give up. Pierre had said Maria is waiting for us. What a future ahead of them, the days to come.

Pierre's hands were dangling beside him. For eight years they had caressed her body. Now Claire was stepping into the misfortune that flowed straight from those hands.

"I'm going to sleep," she announced.

She took a blanket that had been put on a table. She wrapped herself in it, still laughing, and, with a sigh, stretched out below the oil lamp. Pierre did not move.

"I'm sleeping," Claire said.

Pierre also took a blanket, then lay down next to Maria, on the other side of the corridor.

Did Rodrigo Paestra still exist, there, twenty yards from them? Yes.

Translated by Anne Borchardt

Tove Jansson   *Finland, b. 1914*

Tove Jansson was born in a section of Finland where many descendents of Swedish settlers live; called the Finland-Sweden or Fenno-Swedish, this community speaks and writes in Swedish. Her parents were both artists, her mother a painter and illustrator and her father a sculptor; their bohemian lifestyle separated them to some degree from the bourgeois Fenno-Swedish community. Jansson had a happy childhood, with close family ties, and those themes are reflected in her writing.

Jansson's first career was as an artist. She studied art for several years and, like her mother, painted and did illustrations for newspapers and books. She capitalized on this talent in the works for which she is most famous, the Moomin books—children's stories about the Moomintroll family living in Moominvalley—for she illustrated them all. The first of these books, *Småtrollen och den stora översvämningen* (*The Little Trolls and the Great Flood*) was published in 1945 and the eighth and final Moomin book, *Sent i november* (*Moominvalley in November*) in 1971. They have been translated into twenty-five languages, were serialized in a comic strip, first in the *London Evening News* and later syndicated in forty countries, and were made into radio and television programs. These books won Jansson many awards, the most prestigious of which was the Hans Christian Andersen Award in 1963.

Jansson's later work, even her later Moomin books, however, are written primarily for adults. *Bildhuggarens dotter* (*The Sculptor's Daughter*, 1968) is a semiautobiographical novel about the childhood of a girl raised in an artistic environment, seen alternately through the girl's eyes and her grandmother's. Another work heavily influenced by her life was *Sommarboken* (*The Summer Book*, 1972), excerpted below, a novel about a little girl's close relationship with her grandmother, again seen through the child's eyes. This section recounts the family's departure from their summer cottage. *Solstaden* (Sun City, 1974) takes the reader to Florida to explore the alienated, lonely lives of the elderly, which Jansson does with compassion and humor. Jansson published two collections of short stories, *Lyssnerskan* (The Listener, 1971) and *Dockskåpet* (The Doll's House, 1978), both focusing on obsession and mental disturbance and both critically acclaimed. As in all Jansson's books, the visual imagery is precise and acutely observed.

Jansson currently lives on an island in Finland's archipelago.

AUGUST, from THE SUMMER BOOK
from Sommarboken

Every year, the bright Scandinavian summer nights fade away without anyone's noticing. One evening in August you have an errand outdoors, and all of a sudden it's pitch-black. A great warm, dark silence surrounds the house. It is still summer, but the summer is no longer alive. It has come to a standstill; nothing withers, and fall is not ready to begin. There are no stars yet, just darkness. The can of kerosene is brought up from the cellar and left in the hall, and the flashlight is hung up on its peg beside the door.

Not right away, but little by little and incidentally, things begin to shift position in order to follow the progress of the seasons. Day by day, everything moves closer to the house. Sophia's father takes in the tent and the water pump. He removes the buoy and attaches the cable to a cork float. The boat is pulled ashore on a cradle, and the dory is hung upside down behind the woodyard. And so fall begins. A few days later, they dig the potatoes and roll the water barrel up against the wall of the house. Buckets and garden tools move in

toward the house, ornamental pots disappear, Grandmother's parasol and other transitory and attractive objects all change places. The fire extinguisher and the axe, the pick and the snow shovel, appear on the veranda. And at the same time, the whole landscape is transformed.

Grandmother had always liked this great change in August, most of all, perhaps, because of the way it never varied; a place for everything and everything in its place. Now was the time for the traces of habitation to disappear, and, as far as possible, for the island to return to its original condition. The exhausted flower beds were covered with banks of seaweed. The long rains did their leveling and rinsing. All the flowers still in bloom were either red or yellow, strong patches of color above the seaweed. In the woods were a few enormous white roses that blossomed and lived for one day in breathless splendor.

Grandmother's legs ached, which may have been due to the rain, and she couldn't walk around the island as much as she wanted to. But she went out for a little while every day just before dark, and tidied up the ground. She picked up everything that had to do with human beings. She gathered nails and bits of paper and cloth and plastic, pieces of lumber covered with oilspill, and an occasional bottle top. She went down to the shore and built fires where everything burnable could go right ahead and burn, and all the time she felt the island growing cleaner and cleaner, and more and more foreign and distant. It's shaking us off, she thought. It will soon be uninhabited. Almost.

The nights got darker and darker. There was an unbroken chain of navigational lights and beacons along the horizon, and sometimes big boats thumped by in the channel. The sea was motionless.

When the ground was clean, Sophia's father painted all the ring bolts with red lead, and one warm, rainless day he soaked the veranda with seal fat. He oiled the tools and the hinges, and swept the chimney. He put away the nets. He stacked wood against the wall by the stove for next spring and for anyone who might be shipwrecked on the island, and he tied down the woodshed with ropes because it stood so near the high-water mark.

"We have to take in the flower stakes," Grandmother said. "They spoil the landscape." But Sophia's father let them be, for otherwise he wouldn't know what was there in the ground when they came back. Grandmother worried about a lot of things. "Suppose someone lands here," she said. "They always do. They wouldn't know the coarse salt is in the cellar, and the trapdoor may have swelled from the damp. We have to bring up the salt and label it, so they won't think it's sugar. And we ought to put out some more pants—there's nothing worse than wet pants. What if they hang their nets over the flower bed and trample it all down? You never know about roots." A little later, she started worrying about the stovepipe and put up a sign: "Don't close the damper. It might rust shut. If

it doesn't draw, there may be a bird's nest in the chimney—later on in the spring, that is."

"But we'll be back by then," Sophia's father said.

"You never know about birds," Grandmother said. She took down the curtains a week early and covered the south and east windows with disposable paper bedsheets, on which she wrote, "Don't remove the window covers or the fall birds will try to fly right through the house. Use anything you need, but please carry in some more wood. There are tools under the workbench. Enjoy yourselves."

"Why are you in such a rush?" Sophia asked, and her grandmother answered that it was a good idea to do things before you forgot that they had to be done. She set out cigarettes and candles, in case the lamp didn't work, and she hid the barometer, the sleeping bags, and the seashell box under the bed. Later, she brought out the barometer again. She never hid the figurine. Grandmother knew no one understood sculpture, and she thought it wouldn't hurt them to be exposed to a little culture. She also made Papa leave the rugs on the floor, so the room wouldn't look unfriendly over the winter.

Covering two of the windows changed the room, made it secretive and conspiratorial, and, at the same time, very lonely.

Grandmother polished the handle on the door and scoured the garbage pail. The next day, she washed all her clothes out beside the woodyard. Then she was tired and went to the guest room. The guest room grew very crowded with the approach of fall—it was a good place to put all sorts of things that were waiting for spring or were no longer needed. Grandmother liked being surrounded by practical, commonplace things, and before she went to sleep, she studied everything around her: nets, nail kegs, coils of steel wire and rope, sacks full of peat, and other important items. With an odd kind of tenderness, she examined the nameplates of boats long since broken up, some storm indications that had been written on the wall, penciled data on dead seals they had found and a mink they had shot, and she dwelled particularly on the pretty picture of the hermit in his open tent against a sea of desert sand, with his guardian lion in the background. How can I ever leave this room? she thought.

It wasn't easy to get into the room and take her clothes off and open the window for the night air but finally she could lie down and stretch her legs. She blew out the light and listened to Sophia and her father getting ready for bed on the other side of the wall. There was a smell of tar and wet wool and maybe a trace of turpentine, and the sea was still quiet. As Grandmother fell asleep, she remembered the chamberpot under the bed and how much she hated it, this symbol of helplessness. She had accepted it out of pure politeness. A chamberpot is nice to have when it's storming or raining, but the next day you have to carry it clear down to the water, and anything that has to be hidden is a burden.

When she woke up, she lay for a long time and wondered if she should go out or not. It felt as if the night had come right up to the walls and was waiting outside, and her legs ached. The stairs were badly constructed. The steps were too high and too narrow, and then came the rock, which was slippery down toward the woodyard, and then you had to come all the way back again. No sense in lighting a light; it only makes you lose your sense of direction and distance, and the darkness comes closer. Swing your legs over the edge of the bed and wait for your balance to come right. Four steps to the door and open the latch and wait again, then five steps down, holding the handrail. Grandmother wasn't afraid of falling or losing her way, but she knew the darkness

was absolute, and she knew what it was like when you lose your hold and there's nothing left to go by. All the same, she said to herself, I know perfectly well what everything looks like. I don't have to see it. She swung her legs over the edge of the bed and waited for a moment. She took the four careful steps to the door and opened the latch. The night was black, but no longer so warm; there was a fine, sharp chill. She went down the stairs very slowly, turned away from the house, and let go of the railing. It wasn't as hard as she'd expected. As she crouched in the woodyard, she knew exactly where she was, and where the house and the sea and the woods were. From far off in the channel came the thump of a boat sailing past, but she couldn't see the channel lights.

Grandmother sat down on the chopping stump to wait for her balance. It came quickly, but she stayed where she was. The coastal freighter was headed east to Kotka. The sound of its diesel motors gradually died, and the night was as quiet as before. It smelled of fall. A new boat approached, a small boat, probably running on gasoline. It might be a herring boat with an automobile engine—but not this late at night. They always went out right after sunset. In any case, it wasn't in the channel but heading straight out to sea. Its slow thumping passed the island and continued out, farther and farther away, but never stopping.

"Isn't that funny," Grandmother said. "It's only my heart, it's not a herring boat at all." For a long time she wondered if she should go back to bed or stay where she was. She guessed she would stay for a while.

Translated by Thomas Teal

Claire Martin   *Canada, b. 1914*

Claire Martin's foremost work, *Dans un gant de fer* (*In an Iron Glove*), provides us with biographical material sufficient to last a lifetime: in it, Martin recounts the horrors of growing up in a family whose father exerted psychological domination and brute force to oppress and isolate his wife and their four daughters. He sanctioned, and was himself protected, as Mary Jane Green comments, by "the entire patriarchal system of values that derived its authority from the church and [was] administered through the institutions of family and school;"[1] in the latter case, Martin's education by the Ursulines and later the Soeurs de la congrégation de Notre Dame. The autobiography was originally published in two volumes: the first, also known as *La joue gauche* (The Left Cheek, 1965), won the Prix France-Québec (along with Claire Blais' *A Season in the Life of Emmanuel*), and the second, *La Joue droite* (The Right Cheek, 1966), won the Governor General's Prize—both awards for fiction!

Martin herself has commented that "when I first wrote this book, I thought I was relating a story that was typically French Canadian": its popularity, as the Canadian feminist critic Nicole Brossard has suggested in another context, may derive from its incarnation of the "collective schizophrenia"[2] of Quebec society, even while it is criticized by some for exaggerating the brutality of a convent education and Martin's father. Martin also suggests that the book's power rests on this insight: "To be a child or woman will always be like being destitute or colored—a hazardous situation. And it seems that...whenever anyone is strong enough, male enough, rich enough or white enough to persecute the weak, he will gladly do so. But people like that have something ridiculous about them. And the weak look on and laugh." Indeed, Martin brings to her grotesque tale an insouciance and gaiety that, along with a colloquial style, lend the book a tone of conversational intimacy; structured by a series of vignettes and commentary, the book is a Gallic counterpart to Mary McCarthy's *Memories of a Catholic Girlhood* (1959), with its sharp-edged irony and precise architectonics.

Martin began her career writing fiction; after her autobiography she returned to that form, publishing a novel, *Les morts* (The Dead, 1970), and a two-act play, *Moi, je n'étais qu'espoir* (Me, I Was Only Hoping, 1972) based on that work, as well as a short essay, written while Martin was writer-in-residence at the University of Ottawa, describing her youthful fascination with the magic of books, *La petite fille lit* (The Little Girl Is Reading, 1973).

An early feminist, Martin also pursued topics that were traditionally proscribed for Quebec literature. In *Doux-amer* (1960; translated as *Best Man*), for example, Martin portrays a woman who puts her career before love, allows herself infidelity, divorce, and remarriage to a younger man. As traditional roles are reversed, abilities and temperaments—rather than gender—govern behavior.

Martin has also supported writers as a member and past president of Canada's Writer's Guild. Since 1972, she has devoted herself to translating: her translations include the works of Margaret Laurence. Having spent a decade in the south of France, Martin returned in 1983 to live in Quebec City.

from IN AN IRON GLOVE
Dans un gant de fer

At the end of two years my father had had enough of the bachelor life. So he went and cooked up a reconciliation with Mother's confessor—still the same Jesuit—who arrived at my grandparents' loaded with vows and promises on my father's behalf. For his own part he came heavily armed with threats. To listen to him, a woman separated from her husband was responsible for all the sins solitude might lead him into, and that was the only thing that counted. It was enough to terrify the poor woman, all the more so because my father had taken the trouble to write on several occasions to let her know that "he had all the women he needed." Then there were his promises: she would not be beaten again, would have everything she wanted, could see her parents often.

So we left. And a cruel parting it must have been, for I know that Grandmother didn't put much stock in all those fine promises.

To shelter the family my father had bought a large house, well-proportioned but perfectly glacial in winter. The site he chose was a suburb very little frequented in summer and deserted the rest of the year. The building had been put up in the middle of a vast uncleared lot, doubtless to house some schizoid or fugitive from justice. Just what we needed. There was no road to it. To get there you had to take the little shoreline railroad that connected Quebec to La Malbaie. From the house to what one could scarcely call the station— only a platform and a mean shed that stank of urine—there was a muddy path. The closest neighbors lived a quarter of an hour's walk away, more or less. At least they weren't within call. You could have yelled "Help!" and it wouldn't have carried very far. The trap had been sprung and it was to hold us for more than twenty years.

I don't remember anything about the move, but my elder brother and sisters often used to talk about a little sailboat that the previous owner had left in the attic. They put it in a nearby stream and one night the current carried it away. How I dreamt of that sailboat on those interminably long days of my toyless childhood! It made me furious that I couldn't actually remember it, and I couldn't understand how the others could. So Mother explained what memory was, and in the course of our conversation we discovered that while I hadn't forgotten the bathroom where Grandmother used to do my hair when I was two, my sister Dine remembered the kitchen of another house we had left when she was the same age. In both cases the walls were green. Is there some link between the color green and a child's memory? Who knows?

Besides the sailboat, there were four or five huge cardboard boxes in the attic containing monstrous mortuary wreaths of mauve and violet cloth flowers. Mme Gagnon who had sold us the house was supposed to have someone come and pick them up. It was strictly forbidden even so much as to peek into those boxes. However, the flowers pulled out so easily and they made such pretty bouquets that it was no mean temptation. Mme Gagnon, who seemed to have left our shores never to return—I can hardly blame her—never did reclaim her goods, so finally Mother, tired of scolding us, sent the wreaths on to the widow. I can imagine her surprise on receiving this package seven or eight years later. It would be fun to add that during this time she had remarried, but I really can't say.

My parents had come together again in June. In July, Mother became pregnant with her fifth child. What can have been the state of mind of that poor woman, so gentle and frail, when she found herself on her way to producing yet another little misery, a part of whose life, as she well knew, would be abominable.

At all events, she made them solid. And this one had occasion to prove it before he was out of diapers.

If only adults would stop to meditate a little as they go along, on the phenomenon of a child's memory—how exact it is, how early it starts to stock up impressions—perhaps they would behave quite differently for fear of being ashamed one day before this other adult that the child will become. But would he listen to a prompting that might make him forgo the pleasure of anger? My father? Never.

It is as though it all happened yesterday. Mother takes the baby upstairs to put him to bed. My father follows her up. A few seconds later we hear cries and terrifying noises. The baby tumbles down the staircase right to the bottom, followed by Mother who, not being bundled up like her son, takes longer about it. A great deal more. Interminably. We children huddled together in the kitchen not daring to stir. Very young we learned, I don't know how, but we did, that in circumstances like this you had to pretend to see nothing and hear nothing, that you mustn't cry or call out. But all tyrants suffer from a common weakness in system: they cannot prevent those they tyrannize over from thinking. I was three and a half. That's pretty small to choose hatred and scorn.

That evening my father's brother who was, as chance would have it, a practised ear, nose and throat specialist, came to take care of Mother. Her face—I can see it—was black. Her nose was broken and enormous. My uncle looked grim. He knew his big brother, and the story that Mother chose to tell, out of kindness and fear, didn't fool him....

One Sunday morning at sermon time, the chaplain announced that he had a long proclamation to read to us and with an imperial gesture unrolled a crackling scroll. It was the decree—people of my age will remember it well—that forbade dancing in the diocese of Quebec. It was as though the chapel had been hit by lightning! The big girls looked at each other aghast and even the tiny tots were horrified. It should be realized that we were, in general, the offspring of the very cream of what the sisters called "society" in the city of Quebec, and stories about receptions, balls, evening gowns, et cetera, were the staple of our small talk.

> Hereafter, under pain of mortal sin, the waltz, the tango, the foxtrot, the one-step, the two-step, the shimmy....

The list seemed interminable. The chaplain drew a few chuckles with all these tongue-twisters, most of them English, which he mouthed as best he could. You realized that a team of real experts—and it was dizzying to think where they had been unearthed—had taken stock of every solitary thing that bore a name in the whole realm of jiggling to music. Nor was a single obscure polka or bourrée forgotten that nasty-minded people would, of course, immediately discover and put into practice.

The emotion aroused by this decree filled the parlor that Sunday afternoon with a bustle of whispering. What a shame! No, but really, what a rotten shame!

"Pooh! Mother said we'd go dancing in Montreal," said Bérangère with infinite scorn.

And that, in fact, is what people did for a while. Then, since the Chateau Frontenac kept its ballroom open, "for the tourists"—belonging to the Canadian Pacific it had, by that token, acquired a sort of extraterritorial status—little by little Quebec parishioners began to steal in there until, less than five years after the ukase, practically no one paid any attention to it, which may at first sight seem surprising in a populace as docile as ours. However, on second thought, it seems to me that the dance is such a good way for people like us to let off steam that it would have been impossible to forbid it for long. It should be added that, unless I am mistaken, this order was never withdrawn. I draw this, in passing, to the attention of all good citizens of Quebec.

Translated by Philip Stratford

Indira Sant

India, b. 1914

Born Indira Narayan in a rural area in Maharastra, Sant did undergraduate work in Poona, and then became a teacher by profession. Married and widowed young, Sant began writing in 1931, in response to her husband's death. She emerged as one of the most significant contributors to the "new poetry" movement in Marathi in the 1950s, which might be characterized by its concern with literary form and the relationship between art and an intense, often painful inner life. Nonetheless, her poetry continued to be influenced by a close attachment to nature and the romanticism of an earlier generation. Some of her poems also derive from the oral tradition of women's songs in Maharashtra which can perhaps be thought of as giving birth to a female tradition of writing poetry that goes back seven and eight centuries to the poet saints Muktabai, Janabai, and Mirabai of Rajasthan; Bahinabai Chowdhary of Nasik (included in this anthology) is another modern example of this tradition.

The author of six collections of poems up to 1975, Indira Sant won the Sahitya Academy award in 1985 for her *Garbhareshim* (literally, "silk-womb;" a fabric that has a thread of silk running through it, 1982). In her more recent work the spontaneity and lyrical intensity has given way to an increased philosophical sophistication. The poems here are taken from *Snakeskin and Other Poems* (1975), a translation of works drawn from several volumes—*Rangabavari* (Passion for Colors, 1964), *Bāhulyā* (Dolls, 1972), and *Mrgaja* (Mirage, 1978), in respective order of the selections.

Indira Sant currently lives in Belgaum, a small town in Maharastra.

SNAKESKIN
Kāt

Here I am, silent, still,
And so is my reflection;
Clearly defined in the mirror,
I show myself to 'me'.

I do not dare
To outstare that image;
Its tremulous lines
Freeze darkly in the glass;

Should I make the slightest move
To state a thing or two,
The words I suppress
Are formed on its lips;

"Do not let me see again
Even a glimpse of you;
I've been asleep a long time:
Do not wake me up.

Do not stir up
The ashes of my dreams."

"What does this madness mean?
I am not another, you are me."
—But a thick mist separates us
And conceals the mirror!

Here I am, silent, still,
With no one in front of me;
Like a cast-off snakeskin,
The snake out of sight.

Translated by Vrinda Nabar
and Nissim Ezekial

MIDDLE-CLASS JANE
Madhyamavāgi Gargi

Stone of suffering.
Stone of time.
Stone of self-sacrifice.
Love of children as self-defence.
A clean well-swept kitchen.
She protects and maintains the home.
Her name: Mistress of the Household.
                                    Domestic Goddess.
Owner of the Home.[1] Surrounded by it. Bound
                                    to it.
Spinning like a top,
Engrossed and unfulfilled.

The sharp smell of cooking
Spreads everywhere.
And men compose phrases,
Dash off headlines:
The Modern, Independent Woman. Woman's
                                    Progress
Woman's Advance on the Path of Progress.
                                    Etc., etc.[2]
Sweet-sounding phrases.
Reports of progress that reach for the sky.

In the evening,
Twilight-time, exhausted, shifting from hand
                                    to hand
Her hand bag and shopping bags, she returns.
That's Middle-class Jane.
She's the subject of those headlines.
That image of her, carefully carried with her
                                    purse
She throws into the fire
That the tea may be ready sooner.
Her wings are clipped, the tea is poured.

Then at the cooker. The *chappatis*.[3] The spices.
Difficult children and adults. Sullen servants.
Countless threads which bind her tight.
What a drag! She who cooks
Is the one who is cooked.

                    Translated by Vrinda Nabar and
                            Nissim Ezekiel

NOTES (1, 2 by translators)

1. Mistress of Household. Domestic Goddess. Owner of the Home: There is an irony in the original words and phrases which is lost in translation. They are derived from the Sanskrit, embodying traditional notions of feminine sublimity; and they are used in such a way that they imply stereotypes.
2. The Modern, Independent Woman... The irony referred to above is paralleled here in Marathi phrases which echo the English equivalents.
3. Pancakelike wheat bread, usually fried before serving.

AN OBSESSION
Ek Ved

I was once obsessed with
Finding my own way
And wandering through dense forests;
Assessing the wind,
Climbing the hill-tops...

            What remains of it
Is only this:
A framed photograph hung on the wall.

I was once obsessed with
Watching, all by myself,
The sea-birds on the sea-shore,
Rocking on the sea-waves...

            What remains of it
Are mere reflections
In the mirror of memories.

Today
Only darkness obsesses me...
I want to put an end to dreaming,
To be a black stain on the darkness,
            To be dissolved
In its obscurity.

            Translated by Vrinda Nabar and Nissim Ezekiel

RECEIVING
Onjal[1]

To the hungry one[2]
    A handful of rice;
To the thirsty one
    A glass of water.

I have to give:...

To plunge into the self, to pour it out,
    This alone is my strength;
But with you
    I have a longing to receive.

My only hunger
    Is for your silent expressiveness;
My only thirst
    For your flow of feeling.
    Translated by Vrinda Nabar and Nissim Ezekiel

NOTES (by translators)

1. The Marathi word which serves as the title means "The Cupped Hands."
2. To the hungry one...The figurative language of the first four lines in Marathi cannot easily be translated. They represent the idea that the poet throws a handful of rice towards the empty sky as a gesture or symbolic gift. Similarly, the poet would like to present a thimble-ful of water to the thirsty ocean. The later reference to the poet's hunger and thirst become associated with the vastness of the sky and the depth of the ocean.

Ismat Chugtai   *India, b. 1915*

Currently living in Bombay, Ismat Chugtai was born in Uttar Pradesh into a well-to-do Muslim family, one of several older sisters and many brothers, including A.A. Chugtai, also a well-known Urdu writer and an important early influence. At the age of 15, Chugtai managed to avert an arranged marriage by persuading a cousin to offer to marry her. This strategem allowed her to pursue her education, first at Aligarh Muslim University and then, when her father died, at the Isabella Thoburn College in Lucknow. There she received her B.A. and subsequently fought, with six other women, to gain admission to the Baccalaureate of Teaching course, winning the right only by agreeing to *purdah* (veiling). After graduation, Chugtai was appointed headmistress of the Raj Mahal Girls' School in Jodhpur (1939–1940) before going on to become the Inspector of Municipal Schools in Bombay (1941–1943). There she met and married the film director and producer Shahid Lateef, with whom she lived in what she his described as a tumultuous companionship that lasted twenty-four years, until his death in 1967. They have two daughters.

In Bombay, Chugtai began her writing career, opening a new chapter in the history of Urdu literature. Her early novels are *Ziddi* (Stubbornness, 1941) and *Terhi Lakir* (Crooked Line, 1943). She first came into the limelight with the publication of two volumes of short stories, *Kalyan* (Buds, 1945, reprinted 1963) and *Choten* (Wounds, 1943, reprinted 1960). The latter includes "Lihaf" ("The Quilt"), a now-famous story that uses a child narrator to describe the lesbian relationship between a woman confined in the *zenana* (literally, belonging to woman; harem) and her maid servant. For this story Chugtai was charged with obscenity by the Lahore government in 1944; she was later found not guilty. Over and above the legal controversy, the story inspired widespread resentment among the upper classes at its publication; yet critics consider it to be one of her best treatments of that stratum of society, superb in its reticence and suggestiveness. It typifies the originality of her technique (American readers may be reminded of Henry James' *What Maisie Knew*), the new frankness, and the daring treatment of unmentionable themes that Chugtai used to shape the modern short story. Other major collections include *Chui Mui* (Touch Me and I Die, 1952).

Chugtai's criticism of society is not limited to sexual convention, nor is her contribution limited to the short story. Her novel *Ek Katra Khun* (One Drop of Blood, 1975) generated fierce debate because it recreates an event from Muslim religious history, depicting Mohammed's grandsons as champions of oppressed humanity, confronting the tyrannical power of the state.

Though faulted for her unrealistic characters and her failure to digest other influences, Chugtai is deservedly acclaimed for her new subject matter and social concern, her economy of style, and her mastery of the spoken language and dialogue. The story printed here is also evidence of her subversive sense of humor. For her literary contribution in some seventeen volumes, Chugtai has been much recognized, beginning in 1975 with the Government of India Sahitya Academy award and the conferral of the prestigious title of Padma Shri.* Critics writing in English, Madhu Keshwar and Ruth Vanitar, as well as Muhammad Sadiq, have also done much to insure her reputation and make her known to a larger audience.

Chugtai has also had a career as actress, screenplay writer and film-maker. Her movie credits include *Darvaza* (Door), about widow remarriage, and *Sone Ki Chiriya* (Bird of Gold), about an actress exploited by the film industry. She has also done a documentary on the poems of her socialist contemporary, Ali Sardar Jaffri, entitled. *Jawab Aayga* (The Reply will Come).

NOTE

* One in a set of national New Year honors. Padma Bhushan and Padma Vibhushan are higher ones.

ALL FOR A HUSBAND
Ek Shauharki Khātir

And all this happened over the merest trifle. Misfortunes cannot be foreseen. What an unlucky hour it was when I set foot in that train, and stirred up a nest of hornets round my ears! This is how it happened. Last November, I was traveling from Jodhpur to Bombay. Everybody advised me: "Look, don't go. You'll regret it." But when an ant's wings sprout, it flies straight to its destruction.

A long journey and an extra jerky train. Sleep seemed far away, sand flew in through the window. To top it all, solitude. The whole bogey lay empty, like a graveyard filled with row upon row of graves. My heart began to sink. I was fed up with scanning the newspaper. I picked up another. The same news items. Oh God, if I were in a graveyard, at least the corpses might emerge from their graves. Oh God, if only someone would come. Oh God, oh God... I began to pray. All of a sudden, the train stopped, and it was as though an army of locusts had invaded the train. There were more infants and bundles than there were people. The children, as though they had come from famine-stricken villages, fell to nourishing themselves the moment they entered the train. The suckling infants set about it in a businesslike manner while the others moved around, whining and whimpering. As for the bundles, they were tied in such a fashion as to take up the maximum possible space, and refused to stay put anywhere. As you caught hold of one, another fell on your head. I continued to sit on a separate berth at such an angle that if a bundle were to fall on me, my spine would be spared. I value my spine above all the other parts of my body. They say that if your spine breaks, you become a mere lump of flesh.

"Where are you going?" enquired my fellow traveler in an anxious tone, even though she was as yet barely free of the bundles. I hurriedly informed her, and then drew her attention to a heavy bundle which seemed to contain utensils, and was threatening to descend on us at the slightest provocation. The touch of a hand sent the utensils clattering in a manner calculated to strike dread into the boldest heart.

"Where are you coming from?" I told her, with a little less alacrity.

"Are you going to your *maika*?"[1] When one is not married, one's maika is the whole world, and yet is nowhere at all. The question of maika and *sasural*[2] does not arise. Yet her question threw me off balance, and for a moment I wondered in which province there was a danger of my being married.

"Are you going to your husband?"

"No." I began to wish for a change of subject. Why be pitied for nothing at all?

"Oh, then you must be going to your in-laws, isn't it?" What philosophical answers these questions require!

"No—I'm going to Bombay—I-I'm not married," I said, with some trepidation, even though at college I had won first prize for speaking against marriage at a debate, and

even now—in any case, now—well, anyway, that's what I said to her. She gave such a start that the infant was deprived of milk, and instantly began to shriek like a goat being slaughtered. To divert her attention, I tried directing it towards the child, but she just shoved the milk into the child's nose, while she gazed at me with a compassion and kind condescension that cannot be reduced to words. In fact, she looked so affectionate that I was afraid she might gather me into her arms and burst into tears. To cheer her up I bought some roasted gram, but she remained sunk in sorrow. She told me one or two methods of catching a good husband, which, surprisingly, later turned out to be particularly worthless.

My prayers were indeed being answered with a vengeance. Or perhaps the heavenly scribe erred and recorded my submission twice over, for here came another troop of beings. With them came also sticks of sugarcane which had been measured and cut so large as not to fit into any corner of the compartment. They also had rolls of bedding and trunks which refused to stay either on the berths or under them. These ladies created chaos as soon as they arrived. They mercilessly dragged around the trunks and bedding, while the obstinate bundles aforesaid, which had been awaiting this opportunity, promptly fell on the women and children, who then fell on one another.

"Where are you going?" She too seemed deeply concerned.

I told her.

"Where are you coming from?" she next asked, though she was not yet settled, and her *burka* was strangling her. I told her.

"Are you going to your maika or your sasural?" If only I knew! There was no time to think, so I said: "Sasural" in a low tone so as not to be overheard by my other fellow traveler.

"What does your husband do?" Well, I thought, he must be doing something. Why should he roam around, doing nothing? If only he had told me what he does! Well, in any case, he couldn't be unemployed. Just then, she suggested: "In the railways, perhaps...?"

"Yes, he is," I hastened to assure her. A railway man will be fine, I thought. One can get free tickets and explore every part of India. I like their uniform too. Those caps and whistles, green and red flags—how fortunate that I met this nice woman, otherwise I would never have dreamt of a guard or a clerk on...

"What job does he do in the railways?"

"Well, naturally, he'd do a good job, what else?" I hadn't quite realized that it is easy enough to be the wife of a guard but the details might prove a bit too much for me.

"Yes, but what does he do? There are a thousand and one jobs in the railways."

"Oh—whistle—coolie—" I was taken aback, and my eye fell on a coolie weighed down by a large bundle, a bedroll, half a dozen mud pots and two pitchers.

"Coolie—your husband is a coolie?" She too fell prey to a fit of astonishment. I was anxious that we hold this heart-to-heart conversation in low tones, lest my first friend overhear us. Her infant was still happily drinking milk. But once I have made a statement, I always stick to it. In any case, there was little enough to stick to on the present occasion.

"Ye-es, even if he is a coolie, what difference does it make to you?" I said, feeling quite offended.

"Your h-husband, a coolie?"

"So what?" I felt like retorting, "What makes you so jealous? You're welcome to marry a coolie too. Marry ten coolies if you like, who's stopping you—especially if you think coolies are so cheap!" But I restrained myself and pulled a long face.

"However did you get married to a coolie?" she asked, and began to wonder how coolies get married. I wanted to invent something, but when I thought of it, the story of a coolie's marriage seemed very drab, so I said: "Once there was a coolie..."

She listened with attention. "He lived..." I wanted her to say "Hm" or nod her head.

"Then it so happened that one day..." God, if I only knew. I couldn't even recall any story, at that moment. "He was carrying some luggage ..." I wanted her to ask "Whose?" and she did.

"A very beautiful girl's. Then that girl—that girl fell in love with him..."

"Who was the girl?"

Oh my, I never thought of that. Anyway, it hardly matters. There must have been some girl or other. Some beautiful girl.

"And why did she fall in love with a coolie?"

"She fell in love with him because—because—well, how should I know, there must have been some reason. Perhaps he smiled at her..." Just then, a particularly dreadful looking railway employee looked at me and smiled, causing me fervently to hope that I would not actually have to fall in love. After all, I was to appear for an interview. One hears that falling in love reduces one to a terrible condition. And who wants to go around falling in love in unknown territory? Also, I had to stay in Jasimbhai's house, and if there is anything he dreads next to cholera, it is love. Fortunately, the issue was soon forgotten.

"Sister, what are you talking about? Which girl? Who fell in love? I'm asking you how you got married..."

"She is not married, poor thing." My earlier acquaintance had at last overhead us. That is why I kept saying, talk softly, softly—but now I have lost even that coolie.

"At that time I wasn't married..." I hoped to convince her.

"What? you mean you got married sitting in the train?" God, if only that were possible! If only rich, well-placed husbands were on sale instead of hot tea, I would definitely buy one for the journey even if later—later I'd see. And I decided that I would definitely search for a plausible kind of husband. What does one lose? It would work fine. At least, one would not have to cook up fresh lies for each passenger. As soon as someone asks, in a flash you produce your husband!

"My dear, where can you get good boys these days?" she said, despairing of my future. "They demand a car, or a horse carriage. That's the only way to get an earning boy."

I too grew sorrowful. Why can't these boys earn, after all. How many good boys there used to be in earlier times. Like so many carrots and radishes. But now there is not one to bless yourself with. This war has only made things worse. Earlier, at least there were boys enough—earning ones or good-for-nothing ones. Now every man jack of them is rushing off to the war.

"Why don't you get married then?"

"As you please," I answered, like an innocent girl whose parents first arrange her marriage and then ask for her opinion, just to show how liberal they are.

"When will you marry, if you don't marry now?"

"Now—you mean, right now? I think it would perhaps be better if we wait till we reach the junction."

"What?"

"Since you have decided, why delay the auspicious moment?"

"Auspicious? What are you talking about, girl?" She got really upset.

"I'm asking why you don't get married," put in the other.

"Why don't you get married then?" I was getting exasperated so I chose to ignore the presence of her child who was still blissfully sucking away.

"Oo—it seems there's something wrong with your head." She shifted the angle at which she was holding the child, so as to make it clear that he was not merely sleeping in her arms.

"Oh, you mean you are married," I remarked nonchalantly, "When did you get yourself married?"

"My parents got me married. Why would I have got myself married?"

"So you are against marriage? You are right, absolutely right. My parents also went and got married—savages that they were." She

quieted down after this, and took some sweet pancakes out of her basket to console herself.

Oh God, when you answer a prayer, is this the way you go about it? You poor creatures have not a moment's peace. This poor handmaiden of yours was lonely. When she desired company, did you have to start sending such quantities of passengers, and even greater quantities of luggage? Not that I have any right to interfere with your arrangements, but all that I have to say, oh merciful provider, is that you might take into account the tolerance level of your creatures when you are heaping burdens upon them.

I began to feel quite concerned lest my prayer for a husband also be granted after this fashion, and husbands descend upon me, one after another. That would be the end of me. It will be a wonder if I am able to sew buttons on the shirt of one, and serve him cups of tea. How can I possibly endure so many of them, indolent as I am? They say that if you have second thoughts about a letter after you have posted it, you can get it back from the post office by paying a small bribe. If only there was such a system with regard to prayers too! But I had already sent up the prayer, and it was now being answered to my cost.

My new fellow traveler appeared to be sophisticated, and more soft-spoken than was strictly necessary. She seemed to be suffering from some delicate, poetical sickness and also to be in the habit of speaking softly. All in all, I was quite pleased with her.

"Are you going to Hyderabad?" she asked. I was afraid to say no lest she take offense. However, I very politely told her I was going to Bombay.

"You must have come from Ahmedabad?" She seemed adept at filling old bottles with new medicine and cajoling one into drinking it. But she looked so downcast that I could not bring myself to hurt her. So I told her.

"You study there?"

"No. I'm going for an interview."

"My uncle's brother-in-law's aunt lives in

Bombay. You must meet her." I promised faithfully, wondering how I would find the time to go searching for her uncle's brother-in-law's aunt.

"Do your parents live there?"

"No—my..." Before I could complete the sentence, she interposed: "Oh, I see, your husband lives there." Here we were again—what a long detour to come back to the same old terminus—a husband. A man. Indian men may go around cutting off noses, handing out divorces, they may be difficult to secure as husbands, and when they are secured, may turn out to be good-for-nothing whoremongers and gamblers. Yet here are the women all dying for them. Every woman obsessed either with her own or with someone else's husband. The unmarried ones singing songs about a husband, and the married ones crazy about the beloved. The beloved, of course, continues to suck their blood. Such is the situation when the beloved is cruel. If he were to show a little kindness, heaven knows what would happen. I began to think that even the cruelties of husbands may have their advantages.

"Where do you live, in Bombay? How many children do you have?" Here was I, sunk in thought, there was she, proceeding from the husband to the number of children.

"Eight," I remarked, counting the dogs on the platform, "How come there are always more dogs than passengers on platforms?"

"Eight?"

"Yes. Why, what's so surprising about that? If you don't believe me, get off the train and count them for yourself."

"No, how can I break my journey? Of course, if I ever pay a visit to my uncle's brother-in-law's aunt—but—sister, one could never tell by looking at your face..."

"Ah, what can one tell by looking at a face?" I replied, in a philosophical tone. When I feel disgusted with the world, and everything begins to appear dead and dull, I start waxing philosophical.

"How many years have you been married?" she asked, after a pause.

"Four years, three months and..."

"And eight children? Look, sister, I thought OK, maybe it is possible you have eight, but..." She seemed on the verge of tears. I felt sorry for her. But I decided that no matter what happened, I would not be browbeaten any further; otherwise, after the children, she would go on to impose grandchildren too on me. And those other ladies who were so well acquainted with my life history had not yet fallen asleep. We would get involved in another unnecessary exchange of views. Those eight children were already weighing heavy on my spirit.

"Yes, yes, I am telling you there are eight."

"Good God, are they all alive? But sister, how were they born?"

"How do you expect? The same way all children are born, of course."

"I mean, in four years..."

"Oh, I see. That's what you want to know. Well, sometimes two were born together, sometimes three and..."

"What? What?" She gaped at me, and I felt quite offended that she should be so surprised. After all, it was my personal affair, was it not? What difference did it make to her whether someone gave birth to one child or to ten? Of course, what I had been dreading all along was bound to happen. My earlier acquaintances began to show an interest.

"Have you heard this, sister? She has had them sometimes two at a time, and sometimes three—children, I mean..." One of them heard only the word "children," panicked, and hastily began to count her own.

"What's the matter?" enquired the other. When the matter was fully explained, all three of them took offense.

"Just now she said she was not married and now she's started producing two or three children at a time," one of them rebuked me.

"What makes you think I am not married? Heaven preserve me! You must be the unmarried one." The situation began to deteriorate rapidly. A ticket checker passed by.

At least, I have no idea what he was. Every railway employee looks like a ticket checker to me. I leant across to ask him the time. After telling me, he smiled, and off he went, still smiling.

"You said you were traveling alone? And now who is this?"

"He is my daughter's son." Before they could establish some more romantic relationship, I took the decision for myself.

"Daughter's son?" they shrieked in unison.

My God, why have these people determined to take such violent objection to every simple family relationship of mine?

"What does the girl say? That's your daughter's son?"

"So what is it to you?"

"Sister, surely he had gray hair," put in another.

"Must have grayed because of a bad cold," I muttered, and then leant as far out of the window as I could. I was not desirous of committing suicide, and was unpracticed in alighting from a moving train. A harsh world and a distant heaven.

That which is decreed to happen must inevitably happen. When my luggage was being weighed and charged, the clerk asked: "Your name? Your husband's name?"

"*Chugd* (rascal)" I muttered through clenched teeth.

"Chokhe? What an outlandish name." He nudged the other clerk.

Needless to say, when he drew up a receipt that converted me into Mrs. Chokhe, I gave him one across the face with my bag which contained a heavy book. And all this just for a husband.

Translated by Ruth Vanita

NOTES

1. Natal home of a married woman.
2. In-laws' home of a married woman.

Elisabeth Eybers   *South Africa/Holland, b. 1915*

Elisabeth Eybers was born in Klerksdorp, a small town to the west of Johannesburg, in 1915. Shortly after her birth, her family moved to the even smaller town of Schweizer-Reneke, where her father, a clergyman, had been posted, and where Eybers went to school. Although Afrikaans was her native tongue, she attended the anglophone University of the Witwatersrand, obtaining a B.A. (Honors) in 1937, on the basis of her thesis "The Development of Individualism in the Afrikaans Lyric." Also in 1937 she married Albert J. J. Wessels, an aspiring writer and later an influential businessman. The couple had four children, three daughters and a son, and resided in Johannesburg until their separation in 1961. At the time Eybers began writing, while she was working as a journalist in the early 1930s, Afrikaans was just emerging as a written language, having only, in 1925, after a long struggle, achieved recognition as an official language of South Africa, alongside English.

Eybers is widely regarded as among the first significant poets writing in the Afrikaans language. In conjunction with other *Dertigers* (writers of the 1930s) such as N. P. van Wyk Louw, C. M. van den Heever and Uys Krige, she succeeded not only in providing Afrikaans with a poetic vocabulary, but also in constituting the fledgling literature as modernist in its sensibilities, alert and responsive to cultural developments abroad.

Eybers' own poetry is delicate, nuanced, and intuitive, marked by a powerfully meditative stance. Her reflective and carefuly modulated use of narrative irony is at its most effective in her sonnets, a form at which she excels. Her first collection of poems, *Belydenis in die Skemering* (Confession in the Twilight), appeared in 1936, and her impressive oeuvre now includes over a dozen original volumes and several compilations. Eybers has herself translated many of her poems into English, and a selection translated by herself and Olga Kirsch, another well-known Afrikaans poet, has been published under the title *The Quiet Adventure* (1948), the title drawn from Eybers' second published volume, *Die Stil Avontuur* (1939). In 1943, Eybers was awarded the prestigious Hertzog Prize for her first two volumes of poetry, an honor that would be repeated in 1971 for her volume *Onderdak* (Shelter).

With the advent of apartheid in 1948, Eybers found it more and more difficult to continue living and writing in South Africa. Ultimately, the situation began to seem to her intolerable, and when she and her husband separated in 1961, she expressed her dissent by leaving the country and settling in Holland, from where she continues to write in Afrikaans. Eybers' emigration from South Africa was significant because she was one of the first Afrikaner writers to go into exile for political reasons. In this she has been followed by such notable figures as Olga Kirsch, Barend J. Toerien, and Breyten Breytenbach. Despite her emigration, Eybers has continued to be widely read and admired in South Africa. She has twice won the national Central News Agency Prize for Literature (in 1973 and 1978) and in 1972 was awarded an honorary doctorate by the University of the Witwatersrand. Keenly interested in translation, she translated Jules Supervielle's *Le boeuf et l'ane de la creche* (The Ox and the Ass of the Manger) into Afrikaans in 1959. Among Eybers' recent work, the volumes that have attracted most attention have been *Balans* (Balance, 1962), *Onderdak* (Shelter, 1968) and *Kruis of Munt* (Cross or Coin, 1973).

Neil Lazarus

PYGMALION*

No craftsman has been skilfuller than he
with chisel fretting under steadfast knock
to disencumber, bring to light and free
what God holds dungeoned in relentless rock
pending the day it's summoned to escape.
He taps with subtle promise of release
and lustfully pursues the timid shape,
finding, till a stone eyelid stirs, no peace.

Translated by Elisabeth Eybers

SNAIL

My softness heaves its spiralled canopy:
another roof would be too much to bear.
At home I'm sunk, abroad I'm still at sea,
awkward antennae fumble everywhere.

Hermaphrodite the ruttish ocean spewed
up from the ooze, on dry land I endure
a living thirst by day and night renewed,
and know, except slow death, no certain cure.

Translated by Elisabeth Eybers

NOTE

* In Greek mythology, Pygmalion was king of Cyprus; he carved an ivory statue of Galatea, transformed into a living woman by the goldess of love and beauty, Aphrodite.

NARRATIVE

A woman grew, with waiting, over-quiet.
The earth along its spiralled path was spun
through many a day and night, now green,
                                        now dun;
at times she laughed, and then, at times, she
                                        cried.

The years went by. By turns she woke and
                                        slept
through the long hours of night, but every day
she went, as women go, her casual way,
and no one knew what patient tryst she kept.

Hope and despair tread their alternate round
and merge into acceptance, till at length
the years have only quietness in store.

And so at last the narrative has found
in her its happy end; this tranquil strength
is better than the thing she's waiting for.

Translated by Elisabeth Eybers

EMILY DICKINSON

"Essential oils are wrung:
The attar from the rose
Is not expressed by suns alone,
It is the gift of screws"
EMILY DICKINSON

That knowledge which the ruthless screws distil
she could not weigh against the easy truth
that's cheap and readily negotiable:
as time went on, her days grew more aloof.

The years proved meagre as they came and
                                        went;
her narrow, ardent love, commodity
that found no market, still remained unspent:
yearning, forsakenness and ecstasy.

She climbed the scaffolding of loneliness
not to escape from living, but to gain
a perilous glimpse into the universe;
and tunnelled down into the mind's dark mine,
through tortuous shafts descending to obtain
its flawless fragments, glittering, crystalline.

Translated by Elisabeth Eybers

Rina Lasnier   *Canada, b. 1915*

Rina Lasnier's large *oeuvre* is considered one of the major achievements of francophone poetry; Lasnier gives new power to the spiritual tradition of her precursor
Simone Routier (b. 1901) and stands alongside other Canadians of her own
generation, such as Alain Grandbois, Roland Giguère, and Paul-Marie Lapointe.
A founding member of L'Académie canadienne-française, and member of the
Royal Society of Canada, Lasnier won the Quebec Provincial Prize in 1967 and
the Molson Prize in 1971 in recognition of her outstanding contribution to the
humanities.

Having studied in England and at the University of Montreal, where she
obtained degrees in English and French literature, Lasnier began to publish at the
beginning of World War II and achieved her first critical success in 1943 with *La
Mère de nos mères* (The Mother of Our Mothers). In this and such works as
Madones canadiennes (Canadian Madonnas, 1944) and *Notre Dame du pain* (Our
Lady of Sustenance, 1947), Lasnier derived her inspiration from the Marian tradition of the Catholic church, creating female heroines or historical personages
such as the Mohawk convert Kateri Tekakwitha (1656–1680) and Marguerite
Bourgeoys (1620–1700). In *Le chant de la montée* (The Song of the Ascent,
1948), Lasnier turned specifically to the Scriptures, using the story of Jacob

and Rachel in the Book of Genesis to develop a complex work comprised of fifteen cantos that alternate traditional forms with sections of prose poetry.

With the publication of *Escales* (Ports of Call) in 1950, Lasnier marked a new stage in her poetic development: with great virtuosity and precise imagery, she delineated the confrontation between life and death and between the force of love and the flashes of despair which threaten to overwhelm it. In *Mémoires sans jours* (Timeless Memories, 1960), Lasnier continued her experimentation with traditional forms, such as the sonnet, that she had begun in *Présence de l'absence* (The Presence of Absence, 1956), while capturing complex rhythms, especially in a remarkable sequence entitled "Poèmes haitiens." This cycle represents a poetic exploration of the mystery of voodoo. In the three drums of these poems—black, green, and red—various critics have seen the depths of the sea, the surface of the earth, and the blood of life. Likewise, the celebrated poem that opens the first section of the book, "La Malemer," shows Lasnier's ability to use sensuous imagery to convey spiritual experience; Suzanne Paradis has likened its revelation of the poetic art to Rimbaud's "Bateau ivre" ("Ivory Boat") and Baudelaire's *Invitation au voyage* (*Invitation to a Voyage*). *Mémoires* as well as *Les gisants* (Recumbent Statues [on tombstones], 1963) also reveal a certain nostalgia that seems to have gripped Lasnier after a visit to France in 1953–1954.

With *L'arbre blanc* (The White Tree, 1966), Lasnier returned to a *poésie d'un pays*, a "poetry of the country," that endowed nature with symbolic value while remaining true to the specificities of the snowy Québécois landscape. This, along with *La salle des rêves* (The Dream Chamber, 1971), shows Lasnier at the height of her powers. A collected edition of her work appeared the following year, and she has continued to publish, her most recent works being *Entendre l'ombre* (Understanding the Shadow, 1981) and *Voir la nuit* (Seeing the Night, 1981).

THE BODY OF CHRIST
Le Corps du Christ

From his hair matted with clay and with blood
The flawless purity of stars and light

From his tongue without spittle and parables
the spices, honeys, and balms of silence

From his arms held out like hawsers
forests to oppose the thunderstorms

From his blued and lifeless belly
the full currents and plasma of seas

From his feet firm-buttressed and grey
the veinings of rock and unbending metal

From his pious eyelids spread out for our gaze
the pardon that shadows throw on clear justice

From his heart stagnant under the cross
the round shield of the sun before our evil

Body of Christ, lie dormant in your pillaged
                    sleep,
we have all taken from that crucified paradise.

Translated by Fred Cogswell

AT THE WATER'S EDGE
Au bord de l'eau

Because of you, like water I shall kneel;
You will not see me tremble in my dress.
My soul has clasped our image in the pool
And you, a hunter, take as prey my kiss…

Translated by Fred Cogswell

THE DEAF
Les Sourdes

They smothered every living teal
So not to hear the water's sound;
They stoned up springs and brooks in their
zeal

To bury the song underground.

They did not wish to hear the cry
Of rapids on the spray-soaked reef;
They let their hearts' congregation die
On the sands of their disbelief.

Translated by Fred Cogswell

Judith Wright   *Australia, b. 1915*

Judith Wright was the first Australian woman to establish an international reputation as a poet and to have her works regularly studied in Australian schools and universities. In recent years she has acquired a second reputation as an outspoken activist on the issues of nature conservation and Aboriginal rights. Her *The Cry for the Dead* (1981) is a counterhistorical study of the white pioneers' role in the destruction of Aboriginal culture.

Wright was born at Armidale in northern New South Wales, into one of Australia's pioneer pastoral families. Her love of Australia's New England country where she grew up is apparent in much of her early poetry. She also drew on family history for an early prose work, *The Generations of Men* (1955).

In 1936 Wright completed an Arts course at Sydney University. Since 1962, she has been awarded honorary degrees from five Australian universities and taught at the University of Queensland from 1967 to 1968.

Though best known for her poetry, of which ten individual collections, two *Selected Poems* (1963, 1978) and a *Collected Poems* (1971) have so far appeared, Wright has also published a collection of stories, a collection of essays, and four books for children. As well, she has made a valuable contribution to the research and criticism of Australian poetry, particularly through her study *Preoccupations in Australian Poetry* (1964) and her monograph on the colonial poet Charles Harpur (1978). "Woman to Man," below, is a very well-known early poem, from Wright's second collection of the same name, published in 1949. It shows her ability to work with fairly traditional poetic imagery and forms to produce a very personal yet wide-ranging statement. "To Mary Gilmore," to an earlier Australian women poet, is from *Alive: Poems 1971–72* (1973). "Eve to Her Daughters," reprinted here, is from *The Other Half* (1966), is free in form and colloquial in language, and shows the wry humor and the criticism of contemporary society characteristic of Wright's later work.

Elizabeth Webby

WOMAN TO MAN

The eyeless labourer in the night,
the selfless, shapeless seed I hold,
builds for its resurrection day—
silent and swift and deep from sight
foresees the unimagined light.

This is no child with a child's face;
this has no name to name it by:
yet you and I have known it well.
This is our hunter and our chase,
the third who lay in our embrace.

This is the strength that your arm knows,
the arc of flesh that is my breast,
the precise crystals of our eyes.
This is the blood's wild tree that grows
the intricate and folded rose.

This is the maker and the made;
this is the question and reply;
the blind head butting at the dark,
the blaze of light along the blade.
Oh hold me, for I am afraid.

TO MARY GILMORE

Having arranged for the mail and stopped the
                                            papers,
tied loaves of bread Orlando-like* to the tree,
love-messages for birds; suitcase in hand
I pause and regard the irony of me.

Supposed to be fifty-six, hair certainly grey,
stepping out much like sixteen on another
                                            journey
through a very late spring, the conference-
                                    papers packed
as a half-excuse for a double-tongued holiday;
as though I believed—well, then, as though I
                                            believed.
Remember Mary Gilmore, her little son
turned sixty-four, and bald? And Mary playing
her poet's game as though she'd never be done.
This is my place. It isn't far to my grave,
the waiting stone. But still there's life to do
and a taste of spring in the air. Should I sit and
                                            grieve,
Mary, or keep the ink running, like you?

Years have their truths, and each as true as
                                            another.
Salute, Mary. Not long now till we know
the blackened deathly world you once foresaw;
but now—let's live. I pick up my case and go.

NOTE

* Orlando, in Shakespeare's *As You Like It*, wanders
  through the forests of Arden leaving love notes on trees
  for Rosalind.

EVE TO HER DAUGHTERS

It was not I who began it.
Turned out into draughty caves,
hungry so often, having to work for our bread,
hearing the children whining,
I was nevertheless not unhappy.
Where Adam went I was fairly contented to go.
I adapted myself to the punishment: it was my
                                            life.

But Adam, you know...!
He kept on brooding over the insult,
over the trick They had played on us, over the
                                            scolding.
He has discovered a flaw in himself
and he had to make up for it.

Outside Eden the earth was imperfect,
the seasons changed, the game was fleet-footed,
he had to work for our living, and he didn't
                                            like it.

He even complained of my cooking
(it was hard to compete with Heaven).

So he set to work.
The earth must be made a new Eden
with central heating, domesticated animals,
mechanical harvesters, combustion engines,
escalators, refrigerators,
and modern means of communication
and multiplied opportunities for safe investment
and higher education for Abel and Cain
and the rest of the family.
You can see how his pride had been hurt.

In the process he had to unravel everything,
because he believed that mechanism
was the whole secret—he was always
                                    mechanical-minded.

He got to the very inside of the whole machine
exclaiming as he went, So this is how it works!

And now that I know how it works, why, I
                              must have invented it.
As for God and the Other, they cannot be
                              demonstrated,
and what cannot be demonstrated
doesn't exist.
You see, he had always been jealous.

Yes, he got to the centre
where nothing at all can be demonstrated.
And clearly he doesn't exist; but he refuses
to accept the conclusion.
You see, he was always an egotist.

It was warmer than this in the cave;
there was none of this fall-out.
I would suggest, for the sake of the children,
that it's time you took over.

But you are my daughters, you inherit my own
                              faults of character;
you are submissive, following Adam
even beyond existence.
Faults of character have their own logic
and it always works out.
I observed this with Abel and Cain.

Perhaps the whole elaborate fable
right from the beginning
is meant to demonstrate this; perhaps it's the
                              whole secret.

Perhaps nothing exists but our faults?
At least they can be demonstrated.

But it's useless to make
such a suggestion to Adam.
He has turned himself into God,
who is faultless, and doesn't exist.

Natalia Ginzburg   *Italy, b. 1916*

One of the best-known living Italian writers, Natalia Ginzburg was born Natalia
Levi. In 1938 she married Leone Ginzburg, a professor of Russian and French
literature, who died in 1944, a prisoner of the Germans. They had three children.
Although in 1950 she married Gabriele Baldini, a professor of English literature,
she continued to use the name Ginzburg in memory of her first husband.

   Natalia Ginzburg published her first short story in the winter issue, 1933–
1934, of the Florentine journal *Solaria*, and then, in 1942, she published a
collection of short stories *La strada che va in città* (*The Road to the City*, 1942),
under a pseudonym, because of Fascist racial laws (her father was Jewish.) After
the war she began to work for the publisher Einaudi, where she came in contact
with the famous writer Cesare Pavese. *È stato così* (*The Dry Heart*, 1947), a short
novel depicting the disintegration of a marriage from the wife's point of view,
established her as a popular writer not only in Italy but also abroad. Her two
books appeared together in English in 1949, and translations of her major works
followed: *All Our Yesterdays*, also known under the titles *A Light for Fools* and
Dead Yesterdays (*Tutti i nostri ieri*, 1952), a novel based on experiences of the
Fascist period, the war and the resistance; this theme continued in *Le voci della
sera* (*Voices in the Evening*, 1961), which depicts a Piedmontese anti-Fascist family
of factory owners; (*Le piccole virtù* (The Little Virtues, 1962); *Lessico famigliare*
(*Family Sayings*, 1963), memoirs that won the Strega Prize; *Mai devi domandarmi*
(*Never Must You Ask Me*, 1970), a collection of essays; and *Caro Michele* (*No
Way*, 1973). The following story was first included in *Valentino* (1957).

In her prose Ginzburg uses conversational language that is deceptively simple in style and purposely antiliterary. She focuses on seemingly unimportant details of life in order to create a background for her characters, who usually are void of all spiritual values and lack the courage to change their monotonous and unhappy lives. She tends to look at life through the unity of a family that is always middle-class and urban, from her first novel through *Famiglia* (Family, 1977) and *La città e la case* (*The City and the House*, 1985). Therefore it is not surprising that when she turned to biography, she chose the same approach for *La Famiglia Manzoni* (*The Manzoni Family*, 1983).

Ginzburg is also a successful playwright. Her plays *Ti ho sposato per allegria* (I Married You for Fun, 1966), *La segretaria* (The Secretary, 1967), and *Paese di mare* (Seaside Town, 1972) have a bittersweet quality and deal with common, everyday problems dear to the author. One of her plays, *L'inserzione* (*The Advertisement*, 1968), was translated into English and performed by the BBC. Besides the Strega Prize, Ginzburg was awarded the Tempo in 1947, the Veillon in 1952, the Viareggio in 1957, the Marzotto in 1968, the Milan: Club degli Editori in 1969, the Bagutta in 1984, and the Ernest Hemingway Prize in 1985.

Natalia Costa-Zalessow

THE MOTHER
La Madre

Their mother was small and thin, and slightly round-shouldered; she always wore a blue skirt and a red woollen blouse. She had short, curly black hair which she kept oiled to control its bushiness; every day she plucked her eyebrows, making two black fish of them that swam towards her temples; and she used yellow powder on her face. She was very young; how old, they didn't know, but she seemed much younger than the mothers of the boys at school; they were always surprised to see their friends' mothers, how old and fat they were. She smoked a great deal and her fingers were stained with smoke; she even smoked in bed in the evening, before going to sleep. All three of them slept together, in the big double bed with the yellow quilt; their mother was on the side nearest the door, and on the bedside table she had a lamp with its shade wrapped in a red cloth, because at night she read and smoked; sometimes she came in very late, and the boys would wake up and ask her where she had been: she nearly always answered: "At the cinema," or else "With a girl friend of mine;" who this friend was they didn't know, because no woman friend had ever been to the house to see their mother. She told them they must turn the other way while she undressed, they heard the quick rustle of her clothes, and shadows danced on the walls; she slipped into bed beside them, her thin body in its cold silk nightdress, and they moved away from her because she always complained that they came too close and kicked while they slept; sometimes she put out the light so that they should go to sleep and smoked in silence in the darkness.

Their mother was not important. Granny, Grandpa, Aunt Clementina who lived in the country and turned up now and then with chestnuts and maize flour were important; Diomira the maid was important, Giovanni the tubercular porter who made cane chairs was important; all these were very important to the two boys because they were strong people you could trust, strong people in allowing and forbidding, very good at everything they did and always full of wisdom and strength; people who could defend you from storms and robbers. But if they were at home with their mother the boys were frightened, just as if they had been alone; as for allowing or forbidding, she never allowed or forbade anything, at the most she complained in a weary voice: "Don't make such a row because I've got a headache," and if they asked permission to do something or other she answered at once: "Ask Granny," or she said no first and then yes and then no and it was all a muddle. When they went out alone with their mother they felt uncertain and insecure because she always took wrong turnings and had to ask a policeman the way, and then she had such a funny timid way of going into shops to ask for things to buy, and in the shops she always forgot something, gloves or handbag or scarf, and had to go back to look and the boys were ashamed.

Their mother's drawers were untidy and she left all her things scattered about and Diomira grumbled about her when she did out the room in the morning. She even called Granny in to see and together they picked up stockings and clothes and swept up the ash that was scattered all over the place. In the morning their mother went to do the shopping: she came back and flung the string bag on the marble table in the kitchen and took her bicycle and dashed off to the office where she worked. Diomira looked at all the things in the string bag, touched the oranges one by one and the meat, and grumbled and called Granny to see what poor meat it was. Their mother came home at two o'clock when they had all eaten and ate quickly with the newspaper propped up against her glass and then rushed off again to the office on her bicycle and they saw her for a minute at supper again, but after supper she nearly always dashed off.

The boys did their homework in the bedroom. There was their father's picture, large at the head of the bed, with his square black beard and bald head and tortoiseshell-rimmed spectacles, and then another small portrait on the table, with the younger of the boys in his arms. Their father had died when they were very small, they remembered nothing about him: or rather in the older boy's memory there was the shadow of a very distant afternoon, in the country at Aunt Clementina's: his father was pushing him across the meadow in a green wheelbarrow; afterwards he had found some pieces of this wheelbarrow, a handle and a wheel, in Aunt Clementina's attic; when it was new it was a splendid wheelbarrow and he was glad to have it; his father ran along pushing him and his long beard flapped. They knew nothing about their father but they thought he must be the sort of person who is strong and wise in allowing and forbidding; when Grandpa or Diomira got angry with their mother Granny said that they should be sorry for her because she had been very unfortunate, and she said that if Eugenio, the boys' father, had been there she would have been an entirely different woman, whereas she had had the misfortune to lose her husband when she was still young. For a time there had been their father's mother as well, they never saw her because she lived in France but she used to write and send Christmas presents: then in the end she died because she was very old.

At tea-time they ate chestnuts, or bread with oil and vinegar, and then if they had finished their homework they could go and play in the small piazza or among the ruins of the public baths, which had been blown up in an air raid. In the small piazza there were a great many pigeons and they took them bread or got Diomira to give them a paper bag of left-over rice. There they met all the local boys, boys from school and others they met in the youth clubs on Sundays when they had football matches with Don Vigliani, who hitched up his black cassock and kicked. Sometimes they played football in the small piazza too or else cops and robbers. Their grandmother appeared on the balcony occasionally and called to them not to get hurt: it was nice seeing the lighted windows of their home, up there on the third floor, from the dark piazza, and knowing that they could go back there, warm up at the stove and guard themselves from the night. Granny sat in the kitchen with Diomira and mended the linen; Grandpa was in the dining room with his cap on, smoking his pipe. Granny was very fat, and wore black, and on her breast a medal with a picture of Uncle Oreste who had died in the war: she was very good at cooking pizzas and things. Sometimes she took them on her knee, even now when they were quite big boys; she was fat, she had a large soft bosom; from under the neck of her black dress you could see the thick white woollen vest with a scalloped edge which she had made herself. She would take them on her knee and say tender and slightly pitiful-sounding words in dialect; then she would take a long iron hair pin out of her bun and clean their ears, and they would shriek and try to get away and Grandpa would come to the door with his pipe.

Grandpa had taught Greek and Latin at the high school. Now he was pensioned off and was writing a Greek grammar: many of his old pupils used to come and see him now and then. Then Diomira would make coffee; in the lavatory there were exercise book pages with Latin and Greek unseens on them, and his corrections in red and blue. Grandpa had a small white beard, a sort of goatee, and they were not to make a racket because his nerves were tired after all those years at school; he was always rather alarmed because prices kept going up and Granny always had a bit of a row with him in the morning because he was always surprised at the money they needed; he would say that perhaps Diomira pinched the sugar and made coffee in secret and Diomira would hear and rush at him and yell that the coffee was for the students who kept coming; but these were small incidents that quietbed down at once and the boys were not alarmed,

whereas they were alarmed when there was a quarrel between Grandpa and their mother; this happened sometimes if their mother came home very late at night, he would come out of his room with his overcoat over his pyjamas and bare feet, and he and their mother would shout: he said: "I know where you've been, I know where you've been, I know what you are," and their mother said: "What do I care?" and then: "Look, now you've woken the children," and he said: "A fat lot you care what happens to your children. Don't say anything because I know what you are. You're a bitch. You run around at night like the mad bitch you are." And then Granny and Diomira would come out in their nightdresses and push him into his room and say: "Shush, shush," and their mother would get into bed and sob under the bedclothes, her deep sobs echoing in the dark room: the boys thought that Grandpa must be right, they thought their mother was wrong to go to the cinema and to her girl friends at night. They felt very unhappy, frightened and unhappy, and lay huddled close together in the deep, warm, soft bed, and the older boy who was in the middle pushed away so as not to touch his mother's body: there seemed to him something disgusting in his mother's tears, in the wet pillow: he thought: "It gives a chap the creeps when his mother cries." They never spoke between themselves of these rows their mother and Grandpa had, they carefully avoided mentioning them: but they loved each other very much and clung close together at night when their mother cried: in the morning they were faintly embarrassed, because they had hugged so tightly as if to protect themselves, and because there was that thing they didn't want to talk about; besides, they soon forgot that they had been unhappy, the day began and they went to school, and met their friends in the street, and played for a moment at the school door.

In the grey light of morning, their mother got up: with her petticoat wound round her waist she soaped her neck and arms standing bent over the basin: she always tried not to let them see her but in the looking glass they could make out her thin brown shoulders and small naked breasts: in the cold the nipples became dark and protruding, she raised her arms and powdered her armpits: in her armpits she had thick curly hair. When she was completely dressed she started plucking her eyebrows, staring at herself in the mirror from close to and biting her lips hard: then she smothered her face with cream and shook the pink swansdown puff hard and powdered herself: then her face became all yellow. Sometimes she was quite gay in the mornings and wanted to talk to the boys, she asked them about school and their friends and told them things about her time at school: she had a teacher called "Signorina Dirce" and she was an old maid who tried to seem young. Then she put on her coat and picked up her string shopping bag, leant down to kiss the boys and ran out with her scarf wound round her head and her face all perfumed and powdered with yellow powder.

The boys thought it strange to have been born of her. It would have been much less strange to have been born of Granny or Diomira, with their large warm bodies that protected you from fear, that defended you from storms and robbers. It was very strange to think she was their mother, that she had held them for a while in her small womb. Since they learnt that children are in their mother's tummy before being born, they had felt very surprised and also a little ashamed that that womb had once held them. And that she had given them milk from her breasts as well: this was even more unlikely. But now she no longer had small children to feed and cradle, and every day they saw her dash off on her bicycle when the shopping was done, her body jerking away, free and happy. She certainly didn't belong to them: they couldn't count on her. You couldn't ask her anything: there were other mothers, the mothers of their school friends, whom clearly you could ask about all sorts of

things; their friends ran to their mothers when school was over and asked them heaps of things, got their noses blown and their overcoats buttoned, showed their homework and their comics: these mothers were pretty old, with hats or veils or fur collars and they came to talk to the master practically every day: they were people like Granny or like Diomira, large soft imperious bodies of people who didn't make mistakes: people who didn't lose things, who didn't leave their drawers untidy, who didn't come home late at night. But their mother ran off free after the shopping; besides, she was bad at shopping, she got cheated by the butcher and was often given wrong change: she went off and it was impossible to join her where she went, deep down they marvelled at her enormously when they saw her go off: who knows what that office of hers was like, she didn't talk about it much; she had to type and write letters in French and English: who knows, maybe she was pretty good at that.

One day when they were out for a walk with Don Vigliani and with other boys from the youth club, on the way back they saw their mother in a suburban café. She was sitting inside the café; they saw her through the window, and a man was sitting with her. Their mother had laid her tartan scarf on the table and the old crocodile handbag they knew well: the man had a loose light overcoat and a brown moustache and was talking to her and smiling: their mother's face was happy, relaxed and happy, as it never was at home. She was looking at the man and they were holding hands and she didn't see the boys: the boys went on walking beside Don Vigliani who told them all to hurry because they must catch the streetcar: when they were on the streetcar the younger boy moved over to his brother and said: "Did you see Mummy?" and his brother said: "No, I didn't." The younger one laughed softly and said: "Oh yes you did, it was Mummy and there was a man with her." The older boy turned his head away: he was big, nearly thirteen: his younger brother irritated him because he made him feel sorry for him, he couldn't understand why he felt sorry for him but he was sorry for himself as well and he didn't want to think of what he had seen, he wanted to behave as if he had seen nothing.

They said nothing to Granny. In the morning while their mother was dressing the younger boy said: "Yesterday when we were out for a walk with Don Vigliani we saw you and there was a man with you." Their mother jerked round, looking nasty: the black fish on her forehead quivered and met. She said: "But it wasn't me. What an idea. I've got to stay in the office till late in the evening, as you know. Obviously you made a mistake." The older boy then said, in a tired calm voice: "No, it wasn't you. It was someone who looked like you." And both boys realized that the memory must disappear: and they both breathed hard to blow it away.

But the man in the light overcoat once came to the house. He hadn't got his overcoat because it was summer, he wore blue spectacles and a light linen suit, he asked leave to take off his jacket while they had lunch. Granny and Grandpa had gone to Milan to meet some relations and Diomira had gone to her village, so they were alone with their mother. It was then the man came. Lunch was pretty good: their mother had bought nearly everything at the cooked meat shop: there was chicken with chips and this came from the shop: their mother had done the pasta, it was good, only the sauce was a bit burnt. There was wine, too. Their mother was nervous and gay, she wanted to say so much at once: she wanted to talk of the boys to the man and of the man to the boys. The man was called Max and he had been in Africa, he had lots of photographs of Africa and showed them: there was a photograph of a monkey of his, the boys asked him about this monkey a lot; it was so intelligent and so fond of him and had such a funny, pretty way with it when it wanted a sweet. But

he had left it in Africa because it was ill and he was afraid it would die on the steamer. The boys became friendly with this Max. He promised to take them to the cinema one day. They showed him their books, they hadn't got many: he asked them if they had read *Saturnino Farandola* and they said no and he said he would give it to them, and *Robinson delle praterie* as well, as it was very fine. After lunch their mother told them to go and play in the recreation ground. They wished they could stay on with Max. They protested a bit but their mother, and Max too, said they must go; then in the evening when they came home Max was no longer there. Their mother hurriedly prepared the supper, coffee with milk and potato salad: they were happy, they wanted to talk about Africa and the monkey, they were extraordinarily happy and couldn't really understand why: and their mother seemed happy too and told them things, about a monkey she had once seen dancing to a little street organ. And then she told them to go to bed and said she was going out for a minute, they mustn't be scared, there was no reason to be; she bent down to kiss them and told them there was no point in telling Granny and Grandpa about Max because they never liked one inviting people home.

So they stayed on their own with their mother for a few days: they ate unusual things because their mother didn't want to cook, ham and jam and coffee with milk and fried things from the cooked meat shop. Then they washed up together. But when Granny and Grandpa came back the boys felt relieved: the tablecloth was on the dining-room table again, and the glasses and everything there should be: Granny was sitting in her rocking chair again, with her soft body and her smell: Grandma couldn't dash off, she was too old and too fat, it was nice having someone who stayed at home and couldn't ever dash away.

The boys said nothing to Granny about Max. They waited for the book *Saturnino Farandola* and waited for Max to take them to the cinema and show them more photographs of the monkey. Once or twice they asked their mother when they'd be going to the cinema with signor Max. But their mother answered harshly that signor Max had left now. The younger boy asked if he'd gone to Africa. Their mother didn't answer. But he thought he must have gone to Africa to fetch the monkey. He imagined that someday or other he would come and fetch them at school, with a black servant and a monkey in his arms. School began again and Aunt Clementina came to stay with them for awhile; she had brought a bag of pears and apples which they put in the oven to cook with marsala and sugar. Their mother was in a very bad temper and quarrelled continually with Grandpa. She came home late and stayed awake smoking. She had got very much thinner and ate nothing. Her face became ever smaller and yellower, she now put black on her eyelashes too, she spat into a little box and picked up the black where she had spat with a brush; she put on masses of powder, Granny tried to wipe it off her face with a handkerchief and she turned her face away. She hardly ever spoke and when she did it seemed an effort, her voice was so weak. One day she came home in the afternoon at about six o'clock: it was strange, usually she came home much later; she locked herself in the bedroom. The younger boy came and knocked because he needed an exercise book: their mother answered angrily from inside that she wanted to sleep and that they were to leave her in peace: the boy explained timidly that he needed the exercise book; then she came to open up and her face was all swollen and wet: the boy realized she was crying, he went back to Granny and said: "Mummy's crying," and Granny and Aunt Clementina talked quietly together for a long time, they spoke of their mother but you couldn't make out what they were saying.

One night their mother didn't come home. Grandpa kept coming to see, barefoot, with his overcoat over his pajamas; Granny came too and the boys slept badly, they could hear Granny and Grandpa walking about the house, opening and shutting the windows. The boys were very frightened. Then in the morning, they rang up from the police station: their mother had been found dead in a hotel, she had taken poison, she had left a letter: Grandpa and Aunt Clementina went along, Granny shrieked, the boys were sent to an old lady on the floor below who said continually: "Heartless, leaving two babes like this." Their mother was brought home. The boys went to see her when they had her laid out on the bed: Diomira had dressed her in her patent leather shoes and the red silk dress from the time she was married: she was small, a small dead doll.

It was strange to see flowers and candles in the same old room. Diomira and Aunt Clementina and Granny were kneeling and praying: they had said she took the poison by mistake, otherwise the priest wouldn't come and bless her, if he knew she had done it on purpose. Diomira told the boys they must kiss her: they were terribly ashamed and kissed her cold cheek one after the other. Then there was the funeral, it took ages, they crossed the entire town and felt very tired, Don Vigliani was there too and a great many children from school and from the youth club. It was cold, and very windy in the cemetery. When they went home again, Granny started crying and bawling at the sight of the bicycle in the passage: because it was really just like seeing her dashing away, with her free body and her scarf flapping in the wind: Don Vigliani said she was now in heaven, perhaps because he didn't know she had done it on purpose, or he knew and pretended not to: but the boys didn't really know if heaven existed, because Grandpa said no, and Granny said yes, and their mother had once said there was no heaven, with little angels and beautiful music, but that the dead went to a place where they were neither well nor ill, and that where you wish for nothing you rest and are wholly at peace.

The boys went to the country for a time, to Aunt Clementina's. Everyone was very kind to them, and kissed and caressed them, and they were very ashamed. They never spoke together of their mother nor of signor Max either; in the attic at Aunt Clementina's they found the book of *Saturnino Farandola* and they read it over and over and found it very fine. But the older boy often thought of his mother, as he had seen her that day in the café with Max holding her hands and with such a relaxed, happy face; he thought then that maybe their mother had taken poison because Max had gone back to Africa for good. The boys played with Aunt Clementina's dog, a fine dog called Bubi, and they learnt to climb trees, as they couldn't do before. They went bathing in the river, too, and it was nice going back to Aunt Clementina's in the evening and doing crosswords all together. The boys were very happy at Aunt Clementina's. Then they went back to Granny's and were very happy. Granny sat in the rocking chair, and wanted to clean their ears with her hairpins. On Sunday they went to the cemetery, Diomira came too, they bought flowers and on the way back stopped at a bar to have hot punch. When they were in the cemetery, at the grave, Granny prayed and cried, but it was very hard to think that the grave and the crosses and the cemetery had anything to do with their mother, who had been cheated by the butcher and dashed off on her bicycle, and smoked, and took wrong turnings, and sobbed at night. The bed was very big for them now and they had a pillow each. They didn't often think of their mother because it hurt them a little and made them ashamed to think of her. Sometimes they tried to remember how she was, each on his own in silence: and they found it harder and harder to reassemble her short curly hair and the fish on her forehead and her lips: she put on a lot of yellow powder, this they remembered quite well; little by little there was a yellow dot, it was impossible to get the shape of her cheeks and face. Besides, they now realized that they had never loved her much, perhaps she too hadn't loved them much, if she had loved them she wouldn't have taken poison, they had heard Diomira and the porter and the lady on the floor below and so many other people say so. The years went by and the boys grew and so many things happened and that face which they had never loved very much disappeared forever.

Translated by Isabel Quigley

Anne Hébert   *Canada/France, b. 1916*

Considered the founder of modern Quebec poetry, Anne Hébert is claimed by francophone Canada and by France, where she has lived since 1954. Her decision to exile herself is tied to the "difficulty in being and living in this corner of the world which is ours and where man is neither master of himself nor of his land, his language, his religion, his most innate gifts;" it more or less coincides with a decision to be silent about her private life (biographers have little to say about her last thirty years), and a turn in Hébert's work to prose and a highly critical view of French-Canadian society, particularly the sterility of the *haute bourgeoisie* out of which Hébert herself had come. Like Doris Lessing, among others, Hébert has been freed to write about her homeland by achieving a critical distance from it.

Born in a small village just outside Quebec, Hébert was a sickly child who received little formal education; nonetheless, she grew up among the important figures of her day as the daughter of the respected critic Maurice Hébert and the cousin of Hector de Saint-Denys-Garneau, arguably one of the most significant poet-diarists of the modern Francophone literary period. Both in his life and work, and by his premature death in 1943, he exerted the single most important personal and literary influence on Hébert. Together with his work, Hébert's poetry influenced the group known as the *Hexagone* poets, who began writing in the 1950s.

Hébert's poetry may be grouped into two categories: the earliest and middle works, *Les songes en équilibre* (Dreams in Equilibrium, 1942) and *Le tombeau des rois* (*The Tomb of the Kings*, 1953) represent a tragic, existentialist vision; *Mystère de la parole* (*The Mystery of the Word*, 1960) celebrates life and the physical world. *Mystery* mirrors *The Tomb of Kings* from which the first two poems come: the former is an inversion of the latter in theme, structure, and rhythm.

While Hébert won early critical acclaim with her poetry, she first achieved fame as a playwright and popular success with her novels and short stories. The novella *Le Torrent* marked her debut as a prose artist in 1950: apparently because of its violence and perhaps more because of its violent condemnation of Francophone culture, Hébert was unable to find a Canadian publisher. Printed in France, it won the first of many prizes Hébert was to receive, in this instance, from the Royal Academy of Belgium. The novella has justly been called the first true classic of contemporary French-Canadian literature. It was followed by her first novel, *Les chambres de bois* (*The Silent Rooms*, 1958); *Kamouraska* (1970), which was made into a feature film by Claude Jutra; *Les enfants du Sabbat* (*Children of the Black Sabbath*, 1975); *Héloïse* (1980); and most recently, *Les fous de Bassan* (translated as *In the Shadow of the Wind*, 1982), a winner of France's Prix Femina. Her most recent play, written for French radio, was published and translated the same year: *Ile de la demoiselle* (*Maiden Island*, 1979).

Hébert's prose is marked by a highly poetic use of imagery and symbolism; this feature combines with more mundane details in the novels. *Kamouraska*, for example, is based on a historical incident of 1834–1838 involving a man's murder of his lover's husband. *Children of the Black Sabbath*, a story of demonic possession, evokes Quebec society of the 1930s and 1940s. Thus the fiction is the meeting place of history and myth; there, her protagonists confront memories, deeply buried emotions, and the past selves that exert a stranglehold over their current lives. These forces either are integrated into the present or they overwhelm and destroy the characters. The elemental energies thus unleashed ally Hébert's work with other Gothic fiction. It is a Gothic vision distinguished by its mordant social satire.

In one exemplary story, "Un grand mariage," ("A Grand Marriage"), the Lower Town protagonist achieves commercial success and puts the establishment in his debt—for which he exacts one of its daughters in marriage. At the same time, his former Métis love, Délia, returns to "haunt" his house, a maidservant by day and Augustin's lover by night. Illicit and apparently secret, the relationship is exposed for all the community to "read," when Délia, with the last vestige of pride remaining to her, refuses to take communion. From a feminist perspective then, Hébert has created a francophone version of "the madwoman in the attic," converting Délia into a symbol that is a critique of both the sexual and the social repression within society.

CASTLE-LIFE
Vie de Château

This is our ancestors' castle
Without table nor fire
Nor dust nor rug.

The perverse charm of these places
Lies entirely in polished mirrors.

The one occupation possible here
Consists in admiring one's self night and day.

Cast your reflection on stubborn fountains
Your most lasting image without shadow or
                                    color.

See, these mirrors are deep
Like cupboards
Always some corpse lies there under the
                                    silvering
And to cover your reflection at once
Sticks to you like a sea-weed.

It adjusts itself to you, slender and naked,
And counterfeits love in a slow, bitter thrill.
                    Translated by Fred Cogswell

THERE IS SOME ONE, TO BE SURE
Il y a certainement quelqu' un

There is some one, to be sure
Who slaughtered me
Then departed
On tip-toe without
Disrupting his perfect dance

Who forgot to bed me
Who left me standing
And completely tied up
On the rod
My heart in its ancient casket
My pupils the purest
Reflections of water

Who forgot to erase the world's beauty
Around me
Who forgot to close my avid eyes
Allowing thereby my lost passion
                    Translated by Fred Cogswell

EVE
Eve

Queen and undoubted lady crucified
at the farthest city's gates

Tawny owl with nailed wings, disjointed
broken and your wing span pressed down

Sour flesh of green apples, fine juicy orchard,
behold you ruined, flapping in the wind
like a tattered flag

Horny beak, rapacious nose, we will make
you into good-luck charms for pestilent days

We will wear you against death and against
                                    wrath,
scapulars of feathers and shattered bones

Recumbent woman, great anthill under the
                                    larch,
ancient earth riddled by lovers

We invoke you, our first womb, dawn's delicate
face passing between man's ribs
the fierce gates of day

See your husbands and sons rotting every which
                                    way
between your thighs, under a single curse

Mother of Christ, remember your latest-born
daughters, who have neither name nor history,
broken to pieces at birth between two huge
                                    stones

Source of tears and weeping, what live jewels
did you will us for our honor and our care.

Anguish and love, mourning and joy are
                                    celebrated
as equal feasts engraved in all their fullness,
like profound landscapes.

Blind mother, tell us of birth and death
and the brave journey between two savage
                                    glooms,
the world's two poles, the day's axes

Tell us of the tree's evil and its magic,
speak of the garden, God naked and bright,
                                    and sin
as wildly desired as the noon-day shade
                    (continued)

Speak to us of faultless love and the first man
stripped between your arms
Remember your primal passion crowned in the
                                                morning
and like a calmed destiny our face renew

War spreads its ways of terror,
and tied by the same secrets
horror and death and holding hands, the four
                                                elements
armored in flash and thunder stand up like
                                                fierce
offended gods

Sweetness under the iron burns to the bone
its cry transfixes guilt and innocence
pinned by a single sword

Behold us, recognize us, fix on us
Your eyeless gaze, think how our hands play
                                                with chance
as they spin mystery in the evening
like rough wool

The child at our breast is cooling, but man
                                                smells
of burnt bread, and our midday closes over us
like seamless water

From the depths of this unexpected peace
we summon you, Eve, as if we stood upright
supported only by our justified hearts

May your memory break in the sun, and find
                                                again
on your face, at the risk of waking a forgotten
                                                crime,
the shadow of grace like a black beam.

Translated by Fred Cogswell

Toyo Suyemoto   *US, b. 1916*

Toyo Suyemoto Kawakami was one of nine children born into a bilingual family in
California. Her father, an artist, and her mother, a poet, were great influences on
Suyemoto, as she is known. She earned a B.A. from the University of California,
Berkeley, in 1937 and became part of a group of Nisei (second-generation
Japanese) writers who encouraged her to write poetry. During the forced evacua-
tion and internment of Japanese in the United States during World War II,
Suyemoto and her family were moved to the Tanforan Race Track in San Bruno,
California, in 1942, and then to a permanent camp at Topaz, Utah. The family was
interned for three and a half years. In the late 1950s, Suyemoto was selected to
participate in poetry workshops with Randall Jarrell and Karl Shapiro at the
University of Cincinnati. Her poems, essays, and stories appeared in several anthologies and in small West Coast and Hawaiian magazines, including bilingual
Japanese periodicals, and in national literary journals. Recently retired from the
Ohio State University Library system, Suyemoto is divorced, the mother of one
son, and lives in Columbus, Ohio.

English critic David Daiches has written of Suyemoto's poetry: "It is a pleasure to come across a talent both so controlled and so genuine, a use of language at
once delicate and firm." Suyemoto prefers to write precisely compressed formal
verse in the European and Japanese traditions: the double quatrain, the sonnet, the
rondeau, the haiku (or hokku), the tanka, which we have seen in the work of
Yosano Akiko. She cites as influences the American Emily Dickinson, the German

Rainer Maria Rilke, and the Japanese Issa and Basho. Suyemoto continues to write, and "to reflect the change of the seasons and to try to discover symbolic significance in the world about me." Her poems are one reflection of the multi-ethnic strains contributing to American English literature.

Eric Mendelsohn

AFTERTASTE

The honey-mellow taste of summer
Is gone from sunlight, thinned
To lukewarm trickle in the late
October afternoon.

And yet an aftertaste lingers on
The tongue the cool, sharp wind
Of autumn cannot rinse away
Completely, or too soon.

FRAGILITY

Cast no words upon this silence yet
While its slight structure stays intact,
Daring the brash and curious
To half-considered act.

Eggshell could not be more frangible,
Nor feather rest more heavily
Where whisper with a breath may crack
This stillness kept by me.

Once this breaks, I would be lost, deprived
Of frugal comfort that is mine:
Let caution weigh your thought, and then
No words, but some mute sign.

HOKKU

Triangulated,
Dimensions of my world are
Heaven, man and earth.

HOKKU

Stillness of summer—
The eye of the sunflower
Fixed upon the sun.

TANKA

Could words fall like snow,
Perfect in form and meaning,
My thought would whiten
In multiples of pure praise
The very air about you.

HOKKU

A small thing to give,
But I give you the silence
Of moonlight on snow.

HOKKU

The bright moon followed,
But my shadow walked ahead:
I hurried between.

EGG AND STONE

The egg, beside a stone,
Bears no comparison:
The wonderment of each
Is more than shape or touch.

The fragile shelters life,
The hard once grew a leaf,
Compelling mind to know
Far more than eyes can see.

Wei Junyi (Wei Chün-i)   *China, b. 1916*

Wei Junyi was born in Beijing in October 26, 1916. Her father was a professor who had taken part in Sun Yatsen's early revolutionary activities and believed in the equality of women. As a result, Wei Junyi received a good education. Her studies at Qinghua University were interrupted by the outbreak of war with Japan: in 1937, at the age of 21, she joined the revolutionary army in the conviction that the Kuomintang government would never oppose the Japanese army. Thereafter, Wei embarked on three simultaneous careers, including raising her three children.

She began her editorial career working on the periodical *Zhongguo Qingnian* (Chinese Youth) from 1939 to 1946 in Yan'an. Then she served as an editor-reporter in other liberated areas of the north, working both in newspapers and radio. She was in Hebei province preparing the new edition of Chinese Youth when China was liberated, and she soon became chief editor of the magazine. In 1960, she became vice president and associate chief editor of Renmin Wenxue Chuban She, the People's Literature Publishing House.

"Sange Pengyou" ("Three Friends") launched the writing career of Wei Junyi: written, in 1946, the famous story was first published in 1949 in *Renmin Ribao* (The People's Daily), and subsequently included in *Renmin Xiaoshuo Congshu*, (The People's Fiction Series) in the early 1950s, an extensive collection from the liberated areas during the war years. Later it was incorporated into the collection of short stories entitled *Nüren ji* (Women). Early in the story it is suggested that the protagonist's life parallels China's development as a newly emergent Communist state, sloughing off the inequalities—and prerogatives—of an older feudalism. More specifically, it makes use of a socialist realist style that will model the revolutionary consciousness that is to accompany the changed social reality, particularly among the intellectuals sent to work among the peasantry. By showing the disparities between the inner and outer responses of old Wu, Wei honestly reflects the difficulties of intellectuals in adjusting to a situation in which they are no longer the vanguard.

Wei Junyi's other major works include a novel, *Mu Yu Zi* (Mother and Son), the novella collections *Lao Ganbu Biezhuan* (More on the Life of the Old Cadre) and *Guxing Qinren* (The Dear Ones Back Home), essays collected in *Guguo Qing* (A Passion for the Native Land), *Sishui Liu Nian* (How Time Flies), *Lao Caifeng Shouji* (Sketches by an Old Dressmaker), *Qianjinde Jiaoji* (Footprints of Progress), and a reportage collection entitled *Beifangde Hong Xing* (Red Star in the North). Wei recently won a national prize for her novella *Xili* (Baptism).

During the Cultural Revolution, Wei Junyi found herself subject to criticism and then Huifu Mingyu, "rehabilitation." She was sent for three and a half years of manual labor at a cadre re-education "school" (Wu Xi Ganxiao) in Hebei. At the end of this period, Wei was able to return to her work. Although a successful professional woman, she nonetheless sees a long road ahead before women achieve equality in China. At the time of this book's publication, she was recovering from a cerebral hemorrhage.

Shu-ying Tsau

THREE FRIENDS
(San'ge Pengyou)

Dear old friend, did you just arrive here from Beijing? It's been eight years since we parted; had we bumped into each other on the streets, we wouldn't have recognized one another. Don't be surprised, just look at me, don't you think I look like a Beijing street cleaner?

You asked about the changes in my life over the past ten years, didn't you? It seems as long as Chinese history—I don't know where to begin.

Don't overdo it in praising us cadres here in the liberated area, because that makes me blush. Weren't we all the same in the past? Everyone has changed one step at a time. Learn from me? I'm not that great. Good teachers and helpful friends? I can't tell you anything about great men and astonishing heroism. My friends are ordinary people and their changes are ordinary too. Well, let me tell you an anecdote that comes to mind.

In 1943 when I was first assigned to a village to organize mutual-aid teams, I stayed at Liu Jinkuan's house. Liu had recently been commended as a model peasant in Liu Village. I had three friends in this village and the three were different: an intellectual, one of the gentry, and a peasant.

First let me tell you about my peasant friend, the landlord of the house where I stayed, Liu Jinkuan. Friendship naturally was not the word to describe my experience at first. Living there I felt like the Monk Tripitaka on his pilgrimage to the Western Paradise for Buddhist scriptures—in order to succeed, I had to grit my teeth and endure eighty-one different kinds of suffering and privation.[1] I racked my brains trying to become one of them in everyday life so they would not treat me like a stranger. Besides my job, I went to the hills with them every day, conscientiously, to learn about different kinds of millet: the spring sowing, the autumn variety, the selected strain....For months I didn't shave after I got

there. As soon as Liu's wife went back to her parents' home, I moved to his K'ang[2] to sleep next to him. When there was no forage left for his mules, I helped with cutting more; when the yard got dirty I swept it. In packing to come to this village I deliberately did not include any literature. Once here I didn't even dare to brush my teeth any more when I discovered every day the astonished look in the eyes of Liu's mother.

But you can't say that I lived there like an exile. All day long, I was chatting and laughing along with them too. When old Mrs Liu's chickens hatched, I came running and laughing with the first little chick in my hands to show them. When the mule suddenly ate a lot more, I was also so excited that I talked about it with them all evening long. There was a period when even I myself almost believed that I had genuinely changed. But no. Digging the earth or carrying night soil on my shoulders were fine with me, for I only had to grit my teeth to get through it. The one thing, however, about which I could not fool myself, was the continued existence of a private miniature space in my heart. It expanded once I put down the hoe and stopped work, until it grew into a true desolation. Any outside stimulus would be sure to make it worse. I was like a pupil who had received an "A" by using a substitute—if the examination were held right in front of the teacher I would be exposed.

Once, for example, I received a letter from one of my girlfriends living far away. In the letter she said that the sentiment in Chengdu was somewhat like that of Beijing, one could hear the cries of the flower peddlers in the long alleys, and she asked: "How about your life out there?" Within a few days after I received this letter, my feeling of loneliness reached its peak.

One evening I was squatting in the family courtyard next to the stone trough, gazing through the gathering haze at the tip of the tree outside the wall, trying to listen—the stone roller in the yard creaked heavily as old Mrs. Liu, with a loop of thick hemp rope around her shoulder, pushed it, crushing the black soya beans and pressing them into the shape of old coins. Then Liu Jinkuan's wife, standing in the center of the yard, bellowed "Er lao lao lao lao lao...," and immediately a huge black sow and her litter dashed to the stone trough beside me to eat. The sow grunted and the piglets squealed. Comparing the environment I was in with what the letter described, I felt a chill. I couldn't help heaving a sigh. Liu Jinkuan was walking towards me just then and heard my sigh of course. "What are you worrying about, old Wu?" he said. "Ah, must be feeling bad about us losing the piglet again." Then he started telling me how his wife had found it covered with night soil in the latrine that afternoon and he did not know if it would come to or not. Both Liu's wife and mother also joined the discussion, which became the sole topic of the whole evening, at dinner as well as at work. I knew that I should have taken part, but once the lonely feeling came I could never shake it. It turned into a millstone weighing my heart down. I ate in silence and not much either. After putting down my rice bowl, I walked, with my hands clasped behind my back to the center of the yard. Under this sudden attack of loneliness, I forgot everything. One idea was lodged in my mind: "Even Tripitaka needed relaxation on his pilgrimage. I don't have excessive desire but wouldn't it be nice if I could just go somewhere to drive away my cares!" As luck would have it, the village head popped into the courtyard to tell me that the prefectural commissioner's office had sent another intellectual cadre to Liu Village today.

That person was Luo Ping, a specialist in economics. I had met him before in the city but I was not well acquainted with him. To tell you the truth, I detested his ostensibly merry but actually indifferent and perfunctory atti-

tude towards work. Yet—and I didn't know why—as soon as I heard he was coming I got as excited as if, on a desert island, I had suddenly met my family and friends or a long lost soul mate. I sprang up and ran right to the entrance of the village to welcome him. I carried his bag, shouldered his luggage, and hand in hand, we entered the village. Then I got him something to eat and drink and some water so he could wash his feet. That same night I went to the village co-op to keep him company and stayed overnight asking him about this and that, about life in the city. I told him all that I knew about Liu Village, the cadres, the model laborers, the local customs and habits and even about my personal life. He told me about the newly opened art galleries, the new foreigners and so-and-so's lovers' squabbles, etc., things familiar to me, which I found pleasing as if only these things belonged to my own world. Time flew by without my noticing it; when we finally closed our eyes, the cocks were already crowing.

I was very excited talking with him for my mind was carefree. But after I closed my eyes, went half asleep, suddenly a notion leaped to my mind: the scene that night reminded me of one time in 1937 when I was a refugee in Hankou; I dimly recall a similar feeling I had on that occasion—Do you still remember, my friend, what I told you at a movie? I said, "Once I enter the theater—light blue walls all around me, lights off, screen flashing, tuneful soothing jazz in the air—I feel so accustomed to it, so much at home that I imagine I'm free of the sweltering hot, alien Hankou and back in some familiar, exquisite, serene world." These words resurfaced at midnight in Liu Village. I suddenly felt as if someone were standing in a dark corner, making gestures, laughing at me: "Haha! Oho! Here we go again, you haven't changed at all!" I felt I simply had no place to hide from his mockery.

Was it true that I hadn't changed at all?— True enough! Now that my loneliness was gone, and sleeping in an unfamiliar place, I thought of Liu Jinkuan's family. How worried they must have been. Feeling like a deserter, I suffered from insomnia at the co-op. Early that morning I went back to Liu's family with a guilty conscience. That day I labored extraordinarily hard for them.

I went with Liu Jinkuan's mutual-aid team up to the mountains to plant millet. Liu Jinkai and Wang Xiangru were partners, and Liu Jinkuan and I were a team. He ploughed and I filled the furrows with night soil and seeds behind him.

The gentle breeze that follows the Grain Rains wafted through the mountains. The peaks looked like great waves lifted by the wind. Next to the millet field the fresh green wheat seedlings, a few inches high by now, were forming ripples in the breeze. I inhaled deeply to fill my lungs with the boundless fresh air and then exhaled slowly. Hearing me, Liu Jinkuan turned around: "What's the matter with you, old Wu? Why did you sigh?" I answered, "Nothing. I find the fields beautiful, the scenery pleasing!" He said, "Right you are! There's enough moisture in the soil this year. Look at that stretch of wheat field that covers the mountain with its green, how full and neat! I guarantee you'll get good noodles out of this." I too quickly started talking about crops. He tilled the land deep; the turned moist black soil almost buried my feet. It seemed that pockets of fragrance in the rich warm soil were opened, pleasing to the sense of smell. When the sun was high above, I sweated. The uneasy feeling I had from the morning vanished gradually. I asked myself, "Am I not quite happy in the world of red sun and green wheat fields? This is my world too. Why do I have to yearn for the world of light blue walls? Why can't I treat Liu Jinkuan as my close friend? Why...."

I sweated and thought while we were ploughing faster and faster; we drew ahead of Wang Xiangru and Liu Jinkai in no time. I overheard them talking about how the acreage Liu Jinkuan reported owning was the true figure while Chen Faxing lied about his, and was a double-dealer as well when it came to rent reduction.

As if something had just dawned on him, Liu Jinkuan straightened up and said aloud, "Who doesn't know that? He took over the eighteen acres his old man rented from the Huangs but now he's reported it as thirteen acres. Does he want to fool the villagers or Old Wu? Look at Old Wu who gets up early, goes to bed late, works hard with us in the fields. Why? Because he cares about us and he wants us to have a good life. Last night because a piglet of ours fell into the cesspool old Wu was so worried that he couldn't even eat. Old Wu cares for us more than our old folks or our blood brothers do."

My face suddenly felt hot. What he said hit me hard for I was full of remorse over what I had done. As you know even without me telling you, the purpose of my going down to the village was to educate them. Even though Liu was with me all the time—living under the same roof, eating from the same pot—in my mind he was simply the object of my work. He was one of the many objects like one of the stalks of sorghum that covered the mountains. But his attitude toward me was exactly opposite. He really treated me as a close friend, or even better than a close friend.

When I first arrived in the village, Liu's mother told me that he was forty-six years old that year, and his family worked thirty-eight acres counting rented land along with his own. But Liu himself told me later that he was in fact thirty-seven years old, and the land his family worked was eighteen acres more than she had said. His mother lied to me, he said, because she was very backward: she believed rumors; she was afraid her son would be recruited to work for others; she regarded Fourth Lord Huang, the landlord, as her benefactor so she did not want to get a rent reduction from him. Besides this, I also found out about humiliations he had suffered—once he was slapped by Lord Huang's nineteen-year-old concubine, the young lord had had a horse-ride on his back . . . and so on. He always struck me as someone with a strong sense of self-respect, so I don't think it was easy for him to talk about these things, yet he told me, someone with an absolutely different background who had been a complete stranger until a month ago. He made me feel uneasy. Especially the night I went to see Luo Ping in order to escape my loneliness followed by Liu's praise on the mountains the next day—I found what he said hurt me more than criticism. The incident made me reflect on my relation with Liu Jinkuan. Suppose my mother were unwilling to have her rent reduced or secretly blamed the revolution, could I have told the truth to a person like Liu Jinkuan?—Impossible! It was hard to imagine. I had always considered myself a most honest person who would rather be at a disadvantage than take advantage of others. But now, in front of Liu, I felt as if I were the ungrateful man described in popular novels—I looked down on my sworn brother who had entrusted his daughter and son to my care, and went out of my way to claim kinship with high officials in ancient China.

Standing behind him I saw a giant distinct silhouette towering aloft on a mountain slope with the colorful flowering earth beneath and a sunny blue sky above. He looked like a huge pillar separating heaven and earth. In comparison with him, I felt miniscule.

That morning's experience made me serious about becoming Liu's real friend, enjoying his company and kissing loneliness good-bye. As it turned out soon after that I began feeling much more relaxed in Liu Village. My shoulders no longer seemed to be heavily burdened when I was eating, talking, washing my face, and brushing my teeth. You know, a philanthropist who supplies the soup lines for the poor can never be a true friend of the poor who receive his charity, in my opinion. I began to feel happy in Liu Village when I started to feel I was one of the villagers.

I visited Luo Ping again, though. Yet, because of all the time I'd spent with Liu, the gossip about foreigners and other people's marital crises seemed alien to me. At the same time, Luo Ping's "ooh ah, oh wow" style of dealing with people gave me the creeps. I preferred to discuss my problems, no matter whether in my work or personal life, with Liu, who always tried to help me; in dealing with Luo Ping I had to beat around the bush. In Liu's company, I felt the sparkle return to my eyes, and I grew bolder than before. With Liu backing me, I finally was able to get even with the gentry friend.

Now it is time to talk about this gentry friend of mine. He was Liu's landlord, fourth son of the Huang family, named Huang Zonggu. He lived in Liu Village but I got to know him years ago when I attended a governmental affairs meeting. To tell you the truth, whenever I met him in the past I felt somewhat uneasy because this guy had a well-known habit of testing others' knowledge. All of us cadres had experienced this: Huang did not miss a single opportunity to pour out his repertoire of ancient Chinese history and classic poetry. This was the reason why a lot of county cadres were afraid of seeing him. Huang and a few of the older gentry organized a poetry society and because of it they were called "The Culture Club." Thanks to my parents' support I had had a few years of schooling, so I managed to cope with some of the questions and answers. Huang deliberately treated me as his close friend, talking with me in such terms as "we educated ones," "people like us," and often showed his own poems to me and asked for criticism from me. He even wanted me to compose a few poems with him in antiphonal style.[3] You have a fair idea of my knowledge of the classics. All I knew was a few literature textbooks from school and the few poems I translated from classical into modern Chinese for fun. Naturally I was afraid to let the cat out of the bag and become his laughing-stock. In fact, Huang had no interest in my communist ideas, and my dozen years of capitalist education didn't help me appreciate his dated bookish poetic pursuits. Yet the county comrades all said, "Thanks to Wu we can hold our heads up. Otherwise our united front task force would suffer setbacks." I was secretly somewhat pleased to hear the compliment.

Having been sent to Liu Village I knew well enough that I was involved in work at the grassroots level, so I should be close to the peasants but not to the landlords. However I felt it imperative to visit Huang because, like an entertainer on the road, wherever you go you must pay a polite visit to local VIPs, only then can you expect to be successful. I was well received by Huang. I did not realize what a double dealer he was until Liu and I became friends. Huang was a different person in front of county cadres, Liu, and his neighbors. The odd times, when I bumped into him somewhere in the village, he was polite and friendly, often inviting me to his house to compose poems for new peach blossoms. As usual I still had the chills whenever I heard him talking about poems and essays.

Our relationship went on like this till the rent investigation launched by the county demanding that landlords refund the overcharge from last fall's rents. One day Liu, as the head of the Rent Reduction Committee in Liu Village, led tenants with burlap and cotton sacks into Huang's courtyard. That afternoon I rushed to Huang's where the patio—over fifty square feet of black flagstone in the courtyard—was jammed with peasants; even the terrazzo veranda was crowded with them squatting there. The racket could be heard even in the streets.

The three sets of gates from the entrance to the courtyard were all wide open and, unprecedented, there were no vicious dogs to bite you nor were there maids to wait on you. I tiptoed in and saw Huang standing in the middle of the steps with the usual meter-long white copper tobacco pipe in his hands. The only difference was his bony yellow face was swollen, its color verging on a shiny reddish purple like that of his long satin gown. Seeing him stutter with his mouth open made me feel good. I thought of hiding behind people's backs to observe him a little longer but I had

barely found a place before Huang spotted me. His thin eyes glistened as if he had found a savior. He dashed down the steps, approaching me with a loud "Dear Wu, dear Wu, dear comrade Wu!" and he stretched out his hand towards me. I could not shrink back and I had to nod to him and push my way forward toward him. With such a scene unfolding the peasant crowd focused their eyes on us two. People stopped shouting, the courtyard suddenly became quiet and they made way for us.

Huang was grinning peculiarly from ear to ear as he led me to the veranda calling aloud towards the main rooms, the wings and every corner of the yard, "Maid! Chunzi! Maid! We have company! Serve us some tea, will you!" His voice was everywhere. Then he turned around, his face beaming: "I am pleased to see you here, I am really pleased to see you here. I've just done something that I'd love to have your advice on. We haven't chatted for quite a while...."

Talking and smiling like this he seemed oblivious of the existence of the peasant crowd. But could I possibly ignore those hundred pairs of familiar eyes? I clearly sensed that I was the topic of muttered exchanges in the crowd. Liu was standing right at the steps leading to the veranda. As I came close he greeted me "Hi, Wu!" Before I was able to strike up a conversation with him, Huang lifted the felt curtain at the entrance to the living room and bent in my direction while repeating, "Dear Wu, dear Wu!" urging me in to sit. When I refused to go in, he brought a stool out to the edge of the veranda as nonchalant as if we were old buddies.

"Outsiders do not understand this, my dear Wu, but you do! I was born carefree and lazy and never interfere with household affairs, ah, I don't enjoy acquiring land and houses. My family are all muddleheaded and don't know anything about laws. Ah, well, you and I are close friends, naturally you can forgive...."

I was in a rage at being needled like this. His insinuations were obviously meant to undermine my job there. I simply waved my hand to cut him off. But like diarrhea of the mouth or an old vaudevillian's rehearsal of his lines the words went on without a break. Luckily Liu came to my rescue!

Liu suddenly stepped forward interrupting Huang, but saying in a serious voice to me, "Old Wu! why are you and I here?" I suddenly blushed and quickly leaped up from Huang's stool. This was it! Liu Jinkai, Wang Xiangru, and several of their friends surged over the edge of the veranda while the crowd in the yard became restless. Voices were heard—"My stomach is empty!" "Don't play cute"—and quite a few kids wormed in between the adults' legs shouting, "Divide the grain! Divide the grain!" Others shouted, "Take off snow pants, use them as sacks, let's divide the grain now today!"

The Huang family maid bringing two cups of tea on a fine china serving tray was just emerging from the living room when she saw this scene and quickly shrank back behind the felt curtain. I turned around swiftly and stood in front of Liu's group and heard Liu saying, "Let's settle the account with him." I said, "Good!" At this Huang started to get a little nervous, yet he still came over to grab my hand and said "Please do me a favor...."

I lifted my head and saw, above the forced smile, the beady eyes in his bony yellowish face scanning the yard in panic. I suddenly felt that this guy's attempt to use me to pull strings in front of this yard full of peasants was a great insult to me. The old timidity I felt whenever I bumped into him on the street suddenly vanished like snow melting in the spring sun. My head became crystal clear—phooey, why should I be afraid of you? Who do you think you are? You're just a die-hard landlord and illegal usurer! I waved him aside with my hand.

There is no need to tell you what followed after that: Liu's rent reduction movement naturally won the day. Huang wrote a poem because of this incident saying that he collected a little more rent by mistake because like the

Seven Sages of the Bamboo Grove, he was not involved in production.[4] The county cadres and I almost laughed our heads off reading it.

I am positive you know by now who my good teacher and helpful friend is. I think Liu's company was really more beneficial than ten years of schooling! You outsiders always love to exaggerate the achievement of us cadres who wield our pens in the liberated areas, saying that we "have been tempered into steel." Now perhaps you know better. Like anyone else, we had plenty of nostalgia, "dreams," and "loneliness".... What a shame, that I often couldn't distinguish who my friends were and kept forgetting where my feet should have been planted. But with Liu next to me, all such stale stuff was peeled off layer after layer. If you ask about the change in me, this can be considered the change.

Perhaps you're not satisfied? But I told you to begin with that I couldn't offer you any novel tales. This is just an ordinary story that happens eveywhere in our area.

Translated by Shu-ying Tsau

NOTES

1. *Tripitaka*: the sobriquet of Hsuan-tsang (602–664), a Chinese Buddhist monk who undertook a perilous journey to India (629–633) to study the sacred texts before returning to China in 645; his own account of this pilgrimage forms the basis of China's greatest comic novel *Hsi-yu chi* (Record of a Journey to the West; translated as *Monkey*) by Wu Ch'eng-en (1500–ca. 1582), a religious picaresque work that offers a scathing satire of society and Chinese bureaucracy.

2. A structure running along the perimeter of a room and used for daytime seating and for sleeping at night.

3. Poetry in which one person composes stanzas in response to another.

4. *Seven Sages of the Bamboo Grove*: Chinese Chu-Lin Ch'I Hsien, a group of free-thinking Chinese scholars and poets of the mid-third century who banded together to escape from the hypocrisy and corrupt politics of the short-lived Wei-dynasty (220–264) court. Their poems and essays criticize palace life and depict the hardships of country life. Their Taoist-oriented *ch'ing-t'an* ("pure conversation") movement served as a model for later Chinese writers living in troubled times.

Gwendolyn Brooks   *US, b. 1917*

Gwendolyn Brooks was one of the few black poets to achieve general recognition before the 1960s. She won grants from the American Academy of Arts and Letters, two Guggenheim Fellowships, and the first Pulitzer Prize awarded a black artist. She was awarded numerous honorary degrees and was Distinguished Professor of the Arts at the City College of New York. Born in Kansas, Brooks was raised and educated in Chicago. She graduated in 1936 from Wilson Junior College and lived in Chicago with her husband, writer Henry Blakely, and their two children. Succeeding Carl Sandburg in 1968 as the official poet laureate of Illinois, she is also known unofficially, but probably more accurately, as the poet laureate of Chicago. Much of Brooks' poetry, even her highly formal verse, always spoke in ghetto vernacular; in the late 1960s Brooks went further and aligned herself with the surge of black militancy: "I—who have 'gone the gamut' from an almost angry rejection of my dark skin by some of my brainwashed brothers and sisters to a surprized queenhood in the new black sun—am qualified to enter at least the kindergarten of new consciousness now—new consciousness and trudge-toward-progress." Brooks had been known as a poet who "rose" above her blackness; now, to the dismay of some critics, Brooks joined what she called the Black Arts Movement. In tribute to Brooks' support, a group of younger black poets published *To Gwen with Love* (1971), a volume of poems, stories, and essays.

The poems in Brooks' first volume, *A Street in Bronzeville* (1945), tell of the struggles of poor people for spiritual health in the World War II era. Brooks ranges widely through verse forms. Some poems follow from ballad traditions. In others, Brooks flavors the formal diction of Petrarchian sonnets with borrowings from Chicago vernacular. Such poems as the "Ballad of Pearl May Lee," the song of a woman whose man has been seduced by a white woman and then lynched for rape, point to Brooks' future political concerns.

The success of the Pulitzer Prize-winning *Annie Allen* (1949) brought Brooks access to white publications and some financial success. Focused almost novelistically on the coming of age of a single women, *Annie Allen* continues Brooks's experiments with language and form, alluding to but not quite working out the relations between the social responsibilities of the artist and the demands art makes for the sake of art. It contains a section called "The Anniad," a technically demanding miniature epic. Brooks' next book, *Maud Martha* (1953), is her only foray into prose fiction—a loosely connected series of vignettes that again tell the story of a young black girl's coming of age, a process complicated by the soul-deforming pressures of racism.

In her fifth book, *The Bean Eaters* (1960), Brooks steps up the political tempo. "A Bronzeville Mother Loiters in Mississippi. Meanwhile, a Mississippi Mother Burns Bacon" concerns the famous and tragic case of Emmett Till, a 14-year-old black from Chicago who, visiting relatives in Mississippi, was lynched in 1955 for allegedly making advances to a white woman. Another poem, "The Ballad of Rudolph Reed," tells of a black man who moves his family into a white neighborhood—and pays with his life: "His neighbors gathered and kicked his corpse. 'Nigger—' his neighbors said."

In the Mecca (1968), considered by some critics Brooks's breakthrough to overtly political verse, renders in blank verse, free verse, couplets, ballads, sonnets, and other forms the disenchantment and militancy of black America in the 1960s. It includes a three-part poem about the Blackstone Rangers, a long-lived Chicago street gang, for whom Brooks had given writing workshops: "There they are. / Thirty at the corner. / Black, raw, ready. / Sores in the city / that do not want to heal."

The epigraph to the title poem of *Riot* (1968), a volume that begins Brooks' association with the most important black publishing company Broadsides Press, is from Martin Luther King: "A riot is the language of the unheard." The volume is the source of the last selection. *Riot* was followed by *Family Pictures* (1970), *The World of Gwendolyn Brooks* (1971), and Brooks's autobiography, *Report From Part One* (1972), among others. One could say of Brooks that her poetry, too, is written in the language of the unheard.

Eric Mendelsohn

A BRONZEVILLE MOTHER LOITERS IN MISSISSIPPI. MEANWHILE, A MISSISSIPPI MOTHER BURNS BACON

From the first it had been like a
Ballad. It had the beat inevitable, It had the
                                                    blood.
A wildness cut up, and tied in little bunches,
Like the four-line stanzas of the ballads she
                                    had never quite
Understood—the ballads they had set her to,
                                    in school.

Herself: the milk-white maid, the "maid mild"
Of the ballad. Pursued
By the Dark Villain. Rescued by the Fine
                                                    Prince.
The Happiness-Ever-After.
That was worth anything.
It was good to be a "maid mild."
That made the breath go fast.

Her bacon burned. She
Hastened to hide it in the step-on can, and
Drew more strips from the meat case. The eggs
                                    and sour-milk biscuits
Did well. She set out a jar
Of her new quince preserve.

. . .But there was a something about the matter
                            of the Dark Villain.
He should have been older, perhaps.

The hacking down of a villain was more fun to
                                                    think about
When his menace possessed undisputed breadth,
                                                    undisputed height,
And a harsh kind of vice.
And best of all, when his history was cluttered
With the bones of many eaten knights and
                                                    princesses.

The fun was disturbed, then all but nullified
When the Dark Villain was a blackish child
Of fourteen, with eyes still too young to be
                                                    dirty,
And a mouth too young to have lost every
                                                    reminder
Of its infant softness.

That boy must have been surprised! For
These were grown-ups. Grown-ups were
                                    supposed to be wise.
And the Fine Prince—and that other—so tall,
                                    so broad, so
Grown! Perhaps the boy had never guessed
That the trouble with grown-ups was that
        under the magnificent shell of adulthood,
                                                    just under,
Waited the baby full of tantrums.

It occurred to her that there may have been
                                something
Ridiculous in the picture of the Fine Prince
Rushing (rich with the breadth and height and
Mature solidness whose lack, in the Dark
                        Villain, was impressing her,
Confronting her more and more as this first
                                day after the trial
And acquittal wore on) rushing
With his heavy companion to hack down
                                (unhorsed)
That little foe.
So much had happened, she could not
            remember now what that foe had done
Against her, or if anything had been done.
The one thing in the world that she did know
                                and knew
With terrifying clarity was that her
                                composition
Had disintegrated. That, although the pattern
                                prevailed,
The breaks were everywhere. That she could
                                think
Of no thread capable of the necessary
Sew-work.
She made the babies sit in their places at the
                                table.
Then, before calling Him, she hurried
To the mirror with her comb and lipstick. It
                        was necessary
To be more beautiful than ever.
The beautiful wife.
For sometimes she fancied he looked at her as
                                though
Measuring her. As if he considered, Had she
                        been worth It?
Had *she* been worth the blood, the cramped
            cries, the little stuttering bravado,
The gradual dulling of those Negro eyes,
The sudden, overwhelming *little-boyness* in
                                that barn?
Whatever she might feel or half-feel, the lipstick
necessity was something apart. He must never
                                conclude
That she had not been worth It.

He sat down, the Fine Prince, and
Began buttering a biscuit. He looked at his
                                hands.
He twisted in his chair, he scratched his nose.
He glanced again, almost secretly, at his hands.
More papers were in from the North, he
                mumbled. More meddling headlines.
With their pepper-words, "bestiality," and
                        "barbarism," and
"Shocking."
The half-sneers he had mastered for the trial
                        worked across
His sweet and prety face.
What he'd like to do, he explained, was kill
                        them all.
The time lost. The unwanted fame.
Still, it had been fun to show those intruders
A thing or two. To show that snappy-eyed
                        mother,
That sassy, Northern, brown-black——
Nothing could stop Mississippi.
He knew that. Big Fella
Knew that.
And, what was so good, Mississippi knew that.
Nothing and nothing could stop Mississippi.
They could send in their petitions, and scar
Their newspapers with bleeding headlines.
                        Their governors
Could appeal to Washington....
"What I want," the older baby said, "is 'lasses
                        on my jam."
Whereupon the younger baby
Picked up the molasses pitcher and threw
The molasses in his brother's face. Instantly
The Fine Prince leaned across the table and
                        slapped
The small and smiling criminal.
She did not speak. When the Hand
Came down and away, and she could look at
                        her child,
At her baby-child,
She could think only of blood.
Surely her baby's cheek
Had disappeared, and in its place, surely,

Hung a heaviness, a lengthening red, a red that
                had no end.
She shook her head. It was not true, of course.
It was not true at all. The
Child's face was as always, the
Color of the paste in her paste-jar.

She left the table, to the tune of the children's
             lamentations, which were shriller
Than ever. She
Looked out of a window. She said not a word.
                            That
Was one of the new Somethings—
The fear,
Tying her as with iron.

Suddenly she felt his hands upon her. He had
                followed her
To the window. The children whimpering now.
Such bits of tots. And she, their mother,
Could not protect them. She looked at her
                shoulders, still
Gripped in the claim of his hands. She tried,
           but could not resist the idea
That a red ooze was seeping, spreading darkly,
               thickly, slowly,
Over her white shoulders, her own shoulders,
And over all of Earth and Mars.

He whispered something to her, did the Fine
             Prince, something
About love, something about love and night
             and intention.
She heard no hoof-beat of the horse and saw
           no flash of the shining steel.
He pulled her face around to meet
His, and there it was, close close,
For the first time in all those days and nights.
His mouth, wet and red,
So very, very, very red,
Closed over hers.

Then a sickness heaved within her. The
               courtroom Coca-Cola,
The courtroom beer and hate and sweat and
                  drone,
Pushed like a wall against her. She wanted to
               bear it.

But his mouth would not go away and
             neither would the
Decapitated exclamation points in that Other
             Woman's eyes.
She did not scream.
She stood there.
But a hatred for him burst into glorious flower,
And its perfume enclasped them—big,
Bigger than all magnolias.

The last bleak news of the ballad.
The rest of the rugged music.
The last quatrain.

THE LAST QUATRAIN OF THE BALLAD OF EMMETT TILL

After the murder,
After the burial

Emmett's mother is a pretty-faced thing;
           the tint of pulled taffy.
She sits in a red room,
           drinking black coffee.
She kisses her killed boy.
           And she is sorry.
Chaos in windy grays
           through a red prairie.

SPEECH TO THE YOUNG. SPEECH TO THE PROGRESS-TOWARD.

For Nora Brooks Blakely.
For Henry Blakely III.

Say to them,
say to the down-keepers,
the sun-slappers,
the self-soilers,
the harmony-hushers,
"Even if you are not ready for day
it cannot always be night."
You will be right.
For that is the hard home-run.

And remember:
live not for Battles Won.
Live not for The-End-of-the-Song.
Live in the along.

Violeta Parra   *Chile, 1917–1967*

Violeta Parra, poet, folksinger, songwriter, scriptwriter, and actress, was born in the small town of San Carlos in central Chile where she first started writing and performing her music. Greatly disturbed by social injustice and the great suffering of the poor, many of her songs and poems were protest songs that later inspired a whole generation of songwriters throughout the Americas. Parra also did extensive research into the traditional folkmusic of Chile traveling into the remote regions of central and northern Chile to learn and collect the songs, which she then recorded and performed widely. She was immensely popular in the Spanish-speaking world, especially in the 1960s when folk music was popularized by the peace movement.

Parra was also a skilled artist. She was a potter, weaver, ceramicist, painter, and sculptor, and was the first Latin American to have her own (posthumous) show at the Louvre (1969).

The selections below are *canciones* (songs) that Parra wrote and performed. They were collected in *Toda Violeta Parra* (All by Violeta Parra, 1976). One of them, "Gracias a la vida," included here as "I Give Thanks to Life," was made popular in this country when it was recorded by singer Joan Baez.

Violeta Parra is the sister of the eminent poet Nicanor Parra. She had two children. After Parra killed herself in 1967, her poetry was collected in *Decimas: Autobiografia en versos chilenos* (Stanzas: Autobiography in Verse Form, 1970) by her brother, Pablo Neruda, and a third Chilean poet, Pablo de Rokha.

ABOVE THE BURNING SUN
Arriba quemando el sol

When I went to the pampa,
my heart was free and strong,
happy as a mockingbird,
but soon my heart was gone,
first I lost my feathers
and then I lost my song,
and above the burning sun.

When I first saw the miners,
the places where they dwell,
I said to myself, a snail
lives better in its shell,
or the privileged burglar in
a narrow prison cell,
and above the burning sun.

The strings of dingy hovels,
all standing in a row,
the strings of women waiting
to use the water trough,
all carrying their buckets,
their faces filled with woe,
up above, the burning sun.

We went to the company store
to buy our rationed food,
even with twenty items
the discount was no good,
our baskets empty, we returned
to where our lodgings stood,
up above, the burning sun.

(continued)

The pampa is a dry zone,
at least the law says so,
nevertheless, the bottles
of liquor come and go;
of course they're not the poor man's,
contraband, for all I know,
up above, the burning sun.

Should anyone think that I
tell tales in my refrain,
these things happen in Chuqui,
and in Santa Juana, the same,
the miner doesn't realize
the value of his pain,
and above the burning sun.

I went back to Santiago,*
I never got to know
the way the news is broadcast
when the poor man says no,
below, only the dark night,
saltpeter, gold and coal
and above the burning sun.

Translated by Patti Firth

NOTE

* This poem refers to several areas in Chile. The pampa is
a desert in the north called Pampa del Tamacuyal. Chuqui is a copper-mining city in the pampa, while Santa
Juana in south central Chile is known for coal mining.

I GIVE THANKS TO LIFE
Gracias a la vida

I give thanks to life for all it has given me.
It gave me two morning stars, with which I can
                                             see
the difference between black and white perfectly,
and in the night sky the stars shining brilliantly,
and among the multitudes the man loved by me.

I give thanks to life for all it has given me.
It has given me two ears, which effortlessly
record, both night and day, crickets and canaries,
hammers, turbines, barks, sudden squalls upon
                                          the sea,
and my beloved's voice speaks so tenderly.

I give thanks to life for all it has given me.
It has given me the sounds and the ABC's,
with them all the words I can use to think and
                                          speak,
mother, friend, brother, and the light with
                                    which to see
my way to the soul of he who brings love to
                                             me.

I give thanks to life for all it has given me.
It has given me the steps of my tired feet,
with them I traveled through the puddles and
                                         cities,
the beaches and deserts, the mountains and the
                                          fields
and to your house, to your patio and your
                                        street.

I give thanks to life for all it has given me.
It has given me the heart that trembles slightly
when I see the fruit of the human faculties,
when I see the good man, far from iniquity,
when I look deep into your eyes, bright as can
                                             be.

I give thanks to life for all it has given me.
It has given me laughter and given me tears,
so that I may tell happiness from misery,
the two materials that form my melody,
and the song of all of you, the same melody,
and everyone's song, which is my own melody.

Translated by Patti Firth

BECAUSE THE POOR HAVE NO ONE
Porque los pobres no tienen ningún

Because the poor have no one
to turn to, look where they may,
they look up to the heavens
in the endless hope that they
might find that which here on this
earth their brother takes away, Godspeed!
What a life this is we lead, indeed!

Because the poor have no one
to show them compassion,
they call out to the heavens
in search of confession
since their brother will not hear
their hearts' own expression, Godspeed!
What a life this is we lead, indeed!

Because the poor have nothing
in this world their hopes to raise,
they aspire to the next life
all injustice to erase,
for this, all the processions,
the candles, the hymns of praise, Godspeed!
What a life this is we lead, indeed!

From time immemorial
since the invention of hell
to frighten the poor people
with punishment eternal,
and the poor man, innocent,
in his innocence trustful, Godspeed!
What a life this is we lead, indeed!

Heaven holds the reins of power,
the earth and capital,
and the soldiers of the Pope
get their knapsacks well-filled,
and the one who works receives
glory as a muzzle, Godspeed!
What a life this is we lead, indeed!

To continue with the lies
his confessor calls him,
he says that God does not want
any revolution,
contract or labor union,
that these things offend him, Godspeed!
What a life this is we lead, indeed!

Translated by Patti Firth

Christiane Rochefort   *France, b. 1917*

Born in Paris to a family that she has described as being torn apart by internal contradictions, Rochefort explores how women have survived in and revolted against the order of things. Her heroines are often caught between passion and oppression and negotiate a delicate balance of capitulation to desire and pure revolt. Her novel, *Repos du Guerrier* (*Warrior's Rest*, 1948; later made into a film by Roger Vadim), achieved an immediate "succès de scandale" because of its brutally open treatment of an obsessive love affair. Subsequently, Rochefort was inspired by the burgeoning French feminist movement and the student revolts of 1968 in her description of an explosive non-conformity. *Les Petits Enfants du siècle* (1961: translated both as *Children of Heaven* and the awkwardly titled *Josyanne and the Welfare*) drew an unsentimental portrait of an adolescent girl's coming of age in a working-class milieu; neither the protagonist's street savvy nor her awareness of the tensions and betrayals of married life prevent her from falling prey to the romantic idealization of love. In *Les Stances à Sophie* (1963, translated using the somewhat surrealist, slangy title *Cats Don't Care for Money*), the heroine's homosexuality becomes one means of her escape from and revolt against dominant codes of sexuality. In the first section excerpted here, Céline transforms her bohemian character so that Philippe will marry her; in the second section taken from the end of the novel, she is once again—and more consciously than before—subverting the patriarchy. A novel which followed, *Printemps au Parking* (an untranslatable title; literally, Spring at the Parking [Lot]), is noted for its brilliantly satirical depictions of everyday existence in contemporary life. Rochefort's talent for creating utopias is manifest in *Archaos* (1972).

Rochefort experimented heavily for a time with invisible ink and linguistic wordplay; one work in which she practiced these disappearing acts and suggested the paradox of presence/absence was a version of her own life: *Ma vie, revue et corrigée par l'auteur* (My Life, Reviewed and Revised by the Author, 1978). For this experimentation she was flippantly labelled "First Lady of Deconstruction" in an allusion to contemporary philosophical modes of analysis that undermine our traditional concepts of knowledge, order, and reality. She herself more accurately described the book as "an exercise in self-defense." Her more recent work has involved a re-writing of Zola's novels as seen through the eyes of a 14-year-old Punk rocker. In *Le monde est comme deux chevaux* (The World Is like Two Horses, 1984), new style has been replaced by new hair style: "Plus que le mot, le mohawk." (More than the word, the mohawk.)

from CATS DON'T CARE FOR MONEY
Les Stances à Sophie

Why don't you let your hair grow? asked Philippe—six feet one, blond, periwinkle eyes, adorable nose, willful mouth, broad and intelligent forehead, etc.—I'd like you so much better with long hair at least you'd look like a woman, why are you wearing slacks again when you know I like you better in a dress, you love me said Philippe, can't you try to please me just in this little thing. And in that little thing. That shouldn't be such an effort if you really love me said Philippe, what time did you go to bed last night and, if I may ask, what were you up to when you got there, in my opinion you're wasting your time with all those books when you don't remember a word you read anyway. And you still haven't sewed that missing button on your jacket, don't look so surprised, I told you about it last week and I can see it's the same jacket. And with me, the man who only goes out with girls who are impeccably groomed, dressed to the teeth! Me, who would love so much to show you off! I'm telling you all this for your own sake you

know, if I didn't care for you it wouldn't matter to me that your way of life can only lead to disaster, I'd be satisfied to have the same kind of good time with you that most men have with girls who are more or less "free" like you, they're only too happy for you all to remain "free," yes indeed! for them it's not only practical, it's economical, you must know what I mean, you with all your experience. But it just so happens that my interest in you is different, so I try to help you, said Philippe, but you have to make an effort too—hold your fork in the other hand, don't laugh like that it's vulgar, don't roll your bread up that way, it's dirty, stand up straight you smoke too much you're staining your teeth don't drink so much it's not nice for a woman, you don't look too well you should see a doctor. Why don't you look for a regular job instead of doing a lot of odd ones that get you nowhere, honestly your carelessness upsets me, what's going to become of you, you'll ruin your health with all that coffee. Promise me that tomorrow you'll go to bed at midnight, just to please me, said Philippe, if you don't do it for yourself at least do it for me, I wonder what you think you're doing with that bunch of misfits, what do you see in them? They aren't for you, you deserve better than that, if you want to make me happy you'll stop seeing them...If you love me said Philippe, couldn't you do this, that would please me, and not that, which doesn't? It's not so difficult.

Thus spake Philippe, and me, I listened, openmouthed. I drank in his words. I found they made sense.

And anyway, where is this kind of life getting you? Hm? I mean, in the end, where is it getting you?

What could I answer? Nowhere, it's getting me nowhere. But then it isn't intended to get me anywhere, and anyway, get me where? Where is it meant to get me? Well, I don't know. You see, he said, smiling, you see perfectly well that you don't know.

The truth is I don't know anything any more. That man is an Attila. He leaves a desert in his wake. I walk around in a daze. Who am I? What are we doing here? It's a mystery. Oh, those great confused thoughts! he says. It sounds very fine, very poetic, but when you really take a look at them, it's Fogsville. Fogsville, he repeats, pleased with his phrase. Life, you know, life isn't like that, it's much simpler than that, baby. Don't you ever want to lead a normal life? said Philippe.

Normal. What's that? What is a normal life in the world we live in? I'm willing, but what is it?

But Philippe seemed to know. His air of assurance put my uncertainties to flight. Uncertainties are fragile. Since I've known Philippe I've been coming apart at the seams. I'm dissolving, I don't know where I'm going any more, I'm a dust mote in space, and in this state of confusion I have only one place of refuge: his arms. There everything is calm, serene, quiet, and warm. Peace is there, and security.

You see. You see, my little kitten. You need someone. You can't make it all alone. You act proud, but underneath you're just a tiny little girl who needs to be protected, like everybody else. There, there. You see. Doesn't it feel good in my arms?

Oh yes, it feels good! Oh yes. It feels good. That's the trouble. Philippe is strong, he's solid, he's sure. He knows.

He's here. He talks. And poor me I'm listening to him with my mouth hanging open, in a dress, with hair down to my shoulders and my fork in the correct hand. I went to the doctor, I swallowed yellow pills. I arrived on time, relying on the watch he'd given me just for that, which I set ahead so as to be extra sure. I loved him. Some nights I went to bed at midnight so that I could tell him about it the next day, feeling proud of myself and accepting praise from his mouth: That's a good girl, my little kitten, you must keep it up, you'll see how much better you'll feel. I did feel better. I loved him. I cleaned up my damned room when he was coming. He didn't like my room but since he lived in his family's apartment he had to come there to sleep with me. He tried to overlook what he still called my mess, even after all the trouble I'd taken to clean it up; he tried not to see the stuff pinned on the walls, among it several rather indecent portraits of me by obviously different hands, plus some other battle souvenirs which I wasn't hypocrite enough to take down and which bothered him; he'd rather not have seen my bed, because its state of wear and tear seemed to him evidence of previous unmentionable activities, and he particularly hated the spread on which he assumed they had taken place, he found it in dreadful taste and after all the others who preceded him he put his beloved buttocks on it with all the fastidiousness of a virgin, until Christmas, when, on aesthetic grounds, and playing Santa Claus, he gave me a new one, one with no memories, on which he could feel more comfortable. He loved me. He wished me well. And nothing seemed less compatible with all the good things he wanted for me than my way of life, my surroundings, my friends, my habits, my clothes, my hair, my language, my tastes, my ideas, anything which wasn't my true self—that true self which was buried, stifled, hidden, which he loved because he was the only one who knew it, and which was destined to be brought to life by his hands like a pearl wrested from an oyster....And I listened to him, my mouth hanging open, in a dress, with my hair down to the middle of my back. And no earplugs. And he had a lovely voice.

"Did you have a good trip?"

"Wonderful. The weather was beautiful. You can't imagine what weather they have there. You can't even picture it when you're here you're so drowned in soup. Listen, I left under a blue sky. Really blue. Then above Milan we began to see clouds. Just clouds. But then, by the time we got to Paris, I'll never forget it. There, below us, a basin of filth, thick, black, nauseating. Unbearable. Asphyxiating. I said to myself: it isn't possible that people actually live down there. But that's where we landed. In the soup. We literally plunged into it. You couldn't see a thing. Grayness. Nothing. I was terrified, I swear. I said to myself, 'They'll never find the field.'"

"You know perfectly well they have radar."

"That's not the point! Of course I know they have radar! It was an animal fear: I didn't want to go in there! Instinct for self-preservation, probably. Once we landed, I saw it was possible to see after all; I could make out the hangars and that kind of idiotic glass structure, I got out of the plane, everything looked ordinary, as usual, people walked, lived, they didn't seem to be about to crack up—and I was just like them. Only now I know we're living in shit: I saw it with my own eyes from up there. I saw us. Now I see myself. I know that I am walking in shit. No doubt of it. It's no joke. It's proven. I won't forget it again. At every moment I'll be aware of it."

"It's not necessary to cultivate obsessions."

Obsession: being aware of something real. (Note for the Célino-Philippian dictionary.) Function of the word: to make the real thing, which is troublesome, disappear into an imaginary one so that the party can go on. Another example: Atomic Bomb: paranoid obsession of certain sad souls from 1945 to... Function: to suppress the bomb. "Malta does not exist." That dictionary will really be cute. In fact, Célino-Philippian is too restrictive a title for such an important work. It should be more general. It's of public interest. I'll call it the Semantic Dictionary. Dammit, I'm really going to do it! Neo-Bourgeois Semantic Dictionary.

"You seem to have come back from your little trip in good spirits. You've found your tongue."

"Yes. It did me good."

Such is the way of the adulterous woman: she eats, she wipes her mouth, and then she says: it did me good.

What of it: it's true. Philippe even profits by it, I'm nicer. Influenced maybe by their customs down there, not yet readapted to those here. As for in bed, it's going better than before. So, it wasn't quite as perfect as all that?

There are three things outside my reach. And four which I cannot grasp: the flight of an eagle in the sky; the path of a serpent on the rock; the trace of a ship on the sea; and the mark of a man on a woman.

I don't understand either.

The Dictionary is coming along. I've bought the Larousse and Flaubert's *Dictionnaire des Idées Reçus.** One must lean on the Masters, however lightly. And the last-named has a good deal about bull slinging in it too; it's more useful to me than that semester in philology which I thought I should take in a fit of conscience, and whose main result was to inspire Philippe to one of his better efforts, on the theme Here we go again and how on earth do you plan to use that my poor child at your age too, you who never even bothered with a degree in spite of all your so-called learning.

Which is true. Never mind. philology was no help. Why are people so absolutely determined to lose themselves in detail, what form of genius drives them to choose exactly those subjects which are farthest from the essential, what strange aversion keeps them from seeking true knowledge—it is a mystery to me, the mystery of mankind. Only mathematicians are audacious they are so far off, but as soon as you approach the concrete there is only flight, stampede, the Great Myopia. In a moment of wild delirium I even thought of founding a chair; I brought it up to Philippe so as to get a rise out of him, which is always fun. Subject: How Man Thinks. Let it go. I gave up philology, I don't give a damn about it. Aha, I knew it. My Poor Child, you've given this up too, etc., a familiar tune. And what are you doing with all those papers, what's this new whim?

"I'm making a dictionary."

"You're crazy. Better go to bed."

What for?

Because at last I can no longer delude myself. The mechanism still works, but, these evenings, at midnight, in the conjugal bed, the inspiration is lacking. And, sometimes, "I'm tired."

Love.—A: for a woman; total dedication to domestic life, with night service. B: for a man, being satisfied with this.

Love: acceptance and contemplation of Another, as he is, with no requirement of love in return. That's for the Dictionary of the Absolute.

Translated by Helen Eustis

NOTE

* *Larousse*: publisher of standard dictionaries, encyclopedias, and other reference works. *Dictionnaire des Idées Reçues* (Dictionary of Received Ideas), Flaubert's supplement to his unfinished novel *Bouvard et Pécuchet* (1881), frequently published separately. The work is similarly intended to satirize bourgeois philistinism and expose the clichéd language and thought wrought by modern capitalism. Flaubert believed its subtitle might be the "Encyclopedia of Human Stupidity."

Fadwa Tuqan   *Palestine/West Bank, b. 1917*

Fadwa Tuqan was first introduced to poetry as a form of self-expression by her older brother Ibrahim, a well-known nationalist poet. Born in Nablus in 1917, she received her education there and became a noted poet in her own right.

Her first volume of poetry was *Wahdi ma' al-Ayyam* (Alone with the Days), published in Beirut in 1955, when she was 38 years old. Written in the traditional Arabic form of the *qasida*, the monorhymed poems devoted to several recognized themes (eulogy, satire, elegy) or descriptive poems written to or about someone, this early work was influenced by the romantic style evident in the literature of the 1930s.

Although Tuqan's subject matter is primarily love, her writing became increasingly politicized with the intensification of the Arab-Israeli conflict, and Arabic critics have perceived a breakthrough in such works as *Wajadtuha* (I Found It, 1957) and *A'tina Hubban* (Give Us Love, 1960), which, in part, deal with the oppression of the Palestinians. In the former, she describes the sufferings of displaced refugees and in the latter, "Dreams of Remembrance" mingles memories of her brother, who died fighting for the Palestinian cause, with a philosophical meditation on the problem which led him to take such action. In June, 1967,

Tuqan saw her hometown fall to Israeli occupation, and her poetry was further radicalized: *Fida'i wa al'Ard* (Freedom Fighter and the Land, 1968) and *al-Layl wa'l Fursan* (Night and the Knights, 1969) are important examples of her works on the Judeo-Palestinian conflict, part of the literary movement that has come to be called *Al-Adab al-Huzairani* (the June Literature). Yet, as 'Abd al-Muhsin Taha Badr has suggested in discussing her collection *Amam al-Bab-al-Mughlag* (In Front of the Closed Door, 1967), of which the first three poems are excerpts, her work reveals the tension of one who "is trying to rid herself of the old world." (As the selections themselves indicate, Tuqan's greatest emotional energy continues to be absorbed by thwarted personal love.) Other poetic works are "*Ala Qimmet al-Dunya Wahidan* (Alone at the Top of the World, 1973), and *Kabus al Layl wa al-Nahar* (Nightmare in Daylight, 1974) from which "To Etan" is taken.

Late in life, Tuqan turned to prose to sum up her existence and to describe the ways in which her personal life has intersected with the public realm. *Rihia sa'ba, rihia jabaliyya* (A Difficult Journey, A Mountainous Journey, 1985) tells of her personal, political, and literary development, first in British Mandate Palestine in the 1930s and 1940s, then under Jordanian rule in 1948, and finally during the Israeli occupation after 1967.

AFTER THE RELEASE

Neglected, no food and no shelter
No woolen rag to protect me from shivering in
                                          this night
Alone in the deserts of night
My heart trembling with fear
Ever trembling with fear
Ever under the whim of a falling bridge
Or at the mercy of a collapsing roof
My ground ever shaking, tipping over,
     Turning on no axis
Who will save me from this fear
Who will save me from this fear?

                          Translated by Issa J. Boullata

THE LAST KNOCKS

Will You not open this door for me
My hand is exhausted of knocking, knocking
                              at Your door
I have come to Your vastness to beg
Some tranquility
And peace of mind
But Your vastness is closed
In my face, drowned in silence
O Lord of the house

The door was open here
The house was the refuge of all burdened with
                                          grief
The door was open here
And the green olive tree rose high
Embracing the house
The oil lighting without fire
Guiding the steps of him who walks at night
Giving relief to the one crushed by the burden
                                    of the Earth
Flooding him with satisfaction and tranquility
Do You hear me O Lord of the house
After my loss in the deserts
Away from You I have returned to You
But Your vastness is closed
In my face, drowned in silence
Your vastness is shrouded
With the dust of death
If You are here open the door for me
Do not veil Your face from me
See my orphanhood, my loss
Amid the ruins of my collapsing world
The grief of the Earth on my shoulders
And the terrors of a tyrant destiny

                          Translated by Issa J. Boullata

NOTHING IS HERE

In vain, there is no echo, no sound
Come back. Nothing is here but desolation
     silence and the shadow of death.

Translated by Issa J. Boullata

TO ETAN

Aytan fi al-Shabaka al-Fuladhiyya

An Israeli Child
From The Kibbutz Ma'oz Hayim

He falls
under the star that branches
a wild tree in his hands
a web woven with the threads of steel stretching
     walls of blood
around The Dream.
He is caught.
Opening his eyes
Etan, the child, asks,
"How long do we have to watch over this
                    land?"

And time deformed
dragged in khaki, bypasses him
through flames and smoke
sorrows and death.
If only the Star could foretell the truth.

Etan, my child
Like the harbor that is drowning
I can see you drown
through the lie
The bloated dream is a sinking load.
I am afraid for you, my child
to have to grow up in this web of things
to be gradually stripped of
     your human heart and face
you could fall again, my child
     and fall
          and fall
               fading into a fathomless end.

Translated by Kamal Boullata

Tove Ditlevsen   *Denmark, 1918–1976*

Born in the working-class district of Copenhagen, Tove Ditlevsen grew up in a family consisting of her mother, a brother, and her father, who was often unemployed. After completing only the compulsory years of education, she found odd jobs as a housemaid and finally as an office worker. At 21 she married a much older man who was the editor of a literary magazine, in which Ditlevsen's first poem was published. Her first husband also helped her to get *Pigesind* (A Girl's Mind), a collection of poems, published in 1939. Her first novel, *Man gjorde et barn fortraed* (A Child Was Harmed, 1941), about the rape of a child by an older man, was a great success.

Among Ditlevsen's large production of poetry, short stories, novels, and children's books published between the years 1939 and 1973, her memoirs, *Barndom* (Childhood, 1967), *Ungdom* (Youth, 1967), and *Gift* (Married/Poison, 1971), are probably the most read and discussed. Her lifelong struggle, first as a young girl without the support of her family, and later through four marriages, four children, mental illness, alcoholism and drug dependency, during which time she continued writing, is vividly described in these books; she finally ended her life by her own hand after several attempts.

Ditlevsen's poetic style is traditional, with rhymes and simple metaphors. Only in her last collections does she change to a more modernistic style. Her prose is realistic and simple, evocative of the lifestyle of the less fashionable streets of Copenhagen, which she knew and was able to describe so well. Recently she has been "rediscovered" for her feminist themes; several of her works have been translated into English, including a collection of short stories (*Complete Freedom and other Stories*, 1982) and the novel *Tidelig Foraar* (*Early Spring*, 1985). Translations of her poetry have also appeared in various anthologies and literary magazines.

The following poems are from *Den hemmelige rude* (The Secret Pane of Glass, 1961), and *De Voksne* (The Grownups, 1969).

Ingrid Claréus

SUNDAY
Søndag

Nothing ever happens on a Sunday.
You never meet a new love
on a Sunday.
It is the Day of the Distressed.
Boarding-house day or family day.
The woman's most painful hours
when she pictures her lover
with his babies on his knee
while his wife, smiling,
walks in and out with tempting trays,
An accursed day.

Once everything must have been different,
why else should we all of us
look forward to Sunday all week?
When we went to school, perhaps?
But even then the church bells sounded
sorrowful and gray like rain and death.
Even then the voices of the grownups
were weak and toneless as if they fumbled
for Sunday words in vain.

The smell of mold and old bread,
of sleep, rubber boots, and chicory
rose up even then through the stairway,
and the street, stiff, empty, and different
in a desolate way—
the smell of Sunday crammed us
with a fat layer of that disappointment
which follows an expectation
without a particular aim.

But when, then? Somewhere before memory
there was a happiness, an irresistible
                                    expectation,
which no one could yet disappoint.
Then the church bells meant that Father was
                                    home,
the moustache, the dark eyebrows, and the
                                    smell of snuff
was there and stayed there, somewhere near,
and perhaps your young mother's laughter
sounded more merry than on all the other days.

It is Sunday. You never meet
a new love on a Sunday.
You sit in the parlor
rigid and flat like a cardboard figure
in the eyes of the children,
They scrape with their feet
and quarrel listlessly with each other.
"We ought to do something," you say,
"Yes," comes a voice from behind the paper,
Then you both fall silent because everything
                                    you feel
like doing is hidden and secret
and would be unacceptable to the other.
The church bells are ringing.
The nostrils of the children
are filled with a hopeless, inherited smell.
Across their sweet faces moves
a temporary ugliness.
A faded light
is growing in their eyes.

But we all look forward to Sunday
all week, all our lives,
look forward to hundreds
of futile, exhausting, long Sundays.
Family day, boarding-house day,
the hell of secret lovers.
That day when the nauseating grayness of the
                                         grownups
seeps into the children and decides
the incomprehensible Sunday gloom of years
                                    to come.
                        Translated by Knud Mogensen

DIVORCE 3
Skilsmisse 3

It is not easy
to be alone
other people
have impatient
waiting-room eyes.
The floor pulls
your steps away
underneath you.
You move
hand over hand
from hour to hour.
A vocabulary
of around
a hundred words
was not included
in the division of the household.

The craving for
something annoying
the lack of
strong smells.
Cold smoke
in the curtains.
The bed is
too wide now.
Girl friends leave
at potato-boiling time.

Freedom
comes first
with the next train
an unknown
traveler
who doesn't
like children.

The dog is
uneasy
sniffs at
the wrong pants legs
is soon
in heat.

You read books
watch television
take in
nothing
are suddenly
very happy
in the morning
and in despair
before evening.

It's a transition
girl friends say
something you have
to go through.
Weightless as an
astronaut
you float around
in empty rooms
and wait
for the freedom
to do
what you
no longer want to do.
                        Translated by Ann Freeman

SELF-PORTRAIT I
Selvportræt 1

I can not:
cook
wear a hat
make people comfortable
wear jewelry
arrange flowers
remember appointments
thank others for gifts
tip correctly
keep a man
show interest
at meetings for parents.

I can not
stop:
smoking
drinking
eating chocolate
stealing umbrellas
oversleeping
forgetting to remember
birthdays:
and to clean my nails.

Telling people what they
want to hear
giving away secrets
liking
strange places
and psychopaths.

I can:
be alone
wash dishes
read books
form sentences
listen
and be happy
without guilt feelings.

Translated by Ann Freeman

Gloria Fuertes   *Spain, b. 1918*

Gloria Fuertes began her literary career writing poems, stories, and plays for children, and published her first books, *Canciones para niños* (Songs for Children) and *Isla ignorada* (Unknown Island) in 1950. These were very well received by critics and during the next fifteen years Fuertes published five more collections of poetry, two of them prize-winning. *Toda asusta* (Totally Scared, 1958) won first mention in the Concurso International de Poesía Lírica Hispánica (International Competition of Lyric Hispanic Poetry) in Venezuela and *Ni tiro, ni veneno, ni navaja* (Neither Gun, nor Poison, nor Razor, 1965) won the Premio Guipuzcoa in 1965. The following poems are from *Aconsejo beber hilo* (I Advise You to Drink Thread, 1954) and *Cómo atar los bigotes al tigre* (How to Tie the Tiger's Whiskers, 1969); the latter collection won honorable mention for the Premio Vizcaya in 1969. Her immense popularity can be guaged by the fact that her *Antología poética* (Poetic Anthology), is reprinted every two years and her *Obras incompletas* (Incomplete Works, 1975) is now in its seventh edition.

Known as a writer of the working class, Gloria Fuertes deals humorously and realistically with the small details of everyday survival. The theme of women's social struggles figures prominently in her poetry, which is widely available in

English. A recent translation, *Off the Map: Selected Poems* (1984), also reveals her as a poet' of the city; the title suggests the "forest" of the poetic perspective, from which she scrutinizes urban realities.

AUTOBIOGRAPHY
Autobiografía

At the foot of the Cathedral of Burgos
my mother was born.
At the foot of the Cathedral of Madrid
my father was born.
At the foot of my mother I was born
one afternoon in the middle of Spain.
My father was a worker,
my mother was a seamstress.
I wanted to take off with the circus
but I'm only what I am.
When I was little
I went to a reformatory and a free school.
As a kid I was sickly
and summered in a sanatorium,
but now I get around.
I've had at least seven love affairs,
some bad daddies,
and a marvelous appetite.
Now I've got two minor convictions
and a kiss from time to time.
             Translated by Philip Levine and Ada Long

I'M ONLY A WOMAN
Soy sólo una mujer

I'm only a woman, and that's enough,
with a goat and an old car,
a "Praise the Lord" every morning,
and a lecherous fool running the show.

I wish I'd been a designer,
or a raving, sensitive Sappho,*
look at me
here,
lost
among all these slobs.
I say this for anyone who reads me,
I wanted to be a commander without weapons,
to plant my poems on the moon,
but an astronaut beat me to it.

I wanted to be a pusher of peace on earth—
they arrested me on the road—
I'm only a woman, a full-blooded one,
I'm only a woman, and that's enough.
             Translated by Philip Levine and Ada Long

NOTE

* Sappho (fl. 630 B.C.) was the Greek woman poet from
  the island of Lesbos; she was famous for her passionate
  love poetry, much of which was addressed to women.

PLASTIC VIRGIN
Virgen de plástico

With her nylon veil
and electric crown,
with her dry-cell batteries
in her breast, and a dismal smile,
she's on display in all the shops
and on the dusty shelves of poor Catholics.
In New York City, above the bedstead
this white virgin watches over
the washstands of Negroes...
Crossbreed of Fátima and Lourdes,
lightweight model stamped "Made in USA,"
with streaming hair and open hands,
she's washable and shatterproof.
Comes in three colors
—white, pink, and blue—
available in three sizes
though even the big one is small.
There, without angels,
virgin Virgin,
I've felt so bad for you,
pure Virgin of plastic,
I can't bring myself
to ask for one miracle.
             Translated by Philip Levine and Ada Long

Muriel Spark   *UK(Scotland)/Italy, b. 1918*

Muriel Spark was born Muriel Camberg in Edinburgh. Her father was a Jewish engineer, and her mother a Presbyterian with a love of high culture and the flamboyant. Spark was educated at St. James Gillespie's School for Girls, where she began to write poetry. She left Edinburgh at the age of 18 and went to Rhodesia, staying there until 1944 when her six-year marriage to S.O. Spark was dissolved. The marriage produced a son, Robin. Spark then returned to England where she worked for the Foreign Office, in the Political Intelligence Department, distorting the news to lower German morale during World War II. It was her first involvement in fiction writing.

Following World War II, Spark worked as a free-lance journalist in order to support herself as a poet. She was general secretary of the Poetry Society and editor of *The Poetry Review* for a while, and later editor of the journal *European Affairs*. During this period she published several critical works, including *Child of Light: A Reassessment of Mary Wollstonecraft Shelley* (1951), *Emily Brontë: Her Life and Work* (1953), and *John Masefield* (1953).

Spark's career as a popular fiction writer began in the early 1950s as well. In 1951 *The Seraph and the Zambesi*, a short story set in Africa, won *The Observer's* short story competition. At the invitation of Macmillan Publishers, she set to work on a novel, and in 1957, *The Comforters* was published.

The Comforters was the first of Spark's works to be published after her conversion to Roman Catholicism in 1954, and, as all her subsequent works, it shows the influence of her moral vision. *Momenti Mori* (1959), a brilliant comic study of old age, followed.

Spark's novels are, she says, "The novels of a poet," and many critics agree. Yet, she is concerned with more than poetry. At their best, her stories are satirical and wry tales that border on farce.

Of her sixteen novels, by far the most popular is *The Prime of Miss Jean Brodie* (1961), the tragi-comic story of a haughty, self-possessed Scots school teacher at a girls' school in Edinburgh in the 1930s. The work was made into a successful film in the 1950s. Another important work is *The Mandelbaum Gate* (1965), an uncharacteristically long novel about a group of people living in or visiting Jerusalem in 1961, for which she won the James Tait Black Memorial Prize in 1966. Her works have, at times, received mixed criticism. Sometimes they have been accused of being labored so that the intricate plots are not convincing. Her general reputation, however, is that of an original, a crafter of tales that make a statement about the nature of the universe and humanity's place in it. The following story is from *Collected Stories I* (1967).

Dame Muriel Spark was made an Officer in the Order of the British Empire in 1967, and has received numerous awards for radio drama, short stories, and novels, as well as an honorary D. Litt from the University of Strathclyde, Glasgow, Scotland, in 1971. She has resided in Rome since 1967.

John Isom

YOU SHOULD HAVE SEEN THE MESS

I am now more than glad that I did not pass into the Grammar School five years ago, although it was a disappointment at the time. I was always good at English, but not so good at the other subjects!!

I am glad that I went to the Secondary Modern School, because it was only constructed the year before.[1] Therefore, it was much more hygienic than the Grammar School. The Secondary Modern was light and airy, and the walls were painted with a bright, washable, gloss. One day, I was sent over to the Grammar School with a note for one of the teachers, and you should have seen the mess! The corridors were dusty, and I saw dust on the window ledges, which were chipped. I saw into one of the classrooms. It was very untidy in there.

I am also glad that I did not go to the Grammar School, because of what it does to one's habits. This may appear to be a strange remark, at first sight. It is a good thing to have an education behind you, and I do not believe in ignorance, but I have had certain experiences, with educated people, since going out into the world.

I am seventeen years of age, and left school two years ago last month. I had my A certificate for typing, so got my first job, as a junior, in a solicitor's office. Mum was pleased at this, and Dad said it was a first-class start, as it was an old-established firm. I must say that when I went for the interview I was surprised at the windows, and the stairs up to the offices were also far from clean. There was a little waiting room, where some of the elements were missing from the gas fire, and the carpet on the floor was worn. However, Mr. Heygate's office, into which I was shown for the interview, was better. The furniture was old, but it was polished, and there was a good carpet, I will say that. The glass of the bookcase was very clean.

I was to start on the Monday, so along I went. They took me to the general office, where there were two senior shorthand-typists, and a clerk, Mr. Gresham, who was far from smart in appearance. You should have seen the mess!! There was no floor covering whatsoever, and so dusty everywhere. There were shelves all round the room, with old box files on them. The box files were falling to pieces, and all the old papers inside them were crumpled. The worst shock of all was the tea cups. It was my duty to make tea, mornings and afternoons. Miss Bewlay showed me where everything was kept. It was kept in an old orange box, and the cups were all cracked. There were not enough saucers to go round, etc. I will not go into the facilities, but they were also far from hygienic. After three days, I told Mum, and she was upset, most of all about the cracked cups. We never keep a cracked cup, but throw it out, because those cracks can harbour germs. So Mum gave me my own cup to take to the office.

Then at the end of the week, when I got my salary, Mr. Heygate said, "Well, Lorna, what are you going to do with your first pay?" I did not like him saying this, and I nearly passed a comment, but I said, "I don't know." He said, "What do you do in the evenings, Lorna? Do you watch Telly?" I did take this as an insult, because we call it TV, and his remark made me out to be uneducated. I just stood, and did not answer, and he looked surprised. Next day, Saturday, I told Mum and Dad about the facilities, and we decided I should not go back to that job. Also, the desks in the general office were rickety. Dad was indignant, because Mr. Heygate's concern was flourishing, and he had letters after his name.

Everyone admires our flat, because Mum keeps it spotless, and Dad keeps doing things to it. He has done it up all over, and got permission from the Council to re-modernise the kitchen.[2] I well recall the Health Visitor remarking to Mum, "You could eat off your floor, Mrs. Merrified." It is true that you could eat your lunch off Mum's floors, and any hour of the day or night you will find every corner spick and span.

Next, I was sent by the agency to a Publisher's for an interview, because of being good at English. One look was enough!! My next interview was a success, and I am still at Low's Chemical Co. It is a modern block, with a quarter of an hour rest period, morning and afternoon. Mr. Marwood is very smart in appearance. He is well spoken, although he has not got a unversity education behind him. There is special lighting over the desks, and the typewriters are latest models.

So I am happy at Low's. But I have met other people, of an educated type, in the past year, and it has opened my eyes. It so happened that I had to go to the Doctor's house, to fetch a prescription for my young brother, Trevor, when the epidemic was on. I rang the bell, and Mrs. Darby came to the door. She was small, with fair hair, but too long, and a green maternity dress. But she was very nice to me. I had to wait in their livingroom, and you should have seen the state it was in! There were broken toys on the carpet, and the ash trays were full up. There were contemporary pictures on the walls, but the furniture was not contemporary, but old-fashioned, with covers which were past standing up to another wash, I should say. To cut a long story short, Dr. Darby and Mrs. Darby have always been very kind to me, and they meant everything for the best. Dr. Darby is also short and fair, and they have three children, a girl and a boy, and now a baby boy.

When I went that day for the prescription, Dr. Darby said to me, "You look pale, Lorna. It's the London atmosphere. Come on a picnic with us, in the car, on Saturday." After that I went with the Darbys more and more. I liked them, but I did not like the mess, and it was a surprise. But I also kept in with them for the opportunity of meeting people, and Mum and Dad were pleased that I had made nice friends.

So I did not say anything about the cracked lino, and the paintwork all chipped. The children's clothes were very shabby for a doctor, and she changed them out of their school clothes when they came home from school into those worn-out garments. Mum always kept us spotless to go out to play, and I do not like to say it, but those Darby children frequently looked like the Leary family, which the Council evicted from our block, as they were far from houseproud.

One day, when I was there, Mavis (as I called Mrs. Darby by then) put her head out of the window, and shouted to the boy, "John, stop peeing over the cabbages at once. Pee on the lawn." I did not know which way to look. Mum would never say a word like that from the window, and I know for a fact that Trevor would never pass water outside, not even bathing in the sea.

I went there usually at the weekends, but sometimes on weekdays, after supper. They had an idea to make a match for me with a chemist's assistant, whom they had taken up too. He was an orphan, and I do not say there was anything wrong with that. But he was not accustomed to those little extras that I was. He was a good-looking boy, I will say that. So I went once to a dance, and twice to the films with him. To look at, he was quite clean in appearance. But there was only hot water at the weekend at his place, and he said that a bath once a week was sufficient. Jim (as I called Dr. Darby by then) said it was sufficient also, and surprised me. He did not have much money, and I do not hold that against him. But there was no hurry for me, and I could wait for a man in a better position, so that I would not miss those little extras. So he started going out with a girl from the coffee bar, and did not come to the Darbys very much then.

There were plenty of boys at the office, but I will say this for the Darbys, they had lots of friends coming and going, and they had interesting conversation, although sometimes it gave me a surprise, and I did not know where to look. And sometimes they had people who were very down and out, although there is no need to be. But most of the guests were different, so it made a comparison with the boys at the office, who were not so educated in their conversation.

Now it was near the time for Mavis to have her baby, and I was to come in at the weekend, to keep an eye on the children, while the help had her day off. Mavis did not go away to have her baby, but would have it at home, in their double bed, as they did not have twin beds, although he was a Doctor. A girl I knew, in our block, was engaged, but was let down, and even she had her baby in the labour ward. I was sure the bedroom was not hygienic for having a baby, but I did not mention it.

One day, after the baby boy came along, they took me in the car to the country, to see Jim's mother. The baby was put in a carry-cot at the back of the car. He began to cry, and without a word of a lie, Jim said to him over his shoulder, "Oh shut your gob, you little bastard." I did not know what to do, and Mavis was smoking a cigarette. Dad would not dream of saying such a thing to Trevor or I. When we arrived at Jim's mother's place, Jim said, "It's a fourteenth-century cottage, Lorna." I could well believe it. It was very cracked and old, and it made one wonder how Jim could let his old mother live in this tumble-down cottage, as he was so good to everyone else. So Mavis knocked at the door, and the old lady came. There was not much anyone could do to the inside. Mavis said, "Isn't it charming, Lorna?" If that was a joke, it was going too far. I said to the old Mrs. Darby, "Are you going to be rehoused?" but she did not understand this, and I explained how you have to apply to the Council, and keep at them. But it was funny that the Council had not done something already, when they go round condemning. Then old Mrs. Darby said, "My dear, I shall be re-housed in the Grave." I did not know where to look.

There was a carpet hanging on the wall, which I think was there to hide a damp spot. She had a good TV set, I will say that. But some of the walls were bare brick, and the facilities were outside, through the garden. The furniture was far from new.

One Saturday afternoon, as I happened to go to the Darbys, they were just going off to a film, and they took me too. It was the Curzon, and afterwards we went to a flat in Curzon Street. It was a very clean block, I will say that, and there were good carpets at the entrance. The couple there had contemporary furniture, and they also spoke about music. It was a nice place, but there was no Welfare Centre to the flats, where people could go for social intercourse, advice and guidance. But they were well-spoken, and I met Willy Morley, who was an artist. Willy sat beside me, and we had a drink. He was young, dark, with a dark shirt, so one could not see right away if he was clean. Soon after this, Jim said to me, "Willy wants to paint you, Lorna. But you'd better ask your Mum." Mum said it was all right if he was a friend of the Darbys.

I can honestly say that Willy's place was the most unhygienic place I have seen in my life. He said I had an unusual type of beauty, which he must capture. This was when we came back to his place from the restaurant. The light was very dim, but I could see the bed had not been made, and the sheets were far from clean. He said he must paint me, but I told Mavis I did not like to go back there. "Don't you like Willy?" she asked. I could not deny that I liked Willy, in a way. There was something about him, I will say that. Mavis said, "I hope he hasn't been making a pass at you, Lorna." I said he had not done so, which was almost true, because he did not attempt to go to the full extent. It was always unhygienic when I went to Willy's place, and I told him so once, but he said, "Lorna, you are a joy." He had a nice way, and he took me out in his car, which was a good one, but dirty inside, like his place. Jim said one day, "He has pots of money, Lorna," and Mavis said, "You might

make a man of him, as he is keen on you."
They always said Willy came from a good
family.

But I saw that one could not do anything
with him. He would not change his shirt very
often, or get clothes, but he went around like a
tramp, lending people money, as I have seen
with my own eyes. His place was in a terrible
mess, with the empty bottles, and laundry in
the corner. He gave me several gifts over the
period, which I took, as he would have only
given them away, but he never tried to go to
the full extent. He never painted my portrait,
as he was painting fruit on a table all that
time, and they said his pictures were marvellous, and thought Willy and I were getting
married.

One night, when I went home, I was upset
as usual, after Willy's place. Mum and Dad
had gone to bed, and I looked round our
kitchen which is done in primrose and white.

Then I went into the livingroom, where Dad
has done one wall in a patterned paper, deep
rose and white, and the other walls pale rose,
with white wood-work. The suite is new, and
Mum keeps everything beautiful. So it came
to me, all of a sudden, what a fool I was, going
with Willy. I agree to equality, but as to me
marrying Willy, as I said to Mavis, when I
recall his place, and the good carpet gone
greasy, not to mention the paint oozing out of
the tubes, I think it would break my heart to
sink so low.

NOTES

1. A grammar school is attended by those preparing for
   college. The narrator's school prepared its students for
   the work force.
2. The narrator lives in a flat owned and operated by the
   local town council. The rent of these apartments is
   often subsidized because they are occupied by poor,
   usually working class, people.

Sophia de Mello Breyner Andresen   *Portugal, b. 1919*

Sophia de Mello Breyner Andresen is the daughter of an aristocratic family from
the northern Oporto region. She moved to Lisbon to study the classics at the
University and later relocated her life permanently in that city. Sophia (as she is
commonly known) became a recognized poet as early as 1944 but she also earned
a reputation as a political activist. Fiercely antagonistic to the Salazar regime, she
accepted political office as a Socialist member of Parliament in 1975 shortly after
the revolution that put an end to dictatorship. She also served an extended term as
President of the Portuguese Writers' Association in the mid-1970s. Since then,
Sophia has withdrawn from the political arena and has to some extent disappeared
from public view, having decided that a writer's must effective efforts at social
change are those that she makes through her writing. Leaving behind her struggle
on behalf of political prisoners, she has become instead a champion of literacy and
culture for all. To that end, she has re-edited the numerous collections of children's
stories she published earlier.

Sophia de Mello Breyner Andresen's poetry does not fit nicely into any literary
niche. It is informed by a variety of influences: readings in earlier Portuguese
poetry, above all, that of Fernando Pessoa; her studies of the classics; her communion with nature, with the sea in particular. Her poetry is a highly individualized
construct of translucent poetic moments.

Sophia's *oeuvre* consists of the aforementioned collections of children's stories, a number of critical essays, translations of Claudel, Dante, Shakespeare and Euripides, and a dozen books of poetry. The two poems in this anthology are from her early books: *Coral* (1950) and *Mar Novo* (New Sea, 1958). The most recent volumes of poetry are *O Nome das Coisas* (The Name of Things, 1977) and *Navegações* (Navigations, 1983). The earlier poems can best be read in *Antologia* (Anthology, 1978). She is the mother of five, the initial recipients of her early children's stories.

Alice Clemente

LISTEN
Ouve

Listen:
Everything is calm and smooth and sleeping.
The walls apparent, the floor reflecting,
And painted on the glass of the window,
The sky, green emptiness, two trees.
Close your eyes and rest no less profoundly
Than any other thing which never flowered.

Don't touch anything, don't look, don't
                              recollect

One step enough
To shatter the furniture baked
By endless, unused days of sunlight.

Don't remember, don't anticipate.
You do not share the nature of a fruit:
Nothing here that time or sun will ripen.

Translated by Ruth Fainlight

THIS IS THE TIME
Este é o tempo

This is the time
Of a jungle without meaning

Even the blue air coagulates to gratings
And the sun's light becomes obscene.

This the night
Thick with jackals
Weighted with grief

The time when men give up.

Translated by Ruth Fainlight

Louise Bennett   *Jamaica, b. 1919*

Louise Bennett is known not only as a poet, but as a personality emblematic of Jamaican culture. A vivid performer, she gives frequent readings of her poems, often taking on the persona of one of the characters, particularly Miss Mattie. She writes in Jamaican dialect and has been an important force in validating Jamaican culture. Although she has been described as a comic poet, her writing, lighthearted in appearance, is very serious and very political, as we see below in 'Colonization in Reverse," "Jamaican Woman," and "Pass fi White," one of her most famous poems, which captures the tragedy of self-hatred wrought by racism ("She fail her exam, but she passin dere fi white!"). These are from *Selected Poems*.

Bennett was born in Kingston, Jamaica; her father, a baker, died when she was 7 and her mother, a seamstress, supported them both with great difficulty. She started writing her dialect poems in high school and they were so popular that she began performing them for audiences. She also started a Sunday column in the *Gleaner* newspaper. At around the same time, she published her first poetry collection, *Verses in Jamaican Dialect* (1942). Although busy with her writing and performing, Bennett attended Friends' College and finished a course in social work.

In 1945, Bennett won a scholarship to the Royal Academy of Dramatic Art in London. In London, she had her own show on the BBC but left the British capital, despite its promising opportunities, to return to Jamaica. Bennett also lived for a while in the United States where she and Eric Coverly co-directed a folk musical called *Day in Jamaica*.

Bennett married Coverly in 1954 and returned to Jamaica where she worked for the Jamaican Social Welfare Commission, becoming a director in 1959. Her social work, which involved much travel around Jamaica, gave her an opportunity to study the country's folklore and oral traditions, and her rich understanding of her country's cultural heritage has greatly informed her poetry.

Much of Bennett's poetry began as journalism, in newspaper columns and for radio programs. The fact that her writing depends so much on dialogue—its rhythm and tone—has made some critics unwilling to take her seriously as a poet, for they think of her works as being closer to drama. Others complain that her use of Jamaican dialect is "substandard" and shouldn't be encouraged. Since her publication of *Jamaica Labrish* in 1966, however, she has been more widely read and respected and several serious studies have been made of her writing. She is now generally considered one of the most distinguished Caribbean writers. She has received several awards, including an MBE in 1960, the Order of Jamaica in 1974 and an honorary D. Litt from the University of the West Indies in 1983. She has published numerous volumes of her poems and has made several records, many of which appear under her stage name, Miss Lou.

COLONIZATION IN REVERSE

What a joyful news, Miss Mattie;
Ah feel like me heart gwine burs—
Jamaica people colonizin
Englan in reverse.

By de hundred, by de tousan,
From country an from town,
By de ship-load, by de plane-load,
Jamaica is Englan boun.

Dem a pour out a Jamaica;
Everybody future plan
Is fi get a big-time job
An settle in de motherlan.

What a islan! What a people!
Man an woman, ole an young
Jussa pack dem bag an baggage
An tun history upside dung!

Some people doan like travel,
But fi show dem loyalty
Dem all a open up cheap-fare-
To-Englan agency;

An week by week dem shippin off
Dem countryman like fire
Fi immigrate an populate
De seat a de Empire.

Oonoo[1] se how life is funny,
Oonoo see de tunabout?
Jamaica live fi box bread
Out a English people mout.[2]

For when dem catch a Englan
An start play dem different role
Some will settle down to work
An some will settle fi de dole.

Jane seh de dole is not too bad
Because dey payin she
Two pounds a week fi seek a job
Dat suit her dignity.

Me seh Jane will never fine work
At de rate how she dah look
For all day she stay pon Aunt Fan couch
An read love-story book.

What a devilment a Englan!
Dem face war an brave de worse;
But ah wonderin how dem gwine stan
Colonizin in reverse.

NOTES

1. You.
2. Mouth.

JAMAICA OMAN

Jamaica oman cunny,[1] sah!
Is how dem jinnal[2] so?
Look how long dem liberated
An de man dem never know!

Look how long Jamaica oman
—Modder, sister, wife, sweetheart—
Outa road an eena yard deh pon
A dominate her part!

From Maroon Nanny[3] teck her body
Bounce bullet back pon man,
To when nowadays gal-pickney[4] tun
Spellin-Bee champion.[5]

From de grass root to de hill-top,
In profession, skill an trade,
Jamaica oman teck her time
Dah mount an meck de grade.

Some backa man a push, some side-a
Man a hole[6] him han,
Some a lick sense eena man head,
Some a guide him pon him plan!

Neck and neck an foot an foot wid man
She buckle hole her own;
While man a call her "so-so rib"
Oman backbone!

An long before Oman Lib bruck out
Over foreign lan
Jamaica female wasa work
Her liberated plan!

Jamaica oman know she strong,
She know she tallawah,[7]
But she no want her pickney-dem
Fi start call her "Puppa".[8]

So de cunny Jamma oman
Gwan like pants-suit is a style,
An Jamaica man no know she wear
De trousiz all de while!

So Jamaica oman coaxin
Fambly budget from explode
A so Jamaica man a sing
"Oman a heaby load!"

But de cunny Jamma oman
Ban[9] her belly, bite her tongue,
Ketch water, put pot pon fire
An jus dig her toe a grung[10]

For "Oman luck deh a dungle,"[11]
Some rooted more dan some,
But as long as fowl a scratch dungle heap
Oman luck mus come!

Lickle by lickle man start praise her,
Day by day de praise a grow;
So him praise her, so it sweet her,
For she wonder if him know.

NOTES

1. Cunning.
2. Tricky.
3. 18th century Jamaican resistance leader.
4. Child.
5. The winner of the National Spelling Bee has often a woman.
6. Grab.
7. Strong.
8. Father.
9. Binds.
10. Ground.
11. Junk heap.

PASS FI WHITE

Miss Jane jus hear from Merica[1]—
Her daughter proudly write
Fiseh she fail her exam, but
She passin dere fi white!

She seh fi tell de trute she know
Her brain part not so bright—
She couldn pass tru college
So she try fi pass fi white.

She passin wid her work-mate-dem,
She passin wid her boss,
An a nice white bwoy she love dah gwan
Wid her like seh she pass!

But sometime she get fretful and
Her heart start gallop fas
An she bruck out eena cole-sweat
Jussa wonder ef she pass!

Jane get bex,[2] seh she sen de gal
Fi learn bout edication,
It look like seh de gal gawn weh
Gawn work pon her complexion.

She no haffi[3] tan[4] a foreign
Under dat deh strain an fright
For plenty copper-color gal
Deh home yah dah play white.

Her fambily is nayga,[5] but
Dem pedigree is right—
She hope de gal no gawn an tun
No boogooyagga[6] white.

De gal puppa dah laugh an seh
It serve Merica right—
Five year back dem Jim-Crow him, now
Dem pass him pickney white.

Him dah boas all bout de distric
How him daughter is fus-class,
How she smarter dan American
An over deh dah pass!

Some people tink she pass B.A.,
Some tink she pass D.R.—[7]
Wait till dem fine out seh she ongle[8]
Pass de color bar.

NOTES

1. America.
2. Vexed.
3. Have to.
4. Wait.
5. Negro.
6. Low class.
7. Bennett's acronym for doctorate.
8. Only.

Doris Lessing

Rhodesia/UK(England), b. 1919

Doris Lessing, one of England's greatest writers, was born in Khermanshah, Persia, and moved at age 5 to a farm in Southern Rhodesia. Her family was extremely poor and her education was spotty; she went to convent and government schools and, on occasion, studied at home. When 15, she left school entirely and began working as a telephone operator, and later, as a secretary. During those years she became increasingly political and her 1939 marriage to a civil servant could not survive her increasing alienation from the tradition-bound life of the white community in Rhodesia. The marriage lasted only four years, producing two children. In 1945 she married fellow-Communist Gottfried Lessing, a German Jew who was in Africa as a refugee from Hitler. The marriage produced one son. In 1949, they left Rhodesia for England; her husband returned to East Germany shortly afterward to pursue a successful career in the new Communist government.

Lessing's years in Africa had a great influence on her writing. *The Grass is Singing* (1950), Lessing's first novel, is about white farmers in Rhodesia and the horrors of black-white relations there. The five-volume series of semi-autobiographical novels about Martha Quest (*Children of Violence*), published from 1952 to 1969, begins in Lessing's Africa, but, like Lessing, Martha emigrates to England, and the final volume of the quintet, *The Four-Gated City*, sees the destruction of the world from nuclear holocaust. The books create a profoundly realistic picture of a woman's psychological conflicts as she battles to understand her motivations and fights to become independent from the tyranny of sexual oppression.

The Golden Notebook (1962), the most influential of Lessing's books, was written before she had finished the Martha Quest series. Considered by many the first modern feminist novel, it traces the personal and professional life of writer Anna Wulf through her journals, which analyze the growth of her feminist consciousness. The book depicts male-female relationships with great depth and sensitivity.

Beginning in the 1970s, Lessing's novels leave realism for science fiction. Her recent series of books, *Shikasta* (1979), *The Marriages between Zones Three, Four and Five* (1980), *The Sirian Experiments* (1981), and *The Making of the Representative for Planet 8* (1982), are believed by many critics to be considerably weaker than her earlier novels. All Lessing's works have been didactic; indeed, Lessing has argued, in an essay entitled "A Small Personal Voice" (1959), that a writer must be a moral force and present the choices between good and evil that we all face. However, the later books have been accused of sacrificing convincing human interaction and character development for message.

Her most recent novels, however, including *The Diaries of Jane Somers* (1984) and *The Good Terrrorist* (1985), represent a return to realistic storytelling for Lessing, at least for the present. The former, *Jane Somers*, was originally published pseudonymously as a hoax to reveal how difficult it is for new, good writers to gain a readership.

Many of Lessing's numerous short stories have been widely anthologized. Particularly significant stories for women readers are "One Off the Short List," a psychological analysis of compulsive sexual exploitation, and "To Room Nineteen," about a woman's loss of identity in conventional domesticity. The selection, "A Woman on a Roof," is from the collection *A Man and Two Women* (1963).

Lessing won the Somerset Maugham Award in 1954 for *Five: Short Novels* and the Prix Medici in 1976. She has lately been mentioned as a strong candidate for the Nobel Prize.

A WOMAN ON A ROOF

It was during the week of hot sun, that June.

Three men were at work on the roof, where the leads got so hot they had the idea of throwing water on to cool them. But the water steamed, then sizzled; and they made jokes about getting an egg from some woman in the flats under them, to poach it for their dinner. By two it was not possible to touch the guttering they were replacing, and they speculated about what workmen did in regularly hot countries. Perhaps they should borrow kitchen gloves with the egg? They were all a bit dizzy, not used to the heat; and they shed their coats and stood side by side squeezing themselves into a foot-wide patch of shade against a chimney, careful to keep their feet in the thick socks and boots out of the sun. There was a fine view across several acres of roofs. Not far off a man sat in a deck chair reading the newspapers. Then they saw her, between chimneys, about fifty yards away. She lay face down on a brown blanket. They could see the top part of her: black hair, a flushed solid back, arms spread out.

"She's stark naked," said Stanley, sounding annoyed.

Harry, the oldest, a man of about forty-five, said: "Looks like it."

Young Tom, seventeen, said nothing, but he was excited and grinning.

Stanley said: "Someone'll report her if she doesn't watch out."

"She thinks no one can see," said Tom, craning his head all ways to see more.

At this point the woman, still lying prone, brought her two hands up behind her shoulders with the ends of a scarf in them, tied it behind her back, and sat up. She wore a red scarf tied around her breasts and brief red bikini pants. This being the first day of the sun she was white, flushing red. She sat smoking, and did not look up when Stanley let out a wolf whistle. Harry said: "Small things amuse small minds," leading the way back to their part of the roof, but it was scorching. Harry said: "Wait, I'm going to rig up some shade," and disappeared down the skylight into the building. Now that he'd gone, Stanley and Tom went to the farthest point they could to peer at the woman. She had moved, and all they could see were two pink legs stretched on the blanket. They whistled and shouted but the legs did not move. Harry came back with a blanket and shouted: "Come on, then." He sounded irritated with them. They clambered back to him and he said to Stanley: "What

about your missus?" Stanley was newly married, about three months. Stanley said, jeering: "What about my missus?"—preserving his independence. Tom said nothing, but his mind was full of the nearly naked woman. Harry slung the blanket, which he had borrowed from a friendly woman downstairs, from the stem of a television aerial to a row of chimney pots. This shade fell across the piece of gutter they had to replace. But the shade kept moving, they had to adjust the blanket, and not much progress was made. At last some of the heat left the roof, and they worked fast, making up for lost time. First Stanley, then Tom, made a trip to the end of the roof to see the woman. "She's on her back," Stanley said, adding a jest which made Tom snicker, and the older man smile tolerantly. Tom's report was that she hadn't moved, but it was a lie. He wanted to keep what he had seen to himself: he had caught her in the act of rolling down the little red pants over her hips, till they were no more than a small triangle. She was on her back, fully visible, glistening with oil.

Next morning, as soon as they came up, they went to look. She was already there, face down, arms spread out, naked except for the little red pants. She had turned brown in the night. Yesterday she was a scarlet and white woman, today she was a brown woman. Stanley let out a whistle. She lifted her head, startled, as if she'd been asleep, and looked straight over at them. The sun was in her eyes, she blinked and stared, then she dropped her head again. At this gesture of indifference, they all three, Stanley, Tom, and old Harry, let out whistles and yells. Harry was doing it in parody of the younger men, making fun of them, but he was also angry. They were all angry because of her utter indifference to the three men watching her.

"Bitch," said Stanley.

"She should ask us over," said Tom, snickering.

Harry recovered himself and reminded

Stanley: "If she's married, her old man wouldn't like that."

"Christ," said Stanley virtuously, "if my wife lay about like that, for everyone to see, I'd soon stop her."

Harry said, smiling: "How do you know, perhaps she's sunning herself at this very moment?"

"Not a chance, not on our roof." The safety of his wife put Stanley into a good humour, and they went to work. But today it was hotter than yesterday; and several times one or the other suggested they should tell Matthew, the foreman, and ask to leave the roof until the heat wave was over. But they didn't. There was work to be done in the basement of the big block of flats, but up here they felt free, on a different level from ordinary humanity shut in the streets or the buildings. A lot more people came out onto the roofs that day, for an hour at midday. Some married couples sat side by side in deck chairs, the women's legs stockingless and scarlet, the men in vests with reddening shoulders.

The woman stayed on her blanket, turning herself over and over. She ignored them, no matter what they did. When Harry went off to fetch more screws, Stanley said: "Come on." Her roof belonged to a different system of roofs, separated from theirs at one point by about twenty feet. It meant a scrambling climb from one level to another, edging along parapets, clinging to chimneys, while their big boots slipped and slithered, but at last they stood on a small square projecting roof looking straight down at her, close. She sat smoking, reading a book. Tom thought she looked like a poster, or a magazine cover, with the blue sky behind her and her legs stretched out. Behind her a great crane at work on a new building in Oxford Street swung its black arm across the roofs in a great arc. Tom imagined himself at work on the crane, adjusting the arm to swing over and pick her up and swing her back across the sky to drop her near him.

They whistled. She looked up at them, cool and remote, then went on reading. Again, they were furious. Or rather, Stanley was. His sun-heated face was screwed into rage as he whistled again and again, trying to make her look up. Young Tom stopped whistling. He stood beside Stanley, excited, grinning; but he felt as if he were saying to the woman: "Don't associate me with *him*," for his grin was apologetic. Last night he had thought of the unknown woman before he slept, and she had been tender with him. This tenderness he was remembering as he shifted his feet by the jeering, whistling Stanley, and watched the indifferent, healthy brown woman a few feet off, with the gap that plunged to the street between them. Tom thought it was romantic, it was like being high on two hilltops. But there was a shout from Harry, and they clambered back. Stanley's face was hard, really angry. The boy kept looking at him and wondered why he hated the woman so much, for by now he loved her.

They played their little games with the blanket, trying to trap shade to work under; but again it was not until nearly four that they could work seriously, and they were exhausted, all three of them. They were grumbling about the weather, by now. Stanley was in a thoroughly bad humour. When they made their routine trip to see the woman before they packed up for the day, she was apparently asleep, face down, her back all naked save for the scarlet triangle on her buttocks. "I've got a good mind to report her to the police," said Stanley, and Harry said: "What's eating you? What harm's she doing?"

"I tell you, if she was my wife!"

"But she isn't, is she?" Tom knew that Harry, like himself, was uneasy at Stanley's reaction. He was normally a sharp young man, quick at his work, making a lot of jokes, good company.

"Perhaps it will be cooler tomorrow," said Harry.

But it wasn't, it was hotter, if anything, and the weather forecast said the good weather would last. As soon as they were on the roof, Harry went over to see if the woman were there, and Tom knew it was to prevent Stanley going, to put off his bad humour. Harry had grown-up children, a boy the same age as Tom, and the youth trusted and looked up to him.

Harry came back and said: "She's not there."

"I bet her old man has put his foot down," said Stanley, and Harry and Tom caught each other's eyes and smiled behind the young married man's back.

Harry suggested they should get permission to work in the basement, and they did, that day. But before packing up Stanley said: "Let's have a breath of fresh air." Again Harry and Tom smiled at each other as they followed Stanley up to the roof, Tom in the devout conviction that he was there to protect the woman from Stanley. It was about five-thirty, and a calm, full sunlight lay over the roofs. The great crane still swung its black arm from Oxford Street to above their heads. She was not there. Then there was a flutter of white from behind a parapet, and she stood up, in a belted, white dressing gown. She had been there all day, probably, but on a different patch of roof, to hide from them. Stanley did not whistle, he said nothing, but watched the woman bend to collect papers, books, cigarettes, then fold the blanket over her arm. Tom was thinking: If they weren't here, I'd go over and say. . .what? But he knew from his nightly dreams of her that she was kind and friendly. Perhaps she would ask him down to her flat? Perhaps. . . .He stood watching her disappear down the skylight. As she went, Stanley let out a shrill derisive yell; she started, and it seemed as if she nearly fell. She clutched to save herself, they could hear things falling. She looked straight at them, angry. Harry said, facetiously: "Better be careful on those slippery ladders, love." Tom knew he said it to save her from Stanley, but she could not know it. She vanished, frowning. Tom was full of a secret

delight, because he knew her anger was for the others, not for him.

"Roll on some rain," said Stanley, bitter, looking at the blue evening sky.

Next day was cloudless, and they decided to finish the work in the basement. They felt excluded, shut in the grey cement basement fitting pipes, from the holiday atmosphere of London in a heat wave. At lunchtime they came up for some air, but while the married couples, and the men in shirt-sleeves or vests, were there, she was not there, either on her usual patch of roof or where she had been yesterday. They all, even Harry, clambered about, between chimney pots, over parapets, the hot leads stinging their fingers. There was not a sign of her. They took off their shirts and vests and exposed their chests, feeling their feet sweaty and hot. They did not mention the woman. But Tom felt alone again. Last night she had asked him into her flat: it was big and had fitted white carpets and a bed with a padded white leather headtop. She wore a black filmy negligée and her kindness to Tom thickened his throat as he remembered it. He felt she had betrayed him by not being there.

And again after work they climbed up, but still there was nothing to be seen of her. Stanley kept repeating that if it was as hot as this tomorrow he wasn't going to work and that's all there was to it. But they were all there next day. By ten the temperature was in the middle seventies, and it was eighty long before noon. Harry went to the foreman to say it was impossible to work on the leads in that heat; but the foreman said there was nothing else he could put them on, and they'd have to. At midday they stood, silent, watching the skylight on her roof open, and then she slowly emerged in her white gown, holding a bundle of blankets. She looked at them, gravely, then went to the part of the roof where she was hidden from them. Tom was pleased. He felt she was more his when the other men couldn't see her. They had taken off their shirts and vests, but now they put them back again, for they felt the sun bruising their flesh. "She must have the hide of a rhino," said Stanley, tugging at guttering and swearing. They stopped work, and sat in the shade, moving around behind chimney stacks. A woman came to water a yellow window box just opposite them. She was middle-aged, wearing a flowered summer dress. Stanley said to her: "We need a drink more than them." She smiled and said: "Better drop down to the pub quick, it'll be closing in a minute." They exchanged pleasantries, and she left them with a smile and a wave.

"Not like Lady Godiva," said Stanley. "She can give us a bit of a chat and a smile."

"You didn't whistle at *her*," said Tom, reproving.

"Listen to him," said Stanley, "you didn't whistle, then?"

But the boy felt as if he hadn't whistled, as if only Harry and Stanley had. He was making plans, when it was time to knock off work, to get left behind and somehow make his way over to the woman. The weather report said the hot spell was due to break, so he had to move quickly. But there was no chance of being left. The other two decided to knock off work at four, because they were exhausted. As they went down, Tom quickly climbed a parapet and hoisted himself higher by pulling his weight up a chimney. He caught a glimpse of her lying on her back, her knees up, eyes closed, a brown woman lolling in the sun. He slipped and clattered down, as Stanley looked for information: "She's gone down," he said. He felt as if he had protected her from Stanley, and that she must be grateful to him. He could feel the bond between the woman and himself.

Next day, they stood around on the landing below the roof, reluctant to climb up into the heat. The woman who had lent Harry the blanket came out and offered them a cup of tea. They accepted gratefully, and sat around Mrs. Pritchett's kitchen an hour or so, chatting. She was married to an airline pilot. A smart blonde, of about thirty, she had an eye for the handsome sharpfaced Stanley; and the two teased each other while Harry sat in a corner, watching, indulgent, though his expression reminded Stanley that he was married. And young Tom felt envious of Stanley's ease in badinage; felt, too, that Stanley's getting off with Mrs. Pritchett left his romance with the woman on the roof safe and intact.

"I thought they said the heat wave'd break," said Stanley, sullen, as the time approached when they really would have to climb up into the sunlight.

"You don't like it, then?" asked Mrs. Pritchett.

"All right for some," said Stanley. "Nothing to do but lie about as if it was a beach up there. Do you ever go up?"

"Went up once," said Mrs. Pritchett. "But it's a dirty place up there, and it's too hot."

"Quite right too," said Stanley.

Then they went up, leaving the cool neat little flat and friendly Mrs. Pritchett.

As soon as they were up they saw her. The three men looked at her, resentful at her ease in this punishing sun. Then Harry said, because of the expression on Stanley's face: "Come on, we've got to pretend to work, at least."

They had to wrench another length of guttering that ran beside a parapet out of its bed, so that they could replace it. Stanley took it in his two hands, tugged, swore, stood up. "Fuck it," he said, and sat down under a chimney. He lit a cigarette. "Fuck them," he said. "What do they think we are, lizards? I've got blisters all over my hands." Then he jumped up and climbed over the roofs and stood with his back to them. He put his fingers either side of his mouth and let out a shrill whistle. Tom and Harry squatted, not looking at each other, watching him. They could just see the woman's head, the beginnings of her brown shoulders. Stanley whistled again. Then he began stamping with his feet, and whistled and yelled and screamed at the woman, his face getting scarlet. He seemed quite mad, as he stamped and whistled, while the woman did not move, she did not move a muscle.

"Barmy," said Tom.

"Yes," said Harry, disapproving.

Suddenly the older man came to a decision. It was, Tom knew, to save some sort of scandal or real trouble over the woman. Harry stood up and began packing tools into a length of oily cloth. "Stanley," he said, commanding. At first Stanley took no notice, but Harry said: "Stanley, we're packing it in, I'll tell Matthew."

Stanley came back, cheeks mottled, eyes glaring.

"Can't go on like this," said Harry. "It'll break in a day or so. I'm going to tell Matthew we've got sunstroke, and if he doesn't like it, it's too bad." Even Harry sounded aggrieved, Tom noted. The small, competent man, the family man with his grey hair, who was never at a loss, sounded really off balance. "Come on," he said, angry. He fitted himself into the open square in the roof, and went down, watching his feet on the ladder. Then Stanley went, with not a glance at the woman. Then Tom who, his throat beating with excitement, silently promised her in a backward glance: Wait for me, wait, I'm coming.

On the pavement Stanley said: "I'm going home." He looked white now, so perhaps he really did have sunstroke. Harry went off to find the foreman who was at work on the plumbing of some flats down the street. Tom slipped back, not into the building they had been working on, but the building on whose roof the woman lay. He went straight up, no one stopping him. The skylight stood open, with an iron ladder leading up. He emerged onto the roof a couple of yards from her. She sat up, pushing back her black hair with both hands. The scarf across her breasts bound them tight, and brown flesh bulged around it. Her legs were brown and smooth. She stared at him in silence. The boy stood grinning, foolish, claiming the tenderness he expected from her.

"What do you want?" she asked.

"I...I came to...make your acquaint-

ance," he stammered, grinning, pleading with her.

They looked at each other, the slight, scarlet-faced excited boy, and the serious, nearly naked woman. Then, without a word, she lay down on her brown blanket, ignoring him.

"You like the sun, do you?" he enquired of her glistening back.

Not a word. He felt panic, thinking of how she had held him in her arms, stroked his hair, brought him where he sat, lordly, in her bed, a glass of some exhilarating liquor he had never tasted in life. He felt that if he knelt down, stroked her shoulders, her hair, she would turn and clasp him in her arms.

He said: "The sun's all right for you, isn't it?"

She raised her head, set her chin on two small fists. "Go away," she said. He did not move. "Listen," she said, in a slow reasonable voice, where anger was kept in check, though with difficulty; looking at him, her face weary with anger: "If you get a kick out of seeing women in bikinis, why don't you take a sixpenny bus ride to the Lido? You'd see dozens of them, without all this mountaineering."

She hadn't understood him. He felt her unfairness pale him. He stammered: "But I like you, I've been watching you and..."

"Thanks," she said, and dropped her face again, turned away from him.

She lay there. He stood there. She said nothing. She had simply shut him out. He stood, saying nothing at all, for some minutes. He thought: She'll have to say something if I stay. But the minutes went past, with no sign of them in her, except in the tension of her back, her thighs, her arms—the tension of waiting for him to go.

He looked up at the sky, where the sun seemed to spin in heat; and over the roofs where he and his mates had been earlier. He could see the heat quivering where they had worked. "And they expect us to work in these conditions!" he thought, filled with righteous indignation. The woman hadn't moved. A bit of hot wind blew her black hair softly, it shone, and was iridescent. He remembered how he had stroked it last night.

Resentment of her at last moved him off and away down the ladder, through the building, into the street. He got drunk then, in hatred of her.

Next day when he woke the sky was grey.

He looked at the wet grey and thought, vicious: "Well, that's fixed you, hasn't it now? That's fixed you good and proper."

The three men were at work early on the cool leads, surrounded by damp drizzling roofs where no one came to sun themselves, black roofs, slimy with rain. Because it was cool now, they would finish the job that day, if they hurried.

Remedios Varo, Harmonie, *1942, oil on canvas. Courtesy Jeffrey Hoffeld & Co., New York*

Margaréta Liberáki   *Greece, b. 1919*

As Margaréta Liberáki is a very private person, it has been difficult to discover much about her private life. We know she was born in 1919 in Athens and has lived in Paris and Greece. Also, we know she studied law and drawing before turning to writing, publishing her three psychological novels, *Ta Déndra* (The Trees, 1945), *Ta Psáthina Kapélla* (The Straw Hats, 1946), and *O allos Aléxandros* (*The Other Alexander*, 1950), in close succession. Lyberáki's novels focus on her female characters and on male-female relations with *The Other Alexander* being more experimental than the other two.

Liberáki's later work, for which she is primarily known, is for the theater. She wrote six plays between 1954 and 1970, nearly all in both Greek and French. *I Danáides* (The Danaids), one of her most popular, was written in the 1950s, first published in French in 1963, performed at the Centre dramatique de Nanterre (Dramatic Center of Nanterre) in 1973, and published in Greek in 1978. So provocative was this work that the actors who first presented it wrote their own program notes stressing the political overtones of the sexual divisions in the play. I *Yinéka tou Kandávli* (Candaules' Wife, 1954), offers a particularly compelling analysis of disintegration, in which personal, sexual, and political polarities are studied as parallels.

Liberáki is very interested in mythology as a reflection of essential patterns in human behavior, particularly that of destruction and rebirth, which she sees in all facets of human life. In particular, she has gone back to ancient ritual for her texts, in works such as *To Mistírio* (The Mystery, 1976), *I Danáides*, and *Sparagmós* (Rending Asunder, 1970).

To Mistírio, an excerpt of which appears below, is a symbolic political text based on the student occupation of the Athens Polytechnic in November 1973 and its violent repression by the then military government.[1] It takes its title from the Eleusinian Mysteries and embodies the Dionysiac myth of ritual destruction and rebirth. The murdered student, Peter, thus becomes a symbol of his generation and his country. The form of the work, with its sections on Struggle, Passion, Grief, and Rebirth, is that of an initiatory rite. Throughout the text the goddess *Athena* is addressed by her name *in reverse*, Anetha, as a symbol of the need to turn the world inside out.[2]

Christopher Robinson

NOTES

1. In 1967 a coup brought a military dictatorship to power; this repressive government lost a referendum in 1974 and a democratic government replaced it.
2. The Eleusinian mysteries were religious rituals conducted by a sacred cult of the ancient Greek religion. Held at the temple of the goddess Demeter (the goddess of the Earth) in Eleusis, near Athens, these rites were based on the principles of birth and rebirth, also embodied in the ritual dances to Dionysus, the Greek god of fertility, music, and poetry. Athena is the Greek goddess of wisdom and reason.

from THE MYSTERY
To Mistírio

ANETHA THE RED

The statues run with blood when the goddesses menstruate, when they are deflowered, or when they drink your blood. The statue of the goddess is running with blood. Her robe is covered in bloodstains. The blood runs from her thighs (a mass of Greek blood) and turns the grass and the debris around her red—sticks, stones, pieces of iron, shoes, spectacle frames, a coffee pot, a little comb.

Blood is running from my ears. I am ashamed. I find it cheapening. It is because my brain has become detached from its walls and is shaking about. I have a concussion.

After the exodus the threshing floor was deserted, the iron ring remained and grew and embraced the whole of Athens which was now officially declared in a state of siege. There was a curfew after sunset, tanks everywhere, policemen with automatics everywhere—even at the doors of operating theaters—manhunts, arrests, beatings, military marches. The dictatorship had fallen but Fascism was still with us, the arch-Nazi General Ioannides is now in control. The affliction is great.

The last to come out was Christos. On Friday his legs wouldn't hold him any longer. Because of finishing his National Service he hadn't slept for days, so he had fallen asleep in the doorway behind the banana tree and had woken up on Saturday morning. He saw the empty courtyard and the policemen. Some of them were plundering the tinned food and cigarettes, throwing the tins to one another and laughing: others were hosing away the blood. The buildings were empty. Even the last stretcher had gone. The psychiatrist, Dr. Sakellarides, had gone with it: he had been duly beaten up, as had the injured man on the stretcher and the stretcher bearer, before the Black Maria carted them off to Police Headquarters. Christos stroked his close-cropped head, moving his hand around as free-ly as if his arm were growing between his shoulder blades. With a characteristic gesture he scratched his crown like a monkey, told himself, to bolster his confidence, that he looked like a secret policeman, put on an air of indifference and sauntered out.

It was a fine dawn. The army fell into ranks and left victorious, singing "Greece shall never die," while hundreds of policemen cried "Well done, lads!" and clapped. A helicopter was patrolling. Blood and water were running into the drains.

KORALIA'S LAUGHTER

I wasn't aware of them picking me up. When I fell I think I called out "Peter!" and I saw Peter running towards me and heard the burst of firing.

Now I can see soldiers in front of me all the time, I can hear their voices, I can see hundreds of policemen and Peter slain among them. The policemen are calling out to each other "Over here boys, fresh meat!" They are gathering round the pieces of Peter's body and counting them. A girl who looks like Koralia goes to stop them, pushes them out of the way, but they put her in the middle next to the corpse, make a ring round her, and unbutton their flies. They bring their clubs to their open trousers, hold them there with both hands above the dangling flesh and threaten to plunge them into her and tear her apart. When they ask her to save herself by renouncing the dead man, Koralia bursts out laughing. Koralia's laughter spills out of the forecourt and spreads in rings that get wider and wider, like the ripples you make when you throw a stone into the sea. It spreads out into the streets and squares—Kotzia Karaiskaki Koumoundourou —right up to Sacred Way.[1]

Koralia's laughter pierces my eardrums. I

am bleeding. My temples are going to burst.

I must take care of myself, who's going to do it for me, even doctors need treatment here, this place has shifted, lost its coherence and is continually oscillating between the black despair of loss and the exaggerated hope that the stones will become bread, and then back to loss and despair. I've got to get free of my sickness, my brain must get back into place, find its walls again, stop moving about and disturbing me, I'm afraid and dizzy. That's all. All I feel is fear.

People and places suddenly fragment in front of my eyes, nightmare images that tortured me when I was a child come back and torture me again, and I hide under the rugs and weep and am ashamed and dizzy and don't know what to hang on to—opposite me a hand cut off at the wrist is squeezing a bitter orange—what can I hang on to...

THE DERTILISES

I take the Dertilises and I herd them out to graze on a field of thorns. You're to chew and swallow, I tell them. Anyone who spits out so much as one thorn will be punished by grazing here for ever.

I set them to eat glass. One day on the island as a man was going to unload his mule, bottles of wine and beer fell off and the stone steps were covered in pieces of yellow and green glass. That's what the Dertilises are now eating in the middle of Constitution Square, and I am waiting for the moment when the first piece of glass begins to pierce their guts. I'm waiting for the first spasm.

The grazing and the glass are hors d'oeuvres, they are just a foretaste. In a little while all the roads leading to the square will be black with people; a vast silent octopus with tentacles stretching out into the whole basin of Attica is moving forward. They have set out from all over Greece without placards or passwords, but each has a stone. Now they are

circling the square, moving closer and closer round the Dertilises: every citizen silently lifts his stone and hurls it, the Dertilises are buried under the stones.

THE NAPE OF THE POLICEMAN'S NECK

Unknown to the others, in case they think I've gone mad given that they know I know that Peter is dead, I go to the Missing Persons Bureau and give Peter's details and a photograph —of course I don't say that I saw him cut into seven pieces—and I wait, I don't exactly know for what. As the policeman is bending over his cards, I see the nape of his thick milky-white neck and I suddenly want to fall on him and sink my teeth into it. I want to cut him into little strips, without actually doing him the honor of eating him.

THE SECRET POLICEMAN'S EYE

So I want to grab him by the back of the neck with my left hand while my right thumb goes straight for his eyeball to scoop it out, so I can watch it fall out in front of me.

THE CUTTING INTO PIECES

The machine gun makes a line of holes through Peter's body, it tears it limb from limb, then it turns on Cyprus, makes a line of holes down the middle and cuts it in two. The girls bend over searching among the bodies of the dead.

The army makes a line of holes through the students, cuts them in half, the students cry "No partition! No partition."

The island is in pieces. The inhabitants search for the pieces amid the sea. One man is looking for his house, another for his garden, another for a ring. An old woman is looking for two wedding garlands joined with ribbons which have stuck to the seaweed.

THE BURIAL

John, bury my body without my head in a secret ceremony.

A funeral procession with all my fellow students. Anetha heads it with the box in which she has hidden Peter's stolen heart. Behind her are two boys with torches. The burial takes place in an area of clay soil, in a ditch next to a barracks near Hymettus.

At night in Chomateri, a suburb of Athens near Hymettus, they bring other bodies and throw them in and put rubble on top. The workmen leave and soldiers come to do the digging and deal with the rubble.

Night and day in Chile, in a hollow suitable for mass graves which is next to a barracks, they brought the dead in carts, one load after another in piles, and emptied them in.[2]

Translated by Christopher Robinson

NOTES

1. The Sacred Way is the ancient road from Athens to Eleusis followed by initiates to the secret cult of Demeter.
2. In September, 1973 a military coup overthrew the socialist government of Salvador Allende; brutal repression of Allende's supporters and other leftists has continued to this day.

Carson McCullers   *US, 1919–1967*

Although Carson Smith McCullers enjoyed a harmonious family life with a mother who nurtured her daughter's promising eccentricities and although her talent as a young woman was recognized by teachers and publishers alike, her life, as her work reflects, was marked by illness, crossed love, and alcoholism. She twice married the same thwarted writer who escaped a second divorce only by committing suicide in 1953; she chose lovers—both men and women—who were in love with others and thus emotionally unavailable to her. And she continued to drink, even after her first stroke in 1941. Driven to despair by these circumstances and another series of strokes, which left her blind, unable to speak, and permanently paralyzed on the left side, she attempted suicide in 1948. It was not until 1958, when her health again deteriorated badly, that McCullers seemed to have formed a constructive and stable relationship with her psychiatrist, Dr. Mary Mercer, which lasted until McCullers' last stroke and death in 1967.

This difficult, if not tormented, personal life seems to find its counterpoint in the "small-town grotesque" world the reader comes to inhabit in McCullers' fiction. When McCullers was 23, she published *The Heart Is A Lonely Hunter* (1940). John Singer is a deaf mute at the center of a quartet of characters who feel compelled to confide in him, and imagining him as their savior, are desolate when he kills himself. Rich in allegorical detail, the book brought McCullers the praise of such writers as Richard Wright for her full-bodied portrayal of black characters and the friendship of such notables as Tennessee Williams, W.H. Auden, Muriel Rukeyser, Kay Boyle, and Truman Capote. Likewise, the works that followed—*Reflections of a Golden Eye* (1941), *Member of the Wedding* (1946), and, arguably her best work, *The Ballad of the Sad Café* (1951)—clearly belong, to paraphrase her friend Williams, to the tradition of the Awful; they are haunted by death and deformity in the guise of such characters as the impotent Captain Penderton; Allison Langdon, who has cut off her nipples with garden shears;

Cousin Lyman the dwarf; even the sadly disillusioned adolescent, Frankie Adams. Whether such characters are embued with powers of transcendence or redemption has remained a matter of critical contention.

McCullers' work translated successfully to the stage and also to film: *Member of the Wedding* and *Ballad of the Sad Café* were successfully produced on Broadway (although *The Square Root of Wonderful*, 1958, was not well received).

McCullers was a fine short-story writer: in the best of these works, such as "Madame Zilensky and the King of Finland," the selection here, there is a lightness not found elsewhere; the short stories sometimes were a vehicle for McCullers' lyricism, as in the famous "A Tree, A Rock, A Cloud." In them, McCullers also incorporated musical rhythms and motifs (she was something of a child prodigy and had originally come to New York to study music). Printed first in a variety of periodicals, the stories were reissued in a one-volume collection of her work published in 1951; others her sister compiled after McCullers' death under the title *The Mortgaged Heart* (1971).

MADAME ZILENSKY AND THE KING OF FINLAND

To Mr. Brook, the head of the music department at Ryder College, was due all the credit for getting Madame Zilensky on the faculty. The college considered itself fortunate; her reputation was impressive, both as a composer and as a pedagogue. Mr. Brook took on himself the responsibility of finding a house for Madame Zilensky, a comfortable place with a garden, which was convenient to the college and next to the apartment house where he himself lived.

No one in Westbridge had known Madame Zilensky before she came. Mr. Brook had seen her pictures in musical journals, and once he had written to her about the authenticity of a certain Buxtehude manuscript. Also, when it was being settled that she was to join the faculty, they had exchanged a few cables and letters on practical affairs. She wrote in a clear, square hand, and the only thing out of the ordinary in these letters was the fact that they contained an occasional reference to objects and persons altogether unknown to Mr. Brook, such as "the yellow cat in Lisbon" or "poor Heinrich." These lapses Mr. Brook put down to the confusion of getting herself and her family out of Europe.

Mr. Brook was a somewhat pastel person; years of Mozart minutes, of explanations about diminished sevenths and minor triads, had given him a watchful vocational patience. For the most part, he kept to himself. He loathed academic fiddle-faddle and committees. Years before, when the music department had decided to gang together and spend the summer in Salzburg, Mr. Brook sneaked out of the arrangement at the last moment and took a solitary trip to Peru. He had a few eccentricities himself and was tolerant of the peculiarities of others; indeed, he rather relished the ridiculous. Often, when confronted with some grave and incongruous situation, he would feel a little inside tickle, which stiffened his long, mild face and sharpened the light in his gray eyes.

Mr. Brook met Madame Zilensky at the Westbridge station a week before the beginning of the fall semester. He recognized her instantly. She was a tall, straight woman with a pale and haggard face. Her eyes were deeply shadowed and she wore her dark, ragged hair pushed back from her forehead. She had large, delicate hands, which were very grubby. About her person as a whole there was something noble and abstract that made Mr. Brook draw back for a moment and stand nervously undoing his cuff links. In spite of her clothes—a long, black skirt and a broken-down old leather jacket—she made an impression of vague elegance. With Madame Zilensky were three children, boys between the ages of ten and six, all blond, blank-eyed, and beautiful. There was one other person, an old woman who turned out later to be the Finnish servant.

This was the group he found at the station. The only luggage they had with them was two immense boxes of manuscripts, the rest of their paraphernalia having been forgotten in the station at Springfield when they changed trains. That is the sort of thing that can happen to anyone. When Mr. Brook got them all into a taxi, he thought the worst difficulties were over, but Madame Zilensky suddenly tried to scramble over his knees and get out of the door.

"My God!" she said. I left my—how do you say?—my tick-tick-tick—"

"Your watch?" asked Mr. Brook.

"Oh no!" she said vehemently. "You know, my tick-tick-tick," and waved her forefinger from side to side, pendulum fashion.

"Tick-tick," said Mr. Brook, putting his hands to his forehead and closing his eyes. "Could you possibly mean a metronome?"

"Yes! Yes! I think I must have lost it there where we changed trains."

Mr. Brook managed to quiet her. He even said, with a kind of dazed gallantry, that he would get her another one the next day. But at the time he was bound to admit to himself that there was something curious about this panic over a metronome when there was all the rest of the lost luggage to consider.

The Zilensky ménage moved into the house next door, and on the surface everything was all right. The boys were quiet children. Their names were Sigmund, Boris, and Sammy. They were always together and they followed each other around Indian file, Sigmund usually the

first. Among themselves they spoke a desperate-sounding family Esperanto made up of Russian, French, Finnish, German, and English; when other people were around, they were strangely silent. It was not any one thing that the Zilenskys did or said that made Mr. Brook uneasy. There were just little incidents. For example, something about the Zilensky children subconsciously bothered him when they were in a house, and finally he realized that what troubled him was the fact that the Zilensky boys never walked on a rug; they skirted it single file on the bare floor, and if a room was carpeted, they stood in the doorway and did not go inside. Another thing was this: Weeks passed and Madame Zilensky seemed to make no effort to get settled or to furnish the house with anything more than a table and some beds. The front door was left open day and night, and soon the house began to take on a queer, bleak look like that of a place abandoned for years.

The college had every reason to be satisfied with Madame Zilensky. She taught with a fierce insistence. She could become deeply indignant if some Mary Owens or Bernadine Smith would not clean up her Scarlatti trills. She got hold of four pianos for her college studio and set four dazed students to playing Bach fugues together. The racket that came from her end of the department was extraordinary, but Madame Zilensky did not seem to have a nerve in her, and if pure will and effort can get over a musical idea, then Ryder College could not have done better. At night Madame Zilensky worked on her twelfth symphony. She seemed never to sleep; no matter what time of night Mr. Brook happened to look out of his sitting-room window, the light in her studio was always on. No, it was not because of any professional consideration that Mr. Brook became so dubious.

It was in late October when he felt for the first time that something was unmistakably wrong. He had lunched with Madame Zilensky and had enjoyed himself, as she had given him a very detailed account of an African safari she had made in 1928. Later in the afternoon she stopped in at his office and stood rather abstractly in the doorway.

Mr. Brook looked up from his desk and asked, "Is there anything you want?"

"No, thank you," said Madame Zilensky. She had a low, beautiful, sombre voice. "I was only just wondering. You recall the metronome. Do you think perhaps that I might have left it with that French?"

"Who?" asked Mr. Brook.

"Why, that French I was married to," she answered.

"Frenchman," Mr. Brook said mildly. He tried to imagine the husband of Madame Zilensky, but his mind refused. He muttered half to himself, "The father of the children."

"But no," said Madame Zilensky with decision. "The father of Sammy."

Mr. Brook had a swift prescience. His deepest instincts warned him to say nothing further. Still, his respect for order, his conscience, demanded that he ask, "And the father of the other two?"

Madame Zilensky put her hand to the back of her head and ruffled up her short, cropped hair. Her face was dreamy, and for several moments she did not answer. Then she said gently, "Boris is of a Pole who played the piccolo."

"And Sigmund?" he asked. Mr. Brook looked over his orderly desk, with the stack of corrected papers, the three sharpened pencils, the ivory-elephant paperweight. When he glanced up at Madame Zilensky, she was obviously thinking hard. She gazed around at the corners of the room, her brows lowered and her jaw moving from side to side. At last she said, "We were discussing the father of Sigmund?"

"Why, no," said Mr. Brook. "There is no need to do that."

Madame Zilensky answered in a voice both dignified and final. "He was a fellow-countryman."

Mr. Brook really did not care one way or the other. He had no prejudices; people could marry seventeen times and have Chinese children so far as he was concerned. But there was something about this conversation with Madame Zilensky that bothered him. Suddenly he understood. The children didn't look at all like Madame Zilensky, but they looked exactly like each other, and as they all had different fathers, Mr. Brook thought the resemblance astonishing.

But Madame Zilensky had finished with the subject. She zipped up her leather jacket and turned away.

"That is exactly where I left it," she said, with a quick nod. "*Chez* that French."

Affairs in the music department were running smoothly. Mr Brook did not have any serious embarrassments to deal with, such as the harp teacher last year who had finally eloped with a garage mechanic. There was only this nagging apprehension about Madame Zilensky. He could not make out what was wrong in his relations with her or why his feelings were so mixed. To begin with, she was a great globe-trotter, and her conversations were incongruously seasoned with references to far-fetched places. She would go along for days without opening her mouth, prowling through the corridor with her hands in the pockets of her jacket and her face locked in meditation. Then suddenly she would buttonhole Mr. Brook and launch out on a long, volatile monologue, her eyes reckless and bright and her voice warm with eagerness. She would talk about anything or nothing at all. Yet, without exception, there was something queer, in a slanted sort of way, about every episode she ever mentioned. If she spoke of taking Sammy to the barbershop, the impression she created was just as foreign as if she were telling of an afternoon in Bagdad. Mr. Brook could not make it out.

The truth came to him very suddenly, and the truth made everything perfectly clear, or at least clarified the situation. Mr. Brook had come home early and lighted a fire in the little grate in his sitting room. He felt comfortable and at peace that evening. He sat before the fire in his stocking feet, with a volume of William Blake on the table by his side, and he had poured himself a halfglass of apricot brandy. At ten o'clock he was drowsing cozily before the fire, his mind full of cloudy phrases of Mahler and floating half-thoughts. Then all at once, out of this delicate stupor, four words came to his mind: "The King of Finland." The words seemed familiar, but for the first moment he could not place them. Then all at once he tracked them down. He had been walking across the campus that afternoon when Madame Zilensky stopped him and began some preposterous rigmarole, to which he had only half listened; he was thinking about the stack of canons turned in by his counterpoint class. Now the words, the inflections of her voice, came back to him with insidious exactitude. Madame Zilensky had started off with the following remark: "One day, when I was standing in front of a *pâtisserie*, the King of Finland came by in a sled."

Mr. Brook jerked himself up straight in his chair and put down his glass of brandy. The woman was a pathological liar. Almost every word she uttered outside of class was an untruth. If she worked all night, she would go out of her way to tell you she spent the evening at the cinema. If she ate lunch at the Old Tavern, she would be sure to mention that she had lunched with her children at home. The woman was simply a pathological liar, and that accounted for everything.

Mr. Brook cracked his knuckles and got up from his chair. His first reaction was one of exasperation. That day after day Madame Zilensky would have the gall to sit there in his office and deluge him with her outrageous falsehoods! Mr. Brook was intensely provoked. He walked up and down the room, then he went into his kitchenette and made himself a sardine sandwich.

An hour later, as he sat before the fire, his irritation had changed to a scholarly and thoughtful wonder. What he must do, he told himself, was to regard the whole situation impersonally and look on Madame Zilensky as a doctor looks on a sick patient. Her lies were of the guileless sort. She did not dissimulate with any intention to deceive, and the untruths she told were never used to any possible advantage. That was the maddening thing; there was simply no motive behind it all.

Mr. Brook finished off the rest of the brandy. And slowly, when it was almost midnight, a further understanding came to him. The reason for the lies of Madame Zilensky was painful and plain. All her life long Madame Zilensky had worked—at the piano, teaching, and writing those beautiful and immense twelve symphonies. Day and night she had drudged and struggled and thrown her soul into her work, and there was not much of her left over for anything else. Being human, she suffered from this lack and did what she could to make up for it. If she passed the evening bent over a table in the library and later declared that she had spent that time playing cards, it was as though she had managed to do both those things. Through the lies, she lived vicariously. The lies doubled the little of her existence that was left over from work and augmented the little rag end of her personal life.

Mr. Brook looked into the fire, and the face of Madame Zilensky was in his mind—a severe face, with dark, weary eyes and delicately disciplined mouth. He was conscious of a warmth in his chest, and a feeling of pity, protectiveness, and dreadful understanding. For a while he was in a state of lovely confusion.

Later on he brushed his teeth and got into his pajamas. He must be practical. What did this clear up? That French, the Pole with the piccolo, Bagdad? And the children, Sigmund, Boris, and Sammy—who were they? Were they really her children after all, or had she simply rounded them up from somewhere? Mr. Brook polished his spectacles and put them on the table by his bed. He must come to an immediate understanding with her. Otherwise, there would exist in the department a situation which could become most problematical. It was two o'clock. He glanced out of his window and saw that the light in Madame Zilensky's workroom was still on. Mr. Brook got into bed, made terrible faces in the dark, and tried to plan what he would say next day.

Mr. Brook was in his office by eight o'clock. He sat hunched up behind his desk, ready to trap Madame Zilensky as she passed down the corridor. He did not have to wait long, and as soon as he heard her footsteps he called out her name.

Madame Zilensky stood in the doorway. She looked vague and jaded. "How are you? I had such a fine night's rest," she said.

"Pray be seated, if you please," said Mr. Brook. "I would like a word with you."

Madame Zilensky put aside her portfolio and leaned back wearily in the armchair across from him. "Yes?" she asked.

"Yesterday you spoke to me as I was walking across the campus," he said slowly. "And if I am not mistaken, I believe you said something about a pastry shop and the King of Finland. Is that correct?"

Madame Zilensky turned her head to one side and stared retrospectively at a corner of the window sill.

"Something about a pastry shop," he repeated.

Her tired face brightened. "But of course," she said eagerly. "I told you about the time I was standing in front of this shop and the King of Finland—"

"Madame Zilensky!" Mr. Brook cried. "There *is* no King of Finland."

Madame Zilensky looked absolutely blank. Then, after an instant, she started off again. "I was standing in front of Bjarne's *pâtisserie* when I turned away from the cakes and suddenly saw the King of Finland—"

"Madame Zilensky, I just told you that there is no King of Finland."

"In Helsingfors," she started off again desperately, and again he let her get as far as the King, and then no further.

"Finland is a democracy," he said. "You could not possibly have seen the King of Finland. Therefore, what you have just said is an untruth. A pure untruth."

Never afterward could Mr. Brook forget the face of Madame Zilensky at that moment. In her eyes there was astonishment, dismay, and a sort of cornered horror. She had the look of one who watches his whole interior world split open and disintegrate.

"It is a pity," said Mr. Brook with real sympathy.

But Madame Zilensky pulled herself together. She raised her chin and said coldly, "I am a Finn."

"That I do not question," answered Mr. Brook. On second thought, he did question it a little.

"I was born in Finland and I am a Finnish citizen."

"That may very well be," said Mr. Brook in a rising voice.

"In the war," she continued passionately, "I rode a motorcycle and was a messenger."

"Your patriotism does not enter into it."

"Just because I am getting out the first papers—"

"Madame Zilensky!" said Mr. Brook. His hands grasped the edge of the desk. "That is only an irrelevant issue. The point is that you maintained and testified that you saw—that you saw—' But he could nor finish. Her face stopped him. She was deadly pale and there were shadows around her mouth. Her eyes were wide open, doomed, and proud. And Mr. Brook felt suddenly like a murderer. A great commotion of feelings—understanding, remorse, and unreasonable love—made him cover his face with his hands. He could not speak until this agitation in his insides quieted down, and then he said very faintly, "Yes. Of course. The King of Finland. And was he nice?"

An hour later, Mr. Brook sat looking out of the window of his office. The trees along the quiet Westbridge street were almost bare, and the gray buildings of the college had a calm, sad look. As he idly took in the familiar scene, he noticed the Drakes' old Airedale waddling along down the street. It was a thing he had watched a hundred times before, so what was it that struck him as strange? Then he realized with a kind of cold surprise that the old dog was running along backward. Mr. Brook watched the Airedale until he was out of sight, then resumed his work on the canons which had been turned in by the class in counterpoint.

Amrita Pritam   *India, b. 1919*

Amrita Pritam, the most distinguished living writer in the Punjabi language, has published some sixty volumes, beginning with *Thandijān Kirnān* (Cool Rays) in 1935, including poetry, short stories, novels, autobiographies, and other nonfiction prose. Recognized many times for her achievements, initially when she became the first woman to receive the Sahitya Akademy Prize in 1956 for the title poem of *Sunehure* (Messages, 1955), and most recently when she received the Jnanpith Award for *Kagaz te Kanvas* (Paper Was My Canvas, 1973), Pritam is also the recipient of the Padma Shri.* As this goes to press, she is a nominated member of the Rajya Sabha (the Upper House of Legislature). Alternately, periodic efforts have been made to ban her works. Notwithstanding, her wide travels have gained her an appreciative international audience, and her poetry and novels have been translated into Russian, English, and a variety of Indian languages. While Punjabis know her primarily as a poet, her Hindi readership regards her primarily as a prose artist. A special issue of *Mahfil: A Quarterly of South Asian Literature* (1968–1969) devoted to translations and criticism of her work and an interview-article by Ruth Madhu in the feminist *Manushi* (1982) have done much to bring Pritam before an English-speaking audience.

Born in 1919 in Gujranwala, in what is now Pakistan, Pritam was the only child of a school teacher and the eminent writer and devotional poet S. Kartar Singh (Hitkari). Engaged at the age of 4, she was married at 16 to Sardar Gurbaksh Singh, businessman and editor of the Punjabi magazine *Preetlari* (Garland of Love); they had two children. In 1944, she met the poet Sahir Ludhianvi, with whom she maintained an enduring friendship; her undeclared passion of fourteen years for him is recorded in two early poetry collections: *Chaitra* (Name of a month) and *Aag ki baat* (Speaking of Fire). In 1947, when Independence resulted in the partition of India, Pritam moved from Pakistan. In Delhi, she worked from 1949 to 1961 with All-India Radio. In 1960 she divorced her husband; since 1966 she has lived with the painter Imroz. Together they have produced the journal *Nagmani* (The Serpent's Jewel) as a vehicle for international writers as well as for younger Punjabi artists. Pritam herself has made special efforts to publish the work of some Pakistani women poets who were not published in their own country because their work is considered pornographic.

Much of Pritam's work has the dual feminist and nationalist focus that characterizes her own life. *Lamiyān Vātān* (Long Journeys, 1948), excerpts of which are included here, made her famous and expressed the general suffering and grief experienced by Muslim and Hindu alike over the fanaticism that resulted in the division of India and Pakistan. Like her important early novel *Pinjar* (*Skeleton*, 1950), much of this poetry has as its major theme the idea that men take revenge on each other by victimizing women. Yet Pritam's poetry of protest is also combined with an intensely sensuous love poetry that is rich in folk and female idioms.

Less overtly political works show Pritam developing women characters who are becoming aware of their own reconciliation to male dominance. Beginning with *Band Darvāzā* (*The Closed Door*, 1961), and in such novels as *Ik sit aniitaa* (Once There Was an Anita, 1964), *Cakk nambar chatī* (Village 36, 1964), *Dhartii Sāgar te Sipiyān* (Earth, Sea, and Shells, 1965), and *Eriyal* (Aerial, 1968), her heroines move increasingly toward naming their desires and accepting responsibility for their lives. *Aksharon ki Chaya Mein* (In the Shadow of the Alphabet) is a collection of short stories that focus on women's lives and husband-wife relationships, while *Tēsri Aurat* (Third Woman, 1978), a series of six stories, all entitled "Two Women," underline the importance of women's relationships with one another. With two autobiographical works, *Kāla Gulab* (Black Rose, 1968) and *Rasidi Tikat* (translated as *Revenue Stamp*, 1976), Pritam has made herself the subject of her major theme, tracing her own development as a woman and artist.

Pritam's most recent works continue to assert her social and political feminism. *Aurat* (Woman, 1976) is a collection of interviews with women activists and writers, translations of feminist writings, and essays on such topics as the "accidents" in which young wives die of burns, the marriage system, masculinity, and prostitution. *Khari Dhup ka Safar* (Journey Through Burning Heat, 1983) is a historical survey of women writers all over the world and the difficulties and obstacles they encountered in becoming artists.

NOTES

* State honor; the Padma Bhushan and Padma Vibhushan are more important ones. (Literal translation; Lotus Goddess/Lotus Latshme)

TO WARIS SHAH[1] I SAY
Ai Āakhan Waris Shah Nu

Speak from the depths of the grave,
to Waris Shah I say
and add a new page to your saga of love
today.

Once wept a daughter of Punjab
your pen unleashed a million cries,
a million daughters weep today,
to you Waris Shah they turn their eyes.

Awake, decry your Punjab,
O sufferer with those suffering!
Corpses entomb the fields today
the Chenāb is flowing with blood.

Mingled with poison by some,
are the waters of five rivers,
and this torrent of pollution,
unceasingly covers our earth.
And heavy with venom were the winds,
that blew through the forests,
transmuting into a snake,
The reed of each musical branch.
With sting after sting did the serpents
suppress the voice of people.
A moment, so brief, and the limbs of Punjab
turned blue.

Threads snapped from their shuttles
and rent the songs at the throat,
silenced was the spinning wheel's hum,
severed from their gatherings, the women.
Branches heavy with swings,
cracked from peepul trees,
boats laden with trappings,
loosened from anchors to sink.

Despoilers of beauty and love,
each man now turned a Kedu[2]
where can we seek another like
Waris Shah today?

Only you can speak from the grave,
to Waris Shah I say
add another page to your epic of love
today.

Translated by Charles Brasch

NOTES

1. Waris Shah (1755?–1798?): A Muslim mystic poet
   (Sufi), beloved equally by Hindus and Muslims, he
   wrote long, narrative poems called *Qissa*, the most
   famous of which is the archetypal romance *Heer-Ranja*.
2. Kedu was the uncle of Heer who did not let her meet
   her lover Ranja.

SILENCE

A pitcher of thoughts
empty and sad
lies in the niche of my courtyard.
Silence sits thirsty
running its tongue on its lips
begging for a few water-words.

Desire dug a well in my courtyard.
The days strike hammer-strokes.
The nights shovel blades
and years crack like stones.
No water-word sparkles in the pit.

The dark lonely well
sits quiet resting its paw on its chin
chewing the cud of
clods of earth and bits of stones
staring at the silence.

Translated by Balwant Gargi

IMROZ
Imroz

A canvas is spread
On the easel before me.
It seems
As if the patch of color
On the canvas
Swings like red cloth.
And the beast in the man
Raises its horn,
Aims it to strike
And every street, alley, lane
Forms the ring.
Spanish passion rages
In my Punjabi veins—
The myth of Goya,*
Bullfighting
Till death.

Translated by Mahendra Kulasrestha

NOTE

* Goya (1746–1828): One of the greatest painters and
  etchers of his time; legends about bullfighting are associated with his name and bullfighting is the subject of an
  important series of prints which he did—*The Tauro-
  machia* (1815–1816).

AMRITA PRITAM

There was a pain
I inhaled it
Silently,
Like a cigarette.
There are a few songs
I've flicked off
Like ashes
From the cigarette.

Translator unknown

May Swenson

US, b. 1919

May Swenson was born in Utah in 1919 and began her writing career as a reporter. After moving to New York City, where she held various jobs, she became an editor for New Directions in 1959 and served there for the next seven years. She has been since then a poet in residence at various universities. Her awards are many, including a Guggenheim and a Rockefeller Fellowship. Most recently she was awarded a MacArthur Fellowship in 1987. She is a member of the American Institute of Arts and Letters.

Swenson's first books appeared in the 1950s and were collected together with a large number of new poems in the volume *To Mix with Time: New and Selected Poems* (1963). These poems are varied in their interests and subject matter, ranging from philosophical reflections, to travel poems, to cityscapes, most of which are centered in New York City. Swenson's poetry proceeds with a childlike wonder at the forms, at once complex and simple, of nature and the social order, mixed with a sophistication of surfaces and depth. Swenson has developed a style that relies, but not exclusively, on typographical arrangement. She calls her poems "iconographs" and says that the arrangement of the words into geometric patterns occurs only after the poem is formulated. She desires an "object-to-eye encounter" that will precede the reader's engagement with the poem in the traditional "word-by-word" fashion. Clearly this relates her to the work of e.e. cummings, whose poetry is most often identified with modernist experiments in typography and to such later movements as "concrete" or "visual poetry" (though Swenson has not been directly affiliated with either school).

In an early poem such as "Almanac," Swenson can describe accidentally hitting her finger with a hammer and can spin out metaphors that suggest Sylvia Plath's "Cut." She can also ask such perennial questions as "What/is it about/the universa[?]" Hers is a poetry of everyday delights, and these delights are seen in an order that is both familar and lyrical. "Forms faced alike/we dance in some/ frame." In her most recent work, Swenson continues to engage wittily with the colloquial and mundane aspects of life; her fascination with outer space and its exploration is still in evidence in such poems as "The Cross Spider" and "Shuttles." But the chief delights of *In Other Words* are her personal elegy for the poet Elizabeth Bishop (1911–1917), "In the Bodies of Words," and even more significant, a long, philosophical—and sometimes comic—poem, "Banyan." Narrated by Tonto the Monkey, it recounts his adventures with Blondi the Cockatoo as he attempts to learn the purpose of life.

Swenson has written constantly, but only her latest book and *New & Selected Things Taking Shape* (1978) are in print. She has written and edited children's books, incorporating some of her own riddling poems into these volumes. She has also translated the poetry of Tomas Transtömer, the well-known Swedish poet.

Charles Molesworth

EVOLUTION

the stone
would like to be
Alive like me

the rooted tree
longs to be Free

the mute beast
envies my fate
Articulate

on this ball
half dark
half light
i walk Upright
i lie Prone
within the night

beautiful each Shape
to see
wonderful each Thing
to name
here a stone
there a tree
here a river
there a Flame

marvelous to Stroke
the patient beasts
within their yoke

how i Yearn
for the lion
in his den
though he spurn
the touch of men

the longing
that i know
is in the Stone also
it must be

the same that rises
in the Tree
the longing
in the Lion's call
speaks for all

oh to Endure
like the stone
sufficient
to itself alone

or Reincarnate
like the tree
be born each spring
to greenery

or like the lion
without law
to roam the Wild
on velvet paw

but if walking
i meet
a Creature like me
on the street
two-legged
with human face
to recognize
is to Embrace

wonders pale
beauties dim
during my delight
with Him

an Evolution strange
two Tongues touch
exchange
a Feast unknown
to stone
or tree or beast

THE RED BIRD TAPESTRY

Now I put on the thimble of dream
   to stitch among leaves the red node of his
                             body
and fasten here the few beads of his song.

Of the tree a cage of gilded spines
   to palace his scarlet, cathedral his cry,
and a ripple from his beak, I sew,
   a banner bearing seven studs,
this scarf to be the morning that received his
                             stain.

I do with thought instead of actuality
   for it has flown.
With glinting thimble I pull back, pull back
   that freak of scarlet to his throne:

To worship him, enchanted cherry to a tree
   that never bore such fruit—
who tore the veil of possibility
   and swung here for a day,
a never-colored bird, a never-music heard,
   who, doubly wanded then, looped away.

To find, in hollow of my throat, his call,
   and try his note on all the flutes of memory,
until that clear jet rinses me
   that was his single play—
for this I wear his daring and his royal eye.

Now perfected, arrested in absence—
   my needle laid by and spread my hand—
his claws on stems of my fingers fastened,
   rooted my feet and green my brow,
I drink from his beak the seven beads dropping:
   I am the cage that flatters him now.

FRONTISPIECE

In this book I see your face and in your face
your eyes holding the world and all else besides
as a cat's pupils rayed and wide
to what is before them and what more alive
ticks in the shadows flickers in the waves

Your hair in a slow stream curves
from your listening brow
to your ear shaped like a sea-thing found
in that water-haunted house where murmurs
your chaste-fierce name   The vow

the corners your mouth
compelled you to that deep between words and acts
where they cross as sand with salt
There spills the layered light
your sockets lips and nostrils drank

before they sank
On stages of the sea the years tall
tableaus build   The lightouse you commanded
the room the oak and mutable Orlando*
reoccur as the sea's pages to land's mind   The wall

the steep and empty slate
your cane indented until you laid it as a mark
above where the tide would darken
is written in weed and shell how you were sane
when walking you wrapped your face

in the green scarf
the gray
and then the black
The waves carve your hearse and tomb
and toll your voyage out again again

NOTE

* The hero/heroine and title of Virginia Woolf's fable and
  fantasy biography (1928) of Vita Sackville- West.

SURVEY OF THE WHOLE

            World's lopsided
                   That's its trouble
        Don't run in a circle
                   Runs in a loop
          Too much winter
                   In the wrong place
        Too much summer
                   Around the sun

                World's gimpy
                                Been turning so long
            It's lumpy
                            A bad top
        Day's not long enough
                            Spins on a nail
        Night's too long
                            Bent out of kilter
            World's a lemon
                            Wobbles in a loop
        Around the sun
                            It's not an orange
        Won't ever be sweet
                            Turns too fast
        Turns too slow
                            Can't ripen
        Too much desert
                            Too much snow

SWIMMERS

Tossed   then dangled, let go,
by the muscular sea,   made to race—
we are lost,   as the wrestling chest
and glad to be lost   of the sea, itself
in troughs of rough   tangled, tumbles

love. A bath in   in its own embrace.
laughter, our dive   Our limbs like eels
into foam,   are water-boned,
out upslide and float   our faces lost
on the surf of desire.   to difference and

But sucked to the root   contour, as the lapping
of the water-mountain—   crests.
immense—   They cease
about to tip upon us   their charge,
the terror of total   and rock us

delight—   in repeating hammocks
we are towed,   of the releasing
helpless in its   tide—
swell, by hooks   until supine we glide,
of our hair;   on cool green

                smiles
                of an exhaling
                gladiator,
                to the shore
                of sleep.

Andrée Chedid   *Egypt/France, b. 1920*

Of Egyptian-Lebanese parentage, Chedid was born in Cairo, attended high school in Paris, and returned to Egypt for her B.A. She then lived in Lebanon while her husband attended medical school there before she settled permanently in Paris to raise a family. She has two grown children.

Undoubtedly one of the most respected contemporary writers in France, Chedid is also claimed by the Middle East where her work is regularly published as that of a star literary figure.

Admired as a poet, novelist, and playwright, Chedid began her career in English with *Texts for a Countenance* (1949). Other important poetic works include *Double-pays* (Double Country, 1965), *Contre-chant* (Counterpoint, 1968), and *Visage premier* (Primal Face, 1972) from which the poetic texts here are taken, as well as *Cavernes et soleils* (Caverns and Suns, 1979), *Le Coeur suspendu* (The Suspended Heart, 1981), and *Derrière les visages* (Behind the Faces, 1984).

From writing poetry, Chedid moved to short stories and novels that deal with what Chedid calls "the essentials in life..., elementary aspects of nature...love, death and life," as evidenced in the excerpt from *Textes pour le vivant* (Texts for the Living, 1953).[1] Her novels, many of which center around women as queen and worker figures, include *Le sommeil délivré* (*From Sleep Unbound*, 1955), *La cité fertile* (The Fertile City, 1972), and *Néfertiti et le rêve d'Akhnaton* (Nefertiti and the Dream of Akhnaton, 1974). Chedid also took an avid interest in the theater, writing *Bérénice d'Egypte* (1968), *Les nombres* (1968), and *Le montreur* (The Showman, 1969) for the stage.

In her poetry, Chedid engages in the perpetual search for the hidden essence, something more stable and permanent than everyday reality. Chedid does not seek explicitly to disrupt the rules of syntax in her poetry. Her writing breaks new ground in a different way. In *Visage premier* the object of her search is alternately referred to as "face," "life" and "source." Chedid affirms in her poetry the "durée," the process of the search rather than any final resting place, or any illusory grasping of the truth. Although her prose does not fall under the rubric of the cerebral New Novelists who favored a laconic style, it possesses an emotional and lyrical density that also challenges traditional literary forms.

Chedid occupies a unique position between Occidental and Middle Eastern traditions. She is bilingual in French and English as well as being the child of two different Middle Eastern cultures. This duality of cultures and traditions has affected her writing a great deal. Chedid has said that the themes of all her novels are "double," revealing similarities within differences, and building bridges and meeting places where disparate cultures and people confront one another. The novel *L'Autre* (The Other, 1969), for example, illustrates this, operating on two different levels of fact and myth. The story of an old man who rescues a young foreigner (the Other) buried in the rubble of an earthquake, it reveals, at the same time, the rescuer's own painful emergence from obscurity. The problem of "Orientalism" present in all her work, is explicitly articulated in this as well as in her dramatic writings.

In gracing her with many awards, most recently the Louise Labé and Goncourt prizes, the French have also tacitly acknowledged the growing number and influence of Arabs and Africans writing in French today. This process has been as slow and painful as decolonization itself. Although her themes are never directly political, Chedid's literary work has, in many ways, created a space in which these francophone voices may be heard and even recognized.

FOR SURVIVAL
Pour survivre

You shall have, for survival,
Hills of tenderness
The ships of an otherwhere
The delta of love

You shall have, for survival,
The sun of a palm
The draft of a word
The water of the everyday

You shall arrange, for survival,
Braziers   terraces
You'll name the leaf
That enlivens the rock

You shall sing the men
Transfixed by one same breath
Who facing down the mortal shining
Bring their thought to light!

Translated by Marie Ponsot

STEPPING ASIDE
(L'écart)

Often   I inhabit my body
as far as the cavities of my armpits
I cut into this body
to the fingers' limits
I decode my belly
I savor my breath
I navigate in my veins
with blood's speed

The breezes rests on my cheek bones
My hands touch things
Against my flesh your flesh settles me

Often   by being my body
I have lived
And I am living

Often   from a point without place
I glimpse   this body
pounded on by days
assailed by time

Often   from a point without place
I stifle my story
From past to future
I conjugate the horizon

Often   from a point without place
This body   I distance it
And from this very stepping aside
alternately
I live.

Translated by Harriet Zinnes

from TEXTS FOR THE LIVING
Textes pour le vivant

The written word is faithful. More than thought or life, which re-create themselves around the dead like lakes over stone.

And your death—that death which took you this morning to make you into that thing so white, huddled up and hard—it must remain in me, like a gaping hole.

You are there, confined. And the Shadow who knows his victory, who plays his role and lets you play yours, is also there. Allowing you to believe that you are his equal. That you have a chance to escape, if you fight.

Then, despite your heart that is restrained, your eyes that go blind, your face that withdraws, you enter into the battle.

Your breathing builds up again, expands, invades the room. Your living breath, so familiar to these walls.

There is noise, anxiety around you. The voices reach you as if through layers of padding. There are tears and watching eyes. All that, you feel it, but you want to ignore it. To void everything. To be nothing more than this motor which is turning, and turning, and which you must keep on turning.

There you are, working at this breathing, and confident.

Behind you, in his comedy mask, Death wears a smile.

Because in this debate, it is Death who is unobtrusive. Death, who doesn't dare reveal himself, who is driven out of the thoughts, and whose face is unknown.

While you!

With your eyes, your fists, your chest, your shoulders of a fighter, your battle that resounds: it is you, the solid, strong one. The one a child would back.

My besieged, you seem to care only about your body, I fear that there is an island of anguish and of solitude at your center. An island where you find yourself with no recourse, like a cry in the desert, a bird in the palm, or the heart of a beggar.

And I, your companion, I cannot join you. I am a part of your battle, with my blood, and the throbbing of my temples, and I don't know how to let you know. I am your companion, I am your companion and the strength of my love...

The strength of a love!... The strength of a human love, isn't it more than that collapse on the threshold of your body, standing like a prison door?

I am on the other shore, the one where I belong. You, you already have other dimensions.

And side by side, we are as strangers there, like the grass and the stone.

Death is hanging on the edge of your lips. An air of brutality has been added to your pallor. And my useless hand clings to your wrist, where you still live, but so faintly.

Your chest is still. It is your first silence. It looks like peace but it is your defeat. And this quiet, akin to death, your face, weary of the strain, grows to like it.

A tempest of spasms seizes your body, limb by limb. Stiffened like an arc, you fall back into the calm, without a word.

Now you are a thing.

Your body is stone. Your hands are bark and your legs are two stakes.

To look at you, an emptiness rises in me where the tears congeal.

You are white. White as sheets and the snows that persist. White. White and dead, like everything I hate.

Your shoulders are too hard for my living arms. My tenderness grates like a knife of glass.

This death, this life...there they are!

There will be many people, and words.

There will be four candles and roses that will wilt.

There will be tears, regrets, and in a frame, your smile.

There will be nuns with prayers. What do they care about one dead among the dead?

There will be your night on a mild night when the curtains will stir, blown by a nervous wind.

There will be me, distraught, already attached to your face that has softened and rediscovered you.

That will be a ceremony. Gestures and more words that no longer have meaning.

There will be those who will have learned nothing from this new death, and who leave still without a wound.

And you, in your coffin of wood.

The sun, the laughter of children will have disappeared when the lid is lowered, my great stone figure. My white stone figure. My dear figure who is being taken away.

You will be left. Alone, with the other dead. They know what death is.

But you! You, who were still here yesterday, one among us, how are you going to spend this night?

This night when I separate myself from you, when your story ends, when I return to the City...

Translated by Carole Ciano

Rosemary Dobson

Australia, b. 1920

Rosemary Dobson's first collection of poems appeared in 1944. Though she has published other volumes at regular intervals, she has not achieved widespread recognition in Australia for her work, perhaps because she has written few poems on explicitly Australian subjects.

Dobson was born and educated in Sydney, attended art school and worked for a time as an art teacher. The visual arts, especially painting, have remained strong interests and are invoked in many of her better known earlier poems. During World War II she worked as an editor for the then leading Australian publishing house of Angus and Robertson. She later spent several years in England and Europe with her husband, the editor and private-press owner, A.T. Bolton. Since 1972 she has lived in Canberra, the Australian capital.

Dobson has published six individual collections of poetry with the latest, *The Three Fates* (1985), containing some of her best work. A particularly fine sequence celebrates the memory of the poet David Campbell, with whom Dobson translated two volumes of Russian poetry. She has also edited four anthologies, including *Sisters Poets* (1979) for the feminist press, Sisters.

"Cock Crow" and "Amy Caroline" both come from Dobson's fourth collection, *Cock Crow* (1965), and show the use of personal material and the simplification of style that have become even more marked in her recent work.

Elizabeth Webby

COCK CROW

Wanting to be myself, alone,
Between the lit house and the town
I took the road, and at the bridge
Turned back and walked the way I'd come.

Three times I took that lonely stretch,
Three times the dark trees closed me round,
The night absolved me of my bonds
Only my footsteps held the ground.

My mother and my daughter slept,
One life behind and one before,
And I that stood between denied
Their needs in shutting-to the door.

And walking up and down the road
Knew myself, separate and alone,
Cut off from human cries, from pain,
And love that grows about the bone.

Too brief illusion! Thrice for me
I heard the cock crow on the hill,
And turned the handle of the door
Thinking I knew his meaning well.

AMY CAROLINE

My grandmother, living to be ninety, met
Whatever chanced with kindness, held her head
On one side like a sparrow, had a bird's
Bright eyes. At dinner used to set
An extra place for strangers. This was done
She said, in Bendigo and Eaglehawk, it was
A custom she observed. In her thin house
That spoke aloud of every kind of weather
She put out food for lizards, scattered crumbs
For wrens beside the pepper-tree, and saved
The household water for geraniums.
At twilight, at the meditative hour
Perched on the piano-stool, in semi-dark
She liked to strum the songs learnt long ago
In Bendigo and Eaglehawk. She had
Eight children, little money, many griefs.
She was sorry
She never had a jinker* and a horse
To drive about the roads in, of her own.

NOTE

* A two-wheeled racing cart.

Gwen Harwood   *Australia, b. 1920*

Gwen Harwood has not, perhaps, even yet attained the reputation she deserves as one of Australia's leading poets. Factors contributing to this would seem to be her fondness for publishing under pseudonyms, both male and female, her relatively few published volumes, and the fact that she has spent much of her life in Tasmania, far from the literary centers of Sydney and Melbourne.

Harwood was born in Brisbane and, like several other Australian women writers, seemed destined for a career in music rather than literature. In 1945, however, she married William Harwood and moved to Tasmania as a housewife and mother of four children. The frustrations of this new life, as well as her musical interests, are reflected in many of Harwood's poems, including "Suburban Sonnet," reprinted below. A more comic series revolves around the expatriate pianist, Professor Kröte. Harwood has also written five opera librettos for the Australian composer Larry Sitsky and has collaborated on works with others.

Harwood did not begin writing poetry until her late thirties, when she was ill in the hospital. Her first collection, *Poems*, appeared in 1963. It was followed by *Poems: Volume Two* (1968), which included "Suburban Sonnet." The poignant "Father and Child," of which the first part, "Barn Owl," is given here, first appeared in *Selected Poems* (1975). Harwood has since published *The Lion's Bride* (1981). In 1978 she won the Patrick White Literary Award.

Elizabeth Webby

SUBURBAN SONNET

She practises a fugue, though it can matter
to no one now if she plays well or not.
Beside her on the floor two children chatter,
then scream and fight. She hushes them. A pot
boils over. As she rushes to the stove
too late, a wave of nausea overpowers
subject and counter-subject. Zest and love
drain out with soapy water as she scours
the crusted milk. Her veins ache. Once she
                                              played
for Rubinstein, who yawned. The children
                                                      caper
round a sprung mousetrap where a mouse lies
                                                      dead.
When the soft corpse won't move they seem
                                                      afraid.
She comforts them; and wraps it in a paper
featuring: *Tasty dishes from stale bread.*

NOTE
* Artur Rubenstein (1887–1982) was a celebrated pianist.

BARN OWL

Daybreak: the household slept.
I rose, blessed by the sun.
A horny fiend, I crept
out with my father's gun.
Let him dream of a child
obedient, angel-mild—
old No-sayer, robbed of power
by sleep. I knew my prize
who swooped home at this hour
with daylight-riddled eyes
to his place on a high beam
in our old stables, to dream

light's useless time away.
I stood, holding my breath,
in urine-scented hay,
master of life and death,
a wisp-haired judge whose law
would punish beak and claw.

My first shot struck. He swayed,
ruined, beating his only
wing, as I watched, afraid
by the fallen gun, a lonely
child who believed death clean
and final, not this obscene

bundle of stuff that dropped,
and dribbled through loose straw
tangling in bowels, and hopped
blindly closer. I saw
those eyes that did not see
mirror my cruelty

while the wrecked thing that could
not bear the light nor hide
hobbled in its own blood.
My father reached my side,
gave me the fallen gun.
"End what you have begun."

I fired. The blank eyes shone
once into mine, and slept.
I leaned my head upon
my father's arm, and wept,
owl-blind in early sun
for what I had begun.

Ishigaki Rin

Japan, b. 1920

Ishigaki Rin's poetry exhibits what one critic calls a "special combination of a cruel eye and a gentle heart." Her observations of a social and family structure that oppresses while it supports often show a blend of humor and understanding.

Ishigaki's own mother died while she was very young, as did two stepmothers, before a third brought her up. She began writing poetry while still in grammar school. She left school in 1934 and began to work with a major bank, with which she stayed for many years, in order to live independently. During the war she published short stories and some poetry in the journal *Dansō* (Dislocations) that she and a number of other women writers began; but it was after the war that she got her major start as a poet.

After publishing in her union newspaper and in the annual *Ginkōin no shishū* Bank Employees' Poetry Anthology, her first independent collection was *Watakushi no mae ni aru nabe to okama to moeru hi to* (The Pan, the Pot, the Fire I Have Before Me, 1959); here she speaks with clarity and realism of the ordinary happinesses of life while pointing to their costs. Ishigaki's second collection, *Hyōsatsu nado* (Nameplates, etc.), won the nineteenth Mr. H Prize in 1969, for its gentle dissection of the pain and loneliness of everyday life and the superimposed balance of acquiescence and resistance that makes life possible. *Ishigaki Rin Shishū* (The Collected Poetry of Ishigaki Rin, 1971) won the twelfth Tamura Toshiko Prize. *Yūmoa no sakoku* (The Country Closed to Humor, 1973) contains short stories from Ishigaki's early period and miscellaneous essays; the latter include meditations on such diverse subjects as the poet's life as an office worker and the loss of status faced by women as they age.

Among Ishigaki's later writings are the poetry collections *Ryakureki* (Abbreviated Resumé, 1979), *Katei no shi* (Household Poems, 1981), *Yasashii Kotoba* (Gentle Words, 1984), and a prose collection *Honō ni Te o Kazashite* (Warming My Hands at the Fire, 1980).

Phyllis I. Lyons

THE PAN, THE POT, THE FIRE I HAVE BEFORE ME
Watakushi no mae ni aru nabe to okama to moeru hi to

For a long time
these things have always been placed
before us women:

the pan of a reasonable size
suited to the user's strength,
the pot in which it's convenient for rice
to begin to swell and shine, grain by grain,
the heat of the fire inherited from time immemorial—
before these there have always been
mothers, grandmothers, and their mothers.

What measures of love and sincerity
these persons must have poured
into these utensils—
now red carrots,
now black seaweed,
now crushed fish

in the kitchen, always accurately
for morning, noon, and evening, preparations have been made
and before the preparations, in a row, there have always been
some pairs of warm knees and hands.

Ah without those persons waiting
how could women have gone on
cooking so happily?
their unflagging care,
so daily a service they became unconscious of it.

Cooking was mysteriously assigned
to women, as a role,
but I don't think that was unfortunate;
because of that, their knowledge and positions in society
may have lagged behind the times
but it isn't too late:
the things we have before us,

the pan and the pot, and the burning fire,
before these familiar things,
let us study government, economy, literature
as sincerely
as we cook potatoes and meat.

not for vanity and promotion
but so everyone
may serve all
so everyone may work for love.

Translated by Hiroaki Sato

ROOF
Hiroaki Sato

The Japanese house has a low roof,
the poorer the house, the lower the roof;
the low roof
weighs on my back.

What makes the weight of the roof?
I walk away ten steps to look:
what's on top of the house
is not the blue of the sky,
but the thickness of blood.

What holds me and blocks my way,
what confines my strength in its narrowness
and wastes it

my sick father lives on the roof,
my stepmother lives on the roof,
my brothers live on the roof.

The tin roof twangs
when the wind blows,
four hundred square feet at the most,
a gust can easily carry it away—
look, also lying on it,
white radishes, rice,
and the warmth of the bed.

Bear it, they say;
under the weight of this roof
a woman, her spring darkens,
in the distance, the sun sinks.

Translated by Hiroaki Sato

TRAGEDY

A hearse came along the Keihin Route
from the direction in which I was walking.

And,
in the driver's seat and assistant's seat
two men were laughing.
While talking about something or other.
In the assistant's seat the big fellow with the
                                          red face,
really seemed quite happy...
Ha, ha, haaaa...It seemed you could hear his
                                               voice
in his expression.
Laughing.

Quietly the hearse
passed my side
there was one coffin in the rear
passenger without complaint.

Then came three different colored taxis
filled with relatives in mourning clothes.
Riding sadly, downcast...
In that brief second
the funeral procession gently passed me.

"NO!"
Without thinking I turned, raised my hand and
                                            shouted.

As though giving directions to actors,
"Let's do it again,
from the beginning...
Have to start again...."

In the middle of the wide road it was.

Translated by Gregory Campbell

Kath Walker

Kath Walker was the first Aboriginal to write in English and establish a wide readership. She was born near Brisbane, and, like most Aboriginals, experienced the educational and financial disadvantages of racial discrimination.

Leaving school at 13 to work as a servant, she continued to educate herself, serving in the Australian Women's Army during World War II and later working as an adult education tutor. She has been an active campaigner for Aboriginal rights since the 1960s and in 1972 established the Noonuccal-Nughie Education and Cultural Centre at her birthplace, North Stradbroke Island, in order to teach people of all races about the traditional Aboriginal culture of that area.

Walker is best known for her first collection of poems, *We Are Going* (1964), from which the following two selections have been taken. In the title poem, she warns white readers of the destruction of Aboriginal culture and the possible extinction of her race. Other poems protest against white intolerance and cruelty. Walker has also published a second collection of poems, *The Dawn Is at Hand* (1966), and a collection of stories, *Stradbroke Dreamtime* (1972).

Elizabeth Webby

CORROBOREE

Hot day dies, cook time comes.
    Now between the sunset and the sleep-time
Time of playabout.
The hunters paint black bodies by firelight
    with designs of meaning
To dance corroboree.
Now didgeridoo[1] compels with haunting
drone
    eager feet to stamp,
Click sticks click in rhythms to swaying
    bodies
Dancing corroboree.
Like spirit things in from the great
    surrounding dark
Ghost-gums[2] dimly seen stand at
    the edge of light
Watching corroboree.
Eerie the scene in leaping firelight,
Eerie the sounds in that wild setting,
As naked dancers weave stories of the
    tribe
Into corroboree.

NOTES

1. Large hollow pipe made from bamboo or other hollow sapling.
2. The gum, or eucalyptus, tree is common in Australian forests.

WE ARE GOING

For Grannie Coolwell

They came in to the little town
A semi-naked band subdued and silent,
All that remained of their tribe.
They came here to the place of their old bora
    ground[1]
Where now the many white men hurry about
    like ants.
Notice of estate agent reads: "Rubbish May Be
    Tipped Here."
Now it half covers the traces of the old bora
    ring.

(continued)

They sit and are confused, they cannot say
                    their thoughts:
"We are as strangers here now, but the white
                tribe are the strangers.
We belong here, we are of the old ways.
We are the corroboree and the bora ground,
We are the old sacred ceremonies, the laws of
                  the elders.
We are the wonder tales of Dream Time, the
             tribal legends told.[2]
We are the past, the hunts and the laughing
          games, the wandering camp fires.
We are the lightning-bolt over Gaphembah Hill
Quick and terrible,
And the Thunder after him, that loud fellow.
We are the quiet daybreak paling the dark
                   lagoon.

We are the shadow-ghosts creeping back as the
               camp fires burn low.
We are nature and the past, all the old ways
Gone now and scattered.
The scrubs are gone, the hunting and the
                  laughter.
The eagle is gone, the emu and the kangaroo
          are gone from this place.
The bora ring is gone.
The corroboree is gone.
And we are going."

NOTES

1. Place of initiation rites of young Aboriginal boys.
2. Dream Time refers to Aboriginal mythology of the time of creation of the world.
3. The corroboree is an Aboriginal ceremonial dance, accompanied by songs. Dancers are normally painted in clay.

Margherita Guidacci   *Italy, b. 1921*

After obtaining a doctorate in letters from the University of Florence, Margherita Guidacci married the writer Luca Pinna and moved to Rome. They had three sons. She teaches English language and literature at the University of Macerata and has several important translations of various English-language writers to her credit (e.g., Emily Dickinson).

As a poet, Margherita Guidacci was influenced in her formative years by English literature with which she became very familiar. Considered one of the foremost women poets of her generation, her basic inspiration is profoundly spiritual, and her language simple and direct, reflecting an intimate religiosity void of all excessive sentimentality. Her writing is rich in beautiful images, especially of the sea, which frequently turns into a kind of magic emblem. She was awarded the Le Grazie Prize in 1948, the Carducci Prize in 1957, and the Cervia Prize in 1965.

In *La sabbia e l'angelo* (The Sand and the Angel, 1946), her first book of verse, Guidacci depicts the fragility of life during a war not yet forgotten. In the subsequent *Morte del ricco* (Death of the Rich Man, 1955), defined as an *oratorio* and based on a parable from the New Testament, and in *Giorno dei Santi* (Day of the Saints, 1957), the theme of death predominates and assumes the tragically joyous form of Death-Angel in *Paglia e polvere* (Straw and Dust, 1961). Guidacci's tense style and existential themes serve a moral as well as aesthetic purpose in which the author is constantly in search of a superior truth. For example, in *Neurosuite* (*Poems from Neurosuite*, 1970), or a day in the mental hospital, Guidacci looks at modern life as a force that has inflicted the greatest of traumas on human beings, in spite of improved standards of living and technological progress, making the world a true chaos where simple things are but a dream. More subdued are the themes in *Taccuino slavo* (Slavic Notebook, 1976); *Il vuoto e le forme* (Emptiness and Shapes, 1977), which includes a poem written in English; *L'altare di Isenheim* (The Altar of Isenheim, 1980), referring to the triptych of that name by the German Renaissance painter Mathias Grünewald; *Brevi e lunghe: poesie* (Short and Long: Poems, 1980); and *Inno alla gioia* (Hymn to Joy, 1983). Through all her lyric poems Guidacci's main motif remains that of searching for life's meaning in the face of death. The poems offered here are from Guidacci's 1965 collection *Poesie* (Poems), which contain her first three books of poetry.

Natalia Costa-Zalessow

from POEMS
Poesie

1.

The world, offered to you in simile, is easy, you believe, to decipher.
You say: "The sands of time" and "the wind of the soul" and "the pale grass
Of memory." But how, in themselves, do they live,
These things, and sand and grass and wind,
Perhaps lovers alone, and the dead, understand.

2.

But you preserve no trace
Of us. The most powerful ship
Leaves no greater mark
Than the naked body of that tanned
Swimmer or the feet of the seagulls.
Why do you sing if you have no memory?
And what, in you, do we search for eternally
From the other side of memory?

Translated by Claire Siegel

Hisaye Yamamoto   *US, b. 1921*

Hisaye Yamamoto, considered the most accomplished living Asian-American writer, is a Nisei—a second-generation Japanese-American. She was born in California, educated at Compton Junior College and, as mandated by the Japanese Relocation Act, interned in the 1940s in a camp at Poston, Arizona. While she was detained there, her brother was killed in action with U.S. forces in Italy. Granted leave from the camp, Yamamoto went to the East Coast to attend Brown University. She had already begun her journalistic career writing for the *Boston Chronicle*. After the war, she worked for a black newspaper, the *Los Angeles Tribune*, and began to write fiction. Her first published story, "The High-Heeled Shoes," reprinted here, appeared in *Partisan Review* (1948). In 1950 she won a John Hay Whitney Opportunity Fellowship. At about this same time, influenced by Dorothy Day, Yamamoto returned to the East, where she became involved with the Catholic Workers movement, working on their collective farm on Staten Island and writing for their newspaper. In her thirties she married Anthony De Soto and became the mother of five children, one an adopted son.

Yamamoto contributed articles and essays, stories and poems to many periodicals, including *Rafu Shimpo* and other bilingual journals addressed to Japanese Americans. In one of these essays, "Writing," she describes the struggle of Nisei artists for acceptance. Some of her stories focus on the camp experience that traumatized many of her generation; others treat relations between immigrant generations. She refers in her work to a range of literary works, current events, and actual places. Alert to both the preservative and coercive powers of language, Yamamoto captures the interrupted lives of the Nisei, or, as here, the poignant alienation of modern life and the peculiar shape such alienation takes in women's lives.

THE HIGH-HEELED SHOES

In the middle of the morning, the telephone rings. I am the only one at home. I answer it. A man's voice says softly, "Hello, this is Tony."

I don't know anybody named Tony. Nobody else in the house has spoken of knowing any Tony. But the greeting is very warm. It implies, "There is a certain thing which you and I alone know." Evidently he has dialed a wrong number. I tell him so, "You must have the wrong number," and prepare to hang up as soon as I know that he understands.

But the man says this is just the number he wants. To prove it, he recites off the pseudonym by which this household, Garbo-like, goes in the directory, the address, and the phone number. It is a unique name and I know there is probably no such person in the world. I merely tell him a fragment of the truth, that there is no such person at the address, and I am ready to hang up again.

But the man stalls. If there is no such person available, it appears he is willing to talk to me, whoever I am. I am suddenly in a bad humor, suspecting a trap in which I shall be imprisoned uncomfortably by words, words, words, earnestly begging me to try some product or another, the like of which is unknown anywhere else in the world. It isn't that I don't appreciate the unrapturous life a salesman must often lead. And I like to buy things. If I had the money, I would buy a little from every salesman who comes along, after I had permitted him to run ably or ineptly (it doesn't really matter) through the words he has been coached to repeat. Then, not only in the pride of the new acquisition, but in the knowledge that he was temporarily encouraged, my own spirits would gently rise, lifted by the wings of the dove. At each week's end, surrounded knee-deep by my various purchases—the Fuller toothbrush, the receipt for the magazine subscription which will help a girl obtain a nine-week flying course which she eagerly, eagerly wants, the one dozen white eggs fresh from the farm and cheaper than you can get at the corner grocery, the first volume in the indispensable 12-volume Illustrated Encyclopaedia of Home Medicine, the drug sundries totalling at least two dollars which will help guarantee a youngish veteran a permanent job—I could sigh and beam. That would be nice. But I don't have the money, and this coming of ill temper is just as much directed at myself for not having it as it is at the man for probably intending to put me in a position where I shall have to make him a failure.

"And just what is it you want?" I asked impatiently.

The man tells me, as man to woman. In the stark phrasing of his urgent need, I see that the certain thing alluded to by the warmth of his voice is a secret not of the past, but, with my acquiescence, of the near future. I let the receiver take a plunge down onto the hook from approximately a one-foot height. Then, I go outside and pick some pansies for Margarita, as I had been intending to do just before the phone rang. Margarita is the seven-year-old girl next door. She has never known any mother or father, only *tias* and *tios*[1] who share none of her blood. She has a face that looks as if it had been chiseled with utter care out of cream and pale pink marble. Her soft brown hair hangs in plaits as low as her waist. And, these days, because the Catholic school is full and cannot take her, she wanders lonesomely about, with plenty of time for such amenities as dropping in to admire a neighbor's flowers. The pansies I pick for her, lemon yellow, deep purple, clear violet, mottled brown, were transplanted here last year by Wakako and Chester, a young couple we know who have a knack for getting things wholesale, and they are thriving like crazy this Spring, sprawling untidily over their narrow bed and giving no end of blooms.

Later, there is a small, timid rat-tat-tat at the door. It's Margarita, bearing two calla lilies, a couple of clove pinks, and one tall amaryllis stalk with three brilliant brick-red flowers and a bud. She dashes off the porch, down the steps, and around the ivy-sprawled front fence before I can properly thank her. Oh, well. Taking the gift to the service porch, I throw out the wilting brown-edge callas she dashed over with last week, rinse out the blue potato glass, fill it with water, and stick in the new bouquet. But all the time the hands are occupied with these tokens of arrived Spring and knowing Margarita, the mind recalls unlovely, furtive things.

When Mary lived with us, there was a time she left for work in the dark hours of the morning. On one of these mornings, about midway in her lonely walk past the cemetery to the P-car stop, a man came from behind and grabbed her, stopped her mouth with his hand, and, rather arbitrarily, gave her a choice between one kiss and rape. Terrified, she indicated what seemed to be the somewhat lesser requirement. He allowed her to go afterwards, warning her on no account to scream for help or look back, on penalty of death. When she arrived at her place of work, trembling and pale green, her office friends asked whether she was ill, and she told them of her encounter. They advised her to go to the police immediately.

She doubted whether that would help, since she had been unable to see the man. But, persuaded that a report, even incomplete, to the police was her duty to the rest of womankind, she reluctantly went to the nearest station with her story. She came back with the impression that the police had been much amused, that they had actually snickered as she left with their officially regretful shrug over her having given them nothing to go on. She told her boss and he called the police himself and evidently made his influence felt, for we had a caller that evening.

It was I who answered the knock. A policeman stepped in, and, without any preliminaries, asked, "Are you the girl that was raped?"

Making up with enough asperity for a sudden inexplicable lack of aplomb, I said, no, and no one had been raped, *yet*, and called Mary. She and the officer went out on the porch and talked in near whispers for a while. After he left, Mary identified him and his companion as the night patrol for our section of the city. He had promised that they would tell the dawn patrol to be hovering around about the time she left for work each morning. But Mary, nervously trying the dim walk a couple of more times, caught no sign of any kind of patrol. Thereafter, she and the rest of the women of the household took to traveling in style, by taxi, when they were called on to go forth at odd hours. This not only dented our budgets, but made us considerably limit our unescorted evening gadding.

There were similar episodes, fortunately more fleeting. What stayed with me longer than Mary's because it was mine, was the high-heeled shoes. Walking one bright Saturday morning to work along the same stretch that Mary had walked, I noticed a dusty blue, middle-aged sedan parked just ahead. A pair of bare, not especially remarkable legs was crossed in the open doorway, as though the body to them were lying on the front seat, relaxing. I presumed they were a woman's legs, belonging to the wife of some man who had business in the lumberyard just opposite, because they were wearing black high-heeled shoes. As I passed, I glanced at the waiting woman.

My presumption had been rash. It wasn't a woman, but a man, unclothed (except for *the high-heeled shoes, the high-heeled shoes*), and I saw that I was, with frantic gestures, being enjoined to linger awhile. Nothing in my life before had quite prepared for this: some Freud, a smattering of Ellis, lots of Stekel, and fat Krafft-Ebing, in red covers, were on my bookshelves, granted;[2] conversation had explored curiously, and the imagination conjured bizarre scenes at the drop of a casual word. But reading is reading, talking is talking, thinking is thinking, and living is different. Improvising hastily on behavior for the occasion, I chose to pretend as though my heart were repeating Pippa's song,[3] and continued walking, possibly a little faster and a little straighter than I had been, up to the P-car stop. When I got to the printshop, the boss said, "You look rather put upon this morning." I mustered up a feeble smile and nodded, but I couldn't bring myself to speak of the high-heeled shoes. This was nothing so uncomplicated as pure rape, I knew, and the need of the moment was to go away by myself, far from everybody, and think

about things for awhile. But there were galleys and page proofs waiting to be read, and I set to with a sort of dedicated vengeance, for I had recently been reprimanded for getting sloppy again. When the hectic morning of poring over small print was over and my elbows black, letting my thoughts go cautiously but wholly back to the time between leaving the house and boarding the P-car, I found there was not much to think about. I had seen what I had seen. I had, admit it now, been thrown for a sickening loop. That was all. But the incongruity of a naked man in black high-heeled shoes was something the mind could not entirely dismiss, and there were times afterwards when he, never seen again, contributed to a larger perplexity that stirred the lees around and around, before more immediate matters, claiming attention, allowed them to settle again.

There was a man in the theater with groping hands. There was a man on the streetcar with insistent thighs. There was a man who grinned triumphantly and walked quickly away after he trailed one down a drizzly street at dusk and finally succeeded in his aim of thrusting an unexpected hand under one's raincoat.

I remembered them as I plucked the pansies, took them over to Margarita's house, came back home, answered the door, received the amaryllis, the callas, the pinks, and arranged them in the blue potato glass on top of the buffet. I remembered another man, Mohandas Gandhi, probably a stranger to this company, not only because I had been reading on him of late, but because he seemed to be the only unimpeachable authority who had ever been called on to give public advice in this connection. When someone had delicately asked Gandhi, "What is a woman to do when she is attacked by miscreants?," naming the alternatives of violent self-defense and immediate flight, he had replied, "For me, there can be no preparation for violence. All preparation must be for non-violence if courage of the highest type is to be developed. Violence can only be tolerated as being preferable always to cowardice. Therefore I would have no boats ready for flight...." Then he had soared on to the nobler implications of nonviolence, reproaching the world for its cowardice in arming itself with the atomic bomb.

I understood. When I first read these words, I had said, "Why, of course," smiling at the unnecessary alarms of some people. But I had read the words at a rarefied period, forgetting Mary, forgetting the high-heeled shoes. I decided now that the inspiration they gave to his probably feminine questioner was small potatoes. Of all the men suspected of sainthood, Gandhi, measured by his own testimony, should have been able to offer the most concrete comfort here. But he had evaded the issue. In place of the tangible example, vague words. Gandhi, in face of the ubiquitous womanly fear, was a failure. All he had really said was: don't even think about it. Then (I guessed), holding up his strong, bony brown hand, he had shaken his white-fuzzed, compactly-shaped head slowly back and forth and declined to hear the ifs and buts. The rest, as they say, was silence.

But could I have momentarily borrowed Gandhi's attitude to life and death, what would I have done as the man who called himself Tony rang my number? With enough straining, with maybe a resort to urgent, concentrated prayer, could I have found the gentle but effective words to make Tony see that there were more charming ways to spend a morning? I practiced this angle for awhile:

"I'm afraid you *do* have the wrong number." Soberly, hang up. Disconcerting enough, but rather negative.

"It's a nice day for the beach, sir. Why don't you go swimming?—might help you cool off a little." The voice with a compassionate smile. Too flippant.

"There are many lonely women in the world, and there are more acceptable ways to meet them than this. Have you tried joining a Lonely Hearts club? Don't you have any kind of hobby?" Condescending, as though I were forever above his need. Ambiguously worded, too, that last, fraught with the possibility of an abrupt answer.

"Listen, you know you aren't supposed to go around doing things like this. I think I know what made you do it, though, and I think a psychiatrist would help you quite a bit, if you'd cooperate." The enlightened woman's yap. Probably'd hang up on me.

Anyway, it was too late. And, after all, Gandhi was Gandhi, an old man, moreover dead, and I was I, a young woman, more or less alive. Since I was unable to hit on the proper pacifist approach, since, indeed, I doubted the efficacy of the pacifist approach in this crisis, should I, eschewing cowardice, have shouted bitter, indignant words to frighten Tony? Not that, either. Besides, I hadn't gauged his mood. He had spoken casually enough, but there had been an undertone of something. Restrained glee? Playfulness? Confidence? Desperation? I didn't know.

Then, to help protect my sisters, should I have turned toward the official avenues? Was it my responsibility to have responded with pretended warmth, invited him over, and had the police waiting with me when he arrived? Say I had sorrowfully pressed the matter, say Tony were consequently found guilty (of abusing his communication privileges, of course)—the omnipotent they (representing us) would have merely restricted his liberty for awhile, in the name of punishment. What would he have done when he was let go, his debt to society as completely repaid as society, who had created his condition, could make him repay? Telephones in working order abound, with telephone books conveniently alongside them, containing any number of women's names, addresses, and numbers.

And what did Tony do when the sound of my receiver crashed painfully in his ear? Did he laugh and proceed to some other number? His vanity bruised, did he curse? Or perhaps he felt shame, thinking, "My God, what am I doing, what am I doing?" Whatever, what-ever—I knew I had discovered yet another cir-cle to put away with my collection of circles. I was back to what I had started with, the help-less, absolutely useless knowledge that the days and nights must surely be bleak for a man who knew the compulsion to thumb through the telephone directory for a woman's name, any woman's name; that this bleakness, multiplied infinite times (see almost any daily paper), was a great, dark sickness on the earth that no amount of pansies, pinks, or amaryllis, thriv-ing joyously in what garden, however well-ordered and pointed to with pride, could ever begin to assuage.

The telephone rings. Startled, I go warily, wondering whether it might not be Tony again, calling perhaps to avenge the blow to pride by anonymous invective, to raise self-esteem by letting it be known that he is a practical joker. I hold my breath after I say, "Hello?"

It is the familiar voice, slightly querulous but altogether precious, of my aunt Miné. She says I am not to plan anything for supper. She has made something special, ricecakes with Indian bean frosting, as well as pickled fish on vinegard rice. She has also been able to get some yellow-tail, to slice and eat raw. All these things she and Uncle are bringing over this evening. Is about five o'clock too early?

It is possible she wonders at my enthusias-tic appreciation, which is all right, but all out of proportion.

NOTES

1. Spanish for aunts and uncles.
2. Havelock Ellis (1859–1939), Wilhelm Stekel (1888–1942), and Richard von Krafft-Ebing (1840–1902), along with Freud, were recognized medical and psycho-logical authorities on human sexual behavior, and pro-duced massive tomes on the subject, the most famed being Kraft-Ebing's *Psychopathia sexualis* (1886), and Ellis's seven-volume *Studies in the Psychology of Sex* (1897–1928).
3. *Pippa's song*, from Robert Browning's *Pippa Passes* (1841) goes:

> The year's at the spring,
> And day's at the morn;
> Morning's at seven;
> The hillside's dew pearled;
> The lark's on the wing;
> The snail's on the thorn;
> God's in His heaven—
> All's right with the world!

Agustina Bessa-Luís *Portugal, b. 1922*

Agustina Bessa-Luís is generally considered the *doyenne* of contemporary Portu-guese writers. The daughter of landed gentry from the north of Portugal, she is essentially an autodidact who is at the same time one of the best read of Portuguese intellectuals. First published in 1945, she has since produced some twenty-five novels, five plays, four biographies, and countless essays and circumstantial pieces. She has won most of the prestigious literary prizes awarded in her country and has influenced the work of many writers of the next generation. Some of her publi-cations have been adapted for television and film. She herself is interviewed on television with some frequency.

The single most important book by this prolific writer is *A Sibila* (*The Sibyl*, 1954), excerpted below. Bessa-Luís breaks here with nineteenth-century realism and with the neo-realism that dominated the 1940s and 1950s and creates her own presence. All her later work has evolved from this early novel that probes the subliminal reality of her region's inhabitants—women in particular. Her other novels and biographies similarly explore known historical figures as well as fictional ones.

It is often difficult to draw the line between history and fiction in Bessa-Luís' later work; her novels and, indeed, the biographies emerge at the point where history and fiction intersect. The distinction is blurred further by the ubiquitous comments that the author as narrator has inserted into her work. Bessa-Luís use of the story-within-a-story and her departure from conventional conceptions of time and space are features that give her work a thoroughly modern hue. She herself speaks of the pieces as reflections of the oral narrative that surrounded her in childhood and molded her interest in the art of storytelling.

Bessa-Luís' most recent books are: *Os Meninos de Ouro* (The Golden Boys, 1983), a novel based on the life of Francisco de Sá Carneiro, the charismatic leader of the Social Democrats; *Adivinhas de Pedro e Inês* (Riddles of Pedro and Ines, 1983), an inquiry into the fate of the legendary royal lovers of fourteenth-century Portugal; *Um Bicho da Terra* (An Earthworm, 1984), a novel on the life of the embattled Jewish businessman Uriel da Costa, a native of Oporto and later member of the troubled Amsterdam community that produced Rembrandt and Spinoza; and *A Monja de Lisboa* (The Nun from Lisbon, 1985), the story of the controversial Maria de Menezes, a sixteenth-century Portuguese mystic who fell under the scrutiny of the Inquisition.

Agustina Bessa-Luís has a daughter trained in art, and several grandchildren. Her husband reputedly prepares the typescripts of her work for publication.

Alice Clemente

from THE SIBYL
A Sibila

At home, Quina's situation had undergone a profound change. Even before the death of her father. Once, when she was no more than fifteen—gangly, pale, suffering recurring bouts of fatigue, dizzy spells cut short by concoctions of rue—she was suddenly felled by a more serious attack. It was in August, and she had just jumped from the drainage ditch where she had been scrubbing herself clean of caked mud, after having watered the crops, when she fell to the side, unconscious, icy cold, her lips gray. It was the prelude to a long illness. For a year she didn't leave her bed; everyone grew used to thinking of her as an invalid, highly susceptible to short fainting fits which they called attacks, white, drained, speaking softly and smiling unexpectedly into emptiness, clasping for whole afternoons a rosary whose beads, in a rather feverish way, she counted again and again. They thought she would die. They cried over her a great deal, behind closed doors, and her father would always bring her a special something, a silk handkerchief, a packet of biscuits, and sit down beside her to tell her that one day they would go off together to attend the feast of Remedios in Lamego, taking along a packed lunch of codfish croquettes, in whose preparation [Quina's mother] Maria was a specialist, crushing the dried fish with hammer blows on the hearthstone. Quina would smile listlessly.

"It's almost over," said the neighbors, led

by Narcisa Soqueira, who would appear, mournfully muttering herbal recipes and looking vaguely disheartened, for she had intended Quina for her son Augusto, a ragamuffin with a truly foul mouth and a sharp eye for piglets and graftings for the orchard. However, Quina's condition stabilized. At first, she was delirious, seemingly in her death throes, repeating farewells, words of resignation, or merely moving her lips in an infinite, gentle colloquy. This terrified the women, then filled them with a pensive devotion, as they believed the girl supernaturally possessed, whether as victim or elect, they weren't quite sure. Her mother, especially, changed her manner of shoving her about, her general crabbiness, and came to treat her with a deference one might have called zealotry, filled with pride, if anything could be deduced from the succinctness of her words and gestures. The invalid was wrapped in endearments, in pamperings, in an ill-disguised veneration. On the part of Maria, this was perhaps only the rush of tenderness that one feels for a child whose suffering lets us know the intensity of our love. But for Quina, this change in attitude led in a direction that was to define her entire life. She, so little accustomed to caresses that she ended up feeling vexed at being their object, a bit cast out from the confidences and the intimacy of the maternal heart and relegated almost to the plane of a servant, considered just one more in the family, she who contained elements of a powerful personality, reacted in the only way one could expect—her typical reation of "take it or leave it," the conquest of the moment, utilizing for this all her talent for conviction and even affectation. An unleashed passion for the spotlight, albeit within the familial sphere, now revealed itself. She, who until then had imagined herself renouncing respect, attention, love, who had been a little girl eager only to obey, invisible in her very perfection, in her fear of standing out, of going amiss, of arousing criticism or any attention at all, even if complimentary, now understood how her nature resonated to affection, to admiration, and how she expanded in impassioned energy, to the point of flooding all around her with sympathy, with strength, and with an undeniable imperative. She understood this, not in her mind, but in her feelings. She felt that she could never lose that privilege which had suddenly revealed her to be something distinct and quite apart from all the others. The illness became an infirmity, an obstacle to her return to a normal life that would send her back into mediocrity and obscurity; she acquired a manner of expressing herself both sibylline and delicate, which left her listeners in suspense, their souls quivering in a voluptuousness of anticipation, curiosity, and hope. Only close friends came to see her, as news of her condition had been well cloaked to guard against unpleasant gossip, censorious commentaries. And all of them felt a discontentment with themselves, a desire for forgetfulness, austerity, simplicity, and peace, upon entering that room that smelled of apples and corn husks, where Quina lay, gazing at the grandfather clock with its copper pendulum slowly swinging inside the old green and golden case. They thought she would never rise again.

Her uncle José, who was born in the Freixo house, but who had acquired, thanks to the great favors of fortune, the Folgozinho property, a manor house with turrets, an avenue of lindens, a grotto with imitation stalactites of cement, and twenty-two tenants spread over the deep, rich, fertile lands, arrived in September with his daughters. They lived in Porto, and their whirlwind visits to the country were quite infrequent. But this time they stayed longer than usual because Adriana, the eldest, was suffering from anemia, with serious symptoms such as a fever and lack of appetite. There were four girls, two of them still with their hair down, schoolgirl socks, a Liberty sash low on the hips. They spent much time at the Vessada house during this period. They had appeared *en masse*, nice and fresh, with their robes of *voile* and tussor silk, their Irish and Cluny lacework, their parasols full of ruffles and frills, with silk that creaked when they were opened. Quina received them with a fascinated iciness, and watched them trip about with a fluttering of silken things, clasping their skirts in order to go down the kitchen step, revealing a whiteness of embroidered cambric, furbelows, V-shaped lacy inserts and finely pleated muslin, accented with little ribbons of pink satin. They were cheerful, jolly, chirping, filled with the frivolous, innocent charms that come with well-being and good fortune. Quina envied them a great deal. And, as they came filled with that romantic adoration for the country, that curiosity about the rustic, those aspirations toward the simple, full of that enthusiasm of the bourgeois who elude boredom through a willing acceptance of the new, the different, without really adapting to it, they recruited everyone, made countless demands, were always underfoot, peeking in at the Frisian cows in the corrals, presenting sweetmeats to the rag-tail local kids and ox-tongue to the rabbits, which finished them off. They resented Estina, making her stay day after day in Folgozinho, lavishing on her their exuberance, trying to make her wear indoor clothes of princess color with bibwork, braided trimming, and *passementerie*,* combing her hair Phrygian-style, with numerous fluffy curls making an aureole around her brow. Estina said no, she was fed up with those antics, with that fusillade of frivolities, with those bursts of friendly, conspiratorial laughter. And she became impatient to return to her age-worn bench, to plucking plant lice from the cabbage and listening to the crackle of the lard bursting from the iron pots over the fire. But her uncle, rich and of a solemn generosity, thoroughly of "the good old days," had always stood as protector to the Vessada house, even before the death of Francisco Teixeira. Maria was his favorite sister; he possessed, like her, a dry, incorruptible character, and inflexible, authoritarian principles which often earned him some bad feelings. Enthusiastic over the effervescent

ideas of the Republic, he had a house much frequented by politicians, men with a future, champions of revolutionary movements, high-standing men of letters, in an epoch in which art was generally limited to pleasant sentiments and prophetic visions of Utopian communes. Estina suffered greatly in that atmosphere in which one breathed the stench of the solid bourgeoisie, concretely honest, in which girls were initiated into keeping house as if it were a game, and made beds protected by pink cambric aprons, with embroidered kerchiefs in Valencian lace. She was sickened by the food, struck nauseous by the meats soaked in sauces, by the fried eggs, whose raw yolks trembled like a soft abscess, disgusting! Unavoidable contact with the basic problems of life had molded her since earliest childhood, had quickly matured her, had made her incapable of idling at ease with those innocent girls whom comfort had retarded, prolonging for them the time of their infancy.

"This is good for you girls," she would say about a ribbon, a turn of phrase, a taste, an elegance that they wanted her to adopt. And she wouldn't give up her checkered skirt trimmed in black silk, while sighing for her straw hat, which she always would place over her kerchief, whose tips she would fold under the oval crown. In the end, the news that Quina had gotten worse freed her from that oppressive situation.

"Come back, cousin," begged the girls. "We love you." And Adriana, who was to be engaged to one of the promising lions of the opposition's political sphere, gave her as a present a little handkerchief on which she had embroidered a branch and an initial.

"It was meant for Eduardo, but it also works for you, since you are Estina," she said. She kept the handkerchief, and had the kindly discretion not to make clear that her name was Justina, just like her grandmother there in the Freixo house, and that it was the usual thing to call her Estina, like all the others of the region.

She found Quina with shrunken, wasted

features and so weak that just turning her head seemed to exhaust her; her little ring, of braided gold, was loose on her finger, and she amused herself by tightening it with strands of flock from her bedspread. She seemed to regain a bit of energy with the coming of her sister, watching her take up once again her activities, her hat, listening to her tell of the difficulties of her stay in her uncle's house, that disconsolate well-being of watching the days flow by, one's hands crossed in one's lap, in attendance at the parade of unknowns who came to dine, and who left without her being able to remember even their names.

"The devil could have had me there, I was so homesick," she confessed, trying, however, not to be heard by her mother, since for the latter duties did not give one the right to sentimental complaints, and to be agreeable to her brother was, for her and everyone else in the house, a duty.

Towards the beginning of winter, the family decamped from Folgozinho. Maria, with her son Abel, came to see the others off at the station, passing along regards from the girls and a bag of biscuits for the children, which they thanked her for solemnly, but without opening it. They were truly graceful in their long capes lined with Scottish silk, beneath which could be seen beige flannel dresses, sailor-style. Their mother, very beautiful, with orange-tinted hair neatly composed behind her traveling veil, leaned out of the small window, laughing and waving a gloved hand.

"Till next year," she said.

Translated by Alexis Levitin

NOTE

* Braiding.

Mavis Gallant   *Canada/France, b. 1922*

Cosmopolitan *par excellence*, Mavis Gallant (née Young), born in Montreal, was repeatedly uprooted during her childhood, attending some seventeen different schools in Quebec, Ontario, and the eastern United States. After working as a journalist with the *Montreal Standard* (later the *Weekend Magazine*) and as an editor at the National Film Board in the 1940s, and after a brief, unhappy marriage, Gallant has lived most of her adult life as an expatriate in Paris (despite a temporary return to Canada and a stint as writer-in-residence at the University of Toronto in the early 1980s). Publishing regularly in *The New Yorker* since her move to France in 1950, Gallant has earned an international reputation as one of the best short-story writers in the English language. In the past decade, a surge of critical and popular interest in her writing—long neglected by Canadian critics— has led to the reprinting in paperback of her early work, so that her seven short-story collections and two novels are now all readily accessible.

Gallant's journalistic training and her editorial experience with film seem to have influenced the style and structure of her prose, which is verbally pared down, visually exact, and often complex in its cinematic shifting of narrative point of view. Gallant has published some hundred short stories, only a fraction of them collected in her seven books: *The Other Paris* (1956); *My Heart Is Broken* (1964; also published as *An Unmarried Man's Summer*, 1965); *The Pegnitz Junction* (1973); *The End of the World and Other Stories* (1974); *From the Fifteenth District* (1979); *Home Truths* (1981), which won the Governor General's Award, and *Overheard in a Balloon* (1985). Three of these collections each contain a novella: "Its Image in the Mirror," a study of two sisters, in *My Heart is Broken*; the title entry in *The Pegnitz Junction*, a portrait of lovers as strangers; and "Potter," about the incapacity to love, in *From the Fifteenth District*. Gallant has also written a play, *What Is to Be Done?*, and two novels, reprinted by Macmillan in 1983: *Green Water, Green Sky* (1960), which explores the tensions and nuances of the complex mother-daughter bond, and *A Fairly Good Time* (1970), which traces the failure of a cross-cultural marriage. Gallant's nonfiction works include numerous reviews for the *New York Times Book Review*, the introductory essay in *The Affair of Gabrielle Russier* (1971), and *Paris Notebooks: Essays and Reviews* (1986)—the latter two pieces suggesting the depth of Gallant's involvement in contemporary social and political affairs in France, as well as her ongoing concern for women's issues. In this she resembles Genet, her predecessor at the *New Yorker*.

The feelings of deracination and alienation that Gallant experienced in her youth are recurrent themes in her powerfully realistic fiction and are central in the title story of the early *My Heart Is Broken*, presented here.

Wendy Robbins Keitner

MY HEART IS BROKEN

"When that Jean Harlow[1] died," Mrs. Thompson said to Jeannie, "I was on the 83 streetcar with a big, heavy paper parcel in my arms. I hadn't been married for very long, and when I used to visit my mother she'd give me a lot of canned stuff and preserves. I was standing up in the streetcar because nobody'd given me a seat. All the men were unemployed in those days, and they just sat down wherever they happened to be. You wouldn't remember what Montreal was like then. *You* weren't even on earth. To resume what I was saying to you, one of these men sitting down had an American paper—the *Daily News*, I guess it was— and I was sort of leaning over him, and I saw in big print 'JEAN HARLOW DEAD.' You can believe me or not, just as you want to, but that was the most terrible shock I ever had in my life. I never got over it."

Jeannie had nothing to say to that. She lay flat on her back across the bed, with her head toward Mrs. Thompson and her heels just touching the crate that did as a bedside table. Balanced on her flat stomach was an open bottle of coral-pink Cutex nail polish. She held her hands up over her head and with some difficulty applied the brush to the nails of her right hand. Her legs were brown and thin. She wore nothing but shorts and one of her husband's shirts. Her feet were bare.

Mrs. Thompson was the wife of the paymaster in a road-construction camp in northern Quebec. Jeannie's husband was an engineer working on the same project. The road was being pushed through country where nothing had existed until now except rocks and lakes and muskeg. The camp was established between a wild lake and the line of raw dirt that was the road. There were no towns between the camp and the railway spur, sixty miles distant.

Mrs. Thompson, a good deal older than Jeannie, had become her best friend. She was a nice, plain, fat, consoling sort of person, with varicosed legs, shoes unlaced and slit for comfort, blue flannel dressing gown worn at all hours, pudding-bowl haircut, and coarse gray hair. She might have been Jeannie's own mother, or her Auntie Pearl. She rocked her fat self in the rocking chair and went on with what she had to say: "What I was starting off to tell you is you remind me of her, of Jean Harlow. You've got the same teeny mouth, Jeannie, and I think your hair was a whole lot prettier before you started fooling around with it. That peroxide's no good. It splits the ends. I know you're going to tell me it isn't peroxide but something more modern, but the result is the same."

Vern's shirt was spotted with coral-pink that had dropped off the brush. Vern wouldn't mind; at least, he wouldn't say that he minded. If he hadn't objected to anything Jeannie did until now, he wouldn't start off by complaining about a shirt. The campsite outside the uncurtained window was silent and dark. The waning moon would not appear until dawn. A passage of thought made Mrs. Thompson say, "Winter soon."

Jeannie moved sharply and caught the bottle of polish before it spilled. Mrs. Thompson was crazy; it wasn't even September.

"Pretty soon," Mrs. Thompson admitted. "Pretty soon. That's a long season up here, but I'm one person doesn't complain. I've been up here or around here every winter of my married life, except for that one winter Pops was occupying Germany."

"I've been up here seventy-two days," said Jeannie, in her soft voice. "Tomorrow makes seventy-three."

"Is that right?" said Mrs. Thompson, jerking the rocker forward, suddenly snappish. "Is that a fact? Well, who asked you to come up here? Who asked you to come and start counting days like you was in some kind of jail? When you got married to Vern, you must of known where he'd be taking you. He told you, didn't he, that he liked road jobs, construction jobs, and that? Did he tell you, or didn't he?"

"Oh, he told me," said Jeannie.

"You know what, Jeannie?" said Mrs. Thompson. "If you'd of just listened to me, none of this would have happened. I told you that first day, the day you arrived here in your

high-heeled shoes, I said, 'I know this cabin doesn't look much, but all the married men have the same sort of place.' You remember I said that? I said, 'You just get some curtains up and some carpets down and it'll be home.' I took you over and showed you my place, and you said you'd never seen anything so lovely."

"I meant it," said Jeannie. "Your cabin is just lovely. I don't know why, but I never managed to make this place look like yours."

Mrs. Thompson said, "That's plain enough." She looked at the cold grease spattered behind the stove, and the rag of towel over by the sink. "It's partly the experience," she said kindly. She and her husband knew exactly what to take with them when they went on a job, they had been doing it for so many years. They brought boxes for artificial flowers, a brass door knocker, a portable bar decorated with sea shells, a cardboard fireplace that looked real, and an electric fire that sent waves of light rippling over the ceiling and walls. A concealed gramophone played the records they loved and cherished—the good old tunes. They had comic records that dated back to the year 1, and sad soprano records about shipwrecks and broken promises and babies' graves. The first time Jeannie heard one of the funny records, she was scared to death. She was paying a formal call, sitting straight in her chair, with her skirt pulled around her knees. Vern and Pops Thompson were talking about the Army.

"I wish to God I was back," said old Pops.

"Don't I?" said Vern. He was fifteen years older than Jeannie and had been through a lot.

At first there were only scratching and whispering noises, and then a mosquito orchestra started to play, and a dwarf's voice came into the room. "Little Johnnie Green, little Sallie Brown," squealed the dwarf, higher and faster than any human ever could. "Spooning in the park with the grass all around."

"Where is he?" Jeannie cried, while the Thompsons screamed with laughter and Vern smiled. The dwarf sang on: "And each little bird in the treetop high/Sang 'Oh you kid!' and winked his eye."

It was a record that had belonged to Pops Thompson's mother. He had been laughing at it all his life. The Thompsons loved living up north and didn't miss cities or company. Their cabin smelled of cocoa and toast. Over their beds were oval photographs of each other as children, and they had some Teddy bears and about a dozen dolls.

Jeannie capped the bottle of polish, taking care not to press it against her wet nails. She sat up with a single movement and set the bottle down on the bedside crate. Then she turned to face Mrs. Thompson. She sat cross-legged, with her hands outspread before her. Her face was serene.

"Not an ounce of fat on you," said Mrs. Thompson. "You know something? I'm sorry you're going. I really am. Tomorrow you'll be gone. You know that, don't you? You've been counting days, but you won't have to any more. I guess Vern'll take you back to Montreal. What do you think?"

Jeannie dropped her gaze, and began smoothing wrinkles on the bedspread. She muttered something Mrs. Thompson could not understand.

"Tomorrow you'll be gone," Mrs. Thompson continued. "I know it for a fact. Vern is at this moment getting his pay, and borrowing a jeep from Mr. Sherman, and a Polack driver to take you to the train. He sure is loyal to *you*. You know what I heard Mr. Sherman say? He said to Vern, 'If you want to send her off, Vern, you can always stay,' and Vern said, 'I can't very well do that, Mr. Sherman.' And Mr. Sherman said, 'This is the second time you've had to leave a job on account of her, isn't it?,' and then Mr. Sherman said, 'In my opinion, no man by his own self can rape a girl, so there were either two men or else she's invented the whole story.' Then he said, 'Vern, you're either a saint or a

damn fool.' That was all I heard. I came straight over here, Jeannie, because I thought you might be needing me." Mrs. Thompson waited to hear she was needed. She stopped rocking and sat with her feet flat and wide apart. She struck her knees with her open palms and cried, "I *told* you to keep away from the men. I told you it would make trouble, all that being cute and dancing around. I said to you, I remember saying it, I said nothing makes trouble faster in a place like this than a grown woman behaving like a little girl. Don't you remember?"

"I only went out for a walk," said Jeannie. "Nobody'll believe me, but that's all. I went down the road for a walk."

"In high heels?" said Mrs. Thompson. "With a purse on your arm, and a hat on your head? You don't go taking a walk in the bush that way. There's no place to walk *to*. Where'd you think you were going? I could smell Evening in Paris a quarter mile away."

"There's no place to go," said Jeannie, "but what else is there to do? I just felt like dressing up and going out."

"You could have cleaned up your home a bit," said Mrs. Thompson. "There was always that to do. Just look at that sink. That basket of ironing's been under the bed since July. I know it gets boring around here, but you had the best of it. You had the summer. In winter it gets dark around three o'clock. Then the wives have a right to go crazy. I knew one used to sleep the clock around. When her Nembutal ran out, she took about a hundred aspirin. I knew another learned to distill her own liquor, just to kill time. Sometimes the men get so's they don't like the life, and that's death for the wives. But here you had a nice summer, and Vern liked the life."

"He likes it better than anything," said Jeannie. "He liked the Army, but this was his favorite life after that."

"There," said Mrs. Thompson. "You had every reason to be happy. What'd you do if he sent you off alone, now, like Mr. Sherman advised? You'd be alone and you'd have to work. Women don't know when they're well off. Here you've got a good, sensible husband working for you and you don't appreciate it. You have to go and do a terrible thing."

"I only went for a walk," said Jeannie. "That's all I did."

"It's possible," said Mrs. Thompson, "but it's a terrible thing. It's about the worst thing that's ever happened around here. I don't know why you let it happen. A woman can always defend what's precious, even if she's attacked. I hope you remembered to think about bacteria."

"What d'you mean?"

"I mean Javel,[2] or something."

Jeannie looked uncomprehending and then shook her head.

"I wonder what it must be like," said Mrs. Thompson after a time, looking at the dark window. "I mean, think of Berlin and them Russians and all. Think of some disgusting fellow you don't know. Never said hello to, even. Some girls ask for it, though. You can't always blame the man. The man loses his job, his wife if he's got one, everything, all because of a silly girl."

Jeannie frowned, absently. She pressed her nails together, testing the polish. She licked her lips and said, "I was more beaten up, Mrs. Thompson. It wasn't exactly what you think. It was only afterwards I thought to myself, Why, I was raped and everything."

Mrs. Thompson gasped, hearing the word from Jeannie. She said, "Have you got any marks?"

"On my arms. That's why I'm wearing this shirt. The first thing I did was change my clothes."

Mrs. Thompson thought this over, and went on to another thing: "Do you ever think about your mother?"

"Sure."

"Do you pray? If this goes on at nineteen—"

"I'm twenty."

"—what'll you be by the time you're thirty? You've already got a terrible, terrible memory to haunt you all your life."

"I already can't remember it," said Jeannie. "Afterwards I started walking back to camp, but I was walking the wrong way. I met Mr. Sherman. The back of his car was full of coffee, flour, all that. I guess he'd been picking up supplies. He said, 'Well, get in.' He didn't ask any questions at first. I couldn't talk anyway."

"Shock," said Mrs. Thompson wisely.

"You know, I'd have to see it happening to know what happened. All I remember is that first we were only talking..."

"You and Mr. Sherman?"

"No, no, before. When I was taking my walk."

"Don't say who it was," said Mrs. Thompson. "We don't any of us need to know."

"We were just talking, and he got sore all of a sudden and grabbed my arm."

"Don't say the name!" Mrs. Thompson cried.

"Like when I was little, there was this Lana Turner movie. She had two twins. She was just there and then a nurse brought her in the two twins. I hadn't been married or anything, and I didn't know anything, and I used to think if I just kept on seeing the movie I'd know how she got the two twins, you know, and I went, oh, I must have seen it six times, the movie, but in the end I never knew any more. They just brought her the two twins."

Mrs. Thompson sat quite still, trying to make sense of this. "Taking advantage of a woman is a criminal offense," she observed. "I heard Mr. Sherman say another thing, Jeannie. He said, 'If your wife wants to press a charge and talk to some lawyer, let me tell you,' he said, 'you'll never work again anywhere,' he said. Vern said, 'I know that, Mr. Sherman.' And Mr. Sherman said, 'Let me tell you, if any reporters or any investigators start coming around here, they'll get their...they'll never...'

Oh, he was mad. And Vern said, 'I came over to tell you I was quitting, Mr. Sherman.'" Mrs. Thompson had been acting this with spirit, using a quiet voice when she spoke for Vern and a blustering tone for Mr. Sherman. In her own voice, she said, "If you're wondering how I came to hear all this, I was strolling by Mr. Sherman's office window—his bungalow, that is. I had Maureen out in her pram." Maureen was the Thompsons' youngest doll.

Jeannie might not have been listening. She started to tell something else: "You know, where we were before, on Vern's last job, we weren't in a camp. He was away a lot, and he left me in Amos in a hotel. I liked it. Amos isn't all that big, but it's better than here. There was this German in the hotel. He was selling cars. He'd drive me around if I wanted to go to a movie or anything. Vern didn't like him, so we left. It wasn't anybody's fault."

"So he's given up two jobs," said Mrs. Thompson. "One because he couldn't leave you alone, and now this one. Two jobs, and you haven't been married five months. Why should another man be thrown out of work? We don't need to know a thing. I'll be sorry if it was Jimmy Quinn," she went on slowly. "I like that boy. Don't say the name, dear. There's Evans. Susini. Palmer. But it might have been anybody, because you had them all on the boil. So it might have been Jimmy Quinn—let's say—and it could have been

anyone else, too. Well, now let's hope they can get their minds back on the job."

"I thought they all liked me," said Jeannie sadly. "I get along with people. Vern never fights with me."

"Vern never fights with anyone. But he ought to have thrashed *you*."

"If he...you know. I won't say the name. If he'd liked me, I wouldn't have minded. If he'd been friendly. I really mean that. I wouldn't have gone wandering up the road, making all this fuss."

"Jeannie," said Mrs. Thompson, "you don't even know what you're saying."

"He could at least have liked me," said Jeannie. "He wasn't even friendly. It's the first time in my life somebody hasn't liked me. My heart is broken, Mrs. Thompson. My heart is just broken."

She has to cry, Mrs. Thompson thought. She has to have it out. She rocked slowly, tapping her foot, trying to remember how she'd felt about things when she was twenty, wondering if her heart had ever been broken, too.

NOTES

1. Jean Harlow (1911–1937): Famous platinum-blonde movie star of the 1930s whose charm and wit brought glamour to many a depression family.
2. Javel water, a solution of sodium hypochorite, was a common form of disinfectant.

Máire Mhac an tSaoi

Ireland, b. 1922

Born in Dublin, Ireland, in 1922, Máire Mhac an tSaoi was the daughter of Séan MacEntee, Irish revolutionary and founding father of the modern Irish state. She has a distinguished educational background, having attended University College, Dublin, where, in 1941, she was awarded a B.A. in Celtic Studies and Modern Languages, receiving first-class honors and first place in Modern Gaelic, French, and English. She won a Travelling Studentship in Gaelic and English from the National University of Ireland in 1942 to study at the *Institut des Hautes Études* of the University of Paris, but, because of the war, she was unable to go there until 1945. In the interval she worked as a scholar at the Institute for Advanced Studies in Dublin from 1942–1945. She received an M.A. from the National University of Ireland in 1945 and, the following year published *Two Irish Arthurian Romances*, a Gaelic text edited from the original manuscript.

Máire Mhac an tSaoi began her nearly twenty years of diplomatic service in 1947 when she entered the Dublin Ministry of Foreign Affairs as Third Secretary. She served in Paris and Madrid, and then, in 1951, was made Secretary of the Irish Cultural Relations Committee, a post from which she was released in 1952 to work on the compilation of the official modern English/Gaelic dictionary for the Ministry of Education. Several other posts followed, including membership in the Irish Delegation to the General Assembly of the United Nations and, in 1961, an appointment as Permanent Representative of Ireland at the Council of Europe in Strasbourg.

In 1962, Máire Mhac an tSaoi resigned from the Irish Civil Service to marry her senior colleague, the writer Conor Cruise O'Brien, and to accompany him over long periods of residence in Africa, London, and the United States. She has taught courses in Gaelic language and culture at various educational institutions. The couple have two adopted teenaged children of mixed race, part Irish, part African.

Some consider Máire Mhac an tSaoi's published output slight. She has produced, as she puts it, "three slim volumes of verse in Gaelic" entitled *Margadh na Saoire* (The Hiring Fair, 1956), *Codladh an Ghaiscígh* (The Hero's Sleep, 1973), and *An Galar Dubhach* (The Gloomy Sickness, 1980). Her collected works, *An Cion go Seo* (The Sum Till Now) are, at present, in the process of publication. She has also translated poems from classical Gaelic in a collection called *A Heart Full of Thought* (1959); further articles, poems, short stories, essays and translations from her hand have appeared in various newspapers and periodicals. She is currently working on a monograph on the Poet-Earl of Desmond, "a fourteenth-century Hiberno-Norman magnate." Her home is in Howth, near Dublin, in Ireland.

Of the following poems, "Quatrains of Mary Hogan" appeared in The Hiring Fair, "The Hero's Sleep" in a collection of the same name, and "Lament for Seamus Ennis" is included in her current collection.

LAMENT FOR SEAMUS ENNIS, LATE CHAMPION PIPER OF IRELAND[1]

Sunt Lacrimae Rerum—I gcuimhne Shéamuis Ennis

(Slow air)

Sheepeople wheening, wintry their wail;
Fairy wives keening near and away[2]
West to the dune's edge: Donn,[3] spread the tale.

Make the drum's roar a flail—
    Lay on great strokes,
Redoubling each in train,
    Hammers of woe;
This prince, the music waned,
    Seeks his clay home.

Wizards of liss[4] and fort, hosts of the air,
Panicked and routed go, each from his lair;
Boyne's airy pleasure-dome, rainstorm lays bare.

Desert and harpless,
    Tara is grass;[5]
Yet we had argued
    Even such pass
No mortal harm meant—
    No more, alas!

White flowers of repentance the barren staff knew;
The pillar-stones danced to hear Orpheus' tunes;[6]
But, King-piper of Ireland, voice is withheld from you—
    Ever!

Translated by the author
on the basis of a first draft by Canon Coslett Quinn

NOTES

1. Contemporary folklorist and folk musician, recently dead.
2. Sheepeople are fairies in Irish lore; *keening* is dialect for whining.
3. *Donn duimhche*, "Donn of the dune," was the old Irish god of death.
4. Ancient Irish storage place.
5. The prehistoric tombs on the Boyne were believed to be the palaces of the old gods.
6. Orpheus, in Greek mythology, was the fabled musician who could charm animate and inanimate things alike.

QUATRAINS OF MARY HOGAN*
Ceathrúintí Mháire Ní Ógáin

I

Once I am rid of these meshes—
God send it be soon and forever!
It may not be counted unseemly
My peace in your arms to remember.

When prayer becomes possible to me,
With Mass and receipt of Communion,
Oh, who will declare it indecent
To entreat for myself or for you, love?

But, while we await this conclusion,
Do not grow too deeply enamoured,
For I am committed to loosing
All bonds that could ever be fastened.

II

All ban of priest defying,
Indifferent to all
Suspicion, I am lying
Between you and the wall;

Night's winter weather cannot
Reach here to change my mind—
Warm, secret world and narrow,
Within one bed confined;

What is to come we heed not,
Nor what was done before,
The time is ours, my dearest,
And it will last till dawn.

III

So we must reckon a year
That we the one coverlet share,
Difficult now to be clear
What I wanted, for what came prepared?

Mine was a generous love—
You trampled it under your heel—
With never a question at all
If the flesh that was trodden could feel?

Oh, but the body obeys,
For the sake of a long-given word,
But now that the song in the heart has been
                                    stayed
Joy ebbs from our pleasure like tide on the turn.

IV

Infant jealousy feeds at my breast:
I must nurse by day, I must nurse by night;
He's an ugly youngster and teething fast,
And he poisons my veins with his milk-tooth
                                    bite.

Don't let the small wretch separate us—
So sound and healthy as was our mating!
Its warrant was skin to skin that clave, and
Its seal a hand granted every favor.

I have no mind to deny affection
Though doubt takes root in deep dejection—
Do not abuse a good draft mare then,
And she, in her own time, will repair all

V

Oh, what a wonder is pain!
How it gnaws at the cage
Of the ribs! And it will not abate
Or be stated, come night or come day.

Thus it is pain is made known,
You will never be sole or alone,
But will carry your company close
Like a mother her babe in the womb.

VI

"I do not sleep of nights":
It is not much to say,
But who has yet devised
A way to calculate,
Upon the open eye,
How heavy the night's weight?

VII

The night is long!
There were nights once
With you not long—
Which I renounce.

(continued)

Not hard to follow
The road I went;
No longer possible
If I repent.

We lay for mirth
And we rose for gladness—
Practices such
As I must abandon.

Translated by the author

NOTE

* Mary Hogan, the mistress of the eighteenth-century poet
  Donncha Rua Mac Conmara, is the folk protype of the
  maid betrayed.

THE HERO'S SLEEP
Codladh on Ghaiscígh

For an adopted son

Blackberry-sweet the little clustered head!
Small foreign son, my share of this world's
                                                    treasure,
Nest and be welcome underneath my heart;
Nest and be welcome underneath our rafters;
You've come a long way, little morning star.

It is good so to breed, from without:
See my manling, my little bull-calf—
Head him off from the door, trap him safe in
                                                    his bath—

On my word, he's as sound as a trout,
In every limb prospering stoutly,
In strength, and in beauty to crown it.

You took your color from the Autumn
And from the dun rose:
Lovely all yellows! They are your relations—
Look, Conor, here then our son,
Not as his advent was planned,
But as Providence put it in hand.

My small barley hen, let me gather you in:
The night's darkness threatens, the lamp has
                                                    been lit;
The fox is abroad on the roads—
No ill-hap send him snapping to our door,
Where   you shine,   the household's candle,
                            on a   candlestick   of gold!

Asleep beneath my breast
My love has walled you in,
But when your kingly steps go forth,
I dog your path in vain.
What charm will keep you safe?
What talisman prevail?
Is not "No treaty with the white!"
Your proper tribal prayer?

As is a mother's way,
I let my thoughts run on,
And while my mind debates,
You've seized the wooden spoon!
At once my dream is changed
Your hero's light shines round—
Just such another little boy.
They say, was Ulster's Hound.*

Translated by the author

NOTE

* Cuchulain, the mythical Ulster hero.

Nadine Gordimer   *South Africa, b. 1923*

One of the most exceptional living authors writing in English, Nadine Gordimer
was born in 1923, to lower middle-class Jewish parents in the small town of
Springs, outside Johannesburg, South Africa. Both her parents were immigrants to
South Africa, her mother having been born in England, and her father in Lithuania.
Gordimer attended a convent school in Springs, and then went on to a university
education in South Africa. She began to write at a very early age. Indeed, she refers
to herself as "a natural writer."

Living in Springs, a small and fairly isolated town in South Africa, itself fairly isolated and remote from the rest of the world, Gordimer as a young would-be writer experienced a paradoxical form of freedom: "There was the local public library...and I was like a calf in clover there; nobody guided or advised me, nobody told me which books I ought to read if I wanted to become a writer. I read a lot of French and Russian nineteenth-century novels, in translation of course, and I drew, completely unself-consciously, from whatever there was for me to feed on there." This sort of freedom had its price, however. Gordimer's first supposition was that precisely because she lived where she did, her writing would have little to commend it. "I felt that nobody would be interested in the world that I knew, that indeed I wasn't living in the world." The real world was that represented in the novels of Dickens, Hawthorne, and Virginia Woolf, in the light of which Gordimer's local universe could only seem quaint and peripheral. Despite her colonially-induced identification with English culture, she did not live in England; on the other hand, despite the fact that she lived in South Africa, the country and its people remained foreign to her. At the beginning of her career as a writer, the question of cultural identity naturally assumed significant proportions for Gordimer.

Gordimer's first published short story, "Face to Face," appeared in 1949. In stories like "The Train from Rhodesia" and "Ah, Woe Is Me," both from the 1953 collection *The Soft Voice of the Serpent*, and in novels like *The Lying Days* (1953) and *A World of Strangers* (1958), Gordimer presented life in white South Africa as saturated by the exigencies of social reality, and dominated by the large structures of social existence even in its most private and personal moments. Nor were relationships "across the color bar" the only ones inevitably scarred by apartheid. On the contrary, such stories as "Town and Country Lovers" (in *A Soldier's Embrace*, 1980) and "Crimes of Conscience" (in *Something Out There*, 1984) demonstrate in harrowing detail, the overdetermining shadow of apartheid looms over all relationships, blighting their development with its corrosive presence. In *The Late Bourgeois World* (1966), Gordimer suggested that, more typically, intimacy and generosity would be undermined by betrayal and moral cowardice, in accordance with the imperatives of an overarching social logic.

While Gordimer's initial impulse was to define white South African identity, her growing commitment to the cause of black liberation in the country led her first to produce a modernist fiction that was self-consciously critical of the reality it depicted, and then to try and imagine the unimaginable, a "South African revolution" and its aftermath. *A Guest of Honour* (1971), which won the 1972 James Tait Black Memorial Prize, represented a first, tentative step in this direction, and the tendency has been advanced with each succeeding novel. In *The Conservationist* (1974; winner of the Booker Prize for fiction), the central protagonist, a wealthy white industrialist named Mehring, finds his control over his black employees and even over the farmland he owns being undermined through a metaphorical "return of the repressed," as a buried black body is exhumed in a storm—a wind of change—blowing from Mozambique. In *July's People* (1981), the revolution is phrased as having already occurred and its consequences for a "typical" middle-class white family are explored. In the novella *Something Out There*, too, the imminence of radical social transformation is taken for granted, even as Gordimer shows us the fundamental unpreparedness, amounting to pathology, of the local white population. Perhaps the most impressive of these recent novels is *Burger's Daughter* (1979), in which Gordimer focuses upon the struggle of a young white radical, Rosa Burger, to come to terms with the obligations with which history seems to have burdened her. At first, Rosa resents feeling so obligated, and attempts to leave South Africa for Europe. Yet she returns, after recognizing that, for better or worse, it is only as a South African that she can identify herself. Yet in *A Sport of Nature* (1987), which Gordimer has called a "modern picaresque novel,"[2] Gordimer imagines a heroine who has apparently fled to America. Interestingly, too, for the first time, Gordimer identifies her Jewish heritage and probes its legacy in the lives of Hilela and Sasha, the chief characters in the book.

Rosa Burger's return puts one in mind of Gordimer's resolute refusal, despite many offers and opportunities, to leave South Africa. Although she frequently travels abroad, she continues to live in the country where she has been twice married and has brought up her children. Today her work is everywhere admired and respected, and she has been showered with honors, among them the French Grand Aigle d'Or in 1975, the Nelly Sachs Prize of Germany, and an honorary doctorate from the Belgian University of Leuven. Gordimer is an honorary member of the American Academy of Arts and Letters, and an active participant in the affairs of PEN International.

Neil Lazarus

NOTES

1. All quotations, unless otherwise indicated, are drawn from "A Conversation with Nadine Gordimer," in *Salmagundi*, No. 62, Winter 1984, 3–31. The issue also contains a series of critical articles on Gordimer's work.
2. Oral statement at a reading of her work at Queens College, New York City, April 20, 1987.

THE TRAIN FROM RHODESIA

The train came out of the red horizon and bore down towards them over the single straight track.

The stationmaster came out of his little brick station with its pointed chalet roof, feeling the creases in his serge uniform in his legs as well. A stir of preparedness rippled through the squatting native vendors waiting in the dust; the face of a carved wooden animal, eternally surprised, stuck out of a sack. The stationmaster's barefoot children wandered over. From the grey mud huts with the untidy heads that stood within a decorated mud wall, chickens, and dogs with their skin stretched like parchment over their bones, followed the piccanins down to the track. The flushed and perspiring west cast a reflection, faint, without heat, upon the station, upon the tin shed marked "Goods," upon the walled kraal, upon the grey tin house of the stationmaster and upon the sand, that lapped all around from sky to sky, cast little rhythmical cups of shadow, so that the sand became the sea, and closed over the children's black feet softly and without imprint.

The stationmaster's wife sat behind the mesh of her veranda. Above her head the hunk of a sheep's carcass moved slightly, dangling in a current of air.

They waited.

The train called out, along the sky; but there was no answer; and the cry hung on: I'm coming...I'm coming...

The engine flared out now, big, whisking a dwindling body behind it; the track flared out to let it in.

Creaking, jerking, jostling, gasping, the train filled the station.

Here, let me see that one—the young woman curved her body farther out of the corridor window. Missus? smiled the old man, looking at the creatures he held in his hand. From a piece of string on his grey finger hung a tiny woven basket; he lifted it, questioning. No, no, she urged, leaning down towards him, across the height of the train towards the man in the piece of old rug; that one, that one, her hand commanded. It was a lion, carved out of soft dry wood that looked like spongecake; heraldic, black and white, with impressionistic detail burnt in. The old man held it up to her still smiling, not from the heart, but at the customer. Between its vandyke teeth, in the mouth opened in an endless roar too terrible to be heard, it had a black tongue. Look, said the young husband, if you don't mind! And round the neck of the thing, a piece of fur (rat? rabbit? meerkat?); a real mane, majestic, telling you somehow that the artist had delight in the lion.

All up and down the length of the train in the dust the artists sprang, walking bent, like performing animals, the better to exhibit the fantasy held toward the faces on the train. Buck, startled and stiff, staring with round black and white eyes. More lions, standing erect, grappling with strange, thin, elongated warriors who clutched spears and showed no fear in their slits of eyes. How much, they asked from the train, how much?

Give me penny, said the little ones with nothing to sell. The dogs went and sat, quite still, under the dining car, where the train breathed out the smell of meat cooking with onion.

A man passed beneath the arch of reaching arms meeting grey-black and white in the exchange of money for the staring wooden eyes, the stiff wooden legs sticking up in the air; went along under the voices and the bargaining, interrogating the wheels. Past the dogs; glancing up at the dining car where he could stare at the faces, behind glass, drinking beer, two by two, on either side of a uniform railway vase with its pale dead flower. Right to the end, to the guard's van, where the stationmaster's children had just collected their mother's two loaves of bread; to the engine itself, where the stationmaster and the driver stood talking against the steaming complaint of the resting beast.

The man called out to them, something loud and joking. They turned to laugh, in a twirl of steam. The two children careened over the sand, clutching the bread, and burst through the iron gate and up the path through the garden in which nothing grew.

Passengers drew themselves in at the corridor windows and turned into compartments to fetch money, to call someone to look. Those sitting inside looked up: suddenly different, caged faces, boxed in, cut off after the contact of outside. There was an orange a piccanin would like...What about that chocolate? It wasn't very nice...

A girl had collected a handful of the hard kind, that no one liked, out of the chocolate box, and was throwing them to the dogs, over at the dining car. But the hens darted in and swallowed the chocolates, incredibly quick and accurate, before they had even dropped in the dust, and the dogs, a little bewildered, looked up with their brown eyes, not expecting anything.

—No, leave it, said the young woman, don't take it...

Too expensive, too much, she shook her head and raised her voice to the old man, giving up the lion. He held it high where she had handed it to him. No, she said, shaking her head. Three-and-six? insisted her husband, loudly. Yes baas! laughed the old man. *Three and-six?*—the young man was incredulous. Oh leave it—she said. The young man stopped. Don't you want it? he said, keeping his face closed to the old man. No, never mind, she said, leave it. The old native kept his head on one side, looking at them sideways, holding the lion. Three-and-six, he murmured, as old people repeat things to themselves.

The young woman drew her head in. She went into the coupé and sat down. Out of the window, on the other side, there was nothing; sand and bush; a thorn tree. Back through the open doorway, past the figure of her husband in the corridor, there was the station, the voices, wooden animals waving, running feet. Her eye followed the funny little valance of scrolled wood that outlined the chalet roof of the station; she thought of the lion and smiled. That bit of fur round the neck. But the wooden buck, the hippos, the elephants, the baskets that already bulked out of their brown paper under the seat and on the luggage rack! How will they look at home? Where will you put them? What will they mean away from the places you found them? Away from the unreality of the last few weeks? The young man outside. But he is not part of the unreality; he is for good now. Odd...somewhere there was an idea that he, that living with him, was part of the holiday, the strange places.

Outside, a bell rang. The stationmaster was leaning against the end of the train, green flag rolled in readiness. A few men who had got down to stretch their legs sprang onto the train, clinging to the observation platforms, or perhaps merely standing on the iron step, holding the rail; but on the train, safe from the one dusty platform, the one tin house, the empty sand.

There was a grunt. The train jerked. Through the glass the beer drinkers looked out, as if they could not see beyond it. Behind the fly-screen, the stationmaster's wife sat facing back at them beneath the darkening hunk of meat.

There was a shout. The flag dropped out. Joints not yet coordinated, the segmented body of the train heaved and bumped back against itself. It began to move; slowly the scrolled chalet moved past it, the yells of the natives, running alongside, jetted up into the air, fell back at different levels. Staring wooden faces waved drunkenly, there, then gone, questioning for the last time at the windows. Here, one-and-six baas!—As one automatically opens a hand to catch a thrown ball, a man fumbled wildly down his pocket, brought up the shilling and sixpence and threw them out; the old native, gasping, his skinny toes splaying the sand, flung the lion.

The piccanins were waving, the dogs stood, tails uncertain, watching the train go: past the mud huts, where a woman turned to look up from the smoke of the fire, her hand pausing on her hip.

The stationmaster went slowly in under the chalet.

The old native stood, breath blowing out the skin between his ribs, feet tense, balanced in the sand, smiling and shaking his head. In his opened palm, held in the attitude of receiving, was the retrieved shilling and sixpence.

The blind end of the train was being pulled helplessly out of the station.

The young man swung in from the corridor, breathless. He was shaking his head with laughter and triumph. Here! he said. And waggled the lion at her. One-and-six!

What? she said.

He laughed. I was arguing with him for fun, bargaining—when the train had pulled out already, he came tearing after...One-and-six Baas! So there's your lion.

She was holding it away from her, the head with the open jaws, the pointed teeth, the black tongue, the wonderful ruff of fur facing her. She was looking at it with an expression of not seeing, of seeing something different. Her face was drawn up, wryly, like the face of a discomforted child. Her mouth lifted nervously at the corner. Very slowly, cautious, she lifted her finger and touched the mane, where it was joined to the wood.

But how could you, she said. He was shocked by the dismay of her face.

Good Lord, he said, what's the matter?

If you wanted the thing, she said, her voice rising and breaking with the shrill impotence of anger, why didn't you buy it in the first place? If you wanted it, why didn't you pay for it? Why didn't you take it decently, when he offered it? Why did you have to wait for him to run after the train with it, and give him one-and-six? One-and-six!

She was pushing it at him, trying to force him to take the lion. He stood astonished, his hands hanging at his sides.

But you wanted it! You liked it so much?

—It's a beautiful piece of work, she said fiercely, as if to protect it from him.

You liked it so much! You said yourself it was too expensive—

Oh *you*—she said, hopeless and furious. *You*...She threw the lion on to the seat.

He stood looking at her.

She sat down again in the corner and, her face slumped in her hands, stared out of the window. Everything was turning round inside her. One-and-six. One-and-six. One-and-six for the wood and the carving and the sinews of the legs and the switch of the tail. The mouth open like that and the teeth. The black tongue, rolling, like a wave. The mane round the neck. To give one-and-six for that. The heat of shame mounted through her legs and body and sounded in her ears like the sound of sand pouring. Pouring, pouring. She sat there, sick. A weariness, a tastelessness, the discovery of a void made her hands slacken their grip, atrophy emptily, as if the hour was not worth their grasp. She was feeling like this again. She had thought it was something to do with singleness, with being alone and belonging too much to oneself.

She sat there not wanting to move or speak, or to look at anything, even; so that the mood should be associated with nothing, no object, word or sight that might recur and so recall the feeling again...Smut blew in grittily, settled on her hands. Her back remained at exactly the same angle, turned against the young man sitting with his hands drooping between his sprawled legs, and the lion, fallen on its side in the corner.

The train had cast the station like a skin. It called out to the sky, I'm coming, I'm coming; and again, there was no answer.

Dorothy Hewett
Australia, b. 1923

Though Dorothy Hewett first achieved success as a poet, in recent years she has been increasingly recognized as one of Australia's finest dramatists. While not the first Australian woman playwright, Hewett has been the first to achieve a popular as well as a critical success, with numerous productions across the country.

Hewett was born in Western Australia where she grew up on an isolated wheat farm, taking lessons by correspondence until the age of 12. She then attended various schools in Perth and began an Arts degree at the University of Western Australia which, however, she was not to complete until 1961. Many of the turbulent events of her life are reflected in her works, particularly in *The Chapel Perilous* (1972).

Hewett, like many young intellectuals at this time, joined the Communist Party at 19; she attempted suicide at 20 and, at 21, married for the first time. After the death of her son and the breakdown of her marriage, she moved to Sydney where she lived in one of the inner-city slum areas and worked in factories. She drew on these experiences for her only novel, *Bobbin Up* (1959), and her first play, *This Old Man Comes Rolling Home* (1976). During the 1950s Hewett was heavily involved in Communist Party activities in Sydney where she lived with another member of the Party, bearing him three sons.

In 1960 she returned to Perth and married a seaman, Merv Lilley, with whom she had two daughters. After completing her degree, she taught English and Australian Literature at the University of Western Australia for several years, finally moving back to Sydney to work full-time as a writer in 1974.

Hewett has published five collections of poetry, "*Legend of the Green Country*" and "*Grave Fairytale*" coming respectively from the second and third, *Windmill Country* (1968) and *Rapunzel in Surburbia* (1975). They show most of the characteristic features of Hewett's work, such as the use of personal and family experiences and the presentation of controversial subjects through the medium of myth and fantasy. Her poetry is praised for its vigor and frankness especially in its treatment of female sexuality, and for its rich imagery; while it is criticized as self-indulgent and structurally weak.

Hewett's combination of tough subject matter—*Bon-Bons and Roses for Dolly* (1976) provoked a riot in Perth by depicting menstruation on stage—and non-naturalistic style, with much use of music, literary reference and symbolism, have slowed recognition and professional production of her plays. She has written at least fifteen, though many are still unpublished, and finally achieved a popular success with *The Man from Mukinupin* (1979).

Elizabeth Webby

from LEGEND OF THE GREEN COUNTRY

I

September is the spring month bringing tides, swilling green in the harbour mouth,
Turnabout dolphins rolling-backed in the rip and run, the king waves
Swinging the coast, snatching at fishermen from Leeuwin to Norah's Head;
A dangerous month: but I count on an abacus as befits a shopkeeper's daughter.
I never could keep count by modern methods, the ring of the till
Is profit and loss, the ledger, hasped with gold, sits in its heavy dust
On the counter, out front the shopkeeper's sign hangs loose and bangs in the wind,
The name is obliterated, the dog swells and stinks in the gutter,
The golden smell of the beer does not run in the one street, like water;
The windmill head hangs, broken-necked, flapping like a great plain turkey
As the wind rises. . .this was my country, here I go back for nurture
To the dry soaks, to the creeks running salt through the timber,
To the ghosts of the sandalwood cutters, and the blue breath of their fires,
To the navvies[1] in dark blue singlets laying rails in the scrub.

My grandfather rode out, sawing at a hard-mouthed ginger horse,
And a hard heart in him, a dray full of rum and beer, bully-beef and treacle,
Flour and tea, workboots and wideawakes with the corks bobbing for flies;
Counting the campfires in the dusk, counting the men, counting the money,
Counting the sheep from the goats, and the rack rented railway houses.
No wonder I cannot count for the sound of the money-changers,
The sweat and the clink, the land falling into the cash register,
Raped and eroded, thin and black as a myall girl[2] on a railway siding.
He came back, roaring and singing up from the gullies, his beard
Smelt of rum, his money-bag plump as a wild duck under his saddle.
The old horse stumbled in the creek-bed but brought him home,
The dray rattled; as they took him down in the yard he cursed and swore
At the dream, and blubbered for it: next Saturday night he rode his horse
Up the turkey red carpet into the bar, smashing the bottles and glasses,
Tipping the counter, sending the barmaid screaming, her breasts tilting with joy.
The great horse reared and he sang and swore and flung his hat at the sky,
And won his bets, and rode home, satisfied, to a nagging wife and daughter,
Having buried his pain and his lust under the broken bottles.
The publican swept them up in the cold light next morning,
And that was the end of it, they thought, but it wasn't so easy:
There is no end to it and I stand at the mole watching the sea run out,
Or hang over the rails at the Horseshoe Bridge and listen to the tide,
Listen to the earth that pleasured my grandfather with his flocks and acres
Drowned under salt, his orange trees forked bare as unbreeched boys.
Only the apples, little and hard, bitten green and bitter as salt,
They come up in the spring, in the dead orchard they are the fruit
Of our knowledge, and I am Eve, spitting the pips in the eye of the myth-makers.
This is my legend; an old man on a ginger horse who filled his till
And died content with a desert, or so they said: his stone angel
Cost a pretty penny, but the workmanship was faulty, its wings curve
In a great arc over the graveyard, it grows mildewed and dirty,
Its nose is syphilitic, its feet splay like a peasant, its hands
Clasp over its breast like the barmaid who screamed in the pub,
And kissed him, for love, not money, but only once.

II

My grandmother had a bite like a sour green apple,
Little and pitiless she kept the till,
Counted the profits, and stacked the bills of sale.
She bought the shops and the farms, the deeds were hers,
In the locked iron safe with a shower of golden sovereigns.
She never trusted the banks, they failed in the nineties,
She kept her bank notes rolled in the top of her stocking,
Caressingly, while her prices soared and dropped,
Her barometer; crops and wool and railway lines.

(continued)

Each night she read the news by the hurricane lantern,
While the only child wept for love in the washing-up water.
She could argue like a man, politics, finance, banking.
In her rocking chair with her little dangling feet,
Her eyes glittered like broken beer bottle glass.
She kept one eye out for a farmer to spend his money
And a sharp tongue for a borrowing mate of my grandfather's.

Once, long ago, in Swanston Street she "made"
For fashionable ladies, their breasts half bared
And their ankles covered, pads in their hair,
Bustles, bugle beads and jet, dyed ostrich feathers,
You could see their shadows waving from hansom cabs,
And the ghostly wheels turning into Swanston Street.
She had her miracles and quoted them...
Science and Health by Mary Baker Eddy,
She read *The Monitor* while the dust storms whirled,[3]
And marvelled that God was love; it was all clear profit.
She wet the bagging to filter the westerlies,
Planted geraniums and snowdrops under the tank,
And squashed black caterpillars on moonlit forays.
She balanced the ledger and murmured, "God is love,"
Feeling like God, she foreclosed on another farm.

She never read for pleasure, or danced or sang,
Or listened with love, slowly life smote her dumb,
Till she lay in the best bedroom, pleating the quilt,
In a fantasy of ball dresses for Melbourne ladies.
Her eyes were remote as pennies, her sheets stank,
She cackled and counted a mythical till at her days.

III

My father was a black-browed man who rode like an Abo.
The neighbors gossiped, "A touch of the tarbrush there."
He built the farm with his sweat, it lay in the elbow
Of two creeks, thick with wattle and white ti-tree.
At night he blew on the cornet; once, long ago, he'd played
On the pleasure cruises that went up the Yarra on Saturday nights;
The lights bobbed in the muddy water, the girls in white muslin sang "Tipperary."
Now he played in the lonely sleepout, looking out over the flat,
With the smell of creekwater, and a curlew[4] crying like a murdered gin,
Crying all night, till he went out with a shotgun and finished its screaming,
But not his own...he, the mendicant, who married the storekeeper's daughter.

My mother was a dark round girl in a country town,
With down on her lip, her white cambric blouse
Smelt of roses and starch, she was beautiful,
Warm, and frigid in a world of dried-up women,

Aborting themselves with knitting needles on farms.
She wept in the tin humpy at the back of the store,
For the mother who hated, the father who drank
And loved her; then, sadly, she fell in love
And kissed the young accountant who kept the books,
Behind the ledgers, the summer dust on the counters.
He was on the booze, broke all his promises,
Went off to the city and sang in an old spring cart,
"Bottle-oh, Bottle-oh" till his liver gave out
And he died; she married in arum lilies, satin, tulle,
Under the bell that tolled for the storekeeper's daughter.
Men shot themselves in the scrub on her wedding day.
My father brought her wildflowers, rode forty miles,
But he never kissed her like the beautiful bottle-oh,
Boozing in the pub like a fly caught in its amber.

The roof of the hospital cracked like purgatory,
At sunset the birth blood dried on the sheets,
Nobody came to change them, the sun went down,
The pain fell on her body like a beast and mauled it.

She hated the farm, hated the line of wattles
Smudging the creek, kept her hands full of scones,
Boiled the copper, washing out sins in creek water,
Kept sex at bay like the black snake coiled in the garden,
Burning under the African daisies and bridal creeper,
Took her children to bed, he lay alone in the sleep-out,
With a headache and *The Seven Pillars of Wisdom*.[5]
The girls in their picture hats came giggling and singing,
Trailing their hands like willows from the Yarra launches,
Till the dream was nightmare and all his life a regret,
Bought and gelded in an old grey house by a creek-bed.

NOTES

1. Unskilled laborers, often working in construction.
2. A myall is an Australian Aborigine.
3. *Science and Health* (1875) was the first book by Mary Baker Eddy (1821–1910), founder of the Christian Science religion and of the *Christian Science Monitor* in 1908; it is now a highly regarded daily newspaper. *Science and Health*, viewed as divinely inspired, outlined the principles of Eddy's new religion, which taught the art of healing without medicine.
4. An Australian bird.
5. Written by T.E. Lawrence (1888–1935), the book (1926) was the famed British adventurer's account of his experiences in the Middle East in the early twentieth century.

GRAVE FAIRYTALE

I sat in my tower, the seasons whirled,
the sky changed, the river grew
and dwindled to a pool.
The black Witch, light as an eel,
laddered up my hair
to straddle the window-sill.

She was there when I woke, blocking the light,
or in the night, humming, trying on my clothes.
I grew accustomed to her; she was as much a
                                        part of me
as my own self; sometimes I thought, "She *is*
                                        myself!"
a posturing blackness, savage as a cuckoo.

There was no mirror in the tower.

Each time the voice screamed from the thorny
                                        garden

I'd rise and pensively undo the coil,
I felt it switch the ground, the earth tugged at it,
once it returned to me knotted with dead
                                        warm birds,
once wrapped itself three times around the
                                        tower—
            the tower quaked.
Framed in the window, whirling the countryside
with my great net of hair I'd catch a hawk,
            a bird, and once a bear.
One night I woke, the horse pawed at the walls,
the cells was full of light, all my stone house
suffused, the voice called from the calm white
                                        garden,
            "Rapunzel."
I leant across the sill, my plait hissed out
            and spun like hail;
he climbed, slow as a heartbeat, up the stony
                                        side,
we dropped together as he loosed my hair,
his foraging hands tore me from neck to heels:
the witch jumped up my back and beat me to
                                        the wall.
Crouched in a corner I perceived it all,
the thighs jack-knifed apart, the dangling
                                        sword
            thrust home,
pinned like a specimen—to scream with joy.

I watched all night the beasts unsatisfied
roll in their sweat, their guttural cries
made the night thick with sound.
Their shadows gambolled, hunch-backed,
                                        hairy-arsed,
and as she ran four-pawed across the light,
the female dropped coined blood spots on the
                                        floor.

When morning came he put his armour on,
kissing farewell like angels swung on hair.
I heard the metal shoes trample the round
                                        earth
            about my tower.
Three times I lent my hair to the glowing
                                        prince,
hand over hand he climbed, my roots ached,
the blood dribbled on the stone sill.
Each time I saw the framed-faced bully boy
            sick with his triumph.

The third time I hid the shears,
a stab of black ice dripping in my dress.
He rose, his armour glistened in my tears,
the convex scissors snapped,
the glittering coil hissed, and slipped
            through air to undergrowth.
His mouth, like a round O, gaped at his end,
his finger nails ripped out, he clawed through
                                        space.
His horse ran off flank-deep in blown thistles.
Three seasons he stank at the tower's base.
A hawk plucked out his eyes, the ants busied
                                        his brain,
the mud-weed filled his mouth, his great sword
                                        rotted,
his tattered flesh-flags hung on bushes for the
                                        birds.
Bald as a collaborator I sit walled
            in the thumb-nosed tower,
wound round three times with ropes of
                                        autumn leaves.
And the witch...sometimes I idly kick
a little heap of rags across the floor.
I notice it grows smaller every year.

Elizabeth Jolley   *UK(England)/Australia, b. 1923*

Although she has been writing nearly all her life, Elizabeth Jolley's first book did not appear in print until 1976. By 1988, twelve had been published with increasing success, winning for their author several prizes and recognition as one of Australia's leading contemporary novelists.

Jolley was born in Birmingham, England, to an English father and an Austrian mother. This mixed inheritance is reflected in much of Jolley's fiction, as is the theme of the displaced person, reinforced, no doubt, by her own migration to Australia in 1959, when her husband became librarian at the University of Western Australia.

Before her marriage, Jolley had trained and worked as a nurse. Several of her stories and novels have hospital settings, including the story in this anthology, "'Surprise! Surprise!' from Matron," from her first collection *Five Acre Virgin* (1976). This story shows several of the striking characteristics of Jolley's fiction, including her zany, often black, humor, and her tendency to reuse characters and themes; Matron and many of the other characters from this story reappear in others as well as in the novel *Mr. Scobie's Riddle* (1982), which won the *Age* Book of the Year Award and was the first of Jolley's works to be widely acclaimed.

Her first novel, *Palomino* (1980), the most conventional in form and style, won little recognition for its sensitive portrayal of a lesbian relationship. Its themes and settings are reworked in the wonderfully comic *Miss Peabody's Inheritance* (1983) and in the more Gothic *The Well* (1986).

Elizabeth Webby

"SURPRISE! SURPRISE!" FROM MATRON

We are all ready in the dinette, waiting for the ambulance. Lt. Col. Shroud, Reggie we call him, keeps going to the front door.

DOCTORS AND VISITORS
ENTRANCE ONLY
Signed Matron A. Shroud.

"Mind the step!" Matron bawls after him.

"It's all right Amy," he calls back. "I'm not going outside."

She's afraid he'll fall on the broken step out there, it keeps crumbling away a bit more because of the milkman being such a heavy build. Matron says he's ruining the hospital falling all over it every night the way he does.

Mother is one hundred years old today, she had her picture in the paper and a Royal telegram and we are going to have a birthday tea for her off Matron's best white cloth, the one she keeps for Holy Communion. I only hope Mother will realise. Matron has made a birthday cake and has a surprise for mother but she won't say to any of us what it is.

Mother is being brought over specially in the ambulance from the City and District Hospital where she has been getting better from a broken hip. She would keep getting out of bed and then, one day, down she went in her bed socks on the slippery floor even though Matron kept saying patients were not to get out of bed in their wooly socks.

We couldn't have the party at the City and District but here at The Ferns Hospital for the Aged we can do as we like as the place belongs to the Doll and Fingertips, they won it from Matron's brother, the Lt. Col., playing poker. It was hilarious.

"You can still be Matron," they told her, "as we'll need one."

Reggie, the Lt. Col., misses Mother dreadfully so I hope they let her stay once she gets back. He goes all over the place looking for her under beds and in the cupboards.

"I say old sport," he says, "when *is* she coming back? I do sort of miss her you know what?"

The Doll says he's so dumb you can't help liking him. I'm on the day shift now and I don't feel nearly so tired, you really need your beauty sleep, it's the time before midnight that really rests you. Mind you, I usually got a couple of hours on the sofa before the wild life started up in room three. But once the poker was on every night there was no sleep for any of us. It was amazing how my brother and Fingertips were so full of life at their age and Betsy, too, suddenly living it up, painting the terrace red after all those solid years with that good solid husband she had and living that healthy suburban life bringing up her four girls. I got so tired long before they did but of course I was the only one working.

When Mother gets into bed now she gets in like a little girl, climbing in between her sheets with all her treasures filling up the bed and, when she goes to sleep, she lies all curled up with her things, her handbag and the clock and her photographs and her old tin box all round her, and you could think she was just a child there in her bed except that her hair is white and she is all wrinkled and shrivelled up and these treasures aren't what you might call toys.

When I don't see Mother I forget how she is now and my mind goes back to when we were in the valley all those years ago. Once on her birthday she was waiting and waiting for my brother to come. After dreading his visits and always wishing that he would keep away and not keep turning up with Fingertips to get more money from her, there she was watching the empty road, wishing more than anything in the world to see him coming along, passing the gap by the clump of trees and coming on toward the property. After he had taken up with Fingertips he lost interest in the farm and the

jarrah forest he had been so keen to grow. I daresay some of it's still there between the new houses which seemed to spring up as soon as the land was subdivided.

"You can't clean up nature," Mother kept telling my brother. He tried to clean out the creek bed and he was always hacking and cutting and burning off but all the time the castor oil plants and the wild radish and cape weed came back invading and taking over. Trees and branches blew down, wrecking the barn and the fence in places, and every time it rained the top soil washed down the slopes and then the meadow and the bottom paddock were so wet even the cows got bogged. He lost heart and wanted to go back to town, so he went off and only came to see her when he wanted money and then he never came at all. Like on her birthday.

"If only he'd be early!" Mother stood up beside the logs where we'd been sitting waiting all the afternoon. There was a pile of them up a bit from the weatherboard house, they must have been pushed there years ago. From these logs we could see the road. She shaded her eyes with her hand.

"Nature has her own ways," Mother always tried to comfort my brother as everything filled in so quickly when he cleared. Mother worked hard even though the place was not hers and she was only on it by this gentleman's agreement. She stood by when the owner, Dr. Harvey, was having trouble with the bore he had put down. The engineer had come and Mother was out there right on top of them telling them what to do. You could see the doctor felt uneasy to be on his land with us being there, and though he was quiet and very polite while the engineer was trying to get the siphon going, it was clear he was really wishing Mother miles away. There was a great long black plastic pipe all down the slope to the small three-cornered water hole we called the dam, its banks were muddy and trodden down by the few cows left behind from Grandpa's time.

"It's like a stomick wash out," Mother

explained at the top of her voice. "You must get the whole hose full of water before you let it start to run. Fill the hose, pinch it while it fills and then let it go into the dam and it'll start to siphon. Just imagine!" She shouted at them, "water coming up from all that way down under the earth, no trouble at all!" I don't think either of the two men paid any attention to Mother. In a well-bred sort of way they ignored her. Later on that same day Mrs. Harvey and her two children, a boy and a girl, both of them tall grown-up children, came out to the valley. I watched them from behind the barn, they hardly ever came so I wanted to see them close up. They were pale and uneasy walking together round the fence line, the boy and the girl, one each side of their mother, pressed close up to her as if they were needed to help her along with their own bodies. Their eyes looked sad, I thought, and very unfriendly.

"Why do we have to have them on our land?" I heard the boy ask his mother as they passed near where I was standing staring at them. But Mrs. Harvey just went on walking, looking straight ahead as if she had two stones in her head instead of eyes. They all three looked so unhappy, it was because of them looking so unhappy Mother wanted to advise them about everything but they didn't want Mother.

Well my brother never came on that birthday though she was so sure he would, and by that time she was really longing for him to come after wishing for years to be rid of his disagreeable presence. An empty road where you keep expecting to see someone you want to see seems terribly desolate when they don't come. There was a triangle of red gravel over there going steeply off the road where a track went up to some unknown person's place. Mother said the gravel patch was a symbol of complete loneliness and she couldn't bear to look at it any longer and, in the end, we left the log pile and went back down in the dusk to the weatherboard house. The sun had gone from the top of the meadow and that place,

usually so bright, seemed desolate too. My brother the Doll never came and soon after that I left too to go wherever the Doll wanted to go.

There is a commotion in the hall, we all sit up a little more thinking it is Mother coming but it is more like the crash of a bucket and a fall.

"Where's my nurse?" It's Matron, she's just come down. "Who put this pail in such a silly place! Someone has fallen over the pail" it sounds like Mrs. Hailey moaning, "Oh my leg! Oh my poor leg!"

"There dear," Matron comforts her, "just sit down on this chair and vomit." And we can hear Matron clearing away the pail and then all of a sudden Mother is here with us. There she is, very thin and old and very clean straight from the City and District. The noise of the pail stopped us hearing the ambulance.

"They always discharge patients so clean from there," Matron approves, and then she bawls down the passage for the kitchen girl, Jeanette this new one is called, to make the tea.

"Now dears give Mrs. Morgan a hip hip hooray!" Matron squeezes into the dinette beside Mother's wheel chair and Matron sings, "Happy birthday to you!" She wants everyone to join in but no ones does, so Matron sings it all the way to the end by herself.

"Happy birthday to *you*...Happy birthday to *you*...Happy birthday dear Mrs. Morgan Happy birthday to *you*,' and she gives Mother a kiss and we all go to kiss Mother and the Doll takes hold of Mother's handbag.

"Just you let go of that!" Mother says sharply.

"I was just goin' to hold it for you," he says.

"I can hold my own thank you," she says.

"Now dears what about some lovely cake. Isn't this a lovely party dears, give Matron a lovely smile," she says to Mother. But Mother looks round the dinette.

"Where's Betsy?" she says. "Why isn't Betsy here, she is my eldest. Betsy ought to be here."

"Now dear," Matron says in her most sensible voice, "now dear, don't you remember that beautiful funeral. You remember dear don't you, I'm sure every one of us here remembers Mrs. Thompson's beautiful funeral."

So we all have some cake. Fingertips is to hand it round but Mother won't have any from him and she eats my brother's piece. She is hungry after the polony* and mashed potatoes every day in the City and District and she eats nearly all the cake. Reggie can't take his eyes off her.

"We'll just save a teeny piece." Matron puts the plate up on top of the linen cupboard and then there is a ring at the front door.

"Surprise! Surprise!" Matron goes to answer the door and, to our great surprise, she comes back with a very thin old man in a wheel chair, he also is clean as if scrubbed by authority for years. With him are two orderlies in clean, badly-ironed overalls.

"Can we come in?" Matron coyly parts the curtains of the dinette. "Is it all right if we come in?"

"O' course it's all right," Mother says. "I've got my knickers on." Between Mother and the old man there is a moment of recognition. Then is an uneasy pause.

"I thought you was doing life," Mother suddenly says.

"He's very deaf," the orderly eases the chair round.

"I thought you was doing life!" Mother roars at him.

"Yes he was," the orderly begins to explain.

"Well so are we all in a manner of speaking," Matron says. "We are all doing 'life' dears aren't we," she smiles all round the dinette. "Now Mrs. Morgan, give Mr. Morgan a nice birthday smile. Remember dear his birthday is the same as yours and you are both one hundred years old. Just think of it two one hundred birthdays! Hip hip hooray!"

We all sit there staring and clap a bit with our hands but no one cheers with Matron except the Lt. Col. who has to be hushed up because of getting too excited. "Oh I say HOORAY!"

"I thought you was dead," Mother says to Dad. "I thought you was dead," she says really loud but he just sits there with that faint little far away laugh deaf people have. Dad really looks as if his skin has never got dirty, tied to his wheel chair are a cup and plate made of aluminium and a knife, fork and spoon made of the same stuff.

"Why has he got them tied to him?" Mother wants to know.

"He's got used to them so he has them with him now," the orderly explained. "He takes them everywhere."

"Happy birthday!" Matron roars into his ear. Dad just smiles, no teeth, just clean gums, and smiles. "We saved you some birthday cake." Matron reaches up to get it. All this time the Doll and Fingertips have been looking very uneasy: I couldn't help noticing and wondering if it was the toilet they wanted. They half get to their feet and make as if to leave the dinette.

"Sister," Matron says in her most posh voice, "take Mr. Morgan and Mr. Shady to the toilet please." So I get up, and out in the passage Doll says, "Maise we got to get out from here. Quick! We got to!"

"Whatever for, Dad's simple, he can't hurt you."

"It's not that."

I try to reason with my brother.

"Well Mother's not in a bad mood or anything, she'll get over Matron's Surprise and everything'll settle down." We edge down the passage all three together.

"It's not that, it's them! the two men with Dad." The Doll is really agitated, so is Fingertips.

"The big one, that's Bluey he's dumb but is he strong!" Doll says. "And the little one he's little but he's strong too. I never forget a face," Doll says, "not theirs anyhow and I've an idea they won't have forgotten ours! I expect we're still wanted."

"Too right," Fingertips is opening the back door.

"Quick Maise," Doll says, "get us Matron's car key."

"You're not taking her car!"

"For a little while only and it's ours really in a way—"

"Too right!" Fingertips is prancing on the brick path outside the laundry and along by the chicken pen.

"Get us the key," the Doll looks ten years younger in his agitation. "We'll just go off till those cops have took Dad back."

"You're not taking that car," but I go for the key all the same, Matron keeps it on the back of the bathroom door.

In the dinette there is a terrible commotion as Mother has mislaid her handbag. Lt. Col. Reggie is on his hands and knees under the table.

"I'm stuck Amy! Yoohoo Amy I'm stuck, can you move the table?"

But how can Matron move the table with Mrs. Hailey and Mrs. Renfrew and Mother and Dad and the two orderlies who were once exercise-yard cops wedged all round it. Matron herself is stuck as there is hardly room in the dinette for the table and chairs let alone people.

Mother is really carrying on.

"He's pinched my bag," she accuses the old man, she makes a dive at him. "He's pinched my bag and he's sitting on it, look my bag's gone!"

Dad just sits there, he doesn't understand and he's smiling. Mother goes for his legs and the orderlies pull his chair back.

"Now Mrs. Morgan dear," Matron bends over Mother, "Mr. Morgan wouldn't take your bag, would he now, not on your birthday! Remember it's your birthday, lovely old birthday! Happy birthday!"

"I'm telling you he's got my handbag, he thieved it from off me, he'd take anything, you don't do life for nothing," she screams. "Doing life don't change a man," she bawls. "Look at

him, you can see he's a thief and worse!" Matron tries to calm Mother, Mrs. Hailey and Mrs. Renfrew get a bit hysterical too, and Mrs. Hailey begins to take off her clothes.

"Not now dear!" Matron says to her, soothing her as much as she can.

"Pick him up!" Mother screams at the two orderlies, "and just see if my bag isn't under him!" so the frail clean old man who is my Dad, though I don't remember him at all as I never saw him and Mother never ever spoke about him, is lifted up off his chair, his little thin legs dangling in the grey pyjama trousers, he smiles round at everyone and nods his head from up there.

"Higher!" Mother yells. So the orderlies pick him up again like as if he is feather but there is nothing under him except an air cushion for his poor thin bottom and a square of plastic.

"Well I think the lovely birthday party has to come to an end," Matron says and the two orderlies wheel Dad away.

"Poor Dad," I say out loud. "Poor old Dad."

"Why poor?" Mother says. "He's had a long life same as me, if it's a long life we all want."

I help Mrs. Hailey and Mrs. Renfew back to room three and Matron gets her brother, the Lt. Col., from under the table. Mother sits muttering to herself and asks Matron for a glass of water and some bicarbonate of soda as the birthday cake has upset her stomach.

"I never could digest bad cooking," she says.

And then she says can she have a dose of medicinal as she thinks Matron's Surprise has done for her heart.

"Oh my poor heart," she says clutching herself. So Matron gets the brandy from out of her hiding place under the sofa.

"Did they get away?" Mother whispers to me.

"Just for a little while," I say.

"That'll be long enough," Mother says and she sips the medicinal dose slowly.

"Thank you my dear," she says to Matron, "Just fancy silly old me making all that trouble," she says smiling sweetly. "I had my handbag all the time, I didn't realise I was sitting on it! I don't know how I could have been so stupid!" She tugs at herself and pulls out her terrible old handbag.

"Nurse," Matron says to me, "take Mrs. Morgan to room three and help her to bed."

"Thank you for the lovely party," Mother calls out to Matron, "and for the lovely surprise. I never thought I would enjoy myself so much!"

Just when I have tucked Mother into bed I hear the scream of brakes and the tyres on the gravel in the hospital yard. It is the Doll and Fingertips back from their little disappearance ride. The Ferns is all surrounded by cape lilacs, they are all in flower just now and they look like big rain clouds piled up in the sky just outside the windows. There were cape lilacs in the township near the valley where we lived for the last crop, and in those times, when Mother was busy with the sky waiting for rain, she often thought rain was coming but it was only the cape lilacs in clouds of flowers making the sky look as if it was going to pour with rain.

"One of them trees is sure to be a honey tree," Mother says as I arrange her pillow. She suddenly seems old and frail, withered up and small. Years ago when we walked about over the land she would look at the old trees, there were so many bees about. "One of them trees is sure to be filled with honey," she used to say, and she would knock on the bark or press her ear against the trunk to hear the honey dripping slowly, filling the tree.

She was always hoping to find the honey tree, a tree unknown to any human being, which over the years the bees had filled with honey. All the years we lived in the country she hoped to find a hollow tree full of honey.

"Mind you don't get stung!" she says trying to sit up in her bed. "All those bees Mary, just you mind!"

"There's no bees here," I say. "There's no bees and no trees so be quiet do!"

"Where's all my things then?"

"Here," and I stuff them into her bed, the old handbag and the clock and the photographs.

"Where's my tin box?" she asks me. "They're always hiding my tin box."

I get her box, it's probably only full of old dockets from the sale of sour fruit all those years ago. I push the box beside her.

"Thank you my dear," she says and though she calls me Mary I don't know whether she knows I am her daugher or not. And then she says. "I really must pretty myself up a bit in case my son comes," and she fidgets in her bag for her old comb. She wants me to tidy her hair, she says.

"Tell Donald I'm askin' after him? Was that him I heard on the gravel just now?" she asks.

"Yes," I say, "he's back." I push her down under the covers. And she says, poking her head up at me, "The glory of the young men is their strength; and the beauty of old men is the grey head."

"I didn't know you knew the Bible."

"I don't, it's the text for today, Proverbs 20, verse 29, look for yourself, it's in the paper, bottom of the page."

And then she starts to laugh and laugh.

"The only thing is," she says, "he don't have glory and o'course no beauty because he's got a boiled head."

"Bald head you mean."

"Yes like I said a boiled head." And after that she lies down.

When I go out to the backyard with a sheet to put on the clothes line, there is no sign of the Doll and Fingertips and no sign of Matron's car. It must have been another car I heard. I hang out the sheet dripping wet all into my shoes and I can't help wondering when I'll see the Doll again, but more than this, I can't help thinking and thinking will I ever see him again.

NOTE

* A type of sausage.

Denise Levertov   *UK(England)/US, b. 1923*

Denise Levertov was one of two daughers born to Welsh Beatrice Spooner Jones and Russian Paul Philip Levertov, a Christian covert and Anglican priest; this heritage is the subject of Levertov's fine poem "Illustrious Ancestors" (*Overland to the Islands*, 1958). Both her parents were prisoners of war in Leipzig during the First World War; in World War II their house in London was a center for the reception and relocation of Jewish refugees. Levertov served as a civilian nurse. In 1946, she published her first book, *The Double Image*.

Levertov was not to publish again for eleven years, after she had married the American Mitchell Goodman, borne a son Nikolai, and come to live in the United States: she became associated with Charles Olson, Robert Creeley, and Robert Duncan, teachers at the short-lived experimental Black Mountain College, who had published her in their magazine *Origins*. With Duncan, especially, she formed a close friendship, and he influenced her education in the American poetic tradition, discussing with her the contributions of Pound, H.D. (Hilda Doolittle), and most especially Williams Carlos Williams; Duncan also perhaps most clearly recognized her individual talent, commemorating it in "Letters for Denise Levertov: an A muse ment." *Here and Now* reflects Levertov's American experience and represents a concern with capturing the actual and the concrete that she had learned from her reading and had assimilated in her living. This collection was followed by *Overland to the Islands* (1958) and *Eyes at the Back of Our Heads* (1960), which focused on the poet's residence in Mexico, before returning to New York.

Levertov's career reached the height of critical acclaim in the 1960s and 1970s with the publication of *Jacob's Ladder* (1961), *O Taste and See* (1964), and *The Sorrow Dance* (1967). In these works, Levertov moved from an objective poetry to one that offered a subjective crystallization of experience, creating a poetry of "organic form," the poem a manifestation of some ideal order lying behind the chaos of contemporary life. Gaining confidence, she began to depart from brief lyric structures to create longer poetic sequences fusing the personal with the political, the divine with the mundane. As a poet writing about poetry, she produced some of her finest works—both in poetic form and in prose. Such works as "Three Meditations," "Jacob's Ladder," "Song for Ishtar" (reprinted here), "The Film," "The Earth Worm," and "The Cat as Cat" give evidence of her preoccupation with the theme of the poetic imagination, a theme that still can inspire her to some of her best work, as in "Hunting the Phoenix" and "Caedmon" in her most recent *Breathing the Water* (1987). As in "Caedmon" the theme often melds with that of the spiritual life: Levertov has been one of our few poets sympathetic to religion (broadly speaking) and has drawn increasingly on the Hasidic traditions of her father's Jewish heritage as well as the Christian tradition in which she was steeped, for her imagery, motifs, and narratives.

Levertov's work is rarely confessional in the mode of Plath or Sexton. Indeed, in her essay on Sexton's death, Levertov mildly criticizes the image of woman as victim that the confessional mode projects and is eager to disassociate the strength and health of the poetic personality from the destructive elements in Sexton's life. At its best in the title poem of *O Taste and See* and "Stepping Westward," (reprinted here), Levertov's tone is celebratory and sensuous.

Under the pressure of political events, Levertov became an activist, and her activism bred a political poetry, beginning with the controversial "During the Eichmann Trial"[1] and the "Olga Poems," a bittersweet eulogy to her sister. *Relearning the Alphabet* (1970) is her most exclusively and directly political work, including poems that describe Levertov's involvement in the antiwar Free Speech Movement at Berkeley and that focus on such topics as the Vietnam War, draft resisters, the Detroit Riots, and Biafra.[2] "An Interim" and "From a Notebook: October '68–May '69" are remarkable documents of the period and among the best, most complex political poems of the period. *Freeing of the Dust* (1975) is both an unusually confessional work (dealing with her divorce after some twenty years of marriage) and one of her most political, concerned in part with her trip to Hanoi in 1972 with the poet Muriel Rukeyser; out of this came one of Levertov's finest antiwar poems, "The Pilots" (reprinted here). In the section entitled "Age of Terror" in *Candles in Babylon* (1982) and "Prisoners" in *Oblique Prayers* (1984), Levertov shows her continued ability and commitment to find a poetic language: "we stammer in / stammering dread / or parched, utter / silence."

Levertov, a fine craftswoman, is also much concerned with clarifying poetic technique and illuminating poetic tradition both in lectures and essays: the more important of these works includes "Some Notes on Organic Form" (1965) in *The Poet in the World* (1974), which constitutes something of a credo for practitioners of a certain kind of free verse, and "On the Edge of Darkness: What Is Political Poetry" (lecture, 1975) in *Light Up the Cave* (1981), a lucid and nonpartisan discussion. Her own verse is marked by an unusual sensitivity to sonorous effects. In it, she emphasizes the line as a means of establishing a rhythm counterposed to the syntactical unit and of combining with sense to give expression to the poet's inner voice.

Within the last fifteen years, there has been a virtual critical ban on the review of Levertov's works; like Adrienne Rich, she has suffered for the political content of her work, while her spiritual concerns have perhaps alienated her from potential allies. With the latest feminist revival and a concern for the political *and* the spiritual that has been reawakened by some feminist scholars, Levertov's talent and authority are being recognized once again.

NOTES

1. Adolf Eichmann (1906–1962) was a Nazi official tried and hanged by the Israeli Government for crimes against the Jewish people and against humanity. He was the subject of a controversial book by the German-Jewish–American philosopher and critic Hannah Arendt, in which she argued that he was a symbol of the banality of evil.
2. In the summer of 1967, the Detroit community exploded in violence after a racial incident. It followed on similar events that had occurred in Watts, a section of Los Angeles, the previous summer. Both served to legitimate open rebellion against racism and other social inequities. Biafra (1967–1979), a secessionist state from Nigeria established by the Ibo people, was gradually reduced to starvation by Nigerian attacks and blockades; its cause became a rallying cry for many liberal and left-wing groups.

SONG FOR ISHTAR*

The moon is a sow
and grunts in my throat
Her great shining shines through me
so the mud of my hollow gleams
and breaks in silver bubbles

She is a sow
and I a pig and a poet

When she opens her white
lips to devour me I bite back
and laughter rocks the moon

In the black of desire
we rock and grunt, grunt and
shine

NOTE

* An ancient fertility deity, the most widely worshipped
  goddess of the Babylonian and Assyrian cultures, sometimes as a goddess of war. In the Sumerian religion, she
  was called Inanna or Innina.

O TASTE AND SEE*

The world is
not with us enough.
O taste and see

the subway Bible poster said,
meaning **The Lord**, meaning
if anything all that lives
to the imagination's tongue,

grief, mercy, language,
tangerine, weather, to
breathe them, bite,
savor, chew, swallow, transform

into our flesh our
deaths, crossing the street, plum, quince,
living in the orchard and being

hungry and plucking
the fruit.

NOTE

* The poem plays off the sonnet "The World Is Too
  Much With Us" by the English Romantic poet William
  Wordsworth (1770–1850).

STEPPING WESTWARD

What is green in me
darkens, muscadine.

If woman is inconstant,
good, I am faithful to

ebb and flow, I fall
in season and now

is a time of ripening.
If her part

is to be true,
a north star,

good, I hold steady
in the black sky

and vanish by day,
yet burn there

in blue or above
quilts of cloud.

There is no savor
more sweet, more salt

than to be glad to be
what, woman,

and who, myself,
I am, a shadow

that grows longer as the sun
moves, drawn out

on a thread of wonder.
If I bear burdens

they begin to be remembered
as gifts, goods, a basket

of bread that hurts
my shoulders but closes me

in fragrance. I can
eat as I go.

THE PILOTS

Because they were prisoners,
because they were polite and friendly and lonesome and homesick,
because they said Yes, they knew
                          the names of the bombs they dropped
        but didn't say whether they understood what these bombs
                          are designed to do
                          to human flesh, and because
        I didn't ask them, being unable to decide
        whether to ask would serve
        any purpose other than cruelty, and
because since then I met Mrs. Brown, the mother of one of
                                    their fellow prisoners,
and loved her, for she has the same lovingkindness in her
that I saw in Vietnamese women (and men too)
and because my hostility left the room and wasn't there
                          when I thought I needed it
while I was drinking tea with the POW's,

because of all these reasons I hope
they were truly as ignorant,
            as unawakened,
                          as they seemed,
I hope their chances in life up to this point
have been poor,
I hope they can truly be considered
victims of the middle America they come from,
their American Legionnaire fathers, their macho high schools,
their dull skimped Freshman English courses,

for if they did understand precisely
what they were doing, and did it anyway, and would do it again,

then I must learn to distrust
my own preference for trusting people.

then I must learn to question
my own preference for liking people,

then I must learn to keep
my hostility chained to me
so it won't leave me when I need it.

And if it is proved to me
that these men understood their acts,

how shall I ever again
be able to meet the eyes of Mrs. Brown?

Nazik al-Mala'ika   *Iraq/Kuwait, b. 1923*

The daughter of the famous poet Um Nizar, Nazik al-Mala'ika follows in the footseps of a traditionally literary family. Her grandfather was also a poet. Born in Baghdad, Iraq in 1923, she grew up in a wealthy nationalist household, exposed to the colonial policies and culture of the British.

Al-Mala'ika began her studies at the Higher Education Teachers' Training College in Baghdad where she studied Arabic Literature. Later, in the United States, she received her M.A. in English and Comparative Literature from Princeton University. Upon her return to Iraq in the mid-1950s, she began teaching at the University of Mosul in Iraq and also at the University of Basra.

By this time, she was already a noted and somewhat notorious poet, acclaimed by many critics as the first Arab to break away from the classical *qasída* (a traditional poetic structure comparable to the ode in western literature). She was the inspiration of the *Taf'ila*, or free verse movement carried out by various schools in Baghdad. Her first collection of poetry to exhibit this unique free form was entitled *'Ashíqat al-Layl* (The Lover of the Night, 1947), followed by *Shazāyā wa-Ramād* (Splinters and Ashes, 1949), *Qarārat al-Mawjah* (The Bottom of the Wave, 1957), and *Shajarat al-Qamar* (The Moontree, 1968). "I Am," taken from her second and most famous work, reveals the intense subjectivity that is the basis of much of her poetry; in short form, it "indicates the extent of her pessimism and her agonizing sense of life as an overwhelmingly painful riddle." This point of view can be traced historically in such extended works as "Ma'sāt al-Hayāt wa Ughniya līl-Insān" (The Tragedy of Being and A Song to Man [I and II]), which al-Mala'ika published as part of her two-volume collection *Diwān* (Works) in 1970. The poems are different versions written between 1945 and 1946, in 1960, and in 1965 respectively, and thus encapsulate al-Mala'ika's poetic development.

Like many writers of her time and place, al-Mala'ika was also moved to speak out against colonial oppression and particularly against the desecrations against women during periods of war. Both "Washing off Disgrace" and "Jamila," taken from al-Mala'ika's third and fourth volumes, respectively, are justly considered among her signature poems.

With the introduction to *Shazāyā wa-Ramād* in 1949 and the publication of a critical study of free verse, its form and nature, *Qadāyā al-Shi'r al-Mu'āsir* (Issues of Contemporary Poetry, 1954; reprinted 1962), al-Mala'ika laid the theoretical foundations for the free verse movement. The latter, an excerpt from which is reprinted here, was particularly controversial, not because it championed a radically new poetry, but because it seemed to be at least a partial repudiation of al-Mala'ika's previous commitment to it.

In the 1970s, al-Mala'ika moved with her husband and son to Kuwait where she resumed teaching as a professor of Arabic Literature at the University of Kuwait. Her most recent known publication is a sociological work, *al-Tajzi'iyya fī al-Mujtama' al-'Arabi* (Disjunction in Arab Society, 1974). Her writings have also continued to appear in such influential Lebanese journals as *al-Adaab* (Literature), *Shi'r* (Poetry), and *al-'Adīb* (The Writers' Magazine).

I AM
Ana

The night asks me who I am
    Its impenetrable black, its unquiet secret
                            I am
    Its lull rebellious.
    I veil myself with silence
    Wrapping my heart with doubt
    Solemnly, I gaze
    While ages ask me
           who I am.

The wind asks me who I am
    Its bedevilled spirit I am
    Denied by Time, going nowhere
    I journey on and on
    Passing without a pause
    And when reaching an edge
    I think it may be the end
    Of suffering, but then:
          the void.

Time asks me who I am
    A giant enfolding centuries I am
    Later to give new births
    I have created the dim past
    From the bliss of unbound hope
    I push it back into its grave
    To make a new yesterday, its tomorrow
    is ice.

The self asks me who I am
    Baffled, I stare into the dark
    Nothing brings me peace
    I ask, but the answer
    Remains hooded in mirage
    I keep thinking it is near
    Upon reaching it, it dissolves.
              Translated by Kamal Boullata

WASHING OFF DISGRACE
Ghaslān līl-ʿĀr

"Mother!"
A last gasp through her teeth and tears.
The vociferous moan of the night.
Blood gushed.
Her body stabbed staggered.
The waves of her hair
    swayed with crimson mud.
"Mother!"
Only heard by her man of blood.
At dawn
If her twenty years of forlorn hope should call
the meadows and the roseate buds shall echo,
She's gone
washing off disgrace!

Neighborhood women would gossip her story.
The date palms would pass it on the breeze.
It would be heard in the squeaking of every
        weather-beaten door.
and the cobbled stones would whisper:
She's gone
washing off disgrace!

Tomorrow
wiping his dagger before his pals
the butcher bellows,
"Disgrace?
A mere stain on the forehead,
now washed,"
At the tavern
turning to the barman, he yells,
"More wine
and send me that lazy beauty of a nymphet
      you got, the one with the mouth of
                myrrh."
One woman would pour wine
    to a jubilant man
another paid
washing off disgrace!

Women of the neighborhood
women of the village
we knead dough with our tears
    that they may be wellfed

we loosen our braids
        that they may be pleased
We peel the skin of our hands washing their
                        clothes
        that they may be spotless white.
No smile
No joy
No rest
for the glitter of a dagger
             of a father
              of a brother
        is all eyes.
Tomorrow who knows
what deserts may banish
you
washing off disgrace!

Translated by Kamal Boullata

JAMILA*
Nahnu wa Jamila

Yonder you weep
Your hair is loose, your hands are weak
Jamila
But men sang extravagant songs
for you they offered their best
Aren't you drowned in their praise?
Why weep?
        We melted with her smile
        her face and the dimple,
        her braids;
        Our passions were kindled
        with her beauty
        in chains.
We sighed: they made her quench her thirst
        with human blood
        and flames
We were convinced they nailed a heroine to
                      the cross
        and we sang to the glories of
                   martyrdom.
           We will save her, we gasped
        and then drowned amidst our drunken
                     words
        we shouted: Long live Jamila.

They have wounded her with knives
we with words
and the wounds afflicted by one's kin
are deeper than those afflicted by the
                      French
Shame on us
for the doubled wounds of
Jamila.

Translated by Kamal Boullata

NOTE

* Jamila Buhaired is an Algerian woman who was a fighter with the Front for the National Liberation of Algeria (FLN). She was twenty-two when she was wounded in a military confrontation with the French and later arrested. In prison she was subjected to torture several times and on July 15, 1957, condemned to death. Georges Arnaud and Jacques Verges, two Communist supporters of the Algerian Revolution, defended her before world opinion. After her execution, Jamila became the symbol of Algeria's determination to be free. In the mid-1950s every major Arab poet wrote on Jamila. Al-Mala'ika's poem is a reaction. The name itself means "beautiful."

from ISSUES OF CONTEMPORARY POETRY
Qadāyā al-Shi'r al-Mu'āsir

The year 1947 marked the beginning of the free verse movement which was born in Iraq and from Baghdad spread throughout the Arab world. Because of the extremists who answered the call, the movement soon seemed about to engulf all other styles of traditional Arab poetry.

The first free verse poem published was one of my own, "The Cholera," composed in one of the classical quantitative Arabic meters, *al-mutadarik* (al-Khabab). To illustrate, I quote a few lines:

    Dawn has come.
    Listen to the footsteps of the passersby
    In the silence of the early morning—listen,
                      look at
    the procession of mourners.

(continued)

Ten deaths, twenty, . . .
Don't count. Listen to those who are
                                                            weeping.
Listen to the voice of the wretched child.
Dead, dead, the count is lost.
In every house a body lies, mourned by
                                        those who grieve,
No moment of eternity. No moment of
                                                            silence.
This is what the hand of death has done.

Death, death, death . . .
Humanity is complaining, complaining of
                        the deeds of death.[2]

A copy of the magazine containing "The
Cholera" reached Baghdad in 1947, and in the
second half of the same month Badr Shakir
al-Sayyab published a collection in Baghdad
entitled *Azhar Dhabilah* (Withering Flowers).
In the collection was a free verse poem, in
al-Ramal meter, entitled "Was It Love?" In a
footnote to this poem al-Sayyab commented
that this poem was "a sample of the verse that
varies in meter and rhyme."

Al-Sayyab writes:

Is it love that I
Became a slave to wishing
Or is love to repudiate wishes
Or is love a meeting of mouths and a
                                        forgetting of life,
The disappearance of one eye in another
                                        in ecstasy,
Or like a gathering which comes together
                                        only to be
Diminished in the surge of the storm,
Or is it like a shadow in a stream . . .

However, the appearance of these two
poems did not attract much attention from
readers. Two years passed in silence. No free
verse was published in any periodical.

In the summer of 1949 my collection
Shazaya wa-Ramad (Splinters and Ashes) appeared, and a number of free verse poems were
included. In a long introduction to the volume,
I pointed out the importance of the innovations in this poetry, and I tried to explain the
differences between this style of writing and

the two-segment line style.[3] Then I gave an
example of the selection of beats.

The appearance of *Splinters and Ashes*
created a great uproar in the Iraqi press, and
many heated discussions took place in Baghdad literary circles. Many of the reviewers
wrote angry and scornful commentaries, forecasting that the call for free verse would fail
completely. But throughout this uproar, the
majority of the public and of the poets themselves remained silent. Acceptance of the new
forms came about in a quiet way. As soon as
the first early difficult months of the movement
had passed, free verse suddenly began to be
written by young Iraqi poets and to be published in newspapers. The call for free verse
was being answered and was reaching a wider
and wider group . . .

The free verse movement began in rather difficult circumstances and had many obstacles
to overcome. Some of the circumstances were
general and involved the total idea of a new
movement; some are linked with free verse
itself. As for the general circumstances, the free
verse movement was like any new movement
in arts and letters. At first, it was not yet fully
developed as a style, somewhat hesitant, with
the roughness of beginnings, the rawness of
green fruit. This early period was a necessity,
but the movement is still experimental and one
must say that the movement's honesty and zeal
to achieve new forms does not excuse individual poets from slipping now and then and
stumbling into error. But any literary movement that emerges suddenly in certain times
and circumstances is bound to go through long
years of development before it puts down solid
roots, refines its tools, and comes to full
maturity. Such a movement does not emerge
fully grown; it must pass through stages before
it crystallizes. Today its faults appear to us
more clearly, as we see it from a distance and
have explored more completely our new experiences, our new cultural maturity, our widening horizons. . . .

Actually, the movement began to divert

from its earliest stated goal, which was to free poets and poetry from the structures of the past. This is not too surprising. However, there is no need for pessimism about the future of the movement. Historically, this particular poetic movement does not differ from any other movement calling for freedom, whether it is national, social, or literary in character. Throughout the centuries, we have witnessed hundreds of examples of people's revolutions, when an exaggeration in the implementation of the spirit of the revolution led to chaos and degradation at first, until the movement settled into a more stable pattern. Thus, despite some tendencies toward mediocrity, we feel confident of the future of the free verse movement.

Translated by Elizabeth W. Fernea and
Basima Q. Bezirgan

NOTES

1. Free verse, in English prosody, has been defined as "verse, which, although more rhythmic than ordinary prose, is written without rhyme" (M.H. Abrams, rev., *A Glossary of Literary Terms* [New York; Holt, 1957] p. 39). Regarding Arabic poetry, "al-Mala'ika advocated the need for a free verse, in which the meter is based upon the unit of the *taf'ilal* (foot) and the freedom of the poet is secured through his right to vary the *taf'ilal* or the lengths of his lines as he feels most appropriate for the expression of his message" (Mounah A. Khouri and Hamid Algar, eds. and trans., *An Anthology of Modern Arabic Poetry*, [Berkeley: UCPr, 1974], p. 16).

2. I composed it in October 1947, and it was published in the literary magazine *Majallat al-'Urubah* in Beirut, December 1947. The magazine commented on the poem in the same issue. I wrote this poem to express my feeling toward Egypt during its cholera epidemic. I tried to express the sounds of the horses' hoofbeats as they dragged the carriages full of dead bodies through the streets, the victims of the plague in the Rif of Egypt. The necessity of expressing this feeling led me to discover free verse.—N.M.

3. "In the traditional *qasidah* [Arabic poem], each line must consist of an exact number of feet (*tafa'il*), four, six, or eight, which the poet may not increase or decrease throughout his poem. Also, each line must be divided into two equal and balancing hemistiches (*shatrani*). Finally, all lines of the poem must end with exactly the same kind of rhyme, built upon the same rhyming letter" (Mohamed al-Nowaihi, "The Battle of the New Poetry," *Texas Quarterly* 9, no. 2 [Summer 1966]: 148). Very simply put, such poems exhibit terminal rhyme of the pattern aabacada, i.e., an enclosed couplet followed by open couplets.

Claribel Alegría   *Nicaragua/El Salvador, b. 1924*

Daughter of a political exile from Nicaragua (where she was born), Alegría came to El Salvador at 9 months of age and considers it her native country, although she has lived in many countries, including the United States.

Alegría has written in a variety of genres, but is best known for her poetry on political themes. Her recently published *Flores de Volcán* (*Flowers from the Volcano*, 1982) is a bilingual edition of her major works, translated and introduced by Carolyn Forché. It traces the poet's life as it parallels that of El Salvador's tempestuous contemporary history, with images of death and destruction increasingly prevalent.

Alegría's talent as an editor is revealed in her 1962 anthology of Latin American writers, *New Voices of Hispanic America* (1962), includes many who were later to become famous. She won the prestigious Casas de las Américas poetry award in 1978 for *Sobrevivo* (*I Survive*), and her work has been translated into many foreign languages.

The mother of four children, Alegría and her husband (and translator) Darwin J. Flakoll are currently working in Nicaragua on projects concerning the political situation in Central America.

LAUGHING TO DEATH
Muerto de risa

Only eighty dollars
to laugh when I like
and kick off the shoes
that pinch me.
Blood and guns
is only a soap opera
on posters.
A wide-eyed child
looks at me from the wall
"the week of hunger."
I sit myself down in the armchair
in the commercials
I won't have to invent
my own dreams
I close and open my eyes
click
large sofas upholstered
in yellow damask
a child on the sofa
"the weak of hunger
leave your donation in the box."
Automobiles
click
vacuum cleaners
click
in the kitchen now
she smiles at the photographer
makes a tortilla
that she will never eat
click
the foaming cleanser
the washing machine
rinsing the shroud
that will cover her bones
click
click
the commercials are over
I lean back
I relax
Tom and Jerry, finally,
I hear a noise at my side
the same wide eyes
the smile—that same one

looks at me
we laugh
I raise my claws
I grimace
I growl
he grasps his belly
and laughs
and dies.

Translated by Electa Arenal and
Marsha Gabriela Dreyer

WE WERE THREE
Eramos Tres

It was a winter with snow
it was night
today is a day greens
of birds
of sun
a day of ashes
and laments
the wind pushes me
it carries me over the bridge
over the cracked earth
over the dry brook
brimming with plastic and cans
death comes to life
here in Deyá[1]
the brooks
the bridges
my dead lying in wait
at each corner
the innocent grid
of a balcony
the hazy reflection
of my dead
they smile at me from afar
they say goodbye
leave the cemetery
form a wall
my skin
becomes translucent

they knock at my door
they gesture
the bridge was of stone
it was night
our arms entwined
with the swaying of a song
like small frozen clouds
our breath issued
from our mouths
it was a winter with snow
we were three
today the earth is dry
it echoes
my arms fall
I am alone
my dead stand guard
they signal to me
they assault me from the radio
from the newspaper
the wall of my dead
rises
extends from Aconcagua
to Izalco[2]
they continue marking directions

the bridge was of stone
it was night
no one can say
how they died
their persecuted voices
fuse
they died in jail
tortured
my dead rise
they are enraged
the streets are alone
they wink at me
I am a cemetery without a country
there is no room.

Translated by Electa Arenal and
Marsha Gabriela Dreyer

NOTES

1. A small town on Majorca, in the Balearic Islands, where the author lived for many years.
2. Aconcagua in Chile and Izalco in El Salvador are two war-torn nations in Latin America governed by brutal dictatorships.

Lauris Edmond   *New Zealand, b. 1924*

Lauris Edmond, as she noted in a recent autobiographical piece, has "lived two very different lives." On one hand, she was brought up with the expectation of becoming a housewife; on the other hand, she started writing poetry when she was quite young. Although she won a coveted university grant, Edmond chose to pursue a more limited and traditional education at a teachers' college. Soon after graduating she married and settled in the country, eventually raising six children.

In the late 1960s, Edmond was influenced by the woman's movement (she found *The Femine Mystique* particularly inspiring), and she decided to complete her B.A. degree. She finished a second degree and became a high school teacher. By 1975 she was editor of the *Post Primary Teacher's Journal* and separated from her husband.

Edmond did not become a successful writer until relatively late in life. Her first collection of poetry was published when she was 51, and she has been remarkably prolific in the ensuing twelve years, publishing eight volumes in all. Her *Collected Poems* (1984) won the 1985 Commonwealth Poetry Prize. In addition, she has written critical articles and reviews, radio plays, and a novel, *High Country Weather* (1984). "Commercial Traveller," and "Two Birth Poems" exhibit the highly dramatic nature of her poetry; they come from her first collection, *In Middle Air* (1975).

Elizabeth Webby

COMMERCIAL TRAVELLER

Dinner's over. Now he mumbles at
his cigarette, summons the waiter,
scoffs the last fine
sticky drops of wine. "That's better—
damn good in fact. Now coffee
with a touch—here, boy—a smack
of Benedictine." The sweet fire dives
down, but prudently he thinks to peck
back from the tray his extra ten cent
piece (he'll be on the road
tomorrow, no more favours thanks
from this fellow). Now his head
settles grunting back
into copious ease, armchair deep;
the stale public smells lounge
away; he blows smoke rings, a drop
of gravy blots his waistcoat. Inside
his heart waits, famished—no friends come
to talk to greedy boy.
Let him suck his thumb.

TWO BIRTH POEMS

1. A SHIFT OF EMPHASIS

Do not come too close, nor touch
the swollen knot
that tightens round
my multiplicities of pain;
that scream that flies about the room
is mine. I allowed it out.
Keep off. Join the mice in nice
white uniforms running about
with their routines.

It happens here. All my eyes glare,
a thousand fists fight
in the raging darkness of my body—
this smothered yell
comes to kill.
Look out! It cracks me open, it is
the axe that splits the skull—

the knot of blood is cut.

I am broken, scattered,
fragments of me melt and flow—
I am not here; gravity's red centre
has slipped; off course, I roll about
like wind-blown eggshells.

Cradled in the world's lap lies instead
a tiny grey-faced rag of flesh
with a cry as thin as muslin,
and all the power to possess the earth
curled up behind the blindness of its eyes.

2. ZERO POPULATION GROWTH

It was the anonymity I noticed first—
the flowers and I both languishing
in unlit corridors,
banished for recalcitrant
behaviour, minor problems
for the management.

A kind carnation said
"Your water's leaking dear,
you'll have your baby long before the morning."
But still the teacups chattered
while a yellow string of light remained in place
between the supper cups
and our disgrace.
Then a big pain bowled me,
I reeled, sprawled—
Heavens! it would not do!
A flock of nurses flew
to peck protestingly
at a wavering whale
impaled on a lino square.
Even the flowers disdained to smile.

I became incorrigibly plural—
there seemed no end to limbs and things
I could produce; the refuse disposal squad
briskly dismantled, finally towed away
the remains, still seething;
beside me a strange animal
in a basket, breathing.

Later I noticed a small sardonic smile
on the curtain, having a swing;
it chirped "You've done it.
You clever thing."

Janet Frame   *New Zealand, b. 1924*

The recent appearance of her three volumes of autobiography has consolidated Janet Frame's place as the greatest living New Zealand writer. Though it was her fiction that first attracted attention, Frame has also written some remarkable poetry and, with her more accessible autobiographies, has won a whole new audience.

Frame was born in Dunedin, in the far south of New Zealand's South Island. Her father worked for railways, so there were several moves to different small country towns before they settled at Oamaru. With five children in the family, it was a constant struggle to pay the bills. Nevertheless, as we see from her fiction and her autobiographies, Frame's childhood was a time of treasure in spite of the trauma of poverty and the deaths, ten years apart, of two of her sisters by drowning. Her love of language was fostered by her mother, who read and wrote poetry and stories, and encouraged her children to write.

Frame had a successful school career and trained as a teacher at Dunedin Teachers' College and the University of Otago. Afterward, however, she was wrongly diagnosed as a schizophrenic and spent about a decade in and out of mental hospitals. These experiences are reflected in several of her earlier novels, particularly in her second, *Faces in the Water* (1961), excerpted here. Frame underwent many sessions of electric shock therapy and was about to be given a leucotomy when she won a literary award for her first collection of stories, *The Lagoon* (1951). She left the hospital and, living in a garden shed belonging to the eminent writer Frank Sargeson, wrote her first, and still best known, novel, *Owls Do Cry* (1957).

In 1956, fearful that she might be sent back to the hospital, she left for England, living there and in Spain until she returned to New Zealand in 1963. Since 1951, she has published ten novels, four collections of short stories, a volume of poetry, *The Pocket Mirror* (1967), and a children's book, as well as her autobiographies.

Faces in the Water, with its relatively straightforward structure and simple style, is not particularly typical of Frame's later fiction. She has always questioned rigid binary oppositions such as "mad/sane" or "trash/treasure" and this had led to her blurring of the usual distinctions between prose and poetry, "real life" and fiction. Some of her novels, such as *Scented Gardens for the Blind* (1963), and her latest, *Living in the Maniototo* (1979), center on characters who eventually turn out to have been invented by other characters. This is also true of *Daughter Buffalo* (1972), in which an elderly New Zealander seemingly visits New York and has a homosexual relationship with a young American doctor. They adopt as their daughter a buffalo seen in the Central Park Zoo.

Frame's three recent volumes of autobiography—*To the Island* (1982), *An Angel at My Table* (1984), and *The Envoy from Mirror City* (1985)—provide an ideal introduction to both her work and life and are recommended as a starting point for those who wish to become better acquainted with her highly individual prose style and outlook on life.

Elizabeth Webby

from FACES IN THE WATER

They have said that we owe allegiance to Safety, that he is our Red Cross who will provide us with ointment and bandages for our wounds and remove the foreign ideas the glass beads of fantasy the bent hairpins of unreason embedded in our minds. On all the doors which lead to and from the world they have posted warning notices and lists of safety measures to be taken in extreme emergency. Lightning, isolation in the snows of the Antarctic, snake bite, riots, earthquakes. Never sleep in snow. Hide the scissors. Beware of strangers. Lost in a foreign land take your time from the sun and your position from the creeks flowing toward the sea. Don't struggle if you would be rescued from drowning. Suck the snake bite from the wound. When the earth opens and the chimneys topple, run out underneath the sky. But for the final day of destruction when "those that look from the windows shall be darkened" they have provided no slogan. The streets throng with people who panic, looking to the left and the right, covering the scissors, sucking poison from a wound they cannot find, judging their time from the sun's position in the sky when the sun itself has melted and trickles down the ridges of darkness into the hollows of evaporated seas.

Until that day how can we find our path in sleep and dreams and preserve ourselves from their dangerous reality of lightning snakes traffic germs riot earthquakes blizzard and dirt when lice creep like riddles through our minds? Quick, where is the Red Cross God with the ointment and plaster the needle and thread and the clean linen bandages to mummify our festering dreams? Safety First.

I will write about the season of peril. I was put in hospital because a great gap opened in the ice floe between myself and the other people whom I watched, with their world, drifting away through a violet-colored sea where hammerhead sharks in tropical ease swam side by side with the seals and the polar bears. I was alone on the ice. A blizzard came and I grew numb and wanted to lie down and sleep and I would have done so had not the strangers arrived with scissors and cloth bags filled with lice and red-labeled bottles of poison, and other dangers which I had not realized before —mirrors, cloaks, corridors, furniture, square inches, bolted lengths of silence—plain and patterned, free samples of voices. And the strangers, without speaking, put up circular calico tents and camped with me, surrounding me with their merchandise of peril.

But I liked to eat Carmello chocolate because I was lonely. I bought twelve cushions for sixpence. I sat in the cemetery among the chrysanthemums bunched in their brownish water inside slime-coated jam jars. I walked up and down in the dark city, following the gleaming tram lines that held and arrowed the street lights and the trams flashed sudden sparks above my head and made it seem, with rainbow splashes of light, that I looked through tears. But the shopwindows were speaking to me, and the rain too, running down inside the window of the fish shop, and the clean moss and fern inside the florists, and the dowdy droopy two-piece sets and old-fashioned coats hung on the aged plaster models in the cheaper shops that could not afford to light their windows, and crowded their goods together, displayed with large warning tickets painted in red. They all spoke. They said Beware of the Sale, Beware of Bargain Prices. Beware of traffic and germs; if you find a handkerchief hold it up by the tip of the finger and thumb until it is claimed. For a cold in the chest be steamed with Friars' Balsam. Do not sit on the seat of a public lavatory. Danger. Power lines overhead.

I was not yet civilized; I traded my safety for the glass beads of fantasy.

I was a teacher. The headmaster followed me home, he divided his face and body into three in order to threaten me with triple peril, so that three headmasters followed me, one on each side and one at my heels. Once or twice I turned timidly and said, Would you like a star for good conduct? I sat all night in my room, cutting out stars from sheets of gold paper, pasting the stars on the wall and across the door of the landlady's best wardrobe and over the head and face and eyes of her innerspring divan, till the room was papered with stars, furnished as a private night, as a charm against the three headmasters who made me drink tea in sociability every morning in the staff room, and who tiptoed in sand shoes along the marigold border, sprouting pungent advice possibilities and platitudes. With my briberies for good conduct I fancied I held them fast with flour and water in a paper galaxy of approval, when I was really giving to myself alone the hundred rewards, guarantees, safety measures, insurance policies, because I alone was evil, I alone had been seen and heard, had spoken before I was spoken to, had bought fancy biscuits without being told to, and put them down on the wall.

My room stank with sanitary napkins. I did not know where to put them therefore I hid them in the drawer of the landlady's walnut dressing table, in the top drawer, the middle drawer and the bottom drawer; everywhere was the stench of dried blood, of stale food thrown from the shelves of an internal house that was without tenants or furniture or hope of future lease.

The headmaster flapped his wings; he was called a name that sounded like buzzard which gave him power over the dead, to pick the bones of those who lie in the desert.

I swallowed a stream of stars; it was easy; I slept a sleep of good work and conduct excellent.

Perhaps I could have dived into the violet sea and swum across to catch up with the drifting people of the world; yet I thought Safety First, Look to the Left and Look to the Right. The disappearing crowds of people waved their dirty handkerchiefs held, fastidiously, between thumb and forefinger. Such caution! They covered their mouth and nose when they sneezed, but their feet were bare and frozen, and I thought that perhaps they could not afford shoes or stockings, therefore I stayed on my ice floe, not willing to risk the danger of poverty, looking carefully to the left and the right, minding the terrible traffic across the lonely polar desert: until a man with golden hair said, "You need a rest from chrysanthemums and cemeteries and parallel tram lines running down to the sea. You need to escape from sand and lupins and wardrobes and fences. Mrs. Hogg will help you, Mrs. Hogg the Berkshire sow who has had her goiter out, and you should see the stream of cream that flows from the hole in her throat and hear the satisfactory whistling of her breath."

"You have made a mistake," Mrs. Hogg said, standing on tiptoe, her head thrust in the air. "I may have ginger whiskers but there has never been a stream of cream that flows from the hole in my throat. And tell me, what is the difference between geography, electricity, cold feet, a child born without wits and sitting drooling inside a red wooden engine in a concrete yard, and the lament of Guiderius and Aviragus,*

Fear no more that heat o' the sun,
Nor the furious winter's rages...

No exorciser harm thee
Nor no witchcraft charm thee.
Ghost unlaid forebeare thee.
Nothing ill come near thee."

I was afraid of Mrs. Hogg. I could not tell her the difference. I shouted at her,

Loony loony down the line,
Mind your business and I'll mind mine.

What is a loony's business? A loony at Cliffhaven "down the line" where the train stops for twenty minutes to put down and collect the mailbags and to give the travelers a free look at the loonies gathered about, gaping and absorbed?

Tell me, what is the time now? The light-headed school bell is giddily knocking its head against its tongue; am I at school in time? The cherry blossom is budding in its burnished leaves, the velvet-tonsiled snapdragons are in flower, the wind is brushing sunlight into the row of green supple poplars growing outside on the bank, just up the path. I can see them from the windows open only six inches at the bottom and the top, and why are the doors locked by people who wear pink uniforms and carry keys fastened by a knotted cord to their belts and kept inside deep marsupial pockets? Is it after teatime? Violet light, yellow japonica, the children in the street playing hopscotch baseball and marbles until the blotting darkness absorbs even the color from the yellow japonica?

I will put warm woolen socks on the feet of the people in the other world; but I dream and cannot wake, and I am cast over the cliff and hang there by two fingers that are danced and trampled on by the Giant Unreality.

So there was nothing to do but weep. I cried for the snow to melt and powerful councilors to come and tear down the warning notices, and I never answered Mrs. Hogg to tell her the difference for I knew only the similarity that grew with it; the difference dispersed in the air and withered, leaving the fruit of similarity, like a catkin that reveals the hazelnut.

NOTE

* Brothers, and sons of King Cymbeline of Britain who were kidnapped as infants and raised in a cave in Shakespeare's *Cymbeline* (1605).

Henri Cartier-Bresson, Indonesia, *1950, black and white photograph. Courtesy Magnum Photos, Inc., New York*

Friederike Mayröcker

Austria, b. 1924

Friederike Mayröcker is an English teacher and lives in Vienna, where she was born on December 20, 1924. She has written poetry, prose, dramas, and radio plays and ranks among the best of the modern experimentalist poets of Austria. The impulse of her writing is not, according to Mayröcker, located in the radical artistic tendencies of her generation, however, but rather in a far more private sphere. She suggests a connection with her "enclosed" childhood and the net of the family in which she, as an only child, felt both protected and entrapped.

Mayröcker recognizes that every human experience, every new relationship, is preconditioned by past events and relationships—that life is not a logical "story" of successive events. She thus refrains from producing "stories," instead attempting to "narrate" the irresolvable paradox by which successive events become simultaneous in consciousness. Her associative and multidimensional style reflects the wish to capture this simultaneity and assiduously avoids the artificiality of the classical unity of time, place, and plot.

Mayröcker began writing at the age of 15 (in 1939) and published her first poems in 1946 in the avant-garde journal, *Plan*. Since 1954 she has been a close friend of Ernst Jandl, a fellow member of the "Vienna Group," with whom she has co-authored many works (chiefly dramas and radio plays). In the 1970s, Mayröcker produced primarily prose (novels as well as shorter works), returning only recently to poetry. She has toured widely in Europe, the U.S.S.R., and the U.S.A. and spent a year in West Berlin as guest of the German Academic Exchange Service. She has won several literary prizes, including the prestigious Georg Trakl Prize of Salzburg (1977, with Rainer Kunze). She is an ex officio member of the Berlin Academy of Arts.

Marilyn Sibley Fries

EVENING
Abends

Windwhipped bright
Violet rises over
the royal blue height
of my sky, uneasy
the dust settles
and the puddle stares
purple: afar in windows
asters nod in the light
white, white and radiant

Translated by Michael P. Elzay

I CANNOT DRINK YOU
Trinken kann ich dich nicht

I cannot drink you
    and yet would drink you up with my
                            mouth
    because I thirst so for you

I cannot seek you
    and yet would fly over the entire earth
    to be with you

I cannot bed you
    and yet would sleep in snow and wind
    that my cot be free for you

I cannot dream you
    and yet would dream at bright of day
    to see you once again

Translated by Michael P. Elzay

PATRON OF FLAWLESS SERPENT BEAUTY
Schirmherr makelloser Schlangen schönheit

Patron of flawless serpent beauty
exalted keeper of untamable seas
cultivator of the constant fields

you comb the green pelt of the towering forest
wisps of grass thaw around your brow

the long-christened in winter: the crystal icicles
your fist collects in the basins of village ponds
and the silver-eyed warm flocks of birds
nest in your pale arteries

Mighty you are and I fear you greatly
away you gallop on my saddled desires

Translated by Michael Hamburger

Maria Luisa Spaziani   *Italy, b. 1924*

After completing a doctorate in letters in 1948 with a dissertation on Marcel Proust's literary style, Maria Luisa Spaziani began a journalistic career by contributing to various newspapers and periodicals. In 1964 she accepted a teaching position at the University of Messina.

The poems of her first book, *Le acque del sabato* (Saturday's Waters, 1954), technically derive from the Italian hermetic tradition, but with the considerable influence of twentieth-century European poetry. Spaziani subsequently published *Primavera a Parigi* (Spring in Paris, 1954); *Luna lombarda* (Lombard Moon, 1959); *Il gong* (The Gong, 1962), which won the Città di Firenze Prize; *Utilità della memoria* (Utility of Memory, 1966); *L'occhio del ciclone* (The Eye of the Cyclone, 1970), from which the following poems were taken; *Transito con catene* (Transit with Chains, 1977); and *Geometria del disordine* (Geometry of Disorder, 1981).

Spaziani's poems catch the reader's attention on account of their emotional immediacy, which the author succeeds in creating through imagery, capturing sounds and even the silences that fill the world. As a poet, she delineates perfect pictures with a limpidity rare in contemporary poetry. She possesses an impeccable style, enjoyable *per se*, even without the message her poems contain. Moreover, especially in *Geometria del disordine*, she no longer seems to mind the chaos of a terribly violent world, but plunges right into it, almost with joy, following a rational "geometry" or order of her own.

Spaziani's marriage to writer Elemire Zolla produced one daughter. The couple is now separated. She was close friends with the poet Eugenio Montale and carried on a long and fruitful correspondence with him, resulting in over 1,000 letters.

Natalia Costa-Zalessow

from THE EYE OF THE CYCLONE
L'Occhio del Ciclone

1.

Have you seen how still they are on the dark
sea tonight, those ten lanterned fishing boats?
With them, everything is still, waiting for
distant signals from the bottom of the sea.
Roots of the earth's fields; thoughts loosed and
                                        pale;
cries, which, as if frayed in this marsh air, are
                                        lost
in the emptiness; all await that sign.
All the world pauses, the sky's pauses
are longer than a lifetime; everything
waiting for that sign or wonder: ember,
bud sap that rises, plant that descends,
stalk that scarcely believes in its glory
which rules the universe.

2.

Rome has a thousand fountains, and in May
                                        they sing
and thunder, pontificate and roar
almost as if the nearby sea were erupting
from secret mouths. Goddesses, titans,
fluvial divinities, tortoises,
angels and conches and cornucopias.
Perhaps the truth, never pronounced
is, that every street, piazza or alleyway
with its palace, herm, or obelisk,
cathedral or stadium, is a delicate
crust, a sea of sargasso
ready to break and dissolve.
The sea is there, it is here, it boils, furious
from these mouths with their siren's voices.
Rustling of pearls and Medusas,*
it calls the ancient country, sounds again,
announces the reign of the Mothers, makes
ready for some obscure fate, its depths,
its music-filled grottos, its arches
of darkness and triumph.

Translated by Claire Siegel

NOTE

* Medusa was one of the three Gorgons in ancient Greek
mythology. Originally a beautiful woman, she was transformed into a monster with serpents as hair; all who
looked on her turned to stone.

Efua Sutherland   *Ghana, b. 1924*

Efua Theodora Morgue was born at Cape Coast, Ghana, to a family of Christian
converts in 1924. As with many postcolonial subjects who received a Western
education, her literary career involves a journey of discovery of her own people
and their traditions and forms. She began her education at St. Monica's School in
Ghana, a school established by the British. From there, she went on to study at
Teacher Training College, Homerton College, Cambridge. She was also a student
of linguistics at the University of London's School of Oriental and African Studies.

In 1951, Morgue returned to Ghana and, in 1954, married William Sutherland, an American with whom she had three children. Together they established a
school in the Transvolta, and her early writing was devoted to poetry and stories
for children—her first a pictorial essay entitled *The Roadmakers* (1961), followed
by *Playtime in Africa* (1962). Other works for children include the plays *Ananse
and the Dwarf Brigade* and *Two Rhythm Plays*. Her interest in children's literature
complements her engagement in the development of a bilingual society in Ghana.
Sutherland writes: "Some of my writing for children is in both English and Akan; I
am anxious that children are started off bilingually in the schools."

From 1958 to 1961, Sutherland became very active in the theater, establishing
the Ghana Drama Studio at Accra. She also wrote a great deal for Ghanaian radio.
Two of her radio plays, *Foriwa* (1964) and *Edufa* (1966), were performed by the
Ghana Drama Studio and then published in *Okyeama*, an important voice for
African art that she had also helped to found.

The cultural forums she provided were also used to explore her country's
indigenous traditions. Sutherland directed a number of plays based on Ananse
stories; composed with performance in mind, these popular tales demand audience
participation and often include prose or poetry which is chanted by a soloist to a
choral response. Ananse himself is a traditional Ghanaian trickster figure whose
intelligence and perspicacity regarding human nature and psychology does not
leave him invulnerable to human folly, greed, passion, or ambition. He is Everyman. In 1975, Sutherland used this figure in *The Marriage of Anansewa* and
produced the play in both English and Akan. In her preface, she writes, "That
Ananse is, artistically, a medium for society to criticize itself can be seen in the
expression, 'Exterminate Ananse, and society will be ruined.'" The play itself, the
last act of which is reprinted here, concerns Ananse's efforts to marry off his
well-educated daughter; despite her opposition, he has managed to engage her to
four chiefs at once, in a parody of traditional marriage arrangements. The manner
in which he prevents himself from falling victim to his own machinations and
succeeds in pleasing even his daughter may well remind Shakespearean students of
the late romances, *Pericles* and *The Winter's Tale*.

Today, Sutherland has a post as a professor of African Literature and Drama
at the University of Ghana's Institute of African Studies. She is also affiliated with
the School of Drama at Legon and directs the Kusum Agormba, a theater group
based in the Drama Studio of Ghana.

from THE MARRIAGE OF ANANSEWA

CAST

PLAYERS	All performers in the play, grouped together as a unified pool of musicmakers, dancers, actors, *and as a participating audience*. Provision must be made for able song-leaders, one or two drummers and, if possible, a guitarist....
PROPERTY MAN	Serves primarily as property manager, manning a property stand on-stage, and distributing props on cue. In addition, he does scene-setting duties, and is conveniently available as an actor for supporting roles. He can function, if necessary, as a prompter, and quite openly, provided he does it with skilful informality. When *free*, he is responsive to the action of the pool of PLAYERS or of the actors on stage. [Also addressed by his anglicized given name with the honorific title Pa.]
ANANSE	
ANANSEWA	Ananse's daughter
STORYTELLER	
CHIEF-WHO-IS-CHIEF'S MESSENGER	The image of a high-grade diplomat
CHRISTIE	Miss Christina Yamoah, a fashionable woman
GIRLS	About six, of Anansewa's age-group
MESSENGERS	To the "funeral"
1 FROM THE MINES	Two men
2 FROM SAPAASE	One man and two women
3 FROM AKATE	Two men
4 FROM CHIEF-WHO-IS-CHIEF	The "diplomat," another man and two or three women

[STORYTELLER *has come down among the audience, with whom he continues to think the matter over.*]

STORYTELLER: What do you think? All of us have seen this knot that has been tied. How do you suppose Mr. Ananse will untie it? As far as the four chiefs' problem is concerned, since nobody marries a corpse that part of the knot can be considered untied. Moreover, there isn't any law to oblige Ananse to return to them any of the gifts he has received from their hands so far and used to improve his circumstances.

But I ask you, this Dead-and-Alive with whom he is closeted in there, and whom it is impossible to take to the grave; how can he so hide her that nothing of his deceit shall be exposed? What would you do, if you were Ananse?

Should he cause her to vanish?

> To Ouagadougou?
> To Mexico?
> To Kenya?
> Or India?
> Or is it that
> Anansewa herself
> Will now turn to

[*Singing*:] Wind, wind, wind? [*Echo from Anansewa's song.*]

[*Laughing,* STORYTELLER *sits down with the audience. The* PLAYERS *start the song 'I'm Down in a Pit' again, singing it solemnly.* PROPERTY MAN *walks sneakingly in to set two web screens.*]

STORYTELLER: [*Rising and making his way to join the* PLAYERS] That's the nature of Anansegoro. Anansegoro is such that as soon as you release your mind to it it takes you, penetrating where it might not have been possible for you to go. Do you notice that since we started thinking, we also have arrived right where the eye of the story is?

[*The* PLAYERS *increase the volume of their singing.* ANANSE *and* CHRISTIE *sneak in carrying a bed which they set behind the web screens. They communicate in whispers, their movements are speedy. As soon as the bed is in place,* PROPERTY MAN, *in mourning, enters carrying a chair, and is directed by* ANANSE *to sit at the entrance.* CHRISTIE *fetches the clan staff which* ANANSE *gives to* PROPERTY MAN *to hold. Producing a sheet of paper and a pencil from her clothes,* CHRISTIE *reads it and speaks like one suppressing tears.*]

CHRISTIE: I have called Akate and informed Togbe Klu,[1] and they are on their way.

ANANSE: Let your voice quiver a little more so that you'll be in practice.

CHRISTIE: I have called Sapaase Palace and informed them. They say they are on their way.

I have called the Mines and informed them. They may even have arrived already. [*Her voice is now quivering as much as possible.*] I have called Chief-Who-Is-Chief and informed him. [*She sobs.*] Hmmm.

[*The volume of the singing increases and one of the* WOMEN *recites "How could it happen" intermittently in a subdued voice. With great stealth* ANANSE *walks round the bed. The song ceases. He takes a large watch out of his pocket and reads it.*]

ANANSE: The time is up. My soul, Kweku,[2] support me, for I'm weary. Life is really a struggle. Should this moment in which I'm trapped by any chance miscarry, I'm finished. And if care is not taken, I will, moreover, strike the fortune from my daughter's lips and spill it completely. Man is pathetic.

As I stand here, the fear attacking me is overwhelming; still I will take it this way, that I have seized hold of the tail of a wild beast who will bite me if I let go. So I'm holding on to it. What else can I do?

I know that not all my ways can be considered straight. But, before God, I'm not motivated by bad thoughts at this moment. I have a deep fatherly concern for this only child of mine. If the world were not what it is, I would not gamble with such a priceless possession. So what I plead is this: may grace be granted so that from among the four chiefs who desire to marry my child, the one will reveal himself who will love her and take good care of her when I give her to him.

[*He walks slowly to call* ANANSEWA *from the next room. He is indeed weary.*]

Anansewa—a! Come, the time is up.

[*The* PLAYERS *continue singing "I'm Down in a Pit" solemnly.* ANANSEWA *runs in, and throws herself on the bed.* ANANSE *and* CHRISTIE *speedily arrange her. A voice outside calls out "Agoo!" for permission to enter.* CHRISTIE *dashes out.* ANANSE *rushes outside the web screens on tiptoe, and sits on the floor as miserably as possible.* PROPERTY MAN *organises himself. The song ceases as* CHRISTIE *leads in the* MINES MESSENGERS. *They are two men.*]

CHRISTIE: [*As she enters*] Is the elder of the family there? Here are messengers from the Mines.

[ANANSE *groans, and lurches sideways as though he is fainting.* CHRISTIE *dashes across to support him.*]

Pa George! Suppress the agony a little. I have explained what agonising scenes you cannot face. It's because there are customary routines to follow that they feel obliged to come. Respectable messengers, you have permission.

[*She gestures in the direction of the bed, and leads them round it.*]

FIRST MESSENGER: Look, she seems as though she is merely asleep.

CHRISTIE: You see! Anansewa is deceiving us so much. As you look at her, it seems as though she is about to rise any minute. And yet, we know that it's we who are vainly indulging in sweet anticipation.

[ANANSE *groans*.]

Please, Pa George, suppress it a little.

[*She indicates where the* MESSENGERS *should stand*. PROPERTY MAN *moves over to stand by her*.]

FIRST MESSENGER: Respected lady, and you, elder of the family, whom we meet here. We do not like the reason for our coming here, but we are obliged to come. We were in no way expecting that on this day we would come on such a journey. Our royal one, the wealthy paramount Chief of the Mines whose praisename is 'You Are Coming Again, Aren't You,' has had many discussions with his councillors about this marriage he was going to contract. He insisted—against their advice—that if a lady of this quality came into his hands she would give enlightened training to the many children to whom his wives have given birth.

[ANANSE *groans*.]

It has not been our royal one's fortune to hear the news he was expecting. He who is Owner has snatched his property from our royal one's hands.

[ANANSE *groans hard*.]

We will be brief, sir, Our royal one has this to say: that because this lady had not yet become his wife, he cannot give her burial; but that which custom does permit, he is not reluctant to fulfil.

[PROPERTY MAN *carries in the required props. At the mention of each item he hands it over*.]

He sends this bolt of silk; this kente from Bonwire; this dumas cotton cloth. Use them for dressing his lady's bed for her.

He sends this drink, and this bag of money to help her father pay for the funeral in farewell to his lady.

[*The other messenger, receiving the articles one by one from* PROPERTY MAN, *hands them over to* CHRISTIE. *Having received them all she shows them to* ANANSE, *then she enters the screened-off area, places the cloth on the bed, and the drink beside it. Returning, she confers in whispers with* ANANSE, *her mouth close to his ear*.]

CHRISTIE: Respected messengers, Pa Ananse says he has heard the message you bring.

[ANANSE *keels over*. CHRISTIE *quickly holds him up, patting him to comfort him. She breaks into song, and gesturing the* MESSENGERS *to follow her, leads them out*.]

CHRISTIE: Oh really clueless one
      Wailing though I lack skill
      Oh really clueless one.

ANANSE: [*Rising*] Ah! So had my daughter gone into this marriage, this chief's councillors would not have liked it; and she would have gone there to get hated. Very well, I have untied that part of the knot.

[*He and* PROPERTY MAN *sneak in to see if all is well with the bed. They hear* CHRISTIE's *voice calling "Agoo! Agoo!" urgently and dash back to their positions*. CHRISTIE *leads in* SAPAASE MESSENGERS, *two women and a man*.]

CHRISTIE: [*To* PROPERTY MAN] Is the elder of the family there? Here come messengers from Sapaase Palace.

[ANANSE *groans*.]

Pa George! [*She goes over to support him*.] My mothers, this is what I told you about. He is taking it extremely hard.

MALE MESSENGER: Pa Ananse, condolences. We will make it brief. What has to be done must be done, and that is why we came. We are not here to do any agonising things to bruise your pain.

FIRST FEMALE MESSENGER: Oh, where is my lady? Listen, I'll carry you on my back. Place my lady on my back so that I can take her to my chief. Our royal one, you have our sympathy. Pa George, condolences; d'you hear?

[ANANSE *groans*.]

CHRISTIE: Mama, mama, mama. Stop it, stop it, stop it.

[*She starts her song 'Oh Really Clueless One,' gestures in the direction of the bed and leads the* MESSENGERS *to walk round it*.]

SECOND FEMALE MESSENGER: Isn't this as though my lady were merely asleep? Ah, Pa Ananse, my sympathy. Our royal one, sympathy is yours also. My lady, you are lovely. I was campaigning for you so that I could get a beautiful baby from your womb to carry on my back, and display my pride for the purpose of putting to shame a certain bitchy, ugly, somebody who is there in Sapaase Palace.

ANANSE: Stop it. Stop it.

MALE MESSENGER: Very well, sir.

FIRST FEMALE MESSENGER: Alas! My lady, I was anxious for you to come into residence in the top storey of the palace, and then, we would have sent packing downstairs—straight!—that shrew of a woman at large there, who is only waiting to claw out our eyes and scare us away.

[ANANSE *groans*.]

MALE MESSENGER: Enough, mother. [CHRISTIE *points out where they should stand*.] Well, elders of the house whom we meet here, we will be brief. Who likes bitterness? Were we not obliged to come, this journey would have been too bitter and too hard to face. Having come, we are well aware that it is the father who is most afflicted; therefore if you ask us not to do agonising things in his presence, we agree with you.

Had our royal one acquired this lady, a certain nasty beast, who is at large in his home, would have fled on her own accord, and peace would have come to the home.

Truly, we are hurt, because we were paying conscientious attention, as you know. It was as though we were regularly bringing our eggs into storage here, accumulating them for collection later. And the time was just rounding the corner too; but The Implacable One said no. Our eggs have hatched nothingness, leaving us with empty hands.

[ANANSE *groans*.]

I've cut it short, sir. When our royal one discussed the news with his council, some were of the opinion that since this is a case of no-sale-no-payment other families would simply consider the matter concluded. But our particular family is endowed with such compassion that we ourselves would not consider it nice if we did nothing for you. Therefore, what our royal one has to say is this: he has no right to give burial to this child because the head-drink did not come in time to make it a conclusive marriage. You yourselves are well aware that had our royal one not been thoroughly knowledgeable about customary procedure, he would not be occupying his ancient stool. He says that he is not reluctant at all to perform whatever custom he has the right to perform in farewell to the woman he loves.

[*As he names the things they have brought, one woman receives them item by item from* PROPERTY MAN, *and passes them on to* CHRISTIE.]

Here are his silk, his velvet, his white kente cloth, his white striped cloth; place them on his beloved's bed for her to take to the grave. Here is his cash donation of twenty guineas also; spend it on drinks for the funeral. That's the mission that brought us here.

[CHRISTIE *shows* ANANSE *these things and places them on the bed. Returning, she consults him in whispers before she speaks*.]

CHRISTIE: He says he has received your message in full.

[*After a brief hesitation she leads the* MESSENGERS *out, sorrowfully singing her song again*.]

ANANSE: Such verbal agility and trouble-ridden talk.

> The world is dark
> Is dark
> The world is really dark.

[*He rises.*] Had you people got hold of my child, you would have involved her, blameless as she is, in your contention in Sapaase Palace and driven that wild woman of whom you speak to kill her and bereave me for nothing.

It is the Lord I thank, for I would have pushed my child into disaster. All right, I have untied that part of the knot also.

[*He and* PROPERTY MAN *enter the screened area. Almost immediately they hear the clanging of a gong, followed by singing. They fly back to their positions. With "Agoo! Agoo!"* CHRISTIE *leads in* AKATE MESSENGERS, *two men.*]

AKATE MESSENGERS:

> Zoxome mele du yom lo!
> Togbi Klue be, "Zixome mele du yom"
> Kaka made kasia, Ku do aba di
> na Anansewa!
> Amega 'megawo va so di koto,
> ne woa tsoe adi.
> Ao! Anansewa tso da yibo tso
> yi Avli mee!

CHRISTIE: [*She waits for the song to end.*] Elder of the family, you have heard with your own ears. Togbe Klu's messengers have arrived.

[*She indicates a place outside the screens where they move to view* ANANSEWA *through the web. They shake their heads in sorrow and sing again movingly.* ANANSE *groans.*]

CHRISTIE: George, please control yourself so that they can deliver their news.

FIRST MESSENGER: Togbe Ananse and his elders whom we meet here, we come as direct brothers of Togbe Klu IV. In all Akate we are the ones who know what preparations our brother and our chief has endeavoured to make as he awaits Togbe Ananse's child. Our brother was most appreciative of this

lady's training in secretarial work. He was looking forward to having a real helper at last to assist him in building up a substantial business. A helper who would not ruin him as some of his own relatives, I regret to say, have done time and time again to his distress. Look, he is ready to order giant trucks for bringing cattle from Mali. That aside, he has ordered a trawler, for fishing. And the documents for all these were to have been entrusted to his own wife's administration.

[ANANSE *groans.*]

Had this misfortune occurred in the days when Togbe's spirit would quicken at the recital of his praise-name, "Prickly-Pear," Akate town would be in a turmoil that would overflow to this place also. This funeral house wouldn't be so silent.

But these days, he has become a most zealous adherent of a Spiritualist Church, and so when something happens which he cannot fathom he leaves it in God's hands no matter how much he is pained. When he heard the news he wept so much we also wept. But he has left it in God's hands in the same way. He was not even in favour of our coming here. "What was the use," he said. But we said, "No." We have not yet had the vision he has had, which leads him to that point of view. Even if we came to do nothing, we would show our faces here. Togbe Ananse, condolences.

[ANANSE *bows his head;* CHRISTIE *moves over to consult him in whispers.*]

CHRISTIE: He says I should ask you if that is all you have to say.

FIRST MESSENGER: That is all.

CHRISTIE: He says he thanks you for your affection.

MESSENGERS: [*Together*] Boba no lo
                Ha we ga kpe lo

[*They sing their song to the gong as they depart, led by* CHRISTIE, ANANSE *sits staring into the distance; he shakes his head regretfully.*]

ANANSE: Ah! Togbe Klu. You whom I even

forgot sometimes to count among those in the race, lo and behold, it is you who turns out to be the one with such good intentions. You should have given me that understanding, for I had no idea it was your desire to live so well with my child. [*He thinks.*]

Have I allowed your messengers to depart? What if Chief-Who-Is-Chief doesn't come? And if he does, supposing he comes in the manner in which the Mines people and Sapaase people came? What would I do then? If in desperation and torment, I push my child into his hands in that event, I would be pushing her into catastrophe. Oh, has trouble so turned into a fallen tree across my road? Is there no rest at all in this life? Hmm, my mind is exhausted.

[*He moves beside* ANANSEWA. CHRISTIE *shouts 'Agoo!'* ANANSE *darts into hiding behind the web screens.* PROPERTY MAN *rearranges himself.* CHRISTIE *leads in* MESSENGERS OF CHIEF-WHO-IS-CHIEF.]

CHRISTIE: Pa George? [*She doesn't see him.*] Has Pa George gone? [*She sees him.*] Pa George. [*Her voice quivers.*] Your loving ones want you. Indeed, today, I really can't escape dealing with an issue too weighty for my competence.

[ANANSE *leaves the web, and walks out to slump down in his place.*]

My honourable ones, see how miserably he sits. It's he, the father; we are finding it more unbearable to look at him. Had there not been tough-muscled men around to help, we would have buried him instead by now; you would not have met him here alive. A little more delay and you would not have been here in time to view the face of this beloved one of yours either.

ANANSE: Honourable messengers of the great one, have you arrived? I am worth nothing in your sight indeed. I promised you that I would take good care of that precious possession of yours entrusted to me. But I failed to prime my gun and stand firm to defend her.

What shall I say to you? Shall I merely say "Sorry" to you?

[*The* MESSENGERS *whip out their handkerchiefs in unison, and dab their eyes.*]

CHRISTIE: Pa George, don't. My honourable ones, it was for you we were waiting. Because of what the father is doing, we were going to bury the child out of his sight, according to his instructions. Come, then, and view what is yours.

[*She leads them round the bed, wailing in song.*]

Wailing for my child,
Anansewa, don't blame me.
Wailing for my child,
Anansewa, don't blame me.
Wailing,
One, alone, Anansewa.

Don't blame me,
Wailing,
Without skill but wailing,
Anansewa.

[*At the end of the song she points out where the* MESSENGERS *should stand.*]

FIRST MESSENGER: Lady, and elders whom we meet here, forgive us for delaying a little, but the orders which our chief who is so unexpectedly afflicted gave us, enjoined that we should not come on this mission inadequately prepared. Therefore, we were making every effort to assemble everything before setting out. The fires are so totally out, where we come from.

All the way here, we've been painfully regretful. We have this much to say, that if we had been aware that Chief-Who-Is-Chief loved the lady Anansewa with a love so deep we would have seen to settling her by his side without any delay. Had she come to him this might probably not have happened. The time was just rounding the corner too. He has called a meeting of very important people at the palace a week from this very day to fix the day of the wedding and plan all the arrangements before sending word to the lady's father.

What more shall I say to make everyone understand the pathetic plight of our royal one, Chief-Who-Is-Chief?

[ANANSE *keels over and springs up in such agony that* PROPERTY MAN *goes to his aid.*]

CHRISTIE: Sirs, that's what I told you.

FIRST MESSENGER: I will stop there and deliver the message we bring. There is a man who is hailed by the praise-name Fire-Extinguisher. He is Chief-Who-Is-Chief and he has sent us to the respected Mr George K. Ananse.

He says that he makes no error in calling this man his father-in-law, because had Ungenerous Death not snatched this child from his hands, it would be in order so to address him.

This Chief-Who-Is-Chief, who was eager to blend his blood with yours and become a member of your family, wishes me to inform you about this painful grief, and add that he accepts total responsibility for everything concerning the woman who had but one more step to take to enter his home.

Therefore from his hands to yours here are all requirements for her funeral.

[PROPERTY MAN *brings in the things which one of the women receives from him item by item and hands over to* CHRISTIE.]

Here is the ring a husband places on a wife's finger. Here is a bag of money, spend it on the funeral. Here are cloths which any woman who is confidently feminine would select with a careful eye; place them on his beloved one's bed; dumas, white kente, silk kente, velvet, brocade.

The drinks he sends to help his father-in-law with the funeral are in such quantities that we couldn't bring them in here. We needn't even pay attention to that because this...[*He himself receives a bottle from* PROPERTY MAN]...this bottle of Schnapps in my hand is what it is absolutely mandatory for me to place in your hands. His wishes are that this must be the drink with which the farewell libation is poured when his beloved one is being placed in the coffin.

[ANANSE *groans.*]

Finally, it is his desire to do for Ananse-wa what a husband does for a wife. And so he sends his coffin, one made of glass. Place his wife in it for him. [*A momentary hush.*] Lady, bring your elders along, so that I can show you the coffin.

[*The* MESSENGERS *lead* CHRISTIE *and* PROPERTY MAN *to the entrance from where the viewing takes place. Overcome by grief, they whip out their handkerchiefs at the same time and dab their eyes.* ANANSE *springs up, moves over to take a look for himself and wails.*]

ANANSE: Is this my adversity? What have I done that I'm stripped to such nakedness? My child, such was your fortune, and you are so silent? Ah, life does wield a whip that the human being cannot withstand.

[*He falls back into somebody's arms.*]

Ah, sirs, this place has become awesome.

[*It is as though he is going into a trance.*]

Give me drink to pour libation myself.
Give me the drink my child's lover has sent.

[CHRISTIE *hands over the drink to* PROPERTY MAN *who passes it on to* ANANSE. *He is given a glass into which he pours a portion. He moves into the screened-off area, leans against the web and starts the libation.*]

Dependable God,
I'm calling on you,
Earth Efuwa;
Souls who have preceded us,
Come, all of you,
Here is your drink.
What we receive
We share with you.

If you have gone, it does not mean
You have neglected us.
You are with us
In difficulty and in joy.

I am announcing to you
That your grandchild is on her way.
Condolences to you.
Condolences to us.

We know you are there
To give her a welcome embrace.
We know it is to her family she comes,
And that being so,
We should be comforted.
But there is more to it than that,
Ancestors, there is more to it than that.

[*He goes into a trance.*]

You who are lying there!
Anansewa!
I'm calling you!
Listen with the ancestors;

Chief-Who-Is-Chief
The-man-fit-for-a-husband
Has sent his money

[CHRISTIE *places it on the bed.*]

Has sent his cloths

[CHRISTIE *places them on the bed.*]

Has sent his drink
Which I hold in my hand;

A person who is so wise,
A person who so understands what
                                        love is
That though the feast has not yet been
                                        spread
For him to feed,
He has sent his thanks;

See, there stands his coffin
Giving proof of his love,
Giving proof
That for Anansewa's sake
He is doing far more than
What custom prescribes for him;
Anansewa had yet to enter his man's
                                        home
Yet, see how he has done
What a real husband does, in full.

[*He goes into an even deeper trance.*]

Ancestors, I am pleading with you,
If it is your desire
As it is ours
That Chief-Who-Is-Chief
Should marry Anansewa,
See to it that she returns to life!

Wake her!
See to it that Anansewa awakes
And returns to become a bride!

[*He falls into the arms of* PROPERTY MAN *as though he is overcome by contact with the spirits. He sings like a man in a trance.*]

Oh wake, oh wake.

Kweku's child, Anansewa,
Wake, oh wake!

Love is calling you, return,
Wake, oh wake!

Chief-Who-Is-Chief loves you true
Wake, oh wake!

[*He moves swiftly to* ANANSEWA's *side and walks round the bed staring at her. There is a hush.*]

ANANSE: [*Suddenly*] Oh, she is waking. Are there such wonders in the world? My child is waking.

[ANANSEWA *stirs.*]

Does love have such power? Christie, open the doors and let everybody in to see the power of amazing love.

[CHRISTIE *and* PROPERTY MAN *mime opening up the house, and beckon people in. The* PLAYERS *surge all over the place.*]

There is my child, awakened for me by love. How strong love is. Love has awakened my child.

She is rising!
She is rising!
She has risen, complete.

[ANANSEWA *springs out of the bed, causing* MESSENGERS *and all the others to scatter and hover round in bewilderment. But* ANANSE, CHRISTIE *and* PROPERTY MAN *huddle around* ANANSEWA *hugging one another, and shaking hands.*]

ANANSEWA: [*Just like one suddenly woken from a deep sleep*] Father! Where is father? Father.

ANANSE: My lovely child. My one and only daughter. Here I am.

[ANANSEWA *smiles and nestles her head in his bosom.*]

ANANSEWA: Father, I could hear Chief-Who-Is-Chief calling me.

ANANSE: He was indeed calling you. His love has won a victory for us all. [*The guests express much amazement.*] Honourable messengers, I'm dumbfounded. Here, alive, is your precious possession. It is by the grace of the God who never gives us up. I believe that there is nothing better for you to do now than to return to break the news of this miracle to my loving son-in-law, so that his bitterness shall turn to sweetness. Thank you for coming on such a consoling journey.

Friends who brought your compassion in to cover my nakedness in grief, I thank you. By the day of my birth, if our spirits which fled from us return to us, and I don't invite you all to meet here for a great celebration, may no parent call me George Kweku Ananse.

Christie!

CHRISTIE: Georgie!

ANANSE: Rare helper! Supporter, your thanks await you.

[*He hugs* CHRISTIE *and* ANANSEWA.]

STORYTELLER: [*Bursting into laughter and crying out*] That's Kweku all right!

ANANSE: [*Starting*] Goodness! Look, sir, leave the praise-singing alone till some other time, and instead, manage the guests departure for me, to end this whole event right now.

STORYTELLER: [*Still laughing*] I understand you too well. In that case, friends, we will end this Anansegoro right here. Whether you found it interesting or not, do take parts of it away, leaving parts of it with me. We are shaking hands for departure.

[*The* PLAYERS *sing joyfully, shaking hands with* ANANSEWA, CHRISTIE *and* PROPERTY MAN.]

Oh, oh,
Is love's power so strong?
Is love's power so strong?

So strong?
Is love's power so strong?

Let's relate in love
That we may thrive—

True love is rare.

Let's relate in love
That we may thrive—

True giver is rare.

Let's relate in love
That we may thrive—

True helper is rare.

Let's relate in love
That we may thrive—

Thank you, chief so rare.

Let's relate in love
That we may thrive—

Thank you, husband rare.

Let's relate in love
That we may thrive.

CURTAIN

NOTES

1. The first word is an honorific title meaning "leader,"—it precedes the name, in this case, chief of the Akate.
2. Some Ghanaian peoples take a "day name" referring to the day on which they were born. Compare, in Western culture, "Wednesday's Child," for example.

Rosario Castellanos   *Mexico, 1925–1974*

Mary critics consider Rosario Castellanos to be the foremost Latin American feminist writer. Certainly the breadth and scope of her lifetime achievement make her one of the most distinguished Hispanic writers of this century. Ironically, since so few of her works have been translated into English, she is little known in English-speaking countries.

Castellanos wrote poetry, fiction, essays, criticism, and plays. Her novel, *Balún-Canán* (The Nine Guardians, 1957) was considered by some to be the precursor of the Latin American "boom novels" of the 1960s and what has come to be known as magic realism. It was an Indianist novel, and, indeed, the plight of the oppressed Indians in her native Chiapas was, along with women's struggles, a major theme in her opus.

Castellanos received her B.A. in Philosophy at the University of Mexico and went on to do post-graduate work in Spain. Her first published work was her M.A. thesis, *Sobre cultura feminina* (On Feminine Culture, 1950). She then wrote numerous volumes of poetry, two novels about the Tzotzil Indians of Chiapas, three collections of short stories (*Album de Familia* [Family Album, 1971] focusing particularly on women), and four collections of essays. The following essay, "La Mujer y su imagen" (Woman and Her Image) is from a collection entitled *Mujer que sabe latín* (Women Who Know Latin, 1973) and is a compilation of weekly articles about women written for the Mexican daily, *El Excelsior*; Castellanos' major focus in these essays and in her other works is the difficulty of being both a Mexican and a woman. The poems selected are from *Poesía no cres Tú* (Poetry Is Not You, 1972).

Castellanos' life was not a happy or easy one. She was stricken with tuberculosis while young; her first two children died at birth (one other survived); her marriage ended in divorce. These details are relevant, for much of her writing is based, in part, on her personal experiences. Her death too was unfortunate and premature. She accidentally electrocuted herself in Tel Aviv while serving as Mexican Ambassador to the Golda Meier government.

SELF-PORTRAIT
Autorretrato

I am a Mrs.: an appellation
hard to come by, in my case, and more useful
in dealing with people than a title
appended to my name by some academy.

So, then, I display my trophy and repeat:
I am a Mrs.   Fat or thin
according to the movements of the stars
and the cycles of the glands
and other phenomena I don't understand.

Blonde, if I wear a blonde wig.
Or brunette, according to my whim.
(In reality, my hair is getting gray, getting gray.)

I am kind of ugly. It seems to depend to a great
                                                                extent
on how I put on my make-up.

My appearance has changed with time
—but the change is not as great as Weininger*
says there is in the appearance of a genius. I'm
                                                                mediocre.

Which, on the one hand, spares me enemies
and, on the other hand, wins me the devotion
of occasional admirers and friends
who are the kind of men who like to talk on
                                    the telephone
and send long letters of congratulations.

Who slowly sip their whiskeys on the rocks
while chatting about politics and literature.

Girlfriends...well, sometimes...rarely,
and in very tiny doses.
In general, I refuse to look in mirrors.
They would only tell me the usual things:
how badly I dress and how ridiculous
I look when I'm trying to flirt with someone.

I'm the mother of Gabriel. You know, the little
                                                boy
who one day will become an inflexible judge
and maybe also an executioner.
In the meantime I love him.
I write. This poem. And others. And others.
I contribute to journals in my field,
give lectures and classes,
publish weekly articles for a newspaper.

I live opposite the Park, but almost
never look in that direction. And I never
cross the street to take a walk
and breathe and caress
the corrugated bark of the trees.

I know I should listen to music
but frequently avoid it. I know
it's good to see pictures
but never go to exhibitions,
nor theatrical openings, nor the film club.

I prefer to stay here, reading
or, if I turn out the light, thinking
absent-mindedly and puttering a while.

I suffer more out of habit, by inheritance,
like others of my kind,
than for concrete reasons.

I would be happy if I knew how.
I mean, if they'd taught me all the gestures,
the speeches, the scenery.

Instead what they taught me was to cry. But
                                        my crying
mechanism doesn't function as it should
and I never cry at death beds,
nor on momentous occasions, nor when faced
                                with a catastrophe.

I cry when I misplace the statements for my
                                    property tax
or when the rice burns.

Translated by Beth Miller

NOTE

* Otto Weininger (1880–1903). See note on p. 360.

SPEAKING OF GABRIEL
Se habla de Gabriel

Like all my guests my son disturbed me
occupying a place that was my place,
there at the wrong time,
making me split each mouthful in two.

Ugly, sick, bored
I felt him grow at my expense,
rob my blood of its color, add
a secret weight and volume
to my way of being upon this earth.

His body begged mine for birth, to yield to his;
to give him a place in the world,
the provision of time necessary for his history.

I consented. And when he departed through
                                    that wound,
through that unloosening hemorrhage
the last of my aloneness, of looking from behind
                                            a glass
flowed out.

I remained open, manifest
to visitations, to the wind, to presence.

Translated by Maureen Ahern

MEDITATION ON THE BRINK
Meditación en el umbral

No, it's not a solution
to throw oneself under a train like Tolstoy's
                       Anna
or gulp down Madame Bovary's arsenic
or await on the barren heights of Avila the
                       visit
of an angel with a fiery dart
before binding one's veil back over one's head
and starting to act.

Nor to deduce geometric laws by counting
the beams of one's solitary confinement cell
like Sor Juana did. It's not a solution
to write, while company arrives,
in the Austen family living room
or to shut oneself up in the attic
of some New England house
and dream, with the Dickinson's family Bible
under a spinster pillow.

There must be another way that's not named
                       Sappho
or Mesalina or Mary of Egypt
or Magdalene or Clemencia Isaura.*

Another way to be human and free.

Another way to be.

Translated by Maureen Ahern

NOTE

* Anna Karenina and Mme. Bovary, two nineteenth-century heroines from novels of the same names, killed themselves because of disappointment in their adulterous love affairs. Spanish nun St. Teresa de Avila (1515–1582) and Mexican nun Sor Juana de la Cruz (1648–1695) wrote their brilliant works of philosophy and literature from their convents (Sor Juana much of the time in isolation) while the English Jane Austen (1775–1817) wrote many of her great novels in her family parlor and the American Emily Dickinson in her family house in Amherst, Massachusetts. The four writers were unmarried, exchanging, some might say, traditional domestic happiness for creative passion. Sappho, Mesalina, Mary of Egypt, Magdalene, and Clemencia Isaura are probably linked through untraditional sexual behavior. Sappho was said to have been a lesbian; Mesali-

na (fl. A.D. 487), the wife of Claudius I was noted for sexual promiscuity, while fifth-century Mary of Egypt and Mary Magdalene were thought to be repentant sexual sinners. Clemncia Isaura was the thirteenth-century French woman reputed to be the inspiration for troubador poetry.

WOMAN AND HER IMAGE
La Mujer y su imagen

In the course of history (history is an archive of deeds undertaken by men and all that remains outside it belongs to the realm of conjecture, fable, legend, or lie), more than a natural phenomenon, a component of society or a human creature, woman has been myth.

Simone de Beauvoir affirms that a myth always implies a subject that projects its hopes and fears toward a transcending heaven. In our case, man converts whatever is feminine into a receptacle of contradictory moods and places it at a distance from which we are shown a figure that, although varying in form, is monotonous in meaning. And the cumulative mythmaking process manages to conceal its inventions with such opaque density, insert them so deep in the recesses of consciousness and at such remote strata of the past, that it obstructs straightforward observation of the object, or direct knowledge of the being that has been replaced and usurped.

The creator and the spectator of the myth no longer see a woman as a flesh and blood person with certain biological, physiological, and psychological characteristics; much less do they perceive in her the qualities of someone who resembles them in dignity, but is distinct in behavior. Rather, they perceive only the incarnation of some principle, generally sinister, and fundamentally antagonistic.

If we look back at the primitive theogonies that attempt to explain the emergence, existence, and structure of the universe, we find two forces. Instead of complementing each other in harmonious collaboration, they oppose one another in a struggle in which consciousness, willpower, spirit—in short, masculinity—subjugate the feminine, which being immanent passivity, is inertia.

The sun breathes life and the sea reaps its bounty; winds scatter the seed and the earth opens to germination; in a world that places order above chaos, where form saves matter from its inaneness, conflict is inevitably resolved by the triumph of man.

But absolute victory would require the banishment of his opponent. Because that demand has not been met, the victor—who plants his heel on the cervix of the vanquished enemy—feels in each heartbeat, a threat; in each gesture the imminence of flight; and in every move an attempt to revolt.

Fear creates hideous new deliriums. Delusions of the sea devouring the sun at sunset; the earth feeding on offal and corpses; chaos unchained in an enormous surge that arouses the license of the elements, unleashing powers of annihilation that turn the staff of plenty into empty shadows. Fear breeds actions that simultaneously foment its cause and do violence against it.

Thus throughout the centuries, woman has been raised to the altar of the gods, and has breathed the incense of the faithful. That is, when she is not locked up in a gynaeceum or a harem to share the yoke of slavery with her own kind; when she is not confined to the courtyards of the unclean; when she is not branded with the mark of the prostitute; crushed by the servant's burden; expelled from the religious congregation, the political arena, or the university classroom.

This ambivalence of male attitudes is merely superficial. If we examine it closely, we will find an indivisible and constant unity of purpose that is disguised in a multiplicity of ways. For example, suppose that a woman is praised for her beauty. Let us not forget that beauty is an ideal composed and imposed by men, which by strange coincidence corresponds to a series of qualifications that when fulfilled transform the woman who possesses them into a handicapped person; that is, without exaggerating, we might more accurately state, into a thing.

Big strong feet are ugly, they say, but they are good for walking and maintaining an erect posture. In a man, big strong feet are more than permissible, they are obligatory. But in a woman? Even our tritest local troubadors surrender to "a foot as tiny as a thimble." With that foot (which in the China of the mandarins was bound so that it could not develop to its normal size, and in the rest of the civilized world was never subject to any exercise) one cannot go anywhere. Which evidently is what it was all about.

A beautiful woman stretches out on a sofa, exhibiting one of the attributes of her beauty, her small feet, for male admiration, exposing them to his desire. They're covered by a shoe that some glittering fashion mogul has declared to be the expression of elegance, and which possesses all the characteristics that define an instrument of torture. At its widest part it pinches to strangulation; the front ends in unlikely points to which the toes must submit; the heel extends thanks to a spike heel that does not sufficiently support the body to stand on, making balance precarious, a fall easy, and walking impossible. But who, except the suffragettes, dare to use comfortable shoes that respect the laws of anatomy? That's why the suffragettes, in just punishment, are unanimously ridiculed.

There are peoples, like the Arabs, the Dutch, and some Latin Americans, who only concede the title of beautiful to the obese woman. Her food and her sedentary customs earn her that title, at the price, of course, of her health, and her ease of movement. Clumsy, easily tired, she deteriorates from sloth to paralysis.

But there are other more subtle and equally efficient methods to reduce a woman to helplessness: those who would transform her into pure spirit.

As long as this spirit does not keep the company of angels in heaven, she is lodged, alas, in the prison of her body. However in order for the heaviness of this transitory state not to overcome its victim, the body must become as fragile, vulnerable and nonexistent as possible.

Not all women possess the ethereal condition they are supposed to have. Therefore, one must camouflage abundant flesh with choking corsets and eliminate it with extenuating diets. After all, the weaker sex is incapable of picking up the handkerchief she drops, or of opening a book that closes, or of pulling back the lace curtain through which she contemplates the world. Her energy is used up in exhibiting herself to the eyes of the man who applauds her wasp waist, the shadows under her eyes (which if not caused by insomnia or illness can be produced by belladonna), her pallor that reveals a soul sighing to heaven, or the fainting spell of one who cannot bear contact with the brutal realities of everyday life.

Long fingernails prevent the use of hands for work. Complicated hairdos and makeup take up an enormous amount of time, and require the appropriate setting to be properly shown off. One that protects her against the whims of the weather: the rain that ruins the shape of her eyebrows so carefully drawn with a pencil; that erases the rouge so painstakingly, so artistically applied to her cheeks; that dissolves the beautymarks distributed according to a calculated strategy, into ridiculously arbitrary blotches that accent the imperfections of her skin. Or the wind, that blows out curls, irritates her eyes, rumples up her clothes.

The countryside is not the habitat of a beautiful woman, nor is the open air or nature. It's the salon, a temple where she receives the homage of her faithful admirers with the dauntlessness of an idol, an expressionless visage that cannot even demonstrate the single crack of a vain smile because any movement in her face could break into a thousand wrinkles revealing the decline of a star that is, after all, subject to the rigors and ravages of time.

The antithesis of Pygmalion,[1] man does not aspire, by means of beauty, to convert a statue into a living being, but rather a living being into a statue.

What for? To adore her, even though it may be for a brief time, or so we are told. But also, according to what we are not told, in order to immobilize her, to convert any plan of hers into unachievable actions, to avoid risks.

Woman, in her natural state, does not lose her link with the dark powers, irreducible to reason, untamed by technology, that still circulate on this planet, disturbing the logic of events, disorganizing the structured, satirizing the sublime.

Woman not only preserves her link with these dark powers, *she is* a dark power. Nothing will make her change her sign. But she can be reduced in importance, at least, as we have seen, on the aesthetic level, and as we will see, on the ethical level.

Here we are dealing with the concept that Virginia Woolf called, "The Angel in the House," the model of virtue to which every female creature must aspire.[1]

This same English writer defines and describes her in this way: "She was intensely sympathetic. She was immensely charming. She was utterly unselfish. She excelled in the difficult arts of family life. She sacrificed herself daily. If there was chicken, she took the leg; if there was a draft she sat in it—in short she was so constituted that she never had a mind or a wish of her own, but preferred to sympathize always with the minds and wishes of others. Above all—I need not say it—she was pure. Her purity was supposed to be her chief beauty—her blushes, her great grace."

What connotation does purity have in this

case? Of course it's a synonym for ignorance. A radical ignorance of everything that happens in the world, but particularly about matters that have to do with "facts of life" as one so euphemistically alludes to the processes of copulation, reproduction, and perpetuation of the sexual species, among them the human one. But above all, it's ignorance of what the woman herself is.

Thus a rigorous and complex morality is elaborated to protect feminine ignorance from any possible contamination. Woman is a term that acquires an obscene nuance and that is why we should cease using it. We have other much more proper terms available: lady, madam, miss, and why not "The Angel in the House."[2]

A lady is not acquainted with her body by reference, touch, or even sight. When a married woman bathes (that is if she bathes) she keeps her body covered with some modest tunic that is an obstacle to cleanliness and also to vain and pernicious curiosity.

A monster in her own labyrinth, an unmarried woman becomes lost in the meanders of a capricious and invisible intimacy, ruled by principles that "the Other Sex" knows to the point of exactly locating and naming each spot, each turn, predicating the function, importance and limitations of each shape.

An unmarried woman gropes blindly within an anatomy about which she has mistaken notions, stumbling across surprises, terror, scandal, in dark hallways and basements whose secret name belongs to "the Other Sex"; she does not understand, nor should she understand the form that contains her, the function of that which serves as her dwelling, nor is she able to find her way out into open space, light, freedom.

This situation of confinement, which is commonly called innocence or virginity, is apt to last for many years and sometimes for an entire lifetime.

The courage to inquire about herself; the need to become aware of the meaning of her own bodily existence or the unheard of pretention of conferring meaning upon her own spiritual existence is harshly repressed and punished by the social system. This has dictated, once and for all, that the only legitimate feminine attitude is that of waiting.

This is why, from the time a woman is born education works on the given matter in order to adapt it to its destiny and convert it into a morally acceptable entity, in other words, a socially useful one. Thus woman is stripped of her spontaneity of action; forbidden the initiative of decision; taught to obey the commandments of an ethic that is completely alien to her and has no more justification or basis than that of serving the interests, goals, and ends of others.

Sacrificed like Iphigenia[3] on the patriarchal altars, womankind does not die: she waits. The expectation is that of the transition from potential to action: the transformation of moth into butterfly, events that will not take place through mere patience.

Like asceticism for the saints, which is nothing but a prerequisite that does not oblige divine grace to reward it, patience does not oblige chance to dispense or deny the agent which is the active principle and the catalyst of the natural processes: man. Not just any man but rather one anointed by the sacrament of marriage, thanks to which the cycle of development sublimates its profane origin, and attains the required validity. Thus the possibility of fulfillment, sinful in conditions that may not be the ones prescribed, is fulfilled in an atmosphere that renders it acceptable and desirable.

Through the male mediator, woman finds out about her body and its functions, about her person and her obligations only that which is suitable for her and nothing more. Sometimes less. It depends on the generosity, the skill, or the knowledge available to whomever initiates her in the rites of passage.

Moreover, in either a tacit or explicit way, she is thus offered the chance to surpass her limits in a phenomenon that, while it does not erase, at least mitigates the negative signs that mark her, fulfills her needs, and incorporates her into the human nucleus with a letter of genuine citizenship. That phenonemon is maternity.

If motherhood were nothing more than physical birthing, as among animals, it would be anathema. But it is not merely a physical burgeoning because that would imply uncontrollable euphoria, something very distant from the spirit with which society has imbued the perpetuation of life.

In the maternal cavity, a mysterious event takes place—a kind of miracle that, like all miracles, arouses astonishment: it is witnessed by the attendants and experienced by the protagonist "in fear and trembling."[4] Careful. One sudden move, carelessness, an unsatisfied whim and the miracle will not happen. Nine unending months of rest, of dependence upon others, precautions, rites, taboos. Pregnancy is a sickness whose outcome is always catastrophic for whomever suffers it.

You will deliver in pain, the Bible dictates. And if pain does not occur spontaneously, it must be forced out. Repeating the traditional advice, recalling examples, preparing the spirit to provide more room for suffering, inciting moaning and crying; requiring their paroxysmal repetition until that huge cry erupts that splits the neighbors' eardrums even more than the innards of the birthing woman by the newborn.

Is the price paid? Not quite yet. Now the child will become the implacable creditor. Its helplessness will arouse the total abnegation of its mother. She will watch over it while it sleeps; she will eat for it; she will weather the storm in order to shelter it.

Magically, the selfishness that we assume to be characteristic of the human species is rooted out of women. With unbounded plea-

sure, we are assured, a mother outdoes herself for her offspring. She proudly bares the deforming results to her body: she wilts away without melancholy; she hands over what she has stored up without thinking, oh no, not for a single moment, of reciprocity.

Praise be to those dear old gray heads! Eternal glory "to the one who loved us before she knew us." Statues in the squares, days dedicated to her celebration, etc. etc.

Sometimes, like a fly in the ointment, we read on the crime page of the newspaper that someone—and herein follows an appropriate rending of vestments—that some unnatural being has commited the crime of filicide. But it is a tautological case that does not jeopardize any basic principle. (On the contrary, it is the exception that confirms the rule.)

We have mentioned the annulment of women in the realms of the aesthetic and the ethical. Need we allude to something as obvious as the intellectual arena? If ignorance is a virtue, it would be contradictory that, on the one hand, society praise her as it should, and yet, on the other, provide the means to destroy her.

Feasibility is reinforced or derived from concepts. The heart of the argument is that women do not receive instruction because they are incapable of assimilating it.

Leaving aside Schopenhauer's vulgar diatribes, Weininger's esoteric outpourings and Simmel's suspicious equanimity, let us only cite Moebius who, with Germanic tenacity, organized an impressive amount of data in order to prove scientifically, and irrefutably, that woman is "physiologically retarded."[5]

It is not an easy task to explain, one laments, exactly what constitutes mental deficiency. It is something that lies equidistant from imbecility and normality, although for the purpose of designating the latter we do not have an appropriate word at our disposal.

In everyday life, two opposing terms are used: intelligent and stupid. The person who discerns well is intelligent. (In relation to what? But it's rude to interrupt his speech.) The stupid person, on the other hand, is lacking in critical capacity. From the scientific point of view, what is usually called stupidity can be considered as much a morbid anomaly as well as a great reduction in the capacity to discern.

Now, that capacity is linked to bodily characteristics. A small cranium encloses, obviously, a small brain. And a woman's brain is minuscule. Not only are the weight and volume less if we compare them with those of the masculine brain, but the number of circumvolutions are also less. Always. Fatally. Sometimes exaggeratedly. Rudinger[6] (who might this illustrious gentleman be?) found a Bavarian woman who had a kind of brain identical in all respects to that of wild animals. So, why waste ammunition and attempt to impart culture where it is impossible and superfluous!

But M.A. de Neuville, another gentleman as illustrious as Rudinger, takes the podium, to contradict him by making a catalogue of the inventions that our civilization owes to female talent: "Mlle Auerbach has manufactured a comb that allows liquid to reach the scalp directly, simplifying the work of the hairdresser and the maid and permitting elegant persons to possess combs of different essences; Mlle Koller, thinking of smokers and the ladies who imitate them, invented a new wrapper for cigarettes prepared with compressed rose petals; Mlle Doré discovered a new prop machine for the dance with streamers performed by animals: dogs, monkeys, bears; Mlle Aernount, taking pity upon the unfortunate cyclists who ran over rabbits on badly laid cobblestone streets, planned a home velodrome system; Mlle Gronwald discussed the possibility of an aromatic and antiseptic toothpick with a soluble outer coating; Mme Hakin introduced a kind of tie for rubber clogs that prevents confusing and mismatching of the pairs; Mlle Stroemer..."

Enough! We agree with Luis Vives that no one looks for originality of thought, memory, or liberality in women. Because if you search you'll find extravagant cases like the ones we have just listed or the ones that feminists are ready to carry out at a moment's notice.

Let us not allow ourselves to fall into the old trap of trying to change, by a syllogism or a magic spell, the mutilated man—who according to Saint Thomas is woman—into a whole man. Rather let us insist on another problem, which is that in spite of all the domestic techniques, tactics, and strategies used in all latitudes and in all eras by all men, a woman always tends to be a woman, to spin in her own orbit, to govern herself according to a peculiar, untransferable, irrenouncable system of values.

With a strength that bends to no coercion and a stubborness that no argument can persuade, with a persistence that does not diminish in the face of disaster, woman breaks the models that society proposes and imposes upon her in order to achieve her authentic image and consummate herself—and be consumed—in it.

In order to select oneself and place oneself before others one needs to have reached vitally, emotionally or reflectively what Sartre calls a "limit situation"—a situation that due to its intensity, its dramaticism, or its raw metaphysical density is a point of ultimate desperation.

Nuns that tear down the walls of their cells, like Sor Juana or the Portuguese sister; maidens who scorn the guardians of their chastity in order to burn in love like Melibea;[7] lovers who know that abjection is a mask of true power and that domination is a disguise of incurable weakness like Dorotea and Amelia; married women whom boredom leads to madness like Ana de Ozores or to suicide like Anna Karenina, after passing fruitlessly through adultery; married women like Hedda Gabler or the Marquise de Marteuil, who cold bloodedly destroy all that surrounds them and destroy themselves since nothing is forbidden to them because nothing matters; generous prostitutes like la Pintada; old women to whom time has not added hypocrisy like Celestina;[8] lovers whose impetus overcomes their objective like...like all lovers. Each one in her way and in her own circumstances denies the conventional, making the foundations of the establishment tremble, turning hierarchies upside down and achieving authenticity.

The feat of *becoming what one is* (a feat belonging to the privileged whatever their sex or condition) not only demands the discovery of the essential features beneath the spur of passion, dissatisfaction, or surfeit, but above all the rejection of those false images that false mirrors ofter woman in the enclosed gallery where her life takes place.

Smashing to bits the facile composure of features and actions; tossing our reputations to the dogs; affirming our authority over disgrace, scorn, and even death, such is the road that leads from the strictest solitude to total annihilation.

But there was a moment, a decision, and an act in which woman managed to conciliate her behavior with her most secret desires, with her truest forms, with her ultimate substance. And in that conciliation her existence was inserted at the point in the universe befitting her, proving herself to be necessary, and resplendent with meaning, expression, and beauty.

Translated by Maureen Ahern

NOTES

1. Pygmalion, in Greek mythology, was the king of Cyprus, who sculpted a woman out of stone and then fell in love with her.
2. Castellanos borrowed the term "The Angel in the House" from Virginia Woolf's essay "Professions for Women" (Death of the Moths, 1942). Woolf developed her concept in reaction to a popular Victorian poem of idealized domestic life in a poem by Conventry Patmore (1823–1896). The quote is from Woolf's essay.
3. Iphigenia, in Greek mythology, was the daughter of Clytemnestra and Agamemnon who is sacrificed to the goddess Artemis to save her father's fleet.
4. Castellanos is probably referring ironically to Søren Kierkegaard's (1813–1855) book *Fear and Trembling* (1843), in which he writes of the need for people to make ethical choices on the basis of their desire for personal and religious growth without external criteria; this is called a "leap of faith."
5. Along with Otto Weininger, Arthur Schopenhauer (1788–1860), Georg Simmel (1858–1918), and Paul Moebius (1853–1907) all wrote about women's spiritual, mental, and/or psychological inferiority.
6. The two other "eminent" mysoginists referred to by Castellanos are the German scientist Nicolaus Rudinger (1832–1898) and French writer LeMercier de Neuville (1870–1918). The Spanish Lui Vives (1492–1540) was a Renaissance philosopher noted for his empiricist thinking. His *De disciplines libri xx* (Twenty Books on Discipline, 1531) advocated, among other reforms, education for women.
7. The Portuguese sister is probably Mariana Alcoforado (1640–1723) whose letters to her faithless lover were the inspiration for *New Portuguese Letters*, excerpted in this anthology. Medlibea is the ill-fated lover of Calixto, in the fifteenth century Spanish dialogue novel *La Celestina*, presumed to be by Ferdinand de Rojas (1465–1541).
8. Castellanos is cataloguing here female characters in European literature who, for good or ill, defied traditional codes of female behavior.

Clarice Lispector   *Brazil, 1925–1977*

Lispector is probably the most important modern woman writer of Latin America, and certainly one of the most important of either sex in this century. Known for her strong and innovative use of language as a mode of expressing deep psychological realities, Lispector's novels and short stories have been translated into many languages and she is often anthologized.

Although she by no means wrote solely about women, Lispector's characterization of women in existential dilemmas—for example, "Daydreams of a Drunken Woman" and "In the Name of the Rose" from her most important collection of short stories *Laços de família* (*Family Ties*, 1960)—is brilliant. These portraits give startling dramatizations of individual women's attempts to define their existences within the confines of their family and societal structures. The story that follows is from *Family Ties*.

Lispector was born in the Ukraine, while her family was en route to Brazil from Russia. At 16 she entered law school in Rio, and two years later she married a fellow student. His diplomatic career sent them to Italy, Switzerland, and then the United States. The couple had two sons before they separated in 1959.

Her prizes were many, including the Graça Aranha Prize in 1944 for her first novel *Perto do coração selvagem* (Close to the Savage Heart) and the Carmen Dolores Barbosa Prize in 1961 for *A maçã no escuro* (*The Apple in the Dark*). In 1976 she won first prize in the 10th National Literary Competition for her life contribution to Brazilian literature. A year later she died of cancer.

THE BEGINNINGS OF A FORTUNE
Começos de uma fortuna

It was one of those mornings that seem to be suspended in midair...and which come closest to resembling the image we conceive of time.

The veranda was open but the cool air had congealed outside and nothing entered from the garden, as if any influx of air might disturb the harmony. Only some brightly colored flies had penetrated into the dining room and hovered over the sugar bowl. At this hour, Tijuca was still coming to life.

"If only I had some money..." thought Arthur, and the desire for treasure...to possess peacefully, gave his face a detached and thoughtful expression.

"It's not as if I gamble my money."

"That's enough," his mother replied. "Don't you start that nonsense about money again."

In reality he had no wish to start up any pressing discussion that might end up with a solution. A little of the mortification of last night's dinner when his allowance had been discussed, his father mingling authority with understanding and his mother mingling understanding with basic principles—a little of last night's mortification demanded, meantime, some further discussion. But it was quite useless to pursue, for its own sake, the urgency of the previous day. Each night sleep seemed to respond to all his necessities. And in the morning, in contrast to the adults who got up looking sullen and unshaven, each morning he got up looking younger. His hair was untidy, but not in the same way as his father's disheveled appearance, which suggested that something had happened to him during the night. His mother, too, came out of her room looking bedraggled and still drowsy, as if the bitterness of sleep had given her some satisfaction. Until they drank their coffee they were all irritated or pensive, even the maid. This was not the moment to ask for things. But Arthur felt a quiet compulsion to establish his rights in the morning. Each morning he awakened, it was as if he had to recover the previous day— so completely did sleep sever his bonds each night.

"I neither gamble nor waste my money."

"Arthur!" his mother rebuked him sharply, "I have quite enough problems of my own!"

"What problems?" he inquired with sudden interest.

His mother looked at him coldly as if he were a stranger. Yet he was much more of a relation to her than his father, who, in a manner of speaking, had married into the family. She pursed her lips.

"Everybody has their problems, son," she corrected herself, now entering into a new kind of relationship somewhere between the role of mother and teacher. And from that point onward his mother had taken the day in hand. The suggestion of individuality with which he had awakened had now disappeared, and Arthur knew that he could count on her. From the beginning either they always accepted him or reduced him to being himself. When he was a small child they used to play with him, they threw him into the air, smothered him with kisses. Then suddenly they became "individuals"—they put him down and said kindly but already beyond his reach, "That's enough now," and he throbbed with their caresses and all those peals of laughter still in reserve. He would then become cantankerous, and get under their feet, filled with rage which the same instant would turn to delight, sheer delight, if only they would relent.

"Eat up, Arthur," concluded his mother, and once more he knew that he could count on her. So he immediately became more childish and more difficult.

"I also have my problems but no one takes any notice. When I say that I need money one would think that I were asking for money to drink or gamble."

"Since when has it been suggested that it might be for drinking or gambling?" asked his father, coming into the room and making straight for the head of the table. Whatever next? Such presumption!

He had not reckoned on his father's arrival. Bewildered, but accustomed to such moments, he went on.

"But Dad!" his voice became dissonant in a protest that did not quite amount to indignation. To balance the situation, his mother was already won over, tranquilly stirring her coffee, indifferent to the conversation that did not seem to mean anything other than a few more flies to contend with. She waved them from the sugar bowl with a limp hand.

"It is time you were off," his father interrupted. Arthur turned to his mother. But she was spreading butter on her bread, absorbed and happy. She had escaped again. She would say yes to everything without giving it the slightest importance.

Closing the door, he once again had the impression that they were constantly delivering him to life. That is how the street seemed to receive him. "When I have a wife and children, I'll ring the bell on this side of the door and pay them visits and everything will be different," he thought.

Life outside his home was always completely different. Apart from the difference of light—as if only by going out he could really see what time was doing and what dispositions circumstances had taken during the night— apart from the difference of light there was the difference of his whole manner of existence. When he was little his mother used to say, "Away from home he's an angel and at home a devil."

Even now, going through the little front gate, he had become visibly younger and at the same time less of a child—more sensitive and above all without any matter in hand. But with a docile interest. He was not a person who looked for conversation but if someone asked him as now—"Tell me, son, where is the church?"—he gently came to life, inclined his long neck, because they were always shorter than he, and would guide them, attracted by their question, as if there was an exchange of friendship in this encounter and an open field for investigation. He stood carefully observing the woman turn the corner in the direction of the church, patiently responsible for the route she followed.

"But money is made for spending and you know on what," Charlie insisted vehemently.

"I want it for buying things," he replied somewhat vaguely.

"A little bicycle perhaps?" Charlie smiled offensively, blushing at his own mischief.

Arthur smiled wryly, feeling unhappy.

Seated at his school desk he waited for the teacher to get up. When the latter cleared his throat as a preface to the beginning of the lesson, it was the usual well-known signal for the pupils to sit back, open their eyes attentively and think about nothing in particular.

"About nothing," was Arthur's troubled reply to the teacher who questioned him with visible annoyance. "About nothing" was vaguely about an earlier conversation, about tentative plans to go to the movies that evening, about—about money. He *needed* money. But during class, when he found himself obliged to sit still and free of any responsibility, every desire had relaxation as its basis.

"Didn't it dawn upon you right away that Glorinha wanted to be invited to go to the movies?" Charlie asked him, and both of them looked inquisitively in the direction of the girl who was walking away, her satchel under her arm. Thoughtfully, Arthur walked on at his chum's side, observing the stones on the ground.

"If you haven't got enough money for two tickets, I'll loan it to you and you can pay me back later."

As far as he could see, the moment he had some money he would be obliged to use it for a thousand and one things.

"But afterward I'll have to pay you back and I already owe money to Tony's brother," he replied evasively.

"So what? Where's the problem?" insisted the other, ever practical and persuasive.

"So what," he thought with subdued rage, "so what, well it looks as if the moment somebody has any money, everyone comes on the scene ready to help you spend it, and to show you how to get rid of it."

"It looks," he said, trying to not to show his anger, "it looks as if you only need a few coppers and some woman gets the scent of it and pounces on you."

The two of them suddenly smiled at each other. After this he felt much more relaxed and confident. Above all, he felt less oppressed by circumstances. But soon it was already midday and any desire became more pressing and difficult to bear. All during lunch he savagely thought whether or not he should get into debt, and he felt himself ruined.

"Either he is studying too hard or he doesn't eat enough at breakfast," his mother complained. "The point is that he gets up looking fine but by lunch time he appears with this pale face. Then he starts to look drawn and that's always a bad sign."

"It's nothing serious; naturally he gets tired as the day goes on," replied his father cheerfully. Looking at himself in the mirror in the hall before going out, Arthur recognized that he really had the face of one of those young working lads who always look tired. He smiled without moving his lips, satisfaction showing in the depths of his eyes. But at the theater entrance he had little choice but to ask Charlie for a loan because Glorinha was already there, accompanied by another girl.

"Do you prefer to sit at the front or in the middle?" Glorinha asked.

Confronted with this situation, Charlie paid for the friend and Arthur furtively borrowed the money for Glorinha's ticket.

"Looks as if the outing is ruined," he said in passing to Charlie. Immediately afterward he repented having spoken, since his chum had scarcely heard him, taken up as he was with the other girl. There was no need to lower oneself in the eyes of another chap for whom a session at the movies could only be improved by being with a girl.

In fact, the outing was only ruined at the beginning. Soon afterward his body relaxed, he forgot the presence at his side and became absorbed by the film. Only near the middle was he conscious of Glorinha and with a sudden start watched her secretly. With some surprise, he realized that she was not really the little golddigger he had imagined her to be. Glorinha sat there leaning forward, her mouth attentively open. Relieved, Arthur leaned back again in his seat.

Later, however, he wondered whether he had really been exploited or not. And the anguish was so unbearable that he halted in front of a shop window with an expression of horror. His heart was thumping like a piston. In addition to his frightened face, disembodied in the glass of the window, there were saucepans and kitchen utensils that he looked at with a certain familiarity.

"It looks as if I have been exploited," he resolved, and yet he could not superimpose his anger on Glorinha's innocent profile. Gradually the girl's innocence itself became her major crime: so she was exploiting him, she had exploited him and then sat there thoroughly satisfied with herself watching the film? And his eyes filled with tears. "The ungrateful wretch," he thought, awkwardly choosing a word of accusation. As the word was a symbol of complaint rather than anger, he became a little confused and his anger abated. It now seemed to him, looking at it objectively and freely, that she should have been forced to pay for the movie.

But, confronted by his books and notes closed before him, his face brightened.

He no longer heard the doors that banged, the piano of the woman next door, his mother's voice on the telephone. There was a great silence in the room as if in a vault. And the late afternoon gave the impression of morning. He felt remote...so remote, like a giant on the outside with only his absorbed fingers, which kept on turning a pencil backward and forward, penetrating the room. There were moments when he breathed heavily like an old man. The greater part of the time, however, his face barely came to the surface of the air in the room.

"I've already finished my homework!" he called to his mother, who had questioned the noise of running water. Carefully washing his feet in the bath, he reflected that Glorinha's friend was preferable to Glorinha herself. Nor had he made any attempt to observe if Charlie had or had not "taken advantage" of the other girl. At this idea, he quickly stepped out of the bath and paused in front of the mirror above the wash basin—until the tiled floor chilled his wet feet.

No! He had nothing to explain to Charlie and no one would tell him how to spend whatever money he had, and Charlie could believe that he spent it on bicycles. And if he did— what was wrong with that? And if he should never, but never wish to spend his money? And suppose he were to get richer and richer? What's wrong with that? Are you looking for a fight? You think that...

"You may be lost in your thoughts," his mother said, interrupting him, "but at least eat your dinner and try to make some conversation."

Then, suddenly restored to the family circle, he protested. "You always say that one shouldn't talk at the table, and now you want me to talk; you told me not to speak with my mouth full, now...."

"Mind your manners when you are addressing your mother," his father said without severity.

"Dad," Arthur replied meekly, with furrowed eyebrows, "Dad, what is a promissory note?"

"It looks as if high school is not doing you much good," his father said with quiet satisfaction.

"Eat more potatoes, Arthur," persuaded his mother, vainly trying to draw the two men to herself.

"A promissory note," explained his father, pushing away his plate, "is the following: let us suppose that you are in debt...."

Translated by Giovanni Pontiero

Carmen Martín Gaite   *Spain, b. 1925*

Carmen Martín Gaite was born in Salamanca and grew up during the Spanish Civil War. She holds university degrees from both Salamanca and Madrid, and has lived in the latter city during most of her adult life. In 1980, she was a visiting professor at Barnard College and in 1985 at Vassar College.

Martín Gaite is an experimental writer who has worked in a number of styles and modes ranging from neorealism to existentialism to metafiction. From her earliest works on, however, she has reflected an interest in storytelling and the universal human need for a listener. Ever sensitive to the plight of nonconformists in patriarchal society, she has paid particular attention to the status of women both in her literary texts as well as in her essays and history books.

Since winning the National Literary Prize in 1978 for *El cuarto de atrás* (*The Back Room*, 1978), Martín Gaite has achieved international recognition. Other major works of fiction are *Entre Visillos* (From Behind the Curtains), winner of the Nadal Prize for 1957; *Retahilas* (Threads, 1974); and *El cuento de nunca acabar* (Tale without End, 1983). The following story is from the collection *Las Ataduras* (The Ties, 1960).

A STOP ON THE WAY
Un alto an el camino

The child fell asleep a little before they reached Marseilles. There had been a small disagreement among the passengers because some of them wanted the blue light in the compartment left on and others wanted to turn it off. Finally, the most belligerent advocate of the light, a very proper gentleman who until that discussion had neither opened his mouth nor raised his eyes from a very thick book, took his suitcase down from the overhead rack and departed with a snort. From the doorway he uttered an offended "good night, everyone," and once he had gone the others were quiet, as if indifferent to either resolution.

For a few minutes Emilia continued to watch the door. Facing her, her husband was leaning against the window, breathing noisily; she watched him also.

"If it doesn't matter to you," she summed up timidly, addressing the silhouettes of the other passengers, "let's turn out the light. I'm thinking of the boy, who's not feeling well."

A few people stirred slightly, others nodded agreement and still others made vague sounds. But she had already stood up to turn out the light without waiting for an answer.

"Come on, Esteban dear. That man's gone now, so slide over here and make yourself more comfortable," she could be heard saying in the darkness. "That's the way, on Emilia's lap. See how much room there is? Good, that's better, isn't it....? I'll take off your shoes."

The child was probably about six. He began to cry loudly when he was moved, and his crying, half sleepy and half temperamental, occasioned some protest among the other passengers; there were angry shiftings of position. She bent over until she could touch the ear on that head of straight unruly hair as she settled it in her lap.

"But isn't that better? Of course it is. No, no dear; don't cry now," she whispered. "We're coming to Marseilles soon and your daddy doesn't need to wake up. Emilia doesn't want him to; be quiet so Emilia doesn't cry. You don't want her to cry."

"What's wrong with the boy?" his father asked without opening his eyes.

"Nothing, Gino. He's fine, he's just fine."
She buried her hands in Esteban's hair.

"Hush now and go to sleep for heaven's sake, for heaven's sake..." she said, barely pronouncing the words.

There was a long period of silence.

A little before they reached Marseilles Gino was snoring again. During that time—how long she could not guess—Emilia had held her breath, scrutinizing with wide-open, steady eyes the darkness in front of her where she knew her husband was curled up on the other side of the small wooden table; as if she feared his questions might start again at any moment. Her only movement, which was almost imperceptible, was that of her fingers as they combed and uncombed the boy's hair, and her anxiety was focused so intently in the care she put into those caresses that she could feel a kind of magnetic fluid let down and then flow from the tips of her fingers. Her joints had begun to ache from so much tension when Gino's snores allowed her to relax the stiffness of her position. She could not be certain about the first snores and for this reason she listened to them without moving at all, but then he started in on his fuller, more rhythmic snores which were not so loud, and they reassured her completely. She knew Gino's snores well. In five years she had learned to tell them apart. During her long periods of wakefulness they marked the night's slow steps; at those times she was unable to concentrate on anything but that sound and she was incapable of shaking off her surroundings, which snuffed out any other thoughts. Sometimes she was so frightened by her desire to run away or commit murder that she had to wake him so she would not be alone in the night. But that never helped. Gino would get mad because he had been wakened for no good reason and the next morning she would go to confession: "All night, Father, I was thinking about how I could kill him without him being aware of it; when he snores in a certain way I know that I could do something terrible in our bedroom without him being aware of it at all. Even though I don't want to, I'm obsessed by the knowledge that I could do it."

She stopped caressing Esteban's hair; he had fallen asleep too, and she took a deep breath and shifted to the right very slowly. Now she could open the curtain a little and press her face against the glass. They were getting closer; underneath, the iron wheels were turning, ringing. Vague shapes of trees, of rocks, lights from houses. What time would it be?

Someone lit a match and in its glow she could see there was a face awake, watching her—a woman beside Gino—and she wanted to take advantage of its gaze.

"Do you know if it's much further to Marseilles," she asked.

"A little less than five minutes," answered the passenger who had lit the match.

"Is that all? Thanks very much."

"If it won't bother you, I'm going to put the light on for a minute because I have to get down my luggage," another voice said, and the compartment was filled with a dim light.

"Are you going to Marseilles?" asked the woman who was looking so hard at Emilia.

Emilia could make out her face quite well

now and it reminded her of a lizard's face, although she did not know why. Gino was still sleeping soundly; not even the jostling of the suitcase being lowered had disturbed him. Emilia sighed and leaned toward the woman.

"No, no, I'm not going to Marseilles, but . . ."

She scrutinized the woman's face in order to gauge the amount of curiosity in her question and saw that she was still watching her intently. Yes, she would tell her. It was better to tell someone, to have—in some way—an ally. Gino's snores gave her courage.

". . . but the thing is I'd like to get off for a few minutes if I can," she said in a low voice.

"Of course you can; we stop for at least a quarter of an hour."

Through the gap in the curtain, light began to enter from the houses that the train passed as it puffed and slowed its course. The passenger who was getting off took his suitcase into the corridor and some others also left the compartment. They left the door half-open and from the corridor came the rustle of people preparing to alight. The train was leaving the darkness behind and it was gradually surrounded by widening streets and lights. Lights from windows, lampposts, signs, overhead bulbs found their way into the compartment and a few of them settled on Gino's sleeping face, sliding toward his open mouth. But neither the lights nor the increased murmur of people as the train stopped nor even the dry thud of the stop itself wakened him.

The child, on the other hand, complained and stirred in his sleep, but then he covered his eyes with an elbow and was still again.

Everyone was in the corridor now, but Emilia had not gotten up. She did not look at either father or son, she avoided looking at them as she always did when she was afraid of taking part in something. She knew that she could ruin everything with her eyes—the desire they held was so strong. She directed them now toward a large box that was half-hidden behind her suitcase on the overhead rack.

"Didn't you need to get off?" the woman asked her curiously.

"Yes, thank you, but I don't know. . . . I'm worried about the boy. Since he hasn't been feeling well."

The woman looked at Gino.

"Tell your husband. He is your husband, isn't he?"

"Yes, but no, for heaven's sake; he's asleep, he's tired. I'll forget about it, I can forget about it," she concluded in an anguished tone.

The woman with the lizard face leaned toward her.

"Would you like me to sit over there, in your seat? I can take care of the boy for you, if it's not for very long."

"Oh yes. If you would be so kind. You'd be doing me a big favor, a really big favor. Slide over here carefully."

She got up and gave her seat to the other woman. Esteban's head was lifted up and placed in the new lap, but not so carefully that he didn't open his eyes for an instant.

"Where are you going, Emilia?"

"Be quiet for a minute, to deliver a message; be quiet."

"Who'll take care of me? Where's daddy?"

"You can stay with this lady; she's very nice, very good. And with daddy. But be quiet, daddy's asleep."

"You won't be gone long, Emilia?"

"No! Oh I don't know if I should go," Emilia wavered nervously.

"Please go ahead and don't worry, don't be afraid. I get along well with children."

Emilia climbed up on the seat and carefully lowered the cardboard box, looking constantly at her husband and almost bumping him with the package. The child followed her with his eyes.

"What's the lady's name, Emilia?"

"My name's Juana, dear, Juana. But you shouldn't call your mother Emilia; you should call her mommy."

Emilia waved good-bye without speaking and stepped into the corridor.

"She's not my mother, she's daddy's wife," she could hear Esteban saying.

When Emilia entered the station she was struck by its dizzying swarm of activity. Another train kept her from having a good view of the platforms. Vendors selling drinks, pillows, newspapers were her points of reference for gauging distances and trying to fit so many different people into her eyes. The station was enormous! There would never be enough time. As she walked she could feel the warm circle of the compartment she had just left fade behind her and with it she seemed to be losing her balance and refuge. When she had passed the engine of the stopped train, she discovered four more platforms and she left them behind as well, adding them to the distance that worried her so much. Then she entered a very wide space, from which she could see the exits and she stopped there; setting her package on the ground, she took a wrinkled letter from her purse. There was a small map in the letter and she looked at it: "See," Patri's pointed script explained below, "it's really quite simple. Underneath the Dubonet ad." She raised her eyes to a row of flashing green and red signs. It wasn't there. In broken French she asked directions from a boy who passed by carrying some suitcases and he managed to understand her, although she in turn did not understand him. She felt that he was laughing at her, although it did not matter because just at that moment she had seen the name on the sign light up. The letters wriggled beneath a man waving his arms and sitting astride a huge bottle. Good, that must mean...

"Emilia! Over here, Emilia! What a dummy!"

Was that Patri coming to meet her? But how pretty she looked, how well dressed she was! She hesitated a few minutes and the other woman was hugging and shaking her happily. Yes it was Patri.

"Patri, Patri, sister..."

"How are you? I thought you weren't coming. But come on, don't start crying now. Come on, come over here....Shall we sit down?"

"Yes, of course, whatever you want. You know, I thought I was lost."

Bent over by emotion and smallness she let herself be hugged and led. Patri was a great deal taller, and her strong legs walked confidently on high heels. They sat down in a café crowded with people, next to a stand that sold magazines and newspapers.

"What would you like? Coffee?"

Emilia was listening to the confused names coming over the loudspeaker. She heard the whistle of a locomotive. Would Gino have wakened?

"Fine, coffee with cream. Listen, do you think the train will leave without me?"

"No, for heaven's sake. Don't start rushing things. We can sit and relax here for at least ten minutes. I just asked."

Emilia smiled through her tears. She put the box on her knees and a few of the tears slid down her cheeks and fell on the cardboard as she untied the string.

"Please don't cry now."

"I've brought this for you."

"What is it? Give it to me."

"Nothing much. You can open it at home, later. It's some lingerie they make at Gino's factory."

"Lingerie. That's great! Yes, give it to me. Of course I'd rather open it at home."

"The slips are especially pretty. I brought you two of them. I think they're your size. Although you do look heavier."

"Heavier? Don't depress me."

"No, you look terrific like that. You look wonderful. You even look younger."

"It's not likely I look younger, dear, after five years. It has been five years hasn't it?" Emilia nodded yes. "Those five years sure show on you. You're really a wreck."

Their coffee came. Patri crossed her legs and took out a silver cigarette case. She held it out to Emilia who shook her head no.

"Why don't you take care of yourself a little better?" Patri asked, looking at Emilia while she lit her cigarette. "You look tired. Things aren't going well for you, are they?"

"Yes. Yes, they are....It's because of the trip."

"Go on, I know you. How can things be going well for you with that man. You were crazy to fall for him, dear; forgive me for saying that."

"Don't start, Patri. Why would you say a thing like that to me?"

"What do you mean, why would I say a thing like that? Because I've never understood it. A person saddles herself with another woman's child, and who knows what else, when she doesn't know what she's getting into. But you knew well enough what he was like because of poor Anita. She probably died of bitterness."

"I love Gino, even though you might not understand that. He's a good person."

"Good? Well, surely you can't say the way he treats me is good when he doesn't even let me write to you. Come on now, you can't say that's kind. Two sisters who've always been alone, and knowing how much you care about me. Just let him explain why we've not been able to see each other for five years, why the last time I was in Barcelona he was watching you so close you couldn't even give me a hug."

Patri had put out her cigarette with an angry gesture. Emilia lowered her eyes and there was a silence. Then she said with effort:

"It's that you also..."

"What about me?"

"Nothing." Her voice came out timid, fearful of offending. "Well, the life you lead isn't likely to please anyone. Since you left Barcelona, he's heard people say things, things about you, and they're always the same things.

So that you also...put yourself in his place."

"But what does he care? What kind of life does he lead? I'm sure I'm no worse than some of the girlfriends he's had. Forgive me, things might be different now, but he's always had girlfriends."

"He doesn't like you," Emilia said dejectedly. "But it's an impossible situation because you also refuse to see any good in him."

"It's just that I can't stand people like him. I might be a whore, dear, but everyone knows it. I can't stand people who don't practice what they preach.... Forgive me, stop crying. I'm such a creep. But you see I can't stand it when he mistreats you. And I know he does, you're telling me now. I can see it written on your face."

"I'm telling you he doesn't," Emilia protested weakly.

"I wish that were true."

"Besides I have the boy. Gino's always telling him that I'm not his mother, and he does the right thing when you think about it. But I love him as if I were his mother. And he loves me."

Patri looked at her sister's bent profile and listened to her sad warm voice.

"And you, sister, who wouldn't love you. You deserve a prince, the best in this world."

"We aren't meant to be happy in this world, Patri; I've always told you that."

"Be quiet, Emilia, and stop telling me stories. If you could see how I live now. Like a queen. I have everything. A little house... How I wish you could come and see it."

"I'm happy for you. Are you still living with that Michel?"

"Yes. He's been with me a year. He wanted to come and meet you, but I didn't want him to. We can talk better like this, don't you think so?"

"Yes. Do you have any pictures?"

Patri began to rummage in her purse. She looked happy as she rooted through her things. She pulled out three tiny photos and showed them to her sister. The two of them were together on all three. Michel was young and smiling. One photo was taken in the country and they were kissing against a tree trunk.

"He's good-looking. Who took the pictures?"

"It's a camera that takes pictures by itself. Do you really think he's cute?"

"Yes, very cute. And he seems to be in love with you."

"Yes he does love me, Emilia," Patri said enthusiastically. "He really loves me. If it weren't for his mother we'd get married."

"Really?" Emilia asked and her face lit up suddenly. "My God, Patri, do you think you might? That would be wonderful for you. Why don't you give me his mother's address? I can write to her if you want; I'd be happy to. I can tell her what a wonderful person you are."

Patri burst out laughing loudly.

"Come on, Emilia, don't say such things. Who'd want me for a daughter-in-law? You'd do better to make a novena and pray she kicks the bucket soon."

"If she knew you, she'd love you as much as I do."

"I doubt it. And besides it doesn't matter to us. We couldn't be any happier. This way, when we get tired of each other, the door's open. Don't give me that look."

"I'm not giving you any look."

"If you could see what a dreamy little house. With my own refrigerator and everything. Two bedrooms. It's close by, right near the station. Are you sure there isn't time for you to go see it with me?"

Emilia jumped up and looked at the lighted clock at the back of the station. How would she find her train?

"Listen, Patri, I can't; it would be impossible for me to leave. I have to go. How long have we been here?"

"You're right, probably ten minutes have passed. But don't rush. You have time."

"No, no; I don't have time. It's far to my train. Hurry up and kiss me goodbye, for God's sake."

"Wait 'til I pay and I'll go with you."

"No, really I can't wait. If I don't run now, I'll miss it for sure."

"You're going to Milan, aren't you? To see Gino's family."

"Yes. I think it's on the fourth platform. I have to go, Patri, I have to go."

"Don't get so nervous. A person can't live like that, as nervous as you are. Hey, waiter, do you know when the train for Italy leaves?"

The waiter said something very fast while he was picking up their cups.

"My God, what did he say?"

"That it's probably about to leave right now, in a couple of minutes."

"Oh no! A couple of minutes!"

She embraced her sister hurredly and slid from her arms like a rabbit. Patri tried to stop her, telling her to wait, but all Emilia did was turn tearfully, wave her arm, stumble into a porter and finally disappear into the crowd, running at full speed.

She ran wildly, as fast as she could. Counting. Up to sixty makes one minute. Then another sixty, and that would be all. Fifty three...It was really far. Her sides hurt from running. There was a noise as something fell to the ground. An earring. She did not know whether to stop and look for it or go on; she cast a quick glance and didn't see it. One of the earrings from the wedding. Dear God. A hundred fourteen...If she missed the train she'd go back and look for it. She started to run again. The loudspeaker belowed its nasal words.

"The train to Italy?"

"*Celui-là. Il est en train de partir.*"*

She ran even faster and reached the last car, which was already moving. At the risk of falling, she started to climb up. Someone held out a hand.

"Thanks. Is this second class?"

"No, first."

She took a deep breath and leaned against a window. The platforms began to move, taking the people with them. Everything blurred, danced through her tears.

"Don't you feel well, miss?"

"Yes, I'm fine; thank you."

She started to walk. It was a very long train. The passageways between the cars were like quivering tunnels, and in each car she peered into the compartments. From the narrow entrance to her own corridor, she could see Gino leaning from a window; half of his body was sticking out and he was looking down onto the platform. She dried her tears and her legs shook as she approached him. She reached his side just as they were leaving the station and he was drawing in from the window with a worried expression.

"Idiot, you idiot," he said when he saw her, clenching his fists. "How could anyone do the things you do? You sneak off like a thief, leaving the boy in the arms of the first stranger that comes along."

"Be quiet, Gino, don't get mad. I went to the restroom."

"Liar. I know you got off. And I know why."

"Be quiet, Gino, don't make a scene right now."

"Yes I will make a scene, because I feel like it. Anything at all to see that woman. Because you're just like her, and you couldn't live without seeing her."

Emilia pulled open the door to their compartment and went in, stepping over legs in the dark. The woman had already gone back to her own seat and Esteban was huddled against the window, whimpering. She took him in her arms.

"Emilia's here now, darling; don't cry sweetheart."

"He's cried the whole time," Gino said in a harsh voice as he settled into the seat facing hers, "but a lot you cared about him then. You were spellbound listening to that bitch, that slut."

"Daddy, don't scold Emilia; don't scold her, daddy. She's back now."

"Please Gino, don't make Esteban cry, poor thing. You'll be able to say anything you want when we get there. Tomorrow."

"Don't talk about the boy, you hypocrite, the boy means nothing to you," he insisted, beside himself.

Several passengers asked them to be quiet and Gino turned rudely toward his corner, still muttering insults. Emilia's eyes met the eyes of the woman across from her and she nodded a gesture of thanks. Then she settled Esteban in her lap in the same position as before and began to kiss his eyes and hair. She looked again at the familiar, unfriendly compartment, which felt like a coffin to her and at the passengers who all seemed stuffed, petrified in their positions. The train began to move faster as it left Marseilles. They passed quite close to the wall of a building with many windows. Emilia rested her head against the glass. More windows in another wall. She watched them recede. Some were lighted and she could catch glimpses of life inside them. Any one of them could be Patri's. The walls and windows continued a bit longer and were eventually lost to view. The train picked up speed quickly, whistling as it headed into the dark countryside.

Translated by Carol Maier

NOTE

* That one over there. It's about to leave.

Flannery O'Connor   *US, 1925–1964*

An only child, Flannery O'Connor was born in Savannah, Georgia. She graduated from what is now Georgia State College in 1945 and, during a brief stay outside the South, earned an M.F.A. in creative writing at the University of Iowa in 1947, followed by stints at Yaddo, the artists' colony, and in New York City, before returning for good to her mother's birthplace, Milledgeville, Georgia. By 1950, the year she was disabled by lupus, a disease that had killed her father nine years earlier and that would kill her at the age of 39, she had published six stories. The disease challenged her deeply felt Catholicism and transformed her writing, bringing to the fore the existential problem of life and death. "Death," she said, "has always been brother to my imagination." Her writing may be described as Christian grotesque, for in it, opposites are not reconciled, wholeness is not achieved. On the contrary, O'Connor believed that "in us the good is something under construction."

Her first, novel, *Wise Blood* (1952), was received uneasily. Hazel Motes, a paradoxical religious fanatic, sets out to free men from their enslavement to Christ; in the process Motes, in order "to see," blinds himself with lye and becomes a strange, modern version of Christ. In the title story of *A Good Man Is Hard to Find* (1955), another of O'Connor's southern "Christ-haunted" outsiders, the Misfit, a murderous but thoughtful convict, ponders the proposition, as his gang shoots an innocent family in the woods, that there is "no pleasure in life but meanness." Jammed between the possiblity of Christ's existence and the probability of his nonexistence, these characters' obsession with religion takes the ironic form of denying its validity.

In 1959 O'Connor won a Ford Foundation grant and the following year published her second novel, *The Violent Bear It Away*, a tale of atheists and grotesque religious fanatics. *Everything That Rises Must Converge*, published posthumously, features several stories about the conflict between complacent parents and distorted children. Her *Complete Stories* (1972) received the National Book Award, and her stories are seen by many as the most rewarding expression of her art.

A neglected aspect of her work are O'Connor's letters. By her infirmity sentenced to a sedentary life, O'Connor secured a large correspondence with other writers, translators, critics, publishers, friends, and strangers. It constitutes what one critic has called an "epistolary autobiography." *A Habit of Being* (1979) is a major but incomplete selection of her letters edited by her friend Sally Fitzgerald. Another important group can be found in the 1966 edition of *The Added Dimension: The Art and Mind of Flannery O'Connor*, edited by Lewis Lawson and Melvin. J. Friedman. The letters reveal an O'Connor surprisingly different from the author of the fiction, and surprisingly joyful. They also do much to illuminate the artist's literary apprenticeship and literary influence as well as to show the force of Catholicism in O'Connor's life, thought, and writings. Among the samples included here are those to Fitzgerald, to fellow artists, critic Elizabeth Hardwick (Lowell) the poet Robert Lowell, and Maryat Lee, and to "A," an anonymous friend and ten-year correspondent, whom O'Connor never met. The letters themselves show a charming disregard for spelling and grammar and their cadence also shows O'Connor's wry humor, from which neither her mother, Regina, with whom she lived, nor she herself, is exempt.

O'Connor claimed that southern writers wrote about freaks because they could still recognize one. Much criticism has focused on O'Connor's contribution to both the southern literary tradition and that of the grotesque, as well as on her connection with religious writers and thinkers. Dorothy Walters' book (1973) is a helpful introduction, as are those by Gilbert H. Muller and Mike Orvell (both published in 1972).

Eric Mendelsohn

SELECTED LETTERS

TO SALLY AND ROBERT FITZGERALD

Milledgeville
1/25/53

My first issue of *Kenyon Review* came yestiddy and I felt very learned sitting down reading it. There was a chapter of a novel by Randall Jarrell [*Pictures from an Institution*] in it. I suppose you would say it was good Randall Jarrell but it wasn't good fiction. It was of the School of Mary [McCarthy]. The *Kenyon Review* sent me a thoouusand bucks the other day, no note, no nothing; just the dough. My kinfolks think I am a commercial writer now and really they are proud of me. My uncle Louis [Cline] is always bringing me a message from somebody at [his company] who has read *Wise Blood*. The last was: ask her why she don't write about some nice people. Louis says, I told them you wrote what *paid*. There was another message from "the brains of [his] company." He said, yeah it was a good book well written and all that but tell her the next time to write about some rich folks, I'm mighty tired of reading about poor folks...

My mamma has been dickering (negotiating) with [a new farm family] to take the [former farm help's] place. Old man P. looked like he might have had an ancestor back a couple of centuries ago who was at least a decayed gentleman (he wouldn't wear overalls; only khaki) but these...look like they've been joined up with the human race for only a couple of months now. Mrs. W. says she went to school for one day and didn't loin nothin and ain't went back. She has four children and I thought she was one of them. The oldest girl is 14 with a mouth full of snuff. The first time I saw her she had long yellow hair and the next time it was short in an all-over good-for-life permanent and Regina says—they were standing outside the car and we were in—"I see you have a new permanent." "Got it Sad-day," she says and then another pair of hands and eyes pulls up on the window of the car and says, "I'm gonter git me mine next Sad-day." Mam-

ma has one too. I was all set for [them] but he traded with the sawmill man instead of Regina. I hope he gets tired of it and quits though.

The Notre Dame business sounds very good to me. I had some friends who were there and were crazy about it. I visited them but I didn't get to see the university. If sometime next summer proves convenient for you to have me visit you, I would like to come if I am well; but I imagine you will have a crowded schedule, as your prospective children don't always travel by the doctor's clock. If my presence would be convenient at any particular time, I would be pleased to try to manage to have it on hand. My mamma is none too favorable toward any kind of travel for me, or at least nothing longer than two weeks she says, because you know who has to do the nursing when you get sick; and I do. However, I think I will go to New York anyways sometime next summer if it ain't but to spend the week. I am doing fairly well these days, though I am practically bald-headed on top and have a watermelon face. I think that this is going to be permanent. There is another lady in town now with lupus. She went to the hospital a couple of weeks ago and couldn't open her hands but now she is full of ACTH and up cooking her dinner. Now that I know I have the stuff I can take care of myself a lot better. I stay strictly out of the sun and strictly do not take any exercise. No great hardship.

2/1/53

The Maple Oats really send me. I mean they are a heap of improvement over saltless oatmeal, horse biscuit, stewed Kleenex, and the other delicacies that I have been eating. They send Regina too but I think it is because they smell like what the cows here eat. We are going to get Louis to see if he can get them in Atlanta for us. I also like the O'Faoláin[1] book but I like all he writes that I have seen.

The enclosed is a poem. I tell you this. The Poetry Society of Georgia (a social outfit) is offering 50 bucks for one and I thought I would bite but I would like to know first if it works, as they say. Beinst as your occupation is properly poetry, please let me know. This is my first and last. I think it is a filthy habit for a fiction writer to get into. The novel seems to be doing very well. I have a nice gangster of 14 in it named Rufus Florida Johnson. Much more in my line.

My mamma and I have interesting literary discussions like the following which took place over some Modern Library books that I had just ordered:

SHE: "*Mobby Dick*. I've always heard about that."

ME: "*Mow-by Dick*."

SHE: "*Mow-by Dick. The Idiot*.[2] You would get something called *Idiot*. What's it about?"

ME: "An idiot."

I am sending you a subscription to something called the *Shenandoah* that is put out at Washington and Lee University. I told them to begin it with the autumn issue that has a review in it of my book by a man named Brainard Cheney. It also has a review of *The Old Man and the Sea* by Wm. Faulkner, the review I mean, that is nice. He says that Hemingway discovered God the Creator in this one. What part I like in that was where the fish's eye was like a saint in a procession; it sounded to me like he was discovering something new maybe for him.

The Peacock Roosts

The clown-faced peacock
Dragging sixty suns
Barely looks west where
The single one
Goes down in fire.

Bluer than moon-side sky
The trigger head
Circles and backs.
The folded forest squats and flies
The ancient design is raised.

Gripped oak cannot be moved.
This bird looks down
And settles, ready.
Now the leaves can start the wind
That combs these suns

Hung all night in the gold-green silk wood
Or blown straight back until
The single one
Mounting the grey light
Will see the flying forest
Leave the tree and run.

TO ELIZABETH AND ROBERT LOWELL

17 March 1953

I'm glad you liked the story. That is my contribution to Mother's Day throughout the land. I felt I ought to do something like Senator Pappy O'Daniels. He conducted the Light Crust Dough Boys over the radio every Mother's Day and recited an original poem. One went: "I had a mother. I had to have. I lover whether she's good or bad. I lover whether she's live or dead. Whether she's an angel or a old dope head." You poets express yourselves so well in so little space.

I suppose Iowa City is very restful after Europe, it being naturally blank. I always liked it in spite of those sooty tubercular-looking houses. When I was there there was a zoo with two indifferent bears in it and a sign over them that said: "These lions donated by the Iowa City Elks Club." But they had a good collection of game bantams that I used to go and admire, and I admired that electric railroad car that ran to Cedar Rapids.

I am making out fine in spite of any conflicting stories. I have a disease called lupus and I take a medicine called ACTH and I manage well enough to live with both. Lupus is one of those things in the rheumatic department; it comes and goes, when it comes I retire and when it goes, I venture forth. My father had it some twelve or fifteen years ago but at that time there was nothing for it but the undertaker; now it can be controlled with the ACTH. I have enough energy to write with and as that is all I have any business doing anyhow, I can with one eye squinted take it all as a blessing. What you have to measure out, you come to observe closer, or so I tell myself.

Last summer I went to Connecticut to visit the Fitzgeralds and smuggled three live ducks over Eastern Airlines for their children, but I have been inactive criminally since then. My mother and I live on a large place and I have bought me some peafowl and sit on the back steps a good deal studying them. I am going to be the World Authority on Peafowl, and I hope to be offered a chair some day at the Chicken College.

TO "A."

20 July 55

I am very pleased to have your letter. Perhaps it is even more startling to me to find someone who recognizes my work for what I try to make it than it is for you to find a God-conscious writer near at hand. The distance is 87 miles but I feel the spiritual distance is shorter.

I write the way I do because (not though) I am a Catholic. This is a fact and nothing covers it like the bald statement. However, I am a Catholic peculiarly possessed of the modern consciousness, that thing Jung[3] describes as unhistorical, solitary, and guilty. To possess this *within* the Chuch is to bear a burden, the necessary burden for the conscious Catholic. It's to feel the contemporary situation at the ultimate level. I think that the Church is the only thing that is going to make the terrible world we are coming to endurable; the only thing that makes the Church endurable is that it is somehow the body of Christ and that on this we are fed. It seems to be a fact that you have to suffer as much from the Church as for

it but if you believe in the divinity of Christ, you have to cherish the world at the same time that you struggle to endure it. This may explain the lack of bitterness in the stories.

The notice in the *New Yorker* was not only moronic, it was unsigned. It was a case in which it is easy to see that the moral sense has been bred out of certain sections of the population, like the wings have been bred off certain chickens to produce more white meat on them. This is a generation of wingless chickens, which I suppose is what Nietzsche meant when he said God was dead.[4]

I am mighty tired of reading reviews that call *A Good Man* brutal and sarcastic. The stories are hard but they are hard because there is nothing harder or less sentimental than Christian realism. I believe that there are many rough beasts now slouching toward Bethlehem to be born[5] and that I have reported the progress of a few of them, and when I see these stories described as horror stories I am always amused because the reviewer always has hold of the wrong horror.

You were were kind to write me and the measure of my appreciation must be to ask you to write me again. I would like to know who this is who understands my stories.

9 August 55

I have thought of Simone Weil in connection with you almost from the first and I got out this piece I enclose and reread it and the impression was not lessened. In the face of anyone's experience, someone like myself who has had almost no experience, must be humble. I will never have the experience of the convert, or of the one who fails to be converted, or even in all probability of the formidable sinner; but your effort not to be seduced by the Church moves me greatly. God permits it for some reason though it is the devil's greatest work of hallucination. Fr. [Jean] de Menasce told somebody not to come into the Church until he felt it would be an enlargement of his freedom. That is what you are doing and you are right, but do not make your feeling of the voluptuous seductive powers of the Church into a hard shell to protect yourself from her. I suppose it is like marriage, that when you get into it, you find it is the beginning, not the end, of the struggle to make love work.

I think most people come to the Church by means the Church does not allow, else there would be no need their getting to her at all. However, this is true inside as well, as the operation of the Church is entirely set up for the sinner; which creates much misunderstanding among the smug.

I suppose I read Aristotle in college but not to know I was doing it; the same with Plato. I don't have the kind of mind that can carry such beyond the actual reading, i.e., total non-retention has kept my education from being a burden to me. So I couldn't make any judgment on the *Summa*,[6] except to say this: I read it for about twenty minutes every night before I go to bed. If my mother were to come in during this process and say, "Turn off that light. It's late," I with lifted finger and broad bland beatific expression, would reply, "On the contrary, I answer that the light, being eternal and limitless, cannot be turned off. Shut your eyes," or some such thing. In any case, I feel I can personally guarantee that St. Thomas loved God because for the life of me I cannot help loving St. Thomas. His brothers didn't want him to waste himself being a Dominican and so locked him up in a tower and introduced a prostitute into his apartment; her he ran out with a red-hot poker. It would be fashionable today to be in sympathy with the woman, but I am in sympathy with St. Thomas.

I don't know B.R. well, but he came out here one evening and had dessert with us. I have a friend who is very fond of him and so I hear a lot about him and his troubles, of which he seems to be so well supplied that it's a miracle he's still alive. My impression was that he was a very fine and a very proud man. When he was sick about a year ago, I sent him

a copy of St. Bernard's[7] letters and in thanking me, he said he was an agnostic. You are right that he's an anachronism. I guess, strangely cut-off anyway. I wrote to my friend who is so fond of him that perhaps he might be sent something to read that would at least set him thinking in a wider direction, but I am afraid this filled the poor girl with apprehension, she thinking I would probably produce Cardinal Newman[8] or somebody. I had had in mind Gabriel Marcel[9] whose Gifford Lectures I had just read. This girl is a staunch and excellent Presbyterian with a polite horror of anything Romish.

I am highly pleased you noticed the shirts, though it hadn't occurred to me that they suggested the lack of hairshirts. I am chiefly exercised by the hero rampant on the shirt and the always somewhat-less occupying it. This is funny to me. The only embossed one I ever had had a fierce-looking bulldog on it with the word GEORGIA over him. I wore it all the time, it being my policy at that point in life to create an unfavorable impression. My urge for such has to be repressed, as my mother does not approve of making a spectacle of oneself when over thirty.

I have some long and tall thoughts on the subject of God's working through nature, but I will not inflict them on you now. I find I have a habit of announcing the obvious in pompous and dogmatic periods. I like to forget that I'm only a storyteller. Right now I am trying to write a lecture that I have been invited to deliver next spring in Lansing, Mich. to a wholesale gathering of the AAUW [American Association of University Women]. I am trying to write this thing on the justification of distortion in fiction, call it something like "The Freak in Modern Fiction." Anyway, I have it borne in on me that my business is to write and not talk about it. I have ten months to write the lecture in and it is going to take every bit of it. I don't read much modern fiction. I have never read Nelson Algren[10] that you mention. I feel lumpish.

TO "A."

28 August 55

I wish St. Thomas were handy to consult about the fascist business. Of course this word doesn't really exist uncapitalized, so in making it that way you have the advantage of using a word with a private meaning and a public odor: which you must not do. But if it does mean a doubt of the efficacy of love and if this is to be observed in my fiction, then it has to be explained or partly explained by what happens to conviction (I believe love to be efficacious in the loooong run) when it is translated into fiction designed for a public with a predisposition to believe the opposite. This along with the limitations of the writer could account for the negative appearance. But find another word than fascist, for me and St. Thomas too. And totalitarian won't do either. Both St. Thomas and St. John of the Cross, dissimilar as they were, were entirely united by the same belief. The more I read St. Thomas the more flexible he appears to me. Incidentally, St. John would have been able to sit down with the prostitute and said, "Daughter, let us consider this," but St. Thomas doubtless knew his own nature and knew that he had to get rid of her with a poker or she would overcome him. I am not only for St. Thomas here but am in accord with his use of the poker. I call this being tolerantly realistic, not being a fascist.

Another reason for the negative appearance: if you live today you breathe in nihilism. In or out of the Church, it's the gas you breathe. If I hadn't had the Church to fight it with or to tell me the necessity of fighting it, I would be the stinkingest logical positivist[11] you ever saw right now. With such a current to write against, the result almost has to be negative. It does well just to be.

Then another thing, what one has as a born Catholic is something given and accepted before it is experienced. I am only slowly coming to experience things that I have all along accepted. I supposed the fullest writing comes from what has been accepted and experienced both and that I have just not got that far yet all the time. Conviction without experience makes for harshness.

The magazine that had the piece on Simone Weil is called *The Third Hour* and is put out spasmodically (when she can get the money) by a Russian lady named Helene Iswolsky who teaches at Fordham. I used to go with her nephew so I heard considerable about it and ordered some back issues. The old lady is a Catholic of the Eastern Rite persuasion and sort of a one-man Catholic ecumenical movement. The enclosed of Edith Stein[12] came out of there too. I've never read anything E. Stein wrote. None of it that I know of has been translated. There is a new biography by Hilda Graef but I have not seen it. My interest in both of them comes only from what they have done, which overshadows anything they may have written. But I would very much like you to lend me the books of Simone Weil's when you get through with them...

Mrs. Tate is Caroline Gordon Tate, the wife of Allen Tate. She writes fiction as good as anybody, though I have not read much of it myself. They, with John Crowe Ransom and R.P. Warren, were prominent in the '20s in that group at Vanderbilt that called itself the Fugitives. The Fugitives are now here there and yonder. Anyway Mrs. Tate has taught me a lot about writing.

Which brings me to the embarrassing subject of what I have not read and been influenced by. I hope nobody ever asks me in public. If so I intend to look dark and mutter, "Henry James Henry James"—which will be the veriest lie, but no matter. I have not been influenced by the best people. The only good things I read when I was a child were the Greek and Roman myths which I got out of a set of child's encyclopedia called *The Book of Knowledge*. The rest of what I read was Slop with a capital S. The Slop period was followed by the Edgar Allan Poe period which lasted for years and consisted chiefly in a volume called

The Humerous Tales of E.A. Poe. These were mighty humerous—one about a young man who was too vain to wear his glasses and consequently married his grandmother by accident; another about a fine figure of a man who in his room removed wooden arms, wooden legs, hair piece, artificial teeth, voice box, etc. etc.; another about the inmates of a lunatic asylum who take over the establishment and run it to suit themselves. This is an influence I would rather not think about. I went to a progressive high school where one did not read if one did not wish to; I did not wish to (except the *Humerous Tales* etc.). In college I read works of social-science, so-called. The only thing that kept me from being a social-scientist was the grace of God and the fact that I couldn't remember the stuff but a few days after reading it.

I didn't really start to read until I went to Graduate School and then I began to read and write at the same time. When I went to Iowa I had never heard of Faulkner, Kafka, Joyce, much less read them. Then I began to read everything at once, so much so that I didn't have time I suppose to be influenced by any one writer. I read all the Catholic novelists, Mauriac, Bernanos, Bloy, Greene, Waugh; I read all the nuts like Djuna Barnes and Dorothy Richardson and Va. Woolf (unfair to the dear lady of course); I read the best Southern writers like Faulkner and the Tates, K.A. Porter, Eudora Welty and Peter Taylor; read the Russians, not Tolstoy so much but Dostoevsky, Tugenev, Chekhov and Gogol. I became a great admirer of Conrad and have read almost all his fiction. I have totally skipped such people as Dreiser, Anderson (except for a few stories) and Thomas Wolfe. I have learned something from Hawthorne, Flaubert, Balzac and something from Kafka, though I have never been able to finish one of his novels. I've read almost all of Henry James—from a sense of High Duty and because when I read James I feel something is happening to me, in slow motion but happening nevertheless. I admire Dr. Johnson's *Lives of the Poets.* But always

the largest thing that looms up is *The Humerous Tales of Edgar Allan Poe.* I am sure he wrote them all while drunk too.

I have more to say about the figure of Christ as merely human but this has gone on long enough and I will save it. Have you read Romano Guardini?...In my opinion there is nothing like [his book, *The Lord*][13] anywhere, certainly not in this country. I can lend it to you if you would like to see it.

TO MARYAT LEE[14]

19 May 57

Greetings from historic Milledgeville where the ladies and gents wash in separate tubs. Are you sure you haven't caught anything; what I mean is, the blood disease and all, what I mean is there are certain advantages to being stiff-necked? Unadaptability is often a virtue. If I were in Japan, I would be pretty high by the time I left out of there as I wouldn't have washed during the trip. My standard is: when in Rome, do as you done in Milledgeville.

Last Friday week I stood in a receiving line with your brother and sister-in-law for a good hour, pressing the soggy paws of citizens from all over the state who have daughters in college. Your sister-in-law is a whiz bang at it. The guests had their names pinned on them and she never failed to see the name and say it. As for me, my eye was as glazed as the one on the fish served to Mr. K. by the Shinnahon Lines...

Well, you have a decision in front of you if you have to decide whether you will live your whole life with a man. I am sure it requires a metamorphosis for anybody and cannot be done without grace. My prayers are unfeeling but habitual, not to say dogged, and I do include you in them.

I hope you understand that it is not the tooth of the saber-toothed tiger I want, it is the *tiger.* I don't care if it's a old toothless tiger or not, just so it's alive. I intend to start a zoo.

NOTES

1. O'Faoláin, Sean (b. 1900): Irish writer best known for his stories about his country collected in *Midsummer*

Night Madness (1932), *The Heat of the Sun* (1966), and *The Talking Trees* (1971).

2. The book (1868) by the Russian novelist Dostoevsky (1821–1881) concerns a Christ figure whose effect on those around him is tragic.

3. Carl Jung (1875–1961): Swiss psychologist, former disciple of Freud, who became increasingly concerned with the unconscious as a repository of collective meanings, or archetypes.

4. The anti-Christian German philosopher announced this frequently, most famously in *Die frohliche Wissenschaft*, 1882.

5. The last line of "The Second Coming" by the Irish poet William Butler Yeats (1865–1939).

6. *Summa Theologica* (1267–1273) is the major work of one of the greatest figures of the medieval Catholic church, St. Thomas Aquinas (1225–1274). It is a systematic exposition of Christian theology based on the principles of scholasticism and seeks to distinguish two separate and harmonious realms, that of faith and that of science.

7. St. Bernard of Clairvaux (1090?–1153). French clergyman and Doctor of the Church, he founded the Cistercian monastery and preached in the Second Crusade; his views known as *devotio moderna* stress saintliness rather than intellectuality as the means to spiritual progress.

8. John Henry Newman (1801–1890): Englishman responsible for a revival of Catholicism in England known as the Oxford Movement, after his own conversion from Anglicanism. His *Apologia pro vita sua* (1864) is a masterpiece of religious autobiography and his *Idea of a University* (1873) is a classic expression of the importance of a liberal education.

9. Gabriel Marcel (1889?–n.d.): French philosopher, dramatist, and critic: the leading exponent of Christian Existentialism, he introduced the work of the Danish philosopher Søren Kierkegaard to France. In 1969 he won the Prix Goncourt for his novel *Creezy*.

10. Nelson Algren (1909–1981): a neonaturalist writer and member of the Chicago school of realists, whose best novel, *The Man with the Golden Arm* (1949), about dope addiction was made into a film, as was his *A Walk on the Wild Side* (1956); one-time friend and traveling companion of Simone de Beauvoir.

11. One belonging to the philosophical school that rejects metaphysics and believes that only scientifically verifiable statements are meaningful.

12. Edith Stein (1891–1942): a Jewish-born Carmelite nun who died at Auschwitz in the Holocaust, having been seized in a convent in Echt, the Netherlands, by the Nazis and taken there together with her sister, also a Catholic convert. She had sought unsuccessfully to win the support of Pope Pius XI for the defense of the Jews in 1933; in 1987, she was beatified by Pope John Paul II.

13. A life of Christ published in 1937 by the German Catholic philosopher using the insights and method of phenomenology, to apprehend Christ as "pure presence," it is considered a classic by Catholic critics.

14. Maryat Lee (b. 1926): Kentucky-born black dramatist, author of *Dope* (1965) and *Four Men and a Monster* (1969), and founder of the Soul and Latin Theater (1968–1970) in New York City.

Sonja Åkesson   *Sweden, 1926–1977*

Born in Buttle on the Baltic Island of Gotland, where her father was a station master, Sonja Åkesson received only the compulsory six years of education, after which she had to support herself with various occupations, from nursemaid to telephone operator. She married young, had two children, left her husband, and moved with her children to Stockholm. She remarried, and started to write poetry and short stories, after having taken a few classes in "creative writing" at the Stockholm University Extension. After a second divorce, she married the poet Jarl Hammarberg (b. 1940) and published, together with him, two collections of poetry: *Strålande dikter/nej så fan heller* (Splendid Poems/Certainly Not, 1967) and *Kändis* (A Celebrity, 1969), and one play *Hå! vi är på väg* (Ho! We're on Our Way, 1972).

At the time of this collaboration, Sonja Åkesson was already an established poet in Sweden, having made her breakthrough with the collection *Husfrid* (Domestic Peace, 1963), which portrays a housewife trapped at home, unhappy and frustrated. In a poetic style called the "new simplicity" in Sweden, Åkesson created a sensualism that manifested itself in detailed descriptions of trivial, everyday objects and a concentration on the power of language to evoke sights and sounds. Her metaphors are as concrete as objects in a surrealistic painting. Her two most famous poems are included in *Husfrid*: "Vara vit mans slav," (Be White Man's Slave), which became the fighting song of the radical feminist movement in Sweden during the 1960s, and "Självbiografi" (Autobiography), a paraphrase of and reply to the American poet Lawrence Ferlinghetti's (b. 1919) "Autobiography" in *A Coney Island of the Mind* (1958). It is a deliberate attempt to show the other side, to create a dialogue between male and female points of view, to show the differences in the real-life situations of a man and a woman living in essentially the same kind of society during the same period of time. In her later prose and poetry, from the mid-1960s until her death, Åkesson continued to write in an even more confessional style, describing her own alcoholism, drug addiction, and nervous breakdowns.

Named the "national poet of the welfare state," Åkesson enjoyed great popularity during her lifetime. Because of her extraordinary ability to depict, with humor and irony, the life of a typical middle-class, middle-aged housewife, many women in Sweden can easily identify themselves in her poems. But her importance goes beyond that. Her theme is more than the alienation of the housewife in modern society. It is the dilemma for both men and women in coping with the contrasts between reality and an idyllic view of society. Åkesson's collected works are available only in Swedish: *En värk att anpassa, dikter 1957–1965* (A Pain To Live With, 1975); *Ett liv att avverka, dikter 1966–1974* (A Life to Finish, 1976); and *En tid att avliva, prosa 1960–1970* (A Time to Kill, 1978).

Ingrid Claréus

AUTOBIOGRAPHY
Självbiografi

(reply to Ferlinghetti)

I am leading a quiet life
at 83A Queen Street every day.
I blow my kids' noses and polish floors
and copper pots
and make french fries and hot dogs.

I am leading a quiet life
near the subway.
I am a Swede.
I was a Swedish girl.
I read the medical book under the blanket
and was a member of the Baptist
Junior League.
I dreamed of singing in the choir
and singing to the guitar
under the flames of the candles.
I dreamed of singing
to the guitar at the Lucia party.[1]

I owned two records by Alice Babs
and a sports jacket, with a zipper,
that used to be Dad's pants.
I worked in a café
with mirrors and beer
and a pig-sty in the yard.
I can still sense the smell of rats
and raspberry frosting, and of cheese
from the owner who was also a milk tester.

I was a typical brat.
I dug tunnels under the snow.
I sat under a snowing apple tree
waiting for Doomsday.
I was caught in a migrant's shack
on my way home from Junior League.
I took a correspondence course in shorthand
and doodled cover girls
on the pad.

I was in a snowed-in car
picking up Baltic refugees.[2]
Men with mushed-up lungs
crying for water.
A woman with her eye hanging
like a bloody egg down her cheek.

I have eaten sponge cake
at proper meetings of sewing clubs
and sipped carefully chosen wine
with double-breasted
proper literati.
I have attended courses in Transcendental
                                    Meditation[3]
and something in Modern Poetry
where the wife of the right-wing leader
was the only one who spoke up.

I have been caged in a booth
where time refused to be driven out
and tried happiness in a little red cottage
with Love in the guest room
and War in the bed room.
I have never been to the Costa del Sol
or reached the Holy City
and I have no hope of ever getting there.
I have been caged in a bus
and watched kids play bang-bang
on the monument in the Warsaw ghetto.[4]

I have got chilblains at dance-pavillions.
I have lapped up Jularbo Junior
and Rune's Hot Band.
I do not like it much here
but I will not go back
where I came from.
I have always got a lift a lift a lift

I have rested on a bed of agony
with the Little Black Sara.
I have had my mom in heaven
to where you cannot buy a ticket.
And I have seen the butcher in my home town
play the organ with fat, blessed fingers
in a former railroad hotel
while his fiancée wandered about
possessed by a different kind of demon.
I have had a secret affair
with my idol
Clark Gable.

I am leading a quiet life
at 83A Queen Street every day
listening to the neighbor woman chasing
                                    around
with her compulsive broom.
I once left the coziness of a three-room flat
but wound up in another three-room flat.
The inquiries become too much for me.
I have trained myself in adjustment
cover-up and shrewdness.

I have no wings
but a well-developed hunchback.
I hunt for all cracks
as if there were a way out.
I flutter and flutter but my hunchback
stops me in my movements.
Women should not try to find out anything.
They should stay where they are.
My mother always reminds me
of all the things I should be grateful for.

Upset stomach.
I am resting.
I have been around.
I have gone round and round
with my little life,
I have opened wrong doors.
I have seen a conchie[5] rape a check-out girl.
I have seen a cook
drained of her blood
over a garbage can.
I have heard my dying child giggle
strangely
under my strange hand.

I have been sleepless in a small town
where the trees only sighed and sighed.
I have heard more restless trees
lowing like bell-buoys.
I have been brought around snivelling
to all hell's charity institutions.
I have been reduced to pumping machines.
What silence what ticking what pattering!
And the women with their pale hands
entangled in their skeins of yarn.

(continued)

I have seen sculptures of flesh and dreams.
I have seen living stones.
An old grandmother with a raised lantern
give light to the fisherman to land.
A young poet marked by a hopeless illness.
And a girl at an abortion clinic
with a swollen
whitewashed face.
I do not doubt that Sweden
is a land of the Vikings.
I have seen women work eighteen hours a day
for a brass-plated TV-set.
Their dream is the Tonight Show.
They never got to be in the choir.

I am leading a quiet life
at 83A Queen Street every day
practicing my English.
I have read *The Catcher in the Rye*[6]
with the help of a discarded dictionary
and been aware of the deplorable similarity
between a schoolboy in New York
and a housewife in Stockholm
left behind in her awkward manners
in her jerky movements
no saviour.

I scan the editorials every day
making serious attempts
to keep up with the cultural debate.
I see that the Swedish Academy
is made to eat its own prizes.
I see that they have murdered a child
with tranquilizers.
I see that another war is coming
and skim and curse
the pages.
I read the death notices
and feel relief
for those who are gone.

I am looking for a sound soul
in a sound body.
I have saved at least a hundred newspapers
and really intend one day
to seriously take part in the debate.
I see another war roll forth
over the black and white pages.

I ran out in the early dusk
and wanted to put my hand through the sky
but hurried back home
not to burn the potatoes.
I see a similarity between me
and potatoes.
At the slightest cellar light these fumblers
                                    sprout.
But handle with care.
Protect from cold.

I have lived in an alley
too narrow for already reduced breathing.
I have been a dishwasher on a train through
                                    Ångermanland[7]
behind a closed lavatory window.
I have written passionate letters
to unknown addresses.
I have listened to "In the Room of the Mirrors."
I have seen silent children
in starving crowds
from the depths of a movie seat.
I have seen them.
I am a mother.
I was there.
But I did not suffer
enough.

I am a Swede.
I have a health insurance card.[8]
I cry in my room.
I will die of cancer.

I am formed by circumstances.
I am carrying on a war with myself
as a rejected female.
And I have certain plans!
I have a daughter
who should have a future.
I might buy myself a burial plot.
I am only temporarily
a usable household utensil.
I never keep a promise.
I see an expectation
in my childish mirror
as if I should get to have a Christmas tree.

I am leading a quiet life
at 83A Queen Street over the alley every day

looking at the walls.
I think of my sister
who carefully crochets pot holders
from my brother-in-law's
brain convolutions wound into balls.
I think of my brother
who is a cannibal.
I fry my steaks.
I wash my hands.
I have heard the lonely cry
from the half-devoured in the wilderness.
I am the woman.
I was she.
But I did not suffer
enough.

I walked inside and closed my door.
I sit in my comfortable chair.
I visit the staid department stores
where I buy my sterile
props of propriety.
I have written poems with thoughtful
pauses and punctuations.

I change bread into stones.
I feel as if I had my hands tied behind my
                                                back.

I feel as if I had a mute skin
tightened over my face
and fantasize about a small knife
between my teeth.

I have felt
how I vomit my throat
and how my tongue too slipped out
an unusable rag of skin.
Where do I find an instrument
for all my closed-in air?
I am a soiled shoe
in an overcrowded street.
I am a dog without a master
full of persistent love
among indifferent soiled shoes.

I see a similarity between me
and potatoes.
I have felt the rot from within
in the autumn rain.

I have heard married couples
on their custom-made foam rubber mattresses
complain about lost excitements.
I understand their disgust.
I have felt caresses
stick like chewing gum.
I doze by my little wading pool.
I wait
together with bored mothers.
And I see their husbands
come rolling in their VW's
in their worn down wheel tracks.
They have shiny nylon shirts
and small leather cushions behind.
They have idiot-proof chronometers
and looks full of dead flesh
and I feel it
in my own gnawing face.

I am leading a quiet life
reading homages to existence
by someone who did not suffer enough
I chew my own jokes.
I struggle with my tough skin.
I was the ugly duckling
who never changed into a swan.
Did I have a pair of wings then?
I feel the aftereffects of burns.
I pamper my poor hunchback.
I try to find my little knife
way back ruined by rust
and crushed by feet in the yellow grass.

Translated by Ingrid Claréus

NOTES

1. Celebration featuring impersonations of St. Lucia on her name day, December 13, to usher in the Christmas season.
2. In 1940, The Baltic States (Estonia, Latvia, and Lithuania) were made part of the U.S.S.R. Many fled to the neighboring Scandinavian countries.
3. Founded by Indian monk Maharishi Mahesh Yogi in the late 1950s, this method of relaxation became very popular in the West.
4. On April 19, 1943, Jews confined to live in a walled-in section of Poland's capital rebelled against their Nazi jailors. A month later more than 56,000 had been killed.

5. Conscientious objector.
6. A popular novel by American J.D. Salinger (b. 1919), this *bildungsroman* of a teenaged prep school student named Holden Caulfield created a sensation after it was published in 1951 for its open exploration of sexual mores.
7. A historic province in northeastern Sweden.
8. Sweden has a national health system with virtually free medical care for its citizens.

BE WHITE MAN'S SLAVE
Vara vit mans slav

White Man good sometimes, yes
vacuum floors, play cards with kids
on Sundays.

White Man not stand sloppiness.
Swear ugly words
on many days.

White Man not stand Sloppiness
White Man not stand Fried Food.
White Man not stand Dumb Ideas.
White Man have Big Fit
stumble over children's boots.

Be White Man's slave.

Have Other Man's child.
Have White Man's child.
White Man take a hand
support all children
Never be free. Big Debt
to White Man.

White Man make Money at Job.
White Man buy Things.
White Man buy wife.

Wife make gravy.
Wife cook crap.
Wife dump dregs.
Be White Man's slave.

White Man think many Thoughts. Go crazy?
Be White Man's slave.
White Man drink skinful.   Break Things?
Be White Man's slave.

White Man get tired of old breasts old belly
White Man get tired of old wife
tell her go to Hell?
White Man get tired Other Man's child?

Be White Man's slave.
Come   creep on knees
beg
be White Man's slave.

Translated by Richard B. Vowles

Ingeborg Bachmann   *Austria, 1926–1973*

Ingeborg Bachmann is indisputably one of this century's greatest German-language writers, whose extraordinary intellect and profoundly personal perception of her world and her self combined to give her poetry and fiction a remarkable lyrical and expressive power. She was born on June 25, 1926 in Klagenfurt, Austria; her father was a teacher. She studied philosophy, German literature, and psychology at the Universities of Innsbruck, Graz, and Vienna and received her doctorate in 1950 with a dissertation on the reception of Heidegger's philosophy. She composed lyrical poetry under the strong influence of Heidegger and Wittgenstein, grappling often with the particularly modern problem of the linguistic (dis)agreement between sign and thing; later she was to define lyric poetry, however, as "emotion stemming from the experience of suffering," thus hinting at the private aspect of her composition. "Ich schreibe, also bin ich," (I write, therefore I am) she said in the controversial lectures she gave at Frankfurt in 1959–1960. Bachmann chose Rome as her permanent place of residence after 1965, and it was there that she died, as a result of burns suffered in a fire in her apartment, on October 17, 1973.

Bachmann was discovered at the 1952 annual meeting of the then very influential Group 47, a group of writers and critics organized after World War II and influential through the late 1960s in the F.R.G. The Prize of the Group 47, which Bachmann received in 1953, was a fair guarantee of literary fame. In subsequent years she was awarded numerous additional honors, including the Bremen Prize for Literature (1957), the Berlin Critics' Prize (1961), and the Büchner Prize (1964). She published two volumes of poetry, *Die gestundete Zeit* (Borrowed Time, 1953), and *Anrufung des großen Bären* (Invocation of the Big Dipper, 1956), and was the first to hold the guest professorship for poetics at the University of Frankfurt in 1959–1960. Her recognition of the discrepancy between lyrical speech and historical reality led to the cessation of her poetic composition after the publication of the second volume. With rare exceptions ("Ihr Worte" [You Words], a late poem dedicated to Nelly Sachs, and "Keine Delikatessen" [No Delicacies], published in 1968 and included here), she refrained altogether from writing poetry, instead devoting herself to radio plays, opera libretti, translations, and prose. A major selection of her poetry has recently appeared in English.

Currently attracting considerable critical attention, particularly from feminist theoreticians, are Bachmann's prose works, especially the latest ones. Her first collection of stories, *Das dreißigste Jahr* (*The Thirtieth Year*), was published in 1961. The theme begun there concerns the connections between her own personal suffering and historical injustice, particularly regarding the oppression of minorities. This is continued with increased conviction and provocation in the novel *Malina* (1971), planned as the first of an unfinished cycle of novels entitled *Todesarten* (Death Types). Other works intended for this cycle, *Der Fall Franza* (The Case of Franza) and *Requiem für Fanny Goldman* (Requiem for Fanny Goldman), are included as fragments in her posthumously published collected works (1978), and in *Simultan* (1972), translated 1987, the last collection of short stories published before her death.

Marilyn Sibley Fries

NO DELICACIES
Keine Delikatessen

Nothing pleases me anymore.

Should I
dress a metaphor
with an almond blossom?
crucify syntax
on a trick of light?
Who will beat his brains
over such superfluities—

I have learned to be considerate
with the words
that exist
(for the lowest class)

hunger
        disgrace
             tears
and
                    darkness

With unclean sobbing,
with despair
(and I despair even of despair)
of the enormous misery,
the bedridden, the cost of living—
I will get by.

I don't neglect the word
but myself.
The others know
godknows
how to help themselves with words.
I am not my assistant.

Should I
take a thought captive,
lead it into an illuminated sentence cell?
Feed eye and ear
with first-class word tidbits?
Investigate the libido of a vowel,
ascertain the lover's value of our consonants?

Must I,
with this hail-battered head,
with writing cramps in this hand,
under the pressure of three hundred nights,
rip this paper apart,
sweep away the plotted word operas,
destroying thus: I you and he she it

we you?

(Still should. The others should.)

My share, it should be dispersed.

Translated by Mark Anderson

from MALINA

THE THIRD MAN

Malina is supposed to ask about everything. But I answer, without having been asked: this time the place is not Vienna. It is a place that's called Everywhere and Nowhere. The time is not today. Time does not exist anymore, for it could have been yesterday, a long time ago, it can be again, can be always, some things will never have been. There is no standard measure for the units of this time into which other times enter, and there is no standard for the wrong times into which that which never was in time insinuates itself.

Malina is supposed to know everything. But I determine: it is the dreams of last night.

A great window opens up, larger than any window I have seen, but instead of opening onto the yard of our house in the Ungargasse it looks out on a gloomy expanse of clouds. A lake could lie under the clouds. I suspect which lake it might be. But it isn't frozen solid any more, it's no longer free-for-all-night, and the sentimental men's singing clubs that once stood on the ice, in the middle of the lake, have disappeared. And the lake, which cannot be seen, is surrounded by the many cemeteries. There are no crosses on them, but the mist looms thick and ominous above each grave; the graves, the slabs with the inscriptions, are barely discernible. My father stands next to me and withdraws his hand from my shoulder, for gravedigger has walked up to us. My father looks at the old man imperiously, the gravedigger, after this look from my father, turns anxiously to me. He wants to speak, but for a long time only moves his lips in silence, and I hear only his last sentence: This is the cemetery of the murdered daughters.

He should not have said it to me, and I weep bitterly.

The chamber is large and dark, no, it's a reception hall, with dirty walls, it could be in the Hohenstaufen castle in Apulia.[1] For there are no windows and no doors. My father has locked me in, and I want to ask him what he plans to do with me, but again I lack the courage to ask him, and I look around again, for there must be a door, one single door, so that I can get outside, but I realize already there is nothing, no opening, no more openings, for black hoses have been connected to all of them, stuck on all around the walls, attached like gigantic leeches that want to suck something out of the walls. Why didn't I notice the hoses earlier, for they must have been there from the beginning! I was so blind in the half-darkness and felt my way along the walls so as not to lose sight of my father, in order to find a door with him, but now I find him and say: the door, show me the door. My father calmly takes a first hose down from the wall, I see a round hole through which air is blowing in and I duck, my father goes on, taking down one hose after another, and before I can scream I'm already inhaling the gas, more and more gas. I am in the gas chamber, this is it, the world's largest gas chamber, and I'm alone in it. You don't put up a fight in gas. My

father has disappeared, he knew where the door is and didn't show it to me, and while I die, with me dies the wish to see him again and to say the One Thing to him. My father, I say to him, who is no longer there, I would not have betrayed you, I would not have told anyone. You don't put up a fight here.

When it begins the world is already topsy-turvy and I know that I am insane. The elements of the world are still there, but in ghastly combinations such as no one has ever seen. Cars roll around dripping paints, people emerge, grinning larvae, and when they approach me they collapse, are straw dolls, bundles of wire, cardboard figures, and I walk on in this world that is not the world, with clenched fists, outspread arms, in order to fend off the objects, the machines, that come at me and turn to dust, and when fear keeps me from continuing I close my eyes, but the paints, luminous, harsh, raving, spatter me, my face, my bare feet, I open my eyes again to get my bearings, for I want to find my way out of here, then I fly up in the air, for my fingers and toes have swollen into airy heavenly-blue balloons and carry me into heights of never-again in which things are even worse, then they all burst and I fall, fall and stand up, my toes have turned black, I can't walk anymore.

Sire!

My father comes down out of the heavy downpour of colors, he says scornfully: go on, just go on! And I hold my hand in front of my mouth, out of which all my teeth have fallen, they lie insurmountable before me, two curves of marble blocks.

I can't say anything, of course, because I have to get away from my father and over the marble wall, but in a different language I say: Ne! Ne! And in many languages: No! No! Non! Non! Njet! Njet! No! Ném! Ném! Nein! For even in our language I can only say "Nein," beyond that I can find no other word in a language. A rolling contraption, perhaps the ferris wheel, comes at me, scattering excrement from the gondolas, and I say: Ne! Ném! But in order to make me stop shouting my No my father drives his fingers, his short sturdy hard fingers, into my eyes, now I am blind, but I must go on. It's unbearable. So I smile, because my father has reached for my tongue and wants to rip it out so that no one will hear my No here, either, although no one hears me, but before he tears out my tongue the terrible thing happens, a blue gigantic glob flies into my mouth, so that I am unable to utter another sound. My blue, my glorious blue, in which the peacocks strut, and my blue of the distances, my blue coincidence on the horizon! The blue spreads more deeply into me, into my throat, and my father gives a hand and is now tearing my heart and my entrails out of my body, but I can still walk, and I come to the first mushy ice before I get to the eternal ice, and this resounds in me: Is there then nobody left, is there no one here, in this whole world, is there no human being and among brothers, is one worth nothing then, and among

brothers! What is left of me freezes in the ice, is a clump, and I look up to where they, the others, live in the warm world, and the Great Siegfried[2] calls me, quietly at first, and then in the end loudly, impatiently I hear his voice: What are you looking for, what kind of a book do you seek? And I have no voice. What does the Great Siegfried want? He calls from above, ever more clearly: What kind of a book will it be, what is your book going to be?

Suddenly, from the point of the pole from which there is no return I am able to scream: A book about hell. A book about hell!

Translated by Marilyn Sibley Fries

NOTES

1. Castle in the boot of Italy belonging to the German princely family and ruling dynasty of the eleventh to thirteenth centuries; their home as rulers of Sicily from 1194 to 1266.
2. Folk hero of early and medieval German mythology; subsequently the tragic hero of the operatic tetralogy the *Nibelungen* (The Ring of the Nibelungs, 1857–1874) by German composer Richard Wagner (1813–1883); his character was also used by the Nazi ideological machine in the creation of an Aryan mythology.

Annette M'Baye d'Erneville   *Senegal, b. 1926*

Little is known of Annette M'Baye d'Erneville, save that she is one of the few African women to have published her poetry in book form, that she is the founder of an important Senegalese women's magazine, *Awa* (Eva), and that she is one of the women to whom the late Senegalese novelist Mariama Bâ dedicated her first work.

D'Erneville's first poems, originally published in France as *Poèmes africains* (1965) and then in Dakar as *Kaddu* (1966), are dedicated in the later edition mostly to women friends, relatives, and teachers, both African and European, as well as to her son and to her unnamed lover, suggesting a more personal and familiar tone. In one so apparently committed to the liberation of women, it is not surprising to find poems that affirm female solidarity, beauty, and desire. The selections, taken from this collection, are translated from the French.

The book's change of title in migration is similarly suggestive: to Europeans, the poetry objectified the colonial; to blacks, the title evokes their rich oral tradition and presents them as subjects. Many of the poems, such as "Kassacks" and "Labane," celebrate Senegalese rituals and ceremonies, while others deal with the experience of colonialism and oppression. D'Erneville's most recent poems, published in *Chansons pour Laity* (Songs for the Laity, 1976), underscore celebratory ritual and its capacity to serve as a spiritual basis for the creation of a common reader; they are intended for children.

KASSACKS[1]

To Ousmane my son

You are a man, tonight!
You are a man, my son!
   By your bruised flesh
   By your spilled blood
   By your cold glance
   By your immobile thigh.

And your mother remembers
   Her night of love
   Her torn entrails
   Her silent groans
   Her open loins
   The envious looks of her wicked rivals
   The greedy suction of your flower-
                 shaped mouth
   The miraculous amulet that
   —With the help of Allah—
   Has guided your steps to this happy day.

You are a man, tonight!
You are a man, my son!
   By the cutting blade
   By your tried sex[2]
   By your suppressed fear
   By the land of the Ancestors

Gawolo![3] . . . sing of this new man.
Young girls with upright breasts
Cry out his name to the wind.
Selbé N'Diaye,[4] make this little man dance.

You are a man, my son.
You are a man tonight
They are all here:
   Those of your first moon
   Those you call fathers.
Look, look at them well;
They alone are the guardians of the earth
Of the earth that drank your blood.
(Kaolack—August 1958)

Translated by Brian Baer

NOTES

1. Songs of circumcision.
2. The multiple meanings in French of *eprouvé*—"felt," "experienced," "tried," "tested"—create a play on words in the original text that is difficult to translate here; "sex," of course, can refer both to the circumcized genitalia and the masculine sex.
3. A Griot geneologist and singer.
4. The Senegalese equivalent of the noble, brave, and generous knight.

SCULPTURE

To Ndakhte

An athlete's stature!
Perfect curve of the loins!
Suppleness in the contour of the arm!...
But suddenly...the statue takes life
Life and rhythm!
      Rhythm!
Rhythm of a drum that roars,
Rumbles, grows quiet beneath the fingers of
                the master,
This young griot who seems posed for posterity.
(**Sandiara—1956**)

Translated by Brian Baer

LABANE*

Our lost virginities will never be regained.
Never more will we be chosen from princely
beds.

      The Royal Eagle, with his pearly beak
      Digs into the slain hearts
      Ruptures the life roots
      Abandons the remains
      To the rapacious of his court!
      The first drop of blood
      Refreshes him, intoxicates him.

Oh! How pure we would like to be reborn
And let the other at our smooth flanks
Make a gift of his hands!
Would we be worthy of that again!
Oh! Lord! Save us!
(**Diourbel—1963**)

Translated by Brian Baer

NOTE

* The ritual ceremony, held the day before the wedding
night, during which the praises of the young virgin are
sung.

REQUIEM*

To Adrienne d'Erneville
who did not return...

Your final bed was not adorned with roses
Your shroud was neither white silk nor
                maternal cloth
No perfumed water bathed your body
And your tresses were not arranged with a
                comb of gold.

You spoke your fear of the giant bird!
You believed the fork tongue and evil eye!
Who could have thought, seeing you so
                beautiful,
That you were dressing for Lady Death?

Embrace of the night? Kiss of the early
                morning?
The sand of the desert has cast your curves
And burned them to a powder.
(**Paris—1952**)

Translated by Brian Baer

NOTE

* Literally, "rest" in Latin; it may refer to the Roman
Catholic mass for the dead, or more generally, any
lament or dirge.

Marya Fiamengo   *Canada, b. 1926*

Born in Vancouver to Yugoslav parents, Marya Ekaterina Fiamengo received her
B.A. and M.A. (1961) in creative writing from the University of British Columbia,
where she worked under Canadian poet Earle Birney and where, for many years,
she has taught. Reflecting her Slavic origins and her status as a woman—"my kin
and gender"—Fiamengo's poetry deals centrally with such subjects as political
atrocities (including Nazi persecution of the Jews), social injustice, immigrant life
and European values, and the oppression—as well as the indomitable strength—
of women, especially older women.

Understanding that earthly beauty comes to an end, Fiamengo's old women
become a potent source of spiritual enlightenment and nourishment in society.
Fiamengo's best known poem is the powerful title poem of *In Praise of Old
Women* which forges an awesome image of woman, neither as young and innocent
nor as glamorous and sexually liberated, but as a philosopher, a revered elder, a
valuable repository of human wisdom; in it, Fiamengo recovers the ancient goddess
Sophia and reinvents the meaning of "crone."

Formerly married to J. N. Hardman, a sculptor and printmaker, with whom
she had one son, Fiamengo is now divorced. Her career as a poet started with *The
Quality of Halves* (1958), and includes four other books to date: *Overheard at the
Oracle* (1969), *Silt of Iron* (1971), *In Praise of Old Women* (1976), and *North of
the Cold Star* (1978). In addition, her poems have appeared in several anthologies,
including *Forty Women Poets of Canada, Eleven Canadian Poets*, and the *Penguin
Book of Canadian Verse*, as well as in various Canadian periodicals, the English
Envoi, and *Prism International*. In 1975–1976 Fiamengo co-chaired the League of
Canadian Poets.

Wendy Robbins Keitner

IN PRAISE OF OLD WOMEN

Yes, Tadeusz Rozewicz,[1] I too
prefer old women.
They bend over graves
with flowers,
they wash the limbs of the dead,
they count the beads of their rosaries,
they commit no murders
they give advice
or tell fortunes,
they endure.

In Poland, in Russia,
in Asia, in the Balkans,
I see them shawled, kerchiefed
bent-backed, work-wrinkled.

But Tadeusz,
have you been to America?
Where we have no old women.
No Stara Babas,[2]
no haggard Madonnas.

Everyone, Tadeusz, is young in America.
Especially the women
with coifed blue hair
which gleams like the steel
of jets in the daytime sky.
Smooth-skinned at sixty,
second debuts at fifty
renascent
they never grow old in America.

(*continued*)

And we have in America
literate, sexually liberated women
who wouldn't touch a corpse,
who confuse lechery with love,
not out of viciousness
but boringly
out of confusion, neurosis, identity crises.

Tadeusz,
I go to the cemetery
with my mother
one of us stoically old,
the other aging,
and I tell you, Tadeusz,
I will grow old in America.
I will have no second debut.
I will raise my son on old battles,
Kossovo, Neretva, Thermopylae,
Stalingrad and Britain,[3]
and I will wrinkle adamantly in America.

I will put salt in the soup
and I will offer bread and wine
to my friends,
and I will stubbornly praise old women
until their thin taut skins
glow like Ikons ascending on escalators
like Buddhas descending in subways,
and I will liberate all women
to be old in America
because the highest manifestation of wisdom,
Hagia Sophia,[4]
is old and a woman.

NOTES

1. A leading Polish avant-garde writer (b. 1921), whose works depict postwar moral and spiral decay. His play *Stara kobieta wysiadvje* (The Old Woman Broods, 1968), shows modern civilization as a garbage dump.
2. Russian or Polish for old woman.
3. Sites, respectively, in Yugoslavia, Yugoslavia, Greece, Russia, and Great Britain, where in various times in history peoples have fought invaders.
4. Completed in 537 A.D. in Constantinople (now Istanbul), Turkey, this cathedral is one of the most important Byzantine structures extant.

Ibaragi Noriko   *Japan, b. 1926*

Ibaragi Noriko's first literary aspiration was to be a playwright. However, while attending the Imperial Women's College of Pharmacology between 1944 and 1946, she began reading the eighth-century poetry anthology, *Manyōshū* (A Collection of Ten Thousand Leaves); she cites that and the contemporary poet Kaneko Mitsuharu, whom she read extensively after the war, as important influences on her art. After her marriage in 1949, she devoted her attention to writing poetry. She was part of the founding group of the important poetry journal *Kai* (Oar) in 1953. Her first collection, *Taiwa* (Conversations), was published in 1955; *Mienai Haitatsu-fu* (Invisible Mailmen, 1958), from which the first selection comes, followed; *Chinkonka* (Requiem Poems, 1965) was written in memory of her father. (They are the sources of the other poems.) Her many works are noted for their vigorous, unpessimistic, and critical realism.

Ibaragi turned increasingly to prose to explore the nature of language. *Koto no ha sayage* (Clarifying Words, 1975) looks into dialect and poetic language; it asks whether poetry can be taught, and studies the work of the major poets Tanikawa Shuntarō (b. 1931), Ibuse Masuji (b. 1898), and Kaneko Mitsuharu

(b. 1895). Her most recent book, *Hanguru e no tabi* (Travels to Hangul, 1986), speaks of the fifteen years she has spent studying Korean, and is her answer to a self-posed question: "Why is it that when you say you're studying French, everyone nods approvingly, but if you study the language of Japan's closest neighbor, they look at you as if you're crazy?"

Phyllis I. Lyons

WHEN MY BEAUTY WAS AT ITS BEST
Watashi ga Ichiban Kirei datta Toki

When my beauty was at its best
town after town came tumbling down, giving
                                                         us
glimpses of blue sky stuck up in
the least expected places.

When my beauty was at its best
many people around me died
in factories, at sea, on unknown islands, and
I had no chance to make the best of myself.

When my beauty was at its best
I had no young man bringing me lovely presents.
All they did was raise their hands in salute,
                                         and soon
left for the front, leaving me with nothing
                               more than pure looks.

When my beauty was at its best
I was empty-headed,
I was stubborn-hearted,
my limbs were a glossy brown.

When my beauty was at its best
my country was defeated.
"How can that be?"
I strode around the humbled town, my sleeves
                                    rolled up.

When my beauty was at its best
I heard jazz streaming from the radio,
and I plunged myself as rapturously into its
                               sweet melodies
as when I first knew the forbidden pleasure of
                               smoking.

When my beauty was at its best
I was very unhappy
I was very awkward,
I was very, very lonely.

That's why I've decided to live a long time if I
                                        can,
like Monsieur Rouault, the dear old man who
painted those marvelously beautiful pictures in
                                   his old age.
—Yes, in his old age!*

Translated by James Kirkup

NOTE

* Georges Rouault (1871–1958): French Expressionist artist best known for his stained-glass-like religious portraits.

MY CAMERA

My eye
is the lens

My wink,
the shutter

I have a tiny darkroom
surrounded by hair,

and that's why
I don't carry a camera

Do you know, I've many pictures
of you inside me?

Your laughing face in sun filtered through
                                        leaves,
your radiant, chestnut body crossing waves,
lighting a cigarette, in a child-like sleep,
smelling of orchids—in the woods where you
                                   were a lion

In the world, just one; a film library
nobody knows

Translated by Fukuko Kobayashi

OUTRUN

When you feel you've outrun somebody,
without trying to,
or even knowing you were running;
you feel an indefinite loneliness.

One night I outran father,
and cried on a damp pillow without a sound
while he snored, one room over.

And I hate myself for it now.
Hate myself!
I'm not better than he is.

But I outran him,
and like a revelation,
or sword-slash,
it marks a phase of my life.

I wonder if I'll ever give
young friends, nieces, nephews
such a moment.

When you've outrun somebody, you know it.
But if you're outrun, who's to tell you?

Translated by Fukuko Kobayashi

Margaret Laurence   *Canada, 1926–1987*

Like the writer-heroine of her masterpiece, *The Diviners*, Margaret Laurence (née Wemyss), grew up an orphan in a small prairie town, married young and divorced, lived abroad, and disproving Thomas Wolfe's maxim—came home again.* Speaking for a country with historic ties to Britain and France and for a generation of emancipated women who are trying to "have it all"—relation and creation, roots and freedom—Laurence focuses her fiction on the twin pulls of connectedness and independence, making a river that flows both ways the central symbol of her *magnum opus*.

Neepawa, Manitoba, Laurence's birthplace, is recreated in her fictional Manawaka—a microcosm of Canadian society which Laurence portrays as a provincial backwater characterized by narrow-mindedness and class snobbery, but also by heroic strength and personal integrity. Winning a scholarship to United College in Winnipeg in 1944, Laurence initially fled the small town for the city, receiving honors in English and writing for the college paper and later for *The Winnipeg Citizen*. In 1947, she married Jack Laurence, a civil engineer, and moved with him to live briefly in England and then, from 1950 to 1957, in West Africa. The longed-for but also frightening reality of independence she witnessed in the former British colonies of Somalia and Ghana is the subject of much of her early African work: *This Side Jordan* (1960), *The Prophet's Camel Bell* (1963), *A Tree for Poverty* (1954), *The Tomorrow-Tamer* (1963), and *Long Drums and Cannons* (1968).

After a brief return to Canada and separation from her husband, Laurence moved back to England with her two children. The couple divorced in 1969, at which time she moved permanently to the town of Lakefield, Ontario, summering at her cottage (which she christened Manawaka) on the Otonabee River near Peterborough. While her African material first brought her to international attention, her Manawaka novels and stories established Laurence as one of Canada's greatest novelists.

In *The Stone Angel* (1964), *A Jest of God* (1966), *The Fire-Dwellers* (1969), *A Bird in the House* (1970), and *The Diviners* (1974), Laurence explores feminist, national, and postcolonial themes in an attempt, at once deeply personal and nearly universal, to "come to terms with the past." Near the end of her life, Laurence published a collection of essays, *Heart of a Stranger* (1976), and several books for children, among them *The Olden Days Coat* (1979). A measure of her popularity, some of her books have been translated into French, German, Spanish, and Norwegian; numerous paperback editions exist (some with different titles from the original); and films have been produced of *The Fire-Dwellers, A Jest of God* (using its American-edition title of *Rachel, Rachel*), and *The Olden Days Coat*. In Vanessa MacLeod, the central character in the interrelated short stories of *A Bird in the House*, from which the selection here, "The Half-Husky," is taken, Laurence paints a self-portrait of the artist as a young Canadian girl.

Laurence's distinguished career brought her many honors, including the Beta Sigma Phi First Novel Award, two Governor General's Awards (for *A Jest of God* and *The Diviners*), the Molson Prize, and the City of Toronto Award of Merit; she was named Companion of the Order of Canada, B'nai B'rith Toronto Woman of the Year, Fellow of the Royal Society of Canada, and Canadian Booksellers' Association Author of the Year. Laurence received a host of honorary degrees, and her writing is the subject of numerous theses, dissertations, and books. She served as writer in residence at the universities of Toronto, Western Ontario, and Trent, where she held the position of Chancellor from 1981 to 1983.

Wendy Robbins Keitner

NOTE

* *You Can't Go Home Again* (1940) was the second in a three-novel series by American novelist Thomas Wolfe (1900–1938).

THE HALF-HUSKY

When Peter Chorniuk's Wagon clanked slowly into our back yard that September, it never occurred to me that this visit would be different from any other. Peter Chorniuk lived at Galloping Mountain, a hundred miles north of Manawaka, and he was one of the few men from whom it was still possible to buy birch, for the trees were getting scarce. Every autumn he came down to Manawaka and brought a load of birch for our furnace. Birch held the fire better than poplar, but it was expensive and we could afford only the one load, so my grandfather burned a mixture. I watched the man whoa the team and then climb onto the back of the wagon and begin throwing down the cordwood sticks. The powdery white bark was still on and in places had been torn, exposing the pale rust colour of the inner bark. The logs thudded dryly as he flung them down. Later my grandfather and I would have to carry them inside. The plebeian poplar was kept outside, but the birch was stacked in the basement.

I was lying on the roof of the tool-shed, reading. An enormous spruce tree grew beside the shed, and the branches feathered out across the roof, concealing anyone who was perched there. I was fifteen, and getting too old to be climbing on roofs, my mother said.

"Hi, Mr. Chorniuk," I called.

He looked up, and I emerged from the spruce boughs and waved at him. He grinned.

"Hi, Vanessa. Listen, you want a dog, eh?"

"What?" I said. "Has Natasha had pups again?"

"Yeh, that's right," Mr. Chorniuk said. "There's no stopping Natasha. This is her fifth litter. This time she got herself mixed up with a Husky."

"Gee." I was impressed. "The pups are half-Husky? What're they like?"

"Come and see," he beckoned. "I brought one for you."

I slid quickly down from the tool-shed roof onto the fence and then to the ground. The pup was in a cardboard box in the front of the wagon. It was very young and plump, and its fur was short and soft, almost like the down on a chick. It was black, like Natasha, but it had a ruff of white at its throat, and white markings on its head. I picked it up, and it struggled in annoyance, trying to escape, then settled down and sniffed my hands to see if I was friendly.

"Can I really have it?" I asked.

"Sure," Mr. Chorniuk said, "You'll be doing me a favor. What am I going to do with six of them? Everybody up at the mountain's got all the dogs they got any use for. I can't drown them. My wife says I'm crazy. But I'd as soon drown a kid, to tell you the truth. Will your mom let you keep it?"

"Oh sure, *she* will. But—"

"Think *he* won't?" Mr. Chorniuk said, meaning Grandfather Connor. My mother and brother and I had lived in the Brick House with my grandfather ever since the death of my father.

"Well, we'll soon know," I said. "Here he comes now."

Grandfather Connor came striding out of

the house. He was in his late eighties, but he walked straight, carrying his bulky body with an energy that was partly physical and partly sheer determination. His splendid condition, for a man of his age, he attributed to unceasing toil and good habits. He touched neither tobacco nor snuff, he spurned playing cards, and he based his drinking of only tea on the Almighty's contention that wine was a mocker and strong drink was raging. It was a warm day, the leaves turning a clear lemon yellow on the Manitoba maples and the late afternoon sun lighting up the windows of the Brick House like silver foil, but my grandfather was wearing his grey-heather sweater buttoned up to the neck. His face was set in its accustomed expression of displeasure, but it was still a handsome face—strong heavy features, a beaked nose, eyes a chilled blue like snow-shadows.

"Well, Peter, you've brought the wood." It was his habit to begin conversations with a statement of the obvious, so that nothing except agreement was possible.

"Yep. Here it is."

"How much will it be this time?" Grandfather Connor asked.

Mr. Chorniuk told him the price and my grandfather looked stricken. He had never accepted the fact that he could not buy anything for what he paid forty years ago, so he had the permanent conviction that he was being cheated. He began to argue, and Mr. Chorniuk's face assumed a look of purposeful blankness. Just then my grandfather noticed the dog.

"What's that you've got there, Vanessa?"

"Mr. Chorniuk says I can have it, Grandfather. Can I? I promise I'll look after it myself. It wouldn't be any trouble."

"We don't want no dogs around the place," my grandfather said. "They're messy and they're destructive. You'd only be making work for your mother. You might consider her for a change."

"If she says I can, though?" I persisted.

"There's no *if* about it," he decreed flatly.

"Part Husky, that one," Mr. Chorniuk put in, trying to be helpful. "He'd make a good watch dog. Nor worry about pups. It's a him."

"Husky!" Grandfather Connor exclaimed. "I wouldn't trust one of them things as far as I could see it. Tear Roddie to bits, more than likely."

My brother Roderick was five and a half and exceptionally fond of animals. I was pointing this out, arguing hotly and passionately and with no more tact than my grandfather himself, when Roddie and my mother came out into the yard. My brother, sizing up the situation rapidly, added his pleas to mine.

"Aw, come on, Grandfather. Please."

"Can I, Mother?" I begged. "I'll look after him. You won't have to do a thing. Cross my heart."

My mother was always torn between her children and a desire not to provoke my grandfather.

"Well, it's all right as far as I'm concerned," she said uncertainly "but—"

What made my grandfather finally and untypically change his mind was the delay involved.

"Take the blamed thing away, then, Vanessa, for mercy's sake, or this wood won't get unloaded before tomorrow morning. But he's only to go in the basement, mind. If I catch him in the rest of the house, you'll have to get rid of him, understand?"

"Yes, yes!" I fled with the pup. My brother followed.

The pup explored the basement, snuffling around the crate of apples on the floor, burrowing behind the sacks of potatoes and turnips, falling over his own infant-clumsy feet in his attempt to scurry in every direction at once. Roddie and I laughed at him, and then I picked him up to try him in his new bed and he nervously wet all over the blanket.

"What're we going to call him, Vanessa?"

I pondered. Then the name came to me.

"Nanuk."

"*Na-nook*? That's not a name."

"It's an Eskimo name, dopey," I said abruptly.

"Is it really?"

"Sure it is." I had no idea whether it was or not. "Anybody knows that."

"You think you're so smart," my brother said, offended.

"What would you suggest, then?" I asked sarcastically.

"Well, I was thinking of Laddie."

"Laddie! What! A corny old name like that?"

Then I became aware that my own voice carried some disturbing echo of my grandfather's.

"Listen, Laddie's okay for a collie or like that," I amended, "but this one's got to have an Eskimo name, on account of his father being a Husky, see?"

"Yeh, maybe so," my brother said. "Here, Nanuk!"

The pup did not even look up. He seemed too young to own any kind of a name.

Harvey Shinwell delivered our papers. He was a heavily built boy of about sixteen, with colourless eyebrows and a pallid mottled face. After school he would go and pick up the papers from the station and deliver them on his old bicycle. He was somebody who had always been around and whom I had never actually seen. Until that winter.

Nanuk had the run of the yard, but the gates were kept closed. The picket fence was high, and the wooden pieces were driven deep into the earth, so Nanuk could neither get over nor tunnel under. I took him out on walks with me but apart from that he stayed in the yard. This did not mean he was too much confined, however, for our yard was nearly an acre. One day I got home from school just as Harvey Shinwell had come to the gate and thrown the Winnipeg *Free Press* onto our front porch. He didn't get back on his bike immediately. He was standing at the gate, and when I approached along the sidewalk I could see what he was doing.

In his hand he held a short pointed stick. He was poking it through the bars of the gate. On the other side was Nanuk, only four months old, but snarling in a way I had never heard before. He was trying to catch the stick with his teeth, but Harvey withdrew it too quickly. Then Harvey jabbed it in again, and this time it caught Nanuk in the face. He yelped with the pain of it, but he was not driven away. He came back again, trying to get hold of the stick, and once more Harvey with a calm deliberation drove the wooden javelin at the dog.

"What do you think you're doing?" I yelled. "You leave my dog alone, you hear?"

Harvey looked up with a lethargic grin and mounted his bike.

"He tried to bite me," he said. "He's dangerous."

"He is not!" I cried, infuriated. "I saw!"

"Why don't you run and tell your mother, then?" Harvey said, in phony falsetto.

I went inside the yard and knelt in the snow beside Nanuk. He was getting too big for me to lift him. He seemed to have forgotten about the stick. He welcomed me in his usual way, jumping up, taking my wrist gently between his jaws and pretending to bite but holding it so carefully that he never left even the faint marks of his teeth.

I forgot about the stick then, also. Nanuk was enough of a problem because of my grandfather. Their paths hardly ever crossed, but this was only due to the organisational abilities of my mother, who was constantly removing the dog to some place where my grandfather wasn't. Sometimes she would complain irritably about this extra responsibility—"if I'd ever realised, Vanessa, how much work this creature would mean, I'd never have agreed—" and so on. Then I would feel wounded and resentful, and could scarcely bear the fact that the trouble the dog caused her was my fault.

"Okay, give him away," I would storm. "See if I care. Have him chloroformed."

"Maybe I will, then, one of these days," my mother would reply stonily, "and it would serve you right for talking like a lunatic and saying things you don't mean."

Having scared each other more than either of us intended, we would both give in.

"He's really very good," my mother would admit. "And he's company during the day for Roddie."

"Are you sure?" No amount of assurance was ever enough for me. "Are you quite sure you wouldn't rather—"

"Oh yes, of course. It'll be all right, Vanessa. We mustn't worry."

"Yes, Okay," I would say. "We won't, then."

And we would both go our perpetually worrying ways.

Some months later I happened once more to come home just at the moment when Harvey was delivering the paper. This time I saw him from half a block away, and walked along the sidewalk quietly, sticking close to the caragana hedges for concealment. He had half a doughnut in one hand, and in the other a white envelope. He held the doughnut through the iron grille, and when Nanuk came up to the gate, he opened the envelope.

Nanuk screamed. The sound was so sudden and acute that my breath was forced back in upon my lungs. I wondered how many times some kind of tormenting had taken place. I felt the burden of my own neglect. I should have taken it seriously before. I should have watched out for it.

Harvey rode off. When I went to Nanuk and finally calmed him enough to touch him, I found traces of the pepper around his still-closed eyes.

Whenever I tried to work out a plan of counter-attack, my rage would spin me into fantasy—Harvey, fallen into the deepest part of the Wachakwa River, unable to swim, and Nanuk, capable of rescue but waiting for a signal from me. Would I speak or not? Sometimes I let Harvey drown. Sometimes at the last minute I spared him—this was more satisfactory than his death, as it enabled me to feel great-hearted while at the same time enjoying a continuing revenge in the form of Harvey's gibbering remorse. But none of this was much use except momentarily, and when the flamboyant theatre of my mind grew empty again, I still did not know what to do in reality.

I did not tell my mother. I could not face her look of distracted exhaustion at being presented with something else that she was expected to solve and did not know how any more than I. Also, I could not forget what Harvey had said—"Why don't you run and tell your mother?" I began hurrying home from school, so I would get there first. I thought he would not do anything if I were there.

Harvey flipped the newspaper neatly onto the front porch. It landed just at my elbow. I was sitting on the top step. Nanuk was at the gate. I called to him, but he did not seem to hear.

Nanuk was eight months old now, and fully grown. He had changed utterly. His black fur had grown and coarsened, losing the downy quality it used to have, but gaining a marvellous sheen. It rippled silkily across the powerful shoulders that showed the Husky strain in him. The white ruff on his throat and chest was like a lion's plumage. He had a Husky's up-pointed ears and slanted eyes, and his jaws were wolfish.

He was growling now, a deep low sound. Not merely a warning—an open declaration of enmity. He did not try to get over the gate. He remained at a slight distance, his lips drawn back in the devil's grin which I had only seen in pictures of other dogs of his blood, never on Nanuk. Harvey glanced at me, and his face puckered into a smile. He knew he was safe on the other side of the fence. Then, with a speed which caught me off guard, he pulled out a slingshot. The stone was fired before I could get down the steps and as far as the gate. It hit

Nanuk on the throat, where his fur was thick. It did not damage him much, but it drove him wild. He flung himself against the bars of the gate. Harvey was already on his bicycle and pedalling away.

I grabbed the gate handle. Beside me, Nanuk was in a frenzy to get out. He could probably have caught up with the bicycle.

I looked at Nanuk's unrecognisable face, at the fur rising in hackles along the top of his back, at the demented eyes. My hand clenched the gate shut once more. I walked back into the house without looking again at the dog. I went to my room and locked the door. I did not want to see anyone, or talk. I had realised something for the first time. Nanuk had all the muscular force and all the equipment he needed to kill a man. In that second, I had not been sure that he would not do it.

Now I had to tell my mother. She did try, after that, to keep Nanuk inside the house at the time when Harvey delivered the papers. But something was always going wrong. Grandfather Connor let the dog out, claiming that Nanuk was giving the house a foul smell. Or else my mother forgot, and would be apologetic, and this would make me feel worse than if she had said nothing at all.

I tried to get home from school early, but I often forgot and went with my friends to the Regal Café to play the jukebox and drink coffee. On the days when I remembered and put Nanuk safely in the basement, I would watch from the bay window of the living room and see Harvey deposit the paper on the porch. He looked in through the gate, and sometimes he even parked his bike for a moment and waited, to make sure the dog was not there. Then, with an exaggerated shrug, as though he knew he were being observed, he would ride off, his face expressionless.

When I was late, sometimes my brother would report to me.

"Nanuk was out today, Vanessa," he told me one afternoon. "Mum wasn't home. And he wouldn't come when I called him."

"What happened?"

"Harvey—well, he lit a whole bunch of matches all together," my brother said, "and dropped them. I got some water, after, and put it on Nanuk's head. He wasn't burned much, Vanessa, honestly."

I no longer wove intricate dreams in which I either condemned Harvey or magnanimously spared him. What I felt now was not complicated at all. I wanted to injure him, in any way available.

I asked my mother if we could go to the police and get them to warn Harvey off. But she replied that she did not think it would be considered a crime to tease dogs, and in any event she was nervous about going to the police for any reason whatsoever.

Then, unexpectedly, Harvey played into our hands.

I owned a telescope which had once belonged to a MacLeod ancestor who had been in the Royal Navy. It was brass, and it pulled out to three lengths, the largest segment being encased in dark leather interestingly scratched and scuffed with the marks of who-knows-what sea battles or forays into dangerous waters. The lenses were still in perfect condition, and if you sat up in one of our spruce trees you could see every detail of houses two blocks away. I was too old now to climb trees and spy, but my brother often did. One day I found him waiting for me on the front porch.

"Vanessa—" he blurted, "the telescope's gone."

"If you've lost it, Roddie MacLeod, I'll—"

"I never!" he cried. "I left it on the grass near the gate, just for a minute, while I went in to get my rope so I could climb up. Harvey took it. Honest, Vanessa. I was just coming out the front door when I saw him ride off. And when I looked, the telescope was gone."

"Listen, Roddie, you didn't actually see him pick it up?"

"No, but who else could it have been?"

"Did you look carefully for it?"

"Sure, I did," he said indignantly. "Go ahead—look yourself."

I looked, but the telescope wasn't anywhere on the lawn. This time I did not hesitate about telling my mother. This was too good an opportunity to miss. I felt jubilant and excited. I felt like shouting some Highland war-cry, or perhaps whistling *The MacLeod's Praise*. Or quoting some embattled line from Holy Writ. Vengeance is mine, saith the Lord.[1]

"In a way, it's kind of peculiar." I said to my mother, talking so rapidly she could hardly make out what I was saying. "You know, like getting Al Capone[2] on income-tax evasion instead of murder."

"Stop dramatising everything, Vanessa," my mother said, "and let me think for a minute what would be the best thing to do."

"What's all this?" Grandfather Connor demanded crossly, having been roused from his chair by the tumult of my voice.

My mother told him, and he was in no doubt what to do.

"Get your coat on, Vanessa. We're going over there right now."

I looked at him, stunned. Then I shook my head firmly.

"It's a matter for the police."

"Rubbish," my grandfather snapped, unable to acknowledge any authority except his own. "What could Rufus Nolan do that I can't do? He's a fool of a man anyway."

I had not bargained on this. I was out for blood, but I would have preferred someone else to draw it.

"You go, then," I said sullenly. "I don't want to."

"You'd better go with him, Vanessa," my mother said. "Father wouldn't recognise the telescope. He's never had anything to do with it."

"I don't know where Harvey lives," I stalled.

"I know where he lives," my grandfather said. "It's Ada Shinwell's house, at the North End right beside the C.P.R.[3] tracks. Vanessa, for the last time, you get your coat on and come along."

I got my coat on and came along. The North End of Manawaka was full of shacks and shanties, unpainted boards, roofs with half the shingles missing, windows with limp hole-spattered lace curtains or else no curtains at all, chickens milling moronically in yards where the fences had never been lifted when they leaned and the weeds never hacked at or fought down. The cement sidewalks were broken, great chunks heaved up by frost and never repaired, for the Town Council did not pay much attention to this part of town. A few scraggy structures had once been stores but had been deserted when some of the town prospered and moved south, away from the tracks. Now the old signs could still be seen, weathered to peeling pastels, grimy pink that had once shouted crimsonly "Barnes' Grain and Feed," and a mute rotting green that had once boldly been "Thurson's General Store." The windows of these ex-shops were boarded over now, and they were used only as warehouses or roofs over the heads of rodents and tramps.

At the furthest point of the town the C.P.R. station stood, respectably painted in the gloomy maroon colour known as Railway Red, paradoxically neat in the midst of the decrepit buildings around it. Above and beyond the station rose the peaked roofs of the grain elevators, solid and ugly but the closest thing there were to towers here.

I knew Harvey had been brought up by his aunt, his dead mother's sister, but that was all I knew about him. My grandfather went directly to the place. It was a small square frame house with wooden lace along the front porch. At one time it must have been white, but it had not been painted for years. The rust-corroded gate stood open and askew, having apparently once been wrenched off its hinges. In the yard the goldenrod grew, and the tall uncut grass had formed seed-nodules like oats. My grandfather knocked at the door.

"Yes?"

The woman was big and haggard, and her face, wrinkled like elm bark, was spread thickly with a mauvish powder. Her grey hair was snipped short like a man's. She wore a brown tweed skirt which looked as though it had never been cleaned throughout a long life, and a tight-fitting and filthy peach-coloured sweater that betrayed her gaunt and plank-flat body.

"Well, if it ain't Mr. Connor," she said sarcastically.

"Where's your boy, Ada?" my grandfather demanded.

"What's he done?" she asked immediately.

"Stole a telescope. I want it back."

The door opened wider.

"Come in," Harvey's aunt said.

The house was not divided into living room and kitchen. There was one large room on the ground floor and it was used for everything. At one end the black woodstove stood, surrounded by pots and pans hanging on nails from the wall. The table was covered with oilcloth, the worn-off pattern showing only feebly. The dishes from breakfast were still there, the grease stiffened on them, the puddles of egg yolk turned to yellow glue. On the cabinet stood a brown crockery basin with a wooden spoon and batter in it—the pancakes for tonight's meal. The house had that acrid sour-milk and ammonia smell that comes from food left lying around and chamber pots full of urine unemptied until they are overflowing.

In the front part of the room stood two armchairs with the plum velour ripped and stained, and a spineless sofa, sagging in the middle, once blue plush and now grimed to a grey calico. On the sofa sat Harvey. His long legs were thrust forward and his head lolled to one side. He looked as though he were pretending, without much acting ability, to be asleep.

His aunt darted in like a giant darning needle.

"All right, you. Where is it?"

It seemed strange that she would ask him this question straightaway. She never asked him whether or not he had actually taken it.

Harvey did not reply. He lay there on the sofa, his eyes flickering open, then half closing again. His aunt, with an explosive quickness that made me jerk in every nerve, snatched the wooden spoon out of the bowl of batter and hit him across the face.

Harvey's eyes opened a little more, but only a little. The amber slits stared at her, but he did not move. He bore it, that she had hit him like that, and in front of other people. He was not a kid any longer. His shoulders and body looked immensely strong. He could have thrust her hand away, or held her wrists. He could have walked out. But he had not done so. Slowly, with a clown's grin, he wiped the batter off his face.

"All right," she said. "I'll give you one chance more, and that's all. After that, you know what."

I never discovered what final card she held. Would she have turned him over to the Mounties,[4] or thrown him out of the house? It did not really matter. Maybe the threat was one left over from childhood, still believed in by both of them, out of habit. Or maybe there was no specific threat at all, only a matter of one will being able to inflict what it chose upon another.

He lumbered to his feet, and in a few minutes he came back to the room. He threw the telescope on the floor, and he gave me a devastatingly scornful look. Then he sat down on the sofa once more.

His aunt picked up the telescope and handed it to my grandfather. Her voice was a whine, but underneath it there was a desolate anger.

"You're not gonna go to the police, are you? Listen, you got no idea how it's been. What was I supposed to do, left with a kid to look after? Who'd have married me? What man would've taken on that? He's never been

anything but trouble to me. Who do you think he takes after? Some shit nobody but her ever seen."

"I'm not going to the police," my grandfather said aloofly. Then he went away.

"Did you know her, before?" I asked him, when we were walking home.

"No," my grandfather replied without interest. "She was nobody a person would know, to speak of. She was just always around town, that's all."

Harvey's pestering of Nanuk stopped, for soon afterwards he quit school, dropped the paper route, and got a job with Yang Min, the elderly Chinese who kept a small café at the North End, where the railway section hands went for coffee.

For Nanuk, the respite came too late. He had become increasingly suspicious of everyone except the family, and anyone who approached the front gate when he was in the yard was met in the same way, with the low warning growl. If they attempted to open the gate, he would stand there, poised and bristling, waiting for their next move. Their next move became predictable. Whoever it happened to be would quietly close the gate and go away. They would then phone my mother. Sometimes Grandfather Connor would answer the phone. They would tell him about Nanuk, and he would rant at my mother for the rest of the day, saying that all Huskies were savage by nature.

"Listen, Vanessa, I want to talk to you," my mother said. "Grandfather knows someone on a farm out by Freehold who's willing to take Nanuk. It would be a much better place for him. He could run around. And on a farm, he wouldn't be so much of a danger."

I knew there was no point in arguing. It had become inevitable. Nanuk was taken away on a morning when I was at school. I did not say goodbye to him. I did not want to. I mourned for him secretly, but after a while I no longer thought about him so very much.

About a year later, the Starlite Café at the North End was robbed. Yang Min, the old man who owned it, was found unconscious on the floor. He had been badly beaten up.

They caught Harvey quite quickly. He had hopped a freight. The Mounties picked him up only two stops beyond Manawaka.

"Apparently he didn't even try to deny it," my mother said. "Not that it would've done him much good. You'd have thought he would have hidden the money, though, wouldn't you?"

What I said then surprised me as much as it did my mother. I had not known I was going to ask this question. I had not known it was there to be asked.

"Mother—what really happened to Nanuk?"

My mother looked shocked and distressed.

"What makes you think—?"

"Never mind," I said. "Just tell me."

Her voice was almost inaudible, and there was a resignation in it, as though she had given up trying to make everything all right.

"The vet took him," she said, "and chloroformed him. Well, what else could I do, Vanessa? He wasn't safe to go free."

Harvey Shinwell got six years. I never saw him again. I don't know where he went when he got out. Back in, I suppose.

I used to see his aunt occasionally on the street. She was considered safe to go free. Once she said hello to me. I did not reply, although I knew that this was probably not fair, either.

NOTES

1. Actually, "Vengeance is mine; I will repay, saith the Lord." (Romans 12:19).
2. Al Capone (1899–1947): Infamous Chicago gangster, finally imprisoned for tax evasion in 1931.
3. Canadian Pacific Railroad.
4. The Royal Canadian Mounted Police, Canada's federal police force.

Mahasveta Devi

India, b. 1926

Mahasveta Devi was born in Dacca in what is now Bangladesh of a middle-class Bengali family. She received her master's degree in English from Shantiniketan, a famous experimental university founded by the poet Rabindranath Tagore. She began teaching in 1964, at Bijaygarh College in Jadavpur, India, an institution for working-class women. She continued to teach well into the 1980s. Today she is also actively involved in work among the tribals. Both her writings and her political activity make her an influential figure in Bengali life.

A prolific writer of both fiction and journalism, Mahasveta's political concerns began to make themselves a felt part of her creative writing in *Hajar Churashir Ma* (No. 1084's Mother, 1975), a novel which is concerned with the 1967 indigenous revolts in northern West Bengal; there the Munda tribals united with intellectuals, especially young students from Calcutta, to break the unofficial collusion between the government and the landlords, which permitted the latter to circumvent the laws designed to give peasants certain agricultural and political rights. The Naxalite movement swept through Bengal before it was quelled by the Indian government in 1971 in the aftermath of the India-Pakistan war. Though the American critic and translator Gayatri Spivak sees this novel as tied to an "excessively sentimental idiom," it was greeted by its Bengali audience as a significant effort to point the Bengali novel in a new direction. With the publication of *Aranyer Adhikar* (The Rights [or Occupation] of the Forest, 1977), a meticulously researched historical novel about an earlier Munda Insurrection of 1899–1900 for which its author received the Sahitya Academy Award in 1979, Mahasveta became one of the most important writers of contemporary India. One critic has described the work as "fecund, savage, and irresistible." The novel is 'stylistically' important as well: its prose represents a collage of literary, street, and bureaucratic Bengalis, as well as the language of the tribals, and as such, gives voice to many who have hitherto not been "named" in their own language.

Many of Mahasveta's short stories, some of which have been collected in *Agnigarbha* (Womb of Fire, 1978), use women as symbols that reflect more general social oppression: This is true in "Bayen" (literally, "of the left hand;" Witch), which follows and also in "Stanadayani" (The Wet Nurse; Breast Giver, translated in *Truth Tales*), a powerful story that tells of a wet nurse who is literally sucked dry by the rich family she works for as well as by her own husband and children. She dies of breast cancer. The work leaves little doubt that the growing parasite that one day finally sucks her to death is society itself.

Mahasveta has published over fifty works, including a dozen novels, most recently *Murti* (Icon, 1979), *Nairite Megh* (Southwest Monsoon Clouds, 1979), *Chotii Munda evam Tar Tir* (Chotti Munda and His Arrow, 1980), and several very distinguished short stories and plays.

WITCH
Bayen

Bhagirath was very young when his mother was declared a "bayen" and thrown out of the village. A bayen is not an ordinary witch and cannot be killed like an ordinary one, because to kill a bayen means death for your children.

So Chandi was turned into a pariah and put up in a hut by the railside, and Bhagirath was raised by a foster mother, willy-nilly, haphazardly. He never came to know what a real mother is like. Now and then however he did have a glimpse of the shed across the field under the tree where Chandi bayen lived alone, Chandi, who could never be anybody's idea of a mother.

He had also seen the red flag fluttering on her roof from afar, and sometimes in the flaming noon of April, he caught sight of a red-clad figure clanking a piece of tin across the paddy fields towards a dead pond, a dog on its trail. For a bayen has to warn folks of her approach when she moves. For she has but to cast her

eye on a young man or boy before she sucks the blood out of him. So a bayen has to live alone. When she moves, everyone, young and old, moves out of her sight.

One day, and one day alone, Bhagirath saw his father Kalinder talk to the bayen. "Look away son," his father ordered him.

There stood the bayen on tiptoe by the pond. Bhagirath caught the reflection of the red-clad figure in the pond—a sun-bronzed face framed in wild, matted hairs. And eyes that devoured him silently.

No, the bayen did not look at him directly either. She looked at his image as he saw hers in the dark waters, shuddering violently. Bhagirath closed his eyes and clung to his father. "What's made you come here?" hissed his father at her.

"There's no oil for my hair, Gangaputta,[1] no kerosene at home. I'm afraid to be alone."

She was crying, bayen was crying. In the

waters of the pond her eyes appeared, swimming with tears.

"Didn't they send your week's ration on Saturday?"

Every Saturday, someone from the Dom[2] community of the village went to the tree with a week's provision of rice, pulses, salt, oil, etc. for the bayen. Calling on the tree to bear his witness, he would run away as fast as he could.

"The dogs stole all."

"Do you need some money?"

"Who will sell me things?"

"Well, well, I'll buy things. Go away now."

"I can't, I can't live alone . . ."

"Who asked you to be a bayen then? Go!"

And he picked up a handful of mud from the pondside. "Gangaputta, this boy . . . ?"

With an ugly oath he threw it at her. The bayen ran away. "You, you talked to her, father?"

Bhagirath was terrified. For to talk to the bayen meant certain death. And the thought of father dying scared the daylights out of him, because he was sure that his stepmother would turn him out.

"She may well be a bayen now, but she used to be your mother once."

Father's voice grew extraordinarily somber. And Bhagirath felt something rise to his throat. A bayen for a mother! Is bayen a human being then? Hadn't he heard that the bayen raises dead children from the earth, hugs and nurses them? That whole trees dry up instantly the bayen looks at them? And Bhagirath—he, a live boy, born of a bayen's womb? He could think no more. . . . "She used to be a woman, your mother."

"And your wife?"

"Yes, that too."

Something made Kalinder sigh and he added, "I'll tell you all before I die. Don't you worry."

Bhagirath stared in wonder at his father as they walked back along the mud culvert. He had never heard his father speak in that tone before. They were not ordinary Doms. They worked in the cremation grounds, and the municipality allowed only one Dom family to work there. His family used to make bric-a-brac out of canes and bamboosticks, raised poultry in the government farms, made compost out of garbage. Only Kalinder out of the entire Dom community knew how to sign his name—an accomplishment that had recently earned him a job in the subdivisional morgue.

A government job that entitled him to forty-two rupees a month after signing on as Kalinder Gangaputra. Besides, as Bhagirath knew, he also bleached skeletons out of unclaimed bodies, using lime and bleaching powder. A whole skeleton, even the skull or the rib-cage, meant a lot of money.

The morgue official sold the bones to the would-be doctors at a handsome profit. The ten or fifteen rupees that father got out of it was enough for him. He invested the sum in usury and had bought some pigs with the interest.

Father was a respected man in the community. He went to his subdivisional office in shirts and shoes. But now he stared red-eyed, for a long time at the piece of red flag above the bayen's hut burning like a vermillion dot against the saffron-colored horizon.

"She used to be so afraid of the dark," he muttered, "did fate have to make a witch out of her? She's better dead now. But no one can take her life except herself, you know, sonny?"

Kalinder must have been very very sad to talk so much at a time.

"Who makes a bayen out of a person, father?"

"God."

Kalinder glanced warily around to see if any other shadow hovered near Bhagirath in the midday sun. For these bayens are crafty in their art, like any flower girl in the market. If she is keen on having some child, she would walk close by, her face in shadow in spite of the fierce sun all around. Invisible to mortals, she would cast the shadow of her veil on the child as he walked. If the boy died she would chuckle with feigned innocence, "How was I to know? I just tried to make a little shade for him in the heat but there he goes and melts away like butter! Too soft!" Kalinder was relieved to find no shadow of a foul-smelling, red filthy veil anywhere near his son. "What fear, sonny?" he said, "She'd never do you harm."

But Bhagirath was still uncertain. His mind often strayed towards the hut. Be it on the paddyfield, be it on the pasture with the cows, his mind would rush to the railside, if only to see how terror-stricken the bayen was of her loneliness, to see how she put oil on her hair and dried it in the April wind.

But he was too afraid to go.

Perhaps he would never come back if he did. Perhaps she would turn him into a tree or a stone for ever.

He only gazed out for days on end. The sky between the canatim tree and the bayen's hut seemed like a woman's forehead where the red flag, now limp, now flying in the breeze, burned like a vermillion dot. He had a mad wish to rush there, and then, afraid of his own wish, he swiftly traced his way back home.

Curiously enough, no one teased him for being a bayen's son; rather people seemed to treat him with care. For if you treat a bayen's son well, the bayen will be well-disposed toward you; your children will be safe. If you treat him ill, your children will die.

Bhagirath's present mother didn't ill-treat him either. In fact she never betrayed any emotion for him whatsoever. The chief reason being that she didn't have a son. Both her children, Sairavi and Gairabi were daughters. She had no influence over her husband either—first because she hadn't borne him a son, and secondly, because she had such protruding teeth and gums that her lips wouldn't close over. She would hardly go out of the house—"How can I show a face like this?" She would say, "My lips wouldn't close at all.

It makes me look as if I'm smirking all the time. You see, Gangaputta, be sure to cover my face when I die or else they'll say, there goes the buck-toothed wife of the Dom."

Jashi does nothing but work all day— cleans the house, cooks rice, collects wood, makes cowdung cakes for fuel, tends the pigs, picks lice out of her daughters' hair. She calls Bhagirath "boy," have your bath boy, as if there was something very formal between them. For if she didn't take proper care of him, the bayen might kill her daughters by voodoo. Also she knew she would have to depend on Bhagirath for her keep in old age.

Sometimes she would sit, chin in hands, her lips baring her prominent gums, in terror lest the bayen was working voodoo spells on her daughters that very moment or making effigies out of clay. At those times Jashi would look uglier than usual. Kalinder had deliberately married the ugliest girl in the community after the loveliest one he had married before turned out to be a witch.

It is said that Kalinder loved his first wife a good deal. Perhaps it was that love that prompted him to tell Bhagirath about Chandi bayen one day. They were walking along the railtracks. Kalinder had a packet of meat under his arms. It was one of his strange weaknesses that he could not kill the pigs he raised himself. He raised them and sold them to others when he needed some meat. He would get a portion of it from his customer.

"Let's sit a while under the tree, eh?" He asked, as if apologetically, of his thirteen-year-old son, and sat with his back against the trunk of the banyan tree.

"This is the place the robbers go by, isn't it, father?" asked Bhagirath.

Bhagirath went to the government primary school these days. Once his teacher had made them paint a wall poster from a magazine. He had sketched out the letters himself and had made the boys ink them thick. It was from the magazine that Bhagirath had come to know that after the Untouchability Act, 1955, there were no untouchables any more in India. He also learnt that there is a thing called the Constitution of India where it is written, at the very beginning, that all are equal.

The poster still hung on the wall. But Bhagirath and his like knew that their co-students, as well as the teachers liked them to sit a bit apart. None but the very poor and needy from the "lower" castes came to the school. And rightly too. Because there are schools and schools everywhere.

Anyway, the fact is that Bhagirath now spoke a bit differently. His accent had changed a bit; Kalinder was fond of listening to him and often felt himself to be unworthy of his son.

Bhagirath asked him about the robbers. These days the evening trains passing Sonadanga, Palasi, Dhubulia, and other places were often robbed. They came in all shapes and sizes, these robbers...posing as gentlemen, poor students, refugee settlers, or house owners to get an entry into the compartments. Then, at a predetermined place and time they would pull the chain and make the train stop in the darkness. Then in would rush their accomplices from the fields outside. They would loot all they could, beat up and even kill if necessary before disappearing. This banyan tree, particularly, was a favorite haunt after dark.

This is what made Bhagirath ask about the robbers. But Kalinder didn't seem to pay much attention to his words this time. His eyes scoured the bare fields and beyond as if in search of something.

"Sonny," he said, "I used to be a hard and unkind man. But your mother, she was soft, very soft. She cried often. What irony!"

Irony indeed! As if God came and turned the tables in a single day in the Dom community. Chandi became a bayen, a heartless child-hunter. And Kalinder grew gentle. He had to be. If one turns inhuman, disappears beyond the magic portals of the supernatural, the other has to stay behind and make a man out of himself.

About this time Bhagirath understood that his father had something to say to him. He was a bit surprised. His father had talked about the bayen only once before. Why today again?

Kalinder grabbed his son's hand, "What fear?" he said, "Why shouldn't you know what everyone knows about your mother?"

They belonged to the race of cremation attendants, the Gangaputras. They were known as Gangaputras and Gangadasis, men and women who cremated the dead ones on the banks of the Ganges. Any river was the Ganges to them in reverence to the great river. Kalinder would carry bamboo trunks and chop wood in the cremation ground while Chandi worked in the graveyard meant for burial of children, a legacy of their respective posts. The graveyard lay in the north of the village, overlooked by a banyan tree by the lake. In those days, if a child died before five years of age, its body had to be buried, instead of being cremated. Chandi's father used to dig the graves and spread thorn bushes over them to save the dead from the surrounding jackals. Ahoy, ahoy, there! His drunken voice thundered ominously in the dark.

Chandi's father lived almost entirely on liquor and hash. On Saturdays he would go round the village carrying a *thali*[3] in hand. "I am your servant," he would call out. "I am a Gangaputra. May I have my rations, please?"

The villagers were scared of him. They would keep young children out of the way, silently fill his thali and go away.

One day a fair girl with light eyes and reddish hair came instead of him. "I'm Chandi," she announced, "daughter of the Gangaputra. My father is dead. Give me his rations instead."

"Shall you do your father's work then?"
"Yes."
"Aren't you afraid?"
"I'm not."
The word 'fear" was foreign to Chandi. She could understand why parents cried when

their children died. But the dead had to be buried; they couldn't be kept at home. And that was what her job was—simple as that. What was so fearsome or heartless about it? Or if there was any at all, it must surely have been ordained by God himself? At least the Gangaputras had no hand in it? Then why should people detest or fear them so much?

This was the Chandi that Kalinder married. Even in those early days Kalinder was in the bone-business with the morgue official. The bones from the charnel house were used as fertilizers and were expensive as well. Kalinder had money as well as courage. At night he used to return home shouting across the field, "I'm not afraid of anybody! I'm a fire-eater! I've no fear of anyone."

One night he came upon Chandi roaming alone under the banyan tree, lantern in hand. "Hey there!" he said, "Aren't you afraid to the dark?"

"No, I'm a fire-eater too, you see!" And Chandi burst into peals of laughter, which rather surprised him. That very April he married her. Next April Bhagirath was born.

Then one day Chandi came back crying, carrying Bhagirath in her arms.

"They've stoned me, Gangaputta, they said I meant evil."

"Who stoned you?"

"How now! You aren't going to beat them, are you?"

"How dare they?"

Kalinder stopped fencing the yard and almost danced around in rage. "Who dares to stone my wife? How dare he?" He began to swear and curse.

Chandi sat and looked fixedly at him in silence. "I haven't got the heart to do it any more," she said at last, "I haven't got the heart to pick up the spade. But it's God's will. What can I do?"

In wonder she shook her head and looked down at her limbs. Had there been a male member of her father's family, he would have done the job. But there was none. They belonged to the ancient Doms of the cremation

ground. When King Harischandra[4] became a servant, a chandal in the burning ghat, it must have been some ancestor of Chandi who had employed him. When the king regained his kingdom and the ocean-girdled earth was his, he began to dole out large territories.

"And what have you got for us?"

It was the ancient Gangaputra, his voice booming large across the royal court. His likes could never speak in a low voice nor hear one, because the fire of the pyres roared eternally in their ears.

"What do you mean?"

"You've ordained cattle for the brahmins, daily alms for the monks. What have you for us?"

"All the burning-ghats of the world are yours."

"Repeat it."

"All the burning-ghats of the world are yours."

"Swear it!"

"I swear by God."

The ancient Gangaputra raised his hands and danced in wild joy. "Ha!" he shouted, "The burning-ghats for us...all the burning ghats for us. The world's graveyards for us!"

Being one of this particular race herself, could she, Chandi, reject this traditional occupation? And dare she, and let God wreak his wrath upon her?

And yet her fear grew greater everyday. She would turn her face away after digging a grave. Her fear and unease remained even after the grave was well covered with prickly bushes. Any time, any time the legendary fire-mouthed jackal might steal in and start digging away with large paws to get at the body inside.

God...God...God...Chandi would weep softly and rush back home. She would light a lamp and sit praying for Bhagirath. At those times she also prayed for each and every child in the village that each should live forever. This was a weakness that she had newly developed.

Because of her child now, she felt deep pain for every dead child. Her breasts smarted with milk if she stayed too long in the grave-yard now. She silently blamed her father as she dug the graves. He had no call to bring her to this work.

"Get hold of somebody else for this work, respected ones!" She had even said one day, "I'm not fit for this no more..."

But no one in the village seemed to listen. Not even Kalinder, whose dealings in corpses, skin and bone, objects of abhorrence to others, had hardened him. "Scared of false shadows!" he had scoffed at her.

If she cried too hard he would say, "Well, no one's left in your family to do this job for you."

And it was around this time the terrible thing happened. A sister of Kalinder had come for a visit. She had a small daughter who became quite devoted to Chandi. The village was suffering from a severe attack of smallpox at the time. Neither Chandi, nor her people ever went for vaccination. Instead, they relied on appeasing the goddess Sheetala, the deity controlling epidemics. Chandi, accompanied by her sister-in-law, went to pay homage to the goddess carrying the small girl in her arms. The temple of the goddess was a regular affair set up by the coolies from Bihar who had once worked on the railtracks. There was also a regular priest.

As fate would have it, the little girl died a few days later, though not in Chandi's house. But everyone, including the girl's parents, blamed the death on Chandi.

"What, me?"

"Oh, yes, you yourself."

"Not me, for God's sake!" She pleaded with the Doms.

"Who else?"

"Never!" She thundered out, "No harm could ever come of me. Do you know my lineage?"

Then suddenly those people, those craven, superstitious people, lowered their eyes. Someone whispered, "Then how about the milk that spilled out of your breasts as you were piling earth on Tukai's grave?"

"Oh, the fools you are!" She stared at them in wonder and hatred. "Alright," she said after a pause, "I don't care if the rage of my forefathers descends on me. I quit this job from this very day."

"Quit your job?"

"Yes. And let you cowards guard the graves. It's a long time now that I've wanted to leave. The Gangaputta will get a govenment job soon. I needn't stay away at this rotten work any more."

Silencing every mouth, she came back home. She asked Kalinder if he would get a room at his new place of work. "Let's go there. Do you know what they call me?"

It was just to calm her down, just to pacify her with a joke, that he said with a loud laugh, "And what do they call you? A bayen?"

But Chandi started trembling violently. She clutched at the wooden pillar that supported the roof. Excitement, rage, and sorrow made her scream at him. "How could you utter that word, you, and having a son of your own too? Me a bayen? Do I nurse dead children at my breast, do I care for them then, and not for my own son? No, a bayen?"

"Oh, shut up."

Kalinder shouted. For it was dark soon and the time for evil to spread its spell on human beings. It was a time when terrible rage and jealously could easily take hold of an empty stomach and uncooled head. Kalinder knew well the ways of his people.

"I'm not a bayen, oh, I'm not a bayen!!"

Chandi's anguished cry traveled far and wide on raven's wings through the hot winds that reached every nook and corner of the village.

She stopped crying as suddenly as she had begun. "Let's run away somewhere when it's dark." She pleaded with him.

"Where?"

"Just somewhere."

"But where?"

"I don't know."

She took Bhagirath in her arms and crept near him. "Kalinder, come closer," she said, "let me lay my head on your chest." And she said, "I'm so afraid. I'm so afraid to have chucked my forefather's job. Why am I so frightened today? I've a feeling, I'll never see you, nor Bhagirath any more. God! I'm afraid!"

It was here that Kalinder stopped speaking and wiped his eyes. "Now that I look back, you know, sonny, it seems that as if it was God who put those words in her mouth that day."

"What happened next?"

Then for a few days Chandi just sat as if dazed. She puttered about the house a bit and sat a lot with Bhagirath in her arms singing. She burned a lot of incense and lighted lamps about the house and had an air of listening closely at something or other.

Two months passed by uneventfully. No one came to call Chandi to work. There had hardly been any work either. They lived very peacefully, the two of them. Chandi became of a piece again.

"There ought to be some other arrangement for the dead children," she said, "the present one is too bad."

"There will be, by and by. Things are stirring."

Then suddenly she said, "How am I to know if I did it right? You see, for in the nights I seem to hear my father raise his call."

"You hear it?"

"I seem to hear his 'ahoy, ahoy, there!' just as if he were chasing the jackals off the graves."

"Shut up Chandi!" At these words fear grew in Kalinder. Didn't he himself sometimes fear that perhaps Chandi was slowly changing into a witch? Nights when she woke up with a start and seemed to listen to dead children crying in their graves? Perhaps it was true what people were saying? Perhaps it would be better to go to the town after all.

Nor did the Dom community forget her. The Doms were keeping an eye on her, to her complete ignorance. Covertly or overtly, socie-

ty can maintain its vigil if it wants to. There is nothing it cannot do, the society.

And that's how one stormy night, when Kalinder was deep in drunken slumber, his courtyard was filled with people. One of them, Ketan, an uncle of sorts of Chandi, called him up. "Come and see for yourself—whether your wife is a bayen or not."

Stupified, Kalinder sat up and stared at them with sleep-heavy eyes.

"Come out and see, you son of a bitch. You're keeping a bayen for a wife while our children's lives are at stake."

Kalinder came out to see. He saw the burial ground under the banyan tree humming with lights, torches, and people who stood milling around in silence.

"Chandi, you!"

His anguished scream was cut off in mid-air as if with a knife. Everyone looked on in silence.

"Chandi!"

There she was, a sickle in her hand, a lantern burning beside her, a heap of thorn bushes stacked up on one side.

"I was trying to cover holes with these."

"Why, why did you come out?"

"The jackals had stopped their cries suddenly. Something in me said, there they are! Right at the holes, pawing for the bodies."

"You're a bayen!" The villagers raised their chant in awe.

"But there's no one to watch over the dead."

"You're a bayen!"

"It's a job of my forefathers. What do these people know about it?"

"You're a bayen!"

"No, no, I'm not a bayen! I've a son of my own. My breasts are heavy with milk for him. I'm not a bayen. Why, Gangaputta, why don't you tell them, you know best."

Kalinder stared as if entranced, at the dimly lit figure, at the breasts thrust out against the rain-soaked clothes. His mind was scared with pain. Something whispered in him,

"Don't you go near, Kalinder. Go near a snake if you will, a fire even, but not now, not to her, love her as you may. Don't go, or something terrible will happen."

Kalinder stepped forward and looked at Chandi with bloodshot eyes. Then he let out a yell like a beast, "O-ho-ooo! A bayen you are! Whom were you nursing with milk in the grave? O-ho-ooo!'

"Gangaputta! Oh my God!"

The terrible cry that tore out of her seemed to frighten the dead underground, her father's restless spirit and even the ancient Dom who was the forerunner of her race. Perhaps this is how the soul rends the air and the earth when a human being is banished from the human world to the condemned world of the supernatural.

Kalinder rushed to bring out the drum that had belonged to his father-in-law and ran back to the graveyard. He shouted as he beat the drum, "Me, Kalinder Gangaputta, hereby declare that my wife is a bayen, a bayen!"

"Then?" asked Bhagirath.

"Then," my son, she was forced to live alone at Beltala. Afraid as she once was to live alone, she is all alone now. Hush, listen how the bayen sings."

From afar a strange strain of music floated up to them, accompanied by the beat of a tin can. The song seemed to have no words at first but gradually the words distinguished themselves.

"Sleep my darling, sleep, sleep, sleep. . . .
Sleep my darling, sleep. . .sleep. . .!"

Bhagirath knew the song, the song that his stepmother sung to make her daughters sleep.

"Let's go home, sonny. . . ."

Kalinder led a dazed Bhagirath back home. Bhagirath realized that the song entered his soul, mingled in his blood, and reverberated in his ears like some inscrutable pain.

A few days later he made his way to the still pond at noon. For he had heard the sound of the tin and had come rushing.

The shadow of the bayen trembled in the water. The bayen was not looking at him. Her eyes lowered, she was filling the pitcher.

"Haven't you any other cloth to put on?'

The bayen was silent. She had her face turned aside.

"Would you like to wear nice clothes?"

"The son of Gangaputta better go home."

"I. . .I go to school now. I'm a good boy."

"Don't talk to me. I'm a bayen."

"I'm only talking to the shadow."

"Even my shadow is evil. Doesn't the son of Gangaputta know that?"

"I'm not afraid."

"It's high noon now. Young children shouldn't be at large in this heat. Let the boy go home."

"Aren't you afraid to live alone?"

"Afraid? No, I'm not afraid of anything . . . .Why should a bayen be afraid to stay alone?"

"Then what makes you cry?"

"Me, cry!"

"I've heard you."

"He's heard me? To cry?"

Her crimson shadow trembled in the water. Her eyes were full. She wiped them and said, "Let the son of Gangaputta go home and swear never, never to come near the bayen. Or. . .or. . .I'll tell Gangaputta!"

Bhagirath saw her turn back and trace her way along the mud culvert, her hair swirling about her face, her crimson cloth fluttering in the air. He sat alone for a long time by the pond, till the waters became still again. But he couldn't hear the song again.

The bayen on her part sat in silence in her hut, thinking she knew not what. A long while afterwards she raised herself and drew out a broken piece of mirror.

"I'm only a shadow of myself!" She muttered incoherently. She tried to run the comb through her hair. It was impossibly matted.

"Why did the child talk about nice clothes? He was too young then to remember." What should it matter to him, good decent clothes for her? She frowned hard in an attempt to collect her thoughts. It was a long time now that the habit of normal thinking had left her. And now nothing was left but the rustle of the leaves, the whistling of winds, and the sound of the trains—sounds that had muddled up all her thoughts.

Somehow she had a concrete thought today: the child was in for some terrible disaster. And suddenly she felt a very wifely anger at the thoughtlessness of Kalinder. Whose duty was it now to look after the child? Who had to protect him from the witch's eyes?

She rose, lit a lantern, and took to the road. She hurried along the railroad tracks. There was the level crossing, the lineman's cabin. Kalinder, on his way back from work, would turn here and take the mud culvert. As she walked towards it, she saw them. There were people doing something with the tracks.

No, they were piling up bamboo rods on the tracks. The 5-up Lalgola Passenger[5] was due this evening with Wednesday's mailbag. It meant a lot of money. They had been waiting for the loot for a long time.

"Who are you?"

She raised the lantern and swung it by her face. The men looked up, startled, with fear-dilated eyes and ashen faces. She had never seen the people of her community so frightened before. "It's the bayen!"

"So you're piling bamboos, eh, you'd loot the train, eh? What, running away from fear of me? Ha! Throw away these stacks first, or you're done for!"

They couldn't undo what had been done, clear the tracks, prevent the disaster, they couldn't. This is how the society is, this is how it works. It's they who had made her a witch one day with much fanfare and beating of drums. The rain lashed her as she picked up the lantern. She was so helpless, what could she do? If she was a witch now, one with supernatural powers, why wouldn't her servants, the demons of the dark obey her bidding

and stop the train? What could she do now, helpless as she was?

She started running towards the train along the tracks, waving at it wildly in a vain bid to stop it. "Don't come any further, don't. There's a heap of bamboos piled ahead."

The train came bounding like a running child and crashed right into her.

Chandi's name spread far and wide for her heroic self-sacrifice that had saved a major train disaster. Even the government people came to hear of it.

When her body left the morgue, the O.C.[6] accompanied by the B.D.O.[7] came to Kalinder's house.

"The railways department will announce a medal for Chandi Gangadasi, Kalinder. Now I know all about you, you see. She used to live alone, but there must be someone to receive it on her behalf. So I've brought the B.D.O. along."

"It was a brave deed, a real brave deed. Everyone is full of praise. She was your wife?"

Everyone was silent. People looked at one another, scratched their necks in embarrassment, and looked down. Somebody whispered, "Yes sir, she was one of us."

This announcement astonished Bhagirath so much that he looked from one face to another. So they were recognizing her at last?

"Well, the government cannot give it to all of you at the same time."

"Give it to me, sir."

Bhagirath came forward.

"And who are you?"

"She was my mother."

"Really? What's your name, then? What do you do?"

The B.D.O. stared taking notes. Tears streamed down his face as Bhagirath cleared his throat and went on, "Sir, my name is Bhagirath Gangaputra. Kalinder is my father's name. Residence—Dompara. The late Chandi Gangadasi was my mother...the late Chandi Gangadasi...my mother sir, not a witch...

she was never a witch sir...never....''

The B.D.O. stopped writing and stared first at Bhangirath, then at the crowd. The Doms stood silent with eyes down as people condemned, torn with remorse. There was a suffocating and unbearable silence.

Translated by Mahua Bhattacharya

NOTES

1. Also *gangaputra*, traditionally, the name of the guides who led pilgrimages along the banks of the Ganga, or Ganges River, the most sacred of India's rivers.
2. A formerly untouchable caste who worked with corpses and performed certain cremation rites.
3. A flat plate, usually made from brass.
4. In Hindu mythology Harischandra endures Job-like sufferings and gains immortality through good works.
5. A passenger train headed away from the city (up/uptown; down/downtown); in this case, a small district town. The system of numbering is British, in use in India's railway system until approximately 1983.
6. A widely used term in India; it may be compared to "CEO" (Chief Executive Officer) and its increasingly widespread and indiscriminate use.
7. Block Development Officer: Government official responsible for development activities in the administrative division called the "block" that could involve loans for small business/industry; agricultural practices; uplift of untouchables, etc. Mahasveta uses it satirically to suggest the ritualistic function and ineffectiveness of the system.

Ana María Matute   *Spain, b. 1926*

One of Spain's best known contemporary writers, Ana María Matute was born in Barcelona and spent her childhood living half the year in her Catalonian birthplace and half the year in Castilian Madrid, where her mother was raised and where her father had a business. Her convent school education was interrupted by the Spanish Civil War, which disrupted her life as well as those of most other Spanish writers of her time. Nevertheless, Matute was able to nurture her passion for writing and in 1948 published *Los Abel* (The Abels), which was a finalist for the Nadal Prize. She won the coveted Nadal in 1959 for *Primera Memoria* (*School of the Sun*, 1960), the Spanish Critics prize in 1958, the National Literary Prize in 1959 for *Los hijos muertes* (*The Dead Children*, 1958), the Café Gijón Prize for *Fiesta al Noroeste* (Celebration to the Northwest, 1952), the Planeta in 1954 for *Pequeño Teatro* (Little Theater), and several other important prizes as well. She has been translated into many languages and two English-language works have been written about her writing, M.E.W. Jones' *The Literary World of Ana María Matute* and Janet Winecoff Diaz' *Ana María Matute* (1971).

Divorced, with one son, Matute began writing children's stories because she wanted to have something to read to him. She has published numerous books for children, including *El polizón del "Ulises"* (The Cabin Boy of the "Ulysses" 1965), which won the National Prize for Children's Literature, and *Sólo un pie descalzo* (One Shoe Off, 1983), her most recently published work. The following excerpt is from *Los niños tontos* (The Silly Children, 1956), which is not a children's book although children are an important motif in all her work.

from THE SILLY CHILDREN
Los Niños Tontos

THE UGLY GIRL

The girl's face was dark and her eyes were like dark plums. The girl wore her hair parted in two big clumps, braided down both sides of her face. She went to school every day with her notebook crammed with printed letters and a shiny apple for a snack. But the girls at school called after her, "Ugly face," and wouldn't take her hand or want to be with her in jump rope or playing with a hoop. "Go 'way, ugly face." The ugly girl ate her apple, looking at them from a distance, from the acacia trees, next to the wild rosebushes, the gold bees, the malignant ants and the earth hot with sun. There, no one said to her "Go 'way." One day the earth said to her, "You are my color now." They put hawthorne flowers on her head, rag and paper-strip flowers in her mouth, blue and purple ribbons on her wrists. It was very late and they all said, "How beautiful she is." But she went off to her own hot color, to her hidden scents, to her precious hiding place where one plays with the sinking shadows of trees, with unborn flowers and sunflower seeds.

COAL DUST

The girl of the coal yard had black dust on her forehead, on her hands and in her mouth. She stuck her tongue out at the piece of mirror hanging on the window-latch, looked at the roof of her mouth and it seemed to her a sooty chapel. The girl of the coal yard opened the closed spigot that was always leaking small tenuous pearls. The water surged out shattering into a thousand panes of glass against the stone sink. The girl of the coal yard opened the spigot on days when the sun came in, to make the water shine, to make it catch and reflect the stone and the piece of glass. One night the girl of the coal yard woke up because she heard the moon scraping against the shop window. She jumped quickly off her mattress and went to the sink where the black faces of the coal heavers were alternately reflected in it. The whole sky and the whole earth were smeared with black dust filtering in under the doors, through window cracks, killing birds and getting into the stupid mouths that open up like tiny sooty chapels. The girl of the coal yard looked at the moon with intense envy. "If I could only put my hands on the moon," she thought. "If I could wash my face with the moon, and my teeth and my eyes." The girl opened the spigot and as the water rose the moon came down, down until it ducked under the water. Then the girl imitated it. Dawn found the child tightly embracing the moon, at the bottom of the wooden tub.

THE WASHERWOMAN'S SON

The administrator's children threw stones at the washerwoman's son because he was always loaded down with a basket full of clothes, trailing behind his fat mother, on the way to the washing place. The administrator's children whistled when he went by and laughed a lot at seeing his legs which looked like dry wooden pegs, the kind that splits in the heat when you give it a whack. They felt like cracking open his shaven head, as one cuts a prickly melon: that elongated head, scarred, that idiotic head which made them so furious. His mother bathed him one day in an earthen tub and soaped his shaven head—watermelon-head, rock-head, bone-head, block-head—that just had to be broken, once and for all. And the fat lady kissed his smooth scalp and there on the kiss the administrator's sons stoned it and drew blood, as they waited for him, hidden behind the flowering brambles.

THE PASTRY SHOP WINDOW

The small boy with dirty bare feet dreamt every night that he went inside the shop window. Behind the glass were apple pies, red sour cherries, caramel icing, all shining. That small boy always went there trailed by a thin, colorless dog. A profile of a dog.

One night the boy looked up, his eyes strangely wide open. That boy's eyes were varnished with sugar syrup, and the small teeth in his mouth were sharp and eager.

He got to the shop window and leaned his forehead against the glass, which was cold. He felt an intense desolation in the palms of his hands. The lights were all off, and he saw nothing. But that sleepwalking child went back to his hut, with the round pupils of his eyes a honey and toasted sugar color, and very wide open.

The sun came, an enormous sun, and the child saw it come in. He couldn't shut his eyes and he sighed. At that moment a charitable lady showed her head at the door. She was carrying a pot of left-over chickpeas.

"I'm not hungry. I'm not hungry," said the child. And the charitable lady went away scandalized—to tell everybody about it. "I'm not hungry," the child repeated relentlessly.

The small thin dog went away, his heart sunk. He came back, carrying a piece of frost in his mouth, which shone in the sun like a huge chunk of rock candy. The child sucked it all morning, yet with all his nostalgia it didn't melt in his cold mouth.

THE BOY WHO DIDN'T KNOW HOW TO PLAY

There was a boy who didn't know how to play. His mother watched him from the window going back and forth on the dirt paths, his hands still, as if slain and fallen against both sides of his body. The boy didn't like the loud-colored toys, the ball which was so round, the trucks with tiny wheels. He looked at them, touched them and then went to the garden, to the roofless land, his little hands pale white and not very clean, hanging next to his body like strange small mute bells. The mother looked at the child uneasily as he went back and forth with a shadow about his eyes. "If the boy liked to play I wouldn't feel so chill watching him come and go." But the father said, gaily, "He doesn't know how to play, he's not an ordinary boy. He is a boy who thinks."

One day the mother bundled herself up and, hiding behind the trees, followed the child through the rain. When the boy reached the edge of the pond, he squatted and began looking for crickets, caterpillars, baby frogs and worms. He stuck them in a box. Then he sat down on the ground, and took them out one by one. With his dirty tiny nails, almost black, he made a slight noise—crack!—and clipped off their heads.

THE BOY OF THE OVENS

The boy who made ovens out of mud and stones found that they brought him a brother like a little skinned rabbit. What's more, the thing cried.

The boy who made ovens saw everybody's backs. His father's back. The father leaned over the new arrival and spoke to him tenderly. The boy of the ovens wanted to touch his brother's eyes, which were so blind and luminous. But his father slapped his outstretched hand.

At night, when everyone was sleeping, the boy woke up with an obsession. He went to the dark corner of the orchard, gathered dry twigs and heaped them up in his small oven of mud and stones. Then he went into the bedroom, and saw his mother's arm, long and quiet, resting on the sheet. He picked up his brother and carted him away in silence. Then he set the small beloved oven on fire and put the skinned rabbit inside.

Translated by Willis Barnstone

Dhirubhēn Patel

The 1920s and 1930s witnessed unprecedented heights of Indian women's involvement in the national movement for independence. Women led campaigns to burn foreign textiles and support the indigenous industry by wearing homespun *khadi*. Her mother was an active member of the Indian National Congress and Dhirubhēn Patel herself later edited a women's weekly journal in Gujarati and established a publishing company that specialized in books on Gandhian thought. Her story "Lipstick" (1978) has the Gandhian satyagraha movement as a backdrop.

But though Patel grew up in what was one of the most politically charged periods in modern Indian history, little in her writings immediately reflects this public ferment. Nearly all her short stories and novels are set within the family and explore, with subtlety and finesse, the complex, fluctuating, and often contradictory, emotional life of the modern woman. Literary historians classify her fiction as psychological and characterize this movement inward as an important post-independence phase in Indian literature. Women writers played leading roles in this literary movement that took place in the 1950s and 1960s.

Patel's novels, written in a simple, realistic style, invariably center on character, the protagonist often, but not always, a woman. The handling of conflict, of suppressed emotion and sudden outbreaks of turbulent feelings, is sensitive and penetrating. In a well-known story, "Tadh" (Cold, 1978), she explores the anguish of a boy who feels he is responsible for the death of a friend. Her first major novel, *Vadavanal* (Submarine Fires, 1963), has as its theme the jealousy between two sisters and its extraordinary outcome. The heroine in "Darpan" (Mirror, 1977) looks into the mirror only to find the image of a person who doesn't exist. In her major novel thus far, *Sheemlanan Phool* (Flowers of the Sheemlanan Tree, 1976), Patel portrays the widening gulf between a husband and wife caused by the husband's failure to maintain communication at any deeper level than that of sexual intimacy and a long-established daily routine. Patel's originality lies in her awareness that the sheer meaninglessness of such a relationship makes it unbearable; it is not necessarily overt cruelty or infidelity that prompts a woman to take what is in her society the reprehensible step of leaving her husband and home. Though there is some idealization of the wife (other younger women are quickly drawn to her and make her their confidante), she is also shown as uncertain of herself, experiencing doubts and resurgences of love. Ultimately, she returns to her home, but with the knowledge that she has compromised and will never experience the genuine communication she seeks. Some feminist critics may be inclined to criticize Patel for the compromise in the conclusion; but she does not for a moment present Ranna as an erring wife who has been received back by a magnanimous husband. Rather, the husband is shown as incapable of a change in outlook even though he is passionately fond of his wife, and the wife as having acquired a surer knowledge of herself and the choices open to her.

Among Dhirubhēn Patel's other important novels are *Vasno Ankur* (Bamboo Seedling, 1967); *Vavantol* (Hurricane, 1979); *Vamal* (Stunted, 1979); *Ek Bhalo Manas* (A Good Man, 1979); and *Andli Galli* (Blind Alley, 1983). Among her collections of short stories are *Ek Lagan* (A Desire, 1957) and *Vishrambhkatha* (The Revelation, 1966), of which the title story is translated here.

A former college lecturer in English (she holds a postgraduate degree from the University of Bombay), Patel has also written for film, including the international prize-winning *Bhavri Bhavai* (1985).

Susie Tharu

THE REVELATION
Vishrambhkatha

They happened to meet at the Manikarnika Ghat.[1]

Vishwas was thoroughly disgusted. To begin with, he did not believe in rituals. Then the fact that he had had to leave his wife behind added to his irritation. During the journey, he had been subjected to the ordeal of eating all kinds of food. He had thought that things would be better here. But he was wrong. It had been decided that they would have their meals at the house of the family priest. Vishwas did not relish the idea at all.

Looking disdainfully at the devoted mass of humanity surging around, Vishwas pressed his handkerchief to his eyes which smarted with the smoke rising from the funeral pyres. He thought it was shameful that anyone should bathe in dirty water and in the presence of so many people. Momentarily, he tried to forget that Janak Rai and Mangala were his parents.

"What blind faith, what ignorance!" he thought. The scorching heat of the sun and his having been without food since morning only added to the nausea he felt at the incessant clamor of people that grew louder every minute.

"*Yajman Raja ki jai ho!*"[2] A priest came forward to put a mark of sandal paste on his forehead. Vishwas had an impulse to slap the brahmin's face. Somehow, he managed to restrain his hand and looked sternly at the priest. Unperturbed by the look, the brahmin asked: "Babuji, where will you stay?"

"In hell," Vishwas hissed and turned away. His mother, Mangala, was still nowhere to be seen. For quite some time, Vishwas stood there, turning a deaf ear to the continuous chatter of the brahmin. But he could stand it no longer.

Janak Rai had gone back to the rest house after instructing Vishwas to escort Mangala back. For all one knew, he might have settled down to have his meal. Vishwas was hungry and that very thought annoyed him.

What was the world coming to? Here he was, letting his work suffer in order to accompany his parents on this pilgrimage. But neither of them showed the slightest gratitude. Any other mother would surely have cooked a hot meal for her son even if they had been camping somewhere for a couple of days. But his mother did not seem to have time for anyone except her gods and goddesses!

His father was no better. Why could he not order Mangala to cook for them at least once if not twice a day? As a matter of fact, his mother should wash his clothes. How could he go about in such dirty and crumpled clothes?

Time stood still. Only the heat kept increasing. Vishwas almost fainted with hunger and thirst. He was even tired of thinking what he would say to his mother should she appear that very moment. Many of the pilgrims had already bathed and left the Ghat. The brahmins too were preparing to leave after picking up their *chaddars* and sandal paste bowls. Still there was no sign of his mother.

Suddenly, a thought struck Vishwas. After all, this was a place of pilgrimage. Suppose she had lost her way? This sea of humanity—and it was the first time she had left the security of her home and stepped out. Vishwas felt a pang of fear. He burst into sweat. In sheer panic, he cut through the crowd and started looking for his mother. She could not talk in Hindi or give anyone her full name and address. She did not know who the priest was, to whose house she had to go! As these thoughts came to his mind, Vishwas panicked all the more.

The moment Vishwas spotted a woman in a gray sari, he turned in that direction. But either the lady would be too fat or too thin or would be talking in too loud a voice. No one had ever heard his mother talk loudly. At home she stayed engrossed in her household duties—cooking food, hunting for somebody's lost things and quietly listening with bowed head to anyone who chose to talk to her in a raised voice. First, it had been her in-laws, later her husband, and now her son and daughter-in-law.

Vishwas could not recollect any occasion when she had done anything to satisfy her own wish or had contradicted anyone. Whenever she spoke, which she rarely did, her eyes would be lowered and her face would register no emotion. After Vishwas grew up, he had convinced himself that his mother had no personality of her own. She would always remain the way she had been. What would have happened to her without someone to guide her? Pride welled up within him when, in comparison, he thought of his wife, and he felt happy.

He had never found it improper that since his childhood, he had dominated his mother. Even today, as he searched for her amidst these unfamiliar surroundings in an alien city, the thought uppermost in his mind was that of giving her a good scolding the moment he found her.

Honestly, she did not have any sense of time. After all, how long could it take to finish her holy bath and climb those few steps? Prob-ably she was sitting with brahmins performing some *puja*.[3] But how long could that take? Such a long time was enough to wash away the sins of seventeen generations. And—there she was!

Right beside a brahmin's colorful umbrella, two women were standing, each with a hand on the other's shoulder, engaged in what seemed to be a very interesting conversation. For a split second, Vishwas hesitated.

Surely that woman in a gray sari could not be his mother. But there was no doubt she was his mother.

Vishwas was enraged. He rushed in that direction. As he walked, he did not bother who dashed against him, who tumbled, or who cursed.

When he was close enough to her, he called out: "Mother!" But neither of the women looked at him. Both of them were deeply engrossed in their chat. They were in a *samadhi*,[4] as it were. They were not bothered by the scorched earth or the heat of the sun above. The milling crowds did not irritate them. They were oblivious to the grim atmosphere of the Manikarnika Ghat, which proclaimed the transient nature of human experience.

The other woman clapped her hands and said: "Do you remember, Mani, that time when you acted the role of a king in a drama and our Yasoda forgot all her lines?"

"*Namdar . . . Jahanpanah . . . Namdar . . .*"[5] Mangala repeated as if imitating someone. Bent double with laughter, as she recollected her childhood incidents—was that his mother, Mangala? Vishwas stared at her in amazement.

"And Shanti, you were bursting crackers at Diwali and . . ."

"Oh yes, I remember it very well. Had you not pulled me away in time I would surely have burnt to death."

There seemed to be no end to their chatting. It was as if two adolescent girls who were reliving their loving friendship had blossomed to life after a lapse of several years. Tender joys and infinite wonders of those bygone years were reflected once again on the faces of those middle-aged women. Vishwas was flabbergasted as he stood there, listening to them.

After what seemed an eternity, Mangala noticed Vishwas. Almost at once her face froze. She asked nervously: "How long have you been standing here, son?"

"Oh, not very long," Vishwas replied gently.

"It's just that—I met Shanti on the way. Where has your father gone?"

"He has gone back to the rest house. Shall we go now?"

"Yes, let's go." Guiltily, Mangala began to collect her bundle of clothes.

"Give those clothes to me, mother," Vishwas said. Taking the bundle from her, he turned with a smile to the other woman. He said: "Let me carry your bundle as well."

"Take it, my son. God bless you. How can I expect you to recognize me? Your mother and I played as children."

Played...Did his mother ever play with her friends? Was she ever a little girl? Hundreds of unanswered questions sprang up in Vishwas' mind. Unfamiliar feelings surged in his heart like the colors of a rainbow. In his excitement, he turned to say something to his mother. Both of them were lost in their conversation once again.

"Is this your son, Mani? What's his name?"

"Vishwas."

"It's a nice name. Seems to be a good boy too." They walked a few steps together.

Suddenly, Shanti remarked: "He doesn't resemble Vinayak at all."

Shocked, Vishwas looked at his mother. A dark shadow came over her face. She could barely mumble in a quivering voice: "But, Shanti, don't you know the engagement with him was cancelled and I was married elsewhere?"

An uneasy silence gripped all of them. As if with one stroke the beautiful house of cards had come tumbling down before them. The soap bubble with all its radiant colors had suddenly burst. The steps of the Ghat seemed endless. And the heat of the sun overhead became unbearable.

As they reached the top, Mangala composed herself and said: "Son, please give this Masi your father's name and address."

Names and addresses were exchanged. The housewives took leave of each other. But that was only a formality. The real meeting had ended right there on the lowermost step of the Ghat.

Translated by Bina Bhakta

NOTES

1. A ghat is an approach to a river, usually a broad flight of steps. The one referred to is a crowded Benares ghat frequently used for the burning or cremation of the dead.
2. Literally, "Victory to my noble patron," an idiom of thanks for a ritual gift requested by the Brahmin. Brahmins usually make a living by performing ceremonies of various kinds, for which they are traditionally compensated. As society modernizes, life has become difficult for the poorer Brahmins. Patel also means us to see the impatience of the younger generation and the commercialization of the holy places.
3. A ritual of worship.
4. Intense concentration in meditation; a trance in which the meditator is absorbed in the object contemplated. The term is sometimes used today to mean a place where a dead person's ashes are kept.
5. Namdar is a name, Jahanpanah is "Your Majesty" in the Mughal tradition. She's imitating the girl in the play fumbling for her lines.

Barbara Morgan, Martha Graham, Letter to the World, *1940 black and white photograph* © *Barbara Morgan.*

Blanca Varela

Peru, b. 1926

Although born and raised in Lima, Varela has spent considerable time in Paris and New York City and these experiences have influenced her work considerably, both in form and content. Her poetry contains elements of surrealism and existentialism and one of her major themes is the absurdity of existence.

Varela was first brought to the public's attention by Mexican writer Octavio Paz, who compared her poetry to that of the great Peruvian poet César Vallejo.* Although her output is small (she has published only three books of poetry), she is very highly regarded in her native Peru and in the rest of Latin America, where she is frequently the subject of articles and essays.

The following poems are from *Luz del Día* (Light of Day, 1963) and *Valses y Otras Falsas Confesiones* (Waltzes and Other False Confessions, 1972).

NOTE

* Important modernist writer (1892–1938) who exerted a major influence on Peruvian poetry.

MADONNA

The one who'd seen it all turned her face away. She was
proud, made prouder. The mother sitting up in bed, holding
her baby like a cocoon to the sun's last rays.

Just then the nurse brought a dark, swollen breast to the
infant's lips. But he was asleep caring nothing for the sun,
the mystery of a first kiss.

A demanding person might complain about a fleshy tone
in the tile floor, the window's triangle of sky should be more
blue, more like the sky.

And not just that—the child, center of attention, crying
so strangely, the soles of his feet together like a monkey!

The architecture clean, but nothing new—part temple,
part market. Stairs that lead nowhere, windows drowning,
breathing in darkness, tomblike arches, empty benches, curtains
knotted in anger.

And then, cutting across time, the procession of women
with the virtues and secrets of their shoulders. They're all
there. The one whose belly shone like a loaf of hard, white
bread beneath her shroud. The mother with a child behind
her full, comforting hip, protecting himself from the miracle.
The married woman with the childish braid and the conspicuously
mature breasts. And among them, but standing apart, the virgin:
wise as a grandmother, with powerful arms, at the window lost
in thought.

Her back to the scene, the gravest, the sweetest of all.
The strange child in her arms, she seems to know everything.
Love in her rolling eyes, blindness and light in the boy's
plump face.

And in the background, fleeing, an old man climbs
painfully up the stairs. At the top stands a woman, beautifully
dressed, ready to help him gently through the right door.

Translated by Marti Moody

WALTZ OF THE ANGELUS* I
Vals del Angelus I

Look what you've made of me, the poorest saint in the
museum, the one in the last room, next to the johns, the
one with the black wound like an eye under the left temple.
Look what you've made of me, a mother who devours
her brood, who swallows her tears and gets fat,
who should abort with each moon, who bleeds
every day of the year.

I've seen you thus, spilling melted lead in
innocent ears, castrating bulls, dragging
lilies, your immaculate limb, in the slaughterhouse
blood. Disguised as a soothsayer or go-between
in Bastille plaza—you were called Jules
then and your kiss smelled of match and onion.
A general in Bolivia, a tank commander in Vietnam,
an eunuch in the brothels' door of the plaza Mexico.
A formidable strawman at the control panel;
The grand chef of adversity stirring catastrophes
in an immense celestial kettle.
Look what you've made of me.
By your hand I'm in his unavoidable torture
chamber, guided by blood and moans, blind
thanks to the labor and grace of your divine spit.
Look at my skin, that of an aged saint at your breath
rate, look at the sterile drum of my womb. It only
knows the rhythm of anguish, the mute thud of your
womb which makes the prisoner, the fetus, whistle
to the lie.

Translated by Nora Wieser

NOTE

* The Angelus is a prayer recited by Roman Catholics in the morning, at noon, and in the evening to
  celebrate Christ's assumption of human nature.

Monique Bosco   *France/Canada, b. 1927*

A highly accomplished and influential novelist, Monique Bosco published her first
work in France in 1961 (*Un amour maladroit*, Awkward Love); four years later
came *Les Infusoires* (The Infiltrators) followed by *La femme de Loth* (*Lot's Wife*,
1970), which won the Governor General's Award in 1971. She has also published
occasional short stories, poems, dramas, and radio texts. Her most recent novels
evince an interest in revising traditional mythological figures, a signature of the
new *écriture féminine* (feminine writing) that has its origin in the latest wave of
French feminism: *New Medea* (1974), *Charles Lévy, M.D.* (1977), and *Portrait de
Zeus peint par Minerve* (Portrait of Zeus Painted by Minerva [Athena], 1982).

Bosco was born in Vienna to a Jewish mother and French father who then
settled in France where Bosco received her early education until her family escaped
to Canada at the time of the German occupation. She did undergraduate and
graduate work in literature at the University of Montreal. From 1952 to 1959, she
worked abroad as a journalist for Radio Canada. Having received her doctorate in
1953, she returned ten years later to the University of Montreal, where she is

currently professor of Québécois literature. Her most interesting commentary appeared in *Le Devoir*: "Lettre ouverte aux critiques littéraires masculins" (An Open Letter to Male Literary Critics, May 17, 1975).

Influenced by Samuel Beckett and Nathalie Sarraute, Bosco creates alienated characters who are unreal to themselves as well as to others; they often compare themselves to Phèdre and Bérènice, protagonists of Racine's classical tragedies. As Gillian Davies has commented, her heroines—la Petite, Carole, and Hélène—are each the "*femme fictive*," discussed by francophone feminist critic Suzanne Paradis. For all of them, literature is literally a way of being, and it is through fiction that they (re)constitute themselves.

This is especially true for Hélène, the first-person narrator of *Lot's Wife*. The episodically structured and fragmented text is both an agonizing postmortem of a ten-year affair and the confessional autobiography of a Jewish girl whose family fled Vichy France only to pass their child off as a Catholic for the purpose of having her obtain a proper convent education. By using the motif of Lot's wife (Genesis 19:26) and a biblical imagery that draws heavily from the Old Testament, Bosco gives voice to a minority within a minority within a minority—that of a Jewish woman exiled from France and immigrant in the francophone community of an English-dominated Canada.

from LOT'S WIFE
La femme de Loth

From time to time I strike my head against the wall. Shrewd, regular little blows. Like striking a mule. To keep him moving. Time passes. Some hundreds of minutes have gone by without my yielding to the temptation of telephoning you.

You're tired of lying, of this divided existence. I remember something you said. You were sick of this "double life." Cheat! You admit it. *Two lovers have I*, as in that stupid song they used to sing in our parents' day.

You've wasted enough time. One must think of serious things. You are forty, with a wife, children and a good position in life. The cards have been dealt.

Ten years from now, when your interlude of chastity is over, you'll be able to go the pace again—faster than ever. With a pretty girl the same age as your daughter....

Luggage. Passport. I cross the gangway, a traveler like all the others, turning around, confused. Other people's relatives and friends are there, waving their handkerchiefs. I am dreaming. For a moment I thought I saw you among them.

"But Lot's wife looked back, and she became a pillar of salt."

Like that besotted woman, I could wither away in such backward gazing. Through the porthole Montreal looms up mistily. I shall devote the next two months to recording this experience of collapse and flight. I'll force myself to find some meaning in my life through my own words, words to wipe out yours, your cruel sentence of rejection and death. If I find no "extenuating circumstances" I'll put an end to it. "30," as journalists end their copy....

What does all this "history" matter, this past only less hideous than the present? Even as I unwind the skein, the thread escapes me. As if I were telling the story of someone else. This awkward, insignificant little girl is no longer myself, though she resembles me in a few un-couth traits. At present I am at once stronger and infinitely more vulnerable. In those days I was not the active instrument of my fate. To-day, I see that I myself have chosen this trap I'm in and have embraced a thousand humilia-tions to remain there. I am still ready for un-conditional surrender, if it would only restore me to favor....

The road of the past is less painful to follow than the one that lies ahead. So I resume the former, only regretting I have no Bible to hand. For I would like to know why God saw fit to save Lot and his daughters if only they would not look back on their city in flames. I understand Lot's wife all too well.

I too, at this summer's end, may perhaps be turned—through shedding so many tears over the past—into another pillar of salt....

With the end of hostilities I at last grasped what this abominable war had accomplished. Europe in ruins. Persecutions, trials. The shock of these horrors threw me into confusion. My years of self-imposed blindness had cost me dear. With growing fascination I read about the concentration camps and gas chambers in Silesia and Poland.

We had heard in 1940 of my grand-mother's death after a short illness. This was the only time my grandfather communicated with us. "In deference to your mother's last wishes," he wrote. No one told us of his own death. I had inquiries made. He had been picked up in one of the first Paris roundups. I never learned anything more. This bereave-ment was now added to the others. The death of this unknown man seemed at times to cause me more suffering than any of them....

It has always given me a slight surprise to see my shadow on a wall or on the ground. So I had a shadow. And fingerprints too, uniquely mine. Even today I'm not convinced of the reality of my life or the possibility of my death.

I'm trying to pin them both down, to trap them on these sheets of paper. Once I've care-fully described the various stages leading to this necessary, inevitable suicide of mine, I'll go ahead with it. It's the only solution. By ceasing to exist, I will have made my first genu-ine choice as a living person. Exit Hélène....

It's all a matter of getting one's own back. "Feminine" literature has always been prac-tical, pragmatic, utilitarian. For hundreds of years! I was delighted by something in Simone de Beauvoir's *Mémoires*—when she admits having written *L'Invitée* only to score off a rival....

I know what I'm doing. It's not you I'm cast-ing off. Nor any of the people around you. I'm writing these pages simply as a lead-up to the fine ritual murder, the grand symbolic festival when I'll immolate myself in style. I'll kill her, this scabby ewe who spent ten whole years of her life in your shadow, bleating....

The altars of my own people have known other victims. Fatted calves and sheep, offered up with all the usual ceremonies to appease a wrathful God. I've found the way out at last. Alive, I'd have run to answer your faintest call. From now on I won't hear you. Too late you'll see the danger of reducing anyone to absolute dependence. Some day the meekest worm will turn, refusing to be stepped on any longer. There are children, it seems, who cannot feel cold, heat, or pain. Their lives are in constant danger. That was how I lived for a long time, simply unaware of suffering. Now I'm waking up from this long sleep. I can no longer ignore these insults: to remain the accomplice and partner of certain tortures is unworthy of a human being. The path from slavery to com-mon sense is paved with abjurations. I've de-cided to take it....

I'll be a double-goer to the end. A shuffler between love and hate, between the Old Testament and the New. Forswearing both. I don't believe in the Incarnation. Like my ancestors, I think we are awaiting our own Messiah. It was you that I hailed as my saviour. Mary Magdalene was not rejected. But you found my offering ill-timed. And yet my oils and perfumes rejoiced your heart. I feel I am going mad....

"Enough of your blab!" Zazie's phrase[2] recalls me to my task, and none too soon either. "You're dreaming, baby. Go ahead and dive, without all this horsing around."

One likes to polish one's final phrase. Then cast one's bottle of spleen on the waters. These poor pages, the mocking proof that in the long run everything is "literature." Life, love, death. Their portrait and parody. Only a pastime to make us forget the death of passion. The idea of suicide slips away like the lover of a night. *Patience, and shuffle the cards.* Life resumes its hold on the victim of life. I'll go on living.

Translated by John Glassco

NOTES

1. The Guest.
2. An allusion to the well-known heroine of *Zazie dans le métro* (translated and made into a film under the title *Zazie*, 1959) by the French novelist Raymond Queneau (b. 1903).

Luisa Josefina Hernández   *Mexico, b. 1928*

Luisa Hernández studied dramatic theory and writing at Mexico's Universidad Nacional Autónoma with Rodolfo Usigli* and received her degree in literature from there. Since then she has been much honored. She was awarded several research grants, including one from the Rockefeller Foundation to study in the United States, where she spent several years at Columbia University; she has directed theater programs in Cuba and Mexico and received first prize in the Fiestas de Primavera competition for her first play, *Aguardiente de caña* (Cane Liquor, 1950), the El Nacional Prize in 1954 for *Botica Modelo* (Model Drug Store, 1951), a prize from the Festival Dramático of the Instituto Nacional de Bellas Artes for *Los frutos caídos* (Fallen Fruit, 1955).

Hernández's early work is similar to that of fellow Mexican dramatist Elena Garro in her concern for the oppression of women within the family structure. However, her later work shifts its direction, emphasizing more general societal problems. She is known for her sharp psychological portraits and asks to be seen as a "human" rather than a "woman" writer.

The following piece is a selection from *La calle de la gran ocasión* (Street of Bargains, 1962), one of nineteen dialogues each of which focuses on a psychological analysis of its characters.

NOTE

* One of Mexico's premier playwrights (b. 1905).

FLORINDA AND DON GONZALO

*Felice sono nella tua cortesia**
Michelangelo Buonarroti, *Sonetti*

FLORINDA: My name's Florinda and I'm a dressmaker.

DON GONZALO: I'm pleased to meet you, miss. What can I do for you?

FLORINDA: Ah, nothing. Mrs., I'm a widow. You must know that for more than a year I've been living opposite here, in that blue house. I had a quiet moment and I decided to cross over and visit you.

DON GONZALO: Do you want...to sit down?

FLORINDA: No, it isn't necessary. The fact is that I said to myself: "Don Gonzalo spends every afternoon seated in the doorway reading. Perhaps a bit of conversation might suit him."

DON GONZALO: I'm grateful to you.

FLORINDA: No. I was dying to speak with you, because I too feel lonely.

DON GONZALO: Don't you have anyone?

FLORINDA: Two women who help me: one who takes care of the house and the other, a seamstress, who helps with the sewing. But in the afternoon, when they finish working, they go with their families. I certainly don't have a family.

DON GONZALO: I have my brother and his wife, but they have too many things to do to sit down and talk with me. I understand.... I'm somewhat of a nuisance.

FLORINDA: Don't say that!

DON GONZALO: I'm not complaining. It's useless to complain of things which have no remedy. I try to bother them as little as possible. I spend all morning in my room and finally at this time, I come near the door. That's always entertaining. One sees the cars, the people...

FLORINDA: But you don't see anything! All the time I've been living across the street, I've never noticed you raise your eyes from your book.

DON GONZALO: Perhaps. Sometimes I don't feel any curiosity.

FLORINDA: Wrong. Curiosity is the source of many discoveries.

DON GONZALO: Like which ones, for example?

FLORINDA: All inventions, like the sewing machine. What would I do without it?

DON GONZALO: Do you work a lot?

FLORINDA: Several hours a day. When some holiday draws near I work more, even at night. But it doesn't matter. I earn more than I need to live on.

DON GONZALO: That feeling must be very satisfying. I haven't earned a penny in my life.

FLORINDA: But it brings loneliness.

DON GONZALO: Why don't you get married again?

FLORINDA: I've had two suitors, but I don't like them. We widows are difficult to please. We know a great deal about life.

DON GONZALO: I imagine so. Once, I was in love, when I was very young. A friend of the family who used to come every day...we would speak of many things....But, what could only be expected happened.

FLORINDA: And what was that?

DON GONZALO: Her parents found out and they advised her to marry another fellow. She resisted for some time, but she ended by accepting him and I agreed. What kind of life would she have had at my side?

FLORINDA: If the two of you loved one another, a lifetime of love.

DON GONZALO: You're very romantic... Florinda.

FLORINDA: For a widow, yes.

DON GONZALO: Girls want to have a good time, go out, have friends. I'm used to being a burden, but I couldn't have endured being one for my own wife.

FLORINDA: You're very proud, and in order to be happy it's necessary to have humility.

DON GONZALO: Everything is learned too late. There's always time to think; however, to act there's but a moment, only one.

FLORINDA: Don't be a pessimist, Don Gonzalo. Life is long.

DON GONZALO: That's no consolation for me.

FLORINDA: You're so handsome, Don Gonzalo!

DON GONZALO: ...

FLORINDA: Pardon me if I've bothered you. That wasn't my intention. I wouldn't want you to consider it all as lost and to speak without hope. Life...life's miraculous.

DON GONZALO: Do you believe that?

FLORINDA: Yes. Of course one has to do something on his part. Don Gonzalo,...I decided to come to see you after thinking it over for many months. The first time that it occurred to me, I thought that I'd never dare. Then, as time passed I began getting used to the idea, so much so that this morning, I now see it as the most natural thing in the world.

DON GONZALO: Among neighbors, a visit doesn't deserve so many doubts.

FLORINDA: A simple visit, no. But it's a question of something uncommon.

DON GONZALO: What could it be?

FLORINDA: A proposition. I wanted to ask you if you'd like to come to live with me. I'd take care of you, and you on your part would keep me company and we'd have conversations when you desired to speak and when not, I'd resign myself to your handsome presence.

DON GONZALO: Then it's...a proposal of marriage?

FLORINDA: Only in case you wanted to see it that way. I'll be satisfied just with your coming to my house.

DON GONZALO: You're...very touching. Remember that I can't help you in anything and that on the other hand I'd give a lot of bother.

FLORINDA: I've already told you that I earn more money than I spend and that I've time to spare. Do you accept, Don Gonzalo?

DON GONZALO: Tell me, what made you think of it?

FLORINDA: From looking at you so much. I used to look at you from behind the window blinds and then I began to dream of you and

to imagine you so clearly that I almost knew what you were thinking about when you were distracted from your book or when you sighed. Then I opened the window and I sat down there to sew, but you didn't seem to see me and I became very impatient.

DON GONZALO: I did see you.

FLORINDA: Ah!

DON GONZALO: Only...how dare I?

FLORINDA: That had also occurred to me. I thought, "If he has seen me, all the more reason for me to go and speak to him."

DON GONZALO: Won't you be sorry?

FLORINDA: I, Don Gonzalo, am very determined.

DON GONZALO: I'd like to ask one thing of you.

FLORINDA: Whatever you wish.

DON GONZALO: That you marry me.

FLORINDA: Thank you very much, Don Gonzalo. I'll be happy to marry you.

DON GONZALO: And, when...when are you coming for me?

FLORINDA: Well, now. The truth is that I was coming now to pick you up, and I intended to return home with you.

DON GONZALO: Now? Right now?

FLORINDA: As it's a matter of only crossing the street and that's so easy....

DON GONZALO: And, the wedding?

FLORINDA: We'll arrange it there.

DON GONZALO: And, my family?

FLORINDA: We'll inform them later...as it's just across the street.

DON GONZALO: In everything you're a woman of understanding. Let's go.

FLORINDA: Let's go.

DON GONZALO: Be careful in getting off the sidewalk because this wheelchair is getting shakier by the minute.

FLORINDA: Don't worry, Don Gonzalo. Close your eyes and think that the street is a river. I'll let you know when we reach the other shore.

Translated by Francesca Colecchia and Emilio Matao

NOTE

* Happy am I for your courtesy.

Joyce Mansour   *Egypt/France, 1928–1986*

Born of Egyptian parents in Bowden, England, in 1928, Joyce Mansour was soon transplanted to Cairo, where she spent her girlhood and early adult years. Although Mansour's first contacts with the world were through English, "the first language I ever understood in spite of the illiterate hispano-arabo-yiddish entourage of my youth" (*Ça*, p.73), she chose to write in her second language. With the exception of a handful of poems in English and the *Flying Piranha* (1978) written in collaboration with Ted Joan, Mansour has published exclusively in French. By Mansour's own admission her works are autobiographical; however, the life experiences at their source are clothed in fiction or metaphor so outrageous that reality is distorted beyond recognition. In contrast to the exhibitionism of her texts, whose explicit scenarios of sadistic and dark eroticism call to mind *The Story of O*, this self-styled "étrange demoiselle," who died in 1986, kept her personal life well hidden from public view.

In 1953 Mansour left Cairo to settle in Paris, where she discovered both a personal ease and a favorable creative climate. Her ties to Surrealism began in 1954, when her first published volume of poetry (*Cris*, 1953) attracted the attention of reviewers at the Surrealist periodical *Medium*, and brought her into the circle of second-generation Surrealists that was forming around André Breton. An active contributor to the Surrealist reviews *Bief, La Brèche*, and *Archibras*, Mansour also collaborated with Hans Bellmer, Max Walter Svanberg, and Pierre Alechinsky, among others, in the production of illustrated versions of her poetry. Two of her texts figured in *Boîte Alerte*, catalog for the Eighth International Exposition of Surrealism organized around the theme of the erotic (1959–1960).

Mansour's works span a thirty-year period, from 1953 to 1983, and are evenly divided between poetry and prose. The earlier collections of poetry, *Cris* (Cries, 1956) and *Déchirures* (Wounds, 1956) have been reprinted in *Rapaces* (*Birds of Prey*, 1960); *Carré blanc* (Blank Paper, 1965; translated as *Flash Card*, 1978) and *Faire signe au machiniste* (Signal for the Driver to Stop, 1977) followed. Selections here have been taken from *Rapaces* and *Carré blanc*. Mansour's short fiction include *Les gisants satisfaits* (The Satisfied Dead, 1958), *Ça* (Id, 1970), and *Histoires nocives* (Noxious Stories, 1973).

Two of the stories from her editions of short fiction have been translated and included in one of the two studies of the poet by J. H. Mathews, *The Customhouse of Desire* (1975). As the titles of Mansour's fiction suggest, the focus of her creative energies lies in the irrational force of desire gone astray: whether portrayed from the perspective of poet or storyteller, Mansour's loving couples appear as victims of each other's pernicious erotic attraction, and her family figures play out oedipal conflicts to their deadly conclusions. The somber and destructive side of Mansour's writing is, however, redeemed by its very grotesqueness. But while Mansour's persistent black humor and eroticized discourse are often taken for a sign of a surrealist heritage, they may also be seen as elements of a developing feminist expression Mansour shares with other surrealist artists, such as Gisèle Prassinos, Leonora Carrington, or Mimi Parent, who, like Mansour, arrived late to the surrealist scene and whose work overflows the narrow definitions of that movement.

Judith Preckshot

A WOMAN KNEELING IN THE SORRY JELLY
Un femme à genoux dans la gelée triste

A woman kneeling in the sorry jelly
Of her menopause
Was knitting as she thought
Of lambs crucified
To the pleasures of the kitchen
And the long sordid years
Of the great famine
To come

Translated by Albert Herzing

I SAW THE RED ELECTRIC
J'ai vu monter les poils roux électriques

I saw the red electric
Hairs of my cleft
Climb upward toward
My throat of plucked bird
And I laughed
I saw humanity vomit
In the fickle basin of the church
And didn't understand my heart
I saw the camel put on its shirt
And leave without tears for Mecca
With a thousand and one
Sand sellers and
Dark crowds like scaly dragons
But I could not follow them
For sloth won out
Against my ardor
And daily habit reassumed
Its disjointed toe-dance

Translated by Albert Herzing

DESIRE AS LIGHT AS A SHUTTLE
Léger comme une navette, Le Désir

Why weep on the hairless skull of tedium
Odious or otherwise
Esthetic
Argumentative
French-style tedium
I know very well how to sew false eyelashes
                    onto my eyelids
Agate expels hate in the pallor of a glance
I know how to imitate the shadow that closes
                    doors

When love
Clicks its lips standing in the hall
Rereading your letters I think of our walks
The promises of summer lingering Place
                    Dauphine
Yawn under cover
It is already five o'clock
Gone are the kites the docile pawing stones the
                    careless dust
Jumbled is the flower-bed squared like a
                    kerchief

Bogged down the lewd glance
Wool piles up on the clothes rack
Night gurgles inert
A beautiful disorder on my table
Why weep over a bucket of blood
Why forage between the old man's thighs
Venice
I'm ready to cover you
With my woodland hollyhock tongue
Ready to chisel at my pelt
Steal from shopwomen
Jump the ditch with no skirts or blinkers
To sink still moist in your gimcrack arms
Why keep afloat make up have fun
Why answer
Why escape
The memory of your icy sleep
Follows me step by step
When can I see you
Without shedding tears
On me

Translated by Mary Beach

OF SWEET REST
Du doux repos

Quickly take a pen
Write
I will steal I will steal
The orbit of the savage moon
The meager sobs of the waves
Arriving from the other shore
Waves wavelets bandelets & twaddle
Write
Roll between my arms
Like a pebble between sky and the bottom
Of a well
Sand is the shield of the blind
On the parchment of his night
Quickly take some paper
Write
Follow me through the flowerbeds
Trenches crutches thorns
Listen

To the confidences of the rose
Chewed diced anodine
Go ahead write on the back of a tidal wave
Carve your signs
A thousand times enrolled
The mute joy of garbage
Submissive under the veils
Of the aquamarine
Trace
The indelible line
My green heart is smitten o spells of the moon
Sign resolutely with your proud cock
On the helmet & the snail's sealed head-piece
Write sign cross out
I drown in the inkwell of the slightest word
Never

Translated by Mary Beach

Christa Reinig   *Germany/GDR/FRG, b. 1928*

Christa Reinig grew up in the poverty of 1930s Berlin. During World War II she worked in a factory, later as a wreathmaker. She studied art history and archeology and worked for a time as a research assistant at a museum in East Berlin. Her earliest literary sketches date from the years at the end of World War II; she began publishing poems in a satirical G.D.R. journal in 1948 and saw her first story included in a 1951 anthology of new German stories. After 1951, when her publication rights were suspended and a series authored by her for publication in the G.D.R. had been banned, she published exclusively in the F.R.G. In 1964 Reinig was awarded the Bremen Prize for Literature and took that opportunity to immigrate to the F.R.G.; she has lived in Munich since then. As a result of this move, when a tragic back injury left her crippled, she was unable to obtain state support from either Germany. Reinig's poetry is characterized in part by the typical satirical wit of the Berliners, which may, however, be seen as a disguise for the bitterness that lies beneath—the macabre, humor, and nonsense become devices for defending against the horrors of everyday reality. But she is also recognized for a lyrical voice of great poetic power, much evident in her first collection of poems, *Die Steine von Finisterre* (The Stones of Finisterre, 1960). In later poems, notably in *Die Schwalbe von Olevano* (The Sparrow of Olevano, 1969), she begins to abandon her frequent use of allegory and metaphor, preferring instead the shock value of setting everyday individual experiences into linguistic bold relief. The last two poems here are from that volume; the first two selections are found in *Orion trat aus dem Haus*

(Orion Stepped out of the House, 1968), whose central motifs are astrological signs and constellations.

Reinig has also composed radio plays, translated Russian poetry, edited a volume of poems by the nineteenth-century Romantic poet Annette von Droste-Hülshoff (1968), written for children, and published stories and two novels. The first novel, *Die himmlische und die irdische Geometrie* (Heavenly and Earthly Geometry, 1975), is actually an autobiography; the second, *Entmannung* (Unmanning, 1976), is dominated on the one hand by an increasing quality of the fantastic, on the other by a radical feminist perspective that Reinig has assumed in the past decade or so, becoming one of the most prominent (and provocative) spokeswomen for the feminist cause in West Germany. Since that declarative work, she has published three further volumes of poetry and a collection of stories and essays entitled *Der Wolf und die Witwen* (The Wolf and the Widows, 1980).

Marilyn Sibley Fries

MILKY WAY
Milchstraße

The dairy was burning. The fire brigade pushed the pump wagon out of the fire house and clanged away. But since the fire house stood right next to the dairy, the fire brigade would have had nothing to clang about. Therefore they drove out of the village, around the village, and clanged. When they came clanging into the village again the fire house was aflame as well. The hydrant was inside the firehouse. The firemen broke into the dairy, fought their way through smoke and flames, connected the hose to the huge village milk vat, and extinguished the fire. The first suit was filed by the dairy against the insurance company and by the insurance company against the dairy, because neither wanted to pay for the damage. The second suit was filed by the dairy against the fire brigade because the firemen had misappropriated the milk. The third suit was filed by the fire department against the dairy because the dairy company had infringed on the safety regulations and built its dairy too close to the fire house. The fourth suit was filed by the fire department against the state government because the state water department official had improperly installed the hydrant in the fire house. The fifth suit was filed by the state government against the fire department because it had arrived too late at the scene of the fire in violation of the emergency regulations. The sixth suit was filed by the dairy against God Almighty, because He had let the lightning strike. The seventh suit was filed by God Almighty against the fire department because it had made a mess of the heavens.

Translated by Charles L. Findlay

DOLPHIN
Delphin

It's no use, said the keeper, he is too old for sports activities, he has read all the detective stories, and I lose move after move at chess. I am simply no opponent for him. The zoo director spoke into the pool. What else can we do for you, my friend? The dolphin snapped shut the *Critique of Pure Reason** and yawned: While I was still nursing my mother sang to me as a riddle-me-ree that time and space are *a priori*. The solution was: The *Ding-an-sich* is unknowable—Would you like to paint a picture? asked the director, the chimpanzees' exhibition was a great success.— In that case I would not like to paint a picture, said the dolphin, what's all right for a chimpanzee is unworthy of a dolphin.—Would you like to found a new philosophical system, perhaps? The dolphin said: Give me twenty-four hours. I'll consider it. The next day the director returned. Have you thought about it?—Better still, I have accomplished it, said the dolphin, metaphilosophy has been born. Do you happen to have a five-mark piece in your pocket? The dolphin rose out of the water, spun the five-mark piece like a planet, and spoke: All previous philosophemes can be reduced to four. One: This five-mark piece is a five-mark piece and is nothing but a five-mark piece. Two: This five-mark piece is not a five-mark piece, rather is something quite different from a five-mark piece. Three: This five-mark piece is a five-mark piece and is not a five-mark piece. It is both at the same time. Four: This five-mark piece is a five-mark piece and is not a five-mark piece. It is both at once and neither, rather two five-mark pieces equal one ten-mark note, for it is capital and bears interest. Five! Metaphilosophy: If five is equal to ten, one is equal to two. If one is equal to two, one plus one equals two but is equal to three as well, and even four, then one is equal to four; and consequently one plus one equals five equals six equals seven, etc., and following the necessity of the inductive conclusion one plus one equals infinity. One minus one is therefore both one as well as zero and minus one, one plus one minus one is therefore equal to zero and equal to one and two, consequently one plus one equals one minus one equals zero equals one equals infinity. One equals infinity. I am a dolphin. I am one. I am infinity. I am God. The dolphin swallowed the five-mark piece and sank beneath the waves. After the autopsy the director recovered his money.

Translated by Charles L. Findlay

NOTE

* The 1781 text of Immanuel Kant (1724–1804), German philosopher, which stated that the *Ding-an-sich*, the thing-in-itself, that lies beyond experience is unknowable, although we may assume *a priori* (that is, before the fact) knowledge of it.

THE TREE THAT LEARNED TO TALK
Der Baum, der reden lernte

It wasn't aware,
that it was a tree.
They sawed it in two.
The bulldozer could turn.

Out of its stumps it thrusts leaf after leaf,
stuttering,
it gives answers to questions.

Translated by Julia Penn

ODE TO BEING BENUMBED BY THE WIND
Gesang auf die Benommenheit im Wind

He is standing benumbed by the wind.
Wind's taken it.
What was being became wind.
What became wind has been.
Being nothing more.
Being pitiful.
Maybe the stones are merciful.

To be for once.
To be for once not nothing.
Not to be paper.
Paper is impatient.
Paper is not stone.
Stone is benumbedness.

Maybe when the wind blows it's turning into
stone.

Translated by Julia Penn

Ana Maria Hatherly   *Portugal, b. 1929*

Ana Hatherly has a diverse educational background: music study in Portugal, France, and Germany; a degree in Germanic philology from the University of Lisbon; a diploma from the London Film School. This background testifies well to the range of her artistic interests, which was also visible in the series of programs on vanguard art she organized for Portuguese television (1978–1979).

Hatherly has described herself as a writer who is inclined toward the visual arts through experimentation with words. Her poetry is among the most original of her generation in its exploration of the many values of the verbal and the visual in poetry and in poetic prose. The extent to which Hatherly has stretched the fabric of language has been evident in collective exhibits of work by experimental poets such as the one held in 1980 at the National Gallery of Modern Art in Lisbon and also in theatrical representations. She has been particularly conscious of the partnership that is now possible between literature and the mass media: "The syntactical complexity of languages in our day, the interaction of written and pictorial forms, the broad range of available media, among other things, point to a necessary link between art and technology" (Hatherly, Graz Meeting of Artists and Art Critics, Austria, 1978).

Hatherly has published over a dozen books since 1958. The majority are collections of poetry, all well represented in the restrospective anthology *Poesia 1958–1978* (Poetry) published in Lisbon in 1980. There is also a fine prose work *O Mestre* (The Teacher, 1963) and critical works: *PO–EX—Textos Teóricos e Documentos da Poesia Experimental Portuguesa* (PO–EX—Theoretical Texts and Documents of Portuguese Experimental Poetry, 1979). The following works are from *39 Tisanas* (Tisanes, 1969), named for a medicinal herb.

Alice Clemente

TISANE 12

Once upon a time there were two serpents who did not like one another. One day they met on a narrow path and as they disliked each other they devoured one another, mutually. When each devoured the other nothing was left. This traditional tale demonstrates that one must love one's neighbour or else be very careful what one eats.

TISANE 13

Once upon a time there were two ears which lived on top of a cat's head. Tired of spending their lives perked up they frequently lamented their sad fate. Until one day they decided that they no longer wished to live perked up and began to study a way of putting an end to that degrading posture. Said the left ear to the right what if we folded. Said the right what a good idea you do it first so I can see how it's done. The left ear folded. It curled inwards with the utmost determination. It stayed that way for some time until the cat irritated began to scratch the rolled up ear and since it offered resistance the cat stopped scratching only when it perked up again streaming with blood.

Translated by Suzette Macedo

Ursula K. Le Guin   *US, b. 1929*

Ursula Le Guin is one of the few writers in this anthology whose major contributions lie in the traditionally female genre of children's literature and the traditionally male genre of science fiction. Le Guin rechannels science fiction's usual emphasis on technological progress and evolution by the very different resources she brings to bear on it: an anthropological vision derived from her father's profession has embued her work with a respect for difference; knowledge derived from her graduate study of the romance in the Middle Ages and the Renaissance endows it with strong traditional motifs; her personal commitment to Taoism permeates the nondualistic worlds she creates; a concern with the impact of patriarchal politics—on women, on social affairs, and on the earth—leads her to make gender a central theme. By her sensitivity to language, the depth of her characterizations, and the seriousness of the issues she raises, Le Guin has, depending on whether the speaker is an academic critic or a sci-fi buff, either transformed the genre or escaped its boundaries.

Born in Berkeley to anthropologist A.L. Kroeber and writer Theodora, Le Guin was educated at Radcliffe College and Columbia University before winning a Fulbright Scholarship in 1953 to study in France. In the same year, she met and married historian Charles Le Guin. Le Guin has since made her home in Oregon with her husband and three children, devoting herself to writing and occasional teaching.

Rocannon's World (1966) was Le Guin's first novel in what was to become the Hainish cycle, stories related to the various people descended from the original Hainish, who populated the many planets of the universe, including Earth. *Planet of Exile* (1966), *City of Illusions* (1967), *The Left Hand of Darkness* (1969), and *The Dispossessed* (1974) all take place long after these related peoples have been isolated from one another by galactic war and an ensuing dark age and concern, at least in part, efforts to renew contact. While *The Word for World Is Forest* (1972) is Le Guin's most explicitly political work in this cycle, severely condemning colonial exploitation and protesting the Vietnam War, *The Left Hand of Darkness* is her most thorough effort to reconstruct the universe in response to the feminist currents of the period, as she herself acknowledged in her essay "Is Gender Necessary?" The book (winner of several prizes including the prestigious science-fiction Hugo and Nebula awards) is one of Le Guin's most popular works, with over thirty paperback printings.

If the Hainish cycle takes place within recognizable time and space, Le Guin's Earthsea trilogy, originally written for children, is more clearly in the fantasy mode. The trilogy shows her indebtedness to Tolkien, one of the few fantasy or science-fiction writers Le Guin acknowledges as an influence, along with Stanislaw Lem, Philip K. Dick, and Cordwainer Smith. In *A Wizard of Earthsea* (1968), *The Tombs of Atuan* (1971), and *The Farthest Shore* (1972), Le Guin also reveals her talent for naturalizing the supernatural, to paraphrase Robert Scholes.

Le Guin has moved in a variety of directions and worked in genres that blend realism and fantasy. A number of works are set on Le Guin's homeground, such as the satirical *Lathe of Heaven* (1971) and the aptly named *Always Coming Home*

(1985). The latter seems to initiate the Kesh cycle, continued in Le Guin's new collection, *Buffalo Gals and Other Animal Presences* (1987).

Le Guin's short fiction bears radically different relations to the rest of her oeuvre. Some, like those in *The Wind's Twelve Quarters* (1975), represent more-or-less conventional science fiction and fantasy and often prefigure or become part of the novels. Other stories contribute to a broadened definition of what has come to be called speculative fiction. It is a sign of Le Guin's personal success and a radically changed social and literary climate that the stories that comprise *Orsinian Tales* (1976) could not find a publisher in the 1950s and 1960s when she wrote them but were nominated for a National Book Award when they appeared in the following decade. In the book Le Guin creates a world that is historically definable *and* on another plane; one critic has said that it is located in the sick heart of Europe. The pun on Ursinian (the constellation Ursa the Bear and the source of the name Ursula), reinforced by the title of the closing story, reprinted here, is a clue to the territory we find ourselves in. Other collections include *Interfaces* and *Edges* (both 1980) and *The Compass Rose* (1982).

IMAGINARY COUNTRIES

"We can't drive to the river on Sunday," the baron said, "because we're leaving on Friday." The two little ones gazed at him across the breakfast table. Zida said, "Marmalade, please," but Paul, a year older, found in a remote, disused part of his memory a darker dining-room from the windows of which one saw rain falling. "Back to the city?" he asked. His father nodded. And at the nod the sunlit hill outside these windows changed entirely, facing north now instead of south. That day red and yellow ran through the woods like fire, grapes swelled fat on the heavy vines, and the clear, fierce, fenced fields of August stretched themselves out, patient and unboundaried, into the haze of September. Next day Paul knew the moment he woke that it was autumn, and Wednesday. "This is Wednesday," he told Zida, "tomorrow's Thursday, and then Friday when we leave."

"I'm not going to," she replied with indifference, and went off to the Little Woods to work on her unicorn trap. It was made of an egg-crate and many little bits of cloth, with various kinds of bait. She had been making it

ever since they found the tracks, and Paul doubted if she would catch even a squirrel in it. He, aware of time and season, ran full speed to the High Cliff to finish the tunnel there before they had to go back to the city.

Inside the house the baroness's voice dipped like a swallow down the attic stairs. "O Rosa! Where *is* the blue trunk then?" And Rosa not answering, she followed her voice, pursuing it and Rosa and the lost trunk down stairs and ever farther hallways to a joyful reunion at the cellar door. Then from his study the baron heard Tomas and the trunk come grunting upward step by step, while Rosa and the baroness began to empty the children's closets, carrying off little loads of shirts and dresses like delicate, methodical thieves. "What are you doing?" Zida asked sternly, having come back for a coat-hanger in which the unicorn might entangle his hoof. "Packing," said the maid. "Not my things," Zida ordered, and departed. Rosa continued rifling her closet. In his study the baron read on undisturbed except by a sense of regret which rose perhaps from the sound of his wife's sweet, distant voice, perhaps from the quality of the sunlight falling across his desk from the uncurtained window.

In another room his older son Stanislas put a microscope, a tennis racket, and a box full of rocks with their labels coming unstuck into his suitcase, then gave it up. A notebook in his pocket, he went down the cool red halls and stairs, out the door into the vast and sudden sunlight of the yard. Josef, reading under the Four Elms, said, "Where are you off to? It's hot." There was no time for stopping and talking. "Back soon," Stanislas replied politely and went on, up the road in dust and sunlight, past the High Cliff where his half-brother Paul was digging. He stopped to survey the engineering. Roads metalled with white clay zigzagged over the cliff-face. The Citroen and the Rolls were parked near a bridge spanning an erosion-gully. A tunnel had been pierced and was in process of enlargement. "Good tunnel," Stanislas said. Radiant and filthy, the engineer replied, "It'll be ready to drive through this evening, you want to come to the ceremony?" Stanislas nodded, and went on. His road led up a long, high hillslope, but he soon turned from it and, leaping the ditch, entered his kingdom and the kingdom of the trees. Within a few steps all dust and bright light were gone. Leaves overhead and underfoot; an air like green water through which birds swam and the dark trunks rose lifting their burdens, their crowns, towards the other element, the sky. Stanislas went first to the Oak and stretched his arms out, straining to reach a quarter of the way around the trunk. His chest and cheek were pressed against the harsh, scored bark; the smell of it and its shelf-fungi and moss was in his nostrils and the darkness of it in his eyes. It was a bigger thing than he could ever hold. It was very old, and alive, and did not know that he was there. Smiling, he went on quietly, a notebook full of maps in his pocket, among the trees towards yet-uncharted regions of his land.

Josef Brone, who had spent the summer assisting his professor with documentation of the history of the Ten Provinces in the Early Middle Ages, sat uneasily reading in the shade of elms. Country wind blew across the pages, across his lips. He looked up from the Latin chronicle of a battle lost nine hundred years ago to the roofs of the house called Asgard. Square as a box, with a sediment of porches, sheds, and stables, and square to the compass, the house stood in its flat yard; after a while in all directions the fields rose up slowly, turning into hills, and behind them were higher hills, and behind them sky. It was like a white box in a blue and yellow bowl, and Josef, fresh from college and intent upon the Jesuit seminary he would enter in the fall, ready to read documents and make abstracts and copy references, had been embarrassed to find that the baron's family called the place after the home of the northern gods. But this no longer troubled him. So much had happened here that he had not expected, and so little seemed to have been finished. The history was years from completion. In three months he had never found out where Stanislas went, alone, up the road. They were leaving on Friday. Now or never. He got up and followed the boy. The road passed a ten-foot bank, halfway up to which clung the little boy Paul, digging in the dirt with his fingers, making a noise in his throat: rrrm, rrrrm. A couple of toy cars lay at the foot of the bank. Josef followed the road on up the hill and presently began expecting to reach the top, from which he would see where Stanislas had gone. A farm came into sight and went out of sight, the road climbed, a lark went up singing as if very near the sun; but there was no top. The only way to go downhill on this road was to turn around. He did so. As he neared the woods above Asgard a boy leapt out onto the road, quick as a hawk's shadow. Josef called his name, and they met in the white glare of dust. "Where have you been?" asked Josef, sweating.—"In the Great Woods," Stanislas answered, "that grove there." Behind him the trees gathered thick and dark. "Is it cool in there?" Josef asked wistfully. "What do you do in there?"—"Oh, I map trails. Just for the fun of it. It's bigger than it looks." Stanislas hesitated, then added, "You haven't been in it? You might like to see the Oak." Josef followed him over the ditch and through the close green air to the Oak. It was the biggest tree he had ever seen; he had not seen very many. "I suppose it's very old," he said, looking up puzzled at the reach of branches, galaxy after galaxy of green leaves without end. "Oh, a century or two or three or six," said the boy, "see if you can reach around it!" Josef spread out his arms and strained, trying vainly to keep his cheek off the rough bark. "It takes four men to reach around it," Stanislas said. "I call it Yggdrasil.[1] You know. Only of course Yggdrasil was an ash, not an oak. Want to see Loki's Grove?"[2] The road and the hot white sunlight were gone entirely. The young man followed his guide farther into the maze and game of names which was also a real forest: trees, still air, earth. Under tall grey alders above a dry streambed they discussed the tale of the death of Baldur,[3] and Stanislas pointed out to Josef the dark clots, high in the boughs of lesser oaks, of mistletoe. They left the woods and went down the road towards Asgard. Josef walked along stiffly in the dark suit he had bought for his last year at the University, in his pocket a book in a dead language. Sweat ran down his face, he felt very happy. Though he had no maps and was rather late arriving, at least he had walked once through the forest. They passed Paul still burrowing, ignoring the clang of the iron triangle down at the house, which signalled meals, fires, lost children, and other noteworthy events. "Come on, lunch!" Stanislas ordered. Paul slid down the bank and they proceeded, seven, fourteen and twenty-one, sedately to the house.

That afternoon Josef helped the professor pack books, two trunks full of books, a small library of medieval history. Josef liked to read books, not pack them. The professor had asked him, not Tomas, "Lend me a hand with the books, will you?" It was not the kind of work he had expected to do here. He sorted

and lifted and stowed away load after load of resentment in insatiable iron trunks, while the professor worked with energy and interest, swaddling incunabula like babies, handling each volume with affection and despatch. Kneeling with keys he said, "Thanks, Josef! That's that," and lowering the brass catchbars locked away their summer's work, done with, that's that. Josef had done so much here that he had not expected to do, and now nothing was left to do. Disconsolate, he wandered back to the shade of the elms; but the professor's wife, with whom he had not expected to fall in love, was sitting there. "I stole your chair," she said amiably, "sit on the grass." It was more dirt than grass, but they called it grass, and he obeyed. "Rosa and I are worn out," she said, "and I can't bear to think of tomorrow. It's the worst, the next-to-last day—linens and silver and turning dishes upside down and putting out mousetraps and there's always a doll lost and found after everybody's searched for hours under a pile of laundry—and then sweeping the house and locking it all up. And I hate every bit of it, I hate to close this house." Her voice was light and plaintive as a bird's calling in the woods, careless whether anybody heard its plaintiveness, careless of its plaintiveness. "I hope you've liked it here," she said.

"Very much, baroness."

"I hope so. I know Severin has worked you very hard. And we're so disorganized. We and the children and the visitors, we always seem to scatter so, and only meet in passing. . . .I hope it hasn't been distracting." It was true; all summer in tides and cycles the house had been full or half full of visitors, friends of the children, friends of the baroness, friends, colleagues and neighbors of the baron, duck-hunters who slept in the disused stable since the spare bedrooms were full of Polish medieval historians, ladies with broods of children the smallest of whom fell inevitably into the pond about this time of the afternoon. No wonder it was so still, so autumnal now: the rooms vacant, the pond smooth, the hills empty of dispersing laughter.

"I have enjoyed knowing the children," Josef said, "particularly Stanislas." Then he went red as a beet, for Stanislas alone was not her child. She smiled and said with timidity, "Stanislas is very nice. And fourteen—fourteen is such a fearful age, when you find out so fast what you're capable of being, but also what a toll the world expects. . . . He handles it very gracefully. Paul and Zida now, when they get that age they'll lump through it and be tiresome. But Stanislas learned loss so young. . . . When will you enter the seminary?" she asked, moving from the boy to him in one reach of thought. "Next month," he answered looking down, and she asked, "Then you're quite certain it's the life you want to lead?" After a pause and still not looking at her face, though the white of her dress and the green and gold of leaves above her filled his eyes, he said, "Why do you ask, baroness?"

"Because the idea of celibacy terrifies me," she replied, and he wanted to stretch out on the ground flecked with elm leaves like thin oval coins of gold, and die.

"Sterility," she said, "you see, sterility is what I fear, I dread. It is my enemy. I know we have other enemies, but I hate it most, because it makes life less than death. And its allies are horrible: hunger, sickness, deformation, and perversion, and ambition, and the wish to be secure. What on earth are the children doing down there?" Paul had asked Stanislas at lunch if they could play Ragnarok[4] once more. Stanislas had consented, and so was now a Frost Giant storming with roars the ramparts of Asgard represented by a drainage ditch behind the pond. Odin[5] hurled lightning from the walls, and Thor[6]—"Stanislas!" called the mother rising slender and in white from her chair beside the young man, "don't let Zida use the hammer, please."

"I'm Thor, I'm Thor, I got to have a hammer!" Zida screamed. Stanislas intervened briefly, then made ready to storm the ramparts again, with Zida now at his side, on all fours. "She's Fenris the Wolf now," he called up to the mother, his voice ringing through the hot afternoon with the faintest edge of laughter. Grim and stern, one eye shut, Paul gripped his staff and faced the advancing armies of Hel and the Frozen Lands.[7]

"I'm going to find some lemonade for everybody," the baroness said, and left Josef to sink at last face down on the earth, surrendering to the awful sweetness and anguish she had awakened in him, and would it ever sleep again? while down by the pond Odin strove with the icy army on the sunlit battlements of heaven.

Next day only the walls of the house were left standing. Inside it was only a litter of boxes and open drawers and hurrying people carrying things. Tomas and Zida escaped, he, being slow-witted amid turmoil and the only year-round occupant of Asgard, to clean up the yard out of harm's way, and she to the Little Woods all afternoon. At five Paul shrilled from his window, "The car! The car! It's coming!" An enormous black taxi built in 1923 groaned into the yard, feeling its way, its blind, protruding headlamps flashing in the western sun. Boxes, valises, the blue trunk and the two iron trunks were loaded into it by Tomas, Stanislas, Josef, and the taxi-driver from the village, under the agile and efficient supervision of Baron Severin Egideskar, holder of the Follen Chair of Medieval Studies at the University of Krasnoy. "And you'll get us back together with all this at the station tomorrow at eight—right?" The taxi-driver, who had done so each September for seven years, nodded. The taxi laden with the material impediments of seven people lumbered away, changing gears down the road in the weary, sunny stillness of late afternoon, in which the house stood intact once more room after empty room.

The baron now also escaped. Lighting a pipe he strolled slowly but softly, like one escaping, past the pond and past Tomas's chickencoops, along a fence overgrown with ripe wild grasses bowing their heavy, sunlit heads, down to the grove of weeping birch called the Little Woods. "Zida?" he said, pausing in the faint, hot shade shaken by the ceaseless trilling of crickets in the fields around the grove. No answer. In a cloud of blue pipe-smoke he paused again beside an egg-crate decorated with many little bits of figured cloth and colored paper. On the mossy, much-trodden ground in front of it lay a wooden coat hanger. In one of the compartments of the crate was an eggshell painted gold, in another a bit of quartz, in another a breadcrust. Nearby, a small girl lay sound asleep with her shoes off, her rump higher than her head. The baron sat down on the moss near her, relit his pipe, and contemplated the egg-crate. Presently he tickled the soles of the child's feet. She snorted. When she began to wake, he took her onto his lap.

"What is that?"

"A trap for catching a unicorn." She brushed hair and leafmold off her face and arranged herself more comfortably on him.

"Caught any?"

"No."

"Seen any?"

"Paul and I found some tracks."

"Split-hoofed ones, eh?"

She nodded. Delicately through twilight in the baron's imagination walked their neighbor's young white pig, silver between birch trunks.

"Only young girls can catch them, they say," he murmured, and then they sat still for a long time.

"Time for dinner," he said. "All the tablecloths and knives and forks are packed. How shall we eat?"

"With our fingers!" She leapt up, sprang away. "Shoes," he ordered, and laboriously she fitted her small, cool, dirty feet into leather sandals, and then, shouting "Come on, papa!" was off. Quick and yet reluctant, seeming not to follow and yet never far behind her, he came on between the long vague shadows of the birch trees, along the fence, past the chickencoops and the shining pond, into captivity.

They all sat on the ground under the Four Elms. There was cold ham, pickles, cold fried eggplant with salt, hard bread and hard red wine. Elm leaves like thin coins stuck to the bread. The pure, void, windy sky of after-sunset reflected in the pond and in the wine. Stanislas and Paul had a wrestling match and dirt flew over the remains of the ham; the baroness and Rosa, lamenting, dusted the ham. The boys went off to run cars through the tunnel in High Cliff, and discuss what ruin the winter rains might cause. For it would rain. All the nine months they were gone from Asgard rain would beat on the roads and hills, and the tunnel would collapse. Stanislas lifted his head a moment thinking of the Oak in winter when he had never seen it, the roots of the tree that upheld the world drinking dark rain underground. Zida rode clear round the house twice on the shoulders of the unicorn, screaming loudly for pure joy, for eating outside on the ground with fingers, for the first star seen (only from the corner of the eye) over the high fields faint in twilight. Screaming louder with rage she was taken to bed by Rosa, and instantly fell asleep. One by one the stars came out, meeting the eye straight on. One by one the young people went to bed. Tomas with the last half-bottle sang long and hoarsely in the Dorian mode[8] in his room above the stable. Only the baron and his wife remained out in the autumn darkness under leaves and stars.

"I don't want to leave," she murmured.

"Nor I."

"Let's send the books and clothes on back to town, and stay here without them. . . ."

"Forever," he said; but they could not. In the observance of season lies order, which was their realm. They sat on for a while longer, close side by side as lovers of twenty; then rising he said, "Come along, it's late, Freya."[9] They went through darkness to the house, and entered.

In coats and hats, everyone ate bread and drank hot milk and coffee out on the porch in the brilliant early morning. "The car! It's coming!" Paul shouted, dropping his bread in the dirt. Grinding and changing gears, headlamps sightlessly flashing, the taxi came, it was there. Zida stared at it, the enemy within the walls, and began to cry. Faithful to the last to the lost cause of summer, she was carried into the taxi head first, screaming, "I won't go! I don't want to go!" Grinding and changing gears the taxi started. Stanislas's head stuck out of the right front window, the baroness's head out of the left rear, and Zida's red, desolate, and furious face was pressed against the oval back window, so that those three saw Tomas waving good-bye under the white walls of Asgard in the sunlight in the bowl of hills. Paul had no access to a window; but he was already thinking of the train. He saw, at the end of the smoke and the shining tracks, the light of candles in a high dark dining-room, the stare of a rockinghorse in an attic corner, leaves wet with rain overhead on the way to school, and a grey street shortened by a cold, foggy dusk through which shone, remote and festive, the first streetlight of December.

But all this happened a long time ago, nearly forty years ago; I do not know if it happens now, even in imaginary countries. (1935)

NOTES

1. In Norse mythology, the cosmic ash whose branches overhang all the worlds; in some versions, the tree of knowledge.
2. Loki, in Norse mythology, is the mischief maker, father of lies, and evil-doer—the ultimate source of evil and the cause of the destruction of the gods. His association with the grove derives from his personification of forest fire. Loki's offspring is Fenris the Wolf.
3. Odin's son, the Norse god known for his looks and wisdom. He was killed by a shaft of mistletoe and was the first of the gods to die in battle.
4. "The twilight of the gods"; the period of their destruction. In the battle they fight against the Frost Giant, their chief enemy, who with Fenris the Wolf and the tyrannical Queen of Hel, lead the victorious army.
5. One-eyed Norse deity of battle, magic, inspiration, and the dead. In Germanic religion, he is the supreme law-giver and creator of humankind.
6. Norse version of the Thunder God, or God of War. Famed for magic weapons, especially the hammer, the sole protection against the giant.
7. Hel is the prison of death; the Frozen Lands is home to the Giant.
8. Dervied from the basic Western scale, this is one of eight scales used in medieval church music; called the first authentic mode beginning with the tonic D.
9. After the Norse goddess of love, marriage, and fertility.

Antonine Maillet   *Canada, b. 1929*

Born in Bouctouche, New Brunswick, Antonine Maillet lived in Paris in 1963–1964 and again in 1969–1970, before completing her doctorate in Acadian folklore at Laval University and settling in Montreal. Playwright, novelist, and scriptwriter as well as cultural anthropologist, Maillet learned her trade as a fiction writer from pioneer relatives and village entertainers, and at election and school meetings and other social gatherings. A powerful oral tradition provided her with materials for various collections of popular customs, mores, and tales (1968, 1973) and for a discussion of their relation to the literary legacy of Rabelais (1971).*

This effort to capture the Acadian heritage was also the basis of Maillet's "revisionist" literature, which represented a new and vital portrait of Acadians, those original 10,000 French settlers who had been expelled from Nova Scotia by the ruling British. This event is the starting point of *Pélagie-la-charrette*, the story of an Acadian Mother Courage who narrates her people's return from Georgia to

New Brunswick, which earned Maillet the Prix Goncourt in 1979. In Maillet's texts, from the internationally famous *La Sagouine* (1972; translated 1979) to *Evangéline Deusse* (1975) and *Pélagie-la-charrette* (translated 1982), the legendary and ideal heroine immortalized by Longfellow undergoes a metamorphosis; instead, this character represents the harsher facts of exile and return. Along with substituting a more authentic image for the romantic cliché, Maillet restores her characters to their language—a version of the sixteenth-century French of their ancestors—which gives these Acadian women a voice to speak to others and for themselves. Maillet herself is a former nun who renounced the silence of the religious order and became an internationally known writer. Her life and work are thus symbolic of the *prise de parole* (literally, a taking of the word: coming to articulate things not previously said; a new awareness) of the Acadian woman.

Other significant works that are a part of Maillet's project include *Don l'Original* (1972; translated 1979), a rollicking mock-epic fantasy based on folklore and local events in Maillet's native Bouctouche, for which Maillet won the coveted Governor General's Award in 1973; a collection of short stories, the title story of which is translated here and three other novels—*Mariaagélas* (1975), *La Gribouille* (1982), and *Crache à Pic* (1984). In 1982 Maillet also published a history, a play, and a memoir of her childhood that gives particular emphasis to the way she came to be a *raconteuse* (a storyteller); this memoir is entitled *Christophe Cartier de la noisette, dit Nounours* (*Christopher Cartier of Hazelnut, otherwise known as Bear*, 1982).

Through her work, Maillet seems to have energized a new generation of female talents as well as inspiring a more general Acadian literary renaissance, signaled when the publisher Leméac initiated two new series in 1972, one devoted to the oral literature of the Acadians, and the other focusing on the Acadian novel. In recognition for her work, Maillet has been awarded many prizes and honorary doctorates from such prestigious universities as Dalhousie, Toronto, Queen's, and McGill. Her career has moved far from the publication of her first novel, *Pointe-aux-Coques*, which went virtually unnoticed when it appeared in 1958.

NOTE

* François Rabelais (1495?–1553), monk, physician, student of the new learning, the Renaissance author of the bawdy and frequently heretical *Gargantua and Pantagruel* (1532–1552).

BEHIND MY FATHER'S HOUSE
Par derrière chez mon père

Behind my father's house, there is a sweet apple tree, its leaves are green and its fruit is sweet...sweet...oh! so sweet it sends you dreaming of everything that lies behind my father's house. You might say that in the apple tree is the apple; in the apple, the core;[1] in the core, the worm; and in the worm, all our ancestors that the worm has eaten...no. That's too dismal. Let's turn ourselves around and set out feet toward life.

Behind my father's house there is a sweet apple tree, and the tree is in the orchard, and the orchard in the field, and at the end of the field, past the bracken and the raspberry patch, the horizon. And that's where you must go to look at the world. Set out to sea, let the nor'wester bear you away, driving you steadily toward the southeast, and you will travel back in time.

The world is wide, behind my father's house. The world is all space and all time. You can come home through the garden or along the street; but you can also come from the summer or the other seasons. As you wander over the world, you travel back through history. And in history our fathers' lives were acted out.

And so I left my home, my land of dunes and *aboiteaux*,[2] headed for the old world, back down the centuries, seeking the history of my family and my people (and yours) which was written wherever the men who made us went, a history that stretches very far back, behind my father's house.

Behind my father's house and my mother's, they tell me, lies Touraine, the garden of France. It is a lovely green and yellow country whose feet bathe in the Loire: you know, that sweet Loire with its renaissance chateaus. But I'm not here to talk to you of chateaus which haven't really done much for Acadia. No, our people came from these brown clay houses with the slate roofs. And that's not so far. So near, in fact, that one day, while traveling through the hills of Touraine, I suddenly had the urge to stop, like someone returning home to his own country...and go in, go home.

One time or another, you have already gone back like that to your childhood. You go back to your native village, heading straight for the big family home that spots you a long way off and beckons. You can tell it by its air of complicity. And leaning against the rotten trunk of an apple tree or with your arms crossed on the gate, you make the trip once more. The swing, the cherrytrees, the pumpkins, the

cabin, the rhubarb patch, the sandpit, the angelus, Tibi, Mimo, Dolinda, the whole countryside takes shape about you, and your still-hesitating spirit slips all its moorings and lets you sail away.

Then you compose the scenario of the most beautiful drama there is, the only one that interests you deeply, your own life, your own paradise regained. For an hour you live your resurrected childhood, a purified, eternal childhood, laden with memories and pregnant with all the dreams of men. And you have the feeling you possess, in an instant, all lives, since in childhood all are still possible.

The memory game is perhaps the most heartbreaking, but it is the most marvelous one. The possibilities that no longer exist have already been, and therefore belong to us like the treasures of an attic to which we have lost the key. All our life long we look for that key, and that is the most thrilling adventure of man.

And so it happened that day in Touraine. I went back past childhood, farther than behind my father's house, right to my grandfather's grandfather's grandfather's house.

...And I went home, quietly, asking to be excused for arriving a bit late when everyone is already at table. My kinfolk seemed surprised at first to see me again after all those years, but they soon realized that I had come a really long way, that I was that member of the family who had left for Port-Royal on one of the Sieur d'Aulnay's boats,[3] during the grape-harvest, and whom they had been expecting for two or three seasons.

"And how was it over there in the cold country of yours?"

The grandfather it was said that. He had a curly beard and a hoarse voice. But all old men have always had voices and beards like that, and I couldn't manage to place him. Was he the grandfather of this house, or the patriarch of the line I sprang from? So I threw caution to the winds and I replied:

"It was tough at the start. When we arrived in the colony, winter was already beginning. We people of Touraine weren't used to it, you understand. You know, snow, around here...But over there were snow rollers,[4] powder snow, snow squalls..."

"Snow what?"

"Excuse me, that's how we say it. When you're used to the sea, you salt everything with nautical terms; you rig out women, you embark on a load of hay, you moor the senator to his county. In the same way you stick old words on new images: the rollers in the sea become snow rollers; cannon powder, powder snow; and wind squalls, snow squalls. The first Acadians didn't take away enough words with them, from the heart of their Touraine, for all that snow that shrouded them."

"And how did you manage to come through it all so chipper?"

"We had no choice," I told her. "Stand still and you died."

"Sure," she said, "you had to survive. Even when there's nothing but snow to live on, or as we say, *pour tout potage*."[5]

"Why, you know, over there we'd have said *pour tout tripotage*. The language has changed a wee bit."

"Not a particle," said the old man. "You gabble the same jargon as your ancestors, except for your words for snow and your schooner gear."

It was true. We had been talking for an hour about everything, and our tongues had only stumbled over *potage*.

But we didn't stop at the soup course. When we got to the vegetables, they insisted on knowing all about my life out there in the colonies. Had we been happy? and prosperous? Three centuries, just imagine! And I set about telling them about it.

"...Hard times in the beginning...the great days of Grand-Pre...exile...back to the woods...loneliness...loneliness... loneliness..."

"And then what?" asked timidly, candidly, a little girl cousin who couldn't stop twisting her feet around the bars of her chair.

"Then what? Why, after that the Acadians lived like any one else: drinking, eating, sleeping, ploughing the fields, delving in the sea, life that goes from birth to funeral by way of five or six sacraments. Over there we live a fisherman's or a peasant's life like all the peoples of the earth."

Even as I said that, I felt that I wasn't revealing the whole truth: that life, for my people coming back from exile, was not exactly like everyone else's. I thought of those adventurous years in the woods or along the coast, fleeing the enemy any tuft of brush could hide; those years of utter isolation, when history itself remembered nothing any more and went on its merry way as if Acadia were just a mere passing smudge on one of its pages, between two chapters of the chronicles of France and England.

That Acadia, however, was growing a new soul and lived through hours so full of tragedy, comedy, picaresque novels and fantastic tales that history was inadequate to tell her tale and had to call legend to its aid.

My little cousin was asleep. The whole household was frozen still as in the Sleeping Beauty. And I tiptoed out of the brown clay, slate-roofed house that sheltered my ancestors, leaving the door ajar, wondering if I had really entered it.

Translated by John Patterson

NOTES

1. *Coeur* (in the original French text) means either "core" or "heart."
2. *Aboiteau*: "lock" (in a dike), one that opens with the ebb tide and closes when the tide comes in.
3. Charles de Menou Aunay-Charnisay: (ca. 1604–1650) French-born, Lieutenant Governor and informally Governor of Acadia after 1635, he brought families from La Hève to Port Royal to strengthen the colony. Port Royal is the name given by the French to the Annapolis Basin, Nova Scotia.
4. Snow drifts.
5. In all; all told.

Adrienne Rich   *US, b. 1929*

Adrienne Rich's career as poet, activist, and teacher has closely followed the path of the feminist revival of the last few decades; women of her generation are likely to see her life as emblematic. Born into a middle-class Jewish household in Baltimore, educated until the third grade in the family's "very Victorian, pre-Raphaelite" library by her mother, Helen Rich, a composer, and her father, a professor of medicine, Rich graduated from Radcliffe in 1951, married Harvard economist David Conrad in 1953, and lived in Cambridge for thirteen years with her husband and three sons. In the next twenty years she proceeded to make her poetic mark, winning kudos and honors from the largely male world of established poets, the academic establishment, and the mainstream press, apparently, as John Ashbery wrote as late as 1966, "a kind of Emily Dickinson of the suburbs." In fact, Rich was about to separate from her husband and come to New York to teach at Rutgers in New Jersey and at City College, New York, and, in that politically contentious era, forge deep connections among feminist, antiwar, and lesbian politics.

Nonetheless, it still came as something of a shock, when in 1974 Rich won the National Book Award for *Diving into the Wreck*, rejected the award as an individual, and then, in a collective statement written with two other nominees, the black poets Audre Lorde and Alice Walker, accepted it "in the name of all the women in a patriarchal world, and in the name of those who, like us, have been tolerated as token women in this culture, often at great cost and in great pain." Rich spent the next decade excavating a female literary tradition, defining a woman-identified identity, and naming a politics in her poetry and as editor of the important magazine *Sinister Wisdom*. In 1979, she returned to Massachusetts, where she lives with her lover, the West Indian poet Michelle Cliff.

Rich's poetry documents this evolution. Her first volume, *A Change of World* (1951), was selected for the Yale Younger Poets Award by W. H. Auden, who also introduced it: Despite "Storm Warnings" (reprinted here), "the poems a reader will encounter in this book are neatly and modestly dressed, speak quietly but do not mumble, respect their elders but are not cowed by them, and do not tell fibs." Other critics, not so patronizing (nor, ironically, so on target), found Rich's measured, elegant style admirable. As the title poem of her second volume, *The Diamond Cutters* (1955), suggests, the emphasis remained on a chiseled virtuosity. However, in her next book, *Snapshots of a Daughter-in-Law* (1963), Rich declares, "a thinking woman sleeps with monsters." In irregular, experimental stanzas, Rich's poems detail women's anger at the waste of their lives; the title poem appears here.

With the next collections there was "a deepening subjectivity," as her friend and critic Albert Gelpi termed it, as if in answer to Ashbery's comment: "For Rich, however,...[it] does not mean withdrawal, as it did not Dickinson, but on the contrary, a more searching engagement with people and social forces." In *Leaflets: Poems 1965–1968* (1969) and *The Will To Change* (1971), from which "The Burning of Paper Instead of Children" comes, Rich seeks models for future collectivities in the lives of historical women, and, moreover, seeks to determine the precise role of the feminine self. With *Diving into the Wreck* (1973), critics began increasingly to draw battle lines—for and against a poetry that Margaret Atwood says does not "resist the temptation to sloganize" vis-à-vis a poetry that Erica Jong says exhibits a "psychological and organic politics." Even in an increasingly exigent social climate, Rich has chosen the latter road, using poetry for clues to a language beyond patriarchy in such works as *Dream of a Common Language: Poems 1974–77* (1978), *A Wild Patience Has Taken Me This Far* (1981), and *Sources* (1983), a twenty-three-part poem exploring her Jewish heritage and her relationships with her father and her late husband. *The Fact of a Doorframe: Poems Selected and New* (1950–1984) is her most recent review of her oeuvre and contains the last three poems included here. Feminists in the Academy have supported Rich's career. As perhaps the leading American feminist poet of her generation, Rich has been the subject of much critical attention, including books by Charles Altieri (1984), Paula Bennett, and Claire Keyes (both 1986); a collection of reviews and other criticism has also been edited by Jane Roberta Cooper (1984). Nor should Rich's own efforts in creating a prose underpinning for her poetic works be underestimated. It is collected in *Of Woman Born: Motherhood as Experience and Institution* (1976) and *Lies, Secrets, and Silence: Selected Prose 1966–1978* (1979), which includes her important essay, "When We Dead Awaken: Writing as Re-Vision" (1971).

Eric Mendelsohn

STORM WARNINGS

The glass has been falling all the afternoon,
And knowing better than the instrument
What winds are walking overhead, what zone
Of gray unrest is moving across the land,
I leave the book upon a pillowed chair
And walk from window to closed window,
                              watching

Boughs strain against the sky

And think again, as often when the air
Moves inward toward a silent core of waiting,
How with a single purpose time has traveled
By secret currents of the undiscerned
Into this polar realm. Weather abroad
And weather in the heart alike come on
Regardless of prediction.

Between foreseeing and averting change
Lies all the mastery of elements
Which clocks and weatherglasses cannot alter.
Time in the hand is not control of time,
Nor shattered fragments of an instrument
A proof against the wind; the wind will rise,
We can only close the shutters.

I draw the curtains as the sky goes black
And set a match to candles sheathed in glass
Against the keyhold draught, the insistent
                              whine
Of weather through the unsealed aperture.
This is our sole defense against the season;
These are the things that we have learned to do
Who live in trouble regions.

(1951)

SNAPSHOTS OF A DAUGHTER-IN-LAW

1.

You, once a belle in Shreveport,
with henna-colored hair, skin like a peachbud,
still have your dresses copied from that time,
and play a Chopin[1] prelude
called by Cortot: "*Delicious recollections
float like perfume through the memory.*"[2]

Your mind now, mouldering like
                                        wedding-cake,
heavy with useless experience, rich
with suspicion, rumor, fantasy,
crumbling to pieces under the knife-edge
of mere fact. In the prime of your life.

Nervy, glowering, your daughter
wipes the teaspoons, grows another way.

2.

Banging the coffee-pot into the sink
she hears the angels chiding, and looks out
past the raked gardens to the sloppy sky.
Only a week since They said: *Have no
                                        patience.*

The next time it was: *Be insatiable.*
Then: *Save yourself; others you cannot save.*
Sometimes she's let the tapstream scald her
                                        arm,
a match burn to her thumbnail,

or held her hand above the kettle's snout
right in the woolly steam. They are probably
                                        angels,
since nothing hurts her any more, except
each morning's grit blowing into her eyes.

3.

A thinking woman sleeps with monsters.
The beak that grips her, she becomes. And
                                        Nature,
that sprung-lidded, still commodious
steamer-trunk of *tempora* and *mores*[3]
gets stuffed with it all: the mildewed
                                        orange-flowers,
the female pills, the terrible breasts
of Boadicea[4] beneath flat foxes' heads and
                                        orchids.

Two handsome women, gripped in argument,
each proud, acute, subtle, I hear scream
across the cut glass and majolica
like Furies cornered from their prey:
The argument *ad feminam,*[5] all the old knives
that have rusted in my back, I drive in yours,
ma semblable, ma soeur![6]

4.

Knowing themselves too well in one another:
their gifts no pure fruition, but a thorn,
the prick filed sharp against a hint of scorn...
Reading while waiting
for the iron to heat,
writing, *My Life had stood—a Loaded Gun—*[7]
in that Amherst pantry while the jellies boil
                                        and scum,
or, more often,
iron-eyed and beaked and purposed as a bird,
dusting everything on the whatnot everyday of
                                        life.

5.

Dulce ridens, dulce loquens,[8]
she shaves her legs until they gleam
like petrified mammoth-tusk.

6.

When to her lute Corinna sings[9]
neither words nor music are her own;
only the long hair dipping
over her cheek, only the song
of silk against her knees
and these
adjusted in reflections of an eye.

Poised, trembling and unsatisfied, before
an unlocked door, that cage of cages,
tell us, you bird, you tragical machine—
is this *fertilisante douleur?*[10] Pinned down
by love, for you the only natural action,
are you edged more keen
to prise the secrets of the vault? has Nature
                                        shown
her household books to you, daughter-in-law,
that her sons never saw?

7.

"To have in this uncertain world some stay
which cannot be undermined is
of the utmost consequence."[11]
                              Thus wrote
a woman, partly brave and partly good,
who fought with what she partly understood.
Few men about her would or could do more,
hence she was labelled harpy, shrew and whore.

8.

"You all die at fifteen," said Diderot,[12]
and turn part legend, part convention.
Still, eyes inaccurately dream
behind closed windows blankening with steam.
Deliciously, all that we might have been,
all that we were—fire, tears,
wit, taste, martyred ambition—
stirs like the memory of refused adultery
the drained and flagging bosom of our middle
                                        years.

9.

Not that it is done well but
that it is done at all?[13] Yes, think
of the odds! or shrug them off forever.
This luxury of the precocious child,
Time's precious chronic invalid,—
would we, darlings, resign it if we could?
Our blight has been our sinecure:
mere talent was enough for us—
glitter in fragments and rough drafts.

Sigh no more, ladies.
                      Time is male
and in his cups drinks to the fair.
Bemused by gallantry, we hear
our mediocrities over-praised,
indolence read as abnegation,
slattern thought styled intuition,
every lapse forgiven, our crime
only to cast too bold a shadow
or smash the mould straight off.

For that, solitary confinement,
tear gas, attrition shelling.
Few applicants for that honor.

10.

Well,
She's long about her coming, who must be
more merciless to herself than history.
Her mind full to the wind, I see her plunge
breasted and glancing through the currents,
taking the light upon her
at least as beautiful as any boy
or helicopter,
              poised, still coming,
her fine blades making the air wince
but her cargo
no promise then:
delivered
palpable
ours.[14]
(1958–1960)

NOTES

1. Frédéric François Chopin (1810–1849): archetypical Romantic Polish composer and pianist who settled in Paris in 1831.
2. Alfred Cortot (1877–1962): famous French pianist whose notation for Prelude #7, Andantino, A Major appears in the prefatory remarks of his *Chopin: 24 Preludes* (1930).
3. *tempora* and *mores*: literally, "times" and "customs;" an allusion to a phrase in the Classical Latin by the poet Cicero: "Alas! for the degeneracy of our times and the low standards of our morals."
4. Boadicea (d. 61 A.D.): British Queen who led a large though unsuccessful revolt against Roman rule, when Nero's governors confiscated her domain.
5. *ad feminam*: usually, *ad hominem*, a rhetorical or debating strategy of attacking the man (or "person") rather than the merits of the case or weaknesses of the argument itself; here revised by Rich to read: "(to address the attack) against the woman."
6. A female revision of the last line of "Au Lecteur" (To the Reader) by the nineteenth-century French poet Baudelaire to read "Hypocrite reader, my self, my *sister*," rather than "my brother."
7. The first line from the poem by Emily Dickinson; Amherst is the town where the poet was born and raised.
8. Latin for "sweetly laughing, sweetly speaking," from the Classical Latin of Horace (Ode XIX).
9. The first line from the poem by the English Thomas Campion (1567–1620).
10. French for "life-giving sorrow."

11. From Mary Wollstonecraft, *Thoughts on the Education of Daughters* (1787).

12. Denis Diderot (1713–1784): French figure of the Enlightenment who sought to encompass all of human knowledge in the creation of an *Encyclopédie*; he made the statement in a letter to Sophie Volland, his beloved wife, mother of his children, and intellectual companion.

13. An allusion to the notorious remark made by the English writer Samuel Johnson, recorded by his biographer Boswell: "Sir, a woman's preaching is like a dog's walking on his hinder legs. It is not done well; but you are surprized to find it done at all" (July 30, 1763).

14. Rich's note refers to the French text of de Beauvoir's *The Second Sex*: "She comes down from the remoteness of ages, from Thebes, from Crete, from Chichén-Itzá; and she is also the totem set deep in the African jungle; she is a helicopter and a bird; and there is this, the greatest wonder of all: under her tinted hair the forest murmur becomes a thought and words issue from her breasts" (H. M. Parshley, trans.).

THE BURNING OF PAPER INSTEAD OF CHILDREN

I was in danger of verbalizing my moral impulses out of existence.
—Fr. Daniel Berrigan,[1] *on trial in Baltimore.*

1. My neighbor, a scientist and art-collector, telephones me in a state of violent emotion. He tells me that my son and his, aged eleven and twelve, have on the last day of school burned a mathematics text-book in the backyard. He has forbidden my son to come to his house for a week, and has forbidden his own son to leave the house during that time. "The burning of a book," he says, "arouses terrible sensations in me, memories of Hitler; there are few things that upset me so much as the idea of burning a book."

Back there: the library, walled
with green Britannicas
Looking again
in Dürer's *Complete Works*[2]
for MELANCOLIA, the baffled woman

the crocodiles in Herodotus[3]
the Book of the Dead[4]
the *Trial of Jeanne d'Arc,*[5] so blue
I think, It is her color

and they take the book away
because I dream of her too often

love and fear in a house
knowledge of the oppressor
I know it hurts to burn

2. To imagine a time of silence
or few words
a time of chemistry and music

the hollows above your buttocks
traced by my hand
or, *hair is like flesh,* you said

an age of long silence

relief

from this tongue   the slab of limestone
or reinforced concrete
fanatics and traders
dumped on this coast   wildgreen   clayred
that breathed once
in signals of smoke
sweep of the wind

knowledge of the oppressor
this is the oppressor's language

yet I need it to talk to you

3. "People suffer highly in poverty and it takes dignity and intelligence to overcome this suffering. Some of the suffering are: a child did not had dinner last night: a child steal because he did not have money to buy it: to hear a mother say she do not have money to buy food for her children and to see a child without cloth it will make tears in your eyes."[6]

(the fracture of order
the repair of speech
to overcome this suffering)

4. We lie under the sheet
after making love, speaking
of loneliness
relieved in a book
relived in a book
so on that page
the clot and fissure
of it appears
words of a man
in pain
a naked word
entering the clot
a hand grasping
through bars:

deliverance

What happens between us
has happened for centuries
we know it from literature

still it happens

sexual jealousy
outflung hand
beating bed

dryness of mouth
after panting

there are books that describe all this
and they are useless

You walk into the woods behind a house
there in that country
you find a temple
built eighteen hundred years ago
you enter without knowing
what it is you enter
so it is with us

no one knows what may happen
though the books tell everything

burn the texts   said Artaud[7]

5. I am composing on the typewriter late at night, thinking of today. How well we all spoke. A language is a map of our failures. Frederick Douglass wrote an English purer than Milton's.[8] People suffer highly in poverty.

There are methods but we do not use them. Joan, who could not read, spoke some peasant form of French. Some of the suffering are: it is hard to tell the truth; this is America; I cannot touch you now. In America we have only the present tense. I am in danger. You are in danger. The burning of a book arouses no sensation in me. I know it hurts to burn. There are flames of napalm in Catonsville, Maryland. I know it hurts to burn. The typewriter is over-heated, my mouth is burning, I cannot touch you and this is the oppressor's language.
(1968)

NOTES

1. Daniel Berrigan (b.1921): Jesuit priest, political activist, writer; he and his brother Philip became two of the Catonsville Nine, so-called because the group were tried and subsequently imprisoned for breaking into the Selective Service Office in Maryland and burning numerous draft records, as part of the protest against the Vietnam War; one of the atrocities alluded to in the poem is the use of napalm in the bombing of the civilian population.
2. Albrecht Dürer (1471–1528): German painter and engraver; in one of his engravings, he depicted Melancholy as a woman.
3. Greek Historian of the fifth century B.C.
4. Translation of an Egyptian papyrus (of Ani), used more generally to refer to Egyptian funerary literature.
5. Translation of a book of original documents relating to the French peasant girl (1411–1431) and national heroine who, claiming to be inspired by God, rallied French military support for the Dauphin, later Charles VII, against the English. Tried and burned at the stake as a witch, she was later canonized.
6. The prose paragraph was written by one of Rich's students at the City College of New York.
7. Antonin Artaud (1896–1948): French surrealist poet, actor, and director, highly influential in the experimental drama of the 1960s as an advocate of a "theater of cruelty" as a means of breaking through the veneer of civilization and disturbing its complacent assurance.
8. Frederick Douglass (1817?–1895): Black-American abolitionist, the son of a slave, and author of several versions of an autobiography.
    John Milton (1608–1674): English poet, author of *Paradise Lost* (1667); *Aereopagitica* (1664), his classic defence of freedom of the press is considered a model of English prose, but one highly influenced by Latin.

FOR A SISTER

*(Natálya Gorbanévskaya, two years
incarcerated in a Soviet penal mental
asylum for her political activism; and
others)*

I trust none of them. Only my existence
thrown out in the world like a towchain
battered and twisted in many chance
                                         connections,
being pulled this way, pulling in that.

I have to steal the sense of dust on your floor,
milk souring in your pantry
after they came and took you.
I'm forced to guess at the look you threw
                                         backward.

A few paragraphs in the papers,
allowing for printers' errors, wilful omissions,
the trained violence of doctors.
I don't trust them, but I'm learning how to use
                                         them.

Little by little out of the blurred conjectures
your face clears, a sunken marble
slowly cranked up from underwater.
I feel the ropes straining under their load of
                                         despair.

They searched you for contraband, they made
                                         their notations.
A look of intelligence could get you twenty
                                         years.
Better to trace nonexistent circles with your
                                         finger,
try to imitate the smile of the permanently
                                         dulled.

My images. This metaphor for what happens.
A geranium in flames on a green cloth
becomes yours. You, coming home after years
to light the stove, get out the typewriter and
                                         begin again. Your story.

(1972)

Christa Wolf   *Germany/GDR, b. 1929*

Honored with major literary awards in both Germanies, widely translated and
read, Christa Wolf is beyond a doubt the best-known German woman writer of
this or any other century.

Wolf was born in Landsberg on the Warthe (now the Polish town of Gorzów
Wielkopolski) on March 18, 1929; her father, Otto Ihlenfeld, ran a small grocery.
She spent her childhood and youth in that town but fled with her family before the
oncoming Red Army in 1945. Converted to socialism through her reading of
Marx, Wolf joined the Communist Party in 1949, the founding year of the G.D.R.;
she still adheres to the tenets of socialism, although she has indicated some disillusionment with the system under which she lives, most pronouncedly in her participation, with twelve other important G.D.R. writers, in petitioning her government
on behalf of the expatriated songster Wolf Biermann.[1] She studied German Literature in Jena and Leipzig from 1949 to 1953; from 1953 to 1962 she worked as a
research assistant to the German Writers' Union and as an editor for a major
journal and for two publishing houses. A protegé of Anna Seghers, about whom
she has also written, Wolf published her first fictional work, *Moskauer Novelle*
(Moscow Novella) in 1961 and has been a freelance writer since that time. She
lives in Berlin with her husband, Gerhard Wolf. They have two daughters.

The chronological direction of Wolf's work goes against the historical grain:

with each successive major prose work she has moved the temporal locus further back in history. The first novel that brought her immediate recognition, *Der geteilte Himmel* (*Divided Heaven*, 1963), takes place in the early 1960s and is set in the G.D.R. *Nachdenken über Christa T.* (*The Quest for Christa T.*, 1968) was Wolf's next novel and remains perhaps the best known. It occasioned some conflict with the G.D.R. cultural functionaries because of its failure to adhere to established standards of socialist realism. While *The Quest for Christa T.* is set at the end of World War II, *Kindheitsmuster* (*Patterns of Childhood*, 1976) presents an autobiographical attempt to come to terms with the realities of a childhood in the Third Reich. Still further removed historically is *Kein Ort Nirgends* (*No Place on Earth*, 1979), set among the writers of the German Romantic era in 1806 and positing a fictional meeting between two historical characters, Heinrich von Kleist and Karoline von Günderrode. Finally, *Kassandra* (*Cassandra*, 1983) makes a leap back to the beginning of Western civilization and presents the end of the Trojan War as narrated by Cassandra.[2]

With her most recent work, Wolf has relocated herself in the present. *Störfall. Nachrichten eines Tages* (Breakdown. A Day's News, 1987), is a questioning response to the April, 1986 nuclear catastrophe at Chernobyl and is a logical development of her concern expressed elsewhere about modern society's dead-end pursuit of nuclear technology. Wolf creates here a first-person narrator who spends that day listening with one ear to the radio reports and admonitions regarding the nuclear breakdown, with the other to the anticipated ring of the telephone, which will bring her news about the progress of her brother, who on that day is undergoing critical surgery for the removal of a brain tumor. Wolf's skill in suggesting the universal applicability of an apparently intensely personal preoccupation is sustained again in this short piece, which presses the reader into a necessary and unavoidable confrontation with those questions that demand to be asked by all of us, since they concern the survival of the human race.

Wolf's style is fundamentally lyrical, her structure open and multilayered, her didactic message often coined in aphoristic phrases. Wolf's ideas are also expressed through the theoretical essays that often serve as a counterpoint to the novels. "Interview with Myself" (1966), for example, explains and justifies the "subjective authenticity" of *Christa T.*; other essays to be found in *Lesen und Schreiben* (*The Reader and the Writer*, 1971) deal both with individual writers and such topics as the role of the writer in contemporary society or the question of "female" writing. And in the important *Frankfurter Poetik–Vorlesungen* (*Frankfurt Lectures on Poetics*, 1983), Wolf parallels *Kassandra* with an analysis of the patriarchal system that has brought Western civilization to the verge of destruction.

Marilyn Sibley Fries

NOTES

1. See Note to Sarah Kirsch.
2. The prophetess who is forced to see her accurate and dire predictions of disaster ignored.

from INTERVIEW WITH MYSELF
Selbstinterview

Q. What are you reading?

A. The first pages of a new story I am working on, possibly for some considerable time. It will probably be called *Nachdenken über Christa T.* (The Quest for Christa T.)

Q. Can you say something about the subject matter of this story?

A. This is difficult, because there was no "subject matter" that I felt impelled to write about, there is no "region of life" in it that I could call its milieu, no "content," no "plot" that I could describe in a few sentences. I must confess to a purely subjective urge. Someone very close to me died, too young. I don't accept this death. I am looking for some means to defend myself effectively against it. Searching, I write. The result is that I have to pin down this searching, as honestly, as exactly as possible.

Q. Good. But the substance of this search? What will fill the pages of your manuscript?

A. I am forcing my way into the world of this dead person, whom I believe I knew and whom I can only keep hold of if I take on the job of really getting to know her. I am relying not only on deceptive memory but also on material: diaries, letters, sketches of Christa T. that were placed at my disposal after her death. The concrete episodes swim in my memory like small islands—that is the structure of the story.

Q. So you are writing a kind of posthumous biography...

A. That is what I thought at first. Later on, I noticed that the object of my story was not at all, or did not remain so clearly herself, Christa T. I suddenly faced myself. I had not foreseen this. The relations between "us"—Christa T. and the narrator "I"—shifted of themselves into the center; the differences in character and the points at which they touched, the tensions between "us" and the way they dissolved or failed to dissolve. If I were a mathematician I should probably speak of a "function"—

nothing tangible, visible, material, but extraordinarily effective.

Q. At all events, you have now admitted that there are two authentic figures in it—Christa T. and an "I."

A. Have I admitted that? You would be right if, in the final analysis, both characters were not invented...

Q. You spoke of the material you are using. Of recollections.

A. I have been fully in control of the material. I have supplemented memories by invention. I have placed no value at all on faithfulness to documents; I wanted to do justice to the picture I had made for myself of Christa T. This has transformed her, and the "I" that I could not do without.

Q. You stress the subjective elements. Can you nevertheless give something like an idea?

A. After I had started work on it, when the material, the facts, had become familiar and again strange to me, I gradually saw something like a motto, if not an idea. I found it formulated by Becher* and shall use it as a maxim: "For this profound unrest of the human soul is nothing but the premonition and the ability to sense that man has not yet come to himself. This coming-to-oneself—what is it?"

It is a great thought that man does not find peace until he has found himself. I see in this the deep roots of conformity between genuine literature and socialist society: both have the purpose of helping man to realize himself. Like our society, literature adopts the restless especially. To describe people to whom this unrest is foreign as self-satisfied, footling and more than ready to adapt themselves, seems to me tedious and fruitless. But it is sometimes necessary. For example, to show the background against which a restless, productive person stands out, or to define the special quality of his unrest. And also, if this should be the case, why his unrest comes to a halt, why it cannot rise above itself and be fully realized.

Q. I suppose that was the case with Christa T.?

A. You mean because she died so young? Because it is not easy to count the results of her life or point them out? No. I have discovered that she lived fully in the time vouchsafed her.

Q. No mourning, then?

A. Yes, mourning, but not despair or resignation. I regard it as the extreme of anti-resignation if one does not resign onself to death, if one rebels against it.

Q. So you wanted to discover in writing something you did not know before?

A. Yes.

Q. Why do you think it will interest others?

A. I am never sure of this. I can only do my best in posing questions....

Q. You believe literature to be vital?

A. If art did not produce something necessary and new to add to life I do not believe that humanity would for thousands of years have made its great efforts in what we call art, or that the forces needed for it would have been there in times of great material want....

Q. You know our generation's urge to be scientific, to document things.

A. I know and value it, and share it. But our scientific age will not be what it could and must be, if we are to avoid a terrible disaster, if art does not force itself to ask, does not refuse to be distracted from asking the great questions of contemporaries to whom it appeals. To encourage our age to be itself, that is, to constantly change, throughout life, change ourselves through creative work.

Translated by Joan Becker

NOTE

* Johannes R. Becher (1891–1958): Along with Anna Seghers, one of the writers in the generation preceding Wolf's, who played a leading role in the promotion of a socialist literature, ultimately as Minister of Culture and President of the German Academy of Art. His importance and influence are perpetuated to this day in the writers' institute in Leipzig and in the literary prize that bear his name.

Wolf's motto is taken from Becher's journal *Auf andere Art so grosse Hoffnung*. Tagebuch 1950. Eintragungen 1951 (To hope so greatly—in a different way.

Journal of 1950. Entries of 1951) [Berlin/Weimar: Aufbau, 1969, p.224]) The quotation continues: "It is the fulfillment of all the possibilities made available to the human being...."

from THE QUEST FOR CHRISTA T.
Nachdenken über Christa T.

The year is over. The law comes into effect which reminds us to let it go, and we have to abide by that law. Just this one scene, though, which comes up out of memory with such difficulty.

Writing means making things large.

Did she say this, or is memory playing me false? For every statement one needs the place where it was uttered and the moment to match it. Small and petty things, she says, can take care of themselves.

Yes: twilight. I know: morning twilight. The smell of cigarette smoke which must have awakened me. The wall of books on which my glance first falls and which I can't immediately recognize. She's sitting there at the roll-top desk, which is covered with Justus's papers, in her faded red dressing gown, and she's writing: The Big Hope, or The Difficulty of Saying "I."

When I got up I saw the sheet of paper there with my own eyes; but now it has disappeared. Writing means making things large. Yes, it's possibly so: she didn't say it, I read it.

Not disturbing you, am I? she says. Go on sleeping, if you like.

I'm disinclined to believe that I really was asleep. Even if up to this moment I'd forgotten that morning, as one commonly forgets dreams. Even if it makes me mistrustful, coming back to me just now in all clarity and certainty, appearing the way only the most desirable inventions do.

She'd certainly agree to that: for she knew the power that inventions have over us. That morning, the first of the New Year, when she was so wide awake and I was so sleepy, we might have talked about many things, but my mind was too much at rest. I was cradled in the certainty that much was still reversible and attainable, as long as one didn't lose patience and faith in oneself. An untidy confidence had me in its clutches; I believed that all would be well. Only her face, as she leaned over the sheet of paper, seemed strange. Yes, I said— the way one says things, between sleeping and waking, which one doesn't ordinarily say: the same face. I once saw you blowing a trumpet, eighteen years ago.

Curious, she seemed to know.

Her secret, which I'd been looking for all the time we'd known one another, was a secret no longer. What she wanted, in her innermost depths, what she dreamed of and what she'd long ago begun to do, now lay open before me, incontestable and beyond the shadow of a doubt. It seems to me now that we'd known it all along. She certainly hadn't kept the secret fearfully, it was just that she hadn't intruded upon it. Her long hesitation, her experiments with various forms of living, her amateurishness in various realms, all these pointed in the same direction, if only you had the eyes to see. She was trying out the possibilities of life until nothing should be left: that much was understandable.

Among her papers are various fragments written in the third person: *she*, with whom she associated herself, whom she was careful not to name, for what name could she have given her? *She*, who knows she must always be new, and see anew, over and over again; and who can do what she must wish to do. *She*, who knows only the present and won't let herself be deprived of the right to live according to the laws of her own being.

I understand the secret of the third person, who is there without being tangible and who, when circumstances favor her, can bring down more reality upon herself than the first person: I. The difficulty of saying "I."

Was I really asleep? I saw her go by, in all her forms; saw suddenly behind all her transformations the meaning; understood that it's inept to wish for her to arrive and stay anywhere. And I say something to this effect in half sleep. Anyway, she smiles, smokes her cigarette, and writes.

Everything takes a terribly long time with me, she says; but by now we're standing in the small village shop where Justus is having his car repaired, and the wind sweeps through the half-open door, and we ask ourselves at the same moment what this monotonous hammering in the corner and this howling of the wind have to do with our conversation, which concerns time, for I find we haven't got as much time as she takes. But she's suddenly more distinct than she ever was before; and to all of us she gives time for the taking, as long as we know what it's for.

And you know?

She smiles. Go on sleeping, she says.

Then I'm not tired any more either. We walk through the town—red row of barns, church, pharmacy, store, café. It's evening, cold. We're carrying string bags with bottles in them. We look through the windows of the houses we're passing. She knows how the people live who are sitting there beneath the small colored dim standard lamps that have become fashionable in recent years. She knows the taste of the sauté potatoes which are eaten here in the evenings. She understands what the women unwittingly reveal to her, the women who are now closing their doors for the start of the New Year holiday. She tells me stories which are curiously true, although they don't actually happen; but her heroes have the name of the family now gathering before our eyes beneath the electric candles on the Christmas tree, to eat blood sausage and sauerkraut. Christa T. swears that behind the smooth satisfied faces of the parents, of the little boy and the big girl, lurk exactly the same thoughts as the ones which she, in her story, is turning into deeds.

Write, Krischan, why don't you write?— Oh well, she says, well, you know...

She was afraid of the imprecision and ineptness of words. She knew that they do harm, the insidious harm of bypassing life, which she fears almost more than the great catastrophes. She thought life can be wounded by what one says. I know this from Kostia's letter: she must have confessed as much to him, and he alludes to it, having himself now left the irresponsible realm of a merely verbal existence.

We're walking up the stairs to her house, have turned the key in the lock, can hear jazz in the living room and Anna singing softly in the kitchen. As a matter of fact, Christa T. says, perhaps there are one or two things I've got in mind.

I ask Justus.

Yes, he says. I know. She means her sketches. "Around the Lake," she called them. The lake by our house. The villages around. Their story. She visited the local church archives and looked at their documents. It was to be the life of the present, sharply outlined against the background of history. The peasants told her everything, I don't know how she got them to. You should have seen her at the cooperative dance; it was just before she had to go away. She didn't refuse a single dance, but during the intervals she sat at the bar and drew them out—she had the stories coming out of their ears. They didn't need to be asked, because they saw that she wasn't putting them on or acting up but really did almost fall off her stool from laughing when they told her about the gravedigger Hinrichsen's wedding. She made notes; you'll find them.

I didn't find them. Also I didn't find the sheet of paper she'd been writing on that strange morning, which I'd looked at when she was called away by the children and I got up. What I saw wasn't a continuous text, to be sure, only a few notes, and I couldn't figure out the connections. After the curious sentence about the difficulty of saying "I," came the words: "Facts! Stick to the facts." And underneath, in brackets: *But what are facts?*

Facts are the traces left in us by events. That was her view, Gertrud Born says, now Gertrud Dölling. She felt more and more certain about it, I know, the more she thought about it. You see, she was one-sided, of course she was.

Why of course, Gertrud Born?

Then she looks at me as if I didn't under-stand the simplest things. How could every-thing that happens become a fact for each indi-vidual person? She simply sought out the facts that suited her best—as everyone does, she quietly said. Another thing: she had a craving for honesty.

O la la, says Blasing, and he even wags a menacing finger: our eternal dreamer! It was Blasing himself who suggested the game we played that New Year's night between two and three in the morning, when nobody was taking things seriously any more. First he asked the question: what is indispensable for the survival of mankind? Each person wrote his answer on the back of one of Justus's milk-quota forms, folded it and passed it to the next person.

I know her handwriting and afterwards I looked to see what her answer was. Con-science—there it was in her handwriting. Imagination.

It was then that Blasing wagged his finger. O la la, she'd taken it seriously; but she wasn't going to justify herself. She also didn't deny that the exploitation of all the earth's energy resources...No, who'd contradict Blasing on such a point?

Günter walks up to him. Günter sitting with us on the stairs at the university, it's nighttime, a fragrance from the lime trees, what are the lime trees doing here? The order of things is finally falling apart. What I'd like is a little more order, I say, and a little more vision. Then she looks across to me as I lie sleeping there, laughs again, but says quite seriously: Me too.

If only one could believe you mean it, says Günter anxiously, who can tell what you're up to? Then she's astonished, you can see it in her eyes, which withdraw while we go on talking and talking. The puny ego, we say scornfully, sitting on our stairs. The old Adam,* we've finished him off. She says nothing, thinks, thinks, I now know, for years on end until finally, one night in our loggia in Berlin, with the S—Bahn trains thundering by, she says what she thinks: I really don't know. There must be some misunderstanding. All this trouble, just to make sure that every one of us gets to be different—and all so as to get rid of that difference in time too?

I can't accept that, she says, I can't believe in it. Why not? Because one can decide, in certain realms, to regard one thing as true and another as false. Just as people decided, at some time or other, to believe in the good nature of man, because it was helpful to believe it, as a working hypothesis.

Then she talked to me about her students. We were walking from the Marx-Engels Platz to the Alexanderplatz. We stood by the newsstand and let the hundreds of faces go by; we bought the last anemones at the flower shop. Perhaps we're a bit drunk with springtime, I said. But she insisted she was sober and that she knew what she was saying. She said we had a right to invent, to think out inventions that should be audacious but never careless.

Because nothing can become reality unless it has been thought out beforehand.

She was all for reality, that's why she loved the time when real changes were being made. She loved to open up new senses for the sense of a new thing: she wanted to teach her students to be valuable to themselves. I know that she once lost control when one of them looked at her with big eyes and innocently asked: Why? She kept coming back to this: the fact that she hadn't been able to give an answer tormented her for a long time. Was she thinking of this when she wrote, that morning, while I slept, on her piece of paper: *The goal—fullness. Joy. Hard to put a name to it.*

Nothing could be more inappropriate than pity or regret. She did live. She was all there. She was always scared of getting stuck; her shyness and her timidity were the reverse side of her passion for wishing. Now out she came, calm even in the unfulfillment of her wishes, for she had the strength to say: Not yet. She carried many lives around with her, storing them in herself; and in herself she stored many times as well, times in which she lived partially unknown, as was the case in her "real" time; and what is not possible in one

time becomes real in another. But she called all her various times, serenely: Our time.

Writing means making things large. Pulling ourselves together, let's see her writ large. One's wishes are only what one is capable of. Thus her deep and persistent wish guarantees the secret existence of her work: *this long and never-ending journey toward oneself.*

The difficulty of saying "I."

If I were to have to invent her, I wouldn't change her. I'd let her live, among ourselves, whom she, with uncommon knowing, chose as her companions in life. I'd let her sit at the desk, one morning in the twilight, noting the experiences into which the facts of real life had crystallized in her. I'd let her stand up when the children called. Not quench the thirst she always feels. Give her, when she needs it, confidence that her strength was still on the increase; she needed nothing more. I'd gather around her people who were important to her. I'd let her finish the few pages she wanted to leave us, and which, unless we're not utterly deceived, would have been news from the inmost being, that deepest level of being which is harder to reach than the underside of the earth's crust, harder to reach than the stratosphere, because it is more safely guarded: by each one of us.

I'd have let her live.

So that I could sit, as I did that morning, again and again at her table. For Justus who's bringing the coffee pot in, for the children who are speechless with joy because their favorite pastries are on their plates.

Then the sun rose, red and cold. There was snow on the ground. We took our time over breakfast. Stay a while, Christa T. said; but we drove off.

If I'd been allowed to invent us, I'd have given us time to stay.

Translated by Christopher Middleton

NOTE

* In the Old Testament, the father of humankind; according to Christian theology, he is superceded by Christ, who as the new Adam is without sin.

Cécile Cloutier   *Canada, b. 1930*

Perhaps the most remarkable aspect of Cécile Cloutier's life is her immense intellectual curiosity and erudition. She holds a master's degree in philosophy from McMasters University and another in theology from the University of Toronto. For her doctoral work she traveled to France, studying psychology at the University of Tours and esthetics at the University of Paris. She began her teaching career at the University of Ottawa in 1958 and has been a professor of French at the University of Toronto since 1965. She has cofounded the reviews *Emourie, Incidences,* and *Vécrire* and has contributed to numerous periodicals, notably *Liberté, Livres et auteurs canadiens (québécois),* and *Revue d'esthetique de France.* She currently lives in Ontario with her husband, Jerzy Wojciechowski, with whom she has had two daughters.

The author of more than eight collections of poetry. Cloutier established her reputation when her first book, *Mains de sable* (Hands of Sand, 1960) was awarded a prize by a jury headed by the French playwright Jean Cocteau. This imprimateur established her surrealist lineage, one that is reinforced by her association with the *Hexagone* poets, those printed by the eminent Québécois publishing house under the inspired editorship of the poet Gaston Miron.

Despite this lineage, her works seem unmarked either by the dreamlike and irrational mood of surrealism or by the allusion and referentiality of scholarship. Instead, in collections such as *Cuivre et soies* (Copper and Silks, 1964), there are mostly very brief poems characterized by a severe discipline and spare style: they are further defined by a single striking image; or they capture a nuance of feeling through meticulous phrasing and cadence. Critics have noted a greater sensuality and increasing hints of nationalistic sentiment in works published beginning in the late 1960s through the 1970s: *Cannelles et craies* (Cinnamon Sticks and Sticks of Chalk), *Paupières* (Eyelids), *Câblogrammes* (Cablegrams) and *Chaleuils* (an untranslatable neologism).

In the 1980s, Cloutier published a short story—"La Girafe" (The Giraffe, 1984), as well as two more volumes of poetry—*Près* (Near, 1983) and *L'Echangeur* (The Trader, 1985), the last dedicated to her daughters. While reminiscent of *Chaleuils* in its emphasis on bees, sun, and light, Cloutier's latest work puts a new stress on the power of words to transform experience (in the "interchange" between perceiver and perceived) and to create (through puns, double-entendres, and paradox) syntheses impossible in the "real world." More than ever, the poet, along with the child, is the keeper of the dream.

The following poems are from *Cuivre et soies* and *Paupières.*

BY WAY OF ERROR
En guise d'erreur

Man
Has turned sails
One
By
One
And read
The big blue page
Of the sea

Then
He has built up
Some thousands
Of millions
Of miles
Of light cables

And he has given them
Some millions
Of thousands
Of knots

All to tie up the sea

Translated by Fred Cogswell

IF ONLY MY BODY
Si seulement mon corps

If only my body
Did not have a need
For your hand
In order to learn
Its own shape and rhythm

Translated by Fred Cogswell

A LEAF
Une Feuille

I consent
To this speech
Of a tree

Translated by Fred Cogswell

AGAINST MY COUNTRY I TOOK
J'ai pris contre mon pays

Against my country I took
A harsh asphalt vaccine

At journey's end
I discovered exile
By a slight scar

Translated by Fred Cogswell

I WOULD LIKE TO BE TRUE
Je voudrais être vraie

I would like to be true
To the very skin-tip
There where roots grow
If earth were given us

Translated by Fred Cogswell

Margareta Ekström   *Sweden, b. 1930*

Margareta Ekström was born in 1930 to a bourgeois Stockholm family. Her parents were gifted writers and storytellers when, as she tells us, "they were around." She studied literary history and religion, psychology and sociology at the University of Stockholm and since 1960 has worked as a writer and critic. She currently lives in Stockholm and has two teenaged children.

Ekström has been a prolific writer, publishing numerous collections of short stories, for which she has won many awards, as well as poetry, novels, and diaries.

Several individual stories have been translated into English in such publications as *Vogue, London Magazine,* and *Ontario Review.* One volume of stories, *Dödens Barnmorskor* (1975), was recently translated into English (*Death's Midwives,* 1985) with an introduction by Nadine Gordimer, who praises Ekström's great gift for characterization. The selection here, "Lobster in Dinard," delicately portrays a young woman's choice to remain in an adulterous relationship as a way of retaining her freedom.

Of herself, Ekström writes that her main interests are "cooking, astronomy, philosophy, gardening and the enigma of man." Also, she writes that she plans "an autobiography of food and cooking (Food for Thought) and a novel 'Charlotte' [which leans] slightly against Goethe's *Die Wahlverwandtschaften* [Elective Affinities, 1809]." Her major works include two collections of short stories, *Husliga Scener* (Scenes of Domestic Life, 1964) from which the following story was taken, and *Den Femte Årstiden* (The Fifth Season, 1983) and a novel, *Människodjuren* (Human Animals, 1974).

LOBSTER IN DINARD
Hummer i Dinard

"What will you have?" he wondered, looking at her across the large, pale yellow menu.

"Lobster," she said decisively. "It's been on my mind all day; tonight I want lobster."

"You're funny," he said, with the shadow of a smile. "You know what you want."

"Only sometimes. And mostly about food."

"And you even try to be honest," he went on.

"A bad habit from my childhood," she said. "I'm trying to break it."

Outside the windows the sea lay dark and smooth, rolling each wave thinner than the last, and further toward the night. The beach was still warm. Cold and wet met warm and dry with a hiss. The lighthouse on Chateaubriand's island blinked in vain.[1] No ships were tempted into the narrow passage.

A slight draft blew through the window. And no wonder, for this whole part of the hotel was from the turn of the century: the bamboo armchairs, the potted palms, even the waitresses in their enormous Breton folk dresses. Their stiffly-starched bonnet strings threatened to dip graciously into the soup, the sauce, the ripe Brie, and finally to be flambéed with the crêpes and slivered almonds.

She took off her glasses. The cold, old-fashioned light from the ceiling, the slight but tangible draft on her bare arm, the paintings of the waitresses in their younger days, bonnets freshly starched—all this reminded her of a summer villa outside Paris where she had visited her grandmother.

She drew her hand along her arm and felt the hair rising. Then she got back to the menu and found what she had been looking for: "Lobster américaine au gratin,"[2] she said triumphantly. "That's what I want."

Her boldness frightened him a bit. He hemmed and hawed and let his fingers glide along the meat and fish and egg dishes as he mumbled: "Have it, have it...I think I'll have..."

And he settled on lamb.

Then she settled into her chair, let one leg glide over the other, but was careful not to touch him with the tip of her toe. She let her weight fall heavily onto her underarms and felt the paper cloth rustle slightly. Before she had said a word the chilled white wine and hot French bread had been placed before them.

"I recognize that one," she said, pointing at the waitress's back as it receded toward the kitchen. "Second from the left."

"What are you talking about?"

"Haven't you noticed? They've been reproduced—the whole lot of them. Some in gilded frames and some right on the wall. Not al fresco, of course, though maybe al masonite-o," she giggled.

But the pleasure was hers alone.

"You keep changing the subject. Changing my thoughts, my focus. Everything bounces off you tonight. Makes me wonder what's wrong."

"Maybe a concussion," she suggested.

"Cut it out—be serious. I feel like I'm out with a schoolgirl."

"I'm sorry," she said. "I'll pull myself together." But no sooner had she said it than she felt like bursting into laughter. She looked at his smooth white hands which only dared to come halfway out of the cuffs of his perfect, pale blue linen shirt. There they lay on the table, proper as a spinster's, in contrast with her own hands, rough and red from a summer of rowing and sailing.

They had the terrace practically to themselves. At the far end she could see the low-cut back of a young woman's black dress. Her hair was newly done, in a style reminiscent of a straggly artichoke. Over one of her shoulders her escort was visible: thinning hair, impeccably dressed in black, considerably older. There were four tables between them. To their right was the rest of the dining room, dark panelled, white clothed. The hotel owner, a gentleman in his eighties, could sometimes be seen moving between his office and the kitchen, tall and bent with a dark green woollen scarf tied round his neck.

It was off-season. No more boarders, only couples passing through. She drew her hand through her boyish hair.

"You've cut your hair even shorter," he said a bit reproachfully. "But it's pretty like that, too..."

"I don't know how nice it looks," she said, "but it feels good. I don't need a comb or a mirror any more."

On her left she could see their own images and those of the dining room and the costumed waitresses—sometimes real, sometimes painted, it was not always easy to tell which—reflected in the windowpanes. In the background was the sea, breathing heavily, asthmatically. With a quick look she could see herself (no comb or mirror), her tanned arms, her sleeveless black velvet overall. The rest was hidden by the panelled wall.

"Oh, you are so lovely," he said with a touch of irony," but you are somewhere else."

"Let me have my somewhere else to myself," she thought. "Don't shove me into your corner. Soon I'll be lying devoured by our passion, our panting, soon I'll be wriggling like a fish on the hook of desire. Let me be in peace for a little while."

A great deal of serious consideration had preceded this evening. They had set the date long ago, at the beginning of the summer. "In Dinard in September."

"Okay. In Dinard."

It had sounded like a joke. It was so far away. And yet they both knew it would be worth waiting for.

As usual, he had vacationed in Scandinavia with his wife. The children were at camp, exploring caves and making real descents. As usual, she had stayed with her aunt outside Grasse. Her aunt's foster son was twenty now and had taken her on long cruises. Once they went to Marseille. Another time all the way to the Lipari Islands. She had been seasick for the first few days, then she had begun to like it. She had finished her book, *The Black Mirror— The Art of the Silhouette*, on time. It had turned out to be a lovely volume, if a bit too posh, the kind of book people buy as a present. Her publisher, who had given her a very small advance, assured her that he expected it to sell. Now she was between projects, taking a break. She was looking around, tasting and trying: What would she delve into next?

Just as she began to do the research for a tourist guide of Bretagne, their date in Dinard had come round. To her surprise, she felt very little anticipation. But she had the car serviced, filled it and her emergency tank with gas, and left.

His hair was grayer. His wrinkles were broader. He had eaten well in Sweden and Denmark, drunk a lot of *aquavit*. Eel and salmon. Now the curriculum committee awaited him. There would be long conferences in Tours, he said. No, his wife had stayed in Paris.

This was something new. For the first time, they had time. This surprised her. She felt like saying, "I have to be back in Paris the day after tomorrow." But both of them would have taken this as an insult, a demonstration. Not as a fact about her work.

She felt an uncommon surge of melancholy filter in with the cold draft. Just then the lights went down. The sea and the night lurched closer.

It's the electricians' slowdown," he explained. "They're trying to find out how many inches of cold darkness we can stand."

"I can't stand any. My darkness threshold is low today," she thought. But she said nothing.

Then the lobster made its entrance. His leg of lamb crept in behind like an insignificant brown portion of protein. The lobster shone, and exuded aromas. Even in death it raised its huge antennas in arcs of triumph. It had lifted one claw as if to begin a speech. Bits of truffle lay like black marble chips in the puffed, bubbling sauce. Cheese gleamed golden. It smelled of chervil and tarragon and something not readily identifiable. Was it thyme?

She drew in the aromas. She praised and smiled. She exclaimed again and again, "Just look! Isn't it magnificent? It's a real beauty. Did you see how he's holding his claws? What a beauty...a real gentleman!"

He tried to praise the tenderness of the leg of lamb, its garlic perfume. The crispness of the lettuce. He offered her a bite and she unwillingly accepted a piece of cucumber from

his fork. He had forgotten to order bordeaux for himself, sat and waited impatiently for it while his food grew cold.

The lobster illuminated the entire table. It was a red lamp that warmed them.

"You look like you've found a long-lost friend," he said.

"Well, you're here aren't you?" she said, suddenly warm and smiling as if the lobster had supercharged her with a happiness and daring she could communicate to him by gently patting his cheek.

He smiled and seemed to lose his quizzical, ironic skepticism. It was turning into a nice evening after all. He entertained her with political gossip. She told of the Lipari Islands, of a cave with stalactites, of her absent-minded aunt who this summer, too, had served cat food to company for dinner one night. Had opened the wrong tin. The guests couldn't have known by the taste because the meat was well-mixed with tiny onions and roast tomatoes, but to their surprise they discovered bits of gristle and fur in their mouths, spit them out, and found themselves quickly full.

"She has twelve cats now," she said. "It can't go on. Her son figured out that there will be five hundred of them in three years' time. It scared her at first, but then she said: 'That's nothing but a statistic, and statistics always lie. How do you know they'll want so many children?'"

There was a dull laugh from the other table. Had they heard her story? The man with the balding spot lay his fat hand on the young woman's shoulder. She laughed shrilly and deprecatingly. Or invitingly? She seemed to need help. Why had these two met? Where would they be tomorrow?

She wasn't getting full by looking, so finally she assailed her meal. The meat surrendered willingly to her attacks, it had only been lightly restuffed into its shell. It had been removed first, minced and restuffed, and then covered with a layer of au gratin sauce. They had used every bit of the huge lobster. She chewed, her mouth full of fresh, firm, warm lobster meat. She smiled at his night-black eyes as if to convince him that he had not died in vain. She scraped the inside of the shell lovingly, searching for every drop of fat and sauce. She sucked the lobster's narrow wrists with delight and saw the black-framed thumb joint loosen and break, to expose the major and minor ecstasies of the two halves of the claw. She waved the thin bit of cartilage from the larger half like a fan: it was white and delicate and somehow untainted; the au gratin sauce, cheesy and dark brown, voluptuous and creamy, had passed it by, surrounded as it was by the healthy slab of meat, the porcelain-white particles, the rough armor of the shell.

Soon they would go up to their room. The old hotel owner had warned them that the double rooms in the newly renovated wing, the oldest part of the building, were the most expensive rooms in the establishment. Laughing, they had reassured him that his price was exorbitant. If he wanted to offer them a discount, they would readily accept. But they weren't prepared to sacrifice the view of the sea.

She wiped her mouth with the white paper napkin.

"In Sweden," he said," you should have seen the paper napkins! Much better quality than ours!"

"But no lobsters?"

"Well, they had some—but none like that one."

"We should name it!"

When they reached the old-fashioned vestibule where the restaurant wing met the hotel corridors, she said she wanted to take a walk. She was well aware that he despised nocturnal strolls, and added: "I'll be happy to go by myself."

"Don't be too long."

The streets enveloped her like tight but comfortable clothing. She glided along, her steps inaudible. The white wine was alive, it lifted her. But, most importantly, Monsieur Homard[3] walked by her side. His shell clattered elegantly against the cobblestones. He gesticulated with his long antennas, his black buttonhole eyes shifting and turning hither and thither. He was lecturing her on autonomy and independence.

"Suppose," he said, speaking as if he were in her own blood. "Suppose that you had all the time in the world. That you could marry, or live as if you were married...Well, my dear girl, would you be inclined to live in such a bourgeois environment? And where would your love of freedom go? Your adventures?"

She did not reply, but hurried on. She reached the sea. The waves were sleepier. They rinsed slowly, oh so slowly, up onto the sand, almost hesitating to leave it. Half asleep, they rolled back out into the wetness. The lighthouse blinked. Somewhere in the darkness above her he stood waiting, penis angled, prepared to rise chivalrously the moment she entered the room.

She stretched her arms so quickly that M. Homard was frightened and disappeared back down into the sea foam. She recalled T. S. Eliot's crab, scuttling across the floor of the sea. How she had read Eliot on the commuter train and spilt cocoa out of her thermos. How she had lived an entire summer with Eliot's *Quartets*, ignoring the young man from the first-class car who used to come and stare at her with his great sea-green eyes and disappear again without having dared to say a word.

"Freedom," she muttered, squeezing the car key in her pocket. The moonlit streets opened. The buildings pressed together, hiding their inhabitants from her gaze. High above the chimneytops, a flock of migrating birds skimmed past. People got strange interference on their TV sets and wondered why.

She walked and walked. Unwritten poems hummed and rumbled within her. Faces appeared and vanished. She loved them all, and she greeted them as they passed—they only existed in her head. The town was empty. A young man leaned out of a lighted window and looked her way. Beside him hung a model ship, made with exquisite detail. She knew it must be beautiful seen from indoors, illuminated by his red ceiling lamp. She could only see its silhouette.

They stood for a long time, looking at one another without speaking. Finally he laughed and waved: "Come up!"

She smiled and waved back: "Another time. Maybe."

The town was shifting, alive, full of destinies. And she was in its midst. M. Homard was clattering again, but a few steps behind her. He was an old man. When she turned, she saw that he was using a coral cane. He was preaching and warning, but his voice was weak and his words ambiguous. What a life! She swung her arms happily. As she passed her car she gave it a pat and it made her hand black as soot.

He embraced her eagerly and heatedly. They took their time. She thought. "It is better than with anyone else." Outside the sea slept, breathing calmly, deeply. The balcony door was wide open. The fog rolled in. The whole room smelled of seaweed. They sailed away on the soft raft of the double bed.

Just before she fell asleep she saw the lobster wave his claw. But she was no longer sure if it was a cheerful greeting or a signal to stop.

Translated by Linda Schenck

NOTES

1. Dinard is a beach resort in Brittany, France, near the birthplace of the great romantic writer François René de Chateaubriand (1768–1848).
2. Lobster in the shell, with a cheese sauce.
3. French for "Mr. Lobster."
4. The crab is a reference to T. S. Eliot's poem *The Love Song of J. Alfred Prufrock* (1909–1911). *The Four Quartets* (1935–1942) was his last major poetic work.

Svava Jakobsdóttir   *Iceland, b. 1930*

Born in 1930 at Neskaupstad in eastern Iceland, Svava Jakobsdóttir spent part of her childhood in Saskatchewan, Canada, where her father was minister of the Icelandic Lutheran Church. Returning to Reykjavik, Iceland's capital, to finish high school and attend one year of university, she then returned to North America to study English literature at Smith College in Massachusetts, and received her A.B. degree in 1952. She did postgraduate work at Somerville College, Oxford, where she studied Old Icelandic literature, and at Uppsala University in Sweden, doing work there in modern Swedish literature.

Jakobsdóttir has spent her professional life as a diplomat as well as a writer. She worked five years at the Foreign Ministry of Iceland and at the Icelandic Embassy. In 1971 she was elected a member of the Icelandic Parliament, and as Parliamentarian she was a delegate to the United Nations and a member of the Nordic Council. She has also served as Iceland's representative on the Nordic Committee for equality between men and women. In 1979, after two re-elections, she gave up politics to be a full-time writer.

Jakobsdóttir published her first book, a collection of short stories called *Tólf konur* (Twelve Women), in 1965. Since then she has published a novel, *1969*, two more collections of short stories, three full-length plays, of which *Lokaaefing* (Final

Rehearsal) has been produced internationally. She has also written for radio and many of her works have been widely translated. The short story here, "A Story for Children," appeared in her 1967 collection *Veizla undir grjótvegg* (Party under a Stone Wall).

The major themes in Jakobsdóttir's writing focus on women—how they are expected to perform and how they actually do perform in their (usually middle-class) society. Like the character in the following story, many of her female protagonists are searching for their identities, a search often filled with pain and futility.

Jakobsdóttir is a member of the Union of Icelandic Writers and the Icelandic PEN Club. She was awarded a literary prize by the Icelandic Writer's Fund in 1968 and 1982 and the Icelandic Radio's Writer's Fund in 1983. She is also a permanent recipient of a writer's grant awarded annually by the Icelandic state.

Jakobsdóttir has been married since 1955 and lives in Reykjavik with her husband, Jon Hnefill Adalsteinsson, a folklorist. They have one son.

A STORY FOR CHILDREN
Saga handa börnum

For as long as she could remember she had resolved to be true to her nature and devote all her energies to her home and her children. There were several children now and from morning till night she was swamped with work, doing the household chores and caring for the children. She was now preparing supper and waiting for the potatoes to boil. A Danish women's magazine lay on the kitchen bench as if it had been tossed there accidentally; in fact, she kept it there on purpose and sneaked a look at it whenever she got a chance. Without letting the pot of potatoes out of her mind she picked up the magazine and skimmed over Fru Ensom's[1] advice column. This was by no means the column that seemed most interesting to her, but it was usually short. It was possible that it would last just long enough so that the potatoes would be boiling when she finished reading it. The first letter in the column was short: Dear Fru Ensom, I have never lived for anything other than my children and have done everything for them. Now I am left alone and they never visit me. What should I do? Fru Ensom answered: Do more for them.

This was the logical answer, of course. It was perfectly clear that nothing else was possible. She hoped that she wouldn't start writing to the magazines about such obvious things when the time came. No, these columns where people moaned and groaned were not to her liking. The columns which discussed child-rearing and the role of the mother—or rather, *the* column, since both subjects were discussed in one and the same column—were much more positive. The fundamental aspects of child-rearing had of course been familiar to her for quite some time now, but it did happen that she felt weak and fatigued at times. At that point she would leaf through the columns on child-rearing seeking courage and confirmation that she was on the right track in life. She only regretted having less and less time to read.

The uncleaned fish awaited her in the sink and she withstood the temptation to read the child-rearing column this time. She closed the magazine and stood up. She limped a little bit ever since the children had cut off the big toe on her right foot. They had wanted to find out what happened if someone had only nine toes.

Within herself she was proud of her limp and of her children's eagerness to learn, and sometimes she limped even more than was necessary. She now turned the heat down under the potatoes and began cleaning the fish. The kitchen door opened and her little son, who was six years old and had blue eyes and light curly hair, came up to her.

"Mama," he said, and stuck a pin in her arm. She started and almost cut herself with the knife.

"Yes, dear," she said, and reached out her other arm so the child could stick it, too.

"Mama, tell me a story."

She put the knife down, dried her hands and sat down with the child in her lap to tell him a story. She was just about halfway through the story when it occurred to her that one of the other children might suffer psychological harm from not getting supper on time. In the boy's face she tried to see how he would take it if she stopped telling the story. She felt the old indecisiveness taking hold of her and she became distracted from the story. This inability of hers to make decisions had increased with the number of children and the ever-increasing chores. She had begun to fear those moments which interrupted her usual rush from morning to night. More and more often she lost her poise if she stopped to make a decision. The child-rearing columns gave little or no help at such moments, though she tried to call them to mind. They only discussed one problem and one child at a time. Other problems always had to wait until next week.

This time she was spared making a decision. The door opened and all the children crowded into the kitchen. Stjáni, the oldest, was in the lead. At an early age he had shown an admirable interest in both human and animal biology. The boy who had been listening to the story now slid out of her lap and took up a position among his brothers and sisters. They formed a semicircle around her and she looked over each of them one after the other.

"Mama, we want to see what a person's brain looks like."

She looked at the clock.

"Right now?" she asked.

Stjáni didn't answer his mother's question. With a nod of his head and a sharp glance he gave his younger brother a sign, and the younger brother went and got a rope, while Stjáni fastened the saw blade to the handle. The rope was then wrapped around the mother. She felt how the little hands fumbled at her back while the knot was tied. The rope was loose and it wouldn't take much effort to get free. But she was careful not to let it be noticed. He had always been sensitive about how clumsy he was with his hands. Just as Stjáni raised the saw up to her head the image of the children's father came into her mind. She saw him in front of her just as he would appear in a little while: on the threshold of the front door with his briefcase in one hand and his hat in the other. She never saw him except in the front doorway, either on his way out or on his way in. She had once been able to imagine him outside the house among other people or at the office, but now, after the children had been born, they had moved into a new house and he into a new office, and she had lost her bearings. He would come home soon and she still hadn't started frying the fish. The blood had now begun to flow down her head. Stjáni had gotten through with the saw. It seemed to be going well, and fairly quickly. Now and then he stopped as if he were measuring with his eyes just how big the hole had to be. Blood spurted into his face and a curse crossed his lips. He nodded his head and the young brother went immediately and got the mop bucket. They placed it under the hole and soon it was half full. The procedure was over at the exact moment the father appeared in the doorway. He stood motionless for a while and pondered the sight which presented itself to him: his wife tied up, with a hole in her head, the eldest son holding a gray brain in his hand, the curious group of children huddled together, and only one pot on the stove.

"Kids! How can you think of doing this when it's already suppertime?"

He picked up the piece of his wife's skull and snapped it back in just as she was about to bleed to death. Then he took over and soon the children were busy tidying up after themselves. He wiped most of the blood stains off the walls himself before he checked on the pot on the stove. There was a suspicious sound coming from it. The water had boiled away and he took the pot off the stove and set it on the metal counter next to the sink. When he saw the half-cleaned fish in the sink he realized that his wife had still not gotten up from the chair. Puzzled, he knit his brow. It wasn't usual for her to be sitting down when there was so much to do. He went over to her and looked at her attentively. He noticed then that they had forgotten to untie her.

When he had freed her they looked into each other's eyes and smiled. Never was their harmony more deeply felt than when their eyes met in mutual pride over the children.

"Silly urchins," he said, and his voice was filled with the concern and affection that he felt for his family.

Soon afterward they sat down at the table. Everyone except Stjáni. He was in his room studying the brain under a microscope. Meanwhile, his mother kept his supper warm for him in the kitchen. They were all hungry and took to their food briskly; this was an unusually late supper. There was no change to be seen in the mother. She had washed her hair and combed it over the cut before she sat down. Her mild expression displayed the patience and self-denial usual at mealtimes. This expression had first appeared during those years when she served her children first and kept only the smallest and most meager piece for herself. Now the children were big enough so that they could take the best pieces themselves and the expression was actually unnecessary, but it had become an inseparable part of the meal. Before the meal was over Stjáni came in and sat down. The mother went to get his supper. In the kitchen she boned the fish thoroughly be-

fore putting it on the plate. When she picked up the garbage pail to throw the bones away she let out a scream. The brain was right on top of the pail.

The rest of the family rushed out as soon as her scream reached the dining room. The father was in the lead and was quick to discover what was wrong when he saw his wife staring down into the garbage pail. Her scream had died out, but it could still be seen in the contours of her face.

"You think it's a shame to throw it out, don't you, dear?" he asked.

"I don't know," she said and looked at him apologetically. "I didn't think."

"Mama didn't think, mama didn't think, mama didn't think," chanted one of the children who had an especially keen sense of humor.

They all burst out laughing and the laughter seemed to solve the problem. The father said he had an idea; they didn't have to throw the brain out, they could keep it in alcohol.

With that, he put the brain into a clear jar and poured alcohol over it. They brought the jar into the living room and found a place for it on a shelf of knick-knacks. They all agreed it fit well there. Then they finished eating.

There were no noticeable changes in the household routine due to the brain loss. At first a lot of people came to visit. They came to see the brain, and those who had prided themselves on their grandmother's old spinning wheel in the corner of their living room now looked with envy upon the brain upon the shelf. She felt no changes in herself either at first. It hadn't become a bit more difficult for her to do housework or to understand the Danish magazines. Many things even turned out to be easier then before, and situations that earlier had caused her to rack her brain no longer did so. But gradually she began to feel a heaviness in her chest. It seemed as if her lungs no longer had room enough to function and after a year had passed she went to the doctor. A thorough examination revealed that her heart had grown larger *usus innaturalis et adsi-*

dui causa.[2] She asked the doctor to excuse her for having forgotten all the Latin she had learned in school, and patiently he explained to her how the loss of one organ could result in changes in another. Just as a man who loses his sight will acquire a more acute sense of hearing, her heart had increased its activity a good deal when her brain was no longer available. This was a natural development, *lex vitae*,[3] if one may say so—and at that, the doctor laughed—there was no need to fear that such a law could be anything but just. Therefore she didn't have to be afraid. She was in the best of health.

She felt relieved at these words. Lately she had even been afraid that she had only a short time to live, and this fear had become an increasingly loud voice within her breast which said: What will become of them if I die? But now she realized that this voice, whose strength and clarity grew steadily, was no prophecy, but rather the voice of her heart. This knowledge made her happy because the voice of one's heart could be trusted.

The years passed and her heart's voice showed her the way: from the children's rooms and her husband's study to the kitchen and the bedroom. This route was dear to her, and no gust of wind that blew through the front door was ever strong enough to sweep away her tracks. Only one thing aroused fear in her: unexpected changes in the world. The year they changed counter girls at the milk store five times she was never quite all right. But the children grew up. She awoke with a bad dream when her oldest child, Stjáni, began to pack his suitcase to go out into the world. With uncontrollable vehemence she threw herself over the threshold to block his exit. A sucking sound could be heard as the boy stepped on her on his way out. He thought she was moaning and paused a moment and said that she herself was to blame. No one had asked her to lie down there. She smiled as she got up because what he had said wasn't quite right. Her heart had told her to lie there. She had heard the voice clearly and now, as she watched him walk down the street, the voice spoke to her again and said that she could still be glad that she had softened his first steps out into the world. Later on they all left one after the other and she was left alone. She no longer had anything to do in the children's rooms and she would often sit in the easy chair in the living room now. If she looked up, the jar on the shelf came into view, where the brain had stood all these years and, in fact, was almost completely forgotten. Custom had made it commonplace. Sometimes she pondered over it. As far as she could see, it had kept well. But she got less and less pleasure out of looking at it. It reminded her of her children. And gradually she felt that a change was again taking place within herself, but she couldn't bring herself to mention it to her husband. She saw him so seldom lately, and whenever he appeared at home she got up from the chair in a hurry, as if a guest had arrived. One day he brought up the question himself of whether she wasn't feeling well. Pleased, she looked up, but when she saw that he was figuring the accounts at the same time, she became confused in answering (she had never been particularly good in figuring). In her confusion she said she didn't have enough to do. He looked at her amazed and said there were enough things to be done if people only used their brain. Of course he said this without thinking. He knew very well that she didn't have a brain, but she nevertheless took him literally. She took the jar down from the shelf, brought it to the doctor and asked if he thought the brain was still useable. The doctor didn't exclude the possibility of its being of some use, but on the other hand, all organs atrophied after being preserved in alcohol for a long time. Therefore it would be debatable whether it would pay to move it at all; in addition, the *nervi cerebrales*[4] had been left in rather poor shape, and the doctor asked whether some clumsy dolt had actually done the surgery.

"He was so little then, the poor thing," the woman said.

"By the way," said the doctor, "I recall

that you had a highly developed heart."

The woman avoided the doctor's inquiring look and a faint pang of conscience gripped her. And she whispered to the doctor what she hadn't dared hint of to her husband: "My heart's voice has fallen silent."

As she said this she realized why she had come. She unbuttoned her blouse, took it off and laid it neatly on the back of the chair. Her bra went the same way. Then she stood ready in front of the doctor, naked from the waist up. He picked up a scalpel and cut, and a moment later he handed her the gleaming, red heart. Carefully he placed it in her palm and her hands closed around it. Its hesitant beat resembled the fluttering of a bird in a cage. She offered to pay the doctor, but he shook his head and, seeing that she was having difficulty, helped her get dressed. He then offered to call her a taxi since she had so much to carry. She refused, stuffed the brain jar into her shopping bag and slipped the bag over her arm. Then she left with the heart in her hands.

Now began the long march from one child to the next. She first went to see her sons, but found none of them at home. They had all gotten a berth on the ship of state and it was impossible to tell when they would return. Furthermore, they never stayed in home port long enough for there to be time for anything other than begetting children. She withdrew from the bitterness of her daughters-in-law and went to see her oldest daughter, who opened the door herself. A look of astonishment and revulsion came over her face when she saw the slimy, red heart pulsating in her mother's palm, and in her consternation, she slammed the door. This was of course an involuntary reaction and she quickly opened the door again, but she made it clear to her mother that she didn't care at all about her heart; and she wasn't sure it would go with the new furniture in the living room. The mother then realized that it was pointless to continue the march, because her younger daughters had even newer furniture. So she went home. There she filled a jar with alcohol and dropped the heart into it. A deep sucking sound, like a gasp within a human breast, could be heard as the heart sank to the bottom. And now they each stood on the shelf in their own jars, her brain and her heart. But no one came to view them. And the children never came to visit. Their excuse always was that they were too busy. But the truth was that they didn't like the sterile smell that clung to everything in the house.

Translated by Dennis Auburn Hill

NOTES

1. Fru Ensom means "Mrs. Lonesome" in Danish.
2. Latin for a case involving unnatural and persistent use.
3. Latin for "law of life."
4. Latin for "cerebral nerves."

Edna O'Brien   *Ireland/UK(England), b. 1930*

Edna O'Brien's characters are women in search of sexual and sensual fulfillment; they are lonely women struggling, often unsuccessfully, toward independence from their families, their lovers, and the restrictive role models that have formed them, role models that formed their author as well. Born in Taumgraney, County Clare, in the West of Ireland, to parents who were extremely religious, O'Brien describes her years there in her nonfictional work *Mother Ireland* (1970). In 1941, after attending the National School in nearby Scariff, she went to the Convent of Mercy School at Loughrea until 1946, when she migrated to Dublin to go to the Pharmaceutical College. In Dublin she began writing seriously, although she didn't publish her first novel, *The Country Girls*, until 1960, after she had married and moved to London. *The Country Girls* was followed by the second and third parts of the trilogy, *The Lonely Girl* (1962) and *Girls in Their Married Bliss* (1964). Semiautobiographical, the trilogy tells the story of two Irish girls, Kate and Baba, who escape their country and convent upbringing for life in Dublin, later London. *The Lonely Girl* was, in 1964, made into a popular film, *Girl with Green Eyes*. The trilogy was well received by critics, especially for its realism and humor. The books were, however, banned in 1969, along with two more of O'Brien's novels, for obscenity. That her books have been banned in her native Ireland has surely contributed to her popularity. It also places her in the company of other Irish writers such as James Joyce and Frank O'Connor.

O'Brien has since written many other novels, including the highly successful *Night* (1972), which is about a woman who, unlike many of O'Brien's heroines, does achieve independence. O'Brien is well known for her short stories, many originally published in *The New Yorker* and collected in *A Scandalous Woman and Other Stories* (1974), from which the selection here was taken. She has also written plays, including *Virginia* (1981), adapted from Virginia Woolf's diaries.

John Isom

THE CREATURE

She was always referred to as The Creature by the townspeople, the dressmaker for whom she did buttonholing, the sacristan who used to search for her in the pews on the dark winter evenings before locking up, and even the little girl Sally, for whom she wrote out the words of a famine song.[1] Life had treated her rottenly, yet she never complained but always had a ready smile, so that her face with its round rosy cheeks was more like something you could eat or lick; she reminded me of nothing so much as an apple fritter.

I used to encounter her on her way from devotions or from Mass, or having a stroll, and when we passed she smiled, but she never spoke, probably for fear of intruding. I was doing a temporary teaching job in a little town in the west of Ireland and soon came to know that she lived in a tiny house facing a garage that was also the town's fire station. The first time I visited her, we sat in the parlor and looked out on the crooked lettering on the fire-station door. There seemed to be no one in attendance at the station. Nor was there any little muslin curtain to obscure the world, be-cause, as she kept repeating, she had washed it that very day and what a shame. She gave me a glass of rhubarb wine, and we shared the same chair, which was really a wooden seat with a latticed wooden back, that she had got from a rubbish heap and had varnished herself. After varnishing, she had dragged a nail over the wood to give a sort of mottled effect, and you could see where her hand had shaken, because the lines were wavery.

I had come from another part of the country; in fact, I had come to get over a love affair, and since I must have emanated some sort of sadness she was very much at home with me and called me "dearest" when we met and when we were taking leave of one another. After correcting the exercises from school, filling in the roll book, and going for a walk, I would knock on her door and then sit with her in the little room almost devoid of furniture—and devoid even of a plant or a picture—and oftener than not I would be given a glass of rhubarb wine and sometimes a slice of porter cake. She lived alone and had done so for seventeen years. She was a widow and had two children. One daughter farmed in Canada; the son lived about four miles away. She had not set eyes on him for the seventeen years—not since his wife had slung her out—and the children that she had seen as babies were big now, and, as she heard, marvelously handsome. She had a pension and once a year made a journey to the southern end of the country, where her husband's relatives lived in a cottage looking out over the Atlantic.

Her husband had been killed two years after their marriage, shot in the back of a lorry, in an incident that was later described by the British Forces as an accident. She had had to conceal the fact of his death and the manner of his death from her own mother, since her mother had lost a son about the same time, also in combat, and on the very day of her husband's funeral, when the chapel bells were ringing and reringing, she had to pretend it was for a traveling man, a tinker, who had died suddenly. She got to the funeral at the very last minute on the pretext that she was going to see the priest.

She and her husband had lived with her mother. She reared her children in the old farmhouse, eventually told her mother that she, too, was a widow, and as women together they worked and toiled and looked after the stock and milked and churned and kept a sow to whom she gave the name of Bessie. Each year the bonhams[2] would become pets of hers, and follow her along the road to Mass or wherever, and to them, too, she gave pretty names. A migrant workman helped in the summer months, and in the autumn he would kill the pig for their winter meat. The killing of the pig always made her sad, and she reckoned she could hear those roars—each successive roar—over the years, and she would dwell on that, and then tell how a particularly naughty pig stole into the house one time and lapped up the bowls of cream and then lay down on the floor, snoring and belching like a drunken man. The workman slept downstairs on the settle bed, got drunk on Saturdays, and was

the cause of an accident: when he was teaching her son to shoot at targets, the boy shot off three of his own fingers. Otherwise, her life had passed without incident.

When her children came home from school, she cleared half the table for them to do their exercises—she was an untidy woman—then every night she made blancmange[3] for them before sending them to bed. She used to color it red or brown or green as the case may be, and she marveled at these coloring essences almost as much as the children themselves did. She knitted two sweaters each year for them—two identical sweaters of bowneen wool—and she was indeed the proud mother when one was allowed to serve at Mass.

Her finances suffered a dreadful setback when her entire stock contracted foot-and-mouth disease, and to add to her grief she had to see the animals that she so loved die and be buried around the farm, wherever they happened to stagger down. Her lands were disinfected and empty for over a year, and yet she scraped enough to send her children to boarding school and felt lucky in that she got a reduction in the fees because of her reduced circumstances. The parish priest had intervened on her behalf. He admired her and used to joke her on account of the novelettes she so cravenly read. Her children left, her mother died, and she went through a phase of not wanting to see anyone—not even a neighbor—and she reckoned that was her Garden of Gethsemane.[4] She contracted shingles, and one night, dipping into the well for a bucket of water, she looked first at the stars then down at the water and thought how much simpler it would be if she were to drown. Then she remembered being put into the well for sport one time by her brother, and another time having a bucket of water douched over her by a jealous sister, and the memory of the shock of these two experiences and a plea to God made her draw back from the well and hurry up through the nettle garden to the kitchen, where the dog and the fire, at least, awaited her. She went down on her knees and prayed for the strength to go on.

Imagine her joy when, after years of wandering, her son returned from the city, announced that he would become a farmer, and that he was getting engaged to a local girl who worked in the city as a chiropodist. Her gift to them was a patchwork quilt and a special border of cornflowers she planted outside the window, because the bride-to-be was more than proud of her violet-blue eyes and referred to them in one way or another whenever she got the chance. The Creature thought how nice it would be to have a border of complementary flowers outside the window, and how fitting, even though she preferred wallflowers, both for their smell and their softness. When the young couple came home from the honeymoon, she was down on her knees weeding the bed of flowers, and, looking up at the young bride in her veiled hat, she thought an oil painting was no lovelier or no more sumptuous. In secret, she hoped that her daughter-in-law might pare her corns after they had become intimate friends.

Soon she took to going out to the cow-shed to let the young couple be alone, because even by going upstairs she could overhear. It was a small house, and the bedrooms were directly above the kitchen. They quarreled constantly. The first time she heard angry words she prayed that it be just a lovers' quarrel, but such spiteful things were said that she shuddered and remembered her own dead partner and how they had never exchanged a cross word between them. That night she dreamed she was looking for him, and though others knew of his whereabouts they would not guide her. It was not long before she realized that her daughter-in-law was endowed with a sour and heated nature. A woman who automatically bickered over everything—the price of eggs, the best potato plants to put down, even the fields that should be pasture and those that should be reserved for tillage. The women got

on well enough during the day, but rows were inevitable at night when the son came in and, as always, The Creature went out to the cow-shed or down the road while things transpired. Up in her bedroom, she put little swabs of cotton wool in her ears to hide whatever sounds might be forthcoming. The birth of their first child did everything to exacerbate the young woman's nerves, and after three days the milk went dry in her breasts. The son called his mother out to the shed, lit a cigarette for himself, and told her that unless she signed the farm and the house over to him he would have no peace from his young barging wife.

This The Creature did soon after, and within three months she was packing her few belongings and walking away from the house where she had lived for fifty-eight of her sixty years. All she took was her clothing, her aladdin lamp, and a tapestry denoting ships on a hemp-colored sea. It was an heirloom. She found lodgings in the town and was the subject of much curiosity, then ridicule, because of having given her farm over to her son and daughter-in-law. Her son defected on the weekly payment he was supposed to make, but though she took the matter to her solicitor, on the appointed day she did not appear in court and as it happened spent the entire night in the chapel, hiding in the confessional.

Hearing the tale over the months, and how The Creature had settled down and made a soup most days, was saving for an electric blanket, and much preferred winter to summer, I decided to make the acquaintance of her son, unbeknownst to his wife. One evening I followed him to the field where he was driving a tractor. I found a sullen, middle-aged man, who did not dare look at me but proceeded to roll his own cigarette. I recognized him chiefly by the three missing fingers and wondered pointlessly what they had done with them on that dreadful day. He was in the long field where she used to go twice daily with buckets of separated milk, to feed the sucking calves. The house was to be seen behind some trees, and either because of secrecy or nervousness he got off the tractor, crossed over and stood beneath a tree, his back balanced against the knobbled trunk. It was a little hawthorn, and somewhat superstitious, I hesitated to stand under it. Its flowers gave a certain dreaminess to that otherwise forlorn place. There is something gruesome about plowed earth, maybe because it conjures up the grave.

He seemed to know me, and he looked, I thought distastefully, at my patent boots and my tweed cape. He said there was nothing he could do, that the past was the past, and that his mother had made her own life in the town. You would think she had prospered or remarried, his tone was so caustic when he spoke of "her own life." Perhaps he had relied on her to die. I said how dearly she still held him in her thoughts, and he said that she always had a soft heart and if there was one thing in life he hated it was the sodden handkerchief.

With much hedging, he agreed to visit her, and we arranged an afternoon at the end of that week. He called after me to keep it to myself, and I realized that he did not want his wife to know. All I knew about his wife was that she had grown remote, that she had had improvements made on the place—larger windows and a bathroom installed—and that they were never seen together, not even on Christmas morning at chapel.

By the time I called on The Creature that day, it was long after school, and, as usual, she had left the key in the front door for me. I found her dozing in the armchair, very near the stove, her book still in one hand and the fingers of the other hand fidgeting as if she were engaged in some work. Her beautiful embroidered shawl was in a heap on the floor, and the first thing she did when she wakened was to retrieve it and dust it down. I could see that she had come out in some sort of heat rash, and her face resembled nothing so much as a frog's, with her little raisin eyes submerged between pink swollen lids.

At first she was speechless; she just kept shaking her head. But eventually she said that life was a crucible, life was a crucible. I tried consoling her, not knowing what exactly I had to console her about. She pointed to the back door and said things were kiboshed[5] from the very moment he stepped over that threshold. It seems he came up the back garden and found her putting the finishing touches to her hair. Taken by surprise, she reverted to her long-lost state of excitement and could say nothing that made sense except that she thought it was a thief.

When she realized who he was, without giving him time to catch breath, she plied both food and the drink on him, and I could see that he had eaten nothing, because the ox tongue in its mold of jelly was still on the table, untouched. A little whisky bottle lay on its side, empty. She told me how he'd aged and that when she put her hand up to his gray hair he backed away from her as if she'd given him an electric shock. He who hated the soft heart must have hated that touch. She asked for photos of his family, but he had brought none. All he told her was that his daughter was learning to be a mannequin,[6] a and she put her foot in it further by saying there was no need to gild the lily. He had newspapers in the soles of his shoes to keep out the damp, and she took off those damp shoes and tried polishing them. I could see how it all had been, with her jumping up and down trying to please him but in fact just making him edgy. "They were drying on the range," she said, "when he picked them up and put them on." He was gone before she could put a shine on them, and the worst thing was that he had made no promise concerning the future. When she asked, "Will I see you?" he had said, "Perhaps," and she told me that if there was one word in the English vocabulary that scalded her, it was the word "perhaps."

"I did the wrong thing," I said, and, though she didn't nod, I knew that she also was thinking it—that secretly she would consider me from then on as a busybody. All at once I remembered the little hawthorn tree, the bare plowed field, his heart as black and unawakened as the man I had come away to forget, and there was released in me, too, a gigantic and useless sorrow. Whereas for twenty years she had lived on that last high tightrope of hope, it had been taken away from her, leaving her without anyone, without anything, and I wished that I had never punished myself by applying to be a sub in that stagnant, godforsaken little place.

NOTES

1. Song written about the great Irish potato famine (1846–1851).
2. Irish for "young pig."
3. A rich pudding.
4. Place in Jerusabem where Jesus was betrayed by Judas and arrested, while at prayer, after the Last Supper.
5. Slang for "stopped."
6. Model.

Amelia Rosselli   *Italy, b. 1930*

Amelia Rosselli is the daughter of Carlo Rosselli, who, together with his brother Nello, was assassinated on Mussolini's orders in 1937 in France by the French *cagoulards* for being leaders of an antifascist movement in exile.* Rosselli was born in 1930 in France and received the name of her paternal grandmother, who had published some novels and plays in the first decades of the twentieth century. She spent the war years in America and returned to Europe only in 1946 to study in Florence and in London, where her main interest was musical theory. In 1950 she settled in Rome and composed music for theater and films.

As a poet, Rosselli is considered an important member of the Italian contemporary poetic circle. The following poems were taken from *Variazioni belliche* (Bellic Variations, 1964), which was her first book of verse and was followed by *Serie ospedaliera* (Hospital Series, 1969), *Documento* (Document, 1976), *Primi Scritti 1952–1963* (First Writings 1952–1963, 1980), *Impromptu* (Impromptu, 1981) and *Appunti sparsi e persi (1966–1977)* (Scattered and Lost Notes [1966–1977], 1983). A few of her poems have been translated into English and can be found in various anthologies, such as *The New Italian Poetry* (1981).

Rosselli's poems, some semiautobiographical, contain echoes of torments of her generation. Images of the green lawns of the rich recall her life in the United States. Italy seemed a country of barbarians to her, upon her arrival, England a land of quibblers. Her lyrical style contains, at times, a passionate, even violent discourse, expressed in rhythmic form, often transcending normal use of grammar and semantics. The end result is an experimental language rich in creative force that has greatly influenced younger poets in Italy. In 1986 she was made Knight Officer of the Italian Republic and in 1987 the critic Giacinto Spagnoletti published an anthology (*Antologia poetica*) of her opus.

Natalia Costa-Zalessow

NOTE

* Literally "caped ones"; a secret reactionary organization whose goal was to overthrow France's Third Republic and replace it with a right-wing dictatorship.

THREE MARTIAL VARIATIONS
from Variazioni belliche

I

The whole world is widowed if it's true you're still walking
the whole world is widowed if it's true. The whole world is
true if it's true you're still walking, the whole world is
widowed if you're not dying. The whole world is
mine if it's true that you're not living but only
a lantern for my oblique eyes. I was struck blind
by your birth and the new day's importance
is but night because you're distant. I was struck blind
because you're still walking here. Blind because you're walking
and the world is widowed and the world is blind if you're walking
still clutching at my blue sky eyes.

II

Sure of being faithful to you, I betrayed the joy
and suffering in me: equidistant equinox that kept me far
from the sea, from the scent of forests that are your tranquility
my tide of dreams.

III

After the gift of god was the rebirth. After the patience
of the senses all the days collapsed. After China
Ink an elephant was born: joy. After joy
hell came down after paradise the wolf to its den. After
infinity came the merry-go-round. But the lights fell
and the beasts stirred up again, and the wool was ready and the wolf was devoured.
After hunger the boy-child was born, after boredom the lover
wrote his verses. After infinity the merry-go-round
fell after the concussion the ink grew up. The virgin, warm and
sheltered, wrote her verses: and Christ, dying, answered
"don't touch me!" After his verses, Christ devoured the suffering
that afflicted him. After night the whole world's foundation
fell. After boredom the peasant woman who wanted water from the well
deeper than her arms broke the silence with acrid whispers.
After the air descended around her huge body, the daughter
was born with a devastated heart, the birds' suffering born,
desire born and infinity that can't find itself once
it gets lost. We stagger hopefully until in the end the end
fishes up a subservient spirit.

Translated by Kathrine Jason

Nawal al-Saadawi   *Egypt, b. 1930*

Born in 1930 in Kafr Tahla, a small village in the Nile Delta in Egypt, Nawal al-Saadawi first began a career in medicine in the mid-1950s. She did not limit herself to the boundaries of science but began writing short stories, publishing her first collection, *Hanān Qalīl* (A Little Love), in 1962, which was followed in 1964 by *Ta'allamt al-Hubb* (I Learned Love), and in 1965 by *Lahzat Sidq* (A Moment of Truth). A prolific writer, al-Saadawi has continued to publish short stories, collected in *al-Bahithah 'an al-Hubb* (The Quest for Love, 1974), *Mawt al-Rajul al-Wahīd 'ala al-Ard* (Death of the Only Man on Earth, 1976; translated under the title of *God Dies by the Nile*), *Ughnīyat al-Atfāl al-Diyārīyah* (Songs of the Native Children, 1978); and *Mawt Ma 'ali al-Wazir Sābiqan* (*Death of an Ex-Prime Minister*, 1983), from which the following story (originally published in 1969) is taken. Although al-Saadawi has been accused by her critics of a certain stylistic and psychological crudity, her short fiction shows her becoming increasingly nuanced and adept in manipulating point of view. Moreover, her subject matter, reflecting the many different classes of people she has come into contact with and the access she has had to women by virtue of her medical practice and research, is startling, important, and new to Arabic literature.

However controversial her literary production may have seemed, al-Saadawi met with substantial reprisals when she began publishing her nonfiction based on her medical and psychological research on women. The first of these, *al-Mar'a wa al-Jins* (Women and Sex, 1972), a technical treatise on the nature of the hymen, was in effect an effort to demythicize virginity, for which al-Saadawi was dismissed from her positions as Director of Health Education and Editor-in-Chief of the magazine *Health*. As al-Saadawi tells us in the preface to a novel that she later wrote, she considered this "one more consequence of the path I had chosen as a feminist author and novelist whose views were viewed unfavorably by the authorities." Undaunted, she continued to expose the repression of women in the Arab world, sometimes publishing in Lebanon to avoid Egyptian government censorship: *al-Unthā Hiya al-Asl* (The Female Is the Origin, 1974); *al-Rajul wa al-Jins* (Man and Sex, 1975); *al-Wajh al-'Ari lil-Mar' a al-'Arabiyya* (The Naked Face of the Arab Woman, 1977; as well as *al-Mar'a wa al-Sira' al-Nafsi* (Woman and Psychosis, 1977). During this period she also became a member of the United Nations in Addis Ababa, Ethiopia, where she worked as an advisor to women's programs.

It was at the time that al-Saadawi was doing research for this last book, having the opportunity to enter al-Qanatir women's prison, that she met Firdaus, who gives her name to the novel based on her life. Translated as *Woman at Point Zero* (1981), the book tells the story of a woman awaiting execution for the crime of having murdered her pimp. Some eight years after its publication, in September 1981, al-Saadawi published an explicit discussion on the conditions of Muslim women, "Women and Islam," for which she was herself arrested by Egyptian President Anwar Sadat, together with nearly fifteen hundred other Egyptian intellectuals and members of the opposition, and held in the same al-Qanatir prison. *Dhikrayātī fi Sijn al-Nisā* (*Memoirs from the Women's Prison*, 1984) is an autobiographical account of her prison experience, while the work translated as *Twelve Women in One Prison Cell* (1981) is a fictionalized one.

Continuing to work and live with her husband in Egypt, al-Saadawi has increasingly become the spokeswoman for Arab women in the West, especially since the English translations *The Hidden Face of Eve* (*Al-Wajh al-'Āri lī-l-Mar'a al-'Arabiya*, 1980) and *Two Women in One* (*Imrataan fī imra*, 1986) along with the other works mentioned above.

MASCULINE CONFESSION

Pour me another glass of wine, with a lot of ice. Let me talk and don't interrupt me. From time to time you can stroke my head or neck or chest or any part of my body you like, only don't stop me from talking, because I came to you tonight to confess things I can't confess to anyone else, not even to God's agents on earth.

Actually, I don't believe in such agents and I dislike any intermediaries between myself and God. That doesn't mean that I'm proud or arrogant or that I deal haughtily with people. Quite the opposite. I'm humble and compassionate, and I am concerned for all people and for myself as one of them.

My self-concern is limitless, because I love myself. Yes, I confess to you that my only true love is my love of myself. I fell in love with myself the moment my mother gave birth to me. Her eyes shone as she said to my father: It's a boy! I loved my masculinity and from the start I realized it was the reason for my being privileged. I always had to prove its existence, declare it, show it to people to make it clear and visible and so firm that it was not open to doubt.

One day, when I was young, I was standing in the street beside my father, when suddenly a big fat foot trod on my toes. I screamed "ow" in pain. My father looked at me angrily and said harshly: A man never says "ow." Since that day, I have never said "ow." I would hold back the pain and the tears when I was hurt or someone hit me and would brace the muscles of my back and neck and tell myself: I'm a man.

Once, when the doctor was digging his sharp scalpel into the sole of my foot to remove a splinter of glass, I felt my flesh tear and the blood flow. I was drowning in a sea of sweat from so much pain, but I didn't say "ow." That night, when everybody was asleep, I found myself crying in my sleep, softly murmuring "ow, ow" until the morning.

When I awoke, I braced my back and neck muscles, put on my masculinity and wore it proudly, telling myself: I'm a man. What did you say, my dear? My feet and fingers are as soft as yours? That's true. I belong to the leisured class, the bourgeoisie, in other words. I only use my fingers to hold a glass of wine or to sign my name on some papers in the office or to wave to friends. My friends are many, as you know, and I love them all, just as I love all people. In other words, I love nobody. That doesn't mean that I hate them. It's just that I'm always self-concerned, always absorbed in loving myself. I'm ready at any time to defend myself, by any means, even by committing murder.

Don't look at me like that, as though I'm the only criminal on earth. Crime in the lives of us men is a matter of necessity. It's the only possible way for a man to prove he's a man. But since crime calls for bravery or authority, I'm unable to be a criminal. All I have are daydreams in which I imagine myself a bold hero, separating heads from bodies with a rapid blow of my sword. We men have great admiration for murderers. A man cannot admire another man without hating him. That's the reason I feel so ill at ease when I'm amongst important men in authority. And that's why I run away from the company of reputable men and why I feel at ease in the company of disreputable men. But in general, I prefer the company of women. For with a woman, no matter how important she is, one privilege remains mine—my masculinity. What did you say? Please don't interrupt me. Pour me another glass of wine, with a lot of ice, and let me unburden the crimes which weigh on my heart.

I'm not lying to you. All my crimes are human because they have one aim—to prove that I'm a man. No man can prove his masculinity except by beating other men. So I could not avoid entering into the eternal conflict, the conflict with all other men. In conference rooms or in bedrooms, the conflict is one and the same. Since in conference rooms I lack courage and authority, there's nothing left for me other than bedrooms. Don't call me a wolf or a womanizer. No, I'm a married man. I love my wife like I love my mother, with the same sort of spiritual, holy love. In other words, a love in which I take everything and to which I give nothing. That's ideal love. My wife is the only person (and before her it was my mother) with whom I can get angry and at whom I can rage freely. The reason's well known. She can't return my anger in the same way. We men can't show our anger with those who can be angry with us. I am never angry with my boss, but I get angry quickly with my mother. And with my wife I get angry and rage freely, as I do with my children. All of them I provide for and feed and if they got angry with me, they wouldn't find anyone to replace me.

That's what marriage is for. How else would it be possible for a man to give vent to his anger if it weren't for marriage? The poorest man from the lowest social class goes home to his wife, in the end, in order to be angry and to feel that he's a man. What did you say, my dear?

That's why you refused to get married? You're an intelligent woman. I don't think it's only your intelligence that draws me to your bed, you above all other women. So why is it to you especially that I confess, like a man does to his god? Why do I creep from my wife's bed every night to come to you? I'm not lying to you. It's not love, because as I said, I fell in love with myself from the start and that's the beginning and end of it.

The reason, my dear, is that you're the only person with whom I don't have to prove myself a man. That wasn't clear to me in the beginning. I used to ask myself: what ties me to this woman, why do I need her so much? I discovered the reason that night. Do you remember? It was the night I came to you after my shattering defeat to my rival in the election and the violent argument I had with my wife when I found her naked in my friend's arms. I came to you and cried in your arms and as I cried I felt as though the tears had been bottled up inside me, like steam under pressure, ever since the time my father told me off when I was a child and had said: A man never says "ow." That night I saw my tears flow like a river and heard my voice shout "ow" over and over again. When I came to, I found my head at your feet, kneeling at your altar like a person kneels in a house of worship. What did you say, my dear? You saw the first real smile on my face? I told you it was the happiest night of my life? It's true. For the first time in my life, I discovered how stupid I'd been. When I was a boy, I almost lost an eye in a fight to prove myself a man. In my teens, I nearly lost my life on a number of occasions because of my perpetual readiness to compete. As an adult, I almost lost my mental faculties because of my defeat and then my wife's betrayal. But everything changed that night. The false mask which we call masculinity fell away and I began to see my real self. For the first time, I discovered that I did not have to prove to myself or to others that I was a man. What does "man" mean, after all? This discovery was the happiest moment in my life. I was so happy, I began to smother you with kisses, to kiss your feet and rub my nose in them and cry. I found that the taste of my tears and my lowly position at your feet was sweet. What did you say? I confessed my love to you that night? Yes, my dear, I told you that I loved you. But I admit that as soon as I left your place and went back home and then to my office, I felt ashamed of myself. I was ashamed when I realized how I'd revealed to you a hidden part of myself, the feminine part, the part which all men hide as an imperfection. I was so ashamed that I decided never to see you again. But I returned to you the following night and the next night and every night, without a break. I know that I am bound to you by the force of my desire not to be a man but to be myself, as I am. But I'm also bound to this false masculine world. I put on the mask and take my place in the ranks. I play my part. I deliver blows whenever the other cannot hit me and I receive blows from those above me without responding. I suppress my anger until I get home to my wife and I hold back the tears until I come to you. It's a fair division, my dear. Men like us need at least two women. A woman with whom he can get angry and a woman with whom he can cry. What did you

say, my dear? Yes, my wife loves me. She betrayed me because she loves me so much. I wasn't sure of that, but now I'm convinced of it. I am devoted to my wife and desire her more and more. Yes, I desire her more, my dear, because through her I have discovered something new that I couldn't have discovered by myself. I discovered that I'm not the only man on earth. I confess to you that I feel very comforted by this discovery. It's the comfort of surrendering to a fact to which I was unable to surrender before. If men experienced such comfort just once, they'd encourage their wives to betray them as quickly as possible. How many years I lost without this comfort, my dear.

What did you say? I'm very late? Yes, yes. But I'm luckier than others. Some men die believing they're the only one on earth.

What did you say? Women know this from the start? Yes, my dear. Women are smarter than men. A woman always knows that she's not the only woman on earth. Pour me another glass, with a lot of ice. Let me die in your arms and don't interrupt me.

Translated by Shirley Eber

Alice Munro

Canada, b. 1931

Born in the farming community of Wingham, Ontario, during the Great Depression, Alice Munro (née Laidlaw) focuses her fiction on the harsh realities of that time and place, exposing with a surgeon's precision the unglamourous, uneducated, and sometimes downright hostile aspects of small-town life. A regional writer who acknowledges the influence of both Eudora Welty and Katherine Mansfield, Munro writes about fictional communities (Jubilee, Hanratty, Logan) that are nearly identical in their crippling provincialism and distrust of the imagination and the arts; their enforcement of the puritanical values of thrift, hard work, and unpretentiousness; and their allegiance to the cardinal conformist rule that no one is better than anybody else—while being rigidly divided along class lines. Munro is acclaimed critically for the "artless" realism of her prose. William French, an influential literary critic, calls her "one of the great short-story writers of our time."

The daughter of a ne'er-do-well father (who failed at fox farming, among other things) and a mother severely ill with Parkinson's disease, Munro believed that her only escape from rural squalor and poverty lay through education and a good marriage. After studying English for two years at the University of Western Ontario, she left in 1951 to marry James Munro, moving west to Vancouver and Victoria, where he opened a bookstore. In years dominated by the feminine mystique, Munro raised three daughters, while also selling stories to commercial magazines such as *Mayfair* and *Chatelaine* and to literary periodicals including *Tamarack, Canadian Forum*, and *Queen's Quarterly*. In 1976, after twenty-five years of marriage, she and her husband divorced, and Alice Munro returned to Huron County, Ontario, where she was born, settling in the small town of Clinton with her second husband, Gerald Fremlin, a local geographer.

Munro's one novel is the autobiographical *Lives of Girls and Women*, which won a Canadian Bookseller's Award and in 1973 was turned into a Canadian Broadcasting Corporation film starring Munro's daughter Jenny as the heroine. It is the story of Del Jordan, an imaginative girl who refuses to be trapped by other people's expectations of her, also like the young female protagonist of her well-known story "Boys and Girls," which was turned into an Academy-Award-winning short film in 1984.

Munro's five collections of stories are *Dance of the Happy Shades* (1968), which won a Governor General's Award and was translated into French as *Dance des ombres* (1980); *Something I've Been Meaning to Tell You* (1974), from which the following story was taken, winner of a Canada-Australia Literary Prize; *Who Do You Think You Are?* (1978), which appeared in English and American editions as *The Beggar Maid* and in German translation as *Bettlemädchen* (1980); *The Moons of Jupiter* (1982); and *The Progress of Love* (1986). Most of Munro's stories, which appear regularly in *The New Yorker*, are sad, woman-centered sagas describing "streaks of loss and luck," frequently depicting the failure of romances or marriages to which the women have devoted themselves because, like the legendary Beggar Maid, they do "not know how to do without [a man's] love and his promise to look after [them]; [they are] frightened of the world and [are unable] to think up any other plan for [themselves]." What they learn, belatedly, as Munro writes in "Labor Day Dinner," is that "love is not kind or honest and does not contribute to happiness in any reliable way."

Wendy Robbins Keitner

THE FOUND BOAT

At the end of Bell Street, McKay Street, Mayo Street, there was the Flood. It was the Wawanash River, which every spring overflowed its banks. Some springs, say one in every five, it covered the roads on that side of town and washed over the fields, creating a shallow choppy lake. Light reflected off the water made everything bright and cold, as it is in a lakeside town, and woke or revived in people certain vague hopes of disaster. Mostly during the late afternoon and early evening, there were people straggling out to look at it, and discuss whether it was still rising, and whether this time it might invade the town. In general, those under fifteen and over sixty-five were most certain that it would.

Eva and Carol rode out on their bicycles. They left the road—it was the end of Mayo Street, past any houses—and rode right into a field, over a wire fence entirely flattened by the weight of the winter's snow. They coasted a little way before the long grass stopped them, then left their bicycles lying down and went to the water.

"We have to find a log and ride on it," Eva said.

"Jesus, we'll freeze our legs off."

"Jesus, we'll freeze our legs off!" said one of the boys who were there too at the water's edge. He spoke in a sour whine, the way boys imitated girls although it was nothing like the way girls talked. These boys—there were three of them—were all in the same class as Eva and Carol at school and were known to them by name (their names being Frank, Bud and Clayton), but Eva and Carol, who had seen and recognized them from the road, had not spoken to them or looked at them or, even yet, given any sign of knowing they were there. The boys seemed to be trying to make a raft, from lumber they had salvaged from the water.

Eva and Carol took off their shoes and socks and waded in. The water was so cold it sent pain up their legs, like blue electric sparks shooting through their veins, but they went on, pulling their skirts high, tight behind and bunched so they could hold them in front.

"Look at the fat-assed ducks in wading."

"Fat-assed fucks."

Eva and Carol, of course, gave no sign of hearing this. They laid hold of a log and climbed on, taking a couple of boards floating in the water for paddles. There were always things floating around in the Flood—branches, fence-rails, logs, road signs, old lumber; sometimes boilers, washtubs, pots and pans, or even a car seat or stuffed chair, as if somewhere the Flood had got into a dump.

They paddled away from shore, heading out into the cold lake. The water was perfectly clear, they could see the brown grass swimming along the bottom. Suppose it was the sea, thought Eva. She thought of drowned cities and countries. Atlantis. Suppose they were riding in a Viking boat—Viking boats on the Atlantic were more frail and narrow than this log on the Flood—and they had miles of clear sea beneath them, then a spired city, intact as a jewel irretrievable on the ocean floor.

"This is a Viking boat," she said. "I am the carving on the front." She stuck her chest out and stretched her neck, trying to make a curve, and she made a face, putting out her tongue. Then she turned and for the first time took notice of the boys.

"Hey, you sucks!" she yelled at them. "You'd be scared to come out here, this water is ten feet deep!"

"Liar," they answered without interest, and she was.

They steered the log around a row of trees, avoiding floating barbed wire, and got into a little bay created by a natural hollow of the land. Where the bay was now, there would be a pond full of frogs later in the spring, and by the middle of summer there would be no water visible at all, just a low tangle of reeds and bushes, green, to show that mud was still wet around their roots. Larger bushes, willows, grew around the steep bank of this pond and were still partly out of the water. Eva and Carol let the log ride in. They saw a place where something was caught.

It was a boat, or part of one. An old rowboat with most of one side ripped out, the board that had been the seat just dangling. It was pushed up among the branches, lying on what would have been its side, if it had a side, the prow caught high.

Their idea came to them without consultation, at the same time:

"You guys! Hey, you guys!"

"We found you a boat!"

"Stop building your stupid raft and come and look at the boat!"

What surprised them in the first place was that the boys really did come, scrambling overland, half running, half sliding down the bank, wanting to see.

"Hey, where?"

"Where is it, I don't see no boat."

What surprised them in the second place was that when the boys did actually see what boat was meant, this old flood-smashed wreck held up in the branches, they did not understand that they had been fooled, that a joke had been played on them. They did not show a moment's disappointment, but seemed as pleased at the discovery as if the boat had been whole and new. They were already barefoot, because they had been wading in the water to get lumber, and they waded in here without a stop, surrounding the boat and appraising it and paying no attention even of an insulting kind to Eva and Carol who bobbed up and down on their log. Eva and Carol had to call to them.

"How do you think you're going to get it off?"

"It won't float anyway."

"What makes you think it will float?"

"It'll sink. Glub-blub-blub, you'll all be drownded."

The boys did not answer, because they were too busy walking around the boat, pulling at it in a testing way to see how it could be got off with the least possible damage. Frank, who was the most literate, talkative and inept of the three, began referring to the boat as *she*, an affectation which Eva and Carol acknowledged with fish-mouths of contempt.

"She's caught two places. You got to be careful not to tear a hole in her bottom. She's heavier than you'd think."

It was Clayton who climbed up and freed the boat, and Bud, a tall fat boy, who got the weight of it on his back to turn it into the water so that they could half float, half carry it to shore. All this took some time. Eva and Carol abandoned their log and waded out of the water. They walked overland to get their shoes and socks and bicycles. They did not need to come back this way but they came. They stood at the top of the hill, leaning on their bicycles. They did not go on home, but they did not sit down and frankly watch, either. They stood more or less facing each

other, but glancing down at the water and at the boys struggling with the boat, as if they had just halted for a moment out of curiosity, and staying longer than they intended, to see what came of this unpromising project.

About nine o'clock, or when it was nearly dark—dark to people inside the houses, but not quite dark outside—they all returned to town, going along Mayo Street in a sort of procession. Frank and Bud and Clayton came carrying the boat, upside-down, and Eva and Carol walked behind, wheeling their bicycles. The boys' heads were almost hidden in the darkness of the overturned boat, with its smell of soaked wood, cold swampy water. The girls could look ahead and see the street lights in their tin reflectors, a necklace of lights climbing Mayo Street, reaching all the way up to the standpipe. They turned onto Burns Street heading for Clayton's house, the nearest house belonging to any of them. This was not the way home for Eva or for Carol either, but they followed along. The boys were perhaps too busy carrying the boat to tell them to go away. Some younger children were still out playing, playing hopscotch on the sidewalk though they could hardly see. At this time of year the bare sidewalk was still such a novelty and delight. These children cleared out of the way and watched the boat go by with unwilling respect; they shouted questions after it, wanting to know where it came from and what was going to be done with it. No one answered them. Eva and Carol as well as the boys refused to answer or even look at them.

The five of them entered Clayton's yard. The boys shifted weight, as if they were going to put the boat down.

"You better take it round to the back where nobody can see it," Carol said. That was the first thing any of them had said since they came into town.

The boys said nothing but went on, following a mud path between Clayton's house and a leaning board fence. They let the boat down in the back yard.

"It's a stolen boat, you know," said Eva,

mainly for the effect. "It must've belonged to somebody. You stole it."

"You was the ones who stole it then," Bud said, short of breath. "It was you seen it first."

"It was you took it."

"It was all of us then. If one of us gets in trouble then all of us does."

"Are you going to tell anybody on them?" said Carol as she and Eva rode home, along the streets which were dark between the lights now and potholed from winter.

"It's up to you. I won't if you won't."

"I won't if you won't."

They rode in silence, relinquishing something, but not discontented.

The board fence in Clayton's back yard had every so often a post which supported it, or tried to, and it was on these posts that Eva and Carol spent several evenings sitting, jauntily but not very comfortably. Or else they just leaned against the fence while the boys worked on the boat. During the first couple of evenings neighborhood children attracted by the sound of hammering tried to get into the yard to see what was going on, but Eva and Carol blocked their way.

"Who said you could come in here?"

"Just us can come in this yard."

These evenings were getting longer, the air milder. Skipping was starting on the sidewalks. Further along the street there was a row of hard maples that had been tapped. Children drank the sap as fast as it could drip into the buckets. The old man and woman who owned the trees, and who hoped to make syrup, came running out of the house making noises as if they were trying to scare away crows. Finally, every spring, the old man would come out on his porch and fire his shotgun into the air, and then the thieving would stop.

None of those working on the boat bothered about stealing sap, though all had done so last year.

The lumber to repair the boat was picked up here and there, along back lanes. At this time of year things were lying around—old boards and branches, sodden mitts, spoons flung out with the dishwater, lids of pudding pots that had been set in the snow to cool, all the debris that can sift through and survive winter. The tools came from Clayton's cellar— left over, presumably, from the time when his father was alive—and though they had nobody to advise them the boys seemed to figure out more or less the manner in which boats are built, or rebuilt. Frank was the one who showed up with diagrams from books and *Popular Mechanics* magazines. Clayton looked at these diagrams and listened to Frank read the instructions and then went ahead and decided in his own way what was to be done. Bud was best at sawing. Eva and Carol watched everything from the fence and offered criticism and thought up names. The names for the boat that they thought of were: Water Lily, Sea Horse, Flood Queen, and Caro-Eve, after them because they had found it. The boys did not say which, if any, of these names they found satisfactory.

The boat had to be tarred. Clayton heated up a pot of tar on the kitchen stove and brought it out and painted slowly, his thorough way, sitting astride the overturned boat. The other boys were sawing a board to make a new seat. As Clayton worked, the tar cooled and thickened so that finally he could not move the brush any more. He turned to Eva and held out the pot and said, "You can go in and heat this on the stove."

Eva took the pot and went up the back steps. The kitchen seemed black after outside, but it must be light enough to see in, because there was Clayton's mother standing at the ironing board, ironing. She did that for a living, took in wash and ironing.

"Please may I put the tar pot on the stove?" said Eva, who had been brought up to talk politely to parents, even wash-and-iron ladies, and who for some reason especially wanted to make a good impression on Clayton's mother.

"You'll have to poke up the fire then," said Clayton's mother, as if she doubted whether Eva would know how to do that. But Eva could see now, and she picked up the lid with the stove-lifter, and took the poker and poked up a flame. She stirred the tar as it softened. She felt privileged. Then and later. Before she went to sleep a picture of Clayton came to her mind; she saw him sitting astride the boat, tar-painting, with such concentration, delicacy, absorption. She thought of him speaking to her, out of his isolation, in such an ordinary peaceful taking-for-granted voice.

On the twenty-fourth of May, a school holiday in the middle of the week, the boat was carried out of town, a long way now, off the road over fields and fences that had been repaired, to where the river flowed between its normal banks. Eva and Carol, as well as the boys, took turns carrying it. It was launched in the water from a cow-trampled spot between willow bushes that were fresh out in leaf. The boys went first. They yelled with triumph when the boat did float, when it rode amazingly down the river current. The boat was painted black, and green inside, with yellow seats, and a strip of yellow all the way around the outside. There was no name on it, after all. The boys could not imagine that it needed any name to keep it separate from the other boats in the world.

Eva and Carol ran along the bank, carrying bags full of peanut butter-and-jam sandwiches, pickles, bananas, chocolate cake, potato chips, graham crackers stuck together with corn syrup and five bottles of pop to be cooled in the river water. The bottles bumped against their legs. They yelled for a turn.

"If they don't let us they're bastards," Carol said, and they yelled together, "We found it! We found it!"

The boys did not answer, but after a while they brought the boat in, and Carol and Eva came crashing, panting down the bank.

"Does it leak?"

"It don't leak yet."

"We forgot a bailing can," wailed Carol, but nevertheless she got in, with Eva, and Frank pushed them off, crying, "Here's to a Watery Grave!"

And the thing about being in a boat was that it was not solidly bobbing, like a log, but was cupped in the water, so that riding in it was not like being on something in the water, but like being in the water itself. Soon they were all going out in the boat in mixed-up turns, two boys and a girl, two girls and a boy, a girl and a boy, until things were so confused it was impossible to tell whose turn came next, and nobody cared anyway. They went down the river—those who weren't riding, running along the bank to keep up. They passed under two bridges, one iron, one cement. Once they saw a big carp just resting, it seemed to smile at them, in the bridge-shaded water. They did not know how far they had gone on the river, but things had changed—the water had got shallower, and the land flatter. Across an open field they saw a building that looked like a house, abandoned. They dragged the boat up on the bank and tied it and set out across the field.

"That's the old station," Frank said. "That's Pedder Station." The others had heard this name but he was the one who knew, because his father was the station agent in town. He said that this was a station on a branch line that had been torn up, and that there had been a sawmill here, but a long time ago.

Inside the station it was dark, cool. All the windows were broken. Glass lay in shards and in fairly big pieces on the floor. They walked around finding the larger pieces of glass and tramping on them, smashing them, it was like cracking ice on puddles. Some partitions were still in place, you could see where the ticket window had been. There was a bench lying on its side. People had been here, it looked as if people came here all the time, though it was so far from anywhere. Beer bottles and pop bottles were lying around, also cigarette packages, gum and candy wrappers, the paper from a loaf of bread. The walls were covered with dim and fresh pencil and chalk writings and carved with knives.

I LOVE RONNIE COLES

I WANT TO FUCK

KILROY WAS HERE

RONNIE COLES IS AN ASS-HOLE

WHAT ARE YOU DOING HERE?

WAITING FOR A TRAIN

DAWNA   MARY-LOU   BARBARA   JOANNE

It was exciting to be inside this large, dark, empty place, with the loud noise of breaking glass and their voices ringing back from the underside of the roof. They tipped the old beer bottles against their mouths. That reminded them that they were hungry and thirsty and they cleared a place in the middle of the floor and sat down and ate the lunch. They drank the pop just as it was, lukewarm. They ate everything there was and licked the smears of peanut butter and jam off the bread-paper in which the sandwiches had been wrapped.

They played Truth or Dare.

"I dare you to write on the wall, I am a Stupid Ass, and sign your name."

"Tell the truth—what is the worst lie you ever told?"

"Did you ever wet the bed?"

"Did you ever dream you were walking down the street without any clothes on?"

"I dare you to go outside and pee on the railway sign."

It was Frank who had to do that. They could not see him, even his back, but they knew he did it, they heard the hissing sound of his pee. They all sat still, amazed, unable to think of what the next dare would be.

"I dare everybody," said Frank from the doorway, "I dare—Everybody."

"What?"

"Take off all our clothes."

Eva and Carol screamed.

"Anybody who won't do it has to walk—has to *crawl*—around this floor on their hands and knees."

They were all quiet, till Eva said, almost complacently, "What first?"

"Shoes and socks."

"Then we have to go outside, there's too much glass here."

They pulled off their shoes and socks in the doorway, in the sudden blinding sun. The field before them was bright as water. They ran across where the tracks used to go.

That's enough, that's enough," said Carol. "Watch out for thistles!"

"Tops! Everybody take off their tops!"

"I won't! We won't, will we, Eva?"

But Eva was whirling round and round in the sun where the track used to be. "I don't care, I don't care! Truth or Dare! Truth or Dare!"

She unbuttoned her blouse as she whirled, as if she didn't know what her hand was doing, she flung it off.

Carol took off hers. "I wouldn't have done it, if you hadn't!"

"Bottoms!"

Nobody said a word this time, they all bent and stripped themselves. Eva, naked first, started running across the field, and then all the others ran, all five of them running bare through the knee-high hot grass, running towards the river. Not caring now about being caught but in fact leaping and yelling to call attention to themselves, if there was anybody to hear or see. They felt as if they were going to jump off a cliff and fly. They felt that something was happening to them different from anything that had happened before, and it had to do with the boat, the water, the sunlight, the dark ruined station, and each other. They thought of each other now hardly as names or people, but as echoing shrieks, reflections, all bold and white and loud and scandalous, and as fast as arrows. They went running without a break into the cold water and when it came almost to the tops of their legs they fell on it and swam. It stopped their noise. Silence, amazement, came over them in a rush. They dipped and floated and separated, sleek as mink.

Eva stood up in the water her hair dripping, water running down her face. She was waist deep. She stood on smooth stones, her feet fairly wide apart, water flowing between her legs. About a yard away from her Clayton also stood up, and they were blinking the water out of their eyes, looking at each other. Eva did not turn or try to hide; she was quivering from the cold of the water, but also with pride, shame, boldness, and exhilaration.

Clayton shook his head violently, as if he wanted to bang something out of it, then bent over and took a mouthful of river water. He stood up with his cheeks full and made a tight hole of his mouth and shot the water at her as if it was coming out of a hose, hitting her exactly, first one breast and then the other. Water from his mouth ran down her body. He hooted to see it, a loud self-conscious sound that nobody would have expected, from him. The others looked up from wherever they were in the water and closed in to see.

Eva crouched down and slid into the water, letting her head go right under. She swam, and when she let her head out, downstream, Carol was coming after her and the boys were already on the bank, already running into the grass, showing their skinny backs, their white, flat buttocks. They were laughing and saying things to each other but she couldn't hear, for the water in her ears.

"What did he do?" said Carol.

"Nothing."

They crept in to shore. "Let's stay in the bushes till they go," said Eva. "I hate them anyway. I really do. Don't you hate them?"

"Sure," said Carol, and they waited, not very long, until they heard the boys still noisy and excited coming down to the place a bit upriver where they had left the boat. They heard them jump in and start rowing.

"They've got all the hard part, going back," said Eva, hugging herself and shivering violently. "Who cares? Anyway. It never was our boat."

"What if they tell?" said Carol.

"We'll say it's all a lie."

Eva hadn't thought of this solution until she said it, but as soon as she did she felt almost light-hearted again. The ease and scornfulness of it did make them both giggle, and slapping themselves and splashing out of the water they set about developing one of those fits of laughter in which, as soon as one showed signs of exhaustion, the other would snort and start up again, and they would make helpless—soon genuinely helpless—faces at each other and bend over and grab themselves as if they had the worst pain.

Shiraishi Kazuko

Japan, b. 1931

Shiraishi Kazuko was born in Vancouver and moved to Japan as a child, and this special experience of the world undoubtedly has contributed to her poetic voice. Her early poetry was already being published while she was a student in Waseda University's Arts Division. The brilliant, sensually unsettling images of her first poetry collection, *Tamago no furu machi* (Town under a Rainfall of Eggs, 1951) gave almost surrealistic form to her visions of immediate postwar Tokyo. Marriage right after college to a classmate, Shinoda Masahiro (now a major film director), brought a nearly ten-year hiatus to her publishing, as Shinoda apparently discouraged her poetic activities. The failure of the marriage brought Shiraishi back to a public life, as deep involvement in the Tokyo jazz scene, including close relationships with expatriate American jazz musicians, gave new subjects, diction, and rhythms to her poetry. A striking woman, Shiraishi promoted poetry performances, participated in "happenings" at jazz clubs, and appeared on television. Fierce independence, a toughness and frankness about sexuality, and a nondefeatist, unsentimental disillusion run through her works, including *Tora no yūgi* (Tiger's Play, 1960); *Mō sore ijō osoku yatte kite wa ikenai* (You Mustn't Come Any Later Than That, 1963); and *Konban was aramoyō* (Looks Like a Storm Tonight, 1965); this last is the source of the second poem included here. She got the sobriquet "poet of the penis" from her 1970 *Seinaru inja no kisetsu* (Season of Sacred Lust), which won the Mr. H Prize. Her defiant adventurousness is combined with a sensitive control of language and a deep commitment to poetic witness.

Shiraishi has continued to publish prolifically and travel extensively. Her friendship with jazz musicians has continued to be an important inspiration for her work, as can be seen in such works as *Amerikan burakku jāni* (American Black Journey, 1973), *Burakku no asa* (Black Morning, 1974) and *Jazz ni ikiru* (Living in Jazz, 1982). She has been recorded reading her own poetry in Japanese to the improvised accompaniment of black jazz musicians, a work entitled *Dedicated to the Late John Coltrane and other jazz poems*. Shiraishi has done a number of translations into Japanese, including Sandra Hochman's *Endangered Species* (*Koi o kakeru onna*, 1979) and Laurence Houseman's retelling of *Tales from the Arabian Nights* (*Arabian natio*, 1981); movie criticism (*Kawaii otokotachi to kawaii onna-tachi* [Cute Boys and Cute Girls, 1982]); and accounts of travels to Egypt and elsewhere (*Sunazoku kara no tegami* [Letters from Peoples of the Sands, 1984]). Shiraishi has carved out love as her area of expertise in what might be called "advice to young people" books: *Ai no retā kyōshitsu* (Writing Love Letters, 1975) *Koi no sabunoto* (Footnotes on Love, 1976), *Za Raburetā* (The Love Letter, 1983). Recent poetry collections include *Shin dōbutsu shishū* (New Animal Poems, 1983) and *Hi no me o shita otoko* (Man with Eyes of Fire, 1984).

Phyllis I. Lyons

TOWN UNDER A RAINFALL OF EGGS
Tamago no Furu Machi

> While taking a rest in a pool of green lettuces,
> we are showered with a rain of eggs—
> cheap eggs, dear eggs, hard eggs, soft eggs.
> We are showered with babies, boys,
> rats, heroes, monkeys, grasshoppers too, falling
> on church roofs, on playgrounds.
> We hold out our hands in longing, but
> they all, like sorrow, trickle away through our fingers,
> with a funny top hat
> dramatizing the height of a tall building.
> The eggs fall through the chill veins of vegetables too.
> What for?
> (I don't know, don't know, don't know.)
> This is the editorial in our town's local newspaper.

Translated by James Kirkup

BIRD

BYE BYE BLACKBIRD
It is not hundreds of birds nor thousands of birds
But always one bird only that takes wing from within me
Bearing my ugly guts.
Bird,
Every time I conceive you within me
I am made blind, and live a blind existence
Sniffing my way around the world.
I see you only when I have lost you
But then I see my old self die and
A new blind self begin to bud.
On stage, He, changing himself into quite a bird, sings:
BYE BYE BLACKBIRD
Attended by the tens of thousands of ears in his audience.
Then the audience becomes millions of blind wings.
The blind audience has turned into so many ghosts of
Fluttering birds, dancing among the dark seats,
Following the crying of the one bird on stage.
So can anyone tell which is the real bird among
All those ghost birds?   And
BYE BYE BLACKBIRD
What can it be, really, taking wing from here?
The singer himself cannot tell, who is just singing
In ecstasy, feeling, now that something is flying away,
That the real entity may be his smooth rhythm, or may be
The softest loin of his soul, or may be the memory of the
Star of guilty conscience, or may be the warm splash of
Blood out of the tulip-shaped brain of the child seated
Right in the front row.
BYE BYE BLACKBIRD
I am a bird,
Whether I refuse to be myself
Or accept,
Just as long as I am not yet deprived of this
Ever-pecking pointed beak and
A pair of naturally fluttering wings,
I am a bird today,
Making myself into a prayer, piercing the sky
Several times a day, only to be thrust down upon the ground,
Or I am the guts the falling bird is bearing.
Here within myself I have gathered all these fallen birds—huge,
Small, thin and dwarfish, arrogant, gentle: some are still half alive, moaning.
Everyday I perform the bird funeral for them, in which other birds
Strip their flesh to the bones,

(continued)

While
Every day I warm their eggs so as to hatch out the little ones.
Such eggs I warm all the more lovingly and desperately when I know
They will grow into grotesque birds that one day will destroy our future.
BYE BYE BLACKBIRD
I am planning to make that fellow fly away some day, the one
I know will come back and destroy me; yes,
I must expel him so violently that he is bleeding all over,
And then I can really sing for him with all my heart:
BYE BYE BLACKBIRD

Translated by James Kirkup

THE ORIENT IN ME

When I begin writing a poem I do not consciously think that I am Japanese or even that I am an Oriental; but when I finish the poem and examine what I have written, I am constantly surprised to discover in my own work those characteristics of feeling, of "heart," which are distinctively Oriental. Though neither literature in general nor poetry in particular is the product of a specific climate, it is interesting to recognize, especially in one's own word, that the weather of one's inmost soul does, as the years move on, permeate with its singular scent everything that one does.

Generally speaking, there is no word that I more deeply abominate than "nationalism." I don't even like the idea that the Japanese should, by mere superficial observation, appear to be Japanese; or that Americans should look like Americans. I once heard that, during the late war or perhaps soon after it, the highly regarded authority, Yoshida Issui,[1] who was virtually a hermit of poetry, came to be regarded as a traitor to Japan simply because he did not wear military-style puttees. When somebody denounced him as an unpatriotic person by reason of his habit of wearing leather-soled sandals, he turned and answered that criticism with the sharp rejoinder "I am a cosmopolitan." That word, I still consider, is genuinely refreshing; and I continue to believe that any person who produces genuine work must be a cosmopolitan.

I myself am a somewhat outlandish Japanese, having been born in Canada. Though I have always believed it impossible that simply to have passed my childhood in a foreign country should in any way have influenced my writing, I am frequently told that my use of Japanese, my sense of the language, even my ways of thought and of expressing concepts are very different from those of the Japanese people in general. Thus both I and my poetry have long been regarded as outlandish—poems by a somewhat curious Japanese. It was on that account and not, I hope, because my mind was jaundiced that I have perhaps been able to achieve an objective viewpoint, and to write about things Japanese as though I myself were somehow dissociated from Japan. Not unnaturally, it has therefore sometimes occurred to me that I might usefully take advantage of this situation and write an account of what the Japanese really are and, in particular, to try to explore what it means to a Japanese to write a poem in the Japanese language. For it seems to me an irrelevancy when the Japanese, in considering, for instance, Irish or Jewish literature, tend first to ask fundamental questions about the nature of the Jewishness. If Irish literature can only be understood by the Irish or Jewish literature only by Jews, there would seem little point in reading it. It would seem to follow that to believe that only the Japanese can appreciate their language and understand the sensitivities of their literature is a form of self-insulation: a narrow-minded and basically unpleasant form of insularity.

It is neither mere affectation nor from any wish to appear smartly contemporary that I use colloquialisms in my poetry and seek, so far as possible, to avoid using the classical literary language. Just as, when I feel so inclined, I eat *sushi* immediately after eating grilled steak, so I seek to combine in my poetry words drawn not only from English any American slang, but words originating in the vocabularies of the jazz and fashion worlds. Since I integrate into these poems all manner of words, the results are international in the sense that they have no specifically identifiable origins. The United States of America, though it contains some fifty different states, is self-evidently united; and I myself care little how many tens or hundreds of states go to make the unity of my poetry. Where there is no native place, there is my native place; whether on the Lower Nile or in southern Turkey; any place will do. And it is this feeling which lies at the heart of the hippie approach to poetry.

Though *hippie* is the word used to describe a contemporary manifestation, the condition of mind and heart which it describes is as old as humanity. Who was it that in Japan traveled hither and thither like the wind, stacked with but not weighted down by worldly things, convinced that all things earthly were mere transience? Was it not Saigyō?[2] Though I have never read a line of his poetry, the simple truth is that I regard myself, my feeling for the writing of poetry, and my way of life as contemporary manifestations of the same truths as moved that ancient master.

Some four or five years ago I found myself wanting to write a travel poem that had neither a beginning nor an end. It was to be a poem tressed with the hair of an Amazon, dressed like Raquel Welch, and with the heart of a priest though the priest himself was one in the worldly hell. At that time the world of modern jazz included a particularly brilliant tenor saxophonist, John Coltrane, and this man, why I know not, kept blowing music, as it seemed, endlessly. It was not just for five or maybe fifteen minutes. Once this man started blowing, he could not stop for half an hour or an hour or more. His music just flowed on in explanation and admonition of the world. "I cannot blow,." he said, "for a mere three minutes of casual greeting. I simply cannot stop when I wish to express all that I feel in the vast internal world of my spirit." It is the novelists who fashion stories out of the reality in which they live; but a poem does not depend upon a story line or the happenings in the everyday world. For the very source-springs of poetry are existence and reality, and all other things, manifestations of those basic truths, are subsidiary. I was so impressed by this great musician's attitude of soul, his total commitment to living in the world of his art, that I decided to "blow" my own poetry with a similar persistence; to write in a ten-year time-scale with language on soundless paper. If one writes a series of short poems, something is bound to be lost in the intervals between creating and rest, and one is moreover likely to deceive oneself that it is possible similarly to lose oneself, to escape reality. But if one continuously writes poetry as Coltrane continuously emitted music, one can pin down precisely the changing angles of time's passing and, simultaneously, find it delightful that one can neither hide from oneself nor escape reality. I consider myself lucky to have met that American jazzman and to have begun to play a long-breath'd poetry.

The world of art which I thus discovered was not, in fact, American but Oriental. It was that world of the long-sustained ascetic self-discipline of the East. I find it very interesting that, even though I make jazz in poetry, even though I mix outlandish American slang with my native Japanese, still, as the compass needle, however it may waver, inevitably settles down to point north, so my own experiments began to settle down and flow in an easterly direction. I am now deeply moved suddenly to find myself, however proud of my outlandishness, to be traveling jazz-wise in that mainstream of Oriental thinking which leads either to Zen or to the Sword. When I question myself as to the reason for this happiness, the answer e that, at the bottom of it all, I simply do not care for the set of western hearts. This may simply be a question of inborn or inherited taste. Perhaps I am reacting instinctively, perhaps with the animal's instinct for self-preservation, when I testify that there is no other way, not only in respect of poetry but in respect of the whole future of mankind, but to return to the Oriental concept of nothingness; to realize that we are witnessing Mappo, the coming of doomsday, now in the closing period of human civilization.

Translated by Ikuko Atsumi and Graeme Wilson

NOTES

1. Yoshida Issui (1898–1973): A critic, writer of children's short stories, and poet, who began writing in the 1920s. His poetry rejects established poetic standards and is highly anarchistic in form and symbolic in content.
2. Saigyō (1118–1190): One of the foremost male poets in the canon, whose poems are anthologized in the *Shinkokinshū* (1205), the eighth imperial anthology. A devoted priest who frequently went on pilgrimages, his reflective and lyrical poetry is infused with a Buddhist world view, direct observation of nature, and sensitivity drawn from his own life experience.

Sylvia Plath   *US, 1932–1963*

Sylvia Path's short, intense life began in Boston, Massachusetts, where she was born to Otto Plath, a German emigrant and academic, and Auriela, a high-school English teacher. In 1937 the family moved to Winthrop, Massachusetts, and three years later Otto Plath died. The impact on Plath of her father's life and death was huge. Her lifelong inability to live and write in peace are partly traceable to an overbearing father's insistence on perfection and success. In "Daddy," a centerpiece of her largely autobiographical body of poems, Plath depicts her father as a German autocrat and caricature of Nazi terror. The poem was written during the fallout of her marriage to the English poet Ted Hughes; in it Otto Plath is identified with her husband and is made partly accountable for the romantic failure. The failed promises of a gifted life haunted Plath and her poetry to the day of her suicide in 1963.

A precocious, artistic child, Plath had already published by the time she won a scholarship to Smith College in 1950. In 1953 she spent the summer as a guest editor at *Mademoiselle* magazine as reward for winning a short-story contest, but the pressures brought on a nervous breakdown and back home at Wellesley Plath made her first suicide attempt, recounted in *The Bell Jar* (1963), the only novel Plath published. She returned to Smith after psychiatric treatment and graduated summa cum laude in 1955, winning a Fulbright Scholarship to Cambridge University, where she met and married Hughes in 1956. In 1960, back in England after a return to America to teach at Smith and study poetry in a Robert Lowell workshop, Plath bore a daughter, Frieda Rebecca, and Plath's first poetry volume, *The Colossus*, was published. Two years later a son, Nicholas Farrar, was born, but Hughes had begun seeing another woman and the marriage was crumbling. The stress Plath felt in this period dividing her time between artistic and domestic roles was captured in *Three Women: A Monologue for Three Voices* (1962), a radio play that partly shaped the poetic voice for the poems written in the final prolific months of her life.

It is for the poems composed in the months, weeks, and days before her death and collected in *Ariel* that Plath will likely be remembered and evaluated. As Plath moved toward suicide, her poetry became charged. She abandoned the laborious composition process of her early poems and wrote feverishly. The poems in *Ariel* are thus terse, obsessive, and relentlessly intense. As death is embraced, it provides a kind of liberation—sexual, emotional, stylistic—that gives the poems a perverse relish in their own blackness. "Lady Lazarus" again implicates Otto Plath in the author's emotional demise. Behind the poem's direct confrontation with private despair lurk horrific global events; characteristically, Plath's best verse came when it demonstrated her notion that "personal experience shouldn't be a kind of shut box and mirror-looking narcissistic experience" but rather "should be generally relevant to such things as Hiroshima and Dachau and so on." *Ariel* (1965) looks brilliantly in these various directions, as do her other posthumous collections, *Crossing the Water* and *Winter Trees* (both 1971). Plath's *Collected Poems* appeared in 1981.

Plath's critical reputation has been handicapped by a tendency to isolate her in the "confessional school" of poets (along with Allen Ginsburg, Robert Lowell, and Anne Sexton) that emerged after World War II. There is some merit to this classification, but ultimately it does Plath's poetry a disservice. Critical investigation in recent years has discovered strong links between the esthetics of Plath and Virginia Woolf and W. B. Yeats, among others. The constantly shifting images of femininity by which she identifies her poetic personas—a nun, a housekeeper, a pregnant woman suggest an intuitive feminism denied formulation by period convention. Even her suicide and the hard technical virtuosity that presaged it are in Plath's hands vengeful tools at power appropriation. Her lines rage not only about a tragic personal history but against a world that made that history inevitable.

Bill Mullen

THE COURIERS

The word of a snail on the plate of a leaf?
It is not mine. Do not accept it.

Acetic acid in a sealed tin?
Do not accept it. It is not genuine.

A ring of gold with the sun in it?
Lies. Lies and a grief.

Frost on a leaf, the immaculate
Cauldron, talking and crackling

All to itself on the top of each
Of nine black Alps.

A disturbance in mirrors,
The sea shattering its grey one—

Love, Love, my season.

SHEEP IN FOG

The hills step off into whiteness.
People or stars
Regard me sadly, I disappoint them.

The train leaves a line of breath.
O slow
Horse the colour of rust,

Hooves, dolorous bells—
All morning the
Morning has been blackening,

A flower left out.
My bones hold a stillness, the far
Fields melt my heart.

They threaten
To let me through to a heaven
Starless and fatherless, a dark water.

THE APPLICANT

First, are you our sort of a person?
Do you wear
A glass eye, false teeth or a crutch,
A brace or a hook,
Rubber breasts or a rubber crotch,

Stitches to show something's missing? No, no?
                                                    Then
How can we give you a thing?
Stop crying.
Open your hand.
Empty? Empty. Here is a hand

To fill it and willing
To bring teacups and roll away headaches
And do whatever you tell it.
Will you marry it?
It is guaranteed

To thumb shut your eyes at the end
And dissolve of sorrow.
We make new stock from the salt.
I notice you are stark naked.
How about this suit—

Black and stiff, but not a bad fit.
Will you marry it?
It is waterproof, shatterproof, proof
Against fire and bombs through the roof.
Believe me, they'll bury you in it.

Now your head, excuse me, is empty.
I have the ticket for that.
Come here, sweetie, out of the closet.
Well, what do you think of *that*?
Naked as paper to start

But in twenty-five years she'll be silver,
In fifty, gold.
A living doll, everywhere you look.
It can sew, it can cook,
It can talk, talk, talk.

It works, there is nothing wrong with it.
You have a hole, it's a poultice.
You have an eye, it's an image.
My boy, it's your last resort.
Will you marry it, marry it, marry it.

LADY LAZARUS*

I have done it again.
One year in every ten
I manage it—

A sort of walking miracle, my skin
Bright as a Nazi lampshade,
My right foot

A paperweight,
My face a featureless, fine
Jew linen.

Peel off the napkin
O my enemy.
Do I terrify?—

The nose, the eye pits, the full set of teeth?
The sour breath
Will vanish in a day.

Soon, soon the flesh
The grave cave ate will be
At home on me

And I a smiling woman.
I am only thirty.
And like the cat I have nine times to die.

This is Number Three.
What a trash
To annihilate each decade.

What a million filaments.
The peanut-crunching crowd
Shoves in to see

Them unwrap me hand and foot—
The big strip tease,
Gentleman, ladies,

These are my hands,
My knees.
I may be skin and bone,

Nevertheless, I am the same, identical woman.
The first time it happened I was ten.
It was an accident.

The second time I meant
To last it out and not come back at all.
I rocked shut

As a seashell.
They had to call and call
And pick the worms off me like sticky pearls.

Dying
Is an art, like everything else.
I do it exceptionally well.

I do it so it feels like hell.
I do it so it feels real.
I guess you could say I've a call.

It's easy enough to do it in a cell.
It's easy enough to do it and stay put.
It's the theatrical

Comeback in broad day
To the same place, the same face, the same
                                    brute
Amused shout:

"A miracle!"
That knocks me out.
There is a charge

For the eyeing of my scars, there is a charge
For the hearing of my heart—
It really goes.

And there is a charge, a very large charge,
For a word or a touch
Or a bit of blood

Or a piece of my hair or my clothes.
So, so, Herr Doktor.
So, Herr Enemy.

I am your opus,
I am your valuable,
The pure gold baby

That melts to a shriek.
I turn and burn.
Do not think I underestimate your great
                                    concern.

Ash, ash—
You poke and stir.
Flesh, bone, there is nothing there—

A cake of soap,
A wedding ring,
A gold filling.

Herr God, Herr Lucifer,
Beware
Beware.

Out of the ash
I rise with my red hair
And I eat men like air.

NOTE

* In the New Testament, Lazarus was the beggar raised
  from the dead (Luke 16:20—23).

Kōra Rumiko   *Japan, b. 1932*

Kōra Rumiko attended Tokyo Arts College and Keiō University, but withdrew from both. She was active in the radical literary journal *Espoir* (Hope), and has supported translation of African and other Asian literature into Japanese. Kōra has also been a member of the journal *Shisōshiki* (Poetry Organization), a showcase for left-wing poetry. One of her early poetry collections, *Basho* (Place, 1962), won the thirteenth Mr. H. Prize in 1963. Other noteworthy collections are *Seito to tori* (The Student and the Bird, 1958), and *Mienai jimen no ue de* (Over the Invisible Ground, 1970). Kōra has published a number of volumes of critical essays, including *Mono no kotoba* (The Words for Things, 1968) and *Bungaku to mugen na mono* (Literature and the Unbounded, 1972). She has also published fiction. Her terse, unsentimental style is recognized for transcending the lyrical place-boundedness of the traditional Japanese poetic sensibility.

Phyllis I. Lyons

THE TREE
Ki

Within a tree there is a tree which does not yet
                                        exist.

Now its twigs tremble in the wind.

Within a blue sky there is a blue sky which
                                does not yet exist.

Now a bird cuts across its horizon.

Within a body there is a body which does not
                                        yet exist.

Now its sanctuary accumulates fresh blood.

Within a city there is a city which does not
                                        yet exist.

Now its plazas sway before me.

Translated by the author

AWAKENING
Mezame

After objects jostled past me,
trees turned their leaves
and shut me off from the world.

Out of this emptiness,
I touch the hot texture of a cheek;
a naked arm; dark rocks lying everywhere
                                under the earth.

(I escaped the void
and went along the easy curves of leaves in
                                        darkness
towards the border
because you were there;
because you were not there.)

In an atmosphere of heated matter,
I search under my eyelids for a speed
faster than dust falls at dawn.

When clear morning light
opens my eyes from inside,
a crisis also awakens.
My hands mix the unknown breath of objects
with the earth's morning they can't see.

Translated by the author

Ingrid Jonker   *South Africa, 1933–1965*

Ingrid Jonker was born in South Africa in 1933. Her father, Abraham Jonker, was a newspaper editor who went on to become a member of Parliament and an ardent supporter of apartheid and policies of censorship and repression, a stance that pitted him against his daughter. Her mother, Beatrice Cilliers, was from an old Huguenot family with a long history of intellectual attainments. Jonker's parents were separated before her birth, and she was raised by her mother and grandmother in the Cape Town vicinity, often in conditions of real poverty; when her mother died, Ingrid was taken into her father's household at the age of 16.

Jonker had already begun writing poetry, but her work was not published until 1953, when she was 20, under the title *Ontvlugting* (*Escape*). Soon after, she married and, in 1957, bore a child, Simone. Her writing developed rapidly; her use of free verse and surrealistic yet intensely personal imagery brought her far beyond any other poet writing in Afrikaans at the time.

Although Jonker was never politically active, nor did she ever explicitly state that she was a political writer, she did not have the luxury of avoiding politics in a country that was becoming more and more entrenched in the inhuman constrictions of apartheid. In 1960, after the shooting of a black woman and her child at Sharpeville during the riots there, Jonker wrote a poem—"The child who was shot dead by soldiers at Nyanga"; though translated into many languages and winning her international acclaim, the poem could only be published in her own country under the ideologically abbreviated title "The Child." Notwithstanding, it succeeds powerfully in mapping the political terrain of black resistance to apartheid.

Later, the Censorship Bill framed by her father's committee drew her into opposition with writers like herself who wrote in Afrikaans and who began to realize that they had much more to lose than their anglophone colleagues, who could always publish abroad. Unable to avoid a confrontation, Jonker found herself publically disavowed by her father. Though she eventually sought a reconciliation with him, she was rebuffed. About this time, she also became estranged from her husband. Her efforts to publish met with resistance; she only barely succeeded with her second book of poems, *Rook en Oker* (*Smoke and Ocher*, 1963), in which "Begin Summer" and "Daisies in Namaqualand" first appeared.

Jonker became increasingly critical of Afrikaans writing, criticizing it for being "self-pitying and immature." She suffered more and more from a sense of bitterness and despair, and even her passionate love for her daughter did not seem to give her the energy to continue struggling and writing in South Africa. In 1965, she was drowned off the coast of Cape Town in what appeared to be suicide.

A book of poems was published posthumously under the title *Kantelson* (*Setting Sun*, 1965). A volume of collected verse and prose followed on the tenth anniversary of her death. In addition to her poetry, it included Jonker's classic short story "Die Bok" ("The Goat").

Among young writers, Jonker has become almost a cult figure, her passionate and tragic life serving as an example both cautionary and inspirational to those of every color trying to free themselves and their country from the psychic and political burdens of apartheid.

BEGIN SUMMER
Begin somer

(for Simone)

Begin summer and the sea
a broken-open quince
the sky like a child's
balloon
far over the water
Under the sunshades
like stripy sugarsticks
ants of people
and the gay laugh of the bay
has golden teeth

Child with the yellow bucket
and the forgotten pigtail
your mouth surely is a bell
tiny tongue for a clapper
You play on the sun all day
like a ukulele
       Translated by Jack Cope and William Plomer

DAISIES IN NAMAQUALAND
Madeliefies in Namakwaland

Why do we listen still
to the answers of the wild daisies
to the wind to the sun
what has become of the green shrikes

    Behind the closed-up forehead
    where perhaps another shoot falls
    of a drowned springtime
    Behind my shot-down word
    Behind our divided house
    Behind the heart shut against itself
    Behind wire fences, camps, locations
    Behind the silence where unknown
                          languages
    fall like bells at a burial
    Behind our torn-up land

sits the green praying mantis of the veld
and we hear still half-dazed
little blue Namaqualand daisy
something answer, and believe, and know.
       Translated by Jack Cope and William Plomer

THE CHILD WHO WAS SHOT DEAD BY SOLDIERS AT NYANGA
Die kind wat doodgeskiet is deur soldate in Nyanga

The child is not dead
the child lifts his fists against his mother
who shouts Africa! shouts the breath
of freedom and the veld
in the locations of the cordoned heart

The child lifts his fists against his father
in the march of the generations
who shout Africa! shout the breath
of righteousness and blood
in the streets of his embattled pride

The child is not dead
not at Langa nor at Nyanga
not at Orlando nor at Sharpeville
not at the police station at Philippi
where he lies with a bullet through his brain
The child is the dark shadow of the soldiers
on guard with rifles saracens* and batons
the child is present at all assemblies and law-
                                   givings
the child peers through the windows of houses
                 and into the hearts of mothers
this child who just wanted to play in the sun at
                  Nyanga is everywhere
the child grown to a man treks through all
                                    Africa
the child grown into a giant journeys through
                     the whole world

Without a pass
       Translated by Jack Cope and William Plomer

NOTE

* Armor-plated police vehicles.

Irmtraud Morgner

Germany/GDR, b. 1933

Irmtraud Morgner has emerged in the last two decades as one of the most highly regarded authors of the G.D.R. Born in Chemnitz, the daughter of a railroad engineer, Morgner studied German literature at Leipzig from 1952 to 1956, worked thereafter for two years as an assistant editor for a major East German literary journal, and has been a freelance writer since 1953. She is representative of a new generation of East German writers, including Christa Wolf and Sarah Kirsch, who have begun to abandon the narrow definition of realism earlier prevalent in their country to insist instead on a reality expanded by imaginative power and individual experience.

Her 1969 novel, *Hochzeit in Konstantinopel* (Wedding in Constantinople) brought her considerable recognition. Her major work to date, however, is a very long novel (more than seven hundred pages) that shows her at the height of her development and for which she was awarded the prestigious Heinrich Mann Prize of the East German Academy of Arts in 1975: *Leben und Abenteuer der Trobadora Beatriz nach Zeugnissen ihrer Spielfrau Laura. Roman in dreizehn Büchern und sieben Intermezzos* (Life and Adventures of the Troubadour Beatrice as Told by her Minstrel Laura. A Novel in Thirteen Books and Seven Intermezzos [1974]). The thematic core of this novel, in which Beatrice awakens after a sleep of more than eight hundred years and tries to find her way in today's world, is the position of women then and now. Flights of poetic fantasy are accompanied here, as they are in her next major work, *Amanda. Ein Hexenroman* (Amanda. A Witches' Novel [1983]), by very serious references to the historical oppression of the female sex. Organized chiefly according to the esthetic principle of montage, these works argue in their form against the "reality" of a rounded literary work. The form, according to Morgner, must indicate the process of finding the truth. Her montage novels thus become closure-resistant works in progress.

Morgner wants to make a "legendary historical consciousness" accessible to "simple people" whose origins are not recorded—to give them the feeling that they, and their ancestors, also "made history." "Simple people" in this sense are above all women, about whom local history has less to report than about the oppressed males of bygone centuries. The adjective "legendary" points to the prevalence of fantasy, of sensitive imagination on the path back into history. It is not surprising then, that in her latest works, Morgner seeks to reshape archetypal symbols defined by men. In the *Life and Adventures*, she uses Beatrice and Laura, two characters immortalized by the medieval poet Dante and the Renaissance poet Petrarch, as incarnations of sacred and secular love respectively; in *Amanda*, Morgner sets a matriarchal "white magic" against the satanic view of female powers.

The selection included here was written especially for publication in a special G.D.R. issue of the journal *Dimension* (1973).

Marilyn Sibley Fries

LOVE LEGEND
Liebeslegende

1

The news came while I was eating. I failed to understand at first, the meat was tough, the bartender turned away from the counter to tune the radio. He pulled it forward a bit on the cabinet shelf and turned up the volume so that the announcer's voice drowned out the noisy hubbub of talk and dishes, but stood with his ear near the speaker. The sounds abated, increased again, then silence. The back of the cabinet was made of mirror glass. It doubled liquor bottles, packs of cigarettes, the room, the men searched for their faces between display pieces, besides me there were only men in the pub. Their faces were tan up to a line above the brows, their foreheads were pale and had no streaks of lime, Anton reached for the rucksack lying between his boots under the table, I recall it exactly, although years have passed. Even with news of this kind, I knew the men by name. I had been working with them for a short time, our construction site lay on the other side of the river. No one whistled as the stranger entered. He sat down at my table. His hair was conspicuous, similar to a wig, dull, but thicker and not as well-groomed, at first glance black.

2

Two masons had purposely missed their buses. After emptying eight bottles of beer, they got the stranger to play cards. I had another serving. When I lifted my arm to put the bite in my mouth, I felt the soreness in my shoulder. After the second day at work my arm trembled when it wasn't propped on something. We were still watching one another, the workers and I, but no longer warily. After work I sat with them in the pub. They waited for buses, I for evening. The stranger was not one of us. He wrote the scores for the game in small numerals on the edge of a newspaper. He held the pencil with his fingers almost straight. They were shorter than the back of his hand, pale, uncalloused, hairy, thicker toward the edges. After each entry he looked up at the clock with its layers of carved ornamentation, the brown-smoked decorative carvings on the cabinet reached to the ceiling. As soon as I had paid the tab, I joined the card players, ordered a beer, a bottle, the stranger drank from a glass, I envied him. The radio announcer repeated the report on the blockade. The stranger lost two hands. After the other tables were empty, I asked if I might play. The stranger paid the masons their winnings and lined off a new score card on the edge of the newspaper. When I lost for the third time, one of the masons put his hand on my shoulder. His name was Edgar, our brigade called him the swineherd because he supposedly dropped more mortar on the ground while rough-casting than he got on the wall; since then the whole operation has been mechanized. On the tabletop, vibrating from the banging fists, particles of ashes shifted about. The bartender was washing glasses. Edgar took his hand from my shoulder and put it on my knee. The stranger's eyes narrowed. They slanted upward toward the temples. The tabletop was cracked, Edgar had wedged his cards in the crevice. Sometimes he pondered his next play so long that all the flies settled on the smooth-scoured wood. The speaker repeated his announcement of a general mobilization on the Caribbean island. The window fan was blowing the tin dampers and the valance. Edgar breathed into my ear. The stranger coughed. On his forehead protruding veins formed a V above the base of his nose. Black-rimmed iris, ochre-specked on a green background; I put my hand on Edgar's. A cigarette with a long ash still intact hung in the right corner of his mouth, his lips and the right half of his face were stained with nicotine, I scrutinized them. Edgar was in a hurry to go. I got up, held out my hand to the stranger and let him usher me out.

3

We reached the station quickly. It was built on an embankment with two pairs of tracks. We looked at it. He said, "Actually, you could give me a kiss now." His hair burned my hand, he closed his eyes like a woman. I did as I was told. Then we went to the tunnel leading to the platforms. Lights with wire protectors were mounted on the curved ceiling, gutters on the black-painted buttressed walls called a urinal to mind, we looked at the train schedule that was glued on the whitewashed arching walls. "What would you like," he asked. "I want you," I said.

4

"Your place or mire," he asked. "Mine," I said. I had no apartment at the time. During the week I slept in a garret of the House of Culture. On Sundays in my parents' bedroom. When I got the job, I was promised a furnished room somewhere nearby, only a very few of the workers in the county construction unit lived in the little town. My parents lived in Berlin. The House of Culture belonged to the county construction unit. Supposedly, the building had housed a restaurant ruined by poor management, in their spare time volunteers had renovated the ground floor with money from the culture funds, the upstairs had been refurbished with paint. Only the neon signs were burning, weekends, I had a key, the caretaker was a red mountain climber, we trod on the wooden stairs in our stocking feet. The small room had been built under the tapering attic roof and smelled of dust and rubble. A cord with forty watts hung from the ceiling, on the latch of a dormerwindow, my work duds, blue-and-white checkered bed sheets. We bit into each other's lips and whetted our tongues until the saliva ran out of the corners of our mouths, tore at our clothes all the time, climbed out of them, we touched each other's body as if playing an instrument, boards creaked. Loud, when we became one flesh, I tossed my head, clawed down his back probably, the struggle brought us rhythmically,

quickly and relentlessly to the pain. It came, as I heard the cry, and my mouth spoke, I bore the weight of his damp body for a long while. As he raised up, I slid a little to the right, he stretched out on my left side, I looked with pleasure at his face glistening with perspiration. Later I sat up. The skin on his body was taut. A thin layer of fat hid the branching veins. Freckled on the top side of his arms, noticeably muscular around the shoulders and ribs, then indistinct, from the pit of the throat downward hair growing sparsely. Slender hips, concave abdomen, short legs with bony knees, medium-sized genitals. I kissed them.

5

After midnight we thanked each other, introduced ourselves by name, and parted. The next morning, when I heard the caretaker's hiking boot kick the door as usual, my feelings of emptiness were gone. I was astonished, said "yes" as a sign that I was awake, peered at the winding patterns on the slanted wall above me. Every morning I looked at them and had already deciphered a horse and a boot or Italy. A toe print to the left of the horse, I got up, gathered my clothes from the floor, counted. Eighteenth day, light designs, heel prints from shoes and feet, marked the brown-painted boards, cigarette ashes in the washbowl, no water in the pitcher. The caretaker brought up water from the kitchen for the waiter who occupied the next room, I was left to get my supply from the first floor ladies' room, without washing I jumped into my denims. They were stiff with lime at the chest and thighs, the construction site was nearby, during the first few weeks I avoided changing in the construction shack. I was homesick for the site where I had been an apprentice. There were three of us, one woman had married a man from Leuna, another had had a baby, I was the only woman in the unit now who worked on the scaffolding. The brigade grudgingly took me on, according to the regulations protecting workers, women are forbidden to push carts of bricks, for example, directors had given guarantees, when pay for piecework was introduced, the men began to worry about losing money again. That morning Anton and I completed the left gable, at the time we were using one stone, one limestone, in rhythm, of course, as the method developed by our foreman and propagandized in the newspapers was called, our brigade built only two stories, at breakfast talk about piece-work and the blockade. The porter, a woman, brought milk, we were voluntarily committed to abstaining from beer during working hours, no one seemed apprehensive. The odor of Bruno's body arose from my skin. Before evening came, I knew that I loved him.

6

I ate poorly for three days. I hardly slept. Four days later Bruno appeared at the construction site. I didn't see him at first, we were laying concrete, I was operating the lift and could hardly let the crane carriage out of sight, Anton yelled, "Someone to see you." He was my sponsor and had also committed himself to qualifying me politically so that I could go to the university, then he planned to retire. Bruno said, "Let's go." I said, "How." I had remembered him being younger. We ran over the stubblefield to the river. At the bank we fell upon one another. I lay on my back with closed eyes. In reverse position, I observed Bruno. In front of his ears, where the hair was gray, there were crowsfeet, he pulled his shoulders up to chin level, his forearms flanked his head, cupped palms, stretched-out fingers, lips pressed together as if in pain, movement behind tightly closed eyelids, I redoubled my efforts, his face broke open like a wound, his hands closed half-way. Bruno turned his head, I forced grass under my nails, dirt. Toward evening we lay still, Bruno calm, I intoxicated: peace.

7

It lasted until seven. By then we were so cold that we had to leave the river. Reluctantly, we approached the town, avoided the pub, the clubhouse, the semi in which the auxiliary driver was waiting for Bruno. The chestnut trees on the railway embankment were almost bare. We looked at both pairs of tracks. I said, "In Heaven no one would disturb us." "How do you know," Bruno asked. "My grandmother told me," I said. "Let's go," he said. We wanted to bribe the woman at the ticket window with fifty marks. She demanded a hundred because the place did not exist for her. The tickets were 573.20 East German Marks. We were transported on a handcar.

8

As the rails began to bend upward, the angel let the handle go and started the engine. Following orders, Bruno changed over to the other seat. Both seats were parallel to the rails with the backs above the wheels, when the angle of ascent reached more than 160 degrees, we had to fasten our seat belts. The tracks glistened in the darkness, breath turned to snow, when I looked down, it was like being with Bruno, only longer, the angel covered our faces with his wings.

9

Heaven was densely populated. The registration office was located in a skyscraper in the downtown area. The selection process took place in the courtyard. On the basis of fraudulent statements, our petition was granted. We were given robes with holes and referral papers. A camp for the love-making section had been set up in a peaceful area, 789 barracks, *chevaux de frise,** communication trenches. In which unpedigreed dogs of paradise were runners. We were allocated a bed in barrack 361. Unlike the other occupants, we used it regularly. In the beginning. Use of the beds was allowed only if one was clothed and only under medical observation; every third inhabitant was employed by the Celestial Health Department; observation included, among other things, preparing electrocardiograms. In spite of all this, we were blissful. In the beginning. The billeting changed often, married couples were allowed to live in the camp, officially, it was designated as a transit camp. Occasionally, the fellow occupants gave up after the first day. Then their holed robes were burned on the parade ground, accompanied by music, with later conversions the closed gowns were surrendered in the clothing depot. We hardly bothered about camp life, we lay beside each other most of the time, looked at each other. Bruno's beauty had a tinge of ugliness that made it unmistakable, it occupied me. I admired it without effort. In the beginning. During the idle periods, we exchanged speculations about the Cuba crisis, I described equipment frames, door balances, lintels, Bruno talked of grades of gasoline and accidents. After four months there we had our first fight. We blamed the prophylactic health care. At night we knocked down the guard, ran to the outer edge of Heaven, and leaned far over the balustrade. The earth was still blue.

10

We were exposed. For three days we hid in a bunker. When we were put on the list of wanted persons, we fled over the border. After interrogations about morale and materiel in the enemy camp we were welcomed into Hell. A red-winged gentleman decorated us with deserters' medals. With these we were authorized to use all the machines. We chose the three-by-three compartment, air conditioned, maid service, and advanced from stationary, then electronically operated mirrors, to a love detec-

tor, from the ordinary gimbals to programmed gimbals with ninety-two variations, from an organ to a striking mechanism, from a garrotte to a Tantalus machine, a gadget powered by a detector which transformed the appearance, sex, and desires of one's partner. We used the latter to suppress our growing hate. In vain, even the couples who used the most modern aggregates were reduced to poor devils. In a short time there was no difference between them and the group that loitered about in the streets, debated, cursed, and brawled. When I broke Bruno's ring-finger, we decided to return home.

11

Via air lift we reached the little town on earth again. It was spring, the town was still standing, twelve houses had even been built in the meantime, the first person we ran into was the man who delivered coal. We made inquiries, he scrutinized us, remembered finally that the Americans had ended the blockade a long while back, he had forgotten the particulars. We said goodbye and each went to his own station. Due to the shortage of personnel, I returned to my old job immediately. Anton had retired. Bruno visited me once a week, less often after I entered the university. He lives in Dresden now.

Translated by Betty N. Weber

NOTE

* Literally, curly horses; any form of portable wire entanglement, used as a barrier.

Elena Poniatowska   *Mexico, b. 1933*

Elena Poniatowska became famous when, in 1968, she published *La noche de Tlateloco* (Massacre in Mexico), which is meant to be a document, including tape-recorded statements of witnesses, of the 1968 mass murder of student protestors by Mexican policemen in Mexico City. She had, at that time, already published a major novel, *Los cuentos de Lilus Kirkus* (The Stories of Lilus Kirkus, 1967), and in 1969 she wrote her important documentary novel *Hasta no verte, Jesús mío* (*Until I See You, Jesus Dear*), in which she makes a poor, ignorant peasant named Jesusa into a folk hero whose nobility and independence command admiration and respect.

Poniatowska is deeply involved with the journalistic world in Mexico, using reportage and her fiction to express her concern for the rights of the poor, of women, and of those suffering from political oppression. She has two children.

The following story is from her collection *De noche vienes* (You Come From the Night); it had the same title in the Spanish version.

LOVE STORY

Teleca couldn't go to bed: "I'll bet she's gossiping in the doorway."

She peered over the balcony. The empty street leaped at her.

"Then she must have shut herself in the bathroom. She does it because she knows it infuriates me."

She yelled with heartfelt exasperation: "Lupe! Lupe! Lupeeeeeeee!"

The problem was, she couldn't think about anything else; nothing obsessed her like her relationship with Lupe, who could now be heard shuffling around the kitchen.

"Lupe! Where were you?"

"Upstairs, ma'am."

"Doing what at this hour, if you don't mind?"

"Having a bath."

The black hair was dripping down the damp back, the waist, the buttocks; very long hair, now wound up after the shampoo, held up by a red comb, a handful heavy as a horse's mane.

"Didn't you tell me to have a bath every day?"

"But not during your working hours."

The bather looked at her, and Teleca saw the red tree of resentment in her eyes.

"Bring me my breakfast."

"OK."

"That's no way to answer. Say, 'Yes, ma'am.'"

"Uh-huh."

"Say, 'Yes, ma'am,'" Teleca almost shouted.

The woman was silent. Then she seemed to make up her mind: "Yes, ma'am."

Teleca slammed the door as she left the kitchen. In her bedroom, she could do nothing but go from one place to another, pick up one thing after another, put it somewhere else, lose it, pace back and forth next to the door like a caged lion. She couldn't wait for the moment when she could go back to the kitchen, see what Lupe was doing, look at her face, smooth as a river pebble, begin again, choose more tactful words. "I'm going to wait five minutes." She went into the bathroom and brushed her hair furiously. The telephone rang. She thanked the lord for that phone call. Lupe was late in answering, dragged her feet toward the telephone, and slowly came to knock at the door.

"Somebody for you."

Teleca's heart beat faster.

"Say, 'There's a telephone call for you, ma'am.' Besides, you took your time about answering."

That wasn't what she wanted to say. She wanted to assume a serene expression, the smile trembling on her lips, ready to blossom and open. Drops of water were still falling from Lupe's mane. Teleca pushed her aside.

"Who is it? Oh. Arthur! How delightful. Are you all right? Well, just so-so. I feel so nervous. I don't know why, maybe it's the domestic dramas; you know those people just don't understand, however much one would like to approach them, there's just no way, at any rate I can't find one; oh yes. I know there are other topics of conversation, but you see that's my everyday experience and that's what I have to talk about. It helps calm my nerves. ...At the Lady Baltimore? At five? Yes, of course. What fun! Bye-bye...Thanks."

Teleca walked toward the kitchen. "Can it be that a ragged Indian can get me into this state? But...it's impossible. It's not fair! It's this loneliness that's..."

"Lupe, my breakfast."

"Yes, ma'am."

At least she said, "Yes, ma'am." Lupe entered with the tea, the warm egg, the toast, the dazzling white cup, the sugar cubes in a sugar-bowl just as dazzling.

"And the newspaper, isn't it here yet?"

"I'll go see."

"Haven't I told you to bring the paper up first thing in the morning and put it next to my place? It must be sopping."

The servant returned with the *Universal*, her face a mask of itself.

"Lupe, the marmalade. Why don't you put the bitter orange marmalade on the table? The marmalade and the butter."

"Last month you told me not to because you didn't want to get fat."

"But I'm not on a diet anymore."

"OK."

"Not, OK! How many times have I told you to say, 'Yes, ma'am'!"

Teleca tried to concentrate on the headlines; she realized she didn't care, nothing interested her except Lupe, to know what Lupe was thinking, to follow her, stop next to her as she stood at the washtub, look at her strong round arms, her arms, two apple trees extending into leafy twigs—how pretty her fingertips were, wrinkled from the washwater —hear her young voice, juicy as her hands. Lupe must have secretly noticed the power she had over her mistress, because she frowned and curled her lip haughtily, in a temper. When she finished breakfast, Teleca went into the kitchen.

"I'm going to take a bath."

Lupe was silent.

"Keep your ears open for the telephone and the doorbell."

"Uh-huh."

Teleca felt her nerves getting raw; she could have struck her, pulled that damp handful hanging over the Indian, Indian, Indian shoulders. But she also would have liked to see her smile, her eyes bright, cheeks shining— how newly washed brown skin glows!—to hear her ask, in the musical voice of earlier days, "Is everything all right, ma'am?" Everything all right, everything all right...nothing was all right. Teleca made her morning ablutions with Lupe on her mind, forecasting her one P.M. face, the friendly gesture or sparkle in her eye; maybe Lupe will be nice when I leave. She imagined the details: "Lupe, I'm leaving now; remember, I'm not lunching at home today, I'm going to the Güemes, as I told you yesterday," "Yes, ma'am, that's fine, I'll polish the silver. Have a good time, ma'am." Once in a while she'd said, "Have a lovely time." and Teleca still remembered it gratefully. Lupe had stayed with her longer than any other girl. Her solitude made Teleca appreciate the shared hours, the other presence in the house. At first she used the familiar, but when something angered her, she brandished formalities to emphasize the distance. "When I leave, I'll casually tell her to take the radio into the kitchen, so she won't be bored." Teleca thought. "But what's happening to me? I'm paying too much attention to her, as if Lupe were the only person in my life. My nerves are playing tricks on me. What must Lupe think of me? Does she like me? What a close-mouthed woman! She's a blind lump of dough!"

Just at the doorway, Teleca adjusted her hat and said with false gaiety: "Lupe? I'm leaving now. See you at five."

The only answer was the hum of cars in the Avenue of the Insurgents. So Teleca yelled, in a less friendly voice: "Lupe? I'm leaving. Have my tea ready at five, and don't leave streaks on the silverware. Remember now, the polish and a flannel cloth, not soap and a scrub-brush, like last time."

Silence amplified her order.

"Lupe? Lupe, did you hear me?"

"Uh-huh."

The words echoed mournfully, coming perhaps from the kitchen or the ironing board or the inside of a closet or who knows where, from the thick darkness in which Lupe moved, "That squaw, that idiot, that smelly creature, I don't know why I'm worrying about a beast like that." And Teleca marched out. "It will do me good to see some people of my own sort and give up this useless effort to uplift the ones who are past saving." She walked toward the Güemes' house, her dress swirling around her legs, but at the first corner she almost turned back. "I didn't tell her to turn on the radio in the kitchen," and she remembered that slow, heavy, muddy "uh-huh" and thought (with what she imagined to be a pedagogical impulse): "It will do her good. She'll miss me. Of course she'll miss me. It's awful to be alone in a house." She imagined herself in earlier years, alone in her kitchen with no one to teach good manners to, anxiously waiting for the water about to boil furiously in the tea kettle, defenseless against the attack of the bells, ready to start up a conversation with anyone, the

first street vendor, the newspaper boy, yes, yes, like any alley cat; she remembered the warnings she had written for herself in a convent student's angular hand and had stuck up in plain sight, in the kitchen, the hall, not so much because she needed them as to keep her company: "Please close the door," "don't forget to turn off the gas," "check your keys before leaving," "the electricity bill is due the first Friday of every month," "any effort is a success in itself." And in large letters, the numbers that connected her to the outside world. Teleca was ready to scream, anxiety pressing on her heart: "Help, I can't breathe." Or to run as she now ran toward the Güemes' house, where she entered panting, ruffled as a sparrow that takes refuge in the rafters. "How are things? How are things? You look so pretty sitting here!" The Güemes raised startled eyes to their friend's fluttering. What did she mean, "pretty," when they looked like a couple of witches? Teleca immediately asked to use the telephone.

"I forgot to tell Lupe something."

"We're having soufflé to start with. Teleca, don't be long."

"How marvelous, oh how marvelous. I'm so hungry. I'll be right with you."

She took the receiver off the hook. A bell sounded, extended itself on the air, an unanswered signal. How long would that lazy squaw take to answer? Teleca nervously dialed again. The third time was the charm.

"Lupe."

"Uh-huh."

"Haven't I told you . . . . Oh all right, look, I want you to polish my father's polo trophy. It's been ages since you cleaned it and it looks terrible."

"The what?"

"The polo trophy."

"What?"

"Don't you understand? The polo trophy, the tall silver cup with the handles in the form of a swan . . . . I forgot to tell you."

"The biggest cup in the living room?"

"Yes, that one, Lupe." (She almost said, "Dear Lupe," but caught herself.)

"I don't think there's enough polish."

"Why didn't you buy some?"

"You wouldn't let me."

She would have liked to go on talking with Lupe for hours, but the Güemes were calling, "Teleca, Teleca." How dear it was to speak to Lupe through that mouthpiece that fit her hand, without seeing her stubborn, stony, almost impenetrable face. Teleca would often call home to give some advice, to make sure Lupe was there. She would keep on and on until she found her and then scold her: "Where did you go? Who told you you could go out? You can't go out and leave the house empty, like a child! That's why you (addressing an immense caravan of servants, a bevy of women in aprons and braids who were advancing towards her across the desert) are in this state, because you're irresponsible, deformed, stupid, because you have no ambition and no self-respect and don't even want to rise above your lethargy!" She recalled that Lupe never moved a muscle in her face.

"Listen, Lupe, if Mr. Arthur calls, tell him I went to have lunch with the Güemes."

"Didn't you talk to him this morning?"

"Yes, but I forgot to tell him."

"Ah!" said Lupe suspiciously.

"Did you open the bathroom window? The towels have to be aired before it rains. You always forget."

Teleca hated the Güemes for interrupting the dialogue, but she had to give in. "All right, I'll call later to see what has been happening." She heard a murmur that sounded like "uh-huh" and the click of the telephone. "That dirty beast, she hung up on me, she didn't even give me time to say goodbye, but I'll get even, I'll call her after coffee."

The obsessed have the strange power of attracting everyone to the center of their spiral; they press harder and harder, closing tighter at each turn until the circle becomes a single point, a whirling drill. At the table Teleca brought the conversation around to servants—in French, of course, so the good Josephine wouldn't understand.

"Why are servants such idiots?"

"Because if they weren't they wouldn't be servants."

"It's because this is a brutish race. In France, in England, in Spain, servants are different. They know how to behave, they realize to whom they're speaking, they're responsible, they're of a different sort, but these brutes who don't...who don't even have a mat to drop dead on, aren't even grateful for the favor you're doing them."

"I think it's the sun. They're out in the sun so much they've all got sunstroke."

"Or the Spanish Conquest."[1]

"Oh yes, they lost everything with the Conquest, even their sense of shame."

"It's the whole race. They're definitely low on gray matter."

Teleca went on talking without a break until coffee was served. It was her way of being close to Lupe, circling around her, evoking her. One of the Güemes sisters, fat and good-natured, suggested (to block the avalanche): "Why don't we play a little bridge, right now? We can take our coffee with us."

They agreed. At five Teleca cried: "I've got a date with Arthur in the Lady Baltimore at five. How awful! I'll never get there in time. If I'd thought, I would have put it off, since I knew I was having lunch with you."

What really bothered her was not calling Lupe. Now she couldn't. When? Where? There was no way to leave Arthur alone at his table in the tearoom.

"What a shame the chauffeur isn't here, otherwise he could drop you off, Teleca."

"It doesn't matter. I just love taxi drivers."

Over tea, apropos of Teleca's comments, Arthur launched into a long dissertation on the Conquest according to Bernal Diaz del Castillo.[2] That wasn't what she was after. Nobody could give her what she was looking for, nobody but Lupe. Would Arthur ever finish and go away? But Arthur, a dilettante of history, seemed ready to examine everything, down to the U.S. laws on racial segregation. Teleca felt sick to her stomach. Arthur stretched out his arm toward her necklace.

"Look at that chunk of amber hanging from your chain. It's worth ten slaves."

"Because of the worm inside?"

"Precisely. Perhaps, on account of that worm, it's worth fifteen slaves."

"Oh, Arthur, let's go."

Defiantly, without waiting for him, Teleca got up. There was something of the clumsy boy about Teleca that disconcerted Arthur even while it attracted him. Her way of taking the stairs two at a time, her long thin legs that galloped rather than walked, her hipless body, her intent, tea-colored eyes—hadn't they taught her not to stare at people when she was a little girl? Her open smile, from ear to ear, that revealed wide white teeth, strong as grains of corn left out in the sun and wind. Teleca winked, too. "It comes naturally," she said when they reproved her.

"I'm going to play bridge at the Lucerne; I can drop you off in a taxi, Teleca."

"Thanks, Arthur. You're going to play with Novo and Villarrutia? Who's the fourth?"

"Torres Bodet. Haven't you read *The Counterfeiters*[3] yet?"

"I told you I'm very nervous. I can't concentrate."

"If you read it. You'd forget your nerves. Look," said Arthur, pressing his nose against the window, "it's night already. In Mexico, it gets dark all at once. Either there's nothing happening at all and we're absolutely smothered in the thickest boredom, or else we have a catastrophe and everything's over. My God, what a country!"

"It's your country…"

Arthur smiled mockingly. "You're so contradictory, Teleca. This sudden patriotism doesn't suit you. After all, you're always talking about leaving for Spain."

"But meanwhile I stand up for the dark."

"The black holes?"

Teleca didn't answer. She felt a strange sense of solidarity with Lupe. She could kick her, but in front of anyone else she defended passionately anything related to Indians; the earth, the forest, beans, corn, warm stones.

"Look, she hasn't even remembered to turn on the light in the entryway."

Arthur got out of the taxi and stretched out his hand, a soft hand with very pink, fine, thin nails, like a newborn baby's. He bowed low to kiss Teleca's glove.

"Beautiful Teleca."

"She's left the street dark!"

Arthur made his nails dance like lightning bugs.

"Light, more light."

"Please Arthur, try to understand. Your mother takes care of everything for you, you don't understand how hard it is to deal with these people."

Arthur's lips, as rosy as his fingernails, curved in an annoyed grimace. He smiled, and they grew thin to the point of cruelty. Nevertheless, in their natural state they were full, so full that they stuck out.

"Telequita, do some reading. I'll talk to you tomorrow. I want your opinion."

Teleca abruptly stuck her key in the door. She could just glimpse Arthur striking the driver lightly on the shoulder with the handle of his cane, and the taxi drove off.

Teleca strode up the stairs. "Lupe, Lupe! Hasn't anything happened?" She went on up to the second floor. "Lupe?" She passed through the ironing room, the kitchen. "Where has that squaw got to? She must be snoring in her room." "Lupe? Didn't anyone call?" She stopped at the top of the maid's staircase. "Lupe. Lupeeeee!" Teleca never entered the room in the attic. It was one of her rules. "Maybe she's in the library waxing the furniture. I doubt it, but anyway…" She headed for it hopefully. When she opened the door, the bookcases gleamed, and Teleca followed the ray of light with her eyes; in the darkness they acquired the tonality of a Vermeer;[4] some of the corners seemed to float in the air, cutting it, their edges shining; the round arm of a sofa lit up in the darkness, silky and electric as the humped back of a cat. Time polishes, time melts, time shapes. "It smells shut-in. Not only is she not here, she hasn't been here for a long time, even though I ordered her to. What a filthy woman." She went up the stairs again. "Lupe, Lupe." She went flying through the rooms. "Lupe." Again she stood at the foot of the maid's staircase and shouted, shielding her call with both hands, "Lupe!" She had never been so slow in answering. "Smelly old thing. Uppity Indian!" Finally, Teleca decided to climb the stairs. Her heels caught in the iron steps; she almost fell through. Above she heard the water tank dripping. There were no sheets on the washing lines. She burst into the room; it didn't even have a lock. The smell of feet, sweat, and confinement assaulted her and made her gasp in search of breath.

"She must have gone out to buy bread...but...at this hour? She never, never goes at this hour. Besides, I've told her never to leave the house empty. I'm going to get after her, I can't stand having her around, she's bad for me."

She went through the stripped room. She looked for the cartons Lupe had brought her things in. Nothing. She opened the closet. Nothing. The breeze lashed the bare window. At last Teleca had to yield to the evidence. "She's left." She went down the stairway without noticing what she was doing and went directly to her room. The key, yes, the key. No, she didn't take anything. There is the jewelry. She waited a few minutes in the middle of the bedroom, her arms hanging at her sides, not knowing what to do. There was not a sound in the house. Teleca allowed herself to swoon at the feet of her fear, beside herself from the search, her emotion. She tried to encourage herself. "Well, that's better. I'd planned to fire her anyway. She was always

looking down on me. She's saved me a scene. I was bored with that flat nose, anyway. Traitor. It's an ill wind that blows nobody good, or what's that saying? Traitor. It's the best thing that could have happened."

She began by taking off her hat, switching on the bedside lamp, closing the curtains one by one. A rosy light spread through the room. The houses of the rich always glow with a rosy light. Almost euphoric, she went to the kitchen to look for the water pitcher she kept beside her bed at night, and the glass. "Now I'm really going to read *The Counterfeiters*. I didn't plan on eating dinner anyway, so how could it matter?" She came and went, walked through the living room, crossed the dining room, her heels resounding like castanets, up, left, right, turn. "I sound like a flamenco dancing teacher," she told herself affectionately; she put two of the vases of flowers in the hall. "Pig, the water is green, she didn't even change it. Lupe! Lupe! But I must be crazy, she's done me a favor by getting out of here. Yes 'getting out of here,' the way they say it, even though it sounds so ugly." She hung up her coat, or rather tried to, in front of the closet. "Lupe, where are all the hangers? The wooden one for my coat is missing." "I'm obviously delirious, my mind is wandering, I keep talking to that wretch in my mind all the time tomorrow I'll wear lacquer red it's the color that suits me best has that idiot thrown my shoes out? Lupe! Lupe!" Exhausted, Teleca fell to the carpet and rocked her head in her hands. Only then did she notice that her cheeks were wet. She couldn't have been crying all this time! She forced back a sob, "Little Lupe! The best thing for me to do is lie down, take a tranquilizer, tomorrow I'll look for somebody else." Teleca often forgot she had a body—it was so light— but now it was burning, echoing, amplifying all the noises inside. Teleca stretched out her arms to turn back the beautiful, thick damask coverlet that had been her parents'; she did it slowly, carefully, and suddenly, there on the sparkling linen, at the height of the hand-embroidered *A* and *S* interlaced under the family emblem, she saw the excrement, an enormous turd that spread out in concentric circles, in a terrifying rainbow, green, coffee-colored, greenish-yellow, ashy, steaming. In the silence, the stink began to rise.

Years later, when Teleca told Arthur—she had never dared tell anyone—Arthur replied that it was impossible, that Indians were neither vulgar nor scatalogical, much less proctological, that they would never do anything of the kind; no doubt of that, it was not within their patterns of behavior, any researcher of Indian traits could confirm that. Perhaps Lupe had let a delivery boy in, a poor devil corrupted by city ways, a drunk, and between the two of them they thought up that piece of

mischief which, from an impartial point of view, could be considered infantile, but Teleca, protesting, scowling, stubborn, hunched over, insisted.

"No, no, no. It was Lupe's."

Translated by Anne Twitty

NOTES

1. Fernan Cortes' invasion and conquest of Mexico, 1519–1521.
2. Bernal Diaz del Castillo (1492–1581), a Spanish soldier during the Conquest, wrote *Historia Verdadera de la Conquistor de la Nuera-España* (True History of the Conquest of New Spain, 1632).
3. Novel (1925) by French writer André Gide, concerning hypocrisy and horror, betrayal and decadence.
4. Dutch painter (1632–1675) of interior subjects, mainly.

Fay Zwicky   *Australia, b. 1933*

For Fay Zwicky, as for many other women, success as a creative writer has come after success in other careers. Born in Melbourne, she was educated at Melbourne University, where she began publishing poems and stories. She toured as a concert pianist for several years; at the same time, believing that she could not tolerate the stress of performance for a lifetime, she maintained an academic career. Until her recent retirement to concentrate on her writing, she was a Senior Lecturer in English at the University of Western Australia.

"Summer Pogrom" and "Chicken" come from Zwicky's first collection, *Isaac Babel's Fiddle* (1975); the former reflects her strong personal interest in the immigrant experience in Australia and the latter the sharp wit and humor of much of her work. She has since published another collection of poems, *Kaddish* (1982), and a collection of stories, *Hostages* (1983). A dominant concern in her writing has been a metaphysical quest for synthesis of the contemplative and active life. A talented critic and lecturer, Zwicky has published many essays and reviews, some of which have been collected in *The Lyre in the Pawnshop* (1986). She has also edited *Quarry: A Selection of Western Australian Poetry* (1981) and, for the Australian feminist press Sisters, *Journeys* (1982), an anthology of poems by Judith Wright, Rosemary Dobson, Gwen Harwood, and Dorothy Hewett.

Elizabeth Webby

SUMMER POGROM

Spade-bearded Grandfather, squat Lenin[1]
In the snows of Donna Buang.[2]
Your bicycle a wiry crutch, nomadic homburg
Alien, black, correct. Beneath, the curt defiant
Filamented eye. Does it count the dead
Between the Cossack horses' legs in Kovno?[3]

Those dead who sleep in me, me dry
In a garden veiled with myrtle and oleander,
Desert snows that powder memory's track
Scoured by burning winds from eastern rocks,
Flushing the lobes of mind,
Fat white dormant flowrets.

Aggressive under dappled shade, girl in a glove;
Collins Street[4] in autumn,
Mirage of clattering crowds: Why don't you
                                                    speak English?
I don't understand, *I don't understand*!
Sei nicht so ein Dummerchen,[5] nobody cares.
Not for you the upreared hooves of Nikolai,
Eat your icecream, Kleine, *may his soul rot,*
These are good days.

Flared candles; the gift of children; love,
Need fulfilled, a name it has to have—how else
                                                    to feel?
A radiance in the garden, the Electrolux man[6]
                                                    chats,
Cosy spectre of the afternoon's decay.
My eye his eye, the snows of Kovno cover us.
Is that my son bloodied against Isaac the Baker's
                                                    door?

The tepid river's edge, reeds creak, rats' nests
                                                    fold and quiver,
My feet sink in sand; the children splash and
                                                    call, sleek
Little satyrs diamond-eyed reined to summer's
                                                    roundabout,
Hiding from me. Must I excavate you,
Agents of my death? Hushed snows are deep,
                                                    the
Dead lie deep in me.

NOTES

1. Leader (1870–1924) of the Communist Revolution (1917).
2. Australian mountain known for winter sports.
3. City in Lithuania; before World War II it had a large Jewish population which was persecuted by paramilitary Cossacks and victim to bloody masacres known as pogroms.
4. Major thoroughfare in Melbourne.
5. German for "Don't be a silly girl."
6. Vacuum cleaner salesman.

CHICKEN

Tucked snug behind
Proscenium arch a
Baby's stoned to death:
The watchers sit in trembling furs,
Slumped with relief.
Beyond belief!
Come, let's get out before
The peak hour traffic snarls
The bridge. I've got cold chicken
In the fridge for supper—at least
I think I have. Those kids *will*
Gorge themselves. Oh go on.
You can pass! The light's already
Amber, hurry up! I'm dying for a
Cup of tea. Don't talk like that
To me, of all people!
Let's not quarrel, things are
Going so well: Ian's done his maths
And Nigel's sure to top his year.
You've worked so hard with
Him . . . what's that? I
Had to keep her home. You
know that stomach thing she gets.
She'll be all right tomorrow.
Well, the wings have had it but
The breast's still there. Or
Part of it. You must be starving!
Can't see why we push ourselves to
Plays like that although I feel
The writer has a point to make.

(Continued)

Some cake? Oh damn, I
Gave it to that child next door;
I'm sure her mother doesn't
Feed her properly. What's the
Matter? Aren't you feeling well?
It'll pass. There's Dexsal in the
Cupboard and a glass is
Right in front of you.
All right, I'll come up later—
What a mess they leave the

Place! Did you say she was crying?
Probably a dream. It's just a phase
She's going through. I'll go to her.
You go to bed. I can't think
What's the matter with my head.
         There, there, the
Way you cry you'd think I was an
Awful sight. Now be a good girl,
Go to sleep. Good night.

Fleur Adcock   *New Zealand/UK(England) b. 1934*

Fleur Adcock was the first New Zealand woman poet to achieve an international reputation. She was born in New Zealand but spent much of her childhood in England. Returning to New Zealand at the age of 13, Adcock did not feel it was home, and she went back to live in England in 1963.

In the intervening years, Adcock studied languages and classics at Wellington University, getting her B.A. in 1954 and M.A. in 1956. At 18, during her time at university, she married the poet Alister Campbell, with whom she had two sons before the marriage broke up in 1957. With her younger son, Adcock moved to a teaching post at Otago University on the South Island, later becoming a librarian there. She worked as a librarian, in Wellington and later in London, before becoming a full-time writer in 1979.

Adcock attributes much of her love of poetry to her mother, who made up verses and read poems to her as a small child. She began writing early in life, telling stories and inventing imaginary worlds with her younger sister, the New Zealand novelist Marilyn Duckworth. Although she had published a small volume of poems before returning to England, Adcock's breakthrough as a poet came with publication of her second collection, *Tigers* (1967) by Oxford University Press. The poems selected here come from that volume and from *The Eye of the Hurricane* (1969) and show her particular interest in human relationships. As in "For a Five-Year-Old," she characteristically focuses on a specific incident but also makes a statement of wider significance.

Adcock has now published six individual volumes of poetry and a *Selected Poems* (1983). She recently edited anthologies of contemporary New Zealand poetry and of twentieth century women's poetry. Her blend of order, emotion, and fantasy has been widely praised by reviewers.

Elizabeth Webby

WIFE TO HUSBAND

From anger into the pit of sleep
You go with a sudden skid. On me
Stillness falls gradually, a soft
Snowfall, a light cover to keep
Numb for a time the twitching nerves.

Your head on the pillow is turned away;
My face is hidden. But under snow
Shoots uncurl, the green thread curves
Instinctively upwards. Do not doubt
That sense of purpose in mindless flesh:
Between our bodies a warmth grows;
Under the blankets hands move out,
Your back touches my breast, our thighs
Turn to find their accustomed place.

Your mouth is moving over my face:
Do we dare, now, to open our eyes?

FOR A FIVE-YEAR-OLD

A snail is climbing up the window-sill
Into your room, after a night of rain.
You call me in to see, and I explain
That it would be unkind to leave it there:
It might crawl to the floor; we must take care
That no one squashes it. You understand,
And carry it outside, with careful hand,
To eat a daffodil.
I see, then, that a kind of faith prevails:
Your gentleness is moulded still by words
From me, who have trapped mice and shot
                                        wild birds,
From me, who drowned your kittens, who
                                        betrayed
Your closest relatives, and who purveyed
The harshest kind of truth to many another.
But that is how things are: I am your mother,
And we are kind to snails.

INCIDENT

When you were lying on the white sand,
A rock under your head, and smiling,
(Circled by dead shells), I came to you
And you said, reaching to take my hand,
'Lie down.' So for a time we lay
Warm on the sand, talking and smoking,
Easy; while the grovelling sea behind
Sucked at the rocks and measured the day.
Lightly I fell asleep then, and fell
Into a cavernous dream of falling.
It was all the cave-myths, it was all
The myths of tunnel or tower or well—
Alice's rabbit-hole[1] into the ground,
Or the path of Orpheus: a spiral staircase
To hell, furnished with danger and doubt.[2]
Stumbling, I suddenly woke; and found
Water about me. My hair was wet,
And you were sitting on the grey sand,
Waiting for the lapping tide to take me:
Watching, and lighting a cigarette.

NOTES

1. In Lewis Carroll's *Alice in Wonderland* (1865), Alice
   falls into a rabbit hole into a world of strange and
   wonderful adventures.
2. Orpheus, musician of Greek mythology, was allowed to
   descend to hell to retrieve his wife, the nymph Eury-
   dice, as long as he never looked back at her; he did,
   and she disappeared.

Samira 'Azzam

Palestine/Lebanon, 1934–1967

Samira 'Azzam was raised in Palestine until the age of 14 when the British mandate was appropriated by the Jews to create the Israeli state. Like many other upper-class Palestinians, 'Azzam and her family were able to take refuge in other Middle Eastern countries; she was resettled in Jordan and educated there. She married a national of Iraq and published two novels and four collections of short stories before her untimely death in a car accident at the age of 33. Her works include *Al-Sā'ah wa-l-Insān* (The Man and the Clock), *Zill al-Kabīr* (The Great Shadow), *'Id min al-Nafidhah al-Gharbiyah* (Holiday from the Western Window), *Ashyā' Saghīrah* (Little Things), and *Wa-Qisas Ukra* (And Other Stories...).

'Azzam was educated in Western literature, but unlike many of her female peers, she gave more attention to the concrete social realities than to psychological labyrinths of character. In contrast to the highly metaphoric interior dialogues of other writers, she chose to adopt a tone of cool detachment. As the story that follows suggests, the Palestinian theme—a common one in Middle Eastern literature but one that touched her personally—was central to her writing. She often chose to depict the traumas of the political uprooting and separation of people from their home and family members. "'*Amun 'akhar*" ("Another Year") from her second collection, for example, centers on the poignant meeting of a divided family at the Mandelbaum Gate, to which Christian Arabs frequently journeyed during the holy season, until the 1967 Arab-Israeli war closed off such a possibility.

In the selection 'Azzam deals with another aspect of the problem, that of the Palestinian in "exile." To Arab intellectuals and artists, the Palestinian is frequently perceived as the *locus classicus* of the conflict between East and West, the resolution of the Palestinian conflict as the prototype for the Arab world's ability to deal constructively with the problems confronting it. But, as 'Azzam demonstrates, the transformation of the Palestinian into a symbol, on the mundane level, serves only to marginalize the individual and to subject him or her to the worst corruptions of society. From another point of view, the outcome of the story reflects precisely the dilemma to which many writers and critics have pointed. Its title is the same in the original.

Two of 'Azzam's stories are specifically concerned with the emancipation of the Arab woman: "*Al-zill al-Kabīr*" and "*Masīr al-Mar'ah*" (Women's Destiny). As Evelyn Accad, the North-American Arab critic, notes in *Veil of Shame*: "In the first the 'man of her dreams' is a logical impossibility, since the men available are all formed by a male-centered culture which is at odds with her inner world of desire"; in the latter, the effort to refuse one's destiny goes unheeded; precisely because "one" is a woman, the society does not even "see" her or her refusal.

PALESTINIAN

"Give me your identity," he said hesitantly, the words hurting his parched throat. "I shall just look at it and return it to you."

His neighbor did not seem to understand. "I mean your card," he urged, extending his hand with a trace of impatience. "Your identity card."

His nervous hand still extended, the other took out a worn wallet, picked out the card and handed it to him. But before he stepped out of the place his neighbor's voice came from behind him: "And what do you want my identity card for, Palestinian?"

Had the neighbor heard the curse which he murmured in reply he would no doubt have snatched the card back from his fingers. But the Palestinian hastened to his shop, stood behind the grubby counter, opened the card, then thrust his hand into his pocket and took out his own new card. It was green and shiny, its cedar tree bearing healthy, unbent branches—a brand new card which he had received but two weeks before. His picture appeared on one side of it, and every one of its three folded sections bore the round stamp of the Registration Department of the Ministry of Interior, while there was a fourth stamp on the back. Four round, articulate stamps whose vicious circles no suspicion could penetrate, and bearing the signature of the Director and the Superintendant. Embracing each other and interlocked, the signatures had crooked, creased, reinforced lines from which no name could be fathomed—as befits the signatures of all those who held Fate in their hands.

The neighbor's card did not differ from his in anything except in its old, withered look and the specifications of name, age, residence, birthplace and date of birth. It was also different in that it bore signs of rough treatment and too much handling by grubby and careless fingers that did not know how to deal kindly with that which came as a natural birthright, costing its owner no effort or anxiety or doubts or money. It was a card that was not the result of an infuriating, hating, piercing feeling that, in this quarter in which he lived, and where he had opened a grocery shop over ten years ago during which time he sold his wares for cash, on credit, or for nothing when he was cheated, he could not manage to earn for himself a proper name or designation.

For in that corner where his shop was situated—a shop in no way different from most other shops—he was no more than "Palestinian." It was as "Palestinian" that he was identified, designated, cursed when needed. Like that Armenian cobbler whom he had known in his boyhood, and who had spent thirty years of his miserable life trying to catch up with the neighborhood's shoes with patches. No one cared, no one ever needed, even, to know whether he was called Hajop, as an Armenian's name could well be, or Sarkis or Artan. "Armenian" was his full name. Thus he lived and thus he died, his name cutting him off from both the living and the dead. That designation probably had the added effect on him of complete stagnation, for the foreign accent never left his speech and his interest in his surroundings never rose above the level of people's feet!

The two identity cards before him, his finger shifted between them, and the specifications danced before his eyes. A customer came in, but he dismissed him with a sign of his hand, and the latter went away angry and bewildered, not understanding why the man didn't want to sell anything. Meanwhile the newspaper fell to the floor and he picked it up; the headline, printed in red over the pictures of the gang's members, horrified him. But what was the use of reading the story for the fifth or the hundredth time? He would never know more than he already knew, and the man's picture alone was evidence enough—the lean face more than half-covered by the spectacles, the baldness that started right above the spectacles but which did not indicate a satanic brain. As for the rest, he knew only one of them, who had introduced him to that other.

Yes, he was wearing a blue suit when he came into the shop to buy a box of matches costing one "franc." He had taken cigarettes out of his pocket, took one and offered him another, which he declined. The man had smoked half the cigarette while standing on the threshold, his face to the street. Then he turned back and started loitering, like one who wants to be drawn into a conversation, any conversation. But finally he decided to broach the subject openly. He had heard, he said—and did not say how or from whom—that he wanted to be naturalized as a Lebanese. If that was what he wanted, there was only one way. And the price—yes, there was a price—two thousand pounds. A bit more indeed, than people used to pay. But the authorities' attitude was becoming increasingly tough. Besides, the Palestinians have left no stone unturned in their search for family names whose roots extend to Palestine—so much so that those lawyers who got rich out of this naturalization racket were beginning to be let down by the science of genealogy.

Two thousand? too much; or are you going perhaps to link my branch to the trunk of a cedar tree which Solomon omitted to root out when he built himself a Temple in Jerusalem?

Too much. Years ago, indeed, he had refused to pay a quarter of this sum to dig out some forefathers in some good-hearted Lebanese village, or to invent a new life history for his grandfather Abu Salih who, as far as he knew, was born and died in the village of Rama. Not that he had wanted to disown Abu Salih publicly. He only wanted his permission to rectify an accident of geography, freeing him from the term "Palestinian" which tied him to a herd from which all signs of individuality had been obliterated—a term which they used in pity when he refused to be an object of pity, or in anger when there was no

ground for anger, or threateningly whenever his rivals among the small shop owners wanted to give vent to their hatred. That term which they had woven into rumors and gossip by which they sought to interpret events the way they wanted them, rumors which enmeshed him like thin but multiplying threads—a cloud of anxiety which made feel him that he, his shop, his four children and his wife were but playthings for the interpreters of past events, and that his only guarantee against a possible transformation into permanent refugee status was to get naturalized.

This inner urge to get naturalized used to weaken when the threads of rumor became looser and when his fears died down in the round of daily life. It used to grow stronger whenever something happened to shake his tottering existence—for instance when his son left school but could not find work for more than two weeks: the law was quite unequivocal about it and work in government offices and firms was forbidden for those who were not citizens. In the end, the young man had to fly to one of those deserts in which people get together like brothers in misfortune, and whose hardship knew no discrimination despite differences of nationality.

The urge became stronger and stronger whenever he decided to go on a trip, for one reason or another, to his relatives who were scattered here and there, for which he had to wait at the door of some office for a week in order to obtain a pass. When his father, who had lived in his brother's house in Amman, died, he cabled his relatives: "Delay him for a week. Otherwise bury him!" It was the most miserable joke that the man at the telegram counter had ever laughingly listened to.

Two thousand? Too much! The negotiator knits his eyebrows and takes out another cigarette. "You will never get a card for less. I believe you have tried, haven't you?"

Yes, he had tried. His case was kept pending for three years between the promises and excuses of the lawyer, who finally gave up everything except half the costs, which he had received in advance...

"But will it be guaranteed?"

"You won't pay before you hold it in your hand; we get nothing in advance." The man's features relaxed and the shade of a smile appeared on his face. Then he withdrew, his voice still reverberating in the shop, fresh, soft, and sweet. "Think it over, think it over; I shall pass by in a few days."

He did not think it over alone, but tried to make his wife do some of the thinking. "Two thousand?" she asked, horrified. "Man! Is it a Minister's card? Others got it for three hundred or six hundred or even for free."

"Two thousand!" he retorted, not over-convinced of what he was saying but fearful of letting the opportunity slip in this first round. "Because we once thought three hundred was too much. One day we may have to pay ten thousand. Do you want your son to spend his life in an inferno with a temperature of fifty centigrade in summer in a land which knows no winter?"

"Do what you like!" she said, touched on her most sensitive chord. "If it is two thousand, then let it be two thousand. May God's blessing be withheld from that money! That is, if you can find it."

"I will find it if I empty half my window. I shall display that card there, so that people may perhaps know that we have a name!"

It is an attribute of lying that it is decisive in its truthfulness. It was three weeks or four and everything was finished—with lightning speed. He did not meet that man who calls himself "professor" more than once. The latter had jotted down all the details on a piece of paper: the name, the names of wife and children, places of birth, ages. He had said that he would take care of everything, including documents and certificates, and that all he needed was photographs—and the two thousand, of course. The money was not all for himself. Expenses were various, and the partners were even more numerous.

The partners were indeed numerous. Five photographs printed in the paper of five counterfeiters—a gang with all the qualifications, its head a professor and the members no less proficient. And they had, as the paper says, many occupations. *One of them confessed they had forged tens of cards. He was not the only fool; it took many fools to enable justice to take its course. Oh, my grandfather, Abu Salih, you have failed me. Why did you not choose to live twice, once tending an olive grove in Rama and once growing a vineyard at the foot of some Lebanese hill?*

Tear, tear up the newspaper and thrust your finger into the eyes of this "professor" through his dark glasses. But what use would it be tearing up the paper? You will never obliterate the reality of the fraud, or undo the fact that you paid two thousand in return for cardboard and that you acted in concert with counterfeiters and...

How did he fail to realize it? He felt a fire eating through him. Is it not possible that these men have revealed the names of their customers? How stupid! Did he still have any doubts that this would be the ultimate result? Otherwise, how are the authorities to collect the forged cards? Tricked or guilty of complicity? When he paid two thousand which ate up half his window he is tricked. But by the time the truth is put down in the investigation papers he will have consumed himself to the marrow of his bone, and the tale of his foolishness shall be smoke in his neighbors' cigarettes.

Tear it up, tear it up! It is beginning to eat into your flesh. Why do you put it back in your inside pocket? For all the two thousand that it cost, it is not worth more than this newspaper for which you paid only a quarter. Tear it up. Your window will be full one day, and your existence will remain empty until you fill it with something other than fraud and the work of counterfeiters.

Tear it up! Or do you perhaps want more proof? The press trades in lies sometimes, but it does not depict these lies in the form of five photographs of which two you know and will have the pleasure of meeting the others when you are confronted with them.

Are you too cowardly to tear it up even when it rests between your fingers? O tear it up, tear it up, for it is worth no more than the paper on which it is printed. But no, leave it in your inside pocket. Leave it, because tearing it up will hide nothing, obliterate nothing.

He sat down, then stood up. He again sat down and stood up, facing the shop like a blind bull. He turned to face the street. His confusion might be relieved by the rhythm of the life outside, content with its lot, dreaming in nothingness. The gas station emptying its fuel into the bellies of big, shining cars. The fruit seller wiping the dust off his apples and trying to make them as red as possible. The butcher thrusting his knife into the flesh of the dangling carcasses. And the barber working away on the surrendered head, a head that does not exude anxiety, like his own.

Going back into the shop, he turns to the torn newspaper, collects the pieces, makes them into a ball and throws them away. Then he turns his face again to the street, only to see that eternal basket dangling by a rope from the balcony of the second floor, just above the shop. The basket was foolishly dancing under the balcony, and the voice of the neighbor issued from above asking for something. She is forever asking for some item, remembering her shopping lists only in installments...

But this time he does not hear her. Let her shout as much as she likes. He will not sell anybody anything. But the voice does not despair and the basket does not give up. The woman extends her voice across the street, like a bridge, reaching for the boy in the garage opposite and shouting in her drawn-out accent: "Where are you, boy, tell the Palestinian to put a Cola bottle in the basket for me!"

Standing shaking behind the counter, the Palestinian felt the woman's voice pierce through his jacket and reach his inside pocket, reducing the card to shreds, tiny shreds crowding his pocket, without strength or freshness!

Translated by Nissim Rejwan

Kamala Das   *India, b. 1934*

Kamala Nair was born into an affluent joint family in southern Malabar and raised in Calcutta. The only daughter of six children of the respected Malayalam poet Balamani Amma (b. 1909) and the editor and literary critic V. M. Nair, Das nostalgically describes the summers she spent with her maternal grandparents in Nalapet House. The members of this Brahmin family were highly Westernized and at the same time committed to Gandhi's program. The daughter's education, mostly supervised by a stream of governesses and tutors, combined both modern subjects and schooling in traditional lore. At 15 Kamala married a relative of hers—K. Madhava Das, an employee of the Reserve Bank of Bombay—and embarked on a relationship that is described in her autobiography as one that was by turns brutal and indulgent. She gave birth to three sons and turned to writing when her husband developed an intense friendship with another man. A severe heart condition that came on in the 1970s has limited Das's productivity. She currently lives in Trivandrum.

Trilingual, Das generally writes short stories in Malayalam, under the pseudonym of Madhavikutty, and poetry in English; this dualism roughly reflects Das's sense of living in two different worlds and her self-division between two cultures. Das first came to notice as a poet in 1963, when she was awarded the PEN Asian Poetry Prize in Manila. Her first collection, *Summer in Calcutta* (1965), still considered by some to be her best, was followed by *The Descendants* (1967) and *The Old Playhouse* (1973); her collected poems, published in 1985, received the Sahitya Academy Award in 1985. Das had previously won the 1969 Kerala Sahitya Academy Award for her short-story collection *Thannapu* (Cold). With the publication of *Enthe Kathe* (*My Story*, 1975, also translated into fourteen other languages), written during Das's first bout with heart disease, Das explored another genre and gained still more notoriety by discussing her somewhat distant relationships with her famous parents and her extramarital affairs. The confessional element is equally strong in her poetry: although some critics have singled out her work for its urgency and candor, others have faulted it both for its lack of syntactic control and for the egotism which it displays. Despite her limitations, Das has been recognized as bringing a real power to English poetry; she is widely anthologized and has been the subject of numerous studies in English, including three full-length critical works. She continues to publish regularly in *Mathurbhumi* (Motherland), an important Malayalam newspaper; fiction and poetry by major writers and important new ones frequently appear in its weekly magazine. She brought out two collections of short stories in Malayalam, *Enthe Cheru Katha* (My Short Stories, Vol. I and Vol. II) in 1985. Her most recent poetry has dealt with the horror of the civil war in Sri Lanka.

MY GRANDMOTHER'S HOUSE

There is a house now far away where once
I received love. . . . That woman died,
The house withdrew into silence, snakes moved
Among books I was then too young
To read, and my blood turned cold like the
                                              moon.
How often I think of going
There, to peer through blind eyes of windows
                                              or
Just listen to the frozen air,
Or in wild despair, pick an armful of
Darkness to bring it here to lie

Behind my bedroom door like a brooding
Dog. . .you cannot believe, darling,
Can you, that I lived in such a house and
Was proud, and loved. . .I who have lost
My way and beg now at strangers' doors to
Receive love, at least in small change?

AN INTRODUCTION

I don't know politics but I know the names
Of those in power, and can repeat them like
Days of week, or names of months, beginning
                                              with
Nehru.* I am Indian, very brown, born in
Malabar, I speak three languages, write in
Two, dream in one. Don't write in English,
                                         they said,
English is not your mother-tongue. Why not
                                         leave
Me alone, critics, friends, visiting cousins,
Every one of you? Why not let me speak in
Any language I like? The language I speak
Becomes mine, its distortions, its queernesses
All mine, mine alone. It is half English, half
Indian, funny perhaps, but it is honest,
It is as human as I am human, don't
You see? It voices my joys, my longings, my

(continued)

Hopes, and it is useful to me as cawing
Is to crows or roaring to the lions, it
Is human speech, the speech of the mind that is
Here and not there, a mind that sees and hears
                                                    and
Is aware. Not the deaf, blind speech
of trees in storm or of monsoon clouds or of
                                            rain or the
Incoherent mutterings of the blazing
Funeral pyre. I was child, and later they
Told me I grew, for I became tall, my limbs
Swelled and one or two places sprouted hair.
                                                    When
I asked for love, not knowing what else to ask
For, he drew a youth of sixteen into the
Bedroom and closed the door. He did not beat
                                                    me
But my sad woman-body felt so beaten.
The weight of my breasts and womb crushed
                                            me. I shrank
Pitifully. Then . . . I wore a shirt and my
Brother's trousers, cut my hair short and
                                            ignored
My womanliness. Dress in sarees, be girl,
Be wife, they said. Be embroiderer, be cook,
Be a quarreller with servants. Fit in. Oh,
Belong, cried the categorizers, Don't sit
On walls or peep in through our lace-draped
                                            windows.

Be Amy, or be Kamala. Or, better
Still, be Madhavikutty. It is time to
Choose a name, a role. Don't play pretending
                                            games.
Don't play at schizophrenia or be a
Nympho. Don't cry embarassingly loud when
Jilted in love . . . I met a man, loved him. Call
Him not by any name, he is every man
Who wants a woman, just as I am every
Woman who seeks love. In him . . . the hungry
                                            haste
Of rivers, in me . . . the oceans' tireless
Waiting. Who are you, I ask each and
                                            everyone,
The answer is, it is I. Anywhere and
Everywhere, I see the one who calls himself
I; in this world, he is tightly packed like the
Sword in its sheath. It is I who drink lonely
Drinks at twelve, midnight, in hotels of strange
                                            towns,
It is I who laugh, it is I who make love
And then, feel shame, it is I who lie dying
With a rattle in my throat. I am sinner,
I am saint. I am the beloved and the
Betrayed. I have no joys which are not yours,
                                            no
Aches which are not yours. I too call myself I.

NOTE

* Jawaharlal Nehru (1889–1964), first prime minister of
  India (1947–1964).

Diane Di Prima   *US, b. 1934*

Born in Brooklyn into an Italian working-class family, Di Prima attended Swarthmore College from 1951 to 1953 before dropping out to become a writer. Her
subsequent life reads like a record of the shifting currents of America's fringe and
beat culture: early years spent in Greenwich Village coffeehouses connecting with
artists and writers; copublishing *Floating Bear*, a mimeographed monthly poetic journal,
with radical black activist LeRoi Jones (Amiri Baraka) in 1961; a bohemian lifestyle explicitly documented in prose and poetry; wild zeal for the communal life
recorded in works like *Dinners and Nightmare* (1961) dedicated to the author's
"pads & the people who shared them with me"; impermanent marriages, the first

to printer and publisher Alan S. Marlowe in 1962 (divorced 1969), the second to poet Grant Fisher in 1972 (divorced 1975); five children and a period of rural retreat in upstate New York; her 1968 move with family to San Francisco; increasing militancy, active war protest, and publication of *Revolutionary Letters* (1971) dedicated to Bob Dylan; lifelong work in the theater (she was one of the founders of the New York Poets Theater) and numerous experimental productions of her own scripts; continuing small-press publication of novels and poetry through the 1970s, culminating in *Selected Poems: 1956–1976* (1977), the pinnacle thus far of a breathlessly energetic career.

Yet Di Prima's poetry is difficult to classify. It reveals, on one hand, a quotidian modesty and longing for stability uncharacteristic of the Beat Movement to which it undoubtedly belongs. On the other hand, her freedom of form—the abandonment of capitalization, playful abbreviation, the use of "lingo," jive, occasional spatial experimentation on the page—seems more a signature than an experiment. Thus some have seen her as a "domestic" counter to her open-roading Beat contemporaries and others have criticized her work as occasionally mundane.

Yet Di Prima is a self-proclaimed anarchist and her later poems especially reflect a serious radical temper. In "April Fool Birthday Poem for Grandpa," dedicated to the man who introduced her to politics, Di Prima declares the need for revolution, "which is love spelled backwards." In a better, more original poem, "Minnesota Morning Ode" (included here), she invokes Giordano Bruno, a seventeenth-century Italian philosopher burned as a heretic for denouncing the state, and calls for construction of an ideal republic, a "City of the Sun," after the Utopia envisioned by Tommaso Companella (1568–1639), still another philosopher of the Italian Renaissance.

The notion of "transmuting" here suggests yet another of Di Prima's interests: mysticism. Frequent allusions in her poetry to Buddhism and alchemy (she adopted the former as her official religion and helped inspire a revival of the writings of Paracelsus* in the 1960s) seem an attempt to give her often commonplace materials a kind of magic weight. This perhaps explains her later development of a symbolic scheme that has encompassed both her political and her supernatural interests. Her most recent book, *Loba, Parts I–VIII* (1978), evokes a variety of classical myths and feminine deities in an exploration of sexual psychology. Loba, a she-wolf, is an image of both aggression and nurturing, "the archetypal foxfire of the star" and an emblem of the creative impulse. The poem marks an evolution in Di Prima's feminist consciousness and a symbolic transfiguring of a lifetime's passionate experience.

Critical interest in Di Prima has waned in recent years with the passing of the Beat Movement and the subsequent shift away from its fiery cultural activism. She currently lives in San Francisco, where she continues to teach and write.

Bill Mullen

NOTE

* Pseudonym of Philippus von Hohenheim (1473–1541), Swiss-born physician and philosopher whose mystical philosophies were rooted in alchemy and medieval cabalism.

FIRST SNOW, KERHONKSON

for Alan

This, then, is the gift the world has given me
(you have given me)
softly the snow
cupped in hollows
lying on the surface of the pond
matching my long white candles
which stand at the window
which will burn at dusk while the snow
fills up our valley
this hollow
no friend will wander down
no one arriving brown from Mexico
from the sunfields of California, bearing pot
they are scattered now, dead or silent
or blasted to madness
by the howling brightness of our once common
                                                       vision
and this gift of yours—
white silence filling the contours of my life.

AMERICAN INDIAN ART:
FORM AND TRADITION

Were we not fine
were we not all fine
in our buckskin coats, the quillwork, the
buttons & beads?
Were we not fine
were we not all fine

O they have hung our
empty shirts in their cold
marble halls. They have
labeled our baskets, lighted
our masks, disassembled our pipes
in glass cases.
                    (We flashed in those colors
thru the dark woods over the dun plains
in the harsh desert)
                    Where
do they hang our breath? our
bright glance, where is our song now
our sorrow?
(Walker Art Center Minneapolis)

IN MEMORY OF
MY FIRST CHAPATIS*

If we had dope for an excuse, or love,
something bumpier, with ups and downs
(like the chapatis, puffing & going stiff—
I probably overcooked them) to account for
your incessant displeasures.

You stalk around the house, brandishing T-
                                                       squares
you dream of drowning the children
you tell me nine days of the week that you are
                                                       leaving
but you're still here. I can tell by the lump in
                                          my stomach
my unreasonable desire to sleep all the time
so as not to hear you starting the Volkswagen
                                                       Bus
as if it were a Mercedes, zooming out of the
                                                       driveway
The women of the rest of the world have so
                                          much to teach me!
Them in their saris so cool, kneading chapatis
or tortillas, depending on where, kneeling by
                                                       their fires
or by their hibachis, or standing by their wood
                                                       stoves
the women of the rest of the world plait their
                                          hair as I do
but they have more patience, they have put up
                                          a screen
behind which they only dimly discern their
                                                       menfolk
bursting the air with perennial desperations.

NOTE

* Flat fried Indian whole-wheat bread.

MINNESOTA MORNING ODE

for Giordano Bruno

The City of the Sun is coming! I hear it! I smell
                                                it!
here, where they have made even the earth a
                                            jailor
where not even the shadows of animals sneak
                                    over the land
where children are injured & taught to
                            apologize for their scars
the City of the Sun cannot be far now—
(that's what you said then, brother, waiting in
                                            prison
eight years to be burned, to find the sun at last
on the Campo de Fiori—FIELD OF
                            FLOWERS—yes)
how could it be far?
isn't evil at its peak?
(you asked 300 years ago) has not
the descent into matter reached a nadir? &
                                            here
5000 miles later, Northern Minnesota
a forest once, now wasteland
where they mow grass, rake leaves:

I vomit lies like the rest, not knowing
whom to trust, here where betrayal is taught as
                                            virtue
I weep alone for the words I would like to say
& silently put the faces of the old gods
into the hands of the children; hope they
                                recognize them
here in this Christian place, where Christ the
                                            Magus
& Christ the Healer are both forgotten, where
                                        the veil
of the temple is rent, but no resurrection
                                follows...

THE CITY OF THE SUN comes soon, cannot
                                        be far
yet, you are right—what is a millenium
or two to us, brother? The gods can wait
they are strong, they rise—the golden tower
flashing the light of planets, the speaking
                                            statues
that guard its four gates, the holy wind
that carries the spirit of heaven down thru the
                                            stars

it is here! it is here!
I will build it
on this spot. I will build it at Attica[1]
& Wounded Knee[2]
on the Campo de Fiori, at the Vatican:

the strong, bright light of flesh which is the
                                            link
the laughter, which transmutes
(**Minnesota Home School**
Sauk Centre)

NOTES

1. Attica Prison in upstate New York, site of protest in
   1971 by its largely black population against overcrowded and otherwise inhuman conditions; it became
   a symbol of society's betrayal of the poor and of the
   black minority specifically.
2. In 1890, the site in southwestern South Dakota of the
   last major battle of the Indian Wars, in which Amer-
   Indians attempted to retain their rights to the land;
   white troops killed 200 men, women, and children. In
   the Native American movement of the 1960s, Wounded Knee became a rallying cry to oppose oppression.

Malak 'Abd al-Aziz

Egypt, b. ca. 1935

The Egyptian poet Malak 'Abd al-Aziz has produced a number of poetry collections, beginning in 1952 with *Aghānī al-Siba* (Songs of Youth). She apparently did not publish again until 1966, when *Qāla al-Masā'* (The Night Narrated) appeared. Other volumes include *Bahr al-Samt* (Sea of Silence, 1969); *Ann Almisa Qalb al-Ashyā'* (That I Touch the Heart of Things, 1974), from which the following selections are taken; and *Ughniyāt lī-l-Layl* (Songs for the Night, 1978). The writer has also reviewed and critiqued her contemporaries in various Arabic literary magazines.

WE ASKED...
Wa-tasa'alna

We asked...
Keep the pearls in the shells
They should stay at the bottom of the sea,
                                                waiting
Hopefully one day the tide will come
Pulling them from the depths of the sea floor
Casting them upon the shores.
A sunbeam will embrace them,
Penetrating warmly, lingering
In the heart of the oyster...

The light glistens
Pierces the silence and the secrets
The white pearls tremble
Under the sun, they quiver
And it shines on their faces
With the fuel of love, it emanates...

Let the pearls wait for the tide
Until it comes...
Waiting

And we ask
Let the pearls remain in the shells
Did you promise the waves would come?
And wouldn't overflow except on Our shores...
And didn't dispense to lands other than ours...
The only thing it longed for was to embrace
                                                our sand
Thirstily...
Dissolving into it...
Watering it...
Give and take?
We asked...

Translated by Pamela Vittorio

THE FALL
Saqūt

When we entered the bazaars
We saw the veils of rose, of green...
And heard the prattle of the parrots,
Babbling every place.
The same empty words,
Smeared with oil and sweets
So that the artificial taste was concealed
and we proceeded with attentiveness.

At times, I had to dress for the circus,
                                                masked...
We'd stride above the tightrope—alone
And twist over the raised poles
We change colors like a banded chameleon
Which we overcame—and fell upon the truth
Like the sharpened edge of a sword
And we tumbled from above the tightrope,

From the highness of the top, the vertical
                                                height...
Our platform raises, grows higher, higher
Rises higher and rises above the tentpoles, it
                                                springs
And with the touch of a hand
We bared the veils—we unveiled the secret,
And we stood still in the nakedness of the birth
                                                of purity and innocence...
We gleam, we radiate—beneath the sun
in the nakedness of truth.

Translated by Pamela Vittorio

(opposite) Chiao Tsai-yun, Feeding the Ducks, ca. 1960, woodblock print. Courtesy Foreign Languages Press, Bejing

Inger Christensen

Denmark, b. 1935

Inger Christensen was born in 1935 and grew up in a working-class district of a small provincial city in Denmark. Her father was a tailor. She worked as a grade-school teacher before becoming a writer.

Christensen's poetry debut came in 1962 with the collection called *Lys* (Light,) from which "Hvad er min døde sprukne krop" (What Is My Dead Cracked Body) and "Sorg" (Sorrow) were taken, followed by *Graes* (Grass) the next year. During the 1970s she was coeditor of a political-ecological magazine called *Vaekst, Kris, Utopi* (Growth, Crises, Utopia). Up to now, she has published three more books of poetry: the extremely influential *Det* (It, 1969) excerpted below; *Brev i April* (April Letter, 1979) and *Alfabet* (Alphabet, 1981). Apart from poetry, she has also published novels, plays, short stories, essays, and translations. She became a member of the Danish Academy in 1978.

Unlike many of her contemporaries, Christensen is not a confessional poet but rather a highly intellectual one, writing in the modernistic vein and using a simple, poignantly musical language set in a mathematical, logical structure, which has been influenced by Noam Chomsky's linguistic philosophy. Her prose writings include two novels, *Evighedsmaskinen* (The Eternity Machine, 1964) and *Azorno* (1967), as well as a collection of essays, *Del af Labyrinten* (Part of the Labyrinth, 1982), in which she affirms her view of the world and her own creativity.

Considered the foremost woman poet in Denmark today, Christensen shows a keen political awareness in her writing and much concern for the dangerous state of today's world. Although a number of her poems have been translated into English, English-language collections of her poetry have not yet been published.

Ingrid Claréus

WHAT IS MY DEAD CRACKED BODY
Hvad er min døde sprukne krop

What is my dead cracked body?
Ants in snow have nothing to do.
No, poetry, poetry, poetry is my body.
I write it here: what is my body?
And the ants move me, aimlessly,
away, word after word, away.

Translated by Nadia Christensen

SORROW
Sorg

Find the concise
expression for sorrow:
a black slug with slime
and reflex-mechanism
in meaningless order,
just in time the feeler is
out, just in time
pulled in again
and within the body
employed precisely
like an expectant siren
whose descending tone
descends, descends
down through the entire
organism.
O skin,
my outermost
radar screen

Translated by Nadia Christensen

from IT
Det

The Scene 6. connexities

First and foremost the world
means something to me
I take it there are others for whom the
world means something
First and foremost the world
means something to them
Anyone else could have written this
So it surprises me that others
experience something similar
that the constructions put on the world here
others put on the world here and there
in a similar way,
that from the manifold meanings
one very simple ambiguity appears
that even the world is the same
Even the world that has no secrets
before I interfere
Even the world that has no truth
before I interfere
Even the world that finds itself in me
as the stuff we share with each other
the world itself is the same
same old stuff
we share with one another;
in itself of itself for itself
without significance
but out of itself
e.g., here where I act
as one who writes about the world
e.g., here and there where someone or other acts
as one who reads about the world
here and there and everywhere the world is
different and more than it is
like a meaningful interaction.

Translated by Sheila La Farge

Gülten Dayioğlu   *Turkey, b. 1935*

Gülten Dayioğlu was born in 1935 in a village in the province of Kütahya, in western Anatolia, Turkey. Because her father was a government employee, she moved frequently and studied in various parts of Anatolia before graduating from Atatürk Girls' High School in Istanbul. She entered the Faculty of Law of Istanbul University, but chose to take the examination for primary-school teachers before graduating. She taught primary school for fifteen years, until 1977. She now devotes herself full time to writing stories and novels, primarily though not exclusively for young adults. It is for this reason that Dayioğlu is not generally listed among the major Turkish writers. Most recently she has been writing science fiction and is one of very few Turkish writers to embrace this genre. She lives in Istanbul with her husband, who is a lawyer, and youngest son. An older son is also a lawyer.

Her first published collection of stories for adults, in 1970, was entitled *Döl* (The Offspring), the title story of which had won second prize in the Yunus Nadi short story contest of *Cumhuriyet* newspaper for 1964–1965. A second collection, *Geride Kalanlar* (Those Left Behind), was published in 1975 and reissued in 1985. One of the stories in it was adapted for Turkish National Television. The story here, "Yemi Gür Gelen Esekler" ("Like Donkeys Who've Had a Good Feed") is from this collection and is Dayioğlu's first work to appear in English translation. All the stories in this second collection are based on extended interviews carried out by Dayioğlu in her native village, to which she has returned on a regular basis and where she is still accepted as "one of them," despite her present definitely middle class status. Translated into Dutch, Slavic, Swedish, and German, the stories are all related to the question of what happened to the women left in the village when their husbands departed to seek work in Germany.

Regarded as the most successful of children's fiction writers in Turkey, Dayioğlu has produced an oeuvre that includes over thirty story booklets published between 1961 and 1966. Her best-known works are *Dört Kardestiler* (They Were Four Brothers and Sisters), a novel published in 1971 and now made into a ten-part radio play; *Leylek Karda Kaldi* (The Stork Under the Snow), a long story issued in book form by the Turkish Ministry of Culture in 1979 that with her story "Güzel Hanim" ("Pretty Lady") won first and second prizes in the Arkin Children's Literature Contest; and the science fiction works, *Dünya Çocuklarin Olsa* (The Sovereignty of Children, 1981) and *Isin Caği Insanlari* (Men of the Radioactive Era, 1984), the latter published in the prestigious Business Bank (*Is Bankasi*) cultural series.

Ellen Ervin

LIKE DONKEYS WHO'VE HAD A GOOD FEED
Yem Gür Gelen Esekler

The women were sitting around and chatting, at the pool in the public baths. Suddenly they were startled by laughter reverberating in the dome. Emis was driving the young married woman Ceren in front of her, chasing her toward the pool. They jumped into the water right behind each other, all out of breath. They got all tangled up in each other like a ball of wool. Then Ceren got away from Emis. In the pool the chase began again, while they laughed till they choked.

The other women looked at each other as if to ask, "What's going on?"

Granny Hasibe: "What do you think is happening? They're kicking up their heels like donkeys who've had a good feed."

The young woman and her sister-in-law came out of the water a while later, out of breath. Side by side they sat down at the edge of the pool. Their bodies were bright red. Sweat was coursing down their skin in streams. Emis was a tall, large-boned, darkly beautiful woman. Below the waist, she was covered, clothed in long undershorts made of American cloth; her top was bare. Her breasts were tiny for her build. Ceren, in contrast, was very small, with a peaches-and-cream, downy-fresh complexion.

Emis slapped Ceren on the shoulder, meaning "You've gotten away with it."

Ceren chuckled. The women all turned and stared at them, trying to figure out what was going on. One of them couldn't stand it any longer: "What's come over you, girl? Is your donkey having a circumcision party? How come you're bubbling over like a pot of bulghur? Let us in on it so we can laugh, too."

Emis: "This pig-headed Ceren, you know, she grabbed up my waist-cloth when we were getting undressed and just ran off with it. Look, here I am in the steam bath in my underpants. I told her I didn't have an extra pair of undershorts in my things but she didn't listen."

"Emis played this game on me first. Now I'm getting my revenge today," said Ceren, giggling flirtatiously.

Granny Hasibe was the oldest woman in the village. She didn't mince words with anyone. Ceren and Emis's behavior sank in. First she stared hard at both of them. She shook her head from side to side and muttered something under her breath. Then she couldn't stand it any longer and let fly with what she had been turning over in her mind: "What's all this wild stuff about? Anyone seeing you would think you owned the world. Your husbands have been working seven levels underground for years, digging in the mines. But that doesn't bother you in the slightest."

Emis pouted and shrugged her shoulders: "What are we supposed to do? You want us to mourn day and night because our husbands are in Germany?"

"No one's asking you to go into mourning! But this much wild excitement is unsuitable. In the old days back in the village when their husbands were doing their military service married women didn't have the right to open their eyes, even. Our elders would rake us over the coals and say 'a soldier's wife doesn't laugh, she doesn't dance at weddings, she doesn't wear new trousers or use henna.' And you're like soldiers' wives. You don't have husbands around to keep you in line. This much laughing and joking, getting all excited and whinnying never leads to any good. If your husbands hear about it they'll take it out on you."

Emis had begun to get angry: "What are we doing, I'd like to know. We haven't gone and fooled around with some strange men, after all! One or two goods laughs makes a person guilty? Our husbands went to Germany for us to be able to laugh, anyway. We get beautiful, long letters from both of them, telling us 'We're working for you, eat and buy clothes, and have a good time, don't worry about us."

While Emis was talking she nudged Ceren with her elbow every now and then, asking her, "Isn't that so, girl?" and Ceren seconded her sister-in-law with a "Uh huh."

Granny Hasibe's anger had risen. She tried another way to flatten Emis: "Hunh. Who knows what shit they're into, there. They're keeping you happy with a couple of pieces of velvet cloth, three bracelets, and a gold necklace or two."

Emis was determined to hear Granny Hasibe to the end: "Our men can do whatever they want up there. Whatever's left over is enough for me. A real man doesn't wear out! Anyway, we're not interested in velvet and gold necklaces and bracelets like the other young married women. We have other dreams in mind. We're going to move to town when our men get back. We've bought a piece of land there, each of us. Our homes are going to have a lot of rooms and all the rooms will have great big windows. We'll put up rows of shops at the bottom. Our men tell us in their letters, 'If we get fed up we'll move on to the city, what's to hold us back?' Do you understand, Granny? We're a thorn in your side and you're jealous of us, but we're not going to hang around here. We're going to clear out and get away from you all. Just stretch out your legs and sit back and relax."

Granny Hasibe realized she couldn't get the better of Emis. "May God give you what you deserve, girl," she said and put an end to the discussion.

The young women around the pool were bobbing up and down, keeping their eyes fixed on the water. Emis was taken aback by the silence. She wanted to bob up and down with somebody or other and get rid of her feelings. But no one was going along with her. Then a robust voice burst out into a folk song with a lively dance rhythm. Ceren joined her, clapping her hands to the beat. After the first verse of the song ended, Emis shouted, trembling

with rage, "Hey there, girls, why are you silent? Are you dead or something? Come on, let's all sing it."

Most of the young women had husbands abroad. They were all dispirited. They joined in the singing to accommodate Emis, but the melody came out of their mouths like sobs, and they sang a couple of phrases and kept silent for the rest of the time. Emis had no way of controlling the rage swelling up inside her: "Let's dance, come on," she said to Ceren. "These women are finished. They don't know how to do anything but stand around and sigh, their heads bowed, like orphans."

And so the young woman and her sister-in-law sang and danced around to their hearts' content. When Emis began to shake her bare shoulders and sway her hips in the belly dance, Granny Hasibe was too angry to sit still any longer. She got up and left the baths, grumbling and muttering as she went.

Emis and Ceren danced till they were tired out. Then they went over to the basin and soaped their hair. They rubbed themselves down with a loofa cloth, rinsed themselves off and, bundled up in their flowered towels, left the steam bath.

As soon as they had gone, the older women collected in a bunch and started in to gossip as hard as they could. "Well now, they're both going to move to the town," said Zehra, opening the door for talk. Then each of them, one after the other, brought their feelings out into the open.

"They've bought land in the town, both of them."

"Is it really true, though?"

"It's true. It's the custom, now. People who earn a few cents in Germany, they don't like the village any more. They set their sights on the town or the city. Haven't you heard? Why, from our village alone, lots of people have bought houses in the town. People from abroad are smart. Do you think they should just stay in the village and rot like linen on a dung heap?"

"Don't talk like that, dear, my man says when he came back and saw our daughter all bowed and bent over, his heart sank, it's like soldiers' wives in wartime national service, waiting years and years for their husbands, blood and bone marrow all dried up. He swears not to give our other daughters to boys going off to Germany. He says 'not for all the sweets in Damascus.'"

"Uncle Etem's right. What's the use of clothes and money, and bracelets, and a house and a plot of land. Ever since the doors of Germany swung open, the young married women of the village have turned into lice-ridden chickens. The life in them has all gone out, their eyes have no sparkle, their bodies are numb, their speech is thick; every so often they say 'we're sick' and they don't say anything else. The money their husbands send goes to pay the doctors...."

"The other day our Husnu wrote his father. Let's buy a house or a piece of land in town, he said."

"Oh well, it was bound to happen. Go on and leave the village, you too!"

"Everyone who sees the foreigner's money, one by one they'll all go off and desert the village, that's obvious."

"I wouldn't leave my village for anything in the world. I don't care if they give me my weight in gold, and mansions with all the furnishings, I can't break away from this place...."

While the conversations were going on, Granny Hasibe rushed into the steam bath in her clothes, all out of breath. She puckered up her face in disgust and began to speak. "Stones will rain down, stones!"

The women stood up, concerned. "What happened, Granny, why?"

"What more could happen after this? I wish my eyes had clouded over and I hadn't seen it. I hope to God I never see such a thing again, Emis and young Ceren are playing around. I was suspicious anyway but I just couldn't accept it...."

The women spoke out all together: "Come on, tell us. Who are they playing around with?"

Granny Hasibe quieted down her heavy breathing and shook her head slowly: "They're playing around with each other. In fact, Emis is in heat and she's using that bird-brained Ceren."

The women put their hands over their mouths and shrieked, "Aaah!"

Granny Hasibe: "I saw it with my own eyes. I was saying my prayers in the meadow behind the baths. Emis and Ceren came out of the baths. I didn't see them, themselves, but I recognized them by their voices. When I got up from my prayers, I meant to go back to the baths and get my things. But what should I see but the two of them, the girl and her sister-in-law, climbing down to the foot of the bath-house. 'What could they possibly be doing in the dirty water that comes out of the baths?' I thought. And the whole place is filthy down there, it gives you the creeps. 'They're up to something,' I said. My suspicions were gnawing at me. I crossed the wooden bridge right away and crossed to the other side to the slope facing the foot of the baths. I waded in through the poison hemlock, and walked along the stream downhill. When I saw them going into the hollow next to Dombay rock, my curiosity grew by leaps and bounds. I hid among the trees and began to watch from the other side."

"Soooo?" said the women.

"Suddenly, that horse-faced Emis jumped on top of Ceren. She knocked her down to the ground and started kissing her like mad...."

"What happened, what happened then?"

"Then both of them untied their strings and let down their trousers....I completely lost my head. I turned round and rushed back here."

The women spoke all together.

"Yaaa!" they sighed.

Then a short silence fell. Each person there started to evaluate what she had heard, for herself. Zehra broke the silence:

"Look, it had to happen. Two fresh young things without a man for years. Their husbands don't even take an honest to goodness home leave because they're trying to save money. Because of the heat in the steam bath, the women's bodies got all excited, that's obvious. They couldn't wait till they got home. Right next to the rock, they started in to put out their fires immediately. In any case at home what with the old men and old women they probably wouldn't be able to draw a comfortable breath."

Granny Hasibe attacked furiously:

"As for me, I don't know the ins and outs of it, they're sullied now, these women! The great river itself can't wash their sins clean. It's a sin for their men as well, that kind of thing. Their husbands mustn't sleep with them. They must divorce them, is the truth. Curses rain down on the ground such people walk on. Hurry up, let's leave right away and get to them before they've tied up their pants again. Let's all spit in their faces, one after another. . . ."

The women poured a bowl of water over themselves to get rid of the sweat, right away. Then they got dressed immediately and they all started out together on the path toward Dombay rock.

Translated by Ellen Ervin

Sarah Kirsch   *Germany/GDR/FRG, b. 1935*

Sarah Kirsch was born Ingrid Bernstein; her adoption of the name Sarah, the name required of Jewish women during the Third Reich, at her marriage to Rainer Kirsch in 1957 was a clear expression of her stance vis-à-vis Germany's recent past. Kirsch is a member of the "third generation" of East German authors and may be regarded in many ways as typical of that group. She comes from a working-class family (her father was a mechanic), worked for a time in a factory after completing high school, then went to the University at Halle to study biology. Her literary training, and the launching of her literary career, came under the auspices of the Johannes R. Becher Institute for Literature in Leipzig, where she studied from 1963 to 1965. A freelance writer following her completion of training there, she moved after her 1968 divorce to East Berlin but immigrated with a permanent visa to West Berlin in 1977, following the confrontation with East German functionaries due to her radical position in the "Biermann affair" of 1976.* In West Berlin she functioned for a while as the central figure in a group of East German authors and artists who found themselves in western exile following the renewed stringency of the Communist Party in the late 1970s. Kirsch now lives on the Baltic Coast in West Germany and has more or less isolated herself from society.

Kirsch's writings consist in the main of poems, most recently in *La Pagerie* (the name of the estate in France where the poems were written, 1980), of prose poems. *Drachensteigen* (Kite-flying, 1979) was published in West Germany after her emigration and contains work written in East Germany, West Germany, and Italy, including the poignant first poem written after her resettlement in West Berlin, "Der Rest des Fadens" (The Rest of the String). She also wrote and/or edited an important documentary work, *Die Pantherfrau* (The Panther Woman, 1973), a series of tape-recorded protocols in which five East German women report on their lives. It is for her poems, however, that Kirsch has received the highest recognition, including several literary honors, most recently the Austrian Prize for European Literature (1980), the West German Critics' Prize (1982), and the Friedrich Hölderlin Prize (1984). She is also a member of the P.E.N. Club of the Federal Republic of Germany (West Germany).

The tone and theme of many of Kirsch's poems are perhaps best summarized in these lines from one of them: "I knew only myself, and that was too little. Sat there/with me on the bench I in the middle I to the right/and to the left as well..." The dominant attitude of her poetry is one of disappointment and disillusionment bordering on despair. Even her love poetry—as suggested from the first example of her work here—recognizes the fundamental human condition as one of loneliness and isolation and thus combines grief with brief moments of happiness. In "For Droste I Would Gladly Hold a Candle" (published in *Zauber-sprüche* [*Conjurations*, 1973]), she acknowledges, as she does so often elsewhere, her relationship to a precursor (in this case, the early nineteenth-century Romantic poet Annette von Droste-Hülshoff).

Marilyn Sibley Fries

NOTE

* Wolf Biermann (b. 1936), a popular and controversial East German singer and composer of satirical songs and ballads that were often critical of GDR policies, was refused permission to re-enter his country in November, 1976 after a concert tour in West Germany. In immediate protest against their government's action, thirteen of the GDR's leading intellectuals (including Sarah Kirsch and Christa Wolf) formulated and signed a petition which they sent as an open letter to the Central Committee of the Socialist Unity Party and to major newspapers and wire services, both east and west. The protest burgeoned when more than one hundred and fifty individuals (mostly artists and writers) signed the letter or wrote their own statements. The government's retribution was quick; more than half of the thirteen signers were in the Party and have been subsequently expelled or reprimanded. Kirsch, Wolf, and others were censored by the League of Writers, then removed from its leadership.

THEN WE SHALL HAVE NO NEED FOR FIRE
Dann werden wir kein Feuer brauchen

Then we shall have no need of fire
earth will be full of heat
woodland must steam, the oceans
crack—clouds the milky beasts
crowd close: a mammoth tree

The sun is pale in all that shine
the air palpable I hold it close
a high-pitched wind
works at my eyes I do not weep

We amble naked through
apartments doorless shadowless
alone since nobody follows us no one
rest fails: the dogs
are dumb walk unresisting
at my side: their swollen tongues
make no sound are numb

Only heaven about us and foaming rain
cold will never be again, the stones
the leathern flowers our bodies like silk in
                                                    between
radiate heat brightness
is in us we are silver fleshed

Tomorrow you will be with me in paradise

Translated by E. Castendyk Briefs

FOR DROSTE I WOULD GLADLY HOLD A CANDLE
Der Droste würde ich gern Wasser reichen

(for Helga)

For Droste I would gladly hold a candle
Look into old mirrors with her, name
The birds, we direct our eye-glasses
To fields and elder bushes, walk
Sloshingly over the moor, the lapwing calls
Ah, I would say, your Lewin—
Isn't that a horse snorting?

The curl somewhat lighter—and we walk
The gravel path, I the late-born
Would have obliged with scandals—at the
                                    spinet

That stands preciously in the hallway
We play four-handed cavalry songs or
The forbidden ones by Villon
The moon rises—we are alone

The gardner shows us casting
Until Lewin arrives in his carriage
Gives us newspaper proofs, brandies
We pour down our throats, read
Both of us love the bold one, his eyes
Are like green shade-pools, we agree
Thoroughly now on the art of fishing

Translated by Wayne Kvam

Helga M. Novak   *Germany/GDR/FRG, b. 1935*

Helga Novak was born in Berlin, grew up during World War II, and studied journalism and philosophy in the mid-1950s before she followed the path taken by so many of her compatriots in the G.D.R. and went to work—in factories, laboratories, and bookstores. She married an Icelander, with whom she had two children, and lived and worked in Iceland from 1961 to 1965. After traveling in France, Spain, and America, she returned to East Germany to study at the Johannes R. Becher Institute for Literature. She was denied East German citizenship in 1966 and returned to Iceland for a time. She now lives in West Berlin.

Although highly respected for her writings (she won the prestigious Bremen Prize for Literature in 1968), Novak is an outsider in both Germanies—in East Germany because she took socialism at its word and criticized it for not being true to its own demands by pointing to contradictions and refusing to accept power and oppression as necessary manifestations of adjustment in socialist development; in West Germany because her poetic voice and style do not correspond to those of any of her contemporaries there. Her early poems, in which she deals with the victims of Stalinism, a forbidden topic in the G.D.R., were first distributed in the East German underground press and finally published in 1965 in West Germany as *Die Ballade von der reisenden Anna* (The Ballad of Traveling Anna). In subsequent volumes (some four of poetry and two of stories, plus collections of documentary reports, "texts on emancipation," and autobiographical writings) she has continued to deal with victims of oppression, using a narrative style and employing political themes. Most recently she has published prose works: an autobiographical novel, *Die Eisheiligen* (Saints of Ice) in 1979, and *Palisaden* (Palisades), stories and prose, in 1980. Her critical scope has broadened with the years, so that her victimized heroes come to be seen in a social context greater than that of the Marxist society in which she began writing. She is increasingly concerned with loss of individual language brought about by our "society of uniforms," a condition which she views not as an existential problem but as the condition of the underprivileged, of those who live "at the edge." Perhaps her most important work to date is the 1978 poetry volume entitled *Margarete mit dem Schrank* (Margaret with the Closet).

Marilyn Sibley Fries

MAIN POST OFFICE
Hauptpost

It is forenoon. In the main post office there is much activity. I am standing in the lobby. To the right are the telephone booths, to the left the windows. A long, flat counter stretches along the back wall of the lobby. On the counter sit seven or eight typewriters next to one another. They are fastened to the wall with chains. They are available to the public.

Phrases filter from the telephone booths. I catch phrases: We don't exchange artificial limbs, and, You never *can* be reached, and, All full of pimply pimples, and, Well, where do you want to go.

The crowd is rushed for time. The sounds in the main post office swell up, ebb away.

I sit down on a stool in front of a typewriter and write a letter.

I write: I think of you constantly. If you don't come, I am lost.

Behind me two ladies are talking.

I write: It doesn't matter what others are saying, I think you're wonderful, everything about you.

The ladies are talking too loud for me. On my left a man is filling out an information blank. He is typing. He bangs at it.

I write: I like the way you roll your *r*, I could listen to you for hours just because I can't pronounce an *r*.

There are shouts, name-calling, arguments in the lobby. The ladies behind me laugh. The man next to me is reciting his curriculum vitae.

I write: I feel warm flashes up my back, and I get a stomach-ache when I think that we will see one another soon.

The ladies behind me seem to be discussing an acquaintance. They are saying mean things about a third person.

The one lady says: Not a shameful bone in her body.

The other lady says: That's just the way I imagine a slut.

They are bothering me. I pull myself together. I write: First we'll go eat and drink something, and then quick to bed, huh?

One lady says: A real floozy.

The other lady says: We ought to report her.

I turn around and say: Can't you knock your colleague someplace else? The ladies let loose a salvo of laughter. They hold their sides.

I write: You musn't tell anybody what we do. If it's told, then it's over.

There's a tug on my sleeve. Without looking up I say: Pardon me, can't you use another machine?

I write: I would like to go mushroom or amber hunting with you, or feed silver paper to zoo animals, or break display windows full of artificial limbs because they can't be exchanged, or greet blind people on the street just to see...

The ladies behind me have changed the subject. They cry: Yuchhh, and, How mean.

I write: When you come, I'll make myself pretty, too, so pretty that you'll fall over, and I can love you all night long.

Someone hits me on the shoulder. I say: Just a moment, I'll be through in a minute.

One lady says: And all of that in public.

The other lady says: An outright whore.

I write: You, my dearest of dears, I kiss you just all over.

I get a slap on the ear, and another. I am kicked out of the main post office. My hat, my coat are covered with bits of paper. I brush myself off.

Translated by A. Leslie Willson

UNMASKED
demaskiert

when he took off the mask he stopped up the
mouth and eyes
and gathered berries in the papier-mâché shell
o don't throw up your hands in dismay
when the sweetness rises in his face

when he removed his disguise he shut the door
he hung the things in front of the window and
around the light
o don't throw up your hands in dismay
when he begins to dance after the ball

Translated by A. Leslie Willson

GONE OUT
ausgegangen

when I looked for my key today
when I found it in my full purse
the door seemed nailed shut to me
and I did not dare to open it

I broke out the window
I climbed in the window
and patched up the hole
with fresh newspapers

when I looked for a chair
when I had taken off my things
the chair seemed to me to have just three legs
and I did not dare to sit down

I am lying on the floor
and for the first time I see the ceiling sagging
go on and call   knock
even if you climb onto my roof

I am no longer at home

Translated by A. Leslie Willson

Tomioka Taeko   *Japan, b. 1935*

Tomioka Taeko is one of the most multitalented writers active on the Japanese contemporary literary scene, and her excellence has been recognized with a number of literary prizes. She began her literary career as a poet with the collection *Henrei* (Returned Salutation), published in 1957 at her own expense while she was still a student in the English Literature department of Osaka Women's College. This collection won the 1958 Mr. H poetry prize. In 1960 her third volume of poetry, *Monogatari no akuru hi* (The Day After the Tale), won the second Murō Saisei Prize. A first edition of her collected poetry was published in 1967. The cool dryness of her poetic style carried over into her prose when she began writing fiction in the late 1960s. "Ibara no moeru oto" (The Sound of Burning Brambles), a story in her first fiction collection, *Oka ni mukatte hito wa narabu* (Facing the Hills They Stand) was a runner-up for the 1971 Akutagawa Prize, as was "Shikake no aru seibutsu" (Still Life with Working Parts) the following year. Her first novel, *Shokubutsusai* (Plant Festival, 1973), won the fourteenth Tamura Toshiko Prize. The next year, the four-part, semiautobiographical *Meido no kazoku* (Family in Hell) won the 1974 Women's Literature Prize. *Tachikire* (Break-Off) has won the Kawabata Yasunari Prize.

Tomioka has also written extensively as a literary and cultural critic, beginning with the 1968 *Nihon/Nihonjin* (Japan and the Japanese). Related works are

Kōi to geijutsu (Action and Art, 1970); *Watashi no onna kakumei* (My Female Revolution, 1972); *Kotoba no fukō* (The Misfortunes of Language, 1976); and *Shashin no jidai* (The Era of the Photograph, 1979). Other artistic efforts include collaborating with film director Shinoda Masahiro (ex-husband of poet Shiraishi Kazuko) to write the scenario for the film *Shinjū ten no Amijima* (Double Suicide) in 1969, a beautifully crafted modern evocation of the eighteenth-century *bunraku* (puppet play) of the same title; an autobiography, *Seishun zetsubō ondō* (The Despair-of-Youth Rag, 1970); and her first play, *Kekkon kinenbi* (Wedding Anniversary), written and staged in 1973. She has also continued to produce fiction with the novels *Sunadokei no yō ni* (Like Sand in an Hourglass, 1981), *Nami-utsu tochi* (Wave-struck Land, 1983), and *Suijū* (Water Beast, 1985) and the novella and short-story collections *Sūku* (Straw Dog, 1980) and *Tōi sora* (Distant Skies, 1982). Her most recent publication is a joint-authored account of a trip to Europe she took with the female novelist Kōno Taeko, *Arashigaoka futari tabi* (Two to Wuthering Heights,* 1986). Similarly, New York City provides the setting for a number of novellas and poems, commemorating a stay there in the 1960s.

Tomioka's style is characterized by a laconic, sardonic reserve that contains a world of passion, irrationality, even madness. Sexuality—especially in unconventional or asocial forms (see the double-layered incest of *Plant Festival* for example)—is frequently the metaphor she chooses to play out the tensions of power relationships and the bizarreness of human interaction. Her dialogues often draw on the dialect of her native Osaka, though we are also meant to be aware of the techniques that derive from Modernists T. S. Eliot and Gertrude Stein, the latter of whose *Three Lives* Tomioka translated in 1969.

The selections are all from *Onna tomadachi* (Girl Friend, 1964).

Phyllis I. Lyons

NOTE

* The title, taken from Emily Brontë's novel, alludes to Yorkshire, the setting of the book and home of the Brontë family.

STILL LIFE
Seibutsu

Your story is finished.
By the way, today,
what did you have for a snack?
Yesterday your mother said,
I wish I was dead.
You took her hand,
went out, walked around,
viewed a river the color of sand,
viewed a landscape with a river in it.

They call the window the tree of tears in
                                                    France,
said Bonnard's* woman once.
Yesterday you said,
Mom, when did you give birth to me?
Your mother said,
I never gave birth to any living thing.

Translated by Hiroaki Sato

NOTE

* Emile Bonnard (1867–1947), painter, one of whose works is included in this anthology.

GIRLFRIEND
Onna tomodachi

My neighbor
The kept woman recites a sutra[1]
A little past noon
I saw an animal like a donkey
Pass below the window
I saw it through the opening in the curtains
Always through the opening in the curtains
A woman comes to see me
But today she hasn't come yet
Wearing a georgette Annamese dress[2]
The line of her hip attractive to men
She promised to come
Today she hasn't come yet
Today she may have died
The other day
When I traveled with her
At a country antique shop
She wanted an old wood engraving
From Germany or some such place
At a country inn
For the first time with my fingers
I could mess up
The mass of her hair
Like Brigitte Bardot's[3]
We danced
For a long time
Scarlet cheek to cheek
We danced a Viennese waltz
Her transparency
Her optimistic poesy
Occasionally spills like beads of sweat
Which I'd like to mistake for tears
She does not come today
Like my neighbor the kept woman
From midday
I pray aloud
She did not promise
Not to come
You are gone
You who are gone

Translated by Hiroaki Sato

NOTES

1. Treatises relating to the Buddhist tradition.
2. Dress of thin, crinkled cotton of Vietnamese origin.
3. French film actress and sex symbol of the 1960s.

WHO'S AFRAID OF T. S. ELIOT

whether the woman in the next room
has got it over with
without mishap
that's what you are anxious about
the old man said and rose to his feet
all I did was always
just chime in
I didn't want to get involved
I said congratulations
always to everyone
from time to time
I brushed off my shoulders
the many birds perched there
I simply had no grudge
that it would be over
the old man and I cooked and ate
chicken and chrysanthemum greens
the old man sweated
and opened the front of his shirt
Tiresias*

Translated by Hiroaki Sato

NOTE

* In Greek legend, the blind seer. He was given the gift of prophecy by Zeus after Hera had blinded him for his special insight into female sexuality, itself the result of the punishment of having been transformed into a woman.

Monique Wittig   *France/US, b. 1935*

Born in the Haut-Rhin region of France, Monique Wittig moved to Paris, where she studied and worked in publishing. In 1986, under the direction of the theorist Gérard Genette, Wittig completed her dissertation in the social sciences on *le chanteur littéraire* (the literary singer). Radicalized by the events of the 1960s and part of the intellectual and political ferment then disrupting French society, Wittig became a leader in the women's liberation movement that followed. In August 1970, she and Christiane Rochefort, among others, took the historic and more than symbolic action of placing a wreath on the tomb of the unknown soldier in Paris: it was inscribed to the unknown wife of the soldier. In October of the same year, Wittig participated in the founding of the *feministes révolutionnaires* dedicated to the total destruction of the partiarchal order.

Wittig was already something of a celebrity, having published *l'Opoponax* (1964) and *les Guérillères* (1969) with the prestigious house of Editions de Minuit, having been awarded the Prix Medicis and won the critical praise of establishment writers Claude Simon, Alain Robbe-Grillet, and Nathalie Sarraute for her first novel, and having been damned and lauded by numerous critics for her second, indubitably the manifesto for radical feminism and one of the most brilliant works to come out of the women's movement. *Le Corps lesbien* (*The Lesbian Body*, 1969) and *Brouillon pour un dictionnaire des amantes* (literally, Rough Draft for a Dictionary by Lesbians; coauthored with Sande Zeig in 1975 and translated as *Lesbian Peoples: Material for a Dictionary* in 1976) followed, asserting and defining a self-conscious women's writing and lesbian politics-poetics. In 1977, Wittig became part of the radical feminist editorial collective *Questions féministes*, launched under the editorship of Simone de Beauvoir. But by then she had already resettled in northern California and had begun teaching and publishing in English.

Short-story writer, novelist (most recently of *Virgile, non,* 1985), and translator (of the radical philosopher and critic Herbert Marcuse, the Portuguese "Three Marias," and of Djuna Barnes), Wittig has lately turned to drama—*The Constant Journey* was produced in 1984—and increasingly to criticism to frame a "lesbian poetics," the philosophical and theoretical underpinnings of her literary practice and a world in which gender will be unrelated to power and knowledge. Her collected essays and the tentatively titled The Straight Mind: On Ideology and Language should make her ideas available to a wider American audience.

Of her literary achievement, one of her most important critics, Hélène Wenzel, has remarked that with each of her works she has successively appropriated the traditional genres of *bildungsroman*, epic, the "Song of Songs" of the Bible, and the dictionary for feminist-lesbian use. *L'Opoponax*, the earliest of Wittig's writings, from which a selection follows, incarnates "everybody's childhood"; it tells the collective story of girl children's growth and education, their resistance to traditional feminine socialization, their rejection of patriarchy as represented by the language of the Fathers in the Catholic tradition in which they receive their tutelage. Catherine Legrand is the protagonist who achieves her

identity—who says "I," that is—in the language of French feminism; she constitutes herself as the subject of discourse, after she has discovered her love for
another girl, Valerie Borge. She does this using a line from the poet Maurice
Scève's *La Délie*: "Tant je l'amais qu'en elle encore je vis"/I loved her so that in
her I still live. The title of the work is ambiguous: the name of a plant and a variety
of fetid and sweet-smelling resins from plants, it is used variously in the book to
suggest the child's love of language, language's ability to create the world, a
mischievous spirit creating havoc. Wittig herself has said that the "opoponax
appears as a talisman, a sesame to the opening of the world that compels both
words and world to make sense, as a metaphor for the lesbian subject."

In addition to the popularity and social significance of her works, Wittig has
won impressive recognition, including a series of grants from the French Ministry
of Culture and Ministry of Women's Rights. A special issue of *Vlasta* (Spring
1985) is but one scholarly testimony to the critical attention she has been given.

from THE OPOPONAX

You are walking through the tall grass repeating verses that you found in the text book to
yourself, *La nature t'attend dans un silence
austère l'herbe élève à tes pieds son nuage des
soirs.** The sun strikes the tops of the grasses at
an angle, you see its rays go through, the grass
is lighted from beneath, you can see the ocher
shadows or the spaces between the stalks, between the heads, sometimes even between the
sheaths that form them. There are blankets of
light along the ground. The grass and flowers
are getting damp as if water were rising. There
is a smell. Catherine Legrand doesn't know the
names of the weeds that you see caught in the
last light like this. Most of them are of in-
determinate species. You see some that are
long and tall, the elements that make up their
heads look braided, they are hard between
your teeth. Some are feathery like oats except
that the sheaths containing the grain are
smaller more widely spaced and more numerous. You see some that have downy tufts.
Others are pink. There is plain grass. There
are grains that are completely flat, there are
compound umbels. When you run the grass
hits your bare legs. Catherine Legrand's lips
are bloody from the grasses she pulled up
while she ran without looking at them, their
edges are sharp, they have hairs a lighter green

than the rest on both sides, they are so small
that you have to hold the grass right in front
of your face to see them. Catherine Legrand
begins shouting her name with all her might.
You can hear Catherine Legrand, her voice
carries, you can hear it on the hills, people will
rise up and move, on the hills an army will be
on the march and will come toward the cry
which has been heard far and wide. Catherine
Legrand begins shouting other names, Mar-
guerite-Marie Le Monial Anne-Marie Brunet
Sophie Rieux drawing out the syllables modu-
lating them shouting the same name several
times. Catherine Legrand begins shouting the
names of pupils in her class. Several times
Catherine Legrand shouts the names of the
pupils in her class but she doesn't shout the
name of Valerie Borge. The people on the hills
have lain down again. Catherine Legrand
begins to run she jumps over the grasses so
they won't cut her legs. Somebody once told
Catherine Legrand that if she jumps above the
surface of the ground, that if she can just stay
in the air a certain length of time and if the
earth turns beneath her during this time, she
won't fall back in the same place. It's one way
to travel. Catherine Legrand jumps as high as
she can and tries to keep herself up with her
fists. Up there like that you are Gulliver or

Goliath but you fall back in the same place, maybe it's because the earth doesn't turn fast enough. Catherine Legrand walks normally again. The poppies are shapeless, some of them are still in the sun, there is a red haze around them, the daisies don't hold their heads the same way, some are crossways at different angles, some are vertical, the field is all white with them. The end of the field which Catherine Legrand is reaching is mowed. The grass which has been cut today is standing in green piles in which you can see flowers that haven't faded yet. Farther on there are piles of dry grass. You lie on the ground with your head resting on the pile of hay. Your cheeks are scraped by the edges of the grass, pricked by their stems which the scythe has cut off. The heads are dry but the bodies and branches are resting on the damp ground. You hear a dog bark. You don't hear a sound. The vegetation is motionless. The air is still warm. You see that the sky is empty of clouds except at the horizon where the sun is disappearing. Catherine Legrand is drunk from the smell of the grass, she rolls on the ground from one pile to another, she sinks her head into them and inhales. You don't see a house. The cows the heifers the bulls aren't in the fields, they are inside. You don't hear any mooing. Everything is motionless. The light is receding from the grass. A few patches of the field are still struck by it which makes the rest of the field around them look black. So Catherine Legrand gets up and begins to run toward the sun which looks enormous, which looks very close. Catherine Legrand runs through the field, she feels her heart beat, her heart is beating so hard in her chest that you can hear it, you can feel it knocking against your ribs, Catherine Legrand runs toward the sun, her heart rocks back and forth through her body, the blood beats at her temples, in front of her eyes, it's like a fog, the sun begins to beat, you can see the contractions of the blood beaten back, sucked in, passing across the sun, you hear the sun begin to beat harder than your heart on the horizon, back and forth, through Catherine Legrand's body, you hear it, the noise is so loud it explodes in your head, so loud that your heart and the sun explode that Catherine Legrand falls on the ground with her face in the grass. When Catherine Legrand turns over there is no more sun in the sky, her clothes are soaked from the grass or sweat, then a breeze comes up, you see the trees stir, you feel it in the clipped grass, you hear it.

Translated by Helen Weaver

NOTE

* Nature waits for you in austere silence the grass raises the cloud of evenings at your feet.

Assia Djebar   *Algeria/France, b. 1936*

In the city of Cherchell in West Algeria, in 1936, Fatima Zohra Imalayen was born into a traditional Bedouin family, her ancestral roots stemming from the Beni Menacer tribe. Her father, a well-educated man, supported the somewhat atypical education of his daughter, who first studied at the Qur'anic school, then attended the French primary school in Mousaiaville before obtaining her secondary diploma in Blida. In 1955, she became the first Algerian to pass the competitive examination for admission into the Secondary Teachers' Training College at Sèvres.

However, with the onset of the War of Liberation in Algeria (on November 14, 1954), Djebar and other students encountered various forms of discrimination and harassment by the French academy. National solidarity and the summer strike of Algerian students ensued. During this time, Djebar's younger brother was jailed for involvement in the underground, and teaching Djebar failed her examination.

Notwithstanding this academic failure, Djebar became a literary sensation overnight when the prestigious publishing house of Juillard hailed her as another Françoise Sagan and published her first novel *Le soif* (puns on the French words for thirst and mischief; translated as *The Mischief*, 1958), when she was only 20. Though variously criticized as indecent (for its concern with sex, love-making, and abortion) and for its indifference to the Algerian revolution then taking place, Djebar argued that the characters' preoccupation with their individual concerns was to be understood as the consequence of their "occidentalization." Her second novel, *Les impatients*, (The Impatient Ones), however, implicitly responded to this criticism by featuring two female characters who were meant to be "exemplary."

By the time the novel was published in 1958, Djebar had married and followed her husband to Tunisia, where he was a member of the underground. She obtained a diploma in history, began teaching at the University of Rabat, in Morocco's capital, and collaborated on the paper of the National Liberation, *El Moujahid* (The One Who Struggles). In 1962, the same year Algeria gained its independence from the French, she published *Les enfants du nouveau monde* (Children of the New World). Aptly titled, this novel, as critic Evelyne Accad suggests, is markedly different from Djebar's previous work in two ways: for the first time Djebar focuses on political events of the period and shows women whose rebellion is directed toward political goals. Developing some of the characters portrayed in *Les impatients*, she depicts women in the vanguard of the revolution, derived in part from her meeting women soldiers in the Tunisian camps and on the Algerian border.

In 1967 Djebar published *Les alouettes naïves* (Naive Skylarks), from which the selection here is taken, also set at the end of the Algerian war. The book uses a variety of montage and flashback techniques and is otherwise influenced by Lawrence Durrell's *Justine* in tracing the relationships of Omar, Rachid, Nfissa, and Julie as they attempt to reconstruct their lives in the aftermath of the military struggle. In the first section, the opening of the book, Omar's travel home affords a panoramic view of the Tunisian countryside, where he has found his childhood friend Rachid; the second section captures the seaside Tunisian resort where Nfissa and Rachid were wed; the last, the end of the book, shows Nfissa and Rachid, ravaged by their mutual affairs and only partly reconciled to one another.

These works marked the end of one phase of Djebar's career. Thereafter, Djebar turned to other forms, including cinema. In 1974, she returned to Algeria, subsequently divorcing her husband.

After marriage in 1980 to the well-known Algerian poet and writer Malek Alloula, Djebar resettled in Paris and returned to fiction. In *Les femmes d'Alger dans leur appartment* (Women of Algiers in Their Apartment, 1982), she shifted her focus from women in couple relationships to a broad range of contemporary women's experience, especially in women's relations to one another. This new emphasis is also present in her most recent work, *L'amour, la fantasia* (Love, Fantasy, 1985), the first novel in a projected trilogy, which presents a historical panorama of Algerian women from 1830 to the present.

Djebar represents one of the few attempts to penetrate "by fictional means the lives and problems of other women in her culture"; in occupying a moderate stance, she argues for a nonmonolithic view of Moslem women.

from NAIVE SKYLARKS
Les alouettes naïves[1]

It was a day like any other—the harsh sun beat down on our heads as we bumped along the frontier's gravel roads, traveling from sunrise to sunset in an old jeep. We stopped for two, maybe three hours at each refugee camp. My companions would do their work, take note of our needs, and talk with the medical orderly or person in charge. As for me, I was completely caught up in what I was seeing and would throw myself right into it. A furtive smile, a sick person's groan from under a tent, a glance: these are the simple images that remain with me. Then the jeep would start up, a difficult moment. We would raise our hands, whisper a goodbye, and with a jump of the car be off. Seated next to the driver, I finally looked at the war survivors. They were facing us, their backs turned to the horizon. "The frontiers," they calmly said, as if standing up like that against the sky, they were not at the edge of a crater, but were defending themselves against the future. This word resonated with conviction in the hollow biblical eyes of the old people and on the women's tanned faces, especially the old women, who complained in front of us that their supply of snuff was gone, that they couldn't pray with their throats dry for all those days, those days when there was no flour, when the distribution of rations was delayed. Why, they wanted to know. It was up to us to say why. And the young girls, timid Danaïdes[2] dressed by the International Red Cross, exhausted themselves by going to the other side of the hill to fetch water from the only well that wasn't completely dry.

We left a white trail behind us in the dust. From time to time, one of us would give an update of the latest news, announced the evening before by a Liberation Army officer at one of the camps where we had spent the night. He would begin absent-mindedly, knowing all too well that a discussion wouldn't get off the ground. It was too hot and, after six days on the road, we were all tired from the scorching heat before daybreak, the bad roads, and the jeep's rusted motor that broke down once or twice a day, obstinately demanding our attention. During these infernal engine failures, only Ramdane, the driver, seemed happy, whistling a tune from a popular waltz, a memory from the time when he used to go to the St. Stephen Saturday night dance, never suspecting the outbreak of war.

We were all completely fed up then, but no one would admit it. What would have been the use? There were camps to be visited, supply delays to be inventoried, new refugees to be counted and then T. to hurry back to. This time we decided that winter would not take us by surprise.

It was a day like any other, except that on the next day, our trip would be over. We were four men, a little darker and a little thinner, except for Ramdane, who, in addition to his constant cheerfulness, had managed to keep his cheeks round and rosy on top of his lanky body. He was thirty years old, as I was, but he looked ten years younger with his innocent eyes, his carefree air and his lackadaisical walk, which he exaggerated in such a way that he almost limped. We no longer drove on a trail but on a paved road, freshly tarred no doubt, since it looked almost blue under the late afternoon sun. We had arrived at the last camp a short while before. Compared to those we had visited down South, it seemed luxurious. In their flight, the families had managed to bring some of their livestock with them and had built huts out of branches and pounded earth. In the presence of these thatched cottages scattered among the greenness—clusters of broom and pink laurel—we forgot everything, the tents, the sun-scorched plains, the water shortage, and the broken people whom, just days before, we had met all over.

We were approaching our last stop, K., where just a week before, we had spent the night. Behind me the doctor had begun to talk.

He was trying to be scholarly or put on airs to appear so. He recalled K.'s history and, it should be noted, was a gifted storyteller. Listening to him, we forgot that we would have to sleep in that rundown medieval inn with mosquito- and bedbug-infested rooms, because the only hotel in town was closed. It was a ramshackle place, run by an old colonial supporter who had once been linked to a terrorist organization. He had since left but nevertheless refused to sell, a fact that caused the town's young people to gossip as they passed by the open shutters and whispered that the owner was planning to return with his old cohorts.

The doctor was telling how, during the last century, the French had established the little town. Ramdane had stopped whistling, but as soon as the storyteller was finished he began the flat little waltz again. As for me, I listened, but only from time to time and with half an ear. My back hurt, and I watched the little speck in the distance that was K. growing larger. I was anxious to get there, to walk around, to be alone....Suddenly, it occurred to me: young people, in other words, people who have grown insolent in their misery and hope, have no sense of humor.

I was beginning to be irritated by a dull sensation that I felt rising up within me, little by little, during all these days. It was there when I crossed the dusty roads, and as I watched that spectacle I always wanted to flee, each time inventing a new escape tactic—such as not looking at that mass of old people, immobile against the sky, but trying to grasp them, one by one, each in an illusory individuality. However, what they presented to witnesses like myself was their united being, their faith and immobility, an indissoluble chain against the perpetual horizon, a horizon that had not hidden the war. One of them took on the task of announcing their needs in a crude way: the list of those registered for provisions, the number of liters of oil received, or kilos of American surplus cheese, already fermented or spoiled, which, in spite of their

hunger, the women simply could not bring themselves to eat, since they had never tasted cheese except for that which came from their own goats, remembering in a moment yesterday's peace, their houses, homes that were now only ashes.

Yes, I recognized it, that elation that was inevitably crushed, yet each time reborn within me, as though I were still seventeen, outraged and burning with pride. Yesterday, confronted by refugees who had been waiting for three or four years, or this morning, in front of the Roman arch of triumph looming up nobly from the sand: in the face of these hordes and these ruins it would have been easy for me to fall back upon this adolescent romanticism in order to come up with a speech—to talk about the struggle, the upcoming victory, the suffering, and above all about God, as though I were still naive, and about how lucky we were to have been born during the period when our country was about to achieve its liberation. Yet I remained silent, or nearly so, during the entire trip. I even tried to dig up a convincing argument, some bitter flaw to use against myself, ourselves. We were in fact, humorless, yet that laughter, swallowed up somewhere by centuries of slavery and sleep, could resurface tarnished, who knows, maybe some day soon.

I broached this subject with Rachid, whom I had met that evening on a little street in K. In the basement of a dark cheap restaurant and then again that night in the dormitory that we shared with peasants in town for the next day's market, we whispered about our youth, interrupted by six years of war....

Since dawn the odor comes and goes, lingering in the air. The sun, over the course of the day burns through it, dispelling it until the evening. However, if a breeze starts up, the stench quickly becomes unbearable, sending the inhabitants of the neighborhoods nearby into their houses, despite the summer, or into the commercial center of town, near the Gates of Medina. When I come home after work, I often see the passers-by hunched over, their hands covering their mouths and noses. My street turns into a kind of hospital corridor—the people I meet are like patients, up out of bed to vomit. Only the veiled women, their faces protected by a piece of white or black lace, do not alter their step, gently moving their hips that are merely suggested beneath the silk fabric. Alone they glide into the dusk, translucent goddesses . . . .

I don't know why this particular detail comes back to me. Usually, there are so many things about T. that I love, things that struck me from the very start: the medieval-like poetry of its *souks*, the poverty and fragile beauty of its narrow streets, where Italianate flourishes are juxtaposed to the heaviness of Muslim wooden doors, with their patterns chiseled in copper. I love the cheerful carefree air of its inhabitants and also of its objects: a wrought iron window looks out on the square's chestnut trees, a wall inlaid with old ceramic, and further away, beneath a dusty stucco porch, a blind man who sings . . . . Groups of young girls are everywhere, coquettes with a dancing step; the fritter vendors sit cross-legged in front of their fires; jasmine and flower merchants; a blue copper teapot, on top of its burner, left on the sidewalk for a street sweeper; the dark-faced doormen of the fashionable buildings in brown gandoura; here and there, a sigh, a muffled complaint . . . . Here the Orient seems young, a dawn is breaking, not at all as I had known it under other skies—miserable and decadent.

We form a city within the city, we who came from the center of the peninsula, far away, almost from the land where the sun sets. In groups or alone, we are all exiles, waiting and worrying, transplanted into this atmosphere of vice that seems to be the town's age-old heritage. There was a veil of gray sadness and, paradoxically, an enduring hope, entirely out of proportion, given the surroundings. We are destroying the harmony but reawakening the city. I know it. I believe it.

It was somewhere around the time of Rachid's arrival that, I must confess, I began to feel sickened by the lake's stench and began to talk about it. I live in a furnished studio, in one of the few sterile buildings that the owner—an eighty-year-old Jewish lunatic, soon to become my friend—prefers to rent to foreigners passing through, or in a "lasting provisional state" as my compatriots, most of whom are out of work, like to call it among themselves.

They talk about a provisional state. Actually, they are more like those living in the new neighborhoods trying to persuade themselves that the stagnant water will ultimately disappear. This, however, doesn't keep them from admiring the lagoon from behind the windows of the "treno" that takes them to the summer suburbs. That awful stench cursed entire days, and given the seasonal changes and the wind, it grew stronger and stronger, a presence that I sometimes find myself comparing to the war. Because the war is festering inside us and the many journalists—sympathetic to our cause or not, friends or simply observers—who pry combat memories from yesterday's heroes and humanitarian declarations from anonymous leaders, remind me of the flies that swarm around us, feeding off the immense corpse that we are all carrying around within us . . . .

Peace was imminent. Nfissa was preparing for the departure. Already estranged from T., she was ready to repudiate that city of exile and all its uncertainties. Yet she waited, still rooted in the marble house and the village on the water. She imagined how they would cross the frontier on foot, along with the returning hordes and how, taking their time, they would wander through fields of ruin and hope.

Without any reason, Rachid stopped going to the *Journal* and even stopped taking interest in the voyage. One morning, he opened a notebook, turned his back toward Nfissa, and began to write . . . . He thought that he could evoke the war; however, what he evoked was something else entirely.

Behind him, in the past, colors and sounds surfaced, several shadows, a nameless woman's moan, behind him, in the past....Somewhere it was necessary to find a connection....But with what? On the following days, he became further convinced that he had to revive a more distant past. Hammering away, he persisted.

"Why are you writing?" Nfissa finally asks, demanding to know, as though she were saying, "From now on I will never let you escape me, never again."

"Please," she will beg later, "let's sit on the doorstep. Let's do something, watch the others pass by. Let's," she exclaims suddenly, "become nomads again, I will work just like you! It doesn't matter to me as long as we're sleeping together every night, as long as I'm close to you all night and I'm not too tired to take pleasure in our sleep."

Without replying, he takes her in his arms. They lie down together in the bright daylight, yet when he wants to take her, Nfissa feels pierced, withdraws, and senses pain throughout her body....In tears, she pleads, "I want you so much, God knows, but answer my question if you want me to give myself to you."

Rachid was silent, and morning after morning he immersed himself in his new work. "Why? Why?" Nfissa continually harassed him, and Rachid wanted it from her, wanted her demands; yet every night, she continued to turn away from him. During the day, she knew how to smile, showing her face audaciously to the sun and to Rachid, saying with pride, "The death of the child did not break me, no.... Somewhere, something between us is lost forever...." (Yet a voice within her asks, "How long will it last?")

One day Rachid spoke: "A man gets drunk every evening, and afterwards his actions, his words, his feelings disappear in an encroaching dizziness where he falls into the night. But don't you think that somewhere a mirror must preserve those moments?...I am that man who, the next day, looks over for that which is irredeemably lost....I am hunting for myself."

"Will knowing what he did unconsciously tell you something about him?"

"Undoubtedly, but it isn't knowledge he is searching for....Perhaps, quite simply, the fact that a shred of life is completely lost is unbearable to him...."

"Lost because it has been dissolved by memory or was lived without consciousness?"

"I don't know....If I knew I'd be free from the search, don't you think?"

She thought and then said with sudden energy. "If I had lived with you during the war, I would have been your memory, right, and...," she continued, "and we wouldn't be so unhappy."

He responded by saying that it wouldn't have been the same. Actually, was he really so sure?

"Oh yes," he insisted to himself, "I do love her, and this force within me, just how far would it have pushed me?"

Sometimes Rachid found Nfissa a burden, perhaps because he now resented even more the fact that he couldn't separate himself from this need to remember. How could he recover the past if he couldn't find time to be alone and empty? His wife had forbidden him this bitterness and satiation. She wanted only to look forward, insisting that they move ahead quickly and together into the desert. But how could she foresee that this rush into a necessarily opaque future would bring difficulties and Rachid, who was hoping for respite...

It is here that I intervene, I, the narrator, who have followed them step by step up until now, and who, at this moment, when everything is beginning for them, am preparing to cut the thread of their story. Will I be suspected of indulgence toward the blind and trembling woman? The man thinks that he has already felt the weight of his burden, yet it will be she who finally breaks him. Because I know in advance, (an old prejudice?) that the war which ends between peoples is carried on between couples....

However, without any sadness, I will take one last look at them. They are walking in the city, and as always when he wanders, Rachid is searching, questioning himself. An image comes back to him: in a *willaya*, the forest burned to the ground, one solitary tree is left intact. "Will she understand it one day, the fire and the burning?" he asks himself, conscious of Nfissa next to him, imagining that her step has grown lighter.

"My naive skylark" he thinks, suddenly recalling this expression that the French legionnaires gave to their country's prostitute-dancers, to those he himself had once known. This name served as a symbol for the moral decay and for the nameless light burning inside them. . . . The faith that shines in Nfissa's eyes; the drunkenness that will be forgotten the next day, and in the face of such external rotteness, isn't this ignorance justified? . . . In order to keep the flame going, the prostitutes danced in front of the legionnaires.

"And you?" he wondered while looking at Nfissa, "what dance will allow you to play and survive at the same time?"

Understandably, he no longer knows which words are spoken aloud and which remain unspoken during their conversations.

"How I love you!" Nfissa responded.

The surrounding city of T. is stirring, as if the torpor of the lake nearby was competing with the buzzing noise the refugees make in the narrow streets. The declaration of peace had transformed them into menacing flies, constantly looking for an opening in the wall.

The group of women arrived at the river bank. Beyond, to the east, the edge of a little forest at the foot of the mountain could be seen. Since the cease-fire several hours ago, a confused murmur has risen from the little town, from its gardens and white houses. Veiled women poured into the streets. Those who didn't dare go out, like the mother of Omar and her daughters, or those who no longer hoped to find a living son stayed at home. From there, on that first morning, the mountain looked the same but was drowned in silence.

The women stopped in front of the

parched river bed: some hesitant, just standing there, setting down at their feet packets of semolina and honey cakes, hastily prepared during the night. Others, more impatient, took off their babouches *or their old men's shoes and walked on the pebbled floor of the river. Then they appeared, about ten of them, thin, their uniforms covered with dust. Only their silhouettes could be detected and one could only guess from their breathlessness that they had walked all night, rushing down the mountain slopes to be among the first. Already each woman was looking for the image of her son, each heart beating more quickly than the next—but in vain.*

The town's young people were absent, probably dead, yet these resistance fighters had ended up there, hundreds of miles from their original bases. They looked questioningly at the women who were now huddled together, talking feverishly. By the time the oldest woman broke into a shrill cry of victory, the others were already embracing these men with their haggard faces and hunted looks. Alone, separated from the rest, a woman was sobbing.

Two days later, in an Algeria drained of its blood, spring began.

Translated by Astrid Husvedt

NOTES

1. The title contains a manifold pun: it is first the name given to the dancers of the Ouled-Naïl, who originally derived their rhythms from tribal ritual, perhaps sexually related; these performances were corrupted during the period of colonization: thus the title, which may also mean "youthful escapades," is intensified by sexual innuendo. Djebar also attempted both stylistically and thematically to (re)capture the dancer's rhythms, which she saw as parallel to the Algerians' tanage incessant between the past and the present."
2. In Greek mythology, the fifty daughters of Danaüs, king of Argos, who save for one obediently followed their father's command to kill their husbands on their common wedding night; their punishment in the Underworld was to draw water constantly in leaking jars.

Natálya Gorbanévskaya   *USSR/France, b. 1936*

Natálya Gorbanévskaya was born in 1936 and graduated with a degree in philol-ology from Leningrad State University in 1963. She worked in the State Institute of Experimental Design and Technical Research as an engineer and translator. Only a handful of her poems have appeared in official Soviet journals, whereas five collections of her verse have circulated in *samizdat*, and a volume of her poems was published in Frankfurt (1969) and England (1972).

Gorbanévskaya attracted public attention in the Soviet Union and the West with her civil rights activities. In January 1968 she signed a petition protesting the illegalities in the trial of four people arrested for distributing underground publica-tions. After this action she was held against her will in a maternity hospital (she was several months pregnant), then in a prison mental hospital. She described her experiences in the notes "Bezplátnaya meditsínskaya pómoshch," ("Free Health Service", 1969). She did not curtail her activity after her release, for later that year, on August 5, she participated with a handful of others in a peaceful demonstration in Red Square against the Soviet invasion of Czechoslovakia. She was arrested with the others but was soon released because of her 3-month-old child. She then described the demonstration and the arrests in a letter to the world press, for which she was summoned for examination to the Serbsky Institute for Psychia-tric Medicine. The diagnosis read "not responsible for her actions—the possibility of low-profile schizophrenia is not excluded." The case against her was dropped due to her "insanity" and her two small children, and she was placed in her mother's custody (she was not married). Her protest continued in her descriptions of the events of 1968 in the book *Polden* (*Red Square at Noon*, 1969); she was one of the founders of the Action Group for the Defense of Civil Rights in the USSR (founded May 1969); and on August 26, 1969, she again signed a protest against the invasion of Czechoslovakia. On Christmas Eve of that year she was once again arrested. In 1970 she was confined to a psychiatric hospital of a "special type" (for political dissidents) for compulsory treatment, which included painful and danger-ous injections. She was released in 1972 and allowed to emigrate in 1975. She now lives in Paris.

Gorbanévskaya is one of the best of the underground poets. Although her poetry cannot be divorced from her very political actions, her verse is surprisingly apolitical. Rather, her painful political experience is transformed into a highly personal, intense idiom. Her poems thus differ from traditional "prison poetry" in their intimacy, but even her love lyrics contain allusions to her prison experiences. She continues the Russian tradition of the regenerative power of suffering and of affirmation in the face of isolation, pain, despair, and disaster.

Dobrochna Dyrcz-Freeman

NOTHING AT ALL HAPPENS—
I vóvse nétu nichegó—

Nothing at all happens—neither fear,
not stiffening before the executioner:
I let my head fall on the hollowed block,
as on a casual lover's shoulder.

Roll, curly head, over the planed boards,
don't get a splinter in your parted lips:
the boards bruise your temples,
the solemn fanfare sounds in your ears,

the polished copper dazzles the eyes,
the horses' manes toss,—
O, what a day to die on!

Another day dawns sunless,
and in the twilight, half awake, or suffering
from some old fever or some new apocrypha,
my casual lover's shoulder
still smells to me of pine shavings.
(1970)

Translated by Daniel Weissbort

THE FRENCH HORN OF THE TRAIN SIGHS, WEEPS A LITTLE
Vzdókhnet, vspláknet
váltorna elecktríchki

The french horn of the train sighs, weeps a
                                              little,
an unattainable myth.
Through the prison bars a match gleam
                                       trickles,
the whole world is eclipsed.

The horn takes wing, into the night it sweeps.
To flick through tracks
like notes. Oh how am I to reach
that rainy platform!

Forsaken, sleepless, deserted,
deserted without me—
cloud tatters like letters drift down
to your concrete,

and inscribing the puddles with full stops,
with hooks and tails,
their treble voices ring out after
the departed train.
(13 July–10 September 1970, Butyrka Prison)

Translated by Daniel Weissbort

Dacia Maraini   *Italy, b. 1936*

Dacia Maraini, daughter of a famous ethnologist, Fosco Maraini, lived with her family in Japan from 1938 to 1946. She completed her studies in Italy and began a journalistic career as an editorial staff member of *Tempo di letteratura* (Literary Tempo) while contributing to various periodicals and newspapers. As a fiction writer, she started out with a novel *La vacanza* (The Holiday, 1962), a frank treatment of young women's sexual availability, and continued on the same theme with *L'età del malessere* (*The Age of Malaise* or *The Age of Discontent*, 1963), which was awarded the Formentor Prize. Maraini eventually found her calling in the avant-garde and feminist movements, in which she is very active. Her radical rebellion against all traditional feminity, which she casts aside as wrongful masculine imposition, is reflected in all her writings.

Maraini's novel *A memoria* (From Memory, 1967) deals with the torments of an alienation that leads to death. After publishing a collection of short stories, *Mio marito* (My Husband, 1968), from which the following story came, Maraini turned to exploring the life of a social outcast in the novel *Memorie di una ladra* (*Memoirs of a Female Thief*, 1972). In *Donna in guerra* (*Woman at War*, 1975), a novel in diary form, she describes the life of Vannina, a schoolteacher vacationing on an Italian island who comes into contact with the local women, learns about corruption, and gets involved with a group of young radicals. The book is a sociological document of the corrupt life in Southern Italy in the early 1970s and of the rebellion of the young. The subjects of lesbian love and loneliness were treated in her novel *Lettere a Marina* (*Letters to Marina*, 1981).

As a poet, Maraini made her debut in 1966 with *Crudeltà all'aria aperta* (Cruelty in the Open Air, 1966), which was followed by another collection of poems, *Donne mie* (My Women, 1974). Her style is violent and intentionally shocking, as she exhorts women to take possession of their bodies (denied to them since ancient times), and love aggressively, not passively.

Maraini is also very active in the theater. *Viva l'Italia* (Long Live Italy, 1973), was written in 1969 to be performed for the centennial celebration of Italy's unification but was flatly refused on account of its unorthodox treatment of the Garibaldi heroes as oppressors of the landless classes.* Other plays can be found in the collections *Il ricatto a teatro* (Blackmail in the Theater, 1970), *I sogni di Clitennestra* (Clytemnestra's Dreams, 1981), and *Lezioni d'amore* (Love Lessons, 1982). Her plays, mainly performed by the Roman feminist theater Maddalena, have been praised by some critics, who value them for their political commitment despite their coarse language.

Natalia Costa-Zalessow

NOTE

* Guiseppe Garibaldi (1807–1882), one of the chief military leaders of the unification of Italy.

HIBERNATION
Ibernazione

Until a few months ago, I thought of myself as a garden slug. It was true that I slid over things, wounding myself at every move, unable to lift myself above the obstacles. I shared the slug's slow, horizontal movements and its elongated, awkward, expressionless body. But I was anything but smooth and slippery. It was as though I had been skinned. The body which snaked along, bumping into objects and soiling itself on its way was skinless, its inner flesh laid painfully bare. Because of this, I agonized and wandered blindly, dully, in search of the retreat I could never find.

For a while, I obsessively sought consolation in my parents, living with them and never separating myself from them for a moment.

But in truth, they were never really any help to me. When they died, almost simultaneously, I was suddenly on my own.

You might say I learned to live at the very moment of their deaths. In fact, one morning as I sat next to my dying mother's bed, staring at her with eyes kept wide by my pity and disgust, I suddenly felt that I was being hypnotized by the extreme tension and fear and horror of all that was happening to me. My pupils attached themselves to a border of the sheet and fell asleep. But my body was not sleeping, nor was my mind, which kept up its slow, circular work as though digesting rich, heavy foods. My eyes had gone to sleep, taking my senses with them.

I think I must have sat there motionless and absent for more than two hours. When I came back to my senses, I felt rested and relieved, almost strong. In the meantime, my mother had died.

Since that day, I have tried to practice the technique. In the beginning it was difficult. I had trouble reaching the state of tension and nausea which made it possible for me to sleep while awake. But after long and tiresome practice, I have now almost achieved total domination of my body.

When my father died, I still was not in complete command of my sensitivity. I remember that interminable night, spent alternatively between brief intervals of hypnotic sleep and painful expectation. Finally, towards dawn, I began to cry. As the tears slipped down my face and neck, I discovered that all the strength I needed was there, around the eyelids and under the damp eyeballs, between the arch of the eyebrow and the nasal septum. I had only to gather that strength, concentrate it at the center of the iris and project it outward to free myself of all pain.

It was only a few days later that my new life began. I straightened up the house, threw away some old cumbersome furniture, took down the dust-impregnated drapes and washed them, burned all the newspapers and magazines my father had accumulated in the studio where he practiced law, threw away all the old clothes, trinkets, and rubbish littering my mother's drawers and closets.

The money I had inherited was gone after a few weeks, so I set to finding myself a job. A newspaper ad caught my attention and I applied. There were twenty other girls waiting with me but, as soon as I saw them, I knew that I would be chosen. They were all too busy flaunting their beauty, duelling with make-up and boots, while I had done nothing to look like the girl I am: not too young nor too old, neither beautiful nor ugly; diligent, honest, careful, meticulous and serious—all qualities which combine to make a perfect employee for a placement office. Just as I had expected, they examined everyone and then chose me. I was sent off immediately to work at a paper-littered desk.

My colleagues are less pleased with me than my superiors, and at first I disturbed them with my silence and automatic movements, but they have grown accustomed to them and act as though I weren't there. Now and then, they make fun of my punctuality, my meticulous habits, and my absorbed, half-seeing eyes.

The truth is that I am training myself to sleep, even as I work. And I have almost succeeded. Sometimes my awakening is sudden and painful, especially when a colleague touches my shoulder or mistakenly bumps against me or laughs in my ear as a joke. When that happens, I jump up and am overcome by a high fever which fortunately only lasts a few seconds but leaves me exhausted and limp.

When I am not at work, I sit at home in the kitchen and sleep. My eyes stay open and I would even be able to speak or move or perform simple manual tasks, while my pupils suck up all the vigor of my body and suspend it as though in somnolent and immobile limbo.

Sometimes I even forget to eat. A few days ago, I fainted on the street. Fortunately, I didn't hit my head. I had felt it coming and leaned on the bumper of a Fiat 600. Then, a second later, I lost consciousness. When I came to, I was stretched out on a bed at the Emergency Room with a doctor looming over me, measuring my blood pressure. I knew instantly that it was hunger. I hadn't eaten anything for three days. The doctor gave me a lecture and sent me off with a friendly pat on the cheek.

When I got home, I went straight to the refrigerator, where I found some dry and yellowed mozzarella, a plate of frozen spinach and four chicken stock cubes. I put some water on the burner, dissolved the cubes and dropped in the spinach. I ate two plates of it hot and would have eaten something else, but I didn't feel like going downstairs. Tomorrow

I'll have a big meal, I told myself. But the next day I was so busy with my self-hypnosis practice that I forgot the meal and when I got home in the evening, the refrigerator was still empty. So I put a frying pan on the burner, poured a little oil into it and fried the mozzarella, which tasted sour. I ate it with some biscuits I found at the back of the kitchen drawer. They must have been very old because I broke a tooth biting into one of them.

Since then, my waking moments have become fewer and briefer. When I am not awake I sleep, in the weightless, deaf manner which has become natural to me.

Sometimes at night, when the house is dark and silent, I wake up. When that happens, it hurts so much getting my conscience working again that it takes my breath away. So I get up and turn on all the lights and the radio. The noise, the lights, the music and, most of all, the human voices have a power which drops me back into my lucid, somnolent torpor. I go back to bed with the lights on and the radio next to my head on the pillow and I fall asleep.

At seven, the alarm clock starts to trill. Then the part of me that is docile and mechanically machine-like starts up delicately and takes itself through all the necessary motions. I get out of bed, go into the bathroom, wash, dress, go out, take the tram, get off the tram, go into the bar near my office, drink a cappuccino, take the elevator, sit down at my desk, type letters, make phone calls, compile ads for the newspapers, and so forth.

When the holidays come, my sleep grows until it becomes mortal hibernation. Because I don't have to go to the office, I stay in bed all day with the window thrown open and my eyes glued to the house across the street. Sometimes I see children playing with a cat, sometimes a woman in a slip argues with a man in an undershirt. But I don't know if I see the woman in the slip and the man in the undershirt from the kitchen and the children playing with the cat from the bed, or vice versa.

So that I would remember to eat, I hung signs all over the house. On a white card, I wrote, "Eat!" But then I realized that after seeing the sign three or four times, I no longer noticed it. So I decided to change the color of the words and the format of the card every day. But I forgot to do that. Then I got a brilliant idea. I bought cans of meat and distributed them here and there on the floor throughout the house, so that when I stumble over one of them, I lean over and pick it up and this reminds me to eat.

I thought I had gained complete control of myself until the other day, when something happened which shattered all the confidence I had acquired.

I was sitting at my desk in the office doing some accounts. Raising my head, for the first time I noticed the face of the colleague who sits across the room from me. I had never before realized that he was very young; his luminous, melancholy beauty communicated a sense of joy to me that I hadn't felt since childhood. I stared at him so long that finally my eyes tired and emptied out and I returned to my natural state of wakeful sleep.

But when I got home that evening and sat down in front of the kitchen window, the memory of the boy's clear, fresh face came back to me and kept me awake. I tried to remember something else about him—the shape of his shoulders, his teeth, the color of his eyes—but nothing came to me.

This search for details and the effort of remembering kept me awake and disturbed. I couldn't sleep at all that night. I turned on all the lights, danced to tire myself, ate two cans of meat and sucked three eggs, drank some wine and, in a final attempt, lay down on the bed with the radio blasting away on my pillow, but the lights, the food, the voices, and the movements couldn't put me to sleep as they usually do.

So I found a notebook and tried to draw the boy's face on the white paper, exactly as I remembered it. But every face I drew was completely different from the others. I spent the whole night filling up the notebook. The next morning, I dressed earlier than usual and arrived at the office when the door was still locked. I waited on the landing, stamping my feet to ward off the cold.

Just before nine, a young man arrived. Short and bald, he was engulfed in a raincoat of a strange hue somewhere between green and purple. He leaned up against the door, looked at me a moment, and smiled. I responded by lowering my head. And just as I was observing his calm, wide eyes, I realized that he was the boy I had lost my head for the day before. But now, here was this bald, monkey-like man, leering allusively at me as though we shared some secret.

I plastered my eyes to his big, greasy head and it took me only a few seconds to fall back into sleep. I became indifferent to the sight of him; he was just one object among the many objects surrounding me.

After this painful episode, my life returned to its former mechanical state. But I had gained one conviction. The beautiful things I see are my dreams, so I must be very careful never to awaken.

Translated by Kristin Jarratt

Dahlia Ravikovitch

Israel, b. 1936

Dahlia Ravikovitch was born in Israel's Ramat Gan, a suburb of Tel Aviv, and educated at Kibbutz Geva and at a high school in Haifa. She then served in the Israeli army before attending the Hebrew University of Jerusalem, where she studied English literature. After graduating, she taught high school.

She began publishing her poems in her twenties while in the army and has, to date, written five volumes of poetry, including *Ahavat Tapuakh Ha Zahav* (The Love of the Golden Apple, 1959), *Horef Kashe* (A Hard Winter, 1964), and *The Third Book* (1969), from which the following poems are taken. She has also done translations of Yeats, Eliot, and Poe and has written children's books. Lately, she has worked actively for the Israeli peace movement.

Ravikovitch, the best known of contemporary Israeli women poets, is recognized for the biting sarcasm of her often colloquial language and the irony of her themes, which dwell on modern life and manners. She is especially concerned with the alienation of people from one another.

MARIONETTE
ha Marionette

To be a marionette
In this precious gray light before dawn
To sprout up from under the new day
To dive
In lower streams
To be a marionette
A fragile pale porcelain doll
Constrained by strings
To be a marionette

And the strings which bear my life
Are strings of pure silk
A marionette
She too is real
She has memories
Four hundred years ago
There lived Doña Elvira the Duchess of Seville
With her three hundred handmaidens
Each time she cast her eyes

Upon her gossamer silk handkerchief
She saw her destiny:
To be a porcelain puppet
Or a wax doll
Doña Elvira the Duchess of Seville dreamt
                              about late-ripening vines
Her knights always addressed her in subdued
                                             tones
Doña Elvira the Duchess etcetera passed on to
                                         her maker
And left her two sons and daughter
A dubious future
In the precious gray dawn of the twentieth
                                        century
How good it would be to be a marionette
This woman's not responsible for her actions
Says the judge
Her frail heart's gray as the dawn
Her body's constrained by strings.
Translated by Warren Bargad and Stanley F. Chyet

HOW HONG KONG
WAS DESTROYED
Eich Hong Kong nehersa

I'm in Hong Kong.
There's a bay there swarming with snakes.
There are Greeks, Chinamen, and Blacks.
Carnival crocodiles spread their
jaws by the paper lanterns.
Who told you they're carnivorous?
Hordes of people went down to the river.
You've never seen silk like this,
it's redder than poppy petals.

In Hong Kong
the sun rises in the east
and they water the flowers with scented liquids
to enhance their fragrance.
But at night the paper lanterns whip about in
                                         the wind
and if someone's murdered they say:
Was it a Black or a Chinaman?
Did he feel much pain?
Then they toss his body in the river
for all the vermin to eat.

I'm in Hong Kong,
and at night the café lights were lowered.
Outside scores of lanterns were torn apart.
And the earth was bursting and boiling
bursting and boiling
and only I knew
there was nothing in the west
And the paper dragon yawned
but the earth kept bursting.
Hordes of enemies will come here
who've never seen silk in their lives.

But little whores still receive their guests
in stained silk gowns
in little lantern-filled cubicles.
Some of them weep in the morning
over their rancid flesh.
And if someone's killed they say:
Wa-as h-he Black or Chinese?
Poor thing, hope he didn't suffer much.
The first of their guests already come at twilight
like thorns in live flesh.

I'm in Hong Kong
and Hong Kong's on the ocean
suspended like a colored lantern on a hook
at the edge
of the world.
Maybe the dragon will
wrap her in red silk
and drop her
into the starry abyss.
Only the little whores will weep into silk
that men are still
are still
pinching their bellies.

I'm not in Hong Kong
and Hong Kong's not in the world.
Where Hong Kong used to be
there's a single pink stain
half in the sky
and half in the sea.
Translated by Warren Bargad and Stanley F. Chyet

Judith Rodriguez   *Australia, b. 1936*

Born in Perth and brought up in Brisbane, Judith Green Rodriguez is a graduate of
the Universities of Queensland, Australia, and Cambridge, England. She has taught
literature at colleges and universities in Jamaica, London, and Australia and
writing at numerous workshops and classes. She lectures now at the Macarthur
Institute of Higher Education in Sydney, where she lives with her second husband,
the writer Tom Shapcott.

Rodriguez's first short collection came out in a book *Four Poets* (1962) with
contemporary Australian poets, including David Malouf and Rodney Hall. "Nu-
plastik fanfare red" reprinted below, is the title poem of her own first volume,
published in 1973, from which also comes "Frontier Incident." *Water Life* (1976)
contains her linocuts as well as poems; it won the inaugural South Australian
Biennial Prize for Literature. Linocuts figure also in *Shadow on Glass* (1978) and
Mudcrab at Cambaro's (1980), the latter collection winner of the PEN/Peter
Stuyvesant Prize for Poetry. Later books are *Witch Heart* (1982) and *Floridian
Poems* (1986), product of a writer-in-residency at Rollins College in Florida.

Rodriguez has edited several anthologies, including the feminist collection
Mrs. Noah and the Minoan Queen, with her introduction to the poems of six
Australian women (Sisters, Melbourne, 1983). Poetry Editor of *Meanjin* from 1979
to 1982, she now writes a poetry column for the *Sydney Morning Herald*. She is
also author of stories and articles and has received three writing fellowships from
the Literature Board of the Australia Council.

Judith Rodriguez

NU-PLASTIK FANFARE RED

I declare myself:
I am painting my room red.
Because they haven't any
flat red suitable for interiors,
because their acres of colour-card
are snowy with daylight only,
because it will look like Danger! Explosives,
or would you prefer a basement cabaret?
a decent home where Italians moved in,
Como perhaps (yes, I've gilded the mirror)
or simply infernal—

I rejoice to be doing it
with quick-drying plastic,
for small area decoration.
I tear at the wall, brush speeding:
let's expand this limited stuff!
It dries impetuously in patches,
I at edges too late scrub; this is a fight.

I sought the conditions,
and the unbroken wall is yet to come.
Clear stretches screech into clots,
streak into smokiness.
Botched job this, my instant
hell! and no re-sale value, Dad;
cliché too. Well, too bad.

It's satisfying to note
this mix is right for pottery.
(Good glad shock of seeing
that red-figure vases *are*.
Not 4th-edition-earthy, but stab-colour,
new-vein, red-Attis-flower, the full howl.)
My inward amphora!
Even thus shyly to surface:
up we go red, flag-balloon,
broomstick-rocket!
This is a red land, sour

with blood it has not shed,
money not lost, risks evaded,
blood it has forgotten, dried
in furnace airs that vainly
figure (since mines are doing well)
the fire. Torpor
if a disallowed abortion.

Why not a red room?

FRONTIER INCIDENT

The murderers were riding hippogriffs[1]
that bounced and whooped along a foaming
                                    dune.
Too dusty to be truant from a myth,
between his ears each had a great red comb.
The murderers took their weapons from their
                                    hair
and laughed. Their foreheads shone. We were
                                    afraid.
Real knives, real clubs, real boomerangs, real
                                    spears,
real guns, not just something out of Freud.[2]
The sand blew in our eyes, we got no further;
rearing necks tangled the indigo sun.
Fabulously they picnicked on the murder.
Between his ears each had a great red comb.

NOTES

1. Mythological animal with the wings, head, and claws
   of a griffin and the tail and hooves of a horse.
2. Sigmund Freud (1856–1939), the father of modern
   psychology.

Hélène Cixous
Algeria/France, b. 1937

Cixous was born and raised in Oran, Algeria, by Jewish parents. Her mother was from Germany and her father from North Africa. Her childhood was marked by war and the threat of the Holocaust, and the premature death of her father in 1948. It is this part of her life—"the family romance," as one critic puts it, and its relation to her becoming a writer—that she recounts in the prize-winning novel *Dedans* (*Inside*, 1969). She arrived in France in 1955 where she studied English and received her *agrégation* at the remarkable age of 22. (The agrégation is an extremely rigorous competitive national examination given to those who want to teach in the French school system.) She eventually taught at Bordeaux and then Paris. In Paris, she participated in the founding of the experimental university center at Vincennes (now relocated at St. Denis) while writing her doctoral thesis on Joyce. *The Exile of James Joyce* is now considered one of the definitive studies of that writer. Around this time, Cixous began writing fiction as well.

The late 1960s and early 1970s saw a rash of student movements throughout the world. In May of 1968, the upheavals reached their peak in France. Students and professors alike were active politically and intellectually engaged in questioning and overturning traditional academic structures. It was a period of radicalization, and Cixous was in the vanguard of those agitating for change. Breaking new ground in theory as well, she, along with two other well-known critics, Gérard Genette and Tvetan Todorov, established the critical review *Poétique*.

During the 1970s, Cixous became more and more involved in the feminist movement and is today among its most powerful theoreticians, the advocate of what has come to be known as *écriture féminine* (which some would argue relies too heavily on the ideas of Jacques Lacan, the psychoanalyst responsible for "rewriting" Freud). Having allied herself with des Femmes, after 1975 Cixous turned from major male publishers and began printing her works under their imprimatur and in the prestigious organ run by the moderate feminist group Psychanalyse et politique (Psych et po). With *La Jeune née* (*The Newly Born Woman*, 1976) and *La Venue à l'écriture* (The Coming to Writing, 1977), "Le Rire de la Méduse" ("The Laugh of the Medusa," 1975, of which a selection from the revised version is here reprinted) constitutes a trilogy of feminist practice. This now-classic manifesto might be called a prose poem (which evokes Walt Whitman, Emerson, and Thoreau for some American readers), an incitement to action, or a theoretical essay. In it we can see Cixous' favorite gambits: the valorization of femininity and the experimentation with new forms. Cixous tries to create "a language of the body," one which is closer to the unconscious. That is, Cixous hopes that through a new language that represents a new symbolic order, woman will learn to love herself (appropriating her own body through the image of it reflected to her by language as well as by other women).

In this context, Cixous has also argued for and celebrated *both* pregnancy and bisexuality as expressions of *la jouissance*, or the pleasures of the body, which she believes have been repressed by a symbolic patriarchal order; her *Préparatifs de noces au delà de l'abîme* (Preparations for a Marriage Beyond the Abyss, 1978) records the experience of a woman loving women. She has also transposed female mythological figures such as the Medusa into a modern context to affirm the power of these images of and for women. In such works as the revision of Freud, *Le Portrait de Dora* (Portrait of Dora, 1976), *Angst* (1977; translated 1985), the bilingual novel *Vivre l'Orange* (Living the Orange, 1979), and in *Le Livre de Prométhéa* (Promethea's Book, 1983), Cixous has created a new mythology and given voice to what she has called the "Vital Woman." Stylistically, her recent work has been influenced by the works of the Brazilian writer Clarice Lispector.

Although she published another collection of essays *Entre l'écriture* (Between Writing) in 1986, Cixous has turned increasingly to the theatre, making a brilliant début in this genre with her stage version of *Dora*; she also directed her *La prise de l'école de Madubahi* (The Taking of the School of Madubahi, 1986). Her two recent plays, *L'Histoire terrible mais inachevée de Norodom Sihanouk, roi du Cambodge* (The Terrible But Unfinished Story of Norodom Sihanouk, King of Cambodia, 1985) and *L'Indiade ou l'Inde de leurs rêves* (The Indiad, or India of Their Dreams, 1987) have been produced to great critical acclaim.

Beginning in the 1980s, Cixous disassociated herself from political feminist movements, charging them with inadequacy in dispelling the old order. She continues to teach at one of the only centers of feminist studies in France while traveling frequently between France, the United States, and Canada. Her works have had global repercussions on the practice of feminist theory.

from THE LAUGH OF THE MEDUSA
Le rire de la Méduse

I shall speak about women's writing: about *what it will do*. Woman must write her self: must write about women and bring women to writing, from which they have been driven away as violently as from their bodies—for the same reasons, by the same law, with the same fatal goal. Woman must put herself into the text—as into the world and into history—by her own movement.

The future must no longer be determined by the past. I do not deny that the effects of the past are still with us. But I refuse to strengthen them by repeating them, to confer upon them an irremovability the equivalent of destiny, to confuse the biological and the cultural. Anticipation is imperative.

Since these reflections are taking shape in an area just on the point of being discovered, they necessarily bear the mark of our time—a time during which the new breaks away from the old, and, more precisely, the (feminin) new from the old (*la nouvelle de l'ancien*). Thus, as there are no grounds for establishing a discourse, but rather an arid millennial ground to break, what I say has at least two sides and two aims: to break up, to destroy; and to foresee the unforeseeable, to project.

I write this as a woman, toward women. When I say "woman," I'm speaking of woman in her inevitable struggle against conventional man; and of a universal woman subject who must bring women to their senses and to their meaning in history. But first it must be said that in spite of the enormity of the repression that has kept them in the "dark"—that dark which people have been trying to make them accept as their attribute—there is, at this time, no general woman, no one typical woman. What they have *in common* I will say. But what strikes me is the infinite richness of their individual constitutions: you can't talk about *a* female sexuality, uniform, homogeneous, classifiable into codes—any more than you can talk about one unconscious resembling an-

other. Women's imaginary is inexhaustible, like music, painting, writing; their stream of phantasms is incredible.

I have been amazed more than once by a description a woman gave me of a world all her own which she had been secretly haunting since early childhood. A world of searching, the elaboration of a knowledge, on the basis of a systematic experimentation with the bodily functions, a passionate and precise interrogation of her erotogeneity. This practice, extraordinarily rich and inventive, in particular as concerns masturbation, is prolonged or accompanied by a production of forms, a veritable esthetic activity, each stage of rapture inscribing a resonant vision, a composition, something beautiful. Beauty will no longer be forbidden.

I wished that that woman would write and proclaim this unique empire so that other women, other unacknowledged sovereigns, might exclaim: I, too, overflow; my desires have invented new desires, my body knows unheard-of songs. Time and again I, too, have felt so full of luminous torrents that I could burst—burst with forms much more beautiful than those which are put up in frames and sold for a stinking fortune. And I, too, said nothing, showed nothing; I didn't open my mouth, I didn't repaint my half of the world. I was ashamed. I was afraid, and I swallowed my shame and my fear. I said to myself: You are mad! What's the meaning of these waves, these floods, these outbursts? Where is the ebullient, infinite woman who, immersed as she was in her naiveté, kept in the dark about herself, led into self-disdain by the great arm of parental-conjugal phallocentrism, hasn't been ashamed of her strength? Who, surprised and horrified by the fantastic tumult of her drives (for she was made to believe that a well-adjusted normal woman has a...divine composure), hasn't accused herself of being a monster? Who, feeling a funny desire stirring inside her (to sing, to write, to dare to speak, in short, to bring out something new), hasn't thought she was sick? Well, her shameful sickness is that she resists death, that she makes trouble.

And why don't you write? Write! Writing is for you, you are for you: your body is yours, take it. I know why you haven't written. (And why I didn't write before the age of twenty-seven.) Because writing is at once too high, too great for you, it's reserved for the great—that is, for "great men;" and it's "silly." Besides, you've written a little, but in secret. And it wasn't good, because it was in secret, and because you punished yourself for writing, because you didn't go all the way; or because you wrote, irresistibly, as when we would masturbate in secret, not to go further, but to attenuate the tension a bit, just enough to take the edge off. And then as soon as we come, we go and make ourselves feel guilty—so as to be forgiven; or to forget, to bury it until the next time.

Write, let no one hold you back, let nothing stop you: not man; not the imbecilic capitalist machinery, in which publishing houses are the crafty, obsequious relayers of imperatives handed down by an economy that works against us and off our backs; and not *yourself*. Smug-faced readers, managing editors, and big bosses don't like the true texts of women—female-sexed texts. That kind scares them.

I write woman: woman must write woman. And man, man. So only an oblique consideration will be found here of man; it's up to him to say where his masculinity and femininity are at: this will concern us once men have opened their eyes and seen themselves clearly.*

Now women return from afar, from always: from "without," from the heath where witches are kept alive; from below, from beyond "culture"; from their childhood which men have been trying desperately to make them forget, condemning it to "eternal rest." The little girls and their "ill-mannered" bodies immured, well-preserved, intact unto them-

selves, in the mirror. Frigidified. But are they ever seething underneath! What an effort it takes—there's no end to it—for the sex cops to bar their threatening return. Such a display of forces on both sides that the struggle has for centuries been immobilized in the trembling equilibrium of a deadlock....

She [woman] must write her self, because this is the invention of a *new insurgent* writing which, when the moment of her liberation has come, will allow her to carry out the indispensable ruptures and transformations in her history, first at two levels that cannot be separated.

a) Individually. By writing her self, woman will return to the body which has been more than confiscated from her, which has been turned into the uncanny stranger on display—the ailing or dead figure, which so often turns out to be the nasty companion, the cause and location of inhibitions. Censor the body and you censor breath and speech at the same time.

Write your self. Your body must be heard. Only then will the immense resources of the unconscious spring forth. Our naphtha will spread, throughout the world, without dollars —black or gold—nonassessed values that will change the rules of the old game.

To write. An act which will not only "realize" the decensored relation of woman to her sexuality, to her womanly being, giving her access to her native strength; it will give her back her goods, her pleasures, her organs, her immense bodily territories which have been kept under seal; it will tear her away from the superegoized structure in which she has always occupied the place reserved for the guilty (guilty of everything, guilty at every turn: for having desires, for not having any; for being frigid, for being "too hot"; for not being both at once; for being too motherly and not enough; for having children and for not having any; for nursing and for not nursing...)—tear her away by means of this research, this job of analysis and illumination, this emancipation of the marvelous text of her self that she must urgently learn to speak. A woman without a body, dumb, blind, can't possibly be a good fighter. She is reduced to being the servant of the militant male, his shadow. We must kill the false woman who is preventing the live one from breathing. Inscribe the breath of the whole woman.

b) An act that will also be marked by woman's *seizing* the occasion to *speak*, hence her shattering entry into history, which has always been based *on her suppression*. To write and thus to forge for herself the antilogos weapon. To become *at will* the taker and initiator, for her own right, in every symbolic system, in every political process.

It is time for women to start scoring their feats in written and oral language.

Translated Keith Cohen and Paula Cohen

NOTE (by the author)

* Men still have everything to say about their sexuality, and everything to write. For what they have said so far, for the most part, stems from the opposition activity/passivity, from the power relation between a fantasized obligatory virility meant to invade, to colonize, and the consequential phantasm of woman as a "dark continent" to penetrate and to "pacify." (We know what "pacify" means in terms of scotomizing the other and misrecognizing the self.) Conquering her, they've made haste to depart from her borders, to get out of sight, out of body. The way man has of getting out of himself and into her whom he takes not for the other but for his own, deprives him, he knows, of his own bodily territory. One can understand how man, confusing himself with his penis and rushing in for the attack, might feel resentment and fear of being "taken" by the woman, of being lost in her, absorbed, or alone.

Patricia Grace   *New Zealand, b. 1937*

Patricia Grace was the first Maori woman to publish a collection of stories, *Waiariki* (Hot Spring, 1975), and the first to publish a novel, *Mutuwhenua: The Moon Sleeps* (1978). She was born in Wellington, trained as a teacher, and has had seven children while maintaining a career as a teacher and, increasingly, a writer.

Grace's recent publications include two collections of stories, *The Dream Sleepers* (1980) and *Electric City* (1987), and another novel, *Potiki* (Child, 1986). The selection here, "A Way of Talking," from her first collection, reflects the intrinsic racism of the supposedly nonracist white culture in New Zealand, and the beginnings of Maori activism in the 1970s. As well as her notable contribution to the remarkable flowering of Maori writing in English since the early 1970s, Grace has also done much to assist in the parallel reclamation of Maori language and culture. She has written four Maori readers for use in schools and two children's books with texts in both Maori and English. With the artist Robyn Kahukiwa Grace has also produced *Wahine Toa* (1984), a book of Maori myths relating to women. Grace is regarded as the best contemporary New Zealand story writer.

Elizabeth Webby

A WAY OF TALKING

Rose came back yesterday; we went down to the bus to meet her. She's just the same as ever Rose. Talks all the time flat out and makes us laugh with her way of talking. On the way home we kept saying. "E Rohe, you're just the same as ever." It's good having my sister back and knowing she hasn't changed. Rose is the hard-case one in the family, the kamakama[1] one, and the one with the brains.

Last night we stayed up talking till all hours, even Dad and Nanny who usually go to bed after tea. Rose made us laugh telling about the people she knows, and talking off professor this and professor that from varsity. Nanny, Mum, and I had tears running down from laughing; e ta Rose[2] we laughed all night.

At last Nanny got out of her chair and said, "Time for sleeping. The mouths steal the time of the eyes." That's the lovely way she has of talking, Nanny, when she speaks in English. So we went to bed and Rose and I kept our mouths going for another hour or so before falling asleep.

This morning I said to Rose that we'd better go and get her measured for the dress up at Mrs Frazer's. Rose wanted to wait a day or two but I reminded her the wedding was only two weeks away and that Mrs Frazer had three frocks to finish.

"Who's Mrs Frazer anyway," she asked. Then I remembered Rose hadn't met these neighbours though they'd been in the district a few years. Rose had been away at school.

"She's a dressmaker," I looked for words. "She's nice."

"What sort of nice?" asked Rose.

"Rose, don't you say anything funny when we go up there," I said. I know Rose, she's smart. "Don't you get smart." I'm older than Rose but she's the one that speaks out when something doesn't please her. Mum used to say, Rohe you've got the brains but you look to your sister for the sense. I started to feel funny about taking Rose up to Jane Frazer's because Jane often says the wrong thing without knowing.

We got our work done, had a bath and changed, and when Dad came back from the shed we took the station-wagon to drive over to Jane's. Before we left we called out to Mum, "Don't forget to make us a Maori bread for when we get back."

"What's wrong with your own hands," Mum said, but she was only joking. Always when one of us comes home one of the first things she does is make a big Maori bread.

Rose made a good impression with her kamakama ways, and Jane's two nuisance kids took a liking to her straight away. They kept jumping up and down on the sofa to get Rose's attention and I kept thinking what a waste of a good sofa it was, what a waste of a good house for those two nuisance things. I hope when I have kids they won't be so hoha.[3]

I was pleased about Jane and Rose. Jane was asking Rose all sorts of questions about her life in Auckland. About varsity and did Rose join in the marches and demonstrations. Then they went on to talking about fashions and social life in the city, and Jane seemed deeply interested. Almost as though she was jealous of Rose and the way she lived, as though she felt Rose had something better than a lovely house and clothes and everything she needed to make life good for her. I was pleased to see that Jane liked my sister so much, and proud of my sister and her entertaining and friendly ways.

Jane made a cup of coffee when she'd finished measuring Rose for the frock, then packed the two kids outside with a piece of chocolate cake each. We were sitting having coffee when we heard a truck turn in at the bottom of Frazers' drive.

Jane said, "That's Alan. He's been down the road getting the Maoris for scrub cutting."

I felt my face get hot. I was angry. At the same time I was hoping Rose would let the remark pass. I tried hard to think of something to say to cover Jane's words though I'd hardly said a thing all morning. But my tongue seemed to thicken and all I could think of was Rohe don't.

Rose was calm. Not all red and flustered like me. She took a big pull on the cigarette she had lit, squinted her eyes up and blew the smoke out gently. I knew something was coming.

"Don't they have names?"

"What. Who?" Jane was surprised and her face was getting pink.

"The people from down the road whom your husband is employing to cut scrub." Rose the stink thing, she was talking all Pakehafied.[4]

"I don't know any of their names."

I was glaring at Rose because I wanted her to stop but she was avoiding my looks and pretending to concentrate on her cigarette.

"Do they know yours?"

"Mine?"

"Your name."

"Well . . . yes."

"Yet you have never bothered to find out their names or to wonder whether or not they have any."

The silence seemed to bang around in my head for ages and ages. Then I think Jane muttered something about difficulty, but that touchy sister of mine stood up and said, "Come on Hera." And I with my red face and shut mouth followed her out to the station-wagon without a goodbye or anything.

I was so wild with Rose. I was wild. I was determined to blow her up about what she had done, I was determined. But now that we were alone together I couldn't think what to say. Instead I felt an awful big sulk coming on. It has always been my trouble, sulking. Whenever I don't feel sure about something I go into a big fat sulk. We had a teacher at school who used to say to some of us girls, "Speak, don't sulk." She'd say, "You only sulk because you haven't learned how and when to say your minds."

She was right that teacher, yet here I am a young woman about to be married and haven't learned yet how to get the words out. Dad used to say to me, "Look out girlie, you'll stand on your lip."

At last I said, "Rose, you're a stink thing." Tears were on the way. "Gee Rohe, you made me embarrassed." Then Rose said, "Don't worry Honey she's got a thick hide."

These words of Rose's took me by surprise and I realized something about Rose then. What she said made all my anger go away and I felt very sad because it's not our way of talking to each other. Usually we'd say, "Never mind Sis," if we wanted something to be forgotten. But when Rose said, "Don't worry Honey she's got a thick hide," it made her seem a lot older than me, and tougher, and as though she knew much more than me about the world. It made me realize too that underneath her jolly and forthright ways Rose is very hurt. I remembered back to when we were both little and Rose used to play up at school if she didn't like the teacher. She'd get smart and I used to be ashamed and tell Mum on her when we got home, because although she had the brains I was always the well behaved one.

Rose was speaking to me in a new way now. It made me feel sorry for her and for myself. All my life I had been sitting back and letting her do the objecting. Not only me, but Mum and Dad and the rest of the family too. All of us too scared to make known when we had been hurt or slighted. And how can the likes of Jane know when we go round pretending all is well. How can Jane know us?

But then I tried to put another thought into words. I said to Rose, "We do it too. We say, "the Pakeha[5] doctor," or "the Pakeha at the post office," and sometimes we mean it in a bad way."

"Except that we talk like this to each other only. It's not so much what is said, but when and where and in whose presence. Besides, you and I don't speak in this way now, not since we were little. It's the older ones: Mum, Dad, Nanny who have this habit."

Then Rose said something else. "Jane Frazer will still want to be your friend and mine in spite of my embarrassing her today; we're in the fashion."

"What do you mean?"

"It's fashionable for a Pakeha to have a Maori for a friend." Suddenly Rose grinned. Then I heard Jane's voice coming out of that Rohe's mouth and felt a grin of my own coming. "I have friends who are Maoris. They're lovely people. The eldest girl was married recently and I did the frocks. The other girl is at varsity. They're all so *friendly* and so *natural* and their house is absolutely *spotless*."

I stopped the wagon in the drive and when we'd got out Rose started strutting up the path. I saw Jane's way of walking and felt a giggle coming on. Rose walked up Mum's scrubbed steps, "Absolutely spotless." She left her shoes in the porch and bounced into the kitchen. "What did I tell you? Absolutely spotless. And a friendly natural woman taking new bread from the oven."

Mum looked at Rose then at me. "What have you two been up to? Rohe I hope you behaved yourself at that Pakeha place?" But Rose was setting the table. At the sight of Mum's bread she'd forgotten all about Jane and the events of the morning.

When Dad, Heke, and Matiu came in for lunch, Rose, Mum, Nanny and I were already into the bread and the big bowl of hot corn.

"E ta," Dad said. "Let your hardworking father and your two hardworking brothers starve. Eat up."

"The bread's terrible. You men better go down to the shop and get you a shop bread," said Rose.

"Be the day," said Heke.

"Come on my fat Rohe. Move over and make room for your Daddy. Come on my baby shift over."

Dad squeezed himself round behind the table next to Rose. He picked up the bread Rose had buttered for herself and started eating. "The bread's terrible all right," he said. Then Mat and Heke started going on about how awful the corn was and who cooked it and who grew it, who watered it all summer and who pulled out the weeds.

So I joined in the carryings on and forgot about Rose and Jane for the meantime. But I'm not leaving it at that. I'll find some way of letting Rose know I understand and I know it will be difficult for me because I'm not clever the way she is. I can't say things the same and I've never learnt to stick up for myself.

But my sister won't have to be alone again. I'll let her know that.

NOTES

1. Maori for "talkative."
2. An exclamation, such as 'Oh, you!'
3. Maori for "annoying."
4. Europeanized in Maori.
5. European or non-Maori.

Bessie Head   *South Africa/Botswana, 1937–1986*

At the time she died, rather suddenly, of hepatitis in 1986, Bessie Head was just beginning to gain wide acceptance as one of the truly major writers in Africa. Relatively slender though her output was—a total of six works: three novels, a self-styled "African saga," *A Bewitched Crossroad* (1984), a collection of short stories, and the extraordinary and unclassifiable *Serowe: Village of the Rain Wind* (1981)—it seems to demand attention as one of the decisive contributions to contemporary African literature.

Head's life was not an easy one. She was born in Pietermaritzburg, in the province of Natal, South Africa, in 1937, to a white mother and a black father. In the context of South African society, then and now, such a circumstance could not fail to engender drastic consequences. Under South Africa's race laws, Head, as the child of "mixed" parentage, was classified as "coloured." More importantly, her mother was committed to an asylum by her outraged, uncomprehending, and punitive family. She subsequently took her own life, leaving Head to be raised by foster parents until, at age 13, she was sent to a mission school to complete her education. In her searing, largely autobiographical novel *A Question of Power* (1974), Head would return to these developments and their implications.

Upon her graduation from the mission school, Head qualified as a teacher, taught in Natal for a period of four years, and then moved to Johannesburg, where she worked as a journalist on the black Sunday newspaper *Golden City Post*. During her spell in Johannesburg she also contributed to *Drum*, then the most vibrant journalistic and cultural forum in the country.

The early 1960s in South Africa were marked by savage repression and state violence as the ruling National Party attempted to consolidate its power and institute its grand policy of apartheid. In the years following the Sharpeville massacre of 1960, scores of activists and intellectuals left the country to live in exile abroad or elsewhere in Africa. In Head's case, the decision to leave South Africa was made not only against the backdrop of these sociopolitical circumstances but also in the light of a failed marriage. Head applied to the South African authorities for a passport to enable her to travel internationally, but her request was denied. Accordingly, when she was offered a teaching position in neighboring Botswana, she decided to leave South Africa on a one-way exit permit. With her young son she arrived in Botswana in 1964 and, despite the unwelcoming and rather indifferent attitude of the Botswana government, lived there for the rest of her life (with the exception of a four-month stint at the International Writing Program at the University of Iowa in 1977 and a short trip to Denmark in 1980), writing, teaching, and participating as one of a number of refugees in a rural self-sufficiency project at Bamangwato Development Farm. Her involvement in this project, later described in *When Rain Clouds Gather* (1969), was extremely important to her. As she once observed to an interviewer, "In South Africa, all my life I lived in shattered little bits. All those shattered bits began to grow together here... I have a peace against which all the turmoil is worked out." After having been turned down for citizenship in 1977, Head finally became a Botswana national in 1979 when the Botswana government abruptly and unexpectedly reversed its earlier denial.

In Head's work the questions of roots and of identity play a central role. Head has justly been praised for the remarkable dexterity of her evocation of the materiality of everyday existence in rural Botswana, which for all its harshness, is nevertheless perceived as the site and even as the guarantor of community. Yet, as Cecil Abrahams has argued, although Botswana constitutes the "physical and meditative environment" of Head's fiction, it is to South Africa that the broader concerns of her work refer. Among these broader concerns, Abrahams lists "political and spiritual exile, racial hatred and the source of corrupting power and authority."

These concerns are addressed memorably in Head's second and third novels, *Maru* (1971) and *A Question of Power*. As the latter title itself hints, Head's idealism is hostile to institutional power in any form. In *A Question of Power*, thus, Elizabeth, the central protagonist, needs to fight her way free of sexist and racist categories because they possess the power to define her, not only in the eyes of society at large but also in her own eyes, as insane. In its fractures and incoherencies, *A Question of Power* is notoriously difficult to read, but as an exploration of the destructive power of racial and sexual privilege in a broadly colonial context, it is matched only by Jean Rhys's *Wide Sargasso Sea*.

In the late 1970s and early 1980s, perhaps as she began to feel more and more at home in Botswana, Head created characters who are "insiders"; in a volume of her short stories, gathered under the title *The Collector of Treasures* (1977), one of which is reprinted here, the narrator frequently assumes the guise of griot or official storyteller. This tendency is furthered in *Serowe: Village of the Rain Wind*, in which Head, now fully installed as public historian, interviews the inhabitants of Serowe village about their lives and times and weaves the resulting recollections into a narrative sequence that is phrased as a history of Serowe. In this work, one senses that Bessie Head had finally found the home for which she had been searching all her life.

Neil Lazarus

LOOKING FOR A RAIN GOD

It is lonely at the lands where the people go to plough. These lands are vast clearings in the bush, and the wild bush is lonely too. Nearly all the lands are within walking distance from the village. In some parts of the bush where the underground water is very near the surface, people made little rest camps for themselves and dug shallow wells to quench their thirst while on their journey to their own lands. They experienced all kinds of things once they left the village. They could rest at shady watering places full of lush, tangled trees with delicate pale-gold and purple wild flowers springing up between soft green moss and the children could hunt around for wild figs and any berries that might be in season. But from 1958, a seven-year drought fell upon the land and even the watering places began to look as dismal as the dry open thorn-bush country; the leaves of the trees curled up and withered; the moss became dry and hard and, under the shade of the tangled trees, the ground turned a powdery black and white, because there was no rain. People said rather humorously that if you tried to catch the rain in a cup it would only fill a teaspoon. Towards the beginning of the seventh year of drought, the summer had be-

come an anguish to live through. The air was so dry and moisture-free that it burned the skin. No one knew what to do to escape the heat, and tragedy was in the air. At the beginning of that summer, a number of men just went out of their homes and hung themselves to death from trees. The majority of the people had lived off crops, but for two years past they had all returned from the lands with only their rolled-up skin blankets and cooking utensils. Only the charlatans, incanters, and witchdoctors made a pile of money during this time because people were always turning to them in desperation for little talismans and herbs to rub on the plough for the crops to grow and the rain to fall.

The rains were late that year. They came in early November, with a promise of good rain. It wasn't the full, steady downpour of the years of good rain, but thin, scanty, misty rain. It softened the earth and a rich growth of green things sprang up everywhere for the animals to eat. People were called to the village kgotla* to hear the proclamation of the beginning of the ploughing season; they stirred themselves and whole families began to move off to the lands to plough.

The family of the old man, Mokgobja, were among those who left early for the lands. They had a donkey cart and piled everything onto it, Mokgobja—who was over seventy years old; two little girls, Neo and Boseyong; their mother Tiro and an unmarried sister, Nesta; and the father and supporter of the family, Ramadi, who drove the donkey cart. In the rush of the first hope of rain, the man, Ramadi, and the two women, cleared the land of thorn-bush and then hedged their vast ploughing area with this same thorn-bush to protect the future crop from the goats they had brought along for milk. They cleared out and deepened the old well with its pool of muddy water and still in this light, misty rain, Ramadi inspanned two oxen and turned the earth over with a hand plough.

The land was ready and ploughed, waiting for the crops. At night, the earth was alive with insects singing and rustling about in search of food. But suddenly, by mid-November, the rain fled away; the rain-clouds fled away and left the sky bare. The sun danced dizzily in the sky, with a strange cruelty. Each day the land was covered in a haze of mist as the sun sucked up the last drop of moisture out of the earth. The family sat down in despair, waiting and waiting. Their hopes had run so high; the goats had started producing milk, which they had eagerly poured on their porridge, now they ate plain porridge with no milk. It was impossible to plant the corn, maize, pumpkin and water-melon seeds in the dry earth. They sat the whole day in the shadow of the huts and even stopped thinking, for the rain had fled away. Only the children, Neo and Boseyong, were quite happy in their little girl world. They carried on with their game of making house like their mother and chattered to each other in light, soft tones. They made children from sticks around which they tied rags, and scolded them severely in an exact imitation of their own mother. Their voices could be heard scolding the day long: "You stupid thing, when I send you to draw

water, why do you spill half of it out of the bucket!" "You stupid thing! Can't you mind the porridge-pot without letting the porridge burn!" And then they would beat the rag-dolls on their bottoms with severe expressions.

The adults paid no attention to this; they did not even hear the funny chatter; they sat waiting for rain; their nerves were stretched to breaking-point willing the rain to fall out of the sky. Nothing was important, beyond that. All their animals had been sold during the bad years to purchase food, and of all their herd only two goats were left. It was the women of the family who finally broke down under the strain of waiting for rain. It was really the two women who caused the death of the little girls. Each night they started a weird, high-pitched wailing that began on a low, mournful note and whipped up to a frenzy. Then they would stamp their feet and shout as though they had lost their heads. The men sat quiet and self-controlled; it was important for men to maintain their self-control at all times but their nerve was breaking too. They knew the women were haunted by the starvation of the coming year.

Finally, an ancient memory stirred in the old man, Mokgobja. When he was very young and the customs of the ancestors still ruled the land, he had been witness to a rain-making ceremony. And he came alive a little, struggling to recall the details which had been buried by years and years of prayer in a Christian church. As soon as the mists cleared a little, he began consulting in whispers with his youngest son, Ramadi. There was, he said, a certain rain god who accepted only the sacrifice of the bodies of children. Then the rain would fall; then the crops would grow, he said. He explained the ritual and as he talked, his memory became a conviction and he began to talk with unshakable authority. Ramadi's nerves were smashed by the nightly wailing of the women and soon the two men began whispering with the two women. The children continued their game: "You stupid thing! How could you have lost the money on the way to the shop! You must have been playing again!"

After it was all over and the bodies of the two little girls had been spread across the land, the rain did not fall. Instead, there was a deathly silence at night and the devouring heat of the sun by day. A terror, extreme and deep, overwhelmed the whole family. They packed, rolling up their skin blankets and pots, and fled back to the village.

People in the village soon noted the absence of the two little girls. They had died at the lands and were buried there, the family said. But people noted their ashen, terror-stricken faces and a murmur arose. What had killed the children, they wanted to know? And the family replied that they had just died. And people said amongst themselves that it was strange that the two deaths had occurred at the same time. And there was a feeling of great unease at the unnatural looks of the family. Soon the police came around. The family told them the same story of death and burial at the lands. They did not know what the children

had died of. So the police asked to see the graves. At this, the mother of the children broke down and told everything.

Throughout that terrible summer the story of the children hung like a dark cloud of sorrow over the village, and the sorrow was not assuaged when the old man and Ramadi were sentenced to death for ritual murder. All they had on the statute books was that ritual murder was against the law and must be stamped out with the death penalty. The subtle story of strain and starvation and breakdown was inadmissable evidence at court; but all the people who lived off crops knew in their hearts that only a hair's breadth had saved them from sharing a fate similar to that of the Mokgobja family. They could have killed something to make the rain fall.

NOTE

* The village council, which, though deprived of power to allocate land and water rights, remains "the people's place" for discussing human affairs and displaying the wisdom of the elders.

Maria Teresa Horta
Maria Velho da Costa
Maria Isabel Barreno   *Portugal, b. 1937; b. 1938; b. 1939*

The "three Marias" came to their collaborative effort on *Novas Cartas Portuguesas* (*The Three Marias: New Portuguese Letters*, 1974), excerpted below, as established writers, each with a distinct personality. In this work, however, they selected to obliterate their individual identities to produce a work that would be truly an exercise in collaborative writing.

Maria Isabel Barreno began her writing career as the author of sociological studies, coauthoring two books on problems of labor and then working independently on studies of women's issues. She had also tried her hand at fiction, to which she returned after *Novas Cartas Portuguesas*. *A Morte da Mãe* (The Death of the Mother, 1979) is a fictional reconstruction of women's history from prehistoric times to the present. *Inventário de Ana* (Inventory of Ana, 1982) traces the sociopsychological development of Ana in a story that intertwines her life with those of her two friends Josefa and Antónia. In her most recent work *Contos Analógicos* (Analogic Stories), Barreno explores the possibilities of the short story.

Maria Teresa Horta is a woman of catholic interests. She was an active member of the ABC CineClube which produced experimental films in the 1960s. As a poet, she took part in the Poesia-61 group, important exponents of experimental poetry. Fourteen books of her poetry were published between 1960 and 1983. As a novelist, she has published three works, all of them dealing with women's sexual and psychological oppression: *Ambas as Mãos Sobre o Corpo* (Both Hands on Her Body, 1970); *Ana* (1975); *Ema* (1984). She is also a journalist and editor of the feminist magazine *Mulheres* (Women). Maria Teresa Horta is indeed the most radical of all Portuguese feminist writers; with Maria Isabel Barreno she founded the now defunct Women's Liberation Movement.

Of the three, Maria Velho da Costa is the most respected as a novelist. She published her first work, *O Lugar Comum* (The Common Place), in 1966 and has since then published several works that have become modern classics, among them *Maina Mendes* (1969), *Casas Pardas* (Gray Houses, 1977), and *Lucialima*, 1983. Maria Velho da Costa's novels are highly original in their sensitivity to language, its polysemic values in particular; the novels are also original in their form, which is often polyphonic. Da Costa has won important literary prizes for her work and has served as president of the Portuguese Writers' Association (1973–1978). She was in fact serving in that capacity at the time of the "scandalous" appearance of *Novas Cartas Portuguesas*. Maria Velho da Costa was a lecturer of Portugese literature at King's College of the University of London for several years and is now cultural attachée in Cape Verde.

Alice Clemente

from THE THREE MARIAS
Novas Cartas Portuguesas

Extracts from the Diary of Ana Maria, Born in 1940, a Direct Descendant of the Niece of Dona Maria Ana

My ancestor Maria Ana, the philosopher, what point have we reached: if the woman still has nothing, if she exists only through the man, if even the occasional pleasure she receives from him is meager and perverse, what does she risk or what does she stand to lose by rebelling? Revolution is a dangerous game, and the bourgeois citizen taking part in the French Revolution risked everything, even though the objectives of his attack were limited; but what does a woman risk or stand to lose, if none of her needs are satisfied? What, then, were you complaining about? I am well aware that this is not the real problem; I know that this is a false argument; but this whole question is an important one nonetheless.

I am well aware that revolt on the part of the woman is what leads to disruption in every social class; nothing can ever be the same afterwards, neither class relations, nor relations between groups, nor relations between individuals. The very roots of repression must be destroyed, and the basic repression, the one which in my view lies at the very core of the history of the human species, creating the model and giving rise to the myths underlying other repressions, is that of the woman by the man. So long as this situation persists, no understanding between men and women will be possible; even the way we want to bring up our children will be a matter of contention. Everything will have to be entirely different, and we are all afraid. And amid all this, the woman's real problem is not whether she is going to win or lose; it is, rather, the problem of her identity. There is little doubt that in this society there are many things she finds satisfying; but there is even less doubt that the woman (and the man as well) are not aware of how they are manipulated and conditioned. Perfect repression is the sort that is not felt by the person suffering from it, the sort that is unconsciously accepted, thanks to a traditional upbringing spanning many long years, with the result that the mechanisms of repression come to be internalized within the individual, and hence become a source of personal gratification. And if perchance a woman becomes conscious of her enslavement and rejects it, with whom can she identify herself, how can she acquire an identity of her own? Where can she relearn how to be a real person, where can she reinvent the model, the role, the image, the gestures and the words of her life from day to day, the acceptance and the love of others, and the signs of acceptance and love? I am very much aware, Maria Ana, my ancestor, of what you were complaining of, of what you were incapable of: of inventing, all by yourself, the mother, the heroine, the ideology, the myth, the matrix that would give you substance and meaning in the eyes of others, that would open up a path leading to others—if not a path of communication, at least one of shared concerns and anxieties.

And what did you invent in your endeavor to reshape your presence, in your own time and place? You refused a husband, you refused a man, and what this gesture means to us is that you were a spinster, a frustrated, hysterical woman, like all women without a man, writing pretentious texts, just as you would pamper a poodle or take an active part in organized charities were you alive today. And that is the particular coloration you have in my mind's eyes, too, I think that is how you were, at least in part, or perhaps fundamentally, despite the fact that I understand you, and despite the fact that I recognize that I therefore also fear you. Where is there a place to reinvent gestures and words? Everything is permeated with time-hallowed meanings, including our own selves, down to our very bones, our very marrow, even in the case of us women who are attempting to bring about a revolution. Looking at you, Maria Ana, I recognize reluctantly, like everyone else, various facets in you whose colors blend, despite the fact, or perhaps because of the fact, that a number of them were contradictory: the woman who refused to confront others directly, who feared shared pain and experience, a spurned woman whom nobody wanted, perhaps because of your refusal, perhaps not; but in any case a spurned woman is a figure whom society scorns and detests, and in this contempt lies the punishment that we try to escape by surrendering ourselves, without seeking another alternative, since this contempt is more than ample reason for us to cast aspersions on the refusal of a woman to accept a man and instead live by herself, either out of natural inclination or through deliberate choice on her part. Hence we suspect such a refusal of being tinged with bitterness, puritanism, or frigidity, and attach great importance to the consequences of this refusal— loneliness, aridity, frustration—using them as threads to begin weaving the whole pattern all over again: the blame heaped on the woman who lives by herself (if you don't have a man it's because you're puritanical or frigid, and so you're frustrated—and why is it that I presume that you are a virgin?), while at the same time the man who rejects women is surrounded by a certain aura of absurd but haughty superiority. We accept his rejection of what is all too familiar, the exercise of his sex drives on the body of another, his sexual desire that is never questioned (no one will ever presume that he is a virgin even though he may well be one), his sex that is ever visible and complete, whereas the woman who rejects a man always seems to us to be inferior and ignorant, evading an awareness of her sexuality, such as it would be revealed, shaped, and taught to her by a man, fleeing the power of the male as though he were an adversary long since vanquished, avoiding the inevitable defeat that in our heart of hearts we all consider quite natural. Maria Ana, my ancestor, that is how we see you, that is why I am hostile to you despite your being my sister, in this era which many call an age of equality, when women's work is now worth money (though very little) and women's words are now being heard (and misunderstood). Will the day ever come, Maria Ana?

April 13, 1971: a day not purposely chosen—reading articles in an evening "progressive" paper, thought-provoking, instructive reading:

The fashion game—how long are skirts going to be this next summer? Will they stop at calf-length? Professional buyers are playing the game—and placing their bets—the world over; what is at stake is the industry that answers one of the three fundamental needs of humanity—food, clothing, and shelter; the textile and clothing industry brings Italy a billion dollars annual revenue; the fear of buying the wrong thing; a problem that has come to complicate the summer fashion picture is that of "hot pants"; if a daring offensive is not mounted in the field of fashion, these tiny little enemies may well seize this opportunity to strengthen their hold.

A "new chapter" in the special *cinéma-vérité* series—a story that happened yesterday, that is happening today, and will happen tomorrow, so long as there exists a "market" for buying and selling happy hours. This episode was about a lady pianist; her "calling" was to find love without ever becoming attached to a man; but there was one man for whom she was different....

The television critic insisted that it could just as well have been a "doctor" or a "journalist" or an "actor" or a "manufacturer" or a "factory worker" as a pianist; anyone who is alienated, turned into a consumer product.

In the film Catarina, the pianist, sees the possibility of making a new life for herself, of refusing to be turned into an object in such a cruel way, she will stop giving concerts and just make records, and at Christmastime she plans to return to her catalyst-journalist; but she is never reunited with him because the plane that she takes explodes. There had been a discussion following a showing of the film—a male critic, Ramos, had wondered whether a *wanton woman* could ever aspire to love, and a woman critic, Horta, had said that it was called a love story because it was the story of a *lady* pianist rather than a *man* pianist, but the critic maintained that it could just as well have been a "doctor" or a "factory worker" as a pianist (male or female), since the real problem was that of the consumer society, and so he reported that the discussion had turned into a "*dull exchange of banal remarks by ladies sitting eating their little teacakes and drinking their little cups of tea*" (all it takes is to substitute the word "ladies" for "doctors," "journalists," "manufacturers," "factory workers"); you are quite right, Dona Maria, that's terribly ill-bred, isn't that something though, just imagine, won't you have another teacake?

A model is practically a synonym for a candidate aspiring to movie stardom. And this is precisely the case with the [photograph of a] young girl...in a bikini who got herself a role in a film, even though it is a non-speaking role; she will not be required to say a single word; but she's on her way to becoming an actress.

Miss Mozambique arrived in Lisbon wearing a "native costume" (a photograph of the aforementioned beauty with a large group of smiling girls also in native costumes posing on a flight of steps).

Ministry of Finance, General Accounting Department, Personnel Division...announces a competitive examination for Grade 3 administrators, *open to male candidates only*....

The automated kitchen, the invention of a harried man—his wife was in the hospital, and he was staying home to take care of the couple's four children. Markus Beck (a mechanical engineer) tried his best to do all the housework and look after the children, but the dirty dishes in the sink kept piling up higher and higher, foundering in this sea of troubles and tasks (and why did they describe him as "a mechanical engineer whose wife was in the hospital" when they might have said "wife who was pregnant for the fifth time?"), he invented the automated kitchen.

To sum up:

The fashion game to cover or not to cover the
                                                         knee
that is the question: an industry fundamental
                                                        needs
providing food, clothing, and shelter for
                                                     humanity
brings in annual profits of millions of dollars
buyers from all over the world are playing the
                                                        game
clothes designers fear the tiny "hot pants"[1]
                                                       enemy
giving fashion sales a world-wide shot in the
                                                          arm
with long skirts
the latest chapter in the special truth series
happening today, happening tomorrow
as long as there are such things as movies
                                                     markets
the buying and selling of happy hours her
                        calling was to find a man
and the piano and the market and the journalist
                              as long as there is
one for whom she was different and love
the critic is satisfied to substitute the word lady
                          pianist for journalist
or doctor or factory worker and substitute
                                           Dona Maria
for the lady pianist and replace rebellion
by teacakes and can you imagine such a thing
being a critic is ill-bred
model almost synonymous with a role
she won't be required to say a single word
                           she's on her way to being
Miss Native Costume in the general accounting
                                                        office

grade 3 administrators belonging to the male
                                                          sex
needing only a certificate
of proficiency a harried engineer invented
four children and the automated
kitchen
while his wife was in the hospital.

An electronics industry is being developed. Women are being recruited, for their fingers have a delicate touch, thanks to the fine embroidery, the lacework, and other domestic and regional crafts that they have been taught to do—the best possible fingers for assembling electronic equipment. They are paid a mere pittance, since naturally they are unskilled labor, with no specific training for their present jobs as factory workers; it is easy to exploit them, for they are unaware that industry will profit from their already-acquired skills without paying a single extra cent for it; they do not even know that their fingers have been trained, and it seems to them that their lot in life has already changed for the better if someone puts their insignificant female talents to use, being powerless creatures who heretofore have not been good for much of anything, since bearing children doesn't count. Jobs in industry are becoming available for women; that's fine, that proves they're making progress. Equal pay for equal work; but the work is not equal, how is it possible to compare jobs, when men do different things and only women are used for this difficult work in the electronics industry? Young ones, preferably unmarried ones, so that they won't miss work because of family problems. Later it is all quite simple: when they are old enough to get married and have children, or at any rate after having worked for five years or so, they quit; hence the problems of absenteeism, promotions, demands for higher wages are reduced. Replacing personnel is not a problem either; on the contrary, women are already skilled workers when they are hired, and they leave once they're no longer useful, that is to say, when they are exhausted, their eyes ruined, and their nervous systems badly damaged.

Women—and blacks—are also turning up nowadays as workers on road-construction projects and as city street sweepers. Up until recently, these jobs were not regarded as suitable for women. But now that men—white men—no longer want them, because they are backbreaking and pay very badly, they are becoming woman's work.

Merely an example, from which no generalizations can be drawn? On the contrary: this sums up the history of the so-called improvement in the condition of women through access to jobs. But there is also the example of the accountants' jobs for males only; the rules governing competitive examinations for the filling of vacancies in almost all state agencies, where preference is given to men, except for those jobs that they do not want; the various ads in the papers "company seeks female employees...." When we read or hear that "Nowadays women work side by side with men in the most varied sectors of activity," this means, when translated into the terms of the real situation: women today are being utilized in sectors of the labor market, professions, and functions that men have now rejected in favor of others that offer them better working conditions and better pay.

How has the situation of woman changed? Today she is FREE OF LAUNDRY PROBLEMS WITH A WASHING MACHINE. And there are female beauty contests, with the beauties in bathing suits—practically bikinis—turning to the front, to the rear, to the right, to the left. And there is not a single protest from the television critics, some of whom pride themselves on being so "progressive." That's not what people are concerned about, there's no "woman's problem" the real problem lies elsewhere, so why all the fuss? The great majority of middle-class people, who nowadays are no longer landowners, have no appreciable power; the great majority of them make their living by doing intellectual work, by engaging in their liberal or nonliberal profession, lost in a mass society. So who's afraid of an attack on private ownership of the means of production, of an attack on the power elite or pressure groups? Only the very few who would be directly affected. But they all "have" women; and THEREFORE there is no "woman's problem," that's just so much nonsense; that's not the real issue at all. As for the exhibition of human females, not a single protest has been forthcoming from the television critics. It's even a step in the right direction, one of them has said: beauty has ceased to be a sin and ugliness a virtue; it's a public homage to female pulchritude. A woman can buy a washing machine and enter a beauty contest to show off her ass and her legs. How has the situation of the woman changed? Once an object that was a producer, of children and so-called domestic labor, that is to say nonremunerated labor, she has now also become an object that consumes as well, and a consumer product. Once upon a time she was like a piece of farmland, something to make fertile, and now she is commercialized, something to be distributed.

And eroticism, gentlemen, what about eroticism? In almost all the so-called erotic books that are everywhere today, *il n'y a pas de femmes libres, il y a des femmes livrées aux hommes*: there are no women delivered from their bondage, only women delivered over to men. That is the sort of liberation that men offer us; after being the warrior's repose, we are becoming spoils of war. The charwoman who used to clean the office where I work died of septicemia after aborting herself with a stalk of celery, and a few days ago I learned from one of her co-workers that it had been her twenty-third abortion. And a number of years ago a woman friend of mine who is a doctor told me that women who entered the hospital emergency ward with their uteruses perforated, torn to shreds, ruined forever after attempting to abort themselves at home with knitting needles, sticks of wood, cabbage stalks, and anything else they had at hand that would penetrate and scrape, were treated with the greatest of contempt, and that the curettages they were then subjected to were performed without any anesthetic whatsoever, coldly and sadistically, "so as to teach them a lesson." To teach them what lesson, for God's sake?! To teach them that they have been the victims of the contradiction (concealed beneath the mask of what is supposedly their inevitable fate) that society has created between the fecundity-demanded-of-a-woman's womb and the place-denied-women-for-raising-children? Ever since the destiny of the man and the woman irremediably branched off in two opposite directions— but when, o when, did this happen?—the woman has fallen victim not only to all the existential anguish and all the forms of social repression that are the common fate of both men and women, but also to the anguish of her biological destiny, become her drama alone rather than a dramatic experience of our entire species, thereby falling victim to a repression whose instrument is this biological destiny of hers that has been turned into an individual drama. Lovers pass by in pairs and we know that they are irremediably separated one from the other; there is no love between a man and a woman that is worth the pain, for in the love-experience the woman is at the very limits of the agonizing, repressive, and lonely fate that society has invented for her. What good did love do Romeo and Juliet?[2]

Translated by Helen R. Lane

NOTES

1. Very short pants popular in the 1960s.
2. Shakespeare's famous young lovers in the play (ca. 1595) of the same name both killed themselves.

Nancy Spero, To the Revolution, *1983, diptych, collage and ink on paper. Courtesy Josh Baer Gallery, New York*

Michèle Lalonde

Canada, b. 1937

Michèle Lalonde's career epitomizes the way in which feminism and nationalism combined to reinforce one another and reshape francophone literature during the period that has been called the Quiet Revolution (ca. 1960–1970). Published and acclaimed at the age of 21 for the lyric poetry of *Geôles* (Jails), Lalonde subsequently emerged as a voice for the new currents sweeping francophone Canada when she published *Terre des hommes* (Earth of Man, 1967) and recited her poetry with a massed choir and full orchestra conducted by Montreal's André Provost at Expo '67. The title of the book took its name from the theme of that World's Fair and serves as a counterpoint to an essay with the same name written by Gabrielle Roy: the two works symbolize the debate within the francophone community between the older and newer generations regarding its political and cultural role in Canada. With Lalonde, poetry became part of the general ferment in which francophone Canadians asserted their "difference." "Speak White," for instance, was part of a public happening called "Poems and Songs of the Resistance" that toured Quebec with great success in 1968–1969. It reflects the anticolonialism and nationalism that are the common elements of virtually all Lalonde's writing, "a concern with the destiny of her people that places Lalonde in a long and respectable tradition in Québec Letters," as Larry Shouldice has suggested.

The poem makes reference to some of the most significant male writers of British literature as the symbolic shapers of language as well as to some of the major events of British and U.S. history—primarily those relating to the Revolutionary War and events of the 1960s—and to those topographical centers that symbolize America at those periods. Like much political poetry, "Speak White" is also filled with topical references: it embodies the complex relations of language, geography, culture, and action. This selection is in the collection *Défense et illustration de la langue québécoise, suivie de prose et poèmes* (Defense and Illustration of the Québécois Language, followed by Prose and Poems, 1979). The boldfaced words also appear in the original French version, which had the same title.

Lalonde's work is associated with the literary movement known as *poèsie du pays*: this poetry of the country emphasized the distinctiveness of the Québécois identity; unlike members of the older movement of *le terroir*, which also focused on the land, Lalonde, along with such writers as Paul Chamberland, Gatien Lapointe, Yves Prefontaine, and Jean-Guy Pilon, questioned the authority of church, family, and state; they also were concerned with a language that would fully express the distinctive francophone identity of the Canadian people, apart from France as well as from anglophone Canada. Lalonde articulated this stance in an important essay published in 1979—"La Défense et illustration de la langue québécquoise." The essay was part of a debate in which Quebec unilaterally declared its right to use French as its sole official language in 1977. That same year Lalonde published *Dernier recours de Baptiste à Catherine* (Baptiste's Last Appeal to Catherine), a five-act play that traces the oppression of the people of Québéc from 1760 to 1850 and is her effort to reinstall a national history that has been erased by the state and expurgated by the church.

Educated at Harvard and the University of Montreal, Lalonde is married to Dr. Yves Duchastel de Montrouge and is a professor of literature at l'École nationale de théâtre in Montreal. In 1980 she was awarded the Prix Duvernay for the body of her work, and is currently preparing a retrospective collection of her poetry.

SPEAK WHITE
Speak white

Speak white
it is so lovely to listen to you
speaking of **Paradise Lost**
or the anonymous, graceful profile trembling in the sonnets
    of Shakespeare

We are a rude and stammering people
but we are not deaf to the genius of a language
speak with the accent of Milton and Byron and Shelley and Keats
speak white
and please excuse us if in return
we've only our rough ancestral songs
and the chagrin of Nelligan*

speak white
speak of places, this and that
speak to us of the Magna Carta
of the Lincoln Monument
of the cloudy charm of the Thames
of blossom-time on the Potomac
speak to us of your traditions
We are a people who are none too bright
but we are quick to sense
the great significance of crumpets
or the Boston Tea Party

But when you **really speak white**
when you **get down to brass tracks**
to speak of *Better Homes and Gardens*
and the high standard of living
and the Great Society
a little louder then **speak white**

raise your foremens' voices
we are a little hard of hearing
we live too close to the machines
and only hear our heavy breathing over the tools

speak white and loud
so we can hear you clearly
from Saint Henri to Santo Domingo
yes, what a marvellous language
for hiring and firing
for giving the orders
for fixing the hour to be worked to death
and that pause that refreshes
and bucks up the dollar

Speak white
tell us that God is a great big shot
and that we're paid to trust him
speak white
speak to us of production, profits and percentages
speak white
it's a rich language
for buying
but for selling oneself
but for selling one's soul
but for selling oneself

Ah
speak white
big deal
but for telling about
the eternity of a day on strike
for telling the whole
life-story of a nation of caretakers
for coming back home in the evening
at the hour when the sun's gone bust in the alleys
for telling you yes the sun does set yes
every day of our lives to the east of your empires
Nothing's as good as a language of oaths
our mode of expression none too clean
dirtied with oil and with axlegrease

Speak white
feel at home with your words
we are a bitter people
but we'd never reproach a soul
for having a monopoly
on how to improve one's speech

In the sweet tongue of Shakespeare
with the accent of Longfellow
speak a French purely and atrociously white
as in Viet Nam, in the Congo
speak impeccable German
a yellow star between your teeth
speak Russian speak of the right to rule speak of repression
speak white
it's a universal language
we were born to understand it
with its tear-gas phrases
with its billy-club words

(Continued)

Speak white
tell us again about freedom and democracy
We know that liberty is a Black word
as misery is Black
as blood is muddied with the dust of Algiers or of Little Rock
speak white
from Westminister to Washington take turns
speak white as on Wall Street
white as in Watts
Be civilized
and understand our conventional answer
when you ask us politely
how do you do
and we mean to reply
we're doing all right
we're doing fine
we
are not alone
We know now
that we are not alone.

Translated by D. G. Jones

NOTE

* Emile Nelligan (1879–1941): One of the finest Québécois poets, he wrote all of his poems between 16 and 19 years of age, before he was certified insane and confined to a mental hospital. Nelligan's "chagrin" could refer to the suffering of a man often lucidly aware of his madness and sensitive to language or it might refer to the many poems in which Nelligan expresses bitterness at being misunderstood and an object of mockery for his poet contemporaries.

Nélida Piñon
Brazil, b. 1937

Born to a wealthy family in Rio de Janeiro, Nélida Piñon attended high school in Germany and then studied journalism at the Catholic University in Rio. Once her first novel, *Guia mapa do Gabriel Arcanjo* (Guide Map of the Archangel Gabriel, 1961), met with encouraging success, she devoted herself to her writing.

Piñon is the most recent of Brazilian women writers to be known outside of Latin America; her prize-winning novels *Casa de paixão* (House of Passion, 1972), *Tebas do meu coração* (My Beloved Thebes, 1974), and most recently *A força do destino* (The Force of Destiny, 1977) have an international reputation. She is, at the same time, an accomplished short-story writer, as has been evidenced in the acclaimed *Sala de armas* (Fencing Room, 1973), from which comes the following story, and the more recent *O calor das coisas* (The Heat of Things, 1980). Piñon is known for her experimentation with language, her use of mythic, magical literary modes, and bizarre, often humorous plots that explore deeply psychological forces at work in human relationships.

BIRD OF PARADISE
Ave de paraíso

One day each week he used to visit his wife. "To work up passion," as he would say, deeply moved. His wife believed him and welcomed his return with chocolate cake and a pear liqueur made from fruit gathered in their own orchard. The neighbors discussed these rare encounters, but she continued to love him with even greater intensity. The husband, suspecting how difficult life must be for her, begged forgiveness with his eyes, as if reassuring himself that there was no other way in which he ought to love her. He ate her cake but refused everything else even when she tried to insist. He is simply being polite, she thought, concealing herself in his shadow. On one of his visits she had managed to prepare a surprise dinner. The food smelled divine, its flavors redolent of the distant East. The cutlery gleamed on the table alongside the dinner service that had been purchased for their day of celebration when he would open his eyes in sheer delight.

Her husband controlled their existence together by showing his approval. He had always considered her sensitive to harmony and grace. Of this he had become convinced upon their first meeting. She had boarded the tram without any money in her purse for the fare and had looked around her without asking to be rescued from her plight. He had bought her ticket and suggested in a low voice that he, too, needed some assistance. She had smiled and he had held her hand. Apprehensive, she had yielded to his wishes and as he left her safely returned to the door of her home, he promised to return the following day.

"Please do not invite me to dinner because I cannot possibly accept." He sounded so natural, like a fish chastising the sea. She secretly wept, thinking to herself that among so many men, Providence had decreed that she should meet the most difficult man of all. It was the only moment of weakness she showed in her devotion for him. The next day he sent her roses and on the accompanying card there was only one word written—LOVE. She smiled, filled with remorse and rebuking her own infidelity. It was wrong of her to have put him to a similar test, which he, like a true hero, had spurned. On his next visit he made love to her with the passion of a fugitive and he kept on repeating her name in breathless whispers.

Once he disappeared for three months without so much as a letter, telegram, or telephone call. There was nothing left for her in life. There stood the same little table with its red-patterned cover that she herself had embroidered at leisure one Saturday afternoon. There stood their bed with its white linen sheets that she had personally washed, taking great care to avoid using too much bleach in the water. This was their home, which he had suddenly stopped visiting without the slightest warning.

She wandered through the streets in search of him and with each sigh exclaimed, "What is there for a woman without love in her life?"

She had attended the high school in the town where she had been born. The idea of becoming a school teacher had never appealed to her. For as long as she could remember, she had wanted to get married. That was her sole ambition in life. She was afraid that the children of others might sap the strength that was destined for her own flesh and blood. Her mother had tried to persuade her otherwise because they needed the money at home. Her father had lost his job and neither of them was getting any younger. He finished up working behind the counter in a relative's pharmacy. And her mother went out sewing. Meantime, she looked after the household chores since she refused to go out teaching.

This was when she first started to become interested in baking. But the famous recipe for chocolate cake she only acquired much later.

Norma appeared in high spirits wearing a

yellow dress and looking for some help with a pleated skirt from a pattern found by chance in a magazine bought from the news-vendor on the corner. Although she secretly regarded Norma as being a somewhat frivolous young woman who was always trying to persuade her to accompany her to dances where one could find a boyfriend at the drop of a hat, she never permitted herself to criticize her openly. It was through Norma that she met the other girl who was one of Norma's casual acquaintances. Both girls were in the same typing course and both were hoping to work for an American company. They were determined to visit the United States one day and dreamed of strolling up and down Fifth Avenue. Norma's great obsession was the possibility of meeting an American army officer. Both girls lamented that American soldiers no longer visited Brazil as frequently as during the war. Norma's friend who normally had little to say, suddenly asked her, when Norma finally stopped talking: "Why don't you join us?" She was referring to the competitive interviews for secretarial posts with an American company.

She expressed her refusal with a nod. She felt much too embarrassed to explain to them that what she really wanted was to get married. It seemed the easier thing to do and she felt suited to duties of married life.

"Don't tell me...I know...all you want is a good recipe for a chocolate cake," the other girl intervened abruptly.

This time she agreed and she found herself trembling. She asked for the recipe at once with pencil and paper in hand, insisting that Norma's acquaintance should telephone her mother immediately in order to check the ingredients that she could only vaguely remember.

At home, because of the need to economize, it was impossible to try out the recipe. But she consoled herself by thinking—the moment I find someone to love, I shall bake him a cake as a surprise. She always cherished the hope that chocolate cake would be her husband's favorite dessert. Baking a cake only gave one satisfaction if it served to prove one's

love. Norma was intrigued by such simplicity. Years later when the girls had gone their separate ways and gradually lost touch with each other, she was fated to withdraw from the world in order to preserve her love. Norma had once said to her, placing a comforting hand on her shoulder. "This was bound to happen to you," and she was never to see her again. She had wanted to explain and to point out that she was wrong, but Norma simply walked away without once turning back, as relaxed and confident as ever.

When her husband returned home some months later bringing her a pile of presents, he kissed her effusively on the head and the scent that reached her nostrils convinced her that he belonged to some other planet. He tried to make her understand the urgency of his journey and assured her that he had no regrets about going away when he could count on the bliss of their reunion. She found this explanation most flattering and raced to the kitchen before he could entice her into the bedroom. Armed with the necessary ingredients, she set about baking a cake to perfection. She refused to allow him to make love to her unless there was a cake waiting to be eaten afterwards, especially on a special day like this one.

He laughed, amused by her extravagance, feeling that he had no right to argue. He was also anxious that she should feel free to do as she pleased. He waited patiently until she had finished in the kitchen. She then came to him as if reassuring him that she was already resigned to the anguish of his future absence.

She was ever delicate in matters of love and he valued this discretion. He would have repudiated any bold advances on her part capable of destroying forever the illusion of possessing her as if for the first time. Aware of his feeling, she buried her head in the pillow, sobbing quietly.

He called out like King Arthur's steward:* "Women are delightful! Women are delightful!" She knew what he meant by this expression, dried her tears, and meekly submitted herself to his desires. There had never been a time when she refused to fall in with this make-believe and these scenes were often repeated week after week.

He pretended not to notice that the pleasure of this little game might become stale and he did everything possible to renew the thrill. This explains why he loved her so passionately during those first years. His imagination also fed upon the novelty of the experience. Sometimes he adopted different disguises, a false beard and moustache or even a different color of hair. He always returned to the house discreetly, giving people time to guess his real identity. He was reluctant that they should think that he was deliberately deceiving them, but he loved to play tricks on people and then dismiss them with a laugh.

She succumbed with passion, still suffering the pain of his absence. On difficult days her love for him became so intense that she consulted her horoscope in the daily newspaper, hoping that it might reveal the day propitious for baking a chocolate cake to celebrate his return. Up to the end of that year, the oracle had warned her of each successive visit. It never occurred to her to tamper with the dates in order to try to arrange more frequent visits. She respected the system.

At the beginning of the month, however, he suddenly arrived earlier, bringing her some money for domestic expenses and whatever else she might require. He would toss the money into the fruit bowl even when it was already piled high with bananas, pears and apples that she adored because they brought back memories of Christmas. She couldn't explain why but somehow when she ate apples, she thought of herself as an aristocratic young woman who wore imported kid gloves, who spoke fluent French and wore a silk square on her head. The money remained there in the bowl until after he had gone. After his departure she would put it between the pages of her prayer-book. Both of them adored these rituals.

One day he suggested: "Let's go out this evening. We have never been to a cinema together and that is something that we must do before it's too late. Let's go right away." Embracing him tightly she wept for joy: "You are all mine...all mine."

They went but didn't enjoy the film. He censured the love episodes that he found obscene. She agreed with him but her happiness was such that she felt unable to express any strong feelings. They ate ice cream despite his objections. She got some on her dress and he laughed for he adored her rare perceptions and her habit of blundering in little things.

Her mother visited her two or three times a year. She still went out sewing. She enquired discreetly about her husband, a little scared of annoying her daughter. She had never understood that marriage. In church he had forbidden her to wear a wedding dress, claiming that bridal attire should be reserved for the bridegroom alone. After the ceremony, he found her in the bedroom, wearing her white dress, veil, and headdress. On their first night together as husband and wife, she appeared before him dressed as he had always dreamed of her and he closed his eyes for a moment before opening them again in order to make sure that she was still standing by his side...the woman whom he loved.

Deeply moved by her presence, he spoke in the manner that she understood: "You are beautiful. All we need is the chaplain to marry us once more." And when they came to discover each other's body in the night, he persuaded her to relax while he returned the wedding dress that he had bought for her to its hanger in the wardrobe. He assured her that he was incapable of ever conceiving of such things with another woman and she was never to forget those words.

Every time her mother visited her, she asked after her father and how they were getting along but she never ever asked her mother to stay, even though she lived quite some distance away, which meant a long train journey before getting back. During those short visits, her daughter complained of nothing. She seemed completely satisfied with her new life and her mother had never seen a happier woman. She sometimes felt tempted to ask her: "What time do you expect him back?" Or to prolong her visit in order to surprise him when he should arrive home for dinner. But from four-o'clock onwards, her daughter began to get nervous, jumping up at the slightest pretext and pretending to busy herself with this and that. She assured her mother with some vehemence that he was usually late in getting home. As they kissed each other goodbye, her mother always made a point of saying: "You have a lovely home...a really lovely home."

The following week he would question her: "And your mother, hasn't she been to see you lately?" Then she would assume a sad expression and holding him tightly in her arms, she would whisper: "I only have you in the whole wide world." He would kiss her and as if begging her forgiveness, he would say: "I'll be back next Wednesday. Does that make you happy?" She would smile, her face shining with joy, her hair done in the style he preferred. He could detect the first white strands in her hair and he rejoiced in them, thinking to himself: "My little woman is pure...pure... pure..."

One day he could not resist the temptation. He arrived in disguise, his last attempt to deceive the neighbors. In each hand, he was carrying a suitcase. In anticipation she suffered that long journey. She helped him as though he were exhausted and life had asked too much of him. She brought him iced water, regretting that there was no fountain in the garden that she might decorate with mosaic or perhaps even a statue. Her husband drank the water. He removed that mask which she had never once criticized, and assuming a note of feigned independence, he said in a loud voice so that she could overhear him: "The period of trial is over. This time I have come back for good."

His wife, suppressing her deep happiness, looked into his eyes and disappeared quickly into the kitchen. When it came to baking a chocolate cake, no one was her equal.

Translated by Giovanni Pontiero

NOTE

* Arthur was legendary king of England and his brother, Sir Key, was his steward.

Caryl Churchill   *UK(England), b. 1938*

When *Cloud Nine* opened in New York City in 1979, New Yorkers discovered a British playwright who had been actively and prodigiously writing plays and getting them produced since she was 20. Caryl Churchill, born in London, spent the years between 10 and 17 in Montreal, Canada, returning to England to attend Lady Margaret College, Oxford. While at Oxford she had her first two plays produced, *Downstairs* in 1958, and *Having a Wonderful Time* in 1960. Since then she has had a work produced nearly every year, either a play or one of her many radio dramas. Churchill married lawyer David Harter in 1961 and has three sons.

A leftist at Oxford, Churchill has, since the early 1970s, been actively involved with feminism. *Objections to Sex and Violence*, produced at London's avant-garde Royal Court Theater, combined her socialist and feminist interests to present a critique of bourgeois life. Her two subsequent works had their genesis in theater workshops. *Light Shining in Buckingham* (1976) was produced in the Royal Court's experimental upstairs theater and done by the Joint Stock Company. Set in Cromwell's time, it is about six working-class revolutionaries. *Vinegar Tom*

(1976), produced by a feminist group, Monstrous Regiment, uses the historical (seventeenth century) persecution of women as witches as a metaphor for other manifestations of sexism in society.

   Cloud Nine (1979) was the first of Churchill's plays to be presented in the United States. Her most critically successful play, it is a farce about sex roles, hypocrisy, and the double standard, as is *Top Girls*, produced in 1982 in London and at the Public Theater in New York City. *Fen* (1983) and *Soft Cops* (1984) continue Churchill's feminist preoccupations while returning to earlier socialist themes. *Fen* is about ownership of property and what it does to people's emotional lives, and *Soft Cops* is about violence and abuse of authority in its many forms in today's society. The scenes below, from *Owners* (1972), contain many of the themes *Churchill* has used in her dramaturgy. The play was inspired by a scene she witnessed: "I was in an old woman's flat when a young man offering her money to move came round—he was my first image of Worsely...." Marion and Alec came, in part, from the themes of active and passive in the song "Onward Christian Soldiers" and the words "'sitting quietly, doing nothing' in the Zen poem."* Clegg, on the other hand, was informed by Churchill's recent reading of Eva Figes' *Patriarchal Attitudes* (1970). The owners in this play are a real estate tycoon, Marion, and her husband Clegg, a butcher. They have bought the child of Lisa and Alec, the latter Marion's ex-lover and the only "thing" she hasn't been able to own. She has recently bought the apartment house in which Alec and Lisa live, in an attempt to strengthen her hold on Alec.

NOTE

* "Onward Christian Soldiers" is the famous Protestant hymn written by S. Baring-Gould in 1865. The Zen poem referred to is "Sitting quietly, doing nothing./Spring comes and the grass grows by itself.'"

from OWNERS

ACT II, SCENE FIVE

CLEGG *and* LISA *in* CLEGG's *bed, him on top, bouncing up and down under the bedclothes.*

CLEGG: An eye for an eye. A mouth for a mouth. A cunt for a cunt. Vengeance is mine. I will repay. In full.

[*He collapses on her and lies still. After a moment* LISA's *head comes out from under the blanket.*]

LISA: I only came to see the baby.

CLEGG: See him again after.

LISA: You will do all you can for me, won't you?

CLEGG: I just did. What do you want now?

LISA: The baby. You'll sort out the law, sort of thing.

CLEGG [*lifts off her and rolls heavily over onto his back*]: I'm quite puffed. Unaccustomed exertion. They say it's like a five mile run. Or walk is it? Best way of keeping the tum down. Marion's fault I've lost my figure.

LISA: What shall I say to Alec?

CLEGG: Rub it in. Tell him just how marvellously good I was.

LISA: I don't know if I want to tell him at all.

CLEGG: What's the good of it if he never knows? I'll tell him myself. Let him just try and make a fuss. He doesn't know who he's dealing with. What have I had from him that he hasn't had from me? And he's still had most. I've plenty more owing. Plenty more where that come from.

LISA: I feel so funny. I think it must be guilt. Yes I'm sure it is. I felt the same when the headmaster found me behind the apparatus with Nutter Jones. He put his hand right inside my knickers. The headmaster, I mean, in his office. I felt in such a muddle and it all seemed to be my fault though I didn't see what I should have done to make it happen different. And I don't see now. One thing led to so many others. It wasn't really what was in my mind. Nutter Jones come off his motor bike a few years after and smashed his head. He should have worn a helmet. It's always been Alec done it before. I've only ever had to forgive him.

CLEGG: Your turn now. You've every right.

LISA: He's being ever so nice at the moment. Really normal. A perfect husband and father. I'd hate to upset him. I might not tell him about this. Just say I came to see you and you gave me the baby.

CLEGG: No I didn't.

LISA: You will though.

CLEGG: Give you the baby?

LISA: That's what it was for.

CLEGG: What that was for? No it was not. It was my revenge. A teeny little bit of my revenge.

LISA: We agreed before we started.

CLEGG: We did not.

LISA: Half way through then.

CLEGG: Nobody's responsible for what they say in the heat of passion. If I had said at the time, I love you, you wouldn't ever have thought I meant it. So if I said anything it's the same. I don't remember us saying anything. Just heavy breathing and mutters.

LISA: I want my baby.

CLEGG: He's my baby. Marion's bought him a shop.

LISA: Bought him a shop?

CLEGG: A brand new family butcher. Gold lettering. Clegg and Son.

LISA: But he's *my* son.

CLEGG: Lisa, listen to me. I didn't mean to hurt your feelings when I said what I did

was for revenge. I also thought what a very sweet girl you are. I always did look at your bottom in the old days. Nice bit of rump. Marion's more like something for a stew. She's all gristle. But you melt in the mouth.

LISA: You taste like a mouthful of sawdust off your floor. Look at you sweating like a bit of hot fat, which is what you are. With your belly sagging like a black pudding and your poor little pork sausage. Give me my baby.

CLEGG: It's not your nature to be offensive. I understand you being upset. Marion's enough to upset anyone. But if I was to give you the baby I wouldn't dare see her again. I don't care how angry you are, it's nothing like. With Marion it's like a mad person, you don't want to be in the same room, you don't want their attention to fall on you. It's not something I'd expose myself to.

LISA: I'll take him. You can say I took him and you couldn't stop me. She'll believe that. And it's true.

CLEGG: She'd have the police. Or she might commit a crime. She's very near some edge just now and I wouldn't want to push her off. In a mental sense. I don't trust her in a hospital, she takes advantage of the facilities. So just wait, I know a better way. A real winner. I'll admit I do get fed up with him though he is as nice a bit of little baby as you'll see. Turns the scales now at fifteen pounds, and I'm the one fattened him up and no one else. But when I start working again I'll have more important things to think about. A man can't be expected to stay home and look after a baby. He can do it of course because it's not difficult. Even a woman can do it easily. But it is a waste of real abilities.

LISA: I'll take him now.

CLEGG: He's Marion's and my little son, legally adopted. In some states of the United States the penalty for kidnapping is death. I think we can come to an arrangement. Someone's got to look after the little sod while I'm at work, and you won't get Marion stopping home. So maybe, if you're very suitable—I'm not promising anything mind you—you could take care of him for us, on condition you see that he is still my son and will not be stopped by you from following his trade. Because I will not let that shiny new sign over my shop tell a lie.

LISA: So long as I have him.

CLEGG: We'll have to put it carefully to Marion. Where are you going?

LISA: I want to see him.

CLEGG: I didn't say you could get up. You won't be suitable unless you lie flat, did you know that, very feminine and do just as you're told. On your back and underneath is where I like to see a lady. And a man on top. Right on top of the world. Because I know what you ladies like. You like what I give you. I didn't say you mustn't move at all. But just in response.

SCENE SIX

MARION's *office.* ALEC *alone.* CLEGG *comes in with the baby in a carrycot. When he sees* ALEC *he stops, then changes and comes in firmly. At first a silence.*

CLEGG: Some people think they're born lucky. Just walk through. Take what they like. Fall on their feet. I wouldn't count on finding a new flat without a great deal of effort and difficulty.

ALEC: I don't, no.

CLEGG: You say don't, but you do. You think you can do what you like. You think everybody loves you just because one person is out of her mind. You're in for a very nasty shock.

ALEC: Housing is a problem, yes.

CLEGG: Lisa told you about our little plan? How we might let her mind our son part of the time? You've come to take part in the discussion. You feel an interest as the former father. Did she tell you where we talked it over?

ALEC: Yes.

CLEGG: In bed.

ALEC: Yes I can see how it might have happened. She is very upset about the baby.

CLEGG: She's told you, has she? She said she wouldn't. Woman's like that. Deceit is second nature. Due to Eve. But I'm too crafty for them by half. I know their ins and outs. You keep her rather short of it I'd say. Unless it was me that specially appealed to her. Yelping for more. I expect she told you. Or did she not bring out that side of it? I keep myself a little in reserve. You never know what else may turn up. I wouldn't want to waste myself on something as second rate as your wife. She was quite useful. A handy receptacle. But quite disposable after. Isn't that your attitude to Marion?

ALEC: No.

CLEGG: You make a big mistake about Marion. She's not like other women in just one important respect. She is mine. I have invested heavily in Marion and don't intend to lose any part of my profit. She is my flesh. And touching her you touch me. And I will not let myself be touched.

[*Pause*]

You pretend not to notice what I do to Lisa. I can do worse. And touching her I touch you. That's just one of the ways I'll be reaching you. You'll feel me. You'll come limb from limb for me one day. I'll think of you when I'm at work. Chop. Chop. Chop.

[WORSELY *comes in. His wrists, neck and arm are still bandaged. His left leg is in plaster.*]

ALEC: Hurt yourself?

WORSELY: I had a fall. I was climbing down at the time and I slipped.

CLEGG: Down what?

WORSELY: A fire escape.

CLEGG: Were you in a fire?

WORSELY: No. No.

CLEGG: Another time perhaps?

WORSELY: You never know.

CLEGG: I prefer a house that doesn't have any fire escape.

WORSELY: We'll have to talk about it some time. I think we're here to talk about the baby. I don't know why it's all dragged up again. The feelings involved make me quite sick.

CLEGG: How it came up was yesterday afternoon when I was having intercourse with his wife.

WORSELY: Lisa? You?

ALEC: Yes.

WORSELY [to ALEC]: Tell me why you always act so calm.

CLEGG: He's pretending, to try and make me feel I don't matter, but I know I do.

WORSELY: Pretending? Are you?

ALEC: No.

WORSELY: He's not, you know. What he is, is nuts. I wonder what it is Marion sees.

CLEGG: It soon won't matter what he's like. I can tell you what Lisa sees in me.

WORSELY: I'm completely stunned she even looked at you.

CLEGG: Why?

WORSELY: No offence.

CLEGG: Why are you so stunned? She's not Miss World. She's not even Miss South West Islington.

WORSELY: If I'd ever dreamt it was possible and without any rucking from him I'd have had a try myself.

CLEGG: Be my guest.

WORSELY: It's her bottom.

CLEGG: It is definitely her bottom.

WORSELY: It's hard not to go in for this style of talk once it's available. In fact I like Lisa. I feel quite shocked. Is there really no row? Don't get me wrong. I don't like rows very much. I can't stand anything very much. I'm not looking forward to this discussion. It's going to get very high pitched. My head's already aching from it. I don't see why you had to bring the baby. It screws it all up that much tighter. Something's got to snap. Have you had a good look at Marion lately?

CLEGG: She's always very smart and does me credit.

WORSELY: She's not in a good state. [To ALEC:] Interested?

ALEC: I'm sorry to hear it.

WORSELY: You'd better be. She was all right. She was fine. She was a success. Before you turned up again. I thought I might punch you in the face but I don't think you'd notice. And anyway I'd probably fall over. Have you ever tried to kill yourself?

ALEC: No, I don't need to.

WORSELY: Are you dead already? I can't think how else you avoid it. The thought of Marion alone is bad enough and it should be worse for you.

CLEGG: I think it's my role not yours, Worsely, to worry about the state of my wife's health.

WORSELY: Worry, then.

CLEGG: Of course he doesn't need to kill himself. Most of us leave it to something or someone else.

WORSELY: I hear what you say.

CLEGG: You haven't forgotten our little arrangement? The central heating?

WORSELY: The central heating? Yes, that's good.

CLEGG: The financial side is taken care of. I've a cheque here made payable to T. Worsely. Signed Marion Clegg.

WORSELY: Didn't she ask why?

CLEGG: I think she'd better see a doctor.

WORSELY [taking the cheque]: This is very welcome of course. But I'm not quite happy. I have some doubts.

CLEGG: I thought it was going ahead for tonight.

WORSELY: Can we talk about it some other time?

CLEGG: You said you had everything prepared.

WORSELY: I have, yes.

CLEGG: Then what's the problem? I'm counting on it, Worsely.

WORSELY: It's a great idea. There's nothing at all wrong with the idea. Except putting it into practice.

CLEGG: How dare you let me down? Give me the cheque. How dare you?

WORSELY [*giving cheque back*]: I'm very brave.

CLEGG: You're a coward. A woman. A baby.

WORSELY: I didn't say I wouldn't. I'm just having a hesitation.

CLEGG: Then you'd better get moving again, sharpish.

WORSELY: I've too much on. I'm caving in. I owe a great deal to Marion and I don't altogether want to—do anything she'll disapprove of, however much she's—disappointed me.

CLEGG: I shouldn't come into my shop to be served, unless you have good news. With knives to hand the temptation might be irresistible for someone of my hot-blooded disposition. I'm not in a mind for setbacks. I had to have my dog put down.

WORSELY: Whatever for?

CLEGG: He bit me. I was teaching him a trick. I couldn't feel the same to him again. He made himself into just another animal.

[LISA *comes in.*]

LISA: Where is he? [*She goes to the carrycot.*] Can I pick him up?

CLEGG: He's asleep.

LISA: No, he's wakies, my little lamb. What blue blue eyes. Smile for mummy.

CLEGG: Better not. You don't want to get her against you from the start.

LISA: I'll put him down the minute she comes in.

CLEGG: I said leave him. What I like about you is you do what you're told.

WORSELY: You can pick him up later on, Lisa.

LISA: Oh what have you done now? Broken your leg. Were you skiing?

WORSELY: Not exactly, no.

LISA: I hope it doesn't hurt very much. Look at him smile.

WORSELY: When I talk to you it helps me forget the pain.

LISA: My grandmother was a Christian Scientist. Perhaps I've some power of healing. I've never seemed to have any before. I never seem to have any effect on anything. That's why you've got to help me get the baby because I know I can't manage Marion myself.

WORSELY: You can count on me. That's a lie. I wish my head—you haven't any aspirin?

LISA: How many?

WORSELY: Fifty would be nice.

LISA: Three. You will help me won't you? I know she listens to what you say. And Clegg tells me you're really fond of the baby.

WORSELY: The trouble is I'm getting fond of too many people. I'm not against you. That much is clear.

[*He turns away, is seized by* CLEGG.]

CLEGG: We have a contract. I'll sue you for breach. We're sworn to revenge. It's the next step. Oh, Worsely. First him, then her. Then perfect peace.

LISA [*to* ALEC]: We'll get the baby and get out of here, Alec, we'll get far away and have a new life.

ALEC: We may do.

WORSELY: Oh, if my head would stop drumming.

[MARION *comes in.*]

MARION: I know my own mind. The legal position is perfectly clear. What can there possibly be to discuss? I won't have tears, Lisa. Clegg and I are united as the child's parents in our opposition to any interference. Worsely will say the same. You can't pretend Alec wants the baby. It is just your hysteria, Lisa, against the reasonableness of the rest of us.

LISA: I'm not crying this time. Too bad for you. I can see what I'm doing this time.

MARION: Won't you take her home? I have work to do.

LISA: Alec and I both want him. It's just a game to you, Marion. You don't want him really. You just want to win.

MARION: He's legally my child. His name is Clegg.

LISA: But I'm sure it can't really be the law.

Can't we go to a court and tell them I didn't know what I was signing?

MARION: It would take a lot of time. A lot of money. Meanwhile he's used to us and our home. Have you a home that would impress a judge?

LISA: You're only doing it to be cruel to me. Why should you? How can you?

MARION: I shall do as I like. Worsely, please make them all go away.

CLEGG: But Marion, my dear, wait a moment. I'm sure we can come to some arrangement.

MARION: Why should we? We've nothing to gain.

CLEGG: I can't look after him properly in the shop. Suppose we employ Lisa as a daily help to look after him while we're at work.

LISA: In my own home. I'd want him in my own home.

CLEGG: Provided you register with the council as an official babyminder.

MARION: Are you mad, Clegg? Giving him away? Once she's got her hands on him he won't be ours any more. You'll lose your little butcher.

CLEGG: I don't want that. We'd have to have a written agreement about his future.

MARION: There are plenty of people to look after babies. He will have a trained nanny.

CLEGG: But Lisa—

MARION: I said he will have a nanny. Are you going against me, Clegg? It was entirely for you I got the baby. I bought him a shop, for you. If you don't like the arrangements you can go. Clear right off. It would be a delight never to see you again.

LISA: I went to bed with him yesterday afternoon.

MARION: Is she mad?

CLEGG: Well what happened, in a manner of speaking—

MARION: I don't know which of you I'm most sorry for. Perhaps you'd like to take Lisa and the baby and set up house together, Clegg? I'm sure Alec and I wouldn't mind.

CLEGG: No of course I don't want that. It was just—

MARION: Then don't waste my time. Lisa doesn't come into our plans at all.

LISA: Don't let her frighten you Clegg.

MARION: Worsely, please, clear them all out.

WORSELY: One thing, Marion, perhaps...

MARION: Go on.

WORSELY: I don't like to contradict you...

MARION: What?

WORSELY: It might be better for the baby. If it was to go back to Lisa. Entirely.

MARION: Better for the baby? Why?

WORSELY: I don't think you like him very much.

MARION: I adore him.

CLEGG: I'm rather fond of the little chap myself. I wouldn't want to completely give him up.

WORSELY: I like him. More than Clegg does. Far more than you do, Marion. But I'm not saying that makes him mine. Let him go back where he belongs. You're letting yourself go mad, Marion. I've seen you in pieces. I don't know whether I want to smash you up or keep you safe. But you won't get Alec like this. You'll just damage the baby. Keep going, be a success, make a fortune. Use me for anything you like. You can still be magnificent.

[*He bursts into tears.*]

MARION: I think everyone's had their say. None of you has any effect on me.

[LISA *picks up the carrycot and tries to rush out of the door.* CLEGG *grabs her, and they struggle briefly. He gets the carrycot and shuts the door.*]

I think I'm going to send for the police.

CLEGG: The advantage of having Lisa to mind the baby is that if anything should happen to you, his mother, he would have you could say another mother in Lisa, which a nanny however trained could never be.

MARION: Why should anything happen to me Clegg? More than to anyone else?

CLEGG: I must have second sight, Marion. I see you dead within a few weeks.

LISA: Oh what else can I do? Alec.

ALEC: I should like him back.

MARION: Say it again.

ALEC: I should like him back.

MARION: Again.

ALEC: No.

MARION: You'd like him back. Have you actually got a feeling? Put it under glass and it might grow. Wouldn't a different baby be just the same? Do you really mean you prefer your own baby? Next thing we know you'll say you prefer Lisa to me. Or me to Lisa. There's no telling what you might say once you start saying you want something.

ALEC: I should like him back. I can do without.

MARION: I can't do without. He's my bit of you. Not a bit of me. That doesn't matter. Not a bit of Clegg, thank God. But a bit of you.

ALEC: We're leaving the flat.

MARION: Leaving?

ALEC: Leaving London.

MARION: Leaving London?

ALEC: So let us go and take the baby with us.

MARION: Up till now, right up till now, I might have let you have the baby. What is it to me? But if you go it's all I'll have left.

LISA: If you let me mind the baby, Marion, in my own home, we would stay in London for that.

MARION: No. No no no. Very clever but I won't be caught. Leave me if you like but you won't get the baby. I will keep what's mine. The more you want it the more it's worth keeping. But you can't just go like that. I haven't paid you to go. Every one of you thinks I will give in. Because I'm a woman, is it? I'm meant to be kind. I'm meant to understand a woman's feelings wanting her baby back. I don't. I won't. I can be as terrible as anyone. Soldiers have stuck swords through innocents. I can massacre too. Into the furnace. Why shouldn't I be Genghis Khan?* Empires only come by killing. I won't shrink. Not one of you loves me. But he shall grow up to say he does.

NOTE

* Great Mongol leader and conqueror (1167–1227).

Luisa Valenzuela   *Argentina, b. 1938*

Daughter of the popular Argentine writer Luisa Mercedes Levinson, Luisa Valenzuela began her career in the arts early. She started publishing at 15, and before she was 20 she had worked with Jorge Luis Borges at the National Library in Buenos Aires. At 20 she went to Paris to write for the Argentine daily *El Mundo* and later for *La Nación*; there she also wrote programs for French television and radio.

While in Paris, Valenzuela became friendly with writers and critics from *Tel Quel* and other post-Modernist groups who undoubtedly influenced her writing style, which is highly experimental. Often surrealistic, the structure of her work tends to be fragmentary and the imagery mythic or erotic. Also, her work contains a great deal of irony and black humor to express her themes—the need for personal (often female) liberation in an authoritarian, male-dominated culture.

Currently living in New York City, Valenzuela was funded by several grants to come to the United States, including a Fulbright to the International Writers' Program at Iowa; she has been writer-in-residence at Columbia University and at the Center for Inter-American Relations. Several of her works have been translated into English, most recently *Cola de lagartija* (*The Lizard's Tail*, 1983). The following selection is the title story from *Aquí pasan cosas raras* (*Strange Things Happen Here*, 1975).

STRANGE THINGS HAPPEN HERE
Aquí pasan cosas raras

In the café on the corner—every self-respecting café is on a corner, every meeting place is a crossing of two paths (two lives)—Mario and Pedro each order a cup of black coffee and put lots of sugar in it because sugar is free and provides nourishment. Mario and Pedro have been flat broke for some time—not that they're complaining, but it's time they got lucky for a change—and suddenly they see the abandoned brief case, and just by looking at each other they tell themselves that maybe the moment has come. Right here, boys, in the café on the corner, no different from a hundred others.

The brief case is there all by itself on a chair leaning against the table, and nobody has come back to look for it. The neighborhood boys come and go, they exchange remarks that Mario and Pedro don't listen to. There are more of them every day and they have a funny accent, they're from the interior. I wonder what they're doing here, why they've come. Mario and Pedro wonder if someone is going to sit down at the table in the back, move the chair, and find the brief case that they almost love, almost caress and smell and lick and kiss. A man finally comes and sits down at the table alone (and to think that the brief case is probably full of money, and that guy's going to latch on to it for the modest price of a vermouth with lemon, which is what he finally asks for after taking a little while to make up his mind). They bring him the vermouth, along with a whole bunch of appetizers. Which olive, which little piece of cheese will he be raising to his mouth when he spots the brief case on the chair next to his? Pedro and Mario don't even want to think about it and yet it's all they *can* think about. When all is said and done the guy has as much or as little right to the brief case as they do. When all is said and done it's only a question of chance, a table more carefully chosen, and that's it. The guy sips his drink indifferently, swallowing one appetizer or

another; the two of them can't even order another coffee because they're out of dough as might happen to you or to me, more perhaps to me than to you, but that's beside the point now that Pedro and Mario are being tyrannized by a guy who's picking bits of salami out of his teeth with his fingernail as he finishes his drink, not seeing a thing and not listening to what the boys are saying. You see them on street corners. Even Elba said something about it the other day, can you imagine, she's so nearsighted. Just like science fiction, they've landed from another planet even though they look like guys from the interior but with their hair so well combed, they're nice and neat I tell you, and I asked one of them what time it was but didn't get anywhere—they don't have watches of course. Why would they want a watch anyway, you might ask, if they live in a different time from us? I saw them, too. They come out from under the pavement in the streets and that's where they still are and who knows what they're looking for, though we do know that they leave holes in the streets, those enormous potholes they come out of that can't ever be filled in.

The guy with the vermouth isn't listening to them, and neither are Mario and Pedro, who are worrying about a brief case forgotten on a chair that's bound to contain something of value because otherwise it wouldn't have been forgotten just so they could get it, just the two of them, not the guy with the vermouth. He's finished his drink, picked his teeth, left some of the appetizers almost untouched. He gets up from the table, pays, the waiter takes everything off table, puts tip in pocket, wipes table with damp cloth, goes off and, man, the time has come because there's lots going on at the other end of the café and there's nobody at this end and Mario and Pedro know it's now or never.

Mario comes out first with the brief case under his arm and that's why he's the first to see a man's jacket lying on top of a car next to the sidewalk. That is to say, the car is next to the sidewalk, so the jacket lying on the roof is, too. A splendid jacket, of stupendous quality. Pedro sees it too, his legs shake because it's too much of a coincidence, he could sure use a new jacket, especially one with the pockets stuffed with dough. Mario can't work himself up to grabbing it. Pedro can, though with a certain remorse, which gets worse and practically explodes when he sees two cops coming toward them to. . . .

"We found this car on a jacket. This jacket on a car. We don't know what to do with it. The jacket, I mean."

"Well, leave it where you found it then. Don't bother us with things like that, we have more important business to attend to."

More crucial business. Like the persecution of man by man if you'll allow me to use that euphemism. And so the famous jacket is now in Pedro's trembling hands which have picked it up with much affection. He sure needed a jacket like this one, a sports jacket, well lined, lined with cash not silk who cares about silk? With the booty in hand they head back home. They don't have the nerve to take out one of the crisp bills that Mario thought he had glimpsed when he opened the brief case just a hair—spare change to take a taxi or a stinking bus.

They keep an eye peeled to see whether the strange things that are going on here, the things they happened to overhear in the café, have something to do with their two finds. The strange characters either haven't appeared in this part of town or have been replaced: two policemen per corner are too many because there are lots of corners. This is not a gray afternoon like any other, and come to think of it maybe it isn't even a lucky afternoon the way it appears to be. These are the blank faces of a weekday, so different from the blank faces on Sunday. Pedro and Mario have a color now, they have a mask and can feel themselves exist because a brief case (ugly words) and a sports jacket blossomed in their path. (A jacket that's not as new as it appeared to be—threadbare but respectable. That's it: a respectable jacket.) As afternoons go, this isn't an easy one. Something is moving in the air with the howl of the sirens and they're beginning to feel fingered. They see police everywhere, police in the dark hallways, in pairs on all the corners in the city, police bouncing up and down on their motorcycles against traffic as though the proper functioning of the country depended on them, as maybe it does, yes, that's why things are as they are and Mario doesn't dare say that aloud because the brief case has him tongue-tied, not that there's a microphone concealed in it, but what paranoia, when nobody's forcing him to carry it. He could get rid of it in some dark alley—but how can you let go of a fortune that's practically fallen in your lap, even if the fortune's got a load of dynamite inside? He takes a more natural grip on the brief case, holds it affectionately, not as though it were about to explode. At this same moment Pedro decides to put the jacket on and it's a little too big for him but not ridiculous, no not at all. Loose-fitting, yes, but not ridiculous; comfortable, warm, affectionate, just a little bit frayed at the edges, worn. Pedro puts his hands in the pockets of the jacket (*his* pockets) and discovers a few old bus tickets, a dirty handkerchief, several bills, and some coins. He can't bring himself to say anything to Mario and suddenly he turns around to see if they're being followed. Maybe they've fallen into some sort of trap, and Mario must be feeling the same way because he isn't saying a word either. He's whistling between his teeth with the expression of a guy who's been carrying around a ridiculous black brief case like this all his life. The situation doesn't seem quite as bright as it did in the beginning. It looks as though nobody has followed them, but who knows: there are people coming along behind them and maybe somebody left the brief case and the jacket behind for some obscure reason. Mario finally makes up his mind and murmurs to Pedro: Let's not go home, let's go on as if nothing had happened, I

want to see if we're being followed. That's
okay with Pedro. Mario nostalgically remembers the time (an hour ago) when they could
talk out loud and even laugh. The brief case is
getting too heavy and he's tempted once again
to abandon it to its fate. Abandon it without
having had a look at what's inside? Sheer
cowardice.

They walk about aimlessly so as to put
any possible though improbable tail off the
track. It's no longer Pedro and Mario walking,
it's a jacket and a brief case that have turned
into people. They go on walking and finally
the jacket says: "Let's have a drink in a bar.
I'm dying of thirst."

"With all this? Without even knowing
where it came from?"

"Yeah, sure. There's some money in one
pocket." He takes a trembling hand with two
bills in it out of the pocket. A thousand nice
solid pesos. He's not up to rummaging around
in the pockets any more, but he thinks—he
smells—that there's more. They could use a
couple of sandwiches, they can get them in this
café that looks like a nice quiet place.

*A guy says and the other girl's name is
Saturdays there's no bread; anything, I wonder what kind of brainwashing...*In turbulent
times there's nothing like turning your ears on,
though the bad thing about cafés is the din of
voices that drowns out individual voices.

*Listen, you're intelligent enough to under-
stand.*

They allow themselves to be distracted for
a little, they too wonder what kind of brainwashing, and if the guy who was called intelligent believes he is. If it's a question of
believing, they're ready to believe the bit about
the Saturdays without bread, as though they
didn't know that you need bread on Saturday
to make the wafers for mass on Sunday, and
on Sunday you need some wine to get through
the terrible wilderness of workdays.

When a person gets around in the world
—the cafés—with the antennae up he can tune
in on all sorts of confessions and pick up
the most abstruse (most absurd) reasoning pro-

cesses, absolutely necessary because of the
need to be on the alert and through the fault
of these two objects that are alien to them and
yet possess them, envelop them, especially now
when those boys come into the café panting
and sit down at a table with a nothing's-been-
happening-around-here expression on their
faces and take out writing pads, open books,
but it's too late: they bring the police in on
their heels and of course books don't fool the
keen-witted guardians of the law, but instead
get them all worked up. They've arrived in the
wake of the students to impose law and order
and they do, with much pushing and shoving:
your identification papers, come on, come on,
straight out to the paddy wagon waiting outside with its mouth wide open. Pedro and
Mario can't figure out how to get out of there,
how to clear a path for themselves through the
mass of humanity that's leaving the café to its
initial tranquillity. As one of the kids goes out
he drops a little package at Mario's feet, and in
a reflex motion Mario draws the package over
with his foot and hides it behind the famous
brief case leaning against the chair. Suddenly
he's scared: he thinks he's gotten crazy enough
to appropriate anything within reach. Then
he's even more scared: he knows he's done it
to protect the kid, but what if the cops take
it into their head to search *him*? They'd find a
brief case with who knows what inside, an
inexplicable package (suddenly it strikes him
funny, and he hallucinates that the package is
a bomb and sees his leg flying through the
air accompanied out of sympathy by the brief
case, which has burst and is spilling out big
counterfeit bills). All this in the split second
that it took to hide the little package, and
after that nothing. It's better to leave your mind
a blank and watch out for telepathic cops
and things like that. And what was he saying
to himself a thousand years ago when calm
reigned?—a brainwashing; a selfservice brain-
wash so as not to give away what's inside this
crazy head of mine. The kids move off, carted
off with a kick or two from the bluecoats; the
package remains there at the feet of those two

respectable-looking gentlemen, gentlemen with a jacket and a brief case (each of them with one of the two). Respectable gentlemen or two guys very much alone in the peaceful café, gentlemen whom even a club sandwich couldn't console now.

They stand up. Mario knows that if he leaves the little package, the waiter is going to call him back and the jig'll be up. He picks it up, thus adding it to the day's booty but only for a short while; with trembling hands he deposits it in a garbage can on a deserted street. Pedro, who's walking next to him, doesn't understand at all what's going on, but can't work up the strength to ask.

At times, when everything is clear, all sorts of questions can be asked, but in moments like this the mere fact of still being alive condenses everything that is askable and diminishes its value. All they can do is to keep walking, that's all they can do, halting now and then to see for example why that man over there is crying. And the man cries so gently that it's almost sacrilege not to stop and see what the trouble is. It's shop-closing time and the salesgirls heading home are trying to find out what's wrong: their maternal instinct is always ready and waiting, and the man is weeping inconsolably. Finally he manages to stammer: I can't stand it any more. A little knot of people has formed around him with understanding looks on their faces, but they don't understand at all. When he shakes the newspaper and says I can't stand it any more, some people think that he's read the news and the weight of the world is too much for him. They are about to go and leave him to his spinelessness. Finally he manages to explain between hiccups that he's been looking for work for months and doesn't have one peso left for the bus home, nor an ounce of strength to keep on looking.

"Work," Pedro says to Mario. "Come on, this scene's not for us."

"Well, we don't have anything to give him anyway. I wish we did."

Work, work, the others chorus and their hearts are touched, because this word is intelligible whereas tears are not. The man's tears keep boring into the asphalt and who knows what they find, but nobody wonders except maybe him, maybe he's saying to himself, my tears are penetrating the ground and may discover oil. If I die right here and now, maybe I can slip through the holes made by my tears in the asphalt, and in a thousand years I'll have turned into oil so that somebody else like me, in the same circumstances...A fine idea, but the chorus doesn't allow him to become lost in his own thoughts, which—it surmises—are thoughts of death (the chorus is afraid: what an assault it is on the peace of mind of the average citizen, for whom death is something you read about in the newspapers). Lack of work, yes, all of them understand being out of a job and are ready to help him. That's much better than death. And the goodhearted salesgirls from the hardware stores open their purses and take out some crumpled bills, a collection is immediately taken up, the most assertive ones take the others' money and urge them to cough up more. Mario is trying to open the brief case—what treasures can there be inside to share with this guy? Pedro thinks he should have fished out the package that Mario tossed in the garbage can. Maybe it was work tools, spray paint, or the perfect equipment for making a bomb, something to give this guy so that inactivity doesn't wipe him out.

The girls are now pressing the guy to accept the money that's been collected. The guy keeps shrieking that he doesn't want charity. One of the girls explains to him that it's a spontaneous contribution to help his family out while he looks for work with better spirits and a full stomach. The crocodile is now weeping with emotion. The salesgirls feel good, redeemed, and Pedro and Mario decide that this is a lucky sign.

Maybe if they keep the guy company Mario will make up his mind to open the brief case, and Pedro can search the jacket pockets to find their secret contents.

So when the guy is alone again they take him by the arm and invite him to eat with them. The guy hangs back at first, he's afraid of the two of them: they might be trying to get the dough he's just received. He no longer knows if it's true or not that he can't find work or if this is his work—pretending to be desperate so that people in the neighborhood feel sorry for him. The thought suddenly crosses his mind: if it's true that I'm a desperate man and everybody was so good to me, there's no reason why these two won't be. If I pretended to be desperate it means that I'm not a bad actor, and I'm going to get something out of these two as well. He decides they have an odd look about them but seem honest, so the three of them go off to a cheap restaurant together to offer themselves the luxury of some good sausages and plenty of wine.

Three, one of them thinks, is a lucky number. We'll see if something good comes of it.

Why have they spent all this time telling one another their life stories, which maybe are true? The three of them discover an identical need to relate their life stories in full detail, from the time when they were little to these fateful days when so many strange things are happening. The restaurant is near the station and at certain moments they dream of leaving or of derailing a train or something, so as to rid themselves of the tensions building up inside. It's the hour for dreaming and none of the three wants to ask for the check. Neither Pedro nor Mario has said a word about their surprising finds. And the guy wouldn't dream of paying for these two bums' dinners, and besides they invited him.

The tension becomes unbearable and all they have to do is make up their minds. Hours have gone by. Around them the waiters are piling the chairs on the tables, like a scaffolding that is closing in little by little, threatening to swallow them up, because the waiters have felt a sudden urge to build and they keep piling chairs on top of chairs, tables on top of tables, and chairs and then more chairs. They are going to be imprisoned in a net of wooden legs, a tomb of chairs and who knows how many tables. A good end for these three cowards who can't make up their minds to ask for the check. Here they lie: they've paid for seven sausage sandwiches and two pitchers of table wine with their lives. A fair price.

Finally Pedro—Pedro the bold—asks for the check and prays that the money in the outside pockets is enough to cover it. The inside pockets are an inscrutable world even here, shielded by the chairs; the inner pockets form too intricate a labyrinth for him. He would have to live other people's lives if he got into the inside pockets of the jacket, get involved with something that doesn't belong to him, lose himself by stepping into madness.

There is enough money. Friends by now, relieved, the three go out of the restaurant. Pretending to be absent-minded, Mario has left the brief case—too heavy, that's it—amid the intricate construction of chairs and tables piled on top of each other, and he is certain it won't be discovered until the next day. A few blocks farther on, they say good-by to the guy and the two of them walk back to the apartment that they share. They are almost there when Pedro realizes that Mario no longer has the brief case. He then takes off the jacket, folds it affectionately, and leaves it on top of a parked car, its original location. Finally they open the door of the apartment without fear, and go to bed without fear, without money, and without illusions. They sleep soundly, until Mario wakes up with a start, unable to tell whether the bang that has awakened him was real or a dream.

Translated by Helen R. Lane

Katerina Anghéláki-Rooke   *Greece, b. 1939*

Born in Athens in 1939, Katerina Anghéláki-Rooke studied foreign languages (French, Russian, and English) at the universities of Athens, Nice, and Geneva, graduating from the last-named in 1962. That same year she was awarded first prize in the Geneva poetry competition. Other honors included a Ford Foundation Grant in 1922–1923; and 1975–1976, and a Fulbright in 1980–1981. She has taught creative writing at the universities of Iowa, Harvard, Utah, and San Francisco State.

Anghéláki-Rooke has produced a large and highly regarded oeuvre of poetry, starting with *Lýki ke sýnnefa* (Wolves and Clouds, 1963) and including *Magdaliní to megálo thilastikó* (Magdalene the Vast Mammal, 1974), *Enandíos Erotas* (*Counter Love*, 1982, reprinted as *Being and Things On Their Own* in 1986) and *Mnistíres* (Suitors, 1984). *Enandíos Erotas* won second prize in the Academy of Athens poetry competition. The poet Carolyn Kizer praises this book's "evocative power," noting the eroticism in the poetry as "a metaphor for thought." Anghéláki-Rooke's work has also been included in several international anthologies.

As well as writing poetry, she has translated several important modern writers into Greek, including Dylan Thomas, Samuel Beckett, and Edward Albee, and, from Russian, Andrei Voznesensky. She has also translated letters of the Greek poet and novelist Nikos Kazantzakis into English under the title *The Suffering God: Letters from Níkos Kazantzákis* (with Philip Ramp, 1979).

At present she divides her time between Athens and Aegina, where she grows pistachios. Her numerous travel grants have afforded her the opportunity to travel extensively abroad, and she has lived in the United States and England.

Christopher Robinson

THE BODY IS THE VICTORY AND THE DEFEAT OF DREAMS
To Sóma íne i níki ke i ítta ton oníron

The body is the Victory of dreams
when shameless as water
it rises from slumber
marks and scars still asleep
these many signs
its dark olive groves
enamored
cool in the palm.

The body is the Defeat of dreams
as it lies long and empty
(if you shout inside you hear the echo)
with its anemic hair
lovelorn of time
groaning, wounded
hating its motion
its primitive black
fades steadily
waking it's yoked to the briefcase
hanging from it suffering
for hours in the dust.

(*Continued*)

The body is the Victory of dreams
when it puts one foot in front of the other
and gains the solid space.
A place.
A heavy thud.
Death.
When the body gains its place
through death
in the public square
like a wolf with a burning muzzle
it howls "I want"
                    "I can't stand it"
"I threaten—I overthrow"
"My baby's hungry."

The body gives birth to its justice
and defends it.
The body makes the flower
spits out the pip-death
tumbles down, flies
motionless whirls around the cesspool
(motion of the world)
in dream the body is triumphant
or is found naked in the streets
enduring;
it loses its teeth
it trembles erotically
its earth bursts like a watermelon
and it's finished.

Translated by Philip Ramp

TOURISM
Toirismos

My land appeared to me
one morning
like a chunk of bread
tossed in the street
with its doughy crust
covered with ants,
countless, black with sunglasses
fidgeting
with their hands and feet.
Loaded with supplies
they climb the pine planted hills
the breeze of time blows

withered
while thyme barely breathes
and tightens itself
around into empty bottles
and the columns.
Hastily, without passion
they move their hats, antennae
touching whatever fancy
they fancy
the post cards, me,
the brown donkey.
Deserted morning
a haze around the keels
a mute thoughtful
cleaning fish...
Nobody else
empty, me
the ant flocks
strolled, shopped...
Then empty again.
A far away typewriter
as if from the sea
somebody was dictating
the end of the island.
Ant humans
behaving more and more touristically
towards life
they caress without ever
reaching the kernel
insects
they enjoy the luminous intervals
of skin,
but the land is swelling
dropsical
the owl is crippled
while West and East
both blind
poor things
in a ravine
with crows above
excreting on them.
Two old codgers in the countryside
St. Augustine and St. Athanasios*
stammer exorcism, recipes,
their holes draughty with lies
as they tremble from cold.

The consoling lines were broken
the images were transliterated
and were left without glow.

"Strange days down here,"
the foreign girl said,
"no matter how much you suffer
you rejoice with what you see.
The animals emerge from the soil
no hand guides them
they loaf about
they graze colors
and as they stand thoughtful
they are politely swallowed
by night."

Translated by Philip Ramp

NOTE

* St. Augustine (d. 604?), great Catholic theologian and the first archbishop of Canterbury; St. Athanasios (fl. 375), bishop of Alexandria and defender of traditional Church teachings.

Margaret Atwood

Canada, b. 1939

Since, 1967, the year of Canada's centenary, when (at 27) she won the Governor General's Award for *The Circle Game*, Margaret Atwood has become not only the most influential and widely acclaimed writer in Canada but also a national icon. Poet, novelist, short-story writer, editor, and critic, Atwood taps the country's—indeed the century's—primary social and political concerns: feminism, nationalism, ecology, and international violence. Writing with merciless clarity and in powerful images, Atwood has been hailed—by Germaine Greer among others—as one of the most important writers in English today.

At the core of Atwood's diverse, complex, and densely symbolic body of writing lie the dual realities of oppression and liberation, of victimization and survival, of ritualistic drowning, purging, and surfacing; with double vision, she focuses on the numerous parallels between sexual and political exploitation. Repeatedly her female protagonists retreat to a space or time before aggressive patriarchal values made people lose a sacramental vision of the universe. Reaching beyond victor/victim hierarchies, Atwood's central moral imperative would appear to be "open yourself like this and become whole."

Born in 1939 in Ottawa and raised in the bush of northern Ontario and Quebec, where her father's work as an entomologist took the family. Atwood received no formal schooling until the age of 12. She later attended Victoria College, University of Toronto, where she was influenced by mythopoeic poet Jay Macpherson and critic Northrop Frye, completing a B.A. at Toronto in 1961, and an M.A. at Radcliffe College, Cambridge, Massachusetts, in 1962. She married fellow graduate student James Polk, whom she divorced in the early 1970s. The 1970s were enormously productive years during which her landmark book of bitter feminist poems *Power Politics* (1971), her best-selling critical guide to Canadian literature *Survival* (1972), and perhaps her finest novel *Surfacing* (1972) all appeared. Atwood has taught at various Canadian universities, has served as editor and member of the board of directors of House of Anansi Press, and has chaired the Writers Union of Canada; her volunteer work for Amnesty International and for the City of Toronto Zoo has been important as well. She has received numerous awards, including the Union Poetry Prize (1969), Bess Hopkins Prize (1974), Radcliffe Graduate Medal (1980), Molson Prize (1981), a Guggenheim Fellowship Award (1981), and the International Writer's Prize from the Welsh Arts Council (1982), as well as honorary degrees from Trent, Queen's, and Concordia University in Canada, and Smith College in the United States. After nearly a decade living on a farm near Alliston, Ontario, and briefer periods of residence in London and New York, Atwood now makes her home in Toronto, with writer Graeme Gibson and their daughter, Jess.

In the United States, United Kingdom, and Australia, Atwood is best known for her six powerfully symbolic feminist novels, including *The Handmaid's Tale* (1985), *Bodily Harm* (1981), and *Lady Oracle* (1976)—with its epigrammatic answer to the notorious question of what women want: "they wanted multiple orgasms, they wanted the earth to move, but they also wanted help with the dishes." In Canada, however, Atwood's reputation as a complex, incisive, myth-making poet (she has authored a dozen books of poems, including two volumes of *Selected Poems* [1976 and 1986]) surpasses her claims in other fields. Her most enduring poems are those that envision the pioneer past and the primal encounter of the Westernized, masculinized human spirit with the elemental and awesome northern landscape (*The Journals of Susanna Moodie* [1970] holds pride of place), and those that expose the cruelty of sexual politics such as "[you fit into me]" (below). More recently, she has written powerful poems on the theme of the "web of blood" that connects women, especially as mothers and daughters. In her sustained and magnificent attempt to reflect both a postcolonial country that has had no image of itself (as Linda Sandler has suggested) and also the female half of the human race that, likewise, has rarely been entitled to autonomous self-definition, Atwood demonstrates the important truth, expressed by the mother/magician/writer in the poems "Spelling" that: "A word after a word / after a word is power."

"Backdrop Addresses Cowboy" is from *The Animals in That Country* (1968), "Disembarking at Quebec," "Death," and "Further Arrivals" are from *The Journals of Susanna Moodie* (1970), "[you fit into me]" is from *Power Politics* (1971), and "Five Poems for Grandmothers" and "April, Radio, Planting, Easter" are from *Two-Headed Poems* (1978).

Wendy Robbins Keitner

BACKDROP ADDRESSES COWBOY

Starspangled cowboy
sauntering out of the almost-
silly West, on your face
a porcelain grin,
tugging a papier-mâché cactus
on wheels behind you with a string,

you are innocent as a bathtub
full of bullets.

Your righteous eyes, your laconic
trigger-fingers
people the streets with villains:
as you move, the air in front of you
blossoms with targets

and you leave behind you a heroic
trail of desolation:
beer bottles
slaughtered by the side
of the road, bird-
skulls bleaching in the sunset.

I ought to be watching
from behind a cliff or a cardboard storefront
when the shooting starts, hands clasped
in admiration,
but I am elsewhere.

Then what about me

What about the I
confronting you on that border
you are always trying to cross?

I am the horizon
you ride towards, the thing you can never lasso

I am also what surrounds you:
my brain
scattered with your
tincans, bones, empty shells,
the litter of your invasions.

I am the space you desecrate
as you pass through.

DISEMBARKING AT QUEBEC

Is it my clothes, my way of walking,
the things I carry in my hand
—a book, a bag with knitting—
the incongruous pink of my shawl

this space cannot hear

or is it my own lack
of conviction which makes
these vistas of desolation,
long hills, the swamps, the barren sand, the
                                                    glare

of sun on the bone-white
driftlogs, omens of winter,
the moon alien in day-
time a thin refusal

The others leap, shout
            Freedom!

The moving water will not show me
my reflection.

The rocks ignore.

I am a word
in a foreign language.

DEATH OF A YOUNG SON
BY DROWNING

He, who navigated with success
the dangerous river of his own birth
once more set forth

on a voyage of discovery
into the land I floated on
but could not touch to claim.

His feet slid on the bank,
the currents took him;
he swirled with ice and trees in the swollen
                                                        water

and plunged into distant regions,
his head a bathysphere;
through his eyes' thin glass bubbles

he looked out, reckless adventurer
on a landscape stranger than Uranus
we have all been to and some remember.

There was an accident; the air locked,
he was hung in the river like a heart.
They retrieved the swamped body,

cairn of my plans and future charts,
with poles and hooks
from among the nudging logs.

It was spring, the sun kept shining, the new
                                                        grass
lept to solidity;
my hands glistened with details.

After the long trip I was tired of waves.
My foot hit rock. The dreamed sails
collapsed, ragged.

             I planted him in this country
             like a flag.

FURTHER ARRIVALS

After we had crossed the long illness
that was the ocean, we sailed up-river

On the first island
the immigrants threw off their clothes
and danced like sandflies

We left behind one by one
the cities rotting with cholera,
one by one our civilized
distinctions

and entered a large darkness.

It was our own
ignorance we entered.

I have not come out yet

My brain gropes nervous
tentacles in the night, sends out
fears hairy as bears,
demands lamps; or waiting

for my shadowy husband, hears
malice in the trees' whispers.

I need wolf's eyes to see
the truth.

I refuse to look in a mirror.

Whether the wilderness is
real or not
depends on who lives there.

YOU FIT INTO ME

you fit into me
like a hook into an eye

a fish hook
an open eye

from FIVE POEMS FOR GRANDMOTHERS

How little I know
about you finally:

The time you stood
in the nineteenth century
on Yonge Street, a thousand
miles from home, with a brown purse
and a man stole it.

Six children, five who lived.
She never said anything
about those births and the one death;
her mouth closed on a pain
that could neither be told nor ignored.

She used to have such a sense of fun.
Now girls, she would say
when we would tease her.
Her anger though, why
that would curl your hair,
though she never swore,
The worst thing she could say was:
Don't be foolish.

At eighty she had two teeth pulled out
and walked the four miles home
in the noon sun, placing her feet
in her own hunched shadow.

The bibbed print aprons, the shock
of the red lace dress, the pin
I found at six in your second drawer,
made of white beads, the shape of a star.
What did we ever talk about
but food, health and the weather?

Sons branch out, but
one woman leads to another.
Finally I know you
through your daughters,
my mother, her sisters,
and through myself:

Is this you, this edgy joke
I make, are these your long fingers,
your hair of an untidy bird,
is this your outraged
eye, this grip
that will not give up?

APRIL, RADIO, PLANTING, EASTER

In the air-
waves, on the contrary,
there is a lot of noise
but no good news

and there's a limit to how much
you can take of this battering
against the ears without imploding
like some land animal drifting down
into the blackout of ocean, its body
an eye crushed by pliers

so you fashion yourself a helmet
of thickened skin
and move cautiously among the chairs
prepared for ambush,
impervious to the wiry screams
and toy pain of the others.

But there is one rift, one flaw:
that vulnerable bud, knot,
hole in the belly where you were nailed
to the earth forever.

I do not mean *the earth*, I mean the
earth that is here and browns your
feet, thickens your fingers,
unfurls in your brain and in
these onion seedlings
I set in flats lovingly under
a spare window.

We do not walk on the earth
but in it, wading
in that acid sea
where flesh is etched from
molten bone and re-forms.

In this massive tide
warm as liquid
sun, all waves are one
wave; there is no *other*.

Marie-Claire Blais   *Canada, b. 1939*

Marie-Claire Blais was born into a working-class family, the eldest of five children. That she left school at the age of 15 to work in a shoe factory may be Dickenslike apocrypha: Jeannette Urbas tells us that Blais attended business school and worked as a typist to support herself and a room of her own on Rue Ste. Anne in Quebec City, publishing her first novel by the time she was 20 (*La belle bête* [The Beautiful Beast], translated as *Mad Shadows*, 1959). The turning point in her career came when she met the American critic Edmund Wilson, who sponsored her for a Guggenheim and who later wrote the laudatory preface to the English translation for *Une saison dans la vie d'Emmanuel* (*A Season in the Life of Emmanuel*, 1965), which launched her American career. It was this, her sixth book, that made her famous, winning both the Prix France-Québec and France's Prix Medici (1966); an excerpt follows. Like her older contemporary Doris Lessing, Blais has written a trilogy that traces the growth and development of a female artist: *Manuscrits de Pauline Archange* (1968), *Vivre! Vivre!* (1969), and *Les apparences* (translated as *Dürer's Angel*, 1970). In another important and semiautobiographical work, *Les Nuits de l' underground* (*Nights in the Underground*, 1978), Blais depicts an artist's awakening to her lesbianism and with rare optimism, shows it as an alternative to human suffering and isolation; it is a critical addendum to the former works. Like *Manuscrits, Le sourd dans la ville* (*Deaf to the City*, 1980) won the coveted Governor General's Award for its stylistic invention and apocalyptic vision of urban alienation. All told, Blais has published poetry, essays, some twenty-five plays for theater, radio, and television, as well as some fifteen novellas and novels, which include *Visions d'Anna* (1982, translated as *Anna's World*, 1985; *Pierre, La guerre du printemps 81* (Pierre, the War of Spring 81); and *Sommeil d'hiver* (Sleep of Winter, 1984).

Because of her prolific output, her bleak, sometimes grotesque vision of the world, and her experimentation with genre and prose techniques, Blais invites comparison with the American Joyce Carol Oates. Though, like Oates especially concerned with children and adolescents who grow up in families that are callous or indifferent to them, Blais evinces a macabre and surrealist humor along with a lyrical and often dreamlike prose that sets her and her characters in a world apart. Another characteristic of her work is the dominance of sexuality, from the ripening of the young girl in *La belle bête* and the descriptions of masturbation, incest, and pederasty in *Une saison*, to the discussion of gay male relationships in *Le loup* (*The Wolf*, 1972) and gay female relationships in *Les Nuits*. Several critics have suggested that Blais's subject matter and techniques parody various conventions of francophone literature: the psychological novel initiated in Laure Conan's work— part epistolary and part journal; the novels of family and society forming *le terroir* (work using rural settings); and the "orphan subject" that dominates the late-nineteenth-century poetry of the Romantic Emile Nelligan. Yet her works demystify social ideals; and even as they expose the darkness within the human soul and the perversity of human behavior, they display an extraordinary compassion toward the characters exhibiting them.

from A SEASON IN THE LIFE OF EMMANUEL
Une saison dans la vie d'Emmanuel

There was not much to eat, but the father and the elder sons had brutish appetites that filled Grand-mère Antoinette with indignation as she sat there at the end of the table, looking down from a chair that was too high for her. Perched there like a crow, she gave a little curt "Ah" of disapproval every time some froth-coated sliver of food fell from her son-in-law's greedy lips. The men and the boys sat as if in a trance around the table, protecting their plates like so many hoards of treasure, and they ate without raising their eyes. Taking advantage of their miserly silence, Jean-Le Maigre slid under the table on all fours, and sitting there surrounded by the heavy, apparently lifeless legs sloping toward him, he imagined himself lost in the middle of a field of rank-smelling feet, watching the strange movements of those naked extremities beneath the table. Between his father's legs, as though through the dark bannisters of a staircase, he could see his mother coming and going in the kitchen with plates of food. She always looked exhausted and dead-eyed. Her face was the color of the earth. He watched her preparing the thick, greasy food that the men devoured, with customary greed, as fast as she could bring it in. He felt sorry for her. He felt sorry too for those heavy children she carried absent-mindedly around with her every year, dark burdens against her heart. But sometimes he forgot his mother's presence completely and thought only of the companion imprisoned in the cellar, with whom he would later share his evening meal. Grand-mère Antoinette was an accomplice in these thoughts. Salt, cheese, small pieces of food snatched up here and there with a fearless hand, all vanished beneath the table. But meat, no! "If you think," she said to herself, "if you think I'm going to give you meat for Number Seven—no, I'll never consent to that!"

Jean-Le Maigre tickled his grandmother's ankle under the table. "Ah, if he could only live till spring," Grand-mère Antoinette thought.

"December, January, February, if he could only live till March, oh Lord, if he could only live till summer comes...Funerals are such a nuisance for everyone!" But this computation of the months that were still separating her from Jean-Le Maigre's tragic death did not prevent her grandson from behaving as usual like a little devil! Though he was making painful efforts not to betray his presence: fighting down the sharp cough rising in his throat. He was afraid of awakening his father's slumbering wrath. His grandmother was meanwhile imagining the good meal that would follow his funeral. (A consoling image of death, for Monsieur le Curé was so generous toward families in mourning; she could see him already, eating and drinking on her right; and on her left, as though in heaven already, Jean-Le Maigre, clean, his hair neatly combed, and dressed in clothes as white as snow.) There had been so many funerals during the years that Grand-mère Antoinette had reigned in her house, so many little black corpses, in the wintertime, children always disappearing, babies who had lived only a few months, adolescents who had vanished mysteriously in the fall, or in the spring. Grand-mère Antoinette allowed herself to be rocked gently in the swell of all those deaths, suddenly submerged in a great and singular feeling of content.

"Grandma," Jean-Le Maigre begged under the table, "just one piece, just a crumb..."

Grand-mère raised the corner of the tablecloth and saw a great, black eye shining in the darkness. So you're there, are you, she thought, disappointed at finding him still alive as usual, with one hand stretched out toward her, like a dog's paw. But when all was said and done, she'd rather have him like this; yes, it was better than the splendor of a scrubbed and sparkling angel sitting up to that macabre banquet— it was better, this vision of an ordinary Jean-Le Maigre in his rags beneath the table, raising a timid forehead as he begged from her.

Translated by Derek Coltman

Margaret Drabble   *UK(England), b. 1939*

Margaret Drabble, novelist, critic, biographer, editor, and short-story writer, was
born in Yorkshire to a distinguished professional family. Her father was a lawyer
and writer, ahd her mother taught English. Her older sister is the well-known
writer A. S. Byatt, her younger sister is an art historian, and her brother is a lawyer.
Drabble attended Newnham College, Cambridge with a major scholarship, where
she read English literature and graduated with first-class honors in 1960.

Although Drabble began her postuniversity career as an actress with the Royal
Shakespeare Company, she quickly turned to writing and in 1963, in part stimulated by the beginnings of the modern women's movement, published *A Summer
Bird-Cage*, which is about a young woman just out of college and her relationship
with her older sister (a book, understandably, seen as autobiographical by many
readers). Well reviewed, it was followed by four more novels in the next five years,
all extremely popular in England and the United States. The most important of
these early novels is *The Millstone* (1965), about a woman who decides to have a
baby alone. While the early novels analyze the emotional lives of middle-class
women, her later novels, *The Needle's Eye* (1972), *The Realms of Gold* (1975) and
The Ice Age (1977), deal more with universal problems of society. Drabble has also
written several highly regarded works of criticism, including works on William
Wordsworth and Virginia Woolf, and a biography of novelist Arnold Bennett
(1974). She edited the fifth edition of *The Oxford Companion to English Literature* (1985). Moreover, she has written numerous essays for English periodicals,
such as *The New Statesman* and *The Observor*.

Drabble has won many awards, including the E. M. Forster Award (1977) for
The Needle's Eye. She was given an honorary Doctor of Letters from Sheffield
University in 1976 and was made a Commander of the British Empire in 1980.
Formerly married to actor Clive Swift, with whom she had three children, Drabble
is now married to biographer Michael Holroyd.

The following story was first published in *Spare Rib* magazine in 1972.

A SUCCESS STORY

This is a story about a woman. It couldn't
have been told a few years ago: perhaps even
five years ago it couldn't have been told.
Perhaps it can't really be told now. Perhaps I
shouldn't write it, perhaps it's a bad move to
write it. But it's worth risking. Just to see.

This woman was a playwright. She was
one of the few successful women playwrights,
and she had had a hard time on the way up,
for she came from a poor background, from a
part of the country hostile to the arts, from a
family which had never been to the theater in
its life. She wasn't really working class: more
lower middle class, which made her success all
the more remarkable, as her plays didn't have
shock value, they were quite complicated and
delicate. But they worked: they were something new. She made her way up: first of all
she was assistant stagehand at her local repertory, then she worked in the office at a larger
provincial theater as she didn't really have
much interest in life behind the scenes—and all
the while she was writing her plays. The first
one was put on by the rep she was working in,

and it was very much noticed. Kathie (that was her name—Kathie Jones) used to say modestly that it was noticed because she was a woman, and women playwrights were a rarity, and there was something in what she said. But her modesty couldn't explain why she went on writing, professionally, had her plays transferred to the West End, had them filmed, and did really very nicely. She was good at the job, and that was why she succeeded. She was also good, somewhat to her own surprise, at all the things that went along with the job, and which had kept women out of the job for so long: she was good at explaining herself, at arguing with megalomaniac directors, at coolly sticking to her own ideas, at adapting when things really couldn't be made to work. She had good judgment, she was calm and professional, she could stand up for herself.

She was not, of course, world famous, let us not give the impression that she was an international name. No, she was a success in her own country, in her own medium. Some of the gossip columns thought her worth mentioning, some of them didn't. Not that there was much to mention: she was a quiet, hard-working girl, with her own friends, her own circle of close friends—some of them writers, one or two friends from the early days at Grammar School in the Midlands, one or two journalists. She was considered rather exclusive by some, and she was. She didn't much care for a gay social life, partly because she hadn't time, partly because she hadn't been brought up to it and didn't quite know how to cope. She lived with a man who was a journalist, and who traveled a great deal: he was always going off to Brazil and Vietnam and up Everest. He was an exceptionally good-natured man, and they got on well together. Sometimes she was sorry when he went away, but she was always so busy that she didn't miss him much, and anyway it was so interesting when he came back. He, for his part, loved her, and had confidence in her.

So really, one could say that her life had worked out very nicely. She had a job she liked, a reputation, a good relationship, some good friends, a respectable though fluctuating income. At the time of this story, she was in her early thirties, and had written five successful plays and several film scripts. She had a play running at a lucrative little theater in the West End, and was amusing herself by working on a television adaptation of a play by Strindberg. Her man was away: he was in Hungary, but he would be back soon, he would be back at the end of the week. At the moment at which we close in upon her, she was just putting the phone down after speaking to him: they had exchanged news, she had told him what was in his post which she always opened for him, he had said that he loved her and was looking forward to coming back and kissing her all over but particularly between her stockings and her suspenders, if she would please wear such antiquated garments on his return to greet him. Then he told her to enjoy her evening; she was just about to go out to a rather grand party. So she was smiling, as she put down the telephone.

She was quite a nice-looking woman. This we have not mentioned till this point, because it ought not to be of any importance. Or ought it? Well, we shall see. Anyway, she wasn't bad-looking, though she was nothing special. She had rather a long, large-featured face, with a large nose: she had big hands and large bones. Some people thought her beautiful, but others thought she was really plain. You know the type. As a child, she had been plain, as her mother had never tired of saying, and consequently she had no confidence in her appearance at all. Nowadays she didn't care much, she was happy anyway, and as long as her lover continued to take an interest in the serious things of life, like her legs, then she wasn't much interested in looking in the mirror. In fact, she hardly ever did, except to brush her hair, and she wore the same clothes most of the time, until they wore out. But tonight was different. She would have to have a look at herself, at least. So when she'd put the phone down she went into the bathroom to have a look.

Tonight was rather a special, grand sort of party, not the usual kind of thing, so she'd put on her best dress, a long green-blue dress that she'd once thought suited her rather old-fashioned looks. She wasn't so sure, now, she wasn't at all sure what she looked like these days, the older she got the more variable she seemed to be. Not that it mattered much, one way or the other. But one might as well wear one's best dress, once in a while. She'd bought it for one of her own first nights, years ago, and hadn't worn it much since. She didn't go to her own first nights any more, or anyone else's for that matter. It had cost a lot of money, for those days. (Not that she spent much money on clothes now—in fact she spent less.) Staring at herself, hitching it a bit at the shoulder, she wondered whether she'd put it on because she was still, whatever she told herself, slightly nervous about the kind of do she was going to. Surely not. Surely not, these days. Why should she care?

The party she was going to was being given by one of the grandest (socially speaking) theatrical entrepreneurs in London. And there she was going to meet the hero of her childhood dreams. It was all quite romantic. His name was Howard Jago (quite the right sort of name, but people like that have that kind of name) and he was one of the biggest American writers of his generation. He had written plays that made her heart bleed when she was sixteen. They still, oddly enough, moved her profoundly.

She admired him more than she admired any other living writer. He hadn't kept up with the play writing—she knew well enough that playwrights, compared with other writers, have a short working life—but he was now doing screenplays, and also a certain amount of political journalism. He had published a couple of novels, which she had liked immensely: he seemed indefatigable.

When she was a child, she had wanted more than anything to meet him. She had even written him a fan letter telling him so. He did not reply. Probably it never reached him.

She had had several opportunities to meet him before, as he was quite often in Europe, and was published by her publishers. But she had always declined.

Why had she declined? Was she afraid of being bored or disappointed? Afraid of not being disappointed? Was she afraid that he might not have heard of her (when, by the rules of the game, he should have done) or might find her boring? Combing her hair, now, looking at herself in the mirror, she wondered. Perhaps she had simply been too busy, on other occasions: or Dan had been at home and had not wanted to go. He didn't care for grand parties, and neither as a rule did she. They preferred to get very drunk quietly at home among friends: that was their favorite form of social life.

She couldn't work out why she hadn't wanted to meet him before: nor why, now, she had decided that she would.

She put him out of her mind, as she went downstairs and found herself a taxi. There would be plenty of other people there that she would know.

And so indeed there were. She knew nearly everybody, by sight or in person. She thought with some relief, as she looked round the massive house in Belgravia, and its glittering inhabitants—film stars in outre garments, diplomats, writers, cabinet ministers, actors, actresses—she thought that at least she didn't have to feel nervous any more. In a way that took some of the thrill away, but it was much pleasanter to be comfortable than thrilled. Being thrilled had always been so exhausting, and such a letdown in the end. Nowadays, she sought and found more lasting pleasures. Nevertheless, she had been very different once. Ambitious, she must have been, or she wouldn't have found herself here at all, would she? And, as she talked to a friend and kept an eye open for Howard Jago, she said to herself, if I'd known twenty years ago that I would ever find myself here, in a room like this, with people looking like this, I *would* have been delighted. A pity, really, that one couldn't have had that particular thrill then—the thrill of knowing. It wasn't worth much now.

The house was enormous. Tapestries hung on the walls and statues stood in corners. The paintings were by Francis Bacon and Bonnard and Matthew Smith and Braque.*

After a while, she saw her host approaching her. He was leading Howard Jago in her direction: Howard Jago was doing his rounds. He looked as she had imagined him: wild, heavy, irregular, a bit larger than life-size, the kind of man who looks even bigger than he looks on the television. (She had caught a glimpse or two of him on the television.)

"And this," said her host, "is one of the people you particularly asked to meet. This is Kathie Jones."

Kathie smiled, politely. Jago shook her hand.

"I enjoyed your play the other night," said Jago, politely. He looked as though he was being careful. He looked as though he might be a little drunk.

"That's very kind of you," said Kathie. "I must tell you how very much I have always admired your work."

"I've admired it..." and she was going to say, since I was a child, which would have been true, but had to stop herself because it might have been a rude reflection on his age, and went on with "...I've admired it ever since I first found it."

They looked at each other, with assessment, and smiled, civilly. Kathie couldn't think of anything else to say. She had remembered, suddenly, exactly why she hadn't wanted to meet him: she hadn't wanted to meet him because she knew he was a womanizer, she knew it from a friend of hers, an actress, who'd had a bad time with him in New York. He can't help it, her friend had said, he's a real sod, he hates women, you know, but he just has to get off with them, he can't let them alone. . . .

The memory paralyzed her. She wondered why she hadn't thought of it earlier. It was obvious, anyway, from his work, that he had a thing about women, that he didn't like them

and had to have them. He was a great enough writer for it not to matter to her; it was a measure of his greatness, for she did care about such things considerably.

She thought with a sudden nice physical recollection of Dan, who liked women, and loved her in particular, to her great delight.

She stood there, and smiled, and said nothing. Or rather, she said, "And how long are you in London this time, Mr. Jago?"

And he replied, with equal banality. It's all right, she was saying to herself, it's safe. It doesn't matter. (What did she mean by that?)

And as she listened to him, she saw approaching a film actress, a lady of considerable glamour, approaching with some purpose. "Howard, Howard, *there* you are, I *lost* you," she wailed, throwing her arm around his neck, possessively, her bosom heaving, her necklace sparkling: she started to stroke his graying hair, passionately, as she turned to greet Kathie. "Why hello, *Kathie*," she said, "what a surprise, I haven't seen you in *years*. Howard went to see your play, was he telling you?... Oh look, Howard, there's Martin—" and she marched him off: but Kathie Jones had already turned away. Well rid of him, she thought herself. He was drunk: he swayed slightly as Georgina grabbed him. Georgina was well away. She was a young lady with a will of iron. She was quite amusing on some occasions. Kathie wished them joy, and turned to look for a sympathetic friend, thinking as she went that the poor sixteen-year-old child she had been would have been shocked, shocked beyond anything, to have missed the opportunity to ask him, to hear him speak, even, of what he felt about, perhaps, the freedom of the will (one of his themes) and evolution (yet another). She smiled to herself, and went and talked to some publishers. They were much more interesting than Howard Jago had had a chance to be.

It was a couple of hours before he came back to her. She had been enjoying herself. There was plenty to drink, and some very good buffet food, and some people she knew well, and some she hadn't seen for ages: she had been drinking quite steadily, and was sitting on a settee with an actress and her husband and another couple she'd never met before, laughing, very loudly, all of them, choking almost, over some anecdote about a play of hers, when he came back. He was looking more morose than before, and more obviously drunk. As he approached, Kathie made space for him on the settee by her, as he clearly intended to sit: they were still laughing over the story, as he sat. "Hello again," she said, turning to him, secure now, expecting nothing, willing to include him in the circle. "Do you know Jenny, and Bob..."

"Yes, yes," he said crossly, "I know everyone, I've met everyone in this place. I want to get out."

"Why don't you go, then?" asked Kathie, politely, slightly at a loss: and even as she spoke, she saw Georgina bearing down on them. Jago saw her too, and flinched: he rose to his feet, pulling Kathie to hers.

"Come on," he said, "let's get out of here." She was thrilled. She had never heard anyone talk like that except in a movie. And Howard Jago turned his back on Georgina, with calculated offense, and marched Kathie across the room, gripping her elbow, again in a way that she had only seen in the movies.

He paused, as they reached the bar, having shaken off their pursuer.

"You're not alone, are you?" he then said, turning to her with an amazing predictable heavy old-world gallantry. "It's not possible that the best-looking and most intelligent woman in the room could have come here alone, is it?"

"Yes, I'm alone," said Kathie.

"Where's your man, then?"

"He's in Hungary," said Kathie.

"I've had enough of this party," said Howard Jago. "Let's get out of it, for Christ's sake."

"I don't know..." said Kathie. "I should say good bye..."

"There's no need to say good-bye," he said. "Come on. Let's get out."

She hesitated.

He took her arm.

She went.

They went downstairs and looked for a taxi: they found one easily, as it was that kind of district. They got into it. Then he said, again as though in a play or a film written by some playwright infinitely inferior to either of them, "Where shall we go, to my place or yours?"

"Yours," she said. "But only for a little while. I have to get home. I've a script conference in the morning." She was lying.

"Jesus," he said, looking at her legs, actually moving the skirt of her dress so that he could look at her legs, "you've got a beautiful pair of legs."

"They're nothing special," she said, which was true.

They arrived at his hotel, just off Bond Street. They got out, and went into the hotel, and up to his room. He asked the night porter to bring them a drink.

The room was large and expensive. Kathie sat in a chair. So did he. They drank the drink, and talked about the party, and about the people at it—their host, and Georgina, and various other playwrights, and the actress he had made so unhappy in New York the year before. Kathie knew exactly what she was doing: nothing on earth would induce her to get into that bed. She made it clear, as one does make it clear. They laughed a lot, and rang for some more drinks and a sandwich, and talked a lot of nonsense. She felt him move away. He had sense, after all. And when she said she ought to go, he looked at her, and said, "Ah, I'm too old for you, you know."

But he can't have said this with much conviction, or she wouldn't have responded with the awful line she then delivered (which she had said, years before, to an Italian actor in Rome)—"You shouldn't try," she said, smiling falsely, "to seduce innocent girls from the country."

He laughed, also falsely. She kissed him: they parted.

She went down and got a taxi and was in bed and asleep in half an hour.

And that is the end of the story. They were to meet again, over the years, at similar parties, and he was to remark again upon her legs and her looks. They never had any serious conversation. But that isn't part of the story.

The point is: What did she think about this episode? She emerges not too badly from it, anyone would agree. She behaved coolly but not censoriously: she said some silly things, but who doesn't in such a silly situation? She had no regrets on her own behalf, though a few on behalf of that sixteen-year-old girl who had somehow just missed the opportunity of a lifetime. She had grown up so differently from what she had imagined. And she had some regrets about her image of the man. It was spoiled, she had to admit it (not quite forever, because oddly enough some years later she went to see one of his early plays and felt such waves of admiration flowing through her, drowning her resentments, as though his old self were still speaking, and she listening, in some other world without ages). But for years and years, she thought she was never going to be able to take his work seriously again, and when she described the evening to Dan, she was so rude about him and his boorish chauvinist masculine behavior that Dan, who usually sided with her and was as indignant as she was about such matters, actually began to feel quite sorry for Howard Jago, and to take his part. *Poor* Mr. Jago, he would say, fondly, whenever his name came up, *poor* Mr. Jago, he would say, lying safely between Kathie's legs, *what* a disappointing evening, I feel quite sorry for him, picking you, my love.

But that isn't all. It ought to be all, but it isn't. For Kathie, when she told the story to Dan, was lying. She tried to lie when she told it to herself, but she didn't quite succeed. She was an honest woman, and she knew perfectly well that she had received more of a thrill through being picked up by Howard Jago at a party, even picked up as she had been, casually, to annoy another woman—she had re-ceived more of a thrill from this than she would have got from any discussion, however profound, of his work and hers. She would trade the whole of his work, willingly, and all the lasting pleasure it had given, for that silly remark he had made about her legs. She would rather he fancied her, however casually, than talked to her. She would rather he liked her face than her plays.

It's an awful thing to say, but she thought of his face, looking at her, heavy, drunk, sexy, battered, knowing, and wanting her, however idly: and it gave her a permanent satisfaction, that she'd been able to do that to him, that she'd been able to make a man like him look at her in that way. It was better than words, better than friendship.

It's an awful thing to say, but that's how some women are. Even nice, sensible, fulfilled, happy women like Kathie Jones. She would try to excuse herself, sometimes: she would say, I'm only like this because I was a plain child, I need reassurance. But she couldn't fool herself. Really, she knew that she was just a woman, and that's how some women are.

Some people are like that. Some men are like that, too. Howard Jago was exactly like that. People like admiration more than anything. Whatever can one do about it? Perhaps one shouldn't say this kind of thing. One ought not to have said such things, even five years ago, about a woman like Kathie Jones. The opposite case, for political reasons, had to be stated. (This is only a story, and Howard Jago didn't really hate women, any more than Kathie hated men.) But Kathie Jones is all right now. The situation is different, the case is made. We can say what we like about her now, because she's all right. I think.

NOTE

* Influential modern painters, particularly Francis Bacon (b. 1909), Pierre Bonnard (1867–1947), and Georges Braque (1882–1963).

Eigra Lewis Roberts   *UK(Wales), b. 1939*

Eigra Lewis Roberts was born on August 7, 1939, at Blaenau Ffestiniog, a slate-quarrying town in North Wales. She received a B.A. from the University College of North Wales, at Bangor, and taught for three years before becoming a full-time writer. She is married with three children, Sioned, Urien, and Gwydion.

Roberts has published fourteen books, including novels and short stories. Now she works mainly on screenplays for radio and television; she also writes stage plays and programs for school. Her first novel, *Brynhyfryd* (1959), is set in the post–World War II period, which she describes from a woman's point of view. Many of her other works have been female in concern, particularly her biographical writings on the important Welsh writers Ann Griffiths (1975) and Dilys Cadwaladr (1981) and a collection of essays about Welsh women (1975). She has also written a biography of Katherine Mansfield (1981).

Roberts is very highly regarded among writers in Welsh. She has won many awards for prose, poetry, and drama, including the Drama Medal at the National Eisteddfod of Wales (1974), the annual festival of Welsh culture. She has also won the prestigious Garmon award for the best Welsh writer of 1982–1983. The selection here, "An Overdose of Sun," was written in Welsh and published in a collection of short stories entitled *Cudynnau* (Locks [of hair], 1970). It was first published in English in *The Penguin Book of Welsh Short Stories* (1976).

AN OVERDOSE OF SUN
Gormod o Haul

For the first time, ever, she had to move away from the sun. She had suffered it for an hour, only to spite the young ones on the beach. They had made it clear, right from the start, that she was not welcome; that the beach was their playground. They reminded her of the midges that used to swarm above the river on summer evenings. She would challenge the midges, determined to finish her journey, although longing for the feel of ice-cold water on her face. She would have challenged these, too, were it not for the sun.

Now they would assume that it was they, and not the sun, that had made her leave the beach. As she sometimes ran for a bus, the rain splattering against her legs, or as she fought the wind, she was still young. Some people believed that it was the early seasons of the year that showed one at his best. She found it easier to be young in winter, when the little

vigour that remained within her was as evident as an evergreen in an avenue of withered trees. The sun was a cruel thing, revealing one's age as it did the dust on furniture.

Once she had welcomed it, greedily. She would inject it into her flesh, like a drug. If only she could again suck its warmth into her veins and feel it surge through her body. But she had lost her nerve and was afraid of its power.

On the edge of the promenade she was caught in a web of deck chairs, where the middle-aged sat, their legs entwined like cross-stitches. Here the past was bottled like perfume. How pleasant it would be to set her chair amidst them, its canvas between her and the sun. They would accept her as one of them; would let her proceed in their company. And they would willingly let her stop now and again to explore a new smell or to seek its sensation. But she was too heavily burdened and could not hope to catch up with them. Reluctantly, she dragged herself past and made her way towards the benches.

There was room for one, right on the very edge. The beach could not be seen from the benches, only the crown of the sea with the occasional sailing boat woven into it like hair ribbon. Its smell, too, was kept at a distance, and only an echo of it was caught as the gulls hovered above or as a child dripped past. The sun was trapped in the trees overhead. A few lukewarm drops would filter through every now and again.

It was here that the old people sat, a long line of them, linked together like a chain. By her side sat an old woman, her dress hanging loose at the waist; an old woman, flat-chested, long and tough, like a man.

Beyond her sat an old man, his stomach resting on his knees. She knew, if she chose to tickle him under the chin, that a gurgle of laughter would rise from his belly, like bubbles in a lemonade bottle. His eyes were sunken and a faded blue emanated from them, reminding her of the glimmer of light at the far end of a tunnel.

It was strange how men seemed to become gentler as the years passed, while the women became tougher. The men, as they remembered, content with licking the butter off the stale bread; the women eager to touch the bread, to crumble it between their fingers.

What were they looking for, she wondered, here in no man's land? Were old people greedier than they used to be? Her grandmother never ventured farther than the end of the lane. How disappointed she would have been if grandmother had ever insisted on deserting her world. Old people should stay at home, being tempered before their own fires; guarding treasures that they had accumulated over the years.

She, too, should have stayed at home. But others had packed her case and pushed her onto a train. She could see them now, swarming into the station like a retinue; elbowing one another in their eagerness to reach her. Friends who had been neighbours of hers, mind and body; relations who felt that they had a right to her, as blood was thicker than water.

They had tried everything before they had agreed to let her go; the numerous cups of tea, dark and sweet, and the sympathy, arranged delicately, and as sickly as cream cakes.

There was always someone there, as if they had agreed to do shift work. They would have respected a widow. Her memories would have been beautiful enough for her to have been left in their company. But a woman whose husband had left her was like a prisoner whiling away his days in a condemned cell, conscious that one life was coming to an end and that another was beginning; assuming that he could accept such beliefs.

They were ready to stand between her and the fiendish memories that could terrorize her at night. A sister of hers had insisted on lending her a child, as patronizing women share out library books in hospital, to make the sick forget their illness.

But she wanted to dwell on her illness; to remember how and when it had started; what it was like to be healthy. They treated their words as a quarryman would trim his slates, squaring the edges and smoothing the surface so that they would do no harm. They were determined to place a fancy label on her sickness instead of acknowledging it for the cancer it was. But she wanted to scratch the scabs off her memory, making past experiences bleed.

Once, experiences were as easy to acquire as shells on a beach. There was little difference, then, between one shell and another, and in the sun they all had some virtue. She had loaded herself with them. What a shame that no one came around collecting memories as Gypsies collected old rags. What a relief it would be to hang the paper bags on a doorknob and find, in the morning, that the bags and all their contents, had gone.

They expected her to be able to leave her past on the beach for the tide to carry away. Its strength would surely succeed where their tea and sympathy had failed.

But she knew that she would have to follow each memory to its source before it could be aborted from her mind. She would have to see, not the young tree in the garden, but the hole that her husband had dug to uphold its roots in the early days of their marriage. She would have to hear their laughter as the soil yielded to the shoot; she would have to feel their concern when a straight young branch was severed by a storm.

She would have to see, not the bare finger, but the ring that had once adorned it. She would have to remember the cold sweat of his fingers on that challenging wedding day; the dryness and warmth that vibrated within them as their hands touched; remember the terror that she had felt, once, when she thought that the ring was lost; the cold bitting into her finger like chilblains.

If it were not for them, she would, by now, have erased all her husband's finger marks; she would have opened the windows wide, so that the wind would destroy all his echoes. She would have changed the course of the garden paths and would have filled the little pond with dirt and gravel.

Now they were waiting to welcome her back, deaf and dumb, so that they could teach her a fresh vocabulary, lead her into new experiences. She would let them dress and adorn her like a baby doll, and would feel nothing.

One day she would come again, and sit on a bench like this, with the old folk. And she would be flat-chested and wizened, like the old woman by her side. Perhaps she would walk past the people on the edge of the promenade, the ones who were content to place the canvas between themselves and the sun.

Standing there, she would see the beach that supported bold things, like the sun and the young ones. She would return to the bench and sit there, letting the past crumble between her fingers. And she knew now how hard and stale it would be.

Translated by the author

Angela Carter

UK(England), b. 1940

Born in 1940, Angela Carter grew up and went to school in South London. The daughter of a journalist father, Carter did her first writing for a South London newspaper, *The Croydon Advertiser*. At 20 she married and began college at the University of Bristol, receiving her B.A. in English in 1965. She returned to journalism for a short while, writing cultural criticism for, among others, *New Society* and *The New Statesman*.

Carter's first novels are set in Bristol, where she lived after graduating college. Her first, *Shadow Dance* (1966), a detective novel, is set in the Bristol slums and is a grisly story of cruelty and vengeance. *The Magic Toyshop* (1967), which won the Rhys Memorial Prize in 1968, is a novel about the painful passage from innocence to experience of two teenaged siblings imprisoned above a London toyshop. *Several Receptions* (1968), another novel about the violence of modern life, won the Somerset Maugham Award for that year.

As a critique of the realist tradition and what it represents, Carter's next novels depart contemporary settings for more magical terrain. She has talked about leaving the realist tradition at this point for a more mythological direction. *Heroes and Villains* (1969) is a work of what has been called "Gothic science fiction" because it is a fantasy set in a future resembling the Gothic period. Probably her most important novel of this genre is *The Infernal Desire Machine of Dr. Hoffman* (1972), about the search for a machine that will replace reality with fantasy. This work was greatly influenced by the culture of Japan, where Carter lived from 1970 to 1972, as was a collection of short stories published two years later.

Aside from her eight novels, Carter has also written two collections of short stories, a screenplay, children's stories, a volume of poetry, a translation of the French fairy tales of Charles Perrault, and an analysis of sexual morality through an exploration of de Sade's* pornography, called *The Sadeian Woman* (1979). Carter has often been called a Magic Realist, a writer of science fiction, a mythological writer, or even, a Gothic writer. Because one usually finds one or more of these elements in many of her novels and stories, it is hard to say precisely to which genre her works belong. Despite the problem critics seem to have placing her, a problem that has troubled the careers of many writers, Carter has had an increasingly strong following in England and, of late, in the United States, for her violent, intense, often erotic allegories of modern society.

Carter lives with her second husband, a potter, Mark Pearce, and their son, Alexander, near Battersea Park in South London. The selection here is from her collection of short stories, *The Donkey Prince* (1970).

NOTE

* Count Donatien Alphonse Francois de Sade (1740–1814), author of *Justine* (1791) and *Juliette* (1797), both tales of the heroine's subjection to many varieties of physical and emotional cruelty, giving the name to "sadism."

THE DONKEY PRINCE

Many, many years ago, a Queen went for a walk on a mountain. After a while, she grew tired and sat down to rest under a white stone among the tufts of heather. A donkey came up to her and gazed at her with mournful eyes.

"Give me the apple in your pocket," said the donkey. "I've a great craving come upon me for an apple."

The apple the Queen carried in her pocket was no ordinary fruit but a magic apple from the orchard of her father, the King of the West, which he had given her for a wedding present. "Keep the apple safe, and you'll never lose your looks or have a day's illness," he told her. Then he sailed away across the sea in his ship with green sails to attend to his own affairs, which were very extensive.

The Queen felt in her pocket for the apple and wondered how the donkey knew it was

there. She smelled magic and was a little uneasy.

"Much as I'd like to, I can't give you my apple because it was a wedding present from my father," she said. "But if you come back to the palace with me, I'll give you a whole barrelful of fruit."

"It is only the one apple I want," said the donkey. He threw back his head and brayed loudly. Over the rocks came a whole troop of donkeys, jingling with silver bells, and the first one had a white leather saddle on his back.

The donkey who wanted the apple said politely, "Mount and ride, madam. I cannot go with you, so you must come with me."

The Queen saw nothing for it but to climb into the white saddle, and all the donkeys trotted over the heather until they came to a gray place where it was neither night nor day but in-between times. There they saw a hut thatched with turf that was the Donkey Parliament. The hut was lit with storm lanterns and there was a heap of old sacks beside a fire. The smoke from the fire went up through a hole in the ceiling.

The donkey who wanted the apple was the President of the Donkey Parliament, and the heap of sacks was his chair of office, so he sat on it. The hut was crowded with donkeys, and when they saw the Queen riding in, they bellowed and roared. They led her to a bale of clean straw and saw that she was settled comfortably, and then there was a silence.

"Madam," said the President, "though you see us in the shapes of donkeys, my company and I are, in fact, Brown Men of the Hills. Your father transformed us into this shape by a cruel enchantment after my son accidentally transfixed him with an arrow while he was out hunting. If you had given your father's apple to me of your own free will, because of my need, we should have returned to our natural forms at the very first bite I took from it."

At this, the donkeys wept great tears that trickled down their muzzles, and the Queen was so grieved to see their sorrow, she wept with them. She took out the apple and offered it to the President gladly, but he shook his head.

"It is no use now," he said. "Now you want to give us the apple from pity and not of your own free will, and that won't do at all."

"What can I do to help you?" asked the Queen. "There must be something."

"Excuse us while we have a conference," said the President. The three eldest and most venerable donkeys in the gathering rose up and sat beside him on the sacks. While they conversed together in whispers, the Queen sat unhappily in the firelight, for she knew she had failed a test her father had set her to see if her generosity was stronger than her vanity. She had always been excessively proud of her good looks and abundant health.

Finally, the donkey President rose and came to the Queen.

"It is a very great favor we must ask of you," he said. "Such a great favor only our desperate need prompts us to ask."

"I will do all that I can," she said.

"Would you bring up one of our children as your own, in your own palace, as a prince among men?"

She knew it was her father's plan, and she felt so angry with him for trying her so hard that she almost said no. But the donkey eyes around her were so beseeching, she finally said, "Yes, I will, no matter what my husband the King says."

They brought a newborn foal wrapped in a woolen shawl and placed it in her arms.

"The day he finds a man and a woman willing to go through fire and water for him, we shall return to our proper forms," said the President. "You will have to bring him up very well to make him worthy of such devotion. And we shall never be able to thank you enough."

The Queen mounted her white saddle, and the donkeys took her home to the palace. She went into the hall and her ladies flocked around her to peer inside the shawl. They were very much surprised to see a baby with such long ears, such melancholy eyes and such a loud, discordant voice.

"He shall live in the royal nursery and grow up as a prince," said the Queen.

Everybody was astonished but did not say a word aloud, guessing there was some good explanation. She laid the foal in the King's arms.

"This is the heir to the kingdom," she said. "I've promised it will be so, and I can't go back on my word."

Though the King was extremely disconcerted, he accepted his adopted son with good grace, for he respected his wife's strength of mind. Time passed and the donkey went about the palace with cloth of gold on his back. He learned geometry, trigonometry and Greek, since that formed a prince's education in those days, but he never could learn how to hold a pen in his hoof. So he never knew how to write his name, which was Bruno.

He was of such a sweet disposition, so modest and gentle, that he was greatly loved in spite of his unconventional appearance. The King and Queen never had any children of their own, so no ugly problems of succession were raised, and they loved Prince Bruno quite as well as if he were their own flesh and blood.

When Bruno was almost full grown, the Queen lost her magic apple. It fell from her pocket when she was out walking one day, and she did not know where it went. At once the color faded from her face, and besides losing her looks, she became so ill that everyone said she would die. Physicians and surgeons came from many neighboring countries to try to cure her, but nothing brought her back to health.

All day long she lay on her bed with her face to the wall, staring at the wallpaper as if there were wonderful patterns on it that she alone could see.

As the King and the Prince sat sadly together, a bird flew in through the window and perched on the arm of the King's throne.

"The Queen needs her magic apple back again. That's plain to see," said the bird. He had feathers of a startling cherry color flecked with gold.

"But where's her apple? That's the question," said the King.

"A Wild Man found it and took it back to the Savage Mountain where the Wild Men live in mud huts," said the bird.

"Where is the Savage Mountain?" asked the King.

"How should I know?" demanded the bird. "I'm not omniscient." He was a learned bird with a large vocabulary, but he said no more and flew away.

"Wherever it is, I shall find it," said Bruno. So he went out by himself onto the high road out of the kingdom to look for the Savage Mountain, leaving a message to tell the King

where he was going. He met a child who sat on a boulder beside the road, plaiting straw for hats.

"Good morning," said Bruno. "Could you tell me the way to the Savage Mountain?"

The child bit on a straw and stared, but not rudely, only out of curiosity. Bruno realized he was no common sight, with his hairy ears and coat of cloth of gold, so he did not take offense. It was a girl child, but she was so dirty and her rags so nondescript that it was difficult, at first, to tell. Her name was Daisy.

"I heard my mother speak of the Savage Mountain, but she's dead now," said Daisy. "If I think hard, I shall probably remember the way."

"Could you take me there?"

"I daresay. I live with an old woman who works my fingers to the bone with the straw-plaiting, and I'd just a soon go off with you. But we must go down this road to the very end."

With that, she threw her straw away and walked off with him. Soon her feet grew tired.

"May I ride on your back?" she asked. "My legs are getting weary."

Nobody had ever ridden on Bruno's back before because he was a prince. But he did not hesitate, for he saw her feet were bare and the road was very rough.

"With pleasure," he said. She climbed on his back.

"Now I remember the way perfectly," she said. "I recall it in full. But soon the road goes into a bog."

"That's inconvenient," said Bruno.

"We shall see what we shall see," said Daisy.

Just as she had said, they soon arrived at a bog full of mist and smells of decay. Bruno thought they could follow the road no farther. But Daisy got down and gathered rushes and plaited them and laid them on the treacherous ground, which seemed to quake and shiver as they looked at it.

"We shall walk safe now, anyway," she said.

Bruno set his little hooves gingerly on the rushes, and the fragile path held firm. As he went forward, the rush-bridge spread out in front of him and rolled itself up behind, and Daisy wound it up into a ball. By the time they crossed the bog, this ball was very large.

"That is a trick worth knowing," said Bruno.

"A working girl learns a trick or two," said Daisy. "Before us lies a river no man can cross."

"Then how can we cross it?" asked Bruno, almost in despair. She laughed, but not unkindly.

"I'm not a man, I'm a girl. And as for you, you're neither—you're a donkey."

"That's perfectly true," said Bruno bowing his head. "I'd never have thought of that."

"A working girl learns to use her common sense, you know."

They swam the river with ease. On the other side of the river stretched a desolate country where cold winds rushed through grim chasms, and a few trees and bushes, gnarled and stunted by the violence of the elements, clung to the stony soil as if clutching it for dear life with their roots. And still the road went on, though now it was so rough, it was hard to tell the road from the moorland.

"We are approaching the foothills of the Savage Mountain," said Daisy. "Listen and you can hear the Wild Men howl."

Bruno pricked up his enormous ears and heard, carried on the roaring winds, uncouth voices singing outlandish songs in strange harmonies. Since his hearing was extraordinarily good, he also caught another sound. This was the whirr of Wild Men sharpening their knives on grinding stones. But he did not mention this to Daisy, as he thought it would frighten her. Instead, he said, "I think it would be best if you turned back for home now. The Savage Mountain is no place for little girls."

"Nor for foolish donkeys either!" said Daisy angrily. Then they saw by one another's expressions that each had hurt the other's feelings equally, and both were equally sorry.

Daisy flung her arms around Bruno's neck.

"I'd rather go on with you than turn back, no matter what the danger," she said. And they went on as before, though often hungry and cold.

They went up steep paths and down narrow valleys where daylight struggled with darkness. Rain clouds drenched them, and then the rain froze. Bruno had a poor diet of heather and scanty grass, and Daisy found only a few withered roots and berries to eat. But the road still showed no signs of coming to an end.

One morning, as they ate their miserable breakfast, thinking themselves lost and alone in this inhospitable place, a huge knife came flashing through the air and buried itself up to the hilt in the earth beside them.

They saw an enormous figure leaning on an ax and gazing at them from huge red eyes that seemed to spit fire. His long hair was done up in many plaits knotted with strips of leather and hung down to his waist. His beard and moustache were also plaited and reached to the middle of his chest, which was covered with an intricate interlaced pattern of blue-and-red-tattooing.

A leather sack was slung over his shoulder. He wore trousers of wolfskin, and his belt was stuck with many more knives and also daggers. Beside him a mastiff, almost the size of Bruno, sat panting, showing a pink tongue that lolled out for what seemed yards. The newcomer, clearly a Wild Man, was accompanied by his dog, whose name was Hound.

"I see you've noticed my visiting card," said the Wild Man in a menacing voice, showing teeth as white and pointed as splinters of fresh wood.

"Yes, indeed," said Bruno courteously. He and Daisy were not at all afraid, as they were anxious for news of the Wild Men's village.

"I'm sorry, I seem to have interrupted your breakfast," said the Wild Man, who grew less hostile when they showed no fear.

"Such as it is, you are very welcome to share it," invited Daisy, spreading out a handful of greenish blackberries as appetizingly as possible. "But this is all we have, and I'm afraid it's not very nice."

This offer melted the Wild Man's heart. He was not accustomed to generosity from strangers.

"These are friends, Hound," he said to his dog, who at once leaped forward and licked Daisy's face. Then he licked Bruno's muzzle.

"I'd be glad to eat breakfast with you if you allow me to provide the food," said the Wild Man. From his leather sack, he took some oatcakes and a cheese. He sliced them up with one of his wicked knives, and they made a hearty breakfast, for Bruno was fond of oatcakes, too.

"We Wild Men have a bad reputation, but our bark is worse than our bite," said the Wild Man, who was called Hlajki. All the Wild names were full of flinty, uncomfortable j's and k's.

"We live on a harsh mountain and have no time for the soft ways of the valley people. In return, they always expect the worst from us. There's no love lost, I can tell you, and we soon scare them off when they come creeping up to spy on us, full of curiosity to see our Wild ways. But I can tell that you two are different."

Bruno took an instant liking to Hlajki because the Wild Man neither stared at him because he was a donkey, nor cringed and groveled because he was a prince. Hlajki also treated Daisy with beautiful politeness, giving her the largest piece of cheese.

"We're on a mission," confided Bruno.

Hlajki looked grave. "Is it a matter of life and death?"

"My mother's life hangs by a thread."

"Then I'm your man," said Hlajki, swearing by his ax.

"My mother lost her magic apple, and now she is very ill. If she doesn't have her apple back again, they say she'll die. One of the Wild Men found the apple and took it home to his mud dwelling. We have come to fetch it back."

"My own cousin, who is called Klajj, found this apple," said Hlajki. "He brought it into our village, and we clustered around to stare. None of us had seen an apple before, for apple trees won't bear fruit in our climate. Now the apple lies among the other treasures of the Wild Men in the iron safe of our leader, whose name is Terror."

"Do you think he would give it to me if I told him how much depended on it?" asked Bruno.

"No," said Hlajki. "He would kill you with his spear, tan your hide and make himself a pair of trousers from it."

"We shall have to acquire the apple by guile," said Daisy, who was a practical girl. "I shall think of a way. A working girl knows how to use her wits."

She walked up and down, thinking, while Hlajki and Bruno played two-handed whist, for there was a pack of cards at the bottom of Hlajki's sack. Hound sat on the alert in case anyone approached them secretly, for the Wild Men were a very suspicious people. At last Daisy came back, smiling.

"Let me borrow your golden saddlecloth, Bruno," she said.

She wrapped the marvelous stuff around her like a robe and decorated her hair with his gold and jeweled ornaments until she looked like a princess herself, and Bruno, stripped of his finery, looked like any common donkey. You would never have thought she was a girl who plaited straw for a living or that Bruno would inherit a kingdom.

"You are the most beautiful thing I've ever seen upon the Savage Mountain," said Hlajki.

"Take me to your village," she said. "I will beard Terror in his den."

She mounted on Bruno's back, and Hlajki led them to the village, with Hound following them like a dog struck with wonder. The road went right up to the village of the Wild Men and stopped outside Terror's front door, which was surrounded by the skulls of beasts. Their arrival caused considerable commotion among the mud huts of the Wild Men. The Wild Women, with Wild Babies wrapped up in furs, and Wild Children covered with tattooing, all came out to see them, uttering barbaric cries. They gathered about Daisy, fingering her golden robe, their eyes round with awe.

Soon Terror came out of his hut. He was a fearsome sight. He was a head and a half taller then Hlajki and much hairier. His teeth were filed to points as sharp as needles, to show how savage he was. He wore a mantle of bearskin and the antlers of a stag upon his head.

"I am a great magician and will show you some magic tricks," said Daisy.

She took three of the little leather balls the Wild Children played with and began to juggle them so fast you would have thought you saw a hundred of them in the air at the same time. The Wild People fell silent with astonishment and then cheered and applauded loudly.

"Any twopenny-halfpenny conjurer could do as well as that," said Terror. His voice was as dreadful as the beginnings of a storm. "You may impress my wild company who have seen nothing but the Savage Mountain; however, I am a man of travel, and you certainly don't impress me."

Daisy took one of the stone pots in which the Wild People cooked their food and covered it with a fold of her robe. When she brought the pot into the light again, a pink geranium blossomed there. She broke off the flower and gave it to Terror, but he said with a sneer, "It's all done with mirrors. Astonish me. Go on, astonish me. I am so bored with hard times on the Savage Mountain that I'll give you anything you ask for—if you make me astonished."

"Will you give me the apple Hlajki's cousin Klajj found, that is now locked up in your iron safe? said Daisy.

"How do you know about my treasures?" he asked, his face a picture of surprise.

"Because I am the greatest magician in the world," she said. And she took a little wooden whistle from the bosom of her robe.

She began to play a tune of such sweetness that all the Wild People began to cry with pleasure, and even Terror found tears of joy were trickling down his tattooed cheeks. Then a flock of birds appeared, strange and beautiful birds with cherry-colored feathers flecked with gold, and Bruno recognized amongst them the bird who had come to the palace before his travels started.

The birds began to weave a mazy dance in the sky to the music Daisy played, and as they flew they dropped down feathers which turned to rubies when they touched the ground. The Wild People picked up the rubies and treasured them greatly. Then Daisy put down her whistle, and the birds all flew away.

"Bring out the apple," said Terror. "I would give my name, my rank and my reputation as a warrior to possess even a quarter of your magic."

So Daisy took the magic apple, and they went back the way they had come. Now they had plenty of cold meat, oatcakes and cheese which the Wild Men had given them and also the company of Hlajki and Hound, who had vowed by the ax never to leave them. But when the conjuring was over, Terror decided it was a fleeting pleasure compared with the possession of a unique magic apple, and he sent out men to fire the heather and burn the strangers alive.

All the moor behind them became a sea of flame which surged toward them faster than they could run away from it. Hlajki cried out, covered his eyes and began to mutter spells of the Wild Men to protect them, but Daisy said, "I'll make a firebreak." She took matches from her pocket and quickly burned a wide strip of heather. They stood on the charred ground in the heart of a wild fire which roared around them but did not harm them and finally burned itself out.

In this way, Hlajki and Daisy went through fire for Bruno.

So they passed the fire safely, though some sparks singed Hlajki's trousers, and Hound was so shocked at the blaze that he was a much gentler dog in the future and jumped nervously at the slightest sound. They went forward over the fire-blackened country until they reached the river no man could cross. Here the waves washed Hlajki back onto the bank as soon as he tried to swim.

"I shall have to stay on the Savage Mountain all my life and never see you both again," he said, "nor hear the music of your whistle."

Man and dog began to cry, but Bruno said, "Jump on my back." Hlajki sat astride the donkey, though he had never ridden horse nor pony before, and his seat was very shaky. In this fashion, they entered the water. But it was hard going, for Hlajki was of immense stature and his weight pulled Bruno down until it was clear they would both drown if he continued to ride.

"Good night, sweet Prince," said Hlajki simply when he realized what was happening, and he slipped off Bruno's back. He would have sunk beneath the waves straight-away if Bruno had not clasped his beard between his teeth, while Daisy clutched his hair and Hound took hold of his belt. In this manner, they kept him on the surface between them.

So Hlajki and Daisy went through water for Bruno, but it was nearly the death of them all.

As they floundered there, a sudden current in the water threw them high in the air, and Daisy gasped, "I see a ship upon the river."

Floating toward them on the tide came a barge with sails as green as grass. Sailors in green uniforms manned the rigging, and a very old man whose white beard reached to the ground sat on the poop in a chair of carved oak and looking glass. When the barge reached Bruno, Daisy, Hlajki and Hound, the sailors lowered a dinghy and drew them on board. In a few minutes, they stood before the old man, who rose to welcome them.

"I am the King of the West," he said.

Bruno went down on his front legs before him, Daisy curtseyed as she had been taught to do to rich old men, and Hlajki inclined his wild head slightly, for the Wild Men were too proud to bow to anyone. But the dog wagged his tail, sending water everywhere, and the old man smiled.

"Give me the apple, for it is from my own orchard," he said. When he had it safe, he took them into his sumptuous cabin and showed them a mirror.

First this mirror reflected nothing but mist. But soon the mist cleared, and Bruno saw his foster mother in her royal bed at home, waking as if from a refreshing sleep, then taking strong broth hungrily from a cup.

"She's on the high road to health, I'm glad to say," said the King her father. "I can see everything in my magic mirror, but unfortunately my powers of intervention are limited. You had to go through fire and water yourselves."

"Daisy did all the hard work," said Bruno. "A donkey finds it hard to cope with human beings."

But already he was beginning to look more like a man than a donkey.

"I am a greater magician than you, but your talents are certainly wasted in the hat-making industry," said the King to Daisy. "Look in the mirror again."

A fresh cloud of mist blotted out the Queen, and when it blew away, two words in Gothic script appeared in the depths of the glass: *The Future*. Then it showed a young prince in a suit of green velvet, who was plainly Bruno in his true shape. He held Daisy by the hand, and she was wearing a wedding dress. Hlajki in his fur trousers stood beside them as best man, and Hound had his paw on the marriage register, making his mark as a witness. Over their heads, a flock of red-and-gold birds formed a canopy, and the couple was surrounded by a cheering throng of Wild Men, Brown Men of the Hills in their true shapes (small of stature and brown of hue) and the men and women of Bruno's kingdom.

Well, all this came true in the course of time. After Bruno and Daisy were married, the Brown Men returned to their native hills and took up market gardening, for they had given up hunting forever. They always allowed their beasts of burden to wander where they pleased, treating them as equals, which was only right and proper.

Terror's cruelty caused a revolution among the Wild Men, and he was stoned off the Savage Mountain. Hlajki became their new leader, and under his influence, they became gentler by degrees, built themselves houses of wood and thatch, and started eating with knives and forks, which they had never done before.

But all this happened long ago, in another country, and nothing is the same now, of course.

Angela de Hoyos US, b. 1940

Born in Coahuila, Mexico, Angela de Hoyos has lived in San Antonio, Texas, since childhood. She is reticent about her private life but graciously consented to be interviewed by Sonia Saldivar-Hull for this volume. De Hoyos' work provides the major key to the woman who is a product of two worlds, Mexico and the United States, which intersect and emerge in the Chicano culture. As visual artist, as editor, as poet, she seeks to give a name to the indignities and suffering of her people and to nurture the strengths and imagination of the community and individual artists and is well-known for her generosity and support. One of the vehicles through which she has accomplished this support is as general editor of M&A Editions and as coeditor of the journal *Huehuetitlan*.

De Hoyos' poetic history reflects the historical progress of the Chicano's political evolution in recent times. De Hoyos began by writing philosophical poetry that she considered too personal to submit for publication. Eventually some of these early poems found their way to various international journals: "The Mortal Trap" ruminates on the brutality of life, significantly figured as a vengeful woman; "A Matter of Minutes" begins to identify specific historical forces responsible for human suffering. Subsequently collected in a bilingual edition (1976), this work was followed by poems that expressed and reflected a renewed social awareness by Chicanos.

Taking their cue from the black civil rights movement, Chicanos struggled for equal rights in the workplace as well as in the larger political arena. De Hoyos was profoundly affected by her involvement with the Texas farm workers' struggle in the mid-1970s, and in two chapbook collections, *Arise, Chicano! and Other Poems* and *Chicano Poems: for the Barrio* (1975), she sought to expose the cultural imperialism that denigrated the Hispanic culture; at the same time, she appropriated the bilingual language that was her heritage for her poetry.

As in "Chicano" and "Hermano," from *Chicano Poems*, the dual language is used in a variety of subtle and interesting ways: Spanish is used to confide, to express tenderness and solidarity, to lament, while English becomes the language of indictment. Intertwining linguistic threads, the poetry thus embodies what is already thematized—the people of the border live at the boundary, on one hand deprived of their own culture, and on the other denied access to what we all lay claim to. In choosing to write in a collective voice, therefore, de Hoyos assumes the responsibility of the artist to help raise the consciousness of her people. This is evident in the merger of her literary and graphic talents to create poster poetry; a recent example is her tribute to Martin Luther King, Jr., "To Live the Dream" (1987).

Her most recent volume *Woman, Woman* (1985), involves an exploration of the Chicana's struggle against the patriarchy. As in "Lesson in Semantics," de Hoyos asserts that sometimes one has "to spit the word" when speaking of men. But in the final analysis, de Hoyos' political philosophy remains rooted in the belief that the primary fight for the Chicana is that which aligns her with the Chicano working class against the privileged white world, male and female.

THE MORTAL TRAP

Come into the boudoir
of my arms, Life purrs
    to the unsuspecting mortals.

And loving her, beguiled,
we enter.

Whereupon, at every chance
thereafter posturing good-will
    in every glance,
with Brutus-fingered calm she stabs
and stabs
      and stabs
          and stabs
us unto death.

CHICANO

How to paint
    on this page
      the enigma
that furrows
    your sensitive
      brown face
—a sadness,
    porque te llamas
      Juan, y no *John**
as the laws
    of assimilation
      dictate.

BROTHER HERMANO

"Remember the Alamo"
...and my Spanish ancestors
who had the sense to build it.

I was born too late
in a land
that no longer belongs to me
(so it says, right here in this Texas History).

Ay, mi San Antonio de Bexar
cuidad-reina de la frontera,[1]
the long hand of greed
was destined to seize you!
...Qué nadie te oyó cuando caíste,
cuando esos hombres rudos te hurtaron?...[2]
Blind-folded they led you
to a marriage of means
while your Spanish blood
smouldered within you!

Tu cielo
ya no me pertenece.
Ni el Alamo, ni la Villita,
ni el rio que a capricho
por tu mero centro corre.
Ni las misiones
—joyas de tu passado—[3]
    San Juan de Capistrano
    Concepción
    San José
    La Espada

(*continued*)

NOTE

* "Because you are named Juan and not John."

: They belong to a pilgrim
who arrived here only yesterday
whose racist tongue says to me: I hate
Meskins.[4] You're a Meskin. Why don't you
go back to where you came from?
Yes, amigo . . . ! Why don't I? Why don't I
resurrect the Pinta, the Niña and the Santa
                                                    María,
—and you can scare up your little 'Flor de
                                            Mayo'[5]—

so we can all sail back
to where we came from: the motherland
                                            womb.

I was born too late
or perhaps I was born too soon:
It is not yet my time;
this is not yet my home.

I must wait for the conquering barbarian
to learn the Spanish word for love:

HERMANO

NOTES

1. Oh, my San Antonio de Bexar,
   queen-city of the border,
2. Did no one hear you when you fell,
   when those rude men stole you? . . .
3. Your sky
   is no longer mine.
   Not the Alamo, nor la Villita,
   nor the river that capriciously
   runs through your heart.
   Nor the missions
   —jewels of your past
4. Derogatory term for Mexicans.
5. Spanish for "The Mayflower."
                    Notes translated by Sonia Saldivar-Hull

Nafissatou Diallo   *Senegal, 1941–1982*

Nafissatou Diallo was born in Lilene, Senegal, one of five children born to the first wife of a serious and pious Muslim official. As was the custom for all Muslim children, she began her studies at a Koranic school. However, Diallo was permitted to study in a secular school beginning at the age of 7, extremely unusual for someone of her background. She went on to obtain a certificate at the School of Midwifery.

Shortly after she graduated, her father died. It is to him and to her grandmother that she dedicated her first work, an autobiography entitled *De tilène au plateau: une enfance dakaroise* (*A Dakar Childhood*, 1976). Detailing the growth and education of a young girl, the book offers a vivid and often comic dramatization of middle-class Senegalese life as well as the rituals, ceremonies, and traditions of the francophone Islamic world from a child's pour of view; it also captures the transition from village to urban life. Equally significant is Diallo's desire to lift the "taboos of silence that reign over our emotions."

Diallo was married to a Senegalese who received his higher education in Paris; upon their return from Europe, she worked as a midwife and child nurse in Ouagou-Niane. Husband and wife were members of an upwardly mobile class of young, educated men and women who sought a way for Senegal to enter the modern world while preserving the integrity of Senegalese culture and Islam with neither nostalgia nor disdain for the past.

Diallo was committed to fostering solidarity among women, and her writings affirmed the power of womanhood. *La fort maudit* (*The Doomed Fortress*, 1980), dedicated to her three daughters and "to all the mothers of Eternal Africa," is a third-person narrative about a heroic young woman who takes her revenge upon a foreign chief, the conqueror of her people and killer of her lover, by seducing and murdering the despot and then sacrificing her own life. In an extremely rich and complex children's book—*Awa, la petite marchande* (Awa, the Little Fishmonger, 1981), the youthful heroine sacrifices her schooling for a while in order to sell fish with her mother because their family is in financial difficulty. Later, Awa is able to return to her studies and pursue her education in France.

A strange mixture of vital optimism and tragic stoicism, Diallo took her own life at the age of 40.

from A DAKAR CHILDHOOD
De tilène au plateau: une enfance dakaroise

The school year was drawing to a close. I dreaded Thursdays and Sundays, the days when there were no classes and which we spent being de-wormed, since parasites had been discovered in our stools; this wasn't surprising as we were always in contact with sand.

On Mondays and Fridays Mama prepared and bottled five litres of an infusion of garlic. On the mornings when there was no school we queued up in front of her, each holding out a bowl. We drank the infusion with many grimaces and were then sent off to await the results. For several hours we had nothing to eat or drink except a hot decoction made from kinkeliba mixed with some other mysterious ingredients. We did in fact pass an incredible number of ascaris.

Father sent us a picture postcard of Kaaba. "The pilgrimage is going well," he wrote, "but it's exceptionally hot here. Many people have died. Be extra zealous in your prayers. Give generously to the poor. Be good to the children."

Father's whole personality was in those last words. He was the only one in the family who would be able to worry about us children from such a great distance. "Be good to them," said the postcard which was passed from hand to hand and which delighted us youngsters.

At last the end of the pilgrimage was approaching and we prepared to welcome back the traveller. The day of his arrival two rams were slaughtered and several kilos of millet were ground and made into couscous. Relatives and friends sent crates of lemonade. The house was cleaned till it shone; immaculate sheets covered all the beds; we were dressed in our best clothes.

We children were not allowed to go to the airport as there was always such a crush on these occasions when pilgrims returned in large numbers. We waited quietly at home, getting more and more excited every time we heard the noise of a car approaching.

Finally there came the cry, "Here he is! He's here!"

With beating heart I raced to the door and saw my father, majestic in his new pilgrim's attire: he wore a huge cloak embroidered with gold thread and the lamé turban of a "Hadj" on his head. He lifted me off my feet and nearly suffocated me in his embrace. Tears of joy streamed down my cheeks. Generally we were very undemonstrative and kept our feelings of love buried deep in our hearts; to show affection was considered ill-bred, westernized. In my heart of hearts I cursed the way we were brought up, with this strictness, all these scruples and taboos.

That morning my heart overflowed with gratitude to God for bringing Father home safe and sound. Grandmother was in the seventh heaven, trotting briskly hither and thither and petting the pilgrim like a child. To tell the truth Father looked as if he could do with a bit of spoiling and feeding up; he had lost a good deal of weight. This, he said, was quite normal; you were supposed to leave some of your weight behind in Mecca as a symbol of *asaka*, that is the charity to be given to the poor.

The traveller's luggage was unpacked. The jars of *zem-zem* that he had brought back were emptied into basins of water placed outside all the bedrooms. Then we recited verses from the Koran, as laid down for this ritual, made our wishes and drank goblets full of this mixture of holy water from Mecca and Dakar tap-water.

Dressed in our best clothes we waited for the arrival of our visitors whom we welcomed with gifts of dates and sticks of incense. We kept a good look-out for the ones who came for the *ziara*, the pilgrimage, and made a bee-line for them before they even had time to greet anyone.

Father welcomed everyone with a smile. Some of the visitors embraced him; others held his hand in a long grasp, to obtain the benefit of his *baraka*, his spiritual plenitude. From time to time he turned to us to congratulate us on your progress or give us a word of encouragement which warmed our hearts. He personally handed us our share of dates and incense, while our aunts darted disapproving glances at him; if they had been left to share out our dates they would have counted them out one by one. Father always knew who he was dealing with, what was the right thing to do or say, making his presence felt by small gestures, such as giving us children a larger share like this. Naturally he knew that the children always had the worst deal when it came to sharing things out, and that was why we often had recourse to helping ourselves.

Father waited till all the neighbors had left, each one going off with his little packet of incense, then he brought out the presents for the family. The boys got skull-caps which they wore later for the important Korité and Tabaski prayers. For my grandmother and the aunts there were shawls, rosaries, and jars of *tsungël*. We girls received necklaces, rings, and sandals made out of plaited gold thread.

We dug mercilessly into the sacks of dates which the aunts tried every trick to hide from us. We regularly drank our *zem-zem* water in the belief that we were saturating our bodies with holiness. And we felt that this would promote the fulfilment of the wishes that we made.

But I haven't told you about my special supply of *zem-zem*. On the very day of Father's return, in the confusion created by the unpacking, I abstracted from his luggage a jar of the holy Mecca water to keep all for myself, wishing to obtain all its undiluted virtues.

Not finding any other place to drink it without being seen, I locked myself in the lavatory, broke open the top with a knife, coughing hard to cover the noise, fervently pronounced my wishes and drank the bitter liquid down in one gulp. For the next two days I had the most appalling diarrhea.

In those days I never distinguished as far as prayers were concerned, between "clean" and "unclean" places. I was totally ignorant of ablutions and the purifications laid down by our religion. As far as I was concerned God was everywhere. I said my prayers equally well in my bedroom or in the lavatory, where I had the benefit of being left in peace; no one was likely to disturb me there. When I had bad conduct marks at school, I would take refuge in the W.C.* and free from any prying eyes beseech the Lord's help. I can still see myself standing there with outstretched arms, imploring Him, putting all my faith in my prayers, quite unconscious of the aromas that went up to heaven with my petitions.

Translated by Dorothy S. Blair

NOTE

* Water closet, or toilet.

Gwendolyn MacEwen   *Canada, 1941–1987*

Born in Toronto and educated there and in Winnipeg, Gwendolyn MacEwen left school at age 18 to become a writer, having already published a poem in the *Canadian Forum*. Moving to Montreal, she edited the little magazine *Moment* in 1960–1962, married Canadian poet Milton Acorn, and brought out two privately printed collections of poems—*Selah* and *The Drunken Clock*. By 1963, when her first substantial book of poetry—the germane, quasimystical, protofeminist *The Rising Fire*—appeared, along with her first novel, *Julian the Magician*, MacEwen's career was established. She went on to write numerous other books of poetry, including two volumes of selected poems (*Magic Animals*, 1974, and *Earthlight*, 1982); a second novel, *King of Egypt, King of Dreams* (1971); a collection of short stories, *Noman* (1972); two published plays—a verse play "Terror and Erebus" (in *Tamarack Review*, 1974), and a rewriting of Euripides, *Trojan Women* (1981); half a dozen unpublished plays and dramatic documentaries for CBC radio; and two children's books. She was not only one of the most versatile but also one of the most symbolically dense and distinctive of contemporary Canadian women writers.

Even before her short second marriage to Greek singer Nikos Tsingos and her travels to Israel, Egypt, and Greece—the latter described in her memoir *Mermaids and Ikons: A Greek Summer* (1978)—MacEwen had begun to devise a personal iconography, a fantastic amalgam of Jungian, alchemical, kabalistic, and Babylonian imagery. An idiosyncratic mixture of esoteric symbols and colloquial speech, MacEwen's poems are set in a no-man's land between the grotesque realities of contemporary Western civilization and a more ancient realm of fantasy, archetype, and Eastern mythology. MacEwen was inspired typically by a male figure—magician, king, muse—so that her poetry seems both to exorcise private demons and to chart symbolic inner landscapes of the enslaved/autonomous female self.

Her vision united oppositions: destruction/creation, sun/moon, light/dark, waking/dreaming, stasis/process, alienation/enclosure, male/female. As she wrote in the introduction to *Breakfast for Barbarians* (1966): "The key theme of things is the alienation, the exile from our own inventions, and hence from ourselves. Let's say No—rather enclose, absorb. . . ." Though her work has not yet been systematically interpreted along feminist lines, MacEwen, since the early 1960s, was engaged in the process of "recovering" the female self and of finding "home." MacEwen's "Dark Pines Under Water" is from *The Shadow-Maker* (1969)—which won the Governor General's Award; "Meditations of a Seamstress (1) and (2)" from *The Armies of the Moon* (1972).

Wendy Robbins Keitner

DARK PINES UNDER WATER

This land like a mirror turns you inward
And you become a forest in a furtive lake;
The dark pines of your mind reach downward,
You dream in the green of your time,
Your memory is a row of sinking pines.

Explorer, you tell yourself this is not what you
                                            came for
Although it is good here, and green;
You had meant to move with a kind of largeness,
You had planned a heavy grace, an anguished
                                            dream.

But the dark pines of your mind dip deeper
And you are sinking, sinking, sleeper
In an elementary world;
There is something down there and you want
                                            it told.

MEDITATIONS OF A SEAMSTRESS (1)

When it's all too much to handle
and the green seams of the world start fraying,
I drink white wine and sew
like it was going out of style;
        curtains become dresses, dresses
become pillowcovers, clothes
I've worn forever get taken in or out.
Now I can't explain exactly
what comes over me, but when the phone rings
I tell people I'm indisposed;
I refuse to answer the door, I even
neglect my mail.
        (Something vital is at stake,
the Lost Stitch or the Ultimate Armhole,
I don't know what) and hour after hour
on the venerable Singer
I make strong strong seams for my dresses
and my world.
        The wine possesses me
and I sew like a fiend, forgetting to use
the right colors of thread, unable to make
a single straight line;
I know somehow I'm fighting time
and if it's not all done by nightfall
everything will come apart again;
continental shelves will slowly drift into the sea

and earthquakes will tear wide open
the worn-out patches of Asia.
Dusk, a dark needle, stabs the city
and I get visions of chasing fiery spools of thread
mile after mile over highways and fields
until I inhabit some place at the hem of the world
where all the long blue draperies
of skies and rivers wind;
        spiders' webs described
the circling of their frail thoughts forever;
everything fits at last and someone has lined
the thin fabric of this life I wear with grass.

MEDITATIONS OF A SEAMSTRESS (2)

I dream impossible clothes which will confess me
and fall apart miraculous as the Red Sea
to reveal to you the stunning contours of my
mind (you who wear the world with a grace
I will never achieve, invisibly,
like the arcane garment of the emperor).
I dream things not to be worn in this city,
yards of silks which like Isadora's scarf*
may one day choke me, blue tunics held together
by buckles bearing the portraits of lost kings,
vests carved from the skin of frightened deer,
green velvet cloaks in which I may soundlessly
                                            collapse
and succumb to the Forest, sleeves to stress
the arm of the archer, the huntress, Artemis.

Only one dress I made ever came out right—
(it will never happen that way again);
all the way down the front of it
where it opens from the collar to the hem
I sewed the signs of Athens,
a row of obsolete but perfect keys
on a strip of black and gold,
with which you may, O naked emperor,
enter and decode my world.

NOTE

* Isadora Duncan (1877–1927), pioneer of modern dance,
  died when the scarf she was wearing (it was a trademark
  of her dances) strangled her when caught in the wheel of
  her car.

Cristina Peri Rossi   *Uruguay/Spain, b. 1941*

Cristina Peri Rossi is one of the most distinguished of Latin America's younger prose writers. Her novel, *El libro de mis primos* (My Cousins' Book, 1969), won her the Marcha Prize. A collection of short stories, *Los museos abandonados* (The Abandoned Museums, 1968), won the Narrative Prize from Arca Publishers while another short story collection, *La rebelión de los niños* (The Rebellion of the Children, 1976) won the Benito Pérez Galdós Prize. Two other volumes of short stories, *Indicios Pánicos* (Panic Signs, 1970), from which the following selection was taken, and *Viviendo* (Living, 1972), are highly regarded by critics.

Peri Rossi is also recognized as a major poet. She has written seven volumes of poetry since her first, *Ellos los bien nacidos* (Those Well Born, 1968). *Lingüística general* (General Linguistics, 1979) was awarded first prize in the Palma Poetry Competition. The latest is *El deseo del bosque* (The Desire of the Woods, 1980). Her central theme in all her writing is exile, both political and artistic. (She herself lives in Spain). Her poetry can be very erotic, and, like her Uruguayan predecessor Delmira Agustini, she has beneath the surface of her writing a strong current of social protest.

THE TRAPEZE ARTISTS
Los trapecistas

And now, Maria Teresa, until another day.

No more flowers in my room, Maria Teresa, awaiting your arrival. Maria Teresa in the photo album is a little smudged shadow, a spot of liquid that has dried, leaving its yellow flower. Of the photo fixer that testifies forever, Maria Teresa, that your look is the warmest of the looks I might be able to remember, to evoke one day, that your smile for nothing in particular goes with the wind, because you are noble and the features of your face are revealed there forever, so tomorrow your grandchildren may take them up amidst laughter, "Imagine that, the olden days, what funny dresses, those ridiculous fashions, and the poses, always so artificial," or maybe it's the Commissioner in Charge of Investigations who comes to requisition, among the dunes of papers that pile up in my room, The Tracks of That Girl That You Knew and they discover, among yellowed and by now useless clippings, among film programs and bottles of medicine, your features. Maria Teresa, that they're looking for, your face Maria Teresa, food for archives, and they ask me what you've done, what we've done, what we did that day, that that that, that day which I don't remember anymore, when we saw a movie I don't remember which when we went into a horrible cafe where we drank a cup of I don't know what and I don't tell I don't tell or I tell them what I don't know: where you are what you did what we did because the wind and time and Maria Teresa and perhaps if I knew where it is that you are. Better, that way I don't tell them anything. And I took that photograph of you without your knowing it, I pretended the camera wasn't loaded because I sadly intuited the present, because I knew that every minute was a minute and fleeting, so I brandished the camera as in a game, that game that sadly glided between us, and I pressed the shutter that wasn't supposed to expose anything and in the silent intimate complicity of the film—we were like sister and brother—Maria Teresa you were a flower, Maria Teresa sister and friend, fraternal and loving, and suddenly you were a snapshot, a bit of film exposed to the light of your eyes, your profile, and if there had also been a sound track, now I would not only be seeing your smile but also would have recorded your voice, your voice telling me in play, "Please don't play," your voice telling me, "this evening and this evening and this evening," Maria Teresa calling me "crazy crazy crazy crazy baby" and "you are you you are you you are infinite."

What have you done what have we done what did we do the two of us, you alone, separately, separating yourself from me at any moment.

Because

The days crossed each other like opposing armies
and the nights were venereal
Nights of balsam and wakefulness
of bliss and sentinels
of vertigo and caution
we had discovered a new romanticism, we were the pioneers, the prophets of modern feeling.

the huge hemorrage of the Ego suddenly replaced by the always open vein of you of us of them.

The little god of I demolished, we erected the great temple of Everyone; one vertigo is followed by another vertigo,
one martyr by five martyrs
all a question of setting
and volumes;
replace the Roman circus and the lion with the Christian inside
with any street the army and one of us in the center, dancing.

Or, in place of the cross the nails and the martyrdom
the prison torture and death

The *ergastulum*[1] the ghetto the scourge
the jungle barbed wire the *picana*[2]
an unnamed death, "disappeared," "whereabouts unknown," "accidental," "chance," "negligence," "involuntary;"

the same, Maria Teresa, but dressed differently.

The world, yesterday and today, assembled with great complicity, with the blessed help of all, some more or less innocent, with the Inquisition the Popes and the Opus Dei, *The New Yorker*, McNamara, La Falange, The Movement for Peace and the Family, the International Committee for the Conservation of Property, Richard Nixon and the big dailies; James Bond, Brigitte Bardot and Liz Taylor's jewels, all in the same arena, but bear in mind, always set up so that nothing gets disturbed and yesterday's Christians, under another name and a different guise are forced to appear in the arena, under such solemn and voracious lions, such good public servants and heads of families.

The list, Maria Teresa, was already extensive without your name, so it is possible I didn't resign myself to adding yours, to giving them graciously the gift of your look, your smile, your warm skin, the intimacy of your body, the overwhelm-ing communication of your belly, your long, white arms, the soft hills of your breasts with their central lake, your legs two oars rowing softly to either side,

     Maria Teresa, I didn't want to make them that gift, I had the absurd and
                                     impossible desire to dig a hole,

    I had the absurd and impossible desire to open a moat in the middle of history,

     a pit, a ravine,

to construct a place underground for us to take refuge, to hide you, to protect you and to make you promises, to have you forgotten, cared for and showered with attentions.

     Maria Teresa on an island in history,
     Maria Teresa escaped from the book that teaches uninterrupted struggle

Maria Teresa fled from the Bible, from the circus, from the lions, from the pillory of torture, from the war, from the plague, from the siege,

         Maria Teresa to carve out for you a margin to take you away into,
the times are not good, there is death on all sides
and I feared in you, I feared in the others this deathly determinism
this binding oneself to the rules that have been coming true since time
                                 immemorial

    rules that are the wings of an implacable bird.

It flew flew flew
    the bird flew once again, Maria Teresa, and
left
    our house stunned and packed
    our house scrambled and searched
    littled girl undressed
    our house sluggishly inspected
    gave way
    fell
    like a tremendous catastrophe of children
    like the collapse of a palace without support
    without foundations
    our house stunned and made delirious
    by dogs that sniffed around its walls
    like the clawed sex of a child deflowered
    like a vagina plowed.
    Our house trampled underfoot.

      It isn't that I cry over its ashes
       as I do cry
    it's that this hard time
    like old, old bread that I refuse to chew
    is winding me in its smoke
    in its gray soporific
    in its scorn
    This time and its destiny

It's that they're sickening me
I am afraid, Maria Teresa, I tell you this, wherever you may be, to sob, to become
tender and melancholy like a boy who hasn't yet known
a woman
I am afraid of waking up neurotic hypochondriac
and of the anesthetists coming quickly to convince me
that life still isn't that bad
that something always remains
chess bishop or woman
I don't know what
soccer or the possibility of writing in verse
and of your photograph then, Maria Teresa,
being the definitive testimony of the closing of the history.

Your photograph its vague message
making a cemetery in my heart

your photograph

the smile
mounted
on
the back
of your departure

your photograph
and
the Commissioner
searching my house papers books keepsakes the album the herbarium the terrace
the inside of the furniture the refrigerator the photography and film magazines my
address book with phone numbers the phone book with the names underlined the
airlines maps the record jackets the depths of the television the pill boxes the bellies
of your plush dogs and the bed springs.

      Afraid Maria Teresa of the circus.

Translated by Tona Wilson

NOTES

1. Roman slave prison.
2. Electric cattle goad, torture by electric shock.
3. Peri Rossi lists influential people and groups, past and present. The Inquisition was a medieval
   Catholic court to prosecute heretics, especially brutal in Spain; Opus Dei was formed in 1928 by
   priests and laypersons to further Catholicism; *The New Yorker* is a sophisticated weekly founded in
   1925; Robert S. McNamara, Secretary of Defense 1961–1968 is thought responsible for military
   buildup during the Vietnam War; Falange is a shortened name for the fascist party in Spain; 37th
   president, Nixon had a long-standing feud with journalists; Bond is the fictional British master agent
   007; Bardot and Taylor are alluring movie stars.

Ama Ata Aidoo   *Ghana, b. 1942*

Ama Ata Aidoo was born Christina Ama Aidoo in Ghana in 1942. She attended school in Ghana and then went on to the University of Ghana in Legon, where she majored in English literature. While still an undergraduate in Legon, she rapidly achieved recognition when a short story she had submitted won a prize in a competition sponsored by the prestigious Mbari Club in Ibadan and when she wrote and produced her first play, *The Dilemma of a Ghost*, in 1964 (published in 1965).

Building upon this early success, Aidoo then published poetry, short stories, critical essays, and reviews in a variety of literary and cultural journals, both in Africa and the West. A research fellowship at the Institute of African Studies from the University of Ghana enabled her both to continue writing and to develop her research interests in African drama and oral culture. Her second play, *Anowa*, was published in 1969. Whereas *The Dilemma of a Ghost* is set in contemporary Ghana, dramatizing the experiences and difficulties of a black American woman who marries an American-educated Ghanaian man and then returns with him to Ghana, *Anowa* is set in the late nineteenth century, against the backdrop of colonial defeat. The Anowa story is part of Ghanaian legend. A young woman of extraordinary beauty refuses to submit to her parents' wishes concerning her marriage and marries instead a man of her own choosing, only to find her life with him joyless and unfulfilling. Aidoo remembers this story being told to her by her mother. In her play, however, Aidoo not only dramatizes and concretizes the legend of Anowa, she also reconceptualizes it. In *Anowa*, as Lloyd W. Brown has observed, a connection is made between European colonialism and the "masculine authoritarianism" of Kofi, Anowa's husband, whose relentless greed and ambition, initially misunderstood by Anowa, destroys their relationship at its foundations. Anowa emerges, in these terms, as a resolute champion of humane values, committed progressively to a "crusade against entrenched abuses," which, increasingly alone, she can never win.

In 1970, Aidoo published *No Sweetness Here*, the collection of stories for which she is perhaps best known. The title is drawn from a phrase in Ayi Kwei Armah's novel, *The Beautyful [sic] Ones Are Not Yet Born*, for the American edition of which Aidoo had written the introduction: "So much time has gone by, and still there is no sweetness here." Armah had been concerned, in his novel, to focus on the failure of independence in Africa to overturn colonial social relations, and this is a theme to which Aidoo turns directly in her story, "For Whom Things Did Not Change." For the most part, however, the stories in *No Sweetness Here* do not deal with the politics of postcolonialism and the gap between the elite and the masses of the African population; instead, Aidoo's uncluttered, passionate, and lyrical prose is used to convey the vitality and resilience of indigenous cultural forms. Through her valorization of oral culture in such stories as "In the Cutting of a Drink," reprinted here, and "Something to Talk About on the Way to the Funeral," Aidoo presents us with characters who simply cannot be viewed as the mere dispossessed "survivors" of colonialism but must be seen, rather, to display an integrity and resourcefulness that colonialism has quite patently failed to impair.

After the publication of *No Sweetness Here*, Aidoo spent two years away from Ghana. She traveled in Britain, Europe, and East Africa and spent a year at Stanford University on a creative writing scholarship. Returning to Ghana, she took up a position teaching African literature at the University of Cape Coast. Her novel *Our Sister Killjoy*, which had been copyrighted in 1966, was finally published in 1977. The novel, whose experimental form is one of its most striking features, centers on the travels of a young Ghanaian woman, Sissie (the eponymous "Our Sister"), while on a scholarship in Britain and Europe. A collection of new poems by Aidoo was recently published by The College Press in Zimbabwa, under the title *Someone Talking Is Sometime* (1985).

Neil Lazarus

IN THE CUTTING OF A DRINK

I say, my uncles, if you are going to Accra and anyone tells you that the best place for you to drop down is at the Circle, then he has done you good, but...Hm...I even do not know how to describe it....

"Are all these beings that are passing this way and that way human? Did men buy all these cars with money...?"

But my elders, I do not want to waste your time. I looked round and did not find my bag. I just fixed my eyes on the ground and walked on....Do not ask me why. Each time I tried to raise my eyes, I was dizzy from the number of cars which were passing. And I could not stand still. If I did, I felt as if the whole world was made up of cars in motion. There is something somewhere, my uncles. Not desiring to deafen you with too long a story...

I stopped walking just before I stepped into the Circle itself. I stood there for a long time. Then a lorry came along and I beckoned to the driver to stop. Not that it really stopped.

"Where are you going?" he asked me.

"I am going to Mamprobi," I replied. "Jump in," he said, and he started to drive away. Hm...I nearly fell down climbing in. As we went round the thing which was like a big bowl on a very huge stump of wood, I had it in mind to have a good look at it, and later Duayaw told me that it shoots water in the air...but the driver was talking to me, so I could not look at it properly. He told me he himself was not going to Mamprobi but he

was going to the station where I could take a lorry which would be going there....

Yes, my uncles, he did not deceive me. Immediately we arrived at the station I found the driver of a lorry shouting "Mamprobi, Mamprobi." Finally when the clock struck about two-thirty, I was knocking on the door of Duayaw. I did not knock for long when the door opened. Ah, I say, he was fast asleep, fast asleep I say, on a Saturday afternoon.

"How can folks find time to sleep on Saturday afternoons?" I asked myself. We hailed each other heartily. My uncles, Duayaw has done well for himself. His mother Nsedua is a very lucky woman.

"How is it some people are lucky with school and others are not? Did not Mansa go to school with Duayaw here in this very school which I can see for myself? What have we done that Mansa should have wanted to stop going to school?"

But I must continue with my tale....Yes, Duayaw has done well for himself. His room has fine furniture. Only it is too small. I asked him why and he told me he was even lucky to have got that narrow place that looks like a box. It is very hard to find a place to sleep in the city....

He asked me about the purpose of my journey. I told him everything. How, as he himself knew, my sister Mansa had refused to go to school after 'Klase Tri' and how my mother had tried to persuade her to go...

My mother, do not interrupt me, everyone present here knows you tried to do what you could by your daughter.

Yes, I told him how, after she had refused to go, we finally took her to this woman who promised to teach her to keep house and to work with the sewing machine...and how she came home the first Christmas after the woman took her but has never been home again, these twelve years.

Duayaw asked me whether it was my intention then to look for my sister in the city. I told him yes. He laughed saying, "You are funny. Do you think you can find a woman in this place? You do not know where she is staying. You do not even know whether she is married or not. Where can we find her if someone big has married her and she is now living in one of those big bungalows which are some ten miles from the city?"

Do you cry "My Lord," mother? You are surprised about what I said about the marriage? Do not be. I was surprised too, when he talked that way. I too cried "My Lord"...Yes, I too did, mother. But you and I have forgotten that Mansa was born a girl and girls do not take much time to grow. We are thinking of her as we last saw her when she was ten years old. But mother, that is twelve years ago....

Yes, Duayaw told me that she is by now old enough to marry and to do something more than merely marry. I asked him whether he knew where she was and if he knew whether she had any children—"Children?" he cried, and he started laughing, a certain laugh....

I was looking at him all the time he was talking. He told me he was not just discouraging me but he wanted me to see how big and difficult it was, what I proposed to do. I replied that it did not matter. What was necessary was that even if Mansa was dead, her ghost would know that we had not forgotten her entirely. That we had not let her wander in other people's towns and that we had tried to bring her home....

These are useless tears you have started to weep, my mother. Have I said anything to show that she was dead?

Duayaw and I decided on the little things we would do the following day as the beginning of our search. Then he gave me water for my bath and brought me food. He sat by me while I ate and asked me for news of home. I told him that his father has married another woman and of how last year the *akatse* spoiled all our cocoa. We know about that already. When I finished eating, Duayaw asked me to stretch out my bones on the bed and I did. I think I slept fine because when I opened my eyes it was dark. He had switched on his light and there was a woman in the room. He showed me her as a friend but I think she is the girl he wants to marry against the wishes of his people. She is as beautiful as sunrise, but she is not of our tribe....

When Duayaw saw that I was properly awake, he told me it had struck eight o'clock in the evening and his friend had brought some food. The three of us ate together.

Do not say "Ei," uncle, it seems as if people do this thing in the city. A woman prepares a meal for a man and eats it with him. Yes, they do so often.

My mouth could not manage the food. It was prepared from cassava and corn dough, but it was strange food all the same. I tried to do my best. After the meal Duayaw told me we were going for a night out. It was then I remembered my bag. I told him that as matters stood, I could not change my cloth and I could not go out with them. He would not hear of it. "It would certainly be a crime to come to this city and not go out on a Saturday night." He warned me though that there might not be many people, or anybody at all, where we were going who would also be in cloth but I should not worry about that.

Cut me a drink, for my throat is very dry, my uncle....

When we were on the street I could not believe my eyes. The whole place was as clear

as the sky. Some of these lights are very beautiful indeed. Everyone should see them...and
there are so many of them! "Who is paying for
all these lights?" I asked myself. I could not
say that aloud for fear Duayaw would laugh.

We walked through many streets until we
came to a big building where a band was playing. Duayaw went to buy tickets for the three
of us.

You all know that I had not been to anywhere like that before. You must allow me to
say that I was amazed. "Ei, are all these people
children of human beings? And where are they
going? And what do they want?"

Before I went in, I thought the building
was big, but when I went in, I realized the
crowd in it was bigger. Some were in front of a
counter buying drinks, others were dancing...

Yes, that was the case, uncle, we had
gone to a place where they had given a dance,
but I did not know.

Some people were sitting on iron chairs
around iron tables. Duayaw told some people
to bring us a table and chairs and they did. As
soon as we sat down, Duayaw asked us what
we would drink. As for me, I told him *lamlale*
but his woman asked for "Beer"...

Do not be surprised, uncles.

Yes, I remember very well, she asked for
beer. It was not long before Duayaw brought
them. I was too surprised to drink mine. I sat
with my mouth open and watched the daughter of a woman cut beer like a man. The band
had stopped playing for some time and soon
they started again. Duayaw and his woman
went to dance. I sat there and drank my *lamlale*. I cannot describe how they danced.

After some time, the band stopped playing
and Duayaw and his woman came to sit down.
I was feeling cold and I told Duayaw. He said,
"And this is no wonder, have you not been
drinking this women's drink all the time?"

"Does it make one cold?" I asked him.

"Yes," he replied. "Did you not know
that? You must drink beer."

"Yes," I replied. So he bought me beer.

When I was drinking the beer, he told me I
would be warm if I danced.

"You know I cannot dance the way you
people dance," I told him.

"And how do we dance?" he asked me.

"I think you all dance like white men and
as I do not know how that is done, people
would laugh at me," I said. Duayaw started
laughing. He could not contain himself. He
laughed so much his woman asked him what it
was all about. He said something in the white
man's language and they started laughing
again. Duayaw then told me that if people
were dancing, they would be so busy that they
would not have time to watch others dance.
And also, in the city, no one cares if you dance
well or not...

Yes, I danced too, my uncles. I did not
know anyone, that is true. My uncle, do not
say that instead of concerning myself with the
business for which I had gone to the city, I
went dancing. Oh, if you only knew what happened at this place, you would not be saying
this. I would not like to stop somewhere and
tell you the end...I would rather like to put a
rod under the story, as it were, clear off every
little creeper in the bush...

But as we were talking about the dancing,
something made Duayaw turn to look behind
him where four women were sitting by the
table....Oh! he turned his eyes quickly,
screwed his face into something queer which I
could not understand and told me that if I
wanted to dance, I could ask one of those
women to dance with me.

My uncles, I too was very surprised when
I heard that. I asked Duayaw if people who did
not know me would dance with me. He said
"Yes." I lifted my eyes, my uncles, and looked
at those four young women sitting round a
table alone. They were sitting all alone, I say. I
got up.

I hope I am making myself clear, my Uncles, but I was trembling like water in a brass
bowl.

Immediately one of them saw me, she

jumped up and said something in that kind of white man's language which everyone, even those who have not gone to school, speak in the city. I shook my head. She said something else in the language of the people of the place. I shook my head again. Then I heard her ask me in Fante whether I wanted to dance with her. I replied "Yes."

Ei! my little sister, are you asking me a question? Oh! you want to know whether I found Mansa? I do not know...Our uncles have asked me to tell everything that happened there, and you too! I am cooking the whole meal for you, why do you want to lick the ladle now?

Yes, I went to dance with her. I kept looking at her so much I think I was all the time stepping on her feet. I say, she was as black as you and I, but her hair was very long and fell on her shoulders like that of a white woman. I did not touch it but I saw it was very soft. Her lips with that red paint looked like a fresh wound. There was no space between her skin and her dress. Yes, I danced with her. When the music ended. I went back to where I was sitting. I do not know what she told her companions about me, but I heard them laugh.

It was this time that something made me realise that they were all bad women of the city. Duayaw had told me I would feel warm if I danced, yet after I had danced, I was colder than before. You would think someone had poured water on me. I was unhappy thinking about these women. "Have they no homes?" I asked myself. "Do not their mothers like them? God, we are all toiling for our three-pence to buy something to eat...but oh! God! this is no work."

When I thought of my own sister, who was lost, I became a little happy because I felt that although I had not found her, she was nevertheless married to a big man and all was well with her.

When they started to play the band again, I went to the women's table to ask the one with whom I had danced to dance again. But someone had gone with her already. I got one of the two who were still sitting there. She went with me. When we were dancing she asked me whether it was true that I was a Fante. I replied "Yes." We did not speak again. When the band stopped playing, she told me to take her to where they sold things to buy her beer and cigarettes. I was wondering whether I had the money. When we were where the lights were shining brightly, something told me to look at her face. Something pulled at my heart.

"Young woman, is this the work you do?" I asked her.

"Young man, what work do you mean?" she too asked me. I laughed.

"Do you not know what work?" I asked again.

"And who are you to ask me such questions? I say, who are you? Let me tell you that any kind of work is work. You villager, you villager, who are you? she screamed.

I was afraid. People around were looking at us. I laid my hands on her shoulders to calm her down and she hit them away.

"Mansa, Mansa," I said. "Do you not know me?" She looked at me for a long time and started laughing. She laughed, laughed as if the laughter did not come from her stomach. Yes, as if she was hungry.

"I think you are my brother," she said. "Hm."

Oh, my mother and my aunt, oh, little sister, are you all weeping? As for you women!

What is there to weep about? I was sent to find a lost child. I found her a woman.

Cut me a drink...

Any kind of work is work...This is what Mansa told me with a mouth that looked like clotted blood. Any kind of work is work...so do not weep. She will come home this Christmas.

My brother, cut me another drink. Any form of work is work...is work...is work!

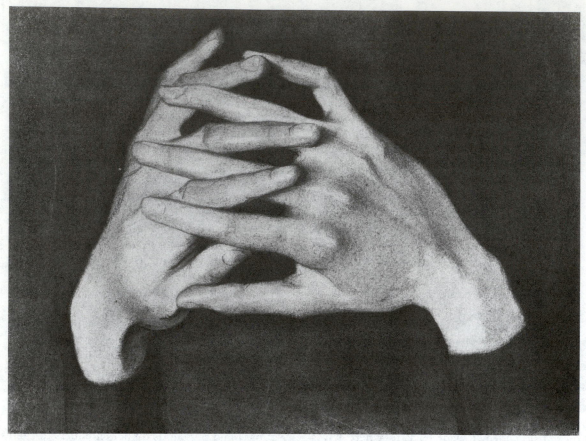

Paula Modersohn-Becker, Study of Two Folded Hands, *ca. 1898, charcoal on paper. Courtesy Kunsthalle, Bremen*

Belkis Cuza Malé

Cuba/US, b. 1942

Born in Guantánamo, Oriente, Cuba, Belkis Cuza Malé began writing poetry at age 15, and by the time she was 20 she had published her first book of poetry, *El viento en la pared* (*Wind on the Wall*, 1962) which received honorable mention in the important Casa do los Américas contest in Havana, as did her second book of poetry, published a year later, *Tiempos de sol* (*Sun Times*, 1963). These early books contain delicate poems about the awakening of creativity and the poetic consciousness. They stand in sharp contrast to her later poems (like those in *Juego de damas* (*Woman on the Front Lines*, 1983), which are concerned with the oppression of women, especially when in a relationship with a man. Unlike many leftist Hispanic writers, Cuza Malé feels that sexual oppression is more serious than racial oppression because women are biologically bound to a maternal role that, by its nature, is extremely restrictive. Jailed briefly in 1971, she left Cuba to live in exile in U.S. as a strong critic of the Castro government. Many of her works since have focused on the theme of exile.

Cuza Malé lives in New Jersey with her husband, poet Heberto Padilla. The couple edits *Linden Lane*, a journal that publishes works by young Hispanic writers. They have four children. The following poems are from *Poésie Cubainé* (1967) and *Nueva poesía Cubana* (New Cuban Poetry).

DEADLY WOMAN
Una mujer fatal

This poem I dedicate to life
to its neighbors the baker, the butcher
and the grocer
to the first, second and third
person singular of the present indicative.

Where does she live, that woman? And where's
                                    her husband?

I sought her address slyly. It wasn't easy.
Her mother had found her a husband, had
                              purchased her
happiness in a tobacconist's as one buys a
                              newspaper.
Chance and the old lady made her.
Then she chose dishonor. Now keeps quet.
                              Poor kid!

Sir—do you know what it's like to retch after
                              retching!

No? Then ask her about it.
Her husband faced up to nothing. They
                              repossessed
the furniture. And little by little she was left
with solitude, with a single cupboard
with her hairpins and a paper flower
alone with the door, the spider on the ceiling
and the gay curtain of her hair. Finally
broken, her face held together by patience.

I lived in her neighborhood
knew the story, the rebellion, and at last
the divorce.
She was absolutely right.
                    Translated by Tom Raworth

I, VIRGINIA WOOLF, FOULMOUTHED IN DEATH
Yo, Virginia Woolf, Desbocada en la Muerte

Loneliness and silence drive
us from the world we live in.
Will anyone look without suspicion
at the waters where I'm rotting?
Where is the beggar who'll steal the only body
                                    I have,
and why will he want to disguise himself in
                              women's clothes?
How much longer must I be the body of this
                              poor devil
who hides out in London under the drizzle?

I mull over my sins,
I know them by heart.
Day after day
then turn off the light,
noisily shutting doors and windows,
and there's no longer a reward for our capture.

Day after day
the world is more inhabitable
now that we don't belong to it any more.

I'm getting old.
Under the mask of a grand, yet defeated, lady
I'm growing old,
I don't find your nose beautiful,
your curiosity insatiable for silence.
Soon winter will go away, never to return,
at least I won't be here to see it.

I'll be so old they'll laugh at me,
I won't understand anything,
they'll be longing for me to die,
so that when everything's over
they'll cover up the mirrors
drag my body downstairs.
make up my new face
and dress me in the clothes of a bride
in the dress they've already washed without me
                                    knowing.

I'm not going to please them.
I'm not going to grow old.
I'm not going to die.
                    Translated by Jorge Guitart and Kevin Power

Ghadah al-Samman   *Syria/Lebanon, b. 1942*

Ghadah al-Samman is one of the most renowned and accomplished writers in the Arab world. Along with such artists as the Lebanese Layla Ba'labakki, the Palestinian Samira Azzam, and the Syrian-Lebanese Colette al-Khuri, she has brought a masterful style to bear on the problem of women in her society and subsequently has used this issue to illuminate more general concerns.

Raised by her father, Ahmad, after her mother, Ruwaiya (also a writer), died, al-Samman received a privileged upbringing despite the poverty of her small Syrian village. Dr. al-Samman supported his daughter's education, ensuring that she learned French and Arabic as well as English, and encouraged her to write. She studied medicine before going on to complete her baccalaureate in English literature at the University of Damascus and her master's degree at the University of Beirut, where she then taught.

Although she began writing in French, in 1962, al-Samman published her first collection of short stories, *Aynak Qadari* (Your Eyes Are My Fate) in Arabic; although the work met with mixed reviews, she was immediately recognized as an important new presence on the Arab literary scene. The titles of her second and third collections are indicative of al-Samman's increasing alienation and despair: *Lā Bahr fī Bayrūt* (There Is No Sea in Beirut, 1963) and *Layl al-Ghurabā'* (Night of Strangers/Foreigners, 1966) evoke a desolate wasteland, one in which there is no possibility of quenching one's thirst for meaning or satisfying one's desire for connection.

"Streetwalker," taken from the former collection, is representative of al-Samman's work during the 1960s. Like her other writing during this period, the story, whose original title literally means "Gypsy Without a Haven," focuses on an upper-class woman and her boredom; she experiences an "identity crisis" in which the desire for self-realization is at war with the primary attachment to the culture that nurtured her development and the standards it imposes. Influenced by such writers as Baudelaire, Mallarmé, and Eliot, al-Samman makes extensive use of symbolism and poetic language (never colloquial language), which nonetheless offers an accurate reflection of the character's state of mind: intense, distracted, and obsessed.

Apparently experiencing deracination and aimless rebellion in her personal life as well, al-Samman spent three years traveling in Europe, studying the cultures and philosophies of the West, while working as a journalist. On her return to Syria in 1966, she found herself subject to a three-month prison sentence, from which she was later pardoned, for having left the country without permission. The crushing defeat of the Arabs during the Israeli-Arab conflict contributed both to a general sense of despair and al-Samman's own pessimism. Increasingly, she also found it difficult to publish, especially because she chose to emphasize issues of female sexuality; she was publicly accused of promiscuity and mental imbalance. Deeply insulted and isolated, al-Samman left Syria to settle in Lebanon.

The decade of the 1970s is marked by a new sense of purpose: al-Samman married and bore a child; *Rahīl al-Marāfi' al-Qadīmah* (Departures for Foreign Ports, 1973) marked a departure for al-Samman in its concern for the poor and its tentative commitment to social solutions as an antidote to individual despair. The year was marked by great productivity, for she also published two other collections—*Hubb* (Love) and *Qisas Hazīrāniyah* (June Stories). And for the first time, al-Samman hazarded the novel, producing in *Bayrūt '75* what one critic has called an almost prophetic anticipation of the Lebanese civil war; in her "lay[ing] bare of the complex roots of the ongoing strife..., Beirut becomes the Arab world in miniature, a microcosmic arena in which Arab society wages war on itself." *Kawābīs Bayrut* (Beirut Nightmares, n.d.) and her *Al-'Amāl Ghayr al-Kamilah* (Incomplete Works, 1979–1980) continue in this vein and present al-Samman's new confidence in challenging Arab society. With her collections *Al-Raghīf Yanbid Ka al-Qalb* (The Loaf Beats Like the Heart, 1979) and *Saffārat Indhar Dākhil Ra'st* (A Warning Siren Inside My Head, 1980), these works also constitute a major contribution to the movement that has come to be called *al-Adab al-Hazīrāni* (The June Literature, 1967–1982), which represents the Arab literary response to the sweeping Israeli victory in 1967.

Al-Samman's most recent works include *al-Bahr Yuhakimu Samakah* (The Sea Prosecutes the Fish) and *Laylat al-Milyār* (A Billion Nights), both published in 1986.

STREETWALKER
Ghajarujija bilā marfa'

Your face speaks to me of vagrancy once again. It brings with it the tang of rainfall on beaches, tender with its sadness and warmth.

Your face. Anguish in the green of your eyes, the lusts of Rome behind your stern features. How long will the beloved curse follow me? When will you no longer appear in the gloom of my room when I put out the light to go to sleep? For it is then that your strange laugh, which smells of your cigarette smoke, comes to me and then I long to dissolve in its scent, disintegrate like a cloud that nobody regrets.

Midnight. The comic program on TV has just finished, and the innocent, unforced laughter of my grandfather and young brothers and sisters has come to an end. I gaze at him, laughing among the children, the expression on his face as naive as theirs in spite of the traces left by the slow, forceful gliding of the vipers of Time. I am deeply fond of him: I long to bring back to his lips the smile that was buried with the body of his only daughter, my mother.

He, too, watches me, with contentment in his eyes as I sit there beside my fiancé, Kamal; his glance steals to my hand lying lifeless in that of Kamal. Lying there only so as to bring a smile to that dear face at any cost.

My weary, broken-down grandfather never once complained of me and my brothers and sisters. Not once did he show any sign of irritation from the day my father left to go to a distant country with a woman who was said to be very beautiful; he left my sick mother behind to die soon after.

In spite of his annoyance at my passion for singing, my grandfather never once tried to stand in my way, though he could not conceal his pleasure the day Kamal, a well-to-do engineer, offered me his heart and fortune. Will I have the strength to go through with it? wearing, for his sake, the mask of an innocent girl? Will I have the strength to go on for the sake of my grandfather's smile?

Your face is a dearly-loved tale of vagrancy; it lures me towards itself, it draws the lost gypsy within me. In your laughter I hear the ring of golden anchor-chains when a vessel strikes landfall. Your arms are my haven, and how can I escape? Night imposes its routine. My grandfather and my brothers and sisters have retired to their rooms; my fiancé has left and every one of my masks has fallen away. I lie in bed and suffer my nightly agony.

I plunge my face under the pillow in search of sleep, for it might be lurking there, but I only find your face—so near...yet so far.

I open my eyes and contemplate the curtains. Sleep might be hiding there. My mind searches behind them...behind the picture... behind the dressing-table...with my eyelashes. I shut out the faint beam of light that steals in through the small window and casts a shadow of bitter reproach over everything—over the image of your face which I see in all things.

It is a procession of faces that I watch in my room—images merging one with the other in my head, thrown up into it by my sleeplessness...a score of incidents, a score of scenes—your face, adored in spite of everything that has happened...yes, in spite of everything. I feel you waking up within my veins as you wake up every night to become one with me, your smile on my lips and the smoke from your cigarette coming out of my mouth.

Those faces, angry vindictive faces, sad faces that scream at me, others that have not yet learnt how to scream. I curse the hallucinations of insomnia. I curse the city of fears it awakens in my head, this weary life of mine torn into shreds of memories...broken up into scattered whirlpools...

There's nothing left for me but to remember...re-live.

The sea lay indolent, glistening, naked and bored, heavy with the rays of the sun on her. You were so considerate, so charming that I quite forgot it was our very first meeting: you, the great composer who could make the city laugh and weep, and I, the young girl who longed to be asked to sing one of your songs.

"This is how I love the sea," I said. "Solid and naked, lazy and bored, and not shrouded in the masked veiling of moonlight. Groaning under the weight of the sun on her bosom, the sun that she loves so much."

"Yes, the sea loves the sun when the sun is far away. Have you noticed the sea by night? She has the face of a person in love, all shadows and fears and sighs.

"And when he is near?"

"She loves him all the more, knowing that he will soon leave. That's what true love is: it's longing, it's the search for security; it's the way to an end, not the end in itself. It reaches its climax the instant before the moment of meeting, then, after a few seconds, it is over."

"What a tragedy. To spend one's life reaching out for a cup that will be the death of us if we don't drink from it. And yet once we take it, and sip from it, we die even so. First it's love and longing that kills us, then it's the lack of love. It kills us simply to know ourselves."

"But you're still so young. Do you really believe what you're saying?"

"I'm afraid so."

"Sing me something! Anything!"

And I sang. I sang of the virgin depths that no man has ever penetrated. I sang of the loneliness that no person has ever escaped.

Every one of us lives isolated in a glass case...each of us talks but not one of us listens. Our life is spent wandering in woods, on seashores, in and out of islands, without haven or retreat. Even when we sight a harbor in the distance, we realize it is not for us.

"There's a strange agony in your voice; there's a bitterness that is deeply stirring. You'll go far. I can understand you so well."

Happy. Happy with our tale of vagrancy. Why do the faces attack me so? Wretched sleeplessness, peeling away from my eyelids the shreds of the happiness we knew. Faces springing out of my weakness and my cowardice, faces that I love and hate. I know what you are. You're part of me. Just as his face is part of me. And like some fabulous beast with two heads, each facing a different way, I'm torn apart. If only sleep could quieten the whirling city within my head. If I could only forget.

Once, when the night was a shimmering fairy tale flowing from your eyes and jetting itself into the sea in front of us, you stretched out your hand, and your palm held a thousand tales of loss. I didn't hesitate. My hand clutched all those tales of deprivation and for the first time I knew the joy of the clouds that moan out thunder when the ecstasy of their meeting rends them. Lightning sprang from our eyes and I felt the fire moving from my hand to my throat. I found it difficult to breathe. But I would not have needed to do any breathing to stay alive, if only we could have stayed like that. I made as if I wanted to pull my hand out of yours, only so that your grip would hold it tighter, so tight that my fingers would knead themselves together and become one single new finger that could join itself to your hand for ever. The delicious battle continued for a few moments, and like a fish that is delighted at being caught, my hand finally relaxed in yours, and you were gentle with it: you took it tenderly by the fingers and brought it close to the red candle on the table we were sitting at, whose soft light crept up the side of your face. I felt its kindness like a book filled with warm words, rich with the glow of harbors basking in the exciting magic of oriental evenings...and I, a tramp in search of a warm harbor.

You pretended to read my palm. You held my hand in yours and your look sank deep into the wilderness of my eyes. You tried to read the unending misery that you saw in them, to smell the tang of the sad rains that pursued the vagrant tramp and to hear the creak of rusty doors that had remained closed too long and round which thorns and creepers had grown, making the place desolate and unattractive.

"I see a bored gypsy," you said.

"Who loves her boredom."

"Who has no home..."

"And who does not wish to have a home because she hates masks. The city is a mask on the face of the wild forest. She is still the daughter of the wilderness."

"There are two men fighting for her. One wants to give her a home..."

"And her mask loves the home; and she wears her mask to bring a smile to the faces of those she loves and feels obliged to."

"As for the other man, he has nothing but a new tale of vagrancy to give."

"That is what she wants. Because a home is a transitory thing, while exile and sorrow are the real truth of human existence."

"She is like a child, searching for fame with her sweet singing voice, but no one knows the deep sorrows she has to bear; she goes on living a life of indifference, of vagrancy, of longing for a tenderness she knows she will never find."

"That is why she loves the man who resembles her, who carries in his face a tale of indifference and vagrancy and tenderness. In loving him, she is idolizing her own self."

"It's an admission of her own artistic narcissism."

"What else do you see in my eyes—my palm, I mean?"

"I see a tramp who loves her quest for a haven more than she loves the haven itself. She will hate it if she finds it—if she has to drop anchor among its rocks."

"I'm sorry for this tramp who drags her anchor and her sorrow along, lost and at sea."

"No you're not: you envy her. Because to you she represents the truth of life: she is a naked totem of human reality. You would be miserable if you let her go."

"What else do you see in my eyes?—I mean, my palm?"

Maybe you saw the truth, for you kept silent.

But why do I go on brooding over everything? This sleeplessness opens up old wounds and with its sorcery raises from their graves old tales, revived with the warm blood gushing from their wounds. What a wasted life! How can I forget?

Your face was aglow with hope when you said to me, "Let's go away together—anywhere."

A splendid plan. Not to have to suffer agonies of jealousy every time I think of your wife lying next to you all through the night and robbing my bosom of your breath, sucking it in from the pillow you share. Always together, tramping about together; your breath would belong to me only and your arms would be a haven for me alone. I saw you out walking one evening, you and your wife and children. I watched you from a distance. I walked behind you like a wolf that had made up its mind to snatch the shepherd away from the fold. Quite simply I longed to tear your wife to pieces—to devour her. I did not hide myself from my own eyes behind a mask of false pity and tenderness. I hated her. Then one of your daughters tripped and fell. I heard her crying, as you bent down to pick her up—so tenderly...and then it was I who wept...cried in the street...cried because of the many times I had fallen down and found no one to lift me up, no father to take hold of me, for he had run away with a woman as lost as I am.

That evening, Kamal offered me his life. I would not have to rob someone else in order to have him. That evening I accepted him, not because of your wife, but because of the little girl that I had once been. I consented so that your daughter would not grow up like me and become a tramp without a haven.

But I cannot believe myself—how can I leave you and go away? What about our happy moments spent together, and the people I used to sing to with your voice in my throat, with your melodies in my heart...the courage you gave me to face them...the sweet taste of conquest, the great success I had when I was able to make strangers respond to the feelings in my breast. I was able, then, to create for myself a huge unknown family with whom I could share my loneliness, my sense of being lost...And you...and the little trifles we shared...and our laughter...

Once when I was sitting beside you in your car which was littered, as always, with the things you kept strewn there, I looked at the streets, the passers-by and the gay shops, and suddenly cried out, "How marvellous!"

"What?" you asked. "Is it some attractive young man?"

"If it were an attractive young man, I would have stifled the sound in my throat."

"A pretty girl, then?"

"If it were, I would have kept quiet and stolen a glance at your face to see if you too were looking at her."

You burst out laughing. You are mine alright. You will look at all faces and still only see me. You will hug dozens of bodies to you, but it will be my hand only that you will feel in yours. You are mine...You were mine. Why do I torture myself so?

What then you sleepless night that is tearing me to pieces? This bed feels heavy to me, as though I were carrying it on my back. I must escape from this bedroom.

I get up...wander through the rooms of the dark house like a murdered ghost that had not been avenged...and the shabby ribbons of my life trail behind me on the floor.

I was sitting in a café with a few friends. The discussion grew heated, one of them addressed the visor-face of the stern-looking girl.

"Tell us," he said. "What shall we do? How shall we distribute the leaflets?"

Full of enthusiasm, the silly fool planned and acted...like an automaton that is under some ideological hypnosis...a city girl with many parts to play and many masks to slip over her face.

But this is my true face, the face of the gypsy who makes fun of other people's idealism. The noise of argument sounds like the buzzing of a gnat in the ears of eternity. Nothing can move the street-woman from her dark, deserted beat as her footsteps stumble along over the rough pavements.

She loves goodness and truth and freedom and the principles that all parties call for; but she does not feel responsible for anything or anyone in this wide world. No one is really interested in anyone else; we are individual grapes that have dropped off an unseen bunch and no legislation or belief or order can put us together again. Why do I contradict myself? How can I explain this overwhelming desire to bring a smile to the lips of my grandfather?

Why is it I care about your daughter and do not wish her to become like me if you were ever to leave her—a gypsy without haven...? Why do I pretend that no ties bind me to anyone?

But this is no pretence—I really do live the life of a comet that loves its loneliness. Maybe it is only my mask that clings to them, the mask of a well-brought up girl which has now molded itself to my face. Who knows what I would find underneath, if I were to pull it off? Has the gypsy's face decayed with time? If I were to fling off my mask would I find I had any face at all?

The image frightens me and I escape from it on to the balcony, with the bubble of feverish faces still pursuing me.

Yesterday morning, the rain washed the windows of Kamal's car as it carried me to view the new house he has prepared for us...the rain wept and wept and the streets and the faces appeared through it, strange and far away like the tearful memory of a tale of cherished vagrancy.

"You've made me so happy," whispered Kamal. "I just can't believe that you'll really be mine in a few days."

I did not tell him that I too could not believe it. I felt like a puppet bound with invisible cords to the finger of a madman who delights in moving us whichever way we do not want to go, thrusting us in directions we do not wish to take, snatching from us all the things we love.

Your face dissolved in the rain...your face and our tales, your melodies and the gypsy who missed her haven when she lost her face...and who lost her face when she realized that the haven was not for her.

"From now on you will sing for me alone," Kamal whispered.

The mask laughed with the joy of a young bride on the threshold of a new life. Your face dissolved in the rain. The day after tomorrow I shall go away with him. When will this night be over? Tired and alone I am, as the gods and the demons are. I go back to my room. I dress, not knowing what I am doing. I go to the street door...I open it to go out....where to?

I go back to my room...exhausted, I fling myself on the bed...The world of insomnia crumbles over my head...the faces leap around, turn, howl, laugh, scream, closer and closer. I fall into a bottomless pit. I give myself up to this indescribable torture—not a pain in one part of the body only, not one that is caused by any one particular idea, but an all-consuming pain, which is tearing at my whole being...I give way.

With difficulty I open my eyes. The gray dawn comes in at the window. Out of my coma I rise, my pain purified like a rock washed clean by the wind and the rain.

I must go out for a walk, alone; this newly-acquired peace needs to be strengthened. I have to resign myself to the fate I had no hand in preparing.

I softly open the street door; my grandfather and brothers and sisters are still fast asleep.

Alone in the street—in the long sad road, where the darkness creeps into corners while the metallic dawn spreads itself over the pavements and shines down off the windows that stand here and there above me, dispersed and staring.

No one is awake: the city is still deep in slumber, enjoying its limited span of death.

And I, a lost tramp in a brazen city of legends weep for a lost haven...weep for roads I am forced to tread and strangers with whom I have to keep company on the journey through life...pretending I am happy and making believe I enjoy being with them.

I see a man in the distance. He is walking slowly at the end of the road. He comes towards me. Nearer. With a stick he taps the ground. My companion in the deserted street...my companion in the brazen city, the companion of my wanderings at dawn...in a dawn that will not brighten. He comes nearer. Lost, he wanders towards me, he does not see me...He is blind. My companion is a blind man, who taps the ground with his stick, walking along unseen ways. Dawn and dusk are all one to him. I feel a strong link between him and me...I walk beside him...He does not hear my footsteps...

I walk beside him and feel my way along with my glances as he feels his with his stick. He walks and talks to himself—it does not matter what he is saying. I also mutter and talk to myself. We walk on and on and at a distance we look like two friends.

A fearful satisfaction fills me. Together we represent the closest of human ties...no pretences, no forced conversation...

Beside the blind man I walk, each one of us talking to himself. The sun rises, people pour out on to the street, a stream of bubbles which are faces fizzing up all around me. I lose my blind man in a side-street.

Translated by Azza Kararah; revised by Lewis Hall.

Khanata Banuna

Morocco, b. 1943

Khanata Banuna was born in Fez, Morocco, in 1943. She has been headmistress of a girls' school in Casablanca. Her literary works are significant in part because they have been written in Arabic, for unlike most Maghrebin authors, she does not publish in French; this signals both a desire to reach an audience educated in indigenous traditions and the existence of a middle-class audience responsive to her subject matter and themes and her philosophical, occasionally introspective style.

Her works include *Li-Yasqut al-Samt* (Down with Silence, 1967), from which the following story has been selected, and three other collections: *Al-Nār wa-al-Ikhtiyār* (The Fire and the Chosen, 1968), *Al-Sūra wa-l-Sawt* (Image and Sound, 1975), and *Al-'Āsifah* (The Tempest, 1979). Her most recent work is a novel entitled *Al-Ghad wa-al-Ghadab* (Tomorrow and the Fury), which was published in 1981.

Banuna is translated into English for the first time here. The short story is a fine example of her stream-of-consciousness technique, with its intense emotional and sexual undertones and unusual architectural and topographical metaphors; the "speaker" is a woman who watches her husband grow distant and lose interest in her. She wants to be free from him, but in the background lies the reality of mores and the legal system that make it difficult if not impossible for women to divorce. In Banuna's later works, these sociopolitical issues come increasingly to the foreground.

Pamela Vittorio

IF ONLY I COULD SMILE
Law Abtasam

The courtyards...and the saga of a past... and all its infinite expanse sinking into my ribs...and your face...that veil, with the shame of a virgin, effaced by the shoulders of a new woman...it gathers you up, carelessly, in the mute space. And here, live the remains of a heart's story—and one not like all hearts...an earthquake it was! Living out its life through the tremor of its destruction with the vigor of a tyrant...and it caused a drop of humanity to dwell within you, possessing the beginnings of man...your ancestor...that is what makes you weep—the dream, the fantasy, the imagination—I chew a morsel, I lost its sweet succulence. And I imagine that I'm chewing its flesh, breaking it into little pieces...and I throw it to the vulturelike beaks of humanity. Then, I move you from that awkward status—it hides you and yet forms you, and because of your burden you drink your ancient wine with the voracity of a woman...in order to lie down with the softness of sorrow in your limbs...in the gigantic step of a man who has hold of his future....

I peruse...and I condense all the faces within your face...and I'm amazed to find you squatting in the shade...confusion dripping on your virgin eyes, and you set your sight on another woman...perhaps you were calling her to come forth? You received her easily, the hills of suffering never possessed you...nor incited abandonment, nor the activity of pain. And you find rest, and in the lowlands of those hills you build your tyranny...like a little Adam who plants his spear in forsaken shores, on some island of Liliputians....

There is the time when I was you—with all the presumptions of someone...and I preserved that someone's cave among the vaults of a temple that witnessed a most magnificent calamity, recounted in silence...I restored you...so that in my opinion you are the hero, who crouches in a meaningless corner of unimportance and sucks on the finger of his childhood in withdrawal...and he is revealed from experience...that other man in you, who used to have hold of his lance and like a hero who disobeyed his quest, spends a short time on an island of terror.

And I return...like a tear petrified in the eyelid of humanity since centuries past. There is the vanishing moment...it descends and I am drowning in it and I emerge to you. And I conquer all the fancies in you, but you inflate yourself with yesterday's likeness and you, on your long journey fervidly begin to pick up your pace...an unexpected, fearful throb in your feet—you perceive a follower... but you keep on walking and I keep on drowning... and I don't know where to?...to blooming lands...to a warm chamber...to a distant corner hiding you from sight.

I wipe away the sweat of jealousy from my brow—and I detest you. The man who sowed the conceitedness of a woman in his path....Then, the shadow plays upon its lyre, a song of eternal sorrow for the agonizing young men...yearning....Opening and closing in the boiling pit, out of which beams radiate...but it is finally defeated, like an imaginary creature whose true essence is discovered...and finds its end...in a soft, womanly harbor in which to rest—not distant; words pouring down with the smoothness of a viper—to the barrenness of my exile.... Discarded...throwing me down into a net of sound, to plant my head in the bosom of something...any bosom? I shed the tears of an envied woman, which seep away....

I seize hold of the faint sound of a whisper...and I search for its source with unexpected courage...and I am amazed that I am not you....But it is clear without the charms of the secrets buried in the wrinkles around the mouth...And the enormous height of an aged forehead—as one of nobility. The obscure view which binds me to you. And where is it? A radical uncertainty within me startles me, to constantly pursue it in every wink of an eye...extending to every courtyard ...and inside everybody's innermost secrets ...even mine.

And before this anniversary, it was yours, and I hung on to it....You slide around me like a beloved fate and you are stuffed in a corner like a reclusive priest who has not yet reached as far as heresy...and it was mine by itself without all the contemplations...until you, ashamed of it, would hide behind a veil of dark glass—smashed by a violent tremor of enraged innards...and in time I realized my shackles which surrounded my thoughtlessness with the violent truth and bound me to a bloody moment of joy...witnessed by a lux-uriant grassy place, and the happy minaret and peaceable smiles...on rose lips...I roam around it to avenge myself....

But...where is it? That moment? The view which wasn't quite complete...spurned by a secret never to ripen—and that's not what frightens me about it. That is the beginning of a timorous sight which is scattered around in a courtyard of eyes that tremble with a love that did not watch the time....

And shall I ever destroy my pride for you? Let myself decline, incessantly on the edge of an existence I don't possess? Should I? Did you eat a gray-haired vengeance and explore the watery seashores with your lumps of affections?

Or did a fierce fire consume it...did I extinguish it by my burning thirst...of long sleeplessness?

Or an avenging frenzy destroyed it...so it became clear...and you stare at the visible, material things with your naked eye...and you see things just as they are...and you fall in love with what will be, and what it will be for you...your hand gropes in certainty... convinces you that you don't deserve any-thing...anything other than weeping insomnia and dragging a legacy of leftovers from past years.

The fangs...and your knife...and years of resolutions...which rip my joints apart... throwing them into a dish for you to eat from ...with a bowed head like a careless cannibal ...and I would like to imbed the fingernails of a tigress in your throat...and cause the youth-ful blood and the words to explode from it... and pour down around my silence in an in-toxicating, prattling sound which drowns you out. Fertilizing...so that it never ends...and I will not be another woman...owned by a crazy young man, while she licks her lips with the blood of victory...in the law of the jungle ....Only, I want to smile...like one normally does...it would be imprinted on my face and for you, a guilty verdict...and if only I could smile...if only I could...I could have your brownness in the cage of my smile and I would imprison you in the verdict which has the other...and you would be free....But I leave your head...delving in tears...I leave the halves of ancient man twisting around like sickles in my nerves....I leave this given word, killing itself in the fold of the hypocrisy which buries it....I leave it, making nonsen-sical lies out of truth...and I leave myself... and perhaps, smile.

Translated by Pamela Vittorio

Ambai (C. S. Lakshmi)   *India, b. 1944*

Ambai started writing at the age of 16. "As I grew up," she tells us, "I was exposed only to the popular Tamil journals which my mother read regularly. I spent a lot of my spare time putting serial stories in order and having them bound. When I began to write...I wrote in the style of whatever I had absorbed from those magazines." Though her early work bears the mark of a conscious stylist and won her many prizes, it is, in comparision to her mature fiction, conventional. Her first book, published in 1962, was a children's adventure story, written for a competition. *Andhi Malai* (Twilight Time, 1967), her second novel, is the story of an idealist who wants to reform life in a village. The woman he falls in love with runs an orphanage. Though this story has an unusual twist, Ambai makes fun of it when she speaks today: "The hero is also a poet; something most heroes are in Tamil novels to this day."

Both her fictional world view and her style have come a long way since, though the touch of the humorist remains the same. Early in 1967 she wrote a long short story, "*Siragugal Muriyum*" (Wings Get Broken) which later became the title piece of her 1976 collection. It was about a sensitive woman married to a crude, insensitive husband. "In my usual manner I sent it to the popular journals and they all sent it back. I put it aside thinking my style must have degenerated due to lack of practice!" Some time later she sent the story to *Kannaiyazhi* (Ring) a leading literary journal in Tamil, in which she has continued to publish regularly. Through the editor she met other writers and critics who discussed Tamil literature with her and encouraged her to write "as I wanted to." Around the same time she joined another group of writers in Madras called *Pregnayi* (Consciousness). She writes: "We read, discussed, fought and grew a lot. It was an important phase of evolution for many of us." The story included in this collection was written during that period, and focuses on a rite of passage for females.

As a writer Ambai never looked back. In 1976 she published her first collection of short stories, *Siragugal Muriyum*. Her 1974–1976 study of women in Tamil literature, *The Face Behind the Mask*, (1984) must have been one of the first extended feminist critical studies undertaken in India. A new collection of her short stories is due shortly. Among them is a hilarious piece about the women in a large family that never seems to stop cooking or eating. She follows in the footsteps of such Tamil women writers as Rajam Krishnan, Anuthama, Saroja Ramamurti, and Lakshmi, who began writing in the 1950s and 1960s, largely on domestic themes. What seems new in Ambai's work is not her realism but her themes and her deft use of symbolism. She inherits her love of music from her mother, a musician, who "had a great zest for life and spread a lot of laughter around her." Her interest in film is shared by her husband, Vishnu Mathur, who is a filmmaker; she scripts his films. She has a doctorate in American Studies. Formerly a teacher at Delhi College, she is currently working on an illustrated social history of women in Tamilnadu. She continues to write fiction, make films, work with women's groups, and "live a quiet, non-competitive, peaceful life in a small apartment overlooking the sea" in Bombay.

Susie Tharu

FALL, MY MOTHER
Amma Oru Kolai Seithāl

When I think of Mother, some incidents, vividly recalled, tug at my heart.

My older sister Kalyani used to have fainting fits. I was not old enough to understand. I was four.

I wake up early one morning I hear a drum. I go to the door to look. Kalyani has been seated on a plank. A man stands before her with a bunch of leaves in his hand. My laughing, gurgling baby brother of a few months is in his crib in the same room with me.

Someone says, "Niranjakshi, go and bring it."

I looked at my mother.

I remember the dark blue sari. She has tied her hair in a knot. She goes into the small room next to mine. She removes the *pallav*[1] of her sari, squeezes out some milk from her breasts into a small cup. Tears pour from her eyes.

Mother rises every day in the dark before dawn to light the fire under the big cauldron in the bathroom.

One morning I see her. The knot of her hair has come undone and it hangs loose. She is squatting, her hair over her cheeks and ears. When the fire is lit and the flames rise, her bent face glows red. That day she is clad in a red sari. Even as I stare, she gets up briskly. Her hair hangs to her knees. Her *pallav* has slid to one side and the hooks of her blouse have come undone to reveal her white breasts, green-veined. She seems to me the daughter of the Fire God, flown in from somewhere. Is she Mother? My own mother?

Why do these lines of the *sloka*[2] come to mind: *Kāli Kālī Mahakālī Bhadrakālī namostu te*?[3]

"Amma...."

Mother turns her head and sees me.

"What are you doing here?"

I cannot speak. The sweat beads up.

They are having a *homa*[4] in the house. Maybe it is the scarlet of her lips or the shining red of her *kumkum*[5]—the flaring flame-shapes appear to be Mother herself. They pour ghee into the fire intoning in elongated, stressed syllables: "*Agnaye Swāhā....*"[6] At the *swāhā* my eyes dart from the fire to her face.

Mother is giving me an oil bath. She has tucked up her sari, showing her smooth white thigh. The green veins show up as she bends and straightens up.

"Amma, why are you so fair? And I am so dark?"

A chuckle.

"Silly, who can be as pretty as you are?"

The events are disjointed. But Mother is the queen in all of them. She is the Fire which purifies, burning up all that is ugly or dirty. At her laughter myriad beauties gather up in a festoon across my mind. She is the Creator. When I lie with my head in her lap, she would stroke me with her long cool fingers and say, "I shall give you dance lessons. You have the right build," or "What lovely thick hair you have," or some such ordinary remark. But something inside me would blossom.

I do not know if it was her design or my own fancies which were responsible for the way I felt about Mother. Nor what it was that she confirmed or created for herself while she planted all these glad blooms in me.

I am 13. My skirts are becoming too short for me. Mother lets out the hem to lengthen them.

Lying with my head in her lap of an evening, I am reminded of something I had read somewhere and I ask her:

"Amma, what is 'coming of age'?"

Silence.

A prolonged silence.

Suddenly she says: "I want you to be just as you are now—romping around in your swirling skirts..."

Mother has gone away to my aunt's. Some people are coming to "see" my cousin Radhu. Mother is not home on that eventful day.

It is Kalyani who gives me an oil bath that *Diwali*[7] day. As she rinses my hair, I look out of the window at the still dark sky and say, "Kalloos, you got me up too early. I do not hear any firecrackers yet."

"I have to have my own bath after finishing with you. You are all of 13 but you cannot manage by yourself. Bend down."

Kalyani is not the patient sort. She rubs my scalp so hard that it hurts.

Mother has made me a skirt in lavender satin for Diwali. My heart had throbbed with excitement as it slithered along on the sewing machine. Mother had to measure me for the skirt.

"Come here. I have to measure you. You have grown." She straightens up and says, "This girl is two inches taller now."

My lavender satin skirt will not be short like the others. It will flow to the floor.

Kalyani pulls me up brusquely and dries my hair. I slip on my chemise and run to the *pūja*[8] room.

Father gives me my new clothes from the pile on a plank at the altar.

"Here, dark one!" That is the way he calls me.

Sometimes when Father says that, I go to the big mirror hanging in the hall and stand looking at myself. I would hear Mother whispering in my ear: "How beautiful you are!"

My satin skirt slithers around me like the fish in Sarala's fish bowl. I put on the velvet blouse and then with *bindi*[9] on my forehead I go to my father.

"Mm....Not bad at all!" he says in mock surprise.

I fetch my crackers but leave them in the front room and run to the *champa* tree. It is my job every morning to gather flowers from the tree. When I fill a basket and bring it to Mother, she would exclaim, wide-eyed, "How much there is!" and dip her fingers in. One could not tell the fingers from the flowers.

My satin skirt hinders my climbing and I cannot get to the top branch. It is still dark. As I climb down a cracker suddenly explodes somewhere and I jump down the last bit, trembling. I rush into the house, panting.

I calm myself, get my crackers and start lighting them. I remember the flowers only after all the crackers are gone.

It is light now.

Holding up the hem of my skirt I pick up the basket lying under the tree. Some flowers have scattered. As I squat to pick them up my skirt spreads out and I notice it has stains on it here and there. Is it from the tree?

I go in calling to my sister. "Kalloos, I have spoilt my new skirt. Will Amma scold me?" I stand there before her holding out the basket of flowers.

Kalyani stares at me for a minute and calling out "Appa" goes out.

Her look and her abrupt departure without even taking the basket from me—a caterpillar wriggles inside of me. I look at my skirt and feel my velvet blouse.

Has anything happened to me?

Please god, nothing has happened to me, has it? Even as I ask myself I know that something has happened. Crackers are going off everywhere. Basket still in hand I stand there shaking, shaking, breath coming fast, lips trembling.

A mighty sob bursts forth.

I want to be with Mother. I want to put my head on her shoulder. Tell her "I am afraid" and cry shamelessly. My mother will stroke my head. Something frightful has happened...

Kalyani returns bringing with her Murukku-Patti, the old widow who sometimes comes to help Mother make *murukkū*.[10]

Patti comes near.

"What is all the tears and fuss about, girl! Is it anything unheard of in the world?"

I understand nothing that she says. My instinct tells me something that makes me shiver. I don't know what to think. From the depths of my being rises a wail of desperate need...Amma...

I think of the time I had got lost when I was five. I am in a big park, walking away from the others, unaware of the darkening evening. Suddenly it is dark. The looming shapes of trees, the quiet, and the noises frighten. It is my father who finds me. But the sobs burst forth only when I see Mother.

Mother holds me close. She strokes me. Murmurs softly, "Nothing happened at all. See, everything is all right now." Her scarlet lips like glowing lines of fire, she puts her face against mine.

I tremble the same way now, feeling lost and frightened.

I sit down, put my head on my knees, and I cry. Something seems to have come to an end. It is like going away leaving something behind, like leaving the theater when they show "The End" on the screen. I feel I am the only one in the whole history of the world who has been so struck down. All the sorrows of my being weighing on my slender, velvet-clad shoulders, I cry.

Why has mother never told me about this on any of those evenings when we were together?

Fear is all I am conscious of. Not the fear you feel of strangers or strange places. It is the tongue-paralyzing fear of coming upon a snake suddenly. It hangs like cobwebs from every cranny of my mind.

I think of the prone figure I had once seen, its blanched lips split. The skull had cracked against a stone. A moment earlier it had been walking ahead of me, a pink, slightly bald head. Now it lay like a cavern, a deep red stream of blood gushing out of its mouth. The blood spattered on the ground and I had stood staring at it. The red spread everywhere, it was in my eyes. Inwardly I screamed again and again, "Oh, the blood! so much of it!" But my tongue uttered no sound. Now I see it all again—the bed of blood, the open mouth, the staring eyes.

How terrifying is blood...blanching lips ...paralyzing limbs...

I need my mother. I need her now to be freed of this fear just as I needed her to hold me close and croon to me when I was frightened of the dark. If only mother were here to put her cool hand on my shoulder and say, "This is something beautiful too."

Kalyani has been sitting next to me and having a cry too. Now she begs, "How long are you going to be at this? Get up now. Please."

"Amma..."

"You know Mother will be back next week. I have just written to her about this. She will be back after they have seen Radhu and talked things over. Now you just get up from there." She was beginning to lose patience. "What a nuisance you are!"

"Tell me what has happened to me."

"There you go again. How many times do you want me to tell you?"

I should not climb trees any more?"

Kalyani raps her knuckles sharply on my head.

"Mule-head! Here I am begging you the last half hour to get up and let me change your clothes and you start asking me this and that." She calls out to Father. "Appa, this girl is being so difficult!"

Father comes. "You mustn't be silly. You must listen to your sister."

When his back is turned. Murukku-Patti adds, "What tantrums! The wretched thing happens to everybody!"

Seven days. Seven days before Mother will be back. Radhu has to be "seen" first.

Seven days of groping in the dark.

One day the ladies from next door and the house opposite call.

"Haven't you given her a *dāvani*[11] to wear, Kalyani?"

"Only after Mother returns, Auntie. This tigress will only listen to her."

"She will begin to behave better now. She will calm down."

Why? What is going to be different from now on?

Why should I have to wear a *dāvani*? Mother had said that day: "Do not change. Be just as you are swirling your skirts..." Why must I change?

Nobody explains anything to me.

They sit around me and talk as though I were a doll. When Father comes they cover themselves and lower their voices.

The fifth day Kalyani hands me a cup of warm oil and says: "Go on, go and have your oil bath."

After a tearful battle in the bathroom with my waist-length hair, I emerge in my chemise to stand before the mirror in the hall.

"You must dress fully in the bathroom hereafter, all right?" says Father.

I close the door after him. I slip off my chemise. The mirror shows me my dark body. Shoulders, arms, chest, waist and soft thighs, somewhat darker than my face. I feel them with my hands. I am not the same girl now? What is Mother going to say?

I put on my school uniform.

When I open the door Kalyani comes. "What will you say when they ask you at school about your staying away?"

I stare at her. My spirits which had picked up at the prospect of going to school, sag again.

"Don't say anything. Just keep mum."

That evening I do not go to the games field. Instead I hide myself behind a thick tree. I had skipped games like this once before. The next day in class Miss Menon had asked, "Who are the fools who did not play last evening?" I had not got up.

"Why didn't you stand up? she had asked.

"But I am not a fool, Miss," I had answered. She wrote "Impertinent" on my report card.

But today even the thought of Miss Menon's scolding does not bother me. Nothing can bother me now but this dreadful thing that has happened to me.

I do not sit there reading Enid Blyton.[12] I ask of the dried leaves falling around me:

"What oh what is it that has happened to me?"

Like the prisoner in the dock with eyes only for the judge's lips, I wait only for what my mother will tell me.

Will she lower her eyes to mine and say, "This that has happened to you is also a beautiful thing?" With a single spark of her smile, she will blow away Murukku-Patti and Kalyani and their frightening insinuations. Mother is different. Where she is, all ugliness is destroyed and only beauty remains. To her beauty is all there is.

I need Mother badly. Something has to be explained. Why I break into a sweat and tremble when I even think of my lavender satin skirt, my tongue turning wooden and immobile, a sudden darkness descends and before one can turn, there is the sound of something hitting against a stone and in the darkness appear a stream of blood and a long stiff body—someone has to explain all this to me in soft, understanding words.

I feel lost, abandoned.

I get up when the gardener calls out and slowly make my way home.

"Why are you so late? Where have you been?"

"Nowhere. Just sat under the tree."

"Alone?"

"Yes."

"You! Are you still a little girl? What if something happens?"

I fling my school bag away. My face flushes. I shut my ears with my hands and scream:

"I will sit there alone, I will! Nothing has happened to me!"

I scream passionately, stressing and stretching each word.

Father and Kalyani stare, shocked.

I go up to the terrace nursing my huff. It will be nice to be alone here with the fragrance from the champa tree. Father and Kalyani must not come here. Just myself and this fragrance. It does not speak and does not touch but feels closer to me than the people in the house. If only they will stop saying things! If only I could see Mother's wide-eyed smile!

When Mother looks at one like that, a warmth spreads inside one. One wants to laugh aloud. Or sing. Mother is Creator. A turn of her head—and the magic of her smile would summon forth all that was joyful, exciting, beautiful.

Kalyani comes up.

"Come and have your dinner, your highness! Amma has spoilt you altogether."

I pout my lips at her and get up.

Mother is back the next morning. The taxi door opens, and my mother, her dark green sari crumpled, comes into the house.

"What is the outcome?" asks father .

"The fellow declined. Said the girl was dark."

"How does your sister feel?"

"She is very disappointed, poor woman."

"We have a dark-skinned daughter too."

Abruptly I go and stand before my mother.

I want to tell her everything myself, more than what Kalyani must have written in her letter. I want to put my lips close to her neck and pour out everything in soft whispers... Tell her of this crawling fear in my heart.

She will explain to me this strange mystery—this choking feeling every night when I go to bed, this alienation from my own body. I look up at her face in hope. She is going to gather me close in her long slender arms. And I am going to bawl out aloud. I shall put my fingers in her hair and cry out loud.

Mother looks at me.

I do not know if she sees me as Radhu for a moment.

"What is your hurry about this wretched thing, girl? We have one more problem on our hands now."

A whiplash of a question.

Whom is she accusing?

Sobs surge soundlessly against my breast.

Mother's lips and nose, her bindi and nose-screw, and her eyes—all appear to spew blood-red tongues of flame.

In the blaze, the cloak of divinity I had clothed her in falls off her, I behold her naked, a mere human mother. The cruel words rise up as sharpened blades and hack blindly at the glad sprouts planted before. Never-to-be-forgotten fears cling to the mind like dark shrouds.

"*Agnaye swaa....haa....*" It was not just the dirt that was burnt away. Buds and blossoms were also scorched.

Translated by Kamala Ramji

NOTES

1. The part of sari that is drawn across the breasts and thrown over the shoulder.
2. A Sanskrit couplet or stanza.
3. Kalī is the black goddess. This *sloka* is an invocation to her, literally translated Kālī, Great Kālī, Gracious Kālī. Bhadrakālī is also an epithet of Durga, the Devi, or goddess in her fierce aspect.
4. A sacred fire; traditionally a sacrificial fire.
5. The red powder traditionally used by a married woman on her forehead.
6. Agnaye Swāhā: An offering to the Fire-God; part of the chant at a Homā.
7. A festival of lights and crackers.
8. A ritual of worship; the pūja room is the special room in the house, usually near the ktichen, where the images of the gods are kept and worshiped each morning.
9. The dot placed on the forehead.
10. A crisp South Indian snack made of rice and lentil flour, delicately spiced, piped into concentric circles and deep fried.
11. A half saree or piece of cloth, about three yards long, worn with a skirt and blouse meant to cover the growing breasts. A girl usually begins wearing it when she first menstruates.
12. A prolific British writer of children's stories, still very popular among young Indian children.

Leilah Assunção   (Maria de Lourdes Torres Assunção)

Brazil, b. 1944

Born in Botuncato in the State of São Paulo, Leilah Assunção, (whose real name is Maria de Lourdes Torres Assunção) is part of the Teatro Novo movement in Brazilian theater, which flourished in the 1960s and 1970s to deal with political, social, and psychological concerns (especially as they affect children and the middle class). She was awarded the Molière Theatre Prize for *Fala baixo, senão eu grito* (Speak Softly, or I'll Scream,1969), and São Paulo's drama critics' award as best Brazilian playwright of that year. A subsequent play, *Jorginho, o machão* (Georgie, Macho Man, 1970), also received theater prizes, whereas *Roda côr de roda* (Pink's Turn, 1975) was banned for two years under Brazil's censorship laws. In October, 1988, her work represented Brazil at the International Woman Playwright Festival at the State University of New York, Buffalo.

Speak Softly has been widely produced in Brazil and abroad. It consists of a dialogue between Mariazinha (Mary), a secretary, and the Man, whose identity is never specified. The two are in Mary's small apartment in São Paulo. It is filled with artifacts of her past, antiques from her once-wealthy family, and dolls and other playthings from her childhood. As the play opens she is singing and talking to the dolls. The man (who may or may not exist and may or may not be a thief or rapist) appears uninvited in her apartment and questions her on her attitudes toward her life. In the passage excerpted here, Mary has almost reached the breaking point, unable to justify her life. After this scene, she and the man destroy the contents of her room and make an imaginary tour of São Paulo, she pretending to be a wealthy woman, a famous movie star, an intellectual, and a beauty. A knock on the door telling her it is time to go to work ends her fantasy and the curtain closes on Mary's animal scream for help; she is unchanged by the night's events.

Amelia Simpson

from SPEAK SOFTLY, OR I'LL SCREAM
Fala baixo, senão eu grito

MAN: Do I hear an offer? All proceeds go to charity! All proceeds go to charity! All proceeds go to ME! Ah, ah, ah, ah, ah. Dong! dong! dong! Do I hear an offer? Do I hear an offer? Tic-toc-tic-toc! Dong! dong! dong! dong! Do I hear an offer? Do I hear an offer? Success. Success. Climb the ladder to success. What will they think of me? Is this money? Is this money?

(*Monologue—the man and sound effects alternate.*)

MAN: Look at the light, look at the butter. You think money grows on trees? You woman chaser! You look like a whore! What'll they think of me? What'll they think of me? Success. Success. Success. Success. Dong! dong! dong! dong! Do I hear an offer? Do I hear an offer? (*Dong! dong! dong! dong!*) Proceeds for charity! All proceeds go to charity! (*Hammers on the table, like a judge, a father.*) (Dong! dong! dong! dong! dong!) Look, the Cathedral clock!

Look, the clock, it's the chimes. (*Dong! dong! dong! dong!*) Do I hear an offer? (*Tic-Toc, Dong! Dong!*) (*Pulls the sheet off the bed, sound effects continually growing louder.*)

MARY: NO!!!

MAN: OLÉ! Do I hear an offer? A table, for the night, for the silent night! Do I hear an offer? Do I hear an offer? Do I hear an offer? An immaculate sheet! Absolutely brand new! Do I hear an offer? Do I hear an offer? Dong! Dong! Dong! (*Washing machine sounds.*) Thousands of uses! Do I hear an offer? Do I hear an offer? The gentleman over there wants to buy a sheet? Look, they've never been used! (*Man holds the sheet; the spotlight is on Mary.*) White, white, white, white! Take it, you won't regret it. Wash and iron, never loses that new look. Go ahead, throw it on the bed, lie down on top of it, this gentleman here will soon be sleeping like a log! Thousands of uses. You can use it as a tablecloth (*Puts it on the china cabinet*), a curtain, a dress, and ...A RUG! Wash and iron, never loses that new look! (*Sound effects: Tic-toc-tic-toc-tic-toc! Dong! Dong! Dong!*) Do I hear an offer? Do I hear an offer? A little imagination and...presto! Half a dozen slips! Bras, panties, hand towels, isn't it incredible! Do I hear an offer? Do I hear an offer? Brand new, immaculate, guaranteed. Never been used, no sir! Nobody can say that you got yourself a used sheet, that "YOUR" house is dirty, that "YOUR" sheet is soiled! Guaranteed! Guaranteed! Do I hear an offer? Do I hear an offer? (*Tic-toc-Dong! Dong! Dong! Dong!*) The gentleman over there prefers the other sheet? The wardrobe? But what's this, my dear sir? This isn't a wardrobe, it's a blue sheet, blue! Just look at this lovely shade of blue! Blue the color of the sea, of the sky! Do I hear an offer? Do I hear an offer? Mary, just look! The birds are climbing, climbing...Who wouldn't prefer sea blue, sky blue? Go on Mary, run! One, two, three, NOW! Go on, Mary, look at

that money! Run! Don't be a slowpoke! Quick, go, go, go! Hurry up! Come on, you snail, you turtle, run, run, run run! Hurry up, swiftly, hurry, hurry.

MARY: All right! I've had enough of this! Out! Get out of here!

MAN: Dong! Dong! Dong! Tic-toc-tic-toc! Do you hear a tic-toc? Do I hear an offer? Do I hear an offer? Balloons, flowers, ribbons, colors! A brand new trunk! (*Takes things out of the trunk.*) Tailored dresses, embroidered dresses! Lace, silk, girdles, garter belts, flowers, flowers, balloons, long ribbons, narrow ribbons, bows, do I hear an offer? Do I hear an offer? Colored balloons, sir? Big and round, just look at them, decorate the house, the yard! This gentleman here doesn't have a colored balloon? A man without a colored balloon is an unhappy man! Your neighbor, sir, has a colored balloon! And bows? Do I hear an offer? Do I hear an offer? (*Dong! Dong! Dong!*) Balloons, ribbons, flowers, handkerchiefs, night tables, ah...He's taken with the china cabinet...But where is it? I don't see it. This is a clock, sir! (*Goes to the china cabinet*) interested in this piece? Yes? It's not for sale, but we can talk about it...Look closely, it's a clock! Keeping time. (*Points*) Look at the lovely hands! The numbers, the workmanship...It runs a little slow but it works (*dong, dong, dong, dong!*). Do I hear an offer? Do I hear an offer? Beautiful balloons, knicknacks! The big clock? (*Opens the clock —money falls out.*) Ah, you little sneak! (*Tosses money in the air.*) Ah, little Mary, I discovered your hiding place. Good thing I'm not on the job today...Do I hear an offer? Do I hear an offer? (*Dong! Dong! Dong!*) What time is it? What time is it? (*Dong! Dong! Dong! Dong! Dong! tic-toc-tic*) The night table, sir? No, that's not for sale. Too bad, it's quite old. (*Opens the table; sounds of washing machines running.*) A place to keep shoes, a diary, medicines, medicines, medicines (*Opens the drawer and pulls out medicines, etc.*). Just look at this change! (*Tosses more money, from inside the table, in the air.*) Thousands of uses. Good for ALL your needs! (*Washers, other machines; tosses more money in the air, then begins to replace everything in the drawers.*) Thousands of uses! (*Takes things out of the drawer again, sits down on top of the night table.*) Do I hear an offer? Do I hear an offer? Tic-toc-tic-toc. The drawer opens and it closes! (*Closes and opens the drawer to the cadence of the voice.*) This drawer has been opening and closing for years. TIC-TOC-TIC-TOC. This drawer has been opening and closing for centuries. Tic-toc-tic-toc. Silent, opening, silent, closing. Tic, Toc, Tic, Toc, TIC-TOC-TIC-TOC-it's on the table! You didn't wash behind your ears! You want to change the world! I'm getting old, I'm getting old. Do you want to send me to the grave? I did everything for you! My God, and what's happening? Nobody hears me? Nobody hears me, nobody hears me... Why was I born? Why was I born? TIC-TOC-TIC-TOC Dong! Dong! Dong! Dong! Do I hear an offer? Do I hear an offer? Everything brand new! Absolutely brand new! Just a little dusty...(*Runs his finger over the night table*). Just a little...(*sound effects: gasping; TIC-TOC continues.*) Well now, little Mary, don't you ever dust your room? Look at all this dust! (*Brushes off the furniture with the sheet.*) A cloud of dust! So much dust...Don't you notice the dust, Mary? Just look at all this dust! On the furniture, the night table, the clock... (*Gasping and tic-toc*). Come over here and look at this dust, Mary. (*She's perplexed but runs a finger over a piece of furniture.*) What a disgrace...Dust, dust, dust. Layers of dust, layers, this must be cleaned up, Mary ...(*Sound effects grow louder: gasping and tic-toc*) dust on the floor, in your bed, on your arm, your nightgown...dust, dust, dust, dust, dust, dust (*tic-toc*), dust and fumes, dust and fumes (*Sound effects: a train*), dust and fumes, dust and fumes. Fumes coming in the window. This isn't

when the train goes by, is it? The little train, spewing fumes...(*Man is controlling the scene, but little by little he too falls under its spell.*) It IS the train! It's the train! The big, black machine, spewing fumes...And the fumes coming in through the window... pouring in, pouring in...the black fumes pouring in...and this dust invading everything...Dust and fumes, dust and fumes, dust and fumes, dust and fumes, dust and fumes, dust and fumes, dust and fumes, dust and fumes. How can you breathe in this air, Mary? Dust and fumes, how can you breathe? Dust and fumes, dust and fumes, dust and fumes, dust and fumes, dust and fumes, dust and fumes, dust and fumes. You can't even see across the room anymore ... It's all dust...dust and fumes (*train growing louder, other sounds continue*). Dust and fumes, dust and fumes...dust and fumes, dust and fumes...Take a deep breath, Mary, a deep breath...(*She holds her breath, dismayed.*) Dust and fumes in every nook and cranny... You're blinded by the dust ...you can't see anything anymore... Dust in your eyes, in your eyelashes, all over the room. Everything is covered with dust and fumes...Thick, black dust, thick and black ...thick, black, thick, black, thick, black, thick, black, thick, black, thick, black, thick, black. Breathe deeply, Mary, breathe...Feel the dust in your nose... breathe...Take a deep breath. Draw dust and fumes deep into yourself...Into your lungs, all the way, thick, black, thick, black ...(*Gasping, train, and tic-toc-tic-toc; he is choking too, sound reaches maximum volume; the train grows louder, it's coming right into the room.*) Thick, black, thick, black, thick, black, thick, black, thick, black, thick, black, thick, black, thick, black, thick, black, thick, black, thick, black, thick, black. Go on, Mary, breathe ...Tic-toc-tic-toc. Where's the tic-toc-tic coming from? (*Mary, choking, runs to the window, opens it, breathes with relief. Sound effects: train whistle coming into the room.*)

(*Pause*)

MARY: (*Softly, exhausted*) From their room...

MAN: (*Tired, slowly*) The train...the train... dong...dong...dong...The Cathedral... the cathedral? (*Smiles, shakes his head.*) The Subway...The Subway...(*Looks at the night table and the sheet.*) Another day... Another day...dong...dong...dong... dong...another day...(*Sound effects: the train whistle, changes into a factory whistle.*) DONG! Look at the time! Look at the time! See the point? Look at the hands of the clock! Don't miss the point, Mary! Don't drop a stitch! A stitch in time! Mary missed the bus and now she's going to miss the boat! (*Factory whistle.*) Time! Time! Time! Time! Look at the hands of the clock! What's the point! DONG! dong! BRRRRR-RRRNG!! (*Buzzer to signal bus to stop.*)

MARY: (*Recovering herself, at the window*) Go away! I've had enough of this! Stop! Get out of here!

MAN: (*Louder*) DONG! DONG! DONG! DONG! BZZZZZZZ!!! (*Pantomiming, enters the office, a forced smile; office sound effects begin, typewriters, growing louder. To the door attendant*) Good morning! (*To the elevator attendant*) Good morning! (*To fellow workers entering the room*) Good morning! Good morning! Good morning! Good morning! Good morning! (*To the clock, grinning now, the boss*) GOOD MORNING!!!! (*Bows, lies down on the floor, gets up; sits down and begins to type; sound effects begin: clack-clack-clack-clack.*) Thank you. Thank you. Thank you. Yes? In room B, please. Have you been taken care of? Union Stores, good morning. One moment, please. Won't it ever be time to go? John had more time put in here (*Sound effects continue: clack-clack-clack.*) That boot-licker. Protection. Thank you. Six-twenty! Only ten minutes to go! That two-bit freckled guy's a creep. So many corrections to do. Connections, protection. Everything alright? Did you see that? Those aren't office clothes. Why not just take off to the beach! (*Sound effects: a fly—bzzz... bzzz...bzzz ...bzzz...; clack-clack-clack-clack.*) Thank you. Thank you. Have you been taken care of? One moment, please. Thank you. (*Brushes a fly off the shoulder; sound effects continue.*) Yes? Thank you. Yes? Thank you. Yes? Yes? Yes? Yes? Yes? (*Shoos away another fly.*) Yes? yes? (*Bzzz ...bzzz...bzzz ...bzzzzzz...bzzzzzz... bzzzzzzzzzzzzzzz.*) Stupid fly (*Brushes it off again, irritated; sound effects: fly and clack clack.*) Look, there he is on your knee! (*Mary swats at the fly.*) Look, there's another... Another fly! Stupid buzzing! (*Alarmed*) Don't these flies bother you? Stupid buzzing ...stupid buzzing...don't you hear it, Mary? (*Sound effects of fly and clack-clack grow louder.*) Swat that fly, Mary!

Translated by Amelia Simpson

Eavan Boland   *Ireland, b. 1944*

Born in Dublin, the youngest of five children, Eavan Boland had an international upbringing. Her father was a distinguished diplomat and scholar in law and classics and her mother a painter who had studied with the post-Expressionists in Paris. The family moved often, and Boland went to a series of convent schools in London, New York City, and, last, in Dublin. She then went to Trinity College in Dublin from 1962–1966 and graduated with first-class honors in English. She was given a junior lectureship at Trinity the year after graduating but after a year gave it up to write full-time; she has continued to teach part-time, at the School of Irish Studies, and also to write journalism for the *Irish Times* on a variety of subjects. She has been married to the writer Kevin Casey since 1969; they have two daughters.

Boland published her first book of poems, *23 Poems* (1962), at 18, paying for their publication with her wages as a housemaid at a Dublin hotel. Her first full-length book of poetry was *New Territory* (1967), which was reasonably well received. Her next book, *The War Horse* (1975), from which the following poems were taken, established her as a major Irish poet. Containing many poems on themes deriving from Ireland's long, tragic history, *The War Horse* is a strong book, one very much informed by Irish politics and culture. Her next two books, *In Her Own Image* (1980) and *Night Feed* (1982), are much more personal, "feminist" books and reflect the writer's personal involvement, through child-bearing, with women's issues. Boland does not, she tells us, want to be seen as a feminist, however; she says that she doesn't speak for all women: "The only person I wish to represent is myself. I happen to live in one place. I happen to be a woman. But my sex and my home are just transient states to what I have to say." Despite this statement, the universality of her vision of woman's reality in these books is a deep and moving one. Boland's latest book of poetry is called *The Journey and Other Poems* (1987).

CHILD OF OUR TIME

(for Aengus)

Yesterday I knew no lullaby
But you have taught me overnight to order
This song, which takes from your final cry
Its tune, from your unreasoned end its reason;
Its rhythm from the discord of your murder
Its motive from the fact you cannot listen.

We who should have known how to instruct
With rhymes for your waking, rhythms for
                                your sleep,
Names for the animals you took to bed,
Tales to distract, legends to protect,
Later an idiom for you to keep
And living, learn, must learn from you, dead.

To make our broken images rebuild
Themselves around your limbs, your broken
Image, find for your sake whose life our idle
Talk has cost, a new language. Child
Of our time, our times have robbed your cradle.
Sleep in a world your final sleep has woken.
September 14, 1974*

NOTE

* The poem eulogizes a child who died during one of the many acts of violence during the last twenty years in Ireland.

SONG

Where in blind files
Bats outsleep the frost
Water slips through stones
Too fast, too fast
For ice; afraid he'd slip
By me I asked him first.

Round as a bracelet
Clasping the wet grass,
An adder drowsed by berries
Which change blood to cess;*
Dreading delay's venom
I risked the first kiss.

My skirt in my hand,
Lifting the hem high
I forded the river there;
Drops splashed my thigh.
Ahead of me at last
He turned at my cry:

"Look how the water comes
Boldly to my side;
See the waves attempt
What you have never tried."
He late that night
Followed the leaping tide.

NOTE

* Success, or luck.

Nancy Morejón   *Cuba, b. 1944*

Nancy Morejón belongs to the first generation to write after the Cuban Revolution; thus, she finds hers themes in the socialist ideals of the Revolution—the class struggle and the attempt to build a new, equal society in Cuba. She is also known as a poet of the city, one who captures vividly life in modern Havana. Sympathetic to feminist ideas, Morejón sees oppression of women a part of the overall class struggle. "My womanhood is reflected in my poetry, but I wouldn't go so far as to call it a style. I think my class origin influences and determines my vision of many phenomena, not only poetry, but culture in general," she has said. Morejón is particularly interested in Cuba's black heritage and the tradition of negritude in Afro-Caribbean literature.

Morejón received her B.A. and M.A. degrees in French literature from the University of Havana and still lives in Havana, working as a poet, translator (from French writers such as René Depestre and Aimée Césaire), critic, and journalist. She began publishing her poems in 1962 with *Mutismos* (Silences) and has since published five more books of poetry, the latest *Octubre imprescindible* (Indispensable October, 1983). Her literary criticism has focused primarily on the works of Cuban poet Nicolás Guillén, and her recent study of his work earned her a UNEAC essay award in 1980. Morejón has also written, with Carmen Gonce, an important study of miners from the Nicaro district of Cuba entitled *Lengua de pájaro* (Bird's Tongue, 1969). The following poems are from *Poésie Cubaine 1959–1966* (1967) and *Nueva poesía Cubana* (New Cuban Poetry, 1969).

SOME PEOPLE/CENTRAL PARK/3.00 P.M.
Parque Central/alguna gente (3:00 P.M.)

he who walks through a park in La Habana[1] great and flourishing
with a lot of white light a lot of white light
that would have driven mad this Van Gogh's sunflower[2]
the white light filling the eyes of the chinese of chinese photographers

he who walks through a park and fails to understand this white light which repeats
itself almost

who fails to understand these hours
makes all the unnecessary trips through and all the side-trips round
the central park of La Habana
he who walks through a park with sacred trees
who passes with his eyes open and closed
loving the Revolution's beat in the eyes
the beat one carries in the eyes and wears at one's belt
he who leans on that light maybe he knows about night and wine

for in the parks and in this one which is central this of La Habana
the old sit on a bench and light a cigar and look at each other talking about the
Revolution and Fidel[3]

the old who sit on benches now and take
the sun and take the sun and take the sun

it's a secret for no one
there go two men with a shabby old briefcase
a plump hand a cry in a gray hat
the old people one sees beside a statue
of the apostle Martí[4] in 1966 in december 1966 the year ending and in the hope
of "liberty's anniversary and a homage to the martyrs" yes
to all men who died among the people and to their blood
to take the sun of afternoon in La Habana Cuba free territory of America

he who walks through the park this way this world the bladder of the Revolution
must sigh
and walk slowly and breathe
and walk lightly and sigh and breathe and walk slowly
and give up his whole life
like with rage
        comrades

Translated by Nathaniel Tarn

NOTES

1. Spanish for Havana, capital of Cuba.
2. A painting (1888) in several versions by post-Impressionist Vincent Van Gogh (1853–1890).
3. The Cuban Revolution (1953–1959), in which populist guerilla forces led by Fidel Castro and Ernesto Che Guevera defeated the government forces of Fulgencio Batista and put in its place Castro's socialist government.
4. Jose Martí (1853–1895), Cuban writer and leader of its early independence movement.

ANGELA DOMINGUEZ HERE!
Presente Angela Dominguez

For my mother's mother

You're a little more light-hearted
singing with troubadors and guitars
in bright shining nights
as bright as your eyes

I see you covered in golden bangles
taking over a bamboo ship
to carry dreams off in your arms
and breathing now in the peace of the grave.

You're the mistress of laughter
        Angela
here in my room
all these years you've been in a portrait and a dry
           flower
faded for the dead

You're the sweetest person I've ever dreamed of

Translated by Jorge Guitart and Kevin Power

Alice Walker   *US, b. 1944*

Alice Walker's life and writings reflect the tensions and ideals of a "womanist"—her own coinage for a black feminist—coming of age in the 1960s, during a period of renewed black consciousness that issued in the activism of the civil rights and black power movements, followed by the women's movement, indebted to the former for both its inspiration and its strategies. Much of her work brings the "double vision" of these perspectives into focus upon "the twin afflictions" of black women's lives—racism and sexism. Yet her works have a larger purpose: they chronicle the fortunes of black Americans in the twentieth century (*The Third Life of Grange Copeland* [1970] and *The Color Purple* span the period from 1920 to 1942; *Meridian* extends this chronology from 1960 to about 1975) in an effort to fashion a usable past that will permit the "survival whole" of Walker's people. Though she began in *The Third Life* by defining the black experience in relation to white society, explaining the cruelties of black men as a consequence of the psychological and economic exploitation of the dominant culture, Walker has increasingly sought to embody the forms of black life on their own terms. It is in this sense that *The Color Purple* represents her most signal achievement, which even her critics recognized transformed "a subliterate dialect [sic] into a medium of remarkable expressiveness, color, and poignancy."

Walker was born into a Georgia sharecropping family, one of eight children. A state rehabilitation scholarship (a childhood accident left her blind in one eye) enabled her to attend Spelman College, the prestigious black women's school in Atlanta, and to complete her education at Sarah Lawrence in New York, graduating in 1965. During this time, an unwanted pregnancy and abortion and a trip to Africa forced Walker to contend with conflicts and myths regarding aspects of her identity both as a woman and as a black. Encouraged by her teacher, the poet Muriel Rukeyser, Walker wrote of these in poetry, eventually included in her first published work, *Once* (1968). Walker returned to the South, first to teach and then to participate in voter registration and welfare rights campaigns, in 1967 marrying Mel Leventhal, a Jewish civil rights lawyer, at a time when the "integrationist" phase of the movement was giving way to an increasingly separationist view and a wave of militancy. She finished her first novel three days after she had given birth to her daughter and only child, about which she has written in "*One* child of One's Own."

Published throughout the 1970s to immediate notice and increasing if controversial acclaim, Walker received teaching appointments to Tugaloo, Wellesley, the University of Massachusetts at Boston, the University of California at Berkeley, and Brandeis. Grants and awards, including fellowships from the Radcliffe Institute (1971–1973) and the Guggenheim Foundation (1977–1978) also enabled her to write. *Revolutionary Petunias and Other Poems* (1971) brought her critical success, and with *Meridian* (1976) she won a wider readership. With *The Color Purple* (1982), Walker found herself the winner of a Pulitzer Prize and the American Book Award; the novel's transformation into a film (1983) with a prize-winning performance by Whoopi Goldberg gave her work an unprecedented audience.

Divorced in 1976, Walker eventually resettled in San Francisco, where she lives with the prominent black social critic and writer Robert Allen. An important collection of her prose, *In Search of Our Mother's Gardens: Womanist Prose* (1983), which constitutes a virtual introduction to the black women's literary movement, thus far caps her career. She is currently at work on another novel.

Even more than in her novels and poetry, Walker's short stories reveal her preoccupation with "exploring the oppressions, the insanities, the loyalties, and the triumphs of black women;"[2] black female critics such as Marie Buncome, Barbara Christian, and Bettye Parker-Smith, especially, continually attest to the stories' powerful, cumulative effect. Collected in *In Love and Trouble* (1973) and *You Can't Keep A Good Woman Down* (1981), they document the great variety of black women, while the titles suggest a shift from mourning their dilemmas to challenging the conventions that oppress them. Perhaps the most famous of these is "Everyday Use" with its quilt motif, while the most controversial are those dealing with highly polemical topics such as abortion, sadomasochism, and interracial rape, as in "Advancing Luna—and Ida B. Wells" and "Porn."

Walker's technique is unobtrusively experimental if not innovative, reflective of female perceptions and genres: critics have frequently commented on the epistolary form of *The Color Purple*; less examination has been given to the kaleidoscopic or mosaic structure of *Meridian* or the way in which Walker weaves the ritual of the marriage ceremony with the thoughts of her female character in "Roselily" as a counterpoint to the distance between promise and fulfillment that is the theme of the story that follows; it is taken from Walker's first collection.

ROSELILY

Dearly Beloved,

She dreams; dragging herself across the world. A small girl in her mother's white robe and veil, knee raised waist high through a bowl of quicksand soup. The man who stands beside her is against this standing on the front porch of her house, being married to the sound of cars whizzing by on highway 61.

we are gathered here

Like cotton to be weighed. Her fingers at the last minute busily removing dry leaves and twigs. Aware it is a superficial sweep. She knows he blames Mississippi for the respectful way the men turn their heads up in the yard, the women stand waiting and knowledgeable, their children held from mischief by teachings from the wrong God. He glares beyond them to the occupants of the cars, white faces glued to promises beyond a country wedding, noses thrust forward like dogs on a track. For him they usurp the wedding.

in the sight of God

Yes, open house. That is what country black folks like. She dreams she does not already have three children. A squeeze around the flowers in her hands chokes off three and four and five years of breath. Instantly she is ashamed and frightened in her superstition. She looks for the first time at the preacher, forces humility into her eyes, as if she believes he is, in fact, a man of God. She can imagine God, a small black boy, timidly pulling the preacher's coattail.

to join this man and this woman

She thinks of ropes, chains, handcuffs, his religion. His place of worship. Where she will be required to sit apart with covered head. In Chicago, a word she hears when thinking of smoke, from his description of what a cinder was, which they never had in Panther Burn. She sees hovering over the heads of the clean neighbors in her front yard black specks falling, clinging, from the sky. But in Chicago. Respect, a chance to build. Her children at last from underneath the detrimental wheel. A chance to be on top. What a relief, she thinks. What a vision, a view, from up so high.

in holy matrimony.

Her fourth child she gave away to the child's father who had some money. Certainly a good job. Had gone to Harvard. Was a good man but weak because good language meant so much to him he could not live with Roselily. Could not abide TV in the living room, five beds in three rooms, no Bach except from four to six on Sunday afternoons. No chess at all. She does not forget to worry about her son among his father's people. She wonders if the New England climate will agree with him. If he will ever come down to Mississippi, as his father did, to try to right the country's wrongs. She wonders if he will be stronger than his father. His father cried off and on throughout her pregnancy. Went to skin and bones. Suffered nightmares, retching and falling out of bed. Tried to kill himself. Later told his wife he found the right baby through friends. Vouched for, the sterling qualities that would make up his character.

It is not her nature to blame. Still, she is not entirely thankful. She supposes New England, the North, to be quite different from what she knows. It seems right somehow to her that people who move there to live return home completely changed. She thinks of the air, the smoke, the cinders. Imagines cinders big as hailstones; heavy, weighing on the people. Wonders how this pressure finds its way into the veins, roping the springs of laughter.

If there's anybody here that knows a reason why

But of course they know no reason why beyond what they daily have come to know.

She thinks of the man who will be her husband, feels shut away from him because of the stiff severity of his plain black suit. His religion. A lifetime of black and white. Of veils. Covered head. It is as if her children are already gone from her. Not dead, but exalted on a pedestal, a stalk that has no roots. She wonders how to make new roots. It is beyond her. She wonders what one does with memories in a brand-new life. This had seemed easy, until she thought of it. "The reasons why... the people who"...she thinks, and does not wonder where the thought is from.

these two should not be joined

She thinks of her mother, who is dead. Dead, but still her mother. Joined. This is confusing. Of her father. A gray old man who sold wild mink, rabbit, fox skins to Sears, Roebuck. He stands in the yard, like a man waiting for a train. Her young sisters stand behind her in smooth green dresses, with flowers in their hands and hair. They giggle, she feels, at the absurdity of the wedding. They are ready for something new. She thinks the man beside her should marry one of them. She feels old. Yoked. An arm seems to reach out from behind her and snatch her backward. She thinks of cemeteries and the long sleep of grandparents mingling in the dirt. She believes that she believes in ghosts. In the soil giving back what it takes.

together

In the city. He sees her in a new way. This she knows, and is grateful. But is it new enough? She cannot always be a bride and virgin, wearing robes and veil. Even now her body itches to be free of satin and voile, organdy and lily of the valley. Memories crash against her. Memories of being bare to the sun. She wonders what it will be like. Not to have to go to a job. Not to work in a sewing plant. Not to worry about learning to sew straight seams in workingmen's overalls, jeans, and dress pants. Her place will be in the home, he has said, repeatedly, promising her rest she had prayed for. But now she wonders. When she is rested, what will she do? They will make babies—she thinks practically about her fine brown body, his strong black one. They will be inevitable. Her hands will be full. Full of what? Babies. She is not comforted.

let him speak

She wishes she had asked him to explain more of what he meant. But she was impatient. Impatient to be done with sewing. With doing everything for three children, alone. Impatient to leave the girls she had known since childhood, their children growing up, their husbands hanging around her, already old, seedy. Nothing about them that she wanted, or needed. The fathers of her children driving by, waving, not waving; reminders of times she would just as soon forget. Impatient to see the South Side, where they would live and build and be respectable and respected and free. Her husband would free her. A romantic hush. Proposal. Promises. A new life! Respectable, reclaimed, renewed. Free! In robe and veil.

or forever hold

She does not even know if she loves him. She loves his sobriety. His refusal to sing just because he knows the tune. She loves his pride. His blackness and his gray car. She loves his understanding of her *condition*. She thinks she loves the effort he will make to redo her into what he truly wants. His love of her makes her completely conscious of how unloved she was before. This is something; though it makes her unbearably sad. Melancholy. She blinks her eyes. Remembers she is finally being married, like other girls. Like other girls, women? Something strains upward behind her eyes. She thinks of the something as a rat trapped, cornered, scurrying to and fro in her head, peering through the windows of her eyes. She wants to live for once. But doesn't know quite what that means. Wonders if she has ever done it. If she ever will. The preacher is odious to her. She wants to strike him out of the way, out of her light, with the back of her hand. It seems to her he has always been standing in front of her, barring her way.

his peace.

The rest she does not hear. She feels a kiss, passionate, rousing, within the general pandemonium. Cars drive up blowing their horns. Firecrackers go off. Dogs come from under the house and begin to yelp and bark. Her husband's hand is like the clasp of an iron gate. People congratulate. Her children press against her. They look with awe and distaste mixed with hope at their new father. He stands curiously apart, in spite of the people crowding about to grasp his free hand. He smiles at them all but his eyes are as if turned inward. He knows they cannot understand that he is not a Christian. He will not explain himself. He feels different, he looks it. The old women thought he was like one of their sons except that he had somehow got away from them. Still a son, not a son. Changed.

She thinks how it will be later in the night in the silvery gray car. How they will spin through the darkness of Mississippi and in the morning be in Chicago, Illinois. She thinks of Lincoln, the president. That is all she knows about the place. She feels ignorant, *wrong*, backward. She presses her worried fingers into his palm. He is standing in front of her. In the crush of well-wishing people, he does not look back.

Sherley Anne Williams   US, b. 1944

Sherley Anne Williams, one of three daughters born in California to a tubercular father and a "worn-out" mother, is a significant figure in the "neo-black" poetry movement, determined, like Alice Walker and their common predecessor Zora Neale Hurston, to forge a black art-for-itself, that does not signify reactively in opposition to white society but actively uncovers and reinforces the meaning of folk rituals.

Receiving a B.A. in history from California State University in Fresno in 1966, Williams undertook graduate studies at Howard University in Washington, D.C., and then taught in the Black Studies Program at Brown University. She completed an M.A. at Brown but chose to forgo a Ph.D., citing the danger of excessive book-learning to a poet. In 1975, Williams was appointed Professor of Literature at the University of California, San Diego, where she currently teaches.

Williams' first book was in the field of literary criticism: *Give Birth to Brightness: A Thematic Study in Neo-Black Literature* (1972), a study of the works of Amiri Baraka (Leroi Jones), James Baldwin, and Ernest Gaines. For black artists to opt for white literary traditions is "to seek their own annihilation," she argues. In this work, she also formulates a canon and charts a typology of the black hero as the basis of a political esthetic and her own literary practice.

The touchstone for Williams is the blues: "In the blues there is some kind of philosophy, a way of looking at the world...We, as writers, are not revealing what the philosophy is. The people who perform the songs do this." Some intellectuals insist on a rift between popular and serious art; for Williams, popular art—blues, jazz, the oral literature of the streets—distills the essence of the black culture of survival. Her two volumes of poetry, *The Peacock Poems* (1975), nominated for the 1976 National Book Award, and *Someone Sweet Angel Chile* (1982), apply the lesson of the blues. The first autobiographical volume, from which the selections are taken, fleshes out Williams' crosscountry travels and her profound feeling for her son. The second begins with a historical narrative set in the 1860s, "Letters From a New England Negro," that points to the never-ending necessity for black women to reinvent themselves. The following section, "Regular Reefer," pays homage to the famous blues woman Bessie Smith (1898?–1937), an icon in the struggle of the doubly oppressed black woman for autonomy.

As in her poetry, Williams' most recent work weaves the themes and rhythms of the blues into its prose. Similarly, *Dessa Rose* (1986), Williams' first foray into fiction, also draws on black history. The novel is based on two separate historical incidents, one in which a pregnant black woman was condemned to death for being one of the leaders of an uprising on a slave coffle in Kentucky in 1829 and the second, in which a white woman living on an isolated plantation in North Carolina harbored runaway slaves in 1830. In uniting the destinies of these two women, Williams offers a revelation of the ties that bind—and liberate—women, and the racial differences that ultimately distinguish their fates.

In all her work, Williams searches for "a new tradition built on a synthesis of black oral traditions and Western literate forms." With *Dessa Rose*, Williams has begun to achieve a popular acclaim that matches the critic's praise.

Eric Mendelsohn

ANY WOMAN'S BLUES

every woman is a victim of the feel blues, too.

> Soft lamp shinin
> > and me alone in the night.
> Soft lamp is shinin
> > and me alone in the night.
> Can't take no one beside me
> > need mo'n jest some man to set me right.
>
> I left many peoples and places
> > tryin not to be alone.
> Left many a person and places
> > I lived my life alone.
> I need to get myself together.
> > Yes, I need to make myself to home.
>
> What's gone can be a window
> > a circle in the eye of the sun.
> What's gone can be a window
> > a circle, well, in the eye of the sun.
> Take the circle from the world, girl,
> > you find the light have gone.
>
> These is old blues
> > and I sing em like any woman do.
> These the old blues
> > and I sing em, sing em, sing em. Just like any woman do.
> My life ain't done yet.
> > Naw. My song ain't through.

HOME

Home, *n. 1.* A house, apartment, or other dwelling serving as the abode of a person or household; residence. *2.* A family or other group dwelling together. *3.* The country, region, city, etc. where one lives. *4.* One's birthplace or residence during formative years. *5.* A place natural or dear because of personal relationships or feelings of comfort and security. *6.* A peaceful place; haven.

I resolved to be very careful about who entered my heart. I didn't put up a sign saying, transients and vagrants not allowed—there is a distinction between a wall and a door, between a turnpike and a path. And shared loved lives, even when the people move on.

> *No, I don't know all the hearts I live in. But I do know the people who live in mine. And I want to be on very good terms with all those who live in my home.*

2 1/2 POEMS: MAKING WHOLE

for Leah King

It be cold   cold   cold
      on yo lip   in yo nose
      freeze the tippa yo ear
      wind sweep the sky blue
      and the day be golden

providence

The campus is an alien thing
      yet even now as I move across it
      the softly voiced calls of How
ya doin   What's hap'nin—Sista
      unsaid and understood—close
      behind me, open before me
      like so many familiar waves in an otherwise
      anonymous sea. Hey now   we call
      Hey now   now   now   now

Now. But we would not be recognized
      and so hurry away leaving the words
      to hang frosty in the chill Rhode Island
      air.

      Watcha doin way up here—I
      watched the slow almost hidden
      smile   half revealing teeth
      crinkling the cold dyed skin.
      I got a fellowship—she said.
      I can dig it—and I'm grinning but her
      retreating back makes me sad.
      I'd know her in Ca'lina   Texas   Luzan
      but we converge here on the Green
      at Brown in Providence.

      We do not meet.

It be cold   cold   cold
   and the wind, Lawd, the wind
      it sweep that sky blue.

conejo

The field fire send up
      a grey trail to the hazy sky.
      Daddy and Bill speak in smoky
      whispers. "Don't get too close by
      the fire. Watch that baby, Ruise."

I move way. This side warm
other side cold. Both
sides can't get warm

at once. Ain' no grapes on the vines. I know
when it be warm, tray grapes turn
brown, crumple in the sun. They juice
be sweet and dusty. The sand burn

yo feet, grit in yo mouth, on yo skin.
The rows of black vines stretch
far as I can see. "There one,
there one," I cry. Bill fetch

the gun to his shoulder and bam! the gopher
dead. "How many you make that?"
"Greens." Daddy spit. "A little
streak-a-lean, streak-a-fat."

It be cold   cold   cold
wind sweep the sky blue
the day be gold.

Yona Wallach   *Israel, 1945–1985*

Born and raised in Israel, Yona Wallach represents the younger, experimental Israeli poets. She lived at Kiryat Ono, co-founded by her father and located outside of Tel Aviv, and published several volumes of poetry, including *Devarim* (Things, 1967), *Shnei Ganim* (Two Gardens, 1969), *Shirim* (Poems, 1975), and *Kol Shirei* (Collected Poems, 1976). Wallach was a very controversial poet during her lifetime. The first woman to express lesbian sentiments in Hebrew, she was almost a cult figure to her generation and was greatly admired for her courageous and forthright challenge to society's "sacred cows," although reviled by the country's religious establishment. Her poems are often erotic, colloquial, sensitive expressions of the pain and sensuality of modern life, especially women's lives. In the years before her death of cancer, she began reaching out in new directions; she wrote lyrics for a rock group, with which she frequently appeared, and cut a record of her songs. The following poems are from *Shnei Ganim.**

NOTE

* Our thanks to Yael Feldman, who provided much of the information for this note.

PREANNUAL POEM
Shir Kedamshnati

It's been suggested there's another sex.
It's good to know that someone knows about it.
If there is another sex, br
ing it here so that we might know it, let's sp
eak frankly, is there or isn't there.
Since by now we're sotired of our wi
ves and our virginal girlfriends and all
the while they show us pictures of th
is other thing and we too fe
el there must be something to it.
And if there is another sex in some other
world new women who know how why do
n't they bring a few here to te
ach our worn out women and may
be they'll also throw open the borders wh
en we're tired and can'tbr
eathe.

Translated by Warren Barged and Stanley F. Chyet

TWO GARDENS
Shnei Ganim

If raisins grew on you from head to toe
I'd pluck them off one by one with my teeth and leave your smooth
White body naked and you'd be naked, how hard it is
To feel naked. But there's something disgusting about that sight
So I say: the greenery here is not repulsive
The greenery here is undulant and sweet, plants of paradise.
Cheery tall-built birds so unlike
People, have you called me unprepared
To look at an animal? Still beset by disgust before curiosity
I think, oh it's nothing limbs it's nothing my blood
And later I run to see only animals so unlike
People. There are no thorns. Everything's soft and lovely.
There are no pits. We're in an eternal garden. The fruits are full
Of themselves. This garden will vanish and no plant will grow like
The plants in this singular garden.
I'm afraid. I see a horizon. My body is disappearing and my soul knows
A horizon's drawing near. There are some very common
Repulsive plants, and there are some people, flesh and
Blood and growth of nails and hair. I see
Them. The earth is flat and small. The flesh and blood are thick and
  alive

The colors are like being, strong and forlorn.
And later we're back in the first garden, round and intertwined.
The sweetness of course is neither like honey nor like sugar
The sweetness is of nectar. And you alone are revealed in the leaves.
If we were somewhere else and I'd call you My Lord
You'd see that I'm as smooth as oil. Or a pearl.
But in this meticulous garden I am light and you are a species.

Translated by Warren Barged and Stanley F. Chyet

Inés Hernandez   *US, b. 1947*

Born in Galveston, Texas, of a Nez Perce Indian mother and a Texas Mexican
father, Inés Hernandez is Nimipu Chicana, mother, grandmother, poet, political
activist, professor, and literary critic and historian. Through the creative act, she
weaves these roles into the fabric of an intense self and a critical perspective of the
external forces shaping that self. Considered a poet in whom the "ideal of a
poet/cultural activist becomes an energetic fact," Hernandez attributes the source
of her creativity, her resistance and insistence, her poetic, activist, and feminist
voice to her ancestral origins.

As a single mother of two sons and a Ford fellow, Hernandez completed her
doctoral studies in English at the University of Houston with her dissertation on
the early twentieth-century poet Sara Estela Ramirez, one of the first dissertations
to undertake highly original research on turn-of-the-century women writers, feminists, and activists (her translations of Ramirez appear in this book). Involved in the
political and cultural arena in Houston, Hernandez was a member of MAYO
(Mexican American Youth Organization)—and as such, one of the founders of
Chicano Studies at the University of Houston—organizer for Raza Unida Party
(and for the woman's caucus within that party), as well as originator and producer/
moderator of the CBS television program *Vamonos* (Let's Go).

In 1975, Hernandez moved from Houston to Austin where she taught at the
University of Texas, creating some of the first courses to focus on Chicanas. She
soon became involved with the group of poets and artists who came to be known
as CASA (Chicanos Artistas Shirviendo Aztlan) as well as with LUChA (League of
United Chicano Artists). Hernandez' first formal poetry readings were part of the
first Festivales Flor Y Canto during the mid-1970s, which were largely responsible
for the encounter and national exposure of young Chicana and Chicano writers. In
the midst of this strong literary artistic community, Hernandez organized and
collaborated in numerous local and national cultural activities and worked collectively in the production of the literary anthologies *'Ta Cincho* and *Festival Flor Y
Canto II*. She also founded and edited *Hembra: Hermanas en movimiento brotan-
do raíces en Aztlán* (Female: Sisters in Movement Sprouting Roots in Aztlan) and,
in 1977, published her first collection of poetry, *Con razón, corazón* (No Wonder,
Heart; revised 1987), from which the poems here come. (Like the work of French-
Canadian Michèle Lalonde, Hernandez's poetry reflects a bilingual tradition. The
boldfaced phrases appear in English in the Spanish version.

After a year as Acting Director of Ethnic Studies at Texas A&I University in Kingsville, Texas, Hernandez moved to Fresno, California, in 1982 to teach at the California State University, where she wrote and directed the play *El dia de Guadalupe* (Day of the Virgin of Guadalupe). She continues to teach at San Francisco State University and at the University of California, Davis. Since her move to California, she has been very involved with the Native American community, especially through her association with DQ University, as a member of its board of directors and, since 1985, as a professor.[1] As part of a segment of the Chicano Indian community who has undertaken spiritual search, Hernandez began her involvement with the Conchero Dance tradition of Mexico and the sweat lodge tradition of the North.[2] Her present struggle centers on contributing to the realization of DQ's dream to become, as Hernandez also envisions, "a true College of the Americas where indigenous peoples from throughout the continent will be able to determine and design their own programs of learning from a native perspective." As she also continues her work with the media, producing "Living on Indian Time" in Berkeley's KPFA and participating in cultural trips such as to Cuba with the Venceremos Brigade, she is preparing for publication her next two collections of poetry, *Abrecaminos: Collected Poems* (Pathfinder) and *War Dance: For All the Skins and All the Meskins.* Through this later poetry and activism, Hernandez sees herself as a cultural worker who forges connections between oppressed peoples in the United States and elsewhere in the world.

Clara Lomas

NOTES

1. DQ University: The ony private American Indian College, established 1971, in Davis, California; the initials refer to a name sacred to the tribes of the Six Nations and to the Aztec tradition.
2. *Conchero* refers to the Aztec's ceremonial dance tradition that dates back to preColumbian times and is said to have been given to the people by Huehuecoyotl (Old Coyote). Also referred to as the *Danza de Conquista*, the "Dance Conquest," the dancer/warriors, men and women, old and young, is seen as both a spiritual act and a model and training for social interaction. There are five major dance ceremonies annually, representing the four directions and center of the universe, but others occur to celebrate some important event or to mark the death of a member of the community.

    The sweat lodge ceremony is a purification ceremony that takes place in a circular building made of willow branches and covered with canvas set aside for that purpose. Heated rocks placed in the center of the lodge are watered to produce steam; along with prayers, song, and other forms of meditation, the ritual is intended to cleanse the participants at every level of their being. To enter the sweat lodge is to enter the womb of Grandmother Earth, the Heart of the Earth, to be healed by her, and to emerge ready once more to proceed with life. Specific practices vary.

I AM A WARRIOR WOMAN
Guerrillera soy

With each drop of my blood
With all my mind and my being
With each sigh
thought
tear and longing

with each rage that I feel
and in each demonstration of love

At whatever moment
that you find me

I am a warrior woman

Translated by the author

PARA TERESA
for Theresa

To you—Theresa
I dedicate these words
that explode from my heart

That day during lunch hour
at Alamo which-had-to-be-its-name
Elementary
my dear people
That day in the bathroom
Door guarded
Myself cornered
I was accused by you, Theresa
You and the rest of your friends
All of you pachucas
You were five in all.

You yelled at me asking why I thought
I was so great
What was I trying to do, you growled
Show you up?
Make the teachers like me, pet me,
Tell me what a credit to my people
   I was?
I was playing right into their hands,
         you challenged
And you would have none of it.
I was to stop.

I was to be like you
I was to play your game of deadly defiance
Arrogance, refusal to submit.
The game in which the winner takes
         nothing
Asks for nothing
Never lets his weaknesses show.

But I didn't understand.
My fear salted with confusion
Charged me to explain to you
I did nothing for the teachers.
I studied for my parents and for my
         grandparents
Who cut out honor roll lists
Whenever their grandchildren's names
                              appeared.

For my shy mother who mastered her terror
to demand her place in mothers' clubs
For my carpenter-father who helped me
         patiently with my math.
For my grandparents who gifted me with pencils
         at Christmas time.
And for myself.
Because I recognized way back then
a tremendous truth
that made of me a rebel
Even though you hadn't noticed
We were not inferior
You and I, and the rest of your friends
and the rest of our people
I knew it the way I knew I was alive
We were good, honorable, brave
Genuine, loyal, strong

And smart.
Mine was a deadly game of defiance,
   also
My contest was to prove
beyond any doubt
that we were not only equal but
         superior to them
That was why I studied.
If I could do it, we all could.
You let me go then,
Your friends unblocked the way
I who-did-not-know-how-to-fight
was not made to engage with you
         who grew-up-fighting
You and I, Theresa
We went in different directions
But we went together.

In sixth grade we did not understand
You with the teased, dyed-black-but-
         reddening hair,
Full petticoats, red lipsticks
And sweaters with the sleeves
pushed up
And me going along with whatever
         my mother wished

(continued)

Certainly never allowed to dye, to
                                    tease, to paint myself
I did not accept your way of anger,
Your judgments
You did not accept mine.

But now, in 1975, when I am twenty-eight
Theresa
I remember you
And you know what—
I understand you
What's more
I respect you
And if you will permit me, I call you sister.

Translated by the author

FOR JANICE, TZILIMAMU'H

I remember mother
that you used to feel

          for flowers
          and little bugs
          and real details
          of our world

I had no rooms of toys

          no barbie dolls
          monopoly sets
          or
          playhouses

that reality brings to

          mind
          my gringa friends
          and the television
          that showed
          me
          what
          I
          had
          not

But you

          made me see
          pain
          that other people
          caused
          terror and
          unkindness

You felt pain

          for a cockroach
          trapped by a spider
          a lame beggar
          who could not walk
          a child with the
          thought of a tear
          in her eyes

And
in spite of it all
we laughed
and invented friends
you even helped me
          entertain them

You read us stories
and later
together
we would go to the
          library
and from there any
          where
and you loved me,

Mother of the Nez Perce
with the laugh of clear
mountain streams
solace for this thirsty
child's soul

Mother of the grandaughter
of your father Ukshanat
          of the chants
of the earth
          of your heart

Mother with the eyes
          of a doe
frightened by crowds
          and cowards
          and sham

Mother of my solitude
          and my song
who with a smile
          gave me the world,

This poem is from your
          daughter.

Liz Lochhead   *UK(Scotland), b. 1947*

Liz Lochhead, considered one of the most important of the "younger" Scottish writers, was born and educated in Motherwell, Lanarkshire, Scotland. In 1965 she entered the Glasgow School of Art, from which she received a diploma in 1970. From 1970 she worked as an art teacher until 1978 when, on receipt of a Scottish Arts Council Fellowship, she devoted herself to writing full-time.

Lochhead is both a playwright and poet. She won the BBC Scotland Prize in 1971 and in 1972 produced the screenplay *Now and Then*. In 1982, she published the play *Blood and Ice*, about the themes of freedom and responsibility in the life of Mary Wollstonecraft Shelley.* However, she is best known critically for her poems; direct in style, often feminist in theme, and erotic in tone, the poems were published in *Memo for Spring* (1972), *Modern Poetry* (1976), from which the selections were taken, and *The Grimm Sisters* (1981). Often writing about the everyday details of life, she has said she "wants [her] poems to be clear. They should make sense to [her] landlady and the man in the corner shop." On the other hand, she wants them to be complex enough to be "pondered over by the academics round at the University if they like to."

NOTE

* Daughter (1797–1851) of Mary Wollstonecraft and William Godwin and author of Frankenstein
  (1818), among many other works.

TODAY

saw the last of my Spanish shampoo
lasted an age now that sharing with you
such a thing of the past is.   Giant size
our brand was always a compromise.
My new one's 'tailored exactly to my needs'
nonspill   protein rich   feeds
body promises to solve my problem hair.
Sweetheart, these days I cannot care

but oh-oh insomniac moonlight
how unhoneyed is my middle of the night.
Oh I can see
you far enough   beyond me
how we'll get back together.
Campsites in Spain   moonlight   heavy
                                        weather
Today saw the end of my Spanish shampoo
          the end of my third month without
                                        you.

POEM FOR MY SISTER

My little sister likes to try my shoes,
to strut in them,
admire her spindle-thin twelve-year-old legs
in this season's styles.
She says they fit her perfectly,
but wobbles
on their high heels, they're
hard to balance.

Tsushima Yūko (Satoko)   *Japan, b. 1947*

Tsushima Yūko is one of Japan's most prominent younger contemporary writers. She bears the mixed blessing of being the daughter of a major writer of the 1930s and 1940s, Dazai Osamu, who committed suicide in 1948. Although Yūko (a penname—her real name is Satoko) never knew her father, critics inevitably invoke his name when they discuss her work. Tsushima began writing around the time she graduated from college, and she first caught public attention with the stories "Requiem" and "Aozora" (Blue Sky), both from 1969. Critics noted her combination of intellectuality and lyrical fantasy. Tsushima has published a number of collections of short stories including *Shanikusai* (Carnival, 1971), *Dōji no kage*, (The Child's Shadow, 1973), and *Yama o hashiru onna* (The Woman Who Runs Through the Mountains, 1980). She has also written such novels as *Ikimono no atsumaru ie* (The House Where Living Creatures Gather, 1973) and *Chōji* (*Child of Fortune*, 1978), for which she won the Women's Literature Prize. She has also won a string of other awards, including the 1979 Noma New Writers Prize for *Hikari no ryōbun* (Territory of Light) and the 1982 Kawaboda Yasunari Prize for *Danmari ichi* (Silent Marketplace). Among her most recent writing is the novel *Hi no kawa no hotori de* (On the Banks of the River of Fire, 1983). A collection of her short stories has recently been published in English under the title *The Shooting Gallery* (1988).

Phyllis I. Lyons

SCATTERING FLOWERS
Hana o maku

Why do they always hound you with flowers when you're dead, my mother once asked me.

It was the day a patient in the room next to hers died. My mother hadn't been in the hospital very long at the time, so she didn't know anything about him; later she learned that he had been quite young. Early that morning she had awakened to some commotion out in the hall. One of the women sharing the room with her went to the door to check it out. She came back tight-lipped, got back into bed, and lay there with her eyes closed. My mother and the other patients in the room had already figured out what had happened. For a while they all lay there pretending to be asleep, she said.

"I like flowers, you know...that's just why I can't understand why they have to use them to decorate a person's death with. The more they grieve, the more the flowers pile up...I hate it how they bury the dead person in them...."

Her face was flushed. It was one of those steamy June days. The green of the weeds in the back garden was dazzling outside the open window and the scent of the grass floated heavily in the hospital room. I spoke hesitantly:

"Maybe if they were red flowers instead of white ones..."

"Red? What a silly thing to say!"

My mother burst out laughing and once more inhaled the scent of the yellow star lilies I had brought her, on the table at her side. She had wanted them the day before. I started to pour out a glass of cold barley tea for her from the thermos. She silently watched my hands.

Suddenly I remembered something: a scene with women dressed in black clothing, lavishly scattering little red flower petals one after another. It was a funeral in the middle of the Egyptian desert, a scene from a movie I'd once seen. I have no idea what kind of flower petals they were. They were a vivid red. The camera was at some distance, so they appeared just as tiny dots. They made me think of bugs. Red shiny bugs swarming and dancing like spray at the edge of the waves.

At the base of a white rocky mountain in the desert, they were interring a corpse. The wall of the cliff was pitted with big semicircles, and deep in each of the hollows was a stone placed as a marker. White stones on a white ground. Everything was white and dried out. The black forms of the women were dots in the hollows, and their shrill, thin crying voices floated out, melting into the sound of the wind. The skirts of their black clothing billowed up higher than their heads, and the red flower petals were cascading all around the rocks. They continued scattering ceaselessly from each woman's hand. The petals were picked up by the wind, and without falling to the ground, they spread out through the sky. As if crawling up the rocky cliff, they spread out wide.

Yanabe's house was in a new housing development in the suburbs. It was one of those cheap, cramped, hunch-shouldered houses you often see pictured in newspapers and advertising flyers. I wanted to look at the house for a while from the gate, but I was worried that I could be seen from inside the house, so I quickly entered the gate without slowing my pace. I pushed the button on the intercom in the narrow vestibule. A voice spoke back immediately. I faced the intercom and identified myself loudly. The voice seemed surprised at the unexpected guest, and I went on to announce my business.

I was kept waiting at the door for about a minute. Two pots of primroses stood side by side at my feet. Maybe because they didn't get much sun, there weren't many flowers, and their color was bad. I rearranged the cloth-wrapped package in my arms that I'd brought from my house and shifted the place of the knot.

Until I'd wrapped up the stuff in the cloth, I'd been confused as to what to do. Should I send it by mail? Or even if I were to take it myself, should I choose a time when Yanabe would be home? But if I went when Yanabe was in, my own husband, who worked in the same company, would be home too. If I were to ask my husband to keep an eye on the house while I went out myself, the thing would get blown up all out of proportion; worse yet, I didn't want to have to let my husband know I was going to Yanabe's. His was the only funeral gift[1] I hadn't left up to the department store to deliver, as I'd done with the others. It's not that I was nostalgic and wanted to use the opportunity to have a nice long chat with him. It was out of curiosity—I wanted somehow, if only briefly, to see for myself the woman who was living with him. That's why his was the only funeral gift I'd taken home. I'd not wanted to admit it to myself and had made excuses to myself. It wouldn't be proper not to give it directly to Yanabe at least, and I could go while I was out that way on some other business....

As each day pursued me, I felt increasingly that I was really getting myself into a mess. You should take care of funeral gifts as soon as possible. Every night for a whole month I'd think, Tomorrow I absolutely must go.

Finally I got myself together, wrapped up the package and left the house. It was after I was on the train that I thought back for the first time in a while on the funerals of my grandmother and mother.

My grandmother's funeral was a simple one, with not a tearful face to be seen. She had been so much work for my husband and me that we felt relief more than anything when she breathed her last. All the same, I had burst out crying at the moment of her death. I mean, that instant is scary, regardless of who's dying. And worse, it resurrected the physical fear I'd felt when my mother died.

After crying for a while, I became aware that I wasn't weeping for my grandmother who lay there before me, but rather was being oppressed by the death of my mother four years earlier. I glanced at my husband sitting tensely beside me and remembered that at the time of Mother's death, Yanabe had set up a strange wailing at my side. That quieted me. When someone dies, the survivors are left in turmoil. Right away, there are piles of things that have to be done. With Mother, too, Yanabe and I had divided up the work and we'd run around like crazy.

As I bowed to Yanabe, who had come to pay a condolence call, I was reminded of our former intimacy, and I couldn't help feeling awkward. Yanabe too had an expression I'd never seen on him, a closed look. It had been nearly a year since I'd last seen him. He left without a single personal word to me. I looked bitterly at his back as he went off. Even though there was no reason for me to be bitter at this late date, I couldn't take my eyes from him as he disappeared into the distance. I mean, Yanabe was nothing more than the man my mother had married when she remarried, and I wasn't even his stepdaughter. We were just three people side by side, Yanabe, and I, and my mother in the middle. When she had died, so had our connection. But we had always done things together: we'd gone out to dinner or the movies, taken trips, played cards. It was always the three of us. A circle of three. So I'd always thought.

Yanabe began to come around while I was in junior high. And then almost ten years later he and my mother had gotten married. In other words, they had apparently waited until I turned twenty. My grandmother and I lived for five years with Yanabe in the house. Sometimes I even called him Father as a joke. We'd been together for so long that I had no compunctions about it.

But within half a year after my mother died, Yanabe suddenly left the house where my grandmother and I were living. At the time, my grandmother told me that Yanabe had been seeing some other woman all the time my mother was in the hospital. There was a kind of warning in her voice. I couldn't believe it. For one thing, where could he have found the time?

While my mother was in the hospital, Yanabe would make room in his schedule at work to go see her every day. There was even one period when he took turns with me staying overnight at the hospital. When he went out, he always told me clearly where I could get in touch with him, in case her condition worsened. Mother had a number of operations, but it seemed that each time death only kept getting closer to her. Yanabe and I read book after book on her illness, we bought questionable drugs and equipment, we even threw ourselves into learning massage therapy. He and I lived through that period as close spiritually as if we were a pair of twins. At least, I'd felt that way.

Even after my mother died, my feelings didn't change. They couldn't have. It's just that, naturally, I stopped being able to call him Father.

The door opened, to a string of "My goodness, how good of you..." I hastily bowed and responded with my own set of clichéd greetings. Not until I had opened the cloth and handed over the package did I look at the woman opposite me. She was small and rather dark, with something about her that made me think of a high school student. She was wearing jeans and looked to be about my age. I tried to leave at that point. The woman quickly asked, as if somehow embarrassed, if I wouldn't stay for a cup of tea, and so I ended up stuck.

I sat down in the foyer and waited for the woman to appear again. The house was quiet. There was a bundle of old newspapers piled on top of the shoe cupboard, and some crumpled paper had fallen on the floor. A pair of women's sandals were tumbled in a corner. I continued to sit there, thinking of nothing, gazing at the sandals and the crumpled paper. I idly recalled my own house while my mother was alive. She was the type who couldn't stand to have even a single breadcrumb on the floor. There had been times when she'd cancel plans to go out to dinner and begin cleaning house. She was always angry at Yanabe, who loved eating. She'd tell him not to eat in such a disgusting fashion.

The woman returned bearing a square tray. She appeared to have made her preparations in a hurry, and some of the tea leaves were spilled on the tray. I looked at her again. There was no resemblance at all in her face to my mother's. Her way of sitting, her way of moving her hands—no resemblance. Rather, somehow she reminded me of one of my friends. She didn't wear any cosmetics and her hair looked as if she'd cut it herself; but far from making her look ugly, it gave her a fresh beauty.

After offering me tea, the woman spoke.

"I saw you once before, Akiko. And so...well, I feel somehow that you aren't a total stranger...."

"When was that?" I snapped back without thinking. I was relieved that she had chosen the topic of conversation for us, and it was as if the tension on my tongue was loosened for the first time. I just wanted to hear what she had to say, whatever it was, and then go home without leaving anything of my own. The woman gazed at the door as she answered.

"Five years ago, no, maybe it was six. Yes, it was the year I joined the company. We passed right by each other just outside the office. He...he was with you."

"He?...You mean Yanabe?..."

The woman nodded lightly and smiled.

"I knew right away that it had to be you because he was there with you. People in the office had told me everything about his family circumstances, you know, he was one of those people that people gossip about. And I had heard that you were the same age as I...You certainly looked bright and taken care of."

"I must have looked an absolute child, right?" I said, as I flipped furiously through my memory, trying to remember what business had taken me to Yanabe's office. Whatever it was, in those days whenever I was with him, I acted as blithe and unsophisticated as a ten-year-old. If it was six years ago, then I would have been twenty-three. My mother was still healthy, she had closed down the haberdashery she'd inherited from my grandfather, and she was enjoying the novelty of spending each day just taking care of me and Yanabe, who were working for different companies.

"Well, yes...I hadn't yet talked to him myself, but I remember it clearly. Even though the sun was out, it was a cold day."

"It was winter, then?"

The woman nodded. "Really, I remember it very clearly...There was no one else around, just the two of you standing there, in front of the big glass door. The glass door caught the sun directly and it was dazzling...I felt quite strange as I watched."

Looking down, I searched for something to say and was finally able to answer. The woman watched me with that same faint smile. My palms started to sweat.

"Well, I did like Yanabe...but when my mother got sick, that was the first time I was actually thankful he'd come to stay with us. Until then, I felt mainly that I had to get along with him for her sake...Of course, thanks to the kind of person he was, she was in fact actually able to die in peace...."

The woman nodded again and then, as if she'd remembered something, swiftly looked back into the house, and then spoke.

"It must have been awful for you, and then on top of it, to lose your grandmother now..."

"Well, yes, it was, but since I didn't have a mother or brothers or sisters, my husband's sister helped me with a lot of it. You must already have heard about it...I mean... from Yanabe..."

"He tells me nothing about you all." She smiled and I smiled with her and nodded. She continued.

"All I knew was your name, from the letter he got from you. But then you got married..."

"Letter?"

"Some legal notice, I guess that's what it was. Please, I'm sorry, but it was a postcard."

"No, no, don't think about it, after all, it was I..."

I finally remembered that Yanabe had spoken to me at the service, about my notification to him of my mother's first anniversary memorial service. After the formal service was over, we stood up, and Yanabe came over and whispered in my ear. He had been sitting in the husband's seat, still as my mother's husband, but in response to my grandmother's strong wishes, her cremated remains had been interred in my grandfather's cemetery plot. I'd checked with Yanabe ahead of time on the legal formalities, but it is possible that he saw it as having been forced on him. My grandmother had told me about it, and so I understood his situation, but all the same, when it came to my mother, I couldn't help needing to rely on him. I was caught up in believing that for one day a year at least, on the anniversary of her death, Yanabe would come to keep me company just as before, as a sort of intimate friend, to talk about her.

—This sounds awful, I guess, but from here on, whenever you have any mail for me, send it to the office, please, I mean, didn't I agree this time to everything you wanted, on the phone?... Understand?—

That's what he'd said to me.

"But then he stopped getting any news at all from you. He must have said something to you about it, right?"

I nodded quickly and then burst out laughing.

"I was just remembering it. And I told him that I didn't care if he even joked about it, but if only he'd tell me about you, we'd be more comfortable together, and even now I might be able to ask to get together with you from time to time...the two of you."

As I spoke, I could hear my own voice as I faced Yanabe. —You're not being fair, to be so secretive. I know all about you now, so it seems even more absurd for you to be so close-mouthed. I mean, the dead are dead, so there's nothing to worry about. All the same, I was surprised. Come on, tell me, what's she like? Come on...

Yanabe and I used to be so close that I could talk to him this way. For example, if I said something like that, he might have teased comfortably, Oh, she's a stunning beauty, you know, and she's such a center of attention that everyone sympathizes with me. No, wait— maybe that's the way he *did* answer. Yanabe and I were always joking with each other, and exchanging insults, and laughing together. There was a certain degree of imitation of the kind of give-and-take he and my mother shared, but it was a lot of fun for me all the same. Once when I was in middle school, a friend of mine came over to play cards while Yanabe was there, and my mother joined us. I got a bit overexcited, and my mother warned me and told Yanabe:

"It's because she's always lonely, that one."

Just hearing that made me feel quite sentimental myself. To have someone there, no matter who, was better than not having anyone. My mother had gotten divorced when I was two, and so I grew up not having a father at all. My grandfather was something of a substitute, but after all, your grandfather is your grandfather. And anyway, he died quite early. It was Yanabe, and not my grandfather, who somehow in some subtle way took that place in my mind, within two or three years after we started being together. Was he an uncle from somewhere? My father? There were lots of times I cursed him for being there. But that didn't usually last long. It was my mother and I who spent our time arguing with each other. My mother and my grandmother. My grandmother and I. We each would go whining and complaining to Yanabe and be comforted. What made me happy was not Yanabe himself but the fact that when he came to visit the atmosphere of the house changed. I used to hope that he'd come to stay with us forever. I wanted to get along with him better than with anyone else. I didn't comprehend what Yanabe was seeing. Until I learned about this woman now before me, I hadn't even tried to understand.

It's not that I wanted to be his lover nor that I wanted to be his daughter. I just wanted to be closer to him. When my mother was hospitalized, I even took it as a point of pride that we had managed to get so intimate. If it had been simply a matter that Yanabe was doing it as a courtesy to someone who came attached to the woman he loved, I couldn't have helped but be consumed by a sense of betrayal. But then, I wonder if I chose the path of "getting along" with Yanabe as my mother's daughter for my own safety.

The thirteen years from when I was thirteen to twenty-six. How long those years were for me, anyway. Should I stay a child? Should I become a cool and collected adult? I could choose only one of these alternatives, and I had been wrapped up in imagining that I'd succeeded in cementing my friendship with Yanabe by remaining a child.

Why wasn't there any way for me to see Yanabe? I felt anew the sense of pain. Why hadn't my grandmother and mother told me the truth, even if it stayed just between us? That whole thirteen years, during which I grew up between my mother and Yanabe: I didn't want them to have meant nothing.

The woman spoke. "He never says anything. I've asked him myself... 'Come on, tell me...what kind of a woman she was....It doesn't matter, I'm just a side issue anyway. I mean, I can't very well do anything silly, considering my situation. I've been conscious right from the start that I'm just someone you let live with you, so it's awful of you not to at least let me know....Come on, even if you pretend you're talking to yourself —but it did no good, he's hopeless."

She stopped speaking, and then turned to pour some fresh tea into the cup behind her.

"Oh, come now...don't call yourself a side issue....Yanabe had to endure a lot all that time. He must have been thinking all the while, 'You've got to be kidding, why should I have to go through this?' So I can imagine how revved up he is. To be able to spend each day doing just as he wants..."

That was a pretty stupid way of putting it, I thought to myself, but all the same, I couldn't help but say it the way I saw it. Maybe speaking the truth always sounds dumb. Yanabe had still been a young man when he began seeing my mother. He probably never dreamed he'd be kept waiting for so long, and besides, he probably never imagined she'd die on him so suddenly and leave him nothing. Yanabe wasn't the sort to want his life to be out of the ordinary. I wonder if, instead of a divorced woman with a child, he'd wanted a child of his own. My mother, anyway, continued to ignore any such thoughts he might have had. She even talked to me about it, when I was in middle school. We both feel that ours is a spiritual love, she'd said. I had believed her absolutely, had even bragged to my friends about it: of course there's such a thing as platonic love, that's what my mother's relationship is, they've never even had sex, you know.

"It doesn't have to have been me, anyone would have done. He's...Even now he seems surprised to find me with him."

The woman's tone of voice was not especially serious. Whether it was that she was finally starting to relax her guard against me or whatever, the movements of her hands gentled. She seemed to have a habit of tucking her hair behind her ears. Again and again she raised her white fingers to the base of her ears.

"Why do you..."

"I'm not saying it out of false modesty. It's true. If I'd been him, I might even have wanted to kill me. How can I say it? Do you know what I mean? I stayed put in a situation where actually I should have taken off right away, and so at least he doesn't forget me. I...He'll never marry again."

"Why?" My mother's already..."

The woman's eyes widened slightly. "Well...I had begun keeping him company from just before your mother died. Did you know? He used to come to make love to me almost every day."

"I'd heard about it from my grandmother ..." I was startled and dropped my glance, just managing to get the words out.

"Right...." The woman sighed. "Your grandmother...Please forgive me, I thought you didn't know anything about it....He, maybe, he's probably forgotten that time himself...he was in a strange state of mind. I had heard about the whole thing from people, that your mother was in the hospital, that she'd been operated on two or three times, and yet I was probably a little crazy then myself. I was the one who made the first moves....This must be awful for you to hear, really....But I just couldn't stand not to say something. I only expressed my sympathies, or something like that, but....Even though he looked as if he would collapse at any moment, he laughed. ...To have to bother with someone like me..."

"Don't....All Yanabe knows how to do is laugh."

"Maybe so....Anyway, after that for quite some time his face was like a hole. Like a hole in the ice. The hole got bigger and bigger...it was...scary..."

The woman looked down at the teapot on the tray and sat silent. I couldn't say anything either. It must have been scary, it just must have been: pure sympathy echoed in my breast. I remembered how I had spontaneously burst into tears at my grandmother's death, even though she had been praying to die quickly.

We had picked up her body from the hospital and were in the midst of making our calls on the neighbors and contacting the undertaker when suddenly my husband and I found ourselves with a period of time when we had nothing to do. Although both our bodies and

nerves ought to have been totally exhausted, we threw off our clothes and clung to each other, beside her corpse. It's not that we were impelled by some need to affirm that we were alive with our own body heat. We had no feeling at all. To borrow the woman's phrase, it's just that at the time we were in a "strange state of mind."

After the first operation, my mother's condition stabilized for a time. She returned home provisionally for a month. Yanabe bought a big American chaise lounge and put it in the sitting room. The slipcover was brightly flowered, like a tropical shirt. My mother complained about how it was in such bad taste, but she spent almost all her time on it. She watched television and ate her meals, and dozed.

I had been imagining how I could make her days as comfortable as possible when she returned from the hospital, and yet by the time a week had passed, I was starting to think it would be better for us all if she'd go back. She was constantly irritable; she had always been the type to say whatever she wanted, but now she just went on and on without stop. What's worse, I was almost her sole target. She started arguing with my grandmother at first, but because I was the one actually taking care of the house in my mother's place, inevitably her irritation focused on me. How I handled the vacuum cleaner, the way I set the table, how I did the laundry, arranged food on the plate, seasoned it, finally even how I moved my fingers, how I walked, how I moved my eyes— nothing pleased her.

When Yanabe came home from work, she'd begin whining: "What a useless daughter I have, you don't know how hard it is on me, how dismal it is when a daughter doesn't understand her mother." Nor at such times did she ever stop haranguing me. If Yanabe defended either me or my grandmother in the slightest, her tears would start and she would accuse him of betraying her: "So you've all gotten to be such good friends while I've been away? Ah yes, I see how it is. I suppose you've already figured out how much the funeral gifts are going to cost. How much is it going to be?"

At which point, Yanabe would start shouting furiously: "You're crazy, we're still trying to figure out how to pay your hospital bills." And she would promptly burst out wailing.

These scenes went on every day. There were times when I couldn't take it anymore. Busier than I'd ever been before and worn out with taking care of the house and nursing my mother at the same time, and the constant detailed abuse from her, I would break down and start crying myself. Even my grandmother and Yanabe joined my mother when she harassed me. Before I realized it, the three of them seemed to have together reached the conclusion that if I weren't such a lazy clod everything would be going just fine. To be sure, I was fairly clumsy. After all, this was the first time in my life I'd had the entire care of the house and simultaneously an invalid to look after. I had been a translator in an office until my mother was hospitalized. I couldn't have been expected to act like a professional housekeeper or a professional nurse. Once I got so upset that I ran out of the house and stayed away all night. I spent the night with a friend from college, crying and blubbering all night. When I returned to the house the next morning, sure enough, my mother and grandmother were waiting tearfully with an interminable sermon they'd prepared.

Our only pleasure was to talk about the picnic Yanabe suggested the three of us should take sometime soon. It couldn't be anywhere far, but we surely could go to some botanical garden in the suburbs. With all her leisure time, my mother enjoyed looking at the maps and choosing places: "I'd love to see the ocean, but then, it would be nice too to take an excursion in the country." Autumn was pretty far advanced, so no matter where we went, we'd be sure to have a pleasant picnic.

The cool, crisp days of Indian summer continued. Still housebound, my mother kept pushing us: "Isn't it okay now? I want to go soon. It doesn't matter where, just let's go soon." And as she fretted, her fever shot up again, and she had to go back to the hospital.

They examined her at the hospital, and she was moved into a room immediately. It was the room next to the one where she'd been before. She sat on the bed but refused to change into her nightgown.

—The weather's so nice, she said.

—You're right, the sky is really pretty.

—Do you suppose they'd let me hold off coming in until tomorrow?

—Why?

—I won't run away, so why don't we call up "Daddy" and have him go somewhere with us. You know, like that family park near here. . . .

—You'll die if you do that.

—Who cares? Don't you know what my illness is?

—What difference does that make? . . . it'll be better in a while.

—You're trying to be smart again. . . . But really, let's go somewhere. If I don't go today, I'll never be able to go anywhere again. Come on, we'll feel great, really. I want to see the sky through the yellow leaves. I want to sit there and eat our picnic as I look up at the yellow and red leaves reaching up to the sky. . . . Didn't we go to the mountains, the three of us, way back? And you were so happy? Have you forgotten?

—Of course I remember! I was a freshman in college.

—That's right. . . we gathered horse chestnuts, and all those pretty leaves. . . and Daddy ate five rice balls. . . . Let's go, Akiko. Just because this is a hospital doesn't mean they have the right to invade my personal freedom. . . . Come on, let's go see the leaves together. . . .

I gave up trying to persuade her to get into bed and went to call Yanabe at the office. As I explained to him how she had to be hospitalized again but she wouldn't get into bed, I could feel my body trembling. The receiver, too, was trembling at my ear. After hanging up, I gazed for a while out the window. The blue sky spread wide, and I could see the moon faintly. It was a quiet, chilly sky. The yellow weeds at ground level looked warm as they swayed back and forth. Red leaves fallen from the trees tumbled lazily in the grass. They looked like soap bubbles. Crimson soap bubbles. I clung to the window sill, supporting my body, which only trembled the harder. It seemed to me that all of it—us, from the moment she'd gotten out of the hospital until just ten minutes earlier—had turned into nothing but a scene inside a soap bubble.

Nothing particularly had happened as far as my mother's condition was concerned, but I must say that I was rather surprised at my own reaction at the time.

I opened my mouth to say these things to the woman. But before I could speak, the woman did.

"Oh, sweetheart, did you wake up?"

I realized for the first time that a child was coming down the hallway, rubbing her eyes. My breath stopped. I was as startled as if I had discovered some impossible beast. My grandmother had not told me that there was a child.

"What is it? Can't you say hello? Come on, say hello...oh, you're still sleepy."

The woman stretched out her arms and drew the child to her lap. The child continued to scrub at her eyes, and peeked out at me. I spoke quickly, matching my tone to the woman's.

"Hello!"

The child continued to say nothing. She looked to be about two, and her hands and feet still had a baby's chubbiness. Her hair was cut straight across in a Dutch bob, and her eyes were huge. She didn't resemble either Yanabe or the woman.

The woman spoke as she stroked the child's head. "If only she'd slept a bit more, it would have been a help....When she's up, I can't get anything done....Come on, the lady'll think you're strange if you don't say hello."

I stood up as I laughed indulgently at the child. "I really have overstayed..."

The woman looked a little surprised as she looked up at me. Deep creases appeared across her brow. I felt that I was seeing her face for the first time.

"No, it's I who have kept you..."

"Well, would you see that Yanabe..."

"Of course. I'll tell him it came by parcel post."

"That's very kind of you....Oh, that's right, I haven't asked anything about him. How is he?"

"Yes, well, mostly okay, he had a light cold recently..." As she answered, the woman stood up, the child in her arms. "Do you mind if I go along to see you off?"

I nodded quickly. I was glad she'd asked. I'd probably never see her again, and I felt somehow that there were still lots of things I wanted to tell her. It's good that she's my own age, I suddenly thought.

The woman and I walked along the road to the station side by side. The child on her back was quiet, only murmuring "Mama" in her mother's ear from time to time.

"...She'll be three in another five months." Looking straight ahead, the woman spoke first. This was a new housing development, so the road ran straight as a line on a chessboard. Maybe that's why the wind is so strong, I mused. The wind was gritty. "It's because of the child, it seems, that he found it hard to stay on at your house....I wanted to tell him that he should stay with you, but...I couldn't. And I didn't blame myself, because it wasn't as if I'd been the one to ask him.... You must have been pretty surprised at the time, right?"

"Yes...pretty surprised. I hadn't expected him to stay with us forever, but I never thought it would be so soon...."

"It really was, wasn't it." The woman

nodded with a bitter smile. "But it's not that I felt I just had to have the baby. It was just because somehow or other I could never imagine having an abortion that it ended up getting born. He seemed to have felt the same way. He never at all wanted to have a baby, you know. As a matter of fact, he even hated me, as my belly began to swell. But...he did accept the idea of the baby, right from the start. Although from the time she was born, he never once gave her the kind of affection he gave you...."

"Oh, come on—I thought that Yanabe was nice to me only to make my mother happy." Once again I wasn't able to gauge the woman's feelings toward me, and I answered swiftly, on my guard.

"Yes...maybe that's just the way fathers are."

"Not at all! Would a true father think like that?"

"...I wonder," the woman responded, not looking at me. "I suppose not,...please, forgive me, for bringing up such strange things. The baby's birthday is in the middle of summer. Do you remember that summer? It was a strange one. From the day she was born we had about a week of solid heat, and then it got cool and stayed that way straight into autumn....She was a big baby, she cried real loud....Once, I forget when, a white towel fell over her face while she was asleep. He discovered it, and stood there for a long time as if he couldn't move. He stood beside the crib like some big ornament...I wondered what was going on, and went over myself to look at the baby, and saw that the towel must have fallen. So I took it off. The thing that was shading her eyes disappeared, and so she started to cry. That big voice of hers. Even the teardrops were huge....When I picked her up to quiet her in my arms, he suddenly got furious—that is, he isn't the type to do anything, but he glared at us out of the corner of his eye and then stormed out of the house.... Later, I realized what he'd been thinking and

how wrong he was....And then, when I understood, I couldn't help feeling my own anger rise. You can't win for losing...." The woman burst out laughing, and so I laughed too. "He really believes that it's manly not to say anything, you see....By the way, how old was your mother when she passed away?"

"Let's see...forty-eight."

"That's how old he is now. I could say that she was quite young, but...."

"You're right—Yanabe *is* young," I said, laughing. My mother had considered it a major character defect that Yanabe looked younger than his age—that, though there'd been only four years between them, it looked like nearly twice that much.

The woman stopped and shifted the child on her back. The child said something that I didn't catch. The woman looked behind and nodded. The child lapsed back into silence. The woman looked over at me and started walking again. She was laughing, a deep frown line between her brows.

"About the time your mother died, he suddenly stopped coming over, although he'd been coming every day, and so I guessed what had happened. I'd known for some time before then that her condition was increasingly precarious, from the expression on his face.... Although I'd figured it out, when I knew for sure that she had died, I found myself considerably unnerved. My relationship with him was predicated on your mother's not dying, while seeming about to die. I...maybe...I was fascinated to see how frightened about it he was. I never once sympathized with him. So I'd not gotten around to thinking about what would happen after your mother died. Two months, three months—I didn't see him. It wasn't interesting to me anymore, and so there shouldn't have been any reason for me to want to see him, and yet....It's a strange business, isn't it?...I don't know anything about funerals. No one close to me has ever died....And so I've wondered what kind of a funeral it was, it must have been quite splendid....Well, anyway, it's not that I'm curious. It's just that I can't help feeling uneasy about it....There are all kinds of funerals, but I'll bet there are fewer than you'd think where the people really do mourn. I can't help feeling that your mother's funeral was especially impressive. Just two participants—you and he. All the same, more splendid than you'd likely ever see. Since he was doing it, he must have gotten together all the flowers he could buy. Huge, scary piles of them....I found myself wanting to see him then, standing there right in the middle of a funeral like that...."

We followed the turning of the road and came onto a shopping street. The child on her back turned her bright, smiling face to me. I smiled back at her. When she smiled, somehow she looked like Yanabe, it seemed to me. The woman continued to speak quietly, looking down at the ground. The station was getting near.

"But since then, I'd forgotten about the funeral. It came back to me after your grandmother's funeral recently. He came home, and most unusual for him, he had one comment about it: 'The smell of incense is all right, but I hate the smell of flowers.' When I heard that, I started to get upset about your mother's funeral all over again. For all the time that had passed, it seemed all the more....I had a dream, too....There was this big, square, deserted building. Like a gymnasium, but the ceiling was real high, and it was dark. Right in the middle, he and you were standing. And white flowers were completely covering the floors and the walls and the ceiling, like bugs. As I watched closely, the white flowers continued to pile up. The ceiling was creaking with the weight of the flowers, threatening to fall at any moment, and yet they continued to pile up. But you and he didn't move. You were sort of dreamy and abstracted, congratulating yourselves on what a good funeral it had been and wondering if there had ever been one like this one....It was an awful dream. If you were to ask me what it was in the dream that gave me the creeps, I couldn't tell you, but

there was just something. It was awful. Not the flowers, but him standing there so dreamy ....Do you follow me?"

The woman suddenly stopped and stood there looking into my face. We were at the foot of the long overpass bridge. Above the bridge was the station. The sound of bells and the public address system came echoing to us from the platform. There were lots of people going past us, but we hadn't hit the rush hour yet, so even though we were standing still, we weren't impeding the flow.

I looked up at the stairs and answered in confusion, "But the actual funeral wasn't so very..."

"What really happened has no bearing on it..." the woman said with a smile, taking the child down from her back, and shrugging her shoulders lightly as if the child had been heavy. "You'll have to excuse me for bringing up such weird topics. I was just thinking myself at that point how much I'd like to meet you. So you really surprised me today. But I'm glad. Don't pay any attention to all these things I've been saying."

"Don't be silly. I should apologize myself, appearing so suddenly...." I bowed my head, laughing easily. As the time for us to part approached, I found myself wanting to think this woman was a good person. From here on, maybe I'd be able to let go of Yanabe, I felt, and a kind of satisfaction grew in me over the day's accomplishment.

"I wish we could meet again, but....By the way, you don't have children, Akiko?"

"No, not so far."

"I see...I keep wondering about such stupid things. Like, why your mother didn't have another child. Of course, I suppose there were all sorts of reasons, but....All the same, I wonder how many possible babies she wasted. But as a result, even he's gotten used to death. He seems to believe that this baby came popping out suddenly from the Mountain of the Dead.[2] She would never have been born if your mother hadn't died, so you can't really say I'm off the mark, can you?...Anyway, this child has come into the world with so much more manure than other children. The blessings of manure—oh, what's the matter, have I said something wrong?"

The woman's words were bad enough; but I felt even angrier at the forced tone. "Of course! How can you say such a horrible thing?"

The woman turned her face away from me and looked down at the child crouching at her feet. I fully intended to leave immediately, but I wanted to say at least something else to her, and I couldn't get my body to move. There was so much feeling welling up in me that I just couldn't find the right words.

"Well then…" In the end, that's all I could get out, and I began walking away. The woman's voice struck my back.

"Take care. Thanks for coming today."

Without turning back, I swiftly climbed the stairs. When I got to the top, I wanted to turn around and look back at the woman and child, but I resisted the impulse and went to the gate. Great surges of feeling roiled within me, and my thoughts were in total confusion. In the past, I had often felt like this when I fought with my mother. She was very good with words, and she would continue to pour an unending stream of sharp words over me as I got more and more confused, until finally in the end she'd always make me cry. Her attack would end at last when she saw the tears. This went on between the two of us even when I was in high school. If only I could cry now as I did then, I'd feel better, I thought.

A kind of furious frustration came over me. I'd been thinking better of her. Why did she have to say such things at this late date about a dead person, even if she was just fantasizing? But then I wondered if maybe she weren't in fact suffering so much that she had to say them. All the same, wasn't she just indulging herself? I didn't even know if I had any right on earth to claim myself as the injured party. Such weariness washed over me that I wanted to squat down on the spot and rest my head between my knees.

Aqua-colored plastic strips had been nailed below the railings on both sides as a safety measure. They were full of holes—perhaps children had done it in mischief. The little strips were all connected, but not one of them had escaped damage. Maybe the strips were too fragile to be used in a place like this; even in the parts that didn't have holes in them, there were long cracks running the length of them, and in places, broken pieces hung down, and it looked quite shabby. Fragments of the same colored stuff lay scattered at my feet. In addition to the danger of falling from the railing to the roadbed below, they could injure people. I hadn't noticed it on the way out. I could see it: children sticking their heads through the holes in the plastic and looking down at the rails, and as they did, their necks got cut, and the blood flowed down, and writhing in pain, they fell onto the tracks. Really, for a second I did actually seem to be seeing such a scene clearly, right before my eyes.

I drew close to the railing and looked down. The many rails gleamed in the evening sun. Cream-colored train cars began to move slowly along them. There were lots of whitish fragments that looked like pieces of the plastic strips, on the rusty gravel. Dandelions had stolen spaces between them and were blooming there.

That's the moment I remembered what my mother had said to me. About why it was that they always hound a person with flowers when he dies.

My mother was afraid of the operations, and she was afraid of the clanking sound of the doctor's metal instruments as he made his rounds.

The quantity of flowers that decorated my mother's funeral was quite a bit beyond the ordinary. As the woman had surmised, that was Yanabe's doing. Hadn't she said anything to him while she was still alive? I too had said nothing when I'd seen him consulting with the florist. The bunches of lilies and roses had stood out especially. Strong-scented flowers.

They had overpowered the incense. Even days after the funeral, the scent of the flowers clung in my nose and wouldn't dissipate. And even now when I smell lilies and roses, I immediately associate the scent with my mother's funeral. Instinctively I screw up my face, as if it were an unpleasant smell. My mother had hated it that they always accompany a person's death with flowers. Even though she hadn't said it, I think she might have been pleased to have been seen off with a funeral like that one in the desert. But the funeral was not for my dead mother. Yanabe had purposely sought out strong-scented flowers and had bought them all up, trying to connect himself anew to my mother through the scent. Wasn't that it?

I'd never had a dream like the woman's. How about Yanabe, I wondered. I could imagine that it might be a continuing dream for him. Flowers that kept increasing in huge masses. Strong-scented white flowers. But then, by kicking them around vigorously, by trampling and crushing them, a baby—according to the woman, a very big baby—had gotten born.

As I left the railing and turned toward the ticket gate it suddenly struck me. How stupid —I hadn't gotten the child's name, or even the woman's. What could the child's name be, I wondered. And a thought popped into my head: Mightn't she let me have the child?

On the train, I clung to the strap and twisted my body to gaze out the window at the evening sky tinged with sunset, in which I painted in imagination a noisily crying baby, floating in a sky filled with white flower petals. Light peach-colored clouds spread before me.

Translated by Phyllis I. Lyons

NOTES

1. By Japanese custom, mourners at a funeral are given memorial gifts (*kōdengaeshi*) by the bereaved family.
2. In popular belief, a mountain of dead bodies in Hell that the souls of the dead must climb.

Marnie Walsh   *US, b. 1947*

Marnie Walsh is a native Dakotan who received her B.A. in History and English from Pennsylvania State University and completed her M.A. in creative writing at the University of New Mexico. In 1975, she published her first novel, *Dolly Purdo*, followed by *The Four Colored Hoop* (1976). The former is a comic novel of the Old West that owes some of its humor to the ways in which it plays off against stereotypes of blacks, Amer-Indians, and women; the latter is a serious attempt to probe the fate of the native American woman. Walsh, like McCullers and Welty, for example, uses grotesque characters, but paints them in pastel colors. Clearly, Walsh's work took its impetus from the ferment amongst Amer-Indians and from the women's movement, as well as such writings as *Little Big Man* (1963) by Thomas Berger that mixed history and fiction, and comedy and tragedy to examine the American experience.

With *A Taste of the Knife* (1976), Walsh turned to poetry: the immediacy and intensity of her poetic work is bounded by a formal control as well as what might be called an epic subjectivity that comes of Walsh's concentration on and use of the points of view of characters who seem to have a historical status and take on almost legendary qualities; they are bonded into a traditional community. The poetry owes something to Walsh's academic knowledge and more to her work on reservations in South Dakota during the 1970s. Since 1984, Walsh has lived in Arizona, somewhat reclusive in her habits and reticent about her current work.

VICKIE LOANS-ARROW, 1973

1

my brother nathan
comes home on leave
from the war on the bus
and we all there to meet him
snow is every place
deep and white
he picks it up in his hands
his eyes dont stop looking at it

2

my brothers friends is there too
george little elk and cousin wayne
who got a new car
from getting his leg shot off
where nathan been
my brother look quiet
when he seen how george
got bad nerves
that make him shake all over
and laugh like he cant close
his mouth no more

3

we all go home
and mama cooks lots to eat
it start to get dark over the snow
nathan go out and watch
he dont make no shadow
i think a shadow on snow
aint good to see anyway
then him and his friends
sit around and drink
say hey lets go to town
they pretty drunk and my brother
fall down in the snow
laughing and white all over
like somebodys ghost

4

he tell us all next morning
he run into his old girl friend
and she take him home
he dont know what happen
to wayne and george
there aint no girls want
no cripples or crazies
so say uncle morris
and nathan get terrible mad
throw his coffee at morris
and hollers goddam whores
goddam bitches
goddam world

5

then my brother run away
out the door in the snow
i follow him and see
he make just a little shadow
even in daytime
and it slides over the snow
like some old owl
he go over the hill to the road
and he the one find the car
that belong to cousin wayne
nathin seen it sticking up
out of the ditch
finds george some ways off
where he drug his self
cousin waynes head stuck half
through the windshield
not shaking no more

(Continued)

6

after that nathan dont talk much
no more and dont go nowhere
just sits to home drunk
then it time he go again
and we all take him to the bus
early in the morning dark
with some pink to the east
well the bus goes with nathan in it
my brother dont look back
dont look out the window
at the shadow running
in the snow beside it.

THOMAS IRON-EYES
BORN *CIRCA* 1840.
DIED 1919,
ROSEBUD AGENCY, S.D.

1

I woke before the day, when the night bird
Knocked three times upon my door
To warn the Other Sleep was coming.
By candlelight I painted the two broad stripes
Of white across my forehead, the three scarlet
                                                                spots
Upon my cheek.   I greased well my braids
With sour fat from the cooking pot, then tied
                                                                them
With a bit of bright string saved for the
                                                        occasion.
From the trunk I took the dress of ceremony,
The breechcloth and the elkskin shirt,
The smoke of their breaths strong in my nose;
Smoke not of this time, this life or place,
But of my youth, of the many lodges I dwelt
                                                            within;
The pony raids, the counting coup;
The smell of grass when it first was green,
And the smell of coming snows, when food
                                                    was plentiful
Within the camp, and ice crept over the rivers.
Carefully I put on the dress, then the leggings
                                                    with scalps,

As thin now and as colorless as the hair
Of sickly animals, sinew-tied along the seams;
And on my feet the red-beaded moccasins
Worn by none but the bravest of warriors.
I lie here, waiting, my dry bones and ancient
                                                                skin
Holding my old heart.
The daystar finds me ready for my journey.

2

Another time, another life, another place,
My people would have wrapped me in
                                                        deerskin,
Sewed me in the finest of furs;
then borne me in honor to the cottonwood
                                                            bier,
Laying at my right hand the sacred pipe,
And at my left the arrows and bow, the lance
I long ago bound with thongs and hung
With the feathers from the eagle's breast.
Below the scaffold of the dead
My pony of the speckled skin and fierce heart
Would be led, and with a blow of the stone ax
Upon his skull, lie down to wait my need.
I would know that far above
In the sacred hoop of the sky
Long-sighted hawks, hanging on silent wings,
Marked my passage.

3

When the Life-Giver hid from the night,
The dark wind would speak to my spirit
And I would arise, taking up my weapons.
Mounting my horse I would follow
The great path over the earth,
The road leading to the Old Grandfathers
Beyond the stars.
I would see the glow of their cooking fires
Bright as arrow tips across the northern sky;
Waiting for me, old friends dance and feast
And play the games of gambling.
Behind me drums would beat, and willow
                                                    whistles cry
Like the doves of spring who nested
In the berry bushes near the river by my village.

I would pause to hear my sons in council
Speaking of my deeds in war, my strength and
                                                        wisdom,
Praising me; knowing my women in their
                                                        sorrow
Were tearing their clothing, their faces bloodied
And smeared with ashes.

4

But I am Thomas.   I am here,
Where no grass grows, no clear rivers run;
Where dirt and despair abound,
Where heat and rain alike rust out
The souls of my people, the roofs of tin;
Where hunger sits in the dooryards,
Where disease, like a serpent, slips from house
                                                        to house.

I am Thomas, waiting for the wagon
To bring the government box of pine;
Waiting for the journey to the burying ground
Below sandy buttes where rattlesnakes
Stink in burrows, and the white man's wooden
                                                        trinities
Stand in crooked rows.

There I shall be put beneath the earth.
There shall my spirit be sealed within
The planks of the coffin.
There I shall not hear the dark wind's cry
To come and ride the starry road
Across the holy circle of the sky.

Gayl Jones   *US, b. 1949*

In the streets and the segregated schools of Lexington, Kentucky, Gayl Jones, poet
and novelist, absorbed the wisdom and rhythm of black vernacular culture. In
1971 she received a B.A. in English from Connecticut College and, by 1975, two
graduate degrees in creative writing from Brown University. She taught creative
writing and Afro-American literature at the University of Michigan from 1975 to
1983, until she left the United States.

Her art is like a blues song, her subjects the terror of incessant sexual warfare,
the obsessive extremes of sexuality and violence, the mingling of pleasure and pain.
In Jones's work, madness is not the affliction of an individual but of a society. In
her first novel, *Corregidora* (1975), the distinction between pain and pleasure,
victim and victimizer is not completely visible. Despite the fact that the blues singer
Ursa Corregidora, a descendent of the incest of the Portuguese slave owner of her
maternal ancestors, is by her husband's violence made sterile, she realizes that the
ritual hatred for men found in the folklore of black women overlooks the perverse
longing of all human beings for their own oppression. James Baldwin remarked
that the novel "dares to confront the absolute terror which lives at the heart of
love."

Jones's second novel, *Eva's Man* (1976), was, like her first, controversial.
Tormented by a lifetime of the sexual malevolence of men, Eva commits a horren-
dous sex crime, which she obsessively recounts from a mental asylum. Gradually
we glimpse the origins of her madness in everyday sexual violence. Some critics
attacked *Eva's Man* for perpetuating sterotypes of black men and women, missing
the point of Jones's attempt to "reclaim such complex, contradictory characters."

White Rat (1977) collects short stories about characters imprisoned in reality. "The Roundhouse" (1975), reprinted here, is an exception, a story of mundane love based loosely on her grandmother's experience. In her narrative poem *Song For Anninho* (1981), a love story placed in seventeenth-century Brazil, Jones again gestures towards the redemptive possibilities of feeling.

THE ROUNDHOUSE

I didn't know what was wrong with him, even after I went to see him. I'd heard at work that he was sick, and asked if he had anybody to do for him. They said he had a room in Will Darcy's rooming house. He didn't have a family, and nobody knew anything about him, and there was no one to take care of him. I hadn't known him long, just three weeks, and we'd never really said more than "Hi." He was a quiet man. He was the kind you feel close to even though you've said no more than "Hi."

I was working at the roundhouse in Garrett, Indiana. Garrett, not Gary. Just after the war, the first one. The roundhouse was where the trains came in. It was our job to polish the parts, and keep the engines shining. I was hired during the war, when they were hiring women. I'd been working a year there, and my kids were going to school, when he came. He never said anything to anybody. He did his work. He did more work than he had to, and he didn't talk to anyone. He looked like a foreigner, reddish brown. Maybe he was a Negro, maybe he was Puerto Rican or something or maybe mixed. People said maybe he couldn't speak English. He never bothered anybody, and nobody bothered him. He came to work and he left work and he never talked. I don't even know if he stopped for lunch.

One day we'd been assigned to the same engine. He was there before I was, polishing away. He looked up when I came. "Hi," I said. He didn't smile. He looked back down. He wasn't being unfriendly. There are some people who just don't talk. I could tell he knew English though. I don't know how but I could tell. He didn't have the look of someone who didn't know the language.

We worked. At lunchtime I quit and started away but saw he was still working. I started to ask, "Aren't you going to have lunch?" but didn't. I thought maybe he wouldn't want me to.

I went and sat down on a bench, eating a sandwich. Some other people were there. Joe McDowell was there.

"Did he say anything to you?" he asked.

"He said 'Hi,'" I said.

"That's more than he said to me," McDowell said. "I worked with him a whole day. Funny thing, though. I didn't feel uncomfortable. Most people don't talk, you feel uncomfortable as hell. With him you don't."

"I know," I said. "It's nice."

"Nobody knows anything about him." McDowell said. "Henderson says he's taken a room over at Darcy's place. That's not far from where you live. I've heard of people that don't talk much. He don't talk at all."

"He probably does when he has to." I said.

"Ask for a job or a room," McDowell said, not sarcastically.

"Anyway, he seems very nice," I said.

McDowell nodded. It was time to start working again. Four more hours. The kids would be home from school.

When five o'clock came, he stopped work, and left. He was practically the first to be gone. It was summer and he didn't need to grab a coat. He rolled down his shirt-sleeves. Neither Darcy's nor where I lived was far from the station, so we both walked home, about a fifteen or twenty minute walk, a half hour on bad days. He walked fast. I didn't try to catch up with him. When I got to the street, he was a block ahead of me. I saw him turn into the rooming house. I passed where he lived and walked a block more up the street.

The next day we walked home the same way, he walking rapidly ahead again. He seemed always in a hurry, even when he worked. He worked hard and fast. It was a wonder the men hadn't got together and told him to slow down, he made the others look bad, but people liked him, though he didn't talk much. As I said, he was walking ahead and turned in at his gate, but when I passed the rooming house this time, he had not gone in the door, but was standing there, his hand on the doorknob, his head turned looking at me. He didn't say anything and went inside. I walked on. I felt funny.

"I knew a switchman I worked with," McDowell was saying then he stopped and looked up.

I looked up. *He* was standing there, looking down at me.

"I want to walk you home," he said to me.

"O—kay," I said, bewildered. Then he walked away. McDowell looked at me and grinned.

When I got outside, he was waiting for me. It had been cooler this morning and he had a jacket slung over his shoulder. He looked down and smiled. We started walking.

"How are you?" I asked.

"Okay," he said.

We walked on.

"I didn't know you came this way," he said, the first time he'd said more than a word or two. "We could have walked together before."

Now I didn't say anything.

"You live a block away from me," he said. I wondered how he knew. "In a house."

"I have two kids," I said.

"You're married?" he asked, as if I might not be.

"I was."

"How do you mean?"

"He died."

"In the war?"

"No."

I was waiting for him to ask how, like most people had, but he didn't. He seemed to feel if I wanted him to know I'd tell him. I wanted him to know. "From alcohol," I said.

"Oh," he said. I guess I hadn't really expected an "I'm sorry" from him either. The platitudes. I guess he didn't do things that way.

Then we were at the boarding house. I was stopping for him to turn in, but he didn't. He took my elbow slightly.

"I'll see you some," he said.

He saw me home, and then went back. I went inside.

"Who's he?" Jean asked. "He's handsome." Jean was my daughter, thirteen, with her hairs in plaits.

"His name's...I don't know his name. He works where I work."

"I haven't seen him before."

"He hasn't walked me home before. Where's Ben?"

"He's in the kitchen."

Ben was my son. He was fourteen. He was light, almost white. Jean was brown. My grandmother had been white. It was hard explaining to people. It was better in Indiana.

"How was school?" I asked.

"The same."

"Much homework?"

"Yes."

Ben came in and said "Hi." I started supper.

"Mama's got a beau," I heard Jean tell Ben.

"I have not," I called. "He works at the roundhouse."

"He walked her home," Jean said, triumphantly. "He's good-looking," she added. "You'll have to check him out."

I didn't hear Ben say anything. I was thinking Ben might like him.

The next day I didn't see him at all, not even after work, and the day after he was not there. I had lunch with McDowell.

"He's probably gone," McDowell said.

"Gone?" I asked.

"You know how it is with them. Come to one town. Hold down a job for a while. Have to keep moving."

"You don't mean he's running from the law?"

"Don't have to be the law."

"What then?"

"Himself. Somebody. How should I know?"

"I didn't know his name," I said.

"James Buchanan Jones, named for the President. Henderson says he calls himself Jake. Wants the people that know him to."

Lunchtime was over. I went back to work.

The next day, McDowell came over to where I was working.

"Henderson says Jake's sick."

"What's wrong?"

"Don't know."

"Hasn't anybody been to see about him?"

"Don't think so. He didn't get close with people."

I frowned and put down the rag and started away. McDowell grabbed my arm.

"Where *you* going?" he asked.

"To see about him."

"The Man won't like it, stopping on the job."

"I don't care."

"You've got two kids."

"Tell him I got sick, Joe."

Joe shook his head slowly.

"It's an hour till lunch," he said.

"All right." I picked up the rag.

He started away.

"Thanks, Joe," I called. He nodded.

At lunchtime I went outside.

"What did the boss say when I didn't come back?" I asked McDowell, the first thing in the morning, before I even started.

"I told him you got sick," he said.

"Thank you."

"How is he?"

"Fever. Wouldn't let me call a doctor. I'm doing what I can. He didn't have any food."

"How are you going to work and take care of him and yourself and the kids?"

"I can manage," I said.

"If you need me you know where to reach me," he said.

"Sure, Joe," I said. I thanked him again. He tapped my arm and went to work. I thought I wouldn't know what to do without him. He had been awfully good to me and the kids.

That afternoon I stopped at the rooming house before going home. I had a bundle with me. A loaf of bread and some curtains. I put the bundle down and went over to him and placed my hand on his forehead. He hadn't been able to shave for about a week now.

"How do you feel?" I asked.

"Better, thanks to you," he said.

"You still have a fever," I said.

I went over to the bundle and started taking the curtains out.

"What are they for? I have curtains," he said.

"Your curtains are ugly," I said.

"They're not, if you don't look at them," he said.

"These you can look at," I said, and started putting the curtains up. The window was small and faced the street. There was only the bed in the room and a chest of drawers, a table and chair.

"Now you won't be able to tell I'm a bachelor," he said.

"I can tell," I said.

I sat down in the chair.

"I've got to go home and fix supper," I said. "I'll be back a little later and bring you something over."

I started up to go but he took one of my hands in both his and said thank you. I smiled and went home.

I went back with some chicken soup. He didn't eat much.

"Your fever's going down," I said. "You couldn't tell by the way you eat, though."

"I never eat much. You have to learn not to."

"Joe McDowell says you're the kind of person that never stays in one place."

"I guess that's right," he said.

"Where are you from?" I asked.

He didn't answer. I didn't press him to.

"You have kids," he said. "What are they like?"

"They're nice," I said.

"You know you live with people a long time and then when somebody asks you what they're like you say they're nice. I guess that's all you can say really." He wasn't being sarcastic.

"I have their pictures," I said. I took out a billfold from my purse and opened it and showed him their pictures.

"The boy's half white," he said.

"Is there a crime against having white blood?" I asked. I was jumpy on that subject.

"The same crime as having black," he said.

"My grandmother," I said.

"You don't have to explain," he said.

"I know," I said.

"They say my mother was a gypsy," he said. "If she showed anybody my picture they would have asked, 'What makes the boy so brown?'"

"You didn't know her?"

"I didn't know her or my father," he said. "I grew up in homes."

"I'm sorry."

He grew angry suddenly. "Don't say you're sorry."

"Okay, Jake." I was hurt.

He touched my hand.

"Don't take it wrong," he said.

"Okay."

I stood up, "I'd better go."

"You're not angry?"

"No, no."

"Promise?"

"I promise."

The next day I saw McDowell for lunch.

"How's he doing?" he asked.

"The fever's almost gone," I said. "I think it's just overwork. He doesn't take care of himself. He doesn't eat."

"He needs a wife," Joe said.

I didn't say anything.

In a couple of days, Jake was well but didn't come back to work again. He had done what McDowell said people like that did.

"You miss him don't you?" McDowell said. "You knew what he'd do. Men like that..."

"Yeah, I know about men like that," I said.

He touched my arm, "I'm sorry," he said.

"Don't be," I said.

When the war was over and the men had come home, the roundhouse had kept some of us on, mostly those who didn't have husbands. Now they were laying some of us off again, or reducing our hours. My hours had been reduced, and what I was making now would hardly buy chicken feed, less more support two kids.

When somebody started paying my grocery bills and coal bills, the first person I thought of was McDowell.

"What are you doing?" I asked Joe. I explained. He said he wasn't doing anything. No, it couldn't be, I decided.

The mysterious bill payments went on for several months. I asked the store not to take any more money, but they said there was nothing they could do about it.

I was in the kitchen fixing supper when the doorbell rang. Jean went to answer it. She came back into the kitchen, smiling.

"Who is it?" I asked.

"Go see," she said.

I frowned and wiped my hands on my apron. I stopped in the doorway to the hall.

"Jake!" I exclaimed. I went over to him. "How are you?"

"Very well," he said. "You look well."

There was a bench in the hall.

"Let's sit down," I said.

He said he'd rather stand, and if things went well then we could sit down. I asked him what he was talking about.

He said he wanted to take care of me. He said I had taken care of him when he was sick, and now he was ready to take care of me.

I looked up at him. He wasn't smiling. He was waiting.

I sat down.

He sat down beside me.

Alice Neel, Self-Portrait, *1980, oil on canvas.*
National Portrait Gallery, Smithsonian Institution, Washington, D.C.

Fawziyya Abu-Khalid

Saudi Arabia, b. 1955

Fawziyya Abu-Khalid was born in the Saudi Arabian capital of Riyadh to a westernized upper-middle-class family. As a young girl she began writing poetry, much of which appeared in a local newspaper. Many of the works written before she was eighteen were included in her first collection published in Lebanon, but *Ilā Matā Yakhtatifūnakī Laylat al-'Urs?* (n.d.), with its provocative, not to say incendiary, title—Until When Will They Go on Raping You on Your Wedding Night?—proved less than acceptable and was banned in Saudi Arabia. The selections are from this volume.

Abu-Khalid studied sociology at the American University in Beirut and continued her education in the United States at Lewis and Clark College in Oregon. Her latest collection, published in 1985, is entitled *Qirā'ah al-Sirr lī-Tārīkh al-Samt al-'Arabī* (Reading the Secret of the History of Arab Silence).

TATTOO WRITING
Al-Kitāba bi-l-Washm

Not with your tribe's spears I write
    for they are dull
    but with my nails
Words without walls.
Sister,
For you I have inscribed
    Love-songs
    weaving the sun's rays
    to your latticed window.

To tell me you accept
    The Tribe's traditions and prescriptions
    is a concession
    to being buried alive.
The noble inch or two
      of tattoo
    over your skin
Shall carve a bottomless night
    into
your flesh.

It pains me
to see The Tribe dwell
in you sprawling
in your college seat not unlike
    your grandmother
    who thought she was
    a lottery ticket won
    at home. A woman
in her twenties
sitting before some tent
shrouded with robes and veils
carrying the spindle
but does not spin.
To hear you talk
about a cloak
the clan's men bought
for you;
to hear your boast
about blue-blood
the heirs
and chip off the old oak tree.
The Sheikh's voice in your voice
cancels
you.

(Continued)

Sister
My kingdom does not claim
        doweries of cows and cattle
thus The Tribe rejects me
for you are their legitimate child
I am the one disavowed
You belong to lords of virgin
        lands
I to seasons bleeding flames.
Should The Tribe's drums and barking
                                        dogs

Shut off your hearing
        the rippling
    of women's
blood

Translated by Kamal Boullata

MOTHER'S INHERITANCE
Man Yuqasimūnī Irth Ummī

Mother,
You did not leave me an inheritance of
                necklaces for a wedding
but a neck
        that towers above the guillotine
Not an embroidered veil for my face
but the eyes of a falcon
        that glitter like the daggers
        in the belts of our men.
Not a piece of land large enough
        to plant a single date palm
but the primal fruit of The Fertile Crescent:*
My Womb.

You let me sleep with all the children
        of our neighborhood
that my agony may give birth
        to new rebels

In the bundle of your will
I thought I could find
        a seed from The Garden of Eden
        that I may plant in my heart
        forsaken by the seasons
Instead
You left me with a sheathless sword
        the name of an obscure child carved
                                on its blade

Every pore in me
        every crack
        opened up:

A sheath.
I plunged the sword into my heart
        but the wall could not contain it
I thrust it into my lungs
        but the window could not box it
I dipped it into my waist
        but the house was too small for it
It lengthened into the streets
        defoliating the decorations
        of official holidays
Tilling asphalt
Announcing the season of
The Coming Feast.

Mother,
Today, they came to confiscate the inheritance
                you left me.
They could not decipher the children's
                                fingerprints
They could not walk the road that stretches
        between the arteries of my heart
        and the cord that feeds the babe
        in every mother's womb.
They seized the children of the neighborhood
        for interrogation
They could not convict the innocence in their
                                        eyes.

They searched my pockets
        took off my clothes
        peeled my skin
But they failed to reach
        the glistening silk that nestles
        the twin doves
        in my breast.

Translated by Kamal Boullata

NOTE

* The Middle East, flanked by the Nile and the Tigris and
Euphrates Rivers; historically and symbolically the
cradle of civilization.

Zabyah Khamis
United Arab Emirates, b. ca. 1958

Zabyah Khamis is one of the few popular poets to emerge from the United Arab Emirates. She works as a broadcaster, and in 1987, was briefly arrested by the security police; although no charges were made, the arrest was believed to have been the result of several articles, including one on the status of women, and poems she had written that were critical of the authorities in the U.A.E. It also came amid a general clampdown on freedom of expression in several Gulf Countries.

Among her recent collections are *Qasā'id Hubb* (Love Odes), written in traditional meters and rhyme, and *Sabābat al-Muhrah al-Umaniyah* (The Yearnings of an Arabian Mare), both published in 1985. She is also credited with a book of short stories entitled *'Urūq al-Jīr wa-l-Hinna* (Veins of Lime and Henna). One of her earlier collections of poetry, *Khtwa Fawq al-Ard* (Footsteps over the Earth, n.d.) is represented by the following selections.

from FADINGS OF MEMORY

I shall see you,
When I decide not to see you
Prisoner of the sleepy pursuit in my soul
The gateway of silence, crouching in the vales
      of the volcano.

I got used to counting the frontiers between
       you and me

Frontiers of a stupid love
The escaping storm
is still between you and me

The dawn is sad
The rain falls
We ignore its source
The salty rains drifted into the circles of sweet
         rain

I held out my hand towards your lips
And your blaming eyes
You were aware that it was the touch before
         last

Between the rails of angry silence...
     Translated by Mona N. Mikhail

THE TEN COMMANDMENTS

Thou shalt not write the names in the sands of
         dust
Which crawling reptiles turn into burning
         coals
Like letters
In the night, thou shalt not depart a stranger
        like a traveling bat
Bored between shores in the eyelids of the sun
Thou shalt not lie, shalt not steal, shalt not
         tyrannize
Thou shalt not commit adultery
Shalt not, shalt not, shalt not, fivefold shalt
         not....

Do not grow trees in them
With green wires
And sparks that spread out in valleys that
       forget the wavings of his forehead
And allows himself the re-drawing of
         fingerprints
No thou shalt not and tenfold thou shalt not
     Translated by Mona N. Mikhail

Loula Anagnostáki   *Greece, contemporary*

Born in Thessalonika, Loula Anagnostáki is a leading Greek playwright with an international reputation; her plays have been translated into English, French, Italian, and Polish and have been broadcast on the radio by the BBC, the RAI (Italian radio) and in Cyprus. Her brother is the left-wing poet Manolis Anagnostákis.

Anagnostáki first came to public attention for her program of one-act plays, *I Dianyktérefsi* (Overnight Stop), *I Póli* (The City), and *I Parélasi* (*The Parade*) by the company of the leading Greek director, Karolos Koun, at the Art Theatre in Athens in 1965. *Níke* (Victory) staged in 1978 by Koun, has been described as a turning point in postmodern Greek theatre, and *I Kaséta* (The Cassette), staged in 1982 by Koun, caused a considerable critical stir.

Anagnostáki's plays are a search for meaning in a world without metaphysical absolutes. In her early plays the characters are searching, in dream and in reality, for a place that will allow them to discover and explore themselves, although they are thwarted at every turn. The relationship of her philosophical position to European existentialist and absurdist thought is evident, but the portraiture of humankind in a permanent state of "exile" makes a typically Greek, concrete image out of the absurdist theme of alienation. In these early plays, Anagnostáki's worldview is not completely negative; the struggle for meaningful human relationships is shown as worth continuing. The frustrated search for meaning also raises the question of the freedom of the individual against society and its oppression. Violence and the threat of violence are ever-present motifs, particularly in *The Parade* and *Antonio*. In *Niké* Anagnostáki has moved to a negative view of human existence as meaningless, but she asserts the individual's right to commit acts, even if negative, which justify his or her being. Self-knowledge, she feels, requires the recognition that humans are free to act, though acts in themselves can have no meaning—thus the pointless circularity of life in *I Kaséta* is broken by the pistol shot that defiantly destroys it at the end.

The following one-acter, *The Parade*, was first performed in the same bill as The City. It was published in 1971 with two other plays under the general title *I Póli* (The City). A brother and sister, aimlessly bickering in their apartment, gradually become fascinated with the preparations for a parade about to go by their window. The brother, who is 17, plays endlessly with militaristic toys. His sister, who is 23, sings and knits. Eventually they are drawn, rather against their will, to the spectacle that is taking place outside. Note that their names are symbolic: Ares, the god of War, and Zoë, the Greek word for life. The excerpt is from the end of the play.

Christopher Robinson

from **THE PARADE**
I Parélasi

ARES: I can't see properly. They're bringing something back. It looks like a cart. [*Uncertainly.*] A cart with wooden bars on its sides and top. I could just see the edge of it and then they stopped it.

[*The dull sound of horse hooves is heard.*]

ZOË: What was that?

ARES: The mounted police. They've just ridden up there, if it actually was the mounted police...I'm not sure any more, I don't recognize their uniforms...[*horses' hooves again.*] They've divided into two ranks, as if to leave a space for the cart to go in between them.

[ZOË *gets up and goes towards him.*]

ZOË: [*In a slightly strange voice*] Go on, what's happening now?

ARES: Wait a moment...There's those people pushing and shoving again. They're trying to get under the ropes...Gently does it...Hey, you there, the man in the flat cap! Where do you think you're going? Get back in there, get back. And the fat lady who's trying to get right in front, yes you, you too, get back to your place, quickly...Oh yes! The boy scouts know their job. The cart is gradually starting to move, it's come right forward—I can't see properly—the man on the horses are in my way. It isn't a cart!...[*Turns to his sister in bewilderment*] Zoë! It's a cage,* a long narrow cage on wheels, and there must be animals inside because they're jumping about and hanging on to the bars.... [*Irritated*] Those wretched mounted police are in the way again!...It's...it's people, Zoë! They've got people in the cage!

ZOË: [*Climbs to the window and also looks out.*] What a crowd!

ARES: There! Look! Where I'm pointing...

ZOË: The square is full...The dogs...Show me where the dogs are...

ARES: Did you see the cage?

ZOË: Where? Where? I can't see...

ARES: Look, there! Over there! Between the horses...

ZOË: Oh yes, black horses. Did you count them?

ARES: [*Crossly*] Look at what I'm trying to show you. What can you see between the two rows of horses?

ZOË: A cage. And there are people in it.

ARES: Did you ever see anything like it!

ZOË: They're naked...Where are the dogs? I want to see the dogs.

ARES: They're old.

ZOË: They've got long hair.

ARES: They're clinging to the bars.

ZOË: They look as if they want to throw themselves out.

ARES: They're as thin as skeletons.

ZOË: They're lunatics, that's what they are, lunatics. They're bringing lunatics to the square...

ARES: Oh no...Oh don't look any more, don't look.

[ZOË *struggles to get free.*]

ZOË: Let go of me. I want to see. [ARES *prevents her.*] What is it? What can you see?

ARES: It's awful...Didn't you notice anything?...

ZOË: No. Tell me quickly, tell me...

ARES: All those people in that cage...they're all maimed...Some have got no legs, some no hands...There's even one without a head, heaven help me. I'm right, he hasn't got a head...But his throat is still moving...

ZOË: [*Hysterically*] Shut the window, quickly, shut it!

ARES: It's not just old people, there are some children with them...There, one of them is holding a child up...Oh!...

ZOË: What? What is it?

ARES: Its face, it's all disfigured, it's burnt...

[*The noise of the crowd comes drifting up.*]

ZOË: [*Blocking her ears*] Shut the window. Shut it!

[ARES *stands quite still. Silence. Immediately afterward there is an enormous din.*]

ZOË [*Continues slowly, in a frightened voice, but with an air of unhealthy curiosity*] What was that noise?

ARES: The crowd surged forward and broke the ropes, they're pouring into the square...But they're stopping them, they're pushing them back again, they're beating them back. The scouts are whipping them with the ends of the snapped ropes, the others have got down off their horses and are beating them with their lances. One of them has got a woman by the hair, he's throwing her to the ground, he's kicking her in the face...[*suddenly bursts into tears*]

ZOË: [*Hysterically*] Get away from the window, get away from it quickly...[*pause*] Go on, what can you see?

ARES: [*Stifling a sob and speaking in a toneless voice*] It's all quiet again. They've all gone back to their places. The square is empty in the middle. There's only the dogs left. And the statue. Even the people in the cage aren't moving...My frien...the fell...the fellow I told you about who let his hair grow long is going up to the statue. He's clapping his hands. They're looking towards the church again. They're bringing someone out. They're dragging him by the hands because he can't walk on his own, he can't see. [*He begins to get caught up in what he is describing again, his voice becomes full of emotion.*] His face is covered with a bandage, that's why they're leading him along, he's stumbling at every step, they're all looking at him...

[*He lets out a stifled cry.*]

ZOË: What is it? What did you see?

ARES: I'm scared.

ZOË: [*Gently trembling*] Why are you scared?

ARES: That man...

ZOË: Go on, go on...

ARES: He's wearing a blue jacket with a yellow pullover underneath...

[ZOË *scrambles up.*]

ZOË: Open the window, I want to see properly...

ARES: Wait...

[*They look at each other.*]

ZOË: [*Quietly*] Is it father?

ARES: What's he doing in the square?

ZOË: He didn't tell us he'd be coming to the parade.

[*Pause*, Ares *gradually turns back to the window.*]

ARES: Look. Now they're uncovering his face.

[*A long pause while they both stare out.*]

ZOË: It isn't him...

ARES: It's a stranger! It was the clothes that confused us.

ZOË: Do you know him?

ARES: No, first time I've seen him.

ZOË: How pale he is. His face is whiter than the bandage he was wearing.

ARES: Look! His hands are tied.

ZOË: So are his feet.

ARES: That's why he keeps stumbling like that...What will they do to him?

ZOË: Oh! They're uncovering the statue. They're uncovering it.

ARES: It isn't a statue.

ZOË: No, it isn't a statue...What is it? Tell me what it is.

ARES: It's a gallows. No, it's not a gallows, it's a guillotine. Like the one they had in the French Revolution, you remember, there's a picture in the history book...[*Gets down, snatches up a book, and leafs through it looking for the illustration as confirmation.*]

ZOË: Ares, that man, the one with the long hair, he's got, he's putting him in there...in *there*, Ares! They're going to kill him. They've made him go down on his knees and they're going to cut his head off...[ARES *rushes to the window.*] And nobody's saying anything...Open the window, call out, do something...

[ARES, *as though in a dream, opens the window. A low buzz of noise is heard.*]

ARES: Hey, you!...Hey!

ZOË: They can't hear.

ARES: They're going...They're leaving the square to go and hide. Can't you see? They're riding them down, they're shooting them...Hey, don't go...They're going to kill him. [*He is almost in tears as a confused hum of voices and a clatter of hooves are heard.*] There's blood on his face.

ZOË: Ares, the dogs! They're setting the dogs on him, all the dogs have hurled themselves on him, they're pulling him to pieces.

ARES: I can't see anything anymore...I can't make anything out...

ZOË: They're tearing him to pieces!

ARES: I can't see anything...I can't make anything out...

ZOË: Ares, get down! Get away from the window!...The man with the long hair is looking at us.

ARES: Yes, he's looking at us. He saw us...

ZOË: He's making a sign to the others. They'll come here, they'll come up here. There! The others are looking this way now! They're coming...Ares, they're coming...Don't, don't come up!...[*She retreats.*]

[ARES, *with an air of coming to his senses, looks around him.*]

ZOË: They're coming up the stairs...They'll break the door down...[*She retreats farther.*] They're coming...they're coming...they're coming.

ARES: [*Rushes to the door, leans his back against it and shouts*] No! No! No!

[ZOË *goes on walking backward like a robot, with her hands held out in front of her, as though to protect herself.*]

ARES: No! No! No!

[*The voices of the mob begin to be covered by triumphal military marches, which eventually dominate completely. At the climax, the music cuts off abruptly and the lights go out.*]

Translated by Christopher Robinson

NOTE

* The word for "cage" is also the word for a "police van" in Greek. This second meaning has to be borne in mind in what follows.

Franca de Armiño   US, fl. 1930s

Presently, little is known about Franca de Armiño; the name may even be pseudonymous.[1] What we do have is the overtly political, Brechtian play *Los hipócritas* which Armino wrote in 1933 and was first produced in New York's Park Palace Theatre on April 15 and 16, 1933, by the Manuel Santigosa Company, a noted Puerto Rican acting company.[2] In her dedication to the play, de Armiño claims that while the play was well received, the Great Depression delayed the play's publication for four years. More likely, however, the overt socialist themes of *Los hipócritas* prevented its publication until 1937.

From the language of the play and from the author's list of works "in progress," we can surmise that de Armiño was an intellectual and a poet as well as a playwright. Her works include *Tragedia Puertorriqueña* (A Puerto Rican Tragedy), "a dramatic comedy of social criticism concerning Hispanic-American customs;" *Aspectos de la Vida* (Aspects of Life), "philosophical essays on life, nature, humanity, and the universe;" and *Luz en Las Tinieblas* (Darkness Illuminated), "poetry on diverse themes" (no dates available).

De Armiño dedicates *Los hipócritas* to the oppressed of the world and to those who work for social change. Following an internationalist agenda, she stresses that her purpose is to make the play adaptable to any country. Although she sets this version in Spain, she encourages future readers and producers to adapt it to fit similar social issues facing workers throughout the world. De Armiño chose to set the play in Spain because of the Spanish Democratic Revolution two years previous in 1931: the people had deposed the King.

Undoubtedly, de Armiño's concerns were more socialist than feminist; the play's action centers around the struggle between the workers of a shoe factory, led by Gerónimo, and the factory owner, Don Severo. Nevertheless, an equally important motif for contemporary feminist readers is Gloria's encounter with the various faces of the patriarchy: the Church, the class system, fascism, and her more immediate master, her father, Don Severo. In love with Gerónimo, Gloria rejects her parents' attempts to marry her off to an impoverished aristocrat, Angelito. De Armiño shows the frailty of the class system when she has the four young people in the play fall in love with people outside their class: Gloria loves Gerónimo and Angelito loves Silberia, a poor orphan who is Doña Inocencia's maid.

The corruption of the capitalists is linked to the corruption of the Church when the priest, Cándido, supposedly in league with Don Severo to convince Gloria to marry Angelito, decides that Gloria's money should come directly to the Church. He recruits Gloria's chaperone, Doña Inocencia, to convince Gloria to enter the convent. In the same room at Don Severo's house, Juan, Gerónimo's as yet unenlightened father, hides and waits for Don Severo in order to beg for his job, which he has lost as a result of Gerónimo's labor activities.

While the play is indeed a comedy and the servants are often objects of comedy, in one scene (4.13) de Armiño further subverts social conventions by having two servants, Elena and Manuel, interpret and comment on the social relevance of the play's action. Manuel compares the packages he carries to the packaging of Gloria in order to sell her to the Duke for his millions and his title. Elena replies that she is glad they are class conscious and do not allow themselves the hypocrisies of capitalism.

Using the didactic, Brechtian techniques familiar to today's audiences of the contemporary Chicano political theater, Teatro Campesino, de Armiño's play is obviously meant to unmask the hypocrisies of capitalism and the patriarchy to her audiences. In the play's final scene, all the actors are on stage for the denouement, in which the characters' ideologically base motives are revealed and a new consciousness is born in this socialist version of the happy ending; and in the way of more traditional romantic comedies, the women also win their men.

Sonia Saldívar-Hull

NOTES

1. The information here is from de Armiño's dedication to the play and from an interview with Nicolás Kanellos, who joins in our search for our literary foremothers; as publisher of Arte Público Press and *The Americas Review* (formerly *Revista Chicano-Riqueña*), he has done much to publish the works of contemporary Puerto Rican and Chicana writers.
2. In the 1920s and 1930s, New York received a wave of exiles from Spain, resulting in the production of many Hispanic plays. Santigosa himself was a Spaniard.

from THE HIPPOCRITES
Los hipócritas

SCENE XVII

[DOÑA INOCENCIA *and* GLORIA *enter the stage through the rear, conversing animatedly, and then sit down on the armchairs next to the center table.*]

DOÑA INOCENCIA: I'm telling you, dear, it's better that you become Jesus Christ's wife . . . .

GLORIA: [*Surprised*] And is Jesus Christ in love with me?

[JUAN *quietly pokes his head out, comically making surprised gestures, and hides again behind the folding screen.*]

DOÑA INOCENCIA: No, dear, no. He loves all of humanity, all his wives . . . Do you understand? He has many wives . . .

GLORIA: [*Sarcastically*] And, who are Jesus Christ's wives? . . .

DOÑA INOCENCIA: The nuns, dear, the nuns . . .

GLORIA: [*Mockingly*] But, tell me, Doña Inocencia, does each one of those wives know that Jesus Christ is a husband of the others, and so polygamous?

DOÑA INOCENCIA: [*Astonished, making the sign of the cross*] Jesus, Holy Mary! Don't say that, dear! Jesus Christ's wives love him spiritually, not physically.

[JUAN *quietly peeks out of his hiding place, comically making gestures of amazement and the sign of the cross as he hides once more.*]

GLORIA: Well, I would not be content with the love of a spirit with no body. Besides, I would never marry a man with so many wives, as Jesus Christ who, according to what you say, is a sultan . . . Prostitution has got to disappear. Women should not be slaves of the brothel. Love should be free, not imposed.

DOÑA INOCENCIA: [*Never before so bewildered, attempting to interrupt* GLORIA *and making the sign of the cross*] Silence, silence, dear . . . do not blaspheme that way . . . Jesus, Holy Mary! But what are you saying? . . .

GLORIA: I am saying that I am marrying Gerónimo, my fiancé; he knows me and I know him . . .

JUAN: [*Pokes his head out of his hideout, more astounded than before, then hiding again with comic gestures, says softly*] But . . . can this be possible? Is this young lady my son's fiancé? The world is upside down!

DOÑA INOCENCIA: [*With character and emphasis*] No, missy, no . . . You are well off and Gerónimo is a poor laborer . . . You have no idea what it means to be Jesus Christ's wife. Except on rare occasions, no one who does not have a dowry . . . can aspire to such an honor . . . You would be highly honored and you would in turn honor your parents . . .

GERÓNIMO: [*Coming out of his hiding place, wrathful, and sarcastically speaking to Doña Inocencia*] So you are the personified innocence about whom I had heard, huh? . . .

DOÑA INOCENCIA: [*Frightened, interrupting him, she gets up and steps back.*] Jesus, Holy Mary! . . . But where has this man come from?

GERÓNIMO: No doubt you are following Father Candido's orders.

DOÑA INOCENCIA: [*Angry*] Me? . . . Lie, you lie. But, how dare you enter this house?

GLORIA: [*Happily yet nervously runs toward Gerónimo*] I am so glad you have arrived! . . . Because of this damned woman I have not been able to get ready. Wait, I'll be right back . . .

GERÓNIMO: Don't take long . . .

DOÑA INOCENCIA: [*Speaking simultaneously as* GLORIA *says the previous lines and attempting to follow her*] Jesus, Holy Mary! . . . Gloria! Gloria! . . . Stay away from that man! What are you doing? Where are you going?

[GERÓNIMO *blocks her way.*]

DOÑA INOCENCIA: [*Confronting him*] Insolent! Let me pass . . .

GERÓNIMO: [*Sarcastically*] So the orders are

to marry Gloria with Jesus Christ, put her in the convent and take the dowry to fill your church's treasury, huh?...ha...ha...ha...Lucrative business!

DOÑA INOCENCIA: [*Angrily speaking simultaneously with Gerónimo*] No, no, no...lie, you lie, you vile scoundrel...My only concern is to have Gloria become Jesus Christ's wife to honor her parents...

GERÓNIMO: [*Sarcastically*] Hypocrite!...You are wasting your time. Gloria is intelligent and does not believe in your sophistic advice...Out! Out of here!...At once!

DOÑA INOCENCIA: [*Defiantly and loudly*] How dare you!...You should be the one to leave. If not, I will call Don Severo...

SCENE XXII

[DON SEVERO *and the* DUKE *enter the stage as* DOÑA AMALIA *speaks to* DOÑA INOCENCIA...]

DON SEVERO: [*Astonished and in a very loud voice*] Amalia! What is this? Gerónimo in this house, and you allow it!

DOÑA AMALIA: [*Nervous and scared*] No, no, Severo, no. I just arrived and, like you, I found him here.

DON SEVERO: [*Speaking to* GERÓNIMO *authoritatively*] Gerómino, get out of my house immediately! [*Meanwhile, the Duke adjusts his monocle as he examines* GERÓNIMO, *up and down, with curiosity.* JUAN *pokes his head out, comically demonstrates fear, and quietly hides again.*]

GERÓNIMO: [*Defiantly and firmly*] Gloria and I are leaving, but not before finding out about your mischievous plotting.

DON SEVERO: [*Authoritatively yells to* GERÓNIMO, *pointing to the* DUKE] You are leaving, but not Gloria. Gloria is the Duke's son's fiancé.

SILBERIA: [*Snapping out of her absorption as she hears* DON SEVERO *speaking, she shrieks*] I am Angelito's fiancé!...

ANGELITO: [*General amazement on stage, as they all turn to look at* SILBERIA *and* ANGELI-

TO. *As he notices his father walking toward him,* ANGELITO *grabs* SILBERIA's *hand and runs with her off stage.*] M...m...my...my...my...fa...fa...fa...ther...er...er...Let's...let's...go...oo...oo!

DUKE: [*Alarmed, he attempts to follow* ANGELITO, *but* GERÓNIMO *blocks his way, while* DON SEVERO *speaks to* GLORIA *softly.*] Angelito!...Angelito!...Where are you going with that plebian? Wait, wait for me, my son.

GERÓNIMO: [*Stopping the* DUKE] Let them go. It's youth rebelling against your old methods.

DUKE: But it's my son! The inheritor of my title! My only hope!...

GERÓNIMO: Your son, yes. But not your slave. What's more, those damned inheritances are condemned to disappear, because they are responsible for having brought divisions and wars between men.

DUKE: [*Resigned to not leaving, he walks toward the couch in front of the folding screen where* JUAN *is hiding.* JUAN *pokes his head out observing and listening in astonishment.*] Damn my luck! All my plans failed! I am ruined!...Ruined! My only solution is suicide!...

[*Overwhelmed, the* DUKE *falls onto the extreme left of the couch, holding his head between his hands. The devout* DOÑA INOCENCIA *and* DOÑA AMALIA *have been praying, their expressions anguished. Meanwhile,* DON SEVERO *has been begging* GLORIA *to marry* ANGELITO. *After her continuous disobedient no's, he desperately holds his hands against his chest, as if suffering an acute pain. Trembling, he moves toward the armchair, holds himself up from its back and with supreme effort yells.*]

DON SEVERO: Gloria!...Gloria!...If you do not marry Angelito, I am doomed, doomed forever!...[*As* GLORIA *hears her father, she indignantly moves away from him, seeking* GERÓNIMO's *protection and taking his arm, while the latter welcomes her happily.*]

JUAN: [*Since he has also heard* DON SEVERO's

words, he resolutely comes out of his hiding-place, wrathful, waving a fist, threatening DON SEVERO *and company.*] Scoundrels! ...To think that I was coming to beg for work. Now I understand your infamies. My son was right in rebelling against this damned capitalism! [*General amazement. The* DUKE *raises his head and, astonished, listens to* JUAN.]

DON SEVERO: [*Sober and trembling, he presses his hand against his heart.*] Ungrateful...

JUAN: [*With irony and defiantly*] And you still want me to thank you for the twenty years you have slavedriven me, paying me slave wages, while you were getting richer. Infamous! Nice solution to my problem! In my old age, after I have given you my best years, you throw me out in the street, with no concern if my family starves to death. And if this were not enough, you also throw my son out for the crime of demanding his rights. You boycott us so that no one in this city will hire us. Is this what you want me to thank you for? [*General amazement. Sober and nervous, incapable of speaking,* DON SEVERO *presses his hand against his heart, demonstrating he is very ill.* DOÑA AMALIA, *the priest, the devout woman, and the* DUKE *get close to him, while* GLORIA *remains close to* GERÓNIMO, *who is stretching out his arms to his father. At this moment, behind the scenes, faraway voices of a multitude are being heard: "Long live the United Front! Long live the Frente Popular! Long live the Social Revolution! ...Long live the strike! Down with fascism!..." These voices increasingly become louder until the curtain falls.*]

Translated by Clara Lomas

Rosario Ferré   *US(Puerto Rico), contemporary*

Daughter of a former governor of Puerto Rico, Rosario Ferré has written poems, essays, and short stories. She is highly regarded in her native country, where she cofounded *Zona de carga y descarga* (Loading Zone), an avant-garde political and literary journal.

Ferré's first publication, in 1976, was the collection of short stories *Papeles de Pandora* (Pandora's Papers). She has also written stories for children and a collection of essays about women writers entitled *Sitio a Eros* (Besieging Eros, 1980). Her major themes, which we can see developed in the following selection, include issues of sex, race, and class.

THE YOUNGEST DOLL

The old aunt had taken her rocking chair out onto the balcony overlooking the cane fields very early as she always did whenever she awoke with the urge to make a doll. As a young girl she used to bathe in the river quite often, but one day when the rain had swollen the current into the lash of a dragon's tail, she had felt a soft feeling of melting snow in the marrow of her bones. Her head submerged in the dark echo chamber of the rocks, she thought she had heard, mingled with the sound of the water, the salt bursts on the faraway beach and felt that her hair had poured out into the sea at last. Precisely at that moment she felt a terrible bite on her calf. They pulled her screaming out of the water and carried her back to the house writhing with pain on a stretcher.

The doctor who examined her assured them that it was nothing; she'd most likely been bitten by a vicious river prawn. Days went by, however, and the wound refused to heal. After a month the doctor had come to the conclusion that the prawn had got into the fleshy part of the calf, where it had evidently begun to fatten. He prescribed a mustard plaster to be applied so that the heat would force the thing out. The aunt spent a whole week with her leg rigid, before her, covered with mustard from ankle to thigh, but when the treatment was over it was discovered that the wound had puffed up even more and was coated with a slimy stone-like substance that would have been impossible to remove without endangering the whole leg. She then became resigned to living with the prawn curled up forever inside the grotto of her calf.

She had been very beautiful, but the prawn that she hid under the long muslin folds of her skirt had stripped her of all vanity. She shut herself up in the house, rejecting all suitors. At first she had dedicated herself to the rearing of her sister's daughters, dragging the monstrous leg about the house with amazing agility. By that time the family was living surrounded by a past that was breaking up all around them with the same impassive musicality with which the crystal chandelier was falling into pieces on the frayed cloth of the dining room table. The girls adored their aunt. She combed their hair, bathed them, and fed them. When she read them stories they would sit around her on the floor and find some way delicately to lift the starched ruffles of her skirt in order to catch a whiff of the odor of ripe sweetsops that the leg gave off when it was at rest.

As the girls grew older the aunt busied herself making dolls for them to play with. At first they were only ordinary dolls, with cotton stuffing and stray buttons sewn on for eyes. But as time went on she refined her art until she had won the respect and reverence of the whole family. The birth of a doll was always the reason for a sacred celebration, which explained why it never occurred to them that the dolls might be sold, not even when the girls were already grown and the family was beginning to fall into need. The aunt had been making the dolls bigger so that they would match the height and measurements of each of the girls. Since there were nine of them and she made a doll of each girl every year, they had to set aside a room in the house as the exclusive quarters of the dolls. By the time the oldest girl had become eighteen there were a hundred twenty-six dolls of all ages in the room. On opening the door one had the feeling of going into a dovecote or the doll room in the tsarina's palace or a warehouse where a long row of tobacco leaves had been spread out to ripen. Nevertheless, the aunt didn't go into the room looking for any of those pleasures. She would throw the bolt and go along lifting up each one of the dolls lovingly, humming to them as she rocked them: "That's what you were like when you were a year old, when you were two, when you were three," reliving the life of each one of them through the empty space they left between her arms.

The day the oldest of the girls turned ten the aunt sat down in her chair facing the cane fields and never got up again. She would rock on the balcony for days on end watching the running tints in the cane leaves pour over the fields like water and she would only come out of her lethargy when the doctor came to see her on those special days or when she woke up with the urge to make a doll. Then she would start shouting for everyone in the house to come help her. The plantation workers could be seen on that day running back and forth to town like merry Inca[1] messengers to buy wax or porcelain clay, lace, needles, spools of thread of all colors. While these errands were being carried out, the aunt would call the girl she'd dreamed about the night before to her room and take her measurements. Then she would make a wax mask of her and cover it with plaster on both sides, like a living face between two dead ones. Then she would let an interminable light-colored little thread of melted wax drain out through a dimple in the chin. The porcelain of the hands and face was always translucent; it had a slight tint of ivory that contrasted with the curdled whiteness of bisque faces. To make the body the aunt would send to the garden for twenty shiny gourds. She would take them in one hand and with an expert whirl of the blade she would slice them into gleaming green leather skulls. Then she would lean them against the railing of the balcony so that the sun and breezes would dry out their cottony gray guano[2] brains. After a few days she would scoop out the contents with a silver spoon and with infinite patience feed it in through the doll's mouth.

The only compromise the aunt made in the creation of the dolls regarding items not of her manufacture was with the glass balls for the eyes. They were mailed from Europe, in all colors, but the aunt didn't consider them usable until they had been submerged for a number of days at the bottom of the stream so they would learn to recognize the slightest stirring of the prawns' antennae. Only then would the rinse them with ammonia and lay them out gleaming like gems on a bed of cotton at the bottom of one of her Dutch cookie tins. The dolls' clothing never varied in spite of the fact that the girls were growing older. She always dressed the youngest in Swiss embroidery and the older ones in silk guipure.[3] On their heads she would always tie the same bow, wide and white and tremulous, like the breast of a dove.

The girls began to get married and leave home. On the wedding day she would present each one with her last doll, kissing the girl on the forehead and saying with a smile, "Here is your Easter." She would reassure the bridegroom by telling him that the doll was only a sentimental ornament, of the kind that in houses of days gone by used to sit on the lid of grand pianos. From up on her balcony the aunt would watch the girl go down the wide front steps of the house for the last time, holding in one hand her modest plaid suitcase and wrapping the other arm around the waist of that exuberant doll made in her image and likeness, shod with kid slippers, with Valencienne pantalettes[4] barely showing under snowy laced skirts. The hands and faces of those dolls, however, could be seen to be less transparent, having the consistency of skim milk. This difference concealed another more subtle one: the wedding doll was never filled with wadding but with honey.

All the other girls had been married and now only the youngest was left at home when the doctor paid the aunt his monthly visit, bringing along his son who had just come back from his medical studies up north. The young man lifted the starched fringe of her skirt and stood looking at the enormous bloated bladder from which a perfumed sperm oozed continuously through the tips of its greenish scales. He took out his stethoscope and listened to it carefully. The aunt thought he was listening for the prawn's breathing to see if it was still alive, and taking his hand tenderly, she placed it over a certain spot so he could feel the constant movement of the antennae. The young man dropped the skirt and stared at his father. "You could have cured this at the start," he told him. "That's true," his father answered, "I only wanted you to come and see the prawn that paid for your education over the past twenty years."

From then on it was the young doctor who visited the old aunt every month. His interest in the youngest girl was soon obvious and the aunt was able to begin her last doll with ample anticipation. He always appeared in his starched collar, his brightly shined shoes, and with the gaudy oriental stickpin of a despicable beggar. After examining the aunt he would sit in the parlor, resting his paper shadow against an oval frame, at the same time as he offered the youngest girl the usual sprig of purple immortelles. She would offer him gingerbread cookies and take the sprig fastidiously with the tips of her fingers as one might pick up a sea urchin turned inside out. She decided to marry him because she was intrigued by his sleepy profile and because she now had an urge to find out what dolphin flesh was like inside.

On her wedding day, when the youngest girl was about to leave the house, she held the doll around the waist and was surprised to find it warm. She forgot about it at once, however, so amazed she was at its artistic excellence. The hands and face were made of the most delicate mikado porcelain. In the half-opened and somewhat sad smile she recognized her complete set of baby teeth. There was, in addition, another special detail. The aunt had encrusted her diamond drop earrings into the eye sockets.

The young doctor took her off to live in town, in a square house that looked like a cement block. He made her sit on the balcony every day so that the people passing on the street would be sure to see that he had married into society. Motionless inside her hot cube, the youngest girl began to suspect that her husband not only had a paper profile but a paper soul as well. Her suspicions were confirmed in a short time. One day he pried the eyes out of the doll with the tip of his scalpel and pawned the earrings for an expensive gold pocket watch with a long embossed chain. From then on the doll remained sitting on the lid of the grand piano, but with its eyelids modestly lowered.

A few months later the young doctor noticed that the doll was missing and asked the youngest girl what she'd done with it. A sisterhood of pious ladies had offered him a goodly amount for the hands and face of mikado porcelain, which they thought would be perfect for the figure of the Virgin on their altarpiece next Lent. The youngest girl answered him that the ants had finally discovered that the doll was filled with honey and had devoured it in a single night. Since the hands and face were made of mikado porcelain, she said, they must have thought they were glazed with sugar and at that very moment were probably breaking their teeth as they furiously gnawed

on fingers and eyelids in some underground burrow. That night the doctor dug up the garden around the house without finding anything.

Years passed and the doctor became a millionaire. He had gathered in all the patients in town who didn't mind paying exorbitant fees in order to get a close look at a legitimate member of the extinct sugar-cane aristocracy. The youngest girl continued to sit on the balcony, motionless in her muslin and lace, always with her eyelids lowered. When her husband's patients, overloaded with necklaces, plumes, and walking sticks, sat near her, settling their rolls of satisfied flesh deep into their chairs with a hubbub of coins, they perceived around them a peculiar smell that made them involuntarily recall the slow supuration of a sweetsop. They would then be seized with an irresistible urge to rub their hands together as if they were honing them.

One thing disturbed the doctor's contentment. He noticed that as he grew older the youngest girl still kept the same firm and porcelained skin that she had had when he would call on her at the big house in the cane fields. One night he decided to go into her room and observe her in her sleep. He noticed that her chest wasn't moving. He then carefully placed his stethoscope over her heart and heard a distant swirl of water. At that moment the doll opened her eyelids and out of the empty sockets of her eyes he saw the furious antennae of the prawns begin to emerge.

Translated by Gregory Rabassa

NOTES

1. South American Indians whose empire, which extended throughout the Andean region, flourished in the fourteenth and fifteenth centuries.
2. Excrement, particularly from birds found along the coast, and used as fertilizer.
3. A kind of lace.
4. Long lacy underpants.

Women's Literary Traditions: Regional Essays

AFRICA

Neil Lazarus

With respect to Africa, the first point to be noted about the century from 1875 to 1975 is that it effectively marks the era of formal European colonialism. Before 1875, the imperial powers, particularly Britain and France but also Portugal, Germany, Belgium, Italy, and Spain, had long been engaged in aggressive interventionist activity in Africa, in terms of which populations were forcibly subordinated and territory seized. In 1884–1885, representatives of these powers met in Berlin, at what became known as the "Scramble for Africa" conference. A blueprint was drawn up for the partition of Africa into discrete "spheres of influence." Each imperial power would be free to act in its "own" sphere of influence as it saw fit. The response of local African populations to European invasion in the ensuing years was, as the British historian Basil Davidson has noted, resistive but unavailing; and it was only in the years following World War II that anticolonial movements began to gather the momentum that would enable them first to challenge and then to topple their European rulers in colony after colony.[1] Egypt only achieved independence in 1952, Ghana only in 1957, Guinea in 1958, Nigeria and Senegal in 1960, Algeria in 1962, Kenya in 1963, Zambia in 1964, Guinea-Bissau in 1974, Angola and Mozambique in 1975, and Zimbabwe as recently as 1980.

In the struggle against colonialism, the participation of women was crucial, and often decisive. In his essay "Algeria Unveiled," the celebrated Antillean psychiatrist and anticolonial revolutionary Frantz Fanon writes about the impact and implications of the changing roles assumed by women activists in the revolution against French occupation in Algeria.[2] The Senegalese writer and filmmaker Sembene Ousmane does much the same in his novel *God's Bits of Wood* (1957), a fictionalized reconstruction of the heroic strike undertaken by African railworkers in French West Africa in 1947–1948. Sembene focuses explicitly on the contribution of women to the success of this strike, suggesting that through their resourcefulness in fending for the community at large during the long months of hunger and deprivation they not only made victory possible but also forged a new self-awareness of the social power they wielded as women. Throughout Africa, in fact, the struggle against colonialism mobilized women as political actors even in those societies in which participation in the political sphere had hitherto been restricted to men.

Colonialism was a brutal and exploitative enterprise, and it visited great destruction upon Africa and African social organization. In parts of Africa, such as the Kenyan "highlands" and much of South Africa, the fabric of social life was torn apart almost completely. Throughout most of the continent, however, colonialism, for all its violence, did not succeed in decimating the forms of indigenous social existence. Despite colonialism, cultures and cultural institutions survived meaningfully. Even as they were being incorporated within and subordinated to an imperial economy, Africans were able to retain their languages and modes of indigenous cultural production. Their cultural activity, thus defined, constituted an integral part of their social life as it was lived; and women, self-evidently, were and have continued to be indispensable to its elaboration. In the oral tradition (within which all of this type of cultural activity was couched), the voice of women has never been silent. Typically, though by no means always, this voice has been collectivistic and generalized. As singers of praise songs, dancers, community poets, and storytellers, African women have characteristically assumed a plural voice, speaking representatively as mothers, daughters, lovers, wives, cultivators, house-keepers. Occasionally, as among the Xhosa of South Africa, women have taken upon themselves the task of speaking on behalf of their communities at large, expressing their society's historical consciousness in its totality.[3]

The significance of the oral tradition in Africa cannot be overstated. In cultures that have historically been nonliterate and in cultures, such as the Hausa of northern Nigeria, in which, since the nineteenth-century, literacy among women has been socially restricted, it is oral culture that provides continuity with the past. In these cultures, it would be quite incorrect to think of orality as a "traditional" form, to be contrasted with the "modernity" of literacy. Oral culture continues to be decisive, the truly popular contemporary medium of artistic expression. The range of its reference is remarkable, extending from praise songs to political satire, from the bawdy to the religious, the formal to the informal and irreverent. Beverly Mack, in an article on Hausa women's poetry, provides us with an example of a contemporary woman poet, Binta Katsina, who "has become known for her song advocating women's participation in the Nigerian work force. In it the entertainer encourages Nigerian women to participate in 'every kind of work,' thus rejecting the northern traditional injunction against women's active public roles."[4] Mack draws attention to the paradoxical position occupied by women poets in Hausa culture: on the one hand, they articulate the experience of Hausa women; on the other, by virtue of their public role as poets, they themselves are unrepresentative of such women. Their "lifestyles deviate from traditional and conservative women's roles...[T]hese women say and do what other Hausa women cannot, criticizing the status quo and encouraging behavior that is not normally condoned."[5]

The bulk of the material included in this volume as "African literature" stems not from the universe of oral, but from that of literate, culture. Most was originally written in English; the remainder has been translated from the French. Throughout the colonial period in Africa, education was administered warily, with an eye toward its potentially radicalizing effect. Literacy was used as a form of social control. Opportunities for formal education were rare, and when these presented themselves, they were conventionally awarded to male students. Since public life became increasingly dependent on a colonial education, women were more or less systematically excluded from this realm. The result was that when, in the first decades of this century, and above all in West and South Africa, nationalist leaders began to make a name for themselves by writing and speaking out against colonial abuses, the overwhelming majority of them were men. In these early years, which extended all the way to 1945, very few African women writing in English, French, or Portuguese managed to make themselves heard.

There were notable exceptions, of course. Adelaide Casely-Hayford (1868–1969) of Sierra Leone was one such. Born into the Creole elite in Freetown, she became an active spokesperson for the nationalist cause in West Africa, following her celebrated husband, the Ghanaian lawyer Joseph Casely-Hayford, author of the first West African novel, *Ethiopia Unbound* (1911), in campaigning for unity, moderation, and a gradual transition to self-government. In her widely anthologized short story "Mista Courifer," she dramatized the political tensions of the early colonial years through the metaphor of a generational clash between a too hot-blooded son and his cautious, law-abiding father. In her later life, Casely-Hayford continued to write, compiling her memoirs, which were eventually published in 1969. A staunch advocate of education, she, with her sister, established a vocational school for girls in Freetown. A second West African, Mabel Dove Danquah (b. 1910), is worthy of mention here too. Like Adelaide Casely-Hayford a nationalist, and like her married to an influential politician (in her case J.B. Danquah), she entered political life after 1945 and became, in 1952, the first woman elected to political office in Ghana. In her many short stories and journalistic articles, Danquah tended to focus on the changing status of women in Ghana.

Other African women who pioneered a literary tradition in these early years included Asma'u (Nana) bint Shehu (1794–1863) of northern Nigeria, who wrote religious verse in Arabic, Fulfulde, and Hausa early in the nineteenth century, and the Swahili writer Siti binti Saad (ca. 1880–1950), whose poetry was composed chiefly with the intent of entertaining its audience. Both Asma'u and Siti binti Saad were unusual among women in receiving Koranic instruction; the latter was apprenticed to the popular Swahili poet Maalim Shabaan (b. ca. 1893). A selection of Siti binti Saad's song-poems, written down before performance, was published in Dar Es Salaam in the collection *Waimbaji wa juzi* (Singers of Yesteryear) in 1966.[6] In Southern Africa, a woman writer, L. Kakaza (ca. 1885–1950), was among a small group of writers responsible for the emergence of Xhosa literature during the first decades of this century. Kakaza is remembered for two works, *Intyatyambo yomzi* (The Flower in the Home, 1913) and *U-Tandiwe wakwa Gcaleka* (Tandiwe, a Girl of the Gcaleka, 1914), both of which reflected an appropriation of the nineteenth-century English novel and which helped to consolidate the emerging ethos of social realist prose fiction in Southern African literature.[7] She was followed by Victoria Swaartbooi (1907–1937), whose *U-Mandisa* (1933), though limited by its autobiographical origins and moralistic tone, marked another advance for women's creativity. Another Xhosa writer, L.T. Futshane (ca. 1915–1951), wrote somewhat later: her *U-Jujuju* (Magic), which appeared in 1938 and *Mhxa ngenqaha* (Mhla in Trouble), published posthumously in 1960, suggest the continuity of a Xhosa literary tradition.

In the years after World War II, after the anticolonial movement gathered momentum, an increasing number of intellectuals in Africa began composing literature in English, French, and Portuguese. Since the colonial education system continued to prefer male over female students, the majority of these new writers were men. A number of women, however—and again, particularly in Anglophone West Africa—managed to rise to prominence as members of this new generation. Two of the most significant of these were Efua Sutherland of Ghana and Flora Nwapa (b. 1931) of Nigeria. The career backgrounds of Sutherland (b. 1924) and Nwapa are similar. They both attended local schools and then traveled to Britain to study education; returning to Africa as "been-to's" (the term popularly used to refer to Africans who have traveled overseas, typically by way of obtaining educational or professional qualifications), they both worked in a variety of different cultural and educational institutions. In their writing, both have been concerned to represent the vitality of indigenous cultural forms, and both have written a number of works for children. The range and quality of Sutherland's work as dramatist, poet, and mixed-media artist are manifested in her bilingual poetry and plays and pictorial essays for children; her radio plays (*Foriwa* [1964] and *Edufa* [1966]); and the comedy *Marriage of Anansewa* (1975), based on the tales of Ananse, the Ghanaian trickster figure and symbol of Everyman. Yet Sutherland's significance cannot be measured in terms of her writing alone. In setting up the Ghana Drama Studio, a local writers' circle, and the important literary magazine, *Okyeame* Sutherland has fostered Ghanaian artists. Nwapa's significance, too, is greater than the sum of its parts. Her first novel, *Efuru* (1966) represented a major breakthrough: it was the first novel by a Nigerian woman to be published and the first novel by an African woman to be published in Britain. A short novel, *Never Again*, was published in 1976 and represents one of the earliest works to focus on the ruinous civil war and its effects upon ordinary Nigerians; but Nwapa's primary energies after the war were devoted to government service, first as Cabinet Minister of Health and Social Welfare responsible for reconstructing social services, and, subsequently, as Commissioner for Lands, Survey and Urban Development in eastern Nigeria. Since then she has set up her own printing press and publishing house. Her fourth novel, *One is Enough* (1981), and several of her works for children have been published by her company, whose general interest is in the continental distribution of works in indigenous African languages. Unlike Sutherland, Nwapa is an ardent feminist and champion of women's rights. It is as a feminist, in fact, that she needs to be read. In their focus upon patriarchal rural communities, novels like *Efuru* and *Idu* (1970) offer a searching critique of the work of such Nigerian male writers as Chinua Achebe and Onuora Nzekwu, in which the exploitation of women in the domestic sphere and the workplace is represented more or less uncritically. In the urban stories of *This Is Lagos and Other Stories* (1971), by the same token, Nwapa may be seen to be offering a repudiation of the masculinist depiction of women presented above all, in Nigeria, by Cyprian Ekwensi and Nkem Nwankwo.

It is possible, in fact, to see in Nwapa's work the point of departure for a writer like Buchi Emecheta (b. 1944), whose prolific output as a novelist since 1972, the date of publication of her first work, *In the Ditch*, has done a great deal to counter the stereotypical image of women in African literature. *In the Ditch* and *Second-Class Citizen* (1974) are both set in London, where Emecheta has lived since the mid-1960s. Her subsequent novels, however, have all been set in Nigeria and, taken together, constitute an uncompromising and austere examination of the hardships under which Nigerian women are living and have been compelled to live. The best of these later works is perhaps *The Joys of Motherhood* (1979), although *Destination Biafra* (1981) has also received considerable attention by virtue of its subject matter. Like Nwapa's *Never Again*, it offers a stinging indictment of the Nigerian civil war. In 1983 Emecheta published *The Double Yoke*, a novel about the contradictory demands placed upon contemporary Nigerian women attempting to advance socially in a hierarchical and male-dominated society. It is interesting to note in this context that Emecheta currently makes her home in Britain and thus, despite frequent visits to Africa, writes essentially as an expatriate. In *The Double Yoke* and elsewhere, she explores the complex issues surrounding women's experience of Western influences in colonial and postcolonial Africa. In common with other Third World women writers, she reaches the conclusion that in certain respects the embrace of Western styles enabled African women to contest the oppressive forms of indigenous patriarchal domination. Emecheta has also written a number of children's books. In 1986, Emecheta published an autobiography, entitled *Head Above Water*.

Other anglophone West African women writers have been able to build upon the achievements of Sutherland and Nwapa. Zulu Sofola (b. 1935) of Nigeria, a playwright and academic who teaches drama in the University of Ibadan, has published several plays, the most notable among them being *Wedlock of the Gods* (1972), which has a traditional setting and concerns the doomed attempt of a young widow to resist the dictates of custom, and *The Wizard of Law* (1975), a satirical farce exposing the crass materialism of the postcolonial urban elite in Nigeria. Ama Ata Aidoo (b. 1942) of Ghana received initial support in her career from Efua Sutherland and has emerged as a major and, like Sofola, an enormously versatile writer. In Aidoo's and Sofola's work there is a turn to the political in a direct sense. Both authors expose the shortcomings of postcolonial society, suggesting that the new elite that has come to power with the collapse of colonialism has in many respects simply stepped into the shoes of the departing British colonizers. The result is that although the nation is nominally independent, it is in fact still overwhelmingly colonial in its organizing structures.

Francophone West African writing remained an almost exclusively male preserve far longer than its anglophone counterpart. Indeed, it was only in 1976 that the first novel in French by an African woman was published. The novel in question, *Le revenant* (The Ghost), was written by Aminata Sow Fall (b. 1941) of Senegal. Set in the postcolonial present, it tells a familiar story of greed, corruption, and materialism among the Senegalese bureaucratic elite. Sow Fall's second novel, *La Grève des Bàttu* (*The Beggars' Strike*, 1979), however, was altogether more momentous. In conjunction with Mariama Bâ's *Une Si Longue Lettre* (*So Long a Letter*, 1980), in fact, it may be said to have propelled women's writing in Senegal to international prominence. *The Beggars' Strike* is a fiercely political novel, centering on the plight of a huge but marginalized and dispossessed stratum of modern Senegalese society, that composed of beggars, the disabled, and the urban unemployed, spawned by the system but neglected by it. The strike referred to in the novel's title is precipitated when a government minister resolves to remove all beggars from the streets of the capital city of an unnamed African nation. The presence of these beggars, it seems, is bad for business and tourism! *The Beggars' Strike* caused considerable controversy in Senegal and was awarded the 1980 Grand Prix Litteraire d'Afrique Noire. It was followed in 1982 by *L'Appel des arènes* (The Appeal of the Arenas). *So Long a Letter* is an equally eloquent work, although altogether different in scope and intent. Written by Mariama Bâ (1929– 1981), it centers on the lives of two privileged Senegalese women, juxtaposing their experiences as members of a class that gains power at independence with their experiences as women, still subordinated to male power. It won the first Noma Award in 1980. Before her death the following year, Bâ completed a second novel, *Un chant écarlate* (*Scarlet Song*). The period immediately following that delimited by this anthology has also produced the highly gifted poetry of Clémentine Nzuji Madiya from Zaire—as evidenced by her first collection, *Lenga* (1976).

In East Africa, writing by women has tended to trace much the same trajectory as that sketched for anglophone West Africa. In the work of such writers as Barbara Kimenye (n.d.) of Uganda, Martha Mvungi (n.d.) of Tanzania, and Rebeka Njau (n.d.) of Kenya, the centrality of the oral tradition is given telling emphasis. The same is true of the writing of Grace Ogot (b. 1930) of Kenya, perhaps the best known of these East African women writers, and, like Flora Nwapa of Nigeria, a figure of considerable social significance. Trained as a nurse in Uganda and Britain, Ogot has been active in the fields of health care, community development, and education. In 1975 she represented Kenya before the General Assembly of the United Nations, and in 1976 she was a Kenyan delegate to UNESCO. She helped to found the Kenyan Writers' Association and has worked in radio and media production. As a writer, she is widely respected for her short stories, of which several volumes have been published. Her first published work, however, was a novel, *The Promised Land* (1966), set in precolonial Kenya and portraying the lives of Luo farmers.

In one respect, recent East African literature shows a marked departure from the West African pattern. A number of writers, men and women, have eschewed the medium of English and have turned instead to Swahili or to one of the several indigenous languages of the region. The most celebrated proponent of such writing is Ngugi wa Thiong'o, but several East African women have followed his lead. Indeed, Micere Mugo (n.d.) of Kenya has collaborated with Ngugi in a number of projects. Together, the two have composed plays in Swahili and Gikuyu. Martha Mvungi, too, has written a novel in Swahili.

To turn one's attention from West or East to Southern Africa is immediately to be made aware of a radical difference in the thrust and impact of the work produced by writers. In the introduction to his anthology *When My Brothers Come Home* (1985), the Malawian poet Frank Chipasula explains the reasons for this difference thus:

> In Central and Southern Africa, more than in West and East Africa, there is a strong relationship between poetry and politics... Most Angolan and Mozambican poets were forged and shaped in the heat of the struggle against Portugal, their common oppressor. This accounts for the thematic, stylistic, and tonal similarities in their poetry. Other poets from this region were also politically active; they, too, have never been exempted from oppression. Because of their dual activities, the poets of Central and Southern Africa have frequently been persecuted, driven into exile, or detained in their own countries, where their poetry has been censored and banned from circulation.[8]

Indeed, no more committed poetry could be imagined than that produced by Noemia de Sousa of Mozambique. Born in Maputo, Mozambique, in 1927, de Sousa was educated in the Portuguese colony and in Brazil. She lived in Lisbon from 1951 to 1964, before exiling herself in France. She is the first African woman writer to achieve a truly international reputation, and her poems, especially "The Poem of Joao" and "If You Want to Know Me," from the collection, *When Bullets Begin to Flower* (1972), are often anthologized.

In South Africa itself, of course, an essentially colonial situation persists to this day. In their writing, South African men and women show the extent to which apartheid reaches into and disfigures even the most naive and private of experiences. Everyday life is saturated by politics. For some writers, such as Bessie Head (1937–1986), the tentacles of apartheid were so crippling that she had to flee to neighboring Botswana before she could realize her potential as a writer. Many South African writers have been compelled to go into exile or, if permitted to remain in the country, have had to endure harrassment, arbitrary detention and often torture, and the confiscation and banning of their work. Miriam Tlali (b. 1930), one such writer, is on record as saying that she simply *assumes*, in sitting down to write, that most of what she produces will be banned. Perhaps surprisingly, under such circumstances, Tlali has indeed continued to be productive. Her first novel, *Muriel at Metropolitan*, was eventually published in 1975 (it had been completed in 1968 but could not at first find a publisher courageous enough to publish it). A second novel, *Amandla*, set in Soweto during the violent riots of 1976, followed in 1980, and several short stories have appeared in *Staffrider*, an influential cultural magazine published in Johannesburg, and often banned.

South Africa, of course, is famously a divided society. In it, however, and despite the rhetoric of apartheid (literally, apartness), the divisions between white and black have not always congealed into the Manicheism that marked such divisions in other colonies in which there was white settlement, such as Algeria, Kenya, and Mozambique. Few people would think seriously of characterizing Albert Camus or Isak Dinesen as African writers, and yet in South Africa and in Zimbabwe there are two white literary traditions, one English, the other Afrikaans, that cannot be regarded as anything other than African. The point of departure for the white English idiom in South Africa, in fact, lies precisely in an explicit differentiation between "expatriate" and "indigenized" consciousness on the part of a remarkable writer, Olive Schreiner (1855–1920). The nature of Schreiner's achievement has often been commented upon. In her work, and above all in her seminal novel *The Story of an African Farm* (1883), she contrived to represent the experience and outlook of a white *African*, not that of a European expatriate in Africa. It was not a matter of being well disposed toward Africa. What distinguished Schreiner from Mary Kingsley (author of *Travels in West Africa*, 1897), Isak Dinesen (1885–1962), or Alyse Simpson (1895–1963, author of *The Land That Never Was*, 1937), was that when she thought of home she thought not of Europe but of Africa. Yet she found she could not use the conventional exoticizing and European vocabulary to describe her world. She needed instead to construct a new vocabulary capable of rendering what she, as a new historical type, saw around her. She was, accordingly, as Stephen Gray has observed, "the first author to think out a blow-by-blow answer to the question: what can South African literature be?"[9] The profundity of Schreiner's answer to this question can be measured by its effect. It is not in the least an exaggeration to say that the entire trajectory of white Southern African literature, from Pauline Smith (1882–1959) to Alan Paton (1903–1988) to Nadine Gordimer (b. 1923) and beyond is literally unthinkable without Schreiner. Not for nothing did Doris Lessing (b. 1919), herself one of the decisive contributors to this tradition, once observe of *The Story of an African Farm* that "it was the first 'real' book I'd met with that had Africa for a setting. Here was the substance of truth, and not from England or Russia or France or America, necessitating all kinds of mental translations, switches, correspondences, but reflecting what I knew and could see."[10]

Yet ultimately it was Schreiner's depiction of the South African landscape as elemental, turbulent, insistently menacing, and incapable of being mastered that her white English literary successors took from her. A cultural paradox is revealed here: for what makes Schreiner's "Africanization" possible is her possession of land, of which the local African population has of course had to be forcibly *dispossessed*. A product of her times, Schreiner never recognized this explicitly in her work, although it is this "guilty secret," arguably, that we see figured in the "overwhelming intransigence"[11] of the landscape, not only in *The Story of an African Farm* but also in Pauline Smith's novel *The Beadle* and her volume of short stories, *The Little Karoo* (both 1926), in Doris Lessing's *The Grass Is Singing* (1950), and in Nadine Gordimer's *The Conservationist* (1974), where the "secret" is brought to the surface and shown for what it is.

In Southern Africa, the alienation of blacks from the land has been complemented, ceaselessly between Schreiner's time and ours, by the forced integration of these same blacks into the urban labor market. White nationalists in the region, from Rhodes to today's apartheid leaders, have always tended to rationalize this state of affairs, speaking of the need to solve what they have chosen to call the "native problem." In literary terms, this position is represented most notoriously by the vicious and bigoted but influential novel, *God's Step-children* (1924), by Sarah Gertrude Millin (1889–1968). For the most part, however, the white English tradition has set its face firmly against racism, although, for obvious reasons, the spector of race has continued to loom obsessively within it. In her short stories set in colonial Rhodesia (*Collected Short Stories*, 1964), as well as in her novel *The Grass Is Singing* (1950), Doris Lessing offers a disturbing picture of the social implications of institutional racism. Focusing both upon rural life and life in the capital city of Salisbury, Lessing reflects powerfully on racial violence, sexual tension, and the troubled intersection of racial and sexual power relations under colonialism.

Very much the same issues are taken up by Nadine Gordimer in her early stories and in several of her novels. *Occasion for Loving* (1963) is particularly important in this respect, because in it Gordimer for the first time moves toward a fundamental critique of the liberal humanism that can be seen to have animated her predecessors, from Schreiner to Lessing and Paton.

As Gordimer's politics have radicalized in the years after the massacre at Sharpeville (1960), in which police fired on an unarmed crowd protesting against the enforcement of pass laws, killing 69 and wounding 180, so her work has tended to come under the scrutiny of the state censors in South Africa. Several of her works have been banned, most controversially *Burger's Daughter* (1979), whose ban has subsequently been lifted. Other white English women writers, followed in Gordimer's footsteps, have been accorded similarly harsh treatment. Sheila Roberts' novel *Johannesburg Requiem* (originally published under the title *He's My Brother* in 1977), was banned shortly after publication. Roberts now lives and teaches in the United States. Her first volume of short stories, *Outside Life's Feast*, won the Olive Schreiner Prize upon its appearance in 1975; and a novel, *The Weekenders*, was published in 1981. Other gifted women writers today include Yvonne Burgess, whose apocalyptic novel *The Strike* was published in 1975, and the novelist and poet Sheila Fugard, author of two volumes of poetry, *Threshold* (1975) and *Mythic Things* (1981), and three novels, *The Castaways* (1972, winner of two prestigious awards), *Rite of Passage*, (1976) and *A Revolutionary Woman* (1983).

The case of Yvonne Burgess is exemplary, for, although she writes in English, she was born an Afrikaner. Her decision to eschew Afrikaans in favor of English reflects a growing conviction among today's Afrikaner intellectuals that their home language, through its social identity as the language of apartheid, has become incompatible with humanitarian thought. The argument is succinctly outlined by Breyten Breytenbach:

> In its present sociological context and political impact Afrikaans bears the stigma of being identified with the policeman, the warder, the judge and the White politician. Afrikaans is the language of oppression and of humiliation, of the boer. Official Afrikaans is the tool of the racist. That is why the majority of South Africans mock and nearly instinctively reject the 'Taal.'[12]

While some Afrikaner writers have fought against the rising tide of censorship that threatens their right to full expression, increasingly those opposed to apartheid have tended to turn to English as a medium of expression. Where they still write in Afrikaans, they subsequently press for the translation of their work into English. This is true, for instance, of Elsa Joubert (b. 1922), whose novel *Die swerfjare van Poppie Nongena* (1979), winner of three prestigious awards in South Africa, has recently appeared in English translation under the title *The Long Journey of Poppie Nongena*. An earlier novel of Joubert's, *Ons wag op die kaptein* (We Await the Captain, 1963), has also been translated, by her husband Klaas Steytler, as *To Die at Sunset*.

That to write Afrikaans should now seem to many authors to represent an insult against humanity is ironic, since it was only sixty years ago that the language succeeded in obtaining recognition for itself as authentic in its own right, and not merely a deformation of Dutch. In 1925 it was promoted to the status of "official" language of South Africa, alongside English. Among its earliest and most significant poets was Elisabeth Eybers (b. 1915), who began writing at a time when Afrikaners prided themselves on their language, viewing it as, in Breytenbach's words, "the youngest prince in the family of Germanic languages."[13] Young writers took upon themselves the task of opening Afrikaans up to experience, of saying in it everything that can or could be said. The unraveling of this idealistic impression of Afrikaans, in the passage from Eybers to Joubert, is perhaps best symbolized in the tragic career of Ingrid Jonker (1933–1965), one of the most creative users of the language, who discovered, however, that Afrikaans poetry that truly attempted to "say everything" would not be tolerated in the ranks of the newly ascendant Afrikaner nationalists. With Jonker's suicide, Afrikaans lost one of its most brilliant and daring voices. The loss has been irreplaceable.

It is difficult to predict the directions that women's writing in Africa are likely to take. In South Africa, certainly, one can predict a proliferation of socially committed work, with the writers concerned defining themselves as social activists through their cultural production. It is interesting to observe, in this respect, that Nelson and Winnie Mandela's daughter, Zindzi, has begun to receive some celebrity as a poet in South Africa.[14] Elsewhere on the continent the decisive issues are likely to remain those that animate contemporary debate: the dialectic of class and gender; the cultural specificity of feminism in the contexts of African societies; the relation between intellectualism and elitism; and the question of linguistic medium. On these and other subjects, there is little consensus; perhaps we ought not to hope for any. For it may well be that the most significant writing of the next several years will be writing that seeks to provide new answers to these weighty but still unresolved questions.

NOTES

In preparing this survey, the following bibliographic sources were consulted: Charlotte Bruner, ed., *Unwinding Threads: Writing by Women in Africa* (London: Heinemann Educational Books, 1983); Frank Mkalawile Chipasula, ed., *When My Brothers Come Home: Poems from Central and Southern Africa* (Middletown, CT: Wesleyan University Press, 1985); Jack Cope and Uys Krige, eds., *The Penguin Book of South African Verse* (Baltimore: Penguin Books, 1968); M.J. Daymond J.U. Jacobs, and Margaret Lenta, eds., *Momentum: On Recent South African Writing* (Pietermaritzburg: University of Natal Press, 1984); J.C. Kannemeyer, *Geskiedenis van die Afrikaanse Literatuur*. 2 vol. (Cape Town and Pretoria: Academica, 1982); Digby Ricci, ed., *Reef of Time: Johannesburg in Writing* (Johannesburg: Ad. Donker, 1986); Malvern van Wyk Smith and Don Maclennan, eds. *Olive Schreiner and After: Essays on Southern African Literature in Honour of Guy Butler* (Cape Town: David Philip, 1983); Hans M. Zell, Carol Bundy, and Virginia Coulon, eds., *A New Readers' Guide to African Literature* (New York: Africana Publishing Corporation, 1983). Except in the case of direct quotations, references to these works, from which much of the information included derives, has not been made in the text.

1. See Basil Davidson, *Modern Africa* (White Plains, NY: Longman, 1983).
2. Frantz Fanon, "Algeria Unveiled," in *A Dying Colonialism*, trans. Haakon Chevalier (New York: Grove Press, 1967), 35–67.
3. See Lloyd W. Brown, *Women Writers in Africa* (Wesport, CT: Greenwood Press, 1981), 14.
4. Beverly Mack, "Songs from Silence: Hausa Women's Poetry," in Carole Boyce Davies and Anne Adams Graves, eds., *Ngambika: Studies of Women in African Literature* (Trenton, NJ: Africa World Press, 1986), 185.
5. Ibid.
6. For information about Asma'u bint Shehu and Situ binti Saad, see Albert S. Gerard, *African Language Literatures. An Introduction to the Literary History of Sub-Saharan Africa* (Washington, DC: Three Continents Press, 1981), 58–9 and 139.

7. For information about L. Kakaza, see Gerard, *African Language Literatures*, 198, and Albert S. Gerard, *Four African Literatures: Xhosa, Sotho, Zulu, Amharic* (Berkeley: University of California Press, 1971), 65.

8. Frank Chipasula, *When My Brothers Come Home. Poems from Central and Southern Africa* (Middletown, CT: Wesleyan University Press, 1985), 4–5.

9. Stephen Gray, *South African Literature: An Introduction* (New York: Harper and Row, 1979), 141.

10. Ibid., 152.

11. Ibid., 150.

12. Breyten Breytenbach, *The True Confessions of an Albino Terrorist* (Johannesburg: Taurus, 1984), 321.

13. "I am not an Afrikaner any more." Interview with Breyten Breytenbach in *Index on Censorship*, 3, 1983, 6.

14. Nelson Mandela, who has been imprisoned since 1962, is President of the African National Congress of South Africa. Winnie Mandela has frequently been detained without trial for long periods and is now under house arrest. Zindzi Mandela has published two volumes of poetry, *Black as I Am* (1978) and *Black and Fourteen* (n.d.).

BIBLIOGRAPHY

Background

Davidson, Basil. *Let Freedom Come*. Boston: Little, Brown, 1978.

Fanon, Frantz. *The Wretched of the Earth*. Trans. Constance Farrington. New York: Grove Press, 1968.

Gutkind, Peter, C.W., and Peter Waterman, eds. *African Social Studies: A Radical Reader*. New York: Monthly Review Press; London: Heinemann Educational Books, 1977.

Hay, Margaret J., and Shared Stichter, eds. *African Women South of the Sahara*. White Plains, NY: Longman, 1984.

Kuzwayo, Ellen. *Call Me Woman*. San Francisco: Spinsters Ink, 1985.

Obbo, Christine. *African Women: Their Struggle for Economic Independence*. London: Zed Press, 1980.

Steady, Filomina Chioma. *Women in Africa*. Cambridge, MA: Schenkman Publishing Co., 1983.

Urdang, Stephanie. *Fighting Two Colonialisms: Women in Guinea-Bissau*. New York: Monthly Review Press, 1979.

Literary Criticism

Ba Shiru (Madison, WI) 12, no. 2 (1987). The entire issue is devoted to women writers in Africa.

Barnett, Ursula A. *A Vision of Order. A Study of Black South African Literature in English (1914–1980)*. London: Sinclair Browne; Amherst: University of Massachusetts Press, 1983.

Berrian, Brenda, and Mildred Mortimer, eds. *Criticial Perspectives on African Women Writers*. Washington, DC: Three Continents Press, Forthcoming.

Brown, Lloyd W. *Women Writers in Black Africa*. Westport, CT: Greenwood Press, 1981.

Clingman, Stephen R. *The Novels of Nadine Gordimer: History from the Inside*. London: Allison and Busby; Johannesburg; Ravan Press, 1986.

Coetzee, J.M., *White Writing. On the Culture of Letters in South Africa*. New Haven, CT: Yale University Press, 1988.

Cope, Jack. *The Adversary Within: Dissident Writers in Afrikaans*. Atlantic Highlands, NJ: Humanities Press, 1982.

Davies, Carol Boyce, and Anne Adams Graves, eds. *Ngambika: Studies of Women in African Literature*. Trenton, NJ: Africa World Press, 1986.

First, Ruth, and Ann Scott. *Olive Schreiner. A Biography*. London: Andre Deutsch, 1980.

Gerard, Albert S. *African Language Literatures: An Introduction to the Literary History of Sub-Saharan Africa.* Washington, DC: Three Continents Press, 1981.

Gerard, Albert S. *Four African Literatures: Xhosa, Sotho, Zulu, Amharic.* Berkeley: University of California Press, 1971.

Jones, Eldred Durosimi, and Eustace Palmer, eds. *African Literature Today,* Vol. 16. London: Heinemann Educational Books; New York: Africana Publishing Company, 1986. The entire volume is devoted to women writers in Africa.

Little, Kenneth. *The Sociology of Urban Women's Image in African Literature.* London: Macmillan, 1980.

Schipper, Mineke, ed. *Unheard Words: Women and Literature in Africa, the Arab World, Asia, the Caribbean and Latin America.* London: Allison and Busby, 1985.

Robert F. Blum, Venetian Lace Makers, *1887, oil on canvas. Cincinnati Art Museum, Gift of Elizabeth S. Potter*

AUSTRALIA AND NEW ZEALAND
Elizabeth Webby

The indigenous peoples of Australia and New Zealand have long traditions of oral literature although much was destroyed, particularly in Australia, following the white invasion. British convicts and their jailers arrived in Australia in 1788 to found the penal colony of New South Wales. Soon after, sealers, whalers, and traders began an unofficial occupation of New Zealand, which became a British possession in 1840.

White settlement of both countries was marked by an extreme imbalance between the sexes. More male than female convicts were transported to Australia; most of the early settlers of New Zealand were men. In both new cultures, too, the emphasis was on traditionally masculine activities: pioneering, exploring, conquering the land and the native peoples. To achieve English domination, a series of wars had to be fought against the Maori in New Zealand. In Australia, a large and often difficult country had to be traversed and mapped. During the second half of the nineteenth century, both countries experienced gold rushes with their attendant social disruptions, including large injections of population, again mostly male.

Until very recently, the literatures of both countries have been perceived and valued very much in terms of how well they reflected this dominant masculine ethos. Australian literature was believed to have come of age in the 1890s with the bush realism of Henry Lawson's stories and the bush romanticism of Banjo Paterson's ballads. New Zealand was thought to have found its own distinctive voice in the 1920s with the idiomatic stories of Frank Sargeson, a writer influenced by Lawson. Literary value was seen to lie in the breaking of ties with Britain, the discovery of unique, local subject matter, and the development of a new, national voice. Country and bush settings were favored over city ones; realism over modernism; simplicity over sophistication. The result was a serious downplaying of the contribution of women writers, particularly those from the nineteenth century and those who wrote against the dominant modes and traditions. It is not surprising that many of the major writers, including Katherine Mansfield, Henry Handel Richardson, and Christina Stead, did most of their work as expatriates.

As in most other English-speaking countries, the strongest contribution of women writers to the literature of Australia and New Zealand has been made in prose, long and short, fiction and nonfiction. Given the nineteenth-century belief that poetry was the highest literary genre, women may have felt less intimidated by prose than poetry. Nineteenth-century playwrights were poorly paid and popular theater even less respectable than the novel. For most of the twentieth century, professional theater hardly existed in New Zealand; in Australia it was dominated by imported plays and performers. So for the many who wrote either to make money or promote a cause, fiction, *the* popular medium of the time, was the obvious choice.

Besides writing for publication in the nineteenth century, many women were also expressing themselves distinctively in letters, diaries, and journals. An increasing number of these are now being published as a result of the growing interest in women's social and cultural history. Less has, so far, been done to unearth women's many contributions published in newspapers and magazines. New writers remain to be uncovered, along with many as yet uncollected stories, novels, articles, and poems by established figures.

The first novel by a woman to be written and published in Australia was *The Guardian* (1838) by Anna Maria Murray (1808–1889). Its Irish setting and use of the Gothic mode doomed it to critical oblivion, as "non-Australian" or "colonial," a fate that was to befall many later works for similar reasons. The first novel to be written and set in Australia was *Clara Morison* (1854) by the noted political and social reformer Catherine Helen Spence (1825–1910). Spence wrote several other novels but stopped when she came to believe she could do more good through journalism and lecturing. She also believed that another South Australian, Catherine Martin (1847–1937), was a much better novelist. Martin's major novel, *An Australian Girl* (1890), an account of a woman tricked into marrying her intellectual inferior, until only recently was dismissed as a "bluestocking romance" for both its form and intellectual focus offended proponents of the dominant mode of democratic realism.

As most Australian novels were published in London (and many still are today), a number of writers felt they had to cater to a broader, English-speaking audience, and it was not surprising to find many books set in more than one country or entirely outside Australia. Such varied settings are characteristic of the work of Rosa Praed (1851–1935), who published over forty novels, ranging from *Policy and Passion* (1881), set in Praed's native Queensland, to *Affinities* (1885), set in London high society and including a character based on Oscar Wilde. Two other leading women novelists of this period are "Tasma" (pseudonym of Jessie Couvreur, 1848–1897), who wrote *Uncle Piper of Piper's Hill* (1889) and five others, and Ada Cambridge (1884–1926). Besides over twenty novels, including *A Marked Man* (1890), Cambridge published a collection of poetry, *Unspoken Thoughts* (1887), presenting some unconventional views on religion and marriage.

The works of Barbara Baynton (1857–1959), and Miles Franklin (1897–1954), however, gained critics' attention *because* of their bush settings. Indeed, Franklin's *My Brilliant Career* (1901) was initially hailed as the first "truly Australian" novel. Since the popular film version of 1979, its spirited heroine, who prefers a career to marriage, has become known and appreciated by an international audience. Franklin was strongly criticized by family and friends, who assumed that she was her heroine and thus felt they were being disparaged; so she published many of her later novels under the less penetrable male pseudonym Brent of Bin Bin.

Franklin's ardent nationalism led her to claim that expatriate Henry Handel Richardson (1870–1946) was not an "Australian writer." Actually, Richardson's historical novel and family saga, *The Fortunes of Richard Mahony*, fits well into the Australian fictional tradition and has received a great deal of critical attention as Australia's first "world-class" novel, while *Maurice Guest* and *The Young Cosima*, set in Europe, have only recently been noticed critically. Another who wrote a goldfields' trilogy,[1] Katharine Susannah Prichard (1883–1969), was in many other respects very different from Richardson. An active Communist, her radical attitudes are also seen in her concern for aborigines and her outspoken presentation of sexuality, especially in *Coonardoo* and her play *Brumby Innes*. The New Zealand-born Jean Devanny (1894–1962) was another who focused on socialism and sexuality; her novels, such as *The Butcher's Shop* (1926), are more strongly feminist than Prichard's.

New Zealand's literary situation differed somewhat from that of Australia. Many of the earliest New Zealand novels were written by women and early gained recognition. Both the fiction and nonfiction, such as *Station Life in New Zealand* (1870), written by Lady Mary Anne Barker (1831–1911), are avowed classics. A major literary figure in nineteenth-century New Zealand was Edith Searle Grossman (1863–1931), a strong advocate of social reform and women's rights. Her novels, set in Australia as well as New Zealand, include *In Revolt* (1893) and *The Heart of the Bush* (1910). Although New Zealand was the first country to give women the vote (in 1893), New Zealand women soon found that the right to vote did not mean independence or equality, as we find in *The Story of a New Zealand River* (1920) by Jane Mander (1877–1949) who was influenced by the South-African-born Olive Schreiner.[2] Like Edith Grossman and Catherine Martin, Mander focused also on the problems that arise in a marriage between an educated woman and an uncultivated, pioneering man (of which there were many in early Australia and New Zealand). The major writers of the period—Katherine Mansfield (1888–1923) and Robin Hyde (1906–1939)—avoided the difficult choices forced on women in a new, pioneering society by leaving for England; others, like Devanny, opted for expatriation to the larger cultural environment of Australia. Hyde's novel *The Godwits Fly* graphically outlines the social and cultural pressures that sent so many writers overseas.

The major Australian novelist of the period from 1920 to 1950, Christina Stead (1902–1983) was also an expatriate for most of her life, and until recently her reputation suffered because of her decision to be a citizen of the world rather than of any one country. Now that all her fiction has been returned to print, it is apparent that she is one of the leading writers of this century, particularly for her novels *The Man Who Loved Children (1940)* and *For Love Alone (1944)*, which display her love for and command of language and show her penetrating insights into the human, especially female, condition. Those women who remained in Australia received support from each other and from the literary critic Nettie Palmer (1885–1964), as Drusilla Modjeska has demonstrated in *Exiles at Home* (1981), so far the only extended study of Australian women writers. Besides Prichard and Devanny, novelists of this period include Eleanor Dark (1901–1985), Henrietta Drake-Brockman (1901–1968), Dymphna Cusack (1902–1981), Eve Langley (1908–1974), Kylie Tennant (1912–1988), and "M. Barnard Eldershaw." The five novels published under this last pseudonym were the result of collaboration between Flora Eldershaw (1897–1956) and Marjorie Barnard (1897–1987). Outstanding among them was the last, *Tomorrow and Tomorrow* (1947), republished in its uncensored version as *Tomorrow, Tomorrow and Tomorrow* (1983), a radical work both in its novel-within-a-novel form and its critique of the apathy and selfishness of Australian society.

Few new Australian women novelists came to prominence in the period from 1950 to 1975, apart from Thea Astley (b. 1925), Elizabeth Harrower (b. 1928), and Shirley Hazzard (b. 1931). Astley has won numerous prizes for her novels and short stories, and her witty, ascerbic style separates her writing from that of most pre-1970s Australian writers. Hazzard, who has lived in New York City for many years, was firmly established critically only with *The Transit of Venus* (1980). For New Zealand, 1951 brought the first book by Janet Frame (b. 1924) now—thanks to the range, originality, and insights of her work—widely regarded as their greatest living writer. The 1950s also saw the first novels of Sylvia Ashton-Warner (1908–1984), whose *Spinster* (1958) and *Teacher* (1963) achieved international success for their frank portrayal of a woman's life, and of Marilyn Duckworth (b. 1935). Two other leading fiction writers, Joy Cowley (b. 1963) and Margaret Sutherland (b. 1941) began publishing in the 1960s and early 1970s.

In the last decade most of the major new writers of fiction in Australia have been women. The strong nationalist feeling associated with the election of a reformist Labor government in 1972 resulted in greater interest in and government sponsorship for local writers and publishers. (Only in 1983 however, did sales of books by local authors exceed those of imported titles.) The feminist movement in the 1970s also encouraged women to write and provided further opportunities for publication and sales, with specialist presses and bookshops. Outstanding among the newer writers are Jessica Anderson (contemp.), Elizabeth Jolley (b. 1923), and Olga Masters (1919–1986), all of whom were over fifty before they were published. Younger women who already have secure reputations include Glenda Adams (b. 1940), Barbara Hanrahan (b. 1939), Beverley Farmer (b. 1941), Helen Garner (b. 1942), Blanche D'Alpuget (b. 1944), Jean Bedford (b. 1946), and Kate Grenville (b. 1950).

The same period in New Zealand has been most notable for the growth of writing by Maoris in both English and Maori, spurred both by feminism and ethnic movements that asserted the rights of minorities. In 1975 Patricia Grace (b. 1937) became the first Maori woman to publish a work of fiction. Of the others who followed, the most outstanding is Keri Hulme (b. 1947). Her novel *the bone people* (1984), brought out by a feminist collective after rejection by commercial publishers, became a local bestseller and went on to win England's prestigious Booker Prize for fiction, chosen over novels by Iris Murdoch and Doris Lessing. A most unusual and highly original novel, *the bone people* is a mixture of fantasy and graphic realism, Maori and English, slang and poetry. Non-Maori women who began publishing fiction in this period include Yvonne de Fresne (b. 1929) and Fiona Kidman (b. 1940).

Though many women wrote, and some published, poetry in Australia during the nineteenth century, the first to achieve much recognition were Mary Gilmore (1864–1962) and Dorothea Mackellar (1885–1968); Mackellar's nationalist "My Country" is one of the best-known Australian poems. Lesbia Harford (1891–1927) wrote poems remarkable for their radical form and subject matter; not surprisingly, they have received little attention until recently. Fortunately this was not the fate of Judith Wright (b. 1915) who, growing up in the country and perhaps influenced by Mary Gilmore, fairly early won recognition for her poems about the bush. Wright has also been actively involved in radical causes, particularly conservation and aboriginal land rights. The latter, naturally, forms a strong theme in the work of Kath Walker (b. 1920) the best-known aboriginal poet. Recognition has been slower for Gwen Harwood (b. 1920) and Rosemary Dobson (b. 1920) who have often chosen to focus on women's relationship to the arts (music for Harwood, painting for Dobson).

As with fiction, there has been a marked increase in the number of women publishing poetry over the last ten years. Besides those represented here, important work has been done by Anne Elder (1918–1976), Jennifer Strauss (b. 1933), J.S. Harry (b. 1939), Kate Llewellyn (b. 1940), Jennifer Rankin (1941–1979), Jennifer Maiden (b. 1949), Susan Hampton (b. 1949), and Gig Ryan (b. 1956). The growing multiculturalism of Australian society, a product of large-scale postwar migration, is reflected in the work of a number of recent writers, most of whom produce prose as well as poetry, such as Antigone Kefala (b. 1935), Anna Couani (b. 1948), Vicki Viidikas (b. 1948), and Ania Walwicz (b. 1951). A particular feature of their work has been an experimental approach to poetic language and form, including a blurring of conventional distinctions between prose and poetry. In his introduction to the recent and controversial *Penguin Book of New Zealand Verse* (1985), Ian Wedde challenges critical orthodoxy by giving a dominant place to women poets as well as including poems written in Maori. The balladist and women's rights activist Jessie Mackay (1864–1938) was the first woman poet to gain recognition. Wedde stresses the significance of Blanche Baughan (1870–1958) as the first poet to deal positively with New Zealand realities. Wedde claims as "one of the great strengths of the process we call 'New Zealand poetry'" the line stretching from Baughan through Ursula Bethell (1874–1945) to Eileen Duggan (1894–1972), Robin Hyde, and Gloria Rawlinson (b. 1918). Other important poets are Ruth France (1913–1967), Ruth Gilbert (b. 1917), Mary Stanley (1919–1980), Ruth Dallas (b. 1919), Janet Frame (b.   ), and Fleur Adcock (b. 1934), the last another expatriate woman now living in England. As in Australia, there has been a big rise since 1975 in the number of women publishing poetry: 1975 produced first collections by Rachel McAlpine (b. 1940), Elizabeth Smither (b. 1941), and Lauris Edmond (b. 1924). In 1985 Edmond's *Selected Poems* won the Commonwealth Poetry Prize. Other notable recent collections have been published by Meg Campbell (b. 1937), Cilla McQueen (b. 1949), Jan Kemp (b. 1949), and Keri Hulme (b. 1924).

Apart from Rosa Praed, who adapted some of her novels for the London stage, there seem to have been no nineteenth-century women playwrights from either country. Many women were, however, associated with the little theater and repertory movements of the first half of the twentieth century. Several in Australia wrote full-length plays; but because opportunities for production were very limited, they made their living in other areas: Betty Roland (b. 1903), Katharine Susannah Prichard, H. Drake-Brockman (1901–1968) and Dymphna Cusack. Mona Brand (b. 1915) and Oriel Gray (b. 1921), both strongly associated with left-wing theater, have written numerous plays, few of which have been published. Similarly, for much of the twentieth century, publication of plays by New Zealand women was limited to one-acters written for amateur groups. In 1957 Stella Jones's *The Tree* was produced in England. It was subsequently given a New Zealand tour by the Wellington Players, the first local professional company.

The most successful Australian woman playwright so far has been Dorothy Hewett (b. 1923), who achieved wide recognition for her historical musical play, *The Man from Mukinupin* (1979) rather than for her earlier, more radical and feminist plays like *The Chapel Perilous* (1972). Since 1980, there has been a marked increase in the number of women writing for the stage—and in professional performances of their plays. Other contemporary feminist playwrights include Doreen Clarke (b. 1928), Jennifer Rankin, Alma De Groen (b. 1941), Jennifer Compton (b. 1949), and Alison Lyssa (b. 1946).

That both De Groen and Compton were originally from New Zealand indicates something of the state of drama there in the 1970s. Local plays did not find large audiences until the late 1970s, and then all the playwrights were male. In 1982, however, Carolyn Burns achieved success with *Objection Overruled*, Hilary Beaton (who reversed the usual pattern by going from Australia to New Zealand) with *Outside In*, Fiona Poole with *In Confidence: Dialogues with Amy Bock*, and Renée (b. 1929) with *Breaking Out*, *Secrets*, and *Setting the Table*. These plays, along with *Wednesday to Come* (1985) and *Pass It On* (1986), have established Renée, a Maori feminist, as one of New Zealand's leading playwrights. Her work is particularly distinguished by its concentration on political issues and use of historical material without ever becoming drearily documentary.

It seems appropriate to end this survey, written when much still needs to be uncovered about women writers from Australia and New Zealand, with a passage from Renée's *Setting the Table*:

> Look we're setting the table. Right? All those women we know about and the hundreds we don't. Well, they got the ingredients ready and cooked the dinner. And now we've got as far as setting the table. Oh I know it seems as though we'll never sit down to the dinner-party. Well, maybe *we* won't. But we'll get the table ready. We and all the ones we don't know about...

NOTES

1. "Goldfields" applies to the many fictional representations of the Australian gold rush, which began in 1851 in New South Wales and by the end of the century had spread through Victoria, Queensland, and West Australia. *The Fortunes of Richard Mahoney* begins in the Ballarat goldfields, northwest of Melbourne, Victoria.
2. *The Story of an African Farm* (1883).

BIBLIOGRAPHY

Background

Bunkle, Phillida, and Beryl Hughes, eds. *Women in New Zealand Society*. Sydney: Allen and Unwin, 1980.

Clark, C.M.H.. *A History of Australia*. 6 vols. Melbourne: Melbourne University Press, 1962–1987.

Dixson, Miriam. *The Real Matilda: Women and Identity in Australia 1788–1975*. Ringwood, Victoria: Penguin Books, 1976, rev. 1984.

Oliver, W.H., ed. *The Oxford History of New Zealand*. Clarendon: Oxford University Press, 1981.

Searle, Geoffrey. *From Deserts the Prophets Come: The Creative Spirit in Australia*. Melbourne: Heinemann, 1973.

Literary Criticism

Dick, Margaret. *The Novels of Kylie Tennant*. Adelaide: Rigby, 1966.

Ferrier, Carole, ed. *Gender, Politics and Fiction: Twentieth Century Australian Women's Novels*. St. Lucia: University of Queensland Press, 1985.

Green, Dorothy. *Henry Handel Richardson and Her Fiction*. Sydney: Allen and Unwin, 1986.

Green H.M. *A History of Australian Literature*. 2 vols. Sydney: Angus and Robertson, 1961.

Hankin, Cherry, ed. *Critical Essays on the New Zealand Novel*. Auckland: Heinemann, 1976.

Hanson, Clare, and Andrew Gurr. *Katherine Mansfield*. London: Macmillan, 1981.

Kramer, Leonie, ed. *The Oxford History of Australian Literature*. Melbourne: Oxford University Press, 1981.

Modjeska, Drusilla. *Exiles at Home: Australian Women Writers, 1925–1945*. Sydney: Angus and Robertson, 1981.

McCormick, E.H. *New Zealand Literature*. London: Oxford University Press, 1959.

Thomson, A.K., ed. *Critical Essays on Judith Wright*. Brisbane: Jacaranda Press, 1968.

Walker, Shirley, ed. *Who is She? Images of Women in Australia Fiction*. St. Lucia: University of Queensland Press, 1983.

Wilde, William H., Joy Hooton, and Barry Andrews, eds. *The Oxford Companion to Australian Literature*. Melbourne: Oxford University Press, 1985.

Australian Writers and their Work (Melbourne: Oxford University Press) has volumes on Ada Cambridge, Tasma and Rosa Praed, Mary Gilmore (in *Three Radicals*), Miles Franklin, Henry Handel Richardson, Katherine Susannah Prichard, Christina Stead, and Judith Wright.

New Zealand Writers and their Work (Wellington: Oxford University Press) has volumes on Mary Ursula Bethell, Eileen Duggan, and Janet Frame.

Twayne's World Authors (Boston: G.K. Hall) has volumes on Miles Franklin, M. Barnard Eldershaw, Eleanor Dark, Christina Stead, Jane Mander, Katherine Mansfield, and Janet Frame, as well as on New Zealand fiction and New Zealand drama.

AUSTRIA AND GERMANY

Marilyn Sibley Fries

They wrote in the isolation of cloisters and family estates; they faced a deep-seated chauvinism that was perpetuated by attitudes, often in writing, of the great thinkers sharing their language. Occasional periods of historical and ideological change allowed greater numbers to come to the fore, but the women writers of the German-speaking countries—represented now by the two Germanies (the Federal Republic [FRG], or West Germany, and the German Democratic Republic [GDR], or East Germany), Austria, and Switzerland—have never been free of antifeminist prejudices in their countries. Opinions denying them intellectual strength or creativity fostered laws that kept them out of high schools until the mid-nineteenth century and out of universities until the end of the nineteenth in Switzerland and the beginning of the twentieth in Germany. In the nineteenth century, the Industrial Revolution moved many out of the home—into the factory.

Until the end of the last century, the origins of their birth were a significant factor in determining which women might enter the field of literature. The women writers of the Romantic period came from the aristocracy and the wealthy bourgeoisie, for instance. It was not until the late nineteenth century, with the beginning of the women's movement and the emergence of a strong socialist faction in German politics, that working-class women began to speak in audible voices. About one hundred years later, however, beginning in the 1960s, women of all social classes writing in German had become a force so dominant in the literary world that at least one German critic was moved to proclaim their activities "a new chapter in German literature" and to devote a book-length study to major figures, whom he credits with providing in their works an alternative to the sterile and cynical resignation of many of their male contemporaries.[1] If we agree to accept this notion of a "new chapter," we might ask just what, from the perspective of *women's* literary history, the preceding chapters contain; and indeed many women writing in Germany today are involved in a concerted effort to trace a female literary lineage and to interpret, or reinterpret, female literary predecessors.

Such diverse women as the philosopher-historian Hannah Arendt, the communist author Anna Seghers, and the Swedish feminist Ellen Key, for instance, have acknowledged the importance for her female successors of Rahel Varnhagen's (1771–1883) life and letters or have explored the critical dilemma of nineteenth-century women poets writing in a hostile environment. Key paid tribute in her laudatory monograph, *Rahel; eine biographische Skizze* (*Rahel Varnhagen: A Portrait*, 1907). Arendt was to follow suit with her own differently motivated *Rahel Varnhagen: Lebensgeschichte einer deutschen Jüdin aus der Romantik* (*Rahel Varnhagen: The Life of a Jewess*, written in Germany in the 1920s, revised and published in England in 1958, Germany in 1959, and the United States in 1974). And Seghers (1900–1983), in a speech during her Parisian exile in 1935, included Varnhagen's contemporary Karoline von Günderode (1780–1806) among the poets she identified as having suffered too greatly from the discrepancy between their own visions and the reality of their times.[2]

These few examples of women responding to women suggest a continuity, forcefully disrupted by the twelve years of Nazi domination (1933–1945) and reestablished in the postwar era by authors such as Ingeborg Drewitz (1923–1986), with her studies on women of the German Romantic period (*Bettina*, 1969; *Berliner Salons*, 1965), Sarah Kirsch (b. 1935), and Christa Wolf (b. 1929). Kirsch's poem cycle *Rückenwind* (Tailwinds, 1977) is devoted in part to the memory of Bettina von Arnim (1788–1859). Wolf's initial curiosity about Seghers' reference to Günderode led to a long-term involvement with these same figures that took the form of essays on Günderode and von Arnim, of an edition of Günderode's works, and of her fictional representation of many important figures of the Romantic era in the narrative *Kein Ort. Nirgends* (*No Place on Earth*, 1979).

The history of these publications and the interests that inspired them help to locate some of the significant moments in the history of women's literature in Germany. The emphasis in this essay is on the women writers of the Romantic era (1800–1830), Realism and Modernism (1860–1933), and the period from about 1960 to the present.

It may seem paradoxical that the anti-Enlightenment Romantic movement provided the intellectual atmosphere necessary for several women to emerge onto the literary and cultural scene in a manner that allows us to identify them as a group. These women were, in the main, born of the intellectually elite and were conscious members of a cultural heritage. Bettina von Arnim, for instance, was the granddaughter of Sophie von La Roche (1730–1807), herself a published novelist, the sister of the famous poet Clemens Brentano, and the wife of the no less renowned Achim von Arnim. Best known for the fictionalization of her early correspondence with Goethe in *Goethe's Correspondence with a Child* (*Goethes Briefwechsel mit einem Kinde*, 1835) and for her tribute in similar form to her close friend Günderode (*Die Günderode*, 1840), Arnim also wrote works that were inspired by the political concerns and activities she shared in her later life with the writers of the politically oppositional literary movement known as Young Germany, most notably *Dies Buch gehört dem König* (This Book Belongs to the King, 1843), which she presented to Friedrich Wilhelm IV; it was one of the earliest records documenting the pitiful conditions of the working poor during the rise of industrialism.

Other women who were connected with the Romantic circle included Dorothea Schlegel (1763–1839) and her sister-in-law, Caroline Schlegel-Schelling (1763–1809). Caroline was the wife of August Wilhelm Schlegel, whom she assisted in his highly regarded translations of Shakespeare, and later of the philosopher F. W. J. von Schelling. Dorothea was the daughter of Moses Mendelssohn and wife of August Wilhelm Schlegel's brother Friedrich; she was an intellectually gifted woman who also translated some writings of Madame de Staël and wrote an unfinished novel, *Florentin* (1801).

Annette von Droste-Hülshoff (1797–1848) was surely the greatest woman poet—indeed, one of the greatest poets altogether—of the nineteenth century. She wrote narrative and lyric poetry in addition to some prose pieces, of which the most notable is the short story *Die Judenbuche* (*The Jew's Beech*, 1842), recognized as one of the great German short stories. One reason for Droste's continuing fascination for us is her poetic revelation of the female subconscious. Her poetry acknowledges the existence of the daemon of the subconscious, which manifests itself in the form of the double (*Doppelgänger*) and expresses the inexpressible desires of eros, lust, and passion. Nature provides the metaphors for her poetic descent into the self.

The revolutionary idealism prompted by the French Revolution that marked the beginning of the nineteenth century was followed by stiff reaction and chauvinism after the Napoleonic Wars and the Congress of Vienna (1815). The Young Germans, whose politically engaged literature was fundamentally oppositional, had their strongest impact in the years from 1830 to 1848. The revolution of March 1848 was again succeeded by a period of conservatism, now strengthened by the increasing bourgeoise and a social stratification newly defined by industrialization.

Isolde Kurz (1853–1944) may be taken as a late example of those who had been nurtured in a democratic spirit under the aegis of the revolution of 1848 only to be dispossessed by the political reaction and social reorganization, elicited by capitalism, that followed. One choice available to a bourgeois woman of the late nineteenth century was travel and independent study: Kurz went to Italy and there pursued her inquiry into the Renaissance. In the *Florentiner Novellen (Florentine Novellas, 1900), Italiensche Erzählungen* (Italian Stories, 1902), and the volumes of poetry that established her literary fame, she embodied Italy as the land of the romantic imagination, spoke of "dead gods," and searched for a love who would be equal to her, "neither master nor a slave." Her largely autobiographical *entwicklungsroman, Vanadis, der Schicksalsweg einer Frau* (Vanadis, The Story of a Woman's Fate, 1931), which her contemporaries called the "female companion to Goethe's *Wilhelm Meister*," is testimony to the end of an age.

Industrialization and its concomitant developments also opened the door to many other women writers, and there began to emerge a body of literature that would soon be perjoratively classified as *Frauenliteratur*, a label that has haunted literature by women since that time. Frequently appearing in serialized form in popular magazines, these works were authored by immensely successful writers such as Hedwig Courths-Mahler (1867–1950) and Eugenie Marlitt (1825–1952). One of the better writers who has been so denigrated was Clara Viebig (1860–1952), a disciple of Zola; her naturalistic novels depicted societal problems in a disturbingly realistic way. Viebig's career is, perhaps, indicative of the direction taken by many serious women writers at the end of the nineteenth and beginning of the twentieth centuries. Unlike most of their predecessors, these women became directly involved in the political and social events of their times; Bettina von Arnim and Louise Alston (1814–1871) who wrote poetry that supported the revolution of 1848, are here exceptions.

In the late nineteenth and early twentieth centuries, women began to fight for the rights of the oppressed, and to demand an end to armed conflict, by publishing political leaflets and pamphlets, founding newspapers, organizing conventions, and speaking out on platforms. Their writings rarely fall into the category of *belles lettres*, but their activities—and the conviction that the pen does indeed wield political power—were important in establishing models for future generations.

The involvement of women in a united political action began around the time of the revolution of 1848. The so-called woman question grew out of the basic issues of the revolution concerning human rights that were brought to the surface by the Industrial Revolution and articulated by philosophers such as Marx and Engels and later August Bebel and Ferdinand Lasalle. While the popular Fanny Lewald-Stahr (1811–1889) emulated the much-admired Rahel Varnhagen in her liberally inclined salon of the later nineteenth century, other women sought a different kind of forum in which to speak. Luise Otto-Peters (1819–1895) edited the militant *Frauen-Zeitung* (Women's Newspaper) from 1849 to 1852 and later the women's journal *Neue Bahnen* (New Paths) and was a founding leader of the Allgemeiner Deutscher Frauenverein (General German Women's Union) in 1865. Peters, who recognized the woman question as a national and social problem and was the first to express demands for equal rights in a programmatic way, is acknowledged as the founder of the German women's movement.

The slightly younger Hedwig Dohm, (1833–1919) was a radical and committed feminist and one of the few from Germany whose prolific writings were translated early into English. Dohm, identified with Bettina von Arnim and Rahel Varnhagen, was an avid reader of George Sand, and wrote on George Eliot; like her German predecessors, she made her Berlin home into an intellectual meeting place. Arguing in her articles that women must have a voice before they can change anything, she focused her attention on suffrage. Dohm's most important writings include "What Pastors Think of Women" (1872), "Jesuitry in the Household" (1873), "The Scientific Emancipation of Women" (1874), and "Nature and Rights of Women" (1876). While her later contemporary Lou Andreas-Salomé (1861–1937) developed a difficult friendship with Friedrich Nietzsche, Dohm wrote a devastating criticism of him and his attitude toward women in "The Anti-Feminists" (1902).

Helene Lange (1848–1930) is regarded by many as the most important figure of the women's movement; she served as a spiritual model particularly to the more moderate wing of the movement. Among her important achievements were the founding of the Allgemeiner Deutscher Lehrerinnenverein in 1890 and the editorship of the magazine *Die Frau* (Woman) from 1893–1930. (She was succeeded in this position by Gertrud Bäumer [1873–1854], who edited the magazine until 1943, making it one of the longest-lived women's journals of the period.) Lange and Bäumer together also edited three volumes of the five-volume *Handbuch der Frauenbewegung* (Handbook of the Women's Movement, 1901–1906). Lange published *Die Frauenbewegung in ihren gegenwärtigen Problemen* (Current Problems of the Women's Movement) in 1908. Finally, like many of the women of the movement, she wrote an autobiography, *Meine Lebenserinnerungen* (Recollections of My Life, 1912).

As evidence of how particular women from particular and disparate backgrounds developed their social consciousness and as insight into the social and political conditions of their times, the autobiographies of activists are perhaps the most generally interesting of their collective production. Lily Braun's (1865–1916) *Memoiren einer Sozialistin* (Memoirs of a Woman Socialist) in two volumes— *Lebensjahre* (Years of Living, 1909) and *Kampfjahre* (Years of Fighting, 1911)— narrates the conversion of an aristocratic woman to socialism. Braun was a cofounder of the newspaper *Die Frauenbewegung* (The Women's Movement, 1895) and wrote novels and political theory. Her work *Die Frauenfrage* (The Woman Question, 1901) was recognized by August Bebel as one of the most important theoretical contributions to the emancipation of women and is today regarded, together with publications by Bebel, Engels, and Zetkin, as a basic reference work on that topic.

Clara Zetkin (1857–1933) was the central figure on the socialist side of the women's movement and was responsible for drawing class lines on the woman question by focusing on the proletariat in *Die Arbeiterinnen und die Frauenfrage der Gegenwart* (The Question of Women Workers and Women in the Present, 1899). She edited the important newspaper *Die Gleichheit* (Equality) from 1891 to 1916 and was the moving force behind the organization of working and socialist women.

Zetkin, like her Austrian contemporary, Adelheid Popp (1869–1939), was from the working class. Popp achieved high recognition with the anonymous publication of her *Jugendgeschichte einer Arbeiterin* (Story of a Working Woman's Youth, 1909). Later editions were published under her name, as were her *Erinnerungen* (Memoirs, 1915) and *Der Weg zur Höhe* (The Path to the Heights, 1929). Popp succeeded Zetkin as the first secretary of the International Women's Committee.

The first women's movement in Germany was eventually torn asunder by the factions representing the bourgeoisie on the one hand, in which the dominant themes were the economic, social, and ethical improvement of the position of woman as mother, and the proletariat on the other, where the arguments centered on the working class and on radical social changes. Helene Stocker (1869–1943) belonged to the left wing of the first group. She founded the Union for Bund für Mutterschutz und Sexualreform (Maternal Protection and Sexual Reform) in 1905 and was editor from 1905 to 1932 of the newspaper *Mutterschutz* (Maternal Protection (after 1908 under the title *Die neue Generation* [The New Generation]). Rosa Luxemburg (1871–1919), today honored by many as a martyr, represents the other extreme. She was not directly involved with the women's movement and must be seen instead as a primary leader in the socialist cause. A brilliant political theoretician, Luxemburg became a leader of the extreme left wing of the German Socialist Party. While imprisoned from 1916 to 1918 for revolutionary activity during the First World War, she wrote the *Spartacus Letters*. With Karl Liebknecht, Luxemburg founded the radical Spartacus League in 1916; this in turn became the German Communist Party in 1918. Both Luxemburg and Liebknecht were murdered by nationalist German soldiers after an abortive Spartacist uprising in January 1919. Her chief work, which presented her theory of imperialism, was *Die Akkumulation des Kapitals* (*Accumulation of Capital*, 1913).

A scholar and intellectual of a different tendency was Luxemburg's contemporary Ricarda Huch (1864–1947), who was one of the most important women writers of the late nineteenth and early twentieth century. She was among the first women to receive a doctorate at a German-speaking institution—although to earn it she had to go to Zurich, where she began studying history in 1887 (no institution of higher education in Germany was open to women before 1908). Huch received her doctorate in 1892 and went on to become a prolific writer, producing not only historical studies but literary criticism, essays, speeches, poems, dramas, novellas, and novels as well. Her study of German Romanticism (1899–1902) still ranks among the major works of literary criticism.

Huch and Luxemburg must be counted among the chief intellects of Germany's early twentieth century. A strong mind that took a different direction was that of Luxemburg's compatriot, Lou Andreas-Salomé (1861–1937), who, like Luxemburg, has assumed mythic proportions, although for a different reason. Andreas-Salomé, who lived in what was then regarded as an unconventional style, was a prototypical liberated woman of exceptional intellect who is best known for her close relationships to Nietzsche, Rilke, and Freud. Her introduction to the fledgling discipline of psychoanalysis is documented in her *In der Schule bei Freud* (*Freud Journal*, 1958), but she became a scholar of the discipline in her own right, producing several articles in which she explored the psyche of women, which was also the major theme of her novels. The correspondence she maintained with Ellen Key, who was mentioned at the outset of this essay, testifies to the international superstructure of the female intellectuals and activists of the period.[3]

The late nineteenth and early twentieth centuries also witnessed the entry of women into the field of fine arts. A forerunner to that era was Paula Modersohn-Becker (1876–1907), who worked and studied at the famous artists' colony Worpswede, near Bremen, and in Paris at the turn of the century. A friend and companion to Rainer Maria Rilke and his wife, student especially of Cézanne, van Gogh, and Gaughin, Modersohn-Becker anticipated German expressionism with a style that deviated markedly from the norm set by her contemporaries. She recorded much about her development as an artist and her life at Worpswede and in Paris in her *Briefe und Tagebuchblätter* (*Letters and Journals*, 1920).

What Modersohn-Becker expressed in her art, women like Varnhagen and von Arnim had expressed in letters and journals, Droste-Hülshoff had revealed in her poetry, and Lou Andreas-Salomé began to discover in her psychoanalytic studies was the sense that women's expression could not, or should not, adhere to the standards, norms, and conventions that apply for male authors. Guided by the ideals of the Enlightenment and its concentration on the human facility to reason, men's writing tended to focus increasingly on *ratio*—a focus intensified by the scientific discoveries of the nineteenth and twentieth centuries—to the eventual apparent exclusion of those aspects of the human mind and experience often attributed to women (emotions, intuition, and so on).

Indeed, those women who achieved critical acclaim created poetry and prose according to established conventions, that is they wrote "like men." As Serke observes:

The path of women into literary history ran via correspondence, journals, and the epistolary novel to the male-determined forms of prose and poetry. Annette von Droste-Hülshoff achieved the first breakthrough.... [But] the 'I' of the poet had to assume masculine behavior in order to achieve recognition.... Even Ricarda Huch, who, in the Third Reich, possessed enough civil courage to proclaim solidarity with the Jewish and socialist authors of whom German society was being "cleansed," narrated history from the perspective of a man. Between her and Droste-Hülshoff lay the first rebellion by German-language women writers.[4]

Serke is referring to the period of the Weimar Republic, Germany's first democracy, which endured on shaky foundations from 1919 to Hitler's assumption of power in 1933. The rebellion that took place not only involved women but was a widespread esthetic revolution whose issue was an astonishing variety of movements, including Dadaism, Futurism, New Objectivity, the Bauhaus, the first blossoming of German film, revolutionary architecture, the continuation of Cubism, Surrealism, and Expressionism—all of this in an extraordinary spirit of liberation from convention of all kinds—political, social, and esthetic. While poets such as Agnes Miegel (1879–1964) and Lulu von Strauss und Torney (1873–1958) continued producing well-conceived and quite popular songs, ballads, and epic poems with traditional rhyme schemes and subjects, others such as novelist Else Lasker-Schüler (1869–1945), poet Claire Goll (1891–1977), and playwright Marie-Luise Fleisser (1901–1974) became members of the artistic bohemia of the times, staunchly maintained their independence by freeing themselves from sexual convention, and produced poems, stories, and plays dealing with women's sensual desires.

This exploration was interrupted by the Third Reich and its aftermath. During the years of Hitler's power, many—most of the best—writers of either sex saw their books banned and burned and were forced into exile, deported to concentration camps, or locked into the silence of "inner emigration." And the immediate postwar years demanded a reckoning with what had happened that did not permit the apparent indulgence of a subjective quest for the self. Any reference to women writers of that period must mention the outlawed and banished. Their works—as is the case with postwar German literature in general—include some of the most powerful writing ever produced in Germany. Nelly Sachs (1891–1970), for instance, a Jewish poet who just barely escaped to Sweden, ranks among the very best poets of the holocaust. Gertrud Kolmar, a Jewish poet of remarkable talent, born in 1894, died in a concentration camp. The exact place and date of her death remain unknown.

Women writers who survived to reenter the literary scene after 1945 dealt with fascism and its aftermath in ways very much determined by their religion and their ideologies.

Forbidden to write in 1936 because she was half Jewish, despite the clear Catholic tendencies of her work, and saved from a worse fate only by her marriage to an "Aryan," Elisabeth Langgässer (1899–1950) published the novel *Das unauslösliche Siegel* (*The Indelible Seal*) in 1946. Written during her enforced silence, the work made her, for a short period, the most famous woman writer in postwar Germany. Her last novel *Märkischer Argonautenfahrt* (Journey of the Frontier Argonauts; translated as *The Quest*, 1950) records the spiritual journey seven people make into the countryside after the collapse of Germany in 1945. The combined references to Christian cosmology, nature, and the myths of the pre-Christian era are used to balance the unredeemed natural world against the world of grace—the recurrent theme of her work.

The Catholic Gertrud von Le Fort (1876–1971) also wrote novels permeated by her Christian beliefs and treated fascism allegorically. Luise Rinser (b. 1911), who was imprisoned for political reasons toward the very end of the war and was released only with the German defeat, recorded her months in a women's detention camp in her *Gefängnistagebuch* (Prison Journal, 1946). Anna Seghers (1900–1983), a socialist and Jew who had achieved recognition already for her early works in the 1920s and is considered by many to rank among the very best of German writers, returned from her Mexican exile to the Soviet-occupied zone in 1947 and continued revealing her commitment to socialist ideology in her socialist realist novels.

In Austria, Erika Mitterer (b. 1906), an admirer and disciple of Rilke, who was able to remain in her country, continued the publication of poems and novels while her Roumanian-born compatriot, the Jew Rose Ausländer (b. 1902), was forced to emigrate to New York and did not return to Europe until 1964; she has resided in Düsseldorf since 1965. Another Austrian, Christine Lavant (1915–1973), deserves recognition for the production of highly original poetry against a background of considerable poverty and under the stress of lifelong disabilities.

The two most recent generations of writers include those for whom the Second World War was an experience of childhood and/or youth and those who were born in the years after the war. For the former, the increasing sense of difference and otherness has come, in many cases, to be the dominant concern of their later writings. This group includes writers such as Ingeborg Drewitz, who wrote novels, stories, essays, and radio plays (a genre, incidentally, that has engaged a great many women writers in this century) in addition to the works mentioned at the outset of this essay. It also includes Gabriele Wohmann (b. 1932) who, since 1958, has published more than fifty works in all genres. A regular participant in the annual meeting of the Group 47[5] beginning in 1960, she has focused on the realm of private lives as the arena in which the conspiratorial and oppressive mechanisms of society are painfully accentuated and experienced. Of similarly extensive production is Ilse Aichinger (b. 1921), whose very Austrian preoccupation with the insufficiency of language has formed the basis for many of her stories, poems, and dialogues.

Recent products from politically committed authors tend to show more concern with form than did those of their similarly engaged predecessors; these works are less tendentious and more "literary," but the strength of the underlying convictions has not lessened. This development is symptomatic of the kind of sophistication that has become possible over the last century: once women's voices could be heard, the voices could become modulated. The most recent generation, finally, may be said to have signaled its position in Verena Stefan's (b. 1947) *Häutungen* (*Shedding*, 1975), a work that, in its introduction, discusses in the manner of contemporary feminist theory how the very language of our society determines opinions and sexual politics.

The woman question as it exists today may be framed differently in socialist GDR and in capitalist FRG, Austria, and Switzerland. Equal rights are constitutionally guaranteed in the GDR, and most women there work outside the home, but Christa Wolf's revelations, the admissions of the women interviewed by Maxie Wander (1933–1977) for her 1977 collection of protocols entitled *Guten Morgen, du Schöne* (Good Morning, You Pretty One) and Irmtraud Morgner's (b. 1933) wildly feminist Troubadora Beatrice's adventures in the GDR give lie to the official positions and examine both the origins and the implementation of patriarchal attitudes. In the West, women have begun to approach the questions from a wider range of angles and disciplines than those embraced by creative forms. Theorists have taken their cues from Virginia Woolf and more recently from French and American feminists; extensive critical attention accompanies the rampant production of literature of all genres in a variety of experimental forms. As society has become more differentiated, so has women's writing permitted more individualistic expression.[6]

NOTES

1. Jürgen Serke, *Frauen Schreiben. Ein neues Kapitel deutschsprachiger Literatur* (Frankfurt am Main: Fischer, 1982).
2. "Vaterlandsliebe" (love of fatherland), given at the First International Writers' Convention on the Defense of Culture; included in *Über Kunst und Wirklichkeit*, Vol. I of *Die Tendenz in der reinen Kunst*, introd. Sigrid Bock (Berlin: Akademie-Verlag, 1970).
3. See Rudolph Binion, *Frau Lou: Nietzsche's Wayward Disciple*, Foreword by Walter Kaufmann (Princeton: Princeton University Press, 1968), 559.
4. Serke, *Frauen Schreiben*, 40. Ricarda Huch's stature was recognized by her election into the prestigious Prussian Academy for Literature, from which she was the *only* member to resign, in public protest, when the Nazis imposed "cultural conformity" on that group in 1933.
5. A loosely-coordinated group of West German authors and critics, whose first meeting in 1947 was prompted by the rigidity of the United States occupying powers, who had banned several publication attempts of the early postwar generation; calling together those involved in literary endeavors it provided at first the only channel for broadcasting their works and exchanging ideas. It held regular meetings for about twenty years and became generally the literary barometer of the FRG, until it disbanded in 1967, recognizing that by its very power, it could no longer practice the democratic liberalism it originally set out to defend.
6. I have relied in writing this paper on several secondary works, some of which (those in English) are listed in the bibliography. Here I should like to acknowledge the German-language sources for this article. They include: Gisela Brinker-Gabler, ed., *Deutsche Dichterinnen vom 16. Jahrhundert bis zur Gegenwart* (Frankfurt am Main: Fischer, 1978); Elke Fredericksen, ed., *Die Frauenfrage in Deutschland, 1865–1915. Texte und Dokumente* (Stuttgart: Reclam, 1981); Elisabeth Friedrichs, *Die deutschsprachigen Schriftstellerinnen des 18. und 19. Jahrhunderts. Ein Lexikon* (Stuttgart: Metzler, 1981); and Gabriele Strecker, *Frauenträume, Frauentränen. Über den deutschen Frauenroman* (Weilheim/Oberbayern: Otto Wilhelm Barth Verlag, 1969). Grateful acknowledgment for assistance at various stages in the preparation of this essay goes to the editors of this volume, Barbara Shollar and Marian Arkin; to my colleagues Sara Lennox, Karen Achberger, and Ingo Seidler; and to various members of the Coalition of Women in German.

BIBLIOGRAPHY

Altbach, Edith Hoshino, Jeanette Clausen, Dagmar Schultz and Naomi Stephan, eds. *German Feminism: Readings in Politics and Literature*. Albany: State University of New York Press, 1984.

Braun, Lily. *Selected Writings on Feminism and Socialism*. Edited and translated by Alfred G. Meyer. Bloomington: Indiana University Press, 1987.

Burkhard, Marianne, and Edith Waldstein, eds. *Women in German Yearbook. Feminist Studies and German Culture*. Vols. I–IV. New York: University Press of America, 1985–1988.

Cocalis, Susan, ed. *The Defiant Muse. German Feminist Poems from the Middle Ages to the Present. A Bilingual Anthology*. New York: Feminist Press. Forthcoming.

———— and Kay Goodman, eds. *Beyond the Eternal Feminine: Critical Essays on Women and German Literature*. Stuttgart: Akademischer Verlag Hans-Dieter Heinz, 1982.

Daviau, Donald G., ed. *Modern Austrian Literature: Special Issue on Austrian Women Writers, Journal of the International Arthur Schnitzler Association* 12, no. 3–4 (1979).

Ecker, Gisela, ed. *Feminist Aesthetics*. Boston: Beacon, 1985.

Fout, John C., ed. *German Women in the Nineteenth Century*. New York: Holmes and Meier, 1984.

Goodman, Katharine. *Dis/Closures. Women's Autobiography in Germany between 1790 and 1914*. New York: Peter Lang, 1986.

Herrmann, Elizabeth Rütschi, and Edna Huttenmaier Spitz. *German Women in the Eighteenth and Nineteenth Centuries. A Social and Literary History*. Bloomington: Indiana University Press, 1986.

Meyer, Alfred G. *The Feminism and Socialism of Lily Braun*. Bloomington: Indiana University Press, 1985.

New German Critique, no. 27 (Fall 1982), Women Writers and Critics.

Resnick, Margery and Isabelle de Courtivron. *Women Writers in Translation: An Annotated Bibliography, 1945–1982*. New York: Garland, 1984.

BRAZIL

Naomi Lindstrom

The writing of Brazilian women has followed a varied course from its discreetly private beginnings through its emergence into the public world of literary life to its continuing evolution into new forms. This essay will describe how this writing began and gained a place in Brazilian literature, and it will indicate the major directions among Brazilian women writers through the years.

Current Brazilian literature features a good number of women writers; in addition, there is a great deal of interest in the ways women's experiences are represented in literature by writers of either sex. Four Brazilian women are recognized as having written classics of national literature: Cecília Meireles (1901–1964), Henriqueta Lisboa (1904–1985), Rachel de Queiroz (b. 1910), and Clarice Lispector (1925–1977). Others, such as Dinah Silveira de Queiroz (1911–1985) and Nélida Piñon (b. 1937) enjoy widespread esteem; the former was the first woman to be awarded the Brazilian Academy of Letter's Machado de Assis Prize, for her novel *A muralha* (*The Women of Brazil*, 1954). Historically, though, Brazilian literature has been slow to make room for women and their work.

In the early part of Brazilian literary history—until 1922, when the country began a massive campaign in favor of cultural advancement and cosmopolitanism—women were not participants in the public side of literary life. Certain women made their mark in literary circles because of their skill as hostesses and conversationalists, their privately displayed wit and knowledge, and their ability to write in such forms as private letters and memoirs or diaries. They were not, however, expected to become "authors" in the public sense. Even now, traces of these chivalric, genteel conventions persist—as, for example in the widespread disinclination to divulge the birthdates of women authors.

The new wave of feminism and the more widespread entry of women into the arts, journalism, and the academic professions have impelled critics to discover what women were writing before they began to appear formally as writers. Two examples from the prehistory of Brazilian women's writing should give an idea of this "lost" literature: Alice Dayrell Brant (1881–1970) kept *Minha vida de menina* (*The Diary of Helena Morley*) between 1893 and 1895. When in 1942 a private edition was printed for Brant's family and close friends, its reputation as a fresh, vital work of social observation quickly spread beyond the intended audience of intimates, and a general edition brought this chronicle of small-town life and family interaction to a wide public. The U.S. poet Elizabeth Bishop became fascinated with the diary and published an English version of it in 1957, which was reissued in 1977. Whereas Brant writes in the tradition of the privately appreciated literary lady—salon belle, hostess, memoirist, or letter writer—Francisca Senhorina da Motta Diniz' (fl. 1880) work is that of a much more rough-and-ready polemical, pamphleteering woman. Motta Diniz was a schoolteacher from Minas Gerais who, during the late nineteenth century, founded small feminist newspapers in various cities of south-central Brazil. Her efforts, such as *O Sexo Femenino* (The Female Sex), which she edited in 1873 in Campanha, and *O Quinze de Novembro do Sexo Femenino* (The Fifteenth of November for the Female Sex, that is, Independence Day), founded in 1890 in Rio de Janeiro, were virtually forgotten until the 1970s' resurgence of feminism.

The general reticence and obscurity of women writers began to end with the coming, in 1922, of Modernism, which meant not only a proliferation of avant-garde movements, but also a vigorous attempt to replace Brazil's cumbersome conventional literary life with an open, cosmopolitan creative scene. Between 1922 and 1930, Brazil went from having virtually no women authors to featuring three women among its first-rank writers. These were the poets Cecília Meireles and Henriqueta Lisboa and the novelist Rachel de Queiroz. Their writing is not fairly described as "women's writing," for their work tended to resemble that of the male writers with whom they were associated, such as Meireles' particular enclave of spiritualistic avant-garde poets and Queiroz's set of regionalist novelists determined to capture realistically the misery of the northeastern region. Of the three, only Queiroz took up women's social problems in a way that may be considered feminist; Lisboa dealt with the theme of woman in a highly abstract, mythic fashion; and it is difficult to identify a distinct woman's element in Meireles' work. Another prominent figure among Brazil's newly emerged women writers, though not as widely celebrated as the three just mentioned, is Dinah Silveira de Queiroz. Over the years she wrote diverse works including short stories, historical novels, children's literature, science fiction, and religious works. She maintained a generally high reputation but did not assume a very defined identity as a writer. In 1980 she became the second woman to be accepted into the Brazilian Academy.

Like Rachel de Queiroz, later women writers often turned to literature to express their social concerns. Maria Clara Machado (b. 1921), for example, has been an actress, dramatist, director, and organizer of Brazilian theater for many years, including periods when theatrical expression was politically difficult. *O menino e o vento* (The Child and the Wind, 1967) criticized schooling and the treatment of children at a time when its liberationist drama was considerably bolder than most Brazilian stage fare. Stella Leonardos de Silva Lima (b. 1923), who worked in children's theater, often with Machado, has also written prose and poetry for both child and adult readers. Involving children in theater, Lima sought to develop a new generation of theatergoers who would expect drama to reflect Brazilian realities rather than follow European patterns. Her writings are critical of the restrictions placed on individual behavior and expression.

Because of the subtle complexity of her existential themes and the variety of narrative techniques employed to convey her material, Clarice Lispector is far and away the most important of the women writers born in the 1920s. Much of her work centers around female characters and their difficulty in becoming autonomous individuals, as does the fiction of Lygia Fagundes Telles (b. 1923), a more popular and accessible writer whose much-read *As meninas* (*The Girl in the Photograph*, 1973) emphasizes the difficulty of entering womanhood when mores are shifting with bewildering rapidity. In 1985 Telles became the third woman admitted to the Brazilian Academy of Letters. The most recent Brazilian woman to win a solid international reputation is Nélida Piñon. In her subtle, mysterious fiction, relations between men and women are a frequent theme.

In recent years, the number of worthwhile women writers on the Brazilian scene has risen impressively. In situating some representative examples of these writers, it is important to avoid forcing them into defined and organized factions or movements within "women's writing," such as has occurred in France over women's expression. As in France, Brazilian literary life contains much theoretical discussion, especially on what might constitute a form of writing distinctive to women, such as female erotics, or the literary presentation of the experience of woman's body. Yet these notions are formulated, aired, and examined rather than argued in factionalistic debate: the essential purpose is not to argue a position but to stimulate thought and literary experiment. In many cases, women writers are still struggling to "get it all said"—that is, simply to express aspects of women's lives that have not previously been expressed publicly. One can, in fact, classify these writers, rather roughly, by their predominant concerns; among these are a broad range of Brazil's social problems, the close examination of female consciousness, woman's involvement in eroticism, and the long-standing tradition of meditative, existential poetry.

The ethnic diversity of Brazil, with its indigenous groups, substantial black population, and varied new immigrants, as well as its descendants of Portuguese colonists, has provided material for women writers. An outstanding representative of Indian-theme writing is Regina Célia Colônia (b. 1942), who has spent time among tribal peoples of the Andes and northern Brazil. *Cancão para o totem* (Song to the Totem, 1975) shows her ability to use tribal lore in an avant-garde poetic prose. Myrtis Campobello (b. 1937) created controversy with her novel *Pele contra pele* (Skin against Skin, 1971), an unflattering look at the treatment accorded blacks in a society that often prides itself on racial equality. Lya Luft (b. 1940), the daughter of Germans, has given special novelistic attention to the situation of the newest Brazilians.

Even when Brazil's women novelists have a knowledgeable and empathetic understanding of the country's indigenous and African heritage, they have typically (more predominantly than men) arisen from the traditional Portuguese stock and the newer "white ethnics." Thus, it was an astonishing literary event, when Carolina Maria de Jesus (1913–1977), a woman of color from the *favela* (the slum zone encircling urban areas) produced the critically esteemed bestseller excerpted in this anthology, *Quarto de despejo* (*Child of the Dark*, 1960).

Class relations and social hierarchy have continued to draw the scrutiny of women writers who are also insightful social critics. A major example is Ruth Bueno (née Goulart, b. 1934), a lawyer specializing in women's rights, on which she has written a noted manual. In her fiction Bueno favors a lyrical prose and explores intimate experience, but these features of her writing do not preclude a sharp critique of society, as can be seen in her science-fiction novel, *Asilo nas torres* (Asylum in the Towers, 1977). Maria Alice Barroso (b. 1926) pursued a conventional social realism early in her career but won her fame when she used innovative novelistic techniques to criticize social arrangements. Her *Um nome para matar* (A Name to Kill, 1967) and *Quem matou Pacífico?* (Who Killed Pacífico?, 1969) show a small town in which a land-owning family attempts to exercise a feudal dominion but is blocked by the resourcefulness of those they would subjugate. A concern with society's rigid organization is also central in the work of the play-wright Leilah Assuncão (b. 1944), whose best-known work, *Fala baixo, senão eu grito* (Speak Softly, or I'll Scream, 1969) is excerpted in this anthology. Teresinka Pereira (Teresinha Alves Pereira, b. 1939) practices a poetry and drama of protest, at times favoring experimental forms to express a beat-generation spirit of freedom and at times focusing on more particular social problems.

Women's personal experience within the constraints of social convention has interested many contemporary authors. Some are involved in exposing the intimate politics of the couple or the family, on the assumption that traditional reticence about the private sphere protects and perpetuates inequalities. Others, following the general lines established by Lispector, scrutinize women's inner experience for what it reveals about the nature of existence. None of these writers could properly be categorized as predominantly feminist, but all show signs of a special concern with the ways in which women register experience. Tânia Faillace (b. 1936) is best represented by the novel *Fuga* (Taking Flight, 1964). Its adolescent female pro-tagonist enters an existential crisis when, just as she is beginning womanhood she discovers that her own feelings and beliefs are much more complex and difficult to define than she had hitherto assumed. Judith Grossman, a poet, critic, and short-story writer with many ties to U.S. literature, created several notable women characters who narrate their own life stories in *A noite estrelada: estórias do interim* (Starry Night: Stories of the Interim, 1977). Renata Pallotini (b. 1938), also known as a poet, has treated in her fiction the complicated balances of power existing between members of a family and partners in a marriage. Rachel Jardim (contemp.) has written short sketches that evoke in detail everyday life in the 1930s and 1940s, especially among contemporary women. Her thematic anthology *Mulheres & mulheres* (Women & Women, 1978), is a showcase for portraits of women characters whose experience reflects both personal and social aspects of existence. Sônia Coutinho (b. 1944) obtained recognition for her short stories with the collections *Nascimento de uma mulher* (Birth of a Woman, 1971) and *Uma certa felicidade* (A Certain Happiness, 1976). She is especially concerned with the disillusionment faced by small-town women who expect to find an idealized liberation in urban life.

Women have lately won attention for their erotic literature, the principal goal of such writing being to assert women's entitlement to express themselves fully. While Brazil is in many respects a very open society in questions of sexuality, as evidenced by the social acceptance of single mothers, gay men, and lesbians, there have been persistent areas of repression, particularly in the public arts, where censorship has run interference. The lifting of many forms of censorship over the past decade, together with a deliberate campaign to assert women's right to erotic expression, resulted in such projects as Márcia Denser's anthologies of erotic stories by women, *Muito prazer* (It's a Great Pleasure, 1983) and *O prazer é todo me* (The Pleasure Is All Mine, 1984) and Olga Savary's (b. 1933) *Carne viva, antologia de poesia erótica* (Raw Flesh, Anthology of Erotic Poetry, 1984), which contains the work of Brazilian authors of both sexes.

Brazilian women poets of promise are extremely numerous. These include poets born in recent decades and others who, though born before 1940, have only with time come to general notice for their work. Minas Gerais, the Brazilian state famous for its outstanding writers (among them Henriqueta Lisboa), has now the exceptional Laïs Correa de Araujo and Celina Ferreira, both born in the late 1920s and both working in the tradition of existential poetry. Adélia Prado (b. 1936), who won public attention with her 1976 collection of poetry *Bagagem* (Baggage), also favors a timeless, meditative poetry. The poetry of all three could profitably be examined for mythic images of women and of female forces in the cosmos.

Other poets deserving mention, among the many currently on the scene, are Jandyra Waters, who emerged as a poet with *Pedras nuas* (Naked Stones, 1974); Lélia Coelho Frota (b. 1937), whose most extensive work is *Poesia lembrada* (Poetry Recollected, 1971); Fúlvia de Carvalho Lopes (b. 1940), who drew praise for her *O ser impossível* (Impossible Being, 1970); and Rita Rodrigo Octávio Moutinho (b. 1951), whose first collection *a hora quieta* (The Still Hour, 1975) was well received.

In sum, although many Brazilian women writers have a strong interest in social criticism, they are unlikely to isolate women's issues. They are more interested in such broad problems as the stratification of society along class and (to some extent) ethnic lines; economic inequalities; the lingering constraints of traditional ideas of propriety; and the damage done by forces working upon Brazil, (such as economic exploitation from abroad). It is not uncommon to hear the statement that a dominant focus specifically on women's issues makes sense only for women in more economically advantaged countries, where social issues other than feminism are less pressing.

BIBLIOGRAPHY

Background

Bello, José Marin. *A History of Modern Brazil, 1889–1964*. Trans. James L. Taylor. Stanford: Stanford University Press, 1966.

Freyre, Gilberto. *The Mansions and the Shanties: The Making of Modern Brazil*. Trans. Harriet de Onis. New York: Knopf, 1966.

Roett, Riordan, ed. *Brazil in the Sixties*. Nashville: Vanderbilt University Press, 1972.

Literary Criticism and Literature

Carlisle, Charles Richard, ed. *Tesserae: A Mosaic of Twentieth Century Brazilian Poetry*. Fort Worth: Latitudes Press, 1984.

Ellison, Fred P. *Brazil's New Novel. Four Northeastern Masters: José Lins do Rego, Jorge Amado, Graciliano Ramos, Raquel de Queiroz*. Berkeley: University of California Press, 1954. Reprint 1980.

Foster, David William, and Roberto Reis, eds. *A Dictionary of Contemporary Brazilian Authors*. Tempe, AZ: Center for Latin American Studies, 1981.

Lowe, Elizabeth. *The City in Brazilian Literature*. Toronto: Associated University Presses/Fairleigh Dickinson University Press, 1982.

CANADA
ANGLOPHONE CANADA[1]
Wendy Robbins Keitner

The Europeans who "discovered" North America, it has been said, were those men who believed least in its existence: merchants and adventurers looking for a northwest ocean passage to the Far East. The continent—inhabited by Inuits and Amer-Indians—that blocked their way gradually became the site of permanent settlements, first French and then English. Eventually bitter trade rivalry, leading to war between Britain and France, resulted both in the decimation of the native peoples (movingly registered in the lamentations of the female "memorizers" of the Nootka oral tradition, for example) and also, notwithstanding the decisive British military victory at the Battle of the Plains of Abraham in 1759, in permanent linguistic, cultural, and religious divisions between anglophone and francophone Canada.

After the American War of Independence in 1776, the immigration of tens of thousands of Loyalist men, women, and children from New England—colonists who chose to remain loyal to Britain and were rewarded with land grants—added another indelible mark on the Canadian character, which is generally seen as more respectful of law and order and less ruggedly individualistic than the American. Loyalist immigration not only strengthened the political, social, and economic dominance of the white Anglo-Saxon Protestant community, but it also determined that Canadian literature in English would represent the confluence of the two main streams in the language—those of Britain and the United States.

Yet, unlike these countries, Canada is not a world power and has a relatively small population—roughly twenty-five million people, equivalent to that of the state of California—in a land of vast expanse; in fact, part of the national psyche is a typically postcolonial sense of national inferiority. The uncivilized wilderness, the insignificant small town, or the "beautiful loser"—the victimized character—all are central symbols in the Canadian imagination. In the work of women writers, an analogy is often drawn between the colonization of the land and other forms of exploitation, between the submerged identity of a country sometimes depicted as a "sleeping giant"—one that had no flag other than the Union Jack until 1965—and the suppressed identity of woman—who was not considered a "person" before the law until 1929.

Canadian literature in English begins in the pre-Confederation or colonial era (about a hundred years before Canada became an independent country in 1867), just after the British conquest of the French and their garrisoning of Quebec; it begins with the writing of a woman—novelist Frances Brooke (1723–1789). Like Brooke, whose epistolary novel of manners *The History of Emily Montague*, set in Quebec, was published in London in 1769, a significant number of other British gentlewomen contributed valuable descriptions of colonial life to early Canadian literature in the form of fiction, diaries, or letters—often exchanged between mothers and daughters: Elizabeth Simcoe (1766–1850); early feminist Anna Jameson (1794–1860); Catharine Parr Traill (1802–1899), author of the practical *The Female Emigrant's Guide* (1854); and her sister, Susanna Moodie (1803–1885), whose *Roughing It in the Bush* (1852) is a classic of pioneer writing. The first Canadian-born novelist to publish was also a woman: Julia Beckwith Hart (1796–1867), author of the romance *St. Ursula's Convent* (1824).

A local dramatic literature began to take shape somewhat later, in the mid-nineteenth century, replacing the well-known English plays that had at first formed the repertoire of garrison theater groups. Again, the beginning of play-writing in English Canada can be traced to the work of a woman: Eliza Lanesford Cushing (1794–1886) published numerous prose and dramatic works on historical and Biblical themes in *The Literary Garland* between 1839 and 1845 (she also edited the influential journal in 1850). A number of other women also wrote and had plays published in this era; some pre-Confederation women's dramatic literature has been recovered—for example, in the volume *Women Pioneers: Canada's Lost Plays* (1979).

No comparable literary archeology has been done in the field of colonial women's poetry, however. Griselda Tonge, Margaret Blennerhasset, Halifax sisters Sarah and Mary E. Herbert (who produced a joint collection of poems, *The Aeolian Harp* [1857], as well as several romantic novels and temperance tales), Clotilda Jennings (*Linden Rhymes*, 1852), and Mary Jane Katzmann (*Frankincense and Myrrh*, 1893) are little more than names in *The Oxford Companion to Canadian Literature*. Only the work of Montreal-born Rosanna Leprohon (1829–1879), whose poems were collected by John Lovell after her death in *The Poetical Works of Mrs. Leprohon (Miss R.E. Mullins)* (1881) and whose novels have become the subject of renewed interest in recent years, has not been forgotten. Leprohon's three novels published during the 1860s—*The Manor House of De Villerai, Antoinette de Mirecourt,* and *Armand Durand*—offer a realistic portrayal of French-English relations, and her essentially feminist views on the education of women and on marriage as a partnership are of special interest. A more comprehensive picture of eighteenth- and nineteenth-century Canadian women's writing remains to be pieced together from the important bibliographic work recently completed by Beth Light and Veronica Strong-Boag in *True Daughters of the North, Canadian Women's History: An Annotated Bibliography* (1980) and that still in progress in the Maritime Women's Archives Project.

The literature of the period following Confederation in 1867 up to World War I must be placed in the context of a new women's history then being made. The "woman question" emerges as a major social and political issue in the decades following the creation of an independent Canada—a fact obscured in traditional histories. Several important women's organizations date from the 1870s and 1880s: women's missionary societies, intended for evangelical work, responded to the urgent need for urban social work; other reformist organizations included the Young Women's Christian Association and the controversial Woman's Christian Temperance Union, which crusaded for both prohibition and women's suffrage. Numerous women's artistic, musical, and literary societies sprang up, as did women's rights associations—the least publicly acceptable element of the club movement in the early years. The first Canadian suffrage organization was founded in 1876 by Dr. Emily Howard Stowe, the first woman physician in Canada, as the Toronto Women's Literary Club; in 1883, it threw off its protective disguise and emerged as the Toronto Women's Suffrage Association. By 1893, a Canadian federation of women's organizations—The National Council of Women of Canada—was formed and took action on such matters as public health, education, adult literacy, factory working conditions, prison reform, and wildlife conservation; in 1900 it compiled a report entitled *Women in Canada*, intended as a handbook of information, to be distributed at the Paris Exhibition, on Canadian women and their work. And, because almost every large city daily had a female journalist writing a regular column or editing a separate women's page by the end of the nineteenth century, Canadians at the time were intensely conscious of the activities of these early female alliances.

In this period of social ferment between Confederation and World War I, two internationally acclaimed Canadian women writers emerged: Sara Jeannette Duncan (1861–1922), who was the first woman to work in the editorial department of a leading Canadian newspaper, wrote numerous plays and novels; Lucy Maud Montgomery (1874–1942) authored one of the world's best-loved children's novels, *Anne of Green Gables* (1908). Another very popular Maritime writer for children is Margaret Marshall Saunders, whose sentimental *Beautiful Joe* (1894), one of her many animal tales, has kept her name alive. Many more novels by women of the time, however, are only now beginning to be investigated. Most contain portraits of traditional women whose lives are centered in family and church, although some present new images of women and describe the technological, industrial, and social changes taking places in their day. Writers to be reassessed include Carrie Jenkins Harris (d. 1903); Alice Jones (1853–1933); Jones' sister, Susan Carleton Jones (1864–1926); Maria Amelia Fytche (1844–1927), author of *Kerchiefs to Hunt Souls* (1896; reprinted, 1980), a novel highly critical of the situation of women, especially as governesses; Lily Dougall (1858–1923), author of a dozen novels and the first editor of *The World Wide*, a Montreal journal of contemporary thought; and May Agnes Fleming (1840–1880), one of the first Canadians to have a career as a writer of popular fiction. Despite the fact that the contemporary literary scene is dominated by powerfully influential women writers, the 200-year-old tradition of female authorship in Canada has received relatively scant critical attention.

While the Anglo-Canadian novel tradition stretches back more than 200 years, and drama nearly 150 years, the poetry tradition, as we know it, is scarcely 100 years old. Here again the beginning is made by a woman. The standard poetry anthologies and literary histories recognize no important poet before Isabella Valancy Crawford (1850–1887) who published only one book in her short lifetime—*Old Spookses' Pass, Malcolm's Katie, and Other Poems* (1884), and whose remarkable mythopoeic powers were not fully appreciated until the 1970s. Other women poets of the period have almost wholly been forgotten: Maritimer Margaret Gill Currie (1843–?); Susie Frances Harrison (1859–1935), whose *Pine, Rose, and Fleur de Lis* (1891) contains a monody on Crawford; and Agnes Ethelwyn Wetherald (1857–1940), who wrote the introduction to J.W. Garvin's *Collected Poems of Isabella Valancy Crawford* (1905). Such works clearly suggest the beginnings of a self-defining female poetic tradition by the turn of the century.

Born in the same year and the same place (Brantford, Ontario) as Sara Jeannette Duncan, E. Pauline Johnson (1861–1913), the daughter of a Mohawk father and an English mother (she later adopted the Indian name Tekahionwake), is the first authentic Indian voice in Canadian literature in English. Johnson left no successor, but the Nootka women's legends collected and "translated" recently by Anne Cameron in *Daughters of Copper Woman* (1981) powerfully extends the West Coast native tradition. This collection contains a creation myth, retells from a native woman's perspective the history of European male conquest, and culminates in a deeply compelling vision of universal sisterhood.

While dramatic literature is the least significant genre in the period, interesting material was produced by such turn-of-the-century playwrights as Agnes Maule Machar (1837–1927), Elizabeth Jane Thompson (1858–1927), Catharine Nina Merritt (1859–1926), Jean Newton McIlwraith (1859–1938), and Sara Anne Curzon (1833–1898). Curzon, an activist, dramatized the controversy surrounding the admission of women to Canadian universities in her 1882 play *The Sweet Girl Graduate* and is remembered as the author of *Laura Secord*, her 1887 play about the young woman who warned the British of an impending American attack during the War of 1812, a play she wrote "to rescue from oblivion the name of a brave woman, and set it in its proper place among the heroes of Canadian history."

The personification of Canadian feminism for the first quarter of the twentieth century is, most obviously, Nellie McClung (1873–1951), popular novelist and political campaigner. During World War I, manpower shortages led to increased female employment in nontraditional jobs, and the Wartime Elections Act of 1917 enfranchised the female relatives of military personnel, significantly broadening the base of the suffragist movement. Building on this, McClung and other suffragists, shortly after the war, not only won for women the right to vote in federal and most provincial elections, but also, in 1929, successfully challenged the British North America Act, which had denied that women were "persons."

The best Canadian poem of the era of the Great Depression is, arguably, *The Wind Our Enemy*, the title poem of Anne Marriott's (b. 1913) first book, published in 1939. Needed are recovery and reevaluation of the work of other women poets in the between-the-wars period: Elizabeth Roberts (1864–1922) and her relative Dorothy Roberts (b. 1906); Florence Randal Livesay (1874–1953); early Modernist Florence Ayscough (1878–1942), who collaborated with the American poet Amy Lowell to produce *Fir-Flower Tablets* (1921); Floris Clarke McLaren (b. 1904), author of *Frozen Fire* (1937); and Louise Morey Bowman (1882–1944), who experimented with free verse. Additionally, a feminist critique needs to be made of the two most successful women poets of the era: Marjorie Pickthall (1883–1922) and Audrey Alexandra Brown (b. 1904), whose writings represent an almost total denial of female experience, but which nonetheless earned the praise of male critics—in 1944 Brown received the Royal Society's Lorne Pierce Medal "for distinguished contributions to Canadian literature." The career of Canada's first major feminist poet, Dorothy Livesay (b. 1909) takes root in the pre-World War II period also, although it does not bear its best fruit until after midcentury; nurturing, and in turn nurtured by, the second wave of the women's movement, her poems about working-class life and women's realities shatter the Victorian mold of the "true woman"—self-sacrificing and beatifically domestic—and strike out in new directions.

In these same years of the Depression, Gwen Pharis Ringwood (1910–1984) emerges as Canada's first major woman dramatist. The author of over sixty plays—dramas, musicals, children's plays, radio plays—Ringwood has been a major force in the development of Canadian drama. Twenty-five of her plays appear in *The Collected Plays of Gwen Pharis Ringwood* (1982). Some of her best works are poetic "folk dramas," such as *Still Stands the House* (1939), a powerful evocation of the severity of prairie life, and *The Deep Has Many Voices* (1967), which again focuses on a strongly realized central female protagonist.

But between-the-wars literature is dominated, finally, by the stunning international success of Mazo de la Roche (1879–1961), whose major triumph was a series of sixteen novels chronicling several generations in the Whiteoaks family; under the sway of a matriarch named Adeline (Gran), the family owns a splendid estate in southern Ontario, of which the focal point is their house, Jalna. As popular in its day as the successful soap operas now (more than eleven million copies have been sold worldwide, and many titles are still in print), the *Jalna* books, created the myth of Canada as a great, good place. Other fiction writers of note are Martha Ostenso (1900–1963); Laura Goodman Salverson (1890–1970); Emily Carr (1871–1945), Canada's most famous woman painter; Irene Baird (1901–1981); Elizabeth Smart (b. 1914); and, especially, Ethel Wilson (1888–1980), whose short stories began to appear in the late 1930s and whose best work, *Swamp Angel* (1954), tracing its female hero's escape from a disastrous marriage to start a new life on a remote lake in northern British Columbia, sets the pattern for several later Canadian women's sagas of self-discovery in the wilderness.

Most of the best work in Canadian literature belongs to the contemporary period, and it is integrally connected with both the nationalist and feminist movements of the late 1950s and the decade of the 1960s. Judy LaMarsh, Canada's first female cabinet minister, appointed by the Liberal government of Lester B. Pearson, prevailed upon him to set up a Royal Commission on the Status of Women; its *Report* (1970) provided a valuable description of, and shocking statistics on, women's inferior status. It concluded: "Perhaps no prejudice in human society is so deeply imbedded or so little understood. To create equality it will be necessary to create a totally new climate, a totally new frame of reference against which every question affecting women can be assessed." The sociopolitical upheaval of the era created an impassioned drive for renewal, providing an impetus which culminated in 1983 in the long overdue "repatriation" from Britain of the Canadian constitution; its new Charter of Rights and Freedoms, whose provisions came into effect in 1985—a landmark year—guarantees women's rights, most particularly native womens' rights, for the first time.

At present, many new directions are being explored by an increasingly large number of women writers. In prose fiction, the most outstanding work has been done by Mavis Gallant (b. 1922), Margaret Laurence (1926–1987), Alice Munro (b. 1931), and Margaret Atwood (b. 1939)—all of whom are represented in this anthology. Other important novelists and short-story writers for whom, unfortunately, space could not be found are Adele Wiseman (b. 1928), who wrote *The Sacrifice* (1956); Sheila Watson (b. 1919), author of *The Double Hook* (1959), the first truly modern Canadian novel; Sylvia Fraser (b. 1935), whose career begins with *Pandora* (1972); and Marian Engel (1933–1985), with whom an overtly feminist fiction begins in *No Clouds of Glory* (1968; reprinted as *Sara Bastard's Notebook* in 1974). Two American-born writers, Audrey Thomas (b. 1935) and Jane Rule (b.

1931), who settled permanently in Canada, deserve special mention. Thomas's autobiographical trilogy—*Mrs. Blood* (1970), *Songs My Mother Taught Me*, (1973), and *Blown Figures* (1974)—and her twin novellas *Munchmeyer and Prospero on the Island* (1971), all written in experimental, discontinuous prose, introduce new themes such as pregnancy, abortion, and miscarriage. Rule's novels—*Desert of the Heart* (1964), *This Is Not For You* (1970), and *Against the Season* (1971)—and her stories collected in *Theme for Diverse Instruments* (1975) introduce the subject of lesbian love. Rule has also written a book about other lesbian writers, *Lesbian Images* (1975). But the best writing by both authors comes in the post-1975 period.

Canadian drama comes into its own in the 1970s and 1980s. Carol Bolt (b. 1941) has emerged as one of Canada's most successful and prolific playwrights. Her early plays—*Buffalo Jump* (1972), *Gabe* (1973), and *Red Emma* (1974)—offer a political reinterpretation of historical events; her most successful play (also adapted for television) is *One Night Stand* (1977), which starts out as a contemporary feminist comedy but ends in senseless violence. Numerous other women playwrights have surfaced recently, among them Joanna Glass (b. 1936); Beverly Simons (b. 1938); Erika Ritter (b. 1948), author of the hit comedy *Automatic Pilot* (1980); and Sharon Pollock (b. 1936), author of *Blood Relations* (1981), which won a Governor General's Award.

In postwar poetry, too, there has been a virtual explosion of talent. Marya Fiamengo (b. 1926) who has written one of the finest poems in the English language on women and aging, "In Praise of Old Women," is represented by this one title. Others poets not represented but also important include Anne Wilkinson (1910–1961), author of *The Hangman Ties the Holly* (1955), whose work forms a bridge between the repression of the female self typical of Audrey Alexandra Brown and the militant feminism of writers after Margaret Atwood; P.K. Page (b. 1916), whose first book, *As Ten As Twenty* (1946), includes the frequently anthologized poem "The Stenographers," which introduces a new subject—female clerical workers in the modern city; Jay MacPherson (b. 1931), who wrote *The Boatman* (1957); the versatile Phyllis Webb (b. 1927); Margaret Avison (b. 1918), whose work reflects a deep Christian spirituality; and Maritime Provinces writer Elizabeth Brewster (b. 1922). More colloquial and expressive poetry is to be found in the work of Jewish writers Miriam Waddington (b. 1917) and Phyllis Gotlieb (b. 1926). Susan Musgrave (b. 1951) published her Haida-inspired *Songs of a Sea-Witch* (1970) at the age of 18; her work, like the experimental writing of Daphne Marlatt (b. 1942) and of Anne Szumigalski (b. 1926), continues in the 1980s. But it is the achievement primarily of Gwendolyn MacEwen (1941–1987)—with her symbolically titled *The Rising Fire* (1963)—Dorothy Livesay, and Margaret Atwood—Canada's extraordinary women of letters—to have developed a truly woman-centered poetics.

In the past decade, all the major novelists and poets of the postwar period have published new work, culminating, perhaps, in the enormously successful dystopia by Atwood, *The Handmaid's Tale* (1985). New writers who have made their debut include novelists Aritha van Herk (*Judith*, 1978) and Australian-born Janette Turner Hospital (*The Ivory Swing*, 1982), both of whom won Seal Book Awards. The increasingly multicultural nature of Canadian society is suggested by works such as Bharati Mukherjee's *Days and Nights in Calcutta* (1977) and *Darkness* (1985); Shirley Faessler's *Everything in the Window* (1979); and Joy

Kogowa's *Obasan* (1981). In poetry this ground is tilled by Mary di Michele in *Mimosa and Other Poems* (1980) and by Kristjana Gunnars in *One-eyed Moon Maps* (1980). Other new poets include lesbian Gwen Hauser, *The Ordinary Invisible Woman* (1978); Erin Mouré, *Empire, York Street* (1979); and—perhaps the best—Roo Borson, author of *Rain* (1980), *A Sad Device* (1981), and *The Whole Night, Coming Home* (1984).

Canadian writing by women, finally, would seem to encompass three reasonably discrete phases of evolution: imitation of foreign and male models, protest against authorities—British parents, American cousins, and Canadian brothers— and free exploration of female experience. The rubric provided by Elaine Showalter's pioneering study of British women's fiction, *A Literature of Their Own*, which divides writers into three chronologically arranged groups—feminine, feminist, and female—is not without relevance to Canadian history.[2] Nor are many of the issues raised by recent feminist critics of American literature such as Emily Stipes Watts and Alicia Suskin Ostriker. But the systematic recovery and detailed reexamination that are called for in the process of "rethinking" Canadian history and "revisioning" the canon of Canadian literature are tasks that have fallen to a still marginalized and regrettably small group of women scholars and critics clustered in the lower ranks of the English departments of most Canadian universities or else working in even greater isolation as private scholars without any institutional affiliation. Important work remains undone, still "waiting the releasing yeast."

NOTES

1. When we refer to anglophone Canada, we are discussing those Canadians writing in English; those writing in French are discussed in the essay on francophone Canada, which follows. Canada is officially a bilingual country.
2. Elaine Showalter, *A Literature of Their Own* (Princeton, N.J.: Princeton University Press, 1977).

BIBLIOGRAPHY

Background

Cleverdon, Catherine L. *The Woman Suffrage Movement in Canada*. Toronto: University of Toronto Press, 1974.

Cook, Ramsay, and Wendy Mitchinson, eds. *The Proper Sphere: Woman's Place in Canadian Society*. Toronto: Oxford University Press, 1976.

Light, Beth, and Veronica Strong-Boag, eds. *True Daughters of the North Canadian Women's History: An Annotated Bibliography* (Toronto: OISE, 1980).

Strong-Boag, Veronica, and Anita Clair Fellman, eds. *Rethinking Canada: The Promise of Women's History*. Toronto: Copp Clark, 1986.

Trofimenkoff, Susan Mann, and Alison Prentice, eds. *The Neglected Majority: Essays in Canadian Women's History*. 2 vols. Toronto: McClelland, 1984.

Literary Criticism

Atwood, Margaret. *Survival*. Toronto: Anansi, 1972.

Canada's Lost Plays, 2 vols. Vol. 1. *The Nineteenth Century*. Ed. Anton Wagner and Richard Plant. Vol. 2. *Women Pioneers*. Ed. Anton Wagner. Toronto: Canadian Theatre Review Publications, 1978, 1979.

Davidson, Arnold E., and Cathy N. Davidson, eds. *The Art of Margaret Atwood: Essays in Criticism*. Toronto: Anansi, 1981.

Klink, Carl F., gen. ed. *Literary History of Canada: Canadian Literature in English*, 2nd ed. 3 vols. Toronto: University of Toronto Press, 1976.

Sorfleet, Robert, ed. *L.M. Montgomery: An Assessment*. Guelph, Ontario: Canadian Children's Press, 1976.

Tausky, Thomas E. *Sara Jeannette Duncan: Novelist of Empire*. Port Credit, Ontario: P.D. Meany, 1980.

Tierney, E. Frank M. *The Crawford Symposium*. Ottawa: University of Ottawa Press, 1979.

Toye, William, gen. ed. *The Oxford Companion to Canadian Literature*. Toronto: Oxford University Press, 1983.

Twayne's World Authors Series (Boston: G.K. Hall) includes volumes on Gwen Pharis Ringwood, Margaret Laurence, and Ethel Wilson.

FRANCOPHONE CANADA
Gillian Davies

> Un visiteur de fâcheuse mémoire a pu dire du peuple canadien-français
> qu'il était un peuple "sans histoire ni litterature."[1]

The selection of French Canadian women writers demonstrates that French Canada does indeed have a literature, one that is intimately linked with its sociopolitical context and its history. The inaccuracy of that visitor's—Lord Durham's—statement is borne out in the dominant themes of a body of literature that, from the beginning, has resonated with the need to affirm national identity and to delineate its specifics. The leading francophone literatures of Quebec and Acadia share this concern.[2]

What is the sociopolitical context of the French Canadian woman writer, and how has this context shaped her material? The American critic Paula Gilbert Lewis, among others, points out the close link between nationalism and feminism in Quebec: "Québécois...feminist writers are still concerned with the problems of class struggle, cultural identity, and linguistic rights that plague the average male Quebecer."[3] Lewis also outlines the evolution from the *prise de conscience* (raised consciousness) of oppression as a native of Quebec—male or female—during the 1960s to the "more clearly focussed form of female/feminist consciousness" of the 1970s and 1980s: it was in 1969 that the Montreal women's liberation movement was founded; in 1970, the Front de Libération des Femmes du Québec published a feminist manifesto; and between 1971 and 1975 the Centre des Femmes edited the first French radical feminist periodical, *Québécoises deboutte*! (Stand Up, Women of Quebec!)

As recently as 1979, it could be asked in what respects Acadia had a literature, if indeed it had one.[4] Can one then speak of a female literary tradition in French Canadian literature? If in Acadia the question is raised, in Quebec there is no such question. While feminist writers and themes began to come to the fore in Quebec in the 1960s, and particularly since 1970, a number of major women writers precede this period.

What is now named the literature of Quebec began to take shape in the mid-nineteenth century. The principal works in the canon are not numerous and almost all are by male authors, the chief genres being poetry and the novel. Félicité Angers (1845–1924) is one of the very few women writers of the period. Under the pseudonym Laure Conan, in 1884 she published *Angéline de Montbrun*, widely recognized as the first psychological novel in French Canada. Recently studies have dealt with the theme of incest in her work and with the question of repression and subversion of desire: Angers' work is now perceived as a great deal more complex, structurally and thematically, than was initially believed.

While other female voices in the nineteenth century are indistinct, the first three decades of the twentieth century produced the work of Marie Le Franc, who earned the Prix Fémina with *Grand-Louis l'Innocent* (1927), and the poets Jovette Bernier, Eva Sénécal, and Simone Routier.

The first novel of Marie Le Franc (1879–1965), *Grand-Louis l'Innocent* (1925), is partly autobiographical; the work was inspired by Le Franc's visit to her native Brittany after twenty years spent in Canada. Eve, haunted by an unhappy Canadian love affair, finds herself involved with Grand-Louis, an amnesiac who comes by chance to her door. She is an intellectual, he a primitive innocent who awakens to the world through her guidance. Eve expresses her conflict about Grand-Louis by projecting it onto the landscape, drawn alternately to the mists of the Breton landscape out of which Grand-Louis appears and to the Canadian storms she associates with her former love, "l'homme du Nord," the man of the North. Resolution is achieved when Eve can finally accept her love for GrandLouis. The mystic fusion between character and landscape and the felt beauty of these physical evocations are essential aspects of Le Franc's novels and poems.

Jovette-Alice Bernier, born in 1900, is the author of five collections of poetry published between 1924 and 1932 and of two novels, *La Chair décevante* (Disappointing Flesh, 1931) and *Non, Monsieur* (1969). She won the Lieutenant Governor's medal in 1929 for her collection of poems *Tout n'est pas dit* (Not Everything Has Been Said). The major themes of her work are love and its deceptions. *La Chair décevante* is the story of the torments an unmarried mother, Didi, undergoes because of the ideological climate of her time and the sacrifices she makes for her son Paul. The work was denounced for its immorality by many critics, for whom, as francophone critic Jacques Cotnam has pointed out, literature was still a question of content rather than one of form; he notes her courage in choosing a theme so controversial for its period.

Eva Sénécal, born in 1905, is a poet—*Un peu d'angoisse...un peu de fièvre* (A Little Anguish..., A Little Fever, 1927) and *La Course dans l'aurore* (Running in the Dawn, 1929) and a novelist—*Dans les ombres* (In the Shadows, 1931) and *Mon Jacques* (1933). Sénécal's poems reflect the postromantic tendencies of the period between the wars. Her first collection is inspired by the external world— animals, plants, the seasons—and by her religious faith. *La Course dans l'aurore* analyzes lyrically and in depth the themes of love, bitterness, and the desire for another spiritual space, "l'ailleurs" (elsewhere). *Dans les ombres* is a psychological novel about the mutual passion between a married Quebec woman and an American stranger. Reflecting a romanticism not present in Sénécal's poems, this novel is also bold in its attack on the constraints of the female condition.

Simone Routier (b. 1901) may be considered a transitional figure and taken as an example of another trend: Like many other francophone intellectuals of her generation, she became an expatriate poet in Paris, achieving immediate fame when her first book won the important Prix David. Routier's poetry between the wars— *Ceux qui seront aimés* (Those Who Will Be Loved, 1931), *Paris-Amour-Deauville* (1932), and *Les Tentations* (Temptations, 1934)—focuses on the theme of love; but it also shows the influence of modernist currents then having an international impact, as well as the spiritual quest which she shared with other Canadian writers, such as Robert Choquette. Subsequent volumes published in the postwar period—*Je te fiancerai* (I Will Become your Fiancée), *Le long voyage* (The Long Journey), and *Les Psaumes du jardin clos* (Psalms From The Cloistered Garden)— took on a deeper philosophical cast in their exploration of the spiritual cosmos. Yet Routier is ultimately a traditionalist. When Thérèse Tardif (b. 1912) published her controversial volume *Désespoir de vieille fille* (An Old Maid's Despair, 1943), which accused church institutions of breeding agony in the faithful, Routier responded by a traditional statement of belief, evading the very questions that Tardif had raised. In contrast, Tardif's work, characterized by a tumultuous, fragmentary style and a passionate forcefulness, is now beginning to be recognized as part of a proto-feminist tradition.[5]

Gabrielle Roy (1909–1983) and Anne Hébert (b. 1916) both published their first works in the 1940s: Roy's *Bonheur d'occasion* (literally, secondhand happiness, translated as *The Tin Flute*) and Hébert's *Les Songes en équilibre* (Dreams in Equilibrium). In this same decade, Adrienne Choquette (1915–1973) published her novel *La Coupe vide* (The Empty Goblet, 1948), and Germaine Guèvremont (1896–1968) produced her seminal work *Le Survenant* (*The Outlander*, 1945). Until the late 1950s, with the publication of such works as Hébert's *Les Chambres de bois* (literally, the wooden rooms, translated as *The Silent Rooms*, 1958), Marie-Claire Blais's *La belle bête*, (literally, the beautiful beast, translated as *Mad Shadows*, 1959), and Claire Martin's collection of short stories *Avec ou sans amour* (With or Without Love, 1958), themes of women's literature had been largely based on traditional values: romantic love, Catholicism, the family, the land.[6]

These works can be seen as the seeds for what was to come: the *Révolution tranquille* began in the period following the death of Premier Maurice Duplessis in 1959. The term refers to the progressive modernization of Quebec society, involving liberation from economic and political domination by the anglophone minority and from the cultural and religious strictures imposed by the Catholic church. This reform movement was accompanied by the first terrorist incidents in 1963; these led to the October crisis of 1970, when the radical Front de Libération du Québec kidnapped a British diplomat and a provincial cabinet minister, assassinating the latter. As a result, the War Measures Act was imposed, civil liberties were suspended, and many leading cultural figures were arrested. However, with the exception of the events of 1970, change and development during the *Révolution tranquille* was nonviolent.

The major issue was autonomy, particularly in matters of culture and language. Departments of Education and Cultural Affairs were established; the people of Quebec claimed, and gained, a greater degree of control in all areas of provincial life. The cultural debate between a dependent French Canada and an independent mother country had already been largely resolved by the end of the 1950s; in the succeeding decades, a more mature, egalitarian relationship had been established.

With the accession to power of the separatist René Lévesque (1923–1987) in 1976, there was a political forum for the debate and resolution of issues of independence that had previously been confined to the domain of artistic expression. Since 1976, Quebec writers have considered themselves distinct from both France and anglophone Canada. A certain level of political reflection continues nevertheless: a *littérature problématique* (problem literature) largely eclipses the *littérature thématique* (literature dealing with more universal themes) of a more settled, if constricted, era.

The profound changes taking place in Quebec society with the advent of the *Révolution tranquille* are reflected in the literature of the period. Writers such as Nicole Brossard (b. 1943) and Madeleine Gagnon (b. 1938) produced works that question certain elemental and established literary processes: writing writes about itself. Transformation of form and content mirror the rupture with an oppressive, traditionalist past. There emerges from the texts of this period the portrait of a woman who ardently desires autonomy; in the process of achieving it, she destroys thematic and formal stereotypes. This deconstruction has its counterpoint in the realm of language. The "language of difference" is both gender-oriented and concerned with indigenous forms of linguistic expression such as *joual* and *chiac*.[7] The term *langagement* encompasses questions of language (Parisian French, or the French of the Academy)—and beyond that—English being the *langue prioritaire* (the first, or supreme, language) against which the feminist engagement in Quebec literature is written. This dual concern with text and context is expressed most vividly in Michéle Lalonde's *Speak White* (1974), included in this anthology, in which a fractured language angrily portrays a fractured identity.

Outstanding in the 1960s are works by the poet Diane Giguère (b. 1937; *Le Temps des jeux* [Playtime] 1961); the novelists Jovette Bernier (1900–1981; *Non, Monsieur*, 1969) and Louise Maheux-Forcier (b. 1929; *Amadou* [a name], 1969); dramatist Françoise Loranger (b. 1913; *Double jeu* [Double Dealing], 1969); and those authors selected for inclusion in the anthology: Claire Martin (b. 1914), Monique Bosco, (b. 1927), Michèle Lalonde (b. 1937), and Marie-Claire Blais (b. 1939).

Prominant among writers not represented are certain leading poets, critics and theorists: Suzanne Paradis (b. 1936), Madeleine Gagnon, and Nicole Brossard. Since the publication in 1959 of *Les Enfants continuels* (Perpetual Children), her first volume of poetry, Suzanne Paradis has published thirteen other collections of poems, ten novels, two essays, a book of short stories, a biography, and numerous critical articles in reviews such as *Liberté* and *Livres et auteurs québécois*. Her literary awards include the France-Québec Prize for *Pour les enfants des morts* (For the Children of the Dead, 1964), and the Governor General's Prize for *Un goût de sel*, (A Taste of Salt, 1983). Paradis's poetry is rich and densely symbolic. In her early poetry, images of women are paradigms of textual genesis. The anguished sentiments of much of her poetry are also present in her fiction. The major themes of death and revolt are reflected in characters' suicides, despair, or madness. The despairing vision in the novel *Les Cormorans* (The Cormorants, 1967) is scarcely mitigated in novels such as *Les Hauts Cris* (The Loud Cries, 1960); *Il ne faut pas sauver les hommes,* (Humanity Should Not Be Saved, 1961), a highly symbolic tale of human suffering with a characteristically lyrical style; and in the short-story collection *François-les-oiseaux*, 1967. Paradis has reworked many of her books, making thematic, structural, and stylistic changes ten or even twenty years later. She herself sees strong links between her novels and her poems. This linking and reworking give her work a seamlessness and timelessness that are reinforced by the virtual absence of historical or geographical referents in her fictional universe.

Brossard's fiction and theory became a rallying point early in the 1970s. She founded the literary journal *La Barre du jour* (At the Helm of the Day; figuratively, at the forefront [of enlightenment], ahead of its time) in 1965 and a monthly newspaper *Les Têtes de pioche* (Pickaxes; figuratively, stubborn as mules) in 1976. Since the mid-1960s, her work has been centered on language and its capacity to transform and deconstruct social codes. She is a radical feminist and has produced work in all the literary genres as well as criticism and theory. Her work stresses the links between the body, language, and social patterns. *Un livre* (A Book, 1970), *Sold-out* (1973), and *L'Amèr* (Seamark; a landmark sighted from the water, 1977; the ambiguous title also plays on the word *la mère*, for mother) are works that synthesize the genres of poetry, the novel and theory and invite the reader to join with the writer in the creation of the text; they explore women's space and its political dimensions in Quebec.

Madeleine Gagnon is a poet, short-story writer, and theorist. *Poélitique* (1975) is a work in which ideological fragments are juxtaposed with political analysis and her own poems. Like Brossard, Gagnon asserts the power of language to transform the sociocultural order. Somewhere between manifesto and poem (the title itself is a neologism combining the words for political and poetic), *Poélitique* exemplifies Gagnon's concerns with problems of gender, class, and individual and collective identity.

L'Euguélionne (1976), by Louky Bersianik (b. 1930), heralds a new stage of feminist writing. The novel, "a vast feminist anti-Bible,"[8] sets the stage for a literary output less concerned with Marxist or independentist issues than with personal explorations of the female condition. Jovette Marchessault's *La Mère des herbes* (Earth Mother, 1980) is an autobiobraphical novel, the second volume in a proposed trilogy, in which the protagonist unravels the origins of her lesbianism and feminism. Her *Triptygne Lesbien* (*Lesbian Triptych*, 1980) is similar in theme and style. The author (b. 1938) has just recently won the esteemed Governor General's Award. Denise Boucher, in the play *Les Fées ont soif* (The Fairies Are Thirsty, 1978), attacks the stereotypes of virgin, mother, and prostitute. She too contributes to this feminist revitalization.

The first history of Acadian literature is subtitled "de rêve en rêve" (from dream to dream): its author, Marguerite Maillet, seems to agree with historian Michel Roy, for whom the literary and artistic production since the 1970s reflects a preoccupation more with a "dead civilization" than with the vitality of Acadian culture.[9]

La Sagouine (literally, the sloven), the protagonist in Antonine Maillet's novel of that name, succinctly states that one of the main issues of Acadian life and letters is that "l'Acadie ain't a country, 'n Acadjen ain't a nationality cause of the fact it ain't written in Joe Graphy's books."[10] The present-day provinces of New Brunswick and Nova Scotia were variously called "Acadie or Nova Scotia"; France and England both, at different times, claimed the Acadian colony under this title, until it was ceded to England at the Treaty of Utrecht in 1713. Acadia is a "dream" in that it never has been a "politically independent and sovereign state."[11]

While the first Acadian literary texts go back to the seventeenth century, the year 1968 is generally recognized as a pivotal one in Acadian socioliterary history. The year saw a critical period of protest among the younger generation. In popular language, their texts, most often poetry, explore this revolt. Another vital year is 1972, when a nationalist party, le Parti acadien, was formed; the first publishing company, Les Editions d'Acadie, was established; and *La Sagouine* came to national prominence. Since then, Acadian cultural life, if one is to judge by the calibre and variety of its literary production, has continued to grow and become more firmly rooted.

New Brunswick, formerly part of Acadia, is the only officially bilingual province in Canada. The Acadian nationalist movement seems to have observed Quebec closely but has not directly emulated its nationalist moves, perhaps because, unike Quebec, francophones are in the minority throughout the Maritime Provinces and the pro-francophone stance of recent provincial governments, in New Brunswick at least, has seemed to provide many of the rights claimed by the more militant Acadian nationalists, particularly in the areas of language and education.

However, historical wrongs are far from forgotten. Virtually all of the work of Antonine Maillet (b. 1929), whose name has become synonymous with Acadian literature, proposes that the past must first be retrieved and then integrated before a culture and a society can flourish autonomously. The historical fact of "la grande chasse"[12] (The Great Expulsion, in which the original French settlers were forced into exile by the distrustful British) of 1755, and a powerful oral tradition of story-telling, legend, and superstition have been the sources from which she draws her material.

This tradition was not the substance of early Acadian women writers—of whom there were indeed few.[13] Of note are Emilie Leblanc, who wrote a celebrated series of letters to the newspaper *Evangéline* between 1895 and 1899 under the name of Marichette, and Josephine Duguay, who in the 1920s and 1930s wrote poems on the themes of nature, religion, and the family under the pseudonym of Glaneuse. Between 1973 and 1982, eighteen women writers, among them the established poet Huguette Légaré, published works of fiction, compared with twenty-six male writers of the same period. But by 1983, more than half were women. In this contemporary group are the *chansons-poèmes* of Angèle Arsenault and Edith Butler and the poems of Roberthe Sénéchal and Dyane Léger (*Graines de fée* [Fairy Grains], 1981). These writers explore the imagination (Léger) and male-female relationships (Arsenault) and examine sociopolitical questions (Sénéchal). Other women have made significant contributions in literary and paraliterary areas: the poets France Daigle, Rose Després, Claire Gagnon, and Anne Cloutier; the folklorists Charlotte Cormier and Catherine Jolicoeur; the historian

Marguerite Michaud; Marguerite Maillet, literary critic and anthologist; and Viola Léger, celebrated *interprète* (interpreter as a performer) of Antonine Maillet's theatrical work.

The immense contribution to Acadian literature made by Antonine Maillet must be acknowledged. However, she has chosen to emphasize the folkloric and mythic elements rather than confronting the present-day forms of alienation and deracination of the Acadian. Moreover, she works in the novel and the theater rather than in poetry, long the predominant genre; it is in the fragmented and violent language of their poems, particularly those of the 1970s, that major, more often male, poets such as Raymond Leblanc, Guy Arsenault, and Herménégilde Chiasson have made important statements. However, as an "adopted" Acadian writer and critic, Henri-Dominique Paratte, states, although contemporary poetry may seem less *engagé* (engaged, involved) than before, the commitment has shifted so that "poetry has become not the ghetto of frustrated desires, but the lyrical unfolding of a richer, more elaborate and self-assured personal universe."[14]

NOTES

1. "A visitor, whom one remembers with anger, said of the French Canadian people that they were a people 'without history or literature.'" In Marguerite Maillet, *Anthologie de textes littéraires acadiens* (Moncton: Editions d'Acadie, 1979), 7.
2. Quebec and Acadia (the maritime region on the east coast of Canada, of which Nova Scotia forms the southernmost point) are the major geographical centers of francophone literature in Canada. As will be discussed later, the indigenous French inhabitants of Acadia were forced to flee the area, many of whom later returned; others settled in scattered communities in New England and established what was to become the Cajun culture of Louisiana.
3. "Introduction," in *Traditionalism, Nationalism and Feminism,* ed. Paula Gilbert Lewis (Westport: Greenwood Press, 1985), 5.
4. Marguerite Maillet, *Anthologie de textes littéraires acadiens* (Moncton: Editions d'Acadie, 1979), 7.
5. See, for example, comments by Barbara Godard in her introduction to Jovette Marchessault's *Lesbian Triptych*, "Flying Away with Language" (Toronto: Women's Press, 1985), 9–28.
6. Liette Gaudreau, "La Voix des femmes pendant la révolution tranquille," in *Le Spectacle de la littérature*, eds. J.-M. Lemelin and Manon Tétrault (Montréal: Triptyque, 1984).
7. Vernacular terms in Quebec and Acadia respectively that generally imply a slack, anglicized, ungrammatical French.
8. Maroussia Hajdukowski-Ahmed, "Louky Bersianik: Feminist Dialogisms," in *Traditionalism, Nationalism and Feminism*, ed. Paula Gilbert Lewis (Westport, CT: Greenwood Press, 1985), 5.
9. Michel Roy, *L'Acadie* (Montréal: Québec/Amérique, 1981), 282.
10. Antonine Maillet, *La Sagouine* (Toronto: Simon and Pierre, 1979), 165.
11. Naomi Griffith, *The Acadians: Creation of a People* (Toronto: McGraw-Hill-Ryerson, 1973), xiii.
12. Roy, 13.
13. Because of the lack of bibliographical sources for much of early Acadian literature, it has proved impossible to provide dates of birth and death for these writers.
14. Henri-Dominique Paratte, *Poésie acadienne contemporaine/Acadian Poetry Now* (Moncton: Les Editions Perce-Neige, 1985), 21.

BIBLIOGRAPHY

Background

Griffiths, Naomi. *The Acadians: Creation of a People*. Toronto: McGraw-Hill Ryerson, 1973.
Saint-Pierre, Gaston, ed. *The French Canadian Experience*. Toronto: MacMillan, 1979.
Thompson, Dale C. *Québec Society and Politics*. Toronto: McClelland and Stewart, 1973.
Wade, Mason. *The French Canadians*. rev. ed. 2 vols. Toronto: Macmillan, 1968.

Literary Criticism

Babby, Ellen. *The Play of Language and Spectacle: a structural reading of selected texts by Gabrielle Roy*. Toronto: ECW Press, 1985.
Gair, Reavley, ed. *A Literary and Linguistic History of New Brunswick*. Fredericton NB: Fiddlehead Poetry Books and Goose Lane Editions, 1985.
Godard, Barbara, Ed. *Gynocritics: feminist approaches to Canadian and Québec Women's writing*. Toronto: ECW Press, 1987.
Hesse, M. G. *Gabrielle Roy*. Boston: Twayne, 1984.
Lewis, Paula Gilbert, ed. *Traditionalism, Nationalism and Feminism*. Westport, CT: Greenwood Press, 1985.
May, Cedric. *Breaking the Silence: The Literature of Québec*. Birmingham, England: University of Birmingham Regional Canadian Studies Centre, 1981.
O'Connell, David. *The French Canadian Novel*. Boston: Twayne, 1986.
Russell, Delbert W. *Anne Hébert*. Boston: Twayne, 1983.
Shouldice, Larry, ed. *Contemporary Québec Criticism*. Toronto: University of Toronto Press, 1979.
Sutherland, Ronald. *Marie-Claire Blais*. Montréal: Forum House, 1970.
Tougas, Gérard. *History of French-Canadian Literature*. Trans. Alta Lind Cook. 2nd. ed. Toronto: Ryerson Press, 1966.
Warwick, John. *The Long Journey: Literary Themes of French Canada*. Toronto: University of Toronto Press, 1968.

CHINA

Katherine Carlitz

Women have been writing in China for almost as long as Chinese history has been recorded: a modern historical bibliography gives the names of over 4,000 women whose writings have been documented, if not always preserved, over the last two millennia.[1] The great bulk of this literature falls into two categories: lyric poetry and the handbook of Confucian virtue for women. Both of these genres were shaped by male-dominated Confucian ideology, the rigidly hierarchical normative description of society resulting from generations of reinterpretation of the teachings of Confucius (551–479 B.C.) and his disciples. Even the sensuous lyrics that women often wrote describing the toilette or the boudoir were written primarily in the Classical Chinese language, whose grammar had been shaped by the tradition of education for public offices that only men could fill. Two personae thus predominated in the writing of Chinese women before this century: the passive beauty conventional in Chinese lyric poetry and the dedicated wife and mother of the Confucian handbooks. And though the passive beauty and the perfect mother echo and reinforce male ideals, the men of letters who compiled local histories regarded even these kinds of women's writings with ambivalence. The Confucian handbooks may have preached submission, but since they are filled with historical references, they testify to a tradition of women's scholarship that required independent, self-directed study. (China's great woman historian Ban Zhao, who lived in the first century A.D., compiled one of the earliest and most influential of these handbooks, the *Nüjie*, or *Instructions for Women*.) The local histories often included special sections about "erudite women," a slightly suspect category, for writing was never a completely acceptable substitute for the needle-work and household management that fulfilled traditional roles. Conventional descriptions of women's lives almost always emphasized "women's work"— needlework—and household management even though the great mass of Chinese women throughout history must have engaged in agricultural labor or local trade to enable their families to survive. And women's needlework could supplement family income, whereas writing could not, for traditional scholarly careers for women did not exist. In this century, however, writing has become an accepted professional vocation for women, and a flowering of modern women's writing that began in the 1920s explored what it meant to be young, Chinese, and female in a way that no poetry, fiction, or drama had done before.

To appreciate this radical change in Chinese women's writing we must first understand certain social changes that took place in China in the years just preceding and following 1900. Since the end of the sixth century the country had been governed primarily by a vast bureaucracy staffed increasingly through the civil service examination system. For centuries before the 1911 republican revolution that overthrew the Qing dynasty, this system had changed little, and it had a profound effect on the nature of literacy and literature. The civil service examinations were overwhelmingly literary, testing the candidates' skill at composing set forms of prose and poetry. Only men could take the examinations and fill public office (women were held responsible for the domestic sphere, raising filial sons who could grow into loyal officials). Over the centuries, education was increasingly geared to success in the examinations, and thus even when girls were very well educated, their education was not seen as leading to any well-defined end. The education of women took place largely in family schools (generally as an adjunct to the education provided for boys) for women could not attend the schools for advanced examination studies that were run by the state or by prominent individuals. The best-educated women tended to be either courtesans, who provided both intellectual and sexual companionship and polished their poetic skills to please their patrons, or the secluded daughters of well-to-do families. (The wealthiest families secluded their daughters the most, in accordance with conventional taboos against their leaving the women's quarters of the household—taboos increasingly difficult to honor as families descended the social ladder and depended on women's productive labor). These courtesans and wealthy daughters must have known prominent officials well and must have been aware of political scandals and upheavals, but they apparently were not motivated to write about realms they could not enter. Women did not produce the important vernacular novels and plays that were major vehicles of social criticism during the Ming (1368–1644) and Qing (1644–1911) dynasties. They did, however, write many of the scriptures associated with the Buddhist-inspired sectarian religious movements of the Ming, movements in which women could and did take leadership roles.

By the late nineteenth century, however, schools for girls were being established, first by Western missionaries and then by Chinese. Women's literacy began gaining male advocates who saw education as a key to reversing the humiliating defeats China was suffering at Western hands. In the first decade of the twentieth century, young women, married and unmarried alike, were among the students the tottering dynasty sent to Japan to gain the skills needed for the modernization of China. Qiu Jin (1875–1907), an ardent nationalist who was executed for her part in an anti-imperial plot, was one of them. Her newspaper *Zhongguo nübao* (Chinese Women's Journal) demonstrates the self-conscious feminism that was beginning to find expression in the cosmopolitan milieu of the newly industrialized cities. Normal schools and colleges were established for women, and young Chinese women began to march in student demonstrations against foreign aggression, to attend unchaperoned political study groups, and to rail against Confucian teachings that restricted them to the home. They still had to contend with overwhelming social prejudice against equipping women to lead independent lives, and the number of women actually affected by the developments described here was very small, but these changes meant that a group of well-educated, urban, and, in many cases, rather Westernized young women would reach their twenties in the 1920s and find themselves faced with the need to create a persona for the modern Chinese woman in the context of modern China's own self-creation.

New literary forms and a new literary language were seen by both sexes as a necessary part of China's modernization, and student demonstrations on May 4, 1919, sparked a thoroughgoing reexamination of traditional Chinese culture by leading young intellectuals. They saw the Classical Chinese language that had been the medium of official and scholarly exchange for over 2,500 years (an elliptical, compressed written form of the language that corresponded to no spoken dialect) as a straitjacket that had helped keep China vulnerable to Western encroachments. (Literary style had often been used to signal political intentions in China, and this twentieth-century emphasis on language reform actually echoed fierce literary debates that had raged during earlier centuries.) Even the traditional literary vernacular of novels and plays was seen as mired in outdated conventions, filled with tag-phrases that echoed the traditional oral storyteller of the marketplace. By the 1920s a literary revolution had taken place, and a modern written vernacular was replacing Classical Chinese as China's main literary language. (The modern vernacular was not created overnight: by now it is a flexible, expressive language, but the written vernacular of the 1920s was still sometimes quite awkward. Since the West was both envied and feared, even Western grammatical forms were imitated on occasion, producing a highly unnatural Chinese syntax.) The "Literary Association" of Peking and Shanghai became the organization of the major literary revolutionaries, and *Short Story* magazine became their voice. A new subjectivity, a new emphasis on the emotional experience of the individual in the modern world, characterized much of this writing. Women published in *Short Story* and similar publications from their very beginning, for the experience of women was one of the heretofore hidden facets of Chinese life that these young intellectuals wanted articulated. For many of these young women writers the 1920s were a brief flowering, ended by marriage or a turn to less emotionally arduous social roles, such as teaching. Still, the women writers described in this essay won immediate recognition and created an enduring identity for the modern, independent women writer. Their number is not great, but their significance is.

We know that by the early 1930s this identity was recognized by the Chinese intellectual community, because books about the "modern Chinese woman writer" began to appear.[2] We see from the biobibliographical descriptions in these books that the theme of romantic love, freely chosen, was the dominant issue for young Chinese women writers, their main expression of the subjectivity of the age. Since this first generation of the "new woman" had been raised in a society where feminine education was still largely training for an arranged marriage, it is not surprising that she wrote about "free love" as a major avenue of self-realization. In her novel *Haibin guren* (The Recluse of the Seashore), Lu Yin (1898–1934) wrote about the conflicts she and her fellow university students felt when they tried to reconcile their modern aspirations with the demands of marriage and the traditional woman's role. There was an avid public for Feng Yuanjun's (b. 1901) poems, essays, and stories that described youthful love and sexual longing with new frankness. Su Xuelin (b. 1987) drew on her student years in France to describe the conflict between love, and duty to one's elders, in her novel *Jixin* (The Bitter Heart). And Ding Ling's (1904–1986) "Shafei nüshi riji" ("Miss Sophie's Diary")[3] created a sensation for its depiction of a woman driven to suicidal despair because of her inability to master her amorous longings. These writers also described the difficult decisions arising from their unprecedented historical situation: Xie Bingying (b. 1903), who went on to write patriotic stories and novels, wrote about the painful choice between a career and motherhood; Chen Ying (b. 1908), who turned to historical scholarship and teaching after publishing a few short stories, wrote about the conflicts between marriage and career. Bing Xin (b. 1900) and Ling Shuhua (b. 1904) stayed aloof from these tumultuous emotions, but their stories, with a domestic setting, pioneered the fictional description of another facet of modern Chinese women's lives by showing the tragicomic qualities of life in upper-class Chinese households, for which "modernity" might be no more than badly applied veneer.

For the women writers who came of age in the 1930s and 1940s, social description became as important as the veiled autobiography that Lu Yin (who wrote one of the books about "modern Chinese women writers" as well as writing fiction) found in many of her contemporaries' works. By this time, the vernacular was firmly established as the literary language, and the heady excitement of China's new "modern age" had been succeeded by worries about the unstable central government, warlord conflicts, civil war, and war with Japan. The Communist Party became a major force among young intellectuals, and it stressed their social responsibility. As left-wing ideology gained adherents, and as these adherents gained in organizational strengths, writers like Ding Ling (1904–1986) and Wei Junyi (b. 1916) wrote about the struggle of intellectuals and peasants to understand each other. Xiao Hong's (1911–1942) keen ear and deadly irony captured the difficulties that traditional China faced in dealing with change, including changes in women's roles. Her account of the treatment of a child bride in *Hulan he zhuan* (Tales of the Hulan River) is a devastating indictment of the old society. During the 1940s, Cao Ming's (b. 1913) *Yuandong li* (Motive Power) brought the world of the male and female industrial worker into modern Chinese fiction. And Chang Ai-ling (b. 1921) continued the genre that Ling Shuhua had pioneered, describing the wealthy urban households that had been displaced by the revolution of 1911. (Despite her expatriation to America, Chang Ai-ling has been a major influence on younger writers from Taiwan, and her excellent stories are omitted from this anthology only because of their length.)[4]

As might be expected from trends already evident in the left-wing writing of the 1930s, the Communist Revolution of 1949 meant the ascendance of "socialist realism" over the subjectivity that had characterized the writing of the 1920s. Now the writer's responsibility was to serve society by articulating the experience of the masses. The central government's increasing control over the organs of publication meant that only socialist realist fiction could find a market. State control over employment was another way in which de facto censorship could be carried out: authors of unacceptable works could lose their livelihood. Ding Ling's socially conscious fiction of the 1940s was a response to the demands of socialist realism; but in the turmoil of the Cultural Revolution of the 1960s and 1970s, when political factional struggles led to an attempt to purge Chinese society of all vestiges of traditional social classes, she was silenced and imprisoned along with many of the older intellectuals whose privileged background had given them the opportunity to participate in the literary revolution of the 1920s. Yet others were able to speak out without retribution. Ru Zhijuan (b. 1925) wrote using a *wanyue* (graceful and restrained) style in her war story "Lilies" (1958) that had been specifically prohibited by the new literary tenets. Her stories on family and motherhood written during the 1960s served to make these themes respectable.[5]

Since many well-to-do families left China in 1949, the Communist Revolution also gave rise to a substantial emigré tradition in Chinese writing. Chang Ai-ling emigrated to Hong Kong in 1952 and then to the West, (where she has lived since

1955, using the name Eileen Chang). Nieh Hua-ling (b. 1926), a long-time resident of Iowa, writes about the China of her youth and the complexities of life in Taiwan. Yü Li-hua writes about the experience of expatriation. Ch'en Jo-hsi (b. 1938), not included here only because she has been widely published elsewhere, is the must culturally complex of these emigré writers. After youth in Taiwan and university education in the United States, she "returned" to the People's Republic of China in 1966 to dedicate herself to the revolution. Disillusioned by the experience of the Cultural Revolution, she went back to Taiwan and eventually came to the United States. Her stories of men and women during the Cultural Revolution, translated into English in a collection titled *The Execution of Mayor Yin* (1978), provide a disturbing account of that whole period.

Some of the women writers who participated in the heady literary ferment of the 1920s and 1930s have been active again in recent years. Ru Zhijuan wrote one of the first published attacks on the catastrophic agricultural policies of the Great Leap Forward in 1958–1959, this time turning to the *haofang* mode. Her willingness to appropriate a traditionally "male"-defined style and subject matter again put her at the literary and feminist forefront. Ding Ling was rehabilitated and allowed to publish and travel after 1978. Wei Junyi in her recent essays, remains as thoughtful and as aware of the difficulties of reconciling one's own views with a changing political line as she was when she wrote the story "Three Friends." The Cultural Revolution was hard on many of these women, coming as they did from the educated and well-to-do families that led China's Republican Revolution, but the literature of the post–Cultural Revolutionary period has—at least at certain moments—echoed the literary world of their youth in its emphasis on the individual's right to her subjective experience. Fiction has, in fact, become one of the primary means of social criticism in the People's Republic of China, and thus while Chinese society as a whole seems to be drawing back from some of the egalitarian aims of the Communist Revolution (stratification of occupation by sex is increasing, with women in the lower-paying jobs), Chinese women's writing today openly criticizes such failures. The hegemony of the political system and the canons of socialist realism make it difficult for writers to suggest alternatives in their fiction, but women like Zhang Jie (b. 1937) and Zhang Kangkang (b. 1950) describe the difficulties young women face in competing with young men for scarce educational resources and the opposition that wives may face from their husbands when they aspire to educational or professional advancement. They make it clear that women can and do understand when Chinese society is unable to fulfill its revolutionary promises to them.

In this century, Chinese women writers have created a body of work that establishes women's experiences in society as a valid literary subject. Changing social conditions will doubtless make it sometimes easier and sometimes more difficult to articulate these experiences, but the women writers of modern China can now draw support from a tradition of their own.

NOTES

1. Hu Wenkai, *Lidai funü zhuzuo kao* (Writings of Women Through the Ages, Shanghai, 1957).

2. Examples are Hu Yubo, *Zhongguo xiandai nü zuojia* (Contemporary Women Writers of China, Shanghai, 1931); and Huang Ying [Lu Yin], *Xiandai Zhongguo nü zuojia* (Women Writers of Contemporary China, Shanghai, 1934).

3. Ding Ling, *Miss Sophie's Diary and Other Stories*. Transl. W. J. F. Jenner, San Francisco: Panda/China Books and Periodicals, 1986.

4. See *The Short Stories of Eileen Chang* (Taipei, 1968). Novels including *Rice-Sprout Song* (New York: Scribner's, 1955) and *The Rouge of the North* (London: Cassell, 1967) are also available.

5. See Perry Link, "Rebels, Victims and Apologists," *New York Times Book Review* (July 6, 1986), 16–17, for a review of her work in translation—*Lilies and Other Stories* (San Francisco: Panda/China Books and Periodicals, 1986).

BIBLIOGRAPHY

Background

Croll, Elisabeth. *Feminism and Socialism in China*. London: Routledge and Kegan Paul, 1978.

Wolf, Margery, and Roxane Witke, eds. *Women in Chinese Society*. Stanford: Stanford University Press, 1975.

Young, Marilyn B., ed. *Women in China*. Ann Arbor: Center for Chinese Studies, University of Michigan, 1973.

Literary Criticism and Literature

Anderson, C.M. *A Study of Two Modern Chinese Authors: Ping Hsin and Ting Ling*. [Ding Ling]. Claremont, CA: n.p., 1954.

Gertlacher, Anna, et al., eds. *Women and Literature in China*. Bochun: Studienverlag Brockmeyer, 1985.

Gibbs, Donald A., and Yun-chen Li. *A Bibliography of Studies and Translations of Modern Chinese Literature: 1918–1942*. Cambridge: East Asian Center, Harvard University Press, 1975.

Hsia, C.T. *A History of Modern Chinese Fiction*. 2nd. ed. New Haven: Yale University Press, 1971.

Kao, George, ed. *Two Writers and the Cultural Revolution*. Hong Kong: The University of Hong Kong. 1980. Includes Ch'en Jo-Hsi.

Winston, L.Y., and Nathan K. Mao, eds. Modern *Chinese Fiction: A Guide to Its Study and Appreciation, Essays and Bibliographies*. Boston: G.K. Hall, 1980.

See also the periodicals *Chinese Literature* (Peking), *The Chinese Pen* (Taipei), and *Renditions* (Hong Kong).

Literary Works

Hsias C.T., Joseph S.M. Lau, and Leo Ou-fan Lee, eds. *Modern Chinese Stories and Novellas, 1919–1949*. New York: Columbia University Press, 1981.

Hsieh, Pengying. *Girl Rebel, An Autobiography*. New York: DaCapo Press, 1975.

Hsu, Vivian Ling, ed. *Born of the Same Roots: Stories of Modern Chinese Women*. Bloomington: Indiana University Press, 1981.

Isaacs, Harold R., ed. *Straw Sandals: Chinese Short Stories, 1918–1933*. Cambridge: MIT Press, 1974. Orig. compiled in 1934.

Link, Perry, ed. *Roses and Thorns: The Second Blooming of the Hundred Flowers in Chinese Fiction, 1979–1980*. Berkeley: University of California Press, 1984.

Nieh, Hua-ling, ed. *Eight Stories by Chinese Women*. Taipei: Heritage Press, 1962.

Seven Contemporary Chinese Women Writers. Preface by Gladys Young. Beijing: Chinese Literature, 1982.

Wang, C.H., and S.M. Lau, eds. *Comprehensive Anthology of Taiwan Literature from 1895 to the Present*. Bloomington: Indiana University Press, forthcoming.

FRANCE

Colette Gaudin

"France is a country," as Germaine Brée remarked, "that has prided itself on a long tradition of successful women writers dating back at least eight hundred years."[1] But in the often-quoted list of about a dozen prestigious names—from the poet Marie de France in the twelfth century to the novelist Colette (1873–1954)—exist enormous gaps. In light of this discontinuity, can we speak legitimately of a tradition?

The years between the Franco-Prussian war of 1870 and World War II offer a perfect illustration of the intermittent recording of literature written by women. Many educated readers of French literature would be hard pressed to cite a single woman writer between George Sand, who died in 1876, and Colette, who published her first novels at the beginning of this century, or between Colette and the generation of Nathalie Sarraute (b. 1900), Simone de Beauvoir (1908–1986), Marguerite Duras (b. 1914), who all became famous after 1945. The century we are considering in this anthology appears divided into two dramatically contrasting parts, the publication of *The Second Sex* in 1949 playing the role of the great divide. In opposition to the present abundance, variety, and visibility of women's works, the previous seventy years seem almost empty. The poets Anna de Noailles (1873–1933), Catherine Pozzi (1882–1934), and Marie Noël (1883–1967), may appear in anthologies; but who still reads the novels of Marguerite Audoux (1863–1937) or Marcelle Tinayre (1872–1948), bestsellers in their time? What happened to the 738 "women of letters" registered in publishers' catalogs in 1908? Were they victims of the normal neglect that regularly befalls a large portion of literary works a few decades after their publication, or is there something particularly detrimental to women's literature in the way it is transmitted as literary culture? If we want to question the apparent silence of women, we have also to interpret the deafness of the literary institution toward them, and sometimes its loquacity.

As surprising as the number of forgotten women writers from 1870 to 1940 is the number of books that periodically tried to save their literature from oblivion. In 1908, for example, Alphonse Séché, deploring the systematic neglect of women, compiled an anthology of a hundred "poétesses," most of them his contemporaries, entitled *Les Muses françaises*. In 1953, a similar rescue operation of thirty women poets was carried out by Marcel Béalu in his anthology of French feminine poetry since 1900. Germaine Brée mentions the second of these works in her study on *Women Writers in France* (1973), wondering why such an apologetic gesture toward "feminine literature" was still necessary in the mid-twentieth century. Her answer points to a paradox that goes well beyond the domain of literature and is still valid today: while French women have gradually won the battle for civic rights since 1946, the year they gained suffrage, the "guiding images" of the culture have not greatly evolved.

Some of these images find comfortable refuge in literary studies under the label of Romanticism. While the Romantic movement in France was embodied in forms as varied as the ironic comedies of Alfred de Musset, the philosophical verses of

Alfred de Vigny, and the epic poetry and colorful drama of Victor Hugo, the Romantic women poets found their inspiration in the lyrical poetry of love, absence, and despair, particularly in Lamartine's *Méditations* (1820). Among them, Marceline Desbordes-Valmore (1786–1859) was the most respected, Delphine de Girardin (1804–1855) the most brilliant, Louise Colet (1810–1876) the most ambitious. These women were almost immediately identified, either in praise or derision, as "the Romantic Muses," a collective designation still used in many contemporary literary histories. At the turn of the century, Charles Maurras (a polemicist and novelist who later founded the ultra-right *Action Française*) updated the notion of the muse in his study of the "Amazones of 1900." Although he lavishly praises the original talents of Renée Vivien (1877–1909), Mme de Régnier (Gérard d'Houville, 1875–1963), Lucie Delarue-Mardrus (1880–1945), and Anna de Noailles, "those feminine heads full of dreamy revolt and feverish meditation," his main purpose is to expose, as their "common principle," the predestined encounter between Romanticism and the "perverse" sincerity of the modern woman. For the nationalist Maurras, Romanticism represents a disease of civilization produced by foreign influences, an excess of imagination, and the disorder of sensitivity. The poetry of these women—of whom three, he is careful to note, were born in foreign lands, while the fourth, "Mme Mardrus," married an Orientalist —is the ultimate expression of that disease. Fascinated and horrified by these "sweet monsters," Maurras issues an apocalyptic warning against their variety of "feminism," "the most brilliant, but also the most threatening for the entire human race."[2]

With illuminating bluntness, Maurras dramatizes the view of women as aliens ("*métèques*") found at the core of the ambivalent judgments that would continue to be passed on women's books in the subsequent decades. While a benevolent paternalism pervades Séché's anthology, a mean condescension characterizes Jean Larnac's *Histoire de la littérature féminine en France* (1929). In both books, Woman is portrayed as the eternal romantic, obsessed with love, incapable of reaching out of herself or dealing with abstractions. The same cliché is expressed gently by Séché, ferociously by Larnac. The former opens a more generous perspective, vaguely echoing Rimbaud's prophecy when he writes "the twentieth century will be the century of Woman."[3] But Larnac is all bitterness. Complaining about the repetitiveness of feminine literature, and at the same time interpreting any sign of rebellion in it as depravity, he concludes that women would have written nothing of value if it were not for the men behind them, or for their "failure" as women.

Larnac may be an "easy target," as Germaine Brée suggests, but his idea that writing represents for women a compensation for a miserable personal life is hard to kill. As late as 1962, in an influential *Histoire vivante de la littérature d'aujourd' hui* (Living History of Contemporary Literature), we find the philosopher Simone Weil (1909–1943), along with Paule Régnier (1890–1950), author of intellectual novels and a profound diary, listed under the category of *Inadaptées* (maladjusted).

Much less colorful in their treatment of women than the works mentioned above, histories of literature in general provide very little or disappointing information about them. In France, the institutionalized discourse of literary history is associated with the name of Gustave Lanson, who, at the end of the nineteenth century, defined a method of systematic erudition inspired by the new "science" of history and applied it to the study of the national literature. He succeeded in imposing this history of literature as *the* academic literary discipline destined to replace the more subjective criticism illustrated by Emile Faguet. Lanson's followers, even more rigid than their master, impressed upon generations of French students an image of literature made up of a succession of schools and great names enshrined in the various *manuels de líttérature* used for teaching.

In almost all literary histories, including the most recent ones, whether inspired by Lanson or by a sociohistorical approach, women writers are either ignored, sparingly mentioned, or listed in senseless enumerations. While a host of secondary and even "minor" male authors are integrated under various labels—names of literary schools (such as *Symbolisme, Parnasse, Ecole Romane*), perspectives, themes, or genres (including the social novel, the psychological novel, regionalism, exoticism, humor)—women appear under "feminine poetry" and the "feminine novel." Time and again, except for "la grande Colette," the names of women of a given period are assembled indiscriminately in paragraphs appended as if in remorse to otherwise significant chapters having nothing to do with women.[4]

In sum, women writers have not only been grouped by their sex. They have also been judged according to their degree of "femininity," the absence or excess of which is found equally disturbing. Literary history has thus done more than marginalize women writers. By subsuming their literature under a stereotyped notion of romanticism, it has reinforced and perpetuated the myth of a feminine essence and effectively frozen "feminine literature" into a nonhistorical category. Rewriting the history of women's writing therefore does not simply entail bringing to light unfairly neglected works; it also means restoring the historical conditions and determinants of women's literature.

A wealth of recent studies do just this.[5] In the domain of historical disciplines, the recent shift from the traditional focus on political and military events toward the study of family, demography, marriage patterns, and food production has contributed to make women less "absent from history."[6] More directly relevant to our subject, comprehensive and well-documented histories of French feminism have revealed both the long and dynamic tradition of the feminist battle for equality and the concomitant antifeminist efforts that, at times succeeded in smothering that tradition.[7] These studies, which give a taste of the energetic and clear prose written by nineteenth-century militant women, are part of a new chapter of history that has directed attention toward the writings of Flora Tristan (1803–1844), Eugénie Niboyet (1797–1889), Suzanne Voilquin (1801–1876), Louise Michel (1830–1905), and those of numerous journalists, pamphleteers, and lecturers (Maria Deraismes, 1824–1894; Paule Minck, 1839–1901; Hubertine Auclert, 1838–1914; Nelly Roussel, 1878–1922; and Hélène Brion, 1887–1962, to name only a few). As a result, biographies and new editions of hard-to-find works have recently been published.

The vitality, tone, and themes of this feminist writing make very clear that the nineteenth century contains some very dark moments in the history of French women. In terms of women's rights, the legacy of the Revolution of 1789 was dismal, apart from modest improvements in primary education and inheritance laws. During the Terror (1793–1794), the political "clubs" where women previously formed and voiced their opinions were closed and most of the champions of sexual equality executed. Then came Napoleon who, as Michèle Sarde says in *Regards sur les françaises* (Perspectives on French Women), made love to and war on women.[8] A very successful war indeed, since the Civil Code promulgated in 1804 embedded in law the principle of the inferiority of women.

In spite of a few changes made during the Third Republic (1871–1940), particularly in the realm of education, the Napoleonic Code set the tone for a long period when women were treated as a commodity—through marriage laws and the regulation of prostitution—and at the same time worshipped for their beauty, sensitivity, and virtues. The celebration of the muse or the Universal Mother seems to have provided an increasingly bourgeois society with exactly the "feminine mystique" it required. The ideal bourgeois woman, devoted to domestic virtues and minor artistic enterprises, indeed appears as a barely disfigured copy of the muse. The dominant pattern of the condition of women remains one of exclusion and confinement: exclusion from the *lycées* (academic high schools) and universities, most literary circles, and all levels of political and economic decision, confinement in the home for the majority, the sweatshop for others, or the *maison de tolérance* (brothel) for the less fortunate.

Under these conditions, it was only through a combination of extraordinary determination and chance that some women managed to gain an education. For the most part, women of the middle class absorbed culture thanks to the development of the press and to the increasing circulation of books. There was a clear separation, often along class lines, between the *poétesses*, accepted as the voice of a male creation, and the women who wrote and fought for social justice and the rights of (working) women. As for George Sand, author of nearly a hundred novels, and her friend Daniel Stern (Marie d'Agoult, 1805–1897), historian and philosopher, they were neither "muses" nor revolutionaries. They pursued, at the price of their social respectability, wide "masculine" intellectual ambitions. George Sand's haughty rejection of her nomination by the feminist paper *La voix des femmes* (The Voice of Women) as their candidate in the 1848 elections shows clearly the ambivalence of her feminism.

When George Sand died in 1876, the Third Republic had just voted on its constitution in the chaotic aftermath of the military defeat of 1870 and the crushing of the popular insurrection known as the Commune of Paris. The bloody repression was not only a defeat of popular forces; it also dealt a cruel blow to the revolutionary feminism illustrated by Louise Michel, one of their main leaders.[9] At that time, she was confined to a disciplinary camp in New Caledonia and most of the other "incendiary women," as they were disparagingly called by those who accused them of setting fires during the Commune, were either dead or in exile. Historians of French feminism agree that 1871 was a significant turning point. It marked the end of revolutionary feminism and the beginning of an era of reformist feminism (sometimes unfairly called "bourgeois"), an era that would last until after World War II.

While Hugo, Verlaine, Rimbaud, and numerous popular song writers celebrated the women of the Commune, the female literature of that period bears almost no trace of the tragic events, not even *La femme d'aujourd'hui* (Today's

Woman), a collection of short plays written in 1880 by the feminist poet Hermance Lesguillon (1812–1882). The exception is of course Louise Michel. In her poems she remains the humanitarian visionary who adopted Victor Hugo as her master but succeeded in conveying the personal vigor of her hopes and her unfailing generosity through simple and vivid images.

Hugo's revolutionary and social Romanticism continued to inspire a few feminists, such as the pacifist Madeleine Vernet (1878–1949). But the favorite genre of women writers of the immediate post-Romantic period remained lyric poetry. Anaïs Segalas (1814–1893), Hugolian in her meditations on death (to the point that one of her pieces was included by mistake in a collection of Hugo's poems), wrote her more original poetry on the simple joys of family life in *Enfantines Poésies à ma fille* (Poems to My Daughter, 1844) and *Poésies pour tous* (Poems for Everyone, 1886). Louisa Siefert (1848–1877) was one of the most elegiac poets of love and solitude (*Poésies inédites* [Unpublished Poems], 1881). Louise Ackermann (1813–1890) followed another romantic vein, however, that of the spiritual rebellion illustrated by poets of despair such as Byron, Shelley, and Vigny. The positivist and evolutionist philosophy pervading her *Poésies philosophiques* (Philosophical Poems, 1874), *Le déluge* (The Flood, 1876), and *Pensées d'une solitaire* (Thoughts of a Solitary Woman, 1883), led critics to characterize her hastily as cold and abstract. There is in fact a great deal of personal passion in her yearning for knowledge and happiness, her denunciation of the absurdity of war, her challenges to Jesus or to Blaise Pascal, and finally in her self-presentation as "the idolatrous mother" of the still unborn "man" of the future.

The *fin de siècle* and the following decades witnessed an extraordinary flourishing of women's writing. This phenomenon is all the more intriguing since this massive and successful production apparently had no impact on the trans-formation of literature. Most of the women writers belonged to the literary establishment, represented by the salons, academies, and literary prizes, and they remained impervious to the various avant garde movements where the modernist sensibility was being forged. They were rich emigrées (Marie Bashkirtseff, Renée Vivien, Anna de Noailles, Hélène Vacaresco), aristocrats (Valentine de Saint-Point; Duchess of Rohan; Gyp, actually Countess of Martel), or women related to prominent literary figures (Gérard d'Houville, daughter of the poet José-Maria de Hérédia and wife of Henri de Régnier; Lucie Delarue-Mardrus, married to the famous translator of *The Thousand and One Nights*; and Rachilde [Marguerite Eymery], wife of the founder of *Le Mercure de France* [The Mercury of France] and herself a renowned critic). Even feminist critics have noted with a certain severity their indifference to the significant literary explorations of the period. For instance, Claudine Chonez—later echoed by Germaine Brée—remarked that "they missed out on surrealism, missed out on the broad movement toward the social novel before 1914, missed out on the sufferings of the century."[10]

To be sure, an impressive number of women poets of the period followed the cult of refined pessimism and precious images inspired by Parnassian and Symbolist masters such as Leconte de Lisle, Sully Prudhomme, and Henri de Régnier. Titles such as *Grisailles et pastels* (Grays and Pastels, 1896) by the Baronne de Baye (1854–?), *Réalités et rêves* (Realities and Dreams, 1901) by Lya Berger (1877–?), or *Gemmes et moires* (Gems and Silks, 1906) by the pseudonymous André Corthis (1885–1952) are representative of the fashionable poetic sensibility of the times. We find many of these works unreadable today for the reason noted by Germaine Brée in her scathing judgment of the most celebrated woman poet, Anna de Noailles. "She is without doubt, and most unfortunately for her own talent, a kind of unadulterated Narcissus, living in her own closed world. She offers us a typical image of a feminine writer."[11]

We must however read further into these works in order to perceive differences through the screen of "feminine" literature. It should be noted first that there were innovative women poets whose accomplishments have been poorly recorded by literary history. Deliberately ignored by the Symbolists and their historians, Marie Krysinska (1864–1908) was the first poet to experiment with free verse. Later, the noisy fame of surrealism and its new "feminine mystique" obscured the contribution of many women artists. The poets Claire Goll (1891–1977) and Céline Arnauld (1895–1952, *Poèmes à claires-voies* [Latticed Poems] 1920) are not even mentioned in the lavish issue of *Obliques* devoted to the "Surrealist Woman" in 1977. The early spontaneous surrealist texts of Gisèle Prassinos (b. 1920), who began writing in 1934, have only recently been collected (*Trouver sans chercher* [Finding Without Looking], 1976).

Moreover, women writers benefited, albeit indirectly, from the atmosphere of freedom and provocation of the period. By 1900, feminism had gradually regained its strength and its voice through the creation of numerous associations, newspapers, and magazines. Women poets and novelists, such as Daniel Lesueur (Jeanne Loiseau, Countess of Agoult, 1860–1921) and Anne Osmont (1872–1953), contributed to *La Fronde* (The Slingshot), the successful and eclectic paper founded by Marguerite Durand (1864–1936) in 1897. The debates over political and social priorities, both within feminist circles and between feminists and Marxist socialists, were made public by the numerous international congresses held in Paris between 1878 and 1913. The spirit of the "incendiary women" lived again in Nelly Roussel's campaign for a reproductive strike and Helène Brion's appeals for pacifism, for which she was sentenced to prison in 1917. In the cosmopolitan high society of *la belle époque* as well as in intellectual circles, feminism had become an object of curiosity, indulgence, or ridicule, in any case a fashionable topic of discussion. The question of the feminine soul, genius, and intelligence was examined, most of the time unfavorably, in the light of the recent biological and psychological sciences. Women of letters did not significantly participate in those discussions. They were either too absorbed in their own emancipation, reassured by their success, or convinced that antifeminism was too vulgar to be worthy of refutation. They were perhaps also "still looking furtively across at men," as Chonez says. Nevertheless, they were beginning to express their emotions and sensuality in their own voices and in a variety of ways.

In their poetry of nature for example, they were moving away from an evasive romantic vocabulary and the association of nature with languid sadness toward more sensuous images. Anna de Noailles's pagan lyricism, played with infinite variations from *Le cœur innombrable* (The Innumerable Heart, 1901) to *L'honneur de souffrir* (The Honor of Suffering, 1927), was often met with sarcasm by critics accusing her of pouring her soul into fruits and vegetables. With more earthy accents and less self-adoration, Marie Dauguet (1865–1942) uses a rich imagery capable of transmuting the most ordinary objects—a manure pile in "Les purins noirs chamarrés d'or" (Gold-laced Manures) from *Les Pastorales*, 1908—into poetic motifs. Hélène Picard (1873–1945) adds a vigor of her own to her poetry of love and nature by playing with prosaic language. As for the stereotype of the sweet and exquisite "Muse of motherhood" (Séché), it was reappropriated and transformed by poets such as Cécile Périn (1877–1959), Cécile Sauvage (1883–1927), and Amélie Murat (1882–1940). By evoking the physical and metaphysical mystery of motherhood at a time when the emancipated woman rejected it as a symbol of dependency, these poets were perhaps the guardians of a domain that would be later fully reclaimed by "writers of the female body."

It was through love poetry that many of these women revealed themselves in the most original and at times most militant manner. The daring expression of their own desire and the physical aspects of love represent a breakthrough in the history of women's literature, as Jeanine Moulin points out in the introduction to her anthology of eight centuries of feminine poetry.[12] Marie Nizet (1859–1922) in *Pour Axel* (For Axel, 1923) and Marguerite Burnat-Provins (1872–1952) in *Le livre pour toi* (The Book for You, 1908) celebrate the body of the man they love and the pains and joys of desire with a sincerity and directness not encountered since Louise Labé (1524–1566). *L'amant* (The Lover) by Marie Dauguet composes a blason of the masculine body as cosmic as the well-known "Union libre" (Free Love) by André Breton. Renée Vivien, the most talented of the women who chose the world of lesbianism sensitively evoked by Colette in *The Pure and the Impure* (1932), wrote highly artistic sapphic poems. Yet this poetic expression of female sensuality was almost totally eclipsed by the quasimonopoly that male writers, in particular the Surrealists after 1920, established over eroticism.

The abundant production of novels by women during the same period ranges from the traditionally sentimental and moralistic literature for adolescents (Zénaïde Fleuriot, 1829–1890) to the bizarre and often macabre tales crafted by Rachilde (1860–1953), who caused a scandal by showing a reversal of sexual roles in *Monsieur Vénus* (1882). Between these two extremes, many novels reveal the new aspirations, emotions, and conflicts of the modern woman of 1900. Extending the domain of the feminine novel to include descriptions of the new professions barely opened to women, Gabrielle Reval (1870–1938) depicts women students and professors as pioneers, while Colette Yver (1874–1953) joins the chorus of male authors who deride the learned woman (*Les Cervelines* [The Brainy Women], 1903; *Princesses de science* [Princesses of Science], 1910). Marcelle Tinayre's *La Rebelle* (1906), set in the feminist and intellectual Paris of 1900, is the most complex of these novels of emancipation.

Anna de Noailles (*Le visage émerveillé* [The Wonderstruck Face], 1904), Gérard d'Houville (*Le temps d'aimer* [Time to love], 1908), and Myriam Harry ([1875–1956]; *L'île de volupté* [The Island of Delight], 1908) create a new type of *jeune fille*, who is charmingly spontaneous, attractive, generally rich and who plays seductively with her new freedom. With more satirical wit, Gyp (1850–1932) transforms the young girl into the impertinent *garçonne* (flapper). In her novels (from *Marie fille-mère* [Mary, the Unmarried Mother], 1909, to *L'ex-Voto*, 1922), Lucie Delarue-Mardrus explores what she calls "l'océanique féminin" (the feminine oceanic dimension), with a more realistic sense of social conditions and with the same compassion she showed in her poems for her often unfortunate "sisters." In contrast to these fashionable works, whose *fin de siècle* style is often too ornate for our modern taste, the autobiographical novels of the former farm servant Marguerite Audoux (*Marie-Claire*, 1910, and *L'atelier de Marie-Claire* [Marie-Claire's Workshop], 1919) shine with stylistic simplicity and authentic emotion.

Colette alone, in this generation of women novelists, succeeded in pulling together the themes of love, nature, and feminine rebellion in a durable and totally original body of work. The young provincial woman who was a famous and scandalous figure in the Paris of *la belle époque* managed to free herself from the literary fashions of the moment: *La retraite sentimentale* (*The Retreat from Love*, 1907) represents her turning point away from both the mannerisms characteristic of the "Amazones" style and a modish licentiousness.

While Colette was unknowingly forging the transition between "feminine" literature and the female literature of the present, a few solitary figures were pursuing their exacting quests: Paule Régnier in her spiritual struggle with faith (*L'abbaye d'Evolayne* [*The Abbey of Evolayne*], 1933), Catherine Pozzi in her fascination with science and poetry (*Peau d'âme* [Soul Skin], 1935). Simone Weil, a university woman, poured into articles and notebooks the meditations on Greek philosophy, Christian spirituality, and social commitment that would be gathered after her death in several influential books. Marguerite Yourcenar (1903–1987), totally apart from any literary circle, was writing her classical short narratives (*Alexis*, 1929; *Le coup de grâce*, 1938), and Nathalie Sarraute was quietly anticipating the revolution in fiction writing that would later be known as the "nouveau roman," or the new novel (*Tropismes*, 1939).

Only after World War II did the improvements in women's education dating from the 1930s—along with other social changes—begin to be felt in the boom of women's literature that preceded the women's movement of the late 1960s. Among a number of excellent novels written by women at that time, some autobiographical works stand out for their depiction of women in daily life. This life is no longer protected by bourgeois comfort but is traversed by the torments of sexuality (*La Bâtarde* by Violette Leduc [1907–1971]); the experiences of war and exile (*J'ai quinze ans et je ne veux pas mourir* by Christine Arnothy [b. 1930]); deportation (*Les bagages de sable* by Anna Langfus [1920–1966]); racism (*Elise ou la vraie vie* by Claire Etcherelli [b. 1934]; and confinement in the working-class suburbs (*Les petits enfants du siècle* by Christiane Rochefort [b. 1917]).

Simone de Beauvoir best captures the spirit of the immediate postwar period in her novel *Les Mandarins* (1954) and in her three-volume *Memoirs*. As for many of her existentialist friends, particularly her companion Jean-Paul Sartre, the war was the shock that awoke her social and political consciousness and shattered the happiness of her personal emancipation. *The Second Sex* was the first to provide a theoretical analysis of the oppression of women and to denounce the mystification of the "eternal feminine" present in every aspect of the socialization of women. To measure the importance and the scope of this book, one could compare it to Daniel

Lesueur's *La condition féminine* (1905), a generous but extremely limited pamphlet that considered only the economic slavery of the working-class woman. If *The Second Sex* still bore traces of an optimistic trust in access to culture as a means of achieving equality, it also gave women an entirely new perspective on the constraints shaping their lives, and on the common—and distinctive—features of their conditions.

The novelty of this renewed militant feminism in France was the active participation of a number of educated women in the intellectual debates of the postexistentialist era. Language and writing came under a close philosophical scrutiny inspired by structuralist, psychoanalytic, and Marxist perspectives. Critics of cultural discourse such as Roland Barthes, Jacques Lacan, and later Jacques Derrida dismantled the belief in a universal thinking subject central to traditional Western thought. Women thinkers found in these philosophies the theoretical elements necessary for demystifying further a culture that inscribed male supremacy in its language.

The most provocative of their texts straddle various genres and disciplines. In a mix of theoretical, fictitious, and lyrical language, writers as different as Hélène Cixous ([b. 1937]; "*Le rire de la Méduse*" ["*The Laugh of the Medusa*"], 1975; *La jeune née*, [*The Newly Born Woman*], 1975), Luce Irigaray (*Speculum de l'autre femme*, [*Speculum of the Other Woman*], 1974), Claudine Herrmann ([b. 1926]; *Les voleuses de langue* [The Tongue Snatchers], 1976), and Annie Leclerc (*Parole de femme* [Woman's Word], 1974) show that the fundamental notions of Western culture, while pretending to be universal, are in fact construed from an exclusively masculine point of view. From that "central" position, women have been treated and described as the silent Other. They have therefore to repossess language in order to break that silence and dispel the mystery imposed on their own desire. These theoreticians have their literary counterparts in the practitioners of *écriture féminine*: Marguerite Duras ([b. 1914]; *Détruire dit-elle*, [*Destroy She Said*], 1969), Joyce Mansour (1928–1986]; *Phallus et momies* [*Phallus and Mummies*], 1969), Monique Wittig ([b. 1935]; *Les guérillères* [*a neologism alluding to female warriors*], 1969), Chantal Chawaf (*Chair chaude* [Hot Flesh], 1976, *Le soleil et la terre* [The Sun and the Earth], 1977), and in some respects Christiane Rochefort (*Archaos* [*a neologism*], 1972).

But many women, beside de Beauvoir, Sarraute, and Yourcenar, remain suspicious of the notion of a women's language. Julia Kristeva (b. 1941) in "Interview" (*Sub-Stance*, 13), and Catherine Clément (b. 1939) in her own section of *La jeune née* express the fear that the insistance on feminine writing might isolate women in a powerless romanticism and unwittingly repeat the exclusion perpetrated by literary history.[13] This debate has brought no theoretical resolution to the question of the specific nature of women's writing, but it has helped to draw attention to the extraordinary expansion of women's creativity that has taken place since the end of World War II. It also contributed to the development of a full-fledged literary criticism, which seems to assure a lasting place for women's literature.

Many other writers born at the turn of the century gained recognition in the postwar period: the Swiss novelist Corinna Bille (1912–1979); Belgian Suzanne Lilar (b. 1901), who opposed Beauvoir's call for emancipation; Elsa Triolet (1896–

1970), whose novels reflect the political turmoil of contemporary history; Béatrice Beck (b. 1914), author of powerful autobiographical novels; and poets such as Andrée Sodenkamp (born in Belgium in 1906), Yanette Delétang-Tardif (1907–1976), and Lise Deharme (1907–1980). The following generation is rich in writers illustrating many variations of feminism, from social and psychological analysis to utopia: Françoise Parturier (b. 1919), Françoise d'Eaubonne (b. 1920), sisters Benoîte Groult (b. 1920) and Flora Groult (b. 1924), Geneviève Gennari (b. 1920), and Marie Cardinal (b. 1929). All genres and styles are also well represented, from the elegantly stylized fiction of Françoise Sagan (b. 1935) to the experimental novels of Lucette Finas (b. 1921), the sensitive and humanistic poetry of Andrée Chedid (b. 1920), and the witty theater of Françoise Dorin (b. 1928). Without adopting feminist themes, many women have considerably broadened the horizon of the traditional novel: Suzanne Prou (b. 1920), Célia Bertin (b. 1920), Simone Jacquemard (b. 1924), Françoise Mallet-Joris (b. 1930), Geneviève Dormann (b. 1933), and Marie Chaix (b. 1942), among many others. The change since 1900 can be measured by the fact that militant literature can no longer be separated from "pleasure literature," if only because the women who assert in their works their right to pleasure are also women who know the world and the battles that have to be fought outside of the "feminine" universe.

In contrast with their American counterparts, French women have generally been more absorbed in the theoretical implications of their writings than in recapturing the history of female writing. Yet, as the female writers of the past become better known—including those who had been previously embalmed in literary history—today's women are looking with more confidence toward their foremothers. Slowly, the gaps in the tradition are being filled.

NOTES

1. Germaine Brée, *Women Writers in France, Variations on a Theme* (New Brunswick, NJ: Rutgers University Press, 1973), 5.
2. Charles Maurras, *L'avenir de l'intelligence* (Paris: Albert Fontemoing, 1905), 221, 225.
3. Alphonse Séché, *Les Muses françaises* (Paris: Louis-Michaud, 1908), 7.
4. A remarkable exception is Robert Sabatier's *Histoire de la poésie française*, 9 vols. (Paris: Albin Michel, 1982). Not only does the author treat women poets fully, he also underlines the past injustices committed toward them and succeeds in avoiding the condescension and uneasiness so common to literary historians. There exists no comparable effort at providing satisfactory and complete information on women novelists in the context of a general literary history. For an ahistorical presentation, see Michel Mercier, *Le roman féminin* (Paris: P.U.F., 1976).
5. Margaret Collins Weitz has compiled an excellent annotated bibliography of these works in *Femmes, Recent Writings on French Women* (Boston: G.K. Hall, 1985).
6. See articles on this subject in *Signs*, 7, no. 1 (1981), particularly Christine Fauré, "Absent from History," 71–80.
7. Maïté Alabistur and Daniel Armogathe, *Histoire du féminisme français* (Paris: Des Femmes, 1977); Jean Rabaut, *Histoire des féminismes français* (Paris: Stock, 1978).
8. Michèle Sarde, *Regards sur les françaises* (Paris: Stock, 1983), 44.
9. This lucid activist and modern woman published her memoirs in 1886; an edited English version appeared in 1981. Her poetic oeuvre was published for the first time only in 1982. See *À Travers la Vie et la Mort* (Paris: Maspero).

10. Claudine Chonez, "Hier, aujourd' hui, demain," in *La Table Ronde* 99 (Mars 1956). Special issue: "La psychologie de la littérature féminine, 61.
11. Brée, 44.
12. Jeanine Moulin, *Huit siècles de poésie féminine* (Paris: Seghers, 1975), 20. See also *The Defiant Muse*, Vol. 1, *French Feminist Poems from the Middle Ages to the Present*, Domna Stanton, ed. (New York: The Feminist Press, 1985); and Evelyne Sullerot, *Women on Love: Eight Centuries of Feminine Writing*, trans. Helen R. Kane (New York: Doubleday, 1979).
13. For an overview of these debates, see Elaine Marks's "Review Essay: Women and Literature in France" (*Signs* 3, no. 4 [Summer 1978], 832–842) and her Introductions I and III, written with Isabelle de Courtivron, in *New French Feminisms* (Amherst: University of Massachusetts Press, 1978).

BIBLIOGRAPHY

Background

Abray J. "Feminism in the French Revolution." *American Historical Review*, 80 (1975), 43–62.
Bidelman, Patrick. *Pariahs Stand Up! The Founding of the Liberal Feminist Movement in France: 1858–1889*. Guilford, CT: Greenwood Press, 1982.
Garcia, Irma. *Promenades Femmilières*. Paris: Editions des Femmes, 1981.
Halimi, Gisele. *The Right to Choose*. Trans. Rosemary Morgan. St. Lucia: University of Queensland Press, 1977. The work of a prominent contemporary leader.
Hause, Steven C. with Anne R. Kenney. *Women's Suffrage and Social Politics in the French Third Republic*. Princeton, NJ: Princeton University Press, 1984.
Marks, Elaine, and Isabelle de Courtivron, eds. *New French Feminisms: An Anthology*. Amherst: University of Massachussetts Press, 1981.
McMillan, James F. *Housewife or Harlot: The Place of Women in French Society, 1870–1940*. New York: St. Martin's Press, 1981.
Muses, Claire G. *French Feminism in the Nineteenth Century*. Albany: SUNY Press, 1984.
Ravenel, Florence Leftwich, *Women and the French Tradition*. New York: Macmillan, 1918.
Singer, Barnett. *Modern France: Mind, Politics, Society, 1870–1970*. Seattle: University of Washington Press, 1981.
Thomas, Edith. *The Women Incendiaries*. Trans. James and Starr Atkinson. New York: George Braziller, 1966.

Literary Criticism and Literature

Gelfand, Elissa D., ed. and transl. *Imagination in Confinement: Women's Writings from French Prisons*. Ithaca, NY: Cornell University Press, 1984.
Grassin, Jean, ed. *Femmes poètes de notre temps*. Carnac, France: Grassin, 1978.
Knapp, Bettina. *French Novelists Speak Out*. Troy, NY: Whitson Publishing Company, 1976. Includes interviews with Andrée Chedid and Françoise Mallet-Joris.
Peyre, Henri. "Contemporary Feminine Literature in France." *Yale French Studies*, 27 (Spring-Summer, 1961).

GREECE

Christopher Robinson

The development of women's writings in modern Greece has been profoundly influenced by the social disadvantages suffered by Greek women until well after the Second World War. The scale of this disadvantage can be measured by the fact that women only received the vote on equal terms with men in 1952, although limited voting rights had been granted in 1930 and extended in 1948. It is also particularly relevant in the present context that as late as 1939 only a small percentage of Greek *boys* went into secondary education: the number of girls receiving more than basic literacy instruction was accordingly infinitesimal up to the start of the Second World War. On the whole, only daughters of the small Europeanized upper class were educationally equipped to express themselves through literature; and even in this social group, no less than among the peasantry, women's personal freedom was also circumscribed by the obligation to marry, the dowry system being essential to the network of economic and political alliances on which the society rested. It is, therefore, unsurprising to find that women writers prior to the 1950s tend to belong by birth or marriage to tight-knit cultural groups: Galateía Kazantzáki (1881–1962) the novelist, for example, was sister of another major novelist, Elli Alexíou (b. 1894) and first wife of the novelist and poet Níkos Kazantzákis; similarly, María Rálli (1905–1976), poet and novelist, was sister of the leading actress Katína Paxinoú and the painter and musician Varvára Konstantopoúlou. Time and again, in what we may call the first and second "waves" of women's writing (1880 to 1920 and 1920 to 1960), we meet similar backgrounds: higher education in Greece or more frequently abroad, usually in literature and sometimes music; a general interest in education and child development, often including experience in teaching; humanitarian work (as for the Red Cross or refugee organizations); and journalism. The growth of a broader urban middle class in the years between the First and Second World Wars modified this pattern to some extent, but only in the 1960s and 1970s has it changed significantly.

One might expect a literature produced by women on a limited social base of this sort to be disregarded by traditional criticism. However, social conditions in Greece had a similarly limiting effect on male writers for a considerable part of the period in question, and women writers were able to command attention from critics because their work constituted a significant proportion of literary production. As early as 1896, Emmanuél Rhoídis caused a critical controversy with an article entitled *Ai gráphousai Ellinídes* (Greek Women Writers) on Arsínoë Papadopoulou. Thereafter, major critics such as Kostis Palamás and Gregorios Xenópoulos regularly reviewed women writers, and women collaborated with the leading male writers on such major periodicals as *Noumás* (1903–1929).

The status accorded to women writers was to some degree protected by an accident of history: the preexistence, which critics could not ignore, of an earlier tradition of female Greek writers stretching from the classical poets Sappho and Corinna to the Byzantine nun Cassia and the Empress Anna Comnena (fl. 1050 A.D.). This tradition tended to be used as grounds for defining, and thereby limiting, notions of "female sensibility," so that male critics could allocate areas of experience such as love and nature to a women's ghetto once they were regarded as "played out" among male poets. Admittedly, two major women writers in the pre–World War II period found it useful to assert their right to be taken seriously by adopting classical pseudonyms—Myrtiótissa (1883–1973) and Melissánthi (b. 1910). But this should be seen in the context of a more widespread use of pseudonyms (for example, the novelist Iréne Athenaía and the poets Chrysánthi Zitsaía and Margaríta Dalmáti), which probably indicates how far women felt obliged by social pressures to divorce their social and creative personas.

Setting aside the essential but anonymous contribution of women to the creation of the large body of Greek folk songs and fairy tales, the history of modern Greek women's writing properly begins with the handful of writers of the Ionian Islands whose work has survived, such as Angelíki Pálli Bartholomaéi (1798–1875) of Corfu, a member of the Italian Academy of Livorno, who wrote a small number of poems in Greek inspired by the 1821 revolution. Unfortunately, in the case of the most prolific and interesting of these women, Elisabét Moutzán Martinéngou (1801–1832), the manuscripts of her plays and other works were destroyed in the Zakynthos earthquake of 1953, and only her fascinating auto-biography (in the censored form published by her son in 1881) survives.

In Greece proper, a typical figure of the same period is Evánthia Kaíri (1779–1886), author of patriotic poetry and of a play on the fall of Missolonghi,[1] *Nikerátos* (1826), which had much success in performance. She belonged to the circle of the educator Adamántios Koraës, with whom she corresponded from an early age and translated French works that he sent her on the education of women, and she was active in trying to enlist the sympathy and aid of foreign women for the Greek cause during the War of Independence (1821–1826). The contribution of Greek women to the formation of a national consciousness at this period has not yet been properly studied.

The first forty years of the new kingdom of Greece (officially established in 1833) have tended to be looked upon retrospectively as a cultural desert. The work of women writers of the mid-century has consequently been forgotten because, like their equally neglected male counterparts, they wrote in an idiom of romantic melancholy on love and nature and in the official (and artificial) form of the Greek language, *katharévousa*.[2] But not all of this work was in fact thematically conventional—Aiani Mazaráki (1838–1892), for example, wrote a poem attacking the unnatural effect of fashion on girls—and much other work certainly needs reassessing, especially the writing of Photeiní Oikonomídou (1856–1883), whose self-descriptive and self-analytical poems include the powerful "Sphallo?" ("Am I wrong?") defending women's aspirations.

The key decade for Greek feminism was 1870 to 1880, when a group of writers founded the feminist journal *Ephimerída ton kyríon* (The Ladies' Newspaper, 1871–1918), which championed, among other issues, the cause of legal reform, with the aim of remedying the dependent status of women (notably the iniquitous effects of the dowry system). Among the influential figures associated with the newspaper was Kallirhöe Parrén (1861–1940), an active figure in the promotion of girls' education and author of various stories including "I Hiraphetiméni" (The Liberated Woman, 1900) and a play *Néa Yinéka* (The New Woman). This journalistic activity seems to have encouraged a wider group of women to publish their writings in the first decade of the new century. Though they mostly produced ostensibly conventional lyric poetry on themes of love and nature, such works need reexamination as examples of women's attempts to use preexisting forms to explore themselves and their relationship to the world around them.

Early women prose writers seem to have concentrated on stories, often with patriotic overtones, portraying Greek rural life (a genre equally popular with male writers between 1880 and 1910). The major prose writer of this period is undoubtedly Penelope Délta (1872–1941), principally known for her contributions to children's literature, which were aimed at stimulating the imagination (not a factor much considered by the Greek school curriculum, then or now), and had their roots in Greek folk traditions, religion, and history. Her novel *Ston keró tou Vulgaroktónou* (In the Time of the Bulgar Slaver, 1911) is a classic of its kind. Delta's patriotism is tainted by the jingoism of the "great idea" (the nationalist vision of restoring Greece to the boundaries of the Byzantine Empire). But her belief in the value of a Greek identity was strong enough to survive the crushing of prewar ideals in the aftermath of the catastrophic campaign of Greece against Turkey (1921–1922) and led her to commit suicide when the Germans entered Athens in 1941. In this way she is typical of the many women writers of the post-1920 period whose works were marked by two major political events, the Asia Minor disaster and the Occupation.[3]

Reassessment of the work of women writers prior to 1920 is hampered by the unavailability of texts. The same is not true of the post-1920 period. The works of such writers as Elli Alexíou, Melpo Axióti (1905–1973), María Rálli, and Ríta Boúmi-Pappá (b. 1906) are now available in "collected" editions. One is at once struck by the quantity and variety of women's writings from the 1920s onward. Only in the theater has the impact of women been slight, and that observation needs to be tempered by the fact that modern Greek theater as a whole has been slow to develop, and male writers have had as little success. Apart from Galateía Kazantzáki's symbolist drama *Enó to plío taxidévei* (While the Ship Sails) based on the image of society as a ship sailing heedless to destruction, which caused a stir when performed by the Greek National Theater in 1933, there were few plays of interest before the Second World War. Since then, however, more women have been experimenting with works for the stage, from the mythological plays of the novelist and playwright Margaríta Liberáki (b. 1919), which explore male/female relations, to the symbolic verse dramas of the poet Zoë Karélli (b. 1901), *M O Diávolos ke i évdomi entolí* (The Devil and the Seventh Commandment, 1955), *Iketídes* (Suppliant Women, 1962), and *Orestes* (1971). The major talent to emerge so far is Loula Anagnostaki (sister of the poet Manólis Anagnostákis), who made her debut as a dramatist in 1965, when Károlos Koun's company, the *Art Theater*, staged a program of her three one-acters. Her plays, reminiscent of the work of both Harold Pinter and the theater of the absurd, with an undercurrent of Freudianism, represent what is, for Greece, one of the first really fruitful modern experimental approaches to drama as a medium.

In narrative prose, women writers have established themselves more solidly. In the 1920s their works tended to follow the prevailing fashion for urban fiction. But in the 1930s—and it has to be remembered that prior to 1930 there were scarcely half a dozen Greek novels of significance by men—women writers made a new impact. In a male-dominated area, the war novel, Tatiána Stávrou introduced what were to be the first of several female perspectives with her collection of stories *Ekíni pou éminan* (Those Who Stayed Behind), describing the fate of the minority Christian communities in Turkey and her novel *I prótes rízes* (First Roots, 1936). Comparable reworking of "male" subgenres can be seen in the slightly later work of Eva Vlámi (b. 1910), who wrote her own versions of the traditional Greek "novel of the sea,"[4] *To chronikó tou Galaxídiou* (Galaxidi: The Fate of a Sea Town, 1947) and *Skeletóvrachos* (1949), and a poetic exploration of the death of the "great idea" in *Ta Ónira tis Angélikas* (Angelica's Dreams, 1958), a work that presents a poetic analogue of the events of the period 1912–1922, with the heroine as a symbol of Greece itself.

But as well as reworking traditional areas, women writers showed an impetus (sadly lacking in the male prose-writers of the 1930s) toward both thematic and stylistic innovation. Galateía Kazantzáki caused a stir with her first novel, *Yinékes* (Women, 1933), by her attempt to express the thoughts, beliefs, characters, and lives of seven women through the pages of their correspondence. Both this and her later works were much influenced by literary realism of a naturalist sort, but the recurrence of the themes of sickness, deprivation, loneliness, and psychological and social subjugation is a facet of acute social observation rather than literary imitation. Her sister, Elli Alexíou, began as a social writer of similar sympathies. Already in her early works her aim to show the pain experienced by the weak (children, the poor, the sick) is reflected in her choice of subjects. Her first book, *Sklirí agónes ya mikrí zoí* (Harsh Struggles for a Little Life, 1931), drew on her experience of working in an orphanage in Palio Phaleron, and her first full novel, *Trito Christianikó Parthenagoyío* (Third Christian Girls' School, 1934), on her experience as a teacher. Alexíou covered the whole range of prose genres in her writing, from novels, stories, and plays to school texts and critical essays. Her pro-Communist beliefs, which took her into exile in France and Eastern Europe after the civil war, led her to a more overtly political commitment, which is seen in the thematically broader canvases of her later novels. Of particular interest is *Parapótami* (Tributaries, 1955), which draws on an atemporal parallel between the struggles of the Greeks against the Turks in Crete and against the Germans in World War II.

The path cleared by women writers of the 1930s was then followed by those starting to write, or developing their writing, in the 1940s. Thus, Lilika Nákou (b. 1903), who came from a cosmopolitan background comparable to Kazantzáki's and Alexíou's, similarly exploited a powerful combination of personal experience and social conscience in her work, from her first major collection of stories, *I kólasi ton pedión* (Children's Hell, 1945), describing the plight of children during the Occupation, and the novel *I Kyría Doremí* (Mrs. Doremi, 1958), a humorous but sharp unmasking of the Greek cultural void, based on her experiences as a music teacher, to the more studied social satire of *Yi tis Viotías* (Boeotian Soil, 1951) and *Ya mia kenoúria zoí* (For a New Life, 1956).

Nakou's work is principally of interest for its subject matter. But the formal experimentalism which had made Kazantzáki's *Yinékes* such a striking work was still to the fore in other women writers. The early works of Melpo Axióti, *Dýskoles nýktes* (Difficult Nights, 1938) and *Thélete na horépsome María* (Shall We Dance Maria, 1940), show a disregard for traditional canons of plot and characterization that make them most easily classifiable as "lyrical fictions" developed around the observation of contemporary society. In the postwar period, Axióti put these qualities to the service of more overtly political ends, as in her major novel, *Eíkostos eónas* (Twentieth Century, 1970), a work portraying Greece as the victim of the twin forces of war and social repression, in which the strength of women in the face of social and personal injustice is a recurrent image. "Lyrical fiction" was used to quite different effect by other writers. María Rálli, who had been writing poetry in the 1930s, also rejected conventional criteria of novelistic realism in her psychological novella *Mia galázia yinéka* (A Blue Woman, 1944); and Galateía Sarándi (b. 1920) made comparable experiments with psychological fiction, starting from the novella *Epistrophí* (Return, 1953) and extending all the way to her most recent novel, *Ta ória* (The Boundaries, 1981), a study of the physical and psychological limits that constrain the modern human.

All these trends have continued in the younger generation of prose writers whose works have overlapped with their established forerunners. The significance of the Asia Minor disaster resounds in the novels of Didó Soteríou, the early works of Tatiána Grítsi-Milliex are firmly rooted in the tradition of Occupation and Resistance literature, and the psychological and social traditions have converged in the novels and stories of Eléni Voískou. In formal experiment it has been Grítsi-Milliex, a writer particularly well versed in European modernism, who has shown the way, from *Imerolóyo* (Diary, 1950) onward, often applying the techniques of the French *new novel* to social purposes that are all too often lacking in French literature (though not in the literature of French Canada). Perhaps Greek women writers have been prepared to break away from conventional restrictions of genre and style precisely because of their need to reject male-created archetypes on a social level.

Despite the range and variety of prose work by Greek women (and I have had no space to look into their contribution to nonfiction), it is in poetry that their achievements have been most widely acknowledged. True, even well-disposed Greek male critics have claimed that women are somehow biologically disposed to write lyric verse and confessional novels. But since poetry has a peculiar place in the hierarchy of Greek cultural values (though honored by all and read by few), and since the Greek male writers whose reputation has spread outside the country are predominantly poets also, it is hardly surprising if such poets as Zoë Karélli and Melissánthi have received substantial critical acclaim. The pioneers in the field, Myrtiótissa and María Polydoúre (1902–1930), instinctively exploited the traditional forms and images of love poetry as a medium to explore their ambiguous relationship to the male-dominated society of their time. Both women expressed their rebellion in "liberated" lifestyles that were at the same time marked by personal and, to a certain extent, cultural submission to the secondary authority of the poets who became their lovers.[5] The complexity of their lives is reflected in their writing.

The next generation of women poets showed a considerable broadening of range. Though frequently basing her writing on personal emotions and rejecting any creative role for the intellect, Zoë Karélli has produced a body of poetry that represents a sustained reflection on the agonies of the human condition. The early works of Melissánthi show a more marked metaphysical tendency, with Biblical influences strong, while her later work has become more concerned with questions of inner freedom. The prolific work of Rita Boúmi-Pappá has taken a more sociopolitical turn. Her first collection, *Ta tragoúdia stin agápi* (Songs to Love, 1930), had an emotional focus; it has been described as one of the two most emotionally powerful works of modern Greek poetry, the other being Melissánthi's *Prophitíes* (Prophecies, 1932). But Boúmi-Pappá was later strongly affected by the hunger and suffering she saw during the Occupation and by the heroism of the Resistance. Her poetry consequently became more socially aware, as for example in her *Hília skotoména korítsia* (A Thousand Murdered Girls, 1963). The civil war, the Cyprus problem, the junta have all fed her poetry with themes, while the classical tradition, Greek history in general, the landscape, and the analysis of the forces at work in life have fed it with images. Her anarchic optimism comes to a head in the prize-winning intergenre text *Morgan Ioánnis, o yálinos prínkipas ke i metamorphósis tou* (John Morgan, the Glass Prince and His Metamorphoses, 1977), where in a mixture of poems and poetic prose Boumi-Pappa explores the theme of the overthrow of contemporary convention—and, since Morgan is not fixed in time and space, of all convention.

The older poets are all writers for whom rhetoric in a positive sense is an inevitable part of poetic expression. Among a slightly younger group there has been a distinct movement against lyricism. Eléni Vakaló (b. 1923), Kiki Dimoulá, and Margaríta Dalmáti all explore, in different ways, consciously bare styles, in which qualities such as ellipsis and irony play a significant part. At the same time, there has been thematic evolution. In particular a number of poets, most prominently Jenny Mastoráki, Katerína Angheláki-Rooke (b. 1939), and Pavlína Pampoúdi (b. 1948) have tackled the issue of gender head on in a variety of ways. Pampoúdi is particularly interesting in her exploration of the self as creator and of the parameters of identity.

For every poet mentioned it would be possible to find a dozen more producing work of comparable interest. There are few male poets currently writing in Greece who have shown the same innovative force as the younger generation of women writers. Perhaps that has been the most striking characteristic of Greek women writers for the past century—a willingness to innovate and explore, thematically and formally, in their effort to identify and develop themselves and their society.

NOTES

1. A town in west central Greece that was captured in 1826 by the Turks during the Greek wars of independence (1821–1829).
2. The literary use of a written form of Greek based on the spoken language (*demotic*) only became standard in poetry in the 1880s and was to take another twenty years to become customary in prose writing. *Katharévousa*, based on the grammar and vocabulary of ancient and Byzantine Greek, had no fixed form and became progressively more archaic as the nineteenth century went on. The struggle between the two forms of written language has dogged Greece ever since 1833 and has been closely bound up with politics, with very negative effects on social and sexual equality (only the educated—that is, the upper class, usually male—segment of the population learned it). As recently as the period 1967–1974, *katharévousa* was reimposed as the language of education.

3. After the defeat of the Greek army in Turkey in 1922, the Turks took their revenge by massacring and pillaging the large and prosperous Greek population in Asia Minor and Pontus. As a result, one and a half million refugees eventually fled to Greece, causing substantial social problems that have still not been entirely resolved. The events of the Italo-German Occupation and the Greek Civil War (1947–1949) that followed the Occupation caused a comparable social trauma.

4. The first Greek prose writers to use demotic at the turn of the present century were very concerned to draw on Greek life and customs for their materials. Not surprisingly, this led to a large number of short stories and novels about life at sea and communities centered on the sea. Typical examples range from A. Karkavítsas' *Lóya tis plóris* (Tales from the Prow, 1899) to S. Myrivílis' *I Panayá i gorgóna* (The Mermaid Madonna, 1949).

5. Myrtiótissa was the lover of the lyrical sonneteer Loréntzos Mavílis (1860–1912) and María Polydoúre of the brilliant but anguished and nihilistic Konstantínos Karyotákis (1896–1928), who committed suicide.

BIBLIOGRAPHY

Background

Journal of Modern Greek Studies 1, no. 1 (May 1983). The issue is entitled "Women and Men in Greece: A Society in Transition" and contains a number of historical and sociological articles as well as literary ones.
Dubisch, Jill. *Gender and Power in Rural Greece*. Princeton: Princeton University Press, 1986.

Literary Criticism and Literature

Relatively little work by modern Greek women writers is available in English, and virtually no critical work has been done on them. The standard history of modern Greek literature—Linos Politis' *A History of Modern Greek Literature* (Oxford University Press, 1973)—hardly mentions women writers. For example, Myrtiótissa and Melissánthi are omitted completely, and Karélli, Liberaki, and Anagnostaki are listed in passing.
Even in Greek there is very little. The best source of information, though it is no means always accurate, is the *Megáli Enkyklopedía Noeellinikís logotechnías* (Great Encyclopaedia of Modern Greek Literature), whose early volumes often contain excepts as well as biographical and critical information.
The standard survey article is Dimitris Yiakos' "Greek women and literature" (Ellinídes tis logotechnías), whose early volumes often contain excepts as well as biographical and critical information.
The basic work on poets is Athina Tarsouli's *Ellinídes piítries* (Greek Women Poets 1857–1940), Athens: n.p., 1951.

Anagnostopoulos, A. "The Poetry of Maria Polydouri: A Selection." *Journal of the Hellenic Diaspora* 5, no. 1 (Spring 1978).
Anghelaki-Rooke, K. "Sex Roles in Modern Greek Poetry." *Journal of Modern Greek Studies* 1 (1983): 141–55. (As well as a critical article, includes text and translations of poems by a selection of contemporary women writers.)
Doulis, Thomas. *Disaster and Fiction: Modern Greek Fiction and the Impact of the Asia Minor Disaster of 1922*. Berkeley: University of California Press, 1977. Includes discussion of Tatiana Stavrou and Dido Sotiriou.
Halls, Aliki. *Greek Modern Theater: Roots and Blossoms*. Ann Arbor: University of Michigan Press, 1981.
Modern Greek Poetry. Trans. intro., comment., notes, Kimon Fiar. Athens, 1982. Contains work by and comment on Karéli, Boumi-Pappa, and Melissánthi.
Robinson, Christopher. "The Comparison of Greek and French Women Poets: Myrtiótissa, Maria Polydouri, Anna de Noailles." *Journal of Modern Greek Studies* 2 (1984): 23–38.

INDIA

Susie Tharu

Indian literature must be one of the few literatures in the world that is written in so many different languages. George Grierson's early twentieth-century linguistic survey lists 225 main languages, while the 1971 census of India names 700 languages and/or dialects spoken by one thousand or more people. This rich miscegeny of language is reflected in the history and the culture too, where traditions mingle and influence each other and differences are celebrated, sometimes in harmony, sometimes in conflict. Major literatures exist in the fifteen nationally recognized languages: Assamese, Bengali, Gujarati, Hindi, Kannada, Kashmiri, Malayalam, Marathi, Oriya, Punjabi, Sanskrit, Sindhi, Tamil, Telugu, and Urdu, as well as in Dogri, English, Konkani, Maithili, Manipuri, Nepali, and Rajastani. Most of these languages have separate scripts. Despite the fact that most people know two or three languages, few readers will have direct access to more than a few of these literatures or the cultural traditions they draw on. If we speak today of an "Indian" literature and include in it writings in English (called Indo-Anglian), it is because the writing of the nineteenth and twentieth centuries emerges out of a shared socioeconomic context and the shared experience of imperialism, nationalism, and urbanization.

The question of whether one can write authentically Indian literature in English is frequently debated. English, some critics claim, is the language of a culturally alienated urban middle class who, like chaffinches, sing only in gilded cages.[1] Its readership too, is obviously limited to a socioeconomically privileged group. Such literature, they argue, can never be the literature of the people or reflect indigenous concerns. Many Indo-Anglian writers (Indians writing in English) agonize over the issue.[2] Others claim that the only truly "national" literature is written in English, regional languages only produced regional literature, and so on. It is also true that those who write in English (Anita Desai [b. 1940], R. K. Narayan [b. 1907], Kamala Markandeya [b. 1924]) had immediate access to an international audience and became widely known, whereas the work of far more popular, more important writers in regional languages is often not available outside their linguistic area.

Additional factors impinge on the situation of the writer and the conditions of creativity for women in India during the period addressed by this book. The second half of the nineteenth century is often spoken of as the "high noon of the empire," for it marked the zenith of colonial exploitation and racist tyranny as much as it did the grandiose extravagance of the Raj. The declaration in 1878 of Queen Victoria as Empress of India was more symbolic than substantive, for by then British power—economic, political and military—was already well entrenched. India with its ancient culture, its vast resources, and its ever-growing market was a jewel, or so the British imagined, that would permanently adorn the Crown. But things were not to turn out so convenient. In 1885, the Indian National Congress was founded. Though this body had little more than the name in common with the one that led the country to political independence in 1947, it signaled the beginnings of middle class opposition to British rule. These were the origins of nationalism, but through its militant, early twentieth-century *Swadeshi* ("of one's own country") phase, which called for the boycott of foreign goods, and support for traditional craftsmen, down to the mass civil disobedience and noncooperation of the *Satyagraha* ("holding onto truth") movement of the 1930s, several strands, including tribal rebellions such as the ones Mahasveti Devi writes about, converge to form the crisscrossing web of what we have come to think of as the Freedom Struggle. The significance of this movement can hardly be overestimated. It challenged an imperial power that had dominated world affairs for well over a century and paved the way for other freedom struggles in Asia and Africa. It is against this backdrop of imperialism and of nationalist growth that we have to view much of Indian literature over the last century or so.

By the 1870s few aspects of life in India were unaffected by colonialism. Worst hit were the peasants, who reeled under the burden of new taxes on land they had traditionally cultivated. Many were victim to the pressures of hunger and debt and had to seek work in British-owned plantations (often as far away as the West Indies). The shadow of famine stalked the century. Social, political, and economic institutions that sustained the society were broken up. Craftsmen and skilled professionals were among those displaced and discredited by the new dispensation. A similar upheaval had taken place at the time of the Industrial Revolution in Europe, but the wage labor that the new factories there had made available was not an alternative for the dislocated peasants here. For many years to come, India, like the other colonies, would only provide the raw materials—and the market—for a growing Western industrial capitalism.

Women's songs—grinding and pounding songs, songs sung on swings, labor songs of all kinds, even lullabies—indicate that though traditional precolonial Indian society was feudal and patriarchal, women were in some ways more central and powerful in these societies than they are even today. This was all the more so in tribal communities, among the lower castes, and in the south of India, where non-Aryan (often matrilineal) cultures still had hold. Though what remains today of those oral art forms is often decorative residues bereft of their historical energy, as with the philosophical songs of Bahinabai Chowdhary (c. 1880–1951), they still evoke an alternative world. With the political and economic upheavals that precipitate the break up of traditional society, the urban centers of commerce and government—Calcutta, Bombay, and Madras—emerged as the new locations for scholarship and the arts. Further, just as the arrival twenty centuries earlier of the nomadic Aryans had initiated a shift from the magnificent visual forms of the predominantly agricultural Indus Valley civilizations to oral literatures, the introduction in the late eighteenth century of the printing press marginalized oral forms and gave written literature a new prominence.

Most of the writers featured in this collection belong to the urban middle class, where the men, if not always the women, had access to English education. Though they were by no means the principal victims of colonial exploitation, this middle class took the brunt of white racism and carried the immediate burden of aggressive and invariably negative European representations of India and Indians. Women too had to find new identities and new voices in this configuration—a configuration made all the more complex because the question of women (and the reform of Hinduism) took on enormous importance at that time.

British administrators and missionaries and Indian social reformers alike denounced "social evils," such as child marriage, the incarceration of young widows, premature consummation, and temple prostitution. They held up as ideal the regard with which Victorian Britain, which was also Christian, treated its women. No society, the British were quick to add, that so abused its women was fit for self-rule.

In the process a very strange thing happened to the question of women. Sensational practices such as *sati* (immolation of the widow at her husband's pyre), widow incarceration, and purdah, which were initially limited to some upper castes and classes, were repeatedly spoken of and consequently established as the "primitive customs" of an entire nation. Ironically, these rites soon became new symbols of social status. For almost half a century, such problems preoccupied the leaders of what has been called the Bengal Renaissance. Issues such as the famines and epidemics that decimated the population seemed to pale in relation to the intensity the woman's question, posed in these grotesque and sensational terms, seemed to acquire.

Two further dimensions of the cultural configuration that emerged at that time are of particular interest to students of women's writing. As the British presence began to consolidate itself politically and militarily after the Sepoy Mutiny of 1857 (reinterpreted by nationalist historiographers as the First War of Indian Independence), imperialism spawned new images of the immediate precolonial period. Eighteenth-century India, which had been the Mecca of European mercantile ambitions, was now increasingly projected as a dark age. Without the modernizing masculine energy the British brought with them, it appeared, India could never have been dragged out of the moral and spiritual morass it had descended into. Nonetheless, India could boast of a golden age in an ancient Hindu civilization held in high esteem by Orientalist scholars and idyllic in its treatment of women.

In many nineteenth-century writings this utopia took on the proportions of a romantic Eden, just as the Victorian "angel in the house" haunted portrayals of Indian women. The lush tropical garden of the Indo-Anglian poet Toru Dutt's (1856–1877) "Baugmaree," named after a place near Calcutta, where her father owned a country house, evokes a very specific sense of the flowers and trees of a lost childhood as paradisical. Victorian ideals of chaste, domestic womanhood influence her rendering of the Mahabharata heroine, Savithri.[3] Inevitably, the question of woman, inflected as it thus was, became (and continued, during later phases of the nationalist struggle, increasingly to be) a highly contested domain, and women, more so women writers, had to step a hazardous and politic path if they were to survive or grow. When we consider that, despite all the dust raised by the reformists, traditional social norms continued to have a powerful hold over women, we appreciate even more the complex guerilla maneuvers women had to make as they established their terrain or even just struggled for survival.

The forms that nineteenth-century women writers seemed most drawn toward are the autobiography and the romantic novel. The new value placed on women as individuals—who suddenly saw their specific lives as significant—resulted in an explosion of such works. Like autobiographies everywhere, most of these writings project the socially applauded contours of a life, in this case the *new* Indian woman's life. But of special interest to us today are details that escape or work against the normalizing pull of such conventional schemes of the self: aspects of her character that were censured, or she felt she had to control, "mistakes" she made, even experiences of sickness, rejection, and mental breakdown. A recurrent theme in these writings is the new scope of marital relationships and of the women's joy in the love and support of progressive husbands. But just as often we find wives speaking of the problems of being married to husbands who break violently with tradition and of the wit and resourcefulness these women have to bring into play as they mediate between orthodox families and rebel sons.

One of the most humorous, moving, and widely read of these is Lakshmibai Tilak's *Smritichitre* (*I Follow After*, 1934–1936). *Janika Grihabahadur Diary* (Diary of a Housewife, ca. 1860), written by the Bengali Kailasabasini Devi (d. 1895), reflects the author's pride in her husband (she even tells us exactly how much he earns as City Magistrate of Calcutta) as well as her confidence in his esteem. Her husband taught her how to read and engaged an English governess from whom Kailasabasini learned English and needlework. Episodes in her private life (the difficulty of finding an educated boy of the same caste for her daughter) are punctuated by her perspective on major public events (such as the Sepoy Mutiny). Kailasabasini's unusual account comes to an abrupt end in 1858 when her husband dies. "My life ends here" she writes, and continues to stay alive for another forty years.

To set against those pictures of marriage as a space of growth and fulfillment we have Binodini Dasi's Bengali *Amar Katha* (My Tale, 1913). Binodini (1863–1941) was an actress who worked with the legendary director Girish Chandra Ghosh (1844–1912) in the Calcutta theater from 1874 to 1886. Her performances have ensured her a reputation as an actress that is perhaps unmatched to this day. She comes through in the diary as courageous and independent. Although she often tells the reader she is a "fallen woman," it is quite clear that she considers herself superior to others who led more conventional lives. The Marathi *Sangate Aike* (Listen, I Am Telling You, 1970) by Hamsa Wadkar (1923–1972) is another personal, intensely felt account of the life of a professional actress.

Among the other early autobiographies of importance are the Bengali *Amar Jiban* (My Life, 1876) by Rasoondari Dasi (1810–after 1880) and *Poorva Katha* (About Earlier Days) by Prasannmayee Devi (1856–1939), as well as the Marathi *Amacya Ayusyathil Kahi Athavani* (Some Reminiscences of Our Life, 1910) by Ramabai Ranade (1862–1924) and *Maze Puran* (My Chronicle, 1944) by Anandibai Karve (1865–1950). Pandita Ramabai's (1858–1922) *The High Caste Hindu Woman* (1887) and *A Testimony* (1917), both written in English, are also autobiographical.[4]

The work of Rokeya Sakawat Hossain (1880–1942), feminist, social activist, and Bengali writer, raises very similar questions. Although she is today considered a writer from Bangladesh, Rokeya died before 1947, when India and Pakistan became independent and separate countries. Formerly East Pakistan, Bangladesh became a separate country in 1971. Rokeya's critique was directed principally against the practice of purdah, but she worked actively and at great personal cost to promote women's education. Her *Avarodhabhasini* (Veiled Women, 1929) is a series of vividly evoked episodes ridiculing purdah and, in the bold and witty utopian projection of Sultana's Dream, she argues that if men are so susceptible to temptation that they have to keep women veiled and secluded, women really ought to take over public life and incarcerate instead the potential aggressors—and in "Sultana's Dream" (1905), that is what they proceed to do. There is no war in this world ruled by the power of the intellect, and science has been turned to the service of humanity. Rokeya's husband, Sakawat, proudly called the story a "terrible revenge" on men.[5] Roushan Jahan, her modern translator, compares her *Maticura* (Bracelet of Pearls, 1905) to Mary Wollstonecraft's *A Vindication of the Rights of Women* (1792).

It is to Rokeya's credit that she was aware that, despite vociferous insistence to the contrary echoing through British India, Western women too were oppressed. In a characteristic gesture she translated Marie Corelli's *Murder of Delicia*, in which a fortune-hunter marries a rich woman and then deserts her.[6]

A certain tension marked the relationship between these early feminists and the Swadeshi phase (1905–1910/11) of the national movement. Swadeshi leaders called for a boycott of foreign goods and a return to traditional life. They revived (and created) popular festivals and cultivated a political idiom with a religious edge. As one might expect, the movement had an immediate and powerful appeal, both with the rural population and with young middle-class men (and behind the scene, women) who were its leaders and supporters. It brought new images of women and new questions to the fore. Women were to uphold the nation and the family and be supportive partners in the fight against imperialism.

In literature, two groups are transitional: the literary circle around Rabindranath Tagore,[7] of which Svarnakumari Devi (1855–1932) was a part and the significant group of women writers who emerged in the Bengali literary community that grew around the influential novelist Saratchandre Chatterjee (1876–1938) in Bhagalpur. Principal among them is Nirupama Devi (1883–1951), a child widow herself and a close friend of Saratchandra's, who wrote several short stories and novels. *Didi* (Older Sister-in-Law, 1915), her best-known novel, is also an important social history of the period, while *Syamali* (1919) is a sensitively developed story of a mute half-wit who blossoms into an intelligent, warm-hearted woman in the love of a young husband (who married her by mistake).

Like Saratchandra Chatterjee himself, who portrayed the suffering of middle-class women with sympathy but never questioned deeply enough to offend or agitate even the most conservative reader, these women writers, beginning in the 1930s and those following until well into the 1960s, break with the public enthusiasms of the earlier generation and move into a more restrained domestic mode.

No history of the freedom struggle fails to mention the major role women played in it. Women of all classes boycotted foreign cloth and spun *khadi* (the handspun, hand-woven cotton and silk that the Gandhians put forward as the solution to a failing village economy). Some peasant and middle-class women joined agrarian struggles said urban trade unions. The Indian National Army, led by Subash Chandra Bose, (1897–1945?) had a whole company of women. Yet women's creative writing at this time seems marked by two surprisingly conservative strains: the domestic realism of fiction and the reflective, often romantic lyric poetry of inner life.

In this context it is notable that Sarojini Naidu (1879–1949) wrote (though some of it was published later) much of her delicate lyric poetry before she met Gandhi and was drawn actively into the freedom struggle.

The Bengali novelist Ashapurna Devi (b. 1909) won a prestigious national literary award (the Jnanpith in 1976) for her *Pratam Pratisruti* (Early Promise, 1964), which is the first in a trilogy of novels that go back to the initial struggles for freedom and education and pick their way through to the lives of women today. Important among her 180 or so other works are *Agni Pariksha* (Ordeal by Fire, 1952), *Galpa Parishat* (Collection of Stories, 1959), and *Svarnalata* (Creeper of Gold, 1966). Her novels are invariably set within the domestic sphere. Realistic plots develop in the security of a wise, warm-hearted narrator who is rarely unsure of anything. History, politics, antagonisms of class or sex almost never intrude into the frame. The world of human relationships appears unchanging—and the implication is, unchangeable, for life will always continue to be played out in its little ironies.

Writers such as Ashapurna Devi, Dhirubhēn Patel (Gujarati, b. 1926), and Nirupama Bargohain (Assamese, b. 1932), are important because they explore in great detail the contours of "ordinary" middle-class women's worlds. Nirmalprabha Bardoloi's (b. 1933) *Dinar Pacat Dina* (Day after Day, 1968) is, as the title implies, a record of the familiar domestic situations from which women's lives take their shape. The Indo-Anglian writers Kamala Markandeya, author of *Nectar in a Sieve* (1954), and Rama Metha, who wrote (1923–1978) *Inside the haveli*, 1976), are later artists in the same mold.

In its acceptance of things-as-they-are, to be endured with courage and nobility, even humor, and its admiration for a traditional way of life, the principal note in the later fiction is a far cry from the sense of possibility, of action and of change that characterized the earlier period. At first glance such works seem conservative, reactionary, confined to spaces and attitudes that had always been sanctioned for women, doing little to question the restrictions. But despite their apparent quietism, these writers are, I believe, very important, for the harshly lit symbolic figures of the old canvases are now replaced with a crowded world in which much more is affirmed and celebrated and the range of fiction expanded. Meanwhile, the issues of woman's freedom and her rights as an individual were kept alive and developed in the fiction of writers such as Lalithambika Antherjanam (1909–1987) who wrote in Malayalan, and the Marathi writer Vivahari Shirulakar (pseudonym of Malatibai Baedekar, b. 1905). Two of Vivahari Shirulkar's works, *Hindolavya* (On the Swing, 1934) and *Virlele Swapna* (The Dream that Disintegrated, 1935), made a major impact in the Marathi world. Her collection of short stories, *Kareanche Vishwas* (The Sighing of Buds, 1933), explores the experiences women face in the context of their new aspirations and provides early hints of rebellion in a woman's world. Reformist concerns also continued to be explored in an important body of women's periodical literature in Gujarati, Hindi, Tamil, Telugu, and Urdu.

Though their work lacks the same scope, a similar pattern may be discerned among major poets such as Mahadevi Verma (b. 1907), Balamani Amma

(b. 1909), Kuntala Kumari Sabat (1900–1938), and Indira Sant (b. 1914). Most of them came into prominence in the 1930s. They write powerful, finely tuned, intensely personal poems of loneliness and suffering, shot through occasionally with the light of relationship (mother-child, lovers, even friends). Even as the novelists were reclaiming a complex outer world, these poets move inward, and their haunting explorations of inner life and the philosophical reflections that mark this poetry expand women's imaginative worlds in a direction often untouched in the earlier writing. There are attempts to re-connect with tradition, as in the echoes of women's folk songs that haunt Indira Sant's carefully modulated poems. Yet all the writers in this group are sophisticated and accomplished formalists. One could also consider Kamala Das (b. 1934) and Amrita Pritam (b. 1917), both major poets of the 1960s, as inheritors of this tradition.

The upper middle-class characters of the Indo-Anglian writer Anita Desai are liminally poised at the edge of old, broken-down worlds. There is no real solution, not even love, to the problems she poses in her carefully crafted books ("a writers writer," she has been called)—only dead ends and formal resolutions. *Voices in the City* (1965) and *Clear Light of Day* (1976) are among her best-known works. Though her domain is more psychological than existential, the Hindi writer, Mannu Bhandari (b. 1931) also portrays in which world a things are uncertain and paradoxical. Her moving and brilliantly constructed *Ap Ki Bunty* (Your Son, Bunty, 1971) portrays a woman who, despite her desire for freedom, chooses to live with a man who makes many demands on her. The novel is written from the point view of her son from an earlier marriage (Bunty) and explores the predicament of the child in these tense "new" relationships. *Mahabhoj* (Death Feast, 1979) is a satire on how politicians exploit the most tragic human situations. Her contemporary, equally well-regarded writer Krishna Sobti (b. 1925) is a meticulous craftsperson and conscious stylist, known for her bold themes. Her influential *Zindaginama* (The Saga of Life, 1979), set on the banks of the River Chenab, portrays life in the Punjab before the partition of India and Pakistan. It was the first time, perhaps, in Hindi literature that the tone and the rhythm of a regional dialect had been so vividly captured. Sobti's *Mitro Marjani* (Damn You, Mitro, 1967) has also been widely commented on. Ismat Chugtai's (b. 1915) mischievous, full-blooded heroines, on the other hand, are drawn from all classes. At first glance they may seem totally different from the pale figures that haunt Indira Sant's or Anita Desai's writing. But like Mitro they too are individuals who construct strong individualist responses to the world around them. They laugh (with the reader) at strictures that would presume to restrain them, and casually put aside oppressive social norms that would have broken lesser beings. In sum, from the late 1960s and into the 1970s women's writing takes on a much wider scope and begins once again to attend more critically to questions related to gender.

Major writers of this period (all four are leading figures in the literatures of their region), the Bengali writer Mahasveta Devi, (b. 1926), the Tamil writer Rajam Krishnan (b. 1925), Muppala Ranganaikamma (b. 1930), who writes in Telugu, and the Urdu Qurratulain Hyder (b. 1928), use the woman's question as emblematic and weave rich tapestries that encompass the lives of peasants, tribals, and workers as well as middle-class women. Though known primarily as a major innovator in form, Hyder also deals with major historical events. *Aag Ka Darya*

(Ocean of Fire, 1962) ranges over 2,500 years of Indian cultural history, and the principal characters reappear in different periods. Muppala Ranganaikamma has written several novels and critical works. Her *Ramayana Vishavriksha* (Ramayana, the Poison Tree, 1974), which is a critique of this important Hindu sacred text[9] from a socialist and feminist point of view, caused an uproar, as did *Janaki Vimukti* (Janaki's Freedom, 1978), a long novel in which Janaki leaves her home and makes a bid to live her life independently. The narrative includes heated discussions on women's issues. Rajam Krishnan writes carefully researched novels set among tribals and salt miners, among others; *Kurinji Then* (Kurinji Honey, 1963) is representative. Her recent work deals sensitively with women's issues.

Since the mid-1970s there have been several important new voices on the scene, and new feminist modulations seem to have emerged in the work of older, more-established writers as well. Women writers, artists, and theater workers have formed groups to support each others' art but also to work together to make plays, paint pictures, and choreograph dances. They have edited oral autobiographies and made important films. Unfortunately, apart from the Tamil story by Ambai (C. S. Lakshmi, b. 1944), little of this ferment, which began in the early 1970s, could be included in this anthology. Among the writers who have made significant contributions are Kundanika Kapadia (Gujarati, b. 1927), Indira Goswami (Assamese, b. 1942), Chhaya Datar (Marathi, b. 1942), Jyotsna Langewal (Marathi), Sara Joseph (Malayalam, b. 1948), Ketaki Kushari Dyson (Bengali), Meena Alexander (English, b. 1951), Lakshmi Kannan (Tamil, b. 1947), and Veena Santeshwar (Kannada, b. 1945).

NOTES

1. Jyotirmoy Datta, "On Caged Chaffinches and Polyglot Parrots," in *10 Years of Quest*, eds. Abu Sayeed Ayyub and Amlan Datta, (Bombay: Manaktalas, 1966), 286−96 and Lal, "Indian Writing in English—A reply to Jyotirmoy Datta," in *10 years*, 297−303.
2. See, for example, Kamala Markandaya, "Why Do We Write in English?" *Adam International Review* (London) 355−360 (1971): 42−43, and Meena Alexander, "Exiled by a Dead Script," in *Contemporary Indian English Verse: An Evaluation*, ed. C. Kulshrestra, (Delhi: Arnold Heinemann, 1980), rpted. in *Journal of South Asia, Literature* (Winter 1986).
3. The *Mahabharata*, a compendium epic of 100,000 couplets, stands at the beginning of Indian literature as *The Iliad* stands at the beginning of Greek and, more broadly, Western literature. As a book (rather than as the repository of an oral tradition), it is usually dated between 400 B.C. and A.D. 400. The "Forest Book" describes the famous story of Savitri, who by her wit and persistence, saves her husband from Yama, the God of Death.
4. This essay cannot do justice to Pandita Ramabai, who may be of particular interest to Americanists because she traveled to America and published an account of it in her native Marathi (1899). A woman of astonishing administrative ability and intellectual power, she was learned enough to debate the woman's question with distinguished Sanskrit scholars. Like that of her younger contemporary Rokeya (discussed in the following section), Pandita's opposition to patriarchal oppressions of the old order brought her into confrontation with emerging nationalist groups, who attacked her personal integrity.
5. Quoted in Roushan Jahan, trans. and ed., *Inside Seclusion: The Avarodhabhasini of*

Rokeya Sakawat Hossain (Dacca: Women for Women, 1981), 20. Also Roushan Jahan and Hannah Papenek, eds. *Sultana's Dream* (New York: Feminist Press, 1988).

6. Marie Corelli (1855–1924) is the pseudonym of the English Mary Mackay, who wrote popular, highly moralistic and sensational novels; she was the favorite novelist of Queen Victoria.

7. Rabindranath Tagore (1861–1941) was a poet, songster, critic, and novelist. Winner of the Nobel Prize in 1913, he is one of the most well-known representatives of modern Indian literature, which synthesized Eastern and Western influences. Though he wrote mostly in Bengali, his works have been widely translated.

8. Women's autobiographies, some available also in English, capture the extent of their involvement. See Vijayalakshmi Pandit, *The Scope of Happiness: A Personal Memoir* (Delhi: Vikas, 1979); Begum Shaista S. Ikramullah, *From Purdah to Parliament* (London: Crescent Press, 1969); Eleanor Morton, *Women Behind Gandhi* (Bombay: Jaico Publishing House, 1961).

9. Ramayana (literally, "the wanderings of Rama") is a unified epic of 24,000 couplets centered around Rama, a righteous king and later an incarnation of Vishnu, one of the great Hindu deities. Believed to be the first work of human origin, and attributed to Valmiki (ca. fourth century), the first poet, the earliest surviving manuscript dates from the eleventh century. Its story is known throughout India and is the basis of many redactions as well as the source of innumerable allusions in other literary works.

BIBLIOGRAPHY

Background

Borthwick, Meredith, ed. *The Changing Role of Women in Bengal: 1849–1905* Princeton: Princeton University Press, 1984.

Chattopadhyay, Kamaladevi. *Indian Women's Battle for Freedom*. Delhi: Abhinav Publications. 1983.

Desai, Neera. *Women in Modern India*. 2nd ed. Bombay: Vora and Co., 1977.

George, K.M., ed. *Comparative Indian Literature*. Madras: Macmillan, Vol. I, 1984, Vol. II, 1985.

Mazumdar, Vina. *Indian Women: From Purdah to Modernity*. New Delhi: Vikas, 1976.

Sarkar, Sumit. *Modern India*. Princeton University Press, Madras: Macmillan, 1982).

Journals that might be consulted include: a special issue on women writers of *Indian Literature*, Sahitya Academy, New Delhi. (24, no. 2, March-April 1986);

Journal of South Asian Literature (earlier entitled *Mahfil*), now published Chicago;

Manushi, A Journal of Women in Society, published in Delhi; and the

Economic and Political Weekly of Bombay (especially valuable is its *Quarterly Review of Women's Studies*, from 1986 on).

Criticism

Kali for Women, ed. *Truth Tales: Contemporary Writing by Indian Women*. Delhi: Kali for Women, 1986.

Lakshmi, C.S. *Women in Tamil Literature*. Delhi: Vikas, 1984.

Mukherjee, Meenakshi. *Realism and Reality. The Novel and Society in India*. New Delhi: Oxford University Press, 1985.

Vaid, Sudesh, and Kumkum Sangari, eds. *Women and Ideology in Modern India*. Delhi: Kali for Women, 1988.

ITALY

Natalia Costa-Zalessow

The presence of women writers in Italian literature has been well known since the second half of the thirteenth century, when the first documented woman poet, Compiuta Donzella, wrote her sonnets and made her contemporaries marvel at her poetic talent. Of course, the number of women authors was very limited in the Middle Ages; no wonder, for during that period literacy was rare and even noblemen preferred being soldiers to writers.

Religion, however, was an important factor of everyday life, and mysticism found many adherents in the thirteenth and fourteenth centuries. Women participated actively in all spiritual movements. Some, like St. Claire (1194–1253), founded convents, distinguishing themselves as able organizers of monastic orders, teachers, and nurses. Others, like Angela da Foligno (ca. 1248–1309), wrote about theological problems or took an active part in political life, striving to bring about peace in a period of general turmoil, as did St. Catherine of Siena (1347–1380), whose letters, dictated to her disciples in the Sienese vernacular, are of great importance to linguists as documents of the spoken language of the time. To the genre of religious, or devotional literature, belong the poems and prose of Caterina Vigri (1413–1463), famous also as a painter and illuminator; the writings of the mystic Caterina Fieschi Adorno (1447–1510); the poems of Tommasina Battista Vernazza (1497–1587); the letters of Caterina dei Ricci (1522–ca. 1590); the mystic meditations of Maria Maddalena de' Pazzi (1566–1607); and the diary of Veronica Giuliani (1660–1727).

During the fifteenth century, as humanistic studies became more prevalent, Neo-Latin literature flowered in Italy, and some Italian women became known as writers of elegant letters and verse in Latin in the style of classic authors. These writings contain defenses of their literary activity and proclaim that women have the same God-given mental abilities as men. From among those who wrote in Italian, the three most famous are Alessandra Macinghi Strozzi (1407–1471), whose letters written from Florence to her sons (in exile in Naples) are still used as a basic source by historians and sociologists of the fifteenth century; Lucrezia Tornabuoni (1425–1482), mother of Lorenzo de' Medici, who left a number of simple but beautiful poems; and Antonia Giannotti Pulci (ca. 1452–?), author of devotional mystery plays.

The sixteenth century brought about great changes in the cultural climate of Italy. Theology was no longer the main emphasis in education. Neo-Platonic philosophy and letters prevailed, and people became interested in literature written in the Italian language (as opposed to Latin). Petrarch and Boccaccio were, respectively, the models for poetry and prose. Aided by the new printing presses that flourished especially in Venice, the Italian literary language was solidified, and Italian literary works, together with those from the visual arts, enjoyed an unprecedented prestige in Europe. Women were again able to profit from this general expansion of cultural activities. The noblewomen of the Italian ruling families (Este of Ferrara, Gonzaga of Mantua, Montefeltro of Urbino) played an important role in shaping Renaissance culture. They were well educated and they engaged in debates with men of letters invited to their courts, where the problem of women's position in society was discussed, resulting in many male-generated treatises. Indeed, Italian feminism was born in this period and was very aggressively defended in later years, when women began to write their *own* treatises. Poetry in the style of Petrarch was the prevailing fashion. It was cultivated by all those who had received an education. Several noblewomen (such as Veronica Gambara [1485–1550] and Vittoria Colonna [1490–1547] distinguished themselves as poets and their poetry became part of the Renaissance literary canon. They served as examples to Isabella di Morra (1520–1546), Laura Bacio Terracina (1519–1577), Chiara Matraini (1515–ca. 1604), and Laura Battiferri Ammannati (1523–1589), who either sent them laudatory sonnets or imitated their poetic style.

Literary ability was not limited, however, to the aristocrats. Courtesans of high standing, reflecting the new Renaissance standard of refinement, showed off their musical ability as well as their erudition. The two most famous are Tullia d'Aragona (ca. 1510–1556) and Veronica Franco (1546–1591), who at times exhibits a fiery feminism in her poems. But the greatest of all the Renaissance women poets remains Gaspara Stampa (ca. 1523–1554), who became a legendary figure after her verses were republished in 1738 by Luisa Bergalli, who compiled the first historical anthology of women poets, in 1726. With so much literary activity by women, it is no wonder that the sixteenth century produced the first anthology of women poets—edited by Ludovico Domenichi in 1559.

The sixteenth century was also an important time for women in the other arts. The painter Sofonisba Anguissola (1528–1626) distinguished herself as a fine portraitist and paved the way for those who came after her, such as Artemisia Gentileschi (1590–1660), Giulia Lama (ca. 1685–after 1753), and Rosalba Carriera (1675–1757). Recognition accorded the talented actress and writer Isabella Canali Andreini (1562–1604) made it easier for other women in the performing arts to gain serious attention. Barbara Strozzi (b. ca. 1619) is considered the most gifted of the composer-singers of the seventeenth century, and in subsequent years women were highly esteemed as performers. Venice had a well-known all-women's choir and orchestra that was part of the musical seminary of the orphanage Ospedale della Pietà, where Antonio Vivaldi taught for several years.

During the late sixteenth and seventeenth centuries, a time in which Baroque extravagance prevailed, political and artistic liberty practically disappeared from Italy, as a consequence of the Spanish hegemony and of the Counter-Reformation. Women's position worsened, as did men's. Despite this, or perhaps as a consequence of it, feminism came of age under the pen of Modesta Pozzo (1555–1592), Lucrezia Marinelli (1571–1653), and Elena Tarabotti (1604–1652), three Venetians who proposed in their works that boys and girls receive equal education. Universities, however, were slow in accepting such ideas. Nevertheless, in 1678 Elena Lucrezia Cornaro Piscopia (1646–1684) became the first woman to be granted a doctorate in philosophy, from the University of Padua, and in the subsequent century, the Age of Reason, which promoted a more active part for women in society, we find not only women with degrees but even female university professors. The most famous was Laura Bassi Verati (1711–1778), who taught experimental physics at the University of Bologna; next came Anna Morandi (1717–1774), professor of anatomy; Clotilde Tambroni (1768–1817), professor of Greek; and Maria Dalle Donne (1777–1842), head of the school of obstetrics; while Maria Gaetana Agnesi (1718–1799) was a notable mathematician who wrote a popular manual on analytical geometry.

Three major literary genres prevailed in eighteenth-century poetry: pastoral poetry, poetic improvisation, and didactic poems. Women were especially active in the Academy of Arcadia, which promoted pastoral poetry. Two of its members, Petronilla Paolini Massimi (1663–1726) and Faustina Maratti Zappi (ca. 1680–1745) were gifted with forceful personal styles. Within this academic framework, the story of Angela Veronese (1779–1847) is unusual. Self-taught, as the daughter of a gardener she grew up among the flowers and trees her father tended for others—indeed, an Arcadian shepherdess transposed into reality. Her autobiography, published in 1826, is a valuable document of the simple life of country folk and the willpower of a girl determined to learn to read and write.

Toward the end of the eighteenth century a new influence swept in from the north and has become known in Italy as Pre-Romanticism. It found its best lyrical representative in Diodata Saluzzo Roero (1774–1840), who succeeded in fusing in her poems and short stories evocative descriptions of moonlit, ruin-filled landscapes with tales of death and a heroic past. (One of her stories deals with the Renaissance poet Gaspara Stampa.)

Highly praised by critics favoring romanticism, her work was not appreciated by supporters of the political movement for unification—the Risorgimento—who preferred fervent patriotic literary works extolling the idea of a united Italy. Many women obliged by writing such patriotic poetry, including Maria Giuseppa Guacci Nobile (1808–1848), Caterina Bon Brenzoni (1813–1856), and Caterina Franceschi Ferrucci (1803–1887). On the other hand, Teresa Albarelli Vordoni (1788–1868), modeling her work on the blank verse of Gaspare Gozzi, used comic realism to describe the miseries of human life and to create a fine social satire in her *Sermoni* (Sermons, 1826), in the tradition of eighteenth-century literature. Erminia Fuà Fusinato (1834–1876), more than any of her contemporaries, embodies a perfect example of patriot, poetess, and educator; she was a typical member of the middle class, which by that time was well established and destined to become the major group from which the proponents of the Risorgimento came. What had been only a literary dream since the Middle Ages did indeed become reality in 1870, when Italy was declared a unified Republic.

During this period the raging debate on women's education was also to have practical consequences. Cristina Trivulzio, Princess of Belgioioso (1808–1871), and the already mentioned Caterina Franceschi Ferrucci, among others, were active proponents of women's education, thus helping prepare the grounds for the passing, in 1879, of the Italian law on compulsory elementary education for all. Nonetheless, Italy, once culturally ahead of the other European countries, was by the late nineteenth century several decades behind the major ones, a fact not only evident in education and industrial progress but also in literature and the degree of women's contribution to it. We do not find original creative fiction in this period but rather memoirs, such as *Ritratti* (Portraits, 1807) by Isabella Teotochi Albrizzi

(1760–1836), which contains penetrating descriptions of important writers and artists whom the author knew, or the exotic *Memorie sull'Egitto* (Egyptian Memoirs, 1841) by Amalia Solla Nizzoli (ca. 1806–ca. 1845), who lived in Egypt from 1819 to 1828. She spoke Arabic and had access to the harem of Defterdar Bey, constable to Pasha Mohammed Ali. No other writer before her had had such firsthand knowledge about women's lives in the Near East.

By the second half of the nineteenth century, women in Italian literature had a long tradition to look back on, even if new obstacles remained to be overcome. Perhaps for this reason Italian women writers did not feel the need to use male pseudonyms, differing thus from other European women writers from other parts of the continent. An exception, but of special interest during this period is Evelina Cattermole Mancini (1849–1896), who wrote under the pen name Contessa Lara. She contributed to the major Italian periodicals and published several books of poetry; *Nuovi versi* (New Verses, 1897) includes her major compositions. No other woman was able to capture the spirit of the decadent society of her days with such precision: Mancini presents almost a photographic documentation, yet a very lyric one. Her only rival was Vittoria Aganoor Pompilj (1855–1910), included in this anthology.

The major contributors to narrative prose in this period are Caterina Percoto (1812–1887), Anna Zuccari (1846–1918), Matilde Serao (1856–1927), and Grazia Deledda (1871–1936). The first, encouraged by the poet Dall'Ongaro, wrote stories describing the simple life of her native Friuli. Following the path set by the great Romantic writer Alessandro Manzoni, Percoto used the realistic mode to create a literature of the common people. Although at times her style is hindered by excessive paternalism, a rigid morality, and naive patriotism, she does succeed in catching aspects of women's daily life. Anna Zuccari's art derives from romanticism and naturalism, although she never felt bound by the narrative form of these movements in her many novels and stories. Praised by the great Italian critic Benedetto Croce as a passionate and idealistic writer, it is not surprising that, like many of her generation still under the influence of the Risorgimento, Zuccari was fervently patriotic and in favor of Italy's intervention in World War I. On the other hand, the younger Matilde Serao, who admired Anna Zuccari and wrote letters to her, did not care about the war but only about the poor mothers whose sons were, like hers, soldiers. Serao was a writer of fiction and a journalist, one who wrested a place for herself in a man's world. Yet her activity was not without precedent in the eighteenth century; she followed after Caterina Cracas (d. 1771), Elisabetta Caminèr Turra (1751–1796), and Eleonora de Fonseca Pimentel (1752–1799), who was executed for her political ideas. Today, women in journalism have their best representative in Oriana Fallaci (b. 1930), who is well known to English-language readers through her popular, informative books. The more famous are *Il sesso inutile* (*The Useless Sex*, 1961), in which she investigates the life and lot of women in various lands; *Penelope alla guerra* (*Penelope at War*, 1966), also dealing with feminist issues; and the two more personal books *Lettera a un bambino mai nato* (*Letter to a Child Never Born*, 1975) and *Un uomo* (*A Man*, 1979).

Grazia Deledda is the only Italian woman writer ever to be awarded the Nobel Prize. It was given to her in 1927 (for the year 1926) in recognition of her simple but powerful prose works, which utilize the setting of her native Sardinia and its folklore. Deledda's characters are still popular with readers, as the frequent reprints of her novels indicate. Besides her, there were many more novelists writing in the first part of this century, such as Marchesa Colombi (pseudonym of Maria Torelli Torriani, 1846–1920), and Carolina Invernizio (1858–1916), author of popular serial stories. Both of these authors have recently received the attention of critics, while others still await their turn. Among other early twentieth century writers we find Clarice Tartufari (1868–1933), Annie Vivanti (1868–1942), Amalia Guglielminetti (1885–1941), and Carola Prosperi (b. 1883), all of whom wrote about the position of modern women in light of social changes. The problem of oppressed Sicilian women was marvelously treated by Maria Messina (1887–1944) in the novel *La casa nel vicolo* (The House in the Alley, 1921) and in some of her short stories, recently rediscovered and republished by the writer Leonardo Sciascia. The same tyrannical ambiance prevailing in Sicilian families reappeared later in the novels of Livia De Stefani (b. 1913), such as *La vigna di uve nere* (*Black Grapes*, 1953), where it serves as background to and cause of the incestuous love between a brother and sister, and *La passione di Rosa* (*Rosa*, 1958), where it underlies the slavish but unappreciated love of the protagonist.

The late nineteenth and early twentieth centuries are considered by some as the golden years of Italian feminism, because of the establishment of the *Unione femminile* (Women's Union), a society that promulgated numerous social activities and promoted the publication of books on women's issues. Rina Faccio (1876–1960), better known as Sibilla Aleramo, was an active member of this society, contributing articles and promoting literacy among the poor by organizing special schools. She was both a poet and a novelist and has remained famous, above all, for her autobiographical novel *Una donna* (*A Woman*, 1906), which dramatized some of the absurdities of Italian marriage laws and the misery and oppression women often suffered in conjugal life, particularly in southern Italy. The book, much lauded by Luigi Pirandello, was widely read and turned Aleramo into a celebrity. She was, however, never able to separate her literary inspiration from her tempestuous private life full of emotional and political turmoil; her leaps from socialism to fascism and finally to communism reflect a restlessness not uncommon among Italian intellectuals.

Another popular writer of that time was Ada Negri (1870–1945), whose poetry achieved its most personal expression in her later work, when she tried to define her condition as a woman. A national heroine of the Fascist regime, she was awarded the Mussolini Prize and made a member of the Italian Academy. Perhaps as a consequence, she is not much read today.

Antonia Pozzi (1912–1938), on the other hand, became known as a poet only after she committed suicide. Posthumously published as *Parole* (Words, 1939), her poems were reprinted in 1943 with a favorable foreword by the esteemed poet Eugenio Montale and gained her the recognition of being the most interesting female voice of the 1930s. Her compositions constitute a personal poetic diary, rich in rhythmic sound and clear images that tend toward the spiritual in their search for truth. A good selection is available in English under the title *Poems* (1955).

Although fascism was a period of great difficulty for most Italian women, the government allegedly promoted laws favoring them, especially working mothers, because the state needed future soldiers. Cultural activities, particularly research into Italy's glorious past, were encouraged, but only as long as women stayed within permitted limits. For example, in 1930 Jolanda De Blasi produced *Antologia delle scrittici italiane dalle origini al 1800* (Anthology of Italian Women Writers from the Beginning to 1800) and *Le scrittrici italiane dalle origini al 1800* (Italian Women Writers from the Beginning to 1800), and between 1940 and 1942 two biographical dictionaries appeared: *Poetesse e scrittrici* (Women Poets and Writers; see Bibliography), and *Eroine, ispiratrici e donne di eccezione* (Heroines, Inspirers, and Exceptional Women). These undertakings were not original but did reflect an Italian literary tradition that the government found useful to promote.

True realism was generally limited to the writings of a small group of openly antifascist writers; most authors preferred the safety of "magic realism," in which a semisurrealistic dreamlike world was created that served to evade the harsh realities of the period. Paola Masino (b. 1908) went beyond this genre to reach true surrealism. Yet realism survived in the tradition of regional naturalism, or *Verismo*. Paola Drigo (1876–1938) concentrated her attention on the lowest and most miserable social classes of the Veneto region, from her first collection of short stories, *La fortuna* (Fortune, 1913), to her best novel, *Maria Zef* (Maria Zef, 1936), whose protagonist is victim of a brutal relationship that matures in a climate of physical and moral degradation.

After 1945, in the new atmosphere of restored liberty and freedom, when women were finally given the right to vote, the tradition of realism experienced a renascence. Renata Viganò (b. 1900) is the only woman to have written a novel, *L'Agnese va a morire* (Agnes is Going to Die, 1949), on the resistance movement. Annamaria Ortese (b. 1915) turned to acute moral and civic polemics with her book *Il mare non bagna Napoli* (The Bay is not Naples, 1953), which won the Viareggio Prize. In this collection of short stories full of gripping pathos, realism borders on surrealism as the author points out the postwar miseries of Naples and its poor, many of whom lived among ruins of the heavily bombed city. Famous is the episode of the little girl who, upon receiving badly needed glasses, sees for the first time the squalor in which she lives. Of a different nature is the exotic realism successfully introduced by Fausta Cialente (b. 1898) in her novels *Cortile a Cleopatra* (A Courtyard in the Cleopatra District, 1936) and *Ballata Levantina* (The Levantines, 1961), both of which reflect the author's observations of the difficult and colorless lives of Moslems and Jews in Egypt, where she lived for twenty-three years with her husband Enrico Terni.

The low-key style and descriptions of monotonous daily routine, typical of Natalia Ginzburg (b. 1916), anthologized here, are also common to the popular Alba De Cespedes (b. 1911), who deals mainly with women's problems within marriage. *Nessuno torna indietro* (There's No Turning Back, 1938) was an international success for its minute examination of eight women, even while it was banned by the Fascist regime in 1940, together with her book *Fuga* (Flight, 1940). In the novel *Dalla parte di lei* (*The Best of Husbands*, 1949), she created a strong female protagonist who kills her husband. Women's search for self-expression is the main theme in most of her novels, including *Quaderno proibito* (*The Secret*, 1952), *Prima e dopo* (*Between Then and Now*, 1955) and *Il rimorso* (*Remorse*, 1963), but in *La bambolona* (*La Bambolona*, 1967), or "the big doll," she shifted to a male protagonist and used a comic plot.

A tendency for simple but profound sentiments can be found in the work of Beatrice Solinas Donghi (b. 1923) and Lalla Romano (b. 1909). The former is a writer of short stories and novels whose best book is perhaps *L'uomo fedele* (The Faithful Man, 1965). Romano intermingles a Proustian evocation of the past and present in her major work, *La penombra che abbiamo attraversato* (The Twilight We Crossed, 1964). Laudomia Bonanni (b. 1908), on the other hand, analyzes with penetrating psychological insight women at the margin of society in *L'imputata* (The Defendant, 1960) and *L'adultera* (The Adulteress, 1964). Also subsumed under the heading of realism is the writing of Milena Milani (b. 1922); she was unsuccessfully taken to court and accused of immorality for the eroticism in her novel, *La ragazza di nome Giulio* (A Girl Called Jules, 1964).

The postwar period is also rich in memoirs of various types, such as Natalia Ginzburg's *Lessico famigliare* (*Family Sayings*, 1963), Susanna Agnelli's *Vestivamo alla marinara* (*We Always Wore Sailor Suits*, 1975), Fausta Cialente's *Le quattro ragazze Wieselberger* (The Four Wieselberger Sisters, 1976), and Anna Banti's (1895–1985) *Un grido lacerante* (A Rending Cry, 1981). In each of these works a different environment is evoked, but all are representative of the turbulent twentieth century: Ginzburg depicts the life of the family of a professor of Jewish origin and their efforts to survive with dignity; Agnelli shows us the private life of rich industrialists during the fascist era and the immediate postwar period; Cialente recreates the turn-of-the-century world of her grandmother and her sisters against the background of the city of Trieste, with its mixed population of Italians, Austrians, and Slavs; while Banti, through her own example, depicts the pains of a woman struggling to hold onto her profession.

The long-standing spiritual tradition was not lost entirely by the postwar generation of poets, for Italy was and still is the center of Roman Catholicism. Therefore, it is not surprising that Alda Merini (b.1931) combined Christian, pagan, and pantheistic motives in her poems *La presenza di Orfeo* (The Presence of Orpheus, 1953) and *Tu sei Pietro; anno 1961* (You Are Peter; Year 1961, 1962). Gilda Musa (b. 1926), on the other hand, started out with a lyrical tone in *Il porto inquieto* (The Restless Port, 1953), but in her subsequent books she tries to reflect directly the difficult nature of modern life in a cement city. Rossana Ombres (b. 1931) makes use of complex cultural traditions in *L'ipotesi di Agar* (Hypothesis of Agar, 1968) and *Le belle statuine* (The Pretty Statuettes, 1975), and Patrizia Cavalli (b. 1947) gives splendor to simple objects through a rich, often arcane use of language in *Le mie poesie non cambieranno il mondo* (My Poems Will Not Change The World, 1974). Armanda Guiducci (b. 1923), after publishing *Poesie per un uomo* (Poems for a Man, 1965), which won the Cittadella "Opera Prima" Prize, assumed a feminist stance in *La mela e il serpente. Autoanalisi di una donna* (The Apple and the Serpent. Autoanalysis of a Woman, 1974). Other women poets, especially of the younger generation, can be found in the anthologies *Donne mie* (My Women, 1976) and *Poesia feminista italiana* (Italian Feminist Poetry, 1978).

In the difficult world of theater, women have not achieved great or lasting fame and, compared to the other literary genres, have contributed less. This in part, may be attributed to the fact that Italy has fewer important playwrights than other European countries, and its dramatic tradition is tied to improvised comedy and opera. But throughout the centuries, women did occasionally write mystery plays, pastoral dramas, opera libretti, tragedies, and comedies, although few of these were ever performed. Today they are remembered only by specialists. There are somewhat more women dramatists in the twentieth century, yet only Natalia Ginzburg and Dacia Maraini (b. 1936) can be considered successful as playwrights. The former writes plays that resemble her stories, that is, dealing with everyday problems; the latter presents polemical political and feminist issues in an aggressive and avantgarde style and is mainly associated with the Maddalena Theater in Rome, which specializes in contemporary plays by women.

With the progress of time and women's increasing literary activity, especially since World War II, it becomes more and more difficult to classify women writers, much less do them justice in a short essay. We can say, however, that women are involved in all literary genres, including journalism, children's literature, and popular biography in narrative form. A prominent writer in the last category was Maria Bellonci (1902–1986), whose books on Lucrezia Borgia and the Gonzaga family are well known in English translations. Also worthy of mention is Lidia Storoni Mazzolani (b. 1911), who has the unusual gift of making an historical or even philological problem into a beautiful story. For example, her book *Una moglie* (A Wife, 1983) is based on a Roman funeral eulogy dictated by a husband for his wife of forty-one years who saved him from proscription in 42 B.C.; it is a touching human episode narrated against the background of the violent historical events witnessed by the couple. However, if we were to judge contemporary writers by their popularity—that is, by how many books they sell—then first place would go to Liala (pseudonym of Liana Negretti Cambiasi, b. 1902), a writer of adventure and romance, who published her first novel in 1931 and her eightieth in 1985.

Although Italian women writers have been recognized as valid contributors to literature since the Renaissance, the general tendency had been to group them together, apart from male writers, a tradition still evident in most anthologies and histories of Italian literature, whereas contemporary criticism has fully integrated them into the mainstream of Italian literature. The problem of classifying them, however, has not been solved completely. Feminist writers want to be treated separately, as a united voice and new force, while well-established women writers tend to shun involvement in feminist publications and prefer to be considered as individual writers, competing with men for a place in literary history. It will be interesting to see how, in the future, this issue will be resolved.

BIBLIOGRAPHY

Background

Bainton, Roland H. *Women of the Reformation in Germany and Italy*. Boston: Beacon, 1974.

Greer, Germaine. *The Obstacle Race*. New York: Farrar Strauss Giroux, 1979.

Kelso, Ruth. *Doctrine of the Lady of the Renaissance*. Urbana: University of Illinois Press, 1978.

Klapisch-Zuber, Christiane. *Women, Family, and Ritual in Renaissance Italy*. Chicago: University of Chicago Press, 1985.

Labalme, Patricia H., ed. *Beyond Their Sex: Learned Women of the European Past*. New York: New York University Press, 1980.

Literary Criticism

Since few books in English are available, it is necessary to list the basic Italian sources.

GENERAL REFERENCE

Dizionario generale degli autori italiani contemporanei. 2 vols. Florence: Vallecchi, 1974.

Enciclopedia biografica e bibliografica italiana. Rome: 1941–42. Series 6: *Poetesse e scrittrici*, Ed. M. Bandini Buti, 2 vols. Istituto Editoriale Italiano. Rome: 1941–42.

Orientamenti culturali—Letteratura italiana: I minori. 4 vols. Milan: Marzorati, 1961–62.

Id.: *I contemporanei*. 6 vols. Milan: Marzorati, 1977.

INDIVIDUAL AUTHORS

Balducci, Carolyn. *A Self-Made Woman: Biography of Nobel-Prize Winner Grazia Deledda*. Boston: Houghton Mifflin, 1975.

Biagini, Enza, *Anna Banti*. Milan: Musia, 1978.

Fava Guzzetta, Lia. *Gianna Manzini*. Florence: La Nuova Italia, 1974.

Gisolfi, Anthony M. *The Essential Matilde Serao*. New York: Las Americas Publishing, 1968.

Marchionne Picchione, Luciana, *Natalia Ginzburg*. Florence: La Nuova Italia, 1978.

Ravanello, Donatella. *scrittura e follia nei romanzi di Elsa Morante*. Venice: Marsilio Editore, 1980.

Venturi, Gianni. *Elsa Morante*. Florence: La Nuova Italia, 1977.

Literary Works

Costa-Zalessow, Natalia. *Scrittici italiane dal XIII al XX secolo: Testi e critica*. Ravenna: Longo, 1982. Includes a detailed bibliography, pp. 21–23, as well as at end of introductions to each author.

Di Nola, Laura, ed. *Poesia femminista italiana*. Rome: Savelli, 1978.

Feldman, Ruth, and Brian Swann, eds. *Italian Poetry Today: Currents and Trends*. St. Paul, MN: New Rivers Press, 1979.

Frabotta, Biancamaria, ed. *Donne in poesia: Antologia della poesia femminile in Italia dal dopoguerra a oggi*. Rome: Savelli, 1977.

JAPAN

Chieko Mulhern

Japanese women have never needed apology or justification for writing. Not only did they participate fully in the art of poetry from the beginning of Japanese literary history in the eighth century, but by A.D. 1000 they had also perfected, if not invented, fiction. Today, nearly ten centuries later, women writers enjoy an equal share in serious literature, matching, or by some recent count surpassing, their male counterparts in quantity and quality of output, critical acclaim, public recognition, and cultural impact.

Japanese literature owes its origin to the sacerdotal function of language. Primitive belief in *kotodama* (the spirit, or the magical power, of the word) survived into the historical period to be preserved in prayers, incantations, and songs, as well as in mythical tales. In transposing diverse oral traditions into written literature, women played a significant role as professional and hereditary reciters assigned to memorize and recount religiohistorical facts and legends from before the beginning of Japan's historical period in the 200s through the early eighth century. It was, however, with the oldest and probably the greatest of Japanese poetic anthologies that individual identities came to prominence. *Man-yōshū* (*Manyoshu*, Collection of Ten Thousand Leaves), compiled in the mid-700s, contains some 4,500 verses by several hundred authors ranging from members of royalty, such as the female *tennō* (emperors) Saimei (thirty-fifth, reigned 655–661) and Jitō (forty-first, reigned 686–697), down to nameless frontier guards and villagers. The oldest verse in it is attributed to Princess Iwa (consort of the legendary sixteenth emperor, alleged to have reigned from 310 to 399). *Manyoshu* boasts many superb women poets: the witty and lyrical Princess Nukada (seventh century); the passionate Lady Kasa (eighth century); and the most prolific as well as gifted Lady Ōtomo of Sakanoue (eighth century). Many of their poems are often quoted today.

In the aristocratic Heian period (784–1185), Japanese culture matured and literature diversified, thanks in no small measure to women's talents and endeavors. The first imperial anthology, *Kokinshū* (*Kokinshu*, Collection of Ancient and Recent Poems, 915), set the standard for the native poetic form of *waka*, a compact lyric verse of thirty-one syllables with the cadence of 5, 7, 5, 7, 7 (the first half of which was to branch off as the seventeen-syllable haiku in the seventeenth century). The collection also immortalized Ono no Komachi, the only woman among the famed "Six Poetic Geniuses" of the tenth century. A mysterious beauty shrouded in the romantic mist of legend, she inspired numerous plays and stories down through the ages. Komachi's poems are highly acclaimed as the epitome of waka art and a poignant representation of the Japanese collective voice lamenting the inevitable passage of time and the unreliability of man's heart, the most dominant and persistent motifs in Japanese literature. Other notable Kokin poetesses are Lady Ise (consort of Emperor Uda, reigned 887–897) and the flamboyant Izumi Shikibu (?–1027), both famous as much for their sensuous apotheosis of love as for their literary skills.

But it was in prose literature that Heian women claimed the greatest achievements and even a virtual monopoly. Japan had had no writing system until the reign of the first female tennō Suiko (thirty-third, reign 592–628), when officially endorsed, imported Chinese characters came into practical use. In the early Heian period, the native script system called *kana* was created to transcribe the Japanese language phonetically, contributing immensely to the refinement of waka poetry, in which the use of Chinese loan words was forbidden. Heian men also learned kana scripts for use in waka poetry, social communictions, and courtship. But for centuries, women were not allowed to study Chinese classics or to write Chinese, which was considered a masculine language unfit for the gentler sex. Chinese continued to be the official and respected language reserved for male aristocrats, much like Latin in medieval Europe.

Ironically and providentially, women's social disadvantage proved literature's gain. While men were struggling with the gramatically rigid and noninflective borrowed language so radically different from their fluid native tongue, women used kana to describe their thoughts and the world around them in the adjective-rich and syntactically protean vernacular. Astonishingly transtemporal as well as transcultural in projecting an honesty of voice and a relentless introspection, women's diaries constitute the bulk of Heian literary masterpieces. Identified only by her sobriquet, court title, or family relationship, many a woman nonetheless etched her individuality on her diary while drawing a realistic tableau of Heian life. The Mother of Michitsuna (?–995?), for example, has bequeathed an incisive testimony to women's resentment against polygamy in *Kagerō nikki* (*Gossamer Diary*), remarkable for its psychological depth, powerful realism, and emotional impact. Equally universal is a young girl's state of mind revealed in *Sarashina nikki* (*As I Cross the Bridge of Dreams*, ca. 1059) by the Daughter of Takasue, mooning over the glittering heroes of romances. She was by no means alone in her addiction to the genre of *monogatari* (tales), which had just been crowned with Japan's grandest work of fiction, *Genji monogatari* (*The Tale of Genji*), completed in its extant form around A.D. 1010 by a court lady known only by the sobriquet Murasaki Shikibu (978?–1014?).

Rivaling *War and Peace* in sheer volume, Joyce in narrative complexity, and Proust in psychoanalytical insight, and featuring an archetypal oedipal son in the person of Prince Genji, this sophisticated tale stands as the undisputed pinnacle of Japanese literature. Until the influx of Western novelistic tradition in the mid-nineteenth century, all subsequent Japanese works in fiction and poetry were inevitably measured against this single work by the daughter and widow of a middle-echelon nobleman-bureaucrat. With its immediate and explosive popularity, even among the highest-ranking men at court, Lady Murasaki became the first author of Japanese fiction to be accorded individual renown in aristocratic circles, where Heian literature was exclusively produced and consumed, most avidly in the salons of empresses and princesses. Among many other famous literary women bred in this milieu were two eleventh-century court-lady poets, Akazome Emon and Ideha no Ben, who have been credited with a forty-chapter work that initiated a new genre called the historical tale; *Eiga monogatari* (*The Tale of Glory*, late-eleventh century) recounts the accomplishments of Regent Fujiwara Michinaga, one of the probable models for Prince Genji.

The literary glory of Japanese women, however, came to an abrupt end with the onset of warrior rule. The samurai eclipsed the imperial court not only in political power but also in cultural leadership for the next seven centuries. During the long medieval period under the Kamakura shogunate (1192–1333) and the Muromachi shogunate (1338–1603), Japan's literary history can cite only a few women by name, such as Princess Shukushi (?–1201) and the Daughter of Shunzei, both prominent in the imperial waka anthology *Shin Kokinshū* (*Shinkokinshu*, New Kokin, 1305). Shunzei's Daughter is also believed to be the author of *Mumyōzōshi* (Nameless Booklet, between 1196 and 1202), which is a unique critique of fiction: beginning with *The Tale of Genji*, it covers many tales preceding and following Lady Murasaki (a mere dozen of them extant) and evaluates women writers by analyzing their characterization, stylistic techniques, and esthetic merits. Literary criticism was apparently considered as feminine a pursuit as fiction writing in premodern Japan. Until a male scholar of English literature published a book in 1885 advocating Western critical theories, this work by Shunzei's Daughter remained the lone example of its kind.

A great many works of fiction continued to be written throughout the medieval period by court ladies or handmaids serving upperclass samurai families. Most of them have been lost, but their existence is at least known thanks to a 1271 collection of waka poems gleaned from many volumes of monogatari. It identifies some one hundred and ninety-five Heian and medieval tales, of which only two dozen are extant today. During the next three centuries, as many as four hundred short stories in the form of richly illustrated booklets and scrolls circulated widely among the samurai aristocracy and the wealthy merchant class. Many were authored and at first orally disseminated by itinerant lay nuns, but all works of fiction prior to the mid-seventeenth century remain anonymous except for *The Tale of Genji*. Frequent battles and isolated residence in manorial fiefs restricted physical mobility and peer interaction of cultured women in the ruling samurai class. Inevitably, significant new genres that emerged in the medieval period were expressly male-oriented, such as war tales, Buddhist hermit literature, and the Nō theatre, in which male actors play female roles.

In the next feudal period (1603–1867), the Tokugawa shogunate adapted the neo-Confucianism of Ming China as its state doctrine and imposed tight control and moralistic strictures on all segments of society, even in the private spheres of life. Most unfortunately, the socially sanctioned view on the education and conduct of women was drafted into a tract entitled *Onnadaigaku* (*The Greater Learning for Women*). This slight volume, commonly attributed to a Confucian physician Kaibara Ekken (1630–1714), dealt a more lasting blow to the Japanese women's collective unconscious and social status than had official ordinances. Girls of middle- and upper-class families were forced to copy and memorize it so as not to forget that "such is the stupidity of the woman's character that it is incumbent on her to distrust herself and to obey her husband," who is her only Heaven, Sun, and Lord. This feudal "feminine mystique" continues to provide contemporary writers with ready motifs and familiar character types while burdening today's women with lingering feelings of guilt and ambivalence.

Meanwhile, deprived of martial opportunities by the long peace and prohibited from engaging in political activities by the repressive shogunate, men in the seventeenth century channeled their interest and energy into artistic pursuits. With the advent of mass production by the woodblock press to replace handcopying, hitherto all but the sole method of making secular books (though Buddhist *sutras*, or scriptural narratives, had been printed since the eighth century), commerical publishing houses emerged, and literature became a full-fledged industry for the first time in Japan's history. But the new genres that proved financially successful were practically off-limits to women: the tales of the red-light district, (a plebeian counterpart to the salons presided over by ranking courtesans); the historical or fantasy adventure yarn; and the all-male Kabuki theater. Even the egalitarian haiku was routinely composed at poetry parties all but inaccessible to most women. The only notable female name in feudal literary history is Chiyo (1703–1775), a nun highly acclaimed in her lifetime for her sensitive haiku, some of which are often quoted today.

It was only after Japan plunged into the modern age with the imperial restoration of 1868 to emerge a parliamentary monarchy that literary horizons opened up again for women. Along with practical knowledge in modern technology and social sciences, Western literature and esthetics made their way into Japan, inspiring the birth in 1887 of Japan's first modern novel, *Ukigumo* (*Floating Cloud*), by a male scholar of Russian, Futabatei Shimei. In the following year, Miyake Kaho (1868–1913) earned a staggering sum equivalent to two-thirds of Japan's per capita net annual income for her *Yabu no uguisu* (Nightingales in the Grove), a novel pitting the "new woman" against the "old woman." Miyake's success helped galvanize many women into taking up fiction writing as a respectable means of making money or propounding some social platform.

In the Meiji period (1868–1912), there were three ways for women to break into the literary world dominated by educated men: to be introduced by influential men related by blood or marriage; to be affiliated with a school or a literary group; or to be tutored and promoted by a leading novelist-critic. Most Meiji women writers made their debut by one of these avenues, but they certainly earned their reputations in their own right. They had much in common. All benefited from advanced learning available to women beyond the universal compulsory education promulgated in 1872. The first major woman writer in modern Japan, Higuchi Ichiyō (1872–1896), studied classical Japanese literature along with Miyake Kaho at an all-female waka school. More women writers, however, owed their intellectual growth to modern Western education provided by Christian women's schools run by American and European missionaries, where courses were often taught in Western languages. Wakamatsu Shizuko (1864–1896; first graduate and first native teacher of the famed Ferris Women's School founded in 1870) contributed to the development of juvenile literature as an independent genre with her critically acclaimed bestseller translation (1890) of *Little Lord Fauntleroy* (1886, by Frances Hodgson Burnett), her own stories for young readers, and her "domestic novels," which added impetus to the ongoing redefinition of women's roles. Another Ferris graduate and teacher, Nakajima Shōen (1863–1901), became a highly placed social activist and the first woman to make public speeches before all-male audiences, but she is also unique as the author of a "political novel," *Sankan no meika* (Blossoms in the Mountain, 1889), whose heroine champions the women's rights movement.

Mostly daughters, sisters, and wives of foremost intellectual leaders and statesmen in the early Meiji period, women writers were welcomed in the battle of the word in politics and literature to oppose the oligarchical government and advocate people's rights. (Since the former samurai class had just lost the right to bear swords, language was the only effective weapon left to them.) Meiji women on their part tackled current social issues as well as new literary theories head on and garnered the interest and admiration of the male readership as well. Instead of female literature constituting a subculture, modern women writers were, and have been ever since, published side by side with men in mainstream literary journals, fiction magazines, and newspapers with nationwide circulation. For over two months in 1889, for example, the major daily newspaper *Yomiuri* serialized *Fujo no kagami* (The Mirror for Women), the first novel by an unknown seventeen-year-old, Kimura Akebono (1872–1889), in which a young heroine carries out Akebono's own frustrated plans to study at Cambridge and returns to open a factory so that Japanese women can have decent employment. Less well known but more courageous was the one-time teacher and journalist Shimizu Shikin (1867–1933), whose last novel, *Imin gakuen* (Immigrant School, 1899), was obviously emulated and closely paralleled by *Hakai, (The Broken Commandment*, 1906, the famed first naturalistic novel in Japan, by a major male writer Shimazaki Tōson) in its plot, key motifs, and the unique theme suggesting a humanistic solution to the savage discrimination against a (formerly outcast) minority, still a taboo topic in Japan today.

Japanese modern fiction almost by definition tended toward realism and naturalism, but a spectacular revolution was needed in poetry to introduce free verse and modernize waka into *tanka* (the same form but with new content and style). Yosano Akiko (1878–1942) became the single most briliant symbol of the poetic renaissance with her first tanka collection, *Midaregami (Tangled Hair,* 1901), which epitomized such romantic ideals as the liberation of emotions and the glorification of women, shaking not only the literary world but society at large. As in the example of Akiko's antiwar poem "My Brother, You Must Not Die," women were able to voice their protest publicly against the heightened jingoistic mood with legal impunity even during the Russo-Japanese War of 1904–1905, ironically turning the feudal feminine mystique to their advantage. A few months earlier than Akiko, for instance, novelist-poet Ōtsuka Naoko (1875–1910) had published her own controversial pacifist poem in a leading intellectual magazine, posing the rhetorical question "Which should be more important to me, my country or my husband?"

Women writers grew even more committed and outspoken in their social concern as waves of radical ideologies and idealistic humanism reached Japan from the West and took root in the literary circles of the Taishō period (1912–1926). Doors to a writing career opened even wider through numerous literary contests, including those for new writers, sponsored by newspapers, intellectual journals, and fiction monthlies, all riding the crest of a publishing boom following the war, which had sparked a surge in the national reading habit. No longer patricians or socialites, most Taishō women entered the literary field by winning contests; they studied Western literature, traveled abroad, joined revolutionary movements, and founded literary or ideological publications to advocate their causes. All Taishō writers were exposed to current Western trends such as socialism and feminism either of the kind glorified by Romanticists or of another dramatized by Ibsen. Inevitably, the celebrated *Seitō* (Blue Stockings, 1911–1916), founded as a women's literary journal by Hiratsuka Raichō (1886–1971) and her stellar associates, launched more political careers of women than literary ones.

Important Taishō women writers are too numerous to list, but typical is the Naturalistic novelist Tamura Toshiko (1884–1945), who won a major newspaper fiction contest in 1911, lived in Vancouver from 1918 to 1936, moved to China in 1938 to publish a Chinese-language journal *Josei* (Female Voice), and has been commemorated by the Tamura Toshiko Prize established in 1961 by and for women writers. The literary careers of many Meiji women had been cut short by early death, many from tuberculosis, or because of the increasing demand of social and domestic obligations attendant on their husbands' rise to the highest positions in their fields. In contrast, a good number of women who emerged in the Taishō period have enjoyed extreme longevity and rich careers into their eighties. Nakamura Teijo (b. 1900) in haiku and Gotō Miyoko (1896–1978) in tanka are both noted for their poignant insights into domestic life and family relationships delineated in a realistic modern style. Another tanka master, Ubukata Tatsue (b. 1905), is an imagist in pursuit of sense perceptions typified by her famous "white imagery." Extremely productive and visible, these women have influenced Japan's large population of amateur poets as judges of reader-contributed poetry columns in leading newspapers and magazines, preparing them for the national tanka contest for the Emperor's Prize awarded every New Year's Day.

Just as prolific and well-known are the writers who are often labeled the "grand dames" of prose literature. A winner of many prizes since 1921, Uno Chiyo (b. 1897) published a number of magazines, wrote many bestselling serious novels, and claimed yet more new readers among younger generations in the mid-1980s with an award-winning bestseller autobiography entitled *Ikiteyuku watashi* (I Go On Living). Nogami Yaeko (1885–1985), a highly respected and versatile novelist of intellectual cast, was posthumously awarded the Japanese Literature Grand Prize for her ambitious last novel *Mori* (Woods, 1982–1985), the greatest laurel in her distinguished eighty-year career that yielded, among other things, timelessly relevant portraits of "women at home" pursuing happiness in mundane settings. Far more accessible in the West is Enchi Fumiko (1905–1986), thanks to the English translations of her profound short stories and two major novels—*Onna zaka* (*The Waiting Years*, 1949–1957), which condemns the hypocrisy of polygamy in the early Meiji period, and *Onna men* (*Masks*, 1958), which plumbs the eerie depths of the modern female psyche. Defying a series of operations for breast and uterine cancers (a subject she was among the first to treat in fiction), Enchi maintained a high standard of production up to her death. In 1985, she was awarded the Order of Culture by the Emperor, postwar Japan's highest honor and one rarely bestowed on women in any field.

The first half (1926–1955) of the current Shōwa period provided a tumultuous stage for what is commonly called the prewar generations of women writers. They fall into two categories, the more radical of which is the proletarians, such as Hirabayashi Taiko (1905–1975) and Sata Ineko (b. 1904), whose experiences with poverty led them to leftist causes. The proletarian women carried on their battle for class equality through underground political activities as well as fiction writing. In the 1930s through World War II, however, serious literature was virtually suspended due to the severely moralistic, ultranationalist censorship and the physical absence of writers, with proletarians in prison and most adult males in war services. In the first decade after the war, while male intellectuals were busy apologizing for compromising their beliefs in cooperating with the militarist regime or in failing to register protest, superior exposés of wartime life and antifascist criticisms in fiction form were penned by women of both leftist and Western humanist persuasions. Notable among them is Miyamoto Yuriko (1899–1951), who had a privileged start in common with Meiji writers but who shared radical convictions with her prewar comrades, as evidenced by her realistic stories.

The second category of prewar women writers were also antimilitarist but basically more dedicated to literature for art's sake than for its utilitarian value: they took up social and women's issues as a viable literary subject matter rather than as a political cause. Hayashi Fumiko (1903–1951) turned the anarchistic ambiance of her impoverished youth into a lyrical eulogy in her diary novel *Hōrōki* (*Record of Wandering*, 1928) and delineated the tragedy of a male-dependent woman in *Ukigumo* (*Drifting Cloud*, 1951), inspired by de Maupassant. Okamoto Kanoko (1889–1939) gave motherhood a sensuous treatment in "Boshi jojō" ("Mother and Son," 1937), and Tsuboi Sakae (1900–1967) stamped the mark of her grassroots humanism on children's stories and her endearing long-selling novel *Nijūshi no hitomi* (*Twenty-four Eyes*, 1951). The line between "pure" literature and popular literature began to blur, as more serious mimetic novels attained both critical acclaim and popular recognition. After producing serious works on war, for instance, Koyama Itoko (b. 1901) earned the twenty-third Naoki Prize, the top award in popular literature established in 1935, for *Shikkō yūyo* (Suspended Sentence, 1950) but also caused two male critics to carry on a serious running debate over experimental techniques in her semidocumentary fiction *Damusaito* (Dam Site, 1954). One of Koyama's popular works has been translated into English and published in New York as *Nagako: Empress of Japan* (*Kōgō-sama*, 1955–1956).

The politics of women's literature have taken different forms in the postwar period. One new subgenre is as unique as it is tragic for deriving from a national cataclysm—the atomic-holocaust literature (*genbaku bungaku*). Proletarian Ōta Yōko (1906–1963) recorded her own experience as a Hiroshima victim in *Shika-bane no machi* (City of Corpses, 1948), banned for three years by the Occupation

Army censorship), and two award-winning works of fiction, *Ningen ranru* (Human Rags, 1951) and *"Han-ningen"* ("Half Human", 1954). A younger writer in the atomic-holocaust subgenre is Hayashi Kyōko (b. 1930), a Nagasaki victim who also represents another subgenre known as colonial literature (*Shokuminichi bungaku*), which is produced by one-time residents of Japanese "colonies" in China and Manchuria focusing on issues such as national identities, Japanese self-image, and the *étrangé* experience.

A new breed of women burst upon the literary scene in the mid-1950s to spearhead the so-called Neo-Heian era. Born in the Shōwa period and university educated, they readily assimilated recent Western literary techniques to create truly individualistic contemporary fiction. The first to attract the spotlight was Sono Ayako (b. 1931), who, featuring intelligent modern women in middle-class settings, aimed to create fictional microcosms in the manner of Charles Dickens, whom she admires. The sensation of 1956, promptly selling out 700,000 copies, was *Banka* (*Elegy*) by Harada Yasuko (b. 1928), which demonstrated her consummate mastery of modern novelistic techniques and introduced a new type of elusive and amoral heroine in a plot admittedly similar to *Bonjour Tristesse* (the translation bears this title, literally, Hello Melancholy, 1954) by Françoise Sagan.

An enormously successful novelist, Ariyoshi Sawako (1931–1984) established her reputation initially with stories dealing with Japanese traditional arts—*Jiuta*, ("Ballad," 1956)—and dynastic sagas of matrilineal family heritage culminating in *Ki no kawa* (*The River Ki*, 1959) and *Hanaoka Seishū no tsuma* (*The Doctor's Wife*, 1967). Ariyoshi's later "investigative novels," based on extensive original research, called public attention to serious problems plaguing contemporary society and made a profound and tangible impact on the national government as well. Ariyoshi's novel *Kōkotsu no hito* (*The Twilight Years*, 1972) on gerontology, and her fight to donate its huge royalties to that cause, resulted in a revision of tax laws, easing restrictions on charitable contributions; and her exposé novel *Fukugō osen* (Compound Pollution, 1975) triggered a discussion in the Diet (Japan's parliament) on industrial pollution control laws, besides raising public awareness and being quoted at court trials by pollution victims' attorney.

Some women writers betray conspicuous influences of European literature and intellectual currents. A rare existentialist, Kurahashi Yumiko (b. 1945), exposes the metaphysical absurdity inherent in the Japanese leftist student movement in *Parutai* ("Partei," 1960)* and continues to deconstruct reality and search for some meaning to existence in antiworlds of the imagination. Perhaps even more primordially cynical is Ōba Minako (b. 1930), who set her award-winning story "Sanbiki no kani" ("Three Crabs," 1968) in the United States, where she had lived as a housewife and college student, to delineate the snobbish ennui and emotional aridity pervading American intellectual circles in scenes reminiscent of T.S. Eliot's *The Cocktail Party*. The most enigmatic of contemporary women writers may be Takahashi Takako (b. 1932), whose fascination with Beaudelaire, Mauriac, and Catholicism tinges her chillingly phantasmogorical stories which focus on the mystical identification and mutual hatred between mother and daughter—*Sōjikei* "Congruent Figures," 1980)—or on the surreal dynamics between the creator and her creation-son— *Ningyō no ai* ("Doll's Love," 1978). Takahashi's story *Kou*

(To Love, 1985) won the Kawabata Yasunari Short Story Award named after Japan's only (and male) winner of the Nobel Prize in literature (in 1968). Disturbingly enigmatic yet explicit, Kōno Taeko (b. 1926) explores the frightening shadows of a housewife's subconscious in *Kani* ("Crabs," 1963) and again in *Saigo no toki* ("Last Time," 1966), or she penetrates female psychopathology in *Ari takaru* (Ants Swarm," 1975). Hellish visions and brooding nihilism are shared by other young women, such as Tsushima Yūko (b. 1947), who exposes apocalyptic nightmares in *Chōji* (*Child of Fortune*, 1978), and Yoshida Tomoko (b. 1934), whose novel *Mumyō chōya* (Unenlightened Long Night, 1970), about madness and the aimlessness of contemporary life, won the Akutagawa Prize. This highest and most coveted honor in serious literature (established together with the Naoki Prize), with the power to propel its biannual recipients into national prominence, has been going increasingly to women in the past two decades. Contemporary women have thus been recognized for initiating new concepts, motifs, and themes.

The daring is evident amongst modern poets as well. Candid use of anatomical words no longer shocks, since Nakajō Fumiko (1922–1954) won a grand prize in 1954 for *Chibusa sōshitsu* (Breasts Lost), a collection of her brilliant tanka exalting and eulogizing her own breasts claimed by cancer. In free verse, Shiraishi Kazuko (b. 1931) shows a revolutionary use of language and a radical treatment of sexual and racial taboos. Two other poets succeeded in fiction as well. With impressive skill, Tomioka Taeko (b. 1935) manipulates the humorous drawl and the breathless run-on pace of her native Osaka dialect in her modernist prose works, juxtaposing existential despair with everyday helplessness. A vanguard of the yet younger set is Kanai Mieko (b. 1947): under the influence of French experimental novels, she has set upon a course of nullifying the traditional differentiation between poetry and fiction, between the writer and her work, and between the observer/narrator and the observed/performer, as illustrated by the endless intermetamorphoses in "Usagi" ("Rabbits," 1976). Among their other contributions, women have been recognized for offering crosscultural perspectives on human relationships as well as penetrating inside views of Western life derived from firsthand observation or personal experience. Yamamoto Michiko (b. 1930) came out with *Betty-san no niwa* (*Betty-san*, 1973), an unsentimental story of the Japanese war bride's stifling life in Sydney with her Australian husband. Following her in the 1980s were a Baptist playwright Mori Reiko (b. 1928) with a novella *Mokkinbaado no iru machi* (The Town Where Mockingbirds Live, 1980), drawing on observations of international marriages in the American Midwest; and longtime New York City resident and painter Kometani Fumiko (b. 1930), who etched a poignant domestic tableau depicting annual Jewish ceremonies and gritty New York in-laws in *Sugikoshi no matsuri* (Passover, 1986). Among the younger generation, Ui Angel (b. 1950) made her debut by winning the Gunzō New Novelist Award for her *Zensōkyoku* (Prelude, 1982), an original manuscript fairly aflame with the intense hatred of a young Japanese woman for her English husband.

In 1975, an eight-volume anthology, *Gendai no joryū bungaku* (Contemporary Literature by Women), collected works by sixty-one award-winning women writers. Since then, their ranks have been swelling steadily. More significantly, women writers have set in motion a major epistemological revolution quite un-precedented in its nature and scope, not only altering the course of Japanese literary history but also threatening the traditional binary view of the human race itself. There is no longer any doubt that the women writers have launched an all-out assault on the long-standing epistemological framework that may be equated with a male-centered or male-defined paradigm.

The first male-created myth to fall was the sanctity of motherhood; symboli-cally the womb has been categorically rejected, abhorred, feared, and hated, most notably in works by Ōba and Takahashi. The mighty male image has been mercilessly minimized and caricaturized into slimy *Suijū* (Water Creatures, 1985) by Tomioka or etherealized into mystical pets by Takahashi, as in her *Higi* (Secret Rite, 1978). The mother-child tie, traditionally viewed as symbiotic throughout life in Japanese culture, has been torn asunder by the extreme manifestation of "man hating" in the metaphor of infanticide (refusal to bear a man's child) in some very recent works by younger women. Now, the male paradigm itself is given the ultimatum by Saegusa Kazuko (b. 1929; also a leading feminist theorist) in her *Hōkai kokuchi* (Annunciation of the Fall, 1985), a middle-class allegory casting a single mother and a male dramatist/adapter of Aeschylus's *Oresteia* trilogy to herald the collapse of the Hellenistic patriarchal system and the return of the Oriental animistic belief in the female as life force.

Japanese women writers have yet to propose a viable and definitive (if not exclusively feminine) paradigm to replace what has been destroyed, but they are making serious efforts. Tsushima recasts woman as *umi no sei* ("birthing sex") into a primordial "great mother" image, fully capable of production and reproduction without male participation. Hikari Agata (b. 1943) redefines and revitalizes the female roles for four pairs of PTA committee members and their children in *Yukkuri Tokyo joshi marason* (Slowly but Steadily, Tokyo Women's Marathon, 1985), setting them on a difficult but rewarding race together. Two of the youngest and most sensational award-winners are totally without self-consciousness or apol-ogy for their sex or sexuality: Nakazawa Kei (b. 1959) lets a teenager discover the dark sea of female physiology through sexual rites of passage in *Umi o kanjiru toki* (When I Feel the Sea, 1978) and *Suiheisenjō nite* (At the Horizon, 1985); and Yamada Eimi (b. 1959) makes a neutral common vocabulary out of English four-letter words and sex objects out of Western men in *Beddotaimu aizu* (Bedtime Eyes, 1985) and *Yubi no tawamure* (Finger Play, 1986).

At present, nevertheless, Japanese women writers are still tentative and ex-perimental in their visions of a future world. Be that as it may, they are undeniably serving as the most articulate and influential leaders not only in updating female cosmology but also in awakening men to reassess the male paradigm as they have never done before. In this sense, contemporary Japanese women are fulfilling their sacerdotal role as effectively as their shamanistic ancestors.

NOTE

* This and the following works have been published in English language anthologies but appeared as separate short novels in Japan.

BIBLIOGRAPHY

Background

Encyclopedia of Japan. Tokyo and New York: Kodansha International Ltd./Harper & Row, 1985.

Hall, John Whitney. *Japan: From Prehistory to Modern Times*. Tokyo and Rutland, VT: Charles E. Tuttle Co., 1973.

Kuwahara, Takeo, *Japan and Western Civilization*. Trans. Tsutomu Kano and Patricia, Murray. Tokyo: University of Tokyo Press, 1983.

Reischauer, Edwin O., and Albert Craig. *Japan: Tradition and Transformation*. Tokyo and Rutland, VT: Charles E. Tuttle Co., 1978.

Reischauer, Edwin O. *Japan: The Story of a Nation*. Tokyo and Rutland, VT: Charles E. Tuttle Co., 1981.

Sansom, George. *The Western World and Japan*. Tokyo and Rutland, VT: Charles E. Tuttle Co., 1950.

Literary Criticism

"Hisamatsu, Sen'ichi. *Biographical Dictionary of Japanese Literature*. Tokyo and New York: Kodansha International Ltd./Harper & Row, 1976.

Kato, Shuichi. *A History of Japanese Literature*. Trans. David Chibbett. Tokyo and New York: Kodansha International Ltd./Harper & Row, 1979.

Keene, Donald. *Dawn to the West: Japanese Literature of the Modern Era*. Vol. 1 [fiction], vol. 2 [poetry, drama, and criticism]. New York: Holt, Reinhart & Winston, 1984.

———. *Japanese Literature: An Introduction for Western Readers*. Tokyo and Rutland, VT: Charles E. Tuttle Co., 1955.

———. *Landscapes and Portraits: Appreciation of Japanese Culture*. Tokyo and New York: Kodansha International Ltd./Harper & Row, 1971.

Konishi, Jin'ichi. *A History of Japanese Literature*. Trans. Aileen Gatten and Nicholas Teele. Princeton: Princeton University Press, 1984.

Lippit, Noriko. *Reality and Fiction in Modern Japanese Literature*. London: MacMillan Press, 1980.

Miyoshi, Masao. *Accomplices of Silence*. Berkeley: Univesity of California Press, 1974.

Mulhern, Chieko, ed. *Japanese Women Writers: A Bio-critical Source Book*. Westport, CT: Greenwood Press (forthcoming).

Swann, Thomas, and Kinya Tsuruta, eds. *Approaches to the Modern Japanese Short Stories*. Tokyo: Waseda University Press, 1982.

Takeda, Katsuhiko, ed. *Essays on Japanese Literature*. Tokyo: Waseda University Press, 1977.

Walker, Janet. *Japanese Novel of the Meiji Period: The Idea of Individualism*. Princeton: Princeton University Press, 1979.

Literary Works

Birnbaum, Phyllis, trans. and ed. *Rabbits, Crabs, Etc.: Stories by Japanese Women*. Honolulu: University of Hawaii Press, 1983.

Gessel, Van C., and Tomone Matsumoto, eds. *The Showa Anthology: Modern Japanese Short Stories*. Vol. 1 (1929–1961) and vol. 2 (1961–1984). Tokyo & New York: Kodansha International Ltd./Harper & Row, 1985.

Hibbett, Howard, ed. *Contemporary Japanese Literature*. Tokyo and Rutland, VT: Charles E. Tuttle Co., 1978.

Keene, Donald, ed. *Modern Japanese Literature: An Anthology*. Tokyo and Rutland, VT: Charles E. Tuttle Co., 1957.

Lippit, Noriko, and Kyoko Selden, eds. *Stories by Contemporary Japanese Women Writers*. Armonk, NY and London: M.E. Sharpe, 1983.

Morris, Ivan. *Modern Japanese Stories*. Tokyo and Rutland, VT: Charles E. Tuttle Co., 1962.

Tanaka, Yuriko, ed. *To Live and To Write: Selections by Japanese Women Writers 1913–1938*. Seattle: The Seal Press, 1987.

Tanaka, Yuriko, and Elizabeth Hanson, eds. *This Kind of Woman: Ten Stories by Japanese Women Writers, 1960–1976*. Stanford: Stanford University Press, 1982.

Ueda, Makoto, ed. *The Mother of Dreams and Other Short Stories*. Tokyo and New York: Kodansha International Ltd./Harper & Row, 1986.

THE MIDDLE EAST

Barbara Harlow

In spring 1923 at the Cairo railway station, Huda Shaarawi (1879–1947) and her travel companion Saiza Nabarawi stepped from their carriage to be greeted by a crowd of waiting women. Huda Shaarawi's first public act on returning to Cairo from an international feminist meeting in Rome was to remove the traditional veil that covered her face. The Egyptian feminist was rewarded with resounding applause from the women who were there that day to witness her historic gesture. Subsequent generations have gone on to accord Huda Shaarawi's symbolic act recognition in the modern history of Arab women as responsible for the unveiling of Egyptian women.[1] Four years earlier, in 1919, Shaarawi and other members of the Women's Central Committee of the Wafd, Egypt's nationalist movement led by Saad Zaghlul, had waged public demonstrations in the streets of Cairo against the British occupation of their country. Although they participated in these demonstrations as veiled women, their confrontation with the armed British forces was less than decorous: violence was averted only at the last minute after a demonstration that lasted for several hours in the blazing sun. Shaarawi and her women compatriots continued to participate through the next decades in the Egyptian nationalist movement, and by the 1930s their political and social activism had expanded to involve a collective Arab feminism.

The necessary connection between national liberation and the women's struggle has characterized much of modern Arab feminism since the latter part of the nineteenth century, from the Wafdist Women's Central Committee, to women's participation in the 1950s in the Algerian war of independence, to the present-day struggle of the Palestinian people for self-determination and a homeland. This history provides the critical context for Arab woman's writing and it is the purpose of this introductory essay to situate the Arabic selections within the sociopolitical transformations in the Arab world over the last century. Europe's imperialist adventures in the Arab world are usually dated from 1798, when Napoleon Bonaparte led a military expedition to Egypt, accompanied by scholars and researchers whose investigations into the geography, demography, and ancient past of the invaded country would eventually produce the multivolume *Description de l'Egypte*. France, however, later lost her suzerainty in Egypt to the British, who officially occupied the debt-ridden country in 1882. In North Africa, or the Maghrib, France meanwhile continued to consolidate her territorial claim, which began in 1830 with a military incursion into Algeria to settle a financial quarrel between the Turkish day of Algiers and the French consul in the city. Following World War I, Britain and France divided between themselves the area of the Levant, or Mashriq, and the Arabian peninsula, thereby creating divisions that resulted, after independence in the 1950s and 1960s, in the Arab nation states as they are known today. Only Palestine/Israel remains contested.

The active role of women in these nationalist movements and liberation organizations and the reciprocal consequences of their nationalist activism for women's liberation and the restructuring of social roles for women underwrites much of the literary production of Arab women in the last century. The combined issue of nationalism and feminism is sung in their poetry, narrated in their novels and stories, and attested to in their essays and journalism. Huda Shaarawi's memoirs recount her evolution as a feminist and political partisan in Egypt. In 1936 Mrs. Matiel E. T. Moggannem published *The Arab Woman and the Palestine Problem*, a history of the women's movement in British Mandate Palestine. Women are likewise given a prominent role in the works of Algerian Assia Djebar, (b. 1936) and the Egyptian Najib Mahfuz's *al-Thuluthiyya* (Trilogy, 1960) "chronicles the lives of a middle class Egyptian family from 1918 to 1944."[2] *Al-Bāb al-maftūh* (The Open Door, 1961) by Latifa al-Zayyat (b. 1926) focuses specifically on a young girl's maturation in the tumultuous 1950s in Egypt. Elsewhere, Palestinian resistance to Israeli occupation continues to figure importantly in women's writing in Palestine/Israel, Lebanon and Jordan. Two novels of Sahar Khalifeh (b. 1941), from the West Bank, *al-Subbār* (Wild Thorns, 1976) and *'Abbād al-shams* (Sunflower, 1980), examine the often conflicted relationship between women's goals and the immediate agenda of the resistance organization. Liana Badr's *Būsla min ajlī 'abbād al-shams* (A Compass for the Sunflower, 1979) is the story of the coming of age of a young Palestinian woman in the resistance following the 1967 war. *Hikāyat Zahra* (The Story of Zahra, 1980), by the Lebanese writer Hanan al-Shaykh (b. 1945), in turn examines the relationship between a Beirut woman and a Palestinian guerilla during the Lebanese civil war.

Misapprehensions in the West of Third World women generally, and Arab women in particular, whose stereotyping has been part of the culture of imperialism, have negatively influenced most of the male academic and some feminist efforts to write women into the historical narrative. Typical of the Western attitudes toward Third World women's history is, as Judith Tucker has pointed out in *Women in Nineteenth Century Egypt*, "the notion that 'progress' for women was imported from the West."[3] As happened elsewhere in the colonized world, in Africa and India for example, the "civilizing mission" was given rhetorical justification through its self-described task of "liberating native women" from confinement within their male-dominated societies. In the Arab world this confinement was formally symbolized for Western observers by the veil and the harem. Studies such as Frantz Fanon's *A Dying Colonialism* (1959), Malek Alloula's *The Colonial Harem* (1981), and Rana Kabbani's (b. 1958) *Europe's Myths of Orient* (1986) have sought not only to criticize the Western attempt to colonize the Arab world through its women but to redirect attention to the struggle waged by these women themselves against what has come to be seen as a "double colonialism," that of Western imperialism no less than the patriarchal traditions of their own societies.

The century defined by the years 1875 and 1975 is an era that is itself divided between the colonialist enterprise and subsequent processes of decolonization in the Arab world. That history is, furthermore, crucial to the evolution of Arab women's intellectual activity. If women's participation in the nationalist struggle over most of that century-long epoch was critical to the development of their own liberation as members of their societies, their continued efforts, albeit not without setbacks, in the postcolonial years have been no less significant in maintaining debate within the newly independent nations. As Monique Gadant has pointed out, "Nationalism asked of women a participation that they were quick to give, they fought and were caught in the trap. For nationalism is frequently conservative, even though it appears to be an inevitable moment of political liberation and economic progress."[4] The efforts to redomesticate women in Algeria, for example, following independence, which were critically challenged by Fadela M'rabet in her 1967 book *Les algériennes* (*Algerian Women*), are still being debated in that country within government forums and by women's oppositional organizations, both Islamic and secular. In Egypt, writers like Nawal al-Saadawi (b. 1930) and Fathyya al-Assal, while often disagreeing with each other, remain constant in their collective opposition to the government's attempt, often under pressure from Islamic revivalism, to reverse the political gains made by women with the new personal status laws in 1979. In the war-ravaged country of Lebanon, women from diverse creeds and confessions met in 1985 to draft a Lebanese Women's Rights Charter, and in the Occupied West Bank and Gaza Strip, committees of working women have been formally established to secure and then to protect the human and civil rights of working Palestinian women. This endeavor has often been supported by progressive Israeli-Jewish women's organizations. In Iraq, women who have themselves been arrested or whose family members are held in Saddam Hussein's prisons are agitating for social and political reform in their country.[5] The women in the newly oil-rich countries of the Gulf area are pressing their changing societies to include them in the development of education, business, journalism and cultural activities. Women's writing in the Arab world is part of this collective challenge.

In the tradition of their literary ancestor Shahrazad, the legendary storyteller of the *Thousand and One Nights*, Arab women are speaking forth in the public arenas of their respective societies. Shahrazad, in the frame story of the popular medieval cycle, was the last of the kingdom's virgins taken by the sultan Shahryar to avenge the multiple transgressions of family, race and class committed by his wife caught in an illicit affair with a black slave. The wife and slave were executed, and the king proceeded to exact further revenge on all the women of his realm, by taking each night a virgin to his bed and beheading her on the following morning. Shahrazad became famous throughout the land when she succeeded in staying her own execution and saving her sisters through the powers of her storytelling, reversing at the same time the hierarchical relationships in the realm of gender and masculine authority.[6]

The Arabic literary tradition is long and distinguished. Predating the emergence of Islam in A.D. 622, the literary language of the pre-Islamic, or Jahiliyya, period has been preserved and has maintained its continuity through the influence of the sacred text of the Quran (Koran), written in Arabic and considered by Muslims to be a poetic and linguistic miracle. Preeminent in that richly varied literary tradition of tales or *maqamāt*, philosophical treatises, and religious exegesis have been the poetic genres. In Jahiliyya times, the poet had a public role to play in the worldly life of the tribe, extolling its exploits, lamenting its dead, praising its leaders, and regretting the days of yore. Poetry has maintained this place of prominence into the twentieth century, only partly supplanted by new forms of expression, such as the novel and autobiography, which accompanied Western intrusion and cultural influence. Poetry, however, both a written and an oral skill in Arabic, continues to captivate audiences and readers throughout the Arab world.

Female poets have, since the classical period, contributed significantly to the development of Arab poetic expression. The *mawwāl*, for example, a form of colloquial poetry sung to the accompaniment of a musical instrument, is considered to have been invented in Harun al-Rashid's court (9th century A.D.) by one of his slave girls. Professional singers and dancers were active bearers of the Arabic poetic tradition. The lullabies sung by Tunisian women and Berber women's songs,[7] the *nabaṭī* verse of Qatari women,[8] and the *ghinnāwa* or "little songs" sung by Bedouin women in Egypt's western desert[9] are all a contributing part of this tradition. They represent as well what Judith Tucker has described as the "world of informal networks, popular culture and the basic forces of production and reproduction."[10]

The voices of women singers, like the Lebanese Fairuz, who sings lyrical verse of her own composition as well as the political poetry of such poets as the Palestinian Mahmud Darwish, are heard in concert, on cassette, and on the radio. The Arab world's most famous singer, however, was undisputedly the Egyptian Umm Kulthum (b. 1910), who for more than four decades sang to Egypt and the rest of the Arab world.[11] In Mahfuz's novel *Miramar* (1967), which condenses into an Alexandrian *pension* the saga of Egypt's postrevolutionary era, a regular occurrence that brought together all the *pension*'s residents was the weekly radio broadcast of Umm Kulthum's recitals. When the singer died in 1975, her funeral, attended by heads of state, is said to have attracted a larger crowd even than that of Gamal Abdel Nasser.

Women have figured just as prominently as writers of poetry. Since al-Khansa', who lived at the time of the prophet Muhammad and challenged male poets in the poetry contests of the time, Arab women composers of poetry have competed with distinction in the literary arena. One Iraqi poet, Nazik al-Mala'ika (b. 1923), is credited with revolutionizing the highly coded and stylistically contained Arabic poetic tradition when she published a poem in "free verse" in 1947 (although this credit is sometimes disputed by proponents of Badr Shakr al-Sayyab). From Fadwa Tuqan's (b. 1917) early poetry in Palestine or the verse of Salma K. Jayyusi (b. a. 1922), also Palestinian, or Etel Adnan (b. 1925) in Lebanon to the poems of Zabyah Khamis (b. ca. 1958) in the United Arab Emirates and of Saudi poet Fawziyya Abu-Khalid (b. 1955), women have continued to reformulate questions of *adab* (which means "culture" as well as "literature") and women's role in contemporary society.

With Western political, military, and economic pressures on the colonized Third World came as well the cultural and literary influences of European letters. In the Arab world, the novel, together with the traditions of realism and naturalism, and the short story made a particular impact. Narrative forms had, of course, existed and been developed in the classical Arabic literature and this narrative tradition was adapted to the new "acculturated forms" of novel and short story from the West, but the legacy of social critique remained an important dimension to that literature. As Denys Johnson-Davies, one of the pioneers in the translation of modern Arabic literature into English, reminded his readers in an interview, in the Arab world "most talent lies to the left of center."[12]

Women's writing has served also to introduce women's issues, both domestic and political, into the public discussion and to nuance these issues according to the specific circumstances of the individual writers' national and historical backgrounds. North African women, for example, from Morocco, Tunisia, and Algeria, write variously in French or Arabic, depending on their generation and education. Thus, writers like Marguerite Taos-Amrouche (1913–1976), the poetess Anna Gréki (1931–1966), or Assia Djebar (b. 1936), who received their schooling during the French occupation of Algeria that effectively destroyed the Arabic school system, compose in French. The younger Moroccan Khanata Banuna (b. 1943) writes in Arabic. The choice of a language in which to write can be both historically conditioned and politically motivated. The francophone writing of the Egyptian Andrée Chedid (b. 1920), like Etel Adnan's Lebanese novel in French, *Sitt Marie Rose* (1978), or the Egyptian Ahdaf Soueif's English-language story collection, *Aisha* (1983), are likewise representative of this bilingual cultural heritage of colonialism. Still another language, that of the cinema, has begun to be developed in recent years by women documentary filmmakers, including Assia Djebar, who has made two films, *La Nouba des femmes du mont Chenoua* (1978) and *La Zerda and the Songs of Forgetting* (1982), and Atiyat al-Abnudi, among whose many films are *Mudhorse* (1971), *The Sad Song of Touha* (1972), and *The Seas of Thirst* (1983).

The issue of language is not, of course, exclusive to women's writing, or even to the Arab world, but it does introduce on the linguistic level of the text the larger historical questions of cultural imperialism and class. These problems are again differently manifested from story to story. As Layla Salah points out in her study of women's writing from the Gulf states, many of the writers in Saudi Arabia or Bahrain, for example, have developed a style that focuses primarily on the expression of personal relationships and psychological needs, a style which Salah refers to as *wijdāni*, or emotional. These needs, however, are conditioned by a social context that is powerfully brought out in such stories as "Her Man" by Ahdaf Soueif (*Aisha*, 1983) and "My World of the Unknown" by Alifa Rifaat (b. 1930; a collection of Rifaat's stories has been translated and published in English under the title *Distant View of a Minaret*, 1983). The personal contradictions lived by Arab women are given a more explicitly political dimension in Etel Adnan's *Sitt Marie Rose*. Although it is called a novel, *Sitt Marie Rose* is based on the true story of Marie Rose Boulos, a Lebanese Christian woman who, having raised her children, returns to the university. Her husband divorces her when she becomes active in political and social issues, such as women's rights, trade unionism, and the Palestinian refugee camps. At the outbreak of the Lebanese civil war, she is living with a Palestinian doctor in West Beirut and directing a school for deaf-mute children in the eastern sector of the divided city. On her way to work one day she is kidnapped by Christian militiamen, who interrogate her before the eyes of the silent children and then execute her. Adnan's novel is a critique of the narrow social codes of gender, race, and class that condemned Sitt Marie Rose to die.

As the Palestinian writer and critic Hanan Awwad points out in her critical study of Ghadah al-Samman (b. 1942) of Syria, *Arab Causes in the Fiction of Ghada al-Samman: 1961–1975* (1983), Arab women writers construct their personal fictions out of the materials provided by the conflicts between traditions and contemporary history. *Khul-Khaal*, for example, the oral history of five Egyptian women collected by Nayra Atiya (1982), exposes the sociocultural pressures on women of Egypt's various classes. These conflicts have been further elaborated with some political emphasis in two very recent collections of Egyptian short stories: Salwa Bakr's *Zīnāt fi jināza al-rā'is* (Ornaments in the President's Funeral Procession, 1985?) and *al-Shaykhūkha* (Old Age, 1986) by Latifa Zayyat.

Prolific and developed though it might be, Arab women's writing has not always found easy access to the still largely male-dominated cultural forums. The case of Layla Balabakki (b. ca. 1936) in Lebanon in 1964 demonstrates well the critical challenge posed by women to the social conventions of an institutionalized literary tradition and the responses such a challenge can provoke. Following the publication in Beirut of her book *Safīnat hanān ila-l-qamar* (*A Spaceship of Tenderness to the Moon*, 1964), Layla Ba' labakki was brought to trial on charges of obscenity and offending the public morality. The story in question dealt with an intimate moment shared by a married couple and described most fully the inner thoughts and unsatisfied longings of the woman. According to the proceedings of the trial, partially reproduced in *Middle Eastern Muslim Women Speak*, the charge related to two sentences in the text of the story. Although the court ultimately decided to halt procedures against the defendant, the questioning reveals the conflicted reasoning behind the trial and some of the difficulties that women face in publishing their work. The court, for example, refused to accept testimony from credentialed intellectuals concerning the literary merit of the work, and even part of the defense of Balabakki dwelt on the fact that she had "left her home and traveled to Paris, where she remained for some time, in an environment totally different from that of her own people."[13] In other words the issue at stake in the Lebanese courtroom was not that of women's writing but that of a woman writing at all.

The pressure of social convention with which Arab women writers must contend is often integral to their writing practice. Nawal al-Saadawi's novel *Firdaus* (*Women at Point Zero*, 1975) and her *Mudhakkirātī fi sijn al-nisā'*, (*Memoirs from the Women's Prison,*' 1984) are a case in point. Another Egyptian female critic and opposition intellectual, Farida al-Naqash, has also published her memoirs of prison under the presidency of Anwar al-Sadat, entitled *al-Sijn: dama'tān...wa warda* (Prison: Two Tears...and a Rose, 1985). Six years earlier, in the occupied West Bank, Raymonda Tawil (b. 1940), a Palestinian journalist, had published *My Home My Prison* (1979) in Hebrew, her account of house arrest and the combined restraints of Arab patriarchal traditions and Israeli military occupation.

Arab women through their writing are not only adding new dimensions to the literary-historical narrative but are reconstituting their personal itineraries as well. In the decades since Huda Sha'arawi privately wrote her memoirs which were published posthumously and in English (reprinted 1987), a significant number of autobiographies by Arab women have begun to appear. In 1969 Umm Kulthum (b. 1910) told her life story to Mahmud Awad; it was published as *Umm Kulthum allāti la ya'rifuha ahad* (*The Umm Kulthum No One Knows*). Leila Khaled (b. 1944), a PFLP commando who participated in the first Palestinian plane hijacking, presented her history under the title *My People Shall Live: The Autobiography of a Revolutionary* (1973). The memoirs of the Lebanese educator Widad Qartas (b. ca. 1909) *Dhikrayyat 1917–1977* (Memoirs, 1982) provide the details of a personal history extending from childhood in a southern Lebanon just feeling the impact of World War I to the outbreak of the Lebanese civil war in Beirut. Qartas's personal history intersects importantly with the political and intellectual trends which radically transformed Lebanon and the Arab world over a period of sixty years. What characterizes these autobiographies of Arab women is the public dimension that attaches to their personal lives no less than to their writing selves. This restructuring of a personal identity through narrative marks also *al-Junūbī* (*The Southerner*, 1986), Abla al-Ruwayni's biography of her late husband Aml Dunql, one of Egypt's most prominent poets of the colloquial language. *al-Junūbī* is, as Fedwa Malti-Douglas has pointed out, as much Abla's story as it is Aml's and as such it engages simultaneously with the complex and intersecting roles of woman, writer-critic, and poet in contemporary Egypt.[14]

In song, poetry, fiction and autobiography, at home and in the public squares, Arab women are representing themselves and their society. They are also involved, as journalists, scholars, anthropologists, and sociologists, in rewriting their own critical history. The influence of colonialism and the imposition of Western cultural paradigms are being reworked now by Arab women according to their own designs and to their own ends as conditioned by the historical specificity of their diverse situations. Nawal al-Saadawi's early influential study of Arab women, *al-Marā'a wa-l-jins* (*Women and Sex*, 1972) was followed by other such investigations. In Morocco, for example, Fatima Mernissi profoundly criticized the institutionalizing of the practice of the veil in Islamic societies. *Beyond the Veil: Male-Female Dynamics in a Modern Muslim Society* (1975) contests the misappropriation of religion in the service of patriarchy in Morocco. Nine years later, under the pseudonym Fatna Sabbah, Mernissi published *Woman in the Muslim Unconscious* (1984).

Arab women anthropologists, often trained in Western universities, have likewise been studying their own societies and cultures and describing the often neglected role of women in Arab culture and society. As one of these social scientists, Lila Abu Lughod, demonstrates in *Veiled Sentiments*, a study of the "little songs" of Egyptian Bedouin women, the dual role of female anthropologist and Arab woman is riddled with contradictions: "I was asking them [the Bedouin women] to be honest, so that I could learn what their lives were like, but at the same time I was unwilling to reveal much about myself. I was presenting them with a persona."[15] These contradictions, however, which figure not only in an Arab female anthropologist's field work but in Arab women's writings more generally, are productive of new possibilities from within the confrontation between First and Third Worlds, and inside the Arab world itself between traditionalism and contemporary challenges. Soraya Altorki, a Saudi anthropologist educated in the West, thus describes her own experience of "fieldwork" among upper-class women in Jiddah: "I was a conscious witness to my own resocialization as an Arab woman. . . ."[16]

NOTES

Please note, where they are known, birthdates are provided for women mentioned. Given the relative difficulty of ascertaining such information in the Middle East, there are numerous cases in which such data must be omitted.

1. See Huda Shaarawi, *The Harem Years: The Memoirs of an Egyptian Feminist*, trans. and intro. Margot Badran (New York: The Feminist Press, 1987).
2. See excerpts from the first volume in *Middle Eastern Muslim Women Speak*, eds. Elizabeth W. Fernea and Basima Q. Bezirgan (Austin: University of Texas Press, 1977), pp. 95–123.
3. Judith Tucker, *Women in Nineteenth Century Egypt* (Cambridge: Cambridge University Press, 1985), p. 3.
4. Monique Gadant, ed., *Women of the Mediterranean*, trans. A.M. Berrett (London: Zed Books, 1986), p. 2.
5. See "Ba'th Terror—Two Personal Accounts" in CARDRI, *Saddam's Iraq: Revolution or Reaction?* (London: Zed Books, 1986), pp. 108–137.
6. See Ferial Ghazoul, *The Arabian Nights: A Structural Analysis* (Cairo: UNESCO, 1980).
7. Fernea and Bezirgan, *Middle Eastern Muslim Women Speak*, pp. 87–93.
8. See Abeer Abu Saud, *Qatari Women: Past and Pressent* (Essex: Longman, 1984), pp. 133–171.
9. See Leila Abu Lughod, *Veiled Sentiments: Honor and Poetry in a Bedouin Society* (Berkeley and Los Angeles: University of California Press, 1986).
10. Tucker, *Women in Nineteenth Century Egypt*, p. 1.
11. Sections of Umm Kulthum's autobiography are included in *Middle Eastern Muslim Women Speak*.
12. "On Translating Arabic Literature: An Interview with Denys Johnson-Davies," *ALIF*, 3 (1983): 86.
13. *Middle Eastern Muslim Women Speak*, p. 287.
14. Fedwa Malti Douglas, "al-Batl wa-l-rāwiya: al-ibad' al-adabi fi *al-Junūbi*" (The Male Hero and the Female Narrator: Literary Creativity in *The Southerner*), *Fusūl*, Summer 1987.
15. Lughod, *Veiled Sentiments*, p. 18.
16. Soraya Altorki, *Women in Saudi Arabia: Ideology and Behavior Among the Elite* (New York: Columbia University Press, 1986), p. 12.

BIBLIOGRAPHY

Background

Abu Saud, Abeer. *Qatari Women: Past and Presnt*. Essex: Longman, 1984.
Alloula, Malek. *The Colonial Harem*. Trans. Myrna and Wlad Godzich. Minneapolis: University of Minnesota Press, 1986.
Altorki, Soraya. *Women in Saudi Arabia: Ideology and Behavior Among the Elite*. New York: Columbia University Press, 1986.
Beck, Lois, and Nikki Keddie, eds. *Women in the Muslim World*. Cambridge: Harvard University Press, 1978.
CARDRI. *Saddom's Irag: Revolution or Reaction?* London: Zed Books, 1986.
Fancon, Frantz. *A Dying Colonialism*. Trans. Haakan Chevalier. New York: Grove Press, 1967.
Fernea, Elizabeth W. and Bezirgan, Basima Q., eds. *Middle Eastern Muslim Women Speak*. Austin, TX: University of Texas Press, 1977.

Fernea, Elizabeth W., ed. *Women and the Family in the Middle East: New Voices of Change.* Austin, TX: University of Texas Press, 1985.

Ghoussoub, Mai. "Feminism—or the Eternal Masculine—in the Arab World." *New Left Review* 161 (1987).

al-Hibri, Aziza, ed. *Women and Islam.* Oxford: Pergamon Press, 1982.

Kabbani, Rana. *Europe's Myths of Orient.* Bloomington, IN: Indiana University Press, 1986.

Malti-Douglas, Fedwa. "al-Batl wa-l-Rāwīyah: al-Ibda' al-Adabi fi *al-Junubi*" (The Male Hero and the Female Narrator: Literary Creativity in *The Southerner*). *Fusul* (1987).

M'rabet, Fadela. *La Femme Algérienne* and *Les Algériennes.* Paris: Maspero, 1969. Single volume.

Shaarawi, Huda. *The Harem Years: The Memoirs of an Egyptian Feminist.* Trans. and intro. Margot Badran. New York: The Feminist Press, 1987.

Tillon, Germaine. *The Republic of Cousins: Women's Oppression in Mediterranean Society,* Trans. Quentin Hoare. London: Al-Saqi Books, 1983.

Tucker, Judith. *Women in Nineteenth Century Egypt.* Cambridge: Cambridge University Press, 1985.

Literary Criticism

Abu Lughod, Lila. *Veiled Sentiments: Honor and Poetry in a Bedouin Society.* Berkeley and Los Angeles: University of California Press, 1986.

Attieh, Aman, ed. and trans. *Saudio Arabian Women Writers.* Washington D.C.: Three Continents Press, forthcoming.

"Bibliography of Arab Women's Writing," *Fusul* (forthcoming). In Arabic.

Boullata, Kamal, ed. *Women of the Fertile Crescent: Modern Poetry by Arab Women.* Washington, D.C.: Three Continents Press, 1978.

Gadant, Monique, ed. *Women of the Mediterranean.* Trans. A.M. Berrett. London: Zed Books, 1986.

Ghazoul, Ferial. *The Arabian Nights: A Structural Study.* Cairo: UNESCO, 1980.

Johnson-Davies, Denys. "On Translating Arabic Literature: An Interview with Denys Johnson Davies." *ALIF* 3 (1983).

Mikhail, Mona. *Images of Arab Women: Fact and Fiction.* Washington D.C.: Three Continents Press, 1978.

PORTUGAL

Alice R. Clemente

From the Middle Ages until modern times, women's writing in Portugal was relatively scarce. It consisted mainly of religious and historical texts produced in convents and was directed at a limited audience. Paradoxically, however, it was the cloister that provided women with the freedom and the education they needed to engage in more creative literary activity. The seventeenth century saw a change in the kind and quality of the nuns' writing and also in its readership.

Three names stand out in the seventeenth century: Soror Violante do Céu, Soror Maria do Céu, and Soror Madalena da Glória. The latter two are known primarily, though not exclusively, for the *exempla* they composed to provide spiritual guidance for their sister nuns. The work of Soror Violante (1602–1693), however, had a broader scope and earned for her a significant position in the ranks of Peninsular Baroque poets. In her own view, Violante's *magnum opus* was *Parnaso Lusitano de Divinos e Humanos Versos* (Lusitanian Parnasus of Secular and Religious Verse, 1733), a substantial collection of religious and panegyrical poems; but for us today and perhaps for her contemporaries also, it is her earlier work, *Rimas Várias* (Poems, 1646), that is of primary interest. A collection of love poems that have much in common with those of her male contemporaries in form and style and in their treatment of the love theme, *Rimas Várias* was well known outside of Portugal, especially to the Spanish writers Lope de Vega and Juan Pérez de Montalbán. The collection may indeed have inspired the apocryphal *Letters of a Portuguese Nun* published in France a few years later.

At the time these nuns were making their mark, and even earlier in fact, a battle was being waged outside convent walls on behalf of women and their rights. João de Barros' *Espelho de Casados* (Mirror of Marriage, 1540), for example, set forth a traditional misogynistic view in its initial pages in order to refute it in the second half of the book; and a few years later, in 1557, Rui Gonçalves, attorney and professor of law, dedicated to the regent, Catarina of Austria, a treatise that analyzed the legal status of women and lamented the fact that women were not eligible to vote or to participate in the legislative process.

That this enlightened view did not take hold is most apparent precisely in the so-called Age of Enlightenment. The country was ruled by a woman, Maria I, from 1777 to 1791; yet little was done to better women's lot. In 1790, for example, Maria issued an order that schools be set up for the education of young girls, but this was not done until 1815. Conservative by nature and education, and psychologically unstable, Maria was incapable of effecting change in the face of opposition. In fact, women's condition worsened, and seclusion in the home became the norm for women of the upper and middle classes during her reign.

Surprisingly, several women were able to escape intellectual imprisonment, notably Teresa Margarida da Silva e Orta (ca. 1711–1793) and Leonor de Almeida, Marquesa de Alorna (1750–1839). Educated in a convent, the first of these women married against her father's wishes; she was disinherited and lived a life of deprivation, encumbered by numerous children. Teresa Margarida da Silva e Orta found solace in literature. At the age of forty she published *Aventuras de*

Diófanes (Adventures of Diofanes, 1752), a feminist novel inspired by the work of the seventeenth-century French writer Fénelon, [*Aventures de Telemaque* (*Adventures of Telemachus*)]. The Marquesa de Alorna was also educated in a convent. She was well connected both in political and cultural circles; she traveled widely and was entertained at the court of Charles III of Spain and at the home of Mme. de Staël in France. Exposed to romanticism while exiled in England for her political activity, she returned home to introduce the new esthetic to her Portuguese contemporaries. The Marquesa de Alorna was the first Portuguese woman outside the royal family to become embroiled in international politics; she was also the first woman to have a lasting impact on the literature of her country, straddling as she did the neoclassical and romantic periods. Her poetry, published posthumously in 1844, is unquestionably the best of its time, though it falls short of the lyrical power of the best Romantics. Alorna's poetry deals with a wide range of themes. There are love poems written in adolescence; poems on the death of her children; songs of absence written from exile in England; patriotic songs; philosophical and religious verse.

In the nineteenth century, the situation for women changed gradually. Liberal ideas growing out of the French Revolution began to take hold in Portugal, and the rise of journalism provided access to culture for larger numbers of readers. Women benefited from both developments. The Civil Code of 1867 addressed some women's issues; others were taken up in the press, specifically in periodicals for and by women. The most important of these was *A Mulher* (Woman), which came out for the first time in January 1883 and published not only literary pieces but reports on feminist successes throughout Europe and America. The experience of Guiomar Torrezão (1844–1898) reveals, however, that the woman writer was not yet a completely acceptable phenomenon. After the death of her father, Torrezão was forced to fend for herself. She resolved her financial difficulties by teaching and writing. In addition to her work as a journalist, this extraordinary woman wrote novels, short stories, plays, and critical essays. Her collection of romantic stories, *Rosas Pálidas* (*Pale Roses*, 1873), went through two editions immediately. A historical novel, *A Família Albergária* (The Boarding-House Family), followed in 1874. Her collection of critical essays, *No Teatro e na Sala* (In the Theater and in the Drawing-room, 1881), appeared with a preface by Camilo Castelo Branco, one of the most distinguished literary figures in nineteenth-century Portugal. Her plays were presented both in Portugal and in Brazil. For several years beginning in 1871, Torrezão also edited a periodical entitled *Almanaque de Senhoras* (Ladies' Almanac), which, according to a contemporary newspaper report, was "to be found in the boudoirs of all the elegant ladies of Portugal and Brazil." The nature of Torrezão's writing was determined by the conservative and conventional tastes of the times. In her critical pieces, however, she did not hesitate to speak to the social and educational needs of women. Torrezão found some notable admirers in her day, not only Castelo Branco but the historian and poet Alexandre Herculano. Another admirer, the short-story writer Fialho de Almeida, commented at the time of Torrezão's death that had she lived in Paris or elsewhere, she would have been considered illustrious but that in Lisbon they considered her almost a comic figure. This observation is supported by other contemporary accounts that attest to the presence of detractors in her life. The fate of this woman has been such that her name is rarely even listed in literary histories or other reference works.

Early in the twentieth century, the consciousness raised by the early journalists in Portugal began to produce visible consequences there, aided by the experiment in republicanism that began in 1910. Gains were made in civil rights and in education. The first woman doctor had appeared in 1891. In 1911, a university chair was given to Carolina Michaëlis de Vasconcelos, the German wife of the Portuguese musicologist and art historian Joaquim de Vasconcelos; in 1913, the first woman lawyer was graduated. It was around this time also that middle-class women began to organize for reform. In 1909, the Republican League of Portuguese Women was formed, with Dr. Adelaide Cabete and the writer Ana de Castro Osório at its helm. In 1914, Dr. Cabete founded the National Council of Portuguese Women, a branch of the International Women's Council. In 1924, the first Congress of Feminism and Education was convoked; the President of Portugal attended and the proceedings were given daily coverage in the press.

The women's movement had as its official voice the journals *A Madrugada* (Dawn) and *Alma Feminina* (Feminine Soul). In the first quarter of the twentieth century, women's writing was in fact predominantly literature directly connected with the women's movement. The most prolific writer was Ana de Castro Osório (1872–1935), essayist, short-story writer, dramatist, and novelist. Her books for children were the first major efforts in this area; one of them was adopted as a textbook in both Portugal and Brazil. However, the distinction of being the first outstanding Portuguese woman writer of the twentieth century must go to Florbela Espanca (1894–1930) whose work is represented in this anthology. Her tortured, erotic sonnets were an immediate success and make her to this day one of the most admired of all Portuguese poets; her complete works are now being reedited.

The advent of the Estado Novo in 1926 (the "New State"; the dictatorship of Salazar) virtually eradicated the hard-earned gains made by women, and they returned to a subordinate position in which they were to languish for over forty years. Women did not stop writing, but the voices that emerged were few and isolated. One of the first was Irene Lisboa (1892–1958) who spoke often of solitude in poems and stories she wrote from the 1930s on to relieve her loneliness as a single woman seriously dedicated to pedagogy. Her work is only now receiving the attention it deserves, for example in *Mulheres Escritoras* (Women Writers, 1980) by Maria Ondina Braga (b. ca. 1930), who is herself a chronicler of the same theme. The latter is the author of several books, among them *A China Fica ao Lado* (China is Next Door, 1968), a collection of short stories that deal with the experience of a young European woman teaching in a girls' school, alone and far from home in the unsettling Eurasian atmosphere of Macao.

Three important writers emerged in the 1950s. The first was Sophia de Mello Breyner Andresen (b. 1919), a daughter of the old northern aristocracy. Influenced by her study of the classics, she began writing poetry that was virtually a hymn to physical reality. Gradually her work acquired a more moral and political cast, as she became preoccupied with the state of her nation. Another product of the fertile Douro region of the North, Agustina Bessa-Luís (b. 1922) emerged as a leading novelist. Her first striking success in 1953 earned her a secure place in literary circles, both national and international; indeed she has become almost a legend. Though her strongest characters are invariably women, the questions she poses through them—and through the men that surround them—sharpen our understanding of the entire human condition. The third voice to emerge in the 1950s was that of the colorful Natália Correia (b. 1923), who has left an indelible mark not only in the realms of poetry, the novel, and theater but in literary scholarship, political writing, and indeed the world of politics itself. A rebellious figure from the start, Correia fought constantly against political repression and for that reason became a victim of oppression herself. In 1966, for example, she was prosecuted for publishing an anthology of erotic poetry. Correia has continued to speak out on subjects ranging from national politics to feminist issues, championing above all the idea of a world in which the feminine principle would prevail, a world turned toward nurturing instead of toward destruction. Of her fourteen books of poetry, the best known perhaps is *Poemas a Rebate* (Poems of Alarm, 1975). *A Madona* (*The Madona*, 1968) and *A Ilha de Circe* (Circe's Island, 1983) are her best known prose works. Of her five plays, *A Pécora* (The Whore) is the one that has attracted most attention. It is an exposé of the exploitation of the credulous in the name of religion. The book was suppressed in 1967 and published only in 1983. Other names could be added—Fernanda Botelho (b. 1926), Maria Judite de Carvalho (b. 1921)—but it was primarily the first three who opened a new chapter in Portuguese women's writing.

Until the late 1960s, Portuguese women, like men, remained subject to the economic and political oppression, as well as to the sexual discrimination, that characterized Salazar's regime. Their role in society was at best that of a partner in survival to their men and, to the extent that there was a resistance movement, a partner in that, too. Gradually, in the late 1960s, conditions began to improve, particularly during the regime of Salazar's successor, Marcelo Caetano. In 1973, the governmental Commission for Social Policy Concerning Women was formed to study the economic and sociopolitical roles of women, but the battle was far from won. A glaring example of the oppression that continued to exist is the case of the three Marias: Maria Teresa Horta (b. 1937) Maria Isabel Barreno (b. 1939), and Maria Velho da Costa (b. 1938). Though all three had begun to publish earlier, along with a growing number of other women writers of the 1960s and early 1970s, such as the poets Ana Hatherly (b. 1929), Fiama Hasse Pais Brandão (b. 1938), Luiza Neto Jorge (b. 1939), and Olga Gonçalves (b. ca. 1930), it was in 1973 that they achieved international fame with their experiment in collective writing: *Novas Cartas Portuguesas* (*New Portugese Letters*). Inspired by the seventeenth-century *Letters of a Portuguese Nun*, the product of this collaborative effort was a complex work that encompassed such diverse concerns as the definition of self and other; the political and social situation of Portugal at that time; and the writing process itself in its relation to the opposition between male and female in society as a whole. The explicit sexuality growing out of the last theme, along with the obvious challenge to traditional social and political values, set the book apart—so much so that it was almost not published. It was published finally with the help of the intrepid Natália Correia, but within a month of publication it was seized by the police and a morals charge was filed against its authors. The international press took up their cause and the international women's movement came to their defense; both helped to ensure that the women were, in time, exonerated. The book was invaluable because it freed women once and for all from the bonds of a male-oriented vision that appropriated certain areas of experience, such as eroticism, for the male writer alone.

The exoneration of the three Marias coincided with a political event that was to change the course of Portuguese history, the bloodless Revolution of April 25, 1974. The country was ripe for change, and women participated in the transformation of society from the beginning. A small number formed the femininist group Movimento de Libertação das Mulheres (Women's Liberation Movement). More importantly, women were incorporated into the new government. Sophia de Melo Breyner Andresen and Natália Correia served terms in Parliament. There was a woman Secretary of State and a bit later an interim Prime Minister, Maria de Loudres Pintasilgo, who in 1985 ran as one of the three candidates for the presidency of Portugal. Pintasilgo was instrumental in institutionalizing reform in the Commission on the Status of Women, which functions directly in connection with the Prime Minister's office. The new Constitution, which took effect on April 25, 1976, guarantees not only full political equality but such rights as maternity leave and equal pay for equal work. As of 1984, abortion was legalized, although under specified conditions.

The social, political, and intellectual freedom of the postrevolutionary period has given the impulse to a veritable flood of writing by women. In addition to the solitary pioneers of the 1950s and to the poets and novelists of the 1960s, all of whom continue to publish prolifically, there is a host of younger talent: Lídia Jorge (b. 1946), Teolinda Gersão (b. ca. 1940), Eduarda Dionísio (b. 1946), Wanda Ramos (b. 1948), Hélia Correia (b. ca. 1940), to mention only a few. Lídia Jorge is the most successful of these up to now. Her first book, *O Dia dos Prodígios* (The Day of the Prodigious Happenings, 1980), has been acclaimed as one of the best novels of the decade following the Revolution, and she has published two more since then: *O Cais das Merendas* (The Snack Wharf, 1982) and *Notícia da Cidade Silvestre* (News of the Wild City, 1984). Women writers have indeed met with such a strong reception from critics and the reading public alike that they can no longer be ignored by historians of Portuguese prose and poetry.

BIBLIOGRAPHY

Background

Figueiredo, Antonio de. *Portugal: Fifty Years of Dictatorship*. New York: Holmes and Meier, 1976.
Gallagher, Tom. *Portugal: a Twentieth-Century Interpretation*. Manchester, NH: Manchester University Press, 1983.
Graham, Lawrence S., and Harry Makler. *Contemporary Portugal: The Revolution and its Antecedents*. Austin: University of Texas Press, 1979.
Graham, Lawrence S., and Douglas L. Wheeler. *In Search of Modern Portugal: The Revolution and its Consequences*. Madison: University of Wisconsin Press, 1983.
Guimarães, Elisa. *Portuguese Women: Past and Present*. Lisbon: Commission on the Status of Women, 1978.
Livermore, Harold V. *A New History of Portugal*. New York: Cambridge University Press, 1976.
Maxwell, Kenneth. *The Press and the Rebirth of Iberian Democracy*. Westport: Greenwood Press, 1983.

Problems of Enlightenment in Portugal: Essays. Minneapolis: Institute for Ideology and Literature, 1984. Includes an article on Teresa Margarida da Silva e Orta.

Literary Criticism

Since there is such a dearth of critical material on Portuguese women writers, the author has included relevant material in Portuguese.

Allegro de Magalhães, Isabel, *O Tempo das Mulheres*. Lisbon, 1987.

Bell, Aubrey F. *Portuguese Literature*. Oxford: Clarendon Press, 1970.

Braga, Maria Ondina. *Mulheres Escritoras*. Lisbon: Livraria Bertrand, 1980.

Brummel, Maria Fernanda. "O Diálogo implécito na técnica narrativa de Olga Gonçalves," *Aufsätze zur Portugiesischen Kulturgeschichte*, 1983.

Correia, Natália. *Antologia da Poesia do Período Barroco*. Lisbon: Moraes Editora, 1982.

Letzring, Maria. "Teresa Margarida da Silva e Orta and the Portuguese Enlightenment," in *Studies in Eighteenth-Century Culture*. Madison: University of Wisconsin Press, 1985.

Lopes, Oscar, and Antonio José Saraiva. *História da Literatura Portuguesa*, 12th ed. Oporto: Porto Editora, 1982.

Machado, Alvaro Manuel. *Agustina Bessa-Luís—O Imaginário Total*. Lisbon: Publicações Dom Quixote, 1983.

Sadlier, Darlene. "Form in *Novas Cartas Portuguesas*," *Novel*, 1986.

Seixo, Maria Alzira. *A Palavra do Romance*. Lisbon: Livros Horizonte, 1986.

———. *Para um Estudo da Expressëo do tempo no Romance Portugues Contemporãneo*, 2nd ed. Lisbon, 1987.

RUSSIA AND THE USSR

Dobrochna Dyrcz-Freeman

Women entered Russian literature as memoirists.[1] Princess Natáliya Dolgorúkaya née Shereméteva (1714–1771) authored the first written eighteenth-century autobiography. Dolgorúkaya followed her financé into exile in Siberia, married him there, and entered a convent when he was executed. She was the first in a long line of women—wives, mothers, sisters—who chronicled the lives and times of their often more famous male counterparts. The eighteenth century also saw the memoirs of Empress Catherine II (1729–1796) and those of the erudite and energetic Ekaterína Dáshkova (1743–1810), who was one of the first women to hold public office in Russia.

In the early nineteenth century, even those women belonging to the privileged classes had very few legal rights, little access to any but the most superficial education, and a social position that was more decorative and spiritual than useful in any broader sense. Marriage was a social and, for poor gentlewomen, financial obligation. The discrepancy between a young woman's emotional expectations, fed by romantic, particularly French, literature, and the reality of a husband chosen for her by her family on the basis of income and social position was often immense and devastating. The one area in which young women expected fulfillment—marriage—became the source of grief. Women's literature of the first half of the nineteenth century reflected the unhappy, often empty lives of these women.

The influence of George Sand and others in her sphere who demanded a woman's right to be meaningfully educated and to choose freely a husband who would be an equal emotional partner can be seen in the works of several women writers of this time. Eléna Andréevna Gán (Hahn) née Fadéeva (pseudonym Zinaída R-va, 1814–1842) wrote highly successful novels and stories about the plight of an educated woman living as an officer's wife amidst the emptiness and vulgarity of a provincial garrison. Yúliya Valeriánovna Zhadóvskaya (1824–1883) depicted the unhappy consequences of social inequality when a woman is not allowed to marry the man she loves. Some of Zhadóvskaya's love laments and poems about shattered dreams became popular romances, set to music by Glinka, among others. In her novel *Seméystvo Tálnikovykh* (The Talnikov Family, 1848), Avdótya Yákovlevna Panáeva (pseudonym N. Stanítsky, 1820–1893) described how the 16-year-old heroine marries the first man who asks her just to escape from her intolerable family. Panáeva also provided an interesting, if sometimes factually unreliable, picture of Russian literary circles in the 1840s and 1850s in her memoirs, *Vospominániya* (1889–1890). Márya Semyónovna Zhúkova's (1804–1855) extremely popular short stories and sketches, set primarily outside of Russia, are notable mostly for their insights into human experience, often undermining romantic clichés. Although her work suffers from sentimentality, which was recognized in her own time, the critic Vissarión Belínsky (1811–1848) nonetheless recommended that more men write like her.

In *Dvoynáya Zhízn* (A Double Life, 1847) by Karolína Kárlovna Pávlova née Jánisch (1807–1893), the emptiness of everyday life in society, described in prose, is countered by the rich inner world of the heroine, rendered in verse. Rediscovered by the Symbolists only at the turn of the century, Pávlova died poor and forgotten, although she was admired early in her life both as a woman and a poet by many of her literary contemporaries, including Púshkin and the Polish poet Adam Mickiewicz. Like Pushkin's Tatiána in *Eugene Onegin*, the characters in Pávlova's work were marked by the noble acceptance of their fate.

The emptiness of life in the upper class was also exposed in such works as Evdókiya Petróvna Rostopchiná's (1811–1858) "Schastlívaya Zhénshchina" (A Happy Woman, 1852). Such exposés continued to the end of the century, and the theme given humorous treatment in the *Mímochka* stories (1883–1893) written by Lídiya Ivánovna Veselítskaya (pseudonym Mme. Mikúlich, 1857–1936).

Not all women conformed to the restrictive societal expectations of the nineteenth century. Nadézhda Andréevna Dúrova (pseudonym A. A. Aleksándrov, 1793–1866) escaped the restrictions of her parents' home and her brief marriage by dressing in men's clothing and joining a Cossack troop. She later fought in the Prussian campaign, was granted a commission, and served as an orderly to Field Marshall Kutúzov while he was pursuing Napoleon back into Europe. In addition to her diaries of her childhood and military service, *Kavaleríst-devítsa: Proisshéstvie v Rossíi* (Cavalry Maiden: It Happened in Russia, 1836) and *Zapíski Aleksándrova: Dobavlénie k Devítse-kavaleríst* (Aleksandrov's Notes: More about the Cavalry Maiden, 1839), Dúrova also wrote conventional romantic fiction.

Some women, however, accepted the social system and their position in it. For example, Nadézhda Stepánovna Sokhánskaya (pseudonyms N. Kokhanóvskaya, Nadézhda S***, and Nadézhda Makárovskaya, 1825–1884) wrote in the tradition of Gógol's "Old-World Landowners" and Aksákov's *Family Chronicle*. Sokhánskaya's glorification of the traditional Russian ideals of family unity and paternal authority placed her in the camp of the Slavophiles. Her stories—with their beautiful descriptions of the life of the landed gentry, as well as glowing accounts of the peasants, their humility, native wisdom, and collectivism—reflected the Slavophile's idealization of pre-Petrine (Peter the Great, ruled 1689–1725) traditions.

The middle of the nineteenth century saw the development of a number of movements that would have far-reaching consequences for the social, historical, and literary future of Russia. The repressive reign of Tsar Nicholas I ended in 1855, and much hope for change was placed in his successor, the more enlightened and at least initially more liberal Alexander II. Maríya Aleksándrovna Vilínskaya-Markóvich (pseudonym Markó Vovchók, 1834–1907) painted an unromanticized picture of freedom-loving, strong peasants victimized by the landowning classes in her folk songs and stories in Ukrainian and Russian. Along with the better-known Turgénev, Vilínskaya-Markóvich was credited by some contemporaries with bringing the peasant into public view, thus contributing to the abolition of serfdom in 1861.

The breakdown of the traditional social order, of which the abolition of serfdom was one indicator, was most vividly seen in the nihilism of the early 1860s. Nihilism, more an ethos than a coherent movement, placed great emphasis on individual emancipation and development, as well as on the potential of science, as the source of inevitable social progress. The female nihilist (*nigilístka*), a serious woman with short hair, plain clothing, glasses, and sometimes smoking a cigarette, was often the object of ridicule because of her drastic break with traditional social norms. It is in nihilism that radical Russian feminism of later decades had its roots.

Populism (*naródnichestvo*) did not acquire its label until the late 1870s, but its roots, too, may be found in the middle of the century, in the work of Aleksándr Ivánovich Hérzen (1812–1870), which led to the movement in the 1870s of "going to the people" (*Khozhdénie v naród*). The work of these dedicated people was based on the assumption that the intelligentsia were morally responsible for acting to improve the lives of the peasants and that peasants could play an important spiritual role in developing a new communal society. The various factions of populism differed in the degree to which they were committed to violence as a weapon in the revolutionary struggle; despite their political differences, all were systematically persecuted and finally suppressed after Alexander II was assassinated in 1881 by members of the People's Will (*Naródnaya vólya*).

All of those movements were, of course, reflected in the literature of the time. For example, the empty lives of upper-class provincial women found in Nadézhda Dmítrevna Khvoshchínskaya's (pseudonym V. Krestóvsky, 1824–1889) early novels, such as *Províntsiya v stárye gódy* (The Provinces in the Old Days, 1853–1856) gave way in later novels to more hopeful portraits of young women helping the peasants, such as in *Bolsháya Medvéditsa* (The Big Dipper, 1870). The politically biting satirical verse of Ánna Pávlovna Barýkova (1839–1893) was used by grassroots activists to politicize the peasants. Elements of folk poetry, in such works as "Skázka pro to, kak tsár Akhreyán khodíl bógu zhálovatsya" (A Tale about how Tsar Akhreyan went to complain to God, 1870s), made Barýkova's verse accessible to and very popular among peasants. An excellent picture of populist activity was given by Véra Nikoláevna Fígner (1852–1942) in her autobiographical works. Fígner also wrote poetry about political prisoners deprived of the ability to continue their work who remained optimistic about the ultimate success of their revolutionary movement. The genre of "prison literature" continues to the present day. Later, Sofíya Vasílevna Kovalévskaya (1850–1891), herself a paragon of the liberated woman—the first Russian woman professor of mathematics, a liberal social activist, a memoirist and prose writer—provided an objectified self-portrait of this generation of Russian feminists in her novel *Nigilístka* (The Nihilist Woman, 1884), and the play "Borbá za schástie" (A Struggle for a Better Lot, 1887).

In the decades from the 1860s to the early 1880s, art had been seen as having predominantly social and political value. Lack of tangible results and the political reaction that followed the Tsar's assassination in 1881 led to the new acceptance of socially uncommitted literature, which opened up new possibilities for artistic expression and experiment. The Russian Silver Age (1890–1917, also known as Symbolism or Modernism) spawned a large number of greater and lesser writers, many of them women.

A religious moralism inspired by Tolstoy can be seen in the later works of Barýkova and Evgéniya Túr (pseudonym of Elizavéta Vasílevna Salhiás de Tournemír, 1815–1892) and was part of a general interest in spirituality at the end of the nineteenth century. In their poetry, for example, Adeláyda Kazimírovna Gértsyk

(d. 1925) searched for the true destiny of Russia in Russian Orthodoxy and in a spiritual renaissance, and Polikséna Sergéevna Solovyóva (pseudonym Allégro, 1867–1924) explored the spiritual depths of humankind that would lay the foundation for a new human being.

The Modernists' obsession with the complex spiritual, emotional and physical manifestations of beauty proved tragic for Elizavéta Ivánovna Dmítrieva (pseudonym Cherubína de Gabriák, d. 1928), whose refined and reserved poetry was greatly admired as long as she was an unseen, mysterious woman. When she appeared in public, her deformed body was ridiculed and she stopped writing. Mírra Aleksándrovna Lokhvítskaya (1869–1905), sometimes known as the Russian Sappho, opened up the sphere of female sensuality in verse. Her writing, as well as that of Zinaída Nikoláevna Gíppius (1869–1945), treated the duality of human existence: spirit and flesh, divine and demonic, ethereal and earthly. Anastasíya Alekséevna Verbítskaya's (1861–1928) novels, such as *Klyuchí schástya* (Keys to Happiness, six books, 1909–1913) and *Ígo lyubví* (The Yoke of Love, 1914–1916) rivaled even those of Tolstoy in popularity due to their uninhibited eroticism; her characters reflected the false morality in the contemporary relationships of the Russian family and of men and women.

Drama was an important genre among the Symbolists, almost all of whom wrote plays. Often experimental, these works departed sharply from the realistic drama of the nineteenth century and had their model rather in Greek and Roman antiquity, medieval mysteries and folk puppet theater. The mystery plays of Lídiya Dmítrevna Zinóveva-Annibál (1866–1907), for example, were designed as dramatic "happenings," during which both actors and audience would achieve a cleansing spiritual renewal.

The alienation felt by many Modernists came in part from their views that urbanization and technology had failed to build a better world. Eleonóra von Nótenberg (pseudonym Eléna Génrikhovna Guró, 1877–1913) represented the opposition between the harmony of nature and the fragmentation of urban life. The impressionistic language of her poetry and prose (she was a painter as well), characterized by neologism often derived from children's language, also related to that of cubo-futurism, of which movement she was an early member.

The Revolution of 1917 and the ensuing civil war drove many writers into emigration. Important and extremely active emigré literary centers, of varied artistic and political affiliations, sprang up in Riga, Tallinn, Warsaw, Prague, Berlin, and Paris. Of particular note among the Parisian emigrés were Nadézhda Aleksándrovna Buchínskaya (pseudonym Nadézhda Téffi, 1872–1952), who was Mirra Lokhvitskaya's younger sister; Nína Nikoláevna Berbérova (b. 1901); Lídiya Davýdovna Chervínskaya (b. 1870); Iraída Gustávovna Ivánova (pseudonym Irína Vladímirovna Odóevtseva, née Heinicke, b. 1901, and returned to Leningrad in 1987); Ánna Semyónovna Prísmanova (1898–1960); and Marína Ivánovna Tsvetáeva (1892–1941). The theme of many of these writers was the alienation of life in emigration, often understood existentially. Significant memoirs of this period include Berbérova's *Kursív móy: avtobiográfiya* (*The Italics are Mine*, 1969; in Russian, 1972); Odóevtseva's *Na beregákh Nevý* (On the Banks of the Neva, 1967) and *Na beregákh Sény* (On the Banks of the Seine, 1983); and Galína

Nikoláevna Kuznetsóva's (1902–1976) *Grásskiy dnevník* (*A Grasse Diary*, 1967) about the Nobel-Prize-winning writer Iván Búnin and his circle.

For those who did not emigrate, the revolution brought even greater changes. The social inequalities of the past were, at least theoretically, eliminated, and writers had the opportunity to participate in the building of a real new society. Aleksándra Kollontái (1872–1952), a truly feminist Russian in word and deed, worked to create the ideally liberated modern woman, a woman free to pursue work and sex openly and without sanctions. Both in her writings (prose, articles, and speeches) and in her own life, Kollontái saw women's major problem as resisting external and internal pressures to be dependent on men.

The variety of literary movements in the 1920s reflected Russian writers' attempts to find an artistic expression appropriate to the new political reality. Acmeism, which arose around 1910 and included Ánna Andréevna Akhmátova (née Gorénko, 1889–1966), Sofíya Yákovlevna Parnók (1885–1933), and Irína Odóevtseva, rejected the Symbolists' obscurity and preoccupation with the "other reality" in favor of clarity of form and the beauty and experiences of this life. The Serapion Brotherhood, with no unifying credo other than the insistence that literature must exist for its own sake and not serve other goals, included the poet Elizavéta Grigórevna Polónskaya (1890–1969). The Constructivists, who believed in saturating art with contemporary imagery and themes, included Véra Mikháylovna Ínber (1890–1972), who made her start in literature with a Symbolist collection of poems in 1914. Perevál (The Divide) was a group of writers in the 1920s devoted to working for the aims of the revolution. Within this group, Ekaterína Strogováya depicted the lack of progressive spirit among the provincial working class. Her style, almost reportage, was presented as if she were taking facts directly from life.

More committed pictures of the "new order" were drawn by others. Though beginning as a Modernist poet, Mariétta Sergéevna Shaginyán (1888–1982) later turned to what she saw as the true "music of the Revolution": the socialist construction of dams and hydroelectric power stations. Lídiya Nikoláevna Seyfúllina (1889–1954) described the emergence of a class of strong peasant women and men who rebel against the crudeness and brutality of the village and herald a new order in such works as *Virinéya* (1924, later made into a successful play) and "Pravonarushiteli" ("The Lawbreakers," 1922).

An unusual treatment of the tragedy of a woman's lot was given in Maríya Mikháylovna Shkápskaya's (1891–1952) striking poetry about motherhood. Her poetry was not published after 1925 because of the Communist party's shift towards the policy that "communist ideology" would be the basic criterion of literature. Although Shkápskaya's poetry was deemed too personal and ideologically irrelevant, she continued to write as a *correspondant-feuilletonist*, providing essay-like sketches for the literary sections of newspapers.

What was only implied by the Party in 1925 became official policy in 1932 with a ban on all literary organizations except for the one, newly created Union of Soviet Writers and the formulation of socialist realism as the only acceptable form of artistic expression. Socialist realism was defined by Stalin as the truthful depiction of that which leads to socialism and in its later development was characterized by *partíynost* (propagation of party policy and ideology), *naródnost* (popular spirit, identified with traditional Russian nationalism), and *idéynost* (idealogical commitment). Given the strict dictates of socialist realism, it is not surprising that the works of some writers met with disapproval. Véra Ínber, for instance, was criticized by the official press for being too concerned with family matters and depicting Soviet reality too superficially and without sufficient heroism. Others, such as Akhmátova, were denied the right to publish; still others were imprisoned or executed in Stalin's purges.

This period was described by Lídiya Kornéevna Chukóvskaya, who, in addition to reminiscences about Akhmátova, wrote about Stalin's purges in *Ólga Petróvna* (translated as *The Deserted House*, 1965) and *Spúsk pod vódu* (*Going Under*, 1972). Two memoirists who wrote about this period have gained much acclaim in the West: Nadézhda Yákovlevna Mandelshtám (1889–1980), and Evgéniya Semyónovna Ginzburg (1896–1980). In *Journey Into the Whirlwind* and *Within the Whirlwind* (Krutóy marshrút, I and II, 1967 and 1978), the latter gives a striking account of arrests, interrogations, trials, jails, and labor camps and also expresses a sense of guilt and expiation for having once been a loyal Communist and thus in some way responsible for Stalin's excesses in the 1930s.

The creative restrictions of socialist realism were slightly relaxed during World War II, and much moving and patriotic verse was written, particularly about the tragic nine-hundred-day siege of Leningrad, during which the city was cut off from supplies of food, fuel, and medicine. Notable is the war poetry of Ánna Akhmátova, Véra Ínber, Ólga Fyódorovna Berggólts (1910–1975), Margaríta Iosífovna Aligér (b. 1915), and Yúliya Drúnina (b. 1925). Although after the war Drúnina wrote largely autobiographical descriptions of life as a wife, mother, and well-adjusted, contented Soviet citizen, the war continued to haunt her, and its imagery lingers, even in her poems about conjugal love. Aligér was also never able to free herself of the war, and her later work talks of the unhappiness of being a survivor as well as her guilt over the horrors of Stalin's purges in the 1930s.

Véra Fyódorovna Panóva's (1905–1973) war novel *Spútniki* (*The Train*, 1945) differed from most Soviet works of this genre in its concentration on the private lives of individuals rather than the heroics of the collective effort. The novel nonetheless won a Stalin Prize (equivalent to the Pulitzer Prize in the United States), and Panóva remained a loyal, officially approved writer, in other works depicting the ideal Soviet woman who is a productive worker and attentive wife and mother. This latter image can also be found in the works of Antonína Koptáeva and others.

Stalin's death in 1953 and Khrushchév's denunciation of him brought a brief thaw in the restrictions on literature, so that such writers as Lyubóv Kábo, Ínna Góff, and Nína Ivánter could write about restless, troubled youths searching to replace the discredited authority of Stalin and the generation that had compromised with him. Galína Evgénevna Volyánskaya's (pseudonym Galína Nikoláeva, 1911–1963) *Bítva v putí* (The Running Battle, 1957) was the first novel to depict Russians' reactions to Stalin's death. In this novel, Nikoláeva rejected Stalinist puritanism and included the new theme (from 1955 on) of Stalinist repression. Pictures of contemporary life, describing (within limits, of course) life as it actually was, were drawn by Olga Dmítrievna Fórsh (1873–1961), who wrote novels and fictionalized memoirs on historical and contemporary themes, mostly with Leningrad as a backdrop; Frída Abrámovna Vígdorova (1915–1965), an educator who wrote about the power of pedagogy and the necessity of allowing children to develop into individuals; and Eléna Sergéevna Vénttsel (pseudonym I. Grékova, b. 1907).

The 1960s saw a poetic revival: poets wrote about artistic estrangement, the poetic transformation of everyday objects, and the richness of the earth and the human spirit. This poetic avant-garde included Yúnna Moríts (b. 1937), Novélla Nikoláevna Matvéeva (b. 1934), Bélla Akhátovna Akhmadúlina (b. 1937), Natálya Gorbanévskaya (b. 1936), Rímma Fyódorovna Kazakóva (b. 1932), as well as M. Borísova, M. Pávlova, T. Zhirmúnskaya, Z. Afanáseva, and E. Ignátova. Akhmadúlina is undoubtedly the best known of these. Her poetry is often compared to Tsvetáeva's in its expression of the irresistible artistic urge and in a controlled hysteria akin to Tsvetáeva's nervous agitation. Another younger poet whose work is inspired by Tsvetáeva and who has in turn been championed by Akhmadúlina is Eléna Shvárts (b. 1949). Few of her works have appeared in the Soviet Union but she is a new star in émigré journals, notable for her variety. One compelling example of her work is "Stárost Knyagíni Dashkóvoy" (The Old Age of Princess Dashkova," 1973): in using the persona of the only woman ever to be appointed a president of an academy of sciences, in this case by Catherine the Great, Shvárts reclaims women's history to explore the significance of the Russian Enlightenment.[2] Gorbanévskaya (*Potéryanny ráy*; Paradise lost, 1965), along with the younger Irína Ratushínskaya (b. 1955), an émigré as of 1987, continue the tradition of "prison poetry."

World War II remains a frequent theme in Soviet literature up to the present day. The loss of a lover or husband during the war had forced many women to become strong and solitary, and throughout the 1960s, 1970s, and 1980s many heroines have been depicted as self-supporting women. Variations on this theme of externally imposed independence (sometimes due to a man's betrayal) can be seen in the prose of I. Grékova, G. Nikoláeva, V. Panóva, Eleonóra Adámova (pseudonym Nóra Adamyán, b. 1910), Natálya Davýdova (b. 1925), Irína Shukhgálter (pseudonym Irína Velembóvskaya, b. 1922), Máya Gánina (b. 1927), and Viktóriya Tókareva (b. 1937). A woman's difficult life, even under seemingly emancipated conditions, was described by Natálya Baránskaya in *Nedélya kak nedélya* (*A Week Like Any Other*, 1969), which is a classic in this genre: Baránskaya's heroine simply cannot handle pursuing a career, running the household, and caring for the children, even with daycare and the occasional help of a loving husband. The heroine of Kséniya Lvóva's *Eléna* (1955) ruins her seemingly good life by having an affair with a married man. Lyubóv Yúnina's "Zhénshchina v odno-kómnatnoy kvartíre" ("Woman in a One-Room Apartment," 1979) finds fulfillment without a man in her life. Yúnina's heroine differs from most others in not needing a personal relationship.

Yet Kollontái's evaluation is still true today: recent fiction and drama (the plays of Lyudmíla Petrushévskaya and Zóya Boguslávskaya) show the emancipated contemporary Soviet woman still longing for a reliable, wise, and strong mate with whom she can share her life. And such topics as poor gynecological care, abuse in prisons, and discrimination against women in upper management and politics are still forbidden to writers in the Soviet Union. Tatyána Mamónova, Tatyána Goricheva, Yúliya Voznesénskaya, and other dissident feminists who emigrated in 1980 discuss these issues in their writing, mostly articles and essays (recently published in a book, *Women and Russia*), but also in some poetry and prose. However, Premier Gorbachev's *perestroika* (rebuilding) is bringing about some radical changes in publishing practices. It is difficult to predict what direction this new freedom will take, or how long it will last, but one might hope that it will allow the *feministki* at home to produce more open, "feminist" critical literature. Some signs of this change are already visible in the appearance in recent years of a number of articles in the popular press on the subject of the "women's problem." One of the best of these is Zóya Boguslávskaya's "Kakíe mý, zhénshchiny?" (What Are We Women Like?) in *Literatúrnaya Gazéta* (The Literary Gazette, August 8, 1987). Very promising developments also include the publication of Petrushevskaya's stories that have not previously been permitted, the staging and popularity of her black comedies in Moscow and other cities, and the appearance in print of such talented and promising young writers as Tatyána Tolstáya (b. 1951) and Larísa Vanééva (b. 1953) to mention only two of many original voices.

Over the past two and a half centuries, women have made contributions in poetry, novels, short stories, plays, and memoirs. They have reflected in style and theme the general development of Russian literature during this entire period. One can detect, however, an evolution of a theme that corresponds to the position of women in Russia and the Soviet Union, and reflects a female perspective.

Throughout the nineteenth century and in some instances until World War II, women's literature in Russia concentrated on the issue of freeing women from the restrictions that their traditional position within the family had imposed upon them. Since World War II, however, it is the family itself that is in jeopardy. With men curiously absent in many works, and barely helpful even when present in others, women are left solely responsible for the survival of the family while at the same time shouldering the same responsibilities as men in work as well as the burdens of everyday life. Liberation that has granted women equal education, equal political responsibility, and equal work has made it extremely difficult for them to cope with their traditional responsibility for the family and its survival. Although the variety of works appearing lately makes it difficult to generalize, there are many examples of the latest women's literature which reflect the conflict of desiring fulfillment in the traditional family, yet being unable to compromise with the disappointments and sacrifices that traditional relationships with men imply. Soviet literary heroines often find that the price for a relationship is too high and, however painful the alternative, they are no longer willing to pay.

NOTES

1. Discussions of women's literature are rare for the Russian language group. Most works discuss the subject of women in Russian literature as the *depiction* of women in literature, largely produced by male authors. In the following essay I have relied mostly on a

scattering of works in those books that are listed in the bibliography. I found Terras'
Handbook particularly valuable, both for its succinct presentation of general literary
movements, and for its discussion of individual authors, and I made frequent use of the
essays found in it.

2. Barbara Heldt, "The Burden of Caring," *The Nation* 244, 23 (June 13, 1987) pp.
820–824.

BIBLIOGRAPHY

Background

Billington, James H. *The Icon and the Axe: An Interpretive History of Russian Culture.* New York:
1966.

Engel, Barbara A. *Mothers and Daughters. Women of the Intelligentsia in Nineteenth-Century Russia.*
Cambridge: Cambridge University Press, 1983.

Engel, Barbara A., and Clifford N. Rosenthal, trans. and eds. *Five Sisters: Women Against the Tsar.*
New York: Knopf, 1975.

Holland, Barbara, ed. *Soviet Sisterhood.* Bloomington: Indiana University Press, 1985.

Mandel, William. *Soviet Women.* Garden City, NY: Anchor Books, 1975.

Stites, Richard. *The Women's Liberation Movement in Russia.* Princeton: Princeton University Press,
1978.

Literary Criticism and Literature

Several anthologies of Russian/USSR literature by women were forthcoming at the time this essay went
to press, including one to be published by Abbeville Press and by Hermitage Press, both of New
York.

Brown, Deming. *Soviet Russian Literature Since Stalin.* Cambridge: Cambridge University Press, 1978.

Brown, Edward J. *Russian Literature Since the Revolution.* Cambridge: Harvard University Press, 1982.

Gasiorowska, Xenia. *Women in Soviet Fiction, 1917–1964.* Madison: University of Wisconsin Press,
1968.

Heldt, Barbara, *Terrible Perfection: Women and Russian Literature.* Bloomington: Indiana University
Press, 1987.

Karlinsky, Simon, and Alfred Appel, Jr., eds. *The Bitter Air of Exile: Russian Writers in the West,
1922–1972.* Berkeley: University of California Press, 1977.

Mirsky, D.S. *A History of Russian Literature.* New York: Knopf, 1964.

Pachmuss, Temira, trans. and ed. *Women Writers in Russian Modernism.* Urbana: University of Illinois
Press, 1978.

Proffer, Carl, and Ellendea Proffer, eds. *Women in Russian Literature. Russian Literature Triquarterly*
9. Ann Arbor: Ardis Publishers, 1974.

Terras, Victor, ed. *Handbook of Russian Literature.* New Haven, CT: Yale University Press, 1985. This
work features individual writers and contains an essay by Xenia Gasiorowska, "Women in Russian
Literature."

Weber, Harry B., ed. *The Modern Encyclopedia of Russian and Soviet Literature.* Gulf Breeze, FL:
Academic International Press, 1977–. This work features individual writers, topics, and an essay by
Irina H. Corten, "Feminism in Russian Literature." This is a multivolume work that is not yet
complete for all letters of the alphabet.

SCANDINAVIA (including Finland and Iceland)

Ingrid Claréus

Literature written by women in Scandinavia dates back to the Viking Age (800–1000). There are several inscriptions written by women in the runic alphabet carved on stones to be found in Denmark, Norway, and Sweden. A famous one is Dynnasteinen (the Dynna Stone) in Norway, which marked a bridge and reads: "Gunvor Trireksdatter made this bridge in memory of her daugher, Astrid; she was the handiest maiden in Hadeland." Thus the mother, by building a bridge, hoped to help save the soul of her daughter. Also Icelandic literature during the Saga period had its share of women writers.

During the later Middle Ages there is one outstanding woman writer, the Swedish Saint Birgitta (1303–1373), who wrote her "Revelations" in Swedish and had them translated into Latin by two of her confessors. Published in 1492, more than one hundred years after her death, for the Vadstena Cloister[1] by Gothab, a German typographer, her revelations deal with both religion and politics. In a rich and sharp language, in a style partly realistic, partly symbolic, Birgitta speaks out against corruption in state and church.

Among the unknown authors of popular ballads, orally composed during the Middle Ages but not written down until the sixteenth century, many were women. Recent research shows that the ballads were composed for the king and his court, that the musicians were men but the singers mostly women, and that the songs were often composed by women, or by men and women in a dialogue form. There are many examples of male chauvinism as well as female glorification to be found in these medieval ballads.

With education among the upper classes growing during the seventeenth century, the number of women writers increased markedly. In Sweden, for example, Queen Christina (1626–1689) turned the country into a showplace of culture, surrounding herself with scientists, philosophers, writers, and artists of international fame (among them the French philosopher René Descartes). She herself wrote diaries, letters, aphorisms, and a biography. In Denmark, Leonora Christina (1621–1698), the daughter of King Christian IV and his mistress Kirstine Munk, wrote her memoirs while imprisoned at Copenhagen's Blue Tower for twenty-two years (1663–1685), accused of helping her husband, Corfitz Ulfeldt, to betray the state. Her most famous work, *Jammersminde* (Memory of Woe), written during her incarceration but published only in 1869, is a heart-rending, realistic account of her sufferings, which, however, never broke her spirit.

While the prevalent literary form for women during the 1600s was the autobiographical prose written by women of the aristocracy, middle-class women of the eighteenth century wrote poetry, often with a religious or didactic purpose. Dorothe Engelbretsdatter (1634–1716) from Bergen, Norway, who wrote mostly religious poems and hymns in a baroque style, using images from her own domestic sphere, was so popular that the king, in 1684, excused her from paying taxes for the rest of her life. The poetry of the Swedish writer Sophia Elisabeth Brenner (1659–1730) provides another example of didactic writing. Her poems, usually composed in the alexandrine meter and depicting everyday life among the bourgeois, were immensely popular.

Scandinavian literature of the eighteenth century, though on the whole rationalistic and neoclassical, was gradually influenced by the trend toward Romanticism already manifested in other parts of Europe, especially in England, France, and Germany. An early Romantic was the important Swedish poet Hedvig Charlotta Nordenflycht (1718–1763), who exercised great influence on the literature and culture of her time through her active participation in literary societies and salons. Named "the Shepherdess of Scandinavia," she wrote a number of love poems: her most famous collection is *Den sörjande turturduvan* (The Mourning Turtle-Dove), published in 1743 in memory of her husband, who died only seven months after their wedding. These poems have been considered by one critic "the first complete expressions of a breakthrough of sentiment during the Age of Enlightenment." In her later poems, Nordenflycht expresses feminist views, demanding education for women, not only in domestic subjects but in literature and the arts as well. Highly educated herself, especially in French literature, she was an admirer of Rousseau,[3] until, in 1758, in a pamphlet against the contemporary French theater, he ascribed its successes to women's taste for shallow pleasures. Deeply wounded by this attack on women, Nordenflycht wrote a long poem, *Fruntimrets försvar* (Defense of Woman) in 1761, hoping to start a dialogue with Rousseau, who, however, never answered her. Another important satirical poet and journalist was Anna Maria Lenngren (1754–1817).

In the early nineteenth century, several important bourgeois women prose writers emerged; their short stories and novels dealt with the home, love, and marriage. In Denmark, for example, Thomasine Gyllembourg (1773–1856) wrote *En Hverdags-Historie* (An Everyday Story, 1828), dealing with marital life in Copenhagen bourgeois society. In that novel and later in *Ægtestand* (Marriage, 1835) she shows compassion for the many women who were married to despotic husbands and speaks out against the double standard in marriage. Her works give us a foretaste of the debate about marriage that was soon to be an important theme during the period of literary naturalism.

In Norway Camilla Collett (1813–1895) wrote the first realistic novel in her country, *Amtmandens Døttre* (The Governor's Daughters, 1854–1855), exposing the plight of middle-class girls. As the first Norwegian novel written from a feminist perspective it naturally became a source of inspiration for the feminist movement as it gradually developed in Norway. Pointing to the lack of educational opportunities for young girls, who were dependent on finding a suitable husband to support them, Collett demands reforms—in this novel and later in her many articles and essays. She is the first woman writer in Norway to work consciously for the emancipation of women.

In Sweden Fredrika Bremer (1801–1865) plays a similar role as Collett. Starting out as a writer of "fireside stories," she became very popular in Sweden and in other parts of the world through translations of her books into English, French, and German. Her early works, dealing with family situations, love, and marriage, keenly expose the limited possibilities for middle-class girls. After her return from a lengthy stay in the United States (1849–1851), she published, in both Swedish and English, her important feminist novel *Hertha* (1856), which puts forward her solutions to improve women's miserable state—especially that of the unmarried, whose position in the home was that of a servant—education and equal legal rights. *Hertha* is the first truly feminist novel in Swedish literature and greatly influenced the debate about "the woman question" in the Swedish parliament and subsequently in legislation. (Unmarried women were granted legal rights at the age of 25 in 1858 but had to wait until 1875 to be admitted to the university.) Mathilde Fibiger (1830–1872), a Danish writer, also wrote critically about the upbringing of young girls. Her novel *Clara Raphael* (1851), written in the form of twelve letters from Clara to a woman friend, discusses problems of love, sexuality, and marriage.

Written and published during the first half of the nineteenth century, Collett's, Bremer's, and Fibiger's novels deal mostly with the emancipation of unmarried women. The novels from the latter half of the century concentrate on the rights of married women, who were still under the guardianship of their husbands. The most prominent women writers of the 1880s and 1890s—the time of "the modern breakthrough" in Scandinavian literature—were Norway's Amalie Skram (1846–1905) and Sweden's Victoria Benedictsson (1850–1888). *Constance Ring* by Skram and *Pengar* (Money) by Benedictsson, both published in 1885, depict marital life within the middle-class family. Both authors condemn the prevailing custom of marrying off the young girl to a much older man without her consent and without her understanding of what it means to be married. Influenced by Ibsen's play *A Doll's House*, in which Nora leaves her husband and their three children to find self-realization, Selma in Pengar also chooses to break up her marriage and to earn her own living, while Constance, after two unfaithful husbands and one lover, sees no other solution for her tragic life than suicide.

In Finland, Minna Canth (1844–1897) is the first distinguished feminist to write in Finnish (the literary language until then had been Swedish). Congruent with her literary interests she was also politically active, and in political activities as well as in her creative writing she lashed out against the injustices of her contemporary society, demanding better conditions for the poor and equal rights for the oppressed. Another Finnish author, Maria Jotuni (1880–1943), excelled as a short-story writer, although she also wrote plays and novels. Her satirical, sometimes bitter writings focus on women in love.

At the end of the nineteenth century Selma Lagerlöf (1858–1940) made her debut with *Gösta Berlings saga* (*The Story of Gösta Berling*, 1891), which was followed by many novels and short stories, one of which is included in this anthology. Lagerlöf received the Nobel Prize for Literature in 1909 and in 1914 became the first woman to be elected to the Swedish Academy. The second Scandinavian woman writer to be awarded the Nobel Prize for Literature was the Norwegian Sigrid Undset (1882–1949) in 1928. Her masterpiece trilogy is *Kristin Lavransdatter* (*Kristin Lavransdatter*, 1920–1922); set in the Middle Ages it describes the life of a strong-willed, passionate woman. Contemporary with Undset but appearing later on the literary scene was Cora Sandel, the pen name of the Norwegian writer Sara Fabricius (1880–1974), who wrote an important trilogy about a young woman's struggle for independence and integrity named *Alberte og Jakob* (*Alberta and Jacob*, 1926), *Alberte og friheten* (*Alberta and Freedom*, 1931), and *Bare Alberte* (*Alberta Alone*, 1939).

Apart from Lagerlöf and Undset, the Danish writer Karen Blixen (1885–1962), published in English-speaking countries under her pseudonym Isak Dinesen, is probably the best known outside of Scandinavia, especially since the popular movie of her autobiographical novel *Out of Africa* (1937) was released in 1985.

The moral debates begun in the 1880s and 1890s about women's place in society went on for a long time in the press and in various publications. Ellen Key (1848–1926), internationally known Swedish educator, essayist, and literary critic, espoused motherhood as the most important role for women—in pamphlets and books like *The Century of the Child* (1905), *Love and Marriage* (1911), and *The Renaissance of Motherhood* (1914). Her thesis was that women should not compete with men in professions that were not "motherly" and should, above all, not work outside of the home as long as their children were young. Not completely conservative, she also stressed that a marriage in which there was no love between the husband and wife was immoral, while any relationship built on love, whether legally entered into or not, was moral. While many women supported Key's opinions, the feminists of the time attacked her, and reactions to many of her ideas can be seen in the literature by women writers of the first half of this century. One of these writers was Elin Wägner (1882–1949), anthologized in this book, author of many novels and short stories with a definite feminist message. She was active in the Swedish suffrage movement both as a journalist and as a public speaker, and when in 1920 Sweden finally gave its women the right to vote—the issue having been raised in Parliament in the 1880s—it was Wägner, together with three other women, who founded the feminist weekly *Tidevarvet* (The Era) to promote women politicians.

With the modernist poet Edith Södergran (1892–1923), Fenno-Swedish literature began to exert an influence on the rest of Scandinavia. Södergran, herself impressed by German and Russian contemporary poets, published *Dikter* (Poems, 1916) and *Septemberlyran* (The September Lyre, 1918). Her verse is unrhymed and full of vivid and visionary images. Some of her poems written between 1916 and 1923 have been translated by, among others, Stina Katchadourian, under the title *Love and Solitude* (1985).

Another Fenno-Swedish writer is novelist Hager Olsson (1893–1978), who was coeditor of the bilingual (Swedish and Finnish) literary journal *Ultra*, a mouthpiece for modernism. Her novel *Träsnidaren och döden* (1940) was translated into English as *The Woodcarver and Death* (1965); its theme is a solitary man's relationship to society, his isolation, and his final salvation through a spirit of fellowship and community with other human beings. A close friend of Edith Södergran, Olsson edited *Ediths brev* (Letters from Edith, 1955). Their contemporary Kerstin Söderholm (1897–1943) wrote delicate poems centering around the differences between human and nature, body and spirit; her diary was published after her death.

Some more recent Fenno-Swedish writers are Solveig von Schoultz (b. 1907), anthologized here; Mirjam Tuominen (1913–1967); Eva Wichman (b. 1908); Tove Jansson, also in this anthology, famous for her children's books about the Moomin family like *Muminpappans bravader* (The Happy Moomin, 1950), *Det osynliga barnet och andra berättelser* (Tales from Moomin Valley, 1963) and *Pappan och havet* (Moomin-papa at Sea, 1966); and Märta Tikkanen (b. 1935), whose collection of poems *Århundradets kärlekssaga* (*Love Story of the Century*, 1984), became a best seller. Tikkanen's novel *Män kan inte våldtas* (Man Rape, 1980) deals with a woman's reactions to being raped.

Among the contemporary generation of women writing in Finnish, Eila Pennanen (b. 1916) is one of her country's most remarkable. The theme of her novels is often the conflict between the inner world of a woman or child and the masculine world outside. Most famous as a short-story writer (five collections were published between 1952 and 1980), she has been compared to Katherine Mansfield. Her compatriot Eeva Kilpi (b. 1928), also a notable short-story writer, treats the situation of the solitary middle-aged woman in *Kesä ja keski-ikäinen nainen* (*Summer and the Middle-aged Woman*, 1949). Marja-Leena Mikkola (b. 1939) writes political and social protest songs, novels, short stories, and documentaries, as well as children's books.

The tradition of strong, independent women characters, manifested in the Icelandic sagas of the Middle Ages, is carried on in the literature of many women writers in Iceland today. The most famous writer of this century is Hulda, the pen name of Unnur Benediktsdottir (1881–1946), who wrote both short stories and poems. Her poetic style borrows from folklore but shows also strong impulses from neo-Romantic and Symbolist movements in literature. Writers like Halldora Björnsson (1907–1968), Asta Sigurdardottir (1930–1970), Valdis Oskarsdottir (b. 1949), and Svava Jakobsdottir (b. 1930) write from a feminist perspective about contemporary social and political issues.

In Denmark Tove Ditlevsen (1917–1976) published her first volume of poems in 1939, and this was followed by many short stories and novels about life in the poorer districts of Copenhagen, where she grew up. Several contemporary Danish women writers have also distinguished themselves—Cecil Bødker (b. 1927), Inger Christensen (b. 1935), and Charlotte Strandgaard (b. 1945) primarily as poets, while Ulla Ryum (b. 1937), Vita Andersen (b. 1944) Suzanne Brøgger (b. 1944) Kirsten Thorup (b. 1942) (whose novel *Baby* [*Baby*, 1973] won the Pegasus Prize in 1979 for the best Danish novel of the 1970s) and Dea Trier Mørch (b. 1941) (whose novel *Vinterbørn* [1976] was translated as *Winter's Child* in 1986) primarily as novelists.

In Norway such poets as Inger Hagerup (1905–1985) and Haldis Moren Vesaas (b. 1907) and prose writers like Torborg Nedreaas (b. 1906), Ebba Haslund (b. 1917), and Bjørg Vik (b. 1935) assert a significant feminist approach in their creative work. Nedreaas' trilogy, *Trylleglasset* (The Magic Glass, 1950), *Musikk fra en blå brønn* (Music from a Blue Well, 1960) and *Ved neste nymåne* (At the Next New Moon, 1971), is an intuitive tale about the psychological growth of a young girl through adolescence and womanhood. Among the youngest of prominent Norwegian writers, Herbjørg Wassmo (b. 1942), Karin Moe (b. 1945), Cecilie Løveid (b. 1951), and Tove Nielsen (b. 1952) are the most promising.

In Sweden, this century has produced many fine writers. Among the older generation are Karin Boye (1901–1941), both poet and prose writer; Moa Martinson (1890–1964), the only proletarian among major Swedish women writers; Agnes von Krusenstjerna (1894–1940), writer of polemic novels about the aristocracy; and Sonja Åkesson (1926–1978). Sara Lidman (b. 1923), Birgitta Trotzig (b. 1929), and Kerstin Ekman (b. 1933) are considered among the foremost of contemporary women writers. Boye's dystopian novel *Kallocain* (*Kallocain*, 1940) gives a terrifying picture of the world in the year 2000, while the poverty and oppression of working-class women are depicted by Moa Martinson in her many novels, one of the best being *Kvinnor och Äppelträd* (*Women and Appletrees* 1933). The equally oppressed middle-class suburban housewife is portrayed by Sonja Åkesson in a "new, simple" style, using colloquial words and expressions, both in her prose and poetry. The prevailing trend of searching for one's roots has been adopted by both Sara Lidman and Kerstin Ekman in their several volumes of novels. Lidman's prose epic *Din tjänare hör* (Thy Servant Listens, 1977), *Vredens barn* (Children of Wrath, 1979), *Nabots sten* (Nabot's Stone, 1981), *Den underbare mannen* (The Wonderful Man, 1983) and *Järnkronan* (The Iron Crown, 1985), about the building of a railroad in Lapland from 1878 to 1894, fills five novels—Ekman's *Häxringarna* (Enchanted Circles, 1974), *Springkällan* (The Spring, 1976), *Änglahuset* (Angel House, 1979) and *En stad av ljus* (A City of Light, 1983)—telling the story of a small central Swedish town and its people from 1870 to 1970, in four volumes.

Other notable Swedish women writers are Margareta Ekström (b. 1930), poet and short-story writer, Birgitta Trotzig (b. 1929) and Agneta Pleijel (b. 1940), and the two poets Siv Arb (b. 1931) and Kristina Lugn (b. 1948), who carry on the tradition of self-revelation and social criticism begun in the poetry of Sonja Åkesson.

The most prominent feature of Scandinavian women's writing is their often autobiographical depiction of female experiences in a male-dominated society. The first feminist novels in the early nineteenth century by Collett, Bremer, and Fibiger lobbied for the education of women, whereas at the end of that century women such as Benedictsson and Skram wrote about the need for women's emancipation and self-realization as compatible with the role of mother and wife. With the twentieth century the topic is expanded and woman's double role as mother/wife and professional is discussed. After finally gaining some legal rights, including suffrage, the political role of women starts to feature, in Scandinavian fiction and in utopian writings by Ellen Key, Elin Wägner, and Karin Boye, a kind of matriarchy that is envisioned as the only solution for the survival of our world.

The feminist movement in Scandinavia during the 1960s and 1970s was followed by a remarkable increase in the output of literature written by women. Although less militant than their sisters in the United States, Scandinavian women have been quite successful in gaining equality under the law, but, as everywhere, many of the old discriminatory attitudes remain and we see these problems mirrored in the many works of literature by women writers. Never before have so many Scandinavian women writers published so profusely and in so many different literary genres as during the last fifty years of this century.

NOTES

1. Cloister founded in 1370 by St. Birgitta in this city in south central Sweden.
2. A line of poetry consisting of twelve syllables.
3. (1712–1778): One of the most influential writers of eighteenth-century France, Rousseau's writings covered such diverse fields as education, ethics, politics, and art.

BIBLIOGRAPHY

Ahokas, J.A. *A History of Finnish Literature*. Bloomington: Indiana University Press, 1973.

Bayerschmidt, Carl F. *Sigrid Undset*. New York: Twayne Publishers, 1970.

Beck, R. *History of Icelandic Poets, 1800–1940*. Ithaca, NY: Cornell University Press, 1950.

Beyer, H. *A History of Norwegian Literature*. New York: New York University Press, 1956.

Borum, P. *Danish Literature: A Short Critical Survey*. Copenhagen: Det Danske Selskab, 1979.

Claudi, J. *Contemporary Danish Authors*. Copenhagen: Det Danske Selskab, 1952.

Dauenhauer, R., and P. Binham. Introduction to *Snow in May: An Anthology of Finnish Writing 1945–72*. Rutherford, NJ: Farleigh Dickenson University Press, 1978.

Downs, B.W. *Modern Norwegian Literature, 1860–1918*. Cambridge: Cambridge University Press, 1966.

Edström, Vivi. *Selma Lagerlöf*. Trans. Barbara Lide. Boston: Twayne Publishers, 1984.

Einarsson, S. *A History of Icelandic Literature*. New York: Johns Hopkins University Press, 1957.

———. *History of Icelandic Prose Writers 1800–1940*. Ithaca, NY: Cornell University Press, 1948.

Hanson, Katherine. *An Everyday Story: Norwegian Women's Fiction*. Seattle: Seal Press, 1984.

Johnsson, E. "Icelandic Literature." In I. Ivask and G. von Wilpert, *World Literature since 1945*. New York: F. Ungar, 1973.

Langbaum, Robert W. *The Gayety of Vision. A Study of Isak Dinesen's Art*. New York: Random House; London: Chatto & Windus, 1964.

Lomas, H. Introduction to *Territorial Song: New Writing in Finland*. London: London Magazine Editions, 1981.

McFarlane, James W. "Sigrid Undset." In *Ibsen and the Temper of Norwegian Literature*. London: Oxford University Press, 1960.

Mitchell, P.M. *A History of Danish Literature*. 2nd ed. New York: Kraus-Thomson Organization, 1971.

Mortensen, B. "Swedish Literature 1870–1950." In E. Bredsdorff et al., *An Introduction to Scandinavian Literature*. Westport, CT: Greenwood Press, 1970.

Printz-Påhlson, G. "Tradition of Contemporary Swedish Poetry." Introduction to *Contemporary Swedish Poetry*. London: Anvil Press Poetry, 1980.

Rossel, Sven H. *A History of Scandinavian Literature 1870–1980*. Minneapolis: University of Minnesota Press, 1981.

Schoolfield, George C. *Edith Södergran: Modernist Poet in Finland*. Westport, CT: Greenwood Press, 1984.

———. Introduction to *Swedo-Finnish Short Stories*. New York: Twayne Publishers, Inc., 1974.

Thurman, Judith. *Isak Dinesen: The Life of a Storyteller*. New York: St. Martin's Press, 1982.

Wamberg, Bodil, ed. *Out of Denmark: Isak Dinesen & Danish Women Writers Today*. Philadelphia: Nordic Books, 1985.

Wilson, Barbara, trans. and intro. *Cora Sandel: Selected Short Stories*. Seattle: Seal Press, 1985.

Wizelius, I. *Swedish Literature 1956–1960*. Stockholm: Swedish Institute, 1960.

SPAIN

Phyllis Zatlin

Although researchers have discovered the names of hundreds of women writing in Spain from the fifteenth century on, prior to the contemporary period only a handful achieved a place of distinction in Spanish literature. There can be no doubt, however, that this select group includes figures of major importance. Saint Teresa of Avila (1515–1582), a mystic and saint who reformed the Carmelite Order, wrote autobiographical and theological essays as well as poetry; her influence extended far beyond the borders of Spain. María de Zayas y Sotomayor (1590–1661) was a champion of women's rights. She is the most representative writer of courtly novels from Spain's golden age. Writing under the male pen name Fernán Caballero, Cecilia Böhl de Faber (1796–1877), on the other hand, defended traditional values and traditional roles for women in her novels. She is credited with starting the *costumbrista* movement (in which writers strove to capture the local color of regional Spain as it invoked images of Spain's national heritage) from which emerged the Spanish realistic novel. Her *La gaviota* (*The Sea Gull*, 1849) is readily available in English translation.

In contrast to Caballero, Cuban-born Gertrudis Gómez de Avellaneda (1814–1873) was an outspoken abolitionist and feminist. An accepted member of the Madrid literary world, she achieved success as a neoclassic dramatist and author of romantic novels and poetry. Her antislavery novel *Sab* (1841) antedates Harriet Beecher Stowe's *Uncle Tom's Cabin* by eleven years. Another ardent defender of women's rights was essayist and reformer Concepción Arenal (1820–1893). Determined to receive an education in spite of the barriers against women, she dressed as a man in order to gain access to the university.

The Iberian peninsula is marked by distinct regions, some of which, like Galicia and Catalonia, have their own languages. In the 1800s, Galicia produced three of Spain's major women writers: Arenal, Rosalía de Castro (1837–1885), and Emilia Pardo Bazán (1851–1921). Of these, the poet Castro was the least recognized during her lifetime. Her relative lack of acclaim may be attributed not only to her being a woman but also to her choosing to live in the provinces and write primarily in Galician rather than in Castilian. Today she is generally regarded, along with Gustavo Adolfo Bécquer, as one of Spain's two most important poets of the nineteenth century. Her reputation has long since eclipsed that of Romantic poet Carolina Coronado (1823–1911), who was more widely known during their lifetimes.

By any measure of achievement, Pardo Bazán is one of the towering figures of Spanish literature. Apparently indefatigable, she traveled and lectured extensively, founded and edited her own journal, and wrote numerous novels, short stories, and essays. She introduced the Spanish intellectual scene to French naturalism and the Russian novel and made a consistent effort throughout her life to improve the status of women. Her best-known novel, *Los pazos de Ulloa* (*The Son of the Bondwoman*, 1886) is available in a recent English-language translation.

While Pardo Bazán's stature has doubtless increased in the decades since her death, the same is not true of novelist Concha Espina (1869–1955). Now somewhat neglected by critics and the general reading public, she nevertheless enjoyed considerable esteem during her lifetime. Indeed she was twice nominated for the Nobel Prize for Literature and once lost the award by only one vote. Her most enduring novel is *El metal de los muertos* (The Metal of the Dead, 1920), a social epic dealing with the conditions in the copper mines of Andalusia.

Pardo Bazán and Espina both tried their hand at playwriting, but it was María Martínez Sierra (1874–1974) who succeeded in following Avellaneda's footsteps as a successful dramatist. Only recently has Martínez Sierra been credited with her achievements, however, for she allowed her husband Greogorio to claim sole authorship for the plays they wrote together, even when she was principal author and the couple was already separated. Several of Martínez Sierra's plays, including the well-known *Canción de cuna* (*Cradle Song*, 1911), were successfully staged in New York.

The early twentieth century, particularly following the establishment of the Second Republic (1931), was a period of great advancement for women in terms of educational, legal, and political rights. Significantly, one of the major forces in the Spanish Communist Party was a woman, Dolores Ibarruri, (b. 1895) *la Pasionaria* (The Passion Flower). Her autobiography, *El unico camino*, (*They Shall Not Pass*, 1963), chronicles the experiences of a young girl from a mining community who came to assume a role in world politics. Nevertheless, while Spanish women were achieving a role of equality in some spheres, few women reached the forefront of the Spanish literary world. Among the writers of the vanguard movements of the 1920s and 1930s there are only two women of prominence: poet and poetry critic Ernestina de Champourcin (b. 1905) and novelist and short-story writer Rosa Chacel (b. 1898). Chacel was one of the many liberal writers and intellectuals who were forced into exile during or following the Spanish civil war (1936–1939). Her recent return to Spain has been marked by an intense critical interest in her narrative art.

The real blossoming of women's literature in Spain has come in the postwar period. When the first Nadal Prize for novels was awarded in 1944 to Carmen Laforet (b. 1921) for her *Nada* (Nothingness), the doors were at last opened to women writers. The Nadal Prize was subsequently awarded to Elena Quiroga (b. 1921) in 1950, Dolores Medio (b. 1914) in 1952, Luisa Forrellad (b. 1930) in 1953, Carmen Martín Gaite (b. 1925) in 1957, and Ana María Matute (b. 1926) in 1959. With the exception of Forrellad, all these women have become important figures in Spanish letters. In 1983 Quiroga joined poet Carmen Conde (b. 1907) to become the second woman elected to the Spanish Royal Academy. Since winning the National Literature Prize of 1978 for her multifaceted metanovel *El cuarto de atrás* (*The Back Room*), Martín Gaite has risen to a position of international stature. Matute is widely anthologized in the United States and has become a very familiar writer to American students of Spanish, both for her short stories and for such novels as *Primera memoria* (*School of the Sun*, 1960). While Laforet, Quiroga, Medio, Martín Gaite, and Matute have followed different paths and differ considerably in style and technique—Quiroga, for example, in the 1950s developed a Faulknerian stream of consciousness style that was atypical of the Spanish novel of the period—they all developed adolescent protagonists and through them presented the experience of growing up female in a repressive society.

The Nadal Prize-winning novelists of the period from 1940 to 1959 were joined by scores of other women authors, too numerous to mention here. The Planeta Prize, also for novels and established in 1952, was won in 1954 by Matute and then in 1956 by Carmen Kurtz (b. 1911), in 1964 by Concha Alós (b. 1926), in 1966 by Marta Portal (b. 1930), and in 1975 by Mercedes Salisachs (b. 1918). Of these, Salisachs has unquestionably enjoyed the greatest popular success, both in Spain and abroad. Her *Una mujer llega al pueblo* (*The Eyes of the Proud*, 1956) has been translated to seven languages. Generally ignored by the critics, Salisachs nevertheless includes among her novels several that are distinguished for their innovative narrative techniques or scathing indictment of contemporary social mores.

Although from Catalonia, Salisachs does not identify with her region or its language. Defying efforts of the Franco regime (1939–1975) to suppress Catalonian culture, a group of women authors did choose to continue in the tradition of their foremothers and write in their native language. Earlier in the century such poets as Caterina Albert (pseudonym Victor Català, 1873–1966) and Clementina Arderiu (1893–1976) had made an important contribution to the cultural richness of their region. In the postwar period Maria Aurelia Capmany (b. 1918) has excelled in novel, theater, and essay, and Teresa Pàmires (b. 1919) has established herself as a major novelist. The long-exiled Mercè Rodoreda (1909–1983), like Chacel, found critical acclaim upon her return to her native land. Her *La plaça del diamant* (*The Time of the Dove*, 1962) is considered by many to be the most important postwar novel written in Catalan and has been made into a film.

The numbers of women writing narrative is certainly equaled by that of women writing poetry, both in Catalan and in Castilian. Conde in her 1971 anthology of poetry written by women in the 1950s included selections from thirty-four poets, among them Aurora de Albornoz (b. 1926), María Victoria Atencia (b. 1931), and Concha Lagos (b. 1913). In addition to Conde herself, however, the major women poets of contemporary Spain are Concha Zardoya (b. 1914) and Gloria Fuertes (b. 1918). The latter in particular has attracted considerable scholarly attention in the United States, and her poetry, marked by its identification with the working class, its concern for women's role in society, and its humor, is readily available in English translation.

In comparison with the short-story writers, novelists, and poets, women dramatists have had a difficult time, even in the postwar period. Dora Sedano (b. 1902) and Julia Maura (1910–1970) were staged successfully with some frequency in the 1940s and 1950s, but in more recent years the only woman dramatist to achieve commercial success has been Ana Diosdado (b. 1938). Born in Argentina, she is the daughter of the late Enrique Diosdado, a highly regarded actor and director, and is herself an actress as well as a multifaceted writer. Her most important stage plays to date are *Olvida los tambores* (Forget the Drums, 1970) and *Usted también podrá disfrutar de ella* (You, Too, Can Enjoy "Her," 1973), both of which number among the dozen longest-running plays by Spanish playwrights on the Madrid stage of the 1970s.

If Madrid was the principal literary center in the early postwar period, in the past decade the focus of activity for women writers and for feminists in particular has shifted to Barcelona. Among the younger Catalonian novelists who have achieved national recognition are Esther Tusquets (b. 1936), Montserrat Roig (b. 1946), Ana María Moix (b. 1947), and Carmen Riera (b. 1948). The most prolific of this group is Roig, a journalist who does her creative writing in Catalan. Castilian translations of such novels as *Ramona, adéu* (Goodby, Ramona, 1972), *El temps de les cireres* (Cherry Time, 1976), and *L'hora violeta* (The Violet Hour, 1980) have become national bestsellers, as have the novels of Tusquets.

Other important novelists who have emerged in democratic Spain include Rosa Montero (b. 1951), also a journalist, and Carmen Gómez Ojea (b. 1945), winner of the Nadal Prize for 1981.

In general this recent generation of novelists is more openly feminist than were the writers of the postwar generation and, freed from the rigid censorship and repressive atmosphere of the earlier period, more able to deal with female sexuality. Indeed, Tusquets' early novels are erotic, replete with descriptions of both lesbian and heterosexual love relationships.

Although Moix in *Julia* (1970) once again treats an adolescent protagonist, there is a general tendency among these writers to present the perspective of the mature woman, particularly in the context of a contemporary society in which women have and demand greater personal and professional freedoms but also find that enduring relationships are harder to sustain. Montero's first novel, *Crónica del desamor* (Chronicle of Indifference, 1979), is a quasidocumentary that reports a long list of the problems facing women today.

In the years since the Spanish Civil War and particularly in the decade since the establishment of a democratic constitutional monarchy (1975), women writers in Spain have flourished, creating a rich and varied literature that speaks both to the Spanish experience and to that of all women in our modern society.

BIBLIOGRAPHY

Background

Brenan, Gerald. *The Spanish Labyrinth*. Cambridge: The University of Cambridge Press, 1943.
Carr, Raymond. *Modern Spain 1875–1980*. Oxford: Oxford University Press, 1980.
Fraser, Ronald. *Blood of Spain: The Experience of Civil War, 1936–1939*. London: Penguin Books, Ltd., 1979.
Jackson, Gabriel. *The Spanish Republic and the Civil War, 1931–39*. Princeton, NJ: Princeton University Press, 1965.
Russell, P.E., ed. *A Companion to Spanish Studies*. London: Methuen & Co., 1973.

Literary Criticism

Bretz, Mary Lee. *Concha Espina*. Twayne World Authors Series 559. Boston: G.K. Hall, 1980.
Díaz, Janet W. *Ana María Matute*. Twayne World Authors Series 152. New York: Twayne Publishers, 1971.
Fox-Lockert, Lucía. *Women Novelists in Spain and Spanish America*. Metuchen, NJ, and London: The Scarecrow Press, 1979.
Hill, Kathleen Kulp. *Rosalía de Castro*. Twayne World Authors Series 446. Boston: G.K. Hall, 1977.
Johnson, Roberta. *Carmen Laforet*. Twayne World Authors Series 601. Boston: G.K. Hall, 1981.
Jones, Margaret E.W. *Dolores Medio*. Twayne World Authors Series 281. New York: Twayne Publishers, 1974.
———. *The Literary World of Ana María Matute*. Studies in Romance Languages 3. Lexington: The University of Kentucky Press, 1970.

O'Connor, Patricia. *Gregorio and María Martinez Sierra*. Twayne World Authors Series 412. Boston: G.K. Hall, 1977.

Pattison, Walter T. *Emilia Pardo Bazán*. Twayne World Author Series 134. New York: Twayne Publishers, 1971.

Servodidio, Mirella, and Marcia Welles, eds. *From Fiction to Metafiction: Essays in Honor of Carmen Martín Gaite*. Lincoln, NE: Society of Twentieth Century Spanish and Spanish American-Studies, 1983.

Zatlin-Boring, Phyllis. *Elena Quiroga*. Twayne World Author Series 459. Boston: G.K. Hall, 1977.

Yan Li, Reader, *1981, oil on canvas. Courtesy the artist and Sabrina Fung, New York*

SPANISH AMERICA

Margarite Fernández Olmos

The region known as Spanish America spans the Rio Grande to Cape Horn and includes a variety of areas such as Mexico, Central America, the Caribbean, and South America. Despite its geographic and cultural diversity, Spanish America shares social institutions and attitudes that took root during its conquest and colonization by the Spanish and, in large measure, continue today, hidden in some cases beneath a veneer of modernity. The majority of its people have not had a voice in shaping its political destiny. Contemporary women authors and feminist social and literary critics are among those who have been suppressed; they are also in the forefront of an ongoing process of ideological and cultural reevaluation taking place in societies that are in crisis situations and searching for other options, new directions. The rediscovery of women authors of the past and the recognition of the valuable contributions of contemporary women are the result of research concerned with reaffirming women as artists whose writing has a great potential to affect the traditional order.

The material conditions Virginia Woolf described as indispensible for female literary creation—economic independence, educational opportunities, and the freedom to express oneself[1]—did not exist for women in Spanish America until the twentieth century and even today are enjoyed by only a small, economically privileged minority of the female population. A collective female literary tradition did not evolve, therefore, until after the modernist movement of the late nineteenth and twentieth centuries. There were, however, important individual figures in earlier periods, such as Sor Juana Inés de la Cruz (1651–1695), the famous nun of colonial Mexico who was called the "Tenth Muse of America." This exceptional woman, admired as much for her literary talent as her fighting spirit, won international fame and distinction in her lifetime and the continuing admiration of critics after her death. A prolific poet whose works are considered the epitome of hispanic Baroque poetry, Sor Juana was no less accomplished in drama and prose. Her essay "Reply to Sor Philotea de la Cruz" (1691) remains a testament to her will to overcome the constraints of the masculinist culture of the time and to her advanced ideas regarding the equality of women. She had to endure the restrictions of convent life and innumerable personal sacrifices in order to assure herself a lifetime of learning and achievement; sadly, not until our own day would other women writers be able to enjoy the same level of literary esteem and status.

The nineteenth century witnessed political independence for the majority of Spanish American nations, whose urge to assert a national identity opened the way for literary experimentation with local themes. The romantic movement's revolutinary spirit inspired the talents of a woman who, because she was female, could identify with the weakest members of her society: the Indian and the black slave. Born in Cuba in 1814, Gertrudis Gómez de Avellaneda is often claimed by both Spanish American and Spanish letters, for in 1838 she traveled to Spain and remained there until her death in 1873. Public scandal and censure marked a lifetime that defied social convention. Avellaneda wrote poems, plays, and novels, among which is her famous work *Sab* (1841), an antislavery novel suggesting a connection that was not lost on other abolitionists: the similarity between the lives of slaves and of women.

It has been said that the nineteenth-century artist in Spanish America could not avoid writing social criticism nor acting "as guide, teacher and conscience of his [or her] country."[2] Although most Spanish Americans were still culturally and artistically dependent on Europe, many artists noticed that there were two Spanish Americas, that of the educated urban minority, with standards and values strongly European, and the Spanish America of the rural masses, with an indigenous or non-European tradition. The ideal of progress and development advocated by the "Europeanized" sector led to their viewing their nations' problems as a struggle between "civilization" (or the European) and "barbarism" (or the native culture). Circumstances forced writers to define the relationship between the artist and society and compelled them to describe and define social conditions.

Among those who would side with the indigenous peoples and use literature as a form of social protest was Clorinda Matto de Turner (1854–1909), a Peruvian who, with her work *Aves sin nido* (*Birds Without a Nest*, 1889), "initiated the novel of social and realistic tendency in Latin America and, at the same time, contributed to the founding of the novelistic form in Peru."[3] Matto de Turner's liberal and anticlerical positions gained her excommunication and exile. *Blanca Sol* (1888), the naturalistic novel by her contemporary compatriot Mercedes Cabello de Carbonera (1845–1909), exposed the decadence of the urban upper classess. Both women benefitted from the revival of the literary circle (the *tertulia*, *salón*, or *velada*), a native tradition that re-emerged at midcentury in Peru to promote and encourage the writing and publication of local authors and provide a reading public for the artist. For women, the tertulia provided a rare opportunity for intellectual political roles in the society. In Lima, Matto de Turner attended the salón presided over by the Argentine author Juana Manuela Gorriti (1819–1892), who also wrote "Indianist" novels. Matto de Turner would later preside over her own.

During the last two decades of the century, the Spanish American elite (with Mexico as a prime example) embraced the Positivist ideology of August Comte,[4] believing it to be the means by which the region could liberate itself from "backward" influences and industrialize the economy. Positivism emphasized material growth and wellbeing and favored a capitalist mentality, regarding private wealth as sacred and as a sure sign of progress. The Positivists sought to offer a scientific solution to the problems of national development; their ideology blinded them, however, to the price society would have to pay for such apparent gains:

> Like so much of the economic and political thought in Latin America then and since, it [positivism] recognized no incompatibility in the imposition of capitalist industrialization in a neofeudal, rural base. With its emphasis on order and hierarchy, positivism assured the elites their venerable privileges, relative prosperity, and selective progress and held out promise of the same to the restless middle sectors. Subsumed was the inferiority of the masses who stood very little chance of "progressing" in a society in which all the institutions repressed them.[5]

Responses to this "selective progress" and to the growing political unrest would be found in the literary and political spheres. The last decade of the century saw the appearance of the first significant Spanish-American literary movement. *Modernismo* emerged as an artistic revolt against bourgeois values and as a rejection of what were considered the archaic literary traditions of the past. Few women are mentioned in connection with this important movement of literary renovation; one is Delmira Agustini (1886–1914), an Uruguayan whose poetry and lifestyle reflect modernism's challenge to literary and social conventions. Agustini's publication in 1914 of a collection of poems entitled *Los cálices vacíos* (Empty Chalices), with its heavily erotic themes, immediately made her a pariah of respectable Montevidean society. In addition to Agustini, however, the female poets most commonly mentioned as the precursors of contemporary women writers—the Argentine Alfonsina Storni (1892–1938), the Uruguayan Juana de Ibarbourou (1897–1979), and the Chilean Gabriela Mistral (1889–1957)—belong to the post-modernist tradition and are considered romantic poets despite individual variations in style and theme. Storni's more famous poems are explicitly feminist in their denunciation of the traditionally dependent role of women in Spanish American society; Ibarbourou's "feminine" poetry of love also express a deep love for the land; Mistral, the first Spanish-American author to receive the Nobel Prize for Literature, in 1945, proclaims in her poetry, among other things, the values of the indigenous peoples in a simple yet powerful language.

The political response that would alter the course of twentieth-century Spanish-American culture was the Mexican Revolution of 1917. Thereafter, nationalism sought indigenous solutions rather than imported programs. Artists reevaluated the non-European elements of the society, and a newly recovered pride and admiration in indigenous peoples and their past inspired the renowned murals and painting of Diego Rivera, José Clemente Orozco, and David Alfaro Siquieros, as well as the newly appreciated paintings of Frida Kahlo. Although the more celebrated novels of the Mexican revolution have been written by men, Nellie Campobello's (b. 1909) *Cartucho* (*Cartridge*, 1931) is a unique and fascinating account of the horrors of the war as seen through the eyes of a child. In areas where the African tradition had formerly been denied or ignored, such as the Caribbean, the reaffirmation of non-European culture would result in the Afro-Caribbean movement of the 1920s and 1930s. The stories of the Cuban author Lydia Cabrera (b. 1900), published in the 1940s, follow in this tradition, searching as they do for an integrated identity that draws upon African popular culture.

Literary movements and trends in Spanish America have characteristically alternated between what until recently had been considered two mutually exclusive and conflicting approaches to artistic expression—nationalism and cosmopolitanism (only two of the numerous designations that are not always clearly defined). For years the male literary establishment debated the merits and pitfalls of these opposing literary and cultural viewpoints. What many failed to perceive until very recently, however, is that very gradually a female tradition in Latin American letters was being forged; it started with the poetry of the literary precursors mentioned above, adding its own unique dimension to the literary production of the area. Significantly, this development coincided with the growth of feminist movements outside Spanish America, and, although few among hispanic authors would have defined themselves as "feminists," the freedom to create and express themselves with an authentic woman's voice was undoubtedly feminist in impulse.

Such women were generally unknown outside the boundaries of their countries or their small literary circles and were not included in the standard anthologies. María Eugenia Vaz Ferreira of Uruguay (1875–1924), for example, was writing in an early modernist style even before Delmira Agustini, and her melancholic verses are the forerunners of Alejandra Pizarnik's macabre death poems. The Salvadoran Claudia Lars (1899–1974) was a prolific writer of delicate yet intense verses whose works spanned the 1930s to the 1970s. Clementina Suárez's (b. 1903) *Corazón sangrante* (Bleeding Heart, 1930) was the first book of poems ever published by a Honduran woman; her strong sensual poetry examines what it is like to be a woman and a mother. Children's literature captured the imagination of Carmen Lyra (1888–1949), whose adaptations opened the world of B'rer Rabbit to the children and the adults of Costa Rica in her enchanting *Cuentos de mi tía Panchita* (Tales of my Aunt Panchita, 1920). Olga Orozco (b. 1920) is an Argentine who began writing in the 1940s and continues today to explore subjects that range from an examination of the fragmented self, as in her poem "Olga Orozco," to an imaginary journey through the parts of the body. The divided personality is also the theme of the poem Puerto Rican Julia de Burgos (1914–1953) dedicated to herself; Burgos' tortuous search for personal authenticity and social justice inspired a rich body of verses written in the 1930s and 1940s that continues to have an impact on Puerto Rican writers of today.

What these women shared was the problem of surviving as writers in a male-dominated profession and the systematic discouragement they felt in their chosen course. A lack of communication between artists has long plagued the Spanish-American writer; for women—outsiders in the literary establishment—the problem was more acute. Even a well-known figure like Victoria Ocampo (1890–1979), the Argentine writer and critic and founder of the prestigious literary journal *Sur* (South, 1931), which helped to disseminate the latest trends in Europe and Spanish America, has testified to the compounded difficulties she had pursuing a career in the arts. Much honored in her later years both within her country and internationally, in 1977 Ocampo became the first woman elected to the Argentine Academy of Letters. The following comments were made during a speech in 1951 to the Argentine Writer's Society upon receiving the Society's prestigious Prize of Honor:

> I hope that women of the future will be spared the type of struggle for existence that I have gone through. A struggle for intellectual existence. It will be a great economy of effort for them. Not that I deny the value of effort. Nothing can be done without it. But there are efforts that wear one out without compensating for the strain—at least not apparently. They are labors of clearing the way. I have taken part in them without succumbing. The rest I did for pleasure.[6]

Although Spanish-American poetry of the 1920s and 1930s was drawing international interest through the works of such authors as Jorge Luis Borges, Pablo Neruda, Gabriela Mistral, and César Vallejo, the Spanish American novel took longer to mature. The "regional" novel of the era documented the problems created by the dichotomy between the marginalized rural sectors and the cosmopolitan cities; the Chilean Marta Brunet (1901–1967) contributed to this genre with her novel *Montaña adentro* (Deep in the Mountain, 1923). At the same time, and particularly in the era between the world wars, the *narrativa fantástica*, or fiction of the fantastic, was being developed as modernization surged through Spanish-American societies. According to the critic Angel Rama, at this juncture women ventured out of poetry and were incorporated into the new literary currents.

> Woman's alienation in Latin America seemed to bridge out towards fantasy in order that through its dark mirrors it could be able to express itself and, in effect, through this medium began to utter its discontents and dissatisfactions...[7]

A withdrawal from the outside world was necessary so women could document the internal territory of their consciousness—thus the publication in 1924 of *Ifigenia, diario de una señorita que se fastidiaba* (Ifigenia, or The Diary of a Young Lady's Boredom) by the Venezuelan Teresa de la Parra (1891–1936) and her *Memorias de Mamá Blanca* (*Mama Blanca's Souvenirs*, 1929). Other works exploring the inner life are *La última niebla* (*House of Mist*, 1934), by the Chilean María Luisa Bombal (1910–1980) and *Personas en la sala* (People in the Parlor, 1950) by Norah Lange (b. 1906). Clara Silva's (b. 1905) existential novel *La sobreviviente* (The Survivor, 1951) is yet another example. Fantasy not only served to express the intimate and the personal but also provided access to the critical and the philosophical, as in, for example, the oneiric short stories of Silvina Ocampo (b. 1903), the sister of Victoria Ocampo, whose prose and poetry are extremely innovative stylistically with their highly symbolic language that often reflects the subconscious of her characters; and those of the Uruguayan Armonía Somers (b. 1914) in her collection *Todos los cuentos* (All the Stories, 1962), which, as Rama writes, "travel the universe of abjection, as Sartre in *Le mur* (*The Wall*), with a natural talent for dealing with states of nausea and moral and physical deterioration."[8] Even bestsellers like *Bodas de cristal* (Crystal Wedding Anniversary, 1952) by the popular Argentine novelist Silvina Bullrich (b. 1915) contain critical commentary regarding the situation of women and, according to Gabriela Mora, demonstrate the affinity between Spanish-American female narrators prior to the 1960s and women from other latitudes:

> Regardless of the countries in which they lived and because of their sex, women were confined to domesticity with the pursuit of love as the only possibility of personal fulfillment...A few works with obvious feminist intent did not fundamentally depart from this conception of the "nature" of women...[they] presented the home as a prison that swallowed up imaginative and sensitive heroines.[9]

The increased participation of women in the workforce of the 1950s, however, was not ignored, as is shown in Marta Brunet's novel *María nadie* (Maria Nobody, 1957), in which the working protagonist pays a heavy price for her independence and rebellion against middle-class prejudice. And it might be said that women's increased involvement with the world also motivated a return to greater realism.

The 1960s were turbulent times in Spanish America, as they were in much of the world. Guerrilla movements inspired by the Cuban Revolution of 1959 demanded the reforms that were always promised but seldom enacted. Writing and research into the nature of political and social problems in the area proliferated; there was also an increased awareness of the relationship between economic and political dependency and underdevelopment. Appeals for change were even heard from the traditionally conservative Catholic church, as socially conscious clergy developed a liberation theology that inspired and supported peoples' demands for social justice. With rare exceptions, however, democratic trends were reversed, and by 1975, three quarters of Spanish-American governments were military dictatorships.

The preoccupation with Spanish-American identity and political commitment, combined with a quest for a more imaginative use of language and imagery, characterize the novels of the so-called Boom of the 1960s. The unprecedented commercial success outside of Spanish America of such authors as Gabriel García Márquez, Mario Vargas Llosa, and Julio Cortazar, and the technical evolution of Spanish-American narrative resulted in the creation of a growing market for writers and publishers and an increase in readership among the Spanish-speaking middle class. Carlos Fuentes, another of the Boom writers and a literary critic, addressed this situation in 1966, explaining that the authors' attempts to reconcile national or local reality with technical and linguistic creativity grow out of a particular historical situation: "We [Spanish-Americans] live in countries where everything remains to be said, but also where the *way* to say all of this has to be discovered.[10]

Increased social consciousness naturally affected the writing of women during this period, although they did not share the commercial success of their male counterparts. One of the most important Spanish-American women writers of this century, the Mexican Rosario Castellanos (1925–1974) is considered by some as the precursor of the internationally famous male authors mentioned above, in her work *Balún Canán* (*The Nine Guardians*, 1951). Poet, dramatist, essayist, and novelist, in *Balún Canán* Castellanos fuses two of her prime interests: the Indian and women. Her thesis on feminine culture, incorporated into her 1973 book of essays, *Mujer que sabe latín* (*Woman Who Knows Latin*), is considered the "intellectual point of departure for the women's liberation movement in Mexico."[11] An examination of the relationship of women to their culture and the structures of power also appear in Elena Garro's (b. 1920) novel *Los recuerdos del porvenir* (*Recollections of Things to Come*, 1963), in which the failures of the Mexican Revolution are exemplified by acts of violence against women conducted in its name, and in her play *Los perros* (*The Dogs*, 1964), in which the commonplace and socially acceptable custom of abduction and rape in rural Mexican society is meant to be viewed as an emblem of women's vulnerability. Another Mexican novelist and playwright, Luisa Josefina Hernández (b. 1928) also focuses on national problems in her writing, expressing the situation of women within a general social context of exploitation and oppression. Similar social scrutiny is embodied in the work of two Argentine authors: Marta Lynch (b. 1929) in her critique of Peronism in *La afombra roja* (The Red Carpet, 1962) and *Al vencedor* (To the Winner, 1965), and Beatriz Guido (b. 1924) in *Fin de fiesta* (The Game is Over, 1958) in which the historical events leading to Peron's rise to power frame her account of the decadent Argentine aristocracy.[12]

While novels and short stories received most of the critical attention in the 1960s, women poets and dramatists continued to pursue their craft in greater numbers. Styles and tones varied greatly. In Cuba, for example, where radical social change was taking place at a rapid pace, writers responded either by participating in the process or rejecting it for exile. Nancy Morejón's (b. 1944) works continue in the tradition of *negritude* (a cultural and political movement of the 1920s that affirmed black identity and consciousness) begun earlier by such poets as Nicolás Guillén, incorporating the ideas and accomplishments of the revolution. Political events would also affect another Cuban poet, Belkis Cuza Malé, whom the experience of exile would link to the countless Spanish American writers who for a variety of reasons have had to leave their countries and, as Malé says, "venture into the voluntary exile of their sensitivity."[13] And beyond the playwrights mentioned above (Castellanos, Garro, and Hernández), the Argentine Griselda Gambaro (b. 1928) and Myrna Casas (b. 1924) in Puerto Rico would also experiment with absurdist techniques in an attempt to come to terms with the equally absurd and often pessimistic reality for Spanish-American women.

The intensity of the desire to express the complexity of Spanish-American reality affected all the arts and contributed to the creation of the New Song Movement, which owed a debt of gratitude to the lonely and untiring efforts of Violeta Parra (1917–1967) in Chile. Poet, songwriter, and artist, Parra's extensive research into the words and music of the common people inspired songs that went beyond the static folklore of the tourism industry to express the genuine hopes, fears, and aspirations of the Chilean people.

Lyrical poets in the 1960s and 1970s explored the personal with images that ranged from the surreal and irrational in Blanca Varela to the obsessive anguish of Alejandra Pizarnik (1935–1972), whose poems of death and terror are often erotic and inaccessible. Poets experimented with language and form, as is apparent in the distinctive poetry of the Mexican Isabel Fraire (b. 1936) and the poetry and philosophical prose of the Costa Rican Carmen Naranjo (b. 1930), whose works have been called a journey towards an *espacio mental*, or mental space.

The decade of the 1970s marks a turning point for women's writing in Spanish America. The resurgence of the international women's movement as well as the political tensions in the region that witnessed the fall of Salvador Allende's socialist government in Chile (1973), the proliferation of military dictatorships and the torture and "disappearance" of political dissidents, and the victory of the Sandinistas in Nicaragua over the dictator Anastasio Somoza (1979) heightened the consciousness of authors and affected the direction of their writing. Women authors began to receive long-overdue critical attention, and although some critics claim that the writing of contemporary women is identical to that of men, others note distinctions in women's use of new approaches to express the old enduring problems: satire and humor to question the nature of power and expose the hypocrisy of traditional ideas regarding the role of women; a frankly and openly erotic stance; an experimental language that "embodies" new and untried human relationships. Perhaps the most compelling indication is the fact that women writers themselves are aware of a difference and of the need, as writer Luisa Valenzuela (b. 1938) has stated, to "effect a radical change...and not follow the rules of inherited, phallocratic language....To measure our words we will use our own scales. And we will be conscious of our bodies when it comes to the body of our writing."[14] The public and the private are no longer clearly delineated; the idea that the personal is political is firmly rooted in the consciousness of contemporary Spanish-American women writers, from the poetry of the Central Americans Claribel Alegría (b. 1924) and Gioconda Belli (b. 1948) to the novels and short stories of Albalucía Angel (b. 1939), Luisa Valenzuela, Cristina Peri Rossi (b. 1941), and Rosario Ferré, including the recent international best-seller *La casa de los espíritus* (*The House of the Spirits*, 1982) by the Chilean Isabel Allende (b. 1942).

Coinciding with this attempt by artists to articulate a "female voice" in literature is the emergence of other voices, a development that constitutes perhaps the most exciting aspect of female literary participation in Spanish America today. The *novela testimonio*, or documentary novel, and other nontraditional forms that have surfaced as a result of the reevaluation of literary conventions have opened literary participation to the great masses of illiterate and semiliterate peoples of the region and permitted other female voices—repressed, ignored, and forgotten for centuries—to be heard. The recuperation and revitalization of genres and new forms of critical analysis have effectively eroded the boundaries between narrative modes and scientific disciplines.

Among the works of this type are the interviews conducted by Margaret Randall (b. 1938) in *Cuban Women Now* (*Mujeres en la revolución*, 1972); the oral autobiography *"Si me permiten hablar..." testimonio de Domitila, una mujer de las minas de Bolivia* (*Let Me Speak! Testimony of Domitila, a Woman of the Bolivian Mines*, 1977) in which the wife of a tin miner, a woman of amazing courage and determination, speaks of her experiences with acute observations of the economic and social causes of her oppression; and *Me llamo Rigoberta Menchú y así me nació la conciencia* (*I...Rigoberta Menchú: An Indian Woman in Guatemala*, 1983), a Guatemalan peasant's oral account of the trials and sufferings of the "colony within," that is, the Indian peoples of Spanish America and their struggle to maintain their culture and their communities.

One of the most famous works of this type is the documentary novel *Hasta no verte Jesús mío* (*Until I see You Jesus Dear*, 1973) by the Mexican author Elena Poniatowska (b. 1933). The novel is based on recorded conversations with Jesusa Palancares, a working-class woman who reveals her varied life during and after the Mexican Revolution with a richness of expression often found in the powerful and creative language of the people. The choice of Jesusa as a protagonist is a conscious effort on Poniatowska's part to incorporate a new feminine voice into the body of Spanish-American literature. Very few poor and working-class women can be found in patriarchal hispanic literature, particularly outside the usual stereotypes. Interestingly, this new approach approximates the original role of oral literature, which was to document and preserve a collective history as an alternative to the official version, giving a voice to the voiceless.

Finally, among those critics concerned with a feminist literary esthetic there exists also a sense that literary criticism in Spanish America must respond to the region's particular reality and objective needs and that a tradition free of European and North American cultural domination must be forged. In the Mexican feminist journal *Fem*, Margara Russoto reacts to Virginia Woolf's essay *A Room of One's Own* in an article entitled "No basta un cuarto propio" ("A Room of One's Own is Not Enough") by asking:

Why isn't a room of one's own enough? Oh, a room of one's own is insecure; highly dangerous; it seduces too much with the possibility of its being corrupted into an object of pure leisure. And 500 pounds a year isn't enough either; not even if it arrives punctually after the death of some aunt. Rich aunts and dead ones are a difficult combination; they are out of fashion; such types are hardly seen at all in our American world. Our aunts get married young, die crazy, or fall in love with Turkish merchants. And on the other hand, inheritance is a literary matter. And many of us, who don't belong to the "class of educated men"—like Virginia Woolf—will never receive an inheritance...

It is not enough then for the old world to tell us what is enough. To point out its deficiencies as if they were our alternatives, carrying beyond their borders an ideal of literature which is absolute and standarized. Here we are and here we will remain: a people without writing, without ancestral libraries, without memory, without enclosures and without money...Our writing is marginal, treacherous, obscure, clandestine. And in this lies our greatest strength and our particular way of naming the reality that we are living today.[12]

Women authors and literary critics in Spanish America, therefore, are in the process of creating new models, always with an eye to recognizing the interplay between what is read and written and what is lived. Far from being disinterested observers, they are embarking on a critique of literary and cultural structures so as to have a direct affect on the condition of women, uncovering the past and the present in order to transcend it.

NOTES

1. See Virginia Woolf, *A Room of One's Own*. (London: Hogarth Press, 1928; repr. New York: Harcourt, 1963).
2. Jean Franco. *The Modern Culture of Latin America: Society and the Artist* (Harmondsworth, England: Penguin, 1970), 11.
3. Elsa Chaney, *Supermadre: Women in Politics in Latin America* (Austin: University of Texas Press, 1979), 53.
4. (1798–1857). French philosopher, his greatest influence has been in the field of sociology.
5. E. Bradford Burns, *Latin America: A Concise Interpretive History* (Englewood Cliffs, NJ: Prentice-Hall, 1982), 146.
6. Victoria Ocampo, "Misfortunes of an Autodidact," *Contemporary Women Authors of Latin America: New Translations*, ed. Doris Meyer and Margarite Fernandez Olmos (Brooklyn, NY: Brooklyn College Press, 1983), 224. Trans. Doris Meyer.
7. Angel Rama, *La novela en America Latina: Panoramas 1920–1980* (Colombia: Insituto Colombiano de Cultura, 1982), 148, All translations are my own unless otherwise noted.
8. Rama, *La* novela, 149.
9. Gabriela Mora, "Latin American Women Writers: A Renewed Approach to Old and New Issues," *The American Book Review 5*, 6 (September-March, 1983): 6.
10. Carlos Fuentes, "Situación del escritor en América Latina," *Mundo Nuevo*, 1 (July 1966): 17.
11. Helene M. Anderson, "Rosario Castellanos and the Structure of Power" in *Contemporary Women Authors of Latin America: Introductory Essays* (New York: Brooklyn College Press, 1983), 22.
12. Juan Perón (1895–1974) was twice president of Argentina (1946–1955 and 1973–1974). His economic and political programs—grounded in a totalitarian, semifascist

government—known as *peronismo*, continues to be extremely influential in Argentinian politics.

13. Belkis Cuza Malé, "A Woman and Her Poems," in *Contemporary Women Authors of Latin America: Introductory Essays*, 95. Translated by Doris Meyer.

14. Luisa Valenzuela, "The Word, That Milk Cow" in *Contemporary Women Authors of Latin America: Introductory Essays*, 96–97. Translated by Doris Meyer.

15. Margara Russoto, "No basta un cuarto propio," *Fem* 6, 21 (February-March 1982):

BIBLIOGRAPHY

Background

Burns, E. Bradford. *Latin America: A Concise Interpretive History*. Englewood Cliffs, NJ: Prentice-Hall, 1982.

Franco, Jean. *The Modern Culture of Latin America: Society and the Artist*. Harmondsworth, England: Penguin, 1970.

Lavrin, Ascension, ed. *Latin American Women: Historical Perspectives*. London: Greenwood Press, 1978.

Nash, June, and Helen I. Safa, Eds. *Sex and Class in Latin America*. New York: Praeger, 1976.

Pescatello, Ann, Ed. *Female and Male in Latin America*. Pittsburgh, PA: University of Pittsburgh Press, 1973.

Literary Bibliographies and Criticism

Alarcon, Norma, and Sylvia Kossnar. *Bibliography of Hispanic Women Writers*. Bloomington, IN: Chicano-Riqueno Studies, 1980.

Cortina, Lynn Ellen Rice. *Spanish-American Women Writers: A Bibliographical Research Checklist*. New York: Garland Publishing, 1983.

Corvalan, Graciela N.V. *Latin American Women Writers in English Translation: A Bibliography*. Los Angeles: California State University Latin America Studies Center, 1980.

Crow, Mary. "Ten Latin American Women Poets." *Colorado State Review* 7, No. 1 (1979): 3–22.

Dorn, Georgette M. "*Four Twentieth-Century Latin American Authors*." SECOLAS Annals, 10 (1979): 125–33.

Fox-Lockert, Lucia. *Women Novelists in Spain and Spanish America*. Metuchen, NJ: Scarecrow Press, 1979.

Garfield, Evelyn Picon. *Women's Voices from Latin America*. Detroit, MI: Wayne State University Press, 1985.

Knaster, Meri. *Women in Spanish America. An Annotated Bibliography from Pre-Conquest to Contemporary Times*. Boston: G.K. Hall, 1977.

Lewald, Ernest. "Aspects of the Modern Argentine Woman: The Fiction of Silvina Bullrich and Marta Lynch." *Chasqui*, 5, no.3 (1976): 19–26.

Meyer, Doris, and Margarite Fernandez Olmos, Eds. *Contemporary Women Authors of Latin America: Introductory Essays and New Translations*. Brooklyn: Brooklyn College Press, 1983.

Miller, Beth, Ed. *Women in Hispanic Literature: Icons and Fallen Idols*. Berkeley: University of California Press, 1983.

Miller, Yvette, and Charles M. Tatum, Eds. *Latin American Women Writers: Yesterday and Today*. Pittsburgh: Latin American Literary Review, 1977.

Mora, Gabriela, and Karen S. Van Hooft, Eds. *Theory and Practice of Feminist Literary Criticism*. Ypsilanti, MI: Bilingual Press, 1982.

Resnick, Margery, and Isabel de Cortivron, Eds. *Women Writers in Translation: An Annotated Bibliography*. New York: Garland Press, 1981.

Rosenbaum, Sidonia. *Modern Women Poets of Spanish America. The Precursors: Delmira Agustini, Gabriela Mistral, Alfonsina Storni, Juana de Ibarbourou*. New York: Hispanic Institute, 1945.

The Latin American Women—Image and Reality. Special Edition. *Revista/Review Interamericana*, 4, no. 2 (1974).

Zapata, Celia Curreas de. "One Hundred Years of Women Writers in Latin America" *Latin American Literary Review*, 3 (1975): 7–16.

THE UNITED KINGDOM AND IRELAND

Marian Arkin

The term "British literature" has all too often been considered synonymous with English literature, and the rich literary traditions of the Irish, Scottish, and Welsh people, traditions that are older and more long lived than that of the English, are, consequently, ignored. Although this essay is, in the main, about literature written by English women—since so much more of it has been produced in England than in these Celtic regions—it also attempts to serve as an introduction, however brief, to writing by women in Scotland, Wales, and Ireland as well, and writing done in Irish, in Scottish Gaelic, in Scots, and in Welsh as well as in English.[1]

Since much writing before the Renaissance (ca. 1500) was done anonymously, it is difficult to know which writers were women, but we can assume, on sociohistorical grounds, there were very few. Women—and indeed most men—of the Middle Ages (A.D. 700 to 1400) received no formal education and were not expected to read and write. Nevertheless, some English women connected with the Church, the major institution of learning at the time, did manage to become literate and to express themselves privately in writing.[2] It was, however, during the Renaissance and the Jacobean period that followed (ca. 1500 to 1700) that women were first allowed to play significant roles in the English literary tradition. These were times of tumultuous change in English society. Feudalism, in which large landholders maintained political control of the country, was replaced by a more centralized, monarchial form of government. Cities and large towns were built up, and a substantial middle class emerged, newly literate in the vernacular of English and with relatively more time and money to spend on the arts. When Henry VIII broke with the Roman Catholic Church in 1534 and established a Church of England governed by the English monarchy, secular literature was welcomed for the first time. Renaissance ideals, developed in the previous century in Europe, became transformed in England into a kind of humanism that fostered nationalism and individualism along with the study of the classics, art, and music. Concomitant with the humanist love of learning, more women were educated and became literate during this period than ever before—although their number was limited to nobility—and this allowed works of quality to be produced by women, including Queen Elizabeth herself (1533–1603), the highly cultured monarch whose poetry and translations reveal her strength and intelligence.

We see in this period the first stirrings of what can be called a female literary tradition. Mary Sidney Herbert, Countess of Pembroke (1561–1621), sister of Sir Phillip Sidney and muse of his *Arcadia*, was a great patron of the arts, and her home a center of English culture. Her most notable work was a translation and versification of over one hundred of the Psalms into English. The family tradition was carried on by her niece, Lady Mary Wroth (fl.1621), known for *Pamphilia to Amphilanthus*, the first English sonnet sequence by a woman, bound together with controversial prose romance, *The Countess of Montgomerie's Urania* (1621), about political intrigue at the court of James I. Another notable woman writer of the Renaissance, Amelia Lanier (1570?–1649), was probably influenced by Mary

Herbert—whom Lanier compared to Minerva, the Roman goddess of wisdom. Possibly the Dark Lady of Shakespeare's sonnets, according to critic A. L. Rowse, Lanier was a poet of considerable talent; moreover, she reveals her feminist sympathies in her long poem *Salve Deus Rex Judaeorum* (Hail to God, King of Jews, 1611), written in English, in which she retells the Adam and Eve story, vindicating Eve and blaming Adam: "Your fault being greater, why should you disdain,/Our being your equals, free from tyranny?" she demands.

Following the Renaissance, literary production by male writers increased, while a renewed prejudice against educating women in any but the fine and domestic arts was revived. Moreover, most women accepted the prevailing value of female "modesty," which precluded any public literary production, and thus even those women who did become literate and express themselves in writing did not consider it ladylike to publish their work.[3] Others who did publish were often ostracized; Margaret Cavendish, Duchess of Newcastle (1623–1674), a woman of great originality and creativity, was ridiculed by her contemporaries and called the "crazy dutchess" for her metaphysical speculations and eccentric dress. We may best remember her for *Female Orations* (1622), in which she analyzes women's lot and quips: "The truth is, we live like bats or owls, labour like beasts, and die like worms." Like Cavendish, Aphra Behn (1640–1689) was reviled during her lifetime and for years after her death by many members of the critical establishment, who thought that the overt sexual references in her works and her independent behavior were not ladylike. Probably the first female writer in English to support herself by writing, Behn produced plays and novels that range from adventures to domestic comedies; her best known play is *The Rover* (1681), and her most famous novel is *Oroonoko, or the History of the Royal Slave* (1688), which, noted for its attention to detail and psychological realism, is often mentioned as a major forerunner of the modern novel.[4] Other women wrote during this time; several, like Hannah Woolley (1623–?), Bathsua Makin (fl. 1673), and Lucy Hutchinson (ca. 1620), complained about the absence of formal education for women and, later on in the century, Lady Mary Chudleigh (1656–1710) produced two strongly feminist books, *The Ladies' Defense, or the Bride-Woman's Counselor* (1702) and *The Female Advocate: or A Plea for the Just Liberty of the Tender Sex and Particularly of Married Women* (1710) the former in response to a sermon by John Sprint, a Nonconformist minister, about the need for women's total subjugation to their husbands.

In literary terms, the next century in England might be referred to as the century of the novel, for it was during the eighteenth-century that the various forms of extended prose fiction began to develop into the form that many now believe best expresses modern life. A new form, one without established conventions, the novel ideally suited the mass entry of English women into the writing profession. Consequently, a majority of eighteenth-century novelists were women. Fanny Burney (1752–1840), one of that century's leading novelists, gave her works such as *Evelina* (1778) and *Cecilia, or Memories of an Heiress* (1782) a degree of realism and cohesiveness hitherto unknown in the genre. (Later, Jane Austen [1775–1817] would take both theme and title of *Pride and Prejudice* [1813] from *Cecilia*.) Other women writers of the eighteenth-century made important contributions to the novel, as well as to other genres: they include Charlotte Smith (1749–1806), prolific nature poet and novelist; Frances Brooke (1724–1789), novelist and dramatist; widely popular Sara Fielding (1710?–1768), novelist (and sister of Henry); novelist and editor of *The Female Spectator* Eliza Haywood (1693–1756); dramatist and novelist Elizabeth Inchbald (1753–1821); Frances Sheridan (1724–1766), playwright and novelist (and mother of playwright Richard Brinsley Sheridan); Mary Delariviere Manley (1663–1724), novelist, playwright, and journalist; and Sarah Robinson Scott (1723–1795), novelist and historian, whose *Millennium Hall* (1762), about a community of women dedicated to good works, was one of the earliest utopian novels.

A flourishing time for the intellect, the eighteenth century refined the ideals and values, literary and philosophical, of the Restoration (of the monarchy in 1660), including a reverence for the learning of antiquity, and an almost religious belief in science and reason. Such ideas, coupled with relative political peace, promoted the nurturing of genius in every field. Moreover, the Industrial Revolution, which occurred in the latter part of the century, prompted the growth of large urban populations—including a substantial and literate middle class (concomitantly helping to reduce the peasantry to poverty and disease). All of these developments created the conditions for middle-class women to publish in considerable numbers. Many of them wrote for and about other women. For example, Mary Astell (1666–1731)—whom her biographer, Ruth Perry, calls "the first English writer for whom the ideas we call 'feminist' were the central focus of sustained analysis"—wrote several books for women, on their education, and on the institution of marriage. Astell was a strong influence on her contemporaries, including Lady Mary Wortley Montagu (1689–1762), who, in turn, gave Astell financial support. Montagu, like Dorothy Osborne, is known best as a writer of letters, including some to her granddaughter cautioning her against marriage; others contain vivid details of life at that time—in Turkey, where she was wife of the English ambassador, and in England, where she was a member of the Enlightenment's literary community. Astell wrote of the superiority of Montagu's letters to travel letters written by men in her preface to a collection of them (1724). Anne Finch, Countess of Winchelsea (1661–1720), was well known in her day for her moving nature poetry, much praised later by Virginia Woolf; many of her poems meditate on the difficulty of being a female poet.

Of all eighteenth-century women writers, however, it was Mary Wollstonecraft (1759–1797) who has had the most extended influence on English feminism. Although she was born and died in the eighteenth century, Wollstonecraft, with her strong commitment to individual endeavor and liberty, was in lifestyle, temperament, and literary production unquestionably a Romantic (Romanticism was the literary period that flourished between 1798 and 1830). At 28 she wrote *Thoughts on the Education of Daughters* (1787), and at 29 *A Vindication of the Rights of Man* (1788), an analysis of the exploitation of the working class in England and her reply to Edmund Burke's *Reflections on the Revolution in France* (1790). She is best known, however, for *A Vindication of the Rights of Woman* (1792), the first critical analysis of women's condition from a feminist perspective and a work whose radical political viewpoint was strongly influenced by the French Revolution she had witnessed firsthand a few years before. In it she writes about women's "barren blooming," which she attributes to "a false system of education gathered from the books written on this subject by men who, considering females rather as women than human creatures, have been more anxious to make them alluring mistresses than affectionate wives and mothers. . . ."

Frankenstein, the main character in the book written by the daughter Wollstonecraft died bearing, Mary Wollstonecraft Godwin Shelley (1797–1851), can be seen as a tragic symbol of the excesses of the Romantic revolution, technology gone wild. Mary Shelley's radical political perspective presents one of the first critiques of modern industrial society as we understand it. *Frankenstein* (1818) was informed by the Gothic tradition that dominated the last decade of the eighteenth century. Influenced by models from German Romanticism, a great many women excelled at the genre; notable was Ann Radcliffe (1764–1823), whose novels— *The Mysteries of Udolpho* (1794) in particular—were a certain influence on Jane Austen's mock-gothic *Northanger Abbey* (written in 1798; published 1818).

The nineteenth century was a great and productive period for English women writers. It was a century in which for the first time numbers of women wrote with a sense of female self-awareness and communality—as we now can read in great and illuminating detail in recent books on the female literary tradition (Ellen Moers' *Literary Women* [1976], Elaine Showalter's *A Literature of Their Own* [1977] and Dale Spender's *Women of Ideas* [1982]). During the nineteenth century, several women writers were finally recognized within their lifetimes as "major authors" by critics and by the reading public and were, accordingly, quoted and feted along with successful males. Spanning both Romantic and Victorian literary periods (the latter named for the woman who ruled England from 1837 to 1901, longer than any other English monarch), it was the century England became "modern," her writers, philosophers, and politicians charged with a progressive spirit and energy that markedly changed the way English people saw and interpreted their daily lives. Nowhere can we understand the complexities of the nineteenth century better than by looking at women's history in it. For nearly every point of conflict, every dynamic movement or event spelled important changes for women: in the workplace—the factories and shops where women labored often twelve to fifteen hours per day for little pay; in the home, where they had few rights when single, none when married; in institutions of higher learning, to which before the late nineteenth century they were not admitted; in the political arena, where women could not hold office or vote. The nineteenth century saw in England the first labor protection acts, the first laws allowing divorced women control of their incomes and custody of their children, the first women's colleges. It was the beginning of "The Cause," of equal rights for women, and many of the famous reformers of the time, like Florence Nightingale (1820–1910), John Stuart Mill (1806–1873), Caroline Norton (1808–1877), and Barbara Bodichon (1827–1891), worked with great commitment to improve women's position in society. The "woman question," the question of what was woman's place in society, was debated by many in essays and fiction and in a number of small magazines on the subject. Coventry Patmore's poem "The Angel in the House" (1854), about woman's role as domestic "angel" of order and harmony, is especially interesting to us because it is addressed so viscerally in the posthumous essay "Professions for Women" (1942) by Virginia Woolf (1882–1941), who writes, "According to the Angel of the House...[women] must charm, they must conciliate, they must—to put it bluntly—tell lies if they are to succeed. Thus, whenever I felt the shadow of her wing or the radiance of her halo upon my page, I took up the inkpot and flung it at her."

Both men and women wrote abundantly and energetically to express their anxiety and eagerness about the great changes taking place around them. Romantic poetry may seem to have dominated the beginning of the century until one remembers it was also the period in which Jane Austen wrote nearly all her novels and Mary Shelley her *Frankenstein*. Jane Austen, Charlotte Brontë (1816–1855), Emily Brontë (1818–1848), and George Eliot (pseudonym of Mary Ann Evans, 1819–1880) were the first "great" women novelists in the English tradition, the earliest to be commonly anthologized, included in college curriculums, analyzed in books of criticism, and depicted in biographies. The century produced significant women poets as well, particularly Christina Rossetti (1830–1894), included in this anthology, and Elizabeth Barrett Browning (1806–1861). Barrett Browning received much critical and public acclaim for *Sonnets from the Portuguese* (1850), *Casa Guidi Windows* (1851), and *Aurora Leigh* (1856), a novel in verse. Her progressive political intelligence, particularly her advocacy of Abolition, women's rights, antipoverty legislation, and Italian unification, is often revealed in her poetry and other writings.[5]

Two other progressive nineteenth-century writers are Harriet Martineau (1802–1876) and Mrs. Elizabeth Cleghorn Gaskell (1810–1865). Martineau, despite poverty and an illness that left her deaf, worked tirelessly for social reform; her radical feminist beliefs are reflected in her many writings, which included the novel *Deerbrook* (1839), numerous volumes of social and political analysis, and the posthumous *Autobiographical Memoirs* (1877), which contains invaluable details about the literary life of her time. Although hardly as zealous or radical as Martineau, Gaskell, daughter and wife of Unitarian ministers, was also committed to reform; *Mary Barton* (1848) is one of the first novels about the working class, although Gaskell is better known for *Cranford* (1853), with its beautifully detailed scenes of country life, and for her loving, albeit controversial, biography of her friend Charlotte Brontë (1857).

The years encompassed by this anthology, starting in the last quarter of the nineteenth century and going on to contemporary times, represent a watershed for English women writers after years of struggle, repression, and censorship, particularly for the middle-class woman who benefitted directly from the social and political transformations in English society. Virginia Woolf, the great spokeswoman for the female author, was born at the beginning of this period and her essays changed the way modern women think about women writers; as a writer of fiction, moreover, Woolf helped to revolutionize the novel.

Woolf began writing in the Edwardian period (1901–1914), a time often referred to as the "golden afternoon" of British history, although it was in fact a period of tremendous national strife. (For example, industrial strikes were frequent, and the Irish question—of Irish independence from England—resulted in bloodshed and lasting bitterness.) The Fabian Society, a distinguished group of socialist thinkers, flourished during this period and its membership, including such notables as G. B. Shaw, Beatrice (1858–1943) and Sidney Webb and Annie Besant (1847–1933), worked vigorously for economic and social reform. Thousands of women took the woman question to the streets, when suffragettes, under the leadership of Emmeline Pankhurst (1858–1928) and her Women's Social and Political Union (founded in 1903), persisted in marching for women's suffrage, despite the frequent arrests and incarceration of many of their number. Inspired by the woman's movement, "new women" novelists, such as Sarah Grand (1854–1943), George Egerton (pseudonym of Mary Chavelita Dunn, 1859–1945), and Elizabeth Robins (1862–1952) wrote novels calling for women's rights. This period was hardly calm in any other way. Brilliant scientific and technological inventions (such as radio, the cinema, the telegraph, and the telephone) changed the lifestyles of the nation, and artists challenged traditional forms while they transformed and "modernized" the arts.

Challenge and revolution were keynotes of the period that followed; the Modern period (1910–1950) was a turbulent and for many Britons a devastating time covering two world wars, the Anglo-Irish war (1919–1921), and worldwide economic depression (1929–1939). It was, moreover, an extraordinarily dynamic time in women's history. Women over 30 got the vote in 1918 (those from 21 to 29 in 1928) and during the world wars were employed in great numbers to fill (often temporarily) jobs vacated by men going to war.[6] The First World War enabled many women, who otherwise wouldn't have, to travel outside of England as nurses and ambulance drivers and to experience some degree of personal independence. The first woman (Lady Astor) took her seat in parliament in 1919,[7] and in 1920 Oxford University finally opened its doors to women. Sexuality became a topic for study and discussion during this period; women's capacity for sexual pleasure was acknowledged, grudgingly, and a woman's right to practice one of the newly developed means of contraception, as well as to exercise sexual preference, was publicly discussed. Indeed in 1928 Radclyffe Hall (1883–1943) published *The Well of Loneliness*, her ground-breaking book about a woman's discovery of her homosexuality.

One of the earliest writers to describe women's sexuality openly in literature was May Sinclair (1863–1946); two of her novels, *The Three Sisters* (1914) and *Mary Oliver* (1919), broke new ground stylistically as well. Written in an early form of stream-of-consciousness, they had a significant influence on the experimental literature of the first half of the twentieth century, known now as modernist writing, as did the fiction of Dorothy Richardson (1873–1957), who published the first volume of her stream-of-consciousness *Pilgrimage* in 1915. The Bloomsbury group was a focal point of early modernism. Centering around Virginia Woolf and her sister, the artist Vanessa Bell (1879–1961) and their husbands, Leonard Woolf and Clive Bell, and including other important writers and thinkers of the day, Bloomsbury, with its estheticist approach to art and literature, encouraged much in the way of modern writing. After they founded Hogarth Press in 1917, the Woolfs published many of the newer experimental writers, such as T. S.

Eliot, Katharine Mansfield (1888–1923), E. M. Forster, and Woolf herself, as well as translations of important European writers, including Sigmund Freud. Much of the writing by and debate about these modernist works appeared in T. S. Eliot's magazine *The Criterion*. Not everyone accepted modernist writing, however, especially in its earliest years. Critic John Middleton Murray, for example, publisher of the influential *The Adelphi*, attacked Woolf's *Jacob's Room* (1922) for having no plot; she responded with her "Mr. Bennett and Mrs. Brown" (1923), which attacked Arnold Bennett and other traditionalists and championed the modernist approach to literature.

World War I (1914–1918) changed England irrevocably, killing and maiming a great many young Englishmen and leaving a legacy of anger and loss in the literature of its survivors. Several women wrote about these war years and the postwar period that followed. Some, like Enid Bagnold (1889–1981; *Diary without Dates*, 1917), Vera Brittain (1896–1970; *Testament of Youth*, 1933) and Radclyffe Hall (*The Well of Loneliness*) describe their wartime experiences as nurses and, in Hall's case, as an ambulance driver, first hand. Others, like Virginia Woolf (*Mrs. Dalloway*, 1925) and Rebecca West (1892–1983; *The Return of the Soldier*, 1918) write about the war from the point of view of those who remained at home.

In the 1920s and 1930s, partially in response to the Russian Revolution (1917), but also a natural outgrowth of progressive ideas from the past half century in England, much English literature reflected a strong sympathy for socialist ideals. Women, having gotten the vote, regrouped around such causes as reproductive rights, economic parity, and world peace. The Six Point Group was an important political action group of the time, and many of its members wrote for the left-wing feminist journal *Time and Tide*: founded in 1920 by Lady Rhondda (Margaret Haig Thomas [1883–1958]), it published many leading feminist writers, including Vera Brittain, regional novelist Winifred Holtby (1898–1935), Cicely Hamilton (1872–1952), founder of the Women Writers Suffrage League in 1908, Rebecca West, and Elizabeth Robins (1862–1952). And in 1928, tireless Ray Strachey (1887–1940) wrote her sociological history of the woman's movement in England, *The Cause*, a witty, moving document of the position of women in England from Mary Wollstonecraft to the years after World War I and an important testimonial to the women and men who helped women achieve some degree of legal and social equality.

In literary criticism, the 1930s marked the beginning of *Scrutiny*, founded by F. R. Leavis and his wife, scholar and critic Q. D. Leavis (1906–1961). A profoundly influential teacher and writer, F. R. Leavis, in the tradition of Victorian critic Matthew Arnold, postulated that literature as a preserver of culture must serve a moral purpose and that it must not be diluted by popular culture or "bad writing," as *he* defined it. Leavis' "Great Tradition" criticism was continually to bump up against the more sociopolitical literary criticism of Marxists, who see art as an artifact of society, to be analyzed for its ability to reveal the social structure of society and, later, of feminists, many of whom see the Leavisite tradition as exclusionary and lending itself to antifemale positions. (For example, if the Great Tradition includes only a select list of established authors, it reflects educational and publishing policies as much as it does those of "literary value"—and so, necessarily, devalues women's literature even as education and publishing devalue women.)

In the 1930s, the English witnessed the buildup of fascism in Europe, in the main with a remarkable degree of passivity. Katharine Burdekin's dystopic *Swastika Night* (1937) is a chilling prophecy of the mysogyny of fascist ideology as was Virginia Woolf's *Three Guineas*, written the following year. During the 1940s England was again immobilized by war, and the literature produced by writers who lived during World War II reflects the devastating effect it had on people's daily lives. For example, Rebecca West, whose journalistic accounts of the coming of Naziism (*Black Lamb and Grey Falcon*, 1941) and the Nuremburg Trials (*A Train of Powder*, 1947 [excerpted here]) are extraordinarily vivid documents, not only as they depict major events but as they capture small details of the events. One of the most celebrated poets of World War II was noncombatant Edith Sitwell (1887–1964), who had earlier achieved fame for her jazz-age poems *Façade* (1923) and *Gold Coast Customs* (1929) and whose poems about the blitz and the atomic bomb renewed her popularity worldwide.

The Modern period saw a great flowering of women writers, many more than we can include in this anthology. Ivy Compton-Burnett (1884–1969), for example, began her extraordinary writing career in 1925 with *Brothers and Sisters* and went on to produce another twenty highly experimental novels, written almost entirely in dialogue, revealing the cruelty and hypocrisy of Victorian households. Vita Sackville-West (1892–1962) has, in the last two decades, become well known for her close friendship with Virginia Woolf (Sackville-West inspired *Orlando*), for her bisexuality, and for her open marriage with her husband, Nigel Nicholson. In her time, she was respected for her novels and poetry, some of it prize-winning, and numerous essays on horticulture, travel, and literature. Greatly influenced by May Sinclair, Rosamund Lehmann's (b. 1901) novels (including *Dusty Answer*, 1927 and *Invitation to the Waltz*, 1932) are important for their frank treatment of women's sexual awakening and the sensual and emotional aspect of women's lives in general. Nancy Mitford (b. 1904) wrote books such as *The Pursuit of Love* (1945) and *Love in a Cold Climate* (1949), noted for their upper-class settings and witty dialogue. Writer Stevie Smith (1902–1971) is best known for her sardonic, epigrammatic poems about middle-class British life. Writing and illustrating the poems during a thirty-year period (1937–1966), Smith performed them to great effect at 1960s poetry readings. Two of the best known women writers of the century carried on and modernized the gothic and romantic traditions of mystery and romance. Agatha Christie (1890–1976) wrote her first detective novel in 1920 (*The Mysterious Affair at Styles*) and went on to produce sixty-six in all. Dorothy Sayers (1893–1957) created the urbane, romantic Lord Peter Wimsey and the wry, intellectual Harriet Vane as hero/detectives of her very successful mystery fiction.

The war, and then postwar anger and depression, preoccupied artistic consciousness in the 1940s and 1950s. Antiwar and antinuclear feeling were high; concern over the unsuccessful Hungarian uprising (1956) and the cold war dominated English thought. "The Movement," which included such poets as Philip

Larkin and Elizabeth Jennings (b. 1926), was a poetic reaction to the chaos and disorder of World War II, stressing as it did "order" and "clarity." The "Angry Young Men," novelists and playwrights (including John Osborne, John Arden, and Alan Sillitoe) created antiheroes who openly rebelled against authority, while many female fiction writers who began writing in the 1950s, novelists such as Barbara Pym (1913–1980) and Elizabeth Taylor (1912–1975), used satire and irony as a way of expressing *their* dissatisfaction with society.

It was in the 1950s that women's writing in England began to reflect a feminist analysis (that is, social and political concern over women's place in society) evidenced in the political essays of the *Time and Tide* writers, among others, in the 1920s and 1930s. The woman who many feel introduced the new wave of feminist writing into England was Rhodesian-bred Doris Lessing (b. 1919); the Martha Quest novels (1952–1969) and *The Golden Notebook* (1962) contain detailed psychological analyses of modern middle-class women struggling to break out of traditional roles and to find ways to live independently in society. Generally, the new woman's movement was slower to develop in Great Britain than in the United States. With the 1970s, however, several now-classic works of socialist feminist theory began appearing, such as Eva Figes' *Patriarchal Attitudes* (1970), Sheila Rowbotham's *Woman's Consciousness: Man's World* (1973), and Juliet Mitchell's *Woman's Estate* (1971) and one could argue that England is in the vanguard of socialist feminism with writers such as Rosemary Jackson, American-born Cora Kaplan, Judith Lowder Newton, and Terry Lovell analyzing the acts of reading and writing as a social construction. *Spare Rib*, a monthly magazine of women's liberation, was first published in 1972, as an outlet for articles by and about women writers, along with *Writing Women*; *Spinster* publishes new writing by lesbians, while *Feminist Review* is an important forum for writing by socialist feminists. Virago Press, which specializes in works by women, and particularly in recovering forgotten female authors, was founded in 1976; later, more radical feminist houses like Pandora, Onlywomen, Woman's Press, and Sheba emerged. Australian-born editor of the *Women's Studies International Forum* Dale Spender has also contributed much to the recovery of British women's history with her important historical works on feminist theorists and intellectuals (see the Bibliography). Her most recent publication is her Mothers of the Novel series (Pandora, 1986) of reprints of lesser known eighteenth-century women novelists. Also, several journals regularly review of women's writing, as do a number of newsletters from local women's groups. Many contemporary women are increasingly recognized for their creative fiction. Some, like Fay Weldon (b. 1933), known for her strongly satiric novels and radio plays, playwrights Pam Gems (b. 1925) and Caryl Churchill (b. 1938), and novelists Angela Carter (b. 1940) and Elaine Feinstein (b. 1930) identify themselves as feminists, as do younger writers like Sara Maitland (b. 1950), Zoë Fairbairns (b. 1948), Michele Roberts, and Michelene Wandor. Others, like novelists A. S. Byatt (b. 1936), sister of Margaret Drabble (b. 1939). Nina Bawden (b. 1925), Susan Hill (b. 1942), and Beryl Bainbridge (b. 1934) are not as outspoken about their sexual politics, although their works reflect in theme and content the changes taking place in "post-Woman's Movement" England.

In stark contrast to the flourishing tradition of writing by women in England stands the literatures of Ireland, Wales, and Scotland. As in England, the post-Norman period (after A.D. 1066) in Ireland failed to nurture the emergence of women writers, although for different historical reasons than in England. Although women under ancient Gaelic law were the legal equals of men, they lost all rights and power under Norman rule. It is thought that some writers of *Danta Gra* (private poems commingling the bardic and courtly styles) were women, although most of these poems, written between 1350 and 1650, were produced anonymously, and many manuscripts were later destroyed by the British; so it is difficult to be certain of women's contribution. One woman thought to have written in this tradition is Brid O'Donnell, a member of the Gaelic aristocracy, but little is known about her.

Gaelic literature was irrevocably weakened in Ireland when the British defeated the Irish at the Battle of Kinsale (1602), thereby destroying the Gaelic aristocracy that had long supported the production of its literature. As a popular language, however, Gaelic did retain a certain vitality,[8] and one of the greatest works in post-Norman Irish was written by a woman: Eibhlin Dubh Ni Chonaill (1747–1805) authored the famous "Caoineadh Airt Ui Laoghaire" (Lament for Art O'Leary, 1773), a tender, angry poem written for the poet's slain husband, which stands as a testimonial to a cruel time in history when Ireland was governed by the harsh British penal laws. Maria Edgeworth (1768–1849), although Irish-born, comes from a very different tradition from Eibhlin Dubh's, that of the Anglo-Irish, those descendents of the English and Scottish colonists who confiscated the land of the defeated native Irish in the early seventeenth century. Edgeworth was educated in England, returning at 15 to live on her father's estate and helping him raise his twenty-one other children. She wrote several books on education, including *Letters to Literary Ladies* (1795), which called for education for women. She is most important, however, for *Castle Rackrent* (1800), a novel about the problem of absentee landlordism; considered the first Irish novel, it was a strong influence on the "Scottish novels" of Sir Walter Scott. Lady Sydney Morgan (1783–1859), writer of many novels and good friends with Mary Shelley and Lady Caroline Lamb (1785–1828), also influenced Scott and was highly regarded by the Romantic poets. Anglo-Irish, like Edgeworth, she is also known for her work supporting Irish emancipation and women's liberation. Indeed, her two-volume history of women, *Woman and Her Master* (1840; repr. 1976), was a beacon of early feminism.

The nineteenth century was, in the main, a catastrophic period in Irish history, for Ireland was visited by a series of famines; the worst, which occurred between 1845 and 1849 and was known as the Great Hunger, was caused by the failure of the potato crop, for one-third of the population of Ireland the only source of food and income. As a result of famine, over a million people died and another million emigrated, reducing the population of the country by one quarter in five years. It was not until the latter part of the nineteenth century that Ireland recovered from this tragedy sufficiently to concentrate on the arts. Then began a remarkable period in Irish literature known as the Irish Revival. Lasting until the 1920s, the Revival is marked by a renewed literary involvement in Irish history, culture, and language.

Feelings of nationalism were very strong during this period and culminated in the Anglo-Irish War (1919–1921) and independence for part of Ireland. One of the most influential Irish writers of this time was the Anglo-Irish Lady Augusta Gregory (1852–1932), playwright, patron of the Irish arts, and cofounder of the Abbey Theatre. The post-Revolutionary period, an especially prolific time for male Irish writers, also saw the early work of two other Anglo-Irishwomen, Elizabeth Bowen (1899–1973) and Molly Keane (b. 1904) while Kate O'Brien (b. 1904), began writing about middle-class Irish-Catholic domestic life in the late 1920s, producing more than a dozen, extremely well-regarded plays and novels.

Women writers in Ireland have been relatively productive in the past few decades, at least those writing in English. Anglo-Irish novelist and philosopher Iris Murdoch (b. 1919) is probably the most distinguished; she has written many fine novels and works of philosophy and, in 1978, won the Booker Prize for her novel *The Sea*. Edna O'Brien (b. 1930) is the best known, but there are many others being read and reviewed, such as novelists Julia O'Faolain (b. 1932) and Jennifer Johnston (b. 1930) and poets Eithne Strong (b. 1923), Eavan Boland (b. 1944) Eileen Ni Chuilleanain (b. 1942), and Madbh McGuckian (b. 1950). Maire Mhac an tSaoi (b. 1922), considered one of the finest poets writing in Irish, is the sole representative in this anthology of the few Irish-language women writers. Works by these writers tend to focus on religion and sexuality, although politics has become an increasingly compelling topic for Irish women writers since the current troubles between Protestants and Catholics in Northern Ireland began in 1969.

Because of its Irish beginnings (Scots migrated from Ireland in the sixth century A.D.), the Gaelic of Ireland was for nearly ten centuries the literary language of the Scottish Highlands and the Western Islands, and Scotland and Ireland shared not only a language but characters and themes to people their legends. Moreover, the classic bardic poetry was the same, for official Scottish poets trained in Ireland. By the sixteenth century, a distinctly Scottish Gaelic literature emerged from the spoken vernacular, probably begun in ballads recited orally. Undoubtedly women participated as writers and singers in this oral culture, although the names of these women are not preserved in history. The translation of the Bible into vernacular Gaelic in the seventeenth century formalized Scottish Gaelic, but as the literature of a sparsely populated region, it has remained a language of a small minority. In contrast is Scots, the Anglo-Saxon–derived language of Lowland Scotland, which became the vernacular of a great majority of the Scottish population during the Renaissance, and until the Reformation in the sixteenth century a fair amount of narrative poetry was written in Scots. The Reformation and ascension of Scottish James I to the English throne in 1603 changed the course of literature written in Scots. An English version of the Bible was widely distributed, and reading in English was encouraged. Moreover, the Court (and thus courtly patronage) moved from Scotland to England. Both events significantly diminished the prestige of Scots as a literary language, a situation that persisted until the eighteenth century, when the first Scots Revival, led by such poets as Allan Ramsey (1686–1758) and Robert Burns (1759–1796) revitalized the use of Scots, which they called "Lallans." The second Scottish Revival began after World War I; popularized by Hugh MacDairmid (Christopher Murray

Grieve, 1892–1978) this movement, for a brief thirty years, breathed new life into poetry written in Scots which MacDairmid modified and called Lallans, after the Scots of the first Revival. Writing in pre-MacDairmid Scots continued, however, and Violet Jacob (1863–1946), Marion Angus (1866–1946), and Helen Cruik-shank (1886–1975) all wrote their poetry in conventional Scots during this period.

Most Scottish prose writers, however, wrote in English. Sir Walter Scott, although he began as a poet, is best known for his immensely popular romances, which in the nineteenth century turned the whole focus of Scottish literature in the direction of the novel. His works, which often included Scottish settings, themes, and dialogues, had a strong influence on Scottish novelist Susan Edmonstone Ferrier (1782–1854), who contributed to the important Scottish journal *Black-wood's Edinburgh Magazine* and wrote novels about contemporary manners, including *Marriage* (1818), *The Inheritance* (1824), and *Destiny* (1831). The latter part of the nineteenth century saw the works of the prolific Margaret Oliphant (1828–1887), who wrote over 100 novels and many articles to support her own and her brother's family. Her major work was a series of novels called *Chronicles of Carlingford* (1863–1876) about a small town outside London. Also writing during this period was Florence Douglas Dixie (1855–1905), a Scottish nationalist who set many of her novels in her native land.

The prose tradition has predominated among modern Anglo-Scottish writers, such as Naomi Mitchison (b. 1897), whose novels, written in English and often set in the past, include *The Corn King and the Spring Queen* (1931), *The Blood of the Martyrs* (1939), and *The Big House* (1950). An important contemporary prose writer is Elspeth Davie (b. 1919), known for her realistic depiction of modern urban life in Scotland. Muriel Spark (b. 1918), an expatriate who is probably the best known Scottish writer today, only occasionally uses Scotland as her setting, although one of her most popular works, *The Prime of Miss Jean Brodie* (1961), is set in the Edinburgh of Spark's birth. Nonetheless, other written arts have not been neglected by Scottish women. On two sides of the coin, Liz Lochhead (b. 1947) is a major force in poetry while Ena Stewart Lamont (b. ca. 1900) will have her 1945 drama, *Men Should Weep*, performed at an International Women's Playwriting Festival in 1988.

Literature in Welsh in its outlines shares much with Scottish-language litera-ture. Vigorous in its bardic form (a form in which only males were trained) in the Middle Ages and the Renaissance, it has had to struggle for survival in the twentieth century. As in Highland Scotland, the translation of the Bible in the sixteenth century fixed the spoken vernacular and allowed for the development of modern literary Welsh, which, while it was spoken by a large majority of the people, was a language without official status. As in seventeenth-century Scotland, many Welsh writers went to London with the ascension of the Welsh Tudor King Henry VII (1457–1509) and wrote in English. The Methodist revival in the eighteenth century, however, gave new energy to Welsh by establishing schools to teach people to read the Welsh Bible, and by the nineteenth century a literature in modern Welsh was highly developed. One of the major writers of the revival was Ann Griffiths (1776–1805), who converted to Methodism at 20 and is known for her intense and passionate hymns—considered some of the most exquisite in Welsh—and for letters written to Methodist minister John Hughes between 1800 and 1804, describing Methodist meetings of the time in vivid detail. Writing half a century later in English was Emily Jane Pfeiffer (1827–1890), called by some the Elizabeth Barret Browning of Wales. Pfeiffer published six volumes of poetry, most important among them *Sonnets and Songs* (1877) and *Under the Aspens* (1882). Another notable Victorian Welsh woman was Amy Dillwyn (1845–1935), idiosyncratic feminist novelist (and businesswoman) whose works tell about the suppressed lives of women of the period. The nineteenth century produced several female members of Welsh nobility who worked to promote the cause of Welsh literature. Lady Charlotte Guest (1802–1895) translated *The Mabinogion* (1846), twelve medieval Welsh stories (some about the Camelot legend) that are of great significance to students of early Welsh culture. Lady Augusta Hall (1802–1896) was a prominent patron of *Cymreigyddion y Fenni*, a cultural society that held important yearly *eisteddfod*.[9] Prose writing in modern Welsh was popularized in the nineteenth century by the founding of several periodicals, including *Yr Amserau* (1843), which merged with the important *Y Faner* (1859); but it was Anna Adaliza Beynon Puddicombe (1836–1908), writing in English under the name of Allen Raine, whose novels, such as *A Welsh Witch* (1902) and *Hearts of Wales* (1905), familiarized the English-speaking reader with Welsh life and customs.

Prose writing is also an area where twentieth-century Welsh women writers excel. Aside from Kate Roberts (1891–1985), who appears in this anthology and is called by some the Thomas Hardy of Wales, several Welsh women have distinguished themselves. Kate Bosse-Griffiths (b. 1910), scholar and novelist, has gained repute for the frank treatment of sexual material in her Welsh-language novels. English-born writer Peggy Eileen Whistler (pseudonym Margiad Evans, 1909–1958 wrote vivid, passionate novels and short stories about the conflicting loyalties of those living in the border lands between Wales and England (for example, *Country Dance*, 1932). Hilda Vaughan's (b. 1892) novels, mainly set in Radnorshire County, where her father was Clerk of the County Council, and, like Evans', written in English, depict the speech and customs of that area of Wales, especially in *The Battle to the Weak* (1925) and *The Invader* (1928). Two distinctive twentieth-century Welsh poets are Brenda Chamberlain (1912–1971), who is anthologized here, and Dilys Cadwaladr (1902–1979), the Welsh-language poet and short-story writer who was the first woman to win the crown at the National Eisteddfod (1953). Gillian Clarke (b. 1937), Marion Eames (b. 1921), and Eigra Lewis Roberts (b. 1939) are fit examples of the vigor of women's participation in the contemporary literary scene in Wales; aside from editing the *Anglo-Welsh Review* from 1976 to 1984, Clarke has published several collections of poetry in English and is highly regarded in Wales and England. Eames, who writes in Welsh, has produced four historical Welsh-language novels on Welsh subjects (two have been translated into English), noted for their psychological realism and historical detail. Roberts, also writing in Welsh, has produced novels about the problems of contemporary women as well as essays about notable women of Wales and biographical works on her countrywomen Ann Griffiths, Dilys Cadwaladr, and New Zealand writer Katherine Mansfield.

One cannot be optimistic about the future of those women writing in the national tongues of Irish, Welsh, Scots, or Scottish Gaelic. Although there have been literary revivals in each of the four languages, the tremendous popularity of English over-shadows all other writing in the United Kingdom and Ireland—and few works get translated into English. Thus, an Irish, Welsh, or Scots writer knows she will have a far smaller readership than she would if she had written in English. For most Celtic language writers, writing in their own tongue is a conscious political deci-sion (for all these writers are bilingual) but also one that will virtually ensure obscurity. Despite this, many fine women writers of this century have made this decision and, despite great odds, have achieved critical prominence.

What the future holds for women writing in English in the United Kingdom remains to be seen. There have been some notable absences from the literary scene. Few works by women of color have been published, except in small magazines, although some writers are emerging. And while Shelagh Delaney's (b. 1939) working-class *A Taste of Honey* (1956) was extremely popular, as were the novels of Nell Dunn (b. 1936; *Up the Junction* 1963, and *Poor Cow* 1967, which vividly capture working-class dialogue), working-class women writers are still rarely heard from in English writing. Many socioeconomic problems plague British society. The class system is everpresent, leaving few spaces in the socioeconomic hierarchy for minorities; the troubles in Ireland persist, dividing the island; and unemployment is high, especially among people of color, who are, in the main, immigrants from former British colonies. Traditionally, women suffer the most in times of economic and/or political distress and are, thus, doubly afflicted. In that dim light, the fact that more women than ever before are publishing in the United Kingdom and Ireland must be seen as a promising sign.

NOTES

1. A brief linguistic history of the United Kingdom and Ireland might be useful here. From ca. 800 B.C. the British Isles were inhabited by Celtic tribes from Europe and in 55 B.C. also by the Roman army of occupation. Angles, Saxons, and Jutes from Northwest Germany invaded England in the sixth and seventh centuries A.D., driving many Celts to what is now Ireland, Scotland, Wales, and Cornwall, and bringing with them a form of English with strong Germanic elements (Old English). This English became so strongly rooted that when in the eleventh century the Normans from France overthrew the Anglo-Saxon princes, they were unable to establish French as more than a language of the court. In 1362, English, then in its Middle form and containing aspects of Norman French and Church Latin as well as traces of Scandinavian languages from the eighth-century Viking invasions, was officially installed as the language of England. When in 1536 England and Wales were joined politically and in 1707 England and Scotland, English became the official language of Scotland and Wales as well.

   According to the Act of Union in 1801, Ireland was considered part of England, until 1921 when Southern Ireland gained its independence from the United Kingdom, establishing the Irish Free State; the six counties of Northern Ireland still remain part of the United Kingdom. Irish (or Gaelic), a branch of Celtic, and English are Ireland's official languages. Scottish Gaelic and Manx, two languages descended from Irish, are still spoken in isolated sections of the Scottish Highlands and the Isle of Man. A form of British (or Brythonic), the other branch of Celtic, is used in rural Wales, and a related form was used in Cornwall until the end of the eighteenth century. From the eleventh century a dialect of English, derived from Anglo-Saxon, called Scots, emerged in Scotland

and during the Renaissance replaced Gaelic as the spoken language of the majority of Lowland Scots. Scots, in its various and unregulated forms, remain the language of many Scottish people.

2. Two such writers were the religious mystics Julian of Norwich (1342–1416?), who vividly recorded her revelations in *A Book of Showings* and Margery Kempe (1373?–?), who dictated the story of her life, *The Book of Margery Kempe*, the first English autobiography, to scribes.

3. For example, Dorothy Osborne (1627–1695) wrote detailed letters, which vividly capture aspects of life at that time, to her future husband, William Temple. In one of her letters Osborne rebukes Margaret Cavendish for her immodesty. Osborne's friend Katherine Phillips (1631–1664), the esteemed poet and playwright known as Orinda in her Scottish literary circle, was horrified when her poems were published without her consent and insisted on their being withdrawn and a public disclaimer issued.

4. Both of these women are described vividly by Virginia Woolf. About Cavendish, Woolf writes in *The Common Reader* (1925): "Garish in her dress, eccentric in her habits, chaste in her conduct, coarse in her speech, she succeeded during her lifetime in drawing upon herself the ridicule of the great and the applause of the learned." In *A Room of One's Own* (1929), Woolf notes Behn's exemplary position: "Now that Aphra Behn had done it, girls could go to their parents and say, You need not give me an allowance, I can make money by my pen."

5. *The Madwoman in the Attic* (1979) by Sandra Gilbert and Susan Gubar gives a trenchant feminist reading of the aforementioned nineteenth-century English woman writers, among others, using the first Mrs. Rochester (from Charlotte Brontë's *Jane Eyre*, 1847) as a symbol of these repressed and entrapped women artists.

6. Many of these jobs were taken away from women after the war was over and social programs instituted to "convince" women that their places were in the home. However, women did make inroads into the male workplace during the wars and these women workers helped to change, irrevocably, the common conception of "women's work."

7. The first woman actually elected to the British Parliament was Irishwoman Constance Marcewicz in 1918. She, however, refused to take her seat as part of the Irish protest against British rule in Ireland.

8. See *An Duanaire* (The Poem Book, 1981), a bilingual anthology of poetry from 1600 to 1900, covering the years between the fall of the Gaelic aristocracy and the emergence of English as Ireland's dominant language.

9. The *eisteddfod* originated as meetings of Welsh bards in medieval times to regulate the complex metric systems of poetry. Revived in the nineteenth century, these gatherings are now a week-long annual cultural competition governed by a national society, although local *eisteddfod* are held all over Wales, suggesting the significance of literary tradition in the cultural life of the country.

BIBLIOGRAPHY

Background

Lewis, Jane. *Women in England*. Bloomington: Indiana University Press, 1984.

Mill, John Stuart. *The Subjection of Women*. 1869. Repr. Harmondsworth, England: Penguin, 1974.

Mitchell, Juliet. *Women, the Longest Revolution*. New York: Pantheon, 1984.

Spender, Dale. *Time and Tide Waits for No Man*. London: Pandora Press, 1984.

Strachey, Ray. *The Cause: A Short History of the Women's Movement in Great Britain*. Bell, 1928, Repr. London: Virago, 1978.

Vicinus, Martha, ed. *A Widening Sphere: Changing Roles of Victorian Women*. Bloomington: Indiana University Press, 1977.

Wollstonecraft, Mary. *A Vindication of the Rights of Women*. 1792. Repr. New York: Norton, 1981.

Woolf, Virginia. *A Room of One's Own*. Hogarth Press, 1928. Repr. New York: Harcourt, 1963, 1974.

Literary History

Albinski, Nan. *The Well-Ordered Paradise: British and American Women's Utopian Fiction*. Beckenham, England: Croom Helm, 1988.

Figes, Eva. *Sex and Subterfuge*: *Women Writers to 1850*. London: Macmillan, 1982.

Gilbert, Sandra M., and Susan Gubar. *Women's Literature: The Tradition in English*. New York: Norton, 1985.

Goreau, Angeline. *The Whole Duty of a Woman: Female Writers in Seventeenth-Century England*, New York: Dial Press, 1985.

Jeffreys, Sheila. *The Spinster and Her Enemies: Feminism and Sexuality, 1880–1930*. London: Pandora Press, 1985.

Ni Chuilleanain, Eileen, ed. *Irish Women: Image and Achievement*. Dublin: Arlen House, 1985.

Rogers, Katherine and William McCarthy. *The Meridian Anthology of Early Women Writers*. New York: New American Library, 1987.

Showalter, Elaine. *A Literature of Their Own: British Women Novelists from Brontë to Lessing*. Princeton, NJ: Princeton University Press, 1977.

Spender, Dale. *Women of Ideas (and What Men Have Done to Them)*. London: Ark, 1983.

Stephens, Meic. *The Oxford Companion to the Literature of Wales*. Oxford: Oxford University Press, 1986.

Literary Criticism

Batslow, Janet, Tony Davies, Rebecca O'Rourke, and Chris Weedon. "Remembering Feminism and the Writing of Women." In *Rewriting English*, 106–139. London: Methuen, 1985.

Freyer, Grattan, ed. *Modern Irish Writing*. Tarrybaun, Bofeanaun, Ballina: Irish Humanities Center, Ltd., 1979.

Gilbert, Sandra, and Susan Gubar. *The Madwoman in the Attic*. New Haven, CT: Yale University Press, 1978.

Schofield, Mary Anne and Cecilia Macheski. *Fetter'd and Free? British Women Novelists 1660–1815*. Columbus: Ohio State University Press, 1986.

Spender, Dale. *Feminist Theorists: Three Centuries of Women's Intellectual Tradition*. London: The Women's Press, 1982.

Wandor, Michelene, ed. *On Gender and Writing*. London: Pandora Press, 1983.

Woolf, Virginia. *Three Guineas*. London: Hogarth Press, 1938. (Repr. New York: Harcourt, 1963).

The Virago Publishing Company (London) has since 1976 been reprinting works by nineteenth- and twentieth-century, predominantly "British" women writers. The Mothers of the Novel reprint series, published by Pandora Press, has, beginning in 1986, reprinted eighteenth- and nineteenth-century, novels. This series, edited by Dale Spender, includes introductions to the novels by contemporary women novelists.

THE UNITED STATES

Barbara Shollar

The extraordinary freedom and feistiness of the American woman has been pointed out by foreign travelers such as Frances Trollope and by Henry James who called her the heiress of all the ages. It is not surprising, then, that she should have played a significant role in the country's literary tradition, although many of her accomplishments have been obliterated from its literary history. Such an essay as this cannot hope to wholly encompass the richness of women's contribution. Instead, it will focus on the feminist tradition and particularly on two periods when feminism was the single greatest impetus to women's writing. The periods from 1875 to approximately 1930, and from 1960 on were informed by a strong women's movement; the possibilities for liberation, as well as the obstacles to its realization, dictated the narrative strategies of women's plots and the symbols and themes of women's poetry.

The period that followed the Civil War was marked by both industrialization and extensive outward movement along a frontier that was closing fast after 1886. At the same time, an extraordinary immigration of largely non-Protestant groups began to swell the cities, bringing with it ideas and customs quite alien to the United States. The disparities between rich and poor were very great; intense labor unrest, agrarian discontent, as well as frequent economic panics, also contributed to a widespread sense of uncertainty.

Yet capitalist industrialization had positive effects for middle-class, white urban women: after 1875 a domestic revolution that included such innovations as gas lighting, municipal water systems, domestic planning, canning, commercial production of ice, as well as commercial laundry machines, and the popularization of the sewing machine freed them from many household burdens. But these women were isolated from two-thirds of the female population who still worked on the farm and in frontier settlements and the nearly 20 percent of the four million women in 1880 who were already a part of the *paid* workforce. Moreover, by 1910, nearly 33 percent of the women in cities—a significant number of them immigrants—worked outside the home; and among black women the figure was probably twice that.

Ideologically, middle-class women were subject to two conflicting forces: the Victorian ideal of femininity and the female ideal of equality that dominated the rhetoric of the women's movement initiated in mid-century and that was recast in more modern terms at the century's end. Antislavery had provided a vocabulary that could be and was adapted to the women's movement; the Civil War gave white women the opportunity to become self-sufficient and to develop skills that they grew reluctant to forswear. This was especially true in the South where a more exaggerated ideal of womanhood had been linked to the Southern cause.[1] The temperance movement, begun in 1874 with the Women's Christian Temperance Union, was the base for women who were not yet prepared to fight the issue of women's equality directly. Not only did it include a vast membership, it also cut across class divisions as no other organization did.

Paradoxically, the domestic sphere to which middle-class women were restricted by the Victorian ideal gave them a base from which to challenge the status of women and the status quo of the larger society. This was paralleled in literature: the local color movement used local landscapes and dialect and drew on communal mores to produce narratives that frequently contested the accepted roles for women and the conventional social arrangements and definitions of reality.

A number of the women who developed this feminist literary tradition were friends and mentors, and they derived ideas from one another. Two women stand at the head of this tradition, one a writer, the other a critical supporter: Harriet Beecher Stowe (1811–1896) and Annie Fields (1834–1915). As the wife of the editor of the newly founded *Atlantic Monthly* (est. 1857), Fields played a significant role in nurturing the talent of such writers as Rose Terry Cooke (1827–1892), Harriet Prescott Spofford (1835–1921), Louise Chandler Moulton (1835–1908), Elizabeth Stuart Phelps Ward (1844–1911), Julia Ward Howe (1819–1910), Sarah Orne Jewett (1849–1909), Alice Brown (1857–1948), and Stowe. Later, the Irish Roman Catholic poet Louise Imogen Guiney (1861–1920) would also find her way into this Anglo-Saxon Protestant circle. Jewett influenced Mary Wilkins Freeman (1852–1930) and subsequently served as a mentor to Willa Cather (1873–1974).[2] This last link is a clear example of the way that the center of the women's literary tradition moved westward and south.

In general, these writers used the short story as the form for their expression, although many of their works are not collections of discrete stories but complexly organized wholes, bound by issues of territorial appropriation and "at homeness" that endow "domestic" concerns with social, political, and metaphysical significance. Alice Brown's *Meadow-Grass: Tales of New England Life* (1895) and *Tiverton Tales* (1899) serve as examples. Thematically, Brown is concerned not to retrieve or sentimentalize the past so much as to underscore its inadequacy to the present, and many of the stories are concerned with individuals' failure or success in meeting change. Thus, one of her few "heroes," Miss Lucindy, seizes the opportunity of her father's death to liberate herself, violating social proprieties by buying gaudy bonnets, riding horses, and most important, adopting and raising a child on her own.

Similarly, Sarah Orne Jewett's *The Country of the Pointed Firs* (1896) privileges the two women in her tales, and their refusal to violate nature is the source of harmony in an otherwise isolated and increasingly alienated community. *The Land of Little Rain* (1903) and *Lost Borders* (1909), works of the neglected southwestern writer Mary Austin (1868–1934), use the Amer-Indian community and its lore as the touchstone of an authentic relation to the land. Both women write feminist-based critiques of the dominant social arrangements and power relationships.

Using the novel form, writers extended the boundaries of what constituted women's sphere, going beyond the portrait of the self-reliant woman that was a staple of popular fiction and developing narratives that had no textual precedents. Their works incarnated a separatist ethic that was sanctioned by both aspects of the Victorian ideal of women—feminine domesticity and equality. Jewett's *A Country Doctor* (1884) is perhaps one of the earliest works about a girl's coming to maturity, a *bildungsroman* that ends not in marriage but in the protagonist's renewed determination to pursue her career in the face of considerable prejudice and discrimination. *A Listener in Babel* (1903) by Vida Scudder (1861–1954) is another such *bildungsroman*. Her friend and lover Florence Converse (1871–1967) was one of the first to present a woman-identified love relationship as an explicit alternative to marriage in *Diana Victrix* (1897). Both Converse in *The Children of Light* (1912) and Charlotte Perkins Gilman (1860–1935) in *What Diantha Did* (1910) depicted cooperative living arrangements that made possible and sustained the careers women forged for themselves.[3]

Another version of the feminist narrative appeared in the works of Myra Kelly (1875–1910), Helen Campbell (1839–1918), and Anna C. Ruddy (n.d.). At the center of the novels by these women is the settlement worker or teacher—obviously types of the "new woman"—who travels into the alien territory of the "other," and whose point of view guides us in the reconstruction of our attitudes toward "those less fortunate than ourselves."[4] These condescending works barely compensated for the rabid prejudices of the time; their real importance lay in sanctioning a wider sphere for women.

But for most middle-class women, careers were alternatives to marriage and marriage meant an effective end to the development of their autonomy and, by extension, to their careers. Kate Chopin's *The Awakening* (1899) was probably the most radical novel of the period. Without apology, Chopin (1851–1904) depicted Edna Pontellier's gradual awakening to her own body and desires; by showing the protagonist's lack of options so clearly, Chopin made her heroine's suicide inevitable. Shortly after Chopin, Edith Wharton (1862–1937) concluded *The House of Mirth* (1905) with the similarly ambiguous suicide of her heroine in a novel that is otherwise quite different from Chopin's in tone, content, and theme.

If the stark realism of the novel pointed to the social traumas of the period, the imaginary worlds described in utopias showed that women remained optimistic and assumed that life could be changed for the better. The genre appeared and dominated the 1890s as part of a larger political ferment in which anarchists, socialists, and other reformers offered their solutions for the difficulties of American life. Women contributed some sixty utopian works, beginning with the Gates trilogy (1868–1887) of Elizabeth Stuart Phelps Ward. Stylistically and structurally innovative, these early developments in speculative fiction experiment with women-centered narratives. Thus, Mary H. Lane (n.d.) first created an all-female society in her *Mizora: A Prophecy* (1889), anticipating the work of Charlotte Perkins Gilman ("Herland," 1915) as well as the feminist utopian revival of the 1970s led by such writers as Ursula Le Guin (b. 1929) and Joanna Russ (b. 1937). Similarly Anna Dodd's *Republic of the Future* (1887) foreshadowed the narrative structures and themes of later dystopias and science fiction. Yet Dodd (n.d.) overtly mocks women's aspirations, while Lane reproduces in feminized form her society's "ideal of Anglo-Saxon racial superiority."[5]

If in creating new worlds, white women drew a condescending and stereotypic portrait of themselves and those groups defined as "the other," then immigrant, indigenous, and black women authored texts that attempted to define their subjective experience. Such writing presented real difficulties, however. The pressure to assimilate during this time was great, and a number of the works are poignant documents of an American identity forged at the price of any identifiable ethnicity. Yet the adoption of the dominant language or rhetoric created the possibility for dialogue and resulted in the first major corpus in American English of what is termed ethnic literature.[6]

In two series, *Idylls of the Gass* (1901) and *A Renegade and Other Tales* (1905), Martha Wolfenstein (1869–1906)[7] recreated the activities of the village of Moritz in the Austrian Empire, and in particular the relationship between the town baker Maryam and her grandson Shimmele. Her 1905 collection, with its numerous variants of gentile-Jewish relationships, and their possibilities for conversion, apostasy, and assimilation, was located in the Old World but suggested the anxieties that haunted Jews in America as much as it reflected her desire to reassure Christian readers. In poetry, too, Emma Lazarus (1849–1887) felt compelled to create a self-conscious ethnic identity in the wake of the pogroms in Europe and anti-Semitic incidents in America: celebrating Jewish history, she demanded that the United States fulfill its destiny as a sanctuary for all exiles.

Other writers marked the conflicts inherent in being what Woodrow Wilson and Theodore Roosevelt called hyphenated Americans. The Sioux Zitkala-Sa (1876–1938), writing as Gertrude Bonnin, began publishing in the *Atlantic Monthly* in 1900. In "The School Days of an Indian Girl," she depicted the painful "journey" of education/assimilation experienced by an ignorant child enticed by adventure and incited by her envy of others. The price of her assimilation, as described by Zitkala-Sa, is the inevitable denigration of personal qualities and customs valued by her Indian culture but scorned or ignored by white society.

The Asian-American literary tradition also began with this century. Sui Sin Far (the pseudonym taken by Edith Eaton, 1867–1914), offspring of an English father and Chinese mother, became not only the first to depict the Chinese positively but also one of the first writers to identify racism and sexism as stemming from the same impulse. In stories published from the 1890s on, some of which were collected in *Mrs. Spring Fragrance*, Sui Sin Far showed women suffering under a double prejudice from whites and from their more Americanized husbands. Using titles such as "The Land of the Free," Sui Sin turned the rhetoric of American democracy against itself; it was an ideal standard against which the legal expulsion of Chinese from their homes in California, hundreds of murders and lynchings, and finally the exclusion of Chinese from this country beginning in 1882 needed to be judged. When Maria Christina Mena (1893–?) began to publish in *Century Magazine*, the Chicana's voice was also added to the multi-ethnic strains of the period.

Blacks during this period fell prey to systematic oppression by Jim Crow laws, were denigrated in racist theories given a scientific basis by Darwinism, and subject to lynchings (the official number put at over 1600 in the 1890s). Predictably, black women writers used fiction as a weapon of protest. Perhaps unwittingly, however, the prototypical image of the light-skinned mulatto heroine to be found in their novels reinforced the notion of the Victorian feminine ideal. Yet the "tragic mulatto" heroine in such works as Frances E. W. Harper's *Iola Leroy* (1892) and Pauline Hopkins' (1895–1930) *Contending Forces* (1900) implicitly indicts sexual as well as racial exploitation; her loyalty to her race (she refused to "pass" as a "white" person) is equally a rejection of the original rape that constitutes her ancestry. As a staunch feminist and indefatigable worker for the rights of her race, Harper (1851–1931) well knew the double burdens under which black women labored and she convincingly expressed this knowledge in her vigorous poems.

Other artists were remolding poetry in their own ways to assert new roles for women: Louise Imogin Guiney depicted flamboyant women and championed a male-identified commitment to will, action, and force in her hymns to a chivalric past; the controversial *Poems of Passion* (1883) by Ella Wheeler Wilcox (1850–1919) inspired an "Erotic School" of writers seeking to break the conventional modes; and Lizette Woodworth Reese (1856–1935) used the pastoral mode and sonnet form to endow domestic scenes with new dignity.

The women who led this first wave of literary feminism at the turn of the century were still operating under the assumptions of the Victorian era. The artists born in the 1870s and 1880s who put their imprint on feminism's second phase, in the first decades of the twentieth century, were far more likely to have had college educations, acquired experience as journalists, and come from the Mid- and Far West and out of the South. Rebelling against the constrictions of small town middle-class life, they participated in a movement known as "the revolt from the village." Their feminism was perhaps narrower and their social concerns broader than that of an earlier generation; the separatist ideal embodied in the concept of sisterhood was not for them the central issue. Yet their accomplishments greatly advanced women's position.

In New York's Greenwich Village, to which women artists all gravitated, if only for brief periods, they found support for their bohemianism and social commitments. There they joined activists like the revolutionary Emma Goldman (1869–1940), the lawyer Crystal Eastman (1881–1928), the nurse and social worker Margaret Sanger (1879–1966), the doctor Josephine Baker (1873–1945), the teacher Henrietta Rodman (n.d.), the writer and war journalist Mary Heaton Vorse (1874–1966), and the younger activist-poet Genevieve Taggard (1894–1948). Together these women pioneered in public health care and child health, organized for birth control, and in 1916 opened the first such clinic in the country, advocated for workers' and women's rights, including the right of women to work after they married, and opposed the suppression of radical political opinion that was to culminate in the Palmer Raids of 1919 and the deportation of radical aliens in 1920. They founded and supported those societies that they believed heralded a new world: the A Club, one of several experimental cooperative living arrangements, frequented by Mark Twain, Theodore Dreiser, Mother Jones (1830–1930), and Maxim Gorky; the Provincetown Players, which was to be the home of Susan Glaspell's (1876–1948) famed *Trifles* as well as Louise Bryant's (1885–1936) symbolist drama *The Game* and Djuna Barnes' (1892–1982) one-act plays; the Congressional Union (1913), which was to become the Women's Party (1916), to fight for an equal rights amendment; the New York Women's Peace Party (1914), later to become the Women's International League for Peace and Freedom. They also participated in the Heterodoxy Club.[8] In addition, these new women founded, helped to publish, edited, and wrote for such magazines as the feminist *Forerunner* (est. 1906 by Charlotte Perkins Gilman), the anarchist *Mother Earth* (est. 1906 by Goldman), and the socialist *Masses*, (1911–1917), the *Woman Rebel* (est. 1914 by Sanger), and the black journal of the newly founded NAACP, *Crisis* (est. 1910, and edited by novelist Jessie Fauset [1882–1961] from 1919 to 1926). Such important journals of poetry as the new *Dial* (1917–1929, edited by Marianne Moore from 1925 to 1929), and the international *Broom* (1921–1923), edited by Lola Ridge, with Harriet Monroe's (1860–1936) *Poetry* (est. 1912), and Margaret Anderson's (1886–1973) *The Little Review* (est. 1914) based in Chicago, were revolutionizing poetry.

In "A Jury of Her Peers" (1916) and the one-act play *Trifles*, on which it is based, Susan Glaspell wrote of a farm woman driven to murder her husband. Banding together in retrospective solidarity, admitting their communal guilt, the neighboring women "acquit" her and keep incriminating evidence from the men who intend to try her in male-dominated courts. In texts that embodied a different, urban "Village," Glaspell and others inscribed the complexities of their heroines living in the modern age. In shifting their focus from a rural to an urban community, these writers also signaled a shift from woman-identified to heterosexual norms; texts increasingly stressed the relations between men and women rather than those among women. Their themes were autonomy and sexual liberation as a symbol of self-definition and self-realization, and the plots provided for divorce as a more humane solution to marital conflict than the murders or suicides that had characterized the novelistic endings of a decade before.

The early Greenwich Village novels by Ellen Glasgow (1873–1945), for example, are awkward, unrealistic, but powerful enunciations about independent women; sexual liaisons are hinted at, if not depicted. Glaspell's *Fidelity* and Vorse's *I've Come to Stay* (both published in 1915) "went further," and permitted their heroines to have sexual relations, live with men who were not their husbands, become pregnant, and consider abortions. Mary Austin's *A Woman of Genius* (1912) is significant in its first-person portrayal of a woman obsessed by her (dramatic) art, which increasingly puts her at odds with her husband and ultimately causes her to desert him. A decade after Glasgow's similar portrayal in *Phases of an Inferior Planet* (1898), Austin daringly refused to impose the divorce and remarriage that had become almost a plot necessity. (In contrast, Edith Wharton, writing from the aristocratic perspective of New York's uptown society, condemned the social-climbing Undine Spragg for using marriage and divorce as barter [*Custom of the Country*, 1913].)

Although divorce had been written into literary texts since 1894, it did not resolve the conflicting claims between (re)marriage and self-realization. Like their somewhat earlier and more radical counterparts, Glaspell and Vorse concluded their novels with marriage because it represented the only sanctioned alternative to the single life, or, especially for working-class women, to prostitution, as suggested in Zoe Beckley's *A Chance to Live* (1917) or *A Daughter of the Morning* (1917) and *Miss Zulu Betts* (1920) by Zona Gale (1874–1938). As late as 1926, Janet Flanner (1892–1978) could see no alternative for her protagonist but to have her accept the "double standard" and forswear her immensely successful career as a set designer in the theater and marry—in the name of love (*The Cubical City*).

The characteristically American genre of autobiography was still another means for women to document and authenticate their professional achievements and frustrations. Elizabeth Stuart Phelps Ward's *Chapters from a Life* (1896) and Elizabeth Blackwell's (1821–1921) memoir of her becoming a doctor (1895) are the precursors to *Twenty Years at Hull House* (1910) by Jane Addams (1860–1935). This new "professionalism" was humorously manifested in *Madeleine* (1919), the autobiography of a prostitute. Though not published until 1972, *Reminiscences* by Mary Hallock Foote (1874–1938), who introduced the frontier West into realistic fiction, is from this period, as is *Plains Woman: The Diary of Martha Farnsworth, 1882–1922* (1986). *Letters of a Woman Homesteader* (1914) by Elinore Stewart (1876–1933) recorded her experiences in staking her claim in Burnt Fork, Wyoming, to suggest alternatives for women immersed in urban poverty. Hers was one of the few indigenous voices to emerge from what began to be noted as the working class.[9]

Three milestones delineated a new poetic consciousness. Sara Teasdale (1884–1933), one of the leaders in the new movement, had published the first twentieth-century anthology of women's poetry in 1917; in the enlarged edition (1928), she wrote: "The decade since 1917 has produced more good poetry by women than any other in the history of the language." Another event equally important in defining a female poetic tradition was the recovery of Emily Dickinson (1830–1886), through the publication of a volume of her work in 1924, followed by the first major biography of her by Genevieve Taggard in 1930. Dickinson's lapidary verse and incisive imagery, as well as her complex personae, coupled with the thrust toward modernism, influenced such diverse writers as Taggard, Dorothy Parker (1893–1967), Toyo Suyemoto (b. 1917), and Amy Lowell (1874–1925) well into the 1930s. Parker gave poetry a new sardonic wit. Lowell, though much derided, championed free verse and experimentation. A third milestone is found in the work of the Irish-born anarchist Lola Ridge (1873–1941), who as early as 1919, developed an androgynous theory of artistic creativity that she articulated in lectures on woman and the creative will (1981).[10]

Women writing in this period were concerned on one hand with craft and objectivity: Edna St. Vincent Millay (1892–1950) refashioned the romantic sonnet; Léonie Adams (b. 1899) drew on Elizabethan forms; Elinor Wylie (1885–1928) turned to seventeenth-century metaphysical verse for her inspiration and Marianne Moore (1887–1972) to prose, both seventeenth century and modern; Mina Loy (1882–1966) worked in a more experimental surrealist mode. By this means, they sloughed off older notions of a "feminine poetry" as mere emotional effusions. On the other hand, female experience, and peculiary female conflicts between creativity (liberation) and traditional femininity (restriction) are often played out in highly symbolic and allusive terms; powerful female figures are invoked as the means of the poet's "uniting herself with the liberated woman of her imagination."

In addition, educated women's persistent concern with worlds other than their own is perhaps best captured by Lola Ridge's *The Ghetto and Other Poems* (1918) and the western writer Janet Lewis's (b. 1903) *The Indian in the Woods* (1922). It also lies behind Alice Corbin's (1881–1949) many volumes of poetry and the important regional collection that she edited in 1928: *The Turquoise Trail: An Anthology of New Mexico Poetry.* But those who were doubly or triply oppressed by race or class as well as gender rarely spoke for themselves. Only one Asian-American, mentored by Harriet Monroe, published a volume of poetry in this period. The title, *Poems in Exile* (1923), by June Fujita (n.d.), suggests how displaced its author felt herself to be, though the poems themselves give little indication of her sense of alienation. Margarette Ball Dickson (1884–?) was one of the few working-class poets (*Gumbo Lilies*, 1924; *Thistledown*, 1928; and *One Man with a Dream*, n.d.).

For black women, the Harlem Renaissance, a period of literary renewal and assertion of a specifically black identity that flourished beginning in the 1920s, seemed to provide a greater impetus to artistic expression than feminism. Yet the African primitivism, widely promulgated by black male artists of the period, tended to associate the female with the barbaric and the erotic; as a consequence women inspired by this renaissance were reluctant to identify themselves wholly with it and found themselves between two worlds. Like white women in the period, they practiced a limited separatist policy, meeting occasionally and sharing subject matter and themes in their work. Georgia Douglas Johnson (1886–1966) was one of several who initially appeared in the pages of *Opportunity* (est. 1923) a black vehicle for the Renaissance, before she won a wider hearing than any black poet since Frances E. Watkins Harper (Harper's verse was published in 1854), with *The Heart of a Woman* (1918), *Bronze* (1922), and *An Autumn Love Cycle* (1926).

Perhaps most important, however, was Anne Spencer (1882–1975). Her influence, which was to extend to the second wave of feminism and the reassertion of black identity in the 1960s, was not limited to her poetic oeuvre, some forty-odd poems that were never published in book form. Her willingness to confront sexism and racism directly and her moral clarity served as the major inspiration to later generations of black poets. These included Margaret Walker (b. 1915), who was awarded the first Pulitzer Prize for Poetry for *For My People* (1942), Gwendolyn Brooks (b. 1917), who also began publishing in the 1940s, and Gloria Oden (b. 1923), who emerged in the early 1950s with *The Naked Frame* and served as an editor of the short-lived *Umber* in Baltimore,[12] as well as those young black women who began to write in greater numbers in the late 1960s and 1970s.

As Henry May has suggested, World War I exposed the moral bankruptcy of the male intellectual community, which lent support to a war that everything in its philosophy opposed.[13] Artists and supporters of the arts experienced an alienation so profound that they have been characterized as a "lost generation"; in the conservative cultural and social climate that followed upon the heels of the war and the approval of the Constitutional amendment of women's right to vote, women, most especially lesbians, recognized that America offered them little in the way of nurture and resources for creativity, and constituted a significant segment of the expatriate community which took up residence primarily in Paris.

Thus, following Gertrude Stein (1874–1946), Nathalie Barney (1876–1972), a well-born Philadelphian, became the center of a lesbian artistic community that included Renée Vivien (1877–1909), Djuna Barnes, and the artist Romaine Brooks

(1874–1970). Janet Flanner, now writing as Genêt for the newly created *New Yorker* (1922), intiated what was to become a significant source of knowledge both about the expatriate community and the French cultural and political scene; on the left bank, Sylvia Beach (1887–1962) and Adrienne Monnier (1892–1955) established the bookshops that became fabled haunts of American artists living abroad and the press that published James Joyce's *Ulysses* (1926) and Pound's *Cantos* (1926). Poet Hilda Doolittle (1886–1961) settled in England with the British writer Bryher (1894–1983). And for various periods, heterosexual writers such as Wharton, Glasgow, Mary Butts (1892–1937), Frances Newman (1833–1928), Katherine Anne Porter (1890–1980), and Kay Boyle (b. 1902) made their way to foreign shores, often with the funds provided by Guggenheim fellowships that became available in the mid-1920s. There they forged the Modernist project, experimenting with radically new styles and subject matter and themes that focused on issues of sexuality and gender.

For those who chose to remain in America, the idealism, community cohesion, and feminist alliances disintegrated. If the feminist question that had so captured the imaginative energies of woman artists now seemed to ebb, partly dissipated by the fragmentation of the women's movement after the victory of the vote, partly vitiated by the suppression of divergent political opinion, it did not do so entirely. It survived to color the ways in which issues of a collective identity were posed and defined, especially in the context of America's emergence as a world power and the end of the second great wave of immigration. Thus, among the best work of this period are a number of historical novels that explore American roots—novels such as Margaret Wilson's (1882–?) *The Able McLaughlins* (1923), Martha Ostenso's (1900–?) *Wild Geese* (1925), Esther Forbe's (1891–1967) *Mirror for Witches* (1928), about the Salem witch trials, and Evelyn Scott's (1893–1963) *The Wave* (1929).

Those who had previously written about the new women's experience in the city returned to the small towns from whence they had come to explore the historical sources of women's successes or failures. Cather's *My Antonia* (1926) is part of this pattern, as is Glaspell's play *The Inheritors* (1921). In the latter, the heroine, involved in a student protest for a Free India movement, finds herself at the same time at odds with the complacent administration of the college and in harmony with the spirit of her grandfathers—a Hungarian refugee and a New England pioneer. Less optimistic, Zona Gale held out little hope for the Midwest, first in *Miss Zulu Betts* (1920; play version, 1921, for which she won the Pulitzer Prize for Drama), and then more tellingly in her less well-known *Faint Perfume* (1923). Glasgow, however, in *Barren Ground* (1925), allowed Dorinda Oakley to be "the victor instead of the victim," triumphing over circumstance. Similarly, the heroines of Katherine Anne Porter heralded a new economic and social order.

In such fine, compelling, and various works as the determinedly naturalistic *The Wind* (1925), the lyrical *Time of Man* (1926) and the realistic *Weeds* (1923), Texan Dorothy Scarborough (1878–1935), Kentucky-born Elizabeth Madox Roberts (1881–1941), and Canadian-born Edith Summers Kelly (1884–1956) rewrote contemporary women's history as they challenged the apparent economic prosperity of the decade. Indeed, poverty marked large segments of the population,

particularly in the city slums, and the largely rural West and South. Elizabeth
Stevenson has suggested that the twenties might well have been labeled the Boll-
weevil Decade, for farming families lost one-third to one-half of their yields.[14] And
from Letty, who is driven to madness by rape and the violence of nature, to Judith,
who gazes out "over the darkening country" that seems "to stretch endlessly,
endlessly," and sees in it "her future life…a sad, dead level of unrelieved monotony," women symbolize both the desolation of the land and bear the brunt of its
privations. If these are not overtly political works, they are at least implicit
critiques of the masculinist myth of the frontier and the West's infinite possibilities
for expansion and paradisiacal retreat. And they articulated themes that were
politicized in the thirties and given class dimensions by such writers as Meridel le
Sueur (b. 1900), Harriette Arnow (b. 1908), and the less well-known Josephine W.
Johnson (b. 1910).

The racial and ethnic dimensions of this revised feminist theme were not
ignored: the black writer Nella Larsen (1893–1963), in *Quicksand* (1928) and
Passing (1929), and the Jewish writer Anzia Yzierska (1880–1970), writing in
Hungry Hearts (1920), *Salome of the Tenements* (1922), and *Bread Givers* (1925),
also questioned the degree to which everyone shared in the American Dream. They
measured, too, the cost of "passing" between two worlds.

Finally it must be said that these revisionist works capture the speech and
customs of a dying world. Many of these writers had in fact made significant
contributions in the areas of folklore. Dorothy Scarborough published two such
books, one collecting black folk songs, the other southern mountain ballads. Other
students, also working at Columbia with the eminent anthropologist Franz Boas,
included Zora Neale Hurston (1891–1960), who did her pioneering studies of her
own Florida community at the end of this decade, and Ella Deloria (1888–1971),
who returned to her home to record the texts of her Dakota people. Similarly
inspired, Elsie Clews Parsons (1875–1971) worked with the Laguna and Zuni
Indians as well as in the South Carolina sea islands; and Margaret Mead (1901–
1975) published her first and seminal work—*Coming of Age in Samoa* (1928).
Others such as Jovita González (fl. 1920–1940) and Fermina Guerra (n.d.) recorded the folklore of the Chicano culture in English and Spanish respectively;
Maria Cadilla de Martínez (1886–1951) transcribed the folklore of Puerto Rico.
Divergent as they may seem, the novels derive their sanction not only for a new
subject matter but also for new methods of style from the disciplines of psychology
and anthropology; they value the languages of folk communities and the human
unconscious that permit the novelist to make use of dialect, stream of consciousness, song and proverb as the means of structuring the narrative and expounding
the tale.

The autobiographical genre also became a vehicle for postwar retrenchment.
While Anglo-Saxon female writers sought their roots in native ideals, immigrant
writers replanted themselves in the new world: similar narrative strategies for such
divergent groups were bound to have rather different implications. Mary Antin's
(1881–1949) *The Promised Land* (1913) was the most hortatory and well-known
expression; Demetra Vaka (1877–1946), journalist, teacher, and activist supporter
of Greek causes, began her writing career by sloughing off the past with *A Child of*

the Orient (1914). These autobiographies were followed by Elizabeth Gertrude Stern's (1889–1954) *My Mother and I* (1917), poignant in its half-conscious recognition that the text by which she declares her cultural independence is one in which she entombs her mother's traditions. Stern's earlier optimism gave way before the experience of anti-semitism and the difficulties of forging an autonomous life and she recast her life a second time in the novel *I am a Woman—and a Jew* (1926). But her defensive apology is a far cry from the prewar Sui Sin Far's scathing "Leaves from the Mental Portfolio of an Eurasian" published in 1909.

Some working-class autobiographers openly challenged the middle-class ethic and idealized versions of modern womanhood. Agnes Smedley (1892–1950) was born in a small town in northern Missouri and was radicalized by her family's subsequent efforts to sustain themselves in the mining camp towns in Colorado. Like Scarborough, Roberts, and Kelly, she described the crippling effects of rural poverty and its consequent affects on the cold relations between men and women in her autobiographical novel *Daughter of Earth* (1929). The haunting Modernist autobiography (*And No Birds Sing*, 1931) of Pauline Leader (fl. 1925–1950), a deaf, Jewish working-class writer, revealed an urban world that was equally spiritually and economically impoverished. Its depiction of a woman alone in the city represents the underside of the middle-class feminist portrait drawn in the twenties and articulates the class conflict in feminist terms, unique in the period.

The decade of the 1960s initiated a movement that lasted well into the 1970s; the formative years did much to shape the writing of the 1980s as well. Following a period of unprecedented affluence for the middle class, many Americans were led by rising expectations to challenge the disparities between rich and poor, and between material wealth and social values. In the civil rights struggles, in the anti-war and peace movements, in the student battles, women forswore "the feminine mystique" and re-emerged in the public sphere, to act as midwives to the "second wave" of feminism.[15]

They defined a new "sexual politics," which argued that the "personal is political": Drawing an analogy to racism, women exposed "sexism." These slogans codified the particular theoretical and historical contribution of this period's feminists and prefaced a more thoroughgoing critique of gender systems as determinants in social, economic, and political structures. In turn, this feminist theory shaped the challenge to traditional sex roles in the public sphere that by 1975 had penetrated the mainstream of American society.

Like their Modernist-feminist foremothers of the early twentieth century, the feminists of the 1960s and 1970s achieved this by coalescing around sexual, economic, and political issues. Thus they organized around reproductive rights (publishing the first feminist sexual/gynocological self-help compendium [*Our Bodies, Ourselves*, 1973], and leading the successful fight to legalize abortion [1973]). To combat increasing poverty levels among women and children as well as widening wage differences between men and women, they organized in factories, health care, and white-collar service industries. Politically, they sought the legal basis for equality through class-action suits. In 1973, having won legal equality in higher education, they re-introduced the Equal Rights Amendment (ERA) into

Congress, fifty years after it had first been submitted. By that time, an organization that could appeal to a broad-based liberal, middle-class and mostly white, constituency had emerged. While adopting some of the rhetoric and "consciousness-raising" tactics of more radical feminist groups, the National Organization for Women (NOW) focused its energies on electoral politics and educational and professional discrimination.

In the academic arena, women worked to establish programs in women's studies. Provided with a communal base, academic women began to do the archival, theoretical, and critical work of renaming and redefining women's roles and contributions to history, literature, the sciences, and the social sciences. Among the most important early literary texts, Mary Ellmann's *Thinking About Women* (1968) and Kate Millet's *Sexual Politics* (1969) forced reconsiderations of gender, as well as literary values based on sex. A second-generation of critics such as Ellen Moers (*Literary Women*, 1976), Elaine Showalter (*A Literature of Their Own*, 1979), and Sandra Gilbert and Susan Gubar (*The Madwoman in the Attic*, 1979) then went on to develop gendered theories of authorship and apply feminist ideas of community in defining a female literary tradition. Noteworthy is the lesbian contribution in this area: lesbian culture had generally been more tolerant of women assuming nontraditional roles, and more committed to a separatist politics than heterosexual society; and in the wake of their own self-affirmation, they established a visible lesbian identity. Lesbianism as a theoretical construct in rethinking female oppression and issues of patriarchy was a significant development in the second wave of feminism, and one which distinguished it from an earlier period. The texts that were of crucial importance in the early stages of the project include those of Mary Daly (*Beyond God the Father: Towards a Philosophy of Women's Liberation*, 1973, and *Gyn/Ecology: The Metaethics of Radical Feminism*, 1978) and Adrienne Rich (*On Lies, Secrets and Silence: Selected Prose, 1966–1978*, 1979). To display the results of their findings, scholars also established The Feminist Press (1971) as well as academic journals, pre-eminently *Women's Studies* (est. 1977) and *Signs* (est. 1975). Feminist work had gained a respectable foothold in Academe.

Women recognized the need to control the means of literary production and distribution. They established feminist periodicals and collectives, became printers and book women, and opened women's bookstores around the country. Again, lesbians frequently took the lead in nurturing the larger feminist community. *Off Our Backs*, based in Washington, D.C., was one of the earliest of many lesbian-feminist newspapers. While it focused on the current political scene, other outlets—Tallahassee's Naiad Press, San Francisco's Diana Press, and Daughters, Inc. of Vermont, to name a few—re-issued the works of older lesbian writers and published that of contemporary radical and lesbian literary women.

Feminism was no less an impetus in creating the female literary renaissance in the 1970s than it had been in the late nineteenth and first third of the twentieth century. Drawing on a newly politicized and woman-identified subculture, women exuberantly celebrated their "differences" and gained mastery over a chaotic history/"herstory." Four writers and their texts signaled the rise of a feminist fiction and exemplified significant feminist themes and topics of the period. Erica

Jong (b. 1942), in her bawdy, comic novel, *Fear of Flying* (1973), reclaimed the female body for sexual pleasure; In *The Women's Room* (1977), Marilyn French (b. 1929) focused on the emergent sisterhood of "dropout" wives and mothers of the 1950s who found themselves on the frontlines of liberation, while Marge Piercy (b. 1936) represented the communal life of the counterculture and challenged definitions of sanity as well as society by merging social realism and prophetic modes (*Small Changes*, 1975; *Woman on the Edge of Time*, 1976); and Rita Mae Brown (b. 1944) introduced the lesbian into mainstream literary history with *Rubyfruit Jungle* (1973), whose feisty heroine put into question all gendered definitions of the self.

There were comparable developments in poetry: from Anne Sexton (1928–1974), who explored the mad consciousness that was the underside of middle-class women's domestic role to Diane Wakoski (b. 1937), whose heroine took to the road within a surreal landscape, poetry trumpeted new expressions of female awareness. The poetic works that placed lesbian identity at the center of self-definition include those of Adrienne Rich (b. 1929), whose "Twenty-One Love Poems" deals with the relation between women loving women and a hostile world. The poetry of New Yorker Audre Lorde (b. 1934; *From a Land Where Other People Live*, 1973; *Coal*, 1976; *Between Ourselves*, 1976) and Californian Pat Parker (b. 1944; *Movement in Black: The Collected Poetry: 1961–1978*, 1978) also defined lesbianism in relation to black identity; and *Edward the Dyke* (1971) and *Work of a Common Woman* (1979) by Judy Grahn (n.d.) put lesbianism in the context of class issues. The recovery of a female poetic tradition influenced many poets and gave them a new self-confidence. The result in the succeeding decade was a poetry of extraordinary virtuosity, coupled with narrative scope and philosophical depth. Amy Clampitt (n.d.) and the younger Gjertrud Schnackenberg (b. 1953), Diane Ackermann (b. 1948), and Jorie Graham (b. 1951), for example, have experimented with poems of ambitious length, while poets such as Marie Ponsot (b. 1921) have metamorphosed traditional forms. Marilyn Hacker (b. 1942), in *Love, Death, and the Changing of the Seasons* (1987), has written an elegant novel in sonnets, and Patricia Dobler (n.d.), in *Talking to Strangers* (1987), has written a verse memoir of a third-generation daughter growing up in an Ohio steel mill town.

In addition to these literary milestones, the period can be defined in terms of several general trends: one major trend is the reemergence of older writers silenced by political suppression and economics; these artists were in turn (re)claimed by a new feminist generation seeking to identify its literary foremothers. Tillie Olsen (b. 1913), for example, published *Tell Me a Riddle*, a collection of stories, in 1961, followed by *Yonnondio*, her unfinished novel of the 1930s, in 1974, and *Silences*, an important contribution to the recovery of still earlier women writers and discussion on why women don't write, in 1978. Similarly, Meridel le Sueur, who had made her mark in the 1930s with journalism and fiction (collected in *Salute to Spring*, 1940), returned to print in 1975. Among her "new" works was *The Girl*, written in 1939 but not published until 1978, which describes a group of women who have banded together to survive the Depression, and who, by narrating the text of their lives, fashion a collective identity. A politics of compassion moved Kay Boyle once again to action and writing. An early critic of militarism in her novel *Generation without Farewell* (1960), Boyle traveled with poets Muriel Rukeyser (1913–1980) and Denise Levertov (b. 1923) to Cambodia on a peace mission in 1966, was twice arrested in 1967 for protesting the war in Vietnam, and was eventually dismissed from the faculty of San Francisco State University for participating in the student and faculty strikes in 1968 and 1969. Her essay collection, *The Long Walk at San Francisco* (1970), maps the moral geography of her opposition.

The second major trend of the period is the movement of the ethnic writer from the margins to the mainstream of women's literary history. Drawing energy from the Black Power movement, the Native American movement, and the repoliticization of the Chicano, Puerto Rican, and Asian-American communities, as well as from the feminist movement, ethnic artists reclaimed the traditions of their communities. They invoked older folklores and indigenous motifs and symbols and mixed poetic and prose genres that were part of those traditions. Since storytellers and legendary figures symbolizing artistic creativity were frequently female, ethnic writers saw the recuperation of their ethnic tradition as but another means of reclaiming their matrilineal heritage.

Among blacks, Paule Marshall (b. 1929) can be credited with introducing the West Indian woman into the American literary narrative. Marshall's *bildungsroman, Brown Girl, Brownstone* (1951) tells the story of a girl of Barbadian parents coming of age in Booklyn. Geography is frequently used to map the personal, cultural, and economic determinants of exploitation and to structure the related stories in *Soul Clap Hands and Sing* (1961) and to define the characters in *The Chosen Place, The Timeless People* (1969). With *The Bluest Eye* (1969), Toni Morrison (b. 1931) made her literary debut. Only in retrospect, did critics recognize the novel's power and stylistic innovation; Morrison coupled the texts of school readers and lyrical internal monologues to present severely "naturalistic" subject matter, the tragic and tormented lives of a black family in the urban ghetto. Her next novel, *Sula* (1974), nourished by the feminist sentiments of the period, emphasized sisterhood. Using fable and allegory, and writing an increasingly magisterial prose in the highly acclaimed—and sometimes controversial—novels *Song of Solomon* (1977), *Tar Baby* (1981), and most recently, *Beloved* (1987), Morrison, like Marshall and others, lent new seriousness to the novel as social critique. Part of a literary renaissance that had its origins in Chicago of the 1960s, and that developed in such places as Watts, Harlem, and Newark, the Black Arts movement was also sustained by poets like Carolyn M. Rodgers (b. 1945), Sonia Sanchez (b. 1934), and Nikki Giovanni (b. 1943).

Two different strains characterize the Asian-American contribution to this period. One defined by Maxine Hong Kingston (b. 1940) in *Warrior Woman* is the recuperation of an ethnic heritage, drawing on family traditions, mythology, and Chinese lore; Kingston "names" her rebellious aunt "No Name Woman," her shaman-doctor mother Brave Orchid, and the heroic warrior woman Fa Mu Lan, on whose back the wrongs of her people was literally inscribed. Kingston writes their stories to show how Chinese women suffered under the burden of their society's traditional gender definitions. Her older contemporary Diana Chang writes out of an opposing strategy. In six novels, beginning with the historical novel, *Frontiers of Love* (1956) and up through *A Perfect Love* (1978), Chang uses Asian and Asian-American characters but rejects racial identity as an adequate index to the self. A similar dichotomy appears in poetic works by Jessica Tarahata Hagedorn (b. 1949; *Dangerous Music*, 1975) and Nellie Wong (b. 1938; *Dreams in Harrison Railroad Park*, 1977). The latter insists on reconstructing an ethnic past and comprehending the mysteries of her parents' and grandparents' experience as part of the project of creating a feminist self; the former, living in eternal migration in a rootless America, can imagine only a postmodern self, selected and constructed from a welter of Spanish, black, and Filipino traditions.

Frequently, male anthropologists and editors had acted as "midwives" to the literary production of Amer-Indians; beginning in the 1970s, native American women in significant numbers authored their own texts. In her short stories and novels, the Amer-Indian writer often concerns herself with the theme of the "mixed breed," the one who stands at the crossroads of two cultures, or the "double self"; she also insists that her story is but a modern version of an older narrative or a tale that already exists, a part of the listener/reader, waiting only to be "told," thus suggesting another double perspective. Leslie Marmon Silko (b. 1948), in such stories as "The Man to Send Rain Clouds" and "Yellow Woman," and in the novel *Ceremony* (1977), shows Indian myth and tradition persisting despite forces that seek to obliterate them, while her poetry evokes images of ancient ritual on the modern landscape (*Laguna Woman*, 1974). Similarly poet-novelist Paula Gunn Allen (b. 1939), having sloughed off an earlier, assimilated self by recounting the death of a marriage in a long poetic sequence (*The Blind Lion*, 1975), turned to fiction (*The Woman Who Owned the Shadows*, 1983) to show an Amer-Indian's reclamation of her heritage and her sexuality as a woman-identified woman.

The final group to contribute to the new mainstream of ethnicity were Chicanas. In 1973, Estela Portillo Trambley (b. 1936) edited the first all-women's issue of a major Chicano journal (*E1 Grito* VII, 1 [September, 1973]). With the *Rain of Scorpions* (1975), she became one of the few Chicanas to publish a book of prose fiction. Despite weaknesses in writing style and a somewhat conservative political stance, the feminist and communal themes found in her stories, novels, as well as the poem (1982) and play (1983) on the Mexican literary heroine, Sor Juana de la Cruz, make Trambley the precursor of what Chicana critic Sonia Saldívar-Woodhull has called the literature of opposition. This literature, which confronts both the oppression of the Chicanos by the Anglo culture *and* the oppression of the Chicanas within the Mexican-American tradition, is exemplified by such writers as Sandra Cisneros (*The House on Mango Street*, 1983) and Cherríe Moraga (*Loving in the War Years*, 1983) who seek to expose the violence and abuse that keep women ignorant and silent within Chicano society. Moraga also deals with contemporary forms of "passing": the Anglo heritage of a mixed breed that enables the protagonist to gain entry to the white institutions that grant power to its initiates and the lesbianism that is rendered invisible by the dominant mythology of heterosexuality. Poets such as Alma Villaneuva (b. 1944: *Bloodroot*, 1977; *Mother, May I*, 1978) and Lorna Dee Cervantes (b. 1954), author of *Emplumada*

(1981) and editor of Mango Press (San Jose, California), were among those women who demanded an active role in the creation of whatever Chicano culture was to be. Others who also reshaped poetry as a major form of Chicana-identified expression include Carmen Tafolla (b. 1951; *Get Your Tortillas Together*, 1975; *Curandera*, 1983), Ana Castillo (*Otro canto*, 1975; *The Invitation*, 1979; *Women Are Not Roses*, 1983; *The Mexquiahuala Letters*, 1986), and Evangelina Vigil (*Thirty an' Seen a Lot*, 1982).

A final trend to note is the rising importance of women in the theater, not only as actresses—traditionally, one of the ways in which women escaped more traditional female social roles—but as directors, producers, and playwrights. Important precursors were Lillian Hellman (1905–1984), whose plays brought a moral seriousness to the stage beginning in the late 1930s, and Lorraine Hansberry (1930–1965), whose *Raisin in the Sun* (1959) made literary history—the first play by a black woman to be produced on Broadway.

Women in theater also created the Greenwich Village avant-garde, in what was to become known as Off-Broadway. Impressarios who developed and directed repertory groups included Judith Malina (b. 1926), who with her husband Julian Beck, founded what is arguably the single most important repertory theater of the 1960s, the Living Theater, and Ellen Stewart (n.d.), who established La Mama in 1962, a vehicle for bringing experimental international plays to the United States. On the west coast, Rachel Rosenthal's (b. 1926) improvisatory Instant Theatre (1956–1966) set the stage for happenings and feminist performance work.

The ferment in drama was to be seen in the works of Rochelle Owens (b. 1936), Adrienne Kennedy (b. 1931, another black writer who chose a more dreamlike and lyrical mode, in contrast with Hansberry's realism), Julie Bovasso (b. 1930), Megan Terry (b. 1932), Maria Irene Fornes (b. 1930), and Rosalyn Drexler (b. 1926). Their works were characterized by experimental, often symbolic styles, nonrealistic and surrealistic subject matter, a sometimes shocking disregard for either dramatic or social propriety, a refusal to separate politics from art, and an intense interest in and use of popular culture that resulted in the blurring between high and low art. Drexler, for instance, makes the television a talking member of the cast, as well as the female protagonist's romantic fantasy in "Softly, and Consider the Nearness" (1967).

Despite the lack of a formal network, still another writer came to the fore who drew her inspiration both from the black movement and the women's movement: Ntozake Shange (b. 1948), in "For Colored Girls Who Have Considered Suicide/ When the Rainbow is Enuf" (1976), adumbrated a new feminist theater. Since then, writers, both experimental and traditional, have told stories of household gods (Momoko Iko), political satire (Joan Holden [b. 1939] writing for the San Francisco Mime Troupe), and feminist fantasy (Lavonne Mueller bringing together Joan of Arc and Susan B. Anthony in "Little Victories"). Of those who have gained more than critical notice, Marsha Norman (b. 1947) stands at the head; her *Getting Out* (1979) is important not only for its subject—the devastating life of a working-class woman who goes crazy and kills a man—but for its innovative staging. Norman went on to win the Pulitzer Prize in 1983 for '*Night, Mother*, a colloquy between mother and daughter before the daughter's suicide.

These then were the women who developed feminist narratives, poetry, and drama beginning in the 1960s. Riding the second wave of feminism, they initiated trends consistent with a new feminist ideology. The themes and subject matter of their literature were woman-identified in the broadest sense, and their works were informed by a female literary tradition and emphasized sisterhood along both horizontal and vertical axes. The women named here stand as a partial fulfillment of Harriet Monroe's 1920 prophesy: "The modern woman has yet to prove her equality as an artist...Perhaps women are just beginning their work in the arts, and the twentieth century may witness an extraordinary development." And indeed it has.

NOTES

1. See Anne Goodwyn Jones, *Tomorrow Is Another Day: The Woman Writer in the South, 1859–1936* (Baton Rouge: Louisiana State University Press, 1981).
2. See Josephine Donovan, *New England Local Color Literature: A Women's Tradition.* (Boston: G.K. Hall, 1972).
3. For the development of separatism as a strategy for women, see Penina Migdal Glazer and Miriam Slater, *Unequal Colleagues: The Entrance of Women into Professions, 1890–1940* (New Brunswick: Rutgers University Press, 1987). See also Nan Bauer Maglin, "Early Feminist Fiction: The Dilemma of Personal Life," *Prospects: Annual Journal of American Cultural Studies* 2:167–191, to whom I am indebted for some of these references.
4. Under this rubric Alice Robbin became one of the earliest to depict urban black life in *Uncle Tom's Tenement* (1886). In *Little Citizens* (1904) and *Little Aliens* (1910), Kelly, drawing on her past teaching experience, depicted the Jewish immigrant. Anna C. Ruddy's 1908 novel, *The Heart of the Stranger* portrays Anglo-American ladies ministering to the immigrants of Little Italy. Glenda Hobbes discusses this narrative strategy in the context of Appalachian fiction in "Starting Out in the Thirties: Harriette Arnow's Literary Genesis," *Literature at the Barricades: The American Writer in the 1930s*, Ralph F. Bogardus and Fred Hobson eds., (University: University of Alabama Press, 1982), pp. 144–161.
5. Jean Pfaelzer, *The Utopian Novel in America, 1886–1896* (Pittsburgh: University of Pittsburgh Press, 1984), pp. 81–85.
6. This essay omits consideration of many women who were part of an oral tradition or who wrote in foreign languages. These traditions are represented in the text. Many American writers addressed both an indigenous population and audiences of a foreign country; two random examples include the French Canadian-American Camille Lessard-Bissonnette (1883–1972), author of *Canuck* (1936), an important novel of francophone working-class life, and the Greek-American Theano Papazoglou-Margaris (n.d.) who wrote in the second quarter of this century.
7. I am indebted for this reference to an unpublished paper by Susan Koppelman.
8. An atypical example of the women's club movement, it was extremely long-lived. Its early members ran the political gamut from founding Communist Party members to staunch Republicans and included artists as well as many of the women responsible for developing theories and doing research in the new academic professions of psychology and education. The personal lives of its members also varied, but all were "pro-women." See Judith Schwarz, *Radical Feminists of Heterodoxy: Greenwich Village, 1912–1940* (Lebanon, New Hampshire: New Victoria Publishers, 1982).
9. Working-class and rural farming women also gave private testimony of their lives,

inscribing new forms of consciousness in letters, journals, and diaries that served as emotional outlets while maintaining familial networks. Rarely published in their own time, works of this period are now available in: Elizabeth Hampsten, ed., *Read This only to Yourself: The Private Writings of Midwestern Women, 1880–1910* (Bloomington: Indiana University Press, 1982), Lillian Schlissel, ed., *Women's Diaries of the Westward Movement* (New York: Schocken Books, 1982), and Joanna Stratton, ed. *Pioneer Mothers: Voices from the Kansas Frontier* (New York: Simon and Schuster, 1981). On the use of the diary genre more generally, see: Margo Culley, ed., *A Day at a Time: The Diary Literature of American Women from 1764 to the Present* (New York: Feminist Press, 1985) and Penelope Franklin, ed., *Private Pages: Diaries of American Women, 1830s–1970s* (New York: Ballentine Books, 1986).

10. See Elaine Sproat, ed., "Woman and the Creative Will," *Michigan Occasional Paper* No. 18 (Spring 1981), in *Michigan Occasional Papers in Women's Studies*, Ann Arbor. This edition of Ridge's work is the only published version.

11. William Drake. *The First Wave: Women Poets in America, 1915–1945* (New York: Macmillan, 1987) p. 115.

12. I am indebted to Marilyn Hacker for this reference.

13. *The End of American Innocence: A Study of the First Years of Our Own Time, 1912–1917* (New York: Quadrangle, 1959).

14. See *The American Twenties: Babbits & Bohemians* (New York: Macmillan, 1970).

15. The feminine mystique was the phrase that Betty Friedan (b. 1921) used (in the book by that title) to define the ideology that equated women's identity and worth with her role as wife and mother, and to which women had fallen prey in the post–World War II decade. The book, which appeared in 1963, seemed to launch the second wave of the women's movement—and was certainly the bible for the National Women's Organization, which Friedan helped to found.

BIBLIOGRAPHY

Background

Berkin, Carol Ruth and Norton, Mary Beth, eds. *Women of America: A History*. Boston: Houghton Mifflin, 1979.

Córdova, Teresa, et. al. *Chicana Voices: Intersections of Class, Race and Gender*. Austin: Center for Mexican American Studies Publications, 1986.

Cott, Nancy F. and Pleck, Elizabeth H., eds. *A Heritage of Her Own: Toward a New Social History of American Women*. New York: Simon and Schuster, 1979.

Gordon, Linda. *Woman's Body, Women's Right: Birth Control in America*. New York: Vintage, 1976.

Hayden, Dolores. *The Grand Domestic Revolution: A History of Feminist Designs for American Homes, Neighborhoods, and Cities*. Cambridge: MIT Press, 1981.

Jones, Jacqueline. *Labor of Love, Labor of Sorrow: Black Women, Work, and the Family from Slavery to the Present*. New York: Basic Books, 1985.

Kessler-Harris, Alice. *Out to Work: A History of Wage-Earning Women in the United States*. Oxford: Oxford University Press, 1982.

Rosenberg, Rosalind. *Beyond Separate Spheres: Intellectual Roots of Modern Feminism*. New Haven, CT: Yale University Press, 1982.

Ryan, Mary P. *Cradle of the Middle Class: The Family in Oneida County, New York, 1790–1865*. Interdisciplinary Perspectives on Modern History, Robert Fogel and Stephan Thernstrom, eds. Cambridge: Cambridge University Press, 1981.

Seller, Maxine Schwartz, ed. *Immigrant Women*. Philadelphia: Temple University Press, 1981.

Stansell, Christine. *City of Women: Sex and Class in New York: 1789–1860*. New York: Knopf, 1986.

Literary Criticism and Literature

See also American Women Writers Series (Rutgers University Press), Radcliffe Biography Series (Addison-Wesley), Western Writers Series (Boise State University), The Schomburg Library of Nineteenth-Century Black Women Writers (Oxford University Press), Black Woman Writers, Beacon Travellers, and Asian Voices Series (Beacon Press). Publishers of significant numbers of texts by women, and especially, ethnic writers include Greenfield Review Press (Greenfield Center, New York), Ahsahta Press (Boise State University), Arte Publico (University of Houston), Kitchen Table: Women of Color Press (New York), and the Feminist Press (City University of New York). Journals are *Amerasia Journal* (Yale and UCLA), *Third Woman, Sun Tracks: An American Indian Literary Magazine* (University of Arizona, Tucson), *Bilingual Review* (York College, New York), and MELUS.

Benstock, Shari. *Women of the Left Bank: Paris, 1900–1940*. University of Texas Press, 1986.

Barolini, Helen, ed. and introd. *The Dream Book: An Anthology of Writings by Italian American Women*. New York: Schocken Books, 1987.

Bataille, Gretchen M. and Kathleen Mullen Sands, eds. and introd. *American Indian Women: Telling Their Lives*. Lincoln: University Press, 1984.

Baym, Nina. *Woman's Fiction: A Guide to Novels by and about Women in America, 1820–1870*. Ithaca: Cornell University Press, 1978.

Dearborn, Mary. *Pocahontas's Daughters: Gender and Ethnicity in American Culture*. New York: Oxford University Press, 1986.

Duke, Maurice, Bryer, Jackson R., and Inge, Thomas M., eds. *American Women Writers: Bibliographical Essays*. Westport, CT: Greenwood Press, 1983.

Evans, Mari, ed. *Black Women Writers (1950–1980): A Critical Evaluation*. Intod. Stephen Henderson. Garden City: Anchor Press/Doubleday, 1984.

Fetterly, Judith. *The Resisting Reader: A Feminist Approach to American Fiction*. Bloomington: Indiana University Press, 1978.

Fetterly, Judith, ed. and introd. *Provisions: A Reader from 19th-Century American Women*. Susan Gubar and Joan Hoff-Wilson, eds. Everywoman Studies in History, Literature, and Culture. Bloomington: Indiana University Press, 1985.

Green, Rayna, ed. *That's What She Said: Contemporary Poetry and Fiction by Native American Women*. Bloomington: Indiana University Press, 1984.

Herrera-Sobek, Maria, ed. *Beyond Stereotypes: The Critical Analysis of Chicana Literature*. Binghamton: Bilingual Press, 1985.

Kim, Elaine H. *Asian American Literature: An Introduction to the Writings and Their Social Context*. Philadelphia: Temple University Press, 1982.

Kolodny, Annette. *The Land Before Her: Fantasy and Experience of the American Frontiers, 1630–1860*. Chapel Hill: University of North Carolina Press, 1984.

Koolish, Lynda. *A Whole New Poetry Beginning Here*. 2 Vols. Ann Arbor: University Microfilms, 1981. Vol. 1 analyzes the women's poetry movement; vol. 2 is a collection of essays by 35 individual poets.

Prenshaw, Peggy Whitman, ed. *Women Writers of the Contemporary South*. Jackson: University of Mississippi Press, 1984.

Stetson, Erlene, ed. *Black Sister: Poetry by Black American Women, 1746–1980*. Bloomington: Indiana University Press, 1984.

Tichi, Cecilia Tichi. *Shifting Gears: Technology, Literature, Culture in Modernist America*. Chapel Hill: University of North Carolina Press, 1987.

Tompkins, Jane. *Sensational Designs: The Cultural Work of American Fiction: 1790–1860*. New York: Oxford University Press, 1985.

Vigil, Evangelina. "Woman of Her Word: Hispanic Women Write." Special Issue of *Revista Chicano-Requeña* (Bloomington, Indiana University Northwest) XI:3–4 (1983).

Writers and Selections by Region

Credits

Wei Junyi, "Three Friends," *Nuren ji* (Sichuan renmin, 1980).

Gwendolyn Brooks, "A Bronzeville Mother Loiters in Mississippi. Meanwhile a Mississippi Mother Burns Bacon" and "The Last Quatrain of the Ballad of Emmet Till," *Blacks*. Copyright © 1987 by the David Company. Reprinted by permission of the author. "Speech to the Young. Speech to the Progress-Toward," *Family Pictures*, 1970, Broadside Press, Detroit.

Fadwa Tuqan, "After the Release," "The Last Knocks," "Nothing Is Here," and "To Etan," *Women of the Fertile Crescent*. Copyright © 1978 by Kamal Boullata. Three Continents Press, Washington, D.C.

Tove Ditlevson, "Sunday," "Divorce 3," and "Self Portrait 1," from *Contemporary Danish Poetry*, L. Jensen, ed., Twayne, 1977.

Gloria Fuertes, "Autobiography," "I'm Only a Woman," and "Plastic Virgin." Copyright © 1984 by Philip Levine and Ada Long. Reprinted from *Off the Map: Selected Poems by Gloria Fuertes* by permission of Wesleyan University Press.

Muriel Spark, "You Should Have Seen the Mess" from *Collected Stories*. Reprinted by permission of David Higham Assoc. Ltd., London.

Sophia de Mello Breyner Andresen, "Listen" and "This Is the Time," translated by R. Fainlight. Reprinted with permission of Carcanet Press Ltd.

Louise Bennett, "Colonization in Reverse," "Jamaica Oman," and "Pass fi White" from *Jamaica Labrish*, Sangster's Jamaica, W.I.

Doris Lessing, "A Woman on a Roof," from *A Man and Two Women*. Copyright © 1958, 1962, and 1963 by Doris Lessing. Reprinted by permission of Simon & Schuster, Inc.

Margaréta Liberáki, from *The Mystery*, pp. 65-70. Copyright © 1977. Kedros Publishing Company, Athens.

Amrita Pritam, "Silence," "To Waris Shah I Say," and "Imroz," *Women Poets of India*. United Writers (1977). Reprinted by permission of the author.

"Evolution" by May Swenson, used by permission of the author, copyright © 1954, renewed 1982, by May Swenson. "The Red Bird Tapestry" by May Swenson, used by permission of the author, copyright © 1958, renewed 1986, by May Swenson. "Frontispiece" by May Swenson, used by permission of the author, copyright © 1956, renewed 1984, by May Swenson, "Survey of the Whole" first published in *The Nation*. "Swimmers" first published in the collection, *Half Sun Half Sleep* by May Swenson. Reprinted by permission of the author, copyright © 1978, © 1967, respectively, by May Swenson.

Andrée Chedid, *Texts for the Living*, Editions Gallimard, Paris, 1953. "In Order to Survive" and "Stepping Aside," *Visage Premier*, 1972. Reprinted by permission of Flammarion et Cie, Paris.

Rosemary Dobson, "Cock Crow" and "Amy Caroline" from *Selected Poems*, © 1973 by Rosemary Dobson. Reprinted by permission of Angus & Robertson Publishers.

Gwen Harwood, "Suburban Sonnet" and "Barn Owl," Selected Poems, © 1975 by Gwen Harwood. Reprinted by permission of Angus & Robertson Publishers.

Ishigaki Rin, "The Pan, the Pot, the Fire I Have Before Me" and "Roof" from *Anthology of Modern Japanese Poets* by Hiroaki Sato (1973). "Tragedy" from *The Poetry of Postwar Japan*, edited by Kijima Hajime. Copyright © 1975 by University of Iowa Press.

Kath Walker, "We Are Going" and "Corroboree," *We Are Going*. Copyright © 1985 by Citadel Press.

Hisaye Yamamoto, "The High-Heeled Shoes" first appeared in *The Partisan Review*, 1948.

Mavis Gallant, "My Heart Is Broken," from *My Heart Is Broken*, Paperjacks, 1976.

Máire Mhac an tSaoi, "Lament for Seamus Ennis," "Quatrains of Mary Hogan," and "The Hero's Sleep" reprinted with permission of the author.

Nadine Gordimer, "The Train from Rhodesia," *Selected Stories*. Copyright © 1952. All rights reserved. Reprinted by permission of Viking Penguin Inc.

Dorothy Hewett, excerpt from *Windmill Country*, Overland with Peter Lydon Publishing, 1968. "Grave Fairytale." Reprinted by permission of University of Western Australia Press.

Elizabeth Jolley, " 'Surprise! Surprise!' from Matron," *Five Acre Virgin*. Copyright © 1976, Viking Penguin Inc.

Denise Levertov, "Song for Ishtar," "O Taste and See," "Stepping Westward," and "The Pilots," from *Poems 1960–1967*, New Directions, 1983.

Nazik al-Mala'ika, "I Am," "Washing Off Disgrace," "Jamila," and "The Beginnings of the Free Verse Movement," from *Issues of Contemporary Poetry*, in *Women of the Fertile Crescent: Modern Poetry* by Arab Women, Kamal Boullata. Reprinted by permission of Three Continents Press.

Lauris Edmond, "Commercial Traveller" and "Two Birth Poems" from *In the Middle Air* (1975), Pegasus Press. Reprinted by permission of Lauris Edmond.

Janet Frame, from *Faces in the Water*, Braziller, 1961.

Friederike Mayröcker, "Evening" and "I Cannot Drink You" from *Dimension*, vol. 1, 3, 1973. Reprinted by permission. "Patron of Flawless Serpent Beauty" from *German Poetry: 1910–1975*, Persea Books, 1976.

Efua Sutherland, "The Marriage of Anansewa," from *The Marriage of Anansewa and Edufa* (Longman African Classics Series), © Efua T. Sutherland 1967, © Longman Group UK Ltd. 1975 and 1987.

Rosario Castellanos, "Self-Portrait," from *Feminist Studies*, vol. 3, no. 3/4 (Spring-Summer 1976). Reprinted by permission of the publisher. "Speaking of Gabriel" translated by Maureen Ahearn, *Denver Quarterly*, 15, 1 (1980). Reprinted by permission. "Meditation on the Brink" reprinted by permission of translator Maureen Ahearn.

Clarice Lispector, "The Beginnings of a Fortune" (translated by Giovanni Pontiero), *Family Ties*, copyright © 1972 by the University of Texas Press. By permission of the publisher.

Flannery O'Connor, "Habit of Being," selections from *The Habit of Being*. Copyright © 1979 by Regina O'Connor. Reprinted by permission of Farrar, Straus and Giroux, Inc.

Sonja Åkesson, "Autobiography" and "Be White Man's Slave," *Scandinavian Review*, no. 3, 1979. Reprinted from *Scandinavian Review*, the Quarterly Journal of the American Scandinavian Foundation.

Ingeborg Bachmann, "No Delicacies," *In the Storm of Roses: Selected Poems*. Copyright © 1968 by Princeton University Press. From *Malina* © Suhrkamp Verlag, Frankfurt-am-Main, 1971. All rights reserved.

Annette M'Baye d'Erneville, "Kassacks," "Sculpture," "Labane," and "Requiem" from *Poèmes Africains*, 1965. Reprinted by permission of Imprimerie A. Diop, Senegal.

Marya Fiamengo, "In Praise of Old Women" from *In Praise of Old Women*, Mosaic Press, 1976.

Ibaragi Noriko, "When My Beauty Was at Its Best" from *Modern Japanese Poetry* translated by James Kirkup, 1978.

Margaret Laurence, "The Half-Husky," from *A Bird in the House*. Used by permission of the Canadian publishers, McClelland and Stewart, Toronto.

Mahasveta Devi, "Witch," reprinted by permission of the author.

Ana María Matute, from *The Silly Children*, W. Barnstone, Artes Hispanicas, 1967.

Dhirubhēn Patel, "The Revelation," *Gujaratic*.

Blanca Varela, "Madonna," "Waltz of the Angelus I," from *Open to the Sun*, N. J. Wieser, ed., Perivale Press, 1980.

Monique Bosco, from *Lot's Wife*, translated by John Glassco, McClelland and Stewart.

Luisa Josefina Hernández, "Florinda and Don Gonzalo." This work originally appeared in "Dialogues" in *Selected Latin American One-Act Plays*, Francesca Colecchia and Julio Matos, editors and translators. Published 1973 by the University of Pittsburgh Press. Used by permission of the publisher.

Joyce Mansour, "A woman kneeling in the sorry jelly," "Desire as Light as a Shuttle," and "Of Sweet Rest" from *Flash Card* (1978), Mary Beach translator. Reprinted by permission of Cherry Valley Editions.

Christa Reinig, "Milky Way," "Dolphin," "The Tree That Learned to Talk" and "Ode to Being Benumbed by the Wind" from *Dimension* II, 2. Copyright © 1969. Used by permission of *Dimension*.

Ana Maria Hatherly, "Tisane 12" and "Tisane 13" translated by Suzette Macedo. Reprinted by permission of Suzette Macedo.

Ursula K. Le Guin, "Imaginary Countries" from *Orsinian Tales* by Ursula Le Guin. Copyright © 1976 by Ursula Le Guin. Reprinted by permission of Harper & Row Publishers, Inc.

Antonine Maillet, "Behind My Father's House," reprinted by permission of translator John F. Patterson.

Adrienne Rich, "Storm Warnings," "Snapshots of a Daughter-in-Law," and "The Burning of Paper Instead of Children," from *The Fact of a Door Frame, Poems Selected and New, 1950–1984*. Copyright © 1981, 1984 by Adrienne Rich. Copyright © 1975, 1978 by W. W. Norton & Company, Inc. Reprinted by permission of W. W. Norton. "For a Sister" is from *Diving Into the Wreck: Poems*, Norton, 1972.

Christa Wolf, "Interview with Myself," *The Reader and the Writer: Essays, Sketches, Memories*. Joan Becker, translator. Reprinted by permission of Seven Seas Press, Berlin.

Cécile Cloutier, "Against My Country I Took" and "I Would Like To Be True," *Paupieres*. Copyright © 1970. Reprinted by permission. Poems from *The Poetry of Modern Quebec: An Anthology*, Harvest House, copyright © 1976.

Margareta Ekström, "Lobster in Dinard," reprinted by permission of the author.

Svava Jakobsdóttir, "A Story for Children," translated by Dennis Auburn Hill. Copyright © 1975 by the American Scandinavian Foundation. All rights reserved.

Edna O'Brien, "The Creature," from *A Fanatic Heart*. Copyright © 1984. Originally appeared in *The New Yorker*, reprinted by permission of Farrar, Straus and Giroux, Inc.

Amelia Rosselli, "Three Martial Variations," Katherine Jason, translator. Reprinted by permission of Garzanti Editore, Milan and Amelia Rosselli.

Nawal al-Saadawi, "Masculine Confession," *Death of an Ex-Minister* translated by Shirley Eber. Copyright © 1987, used by permission of Methuen London Ltd.

Katerina Angheláki-Rooke, "The Body Is the Victory and the Defeat of Dreams" and "Tourism." Reprinted by permission of the author.

Margaret Atwood, "Backdrop Addresses Cowboy," from *Animals in That Country,* © 1968 Oxford University Press, Canada; "Disembarking at Quebec," "Death of a Young Son by Drowning," and "Further Arrivals," from *The Journals of Susanna Moodie,* © 1970 Oxford University Press, Canada; "you fit into me" from *Power Politics,* © 1971 Margaret Atwood, reprinted by permission of House of Anansi Press, Toronto; "Five Poems for Grandmothers" and "April, Radio, Planting, Easter" from *Two-Headed Poems,* 1978 by Margaret Atwood.

Marie-Claire Blais, "A Season in the Life of Emmanuel," copyright © 1966 by Marie-Claire Blais. Reprinted by permission of Farrar, Straus and Giroux, Inc.

Margaret Drabble, "A Success Story," *Spare Rib Magazine,* London, 1972.

Eigra Lewis Roberts, "An Overdose of Sun," from *A Penguin Book of Welsh Short Stories,* Penguin, 1970.

Angela Carter, "The Donkey Prince," Heinemann Publishers. Reprinted by permission of Elaine Markson, agent.

Angela de Hoyos, "The Mortal Trap," from *Selected Poems/Selecciones,* Dezkalzo Press, San Antonio, Texas, 1979. "Chicano" and "Brother Hermano" from *Chicano Poems: For the Barrio,* Backstage Books, Bloomington, Indiana, 1975.

Nafissatou Diallo, "A Dakar Childhood," reprinted by permission of Longman Group Ltd. UK.

Gwendolyn MacEwen, "Dark Pines Under Water," from *The Shadow Maker,* 1969 and "Meditations of a Seamstress 1 and 2" from *The Armies of the Moon,* 1972. Macmillan, Toronto.

Cristina Peri Rossi, "The Trapeze Artists," from *Indicios Panicos,* Editorial Bruguera, Barcelona.

Ama Ata Aidoò, "In the Cutting of a Drink," from *No Sweetness Here,* copyright © 1971 by Ama Ata Aidoo. Reprinted by permission of Curtis Brown Associates.

Belkis Cuza Malé, "Deadly Women," and "I, Virginia Woolf, Foulmouthed in Death," *Latin American Literary Review,* vol. IV, no. 82, Spring-Summer. Reprinted by permission.

Ghadah al-Samman, "Street Walker," *Arabic Writing Today: The Short Story,* 1968. Reprinted by permission of American Research Center, Egypt.

Khanata Banuna, "If Only I Could Smile," from *Down with Silence,* 1967.

Ambai, "Fall, My Mother," translated by Kamela Ramji, reprinted by permission of the author.

Evan Boland, "Child of Our Time" and "Song" from *The Journey and Other Poems* (1987). Reprinted by permission of Carcanet Press, New York City.

Nancy Morejon, "Angela Dominguez Here!" *Latin American Literary Review,* vol. IV, no. 8, Spring-Summer, 1978. Reprinted by permission.

Alice Walker, "Roselily," from *In Love and Trouble,* copyright © 1972 by Alice Walker. Reprinted by permission of Harcourt Brace Jovanovich, Inc.

Sherley Anne Williams, "Any Woman's Blues," "Home," and "2½ Poems: Making Whole," copyright © 1975 by Sherley Williams. Reprinted from *The Peacock Poems* by permission of Wesleyan University Press.

Yona Wallach, "Preannual Poem" and "Two Gardens" from *Israeli Poetry,* W. Barget and S. Chyet, ed. University of Iowa Press, 1986.

Liz Lochhead, "Today" and "Poem for My Sister," from *Modern Poetry,* Carcanet Press.

Tsushima Yuko, "Scattering Flowers," reprinted by permission of translator Phyllis I. Lyons.

Marnie Walsh, "Vickie Loans-Arrow, 1973" and "Thomas Iron-Eyes, Born *circa* 1840. Died 1919, Rosebud Agency, S.D." from *A Taste of the Knife,* Ahsahta Press. Reprinted by permission of Marnie Walsh.

Gayl Jones, "The Roundhouse," from *White Rat: Short Stories,* copyright © 1977 by Gayl Jones. Reprinted by permission of Random House, Inc.

Fawziyya Abu-Khalid, "Tattoo Writing" and "Mother's Inheritance" from *Women of the Fertile Crescent: Modern Poetry of Arab Women.* Copyright © 1978 by Three Continents Press.

Zabyah Khamis, "Fadings of Memory" and "The Ten Commandments" from *Footsteps Over the Earth.*

Loula Anagnostáki, from *The Parade,* in *The City,* Kedros Publishing, Athens, 1971.

Franca de Armiño, from *The Hippocrites,* Modernistic Editorial Publishing, 1937.

Rosario Ferré, "The Youngest Doll," first published in *The Kenyon Review—New Series,* Winter 1980, vol. II, no. 1. Copyright © by Kenyon College. Reprinted by permission of author and publisher.

Index of Writers and Selections